THE INTERLINEAR

NRSV- NIV

PARALLEL
NEW TESTAMENT
IN GREEK
AND ENGLISH

THE INTERLINEAR

NRSV-
NIV

PARALLEL
NEW TESTAMENT
IN GREEK
AND ENGLISH

ALFRED MARSHALL

ZondervanPublishingHouse
Academic and Professional Books
Grand Rapids, Michigan

A Division of HarperCollinsPublishers

The Interlinear NRSV-NIV Parallel New Testament in Greek and English
Copyright © 1993 by Zondervan Publishing House

Requests for information should be addressed to:
Zondervan Publishing House
Grand Rapids, Michigan 49530

Library of Congress Cataloging-in-Publication Data

Bible. N. T. Greek. 1993
    The interlinear NRSV-NIV parallel New Testament in Greek and English
      p.   cm.
    ISBN 0-310-40160-7
    1. Bible. N. T.—Interlinear translations, English. I. Marshall, Alfred. II.
Bible. N. T. English. New Revised Standard. 1993. III. Bible. N. T. English. New
International. 1993. IV. Title.
    BS1965.5 19993
    225.4'8–dc20   93-37364
                                                        CIP

Previously published in 1990 as The NRSV-NIV Parallel New Testament in Greek
and English.

Scripture taken from the HOLY BIBLE: NEW INTERNATIONAL VERSION®
(North American Edition). Copyright © 1973, 1978, 1984, by the International Bible
Society. Used by permission of Zondervan Publishing House.

The "NIV" and "New International Version" trademarks are registered in the
United States Patent and Trademark Office by the International Bible Society. Use
of either trademark requires the permission of International Bible Society.

Printed in the United States of America

      01 02 03 04 /DC/ 15 14 13 12 11 10 9 8 7 6

This edition is printed on acid-free paper and meets the American National
Standards Institute Z39.48 standard.

Introduction to the
Interlinear Greek Text and Translation

THE GREEK TEXT

THE text of the Greek New Testament has come down to us in various manuscripts, printing not being invented until the fifteenth century and Erasmus not publishing his Greek New Testament until 1516. Some of these manuscripts are more important than others (age not necessarily being indicative of importance). The study of the various manuscript copies, and the assessment of their individual value in attempting to reconstruct the original as nearly as possible, constitutes the science of textual criticism. For those who wish to study this seriously there are many books available; it is sufficient to say here that, after Erasmus, a great number of scholars have, over a long period, applied themselves to the task of constructing a reliable text out of the mass of various readings that have arisen from copying and making copies from copies of the old manuscripts (scholars such as Mill, Stephens, Griesbach, Lachmann, Tischendorf, Tregelles, and Alford).

The Greek text used in this book is that of the 21st edition of Eberhard Nestle's *Novum Testamentum Graece,* based on the study and critical research of generations of scholars, except that John 7:53–8:11 is not in that text but is relegated to the foot of the page as a critical note. It is here retained in the text. The critical notes of Nestle's work, which enable students to follow the reasons for variations in the text, have been omitted as being outside the scope of this publication. The student who requires these critical notes is referred to the Greek edition published in Great Britain by the British and Foreign Bible Society and in Germany (Stuttgart) by Privilegierte Württembergische Bibelanstalt, by whose permission this recension is used.

Square brackets are found in certain places in the Greek text.

These indicate only that, according to Nestle, some editors include and others omit the word or words so enclosed. Translation has been made here in the usual way.

Avoiding interpretation, then, we give some details of how we have proceeded in the matter of a literal translation. These should be studied and understood if proper use is to be made of this attempt to promote an intelligent reading of the Greek New Testament.

THE ENGLISH TRANSLATION

The Wording in General

The relationship between the Greek text and the interlinear English is as follows: Greek words not required in the translation into English are (a) represented by a short dash, as for example the definite article with proper names. Alternatively (b) italic type is used to show that words or even in some cases letters are not really needed for an idiomatic English rendering. For example, "man" is sometimes redundant (as in Matt. 20:1; Acts 2:22). On the other hand, words supplied in English for which there is no Greek equivalent are placed in square brackets [. . .]. Naturally, there will be differences of judgment as to this practice in the passages involved.

The modern form for the third person singular of verbs (present indicative) has been used (loves) in place of the now obsolete -(e)th (loveth); but the older "ye" has been retained for the nominative ("you" for the oblique cases) of the second person plural pronoun; and "thou" (thee), not "you," for the second person singular. It is a loss that in modern English these differences have disappeared; so unaccustomed are we now to them that even the average reader of the Authorized Version misses the point of Luke 22:31. The loss is even more to be regretted when God is addressed as "You."

Where some word other than the strictly literal one seems to be needed in the translation, the former is printed in parentheses immediately after the latter—e.g., Matthew 10:17, "beware from (of) men."

Occasionally it is not feasible to give a literal rendering without undue explanation; some idiomatic word or phrase has to be used. There are only a few of such passages, and they are indicated by the mark †.

There are a number of Greek phrases, other than where † is used, which are to be taken as a whole, not word for word:

ἐπὶ τὸ αὐτό = "on the same" = "together"
διὰ τοῦτο = "because-of this" = "therefore"
ἵνα μή = "in-order-that not" = "lest"
καθ᾽ ὑπερβολήν = "by-way-of excess" = "excessively"

Εὐαγγελίζω. This and its cognate noun have been anglicized (evangelize, evangel). But while we can "evangelize" a city, we do not "evangelize" a person or a subject; so we must speak of "preaching (good tidings) to" a person or of "preaching" a subject. We can, of course, speak of "evangelizing" absolutely as in 1 Corinthians 1:17. Ellicott on 1 Thessalonians 3:6 has some useful information for the student.

Verbs

The ending of a Greek verb normally indicates the person (1st, 2nd, or 3rd, sing. or pl.). If the pronoun is separately expressed, this can be clearly seen in the interlinear translation.

Where there is more than one subject of a verb, Greek will often put the verb in the singular to agree with the nearest subject. This is not in accordance with English grammar, which requires a plural verb if there is more than one subject. In Revelation 9:2, "sun" and "air" call for the plural "were darkened," as in the Authorized Version. But the Greek verb is in the singular. It is sometimes typographically possible to indicate the difference of grammatical usage.

A peculiarity of Greek construction is that a neuter plural subject may take a singular verb; but this is by no means invariable, and there appears to be no rule to go by. In translating, the position is sometimes shown by the use of an italic letter for the ending of the verb ([they] commit*s*); at other times the alternative is given in parenthesis (is(are)). But there are places where neither course is possible without taking up too much space, and the matter is left to the intelligence of the reader.

The subjunctive mood is dying out in English, and no attempt has been made to represent consistently the Greek mood, except by the use of the analytic form "I may . . . ," with its related optative (of which latter there are only thirty-seven examples in the New Testament, fifteen of these being the familiar γένοιτο = "may it be"). But such words as ἵνα and compounds of ἄν (ὅταν, ἐάν), etc., introducing a subjective or hypothetical element into a verbal idea, must be followed by the subjunctive mood.

The Greek perfect can generally be taken as represented by an English present—a past action continuing in its effect down to the present, in contrast to an action wholly in the past. But in a literal translation the English perfect has been retained. In John 11:27, the Authorized Version is idiomatically correct, but the Revised Version is literally so (πεπίστευκα = "I have believed"); compare 2 Timothy 1:12, where the Authorized Version adopts the literal equivalent. So, for example, τετέλεσται = "it has been finished" = "it is finished." In participles, italics show that the auxiliary verbs may be dispensed with in English.

The interlinear translation has introduced a comma after "Behold" in a number of places. The reason for this is as follows. The Greek ἰδού (or other form), properly an imperative of the defective verb ὁράω, is used as an exclamation, as is its English equivalent. That is to say, it is not then an active verb taking a direct object in the accusative case; it is simply exclamatory and is followed by a noun in the nominative, with its predicate or complement understood. For example, in John 1:29, there is no command to behold the Lamb of God; instead, the idea is, "Look! [there goes]. . . ." The position is different in such passages as Matthew 28:6 and Romans 11:22, where there is a command.

Greek will often use a preposition in a compound verb and then repeat it (or use one similar) before a noun in the same sentence; in such passages the preposition would not be used twice in English. But in such a phrase as εἰσέρχεσθαι εἰς οἶκον we can say "to enter into a house" (the counterpart in French being *entrer dans une maison*). We can indeed say simply "to enter a house." Another exception would be ἀπέρχεσθαι ἀπό ("to go away from"). But διαφέρειν διὰ τοῦ ἱεροῦ means "to carry *through* through the temple" (e.g., Mark 11:16).

Necessity or compulsion is most frequently expressed by the use of an impersonal verb (or a verb used impersonally), with the person concerned in the accusative as the object of the verb (δεῖ με = "it behoves me" = "I must").

Participles

Greek is "a participle-loving language," said the late A. T. Robertson, and it uses this part of speech much more frequently than we do, and in different ways.

To begin with, it is absolutely essential to grasp the distinction between *continuous, momentary,* and *completed* action. The first is commonly, but wrongly, spoken of as a present participle, the second as an aorist (which does not mean "past"), and the third as a perfect. (There is a rare future participle—continuous in the future.)

1. A participle may be used as an adjective qualifying a noun,

just as in English (e.g., 1 Thess. 1:9—"a living God"; Heb. 7:8—"dying men"). This is so simple as not to need further remark.

2. A participle may be used, again as in English, as a verb to describe some action (e.g., Acts 9:39—"all the widows stood by . . . weeping and showing. . .").

3. A participle may be used, with the definite article, with, say, "one" understood, where we should use a noun or a relative phrase (e.g., frequently, ὁ πιστεύων = "the [one] believing" = "the believer" *or* "he who believes"). Here the participle is continuous; in Luke 1:45, it is momentary (and, naturally, feminine in gender, referring to Mary's one act of faith at the Annunciation). If two participles are used with but one definite article, as in John 5:24, the meaning is that one person is doubly described, not two persons doing two things. This feature has been preserved in our translation.

4. Very frequently indeed, where in English we use two or more finite verbs to describe associated actions, Greek will use participles and only one finite verb for the main action. But here judgment is necessary to distinguish two (or more) simultaneous actions from consecutive ones; and as we have no aorist participle in English the matter is not always free from difficulty. In Acts 10:34 ("Peter opening his mouth said") the two actions were obviously simultaneous! Likewise, Acts 1:24 ("Praying they said"). But sometimes one action must be completed before another could begin (e.g., Luke 22:17—"having given thanks, he said . . ."). Here the act of giving thanks to God would be complete before Jesus addressed His disciples; therefore the aorist participle must be represented in English by the analytic "having given thanks." That this is not unimportant is shown by Matthew 26:30 ("having sung a hymn they went out"). To translate the aorist participle here by "singing a hymn" would certainly convey the idea that the singing occurred as they went out. In Acts 21:14, it is not easy to see how the keeping silence and the saying could be contemporaneous ("Having said, The will of the Lord be done, we kept silence"). These few examples should, we think, suffice to show the principles involved.

Negatives

As the negatives οὐ(κ) (categorical) and μή (hypothetical) are easily recognizable, it has not been thought necessary always to render them separately, but they are included with any verb with which they may be used. But whereas in English the negative follows the verb, in Greek it precedes (e.g., Matt. 3:11). If such a phrase happens to be broken at the end of a line, this course has not been feasible.

The double negative οὐ μή has been consistently rendered "by no means."

Incidentally, though of importance, these two negative particles, or their compounds, when introducing questions, expect different answers. οὐ appeals to the fact, anticipating "Yes, it is so" (e.g., John 11:9, "Are there not twelve hours of the day?"). The answer would be "Yes, there are." On the contrary, μή denies the suggestion and expects the reply "No, it is not so"; or, if not so explicit as that, doubts whether it is so (e.g., John 18:35). The form of the question in the Authorized Version and the Revised Version indicates that Pilate was asking for information, whereas he was rejecting the idea with scorn and contempt—"I am not a Jew [am I]?" The answer, if any, would be—"No, certainly not." This distinction is largely overlooked in the English Versions. To assist to the correct nuance of thought, in such places the latter negative in the interlinear translation is italicized, and the reader must read into the original what is intended; the result is sometimes surprising. An article in *The Bible Translator* for January 1953 may be consulted.

While on the subject of negatives, Greek favors the use of two such, one strengthening the other. In such sentences the second negative has to be replaced in English by a positive (e.g., Matt. 22:46).

Nouns

In familiar proper names there will appear some inconsistency, a compromise between the actual spellings preferred by Nestle and the Authorized Version; but this is of no great importance.

In Greek, gender belongs to the word and not necessarily to what is indicated by the word; whereas, of course, in English we keep the ideas of masculine, feminine, and neuter to men, women, and inanimate things respectively—English, by the way, being the only great modern language to do so. Allowance must be made for this in translating; sometimes it is possible to transfer the idea from one language to another. The note to Revelation 13:1 may be consulted.

It has not been considered necessary always to indicate the order of a noun and its adjective; a knowledge of English is sufficient for this. But where there is any risk of ambiguity, small superior figures indicate the order in which the words should be read.

Adjectives

The construction of the demonstrative adjectives is peculiar in Greek. The definite article is used as well as the demonstrative adjective in one of two possible positions: either—

$$\text{οὗτος ὁ οἶκος}$$
this *the* house

or—

$$\text{ὁ οἶκος οὗτος}$$
the house this

The definite article is of course not wanted in English, and the proper translation of the phrase is obvious—"this house." Similarly ἐκεῖνος ("that"). It is sometimes possible typographically to treat the three-word phrase as a whole, with the idiomatic translation underneath.

There is no indefinite article in Greek. The use of it in translation is a matter of individual judgment. The numeral "one" is sometimes found; whether this means that just one, and no more, is to be understood is again open to argument (e.g., Matt. 21:19; 26:69). We have inserted "a" or "an" as a matter of course where it seems called for.

The definite article must sometimes be rendered by a pronoun or a possessive adjective. This is particularly so where parts of the body are indicated (e.g., Matt. 8:3). Sometimes it is used "pronominally"—that is, it must be rendered "he" (or otherwise according to the gender) or "they" (e.g., Mark 10:4).

Similarly, the definite article is used in Greek with a possessive adjective, as in Matthew 18:20—

$$\text{εἰς τὸ ἐμὸν ὄνομα}$$
in *the* my name

or, alternatively, the construction may be, say—

$$\text{εἰς τὸ ὄνομα τὸ ἐμόν}$$
in *the* name *the* my

This remark applies only to the first and second persons, singular and plural, not to the third, where the only possible construction in this respect would be "in the name of him/her/them." This has been followed literally, as the reader can always make the necessary English construction for himself. Occasionally such a construction as "in the name of me" will be found, meaning the same thing.

The neuter form of an adjective may be used as an adverb. In John 19:35, ἀληθῆ is the neuter of ἀληθής ("true") and must be rendered "truly." So πρῶτον ("firstly"), though "first" is quite often used in English as an adverb. Conversely, an adverb may be used as an adjective (e.g., νῦν, "now" = "present").

The word ταῦτα ("these things," neuter plural) might be rendered by the singular "this," as in the common phrase μετὰ ταῦτα ("after this"); but this liberty has not been taken in the present literal translation.

The gender of an adjective may demand "man," "woman," or "thing" to be supplied (e.g., Matt. 9:27—"two blind men").

There is the *genitive of quality,* of which there are many examples in the New Testament. If in English we say "a man of courage" or "an act of kindness," this is equivalent to "a courageous man" or "a kind act" respectively. We have translated literally, with an occasional footnote where this construction is not generally recognized.

As "first" is used as an adverb as well as "firstly," it has not been thought necessary always to print "first*ly*"; the matter is of no great importance.

Particles

A number of Greek particles are said to be "post-positive"— that is to say, they cannot stand as the first word in a sentence but are found in the second, third, or even the fourth place. Such words must of course be taken first in English; but it has not been thought necessary to show this, as the construction is sufficiently obvious. They include γάρ ("for"), δέ ("and, but, now"), οὖν ("therefore," which can be post-positive in English), τις (a certain), μέν (indeed), and γε ("really"—generally too subtle to be reproduced in English).

μέν . . . δέ. These two particles, in contrasted clauses, are not translatable literally, unless "indeed . . . but" be used, as we have done in some places. But by adopting the phrases "on the one hand . . . on the other" the contrast is brought out. These particles are, in fact, somewhat elusive as to their force. See John 19:24, 32, where μέν has been left untranslated—an example of the difficulty of rendering it satisfactorily in a literal translation.

The word ὅτι as a conjunction, when meaning "that," is used to introduce spoken words as recorded; it is then known as the "recitative ὅτι." In English the original present tense of any verb would in such a construction ("indirect speech") be changed to the past—e.g., "He said that the man was a liar." But Greek retains the original tense as actually used. What the speaker really said was "The man is a liar." The conjunction thus becomes superfluous and the reported words would in modern usage be put within quotation marks, as above. These, however, are not used in this translation (e.g., Matt. 21:3).

Strictly speaking, ἵνα is a "telic" particle—that is, it denotes purpose (τέλος, "an end"); hence a full translation is "in order that." But inasmuch as in New Testament times there was a tendency to use it where ὅτι would be expected, it sometimes means no more than the conjunction "that" (e.g., Matt. 5:29). Sometimes, then, where there may be room for difference of opinion as to its precise force, or even where there is none, "*in order* that" will be found in the literal translation.

Idiomatic constructions

There are five idiomatic Greek constructions that, being of frequent occurrence, call for explanation.

a. The *genitive absolute*. This is made up of a participle and a noun or pronoun, both in the genitive case and agreeing otherwise as well but having no grammatical relation to the context. It is used to indicate time during which, at which, or connected with which something takes place. The close of such a Greek phrase is shown by the superior letter a (e.g., Luke 3:1). There are variations of this. In Luke 12:36, two participles are used with no noun; it has to be supplied from the context. So also 2 Corinthians 7:15, and see the note on Romans 9:11 under "Notes on Particular Passages" below.

b. The *accusative* (or other case) *and infinitive*. Here what is in English the subject of the verb (the doer of the action) is put in the accusative (or other) case, and the verb itself is put in the infinitive. A superior letter b closes such a phrase (e.g., Luke 1:21).

c. The *dative of possession*. The possessor is put in the dative case. The idea may be grasped by comparing our English way of saying that a thing "belongs to so-and-so." The superior letter c shows this idiom (e.g., Luke 1:5, 7, 14).

d. The *genitive of purpose* or *result*. The infinitive of a verb is in the genitive case, as shown by the preceding definite article. The article itself can be ignored. Again the appropriate letter d shows the existence of the idiom (e.g., Matt. 2:13). The same idea can be shown without any article (e.g., Matt. 4:1).

e. The *dative of time*. This shows a point of time "in" or "at" which a thing happens (ἐν may or may not be used). The letter e indicates this (e.g., Luke 2:43; 18:35).

The constructions b and e can sometimes be combined (e.g., Luke 1:8).

Notes on Particular Passages

Mark 10:11—An article by Dr. Nigel Turner in *The Bible Translator* for October 1956 gives good reasons for understanding the verse thus, αὐτήν referring to the last woman mentioned (ἄλλην).

Mark 14:6—The ἐν here is somewhat puzzling. The parallel in Matthew (26:10) has εἰς, which would mean "to," "toward," or "for"; and Mark's ἐν must then be taken as equivalent in meaning to εἰς. This may throw light on 1 John 4:16.

Luke 7:14—It does not seem right to insist here on the passive voice of ἐγέρθητι (cf. 8:54 and, in another connection, 11:8). But our Lord "was raised," as are the dead generally; they do not "rise"; (see 1 Cor. 15, etc.).

John 8:25—"The answer of Jesus is one of the most disputed passages in the Gospel" (Godet). Nestle punctuates as a question; hence we have given what appears to be a reasonable rendering interrogatively.

Acts 7:46—The word οἴκῳ is a manuscript variant for θεῷ. There is some uncertainty as to how this reading arose; see the Authorized Version. Has Psalm 24:6, text and margin, any bearing on the matter?

Acts 18:10—The words λαὸς πολύς must not be understood as meaning "many persons." λαός is the regular word for the chosen people, Israel (almost without exception). Here in Corinth was to be a new community, taking the place of the Jewish population. So translate it "a great people."

Romans 1:12—This refers to their faith (= "confidence") in one another—Paul and his readers. "Mutual" is correct in Authorized Version, but it is generally misunderstood as being equivalent to "common," which it is not.

Romans 9:11—There is no noun agreeing with the two participles. But it is nevertheless a "genitive absolute" construction. The Authorized Version supplies the subject.

2 Corinthians 11:28—There is another view of Paul's words here. The word ἐπίστασις occurs in the New Testament only here and in Acts 24:12. The related noun ἐπιστάτης ("one standing over,"

"superintendent," "master") is peculiar to Luke (six times in his Gospel). Then there is a variant reading in our verse, μου instead of μοι. So the meaning may be—"my daily superintendence *or* attention." This would bring it into line with the remainder of the verse.

Philippians 3:16—This is, according to Burton, the only certain use in the New Testament of the "imperatival infinitive," Romans 12:15 being a probable example. Moulton thinks it highly probable in Titus 2:1–10. The epistolary χαίρειν (Acts 15:23; 23:26; James 1:1) is said to be the same in origin, though a verb of bidding may be assumed, as in fact we do find in 2 John 10, 11. Compare the French warning in railway carriages—*Ne pas se pencher au dehors*. In English we have such a full expression as "You are 'to do' so and so" (e.g., 2 Thess. 3:14). If Nestle's text is accepted here, it is an additional instance to those given under Philippians 3:16 above, though with a negative as a prohibition. (Textus Receptus, etc., give a plain imperative.) But perhaps we may insert "so as" ("mark this man, so as not to mix with him").

2 Timothy 4:3—The construction of the last three words of this verse is difficult. "Having itching ears" may be a workable paraphrase, but it cannot be said to represent literally the actual Greek. There is no word for "having"; and there is nothing corresponding to "itching" as a participial adjective qualifying "ears." τὴν ἀκοήν is accusative singular, the object of a verb—and the only verb is the participle that precedes. This is masculine plural, agreeing with διδασκάλους, and, while this latter is accusative, whereas the participle is nominative, this must be taken as an example of rational rather than grammatical concord. It is the teachers who "tickle" the ears of those concerned.

Hebrews 2:10—That is, it is God who perfected Jesus Christ (the author, or captain, of our salvation) by means of sufferings, whose work it is to lead many sons to glory; ἀγαγόντα ("leading," referring to Jesus) agrees with ἀρχηγόν, not with αὐτῷ ("him," i.e., God). Besides, there is a parallel between Joshua and Jesus, as both leaders of their peoples. In fine, it is the function of a captain to lead, and Jesus is the leader here.

Hebrews 9:16–17—We are aware of the problem in regard to διαθήκη in this passage; but this translation is no place for purporting to settle a question that has divided commentators. It must suffice to say that we have translated the word consistently as "covenant"; the

idea of a legatee receiving something on the death of a testator by
reason of the latter's having made a "testament" or "will" is, so far
as we can see, quite non-biblical. The covenant victim, then, is "the
one making covenant," unless the person establishing the covenant
is to be understood as identifying himself with it; and the covenant is
in fact ratified over the dead body or bodies. But other views are
taken of the matter.

James 2:1—This is an example of two genitives in apposition. There
are other instances of such a construction. In Colossians 1:18, the
meaning must be "of the body (,) *of* the church"—the body is the
church, as verse 24 says. Colossians 2:2 has "of God, of Christ."
For Romans 11:17, see the note at that place. Regarding John 8:44
("of the father (,) *of* the devil"), their father was the Devil.

Revelation 16:14—The word "Almighty" is not an adjective but
another noun in apposition.

NOTE on Matthew 16:3; 27:65; Luke 12:56; Acts 21:37; 1 Thessalonians 4:4; 1 Timothy 3:5; James 4:17; 2 Peter 2:9—As in French, so
in the Greek of the New Testament, we have the idea of "to know
(how) to do" a thing as being the same as "to be able to do" it. But
while the French use only *savoir*, not *connaître,* in this way, both
γινώσκω and οἶδα have this meaning in the New Testament. In fact,
it is the former in Matthew 16:3 and the latter in the parallel in Luke
(12:56). So, in French, *Savez-vous nager?* = Know you to swim? =
Can you swim? In all the above passages this seems to be the
meaning. It may be noted that the Authorized Version so renders the
verbs in some passages, in others giving "know how." The instance
in James 4:17 may be arguable. Philippians 4:12 also may be
considered, and Matthew 7:11 = Luke 11:13.

The New Revised Standard Version

To the Reader

This preface is addressed to you by the Committee of translators, who wish to explain, as briefly as possible, the origin and character of our work. The publication of our revision is yet another step in the long, continual process of making the Bible available in the form of the English language that is most widely current in our day. To summarize in a single sentence: the New Revised Standard Version of the Bible is an authorized revision of the Revised Standard Version, published in 1952, which was a revision of the American Standard Version, published in 1901, which, in turn, embodied earlier revisions of the King James Version, published in 1611.

The need for issuing a revision of the Revised Standard Version of the Bible arises from three circumstances: (*a*) the acquisition of still older Biblical manuscripts, (*b*) further investigation of linguistic features of the text, and (*c*) changes in preferred English usage. Consequently, in 1974 the Policies Committee of the Revised Standard Version, which is a standing committee of the National Council of the Churches of Christ in the U.S.A., authorized the preparation of a revision of the entire RSV Bible.

For the New Testament the Committee has based its work on the most recent edition of *The Greek New Testament,* prepared by an interconfessional and international committee and published by the United Bible Societies (1966; 3rd ed. corrected, 1983; information concerning changes to be introduced into the critical apparatus of the forthcoming 4th edition was available to the Committee). As in that edition, double brackets are used to enclose a few passages that are generally regarded to be later additions to their text, but which we have retained because of their evident antiquity and their importance in the textual tradition. Only in very rare instances have we replaced the text or the punctuation of the Bible Societies' edition by an alternative that seemed to us to be superior. Here and there in the footnotes the phrase, "Other ancient authorities read," identifies alternative readings preserved by Greek manuscripts and early versions. Alternative renderings of the text are indicated by the word "Or."

As for the style of English adopted for the present revision, among the mandates given to the Committee in 1980 by the Division of Education and Ministry of the National Council of Churches of Christ (which now holds the copyright of the RSV Bible) was the directive to continue in the tradition of the King James Bible, but to introduce such changes as are warranted on the basis of accuracy, clarity, euphony, and current English usage. Within the constraints set by the original texts and by the mandates of the Division, the Committee has followed the maxim, "As literal as possible, as free as necessary." As a consequence, the New Revised Standard Version (NRSV) remains essentially a literal translation. Paraphrastic renderings have been adopted only sparingly, and then chiefly to compensate for a deficiency in the English language—the lack of a common gender third person singular pronoun.

During the almost half a century since the publication of the RSV, many in the churches have become sensitive to the danger of linguistic sexism arising from the inherent bias of the English language towards the masculine gender, a bias that in the case of the Bible has often restricted or obscured the meaning of the original text. The mandates from the Division specified that, in references to men and women, masculine-oriented language should be eliminated as far as this can be done without altering passages that reflect the historical situation of ancient patriarchal culture. As can be appreciated, more than once the Committee found that the several, mandates stood in tension and even in conflict. The various concerns had to be balanced case by case in order to provide a faithful and acceptable rendering without using contrived English. In the vast majority of cases, however, inclusiveness has been attained by simple rephrasing or by introducing plural forms when this does not distort the meaning of the passage. Of course, in narrative and in parable no attempt was made to generalize the sex of individual persons.

It will be seen that in prayers addressed to God the archaic second person singular pronouns (*thee, thou, thine*) and verb forms (*art, hast, hadst*) are no longer used. Although some readers may regret this change, it should be pointed out that in the original languages neither the Old Testament nor the New makes any linguistic distinction between addressing a human being and addressing the Deity. Furthermore, in the tradition of the King James Version one will not expect to find the use of capital letters for pronouns that refer to the Deity—such capitalization is an unnecessary innovation that has only recently been introduced into a few

English translations of the Bible. Finally, we have left to the discretion of the licensed publishers such matters as section headings, cross-references, and clues to the pronunciation of proper names.

This new version seeks to preserve all that is best in the English Bible as it has been known and used through the years. It is intended for use in public reading and congregational worship, as well as in private study, instruction, and meditation. We have resisted the temptation to introduce terms and phrases that merely reflect current moods, and have tried to put the message of the Scriptures in simple, enduring words and expressions that are worthy to stand in the great tradition of the King James Bible and its predecessors. It is the hope and prayer of the translators that this version of the Bible may continue to hold a large place in congregational life and to speak to all readers, young and old alike, helping them to understand and believe and respond to its message.

For the Committee,
BRUCE M. METZGER

The New International Version

The New International Version of the New Testament, first published in 1973, is a completely new translation made by many scholars working directly from the Greek. The Greek text used in the work of translation was an eclectic one. Where existing texts differ, the translators made their choice of readings in accord with sound principles of textual criticism. Footnotes call attention to places where there was uncertainty about what constituted the original text. These have been introduced by the phrase "Some MSS add (*or* omit *or* read)."

As in all translations of the Scriptures, the precise meaning of the original text could not in every case be determined. In important instances of this kind, footnotes introduced by "Or" suggest an alternate rendering of the text. In the translation itself, brackets were occasionally used to indicate words or phrases supplied for clarification.

Certain convictions and aims guided the translators. They were all committed to the full authority and complete trustworthiness of the Scriptures. Therefore, their first concern was the accuracy of the translation and its fidelity to the thought of the New Testament writers. While they weighed the significance of the lexical and grammatical details of the Greek text, they strove for more than a word-for-word translation. Because thought patterns and syntax differ from language to language, faithful communication of the meaning of the writers of the New Testament demanded frequent modifications in sentence structure and constant regard for the contextual meanings of words.

Concern for clarity of style—that it should be idiomatic without being idiosyncratic, contemporary without being dated—also motivated the translators and their consultants. They consistently aimed at simplicity of expression, with sensitive attention to the connotation and sound of the chosen word. At the same time, they endeavored to avoid a sameness of style in order to reflect the varied styles and moods of the New Testament writers.

As for the omission of the pronouns "thou," "thee," and

"thine" in reference to the Deity, the translators felt that to retain these archaisms (along with the strange verb forms, such as *doest, wouldest,* and *hadst*) would have violated their aim of faithful translation. The Greek text uses no special pronouns to express reverence for God and Christ. Scripture is not enhanced by keeping, as a special mode of addressing Deity, forms that in the day of the King James Bible were simply the regular pronouns and verbs used in everyday speech, whether referring to God or to man.

The Greek Alphabet

A	α	Alpha	a	
B	β	Beta	b	
Γ	γ	Gamma	g	hard, as in be*g*in[1]
Δ	δ	Delta	d	
E	ε	Epsilon	e	short, as in m*e*t
Z	ζ	Zeta	z	
H	η	Eta	e	long, as in sc*e*ne
Θ	θ	Theta	th	as in *th*in
I	ι	Iota	i	
K	κ	Kappa	k	
Λ	λ	Lambda	l	
M	μ	Mu	m	
N	ν	Nu	n	
Ξ	ξ	Xi	x	
O	o	Omicron	o	short, as in l*o*t
Π	π	Pi	p	
P	ρ	Rho	r	
Σ	σ, *final s*	Sigma	s[2]	
T	τ	Tau	t	
Υ	υ	Upsilon	u	
Φ	φ	Phi	ph	
X	χ	Chi	ch	hard, as in lo*ch*
Ψ	ψ	Psi	ps	
Ω	ω	Omega	o	long, as in thr*o*ne

[1]Except that before κ, χ or another γ, it is nasal—ng, as in a*n*chor.
[2]Sharp as in thi*s*, but flat before β or μ, as in a*s*bestos, di*s*mal.

The left-hand column contains the NRSV text, the right-hand column, the NIV text.

Matthew
Chapter 1
The Genealogy of Jesus the Messiah

AN account of the genealogy[a] of Jesus the Messiah,[b] the son of David, the son of Abraham. 2 Abraham was the father of Isaac, and Isaac the father of Jacob, and Jacob the father of Judah and his brothers, 3and Judah the father of Perez and Zerah by Tamar, and Perez the father of Hezron, and Hezron the father of Aram, 4and Aram the father of Aminadab, and Aminadab the father of Nahshon, and Nahshon the father of Salmon, 5and Salmon the father of Boaz by Rahab, and Boaz the father of Obed by Ruth, and Obed the father of Jesse, 6and Jesse the father of King David.

And David was the father of Solomon by the wife of Uriah, 7and Solomon the father of Rehoboam, and Rehoboam the father of Abijah, and Abijah the father of Asaph,[c] 8and Asaph[c] the father of Jehoshaphat, and Jehoshaphat the father of Joram, and Joram the father of Uzziah, 9and Uzziah the father of Jotham, and Jotham the father of Ahaz, and Ahaz the father of Hezekiah, 10and Hezekiah the father of Manasseh, and Manasseh the father of Amos,[d] and Amos[d] the father of Josiah, 11and Josiah the father of Jechoniah and his brothers, at the time of the deportation to Babylon.

12 And after the deportation to Babylon: Jechoniah was the father of Salathiel, and Salathiel the father of Zerubbabel, 13and Zerubbabel the father of Abiud, and Abiud the father of Eliakim, and Eliakim the

[a] Or birth
[b] Or Jesus Christ
[c] Other ancient authorities read Asa
[d] Other ancient authorities read Amon

ΚΑΤΑ ΜΑΘΘΑΙΟΝ
According to Matthew

1 Βίβλος γενέσεως Ἰησοῦ Χριστοῦ
[The] book of [the] generation of Jesus Christ
υἱοῦ Δαυὶδ υἱοῦ Ἀβραάμ.
son of David son of Abraham.

2 Ἀβραὰμ ἐγέννησεν τὸν Ἰσαάκ, Ἰσαὰκ δὲ
Abraham begat - Isaac, and Isaac
ἐγέννησεν τὸν Ἰακώβ, Ἰακὼβ δὲ ἐγέννησεν τὸν
begat - Jacob, and Jacob begat -
Ἰούδαν καὶ τοὺς ἀδελφοὺς αὐτοῦ, 3 Ἰούδας δὲ
Judas and the brothers of him, and Judas
ἐγέννησεν τὸν Φάρες καὶ τὸν Ζάρα ἐκ τῆς
begat - Phares and - Zara out of -
Θαμάρ, Φάρες δὲ ἐγέννησεν τὸν Ἐσρώμ,
Thamar, and Phares begat - Esrom,
Ἐσρὼμ δὲ ἐγέννησεν τὸν Ἀράμ, 4 Ἀρὰμ δὲ
and Esrom begat - Aram, and Aram
ἐγέννησεν τὸν Ἀμιναδάβ, Ἀμιναδὰβ δὲ
begat - Aminadab, and Aminadab
ἐγέννησεν τὸν Ναασσών, Ναασσὼν δὲ ἐγέννησεν
begat - Naasson, and Naasson begat
τὸν Σαλμών, 5 Σαλμὼν δὲ ἐγέννησεν τὸν Βόες
- Salmon, and Salmon begat - Booz
ἐκ τῆς Ῥαχάβ, Βόες δὲ ἐγέννησεν τὸν Ἰωβὴδ
out of - Rachab, and Booz begat - Obed
ἐκ τῆς Ῥούθ, Ἰωβὴδ δὲ ἐγέννησεν τὸν Ἰεσσαί,
out of - Ruth, and Obed begat - Jesse,
6 Ἰεσσαὶ δὲ ἐγέννησεν τὸν Δαυὶδ τὸν βασιλέα.
and Jesse begat - David the king.
Δαυὶδ δὲ ἐγέννησεν τὸν Σολομῶνα ἐκ τῆς
And David begat - Solomon out of the

τοῦ Οὐρίου, 7 Σολομὼν δὲ ἐγέννησεν
[one who had been the wife]- of Uriah, and Solomon begat
τὸν Ῥοβοάμ, Ῥοβοὰμ δὲ ἐγέννησεν τὸν
- Roboam, and Roboam begat -
Ἀβιά, Ἀβιὰ δὲ ἐγέννησεν τὸν Ἀσάφ, 8 Ἀσὰφ
Abia, and Abia begat - Asaph, and Asaph
δὲ ἐγέννησεν τὸν Ἰωσαφάτ, Ἰωσαφὰτ
begat - Josaphat, and Josaphat
ἐγέννησεν τὸν Ἰωράμ, Ἰωρὰμ δὲ ἐγέννησεν τὸν
begat - Joram, and Joram begat -
Ὀζίαν, 9 Ὀζίας δὲ ἐγέννησεν τὸν Ἰωαθάμ,
Ozias, and Ozias begat - Joatham,
Ἰωαθὰμ δὲ ἐγέννησεν τὸν Ἀχάζ, Ἀχὰζ δὲ
and Joatham begat - Achaz, and Achaz
ἐγέννησεν τὸν Ἐζεκίαν, 10 Ἐζεκίας δὲ
begat - Hezekias, and Hezekias
ἐγέννησεν τὸν Μανασσῆ, Μανασσῆς δὲ ἐγέννησεν
begat - Manasses, and Manasses begat
τὸν Ἀμώς, Ἀμὼς δὲ ἐγέννησεν τὸν Ἰωσίαν,
- Amos, and Amos begat - Josias,
11 Ἰωσίας δὲ ἐγέννησεν τὸν Ἰεχονίαν καὶ
and Josias begat - Jechonias and
τοὺς ἀδελφοὺς αὐτοῦ ἐπὶ τῆς μετοικεσίας
the brothers of him at the deportation
Βαβυλῶνος. 12 Μετὰ δὲ τὴν μετοικεσίαν
of Babylon. And after the deportation
Βαβυλῶνος Ἰεχονίας ἐγέννησεν τὸν Σαλαθιήλ,
of Babylon Jechonias begat - Salathiel,
Σαλαθιὴλ δὲ ἐγέννησεν τὸν Ζοροβαβέλ,
and Salathiel begat - Zorobabel,
13 Ζοροβαβὲλ δὲ ἐγέννησεν τὸν Ἀβιούδ,
and Zorobabel begat - Abiud,
Ἀβιοὺδ δὲ ἐγέννησεν τὸν Ἐλιακίμ, Ἐλιακὶμ δὲ
and Abiud begat - Eliakim, and Eliakim

Matthew
Chapter 1
The Genealogy of Jesus

A RECORD of the genealogy of Jesus Christ the son of David, the son of Abraham:

2Abraham was the father of Isaac,
Isaac the father of Jacob,
Jacob the father of Judah and his brothers,
3Judah the father of Perez and Zerah, whose mother was Tamar,
Perez the father of Hezron,
Hezron the father of Ram,
4Ram the father of Amminadab,
Amminadab the father of Nahshon,
Nahshon the father of Salmon,
5Salmon the father of Boaz, whose mother was Rahab,
Boaz the father of Obed, whose mother was Ruth,
Obed the father of Jesse,
6and Jesse the father of King David.

David was the father of Solomon, whose mother had been Uriah's wife,
7Solomon the father of Rehoboam,
Rehoboam the father of Abijah,
Abijah the father of Asa,
8Asa the father of Jehoshaphat,
Jehoshaphat the father of Jehoram,
Jehoram the father of Uzziah,
9Uzziah the father of Jotham,
Jotham the father of Ahaz,
Ahaz the father of Hezekiah,
10Hezekiah the father of Manasseh,
Manasseh the father of Amon,
Amon the father of Josiah,
11and Josiah the father of Jeconiah[a] and his brothers at the time of the exile to Babylon.

12After the exile to Babylon:
Jeconiah was the father of Shealtiel,
Shealtiel the father of Zerubbabel,
13Zerubbabel the father of Abiud,
Abiud the father of Eliakim,
Eliakim the father of

[a]11 That is, Jehoiachin; also in verse 12

father of Azor, 14 and Azor the father of Zadok, and Zadok the father of Achim, and Achim the father of Eliud, 15 and Eliud the father of Eleazar, and Eleazar the father of Matthan, and Matthan the father of Jacob, 16 and Jacob the father of Joseph the husband of Mary, of whom Jesus was born, who is called the Messiah. e

17 So all the generations from Abraham to David are fourteen generations; and from David to the deportation to Babylon, fourteen generations; and from the deportation to Babylon to the Messiah, e fourteen generations.

The Birth of Jesus the Messiah

18 Now the birth of Jesus the Messiah b took place in this way. When his mother Mary had been engaged to Joseph, but before they lived together, she was found to be with child from the Holy Spirit. 19 Her husband Joseph, being a righteous man and unwilling to expose her to public disgrace, planned to dismiss her quietly. 20 But just when he had resolved to do this, an angel of the Lord appeared to him in a dream and said, "Joseph, son of David, do not be afraid to take Mary as your wife, for the child conceived in her is from the Holy Spirit. 21 She will bear a son, and you are to name him Jesus, for he will save his people from their sins." 22 All this took place to fulfill what had been spoken by the Lord through the prophet:
23 "Look, the virgin
    shall conceive
    and bear a son,

e Or the Christ

ἐγέννησεν τὸν Ἀζώρ, 14 Ἀζὼρ δὲ ἐγέννησεν
begat   -   Azor,   and Azor   begat

τὸν Σαδώκ, Σαδὼκ δὲ ἐγέννησεν τὸν Ἀχίμ,
-   Sadoc,   and Sadoc   begat   -   Achim,

Ἀχὶμ δὲ ἐγέννησεν τὸν Ἐλιούδ, 15 Ἐλιοὺδ δὲ
and Achim   begat   -   Eliud,   and Eliud

ἐγέννησεν τὸν Ἐλεαζάρ, Ἐλεαζὰρ δὲ ἐγέννησεν
begat   -   Eleazar,   and Eleazar   begat

τὸν Ματθάν, Ματθὰν δὲ ἐγέννησεν τὸν Ἰακώβ,
-   Matthan,   and Matthan   begat   -   Jacob,

16 Ἰακὼβ δὲ ἐγέννησεν τὸν Ἰωσὴφ τὸν ἄνδρα
and Jacob   begat   -   Joseph   the husband

Μαρίας, ἐξ ἧς ἐγεννήθη Ἰησοῦς ὁ λεγόμενος
of Mary, of whom   was born   Jesus the [one] called

Χριστός.
Christ.

17 Πᾶσαι οὖν αἱ γενεαὶ ἀπὸ Ἀβραὰμ
Therefore all   the generations from   Abraham

ἕως Δαυὶδ γενεαὶ δεκατέσσαρες, καὶ ἀπὸ
until   David generations   fourteen,   and from

Δαυὶδ ἕως τῆς μετοικεσίας Βαβυλῶνος γενεαὶ
David until the   deportation   of Babylon generations

δεκατέσσαρες, καὶ ἀπὸ τῆς μετοικεσίας Βαβυ-
fourteen,   and from the   deportation   of Baby-

λῶνος ἕως τοῦ Χριστοῦ γενεαὶ δεκατέσσαρες.
lon   until the   Christ generations   fourteen.

18 Τοῦ δὲ Ἰησοῦ Χριστοῦ ἡ γένεσις
- Now   of Jesus   Christ the   birth

οὕτως ἦν. μνηστευθείσης τῆς μητρὸς αὐτοῦ
thus   was.   Being betrothed the   mother   of him
=When his mother Mary was betrothed

Μαρίας τῷ Ἰωσήφ, πρὶν ἢ συνελθεῖν αὐτοὺς
Mary   -   to Joseph,   before to come together them
=before they came together

εὑρέθη ἐν γαστρὶ ἔχουσα ἐκ πνεύματος
she was found in   womb   having of(by) [the] Spirit
= she was pregnant

ἁγίου. 19 Ἰωσὴφ δὲ ὁ ἀνὴρ αὐτῆς,
Holy.   Now Joseph   the husband of her,

δίκαιος ὢν καὶ μὴ θέλων αὐτὴν δειγμα-
just   being and not   wishing her to hold up as an

τίσαι, ἐβουλήθη λάθρα ἀπολῦσαι αὐτήν.
example,   resolved   secretly to dismiss   her.

20 ταῦτα δὲ αὐτοῦ ἐνθυμηθέντος, ἰδοὺ
But these things   him   thinking on,   behold
=while he thought on these things,

ἄγγελος κυρίου κατ' ὄναρ ἐφάνη
an angel   of [the] Lord by   a dream   appeared

αὐτῷ λέγων· Ἰωσὴφ υἱὸς Δαυίδ, μὴ
to him saying: Joseph   son   of David, not

φοβηθῇς παραλαβεῖν Μαρίαν τὴν
fear thou   to take   Mary   the

γυναῖκά σου· τὸ γὰρ ἐν αὐτῇ γεννηθὲν
wife   of thee;   for the thing in   her   begotten

ἐκ πνεύματός ἐστιν ἁγίου. 21 τέξεται δὲ
of [the] Spirit   is   Holy.   And she will bear

υἱόν, καὶ καλέσεις τὸ ὄνομα αὐτοῦ
a son,   and thou shalt call the   name   of him

Ἰησοῦν· αὐτὸς γὰρ σώσει τὸν λαὸν
Jesus;   for he   will save   the   people

αὐτοῦ ἀπὸ τῶν ἁμαρτιῶν αὐτῶν. 22 Τοῦτο δὲ
of him from the   sins   of them.   Now this

ὅλον γέγονεν ἵνα πληρωθῇ τὸ ῥηθὲν
all has occurred in order that might be fulfilled the [thing] spoken

ὑπὸ κυρίου διὰ τοῦ προφήτου λέγοντος·
by   [the] Lord through the   prophet   saying:

23 ἰδοὺ ἡ παρθένος ἐν γαστρὶ ἕξει
Behold the   virgin   in   womb   will have

Azor,
14 Azor the father of Zadok,
Zadok the father of Akim,
Akim the father of Eliud,
15 Eliud the father of Eleazar,
Eleazar the father of Matthan,
Matthan the father of Jacob,
16 and Jacob the father of Joseph, the husband of Mary, of whom was born Jesus, who is called Christ.
17 Thus there were fourteen generations in all from Abraham to David, fourteen from David to the exile to Babylon, and fourteen from the exile to the Christ. b

The Birth of Jesus Christ

18 This is how the birth of Jesus Christ came about: His mother Mary was pledged to be married to Joseph, but before they came together, she was found to be with child through the Holy Spirit. 19 Because Joseph her husband was a righteous man and did not want to expose her to public disgrace, he had in mind to divorce her quietly. 20 But after he had considered this, an angel of the Lord appeared to him in a dream and said, "Joseph son of David, do not be afraid to take Mary home as your wife, because what is conceived in her is from the Holy Spirit. 21 She will give birth to a son, and you are to give him the name Jesus, c because he will save his people from their sins." 22 All this took place to fulfill what the Lord had said through the prophet: 23 "The virgin will be with child and will give birth to a son, and they will call

b 17 Or Messiah. "The Christ" (Greek) and "the Messiah" (Hebrew) both mean "the Anointed One."
c 21 Jesus is the Greek form of Joshua, which means the LORD saves.

and they shall name him Emmanuel," which means, "God is with us." 24 When Joseph awoke from sleep, he did as the angel of the Lord commanded him; he took her as his wife, 25 but had no marital relations with her until she had borne a son;*f* and he named him Jesus.

Chapter 2

The Visit of the Wise Men

IN the time of King Herod, after Jesus was born in Bethlehem of Judea, wise men*g* from the East came to Jerusalem, 2 asking, "Where is the child who has been born king of the Jews? For we observed his star at its rising,*h* and have come to pay him homage." 3 When Herod heard this, he was frightened, and all Jerusalem with him; 4 and calling together all the chief priests and scribes of the people, he inquired of them where the Messiah*e* was to be born. They told him, "In Bethlehem of Judea; for so it has been written by the prophet:

6 'And you, Bethlehem,
  in the land
  of Judah,
 are by no means
  least among the
  rulers of Judah;
 for from you shall
  come a ruler
 who is to shepherd*i*
  my
  people Israel.' "

7 Then Herod secretly called for the wise men*j* and learned from them the exact time when the star had appeared. 8 Then he sent them to Bethlehem, saying, "Go and search dili-

f Other ancient authorities read *her firstborn son*
g Or *astrologers*; Gk *magi*
h Or *in the East*
i Or *rule*
j Or *astrologers*; Gk *magi*

Center column (interlinear)

καὶ τέξεται υἱόν, καὶ καλέσουσιν τὸ
and will bear a son, and they will call the

ὄνομα αὐτοῦ Ἐμμανουήλ, ὅ ἐστιν
name of him Emmanuel, which is

μεθερμηνευόμενον μεθ᾽ ἡμῶν ὁ θεός.
being interpreted with us - God.

24 ἐγερθεὶς δὲ [ὁ] Ἰωσὴφ ἀπὸ τοῦ
Then *being raised - *Joseph from the(his)

ὕπνου ἐποίησεν ὡς προσέταξεν αὐτῷ ὁ
sleep did as bade him the

ἄγγελος κυρίου, καὶ παρέλαβεν τὴν
angel of [the] Lord, and took the

γυναῖκα αὐτοῦ· 25 καὶ οὐκ ἐγίνωσκεν
wife of him; and knew not

αὐτὴν ἕως [οὗ] ἔτεκεν υἱόν· καὶ ἐκάλεσεν
her until she bore a son; and he called

τὸ ὄνομα αὐτοῦ Ἰησοῦν.
the name of him Jesus.

2 Τοῦ δὲ Ἰησοῦ γεννηθέντος ἐν Βηθλέεμ
- Now Jesus having been born*a* in Bethlehem
=when Jesus was born

τῆς Ἰουδαίας ἐν ἡμέραις Ἡρῴδου τοῦ
- of Judæa in [the] days of Herod the

βασιλέως, ἰδοὺ μάγοι ἀπὸ ἀνατολῶν
king, behold magi from [the] east

παρεγένοντο εἰς Ἱεροσόλυμα 2 λέγοντες·
arrived in Jerusalem saying:

ποῦ ἐστιν ὁ τεχθεὶς βασιλεὺς τῶν
Where is the [one] born king of the

Ἰουδαίων; εἴδομεν γὰρ αὐτοῦ τὸν ἀστέρα
Jews? for we saw of him the star

ἐν τῇ ἀνατολῇ, καὶ ἤλθομεν προσκυνῆσαι
in the east, and came to worship

αὐτῷ. 3 ἀκούσας δὲ ὁ βασιλεὺς Ἡρῴδης
him. Now hearing [this] the king Herod

ἐταράχθη, καὶ πᾶσα Ἱεροσόλυμα μετ᾽
was troubled, and all Jerusalem with

αὐτοῦ, 4 καὶ συναγαγὼν πάντας τοὺς
him, and having assembled all the

ἀρχιερεῖς καὶ γραμματεῖς τοῦ λαοῦ
chief priests and scribes of the people

ἐπυνθάνετο παρ᾽ αὐτῶν ποῦ ὁ χριστὸς
he inquired from them where the Christ

γεννᾶται. 5 οἱ δὲ εἶπαν αὐτῷ· ἐν
is being born. And they told him: In

Βηθλέεμ τῆς Ἰουδαίας· οὕτως γὰρ
Bethlehem - of Judæa; for thus

γέγραπται διὰ τοῦ προφήτου· 6 καὶ
it has been written through the prophet: And

σὺ Βηθλέεμ, γῆ Ἰούδα, οὐδαμῶς ἐλαχίστη
thou Bethlehem, land of Juda, *not at all *least

εἶ ἐν τοῖς ἡγεμόσιν Ἰούδα. ἐκ σοῦ γὰρ
*art among the governors of Juda. For out of thee

ἐξελεύσεται ἡγούμενος, ὅστις ποιμανεῖ
will come forth a governor, who will shepherd

τὸν λαόν μου τὸν Ἰσραήλ.
the people of me the Israel.

7 Τότε Ἡρῴδης λάθρα καλέσας τοὺς
Then Herod secretly calling the

μάγους ἠκρίβωσεν παρ᾽ αὐτῶν. τὸν
magi inquired carefully from them the

χρόνον τοῦ φαινομένου ἀστέρος, 8 καὶ
time of the appearing star, and

πέμψας αὐτοὺς εἰς Βηθλέεμ εἶπεν·
sending them to Bethlehem said:

him Immanuel"*d*—which means, "God with us." 24 When Joseph woke up, he did what the angel of the Lord had commanded him and took Mary home as his wife. 25 But he had no union with her until she gave birth to a son. And he gave him the name Jesus.

Chapter 2

The Visit of the Magi

AFTER Jesus was born in Bethlehem in Judea, during the time of King Herod, Magi*e* from the east came to Jerusalem 2 and asked, "Where is the one who has been born king of the Jews? We saw his star in the east*f* and have come to worship him."
3 When King Herod heard this he was disturbed, and all Jerusalem with him. 4 When he had called together all the people's chief priests and teachers of the law, he asked them where the Christ*g* was to be born. 5 "In Bethlehem in Judea," they replied, "for this is what the prophet has written:

6 " 'But you, Bethlehem,
  in the land of Judah,
 are by no means least
  among the rulers of
  Judah;
 for out of you will come
  a ruler
 who will be the
  shepherd of my
  people Israel.' "*h*

7 Then Herod called the Magi secretly and found out from them the exact time the star had appeared. 8 He sent them to Bethlehem and said, "Go and

d 23 Isaiah 7:14
e 1 Traditionally *Wise Men*
f 2 Or *star when it rose*
g 4 Or *Messiah*
h 6 Micah 5:2

gently for the child; and when you have found him, bring me word so that I may also go and pay him homage." 9 When they had heard the king, they set out; and there, ahead of them, went the star that they had seen at its rising,[k] until it stopped over the place where the child was. 10 When they saw that the star had stopped,[l] they were overwhelmed with joy. 11 On entering the house, they saw the child with Mary his mother; and they knelt down and paid him homage. Then, opening their treasure chests, they offered him gifts of gold, frankincense, and myrrh. 12 And having been warned in a dream not to return to Herod, they left for their own country by another road.

The Escape to Egypt

13 Now after they had left, an angel of the Lord appeared to Joseph in a dream and said, "Get up, take the child and his mother, and flee to Egypt, and remain there until I tell you; for Herod is about to search for the child, to destroy him." 14 Then Joseph[m] got up, took the child and his mother by night, and went to Egypt, 15 and remained there until the death of Herod. This was to fulfill what had been spoken by the Lord through the prophet, "Out of Egypt I have called my son."

The Massacre of the Infants

16 When Herod saw that he had been tricked by the wise men,[j] he was infuriated, and he sent and killed all the children in and around Bethlehem who

---

πορευθέντες ἐξετάσατε ἀκριβῶς περὶ τοῦ
Going   question ye   carefully concerning the

παιδίου· ἐπὰν δὲ εὕρητε, ἀπαγγείλατέ
child;   and when ye find,   report

μοι, ὅπως κἀγὼ ἐλθὼν προσκυνήσω αὐτῷ.
to me, so that I also coming may worship him.

9 οἱ δὲ ἀκούσαντες τοῦ βασιλέως ἐπορεύθησαν·
So they hearing   the   king   went;

καὶ ἰδοὺ ὁ ἀστήρ, ὃν εἶδον ἐν τῇ
and behold the star, which they saw in the

ἀνατολῇ, προῆγεν αὐτοὺς ἕως ἐλθὼν
east,   went before them   until coming

ἐστάθη ἐπάνω οὗ ἦν τὸ παιδίον. **10** ἰδόντες
it stood over where was the child.   [2]seeing

δὲ τὸν ἀστέρα ἐχάρησαν χαρὰν μεγάλην
[1]And the star   they rejoiced [with] a joy great

σφόδρα. **11** καὶ ἐλθόντες εἰς τὴν οἰκίαν
exceedingly.   And coming   into the house

εἶδον τὸ παιδίον μετὰ Μαρίας τῆς μητρὸς
they saw the child with Mary the mother

αὐτοῦ, καὶ πεσόντες προσεκύνησαν αὐτῷ,
of him, and falling they worshipped him,

καὶ ἀνοίξαντες τοὺς θησαυροὺς αὐτῶν
and opening   the treasures   of them

προσήνεγκαν αὐτῷ δῶρα, χρυσὸν καὶ
they offered to him gifts, gold   and

λίβανον καὶ σμύρναν. **12** καὶ χρηματισθέντες
frankincense and myrrh.   And having been warned

κατ' ὄναρ μὴ ἀνακάμψαι πρὸς Ἡρώδην,
by a dream not to return to Herod,

δι' ἄλλης ὁδοῦ ἀνεχώρησαν εἰς τὴν
by another way they departed to the

χώραν αὐτῶν.
country of them.

13 Ἀναχωρησάντων δὲ αὐτῶν, ἰδοὺ
Now having departed   them,[a] behold
= when they had departed,

ἄγγελος κυρίου φαίνεται κατ' ὄναρ τῷ
an angel of [the] Lord appears by a dream –

Ἰωσὴφ λέγων· ἐγερθεὶς παράλαβε τὸ
to Joseph saying: Rising   take thou the

παιδίον καὶ τὴν μητέρα αὐτοῦ, καὶ φεῦγε
child   and the mother of him, and flee

εἰς Αἴγυπτον, καὶ ἴσθι ἐκεῖ ἕως ἂν εἴπω
into Egypt,   and be there until   I tell

σοι· μέλλει γὰρ Ἡρῴδης ζητεῖν τὸ παιδίον τοῦ
thee; for [2]is about [1]Herod to seek the child

ἀπολέσαι αὐτό. **14** ὁ δὲ ἐγερθεὶς παρέλαβεν
to destroy[d] him.   So he rising   took

τὸ παιδίον καὶ τὴν μητέρα αὐτοῦ
the child   and the mother of him

νυκτὸς καὶ ἀνεχώρησεν εἰς Αἴγυπτον,
of(by) night and departed   to Egypt,

15 καὶ ἦν ἐκεῖ ἕως τῆς τελευτῆς Ἡρῴδου·
and was there until the death   of Herod;

ἵνα πληρωθῇ τὸ ῥηθὲν ὑπὸ κυρίου
in order that might be fulfilled the [thing] spoken by [the] Lord

διὰ τοῦ προφήτου λέγοντος· ἐξ
through the prophet   saying: Out of

Αἰγύπτου ἐκάλεσα τὸν υἱόν μου.
Egypt   I called the son of me.

16 Τότε Ἡρῴδης ἰδὼν ὅτι ἐνεπαίχθη
Then Herod   seeing that he was mocked

ὑπὸ τῶν μάγων ἐθυμώθη λίαν, καὶ
by the magi   was angered exceedingly, and

ἀποστείλας ἀνεῖλεν πάντας τοὺς παῖδας
sending   killed all   the boy-children

---

make a careful search for the child. As soon as you find him, report to me, so that I too may go and worship him."

9 After they had heard the king, they went on their way, and the star they had seen in the east[i] went ahead of them until it stopped over the place where the child was. 10 When they saw the star, they were overjoyed. 11 On coming to the house, they saw the child with his mother Mary, and they bowed down and worshiped him. Then they opened their treasures and presented him with gifts of gold and of incense and of myrrh. 12 And having been warned in a dream not to go back to Herod, they returned to their country by another route.

The Escape to Egypt

13 When they had gone, an angel of the Lord appeared to Joseph in a dream. "Get up," he said, "take the child and his mother and escape to Egypt. Stay there until I tell you, for Herod is going to search for the child to kill him."

14 So he got up, took the child and his mother during the night and left for Egypt, 15 where he stayed until the death of Herod. And so was fulfilled what the Lord had said through the prophet: "Out of Egypt I called my son."[j]

16 When Herod realized that he had been outwitted by the Magi, he was furious, and he gave orders to kill all the boys in Bethle-

---

[k] Or *in the East*
[l] Gk *saw the star*
[m] Gk *he*

[i] 9 Or *seen when it rose*
[j] 15 Hosea 11:1

were two years old or un-
der, according to the time
that he had learned from
the wise men.ʲ 17 Then was
fulfilled what had been spoken through the prophet
Jeremiah:
18 "A voice was heard in
    Ramah,
    wailing and loud
      lamentation,
    Rachel weeping for
      her children;
    she refused to be
      consoled,
    because they are
      no more."

The Return from Egypt

19 When Herod died, an
angel of the Lord suddenly
appeared in a dream to Joseph in Egypt and said,
20 "Get up, take the child
and his mother, and go to
the land of Israel, for those
who were seeking the
child's life are dead."
21 Then Josephᵐ got up,
took the child and his mother, and went to the land of
Israel. 22 But when he
heard that Archelaus was
ruling over Judea in place
of his father Herod, he was
afraid to go there. And after
being warned in a dream,
he went away to the district
of Galilee. 23 There he
made his home in a town
called Nazareth, so that
what had been spoken
through the prophets might
be fulfilled, "He will be
called a Nazorean."

τοὺς ἐν Βηθλέεμ καὶ ἐν πᾶσι τοῖς
— in Bethlehem and in all the
ὁρίοις αὐτῆς ἀπὸ διετοῦς καὶ κατωτέρω,
districts of it from two years and under,
κατὰ τὸν χρόνον ὃν ἠκρίβωσεν παρὰ τῶν
according to the time which he strictly inquired from the
μάγων. 17 τότε ἐπληρώθη τὸ ῥηθὲν διὰ
magi. Then was fulfilled the [thing] spoken through
Ἰερεμίου τοῦ προφήτου λέγοντος· 18 φωνὴ
Jeremiah the prophet saying: A voice
ἐν Ῥαμὰ ἠκούσθη, κλαυθμὸς καὶ ὀδυρμὸς
in Rama was heard, weeping and mourning
πολύς· Ῥαχὴλ κλαίουσα τὰ τέκνα αὐτῆς,
much; Rachel weeping for the children of her,
καὶ οὐκ ἤθελεν παρακληθῆναι, ὅτι
and would not to be comforted, because
οὐκ εἰσίν.
they are not.

19 Τελευτήσαντος δὲ τοῦ Ἡρῴδου, ἰδοὺ
But dying — Herod,ᵃ behold
= Herod having died,
ἄγγελος κυρίου φαίνεται κατ᾽ ὄναρ τῷ
an angel of [the] Lord appears by a dream
Ἰωσὴφ ἐν Αἰγύπτῳ 20 λέγων· ἐγερθεὶς
to Joseph in Egypt saying: Rising
παράλαβε τὸ παιδίον καὶ τὴν μητέρα
take thou the child and the mother
αὐτοῦ, καὶ πορεύου εἰς γῆν Ἰσραήλ·
of him, and go into [the] land of Israel;
τεθνήκασιν γὰρ οἱ ζητοῦντες τὴν ψυχὴν
for have died the [ones] seeking the life
τοῦ παιδίου. 21 ὁ δὲ ἐγερθεὶς παρέλαβεν
of the child. So he rising took
τὸ παιδίον καὶ τὴν μητέρα αὐτοῦ καὶ
the child and the mother of him and
εἰσῆλθεν εἰς γῆν Ἰσραήλ. 22 ἀκούσας δὲ
entered into [the] land of Israel. But hearing
ὅτι Ἀρχέλαος βασιλεύει τῆς Ἰουδαίας
that Archelaus reigns over — Judæa
ἀντὶ τοῦ πατρὸς αὐτοῦ Ἡρῴδου ἐφοβήθη
instead of the father of him Herod he feared
ἐκεῖ ἀπελθεῖν· χρηματισθεὶς δὲ κατ᾽
there to go; and being warned by
ὄναρ ἀνεχώρησεν εἰς τὰ μέρη τῆς
a dream he departed into the parts —
Γαλιλαίας, 23 καὶ ἐλθὼν κατῴκησεν εἰς
of Galilee, and coming dwelt in
πόλιν λεγομένην Ναζαρέθ· ὅπως πληρωθῇ
a city called Nazareth; so that was fulfilled
τὸ ῥηθὲν διὰ τῶν προφητῶν ὅτι
the [thing] spoken through the prophets[,] —
Ναζωραῖος κληθήσεται.
A Nazarene he shall be called.

---

hem and its vicinity who
were two years old and under, in accordance with the
time he had learned from
the Magi. 17 Then what was
said through the prophet
Jeremiah was fulfilled:

18 "A voice is heard in
    Ramah,
    weeping and great
      mourning,
    Rachel weeping for her
      children
    and refusing to be
      comforted,
    because they are no
      more."ᵏ

The Return to Nazareth

19 After Herod died, an
angel of the Lord appeared
in a dream to Joseph in
Egypt 20 and said, "Get up,
take the child and his mother and go to the land of Israel, for those who were trying to take the child's life
are dead."
21 So he got up, took the
child and his mother and
went to the land of Israel.
22 But when he heard that
Archelaus was reigning in
Judea in place of his father
Herod, he was afraid to go
there. Having been warned
in a dream, he withdrew to
the district of Galilee, 23 and
he went and lived in a town
called Nazareth. So that was
fulfilled what was said
through the prophets: "He
will be called a Nazarene."

Chapter 3

*The Proclamation of John
the Baptist*

IN those days John the
  Baptist appeared in the
wilderness of Judea, pro-
claiming, 2 "Repent, for the
kingdom of heaven has
come near."ⁿ 3 This is the
one of whom the prophet
Isaiah spoke when he said,
  "The voice of one
    crying out in

ⁿ Or is at hand

---

3 Ἐν δὲ ταῖς ἡμέραις ἐκείναις παραγίνεται
Now in — days those arrives
Ἰωάννης ὁ βαπτιστὴς κηρύσσων ἐν τῇ
John the Baptist proclaiming in the
ἐρήμῳ τῆς Ἰουδαίας, 2 λέγων· μετανοεῖτε·
wilderness — of Judæa, saying: Repent ye;
ἤγγικεν γὰρ ἡ βασιλεία τῶν οὐρανῶν.
for has come near the kingdom of the heavens.
3 οὗτος γάρ ἐστιν ὁ ῥηθεὶς διὰ Ἠσαΐου
For this is the [one] spoken [of] through Isaiah
τοῦ προφήτου λέγοντος· φωνὴ βοῶντος
the prophet saying: A voice of [one] crying

Chapter 3

*John the Baptist Prepares
the Way*

IN those days John the
  Baptist came, preaching
in the Desert of Judea 2 and
saying, "Repent, for the
kingdom of heaven is
near." 3 This is he who was
spoken of through the
prophet Isaiah:

  "A voice of one calling

ᵏ18 Jer. 31:15

the wilderness:
'Prepare the way of
the Lord,
make his paths
straight.' "
4 Now John wore clothing
of camel's hair with a leather belt around his waist,
and his food was locusts
and wild honey. 5 Then the
people of Jerusalem and all
Judea were going out to
him, and all the region
along the Jordan, 6 and they
were baptized by him in the
river Jordan, confessing
their sins.
7 But when he saw
many Pharisees and Saddu-
cees coming for baptism,
he said to them, "You
brood of vipers! Who
warned you to flee from the
wrath to come? 8 Bear fruit
worthy of repentance. 9 Do
not presume to say to yourselves, 'We have Abraham
as our ancestor'; for I tell
you, God is able from these
stones to raise up children
to Abraham. 10 Even now
the ax is lying at the root of
the trees; every tree therefore that does not bear
good fruit is cut down and
thrown into the fire.
11 "I baptize you with[o]
water for repentance, but
one who is more powerful
than I is coming after me; I
am not worthy to carry his
sandals. He will baptize
you with[o] the Holy Spirit
and fire. 12 His winnowing
fork is in his hand, and he
will clear his threshing
floor and will gather his
wheat into the granary; but
the chaff he will burn with
unquenchable fire."

ἐν   τῇ   ἐρήμῳ·   ἐτοιμάσατε   τὴν   ὁδὸν
in   the   wilderness: Prepare ye   the   way

κυρίου,   εὐθείας   ποιεῖτε   τὰς   τρίβους
of [the] Lord,   straight   make   the   paths

αὐτοῦ.   4 Αὐτὸς   δὲ   ὁ   Ἰωάννης·   εἶχεν
of him.   Now ²himself   -   ¹John   had

τὸ   ἔνδυμα   αὐτοῦ   ἀπὸ   τριχῶν   καμήλου
the   raiment   of him   from   hairs   of a camel

καὶ   ζώνην   δερματίνην   περὶ   τὴν   ὀσφὺν
and   a girdle   leathern   round   the   loin[s]

αὐτοῦ·   ἡ   δὲ   τροφὴ   ἦν   αὐτοῦ   ἀκρίδες
of him;   and the   food   ²was   ¹of him   locusts

καὶ   μέλι   ἄγριον.   5 Τότε   ἐξεπορεύετο   πρὸς
and   honey   wild.   Then   went out   to

αὐτὸν   Ἱεροσόλυμα   καὶ   πᾶσα   ἡ   Ἰουδαία
him   Jerusalem   and   all   -   Judæa

καὶ   πᾶσα   ἡ   περίχωρος   τοῦ   Ἰορδάνου,
and   all   the   neighbourhood   of the   Jordan,

6 καὶ   ἐβαπτίζοντο   ἐν   τῷ   Ἰορδάνῃ   ποταμῷ
and   were baptized   in   the   Jordan   river

ὑπ'   αὐτοῦ   ἐξομολογούμενοι   τὰς   ἁμαρτίας
by   him   confessing   the   sins

αὐτῶν.   7 Ἰδὼν   δὲ   πολλοὺς   τῶν
of them.   And seeing   many   of the

Φαρισαίων   καὶ   Σαδδουκαίων   ἐρχομένους
Pharisees   and   Sadducees   coming

ἐπὶ   τὸ   βάπτισμα   εἶπεν   αὐτοῖς·   γεννήματα
to   the   baptism   he said   to them: Offspring

ἐχιδνῶν,   τίς   ὑπέδειξεν   ὑμῖν   φυγεῖν   ἀπὸ
of vipers,   who   warned   you   to flee   from

τῆς   μελλούσης   ὀργῆς;   8 ποιήσατε   οὖν
the   coming   wrath?   Produce   therefore

καρπὸν   ἄξιον   τῆς   μετανοίας·   9 καὶ
fruit   worthy   -   of repentance;   and

μὴ   δόξητε   λέγειν   ἐν   ἑαυτοῖς·   πατέρα
think not   to say   among   [your]selves: ²[as] father

ἔχομεν   τὸν   Ἀβραάμ·   λέγω   γὰρ   ὑμῖν   ὅτι
¹We have   -   ¹Abraham;   for I tell   you   that

δύναται   ὁ   θεὸς   ἐκ   τῶν   λίθων   τούτων
²is able   -   ¹God   out of   -   stones   these

ἐγεῖραι   τέκνα   τῷ   Ἀβραάμ.   10 ἤδη   δὲ
to raise   children   -   to Abraham.   And already

ἡ   ἀξίνη   πρὸς   τὴν   ῥίζαν   τῶν   δένδρων
the   axe   at   the   root   of the   trees

κεῖται·   πᾶν   οὖν   δένδρον   μὴ   ποιοῦν
is laid;   therefore every   tree   not   producing

καρπὸν   καλὸν   ἐκκόπτεται   καὶ   εἰς   πῦρ
fruit   good   is cut down   and   into [the] fire

βάλλεται.   11 ἐγὼ   μὲν   ὑμᾶς   βαπτίζω
is cast.   I   indeed   you   baptize

ἐν   ὕδατι   εἰς   μετάνοιαν·   ὁ   δὲ
in   water   to   repentance;   but the [one]

ὀπίσω   μου   ἐρχόμενος   ἰσχυρότερός   μού
after   me   coming   ²stronger ³[than]   ⁴I

ἐστιν,   οὗ   οὐκ   εἰμὶ   ἱκανὸς   τὰ   ὑποδήματα
¹is,   of whom   I am not   worthy   the   sandals

βαστάσαι·   αὐτὸς   ὑμᾶς   βαπτίσει   ἐν   πνεύματι
to bear;   he   ²you   ¹will baptize   in   [the] Spirit

ἁγίῳ   καὶ   πυρί·   12 οὗ   τὸ   πτύον   ἐν   τῇ
Holy   and   fire;   of whom   the   fan [is]   in   the

χειρὶ   αὐτοῦ,   καὶ   διακαθαριεῖ   τὴν   ἅλωνα
hand   of him,   and he will thoroughly cleanse   the threshing-floor

αὐτοῦ,   καὶ   συνάξει   τὸν   σῖτον   αὐτοῦ
of him,   and   will gather   the   wheat   of him

εἰς   τὴν   ἀποθήκην,   τὸ   δὲ   ἄχυρον   κατα-
into   the   barn,   but the   chaff   he will

---

in the desert,
'Prepare the way for the
Lord,
make straight paths for
him.' "[l]
4 John's clothes were
made of camel's hair, and
he had a leather belt around
his waist. His food was locusts and wild honey. 5 People went out to him from
Jerusalem and all Judea
and the whole region of the
Jordan. 6 Confessing their
sins, they were baptized by
him in the Jordan River.
7 But when he saw many
of the Pharisees and Sadducees coming to where he
was baptizing, he said to
them: "You brood of vi-
pers! Who warned you to
flee from the coming
wrath? 8 Produce fruit in
keeping with repentance.
9 And do not think you can
say to yourselves, 'We
have Abraham as our fa-
ther.' I tell you that out of
these stones God can raise
up children for Abraham.
10 The ax is already at the
root of the trees, and every
tree that does not produce
good fruit will be cut down
and thrown into the fire.
11 "I baptize you with[m]
water for repentance. But
after me will come one who
is more powerful than I,
whose sandals I am not fit
to carry. He will baptize
you with the Holy Spirit
and with fire. 12 His winnowing fork is in his hand,
and he will clear his threshing floor, gathering his
wheat into the barn and
burning up the chaff with

---

[o] Or in

[l] 3 Isaiah 40:3
[m] 11 Or in

The Baptism of Jesus

13 Then Jesus came from Galilee to John at the Jordan, to be baptized by him. 14 John would have prevented him, saying, "I need to be baptized by you, and do you come to me?" 15 But Jesus answered him, "Let it be so now; for it is proper for us in this way to fulfill all righteousness." Then he consented. 16 And when Jesus had been baptized, just as he came up from the water, suddenly the heavens were opened to him and he saw the Spirit of God descending like a dove and alighting on him. 17 And a voice from heaven said, "This is my Son, the Beloved,*p* with whom I am well pleased."

καύσει πυρὶ ἀσβέστῳ.
consume with fire unquenchable.

13 Τότε παραγίνεται ὁ Ἰησοῦς ἀπὸ τῆς
Then arrives — Jesus from —

Γαλιλαίας ἐπὶ τὸν Ἰορδάνην πρὸς τὸν
Galilee at the Jordan to —

Ἰωάννην τοῦ βαπτισθῆναι ὑπ' αὐτοῦ.
John — to be baptized[d] by him.

14 ὁ δὲ διεκώλυεν αὐτὸν λέγων· ἐγὼ
But he forbade him saying: I

χρείαν ἔχω ὑπὸ σοῦ βαπτισθῆναι, καὶ σὺ
¹need ¹have ⁴by ⁵thee ²to be baptized, and thou

ἔρχῃ πρός μέ; 15 ἀποκριθεὶς δὲ ὁ
comest to me? But answering —

Ἰησοῦς εἶπεν αὐτῷ· ἄφες ἄρτι· οὕτως γὰρ
Jesus said to him: Permit now; for thus

πρέπον ἐστὶν ἡμῖν πληρῶσαι πᾶσαν
²fitting ¹it is to us to fulfil all

δικαιοσύνην. τότε ἀφίησιν αὐτόν.
righteousness. Then he permits him.

16 βαπτισθεὶς δὲ ὁ Ἰησοῦς εὐθὺς ἀνέβη
And having been baptized - Jesus immediately went up

ἀπὸ τοῦ ὕδατος· καὶ ἰδοὺ ἠνεῴχθησαν
from the water; and behold ²were opened

οἱ οὐρανοί, καὶ εἶδεν πνεῦμα θεοῦ
¹the ²heavens, and he saw [the] Spirit of God

καταβαῖνον ὡσεὶ περιστεράν, ἐρχόμενον ἐπ'
coming down as a dove, coming upon

αὐτόν· 17 καὶ ἰδοὺ φωνὴ ἐκ τῶν
him; and behold a voice out of the

οὐρανῶν λέγουσα· οὗτός ἐστιν ὁ υἱός
heavens saying: This is the son

μου ὁ ἀγαπητός, ἐν ᾧ εὐδόκησα.
of me the beloved, in whom I was well pleased.

unquenchable fire."

The Baptism of Jesus

13 Then Jesus came from Galilee to the Jordan to be baptized by John. 14 But John tried to deter him, saying, "I need to be baptized by you, and do you come to me?" 15 Jesus replied, "Let it be so now; it is proper for us to do this to fulfill all righteousness." Then John consented.

16 As soon as Jesus was baptized, he went up out of the water. At that moment heaven was opened, and he saw the Spirit of God descending like a dove and lighting on him. 17 And a voice from heaven said, "This is my Son, whom I love; with him I am well pleased."

Chapter 4

The Temptation of Jesus

THEN Jesus was led up by the Spirit into the wilderness to be tempted by the devil. 2 He fasted forty days and forty nights, and afterwards he was famished. 3 The tempter came and said to him, "If you are the Son of God, command these stones to become loaves of bread." 4 But he answered, 'One does not live by bread alone, but by every word that comes from the mouth of God.' "

5 Then the devil took him to the holy city and placed him on the pinnacle of the temple, 6 saying to him, "If you are the Son of

4 Τότε ὁ Ἰησοῦς ἀνήχθη εἰς τὴν
Then — Jesus was led up into the

ἔρημον ὑπὸ τοῦ πνεύματος πειρασθῆναι
wilderness by the Spirit to be tempted

ὑπὸ τοῦ διαβόλου. 2 καὶ νηστεύσας ἡμέρας
by the devil. And having fasted days

τεσσεράκοντα καὶ τεσσεράκοντα νύκτας
forty and forty nights

ὕστερον ἐπείνασεν. 3 καὶ προσελθὼν ὁ
afterward he hungered. And approaching the

πειράζων εἶπεν αὐτῷ· εἰ υἱὸς εἶ τοῦ
tempting [one] said to him: If Son thou art of

θεοῦ, εἰπὲ ἵνα οἱ λίθοι οὗτοι ἄρτοι
of God, say *in order* that - stones these ²loaves

γένωνται. 4 ὁ δὲ ἀποκριθεὶς εἶπεν·
¹may become. But he answering said:

γέγραπται· οὐκ ἐπ' ἄρτῳ μόνῳ ζήσεται
It has been written: Not on bread only shall live

ὁ ἄνθρωπος, ἀλλ' ἐπὶ παντὶ ῥήματι
- man, but on every word

ἐκπορευομένῳ διὰ στόματος θεοῦ. 5 Τότε
proceeding through [the] mouth of God. Then

παραλαμβάνει αὐτὸν ὁ διάβολος εἰς τὴν
takes him the devil into the

ἁγίαν πόλιν, καὶ ἔστησεν αὐτὸν ἐπὶ τὸ
holy city, and stood him on the

πτερύγιον τοῦ ἱεροῦ, 6 καὶ λέγει αὐτῷ·
wing of the temple, and says to him:

Chapter 4

The Temptation of Jesus

THEN Jesus was led by the Spirit into the desert to be tempted by the devil. 2 After fasting forty days and forty nights, he was hungry. 3 The tempter came to him and said, "If you are the Son of God, tell these stones to become bread."

4 Jesus answered, "It is written: 'Man does not live on bread alone, but on every word that comes from the mouth of God.'*n*"

5 Then the devil took him to the holy city and had him stand on the highest point of the temple. 6 "If you are

p Or *my beloved Son*

n4 Deut. 8:3

God, throw yourself down;
for it is written,
'He will command his
    angels
    concerning you,'
and 'On their hands
    they will bear
    you up,
so that you will not
    dash your foot
    against a
    stone.' "
7 Jesus said to him, "Again
it is written, 'Do not put the
Lord your God to the
test.' "
8 Again, the devil took
him to a very high moun-
tain and showed him all the
kingdoms of the world and
their splendor; 9 and he said
to him, "All these I will give
you, if you will fall down
and worship me." 10 Jesus
said to him, "Away with
you, Satan! for it is written,
'Worship the Lord
    your God,
    and serve only
    him.' "
11 Then the devil left him,
and suddenly angels came
and waited on him.

*Jesus Begins His Ministry
in Galilee*

12 Now when Jesus *q*
heard that John had been
arrested, he withdrew to
Galilee. 13 He left Nazareth
and made his home in Ca-
pernaum by the sea, in the
territory of Zebulun and
Naphtali, 14 so that what
had been spoken through
the prophet Isaiah might be
fulfilled:
15 "Land of Zebulun,
    land of
    Naphtali,
    on the road by the
        sea, across the
        Jordan, Galilee
        of the
        Gentiles—
16 the people who sat in
        darkness
    have seen a great
        light,
    and for those who sat
        in the region
        and shadow of
        death
    light has dawned."
17 From that time Jesus began to proclaim, "Repent,
for the kingdom of heaven
has come near." *r*

εἰ   υἱὸς   εἶ   τοῦ   θεοῦ,   βάλε   σεαυτὸν
If   Son   thou art   -   of God,   cast   thyself
κάτω·   γέγραπται   γὰρ   ὅτι   τοῖς   ἀγγέλοις
down;   for it has been written[,]   -   To the   angels
αὐτοῦ   ἐντελεῖται   περὶ   σοῦ καὶ ἐπὶ χειρῶν
of him   he will give command   concerning   thee   and on   hands
ἀροῦσίν   σε,   μήποτε   προσκόψῃς   πρὸς
they will bear   thee,   lest   thou strike   against
λίθον   τὸν   πόδα   σου.   7 ἔφη   αὐτῷ   ὁ
a stone   the   foot   of thee.   Said   to him   -
Ἰησοῦς·   πάλιν   γέγραπται·   οὐκ   ἐκπειράσεις
Jesus: Again it has been written: Not overtempt shalt thou
κύριον   τὸν   θεόν   σου.   8 Πάλιν   παρα-
[the] Lord   the   God   of thee.   Again
λαμβάνει   αὐτὸν   ὁ   διάβολος   εἰς   ὄρος
takes   him   the   devil   to   a mountain
ὑψηλὸν   λίαν,   καὶ   δείκνυσιν   αὐτῷ   πάσας
high   exceedingly,   and   shows   him   all
τὰς   βασιλείας   τοῦ   κόσμου   καὶ   τὴν
the   kingdoms   of the   world   and   the
δόξαν   αὐτῶν,   9 καὶ   εἶπεν   αὐτῷ·   ταῦτά
glory   of them,   and   said   to him: These things
σοι   πάντα   δώσω,   ἐὰν   πεσὼν   προσκυνήσῃς
to thee   all   I will give,   if   falling   thou wilt worship
μοι.   10 τότε   λέγει   αὐτῷ   ὁ   Ἰησοῦς·
me.   Then   says   to him   -   Jesus:
ὕπαγε,   σατανᾶ·   γέγραπται   γάρ·   κύριον
Go,   Satan;   for it has been written: [The] Lord
τὸν   θεόν   σου   προσκυνήσεις   καὶ   αὐτῷ
the   God   of thee   thou shalt worship   and   him
μόνῳ   λατρεύσεις.   11 Τότε   ἀφίησιν   αὐτὸν
only   thou shalt serve.   Then   leaves   him
ὁ   διάβολος,   καὶ   ἰδοὺ   ἄγγελοι   προσῆλθον
the   devil,   and   behold   angels   approached
καὶ   διηκόνουν   αὐτῷ.
and   ministered   to him.
12 Ἀκούσας   δὲ   ὅτι   Ἰωάννης   παρεδόθη
Now hearing   that   John   was delivered up
ἀνεχώρησεν   εἰς   τὴν   Γαλιλαίαν.   13 καὶ
he departed   to   -   Galilee.   And
καταλιπὼν   τὴν   Ναζαρὰ   ἐλθὼν   κατῴκησεν
leaving   -   Nazareth   coming   he dwelt
εἰς   Καφαρναοὺμ   τὴν   παραθαλασσίαν   ἐν
in   Capernaum   -   beside the sea   in [the]
ὁρίοις   Ζαβουλὼν   καὶ   Νεφθαλίμ·   14 ἵνα
districts   of Zebulon   and   Naphthali;   in order that
πληρωθῇ   τὸ   ῥηθὲν   διὰ   Ἡσαΐου
might be fulfilled   the [thing]   spoken   through   Isaiah
τοῦ   προφήτου   λέγοντος·   15 γῆ   Ζαβουλὼν
the   prophet   saying: Land   of Zebulon
καὶ   γῆ   Νεφθαλίμ,   ὁδὸν   θαλάσσης,
and   land   of Naphthali,   way   of [the] sea,
πέραν   τοῦ   Ἰορδάνου,   Γαλιλαία   τῶν   ἐθνῶν,
beyond   the   Jordan,   Galilee   of the   nations,
16 ὁ   λαὸς   ὁ   καθήμενος   ἐν   σκοτίᾳ   φῶς
the   people   -   sitting   in   darkness   'light
εἶδεν   μέγα,   καὶ   τοῖς   καθημένοις   ἐν
'saw   'a great,   and   to the [ones]   sitting   in
χώρᾳ   καὶ   σκιᾷ   θανάτου,   φῶς   ἀνέτειλεν
a land   and   shadow   of death,   light   sprang up
αὐτοῖς.
to them.
17 Ἀπὸ   τότε   ἤρξατο   ὁ   Ἰησοῦς   κηρύσσειν
From   then   began   -   Jesus   to proclaim
καὶ   λέγειν·   μετανοεῖτε·   ἤγγικεν   γὰρ
and   to say: Repent ye;   for has drawn near

---

the Son of God," he said,
"throw yourself down. For
it is written:

" 'He will command his
    angels concerning
    you,
and they will lift you
    up in their hands,
so that you will not
    strike your foot
    against a stone.' *o*"

7 Jesus answered him, "It
is also written: 'Do not put
the Lord your God to the
test.' *p*"
8 Again, the devil took
him to a very high moun-
tain and showed him all the
kingdoms of the world and
their splendor. 9 "All this I
will give you," he said, "if
you will bow down and
worship me."
10 Jesus said to him,
"Away from me, Satan!
For it is written: 'Worship
the Lord your God, and
serve him only.' *q*"
11 Then the devil left him,
and angels came and at-
tended him.

Jesus Begins to Preach

12 When Jesus heard that
John had been put in prison, he returned to Galilee.
13 Leaving Nazareth, he
went and lived in Caper-
naum, which was by the lake
in the area of Zebulun and
Naphtali— 14 to fulfill what
was said through the
prophet Isaiah:

15 "Land of Zebulun and
    land of Naphtali,
    the way to the sea,
    along the Jordan,
    Galilee of the
    Gentiles—
16 the people living in
    darkness
    have seen a great light;
on those living in the
    land of the shadow
    of death
    a light has dawned." *r*

17 From that time on Jesus
began to preach, "Repent,
for the kingdom of heaven
is near."

---

q Gk *he*
r Or *is at hand*

o 6 Psalm 91:11,12
p 7 Deut. 6:16
q 10 Deut. 6:13
r 16 Isaiah 9:1,2

Jesus Calls the First Disciples

18 As he walked by the Sea of Galilee, he saw two brothers, Simon, who is called Peter, and Andrew his brother, casting a net into the sea—for they were fishermen. 19 And he said to them, "Follow me, and I will make you fish for people." 20 Immediately they left their nets and followed him. 21 As he went from there, he saw two other brothers, James son of Zebedee and his brother John, in the boat with their father Zebedee, mending their nets, and he called them. 22 Immediately they left the boat and their father, and followed him.

Jesus Ministers to Crowds of People

23 Jesus[s] went throughout Galilee, teaching in their synagogues and proclaiming the good news[t] of the kingdom and curing every disease and every sickness among the people. 24 So his fame spread throughout all Syria, and they brought to him all the sick, those who were afflicted with various diseases and pains, demoniacs, epileptics, and paralytics, and he cured them. 25 And great crowds followed him from Galilee, the Decapolis, Jerusalem, Judea, and from beyond the Jordan.

Chapter 5

The Beatitudes

W HEN Jesus[a] saw the crowds, he went up the mountain; and after he

[s] Gk He
[t] Gk gospel

ἡ βασιλεία τῶν οὐρανῶν.
the kingdom of the heavens.

18 Περιπατῶν δὲ παρὰ τὴν θάλασσαν
And walking beside the sea

τῆς Γαλιλαίας εἶδεν δύο ἀδελφούς, Σίμωνα
of Galilee he saw two brothers, Simon

τὸν λεγόμενον Πέτρον καὶ Ἀνδρέαν τὸν
- called Peter and Andrew the

ἀδελφὸν αὐτοῦ, βάλλοντας ἀμφίβληστρον εἰς
brother of him, casting a net into

τὴν θάλασσαν· ἦσαν γὰρ ἁλεεῖς. 19 καὶ
the sea; for they were fishers. And

λέγει αὐτοῖς· δεῦτε ὀπίσω μου, καὶ
he says to them: Come after me, and

ποιήσω ὑμᾶς ἁλεεῖς ἀνθρώπων. 20 οἱ
I will make you fishers of men. ²they

δὲ εὐθέως ἀφέντες τὰ δίκτυα ἠκολούθη-
¹And immediately leaving the nets fol-

σαν αὐτῷ. 21 Καὶ προβὰς ἐκεῖθεν εἶδεν
lowed him. And going on thence he saw

ἄλλους δύο ἀδελφούς, Ἰάκωβον τὸν τοῦ
other two brothers, James the [son] -

Ζεβεδαίου καὶ Ἰωάννην τὸν ἀδελφὸν
of Zebedee and John the brother

αὐτοῦ, ἐν τῷ πλοίῳ μετὰ Ζεβεδαίου τοῦ
of him, in the boat with Zebedee the

πατρὸς αὐτῶν καταρτίζοντας τὰ δίκτυα
father of them mending the nets

αὐτῶν· καὶ ἐκάλεσεν αὐτούς. 22 οἱ δὲ
of them; and he called them. And they

εὐθέως ἀφέντες τὸ πλοῖον καὶ τὸν
immediately leaving the boat and the

πατέρα αὐτῶν ἠκολούθησαν αὐτῷ.
father of them followed him.

23 Καὶ περιῆγεν ἐν ὅλῃ τῇ Γαλιλαίᾳ,
And he went about in all - Galilee,

διδάσκων ἐν ταῖς συναγωγαῖς αὐτῶν
teaching in the synagogues of them

καὶ κηρύσσων τὸ εὐαγγέλιον τῆς βασιλείας
and proclaiming the gospel of the kingdom

καὶ θεραπεύων πᾶσαν νόσον καὶ πᾶσαν
and healing every disease and every

μαλακίαν ἐν τῷ λαῷ. 24 καὶ ἀπῆλθεν ἡ
illness among the people. And went the

ἀκοὴ αὐτοῦ εἰς ὅλην τὴν Συρίαν· καὶ
report of him into all - Syria; and

προσήνεγκαν αὐτῷ πάντας τοὺς κακῶς
they brought to him all the [ones] ²ill
                                       =those who were ill

ἔχοντας ποικίλαις νόσοις καὶ βασάνοις
¹having ²various ³diseases ⁴and ⁵tortures

συνεχομένους, δαιμονιζομένους καὶ σεληνιαζ-
¹suffering from, demon-possessed and luna-

ομένους καὶ παραλυτικούς, καὶ ἐθεράπευσεν
tics and paralysed, and he healed

αὐτούς. 25 καὶ ἠκολούθησαν αὐτῷ ὄχλοι
them. And ³followed ⁴him ²crowds

πολλοὶ ἀπὸ τῆς Γαλιλαίας καὶ Δεκαπόλεως
¹many from - Galilee and Decapolis

καὶ Ἰεροσολύμων καὶ Ἰουδαίας καὶ πέραν
and Jerusalem and Judæa and beyond

τοῦ Ἰορδάνου.
the Jordan.

5 Ἰδὼν δὲ τοὺς ὄχλους ἀνέβη εἰς
And seeing the crowds he went up into

The Calling of the First Disciples

18As Jesus was walking beside the Sea of Galilee, he saw two brothers, Simon called Peter and his brother Andrew. They were casting a net into the lake, for they were fishermen. 19"Come, follow me," Jesus said, "and I will make you fishers of men." 20At once they left their nets and followed him.

21Going on from there, he saw two other brothers, James son of Zebedee and his brother John. They were in a boat with their father Zebedee, preparing their nets. Jesus called them, 22and immediately they left the boat and their father and followed him.

Jesus Heals the Sick

23Jesus went throughout Galilee, teaching in their synagogues, preaching the good news of the kingdom, and healing every disease and sickness among the people. 24News about him spread all over Syria, and people brought to him all who were ill with various diseases, those suffering severe pain, the demon-possessed, those having seizures, and the paralyzed, and he healed them. 25Large crowds from Galilee, the Decapolis,[s] Jerusalem, Judea and the region across the Jordan followed him.

Chapter 5

The Beatitudes

N OW when he saw the crowds, he went up

[s]25 That is, the Ten Cities

sat down, his disciples came to him. 2Then he began to speak, and taught them, saying:

3 "Blessed are the poor in spirit, for theirs is the kingdom of heaven.

4 "Blessed are those who mourn, for they will be comforted.

5 "Blessed are the meek, for they will inherit the earth.

6 "Blessed are those who hunger and thirst for righteousness, for they will be filled.

7 "Blessed are the merciful, for they will receive mercy.

8 "Blessed are the pure in heart, for they will see God.

9 "Blessed are the peacemakers, for they will be called children of God.

10 "Blessed are those who are persecuted for righteousness' sake, for theirs is the kingdom of heaven.

11 "Blessed are you when people revile you and persecute you and utter all kinds of evil against you falsely[u] on my account. 12Rejoice and be glad, for your reward is great in heaven, for in the same way they persecuted the prophets who were before you.

Salt and Light

13 "You are the salt of the earth; but if salt has lost its taste, how can its saltiness be restored? It is no longer good for anything, but is thrown out and trampled under foot.

14 "You are the light of the world. A city built on a hill cannot be hid. 15No one after lighting a lamp puts it under the bushel basket, but on the lampstand, and it gives light to all in the house. 16In the same way,

---

τὸ ὄρος· καὶ καθίσαντος αὐτοῦ προσῆλθαν
the mountain; and sitting him[a] [a]approached
                      = when he sat

αὐτῷ οἱ μαθηταὶ αὐτοῦ· 2 καὶ ἀνοίξας τὸ
[a]to him [the] [a]disciples [a]of him; and opening the

στόμα αὐτοῦ ἐδίδασκεν αὐτοὺς λέγων·
mouth of him he taught them saying:

3 Μακάριοι οἱ πτωχοὶ τῷ πνεύματι,
Blessed [are] the poor - in spirit,

ὅτι αὐτῶν ἐστιν ἡ βασιλεία τῶν οὐρανῶν.
for of them is the kingdom of the heavens.

4 μακάριοι οἱ πενθοῦντες, ὅτι αὐτοὶ
Blessed [are] the mourning [ones], for they

παρακληθήσονται. 5 μακάριοι οἱ πραεῖς,
shall be comforted. Blessed [are] the meek,

ὅτι αὐτοὶ κληρονομήσουσιν τὴν γῆν.
for they shall inherit the earth.

6 μακάριοι οἱ πεινῶντες καὶ διψῶντες
Blessed [are] the hungering and thirsting [ones] [after]

τὴν δικαιοσύνην, ὅτι αὐτοὶ χορτασ-
- righteousness, for they shall be

θήσονται. 7 μακάριοι οἱ ἐλεήμονες, ὅτι
satisfied. Blessed [are] the merciful, for

αὐτοὶ ἐλεηθήσονται. 8 μακάριοι οἱ καθαροὶ
they shall obtain mercy. Blessed [are] the clean

τῇ καρδίᾳ, ὅτι αὐτοὶ τὸν θεὸν ὄψονται.
- in heart, for they - [a]God [a]shall see.

9 μακάριοι οἱ εἰρηνοποιοί, ὅτι [αὐτοὶ]
Blessed [are] the peacemakers, for they

υἱοὶ θεοῦ κληθήσονται. 10 μακάριοι οἱ
sons of God shall be called. Blessed [are] the [ones]

δεδιωγμένοι ἕνεκεν δικαιοσύνης, ὅτι αὐτῶν
having been persecuted for the sake of righteousness, for of them

ἐστιν ἡ βασιλεία τῶν οὐρανῶν. 11 μακάριοι
is the kingdom of the heavens. Blessed

ἐστε ὅταν ὀνειδίσωσιν ὑμᾶς καὶ διώξωσιν
are ye when they reproach you and persecute

καὶ εἴπωσιν πᾶν πονηρὸν καθ' ὑμῶν
and say all evil against you

ψευδόμενοι ἕνεκεν ἐμοῦ. 12 χαίρετε
lying for the sake of me. Rejoice

καὶ ἀγαλλιᾶσθε, ὅτι ὁ μισθὸς ὑμῶν
and be glad, because the reward of you [is]

πολὺς ἐν τοῖς οὐρανοῖς· οὕτως γὰρ
much in the heavens; for thus

ἐδίωξαν τοὺς προφήτας τοὺς πρὸ
they persecuted the prophets - before

ὑμῶν.
you.

13 Ὑμεῖς ἐστε τὸ ἅλας τῆς γῆς· ἐὰν δὲ
Ye are the salt of the earth; but if

τὸ ἅλας μωρανθῇ, ἐν τίνι ἁλισθήσεται;
the salt be tainted, by what shall it be salted?

εἰς οὐδὲν ἰσχύει ἔτι εἰ μὴ βληθὲν ἔξω
for nothing is it strong longer except being cast out

καταπατεῖσθαι ὑπὸ τῶν ἀνθρώπων. 14 Ὑμεῖς
to be trodden down by - men. Ye

ἐστε τὸ φῶς τοῦ κόσμου. οὐ δύναται
are the light of the world. [a]Not [a]can

πόλις κρυβῆναι ἐπάνω ὄρους κειμένη·
[a]a city [a]to be hid [a]on [a]a mountain [a]set;

15 οὐδὲ καίουσιν λύχνον καὶ τιθέασιν
nor do they light a lamp and place

αὐτὸν ὑπὸ τὸν μόδιον, ἀλλ' ἐπὶ τὴν
it under the bushel, but on the

λυχνίαν, καὶ λάμπει πᾶσιν τοῖς ἐν τῇ
lampstand, and it lightens all the [ones] in the

---

on a mountainside and sat down. His disciples came to him, and he began to teach them, saying:

3"Blessed are the poor in spirit,
  for theirs is the
  kingdom of heaven.
4Blessed are those who
  mourn,
  for they will be
  comforted.
5Blessed are the meek,
  for they will inherit the
  earth.
6Blessed are those who
  hunger and thirst for
  righteousness,
  for they will be filled.
7Blessed are the merciful,
  for they will be shown
  mercy.
8Blessed are the pure in
  heart,
  for they will see God.
9Blessed are the
  peacemakers,
  for they will be called
  sons of God.
10Blessed are those who
  are persecuted
  because of
  righteousness,
  for theirs is the
  kingdom of heaven.

11"Blessed are you when people insult you, persecute you and falsely say all kinds of evil against you because of me. 12Rejoice and be glad, because great is your reward in heaven, for in the same way they persecuted the prophets who were before you.

Salt and Light

13"You are the salt of the earth. But if the salt loses its saltiness, how can it be made salty again? It is no longer good for anything, except to be thrown out and trampled by men.

14"You are the light of the world. A city on a hill cannot be hidden. 15Neither do people light a lamp and put it under a bowl. Instead they put it on its stand, and it gives light to everyone in

---

[u] Other ancient authorities lack *falsely*

let your light shine before others, so that they may see your good works and give glory to your Father in heaven.

The Law and the Prophets

17 "Do not think that I have come to abolish the law or the prophets; I have come not to abolish but to fulfill. 18 For truly I tell you, until heaven and earth pass away, not one letter,ᵛ not one stroke of a letter, will pass from the law until all is accomplished. 19 Therefore, whoever breaksʷ one of the least of these commandments, and teaches others to do the same, will be called least in the kingdom of heaven; but whoever does them and teaches them will be called great in the kingdom of heaven. 20 For I tell you, unless your righteousness exceeds that of the scribes and Pharisees, you will never enter the kingdom of heaven.

Concerning Anger

21 "You have heard that it was said to those of ancient times, 'You shall not murder'; and 'whoever murders shall be liable to judgment.' 22 But I say to you that if you are angry with a brother or sister,ˣ you will be liable to judgment; and if you insultʸ a brother or sister,ᶻ you will be liable to the council; and if you say, 'You fool,' you will be liable to the hellᵃ of fire. 23 So when you are offering your gift at the altar, if you remember that your brother or sisterᵇ has something against you,

---

οἰκίᾳ. 16 οὕτως λαμψάτω τὸ φῶς ὑμῶν
house. Thus let shine the light of you

ἔμπροσθεν τῶν ἀνθρώπων, ὅπως ἴδωσιν
before — men, so that they may see

ὑμῶν τὰ καλὰ ἔργα καὶ δοξάσωσιν
of you the good works and may glorify

τὸν πατέρα ὑμῶν τὸν ἐν τοῖς οὐρανοῖς.
the Father of you — in the heavens.

17 Μὴ νομίσητε ὅτι ἦλθον καταλῦσαι
Think not that I came to destroy

τὸν νόμον ἢ τοὺς προφήτας· οὐκ ἦλθον
the law or the prophets; I came not

καταλῦσαι ἀλλὰ πληρῶσαι. 18 ἀμὴν γὰρ
to destroy but to fulfil. For truly

λέγω ὑμῖν, ἕως ἂν παρέλθῃ ὁ οὐρανὸς
I say to you, until pass away the heaven

καὶ ἡ γῆ, ἰῶτα ἓν ἢ μία κεραία οὐ
and the earth, iota one or one point by no

μὴ παρέλθῃ ἀπὸ τοῦ νόμου, ἕως ἂν
means shall pass away from the law, until

πάντα γένηται. 19 ὃς ἐὰν οὖν λύσῃ
all things come to pass. *Whoever ¹therefore breaks

μίαν τῶν ἐντολῶν τούτων τῶν ἐλαχίστων
one — commandments of these the least

καὶ διδάξῃ οὕτως τοὺς ἀνθρώπους, ἐλάχιστος
and teaches thus — men, least

κληθήσεται ἐν τῇ βασιλείᾳ τῶν οὐρανῶν·
he shall be called in the kingdom of the heavens;

ὃς δ' ἂν ποιήσῃ καὶ διδάξῃ, οὗτος
but whoever does and teaches, this [one]

μέγας κληθήσεται ἐν τῇ βασιλείᾳ τῶν
great shall be called in the kingdom of the

οὐρανῶν. 20 λέγω γὰρ ὑμῖν ὅτι ἐὰν μὴ
heavens. For I tell you that except

περισσεύσῃ ὑμῶν ἡ δικαιοσύνη πλεῖον
shall exceed of you the righteousness more [than] [that]

τῶν γραμματέων καὶ Φαρισαίων, οὐ μὴ
of the scribes and Pharisees, by no means

εἰσέλθητε εἰς τὴν βασιλείαν τῶν οὐρανῶν.
shall ye enter into the kingdom of the heavens.

21 Ἠκούσατε ὅτι ἐρρέθη τοῖς ἀρχαίοις·
Ye heard that it was said to the ancients:

οὐ φονεύσεις· ὃς δ' ἂν φονεύσῃ,
Thou shalt not kill; and whoever kills,

ἔνοχος ἔσται τῇ κρίσει. 22 ἐγὼ δὲ
liable shall be to the judgment. But I

λέγω ὑμῖν ὅτι πᾶς ὁ ὀργιζόμενος τῷ
tell you that everyone being angry with the

ἀδελφῷ αὐτοῦ ἔνοχος ἔσται τῇ κρίσει·
brother of him liable shall be to the judgment;

ὃς δ' ἂν εἴπῃ τῷ ἀδελφῷ αὐτοῦ ῥακά,
and whoever says to the brother of him[,] Raca,

ἔνοχος ἔσται τῷ συνεδρίῳ· ὃς δ' ἂν εἴπῃ
liable shall be to the council; and whoever says[,]

μωρέ, ἔνοχος ἔσται εἰς τὴν γέενναν
Fool, liable shall be to the gehenna

τοῦ πυρός. 23 ἐὰν οὖν προσφέρῃς τὸ
— of fire. Therefore if thou bringest the

δῶρόν σου ἐπὶ τὸ θυσιαστήριον κἀκεῖ
gift of thee to the altar and there

μνησθῇς ὅτι ὁ ἀδελφός σου ἔχει τι
rememberest that the brother of thee has something

κατὰ σοῦ, 24 ἄφες ἐκεῖ τὸ δῶρόν σου
against thee, leave there the gift of thee

ἔμπροσθεν τοῦ θυσιαστηρίου, καὶ ὕπαγε
before the altar, and go

---

the house. 16 In the same way, let your light shine before men, that they may see your good deeds and praise your Father in heaven.

The Fulfillment of the Law

17 "Do not think that I have come to abolish the Law or the Prophets; I have not come to abolish them but to fulfill them. 18 I tell you the truth, until heaven and earth disappear, not the smallest letter, not the least stroke of a pen, will by any means disappear from the Law until everything is accomplished. 19 Anyone who breaks one of the least of these commandments and teaches others to do the same will be called least in the kingdom of heaven, but whoever practices and teaches these commands will be called great in the kingdom of heaven. 20 For I tell you that unless your righteousness surpasses that of the Pharisees and the teachers of the law, you will certainly not enter the kingdom of heaven.

Murder

21 "You have heard that it was said to the people long ago, 'Do not murder,ᵗ and anyone who murders will be subject to judgment.' 22 But I tell you that anyone who is angry with his brotherᵘ will be subject to judgment. Again, anyone who says to his brother, 'Raca,'ᵛ is answerable to the Sanhedrin. But anyone who says, 'You fool!' will be in danger of the fire of hell.

23 "Therefore, if you are offering your gift at the altar and there remember that your brother has something against you, 24 leave

---

ᵛ Gk one iota
ʷ Or annuls
ˣ Gk a brother; other ancient authorities add without cause
ʸ Gk say Raca to (an obscure term of abuse)
ᶻ Gk a brother
ᵃ Gk Gehenna
ᵇ Gk your brother

ᵗ21 Exodus 20:13
ᵘ22 Some manuscripts brother without cause
ᵛ22 An Aramaic term of contempt

24 leave your gift there before the altar and go; first be reconciled to your brother or sister,^b and then come and offer your gift. 25 Come to terms quickly with your accuser while you are on the way to court^c with him, or your accuser may hand you over to the judge, and the judge to the guard, and you will be thrown into prison. 26 Truly I tell you, you will never get out until you have paid the last penny.

Concerning Adultery

27 "You have heard that it was said, 'You shall not commit adultery.' 28 But I say to you that everyone who looks at a woman with lust has already committed adultery with her in his heart. 29 If your right eye causes you to sin, tear it out and throw it away; it is better for you to lose one of your members than for your whole body to be thrown into hell.^a 30 And if your right hand causes you to sin, cut it off and throw it away; it is better for you to lose one of your members than for your whole body to go into hell.^a

Concerning Divorce

31 "It was also said, 'Whoever divorces his wife, let him give her a certificate of divorce.' 32 But I say to you that anyone who divorces his wife, except on the ground of unchastity, causes her to commit adultery; and whoever marries a divorced woman commits adultery.

Concerning Oaths

33 "Again, you have heard that it was said to those of ancient times, 'You shall not swear falsely, but carry out the vows you have made to the Lord.' 34 But I say to you, Do not swear at all, either by heaven, for it is the throne of God, 35 or by the

^c Gk lacks *to court*

πρῶτον διαλλάγηθι τῷ ἀδελφῷ σου, καὶ
first be reconciled to the brother of thee, and

τότε ἐλθὼν πρόσφερε τὸ δῶρόν σου.
then coming offer the gift of thee.

25 ἴσθι εὐνοῶν τῷ ἀντιδίκῳ σου
Be well disposed to the opponent of thee

ταχὺ ἕως ὅτου εἶ μετ' αὐτοῦ ἐν τῇ
quickly while thou art with him in the

ὁδῷ· μήποτέ σε παραδῷ ὁ ἀντίδικος τῷ
way; lest ⁴thee ²deliver ¹the ³opponent to the

κριτῇ καὶ ὁ κριτὴς τῷ ὑπηρέτῃ, καὶ
judge and the judge to the attendant, and

εἰς φυλακὴν βληθήσῃ· 26 ἀμὴν λέγω
into prison thou be cast; truly I say

σοι, οὐ μὴ ἐξέλθῃς ἐκεῖθεν ἕως ἂν
to thee, by no means shalt thou come out thence until

ἀποδῷς τὸν ἔσχατον κοδράντην.
thou repayest the last farthing.

27 Ἠκούσατε ὅτι ἐρρέθη· οὐ μοιχεύσεις.
Ye heard that it was said: Thou shalt not commit adultery.

28 ἐγὼ δὲ λέγω ὑμῖν ὅτι πᾶς ὁ βλέπων
But I tell you that everyone seeing

γυναῖκα πρὸς τὸ ἐπιθυμῆσαι [αὐτὴν]
a woman with a view - to desire her

ἤδη ἐμοίχευσεν αὐτὴν ἐν τῇ καρδίᾳ
already committed adultery with her in the heart

αὐτοῦ. 29 εἰ δὲ ὁ ὀφθαλμός σου ὁ δεξιὸς
of him. So if the ²eye ³of thee - ¹right

σκανδαλίζει σε, ἔξελε αὐτὸν καὶ βάλε
⁴causes ⁵to stumble ⁶thee, pluck out it and cast

ἀπὸ σοῦ· συμφέρει γάρ σοι ἵνα ἀπόληται·
from thee; for it is expedient for thee that ⁵perish

ἐν τῶν μελῶν σου καὶ μὴ ὅλον τὸ
¹one ²of the ³members ⁴of thee and not all the

σῶμά σου βληθῇ εἰς γέενναν. 30 καὶ
body of thee be cast into gehenna. And

εἰ ἡ δεξιά σου χείρ σκανδαλίζει σε, ἔκκοψον
if the ¹right ²of thee ³hand ⁴causes ⁵to stumble ⁶thee, cut out

αὐτὴν καὶ βάλε ἀπὸ σοῦ· συμφέρει γάρ
it and cast from thee; for it is expedient

σοι ἵνα ἀπόληται ἓν τῶν μελῶν σου
for thee that ⁵perish ¹one ²of the ³members ⁴of thee

καὶ μὴ ὅλον τὸ σῶμά σου εἰς γέενναν
and not all the body of thee into gehenna

ἀπέλθῃ. 31 Ἐρρέθη δέ· ὃς ἂν ἀπολύσῃ
go away. And it was said: Whoever dismisses

τὴν γυναῖκα αὐτοῦ, δότω αὐτῇ ἀποστάσιον.
the wife of him, let him give her a bill of divorce.

32 ἐγὼ δὲ λέγω ὑμῖν ὅτι πᾶς ὁ ἀπολύων
But I tell you that everyone dismissing

τὴν γυναῖκα αὐτοῦ παρεκτὸς λόγου
the wife of him apart from a matter

πορνείας ποιεῖ αὐτὴν μοιχευθῆναι,
of fornication makes her to commit adultery,

καὶ ὃς ἐὰν ἀπολελυμένην γαμήσῃ,
and whoever ²a dismissed [woman] ¹marries,

μοιχᾶται. 33 Πάλιν ἠκούσατε ὅτι ἐρρέθη
commits adultery. Again ye heard that it was said

τοῖς ἀρχαίοις· οὐκ ἐπιορκήσεις, ἀποδώσεις
to the ancients: Thou shalt not perjure, ²shalt repay

δὲ τῷ κυρίῳ τοὺς ὅρκους σου. 34 ἐγὼ δὲ
¹but to the Lord the oaths of thee. But I

λέγω ὑμῖν μὴ ὀμόσαι ὅλως· μήτε ἐν τῷ
tell you not to swear at all; neither by the

οὐρανῷ, ὅτι θρόνος ἐστὶν τοῦ θεοῦ·
heaven, because [the] throne it is - of God;

---

your gift there in front of the altar. First go and be reconciled to your brother; then come and offer your gift. 25 "Settle matters quickly with your adversary who is taking you to court. Do it while you are still with him on the way, or he may hand you over to the judge, and the judge may hand you over to the officer, and you may be thrown into prison. 26 I tell you the truth, you will not get out until you have paid the last penny.^w

Adultery

27 "You have heard that it was said, 'Do not commit adultery.'^x 28 But I tell you that anyone who looks at a woman lustfully has already committed adultery with her in his heart. 29 If your right eye causes you to sin, gouge it out and throw it away. It is better for you to lose one part of your body than for your whole body to be thrown into hell. 30 And if your right hand causes you to sin, cut it off and throw it away. It is better for you to lose one part of your body than for your whole body to go into hell.

Divorce

31 "It has been said, 'Anyone who divorces his wife must give her a certificate of divorce.'^y 32 But I tell you that anyone who divorces his wife, except for marital unfaithfulness, causes her to become an adulteress, and anyone who marries the divorced woman commits adultery.

Oaths

33 "Again, you have heard that it was said to the people long ago, 'Do not break your oath, but keep the oaths you have made to the Lord.' 34 But I tell you, Do not swear at all: either by heaven, for it is God's throne; 35 or by the earth,

^w 26 Greek *kodrantes*
^x 27 Exodus 20:14
^y 31 Deut. 24:1

earth, for it is his footstool, or by Jerusalem, for it is the city of the great King. 36And do not swear by your head, for you cannot make one hair white or black. 37Let your word be 'Yes, Yes' or 'No, No'; anything more than this comes from the evil one. [d]

Concerning Retaliation

38 "You have heard that it was said, 'An eye for an eye and a tooth for a tooth.' 39But I say to you, Do not resist an evildoer. But if anyone strikes you on the right cheek, turn the other also; 40and if anyone wants to sue you and take your coat, give your cloak as well. 41and if anyone forces you to go one mile, go also the second mile. 42Give to everyone who begs from you, and do not refuse anyone who wants to borrow from you.

Love for Enemies

43 "You have heard that it was said, 'You shall love your neighbor and hate your enemy.' 44But I say to you, Love your enemies and pray for those who persecute you, 45so that you may be children of your Father in heaven; for he makes his sun rise on the evil and on the good, and sends rain on the righteous and on the unrighteous. 46For if you love those who love you, what reward do you have? Do not even the tax collectors do the same? 47And if you greet only your brothers and sisters, [e] what more are you doing than others? Do not even

---

35 μήτε   ἐν   τῇ   γῇ,   ὅτι   ὑποπόδιόν
nor   by   the   earth, because   footstool

ἐστιν   τῶν   ποδῶν   αὐτοῦ·   μήτε   εἰς
it is   of the   feet   of him;   nor   by

'Ιεροσόλυμα,   ὅτι   πόλις   ἐστὶν   τοῦ   μεγάλου
Jerusalem,   because city   it is   of the   great

βασιλέως·   **36** μήτε   ἐν   τῇ   κεφαλῇ   σου
King;   nor   by   the   head   of thee

ὀμόσῃς,   ὅτι   οὐ   δύνασαι   μίαν   τρίχα
swear,   because thou canst not   one   hair

λευκὴν   ποιῆσαι   ἢ   μέλαιναν.   **37** ἔστω
white   to make   or   black.   ¹let ²be

δὲ   ὁ   λόγος   ὑμῶν   ναὶ   ναί,   οὐ   οὔ·
¹But ²the   ⁴word   ⁵of you   Yes   yes,   No   no;

τὸ   δὲ   περισσὸν   τούτων   ἐκ   τοῦ   πονηροῦ
for the   excess   of these   of   -   evil

ἐστιν.   **38** Ἠκούσατε   ὅτι   ἐρρέθη·   ὀφθαλμὸν
is.   Ye heard   that   it was said: An eye

ἀντὶ   ὀφθαλμοῦ   καὶ   ὀδόντα   ἀντὶ   ὀδόντος.
instead of   an eye   and   a tooth   instead of   a tooth.

39 ἐγὼ   δὲ   λέγω   ὑμῖν   μὴ   ἀντιστῆναι
But I   tell   you   not   to oppose

τῷ   πονηρῷ·   ἀλλ'   ὅστις   σε   ῥαπίζει   εἰς
-      evil;   but   who   thee   strikes   on

τὴν   δεξιὰν   σιαγόνα   [σου],   στρέψον   αὐτῷ
the   right   cheek   of thee,   turn   to him

καὶ   τὴν   ἄλλην·   **40** καὶ   τῷ   θέλοντί
also   the   other;   and   to the [one]   wishing

σοι   κριθῆναι   καὶ   τὸν   χιτῶνά   σου   λαβεῖν,
thee   to judge   and   the   tunic   of thee   to take,

ἄφες   αὐτῷ   καὶ   τὸ   ἱμάτιον·   **41** καὶ
allow   him   also   the   [outer] garment;   and

ὅστις   σε   ἀγγαρεύσει   μίλιον   ἕν,   ὕπαγε
who   ²thee   ¹shall impress   ⁴mile   ³one,   go

μετ'   αὐτοῦ   δύο.   **42** τῷ   αἰτοῦντί
with   him   two.   To the [one]   asking

σε   δός,   καὶ   τὸν   θέλοντα   ἀπὸ   σοῦ
thee   give,   and   the [one]   wishing   from   thee

δανείσασθαι   μὴ   ἀποστραφῇς.   **43** Ἠκούσατε
to borrow   turn not away.   Ye heard

ὅτι   ἐρρέθη·   ἀγαπήσεις   τὸν   πλησίον   σου
that   it was said: Thou shalt love   the   neighbour   of thee

καὶ   μισήσεις   τὸν   ἐχθρόν   σου.   **44** ἐγὼ
and   thou shalt hate   the   enemy   of thee.   ²I

δὲ   λέγω   ὑμῖν·   ἀγαπᾶτε   τοὺς   ἐχθροὺς
¹But   tell   you: Love ye   the   enemies

ὑμῶν   καὶ   προσεύχεσθε   ὑπὲρ   τῶν
of you   and   pray ye   for   the [ones]

διωκόντων   ὑμᾶς·   **45** ὅπως   γένησθε   υἱοὶ
persecuting   you;   so that ye may become   sons

τοῦ   πατρὸς   ὑμῶν   τοῦ   ἐν   οὐρανοῖς,
of the   Father   of you   -   in   heavens,

ὅτι   τὸν   ἥλιον   αὐτοῦ   ἀνατέλλει   ἐπὶ
because   the   sun   of him   he makes to rise   on

πονηροὺς   καὶ   ἀγαθοὺς   καὶ   βρέχει   ἐπὶ
evil men   and   good   and   rains   on

δικαίους   καὶ   ἀδίκους.   **46** ἐὰν   γὰρ
just men   and   unjust.   For if

ἀγαπήσητε   τοὺς   ἀγαπῶντας   ὑμᾶς,   τίνα
ye love   the [ones]   loving   you,   what

μισθὸν   ἔχετε;   οὐχὶ   καὶ   οἱ   τελῶναι   τὸ
reward   have ye?   ²not   ³even   ⁴the   ⁵tax-collectors   ⁶the

αὐτὸ   ποιοῦσιν;   **47** καὶ   ἐὰν   ἀσπάσησθε
⁷same   ¹do?   and   if   ye greet

τοὺς   ἀδελφοὺς   ὑμῶν   μόνον,   τί   περισσὸν
the   brothers   of you   only,   what   excess

---

for it is his footstool; or by Jerusalem, for it is the city of the Great King. 36And do not swear by your head, for you cannot make even one hair white or black. 37Simply let your 'Yes' be 'Yes,' and your 'No,' 'No'; anything beyond this comes from the evil one.

An Eye for an Eye

38"You have heard that it was said, 'Eye for eye, and tooth for tooth.' [c] 39But I tell you, Do not resist an evil person. If someone strikes you on the right cheek, turn to him the other also. 40And if someone wants to sue you and take your tunic, let him have your cloak as well. 41If someone forces you to go one mile, go with him two miles. 42Give to the one who asks you, and do not turn away from the one who wants to borrow from you.

Love for Enemies

43"You have heard that it was said, 'Love your neighbor[a] and hate your enemy.' 44But I tell you: Love your enemies[b] and pray for those who persecute you, 45that you may be sons of your Father in heaven. He causes his sun to rise on the evil and the good, and sends rain on the righteous and the unrighteous. 46If you love those who love you, what reward will you get? Are not even the tax collectors doing that? 47And if you greet only your brothers, what are you doing more than others? Do not even pagans

---

[d] Or evil
[e] Gk your brothers

[c]38 Exodus 21:24; Lev. 24:20; Deut. 19:21
[a]43 Lev. 19:18
[b]44 Some late manuscripts enemies, bless those who curse you, do good to those who hate you

the Gentiles do the same? 48 Be perfect, therefore, as your heavenly Father is perfect.

ποιεῖτε; οὐχὶ καὶ οἱ ἐθνικοὶ τὸ αὐτὸ
do ye?   ²not ³even ⁴the ⁵gentiles ⁶the ⁷same
ποιοῦσιν; 48 Ἔσεσθε οὖν ὑμεῖς τέλειοι
¹do?   Be therefore ye perfect
ὡς ὁ πατὴρ ὑμῶν ὁ οὐράνιος τέλειός
as the ²Father ³of you - ¹heavenly perfect
ἐστιν.
is.

do that? 48 Be perfect, therefore, as your heavenly Father is perfect.

Chapter 6

Concerning Almsgiving

"BEWARE of practicing your piety before others in order to be seen by them; for then you have no reward from your Father in heaven.

2 "So whenever you give alms, do not sound a trumpet before you, as the hypocrites do in the synagogues and in the streets, so that they may be praised by others. Truly I tell you, they have received their reward. 3 But when you give alms, do not let your left hand know what your right hand is doing, 4 so that your alms may be done in secret; and your Father who sees in secret will reward you.ᶠ

Concerning Prayer

5 "And whenever you pray, do not be like the hypocrites; for they love to stand and pray in the synagogues and at the street corners, so that they may be seen by others. Truly I tell you, they have received their reward. 6 But whenever you pray, go into your room and shut the door and pray to your Father who is in secret; and your Father who sees in secret will reward you.ᶠ

7 "When you are praying, do not heap up empty phrases as the Gentiles do; for they think that they will be heard because of their many words. 8 Do not be

6 Προσέχετε δὲ τὴν δικαιοσύνην ὑμῶν
  And take ye heed the righteousness of you
μὴ ποιεῖν ἔμπροσθεν τῶν ἀνθρώπων πρὸς
not to do in front of - men with a view to
τὸ θεαθῆναι αὐτοῖς· εἰ δὲ μή γε, μισθὸν
- to be seen by them; otherwise, reward
οὐκ ἔχετε παρὰ τῷ πατρὶ ὑμῶν τῷ
have not with the Father of you -
ἐν τοῖς οὐρανοῖς. 2 Ὅταν οὖν ποιῇς
in the heavens. ²When ¹therefore thou doest
ἐλεημοσύνην, μὴ σαλπίσῃς ἔμπροσθέν σου,
alms, sound not a trumpet before thee,
ὥσπερ οἱ ὑποκριταὶ ποιοῦσιν ἐν ταῖς
as the hypocrites do in the
συναγωγαῖς καὶ ἐν ταῖς ῥύμαις, ὅπως
synagogues and in the streets, so that
δοξασθῶσιν ὑπὸ τῶν ἀνθρώπων· ἀμὴν
they may be glorified by - men; truly
λέγω ὑμῖν, ἀπέχουσιν τὸν μισθὸν αὐτῶν.
I tell you, they have the reward of them.
3 σοῦ δὲ ποιοῦντος ἐλεημοσύνην μὴ
But thee doingᵃ alms not
= when thou doest
γνώτω ἡ ἀριστερά σου τί ποιεῖ ἡ
let know the left [hand] of thee what does the
δεξιά σου, 4 ὅπως ᾖ σου ἡ ἐλεημοσύνη
right of thee, so that ¹may be ²of thee ¹the ⁴alms
ἐν τῷ κρυπτῷ· καὶ ὁ πατήρ σου
in - secret; and the Father of thee
ὁ βλέπων ἐν τῷ κρυπτῷ ἀποδώσει σοι.
the [one] seeing in - secret will repay thee.
5 Καὶ ὅταν προσεύχησθε, οὐκ ἔσεσθε
And when ye pray, be not ye
ὡς οἱ ὑποκριταί· ὅτι φιλοῦσιν ἐν ταῖς
as the hypocrites; because they love in the
συναγωγαῖς καὶ ἐν ταῖς γωνίαις τῶν
synagogues and in the corners of the
πλατειῶν ἑστῶτες προσεύχεσθαι, ὅπως
open streets standing to pray, so that
φανῶσιν τοῖς ἀνθρώποις· ἀμὴν λέγω
they may appear - to men; truly I tell
ὑμῖν, ἀπέχουσιν τὸν μισθὸν αὐτῶν. 6 σὺ
you, they have the reward of them. ⁴thou
δὲ ὅταν προσεύχῃ, εἴσελθε εἰς τὸ ταμιεῖον
¹But ³when ⁴prayest, enter into the private room
σου καὶ κλείσας τὴν θύραν σου πρόσευξαι
of thee and having shut the door of thee pray
τῷ πατρί σου τῷ ἐν τῷ κρυπτῷ·
to the Father of thee the [one] in - secret;
καὶ ὁ πατήρ σου ὁ βλέπων ἐν τῷ
and the Father of thee the [one] seeing in -
κρυπτῷ ἀποδώσει σοι. 7 Προσευχόμενοι δὲ
secret will repay thee. But praying
μὴ βατταλογήσητε ὥσπερ οἱ ἐθνικοί·
do not utter empty words as the gentiles;
δοκοῦσιν γὰρ ὅτι ἐν τῇ πολυλογίᾳ αὐτῶν
for they think that in the much speaking of them

Chapter 6

Giving to the Needy

"BE careful not to do your 'acts of righteousness' before men, to be seen by them. If you do, you will have no reward from your Father in heaven.

2 "So when you give to the needy, do not announce it with trumpets, as the hypocrites do in the synagogues and on the streets, to be honored by men. I tell you the truth, they have received their reward in full. 3 But when you give to the needy, do not let your left hand know what your right hand is doing, 4 so that your giving may be in secret. Then your Father, who sees what is done in secret, will reward you.

Prayer

5 "And when you pray, do not be like the hypocrites, for they love to pray standing in the synagogues and on the street corners to be seen by men. I tell you the truth, they have received their reward in full. 6 But when you pray, go into your room, close the door and pray to your Father, who is unseen. Then your Father, who sees what is done in secret, will reward you. 7 And when you pray, do not keep on babbling like pagans, for they think they will be heard because of their many words. 8 Do

ᶠ Other ancient authorities add openly

like them, for your Father knows what you need before you ask him.
9 "Pray then in this way:

Our Father in heaven, hallowed be your name,
10 Your kingdom come.
Your will be done, on earth as it is in heaven.
11 Give us this day our daily bread. *g*
12 And forgive us our debts, as we also have forgiven our debtors.
13 And do not bring us to the time of trial, *h* but rescue us from the evil one. *i*
14 For if you forgive others their trespasses, your heavenly Father will also forgive you; 15 but if you do not forgive others, neither will your Father forgive your trespasses.

Concerning Fasting

16 "And whenever you fast, do not look dismal, like the hypocrites, for they disfigure their faces so as to show others that they are fasting. Truly I tell you, they have received their reward. 17 But when you fast, put oil on your head and wash your face, 18 so that your fasting may be seen not by others but by your Father who is in secret; and your Father who sees in secret will reward you. *f*

Concerning Treasures

19 "Do not store up for yourselves treasures on earth, where moth and rust *j* consume and where thieves break in and steal; 20 but store up for your-

Middle column (interlinear Greek):

εἰσακουσθήσονται. 8 μὴ οὖν ὁμοιωθῆτε
they will be heard.   Not therefore be ye like

αὐτοῖς· οἶδεν γὰρ [ὁ θεὸς] ὁ πατὴρ
them;   for *knows* – *God* *the* *Father*

ὑμῶν ὧν χρείαν ἔχετε πρὸ τοῦ ὑμᾶς
of you of what things *need* *ye have before* – *you*

αἰτῆσαι αὐτόν. 9 οὕτως οὖν προσεύχεσθε
to ask *him.* *Thus* *therefore* *pray*

ὑμεῖς· Πάτερ ἡμῶν ὁ ἐν τοῖς οὐρανοῖς·
ye: Father of us the [one] in   the   heavens:

Ἁγιασθήτω τὸ ὄνομά σου· 10 ἐλθάτω
Let it be hallowed the   name   of thee;   let it come

ἡ βασιλεία σου· γενηθήτω τὸ θέλημά σου,
the kingdom of thee; let it come about the   will   of thee,

ὡς ἐν οὐρανῷ καὶ ἐπὶ γῆς· 11 Τὸν
as   in heaven   also   on   earth;   The

ἄρτον ἡμῶν τὸν ἐπιούσιον δὸς ἡμῖν
bread *of us* – *daily* *give* *to us*

σήμερον· 12 καὶ ἄφες ἡμῖν τὰ ' ὀφειλή-
to-day;   and forgive us   the   debts

ματα ἡμῶν, ὡς καὶ ἡμεῖς ἀφήκαμεν
of us,   as   indeed   we   forgave

τοῖς ὀφειλέταις ἡμῶν· 13 καὶ μὴ εἰσενέγκῃς
the   debtors   of us;   and not   bring

ἡμᾶς εἰς πειρασμόν, ἀλλὰ ῥῦσαι ἡμᾶς ἀπὸ
us   into temptation,   but   rescue   us   from

τοῦ πονηροῦ. 14 Ἐὰν γὰρ ἀφῆτε τοῖς
–   evil.   For if   ye forgive   –

ἀνθρώποις τὰ παραπτώματα αὐτῶν, ἀφήσει
men   the   trespasses   of them, will forgive

καὶ ὑμῖν ὁ πατὴρ ὑμῶν ὁ οὐράνιος·
also   you   the *Father* *of you* – *heavenly*:

15 ἐὰν δὲ μὴ ἀφῆτε τοῖς ἀνθρώποις,
but if   ye forgive not   –   men,

οὐδὲ ὁ πατὴρ ὑμῶν ἀφήσει τὰ παραπτώ-
neither the   Father   of you will forgive the   tres-

ματα ὑμῶν. 16 Ὅταν δὲ νηστεύητε,
passes   of you.   And when   ye fast,

μὴ γίνεσθε ὡς οἱ ὑποκριταὶ σκυθρωποί·
be not   as   the   hypocrites   gloomy;

ἀφανίζουσιν γὰρ τὰ πρόσωπα αὐτῶν
for they disfigure   the   faces   of them

ὅπως φανῶσιν τοῖς ἀνθρώποις νηστεύοντες·
so that they may appear –   to men   fasting;

ἀμὴν λέγω ὑμῖν, ἀπέχουσιν τὸν μισθὸν
truly   I tell   you,   they have   the   reward

αὐτῶν. 17 σὺ δὲ νηστεύων ἄλειψαί σου
of them.   But thou   fasting   anoint   of thee

τὴν κεφαλὴν καὶ τὸ πρόσωπόν σου νίψαι,
the   head   and the   face   of thee   wash,

18 ὅπως μὴ φανῇς τοῖς ἀνθρώποις νηστεύων
so that appearest not –   to men   fasting

ἀλλὰ τῷ πατρί σου τῷ ἐν τῷ κρυφαίῳ·
but   to the   Father of thee the [one] in   –   secret;

καὶ ὁ πατήρ σου ὁ βλέπων ἐν τῷ
and   the   Father   of thee   the [one] seeing   in   –

κρυφαίῳ ἀποδώσει σοι.
secret   will repay   thee.

19 Μὴ θησαυρίζετε ὑμῖν θησαυροὺς
Do not lay up *treasure*   for you   *treasures*

ἐπὶ τῆς γῆς, ὅπου σὴς καὶ βρῶσις
on   the   earth,   where   moth   and   rust

ἀφανίζει, καὶ ὅπου κλέπται διορύσσουσιν
removes,   and   where   thieves   dig through

καὶ κλέπτουσιν· 20 θησαυρίζετε δὲ ὑμῖν
and   steal;   but lay up *treasure*   for you

not be like them, for your Father knows what you need before you ask him.
9 "This, then, is how you should pray:

" 'Our Father in heaven, hallowed be your name,
10 your kingdom come, your will be done on earth as it is in heaven.
11 Give us today our daily bread.
12 Forgive us our debts, as we also have forgiven our debtors.
13 And lead us not into temptation, but deliver us from the evil one. *c'*

14 For if you forgive men when they sin against you, your heavenly Father will also forgive you. 15 But if you do not forgive men their sins, your Father will not forgive your sins.

Fasting

16 "When you fast, do not look somber as the hypocrites do, for they disfigure their faces to show men they are fasting. I tell you the truth, they have received their reward in full. 17 But when you fast, put oil on your head and wash your face, 18 so that it will not be obvious to men that you are fasting, but only to your Father, who is unseen; and your Father, who sees what is done in secret, will reward you.

Treasures in Heaven

19 "Do not store up for yourselves treasures on earth, where moth and rust destroy, and where thieves break in and steal. 20 But store up for yourselves

g Or *our bread for tomorrow*
h Or *us into temptation*
i Or *from evil.* Other ancient authorities add, in some form. *For the kingdom and the power and the glory are yours forever. Amen.*
j Gk *eating*

c 13 Or *from evil*; some late manuscripts *one*, / *for yours is the kingdom and the power and the glory forever. Amen.*

selves treasures in heaven, where neither moth nor rust[j] consumes and where thieves do not break in and steal. 21 For where your treasure is, there your heart will be also.

The Sound Eye

22 "The eye is the lamp of the body. So, if your eye is healthy, your whole body will be full of light; 23 but if your eye is unhealthy, your whole body will be full of darkness. If then the light in you is darkness, how great is the darkness!

Serving Two Masters

24 "No one can serve two masters; for a slave will either hate the one and love the other, or be devoted to the one and despise the other. You cannot serve God and wealth.[k]

Do Not Worry

25 "Therefore I tell you, do not worry about your life, what you will eat or what you will drink,[l] or about your body, what you will wear. Is not life more than food, and the body more than clothing? 26 Look at the birds of the air; they neither sow nor reap nor gather into barns, and yet your heavenly Father feeds them. Are you not of more value than they? 27 And can any of you by worrying add a single hour to your span of life?[m] 28 And why do you worry about clothing? Consider the lilies of the field, how they grow; they neither toil nor spin, 29 yet I tell you, even Solomon in all his glory was not clothed like one of these. 30 But if God so clothes the grass of the

---

θησαυροὺς ἐν οὐρανῷ, ὅπου οὔτε σὴς
treasures in heaven, where neither moth

οὔτε βρῶσις ἀφανίζει, καὶ ὅπου κλέπται
nor rust removes, and where thieves

οὐ διορύσσουσιν οὐδὲ κλέπτουσιν· 21 ὅπου
do not dig through nor steal; ¹where

γάρ ἐστιν ὁ θησαυρός σου, ἐκεῖ
¹for is the treasure of thee, there

ἔσται καὶ ἡ καρδία σου. 22 Ὁ λύχνος
will be also the heart of thee. The lamp

τοῦ σώματός ἐστιν ὁ ὀφθαλμός. ἐὰν οὖν
of the body is the eye. ²If ¹therefore

ᾖ ὁ ὀφθαλμός σου ἁπλοῦς, ὅλον τὸ σῶμά
⁴be ¹the ²eye ³of thee single, all the body

σου φωτεινὸν ἔσται· 23 ἐὰν δὲ ὁ
of thee shining will be; but if the

ὀφθαλμός σου πονηρὸς ᾖ, ὅλον τὸ σῶμά
eye of thee evil be, all the body

σου σκοτεινὸν ἔσται. εἰ οὖν τὸ φῶς
of thee dark will be. ²If ¹therefore the light

τὸ ἐν σοὶ σκότος ἐστιν, τὸ σκότος
- in thee darkness is, the darkness

πόσον. 24 Οὐδεὶς δύναται δυσὶ κυρίοις
how great. No one can two lords

δουλεύειν· ἢ γὰρ τὸν ἕνα μισήσει καὶ
to serve; for either the one he will hate and

τὸν ἕτερον ἀγαπήσει, ἢ ἑνὸς ἀνθέξεται
the other he will love, or one he will hold to

καὶ τοῦ ἑτέρου καταφρονήσει. οὐ δύνασθε
and the other he will despise. Ye cannot

θεῷ δουλεύειν καὶ μαμωνᾷ. 25 Διὰ
God to serve and mammon. There-

τοῦτο λέγω ὑμῖν, μὴ μεριμνᾶτε τῇ
fore I say to you: Be not anxious for the

ψυχῇ ὑμῶν τί φάγητε [ἢ τί πίητε],
life of you[,] what ye may eat or what ye may drink,

μηδὲ τῷ σώματι ὑμῶν τί ἐνδύσησθε.
nor the body of you[,] what ye may put on.

οὐχὶ ἡ ψυχὴ πλεῖόν ἐστιν τῆς τροφῆς καὶ τὸ
²not ³the ⁴life ⁵more ¹Is [than] the food and the

σῶμα τοῦ ἐνδύματος; 26 ἐμβλέψατε εἰς
body [than] the raiment? Look ye at

τὰ πετεινὰ τοῦ οὐρανοῦ, ὅτι οὐ σπείρουσιν
the birds — of heaven, that they sow not

οὐδὲ θερίζουσιν οὐδὲ συνάγουσιν εἰς
nor reap nor gather into

ἀποθήκας, καὶ ὁ πατὴρ ὑμῶν ὁ οὐράνιος
barns, and the ²Father ³of you — ¹heavenly

τρέφει αὐτά· οὐχ ὑμεῖς μᾶλλον διαφέρετε
feeds them; do not ye more excel

αὐτῶν; 27 τίς δὲ ἐξ ὑμῶν μεριμνῶν
them? But who of you being anxious

δύναται προσθεῖναι ἐπὶ τὴν ἡλικίαν αὐτοῦ
can to add to the stature of him

πῆχυν ἕνα; 28 καὶ περὶ ἐνδύματος τί
cubit one? and concerning clothing why

μεριμνᾶτε; καταμάθετε τὰ κρίνα τοῦ ἀγροῦ,
be ye anxious? consider the lilies of the field,

πῶς αὐξάνουσιν· οὐ κοπιῶσιν οὐδὲ
how they grow; they labour not nor

νήθουσιν· 29 λέγω δὲ ὑμῖν ὅτι οὐδὲ Σολομὼν
spin; but I tell you that not Solomon

ἐν πάσῃ τῇ δόξῃ αὐτοῦ περιεβάλετο ὡς
in all the glory of him was clothed as

ἓν τούτων. 30 εἰ δὲ τὸν χόρτον τοῦ
one of these. But if the grass of the

---

treasures in heaven, where moth and rust do not destroy, and where thieves do not break in and steal. 21 For where your treasure is, there your heart will be also.

22 "The eye is the lamp of the body. If your eyes are good, your whole body will be full of light. 23 But if your eyes are bad, your whole body will be full of darkness. If then the light within you is darkness, how great is that darkness!

24 "No one can serve two masters. Either he will hate the one and love the other, or he will be devoted to the one and despise the other. You cannot serve both God and Money.

Do Not Worry

25 "Therefore I tell you, do not worry about your life, what you will eat or drink; or about your body, what you will wear. Is not life more important than food, and the body more important than clothes? 26 Look at the birds of the air; they do not sow or reap or store away in barns, and yet your heavenly Father feeds them. Are you not much more valuable than they? 27 Who of you by worrying can add a single hour to his life[d]?

28 "And why do you worry about clothes? See how the lilies of the field grow. They do not labor or spin. 29 Yet I tell you that not even Solomon in all his splendor was dressed like one of these. 30 If that is

---

k Gk mammon
l Other ancient authorities lack or what you will drink
m Or add one cubit to your height

d27 Or single cubit to his height

field, which is alive today and tomorrow is thrown into the oven, will he not much more clothe you— you of little faith? 31 Therefore do not worry, saying, 'What will we eat?' or 'What will we drink?' or 'What will we wear?' 32 For it is the Gentiles who strive for all these things; and indeed your heavenly Father knows that you need all these things. 33 But strive first for the kingdom of God*n* and his*o* righteousness, and all these things will be given to you as well. 34 "So do not worry about tomorrow, for tomorrow will bring worries of its own. Today's trouble is enough for today.

ἀγροῦ	σήμερον	ὄντα	καὶ	αὔριον	εἰς
field	to-day	being	and	to-morrow	into

κλίβανον	βαλλόμενον	ὁ	θεὸς	οὕτως
an oven	being thrown	–	God	thus

ἀμφιέννυσιν,	οὐ	πολλῷ	μᾶλλον	ὑμᾶς,
clothes,	not	much	more	you,

ὀλιγόπιστοι;	31 μὴ	οὖν	μεριμνήσητε
little-faiths?	Therefore	be ye	not anxious

λέγοντες·	τί	φάγωμεν;	ἤ·	τί
saying:	What	may we eat?	or:	what

πίωμεν;	ἤ·	τί	περιβαλώμεθα;	32 πάντα
may we drink?	or:	What	may we put on?	*all

γὰρ	ταῦτα	τὰ	ἔθνη	ἐπιζητοῦσιν·	οἶδεν
*for	these things	the	nations	seek after;	*knows

γὰρ	ὁ	πατὴρ	ὑμῶν	ὁ	οὐράνιος	ὅτι
*for	²the	⁴Father	⁵of you	–	³heavenly	that

χρῄζετε	τούτων	ἁπάντων.	33 ζητεῖτε δὲ
ye need	these things	of all.	But seek ye

πρῶτον	τὴν	βασιλείαν	καὶ	τὴν	δικαιοσύνην
first	the	kingdom	and	the	righteousness

αὐτοῦ,	καὶ	ταῦτα	πάντα	προστεθήσεται
of him,	and	these things	all	shall be added

ὑμῖν.	34 μὴ	οὖν	μεριμνήσητε	εἰς	τὴν
to you.	Therefore	be ye	not anxious	for	the

αὔριον,	ἡ	γὰρ	αὔριον	μεριμνήσει
morrow,	for the		morrow	will be anxious

ἑαυτῆς·	ἀρκετὸν	τῇ	ἡμέρᾳ	ἡ	κακία	αὐτῆς.
of itself;	sufficient	to the	day	the	evil	of it.

how God clothes the grass of the field, which is here today and tomorrow is thrown into the fire, will he not much more clothe you, O you of little faith? 31 So do not worry, saying, 'What shall we eat?' or 'What shall we drink?' or 'What shall we wear?' 32 For the pagans run after all these things, and your heavenly Father knows that you need them. 33 But seek first his kingdom and his righteousness, and all these things will be given to you as well. 34 Therefore do not worry about tomorrow, for tomorrow will worry about itself. Each day has enough trouble of its own.

Chapter 7

Judging Others

" DO not judge, so that you may not be judged. 2 For with the judgment you make you will be judged, and the measure you give will be the measure you get. 3 Why do you see the speck in your neighbor's*p* eye, but do not notice the log in your own eye? 4 Or how can you say to your neighbor,*q* 'Let me take the speck out of your eye,' while the log is in your own eye? 5 You hypocrite, first take the log out of your own eye, and then you will see clearly to take the speck out of your neighbor's*p* eye.

Profaning the Holy

6 "Do not give what is holy to dogs; and do not throw your pearls before swine, or they will trample them under foot and turn and maul you.

Ask, Search, Knock

7 "Ask, and it will be given you; search, and you

7 Μὴ	κρίνετε,	ἵνα	μὴ	κριθῆτε·	2 ἐν	ᾧ
Judge not,		lest		ye be judged;	²with	*what

γὰρ	κρίματι	κρίνετε	κριθήσεσθε,	καὶ
*for	judgment	ye judge	ye shall be judged,	and

ἐν	ᾧ	μέτρῳ	μετρεῖτε	μετρηθήσεται	ὑμῖν.
with	what	measure	ye measure	it shall be measured	to you.

3 τί	δὲ	βλέπεις	τὸ	κάρφος	τὸ	ἐν
And why		seest thou	the	chip	–	in

τῷ	ὀφθαλμῷ	τοῦ	ἀδελφοῦ	σου,	τὴν
the	eye	of the	brother	of thee,	*the

δὲ	ἐν	τῷ	σῷ	ὀφθαλμῷ	δοκὸν	οὐ	κατα-
¹but	⁴in	–	⁵thine	⁶eye	³beam	thou	consider-

νοεῖς;	4 ἤ	πῶς	ἐρεῖς	τῷ	ἀδελφῷ	σου·
est not?	or	how	wilt thou say	to the	brother	of thee:

ἄφες	ἐκβάλω	τὸ	κάρφος	ἐκ	τοῦ	ὀφθαλμοῦ
Allow [that] I may pluck *out*		the	chip	out of	the	eye

σου,	καὶ	ἰδοὺ	ἡ	δοκὸς	ἐν	τῷ	ὀφθαλμῷ
of thee,	and	behold	the	beam	in	the	eye

σου;	5 ὑποκριτά,	ἔκβαλε	πρῶτον	ἐκ	τοῦ
of thee?	hypocrite,	pluck *out*	first	out of	the

ὀφθαλμοῦ	σου	τὴν	δοκόν,	καὶ	τότε
eye	of thee	the	beam,	and	then

διαβλέψεις	ἐκβαλεῖν	τὸ	κάρφος	ἐκ
thou wilt see clearly	to pluck *out*	the	chip	out of

τοῦ	ὀφθαλμοῦ	τοῦ	ἀδελφοῦ	σου.	6 Μὴ
the	eye	of the	brother	of thee.	not

δῶτε	τὸ	ἅγιον	τοῖς	κυσίν,	μηδὲ	βάλητε
Give	the	holy	to the	dogs,	neither	cast

τοὺς	μαργαρίτας	ὑμῶν	ἔμπροσθεν	τῶν
the	pearls	of you	before	the

χοίρων,	μήποτε	καταπατήσουσιν	αὐτοὺς
pigs,	lest	they will trample	them

ἐν	τοῖς	ποσὶν	αὐτῶν	καὶ	στραφέντες
with	the	feet	of them	and	turning

ῥήξωσιν	ὑμᾶς.	7 Αἰτεῖτε,	καὶ	δοθήσεται
may rend	you.	Ask,	and	it shall be given

Chapter 7

Judging Others

" DO not judge, or you too will be judged. 2 For in the same way you judge others, you will be judged, and with the measure you use, it will be measured to you.

3 "Why do you look at the speck of sawdust in your brother's eye and pay no attention to the plank in your own eye? 4 How can you say to your brother, 'Let me take the speck out of your eye,' when all the time there is a plank in your own eye? 5 You hypocrite, first take the plank out of your own eye, and then you will see clearly to remove the speck from your brother's eye.

6 "Do not give dogs what is sacred; do not throw your pearls to pigs. If you do, they may trample them under their feet, and then turn and tear you to pieces.

Ask, Seek, Knock

7 "Ask and it will be given

n Other ancient authorities lack *of God*
o Or *its*
p Gk *brother's*
q Gk *brother*

will find; knock, and the door will be opened for you. 8For everyone who asks receives, and everyone who searches finds, and for everyone who knocks, the door will be opened. 9Is there anyone among you who, if your child asks for bread, will give a stone? 10Or if the child asks for a fish, will give a snake? 11If you then, who are evil, know how to give good gifts to your children, how much more will your Father in heaven give good things to those who ask him!

The Golden Rule

12 "In everything do to others as you would have them do to you; for this is the law and the prophets.

The Narrow Gate

13 "Enter through the narrow gate; for the gate is wide that leads to destruction,[r] and there are many who take it. 14For the gate is narrow and the road is hard that leads to life, and there are few who find it.

A Tree and Its Fruit

15 "Beware of false prophets, who come to you in sheep's clothing but inwardly are ravenous wolves. 16You will know them by their fruits. Are grapes gathered from thorns, or figs from thistles? 17In the same way, every good tree bears good fruit, but the bad tree bears bad fruit. 18A good tree cannot bear bad fruit, nor can a bad tree bear good fruit. 19Every tree that

---

ὑμῖν· ζητεῖτε, καὶ εὑρήσετε· κρούετε,
to you; seek, and ye shall find; knock,

καὶ ἀνοιγήσεται ὑμῖν. 8 πᾶς γὰρ ὁ αἰτῶν
and it shall be opened to you. For every asking [one]

λαμβάνει, καὶ ὁ ζητῶν εὑρίσκει, καὶ
receives, and the seeking [one] finds, and

τῷ κρούοντι ἀνοιγήσεται. 9 ἢ τίς ἐστιν
to the knocking [one] it shall be opened. Or ¹what ²is there

ἐξ ὑμῶν ἄνθρωπος, ὃν αἰτήσει ὁ υἱὸς
⁴of ⁵you ³man, whom ⁶will ask ¹the ⁸son

αὐτοῦ ἄρτον, μὴ λίθον ἐπιδώσει αὐτῷ;
⁷of him ⁹a loaf, not a stone he will give him?

10 ἢ καὶ ἰχθὺν αἰτήσει, μὴ ὄφιν ἐπιδώσει
or also a fish he will ask, not a serpent he will give

αὐτῷ; 11 εἰ οὖν ὑμεῖς πονηροὶ ὄντες
him? If therefore ye ²evil ¹being

οἴδατε· δόματα ἀγαθὰ διδόναι τοῖς τέκνοις
know ²gifts ³good ¹to give to the children

ὑμῶν, πόσῳ μᾶλλον ὁ πατὴρ ὑμῶν ὁ
of you, how much more the Father of you –

ἐν τοῖς οὐρανοῖς δώσει ἀγαθὰ τοῖς
in the heavens will give good things to the [ones]

αἰτοῦσιν αὐτόν. 12 Πάντα οὖν ὅσα ἐὰν
asking him. All things therefore as many soever as

θέλητε ἵνα ποιῶσιν ὑμῖν οἱ ἄνθρωποι,
ye wish that may do to you – men,

οὕτως καὶ ὑμεῖς ποιεῖτε αὐτοῖς· οὗτος
thus also ye do to them; ²this

γάρ ἐστιν ὁ νόμος καὶ οἱ προφῆται.
¹for is the law and the prophets.

13 Εἰσέλθατε διὰ τῆς στενῆς πύλης·
Enter ye in through the narrow gate;

ὅτι πλατεῖα [ἡ πύλη] καὶ εὐρύχωρος
because wide [the gate] and broad

ἡ ὁδὸς ἡ ἀπάγουσα εἰς τὴν ἀπώλειαν,
the way – leading away to – destruction,

καὶ πολλοί εἰσιν οἱ εἰσερχόμενοι δι'
and many are the [ones] going in through

αὐτῆς· 14 ὅτι στενὴ ἡ πύλη καὶ ·τεθλιμ-
it; because strait the gate and made

μένη ἡ ὁδὸς ἡ ἀπάγουσα εἰς τὴν ζωήν,
narrow the way – leading away to – life,

καὶ ὀλίγοι εἰσὶν οἱ εὑρίσκοντες αὐτήν.
and few are the [ones] finding it.

15 Προσέχετε ἀπὸ τῶν ψευδοπροφητῶν,
Beware from(of) – false prophets,

οἵτινες ἔρχονται πρὸς ὑμᾶς ἐν ἐνδύμασι
who come to you in clothes

προβάτων, ἔσωθεν δέ εἰσιν λύκοι ἅρπαγες.
of sheep, but within are wolves greedy.

16 ἀπὸ τῶν καρπῶν αὐτῶν ἐπιγνώσεσθε
From the fruits of them ye will know

αὐτούς. μήτι συλλέγουσιν ἀπὸ ἀκανθῶν σταφυλὰς
them. They do not gather from thorns grapes

ἢ ἀπὸ τριβόλων σῦκα; 17 οὕτως πᾶν
or from thistles figs? So ¹every

δένδρον ἀγαθὸν καρποὺς καλοὺς ποιεῖ,
²tree ³good ⁴fruits ⁵good ⁶produces,

τὸ δὲ σαπρὸν δένδρον καρποὺς πονηροὺς
but the corrupt tree fruits evil

ποιεῖ. 18 οὐ δύναται δένδρον ἀγαθὸν
produces. ²Cannot ³tree ¹a good

καρποὺς πονηροὺς ἐνεγκεῖν, οὐδὲ δένδρον
⁴fruits ⁵evil ⁶to bear, nor ⁷tree

σαπρὸν καρποὺς καλοὺς ἐνεγκεῖν. 19 πᾶν
¹a corrupt ⁶fruits ⁵good ³to bear. Every

---

to you; seek and you will find; knock and the door will be opened to you. 8For everyone who asks receives; he who seeks finds; and to him who knocks, the door will be opened.

9"Which of you, if his son asks for bread, will give him a stone? 10Or if he asks for a fish, will give him a snake? 11If you, then, though you are evil, know how to give good gifts to your children, how much more will your Father in heaven give good gifts to those who ask him! 12So in everything, do to others what you would have them do to you, for this sums up the Law and the Prophets.

The Narrow and Wide Gates

13"Enter through the narrow gate. For wide is the gate and broad is the road that leads to destruction, and many enter through it. 14But small is the gate and narrow the road that leads to life, and only a few find it.

A Tree and Its Fruit

15"Watch out for false prophets. They come to you in sheep's clothing, but inwardly they are ferocious wolves. 16By their fruit you will recognize them. Do people pick grapes from thornbushes, or figs from thistles? 17Likewise every good tree bears good fruit, but a bad tree bears bad fruit. 18A good tree cannot bear bad fruit, and a bad tree cannot bear good fruit.

---

r Other ancient authorities read *for the road is wide and easy* does not bear good fruit is cut down and thrown into the fire. 20 Thus you will know them by their fruits.

Concerning Self-Deception

21 "Not everyone who says to me, 'Lord, Lord,' will enter the kingdom of heaven, but only the one who does the will of my Father in heaven. 22 On that day many will say to me, 'Lord, Lord, did we not prophesy in your name, and cast out demons in your name, and do many deeds of power in your name?' 23 Then I will declare to them, 'I never knew you; go away from me, you evildoers.'

Hearers and Doers

24 "Everyone then who hears these words of mine and acts on them will be like a wise man who built his house on rock. 25 The rain fell, the floods came, and the winds blew and beat on that house, but it did not fall, because it had been founded on rock. 26 And everyone who hears these words of mine and does not act on them will be like a foolish man who built his house on sand. 27 The rain fell, and the floods came, and the winds blew and beat against that house, and it fell—and great was its fall!"

28 Now when Jesus had finished saying these

δένδρον μὴ ποιοῦν καρπὸν καλὸν ἐκκόπτεται
tree   not producing   fruit   good   is cut down

καὶ εἰς πῦρ βάλλεται. 20 ἄρα γε ἀπὸ
and into fire is cast.   Therefore   from

τῶν καρπῶν αὐτῶν ἐπιγνώσεσθε αὐτούς.
the fruits   of them   ye will know   them.

21 Οὐ πᾶς ὁ λέγων μοι κύριε κύριε,
Not everyone saying to me Lord[,] Lord,

εἰσελεύσεται εἰς τὴν βασιλείαν τῶν οὐρανῶν,
will enter into the kingdom of the heavens,

ἀλλ' ὁ ποιῶν τὸ θέλημα τοῦ πατρός
but the [one] doing the will of the Father

μου τοῦ ἐν τοῖς οὐρανοῖς. 22 πολλοί
of me - in the heavens.   Many

ἐροῦσίν μοι ἐν ἐκείνῃ τῇ ἡμέρᾳ· κύριε
will say to me in that the day· Lord[,]

κύριε, οὐ τῷ σῷ ὀνόματι ἐπροφητεύσαμεν,
Lord, not - in thy name we prophesied,

καὶ τῷ σῷ ὀνόματι δαιμόνια ἐξεβάλομεν,
and - in thy name demons we expelled,

καὶ τῷ σῷ ὀνόματι δυνάμεις πολλὰς
and - in thy name mighty works many

ἐποιήσαμεν; 23 καὶ τότε ὁμολογήσω
did?   and then I will declare

αὐτοῖς ὅτι οὐδέποτε ἔγνων ὑμᾶς· ἀπο-
to them[,] - Never I knew you; de-

χωρεῖτε ἀπ' ἐμοῦ οἱ ἐργαζόμενοι τὴν
part from me the [ones] working the

ἀνομίαν.
lawlessness.

24 Πᾶς οὖν ὅστις ἀκούει μου τοὺς
Everyone therefore who hears of me -

λόγους τούτους καὶ ποιεῖ αὐτούς,
words these and does them,

ὁμοιωθήσεται ἀνδρὶ φρονίμῳ, ὅστις ᾠκοδό-
shall be likened man to a prudent, who built

μησεν αὐτοῦ τὴν οἰκίαν ἐπὶ τὴν πέτραν.
of him the house on the rock.

25 καὶ κατέβη ἡ βροχὴ καὶ ἦλθον οἱ
And came down the rain and came the

ποταμοὶ καὶ ἔπνευσαν οἱ ἄνεμοι καὶ
rivers and blew the winds and

προσέπεσαν τῇ οἰκίᾳ ἐκείνῃ, καὶ οὐκ
fell against - house that, and not

ἔπεσεν· τεθεμελίωτο γὰρ ἐπὶ τὴν
it fell; for it had been founded on the

πέτραν. 26 καὶ πᾶς ὁ ἀκούων μου
rock.   And everyone hearing of me

τοὺς λόγους τούτους καὶ μὴ ποιῶν
- words these and not doing

αὐτοὺς ὁμοιωθήσεται ἀνδρὶ μωρῷ, ὅστις
them shall be likened man to a foolish, who

ᾠκοδόμησεν αὐτοῦ τὴν οἰκίαν ἐπὶ τὴν
built of him the house on the

ἄμμον. 27 καὶ κατέβη ἡ βροχὴ καὶ
sand.   And came down the rain and

ἦλθον οἱ ποταμοὶ καὶ ἔπνευσαν οἱ
came the rivers and blew the

ἄνεμοι καὶ προσέκοψαν τῇ οἰκίᾳ ἐκείνῃ,
winds and beat against - house that,

καὶ ἔπεσεν, καὶ ἦν ἡ πτῶσις αὐτῆς
and it fell, and was the fall of it

μεγάλη.
great.

28 Καὶ ἐγένετο ὅτε ἐτέλεσεν ὁ Ἰησοῦς
And it came to pass when finished - Jesus

---

19 Every tree that does not bear good fruit is cut down and thrown into the fire. 20 Thus, by their fruit you will recognize them.

21 "Not everyone who says to me, 'Lord, Lord,' will enter the kingdom of heaven, but only he who does the will of my Father who is in heaven. 22 Many will say to me on that day, 'Lord, Lord, did we not prophesy in your name, and in your name drive out demons and perform many miracles?' 23 Then I will tell them plainly, 'I never knew you. Away from me, you evildoers!'

The Wise and Foolish Builders

24 "Therefore everyone who hears these words of mine and puts them into practice is like a wise man who built his house on the rock. 25 The rain came down, the streams rose, and the winds blew and beat against that house; yet it did not fall, because it had its foundation on the rock. 26 But everyone who hears these words of mine and does not put them into practice is like a foolish man who built his house on sand. 27 The rain came down, the streams rose, and the winds blew and beat against that house, and it fell with a great crash."

28 When Jesus had finished saying

things, the crowds were astounded at his teaching, 29 for he taught them as one having authority, and not as their scribes.

Chapter 8

Jesus Cleanses a Leper

WHEN Jesus[s] had come down from the mountain, great crowds followed him; 2 and there was a leper[t] who came to him and knelt before him, saying, "Lord, if you choose, you can make me clean." 3 He stretched out his hand and touched him, saying, "I do choose. Be made clean!" Immediately his leprosy[t] was cleansed. 4 Then Jesus said to him, "See that you say nothing to anyone; but go, show yourself to the priest, and offer the gift that Moses commanded, as a testimony to them."

Jesus Heals a Centurion's Servant

5 When he entered Capernaum, a centurion came to him, appealing to him 6 and saying, "Lord, my servant is lying at home paralyzed, in terrible distress." 7 And he said to him, "I will come and cure him." 8 The centurion answered, "Lord, I am not worthy to have you come under my roof; but only speak the word, and my servant will be healed. 9 For I also am a man under authority, with soldiers under me; and I say to one, 'Go,' and he goes, and to another, 'Come,' and he comes, and to my slave, 'Do this,' and the slave does it." 10 When Jesus heard him, he was amazed and said to those who followed him, "Truly I tell you, in no one[u] in Isra-

---

τοὺς λόγους τούτους, ἐξεπλήσσοντο οἱ
\- words these, were astounded the
ὄχλοι ἐπὶ τῇ διδαχῇ αὐτοῦ· 29 ἦν γὰρ
crowds at the teaching of him; for he was
διδάσκων αὐτοὺς ὡς ἐξουσίαν ἔχων, καὶ
teaching them as authority having, and
οὐχ ὡς οἱ γραμματεῖς αὐτῶν.
not as the scribes of them.

8 Καταβάντος δὲ αὐτοῦ ἀπὸ τοῦ ὄρους
And coming down him[a] from the mountain
= as he came down
ἠκολούθησαν αὐτῷ ὄχλοι πολλοί. 2 καὶ
followed him crowds many. And
ἰδοὺ λεπρὸς προσελθὼν προσεκύνει αὐτῷ
behold a leper approaching worshipped him
λέγων· κύριε, ἐὰν θέλῃς, δύνασαί με
saying: Lord, if thou art willing, thou art able me
καθαρίσαι. 3 καὶ ἐκτείνας τὴν χεῖρα
to cleanse. And stretching out the(his) hand
ἥψατο αὐτοῦ λέγων· θέλω, καθαρίσθητι.
he touched him saying: I am willing, be thou cleansed.
καὶ εὐθέως ἐκαθαρίσθη αὐτοῦ ἡ λέπρα.
And immediately was cleansed of him the leprosy.
4 καὶ λέγει αὐτῷ ὁ Ἰησοῦς· ὅρα μηδενὶ
And says to him - Jesus: See to no one
εἴπῃς, ἀλλὰ ὕπαγε σεαυτὸν δεῖξον τῷ
thou tellest, but go thyself show to the
ἱερεῖ καὶ προσένεγκον τὸ δῶρον ὃ
priest and offer the gift which
προσέταξεν Μωϋσῆς, εἰς μαρτύριον αὐτοῖς.
commanded Moses, for a testimony to them.
5 Εἰσελθόντος δὲ αὐτοῦ εἰς Καφαρναοὺμ
And entering him[a] into Capernaum,
προσῆλθεν αὐτῷ ἑκατόνταρχος παρακαλῶν
approached to him a centurion beseeching
αὐτὸν 6 καὶ λέγων· κύριε, ὁ παῖς μου
him and saying: Lord, the boy of me
βέβληται ἐν τῇ οἰκίᾳ παραλυτικός,
has been laid [aside] in the house a paralytic,
δεινῶς βασανιζόμενος. 7 λέγει αὐτῷ·
terribly being tortured. He says to him:
ἐγὼ ἐλθὼν θεραπεύσω αὐτόν. 8 ἀποκριθεὶς
I coming will heal him. answering
δὲ ὁ ἑκατόνταρχος ἔφη· κύριε, οὐκ εἰμὶ
But the centurion said: Lord, I am not
ἱκανὸς ἵνα μου ὑπὸ τὴν στέγην εἰσέλθῃς·
worthy that of me under the roof thou mayest enter;
ἀλλὰ μόνον εἰπὲ λόγῳ, καὶ ἰαθήσεται ὁ παῖς
but only say in a word, and will be healed the boy
μου. 9 καὶ γὰρ ἐγὼ ἄνθρωπός εἰμι
of me. *also ¹For ¹I ᵃa man ᵃam
ὑπὸ ἐξουσίαν, ἔχων ὑπ' ἐμαυτὸν στρατιώτας,
under authority, having under myself soldiers,
καὶ λέγω τούτῳ· πορεύθητι, καὶ πορεύεται,
and I say to this: Go, and he goes,
καὶ ἄλλῳ· ἔρχου, καὶ ἔρχεται, καὶ τῷ
and to another: Come, and he comes, and to the
δούλῳ μου· ποίησον τοῦτο, καὶ ποιεῖ.
slave of me: Do this, and he does [it].
10 ἀκούσας δὲ ὁ Ἰησοῦς ἐθαύμασεν
And hearing - Jesus marvelled
καὶ εἶπεν τοῖς ἀκολουθοῦσιν· ἀμὴν λέγω
and said to the [ones] following: Truly I tell

---

ished saying these things, the crowds were amazed at his teaching, 29 because he taught as one who had authority, and not as their teachers of the law.

Chapter 8

The Man With Leprosy

WHEN he came down from the mountainside, large crowds followed him. 2 A man with leprosy[e] came and knelt before him and said, "Lord, if you are willing, you can make me clean." 3 Jesus reached out his hand and touched the man. "I am willing," he said. "Be clean!" Immediately he was cured[f] of his leprosy. 4 Then Jesus said to him, "See that you don't tell anyone. But go, show yourself to the priest and offer the gift Moses commanded, as a testimony to them."

The Faith of the Centurion

5 When Jesus had entered Capernaum, a centurion came to him, asking for help. 6 "Lord," he said, "my servant lies at home paralyzed and in terrible suffering." 7 Jesus said to him, "I will go and heal him." 8 The centurion replied, "Lord, I do not deserve to have you come under my roof. But just say the word, and my servant will be healed. 9 For I myself am a man under authority, with soldiers under me. I tell this one, 'Go,' and he goes; and that one, 'Come,' and he comes. I say to my servant, 'Do this,' and he does it." 10 When Jesus heard this, he was astonished and said to those following him, "I tell you the truth, I have not

---

[s] Gk he
[t] The terms leper and leprosy can refer to several diseases
[u] Other ancient authorities read Truly I tell you, not even

[e]2 The Greek word was used for various diseases affecting the skin—not necessarily leprosy.
[f]3 Greek made clean

el have I found such faith. 11I tell you, many will come from east and west and will eat with Abraham and Isaac and Jacob in the kingdom of heaven, 12while the heirs of the kingdom will be thrown into the outer darkness, where there will be weeping and gnashing of teeth." 13And to the centurion Jesus said, "Go; let it be done for you according to your faith." And the servant was healed in that hour.

Jesus Heals Many at Peter's House

14 When Jesus entered Peter's house, he saw his mother-in-law lying in bed with a fever; 15he touched her hand, and the fever left her, and she got up and began to serve him. 16That evening they brought to him many who were possessed with demons; and he cast out the spirits with a word, and cured all who were sick. 17This was to fulfill what had been spoken through the prophet Isaiah, "He took our infirmities and bore our diseases."

Would-Be Followers of Jesus

18 Now when Jesus saw great crowds around him, he gave orders to go over to the other side. 19A scribe then approached and said, "Teacher, I will follow you wherever you go." 20And Jesus said to him, "Foxes have holes, and birds of the air have nests; but the Son of Man has nowhere to lay

---

ὑμῖν, παρ' οὐδενὶ τοσαύτην πίστιν ἐν τῷ
you, from no one such faith in -

'Ισραὴλ εὗρον. 11 λέγω δὲ ὑμῖν ὅτι
Israel I found. And I say you that

πολλοὶ ἀπὸ ἀνατολῶν καὶ δυσμῶν ἥξουσιν
many from east and west will come

καὶ ἀνακλιθήσονται μετὰ 'Αβραὰμ καὶ
and will recline with Abraham and

'Ισαὰκ καὶ 'Ιακὼβ ἐν τῇ βασιλείᾳ τῶν
Isaac and Jacob in the kingdom of the

οὐρανῶν· 12 οἱ δὲ υἱοὶ τῆς βασιλείας
heavens; but the sons of the kingdom

ἐκβληθήσονται εἰς τὸ σκότος τὸ ἐξώτερον·
will be cast out into the darkness - outer;

ἐκεῖ ἔσται ὁ κλαυθμὸς καὶ ὁ βρυγμὸς
there will be the weeping and the gnashing

τῶν ὀδόντων. 13 καὶ εἶπεν ὁ 'Ιησοῦς τῷ
of the teeth. And said - Jesus to the

ἑκατοντάρχῃ· ὕπαγε, ὡς ἐπίστευσας γενη-
centurion: Go, as thou believedst let it

θήτω σοι. καὶ ἰάθη ὁ παῖς ἐν τῇ
be to thee. And was healed the boy in -

ὥρᾳ ἐκείνῃ.
hour that.

14 Καὶ ἐλθὼν ὁ 'Ιησοῦς εἰς τὴν οἰκίαν
And coming - Jesus into the house

Πέτρου εἶδεν τὴν πενθερὰν αὐτοῦ βεβλη-
of Peter he saw the mother-in-law of him *having been*

μένην καὶ πυρέσσουσαν· 15 καὶ ἥψατο
laid [aside] and fever-stricken; and he touched

τῆς χειρὸς αὐτῆς, καὶ ἀφῆκεν αὐτὴν ὁ
the hand of her, and left her the

πυρετός· καὶ ἠγέρθη, καὶ διηκόνει αὐτῷ.
fever; and she arose, and ministered to him.

16 'Οψίας δὲ γενομένης προσήνεγκαν
And evening coming[a] they brought
= when evening came

αὐτῷ δαιμονιζομένους πολλούς· καὶ ἐξέβαλεν
to him *being* demon-possessed many; and he expelled

τὰ πνεύματα λόγῳ, καὶ πάντας τοὺς
the spirits with a word, and all the [ones]
= those

κακῶς ἔχοντας ἐθεράπευσεν· 17 ὅπως
ill having he healed; so that
who were ill

πληρωθῇ τὸ ῥηθὲν διὰ 'Ησαΐου τοῦ
was fulfilled the [thing] spoken through Isaiah the

προφήτου λέγοντος· αὐτὸς τὰς ἀσθενείας
prophet saying: He the weaknesses

ἡμῶν ἔλαβεν καὶ τὰς νόσους ἐβάστασεν.
of us took and the diseases he bore.

18 'Ιδὼν δὲ ὁ 'Ιησοῦς ὄχλον περὶ
But ²seeing - ¹Jesus a crowd around

αὐτὸν ἐκέλευσεν ἀπελθεῖν εἰς τὸ πέραν.
him commanded to go away to the other side.

19 Καὶ προσελθὼν εἷς γραμματεὺς εἶπεν
And approaching one scribe said

αὐτῷ· διδάσκαλε, ἀκολουθήσω σοι
to him: Teacher, I will follow thee

ὅπου ἐὰν ἀπέρχῃ. 20 καὶ λέγει αὐτῷ
wherever thou mayest go. And says to him

ὁ 'Ιησοῦς· αἱ ἀλώπεκες φωλεοὺς ἔχουσιν
- Jesus: The foxes holes have

καὶ τὰ πετεινὰ τοῦ οὐρανοῦ κατα-
and the birds of the heaven nests,

σκηνώσεις, ὁ δὲ υἱὸς τοῦ ἀνθρώπου
but the Son - of man

---

found anyone in Israel with such great faith. 11I say to you that many will come from the east and the west, and will take their places at the feast with Abraham, Isaac and Jacob in the kingdom of heaven. 12But the subjects of the kingdom will be thrown outside, into the darkness, where there will be weeping and gnashing of teeth."

13Then Jesus said to the centurion, "Go! It will be done just as you believed it would." And his servant was healed at that very hour.

Jesus Heals Many

14When Jesus came into Peter's house, he saw Peter's mother-in-law lying in bed with a fever. 15He touched her hand and the fever left her, and she got up and began to wait on him.

16When evening came, many who were demon-possessed were brought to him, and he drove out the spirits with a word and healed all the sick. 17This was to fulfill what was spoken through the prophet Isaiah:

"He took up our
    infirmities
and carried our
    diseases."[g]

The Cost of Following Jesus

18When Jesus saw the crowd around him, he gave orders to cross to the other side of the lake. 19Then a teacher of the law came to him and said, "Teacher, I will follow you wherever you go."

20Jesus replied, "Foxes have holes and birds of the air have nests, but the Son of Man has no place to lay

g17 Isaiah 53:4

his head." 21 Another of his disciples said to him, "Lord, first let me go and bury my father." 22 But Jesus said to him, "Follow me, and let the dead bury their own dead."

Jesus Stills the Storm

23 And when he got into the boat, his disciples followed him. 24 A windstorm arose on the sea, so great that the boat was being swamped by the waves; but he was asleep. 25 And they went and woke him up, saying, "Lord, save us! We are perishing!" 26 And he said to them, "Why are you afraid, you of little faith?" Then he got up and rebuked the winds and the sea; and there was a dead calm. 27 They were amazed, saying, "What sort of man is this, that even the winds and the sea obey him?"

Jesus Heals the Gadarene Demoniacs

28 When he came to the other side, to the country of the Gadarenes,ᵛ two demoniacs coming out of the tombs met him. They were so fierce that no one could pass that way. 29 Suddenly they shouted, "What have you to do with us, Son of God? Have you come here to torment us before the time?" 30 Now a large herd of swine was feeding at some distance from them. 31 The demons begged him, "If you cast us out, send us into the herd of swine."

οὐκ ἔχει ποῦ τὴν κεφαλὴν κλίνῃ.
has not where the(his) head he may lay.

21 ἕτερος δὲ τῶν μαθητῶν εἶπεν
And another of the disciples said

αὐτῷ· κύριε, ἐπίτρεψόν μοι πρῶτον
to him: Lord, allow me first

ἀπελθεῖν καὶ θάψαι τὸν πατέρα μου.
to go away and bury the father of me.

22 ὁ δὲ Ἰησοῦς λέγει αὐτῷ· ἀκολούθει
- But Jesus says to him: Follow thou

μοι, καὶ ἄφες τοὺς νεκροὺς θάψαι τοὺς
me, and leave the dead to bury the

ἑαυτῶν νεκρούς.
of themselves dead.

23 Καὶ ἐμβάντι αὐτῷ εἰς τὸ πλοῖον,
And embarking himᵉ in the ship,
= as he embarked

ἠκολούθησαν αὐτῷ οἱ μαθηταὶ αὐτοῦ.
followed him the disciples of him.

24 καὶ ἰδοὺ σεισμὸς μέγας ἐγένετο ἐν
And behold storm a great there was in

τῇ θαλάσσῃ, ὥστε τὸ πλοῖον καλύπτ-
the sea, so as the ship to be en-

εσθαι ὑπὸ τῶν κυμάτων· αὐτὸς δὲ ἐκάθευδεν.
veloped by the waves; but he was sleeping.

25 καὶ προσελθόντες ἤγειραν αὐτὸν λέγοντες·
And approaching they roused him saying:

κύριε, σῶσον, ἀπολλύμεθα. **26** καὶ λέγει
Lord, save, we are perishing. And he says

αὐτοῖς· τί δειλοί ἐστε, ὀλιγόπιστοι;
to them: Why fearful are ye, little-faiths?

τότε ἐγερθεὶς ἐπετίμησεν τοῖς ἀνέμοις καὶ
Then rising he rebuked the winds and

τῇ θαλάσσῃ, καὶ ἐγένετο γαλήνη μεγάλη.
the sea, and there was calm a great.

27 οἱ δὲ ἄνθρωποι ἐθαύμασαν λέγοντες·
And the men marvelled saying:

ποταπός ἐστιν οὗτος, ὅτι καὶ οἱ ἄνεμοι
Of what sort is this [man], that even the winds

καὶ ἡ θάλασσα αὐτῷ ὑπακούουσιν;
and the sea him obey?

28 Καὶ ἐλθόντος αὐτοῦ εἰς τὸ πέραν εἰς
And coming himᵃ to the other side into
= when he came

τὴν χώραν τῶν Γαδαρηνῶν ὑπήντησαν
the country of the Gadarenes met

αὐτῷ δύο δαιμονιζόμενοι ἐκ τῶν μνημείων
him two demon-possessed out of the tombs

ἐξερχόμενοι, χαλεποὶ λίαν, ὥστε μὴ
coming out, dangerous exceedingly, so as not

ἰσχύειν τινὰ παρελθεῖν διὰ τῆς ὁδοῦ
to be able anyoneᵇ to pass through - way

ἐκείνης. **29** καὶ ἰδοὺ ἔκραξαν λέγοντες·
that. And behold they cried out saying:

τί ἡμῖν καὶ σοί, υἱὲ τοῦ θεοῦ; ἦλθες
What to us and to thee, Son - of God? camest thou

ὧδε πρὸ καιροῦ βασανίσαι ἡμᾶς; **30** ἦν
here before [the] time to torture us? there was

δὲ μακρὰν ἀπ' αὐτῶν ἀγέλη χοίρων
Now far off from them a herd pigs

πολλῶν βοσκομένη. **31** οἱ δὲ δαίμονες
of many feeding. And the demons

παρεκάλουν αὐτὸν λέγοντες· εἰ ἐκβάλλεις
besought him saying: If thou expellest

ἡμᾶς, ἀπόστειλον ἡμᾶς εἰς τὴν ἀγέλην
us, send us into the herd

---

his head."
21 Another disciple said to him, "Lord, first let me go and bury my father." 22 But Jesus told him, "Follow me, and let the dead bury their own dead."

Jesus Calms the Storm

23 Then he got into the boat and his disciples followed him. 24 Without warning, a furious storm came up on the lake, so that the waves swept over the boat. But Jesus was sleeping. 25 The disciples went and woke him, saying, "Lord, save us! We're going to drown!"

26 He replied, "You of little faith, why are you so afraid?" Then he got up and rebuked the winds and the waves, and it was completely calm.

27 The men were amazed and asked, "What kind of man is this? Even the winds and the waves obey him!"

The Healing of Two Demon-possessed Men

28 When he arrived at the other side in the region of the Gadarenes,ʰ two demon-possessed men coming from the tombs met him. They were so violent that no one could pass that way. 29 "What do you want with us, Son of God?" they shouted. "Have you come here to torture us before the appointed time?"

30 Some distance from them a large herd of pigs was feeding. 31 The demons begged Jesus, "If you drive us out, send us into the herd of pigs."

ᵛ Other ancient authorities read *Gergesenes*; others, *Gerasenes*

ʰ28 Some manuscripts *Gergesenes*; others *Gerasenes*

32 And he said to them, "Go!" So they came out and entered the swine; and suddenly, the whole herd rushed down the steep bank into the sea and perished in the water. 33 The swineherds ran off, and on going into the town, they told the whole story about what had happened to the demoniacs. 34 Then the whole town came out to meet Jesus; and when they saw him, they begged him to leave their neighborhood. 1 And after getting into a boat he crossed the sea and came to his own town.

Jesus Heals a Paralytic

2 And just then some people were carrying a paralyzed man lying on a bed. When Jesus saw their faith, he said to the paralytic, "Take heart, son; your sins are forgiven." 3 Then some of the scribes said to themselves, "This man is blaspheming." 4 But Jesus, perceiving their thoughts, said, "Why do you think evil in your hearts? 5 For which is easier, to say, 'Your sins are forgiven,' or to say, 'Stand up and walk'? 6 But so that you may know that the Son of Man has authority on earth to forgive sins"—he then said to the paralytic— "Stand up, take your bed and go to your home." 7 And he stood up and went to his home. 8 When the crowds saw it, they were filled with awe, and they glorified God, who had given such authority to human beings.

τῶν χοίρων. 32 καὶ εἶπεν αὐτοῖς·
of the pigs. And he said to them:

ὑπάγετε. οἱ δὲ ἐξελθόντες ἀπῆλθον εἰς
Go ye. So the coming out [ones] went away into

τοὺς χοίρους· καὶ ἰδοὺ ὥρμησεν πᾶσα ἡ
the pigs; and behold rushed all the

ἀγέλη κατὰ τοῦ κρημνοῦ εἰς τὴν θάλασσαν,
herd down the precipice into the sea,

καὶ ἀπέθανον ἐν τοῖς ὕδασιν. 33 οἱ
and died in the waters. the

δὲ βόσκοντες ἔφυγον, καὶ ἀπελθόντες
But feeding [ones] fled, and going away

εἰς τὴν πόλιν ἀπήγγειλαν πάντα καὶ
into the city reported all things and

τὰ τῶν δαιμονιζομένων. 34 καὶ ἰδοὺ
the [things] of the demon-possessed [ones]. And behold

πᾶσα ἡ πόλις ἐξῆλθεν εἰς ὑπάντησιν
all the city came out with a view to a meeting [with]

τῷ Ἰησοῦ, καὶ ἰδόντες αὐτὸν παρεκάλεσαν
- Jesus, and seeing ²him ¹besought

ὅπως μεταβῇ ἀπὸ τῶν ὁρίων αὐτῶν.
so that he might remove from the borders of them.

---

9 Καὶ ἐμβὰς εἰς πλοῖον διεπέρασεν,
And embarking in a ship he crossed over,

καὶ ἦλθεν εἰς τὴν ἰδίαν πόλιν. 2 Καὶ
and came into the(his) own city. And

ἰδοὺ προσέφερον αὐτῷ παραλυτικὸν ἐπὶ
behold they brought to him a paralytic on

κλίνης βεβλημένον. καὶ ἰδὼν ὁ Ἰησοῦς
a mattress *having been* laid. And ²seeing - ¹Jesus

τὴν πίστιν αὐτῶν εἶπεν τῷ παραλυτικῷ·
the faith of them said to the paralytic:

θάρσει, τέκνον, ἀφίενταί σου αἱ ἁμαρτίαι.
Be of good cheer, child, are forgiven of thee the sins.

3 καὶ ἰδού τινες τῶν γραμματέων εἶπαν
And behold some of the scribes said

ἐν ἑαυτοῖς· οὗτος βλασφημεῖ. 4 καὶ
among themselves: This [man] blasphemes. And

εἰδὼς ὁ Ἰησοῦς τὰς ἐνθυμήσεις αὐτῶν
¹knowing - ²Jesus the thoughts of them

εἶπεν· ἱνατί ἐνθυμεῖσθε πονηρὰ ἐν ταῖς
said: Why think ye evil things in the

καρδίαις ὑμῶν; 5 τί γάρ ἐστιν εὐκοπώ-
hearts of you? for which is easier,

τερον, εἰπεῖν· ἀφίενταί σου αἱ ἁμαρτίαι, ἢ
to say: ⁴are forgiven ²of thee ¹The ³sins, or

εἰπεῖν· ἔγειρε καὶ περιπάτει; 6 ἵνα δὲ
to say: Rise and walk? But in order that

εἰδῆτε ὅτι ἐξουσίαν ἔχει ὁ υἱὸς τοῦ
ye may know that authority has the Son -

ἀνθρώπου ἐπὶ τῆς γῆς ἀφιέναι ἁμαρτίας—
of man on the earth to forgive sins—

τότε λέγει τῷ παραλυτικῷ· ἔγειρε ἀρόν
then he says to the paralytic: Rise[,] take

σου τὴν κλίνην καὶ ὕπαγε εἰς τὸν οἶκόν
of thee the mattress and go to the house

σου. 7 καὶ ἐγερθεὶς ἀπῆλθεν εἰς τὸν
of thee. And rising he went away to the

οἶκον αὐτοῦ. 8 ἰδόντες δὲ οἱ ὄχλοι
house of him. But seeing the crowds

ἐφοβήθησαν καὶ ἐδόξασαν τὸν θεὸν τὸν
feared and glorified - God the [one]

δόντα ἐξουσίαν τοιαύτην τοῖς ἀνθρώποις.
giving ²authority ¹such to men.

Chapter 9

Jesus Heals a Paralytic

JESUS stepped into a boat, crossed over and came to his own town. 2 Some men brought to him a paralytic, lying on a mat. When Jesus saw their faith, he said to the paralytic, "Take heart, son; your sins are forgiven."

3 At this, some of the teachers of the law said to themselves, "This fellow is blaspheming!"

4 Knowing their thoughts, Jesus said, "Why do you entertain evil thoughts in your hearts? 5 Which is easier: to say, 'Your sins are forgiven,' or to say, 'Get up and walk'? 6 But so that you may know that the Son of Man has authority on earth to forgive sins. . . ." Then he said to the paralytic, "Get up, take your mat and go home." 7 And the man got up and went home. 8 When the crowd saw this, they were filled with awe; and they praised God, who had given such authority to men.

32 He said to them, "Go!" So they came out and went into the pigs, and the whole herd rushed down the steep bank into the lake and died in the water. 33 Those tending the pigs ran off, went into the town and reported all this, including what had happened to the demon-possessed men. 34 Then the whole town went out to meet Jesus. And when they saw him, they pleaded with him to leave their region.

The Call of Matthew

9 As Jesus was walking along, he saw a man called Matthew sitting at the tax booth; and he said to him, "Follow me." And he got up and followed him.

10 And as he sat at dinner[w] in the house, many tax collectors and sinners came and were sitting[x] with him and his disciples. 11 When the Pharisees saw this, they said to his disciples, "Why does your teacher eat with tax collectors and sinners?" 12 But when he heard this, he said, "Those who are well have no need of a physician, but those who are sick. 13 Go and learn what this means, 'I desire mercy, not sacrifice.' For I have come to call not the righteous but sinners."

The Question about Fasting

14 Then the disciples of John came to him, saying, "Why do we and the Pharisees fast often,[y] but your disciples do not fast?" 15 And Jesus said to them, "The wedding guests cannot mourn as long as the bridegroom is with them, can they? The days will come when the bridegroom is taken away from them, and then they will fast. 16 No one sews a piece of unshrunk cloth on an old cloak, for the patch pulls away from the cloak, and a worse tear is made. 17 Neither is new wine put into old wineskins; otherwise, the skins burst, and the

---

9 Καὶ παράγων ὁ Ἰησοῦς ἐκεῖθεν εἶδεν
And ⁸passing by – ¹Jesus thence saw
ἄνθρωπον καθήμενον ἐπὶ τὸ τελώνιον,
a man sitting at the custom house,
Μαθθαῖον λεγόμενον, καὶ λέγει αὐτῷ·
Matthew named, and says to him:
ἀκολούθει μοι. καὶ ἀναστὰς ἠκολούθησεν
Follow me. And rising up he followed
αὐτῷ. 10 Καὶ ἐγένετο αὐτοῦ ἀνακει-
him. And it came to pass him reclin-
=as he was reclining
μένου ἐν τῇ οἰκίᾳ, καὶ ἰδοὺ πολλοὶ
ing⁸ in the house, and behold many
τελῶναι καὶ ἁμαρτωλοὶ ἐλθόντες συνανέκειντο
tax-collectors and sinners coming reclined at table with
τῷ Ἰησοῦ καὶ τοῖς μαθηταῖς αὐτοῦ.
– Jesus and the disciples of him.
11 καὶ ἰδόντες οἱ Φαρισαῖοι ἔλεγον τοῖς
And ⁸seeing ¹the ²Pharisees said to the
μαθηταῖς αὐτοῦ· διὰ τί μετὰ τῶν τελωνῶν
disciples of him: Why with – tax-collectors
καὶ ἁμαρτωλῶν ἐσθίει ὁ διδάσκαλος ὑμῶν;
and sinners eats the teacher of you?
12 ὁ δὲ ἀκούσας εἶπεν· οὐ χρείαν
But he hearing said: Not need
ἔχουσιν οἱ ἰσχύοντες ἰατροῦ ἀλλ' οἱ
have the [ones] being strong of a physician but the [ones]
=those
κακῶς ἔχοντες. 13 πορευθέντες δὲ μάθετε
ill having. But going learn ye
who are ill
τί ἐστιν· ἔλεος θέλω καὶ οὐ θυσίαν· οὐ
what it is: Mercy I desire and not sacrifice; not
γὰρ ἦλθον καλέσαι δικαίους ἀλλὰ
for I came to call righteous [people] but
ἁμαρτωλούς.
sinners.
14 Τότε προσέρχονται αὐτῷ οἱ μαθηταὶ
Then approach to him the disciples
Ἰωάννου λέγοντες· διὰ τί ἡμεῖς καὶ οἱ
of John saying: Why we and the
Φαρισαῖοι νηστεύομεν, οἱ δὲ μαθηταί
Pharisees fast, but the disciples
σου οὐ νηστεύουσιν; 15 καὶ εἶπεν
of thee fast not? And said
αὐτοῖς ὁ Ἰησοῦς· μὴ δύνανται οἱ
to them – Jesus: not Can the
υἱοὶ τοῦ νυμφῶνος πενθεῖν, ἐφ' ὅσον
sons of the bridechamber to mourn, so long as
μετ' αὐτῶν ἐστιν ὁ νυμφίος; ἐλεύσονται
with them is the bridegroom? ⁸will come
δὲ ἡμέραι ὅταν ἀπαρθῇ ἀπ' αὐτῶν ὁ
¹but days when is taken away from them the
νυμφίος, καὶ τότε νηστεύσουσιν. 16 οὐδεὶς
bridegroom, and then they will fast. no one
δὲ ἐπιβάλλει ἐπίβλημα ῥάκους ἀγνάφου
Now puts on a patch cloth of unfulled
ἐπὶ ἱματίῳ παλαιῷ· αἴρει γὰρ τὸ
on garment an old; for takes away the
πλήρωμα αὐτοῦ ἀπὸ τοῦ ἱματίου, καὶ
fullness of it from the garment, and
χεῖρον σχίσμα γίνεται. 17 οὐδὲ
a worse rent becomes. Neither
βάλλουσιν οἶνον νέον εἰς ἀσκοὺς
do they put wine new into wineskins
παλαιούς· εἰ δὲ μή γε, ῥήγνυνται
old; otherwise, are burst

The Calling of Matthew

9 As Jesus went on from there, he saw a man named Matthew sitting at the tax collector's booth. "Follow me," he told him, and Matthew got up and followed him.

10 While Jesus was having dinner at Matthew's house, many tax collectors and "sinners" came and ate with him and his disciples. 11 When the Pharisees saw this, they asked his disciples, "Why does your teacher eat with tax collectors and 'sinners'?" 12 On hearing this, Jesus said, "It is not the healthy who need a doctor, but the sick. 13 But go and learn what this means: 'I desire mercy, not sacrifice.'[i] For I have not come to call the righteous, but sinners."

Jesus Questioned About Fasting

14 Then John's disciples came and asked him, "How is it that we and the Pharisees fast, but your disciples do not fast?" 15 Jesus answered, "How can the guests of the bridegroom mourn while he is with them? The time will come when the bridegroom will be taken from them; then they will fast. 16 "No one sews a patch of unshrunk cloth on an old garment, for the patch will pull away from the garment, making the tear worse. 17 Neither do men pour new wine into old wineskins. If they do, the skins will burst, the wine

---

w Gk reclined
x Gk were reclining
y Other ancient authorities lack often

i 13 Hosea 6:6

wine is spilled, and the skins are destroyed; but new wine is put into fresh wineskins, and so both are preserved."

A Girl Restored to Life and a Woman Healed

18 While he was saying these things to them, suddenly a leader of the synagogue[z] came in and knelt before him, saying, "My daughter has just died; but come and lay your hand on her, and she will live." 19 And Jesus got up and followed him, with his disciples. 20 And suddenly a woman who had been suffering from hemorrhages for twelve years came up behind him and touched the fringe of his cloak, 21 for she said to herself, "If I only touch his cloak, I will be made well." 22 Jesus turned, and seeing her he said, "Take heart, daughter; your faith has made you well." And instantly the woman was made well. 23 When Jesus came to the leader's house and saw the flute players and the crowd making a commotion, 24 he said, "Go away; for the girl is not dead but sleeping." And they laughed at him. 25 But when the crowd had been put outside, he went in and took her by the hand, and the girl got up. 26 And the report of this spread throughout that district.

Jesus Heals Two Blind Men

27 As Jesus went on from there, two blind men followed him, crying loudly, "Have mercy on us, Son of David!" 28 When he entered the house, the blind

---

οἱ ἀσκοί, καὶ ὁ οἶνος ἐκχεῖται καὶ
the wineskins, and the wine is poured out and
οἱ ἀσκοὶ ἀπόλλυνται. ἀλλὰ βάλλουσιν
the wineskins are destroyed. But they put
οἶνον νέον εἰς ἀσκοὺς καινούς, καὶ
wine new into wineskins fresh, and
ἀμφότεροι συντηροῦνται.
both are preserved.

18 Ταῦτα αὐτοῦ λαλοῦντος αὐτοῖς,
These things him speaking[a] to them,
= As he was speaking these things
ἰδοὺ ἄρχων [εἷς] προσελθὼν προσ-
behold ruler one approaching wor-
εκύνει αὐτῷ λέγων ὅτι ἡ θυγάτηρ
shipped him saying[,] that The daughter
μου ἄρτι ἐτελεύτησεν· ἀλλὰ ἐλθὼν
of me just now died; but coming
ἐπίθες τὴν χεῖρά σου ἐπ' αὐτήν,
lay on the hand of thee on her,
καὶ ζήσεται. 19 καὶ ἐγερθεὶς ὁ Ἰησοῦς
and she will live. And rising — Jesus
ἠκολούθει αὐτῷ καὶ οἱ μαθηταὶ αὐτοῦ.
followed him[,] also the disciples of him.
20 Καὶ ἰδοὺ γυνὴ αἱμορροοῦσα
And behold a woman suffering from a flow of blood
δώδεκα ἔτη προσελθοῦσα ὄπισθεν ἥψατο
twelve years approaching behind touched
τοῦ κρασπέδου τοῦ ἱματίου αὐτοῦ·
the fringe of the garment of him;
21 ἔλεγεν γὰρ ἐν ἑαυτῇ· ἐὰν μόνον
for she was saying in herself: If only
ἅψωμαι τοῦ ἱματίου αὐτοῦ, σωθήσομαι.
I may touch the garment of him, I shall be healed.
22 ὁ δὲ Ἰησοῦς στραφεὶς καὶ ἰδὼν
— And Jesus turning and seeing
αὐτὴν εἶπεν· θάρσει, θύγατερ· ἡ
her said: Be of good cheer, daughter; the
πίστις σου σέσωκέν σε. καὶ ἐσώθη
faith of thee has healed thee. And was healed
ἡ γυνὴ ἀπὸ τῆς ὥρας ἐκείνης. 23 Καὶ
the woman from — hour that. And
ἐλθὼν ὁ Ἰησοῦς εἰς τὴν οἰκίαν τοῦ ἄρχοντος
coming — Jesus into the house of the ruler
καὶ ἰδὼν τοὺς αὐλητὰς καὶ τὸν ὄχλον
and seeing the flute-players and the crowd
θορυβούμενον 24 ἔλεγεν· ἀναχωρεῖτε· οὐ
terrified he said: Depart ye; not
γὰρ ἀπέθανεν τὸ κοράσιον ἀλλὰ καθεύδει.
for died the girl but sleeps.
καὶ κατεγέλων αὐτοῦ. 25 ὅτε δὲ
And they ridiculed him. But when
ἐξεβλήθη ὁ ὄχλος, εἰσελθὼν ἐκράτησεν
was put out the crowd, entering he took hold of
τῆς χειρὸς αὐτῆς, καὶ ἠγέρθη τὸ κορά-
the hand of her, and was raised the girl.
σιον. 26 καὶ ἐξῆλθεν ἡ φήμη αὕτη
And went out ‒ report this
εἰς ὅλην τὴν γῆν ἐκείνην. 27 Καὶ
into all ‒ land that. And
παράγοντι ἐκεῖθεν τῷ Ἰησοῦ ἠκολούθησαν
passing by thence ‒ Jesus[e] followed
= as Jesus passed by thence
δύο τυφλοὶ κράζοντες καὶ λέγοντες· ἐλέησον
two blind men crying out and saying: Pity
ἡμᾶς, υἱὸς Δαυίδ. 28 ἐλθόντι δὲ εἰς
us, son of David. And coming[e] into
= when he came

---

will run out and the wineskins will be ruined. No, they pour new wine into new wineskins, and both are preserved."

A Dead Girl and a Sick Woman

18 While he was saying this, a ruler came and knelt before him and said, "My daughter has just died. But come and put your hand on her, and she will live." 19 Jesus got up and went with him, and so did his disciples. 20 Just then a woman who had been subject to bleeding for twelve years came up behind him and touched the edge of his cloak. 21 She said to herself, "If I only touch his cloak, I will be healed." 22 Jesus turned and saw her. "Take heart, daughter," he said, "your faith has healed you." And the woman was healed from that moment. 23 When Jesus entered the ruler's house and saw the flute players and the noisy crowd, 24 he said, "Go away. The girl is not dead but asleep." But they laughed at him. 25 After the crowd had been put outside, he went in and took the girl by the hand, and she got up. 26 News of this spread through all that region.

Jesus Heals the Blind and Mute

27 As Jesus went on from there, two blind men followed him, calling out, "Have mercy on us, Son of David!" 28 When he had gone indoors, the blind men came

---

men came to him; and Jesus said to them, "Do you believe that I am able to do this?" They said to him, "Yes, Lord." 29 Then he touched their eyes and said, "According to your faith let it be done to you." 30 And their eyes were opened. Then Jesus sternly ordered them, "See that no one knows of this." 31 But they went away and spread the news about him throughout that district.

Jesus Heals One Who Was Mute

32 After they had gone away, a demoniac who was mute was brought to him. 33 And when the demon had been cast out, the one who had been mute spoke; and the crowds were amazed and said, "Never has anything like this been seen in Israel." 34 But the Pharisees said, "By the ruler of the demons he casts out the demons." [a]

The Harvest Is Great, the Laborers Few

35 Then Jesus went about all the cities and villages, teaching in their synagogues, and proclaiming the good news of the kingdom, and curing every disease and every sickness. 36 When he saw the crowds, he had compassion for them, because they were harassed and helpless, like sheep without a shepherd. 37 Then he said to his disciples, "The harvest is plentiful, but the laborers are few; 38 therefore ask the Lord of the harvest to send out laborers into his harvest."

τὴν οἰκίαν προσῆλθον αὐτῷ οἱ τυφλοί,
the house approached to him the blind men,

καὶ λέγει αὐτοῖς ὁ Ἰησοῦς· πιστεύετε
and says to them - Jesus: Believe ye

ὅτι δύναμαι τοῦτο ποιῆσαι; λέγουσιν
that I can this to do? They say

αὐτῷ· ναί, κύριε. 29 τότε ἥψατο τῶν
to him: Yes, Lord. Then he touched the

ὀφθαλμῶν αὐτῶν λέγων· κατὰ τὴν
eyes of them saying: According to the

πίστιν ὑμῶν γενηθήτω ὑμῖν. 30 καὶ
faith of you let it be to you. And

ἠνεῴχθησαν αὐτῶν οἱ ὀφθαλμοί. καὶ
were opened of them the eyes. And

ἐνεβριμήθη αὐτοῖς ὁ Ἰησοῦς λέγων·
sternly admonished them - Jesus saying:

ὁρᾶτε μηδεὶς γινωσκέτω. 31 οἱ δὲ
See ²no one ¹let ³know. But they

ἐξελθόντες διεφήμισαν αὐτὸν ἐν ὅλῃ
going out spread about him in all

τῇ γῇ ἐκείνῃ. 32 Αὐτῶν δὲ ἐξερχομένων,
- land that. And them going out,ᵃ
= as they were going out,

ἰδοὺ προσήνεγκαν αὐτῷ κωφὸν δαι-
behold they brought to him a dumb man being

μονιζόμενον. 33 καὶ ἐκβληθέντος τοῦ
demon-possessed. And being expelled the
= when the demon was expelled

δαιμονίου ἐλάλησεν ὁ κωφός. καὶ ἐθαύμασαν
demonᵃ spoke the dumb man. And marvelled

οἱ ὄχλοι λέγοντες· οὐδέποτε ἐφάνη οὕτως
the crowds saying: Never it appeared thus

ἐν τῷ Ἰσραήλ. 34 οἱ δὲ Φαρισαῖοι
in - Israel. But the Pharisees

ἔλεγον· ἐν τῷ ἄρχοντι τῶν δαιμονίων
said: By the ruler of the demons

ἐκβάλλει τὰ δαιμόνια.
he expels the demons.

35 Καὶ περιῆγεν ὁ Ἰησοῦς τὰς
And went about - Jesus the

πόλεις πάσας καὶ τὰς κώμας, διδάσκων
cities all and the villages, teaching

ἐν ταῖς συναγωγαῖς αὐτῶν καὶ κηρύσσων
in the synagogues of them and proclaiming

τὸ εὐαγγέλιον τῆς βασιλείας καὶ θεραπεύων
the gospel of the kingdom and healing

πᾶσαν νόσον καὶ πᾶσαν μαλακίαν.
every disease and every illness.

36 Ἰδὼν δὲ τοὺς ὄχλους ἐσπλαγχνίσθη
And seeing the crowds he was filled with tenderness

περὶ αὐτῶν, ὅτι ἦσαν ἐσκυλμένοι καὶ
concerning them, because they were distressed and

ἐρριμμένοι ὡσεὶ πρόβατα μὴ ἔχοντα
prostrate as sheep not having

ποιμένα. 37 τότε λέγει τοῖς μαθηταῖς
a shepherd. Then he says to the disciples

αὐτοῦ· ὁ μὲν θερισμὸς πολύς, οἱ δὲ
of him: Indeed the harvest [is] much, but the

ἐργάται ὀλίγοι· 38 δεήθητε οὖν τοῦ κυρίου
workmen few; pray ye therefore the Lord

τοῦ θερισμοῦ ὅπως ἐκβάλῃ
of the harvest so that he may thrust forth

ἐργάτας εἰς τὸν θερισμὸν αὐτοῦ. 10 Καὶ
workmen into the harvest of him. And

---

to him, and he asked them, "Do you believe that I am able to do this?"

"Yes, Lord," they replied.

29 Then he touched their eyes and said, "According to your faith will it be done to you"; 30 and their sight was restored. Jesus warned them sternly, "See that no one knows about this." 31 But they went out and spread the news about him all over that region.

32 While they were going out, a man who was demon-possessed and could not talk was brought to Jesus. 33 And when the demon was driven out, the man who had been mute spoke. The crowd was amazed and said, "Nothing like this has ever been seen in Israel."

34 But the Pharisees said, "It is by the prince of demons that he drives out demons."

The Workers Are Few

35 Jesus went through all the towns and villages, teaching in their synagogues, preaching the good news of the kingdom and healing every disease and sickness. 36 When he saw the crowds, he had compassion on them, because they were harassed and helpless, like sheep without a shepherd. 37 Then he said to his disciples, "The harvest is plentiful but the workers are few. 38 Ask the Lord of the harvest, therefore, to send out workers into his harvest field."

---

[a] Other ancient authorities lack this verse

Chapter 10

The Twelve Apostles

THEN Jesus[b] summoned his twelve disciples and gave them authority over unclean spirits, to cast them out, and to cure every disease and every sickness. 2 These are the names of the twelve apostles: first, Simon, also known as Peter, and his brother Andrew; James son of Zebedee, and his brother John; 3 Philip and Bartholomew; Thomas and Matthew the tax collector; James son of Alphaeus, and Thaddaeus;[c] 4 Simon the Cananaean, and Judas Iscariot, the one who betrayed him.

The Mission of the Twelve

5 These twelve Jesus sent out with the following instructions: "Go nowhere among the Gentiles, and enter no town of the Samaritans, 6 but go rather to the lost sheep of the house of Israel. 7 As you go, proclaim the good news, 'The kingdom of heaven has come near.'[d] 8 Cure the sick, raise the dead, cleanse the lepers,[e] cast out demons. You received without payment; give without payment. 9 Take no gold, or silver, or copper in your belts, 10 no bag for your journey, or two tunics, or sandals, or a staff; for laborers deserve their food. 11 Whatever town or village you enter, find out who in it is worthy, and stay there until you leave.

προσκαλεσάμενος　τοὺς　δώδεκα　μαθητὰς
calling forward　the　twelve　disciples

αὐτοῦ　ἔδωκεν　αὐτοῖς　ἐξουσίαν　πνευμάτων
of him　he gave　to them　authority　of(over) spirits

ἀκαθάρτων　ὥστε　ἐκβάλλειν　αὐτά,　καὶ
unclean　so as　to expel　them,　and

θεραπεύειν　πᾶσαν　νόσον　καὶ　πᾶσαν　μαλα-
to heal　every　disease　and　every　ill-

κίαν.　2 Τῶν　δὲ　δώδεκα　ἀποστόλων
ness.　Now of the　twelve　apostles

τὰ　ὀνόματά　ἐστιν　ταῦτα·　πρῶτος　Σίμων
the　names　is(are)　these:　first　Simon

ὁ　λεγόμενος　Πέτρος　καὶ　'Ανδρέας　ὁ
the [one]　named　Peter　and　Andrew　the

ἀδελφὸς　αὐτοῦ,　καὶ　'Ιάκωβος　ὁ　τοῦ
brother　of him,　and　James　the [son] –

Ζεβεδαίου　καὶ　'Ιωάννης　ὁ　ἀδελφὸς　αὐτοῦ,
of Zebedee　and　John　the　brother　of him,

3 Φίλιππος　καὶ　Βαρθολομαῖος,　Θωμᾶς
Philip　and　Bartholomew,　Thomas

καὶ　Ματθαῖος　ὁ　τελώνης,　'Ιάκωβος
and　Matthew　the　tax-collector,　James

ὁ　τοῦ　'Αλφαίου　καὶ　Θαδδαῖος,　4 Σίμων
the [son] –　of Alphæus　and　Thaddæus,　Simon

ὁ　Καναναῖος　καὶ　'Ιούδας　ὁ　'Ισκαριώτης
the　Cananæan　and　Judas　–　Iscariot

ὁ　καὶ　παραδοὺς　αὐτόν.　5 Τούτους
the [one] also　betraying　him.　These

τοὺς　δώδεκα　ἀπέστειλεν　ὁ　'Ιησοῦς
–　twelve　sent forth　–　Jesus

παραγγείλας　αὐτοῖς　λέγων·
giving charge　to them　saying:

Εἰς　ὁδὸν　ἐθνῶν　μὴ　ἀπέλθητε,　καὶ
Into [the]　way　of [the] nations　go ye not,　and

εἰς　πόλιν　Σαμαριτῶν　μὴ　εἰσέλθητε·
into　a city　of Samaritans　enter not;

6 πορεύεσθε　δὲ　μᾶλλον　πρὸς　τὰ　πρόβατα
but go　rather　unto　the　sheep

τὰ　ἀπολωλότα　οἴκου　'Ισραήλ.　7 πορευ-
the　lost　of [the] house of Israel.　And

όμενοι　δὲ　κηρύσσετε　λέγοντες　ὅτι　ἤγγικεν
going　proclaim ye　saying[,]　– has drawn near

ἡ　βασιλεία　τῶν　οὐρανῶν.　8 ἀσθενοῦντας
The　kingdom　of the　heavens.　Ailing [ones]

θεραπεύετε,　νεκροὺς　ἐγείρετε,　λεπροὺς
heal ye,　dead [ones]　raise,　lepers

καθαρίζετε,　δαιμόνια　ἐκβάλλετε·　δωρεὰν
cleanse,　demons　expel;　freely

ἐλάβετε,　δωρεὰν　δότε.　9 Μὴ　κτήσησθε
ye received,　freely　give.　Do not provide

χρυσὸν　μηδὲ　ἄργυρον　μηδὲ　χαλκὸν　εἰς
gold　nor　silver　nor　brass　in

τὰς　ζώνας　ὑμων,　10 μὴ　πήραν　εἰς　ὁδὸν
the　girdles　of you,　not　a wallet　for [the] way

μηδὲ　δύο　χιτῶνας　μηδὲ　ὑποδήματα　μηδὲ
nor　two　tunics　nor　sandals　nor

ῥάβδον·　ἄξιος　γὰρ　ὁ　ἐργάτης　τῆς
a staff;　for worthy [is]　the　workman　of the

τροφῆς　αὐτοῦ.　11 εἰς　ἣν　δ᾽　ἂν　πόλιν
food　of him.　And into whatever　city

ἢ　κώμην　εἰσέλθητε,　ἐξετάσατε　τίς　ἐν
or　village　ye may enter,　inquire　who　in

αὐτῇ　ἄξιός　ἐστιν·　κἀκεῖ　μείνατε　ἕως　ἂν
it　worthy　is;　and there　remain　until

Chapter 10

Jesus Sends Out the Twelve

HE called his twelve disciples to him and gave them authority to drive out evil[j] spirits and to heal every disease and sickness.

2 These are the names of the twelve apostles: first, Simon (who is called Peter) and his brother Andrew; James son of Zebedee, and his brother John; 3 Philip and Bartholomew; Thomas and Matthew the tax collector; James son of Alphaeus, and Thaddaeus; 4 Simon the Zealot and Judas Iscariot, who betrayed him.

5 These twelve Jesus sent out with the following instructions: "Do not go among the Gentiles or enter any town of the Samaritans. 6 Go rather to the lost sheep of Israel. 7 As you go, preach this message: 'The kingdom of heaven is near.' 8 Heal the sick, raise the dead, cleanse those who have leprosy,[k] drive out demons. Freely you have received, freely give. 9 Do not take along any gold or silver or copper in your belts; 10 take no bag for the journey, or extra tunic, or sandals or a staff; for the worker is worth his keep.

11 "Whatever town or village you enter, search for some worthy person there and stay at his house until

---

[b] Gk he
[c] Other ancient authorities read Lebbaeus, or Lebbaeus called Thaddaeus
[d] Or is at hand
[e] The terms leper and leprosy can refer to several diseases

12 As you enter the house, greet it. 13 If the house is worthy, let your peace come upon it; but if it is not worthy, let your peace return to you. 14 If anyone will not welcome you or listen to your words, shake off the dust from your feet as you leave that house or town. 15 Truly I tell you, it will be more tolerable for the land of Sodom and Gomorrah on the day of judgment than for that town.

Coming Persecutions

16 "See, I am sending you out like sheep into the midst of wolves; so be wise as serpents and innocent as doves. 17 Beware of them, for they will hand you over to councils and flog you in their synagogues; 18 and you will be dragged before governors and kings because of me, as a testimony to them and the Gentiles. 19 When they hand you over, do not worry about how you are to speak or what you are to say; for what you are to say will be given to you at that time; 20 for it is not you who speak, but the Spirit of your Father speaking through you. 21 Brother will betray brother to death, and a father his child, and children will rise against parents and have them put to death; 22 and you will be hated by all because of my name. But the one who endures to the end will be saved. 23 When they persecute you in one town, flee

---

ἐξέλθητε. 12 εἰσερχόμενοι δὲ εἰς τὴν
ye may go out.　　And entering　　into　the

οἰκίαν ἀσπάσασθε αὐτήν· 13 καὶ ἐὰν μὲν
house　　greet　　　it;　　　and　if　indeed

ᾖ ἡ οἰκία ἀξία, ἐλθάτω ἡ εἰρήνη ὑμῶν
be the house worthy, let come the peace of you

ἐπ' αὐτήν· ἐὰν δὲ μὴ ᾖ ἀξία, ἡ εἰρήνη
on　it;　but if　it be not　worthy, the　peace

ὑμῶν πρὸς ὑμᾶς ἐπιστραφήτω. 14 καὶ
of you　unto　you　　let return.　　And

ὃς ἂν μὴ δέξηται ὑμᾶς μηδὲ ἀκούσῃ
whoever may not receive　you　nor　hear

τοὺς λόγους ὑμῶν, ἐξερχόμενοι ἔξω
the　words　of you,　going out　outside

τῆς οἰκίας ἢ τῆς πόλεως ἐκείνης ἐκτινά-
-　house　or　-　city　that　shake

ξατε τὸν κονιορτὸν τῶν ποδῶν ὑμῶν.
off　the　dust　of the　feet　of you.

15 ἀμὴν λέγω ὑμῖν, ἀνεκτότερον ἔσται
Truly I tell you,　more tolerable it will be [for]

γῇ Σοδόμων καὶ Γομόρρων ἐν ἡμέρᾳ κρίσεως
[the] land of Sodom and Gomorra in [the] day of judgment

ἢ τῇ πόλει ἐκείνῃ. 16 Ἰδοὺ ἐγὼ
than [for]　-　city　that.　　Behold　I

ἀποστέλλω ὑμᾶς ὡς πρόβατα ἐν μέσῳ
send forth　you　as　sheep　in [the] midst

λύκων· γίνεσθε οὖν φρόνιμοι ὡς οἱ
of wolves;　be ye　therefore prudent　as　-

ὄφεις καὶ ἀκέραιοι ὡς αἱ περιστεραί.
serpents and　harmless　as　-　doves.

17 Προσέχετε δὲ ἀπὸ τῶν ἀνθρώπων·
And beware　　from (of)　-　　men;

παραδώσουσιν γὰρ ὑμᾶς εἰς συνέδρια,
for they will deliver up　you　to　councils,

καὶ ἐν ταῖς συναγωγαῖς αὐτῶν μαστιγώ-
and in the　synagogues　of them　they will

σουσιν ὑμᾶς· 18 καὶ ἐπὶ ἡγεμόνας δὲ καὶ
scourge　you;　and before leaders and also

βασιλεῖς ἀχθήσεσθε ἕνεκεν ἐμοῦ, εἰς
kings　ye will be led　for the sake of　me,　for

μαρτύριον αὐτοῖς καὶ τοῖς ἔθνεσιν.
a testimony　to them　and　to the　nations.

19 ὅταν δὲ παραδῶσιν ὑμᾶς, μὴ μεριμνή-
But when　they deliver up　you,　do not be

σητε πῶς ἢ τί λαλήσητε· δοθήσεται
anxious how　or what ye may say;　[1]it will be given

γὰρ ὑμῖν ἐν ἐκείνῃ τῇ ὥρᾳ τί λαλήσητε·
[1]for to you in　that　-　hour what ye may say;

20 οὐ γὰρ ὑμεῖς ἐστε οἱ λαλοῦντες,
for not　ye　are the [ones]　speaking,

ἀλλὰ τὸ πνεῦμα τοῦ πατρὸς ὑμῶν τὸ
but　the　Spirit　of the　Father　of you the [one]

λαλοῦν ἐν ὑμῖν. 21 παραδώσει δὲ
speaking in　you.　And [1]will deliver up

ἀδελφὸς • ἀδελφὸν εἰς θάνατον καὶ πατὴρ
[1]brother　brother　to　death　and　father

τέκνον, καὶ ἐπαναστήσονται τέκνα ἐπὶ
child,　and　will stand up　children against

γονεῖς καὶ θανατώσουσιν αὐτούς. 22 καὶ
parents and　put to death　them.　And

ἔσεσθε μισούμενοι ὑπὸ πάντων διὰ
ye will be　being hated　by　all men on account of

τὸ ὄνομά μου· ὁ δὲ ὑπομείνας εἰς
the　name　of me; but the [one]　enduring　to

τέλος, οὗτος σωθήσεται. 23 ὅταν δὲ
[the] end,　this　will be saved.　But when

---

you leave. 12 As you enter the home, give it your greeting. 13 If the home is deserving, let your peace rest on it; if it is not, let your peace return to you. 14 If anyone will not welcome you or listen to your words, shake the dust off your feet when you leave that home or town. 15 I tell you the truth, it will be more bearable for Sodom and Gomorrah on the day of judgment than for that town. 16 I am sending you out like sheep among wolves. Therefore be as shrewd as snakes and as innocent as doves.

17 "Be on your guard against men; they will hand you over to the local councils and flog you in their synagogues. 18 On my account you will be brought before governors and kings as witnesses to them and to the Gentiles. 19 But when they arrest you, do not worry about what to say or how to say it. At that time you will be given what to say, 20 for it will not be you speaking, but the Spirit of your Father speaking through you.

21 "Brother will betray brother to death, and a father his child; children will rebel against their parents and have them put to death. 22 All men will hate you because of me, but he who stands firm to the end will be saved. 23 When you are

to the next; for truly I tell you, you will not have gone through all the towns of Israel before the Son of Man comes.

24 "A disciple is not above the teacher, nor a slave above the master; 25 it is enough for the disciple to be like the teacher, and the slave like the master. If they have called the master of the house Beelzebul, how much more will they malign those of his household!

Whom to Fear

26 "So have no fear of them; for nothing is covered up that will not be uncovered, and nothing secret that will not become known. 27 What I say to you in the dark, tell in the light; and what you hear whispered, proclaim from the housetops. 28 Do not fear those who kill the body but cannot kill the soul; rather fear him who can destroy both soul and body in hell.*f* 29 Are not two sparrows sold for a penny? Yet not one of them will fall to the ground apart from your Father. 30 And even the hairs of your head are all counted. 31 So do not be afraid; you are of more value than many sparrows.

32 "Everyone therefore who acknowledges me before others, I also will acknowledge before my Father in heaven; 33 but whoever denies me before others, I also will deny before my Father in heaven.

διώκωσιν ὑμᾶς ἐν τῇ πόλει ταύτῃ,
they persecute you in - city this,

φεύγετε εἰς τὴν ἑτέραν· ἀμὴν γὰρ
flee ye to [an]other; for truly

λέγω ὑμῖν, οὐ μὴ τελέσητε τὰς πόλεις
I tell you, by no means ye will complete the cities

[τοῦ] Ἰσραὴλ ἕως ἔλθῃ ὁ υἱὸς τοῦ ἀν-
- of Israel until comes the Son - of

θρώπου. 24 Οὐκ ἔστιν μαθητὴς ὑπὲρ
man. not is A disciple above

τὸν διδάσκαλον οὐδὲ δοῦλος ὑπὲρ τὸν
the teacher nor a slave above the

κύριον αὐτοῦ. 25 ἀρκετὸν τῷ μαθητῇ
lord of him. Enough for the disciple

ἵνα γένηται ὡς ὁ διδάσκαλος αὐτοῦ,
that he be as the teacher of him,

καὶ ὁ δοῦλος ὡς ὁ κύριος αὐτοῦ. εἰ
and the slave as the lord of him. If

τὸν οἰκοδεσπότην Βεεζεβοὺλ ἐπεκάλεσαν,
the housemaster Beelzebub they called,

πόσῳ μᾶλλον τοὺς οἰκιακοὺς αὐτοῦ.
how much more the members of [the] household of him.

26 μὴ οὖν φοβηθῆτε αὐτούς· οὐδὲν γὰρ
Therefore fear ye not them; for nothing

ἐστιν κεκαλυμμένον ὃ οὐκ ἀποκαλυφ-
is *having been* veiled which will not be un-

θήσεται, καὶ κρυπτὸν ὃ οὐ γνωσθήσεται.
veiled, and hidden which will not be made known.

27 ὃ λέγω ὑμῖν ἐν τῇ σκοτίᾳ, εἴπατε
What I say to you in the darkness, say ye

ἐν τῷ φωτί· καὶ ὃ εἰς τὸ οὖς ἀκούετε,
in the light; and what in the ear ye hear,

κηρύξατε ἐπὶ τῶν δωμάτων. 28 καὶ
proclaim on the housetops. And

μὴ φοβεῖσθε ἀπὸ τῶν ἀποκτεννόντων
do not fear - the [ones] killing

τὸ σῶμα, τὴν δὲ ψυχὴν μὴ δυναμένων
the body, but the soul not *being* able

ἀποκτεῖναι· φοβεῖσθε δὲ μᾶλλον τὸν
to kill; but fear ye rather the [one]

δυνάμενον καὶ ψυχὴν καὶ σῶμα ἀπολέσαι
being able both soul and body to destroy

ἐν γεέννῃ. 29 οὐχὶ δύο στρουθία ἀσσα-
in gehenna. Not two sparrows of(for) a

ρίου πωλεῖται; καὶ ἓν ἐξ αὐτῶν οὐ
farthing are sold? and one of them not

πεσεῖται ἐπὶ τὴν γῆν ἄνευ τοῦ πατρὸς
will fall on the earth without the Father

ὑμῶν. 30 ὑμῶν δὲ καὶ αἱ τρίχες τῆς
of you. But of you even the hairs of the

κεφαλῆς πᾶσαι ἠριθμημέναι εἰσίν. 31 μὴ
head all *having been* numbered are. not

οὖν φοβεῖσθε· πολλῶν στρουθίων διαφέρετε
Therefore fear ye; ³many ⁴sparrows ²excel

ὑμεῖς. 32 Πᾶς οὖν ὅστις ὁμολογήσει
¹ye. Everyone therefore who shall confess

ἐν ἐμοὶ ἔμπροσθεν τῶν ἀνθρώπων,
- me before - men,

ὁμολογήσω κἀγὼ ἐν αὐτῷ ἔμπροσθεν
will confess I also - him before

τοῦ πατρός μου τοῦ ἐν τοῖς οὐρανοῖς·
the Father of me - in the heavens;

33 ὅστις δ' ἂν ἀρνήσηται με ἔμπροσθεν
and whoever denies me before

τῶν ἀνθρώπων, ἀρνήσομαι κἀγὼ αὐτὸν
- men, will deny I also him

---

persecuted in one place, flee to another. I tell you the truth, you will not finish going through the cities of Israel before the Son of Man comes.

24 "A student is not above his teacher, nor a servant above his master. 25 It is enough for the student to be like his teacher, and the servant like his master. If the head of the house has been called Beelzebub,*l* how much more the members of his household!

26 "So do not be afraid of them. There is nothing concealed that will not be disclosed, or hidden that will not be made known. 27 What I tell you in the dark, speak in the daylight; what is whispered in your ear, proclaim from the roofs. 28 Do not be afraid of those who kill the body but cannot kill the soul. Rather, be afraid of the One who can destroy both soul and body in hell. 29 Are not two sparrows sold for a penny*m*? Yet not one of them will fall to the ground apart from the will of your Father. 30 And even the very hairs of your head are all numbered. 31 So don't be afraid; you are worth more than many sparrows.

32 "Whoever acknowledges me before men, I will also acknowledge him before my Father in heaven. 33 But whoever disowns me before men, I will disown

---

Not Peace, but a Sword

34 "Do not think that I have come to bring peace to the earth; I have not come to bring peace, but a sword. 35 For I have come to

set a man against his father,
and a daughter against her mother,
and a daughter-in-law against her mother-in-law;

36 and one's foes will be members of one's own household.

37 Whoever loves father or mother more than me is not worthy of me; and whoever loves son or daughter more than me is not worthy of me; 38 and whoever does not take up the cross and follow me is not worthy of me. 39 Those who find their life will lose it, and those who lose their life for my sake will find it.

Rewards

40 "Whoever welcomes you welcomes me, and whoever welcomes me welcomes the one who sent me. 41 Whoever welcomes a prophet in the name of a prophet will receive a prophet's reward; and whoever welcomes a righteous person in the name of a righteous person will receive the reward of the righteous; 42 and whoever gives even a cup of cold water to one of these little ones in the name of a disciple—truly I tell you, none of these will lose their reward."

ἔμπροσθεν τοῦ πατρός μου τοῦ ἐν
before   the   Father of me the   in

τοῖς οὐρανοῖς. 34 Μὴ νομίσητε ὅτι
the heavens.   Do not suppose that

ἦλθον βαλεῖν εἰρήνην ἐπὶ τὴν γῆν· οὐκ ἦλθον
I came to bring peace on the earth; I came not

βαλεῖν εἰρήνην ἀλλὰ μάχαιραν. 35 ἦλθον γὰρ
to bring peace but   a sword.   For I came

διχάσαι ἄνθρωπον κατὰ τοῦ πατρὸς
to make hostile a man   against the father

αὐτοῦ καὶ θυγατέρα κατὰ τῆς μητρὸς
of him and a daughter against the mother

αὐτῆς καὶ νύμφην κατὰ τῆς πενθερᾶς
of her and a bride against the mother-in-law

αὐτῆς, 36 καὶ ἐχθροὶ τοῦ ἀνθρώπου οἱ
of her,   and [the] enemies of a man the

οἰκιακοὶ αὐτοῦ. 37 Ὁ φιλῶν πατέρα
members of [the] household of him. The [one] loving father

ἢ μητέρα ὑπὲρ ἐμὲ οὐκ ἔστιν μου ἄξιος·
or mother beyond me is not   of me worthy;

καὶ ὁ φιλῶν υἱὸν ἢ θυγατέρα ὑπὲρ
and the [one] loving son or daughter beyond

ἐμὲ οὐκ ἔστιν μου ἄξιος· 38 καὶ ὃς
me is not   of me worthy;   and [he] who

οὐ λαμβάνει τὸν σταυρὸν αὐτοῦ καὶ
takes not the   cross   of him and

ἀκολουθεῖ ὀπίσω μου, οὐκ ἔστιν μου
follows   after me,   is not   of me

ἄξιος. 39 ὁ εὑρὼν τὴν ψυχὴν αὐτοῦ
worthy.   The [one] finding the life of him

ἀπολέσει αὐτήν, καὶ ὁ ἀπολέσας τὴν
will lose it,   and the [one] losing the

ψυχὴν αὐτοῦ ἕνεκεν ἐμοῦ εὑρήσει αὐτήν.
life of him for the sake of me will find it.

40 Ὁ δεχόμενος ὑμᾶς ἐμὲ δέχεται, καὶ
The [one] receiving you me receives, and

ὁ ἐμὲ δεχόμενος δέχεται τὸν
the [one] me receiving receives the [one]

ἀποστείλαντά με. 41 ὁ δεχόμενος προ-
having sent me.   The [one] receiving a pro-

φήτην εἰς ὄνομα προφήτου μισθὸν
phet in [the] name of a prophet [the] reward

προφήτου λήμψεται, καὶ ὁ δεχόμενος
of a prophet will receive, and the [one] receiving

δίκαιον εἰς ὄνομα δικαίου μισθὸν
a righteous man in [the] name of a righteous man [the] reward

δικαίου λήμψεται. 42 καὶ ὃς ἐὰν ποτίσῃ
of a righteous man will receive. And whoever gives to drink

ἕνα τῶν μικρῶν τούτων ποτήριον ψυχροῦ
one - of these little [ones] a cup of cold water

μόνον εἰς ὄνομα μαθητοῦ, ἀμὴν λέγω ὑμῖν,
only in [the] name of a disciple, truly I tell you,

οὐ μὴ ἀπολέσῃ τὸν μισθὸν αὐτοῦ.
on no account will he lose the reward of him.

---

him before my Father in heaven.

34 "Do not suppose that I have come to bring peace to the earth. I did not come to bring peace, but a sword. 35 For I have come to turn

" 'a man against his father,
a daughter against her mother,
a daughter-in-law against her mother-in-law—

36 a man's enemies will be the members of his own household.' [n]

37 "Anyone who loves his father or mother more than me is not worthy of me; anyone who loves his son or daughter more than me is not worthy of me; 38 and anyone who does not take his cross and follow me is not worthy of me. 39 Whoever finds his life will lose it, and whoever loses his life for my sake will find it.

40 "He who receives you receives me, and he who receives me receives the one who sent me. 41 Anyone who receives a prophet because he is a prophet will receive a prophet's reward, and anyone who receives a righteous man because he is a righteous man will receive a righteous man's reward. 42 And if anyone gives even a cup of cold water to one of these little ones because he is my disciple, I tell you the truth, he will certainly not lose his reward."

Chapter 11

NOW when Jesus had finished instructing his twelve disciples, he went on from there to teach and proclaim his message in their cities.

---

11 Καὶ ἐγένετο ὅτε ἐτέλεσεν ὁ
And   it came to pass when ended

Ἰησοῦς διατάσσων τοῖς δώδεκα μαθηταῖς
Jesus giving charge to the twelve disciples

αὐτοῦ, μετέβη ἐκεῖθεν τοῦ διδάσκειν
of him, he removed thence -   to teach [d]

καὶ κηρύσσειν ἐν ταῖς πόλεσιν αὐτῶν.
and to proclaim [d] in the cities of them.

Chapter 11

Jesus and John the Baptist

AFTER Jesus had finished instructing his twelve disciples, he went on from there to teach and preach in the towns of Galilee. [o]

n36 Micah 7:6
o1 Greek in their towns

Messengers from John the Baptist

2 When John heard in prison what the Messiah[g] was doing, he sent word by his[h] disciples [3]and said to him, "Are you the one who is to come, or are we to wait for another?" [4]Jesus answered them, "Go and tell John what you hear and see: [5]the blind receive their sight, the lame walk, the lepers[i] are cleansed, the deaf hear, the dead are raised, and the poor have good news brought to them. [6]And blessed is anyone who takes no offense at me."

Jesus Praises John the Baptist

7 As they went away, Jesus began to speak to the crowds about John: "What did you go out into the wilderness to look at? A reed shaken by the wind? [8]What then did you go out to see? Someone[j] dressed in soft robes? Look, those who wear soft robes are in royal palaces. [9]What then did you go out to see? A prophet?[k] Yes, I tell you, and more than a prophet. [10]This is the one about whom it is written,

'See, I am sending my
    messenger
    ahead of you,
who will prepare
    your way
    before you.'

[11]Truly I tell you, among those born of women no one has arisen greater than John the Baptist; yet the least in the kingdom of heaven is greater than he. [12]From the days of John the Baptist until now, the kingdom of heaven has suffered violence,[l] and the violent take it by force. [13]For all the prophets and the law prophesied until John

[g] Or the Christ
[h] Other ancient authorities read two of his
[i] The terms leper and leprosy can refer to several diseases
[j] Or Why then did you go out? To see someone
[k] Other ancient authorities read Why then did you go out? To see a prophet?
[l] Or has been coming violently

---

2 Ὁ δὲ Ἰωάννης ἀκούσας ἐν τῷ
   - But   John   hearing   in   the
δεσμωτηρίῳ τὰ ἔργα τοῦ Χριστοῦ,
  prison   the   works   -   of Christ,
πέμψας διὰ τῶν μαθητῶν αὐτοῦ 3 εἶπεν
sending through   the   disciples   of him   said
αὐτῷ· σὺ εἶ ὁ ἐρχόμενος, ἢ ἕτερον
to him: Thou art   the   coming [one],   or   another
προσδοκῶμεν; 4 καὶ ἀποκριθεὶς ὁ
may we expect?   And   answering   -
Ἰησοῦς εἶπεν αὐτοῖς· πορευθέντες ἀπαγ-
Jesus   said   to them: Going   re-
γείλατε Ἰωάννῃ ἃ ἀκούετε καὶ βλέπετε·
port   to John [the things] which ye hear and   see:
5 τυφλοὶ ἀναβλέπουσιν καὶ χωλοὶ
  blind men   see again   and   lame men
περιπατοῦσιν, λεπροὶ καθαρίζονται καὶ κωφοὶ
  walk,   lepers   are cleansed   and deaf men
ἀκούουσιν, καὶ νεκροὶ ἐγείρονται καὶ
  hear,   and   dead men   are raised   and
πτωχοὶ εὐαγγελίζονται· 6 καὶ μακάριός
poor men   are evangelized;   and   blessed
ἐστιν ὃς ἐὰν μὴ σκανδαλισθῇ ἐν ἐμοι.
  is   whoever   is not offended   in   me.
7 Τούτων δὲ πορευομένων ἤρξατο ὁ
And these   going[a]   began   -
= as these were going
Ἰησοῦς λέγειν τοῖς ὄχλοις περὶ Ἰωάννου·
Jesus   to say   to the   crowds concerning John:
τί ἐξήλθατε εἰς τὴν ἔρημον θεάσασθαι;
What went ye out   into   the   wilderness   to see?
κάλαμον ὑπὸ ἀνέμου σαλευόμενον; 8 ἀλλὰ
a reed   by   wind   being shaken?   But
τί ἐξήλθατε ἰδεῖν; ἄνθρωπον ἐν μαλακοῖς
what went ye out to see?   a man   in   soft material
ἠμφιεσμένον; ἰδοὺ οἱ τὰ μαλακὰ
having been clothed? Behold[,] the [ones]   -   soft material
φοροῦντες ἐν τοῖς οἴκοις τῶν βασιλέων. 9 ἀλλὰ
wearing [are] in   the   houses   -   of kings.   But
τί ἐξήλθατε; προφήτην ἰδεῖν; ναὶ λέγω
why went ye out?   a prophet   to see? Yes[,]   I tell
ὑμῖν, καὶ περισσότερον προφήτου. 10 οὗτός
you,   and   more [than] a prophet.   This
ἐστιν περὶ οὗ γέγραπται· ἰδοὺ ἐγὼ
is he concerning whom it has been written: Behold[,] I
ἀποστέλλω τὸν ἄγγελόν μου πρὸ προσώπου
send forth   the   messenger   of me before [the] face
σου, ὃς κατασκευάσει τὴν ὁδόν σου
of thee, who   will prepare   the   way   of thee
ἔμπροσθέν σου. 11 ἀμὴν λέγω ὑμῖν,
  before   thee.   Truly   I tell   you,
οὐκ ἐγήγερται ἐν γεννητοῖς γυναικῶν
there has not arisen   among [those] born   of women
μείζων Ἰωάννου τοῦ βαπτιστοῦ· ὁ δὲ
a greater [than] John   the   Baptist;   but the
μικρότερος ἐν τῇ βασιλείᾳ τῶν οὐρανῶν
  lesser   in   the   kingdom   of the   heavens
μείζων αὐτοῦ ἐστιν. 12 ἀπὸ δὲ τῶν
greater [than]   he   is.   And from   the
ἡμερῶν Ἰωάννου τοῦ βαπτιστοῦ ἕως
  days   of John   the   Baptist   until
ἄρτι ἡ βασιλεία τῶν οὐρανῶν βιάζεται,
now the kingdom   of the   heavens   is forcibly treated,
καὶ βιασταὶ ἁρπάζουσιν αὐτήν. 13 πάντες γὰρ
and forceful men   seize   it.   For all
οἱ προφῆται καὶ ὁ νόμος ἕως
the   prophets   and   the   law   until

---

[2]When John heard in prison what Christ was doing, he sent his disciples [3]to ask him, "Are you the one who was to come, or should we expect someone else?"

[4]Jesus replied, "Go back and report to John what you hear and see: [5]The blind receive sight, the lame walk, those who have leprosy[p] are cured, the deaf hear, the dead are raised, and the good news is preached to the poor. [6]Blessed is the man who does not fall away on account of me."

[7]As John's disciples were leaving, Jesus began to speak to the crowd about John: "What did you go out into the desert to see? A reed swayed by the wind? [8]If not, what did you go out to see? A man dressed in fine clothes? No, those who wear fine clothes are in kings' palaces. [9]Then what did you go out to see? A prophet? Yes, I tell you, and more than a prophet. [10]This is the one about whom it is written:

"'I will send my
    messenger ahead of
    you,
who will prepare your
    way before you.'[q]

[11]I tell you the truth: Among those born of women there has not risen anyone greater than John the Baptist; yet he who is least in the kingdom of heaven is greater than he. [12]From the days of John the Baptist until now, the kingdom of heaven has been forcefully advancing, and forceful men lay hold of it. [13]For all the Prophets and the Law prophesied until John.

[p]5 The Greek word was used for various diseases affecting the skin—not necessarily leprosy.
[q]10 Mal. 3:1

came; [14] and if you are willing to accept it, he is Elijah who is to come. [15] Let anyone with ears [m] listen!

[16] "But to what will I compare this generation? It is like children sitting in the marketplaces and calling to one another,

[17] 'We played the flute
for you, and you
did not dance;
we wailed, and you
did not mourn.'

[18] For John came neither eating nor drinking, and they say, 'He has a demon'; [19] the Son of Man came eating and drinking, and they say, 'Look, a glutton and a drunkard, a friend of tax collectors and sinners!' Yet wisdom is vindicated by her deeds." [n]

*Woes to Unrepentant
Cities*

[20] Then he began to reproach the cities in which most of his deeds of power had been done, because they did not repent. [21] "Woe to you, Chorazin! Woe to you, Bethsaida! For if the deeds of power done in you had been done in Tyre and Sidon, they would have repented long ago in sackcloth and ashes. [22] But I tell you, on the day of judgment it will be more tolerable for Tyre and Sidon than for you. [23] And you, Capernaum,
will you be exalted to
heaven?
No, you will be
brought down
to Hades.
For if the deeds of power done in you had been done in Sodom, it would have remained until this day. [24] But I tell you that on the day of judgment it will be more tolerable for the land of Sodom than for you."

Jesus Thanks His Father

[25] At that time Jesus said, "I thank [o] you, Fa-

’Ιωάννου ἐπροφήτευσαν·
John   prophesied;
δέξασθαι,   αὐτός ἐστιν
to receive [it or him], he is
ἔρχεσθαι.   15 ὁ ἔχων
to come.   The [one] having
16 Τίνι δὲ ὁμοιώσω
But to what   shall I liken
ὁμοία ἐστὶν παιδίοις
Like   it is   to children
ἀγοραῖς ἃ
marketplaces who
17 λέγουσιν·
say:
ὠρχήσασθε· ἐθρηνήσαμεν
ye did dance;   we lamented
18 ἦλθεν γὰρ ’Ιωάννης
For came   John
πίνων,   καὶ λέγουσιν·
drinking, and they say:
19 ἦλθεν ὁ υἱὸς τοῦ
Came   the Son   of
πίνων,   καὶ λέγουσιν·
drinking, and they say:
φάγος καὶ οἰνοπότης,
gluttonous and a wine-drinker,
ἁμαρτωλῶν. καὶ ἐδικαιώθη
of sinners.   And was(is) justified
τῶν ἔργων αὐτῆς.
the   works of her.
20 Τότε ἤρξατο
Then   he began
ἐν αἷς ἐγένοντο
in which happened
αὐτοῦ, ὅτι οὐ μετενόησαν·
of him, because they repented not:
Χοραζίν· οὐαί σοι,
Chorazin; woe to thee,
ἐν Τύρῳ καὶ Σιδῶνι
in Tyre and Sidon
αἱ γενόμεναι ἐν
-   having happened in
ἐν σάκκῳ καὶ
in sackcloth and
22 πλὴν λέγω ὑμῖν,
However I tell   you,
ἀνεκτότερον ἔσται
more tolerable it will be
ὑμῖν. 23 καὶ σύ,
for you.   And thou,
ἕως οὐρανοῦ ὑψωθήσῃ;
as far as heaven wast thou exalted?
καταβήσῃ· ὅτι εἰ ἐν
thou shalt descend; because if in
αἱ δυνάμεις αἱ γενόμεναι
the powerful deeds - having happened
ἔμεινεν ἂν μέχρι τῆς
it would have remained until
λέγω ὑμῖν ὅτι γῇ
I tell   you that for [the] land
ἔσται ἐν ἡμέρα κρίσεως
it will be in [the] day of judgment
25 Ἐν ἐκείνῳ τῷ
At   that   the
ὁ ’Ιησοῦς εἶπεν·
-   Jesus   said:

14 καὶ εἰ θέλετε
and if ye are willing
αὐτός ἐστιν ’Ηλίας ὁ μέλλων
he is Elias the [one] about
ὦτα ἀκουέτω.
ears   let him hear.
τὴν γενεὰν ταύτην;
-   generation this?
καθημένοις ἐν ταῖς
sitting   in the
προσφωνοῦντα τοῖς ἑτέροις
calling to   the   others
ηὐλήσαμεν ὑμῖν καὶ οὐκ
We piped   to you and not
καὶ οὐκ ἐκόψασθε.
and   ye did not mourn.
μήτε ἐσθίων μήτε
neither eating nor
δαιμόνιον ἔχει.
a demon   He has.
ἀνθρώπου ἐσθίων καὶ
man   eating and
ἰδοὺ ἄνθρωπος
Behold[,]   a man
τελωνῶν φίλος καὶ
of tax-collectors a friend and
ἡ σοφία ἀπὸ
-   wisdom from(by)
ὀνειδίζειν τὰς πόλεις
to reproach the cities
αἱ πλεῖσται δυνάμεις
the very many powerful deeds
21 οὐαί σοι,
Woe to thee,
Βηθσαϊδά· ὅτι εἰ
Bethsaida· because if
ἐγένοντο αἱ δυνάμεις
happened the powerful deeds
ὑμῖν, πάλαι ἂν
you, long ago -
σποδῷ μετενόησαν.
ashes they would have repented.
Τύρῳ καὶ Σιδῶνι
For Tyre and for Sidon
ἐν [the] ἡμέρα κρίσεως ἢ
in [the] day of judgment than
Καφαρναούμ, μὴ
Capernaum,   not
ἕως ᾅδου
as far as hades
Σοδόμοις ἐγενήθησαν
Sodom   happened
ἐν σοί,
in   thee,
σήμερον. 24 πλὴν
to-day.   However
Σοδόμων ἀνεκτότερον
of Sodom   more tolerable
ἢ σοί.
than for thee.
καιρῷ ἀποκριθεὶς
time   answering
ἐξομολογοῦμαί σοι,
I give thanks   to thee,

---

[14] And if you are willing to accept it, he is the Elijah who was to come. [15] He who has ears, let him hear.

[16] "To what can I compare this generation? They are like children sitting in the marketplaces and calling out to others:

[17] "'We played the flute
for you,
and you did not dance;
we sang a dirge,
and you did not
mourn.'

[18] For John came neither eating nor drinking, and they say, 'He has a demon.' [19] The Son of Man came eating and drinking, and they say, 'Here is a glutton and a drunkard, a friend of tax collectors and "sinners."' But wisdom is proved right by her actions."

*Woe on Unrepentant
Cities*

[20] Then Jesus began to denounce the cities in which most of his miracles had been performed, because they did not repent. [21] "Woe to you, Korazin! Woe to you, Bethsaida! If the miracles that were performed in you had been performed in Tyre and Sidon, they would have repented long ago in sackcloth and ashes. [22] But I tell you, it will be more bearable for Tyre and Sidon on the day of judgment than for you. [23] And you, Capernaum, will you be lifted up to the skies? No, you will go down to the depths. [r] If the miracles that were performed in you had been performed in Sodom, it would have remained to this day. [24] But I tell you that it will be more bearable for Sodom on the day of judgment than for you."

Rest for the Weary

[25] At that time Jesus said, "I praise you, Father, Lord

---

[m] Other ancient authorities add *to
hear*
[n] Other ancient authorities read
children
[o] Or *praise*
[r] 23 Greek *Hades*

ther, Lord of heaven and earth, because you have hidden these things from the wise and the intelligent and have revealed them to infants; 26 yes, Father, for such was your gracious will. *p* 27 All things have been handed over to me by my Father; and no one knows the Son except the Father, and no one knows the Father except the Son and anyone to whom the Son chooses to reveal him. 28 "Come to me, all you that are weary and are carrying heavy burdens, and I will give you rest. 29 Take my yoke upon you, and learn from me; for I am gentle and humble in heart, and you will find rest for your souls. 30 For my yoke is easy, and my burden is light."

πάτερ, κύριε τοῦ οὐρανοῦ καὶ τῆς γῆς,
Father, lord of the heaven and of the earth,
ὅτι ἔκρυψας ταῦτα ἀπὸ σοφῶν καὶ συνε-
because thou hiddest these things from wise and intel-
τῶν, καὶ ἀπεκάλυψας αὐτὰ νηπίοις·
ligent men, and didst reveal them to infants:
26 ναί, ὁ πατήρ, ὅτι οὕτως εὐδοκία
yes, - Father, because thus good pleasure
ἐγένετο ἔμπροσθέν σου. 27 Πάντα μοι
it was before thee. All things to me
παρεδόθη ὑπὸ τοῦ πατρός μου, καὶ
were delivered by the Father of me, and
οὐδεὶς ἐπιγινώσκει τὸν υἱὸν εἰ μὴ ὁ
no one fully knows the Son except the
πατήρ, οὐδὲ τὸν πατέρα τις ἐπιγινώσκει
Father, neither the Father anyone fully knows
εἰ μὴ ὁ υἱὸς καὶ ᾧ ἐὰν βούληται ὁ
except the Son and [he] to whom if wills the
υἱὸς ἀποκαλύψαι. 28 Δεῦτε πρός με
Son to reveal. Come unto me
πάντες οἱ κοπιῶντες καὶ πεφορτισμένοι,
all the [ones] labouring and *having been* burdened,
κἀγὼ ἀναπαύσω ὑμᾶς. 29 ἄρατε τὸν
and I will rest you. Take the
ζυγόν μου ἐφ᾽ ὑμᾶς καὶ μάθετε ἀπ᾽
yoke of me on you and learn from
ἐμοῦ, ὅτι πραΰς εἰμι καὶ ταπεινὸς τῇ
me, because meek I am and lowly
καρδίᾳ, καὶ εὑρήσετε ἀνάπαυσιν ταῖς
in heart, and ye will find rest to the
ψυχαῖς ὑμῶν· 30 ὁ γὰρ ζυγός μου
souls of you; for the yoke of me
χρηστὸς καὶ τὸ φορτίον μου ἐλαφρόν
gentle and the burden of me light
ἐστιν.
is.

of heaven and earth, because you have hidden these things from the wise and learned, and revealed them to little children. 26 Yes, Father, for this was your good pleasure. 27 "All things have been committed to me by my Father. No one knows the Son except the Father, and no one knows the Father except the Son and those to whom the Son chooses to reveal him. 28 "Come to me, all you who are weary and burdened, and I will give you rest. 29 Take my yoke upon you and learn from me, for I am gentle and humble in heart, and you will find rest for your souls. 30 For my yoke is easy and my burden is light."

Chapter 12

Plucking Grain on the Sabbath

AT that time Jesus went through the grainfields on the sabbath; his disciples were hungry, and they began to pluck heads of grain and to eat. 2 When the Pharisees saw it, they said to him, "Look, your disciples are doing what is not lawful to do on the sabbath." 3 He said to them, "Have you not read what David did when he and his companions were hungry? 4 He entered the house of God and ate the bread of the Presence, which it was not lawful for him or his companions to eat, but only for the priests. 5 Or have you not read in the

12 Ἐν ἐκείνῳ τῷ καιρῷ ἐπορεύθη ὁ
At that - time went -
Ἰησοῦς τοῖς σάββασιν διὰ τῶν σπορίμων·
Jesus on the sabbath through the cornfields;
οἱ δὲ μαθηταὶ αὐτοῦ ἐπείνασαν, καὶ
and the disciples of him hungered, and
ἤρξαντο τίλλειν στάχυας καὶ ἐσθίειν.
began to pluck ears [of corn] and to eat.
2 οἱ δὲ Φαρισαῖοι ἰδόντες εἶπαν αὐτῷ·
But the Pharisees seeing said to him:
ἰδοὺ οἱ μαθηταί σου ποιοῦσιν ὃ οὐκ
Behold[,] the disciples of thee are doing what not
ἔξεστιν ποιεῖν ἐν σαββάτῳ. 3 ὁ δὲ
it is lawful to do on a sabbath. And he
εἶπεν αὐτοῖς· οὐκ ἀνέγνωτε τί ἐποίησεν
said to them: Did ye not read what did
Δαυίδ, ὅτε ἐπείνασεν καὶ οἱ μετ᾽
David, when he hungered and the [ones] with
αὐτοῦ; 4 πῶς εἰσῆλθεν εἰς τὸν οἶκον
him? how he entered into the house
τοῦ θεοῦ καὶ τοὺς ἄρτους τῆς προ-
- of God and the loaves of the set-
θέσεως ἔφαγον, ὃ οὐκ ἐξὸν ἦν αὐτῷ
ting forth ate, which not lawful it was for him
φαγεῖν οὐδὲ τοῖς μετ᾽ αὐτοῦ, εἰ μὴ
to eat neither the [ones] with him, except
τοῖς ἱερεῦσιν μόνοις; 5 ἢ οὐκ ἀνέγνωτε
for the priests only? or did ye not read

Chapter 12

Lord of the Sabbath

AT that time Jesus went through the grainfields on the Sabbath. His disciples were hungry and began to pick some heads of grain and eat them. 2 When the Pharisees saw this, they said to him, "Look! Your disciples are doing what is unlawful on the Sabbath." 3 He answered, "Haven't you read what David did when he and his companions were hungry? 4 He entered the house of God, and he and his companions ate the consecrated bread— which was not lawful for them to do, but only for the priests. 5 Or haven't you

p Or for so it was well-pleasing in your sight

law that on the sabbath the priests in the temple break the sabbath and yet are guiltless? 6 I tell you, something greater than the temple is here. 7 But if you had known what this means, 'I desire mercy, and not sacrifice, you would not have condemned the guiltless. 8 For the Son of Man is lord of the sabbath."

The Man with a Withered Hand

9 He left that place and entered their synagogue; 10 a man was there with a withered hand, and they asked him, "Is it lawful to cure on the sabbath?" so that they might accuse him. 11 He said to them, "Suppose one of you has only one sheep and it falls into a pit on the sabbath; will you not lay hold of it and lift it out? 12 How much more valuable is a human being than a sheep! So it is lawful to do good on the sabbath." 13 Then he said to the man, "Stretch out your hand." He stretched it out, and it was restored, as sound as the other. 14 But the Pharisees went out and conspired against him, how to destroy him.

God's Chosen Servant

15 When Jesus became aware of this, he departed. Many crowds[a] followed him, and he cured all of them, 16 and he ordered them not to make him known. 17 This was to fulfill what had been spoken through the prophet Isaiah:
18 "Here is my servant,
   whom I
     have chosen,
my beloved, with
   whom my soul
   is well pleased.
I will put my Spirit
   upon him,

ἐν τῷ νόμῳ ὅτι τοῖς σάββασιν οἱ
in the law that on the sabbaths the
ἱερεῖς ἐν τῷ ἱερῷ τὸ σάββατον βεβηλοῦ-
priests in the temple the sabbath pro-
σιν καὶ ἀναίτιοί εἰσιν; 6 λέγω δὲ
fane and guiltless are? And I tell
ὑμῖν ὅτι τοῦ ἱεροῦ μεῖζόν ἐστιν ὧδε.
you that [than] the temple a greater [thing] is here.
7 εἰ δὲ ἐγνώκειτε τί ἐστιν· ἔλεος
But if ye had known what it is: Mercy
θέλω καὶ οὐ θυσίαν, οὐκ ἂν κατε-
I desire and not sacrifice, ye would not have
δικάσατε τοὺς ἀναιτίους. 8 κύριος γάρ
condemned the guiltless. For Lord
ἐστιν τοῦ σαββάτου ὁ υἱὸς τοῦ ἀνθρώπου.
is of the sabbath the Son - of man.
9 Καὶ μεταβὰς ἐκεῖθεν ἦλθεν εἰς τὴν
And removing thence he came into the
συναγωγὴν αὐτῶν. 10 καὶ ἰδοὺ ἄνθρωπος
synagogue of them. And behold[,] a man
χεῖρα ἔχων ξηράν· καὶ ἐπηρώτησαν αὐτὸν
[his] hand having ¹withered· and they questioned him
λέγοντες· εἰ ἔξεστιν τοῖς σάββασιν
saying: If it is lawful on the sabbaths
θεραπεῦσαι; ἵνα κατηγορήσωσιν αὐτοῦ.
to heal? in order that they might accuse him.
11 ὁ δὲ εἶπεν αὐτοῖς· τίς ἔσται ἐξ
So he said to them: ¹What ²will there be ³of
ὑμῶν ἄνθρωπος ὃς ἕξει πρόβατον ἕν,
⁵you ⁴man who will have sheep one,
καὶ ἐὰν ἐμπέσῃ τοῦτο τοῖς σάββασιν
and if ²fall in ¹this on the sabbaths
εἰς βόθυνον, οὐχὶ κρατήσει αὐτὸ καὶ
into a ditch, will he not lay hold of it and
ἐγερεῖ; 12 πόσῳ οὖν διαφέρει ἄνθρωπος
raise? By how much then surpasses a man
προβάτου. ὥστε ἔξεστιν τοῖς σάββασιν
a sheep. So that it is lawful on the sabbaths
καλῶς ποιεῖν. 13 τότε λέγει τῷ ἀνθρώπῳ·
well to do. Then he says to the man:
ἔκτεινόν σου τὴν χεῖρα. καὶ ἐξέτεινεν,
Stretch forth of thee the hand. And he stretched forth,
καὶ ἀπεκατεστάθη ὑγιὴς ὡς ἡ ἄλλη.
and it was restored healthy as the other.
14 ἐξελθόντες δὲ οἱ Φαρισαῖοι συμβούλιον
And going out the Pharisees counsel
ἔλαβον κατ' αὐτοῦ, ὅπως αὐτὸν ἀπολέ-
took against him, so as him they might
σωσιν. 15 Ὁ δὲ Ἰησοῦς γνοὺς ἀνε-
destroy. - But Jesus knowing de-
χώρησεν ἐκεῖθεν. καὶ ἠκολούθησαν αὐτῷ
parted thence. And followed him
πολλοί, καὶ ἐθεράπευσεν αὐτοὺς πάντας,
many, and he healed them all,
16 καὶ ἐπετίμησεν αὐτοῖς ἵνα μὴ φανερὸν
and warned them that ³not ⁴manifest
αὐτὸν ποιήσωσιν· 17 ἵνα πληρωθῇ τὸ
⁵him ¹they ²should ⁵make; that might be fulfilled the [thing]
ῥηθὲν διὰ Ἡσαίου τοῦ προφήτου
spoken through Isaiah the prophet
λέγοντος· 18 ἰδοὺ ὁ παῖς μου ὃν
saying: Behold[,] the servant of me whom
ἡρέτισα, ὁ ἀγαπητός μου ὃν εὐδόκησεν
I chose, the beloved of me [with] whom was well pleased
ἡ ψυχή μου· θήσω τὸ πνεῦμα μου ἐπ'
the soul of me; I will put the spirit of me on

---

read in the Law that on the Sabbath the priests in the temple desecrate the day and yet are innocent? 6 I tell you that one[s] greater than the temple is here. 7 If you had known what these words mean, 'I desire mercy, not sacrifice,'[t] you would not have condemned the innocent. 8 For the Son of Man is Lord of the Sabbath."

9 Going on from that place, he went into their synagogue, 10 and a man with a shriveled hand was there. Looking for a reason to accuse Jesus, they asked him, "Is it lawful to heal on the Sabbath?"

11 He said to them, "If any of you has a sheep and it falls into a pit on the Sabbath, will you not take hold of it and lift it out? 12 How much more valuable is a man than a sheep! Therefore it is lawful to do good on the Sabbath."

13 Then he said to the man, "Stretch out your hand." So he stretched it out and it was completely restored, just as sound as the other. 14 But the Pharisees went out and plotted how they might kill Jesus.

God's Chosen Servant

15 Aware of this, Jesus withdrew from that place. Many followed him, and he healed all their sick, 16 warning them not to tell who he was. 17 This was to fulfill what was spoken through the prophet Isaiah:

18 "Here is my servant
   whom I have
     chosen,
  the one I love, in
   whom I delight;
 I will put my Spirit on
   him,

---

[a] Other ancient authorities lack crowds

[s] Or something; also in verses 41 and 42
[t] Hosea 6:6

and he will proclaim justice to the Gentiles.

19 He will not wrangle or cry aloud, nor will anyone hear his voice in the streets.

20 He will not break a bruised reed or quench a smoldering wick until he brings justice to victory.

21 And in his name the Gentiles will hope."

Jesus and Beelzebul

22 Then they brought to him a demoniac who was blind and mute; and he cured him, so that the one who had been mute could speak and see. 23 All the crowds were amazed and said, "Can this be the Son of David?" 24 But when the Pharisees heard it, they said, "It is only by Beelzebul, the ruler of the demons, that this fellow casts out the demons." 25 He knew what they were thinking and said to them, "Every kingdom divided against itself is laid waste, and no city or house divided against itself will stand. 26 If Satan casts out Satan, he is divided against himself; how then will his kingdom stand? 27 If I cast out demons by Beelzebul, by whom do your own exorcists' cast them out? Therefore they will be your judges. 28 But if it is by the Spirit of God that I cast out demons, then the kingdom of God has come to you. 29 Or how can one enter a strong man's house and plunder his property, with-

αὐτόν, καὶ κρίσιν τοῖς ἔθνεσιν ἀπαγγελεῖ.
him, and judgment to the nations he will announce.

19 οὐκ ἐρίσει οὐδὲ κραυγάσει, οὐδὲ
He will not strive nor will shout, nor

ἀκούσει τις ἐν ταῖς πλατείαις τὴν
will hear anyone in the streets the

φωνὴν αὐτοῦ. **20** κάλαμον συντετριμμένον
voice of him. A reed having been bruised

οὐ κατεάξει καὶ λίνον τυφόμενον οὐ
he will not break and flax smoking not

σβέσει, ἕως ἂν ἐκβάλῃ εἰς νῖκος τὴν
he will quench, until he put forth to victory the

κρίσιν. **21** καὶ τῷ ὀνόματι αὐτοῦ ἔθνη
judgment. And in the name of him nations

ἐλπιοῦσιν.
will hope.

22 Τότε προσηνέχθη αὐτῷ δαιμονιζ-
Then was brought to him a demon-

όμενος τυφλὸς καὶ κωφός· καὶ ἐθεράπευσεν
possessed man blind and dumb; and he healed

αὐτόν, ὥστε τὸν κωφὸν λαλεῖν καὶ
him, so as the dumb to speak and

βλέπειν. **23** καὶ ἐξίσταντο πάντες οἱ
to see[b]. And were astonished all the

ὄχλοι καὶ ἔλεγον· μήτι οὗτός ἐστιν ὁ
crowds and said: not This is the

υἱὸς Δαυίδ; **24** οἱ δὲ Φαρισαῖοι ἀκού-
son of David? But the Pharisees hear-

σαντες εἶπον· οὗτος οὐκ ἐκβάλλει τὰ
ing said: This man does not expel the

δαιμόνια εἰ μὴ ἐν τῷ Βεεζεβοὺλ ἄρχοντι
demons except by - Beelzebub ruler

τῶν δαιμονίων. **25** εἰδὼς δὲ τὰς ἐνθυμήσεις
of the demons. But knowing the thoughts

αὐτῶν εἶπεν αὐτοῖς· πᾶσα βασιλεία
of them he said to them: Every kingdom

μερισθεῖσα καθ' ἑαυτῆς ἐρημοῦται,
divided against itself is brought to desolation,

καὶ πᾶσα πόλις ἢ οἰκία μερισθεῖσα καθ'
and every city or house divided against

ἑαυτῆς οὐ σταθήσεται. **26** καὶ εἰ
itself will not stand. And if

ὁ σατανᾶς τὸν σατανᾶν ἐκβάλλει, ἐφ'
- Satan 'Satan 'expels, against

ἑαυτὸν ἐμερίσθη· πῶς οὖν σταθή-
himself he was(is) divided; how therefore will

σεται ἡ βασιλεία αὐτοῦ; **27** καὶ εἰ
stand the kingdom of him? And if

ἐγὼ ἐν Βεεζεβοὺλ ἐκβάλλω τὰ δαιμόνια,
I by Beelzebub expel the demons,

οἱ υἱοὶ ὑμῶν ἐν τίνι ἐκβάλλουσιν;
the sons of you by what do they expel?

διὰ τοῦτο αὐτοὶ κριταὶ ἔσονται ὑμῶν.
therefore they judges shall be of you.

28 εἰ δὲ ἐν πνεύματι θεοῦ ἐγὼ
But if by [the] Spirit of God I

ἐκβάλλω τὰ δαιμόνια, ἄρα ἔφθασεν
expel the demons, then came

ἐφ' ὑμᾶς ἡ βασιλεία τοῦ θεοῦ. **29** ἢ
upon you the kingdom of God. Or

πῶς δύναταί τις εἰσελθεῖν εἰς τὴν
how can anyone to enter into the

οἰκίαν τοῦ ἰσχυροῦ καὶ τὰ σκεύη αὐτοῦ
house of the strong man and the vessels of him

and he will proclaim justice to the nations.

19 He will not quarrel or cry out; no one will hear his voice in the streets.

20 A bruised reed he will not break, and a smoldering wick he will not snuff out, till he leads justice to victory.

21 In his name the nations will put their hope."[u]

Jesus and Beelzebub

22 Then they brought him a demon-possessed man who was blind and mute, and Jesus healed him, so that he could both talk and see. 23 All the people were astonished and said, "Could this be the Son of David?"

24 But when the Pharisees heard this, they said, "It is only by Beelzebub,[v] the prince of demons, that this fellow drives out demons."

25 Jesus knew their thoughts and said to them, "Every kingdom divided against itself will be ruined, and every city or household divided against itself will not stand. 26 If Satan drives out Satan, he is divided against himself. How then can his kingdom stand? 27 And if I drive out demons by Beelzebub, by whom do your people drive them out? So then, they will be your judges. 28 But if I drive out demons by the Spirit of God, then the kingdom of God has come upon you.

29 "Or again, how can anyone enter a strong man's house and carry off

out first tying up the strong man? Then indeed the house can be plundered. 30 Whoever is not with me is against me, and whoever does not gather with me scatters. 31 Therefore I tell you, people will be forgiven for every sin and blasphemy, but blasphemy against the Spirit will not be forgiven. 32 Whoever speaks a word against the Son of Man will be forgiven, but whoever speaks against the Holy Spirit will not be forgiven, either in this age or in the age to come.

A Tree and Its Fruit

33 "Either make the tree good, and its fruit good; or make the tree bad, and its fruit bad; for the tree is known by its fruit. 34 You brood of vipers! How can you speak good things, when you are evil? For out of the abundance of the heart the mouth speaks. 35 The good person brings good things out of a good treasure, and the evil person brings evil things out of an evil treasure. 36 I tell you, on the day of judgment you will have to give an account for every careless word you utter; 37 for by your words you will be justified, and by your words you will be condemned."

The Sign of Jonah

38 Then some of the scribes and Pharisees said to him, "Teacher, we wish to see a sign from you."

ἁρπάσαι, ἐὰν μὴ πρῶτον δήσῃ τὸν
to seize,   if   not   first   he binds   the

ἰσχυρόν; καὶ τότε τὴν οἰκίαν αὐτοῦ
strong man?   and   then   the   house   of him

διαρπάσει. 30 ὁ μὴ ὢν μετ' ἐμοῦ
he will plunder.   The [one] not   being   with   me

κατ' ἐμοῦ ἐστιν, καὶ ὁ μὴ συνάγων μετ'
against   me   is,   and the [one] not   gathering   with

ἐμοῦ σκορπίζει. 31 Διὰ τοῦτο λέγω
me   scatters.   Therefore   I tell

ὑμῖν, πᾶσα ἁμαρτία καὶ βλασφημία
you,   all   sin   and   blasphemy

ἀφεθήσεται τοῖς ἀνθρώποις, ἡ δὲ τοῦ
will be forgiven   -   to men,   but the   of the

πνεύματος βλασφημία οὐκ ἀφεθήσεται.
Spirit   blasphemy   will not be forgiven.

32 καὶ ὃς ἐὰν εἴπῃ λόγον κατὰ τοῦ
And   whoever   speaks   a word   against   the

υἱοῦ τοῦ ἀνθρώπου, ἀφεθήσεται αὐτῷ·
Son   -   of man,   it will be forgiven   to him;

ὃς δ' ἂν εἴπῃ κατὰ τοῦ πνεύματος
but whoever   speaks   against   the   Spirit

τοῦ ἁγίου, οὐκ ἀφεθήσεται αὐτῷ
-   Holy,   it will not be forgiven   to him

οὔτε ἐν τούτῳ τῷ αἰῶνι οὔτε ἐν τῷ
neither   in   this   -   age   nor   in   the [one]

μέλλοντι. 33 Ἢ ποιήσατε τὸ δένδρον
coming.   Either   make   the   tree

καλὸν καὶ τὸν καρπὸν αὐτοῦ καλόν,
good   and   the   fruit   of it   good,

ἢ ποιήσατε τὸ δένδρον σαπρὸν καὶ τὸν
or   make   the   tree   bad   and   the

καρπὸν αὐτοῦ σαπρόν· ἐκ γὰρ τοῦ
fruit   of it   bad;   for of (by)   the

καρποῦ τὸ δένδρον γινώσκεται. 34 γεννή-
fruit   the   tree   is known.   Off-

ματα ἐχιδνῶν, πῶς δύνασθε ἀγαθὰ λαλεῖν
spring   of vipers,   how   can ye   good things   to speak

πονηροὶ ὄντες; ἐκ γὰρ τοῦ περισ-
²evil   ¹being?   for out of   the   abund-

σεύματος τῆς καρδίας τὸ στόμα λαλεῖ.
ance   of the   heart   the   mouth   speaks.

35 ὁ ἀγαθὸς ἄνθρωπος ἐκ τοῦ ἀγαθοῦ
The   good   man   out of   the   good

θησαυροῦ ἐκβάλλει ἀγαθά, καὶ ὁ πονηρὸς
treasure   puts forth   good things,   and   the   evil

ἄνθρωπος ἐκ τοῦ πονηροῦ θησαυροῦ
man   out of   the   evil   treasure

ἐκβάλλει πονηρά. 36 λέγω δὲ
puts forth   evil things.   But I tell

ὑμῖν ὅτι πᾶν ῥῆμα ἀργὸν ὃ λαλήσουσιν
you   that   every   word   idle   which   will speak

οἱ ἄνθρωποι, ἀποδώσουσιν περὶ αὐτοῦ
-   men,   they will render   concerning   it

λόγον ἐν ἡμέρᾳ κρίσεως· 37 ἐκ γὰρ
account   in [the] day   of judgment;   for of (by)

τῶν λόγων σου δικαιωθήσῃ, καὶ ἐκ
the   words   of thee   thou wilt be justified,   and   of (by)

τῶν λόγων σου καταδικασθήσῃ.
the   words   of thee   thou wilt be condemned.

38 Τότε ἀπεκρίθησαν αὐτῷ τινες τῶν
Then   answered   him   some   of the

γραμματέων καὶ Φαρισαίων λέγοντες·
scribes   and   Pharisees   saying:

διδάσκαλε, θέλομεν ἀπὸ σοῦ σημεῖον ἰδεῖν.
Teacher,   we wish   from   thee   a sign   to see.

his possessions unless he first ties up the strong man? Then he can rob his house. 30 "He who is not with me is against me, and he who does not gather with me scatters. 31 And so I tell you, every sin and blasphemy will be forgiven men, but the blasphemy against the Spirit will not be forgiven. 32 Anyone who speaks a word against the Son of Man will be forgiven, but anyone who speaks against the Holy Spirit will not be forgiven, either in this age or in the age to come.

33 "Make a tree good and its fruit will be good, or make a tree bad and its fruit will be bad, for a tree is recognized by its fruit. 34 You brood of vipers, how can you who are evil say anything good? For out of the overflow of the heart the mouth speaks. 35 The good man brings good things out of the good stored up in him, and the evil man brings evil things out of the evil stored up in him. 36 But I tell you that men will have to give account on the day of judgment for every careless word they have spoken. 37 For by your words you will be acquitted, and by your words you will be condemned."

The Sign of Jonah

38 Then some of the Pharisees and teachers of the law said to him, "Teacher, we want to see a miraculous sign from you."

39 But he answered them, "An evil and adulterous generation asks for a sign, but no sign will be given to it except the sign of the prophet Jonah. 40 For just as Jonah was three days and three nights in the belly of the sea monster, so for three days and three nights the Son of Man will be in the heart of the earth. 41 The people of Nineveh will rise up at the judgment with this generation and condemn it, because they repented at the proclamation of Jonah, and see, something greater than Jonah is here! 42 The queen of the South will rise up at the judgment with this generation and condemn it, because she came from the ends of the earth to listen to the wisdom of Solomon, and see, something greater than Solomon is here!

The Return of the Unclean Spirit

43 "When the unclean spirit has gone out of a person, it wanders through waterless regions looking for a resting place, but it finds none. 44 Then it says, 'I will return to my house from which I came.' When it comes, it finds it empty, swept, and put in order. 45 Then it goes and brings along seven other spirits more evil than itself, and they enter and live there; and the last state of that person is worse than the first. So will it be also with this evil generation."

The True Kindred of Jesus

46 While he was still speaking to the crowds, his

---

39 ὁ   δὲ   ἀποκριθεὶς   εἶπεν   αὐτοῖς·
But he   answering   said   to them:

γενεὰ   πονηρὰ   καὶ   μοιχαλὶς   σημεῖον
generation An evil   and   adulterous   a sign

ἐπιζητεῖ,   καὶ   σημεῖον   οὐ   δοθήσεται
seeks,   and   a sign   shall not be given

αὐτῇ   εἰ   μὴ   τὸ   σημεῖον   Ἰωνᾶ   τοῦ
to it   except   the   sign   of Jonas

προφήτου. **40** ὥσπερ   γὰρ   ἦν   Ἰωνᾶς
prophet.   For as   was   Jonas

ἐν τῇ κοιλίᾳ τοῦ κήτους τρεῖς ἡμέρας
in the belly   of the sea monster three days

καὶ τρεῖς νύκτας, οὕτως ἔσται ὁ υἱὸς
and three nights,   so   will be the Son

τοῦ ἀνθρώπου ἐν τῇ καρδίᾳ τῆς γῆς
-    of man   in the heart   of the earth

τρεῖς ἡμέρας καὶ τρεῖς νύκτας. **41** ἄνδρες
three days   and three nights.   Men

Νινευῖται ἀναστήσονται ἐν τῇ κρίσει
Ninevites   will stand up   in the judgment

μετὰ τῆς γενεᾶς ταύτης καὶ κατα-
with   -   generation this   and will

κρινοῦσιν αὐτήν· ὅτι μετενόησαν εἰς τὸ
condemn   it;   because they repented at the

κήρυγμα Ἰωνᾶ, καὶ ἰδοὺ πλεῖον   Ἰωνᾶ
proclamation of Jonas, and behold a greater thing [than] Jonas

ὧδε. **42** βασίλισσα νότου   ἐγερθήσεται
[is] here.   [The] queen of [the] south will be raised

ἐν τῇ κρίσει μετὰ τῆς γενεᾶς ταύτης
in the judgment with   -   generation this

καὶ κατακρινεῖ αὐτήν· ὅτι ἦλθεν ἐκ
and will condemn it;   because she came out of

τῶν περάτων τῆς γῆς ἀκοῦσαι τὴν σοφίαν
the limits   of the earth to hear the wisdom

Σολομῶνος, καὶ ἰδοὺ πλεῖον Σολομῶνος
of Solomon, and behold a greater thing [than] Solomon

ὧδε. **43** Ὅταν δὲ τὸ ἀκάθαρτον πνεῦμα
[is] here.   Now when the unclean   spirit

ἐξέλθῃ ἀπὸ τοῦ ἀνθρώπου, διέρχεται δι'
goes out from   -   a man,   he goes through

ἀνύδρων τόπων ζητοῦν ἀνάπαυσιν, καὶ
dry   places seeking rest,   and

οὐχ εὑρίσκει. **44** τότε λέγει· εἰς τὸν
finds not.   Then   he says: Into the

οἶκόν μου ἐπιστρέψω ὅθεν ἐξῆλθον·
house of me I will return whence I came out;

καὶ ἐλθὸν εὑρίσκει σχολάζοντα [καὶ]
and coming he finds [it] standing empty and

σεσαρωμένον καὶ κεκοσμημένον. **45** τότε
having been swept and having been furnished. Then

πορεύεται καὶ παραλαμβάνει μεθ' ἑαυτοῦ
he goes   and   takes   with himself

ἑπτὰ ἕτερα πνεύματα πονηρότερα ἑαυτοῦ,
seven other spirits   more evil [than] himself,

καὶ εἰσελθόντα κατοικεῖ ἐκεῖ· καὶ
and entering   dwells   there;   and

γίνεται τὰ ἔσχατα τοῦ ἀνθρώπου ἐκείνου
becomes the last things -   man   of that

χείρονα τῶν πρώτων. οὕτως ἔσται
worse [than] the first.   Thus   it will be

καὶ τῇ γενεᾷ ταύτῃ τῇ πονηρᾷ.
also - 'generation 'to this - 'evil.

46 Ἔτι αὐτοῦ λαλοῦντος τοῖς ὄχλοις,
Yet   him   speaking*   to the crowds,
=While he was still speaking

---

39 He answered, "A wicked and adulterous generation asks for a miraculous sign! But none will be given it except the sign of the prophet Jonah. 40 For as Jonah was three days and three nights in the belly of a huge fish, so the Son of Man will be three days and three nights in the heart of the earth. 41 The men of Nineveh will stand up at the judgment with this generation and condemn it; for they repented at the preaching of Jonah, and now one w greater than Jonah is here. 42 The Queen of the South will rise at the judgment with this generation and condemn it; for she came from the ends of the earth to listen to Solomon's wisdom, and now one greater than Solomon is here.
43 "When an evil x spirit comes out of a man, it goes through arid places seeking rest and does not find it. 44 Then it says, 'I will return to the house I left.' When it arrives, it finds the house unoccupied, swept clean and put in order. 45 Then it goes and takes with it seven other spirits more wicked than itself, and they go in and live there. And the final condition of that man is worse than the first. That is how it will be with this wicked generation."

Jesus' Mother and Brothers

46 While Jesus was still talking to the crowd, his

---

w 41 Or something; also in verse 42
x 43 Greek unclean

mother and his brothers were standing outside, wanting to speak to him. [47] Someone told him, "Look, your mother and your brothers are standing outside, wanting to speak to you." [s] [48] But to the one who had told him this, Jesus [t] replied, "Who is my mother, and who are my brothers?" [49] And pointing to his disciples, he said, "Here are my mother and my brothers! [50] For whoever does the will of my Father in heaven is my brother and sister and mother."

ἰδοὺ ἡ μήτηρ καὶ οἱ ἀδελφοὶ αὐτοῦ
behold the mother and the brothers of him

εἰστήκεισαν ἔξω ζητοῦντες αὐτῷ λαλῆσαι.
stood outside seeking to him to speak.

47 [εἶπεν δέ τις αὐτῷ· ἰδοὺ ἡ μήτηρ
And said someone to him: Behold[,] the mother

σου καὶ οἱ ἀδελφοί σου ἔξω ἑστήκασιν
of thee and the brothers of thee outside are standing

ζητοῦντές σοι λαλῆσαι.] **48** ὁ δὲ
seeking to thee to speak.] And he

ἀποκριθεὶς εἶπεν τῷ λέγοντι αὐτῷ· τίς
answering said to the [one] saying to him: Who

ἐστιν ἡ μήτηρ μου, καὶ τίνες εἰσίν οἱ
is the mother of me, and who are the

ἀδελφοί μου; **49** καὶ ἐκτείνας τὴν
brothers of me? And stretching forth the

χεῖρα [αὐτοῦ] ἐπὶ τοὺς μαθητὰς αὐτοῦ
hand of him on the disciples of him

εἶπεν· ἰδοὺ ἡ μήτηρ μου καὶ οἱ ἀδελφοί
he said: Behold[,] the mother of me and the brothers

μου. **50** ὅστις γὰρ ἂν ποιήσῃ τὸ θέλημα
of me. For whoever does the will

τοῦ πατρός μου τοῦ ἐν οὐρανοῖς, αὐτός
of the Father of me – in heavens, he

μου ἀδελφὸς καὶ ἀδελφὴ καὶ μήτηρ ἐστίν.
of me brother and sister and mother is.

mother and brothers stood outside, wanting to speak to him. [47] Someone told him, "Your mother and brothers are standing outside, wanting to speak to you." [y] [48] He replied to him, "Who is my mother, and who are my brothers?" [49] Pointing to his disciples, he said, "Here are my mother and my brothers. [50] For whoever does the will of my Father in heaven is my brother and sister and mother."

Chapter 13

The Parable of the Sower

THAT same day Jesus went out of the house and sat beside the sea. [2] Such great crowds gathered around him that he got into a boat and sat there, while the whole crowd stood on the beach. [3] And he told them many things in parables, saying: "Listen! A sower went out to sow. [4] And as he sowed, some seeds fell on the path, and the birds came and ate them up. [5] Other seeds fell on rocky ground, where they did not have much soil, and they sprang up quickly, since they had no depth of soil. [6] But when the sun rose, they were scorched; and since they had no root, they withered away. [7] Other seeds fell among thorns, and the thorns grew up and choked

13 Ἐν τῇ ἡμέρᾳ ἐκείνῃ ἐξελθὼν ὁ
On – day that going out of –

Ἰησοῦς τῆς οἰκίας ἐκάθητο παρὰ τὴν
Jesus of the house sat beside the

θάλασσαν· **2** καὶ συνήχθησαν πρὸς αὐτὸν
sea; and were assembled to him

ὄχλοι πολλοί, ὥστε αὐτὸν εἰς πλοῖον
crowds many, so as him into a ship
=so that embarking in a ship he sat,

ἐμβάντα καθῆσθαι, καὶ πᾶς ὁ ὄχλος
embarking to sit[b], and all the crowd

ἐπὶ τὸν αἰγιαλὸν εἰστήκει. **3** καὶ ἐλάλησεν
on the beach stood. And he spoke

αὐτοῖς πολλὰ ἐν παραβολαῖς λέγων·
to them many things in parables saying:

Ἰδοὺ ἐξῆλθεν ὁ σπείρων τοῦ σπείρειν.
Behold went out the [one] sowing – to sow[d].

4 καὶ ἐν τῷ σπείρειν αὐτὸν ἃ μὲν
And in the to sow him[e] some indeed
=as he sowed

ἔπεσεν παρὰ τὴν ὁδόν, καὶ ἐλθόντα τὰ
fell beside the way, and coming the

πετεινὰ κατέφαγεν αὐτά. **5** ἄλλα δὲ
birds devoured them. But others

ἔπεσεν ἐπὶ τὰ πετρώδη ὅπου οὐκ
fell on the rocky places where not

εἶχεν γῆν πολλήν, καὶ εὐθέως ἐξανέτειλεν
it had earth much, and immediately it sprang up

διὰ τὸ μὴ ἔχειν βάθος γῆς· **6** ἡλίου
on account of the not to have depth of earth; [the] sun
=because it had not

δὲ ἀνατείλαντος ἐκαυματίσθη, καὶ διὰ
But having risen[a] it was scorched, and on account of
=when the sun rose   =because

τὸ μὴ ἔχειν ῥίζαν ἐξηράνθη. **7** ἄλλα δὲ
the not to have root it was dried up. But others
it had not

ἔπεσεν ἐπὶ τὰς ἀκάνθας, καὶ ἀνέβησαν
fell on the thorns, and came up

Chapter 13

The Parable of the Sower

THAT same day Jesus went out of the house and sat by the lake. [2] Such large crowds gathered around him that he got into a boat and sat in it, while all the people stood on the shore. [3] Then he told them many things in parables, saying: "A farmer went out to sow his seed. [4] As he was scattering the seed, some fell along the path, and the birds came and ate it up. [5] Some fell on rocky places, where it did not have much soil. It sprang up quickly, because the soil was shallow. [6] But when the sun came up, the plants were scorched, and they withered because they had no root. [7] Other seed fell among thorns, which grew

[s] Other ancient authorities lack verse 47
[t] Gk he

[y] 47 Some manuscripts do not have verse 47.

them. 8Other seeds fell on good soil and brought forth grain, some a hundredfold, some sixty, some thirty. 9Let anyone with ears[u] listen!"

The Purpose of the Parables

10 Then the disciples came and asked him, "Why do you speak to them in parables?" 11He answered, "To you it has been given to know the secrets[v] of the kingdom of heaven, but to them it has not been given. 12For to those who have, more will be given, and they will have an abundance; but from those who have nothing, even what they have will be taken away. 13The reason I speak to them in parables is that 'seeing they do not perceive, and hearing they do not listen, nor do they understand.' 14With them indeed is fulfilled the prophecy of Isaiah that says:
'You will indeed
    listen, but never
        understand,
and you will indeed
    look, but never
        perceive.
15 For this people's
        heart has
        grown dull,
    and their ears are
        hard of hearing,
    and they have
        shut their eyes;
so that they might
        not look with
        their eyes,
    and listen with their
        ears,
    and understand with
        their heart and
        turn—
    and I would heal
        them.'

16But blessed are your eyes, for they see, and your ears, for they hear. 17Truly I tell you, many prophets and righteous people longed to see what you see, but did not see it, and to hear what you hear, but did not hear it.

αἱ ἄκανθαι καὶ ἀπέπνιξαν αὐτά. 8 ἄλλα δὲ
the thorns and choked them. And others
ἔπεσεν ἐπὶ τὴν γῆν τὴν καλὴν καὶ
fell on the earth - good and
ἐδίδου καρπόν, ὃ μὲν ἑκατόν, ὃ δὲ
gave fruit, the one a hundred, the other
ἑξήκοντα, ὃ δὲ τριάκοντα. 9 ὁ ἔχων
sixty, the other thirty. The [one] having
ὦτα ἀκουέτω. 10 Καὶ προσελθόντες οἱ
ears let him hear. And approaching the
μαθηταὶ εἶπαν αὐτῷ· διὰ τί ἐν παρα-
disciples said to him: Why in par-
βολαῖς λαλεῖς αὐτοῖς; 11 ὁ δὲ
ables speakest thou to them? And he
ἀποκριθεὶς εἶπεν· ὅτι ὑμῖν δέδοται
answering said: Because to you it has been given
γνῶναι τὰ μυστήρια τῆς βασιλείας τῶν
to know the mysteries of the kingdom of the
οὐρανῶν, ἐκείνοις δὲ οὐ δέδοται. 12 ὅστις
heavens, but to those it has not been given. [he] who
γὰρ ἔχει, δοθήσεται αὐτῷ καὶ περισ-
For has, it will be given to him and he will
σευθήσεται· ὅστις δὲ οὐκ ἔχει, καὶ
have abundance; but [he] who has not, even
ὃ ἔχει ἀρθήσεται ἀπ’ αὐτοῦ. 13 διὰ
what he has will be taken from him. There-
τοῦτο ἐν παραβολαῖς αὐτοῖς λαλῶ, ὅτι
fore in parables to them I speak, because
βλέποντες οὐ βλέπουσιν καὶ ἀκούοντες
seeing they see not and hearing
οὐκ ἀκούουσιν οὐδὲ συνιοῦσιν. 14 καὶ
they hear not neither understand. And
ἀναπληροῦται αὐτοῖς ἡ προφητεία Ἡσαΐου
is fulfilled in them the prophecy of Isaiah
ἡ λέγουσα· ἀκοῇ ἀκούσετε καὶ οὐ μὴ
- saying: In hearing ye will hear and by no means
συνῆτε, καὶ βλέποντες βλέψετε
understand, and seeing ye will see
καὶ οὐ μὴ ἴδητε. 15 ἐπαχύνθη γὰρ
and by no means perceive. For waxed gross
ἡ καρδία τοῦ λαοῦ τούτου, καὶ τοῖς
the heart - people of this, and with the
ὠσὶν βαρέως ἤκουσαν, καὶ τοὺς ὀφθαλμοὺς
ears heavily they heard, and the eyes
αὐτῶν ἐκάμμυσαν· μήποτε ἴδωσιν τοῖς
of them they closed; lest they see with the
ὀφθαλμοῖς καὶ τοῖς ὠσὶν ἀκούσωσιν
eyes and with the ears hear
καὶ τῇ καρδίᾳ συνῶσιν καὶ ἐπιστρέψωσιν,
and with the heart understand and turn back,
καὶ ἰάσομαι αὐτούς. 16 ὑμῶν δὲ μακάριοι
and I will heal them. But of you blessed
οἱ ὀφθαλμοὶ ὅτι βλέπουσιν, καὶ τὰ
the eyes because they see, and the
ὦτα [ὑμῶν] ὅτι ἀκούουσιν. 17 ἀμὴν
ears of you because they hear. truly
γὰρ λέγω ὑμῖν ὅτι πολλοὶ προφῆται καὶ
For I say to you that many prophets and
δίκαιοι ἐπεθύμησαν ἰδεῖν ἃ
righteous men desired to see [the things] which
βλέπετε καὶ οὐκ εἶδαν, καὶ ἀκοῦσαι
ye see and did not see, and to hear
ἃ ἀκούετε καὶ οὐκ ἤκουσαν.
[the things] which ye hear and did not hear.

up and choked the plants. 8Still other seed fell on good soil, where it produced a crop—a hundred, sixty or thirty times what was sown. 9He who has ears, let him hear."

10The disciples came to him and asked, "Why do you speak to the people in parables?"

11He replied, "The knowledge of the secrets of the kingdom of heaven has been given to you, but not to them. 12Whoever has will be given more, and he will have an abundance. Whoever does not have, even what he has will be taken from him. 13This is why I speak to them in parables:

"Though seeing, they do
    not see;
though hearing, they
    do not hear or
    understand.

14In them is fulfilled the prophecy of Isaiah:

" 'You will be ever
    hearing but never
        understanding;
you will be ever seeing
    but never
        perceiving.
15For this people's heart
        has become
        calloused;
    they hardly hear with
        their ears,
    and they have closed
        their eyes.
Otherwise they might
    see with their eyes,
    hear with their ears,
    understand with their
        hearts
and turn, and I would
    heal them.'[z]

16But blessed are your eyes because they see, and your ears because they hear. 17For I tell you the truth, many prophets and righteous men longed to see what you see but did not see it, and to hear what you hear but did not hear it.

---

u Other ancient authorities add to hear
v Or mysteries
z15 Isaiah 6:9,10

The Parable of the Sower Explained

18 "Hear then the parable of the sower. 19When anyone hears the word of the kingdom and does not understand it, the evil one comes and snatches away what is sown in the heart; this is what was sown on the path. 20 As for what was sown on rocky ground, this is the one who hears the word and immediately receives it with joy; 21 yet such a person has no root, but endures only for a while, and when trouble or persecution arises on account of the word, that person immediately falls away. w 22 As for what was sown among thorns, this is the one who hears the word, but the cares of the world and the lure of wealth choke the word, and it yields nothing. 23 But as for what was sown on good soil, this is the one who hears the word and understands it, who indeed bears fruit and yields, in one case a hundredfold, in another sixty, and in another thirty."

The Parable of Weeds among the Wheat

24 He put before them another parable: "The kingdom of heaven may be compared to someone who sowed good seed in his field; 25 but while everybody was asleep, an enemy came and sowed weeds among the wheat, and then went away. 26 So when the plants came up and bore grain, then the weeds appeared as well. 27 And the slaves of the householder came and said to him,

---

18 Ὑμεῖς οὖν ἀκούσατε τὴν παραβολὴν
   ³Ye   ¹therefore   ¹hear   the   parable

τοῦ σπείραντος. **19** Παντὸς ἀκούοντος
of the   sowing [one].   Everyone   hearing⁰
                        = When anyone hears

τὸν λόγον τῆς βασιλείας καὶ μὴ συνιέντος
the   word   of the   kingdom   and   not understanding⁰
                             = does not understand

ἔρχεται ὁ πονηρὸς καὶ ἁρπάζει τὸ
comes   the   evil one   and   seizes the [thing]

ἐσπαρμένον ἐν τῇ καρδίᾳ αὐτοῦ· οὗτός
having been sown   in   the   heart   of him;   this

ἐστιν ὁ παρὰ τὴν ὁδὸν σπαρείς. **20** ὁ [word]
is   the [word]   by   the   way   sown.   the [word]

δὲ ἐπὶ τὰ πετρώδη σπαρείς, οὗτός ἐστιν
And on   the   rocky places   sown,   this   is

ὁ τὸν λόγον ἀκούων καὶ εὐθὺς μετὰ
the [one]   ⁸the   ⁹word   ¹hearing   and immediately with

χαρᾶς λαμβάνων αὐτόν· **21** οὐκ ἔχει δὲ
joy   receiving   it;   but he has not

ῥίζαν ἐν ἑαυτῷ ἀλλὰ πρόσκαιρός ἐστιν,
root   in   himself   but   short-lived   is,

γενομένης δὲ θλίψεως ἢ διωγμοῦ
and occurring   tribulation   or   persecution⁰
     = when tribulation or persecution occurs

διὰ τὸν λόγον εὐθὺς σκανδαλίζεται.
on account of the   word   immediately   he is offended.

22 ὁ δὲ εἰς τὰς ἀκάνθας σπαρείς, οὗτός
But the [word]   in   the   thorns   sown,   this

ἐστιν ὁ τὸν λόγον ἀκούων, καὶ ἡ
is   the [one]   ⁸the   ⁹word   ¹hearing,   and   the

μέριμνα τοῦ αἰῶνος καὶ ἡ ἀπάτη
anxiety   of the   age   and   the   deceit

τοῦ πλούτου συμπνίγει τὸν λόγον, καὶ
-   of riches   chokes   the   word,   and

ἄκαρπος γίνεται. **23** ὁ δὲ ἐπὶ τὴν
unfruitful   it becomes.   And the [word]   on   the

καλὴν γῆν σπαρείς, οὗτός ἐστιν ὁ
good   earth   sown,   this   is   the [one]

τὸν λόγον ἀκούων καὶ συνιείς, ὃς
⁴the   ⁸word   ¹hearing   ²and   ³understanding,   who

δὴ καρποφορεῖ καὶ ποιεῖ ὃ μὲν ἑκατόν,
indeed   bears fruit   and   produces   one indeed   a hundred,

ὃ δὲ ἑξήκοντα, ὃ δὲ τριάκοντα.
the other   sixty,   the other   thirty.

24 Ἄλλην παραβολὴν παρέθηκεν αὐτοῖς
   Another   parable   he set before   them

λέγων· ὡμοιώθη ἡ βασιλεία τῶν
saying: was(is) likened   The   kingdom   of the

οὐρανῶν ἀνθρώπῳ σπείραντι καλὸν σπέρμα
heavens   to a man   sowing   good   seed

ἐν τῷ ἀγρῷ αὐτοῦ. **25** ἐν δὲ τῷ
in   the   field   of him.   But in   the
                       = while men slept

καθεύδειν τοὺς ἀνθρώπους ἦλθεν αὐτοῦ
to sleep   -   men⁰   came   of him

ὁ ἐχθρὸς καὶ ἐπέσπειρεν ζιζάνια ἀνὰ μέσον
the   enemy   and   oversowed   tares   in between

τοῦ σίτου καὶ ἀπῆλθεν. **26** ὅτε δὲ
the   wheat   and   went away.   But when

ἐβλάστησεν ὁ χόρτος καὶ καρπὸν
sprouted   the   grass   and   fruit

ἐποίησεν, τότε ἐφάνη καὶ τὰ ζιζάνια.
produced,   then   appeared   also   the   tares.

27 προσελθόντες δὲ οἱ δοῦλοι τοῦ οἰκο-
   So approaching   the   slaves   of the   house-

18"Listen then to what the parable of the sower means: 19When anyone hears the message about the kingdom and does not understand it, the evil one comes and snatches away what was sown in his heart. This is the seed sown along the path. 20The one who received the seed that fell on rocky places is the man who hears the word and at once receives it with joy. 21But since he has no root, he lasts only a short time. When trouble or persecution comes because of the word, he quickly falls away. 22The one who received the seed that fell among the thorns is the man who hears the word, but the worries of this life and the deceitfulness of wealth choke it, making it unfruitful. 23But the one who received the seed that fell on good soil is the man who hears the word and understands it. He produces a crop, yielding a hundred, sixty or thirty times what was sown."

The Parable of the Weeds

24Jesus told them another parable: "The kingdom of heaven is like a man who sowed good seed in his field. 25But while everyone was sleeping, his enemy came and sowed weeds among the wheat, and went away. 26When the wheat sprouted and formed heads, then the weeds also appeared.

27"The owner's servants came to him and said, 'Sir,

ʷ Gk *stumbles*

'Master, did you not sow good seed in your field? Where, then, did these weeds come from?' 28 He answered, 'An enemy has done this.' The slaves said to him, 'Then do you want us to go and gather them?' 29 But he replied, 'No; for in gathering the weeds you would uproot the wheat along with them. 30 Let both of them grow together until the harvest; and at harvest time I will tell the reapers, Collect the weeds first and bind them in bundles to be burned, but gather the wheat into my barn.' "

The Parable of the Mustard Seed

31 He put before them another parable: "The kingdom of heaven is like a mustard seed that someone took and sowed in his field; 32 it is the smallest of all the seeds, but when it has grown it is the greatest of shrubs and becomes a tree, so that the birds of the air come and make nests in its branches."

The Parable of the Yeast

33 He told them another parable: "The kingdom of heaven is like yeast that a woman took and mixed in with[x] three measures of flour until all of it was leavened."

The Use of Parables

34 Jesus told the crowds all these things in parables; without a parable he told them nothing. 35 This was to fulfill what had been spoken through the prophet:[y]
"I will open my
     mouth to speak
     in parables;

δεσπότου εἶπον αὐτῷ· κύριε, οὐχὶ καλὸν
master said to him: Lord, not good
σπέρμα ἔσπειρας ἐν τῷ σῷ ἀγρῷ;
seed sowedst thou in - thy field?
πόθεν οὖν ἔχει ζιζάνια; 28 ὁ δὲ ἔφη
whence then has it tares? And he said
αὐτοῖς· ἐχθρὸς ἄνθρωπος τοῦτο ἐποίησεν.
to them: An enemy *man* this did.
οἱ δὲ δοῦλοι αὐτῷ λέγουσιν· θέλεις
So the slaves to him say: Willest thou
οὖν ἀπελθόντες συλλέξωμεν αὐτά; 29 ὁ
then going away we may collect them? he
δέ φησιν· οὔ, μήποτε συλλέγοντες τὰ
But says: No, lest collecting the
ζιζάνια ἐκριζώσητε ἅμα αὐτοῖς τὸν
tares ye should root up together with them the
σῖτον. 30 ἄφετε συναυξάνεσθαι ἀμφότερα
wheat. Leave to grow together both
ἕως τοῦ θερισμοῦ· καὶ ἐν καιρῷ τοῦ
until the harvest; and in time of the
θερισμοῦ ἐρῶ τοῖς θερισταῖς· συλλέξατε
harvest I will say to the reapers: Collect ye
πρῶτον τὰ ζιζάνια καὶ δήσατε αὐτὰ
first the tares and bind them
εἰς δέσμας πρὸς τὸ κατακαῦσαι αὐτά,
in bundles - - to burn them,
τὸν δὲ σῖτον συναγάγετε εἰς τὴν ἀποθήκην
but the wheat gather ye into the barn
μου. 31 Ἄλλην παραβολὴν παρέθηκεν
of me. Another parable he set before
αὐτοῖς λέγων· ὁμοία ἐστὶν ἡ βασιλεία
them saying: Like is the kingdom
τῶν οὐρανῶν κόκκῳ σινάπεως, ὃν
of the heavens to a grain of mustard, which
λαβὼν ἄνθρωπος ἔσπειρεν ἐν τῷ ἀγρῷ
¹taking ¹a man sowed in the field
αὐτοῦ· 32 ὃ μικρότερον μέν ἐστιν
of him; which less indeed is
πάντων τῶν σπερμάτων, ὅταν δὲ
[than] all the seeds, but when
αὐξηθῇ, μεῖζον τῶν λαχάνων ἐστὶν
it grows, greater [than] the herbs it is
καὶ γίνεται δένδρον, ὥστε ἐλθεῖν τὰ
and becomes a tree, so as to come the
πετεινὰ τοῦ οὐρανοῦ καὶ κατασκηνοῦν
birds of the heaven and dwell
ἐν τοῖς κλάδοις αὐτοῦ. 33 Ἄλλην
in the branches of it. Another
παραβολὴν ἐλάλησεν αὐτοῖς· ὁμοία
parable he spoke to them: Like
ἐστὶν ἡ βασιλεία τῶν οὐρανῶν ζύμῃ,
is the kingdom of the heavens to leaven,
ἣν λαβοῦσα γυνὴ ἐνέκρυψεν εἰς ἀλεύρου
which ¹taking ¹a woman hid in ¹of meal
σάτα τρία, ἕως οὗ ἐζυμώθη ὅλον.
¹measures ¹three, until was leavened [the] whole.
34 Ταῦτα πάντα ἐλάλησεν ὁ Ἰησοῦς ἐν
These things all spoke - Jesus in
παραβολαῖς τοῖς ὄχλοις, καὶ χωρὶς παραβολῆς
parables to the crowds, and without a parable
οὐδὲν ἐλάλει αὐτοῖς· 35 ὅπως πληρωθῇ
nothing he spoke to them; so that was fulfilled
τὸ ῥηθὲν διὰ τοῦ προφήτου λέγοντος·
the [thing] spoken through the prophet saying:
ἀνοίξω ἐν παραβολαῖς τὸ στόμα μου,
I will open in parables the mouth of me,

---

didn't you sow good seed in your field? Where then did the weeds come from?'
28 " 'An enemy did this,' he replied.
"The servants asked him, 'Do you want us to go and pull them up?'
29 " 'No,' he answered, 'because while you are pulling the weeds, you may root up the wheat with them. 30 Let both grow together until the harvest. At that time I will tell the harvesters: First collect the weeds and tie them in bundles to be burned; then gather the wheat and bring it into my barn.' "

The Parables of the Mustard Seed and the Yeast

31 He told them another parable: "The kingdom of heaven is like a mustard seed, which a man took and planted in his field. 32 Though it is the smallest of all your seeds, yet when it grows, it is the largest of garden plants and becomes a tree, so that the birds of the air come and perch in its branches."

33 He told them still another parable: "The kingdom of heaven is like yeast that a woman took and mixed into a large amount[a] of flour until it worked all through the dough."

34 Jesus spoke all these things to the crowd in parables; he did not say anything to them without using a parable. 35 So was fulfilled what was spoken through the prophet:

"I will open my mouth
     in parables,

---

[x] Gk hid in
[y] Other ancient authorities read the prophet Isaiah

[a] 33 Greek three satas (probably about 1/2 bushel or 22 liters)

I will proclaim what
has been hidden
from the
foundation of
the world." [z]

*Jesus Explains the
Parable of the Weeds*

36 Then he left the
crowds and went into the
house. And his disciples
approached him, saying,
"Explain to us the parable
of the weeds of the field."
[37] He answered, "The one
who sows the good seed is
the Son of Man; [38] the field
is the world, and the good
seed are the children of the
kingdom; the weeds are the
children of the evil one,
[39] and the enemy who
sowed them is the devil; the
harvest is the end of the
age, and the reapers are angels. [40] Just as the weeds
are collected and burned up
with fire, so will it be at the
end of the age. [41] The Son
of Man will send his angels,
and they will collect out of
his kingdom all causes of
sin and all evildoers, [42] and
they will throw them into
the furnace of fire, where
there will be weeping and
gnashing of teeth. [43] Then
the righteous will shine like
the sun in the kingdom of
their Father. Let anyone
with ears [a] listen!

Three Parables

44 "The kingdom of
heaven is like treasure hid-

ἐρεύξομαι κεκρυμμένα ἀπὸ καταβολῆς.
I will utter things having been hidden from [the] foundation.

36 Τότε ἀφεὶς τοὺς ὄχλους ἦλθεν
Then sending away the crowds he came

εἰς τὴν οἰκίαν. Καὶ προσῆλθον αὐτῷ
into the house. And approached to him

οἱ μαθηταὶ αὐτοῦ λέγοντες· διασάφησον
the disciples of him saying: Explain thou

ἡμῖν τὴν παραβολὴν τῶν ζιζανίων τοῦ
to us the parable of the tares of the

ἀγροῦ. 37 ὁ δὲ ἀποκριθεὶς εἶπεν· ὁ
field. And he answering said: The [one]

σπείρων τὸ καλὸν σπέρμα ἐστὶν ὁ
sowing the good seed is the

υἱὸς τοῦ ἀνθρώπου· 38 ὁ δὲ ἀγρός
Son - of man; and the field

ἐστιν ὁ κόσμος· τὸ δὲ καλὸν σπέρμα,
is the world; and the good seed,

οὗτοί εἰσιν οἱ υἱοὶ τῆς βασιλείας· τὰ δὲ
these are the sons of the kingdom; and the

ζιζάνιά εἰσιν οἱ υἱοὶ τοῦ πονηροῦ, 39 ὁ
tares are the sons of the evil [one], the

δὲ ἐχθρὸς ὁ σπείρας αὐτά ἐστιν ὁ
and enemy the [one] sowing them is the

διάβολος· ὁ δὲ θερισμὸς συντέλεια
devil; and the harvest [the] completion

αἰῶνός ἐστιν, οἱ δὲ θερισταὶ ἄγγελοί
of [the] age is, and the reapers angels

εἰσιν. 40 ὥσπερ οὖν συλλέγεται τὰ
are. As therefore are collected the

ζιζάνια καὶ πυρὶ κατακαίεται, οὕτως
tares and with fire are consumed, thus

ἔσται ἐν τῇ συντελείᾳ τοῦ αἰῶνος·
it will be at the completion of the age;

41 ἀποστελεῖ ὁ υἱὸς τοῦ ἀνθρώπου
will send forth the Son - of man

τοὺς ἀγγέλους αὐτοῦ, καὶ συλλέξουσιν
the angels of him, and they will collect

ἐκ τῆς βασιλείας αὐτοῦ πάντα
out of the kingdom of him all

τὰ σκάνδαλα καὶ τοὺς ποιοῦντας
the things leading to sin and the [ones] doing

τὴν ἀνομίαν, 42 καὶ βαλοῦσιν αὐτοὺς εἰς
- lawlessness, and will cast them into

τὴν κάμινον τοῦ πυρός· ἐκεῖ ἔσται ὁ
the furnace - of fire; there will be the

κλαυθμὸς καὶ ὁ βρυγμὸς τῶν ὀδόντων.
wailing and the gnashing of the teeth.

43 τότε οἱ δίκαιοι ἐκλάμψουσιν ὡς ὁ
Then the righteous will shine forth as the

ἥλιος ἐν τῇ βασιλείᾳ τοῦ πατρὸς
sun in the kingdom of the Father

αὐτῶν. ὁ ἔχων ὦτα ἀκουέτω.
of them. The [one] having ears let him hear.

44 Ὁμοία ἐστὶν ἡ βασιλεία τῶν
Like is the kingdom of the

οὐρανῶν θησαυρῷ κεκρυμμένῳ ἐν τῷ
heavens to treasure having been hidden in the

ἀγρῷ, ὃν εὑρὼν ἄνθρωπος ἔκρυψεν, καὶ
field, which [2]finding [1]a man hid, and

ἀπὸ τῆς χαρᾶς αὐτοῦ ὑπάγει καὶ πωλεῖ
from the joy of him goes and sells

ὅσα ἔχει καὶ ἀγοράζει τὸν ἀγρὸν
what things he has and buys - field

ἐκεῖνον. 45 Πάλιν ὁμοία ἐστὶν ἡ
that. Again like is the

I will utter things
hidden since the
creation of the
world." [b]

*The Parable of the Weeds
Explained*

[36] Then he left the crowd
and went into the house.
His disciples came to him
and said, "Explain to us
the parable of the weeds in
the field."
[37] He answered, "The one
who sowed the good seed is
the Son of Man. [38] The field
is the world, and the good
seed stands for the sons of
the kingdom. The weeds
are the sons of the evil one,
[39] and the enemy who sows
them is the devil. The harvest is the end of the age,
and the harvesters are angels.
[40] "As the weeds are
pulled up and burned in the
fire, so it will be at the end
of the age. [41] The Son of
Man will send out his an-
gels, and they will weed out
of his kingdom everything
that causes sin and all who
do evil. [42] They will throw
them into the fiery furnace,
where there will be weep-
ing and gnashing of teeth.
[43] Then the righteous will
shine like the sun in the
kingdom of their Father.
He who has ears, let him
hear.

*The Parables of the
Hidden Treasure and the
Pearl*

[44] "The kingdom of heav-

---

[z] Other ancient authorities lack *of
the world*
[a] Other ancient authorities add *to
hear*

[b] 35 Psalm 78:2

den in a field, which someone found and hid; then in his joy he goes and sells all that he has and buys that field.

45 "Again, the kingdom of heaven is like a merchant in search of fine pearls; 46 on finding one pearl of great value, he went and sold all that he had and bought it.

47 "Again, the kingdom of heaven is like a net that was thrown into the sea and caught fish of every kind; 48 when it was full, they drew it ashore, sat down, and put the good into baskets but threw out the bad. 49 So it will be at the end of the age. The angels will come out and separate the evil from the righteous 50 and throw them into the furnace of fire, where there will be weeping and gnashing of teeth.

Treasures New and Old

51 "Have you understood all this?" They answered, "Yes." 52 And he said to them, "Therefore every scribe who has been trained for the kingdom of heaven is like the master of a household who brings out of his treasure what is new and what is old." 53 When Jesus had finished these parables, he left that place.

The Rejection of Jesus at Nazareth

54 He came to his hometown and began to teach the people[b] in their synagogue, so that they were astounded and said, "Where did this man get this wisdom and these deeds of power? 55 Is not this the carpenter's son? Is not his mother called Mary? And are not his brothers James and Joseph and Simon and Judas?

βασιλεία   τῶν   οὐρανῶν   ἐμπόρῳ   ζητοῦντι
kingdom   of the   heavens   to a merchant   seeking
καλοὺς   μαργαρίτας·   46 εὑρὼν   δὲ   ἕνα   πολύτιμον
beautiful   pearls;   and finding   one   valuable
μαργαρίτην   ἀπελθὼν   πέπρακεν   πάντα
pearl   going away   sold   all things
ὅσα   εἶχεν   καὶ   ἠγόρασεν   αὐτόν.
what   he had   and   bought   it.
47 Πάλιν   ὁμοία   ἐστὶν   ἡ   βασιλεία   τῶν
Again   like   is   the   kingdom   of the
οὐρανῶν   σαγήνη   βληθείσῃ   εἰς   τὴν   θάλασσαν
heavens   to a net   cast   into   the   sea
καὶ   ἐκ   παντὸς   γένους   συναγαγούσῃ·
and   of   every   kind   gathering;
48 ἣν   ὅτε   ἐπληρώθη   ἀναβιβάσαντες   ἐπὶ
which   when   it was filled   bringing up   onto
τὸν   αἰγιαλὸν   καὶ   καθίσαντες   συνέλεξαν
the   shore   and   sitting   collected
τὰ   καλὰ   εἰς   ἄγγη,   τὰ   δὲ   σαπρὰ   ἔξω
the   good   into   vessels,   but the   bad   out
ἔβαλον.   49 οὕτως   ἔσται   ἐν   τῇ   συντελείᾳ
cast.   Thus   it will be   at   the   completion
τοῦ   αἰῶνος·   ἐξελεύσονται   οἱ   ἄγγελοι   καὶ
of the   age;   will go forth   the   angels   and
ἀφοριοῦσιν   τοὺς   πονηροὺς   ἐκ   μέσου
will separate   the   evil men   from [the] midst
τῶν   δικαίων,   50 καὶ   βαλοῦσιν   αὐτοὺς
of the   righteous,   and   will cast   them
εἰς   τὴν   κάμινον   τοῦ   πυρός·   ἐκεῖ
into   the   furnace   -   of fire;   there
ἔσται   ὁ   κλαυθμὸς   καὶ   ὁ   βρυγμὸς   τῶν
will be   the   wailing   and   the   gnashing   of the
ὀδόντων.   51 Συνήκατε   ταῦτα   πάντα;
teeth.   Did ye understand   [1]these things   [1]all?
λέγουσιν   αὐτῷ·   ναί.   52 ὁ   δὲ   εἶπεν
They say   to him: Yes.   So he   said
αὐτοῖς·   διὰ   τοῦτο   πᾶς   γραμματεὺς
to them: Therefore   every   scribe
μαθητευθεὶς   τῇ   βασιλείᾳ   τῶν   οὐρανῶν
made a disciple   to the   kingdom   of the   heavens
ὅμοιός   ἐστιν   ἀνθρώπῳ   οἰκοδεσπότῃ,
like   is   to a man   a housemaster,
ὅστις   ἐκβάλλει   ἐκ   τοῦ   θησαυροῦ
who   puts forth   out of   the   treasure
αὐτοῦ   καινὰ   καὶ   παλαιά.
of him   new   and   old things.
53 Καὶ   ἐγένετο   ὅτε   ἐτέλεσεν   ὁ
And   it came to pass   when   ended   -
Ἰησοῦς   τὰς   παραβολὰς   ταύτας,   μετῆρεν
Jesus   -   parables   these,   he removed
ἐκεῖθεν.   54 καὶ   ἐλθὼν   εἰς   τὴν   πατρίδα
thence.   And   coming   into   the   native town
αὐτοῦ   ἐδίδασκεν   αὐτοὺς   ἐν   τῇ   συνα-
of him   he taught   them   in   the   syna-
γωγῇ   αὐτῶν,   ὥστε   ἐκπλήσσεσθαι   αὐτοὺς
gogue   of them,   so as   to be astounded   them
    = so that they were astounded
καὶ   λέγειν·   πόθεν   τούτῳ   ἡ   σοφία   αὕτη
and   to say[b]:   Whence   to this man   -   wisdom   this
and said:
καὶ   αἱ   δυνάμεις;   55 οὐχ   οὗτός   ἐστιν
and   the   powerful deeds?   not   this man   is
ὁ   τοῦ   τέκτονος   υἱός;   οὐχ   ἡ   μήτηρ
the   of the   carpenter   son?   not   the   mother
αὐτοῦ   λέγεται   Μαριὰμ   καὶ   οἱ   ἀδελφοὶ
of him   called   Mary   and   the   brothers
αὐτοῦ   Ἰάκωβος   καὶ   Ἰωσὴφ   καὶ   Σίμων
of him   James   and   Joseph   and   Simon

---

en is like treasure hidden in a field. When a man found it, he hid it again, and then in his joy went and sold all he had and bought that field.

45 "Again, the kingdom of heaven is like a merchant looking for fine pearls. 46 When he found one of great value, he went away and sold everything he had and bought it.

The Parable of the Net

47 "Once again, the kingdom of heaven is like a net that was let down into the lake and caught all kinds of fish. 48 When it was full, the fishermen pulled it up on the shore. Then they sat down and collected the good fish in baskets, but threw the bad away. 49 This is how it will be at the end of the age. The angels will come and separate the wicked from the righteous 50 and throw them into the fiery furnace, where there will be weeping and gnashing of teeth.

51 "Have you understood all these things?" Jesus asked.

"Yes," they replied.

52 He said to them, "Therefore every teacher of the law who has been instructed about the kingdom of heaven is like the owner of a house who brings out of his storeroom new treasures as well as old."

A Prophet Without Honor

53 When Jesus had finished these parables, he moved on from there. 54 Coming to his hometown, he began teaching the people in their synagogue, and they were amazed. "Where did this man get this wisdom and these miraculous powers?" they asked. 55 "Isn't this the carpenter's son? Isn't his mother's name Mary, and aren't his brothers James, Joseph,

---

[b] Gk *them*

56 And are not all his sisters with us? Where then did this man get all this?" 57 And they took offense at him. But Jesus said to them, "Prophets are not without honor except in their own country and in their own house." 58 And he did not do many deeds of power there, because of their unbelief.

καὶ　　'Ιούδας;　　**56** καὶ　αἱ　ἀδελφαὶ　αὐτοῦ
and　　Judas?　　　and　the　sisters　of him

οὐχὶ　πᾶσαι　πρὸς　ἡμᾶς　εἰσιν;　πόθεν
not　all　with　us　are?　Whence

οὖν　τούτῳ　ταῦτα　πάντα;　**57** καὶ
then　to this man　these things　all?　And

ἐσκανδαλίζοντο　ἐν　αὐτῷ.　ὁ δὲ　'Ιησοῦς
they were offended　in　him.　- But　Jesus

εἶπεν　αὐτοῖς·　οὐκ　ἔστιν　προφήτης
said　to them:　ᵃnot　ᵇis　¹A prophet

ἄτιμος　εἰ μὴ　ἐν　τῇ　πατρίδι　καὶ
unhonoured　except　in　the(his)　native town　and

ἐν τῇ οἰκίᾳ αὐτοῦ.　**58** καὶ οὐκ ἐποίησεν ἐκεῖ
in the　house　of him.　And　not　he did　there

δυνάμεις　πολλὰς　διὰ　τὴν　ἀπιστίαν　αὐτῶν.
powerful deeds　many　because of the　unbelief　of them.

Simon and Judas? 56 Aren't all his sisters with us? Where then did this man get all these things?" 57 And they took offense at him. But Jesus said to them, "Only in his hometown and in his own house is a prophet without honor." 58 And he did not do many miracles there because of their lack of faith.

Chapter 14

The Death of John the Baptist

AT that time Herod the ruler[c] heard reports about Jesus; 2 and he said to his servants, "This is John the Baptist; he has been raised from the dead, and for this reason these powers are at work in him." 3 For Herod had arrested John, bound him, and put him in prison on account of Herodias, his brother Philip's wife,[d] 4 because John had been telling him, "It is not lawful for you to have her." 5 Though Herod[e] wanted to put him to death, he feared the crowd, because they regarded him as a prophet. 6 But when Herod's birthday came, the daughter of Herodias danced before the company, and she pleased Herod 7 so much that he promised on oath to grant her whatever she might ask. 8 Prompted by her mother, she said, "Give me the head of John the Baptist here on a platter." 9 The king was grieved, yet out of regard for his oaths and for the guests, he commanded it to be given; 10 he sent and had John beheaded in the pris-

---

14 'Εν　ἐκείνῳ　τῷ　καιρῷ　ἤκουσεν
At　that　-　time　heard

'Ηρῴδης　ὁ　τετραάρχης　τὴν　ἀκοὴν　'Ιησοῦ,
Herod　the　tetrarch　the　report　of Jesus,

2 καὶ　εἶπεν　τοῖς　παισὶν　αὐτοῦ·　οὗτός
and　said　to the　servants　of him:　This

ἐστιν　'Ιωάννης　ὁ　βαπτιστής·　αὐτὸς
is　John　the　Baptist;　he

ἠγέρθη　ἀπὸ　τῶν　νεκρῶν,　καὶ　διὰ　τοῦτο
was raised　from　the　dead,　and　therefore

αἱ　δυνάμεις　ἐνεργοῦσιν　ἐν　αὐτῷ.
the　powerful deeds　operate　in　him.

3 'Ο　γὰρ　'Ηρῴδης　κρατήσας　τὸν　'Ιωάννην
- For　Herod　seizing　the　John

ἔδησεν　καὶ　ἐν　φυλακῇ　ἀπέθετο　διὰ
bound　and　in　prison　put away　on account of

'Ηρῳδιάδα　τὴν　γυναῖκα　Φιλίππου　τοῦ
Herodias　the　wife　of Philip　the

ἀδελφοῦ　αὐτοῦ·　**4** ἔλεγεν　γὰρ　ὁ　'Ιωάννης
brother　of him:　for said　John

αὐτῷ·　οὐκ　ἔξεστιν　σοι　ἔχειν　αὐτήν.
to him:　It is not lawful　for thee　to have　her.

5 καὶ　θέλων　αὐτὸν　ἀποκτεῖναι　ἐφοβήθη
And　wishing　him　to kill　he feared

τὸν　ὄχλον,　ὅτι　ὡς　προφήτην　αὐτὸν
the　crowd,　because　as　a prophet　him

εἶχον.　**6** γενεσίοις　δὲ　γενομένοις　τοῦ
they had.　Now on the birthday　occurring⁰　-

'Ηρῴδου　ὠρχήσατο　ἡ　θυγάτηρ　τῆς
of Herod　danced　the　daughter　of the

'Ηρῳδιάδος　ἐν　τῷ　μέσῳ　καὶ　ἤρεσεν
of Herodias　in　the　midst　and　pleased

τῷ 'Ηρῴδῃ,　**7** ὅθεν　μεθ'　ὅρκου　ὡμολόγησεν
- Herod,　whence　with　an oath　he promised

αὐτῇ　δοῦναι　ὃ　ἐὰν　αἰτήσηται.　**8** ἡ　δὲ
ᵇher　¹to give　whatever　she might ask.　So she

προβιβασθεῖσα　ὑπὸ　τῆς　μητρὸς　αὐτῆς·
being instructed　by　the　mother　of her:

δός　μοι,　φησίν,　ὧδε　ἐπὶ　πίνακι　τὴν
Give　me,　she says,　here　on　a platter　the

κεφαλὴν　'Ιωάννου　τοῦ　βαπτιστοῦ.　**9** καὶ
head　of John　the　Baptist.　And

λυπηθεὶς　ὁ　βασιλεὺς　διὰ　τοὺς
being grieved　the　king　on account of　the

ὅρκους　καὶ　τοὺς　συνανακειμένους
oaths　and　the [ones]　reclining at table with [him]

ἐκέλευσεν　δοθῆναι,　**10** καὶ　πέμψας
he commanded　to be given,　and　sending

Chapter 14

John the Baptist Beheaded

AT that time Herod the tetrarch heard the reports about Jesus, 2 and he said to his attendants, "This is John the Baptist; he has risen from the dead! That is why miraculous powers are at work in him." 3 Now Herod had arrested John and bound him and put him in prison because of Herodias, his brother Philip's wife, 4 for John had been saying to him: "It is not lawful for you to have her." 5 Herod wanted to kill John, but he was afraid of the people, because they considered him a prophet. 6 On Herod's birthday the daughter of Herodias danced for them and pleased Herod so much 7 that he promised with an oath to give her whatever she asked. 8 Prompted by her mother, she said, "Give me here on a platter the head of John the Baptist." 9 The king was distressed, but because of his oaths and his dinner guests, he ordered that her request be granted 10 and had John

---

c Gk tetrarch
d Other ancient authorities read his brother's wife
e Gk he

on. 11 The head was brought on a platter and given to the girl, who brought it to her mother. 12 His disciples came and took the body and buried it; then they went and told Jesus.

Feeding the Five Thousand

13 Now when Jesus heard this, he withdrew from there in a boat to a deserted place by himself. But when the crowds heard it, they followed him on foot from the towns. 14 When he went ashore, he saw a great crowd; and he had compassion for them and cured their sick. 15 When it was evening, the disciples came to him and said, "This is a deserted place, and the hour is now late; send the crowds away so that they may go into the villages and buy food for themselves." 16 Jesus said to them, "They need not go away; you give them something to eat." 17 They replied, "We have nothing here but five loaves and two fish." 18 And he said, "Bring them here to me." 19 Then he ordered the crowds to sit down on the grass. Taking the five loaves and the two fish, he looked up to heaven, and blessed and broke the loaves, and gave them to the disciples, and the disciples gave them to the crowds. 20 And all ate and were filled; and they took up what was left over of the

---

ἀπεκεφάλισεν Ἰωάννην ἐν τῇ φυλακῇ.
beheaded   John   in   the prison.

11 καὶ ἠνέχθη ἡ κεφαλὴ αὐτοῦ ἐπὶ
   And   was brought the head   of him on

πίνακι καὶ ἐδόθη τῷ κορασίῳ, καὶ
a platter and was given to the maid,   and

ἤνεγκεν τῇ μητρὶ αὐτῆς. 12 καὶ
she brought [it] to the mother of her.   And

προσελθόντες οἱ μαθηταὶ αὐτοῦ ἦραν τὸ
⁴approaching ¹the ²disciples ³of him took the

πτῶμα καὶ ἔθαψαν αὐτόν, καὶ ἐλθόντες
corpse and buried   him,   and coming

ἀπήγγειλαν τῷ Ἰησοῦ. 13 Ἀκούσας δὲ
reported   - to Jesus.   And ²hearing

ὁ Ἰησοῦς ἀνεχώρησεν ἐκεῖθεν ἐν
- ¹Jesus   departed   thence   in

πλοίῳ εἰς ἔρημον τόπον κατ᾽ ἰδίαν·
a ship to a desert   place   privately;

καὶ ἀκούσαντες οἱ ὄχλοι ἠκολούθησαν
and ²hearing   ¹the ²crowds   followed

αὐτῷ πεζῇ ἀπὸ τῶν πόλεων. 14 Καὶ
him   afoot from   the   cities.   And

ἐξελθὼν εἶδεν πολὺν ὄχλον, καὶ
going forth he saw a much crowd,   and

ἐσπλαγχνίσθη ἐπ᾽ αὐτοῖς καὶ
was filled with tenderness over them   and

ἐθεράπευσεν τοὺς ἀρρώστους αὐτῶν.
healed   the   sick   of them.

15 ὀψίας δὲ γενομένης προσῆλθον αὐτῷ
   Now evening coming on*   approached to him
   —when evening came on

οἱ μαθηταὶ λέγοντες· ἔρημός ἐστιν
the disciples saying: Desert   is the

τόπος καὶ ἡ ὥρα ἤδη παρῆλθεν·
place   and the hour already passed;

ἀπόλυσον οὖν τοὺς ὄχλους, ἵνα ἀπελθόντες
dismiss therefore the crowds,   that going away

εἰς τὰς κώμας ἀγοράσωσιν ἑαυτοῖς
into the villages they may buy   for themselves

βρώματα. 16 ὁ δὲ Ἰησοῦς εἶπεν αὐτοῖς·
foods.   - But Jesus   said to them:

οὐ χρείαν ἔχουσιν ἀπελθεῖν· δότε
Not need they have to go away;   give

αὐτοῖς ὑμεῖς φαγεῖν. 17 οἱ δὲ λέγουσιν
them   ye   to eat.   But they   say

αὐτῷ· οὐκ ἔχομεν ὧδε εἰ μὴ πέντε
to him: We have not here except   five

ἄρτους καὶ δύο ἰχθύας. 18 ὁ δὲ εἶπεν·
loaves and two fishes.   And he said:

φέρετέ μοι ὧδε αὐτούς. 19 καὶ κελεύσας
Bring to me here them.   And having commanded

τοὺς ὄχλους ἀνακλιθῆναι ἐπὶ τοῦ χόρτου,
the crowds   to recline   on the grass,

λαβὼν τοὺς πέντε ἄρτους καὶ τοὺς δύο
taking the five loaves   and the two

ἰχθύας, ἀναβλέψας εἰς τὸν οὐρανὸν
fishes, looking up   to -   heaven

εὐλόγησεν, καὶ κλάσας ἔδωκεν τοῖς
he blessed,   and breaking gave to the

μαθηταῖς τοὺς ἄρτους, οἱ δὲ μαθηταὶ
disciples the loaves,   and the disciples

τοῖς ὄχλοις. 20 καὶ ἔφαγον πάντες καὶ
to the crowds,   And ate   all   and

ἐχορτάσθησαν· καὶ ἦραν τὸ περισσεῦον
were satisfied;   and they took the excess

---

beheaded in the prison. 11 His head was brought in on a platter and given to the girl, who carried it to her mother. 12 John's disciples came and took his body and buried it. Then they went and told Jesus.

Jesus Feeds the Five Thousand

13 When Jesus heard what had happened, he withdrew by boat privately to a solitary place. Hearing of this, the crowds followed him on foot from the towns. 14 When Jesus landed and saw a large crowd, he had compassion on them and healed their sick.

15 As evening approached, the disciples came to him and said, "This is a remote place, and it's already getting late. Send the crowds away, so they can go to the villages and buy themselves some food."

16 Jesus replied, "They do not need to go away. You give them something to eat."

17 "We have here only five loaves of bread and two fish," they answered.

18 "Bring them here to me," he said. 19 And he directed the people to sit down on the grass. Taking the five loaves and the two fish and looking up to heaven, he gave thanks and broke the loaves. Then he gave them to the disciples, and the disciples gave them to the people. 20 They all ate and were satisfied, and the disciples picked up twelve

broken pieces, twelve baskets full. 21 And those who ate were about five thousand men, besides women and children.

Jesus Walks on the Water

22 Immediately he made the disciples get into the boat and go on ahead to the other side, while he dismissed the crowds. 23 And after he had dismissed the crowds, he went up the mountain by himself to pray. When evening came, he was there alone, 24 but by this time the boat, battered by the waves, was far from the land,*f* for the wind was against them. 25 And early in the morning he came walking toward them on the sea. 26 But when the disciples saw him walking on the sea, they were terrified, saying, "It is a ghost!" And they cried out in fear. 27 But immediately Jesus spoke to them and said, "Take heart, it is I; do not be afraid."

28 Peter answered him, "Lord, if it is you, command me to come to you on the water." 29 He said, "Come." So Peter got out of the boat, started walking on the water, and came toward Jesus. 30 But when he noticed the strong wind,*g* he became frightened, and beginning to sink, he cried out, "Lord, save me!" 31 Jesus immediately reached out his hand and caught him, saying to him, "You of little faith, why did

---

τῶν κλασμάτων, δώδεκα κοφίνους πλήρεις.
of the fragments, twelve baskets full.

21 οἱ δὲ ἐσθίοντες ἦσαν ἄνδρες ὡσεὶ
And the [ones] eating were men about

πεντακισχίλιοι χωρὶς γυναικῶν καὶ
five thousand apart from women and

παιδίων. 22 Καὶ [εὐθέως] ἠνάγκασεν
children. And immediately he constrained

τοὺς μαθητὰς ἐμβῆναι εἰς τὸ πλοῖον
the disciples to embark in the ship

καὶ προάγειν αὐτὸν εἰς τὸ πέραν,
and to go before him to the other side,

ἕως οὗ ἀπολύσῃ τοὺς ὄχλους. 23 Καὶ
until he should dismiss the crowds. And

ἀπολύσας τοὺς ὄχλους ἀνέβη εἰς τὸ
having dismissed the crowds he went up into the

ὄρος κατ᾽ ἰδίαν προσεύξασθαι. ὀψίας
mountain privately to pray. evening
— And when

δὲ γενομένης μόνος ἦν ἐκεῖ. 24 τὸ δὲ
And coming on* alone he was there. But the
evening came on

πλοῖον ἤδη σταδίους πολλοὺς ἀπὸ τῆς
ship now furlongs many from the

γῆς ἀπεῖχεν, βασανιζόμενον ὑπὸ τῶν
land was away, being distressed by the

κυμάτων, ἦν γὰρ ἐναντίος ὁ ἄνεμος.
waves, ⁴was ¹for ²contrary ³the ⁵wind.

25 τετάρτῃ δὲ φυλακῇ τῆς νυκτὸς
Now in [the] fourth watch of the night

ἦλθεν πρὸς αὐτοὺς περιπατῶν ἐπὶ τὴν
he came toward them walking on the

θάλασσαν. 26 οἱ δὲ μαθηταὶ ἰδόντες
sea. And the disciples seeing

αὐτὸν ἐπὶ τῆς θαλάσσης περιπατοῦντα
him on the sea walking

ἐταράχθησαν λέγοντες ὅτι φάντασμά
were troubled saying[,] - A phantasm

ἐστιν, καὶ ἀπὸ τοῦ φόβου ἔκραξαν.
it is, and from fear they cried out.

27 εὐθὺς δὲ ἐλάλησεν [ὁ Ἰησοῦς]
But immediately spoke Jesus

αὐτοῖς λέγων· θαρσεῖτε, ἐγώ εἰμι·
to them saying: Be of good cheer, I am;

μὴ φοβεῖσθε. 28 ἀποκριθεὶς δὲ αὐτῷ ὁ
do not fear. And answering him -

Πέτρος εἶπεν· κύριε, εἰ σὺ εἶ, κέλευσόν
Peter said: Lord, if thou art, command

με ἐλθεῖν πρὸς σὲ ἐπὶ τὰ ὕδατα. 29 ὁ
me to come to thee on the waters. he

δὲ εἶπεν· ἐλθέ. καὶ καταβὰς ἀπὸ τοῦ
And said: Come. And going down from the

πλοίου Πέτρος περιπάτησεν ἐπὶ τὰ ὕδατα
ship Peter walked on the waters

καὶ ἦλθεν πρὸς τὸν Ἰησοῦν. 30 βλέπων δὲ
and came toward - Jesus. But seeing

τὸν ἄνεμον ἐφοβήθη, καὶ ἀρξάμενος
the wind he was afraid, and beginning

καταποντίζεσθαι ἔκραξεν λέγων·
to sink he cried out saying:

κύριε, σῶσόν με. 31 εὐθέως δὲ ὁ
Lord, save me. And immediately -

Ἰησοῦς ἐκτείνας τὴν χεῖρα ἐπελάβετο
Jesus stretching out the(his) hand took hold

αὐτοῦ, καὶ λέγει αὐτῷ· ὀλιγόπιστε,
of him, and says to him: Little-faith,

---

basketfuls of broken pieces that were left over. 21 The number of those who ate was about five thousand men, besides women and children.

Jesus Walks on the Water

22 Immediately Jesus made the disciples get into the boat and go on ahead of him to the other side, while he dismissed the crowd. 23 After he had dismissed them, he went up on a mountainside by himself to pray. When evening came, he was there alone, 24 but the boat was already a considerable distance*c* from land, buffeted by the waves because the wind was against it.

25 During the fourth watch of the night Jesus went out to them, walking on the lake. 26 When the disciples saw him walking on the lake, they were terrified. "It's a ghost," they said, and cried out in fear.

27 But Jesus immediately said to them: "Take courage! It is I. Don't be afraid."

28 "Lord, if it's you," Peter replied, "tell me to come to you on the water."

29 "Come," he said.

Then Peter got down out of the boat, walked on the water and came toward Jesus. 30 But when he saw the wind, he was afraid and, beginning to sink, cried out, "Lord, save me!"

31 Immediately Jesus reached out his hand and caught him. "You of little

---

f Other ancient authorities read *was out on the sea*
g Other ancient authorities read *the wind*

c 24 Greek *many stadia*

you doubt?" 32When they got into the boat, the wind ceased. 33And those in the boat worshipped him, saying, "Truly you are the Son of God."

Jesus Heals the Sick in Gennesaret

34 When they had crossed over, they came to land at Gennesaret. 35 After the people of that place recognized him, they sent word throughout the region and brought all who were sick to him, 36and begged him that they might touch even the fringe of his cloak; and all who touched it were healed.

εἰς τί ἐδίστασας;
why didst thou doubt?

32 καὶ ἀναβάντων
And going up
= as they went up

αὐτῶν εἰς τὸ πλοῖον ἐκόπασεν ὁ ἄνεμος.
them into the ship ceased the wind.

33 οἱ δὲ ἐν τῷ πλοίῳ προσεκύνησαν αὐτῷ
And the [ones] in the ship worshipped him

λέγοντες· ἀληθῶς θεοῦ υἱὸς εἶ. 34 Καὶ
saying: Truly of God Son thou art. And

διαπεράσαντες ἦλθον ἐπὶ τὴν γῆν εἰς
crossing over they came onto the land to

Γεννησαρέτ. 35 καὶ ἐπιγνόντες αὐτὸν
Gennesaret. And recognizing him

οἱ ἄνδρες τοῦ τόπου ἐκείνου ἀπέστειλαν
the men - place of that sent

εἰς ὅλην τὴν περίχωρον ἐκείνην, καὶ
into - the neighbourhood that, and

προσήνεγκαν αὐτῷ πάντας τοὺς κακῶς
brought to him all the [ones] ill
= those who were ill,

ἔχοντας, 36 καὶ παρεκάλουν αὐτὸν ἵνα
having, and besought him that

μόνον ἅψωνται τοῦ κρασπέδου τοῦ
only they might touch the fringe the

ἱματίου αὐτοῦ· καὶ ὅσοι ἥψαντο διεσώθησαν.
garment of him; and as many as touched were completely healed.

---

faith," he said, "why did you doubt?"
32And when they climbed into the boat, the wind died down. 33Then those who were in the boat worshiped him, saying, "Truly you are the Son of God."
34When they had crossed over, they landed at Gennesaret. 35And when the men of that place recognized Jesus, they sent word to all the surrounding country. People brought all their sick to him 36and begged him to let the sick just touch the edge of his cloak, and all who touched him were healed.

Chapter 15

The Tradition of the Elders

THEN Pharisees and scribes came to Jesus from Jerusalem and said, 2"Why do your disciples break the tradition of the elders? For they do not wash their hands before they eat." 3He answered them, "And why do you break the commandment of God for the sake of your tradition? 4For God said,[h] 'Honor your father and your mother,' and, 'Whoever speaks evil of father or mother must surely die.' 5But you say that whoever tells father or mother, 'Whatever support you might have had from me is given to God,'[i] then that person need not honor the father.[j] 6So, for the sake of your tradition, you make void the word[k] of God. 7You hypocrites! Isaiah prophesied rightly about you when he said:
8 'This people honors me with

Chapter 15

15 Τότε προσέρχονται τῷ Ἰησοῦ
Then approach - to Jesus

ἀπὸ Ἱεροσολύμων Φαρισαῖοι καὶ γραμματεῖς
from Jerusalem Pharisees and scribes

λέγοντες· 2 διὰ τί οἱ μαθηταί σου
saying: Why the disciples of thee

παραβαίνουσιν τὴν παράδοσιν τῶν
transgress the tradition of the

πρεσβυτέρων; οὐ γὰρ νίπτονται τὰς χεῖρας
elders? for not they wash the(ir) hands

ὅταν ἄρτον ἐσθίωσιν. 3 ὁ δὲ ἀπο-
whenever bread they eat. And he answer-

κριθεὶς εἶπεν αὐτοῖς· διὰ τί καὶ ὑμεῖς
ing said to them: Why indeed ye

παραβαίνετε τὴν ἐντολὴν τοῦ θεοῦ
transgress the commandment - of God

διὰ τὴν παράδοσιν ὑμῶν; 4 ὁ γὰρ
on account of the tradition of you? - For

θεὸς εἶπεν· τίμα τὸν πατέρα καὶ τὴν
God said: Honour the father and the

μητέρα, καί· ὁ κακολογῶν πατέρα
mother, and: The [one] speaking evil of father

ἢ μητέρα θανάτῳ τελευτάτω. 5 ὑμεῖς δὲ
or mother by death let him die. But ye

λέγετε· ὃς ἂν εἴπῃ τῷ πατρὶ ἢ
say: Whoever says to the(his) father or

τῇ μητρί· δῶρον ὃ ἐὰν ἐξ ἐμοῦ
to the(his) mother: A gift whatever by me

ὠφελήθης, 6 οὐ μὴ τιμήσει τὸν
thou mightest be owed, by no means shall he honour the

πατέρα αὐτοῦ ἢ τὴν μητέρα αὐτοῦ·
father of him or the mother of him;

καὶ ἠκυρώσατε τὸν λόγον τοῦ θεοῦ
and ye annulled the word - of God

διὰ τὴν παράδοσιν ὑμῶν. 7 ὑποκρι-
on account of the tradition of you. Hypocrites,

ταί, καλῶς ἐπροφήτευσεν περὶ ὑμῶν
  well prophesied concerning you

Ἡσαΐας λέγων· 8 ὁ λαὸς οὗτος τοῖς
Isaiah saying: This people with the

Clean and Unclean

THEN some Pharisees and teachers of the law came to Jesus from Jerusalem and asked, 2"Why do your disciples break the tradition of the elders? They don't wash their hands before they eat!"
3Jesus replied, "And why do you break the command of God for the sake of your tradition? 4For God said, 'Honor your father and mother'[d] and 'Anyone who curses his father or mother must be put to death.'[e] 5But you say that if a man says to his father or mother, 'Whatever help you might otherwise have received from me is a gift devoted to God,' 6he is not to 'honor his father'[f] with it. Thus you nullify the word of God for the sake of your tradition. 7You hypocrites! Isaiah was right when he prophesied about you:
8" 'These people honor

---

h Other ancient authorities read *commanded, saying*
i Or *is an offering*
j Other ancient authorities add *or the mother*
k Other ancient authorities read *law*; others, *commandment*

d4 Exodus 20:12; Deut. 5:16
e4 Exodus 21:17; Lev. 20:9
f6 Some manuscripts *father or his mother*

their lips,
but their hearts are
far from me;
9 in vain do they
worship me,
teaching human
precepts as
doctrines.' ''

Things That Defile

10 Then he called the crowd to him and said to them, "Listen and understand; 11 it is not what goes into the mouth that defiles a person, but it is what comes out of the mouth that defiles." 12 Then the disciples approached and said to him, "Do you know that the Pharisees took offense when they heard what you said?" 13 He answered, "Every plant that my heavenly Father has not planted will be uprooted. 14 Let them alone; they are blind guides of the blind.*j* And if one blind person guides another, both will fall into a pit." 15 But Peter said to him, "Explain this parable to us." 16 Then he said, "Are you also still without understanding? 17 Do you not see that whatever goes into the mouth enters the stomach, and goes out into the sewer? 18 But what comes out of the mouth proceeds from the heart, and this is what defiles. 19 For out of the heart come evil intentions, murder, adultery, fornication, theft, false witness, slander. 20 These are what defile a person, but to eat with unwashed hands does not defile."

The Canaanite Woman's Faith

21 Jesus left that place and went away to the district of Tyre and Sidon.

χείλεσίν με τιμᾷ, ἡ δὲ καρδία αὐτῶν
lips   me   honours,   but the   heart   of them

πόρρω ἀπέχει ἀπ' ἐμοῦ· 9 μάτην δὲ
far   is away   from   me;   and vainly

σέβονται με, διδάσκοντες διδασκαλίας
they worship   me,   teaching   teachings

ἐντάλματα ἀνθρώπων. 10 Καὶ προσκαλε-
ordinances   of men.   And   calling

σάμενος τὸν ὄχλον εἶπεν αὐτοῖς·
forward   the   crowd   he said   to them:

ἀκούετε καὶ συνίετε· 11 οὐ τὸ εἰσερχ-
Hear ye   and   understand: Not the [thing] enter-

όμενον εἰς τὸ στόμα κοινοῖ τὸν ἄνθρωπον,
ing   into   the   mouth   defiles   the   man,

ἀλλὰ τὸ ἐκπορευόμενον ἐκ τοῦ στόματος,
but the [thing]   coming forth   out of   the   mouth,

τοῦτο κοινοῖ τὸν ἄνθρωπον. 12 Τότε
this   defiles   the   man.   Then

προσελθόντες οἱ μαθηταὶ λέγουσιν αὐτῷ·
approaching   the   disciples   say   to him:

οἶδας ὅτι οἱ Φαρισαῖοι ἀκούσαντες τὸν
Dost thou know that the   Pharisees   hearing   the

λόγον ἐσκανδαλίσθησαν; 13 ὁ δὲ ἀπο-
saying   were offended?   And he   answer-

κριθεὶς εἶπεν· πᾶσα φυτεία ἣν οὐκ
ing   said: Every   plant   which   not

ἐφύτευσεν ὁ πατήρ μου ὁ οὐράνιος ἐκριζω-
planted   the Father of me –   heavenly   shall be

θήσεται. 14 ἄφετε αὐτούς· τυφλοί εἰσιν
uprooted.   Leave   them;   blind   they are

ὁδηγοὶ τυφλῶν· τυφλὸς δὲ τυφλὸν
leaders   of blind;   *a blind man   *and *a blind man

ἐὰν ὁδηγῇ, ἀμφότεροι εἰς βόθυνον πεσοῦνται.
*if   *leads,   both   into   a ditch   will fall.

15 Ἀποκριθεὶς δὲ ὁ Πέτρος εἶπεν αὐτῷ·
And answering   –   Peter   said   to him:

φράσον ἡμῖν τὴν παραβολήν. 16 ὁ δὲ
Explain   to us   the   parable.   So he

εἶπεν· ἀκμὴν καὶ ὑμεῖς ἀσύνετοι
said: Thus   also   ye   unintelligent

ἐστε; 17 οὐ νοεῖτε ὅτι πᾶν τὸ
are?   Do ye not understand that   everything

εἰσπορευόμενον εἰς τὸ στόμα εἰς τὴν
entering   into   the   mouth   into   the

κοιλίαν χωρεῖ καὶ εἰς ἀφεδρῶνα ἐκβάλλεται;
stomach   goes   and into   a drain   is cast out?

18 τὰ δὲ ἐκπορευόμενα ἐκ τοῦ
but the things   coming forth   out of   the

στόματος ἐκ τῆς καρδίας ἐξέρχεται,
mouth   out of   the   heart   comes forth,

κἀκεῖνα κοινοῖ τὸν ἄνθρωπον. 19 ἐκ
and those   defiles   the   man.   out of

γὰρ τῆς καρδίας ἐξέρχονται διαλογισμοὶ
For   the   heart   come forth   thoughts

πονηροί, φόνοι, μοιχεῖαι, πορνεῖαι, κλοπαί,
evil,   murders,   adulteries,   fornications,   thefts,

ψευδομαρτυρίαι, βλασφημίαι. 20 ταῦτά
false witnessings,   blasphemies.   These things

ἐστιν τὰ κοινοῦντα τὸν ἄνθρωπον·
is(are)   the [ones]   defiling   the   man;

τὸ δὲ ἀνίπτοις χερσὶν φαγεῖν οὐ
–   but   with unwashed   hands   to eat   not

κοινοῖ τὸν ἄνθρωπον.
defiles   the   man.

21 Καὶ ἐξελθὼν ἐκεῖθεν ὁ Ἰησοῦς
And   going forth   thence   –   Jesus

---

me with their lips,
but their hearts are far from
me.
9 They worship me in
vain;
their teachings are but
rules taught by
men.'*g*''

10 Jesus called the crowd to him and said, "Listen and understand. 11 What goes into a man's mouth does not make him 'unclean,' but what comes out of his mouth, that is what makes him 'unclean.' ''

12 Then the disciples came to him and asked, "Do you know that the Pharisees were offended when they heard this?''

13 He replied, "Every plant that my heavenly Father has not planted will be pulled up by the roots. 14 Leave them; they are blind guides.*h* If a blind man leads a blind man, both will fall into a pit.''

15 Peter said, "Explain the parable to us.''

16 "Are you still so dull?'' Jesus asked them. 17 "Don't you see that whatever enters the mouth goes into the stomach and then out of the body? 18 But the things that come out of the mouth come from the heart, and these make a man 'unclean.' 19 For out of the heart come evil thoughts, murder, adultery, sexual immorality, theft, false testimony, slander. 20 These are what make a man 'unclean'; but eating with unwashed hands does not make him 'unclean.' ''

The Faith of the Canaanite Woman

21 Leaving that place, Jesus withdrew to the re-

---

j Other ancient authorities lack *of the blind*

g 9 Isaiah 29:13
h 14 Some manuscripts *guides of the blind*

22 Just then a Canaanite woman from that region came out and started shouting, "Have mercy on me, Lord, Son of David; my daughter is tormented by a demon." 23 But he did not answer her at all. And his disciples came and urged him, saying, "Send her away, for she keeps shouting after us." 24 He answered, "I was sent only to the lost sheep of the house of Israel." 25 But she came and knelt before him, saying, "Lord, help me." 26 He answered, "It is not fair to take the children's food and throw it to the dogs." 27 She said, "Yes, Lord, yet even the dogs eat the crumbs that fall from their masters' table." 28 Then Jesus answered her, "Woman, great is your faith! Let it be done for you as you wish." And her daughter was healed instantly.

Jesus Cures Many People

29 After Jesus had left that place, he passed along the Sea of Galilee, and he went up the mountain, where he sat down. 30 Great crowds came to him, bringing with them the lame, the maimed, the blind, the mute, and many others. They put them at his feet, and he cured them, 31 so that the crowd was amazed when they saw the mute speaking, the maimed

---

ἀνεχώρησεν εἰς τὰ μέρη Τύρου καὶ
departed into the parts of Tyre and

Σιδῶνος. 22 καὶ ἰδοὺ γυνὴ Χαναναία
Sidon. And behold woman a Canaanite

ἀπὸ τῶν ὁρίων ἐκείνων ἐξελθοῦσα
from — borders those coming forth

ἔκραζεν λέγουσα· ἐλέησόν με, κύριε
cried out saying: Pity me, Lord[,]

υἱὸς Δαυίδ· ἡ θυγάτηρ μου κακῶς
son of David; the daughter of me badly

δαιμονίζεται. 23 ὁ δὲ οὐκ ἀπεκρίθη
is demon-possessed. But he answered not

αὐτῇ λόγον. καὶ προσελθόντες οἱ μαθηταὶ
her a word. And approaching the disciples

αὐτοῦ ἠρώτων αὐτὸν λέγοντες· ἀπόλυσον
of him besought him saying: Dismiss

αὐτήν, ὅτι κράζει ὄπισθεν ἡμῶν. 24 ὁ
her, because she is crying out behind us. he

δὲ ἀποκριθεὶς εἶπεν· οὐκ ἀπεστάλην
But answering said: I was not sent

εἰ μὴ εἰς τὰ πρόβατα τὰ ἀπολωλότα
except to the sheep — lost

οἴκου Ἰσραήλ. 25 ἡ δὲ ἐλθοῦσα
of [the] house of Israel. But she coming

προσεκύνει αὐτῷ λέγουσα· κύριε, βοήθει
worshipped him saying: Lord, help

μοι. 26 ὁ δὲ ἀποκριθεὶς εἶπεν· οὐκ
me. But he answering said: not

ἔστιν καλὸν λαβεῖν τὸν ἄρτον τῶν τέκνων
It is good to take the bread of the children

καὶ βαλεῖν τοῖς κυναρίοις. 27 ἡ δὲ
and to throw to the dogs. And she

εἶπεν· ναί, κύριε· καὶ γὰρ τὰ κυνάρια
said: Yes, Lord; but even the dogs

ἐσθίει ἀπὸ τῶν ψιχίων τῶν πιπτόντων
eats from the crumbs — falling

ἀπὸ τῆς τραπέζης τῶν κυρίων αὐτῶν.
from the table of the masters of them.

28 τότε ἀποκριθεὶς ὁ Ἰησοῦς εἶπεν αὐτῇ·
Then answering — Jesus said to her:

ὦ γύναι, μεγάλη σου ἡ πίστις· γενηθήτω
O woman, great of thee the faith; let it be

σοι ὡς θέλεις. καὶ ἰάθη ἡ
to thee as thou desirest. And was healed the

θυγάτηρ αὐτῆς ἀπὸ τῆς ὥρας ἐκείνης.
daughter of her from — hour that.

29 Καὶ μεταβὰς ἐκεῖθεν ὁ Ἰησοῦς
And removing thence — Jesus

ἦλθεν παρὰ τὴν θάλασσαν τῆς Γαλιλαίας,
came by the sea of Galilee,

καὶ ἀναβὰς εἰς τὸ ὄρος ἐκάθητο ἐκεῖ.
and going up into the mountain he sat there.

30 καὶ προσῆλθον αὐτῷ ὄχλοι πολλοὶ ἔχοντες
And approached to him crowds many having

μεθ᾽ ἑαυτῶν χωλούς, κυλλούς, τυφλούς,
with themselves lame, maimed, blind,

κωφούς, καὶ ἑτέρους πολλούς, καὶ ἔρριψαν
dumb, and others many, and cast

αὐτοὺς παρὰ τοὺς πόδας αὐτοῦ· καὶ
them at the feet of him; and

ἐθεράπευσεν αὐτούς· 31 ὥστε τὸν ὄχλον
he healed them; so as the crowd
=so that the crowd marvelled

θαυμάσαι[b] βλέποντας κωφοὺς λαλοῦντας,
to marvel seeing dumb men speaking,

---

gion of Tyre and Sidon. 22 A Canaanite woman from that vicinity came to him, crying out, "Lord, Son of David, have mercy on me! My daughter is suffering terribly from demon-possession."
23 Jesus did not answer a word. So his disciples came to him and urged him, "Send her away, for she keeps crying out after us."
24 He answered, "I was sent only to the lost sheep of Israel."
25 The woman came and knelt before him. "Lord, help me!" she said.
26 He replied, "It is not right to take the children's bread and toss it to their dogs."
27 "Yes, Lord," she said, "but even the dogs eat the crumbs that fall from their masters' table."
28 Then Jesus answered, "Woman, you have great faith! Your request is granted." And her daughter was healed from that very hour.

Jesus Feeds the Four Thousand

29 Jesus left there and went along the Sea of Galilee. Then he went up on a mountainside and sat down. 30 Great crowds came to him, bringing the lame, the blind, the crippled, the mute and many others, and laid them at his feet; and he healed them. 31 The people were amazed when they saw the mute speaking, the crippled

whole, the lame walking, and the blind seeing. And they praised the God of Israel.

Feeding the Four Thousand

32 Then Jesus called his disciples to him and said, "I have compassion for the crowd, because they have been with me now for three days and have nothing to eat; and I do not want to send them away hungry, for they might faint on the way." 33 The disciples said to him, "Where are we to get enough bread in the desert to feed so great a crowd?" 34 Jesus asked them, "How many loaves have you?" They said, "Seven, and a few small fish." 35 Then ordering the crowd to sit down on the ground, 36 he took the seven loaves and the fish; and after giving thanks he broke them and gave them to the disciples, and the disciples gave them to the crowds. 37 And all of them ate and were filled; and they took up the broken pieces left over, seven baskets full. 38 Those who had eaten were four thousand men, besides women and children. 39 After sending away the crowds, he got into the boat and went to the region of Magadan. [m]

κυλλοὺς ὑγιεῖς καὶ χωλοὺς περιπατοῦντας
maimed whole and lame walking

καὶ τυφλοὺς βλέποντας· καὶ ἐδόξασαν
and blind seeing; and they glorified

τὸν θεὸν Ἰσραήλ. 32 Ὁ δὲ Ἰησοῦς
the God of Israel. – And Jesus

προσκαλεσάμενος τοὺς μαθητὰς αὐτοῦ
calling forward the disciples of him

εἶπεν· σπλαγχνίζομαι ἐπὶ τὸν ὄχλον,
said: I am filled with tenderness over the crowd,

ὅτι ἤδη ἡμέραι τρεῖς προσμένουσίν
because now days three they remain

μοι καὶ οὐκ ἔχουσιν τί φάγωσιν·
with me and have not anything they may eat;

καὶ ἀπολῦσαι αὐτοὺς νήστεις οὐ θέλω,
and to dismiss them without food I am not willing,

μήποτε ἐκλυθῶσιν ἐν τῇ ὁδῷ. 33 καὶ
lest they fail in the way. And

λέγουσιν αὐτῷ οἱ μαθηταί· πόθεν
say to him the disciples: Whence

ἡμῖν ἐν ἐρημίᾳ ἄρτοι τοσοῦτοι ὥστε
to us in a desert loaves so many so as

χορτάσαι ὄχλον τοσοῦτον; 34 καὶ λέγει
to satisfy a crowd so great? And says

αὐτοῖς ὁ Ἰησοῦς· πόσους ἄρτους ἔχετε;
to them – Jesus: How many loaves have ye?

οἱ δὲ εἶπαν· ἑπτά, καὶ ὀλίγα ἰχθύδια.
And they said: Seven, and a few fishes.

35 καὶ παραγγείλας τῷ ὄχλῳ ἀναπεσεῖν
And having enjoined the crowd to recline

ἐπὶ τὴν γῆν 36 ἔλαβεν τοὺς ἑπτὰ
on the ground he took the seven

ἄρτους καὶ τοὺς ἰχθύας καὶ εὐχαριστήσας
loaves and the fishes and giving thanks

ἔκλασεν καὶ ἐδίδου τοῖς μαθηταῖς, οἱ δὲ
he broke and gave to the disciples, and the

μαθηταὶ τοῖς ὄχλοις. 37 καὶ ἔφαγον πάντες
disciples to the crowds. And ate all

καὶ ἐχορτάσθησαν, καὶ τὸ περισσεῦον τῶν
and were satisfied, and the excess of the

κλασμάτων ἦραν, ἑπτὰ σπυρίδας πλήρεις.
fragments they took, seven baskets full.

38 οἱ δὲ ἐσθίοντες ἦσαν τετρακισχίλιοι
And the [ones] eating were four thousand

ἄνδρες χωρὶς γυναικῶν καὶ παιδίων.
men apart from women and children.

39 Καὶ ἀπολύσας τοὺς ὄχλους ἐνέβη εἰς
And having dismissed the crowds he embarked in

τὸ πλοῖον, καὶ ἦλθεν εἰς τὰ ὅρια Μαγαδάν.
the ship, and came into the borders of Magadan.

made well, the lame walking and the blind seeing. And they praised the God of Israel.

32 Jesus called his disciples to him and said, "I have compassion for these people; they have already been with me three days and have nothing to eat. I do not want to send them away hungry, or they may collapse on the way."

33 His disciples answered, "Where could we get enough bread in this remote place to feed such a crowd?"

34 "How many loaves do you have?" Jesus asked.

"Seven," they replied, "and a few small fish."

35 He told the crowd to sit down on the ground. 36 Then he took the seven loaves and the fish, and when he had given thanks, he broke them and gave them to the disciples, and they in turn to the people. 37 They all ate and were satisfied. Afterward the disciples picked up seven basketfuls of broken pieces that were left over. 38 The number of those who ate was four thousand, besides women and children. 39 After Jesus had sent the crowd away, he got into the boat and went to the vicinity of Magadan.

Chapter 16

The Demand for a Sign

THE Pharisees and Sadducees came, and to test Jesus [n] they asked him to show him a sign from heaven. 2 He answered them, "When it is evening, you say, 'It will be fair weather, for the sky is red.' 3 And in the morning, 'It will be stormy today, for the sky is red and threatening.' You know how to interpret the appearance of the sky, but you cannot in-

16 Καὶ προσελθόντες οἱ Φαρισαῖοι καὶ
And approaching the Pharisees and

Σαδδουκαῖοι πειράζοντες ἐπηρώτησαν αὐτὸν
Sadducees tempting asked him

σημεῖον ἐκ τοῦ οὐρανοῦ ἐπιδεῖξαι
a sign out of the heaven to show

αὐτοῖς. 2 ὁ δὲ ἀποκριθεὶς εἶπεν αὐτοῖς·
to them. But he answering said to them:

[ὀψίας γενομένης λέγετε· εὐδία,
Evening coming on= ye say: Fair weather,
=When evening comes on

πυρράζει γὰρ ὁ οὐρανός· 3 καὶ πρωΐ·
for is red the heaven(sky); and in the morning:

σήμερον χειμών, πυρράζει γὰρ στυγνάζων
To-day stormy weather, for is red being overcast

Chapter 16

The Demand for a Sign

THE Pharisees and Sadducees came to Jesus and tested him by asking him to show them a sign from heaven.

2 He replied, [i] "When evening comes, you say, 'It will be fair weather, for the sky is red,' 3 and in the

[i]2 Some early manuscripts do not have the rest of verse 2 and all of verse 3.

terpret the signs of the times. *o* 4 An evil and adulterous generation asks for a sign, but no sign will be given to it except the sign of Jonah." Then he left them and went away.

The Yeast of the Pharisees and Sadducees

5 When the disciples reached the other side, they had forgotten to bring any bread. 6 Jesus said to them, "Watch out, and beware of the yeast of the Pharisees and Sadducees." 7 They said to one another, "It is because we have brought no bread." 8 And becoming aware of it, Jesus said, "You of little faith, why are you talking about having no bread? 9 Do you still not perceive? Do you not remember the five loaves for the five thousand, and how many baskets you gathered? 10 Or the seven loaves for the four thousand, and how many baskets you gathered? 11 How could you fail to perceive that I was not speaking about bread? Beware of the yeast of the Pharisees and Sadducees!" 12 Then they understood that he had not told them to beware of the yeast of bread, but of the teaching of the Pharisees and Sadducees.

Peter's Declaration about Jesus

13 Now when Jesus came into the district of Caesarea Philippi, he asked his disciples, "Who do people say that the Son of Man is?" 14 And they said, "Some say John the Baptist, but others Elijah, and still others Jeremiah or one of the prophets." 15 He said to them, "But who do you

ὁ οὐρανός. τὸ μὲν πρόσωπον τοῦ
the heaven(sky). The - face of the
οὐρανοῦ γινώσκετε διακρίνειν, τὰ δὲ
heaven(sky) ye know* to discern, but the
σημεῖα τῶν καιρῶν οὐ δύνασθε;] 4 γενεὰ
signs of the times can ye not? A generation
πονηρὰ καὶ μοιχαλὶς σημεῖον ἐπιζητεῖ,
evil and adulterous a sign seeks,
καὶ σημεῖον οὐ δοθήσεται αὐτῇ εἰ μὴ
and a sign shall be given to it except
τὸ σημεῖον Ἰωνᾶ. καὶ καταλιπὼν αὐτοὺς
the sign of Jonah. And leaving them
ἀπῆλθεν. 5 Καὶ ἐλθόντες οἱ μαθηταὶ εἰς
he went away. And coming the disciples to
τὸ πέραν ἐπελάθοντο ἄρτους λαβεῖν.
the other side they forgot loaves to take.
ὁ δὲ Ἰησοῦς εἶπεν αὐτοῖς· 6 ὁρᾶτε καὶ
- And Jesus said to them: Beware and
προσέχετε ἀπὸ τῆς ζύμης τῶν Φαρισαίων
take heed from the leaven of the Pharisees
καὶ Σαδδουκαίων. 7 οἱ δὲ διελογίζοντο
and Sadducees. But they reasoned
ἐν ἑαυτοῖς λέγοντες ὅτι ἄρτους οὐκ
among themselves saying[:] - Loaves not
ἐλάβομεν. 8 γνοὺς δὲ ὁ Ἰησοῦς εἶπεν·
we took. But knowing - Jesus said:
τί διαλογίζεσθε ἐν ἑαυτοῖς, ὀλιγόπιστοι,
Why reason ye among yourselves, little-faiths,
ὅτι ἄρτους οὐκ ἔχετε; 9 οὔπω νοεῖτε,
because loaves ye have not? Do ye not yet understand,
οὐδὲ μνημονεύετε τοὺς πέντε ἄρτους τῶν
neither remember ye the five loaves of the
πεντακισχιλίων καὶ πόσους κοφίνους
five thousand and how many baskets
ἐλάβετε; 10 οὐδὲ τοὺς ἑπτὰ ἄρτους τῶν
ye took? Neither the seven loaves of the
τετρακισχιλίων καὶ πόσας σπυρίδας
four thousand and how many baskets
ἐλάβετε; 11 πῶς οὐ νοεῖτε ὅτι οὐ
ye took? How do ye not understand that not
περὶ ἄρτων εἶπον ὑμῖν; προσέχετε δὲ ἀπὸ
concerning loaves I said to you? But take heed from
τῆς ζύμης τῶν Φαρισαίων καὶ Σαδ-
the leaven of the Pharisees and Sad-
δουκαίων. 12 τότε συνῆκαν ὅτι οὐκ
ducees. Then they understood that not
εἶπεν προσέχειν ἀπὸ τῆς ζύμης [τῶν
he said to take heed from the leaven of the
ἄρτων], ἀλλὰ ἀπὸ τῆς διδαχῆς τῶν
loaves, but from the teaching of the
Φαρισαίων καὶ Σαδδουκαίων.
Pharisees and Sadducees.
13 Ἐλθὼν δὲ ὁ Ἰησοῦς εἰς τὰ μέρη
And coming - Jesus into the parts
Καισαρείας τῆς Φιλίππου ἠρώτα τοὺς
of Cæsarea - of Philip he questioned the
μαθητὰς αὐτοῦ λέγων· τίνα λέγουσιν οἱ
disciples of him saying: Whom say -
ἄνθρωποι εἶναι τὸν υἱὸν τοῦ ἀνθρώπου;
men to be the Son - of man?
14 οἱ δὲ εἶπαν· οἱ μὲν Ἰωάννην τὸν
And they said: Some indeed John the
βαπτιστήν, ἄλλοι δὲ Ἡλίαν, ἕτεροι δὲ
Baptist, and others Elias, and others
Ἰερεμίαν ἢ ἕνα τῶν προφητῶν. 15 λέγει
Jeremias or one of the prophets. He says

morning, 'Today it will be stormy, for the sky is red and overcast.' You know how to interpret the appearance of the sky, but you cannot interpret the signs of the times. 4 A wicked and adulterous generation looks for a miraculous sign, but none will be given it except the sign of Jonah." Jesus then left them and went away.

The Yeast of the Pharisees and Sadducees

5 When they went across the lake, the disciples forgot to take bread. 6 "Be careful," Jesus said to them. "Be on your guard against the yeast of the Pharisees and Sadducees." 7 They discussed this among themselves and said, "It is because we didn't bring any bread." 8 Aware of their discussion, Jesus asked, "You of little faith, why are you talking among yourselves about having no bread? 9 Do you still not understand? Don't you remember the five loaves for the five thousand, and how many basketfuls you gathered? 10 Or the seven loaves for the four thousand, and how many basketfuls you gathered? 11 How is it you don't understand that I was not talking to you about bread? But be on your guard against the yeast of the Pharisees and Sadducees." 12 Then they understood that he was not telling them to guard against the yeast used in bread, but against the teaching of the Pharisees and Sadducees.

Peter's Confession of Christ

13 When Jesus came to the region of Caesarea Philippi, he asked his disciples, "Who do people say the Son of Man is?"

14 They replied, "Some say John the Baptist; others say Elijah; and still others, Jeremiah or one of the prophets."

*See note on page xvi. Note the use in the next line of δύνασθε.

say that I am?" 16 Simon Peter answered, "You are the Messiah, p the Son of the living God." 17 And Jesus answered him, "Blessed are you, Simon son of Jonah! For flesh and blood has not revealed this to you, but my Father in heaven. 18 And I tell you, you are Peter, q and on this rock r I will build my church, and the gates of Hades will not prevail against it. 19 I will give you the keys of the kingdom of heaven, and whatever you bind on earth will be bound in heaven, and whatever you loose on earth will be loosed in heaven." 20 Then he sternly ordered the disciples not to tell anyone that he was s the Messiah. p

Jesus Foretells His Death and Resurrection

21 From that time on, Jesus began to show his disciples that he must go to Jerusalem and undergo great suffering at the hands of the elders and chief priests and scribes, and be killed, and on the third day be raised. 22 And Peter took him aside and began to rebuke him, saying, "God forbid it, Lord! This must never happen to you." 23 But he turned and said to Peter, "Get behind me, Satan! You are a stumbling block to me; for you are setting your mind not on divine things but on human things."

The Cross and Self-Denial

24 Then Jesus told his disciples, "If any want to

αὐτοῖς· ὑμεῖς δὲ τίνα με λέγετε εἶναι;
to them: But ²ye ¹whom ⁴me ²say   to be?

16 ἀποκριθεὶς δὲ Σίμων Πέτρος εἶπεν·
  And answering   Simon   Peter   said:

17 σὺ εἶ ὁ χριστὸς ὁ υἱὸς τοῦ θεοῦ
Thou art the   Christ   the   Son   -   of God

τοῦ ζῶντος. ἀποκριθεὶς δὲ ὁ Ἰησοῦς
of the   living.   And answering   -   Jesus

εἶπεν αὐτῷ· μακάριος εἶ, Σίμων
said   to him: Blessed   art thou,   Simon

Βαριωνᾶ, ὅτι σὰρξ καὶ αἷμα οὐκ ἀπεκά-
Barjonas, because flesh   and   blood   not   did not

λυψέν σοι ἀλλ' ὁ πατήρ μου ὁ ἐν
reveal   to thee   but   the   Father   of me   -   in

τοῖς οὐρανοῖς. 18 κἀγὼ δέ σοι λέγω
the   heavens.   And I also   to thee   say[,]

ὅτι σὺ εἶ Πέτρος, καὶ ἐπὶ ταύτῃ τῇ
-   Thou art   Peter,   and   on   this   the

πέτρᾳ οἰκοδομήσω μου τὴν ἐκκλησίαν,
rock   I will build   of me   the   church,

καὶ πύλαι ᾅδου οὐ κατισχύσουσιν
and   [the] gates   of hades   will not prevail against

αὐτῆς. 19 δώσω σοι τὰς κλεῖδας τῆς
it.   I will give thee   the   keys   of the

βασιλείας τῶν οὐρανῶν, καὶ ὃ ἐὰν
kingdom   of the   heavens,   and   whatever

δήσῃς ἐπὶ τῆς γῆς ἔσται δεδεμένον ἐν τοῖς
thou bindest on   the   earth shall be *having been* bound in   the

οὐρανοῖς, καὶ ὃ ἐὰν λύσῃς ἐπὶ τῆς
heavens,   and   whatever   thou loosest on   the

γῆς ἔσται λελυμένον ἐν τοῖς οὐρανοῖς.
earth   shall be *having been* loosed in   the   heavens.

20 τότε ἐπετίμησεν τοῖς μαθηταῖς ἵνα
Then   he warned   the   disciples   that

μηδενὶ εἴπωσιν ὅτι αὐτός ἐστιν ὁ
to no one   they should tell   that   he   is   the

χριστός.
Christ.

21 Ἀπὸ τότε ἤρξατο Ἰησοῦς Χριστὸς
From   then   began   Jesus   Christ

δεικνύειν τοῖς μαθηταῖς αὐτοῦ ὅτι δεῖ
to show   to the   disciples   of him   that it behoves

αὐτὸν εἰς Ἱεροσόλυμα ἀπελθεῖν καὶ
him   to   Jerusalem   to go   and

πολλὰ παθεῖν ἀπὸ τῶν πρεσβυτέρων καὶ
many things to suffer   from   the   elders   and

ἀρχιερέων καὶ γραμματέων καὶ ἀποκτανθῆναι
chief priests   and   scribes   and   to be killed

καὶ τῇ τρίτῃ ἡμέρᾳ ἐγερθῆναι. 22 καὶ
and on the   third   day   to be raised.   And

προσλαβόμενος αὐτὸν ὁ Πέτρος ἤρξατο
taking   him   -   Peter   began

ἐπιτιμᾶν αὐτῷ λέγων· ἵλεώς σοι,
to rebuke   him   saying: Propitious to thee,
                                   = May God help thee,

κύριε· οὐ μὴ ἔσται σοι τοῦτο. 23 ὁ δὲ
Lord: by no means shall be to thee   this.   But he

στραφεὶς εἶπεν τῷ Πέτρῳ· ὕπαγε ὀπίσω
turning   said   to   Peter: Go   behind

μου, σατανᾶ· σκάνδαλον εἶ ἐμοῦ,
me,   Satan;   an offence   thou art   of me,

ὅτι οὐ φρονεῖς τὰ τοῦ θεοῦ
because   thou thinkest not   the things   -   of God

ἀλλὰ τὰ τῶν ἀνθρώπων. 24 Τότε ὁ
but   the things   -   of men.   Then   -

Ἰησοῦς εἶπεν τοῖς μαθηταῖς αὐτοῦ· εἴ
Jesus   said   to the   disciples   of him: If

15 "But what about you?" he asked. "Who do you say I am?"
16 Simon Peter answered, "You are the Christ, j the Son of the living God."
17 Jesus replied, "Blessed are you, Simon son of Jonah, for this was not revealed to you by man, but by my Father in heaven. 18 And I tell you that you are Peter, k and on this rock I will build my church, and the gates of Hades l will not overcome it. m 19 I will give you the keys of the kingdom of heaven; whatever you bind on earth will be n bound in heaven, and whatever you loose on earth will be n loosed in heaven." 20 Then he warned his disciples not to tell anyone that he was the Christ.

Jesus Predicts His Death

21 From that time on Jesus began to explain to his disciples that he must go to Jerusalem and suffer many things at the hands of the elders, chief priests and teachers of the law, and that he must be killed and on the third day be raised to life.
22 Peter took him aside and began to rebuke him. "Never, Lord!" he said. "This shall never happen to you!"
23 Jesus turned and said to Peter, "Get behind me, Satan! You are a stumbling block to me; you do not have in mind the things of God, but the things of men."
24 Then Jesus said to his disciples, "If anyone

p Or *the Christ*
q Gk *Petros*
r Gk *petra*
s Other ancient authorities add *Jesus*

j 16 Or *Messiah*; also in verse 20
k 18 *Peter* means *rock.*
l 18 Or *hell*
m 18 Or *not prove stronger than it*
n 19 Or *have been*

become my followers, let them deny themselves and take up their cross and follow me. 25 For those who want to save their life will lose it, and those who lose their life for my sake will find it. 26 For what will it profit them if they gain the whole world but forfeit their life? Or what will they give in return for their life? 27 "For the Son of Man is to come with his angels in the glory of his Father, and then he will repay everyone for what has been done. 28 Truly I tell you, there are some standing here who will not taste death before they see the Son of Man coming in his kingdom."

τις θέλει ὀπίσω μου ἐλθεῖν, ἀπαρνησάσθω
anyone wishes after me to come, let him deny
ἑαυτὸν καὶ ἀράτω τὸν σταυρὸν αὐτοῦ,
himself and let him take the cross of him,
καὶ ἀκολουθείτω μοι. **25** ὃς γὰρ ἐὰν
and let him follow me. For whoever
θέλῃ τὴν ψυχὴν αὐτοῦ σῶσαι, ἀπολέσει
wishes the life of him to save, he will lose
αὐτήν· ὃς δ' ἂν ἀπολέσῃ τὴν ψυχὴν
it; and whoever loses the life
αὐτοῦ ἕνεκεν ἐμοῦ, εὑρήσει αὐτήν. **26** τί
of him for the sake of me, he will find it. what
γὰρ ὠφεληθήσεται ἄνθρωπος, ἐὰν τὸν
For will be benefited a man, if the
κόσμον ὅλον κερδήσῃ, τὴν δὲ ψυχὴν
world whole he should gain, but the soul
αὐτοῦ ζημιωθῇ; ἢ τί δώσει ἄνθρωπος
of him loses? or what will give a man
ἀντάλλαγμα τῆς ψυχῆς αὐτοῦ; **27** μέλλει
an exchange of the soul of him? is about
γὰρ ὁ υἱὸς τοῦ ἀνθρώπου ἔρχεσθαι ἐν τῇ
For the Son - of man to come in the
δόξῃ τοῦ πατρὸς αὐτοῦ μετὰ τῶν ἀγγέλων
glory of the Father of him with the angels
αὐτοῦ, καὶ τότε ἀποδώσει ἑκάστῳ
of him, and then he will reward to each man
κατὰ τὴν πρᾶξιν αὐτοῦ. **28** ἀμὴν λέγω
according to the conduct of him. Truly I say
ὑμῖν ὅτι εἰσίν τινες τῶν ὧδε ἑστώτων
to you[,] - There are some of the [ones] here standing
οἵτινες οὐ μὴ γεύσωνται θανάτου ἕως ἂν
who by no means may taste of death until
ἴδωσιν τὸν υἱὸν τοῦ ἀνθρώπου ἐρχόμενον
they see the Son - of man coming
ἐν τῇ βασιλείᾳ αὐτοῦ.
in the kingdom of him.

would come after me, he must deny himself and take up his cross and follow me. 25 For whoever wants to save his life *o* will lose it, but whoever loses his life for me will find it. 26 What good will it be for a man if he gains the whole world, yet forfeits his soul? Or what can a man give in exchange for his soul? 27 For the Son of Man is going to come in his Father's glory with his angels, and then he will reward each person according to what he has done. 28 I tell you the truth, some who are standing here will not taste death before they see the Son of Man coming in his kingdom."

Chapter 17

The Transfiguration

SIX days later, Jesus took with him Peter and James and his brother John and led them up a high mountain, by themselves. 2 And he was transfigured before them, and his face shone like the sun, and his clothes became dazzling white. 3 Suddenly there appeared to them Moses and Elijah, talking with him. 4 Then Peter said to Jesus, "Lord, it is good for us to be here; if you wish, I *t* will make three dwellings *u* here, one for you, one for Moses, and one for Elijah." 5 While he was still speak-

17 Καὶ μεθ' ἡμέρας ἓξ παραλαμβάνει ὁ
And after days six takes -
Ἰησοῦς τὸν Πέτρον καὶ Ἰάκωβον καὶ
Jesus - Peter and James and
Ἰωάννην τὸν ἀδελφὸν αὐτοῦ, καὶ ἀναφέρει
John the brother of him, and leads up
αὐτοὺς εἰς ὄρος ὑψηλὸν κατ' ἰδίαν. **2** καὶ
them to mountain a high privately. And
μετεμορφώθη ἔμπροσθεν αὐτῶν, καὶ
he was transfigured before them, and
ἔλαμψεν τὸ πρόσωπον αὐτοῦ ὡς ὁ ἥλιος,
shone the face of him as the sun,
τὰ δὲ ἱμάτια αὐτοῦ ἐγένετο λευκὰ ὡς
and the garments of him became white as
τὸ φῶς. **3** καὶ ἰδοὺ ὤφθη αὐτοῖς Μωϋσῆς
the light. And behold was seen by them Moses
καὶ Ἡλίας συλλαλοῦντες μετ' αὐτοῦ.
and Elias conversing with him.
4 ἀποκριθεὶς δὲ ὁ Πέτρος εἶπεν τῷ
And answering - Peter said
Ἰησοῦ· κύριε, καλόν ἐστιν ἡμᾶς ὧδε
to Jesus: Lord, good it is us here
εἶναι· εἰ θέλεις, ποιήσω ὧδε τρεῖς
to be; if thou willest, I will make here three
σκηνάς, σοὶ μίαν καὶ Μωϋσεῖ
tents, for thee one and for Moses
μίαν καὶ Ἡλίᾳ μίαν. **5** ἔτι αὐτοῦ
one and for Elias one. Yet him
    = While he was yet

Chapter 17

The Transfiguration

AFTER six days Jesus took with him Peter, James and John the brother of James, and led them up a high mountain by themselves. 2 There he was transfigured before them. His face shone like the sun, and his clothes became as white as the light. 3 Just then there appeared before them Moses and Elijah, talking with Jesus.

4 Peter said to Jesus, "Lord, it is good for us to be here. If you wish, I will put up three shelters—one for you, one for Moses and one for Elijah."

5 While he was still speak-

o 25 The Greek word means either *life* or *soul*; also in verse 26.

ing, suddenly a bright cloud overshadowed them, and from the cloud a voice said, "This is my Son, the Beloved;ᵛ with him I am well pleased; listen to him!" 6When the disciples heard this, they fell to the ground and were overcome by fear. 7But Jesus came and touched them, saying, "Get up and do not be afraid." 8And when they looked up, they saw no one except Jesus himself alone.

9 As they were coming down the mountain, Jesus ordered them, "Tell no one about the vision until after the Son of Man has been raised from the dead." 10And the disciples asked him, "Why, then, do the scribes say that Elijah must come first?" 11He replied, "Elijah is indeed coming and will restore all things; 12but I tell you that Elijah has already come, and they did not recognize him, but they did to him whatever they pleased. So also the Son of Man is about to suffer at their hands." 13Then the disciples understood that he was speaking to them about John the Baptist.

Jesus Cures a Boy with a Demon

14 When they came to the crowd, a man came to him, knelt before him, 15and said, "Lord, have mercy on my son, for he is an epileptic and he suffers terribly; he often falls into the fire and often into the water. 16And I brought him to your disciples, but they could not cure him."

λαλοῦντος, ἰδοὺ νεφέλη φωτεινὴ ἐπεσκίασεν
speakingᵃ, behold cloud a bright overshadowed
speaking,

αὐτούς, καὶ ἰδοὺ φωνὴ ἐκ τῆς νεφέλης
them, and behold a voice out of the cloud

λέγουσα· οὗτός ἐστιν ὁ υἱός μου ὁ
saying: This is the son of me the

ἀγαπητός, ἐν ᾧ εὐδόκησα· ἀκούετε
beloved, in whom I was well pleased; hear ye

αὐτοῦ. 6 καὶ ἀκούσαντες οἱ μαθηταὶ
him. And hearing the disciples

ἔπεσαν ἐπὶ πρόσωπον αὐτῶν καὶ
fell on [the] face[s] of them and

ἐφοβήθησαν σφόδρα. 7 καὶ προσῆλθεν ὁ
feared exceedingly. And approached -

Ἰησοῦς καὶ ἁψάμενος αὐτῶν εἶπεν·
Jesus and touching them said:

ἐγέρθητε καὶ μὴ φοβεῖσθε. 8 ἐπάραντες δὲ
Rise and do not fear. And lifting up

τοὺς ὀφθαλμοὺς αὐτῶν οὐδένα εἶδον εἰ
the eyes of them no one they saw ex-

μὴ αὐτὸν Ἰησοῦν μόνον. 9 Καὶ κατα-
cept himself Jesus only. And com-
= as

βαινόντων αὐτῶν ἐκ τοῦ ὄρους ἐνετείλατο
ing down themᵃ out of the mountain enjoined
they were coming down

αὐτοῖς ὁ Ἰησοῦς λέγων· μηδενὶ εἴπητε
them - Jesus saying: To no one tell

τὸ ὅραμα ἕως οὗ ὁ υἱὸς τοῦ ἀνθρώπου
the vision until the Son - of man

ἐκ νεκρῶν ἐγερθῇ. 10 Καὶ ἐπηρώτησαν
out of dead be raised. And questioned

αὐτὸν οἱ μαθηταὶ λέγοντες· τί οὖν
him the disciples saying: Why then

οἱ γραμματεῖς λέγουσιν ὅτι Ἠλίαν δεῖ
the scribes say that ¹Elias ¹it behoves

ἐλθεῖν πρῶτον; 11 ὁ δὲ ἀποκριθεὶς εἶπεν·
to come first? And he answering said:

Ἠλίας μὲν ἔρχεται καὶ ἀποκαταστήσει
Elias indeed is coming and will restore

πάντα· 12 λέγω δὲ ὑμῖν ὅτι Ἠλίας
all things; but I tell you that Elias

ἤδη ἦλθεν, καὶ οὐκ ἐπέγνωσαν
already came, and they did not recognize

αὐτόν, ἀλλ' ἐποίησαν ἐν αὐτῷ ὅσα
him, but did by him whatever things

ἠθέλησαν· οὕτως καὶ ὁ υἱὸς τοῦ ἀνθρώπου
they wished; thus also the Son - of man

μέλλει πάσχειν ὑπ' αὐτῶν. 13 τότε
is about to suffer by them. Then

συνῆκαν οἱ μαθηταὶ ὅτι περὶ
understood the disciples that concerning

Ἰωάννου τοῦ βαπτιστοῦ εἶπεν αὐτοῖς.
John the Baptist he spoke to them.

14 Καὶ ἐλθόντων πρὸς τὸν ὄχλον προσ-
And [they] coming to the crowd ap-

ῆλθεν αὐτῷ ἄνθρωπος γονυπετῶν αὐτὸν
proached· to him a man falling on knees to him

15 καὶ λέγων· κύριε, ἐλέησόν μου τὸν
and saying: Lord, pity of me the

υἱόν, ὅτι σεληνιάζεται καὶ κακῶς ἔχει·
son, because he is moonstruck and ill has·
= is ill;

πολλάκις γὰρ πίπτει εἰς τὸ πῦρ καὶ
for often he falls into the fire and

πολλάκις εἰς τὸ ὕδωρ. 16 καὶ προσήνεγκα
often into the water. And I brought

αὐτὸν τοῖς μαθηταῖς σου, καὶ οὐκ
him to the disciples of thee, and not

---

ing, a bright cloud enveloped them, and a voice from the cloud said, "This is my Son, whom I love; with him I am well pleased. Listen to him!" 6When the disciples heard this, they fell face-down to the ground, terrified. 7But Jesus came and touched them. "Get up," he said. "Don't be afraid." 8When they looked up, they saw no one except Jesus.

9As they were coming down the mountain, Jesus instructed them, "Don't tell anyone what you have seen, until the Son of Man has been raised from the dead." 10The disciples asked him, "Why then do the teachers of the law say that Elijah must come first?" 11Jesus replied, "To be sure, Elijah comes and will restore all things. 12But I tell you, Elijah has already come, and they did not recognize him, but have done to him everything they wished. In the same way the Son of Man is going to suffer at their hands." 13Then the disciples understood that he was talking to them about John the Baptist.

The Healing of a Boy With a Demon

14When they came to the crowd, a man approached Jesus and knelt before him. 15"Lord, have mercy on my son," he said. "He has seizures and is suffering greatly. He often falls into the fire or into the water. 16I brought him to your disciples, but they could not

---

ᵛ Or my beloved Son

17 Jesus answered, "You faithless and perverse generation, how much longer must I be with you? How much longer must I put up with you? Bring him here to me." 18 And Jesus rebuked the demon,[w] and it[x] came out of him, and the boy was cured instantly. 19 Then the disciples came to Jesus privately and said, "Why could we not cast it out?" 20 He said to them, "Because of your little faith. For truly I tell you, if you have faith the size of a[y] mustard seed, you will say to this mountain, 'Move from here to there,' and it will move; and nothing will be impossible for you."[z]

Jesus Again Foretells His Death and Resurrection

22 As they were gathering[a] in Galilee, Jesus said to them, "The Son of Man is going to be betrayed into human hands, 23 and they will kill him, and on the third day he will be raised." And they were greatly distressed.

Jesus and the Temple Tax

24 When they reached Capernaum, the collectors of the temple tax[b] came to Peter and said, "Does your teacher not pay the temple tax?"[b] 25 He said, "Yes, he does." And when he came home, Jesus spoke of it first, asking, "What do you think, Simon? From whom do kings of the earth take toll or tribute? From their children or from others?"

Middle column (interlinear)

ἠδυνήθησαν αὐτὸν θεραπεῦσαι. **17** ἀπο-
they were able him to heal. an-

κριθεὶς δὲ ὁ Ἰησοῦς εἶπεν· ὦ γενεὰ
swering And - Jesus said: O generation

ἄπιστος καὶ διεστραμμένη, ἕως πότε
unbelieving and *having been* perverted, until when

μεθ' ὑμῶν ἔσομαι; ἕως πότε
with you shall I be? until when

ἀνέξομαι ὑμῶν; φέρετέ μοι αὐτὸν
shall I endure you? bring to me him

ὧδε. **18** καὶ ἐπετίμησεν αὐτῷ ὁ Ἰησοῦς,
here. And rebuked it - Jesus,

καὶ ἐξῆλθεν ἀπ' αὐτοῦ τὸ δαιμόνιον,
and came out from him the demon,

καὶ ἐθεραπεύθη ὁ παῖς ἀπὸ τῆς ὥρας
and was healed the boy from the hour

ἐκείνης. **19** Τότε προσελθόντες οἱ μαθηταὶ
that. Then ²approaching ¹the ³disciples

τῷ Ἰησοῦ κατ' ἰδίαν εἶπον· διὰ
- to Jesus privately said: Why

τί ἡμεῖς οὐκ ἠδυνήθημεν ἐκβαλεῖν αὐτό;
we were not able to expel it?

20 ὁ δὲ λέγει αὐτοῖς· διὰ τὴν ὀλιγο-
And he says to them: Because of the little

πιστίαν ὑμῶν· ἀμὴν γὰρ λέγω ὑμῖν, ἐὰν
faith of you; for truly I say to you, if

ἔχητε πίστιν ὡς κόκκον σινάπεως,
ye have faith as a grain of mustard,

ἐρεῖτε τῷ ὄρει τούτῳ· μετάβα
ye will say - mountain to this: Remove

ἔνθεν ἐκεῖ, καὶ μεταβήσεται, καὶ οὐδὲν
hence there, and it will be removed, and nothing

ἀδυνατήσει ὑμῖν. ‡
will be impossible to you.

22 Συστρεφομένων δὲ αὐτῶν ἐν τῇ
And strolling them* in -
=as they were strolling

Γαλιλαίᾳ εἶπεν αὐτοῖς ὁ Ἰησοῦς· μέλλει
Galilee said to them - Jesus: is about

ὁ υἱὸς τοῦ ἀνθρώπου παραδίδοσθαι εἰς
The Son - of man to be delivered into

χεῖρας ἀνθρώπων, **23** καὶ ἀποκτενοῦσιν
[the] hands of men, and they will kill

αὐτόν, καὶ τῇ τρίτῃ ἡμέρᾳ ἐγερθήσεται.
him, and on the third day he will be raised.

καὶ ἐλυπήθησαν σφόδρα.
And they were grieved exceedingly.

24 Ἐλθόντων δὲ αὐτῶν εἰς Καφαρναοὺμ
And coming them* to Capernaum
=when they came

προσῆλθον οἱ τὰ δίδραχμα λαμβάνοντες
approached the [ones] the didrachmæ receiving

τῷ Πέτρῳ καὶ εἶπαν· ὁ διδάσκαλος
- Peter and said: The teacher

ὑμῶν οὐ τελεῖ δίδραχμα; λέγει· ναί.
of you not pays drachmae? He says: Yes.

25 καὶ ἐλθόντα εἰς τὴν οἰκίαν προ-
And ⁴coming ⁵into ⁶the ⁷house ¹pre-

έφθασεν αὐτὸν ὁ Ἰησοῦς λέγων· τί σοι
ceded ³him ²Jesus saying: What to thee

δοκεῖ, Σίμων; οἱ βασιλεῖς τῆς γῆς
seems it, Simon? the kings of the earth

ἀπὸ τίνων λαμβάνουσιν τέλη ἢ κῆνσον;
from whom do they take toll or poll-tax?

ἀπὸ τῶν υἱῶν αὐτῶν ἢ ἀπὸ τῶν ἀλλοτρίων;
from the sons of them or from - strangers?

heal him."

17"O unbelieving and perverse generation," Jesus replied, "how long shall I stay with you? How long shall I put up with you? Bring the boy here to me." 18 Jesus rebuked the demon, and it came out of the boy, and he was healed from that moment.

19 Then the disciples came to Jesus in private and asked, "Why couldn't we drive it out?"

20 He replied, "Because you have so little faith. I tell you the truth, if you have faith as small as a mustard seed, you can say to this mountain, 'Move from here to there' and it will move. Nothing will be impossible for you.[p]

22 When they came together in Galilee, he said to them, "The Son of Man is going to be betrayed into the hands of men. 23 They will kill him, and on the third day he will be raised to life." And the disciples were filled with grief.

The Temple Tax

24 After Jesus and his disciples arrived in Capernaum, the collectors of the two-drachma tax came to Peter and asked, "Doesn't your teacher pay the temple tax[q]?"

25"Yes, he does," he replied.

When Peter came into the house, Jesus was the first to speak. "What do you think, Simon?" he asked. "From whom do the kings of the earth collect duty and taxes—from their own sons or from others?"

Footnotes

*w Gk it or him
*x Gk the demon
*y Gk faith as a grain of
*z Other ancient authorities add verse 21, But this kind does not come out except by prayer and fasting
*a Other ancient authorities read living
*b Gk didrachma

‡ Verse 21 omitted by Nestle; cf. NIV

*p 20 Some manuscripts you. 21 But this kind does not go out except by prayer and fasting.
*q 24 Greek the two drachmas

26 When Peter[c] said, "From others," Jesus said to him, "Then the children are free. 27 However, so that we do not give offense to them, go to the sea and cast a hook; take the first fish that comes up; and when you open its mouth, you will find a coin;[d] take that and give it to them for you and me."

26 εἰπόντος δέ· ἀπὸ τῶν ἀλλο-
and [he] saying*: From - strangers,
=when he said :

τρίων, ἔφη αὐτῷ ὁ Ἰησοῦς· ἄρα γε
said to him - Jesus: Then

ἐλεύθεροί εἰσιν οἱ υἱοί. 27 ἵνα δὲ μὴ
free are the sons. But lest

σκανδαλίσωμεν αὐτούς, πορευθεὶς εἰς
we should offend them, going to

θάλασσαν βάλε ἄγκιστρον καὶ τὸν
[the] sea cast a hook and the

ἀναβάντα πρῶτον ἰχθὺν ἆρον, καὶ ἀνοίξας
²coming up ³first ¹fish take, and opening

τὸ στόμα αὐτοῦ εὑρήσεις στατῆρα·
the mouth of it thou wilt find a stater;

ἐκεῖνον λαβὼν δὸς αὐτοῖς ἀντὶ ἐμοῦ καὶ
that taking give them for me and

σοῦ.
thee.

26 "From others," Peter answered.
"Then the sons are exempt," Jesus said to him. 27 "But so that we may not offend them, go to the lake and throw out your line. Take the first fish you catch; open its mouth and you will find a four-drachma coin. Take it and give it to them for my tax and yours."

Chapter 18

True Greatness

AT that time the disciples came to Jesus and asked, "Who is the greatest in the kingdom of heaven?" 2 He called a child, whom he put among them, 3 and said, "Truly I tell you, unless you change and become like children, you will never enter the kingdom of heaven. 4 Whoever becomes humble like this child is the greatest in the kingdom of heaven. 5 Whoever welcomes one such child in my name welcomes me.

Temptations to Sin

6 "If any of you put a stumbling block before one of these little ones who believe in me, it would be better for you if a great millstone were fastened around your neck and you were drowned in the depth of the sea. 7 Woe to the world because of stumbling blocks! Occasions for stumbling are bound to come, but woe to the one by whom the stumbling block comes! 8 "If your hand or your foot causes you to stumble, cut it off and throw it away;

18 Ἐν ἐκείνῃ τῇ ὥρᾳ προσῆλθον οἱ
In that - hour approached the

μαθηταὶ τῷ Ἰησοῦ λέγοντες· τίς ἄρα
disciples - to Jesus saying: Who then

μείζων ἐστὶν ἐν τῇ βασιλείᾳ τῶν οὐρανῶν;
greater is in the kingdom of the heavens?

2 καὶ προσκαλεσάμενος παιδίον ἔστησεν
And calling forward a child he set

αὐτὸ ἐν μέσῳ αὐτῶν 3 καὶ εἶπεν· ἀμὴν
him in [the] midst of them and said: Truly

λέγω ὑμῖν, ἐὰν μὴ στραφῆτε καὶ
I say to you, except ye turn and

γένησθε ὡς τὰ παιδία, οὐ μὴ
become as - children, by no means

εἰσέλθητε εἰς τὴν βασιλείαν τῶν
may ye enter into the kingdom of the

οὐρανῶν. 4 ὅστις οὖν ταπεινώσει ἑαυτὸν
heavens. ²[he] who ¹Therefore will humble himself

ὡς τὸ παιδίον τοῦτο, οὗτός ἐστιν ὁ
as - child this, this [one] is the

μείζων ἐν τῇ βασιλείᾳ τῶν οὐρανῶν.
greater in the kingdom of the heavens.

5 καὶ ὃς ἐὰν δέξηται ἓν παιδίον
And whoever receives one child

τοιοῦτο ἐπὶ τῷ ὀνόματί μου, ἐμὲ δέχεται·
such on(in) the name of me, me receives;

6 ὃς δ᾽ ἂν σκανδαλίσῃ ἕνα τῶν
and whoever offends one of the

μικρῶν τούτων τῶν πιστευόντων εἰς ἐμέ,
little [ones] of these - believing in me,

συμφέρει αὐτῷ ἵνα κρεμασθῇ μύλος
it is expedient for him that be hanged an upper

ὀνικὸς περὶ τὸν τράχηλον αὐτοῦ καὶ
millstone round the neck of him and

καταποντισθῇ ἐν τῷ πελάγει τῆς θαλάσσης.
he be drowned in the depth of the sea.

7 Οὐαὶ τῷ κόσμῳ ἀπὸ τῶν σκανδάλων·
Woe to the world from - offences;

ἀνάγκη γὰρ ἐλθεῖν τὰ σκάνδαλα, πλὴν
for [it is] a necessity to come - offences, but

οὐαὶ τῷ ἀνθρώπῳ δι᾽ οὗ τὸ σκάνδαλον
woe to the man through whom the offence

ἔρχεται. 8 Εἰ δὲ ἡ χείρ σου ἢ ὁ
comes. Now if the hand of thee or the

πούς σου σκανδαλίζει σε, ἔκκοψον αὐτὸν
foot of thee offends thee, cut off it

Chapter 18

The Greatest in the Kingdom of Heaven

AT that time the disciples came to Jesus and asked, "Who is the greatest in the kingdom of heaven?"
2 He called a little child and had him stand among them. 3 And he said: "I tell you the truth, unless you change and become like little children, you will never enter the kingdom of heaven. 4 Therefore, whoever humbles himself like this child is the greatest in the kingdom of heaven.
5 "And whoever welcomes a little child like this in my name welcomes me. 6 But if anyone causes one of these little ones who believe in me to sin, it would be better for him to have a large millstone hung around his neck and to be drowned in the depths of the sea.
7 "Woe to the world because of the things that cause people to sin! Such things must come, but woe to the man through whom they come! 8 If your hand or your foot causes you to sin cut it off and throw it away.

[c] Gk he
[d] Gk stater; the stater was worth two didrachmas

it is better for you to enter life maimed or lame than to have two hands or two feet and to be thrown into the eternal fire. 9And if your eye causes you to stumble, tear it out and throw it away; it is better for you to enter life with one eye than to have two eyes and to be thrown into the hell*e* of fire.

The Parable of the Lost Sheep

10 "Take care that you do not despise one of these little ones; for, I tell you, in heaven their angels continually see the face of my Father in heaven.*f* 12What do you think? If a shepherd has a hundred sheep, and one of them has gone astray, does he not leave the ninety-nine on the mountains and go in search of the one that went astray? 13And if he finds it, truly I tell you, he rejoices over it more than over the ninety-nine that never went astray. 14So it is not the will of your*g* Father in heaven that one of these little ones should be lost.

Reproving Another Who Sins

15 "If another member of the church*h* sins against you,*i* go and point out the fault when the two of you are alone. If the member listens to you, you have regained that one.*j* 16But if you are not listened to, take one or two others along with you, so that every word may be confirmed by the evidence of two or three witnesses. 17If the member refuses to listen to them, tell it to the church; and if the offender refuses

καὶ βάλε ἀπὸ σοῦ· καλόν σοί ἐστιν
and cast from thee; good for thee it is
εἰσελθεῖν εἰς τὴν ζωὴν κυλλὸν ἢ χωλόν,
to enter into – life maimed or lame,
ἢ δύο χεῖρας ἢ δύο πόδας ἔχοντα βληθῆναι
than two hands or two feet having to be cast
εἰς τὸ πῦρ τὸ αἰώνιον. 9 καὶ εἰ ὁ
into the fire – eternal. And if the
ὀφθαλμός σου σκανδαλίζει σε, ἔξελε αὐτὸν
eye of thee offends thee, pluck out it
καὶ βάλε ἀπὸ σοῦ· καλόν σοί ἐστιν
and cast from thee; good for thee it is
μονόφθαλμον εἰς τὴν ζωὴν εἰσελθεῖν, ἢ
one-eyed into the life to enter, than
δύο ὀφθαλμοὺς ἔχοντα βληθῆναι εἰς
two eyes having to be cast into
τὴν γέενναν τοῦ πυρός. 10 Ὁρᾶτε μὴ
the gehenna – of fire. See [that] not
καταφρονήσητε ἑνὸς τῶν μικρῶν τούτων·
ye despise one – little [ones] of these;
λέγω γὰρ ὑμῖν ὅτι οἱ ἄγγελοι αὐτῶν
for I tell you that the angels of them
ἐν οὐρανοῖς διὰ παντὸς βλέπουσι τὸ
in heavens always see the
πρόσωπον τοῦ πατρός μου τοῦ ἐν οὐρανοῖς.‡
face of the Father of me – in heavens.
12 Τί ὑμῖν δοκεῖ; ἐὰν γένηταί τινι
What to you seems it? if there be to any
= any man has
ἀνθρώπῳ ἑκατὸν πρόβατα καὶ πλανηθῇ
man*e* a hundred sheep and wanders
ἐν ἐξ αὐτῶν, οὐχὶ ἀφήσει τὰ ἐνενήκοντα
one of them, will he not leave the ninety-
ἐννέα ἐπὶ τὰ ὄρη καὶ πορευθεὶς ζητεῖ τὸ
nine on the mountains and going seeks the
πλανώμενον; 13 καὶ ἐὰν γένηται
wandering [one]? And if he happens
εὑρεῖν αὐτό, ἀμὴν λέγω ὑμῖν ὅτι
to find it, truly I say to you that
χαίρει ἐπ' αὐτῷ μᾶλλον ἢ ἐπὶ τοῖς
he rejoices over it more than over the
ἐνενήκοντα ἐννέα τοῖς μὴ πεπλανημένοις.
ninety-nine – not having wandered.
14 οὕτως οὐκ ἔστιν θέλημα ἔμπροσθεν
So it is not [the] will before
τοῦ πατρὸς ὑμῶν τοῦ ἐν οὐρανοῖς ἵνα
the Father of you – in heaven*s* that
ἀπόληται ἓν τῶν μικρῶν τούτων.
should perish one – little [ones] of these.
15 Ἐὰν δὲ ἁμαρτήσῃ ὁ ἀδελφός σου,
Now if sins the brother of thee,
ὕπαγε ἔλεγξον αὐτὸν μεταξὺ σοῦ καὶ
go reprove him between thee and
αὐτοῦ μόνου. ἐὰν σου ἀκούσῃ, ἐκέρδησας
him alone. If thee he hears, thou gainedst
τὸν ἀδελφόν σου· 16 ἐὰν δὲ μὴ
the brother of thee; but if not
ἀκούσῃ, παράλαβε μετὰ σοῦ ἔτι ἕνα ἢ
he hears, take with thee more one or
δύο, ἵνα ἐπὶ στόματος δύο μαρτύρων
two, that on(by) [the] mouth of two witnesses
ἢ τριῶν σταθῇ πᾶν ῥῆμα· 17 ἐὰν δὲ
or three may be established every word; but if
παρακούσῃ αὐτῶν, εἰπὸν τῇ ἐκκλησίᾳ·
he refuses to hear them, tell to the church;

It is better for you to enter life maimed or crippled than to have two hands or two feet and be thrown into eternal fire. 9And if your eye causes you to sin, gouge it out and throw it away. It is better for you to enter life with one eye than to have two eyes and be thrown into the fire of hell.

The Parable of the Lost Sheep

10"See that you do not look down on one of these little ones. For I tell you that their angels in heaven always see the face of my Father in heaven.*r*
12"What do you think? If a man owns a hundred sheep, and one of them wanders away, will he not leave the ninety-nine on the hills and go to look for the one that wandered off? 13And if he finds it, I tell you the truth, he is happier about that one sheep than about the ninety-nine that did not wander off. 14In the same way your Father in heaven is not willing that any of these little ones should be lost.

A Brother Who Sins Against You

15"If your brother sins against you,*s* go and show him his fault, just between the two of you. If he listens to you, you have won your brother over. 16But if he will not listen, take one or two others along, so that 'every matter may be established by the testimony of two or three witnesses.'*t* 17If he refuses to listen to them, tell it to the

e Gk Gehenna
f Other ancient authorities add verse 11. For the Son of Man came to save the lost
g Other ancient authorities read my
h Gk If your brother
i Other ancient authorities lack against you
j Gk the brother

‡ Ver. 11 omitted by Nestle; *cf.* NIV note.

*r*10 Some manuscripts heaven.
11 The Son of Man came to save what was lost.
*s*15 Some manuscripts do not have against you.
*t*16 Deut. 19:15

to listen even to the church, let such a one be to you as a Gentile and a tax collector. 18 Truly I tell you, whatever you bind on earth will be bound in heaven, and whatever you loose on earth will be loosed in heaven. 19 Again, truly I tell you, if two of you agree on earth about anything you ask, it will be done for you by my Father in heaven. 20 For where two or three are gathered in my name, I am there among them."

Forgiveness

21 Then Peter came and said to him, "Lord, if another member of the church[k] sins against me, how often should I forgive? As many as seven times?" 22 Jesus said to him, "Not seven times, but, I tell you, seventy-seven[l] times.

The Parable of the Unforgiving Servant

23 "For this reason the kingdom of heaven may be compared to a king who wished to settle accounts with his slaves. 24 When he began the reckoning, one who owed him ten thousand talents[m] was brought to him; 25 and, as he could not pay, his lord ordered him to be sold, together with his wife and children and all his possessions, and payment to be made. 26 So the slave fell on his knees before him, saying, 'Have patience with me, and I will pay you everything.' 27 And out of pity for him, the lord of that slave released him and forgave him the debt.

---

k Gk *if my brother*
l Or *seventy times seven*
m A talent was worth more than fifteen years' wages of a laborer

---

ἐὰν δὲ καὶ τῆς ἐκκλησίας παρακούσῃ,
and if even the church he refuses to hear,
ἔστω σοι ὥσπερ ὁ ἐθνικὸς καὶ
let him be to thee as the gentile and
ὁ τελώνης. 18 Ἀμὴν λέγω ὑμῖν,
the tax-collector. Truly I say to you,
ὅσα ἐὰν δήσητε ἐπὶ τῆς γῆς ἔσται
whatever things ye bind on the earth shall be
δεδεμένα ἐν οὐρανῷ, καὶ ὅσα ἐὰν
having been bound in heaven, and whatever things
λύσητε ἐπὶ τῆς γῆς ἔσται λελυμένα
ye loose on the earth shall be having been loosed
ἐν οὐρανῷ. 19 Πάλιν [ἀμὴν] λέγω
in heaven. Again truly I say
ὑμῖν ὅτι ἐὰν δύο συμφωνήσωσιν ἐξ
to you that if two agree of
ὑμῶν ἐπὶ τῆς γῆς περὶ παντὸς πράγ-
you on the earth concerning every
ματος οὗ ἐὰν αἰτήσωνται, γενήσεται
thing whatever they ask, it shall be
αὐτοῖς παρὰ τοῦ πατρός μου τοῦ ἐν
to them from the Father of me – in
οὐρανοῖς. 20 οὗ γὰρ εἰσιν δύο ἢ τρεῖς
heavens. For where are two or three
συνηγμένοι εἰς τὸ ἐμὸν ὄνομα, ἐκεῖ εἰμι
having been assembled in – my name, there I am
ἐν μέσῳ αὐτῶν.
in [the] midst of them.
21 Τότε προσελθὼν ὁ Πέτρος εἶπεν
Then approaching – Peter said
αὐτῷ· κύριε, ποσάκις ἁμαρτήσει εἰς
to him: Lord, how often will sin against
ἐμὲ ὁ ἀδελφός μου καὶ ἀφήσω αὐτῷ;
me the brother of me and I will forgive him?
ἕως ἑπτάκις; 22 λέγει αὐτῷ ὁ Ἰησοῦς·
until seven times? says to him – Jesus:
οὐ λέγω σοι ἕως ἑπτάκις, ἀλλὰ
I tell not to thee until seven times, but
ἕως ἑβδομηκοντάκις ἑπτά. 23 Διὰ τοῦτο
until seventy times seven. Therefore
ὡμοιώθη ἡ βασιλεία τῶν οὐρανῶν
was(is) likened the kingdom of the heavens
ἀνθρώπῳ βασιλεῖ, ὃς ἠθέλησεν συνᾶραι
to a man a king, who wished to take
λόγον μετὰ τῶν δούλων αὐτοῦ. 24 ἀρξα-
account with the slaves of him. And
μένου δὲ αὐτοῦ συναίρειν, προσήχθη
beginning him[a] to take, [b]was brought forward
=as he began
εἷς αὐτῷ ὀφειλέτης μυρίων ταλάντων.
[1]one [a]to him [2]debtor [3]of ten thousand [4]talents.
25 μὴ ἔχοντος δὲ αὐτοῦ ἀποδοῦναι, ἐκέλευσεν
And not having him[a] to repay, commanded
=as he had not
αὐτὸν ὁ κύριος πραθῆναι καὶ τὴν
him the lord to be sold and the(his)
γυναῖκα καὶ τὰ τέκνα καὶ πάντα ὅσα
wife and – children and all things whatever
ἔχει, καὶ ἀποδοθῆναι. 26 πεσὼν οὖν ὁ
he has, and to be repaid. Falling therefore the
δοῦλος προσεκύνει αὐτῷ λέγων· μακρο-
slave did obeisance to him saying: Defer
θύμησον ἐπ' ἐμοί, καὶ πάντα ἀποδώσω
anger over me, and all things I will repay
σοι. 27 σπλαγχνισθεὶς δὲ ὁ κύριος τοῦ
thee. And filled with tenderness the lord –
δούλου ἐκείνου ἀπέλυσεν αὐτόν, καὶ τὸ
slave of that released him, and the

---

church; and if he refuses to listen even to the church, treat him as you would a pagan or a tax collector. 18 "I tell you the truth, whatever you bind on earth will be[u] bound in heaven, and whatever you loose on earth will be[u] loosed in heaven.

19 "Again, I tell you that if two of you on earth agree about anything you ask for, it will be done for you by my Father in heaven. 20 For where two or three come together in my name, there am I with them."

The Parable of the Unmerciful Servant

21 Then Peter came to Jesus and asked, "Lord, how many times shall I forgive my brother when he sins against me? Up to seven times?"

22 Jesus answered, "I tell you, not seven times, but seventy-seven times.[v]

23 "Therefore, the kingdom of heaven is like a king who wanted to settle accounts with his servants. 24 As he began the settlement, a man who owed him ten thousand talents[w] was brought to him. 25 Since he was not able to pay, the master ordered that he and his wife and his children and all that he had be sold to repay the debt.

26 "The servant fell on his knees before him. 'Be patient with me,' he begged, 'and I will pay back everything.' 27 The servant's master took pity on him,

---

u 18 Or *have been*
v 22 Or *seventy times seven*
w 24 That is, millions of dollars

28 But that same slave, as he went out, came upon one of his fellow slaves who owed him a hundred denarii;[n] and seizing him by the throat, he said, 'Pay what you owe.' 29 Then his fellow slave fell down and pleaded with him, 'Have patience with me, and I will pay you.' 30 But he refused; then he went and threw him into prison until he would pay the debt. 31 When his fellow slaves saw what had happened, they were greatly distressed, and they went and reported to their lord all that had taken place. 32 Then his lord summoned him and said to him, 'You wicked slave! I forgave you all that debt because you pleaded with me. 33 Should you not have had mercy on your fellow slave, as I had mercy on you?' 34 And in anger his lord handed him over to be tortured until he would pay his entire debt. 35 So my heavenly Father will also do to every one of you, if you do not forgive your brother or sister[o] from your heart."

δάνειον ἀφῆκεν αὐτῷ. 28 ἐξελθὼν δὲ
loan forgave him. But going out

ὁ δοῦλος ἐκεῖνος εὗρεν ἕνα τῶν
- slave that found one of the

συνδούλων αὐτοῦ, ὃς ὤφειλεν αὐτὸν ἑκατὸν
fellow-slaves of him, who owed him a hundred

δηνάρια, καὶ κρατήσας αὐτὸν ἔπνιγεν
denarii, and seizing him throttled

λέγων· ἀπόδος εἴ τι ὀφείλεις.
saying: Repay if something thou owest.

29 πεσὼν οὖν ὁ σύνδουλος αὐτοῦ παρε-
Falling therefore the fellow-slave of him be-

κάλει αὐτὸν λέγων· μακροθύμησον ἐπ᾽
sought him saying: Defer anger over

ἐμοί, καὶ ἀποδώσω σοι. 30 ὁ δὲ οὐκ
me, and I will repay thee. But he not

ἤθελεν, ἀλλὰ ἀπελθὼν ἔβαλεν αὐτὸν εἰς
wished, but going away threw him into

φυλακὴν ἕως ἀποδῷ τὸ ὀφειλόμενον.
prison until he should repay the thing owing.

31 ἰδόντες οὖν οἱ σύνδουλοι αὐτοῦ τὰ
Seeing therefore the fellow-slaves of him the things

γενόμενα ἐλυπήθησαν σφόδρα, καὶ
having taken place they were grieved exceedingly, and

ἐλθόντες διεσάφησαν τῷ κυρίῳ ἑαυτῶν
coming explained to the lord of themselves

πάντα τὰ γενόμενα. 32 τότε προσ-
all the things having taken place. Then ¹call-

καλεσάμενος αὐτὸν ὁ κύριος αὐτοῦ λέγει
ing ²forward ³him the lord of him says

αὐτῷ· δοῦλε πονηρέ, πᾶσαν τὴν ὀφειλὴν
to him: ²Slave ¹wicked, all - debt

ἐκείνην ἀφῆκά σοι, ἐπεὶ παρεκάλεσάς με·
that I forgave thee, since thou besoughtest me;

33 οὐκ ἔδει καὶ σὲ ἐλεῆσαι τὸν
did it not behove also thee to pity the

σύνδουλόν σου, ὡς κἀγὼ σὲ ἠλέησα;
fellow-slave of thee, as I also thee pitied?

34 καὶ ὀργισθεὶς ὁ κύριος αὐτοῦ
And being angry the lord of him

παρέδωκεν αὐτὸν τοῖς βασανισταῖς ἕως οὗ
delivered him to the tormentors until

ἀποδῷ πᾶν τὸ ὀφειλόμενον αὐτῷ.
he should repay all the thing owing to him.

35 Οὕτως καὶ ὁ πατήρ μου ὁ οὐράνιος
Thus also the Father of me the heavenly

ποιήσει ὑμῖν, ἐὰν μὴ ἀφῆτε ἕκαστος
will do to you, unless ye forgive each one

τῷ ἀδελφῷ αὐτοῦ ἀπὸ τῶν καρδιῶν
the brother of him from the hearts

ὑμῶν.
of you.

canceled the debt and let him go.
28 "But when that servant went out, he found one of his fellow servants who owed him a hundred denarii.[x] He grabbed him and began to choke him. 'Pay back what you owe me!' he demanded.
29 "His fellow servant fell to his knees and begged him, 'Be patient with me, and I will pay you back.'
30 "But he refused. Instead, he went off and had the man thrown into prison until he could pay the debt.
31 When the other servants saw what had happened, they were greatly distressed and went and told their master everything that had happened.
32 "Then the master called the servant in. 'You wicked servant,' he said, 'I canceled all that debt of yours because you begged me to.
33 Shouldn't you have had mercy on your fellow servant just as I had on you?'
34 In anger his master turned him over to the jailers to be tortured, until he should pay back all he owed.
35 "This is how my heavenly Father will treat each of you unless you forgive your brother from your heart."

[n] The denarius was the usual day's wage for a laborer
[o] Gk brother

Chapter 19

Teaching about Divorce

WHEN Jesus had finished saying these things, he left Galilee and went to the region of Judea beyond the Jordan. 2 Large crowds followed him, and he cured them there.

19 Καὶ ἐγένετο ὅτε ἐτέλεσεν ὁ
And it came to pass when ended -

Ἰησοῦς τοὺς λόγους τούτους, μετῆρεν
Jesus - words these, he removed

ἀπὸ τῆς Γαλιλαίας καὶ ἦλθεν εἰς τὰ
from - Galilee and came into the

ὅρια τῆς Ἰουδαίας πέραν τοῦ Ἰορδάνου.
borders of Judæa across the Jordan.

2 καὶ ἠκολούθησαν αὐτῷ ὄχλοι πολλοί,
And followed him crowds many,

καὶ ἐθεράπευσεν αὐτοὺς ἐκεῖ.
and he healed them there.

Chapter 19

Divorce

WHEN Jesus had finished saying these things, he left Galilee and went into the region of Judea to the other side of the Jordan. 2 Large crowds followed him, and he healed them there.

[x] 28 That is, a few dollars

3 Some Pharisees came to him, and to test him they asked, "Is it lawful for a man to divorce his wife for any cause?" ⁴He answered, "Have you not read that the one who made them at the beginning 'made them male and female,' ⁵and said, 'For this reason a man shall leave his father and mother and be joined to his wife, and the two shall become one flesh'? ⁶So they are no longer two, but one flesh. Therefore what God has joined together, let no one separate." ⁷They said to him, "Why then did Moses command us to give a certificate of dismissal and to divorce her?" ⁸He said to them, "It was because you were so hard-hearted that Moses allowed you to divorce your wives, but from the beginning it was not so. ⁹And I say to you, whoever divorces his wife, except for unchastity, and marries another commits adultery."ᵖ

10 His disciples said to him, "If such is the case of a man with his wife, it is better not to marry." ¹¹But he said to them, "Not everyone can accept this teaching, but only those to whom it is given. ¹²For there are eunuchs who have been so from birth, and there are eunuchs who have been made eunuchs by others, and there are eunuchs who have made themselves eunuchs for the sake of the kingdom of heaven. Let anyone accept this who can."

---

3 Καὶ　προσῆλθον　αὐτῷ　Φαρισαῖοι
And　approached　to him　Pharisees

πειράζοντες　αὐτὸν　καὶ　λέγοντες·　εἰ　ἔξεστιν
tempting　him　and　saying:　If　it is lawful

ἀπολῦσαι　τὴν　γυναῖκα　αὐτοῦ　κατὰ　πᾶσαν
to dismiss　the　wife　of him　for　every

αἰτίαν;　4 ὁ　δὲ　ἀποκριθεὶς　εἶπεν·　οὐκ
cause?　And he　answering　said:　not

ἀνέγνωτε　ὅτι　ὁ　κτίσας　ἀπ᾽
Did ye read　that　the [one]　creating　from

ἀρχῆς　ἄρσεν　καὶ　θῆλυ　ἐποίησεν　αὐτούς;
[the] beginning　male　and　female　made　them?

5 καὶ　εἶπεν·　ἕνεκα　τούτου　καταλείψει
And　he said:　For the sake　of this　shall leave

ἄνθρωπος　τὸν　πατέρα　καὶ　τὴν　μητέρα
a man　the(his)　father　and　the(his)　mother

καὶ　κολληθήσεται　τῇ　γυναικὶ　αὐτοῦ,
and　shall cleave　to the　wife　of him,

καὶ　ἔσονται　οἱ　δύο　εἰς　σάρκα　μίαν·
and　¹shall be　¹the　²two　³in　⁵flesh　⁴one;

6 ὥστε　οὐκέτι　εἰσὶν　δύο　ἀλλὰ　σὰρξ　μία.
so as　no longer　are they　two　but　flesh　one.

ὃ　οὖν　ὁ　θεὸς　συνέζευξεν,　ἄνθρωπος
What therefore　–　God　yoked together,　a man

μὴ　χωριζέτω.　7 λέγουσιν　αὐτῷ·　τί　οὖν
let not separate.　They say　to him:　Why then

Μωϋσῆς　ἐνετείλατο　δοῦναι　βιβλίον　ἀπο-
¹Moses　¹did ²enjoin　to give　a document　of

στασίου　καὶ　ἀπολῦσαι;　8 λέγει　αὐτοῖς·
divorce　and　to dismiss?　He says　to them:

ὅτι　Μωϋσῆς　πρὸς　τὴν　σκληροκαρδίαν
–　Moses　in view of　the　obduracy

ὑμῶν　ἐπέτρεψεν　ὑμῖν　ἀπολῦσαι　τὰς
of you　allowed　you　to dismiss　the

γυναῖκας　ὑμῶν·　ἀπ᾽　ἀρχῆς　δὲ　οὐ
wives　of you;　but from [the] beginning　not

γέγονεν　οὕτως.　9 λέγω　δὲ　ὑμῖν　ὅτι
it has been　so.　But I say　to you　that

ὃς　ἂν　ἀπολύσῃ　τὴν　γυναῖκα　αὐτοῦ
whoever　dismisses　the　wife　of him

μὴ　ἐπὶ　πορνείᾳ　καὶ　γαμήσῃ　ἄλλην,
not　of(for)　fornication　and　marries　another,

μοιχᾶται.　10 λέγουσιν　αὐτῷ　οἱ　μαθηταί·
commits adultery.　Say　to him　the　disciples:

εἰ　οὕτως　ἐστὶν　ἡ　αἰτία　τοῦ　ἀνθρώπου
If　so　is　the　cause of the　man

μετὰ　τῆς　γυναικός,　οὐ　συμφέρει　γαμῆσαι.
with　the　wife,　it is not expedient　to marry.

11 ὁ　δὲ　εἶπεν　αὐτοῖς·　οὐ　πάντες　χωροῦσιν
And　he　said　to them:　Not all men　grasp

τὸν　λόγον　τοῦτον,　ἀλλ᾽　οἷς　δέδοται.
–　saying　this,　but [those] to whom　it has been given.

12 εἰσὶν　γὰρ　εὐνοῦχοι　οἵτινες　ἐκ　κοιλίας
For there are　eunuchs　who　from [the] womb

μητρὸς　ἐγεννήθησαν　οὕτως,　καὶ　εἰσὶν
of a mother　were born　so,　and　there are

εὐνοῦχοι　οἵτινες　εὐνουχίσθησαν　ὑπὸ　τῶν
eunuchs　who　were made eunuchs　by　–

ἀνθρώπων,　καὶ　εἰσὶν　εὐνοῦχοι　οἵτινες
men,　and　there are　eunuchs　who

εὐνούχισαν　ἑαυτοὺς　διὰ　τὴν
made eunuchs　themselves　on account of　the

βασιλείαν　τῶν　οὐρανῶν.　ὁ　δυνάμενος
kingdom　of the　heavens.　The [one]　being able

χωρεῖν　χωρείτω.
to grasp [it]　let him grasp.

---

³Some Pharisees came to him to test him. They asked, "Is it lawful for a man to divorce his wife for any and every reason?"

⁴"Haven't you read," he replied, "that at the beginning the Creator 'made them male and female,'ʸ ⁵and said, 'For this reason a man will leave his father and mother and be united to his wife, and the two will become one flesh'ᶻ? ⁶So they are no longer two, but one. Therefore what God has joined together, let man not separate."

⁷"Why then," they asked, "did Moses command that a man give his wife a certificate of divorce and send her away?"

⁸Jesus replied, "Moses permitted you to divorce your wives because your hearts were hard. But it was not this way from the beginning. ⁹I tell you that anyone who divorces his wife, except for marital unfaithfulness, and marries another woman commits adultery."

¹⁰The disciples said to him, "If this is the situation between a husband and wife, it is better not to marry."

¹¹Jesus replied, "Not everyone can accept this word, but only those to whom it has been given. ¹²For some are eunuchs because they were born that way; others were made that way by men; and others have renounced marriageᵃ because of the kingdom of heaven. The one who can accept this should accept it."

ᵖ Other ancient authorities read *except on the ground of unchastity, causes her to commit adultery;* others add at the end of the verse *and he who marries a divorced woman commits adultery*

ʸ4 Gen. 1:27
ᶻ5 Gen. 2:24
ᵃ12 Or *have made themselves eunuchs*

Jesus Blesses Little Children

13 Then little children were being brought to him in order that he might lay his hands on them and pray. The disciples spoke sternly to those who brought them; 14 but Jesus said, "Let the little children come to me, and do not stop them; for it is to such as these that the kingdom of heaven belongs." 15 And he laid his hands on them and went on his way.

The Rich Young Man

16 Then someone came to him and said, "Teacher, what good deed must I do to have eternal life?" 17 And he said to him, "Why do you ask me about what is good? There is only one who is good. If you wish to enter into life, keep the commandments." 18 He said to him, "Which ones?" And Jesus said, "You shall not murder; You shall not commit adultery; You shall not steal; You shall not bear false witness; 19 Honor your father and mother; also, You shall love your neighbor as yourself." 20 The young man said to him, "I have kept all these;[q] what do I still lack?" 21 Jesus said to him, "If you wish to be perfect, go, sell your possessions, and give the money[r] to the poor, and you will have treasure in heaven; then come, follow me." 22 When the young man heard this word, he went away grieving, for he had many possessions.

23 Then Jesus said to his disciples, "Truly I tell you, it will be hard for a rich person to enter the kingdom of heaven. 24 Again I tell you, it is easier for a camel to go through the eye of a needle than for

---

13 Τότε προσηνέχθησαν αὐτῷ παιδία,
Then were brought to him children,

ἵνα τὰς χεῖρας ἐπιθῇ αὐτοῖς καὶ
that the(his) hands he should put on them and

προσεύξηται· οἱ δὲ μαθηταὶ ἐπετίμησαν
pray; but the disciples rebuked

αὐτοῖς. 14 ὁ δὲ Ἰησοῦς εἶπεν· ἄφετε
them. - But Jesus said: Permit

τὰ παιδία καὶ μὴ κωλύετε αὐτὰ ἐλθεῖν
the children and do not prevent them to come

πρός με· τῶν γὰρ τοιούτων ἐστὶν ἡ
unto me; - for of such is the

βασιλεία τῶν οὐρανῶν. 15 καὶ ἐπιθεὶς
kingdom of the heavens. And putting on

τὰς χεῖρας αὐτοῖς ἐπορεύθη ἐκεῖθεν.
the(his) hands on them he went thence.

16 Καὶ ἰδοὺ εἷς προσελθὼν αὐτῷ εἶπεν·
And behold one approaching to him said:

διδάσκαλε, τί ἀγαθὸν ποιήσω ἵνα
Teacher, what good thing may I do that

σχῶ ζωὴν αἰώνιον; ὁ δὲ εἶπεν αὐτῷ·
I may have life eternal? And he said to him:

17 τί με ἐρωτᾷς περὶ τοῦ ἀγαθοῦ;
Why me questionest thou concerning the good?

εἷς ἐστιν ὁ ἀγαθός· εἰ δὲ θέλεις εἰς
one is the good; but if thou wishest into

τὴν ζωὴν εἰσελθεῖν, τήρει τὰς ἐντολάς.
- life to enter, keep the commandments.

18 λέγει αὐτῷ· ποίας; ὁ δὲ Ἰησοῦς
He says to him: Which? - And Jesus

ἔφη· τὸ οὐ φονεύσεις, οὐ μοιχεύσεις,
said: - Thou shalt not kill, Thou shalt not commit adultery,

οὐ κλέψεις, οὐ ψευδομαρτυρήσεις,
Thou shalt not steal, Thou shalt not bear false witness,

19 τίμα τὸν πατέρα καὶ τὴν μητέρα,
Honour the(thy) father and the(thy) mother,

καὶ ἀγαπήσεις τὸν πλησίον σου ὡς
and Thou shalt love the neighbour of thee as

σεαυτόν. 20 λέγει αὐτῷ ὁ νεανίσκος·
thyself. Says to him the young man:

ταῦτα πάντα ἐφύλαξα· τί ἔτι ὑστερῶ;
These things all I kept; what yet do I lack?

21 ἔφη αὐτῷ ὁ Ἰησοῦς· εἰ θέλεις τέλειος
Said to him - Jesus: If thou wishest perfect

εἶναι, ὕπαγε πώλησόν σου τὰ ὑπάρχοντα
to be, go sell of thee the belongings

καὶ δὸς πτωχοῖς, καὶ ἕξεις
and give to [the] poor, and thou shalt have

θησαυρὸν ἐν οὐρανοῖς, καὶ δεῦρο ἀκολούθει
treasure in heavens, and come follow

μοι. 22 ἀκούσας δὲ ὁ νεανίσκος τὸν
me. But hearing the young man -

λόγον [τοῦτον] ἀπῆλθεν λυπούμενος·
word this went away grieving;

ἦν γὰρ ἔχων κτήματα πολλά. 23 Ὁ
for he was having possessions many.

δὲ Ἰησοῦς εἶπεν τοῖς μαθηταῖς αὐτοῦ·
So Jesus said to the disciples of him:

ἀμὴν λέγω ὑμῖν ὅτι πλούσιος δυσκόλως
Truly I tell you that a rich man hardly

εἰσελεύσεται εἰς τὴν βασιλείαν τῶν
will enter into the kingdom of the

οὐρανῶν. 24 πάλιν δὲ λέγω ὑμῖν,
heavens. And again I tell you,

εὐκοπώτερόν ἐστιν κάμηλον διὰ τρήματος
easier it is a camel through [the] eye

The Little Children and Jesus

13 Then little children were brought to Jesus for him to place his hands on them and pray for them. But the disciples rebuked those who brought them.

14 Jesus said, "Let the little children come to me, and do not hinder them, for the kingdom of heaven belongs to such as these." 15 When he had placed his hands on them, he went on from there.

The Rich Young Man

16 Now a man came up to Jesus and asked, "Teacher, what good thing must I do to get eternal life?"

17 "Why do you ask me about what is good?" Jesus replied. "There is only One who is good. If you want to enter life, obey the commandments."

18 "Which ones?" the man inquired.

Jesus replied, " 'Do not murder, do not commit adultery, do not steal, do not give false testimony, 19 honor your father and mother,'[b] and 'love your neighbor as yourself.'[c]"

20 "All these I have kept," the young man said. "What do I still lack?"

21 Jesus answered, "If you want to be perfect, go, sell your possessions and give to the poor, and you will have treasure in heaven. Then come, follow me."

22 When the young man heard this, he went away sad, because he had great wealth.

23 Then Jesus said to his disciples, "I tell you the truth, it is hard for a rich man to enter the kingdom of heaven. 24 Again I tell you, it is easier for a camel to go through the eye of a

---

q Other ancient authorities add *from my youth*
r Gk lacks *the money*

b19 Exodus 20:12-16; Deut. 5:16-20
c19 Lev. 19:18

someone who is rich to enter the kingdom of God." 25When the disciples heard this, they were greatly astounded and said, "Then who can be saved?" 26But Jesus looked at them and said, "For mortals it is impossible, but for God all things are possible."

27 Then Peter said in reply, "Look, we have left everything and followed you. What then will we have?" 28Jesus said to them, "Truly I tell you, at the renewal of all things, when the Son of Man is seated on the throne of his glory, you who have followed me will also sit on twelve thrones, judging the twelve tribes of Israel. 29And everyone who has left houses or brothers or sisters or father or mother or children or fields, for my name's sake, will receive a hundredfold,*s* and will inherit eternal life. 30But many who are first will be last, and the last will be first.

ῥαφίδος   εἰσελθεῖν   ἤ   πλούσιον   εἰς   τὴν
of a needle   to enter   than   a rich man   into   the

βασιλείαν   τοῦ   θεοῦ.   25 ἀκούσαντες   δὲ
kingdom   -   of God.   And hearing

οἱ   μαθηταὶ   ἐξεπλήσσοντο   σφόδρα
the   disciples   were astounded   exceedingly

λέγοντες·   τίς   ἄρα   δύναται   σωθῆναι;
saying: Who   then   can   to be saved?

26 ἐμβλέψας   δὲ   ὁ   Ἰησοῦς   εἶπεν
And looking upon   -   Jesus   said

αὐτοῖς·   παρὰ   ἀνθρώποις   τοῦτο   ἀδύνατόν
to them: With   men   this   impossible

ἐστιν,   παρὰ   δὲ   θεῷ   πάντα   δυνατά.
is,   but with   God   all things [are] possible.

27 Τότε   ἀποκριθεὶς   ὁ   Πέτρος   εἶπεν   αὐτῷ·
Then   answering   -   Peter   said   to him:

ἰδοὺ   ἡμεῖς   ἀφήκαμεν   πάντα   καὶ
Behold   we   left   all things   and

ἠκολουθήσαμέν   σοι·   τί   ἄρα   ἔσται
followed   thee;   what   then   shall be

ἡμῖν;   28 ὁ   δὲ   Ἰησοῦς   εἶπεν   αὐτοῖς·
to us°?   -   And   Jesus   said   to them:
                         =shall we have?

ἀμὴν   λέγω   ὑμῖν   ὅτι   ὑμεῖς   οἱ   ἀκολουθή-
Truly   I tell   you   that   ye   the [ones]   having

σαντές   μοι,   ἐν   τῇ   παλιγγενεσίᾳ,   ὅταν
followed   me,   in   the   regeneration,   when

καθίσῃ   ὁ   υἱὸς   τοῦ   ἀνθρώπου   ἐπὶ   θρόνου
sits   the Son   -   of man   on [the] throne

δόξης   αὐτοῦ,   καθήσεσθε   καὶ   αὐτοὶ   ἐπὶ
of glory   of him,   ye will sit   also   [your]selves   on

δώδεκα   θρόνους   κρίνοντες   τὰς   δώδεκα
twelve   thrones   judging   the   twelve

φυλὰς   τοῦ   Ἰσραήλ.   29 καὶ   πᾶς   ὅστις
tribes   -   of Israel.   And   everyone   who

ἀφῆκεν   οἰκίας   ἢ   ἀδελφοὺς   ἢ   ἀδελφὰς   ἢ
left   houses   or   brothers   or   sisters   or

πατέρα   ἢ   μητέρα   ἢ   τέκνα   ἢ   ἀγροὺς
father   or   mother   or   children   or   fields

ἕνεκεν   τοῦ   ἐμοῦ   ὀνόματος,   πολλαπλα-
for the sake of   -   my   name,   mani-

σίονα   λήμψεται   καὶ   ζωὴν   αἰώνιον
fold   will receive   and   life   eternal

κληρονομήσει.   30 Πολλοὶ   δὲ   ἔσονται   πρῶτοι
will inherit.   But many   ²will be   ¹first

ἔσχατοι   καὶ   ἔσχατοι   πρῶτοι.
²last   and   last   first.

---

needle than for a rich man to enter the kingdom of God." 25When the disciples heard this, they were greatly astonished and asked, "Who then can be saved?" 26Jesus looked at them and said, "With man this is impossible, but with God all things are possible."

27Peter answered him, "We have left everything to follow you! What then will there be for us?" 28Jesus said to them, "I tell you the truth, at the renewal of all things, when the Son of Man sits on his glorious throne, you who have followed me will also sit on twelve thrones, judging the twelve tribes of Israel. 29And everyone who has left houses or brothers or sisters or father or mother*d* or children or fields for my sake will receive a hundred times as much and will inherit eternal life. 30But many who are first will be last, and many who are last will be first.

Chapter 20

The Laborers in the Vineyard

" "FOR the kingdom of heaven is like a landowner who went out early in the morning to hire laborers for his vineyard. 2After agreeing with the laborers for the usual daily wage,*t* he sent them into his vineyard. 3When he went out about nine o'clock, he saw others standing idle in the marketplace; 4and he said to them,

---

20 Ὁμοία   γάρ   ἐστιν   ἡ   βασιλεία   τῶν
For like   is   the   kingdom   of the

οὐρανῶν   ἀνθρώπῳ   οἰκοδεσπότῃ,   ὅστις
heavens   to a man   a housemaster,   who

ἐξῆλθεν   ἅμα   πρωὶ   μισθώσασθαι
went out   early in the morning   to hire

ἐργάτας   εἰς   τὸν   ἀμπελῶνα   αὐτοῦ.   2 συμ-
workmen   in   the   vineyard   of him.   And

φωνήσας   δὲ   μετὰ   τῶν   ἐργατῶν   ἐκ   δηναρίου
agreeing   with   the   workmen   out of(for) a denarius

τὴν   ἡμέραν   ἀπέστειλεν   αὐτοὺς   εἰς   τὸν
the   day   he sent   them   into   the

ἀμπελῶνα   αὐτοῦ.   3 καὶ   ἐξελθὼν   περὶ
vineyard   of him.   And   going out   about

τρίτην   ὥραν   εἶδεν   ἄλλους   ἑστῶτας
[the] third   hour   he saw   others   standing

ἐν   τῇ   ἀγορᾷ   ἀργούς,   4 καὶ   ἐκείνοις
in   the   marketplace   idle,   and   to those

Chapter 20

The Parable of the Workers in the Vineyard

" "FOR the kingdom of heaven is like a landowner who went out early in the morning to hire men to work in his vineyard. 2He agreed to pay them a denarius for the day and sent them into his vineyard.

3"About the third hour he went out and saw others standing in the marketplace doing nothing. 4He told them, 'You also go and

---

s Other ancient authorities read *manifold*
t Gk *a denarius*

d 29 Some manuscripts *mother or wife*

'You also go into the vineyard, and I will pay you whatever is right.' So they went. 5When he went out again about noon and about three o'clock, he did the same. 6And about five o'clock he went out and found others standing around; and he said to them, 'Why are you standing here idle all day?' 7They said to him, 'Because no one has hired us.' He said to them, 'You also go into the vineyard.' 8When evening came, the owner of the vineyard said to his manager, 'Call the laborers and give them their pay, beginning with the last and then going to the first.' 9When those hired about five o'clock came, each of them received the usual daily wage.[u] 10Now when the first came, they thought they would receive more; but each of them also received the usual daily wage.[u] 11And when they received it, they grumbled against the landowner, 12saying, 'These last worked only one hour, and you have made them equal to us who have borne the burden of the day and the scorching heat.' 13But he replied to one of them, 'Friend, I am doing you no wrong; did you not agree with me for the usual daily wage?[u] 14Take what belongs to you and go; I choose to give to this last the same as I give to you. 15Am I not allowed to do what I choose with what belongs to me? Or are you envious because I am generous?'[v] 16So the last will

εἶπεν· ὑπάγετε καὶ ὑμεῖς εἰς τὸν
said: Go also ye into the

ἀμπελῶνα, καὶ ὃ ἐὰν ᾖ δίκαιον δώσω
vineyard, and whatever may be just I will give

ὑμῖν. οἱ δὲ ἀπῆλθον. 5 πάλιν [δὲ]
you. And they went. And again

ἐξελθὼν περὶ ἕκτην καὶ ἐνάτην ὥραν
going out about [the] sixth and [the] ninth hour

ἐποίησεν ὡσαύτως. 6 περὶ δὲ τὴν
he did similarly. And about the

ἑνδεκάτην ἐξελθὼν εὗρεν ἄλλους ἑστῶτας,
eleventh going out he found others standing,

καὶ λέγει αὐτοῖς· τί ὧδε ἑστήκατε
and says to them: Why here stand ye

ὅλην τὴν ἡμέραν ἀργοί; 7 λέγουσιν αὐτῷ·
all the day idle? They say to him:

ὅτι οὐδεὶς ἡμᾶς ἐμισθώσατο. λέγει αὐτοῖς·
Because no one us hired. He says to them:

ὑπάγετε καὶ ὑμεῖς εἰς τὸν ἀμπελῶνα.
Go also ye into the vineyard.

8 ὀψίας δὲ γενομένης λέγει ὁ κύριος
And evening having come[a] says the lord
= when evening had come

τοῦ ἀμπελῶνος τῷ ἐπιτρόπῳ αὐτοῦ·
of the vineyard to the steward of him:

κάλεσον τοὺς ἐργάτας καὶ ἀπόδος τὸν
Call the workmen and pay the

μισθόν, ἀρξάμενος ἀπὸ τῶν ἐσχάτων
wage, beginning from the last ones

ἕως τῶν πρώτων. 9 ἐλθόντες δὲ οἱ
until the first. And coming the [ones]

περὶ τὴν ἑνδεκάτην ὥραν ἔλαβον ἀνὰ
about the eleventh hour received each

δηνάριον. 10 καὶ ἐλθόντες οἱ πρῶτοι
a denarius. And coming the first

ἐνόμισαν ὅτι πλεῖον λήμψονται· καὶ
supposed that more they will receive; and

ἔλαβον τὸ ἀνὰ δηνάριον καὶ αὐτοί.
they received the [2]each [1]denarius also [them]selves.

11 λαβόντες δὲ ἐγόγγυζον κατὰ τοῦ
And receiving they grumbled against the

οἰκοδεσπότου λέγοντες· 12 οὗτοι οἱ ἔσχατοι
housemaster saying: These – last

μίαν ὥραν ἐποίησαν, καὶ ἴσους αὐτοὺς
one hour wrought, and equal them

ἡμῖν ἐποίησας τοῖς βαστάσασι τὸ
to us thou madest the [ones] having borne the

βάρος τῆς ἡμέρας καὶ τὸν καύσωνα.
burden of the day and the heat.

13 ὁ δὲ ἀποκριθεὶς ἑνὶ αὐτῶν εἶπεν·
But he answering one of them said:

ἑταῖρε, οὐκ ἀδικῶ σε· οὐχὶ
Comrade, I do not injure thee; not

δηναρίου συνεφώνησάς μοι; 14 ἆρον
of(for) a denarius thou didst agree with me? take

τὸ σὸν καὶ ὕπαγε· θέλω δὲ
the thine and go; but I wish
= that which is thine

τούτῳ τῷ ἐσχάτῳ δοῦναι ὡς καὶ
to this – last man to give as also

σοί· 15 οὐκ ἔξεστίν μοι ὃ θέλω
to thee; is it not lawful to me what I wish

ποιῆσαι ἐν τοῖς ἐμοῖς; ἢ ὁ
to do among the my things? or the

ὀφθαλμός σου πονηρός ἐστιν ὅτι ἐγὼ
eye of thee evil is because I

work in my vineyard, and I will pay you whatever is right.' 5So they went.

"He went out again about the sixth hour and the ninth hour and did the same thing. 6About the eleventh hour he went out and found still others standing around. He asked them, 'Why have you been standing here all day long doing nothing?'

7"'Because no one has hired us,' they answered.

"He said to them, 'You also go and work in my vineyard.'

8"When evening came, the owner of the vineyard said to his foreman, 'Call the workers and pay them their wages, beginning with the last ones hired and going on to the first.'

9"The workers who were hired about the eleventh hour came and each received a denarius. 10So when those came who were hired first, they expected to receive more. But each one of them also received a denarius. 11When they received it, they began to grumble against the landowner. 12These men who were hired last worked only one hour,' they said, 'and you have made them equal to us who have borne the burden of the work and the heat of the day.'

13"But he answered one of them, 'Friend, I am not being unfair to you. Didn't you agree to work for a denarius? 14Take your pay and go. I want to give the man who was hired last the same as I gave you. 15Don't I have the right to do what I want with my own money? Or are you envious because I am generous?'

---

[u] Gk a denarius
[v] Gk is your eye evil because I am good?

be first, and the first will be last." [w]

A Third Time Jesus Foretells His Death and Resurrection

17 While Jesus was going up to Jerusalem, he took the twelve disciples aside by themselves, and said to them on the way, 18 "See, we are going up to Jerusalem, and the Son of Man will be handed over to the chief priests and scribes, and they will condemn him to death; 19 then they will hand him over to the Gentiles to be mocked and flogged and crucified; and on the third day he will be raised."

The Request of the Mother of James and John

20 Then the mother of the sons of Zebedee came to him with her sons, and kneeling before him, she asked a favor of him. 21 And he said to her, "What do you want?" She said to him, "Declare that these two sons of mine will sit, one at your right hand and one at your left, in your kingdom." 22 But Jesus answered, "You do not know what you are asking. Are you able to drink the cup that I am about to drink?" [x] They said to him, "We are able." 23 He said to them, "You will indeed drink my cup, but to sit at my right hand and at my left, this is not mine to grant, but it is for those for whom it has been prepared by my Father."

24 When the ten heard it, they were angry with the two brothers. 25 But Jesus called them to him and said, "You know that the rulers of the Gentiles lord it over them, and their great

[w] Other ancient authorities add *for many are called but few are chosen*
[x] Other ancient authorities add *or to be baptized with the baptism that I am baptized with?*

ἀγαθός εἰμι; **16** Οὕτως ἔσονται οἱ ἔσχατοι
good am?   Thus   will be   the   last [ones]
πρῶτοι καὶ οἱ πρῶτοι ἔσχατοι.
first   and   the   first   last.

17 Μέλλων δὲ ἀναβαίνειν Ἰησοῦς εἰς
And being about   to go up   Jesus   to
Ἱεροσόλυμα παρέλαβεν τοὺς δώδεκα κατ᾽
Jerusalem   he took   the   twelve   private-
ἰδίαν, καὶ ἐν τῇ ὁδῷ εἶπεν αὐτοῖς·
ly,   and   in   the   way   said   to them:
18 ἰδοὺ ἀναβαίνομεν εἰς Ἱεροσόλυμα, καὶ
Behold   we are going up   to   Jerusalem,   and
ὁ υἱὸς τοῦ ἀνθρώπου παραδοθήσεται τοῖς
the Son   -   of man   will be delivered   to the
ἀρχιερεῦσιν καὶ γραμματεῦσιν, καὶ κατα-
chief priests   and   scribes,   and   they will
κρινοῦσιν αὐτὸν εἰς θάνατον, **19** καὶ
condemn   him   to   death,   and
παραδώσουσιν αὐτὸν τοῖς ἔθνεσιν εἰς
they will deliver   him   to the   nations   for
τὸ ἐμπαῖξαι καὶ μαστιγῶσαι καὶ
-   to mock   and   to scourge   and
σταυρῶσαι, καὶ τῇ τρίτῃ ἡμέρα ἐγερθή-
to crucify,   and   on the   third   day   he will be
σεται.
raised.

20 Τότε προσῆλθεν αὐτῷ ἡ μήτηρ τῶν
Then   approached   *to* him   the   mother   of the
υἱῶν Ζεβεδαίου μετὰ τῶν υἱῶν αὐτῆς
sons   of Zebedee   with   the   sons   of her
προσκυνοῦσα καὶ αἰτοῦσά τι ἀπ᾽ αὐτοῦ.
doing obeisance   and   asking   something   from   him.
21 ὁ δὲ εἶπεν αὐτῇ· τί θέλεις; λέγει
And he   said   to her: What wishest thou?   She says
αὐτῷ· εἰπὲ ἵνα καθίσωσιν οὗτοι οἱ
to him: Say   that   may sit   these   the
δύο υἱοί μου εἷς ἐκ δεξιῶν καὶ εἷς
two   sons   of me   one   on [the] right   and   one
ἐξ εὐωνύμων σου ἐν τῇ βασιλείᾳ
on [the] left   of thee   in   the   kingdom
σου. **22** ἀποκριθεὶς δὲ ὁ Ἰησοῦς
of thee.   And answering   -   Jesus
εἶπεν· οὐκ οἴδατε τί αἰτεῖσθε.
said: Ye know not   what   ye ask.
δύνασθε πιεῖν τὸ ποτήριον ὃ ἐγὼ
Can ye   to drink   the   cup   which   I
μέλλω πίνειν; λέγουσιν αὐτῷ· δυνάμεθα.
am about   to drink?   They say   to him: We can.
23 λέγει αὐτοῖς· τὸ μὲν ποτήριόν μου
He says   to them: Indeed the   cup   of me
πίεσθε, τὸ δὲ καθίσαι ἐκ δεξιῶν
ye shall drink,   -   but   to sit   on [the] right
μου καὶ ἐξ εὐωνύμων οὐκ ἔστιν
of me   and   on [the] left   is not
ἐμὸν τοῦτο δοῦναι, ἀλλ᾽ οἷς ἡτοί-
mine   this   to give,   but   to whom   it has
μασται ὑπὸ τοῦ πατρός μου. **24** καὶ
been prepared by   the   Father   of me.   And
ἀκούσαντες οἱ δέκα ἠγανάκτησαν περὶ
hearing   the   ten   were incensed   about
τῶν δύο ἀδελφῶν. **25** ὁ δὲ Ἰησοῦς
the   two   brothers.   -   So   Jesus
προσκαλεσάμενος αὐτοῖς εἶπεν· οἴδατε
calling forward   them   said: Ye know
ὅτι οἱ ἄρχοντες τῶν ἐθνῶν κατακυριεύουσιν
that the   rulers   of the nations   lord it over

---

16 "So the last will be first, and the first will be last."

Jesus Again Predicts His Death

17 Now as Jesus was going up to Jerusalem, he took the twelve disciples aside and said to them, 18 "We are going up to Jerusalem, and the Son of Man will be betrayed to the chief priests and the teachers of the law. They will condemn him to death 19 and will turn him over to the Gentiles to be mocked and flogged and crucified. On the third day he will be raised to life!"

A Mother's Request

20 Then the mother of Zebedee's sons came to Jesus with her sons and, kneeling down, asked a favor of him.

21 "What is it you want?" he asked.

She said, "Grant that one of these two sons of mine may sit at your right and the other at your left in your kingdom."

22 "You don't know what you are asking," Jesus said to them. "Can you drink the cup I am going to drink?"

"We can," they answered.

23 Jesus said to them, "You will indeed drink from my cup, but to sit at my right or left is not for me to grant. These places belong to those for whom they have been prepared by my Father."

24 When the ten heard about this, they were indignant with the two brothers. 25 Jesus called them together and said, "You know that the rulers of the Gentiles lord it over them, and

ones are tyrants over them. 26 It will not be so among you; but whoever wishes to be great among you must be your servant, 27 and whoever wishes to be first among you must be your slave; 28 just as the Son of Man came not to be served but to serve, and to give his life a ransom for many."

Jesus Heals Two Blind Men

29 As they were leaving Jericho, a large crowd followed him. 30 There were two blind men sitting by the roadside. When they heard that Jesus was passing by, they shouted, "Lord, ʸ have mercy on us, Son of David!" 31 The crowd sternly ordered them to be quiet; but they shouted even more loudly, "Have mercy on us, Lord, Son of David!" 32 Jesus stood still and called them, saying, "What do you want me to do for you?" 33 They said to him, "Lord, let our eyes be opened." 34 Moved with compassion, Jesus touched their eyes. Immediately they regained their sight and followed him.

Chapter 21

Jesus' Triumphal Entry into Jerusalem

WHEN they had come near Jerusalem and had reached Bethphage, at the Mount of Olives, Jesus sent two disciples, 2 saying to them, "Go into the village ahead of you, and immediately you will find a donkey tied, and a colt with her; untie them and bring them to me. 3 If anyone says anything to you, just

ʸ Other ancient authorities lack Lord

αὐτῶν καὶ οἱ μεγάλοι κατεξουσιάζουσιν
them and the great ones have authority over

αὐτῶν. **26** οὐχ οὕτως ἐστιν ἐν ὑμῖν·
them, Not thus is it among you;

ἀλλ' ὃς ἐὰν θέλῃ ἐν ὑμῖν μέγας γενέσθαι,
but whoever wishes among you great to become,

ἔσται ὑμῶν διάκονος, **27** καὶ ὃς ἂν
will be of you servant, and whoever

θέλῃ ἐν ὑμῖν εἶναι πρῶτος, ἔσται ὑμῶν
wishes among you to be first, he shall be of you

δοῦλος· **28** ὥσπερ ὁ υἱὸς τοῦ ἀνθρώπου
slave; as the Son of man

οὐκ ἦλθεν διακονηθῆναι, ἀλλὰ διακο-
came not to be served, but to

νῆσαι καὶ δοῦναι τὴν ψυχὴν αὐτοῦ
serve and to give the life of him

λύτρον ἀντὶ πολλῶν.
a ransom instead of many.

29 Καὶ ἐκπορευομένων αὐτῶν ἀπὸ Ἰεριχὼ
And going out themᵃ from Jericho
=as they were going out

ἠκολούθησεν αὐτῷ ὄχλος πολύς. **30** καὶ
followed him crowd a much. And

ἰδοὺ δύο τυφλοὶ καθήμενοι παρὰ τὴν
behold two blind men sitting beside the

ὁδόν, ἀκούσαντες ὅτι Ἰησοῦς παράγει,
way, hearing that Jesus is passing by,

ἔκραξαν λέγοντες· κύριε, ἐλέησον ἡμᾶς,
cried out saying: Lord, pity us,

υἱὸς Δαυίδ. **31** ὁ δὲ ὄχλος ἐπετίμησεν
son of David. But the crowd rebuked

αὐτοῖς ἵνα σιωπήσωσιν· οἱ δὲ μεῖζον
them that they should be silent; but they more

ἔκραξαν λέγοντες· κύριε, ἐλέησον ἡμᾶς,
cried out saying: Lord, pity us,

υἱὸς Δαυίδ. **32** καὶ στὰς ὁ Ἰησοῦς
son of David. And standing Jesus

ἐφώνησεν αὐτοὺς καὶ εἶπεν· τί θέλετε
called them and said: What wish ye

ποιήσω ὑμῖν; **33** λέγουσιν αὐτῷ· κύριε,
I may do to you? They say to him: Lord,

ἵνα ἀνοιγῶσιν οἱ ὀφθαλμοὶ ἡμῶν.
that may be opened the eyes of us.

34 σπλαγχνισθεὶς δὲ ὁ Ἰησοῦς ἥψατο
And being filled with tenderness - Jesus touched

τῶν ὀμμάτων αὐτῶν, καὶ εὐθέως ἀνέβλεψαν
the eyes of them, and immediately they saw again

καὶ ἠκολούθησαν αὐτῷ.
and followed him.

21 Καὶ ὅτε ἤγγισαν εἰς Ἰεροσόλυμα
And when they drew near to Jerusalem

καὶ ἦλθον εἰς Βηθφαγὴ εἰς τὸ ὄρος τῶν
and came to Bethphage to the mount of the

ἐλαιῶν, τότε Ἰησοῦς ἀπέστειλεν δύο
olives, then Jesus sent two

μαθητὰς **2** λέγων αὐτοῖς· πορεύεσθε εἰς
disciples telling them: Go ye into

τὴν κώμην τὴν κατέναντι ὑμῶν, καὶ εὐθὺς
the village - opposite you, and at once

εὑρήσετε ὄνον δεδεμένην καὶ πῶλον μετ'
ye will find an ass *having been* tied and a colt with

αὐτῆς· λύσαντες ἀγάγετέ μοι. **3** καὶ ἐάν
her/it; loosening bring to me. And if

τις ὑμῖν εἴπῃ τι, ἐρεῖτε ὅτι ὁ
anyone to you says anything, ye shall say[,] - The

---

their high officials exercise authority over them. 26 Not so with you. Instead, whoever wants to become great among you must be your servant, 27 and whoever wants to be first must be your slave— 28 just as the Son of Man did not come to be served, but to serve, and to give his life as a ransom for many."

Two Blind Men Receive Sight

29 As Jesus and his disciples were leaving Jericho, a large crowd followed him. 30 Two blind men were sitting by the roadside, and when they heard that Jesus was going by, they shouted, "Lord, Son of David, have mercy on us!" 31 The crowd rebuked them and told them to be quiet, but they shouted all the louder, "Lord, Son of David, have mercy on us!" 32 Jesus stopped and called them. "What do you want me to do for you?" he asked. 33 "Lord," they answered, "we want our sight." 34 Jesus had compassion on them and touched their eyes. Immediately they received their sight and followed him.

Chapter 21

The Triumphal Entry

AS they approached Jerusalem and came to Bethphage on the Mount of Olives, Jesus sent two disciples, 2 saying to them, "Go to the village ahead of you, and at once you will find a donkey tied there, with her colt by her. Untie them and bring them to me. 3 If anyone says anything to you, tell him that the Lord

say this, 'The Lord needs them.' And he will send them immediately.ᶜ"
4 This took place to fulfill what had been spoken through the prophet, saying,
5 "Tell the daughter of Zion,
Look, your king is coming to you, humble, and mounted on a donkey, and on a colt, the foal of a donkey."
6 The disciples went and did as Jesus had directed them, 7 they brought the donkey and the colt, and put their cloaks on them, and he sat on them. 8 A very large crowdᵃ spread their cloaks on the road, and others cut branches from the trees and spread them on the road. 9 The crowds that went ahead of him and that followed were shouting,
"Hosanna to the Son of David!
Blessed is the one who comes in the name of the Lord!
Hosanna in the highest heaven!"
10 When he entered Jerusalem, the whole city was in turmoil, asking, "Who is this?" 11 The crowds were saying, "This is the prophet Jesus from Nazareth in Galilee."

Jesus Cleanses the Temple

12 Then Jesus entered the templeᵇ and drove out all who were selling and buying in the temple, and he overturned the tables of the money changers and the seats of those who sold doves. 13 He said to them, "It is written,
'My house shall be called a house of prayer';
but you are making it a den of robbers."
14 The blind and the lame came to him in the

κύριος αὐτῶν χρείαν ἔχει· εὐθὺς δὲ
Lord of them need has; and immediately
ἀποστελεῖ αὐτούς. 4 Τοῦτο δὲ γέγονεν
he will send them. Now this has happened
ἵνα πληρωθῇ τὸ ῥηθὲν διὰ τοῦ
that might be fulfilled the thing spoken through the
προφήτου λέγοντος· 5 εἴπατε τῇ θυγατρὶ
prophet saying: Tell ye the daughter
Σιών· ἰδοὺ ὁ βασιλεύς σου ἔρχεταί σοι
of Zion: Behold[,] the king of thee comes to thee
πραῢς καὶ ἐπιβεβηκὼς ἐπὶ ὄνον καὶ ἐπὶ
meek and having mounted on an ass and on
πῶλον υἱὸν ὑποζυγίου. 6 πορευθέντες δὲ
a colt son(foal) of an ass. And going
οἱ μαθηταὶ καὶ ποιήσαντες καθὼς συνέταξεν
the disciples and doing as directed
αὐτοῖς ὁ Ἰησοῦς 7 ἤγαγον τὴν ὄνον καὶ
them – Jesus they brought the ass and
τὸν πῶλον, καὶ ἐπέθηκαν ἐπ' αὐτῶν
the colt, and put on on them
τὰ ἱμάτια, καὶ ἐπεκάθισεν ἐπάνω αὐτῶν.
the(ir) garments, and he sat on on them.
8 ὁ δὲ πλεῖστος ὄχλος ἔστρωσαν ἑαυτῶν
And the very large crowd strewed of themselves
τὰ ἱμάτια ἐν τῇ ὁδῷ, ἄλλοι δὲ ἔκοπτον
the garments in the way, and others cut
κλάδους ἀπὸ τῶν δένδρων καὶ ἐστρών-
branches from the trees and strewed
νυον ἐν τῇ ὁδῷ. 9 οἱ δὲ ὄχλοι οἱ
in the way. And the crowds the [ones]
προάγοντες αὐτὸν καὶ οἱ ἀκολουθοῦντες
going before him and the [ones] following
ἔκραζον λέγοντες· ὡσαννὰ τῷ υἱῷ Δαυίδ·
cried out saying: Hosanna to the son of David;
εὐλογημένος ὁ ἐρχόμενος ἐν ὀνόματι
blessed the [one] coming in [the] name
κυρίου· ὡσαννὰ ἐν τοῖς ὑψίστοις. 10 καὶ
of [the] Lord; hosanna in the highest [places]. And
εἰσελθόντος αὐτοῦ εἰς Ἰεροσόλυμα ἐσείσθη
entering him into Jerusalem was shaken
=as he entered
πᾶσα ἡ πόλις λέγουσα· τίς ἐστιν οὗτος;
all the city saying: Who is this?
11 οἱ δὲ ὄχλοι ἔλεγον· οὗτός ἐστιν ὁ
And the crowds said: This is the
προφήτης Ἰησοῦς ὁ ἀπὸ Ναζαρὲθ τῆς
prophet Jesus the [one] from Nazareth –
Γαλιλαίας.
of Galilee.
12 Καὶ εἰσῆλθεν Ἰησοῦς εἰς τὸ ἱερὸν
And entered Jesus into the temple
καὶ ἐξέβαλεν πάντας τοὺς πωλοῦντας καὶ
and cast out all the [ones] selling and
ἀγοράζοντας ἐν τῷ ἱερῷ, καὶ τὰς τραπέζας
buying in the temple, and the tables
τῶν κολλυβιστῶν κατέστρεψεν καὶ τὰς
of the money-changers he overturned and the
καθέδρας τῶν πωλούντων τὰς περιστεράς,
seats of the [ones] selling the doves,
13 καὶ λέγει αὐτοῖς· γέγραπται· ὁ οἶκός
and says to them: It has been written: The house
μου οἶκος προσευχῆς κληθήσεται, ὑμεῖς
of me a house of prayer shall be called, ᵇye
δὲ αὐτὸν ποιεῖτε σπήλαιον λῃστῶν. 14 Καὶ
ᵇbut ⁴it ²are making a den of robbers. And
προσῆλθον αὐτῷ τυφλοὶ καὶ χωλοὶ ἐν τῷ
approached to him blind and lame [ones] in the

---

needs them, and he will send them right away."
4 This took place to fulfill what was spoken through the prophet:
5 "Say to the Daughter of Zion,
'See, your king comes to you,
gentle and riding on a donkey,
on a colt, the foal of a donkey.' "ᵉ
6 The disciples went and did as Jesus had instructed them. 7 They brought the donkey and the colt, placed their cloaks on them, and Jesus sat on them. 8 A very large crowd spread their cloaks on the road, while others cut branches from the trees and spread them on the road. 9 The crowds that went ahead of him and those that followed shouted,
"Hosannaᶠ to the Son of David!"
"Blessed is he who comes in the name of the Lord!"ᵍ
"Hosannaᶠ in the highest!"
10 When Jesus entered Jerusalem, the whole city was stirred and asked, "Who is this?"
11 The crowds answered, "This is Jesus, the prophet from Nazareth in Galilee."

Jesus at the Temple

12 Jesus entered the temple area and drove out all who were buying and selling there. He overturned the tables of the money changers and the benches of those selling doves. 13 "It is written," he said to them, " 'My house will be called a house of prayer,'ʰ but you are making it a 'den of robbers.'ⁱ"
14 The blind and the lame came to him at the temple,

ᶜOr 'The Lord needs them and will send them back immediately.'
ᵃOr Most of the crowd
ᵇOther ancient authorities add of God

ᵉ5 Zech. 9:9
ᶠ9 A Hebrew expression meaning "Save!" which became an exclamation of praise; also in verse 15
ᵍ9 Psalm 118:26
ʰ13 Isaiah 56:7
ⁱ13 Jer. 7:11

temple, and he cured them.
15 But when the chief priests and the scribes saw the amazing things that he did, and heard[c] the children crying out in the temple, "Hosanna to the Son of David," they became angry 16 and said to him, "Do you hear what these are saying?" Jesus said to them, "Yes; have you never read, 'Out of the mouths of infants and nursing babies you have prepared praise for yourself'?"

17 He left them, went out of the city to Bethany, and spent the night there.

Jesus Curses the Fig Tree

18 In the morning, when he returned to the city, he was hungry. 19 And seeing a fig tree by the side of the road, he went to it and found nothing at all on it but leaves. Then he said to it, "May no fruit ever come from you again!" And the fig tree withered at once. 20 When the disciples saw it, they were amazed, saying, "How did the fig tree wither at once?" 21 Jesus answered them, "Truly I tell you, if you have faith and do not doubt, not only will you do what has been done to the fig tree, but even if you say to this mountain, 'Be lifted up and thrown into the sea,' it will be done. 22 Whatever you ask for in prayer with faith, you will receive."

The Authority of Jesus Questioned

23 When he entered the temple, the chief priests and the elders of the people came to him as he was teaching, and said, "By what authority are you doing these things, and who gave you this authority?"

ἱερῷ, καὶ ἐθεράπευσεν αὐτούς. 15 ἰδόντες
temple, and he healed them. ᵗseeing
δὲ οἱ ἀρχιερεῖς καὶ οἱ γραμματεῖς τὰ
¹But ²the ³chief priests ⁴and ⁵the ⁶scribes the
θαυμάσια ἃ ἐποίησεν καὶ τοὺς παῖδας
marvels which he did and the children
τοὺς κράζοντας ἐν τῷ ἱερῷ καὶ λέγοντας·
- crying out in the temple and saying:
ὡσαννὰ τῷ υἱῷ Δαυίδ, ἠγανάκτησαν, 16 καὶ
Hosanna to the son of David, they were incensed, and
εἶπαν αὐτῷ· ἀκούεις τί οὗτοι λέγουσιν;
said to him: Hearest thou what these are saying?
ὁ δὲ Ἰησοῦς λέγει αὐτοῖς· ναί· οὐδέποτε
- And Jesus says to them: Yes; never
ἀνέγνωτε ὅτι ἐκ στόματος νηπίων καὶ
did ye read[,] - Out of [the] mouth of infants and
θηλαζόντων κατηρτίσω αἶνον; 17 Καὶ
sucking [ones] thou didst prepare praise! And
καταλιπὼν αὐτοὺς ἐξῆλθεν ἔξω τῆς
leaving them he went forth outside the
πόλεως εἰς Βηθανίαν, καὶ ηὐλίσθη ἐκεῖ.
city to Bethany, and lodged there.
18 Πρωῒ δὲ ἐπαναγαγὼν εἰς τὴν πόλιν
Now early going up to the city
ἐπείνασεν. 19 καὶ ἰδὼν συκῆν μίαν ἐπὶ τῆς
he hungered. And seeing fig-tree one on the
ὁδοῦ ἦλθεν ἐπ' αὐτήν, καὶ οὐδὲν εὗρεν
way he went up(to) it, and nothing found
ἐν αὐτῇ εἰ μὴ φύλλα μόνον, καὶ λέγει
in it except leaves only, and says
αὐτῇ· οὐ μηκέτι ἐκ σοῦ καρπὸς γένηται
to it: Never of thee fruit may be
εἰς τὸν αἰῶνα. καὶ ἐξηράνθη παραχρῆμα
to the age. And was dried up instantly
ἡ συκῆ. 20 καὶ ἰδόντες οἱ μαθηταὶ
the fig-tree. And seeing the disciples
ἐθαύμασαν λέγοντες· πῶς παραχρῆμα
marvelled saying: How instantly
ἐξηράνθη ἡ συκῆ; 21 ἀποκριθεὶς δὲ ὁ
was withered the fig-tree? And answering -
Ἰησοῦς εἶπεν αὐτοῖς· ἀμὴν λέγω ὑμῖν,
Jesus said to them: Truly I say to you,
ἐὰν ἔχητε πίστιν καὶ μὴ διακριθῆτε,
If ye have faith and do not doubt,
οὐ μόνον τὸ τῆς συκῆς ποιήσετε, ἀλλὰ
not only the* of the fig-tree ye will do, but
κἂν τῷ ὄρει τούτῳ εἴπητε· ἄρθητι
also if - mountain to this ye say: Be thou taken
καὶ βλήθητι εἰς τὴν θάλασσαν, γενήσεται·
and cast into the sea, it shall be;
22 καὶ πάντα ὅσα ἂν αἰτήσητε ἐν τῇ
and all things whatever ye may ask in -
προσευχῇ πιστεύοντες λήμψεσθε.
prayer believing ye shall receive.
23 Καὶ ἐλθόντος αὐτοῦ εἰς τὸ ἱερὸν
And coming him* into the temple
=as he came
προσῆλθον αὐτῷ διδάσκοντι οἱ ἀρχιερεῖς
approached to him teaching* the chief priests
=while he taught
καὶ οἱ πρεσβύτεροι τοῦ λαοῦ λέγοντες·
and the elders of the people saying:
ἐν ποίᾳ ἐξουσίᾳ ταῦτα ποιεῖς; καὶ
By what authority these things doest thou? and
τίς σοι ἔδωκεν τὴν ἐξουσίαν ταύτην;
who thee gave - authority this?

---

and he healed them. 15 But when the chief priests and the teachers of the law saw the wonderful things he did and the children shouting in the temple area, "Hosanna to the Son of David," they were indignant.

16 "Do you hear what these children are saying?" they asked him.

"Yes," replied Jesus, "have you never read,

" 'From the lips of children and infants you have ordained praise'*?"

17 And he left them and went out of the city to Bethany, where he spent the night.

The Fig Tree Withers

18 Early in the morning, as he was on his way back to the city, he was hungry. 19 Seeing a fig tree by the road, he went up to it but found nothing on it except leaves. Then he said to it, "May you never bear fruit again!" Immediately the tree withered.

20 When the disciples saw this, they were amazed. "How did the fig tree wither so quickly?" they asked.

21 Jesus replied, "I tell you the truth, if you have faith and do not doubt, not only can you do what was done to the fig tree, but also you can say to this mountain, 'Go, throw yourself into the sea,' and it will be done. 22 If you believe, you will receive whatever you ask for in prayer."

The Authority of Jesus Questioned

23 Jesus entered the temple courts, and, while he was teaching, the chief priests and the elders of the people came to him. "By what authority are you doing these things?" they asked. "And who gave you this authority?"

---

24 Jesus said to them, "I will also ask you one question; if you tell me the answer, then I will also tell you by what authority I do these things. 25 Did the baptism of John come from heaven, or was it of human origin?" And they argued with one another, "If we say, 'From heaven,' he will say to us, 'Why then did you not believe him?' 26 But if we say, 'Of human origin,' we are afraid of the crowd; for all regard John as a prophet." 27 So they answered Jesus, "We do not know." And he said to them, "Neither will I tell you by what authority I am doing these things.

The Parable of the Two Sons

28 "What do you think? A man had two sons; he went to the first and said, 'Son, go and work in the vineyard today.' 29 He answered, 'I will not'; but later he changed his mind and went. 30 The father[d] went to the second and said the same; and he answered, 'I go, sir'; but he did not go. 31 Which of the two did the will of his father?" They said, "The first." Jesus said to them, "Truly I tell you, the tax collectors and the prostitutes are going into the kingdom of God ahead of you. 32 For John came to you in the way of righteousness and you did not believe him, but the tax collectors and the prostitutes believed him; and even after you saw it, you did not change your minds and believe him.

The Parable of the Wicked Tenants

33 "Listen to another parable. There was a land-

24 ἀποκριθεὶς δὲ ὁ Ἰησοῦς εἶπεν αὐτοῖς·
And answering – Jesus said to them:
ἐρωτήσω ὑμᾶς κἀγὼ λόγον ἕνα, ὃν
will question you I also word one, which
ἐὰν εἴπητέ μοι, κἀγὼ ὑμῖν ἐρῶ ἐν ποίᾳ
if ye tell me, I also you will tell by what
ἐξουσίᾳ ταῦτα ποιῶ· 25 τὸ βάπτισμα
authority these things I do: The baptism
τὸ Ἰωάννου πόθεν ἦν; ἐξ οὐρανοῦ ἢ
– of John whence was it? from heaven or
ἐξ ἀνθρώπων; οἱ δὲ διελογίζοντο ἐν
from men? And they reasoned among
ἑαυτοῖς λέγοντες· ἐὰν εἴπωμεν· ἐξ οὐρανοῦ,
themselves saying: If we say: From heaven,
ἐρεῖ ἡμῖν· διὰ τί οὖν οὐκ ἐπιστεύσατε
he will say to us: Why then believed ye not
αὐτῷ; 26 ἐὰν δὲ εἴπωμεν· ἐξ ἀνθρώπων,
him? But if we say: From men,
φοβούμεθα τὸν ὄχλον· πάντες γὰρ ὡς
we fear the crowd: for all as
προφήτην ἔχουσιν τὸν Ἰωάννην. 27 καὶ
a prophet have – John. And
ἀποκριθέντες τῷ Ἰησοῦ εἶπαν· οὐκ
answering – Jesus they said: We do
οἴδαμεν. ἔφη αὐτοῖς καὶ αὐτός· οὐδὲ
not know. said to them also He: Neither
ἐγὼ λέγω ὑμῖν ἐν ποίᾳ ἐξουσίᾳ ταῦτα
I tell you by what authority these things
ποιῶ. 28 Τί δὲ ὑμῖν δοκεῖ; ἄνθρωπος
I do. But what to you seems it? A man
εἶχεν τέκνα δύο· προσελθὼν τῷ πρώτῳ
had children two; approaching to the first
εἶπεν· τέκνον, ὕπαγε σήμερον ἐργάζου ἐν
he said: Child, go to-day work in
τῷ ἀμπελῶνι. 29 ὁ δὲ ἀποκριθεὶς εἶπεν·
the vineyard. But he answering said:
ἐγὼ κύριε, καὶ οὐκ ἀπῆλθεν. 30 προσ-
I [go], lord, and went not. And
ελθὼν δὲ τῷ δευτέρῳ εἶπεν ὡσαύτως.
approaching to the second he said similarly.
ὁ δὲ ἀποκριθεὶς εἶπεν· οὐ θέλω, ὕστερον
And he answering said: I will not, later
μεταμεληθεὶς ἀπῆλθεν. 31 τίς ἐκ τῶν δύο
repenting he went. Which of the two
ἐποίησεν τὸ θέλημα τοῦ πατρός; λέγουσιν·
did the will of the father? They say:
ὁ ὕστερος. λέγει αὐτοῖς ὁ Ἰησοῦς· ἀμὴν
The latter. Says to them – Jesus: Truly
λέγω ὑμῖν ὅτι οἱ τελῶναι καὶ αἱ πόρναι
I tell you[,] – The tax-collectors and the harlots
προάγουσιν ὑμᾶς εἰς τὴν βασιλείαν τοῦ
are going before you into the kingdom –
θεοῦ. 32 ἦλθεν γὰρ Ἰωάννης πρὸς ὑμᾶς
of God. For came John to you
ἐν ὁδῷ δικαιοσύνης, καὶ οὐκ ἐπιστεύσατε
in a way of righteousness, and ye believed not
αὐτῷ· οἱ δὲ τελῶναι καὶ αἱ πόρναι
him; but the tax-collectors and the harlots
ἐπίστευσαν αὐτῷ· ὑμεῖς δὲ ἰδόντες οὐδὲ
believed him; but ye seeing not
μετεμελήθητε ὕστερον τοῦ πιστεῦσαι αὐτῷ.
repented later – to believe[d] him.
= so as to believe

33 Ἄλλην παραβολὴν ἀκούσατε. Ἄνθρωπος
Another parable hear ye. A man

24 Jesus replied, "I will also ask you one question. If you answer me, I will tell you by what authority I am doing these things. 25 John's baptism—where did it come from? Was it from heaven, or from men?"

They discussed it among themselves and said, "If we say, 'From heaven,' he will ask, 'Then why didn't you believe him?' 26 But if we say, 'From men'—we are afraid of the people, for they all hold that John was a prophet."

27 So they answered Jesus, "We don't know."

Then he said, "Neither will I tell you by what authority I am doing these things.

The Parable of the Two Sons

28 "What do you think? There was a man who had two sons. He went to the first and said, 'Son, go and work today in the vineyard.'

29 "'I will not,' he answered, but later he changed his mind and went.

30 "Then the father went to the other son and said the same thing. He answered, 'I will, sir,' but he did not go.

31 "Which of the two did what his father wanted?"

"The first," they answered.

Jesus said to them, "I tell you the truth, the tax collectors and the prostitutes are entering the kingdom of God ahead of you. 32 For John came to you to show you the way of righteousness, and you did not believe him, but the tax collectors and the prostitutes did. And even after you saw this, you did not repent and believe him.

The Parable of the Tenants

33 "Listen to another parable: There was a landown-

[d] Gk He

---

* Some such word as 'sign' must be supplied.

owner who planted a vineyard, put a fence around it, dug a wine press in it, and built a watchtower. Then he leased it to tenants and went to another country. 34 When the harvest time had come, he sent his slaves to the tenants to collect his produce. 35 But the tenants seized his slaves and beat one, killed another, and stoned another. 36 Again he sent other slaves, more than the first; and they treated them in the same way. 37 Finally he sent his son to them, saying, 'They will respect my son.' 38 But when the tenants saw the son, they said to themselves, 'This is the heir; come, let us kill him and get his inheritance.' 39 So they seized him, threw him out of the vineyard, and killed him. 40 Now when the owner of the vineyard comes, what will he do to those tenants?" 41 They said to him, "He will put those wretches to a miserable death, and lease the vineyard to other tenants who will give him the produce at the harvest time."

42 Jesus said to them, "Have you never read in the scriptures:

'The stone that the
    builders rejected
has become the
    cornerstone;*e*
this was the Lord's
    doing,
and it is amazing in
    our eyes'?

43 Therefore I tell you, the kingdom of God will be taken away from you and given to a people that pro-

---

ἦν οἰκοδεσπότης ὅστις ἐφύτευσεν ἀμπελῶνα,
there was a housemaster who planted a vineyard,

καὶ φραγμὸν αὐτῷ περιέθηκεν καὶ ὤρυξεν
and ²a hedge ³it ¹put round and dug

ἐν αὐτῷ ληνὸν καὶ ᾠκοδόμησεν πύργον,
in it a winepress and built a tower,

καὶ ἐξέδοτο αὐτὸν γεωργοῖς, καὶ ἀπεδή-
and let it to husbandmen, and departed.

μησεν. 34 ὅτε δὲ ἤγγισεν ὁ καιρὸς τῶν
And when drew near the time of the

καρπῶν, ἀπέστειλεν τοὺς δούλους αὐτοῦ
fruits, he sent the slaves of him

πρὸς τοὺς γεωργοὺς λαβεῖν τοὺς καρποὺς
to the husbandmen to receive the fruits

αὐτοῦ. 35 καὶ λαβόντες οἱ γεωργοὶ
of it. And ²taking ¹the ²husbandmen

τοὺς δούλους αὐτοῦ ὃν μὲν ἔδειραν, ὃν
the slaves of him this one they flogged, that

δὲ ἀπέκτειναν, ὃν δὲ ἐλιθοβόλησαν. 36 πάλιν
one they killed, another they stoned. Again

ἀπέστειλεν ἄλλους δούλους πλείονας τῶν
he sent other slaves more [than] the

πρώτων, καὶ ἐποίησαν αὐτοῖς ὡσαύτως.
first [ones], and they did to them similarly.

37 ὕστερον δὲ ἀπέστειλεν πρὸς αὐτοὺς
But later he sent to them

τὸν υἱὸν αὐτοῦ λέγων· ἐντραπήσονται
the son of him saying: They will reverence

τὸν υἱόν μου. 38 οἱ δὲ γεωργοὶ ἰδόντες
the son of me. But the husbandmen seeing

τὸν υἱὸν εἶπον ἐν ἑαυτοῖς· οὗτός ἐστιν
the son said among themselves: This is

ὁ κληρονόμος· δεῦτε ἀποκτείνωμεν αὐτὸν
the heir; come[,] let us kill him

καὶ σχῶμεν τὴν κληρονομίαν αὐτοῦ·
and let us possess the inheritance of him;

39 καὶ λαβόντες αὐτὸν ἐξέβαλον ἔξω τοῦ
and taking ²him ¹they cast out outside the

ἀμπελῶνος καὶ ἀπέκτειναν. 40 ὅταν οὖν
vineyard and killed. When therefore

ἔλθῃ ὁ κύριος τοῦ ἀμπελῶνος, τί ποιήσει
comes the lord of the vineyard, what will he do

τοῖς γεωργοῖς ἐκείνοις; 41 λέγουσιν αὐτῷ·
- husbandmen to those? They say to him:

κακοὺς κακῶς ἀπολέσει αὐτούς, καὶ τὸν
Bad men badly he will destroy them, and the

ἀμπελῶνα ἐκδώσεται ἄλλοις γεωργοῖς,
vineyard he will give out to other husbandmen,

οἵτινες ἀποδώσουσιν αὐτῷ τοὺς καοποὺς
who will render to him the fruits

ἐν τοῖς καιροῖς αὐτῶν. 42 λέγει αὐτοῖς ὁ
in the seasons of them. Says to them -

Ἰησοῦς· οὐδέποτε ἀνέγνωτε ἐν ταῖς
Jesus: Did ye never read in the

γραφαῖς· λίθον ὃν ἀπεδοκίμασαν οἱ
scriptures: A stone which rejected the

οἰκοδομοῦντες, οὗτος ἐγενήθη εἰς κεφαλὴν
building [ones], this became head

γωνίας· παρὰ κυρίου ἐγένετο αὕτη, καὶ
of [the] corner; from [the] Lord became this, and

ἔστιν θαυμαστὴ ἐν ὀφθαλμοῖς ἡμῶν; 43 διὰ
it is marvellous in [the] eyes of us? There-

τοῦτο λέγω ὑμῖν ὅτι ἀρθήσεται ἀφ' ὑμῶν
fore I tell you[,] - will be taken from you

ἡ βασιλεία τοῦ θεοῦ καὶ δοθήσεται
The kingdom of God and will be given

---

er who planted a vineyard. He put a wall around it, dug a winepress in it and built a watchtower. Then he rented the vineyard to some farmers and went away on a journey. 34 When the harvest time approached, he sent his servants to the tenants to collect his fruit.

35 "The tenants seized his servants; they beat one, killed another, and stoned a third. 36 Then he sent other servants to them, more than the first time, and the tenants treated them the same way. 37 Last of all, he sent his son to them. 'They will respect my son,' he said.

38 "But when the tenants saw the son, they said to each other, 'This is the heir. Come, let's kill him and take his inheritance.' 39 So they took him and threw him out of the vineyard and killed him.

40 "Therefore, when the owner of the vineyard comes, what will he do to those tenants?"

41 "He will bring those wretches to a wretched end," they replied, "and he will rent the vineyard to other tenants, who will give him his share of the crop at harvest time."

42 Jesus said to them, "Have you never read in the Scriptures:

" 'The stone the builders
    rejected
has become the
    capstone*k*;
the Lord has done this,
and it is marvelous in
    our eyes'*l*?

43 "Therefore I tell you that the kingdom of God will be taken away from you and given to a people

---

e Or keystone

*k*42 Or cornerstone
*l*42 Psalm 118:22,23

duces the fruits of the kingdom.[f] 44 The one who falls on this stone will be broken to pieces; and it will crush anyone on whom it falls."[g]

45 When the chief priests and the Pharisees heard his parables, they realized that he was speaking about them. 46 They wanted to arrest him, but they feared the crowds, because they regarded him as a prophet.

Chapter 22

The Parable of the Wedding Banquet

ONCE more Jesus spoke to them in parables, saying: 2 "The kingdom of heaven may be compared to a king who gave a wedding banquet for his son. 3 He sent his slaves to call those who had been invited to the wedding banquet, but they would not come. 4 Again he sent other slaves, saying, 'Tell those who have been invited: Look, I have prepared my dinner, my oxen and my fat calves have been slaughtered, and everything is ready; come to the wedding banquet.' 5 But they made light of it and went away, one to his farm, another to his business, 6 while the rest seized his slaves, mistreated them, and killed them. 7 The king was enraged. He sent his troops, destroyed those murderers, and burned their city. 8 Then he said to his slaves, 'The wedding is ready, but those invited were not worthy. 9 Go therefore into the main streets, and invite everyone you find to the wed-

---

ἔθνει ποιοῦντι τοὺς καρποὺς αὐτῆς.
to a nation producing the fruits of it.
44 [καὶ ὁ πεσὼν ἐπὶ τὸν λίθον τοῦτον
And the[one] falling on - stone this
συνθλασθήσεται· ἐφ' ὃν δ' ἂν πέσῃ,
will be broken in pieces; but on whomever it falls,
λικμήσει αὐτόν.] 45 Καὶ ἀκούσαντες οἱ
it will crush him.] And hearing the
ἀρχιερεῖς καὶ οἱ Φαρισαῖοι τὰς παραβολὰς
chief priests and the Pharisees the parables
αὐτοῦ ἔγνωσαν ὅτι περὶ αὐτῶν λέγει·
of him they knew that concerning them he tells;
46 καὶ ζητοῦντες αὐτὸν κρατῆσαι ἐφοβήθησαν
and seeking him to seize they feared
τοὺς ὄχλους, ἐπεὶ εἰς προφήτην αὐτὸν εἶχον.
the crowds, since for a prophet him they had.

22 Καὶ ἀποκριθεὶς ὁ Ἰησοῦς πάλιν
And answering - Jesus again
εἶπεν ἐν παραβολαῖς αὐτοῖς λέγων·
spoke in parables to them saying:
2 ὡμοιώθη ἡ βασιλεία τῶν οὐρανῶν
Was(is) likened the kingdom of the heavens
ἀνθρώπῳ βασιλεῖ, ὅστις ἐποίησεν γάμους
to a man a king, who made a wedding feast
τῷ υἱῷ αὐτοῦ. 3 καὶ ἀπέστειλεν τοὺς
for the son of him. And he sent the
δούλους αὐτοῦ καλέσαι τοὺς κεκλημένους
slaves of him to call the[ones] having been invited
εἰς τοὺς γάμους, καὶ οὐκ ἤθελον ἐλθεῖν.
to the feast, and they wished not to come.
4 πάλιν ἀπέστειλεν ἄλλους δούλους λέγων·
Again he sent other slaves saying:
εἴπατε τοῖς κεκλημένοις· ἰδοὺ τὸ
Tell the[ones] having been invited: Behold[,] the
ἄριστόν μου ἡτοίμακα, οἱ ταῦροί μου
supper of me I have prepared, the oxen of me
καὶ τὰ σιτιστὰ τεθυμένα, καὶ πάντα
and the fatted beasts having been killed, and all things
ἕτοιμα· δεῦτε εἰς τοὺς γάμους. 5 οἱ δὲ
[are] ready; come to the feast. But they
ἀμελήσαντες ἀπῆλθον, ὃς μὲν εἰς τὸν
not caring went off, one to the(his)
ἴδιον ἀγρόν, ὃς δὲ ἐπὶ τὴν ἐμπορίαν
own field, another on the trading
αὐτοῦ· 6 οἱ δὲ λοιποὶ κρατήσαντες
of him; and the rest seizing
τοὺς δούλους αὐτοῦ ὕβρισαν καὶ ἀπέκτειναν.
the slaves of him insulted and killed.
7 ὁ δὲ βασιλεὺς ὠργίσθη, καὶ πέμψας
So the king became angry, and sending
τὰ στρατεύματα αὐτοῦ ἀπώλεσεν τοὺς
the armies of him destroyed -
φονεῖς ἐκείνους καὶ τὴν πόλιν αὐτῶν
murderers those and the city of them
ἐνέπρησεν. 8 τότε λέγει τοῖς δούλοις
burned. Then he says to the slaves
αὐτοῦ· ὁ μὲν γάμος ἕτοιμός ἐστιν, οἱ δὲ
of him: Indeed the feast ready is, but the[ones]
κεκλημένοι οὐκ ἦσαν ἄξιοι· 9 πορεύεσθε
having been invited were not worthy; go ye
οὖν ἐπὶ τὰς διεξόδους τῶν ὁδῶν, καὶ
therefore onto the partings of the ways, and
ὅσους ἐὰν εὕρητε καλέσατε εἰς τοὺς
as many as ye find call to the

---

who will produce its fruit. 44 He who falls on this stone will be broken to pieces, but he on whom it falls will be crushed."[m]

45 When the chief priests and the Pharisees heard Jesus' parables, they knew he was talking about them. 46 They looked for a way to arrest him, but they were afraid of the crowd because the people held that he was a prophet.

Chapter 22

The Parable of the Wedding Banquet

JESUS spoke to them again in parables, saying: 2 "The kingdom of heaven is like a king who prepared a wedding banquet for his son. 3 He sent his servants to those who had been invited to the banquet to tell them to come, but they refused to come.

4 "Then he sent some more servants and said, 'Tell those who have been invited that I have prepared my dinner: My oxen and fattened cattle have been butchered, and everything is ready. Come to the wedding banquet.'

5 "But they paid no attention and went off—one to his field, another to his business. 6 The rest seized his servants, mistreated them and killed them. 7 The king was enraged. He sent his army and destroyed those murderers and burned their city.

8 "Then he said to his servants, 'The wedding banquet is ready, but those I invited did not deserve to come. 9 Go to the street corners and invite to the banquet anyone you find.' 10 So

---

[f] Gk the fruits of it
[g] Other ancient authorities lack verse 44

[m] 44 Some manuscripts do not have verse 44.

ding banquet.' ¹⁰Those slaves went out into the streets and gathered all whom they found, both good and bad; so the wedding hall was filled with guests.

11 "But when the king came in to see the guests, he noticed a man there who was not wearing a wedding robe, ¹²and he said to him, 'Friend, how did you get in here without a wedding robe?' And he was speechless. ¹³Then the king said to the attendants, 'Bind him hand and foot, and throw him into the outer darkness, where there will be weeping and gnashing of teeth.' ¹⁴For many are called, but few are chosen."

The Question about Paying Taxes

15 Then the Pharisees went and plotted to entrap him in what he said. ¹⁶So they sent their disciples to him, along with the Herodians, saying, "Teacher, we know that you are sincere, and teach the way of God in accordance with truth, and show deference to no one; for you do not regard people with partiality. ¹⁷Tell us, then, what you think. Is it lawful to pay taxes to the emperor, or not?" ¹⁸But Jesus, aware of their malice, said, "Why are you putting me to the test, you hypocrites? ¹⁹Show me the coin used for the tax." And they brought him a denarius. ²⁰Then he said to them, "Whose head is this, and whose title?" ²¹They answered, "The emperor's.

γάμους.   10 καὶ   ἐξελθόντες   οἱ   δοῦλοι
feast.   And   going forth   –   slaves

ἐκεῖνοι   εἰς   τὰς   ὁδοὺς   συνήγαγον   πάντας
those   into   the   ways   assembled   all

οὓς   εὗρον,   πονηρούς   τε   καὶ   ἀγαθούς·
whom they found,   both bad   and   good;

καὶ   ἐπλήσθη   ὁ   νυμφὼν   ἀνακειμένων.
and   was filled   the wedding chamber   of(with) reclining [ones].

11 εἰσελθὼν   δὲ   ὁ   βασιλεὺς   θεάσασθαι
But entering   the   king   to behold

τοὺς   ἀνακειμένους   εἶδεν   ἐκεῖ
the   reclining [ones]   he saw   there

ἄνθρωπον   οὐκ   ἐνδεδυμένον   ἔνδυμα   γάμου·
a man   not   *having been* dressed[in]   a dress   of wedding;

12 καὶ   λέγει   αὐτῷ·   ἑταῖρε,   πῶς
and   he says   to him: Comrade,   how

εἰσῆλθες   ὧδε   μὴ   ἔχων   ἔνδυμα   γάμου;
enteredst thou   here   not   having   a dress   of wedding?

ὁ   δὲ   ἐφιμώθη.   13 τότε   ὁ   βασιλεὺς
And he   was silenced.   Then   the   king

εἶπεν   τοῖς   διακόνοις·   δήσαντες   αὐτοῦ
said   to the   servants: Binding   of him

πόδας   καὶ   χεῖρας   ἐκβάλετε   αὐτὸν
feet   and   hands   throw out   him

εἰς   τὸ   σκότος   τὸ   ἐξώτερον·   ἐκεῖ   ἔσται
into   the   darkness   –   outer;   there   will be

ὁ   κλαυθμὸς   καὶ   ὁ   βρυγμὸς   τῶν
the   wailing   and   the   gnashing   of the

ὀδόντων.   14 Πολλοὶ   γάρ   εἰσιν   κλητοί,
teeth.   For many   are   called,

ὀλίγοι   δὲ   ἐκλεκτοί.
but few   chosen.

15 Τότε   πορευθέντες   οἱ   Φαρισαῖοι   συμ-
Then   going   the   Pharisees   coun-

βούλιον   ἔλαβον   ὅπως   αὐτὸν   παγιδεύσωσιν
sel   took   so as   him   they might ensnare

ἐν   λόγῳ.   16 καὶ   ἀποστέλλουσιν   αὐτῷ
in   a word.   And   they send   to him

τοὺς   μαθητὰς   αὐτῶν   μετὰ   τῶν   Ἡρω-
the   disciples   of them   with   the   Hero-

διανῶν   λέγοντας·   διδάσκαλε,   οἴδαμεν
dians   saying: Teacher,   we know

ὅτι   ἀληθὴς   εἶ   καὶ   τὴν   ὁδὸν   τοῦ
that   truthful   thou art   and   the   way   –

θεοῦ   ἐν   ἀληθείᾳ   διδάσκεις,   καὶ   οὐ
of God   in   truth   thou teachest,   and   not

μέλει   σοι   περὶ   οὐδενός,   οὐ   γὰρ
it concerns   to thee   about   no one(anyone),   ²not   ¹for

βλέπεις   εἰς   πρόσωπον   ἀνθρώπων·
²thou lookest   to   face   of men;

17 εἰπὸν   οὖν   ἡμῖν,   τί   σοι   δοκεῖ;
tell   therefore   us,   what   to thee   seems it?

ἔξεστιν   δοῦναι   κῆνσον   Καίσαρι   ἢ   οὔ;
is it lawful   to give   tribute   to Cæsar   or   no?

18 γνοὺς   δὲ   ὁ   Ἰησοῦς   τὴν   πονηρίαν
But knowing   –   Jesus   the   wickedness

αὐτῶν   εἶπεν·   τί   με   πειράζετε,   ὑποκριταί;
of them   said: Why   me   tempt ye,   hypocrites?

19 ἐπιδείξατέ   μοι   τὸ   νόμισμα   τοῦ   κήνσου.
Show   me   the   money   of the   tribute.

οἱ   δὲ   προσήνεγκαν   αὐτῷ   δηνάριον.   20 καὶ
And they   brought   to him   a denarius.   And

λέγει   αὐτοῖς·   τίνος   ἡ   εἰκὼν   αὕτη
he says   to them: Of whom   –   image   this

καὶ   ἡ   ἐπιγραφή;   21 λέγουσιν·   Καίσαρος.
and   –   superscription?   They say: Of Cæsar.

---

the servants went out into the streets and gathered all the people they could find, both good and bad, and the wedding hall was filled with guests.

¹¹"But when the king came in to see the guests, he noticed a man there who was not wearing wedding clothes. ¹²'Friend,' he asked, 'how did you get in here without wedding clothes?' The man was speechless.

¹³"Then the king told the attendants, 'Tie him hand and foot, and throw him outside, into the darkness, where there will be weeping and gnashing of teeth.'

¹⁴"For many are invited, but few are chosen."

Paying Taxes to Caesar

¹⁵Then the Pharisees went out and laid plans to trap him in his words. ¹⁶They sent their disciples to him along with the Herodians. "Teacher," they said, "we know you are a man of integrity and that you teach the way of God in accordance with the truth. You aren't swayed by men, because you pay no attention to who they are. ¹⁷Tell us then, what is your opinion? Is it right to pay taxes to Caesar or not?"

¹⁸But Jesus, knowing their evil intent, said, "You hypocrites, why are you trying to trap me? ¹⁹Show me the coin used for paying the tax." They brought him a denarius, ²⁰and he asked them, "Whose portrait is this? And whose inscription?"

²¹"Caesar's," they replied.

Then he said to them,

Then he said to them, "Give therefore to the emperor the things that are the emperor's, and to God the things that are God's." 22 When they heard this, they were amazed; and they left him and went away.

The Question about the Resurrection

23 The same day some Sadducees came to him, saying there is no resurrection;[h] and they asked him a question, saying, 24 "Teacher, Moses said, 'If a man dies childless, his brother shall marry the widow, and raise up children for his brother.' 25 Now there were seven brothers among us; the first married, and died childless, leaving the widow to his brother. 26 The second did the same, so also the third, down to the seventh. 27 Last of all, the woman herself died. 28 In the resurrection, then, whose wife of the seven will she be? For all of them had married her."

29 Jesus answered them, "You are wrong, because you know neither the scriptures nor the power of God. 30 For in the resurrection they neither marry nor are given in marriage, but are like angels[i] in heaven. 31 And as for the resurrection of the dead, have you not read what was said to you by God, 32 'I am the God of Abraham, and the God of Isaac, and the God of Jacob'? He is God not of the dead, but of the living." 33 And when the crowd heard it, they were astounded at his teaching.

The Greatest Commandment

34 When the Pharisees heard that he had silenced

h Other ancient authorities read *who say that there is no resurrection*
i Other ancient authorities add *of God*

τότε λέγει αὐτοῖς· ἀπόδοτε οὖν τὰ
Then he says to them: Render then the things

Καίσαρος Καίσαρι καὶ τὰ τοῦ θεοῦ
of Cæsar to Cæsar and the things – of God

τῷ θεῷ. 22 καὶ ἀκούσαντες ἐθαύμασαν,
– to God. And hearing they marvelled,

καὶ ἀφέντες αὐτὸν ἀπῆλθαν.
and leaving him went away.

23 Ἐν ἐκείνῃ τῇ ἡμέρᾳ προσῆλθον
On that – day approached

αὐτῷ Σαδδουκαῖοι, λέγοντες μὴ εἶναι
to him Sadducees, saying not to be

ἀνάστασιν, καὶ ἐπηρώτησαν αὐτὸν
a resurrection, and questioned him

24 λέγοντες· διδάσκαλε, Μωϋσῆς εἶπεν·
saying: Teacher, Moses said:

ἐάν τις ἀποθάνῃ μὴ ἔχων τέκνα,
If any man dies not having children,

ἐπιγαμβρεύσει ὁ ἀδελφὸς αὐτοῦ τὴν
shall take to wife after the brother of him the

γυναῖκα αὐτοῦ καὶ ἀναστήσει σπέρμα
wife of him and shall raise up seed

τῷ ἀδελφῷ αὐτοῦ. 25 ἦσαν δὲ παρ᾽
to the brother of him. Now there were with

ἡμῖν ἑπτὰ ἀδελφοί· καὶ ὁ πρῶτος
us seven brothers; and the first

γήμας ἐτελεύτησεν, καὶ μὴ ἔχων
having married died, and not having

σπέρμα ἀφῆκεν τὴν γυναῖκα αὐτοῦ τῷ
seed left the wife of him to the

ἀδελφῷ αὐτοῦ· 26 ὁμοίως καὶ ὁ δεύτερος
brother of him; likewise also the second

καὶ ὁ τρίτος, ἕως τῶν ἑπτά. 27 ὕστερον
and the third, until the seven. last

δὲ πάντων ἀπέθανεν ἡ γυνή. 28 ἐν τῇ
And of all died the woman. In the

ἀναστάσει οὖν τίνος τῶν ἑπτὰ ἔσται
resurrection then of which of the seven will she be

γυνή; πάντες γὰρ ἔσχον αὐτήν. 29 ἀπο-
wife? for all had her. an-

κριθεὶς δὲ ὁ Ἰησοῦς εἶπεν αὐτοῖς·
swering And – Jesus said to them:

πλανᾶσθε μὴ εἰδότες τὰς γραφὰς μηδὲ
Ye err not knowing the scriptures nor

τὴν δύναμιν τοῦ θεοῦ. 30 ἐν γὰρ τῇ
the power – of God. For in the

ἀναστάσει οὔτε γαμοῦσιν οὔτε γαμίζονται,
resurrection neither they marry nor are given in marriage,

ἀλλ᾽ ὡς ἄγγελοι ἐν τῷ οὐρανῷ εἰσιν.
but as angels in *the* heaven are.

31 περὶ δὲ τῆς ἀναστάσεως τῶν νεκρῶν
But concerning the resurrection of the dead

οὐκ ἀνέγνωτε τὸ ῥηθὲν ὑμῖν ὑπὸ
did ye not read the thing said to you by

τοῦ θεοῦ λέγοντος· 32 ἐγώ εἰμι ὁ θεὸς
– God saying: I am the God

Ἀβραὰμ καὶ ὁ θεὸς Ἰσαὰκ καὶ ὁ θεὸς
of Abraham and the God of Isaac and the God

Ἰακώβ; οὐκ ἔστιν [ὁ] θεὸς νεκρῶν
of Jacob? He is not the God of dead men

ἀλλὰ ζώντων. 33 καὶ ἀκούσαντες οἱ ὄχλοι
but of living [ones]. And hearing the crowds

ἐξεπλήσσοντο ἐπὶ τῇ διδαχῇ αὐτοῦ.
were astounded over(at) the teaching of him.

34 Οἱ δὲ Φαρισαῖοι ἀκούσαντες ὅτι
But the Pharisees hearing that

"Give to Caesar what is Caesar's, and to God what is God's."
22 When they heard this, they said, "We are amazed." So they left him and went away.

Marriage at the Resurrection

23 That same day the Sadducees, who say there is no resurrection, came to him with a question. 24 "Teacher," they said, "Moses told us that if a man dies without having children, his brother must marry the widow and have children for him. 25 Now there were seven brothers among us. The first since he had no children, he left his wife to his brother. 26 The same thing happened to the second and third brother, right on down to the seventh. 27 Finally, the woman died. 28 Now then, at the resurrection, whose wife will she be of the seven, since all of them were married to her?"

29 Jesus replied, "You are in error because you do not know the Scriptures or the power of God. 30 At the resurrection people will neither marry nor be given in marriage; they will be like the angels in heaven. 31 But about the resurrection of the dead—have you not read what God said to you, 32 'I am the God of Abraham, the God of Isaac, and the God of Jacob'[n]? He is not the God of the dead but of the living."

33 When the crowds heard this, they were astonished at his teaching.

The Greatest Commandment

34 Hearing that Jesus had silenced the Sadducees, the

n 32 Exodus 3:6

the Sadducees, they gathered together, 35 and one of them, a lawyer, asked him a question to test him. 36 "Teacher, which commandment in the law is the greatest?" 37 He said to him, " 'You shall love the Lord your God with all your heart, and with all your soul, and with all your mind.' 38 This is the greatest and first commandment. 39 And a second is like it: 'You shall love your neighbor as yourself.' 40 On these two commandments hang all the law and the prophets."

The Question about David's Son

41 Now while the Pharisees were gathered together, Jesus asked them this question: 42 "What do you think of the Christ?[j] Whose son is he?" They said to him, "The son of David." 43 He said to them, "How is it then that David by the Spirit[k] calls him Lord, saying,

44 'The Lord said to my Lord,
"Sit at my right hand,
until I put your
enemies under
your feet" '?

45 If David thus calls him Lord, how can he be his son?" 46 No one was able to give him an answer, nor from that day did anyone dare to ask him any more questions.

ἐφίμωσεν   τοὺς   Σαδδουκαίους,   συνήχθησαν
he silenced   the   Sadducees,   were assembled

ἐπὶ   τὸ   αὐτό,   35 καὶ   ἐπηρώτησεν   εἷς
together,   and   [b]questioned   [a]one

ἐξ   αὐτῶν   νομικὸς   πειράζων   αὐτόν·   36 δι-
[a]of [a]them   [a]a lawyer [b]tempting   him: Teach-

δάσκαλε,   ποία   ἐντολὴ   μεγάλη   ἐν   τῷ
er,   what commandment [is] great   in   the

νόμῳ;   37 ὁ   δὲ   ἔφη   αὐτῷ·   ἀγαπήσεις
law?   And he   said   to him: Thou shalt love

κύριον   τὸν   θεόν   σου   ἐν   ὅλῃ   τῇ   καρδίᾳ
[the] Lord the   God of thee with   all   the   heart

σου   καὶ   ἐν   ὅλῃ   τῇ   ψυχῇ   σου   καὶ   ἐν
of thee and   with   all   the   soul   of thee   and   with

ὅλῃ   τῇ   διανοίᾳ   σου.   38 αὕτη   ἐστιν   ἡ
all   the   understanding of thee.   This   is   the

μεγάλη   καὶ   πρώτη   ἐντολή.   39 δευτέρα
great   and   first   commandment.   [The] second

ὁμοία   αὐτῇ·   ἀγαπήσεις   τὸν   πλησίον   σου
[is] like to it: Thou shalt love the   neighbour of thee

ὡς   σεαυτόν.   40 ἐν   ταύταις   ταῖς   δυσὶν   ἐντολαῖς
as   thyself.   In(on) these   -   two   commandments

ὅλος   ὁ   νόμος   κρέμαται   καὶ   οἱ   προφῆται.
all   the   law   hangs   and   the   prophets.

41 Συνηγμένων   δὲ   τῶν   Φαρισαίων
And having assembled   the   Pharisees[a]
= when the Pharisees were assembled

ἐπηρώτησεν   αὐτοὺς   ὁ   Ἰησοῦς   42 λέγων·   τι
questioned   them   -   Jesus   saying: What

ὑμῖν   δοκεῖ   περὶ   τοῦ   χριστοῦ;   τίνος
to you   seems it concerning the   Christ?   of whom

υἱός   ἐστιν;   λέγουσιν   αὐτῷ·   τοῦ   Δαυίδ.
son   is he?   They say   to him: -   Of David.

43 λέγει   αὐτοῖς·   πῶς   οὖν   Δαυὶδ   ἐν
He says   to them: How   then   David   in

πνεύματι   καλεῖ   αὐτὸν   κύριον   λέγων·
spirit   calls   him   Lord   saying:

44 εἶπεν   κύριος   τῷ   κυρίῳ   μου·
Said   [the] Lord to the   Lord   of me:

κάθου   ἐκ   δεξιῶν   μου   ἕως   ἂν   θῶ   τοὺς
Sit   on [the] right of me   until   I put   the

ἐχθρούς   σου   ὑποκάτω   τῶν   ποδῶν   σου;
enemies   of thee underneath   the   feet   of thee?

45 εἰ   οὖν   Δαυὶδ   καλεῖ   αὐτὸν   κύριον,   πῶς
If   then   David   calls   him   Lord,   how

υἱὸς   αὐτοῦ   ἐστιν;   46 καὶ   οὐδεὶς   ἐδύνατο
son   of him   is he?   And   no one   was able

ἀποκριθῆναι   αὐτῷ   λόγον   οὐδὲ   ἐτόλμησέν
to answer   him   a word   nor   dared

τις   ἀπ᾽   ἐκείνης   τῆς   ἡμέρας   ἐπερωτῆσαι
anyone from   that   -   day   to question

αὐτὸν   οὐκέτι.
him   no(any) more.

Pharisees got together. 35 One of them, an expert in the law, tested him with this question: 36 "Teacher, which is the greatest commandment in the Law?"

37 Jesus replied: " 'Love the Lord your God with all your heart and with all your soul and with all your mind.'[o] 38 This is the first and greatest commandment. 39 And the second is like it: 'Love your neighbor as yourself.'[p] 40 All the Law and the Prophets hang on these two commandments."

Whose Son Is the Christ?

41 While the Pharisees were gathered together, Jesus asked them, 42 "What do you think about the Christ[q]? Whose son is he?"

"The son of David," they replied.

43 He said to them, "How is it then that David, speaking by the Spirit, calls him 'Lord'? For he says,

44 " 'The Lord said to my Lord:
"Sit at my right hand
until I put your enemies
under your feet." '[r]

45 If then David calls him 'Lord,' how can he be his son?" 46 No one could say a word in reply, and from that day on no one dared to ask him any more questions.

Chapter 23

Jesus Denounces Scribes and Pharisees

THEN Jesus said to the crowds and to his disciples, 2 "The scribes and the Pharisees sit on Moses' seat; 3 therefore, do whatever they teach you and follow it; but do not do as they do, for they do not practice

---

23 Τότε   ὁ   Ἰησοῦς   ἐλάλησεν   τοῖς   ὄχλοις
Then   -   Jesus   spoke   to the   crowds

καὶ   τοῖς   μαθηταῖς   αὐτοῦ   2 λέγων·   ἐπὶ
and   to the   disciples   of him   saying: On

τῆς   Μωϋσέως   καθέδρας   ἐκάθισαν   οἱ
the   of Moses   seat   sat   the

γραμματεῖς   καὶ   οἱ   Φαρισαῖοι.   3 πάντα
scribes   and   the   Pharisees.   All things

οὖν   ὅσα   ἐὰν   εἴπωσιν   ὑμῖν   ποιήσατε
therefore whatever they may tell   you   do ye

καὶ   τηρεῖτε,   κατὰ   δὲ   τὰ   ἔργα   αὐτῶν
and   keep,   but according to the   works   of them

Chapter 23

Seven Woes

THEN Jesus said to the crowds and to his disciples: 2 "The teachers of the law and the Pharisees sit in Moses' seat. 3 So you must obey them and do everything they tell you. But do not do what they do, for

---

[j] Or Christ
[k] Gk in spirit

[o]37 Deut. 6:5
[p]39 Lev. 19:18
[q]42 Or Messiah
[r]44 Psalm 110:1

what they teach. 4They tie up heavy burdens, hard to bear,[l] and lay them on the shoulders of others; but they themselves are unwilling to lift a finger to move them. 5They do all their deeds to be seen by others; for they make their phylacteries broad and their fringes long. 6They love to have the place of honor at banquets and the best seats in the synagogues, 7and to be greeted with respect in the marketplaces, and to have people call them rabbi. 8But you are not to be called rabbi, for you have one teacher, and you are all students.[m] 9And call no one your father on earth, for you have one Father—the one in heaven. 10Nor are you to be called instructors, for you have one instructor, the Messiah.[n] 11The greatest among you will be your servant. 12All who exalt themselves will be humbled, and all who humble themselves will be exalted.

13 "But woe to you, scribes and Pharisees, hypocrites! For you lock people out of the kingdom of heaven. For you do not go in yourselves, and when others are going in, you stop them.[o] 15Woe to you, scribes and Pharisees, hypocrites! For you cross sea and land to make a single convert, and you make the new convert twice as much a child of hell[p] as yourselves.

16 "Woe to you, blind

μὴ ποιεῖτε· λέγουσιν γὰρ καὶ οὐ ποιοῦσιν.
do ye not;   for they say   and   do not.

4 δεσμεύουσιν δὲ φορτία βαρέα καὶ
And they bind   burdens   heavy   and

ἐπιτιθέασιν ἐπὶ τοὺς ὤμους τῶν ἀνθρώπων,
put on   on the   shoulders   - of men,

αὐτοὶ δὲ τῷ δακτύλῳ αὐτῶν οὐ
but they   with the   finger   of them   not

θέλουσιν κινῆσαι αὐτά. 5 πάντα δὲ
are willing   to move   them.   But all

τὰ ἔργα αὐτῶν ποιοῦσιν πρὸς τὸ θεαθῆναι
the works   of them   they do   for   -   to be seen

τοῖς ἀνθρώποις· πλατύνουσιν γὰρ τὰ
-   by men;   for they broaden   the

φυλακτήρια αὐτῶν καὶ μεγαλύνουσιν τὰ
phylacteries   of them   and   enlarge   the

κράσπεδα, 6 φιλοῦσιν δὲ τὴν πρωτο-
fringes,   and they like   the   chief

κλισίαν ἐν τοῖς δείπνοις καὶ τὰς πρωτο-
place   in the   suppers   and   the   chief

καθεδρίας ἐν ταῖς συναγωγαῖς 7 καὶ τοὺς
seats   in the   synagogues .   and   the

ἀσπασμοὺς ἐν ταῖς ἀγοραῖς καὶ
greetings   in   the   marketplaces   and

καλεῖσθαι ὑπὸ τῶν ἀνθρώπων ῥαββί.
to be called   by   -   men   rabbi.

8 ὑμεῖς δὲ μὴ κληθῆτε ῥαββί· εἷς γὰρ
But ye   be not called   rabbi;   for one

ἐστιν ὑμῶν ὁ διδάσκαλος, πάντες δὲ ὑμεῖς
is   of you the   teacher,   and all   ye

ἀδελφοί ἐστε. 9 καὶ πατέρα μὴ καλέσητε
brothers   are.   And   father   call ye not

ὑμῶν ἐπὶ τῆς γῆς· εἷς γάρ ἐστιν
of you   on   the   earth;   for one   is

ὑμῶν ὁ πατὴρ ὁ οὐράνιος. 10 μηδὲ
of you   the   Father   -   heavenly.   Neither

κληθῆτε καθηγηταί, ὅτι καθηγητὴς
be ye called   leaders,   because   leader

ὑμῶν ἐστιν εἷς ὁ Χριστός. 11 ὁ δὲ
of you   is   one   the   Christ.   And the

μείζων ὑμῶν ἔσται ὑμῶν διάκονος.
greater   of you   shall be   of you   servant.

12 Ὅστις δὲ ὑψώσει ἑαυτὸν ταπεινωθήσεται,
And [he] who   will exalt   himself   shall be humbled,

καὶ ὅστις ταπεινώσει ἑαυτὸν ὑψωθήσεται.
and   [he] who   will humble   himself   shall be exalted.

13 Οὐαὶ δὲ ὑμῖν, γραμματεῖς καὶ Φαρισαῖοι
But woe   to you,   scribes   and   Pharisees

ὑποκριταί, ὅτι κλείετε τὴν βασιλείαν
hypocrites,   because   ye shut   the   kingdom

τῶν οὐρανῶν ἔμπροσθεν τῶν ἀνθρώπων·
of the   heavens   before   -   men;

ὑμεῖς γὰρ οὐκ εἰσέρχεσθε, οὐδὲ τοὺς
for ye   do not enter,   nor the [ones]

εἰσερχομένους ἀφίετε εἰσελθεῖν.‡ 15 Οὐαὶ
entering   do ye allow   to enter.   Woe

ὑμῖν, γραμματεῖς καὶ Φαρισαῖοι ὑποκριταί,
to you,   scribes   and   Pharisees   hypocrites,

ὅτι περιάγετε τὴν θάλασσαν καὶ τὴν
because   ye go about   the   sea   and   the

ξηρὰν ποιῆσαι ἕνα προσήλυτον, καὶ ὅταν
dry [land]   to make   one   proselyte,   and   when

γένηται, ποιεῖτε αὐτὸν υἱὸν γεέννης διπλό-
he becomes,   ye make   him   a son of gehenna   twofold

τερον ὑμῶν. 16 Οὐαὶ ὑμῖν, ὁδηγοὶ τυφλοὶ
more [than] you.   Woe   to you,   leaders   blind

---

they do not practice what they preach. 4They tie up heavy loads and put them on men's shoulders, but they themselves are not willing to lift a finger to move them.

5"Everything they do is done for men to see: They make their phylacteries[s] wide and the tassels on their garments long; 6they love the place of honor at banquets and the most important seats in the synagogues; 7they love to be greeted in the marketplaces and to have men call them 'Rabbi.'

8"But you are not to be called 'Rabbi,' for you have only one Master and you are all brothers. 9And do not call anyone on earth 'father,' for you have one Father, and he is in heaven. 10Nor are you to be called 'teacher,' for you have one Teacher, the Christ.[t] 11The greatest among you will be your servant. 12For whoever exalts himself will be humbled, and whoever humbles himself will be exalted.

13"Woe to you, teachers of the law and Pharisees, you hypocrites! You shut the kingdom of heaven in men's faces. You yourselves do not enter, nor will you let those enter who are trying to.[u]

15"Woe to you, teachers of the law and Pharisees, you hypocrites! You travel over land and sea to win a single convert, and when he becomes one, you make him twice as much a son of hell as you are.

16"Woe to you, blind

---

[l] Other ancient authorities lack *hard to bear*
[m] Gk *brothers*
[n] Or *the Christ*
[o] Other authorities add here (or after verse 12) verse 14, *Woe to you, scribes and Pharisees, hypocrites! For you devour widows' houses and for the sake of appearance you make long prayers; therefore you will receive the greater condemnation*
[p] Gk *Gehenna*

[s]5 That is, boxes containing Scripture verses, worn on forehead and arm
[t]10 Or *Messiah*
[u]13 Some manuscripts *to.* 14*Woe to you, teachers of the law and Pharisees, you hypocrites! You devour widows' houses and for a show make lengthy prayers. Therefore you will be punished more severely.*

guides, who say, 'Whoever swears by the sanctuary is bound by nothing, but whoever swears by the gold of the sanctuary is bound by the oath.' 17 You blind fools! For which is greater, the gold or the sanctuary that has made the gold sacred? 18 And you say, 'Whoever swears by the altar is bound by nothing, but whoever swears by the gift that is on the altar is bound by the oath.' 19 How blind you are! For which is greater, the gift or the altar that makes the gift sacred? 20 So whoever swears by the altar, swears by it and by everything on it; 21 and whoever swears by the sanctuary, swears by it and by the one who dwells in it; 22 and whoever swears by heaven, swears by the throne of God and by the one who is seated upon it.

23 "Woe to you, scribes and Pharisees, hypocrites! For you tithe mint, dill, and cummin, and have neglected the weightier matters of the law: justice and mercy and faith. It is these you ought to have practiced without neglecting the others. 24 You blind guides! You strain out a gnat but swallow a camel!

25 "Woe to you, scribes and Pharisees, hypocrites! For you clean the outside of the cup and of the plate, but inside they are full of greed and self-indulgence. 26 You blind Pharisee! First clean the inside of the cup,^q so that the outside also may become clean.

27 "Woe to you, scribes and Pharisees, hypocrites! For you are like whitewashed tombs, which on

οἱ λέγοντες· ὃς ἂν ὀμόσῃ ἐν τῷ ναῷ,
the [ones] saying: Whoever swears by the shrine,
οὐδέν ἐστιν· ὃς δ' ἂν ὀμόσῃ ἐν τῷ χρυσῷ
nothing it is; but whoever swears by the gold
τοῦ ναοῦ, ὀφείλει. 17 μωροὶ καὶ τυφλοί,
of the shrine, he owes. Fools and blind,
τίς γὰρ μείζων ἐστιν, ὁ χρυσὸς ἢ ὁ ναὸς
for which greater is, the gold or the shrine
ὁ ἁγιάσας τὸν χρυσόν; 18 καὶ· ὃς ἂν
- sanctifying the gold? And: whoever
ὀμόσῃ ἐν τῷ θυσιαστηρίῳ, οὐδέν ἐστιν·
swears by the altar, nothing it is;
ὃς δ' ἂν ὀμόσῃ ἐν τῷ δώρῳ τῷ ἐπάνω
but whoever swears by the gift - upon
αὐτοῦ, ὀφείλει. 19 τυφλοί, τί γὰρ μεῖζον,
it, he owes. Blind, for which [is] greater,
τὸ δῶρον ἢ τὸ θυσιαστήριον τὸ
the gift or the altar the
ἁγιάζον τὸ δῶρον; 20 ὁ οὖν ὀμόσας
sanctifying the gift? Therefore the [one] swearing
ἐν τῷ θυσιαστηρίῳ ὀμνύει ἐν αὐτῷ καὶ
by the altar swears by it and
ἐν πᾶσι τοῖς ἐπάνω αὐτοῦ· 21 καὶ ὁ
by all the things upon it; and the [one]
ὀμόσας ἐν τῷ ναῷ ὀμνύει ἐν αὐτῷ
swearing by the shrine swears by it
καὶ ἐν τῷ κατοικοῦντι αὐτόν· 22 καὶ
and by the [one] inhabiting it; and
ὁ ὀμόσας ἐν τῷ οὐρανῷ ὀμνύει ἐν τῷ
the [one] swearing by the heaven swears by the
θρόνῳ τοῦ θεοῦ καὶ ἐν τῷ καθημένῳ
throne - of God and by the [one] sitting
ἐπάνω αὐτοῦ. 23 Οὐαὶ ὑμῖν, γραμματεῖς
upon it. Woe to you, scribes
καὶ Φαρισαῖοι ὑποκριταί, ὅτι ἀποδεκατοῦτε
and Pharisees hypocrites, because ye tithe
τὸ ἡδύοσμον καὶ τὸ ἄνηθον καὶ τὸ
the mint and the dill and the
κύμινον, καὶ ἀφήκατε τὰ βαρύτερα
cummin, and ye [have] left the heavier things
τοῦ νόμου, τὴν κρίσιν καὶ τὸ ἔλεος
of the law, the judgment and the mercy
καὶ τὴν πίστιν· ταῦτα δὲ ἔδει ποιῆσαι
and faith; but these things it behoved to do
κἀκεῖνα μὴ ἀφεῖναι. 24 ὁδηγοὶ τυφλοί,
and those not to leave. Leaders blind,
οἱ διϋλίζοντες τὸν κώνωπα, τὴν δὲ
the [ones] straining the gnat, but ¹the
κάμηλον καταπίνοντες. 25 Οὐαὶ ὑμῖν,
¹camel ¹swallowing. Woe to you,
γραμματεῖς καὶ Φαρισαῖοι ὑποκριταί, ὅτι
scribes and Pharisees hypocrites, because
καθαρίζετε τὸ ἔξωθεν τοῦ ποτηρίου καὶ
ye cleanse the outside of the cup and
τῆς παροψίδος, ἔσωθεν δὲ γέμουσιν ἐξ
the dish, but within they are full of
ἁρπαγῆς καὶ ἀκρασίας. 26 Φαρισαῖε τυφλέ,
robbery and intemperance. Pharisee blind,
καθάρισον πρῶτον τὸ ἐντὸς τοῦ ποτηρίου
cleanse thou first the inside of the cup
ἵνα γένηται καὶ τὸ ἐκτὸς αὐτοῦ καθαρόν.
that may be also the outside of it clean.
27 Οὐαὶ ὑμῖν, γραμματεῖς καὶ Φαρισαῖοι
Woe to you, scribes and Pharisees
ὑποκριταί, ὅτι παρομοιάζετε τάφοις κεκονια-
hypocrites, because ye resemble graves having been

guides! You say, 'If anyone swears by the temple, it means nothing; but if anyone swears by the gold of the temple, he is bound by his oath.' 17 You blind fools! Which is greater: the gold, or the temple that makes the gold sacred? 18 You also say, 'If anyone swears by the altar, it means nothing; but if anyone swears by the gift on it, he is bound by his oath.' 19 You blind men! Which is greater: the gift, or the altar that makes the gift sacred? 20 Therefore, he who swears by the altar swears by it and by everything on it. 21 And he who swears by the temple swears by it and by the one who dwells in it. 22 And he who swears by heaven swears by God's throne and by the one who sits on it.

23 "Woe to you, teachers of the law and Pharisees, you hypocrites! You give a tenth of your spices—mint, dill and cummin. But you have neglected the more important matters of the law—justice, mercy and faithfulness. You should have practiced the latter, without neglecting the former. 24 You blind guides! You strain out a gnat but swallow a camel.

25 "Woe to you, teachers of the law and Pharisees, you hypocrites! You clean the outside of the cup and dish, but inside they are full of greed and self-indulgence. 26 Blind Pharisee! First clean the inside of the cup and dish, and then the outside also will be clean.

27 "Woe to you, teachers of the law and Pharisees, you hypocrites! You are like whitewashed tombs,

^qOther ancient authorities add *and of the plate*

‡ Ver. 14 omitted by Nestle; *cf.* NIV footnote.

the outside look beautiful, but inside they are full of the bones of the dead and of all kinds of filth. 28 So you also on the outside look righteous to others, but inside you are full of hypocrisy and lawlessness.

29 "Woe to you, scribes and Pharisees, hypocrites! For you build the tombs of the prophets and decorate the graves of the righteous, 30 and you say, 'If we had lived in the days of our ancestors, we would not have taken part with them in shedding the blood of the prophets.' 31 Thus you testify against yourselves that you are descendants of those who murdered the prophets. 32 Fill up, then, the measure of your ancestors. 33 You snakes, you brood of vipers! How can you escape being sentenced to hell?^r 34 Therefore I send you prophets, sages, and scribes, some of whom you will kill and crucify, and some you will flog in your synagogues and pursue from town to town, 35 so that upon you may come all the righteous blood shed on earth, from the blood of righteous Abel to the blood of Zechariah son of Barachiah, whom you murdered between the sanctuary and the altar. 36 Truly I tell you, all this will come upon this generation.

The Lament over Jerusalem

37 "Jerusalem, Jerusalem, the city that kills the prophets and stones those who are sent to it! How often have I desired to gather your children together as a

^r Gk Gehenna

μένοις, οἵτινες ἔξωθεν μὲν φαίνονται
whitewashed, who(which) outwardly indeed appear

ὡραῖοι, ἔσωθεν δὲ γέμουσιν ὀστέων
beautiful, but within they are full of bones

νεκρῶν καὶ πάσης ἀκαθαρσίας. 28 οὕτως
of dead men and of all uncleanness. Thus

καὶ ὑμεῖς ἔξωθεν μὲν φαίνεσθε τοῖς
also ye outwardly indeed appear -

ἀνθρώποις δίκαιοι, ἔσωθεν δέ ἐστε μεστοὶ
to men righteous, but within ye are full

ὑποκρίσεως καὶ ἀνομίας. 29 Οὐαὶ ὑμῖν,
of hypocrisy and of lawlessness. Woe to you

γραμματεῖς καὶ Φαρισαῖοι ὑποκριταί,
scribes and Pharisees hypocrites,

ὅτι οἰκοδομεῖτε τοὺς τάφους τῶν προφητῶν
because ye build the graves of the prophets

καὶ κοσμεῖτε τὰ μνημεῖα τῶν δικαίων,
and adorn the monuments of the righteous,

30 καὶ λέγετε· εἰ ἤμεθα ἐν ταῖς ἡμέραις
and say: If we were in the days

τῶν πατέρων ἡμῶν, οὐκ ἂν ἤμεθα
of the fathers of us, we would not have been

αὐτῶν κοινωνοὶ ἐν τῷ αἵματι τῶν προ-
of them partakers in the blood of the pro-

φητῶν. 31 ὥστε μαρτυρεῖτε ἑαυτοῖς ὅτι
phets. So ye witness to [your]selves that

υἱοί ἐστε τῶν φονευσάντων τοὺς προφήτας.
sons ye are of the [ones] having killed the prophets.

32 καὶ ὑμεῖς πληρώσατε τὸ μέτρον τῶν
And 'ye 'fulfil the measure of the

πατέρων ὑμῶν. 33 ὄφεις, γεννήματα ἐχιδνῶν,
fathers of you. Serpents, offspring of vipers,

πῶς φύγητε ἀπὸ τῆς κρίσεως τῆς γεέννης;
how escape ye from the judgment - of gehenna?

34 διὰ τοῦτο ἰδοὺ ἐγὼ ἀποστέλλω πρὸς
Therefore behold I send to

ὑμᾶς προφήτας καὶ σοφοὺς καὶ γραμ-
you prophets and wise men and scribes;

ματεῖς· ἐξ αὐτῶν ἀποκτενεῖτε καὶ
of them ye will kill and

σταυρώσετε, καὶ ἐξ αὐτῶν μαστιγώσετε
will crucify, and of them ye will scourge

ἐν ταῖς συναγωγαῖς ὑμῶν καὶ διώξετε
in the synagogues of you and will persecute

ἀπὸ πόλεως εἰς πόλιν· 35 ὅπως ἔλθῃ
from city to city; so comes

ἐφ᾽ ὑμᾶς πᾶν αἷμα δίκαιον ἐκχυννόμενον
on you all blood righteous being shed

ἐπὶ τῆς γῆς ἀπὸ τοῦ αἵματος Ἄβελ τοῦ
on the earth from the blood of Abel the

δικαίου ἕως τοῦ αἵματος Ζαχαρίου υἱοῦ
righteous until the blood of Zacharias son

Βαραχίου, ὃν ἐφονεύσατε μεταξὺ τοῦ ναοῦ
Barachias, whom ye murdered between the shrine

καὶ τοῦ θυσιαστηρίου. 36 ἀμὴν λέγω
and the altar. Truly I tell

ὑμῖν, ἥξει ταῦτα πάντα ἐπὶ τὴν
you, will come all these things on -

γενεὰν ταύτην. 37 Ἰερουσαλὴμ Ἰερουσαλήμ,
generation this. Jerusalem Jerusalem,

ἡ ἀποκτείνουσα τοὺς προφήτας καὶ
the [one] killing the prophets and

λιθοβολοῦσα τοὺς ἀπεσταλμένους πρὸς αὐτήν,
stoning the [ones] sent to her,

ποσάκις ἠθέλησα ἐπισυναγαγεῖν τὰ τέκνα
how often I wished to gather the children

which look beautiful on the outside but on the inside are full of dead men's bones and everything unclean. 28 In the same way, on the outside you appear to people as righteous but on the inside you are full of hypocrisy and wickedness.

29 "Woe to you, teachers of the law and Pharisees, you hypocrites! You build tombs for the prophets and decorate the graves of the righteous. 30 And you say, 'If we had lived in the days of our forefathers, we would not have taken part with them in shedding the blood of the prophets.' 31 So you testify against yourselves that you are the descendants of those who murdered the prophets. 32 Fill up, then, the measure of the sin of your forefathers! 33 "You snakes! You brood of vipers! How will you escape being condemned to hell? 34 Therefore I am sending you prophets and wise men and teachers. Some of them you will kill and crucify; others you will flog in your synagogues and pursue from town to town. 35 And so upon you will come all the righteous blood that has been shed on earth, from the blood of righteous Abel to the blood of Zechariah son of Berekiah, whom you murdered between the temple and the altar. 36 I tell you the truth, all this will come upon this generation.

37 "O Jerusalem, Jerusalem, you who kill the prophets and stone those sent to you, how often I have longed to gather your

hen gathers her brood under her wings, and you were not willing! 38 See, your house is left to you, desolate. s 39 For I tell you, you will not see me again until you say, 'Blessed is the one who comes in the name of the Lord.' "

Chapter 24

The Destruction of the Temple Foretold

AS Jesus came out of the temple and was going away, his disciples came to point out to him the buildings of the temple. 2 Then he asked them, "You see all these, do you not? Truly I tell you, not one stone will be left here upon another; all will be thrown down."

Signs of the End of the Age

3 When he was sitting on the Mount of Olives, the disciples came to him privately, saying, "Tell us, when will this be, and what will be the sign of your coming and of the end of the age?" 4 Jesus answered them, "Beware that no one leads you astray. 5 For many will come in my name, saying, 'I am the Messiah!' t and they will lead many astray. 6 And you will hear of wars and rumors of wars; see that you are not alarmed; for this must take place, but the end is not yet. 7 For nation will rise against nation, and kingdom against kingdom, and there will be famines u and earthquakes in various places; 8 all this is but the beginning of the birthpangs.

Persecutions Foretold

9 "Then they will hand you over to be tortured and will put you to death, and

s Other ancient authorities lack desolate
t Or the Christ
u Other ancient authorities add and pestilences

σου,　ὃν　τρόπον　ὄρνις　ἐπισυνάγει　τὰ
of thee,　as　　a bird　gathers　the

νοσσία　[αὐτῆς]　ὑπὸ　τὰς　πτέρυγας,　καὶ
young　of her　under the(her)　wings,　and

οὐκ　ἠθελήσατε.　38 ἰδοὺ　ἀφίεται　ὑμῖν　ὁ
ye wished not.　Behold　is left　to you the

οἶκος　ὑμῶν.　39 λέγω　γὰρ　ὑμῖν,　οὐ　μὴ
house　of you.　For I tell　you, by no means

με　ἴδητε　ἀπ'　ἄρτι　ἕως　ἂν　εἴπητε·
me　ye see　from　now　until　ye say:

εὐλογημένος　ὁ　ἐρχόμενος　ἐν　ὀνόματι
Blessed　the [one]　coming　in　[the] name

κυρίου.
of [the] Lord.

24 Καὶ　ἐξελθὼν　ὁ　Ἰησοῦς　ἀπὸ　τοῦ
And　going forth　-　Jesus　from　the

ἱεροῦ　ἐπορεύετο,　καὶ　προσῆλθον　οἱ　μαθηταὶ
temple　went,　and　⁴approached　¹the　²disciples

αὐτοῦ　ἐπιδεῖξαι　αὐτῷ　τὰς　οἰκοδομὰς
³of him　to show　him　the　buildings

τοῦ　ἱεροῦ.　2 ὁ　δὲ　ἀποκριθεὶς　εἶπεν
of the　temple.　And he　answering　said

αὐτοῖς·　οὐ　βλέπετε　ταῦτα　πάντα;　ἀμὴν　ἐπὶ
to them:　See ye not　all these things?　Truly

λέγω　ὑμῖν,　οὐ　μὴ　ἀφεθῇ　ὧδε　λίθος　ἐπὶ
I tell　you,　by no means will be left here　stone　on

λίθον　ὃς　οὐ　καταλυθήσεται.　3 Καθημένου
stone　which　shall not be overthrown.　sitting

δὲ　αὐτοῦ　ἐπὶ　τοῦ　ὄρους　τῶν　ἐλαιῶν
and　him·　on　the　mount　of the　olives
= And as he sat

προσῆλθον　αὐτῷ　οἱ　μαθηταὶ　κατ'　ἰδίαν
approached　to him　the　disciples　privately

λέγοντες·　εἰπὲ　ἡμῖν,　πότε　ταῦτα　ἔσται,
saying:　Tell　us,　when these things　will be,

καὶ　τί　τὸ　σημεῖον　τῆς　σῆς　παρουσίας
and　what the　sign　-　of thy　presence

καὶ　συντελείας　τοῦ　αἰῶνος;　4 καὶ　ἀπο-
and of [the] completion of the　age?　And answer-

κριθεὶς　ὁ　Ἰησοῦς　εἶπεν　αὐτοῖς·　βλέπετε
ing　-　Jesus　said　to them:　See ye

μή　τις　ὑμᾶς　πλανήσῃ.　5 πολλοὶ　γὰρ
not(lest) anyone ³you　¹cause ²to err.　For many

ἐλεύσονται　ἐπὶ　τῷ　ὀνόματί　μου　λέγοντες·
will come　on(in)　the　name　of me　saying:

ἐγώ　εἰμι　ὁ　χριστός,　καὶ　πολλοὺς　πλανή-
I　am　the　Christ,　and　²many　¹will cause

σουσιν.　6 μελλήσετε　δὲ　ἀκούειν　πολέ-
³to err.　But ye will be about　to hear　[of]

μους　καὶ　ἀκοὰς　πολέμων·　ὁρᾶτε　μὴ
wars　and　rumours　of wars;　see　not

θροεῖσθε·　δεῖ　γὰρ　γενέσθαι,　ἀλλ'
ye are disturbed; for it behoves　to happen,　but

οὔπω　ἐστὶν　τὸ　τέλος.　7 ἐγερθήσεται　γὰρ
not yet　is　the　end.　For will be raised

ἔθνος　ἐπὶ　ἔθνος　καὶ　βασιλεία　ἐπὶ　βασιλείαν,
nation against nation　and　kingdom against kingdom,

καὶ　ἔσονται　λιμοὶ　καὶ　σεισμοὶ
and　there will be　famines　and　earthquakes

κατὰ　τόπους·　8 πάντα　δὲ　ταῦτα　ἀρχὴ
throughout places;　but all these things [are] beginning

ὠδίνων.　9 τότε　παραδώσουσιν　ὑμᾶς
of birth-pangs.　Then　they will deliver　you

εἰς　θλῖψιν　καὶ　ἀποκτενοῦσιν　ὑμᾶς,
to　affliction　and　will kill　you,

---

children together, as a hen gathers her chicks under her wings, but you were not willing. 38 Look, your house is left to you desolate. 39 For I tell you, you will not see me again until you say, 'Blessed is he who comes in the name of the Lord.' v "

Chapter 24

Signs of the End of the Age

JESUS left the temple and was walking away when his disciples came up to him to call his attention to its buildings. 2 "Do you see all these things?" he asked. "I tell you the truth, not one stone here will be left on another; every one will be thrown down."

3 As Jesus was sitting on the Mount of Olives, the disciples came to him privately. "Tell us," they said, "when will this happen, and what will be the sign of your coming and of the end of the age?"

4 Jesus answered: "Watch out that no one deceives you. 5 For many will come in my name, claiming, 'I am the Christ,' w' and will deceive many. 6 You will hear of wars and rumors of wars, but see to it that you are not alarmed. Such things must happen, but the end is still to come. 7 Nation will rise against nation, and kingdom against kingdom. There will be famines and earthquakes in various places. 8 All these are the beginning of birth pains.

9 "Then you will be handed over to be persecuted and put to death, and you

v 39 Psalm 118:26
w 5 Or Messiah; also in verse 23

you will be hated by all nations because of my name. 10Then many will fall away,ᵛ and they will betray one another and hate one another. 11And many false prophets will arise and lead many astray. 12And because of the increase of lawlessness, the love of many will grow cold. 13But the one who endures to the end will be saved. 14And this good newsʷ of the kingdom will be proclaimed throughout the world, as a testimony to all the nations; and then the end will come.

The Desolating Sacrilege

15 "So when you see the desolating sacrilege standing in the holy place, as was spoken of by the prophet Daniel (let the reader understand), 16then those in Judea must flee to the mountains; 17the one on the housetop must not go down to take what is in the house; 18the one in the field must not turn back to get a coat. 19Woe to those who are pregnant and to those who are nursing infants in those days! 20Pray that your flight may not be in winter or on a sabbath. 21For at that time there will be great suffering, such as has not been from the beginning of the world until now, no, and never will be. 22And if those days had not been cut short, no one would be saved; but for the sake of the elect those days will be cut short. 23Then if anyone says, 'Look! Here is the Messiah!'ˣ or

---

καὶ ἔσεσθε μισούμενοι ὑπὸ πάντων
and ye will be being hated by all

τῶν ἐθνῶν διὰ τὸ ὄνομά μου.
the nations because of the name of me.

10 καὶ τότε σκανδαλισθήσονται πολλοὶ καὶ
And then will be offended many and

ἀλλήλους παραδώσουσιν καὶ μισήσουσιν
one another will deliver and they will hate

ἀλλήλους· **11** καὶ πολλοὶ ψευδοπροφῆται
one another; and many false prophets

ἐγερθήσονται καὶ πλανήσουσιν πολλούς·
will be raised and will cause to err many;

12 καὶ διὰ τὸ πληθυνθῆναι τὴν
and because of - to be increased the

ἀνομίαν ψυγήσεται ἡ ἀγάπη τῶν
lawlessness will grow cold the love of the

πολλῶν. **13** ὁ δὲ ὑπομείνας εἰς τέλος,
many. But the [one] enduring to [the] end,

οὗτος σωθήσεται. **14** καὶ κηρυχθήσεται
this will be saved. And will be proclaimed

τοῦτο τὸ εὐαγγέλιον τῆς βασιλείας
this - gospel of the kingdom

ἐν ὅλῃ τῇ οἰκουμένῃ εἰς μαρτύριον
in all the inhabited earth for a testimony

πᾶσιν τοῖς ἔθνεσιν, καὶ τότε ἥξει τὸ
to all the nations, and then will come the

τέλος. **15** Ὅταν οὖν ἴδητε τὸ
end. When therefore ye see the

βδέλυγμα τῆς ἐρημώσεως τὸ ῥηθὲν διὰ
abomination - of desolation - spoken through

Δανιὴλ τοῦ προφήτου ἑστὸς ἐν τόπῳ
Daniel the prophet stand in place

ἁγίῳ, ὁ ἀναγινώσκων νοείτω,
holy, the [one] reading let him understand,

16 τότε οἱ ἐν τῇ Ἰουδαίᾳ φευγέτωσαν
then the [ones] in - Judæa let them flee

εἰς τὰ ὄρη, **17** ὁ ἐπὶ τοῦ δώματος μὴ
to the mountains, the [one] on the housetop let him

καταβάτω ἆραι τὰ ἐκ τῆς οἰκίας αὐτοῦ,
not come down to take the things out of the house of him,

18 καὶ ὁ ἐν τῷ ἀγρῷ μὴ ἐπιστρεψάτω
and the [one] in the field let him not turn back

ὀπίσω ἆραι τὸ ἱμάτιον αὐτοῦ. **19** οὐαὶ
behind to take the garment of him. woe

δὲ ταῖς ἐν γαστρὶ ἐχούσαις καὶ ταῖς
And to the women in womb having and to the [ones]
= the pregnant women

θηλαζούσαις ἐν ἐκείναις ταῖς ἡμέραις.
giving suck in those - days.

20 προσεύχεσθε δὲ ἵνα μὴ γένηται ἡ
And pray ye lest happen the

φυγὴ ὑμῶν χειμῶνος μηδὲ σαββάτῳ·
flight of you of(in) winter nor on a sabbath;

21 ἔσται γὰρ τότε θλῖψις μεγάλη, οἵα οὐ
for will be then affliction great, such as not

γέγονεν ἀπ᾽ ἀρχῆς κόσμου ἕως
has happened from [the] beginning of [the] world until

τοῦ νῦν οὐδ᾽ οὐ μὴ γένηται. **22** καὶ
- now neither by no means may happen. And

εἰ μὴ ἐκολοβώθησαν αἱ ἡμέραι ἐκεῖναι,
except were cut short the days those,

οὐκ ἂν ἐσώθη πᾶσα σάρξ· διὰ δὲ τοὺς
not - was saved all flesh; but on account of the
= no flesh would be saved;

ἐκλεκτοὺς κολοβωθήσονται αἱ ἡμέραι ἐκεῖναι.
chosen will be cut short - days those.

23 τότε ἐάν τις ὑμῖν εἴπῃ· ἰδοὺ ὧδε
Then if anyone to you says: Behold here

---

will be hated by all nations because of me. 10At that time many will turn away from the faith and will betray and hate each other, 11and many false prophets will appear and deceive many people. 12Because of the increase of wickedness, the love of most will grow cold, 13but he who stands firm to the end will be saved. 14And this gospel of the kingdom will be preached in the whole world as a testimony to all nations, and then the end will come.

15"So when you see standing in the holy place 'the abomination that causes desolation,'ˣ spoken of through the prophet Daniel—let the reader understand—16then let those who are in Judea flee to the mountains. 17Let no one on the roof of his house go down to take anything out of the house. 18Let no one in the field go back to get his cloak. 19How dreadful it will be in those days for pregnant women and nursing mothers! 20Pray that your flight will not take place in winter or on the Sabbath. 21For then there will be great distress, unequaled from the beginning of the world until now—and never to be equaled again. 22If those days had not been cut short, no one would survive, but for the sake of the elect those days will be shortened. 23At that time if anyone says to you, 'Look, here is the Christ!'

ᵛ Or *stumble*
ʷ Or *gospel*
ˣ Or *the Christ*

ˣ15 Daniel 9:27; 11:31; 12:11

'There he is!'—do not believe it. 24 For false messiahs[y] and false prophets will appear and produce great signs and omens, to lead astray, if possible, even the elect. 25 Take note, I have told you beforehand. 26 So, if they say to you, 'Look! He is in the wilderness,' do not go out. If they say, 'Look! He is in the inner rooms,' do not believe it. 27 For as the lightning comes from the east and flashes as far as the west, so will be the coming of the Son of Man. 28 Wherever the corpse is, there the vultures will gather.

The Coming of the Son of Man

29 "Immediately after the suffering of those days the sun will be darkened,
and the moon will not give
its light;
the stars will fall from heaven,
and the powers of heaven will
be shaken.
30 Then the sign of the Son of Man will appear in heaven, and then all the tribes of the earth will mourn, and they will see 'the Son of Man coming on the clouds of heaven' with power and great glory. 31 And he will send out his angels with a loud trumpet call, and they will gather his elect from the four winds, from one end of heaven to the other.

The Lesson of the Fig Tree

32 "From the fig tree learn its lesson: as soon as its branch becomes tender and puts forth its leaves, you know that summer is near. 33 So also, when you

ὁ   χριστός,   ἤ·   ὧδε,   μὴ   πιστεύσητε·
the   Christ,   or: Here,   do not believe;
24 ἐγερθήσονται   γὰρ   ψευδόχριστοι   καὶ
for will be raised   false Christs   and
ψευδοπροφῆται,   καὶ   δώσουσιν   σημεῖα   μεγάλα
false prophets,   and   they will give   signs   great
καὶ   τέρατα,   ὥστε   πλανῆσαι,   εἰ   δυνατόν,
and   marvels,   so as   to cause to err,   if   possible,
καὶ   τοὺς   ἐκλεκτούς.   25 ἰδοὺ   προείρηκα
even   the   chosen.   Behold I have before told
ὑμῖν.   26 ἐὰν   οὖν   εἴπωσιν   ὑμῖν·   ἰδοὺ
you.   If   therefore   they say   to you: Behold
ἐν   τῇ   ἐρήμῳ   ἐστίν,   μὴ   ἐξέλθητε·   ἰδοὺ
in   the   desert   he is,   go not ye forth;   Behold
ἐν   τοῖς   ταμιείοις,   μὴ   πιστεύσητε·
in   the   private rooms,   do not ye believe;
27 ὥσπερ   γὰρ   ἡ   ἀστραπὴ   ἐξέρχεται   ἀπὸ
for as   the   lightning   comes forth   from
ἀνατολῶν   καὶ   φαίνεται   ἕως   δυσμῶν,
[the] east   and   shines   unto   [the] west,
οὕτως   ἔσται   ἡ   παρουσία   τοῦ   υἱοῦ
so   will be   the   presence   of the   Son
τοῦ   ἀνθρώπου·   28 ὅπου   ἐὰν   ᾖ   τὸ
-       of man;   wherever   may be   the
πτῶμα,   ἐκεῖ   συναχθήσονται   οἱ   ἀετοί.
carcase,   there   will be assembled   the   eagles.
29 Εὐθέως   δὲ   μετὰ   τὴν   θλῖψιν   τῶν
And immediately   after   the   affliction   -
ἡμερῶν   ἐκείνων   ὁ   ἥλιος   σκοτισθήσεται,
days   of those   the   sun   will be darkened,
καὶ   ἡ   σελήνη   οὐ   δώσει   τὸ   φέγγος
and   the   moon   will not give   the   light
αὐτῆς,   καὶ   οἱ   ἀστέρες   πεσοῦνται   ἀπὸ   τοῦ
of her,   and   the   stars   will fall   from   -
οὐρανοῦ,   καὶ   αἱ   δυνάμεις   τῶν   οὐρανῶν
heaven,   and   the   powers   of the   heavens
σαλευθήσονται.   30 καὶ   τότε   φανήσεται
will be shaken.   And   then   will appear
τὸ   σημεῖον   τοῦ   υἱοῦ   τοῦ   ἀνθρώπου   ἐν
the   sign   of the   Son   -   of man   in
οὐρανῷ,   καὶ   τότε   κόψονται   πᾶσαι   αἱ
heaven,   and   then   will bewail   all   the
φυλαὶ   τῆς   γῆς   καὶ   ὄψονται   τὸν   υἱὸν
tribes   of the   land   and   they will see   the   Son
τοῦ   ἀνθρώπου   ἐρχόμενον   ἐπὶ   τῶν
-       of man   coming   on   the
νεφελῶν   τοῦ   οὐρανοῦ   μετὰ   δυνάμεως   καὶ
clouds   -   of heaven   with   power   and
δόξης   πολλῆς·   31 καὶ   ἀποστελεῖ   τοὺς
glory   much;   and   he will send   the
ἀγγέλους   αὐτοῦ   μετὰ   σάλπιγγος   μεγάλης,
angels   of him   with   trumpet   a great,
καὶ   ἐπισυνάξουσιν   τοὺς   ἐκλεκτοὺς   αὐτοῦ
and   they will assemble   the   chosen   of him
ἐκ   τῶν   τεσσάρων   ἀνέμων   ἀπ'   ἄκρων
out of   the   four   winds   from [the]   extremities
οὐρανῶν   ἕως   [τῶν]   ἄκρων   αὐτῶν.   32 Ἀπὸ
of [the] heavens   unto   the   extremities of them.   from
δὲ   τῆς   συκῆς   μάθετε   τὴν   παραβολήν·
Now   the   fig-tree   learn ye   the   parable:
ὅταν   ἤδη   ὁ   κλάδος   αὐτῆς   γένηται   ἁπαλὸς
When   now   the   branch   of it   becomes   tender
καὶ   τὰ   φύλλα   ἐκφύῃ,   γινώσκετε   ὅτι
and   the   leaves   it puts forth,   ye know   that
ἐγγὺς   τὸ   θέρος·   33 οὕτως   καὶ   ὑμεῖς
near [is]   the   summer;   so   also   ye

or, 'There he is!' do not believe it. 24 For false Christs and false prophets will appear and perform great signs and miracles to deceive even the elect—if that were possible. 25 See, I have told you ahead of time.
26 "So if anyone tells you, 'There he is, out in the desert,' do not go out; or, 'Here he is, in the inner rooms,' do not believe it. 27 For as lightning that comes from the east is visible even in the west, so will be the coming of the Son of Man. 28 Wherever there is a carcass, there the vultures will gather.
29 "Immediately after the distress of those days

" 'the sun will be
darkened,
and the moon will not
give its light;
the stars will fall from
the sky,
and the heavenly
bodies will be
shaken.'[y]

30 "At that time the sign of the Son of Man will appear in the sky, and all the nations of the earth will mourn. They will see the Son of Man coming on the clouds of the sky, with power and great glory. 31 And he will send his angels with a loud trumpet call, and they will gather his elect from the four winds, from one end of the heavens to the other.
32 "Now learn this lesson from the fig tree: As soon as its twigs get tender and its leaves come out, you know that summer is near. 33 Even so, when you see all

[y] Or *christs*

[y] 29 Isaiah 13:10; 34:4

see all these things, you know that he^z is near, at the very gates. ³⁴Truly I tell you, this generation will not pass away until all these things have taken place. ³⁵Heaven and earth will pass away, but my words will not pass away.

The Necessity for Watchfulness

36 "But about that day and hour no one knows, neither the angels of heaven, nor the Son,^{a} but only the Father. ³⁷For as the days of Noah were, so will be the coming of the Son of Man. ³⁸For as in those days before the flood they were eating and drinking, marrying and giving in marriage, until the day Noah entered the ark, ³⁹and they knew nothing until the flood came and swept them all away, so too will be the coming of the Son of Man. ⁴⁰Then two will be in the field; one will be taken and one will be left. ⁴¹Two women will be grinding meal together; one will be taken and one will be left. ⁴²Keep awake therefore, for you do not know on what day^b your Lord is coming. ⁴³But understand this: if the owner of the house had known in what part of the night the thief was coming, he would have stayed awake and would not have let his house be broken into. ⁴⁴Therefore you also must be ready, for the Son of Man is coming at an unexpected hour.

The Faithful or the Unfaithful Slave

45 "Who then is the faithful and wise slave, whom his master has put in charge of his household, to

---

ὅταν ἴδητε πάντα ταῦτα, γινώσκετε ὅτι
when ye see all these things, know that

ἐγγύς ἐστιν ἐπὶ θύραις. 34 ἀμὴν λέγω
near it is on(at) [the] doors. Truly I tell

ὑμῖν ὅτι οὐ μὴ παρέλθῃ ἡ γενεὰ
you that by no means passes away – generation

αὕτη ἕως ἂν πάντα ταῦτα γένηται.
this until all these things happens.

35 ὁ οὐρανὸς καὶ ἡ γῆ παρελεύσεται, οἱ
The heaven and the earth will pass away, ¹the

δὲ λόγοι μου οὐ μὴ παρέλθωσιν. 36 Περὶ
¹but words of me by no means may pass away. concerning

δὲ τῆς ἡμέρας ἐκείνης καὶ ὥρας οὐδεὶς
But – day that and hour no one

οἶδεν, οὐδὲ οἱ ἄγγελοι τῶν οὐρανῶν
knows, neither the angels of the heavens

οὐδὲ ὁ υἱός, εἰ μὴ ὁ πατὴρ μόνος.
nor the Son, except the Father only.

37 ὥσπερ γὰρ αἱ ἡμέραι τοῦ Νῶε, οὕτως
For as the days – of Noah, so

ἔσται ἡ παρουσία τοῦ υἱοῦ τοῦ ἀνθρώπου.
will be the presence of the Son – of man.

38 ὡς γὰρ ἦσαν ἐν ταῖς ἡμέραις
For as they were in – days

[ἐκείναις] ταῖς πρὸ τοῦ κατακλυσμοῦ
those the [ones] before the flood

τρώγοντες καὶ πίνοντες, γαμοῦντες καὶ
eating and drinking, marrying and

γαμίζοντες, ἄχρι ἧς ἡμέρας εἰσῆλθεν
being given in marriage, until which day entered

Νῶε εἰς τὴν κιβωτόν, 39 καὶ οὐκ ἔγνωσαν
Noah into the ark, and knew not

ἕως ἦλθεν ὁ κατακλυσμὸς καὶ ἦρεν
until came the flood and took

ἅπαντας, οὕτως ἔσται καὶ ἡ παρουσία
all, so will be also the presence

τοῦ υἱοῦ τοῦ ἀνθρώπου 40 τότε ἔσονται
of the Son – of man. Then will be

δύο ἐν τῷ ἀγρῷ, εἷς παραλαμβάνεται
two men in the field, one is taken

καὶ εἷς ἀφίεται· 41 δύο ἀλήθουσαι
and one is left; two women grinding

ἐν τῷ μύλῳ, μία παραλαμβάνεται καὶ
in(at) the mill, one is taken and

μία ἀφίεται. 42 γρηγορεῖτε οὖν, ὅτι
one is left. Watch ye therefore, because

οὐκ οἴδατε ποίᾳ ἡμέρᾳ ὁ κύριος
ye know not on what day the lord

ὑμῶν ἔρχεται. 43 Ἐκεῖνο δὲ γινώσκετε
of you is coming. And that know ye

ὅτι εἰ ᾔδει ὁ οἰκοδεσπότης ποίᾳ
that if knew the housemaster in what

φυλακῇ ὁ κλέπτης ἔρχεται, ἐγρηγόρησεν
watch the thief is coming, he would have

ἂν καὶ οὐκ ἂν εἴασεν διορυχθῆναι
watched and would not have allowed to be dug through

τὴν οἰκίαν αὐτοῦ. 44 διὰ τοῦτο καὶ
the house of him. Therefore also

ὑμεῖς γίνεσθε ἕτοιμοι, ὅτι ᾗ οὐ δοκεῖτε
ye be ready, because ¹in which ²ye think not

ὥρᾳ ὁ υἱὸς τοῦ ἀνθρώπου ἔρχεται. 45 Τίς
²hour the Son – of man comes. Who

ἄρα ἐστὶν ὁ πιστὸς δοῦλος καὶ φρόνιμος
then is the faithful slave and prudent

ὃν κατέστησεν ὁ κύριος ἐπὶ τῆς οἰκετείας
whom appointed the lord over the household

---

these things, you know that it^z is near, right at the door. ³⁴I tell you the truth, this generation^a will certainly not pass away until all these things have happened. ³⁵Heaven and earth will pass away, but my words will never pass away.

The Day and Hour Unknown

36 "No one knows about that day or hour, not even the angels in heaven, nor the Son,^{b} but only the Father. ³⁷As it was in the days of Noah, so it will be at the coming of the Son of Man. ³⁸For in the days before the flood, people were eating and drinking, marrying and giving in marriage, up to the day Noah entered the ark; ³⁹and they knew nothing about what would happen until the flood came and took them all away. That is how it will be at the coming of the Son of Man. ⁴⁰Two men will be in the field; one will be taken and the other left. ⁴¹Two women will be grinding with a hand mill; one will be taken and the other left.

42 "Therefore keep watch, because you do not know on what day your Lord will come. ⁴³But understand this: If the owner of the house had known at what time of night the thief was coming, he would have kept watch and would not have let his house be broken into. ⁴⁴So you also must be ready, because the Son of Man will come at an hour when you do not expect him.

45 "Who then is the faithful and wise servant, whom the master has put in charge of the servants in his

---

^{z} Or it
^{a} Other ancient authorities lack nor the Son
^{b} Other ancient authorities read at what hour

^{z}33 Or he
^{a}34 Or race
^{b}36 Some manuscripts do not have nor the Son.

give the other slaves^c their allowance of food at the proper time? 46Blessed is that slave whom his master will find at work when he arrives. 47Truly I tell you, he will put that one in charge of all his possessions. 48But if that wicked slave says to himself, 'My master is delayed,' 49and he begins to beat his fellow slaves, and eats and drinks with drunkards, 50the master of that slave will come on a day when he does not expect him and at an hour that he does not know. 51He will cut him in pieces^d and put him with the hypocrites, where there will be weeping and gnashing of teeth.

αὐτοῦ τοῦ δοῦναι αὐτοῖς τὴν τροφὴν ἐν
of him - to give^d to them the food in

καιρῷ; 46 μακάριος ὁ δοῦλος ἐκεῖνος ὃν
season? blessed [is] - slave that whom

ἐλθὼν ὁ κύριος αὐτοῦ εὑρήσει οὕτως
coming the lord of him will find so

ποιοῦντα· 47 ἀμὴν λέγω ὑμῖν ὅτι ἐπὶ
doing; truly I tell you that over

πᾶσιν · τοῖς ὑπάρχουσιν αὐτοῦ καταστήσει
all the goods of him he will appoint

αὐτόν. 48 ἐὰν δὲ εἴπῃ ὁ κακὸς δοῦλος
him. But if says - wicked slave

ἐκεῖνος ἐν τῇ καρδίᾳ αὐτοῦ· χρονίζει
that in the heart of him: Delays

μου ὁ κύριος, 49 καὶ ἄρξηται τύπτειν
of me the lord, and begins to strike

τοὺς συνδούλους αὐτοῦ, ἐσθίῃ δὲ καὶ
the fellow-slaves of him, and eats and

πίνῃ μετὰ τῶν μεθυόντων, 50 ἥξει ὁ
drinks with the [ones] being drunk, will come the

κύριος τοῦ δούλου ἐκείνου ἐν ἡμέρᾳ ᾗ
lord - slave of that on a day on which

οὐ προσδοκᾷ καὶ ἐν ὥρᾳ ᾗ οὐ
he does not expect and in an hour in which not

γινώσκει, 51 καὶ διχοτομήσει αὐτόν,
he knows, and will cut asunder him,

καὶ τὸ μέρος αὐτοῦ μετὰ τῶν
and the portion of him with the

ὑποκριτῶν θήσει· ἐκεῖ ἔσται ὁ
hypocrites will place; there will be the

κλαυθμὸς καὶ ὁ βρυγμὸς τῶν ὀδόντων.
wailing and the gnashing of the teeth.

household to give them their food at the proper time? 46It will be good for that servant whose master finds him doing so when he returns. 47I tell you the truth, he will put him in charge of all his possessions. 48But suppose that servant is wicked and says to himself, 'My master is staying away a long time,' 49and he then begins to beat his fellow servants and to eat and drink with drunkards. 50The master of that servant will come on a day when he does not expect him and at an hour he is not aware of. 51He will cut him to pieces and assign him a place with the hypocrites, where there will be weeping and gnashing of teeth.

Chapter 25

The Parable of the Ten Bridesmaids

' 'THEN the kingdom of heaven will be like this. Ten bridesmaids^e took their lamps and went to meet the bridegroom.^f 2Five of them were foolish, and five were wise. 3When the foolish took their lamps, they took no oil with them; 4but the wise took flasks of oil with their lamps. 5As the bridegroom was delayed, all of them became drowsy and slept. 6But at midnight there was a shout, 'Look! Here is the bridegroom! Come out to meet him.' 7Then all those bridesmaids^e got up and

25 Τότε ὁμοιωθήσεται ἡ βασιλεία
Then shall be likened the kingdom

τῶν οὐρανῶν δέκα παρθένοις, αἵτινες
of the heavens to ten virgins, who

λαβοῦσαι τὰς λαμπάδας ἑαυτῶν ἐξῆλθον
taking the lamps of them* went forth

εἰς ὑπάντησιν τοῦ νυμφίου. 2 πέντε δὲ
to a meeting of the bridegroom. Now five

ἐξ αὐτῶν ἦσαν μωραὶ καὶ πέντε φρόνιμοι.
of them were foolish and five prudent.

3 αἱ γὰρ μωραὶ λαβοῦσαι τὰς λαμπάδας
For the foolish [ones] taking the lamps

οὐκ ἔλαβον μεθ' ἑαυτῶν ἔλαιον.
did not take with them oil.

4 αἱ δὲ φρόνιμοι ἔλαβον ἔλαιον ἐν
But the prudent [ones] took oil in

τοῖς ἀγγείοις μετὰ τῶν λαμπάδων ἑαυτῶν.
the vessels with the lamps of them.

5 χρονίζοντος δὲ τοῦ νυμφίου ἐνύσταξαν
But delaying the bridegroom^a slumbered
=while the bridegroom delayed

πᾶσαι καὶ ἐκάθευδον. 6 μέσης δὲ
all and slept. And of(in) [the] middle

νυκτὸς κραυγὴ γέγονεν· ἰδοὺ ὁ
of [the] night a cry there has been: Behold[,] the

νυμφίος, ἐξέρχεσθε εἰς ἀπάντησιν. 7 τότε
bridegroom, go ye forth to a meeting. Then

ἠγέρθησαν πᾶσαι αἱ παρθένοι ἐκεῖναι
were raised all - virgins those

Chapter 25

The Parable of the Ten Virgins

' 'AT that time the kingdom of heaven will be like ten virgins who took their lamps and went out to meet the bridegroom. 2Five of them were foolish and five were wise. 3The foolish ones took their lamps but did not take any oil with them. 4The wise, however, took oil in jars along with their lamps. 5The bridegroom was a long time in coming, and they all became drowsy and fell asleep. 6'At midnight the cry rang out: 'Here's the bridegroom! Come out to meet him!' 7'Then all the virgins

^c Gk to give them
^d Or cut him off
^e Gk virgins
^f Other ancient authorities add and the bride

*Here, and in the three following occurrences, as elsewhere, the strict meaning is emphatic or reflexive—'of themselves'; but this cannot be insisted on.

trimmed their lamps. 8The foolish said to the wise, 'Give us some of your oil, for our lamps are going out.' 9But the wise replied, 'No! there will not be enough for you and for us; you had better go to the dealers and buy some for yourselves.' 10And while they went to buy it, the bridegroom came, and those who were ready went with him into the wedding banquet; and the door was shut. 11Later the other bridesmaids g came also, saying, 'Lord, lord, open to us.' 12But he replied, 'Truly I tell you, I do not know you.' 13Keep awake therefore, for you know neither the day nor the hour. h

The Parable of the Talents

14 "For it is as if a man, going on a journey, summoned his slaves and entrusted his property to them; 15to one he gave five talents, i to another two, to another one, to each according to his ability. Then he went away. 16The one who had received the five talents went off at once and traded with them, and made five more talents. 17In the same way, the one who had the two talents made two more talents. 18But the one who had received the one talent went off and dug a hole in the ground and hid his master's money. 19After a long time the master of those slaves came and settled accounts with them. 20Then the one

---

καὶ   ἐκόσμησαν   τὰς   λαμπάδας   ἑαυτῶν.
and   trimmed   the   lamps   of them.

8 αἱ   δὲ   μωραὶ   ταῖς   φρονίμοις   εἶπαν·
So the   foolish [ones]   to the   prudent   said:

δότε   ἡμῖν   ἐκ   τοῦ   ἐλαίου   ὑμῶν,   ὅτι
Give   us   of   the   oil   of you, because

αἱ   λαμπάδες   ἡμῶν   σβέννυνται.   9 ἀπεκρί-
the   lamps   of us   are being quenched.   But

θησαν   δὲ   αἱ   φρόνιμοι   λέγουσαι·   μήποτε
answered   the   prudent   saying: Lest

οὐ   μὴ   ἀρκέσῃ   ἡμῖν   καὶ   ὑμῖν·
by no means   it suffices   to us   and   to you;

πορεύεσθε   μᾶλλον   πρὸς   τοὺς   πωλοῦντας
go ye   rather   to   the [ones]   selling

καὶ   ἀγοράσατε   ἑαυταῖς.   10 ἀπερχομένων
and   buy   for [your]selves.   And going
= as they

δὲ   αὐτῶν   ἀγοράσαι   ἦλθεν   ὁ   νυμφίος,
away   them   to buy   came   the   bridegroom,
were going away

καὶ   αἱ   ἕτοιμοι   εἰσῆλθον   μετ'   αὐτοῦ
and   the   ready [ones]   went in   with   him

εἰς   τοὺς   γάμους,   καὶ   ἐκλείσθη   ἡ
to   the   wedding festivities, and   was shut   the

θύρα.   11 ὕστερον   δὲ   ἔρχονται   καὶ   αἱ
door.   Then later   come   also   the

λοιπαὶ   παρθένοι   λέγουσαι·   κύριε   κύριε,
remaining   virgins   saying: Lord[,]   Lord,

ἄνοιξον   ἡμῖν.   12 ὁ   δὲ   ἀποκριθεὶς   εἶπεν·
open   to us.   But he   answering   said:

ἀμὴν   λέγω   ὑμῖν,   οὐκ   οἶδα   ὑμᾶς.
Truly   I say   to you,   I know not   you.

13 Γρηγορεῖτε   οὖν,   ὅτι   οὐκ   οἴδατε
Watch ye   therefore, because   ye know not

τὴν   ἡμέραν   οὐδὲ   τὴν   ὥραν.   14 Ὥσπερ
the   day   nor   the   hour.   as

γὰρ   ἄνθρωπος   ἀποδημῶν   ἐκάλεσεν
For   a man   going from home   called

τοὺς   ἰδίους   δούλους   καὶ   παρέδωκεν   αὐτοῖς
the(his)   own   slaves   and   delivered   to them

τὰ   ὑπάρχοντα   αὐτοῦ,   15 καὶ   ᾧ   μὲν   ἔδωκεν
the   goods   of him,   and   to one   he gave

πέντε   τάλαντα,   ᾧ   δὲ   δύο,   ᾧ   δὲ
five   talents,   to another   two,   to another

ἕν,   ἑκάστῳ   κατὰ   τὴν   ἰδίαν   δύναμιν,
one,   to each   according to the(his)   own   ability,

καὶ   ἀπεδήμησεν.   16 εὐθέως   πορευθεὶς
and   went from home.   Immediately   going

ὁ   τὰ   πέντε   τάλαντα   λαβὼν   ἠργάσατο
the [one] the   five   talents   receiving   traded

ἐν   αὐτοῖς   καὶ   ἐκέρδησεν   ἄλλα
in   them   and   gained   other

πέντε·   17 ὡσαύτως   ὁ   τὰ   δύο   ἐκέρδησεν
five;   similarly   the [one] the   two   gained
[receiving]

ἄλλα   δύο.   18 ὁ   δὲ   τὸ   ἓν   λαβὼν
other   two.   But the [one]   the   one   receiving

ἀπελθὼν   ὤρυξεν   γῆν   καὶ   ἔκρυψεν
going away   dug   earth   and   hid

τὸ   ἀργύριον   τοῦ   κυρίου   αὐτοῦ.
the   silver   of the   lord   of him.

19 μετὰ   δὲ   πολὺν   χρόνον   ἔρχεται   ὁ
Then after   much   time   comes   the

κύριος   τῶν   δούλων   ἐκείνων   καὶ   συναίρει
lord   –   slaves   of those   and   takes

λόγον   μετ'   αὐτῶν.   20 καὶ   προσελθὼν
account   with   them.   And   approaching

---

woke up and trimmed their lamps. 8The foolish ones said to the wise, 'Give us some of your oil; our lamps are going out.'

9"'No,' they replied, 'there may not be enough for both us and you. Instead, go to those who sell oil and buy some for yourselves.'

10"But while they were on their way to buy the oil, the bridegroom arrived. The virgins who were ready went in with him to the wedding banquet. And the door was shut.

11"Later the others also came. 'Sir! Sir!' they said. 'Open the door for us!'

12"But he replied, 'I tell you the truth, I don't know you.'

13"Therefore keep watch, because you do not know the day or the hour.

The Parable of the Talents

14"Again, it will be like a man going on a journey, who called his servants and entrusted his property to them. 15To one he gave five talents c of money, to another two talents, and to another one talent, each according to his ability. Then he went on his journey. 16The man who had received the five talents went at once and put his money to work and gained five more. 17So also, the one with the two talents gained two more. 18But the man who had received the one talent went off, dug a hole in the ground and hid his master's money.

19"After a long time the master of those servants returned and settled accounts

---

g Gk *virgins*
h Other ancient authorities add *in which the Son of Man is coming*
i A talent was worth more than fifteen years' wages of a laborer

c15 A talent was worth more than a thousand dollars.

who had received the five talents came forward, bringing five more talents, saying, 'Master, you handed over to me five talents; see, I have made five more talents.' 21 His master said to him, 'Well done, good and trustworthy slave; you have been trustworthy in a few things, I will put you in charge of many things; enter into the joy of your master.' 22 And the one with the two talents also came forward, saying, 'Master, you handed over to me two talents; see, I have made two more talents.' 23 His master said to him, 'Well done, good and trustworthy slave; you have been trustworthy in a few things, I will put you in charge of many things; enter into the joy of your master.' 24 Then the one who had received the one talent also came forward, saying, 'Master, I knew that you were a harsh man, reaping where you did not sow, and gathering where you did not scatter seed; 25 so I was afraid, and I went and hid your talent in the ground. Here you have what is yours.' 26 But his master replied, 'You wicked and lazy slave! You knew, did you, that I reap where I did not sow, and gather where I did not scatter? 27 Then you ought to have invested my money with the bankers, and on my return I would have received what was my own with interest. 28 So take the talent from him, and give it to the one with the ten talents. 29 For to all those who have, more will be given,

ὁ　τὰ　πέντε　τάλαντα　λαβὼν　προσ-
the [one] the　five　talents　receiving　brought

ἤνεγκεν　ἄλλα　πέντε　τάλαντα　λέγων·　κύριε,
other　five　talents　saying:　Lord,

πέντε　τάλαντά　μοι　παρέδωκας·　ἴδε　ἄλλα
five　talents　to me thou deliveredst;　behold　other

πέντε　τάλαντα　ἐκέρδησα.　21 ἔφη　αὐτῷ
five　talents　I gained.　Said　to him

ὁ　κύριος　αὐτοῦ·　εὖ,　δοῦλε　ἀγαθὲ　καὶ
the　lord　of him:　Well,　slave　good　and

πιστέ,　ἐπὶ　ὀλίγα　ἦς　πιστός,
faithful,　over　a few things　thou wast　faithful,

ἐπὶ　πολλῶν　σε　καταστήσω·　εἴσελθε
over　many　thee　I will set;　enter thou

εἰς　τὴν　χαρὰν　τοῦ　κυρίου　σου.　22 προσ-
into　the　joy　of the　lord　of thee.　Ap-

ελθὼν　καὶ　ὁ　τὰ　δύο　τάλαντα
proaching　also　the [one] the　two　talents
　　　　　　　　[having received]

εἶπεν·　κύριε,　δύο　τάλαντά　μοι
said:　Lord,　two　talents　to me

παρέδωκας·　ἴδε　ἄλλα　δύο　τάλαντα
thou deliveredst;　behold　other　two　talents

ἐκέρδησα.　23 ἔφη　αὐτῷ　ὁ　κύριος　αὐτοῦ·
I gained.　Said　to him the　lord　of him:

εὖ,　δοῦλε　ἀγαθὲ　καὶ　πιστέ,　ἐπὶ
Well,　slave　good　and　faithful,　over

ὀλίγα　ἦς　πιστός,　ἐπὶ　πολλῶν
a few things　thou wast　faithful,　over　many

σε　καταστήσω·　εἴσελθε　εἰς　τὴν
thee　I will set;　enter thou　into　the

χαρὰν　τοῦ　κυρίου　σου.　24 προσ-
joy　of the　lord　of thee.　ap-

ελθὼν　δὲ　καὶ　ὁ　τὸ　ἓν　τάλαντον
proaching　And　also　the [one] the　one　talent

εἰληφὼς　εἶπεν·　κύριε,　ἔγνων　σε
having received　said:　Lord,　I knew　thee

ὅτι　σκληρὸς　εἶ　ἄνθρωπος,　θερίζων
that　²a hard　¹thou art　³man,　reaping

ὅπου　οὐκ　ἔσπειρας,　καὶ　συνάγων
where　thou didst not sow,　and　gathering

ὅθεν　οὐ　διεσκόρπισας·　25 καὶ　φοβηθεὶς
whence　thou didst not scatter;　and　fearing

ἀπελθὼν　ἔκρυψα　τὸ　τάλαντόν　σου
going away　I hid　the　talent　of thee

ἐν　τῇ　γῇ·　ἴδε　ἔχεις　τὸ　σόν.
in　the　earth;　behold　thou hast　the　thine.

26 ἀποκριθεὶς　δὲ　ὁ　κύριος　αὐτοῦ　εἶπεν
And answering　the　lord　of him　said

αὐτῷ·　πονηρὲ　δοῦλε　καὶ　ὀκνηρέ,
to him:　Evil　slave　and　slothful,

ἤδεις　ὅτι　θερίζω　ὅπου　οὐκ　ἔσπειρα,
thou knewest that　I reap　where　I sowed not,

καὶ　συνάγω　ὅθεν　οὐ　διεσκόρπισα;
and　I gather　whence　I did not scatter?

27 ἔδει　σε　οὖν　βαλεῖν　τὰ　ἀργύριά
it behoved　thee　therefore　to put　the　silver pieces

μου　τοῖς　τραπεζίταις,　καὶ　ἐλθὼν　ἐγὼ
of me　to the　bankers,　and　coming　I

ἐκομισάμην　ἂν　τὸ　ἐμὸν　σὺν　τόκῳ.
would have received　the　mine　with　interest.

28 ἄρατε　οὖν　ἀπ᾽　αὐτοῦ　τὸ　τάλαντον
Take　therefore　from　him　the　talent

καὶ　δότε　τῷ　ἔχοντι　τὰ　δέκα　τάλαντα·
and　give　to the [one] having　the　ten　talents;

29 τῷ　γὰρ　ἔχοντι　παντὶ　δοθήσεται　καὶ
for to　²having　¹everyone　will be given　and

with them. 20 The man who had received the five talents brought the other five. 'Master,' he said, 'you entrusted me with five talents. See, I have gained five more.'

21 "His master replied, 'Well done, good and faithful servant! You have been faithful with a few things; I will put you in charge of many things. Come and share your master's happiness!'

22 "The man who had the two talents also came. 'Master,' he said, 'you entrusted me with two talents; see, I have gained two more.'

23 "His master replied, 'Well done, good and faithful servant! You have been faithful with a few things; I will put you in charge of many things. Come and share your master's happiness!'

24 "Then the man who had received the one talent came. 'Master,' he said, 'I knew that you are a hard man, harvesting where you have not sown and gathering where you have not scattered seed. 25 So I was afraid and went out and hid your talent in the ground. See, here is what belongs to you.'

26 "His master replied, 'You wicked, lazy servant! So you knew that I harvest where I have not sown and gather where I have not scattered seed? 27 Well then, you should have put my money on deposit with the bankers, so that when I returned I would have received it back with interest.

28 " 'Take the talent from him and give it to the one who has the ten talents. 29 For everyone who has will be given more, and he

and they will have an abundance; but from those who have nothing, even what they have will be taken away. 30 As for this worthless slave, throw him into the outer darkness, where there will be weeping and gnashing of teeth.'

The Judgment of the Nations

31 "When the Son of Man comes in his glory, and all the angels with him, then he will sit on the throne of his glory. 32 All the nations will be gathered before him, and he will separate people one from another as a shepherd separates the sheep from the goats, 33 and he will put the sheep at his right hand and the goats at the left. 34 Then the king will say to those at his right hand, 'Come, you that are blessed by my Father, inherit the kingdom prepared for you from the foundation of the world; 35 for I was hungry and you gave me food, I was thirsty and you gave me something to drink, I was a stranger and you welcomed me, 36 I was naked and you gave me clothing, I was sick and you took care of me, I was in prison and you visited me.' 37 Then the righteous will answer him, 'Lord, when was it that we saw you hungry and gave you food, or thirsty and gave you something to drink? 38 And when was it that we saw you a stranger and welcomed you, or naked and gave you clothing? 39 And when was it that we saw you sick or in prison and visited you?' 40 And the king will answer them, 'Truly I tell you, just

περισσευθήσεται· τοῦ δὲ μὴ ἔχοντος
he will have abundance; but from the [one] not having
καὶ ὃ ἔχει ἀρθήσεται ἀπ᾽ αὐτοῦ.
even what he has will be taken from him.
30 καὶ τὸν ἀχρεῖον δοῦλον ἐκβάλετε εἰς
And the useless slave cast ye out into
τὸ σκότος τὸ ἐξώτερον· ἐκεῖ ἔσται ὁ
the darkness - outer; there will be the
κλαυθμὸς καὶ ὁ βρυγμὸς τῶν ὀδόντων
wailing and the gnashing of the teeth.
31 Ὅταν δὲ ἔλθῃ ὁ υἱὸς τοῦ ἀνθρώπου
And when comes the Son - of man
ἐν τῇ δόξῃ αὐτοῦ καὶ πάντες οἱ ἄγγελοι
in the glory of him and all the angels
μετ᾽ αὐτοῦ, τότε καθίσει ἐπὶ θρόνου
with him, then he will sit on a throne
δόξης αὐτοῦ· **32** καὶ συναχθήσονται
of glory of him; and will be assembled
ἔμπροσθεν αὐτοῦ πάντα τὰ ἔθνη, καὶ
before him all the nations, and
ἀφορίσει αὐτοὺς ἀπ᾽ ἀλλήλων, ὥσπερ
he will separate them from one another, as
ὁ ποιμὴν ἀφορίζει τὰ πρόβατα ἀπὸ
the shepherd separates the sheep from
τῶν ἐρίφων, **33** καὶ στήσει τὰ μὲν
the goats, and will set the -
πρόβατα ἐκ δεξιῶν αὐτοῦ, τὰ δὲ ἐρίφια
sheep on [the] right of him, but the goats
ἐξ εὐωνύμων. **34** τότε ἐρεῖ ὁ
on [the] left. Then will say the
βασιλεὺς τοῖς ἐκ δεξιῶν αὐτοῦ·
king to the [ones] on [the] right of him:
δεῦτε οἱ εὐλογημένοι τοῦ πατρός μου,
Come the [ones] blessed of the Father of me,
κληρονομήσατε τὴν ἡτοιμασμένην ὑμῖν
inherit ye the ¹having been prepared ²for you
βασιλείαν ἀπὸ καταβολῆς κόσμου.
¹kingdom from [the] foundation of [the] world.
35 ἐπείνασα γὰρ καὶ ἐδώκατέ μοι
For I hungered and ye gave me
φαγεῖν, ἐδίψησα , καὶ ἐποτίσατέ με,
to eat, I thirsted and ye gave ²drink ¹me,
ξένος ἤμην καὶ συνηγάγετέ με,
a stranger I was and ye entertained me,
36 γυμνὸς καὶ περιεβάλετέ με, ἠσθένησα
naked and ye clothed me, I ailed
καὶ ἐπεσκέψασθέ με, ἐν φυλακῇ ἤμην
and ye visited me, in prison I was
καὶ ἤλθατε πρός με. **37** τότε ἀποκριθή-
and ye came to me. Then will
σονται αὐτῷ οἱ δίκαιοι λέγοντες· κύριε,
answer him the righteous saying: Lord,
πότε σε εἴδομεν πεινῶντα καὶ ἐθρέψαμεν,
when thee saw we hungering and fed,
ἢ διψῶντα καὶ ἐποτίσαμεν; **38** πότε δέ
or thirsting and gave drink? and when
σε εἴδομεν ξένον καὶ συνηγάγομεν,
thee saw we a stranger and entertained,
ἢ γυμνὸν καὶ περιεβάλομεν; **39** πότε δέ
or naked and clothed? and when
σε εἴδομεν ἀσθενοῦντα ἢ ἐν φυλακῇ καὶ
thee saw we ailing or in prison and
ἤλθομεν πρὸς σέ; **40** καὶ ἀποκριθεὶς ὁ
came to thee? And answering the
βασιλεὺς ἐρεῖ αὐτοῖς· ἀμὴν λέγω
king will say to them: Truly I tell

will have an abundance. Whoever does not have, even what he has will be taken from him. 30 And throw that worthless servant outside, into the darkness, where there will be weeping and gnashing of teeth.'

The Sheep and the Goats

31 "When the Son of Man comes in his glory, and all the angels with him, he will sit on his throne in heavenly glory. 32 All the nations will be gathered before him, and he will separate the people one from another as a shepherd separates the sheep from the goats. 33 He will put the sheep on his right and the goats on his left. 34 Then the King will say to those on his right, 'Come, you who are blessed by my Father; take your inheritance, the kingdom prepared for you since the creation of the world. 35 For I was hungry and you gave me something to eat, I was thirsty and you gave me something to drink, I was a stranger and you invited me in, 36 I needed clothes and you clothed me, I was sick and you looked after me, I was in prison and you came to visit me.' 37 "Then the righteous will answer him, 'Lord, when did we see you hungry and feed you, or thirsty and give you something to drink? 38 When did we see you a stranger and invite you in, or needing clothes and clothe you? 39 When did we see you sick or in prison and go to visit you?' 40 "The King will reply, 'I tell you the truth, whatever

as you did it to one of the least of these who are members of my family,ʲ you did it to me.' ⁴¹Then he will say to those at his left hand, 'You that are accursed, depart from me into the eternal fire prepared for the devil and his angels; ⁴²for I was hungry and you gave me no food, I was thirsty and you gave me nothing to drink, ⁴³I was a stranger and you did not welcome me, naked and you did not give me clothing, sick and in prison and you did not visit me.' ⁴⁴Then they also will answer, 'Lord, when was it that we saw you hungry or thirsty or a stranger or naked or sick or in prison, and did not take care of you?' ⁴⁵Then he will answer them, 'Truly I tell you, just as you did not do it to one of the least of these, you did not do it to me.' ⁴⁶And these will go away into eternal punishment, but the righteous into eternal life."

ὑμῖν, ἐφ᾽ ὅσον ἐποιήσατε ἑνὶ τούτων	you, inasmuch as ye did to one of these
τῶν ἀδελφῶν μου τῶν ἐλαχίστων, ἐμοὶ	- brothers of me the least, to me
ἐποιήσατε. 41 τότε ἐρεῖ καὶ τοῖς ἐξ	ye did. Then he will say also to the [ones] on
εὐωνύμων· πορεύεσθε ἀπ᾽ ἐμοῦ κατ-	[the] left: Go from me having been
ηραμένοι εἰς τὸ πῦρ τὸ αἰώνιον	cursed [ones] into the fire the eternal
τὸ ἡτοιμασμένον τῷ διαβόλῳ καὶ τοῖς	- having been prepared for the devil and the
ἀγγέλοις αὐτοῦ. 42 ἐπείνασα γὰρ καὶ	angels of him. For I hungered and
οὐκ ἐδώκατέ μοι φαγεῖν, ἐδίψησα	ye gave not me to eat, I thirsted
καὶ οὐκ ἐποτίσατέ με, 43 ξένος	and ye ¹gave ²not ⁴drink ³me, a stranger
ἤμην καὶ οὐ συνηγάγετέ με, γυμνὸς	I was and ye entertained not me, naked
καὶ οὐ περιεβάλετέ με, ἀσθενὴς καὶ ἐν	and ye clothed not me, ill and in
φυλακῇ καὶ οὐκ ἐπεσκέψασθέ με. 44 τότε	prison and ye visited not me. Then
ἀποκριθήσονται καὶ αὐτοὶ λέγοντες· κύριε,	will answer also they saying: Lord,
πότε σε εἴδομεν πεινῶντα ἢ διψῶντα ἢ	when thee saw we hungering or thirsting or
ξένον ἢ γυμνὸν ἢ ἀσθενῆ ἢ ἐν φυλακῇ	a stranger or naked or ill or in prison
καὶ οὐ διηκονήσαμέν σοι; 45 τότε	and did not minister to thee? Then
ἀποκριθήσεται αὐτοῖς λέγων· ἀμὴν λέγω	he will answer them saying: Truly I tell
ὑμῖν, ἐφ᾽ ὅσον οὐκ ἐποιήσατε ἑνὶ	you, inasmuch as ye did not to one
τούτων τῶν ἐλαχίστων, οὐδὲ ἐμοὶ	of these - least [ones], neither to me
ἐποιήσατε. 46 καὶ ἀπελεύσονται οὗτοι εἰς	ye did. And will go away these into
κόλασιν αἰώνιον, οἱ δὲ δίκαιοι εἰς	punishment eternal, but the righteous into
ζωὴν αἰώνιον.	life eternal.

you did for one of the least of these brothers of mine, you did for me.' ⁴¹"Then he will say to those on his left, 'Depart from me, you who are cursed, into the eternal fire prepared for the devil and his angels. ⁴²For I was hungry and you gave me nothing to eat, I was thirsty and you gave me nothing to drink, ⁴³I was a stranger and you did not invite me in, I needed clothes and you did not clothe me, I was sick and in prison and you did not look after me.' ⁴⁴"They also will answer, 'Lord, when did we see you hungry or thirsty or a stranger or needing clothes or sick or in prison, and did not help you?' ⁴⁵"He will reply, 'I tell you the truth, whatever you did not do for one of the least of these, you did not do for me.' ⁴⁶"Then they will go away to eternal punishment, but the righteous to eternal life."

Chapter 26

The Plot to Kill Jesus

WHEN Jesus had finished saying all these things, he said to his disciples, ²"You know that after two days the Passover is coming, and the Son of Man will be handed over to be crucified."

3 Then the chief priests and the elders of the people gathered in the palace of the high priest, who was called Caiaphas, ⁴and they conspired to arrest Jesus

26 Καὶ ἐγένετο ὅτε ἐτέλεσεν ὁ	And it came to pass when ended -
Ἰησοῦς πάντας τοὺς λόγους τούτους,	Jesus all - words these,
εἶπεν τοῖς μαθηταῖς αὐτοῦ· 2 οἴδατε	he said to the disciples of him: Ye know
ὅτι μετὰ δύο ἡμέρας τὸ πάσχα γίνεται,	that after two days the passover occurs,
καὶ ὁ υἱὸς τοῦ ἀνθρώπου παραδίδοται εἰς	and the Son of man is delivered -
τὸ σταυρωθῆναι. 3 Τότε συνήχθησαν οἱ	- to be crucified. Then were assembled the
ἀρχιερεῖς καὶ οἱ πρεσβύτεροι τοῦ λαοῦ	chief priests and the elders of the people
εἰς τὴν αὐλὴν τοῦ ἀρχιερέως τοῦ	in the court of the high priest -
λεγομένον Καϊαφᾶ, 4 καὶ συνεβουλεύ-	named Caiaphas, and con-
σαντο ἵνα τὸν Ἰησοῦν δόλῳ κρατή-	sulted that - Jesus by guile they might

Chapter 26

The Plot Against Jesus

WHEN Jesus had finished saying all these things, he said to his disciples, ²"As you know, the Passover is two days away —and the Son of Man will be handed over to be crucified."

³Then the chief priests and the elders of the people assembled in the palace of the high priest, whose name was Caiaphas, ⁴and they plotted to arrest Jesus

ʲGk these my brothers

by stealth and kill him. 5 But they said, "Not during the festival, or there may be a riot among the people."

The Anointing at Bethany

6 Now while Jesus was at Bethany in the house of Simon the leper, [k] 7 a woman came to him with an alabaster jar of very costly ointment, and she poured it on his head as he sat at the table. 8 But when the disciples saw it, they were angry and said, "Why this waste? 9 For this ointment could have been sold for a large sum, and the money given to the poor." 10 But Jesus, aware of this, said to them, "Why do you trouble the woman? She has performed a good service for me. 11 For you always have the poor with you, but you will not always have me. 12 By pouring this ointment on my body she has prepared me for burial. 13 Truly I tell you, wherever this good news [l] is proclaimed in the whole world, what she has done will be told in remembrance of her."

Judas Agrees to Betray Jesus

14 Then one of the twelve, who was called Judas Iscariot, went to the chief priests 15 and said, "What will you give me if I betray him to you?" They paid him thirty pieces of silver. 16 And from that moment he began to look for an opportunity to betray him.

The Passover with the Disciples

17 On the first day of Unleavened Bread the disciples came to Jesus, saying, "Where do you want us to make the preparations for you to eat the Passover?" 18 He said, "Go into

σωσιν καὶ ἀποκτείνωσιν· 5 ἔλεγον δέ·
seize and might kill; but they said:

μὴ ἐν τῇ ἑορτῇ, ἵνα μὴ θόρυβος
Not at the feast, lest a disturbance

γένηται ἐν τῷ λαῷ.
occurs among the people.

6 Τοῦ δὲ Ἰησοῦ γενομένου ἐν Βηθανίᾳ
- And Jesus being[a] in Bethany
=when Jesus was

ἐν οἰκίᾳ Σίμωνος τοῦ λεπροῦ,
in [the] house of Simon the leper,

7 προσῆλθεν αὐτῷ γυνὴ ἔχουσα ἀλάβαστρον
approached to him a woman having an alabaster phial

μύρου βαρυτίμου καὶ κατέχεεν ἐπὶ
of ointment very expensive and poured [it] on

τῆς κεφαλῆς αὐτοῦ ἀνακειμένου. 8 ἰδόντες
the head of him reclining. And see-

δὲ οἱ μαθηταὶ ἠγανάκτησαν λέγοντες·
ing the disciples were angry saying:

εἰς τί ἡ ἀπώλεια αὕτη; 9 ἐδύνατο γὰρ
To what - waste this? for could

τοῦτο πραθῆναι πολλοῦ καὶ δοθῆναι
this to be sold of(for) much and to be given

πτωχοῖς. 10 γνοὺς δὲ ὁ Ἰησοῦς εἶπεν
to poor. And knowing - Jesus said

αὐτοῖς· τί κόπους παρέχετε τῇ γυναικί;
to them: Why trouble ye the woman?

ἔργον γὰρ καλὸν ἠργάσατο εἰς ἐμέ·
for work a good she wrought to me:

11 πάντοτε γὰρ τοὺς πτωχοὺς ἔχετε μεθ᾽
for always the poor ye have with

ἑαυτῶν, ἐμὲ δὲ οὐ πάντοτε ἔχετε·
yourselves, but me not always ye have;

12 βαλοῦσα γὰρ αὕτη τὸ μύρον τοῦτο
for ²putting ¹this woman - ⁴ointment ³this

ἐπὶ τοῦ σώματός μου πρὸς τὸ ἐνταφιάσαι
on the body of me for - to bury

με ἐποίησεν. 13 ἀμὴν λέγω ὑμῖν, ὅπου
me she did. Truly I tell you, wher-

ἐὰν κηρυχθῇ τὸ εὐαγγέλιον τοῦτο ἐν
ever is proclaimed - gospel this in

ὅλῳ τῷ κόσμῳ, λαληθήσεται καὶ ὃ
all the world, will be spoken also what

ἐποίησεν αὕτη εἰς μνημόσυνον αὐτῆς.
did this woman for a memorial of her.

14 Τότε πορευθεὶς εἷς τῶν δώδεκα, ὁ
Then going one of the twelve, the [one]

λεγόμενος Ἰούδας Ἰσκαριώτης, πρὸς
named Judas Iscariot, to

τοὺς ἀρχιερεῖς 15 εἶπεν· τί θέλετέ μοι
the chief priests he said: What are ye willing me

δοῦναι, κἀγὼ ὑμῖν παραδώσω αὐτόν;
to give, and I to you will deliver him?

οἱ δὲ ἔστησαν αὐτῷ τριάκοντα ἀργύρια.
And they weighed him thirty pieces of silver.

16 καὶ ἀπὸ τότε ἐζήτει εὐκαιρίαν ἵνα
And from then he sought opportunity that

αὐτὸν παραδῷ.
him he might deliver.

17 Τῇ δὲ πρώτῃ τῶν ἀζύμων
Now on the first [day] - of unleavened bread

προσῆλθον οἱ μαθηταὶ τῷ Ἰησοῦ
approached the disciples - to Jesus

λέγοντες· ποῦ θέλεις ἑτοιμάσωμέν
saying: Where willest thou we may prepare

σοι φαγεῖν τὸ πάσχα; 18 ὁ δὲ
for thee to eat the passover? So he

Jesus Anointed at Bethany

6 While Jesus was in Bethany in the home of a man known as Simon the Leper, 7 a woman came to him with an alabaster jar of very expensive perfume, which she poured on his head as he was reclining at the table.

8 When the disciples saw this, they were indignant. "Why this waste?" they asked. 9 "This perfume could have been sold at a high price and the money given to the poor."

10 Aware of this, Jesus said to them, "Why are you bothering this woman? She has done a beautiful thing to me. 11 The poor you will always have with you, but you will not always have me. 12 When she poured this perfume on my body, she did it to prepare me for burial. 13 I tell you the truth, wherever this gospel is preached throughout the world, what she has done will also be told, in memory of her."

Judas Agrees to Betray Jesus

14 Then one of the Twelve—the one called Judas Iscariot—went to the chief priests 15 and asked, "What are you willing to give me if I hand him over to you?" So they counted out for him thirty silver coins. 16 From then on Judas watched for an opportunity to hand him over.

The Lord's Supper

17 On the first day of the Feast of Unleavened Bread, the disciples came to Jesus and asked, "Where do you want us to make preparations for you to eat the Passover?"

---

[k] The terms *leper* and *leprosy* can refer to several diseases
[l] Or *gospel*

the city to a certain man, and say to him, 'The Teacher says, My time is near; I will keep the Passover at your house with my disciples.' " 19 So the disciples did as Jesus had directed them, and they prepared the Passover meal.

20 When it was evening, he took his place with the twelve;[m] 21 and while they were eating, he said, "Truly I tell you, one of you will betray me." 22 And they became greatly distressed and began to say to him one after another, "Surely not I, Lord?" 23 He answered, "The one who has dipped his hand into the bowl with me will betray me. 24 The Son of Man goes as it is written of him, but woe to that one by whom the Son of Man is betrayed! It would have been better for that one not to have been born." 25 Judas, who betrayed him, said, "Surely not I, Rabbi?" He replied, "You have said so."

The Institution of the Lord's Supper

26 While they were eating, Jesus took a loaf of bread, and after blessing it he broke it, gave it to the disciples, and said, "Take, eat; this is my body." 27 Then he took a cup, and after giving thanks he gave it to them, saying, "Drink from it, all of you; 28 this is my blood of the[n] covenant, which is poured out for many for the forgiveness of sins. 29 I tell you, I

εἶπεν· ὑπάγετε εἰς τὴν πόλιν πρὸς
said: Go ye into the city to

τὸν δεῖνα καὶ εἴπατε αὐτῷ· ὁ
such a one and say to him: The

διδάσκαλος λέγει· ὁ καιρός μου
teacher says: The time of me

ἐγγύς ἐστιν· πρὸς σὲ ποιῶ τὸ πάσχα
near is; with thee I make the passover

μετὰ τῶν μαθητῶν μου. 19 καὶ ἐποίησαν
with the disciples of me. And did

οἱ μαθηταὶ ὡς συνέταξεν αὐτοῖς ὁ
the disciples as enjoined them -

Ἰησοῦς, καὶ ἡτοίμασαν τὸ πάσχα. 20 Ὀψίας
Jesus, and prepared the passover. evening

δὲ γενομένης ἀνέκειτο μετὰ τῶν δώδεκα
And coming = when evening came he reclined with the twelve

[μαθητῶν]. 21 καὶ ἐσθιόντων αὐτῶν εἶπεν·
disciples. And = as they were eating them[a] he said:

ἀμὴν λέγω ὑμῖν ὅτι εἷς ἐξ ὑμῶν παρα-
Truly I tell you that one of you

δώσει με. 22 καὶ λυπούμενοι σφόδρα
betray me. And grieving exceedingly

ἤρξαντο λέγειν αὐτῷ εἷς ἕκαστος·
they began to say to him [a]one [a]each:

μήτι ἐγώ εἰμι, κύριε; 23 ὁ δὲ ἀποκριθεὶς
Not I am, Lord? = It is not I, And he answering

εἶπεν· ὁ ἐμβάψας μετ' ἐμοῦ τὴν
said: The [one] dipping with me the(his)

χεῖρα ἐν τῷ τρυβλίῳ, οὗτός με παρα-
hand in the dish, this man me will

δώσει. 24 ὁ μὲν υἱὸς τοῦ ἀνθρώπου
betray. Indeed the Son - of man

ὑπάγει καθὼς γέγραπται περὶ αὐτοῦ,
goes as it has been written concerning him,

οὐαὶ δὲ τῷ ἀνθρώπῳ ἐκείνῳ δι'
but woe - man to that through

οὗ ὁ υἱὸς τοῦ ἀνθρώπου παραδίδοται·
whom the Son - of man is betrayed:

καλὸν ἦν αὐτῷ εἰ οὐκ ἐγεννήθη
good were it for him if was not born

ὁ ἄνθρωπος ἐκεῖνος. 25 ἀποκριθεὶς δὲ
- man that. And answering

Ἰούδας ὁ παραδιδοὺς αὐτὸν εἶπεν·
Judas the [one] betraying him said:

μήτι ἐγώ εἰμι, ῥαββί; λέγει αὐτῷ·
Not I am, rabbi? He says to him: = It is not I,

σὺ εἶπας. 26 Ἐσθιόντων δὲ αὐτῶν
Thou saidst. And eating them[a] = as they were eating

λαβὼν ὁ Ἰησοῦς ἄρτον καὶ εὐλογήσας
taking - Jesus a loaf and blessing

ἔκλασεν καὶ δοὺς τοῖς μαθηταῖς εἶπεν·
he broke and giving to the disciples said:

λάβετε φάγετε· τοῦτό ἐστιν τὸ σῶμά
Take ye[,] eat ye; this is the body

μου. 27 καὶ λαβὼν ποτήριον καὶ εὐχαρι-
of me. And taking a cup and giving

στήσας ἔδωκεν αὐτοῖς λέγων· πίετε ἐξ
thanks he gave to them saying: Drink ye of

αὐτοῦ πάντες· 28 τοῦτο γάρ ἐστιν τὸ
it all; for this is the

αἷμά μου τῆς διαθήκης τὸ περὶ πολλῶν
blood of me of the covenant the [blood] concerning many

ἐκχυννόμενον εἰς ἄφεσιν ἁμαρτιῶν. 29 λέγω
being shed for forgiveness of sins. I tell

---

18 He replied, "Go into the city to a certain man and tell him, 'The Teacher says: My appointed time is near. I am going to celebrate the Passover with my disciples at your house.' " 19 So the disciples did as Jesus had directed them and prepared the Passover.

20 When evening came, Jesus was reclining at the table with the Twelve. 21 And while they were eating, he said, "I tell you the truth, one of you will betray me."

22 They were very sad and began to say to him one after the other, "Surely not I, Lord?"

23 Jesus replied, "The one who has dipped his hand into the bowl with me will betray me. 24 The Son of Man will go just as it is written about him. But woe to that man who betrays the Son of Man! It would be better for him if he had not been born."

25 Then Judas, the one who would betray him, said, "Surely not I, Rabbi?"

Jesus answered, "Yes, it is you."[d]

26 While they were eating, Jesus took bread, gave thanks and broke it, and gave it to his disciples, saying, "Take and eat; this is my body."

27 Then he took the cup, gave thanks and offered it to them, saying, "Drink from it, all of you. 28 This is my blood of the[e] covenant, which is poured out for many for the forgiveness of

---

will never again drink of this fruit of the vine until that day when I drink it new with you in my Father's kingdom."
30 When they had sung the hymn, they went out to the Mount of Olives.

Peter's Denial Foretold

31 Then Jesus said to them, "You will all become deserters because of me this night; for it is written,
'I will strike the shepherd,
and the sheep of the flock will be scattered.'
32 But after I am raised up, I will go ahead of you to Galilee." 33 Peter said to him, "Though all become deserters because of you, I will never desert you." 34 Jesus said to him, "Truly I tell you, this very night, before the cock crows, you will deny me three times." 35 Peter said to him, "Even though I must die with you, I will not deny you." And so said all the disciples.

Jesus Prays in Gethsemane

36 Then Jesus went with them to a place called Gethsemane; and he said to his disciples, "Sit here while I go over there and pray." 37 He took with him Peter and the two sons of Zebedee, and began to be grieved and agitated. 38 Then he said to them, "I am deeply grieved, even to death; remain here, and stay awake with me." 39 And going a little farther, he threw himself on the ground and prayed, "My Father, if it is possible, let

---

δὲ ὑμῖν, οὐ μὴ πίω ἀπ᾽ ἄρτι ἐκ
And you, by no means will I drink from now of
τούτου τοῦ γενήματος τῆς ἀμπέλου ἕως
this - fruit of the vine until
τῆς ἡμέρας ἐκείνης ὅταν αὐτὸ πίνω μεθ᾽
- day that when it I drink with
ὑμῶν καινὸν ἐν τῇ βασιλείᾳ τοῦ πατρός
you new in the kingdom of the Father
μου.
of me.

30 Καὶ ὑμνήσαντες ἐξῆλθον εἰς τὸ
And having sung a hymn they went forth to the
ὄρος τῶν ἐλαιῶν. 31 Τότε λέγει αὐτοῖς ὁ
mount of the olives. Then says to them -
Ἰησοῦς· πάντες ὑμεῖς σκανδαλισθήσεσθε
Jesus: All ye will be offended
ἐν ἐμοὶ ἐν τῇ νυκτὶ ταύτῃ· γέγραπται
in me to-night; it has been written
γάρ· πατάξω τὸν ποιμένα, καὶ δια-
for: I will strike the shepherd, and will
σκορπισθήσονται τὰ πρόβατα τῆς ποίμνης·
be scattered the sheep of the flock;
32 μετὰ δὲ τὸ ἐγερθῆναί με προάξω
but after the to be raised me[b] I will go before
                               = I am raised
ὑμᾶς εἰς τὴν Γαλιλαίαν. 33 ἀποκριθεὶς
you to - Galilee. answering
δὲ ὁ Πέτρος εἶπεν αὐτῷ· εἰ πάντες
And - Peter said to him: If all men
σκανδαλισθήσονται ἐν σοί, ἐγὼ οὐδέποτε
shall be offended in thee, I never
σκανδαλισθήσομαι. 34 ἔφη αὐτῷ ὁ Ἰησοῦς·
will be offended. Said to him - Jesus:
ἀμὴν λέγω σοι ὅτι ἐν ταύτῃ τῇ νυκτὶ
Truly I tell thee that in this the to-night
πρὶν ἀλέκτορα φωνῆσαι τρὶς ἀπαρνήσῃ
before a cock to crow[b] three times thou wilt deny
με. 35 λέγει αὐτῷ ὁ Πέτρος· κἂν
me. Says to him - Peter: Even if
δέῃ με σὺν σοὶ ἀποθανεῖν, οὐ μή σε
it behoves me with thee to die, by no means thee
          = I must die with thee.
ἀπαρνήσομαι. ὁμοίως καὶ πάντες οἱ
I will deny. Likewise also all the
μαθηταὶ εἶπαν.
disciples said.

36 Τότε ἔρχεται μετ᾽ αὐτῶν ὁ Ἰησοῦς
Then comes with them - Jesus
εἰς χωρίον λεγόμενον Γεθσημανί, καὶ λέγει
to a piece of land called Gethsemane, and says
τοῖς μαθηταῖς· καθίσατε αὐτοῦ ἕως οὗ
to the disciples: Sit ye here until
ἀπελθὼν ἐκεῖ προσεύξωμαι. 37 καὶ παρα-
going away there I may pray. And tak-
λαβὼν τὸν Πέτρον καὶ τοὺς δύο υἱοὺς
ing - Peter and the two sons
Ζεβεδαίου ἤρξατο λυπεῖσθαι καὶ ἀδημονεῖν.
of Zebedee he began to grieve and to be distressed.
38 τότε λέγει αὐτοῖς· περίλυπός ἐστιν
Then he says to them: Deeply grieved is
ἡ ψυχή μου ἕως θανάτου· μείνατε
the soul of me unto death; remain ye
ὧδε καὶ γρηγορεῖτε μετ᾽ ἐμοῦ. 39 καὶ
here and watch ye with me. And
προελθὼν μικρὸν ἔπεσεν ἐπὶ πρόσωπον
going forward a little he fell on [the] face
αὐτοῦ προσευχόμενος καὶ λέγων· πάτερ
of him praying and saying: Father

---

sins. 29 I tell you, I will not drink of this fruit of the vine from now on until that day when I drink it anew with you in my Father's kingdom."
30 When they had sung a hymn, they went out to the Mount of Olives.

Jesus Predicts Peter's Denial

31 Then Jesus told them, "This very night you will all fall away on account of me, for it is written:
" 'I will strike the shepherd,
and the sheep of the flock will be scattered.'[f]
32 But after I have risen, I will go ahead of you into Galilee."
33 Peter replied, "Even if all fall away on account of you, I never will."
34 "I tell you the truth," Jesus answered, "this very night, before the rooster crows, you will disown me three times."
35 But Peter declared, "Even if I have to die with you, I will never disown you." And all the other disciples said the same.

Gethsemane

36 Then Jesus went with his disciples to a place called Gethsemane, and he said to them, "Sit here while I go over there and pray." 37 He took Peter and the two sons of Zebedee along with him, and he began to be sorrowful and troubled. 38 Then he said to them, "My soul is overwhelmed with sorrow to the point of death. Stay here and keep watch with me."
39 Going a little farther, he fell with his face to the ground and prayed, "My

this cup pass from me; yet not what I want but what you want." 40 Then he came to the disciples and found them sleeping; and he said to Peter, "So, could you not stay awake with me one hour? 41 Stay awake and pray that you may not come into the time of trial;⁰ the spirit indeed is willing, but the flesh is weak." 42 Again he went away for the second time and prayed, "My Father, if this cannot pass unless I drink it, your will be done." 43 Again he came and found them sleeping, for their eyes were heavy. 44 So leaving them again, he went away and prayed for the third time, saying the same words. 45 Then he came to the disciples and said to them, "Are you still sleeping and taking your rest? See, the hour is at hand, and the Son of Man is betrayed into the hands of sinners. 46 Get up, let us be going. See, my betrayer is at hand."

The Betrayal and Arrest of Jesus

47 While he was still speaking, Judas, one of the twelve, arrived; with him was a large crowd with swords and clubs, from the chief priests and the elders of the people. 48 Now the betrayer had given them a sign, saying, "The one I will kiss is the man; arrest him." 49 At once he came up to Jesus and said, "Greetings, Rabbi!" and kissed him. 50 Jesus said to

μου, εἰ δυνατόν ἐστιν, παρελθάτω ἀπ'
of me, if possible it is, let pass from
ἐμοῦ τὸ ποτήριον τοῦτο· πλὴν οὐχ
me - cup this; yet not
ὡς ἐγὼ θέλω ἀλλ' ὡς σύ. 40 καὶ
as I will but as thou. And
ἔρχεται πρὸς τοὺς μαθητὰς καὶ εὑρίσκει
he comes to the disciples and finds
αὐτοὺς καθεύδοντας, καὶ λέγει τῷ Πέτρῳ·
them sleeping, and says - to Peter:
οὕτως οὐκ ἰσχύσατε μίαν ὥραν
So were ye not able one hour
γρηγορῆσαι μετ' ἐμοῦ; 41 γρηγορεῖτε καὶ
to watch with me? Watch ye and
προσεύχεσθε, ἵνα μὴ εἰσέλθητε εἰς
pray, lest ye enter into
πειρασμόν· τὸ μὲν πνεῦμα πρόθυμον,
temptation; indeed the spirit [is] eager,
ἡ δὲ σὰρξ ἀσθενής. 42 πάλιν ἐκ
but the flesh weak. Again
δευτέρου ἀπελθὼν προσηύξατο λέγων·
second [time] going away he prayed saying:
πάτερ μου, εἰ οὐ δύναται τοῦτο παρελθεῖν
Father of me, if cannot this to pass away
ἐὰν μὴ αὐτὸ πίω, γενηθήτω τὸ θέλημά
except I drink, let be done the will
σου. 43 καὶ ἐλθὼν πάλιν εὗρεν αὐτοὺς
of thee. And coming again he found them
καθεύδοντας, ἦσαν γὰρ αὐτῶν οἱ ὀφθαλμοὶ
sleeping, for were of them the eyes
βεβαρημένοι. 44 καὶ ἀφεὶς αὐτοὺς πάλιν
having been burdened. And leaving them again
ἀπελθὼν προσηύξατο ἐκ τρίτου, τὸν
going away he prayed a third [time], the
αὐτὸν λόγον εἰπὼν πάλιν. 45 τότε ἔρχεται
same word saying again. Then he comes
πρὸς τοὺς μαθητὰς καὶ λέγει αὐτοῖς·
to the disciples and says to them:
καθεύδετε λοιπὸν καὶ ἀναπαύεσθε·
Sleep ye now and rest;
ἰδοὺ ἤγγικεν ἡ ὥρα καὶ ὁ υἱὸς τοῦ
behold has drawn near the hour and the Son -
ἀνθρώπου παραδίδοται εἰς χεῖρας
of man is betrayed into [the] hands
ἁμαρτωλῶν. 46 ἐγείρεσθε, ἄγωμεν· ἰδοὺ
of sinners. Rise ye, let us be going; behold
ἤγγικεν ὁ παραδιδούς με.
has drawn near the [one] betraying me.

47 Καὶ ἔτι αὐτοῦ λαλοῦντος, ἰδοὺ
And still him speaking,ª behold
= while he was still speaking,
Ἰούδας εἷς τῶν δώδεκα ἦλθεν, καὶ μετ'
Judas one of the twelve came, and with
αὐτοῦ ὄχλος πολὺς μετὰ μαχαιρῶν καὶ
him crowd a much with swords and
ξύλων ἀπὸ τῶν ἀρχιερέων καὶ πρεσβυτέρων
clubs from the chief priests and elders
τοῦ λαοῦ. 48 ὁ δὲ παραδιδοὺς αὐτὸν ἔδωκεν
of the people. Now the [one] betraying him gave
αὐτοῖς σημεῖον λέγων· ὃν ἂν φιλήσω
them a sign saying: Whomever I may kiss
αὐτός ἐστιν· κρατήσατε αὐτόν. 49 καὶ
he it is; seize ye him. And
εὐθέως προσελθὼν τῷ Ἰησοῦ εἶπεν· χαῖρε,
immediately approaching - to Jesus he said: Hail,
ῥαββί, καὶ κατεφίλησεν αὐτόν. 50 ὁ
rabbi, and affectionately kissed him. -

Father, if it is possible, may this cup be taken from me. Yet not as I will, but as you will."
40 Then he returned to his disciples and found them sleeping. "Could you men not keep watch with me for one hour?" he asked Peter. 41 "Watch and pray so that you will not fall into temptation. The spirit is willing, but the body is weak."
42 He went away a second time and prayed, "My Father, if it is not possible for this cup to be taken away unless I drink it, may your will be done."
43 When he came back, he again found them sleeping, because their eyes were heavy. 44 So he left them and went away once more and prayed the third time, saying the same thing.
45 Then he returned to the disciples and said to them, "Are you still sleeping and resting? Look, the hour is near, and the Son of Man is betrayed into the hands of sinners. 46 Rise, let us go! Here comes my betrayer!"

Jesus Arrested

47 While he was still speaking, Judas, one of the Twelve, arrived. With him was a large crowd armed with swords and clubs, sent from the chief priests and the elders of the people. 48 Now the betrayer had arranged a signal with them: "The one I kiss is the man; arrest him." 49 Going at once to Jesus, Judas said, "Greetings, Rabbi!" and kissed him.

⁰ Or into temptation

him, "Friend, do what you are here to do." Then they came and laid hands on Jesus and arrested him. 51 Suddenly, one of those with Jesus put his hand on his sword, drew it, and struck the slave of the high priest, cutting off his ear. 52 Then Jesus said to him, "Put your sword back into its place; for all who take the sword will perish by the sword. 53 Do you think that I cannot appeal to my Father, and he will at once send me more than twelve legions of angels? 54 But how then would the scriptures be fulfilled, which say it must happen in this way?" 55 At that hour Jesus said to the crowds, "Have you come out with swords and clubs to arrest me as though I were a bandit? Day after day I sat in the temple teaching, and you did not arrest me. 56 But all this has taken place, so that the scriptures of the prophets may be fulfilled." Then all the disciples deserted him and fled.

Jesus before the High Priest

57 Those who had arrested Jesus took him to Caiaphas the high priest, in whose house the scribes and the elders had gathered. 58 But Peter was following him at a distance, as far as the courtyard of the high priest; and going inside, he sat with the guards in order to see how this would end. 59 Now the chief priests and the whole council were looking for false testimony against

---

δὲ   'Ιησοῦς   εἶπεν   αὐτῷ·   ἑταῖρε,
But   Jesus   said   to him: Comrade, [do that]

ἐφ' ὃ   πάρει.   τότε   προσελθόντες   ἐπέβαλον
on what thou art here.   Then   approaching   they laid on

τὰς   χεῖρας   ἐπὶ   τὸν   'Ιησοῦν   καὶ   ἐκράτησαν
the(ir)   hands   on   -   Jesus   and   seized

αὐτόν.   51 καὶ   ἰδοὺ   εἷς   τῶν   μετὰ
him.   And   behold   one   of the [ones]   with

'Ιησοῦ   ἐκτείνας   τὴν   χεῖρα   ἀπέσπασεν
Jesus   stretching out   the(his)   hand   drew

τὴν   μάχαιραν   αὐτοῦ,   καὶ   πατάξας   τὸν
the   sword   of him,   and   striking   the

δοῦλος   τοῦ   ἀρχιερέως   ἀφεῖλεν   αὐτοῦ   τὸ
slave   of the   high priest   cut off   of him   the

ὠτίον.   52 τότε   λέγει   αὐτῷ   ὁ   'Ιησοῦς·
ear.   Then   says   to him   -   Jesus:

ἀπόστρεψον   τὴν   μάχαιράν   σου   εἰς   τὸν
Put back   the   sword   of thee   into   the

τόπον   αὐτῆς·   πάντες   γὰρ   οἱ   λαβόντες
place   of it;   for all   the [ones]   taking

μάχαιραν   ἐν   μαχαίρῃ   ἀπολοῦνται.   53 ἢ
a sword   by   a sword   will perish.

δοκεῖς   ὅτι   οὐ   δύναμαι   παρακαλέσαι
thinkest thou   that   I cannot   *to ask*

τὸν   πατέρα   μου,   καὶ   παραστήσει   μοι
the   Father   of me,   and   he will provide   me

ἄρτι   πλείω   δώδεκα   λεγιῶνας   ἀγγέλων;
now   more [than] twelve   legions   of angels?

54 πῶς   οὖν   πληρωθῶσιν   αἱ   γραφαὶ   ὅτι
how   then   may be fulfilled   the   scriptures   that

οὕτως   δεῖ   γενέσθαι;   55 Ἐν   ἐκείνῃ   τῇ   ὥρᾳ
thus   it must be?   In   that   -   hour

εἶπεν   ὁ   'Ιησοῦς   τοῖς   ὄχλοις·   ὡς   ἐπὶ
said   -   Jesus   to the   crowds: As against

λῃστὴν   ἐξήλθατε   μετὰ   μαχαιρῶν   καὶ
a robber   came ye forth   with   swords   and

ξύλων   συλλαβεῖν   με;   καθ'   ἡμέραν   ἐν
clubs   to take   me?   daily   in

τῷ   ἱερῷ   ἐκαθεζόμην   διδάσκων,   καὶ   οὐκ
the   temple   I sat   teaching,   and   not

ἐκρατήσατέ   με.   56 τοῦτο   δὲ   ὅλον
ye seized   me.   But this   all

γέγονεν   ἵνα   πληρωθῶσιν   αἱ   γραφαὶ
has come to pass   that   may be fulfilled   the   scriptures

τῶν   προφητῶν.   Τότε   οἱ   μαθηταὶ   πάντες
of the   prophets.   Then   the   disciples   all

ἀφέντες   αὐτὸν   ἔφυγον.
leaving   him   fled.

57 Οἱ   δὲ   κρατήσαντες   τὸν   'Ιησοῦν
But the [ones]   having seized   -   Jesus

ἀπήγαγον   πρὸς   Καϊάφαν   τὸν   ἀρχιερέα,
led [him] away   to   Caiaphas   the   high priest,

ὅπου   οἱ   γραμματεῖς   καὶ   οἱ   πρεσβύτεροι
where   the   scribes   and   the   elders

συνήχθησαν.   58 ὁ   δὲ   Πέτρος   ἠκολούθει
were assembled.   -   And   Peter   followed

αὐτῷ   [ἀπὸ]   μακρόθεν   ἕως   τῆς   αὐλῆς
him   from   afar   up to   the   court

τοῦ   ἀρχιερέως,   καὶ   εἰσελθὼν   ἔσω   ἐκάθητο
of the   high priest,   and   entering   within   sat

μετὰ   τῶν   ὑπηρετῶν   ἰδεῖν   τὸ   τέλος.
with   the   attendants   to see   the   end.

59 Οἱ   δὲ   ἀρχιερεῖς   καὶ   τὸ   συνέδριον
And the   chief priests   and   the   council

ὅλον   ἐζήτουν   ψευδομαρτυρίαν   κατὰ   τοῦ
whole   sought   false witness   against   -

---

50 Jesus replied, "Friend, do what you came for."g Then the men stepped forward, seized Jesus and arrested him. 51 With that, one of Jesus' companions reached for his sword, drew it out and struck the servant of the high priest, cutting off his ear. 52 "Put your sword back in its place," Jesus said to him, "for all who draw the sword will die by the sword. 53 Do you think I cannot call on my Father, and he will at once put at my disposal more than twelve legions of angels? 54 But how then would the Scriptures be fulfilled that say it must happen in this way?"

55 At that time Jesus said to the crowd, "Am I leading a rebellion, that you have come out with swords and clubs to capture me? Every day I sat in the temple courts teaching, and you did not arrest me. 56 But this has all taken place that the writings of the prophets might be fulfilled." Then all the disciples deserted him and fled.

Before the Sanhedrin

57 Those who had arrested Jesus took him to Caiaphas, the high priest, where the teachers of the law and the elders had assembled. 58 But Peter followed him at a distance, right up to the courtyard of the high priest. He entered and sat down with the guards to see the outcome.

59 The chief priests and the whole Sanhedrin were looking for false evidence against Jesus so that they

g50 Or "Friend, why have you come?"

Jesus so that they might put him to death, 60but they found none, though many false witnesses came forward. At last two came forward 61and said, "This fellow said, 'I am able to destroy the temple of God and to build it in three days.' " 62The high priest stood up and said, "Have you no answer? What is it that they testify against you?" 63But Jesus was silent. Then the high priest said to him, "I put you under oath before the living God, tell us if you are the Messiah,*p* the Son of God." 64Jesus said to him, "You have said so. But I tell you,

From now on you will see the
Son of Man
seated at the right
hand of Power
and coming on the
clouds
of heaven."

65Then the high priest tore his clothes and said, "He has blasphemed! Why do we still need witnesses? You have now heard his blasphemy. 66What is your verdict?" They answered, "He deserves death." 67Then they spat in his face and struck him; and some slapped him, 68saying, "Prophesy to us, you Messiah!*p* Who is it that struck you?"

Peter's Denial of Jesus

69 Now Peter was sitting outside in the courtyard. A servant-girl came to him and said, "You also were with Jesus the Galilean." 70But he denied it before all of them, saying, "I do not know what you are talking about." 71When he went out to the porch, another servant-girl saw him, and she said to the bystand-

---

Ἰησου ὅπως αὐτὸν θανατώσωσιν, 60 καὶ
Jesus so as him they might put to death, and
οὐχ εὗρον πολλῶν προσελθόντων
did not find[,] many approaching
=when many false witnesses approached.
ψευδομαρτύρων. ὕστερον δὲ προσελθόντες
false witnesses*. But later approaching
δύο 61 εἶπαν· οὗτος ἔφη· δύναμαι κατα-
two said: This man said: I can to de-
λῦσαι τὸν ναὸν τοῦ θεοῦ καὶ διὰ τριῶν
stroy the shrine of God and through(after) three
ἡμερῶν οἰκοδομῆσαι. 62 καὶ ἀναστὰς
days to build. And standing up
ὁ ἀρχιερεὺς εἶπεν αὐτῷ· οὐδὲν
the high priest said to him: Nothing
ἀποκρίνῃ, τί οὗτοί σου κατα-
answerest thou, what these men thee give
μαρτυροῦσιν; 63 ὁ δὲ Ἰησοῦς ἐσιώπα.
evidence against? - But Jesus remained silent.
καὶ ὁ ἀρχιερεὺς εἶπεν αὐτῷ· ἐξορκίζω
And the high priest said to him: I adjure
σε κατὰ τοῦ θεοῦ τοῦ ζῶντος ἵνα ἡμῖν
thee by God the living that us
εἴπῃς εἰ σὺ εἶ ὁ χριστὸς ὁ υἱὸς τοῦ
thou tell if thou art the Christ the Son -
θεοῦ. 64 λέγει αὐτῷ ὁ Ἰησοῦς· σὺ εἶπας·
of God. Says to him - Jesus: Thou saidst;
πλὴν λέγω ὑμῖν, ἀπ' ἄρτι ὄψεσθε τὸν
yet I tell you, from now ye will see the
υἱὸν τοῦ ἀνθρώπου καθήμενον ἐκ
Son - of man sitting on [the]
δεξιῶν τῆς δυνάμεως καὶ ἐρχόμενον
right [hand] of the power and coming
ἐπὶ τῶν νεφελῶν τοῦ οὐρανοῦ. 65 τότε
on the clouds - of heaven. Then
ὁ ἀρχιερεὺς διέρρηξεν τὰ ἱμάτια αὐτοῦ
the high priest rent the garments of him
λέγων· ἐβλασφήμησεν· τί ἔτι χρείαν ἔχομεν
saying: He blasphemed; what yet need have we
μαρτύρων; ἴδε νῦν ἠκούσατε τὴν βλασφη-
of witnesses? behold now ye heard the blas-
μίαν· 66 τί ὑμῖν δοκεῖ; οἱ δὲ ἀπο-
phemy; what to you seems it? And they answer-
κριθέντες εἶπαν· ἔνοχος θανάτου ἐστίν.
ing said: Liable of(to) death he is.
67 Τότε ἐνέπτυσαν εἰς τὸ πρόσωπον αὐτοῦ
Then they spat in the face of him
καὶ ἐκολάφισαν αὐτόν, οἱ δὲ
and violently maltreated him, and they
ἐρράπισαν 68 λέγοντες· προφήτευσον ἡμῖν,
slapped [him] saying: Prophesy thou to us,
χριστέ, τίς ἐστιν ὁ παίσας σε;
Christ, who is it the [one] having struck thee?
69 Ὁ δὲ Πέτρος ἐκάθητο ἔξω ἐν
- And Peter sat outside in
τῇ αὐλῇ· καὶ προσῆλθεν αὐτῷ μία
the court; and approached to him one
παιδίσκη λέγουσα· καὶ σὺ ἦσθα μετὰ
maidservant saying: Also thou wast with
Ἰησοῦ τοῦ Γαλιλαίου. 70 ὁ δὲ ἠρνήσατο
Jesus the Galilæan. But he denied
ἔμπροσθεν πάντων λέγων· οὐκ οἶδα
before all saying: I know not
τί λέγεις. 71 ἐξελθόντα δὲ εἰς τὸν
what thou sayest. And *going out *into *the
πυλῶνα εἶδεν αὐτὸν ἄλλη καὶ λέγει
*porch *saw *him *another and says

---

could put him to death. 60But they did not find any, though many false witnesses came forward. Finally two came forward 61and declared, "This fellow said, 'I am able to destroy the temple of God and rebuild it in three days.' " 62Then the high priest stood up and said to Jesus, "Are you not going to answer? What is this testimony that these men are bringing against you?" 63But Jesus remained silent.

The high priest said to him, "I charge you under oath by the living God: Tell us if you are the Christ,*h* the Son of God."

64"Yes, it is as you say," Jesus replied. "But I say to all of you: In the future you will see the Son of Man sitting at the right hand of the Mighty One and coming on the clouds of heaven."

65Then the high priest tore his clothes and said, "He has spoken blasphemy! Why do we need any more witnesses? Look, now you have heard the blasphemy. 66What do you think?"

"He is worthy of death," they answered.

67Then they spit in his face and struck him with their fists. Others slapped him 68and said, "Prophesy to us, Christ. Who hit you?"

Peter Disowns Jesus

69Now Peter was sitting out in the courtyard, and a servant girl came to him. "You also were with Jesus of Galilee," she said.

70But he denied it before them all. "I don't know what you're talking about," he said.

71Then he went out to the gateway, where another girl saw him and said to the

---

p Or Christ

7porch ²saw ³him ¹another and says

h63 Or Messiah; also in verse 68

ers, "This man was with Jesus of Nazareth."[q] 72 Again he denied it with an oath, "I do not know the man." 73 After a little while the bystanders came up and said to Peter, "Certainly you are also one of them, for your accent betrays you." 74 Then he began to curse, and he swore an oath, "I do not know the man!" At that moment the cock crowed. 75 Then Peter remembered what Jesus had said: "Before the cock crows, you will deny me three times." And he went out and wept bitterly.

τοῖς	ἐκεῖ·	οὗτος	ἦν	μετὰ	Ἰησοῦ	τοῦ
to the [ones]	there:	This man	was	with	Jesus	the

Ναζωραίου.	**72** καὶ	πάλιν	ἠρνήσατο
Nazarene.	And	again	he denied

μετὰ	ὅρκου	ὅτι	οὐκ	οἶδα	τὸν	ἄνθρωπον.
with	an oath[,]	-	I know not	the	man.	

73 μετὰ	μικρὸν	δὲ	προσελθόντες	οἱ
And after a little			approaching	the [ones]

ἑστῶτες	εἶπον	τῷ	Πέτρῳ·	ἀληθῶς	καὶ
standing	said	-	to Peter:	Truly	also

σὺ	ἐξ	αὐτῶν	εἶ,	καὶ	γὰρ	ἡ	λαλιά	σου
thou	of	them	art,	for indeed		the	speech	of thee

δῆλόν	σε	ποιεῖ.	**74** τότε	ἤρξατο	καταθε-
manifest	thee	makes.	Then	he began	to

ματίζειν	καὶ	ὀμνύειν	ὅτι	οὐκ	οἶδα	τὸν
curse	and	to swear[,]	-	I know not	the

ἄνθρωπον.	καὶ	εὐθὺς	ἀλέκτωρ	ἐφώνησεν
man.	And immediately	a cock	crowed.

75 καὶ	ἐμνήσθη	ὁ	Πέτρος	τοῦ	ῥήματος
And	remembered	-	Peter	the	word

Ἰησοῦ	εἰρηκότος	ὅτι	πρὶν	ἀλέκτορα
of Jesus	having said[,]	-	Before	a cock

φωνῆσαι	τρὶς	ἀπαρνήσῃ	με·	καὶ
to crow[b]	three times	thou wilt deny	me;	and

ἐξελθὼν	ἔξω	ἔκλαυσεν	πικρῶς.
going forth	outside	he wept	bitterly.

people there, "This fellow was with Jesus of Nazareth." 72 He denied it again, with an oath: "I don't know the man!" 73 After a little while, those standing there went up to Peter and said, "Surely you are one of them, for your accent gives you away." 74 Then he began to call down curses on himself and he swore to them, "I don't know the man!" Immediately a rooster crowed. 75 Then Peter remembered the word Jesus had spoken: "Before the rooster crows, you will disown me three times." And he went outside and wept bitterly.

Chapter 27

Jesus Brought before Pilate

WHEN morning came, all the chief priests and the elders of the people conferred together against Jesus in order to bring about his death. 2 They bound him, led him away, and handed him over to Pilate the governor.

The Suicide of Judas

3 When Judas, his betrayer, saw that Jesus[r] was condemned, he repented and brought back the thirty pieces of silver to the chief priests and the elders. 4 He said, "I have sinned by betraying innocent[s] blood." But they said, "What is that to us? See to it yourself." 5 Throwing down the pieces of silver in the temple, he departed; and he went and hanged himself. 6 But the chief priests, taking the pieces of silver, said, "It is not lawful to put them into the treasury, since they are blood money." 7 After conferring together, they used them to buy the potter's field as a place to bury for-

---

27 Πρωΐας	δὲ	γενομένης	συμβούλιον
And early morning		coming[a]	counsel
= when early morning came			

ἔλαβον	πάντες	οἱ	ἀρχιερεῖς	καὶ	οἱ
took	all	the	chief priests	and	the

πρεσβύτεροι	τοῦ	λαοῦ	κατὰ	τοῦ
elders	of the	people	against	-

Ἰησοῦ	ὥστε	θανατῶσαι	αὐτόν·	**2** καὶ
Jesus	so as	to put to death	him;	and

δήσαντες	αὐτὸν	ἀπήγαγον	καὶ	παρ-
having bound	him	they led away	and	de-

έδωκαν	Πιλάτῳ	τῷ	ἡγεμόνι.	**3** Τότε
livered	to Pilate	the	governor.	Then

ἰδὼν	Ἰούδας	ὁ	παραδοὺς	αὐτὸν
[5]seeing	[1]Judas	[2]the [one]	[3]having betrayed	[4]him

ὅτι	κατεκρίθη,	μεταμεληθεὶς	ἔστρεψεν	τὰ
that	he was condemned,	repenting	returned	the

τριάκοντα	ἀργύρια	τοῖς	ἀρχιερεῦσιν
thirty	pieces of silver	to the	chief priests

καὶ	πρεσβυτέροις	**4** λέγων·	ἥμαρτον
and	elders	saying:	I sinned

παραδοὺς	αἷμα	ἀθῷον.	οἱ	δὲ	εἶπαν·
betraying	blood	innocent.	But they		said:

τί	πρὸς	ἡμᾶς;	σὺ	ὄψῃ.	**5** καὶ	ῥίψας
What	to	us?	thou	shalt see [to it].	And	tossing

τὰ	ἀργύρια	εἰς	τὸν	ναὸν	ἀν-
the	pieces of silver	into	the	shrine	he

ἐχώρησεν,	καὶ	ἀπελθὼν	ἀπήγξατο.	**6** οἱ
departed,	and	going away	hanged himself.	the

δὲ	ἀρχιερεῖς	λαβόντες	τὰ	ἀργύρια	εἶπαν·
But	chief priests	taking	the	pieces of silver	said:

οὐκ	ἔξεστιν	βαλεῖν	αὐτὰ	εἰς	τὸν
It is not lawful		to put	them	into	the

κορβανᾶν,	ἐπεὶ	τιμὴ	αἵματός	ἐστιν.
treasury,	since	price	of blood	it is.

7 συμβούλιον	δὲ	λαβόντες	ἠγόρασαν	ἐξ
So counsel		taking	they bought	of (with)

αὐτῶν	τὸν	ἀγρὸν	τοῦ	κεραμέως	εἰς	ταφὴν
them	the	field	of the	potter	for	burial

Chapter 27

Judas Hangs Himself

EARLY in the morning, all the chief priests and the elders of the people came to the decision to put Jesus to death. 2 They bound him, led him away and handed him over to Pilate, the governor.

3 When Judas, who had betrayed him, saw that Jesus was condemned, he was seized with remorse and returned the thirty silver coins to the chief priests and the elders. 4 "I have sinned," he said, "for I have betrayed innocent blood."

"What is that to us?" they replied. "That's your responsibility."

5 So Judas threw the money into the temple and left. Then he went away and hanged himself.

6 The chief priests picked up the coins and said, "It is against the law to put this into the treasury, since it is blood money." 7 So they decided to use the money to buy the potter's field as a burial place for foreigners.

---

[q] Gk the Nazorean
[r] Gk he
[s] Other ancient authorities read righteous

eigners. 8 For this reason that field has been called the Field of Blood to this day. 9 Then was fulfilled what had been spoken through the prophet Jeremiah,[t] "And they took[u] the thirty pieces of silver, the price of the one on whom a price had been set,[v] on whom some of the people of Israel had set a price, 10 and they gave[w] them for the potter's field, as the Lord commanded me."

Pilate Questions Jesus

11 Now Jesus stood before the governor; and the governor asked him, "Are you the King of the Jews?" Jesus said, "You say so." 12 But when he was accused by the chief priests and elders, he did not answer. 13 Then Pilate said to him, "Do you not hear how many accusations they make against you?" 14 But he gave him no answer, not even to a single charge, so that the governor was greatly amazed.

Barabbas or Jesus?

15 Now at the festival the governor was accustomed to release a prisoner for the crowd, anyone whom they wanted. 16 At that time they had a notorious prisoner, called Jesus[x] Barabbas. 17 So after they had gathered, Pilate said to them, "Whom do you want me to release for you, Jesus[x] Barabbas or Jesus who is called the Messiah?"[y] 18 For he realized that it was out of jealousy that they had handed him over. 19 While he was sitting on the judgment seat, his wife sent word to him, "Have nothing to do with that innocent man, for today I have suffered a great deal because of a dream

---

τοῖς　ξένοις.　8 διὸ　ἐκλήθη　ὁ　ἀγρὸς
for the　strangers.　Wherefore　was called　-　field
ἐκεῖνος　ἀγρὸς　αἵματος　ἕως　τῆς　σήμερον.
that　Field　of blood　until　-　to-day.
9 τότε　ἐπληρώθη　τὸ　ῥηθὲν　διὰ
Then　was fulfilled　the [thing]　spoken　through
Ἰερεμίου　τοῦ　προφήτου　λέγοντος·　καὶ
Jeremiah　the　prophet　saying:　And
ἔλαβον　τὰ　τριάκοντα　ἀργύρια,　τὴν
they took　the　thirty　pieces of silver,　the
τιμὴν　τοῦ　τετιμημένου　ὃν　ἐτιμήσαντο
price　of the [one] having been priced　whom　they priced
ἀπὸ　υἱῶν　Ἰσραήλ,　10 καὶ　ἔδωκαν
from [the] sons　of Israel,　and　gave
αὐτὰ　εἰς　τὸν　ἀγρὸν　τοῦ　κεραμέως,　καθὰ
them　for　the　field　of the　potter,　as
συνέταξέν　μοι　κύριος.　11 Ὁ　δὲ
directed　me　[the] Lord.　-　And
Ἰησοῦς　ἐστάθη　ἔμπροσθεν　τοῦ　ἡγεμόνος·
Jesus　stood　before　the　governor;
καὶ　ἐπηρώτησεν　αὐτὸν　ὁ　ἡγεμὼν　λέγων·
and　questioned　him　the　governor　saying:
σὺ　εἶ　ὁ　βασιλεὺς　τῶν　Ἰουδαίων;　ὁ δὲ
Thou art　the　king　of the　Jews?　- And
Ἰησοῦς　ἔφη·　σὺ　λέγεις.　12 καὶ　ἐν
Jesus　said:　Thou　sayest.　And　in
τῷ　κατηγορεῖσθαι　αὐτὸν　ὑπὸ　τῶν
the　to be accused = as he was accused　him[e]　by　the
ἀρχιερέων　καὶ　πρεσβυτέρων　οὐδὲν
chief priests　and　elders　nothing
ἀπεκρίνατο. 13 τότε λέγει αὐτῷ ὁ Πιλᾶτος·
he answered.　Then　says　to him　-　Pilate:
οὐκ　ἀκούεις　πόσα　σου　κατα-
Hearest thou not　what things　[a]thee　[1]they
μαρτυροῦσιν;　14 καὶ　οὐκ　ἀπεκρίθη　αὐτῷ
[2]give evidence against?　And　he answered not　him
πρὸς　οὐδὲ　ἓν　ῥῆμα,　ὥστε　θαυμάζειν
to　not　one　word,　so as = so that the governor marvelled　to marvel
τὸν　ἡγεμόνα　λίαν.　15 Κατὰ　δὲ　ἑορτὴν
the　governor[b] exceedingly.　Now at　a feast
εἰώθει　ὁ　ἡγεμὼν　ἀπολύειν　ἕνα　τῷ　ὄχλῳ
was accustomed　the　governor　to release　[a]one [1]to the [2]crowd
δέσμιον　ὃν·　ἤθελον.　16 εἶχον　δὲ　τότε
[4]prisoner　whom　they wished.　And they had　then
δέσμιον　ἐπίσημον　λεγόμενον　Βαραββᾶν.
prisoner　a notable　named　Barabbas.
17 συνηγμένων　οὖν　αὐτῶν　εἶπεν　αὐτοῖς
Therefore having assembled　them[a]　said　to them
= when they were assembled
ὁ　Πιλᾶτος·　τίνα　θέλετε　ἀπολύσω
-　Pilate:　Whom　do ye wish　I may release
ὑμῖν,　[τὸν]　Βαραββᾶν　ἢ　Ἰησοῦν　τὸν
to you,　-　Barabbas　or　Jesus　-
λεγόμενον　χριστόν;　18 ᾔδει　γὰρ　ὅτι
called　Christ?　for he knew　that
διὰ　φθόνον　παρέδωκαν　αὐτόν.　19 Καθη-
because of envy　they delivered　him.　sit-
μένου　δὲ　αὐτοῦ　ἐπὶ　τοῦ　βήματος
ting　Now　him[a]　on　the　tribunal
= Now as he sat
ἀπέστειλεν　πρὸς　αὐτὸν　ἡ　γυνὴ　αὐτοῦ
sent　to　him　the　wife　of him
λέγουσα·　μηδὲν　σοὶ　καὶ　τῷ　δικαίῳ
saying:　Nothing　to thee　and　just man
ἐκείνῳ·　πολλὰ　γὰρ　ἔπαθον　σήμερον　κατ'
to that;　for many things　I suffered　to-day　by

---

8 That is why it has been called the Field of Blood to this day. 9 Then what was spoken by Jeremiah the prophet was fulfilled: "They took the thirty silver coins, the price set on him by the people of Israel, 10 and they used them to buy the potter's field, as the Lord commanded me."[i]

Jesus Before Pilate

11 Meanwhile Jesus stood before the governor, and the governor asked him, "Are you the king of the Jews?"

"Yes, it is as you say," Jesus replied.

12 When he was accused by the chief priests and the elders, he gave no answer. 13 Then Pilate asked him, "Don't you hear the testimony they are bringing against you?" 14 But Jesus made no reply, not even to a single charge—to the great amazement of the governor.

15 Now it was the governor's custom at the Feast to release a prisoner chosen by the crowd. 16 At that time they had a notorious prisoner, called Barabbas. 17 So when the crowd had gathered, Pilate asked them, "Which one do you want me to release to you: Barabbas, or Jesus who is called Christ?" 18 For he knew it was out of envy that they had handed Jesus over to him.

19 While Pilate was sitting on the judge's seat, his wife sent him this message: "Don't have anything to do with that innocent man, for I have suffered a great deal

---

[t] Other ancient authorities read *Zechariah* or *Isaiah*
[u] Or *I took*
[v] Or *the price of the precious One*
[w] Other ancient authorities read *I gave*
[x] Other ancient authorities lack *Jesus*
[y] Or *the Christ*

[i]10 See Zech. 11:12,13; Jer. 19:1-13; 32:6-9.

about him." 20 Now the chief priests and the elders persuaded the crowds to ask for Barabbas and to have Jesus killed. 21 The governor again said to them, "Which of the two do you want me to release for you?" And they said, "Barabbas." 22 Pilate said to them, "Then what should I do with Jesus who is called the Messiah?" y All of them said, "Let him be crucified!" 23 Then he asked, "Why, what evil has he done?" But they shouted all the more, "Let him be crucified!"

Pilate Hands Jesus over to Be Crucified

24 So when Pilate saw that he could do nothing, but rather that a riot was beginning, he took some water and washed his hands before the crowd, saying, "I am innocent of this man's blood; z see to it yourselves." 25 Then the people as a whole answered, "His blood be on us and on our children!" 26 So he released Barabbas for them; and after flogging Jesus, he handed him over to be crucified.

The Soldiers Mock Jesus

27 Then the soldiers of the governor took Jesus into the governor's headquarters, a and they gathered the whole cohort around him. 28 They stripped him and put a scarlet robe on him, 29 and after twisting some thorns into a crown, they put it on his head. They put a reed in his right hand and knelt before him and mocked him, saying, "Hail, King of the Jews!" 30 They spat on him, and took the reed and struck him on the head. 31 After mocking him, they

z Other ancient authorities read *this righteous blood,* or *this righteous man's blood*
a Gk *the praetorium*

ὄναρ   δι᾽   αὐτόν.　**20** Οἱ δὲ ἀρχιερεῖς
a dream because of him.　　　But the　 chief priests

καὶ   οἱ   πρεσβύτεροι   ἔπεισαν   τοὺς
and the   elders   persuaded   the

ὄχλους   ἵνα   αἰτήσωνται   τὸν Βαραββᾶν,
crowds that they should ask   -   Barabbas,

τὸν δὲ ᾽Ιησοῦν ἀπολέσωσιν.　**21** ἀπο-
 - and Jesus should destroy.　　　So

κριθεὶς   δὲ   ὁ   ἡγεμὼν   εἶπεν   αὐτοῖς·
answering   the governor   said   to them:

τίνα θέλετε ἀπὸ τῶν δύο ἀπολύσω
Which do ye wish from the two I may release

ὑμῖν;   οἱ   δὲ   εἶπαν·   τὸν   Βαραββᾶν.
to you? And they   said: -   Barabbas.

22 λέγει αὐτοῖς ὁ Πιλᾶτος· τί οὖν
 Says   to them   -   Pilate: What then

ποιήσω ᾽Ιησοῦν τὸν λεγόμενον χριστόν;
may I do [to] Jesus   -   called   Christ?

λέγουσιν πάντες·   σταυρωθήτω.　**23** ὁ δὲ
They say   all: Let him be crucified.　　 But he

ἔφη· τί γὰρ κακὸν ἐποίησεν;   οἱ   δὲ
said: Why what evil   did he?   But they

περισσῶς ἔκραζον λέγοντες· σταυρω-
 more   cried out   saying: Let him be

θήτω.　**24** ἰδὼν δὲ ὁ Πιλᾶτος ὅτι οὐδὲν
crucified.　 And seeing   - Pilate   that nothing

ὠφελεῖ ἀλλὰ μᾶλλον θόρυβος γίνεται,
is gained but rather   an uproar   occurs,

λαβὼν ὕδωρ ἀπενίψατο τὰς χεῖρας
taking water he washed the(his) hands

κατέναντι τοῦ ὄχλου λέγων· ἀθῷός
in front of the   crowd   saying: Innocent

εἰμι ἀπὸ τοῦ αἵματος τούτου· ὑμεῖς
I am from the   blood   of this man; ye

ὄψεσθε.　**25** καὶ ἀποκριθεὶς πᾶς ὁ λαὸς
will see [to it].　And answering   all the people

εἶπεν· τὸ αἷμα αὐτοῦ ἐφ᾽ ἡμᾶς καὶ
said: The blood of him on   us   and

ἐπὶ τὰ τέκνα ἡμῶν.　**26** τότε ἀπέλυσεν
on the children of us.　　 Then he released

αὐτοῖς τὸν Βαραββᾶν, τὸν δὲ ᾽Ιησοῦν
to them   -   Barabbas,   -   but Jesus

φραγελλώσας παρέδωκεν ἵνα σταυρωθῇ.
having scourged he delivered that he might be crucified.

27 Τότε οἱ στρατιῶται τοῦ ἡγεμόνος
 Then the soldiers   of the   governor

παραλαβόντες τὸν ᾽Ιησοῦν εἰς τὸ πραιτώ-
having taken   -   Jesus   into the   præ-

ριον συνήγαγον ἐπ᾽ αὐτὸν ὅλην τὴν
torium assembled against him   all   the

σπεῖραν.　**28** καὶ ἐκδύσαντες αὐτὸν χλαμίδα
 band.　　 And stripping   him   cloak

κοκκίνην περιέθηκαν αὐτῷ,　**29** καὶ
a purple   they placed round him,　　and

πλέξαντες στέφανον ἐξ ἀκανθῶν ἐπέθηκαν
having plaited a crown of thorns they placed [it] on

ἐπὶ τῆς κεφαλῆς αὐτοῦ καὶ κάλαμον
on the   head   of him and   a reed

ἐν τῇ δεξιᾷ αὐτοῦ, καὶ γονυπετή-
in the right [hand] of him, and   bowing

σαντες ἔμπροσθεν αὐτοῦ ἐνέπαιξαν αὐτῷ
the knee in front of   him   mocked   at him

λέγοντες· χαῖρε, βασιλεῦ τῶν ᾽Ιουδαίων,
 saying: Hail,   king   of the   Jews,

30 καὶ ἐμπτύσαντες εἰς αὐτὸν ἔλαβον
 and   spitting   at   him   took

---

today in a dream because of him."

20 But the chief priests and the elders persuaded the crowd to ask for Barabbas and to have Jesus executed.

21 "Which of the two do you want me to release to you?" asked the governor.

"Barabbas," they answered.

22 "What shall I do, then, with Jesus who is called Christ?" Pilate asked.

They all answered, "Crucify him!"

23 "Why? What crime has he committed?" asked Pilate.

But they shouted all the louder, "Crucify him!"

24 When Pilate saw that he was getting nowhere, but that instead an uproar was starting, he took water and washed his hands in front of the crowd. "I am innocent of this man's blood," he said. "It is your responsibility!"

25 All the people answered, "Let his blood be on us and on our children!"

26 Then he released Barabbas to them. But he had Jesus flogged, and handed him over to be crucified.

The Soldiers Mock Jesus

27 Then the governor's soldiers took Jesus into the Praetorium and gathered the whole company of soldiers around him. 28 They stripped him and put a scarlet robe on him, 29 and then twisted together a crown of thorns and set it on his head. They put a staff in his right hand and knelt in front of him and mocked him. "Hail, king of the Jews!" they said. 30 They spit on him, and took the staff and struck him on the head again and again. 31 After they had mocked him, they

stripped him of the robe and put his own clothes on him. Then they led him away to crucify him.

The Crucifixion of Jesus

32 As they went out, they came upon a man from Cyrene named Simon; they compelled this man to carry his cross. 33 And when they came to a place called Golgotha (which means Place of a Skull), 34 they offered him wine to drink, mixed with gall; but when he tasted it, he would not drink it. 35 And when they had crucified him, they divided his clothes among themselves by casting lots;[b] 36 then they sat down there and kept watch over him. 37 Over his head they put the charge against him, which read, "This is Jesus, the King of the Jews."

38 Then two bandits were crucified with him, one on his right and one on his left. 39 Those who passed by derided[c] him, shaking their heads 40 and saying, "You who would destroy the temple and build it in three days, save yourself! If you are the Son of God, come down from the cross." 41 In the same way the chief priests also, along with the scribes and elders, were mocking him, saying, 42 "He saved others; he cannot save himself.[d] He is the King of Israel; let him come down from the cross now, and we will believe in him. 43 He trusts in God; let God deliv-

---

τὸν κάλαμον καὶ ἔτυπτον εἰς τὴν κεφαλὴν
the reed and struck at the head

αὐτοῦ. 31 καὶ ὅτε ἐνέπαιξαν αὐτῷ,
of him. And when they mocked at him,

ἐξέδυσαν αὐτὸν τὴν χλαμύδα καὶ ἐνέδυσαν
they took off him the cloak and put on

αὐτὸν τὰ ἱμάτια αὐτοῦ, καὶ ἀπήγαγον
him the garments of him, and led away

αὐτὸν εἰς τὸ σταυρῶσαι. 32 Ἐξερχόμενοι
him - - to crucify. going forth

δὲ εὗρον ἄνθρωπον Κυρηναῖον, ὀνό-
And they found a man a Cyrenian, by

ματι Σίμωνα· τοῦτον ἠγγάρευσαν ἵνα
name Simon; this man they impressed that

ἄρῃ τὸν σταυρὸν αὐτοῦ. 33 Καὶ
he should bear the cross of him. And

ἐλθόντες εἰς τόπον λεγόμενον Γολγοθά,
coming to a place called Golgotha,

ὃ ἐστιν κρανίου τόπος λεγόμενος,
which is ²of a skull ³A place ¹called,

34 ἔδωκαν αὐτῷ πιεῖν οἶνον μετὰ
they gave him to drink wine with

χολῆς μεμιγμένον· καὶ γευσάμενος οὐκ
gall having been mixed; and tasting not

ἠθέλησεν πιεῖν. 35 σταυρώσαντες δὲ
he would to drink. And having crucified

αὐτὸν διεμερίσαντο τὰ ἱμάτια αὐτοῦ
him they divided the garments of him

βάλλοντες κλῆρον, 36 καὶ καθήμενοι ἐτήρουν
casting a lot, and sitting they guarded

αὐτὸν ἐκεῖ. 37 καὶ ἐπέθηκαν ἐπάνω
him there. And they placed on above

τῆς κεφαλῆς αὐτοῦ τὴν αἰτίαν αὐτοῦ
the head of him the charge of him

γεγραμμένην· ΟΥΤΟΣ ΕΣΤΙΝ ΙΗΣΟΥΣ
having been written: THIS IS JESUS

Ο ΒΑΣΙΛΕΥΣ ΤΩΝ ΙΟΥΔΑΙΩΝ. 38 Τότε
THE KING OF THE JEWS. Then

σταυροῦνται σὺν αὐτῷ δύο λῃσταί,
are crucified with him two robbers,

εἷς ἐκ δεξιῶν καὶ εἷς ἐξ εὐωνύμων.
one on [the] right and one on [the] left.

39 Οἱ δὲ παραπορευόμενοι ἐβλασφήμουν
And the [ones] passing by blasphemed

αὐτὸν κινοῦντες τὰς κεφαλὰς αὐτῶν
him wagging the heads of them

40 καὶ λέγοντες· ὁ καταλύων τὸν ναὸν
and saying: The [one] destroying the shrine

καὶ ἐν τρισὶν ἡμέραις οἰκοδομῶν,
and in three days building [it],

σῶσον σεαυτόν, εἰ υἱὸς εἶ τοῦ θεοῦ,
save thyself, if Son thou art - of God,

καὶ κατάβηθι ἀπὸ τοῦ σταυροῦ. 41 ὁμοίως
and come down from the cross. Likewise

[καὶ] οἱ ἀρχιερεῖς ἐμπαίζοντες μετὰ
also the chief priests mocking with

τῶν γραμματέων καὶ πρεσβυτέρων ἔλεγον
the scribes and elders said:

42 ἄλλους ἔσωσεν, ἑαυτὸν οὐ δύναται
Others he saved, himself he cannot

σῶσαι· βασιλεὺς Ἰσραήλ ἐστιν,
to save; King of Israel he is,

καταβάτω νῦν ἀπὸ τοῦ σταυροῦ καὶ
let him come down now from the cross and

πιστεύσομεν ἐπ' αὐτόν. 43 πέποιθεν
we will believe on him. He has trusted

---

took off the robe and put his own clothes on him. Then they led him away to crucify him.

The Crucifixion

32 As they were going out, they met a man from Cyrene, named Simon, and they forced him to carry the cross. 33 They came to a place called Golgotha (which means The Place of the Skull). 34 There they offered Jesus wine to drink, mixed with gall; but after tasting it, he refused to drink it. 35 When they had crucified him, they divided up his clothes by casting lots.[j] 36 And sitting down, they kept watch over him there. 37 Above his head they placed the written charge against him: THIS IS JESUS, THE KING OF THE JEWS. 38 Two robbers were crucified with him, one on his right and one on his left. 39 Those who passed by hurled insults at him, shaking their heads 40 and saying, "You who are going to destroy the temple and build it in three days, save yourself! Come down from the cross, if you are the Son of God!" 41 In the same way the chief priests, the teachers of the law and the elders mocked him. 42 "He saved others," they said, "but he can't save himself! He's the King of Israel! Let him come down now from the cross, and we will believe in him. 43 He trusts in God.

---

[b] Other ancient authorities add *in order that what had been spoken through the prophet might be fulfilled,* "They divided my clothes among themselves, and for my clothing they cast lots."

[c] Or *blasphemed*

[d] Or *is he unable to save himself?*

---

[j] 35 A few late manuscripts *lots that the word spoken by the prophet might be fulfilled: "They divided my garments among themselves and cast lots for my clothing"* (Psalm 22:18)

er him now, if he wants to; for he said, 'I am God's Son.' " 44 The bandits who were crucified with him also taunted him in the same way.

The Death of Jesus

45 From noon on, darkness came over the whole land^e until three in the afternoon. 46 And about three o'clock Jesus cried with a loud voice, "Eli, Eli, lema sabachthani?" that is, "My God, my God, why have you forsaken me?" 47 When some of the bystanders heard it, they said, "This man is calling for Elijah." 48 At once one of them ran and got a sponge, filled it with sour wine, put it on a stick, and gave it to him to drink. 49 But the others said, "Wait, let us see whether Elijah will come to save him."^f 50 Then Jesus cried again with a loud voice and breathed his last.^g 51 At that moment the curtain of the temple was torn in two, from top to bottom. The earth shook, and the rocks were split. 52 The tombs were also opened, and many bodies of the saints who had fallen asleep were raised. 53 After his resurrection they came out of the tombs and entered the holy city and appeared to many. 54 Now when the centurion and those with him, who were keeping watch over Jesus, saw the earthquake and what took place, they were terrified and said, "Truly this man was God's Son!"^h 55 Many women were

ἐπὶ τὸν θεόν, ῥυσάσθω νῦν εἰ θέλει
on - God, let him rescue now if he wants

αὐτόν· εἶπεν γὰρ ὅτι θεοῦ εἰμι υἱός.
him; for he said[,] - of God I am Son.

44 τὸ δ' αὐτὸ καὶ οἱ λῃσταὶ οἱ συσταυρω-
And the same also the robbers - crucified

θέντες σὺν αὐτῷ ὠνείδιζον αὐτόν. 45 Ἀπὸ
with with him reproached him. from

δὲ ἕκτης ὥρας σκότος ἐγένετο ἐπὶ
Now [the] sixth hour darkness occurred over

πᾶσαν τὴν γῆν ἕως ὥρας ἐνάτης.
all the land until hour [the] ninth.

46 περὶ δὲ τὴν ἐνάτην ὥραν ἀνεβόησεν ὁ
And about the ninth hour cried out

Ἰησοῦς φωνῇ μεγάλῃ λέγων· ἠλὶ ἠλὶ
Jesus voice with a great saying: Eli Eli

λεμὰ σαβαχθάνι; τοῦτ' ἔστιν· θεέ μου
lema sabachthani? this is: God of me,

θεέ μου, ἱνατί με ἐγκατέλιπες; 47 τινὲς
God of me, why me didst thou forsake? some

δὲ τῶν ἐκεῖ ἑστηκότων ἀκούσαντες
And of the [ones] there standing hearing

ἔλεγον ὅτι Ἡλίαν φωνεῖ οὗτος.
said[,] Elias calls this man.

48 καὶ εὐθέως δραμὼν εἷς ἐξ αὐτῶν καὶ
And immediately running one of them and

λαβὼν σπόγγον πλήσας τε ὄξους καὶ
taking a sponge and filling of(with) vinegar and

περιθεὶς καλάμῳ ἐπότιζεν αὐτόν.
putting [it] round a reed gave to drink him.

49 οἱ δὲ λοιποὶ εἶπαν· ἄφες ἴδωμεν
But the rest said: Leave[,] let us see

εἰ ἔρχεται Ἡλίας σώσων αὐτόν. 50 ὁ
if comes Elias saving him.

δὲ Ἰησοῦς πάλιν κράξας φωνῇ
And Jesus again crying out voice

μεγάλῃ ἀφῆκεν τὸ πνεῦμα. 51 Καὶ
with a great released the(his) spirit. And

ἰδοὺ τὸ καταπέτασμα τοῦ ναοῦ ἐσχίσθη
behold the veil of the shrine was rent

[ἀπ'] ἄνωθεν ἕως κάτω εἰς δύο, καὶ ἡ
from above to below in two, and the

γῆ ἐσείσθη, καὶ αἱ πέτραι ἐσχί-
earth was shaken, and the rocks were

θησαν, 52 καὶ τὰ μνημεῖα ἀνεῴχθησαν
rent, and the tombs were opened

καὶ πολλὰ σώματα τῶν κεκοιμημένων
and many bodies of the having fallen asleep

ἁγίων ἠγέρθησαν· 53 καὶ ἐξελθόντες
saints were raised; and coming forth

ἐκ τῶν μνημείων μετὰ τὴν ἔγερσιν
out of the tombs after the rising

αὐτοῦ εἰσῆλθον εἰς τὴν ἁγίαν πόλιν καὶ
of him entered into the holy city and

ἐνεφανίσθησαν πολλοῖς. 54 Ὁ δὲ ἑκατόν-
appeared to many. And the centu-

ταρχος καὶ οἱ μετ' αὐτοῦ τηροῦντες
rion and the [ones] with him guarding

τὸν Ἰησοῦν ἰδόντες τὸν σεισμὸν καὶ
- Jesus seeing the earthquake and

τὰ γινόμενα ἐφοβήθησαν σφόδρα,
the things happening feared exceedingly,

λέγοντες· ἀληθῶς θεοῦ υἱὸς ἦν οὗτος.
saying: Truly of God Son was this man.

55 Ἦσαν δὲ ἐκεῖ γυναῖκες πολλαὶ
Now there were there women many

Let God rescue him now if he wants, for he said, 'I am the Son of God.' " 44 In the same way the robbers who were crucified with him also heaped insults on him.

The Death of Jesus

45 From the sixth hour until the ninth hour darkness came over all the land. 46 About the ninth hour Jesus cried out in a loud voice, "Eloi, Eloi,^k lama sabachthani?"—which means, "My God, my God, why have you forsaken me?"^l 47 When some of those standing there heard this, they said, "He's calling Elijah." 48 Immediately one of them ran and got a sponge. He filled it with wine vinegar, put it on a stick, and offered it to Jesus to drink. 49 The rest said, "Now leave him alone. Let's see if Elijah comes to save him." 50 And when Jesus had cried out again in a loud voice, he gave up his spirit. 51 At that moment the curtain of the temple was torn in two from top to bottom. The earth shook and the rocks split. 52 The tombs broke open and the bodies of many holy people who had died were raised to life. 53 They came out of the tombs, and after Jesus' resurrection they went into the holy city and appeared to many people. 54 When the centurion and those with him who were guarding Jesus saw the earthquake and all that had happened, they were terrified, and exclaimed, "Surely he was the Son^m of God!" 55 Many women were

---

^e Or earth
^f Other ancient authorities add *And another took a spear and pierced his side, and out came water and blood*
^g Or *gave up his spirit*
^h Or *a son of God*

^k 46 Some manuscripts *Eli, Eli*
^l 46 Psalm 22:1
^m 54 Or *a son*

also there, looking on from a distance; they had followed Jesus from Galilee and had provided for him. 56 Among them were Mary Magdalene, and Mary the mother of James and Joseph, and the mother of the sons of Zebedee.

The Burial of Jesus

57 When it was evening, there came a rich man from Arimathea, named Joseph, who was also a disciple of Jesus. 58 He went to Pilate and asked for the body of Jesus; then Pilate ordered it to be given to him. 59 So Joseph took the body and wrapped it in a clean linen cloth 60 and laid it in his own new tomb, which he had hewn in the rock. He then rolled a great stone to the door of the tomb and went away. 61 Mary Magdalene and the other Mary were there, sitting opposite the tomb.

The Guard at the Tomb

62 The next day, that is, after the day of Preparation, the chief priests and the Pharisees gathered before Pilate 63 and said, "Sir, we remember what that impostor said while he was still alive, 'After three days I will rise again.' 64 Therefore command the tomb to be made secure until the third day; otherwise his disciples may go and steal him away, and tell the people, 'He has been raised from the dead,' and the last deception would be worse than the first." 65 Pilate said to them, "You have a

ἀπὸ μακρόθεν θεωροῦσαι, αἵτινες ἠκολού-
from afar beholding, who followed

θησαν τῷ Ἰησοῦ ἀπὸ τῆς Γαλιλαίας
- Jesus from - Galilee

διακονοῦσαι αὐτῷ· 56 ἐν αἷς ἦν
ministering to him; among whom was

Μαρία ἡ Μαγδαληνή, καὶ Μαρία ἡ
Mary the Magdalene, and Mary the

τοῦ Ἰακώβου καὶ Ἰωσὴφ μήτηρ, καὶ ἡ
- of James and of Joseph mother, and the

μήτηρ τῶν υἱῶν Ζεβεδαίου.
mother of the sons of Zebedee.

57 Ὀψίας δὲ γενομένης ἦλθεν ἄνθρωπος
Now evening having come[a] came man
= when evening had come

πλούσιος ἀπὸ Ἀριμαθαίας, τοὔνομα Ἰωσήφ,
a rich from Arimathæa, the name Joseph,

ὃς καὶ αὐτὸς ἐμαθητεύθη τῷ Ἰησοῦ·
who also himself was discipled - to Jesus;

58 οὗτος προσελθὼν τῷ Πιλάτῳ ἠτήσατο
this man approaching - to Pilate asked

τὸ σῶμα τοῦ Ἰησοῦ. τότε ὁ Πιλᾶτος
the body - of Jesus. Then - Pilate

ἐκέλευσεν ἀποδοθῆναι. 59 καὶ λαβὼν
commanded [it] to be given [him]. And taking

τὸ σῶμα ὁ Ἰωσὴφ ἐνετύλιξεν αὐτὸ [ἐν]
the body - Joseph wrapped it in

σινδόνι καθαρᾷ, 60 καὶ ἔθηκεν αὐτὸ ἐν
sheet a clean, and placed it in

τῷ καινῷ αὐτοῦ μνημείῳ ὃ ἐλατό-
the new of him tomb which he

μησεν ἐν τῇ πέτρᾳ, καὶ προσκυλίσας
hewed in the rock, and having rolled to

λίθον μέγαν τῇ θύρᾳ τοῦ μνημείου
stone a great to the door of the tomb

ἀπῆλθεν. 61 Ἦν δὲ ἐκεῖ Μαριὰμ
went away. And there was there Mary

ἡ Μαγδαληνὴ καὶ ἡ ἄλλη Μαρία,
the Magdalene and the other Mary,

καθήμεναι ἀπέναντι τοῦ τάφου. 62 Τῇ
sitting opposite the grave. on the

δὲ ἐπαύριον, ἥτις ἐστὶν μετὰ τὴν παρα-
And morrow, which is after the prepara-

σκευήν, συνήχθησαν οἱ ἀρχιερεῖς
tion, were assembled the chief priests

καὶ οἱ Φαρισαῖοι πρὸς Πιλᾶτον 63 λέ-
and the Pharisees to Pilate say-

γοντες· κύριε, ἐμνήσθημεν ὅτι ἐκεῖνος
ing: Sir, we remembered that that

ὁ πλάνος εἶπεν ἔτι ζῶν· μετὰ τρεῖς
- deceiver said yet living: After three

ἡμέρας ἐγείρομαι. 64 κέλευσον οὖν
days I am raised. Command therefore

ἀσφαλισθῆναι τὸν τάφον ἕως τῆς
to be made fast the grave until the

τρίτης ἡμέρας, μήποτε ἐλθόντες οἱ μαθηταὶ
third day, lest coming the disciples

κλέψωσιν αὐτὸν καὶ εἴπωσιν τῷ λαῷ·
may steal him and may say to the people:

ἠγέρθη ἀπὸ τῶν νεκρῶν, καὶ ἔσται
He was raised from the dead, and will be

ἡ ἐσχάτη πλάνη χείρων τῆς πρώτης.
the last deceit worse [than] the first.

65 ἔφη αὐτοῖς ὁ Πιλᾶτος· ἔχετε κου-
Said to them - Pilate: Ye have a

there, watching from a distance. They had followed Jesus from Galilee to care for his needs. 56 Among them were Mary Magdalene, Mary the mother of James and Joses, and the mother of Zebedee's sons.

The Burial of Jesus

57 As evening approached, there came a rich man from Arimathea, named Joseph, who had himself become a disciple of Jesus. 58 Going to Pilate, he asked for Jesus' body, and Pilate ordered that it be given to him. 59 Joseph took the body, wrapped it in a clean linen cloth, 60 and placed it in his own new tomb that he had cut out of the rock. He rolled a big stone in front of the entrance to the tomb and went away. 61 Mary Magdalene and the other Mary were sitting there opposite the tomb.

The Guard at the Tomb

62 The next day, the one after Preparation Day, the chief priests and the Pharisees went to Pilate. 63 "Sir," they said, "we remember that while he was still alive that deceiver said, 'After three days I will rise again.' 64 So give the order for the tomb to be made secure until the third day. Otherwise, his disciples may come and steal the body and tell the people that he has been raised from the dead. This last deception will be worse than the first."

65 "Take a guard," Pilate answered. "Go, make the

guard[i] of soldiers; go, make it as secure as you can."[j] 66 So they went with the guard and made the tomb secure by sealing the stone.

Chapter 28

The Resurrection of Jesus

AFTER the sabbath, as the first day of the week was dawning, Mary Magdalene and the other Mary went to see the tomb. 2 And suddenly there was a great earthquake; for an angel of the Lord, descending from heaven, came and rolled back the stone and sat on it. 3 His appearance was like lightning, and his clothing white as snow. 4 For fear of him the guards shook and became like dead men. 5 But the angel said to the women, "Do not be afraid; I know that you are looking for Jesus who was crucified. 6 He is not here; for he has been raised, as he said. Come, see the place where he[k] lay. 7 Then go quickly and tell his disciples, 'He has been raised from the dead,[l] and indeed he is going ahead of you to Galilee; there you will see him.' This is my message for you." 8 So they left the tomb quickly with fear and great joy, and ran to tell his disciples. 9 Suddenly Jesus met them and said, "Greetings!" And they came to him, took hold of his feet, and worshiped him. 10 Then

στωδίαν· ὑπάγετε ἀσφαλίσασθε ὡς οἴδατε.
guard; go ye make fast as ye know*.

66 οἱ δὲ πορευθέντες ἠσφαλίσαντο τὸν
And they going made fast the

τάφον σφραγίσαντες τὸν λίθον μετὰ τῆς
grave sealing the stone with the

κουστωδίας.
guard.

28 Ὀψὲ δὲ σαββάτων, τῇ ἐπιφωσκούσῃ
But late of [the] sabbaths, at the drawing on

εἰς μίαν σαββάτων, ἦλθεν Μαριὰμ ἡ
toward one of [the] sabbaths, came Mary the
= the first day of the week,

Μαγδαληνὴ καὶ ἡ ἄλλη Μαρία θεωρῆσαι
Magdalene and the other Mary to view

τὸν τάφον. 2 καὶ ἰδοὺ σεισμὸς ἐγένετο
the grave. And behold earthquake occurred

μέγας· ἄγγελος γὰρ κυρίου καταβὰς
a great; for an angel of [the] Lord descending

ἐξ οὐρανοῦ καὶ προσελθὼν ἀπεκύλισεν
out of heaven and approaching rolled away

τὸν λίθον καὶ ἐκάθητο ἐπάνω αὐτοῦ.
the stone and sat upon it.

3 ἦν δὲ ἡ εἰδέα αὐτοῦ ὡς ἀστραπή,
And was the appearance of him as lightning,

καὶ τὸ ἔνδυμα αὐτοῦ λευκὸν ὡς χιών.
and the dress of him white as snow.

4 ἀπὸ δὲ τοῦ φόβου αὐτοῦ ἐσείσθησαν
And from the fear of him were shaken

οἱ τηροῦντες καὶ ἐγενήθησαν ὡς
the [ones] guarding and they became as

νεκροί. 5 ἀποκριθεὶς δὲ ὁ ἄγγελος
dead. And answering the angel

εἶπεν ταῖς γυναιξίν· μὴ φοβεῖσθε ὑμεῖς·
said to the women: Fear not ye;

οἶδα γὰρ ὅτι Ἰησοῦν τὸν ἐσταυρω-
for I know that Jesus the [one] having been

μένον ζητεῖτε· 6 οὐκ ἔστιν ὧδε·
crucified ye seek; he is not here;

ἠγέρθη γὰρ καθὼς εἶπεν· δεῦτε ἴδετε τὸν
for he was raised as he said; come see ye the

τόπον ὅπου ἔκειτο. 7 καὶ ταχὺ πορευθεῖσαι
place where he lay. And quickly going

εἴπατε τοῖς μαθηταῖς αὐτοῦ ὅτι ἠγέρθη
tell the disciples of him that he was raised

ἀπὸ τῶν νεκρῶν, καὶ ἰδοὺ προάγει ὑμᾶς
from the dead, and behold he goes before you

εἰς τὴν Γαλιλαίαν, ἐκεῖ αὐτὸν ὄψεσθε.
to - Galilee, there him ye will see.

ἰδοὺ εἶπον ὑμῖν. 8 καὶ ἀπελθοῦσαι ταχὺ
Behold I told you. And going away quickly

ἀπὸ τοῦ μνημείου μετὰ φόβου καὶ χαρᾶς
from the tomb with fear and joy

μεγάλης ἔδραμον ἀπαγγεῖλαι τοῖς
great they ran to announce to the

μαθηταῖς αὐτοῦ. 9 καὶ ἰδοὺ Ἰησοῦς
disciples of him. And behold Jesus

ὑπήντησεν αὐταῖς λέγων· χαίρετε. αἱ δὲ
met them saying: Hail. And they

προσελθοῦσαι ἐκράτησαν αὐτοῦ τοὺς πόδας
approaching held of him the feet

καὶ προσεκύνησαν αὐτῷ. 10 τότε λέγει
and worshipped him. Then says

tomb as secure as you know how." 66 So they went and made the tomb secure by putting a seal on the stone and posting the guard.

Chapter 28

The Resurrection

AFTER the Sabbath, at dawn on the first day of the week, Mary Magdalene and the other Mary went to look at the tomb.

2 There was a violent earthquake, for an angel of the Lord came down from heaven and, going to the tomb, rolled back the stone and sat on it. 3 His appearance was like lightning, and his clothes were white as snow. 4 The guards were so afraid of him that they shook and became like dead men.

5 The angel said to the women, "Do not be afraid, for I know that you are looking for Jesus, who was crucified. 6 He is not here; he has risen, just as he said. Come and see the place where he lay. 7 Then go quickly and tell his disciples: 'He has risen from the dead and is going ahead of you into Galilee. There you will see him.' Now I have told you."

8 So the women hurried away from the tomb, afraid yet filled with joy, and ran to tell his disciples. 9 Suddenly Jesus met them. "Greetings," he said. They came to him, clasped his feet and worshiped him.

[i] Or Take a guard
[j] Gk you know how
[k] Other ancient authorities read the Lord
[l] Other ancient authorities lack from the dead

* can. See note on page xviii.

Jesus said to them, "Do not be afraid; go and tell my brothers to go to Galilee; there they will see me."

The Report of the Guard

11 While they were going, some of the guard went into the city and told the chief priests everything that had happened. 12 After the priests[m] had assembled with the elders, they devised a plan to give a large sum of money to the soldiers, 13 telling them, "You must say, 'His disciples came by night and stole him away while we were asleep.' 14 If this comes to the governor's ears, we will satisfy him and keep you out of trouble." 15 So they took the money and did as they were directed. And this story is still told among the Jews to this day.

The Commissioning of the Disciples

16 Now the eleven disciples went to Galilee, to the mountain to which Jesus had directed them. 17 When they saw him, they worshiped him; but some doubted. 18 And Jesus came and said to them, "All authority in heaven and on earth has been given to me. 19 Go therefore and make disciples of all nations, baptizing them in the name of the Father and of the Son and of the Holy Spirit, 20 and teaching them to obey everything that I have commanded you. And remember, I am with you always, to the end of the age."[n]

αὐταῖς ὁ Ἰησοῦς· μὴ φοβεῖσθε· ὑπάγετε
to them — Jesus: Fear ye not; go ye

ἀπαγγείλατε τοῖς ἀδελφοῖς μου ἵνα
announce to the brothers of me that

ἀπέλθωσιν εἰς τὴν Γαλιλαίαν, κἀκεῖ
they may go away into — Galilee, and there

με ὄψονται. 11 Πορευομένων δὲ αὐτῶν[a]
me they will see. And going them[a]
= as they were going

ἰδού τινες τῆς κουστωδίας ἐλθόντες εἰς
behold some of the guard coming into

τὴν πόλιν ἀπήγγειλαν τοῖς ἀρχιερεῦσιν
the city announced to the chief priests

ἅπαντα τὰ γενόμενα. 12 καὶ συν-
all the things having happened. And being

αχθέντες μετὰ τῶν πρεσβυτέρων συμβούλιόν[a]
assembled with the elders counsel[a]

τε λαβόντες ἀργύρια ἱκανὰ ἔδωκαν τοῖς
[1]and [2]taking silver enough gave to the

στρατιώταις, 13 λέγοντες· εἴπατε ὅτι οἱ
soldiers, saying: Say ye that the

μαθηταὶ αὐτοῦ νυκτὸς ἐλθόντες ἔκλεψαν
disciples of him of(by) night coming stole

αὐτὸν ἡμῶν κοιμωμένων. 14 καὶ ἐὰν
him we sleeping.[a] And if
= while we slept.

ἀκουσθῇ τοῦτο ἐπὶ τοῦ ἡγεμόνος,
be heard this before the governor,

ἡμεῖς πείσομεν καὶ ὑμᾶς ἀμερίμνους
we will persuade and you free from anxiety

ποιήσομεν. 15 οἱ δὲ λαβόντες ἀργύρια
we will make. And they taking silver

ἐποίησαν ὡς ἐδιδάχθησαν. Καὶ διεφη-
did as they were taught. And was spread

μίσθη ὁ λόγος οὗτος παρὰ Ἰουδαίοις
about — saying this by Jews

μέχρι τῆς σήμερον [ἡμέρας]. 16 Οἱ δὲ
until to-day. So the

ἔνδεκα μαθηταὶ ἐπορεύθησαν εἰς τὴν
eleven disciples went to —

Γαλιλαίαν, εἰς τὸ ὄρος οὗ ἐτάξατο
Galilee, to the mountain where appointed

αὐτοῖς ὁ Ἰησοῦς, 17 καὶ ἰδόντες αὐτὸν
them — Jesus, and seeing him

προσεκύνησαν, οἱ δὲ ἐδίστασαν. 18 καὶ
they worshipped, but some doubted. And

προσελθὼν ὁ Ἰησοῦς ἐλάλησεν αὐτοῖς
approaching — Jesus talked with them

λέγων· ἐδόθη μοι πᾶσα ἐξουσία ἐν
saying: was given to me All authority in

οὐρανῷ καὶ ἐπὶ [τῆς] γῆς. 19 πορευθέντες
heaven and on the earth. Going

οὖν μαθητεύσατε πάντα τὰ ἔθνη, βαπτίζ-
therefore disciple ye all the nations, baptiz-

οντες αὐτοὺς εἰς τὸ ὄνομα τοῦ πατρὸς
ing them in the name of the Father

καὶ τοῦ υἱοῦ καὶ τοῦ ἁγίου πνεύματος,
and of the Son and of the Holy Spirit,

20 διδάσκοντες αὐτοὺς τηρεῖν πάντα
teaching them to observe all things

ὅσα ἐνετειλάμην ὑμῖν· καὶ ἰδοὺ ἐγὼ
whatever I gave command to you; and behold I

μεθ' ὑμῶν εἰμι πάσας τὰς ἡμέρας ἕως
with you am all the days until

τῆς συντελείας τοῦ αἰῶνος.
the completion of the age.

---

10 Then Jesus said to them, "Do not be afraid. Go and tell my brothers to go to Galilee; there they will see me."

The Guards' Report

11 While the women were on their way, some of the guards went into the city and reported to the chief priests everything that had happened. 12 When the chief priests had met with the elders and devised a plan, they gave the soldiers a large sum of money, 13 telling them, "You are to say, 'His disciples came during the night and stole him away while we were asleep.' 14 If this report gets to the governor, we will satisfy him and keep you out of trouble." 15 So the soldiers took the money and did as they were instructed. And this story has been widely circulated among the Jews to this very day.

The Great Commission

16 Then the eleven disciples went to Galilee, to the mountain where Jesus had told them to go. 17 When they saw him, they worshiped him; but some doubted. 18 Then Jesus came to them and said, "All authority in heaven and on earth has been given to me. 19 Therefore go and make disciples of all nations, baptizing them in[n] the name of the Father and of the Son and of the Holy Spirit, 20 and teaching them to obey everything I have commanded you. And surely I am with you always, to the very end of the age."

---

[m] Gk *they*
[n] Other ancient authorities add *Amen*

[n] 19 Or *into*; see Acts 8:16; 19:5; Romans 6:3; 1 Cor. 1:13; 10:2 and Gal. 3:27.

Chapter 1

The Proclamation of John the Baptist

THE beginning of the good news[a] of Jesus Christ, the Son of God.[b]
2 As it is written in the prophet Isaiah,[c]
"See, I am sending
my messenger
ahead of you,[d]
who will prepare
your way;
3 the voice of one
crying out in the
wilderness:
'Prepare the way of
the Lord,
make his paths
straight,'"
4 John the baptizer appeared[e] in the wilderness, proclaiming a baptism of repentance for the forgiveness of sins. 5 And people from the whole Judean countryside and all the people of Jerusalem were going out to him, and were baptized by him in the river Jordan, confessing their sins. 6 Now John was clothed with camel's hair, with a leather belt around his waist, and he ate locusts and wild honey. 7 He proclaimed, "The one who is more powerful than I is coming after me; I am not worthy to stoop down and untie the thong of his sandals. 8 I have baptized you with[f] water; but he will baptize you with[f] the Holy Spirit."

The Baptism of Jesus

9 In those days Jesus came from Nazareth of Galilee and was baptized by John in the Jordan. 10 And just as he was coming up out of the water, he saw the heavens torn apart and the Spirit descending like a dove on him. 11 And a voice came from heaven, "You are my Son, the Beloved;[g] with you I am well pleased."

The Temptation of Jesus

12 And the Spirit immediately drove him out into the wilderness. 13 He was in the wilderness forty days, tempted by Satan; and he was with the wild beasts; and the angels waited on him.

---

[a] Or gospel
[b] Other ancient authorities lack the Son of God
[c] Other ancient authorities read in the prophets
[d] Gk before your face
[e] Other ancient authorities read John was baptizing
[f] Or in
[g] Or my beloved Son

---

1 Ἀρχὴ τοῦ εὐαγγελίου Ἰησοῦ Χριστοῦ.
[The] beginning of the gospel of Jesus Christ.
2 Καθὼς γέγραπται ἐν τῷ Ἠσαΐᾳ τῷ
As it has been written in - Isaiah the
προφήτῃ· ἰδοὺ ἀποστέλλω τὸν ἄγγελόν μου
prophet: Behold[,] I send the messenger of me
πρὸ προσώπου σου, ὃς κατασκευάσει τὴν ὁδόν
before [the] face of thee, who will prepare the way
σου· 3 φωνὴ βοῶντος ἐν τῇ ἐρήμῳ· ἑτοιμάσατε
of thee; a voice of [one] crying in the desert: Prepare ye
τὴν ὁδὸν κυρίου, εὐθείας ποιεῖτε τὰς τρίβους
the way of [the] Lord, straight make the paths
αὐτοῦ, 4 ἐγένετο Ἰωάννης ὁ βαπτίζων ἐν τῇ
of him, came John the [one] baptizing in the
ἐρήμῳ κηρύσσων βάπτισμα μετανοίας εἰς
desert proclaiming a baptism of repentance for
ἄφεσιν ἁμαρτιῶν. 5 καὶ ἐξεπορεύετο πρὸς
forgiveness of sins. And went out to
αὐτὸν πᾶσα ἡ Ἰουδαία χώρα καὶ οἱ Ἱεροσο-
him all the Judæan country and the Jerusa-
λυμῖται πάντες, καὶ ἐβαπτίζοντο ὑπ' αὐτοῦ
lemites all, and were baptized by him
ἐν τῷ Ἰορδάνῃ ποταμῷ ἐξομολογούμενοι τὰς
in the Jordan river confessing the
ἁμαρτίας αὐτῶν. 6 καὶ ἦν ὁ Ἰωάννης
sins of them. And was - John
ἐνδεδυμένος τρίχας καμήλου καὶ ζώνην
having been clothed [in] hairs of a camel and girdle
δερματίνην περὶ τὴν ὀσφὺν αὐτοῦ, καὶ ἔσθων
a leathern round the loin[s] of him, and eating
ἀκρίδας καὶ μέλι ἄγριον. 7 καὶ ἐκήρυσσεν
locusts and honey wild. And he proclaimed
λέγων· ἔρχεται ὁ ἰσχυρότερός μου ὀπίσω
saying: Comes the [one] stronger of me after
= than I
[μου], οὗ οὐκ εἰμὶ ἱκανὸς κύψας λῦσαι
me, of whom I am not competent stooping to loosen
τὸν ἱμάντα τῶν ὑποδημάτων αὐτοῦ. 8 ἐγὼ
the thong of the sandals of him. I
ἐβάπτισα ὑμᾶς ὕδατι, αὐτὸς δὲ βαπτίσει ὑμᾶς
baptized you in water, but he will baptize you
πνεύματι ἁγίῳ.
Spirit in [the] Holy.
9 Καὶ ἐγένετο ἐν ἐκείναις ταῖς ἡμέραις
And it came to pass in those - days
ἦλθεν Ἰησοῦς ἀπὸ Ναζαρὲθ τῆς Γαλιλαίας
came Jesus from Nazareth - of Galilee
καὶ ἐβαπτίσθη εἰς τὸν Ἰορδάνην ὑπὸ
and was baptized in the Jordan by
Ἰωάννου. 10 καὶ εὐθὺς ἀναβαίνων ἐκ τοῦ
John. And immediately going up out of the
ὕδατος εἶδεν σχιζομένους τοὺς οὐρανοὺς
water he saw being rent the heavens
καὶ τὸ πνεῦμα ὡς περιστερὰν καταβαῖνον
and the Spirit as a dove coming down
εἰς αὐτόν· 11 καὶ φωνὴ [ἐγένετο] ἐκ τῶν
to him; and a voice there was out of the
οὐρανῶν· σὺ εἶ ὁ υἱός μου ὁ ἀγαπητός,
heavens: Thou art the Son of me the beloved,
ἐν σοὶ εὐδόκησα. 12 Καὶ εὐθὺς τὸ
in thee I was well pleased. And immediately the
πνεῦμα αὐτὸν ἐκβάλλει εἰς τὴν ἔρημον.
Spirit him thrusts forth into the desert.
13 καὶ ἦν ἐν τῇ ἐρήμῳ τεσσεράκοντα
And he was in the desert forty
ἡμέρας πειραζόμενος ὑπὸ τοῦ σατανᾶ, καὶ
days being tempted by - Satan, and
ἦν μετὰ τῶν θηρίων, καὶ οἱ ἄγγελοι
was with the wild beasts, and the angels

Chapter 1

John the Baptist Prepares the Way

THE beginning of the gospel about Jesus Christ, the Son of God.[a]

2 It is written in Isaiah the prophet:

"I will send my
messenger ahead of
you,
who will prepare your
way"[b]—
3 "a voice of one calling in
the desert,
'Prepare the way for the
Lord,
make straight paths for
him.'"[c]

4 And so John came, baptizing in the desert region and preaching a baptism of repentance for the forgiveness of sins. 5 The whole Judean countryside and all the people of Jerusalem went out to him. Confessing their sins, they were baptized by him in the Jordan River. 6 John wore clothing made of camel's hair, with a leather belt around his waist, and he ate locusts and wild honey. 7 And this was his message: "After me will come one more powerful than I, the thongs of whose sandals I am not worthy to stoop down and untie. 8 I baptize you with[d] water, but he will baptize you with the Holy Spirit."

The Baptism and Temptation of Jesus

9 At that time Jesus came from Nazareth in Galilee and was baptized by John in the Jordan. 10 As Jesus was coming up out of the water, he saw heaven being torn open and the Spirit descending on him like a dove. 11 And a voice came from heaven: "You are my Son, whom I love; with you I am well pleased."

12 At once the Spirit sent him out into the desert, 13 and he was in the desert forty days, being tempted by Satan. He was with the wild animals, and angels attended him.

---

[a] 1 Some manuscripts do not have the Son of God.
[b] 2 Mal. 3:1
[c] 3 Isaiah 40:3
[d] 8 Or in

The Beginning of the Galilean Ministry

14 Now after John was arrested, Jesus came to Galilee, proclaiming the good news[a] of God,[h] 15 and saying, "The time is fulfilled, and the kingdom of God has come near;[i] repent, and believe in the good news."[a]

Jesus Calls the First Disciples

16 As Jesus passed along the Sea of Galilee, he saw Simon and his brother Andrew casting a net into the sea—for they were fishermen. 17 And Jesus said to them, "Follow me and I will make you fish for people." And immediately they left their nets and followed him. 19 As he went a little farther, he saw James son of Zebedee and his brother John, who were in their boat mending the nets. 20 Immediately he called them; and they left their father Zebedee in the boat with the hired men, and followed him.

The Man with an Unclean Spirit

21 They went to Capernaum; and when the sabbath came, he entered the synagogue and taught. 22 They were astounded at his teaching, for he taught them as one having authority, and not as the scribes. 23 Just then there was in their synagogue a man with an unclean spirit, 24 and he cried out, "What have you to do with us, Jesus of Nazareth? Have you come to destroy us? I know who you are, the Holy One of God." 25 But Jesus rebuked him, saying, "Be silent, and

---

διηκόνουν αὐτῷ.
ministered to him.

14 Καὶ   μετὰ   τὸ   παραδοθῆναι   τὸν
And   after   the   to be delivered   –
= after John was delivered

'Ιωάννην   ἦλθεν   ὁ   'Ιησοῦς   εἰς   τὴν   Γαλιλαίαν
John[b]   came   –   Jesus   into   –   Galilee

κηρύσσων   τὸ   εὐαγγέλιον   τοῦ   θεοῦ   **15** [καὶ
proclaiming   the   gospel   –   of God   and

λέγων],   ὅτι   πεπλήρωται   ὁ   καιρὸς   καὶ
saying,   –   Has been fulfilled   the   time   and

ἤγγικεν   ἡ   βασιλεία   τοῦ   θεοῦ·   μετανοεῖτε
has drawn near   the   kingdom   –   of God;   repent ye

καὶ   πιστεύετε   ἐν   τῷ   εὐαγγελίῳ.   **16** Καὶ
and   believe   in   the   gospel.   And

παράγων   παρὰ   τὴν   θάλασσαν   τῆς   Γαλιλαίας
passing along   beside   the   sea   –   of Galilee

εἶδεν   Σίμωνα   καὶ   'Ανδρέαν   τὸν   ἀδελφὸν
he saw   Simon   and   Andrew   the   brother

Σίμωνος   ἀμφιβάλλοντας   ἐν   τῇ   θαλάσσῃ·
of Simon   casting [a net]   in   the   sea;

ἦσαν   γὰρ   ἁλεεῖς.   **17** καὶ   εἶπεν   αὐτοῖς
for they were   fishers.   And   said   to them

ὁ   'Ιησοῦς·   δεῦτε   ὀπίσω   μου,   καὶ   ποιήσω
–   Jesus: Come   after   me,   and   I will make

ὑμᾶς   γενέσθαι   ἁλεεῖς   ἀνθρώπων.   **18** καὶ
you   to become   fishers   of men.   And

εὐθὺς   ἀφέντες   τὰ   δίκτυα   ἠκολούθησαν
immediately   leaving   the   nets   they followed

αὐτῷ.   **19** Καὶ   προβὰς   ὀλίγον   εἶδεν
him.   And   going forward   a little   he saw

'Ιάκωβον   τὸν   τοῦ   Ζεβεδαίου   καὶ   'Ιωάννην
James   the [son]   of Zebedee   and   John

τὸν   ἀδελφὸν   αὐτοῦ   καὶ   αὐτοὺς   ἐν   τῷ
the   brother   of him   even   them   in   the

πλοίῳ   καταρτίζοντας   τὰ   δίκτυα.   **20** καὶ
ship   mending   the   nets.   And

εὐθὺς   ἐκάλεσεν   αὐτούς·   καὶ   ἀφέντες   τὸν
immediately   he called   them;   and   leaving   the

πατέρα   αὐτῶν   Ζεβεδαῖον   ἐν   τῷ   πλοίῳ
father   of them   Zebedee   in   the   ship

μετὰ   τῶν   μισθωτῶν   ἀπῆλθον   ὀπίσω   αὐτοῦ.
with   the   hired servants   they went   after   him.

21 Καὶ   εἰσπορεύονται   εἰς   Καφαρναούμ·
And   they enter   into   Capernaum;

καὶ   εὐθὺς   τοῖς   σάββασιν   εἰσελθὼν
and   immediately   on the   sabbaths   entering

εἰς   τὴν   συναγωγὴν   ἐδίδασκεν.   **22** καὶ
into   the   synagogue   he taught.   And

ἐξεπλήσσοντο   ἐπὶ   τῇ   διδαχῇ   αὐτοῦ·   ἦν
they were astounded   on(at)   the   teaching   of him;   [a]he was

γὰρ   διδάσκων   αὐτοὺς   ὡς   ἐξουσίαν   ἔχων,
[a]for   teaching   them   as   authority   having,

καὶ   οὐχ   ὡς   οἱ   γραμματεῖς.   **23** Καὶ   εὐθὺς
and   not   as   the   scribes.   And immediately

ἦν   ἐν   τῇ   συναγωγῇ   αὐτῶν   ἄνθρωπος
there was   in   the   synagogue   of them   a man

ἐν   πνεύματι   ἀκαθάρτῳ,   καὶ   ἀνέκραξεν
in   spirit   an unclean,   and   he cried out

24 λέγων·   τί   ἡμῖν   καὶ   σοί,   'Ιησοῦ
saying: What   to us   and   to thee,   Jesus

Ναζαρηνέ;   ἦλθες   ἀπολέσαι   ἡμᾶς;   οἶδά
Nazarene?   camest thou   to destroy   us?   I know

σε   τίς   εἶ,   ὁ   ἅγιος   τοῦ   θεοῦ.   **25** καὶ
thee   who thou art,   the   holy [one]   –   of God.   And

ἐπετίμησεν   αὐτῷ   ὁ   'Ιησοῦς   [λέγων]·
rebuked   him   –   Jesus   saying:

The Calling of the First Disciples

14 After John was put in prison, Jesus went into Galilee, proclaiming the good news of God. 15 "The time has come," he said. "The kingdom of God is near. Repent and believe the good news!"

16 As Jesus walked beside the Sea of Galilee, he saw Simon and his brother Andrew casting a net into the lake, for they were fishermen. 17 "Come, follow me," Jesus said, "and I will make you fishers of men." 18 At once they left their nets and followed him.

19 When he had gone a little farther, he saw James son of Zebedee and his brother John in a boat, preparing their nets. 20 Without delay he called them, and they left their father Zebedee in the boat with the hired men and followed him.

Jesus Drives Out an Evil Spirit

21 They went to Capernaum, and when the Sabbath came, Jesus went into the synagogue and began to teach. 22 The people were amazed at his teaching, because he taught them as one who had authority, not as the teachers of the law. 23 Just then a man in their synagogue who was possessed by an evil[e] spirit cried out, 24 "What do you want with us, Jesus of Nazareth? Have you come to destroy us? I know who you are—the Holy One of God!"

25 "Be quiet!" said Jesus

---

[h] Other ancient authorities read of the kingdom
[i] Or is at hand

[e]23 Greek unclean; also in verses 26 and 27

come out of him!" 26 And the unclean spirit, convulsing him and crying with a loud voice, came out of him. 27 They were all amazed, and they kept on asking one another, "What is this? A new teaching—with authority! He^j commands even the unclean spirits, and they obey him." 28 At once his fame began to spread throughout the surrounding region of Galilee.

Jesus Heals Many at Simon's House

29 As soon as they^k left the synagogue, they entered the house of Simon and Andrew, with James and John. 30 Now Simon's mother-in-law was in bed with a fever, and they told him about her at once. 31 He came and took her by the hand and lifted her up. Then the fever left her, and she began to serve them.

32 That evening, at sundown, they brought to him all who were sick or possessed with demons. 33 And the whole city was gathered around the door. 34 And he cured many who were sick with various diseases, and cast out many demons; and he would not permit the demons to speak, because they knew him.

A Preaching Tour in Galilee

35 In the morning, while it was still very dark, he got up and went out to a deserted place, and there he prayed. 36 And Simon and his companions hunted for him. 37 When they found him, they said to him, "Everyone is searching for you." 38 He answered, "Let us go on to the neighboring

φιμώθητι καὶ ἔξελθε [ἐξ αὐτοῦ]. 26 καὶ
Be quiet and come out of him. And

σπαράξαν αὐτὸν τὸ πνεῦμα τὸ ἀκάθαρτον
throwing him the spirit the unclean

καὶ φωνῆσαν φωνῇ μεγάλῃ ἐξῆλθεν ἐξ
and shouting voice with a great he came out out of

αὐτοῦ. 27 καὶ ἐθαμβήθησαν ἅπαντες, ὥστε
him. And were astounded all, so as = so that

συζητεῖν αὐτοὺς λέγοντας· τί ἐστιν τοῦτο;
to debate them^b saying: What is this? they debated

διδαχὴ καινὴ κατ' ἐξουσίαν· καὶ τοῖς
teaching a new by authority; and the

πνεύμασι τοῖς ἀκαθάρτοις ἐπιτάσσει, καὶ
spirits the unclean he commands, and

ὑπακούουσιν αὐτῷ. 28 καὶ ἐξῆλθεν ἡ
they obey him. And went forth the

ἀκοὴ αὐτοῦ εὐθὺς πανταχοῦ εἰς ὅλην
report of him immediately everywhere into all

τὴν περίχωρον τῆς Γαλιλαίας. 29 Καὶ
the neighbourhood - of Galilee. And

εὐθὺς ἐκ τῆς συναγωγῆς ἐξελθόντες ἦλθον
immediately out of the synagogue going forth they came

εἰς τὴν οἰκίαν Σίμωνος καὶ Ἀνδρέου
into the house of Simon and Andrew

μετὰ Ἰακώβου καὶ Ἰωάννου. 30 ἡ δὲ
with James and John. Now the

πενθερὰ Σίμωνος κατέκειτο πυρέσσουσα.
mother-in-law of Simon was laid [aside] fever-stricken.

καὶ εὐθὺς λέγουσιν αὐτῷ περὶ αὐτῆς.
and immediately they tell him about her.

31 καὶ προσελθὼν ἤγειρεν αὐτὴν κρατήσας
And approaching he raised her holding

τῆς χειρός καὶ ἀφῆκεν αὐτὴν ὁ πυρετός,
the(her) hand; and left her the fever,

καὶ διηκόνει αὐτοῖς. 32 Ὀψίας δὲ γενο-
and she served them. And evening com- = when evening

μένης, ὅτε ἔδυσεν ὁ ἥλιος, ἔφερον πρὸς
ing,^a when set the sun, they brought to came,

αὐτὸν πάντας τοὺς κακῶς ἔχοντας καὶ
him all the [ones] ill having and = those who were ill

τοὺς δαιμονιζομένους· 33 καὶ ἦν ὅλη ἡ
the being demon-possessed; and was all the

πόλις ἐπισυνηγμένη πρὸς τὴν θύραν.
city having been assembled at the door.

34 καὶ ἐθεράπευσεν πολλοὺς κακῶς ἔχοντας
And he healed many ill having = who were ill

ποικίλαις νόσοις, καὶ δαιμόνια πολλὰ
with various diseases, and demons many

ἐξέβαλεν, καὶ οὐκ ἤφιεν λαλεῖν τὰ δαιμόνια,
he expelled, and did not allow to speak the demons,

ὅτι ᾔδεισαν αὐτόν. 35 Καὶ πρωῒ ἔννυχα
because they knew him. And ^aearly ^iin the night

λίαν ἀναστὰς ἐξῆλθεν καὶ ἀπῆλθεν εἰς
^ivery ^irising up he went out and went away to

ἔρημον τόπον, κἀκεῖ προσηύχετο. 36 καὶ
a desert place, and there prayed. And

κατεδίωξεν αὐτὸν Σίμων καὶ οἱ μετ'
hunted down him Simon and the [ones] with

αὐτοῦ, καὶ εὗρον αὐτὸν καὶ λέγουσιν
him, and found him and say

αὐτῷ 37 ὅτι πάντες ζητοῦσίν σε. 38 καὶ
to him[,] All are seeking thee. And

λέγει αὐτοῖς· ἄγωμεν ἀλλαχοῦ εἰς τὰς
he says to them: Let us go elsewhere into the

sternly. "Come out of him!" 26 The evil spirit shook the man violently and came out of him with a shriek.

27 The people were all so amazed that they asked each other, "What is this? A new teaching—and with authority! He even gives orders to evil spirits and they obey him." 28 News about him spread quickly over the whole region of Galilee.

Jesus Heals Many

29 As soon as they left the synagogue, they went with James and John to the home of Simon and Andrew. 30 Simon's mother-in-law was in bed with a fever, and they told Jesus about her. 31 So he went to her, took her hand and helped her up. The fever left her and she began to wait on them.

32 That evening after sunset the people brought to Jesus all the sick and demon-possessed. 33 The whole town gathered at the door, 34 and Jesus healed many who had various diseases. He also drove out many demons, but he would not let the demons speak because they knew who he was.

Jesus Prays in a Solitary Place

35 Very early in the morning, while it was still dark, Jesus got up, left the house and went off to a solitary place, where he prayed. 36 Simon and his companions went to look for him, 37 and when they found him, they exclaimed: "Everyone is looking for you!"

38 Jesus replied, "Let us go somewhere else—to the

^j Or A new teaching! With authority he
^k Other ancient authorities read he

towns, so that I may proclaim the message there also; for that is what I came out to do." 39 And he went throughout Galilee, proclaiming the message in their synagogues and casting out demons.

Jesus Cleanses a Leper

40 A leper[l] came to him begging him, and kneeling[m] he said to him, "If you choose, you can make me clean." 41 Moved with pity,[n] Jesus[o] stretched out his hand and touched him, and said to him, "I do choose. Be made clean!" 42 Immediately the leprosy[l] left him, and he was made clean. 43 After sternly warning him he sent him away at once, 44 saying to him, "See that you say nothing to anyone; but go, show yourself to the priest, and offer for your cleansing what Moses commanded, as a testimony to them." 45 But he went out and began to proclaim it freely, and to spread the word, so that Jesus[o] could no longer go into a town openly, but stayed out in the country; and people came to him from every quarter.

Chapter 2

Jesus Heals a Paralytic

WHEN he returned to Capernaum after some days, it was reported that he was at home. 2 So many gathered around that there was no longer room for them, not even in front of the door; and he was speaking the word to them. 3 Then some people[p] came, bringing to him a paralyzed man, carried by four of them. 4 And when they could not bring him to Jesus because of the crowd, they removed the roof above him; and after having dug through it, they let down the mat on which

[l] The terms leper and leprosy can refer to several diseases
[m] Other ancient authorities lack kneeling
[n] Other ancient authorities read anger
[o] Gk he
[p] Gk they

Middle column (interlinear)

ἐχομένας κωμοπόλεις, ἵνα καὶ ἐκεῖ
neighbouring   towns,   that also there
κηρύξω· εἰς τοῦτο γὰρ ἐξῆλθον. 39 καὶ
I may proclaim; for for this [purpose] I came forth.   And
ἦλθεν κηρύσσων εἰς τὰς συναγωγὰς αὐτῶν
he came proclaiming   in the   synagogues   of them
εἰς ὅλην τὴν Γαλιλαίαν καὶ τὰ δαιμόνια
in all   -   Galilee   and the   demons
ἐκβάλλων.
expelling.

40 Καὶ ἔρχεται πρὸς αὐτὸν λεπρὸς
And comes   to   him   a leper
παρακαλῶν αὐτὸν καὶ γονυπετῶν λέγων
beseeching   him and falling on [his] knees saying
αὐτῷ ὅτι ἐὰν θέλῃς δύνασαί με καθαρίσαι.
to him[,] - If thou art willing thou art able me to cleanse.
41 καὶ σπλαγχνισθεὶς ἐκτείνας τὴν
And being filled with tenderness stretching forth the(his)
χεῖρα αὐτοῦ ἥψατο καὶ λέγει αὐτῷ· θέλω,
hand him[1] he touched and says to him: I am willing,
καθαρίσθητι. 42 καὶ εὐθὺς ἀπῆλθεν ἀπ᾽
be thou cleansed.   And immediately departed   from
αὐτοῦ ἡ λέπρα, καὶ ἐκαθαρίσθη. 43 καὶ
him   the leprosy, and   he was cleansed.   And
ἐμβριμησάμενος αὐτῷ εὐθὺς ἐξέβαλεν αὐτόν,
sternly admonishing him immediately he put out   him,
44 καὶ λέγει αὐτῷ· ὅρα μηδενὶ μηδὲν
and says to him: See no one no(any)thing
εἴπῃς, ἀλλὰ ὕπαγε σεαυτὸν δεῖξον τῷ
thou tellest, but go thyself show to the
ἱερεῖ καὶ προσένεγκε περὶ τοῦ καθαρισμοῦ σου
priest and   offer   concerning the   cleansing   of thee
ἃ προσέταξεν Μωϋσῆς, εἰς μαρτύριον
[the things] which commanded Moses,   for a testimony
αὐτοῖς. 45 ὁ δὲ ἐξελθὼν ἤρξατο κηρύσσειν
to them.   But he going out began   to proclaim
πολλὰ καὶ διαφημίζειν τὸν λόγον, ὥστε
many things and to spread about the matter,   so as
= so that
μηκέτι αὐτὸν δύνασθαι φανερῶς εἰς πόλιν
no longer him to be able[b] openly into a city
he was no longer able
εἰσελθεῖν, ἀλλ᾽ ἔξω ἐπ᾽ ἐρήμοις τόποις
to enter,   but outside on(in) desert   places
ἦν· καὶ ἤρχοντο πρὸς αὐτὸν πάντοθεν.
he was; and they came   to   him from all directions.

2 Καὶ εἰσελθὼν πάλιν εἰς Καφαρναοὺμ
And entering   again into   Capernaum
δι᾽ ἡμερῶν ἠκούσθη ὅτι ἐν οἴκῳ ἐστίν.
through days it was heard that at home he is(was).
= after [some] days
2 καὶ συνήχθησαν πολλοί, ὥστε μηκέτι
And   were assembled   many,   so as no longer
χωρεῖν μηδὲ τὰ πρὸς τὴν θύραν, καὶ
to have room not -   at the   door,   and
ἐλάλει αὐτοῖς τὸν λόγον. 3 καὶ ἔρχονται
he spoke to them the   word.   And they come
φέροντες πρὸς αὐτὸν παραλυτικὸν αἰρόμενον
carrying   to   him   a paralytic   being borne
ὑπὸ τεσσάρων. 4 καὶ μὴ δυνάμενοι
by   four [men].   And not being able
προσενέγκαι αὐτῷ διὰ τὸν ὄχλον
to bring   to him because of the   crowd
ἀπεστέγασαν τὴν στέγην ὅπου ἦν, καὶ
they unroofed   the   roof where he was, and
ἐξορύξαντες χαλῶσι τὸν κράβατον ὅπου ὁ
having opened up they lower the   mattress   where the

nearby villages—so I can preach there also. That is why I have come." 39 So he traveled throughout Galilee, preaching in their synagogues and driving out demons.

A Man With Leprosy

40 A man with leprosy[f] came to him and begged him on his knees, "If you are willing, you can make me clean." 41 Filled with compassion, Jesus reached out his hand and touched the man. "I am willing," he said. "Be clean!" 42 Immediately the leprosy left him and he was cured. 43 Jesus sent him away at once with a strong warning: 44 "See that you don't tell this to anyone. But go, show yourself to the priest and offer the sacrifices that Moses commanded for your cleansing, as a testimony to them." 45 Instead he went out and began to talk freely, spreading the news. As a result, Jesus could no longer enter a town openly but stayed outside in lonely places. Yet the people still came to him from everywhere.

Chapter 2

Jesus Heals a Paralytic

A FEW days later, when Jesus again entered Capernaum, the people heard that he had come home. 2 So many gathered that there was no room left, not even outside the door, and he preached the word to them. 3 Some men came, bringing to him a paralytic, carried by four of them. 4 Since they could not get him to Jesus because of the crowd, they made an opening in the roof above Jesus and, after digging through it, lowered the mat the par-

[f] 40 The Greek word was used for various diseases affecting the skin—not necessarily leprosy.

the paralytic lay. ⁵When Jesus saw their faith, he said to the paralytic, "Son, your sins are forgiven." ⁶Now some of the scribes were sitting there, questioning in their hearts, ⁷"Why does this fellow speak in this way? It is blasphemy! Who can forgive sins but God alone?" ⁸At once Jesus perceived in his spirit that they were discussing these questions among themselves; and he said to them, "Why do you raise such questions in your hearts? ⁹Which is easier, to say to the paralytic, 'Your sins are forgiven,' or to say, 'Stand up and take your mat and walk'? ¹⁰But so that you may know that the Son of Man has authority on earth to forgive sins"—he said to the paralytic— ¹¹"I say to you, stand up, take your mat and go to your home." ¹²And he stood up, and immediately took the mat and went out before all of them; so that they were all amazed and glorified God, saying, "We have never seen anything like this!"

Jesus Calls Levi

13 Jesus*�q* went out again beside the sea; the whole crowd gathered around him, and he taught them. ¹⁴As he was walking along, he saw Levi son of Alphaeus sitting at the tax booth, and he said to him, "Follow me." And he got up and followed him.

15 And as he sat at dinner*ʳ* in Levi's*ˢ* house, many tax collectors and

---

παραλυτικὸς κατέκειτο. 5 καὶ ἰδὼν ὁ
paralytic was lying. And seeing

'Ιησοῦς τὴν πίστιν αὐτῶν λέγει τῷ
Jesus the faith of them he says to the

παραλυτικῷ· τέκνον, ἀφίενταί σου αἱ
paralytic: Child, are forgiven of thee the

ἁμαρτίαι. 6 ἦσαν δέ τινες τῶν γραμματέων
sins. Now there were some of the scribes

ἐκεῖ καθήμενοι καὶ διαλογιζόμενοι ἐν ταῖς
there sitting and reasoning in the

καρδίαις αὐτῶν· 7 τί οὗτος οὕτως λαλεῖ;
hearts of them: Why this [man] thus speaks?

βλασφημεῖ· τίς δύναται ἀφιέναι ἁμαρτίας
he blasphemes; who can *to* forgive sins

εἰ μὴ εἷς ὁ θεός; 8 καὶ εὐθὺς ἐπιγνοὺς
except one[,] – God? And immediately knowing

ὁ 'Ιησοῦς τῷ πνεύματι αὐτοῦ ὅτι οὕτως
– Jesus in the spirit of him that thus

διαλογίζονται ἐν ἑαυτοῖς, λέγει αὐτοῖς·
they reason among themselves, he says to them:

τί ταῦτα διαλογίζεσθε ἐν ταῖς καρδίαις
Why these things reason ye in the hearts

ὑμῶν; 9 τί ἐστιν εὐκοπώτερον, εἰπεῖν
of you? What is easier, to say

τῷ παραλυτικῷ· ἀφίενταί σου αἱ ἁμαρτίαι,
to the paralytic: are forgiven of thee the sins,

ἢ εἰπεῖν· ἔγειρε καὶ ἆρον τὸν κράβατόν·
or to say: Rise and take the mattress

σου καὶ περιπάτει; 10 ἵνα δὲ εἰδῆτε
of thee and walk? But that ye may know

ὅτι ἐξουσίαν ἔχει ὁ υἱὸς τοῦ ἀνθρώπου
that authority has the Son – of man

ἀφιέναι ἁμαρτίας ἐπὶ τῆς γῆς,—λέγει τῷ
to forgive sins on the earth,—he says to the

παραλυτικῷ· 11 σοὶ λέγω, ἔγειρε ἆρον
paralytic: To thee I say, rise[,] take

τὸν κράβατόν σου καὶ ὕπαγε εἰς τὸν
the mattress of thee and go to the

οἰκόν σου. 12 καὶ ἠγέρθη καὶ εὐθὺς
house of thee. And he arose and immediately

ἄρας τὸν κράβατον ἐξῆλθεν ἔμπροσθεν
taking the mattress he went forth before

πάντων, ὥστε ἐξίστασθαι πάντας καὶ
all, so as to be astonished all and
= so that they were all astonished and glorified

δοξάζειν τὸν θεὸν λέγοντας ὅτι οὕτως
to glorify*ᵇ* – God saying[,] – Thus

οὐδέποτε εἴδαμεν.
never we saw.

13 Καὶ ἐξῆλθεν πάλιν παρὰ τὴν θάλασσαν·
And he went forth again by the sea;

καὶ πᾶς ὁ ὄχλος ἤρχετο πρὸς αὐτόν,
and all the crowd came to him,

καὶ ἐδίδασκεν αὐτούς. 14 Καὶ παράγων
and he taught them. And passing along

εἶδεν Λευὶν τὸν τοῦ 'Αλφαίου καθήμενον
he saw Levi the [son] – Alphæus sitting

ἐπὶ τὸ τελώνιον, καὶ λέγει αὐτῷ· ἀκολούθει
on(in *or* at) the custom house, and says to him: Follow

μοι. καὶ ἀναστὰς ἠκολούθησεν αὐτῷ.
me. And rising up he followed him.

15 Καὶ γίνεται κατακεῖσθαι αὐτὸν ἐν τῇ
And it comes to pass to recline him*ᵇ* in the
= he reclines

οἰκίᾳ αὐτοῦ, καὶ πολλοὶ τελῶναι καὶ
house of him, and many tax-collectors and

---

alyzed man was lying on. ⁵When Jesus saw their faith, he said to the paralytic, "Son, your sins are forgiven." ⁶Now some teachers of the law were sitting there, thinking to themselves, ⁷"Why does this fellow talk like that? He's blaspheming! Who can forgive sins but God alone?" ⁸Immediately Jesus knew in his spirit that this was what they were thinking in their hearts, and he said to them, "Why are you thinking these things? ⁹Which is easier: to say to the paralytic, 'Your sins are forgiven,' or to say, 'Get up, take your mat and walk'? ¹⁰But that you may know that the Son of Man has authority on earth to forgive sins . . . ." He said to the paralytic, ¹¹"I tell you, get up, take your mat and go home." ¹²He got up, took his mat and walked out in full view of them all. This amazed everyone and they praised God, saying, "We have never seen anything like this!"

The Calling of Levi

¹³Once again Jesus went out beside the lake. A large crowd came to him, and he began to teach them. ¹⁴As he walked along, he saw Levi son of Alphaeus sitting at the tax collector's booth. "Follow me," Jesus told him, and Levi got up and followed him.

¹⁵While Jesus was having dinner at Levi's house, many tax collectors and

---

�q Gk *He*
ʳ Gk *reclined*
ˢ Gk *his*

sinners were also sitting[t] with Jesus and his disciples—for there were many who followed him. [16]When the scribes of[u] the Pharisees saw that he was eating with sinners and tax collectors, they said to his disciples, "Why does he eat[v] with tax collectors and sinners?" [17]When Jesus heard this, he said to them, "Those who are well have no need of a physician, but those who are sick; I have come to call not the righteous but sinners."

The Question about Fasting

18 Now John's disciples and the Pharisees were fasting; and people[p] came and said to him, "Why do John's disciples and the disciples of the Pharisees fast, but your disciples do not fast?" [19]Jesus said to them, "The wedding guests cannot fast while the bridegroom is with them, can they? As long as they have the bridegroom with them, they cannot fast. [20]The days will come when the bridegroom is taken away from them, and then they will fast on that day. 21 "No one sews a piece of unshrunk cloth on an old cloak; otherwise, the patch pulls away from it, the new from the old, and a worse tear is made. [22]And no one puts new wine into old wineskins; otherwise, the wine will burst the skins, and the wine is lost, and so are the skins; but one puts new wine into fresh wineskins."[w]

Pronouncement about the Sabbath

23 One sabbath he was going through the grain-

ἁμαρτωλοὶ συνανέκειντο τῷ Ἰησοῦ καὶ
sinners　reclined with　-　Jesus　and
τοῖς μαθηταῖς αὐτοῦ· ἦσαν γὰρ πολλοί,
the　disciples　of him;　for there were　many,
καὶ ἠκολούθουν αὐτῷ. 16 καὶ οἱ γραμματεῖς
and　they followed　him.　And the　scribes
τῶν Φαρισαίων ἰδόντες ὅτι ἐσθίει
of the　Pharisees　seeing　that　he eats(ate)
μετὰ τῶν ἁμαρτωλῶν καὶ τελωνῶν ἔλεγον
with　-　sinners　and tax-collectors　said
τοῖς μαθηταῖς αὐτοῦ· ὅτι μετὰ τῶν
to the　disciples　of him:　-　With　-
τελωνῶν καὶ ἁμαρτωλῶν ἐσθίει; 17 καὶ
tax-collectors　and　sinners　does he eat?　And
ἀκούσας ὁ Ἰησοῦς λέγει αὐτοῖς [ὅτι] οὐ
hearing　-　Jesus　says　to them[,]　-　Not
χρείαν ἔχουσιν οἱ ἰσχύοντες ἰατροῦ ἀλλ'
need　have the [ones] being strong of a physician　but
οἱ κακῶς ἔχοντες· οὐκ ἦλθον καλέσαι
the [ones] ill　having;　I came not　to call
= those who are ill;
δικαίους ἀλλὰ ἁμαρτωλούς. 18 Καὶ ἦσαν
righteous men but　sinners.　And　[1]were
οἱ μαθηταὶ Ἰωάννου καὶ οἱ Φαρισαῖοι
[1]the [2]disciples [3]of John [4]and [5]the [6]Pharisees
νηστεύοντες. καὶ ἔρχονται καὶ λέγουσιν
[7]fasting.　And　they come　and　say
αὐτῷ· διὰ τί οἱ μαθηταὶ Ἰωάννου καὶ
to him:　Why　the　disciples　of John　and
οἱ μαθηταὶ τῶν Φαρισαίων νηστεύουσιν,
the　disciples　of the　Pharisees　fast,
οἱ δὲ σοὶ μαθηταὶ οὐ νηστεύουσιν; 19 καὶ
-　but thy　disciples　do not fast?　And
εἶπεν αὐτοῖς ὁ Ἰησοῦς· μὴ δύνανται οἱ
said　to them　-　Jesus:　not　can　the
υἱοὶ τοῦ νυμφῶνος, ἐν ᾧ ὁ νυμφίος
sons　of the　bridechamber,　while[f]　the　bridegroom
μετ' αὐτῶν ἐστιν, νηστεύειν; ὅσον χρόνον
with　them　is,　to fast?　what　time
ἔχουσιν τὸν νυμφίον μετ' αὐτῶν, οὐ
they have　the　bridegroom　with　them,　not
δύνανται νηστεύειν. 20 ἐλεύσονται δὲ ἡμέραι
they can　to fast.　But will come　days
ὅταν ἀπαρθῇ ἀπ' αὐτῶν ὁ νυμφίος, καὶ
when　taken away from　them　the bridegroom,　and
τότε νηστεύσουσιν ἐν ἐκείνῃ τῇ ἡμέρᾳ.
then　they will fast　in　that　-　day.
21 Οὐδεὶς ἐπίβλημα ῥάκους ἀγνάφου ἐπιράπτει
No one　a patch　cloth　of unfulled　sews
ἐπὶ ἱμάτιον παλαιόν· εἰ δὲ μή, αἴρει
on　garment　an old;　otherwise,　[1]takes
τὸ πλήρωμα ἀπ' αὐτοῦ τὸ καινὸν τοῦ
[4]the [2]fulness [3]from　itself [1]the [1]new [1]the
παλαιοῦ, καὶ χεῖρον σχίσμα γίνεται. 22 καὶ
[6]old,　and　a worse　rent　occurs.　And
οὐδεὶς βάλλει οἶνον νέον εἰς ἀσκοὺς παλαιούς·
no one　puts　wine　new　into wineskins　old;
εἰ δὲ μή, ῥήξει ὁ οἶνος τοὺς ἀσκούς,
otherwise,　[3]will burst [1]the [2]wine　the　wineskins,
καὶ ὁ οἶνος ἀπόλλυται καὶ οἱ ἀσκοί.
and　the　wine　perishes　and　the wineskins.
[ἀλλὰ οἶνον νέον εἰς ἀσκοὺς καινούς.]
But　wine　new　into wineskins　fresh.
23 Καὶ ἐγένετο αὐτὸν ἐν τοῖς σάββασιν
And it came to pass him　on　the　sabbaths
= as he passed on the sabbath

"sinners" were eating with him and his disciples, for there were many who followed him. [16]When the teachers of the law who were Pharisees saw him eating with the "sinners" and tax collectors, they asked his disciples: "Why does he eat with tax collectors and 'sinners'?"

[17]On hearing this, Jesus said to them, "It is not the healthy who need a doctor, but the sick. I have not come to call the righteous, but sinners."

Jesus Questioned About Fasting

[18]Now John's disciples and the Pharisees were fasting. Some people came and asked Jesus, "How is it that John's disciples and the disciples of the Pharisees are fasting, but yours are not?"

[19]Jesus answered, "How can the guests of the bridegroom fast while he is with them? They cannot, so long as they have him with them. [20]But the time will come when the bridegroom will be taken from them, and on that day they will fast.

[21]"No one sews a patch of unshrunk cloth on an old garment. If he does, the new piece will pull away from the old, making the tear worse. [22]And no one pours new wine into old wineskins. If he does, the wine will burst the skins, and both the wine and the wineskins will be ruined. No, he pours new wine into new wineskins."

Lord of the Sabbath

[23]One Sabbath Jesus was going through the grain-

---

[t] Gk reclining
[u] Other ancient authorities read and
[v] Other ancient authorities add and drink
[w] Other ancient authorities lack but one puts new wine into fresh wineskins

fields; and as they made their way his disciples began to pluck heads of grain. 24The Pharisees said to him, "Look, why are they doing what is not lawful on the sabbath?" 25And he said to them, "Have you never read what David did when he and his companions were hungry and in need of food? 26He entered the house of God, when Abiathar was high priest, and ate the bread of the Presence, which it is not lawful for any but the priests to eat, and he gave some to his companions." 27Then he said to them, "The sabbath was made for humankind, and not humankind for the sabbath; 28so the Son of Man is lord even of the sabbath."

παραπορεύεσθαι διὰ τῶν σπορίμων, καὶ
to pass^b   through   the   cornfields,   and

οἱ μαθηταὶ αὐτοῦ ἤρξαντο ὁδὸν ποιεῖν
the   disciples   of him   began   way   to make

τίλλοντες τοὺς στάχυας. 24 καὶ οἱ Φαρισαῖοι
plucking   the   ears of corn.   And the   Pharisees

ἔλεγον αὐτῷ· ἴδε τί ποιοῦσιν τοῖς σάββασιν
said   to him: Behold[,] why   do   on the   sabbath*s*

ὃ οὐκ ἔξεστιν; 25 καὶ λέγει αὐτοῖς·
what   is not lawful?   And   he says   to them:

οὐδέποτε ἀνέγνωτε τί ἐποίησεν Δαυίδ,
never   read ye   what   did   David,

ὅτε χρείαν ἔσχεν καὶ ἐπείνασεν αὐτὸς
when   need   he had   and   hungered   he

καὶ οἱ μετ' αὐτοῦ; 26 [πῶς] εἰσῆλθεν
and the [ones] with   him?   how   he entered

εἰς τὸν οἶκον τοῦ θεοῦ ἐπὶ 'Αβιαθὰρ
into   the   house   – of God on(in the days of) Abiathar

ἀρχιερέως καὶ τοὺς ἄρτους τῆς προθέσεως
high priest   and   the   loaves   of the   setting forth

ἔφαγεν, οὓς οὐκ ἔξεστιν φαγεῖν εἰ μὴ
ate,   which   it is not lawful   to eat   except

τοὺς ἱερεῖς, καὶ ἔδωκεν καὶ τοῖς σὺν
the   priests,   and   gave   also to the [ones] with

αὐτῷ οὖσιν; 27 καὶ ἔλεγεν αὐτοῖς·
him   being?   And   he said   to them:

τὸ σάββατον διὰ τὸν ἄνθρωπον ἐγένετο,
The   sabbath   on account of   –   man   was,

καὶ οὐχ ὁ ἄνθρωπος διὰ τὸ σάββατον·
and   not   –   man on account of the   sabbath;

28 ὥστε κύριός ἐστιν ὁ υἱὸς τοῦ ἀνθρώπου
   so as   Lord   is   the   Son   –   of man

καὶ τοῦ σαββάτου.
also   of the   sabbath.

---

fields, and as his disciples walked along, they began to pick some heads of grain. 24The Pharisees said to him, "Look, why are they doing what is unlawful on the Sabbath?"

25He answered, "Have you never read what David did when he and his companions were hungry and in need? 26In the days of Abiathar the high priest, he entered the house of God and ate the consecrated bread, which is lawful only for priests to eat. And he also gave some to his companions."

27Then he said to them, "The Sabbath was made for man, not man for the Sabbath. 28So the Son of Man is Lord even of the Sabbath."

Chapter 3

The Man with a Withered Hand

AGAIN he entered the synagogue, and a man was there who had a withered hand. 2They watched him to see whether he would cure him on the sabbath, so that they might accuse him. 3And he said to the man who had the withered hand, "Come forward." 4Then he said to them, "Is it lawful to do good or to do harm on the sabbath, to save life or to kill?" But they were silent. 5He looked around at them with anger; he was grieved at their hardness of heart and said to the man, "Stretch out your hand." He stretched it out, and his hand was restored. 6The Pharisees went out and immediately conspired with

---

3 Καὶ εἰσῆλθεν πάλιν εἰς συναγωγήν.
  And   he entered   again   into   a synagogue.

καὶ ἦν ἐκεῖ ἄνθρωπος ἐξηραμμένην ἔχων
And there was there   a man   ⁴*having been* withered ¹having

τὴν χεῖρα· 2 καὶ παρετήρουν αὐτὸν εἰ
²the   ³hand;   and they watched carefully   him   if

τοῖς σάββασιν θεραπεύσει αὐτόν, ἵνα
on the   sabbath*s*   he will heal   him,   that

κατηγορήσωσιν αὐτοῦ. 3 καὶ λέγει τῷ
they might accuse   him.   And   he says   to the

ἀνθρώπῳ τῷ τὴν χεῖρα ἔχοντι ξηράν·
man   –   the   hand   having   dry:

ἔγειρε εἰς τὸ μέσον. 4 καὶ λέγει αὐτοῖς·
Rise   into the   midst.   And   he says   to them:

ἔξεστιν τοῖς σάββασιν ἀγαθὸν ποιῆσαι
Lawful   on the   sabbath*s*   good   to do

ἢ κακοποιῆσαι, ψυχὴν σῶσαι ἢ ἀποκτεῖναι;
or   to do evil,   life   to save   or   to kill?

οἱ δὲ ἐσιώπων. 5 καὶ περιβλεψάμενος
But they   were silent.   And   looking round

αὐτοὺς μετ' ὀργῆς, συλλυπούμενος ἐπὶ
[on] them   with   anger,   being greatly grieved   on(at)

τῇ πωρώσει τῆς καρδίας αὐτῶν, λέγει
the   hardness   of the   heart   of them,   he says

τῷ ἀνθρώπῳ· ἔκτεινον τὴν χεῖρα. καὶ
to the   man: Stretch forth   the   hand.   And

ἐξέτεινεν, καὶ ἀπεκατεστάθη ἡ χεὶρ αὐτοῦ.
he stretched forth, and   was restored   the   hand   of him.

6 καὶ ἐξελθόντες οἱ Φαρισαῖοι εὐθὺς μετὰ
  And   going forth   the   Pharisees   immediately   with

Chapter 3

ANOTHER time he went into the synagogue, and a man with a shriveled hand was there. 2Some of them were looking for a reason to accuse Jesus, so they watched him closely to see if he would heal him on the Sabbath. 3Jesus said to the man with the shriveled hand, "Stand up in front of everyone."

4Then Jesus asked them, "Which is lawful on the Sabbath: to do good or to do evil, to save life or to kill?" But they remained silent.

5He looked around at them in anger and, deeply distressed at their stubborn hearts, said to the man, "Stretch out your hand." He stretched it out, and his hand was completely restored. 6Then the Pharisees went out and began to plot

the Herodians against him, how to destroy him.

A Multitude at the Seaside

7 Jesus departed with his disciples to the sea, and a great multitude from Galilee followed him; 8 hearing all that he was doing, they came to him in great numbers from Judea, Jerusalem, Idumea, beyond the Jordan, and the region around Tyre and Sidon. 9 He told his disciples to have a boat ready for him because of the crowd, so that they would not crush him; 10 for he had cured many, so that all who had diseases pressed upon him to touch him. 11 Whenever the unclean spirits saw him, they fell down before him and shouted, "You are the Son of God!" 12 But he sternly ordered them not to make him known.

Jesus Appoints the Twelve

13 He went up the mountain and called to him those whom he wanted, and they came to him. 14 And he appointed twelve, whom he also named apostles,ˣ to be with him, and to be sent out to proclaim the message, 15 and to have authority to cast out demons. 16 So he appointed the twelve:ʸ Simon (to whom he gave the name Peter); 17 James son of Zebedee and John the brother of James (to whom he gave the name Boanerges, that is, Sons of Thunder); 18 and Andrew, and Philip, and Bartholomew, and Matthew, and Thomas, and James son of Alphaeus, and Thaddaeus, and Si-

ˣ Other ancient authorities lack *whom he also named apostles*
ʸ Other ancient authorities lack *So he appointed the twelve*

Middle column (interlinear)

τῶν Ἡρωδιανῶν συμβούλιον ἐδίδουν κατ᾽
the Herodians counsel gave against

αὐτοῦ, ὅπως αὐτὸν ἀπολέσωσιν.
him, that him they might destroy.

7 Καὶ ὁ Ἰησοῦς μετὰ τῶν μαθητῶν
And — Jesus with the disciples

αὐτοῦ ἀνεχώρησεν πρὸς τὴν θάλασσαν·
of him departed to the sea;

καὶ πολὺ πλῆθος ἀπὸ τῆς Γαλιλαίας
and a much(great) multitude from — Galilee

ἠκολούθησεν· καὶ ἀπὸ τῆς Ἰουδαίας **8** καὶ
followed; and from — Judæa and

ἀπὸ Ἱεροσολύμων καὶ ἀπὸ τῆς Ἰδουμαίας
from Jerusalem and from — Idumæa

καὶ πέραν τοῦ Ἰορδάνου καὶ περὶ Τύρον
and beyond the Jordan and round Tyre

καὶ Σιδῶνα, πλῆθος πολύ, ἀκούοντες ὅσα
and Sidon, multitude a much(great), hearing what things

ποιεῖ, ἦλθον πρὸς αὐτόν. **9** καὶ εἶπεν
he does, came to him. And he told

τοῖς μαθηταῖς αὐτοῦ ἵνα πλοιάριον προσκαρτερῇ
the disciples of him that a boat should remain near

αὐτῷ διὰ τὸν ὄχλον, ἵνα μὴ θλίβωσιν
him because of the crowd, lest they should press upon

αὐτόν· **10** πολλοὺς γὰρ ἐθεράπευσεν, ὥστε
him; for many he healed, so as

ἐπιπίπτειν αὐτῷ ἵνα αὐτοῦ ἅψωνται
to fall upon him that him they might touch

ὅσοι εἶχον μάστιγας. **11** καὶ τὰ πνεύματα
as many as had plagues. And the spirits

τὰ ἀκάθαρτα, ὅταν αὐτὸν ἐθεώρουν, προσέπιπτον
— unclean, when him they saw, fell before

αὐτῷ καὶ ἔκραζον λέγοντα ὅτι σὺ εἶ ὁ
him and cried out saying[,] — Thou art the

υἱὸς τοῦ θεοῦ. **12** καὶ πολλὰ ἐπετίμα
Son — of God. And much he warned

αὐτοῖς ἵνα μὴ αὐτὸν φανερὸν ποιήσωσιν.
them that not him manifest they should make.

13 Καὶ ἀναβαίνει εἰς τὸ ὄρος, καὶ
And he goes up into the mountain, and

προσκαλεῖται οὓς ἤθελεν αὐτός, καὶ
calls to [him] [those] whom wished he, and

ἀπῆλθον πρὸς αὐτόν. **14** καὶ ἐποίησεν δώδεκα
they went to him. And he made twelve

ἵνα ὦσιν μετ᾽ αὐτοῦ, καὶ ἵνα ἀποστέλλῃ
that they might be with him, and that he might send

αὐτοὺς κηρύσσειν **15** καὶ ἔχειν ἐξουσίαν
them to proclaim and to have authority

ἐκβάλλειν τὰ δαιμόνια· **16** καὶ ἐποίησεν
to expel the demons; and he made

τοὺς δώδεκα, καὶ ἐπέθηκεν ὄνομα τῷ
the twelve, and he added a name —

Σίμωνι Πέτρον· **17** καὶ Ἰάκωβον τὸν τοῦ
to Simon[,] Peter; and James the [son] of

Ζεβεδαίου καὶ Ἰωάννην τὸν ἀδελφὸν τοῦ
of Zebedee and John the brother of

Ἰακώβου, καὶ ἐπέθηκεν αὐτοῖς ὄνομα
of James, and he added to them a name[,]

Βοανηργές, ὅ ἐστιν υἱοὶ βροντῆς· **18** καὶ
Boanerges, which is sons of thunder; and

Ἀνδρέαν καὶ Φίλιππον καὶ Βαρθολομαῖον
Andrew and Philip and Bartholomew

καὶ Ματθαῖον καὶ Θωμᾶν καὶ Ἰάκωβον
and Matthew and Thomas and James

τὸν τοῦ Ἀλφαίου καὶ Θαδδαῖον καὶ
the [son] — of Alphæus and Thaddæus and

with the Herodians how they might kill Jesus.

Crowds Follow Jesus

7 Jesus withdrew with his disciples to the lake, and a large crowd from Galilee followed. 8 When they heard all he was doing, many people came to him from Judea, Jerusalem, Idumea, and the regions across the Jordan and around Tyre and Sidon. 9 Because of the crowd he told his disciples to have a small boat ready for him, to keep the people from crowding him. 10 For he had healed many, so that those with diseases were pushing forward to touch him. 11 Whenever the evilᵍ spirits saw him, they fell down before him and cried out, "You are the Son of God." 12 But he gave them strict orders not to tell who he was.

The Appointing of the Twelve Apostles

13 Jesus went up on a mountainside and called to him those he wanted, and they came to him. 14 He appointed twelve—designating them apostlesʰ—that they might be with him and that he might send them out to preach 15 and to have authority to drive out demons. 16 These are the twelve he appointed: Simon (to whom he gave the name Peter); 17 James son of Zebedee and his brother John (to them he gave the name Boanerges, which means Sons of Thunder); 18 Andrew, Philip, Bartholomew, Matthew, Thomas, James son of Alphaeus, Thaddaeus, Simon the

ᵍ11 Greek *unclean*; also in verse 30
ʰ14 Some manuscripts do not have *designating them apostles*.

mon the Cananaean, 19 and Judas Iscariot, who betrayed him.

Jesus and Beelzebul

Then he went home; 20 and the crowd came together again, so that they could not even eat. 21 When his family heard it, they went out to restrain him, for people were saying, "He has gone out of his mind." 22 And the scribes who came down from Jerusalem said, "He has Beelzebul, and by the ruler of the demons he casts out demons." 23 And he called them to him, and spoke to them in parables, "How can Satan cast out Satan? 24 If a kingdom is divided against itself, that kingdom cannot stand. 25 And if a house is divided against itself, that house will not be able to stand. 26 And if Satan has risen up against himself and is divided, he cannot stand, but his end has come. 27 But no one can enter a strong man's house and plunder his property without first tying up the strong man; then indeed the house can be plundered. 28 "Truly I tell you, people will be forgiven for their sins and whatever blasphemies they utter; 29 but whoever blasphemes against the Holy Spirit can never have forgiveness, but is guilty of an eternal sin"— 30 for they had said, "He has an unclean spirit."

The True Kindred of Jesus

31 Then his mother and his brothers came; and standing outside, they sent to him and called him. 32 A

Σίμωνα τὸν Καναναῖον 19 καὶ Ἰούδαν
Simon　the　Cananæan　and　Judas

Ἰσκαριώθ, ὃς καὶ παρέδωκεν αὐτόν.
Iscariot,　who　indeed　betrayed　him.

20 Καὶ ἔρχεται εἰς οἶκον· καὶ συνέρχεται
And　he comes　into　a house;　and　comes together

πάλιν [ὁ] ὄχλος, ὥστε μὴ δύνασθαι
again　the　crowd,　so as　not　to be able
　　　　　　　　　　　= so that they were not able

αὐτοὺς μηδὲ ἄρτον φαγεῖν. 21 καὶ ἀκούσαντες
them[b] *not*　bread　to eat.　And　hearing

οἱ παρ' αὐτοῦ ἐξῆλθον κρατῆσαι αὐτόν·
the[ones] with　him　went forth　to seize　him;
= his relations

ἔλεγον γὰρ ὅτι ἐξέστη. 22 καὶ οἱ
for they said[,]　– He is beside himself.　And　the

γραμματεῖς οἱ ἀπὸ Ἱεροσολύμων καταβάντες
scribes　–　from　Jerusalem　coming down

ἔλεγον ὅτι Βεεζεβοὺλ ἔχει, καὶ ὅτι ἐν
said[,]　–　Beelzebub　he has, and[,]　–　By

τῷ ἄρχοντι τῶν δαιμονίων ἐκβάλλει τὰ
the　ruler　of the　demons　he expels　the

δαιμόνια. 23 καὶ προσκαλεσάμενος αὐτοὺς
demons.　And　calling to [him]　them

ἐν παραβολαῖς ἔλεγεν αὐτοῖς· πῶς δύναται
in　parables　he said　to them:　How　can

σατανᾶς σατανᾶν ἐκβάλλειν; 24 καὶ ἐὰν
Satan　[1]Satan　[1]to expel ?　and　if

βασιλεία ἐφ' ἑαυτὴν μερισθῇ, οὐ δύναται
a kingdom　against　itself　be divided,　cannot

σταθῆναι ἡ βασιλεία ἐκείνη· 25 καὶ ἐὰν
stand　–　kingdom　that;　and　if

οἰκία ἐφ' ἑαυτὴν μερισθῇ, οὐ δυνήσεται
a house　against　itself　be divided,　will not be able

ἡ οἰκία ἐκείνη στῆναι. 26 καὶ εἰ ὁ
–　house　that　to stand.　And　if　–

σατανᾶς ἀνέστη ἐφ' ἑαυτὸν καὶ ἐμερίσθη,
Satan　stood up　against　himself　and　was divided,

οὐ δύναται στῆναι ἀλλὰ τέλος ἔχει.
he cannot　to stand　but　an end　has.

27 ἀλλ' οὐ δύναται οὐδεὶς εἰς τὴν οἰκίαν
But　cannot　no(any)one　into　the　house

τοῦ ἰσχυροῦ εἰσελθὼν τὰ σκεύη αὐτοῦ
of the strong man　entering　the　goods　of him

διαρπάσαι, ἐὰν μὴ πρῶτον τὸν ἰσχυρὸν
to plunder,　unless　first　the　strong man

δήσῃ, καὶ τότε τὴν οἰκίαν αὐτοῦ διαρπάσει.
he bind,　and　then　the　house　of him　he will plunder.

28 Ἀμὴν λέγω ὑμῖν ὅτι πάντα ἀφεθήσεται
Truly　I tell　you　that　all　will be forgiven

τοῖς υἱοῖς τῶν ἀνθρώπων τὰ ἁμαρτήματα
to the　sons　–　of men　the　sins

καὶ αἱ βλασφημίαι, ὅσα ἐὰν βλασφημήσωσιν·
and the　blasphemies,　whatever　they may blaspheme;

29 ὃς δ' ἂν βλασφημήσῃ εἰς τὸ πνεῦμα
but whoever　blasphemes　against　the　Spirit

τὸ ἅγιον, οὐκ ἔχει ἄφεσιν εἰς τὸν αἰῶνα,
–　Holy,　has not　forgiveness　unto　the　age,

ἀλλὰ ἔνοχός ἐστιν αἰωνίου ἁμαρτήματος.
but　liable　is　of an eternal　sin.

30 ὅτι ἔλεγον· πνεῦμα ἀκάθαρτον ἔχει.
Because　they said:　spirit　an unclean　he has.

31 Καὶ ἔρχονται ἡ μήτηρ αὐτοῦ καὶ οἱ
And　come　the　mother　of him　and the

ἀδελφοὶ αὐτοῦ, καὶ ἔξω στήκοντες ἀπέστειλαν
brothers　of him,　and outside　standing　sent

πρὸς αὐτὸν καλοῦντες αὐτόν. 32 καὶ
to　him　calling　him.　And

Zealot 19 and Judas Iscariot, who betrayed him.

Jesus and Beelzebub

20 Then Jesus entered a house, and again a crowd gathered, so that he and his disciples were not even able to eat. 21 When his family heard about this, they went to take charge of him, for they said, "He is out of his mind."

22 And the teachers of the law who came down from Jerusalem said, "He is possessed by Beelzebub![*i*] By the prince of demons he is driving out demons."

23 So Jesus called them and spoke to them in parables: "How can Satan drive out Satan? 24 If a kingdom is divided against itself, that kingdom cannot stand. 25 If a house is divided against itself, that house cannot stand. 26 And if Satan opposes himself and is divided, he cannot stand; his end has come. 27 In fact, no one can enter a strong man's house and carry off his possessions unless he first ties up the strong man. Then he can rob his house. 28 I tell you the truth, all the sins and blasphemies of men will be forgiven them. 29 But whoever blasphemes against the Holy Spirit will never be forgiven; he is guilty of an eternal sin."

30 He said this because they were saying, "He has an evil spirit."

Jesus' Mother and Brothers

31 Then Jesus' mother and brothers arrived. Standing outside, they sent someone in to call him. 32 A crowd

i 22 Greek Beezeboul or Beelzeboul

crowd was sitting around him; and they said to him, "Your mother and your brothers and sisters[z] are outside, asking for you." [33] And he replied, "Who are my mother and my brothers?" [34] And looking at those who sat around him, he said, "Here are my mother and my brothers! [35] Whoever does the will of God is my brother and sister and mother."

ἐκάθητο περὶ αὐτὸν ὄχλος, καὶ λέγουσιν
sat   round   him   a crowd,   and   they say

αὐτῷ· ἰδοὺ ἡ μήτηρ σου καὶ οἱ ἀδελφοί
to him: Behold[,] the mother of thee and the brothers

σου καὶ αἱ ἀδελφαί σου ἔξω ζητοῦσίν σε.
of thee and the sisters of thee outside seek thee.

33 καὶ ἀποκριθεὶς αὐτοῖς λέγει· τίς ἐστιν
And answering them he says: Who is

ἡ μήτηρ μου καὶ οἱ ἀδελφοί; **34** ·καὶ
the mother of me and the brothers? And

περιβλεψάμενος τοὺς περὶ αὐτὸν κύκλῳ
looking round [at] the [ones] round him in a circle

καθημένους λέγει· ἴδε ἡ μήτηρ ου
sitting he says: Behold[,] the mother of me

καὶ οἱ ἀδελφοί μου. **35** ὃς ἂν ποιήσῃ τὸ
and the brothers of me. Whoever does the

θέλημα τοῦ θεοῦ, οὗτος ἀδελφός μου
will - of God, this one brother of me

καὶ ἀδελφὴ καὶ μήτηρ ἐστίν.
and sister and mother is.

was sitting around him, and they told him, "Your mother and brothers are outside looking for you." [33] "Who are my mother and my brothers?" he asked. [34] Then he looked at those seated in a circle around him and said, "Here are my mother and my brothers! [35] Whoever does God's will is my brother and sister and mother."

Chapter 4

The Parable of the Sower

AGAIN he began to teach beside the sea. Such a very large crowd gathered around him that he got into a boat on the sea and sat there, while the whole crowd was beside the sea on the land. [2] He began to teach them many things in parables, and in his teaching he said to them: [3] "Listen! A sower went out to sow. [4] And as he sowed, some seed fell on the path, and the birds came and ate it up. [5] Other seed fell on rocky ground, where it did not have much soil, and it sprang up quickly, since it had no depth of soil. [6] And when the sun rose, it was scorched; and since it had no root, it withered away. [7] Other seed fell among thorns, and the thorns grew up and choked it, and it yielded no grain. [8] Other seed fell into good soil and brought forth

4 Καὶ πάλιν ἤρξατο διδάσκειν παρὰ τὴν
And again he began to teach by the

θάλασσαν· καὶ συνάγεται πρὸς αὐτὸν ὄχλος
sea; and is assembled to him crowd

πλεῖστος, ὥστε αὐτὸν εἰς πλοῖον ἐμβάντα
a very large, so as him in a ship embarking
= so that embarking in a ship he sat

καθῆσθαι ἐν τῇ θαλάσσῃ, καὶ πᾶς ὁ
to sit[b] in the sea, and all the

ὄχλος πρὸς τὴν θάλασσαν ἐπὶ τῆς γῆς
crowd toward the sea on the land

ἦσαν. **2** καὶ ἐδίδασκεν αὐτοὺς ἐν παραβολαῖς
were. And he taught them in parables

πολλά, καὶ ἔλεγεν αὐτοῖς ἐν τῇ διδαχῇ
many things, and said to them in the teaching

αὐτοῦ· **3** ἀκούετε. ἰδοὺ ἐξῆλθεν ὁ σπείρων
of him: Hear ye. Behold[,] went out the [one] sowing

σπεῖραι. **4** καὶ ἐγένετο ἐν τῷ σπείρειν
to sow. And it came to pass in the to sow[e]
= as he sowed

ὃ μὲν ἔπεσεν παρὰ τὴν ὁδόν, καὶ ἦλθεν
some fell by the way, and came

τὰ πετεινὰ καὶ κατέφαγεν αὐτό. **5** καὶ
the birds and devoured it. And

ἄλλο ἔπεσεν ἐπὶ τὸ πετρῶδες ὅπου οὐκ
other fell on the rocky place where not

εἶχεν γῆν πολλήν, καὶ εὐθὺς ἐξανέτειλεν
it had earth much, and immediately it sprang up

διὰ τὸ μὴ ἔχειν βάθος γῆς·
on account of the not to have depth of earth;
= because it had no depth of earth;

6 καὶ ὅτε ἀνέτειλεν ὁ ἥλιος ἐκαυματίσθη, καὶ
and when rose the sun it was scorched, and

διὰ τὸ μὴ ἔχειν ῥίζαν ἐξηράνθη. **7** καὶ
on account of the not to have root it was withered. And
= because it had no root

ἄλλο ἔπεσεν εἰς τὰς ἀκάνθας, καὶ ἀνέβησαν
other fell among the thorns, and came up

αἱ ἄκανθαι καὶ συνέπνιξαν αὐτό, καὶ
the thorns and choked it, and

καρπὸν οὐκ ἔδωκεν. **8** καὶ ἄλλα ἔπεσεν
fruit it gave not. And others fell

εἰς τὴν γῆν τὴν καλὴν καὶ ἐδίδου καρπὸν
into the earth - good and gave fruit

Chapter 4

The Parable of the Sower

AGAIN Jesus began to teach by the lake. The crowd that gathered around him was so large that he got into a boat and sat in it out on the lake, while all the people were along the shore at the water's edge. [2] He taught them many things by parables, and in his teaching said: [3] "Listen! A farmer went out to sow his seed. [4] As he was scattering the seed, some fell along the path, and the birds came and ate it up. [5] Some fell on rocky places, where it did not have much soil. It sprang up quickly, because the soil was shallow. [6] But when the sun came up, the plants were scorched, and they withered because they had no root. [7] Other seed fell among thorns, which grew up and choked the plants, so that they did not bear grain. [8] Still other seed fell on good soil. It came up,

[z] Other ancient authorities lack *and sisters*

grain, growing up and increasing and yielding thirty and sixty and a hundredfold." 9And he said, "Let anyone with ears to hear listen!"

The Purpose of the Parables

10 When he was alone, those who were around him along with the twelve asked him about the parables. 11 And he said to them, "To you has been given the secret[a] of the kingdom of God, but for those outside, everything comes in parables; 12 in order that

  'they may indeed
    look, but not
    perceive,
  and may indeed
    listen, but not
    understand;
  so that they may not
    turn again and
    be forgiven.' "

13 And he said to them, "Do you not understand this parable? Then how will you understand all the parables? 14 The sower sows the word. 15 These are the ones on the path where the word is sown: when they hear, Satan immediately comes and takes away the word that is sown in them. 16 And these are the ones sown on rocky ground: when they hear the word, they immediately receive it with joy. 17 But they have no root, and endure only for a while; then, when trouble or persecution arises on account of the word, immediately they fall away.[b] 18 And others are those sown among the thorns: these are the ones who hear the word, 19 but the cares of the world, and the lure of wealth, and the desire for other things come in and choke the word, and it yields nothing. 20 And these are the ones

ἀναβαίνοντα καὶ αὐξανόμενα καὶ ἔφερεν
coming up   and   growing   and   bore

εἰς τριάκοντα καὶ ἐν ἐξήκοντα καὶ ἐν
in   thirty   and in   sixty   and in

ἑκατόν.   9 καὶ   ἔλεγεν· ὃς   ἔχει   ὦτα
a hundred.   And   he said: Who   has   ears

ἀκούειν ἀκουέτω.   10 Καὶ   ὅτε   ἐγένετο
to hear   let him hear.   And   when   he was

κατὰ μόνας, ἠρώτων αὐτὸν οἱ περὶ
alone,†   asked   him   the [ones] round

αὐτὸν σὺν τοῖς δώδεκα τὰς παραβολάς.
him   with   the   twelve   the   parables.

11 καὶ ἔλεγεν αὐτοῖς· ὑμῖν τὸ μυστήριον
And   he said   to them: To you the   mystery

δέδοται τῆς βασιλείας τοῦ θεοῦ· ἐκείνοις δὲ
has been given of the   kingdom   - of God; but to those

τοῖς ἔξω ἐν παραβολαῖς τὰ πάντα
the [ones] outside in   parables   -   all things

γίνεται,   12 ἵνα βλέποντες βλέπωσιν καὶ
is(are),   that   seeing   they may see   and

μὴ ἴδωσιν, καὶ ἀκούοντες ἀκούωσιν καὶ
not   perceive,   and   hearing   they may hear   and

μὴ συνιῶσιν, μήποτε ἐπιστρέψωσιν καὶ
not   understand,   lest   they should turn   and

ἀφεθῇ αὐτοῖς.   13 καὶ λέγει αὐτοῖς·
it should be forgiven them.   And   he says   to them:

οὐκ οἴδατε τὴν παραβολὴν ταύτην, καὶ πῶς
Know ye not   -   parable   this,   and how

πάσας τὰς παραβολὰς γνώσεσθε;   14 ὁ
all   the   parables   will ye know?   The [one]

σπείρων τὸν λόγον σπείρει.   15 οὗτοι δέ εἰσιν
sowing ²the ³word ¹sows.   And these   are

οἱ παρὰ τὴν ὁδόν, ὅπου σπείρεται ὁ
the [ones] by   the   way,   where   is sown   the

λόγος, καὶ ὅταν ἀκούσωσιν, εὐθὺς ἔρχεται
word,   and   when   they hear,   immediately comes

ὁ σατανᾶς καὶ αἴρει τὸν λόγον τὸν
-   Satan   and   takes   the   word   -

ἐσπαρμένον εἰς αὐτούς.   16 καὶ οὗτοί εἰσιν
having been sown in   them.   And   these   are

ὁμοίως οἱ ἐπὶ τὰ πετρώδη σπειρόμενοι,
likewise the [ones] on   the   rocky places   being sown,

οἳ ὅταν ἀκούσωσιν τὸν λόγον εὐθὺς
who   when   they hear   the   word immediately

μετὰ χαρᾶς λαμβάνουσιν αὐτόν,   17 καὶ
with   joy   receive   it,   and

οὐκ ἔχουσιν ῥίζαν ἐν ἑαυτοῖς ἀλλὰ
have not   root   in   themselves   but

πρόσκαιροί εἰσιν, εἶτα γενομένης θλίψεως
shortlived   are,   then   happening   affliction
             = when affliction or persecution happens

ἢ διωγμοῦ διὰ τὸν λόγον εὐθὺς
or   persecution³ on account of the   word immediately

σκανδαλίζονται.   18 καὶ ἄλλοι εἰσὶν οἱ εἰς
they are offended.   And   others   are the [ones] among

τὰς ἀκάνθας σπειρόμενοι· οὗτοί εἰσιν οἱ
the   thorns   being sown;   these   are the [ones]

τὸν λόγον ἀκούσαντες,   19 καὶ αἱ μέριμναι
the   word   hearing,   and the   cares

τοῦ αἰῶνος καὶ ἡ ἀπάτη τοῦ πλούτου
of the   age   and   the deceitfulness   -   of riches

καὶ αἱ περὶ τὰ λοιπὰ ἐπιθυμίαι
and   ¹the   ²about   ⁴the   ⁵other things   ³desires

εἰσπορευόμεναι συμπνίγουσιν τὸν λόγον, καὶ
coming in   choke   the   word,   and

ἄκαρπος γίνεται.   20 καὶ ἐκεῖνοί εἰσιν
unfruitful   it becomes.   And   those   are

grew and produced a crop, multiplying thirty, sixty, or even a hundred times."

9Then Jesus said, "He who has ears to hear, let him hear."

10When he was alone, the Twelve and the others around him asked him about the parables. 11He told them, "The secret of the kingdom of God has been given to you. But to those on the outside everything is said in parables 12so that,

  " 'they may be ever
    seeing but never
    perceiving,
  and ever hearing but
    never
    understanding;
  otherwise they might
    turn and be
    forgiven!'ʲ"

13Then Jesus said to them, "Don't you understand this parable? How then will you understand any parable? 14The farmer sows the word. 15Some people are like seed along the path, where the word is sown. As soon as they hear it, Satan comes and takes away the word that was sown in them. 16Others, like seed sown on rocky places, hear the word and at once receive it with joy. 17But since they have no root, they last only a short time. When trouble or persecution comes because of the word, they quickly fall away. 18Still others, like seed sown among thorns, hear the word; 19but the worries of this life, the deceitfulness of wealth and the desires for other things come in and choke the word, making it unfruitful. 20Others, like seed sown on

a Or mystery
b Or stumble

ʲ12 Isaiah 6:9,10

sown on the good soil: they hear the word and accept it and bear fruit, thirty and sixty and a hundredfold."

A Lamp under a Bushel Basket

21 He said to them, "Is a lamp brought in to be put under the bushel basket, or under the bed, and not on the lampstand? 22 For there is nothing hidden, except to be disclosed; nor is anything secret, except to come to light. 23 Let anyone with ears to hear listen!" 24 And he said to them, "Pay attention to what you hear; the measure you give will be the measure you get, and still more will be given you. 25 For to those who have, more will be given; and from those who have nothing, even what they have will be taken away."

The Parable of the Growing Seed

26 He also said, "The kingdom of God is as if someone would scatter seed on the ground, 27 and would sleep and rise night and day, and the seed would sprout and grow, he does not know how. 28 The earth produces of itself, first the stalk, then the head, then the full grain in the head. 29 But when the grain is ripe, at once he goes in with his sickle, because the harvest has come."

The Parable of the Mustard Seed

30 He also said, "With what can we compare the kingdom of God, or what parable will we use for it? 31 It is like a mustard seed, which, when sown upon the ground, is the smallest of all the seeds on earth; 32 yet when it is sown it grows up and becomes the greatest of all shrubs, and puts forth large branches,

Middle column (interlinear)

οἱ ἐπὶ τὴν γῆν τὴν καλὴν σπαρέντες,
the [ones] on the earth - good sown,

οἵτινες ἀκούουσιν τὸν λόγον καὶ παραδέχονται
who hear the word and welcome [it]

καὶ καρποφοροῦσιν ἐν τριάκοντα καὶ ἐν
and bear fruit in thirty and in

ἐξήκοντα καὶ ἐν ἑκατόν. 21 Καὶ ἔλεγεν
sixty and in a hundred. And he said

αὐτοῖς ὅτι μήτι ἔρχεται ὁ λύχνος ἵνα
to them[,] - not Comes the lamp that

ὑπὸ τὸν μόδιον τεθῇ ἢ ὑπὸ τὴν
under the bushel it may be placed or under the

κλίνην; οὐχ ἵνα ἐπὶ τὴν λυχνίαν
couch? not that on the lampstand

τεθῇ; 22 οὐ γάρ ἐστίν τι κρυπτόν,
it may be placed? For there is not anything hidden,

ἐὰν μὴ ἵνα φανερωθῇ· οὐδὲ ἐγένετο
except that it may be manifested; nor became

ἀπόκρυφον, ἀλλ' ἵνα ἔλθῃ εἰς φανερόν.
covered, but that it may come into [the] open.

23 εἰ τις ἔχει ὦτα ἀκούειν ἀκουέτω.
If anyone has ears to hear let him hear.

24 Καὶ ἔλεγεν αὐτοῖς· βλέπετε τί
And he said to them: Take heed what

ἀκούετε. ἐν ᾧ μέτρῳ μετρεῖτε
ye hear. With what measure ye measure

μετρηθήσεται ὑμῖν, καὶ προστεθήσεται ὑμῖν.
it will be measured to you, and it will be added to you.

25 ὃς γὰρ ἔχει, δοθήσεται αὐτῷ· καὶ ὃς
For [he] who has, it will be given to him; and who

οὐκ ἔχει, καὶ ὃ ἔχει ἀρθήσεται ἀπ'
has not, even what he has will be taken from

αὐτοῦ. 26 Καὶ ἔλεγεν· οὕτως ἐστὶν ἡ
him. And he said: Thus is the

βασιλεία τοῦ θεοῦ, ὡς ἄνθρωπος βάλῃ
kingdom - of God, as a man might cast

τὸν σπόρον ἐπὶ τῆς γῆς, 27 καὶ καθεύδῃ
the seed on the earth, and might sleep

καὶ ἐγείρηται νύκτα καὶ ἡμέραν, καὶ ὁ
and rise night and day, and the

σπόρος βλαστᾷ καὶ μηκύνηται ὡς οὐκ
seed sprouts and lengthens as not

οἶδεν αὐτός. 28 αὐτομάτη ἡ γῆ καρποφορεῖ,
knows he. Of its own accord the earth bears fruit,

πρῶτον χόρτον, εἶτεν στάχυν, εἶτεν πλήρης
first grass, then an ear, then full

σῖτος ἐν τῷ στάχυϊ. 29 ὅταν δὲ παραδοῖ
corn in the ear. But when permits

ὁ καρπός, εὐθὺς ἀποστέλλει τὸ δρέπανον,
the fruit, immediately he sends (puts) forth the sickle,

ὅτι παρέστηκεν ὁ θερισμός. 30 Καὶ ἔλεγεν·
because has come the harvest. And he said:

πῶς ὁμοιώσωμεν τὴν βασιλείαν τοῦ θεοῦ,
How may we liken the kingdom - of God,

ἢ ἐν τίνι αὐτὴν παραβολῇ θῶμεν; 31 ὡς
or by ¹what ⁴it ²parable ³may we place? As

κόκκῳ σινάπεως, ὃς ὅταν σπαρῇ ἐπὶ τῆς
a grain of mustard, which when it is sown on the

γῆς, μικρότερον ὂν πάντων τῶν σπερμάτων
earth, smaller being [than] all the seeds

τῶν ἐπὶ τῆς γῆς, 32 καὶ ὅταν σπαρῇ,
- on the earth, and when it is sown,

ἀναβαίνει καὶ γίνεται μεῖζον πάντων τῶν
comes up and becomes greater [than] all the

λαχάνων, καὶ ποιεῖ κλάδους μεγάλους,
herbs, and makes branches great,

good soil, hear the word, accept it, and produce a crop—thirty, sixty or even a hundred times what was sown."

A Lamp on a Stand

21 He said to them, "Do you bring in a lamp to put it under a bowl or a bed? Instead, don't you put it on its stand? 22 For whatever is hidden is meant to be disclosed, and whatever is concealed is meant to be brought out into the open. 23 If anyone has ears to hear, let him hear."

24 "Consider carefully what you hear," he continued. "With the measure you use, it will be measured to you—and even more. 25 Whoever has will be given more; whoever does not have, even what he has will be taken from him."

The Parable of the Growing Seed

26 He also said, "This is what the kingdom of God is like. A man scatters seed on the ground. 27 Night and day, whether he sleeps or gets up, the seed sprouts and grows, though he does not know how. 28 All by itself the soil produces grain—first the stalk, then the head, then the full kernel in the head. 29 As soon as the grain is ripe, he puts the sickle to it, because the harvest has come."

The Parable of the Mustard Seed

30 Again he said, "What shall we say the kingdom of God is like, or what parable shall we use to describe it? 31 It is like a mustard seed, which is the smallest seed you plant in the ground. 32 Yet when planted, it grows and becomes the largest of all garden plants,

so that the birds of the air can make nests in its shade.''

The Use of Parables

33 With many such parables he spoke the word to them, as they were able to hear it; [34] he did not speak to them except in parables, but he explained everything in private to his disciples.

Jesus Stills a Storm

35 On that day, when evening had come, he said to them, ''Let us go across to the other side.'' [36] And leaving the crowd behind, they took him with them in the boat, just as he was. Other boats were with him. [37] A great windstorm arose, and the waves beat into the boat, so that the boat was already being swamped. [38] But he was in the stern, asleep on the cushion; and they woke him up and said to him, ''Teacher, do you not care that we are perishing?'' [39] He woke up and rebuked the wind, and said to the sea, ''Peace! Be still!'' Then the wind ceased, and there was a dead calm. [40] He said to them, ''Why are you afraid? Have you still no faith?'' [41] And they were filled with great awe and said to one another, ''Who then is this, that even the wind and the sea obey him?''

ὥστε δύνασθαι ὑπὸ τὴν σκιὰν αὐτοῦ τὰ
so as   to be able   under   the   shade   of it   the
= so that the birds of heaven are able to dwell under its shade.

πετεινὰ τοῦ οὐρανοῦ κατασκηνοῦν. 33 Καὶ
birds   -   of heaven   to dwell.[b]   And

τοιαύταις παραβολαῖς πολλαῖς ἐλάλει αὐτοῖς
[a]such   [a]parables   [1]in many   he spoke   to them

τὸν λόγον, καθὼς ἠδύναντο ἀκούειν·
the   word,   as   they were able   to hear;

34 χωρὶς δὲ παραβολῆς οὐκ ἐλάλει αὐτοῖς,
and without   a parable   he spoke not   to them,

κατ' ἰδίαν δὲ τοῖς ἰδίοις μαθηταῖς ἐπέλυεν
but privately   to the(his) own   disciples   he explained

πάντα.
all things.

35 Καὶ λέγει αὐτοῖς ἐν ἐκείνῃ τῇ
And   he says   to them   on   that   -

ἡμέρᾳ ὀψίας γενομένης· διέλθωμεν εἰς τὸ
day   evening   having come[a]: Let us pass over   to   the
= when evening had come:

πέραν. 36 καὶ ἀφέντες τὸν ὄχλον
other side.   And   leaving   the   crowd

παραλαμβάνουσιν αὐτὸν ὡς ἦν ἐν τῷ
they take   him   as he was   in   the

πλοίῳ, καὶ ἄλλα πλοῖα ἦν μετ' αὐτοῦ.
ship,   and   other   ships   were   with   him.

37 καὶ γίνεται λαῖλαψ μεγάλη ἀνέμου,
And   occurs   storm   a great   of wind,

καὶ τὰ κύματα ἐπέβαλλεν εἰς τὸ πλοῖον,
and   the   waves   struck   into   the   ship,

ὥστε ἤδη γεμίζεσθαι τὸ πλοῖον. 38 καὶ
so as   now   to be filled   the   ship.[b]   And

αὐτὸς ἦν ἐν τῇ πρύμνῃ ἐπὶ τὸ
he   was   in   the   stern   on   the

προσκεφάλαιον καθεύδων. καὶ ἐγείρουσιν
pillow   sleeping.   And   they rouse

αὐτὸν καὶ λέγουσιν αὐτῷ· διδάσκαλε, οὐ μέλει
him   and   say   to him: Teacher,   matters it not

σοι ὅτι ἀπολλύμεθα; 39 καὶ διεγερθεὶς
to thee that   we are perishing?   And   being roused

ἐπετίμησεν τῷ ἀνέμῳ καὶ εἶπεν τῇ
he rebuked   the   wind   and   said   to the

θαλάσσῃ· σιώπα, πεφίμωσο. καὶ ἐκόπασεν
sea: Be quiet,   be muzzled.   And   dropped

ὁ ἄνεμος, καὶ ἐγένετο γαλήνη μεγάλη.
the   wind,   and   there was   calm   a great.

40 καὶ εἶπεν αὐτοῖς· τί δειλοί ἐστε
And   he said   to them: Why   fearful   are ye

οὕτως; πῶς οὐκ ἔχετε πίστιν; 41 καὶ
thus ?   how   have ye not   faith ?   And

ἐφοβήθησαν φόβον μέγαν, καὶ ἔλεγον πρὸς
they feared   fear   a great,   and   said   to

ἀλλήλους· τίς ἄρα οὗτός ἐστιν, ὅτι καὶ
one another: Who   then   this man   is,   that   both

ὁ ἄνεμος καὶ ἡ θάλασσα ὑπακούει αὐτῷ;
the   wind   and   the   sea   obeys   him ?

5 Καὶ ἦλθον εἰς τὸ πέραν τῆς θαλάσσης
And   they came to   the other side   of the   sea

εἰς τὴν χώραν τῶν Γερασηνῶν. 2 καὶ
into   the   country   of the   Gerasenes.   And

ἐξελθόντος αὐτοῦ ἐκ τοῦ πλοίου, [εὐθὺς]
coming out   him[a]   out of the   ship,   immediately
= as he came out

ὑπήντησεν αὐτῷ ἐκ τῶν μνημείων ἄνθρωπος
met   him   out of   the   tombs   a man

---

with such big branches that the birds of the air can perch in its shade.''

[33] With many similar parables Jesus spoke the word to them, as much as they could understand. [34] He did not say anything to them without using a parable. But when he was alone with his own disciples, he explained everything.

Jesus Calms the Storm

[35] That day when evening came, he said to his disciples, ''Let us go over to the other side.'' [36] Leaving the crowd behind, they took him along, just as he was, in the boat. There were also other boats with him. [37] A furious squall came up, and the waves broke over the boat, so that it was nearly swamped. [38] Jesus was in the stern, sleeping on a cushion. The disciples woke him and said to him, ''Teacher, don't you care if we drown?''

[39] He got up, rebuked the wind and said to the waves, ''Quiet! Be still!'' Then the wind died down and it was completely calm.

[40] He said to his disciples, ''Why are you so afraid? Do you still have no faith?''

[41] They were terrified and asked each other, ''Who is this? Even the wind and the waves obey him!''

Chapter 5 (left)

Jesus Heals the Gerasene Demoniac

THEY came to the other side of the sea, to the country of the Gerasenes.[c] [2] And when he had stepped out of the boat, immediately a man out of the tombs

---

Chapter 5

The Healing of a Demon-possessed Man

THEY went across the lake to the region of the Gerasenes.[k] [2] When Jesus got out of the boat, a man with an evil[l] spirit came from the tombs to

with an unclean spirit met him. ³He lived among the tombs; and no one could restrain him any more, even with a chain; ⁴for he had often been restrained with shackles and chains, but the chains he wrenched apart, and the shackles he broke in pieces; and no one had the strength to subdue him. ⁵Night and day among the tombs and on the mountains he was always howling and bruising himself with stones. ⁶When he saw Jesus from a distance, he ran and bowed down before him; ⁷and he shouted at the top of his voice, "What have you to do with me, Jesus, Son of the Most High God? I adjure you by God, do not torment me." ⁸For he had said to him, "Come out of the man, you unclean spirit!" ⁹Then Jesus*d* asked him, "What is your name?" He replied, "My name is Legion; for we are many." ¹⁰He begged him earnestly not to send them out of the country. ¹¹Now there on the hillside a great herd of swine was feeding; ¹²and the unclean spirits*e* begged him, "Send us into the swine; let us enter them." ¹³So he gave them permission. And the unclean spirits came out and entered the swine; and the herd, numbering about two thousand, rushed down the steep bank into the sea, and were drowned in the sea.

14 The swineherds ran off and told it in the city and in the country. Then people came to see what it was that

ἐν πνεύματι ἀκαθάρτῳ, 3 ὃς τὴν κατοίκησιν
in(with) spirit an unclean, who the(his) dwelling

εἶχεν ἐν τοῖς μνήμασιν, καὶ οὐδὲ ἁλύσει
had among the tombs, and not with a chain
=no one any more

οὐκέτι οὐδεὶς ἐδύνατο αὐτὸν δῆσαι, 4 διὰ
no longer no one was able him to bind, on account of
was able to bind him with a chain, = because

τὸ αὐτὸν πολλάκις πέδαις καὶ ἁλύσεσιν
the him often with fetters and chains
he had often been bound with fetters and chains, and . . .

δεδέσθαι, καὶ διεσπάσθαι ὑπ' αὐτοῦ τὰς
to have been bound, and to be burst by him the

ἁλύσεις καὶ τὰς πέδας συντετρίφθαι, καὶ
chains and the fetters to have been broken, and

οὐδεὶς ἴσχυεν αὐτὸν δαμάσαι· 5 καὶ
no one was able him to subdue; and

διὰ παντὸς νυκτὸς καὶ ἡμέρας ἐν τοῖς μνήμασιν
always of(by) night and day among the tombs

καὶ ἐν τοῖς ὄρεσιν ἦν κράζων καὶ
and in the mountains he was crying out and

κατακόπτων ἑαυτὸν λίθοις. 6 καὶ ἰδὼν
cutting himself with stones. And seeing

τὸν Ἰησοῦν ἀπὸ μακρόθεν ἔδραμεν καὶ
— Jesus from afar he ran and

προσεκύνησεν αὐτόν, 7 καὶ κράξας φωνῇ
worshipped him, and crying out with a voice

μεγάλῃ λέγει· τί ἐμοὶ καὶ σοί, Ἰησοῦ
great(loud) he says: What to me and to thee, Jesus

υἱὲ τοῦ θεοῦ τοῦ ὑψίστου; ὁρκίζω σε
Son – of God the most high? I adjure thee

τὸν θεόν, μή με βασανίσῃς. 8 ἔλεγεν
– by God, not me thou mayest torment. he said

γὰρ αὐτῷ· ἔξελθε τὸ πνεῦμα τὸ ἀκάθαρτον
For to him: Come out the spirit – unclean

ἐκ τοῦ ἀνθρώπου. 9 καὶ ἐπηρώτα αὐτόν·
out of the man. And he questioned him:

τί ὄνομά σοι; καὶ λέγει αὐτῷ· λεγιὼν
What name to thee? And he says to him: Legion
= What name hast thou ? = My

ὄνομά μοι, ὅτι πολλοί ἐσμεν. 10 καὶ
name to me,* because many we are. And
name is Legion,

παρεκάλει αὐτὸν πολλὰ ἵνα μὴ αὐτὰ
he besought him much that not them

ἀποστείλῃ ἔξω τῆς χώρας. 11 ἦν δὲ
he would send outside the country. Now there was

ἐκεῖ πρὸς τῷ ὄρει ἀγέλη χοίρων μεγάλη
there near the mountain herd of pigs a great

βοσκομένη· 12 καὶ παρεκάλεσαν αὐτὸν
feeding; and they besought him

λέγοντες· πέμψον ἡμᾶς εἰς τοὺς χοίρους,
saying: Send us into the pigs,

ἵνα εἰς αὐτοὺς εἰσέλθωμεν. 13 καὶ ἐπέτρεψεν
that into them we may enter. And he allowed

αὐτοῖς. καὶ ἐξελθόντα τὰ πνεύματα τὰ
them. And coming out the spirits –

ἀκάθαρτα εἰσῆλθον εἰς τοὺς χοίρους, καὶ
unclean entered into the pigs, and

ὥρμησεν ἡ ἀγέλη κατὰ τοῦ κρημνοῦ εἰς
rushed the herd down the precipice into

τὴν θάλασσαν, ὡς δισχίλιοι, καὶ ἐπνίγοντο
the sea, about two thousand, and were choked

ἐν τῇ θαλάσσῃ. 14 καὶ οἱ βόσκοντες
in the sea. And the [ones] feeding

αὐτοὺς ἔφυγον καὶ ἀπήγγειλαν εἰς τὴν
them fled and reported in the

πόλιν καὶ εἰς τοὺς ἀγρούς· καὶ ἦλθον
city and in the fields; and they came

meet him. ³This man lived in the tombs, and no one could bind him any more, not even with a chain. ⁴For he had often been chained hand and foot, but he tore the chains apart and broke the irons on his feet. No one was strong enough to subdue him. ⁵Night and day among the tombs and in the hills he would cry out and cut himself with stones.

⁶When he saw Jesus from a distance, he ran and fell on his knees in front of him. ⁷He shouted at the top of his voice, "What do you want with me, Jesus, Son of the Most High God? Swear to God that you won't torture me!" ⁸For Jesus had said to him, "Come out of this man, you evil spirit!"

⁹Then Jesus asked him, "What is your name?"

"My name is Legion," he replied, "for we are many." ¹⁰And he begged Jesus again and again not to send them out of the area.

¹¹A large herd of pigs was feeding on the nearby hillside. ¹²The demons begged Jesus, "Send us among the pigs; allow us to go into them." ¹³He gave them permission, and the evil spirits came out and went into the pigs. The herd, about two thousand in number, rushed down the steep bank into the lake and were drowned.

¹⁴Those tending the pigs ran off and reported this in the town and countryside, and the people went out to

d Gk he
e Gk they

had happened. 15They came to Jesus and saw the demoniac sitting there, clothed and in his right mind, the very man who had had the legion; and they were afraid. 16Those who had seen what had happened to the demoniac and to the swine reported it. 17Then they began to beg Jesus*f* to leave their neighborhood. 18As he was getting into the boat, the man who had been possessed by demons begged him that he might be with him. 19But Jesus*d* refused, and said to him, "Go home to your friends, and tell them how much the Lord has done for you, and what mercy he has shown you." 20And he went away and began to proclaim in the Decapolis how much Jesus had done for him; and everyone was amazed.

A Girl Restored to Life and a Woman Healed

21 When Jesus had crossed again in the boat*g* to the other side, a great crowd gathered around him; and he was by the sea. 22Then one of the leaders of the synagogue named Jairus came and, when he saw him, fell at his feet 23and begged him repeatedly, "My little daughter is at the point of death. Come and lay your hands on her, so that she may be made well, and live." 24So he went with him.

And a large crowd followed him and pressed in on him. 25Now there was a woman who had been suffering from hemorrhages for twelve years. 26She had endured much under many physicians, and had spent all that she had; and she was no better, but rather

---

ἰδεῖν τί ἐστιν τὸ γεγονός. 15 καὶ
to see what is the thing having happened. And

ἔρχονται πρὸς τὸν Ἰησοῦν, καὶ θεωροῦσιν τὸν
they come to - Jesus, and see the

δαιμονιζόμενον καθήμενον ἱματισμένον καὶ
demon-possessed man sitting *having been* clothed and

σωφρονοῦντα, τὸν ἐσχηκότα τὸν λεγιῶνα,
being in his senses, the man having had the legion,

καὶ ἐφοβήθησαν. 16 καὶ διηγήσαντο αὐτοῖς οἱ
and they were afraid. And related to them the [ones]

ἰδόντες πῶς ἐγένετο τῷ δαιμονιζομένῳ
seeing how it happened to the demon-possessed man

καὶ περὶ τῶν χοίρων. 17 καὶ ἤρξαντο
and about the pigs. And they began

παρακαλεῖν αὐτὸν ἀπελθεῖν ἀπὸ τῶν ὁρίων
to beseech him to depart from the territory

αὐτῶν. 18 καὶ ἐμβαίνοντος αὐτοῦ εἰς τὸ
of them. And embarking him* in the
                    = as he embarked

πλοῖον παρεκάλει αὐτὸν ὁ δαιμονισθεὶς
ship besought him the [one] demon-possessed

ἵνα μετ' αὐτοῦ ᾖ. 19 καὶ οὐκ ἀφῆκεν
that with him he might be. And he permitted not

αὐτόν, ἀλλὰ λέγει αὐτῷ· ὕπαγε εἰς τὸν
him, but says to him: Go to the

οἶκόν σου πρὸς τοὺς σούς, καὶ ἀπάγγειλον
house of thee to the thine, and report
           = thy people,

αὐτοῖς ὅσα ὁ κύριός σοι πεποίηκεν καὶ
to them what things the Lord to thee has done and

ἠλέησέν σε. 20 καὶ ἀπῆλθεν καὶ ἤρξατο
pitied thee. And he departed and began

κηρύσσειν ἐν τῇ Δεκαπόλει ὅσα ἐποίησεν
to proclaim in - Decapolis what things did

αὐτῷ ὁ Ἰησοῦς, καὶ πάντες ἐθαύμαζον.
to him - Jesus, and all men marvelled.

21 Καὶ διαπεράσαντος τοῦ Ἰησοῦ* ἐν τῷ
And crossing over - Jesus in the
           = when Jesus had crossed over

πλοίῳ πάλιν εἰς τὸ πέραν συνήχθη ὄχλος
ship again to the other side was assembled crowd

πολὺς ἐπ' αὐτόν, καὶ ἦν παρὰ τὴν θάλασσαν.
a much(great) to him, and he was by the sea.

22 Καὶ ἔρχεται εἷς τῶν ἀρχισυναγώγων,
And comes one of the synagogue chiefs,

ὀνόματι Ἰάϊρος, καὶ ἰδὼν αὐτὸν πίπτει
by name Jairus, and seeing him falls

πρὸς τοὺς πόδας αὐτοῦ, 23 καὶ παρακαλεῖ
at the feet of him, and beseeches

αὐτὸν πολλὰ λέγων ὅτι τὸ θυγάτριόν μου
him much saying[,] - The daughter of me

ἐσχάτως ἔχει, ἵνα ἐλθὼν ἐπιθῇς
is at the point of death,† that coming thou mayest lay *on*

τὰς χεῖρας αὐτῇ, ἵνα σωθῇ καὶ ζήσῃ.
the(thy) hands on her, that she may be healed and may live.

24 καὶ ἀπῆλθεν μετ' αὐτοῦ. καὶ ἠκολούθει αὐτῷ
And he went with him. And followed him

ὄχλος πολύς, καὶ συνέθλιβον αὐτόν. 25 Καὶ
crowd a much(great), and pressed upon him. And

γυνὴ οὖσα ἐν ῥύσει αἵματος δώδεκα
a woman being in a flow of blood twelve
          = having

ἔτη, 26 καὶ πολλὰ παθοῦσα ὑπὸ πολλῶν
years, and many things suffering by many

ἰατρῶν καὶ δαπανήσασα τὰ παρ' αὐτῆς
physicians and having spent *the* with her

πάντα, καὶ μηδὲν ὠφεληθεῖσα ἀλλὰ μᾶλλον
all things, and nothing having been profited but rather

---

see what had happened. 15When they came to Jesus, they saw the man who had been possessed by the legion of demons, sitting there, dressed and in his right mind; and they were afraid. 16Those who had seen it told the people what had happened to the demon-possessed man—and told about the pigs as well. 17Then the people began to plead with Jesus to leave their region.

18As Jesus was getting into the boat, the man who had been demon-possessed begged to go with him. 19Jesus did not let him, but said, "Go home to your family and tell them how much the Lord has done for you, and how he has had mercy on you." 20So the man went away and began to tell in the Decapolis*m* how much Jesus had done for him. And all the people were amazed.

A Dead Girl and a Sick Woman

21When Jesus had again crossed over by boat to the other side of the lake, a large crowd gathered around him while he was by the lake. 22Then one of the synagogue rulers, named Jairus, came there. Seeing Jesus, he fell at his feet 23and pleaded earnestly with him, "My little daughter is dying. Please come and put your hands on her so that she will be healed and live." 24So Jesus went with him.

A large crowd followed and pressed around him. 25And a woman was there who had been subject to bleeding for twelve years. 26She had suffered a great deal under the care of many doctors and had spent all

---

f Gk *him*
g Other ancient authorities lack *in the boat*

m 20 That is, the Ten Cities

grew worse. 27 She had heard about Jesus, and came up behind him in the crowd and touched his cloak, 28 for she said, "If I but touch his clothes, I will be made well." 29 Immediately her hemorrhage stopped; and she felt in her body that she was healed of her disease. 30 Immediately aware that power had gone forth from him, Jesus turned about in the crowd and said, "Who touched my clothes?" 31 And his disciples said to him, "You see the crowd pressing in on you; how can you say, 'Who touched me?' " 32 He looked all around to see who had done it. 33 But the woman, knowing what had happened to her, came in fear and trembling, fell down before him, and told him the whole truth. 34 He said to her, "Daughter, your faith has made you well; go in peace, and be healed of your disease."

35 While he was still speaking, some people came from the leader's house to say, "Your daughter is dead. Why trouble the teacher any further?" 36 But overhearing*h* what they said, Jesus said to the leader of the synagogue, "Do not fear, only believe." 37 He allowed no one to follow him except Peter, James, and John, the brother of James. 38 When they came to the house of the leader of the synagogue, he saw a commotion, people weeping and wailing loudly. 39 When he had entered, he said to them, "Why do you make a commotion and weep? The child is not dead

h Or *ignoring*: other ancient authorities read *hearing*

Center column (Greek interlinear)

εἰς τὸ χεῖρον ἐλθοῦσα, 27 ἀκούσασα τὰ
to the worse having come, hearing the things

περὶ τοῦ Ἰησοῦ, ἐλθοῦσα ἐν τῷ ὄχλῳ
about – Jesus, coming in the crowd

ὄπισθεν ἥψατο τοῦ ἱματίου αὐτοῦ· 28 ἔλεγεν
behind touched the garment of him; she said[,]

γὰρ ὅτι ἐὰν ἅψωμαι κἂν τῶν ἱματίων
for – If I may touch even the garments

αὐτοῦ, σωθήσομαι. 29 καὶ εὐθὺς ἐξηράνθη
of him, I shall be healed. And immediately was dried up

ἡ πηγὴ τοῦ αἵματος αὐτῆς, καὶ ἔγνω
the fountain of the blood of her, and she knew

τῷ σώματι ὅτι ἴαται ἀπὸ τῆς
in the(her) body that she is(was) cured from the

μάστιγος. 30 καὶ εὐθὺς ὁ Ἰησοῦς ἐπιγνοὺς ἐν
plague. And immediately – Jesus knowing in

ἑαυτῷ τὴν ἐξ αὐτοῦ δύναμιν ἐξελθοῦσαν,
himself the ¹the ⁶out of ⁵him ²power ³going forth,

ἐπιστραφεὶς ἐν τῷ ὄχλῳ ἔλεγεν· τίς μου ἥψατο τῶν
turning in the crowd said: Who of me touched the

ἱματίων; 31 καὶ ἔλεγον αὐτῷ οἱ μαθηταὶ
garments? And said to him the disciples

αὐτοῦ· βλέπεις τὸν ὄχλον συνθλίβοντά σε,
of him: Thou seest the crowd pressing upon thee,

καὶ λέγεις· τίς μου ἥψατο; 32 καὶ
and thou sayest: Who me touched? And

περιεβλέπετο ἰδεῖν τὴν τοῦτο ποιήσασαν.
he looked round to see the [one] this having done.

33 ἡ δὲ γυνὴ φοβηθεῖσα καὶ τρέμουσα,
And the woman fearing and trembling,

εἰδυῖα ὃ γέγονεν αὐτῇ, ἦλθεν καὶ προσέ-
knowing what has happened to her, came and fell

πεσεν αὐτῷ καὶ εἶπεν αὐτῷ πᾶσαν τὴν ἀλήθειαν.
before him and told him all the truth.

34 ὁ δὲ εἶπεν αὐτῇ· θυγάτηρ, ἡ πίστις
And he said to her: Daughter, the faith

σου σέσωκέν σε· ὕπαγε εἰς εἰρήνην, καὶ
of thee has healed thee; go in peace, and

ἴσθι ὑγιὴς ἀπὸ τῆς μάστιγός σου. 35 Ἔτι
be whole from the plague of thee. Still
                                = While

αὐτοῦ λαλοῦντος ἔρχονται ἀπὸ τοῦ
him speaking* they come from the
he was still speaking

ἀρχισυναγώγου λέγοντες ὅτι ἡ θυγάτηρ
synagogue chief saying[,] – The daughter

σου ἀπέθανεν· τί ἔτι σκύλλεις τὸν διδάσκαλον;
of thee died; why still troublest thou the teacher?

36 ὁ δὲ Ἰησοῦς παρακούσας τὸν λόγον
– But Jesus overhearing the word

λαλούμενον λέγει τῷ ἀρχισυναγώγῳ· μὴ
being spoken says to the synagogue chief: not

φοβοῦ, μόνον πίστευε. 37 καὶ οὐκ ἀφῆκεν
Fear, only believe. And he allowed not

οὐδένα μετ' αὐτοῦ συνακολουθῆσαι εἰ μὴ
no(any)one with him to accompany except

τὸν Πέτρον καὶ Ἰάκωβον καὶ Ἰωάννην
– Peter and James and John

τὸν ἀδελφὸν Ἰακώβου. 38 καὶ ἔρχονται
the brother of James. And they come

εἰς τὸν οἶκον τοῦ ἀρχισυναγώγου, καὶ
into the house of the synagogue chief, and

θεωρεῖ θόρυβον, καὶ κλαίοντάς καὶ
he sees an uproar, and [men] weeping and

ἀλαλάζοντας πολλά, 39 καὶ εἰσελθὼν λέγει
crying aloud much, and entering he says

αὐτοῖς· τί θορυβεῖσθε καὶ κλαίετε; τὸ
to them: Why make ye an uproar and weep? the

she had, yet instead of getting better she grew worse. 27 When she heard about Jesus, she came up behind him in the crowd and touched his cloak, 28 because she thought, "If I just touch his clothes, I will be healed." 29 Immediately her bleeding stopped and she felt in her body that she was freed from her suffering.

30 At once Jesus realized that power had gone out from him. He turned around in the crowd and asked, "Who touched my clothes?"

31 "You see the people crowding against you," his disciples answered, "and yet you can ask, 'Who touched me?' "

32 But Jesus kept looking around to see who had done it. 33 Then the woman, knowing what had happened to her, came and fell at his feet and, trembling with fear, told him the whole truth. 34 He said to her, "Daughter, your faith has healed you. Go in peace and be freed from your suffering."

35 While Jesus was still speaking, some men came from the house of Jairus, the synagogue ruler. "Your daughter is dead," they said. "Why bother the teacher any more?"

36 Ignoring what they said, Jesus told the synagogue ruler, "Don't be afraid; just believe."

37 He did not let anyone follow him except Peter, James and John the brother of James. 38 When they came to the home of the synagogue ruler, Jesus saw a commotion, with people crying and wailing loudly. 39 He went in and said to them, "Why all this com-

but sleeping." 40 And they laughed at him. Then he put them all outside, and took the child's father and mother and those who were with him, and went in where the child was. 41 He took her by the hand and said to her, "Talitha cum," which means, "Little girl, get up!" 42 And immediately the girl got up and began to walk about (she was twelve years of age). At this they were overcome with amazement. 43 He strictly ordered them that no one should know this, and told them to give her something to eat.

παιδίον	οὐκ	ἀπέθανεν	ἀλλὰ	καθεύδει.
child		did not die	but	sleeps.

40 καὶ	κατεγέλων	αὐτοῦ.	αὐτὸς	δὲ	ἐκβαλὼν
And	they ridiculed	him.	But he		putting out

πάντας	παραλαμβάνει	τὸν	πατέρα	τοῦ
all	takes	the	father	of the

παιδίου	καὶ	τὴν	μητέρα	καὶ	τοὺς	μετ'
child	and	the	mother	and	the [ones]	with

αὐτοῦ,	καὶ	εἰσπορεύεται	ὅπου	ἦν	τὸ
him,	and	goes in	where	was	the

παιδίον.	41 καὶ	κρατήσας	τῆς	χειρὸς
child.	And	taking hold	of the	hand

τοῦ	παιδίου	λέγει	αὐτῇ·	ταλιθὰ	κοῦμ,	ὅ
of the	child	he says	to her:	Talitha	koum,	which

ἐστιν	μεθερμηνευόμενον·	τὸ	κοράσιον,	σοὶ
is	being interpreted:	-	Maid,	to thee

λέγω,	ἔγειρε.	42 καὶ	εὐθὺς	ἀνέστη	τὸ
I say,	arise.	And immediately	rose up	the

κοράσιον	καὶ	περιεπάτει·	ἦν	γὰρ
maid	and	walked;	for she was

ἐτῶν	δώδεκα.	καὶ	ἐξέστησαν	εὐθὺς
[of the age] of years	twelve.	And they were astonished immediately
		=immediately they were exceedingly astonished.		

ἐκστάσει	μεγάλῃ.	43 καὶ	διεστείλατο
astonishment	with a great.	And	he ordered

αὐτοῖς	πολλὰ	ἵνα	μηδεὶς	γνοῖ	τοῦτο,	καὶ
them	much	that	no one should know	this,	and

εἶπεν	δοθῆναι	αὐτῇ	φαγεῖν.
told	to be given	to her	to eat.
	=[them] to give her [something] to eat.		

motion and wailing? The child is not dead but asleep." 40 But they laughed at him.

After he put them all out, he took the child's father and mother and the disciples who were with him, and went in where the child was. 41 He took her by the hand and said to her, "Talitha koum!" (which means, "Little girl, I say to you, get up!"). 42 Immediately the girl stood up and walked around (she was twelve years old). At this they were completely astonished. 43 He gave strict orders not to let anyone know about this, and told them to give her something to eat.

Chapter 6

The Rejection of Jesus at Nazareth

HE left that place and came to his hometown, and his disciples followed him. 2 On the sabbath he began to teach in the synagogue, and many who heard him were astounded. They said, "Where did this man get all this? What is this wisdom that has been given to him? What deeds of power are being done by his hands! 3 Is not this the carpenter, the son of Mary[i] and brother of James and Joses and Judas and Simon, and are not his sisters here with us?" And they took offense[j] at him. 4 Then Jesus said to them, "Prophets are not without honor, except in their hometown, and among their own kin, and in their own house." 5 And he could do no deed of power

6 Καὶ	ἐξῆλθεν	ἐκεῖθεν,	καὶ	ἔρχεται	εἰς
And	he went forth	thence,	and	comes	into

τὴν	πατρίδα	αὐτοῦ,	καὶ	ἀκολουθοῦσιν
the	native place	of him,	and	follow

αὐτῷ	οἱ	μαθηταὶ	αὐτοῦ.	2 καὶ	γενομένου
him	the	disciples	of him.	And	coming
					= when

σαββάτου	ἤρξατο	διδάσκειν	ἐν	τῇ	συναγωγῇ·
a sabbath	he began	to teach	in	the	synagogue;
a sabbath came					

καὶ	οἱ	πολλοὶ	ἀκούοντες	ἐξεπλήσσοντο
and	the	many	hearing	were astonished

λέγοντες·	πόθεν	τούτῳ	ταῦτα,	καὶ	τίς	ἡ
saying:	Whence	to this man	these things,	and	what	the

σοφία	ἡ	δοθεῖσα	τούτῳ;	καὶ	αἱ	δυνάμεις
wisdom	-	given	to this(him)?	And	the	powerful deeds

τοιαῦται	διὰ	τῶν	χειρῶν	αὐτοῦ	γινόμεναι;
such	through	the	hands	of him	coming about?

3 οὐχ	οὗτός	ἐστιν	ὁ	τέκτων,	ὁ	υἱὸς
¹Not	²this man	¹is	the	carpenter,	the	son

τῆς	Μαρίας	καὶ	ἀδελφὸς	Ἰακώβου	καὶ
of Mary		and	brother	of James	and

Ἰωσῆτος	καὶ	Ἰούδα	καὶ	Σίμωνος;	καὶ
Joses	and	Judas	and	Simon?	and

οὐκ	εἰσὶν	αἱ	ἀδελφαὶ	αὐτοῦ	ὧδε	πρὸς
²not	¹are	the	sisters	of him	here	with

ἡμᾶς;	καὶ	ἐσκανδαλίζοντο	ἐν	αὐτῷ.	4 καὶ
us?	and	they were offended	in(at)	him.	And

ἔλεγεν	αὐτοῖς	ὁ	Ἰησοῦς	ὅτι	οὐκ	ἔστιν
said	to them	-	Jesus[,]	-	²not	¹is

προφήτης	ἄτιμος	εἰ	μὴ	ἐν	τῇ	πατρίδι
¹A prophet	unhonoured	except	in	the	native place

αὐτοῦ	καὶ	ἐν	τοῖς	συγγενεῦσιν	αὐτοῦ
of him	and	among	the	relatives	of him

καὶ	ἐν	τῇ	οἰκίᾳ	αὐτοῦ.	5 καὶ	οὐκ
and	in	the	house	of him.	And	not

Chapter 6

A Prophet Without Honor

JESUS left there and went to his hometown, accompanied by his disciples. 2 When the Sabbath came, he began to teach in the synagogue, and many who heard him were amazed.

"Where did this man get these things?" they asked. "What's this wisdom that has been given him, that he even does miracles! 3 Isn't this the carpenter? Isn't this Mary's son and the brother of James, Joseph,[n] Judas and Simon? Aren't his sisters here with us?" And they took offense at him.

4 Jesus said to them, "Only in his hometown, among his relatives and in his own house is a prophet without honor." 5 He could

i Other ancient authorities read son of the carpenter and of Mary
j Or stumbled

n3 Greek Joses, *a variant of* Joseph

there, except that he laid his hands on a few sick people and cured them. 6 And he was amazed at their unbelief.

The Mission of the Twelve

Then he went about among the villages teaching. 7 He called the twelve and began to send them out two by two, and gave them authority over the unclean spirits. 8 He ordered them to take nothing for their journey except a staff; no bread, no bag, no money in their belts; 9 but to wear sandals and not to put on two tunics. 10 He said to them, "Wherever you enter a house, stay there until you leave the place. 11 If any place will not welcome you and they refuse to hear you, as you leave, shake off the dust that is on your feet as a testimony against them." 12 So they went out and proclaimed that all should repent. 13 They cast out many demons, and anointed with oil many who were sick and cured them.

The Death of John the Baptist

14 King Herod heard of it, for Jesus' *k* name had become known. Some were *l* saying, "John the baptizer has been raised from the dead; and for this reason these powers are at work in him." 15 But others said, "It is Elijah." And others said, "It is a prophet, like one of the prophets of old." 16 But when Herod heard of it, he said, "John, whom I beheaded, has been raised." 17 For Herod himself had sent men who arrested John, bound him, and put

ἐδύνατο ἐκεῖ ποιῆσαι οὐδεμίαν δύναμιν,
he could there *to do* no(any) powerful deed,
εἰ μὴ ὀλίγοις ἀρρώστοις ἐπιθεὶς τὰς
except *on* a few sick [ones] laying on the(his)
χεῖρας ἐθεράπευσεν. 6 καὶ ἐθαύμασεν διὰ
hands he healed. And he marvelled because of
τὴν ἀπιστίαν αὐτῶν.
the unbelief of them.
Καὶ περιῆγεν τὰς κώμας κύκλῳ
And he went round the villages in circuit
διδάσκων. 7 Καὶ προσκαλεῖται τοὺς δώδεκα,
teaching. And he calls to [him] the twelve,
καὶ ἤρξατο αὐτοὺς ἀποστέλλειν δύο δύο,
and began them to send forth two [by] two,
καὶ ἐδίδου αὐτοῖς ἐξουσίαν τῶν πνευμάτων
and gave them authority the spirits
τῶν ἀκαθάρτων, 8 καὶ παρήγγειλεν αὐτοῖς
- of(over) unclean, and charged them
ἵνα μηδὲν αἴρωσιν εἰς ὁδὸν εἰ μὴ ῥάβδον
that nothing they should take in [the] way except a staff
μόνον, μὴ ἄρτον, μὴ πήραν, μὴ εἰς τὴν
only, not bread, not a wallet, not in the
ζώνην χαλκόν, 9 ἀλλὰ ὑποδεδεμένους σανδάλια,
girdle copper [money], but having had tied on sandals,
καὶ μὴ ἐνδύσησθε δύο χιτῶνας. 10 καὶ
and do not put on two tunics. And
ἔλεγεν αὐτοῖς· ὅπου ἐὰν εἰσέλθητε εἰς
he said to them: Wherever ye enter into
οἰκίαν, ἐκεῖ μένετε ἕως ἂν ἐξέλθητε
a house, there remain until ye go out
ἐκεῖθεν. 11 καὶ ὃς ἂν τόπος μὴ δέξηται
thence. And whatever place receives not
ὑμᾶς μηδὲ ἀκούσωσιν ὑμῶν, ἐκπορευόμενοι
you nor they hear you, going out
ἐκεῖθεν ἐκτινάξατε τὸν χοῦν τὸν ὑποκάτω
thence shake off the dust - under
τῶν ποδῶν ὑμῶν εἰς μαρτύριον αὐτοῖς.
the feet of you for a testimony to them.
12 Καὶ ἐξελθόντες ἐκήρυξαν ἵνα μετανοῶσιν,
And going forth they proclaimed that men should repent,
13 καὶ δαιμόνια πολλὰ ἐξέβαλλον, καὶ
and demons many they expelled, and
ἤλειφον ἐλαίῳ πολλοὺς ἀρρώστους καὶ
anointed with oil many sick [ones] and
ἐθεράπευον.
healed.
14 Καὶ ἤκουσεν ὁ βασιλεὺς Ἡρῴδης,
And heard the king Herod,
φανερὸν γὰρ ἐγένετο τὸ ὄνομα αὐτοῦ, καὶ
for manifest became the name of him, and
ἔλεγον ὅτι Ἰωάννης ὁ βαπτίζων ἐγήγερται
they said[,] - John the baptizing [one] has been raised
ἐκ νεκρῶν, καὶ διὰ τοῦτο ἐνεργοῦσιν αἱ
from [the] dead, and therefore operate the
δυνάμεις ἐν αὐτῷ. 15 ἄλλοι δὲ ἔλεγον
powerful deeds in him. But others said[,]
ὅτι Ἠλίας ἐστίν· ἄλλοι δὲ ἔλεγον ὅτι
- Elias it/he is; and [yet] others said[,]
προφήτης ὡς εἷς τῶν προφητῶν. 16 ἀκούσας δὲ
A prophet as one of the prophets. But hearing
ὁ Ἡρῴδης ἔλεγεν· ὃν ἐγὼ ἀπεκεφάλισα
- Herod said: ²whom ¹I ⁴beheaded
Ἰωάννην, οὗτος ἠγέρθη. 17 Αὐτὸς γὰρ ὁ
³John, this was raised. For ³himself - ¹
Ἡρῴδης ἀποστείλας ἐκράτησεν τὸν Ἰωάννην
¹Herod sending seized - John

not do any miracles there, except lay his hands on a few sick people and heal them. 6 And he was amazed at their lack of faith.

Jesus Sends Out the Twelve

Then Jesus went around teaching from village to village. 7 Calling the Twelve to him, he sent them out two by two and gave them authority over evil *o* spirits.
8 These were his instructions: "Take nothing for the journey except a staff —no bread, no bag, no money in your belts. 9 Wear sandals but not an extra tunic. 10 Whenever you enter a house, stay there until you leave that town. 11 And if any place will not welcome you or listen to you, shake the dust off your feet when you leave, as a testimony against them."
12 They went out and preached that people should repent. 13 They drove out many demons and anointed many sick people with oil and healed them.

John the Baptist Beheaded

14 King Herod heard about this, for Jesus' name had become well known. Some were saying, *p* "John the Baptist has been raised from the dead, and that is why miraculous powers are at work in him."
15 Others said, "He is Elijah."
And still others claimed, "He is a prophet, like one of the prophets of long ago."
16 But when Herod heard this, he said, "John, the man I beheaded, has been raised from the dead!"
17 For Herod himself had given orders to have John

---

k Gk *his*
l Other ancient authorities read *He was*

o 7 Greek *unclean*
p 14 Some early manuscripts *He was saying*

him in prison on account of Herodias, his brother Philip's wife, because Herod[m] had married her. 18 For John had been telling Herod, "It is not lawful for you to have your brother's wife." 19 And Herodias had a grudge against him, and wanted to kill him. But she could not, 20 for Herod feared John, knowing that he was a righteous and holy man, and he protected him. When he heard him, he was greatly perplexed;[n] and yet he liked to listen to him. 21 But an opportunity came when Herod on his birthday gave a banquet for his courtiers and officers and for the leaders of Galilee. 22 When his daughter Herodias[o] came in and danced, she pleased Herod and his guests; and the king said to the girl, "Ask me for whatever you wish, and I will give it." 23 And he solemnly swore to her, "Whatever you ask me, I will give you, even half of my kingdom." 24 She went out and said to her mother, "What should I ask for?" She replied, "The head of John the baptizer." 25 Immediately she rushed back to the king and requested, "I want you to give me at once the head of John the Baptist on a platter." 26 The king was deeply grieved; yet out of regard for his oaths and for the guests, he did not want to refuse her. 27 Immediately the king sent a soldier of the

καὶ ἔδησεν αὐτὸν ἐν φυλακῇ διὰ Ἡρῳδιάδα
and bound him in prison because of Herodias
τὴν γυναῖκα Φιλίππου τοῦ ἀδελφοῦ αὐτοῦ,
the wife of Philip the brother of him,
ὅτι αὐτὴν ἐγάμησεν· 18 ἔλεγεν γὰρ ὁ
because her he married; for said the
Ἰωάννης τῷ Ἡρῴδη ὅτι οὐκ ἔξεστίν
John - to Herod[,] It is not lawful
σοι ἔχειν τὴν γυναῖκα τοῦ ἀδελφοῦ σου.
for thee to have the wife of the brother of thee.
19 ἡ δὲ Ἡρῳδιὰς ἐνεῖχεν αὐτῷ καὶ
- Now Herodias had a grudge against him and
ἤθελεν αὐτὸν ἀποκτεῖναι, καὶ οὐκ ἠδύνατο·
wished ᵃhim ¹to kill, and could not;
20 ὁ γὰρ Ἡρῴδης ἐφοβεῖτο τὸν Ἰωάννην,
- for Herod feared - John.
εἰδὼς αὐτὸν ἄνδρα δίκαιον καὶ ἅγιον, καὶ
knowing him a man just and holy, and
συνετήρει αὐτόν, καὶ ἀκούσας αὐτοῦ πολλὰ
kept safe him, and hearing him much
                                 = was
ἠπόρει, καὶ ἡδέως αὐτοῦ ἤκουεν. 21 καὶ
was in difficulties, and gladly him heard. And
in great difficulties,
γενομένης ἡμέρας εὐκαίρου ὅτε Ἡρῴδης
coming day a suitableᵃ when Herod
= when a suitable day came
τοῖς γενεσίοις αὐτοῦ δεῖπνον ἐποίησεν τοῖς
on the birthday festivities of him a supper made for the
μεγιστᾶσιν αὐτοῦ καὶ τοῖς χιλιάρχοις καὶ
courtiers of him and the chiliarchs and
τοῖς πρώτοις τῆς Γαλιλαίας, 22 καὶ
the chief men - of Galilee, and
εἰσελθούσης τῆς θυγατρὸς αὐτῆς τῆς
entering the daughter ¹of herself -
= when the daughter of Herodias herself entered and danced,
Ἡρῳδιάδος καὶ ὀρχησαμένης, ἤρεσεν τῷ
¹of Herodias and dancing,ᵃ she pleased -
Ἡρῴδη καὶ τοῖς συνανακειμένοις. ὁ δὲ
Herod and the [ones] reclining with [him]. And the
βασιλεὺς εἶπεν τῷ κορασίῳ· αἴτησόν με
king said to the girl: Ask me
ὃ ἐὰν θέλῃς, καὶ δώσω σοι· 23 καὶ
whatever thou wishest, and I will give thee; and
ὤμοσεν αὐτῇ ὅτι ὃ ἐὰν αἰτήσῃς δώσω
he swore to her[,] - Whatever thou askest I will give
σοι ἕως ἡμίσους τῆς βασιλείας μου.
thee up to half of the kingdom of me.
24 καὶ ἐξελθοῦσα εἶπεν τῇ μητρὶ αὐτῆς·
And going out she said to the mother of her:
τί αἰτήσωμαι; ἡ δὲ εἶπεν· τὴν κεφαλὴν
What may I ask? And she said: The head
Ἰωάννου τοῦ βαπτίζοντος. 25 καὶ
of John the [one] baptizing. And
εἰσελθοῦσα εὐθὺς μετὰ σπουδῆς πρὸς τὸν
entering immediately with haste to the
βασιλέα ᾐτήσατο λέγουσα· θέλω ἵνα ἐξαυτῆς
king she asked saying: I wish that at once
δῷς μοι ἐπὶ πίνακι τὴν κεφαλὴν Ἰωάννου
thou mayest give me on a dish the head of John
τοῦ βαπτιστοῦ. 26 καὶ περίλυπος γενόμενος
the Baptist. And deeply grieved becoming
ὁ βασιλεὺς διὰ τοὺς ὅρκους καὶ τοὺς
the king because of the oaths and the [ones]
ἀνακειμένους οὐκ ἠθέλησεν ἀθετῆσαι αὐτήν.
reclining did not wish to reject her.
27 καὶ εὐθὺς ἀποστείλας ὁ βασιλεὺς
And immediately ᵃsending ¹the ᵃking

arrested, and he had him bound and put in prison. He did this because of Herodias, his brother Philip's wife, whom he had married. 18 For John had been saying to Herod, "It is not lawful for you to have your brother's wife." 19 So Herodias nursed a grudge against John and wanted to kill him. But she was not able to, 20 because Herod feared John and protected him, knowing him to be a righteous and holy man. When Herod heard John, he was greatly puzzled[q]; yet he liked to listen to him. 21 Finally the opportune time came. On his birthday Herod gave a banquet for his high officials and military commanders and the leading men of Galilee. 22 When the daughter of Herodias came in and danced, she pleased Herod and his dinner guests.

The king said to the girl, "Ask me for anything you want, and I'll give it to you." 23 And he promised her with an oath, "Whatever you ask I will give you, up to half my kingdom." 24 She went out and said to her mother, "What shall I ask for?"

"The head of John the Baptist," she answered.

25 At once the girl hurried in to the king with the request: "I want you to give me right now the head of John the Baptist on a platter."

26 The king was greatly distressed, but because of his oaths and his dinner guests, he did not want to refuse her. 27 So he immediately sent an executioner

[m] Gk he
[n] Other ancient authorities read he did many things
[o] Other ancient authorities read the daughter of Herodias herself
[q] 20 Some early manuscripts he did many things

guard with orders to bring John's[p] head. He went and beheaded him in the prison, 28brought his head on a platter, and gave it to the girl. Then the girl gave it to her mother. 29When his disciples heard about it, they came and took his body, and laid it in a tomb.

Feeding the Five Thousand

30 The apostles gathered around Jesus, and told him all that they had done and taught. 31He said to them, "Come away to a deserted place all by yourselves and rest a while." For many were coming and going, and they had no leisure even to eat. 32And they went away in the boat to a deserted place by themselves. 33Now many saw them going and recognized them, and they hurried there on foot from all the towns and arrived ahead of them. 34As he went ashore, he saw a great crowd; and he had compassion for them, because they were like sheep without a shepherd; and he began to teach them many things. 35When it grew late, his disciples came to him and said, "This is a deserted place, and the hour is now very late; 36send them away so that they may go into the surrounding country and villages and buy something for themselves to eat." 37But he answered them, "You give them something to eat." They said to him, "Are we to go

σπεκουλάτορα ἐπέταξεν ἐνέγκαι τὴν κεφαλὴν
an executioner   gave order   to bring   the   head

αὐτοῦ.   καὶ   ἀπελθὼν   ἀπεκεφάλισεν   αὐτὸν
of him.   And   going   he beheaded   him

ἐν τῇ φυλακῇ, 28 καὶ ἤνεγκεν τὴν κεφαλὴν
in the prison,   and brought   the   head

αὐτοῦ ἐπὶ πίνακι καὶ ἔδωκεν αὐτὴν τῷ
of him   on   a dish   and   gave   it   to the

κορασίῳ, καὶ τὸ κοράσιον ἔδωκεν αὐτὴν
girl,   and the   girl   gave   it

τῇ μητρὶ αὐτῆς. 29 καὶ ἀκούσαντες οἱ
to the mother of her.   And   hearing   the

μαθηταὶ αὐτοῦ ἦλθαν καὶ ἦραν τὸ πτῶμα
disciples   of him   went   and took the corpse

αὐτοῦ καὶ ἔθηκαν αὐτὸ ἐν μνημείῳ.
of him and   put   it   in   a tomb.

30 Καὶ συνάγονται οἱ ἀπόστολοι πρὸς
And   assemble   the   apostles   to

τὸν Ἰησοῦν, καὶ ἀπήγγειλαν αὐτῷ πάντα
–   Jesus,   and   reported   to him all things

ὅσα ἐποίησαν καὶ ὅσα ἐδίδαξαν. 31 καὶ
which they did   and which they taught.   And

λέγει αὐτοῖς· δεῦτε ὑμεῖς αὐτοὶ κατ'
he says to them: Come   ye   [your]selves pri-

ἰδίαν εἰς ἔρημον τόπον καὶ ἀναπαύσασθε ὀλίγον.
vately to a desert   place   and   rest   a little.

ἦσαν γὰρ οἱ ἐρχόμενοι καὶ οἱ
For ²were ³the [ones] ⁴coming ⁵and ⁶the [ones]

ὑπάγοντες πολλοί, καὶ οὐδὲ φαγεῖν
⁷going   ¹many,   and   not   to eat

εὐκαίρουν. 32 καὶ ἀπῆλθον ἐν τῷ πλοίῳ
they had opportunity. And they went away in the   ship

εἰς ἔρημον τόπον κατ' ἰδίαν. 33 καὶ
to a desert place   privately.   And

εἶδον αὐτοὺς ὑπάγοντας καὶ ἐπέγνωσαν
²saw   ³them   ⁴going   ⁵and   ⁶knew

πολλοί, καὶ πεζῇ ἀπὸ πασῶν τῶν πόλεων
¹many,   and on foot from   all   the   cities

συνέδραμον ἐκεῖ καὶ προῆλθον αὐτούς.
ran together   there and came before   them.

34 Καὶ ἐξελθὼν εἶδεν πολὺν ὄχλον, καὶ
And going forth he saw a much(great) crowd, and

ἐσπλαγχνίσθη ἐπ' αὐτοὺς ὅτι ἦσαν ὡς
had compassion   on   them because they were as

πρόβατα μὴ ἔχοντα ποιμένα, καὶ ἤρξατο
sheep   not having   a shepherd, and   he began

διδάσκειν αὐτοὺς πολλά. 35 Καὶ ἤδη ὥρας
to teach   them   many things.   And now an hour
= it being

πολλῆς γενομένης προσελθόντες αὐτῷ οἱ
much   coming⁸   approaching   to him the
late

μαθηταὶ αὐτοῦ ἔλεγον ὅτι ἔρημός ἐστιν
disciples   of him said[,]   –   Desert   is

ὁ τόπος καὶ ἤδη ὥρα πολλή· 36 ἀπόλυσον
the place and now hour a much;   dismiss
= it is late:

αὐτούς, ἵνα ἀπελθόντες εἰς τοὺς κύκλῳ
them,   that going away   to the round about

ἀγροὺς καὶ κώμας ἀγοράσωσιν ἑαυτοῖς τί
fields   and villages they may buy for themselves what

φάγωσιν. 37 ὁ δὲ ἀποκριθεὶς εἶπεν αὐτοῖς·
they may eat.   But he   answering   said to them:

δότε αὐτοῖς ὑμεῖς φαγεῖν. καὶ λέγουσιν
Give them   ye   to eat.   And they say

with orders to bring John's head. The man went, beheaded John in the prison, 28and brought back his head on a platter. He presented it to the girl, and she gave it to her mother. 29On hearing of this, John's disciples came and took his body and laid it in a tomb.

Jesus Feeds the Five Thousand

30The apostles gathered around Jesus and reported to him all they had done and taught. 31Then, because so many people were coming and going that they did not even have a chance to eat, he said to them, "Come with me by yourselves to a quiet place and get some rest." 32So they went away by themselves in a boat to a solitary place. 33But many who saw them leaving recognized them and ran on foot from all the towns and got there ahead of them. 34When Jesus landed and saw a large crowd, he had compassion on them, because they were like sheep without a shepherd. So he began teaching them many things.

35By this time it was late in the day, so his disciples came to him. "This is a remote place," they said, "and it's already very late. 36Send the people away so they can go to the surrounding countryside and villages and buy themselves something to eat." 37But he answered, "You give them something to eat."

They said to him, "That

and buy two hundred denarii*q* worth of bread, and give it to them to eat?" ³⁸And he said to them, "How many loaves have you? Go and see." When they had found out, they said, "Five, and two fish." ³⁹Then he ordered them to get all the people to sit down in groups on the green grass. ⁴⁰So they sat down in groups of hundreds and of fifties. ⁴¹Taking the five loaves and the two fish, he looked up to heaven, and blessed and broke the loaves, and gave them to his disciples to set before the people; and he divided the two fish among them all. ⁴²And all ate and were filled; ⁴³and they took up twelve baskets full of broken pieces and of the fish. ⁴⁴Those who had eaten the loaves numbered five thousand men.

Jesus Walks on the Water

45 Immediately he made his disciples get into the boat and go on ahead to the other side, to Bethsaida, while he dismissed the crowd. ⁴⁶After saying farewell to them, he went up on the mountain to pray. ⁴⁷When evening came, the boat was out on the sea, and he was alone on the land. ⁴⁸When he saw that they were straining at the oars against an adverse wind, he came towards them early in the morning, walking on the sea. He intended to pass them by. ⁴⁹But when they saw him walking on the sea, they thought it was a ghost and cried out; ⁵⁰for they all saw

---

αὐτῷ· ἀπελθόντες ἀγοράσωμεν δηναρίων
to him: Going away   may we buy   ²of(for) ⁴denarii

διακοσίων ἄρτους, καὶ δώσομεν αὐτοῖς
¹two hundred   ¹loaves,   and   shall we give   them

φαγεῖν; 38 ὁ δὲ λέγει αὐτοῖς· πόσους
to eat?   38 And he   says   to them: How many

ἔχετε ἄρτους; ὑπάγετε ἴδετε. καὶ γνόντες
have ye   loaves?   Go   see.   And   knowing

λέγουσιν· πέντε, καὶ δύο ἰχθύας. 39 καὶ
they say: Five,   and   two   fishes.   39 And

ἐπέταξεν αὐτοῖς ἀνακλιθῆναι πάντας συμπόσια
he instructed   them   to recline   all   companies

συμπόσια ἐπὶ τῷ χλωρῷ χόρτῳ. 40 καὶ
companies   on   the   green   grass.   40 And

ἀνέπεσαν πρασιαὶ πρασιαὶ κατὰ ἑκατὸν
they reclined   groups   groups   by   a hundred

καὶ κατὰ πεντήκοντα. 41 καὶ λαβὼν τοὺς
and   by   fifty.   41 And   taking   the

πέντε ἄρτους καὶ τοὺς δύο ἰχθύας,
five   loaves   and   the   two   fishes,

ἀναβλέψας εἰς τὸν οὐρανὸν εὐλόγησεν καὶ
looking up   to   -   heaven   he blessed   and

κατέκλασεν τοὺς ἄρτους καὶ ἐδίδου τοῖς
broke   the   loaves   and   gave   to the

μαθηταῖς ἵνα παρατιθῶσιν αὐτοῖς, καὶ
disciples   that   they might set before   them,   and

τοὺς δύο ἰχθύας ἐμέρισεν πᾶσιν. 42 καὶ
the   two   fishes   he divided   to all.   42 And

ἔφαγον πάντες καὶ ἐχορτάσθησαν, 43 καὶ
they ate   all   and   were satisfied,   43 and

ἦραν κλάσματα δώδεκα κοφίνων πληρώματα
they took fragments   twelve   ²of baskets   ¹fullnesses

καὶ ἀπὸ τῶν ἰχθύων 44 καὶ ἦσαν οἱ
and   from   the   fishes.   44 And   were   the

φαγόντες τοὺς ἄρτους πεντακισχίλιοι ἄνδρες.
[ones] eating   the   loaves   five thousand   males.

45 Καὶ εὐθὺς ἠνάγκασεν τοὺς μαθητὰς
  And   immediately   he constrained   the   disciples

αὐτοῦ ἐμβῆναι εἰς τὸ πλοῖον καὶ προάγειν
of him   to embark   in   the   ship   and to go before

εἰς τὸ πέραν πρὸς Βηθσαϊδάν, ἕως αὐτὸς
to   the other side   to   Bethsaida,   until   he

ἀπολύει τὸν ὄχλον. 46 καὶ ἀποταξάμενος
dismisses   the   crowd.   46 And   having said farewell

αὐτοῖς ἀπῆλθεν εἰς τὸ ὄρος προσεύξασθαι.
to them   he went away   to   the   mountain   to pray.

47 καὶ ὀψίας γενομένης ἦν τὸ πλοῖον ἐν
  And   evening   coming on*a*   was   the   ship   in
    = when evening came on

μέσῳ τῆς θαλάσσης, καὶ αὐτὸς μόνος ἐπὶ
[the] midst of the   sea,   and   he   alone   on

τῆς γῆς. 48 καὶ ἰδὼν αὐτοὺς βασανιζομένους
the land.   48 And seeing   them   being distressed

ἐν τῷ ἐλαύνειν, ἦν γὰρ ὁ ἄνεμος ἐναντίος
in   the   to row,   ⁴was   ¹for   ²the -   ²wind   contrary
    = rowing,

αὐτοῖς, περὶ τετάρτην φυλακὴν τῆς νυκτὸς
to them,   about   [the] fourth   watch   of the   night

ἔρχεται πρὸς αὐτοὺς περιπατῶν ἐπὶ τῆς
he comes   toward   them   walking   on   the

θαλάσσης· καὶ ἤθελεν παρελθεῖν αὐτούς.
sea;   and   wished   to go by   them.

49 οἱ δὲ ἰδόντες αὐτὸν ἐπὶ τῆς θαλάσσης
  But they   seeing   him   on   the   sea

περιπατοῦντα ἔδοξαν ὅτι φάντασμά ἐστιν,
walking   thought   that   a phantasm   it is(was),

---

would take eight months of a man's wages*r*! Are we to go and spend that much on bread and give it to them to eat?"
³⁸"How many loaves do you have?" he asked. "Go and see."

When they found out, they said, "Five—and two fish."

³⁹Then Jesus directed them to have all the people sit down in groups on the green grass. ⁴⁰So they sat down in groups of hundreds and fifties. ⁴¹Taking the five loaves and the two fish and looking up to heaven, he gave thanks and broke the loaves. Then he gave them to his disciples to set before the people. He also divided the two fish among them all. ⁴²They all ate and were satisfied, ⁴³and the disciples picked up twelve basketfuls of broken pieces of bread and fish. ⁴⁴The number of the men who had eaten was five thousand.

Jesus Walks on the Water

⁴⁵Immediately Jesus made his disciples get into the boat and go on ahead of him to Bethsaida, while he dismissed the crowd. ⁴⁶After leaving them, he went up on a mountainside to pray.

⁴⁷When evening came, the boat was in the middle of the lake, and he was alone on land. ⁴⁸He saw the disciples straining at the oars, because the wind was against them. About the fourth watch of the night he went out to them, walking on the lake. He was about to pass by them, ⁴⁹but when they saw him walking on the lake, they thought he was a ghost. They cried

---

q The denarius was the usual day's wage for a laborer

r 37 Greek take two hundred denarii

him and were terrified. But immediately he spoke to them and said, "Take heart, it is I; do not be afraid." 51 Then he got into the boat with them and the wind ceased. And they were utterly astounded, 52 for they did not understand about the loaves, but their hearts were hardened.

Healing the Sick in Gennesaret

53 When they had crossed over, they came to land at Gennesaret and moored the boat. 54 When they got out of the boat, people at once recognized him, 55 and rushed about that whole region and began to bring the sick on mats to wherever they heard he was. 56 And wherever he went, into villages or cities or farms, they laid the sick in the marketplaces, and begged him that they might touch even the fringe of his cloak; and all who touched it were healed.

καὶ ἀνέκραξαν· **50** πάντες γὰρ αὐτὸν εἶδαν
and   cried out;   for all   him   saw

καὶ ἐταράχθησαν. ὁ δὲ εὐθὺς ἐλάλησεν
and   were troubled.   But he immediately   talked

μετ᾽ αὐτῶν, καὶ λέγει αὐτοῖς· θαρσεῖτε,
with   them,   and   says   to them: Be of good cheer,

ἐγώ εἰμι· μὴ φοβεῖσθε. **51** καὶ ἀνέβη
I   am;   be ye not afraid.   And he went up

πρὸς αὐτοὺς εἰς τὸ πλοῖον, καὶ ἐκόπασεν
to   them   into the   ship,   and   ceased

ὁ ἄνεμος· καὶ λίαν ἐκ περισσοῦ ἐν ἑαυτοῖς
the   wind;   and very much exceedingly   in themselves

ἐξίσταντο· **52** οὐ γὰρ συνῆκαν ἐπὶ
they were astonished ;   for they did not understand concerning

τοῖς ἄρτοις ἀλλ᾽ ἦν αὐτῶν ἡ καρδία
the   loaves,   but   was   of them   the   heart

πεπωρωμένη. **53** Καὶ διαπεράσαντες ἐπὶ
having been hardened.   And   crossing over   *onto

τὴν γῆν ἦλθον εἰς Γεννησαρὲτ καὶ
*the   *land *they came   to   Gennesaret   and

προσωρμίσθησαν. **54** καὶ ἐξελθόντων αὐτῶν
anchored.   And   coming *out*   them*
                                  = as they came

ἐκ τοῦ πλοίου εὐθὺς ἐπιγνόντες αὐτὸν
out of the   ship   immediately   knowing   him

55 περιέδραμον ὅλην τὴν χώραν ἐκείνην
they ran round   all   -   country   that

καὶ ἤρξαντο ἐπὶ τοῖς κραβάτοις τοὺς
and   began   on   the   pallets   the [ones]
                                       = those

κακῶς ἔχοντας περιφέρειν, ὅπου ἤκουον
ill   having   to carry round,   where   they heard
who were ill

ὅτι ἐστίν. **56** καὶ ὅπου ἂν εἰσεπορεύετο
that he is(was).   And   wherever   he entered

εἰς κώμας ἢ εἰς πόλεις ἢ εἰς ἀγρούς,
into villages   or into   cities   or   into   country,

ἐν ταῖς ἀγοραῖς ἐτίθεσαν τοὺς ἀσθενοῦντας,
in   the   marketplaces they put   the   ailing [ones],

καὶ παρεκάλουν αὐτὸν ἵνα κἂν τοῦ
and   besought   him   that if even   the

κρασπέδου τοῦ ἱματίου αὐτοῦ ἅψωνται·
fringe   of the   garment   of him they might touch;

καὶ ὅσοι ἂν ἥψαντο αὐτοῦ ἐσῴζοντο.
and   as many as   touched   him   were healed.

---

out, 50 because they all saw him and were terrified. Immediately he spoke to them and said, "Take courage! It is I. Don't be afraid." 51 Then he climbed into the boat with them, and the wind died down. They were completely amazed, 52 for they had not understood about the loaves; their hearts were hardened.

53 When they had crossed over, they landed at Gennesaret and anchored there. 54 As soon as they got out of the boat, people recognized Jesus. 55 They ran throughout that whole region and carried the sick on mats to wherever they heard he was. 56 And wherever he went—into villages, towns or countryside—they placed the sick in the marketplaces. They begged him to let them touch even the edge of his cloak, and all who touched him were healed.

Chapter 7

The Tradition of the Elders

NOW when the Pharisees and some of the scribes who had come from Jerusalem gathered around him, 2 they noticed that some of his disciples were eating with defiled hands, that is, without washing them. 3 (For the Pharisees, and all the Jews, do not eat unless they thoroughly wash their hands,[r] thus observing the tradition of the elders; 4 and they do not eat anything from the market unless they wash it;[s] and there are also many

[r] Meaning of Gk uncertain
[s] Other ancient authorities read *and when they come from the marketplace, they do not eat unless they purify themselves*

---

7 Καὶ συνάγονται πρὸς αὐτὸν οἱ Φαρισαῖοι
And   assemble   to   him   the   Pharisees

καὶ τινες τῶν γραμματέων ἐλθόντες ἀπὸ
and   some   of the   scribes   coming   from

Ἱεροσολύμων. **2** καὶ ἰδόντες τινὰς τῶν
Jerusalem.   And   seeing   some   of the

μαθητῶν αὐτοῦ ὅτι κοιναῖς χερσίν, τοῦτ᾽
disciples of him   that with unclean   hands,   this

ἔστιν ἀνίπτοις, ἐσθίουσιν τοὺς ἄρτους,
is   unwashed,   they eat   the   bread,

3 — οἱ γὰρ Φαρισαῖοι καὶ πάντες οἱ
— for the   Pharisees   and   all   the

Ἰουδαῖοι ἐὰν μὴ πυγμῇ νίψωνται τὰς
Jews   unless   with [the] fist they wash   the
                = ? carefully

χεῖρας οὐκ ἐσθίουσιν, κρατοῦντες τὴν
hands   eat not,   holding   the

παράδοσιν τῶν πρεσβυτέρων, **4** καὶ ἀπ᾽
tradition   of the   elders,   and   from

ἀγορᾶς ἐὰν μὴ ῥαντίσωνται οὐκ ἐσθίουσιν, καὶ
marketplaces unless   they sprinkle   they eat not,   and

Chapter 7

Clean and Unclean

THE Pharisees and some of the teachers of the law who had come from Jerusalem gathered around Jesus and 2 saw some of his disciples eating food with hands that were "unclean," that is, unwashed. 3 (The Pharisees and all the Jews do not eat unless they give their hands a ceremonial washing, holding to the tradition of the elders. 4 When they come from the marketplace they do not eat unless they wash. And other traditions that they observe, the washing of cups, pots, and bronze kettles. *t)* 5 So the Pharisees and the scribes asked him, "Why do your disciples not live *u* according to the tradition of the elders, but eat with defiled hands?" 6 He said to them, "Isaiah prophesied rightly about you hypocrites, as it is written,

'This people honors
    me with
    their lips,
but their hearts are
    far from me;
7 in vain do they
    worship me,
teaching human
    precepts as
    doctrines.'

8 You abandon the commandment of God and hold to human tradition."

9 Then he said to them, "You have a fine way of rejecting the commandment of God in order to keep your tradition! 10 For Moses said, 'Honor your father and your mother'; and, 'Whoever speaks evil of father or mother must surely die.' 11 But you say that if anyone tells father or mother, 'Whatever support you might have had from me is Corban' (that is, an offering to God *v*)— 12 then you no longer permit doing anything for a father or mother, 13 thus making void the word of God through your tradition that you have handed on. And you do many things like this."

14 Then he called the crowd again and said to them, "Listen to me, all of you, and understand: 15 there is nothing outside a person that by going in can defile, but the things that come out are what defile." *w*

---

t Other ancient authorities add and beds
u Gk walk
v Gk lacks to God
w Other ancient authorities add verse 16, "Let anyone with ears to hear listen"

ἄλλα πολλά ἐστιν ἃ παρέλαβον κρατεῖν,
other things many there are which they received to hold,

βαπτισμοὺς ποτηρίων καὶ ξεστῶν καὶ
washings of cups and of utensils and

χαλκίων, — 5 καὶ ἐπερωτῶσιν αὐτὸν οἱ
of bronze vessels, — and questioned him the

Φαρισαῖοι καὶ οἱ γραμματεῖς· διὰ τί
Pharisees and the scribes: Why

οὐ περιπατοῦσιν οἱ μαθηταί σου κατὰ τὴν
walk not the disciples of thee according to the

παράδοσιν τῶν πρεσβυτέρων, ἀλλὰ κοιναῖς
tradition of the elders, but with unclean

χερσὶν ἐσθίουσιν τὸν ἄρτον; 6 ὁ δὲ εἶπεν
hands eat - bread? And he said

αὐτοῖς· καλῶς ἐπροφήτευσεν Ἡσαΐας περὶ
to them: Well prophesied Esaias concerning

ὑμῶν τῶν ὑποκριτῶν, ὡς γέγραπται ὅτι –
you the hypocrites, as it has been written[:] –

οὗτος ὁ λαὸς τοῖς χείλεσίν με τιμᾷ,
This – people with the lips me honours,

ἡ δὲ καρδία αὐτῶν πόρρω ἀπέχει ἀπ᾽
but the heart of them ²is ³away ¹far from

ἐμοῦ· 7 μάτην δὲ σέβονταί με, διδάσκοντες
me; and in vain they worship me, teaching

διδασκαλίας ἐντάλματα ἀνθρώπων. 8 ἀφέντες
teachings [which are] commands of men. Leaving

τὴν ἐντολὴν τοῦ θεοῦ κρατεῖτε τὴν
the commandment – of God ye hold the

παράδοσιν τῶν ἀνθρώπων. 9 καὶ ἔλεγεν
tradition – of men. And he said

αὐτοῖς· καλῶς ἀθετεῖτε τὴν ἐντολὴν τοῦ
to them: Well ye set aside the commandment –

θεοῦ, ἵνα τὴν παράδοσιν ὑμῶν τηρήσητε.
of God, that the tradition of you ye may keep.

10 Μωϋσῆς γὰρ εἶπεν· τίμα τὸν πατέρα σου
For Moses said: Honour the father of thee

καὶ τὴν μητέρα σου, καί· ὁ κακολογῶν
and the mother of thee, and: The [one] speaking evil of

πατέρα ἢ μητέρα θανάτῳ τελευτάτω. 11 ὑμεῖς
father or mother by death let him end(die). ye

δὲ λέγετε· ἐὰν εἴπῃ ἄνθρωπος τῷ πατρὶ
But say: If says a man to the(his) father

ἢ τῇ μητρί· κορβᾶν, ὅ ἐστιν δῶρον,
or to the mother: Korban, which is a gift,

ὃ ἐὰν ἐξ ἐμοῦ ὠφεληθῇς, 12 οὐκέτι ἀφίετε
whatever by me thou mightest profit, no longer ye allow

αὐτὸν οὐδὲν ποιῆσαι τῷ πατρὶ ἢ τῇ
him no(any)thing to do for the father or the

μητρί, 13 ἀκυροῦντες τὸν λόγον τοῦ θεοῦ
mother, annulling the word – of God

τῇ παραδόσει ὑμῶν ᾗ παρεδώκατε· καὶ
by the tradition of you which ye received; and

παρόμοια τοιαῦτα πολλὰ ποιεῖτε. 14 Καὶ
²similar things ²such ¹many ye do. And

προσκαλεσάμενος πάλιν τὸν ὄχλον ἔλεγεν
calling to [him] again the crowd he said

αὐτοῖς· ἀκούσατέ μου πάντες καὶ σύνετε.
to them: Hear ye me all and understand.

15 οὐδέν ἐστιν ἔξωθεν τοῦ ἀνθρώπου
Nothing there is from without – a man

εἰσπορευόμενον εἰς αὐτὸν ὃ δύναται κοινῶσαι
entering into him which can to defile

αὐτόν· ἀλλὰ τὰ ἐκ τοῦ ἀνθρώπου ἐκπο-
him; but the things out of – a man coming

---

they observe many other traditions, such as the washing of cups, pitchers and kettles. *s)*
5 So the Pharisees and teachers of the law asked Jesus, "Why don't your disciples live according to the tradition of the elders instead of eating their food with 'unclean' hands?"
6 He replied, "Isaiah was right when he prophesied about you hypocrites; as it is written:

" 'These people honor
    me with their lips,
but their hearts are far
    from me.
7 They worship me in
    vain;
    their teachings are but
    rules taught by
    men.' *t*

8 You have let go of the commands of God and are holding on to the traditions of men."

9 And he said to them: "You have a fine way of setting aside the commands of God in order to observe *u* your own traditions! 10 For Moses said, 'Honor your father and your mother,' *v* and, 'Anyone who curses his father or mother must be put to death.' *w* 11 But you say that if a man says to his father or mother: 'Whatever help you might otherwise have received from me is Corban' (that is, a gift devoted to God), 12 then you no longer let him do anything for his father or mother. 13 Thus you nullify the word of God by your tradition that you have handed down. And you do many things like that."

14 Again Jesus called the crowd to him and said, "Listen to me, everyone, and understand this. 15 Nothing outside a man can make him 'unclean' by going into him. Rather, it is what comes out of a man

---

s 4 Some early manuscripts pitchers, kettles and dining couches
t 6,7 Isaiah 29:13
u 9 Some manuscripts set up
v 10 Exodus 20:12; Deut. 5:16
w 10 Exodus 21:17; Lev. 20:9

17 When he had left the crowd and entered the house, his disciples asked him about the parable. 18 He said to them, "Then do you also fail to understand? Do you not see that whatever goes into a person from outside cannot defile, 19 since it enters, not the heart but the stomach, and goes out into the sewer?" (Thus he declared all foods clean.) 20 And he said, "It is what comes out of a person that defiles. 21 For it is from within, from the human heart, that evil intentions come: fornication, theft, murder, 22 adultery, avarice, wickedness, deceit, licentiousness, envy, slander, pride, folly. 23 All these evil things come from within, and they defile a person."

The Syrophoenician Woman's Faith

24 From there he set out and went away to the region of Tyre.ˣ He entered a house and did not want anyone to know he was there. Yet he could not escape notice, 25 but a woman whose little daughter had an unclean spirit immediately heard about him, and she came and bowed down at his feet. 26 Now the woman was a Gentile, of Syrophoenician origin. She begged him to cast the demon out of her daughter. 27 He said to her, "Let the children be fed first, for it is not fair to take the children's food and throw it to the dogs." 28 But she an-

---

ρευόμενά ἐστιν τὰ κοινοῦντα τὸν ἄνθρωπον. ‡
forth　are the [ones]　defiling　-　a man.

17 Καὶ ὅτε εἰσῆλθεν εἰς οἶκον ἀπὸ τοῦ
And when he entered into a house from the

ὄχλου, ἐπηρώτων αὐτὸν οἱ μαθηταὶ αὐτοῦ
crowd,　questioned　him　the　disciples　of him

τὴν παραβολήν. **18** καὶ λέγει αὐτοῖς·
the　parable.　And he says　to them:

οὕτως καὶ ὑμεῖς ἀσύνετοί ἐστε; οὐ
Thus also　ye　undiscerning　are?　do ye not

νοεῖτε ὅτι πᾶν τὸ ἔξωθεν εἰσπορευόμενον
understand that everything from without　entering

εἰς τὸν ἄνθρωπον οὐ δύναται αὐτὸν
into　the　man　cannot　him

κοινῶσαι, **19** ὅτι οὐκ εἰσπορεύεται αὐτοῦ
to defile,　because　it enters not　of him

εἰς τὴν καρδίαν ἀλλ' εἰς τὴν κοιλίαν,
into　the　heart　but　into　the　belly,

καὶ εἰς τὸν ἀφεδρῶνα ἐκπορεύεται, καθα-
and into the　drain　goes out,　purg-

ρίζων πάντα τὰ βρώματα; **20** ἔλεγεν δὲ
ing　all　-　foods?　And he said[,]

ὅτι τὸ ἐκ τοῦ ἀνθρώπου ἐκπορευόμενον,
The thing out of　-　a man　coming forth,

ἐκεῖνο κοινοῖ τὸν ἄνθρωπον. **21** ἔσωθεν
that　defiles　-　a man.　from within

γὰρ ἐκ τῆς καρδίας τῶν ἀνθρώπων
For　out of　the　heart　-　of men

οἱ διαλογισμοὶ οἱ κακοὶ ἐκπορεύονται,
-　thoughts　evil　come forth,

πορνεῖαι, κλοπαί, φόνοι, **22** μοιχεῖαι,
fornications,　thefts,　murders,　adulteries,

πλεονεξίαι, πονηρίαι, δόλος, ἀσέλγεια, ὀφθαλμὸς
greedinesses,　iniquities,　deceit,　lewdness,　eye

πονηρός, βλασφημία, ὑπερηφανία, ἀφροσύνη·
an evil,　blasphemy,　arrogance,　foolishness;

23 πάντα ταῦτα τὰ πονηρὰ ἔσωθεν ἐκπορεύεται
all　these　-　evil things from within　comes forth

καὶ κοινοῖ τὸν ἄνθρωπον.
and　defile　-　a man.

24 Ἐκεῖθεν δὲ ἀναστὰς ἀπῆλθεν εἰς τὰ ὅρια
And thence　rising up　he went away into the district

Τύρου. Καὶ εἰσελθὼν εἰς οἰκίαν οὐδένα ἤθελεν
of Tyre.　And　entering　into a house　no one he wished

γνῶναι, καὶ οὐκ ἠδυνάσθη λαθεῖν· **25** ἀλλ'
to know,　and　could not　to be hidden;　but

εὐθὺς ἀκούσασα γυνὴ περὶ αὐτοῦ, ἧς
immediately ˢhearing ¹a woman about him, of whom = whose

εἶχεν τὸ θυγάτριον αὐτῆς πνεῦμα ἀκάθαρτον,
had the　daughter　of her　spirit　an unclean,
daughter had

ἐλθοῦσα προσέπεσεν πρὸς τοὺς πόδας αὐτοῦ·
coming　fell　at　the　feet　of him;

26 ἡ δὲ γυνὴ ἦν Ἑλληνίς, Συροφοινίκισσα
and the woman was　a Greek,　a Syrophenician

τῷ γένει· καὶ ἠρώτα αὐτὸν ἵνα τὸ
-　by race;　and　she asked　him　that　the

δαιμόνιον ἐκβάλῃ ἐκ τῆς θυγατρὸς αὐτῆς.
demon　he would expel out of the　daughter　of her.

27 καὶ ἔλεγεν αὐτῇ· ἄφες πρῶτον
And　he said　to her:　Permit　first

χορτασθῆναι τὰ τέκνα· οὐ γάρ ἐστιν καλὸν
to be satisfied　the children;　for it is not　good

λαβεῖν τὸν ἄρτον τῶν τέκνων καὶ τοῖς
to take　the　bread　of the　children and　to the

---

that makes him 'unclean.'ˣ 17 After he had left the crowd and entered the house, his disciples asked him about this parable. 18 "Are you so dull?" he asked. "Don't you see that nothing that enters a man from the outside can make him 'unclean'? 19 For it doesn't go into his heart but into his stomach, and then out of his body." (In saying this, Jesus declared all foods "clean.")
20 He went on: "What comes out of a man is what makes him 'unclean.' 21 For from within, out of men's hearts, come evil thoughts, sexual immorality, theft, murder, adultery, 22 greed, malice, deceit, lewdness, envy, slander, arrogance and folly. 23 All these evils come from inside and make a man 'unclean.'"

The Faith of a Syrophoenician Woman

24 Jesus left that place and went to the vicinity of Tyre.ʸ He entered a house and did not want anyone to know it; yet he could not keep his presence secret. 25 In fact, as soon as she heard about him, a woman whose little daughter was possessed by an evilᶻ spirit came and fell at his feet. 26 The woman was a Greek, born in Syrian Phoenicia. She begged Jesus to drive the demon out of her daughter. 27 "First let the children eat all they want," he told her, "for it is not right to take the children's bread and toss it to their dogs."

ˣ15 Some early manuscripts *'unclean.'* 16If anyone has ears to hear, let him hear.
ʸ24 Many early manuscripts *Tyre and Sidon*
ᶻ25 Greek *unclean*

swered him, "Sir,ʸ even the dogs under the table eat the children's crumbs." 29 Then he said to her, "For saying that, you may go—the demon has left your daughter." 30 So she went home, found the child lying on the bed, and the demon gone.

Jesus Cures a Deaf Man

31 Then he returned from the region of Tyre, and went by way of Sidon towards the Sea of Galilee, in the region of the Decapolis. 32 They brought to him a deaf man who had an impediment in his speech; and they begged him to lay his hand on him. 33 He took him aside in private, away from the crowd, and put his fingers into his ears, and he spat and touched his tongue. 34 Then looking up to heaven, he sighed and said to him, "Ephphatha," that is, "Be opened." 35 And immediately his ears were opened, his tongue was released, and he spoke plainly. 36 Then Jesusᶻ ordered them to tell no one; but the more he ordered them, the more zealously they proclaimed it. 37 They were astounded beyond measure, saying, "He has done everything well; he even makes the deaf to hear and the mute to speak."

κυναρίοις βαλεῖν. 28 ἡ δὲ ἀπεκρίθη καὶ
dogs to throw [it]. And she answered and

λέγει αὐτῷ· ναί, κύριε· καὶ τὰ κυνάρια
says to him: Yes, Lord; and yet the dogs

ὑποκάτω τῆς τραπέζης ἐσθίουσιν ἀπὸ τῶν
under the table eat from the

ψιχίων τῶν παιδίων. 29 καὶ εἶπεν αὐτῇ·
crumbs of the children. And he said to her:

διὰ τοῦτον τὸν λόγον ὕπαγε, ἐξελήλυθεν
Because of this — word go, has gone forth

ἐκ τῆς θυγατρός σου τὸ δαιμόνιον. 30 καὶ
out of the daughter of thee the demon. And

ἀπελθοῦσα εἰς τὸν οἶκον αὐτῆς εὗρεν τὸ
going away to the house of her she found the

παιδίον βεβλημένον ἐπὶ τὴν κλίνην καὶ τὸ
child *having been* laid on the couch and the

δαιμόνιον ἐξεληλυθός. 31 Καὶ πάλιν ἐξελθὼν
demon having gone forth. And again going forth

ἐκ τῶν ὁρίων Τύρου ἦλθεν διὰ Σιδῶνος
out of the district of Tyre he came through Sidon

εἰς τὴν θάλασσαν τῆς Γαλιλαίας ἀνὰ
to the sea — of Galilee in the

μέσον τῶν ὁρίων Δεκαπόλεως. 32 Καὶ
midst of the district of Decapolis. And

φέρουσιν αὐτῷ κωφὸν καὶ μογιλάλον, καὶ
they bring to him a man deaf and speaking with difficulty, and

παρακαλοῦσιν αὐτὸν ἵνα ἐπιθῇ αὐτῷ τὴν
they beseech him that he would put *on* on him the(his)

χεῖρα. 33 καὶ ἀπολαβόμενος αὐτὸν ἀπὸ
hand. And taking away him from

τοῦ ὄχλου κατ' ἰδίαν ἔβαλεν τοὺς δακτύλους
the crowd privately he put the fingers

αὐτοῦ εἰς τὰ ὦτα αὐτοῦ καὶ πτύσας
of him into the ears of him and spitting

ἥψατο τῆς γλώσσης αὐτοῦ, 34 καὶ
he touched the tongue of him, and

ἀναβλέψας εἰς τὸν οὐρανὸν ἐστέναξεν,
looking up to — heaven he groaned,

καὶ λέγει αὐτῷ· ἐφφαθά, ὅ ἐστιν διανοίχθητι.
and says to him: Ephphatha, which is Be thou opened.

35 καὶ ἠνοίγησαν αὐτοῦ αἱ ἀκοαί, καὶ
And were opened of him the ears, and

εὐθὺς ἐλύθη ὁ δεσμὸς τῆς γλώσσης αὐτοῦ,
immediately was loosened the bond of the tongue of him,

καὶ ἐλάλει ὀρθῶς. 36 καὶ διεστείλατο
and he spoke correctly. And he ordered

αὐτοῖς ἵνα μηδενὶ λέγωσιν· ὅσον δὲ
them that no one they should tell; but as much as

αὐτοῖς διεστέλλετο, αὐτοὶ μᾶλλον περισσότερον
them he ordered, they more exceedingly

ἐκήρυσσον. 37 καὶ ὑπερπερισσῶς ἐξεπλήσσοντο
proclaimed. And most exceedingly they were astounded

λέγοντες· καλῶς πάντα πεποίηκεν, καὶ
saying: Well all things he has done, both

τοὺς κωφοὺς ποιεῖ ἀκούειν καὶ ἀλάλους
the deaf he makes to hear and dumb

λαλεῖν.
to speak.

28 "Yes, Lord," she replied, "but even the dogs under the table eat the children's crumbs."
29 Then he told her, "For such a reply, you may go; the demon has left your daughter."
30 She went home and found her child lying on the bed, and the demon gone.

The Healing of a Deaf and Mute Man

31 Then Jesus left the vicinity of Tyre and went through Sidon, down to the Sea of Galilee and into the region of the Decapolis.ᵃ 32 There some people brought to him a man who was deaf and could hardly talk, and they begged him to place his hand on the man.
33 After he took him aside, away from the crowd, Jesus put his fingers into the man's ears. Then he spit and touched the man's tongue. 34 He looked up to heaven and with a deep sigh said to him, "*Ephphatha!*" (which means, "Be opened!"). 35 At this, the man's ears were opened, his tongue was loosened and he began to speak plainly.
36 Jesus commanded them not to tell anyone. But the more he did so, the more they kept talking about it.
37 People were overwhelmed with amazement. "He has done everything well," they said. "He even makes the deaf hear and the mute speak."

Chapter 8

Feeding the Four Thousand

I N those days when there was again a great crowd without anything to eat, he called his disciples and said to them, 2 "I have compassion for the crowd, because

8 Ἐν ἐκείναις ταῖς ἡμέραις πάλιν πολλοῦ
In those — days again a much(great)
= there being

ὄχλου ὄντος καὶ μὴ ἐχόντων τί φάγωσιν,
crowd being* and not having* anything they might eat,
a great crowd

προσκαλεσάμενος τοὺς μαθητὰς λέγει αὐτοῖς·
calling to [him] the disciples he says to them:

Chapter 8

Jesus Feeds the Four Thousand

D URING those days another large crowd gathered. Since they had nothing to eat, Jesus called his disciples to him and

ʸ Or *Lord*: other ancient authorities prefix *Yes*
ᶻ Gk *he*

ᵃ 31 That is, the Ten Cities

they have been with me now for three days and have nothing to eat. 3 If I send them away hungry to their homes, they will faint on the way—and some of them have come from a great distance." 4 His disciples replied, "How can one feed these people with bread here in the desert?" 5 He asked them, "How many loaves do you have?" They said, "Seven." 6 Then he ordered the crowd to sit down on the ground; and he took the seven loaves, and after giving thanks he broke them and gave them to his disciples to distribute; and they distributed them to the crowd. 7 They had also a few small fish; and after blessing them, he ordered that these too should be distributed. 8 They ate and were filled; and they took up the broken pieces left over, seven baskets full. 9 Now there were about four thousand people. And he sent them away. 10 And immediately he got into the boat with his disciples and went to the district of Dalmanutha. *a*

The Demand for a Sign

11 The Pharisees came and began to argue with him, asking him for a sign from heaven, to test him. 12 And he sighed deeply in his spirit and said, "Why does this generation ask for a sign? Truly I tell you, no sign will be given to this generation." 13 And he left them, and getting into the boat again, he went across to the other side.

The Yeast of the Pharisees and of Herod

14 Now the disciples *b* had forgotten to bring any bread; and they had only one loaf with them in the boat. 15 And he cautioned them, saying, "Watch

---

2 σπλαγχνίζομαι ἐπὶ τὸν ὄχλον, ὅτι ἤδη
I have compassion   on   the   crowd, because now
ἡμέραι τρεῖς προσμένουσίν μοι καὶ οὐκ
days   three   they remain with   me   and not
ἔχουσιν τί φάγωσιν· 3 καὶ ἐὰν ἀπολύσω
they have anything they may eat;   and   if   I dismiss
αὐτοὺς νήστεις εἰς οἶκον αὐτῶν, ἐκλυθήσονται
them   fasting   to   house of them,   they will faint
ἐν τῇ ὁδῷ· καί τινες αὐτῶν ἀπὸ μακρόθεν
in the way;   and some of them from afar
εἰσίν. 4 καὶ ἀπεκρίθησαν αὐτῷ οἱ μαθηταὶ
are.   And   answered   him the disciples
αὐτοῦ ὅτι πόθεν τούτους δυνήσεταί τις
of him[,] – ¹Whence ²these people ⁴will ⁵be able ³anyone
ὧδε χορτάσαι ἄρτων ἐπ᾽ ἐρημίας; 5 καὶ
⁸here ⁶to satisfy ⁷of(with) loaves ⁹on(in) ¹⁰a desert ?   And
ἠρώτα αὐτούς· πόσους ἔχετε ἄρτους;
he asked   them: How many   have ye loaves ?
οἱ δὲ εἶπαν· ἑπτά. 6 καὶ παραγγέλλει τῷ
And they   said: Seven.   And   he commands the
ὄχλῳ ἀναπεσεῖν ἐπὶ τῆς γῆς· καὶ λαβὼν
crowd   to recline on   the ground; and taking
τοὺς ἑπτὰ ἄρτους εὐχαριστήσας ἔκλασεν
the   seven   loaves giving thanks he broke
καὶ ἐδίδου τοῖς μαθηταῖς αὐτοῦ ἵνα
and   gave to the disciples of him that
παρατιθῶσιν, καὶ παρέθηκαν τῷ ὄχλῳ.
they might serve, and   they served the   crowd.
7 καὶ εἶχον ἰχθύδια ὀλίγα· καὶ εὐλογήσας
And they had   fishes a few; and blessing
αὐτὰ εἶπεν καὶ ταῦτα παρατιθέναι. 8 καὶ
them he told also these to be served.   And
ἔφαγον καὶ ἐχορτάσθησαν, καὶ ἦραν
they ate and   were satisfied,   and   took
περισσεύματα κλασμάτων, ἑπτὰ σπυρίδας.
excesses   of fragments, seven baskets.
9 ἦσαν δὲ ὡς τετρακισχίλιοι. καὶ ἀπέλυσεν
Now they were about four thousand. And he dismissed
αὐτούς. 10 Καὶ εὐθὺς ἐμβὰς εἰς τὸ
them.   And immediately embarking in the
πλοῖον μετὰ τῶν μαθητῶν αὐτοῦ
ship   with the   disciples of him
ἦλθεν εἰς τὰ μέρη Δαλμανουθά.
he came into the   region of Dalmanutha.
11 Καὶ ἐξῆλθον οἱ Φαρισαῖοι καὶ ἤρξαντο
And came forth the Pharisees and began
συζητεῖν αὐτῷ, ζητοῦντες παρ᾽ αὐτοῦ
to debate with him, seeking from him
σημεῖον ἀπὸ τοῦ οὐρανοῦ, πειράζοντες
a sign   from   –   heaven,   tempting
αὐτόν. 12 καὶ ἀναστενάξας τῷ πνεύματι
him.   And   groaning   in the   spirit
αὐτοῦ λέγει· τί ἡ γενεὰ αὕτη ζητεῖ
of him he says: Why – ²generation ¹this ³does ⁴seek
σημεῖον; ἀμὴν λέγω ὑμῖν, εἰ δοθήσεται
a sign ? Truly I tell you,   if will be given
τῇ γενεᾷ ταύτῃ σημεῖον. 13 καὶ ἀφεὶς
– generation to this a sign.   And leaving
αὐτοὺς πάλιν ἐμβὰς ἀπῆλθεν εἰς τὸ
them   again embarking he went away to the
πέραν. 14 Καὶ ἐπελάθοντο λαβεῖν ἄρτους,
other side.   And   they forgot   to take   loaves,
καὶ εἰ μὴ ἕνα ἄρτον οὐκ εἶχον μεθ᾽
and except one   loaf they had not with
ἑαυτῶν ἐν τῷ πλοίῳ. 15 καὶ διεστέλλετο
themselves in the ship.   And he charged

---

said, 2 "I have compassion for these people; they have already been with me three days and have nothing to eat. 3 If I send them home hungry, they will collapse on the way, because some of them have come a long distance."

4 His disciples answered, "But where in this remote place can anyone get enough bread to feed them?"

5 "How many loaves do you have?" Jesus asked.

"Seven," they replied.

6 He told the crowd to sit down on the ground. When he had taken the seven loaves and given thanks, he broke them and gave them to his disciples to set before the people, and they did so. 7 They had a few small fish as well; he gave thanks for them also and told the disciples to distribute them. 8 The people ate and were satisfied. Afterward the disciples picked up seven basketfuls of broken pieces that were left over. 9 About four thousand men were present. And having sent them away, 10 he got into the boat with his disciples and went to the region of Dalmanutha.

11 The Pharisees came and began to question Jesus. To test him, they asked him for a sign from heaven. 12 He sighed deeply and said, "Why does this generation ask for a miraculous sign? I tell you the truth, no sign will be given to it." 13 Then he left them, got back into the boat and crossed to the other side.

The Yeast of the Pharisees and Herod

14 The disciples had forgotten to bring bread, except for one loaf they had with them in the boat. 15 "Be careful," Jesus

---

a Other ancient authorities read *Mageda* or *Magdala*
b Gk *they*

out—beware of the yeast of the Pharisees and the yeast of Herod."[c] [16]They said to one another, "It is because we have no bread." [17]And becoming aware of it, Jesus said to them, "Why are you talking about having no bread? Do you still not perceive or understand? Are your hearts hardened? [18]Do you have eyes, and fail to see? Do you have ears, and fail to hear? And do you not remember? [19]When I broke the five loaves for the five thousand, how many baskets full of broken pieces did you collect?" They said to him, "Twelve." [20]"And the seven for the four thousand, how many baskets full of broken pieces did you collect?" And they said to him, "Seven." [21]Then he said to them, "Do you not yet understand?"

Jesus Cures a Blind Man at Bethsaida

[22] They came to Bethsaida. Some people[d] brought a blind man to him and begged him to touch him. [23]He took the blind man by the hand and led him out of the village; and when he had put saliva on his eyes and laid his hands on him, he asked him, "Can you see anything?" [24]And the man[e] looked up and said, "I can see people, but they look like trees, walking." [25]Then Jesus[e] laid his hands on his eyes again; and he looked intently and his sight was restored, and he saw everything clearly. [26]Then he sent him away to his home, saying, "Do not even go into the village."[f]

Peter's Declaration about Jesus

[27] Jesus went on with his disciples to the villages of Caesarea Philippi; and

αὐτοῖς	λέγων·	ὁρᾶτε,	βλέπετε	ἀπὸ	τῆς
them	saying :	See, = Beware of	look ye	from	the
ζύμης	τῶν	Φαρισαίων	καὶ	τῆς	ζύμης
leaven	of the	Pharisees	and	of the	leaven

'Ηρώδου. 16 καὶ διελογίζοντο πρὸς ἀλλήλους
of Herod. And they reasoned with one another

ὅτι ἄρτους οὐκ ἔχουσιν. 17 καὶ γνοὺς
because loaves they have(had) not. And knowing

λέγει αὐτοῖς· τί διαλογίζεσθε ὅτι ἄρτους
he says to them: Why reason ye because loaves

οὐκ ἔχετε; οὔπω νοεῖτε οὐδὲ συνίετε;
ye have not? not yet understand ye nor realize?

πεπωρωμένην ἔχετε τὴν καρδίαν ὑμῶν;
having been hardened have ye the heart of you?

18 ὀφθαλμοὺς ἔχοντες οὐ βλέπετε, καὶ
eyes having see ye not, and

ὦτα ἔχοντες οὐκ ἀκούετε; καὶ
ears having hear ye not? and

οὐ μνημονεύετε, 19 ὅτε τοὺς πέντε ἄρτους
do ye not remember, when the five loaves

ἔκλασα εἰς τοὺς πεντακισχιλίους, πόσους
I broke to the five thousand, how many

κοφίνους κλασμάτων πλήρεις ἤρατε; λέγουσιν
baskets of fragments full ye took? They say

αὐτῷ· δώδεκα. 20 ὅτε τοὺς ἑπτὰ εἰς
to him: Twelve. When the seven to

τοὺς τετρακισχιλίους, πόσων σπυρίδων
the four thousand, [3]of how many [2]baskets

πληρώματα κλασμάτων ἤρατε; καὶ λέγουσιν·
[1]fullnesses [4]of fragments ye took? And they say:

ἑπτά. 21 καὶ ἔλεγεν αὐτοῖς· οὔπω συνίετε;
Seven. And he said to them: Not yet do ye realize?

22 Καὶ ἔρχονται εἰς Βηθσαϊδάν. Καὶ
And they come to Bethsaida. And

φέρουσιν αὐτῷ τυφλόν, καὶ παρακαλοῦσιν
they bring to him a blind man, and beseech

αὐτὸν ἵνα αὐτοῦ ἅψηται. 23 καὶ ἐπιλαβόμενος
him that him he would touch. And laying hold of

τῆς χειρὸς τοῦ τυφλοῦ ἐξήνεγκεν αὐτὸν
the hand of the blind man he led forth him

ἔξω τῆς κώμης, καὶ πτύσας εἰς τὰ
outside the village, and spitting in the

ὄμματα αὐτοῦ, ἐπιθεὶς τὰς χεῖρας αὐτῷ,
eyes of him, putting on the hands on him,

ἐπηρώτα αὐτόν· εἴ τι βλέπεις; 24 καὶ
questioned him: If anything thou seest? And

ἀναβλέψας ἔλεγεν· βλέπω τοὺς ἀνθρώπους,
looking up he said: I see - men,

ὅτι ὡς δένδρα ὁρῶ περιπατοῦντας.
that as trees I behold walking.

25 εἶτα πάλιν ἐπέθηκεν τὰς χεῖρας ἐπὶ
Then again he put on the hands on

τοὺς ὀφθαλμοὺς αὐτοῦ, καὶ διέβλεψεν καὶ
the eyes of him, and he looked steadily and

ἀπεκατέστη, καὶ ἐνέβλεπεν τηλαυγῶς ἅπαντα.
was restored, and saw clearly all things.

26 καὶ ἀπέστειλεν αὐτὸν εἰς οἶκον αὐτοῦ
And he sent him to house of him

λέγων· μηδὲ εἰς τὴν κώμην εἰσέλθῃς.
saying: Not into the village thou mayest enter.

27 Καὶ ἐξῆλθεν ὁ Ἰησοῦς καὶ οἱ μαθηταὶ
And went forth - Jesus and the disciples

αὐτοῦ εἰς τὰς κώμας Καισαρείας τῆς
of him to the villages of Cæsarea -

warned them. "Watch out for the yeast of the Pharisees and that of Herod." [16]They discussed this with one another and said, "It is because we have no bread." [17]Aware of their discussion, Jesus asked them: "Why are you talking about having no bread? Do you still not see or understand? Are your hearts hardened? [18]Do you have eyes but fail to see, and ears but fail to hear? And don't you remember? [19]When I broke the five loaves for the five thousand, how many basketfuls of pieces did you pick up?" "Twelve," they replied. [20]"And when I broke the seven loaves for the four thousand, how many basketfuls of pieces did you pick up?" They answered, "Seven." [21]He said to them, "Do you still not understand?"

The Healing of a Blind Man at Bethsaida

[22]They came to Bethsaida, and some people brought a blind man and begged Jesus to touch him. [23]He took the blind man by the hand and led him outside the village. When he had spit on the man's eyes and put his hands on him, Jesus asked, "Do you see anything?" [24]He looked up and said, "I see people; they look like trees walking around." [25]Once more Jesus put his hands on the man's eyes. Then his eyes were opened, his sight was restored, and he saw everything clearly. [26]Jesus sent him home, saying, "Don't go into the village.[b]"

Peter's Confession of Christ

[27]Jesus and his disciples went on to the villages around Caesarea Philippi.

[c] Other ancient authorities read *the Herodians*
[d] Gk *They*
[e] Gk *he*
[f] Other ancient authorities add *or tell anyone in the village*

[b]26 Some manuscripts *Don't go and tell anyone in the village*

on the way he asked his disciples, "Who do people say that I am?" 28 And they answered him, "John the Baptist; and others, Elijah; and still others, one of the prophets." 29 He asked them, "But who do you say that I am?" Peter answered him, "You are the Messiah." *g* 30 And he sternly ordered them not to tell anyone about him.

Jesus Foretells His Death and Resurrection

31 Then he began to teach them that the Son of Man must undergo great suffering, and be rejected by the elders, the chief priests, and the scribes, and be killed, and after three days rise again. 32 He said all this quite openly. And Peter took him aside and began to rebuke him. 33 But turning and looking at his disciples, he rebuked Peter and said, "Get behind me, Satan! For you are setting your mind not on divine things but on human things."

34 He called the crowd with his disciples, and said to them, "If any want to become my followers, let them deny themselves and take up their cross and follow me. 35 For those who want to save their life will lose it, and those who lose their life for my sake, and for the sake of the gospel, *h* will save it. 36 For what will it profit them to gain the whole world and forfeit their life? 37 Indeed, what can they give in return for their life? 38 Those who are

g Or the Christ
h Other ancient authorities read lose their life for the sake of the gospel

---

Φιλίππου· καὶ ἐν τῇ ὁδῷ ἐπηρώτα τοὺς
of Philip; and in the way he questioned the

μαθητὰς αὐτοῦ λέγων αὐτοῖς· τίνα με
disciples of him saying to them: Whom me

λέγουσιν οἱ ἄνθρωποι εἶναι; 28 οἱ δὲ
say — men to be? And they

εἶπαν αὐτῷ λέγοντες ὅτι Ἰωάννην τὸν
told him saying[,] — John the

βαπτιστήν, καὶ ἄλλοι Ἠλίαν, ἄλλοι δὲ
Baptist, and others Elias, but others[,]

ὅτι εἷς τῶν προφητῶν. 29 καὶ αὐτὸς
— one of the prophets. And he

ἐπηρώτα αὐτούς· ὑμεῖς δὲ τίνα με λέγετε
questioned them: But ye whom me say ye

εἶναι; ἀποκριθεὶς ὁ Πέτρος λέγει αὐτῷ·
to be? Answering — Peter says to him:

σὺ εἶ ὁ χριστός. 30 καὶ ἐπετίμησεν
Thou art the Christ. And he warned

αὐτοῖς ἵνα μηδενὶ λέγωσιν περὶ αὐτοῦ.
them that no one they might tell about him.

31 Καὶ ἤρξατο διδάσκειν αὐτοὺς ὅτι δεῖ
And he began to teach them that it behoves

τὸν υἱὸν τοῦ ἀνθρώπου πολλὰ παθεῖν,
the Son — of man many things to suffer,

καὶ ἀποδοκιμασθῆναι ὑπὸ τῶν πρεσβυτέρων
and to be rejected by the elders

καὶ τῶν ἀρχιερέων καὶ τῶν γραμματέων
and the chief priests and the scribes

καὶ ἀποκτανθῆναι καὶ μετὰ τρεῖς ἡμέρας
and to be killed and after three days

ἀναστῆναι· 32 καὶ παρρησίᾳ τὸν λόγον
to rise again; and openly the word

ἐλάλει. καὶ προσλαβόμενος ὁ Πέτρος
he spoke. And ¹taking ⁴aside — ¹Peter

αὐτὸν ἤρξατο ἐπιτιμᾶν αὐτῷ. 33 ὁ δὲ
²him began to rebuke him. But he

ἐπιστραφεὶς καὶ ἰδὼν τοὺς μαθητὰς αὐτοῦ
turning round and seeing the disciples of him

ἐπετίμησεν Πέτρῳ καὶ λέγει· ὕπαγε ὀπίσω
rebuked Peter and says: Go behind

μου, σατανᾶ, ὅτι οὐ φρονεῖς τὰ τοῦ
me, Satan, because thou mindest not the things —

θεοῦ ἀλλὰ τὰ τῶν ἀνθρώπων. 34 Καὶ
of God but the things — of men. And

προσκαλεσάμενος τὸν ὄχλον σὺν τοῖς μαθηταῖς
calling to [him] the crowd with the disciples

αὐτοῦ εἶπεν αὐτοῖς· εἴ τις θέλει ὀπίσω
of him he said to them: If anyone wishes after

μου ἐλθεῖν, ἀπαρνησάσθω ἑαυτὸν καὶ ἀράτω
me to come, let him deny himself and take

τὸν σταυρὸν αὐτοῦ, καὶ ἀκολουθείτω μοι.
the cross of him, and let him follow me.

35 ὃς γὰρ ἐὰν θέλῃ τὴν ψυχὴν αὐτοῦ σῶ-
For whoever wishes the life of him to

σαι, ἀπολέσει αὐτήν· ὃς δ' ἂν ἀπολέσει
save, will lose it; but whoever will lose

τὴν ψυχὴν αὐτοῦ ἕνεκεν ἐμοῦ καὶ τοῦ
the life of him for the sake of me and the

εὐαγγελίου, σώσει αὐτήν. 36 τί γὰρ ὠφελεῖ
gospel, will save it. For what profits

ἄνθρωπον κερδῆσαι τὸν κόσμον ὅλον καὶ
a man to gain the world whole and

ζημιωθῆναι τὴν ψυχὴν αὐτοῦ; 37 τί γὰρ
to be fined the soul of him? For what

δοῖ ἄνθρωπος ἀντάλλαγμα τῆς ψυχῆς αὐτοῦ;
might give a man an exchange of the soul of him?

On the way he asked them, "Who do people say I am?"

28 They replied, "Some say John the Baptist; others say Elijah; and still others, one of the prophets."

29 "But what about you?" he asked. "Who do you say I am?"

Peter answered, "You are the Christ. *c*"

30 Jesus warned them not to tell anyone about him.

Jesus Predicts His Death

31 He then began to teach them that the Son of Man must suffer many things and be rejected by the elders, chief priests and teachers of the law, and that he must be killed and after three days rise again. 32 He spoke plainly about this, and Peter took him aside and began to rebuke him.

33 But when Jesus turned and looked at his disciples, he rebuked Peter. "Get behind me, Satan!" he said. "You do not have in mind the things of God, but the things of men."

34 Then he called the crowd to him along with his disciples and said: "If anyone would come after me, he must deny himself and take up his cross and follow me. 35 For whoever wants to save his life *d* will lose it, but whoever loses his life for me and for the gospel will save it. 36 What good is it for a man to gain the whole world, yet forfeit his soul? 37 Or what can a man give in exchange for his soul? 38 If anyone is

c 29 Or Messiah. "The Christ" (Greek) and "the Messiah" (Hebrew) both mean "the Anointed One."
d 35 The Greek word means either life or soul; also in verse 36.

ashamed of me and of my words[i] in this adulterous and sinful generation, of them the Son of Man will also be ashamed when he comes in the glory of his Father with the holy angels." [1]And he said to them, "Truly I tell you, there are some standing here who will not taste death until they see that the kingdom of God has come with[j] power."

The Transfiguration

2 Six days later, Jesus took with him Peter and James and John, and led them up a high mountain apart, by themselves. And he was transfigured before them, [3]and his clothes became dazzling white, such as no one[k] on earth could bleach them. [4]And there appeared to them Elijah with Moses, who were talking with Jesus. [5]Then Peter said to Jesus, "Rabbi, it is good for us to be here; let us make three dwellings,[l] one for you, one for Moses, and one for Elijah." [6]He did not know what to say, for they were terrified. [7]Then a cloud overshadowed them, and from the cloud there came a voice, "This is my Son, the Beloved;[m] listen to him!" [8]Suddenly when they looked around, they saw no one with them any more, but only Jesus.

The Coming of Elijah

9 As they were coming down the mountain, he ordered them to tell no one

---

38 ὃς γὰρ ἐὰν ἐπαισχυνθῇ με καὶ
For whoever   is ashamed of   me   and
τοὺς ἐμοὺς λόγους ἐν τῇ γενεᾷ ταύτῃ
-    my   words   in -   generation this
τῇ μοιχαλίδι καὶ ἁμαρτωλῷ, καὶ ὁ
-   adulterous and   sinful,   also the
υἱὸς τοῦ ἀνθρώπου ἐπαισχυνθήσεται αὐτόν,
Son   -   of man   will be ashamed of   him,
ὅταν ἔλθῃ ἐν τῇ δόξῃ τοῦ πατρὸς
when he comes in the glory of the   Father
αὐτοῦ μετὰ τῶν ἀγγέλων τῶν ἁγίων.
of him with   the   angels   -   holy.

9 καὶ ἔλεγεν αὐτοῖς· ἀμὴν λέγω ὑμῖν
And   he said   to them: Truly I tell   you
ὅτι εἰσίν τινες ὧδε τῶν ἑστηκότων
that there are some here of the [ones] standing
οἵτινες οὐ μὴ γεύσωνται θανάτου ἕως ἂν
who by no means may taste of death   until
ἴδωσιν τὴν βασιλείαν τοῦ θεοῦ ἐληλυθυῖαν
they see the   kingdom   -   of God   having come
ἐν δυνάμει.
in power.

2 Καὶ μετὰ ἡμέρας ἓξ παραλαμβάνει
And   after   days   six   takes
ὁ Ἰησοῦς τὸν Πέτρον καὶ τὸν Ἰάκωβον
- Jesus   -   Peter   and   -   James
καὶ Ἰωάννην, καὶ ἀναφέρει αὐτοὺς εἰς
and John,   and   leads up   them   into
ὄρος ὑψηλὸν κατ᾽ ἰδίαν μόνους. καὶ
mountain a high   privately   alone.   And
μετεμορφώθη ἔμπροσθεν αὐτῶν, **3** καὶ τὰ
he was transfigured before   them,   and the
ἱμάτια αὐτοῦ ἐγένετο στίλβοντα λευκὰ λίαν,
garments of him became   gleaming   white exceedingly,
οἷα γναφεὺς ἐπὶ τῆς γῆς οὐ δύναται
such as fuller   on the earth   cannot
οὕτως λευκᾶναι. **4** καὶ ὤφθη αὐτοῖς Ἠλίας
so   to whiten.   And appeared to them   Elias
σὺν Μωϋσεῖ, καὶ ἦσαν συλλαλοῦντες τῷ
with Moses,   and they were   conversing with
Ἰησοῦ. **5** καὶ ἀποκριθεὶς ὁ Πέτρος λέγει
Jesus.   And   answering   -   Peter   says
τῷ Ἰησοῦ· ῥαββί, καλόν ἐστιν ἡμᾶς ὧδε
- to Jesus: Rabbi, good   it is   us   here
εἶναι, καὶ ποιήσωμεν τρεῖς σκηνάς, σοὶ
to be, and   let us make   three   tents,   for thee
μίαν καὶ Μωϋσεῖ μίαν καὶ Ἠλίᾳ μίαν.
one   and for Moses   one and for Elias one.
6 οὐ γὰρ ᾔδει τί ἀποκριθῇ· ἔκφοβοι γὰρ
For he knew not what he answered; for exceedingly afraid
ἐγένοντο. **7** καὶ ἐγένετο νεφέλη ἐπισκιάζουσα
they became.   And there came a cloud overshadowing
αὐτοῖς, καὶ ἐγένετο φωνὴ ἐκ τῆς νεφέλης·
them,   and there came a voice out of the   cloud:
οὗτός ἐστιν ὁ υἱός μου ὁ ἀγαπητός,
This   is   the Son of me the beloved,
ἀκούετε αὐτοῦ. **8** καὶ ἐξάπινα περιβλεψάμενοι
hear ye   him.   And suddenly   looking round
οὐκέτι οὐδένα εἶδον εἰ μὴ τὸν Ἰησοῦν
no longer no(any)one they saw except   -   Jesus
μόνον μεθ᾽ ἑαυτῶν. **9** Καὶ καταβαινόντων
only   with themselves.   And   coming down
                                    = as they came down
αὐτῶν ἐκ τοῦ ὄρους διεστείλατο αὐτοῖς
them   out of the   mountain   he ordered   them

---

ashamed of me and my words in this adulterous and sinful generation, the Son of Man will be ashamed of him when he comes in his Father's glory with the holy angels."

Chapter 9

[A]ND he said to them, "I tell you the truth, some who are standing here will not taste death before they see the kingdom of God come with power."

The Transfiguration

[2]After six days Jesus took Peter, James and John with him and led them up a high mountain, where they were all alone. There he was transfigured before them. [3]His clothes became dazzling white, whiter than anyone in the world could bleach them. [4]And there appeared before them Elijah and Moses, who were talking with Jesus.

[5]Peter said to Jesus, "Rabbi, it is good for us to be here. Let us put up three shelters—one for you, one for Moses and one for Elijah." [6](He did not know what to say, they were so frightened.)

[7]Then a cloud appeared and enveloped them, and a voice came from the cloud: "This is my Son, whom I love. Listen to him!"

[8]Suddenly, when they looked around, they no longer saw anyone with them except Jesus.

[9]As they were coming down the mountain, Jesus gave them orders not to tell

---

[i] Other ancient authorities read *and of mine*
[j] Or *in*
[k] Gk *no fuller*
[l] Or *tents*
[m] Or *my beloved Son*

about what they had seen, until after the Son of Man had risen from the dead. [10] So they kept the matter to themselves, questioning what this rising from the dead could mean. [11] Then they asked him, "Why do the scribes say that Elijah must come first?" [12] He said to them, "Elijah is indeed coming first to restore all things. How then is it written about the Son of Man, that he is to go through many sufferings and be treated with contempt? [13] But I tell you that Elijah has come, and they did to him whatever they pleased, as it is written about him."

The Healing of a Boy with a Spirit

[14] When they came to the disciples, they saw a great crowd around them, and some scribes arguing with them. [15] When the whole crowd saw him, they were immediately overcome with awe, and they ran forward to greet him. [16] He asked them, "What are you arguing about with them?" [17] Someone from the crowd answered him, "Teacher, I brought you my son; he has a spirit that makes him unable to speak; [18] and whenever it seizes him, it dashes him down; and he foams and grinds his teeth and becomes rigid; and I asked your disciples to cast it out, but they could not do so." [19] He answered them, "You faithless generation, how much longer must I be among you? How much longer must I put up with you? Bring him to me." [20] And they brought the boy[n] to him. When the spirit saw him, immediately it convulsed the boy,[n] and

[n] Gk him

ἵνα μηδενὶ ἃ εἶδον διηγήσωνται,
that to no one [the] things which they saw they should relate,

εἰ μὴ ὅταν ὁ υἱὸς τοῦ ἀνθρώπου ἐκ νεκρῶν
except when the Son - of man out of [the] dead

ἀναστῇ. 10 καὶ τὸν λόγον ἐκράτησαν πρὸς
should rise. And the word they held to

ἑαυτοὺς συζητοῦντες τί ἐστιν τὸ ἐκ
themselves debating what is the " out of

νεκρῶν ἀναστῆναι. 11 Καὶ ἐπηρώτων αὐτὸν
[the] dead to rise. And they questioned him

λέγοντες· ὅτι λέγουσιν οἱ γραμματεῖς ὅτι
saying: Why say the scribes that

Ἠλίαν δεῖ ἐλθεῖν πρῶτον; 12 ὁ δὲ ἔφη
Elias it behoves to come first? And he said

αὐτοῖς· Ἠλίας μὲν ἐλθὼν πρῶτον
to them: Elias indeed coming first

ἀποκαθιστάνει πάντα· καὶ πῶς γέγραπται
restores all things; and how has it been written

ἐπὶ τὸν υἱὸν τοῦ ἀνθρώπου, ἵνα πολλὰ
on(concerning) the Son - of man, that many things

πάθῃ καὶ ἐξουδενηθῇ; 13 ἀλλὰ λέγω ὑμῖν
he should suffer and be set at naught? But I tell you

ὅτι καὶ Ἠλίας ἐλήλυθεν, καὶ ἐποίησαν
that indeed Elias has come, and they did

αὐτῷ ὅσα ἤθελον, καθὼς γέγραπται
to him what they wished, as it has been written

ἐπ' αὐτόν.
on(concerning) him.

14 Καὶ ἐλθόντες πρὸς τοὺς μαθητὰς
And coming to the disciples

εἶδον ὄχλον πολὺν περὶ αὐτοὺς καὶ
they saw crowd a much(great) around them and

γραμματεῖς συζητοῦντας πρὸς αὐτούς.
scribes debating with them.

15 καὶ εὐθὺς πᾶς ὁ ὄχλος ἰδόντες αὐτὸν
And immediately all the crowd seeing him

ἐξεθαμβήθησαν, καὶ προστρέχοντες ἠσπάζοντο
were greatly astonished, and running up to greeted

αὐτόν. 16 καὶ ἐπηρώτησεν αὐτούς· τί
him. And he questioned them: What

συ[ζ]ητεῖτε πρὸς αὐτούς; 17 καὶ ἀπεκρίθη
are ye debating with them? And answered

αὐτῷ εἷς ἐκ τοῦ ὄχλου· διδάσκαλε,
him one of the crowd: Teacher,

ἤνεγκα τὸν υἱόν μου πρὸς σέ, ἔχοντα
I brought the son of me to thee, having

πνεῦμα ἄλαλον· 18 καὶ ὅπου ἐὰν αὐτὸν
spirit a dumb; and wherever him

καταλάβῃ, ῥήσσει αὐτόν, καὶ ἀφρίζει καὶ
it seizes, it tears him, and he foams and

τρίζει τοὺς ὀδόντας καὶ ξηραίνεται· καὶ
grinds the(his) teeth and he wastes away; and

εἶπα τοῖς μαθηταῖς σου ἵνα αὐτὸ
I told the disciples of thee that it

ἐκβάλωσιν, καὶ οὐκ ἴσχυσαν. 19 ὁ δὲ
they might expel, and they were not able. And he

ἀποκριθεὶς αὐτοῖς λέγει· ὦ γενεὰ ἄπιστος,
answering them says: O generation unbelieving,

ἕως πότε πρὸς ὑμᾶς ἔσομαι; ἕως πότε
until when with you shall I be? how long
= how long

ἀνέξομαι ὑμῶν; φέρετε αὐτὸν πρός με.
shall I endure you? bring him to me.

20 καὶ ἤνεγκαν αὐτὸν πρὸς αὐτόν. καὶ
And they brought him to him. And

ἰδὼν αὐτὸν τὸ πνεῦμα εὐθὺς συνεσπάραξεν
seeing him the spirit immediately violently threw

anyone what they had seen until the Son of Man had risen from the dead. [10]They kept the matter to themselves, discussing what "rising from the dead" meant.

[11]And they asked him, "Why do the teachers of the law say that Elijah must come first?"

[12]Jesus replied, "To be sure, Elijah does come first, and restores all things. Why then is it written that the Son of Man must suffer much and be rejected? [13]But I tell you, Elijah has come, and they have done to him everything they wished, just as it is written about him."

The Healing of a Boy With an Evil Spirit

[14]When they came to the other disciples, they saw a large crowd around them and the teachers of the law arguing with them. [15]As soon as all the people saw Jesus, they were overwhelmed with wonder and ran to greet him.

[16]"What are you arguing with them about?" he asked.

[17]A man in the crowd answered, "Teacher, I brought you my son, who is possessed by a spirit that has robbed him of speech. [18]Whenever it seizes him, it throws him to the ground. He foams at the mouth, gnashes his teeth and becomes rigid. I asked your disciples to drive out the spirit, but they could not."

[19]"O unbelieving generation," Jesus replied, "how long shall I stay with you? How long shall I put up with you? Bring the boy to me."

[20]So they brought him. When the spirit saw Jesus, it immediately threw the boy into a convulsion. He

he fell on the ground and rolled about, foaming at the mouth. 21 Jesus⁰ asked the father, "How long has this been happening to him?" And he said, "From childhood. 22 It has often cast him into the fire and into the water, to destroy him; but if you are able to do anything, have pity on us and help us." 23 Jesus said to him, "If you are able!— All things can be done for the one who believes." 24 Immediately the father of the child cried out, ᵖ "I believe; help my unbelief!" 25 When Jesus saw that a crowd came running together, he rebuked the unclean spirit, saying to it, "You spirit that keeps this boy from speaking and hearing, I command you, come out of him, and never enter him again!" 26 After crying out and convulsing him terribly, it came out, and the boy was like a corpse, so that most of them said, "He is dead." 27 But Jesus took him by the hand and lifted him up, and he was able to stand. 28 When he had entered the house, his disciples asked him privately, "Why could we not cast it out?" 29 He said to them, "This kind can come out only through prayer."�q

Jesus Again Foretells His Death and Resurrection

30 They went on from there and passed through Galilee. He did not want anyone to know it; 31 for he was teaching his disciples, saying to them, "The Son of Man is to be betrayed into human hands, and they will kill him, and three days after being killed, he will rise again." 32 But they did

---

αὐτόν, καὶ πεσὼν ἐπὶ τῆς γῆς ἐκυλίετο
him, and falling on the earth he wallowed
ἀφρίζων. 21 καὶ ἐπηρώτησεν τὸν πατέρα
foaming. And he questioned the father
αὐτοῦ· πόσος χρόνος ἐστὶν ὡς τοῦτο
of him: What time is it while this
γέγονεν αὐτῷ; ὁ δὲ εἶπεν· ἐκ παιδιόθεν·
has happened to him? And he said: From childhood;
22 καὶ πολλάκις καὶ εἰς πῦρ αὐτὸν
and often both into fire him
ἔβαλεν καὶ εἰς ὕδατα ἵνα ἀπολέσῃ αὐτόν· ἀλλ'
it threw and into waters that it may destroy him; but
εἴ τι δύνῃ, βοήθησον ἡμῖν σπλαγχνισθεὶς
if anything thou canst, help us having compassion
ἐφ' ἡμᾶς. 23 ὁ δὲ Ἰησοῦς εἶπεν αὐτῷ· τὸ εἰ
on us. - And Jesus said to him: The "if
δύνῃ, πάντα δυνατὰ τῷ πιστεύοντι.
thou canst," all things possible to the [one] believing.
24 εὐθὺς κράξας ὁ πατὴρ τοῦ παιδίου
Immediately crying out the father of the child
ἔλεγεν· πιστεύω· βοήθει μου τῇ ἀπιστίᾳ.
said: I believe; help thou of me the unbelief.
25 ἰδὼν δὲ ὁ Ἰησοῦς ὅτι ἐπισυντρέχει
And ²seeing - ¹Jesus that is(was) running together
ὄχλος, ἐπετίμησεν τῷ πνεύματι τῷ ἀκαθάρτῳ
a crowd, rebuked the spirit - unclean
λέγων αὐτῷ· τὸ ἄλαλον καὶ κωφὸν
saying to it: - Dumb and deaf
πνεῦμα, ἐγὼ ἐπιτάσσω σοι, ἔξελθε ἐξ
spirit, I command thee, come forth out of
αὐτοῦ καὶ μηκέτι εἰσέλθῃς εἰς αὐτόν.
him and no more mayest thou enter into him.
26 καὶ κράξας καὶ πολλὰ σπαράξας
And crying out and much convulsing [him]
ἐξῆλθεν· καὶ ἐγένετο ὡσεὶ νεκρός, ὥστε
it came out; and he was as dead, so as
τοὺς πολλοὺς λέγειν ὅτι ἀπέθανεν. 27 ὁ
- many to sayᵇ that he died.
= many said
δὲ Ἰησοῦς κρατήσας τῆς χειρὸς αὐτοῦ
But Jesus taking hold of the hand of him
ἤγειρεν αὐτόν, καὶ ἀνέστη. 28 καὶ
raised him, and he stood up. And
εἰσελθόντος αὐτοῦ εἰς οἶκον οἱ μαθηταὶ
entering himᵃ into a house the disciples
=when he entered
αὐτοῦ κατ' ἰδίαν ἐπηρώτων αὐτόν· ὅτι
of him privately questioned him: Why
ἡμεῖς οὐκ ἠδυνήθημεν ἐκβαλεῖν αὐτό;
we were not able to expel it?
29 καὶ εἶπεν αὐτοῖς· τοῦτο τὸ γένος ἐν
And he told them: This - kind by
οὐδενὶ δύναται ἐξελθεῖν εἰ μὴ ἐν προσευχῇ.
nothing can *to* come out except by prayer.
30 Κἀκεῖθεν ἐξελθόντες παρεπορεύοντο διὰ
And thence going forth they passed through
τῆς Γαλιλαίας, καὶ οὐκ ἤθελεν ἵνα
- Galilee, and he wished not that
τις γνοῖ· 31 ἐδίδασκεν γὰρ τοὺς μαθητὰς
anyone should know; for he was teaching the disciples
αὐτοῦ, καὶ ἔλεγεν αὐτοῖς ὅτι ὁ υἱὸς τοῦ
of him, and told them[,] - The Son
ἀνθρώπου παραδίδοται εἰς χεῖρας ἀνθρώπων,
of man is betrayed into [the] hands of men,
καὶ ἀποκτενοῦσιν αὐτόν, καὶ ἀποκτανθεὶς
and they will kill him, and being killed
μετὰ τρεῖς ἡμέρας ἀναστήσεται. 32 οἱ
after three days he will rise up. they

---

fell to the ground and rolled around, foaming at the mouth.
21 Jesus asked the boy's father, "How long has he been like this?"
"From childhood," he answered. 22 "It has often thrown him into fire or water to kill him. But if you can do anything, take pity on us and help us."
23 "'If you can'?" said Jesus. "Everything is possible for him who believes."
24 Immediately the boy's father exclaimed, "I do believe; help me overcome my unbelief!"
25 When Jesus saw that a crowd was running to the scene, he rebuked the evilᵉ spirit. "You deaf and mute spirit," he said, "I command you, come out of him and never enter him again."
26 The spirit shrieked, convulsed him violently and came out. The boy looked so much like a corpse that many said, "He's dead." 27 But Jesus took him by the hand and lifted him to his feet, and he stood up.
28 After Jesus had gone indoors, his disciples asked him privately, "Why couldn't we drive it out?"
29 He replied, "This kind can come out only by prayer.ᶠ"
30 They left that place and passed through Galilee. Jesus did not want anyone to know where they were, 31 because he was teaching his disciples. He said to them, "The Son of Man is going to be betrayed into the hands of men. They will kill him, and after three days he will rise." 32 But

---

⁰ Gk *He*
ᵖ Other ancient authorities add *with tears*
q Other ancient authorities add *and fasting*

ᵉ25 Greek *unclean*
ᶠ29 Some manuscripts *prayer and fasting*

not understand what he was saying and were afraid to ask him.

Who Is the Greatest?

33 Then they came to Capernaum; and when he was in the house he asked them, "What were you arguing about on the way?" 34 But they were silent, for on the way they had argued with one another who was the greatest. 35 He sat down, called the twelve, and said to them, "Whoever wants to be first must be last of all and servant of all." 36 Then he took a little child and put it among them; and taking it in his arms, he said to them, 37 "Whoever welcomes one such child in my name welcomes me, and whoever welcomes me welcomes not me but the one who sent me."

Another Exorcist

38 John said to him, "Teacher, we saw some-one*ʳ* casting out demons in your name, and we tried to stop him, because he was not following us." 39 But Jesus said, "Do not stop him; for no one who does a deed of power in my name will be able soon afterward to speak evil of me. 40 Whoever is not against us is for us. 41 For truly I tell you, whoever gives you a cup of water to drink because you bear the name of Christ will by no means lose the reward.

Temptations to Sin

42 "If any of you put a stumbling block before one of these little ones who believe in me,*ˢ* it would be better for you if a great millstone were hung around your neck and you were thrown into the sea. 43 If your hand causes you to stumble, cut it off; it is better for you to enter life

---

δὲ ἠγνόουν τὸ ῥῆμα, καὶ ἐφοβοῦντο
But did not know the word, and feared

αὐτὸν ἐπερωτῆσαι.
him to question.

33 Καὶ ἦλθον εἰς Καφαρναούμ. Καὶ
And they came to Capernaum. And

ἐν τῇ οἰκίᾳ γενόμενος ἐπηρώτα αὐτούς·
in the house being he questioned them:

τί ἐν τῇ ὁδῷ διελογίζεσθε; 34 οἱ δὲ
What in the way were ye debating? And they

ἐσιώπων· ²with ¹one another ¹for they debated
were silent;

ἐν τῇ ὁδῷ τίς μείζων. 35 καὶ καθίσας
in the way who [was] greater. And sitting

ἐφώνησεν τοὺς δώδεκα καὶ λέγει αὐτοῖς·
he called the twelve and says to them:

εἴ τις θέλει πρῶτος εἶναι, ἔσται πάντων
If anyone wishes first to be, he shall be of all

ἔσχατος καὶ πάντων διάκονος. 36 καὶ
last and of all servant. And

λαβὼν παιδίον ἔστησεν αὐτὸ ἐν [τῷ] μέσῳ
taking a child he set it(him) in [the] midst

αὐτῶν, καὶ ἐναγκαλισάμενος αὐτὸ εἶπεν
of them, and folding in [his] arms it he said

αὐτοῖς· 37 ὃς ἂν ἓν τῶν τοιούτων παιδίων
to them: Whoever one — of such children

δέξηται ἐπὶ τῷ ὀνόματί μου, ἐμὲ δέχεται·
receives on(in) the name of me, me receives;

καὶ ὃς ἂν ἐμὲ δέχηται, οὐκ ἐμὲ δέχεται
and whoever me receives, not me receives

ἀλλὰ τὸν ἀποστείλαντά με. 38 Ἔφη αὐτῷ
but the [one] having sent me. Said to him

ὁ Ἰωάννης· διδάσκαλε, εἴδομέν τινα ἐν
— John: Teacher, we saw someone in

τῷ ὀνόματί σου ἐκβάλλοντα δαιμόνια, ὃς
the name of thee expelling demons, who

οὐκ ἀκολουθεῖ ἡμῖν, καὶ ἐκωλύομεν αὐτόν,
does not follow us, and we forbade him,

ὅτι οὐκ ἠκολούθει ἡμῖν. 39 ὁ δὲ Ἰησοῦς
because he was not following us. — But Jesus

εἶπεν· μὴ κωλύετε αὐτόν· οὐδεὶς γὰρ
said: Do not forbid him: for no one

ἔστιν ὃς ποιήσει δύναμιν ἐπὶ τῷ ὀνόματί
there is who shall do a mighty work on(in) the name

μου καὶ δυνήσεται ταχὺ κακολογῆσαί με·
of me and will be able quickly to speak evil of me;

40 ὃς γὰρ οὐκ ἔστιν καθ᾽ ἡμῶν, ὑπὲρ
for who is not against us, for

ἡμῶν ἐστιν. 41 Ὃς γὰρ ἂν ποτίσῃ
us is. For whoever ¹gives ²drink

ὑμᾶς ποτήριον ὕδατος ἐν ὀνόματι, ὅτι
²you a cup of water in [the] name, because

Χριστοῦ ἐστε, ἀμὴν λέγω ὑμῖν ὅτι
of Christ ye are, truly I tell you that

οὐ μὴ ἀπολέσῃ τὸν μισθὸν αὐτοῦ. 42 Καὶ
by no means he will lose the reward of him. And

ὃς ἂν σκανδαλίσῃ ἕνα τῶν μικρῶν τούτων
whoever offends one — ³little [ones] ¹of these

τῶν πιστευόντων, καλόν ἐστιν αὐτῷ μᾶλλον
— ²believing, good is it for him rather

εἰ περίκειται μύλος ὀνικὸς περὶ τὸν
if be laid *round* a [heavy] millstone round the

τράχηλον αὐτοῦ καὶ βέβληται εἰς τὴν
neck of him and he be thrown into the

θάλασσαν. 43 Καὶ ἐὰν σκανδαλίσῃ σε ἡ
sea. And if offends thee the

---

they did not understand what he meant and were afraid to ask him about it.

Who Is the Greatest?

33 They came to Capernaum. When he was in the house, he asked them, "What were you arguing about on the road?" 34 But they kept quiet because on the way they had argued about who was the greatest.

35 Sitting down, Jesus called the Twelve and said, "If anyone wants to be first, he must be the very last, and the servant of all."

36 He took a little child and had him stand among them. Taking him in his arms, he said to them, 37 "Whoever welcomes one of these little children in my name welcomes me; and whoever welcomes me does not welcome me but the one who sent me."

Whoever Is Not Against Us Is for Us

38 "Teacher," said John, "we saw a man driving out demons in your name and we told him to stop, because he was not one of us."

39 "Do not stop him," Jesus said. "No one who does a miracle in my name can in the next moment say anything bad about me, 40 for whoever is not against us is for us. 41 I tell you the truth, anyone who gives you a cup of water in my name because you belong to Christ will certainly not lose his reward.

Causing to Sin

42 "And if anyone causes one of these little ones who believe in me to sin, it would be better for him to be thrown into the sea with a large millstone tied around his neck. 43 If your hand causes you to sin, cut

---

ʳ Other ancient authorities add *who does not follow us*
ˢ Other ancient authorities lack *in me*

maimed than to have two hands and to go to hell,[t] to the unquenchable fire.[u] 45 And if your foot causes you to stumble, cut it off; it is better for you to enter life lame than to have two feet and to be thrown into hell.[t,u] 47 And if your eye causes you to stumble, tear it out; it is better for you to enter the kingdom of God with one eye than to have two eyes and to be thrown into hell,[t] 48 where their worm never dies, and the fire is never quenched.

49 "For everyone will be salted with fire.[v] 50 Salt is good; but if salt has lost its saltiness, how can you season it?[w] Have salt in yourselves, and be at peace with one another."

χείρ σου, ἀπόκοψον αὐτήν· καλόν ἐστίν
hand of thee, cut off it; good is it
σε κυλλόν εἰσελθεῖν εἰς τὴν ζωήν, ἢ τὰς
thee maimed to enter into - life, than the
δύο χεῖρας ἔχοντα ἀπελθεῖν εἰς τὴν
two hands having to go away into -
γέενναν, εἰς τὸ πῦρ τὸ ἄσβεστον.‡ 45 καὶ
gehenna, into the fire the unquenchable. And
ἐὰν ὁ πούς σου σκανδαλίζῃ σε, ἀπόκοψον
if the foot of thee offends thee, cut off
αὐτόν· καλόν ἐστίν σε εἰσελθεῖν εἰς τὴν
it; good is it thee to enter into -
ζωὴν χωλόν, ἢ τοὺς δύο πόδας ἔχοντα
life lame, than the two feet having
βληθῆναι εἰς τὴν γέενναν.‡ 47 καὶ ἐὰν ὁ
to be cast into - gehenna. And if the
ὀφθαλμός σου σκανδαλίζῃ σε, ἔκβαλε αὐτόν·
eye of thee offends thee, cast out it;
καλόν σέ ἐστιν μονόφθαλμον εἰσελθεῖν εἰς
good thee is it one-eyed to enter into
τὴν βασιλείαν τοῦ θεοῦ, ἢ δύο ὀφθαλμοὺς
the kingdom - of God, than two eyes
ἔχοντα βληθῆναι εἰς τὴν γέενναν, 48 ὅπου
having to be cast into - gehenna, where
ὁ σκώληξ αὐτῶν οὐ τελευτᾷ καὶ τὸ
the worm of them dies not and the
πῦρ οὐ σβέννυται. 49 Πᾶς γὰρ πυρὶ
fire is not quenched. For everyone with fire
ἁλισθήσεται. 50 καλὸν τὸ ἅλας· ἐὰν δὲ
shall be salted. Good [is] - salt; but if
τὸ ἅλας ἄναλον γένηται, ἐν τίνι αὐτὸ
- salt saltless becomes, by what it
ἀρτύσετε; ἔχετε ἐν ἑαυτοῖς ἅλα καὶ
will ye season? Have in yourselves salt and
εἰρηνεύετε ἐν ἀλλήλοις.
be at peace among one another.

---

it off. It is better for you to enter life maimed than with two hands to go into hell, where the fire never goes out.[g] 45 And if your foot causes you to sin, cut it off. It is better for you to enter life crippled than to have two feet and be thrown into hell.[h] 47 And if your eye causes you to sin, pluck it out. It is better for you to enter the kingdom of God with one eye than to have two eyes and be thrown into hell, 48 where

  " 'their worm does not die,
    and the fire is not quenched.'[i]

49 Everyone will be salted with fire.
50 "Salt is good, but if it loses its saltiness, how can you make it salty again? Have salt in yourselves, and be at peace with each other."

Chapter 10
Teaching about Divorce

HE left that place and went to the region of Judea and[x] beyond the Jordan. And crowds again gathered around him; and, as was his custom, he again taught them.

2 Some Pharisees came, and to test him they asked, "Is it lawful for a man to divorce his wife?" 3 He answered them, "What did Moses command you?" 4 They said, "Moses allowed a man to write a certificate of dismissal and to divorce her." 5 But Jesus said to them, "Because of your hardness of heart he wrote this commandment for you. 6 But from the beginning of creation, 'God made them male and female.' 7 'For this reason a

---

10 Καὶ ἐκεῖθεν ἀναστὰς ἔρχεται εἰς τὰ
And thence rising up he comes into the
ὅρια τῆς Ἰουδαίας καὶ πέραν τοῦ
territory of Judæa and beyond the
Ἰορδάνου, καὶ συμπορεύονται πάλιν ὄχλοι
Jordan, and ²go with ¹again ²crowds
πρὸς αὐτόν, καὶ ὡς εἰώθει πάλιν ἐδίδασκεν
⁴with ⁵him, and as he was wont again he taught
αὐτούς. 2 Καὶ προσελθόντες Φαρισαῖοι
them. And ²approaching ¹Pharisees
ἐπηρώτων αὐτὸν εἰ ἔξεστιν ἀνδρὶ γυναῖκα
questioned him if it is(was) lawful for a man a wife
ἀπολῦσαι, πειράζοντες αὐτόν. 3 ὁ δὲ
to dismiss, testing him. And he
ἀποκριθεὶς εἶπεν αὐτοῖς· 4 τί ὑμῖν ἐνετείλατο
answering said to them: What you ordered
Μωϋσῆς; οἱ δὲ εἶπαν· ἐπέτρεψεν Μωϋσῆς
Moses? And they said: permitted Moses
βιβλίον ἀποστασίου γράψαι καὶ ἀπολῦσαι.
a roll of divorce to write and to dismiss.
5 ὁ δὲ Ἰησοῦς εἶπεν αὐτοῖς· πρὸς τὴν
- And Jesus said to them: For the
σκληροκαρδίαν ὑμῶν ἔγραψεν ὑμῖν τὴν
hardheartedness of you he wrote to you -
ἐντολὴν ταύτην. 6 ἀπὸ δὲ ἀρχῆς κτίσεως
this commandment. But from [the] beginning of creation

‡ Verse 44 omitted by Nestle; cf. NIV footnote.

‡ Verse 46 omitted by Nestle; cf. NIV footnote.

Chapter 10
Divorce

JESUS then left that place and went into the region of Judea and across the Jordan. Again crowds of people came to him, and as was his custom, he taught them.
2 Some Pharisees came and tested him by asking, "Is it lawful for a man to divorce his wife?"
3 "What did Moses command you?" he replied.
4 They said, "Moses permitted a man to write a certificate of divorce and send her away."
5 "It was because your hearts were hard that Moses wrote you this law," Jesus replied. 6 "But at the beginning of creation God

---

[t] Gk Gehenna
[u] Verses 44 and 46 (which are identical with verse 48) are lacking in the best ancient authorities
[v] Other ancient authorities either add or substitute and every sacrifice will be salted with salt
[w] Or how can you restore its saltiness?
[x] Other ancient authorities lack and

[g]43 Some manuscripts out. [44]where / " 'their worm does not die, / and the fire is not quenched.'
[h]45 Some manuscripts hell, [46]where / " 'their worm does not die, / and the fire is not quenched.'
[i]48 Isaiah 66:24

man shall leave his father and mother and be joined to his wife,[y] [8]and the two shall become one flesh.' So they are no longer two, but one flesh. [9]Therefore what God has joined together, let no one separate."

[10] Then in the house the disciples asked him again about this matter. [11]He said to them, "Whoever divorces his wife and marries another commits adultery against her; [12]and if she divorces her husband and marries another, she commits adultery."

Jesus Blesses Little Children

[13] People were bringing little children to him in order that he might touch them; and the disciples spoke sternly to them. [14]But when Jesus saw this, he was indignant and said to them, "Let the little children come to me; do not stop them; for it is to such as these that the kingdom of God belongs. [15]Truly I tell you, whoever does not receive the kingdom of God as a little child will never enter it." [16]And he took them up in his arms, laid his hands on them, and blessed them.

The Rich Man

[17] As he was setting out on a journey, a man ran up and knelt before him, and asked him, "Good Teacher, what must I do to inherit eternal life?" [18]Jesus said to him, "Why do you call me good? No one is good but God alone. [19]You know the commandments: 'You shall not murder; You shall not commit adultery; You shall not steal; You shall not bear false witness; You shall not defraud; Honor your father and mother.'" [20]He said to him, "Teacher, I have kept all these since my youth."

ἄρσεν καὶ θῆλυ ἐποίησεν αὐτούς· 7 ἕνεκεν
male and female he made them; for the sake of

τούτου καταλείψει ἄνθρωπος τὸν πατέρα
this shall leave a man the father

αὐτοῦ καὶ τὴν μητέρα, 8 καὶ ἔσονται
of him and the mother, and shall be

οἱ δύο εἰς σάρκα μίαν· ὥστε οὐκέτι
the two - flesh one; so as no longer

εἰσὶν δύο ἀλλὰ μία σάρξ. 9 ὃ οὖν ὁ
are they two but one flesh. What then -

θεὸς συνέζευξεν, ἄνθρωπος μὴ χωριζέτω.
God yoked together, ³man ²not ¹let ⁴separate.

10 καὶ εἰς τὴν οἰκίαν πάλιν οἱ μαθηταὶ
And in the house again the disciples

περὶ τούτου ἐπηρώτων αὐτόν. 11 καὶ
about this questioned him. And

λέγει αὐτοῖς· ὃς ἂν ἀπολύσῃ τὴν γυναῖκα
he says to them: Whoever dismisses the wife

αὐτοῦ καὶ γαμήσῃ ἄλλην, μοιχᾶται ἐπ'
of him and marries another, commits adultery with

αὐτήν· 12 καὶ ἐὰν αὐτὴ ἀπολύσασα τὸν
her; and if she having dismissed the

ἄνδρα αὐτῆς γαμήσῃ ἄλλον, μοιχᾶται.
husband of her marries another, she commits adultery.

13 Καὶ προσέφερον αὐτῷ παιδία ἵνα
And they brought to him children that

αὐτῶν ἅψηται· οἱ δὲ μαθηταὶ ἐπετίμησαν
them he might touch; but the disciples rebuked

αὐτοῖς. 14 ἰδὼν δὲ ὁ Ἰησοῦς ἠγανάκτησεν
them. But ²seeing - ¹Jesus was angry

καὶ εἶπεν αὐτοῖς· ἄφετε τὰ παιδία
and said to them: Allow the children

ἔρχεσθαι πρός με, μὴ κωλύετε αὐτά·
to come to me, do not prevent them;

τῶν γὰρ τοιούτων ἐστὶν ἡ βασιλεία τοῦ
- for of such is the kingdom -

θεοῦ. 15 ἀμὴν λέγω ὑμῖν, ὃς ἂν
of God. Truly I tell you, whoever

μὴ δέξηται τὴν βασιλείαν τοῦ θεοῦ ὡς
receives not the kingdom - of God as

παιδίον, οὐ μὴ εἰσέλθῃ εἰς αὐτήν. 16 καὶ
a child, by no means may enter into it. And

ἐναγκαλισάμενος αὐτὰ κατευλόγει τιθεὶς τὰς
folding in [his] arms them he blesses putting the(his)

χεῖρας ἐπ' αὐτά.
hands on them.

17 Καὶ ἐκπορευομένου αὐτοῦ εἰς ὁδὸν
And going forth himᵃ into [the] way
= as he went forth

προσδραμὼν εἷς καὶ γονυπετήσας αὐτὸν
running to one and kneeling to him

ἐπηρώτα αὐτόν· διδάσκαλε ἀγαθέ, τί ποιήσω
questioned him: Teacher good, what may I do

ἵνα ζωὴν αἰώνιον κληρονομήσω; 18 ὁ δὲ
that life eternal I may inherit ? - And

Ἰησοῦς εἶπεν αὐτῷ· τί με λέγεις ἀγαθόν;
Jesus said to him: Why me callest thou good ?

οὐδεὶς ἀγαθὸς εἰ μὴ εἷς ὁ θεός. 19 τὰς ἐντολὰς
no one good except one - God. The commandments

οἶδας· μὴ φονεύσῃς, μὴ μοιχεύσῃς,
thou knowest: Do not kill, Do not commit adultery,

μὴ κλέψῃς, μὴ ψευδομαρτυρήσῃς, μὴ
Do not steal, Do not bear false witness, Do

ἀποστερήσῃς, τίμα τὸν πατέρα σου καὶ
not defraud, Honour the father of thee and

τὴν μητέρα. 20 ὁ δὲ ἔφη αὐτῷ· διδάσκαλε,
the mother. And he said to him: Teacher,

'made them male and female.'ʲ 7'For this reason a man will leave his father and mother and be united to his wife,ᵏ 8and the two will become one flesh.'ˡ So they are no longer two, but one. 9Therefore what God has joined together, let man not separate."

10When they were in the house again, the disciples asked Jesus about this. 11He answered, "Anyone who divorces his wife and marries another woman commits adultery against her. 12And if she divorces her husband and marries another man, she commits adultery."

The Little Children and Jesus

13People were bringing little children to Jesus to have him touch them, but the disciples rebuked them. 14When Jesus saw this, he was indignant. He said to them, "Let the little children come to me, and do not hinder them, for the kingdom of God belongs to such as these. 15I tell you the truth, anyone who will not receive the kingdom of God like a little child will never enter it." 16And he took the children in his arms, put his hands on them and blessed them.

The Rich Young Man

17As Jesus started on his way, a man ran up to him and fell on his knees before him. "Good teacher," he asked, "what must I do to inherit eternal life?"

18"Why do you call me good?" Jesus answered. "No one is good—except God alone. 19You know the commandments: 'Do not murder, do not commit adultery, do not steal, do not give false testimony, do not defraud, honor your father and mother.'ᵐ"

20"Teacher," he declared, "all these I have

ʸ Other ancient authorities lack *and be joined to his wife*

ʲ6 Gen. 1:27
ᵏ7 Some early manuscripts do not have *and be united to his wife.*
ˡ8 Gen. 2:24
ᵐ19 Exodus 20:12-16; Deut. 5:16-20

21 Jesus, looking at him, loved him and said, "You lack one thing; go, sell what you own, and give the money[z] to the poor, and you will have treasure in heaven; then come, follow me." 22 When he heard this, he was shocked and went away grieving, for he had many possessions.

23 Then Jesus looked around and said to his disciples, "How hard it will be for those who have wealth to enter the kingdom of God!" 24 And the disciples were perplexed at these words. But Jesus said to them again, "Children, how hard it is[a] to enter the kingdom of God! 25 It is easier for a camel to go through the eye of a needle than for someone who is rich to enter the kingdom of God." 26 They were greatly astounded and said to one another,[b] "Then who can be saved?" 27 Jesus looked at them and said, "For mortals it is impossible, but not for God; for God all things are possible."

28 Peter began to say to him, "Look, we have left everything and followed you." 29 Jesus said, "Truly I tell you, there is no one who has left house or brothers or sisters or mother or father or children or fields, for my sake and for the sake of the good news,[c] 30 who will not receive a hundredfold now in this age—houses, brothers and sisters, mothers and

---

ταῦτα πάντα ἐφυλαξάμην ἐκ νεότητός μου.
all these things I observed from youth of me.

21 ὁ δὲ Ἰησοῦς ἐμβλέψας αὐτῷ ἠγάπησεν
- But Jesus looking at him loved

αὐτὸν καὶ εἶπεν αὐτῷ· ἕν σε ὑστερεῖ·
him and said to him: One thing thee is wanting:

ὕπαγε, ὅσα ἔχεις πώλησον καὶ δὸς [τοῖς]
go, what things thou hast sell and give to the

πτωχοῖς, καὶ ἔξεις θησαυρὸν ἐν οὐρανῷ,
poor, and thou wilt have treasure in heaven,

καὶ δεῦρο ἀκολούθει μοι. 22 ὁ δὲ στυγνάσας
and come follow me. But he being sad

ἐπὶ τῷ λόγῳ ἀπῆλθεν λυπούμενος, ἦν
at the word went away grieving, ²he was

γὰρ ἔχων κτήματα πολλά. 23 Καὶ
¹for having possessions many. And

περιβλεψάμενος ὁ Ἰησοῦς λέγει τοῖς
looking round - Jesus says to the

μαθηταῖς αὐτοῦ· πῶς δυσκόλως οἱ τὰ
disciples of him: How hardly the [ones] the

χρήματα ἔχοντες εἰς τὴν βασιλείαν τοῦ
riches having into the kingdom -

θεοῦ εἰσελεύσονται. 24 οἱ δὲ μαθηταὶ
of God shall enter. And the disciples

ἐθαμβοῦντο ἐπὶ τοῖς λόγοις αὐτοῦ. ὁ δὲ
were amazed at the words of him. - And

Ἰησοῦς πάλιν ἀποκριθεὶς λέγει αὐτοῖς·
Jesus again answering says to them:

τέκνα, πῶς δύσκολόν ἐστιν εἰς τὴν
Children, how hard it is into the

βασιλείαν τοῦ θεοῦ εἰσελθεῖν· 25 εὐκοπώτερόν
kingdom - of God to enter; easier

ἐστιν κάμηλον διὰ τῆς τρυμαλιᾶς τῆς
it is a camel through the eye -

ῥαφίδος διελθεῖν ἢ πλούσιον εἰς τὴν
of a needle to go through than a rich man into the

βασιλείαν τοῦ θεοῦ εἰσελθεῖν. 26 οἱ δὲ
kingdom - of God to enter. But they

περισσῶς ἐξεπλήσσοντο λέγοντες πρὸς
exceedingly were astonished saying to

ἑαυτούς· καὶ τίς δύναται σωθῆναι;
themselves: And who can to be saved?

27 ἐμβλέψας αὐτοῖς ὁ Ἰησοῦς λέγει· παρὰ
Looking at them - Jesus says: With

ἀνθρώποις ἀδύνατον, ἀλλ' οὐ παρὰ θεῷ·
men [it is] impossible, but not with God;

πάντα γὰρ δυνατὰ παρὰ τῷ θεῷ. 28 Ἤρξατο
for all things [are] possible with - God. Began

λέγειν ὁ Πέτρος αὐτῷ· ἰδοὺ ἡμεῖς ἀφήκαμεν
to say - Peter to him: Behold [,] we left

πάντα καὶ ἠκολουθήκαμέν σοι. 29 ἔφη ὁ
all things and have followed thee. Said -

Ἰησοῦς· ἀμὴν λέγω ὑμῖν, οὐδεὶς ἐστιν
Jesus: Truly I tell you, no one there is

ὃς ἀφῆκεν οἰκίαν ἢ ἀδελφοὺς ἢ ἀδελφὰς
who left house or · brothers or sisters

ἢ μητέρα ἢ πατέρα ἢ τέκνα ἢ ἀγροὺς
or mother or father or children or fields

ἕνεκεν ἐμοῦ καὶ ἕνεκεν τοῦ εὐαγγελίου,
for the sake of me and for the sake of the gospel,

30 ἐὰν μὴ λάβῃ ἑκατονταπλασίονα νῦν
but he receives a hundredfold now

ἐν τῷ καιρῷ τούτῳ οἰκίας καὶ ἀδελφοὺς
in - this time houses and brothers

καὶ ἀδελφὰς καὶ μητέρας καὶ τέκνα καὶ
and sisters and mothers and children and

---

21 Jesus looked at him and loved him. "One thing you lack," he said. "Go, sell everything you have and give to the poor, and you will have treasure in heaven. Then come, follow me."

22 At this the man's face fell. He went away sad, because he had great wealth.

23 Jesus looked around and said to his disciples, "How hard it is for the rich to enter the kingdom of God!"

24 The disciples were amazed at his words. But Jesus said again, "Children, how hard it is[n] to enter the kingdom of God! 25 It is easier for a camel to go through the eye of a needle than for a rich man to enter the kingdom of God."

26 The disciples were even more amazed, and said to each other, "Who then can be saved?"

27 Jesus looked at them and said, "With man this is impossible, but not with God; all things are possible with God."

28 Peter said to him, "We have left everything to follow you!"

29 "I tell you the truth," Jesus replied, "no one who has left home or brothers or sisters or mother or father or children or fields for me and the gospel 30 will fail to receive a hundred times as much in this present age (homes, brothers, sisters, mothers, children and

---

[z] Gk lacks the money
[a] Other ancient authorities add for those who trust in riches
[b] Other ancient authorities read to him
[c] Or gospel

[n] 24 Some manuscripts is for those who trust in riches

children, and fields with persecutions—and in the age to come eternal life. 31 But many who are first will be last, and the last will be first."

A Third Time Jesus Foretells His Death and Resurrection

32 They were on the road, going up to Jerusalem, and Jesus was walking ahead of them; they were amazed, and those who followed were afraid. He took the twelve aside again and began to tell them what was to happen to him, 33 saying, "See, we are going up to Jerusalem, and the Son of Man will be handed over to the chief priests and the scribes, and they will condemn him to death; then they will hand him over to the Gentiles; 34 they will mock him, and spit upon him, and flog him, and kill him; and after three days he will rise again."

The Request of James and John

35 James and John, the sons of Zebedee, came forward to him and said to him, "Teacher, we want you to do for us whatever we ask of you." 36 And he said to them, "What is it you want me to do for you?" 37 And they said to him, "Grant us to sit, one at your right hand and one at your left, in your glory." 38 But Jesus said to them, "You do not know what you are asking. Are you able to drink the cup that I drink, or be baptized with the baptism that I am baptized with?" 39 They replied, "We are able." Then Jesus said to them, "The cup that I drink you will drink; and with the baptism with which I am baptized, you will be baptized; 40 but

---

ἀγροὺς μετὰ διωγμῶν, καὶ ἐν τῷ αἰῶνι
fields   with persecutions, and in the age

τῷ ἐρχομένῳ ζωὴν αἰώνιον. 31 πολλοὶ δὲ
— coming   life eternal.   And ¹many

ἔσονται πρῶτοι ἔσχατοι καὶ οἱ ἔσχατοι
²will be ³first ⁴last   and the last

πρῶτοι.
first.

32 ⁵Ησαν δὲ ἐν τῇ ὁδῷ ἀναβαίνοντες
   Now they were in the way going up

εἰς Ἱεροσόλυμα, καὶ ἦν προάγων αὐτοὺς
to Jerusalem,   and was going before them

ὁ Ἰησοῦς, καὶ ἐθαμβοῦντο, οἱ δὲ
- Jesus,   and they were astonished, and the

ἀκολουθοῦντες ἐφοβοῦντο. καὶ παραλαβὼν
[ones] following were afraid. And taking

πάλιν τοὺς δώδεκα ἤρξατο αὐτοῖς λέγειν
again the twelve he began them to tell

τὰ μέλλοντα αὐτῷ συμβαίνειν, 33 ὅτι ἰδοὺ
the things about to him to happen,   — Behold

ἀναβαίνομεν εἰς Ἱεροσόλυμα, καὶ ὁ υἱὸς
we are going up to Jerusalem,   and the Son

τοῦ ἀνθρώπου παραδοθήσεται τοῖς
- of man   will be betrayed to the

ἀρχιερεῦσιν καὶ τοῖς γραμματεῦσιν, καὶ
chief priests and to the scribes,   and

κατακρινοῦσιν αὐτὸν θανάτῳ καὶ παραδώσουσιν
they will condemn him to death and will deliver

αὐτὸν τοῖς ἔθνεσιν 34 καὶ ἐμπαίξουσιν
him to the nations   and they will mock

αὐτῷ καὶ ἐμπτύσουσιν αὐτῷ καὶ μαστι-
him   and will spit at   him and will

γώσουσιν αὐτὸν καὶ ἀποκτενοῦσιν, καὶ
scourge   him and will kill,   and

μετὰ τρεῖς ἡμέρας ἀναστήσεται.
after three days   he will rise again.

35 Καὶ προσπορεύονται αὐτῷ Ἰάκωβος
   And approach   to him James

καὶ Ἰωάννης οἱ [δύο] υἱοὶ Ζεβεδαίου
and John the two   sons of Zebedee

λέγοντες αὐτῷ· διδάσκαλε, θέλομεν ἵνα ὃ ἐὰν
saying   to him: Teacher, we wish that whatever

αἰτήσωμέν σε ποιήσῃς ἡμῖν. 36 ὁ
we may ask thee thou mayest do for us.   he

δὲ εἶπεν αὐτοῖς· τί θέλετέ με ποιήσω
And said to them: What wish ye me I may do

ὑμῖν; 37 οἱ δὲ εἶπαν αὐτῷ· δὸς ἡμῖν
for you?   And they said to him: Give us

ἵνα εἷς σου ἐκ δεξιῶν καὶ εἷς ἐξ
that one of thee out of(on) [the] right and one on
              = on thy right

ἀριστερῶν καθίσωμεν ἐν τῇ δόξῃ σου.
[thy] left we may sit in the glory of thee.

38 ὁ δὲ Ἰησοῦς εἶπεν αὐτοῖς· οὐκ οἴδατε
   - And Jesus said to them: Ye know not

τί αἰτεῖσθε. δύνασθε πιεῖν τὸ ποτήριον
what ye ask. Can ye to drink the cup

ὃ ἐγὼ πίνω, ἢ τὸ βάπτισμα ὃ ἐγὼ
which I drink, or the baptism which I

βαπτίζομαι βαπτισθῆναι; 39 οἱ δὲ εἶπαν
am baptized to be baptized [with]? And they said

αὐτῷ· δυνάμεθα. ὁ δὲ Ἰησοῦς εἶπεν
to him: We can. - And Jesus said

αὐτοῖς· τὸ ποτήριον ὃ ἐγὼ πίνω πίεσθε,
to them: The cup which I drink shall ye drink,

καὶ τὸ βάπτισμα ὃ ἐγὼ βαπτίζομαι
and the baptism which I am baptized [with]

---

fields—and with them, persecutions) and in the age to come, eternal life. 31 But many who are first will be last, and the last first."

Jesus Again Predicts His Death

32 They were on their way up to Jerusalem, with Jesus leading the way, and the disciples were astonished, while those who followed were afraid. Again he took the Twelve aside and told them what was going to happen to him. 33 "We are going up to Jerusalem," he said, "and the Son of Man will be betrayed to the chief priests and teachers of the law. They will condemn him to death and will hand him over to the Gentiles, 34 who will mock him and spit on him, flog him and kill him. Three days later he will rise."

The Request of James and John

35 Then James and John, the sons of Zebedee, came to him. "Teacher," they said, "we want you to do for us whatever we ask." 36 "What do you want me to do for you?" he asked. 37 They replied, "Let one of us sit at your right and the other at your left in your glory." 38 "You don't know what you are asking," Jesus said. "Can you drink the cup I drink or be baptized with the baptism I am baptized with?" 39 "We can," they answered. Jesus said to them, "You will drink the cup I drink and be baptized with the baptism I am baptized

to sit at my right hand or at my left is not mine to grant, but it is for those for whom it has been prepared."

41 When the ten heard this, they began to be angry with James and John. 42 So Jesus called them and said to them, "You know that among the Gentiles those whom they recognize as their rulers lord it over them, and their great ones are tyrants over them. 43 But it is not so among you; but whoever wishes to become great among you must be your servant, 44 and whoever wishes to be first among you must be slave of all. 45 For the Son of Man came not to be served but to serve, and to give his life a ransom for many."

The Healing of Blind Bartimaeus

46 They came to Jericho. As he and his disciples and a large crowd were leaving Jericho, Bartimaeus son of Timaeus, a blind beggar, was sitting by the roadside. 47 When he heard that it was Jesus of Nazareth, he began to shout out and say, "Jesus, Son of David, have mercy on me!" 48 Many sternly ordered him to be quiet, but he cried out even more loudly, "Son of David, have mercy on me!" 49 Jesus stood still and said, "Call him here." And they called the blind man, saying to him, "Take heart; get up, he is calling you." 50 So throwing off his cloak, he sprang up and came to Jesus. 51 Then Jesus said to him, "What do you want me to do for you?" The

βαπτισθήσεσθε· **40** τὸ δὲ καθίσαι ἐκ δεξιῶν
ye shall be baptized;   –   but   to sit   on   right

μου ἢ ἐξ εὐωνύμων οὐκ ἔστιν ἐμὸν
of me   or   on   [my] left   is not   mine

δοῦναι, ἀλλ' οἷς ἡτοίμασται. **41** Καὶ
to give,   but   for whom it has been prepared.   And

ἀκούσαντες οἱ δέκα ἤρξαντο ἀγανακτεῖν
³hearing   ¹the   ²ten   began   to be incensed

περὶ Ἰακώβου καὶ Ἰωάννου. **42** καὶ
about   James   and   John.   And

προσκαλεσάμενος αὐτοὺς ὁ Ἰησοῦς λέγει
¹calling ³to ⁴[him]   ²them   –   Jesus   says

αὐτοῖς· οἴδατε ὅτι οἱ δοκοῦντες ἄρχειν
to them: Ye know   that   the [ones]   thinking   to rule

τῶν ἐθνῶν κατακυριεύουσιν αὐτῶν καὶ
the   nations   lord it over   them   and

οἱ μεγάλοι αὐτῶν κατεξουσιάζουσιν αὐτῶν.
the great [ones] of them   exercise authority over   them.

43 οὐχ οὕτως δέ ἐστιν ἐν ὑμῖν· ἀλλ'
²not   ³so   ¹But   is it   among you;   but

ὃς ἂν θέλῃ μέγας γενέσθαι ἐν ὑμῖν,
whoever   wishes   great   to become   among   you,

ἔσται ὑμῶν διάκονος, **44** καὶ ὃς ἂν
shall be   of you   servant,   and   whoever

θέλῃ ἐν ὑμῖν εἶναι πρῶτος, ἔσται πάντων
wishes   among you   to be   first,   shall be   of all

δοῦλος· **45** καὶ γὰρ ὁ υἱὸς τοῦ ἀνθρώπου
slave;   for even   the   Son   –   of man

οὐκ ἦλθεν διακονηθῆναι ἀλλὰ διακονῆσαι
did not come   to be served   but   to serve

καὶ δοῦναι τὴν ψυχὴν αὐτοῦ λύτρον ἀντὶ
and to give   the   life   of him   a ransom   instead of

πολλῶν.
many.

46 Καὶ ἔρχονται εἰς Ἰεριχώ. Καὶ
And   they come   to   Jericho.   And

ἐκπορευομένου αὐτοῦ ἀπὸ Ἰεριχὼ καὶ τῶν
going out   him^a   from   Jericho   and   the
= as he was going out

μαθητῶν αὐτοῦ καὶ ὄχλου ἱκανοῦ ὁ υἱὸς
disciples^a   of him   and   crowd a considerable^a   the   son

Τιμαίου Βαρτιμαῖος, τυφλὸς προσαίτης,
of Timæus   Bartimæus,   a blind   beggar,

ἐκάθητο παρὰ τὴν ὁδόν. **47** καὶ ἀκούσας
sat   by   the   way.   And   hearing

ὅτι Ἰησοῦς ὁ Ναζαρηνός ἐστιν ἤρξατο
that   Jesus   the   Nazarene   it is(was)   he began

κράζειν καὶ λέγειν· υἱὲ Δαυὶδ Ἰησοῦ,
to cry out   and   to say: Son   of David   Jesus,

ἐλέησόν με. **48** καὶ ἐπετίμων αὐτῷ πολλοὶ
pity   me.   And   rebuked   him   many

ἵνα σιωπήσῃ· ὁ δὲ πολλῷ μᾶλλον ἔκραζεν·
that he should be quiet. But he   much   more   cried out:

υἱὲ Δαυίδ, ἐλέησόν με. **49** καὶ στὰς
Son   of David,   pity   me.   And   standing

ὁ Ἰησοῦς εἶπεν· φωνήσατε αὐτόν. καὶ
–   Jesus   said: Call   him.   And

φωνοῦσιν τὸν τυφλὸν λέγοντες αὐτῷ·
they call   the   blind man   saying   to him:

θάρσει, ἔγειρε, φωνεῖ σε. **50** ὁ δὲ
Be of good courage,   rise,   he calls   thee.   So he

ἀποβαλὼν τὸ ἱμάτιον αὐτοῦ ἀναπηδήσας ἦλθεν
throwing away   the   garment   of him   leaping up   came

πρὸς τὸν Ἰησοῦν. **51** καὶ ἀποκριθεὶς αὐτῷ ὁ
to   –   Jesus.   And   answering   him   –

Ἰησοῦς εἶπεν· τί σοι θέλεις ποιήσω;
Jesus   said: What for thee   wishest thou   I may do?

with, 40 but to sit at my right or left is not for me to grant. These places belong to those for whom they have been prepared."
41 When the ten heard about this, they became indignant with James and John. 42 Jesus called them together and said, "You know that those who are regarded as rulers of the Gentiles lord it over them, and their high officials exercise authority over them. 43 Not so with you. Instead, whoever wants to become great among you must be your servant, 44 and whoever wants to be first must be slave of all. 45 For even the Son of Man did not come to be served, but to serve, and to give his life as a ransom for many."

Blind Bartimaeus Receives His Sight

46 Then they came to Jericho. As Jesus and his disciples, together with a large crowd, were leaving the city, a blind man, Bartimaeus (that is, the Son of Timaeus), was sitting by the roadside begging. 47 When he heard that it was Jesus of Nazareth, he began to shout, "Jesus, Son of David, have mercy on me!"
48 Many rebuked him and told him to be quiet, but he shouted all the more, "Son of David, have mercy on me!"
49 Jesus stopped and said, "Call him."
So they called to the blind man, "Cheer up! On your feet! He's calling you." 50 Throwing his cloak aside, he jumped to his feet and came to Jesus.
51 "What do you want me to do for you?" Jesus asked him.

blind man said to him, "My teacher,[d] let me see again." [52] Jesus said to him, "Go; your faith has made you well." Immediately he regained his sight and followed him on the way.

ὁ   δὲ   τυφλὸς   εἶπεν   αὐτῷ·   ῥαββουνί,   ἵνα
And the   blind man   said   to him: Rabboni,   that
ἀναβλέψω.   52 καὶ   ὁ   Ἰησοῦς   εἶπεν   αὐτῷ·
I may see again.   And   –   Jesus   said   to him:
ὕπαγε,   ἡ   πίστις   σου   σέσωκέν   σε.   καὶ
Go,   the   faith   of thee   has healed   thee.   And
εὐθὺς   ἀνέβλεψεν,   καὶ   ἠκολούθει   αὐτῷ   ἐν
immediately   he saw again,   and   followed   him   in
τῇ   ὁδῷ.
the   way.

The blind man said, "Rabbi, I want to see." [52]"Go," said Jesus, "your faith has healed you." Immediately he received his sight and followed Jesus along the road.

Chapter 11

Jesus' Triumphal Entry into Jerusalem

WHEN they were approaching Jerusalem, at Bethphage and Bethany, near the Mount of Olives, he sent two of his disciples [2] and said to them, "Go into the village ahead of you, and immediately as you enter it, you will find tied there a colt that has never been ridden; untie it and bring it. [3] If anyone says to you, 'Why are you doing this?' just say this, 'The Lord needs it and will send it back here immediately.'" [4] They went away and found a colt tied near a door, outside in the street. As they were untying it, [5] some of the bystanders said to them, "What are you doing, untying the colt?" [6] They told them what Jesus had said; and they allowed them to take it. [7] Then they brought the colt to Jesus and threw their cloaks on; and he sat on it. [8] Many people spread their cloaks on the road, and others spread leafy branches that they had cut in the fields. [9] Then those who went ahead and those who followed were shouting,

"Hosanna!
Blessed is the one
who comes in
the name of the
Lord!
[10] Blessed is the
coming kingdom
of our ancestor
David!
Hosanna in the
highest heaven!"

11 Καὶ   ὅτε   ἐγγίζουσιν   εἰς   Ἱεροσόλυμα
And   when   they draw near   to   Jerusalem
εἰς   Βηθφαγὴ   καὶ   Βηθανίαν   πρὸς   τὸ
to   Bethphage   and   Bethany   at   the
ὄρος   τῶν   ἐλαιῶν,   ἀποστέλλει   δύο   τῶν
mount   of the   olives,   he sends   two   of the
μαθητῶν   αὐτοῦ   2 καὶ   λέγει   αὐτοῖς·   ὑπάγετε
disciples   of him   and   tells   them: Go ye
εἰς   τὴν   κώμην   τὴν   κατέναντι   ὑμῶν,   καὶ
into   the   village   –   opposite   you,   and
εὐθὺς   εἰσπορευόμενοι   εἰς   αὐτὴν   εὑρήσετε
immediately   entering   into   it   ye will find
πῶλον   δεδεμένον   ἐφ'   ὃν   οὐδεὶς   οὔπω
a colt   having been tied   on   which   [1]no one   [2]not yet
ἀνθρώπων   ἐκάθισεν·   λύσατε   αὐτὸν   καὶ
[3]of men   [4]sat: loosen   it   and
φέρετε.   3 καὶ   ἐάν   τις   ὑμῖν   εἴπῃ·   τί
bring.   And   if   anyone   to you   says: Why
ποιεῖτε   τοῦτο;   εἴπατε·   ὁ   κύριος   αὐτοῦ
do ye   this?   say: The   Lord   of it
χρείαν   ἔχει,   καὶ   εὐθὺς   αὐτὸν   ἀποστέλλει
need   has,   and   immediately   it   he sends
πάλιν   ὧδε.   4 καὶ   ἀπῆλθον   καὶ   εὗρον
again   here.   And   they went   and   found
πῶλον   δεδεμένον   πρὸς   θύραν   ἔξω   ἐπὶ
a colt   having been tied   at   a door   outside   on
τοῦ   ἀμφόδου,   καὶ   λύουσιν   αὐτόν.   5 καὶ
the   open street,   and   they loosen   it.   And
τινες   τῶν   ἐκεῖ   ἑστηκότων   ἔλεγον   αὐτοῖς·
some   of the [ones]   there   standing   said   to them:
τί   ποιεῖτε   λύοντες   τὸν   πῶλον;   6 οἱ   δὲ
What   do ye   loosening   the   colt?   And they
εἶπαν   αὐτοῖς   καθὼς   εἶπεν   ὁ   Ἰησοῦς·
said   to them   as   said   –   Jesus;
καὶ   ἀφῆκαν   αὐτούς.   7 καὶ   φέρουσιν   τὸν
and   they let go   them.   And   they bring   the
πῶλον   πρὸς   τὸν   Ἰησοῦν,   καὶ   ἐπιβάλλουσιν
colt   to   –   Jesus,   and   they throw on
αὐτῷ   τὰ   ἱμάτια   αὐτῶν,   καὶ   ἐκάθισεν
it   the   garments   of them,   and   he sat
ἐπ'   αὐτόν.   8 καὶ   πολλοὶ   τὰ   ἱμάτια   αὐτῶν
on   it.   And   many   the   garments   of them
ἔστρωσαν   εἰς   τὴν   ὁδόν,   ἄλλοι   δὲ   στιβάδας,
strewed   in   the   way,   and others   wisps of twigs,
κόψαντες   ἐκ   τῶν   ἀγρῶν.   9 καὶ   οἱ
cutting   out of   the   fields.   And the [ones]
προάγοντες   καὶ   οἱ   ἀκολουθοῦντες   ἔκραζον·
going before   and the [ones]   following   cried out:
ὡσαννά·   εὐλογημένος   ὁ   ἐρχόμενος   ἐν
Hosanna;   blessed   the [one]   coming   in
ὀνόματι   κυρίου·   10 εὐλογημένη   ἡ   ἐρχομένη
[the] name   of [the] Lord;   blessed   the   coming
βασιλεία   τοῦ   πατρὸς   ἡμῶν   Δαυίδ·   ὡσαννὰ
kingdom   of the   father   of us   David;   Hosanna

Chapter 11

The Triumphal Entry

AS they approached Jerusalem and came to Bethphage and Bethany at the Mount of Olives, Jesus sent two of his disciples, [2]saying to them, "Go to the village ahead of you, and just as you enter it, you will find a colt tied there, which no one has ever ridden. Untie it and bring it here. [3]If anyone asks you, 'Why are you doing this?' tell him, 'The Lord needs it and will send it back here shortly.'"

[4]They went and found a colt outside in the street, tied at a doorway. As they untied it, [5]some people standing there asked, "What are you doing, untying that colt?" [6]They answered as Jesus had told them to, and the people let them go. [7]When they brought the colt to Jesus and threw their cloaks over it, he sat on it. [8]Many people spread their cloaks on the road, while others spread branches they had cut in the fields. [9]Those who went ahead and those who followed shouted,

"Hosanna![o]"

"Blessed is he who
comes in the name
of the Lord!"[p]

[10]"Blessed is the coming
kingdom of our
father David!"

"Hosanna in the
highest!"

---

[d] Aramaic *Rabbouni*

[o]9 A Hebrew expression meaning "Save!" which became an exclamation of praise; also in verse 10

[p]9 Psalm 118:25,26

11 Then he entered Jerusalem and went into the temple; and when he had looked around at everything, as it was already late, he went out to Bethany with the twelve.

Jesus Curses the Fig Tree

12 On the following day, when they came from Bethany, he was hungry. 13 Seeing in the distance a fig tree in leaf, he went to see whether perhaps he would find anything on it. When he came to it, he found nothing but leaves, for it was not the season for figs. 14 He said to it, "May no one ever eat fruit from you again." And his disciples heard it.

Jesus Cleanses the Temple

15 Then they came to Jerusalem. And he entered the temple and began to drive out those who were selling and those who were buying in the temple, and he overturned the tables of the money changers and the seats of those who sold doves; 16 and he would not allow anyone to carry anything through the temple. 17 He was teaching and saying, "Is it not written,

'My house shall be
called a house
of prayer for all
the nations'?
But you have made
it a den
of robbers."

18 And when the chief priests and the scribes heard it, they kept looking for a way to kill him; for they were afraid of him, because the whole crowd was spellbound by his teaching. 19 And when evening came, Jesus and his disciplesᵉ went out of the city.

The Lesson from the Withered Fig Tree

20 In the morning as they passed by, they saw the fig tree withered away to its roots. 21 Then Peter remembered and said to him, "Rabbi, look! The fig tree that you cursed has withered." 22 Jesus an-

---

ἐν τοῖς ὑψίστοις. 11 Καὶ εἰσῆλθεν εἰς
in the highest [places]. ₂And he entered into
'Ιεροσόλυμα εἰς τὸ ἱερόν· καὶ περιβλεψάμενος
Jerusalem into the temple; and looking round at
πάντα, ὀψὲ ἤδη οὔσης τῆς ὥρας, ἐξῆλθεν
all things, ³late ⁴now ³being ¹the ²hour,ᵃ he went forth
εἰς Βηθανίαν μετὰ τῶν δώδεκα.
to Bethany with the twelve.
12 Καὶ τῇ ἐπαύριον ἐξελθόντων αὐτῶνᵃ
And on the morrow going forth them
= as they went forth
ἀπὸ Βηθανίας ἐπείνασεν. 13 καὶ ἰδὼν
from Bethany he hungered. And seeing
συκῆν ἀπὸ μακρόθεν ἔχουσαν φύλλα ἦλθεν
a fig-tree from afar having leaves he came
εἰ ἄρα τι εὑρήσει ἐν αὐτῇ, καὶ ἐλθὼν
if perhaps something he will find in it, and coming
ἐπ' αὐτὴν οὐδὲν εὗρεν εἰ μὴ φύλλα·
upon it nothing he found except leaves;
ὁ γὰρ καιρὸς οὐκ ἦν σύκων. 14 καὶ
for the time was not of figs. And
ἀποκριθεὶς εἶπεν αὐτῇ· μηκέτι εἰς τὸν
answering he said to it: No more to the
αἰῶνα ἐκ σοῦ μηδεὶς καρπὸν φάγοι.
age of thee no one fruit may eat.
= May no one eat fruit of thee for ever.
καὶ ἤκουον οἱ μαθηταὶ αὐτοῦ. 15 Καὶ
And ⁴heard ¹the ²disciples ³of him. And
ἔρχονται εἰς 'Ιεροσόλυμα. Καὶ εἰσελθὼν
they come to Jerusalem. And entering
εἰς τὸ ἱερὸν ἤρξατο ἐκβάλλειν τοὺς
into the temple he began to cast out the [ones]
πωλοῦντας καὶ τοὺς ἀγοράζοντας ἐν τῷ
selling and the [ones] buying in the
ἱερῷ, καὶ τὰς τραπέζας τῶν κολλυβιστῶν
temple, and the tables of the moneychangers
καὶ τὰς καθέδρας τῶν πωλούντων τὰς
and the seats of the [ones] selling the
περιστερὰς κατέστρεψεν, 16 καὶ οὐκ ἤφιεν
doves he overturned, and did not permit
ἵνα τις διενέγκῃ σκεῦος διὰ τοῦ
that anyone should carry *through* a vessel through the
ἱεροῦ, 17 καὶ ἐδίδασκεν καὶ ἔλεγεν αὐτοῖς· οὐ
temple, and taught and said to them: Not
γέγραπται ὅτι ὁ οἶκός μου οἶκος προσευχῆς
has it been written that the house of me a house of prayer
κληθήσεται πᾶσιν τοῖς ἔθνεσιν; ὑμεῖς δὲ
shall be called for all the nations? but ye
πεποιήκατε αὐτὸν σπήλαιον λῃστῶν. 18 καὶ
have made it a den of robbers. And
ἤκουσαν οἱ ἀρχιερεῖς καὶ οἱ γραμματεῖς,
⁶heard ¹the ²chief priests ³and ⁴the ⁵scribes,
καὶ ἐζήτουν πῶς αὐτὸν ἀπολέσωσιν·
and they sought how him they might destroy;
ἐφοβοῦντο γὰρ αὐτόν, πᾶς γὰρ ὁ ὄχλος
for they feared him, for all the crowd
ἐξεπλήσσετο ἐπὶ τῇ διδαχῇ αὐτοῦ. 19 Καὶ
was astounded at the teaching of him. And
ὅταν ὀψὲ ἐγένετο, ἐξεπορεύοντο ἔξω τῆς
when late it became, they went forth outside the
πόλεως. 20 Καὶ παραπορευόμενοι πρωῒ
city. And passing along early
εἶδον τὴν συκῆν ἐξηραμμένην ἐκ ῥιζῶν.
they saw the fig-tree *having been* withered from [the] roots.
21 καὶ ἀναμνησθεὶς ὁ Πέτρος λέγει αὐτῷ·
And ²remembering – ¹Peter says to him:
ῥαββί, ἴδε ἡ συκῆ ἦν κατηράσω
Rabbi, behold[,] the fig-tree which thou cursedst

---

11 Jesus entered Jerusalem and went to the temple. He looked around at everything, but since it was already late, he went out to Bethany with the Twelve.

Jesus Clears the Temple

12 The next day as they were leaving Bethany, Jesus was hungry. 13 Seeing in the distance a fig tree in leaf, he went to find out if it had any fruit. When he reached it, he found nothing but leaves, because it was not the season for figs. 14 Then he said to the tree, "May no one ever eat fruit from you again." And his disciples heard him say it.

15 On reaching Jerusalem, Jesus entered the temple area and began driving out those who were buying and selling there. He overturned the tables of the money changers and the benches of those selling doves, 16 and would not allow anyone to carry merchandise through the temple courts. 17 And as he taught them, he said, "Is it not written:

" 'My house will be
called
a house of prayer for
all nations'ᵍ?
But you have made it 'a den
of robbers.'ʳ"

18 The chief priests and the teachers of the law heard this and began looking for a way to kill him, for they feared him, because the whole crowd was amazed at his teaching.

19 When evening came, theyˢ went out of the city.

The Withered Fig Tree

20 In the morning, as they went along, they saw the fig tree withered from the roots. 21 Peter remembered and said to Jesus, "Rabbi, look! The fig tree you cursed has withered!"

---

swered them, "Have[f] faith in God. 23 Truly I tell you, if you say to this mountain, 'Be taken up and thrown into the sea,' and if you do not doubt in your heart, but believe that what you say will come to pass, it will be done for you. 24 So I tell you, whatever you ask for in prayer, believe that you have received[g] it, and it will be yours.

25 "Whenever you stand praying, forgive, if you have anything against anyone; so that your Father in heaven may also forgive you your trespasses."[h]

Jesus' Authority Is Questioned

27 Again they came to Jerusalem. As he was walking in the temple, the chief priests, the scribes, and the elders came to him 28 and said, "By what authority are you doing these things? Who gave you this authority to do them?" 29 Jesus said to them, "I will ask you one question; answer me, and I will tell you by what authority I do these things. 30 Did the baptism of John come from heaven, or was it of human origin? Answer me." 31 They argued with one another, "If we say, 'From heaven,' he will say, 'Why then did you not believe him?' 32 But shall we say, 'Of human origin'?"— they were afraid of the crowd, for all regarded John as truly a prophet. 33 So they answered Jesus, "We do not know." And Jesus said to them, "Neither will I tell you by what authority I am doing these things."

ἐξήρανται. **22** καὶ ἀποκριθεὶς ὁ Ἰησοῦς λέγει
has been withered.   And   answering –   Jesus   says

αὐτοῖς· ἔχετε πίστιν θεοῦ. **23** ἀμὴν λέγω ὑμῖν
to them: Have [the] faith of God.   Truly   I tell   you

ὅτι ὃς ἂν εἴπῃ τῷ ὄρει τούτῳ· ἄρθητι
that whoever says – mountain to this: Be thou taken

καὶ βλήθητι εἰς τὴν θάλασσαν, καὶ μὴ
and be thou cast into the sea, and not

διακριθῇ ἐν τῇ καρδίᾳ αὐτοῦ ἀλλὰ πιστεύῃ
doubts in the heart of him but believes

ὅτι ὃ λαλεῖ γίνεται, ἔσται αὐτῷ. **24** διὰ
that what he says happens, it will be to him.[e] There-
= he will have it.

τοῦτο λέγω ὑμῖν, πάντα ὅσα προσεύχεσθε
fore I tell you, all things which ye pray

καὶ αἰτεῖσθε, πιστεύετε ὅτι ἐλάβετε, καὶ
and ask, believe that ye received, and

ἔσται ὑμῖν, **25** καὶ ὅταν στήκετε
it will be to you.[e] And when ye stand
= ye will have it.

προσευχόμενοι, ἀφίετε εἴ τι ἔχετε κατά
praying, forgive if anything ye have against

τινος, ἵνα καὶ ὁ πατὴρ ὑμῶν ὁ ἐν τοῖς
anyone, that also the Father of you – in the

οὐρανοῖς ἀφῇ ὑμῖν τὰ παραπτώματα ὑμῶν.‡
heavens may forgive you the trespasses of you.

27 Καὶ ἔρχονται πάλιν εἰς Ἱεροσόλυμα.
And they come again to Jerusalem.

καὶ ἐν τῷ ἱερῷ περιπατοῦντος αὐτοῦ
And in the temple walking him[a]
= as he walked

ἔρχονται πρὸς αὐτὸν οἱ ἀρχιερεῖς καὶ οἱ
come to him the chief priests and the

γραμματεῖς καὶ οἱ πρεσβύτεροι, **28** καὶ
scribes and the elders, and

ἔλεγον αὐτῷ· ἐν ποίᾳ ἐξουσίᾳ ταῦτα
said to him: By what authority these things

ποιεῖς; ἢ τίς σοι ἔδωκεν τὴν ἐξουσίαν
doest thou ? or who thee gave the authority

ταύτην ἵνα ταῦτα ποιῇς; **29** ὁ δὲ Ἰησοῦς
this that these things thou mayest do ? – And Jesus

εἶπεν αὐτοῖς· ἐπερωτήσω ὑμᾶς ἕνα λόγον,
said to them: I will question you one word,

καὶ ἀποκρίθητέ μοι, καὶ ἐρῶ ὑμῖν ἐν
and answer ye me, and I will tell you by

ποίᾳ ἐξουσίᾳ ταῦτα ποιῶ. **30** τὸ βάπτισμα
what authority these things I do. The baptism

τὸ Ἰωάννου ἐξ οὐρανοῦ ἦν ἢ ἐξ ἀνθρώπων;
– of John of heaven was it or of men ?

ἀποκρίθητέ μοι. **31** καὶ διελογίζοντο πρὸς
answer ye me. And they debated with

ἑαυτοὺς λέγοντες· ἐὰν εἴπωμεν· ἐξ οὐρανοῦ,
themselves saying: If we say: Of heaven,

ἐρεῖ· διὰ τί οὖν οὐκ ἐπιστεύσατε αὐτῷ;
he will say: Why then did ye not believe him ?

32 ἀλλὰ εἴπωμεν· ἐξ ἀνθρώπων;—ἐφοβοῦντο
But may we say: Of men ? — they feared

τὸν ὄχλον· ἅπαντες γὰρ εἶχον τὸν Ἰωάννην
the crowd: for all men held the John

ὄντως ὅτι προφήτης ἦν. **33** καὶ
²really ¹that ³a prophet ⁴he was. And

ἀποκριθέντες τῷ Ἰησοῦ λέγουσιν· οὐκ
answering – Jesus they say: not

οἴδαμεν. καὶ ὁ Ἰησοῦς λέγει αὐτοῖς·
We know. And – Jesus says to them:

οὐδὲ ἐγὼ λέγω ὑμῖν ἐν ποίᾳ ἐξουσίᾳ
Neither I tell you by what authority

‡ Verse 26 omitted by Nestle; cf. NIV footnote.

---

22 "Have[i] faith in God," Jesus answered. 23 "I tell you the truth, if anyone says to this mountain, 'Go, throw yourself into the sea,' and does not doubt in his heart but believes that what he says will happen, it will be done for him. 24 Therefore I tell you, whatever you ask for in prayer, believe that you have received it, and it will be yours. 25 And when you stand praying, if you hold anything against anyone, forgive him, so that your Father in heaven may forgive you your sins. ⁿ"

The Authority of Jesus Questioned

27 They arrived again in Jerusalem, and while Jesus was walking in the temple courts, the chief priests, the teachers of the law and the elders came to him. 28 "By what authority are you doing these things?" they asked. "And who gave you authority to do this?"

29 Jesus replied, "I will ask you one question. Answer me, and I will tell you by what authority I am doing these things. 30 John's baptism—was it from heaven, or from men? Tell me!"

31 They discussed it among themselves and said, "If we say, 'From heaven,' he will ask, 'Then why didn't you believe him?' 32 But if we say, 'From men' . . . ." (They feared the people, for everyone held that John really was a prophet.)

33 So they answered Jesus, "We don't know." Jesus said, "Neither will I tell you by what authority I am doing these things."

---

[f] Other ancient authorities read "If you have
[g] Other ancient authorities read are receiving
[h] Other ancient authorities add verse 26, "But if you do not forgive, neither will your Father in heaven forgive your trespasses."

[i]22 Some early manuscripts If you have
ⁿ25 Some manuscripts sins. 26But if you do not forgive, neither will your Father who is in heaven forgive your sins.

Chapter 12

The Parable of the Wicked Tenants

THEN he began to speak to them in parables. "A man planted a vineyard, put a fence around it, dug a pit for the wine press, and built a watchtower; then he leased it to tenants and went to another country. 2 When the season came, he sent a slave to the tenants to collect from them his share of the produce of the vineyard. 3 But they seized him, and beat him, and sent him away empty-handed. 4 And again he sent another slave to them; this one they beat over the head and insulted. 5 Then he sent another, and that one they killed. And so it was with many others; some they beat, and others they killed. 6 He had still one other, a beloved son. Finally he sent him to them, saying, 'They will respect my son.' 7 But those tenants said to one another, 'This is the heir; come, let us kill him, and the inheritance will be ours.' 8 So they seized him, killed him, and threw him out of the vineyard. 9 What then will the owner of the vineyard do? He will come and destroy the tenants and give the vineyard to others. 10 Have you not read this scripture:

'The stone that the
    builders rejected
has become the
    cornerstone;[i]
11 this was the Lord's
    doing,
and it is amazing in
    our eyes'?"

12 When they realized that he had told this parable against them, they wanted to arrest him, but they

---

ταῦτα   ποιῶ.   **12** Καὶ   ἤρξατο   αὐτοῖς   ἐν
these things I do.   And   he began   to them   in

παραβολαῖς   λαλεῖν.   ἀμπελῶνα   ἄνθρωπος
parables   to speak.   ³a vineyard   ¹A man

ἐφύτευσεν,   καὶ   περιέθηκεν   φραγμὸν   καὶ   ὤρυξεν
²planted,   and   put round [it]   a hedge   and   dug

ὑπολήνιον   καὶ   ᾠκοδόμησεν   πύργον,   καὶ
a winepress   and   built   a tower,   and

ἐξέδοτο   αὐτὸν   γεωργοῖς,   καὶ   ἀπεδήμησεν.
let out   it   to husbandmen,   and   went away.

2 καὶ   ἀπέστειλεν   πρὸς   τοὺς   γεωργοὺς   τῷ
And   he sent   to   the   husbandmen   at the

καιρῷ   δοῦλον,   ἵνα   παρὰ   τῶν   γεωργῶν
time   a slave,   that   from   the   husbandmen

λάβῃ   ἀπὸ   τῶν   καρπῶν   τοῦ   ἀμπελῶνος·
he might from(of)   the   fruits   of the   vineyard;
receive

3 καὶ   λαβόντες   αὐτὸν   ἔδειραν   καὶ   ἀπέστειλαν
And   taking   him   they beat   and   sent away

κενόν.   **4** καὶ   πάλιν   ἀπέστειλεν   πρὸς   αὐτοὺς
empty.   And   again   he sent   to   them

ἄλλον   δοῦλον·   κἀκεῖνον   ἐκεφαλαίωσαν   καὶ
another   slave;   and that one   they wounded in the head and

ἠτίμασαν.   **5** καὶ   ἄλλον   ἀπέστειλεν·   κἀκεῖνον
insulted.   And   another   he sent;   and that one

ἀπέκτειναν,   καὶ   πολλοὺς   ἄλλους,   οὓς   μὲν
they killed,   and   many   others,   ²some

δέροντες,   οὓς   δὲ   ἀποκτέννοντες.   **6** ἔτι   ἕνα
¹beating,   ²others   ¹killing.   Still   one

εἶχεν,   υἱὸν   ἀγαπητόν·   ἀπέστειλεν   αὐτὸν
he had,   a son   beloved;   he sent   him

ἔσχατον   πρὸς   αὐτοὺς   λέγων   ὅτι   ἐντραπήσονται
last   to   them   saying[,]   -   They will reverence

τὸν   υἱόν   μου.   **7** ἐκεῖνοι   δὲ   οἱ   γεωργοὶ
the   son   of me.   But those   -   husbandmen

πρὸς   ἑαυτοὺς   εἶπαν   ὅτι   οὗτός   ἐστιν   ὁ
to   themselves   said[,]   -   This   is   the

κληρονόμος·   δεῦτε   ἀποκτείνωμεν   αὐτόν,   καὶ
heir;   come[,]   let us kill   him,   and

ἡμῶν   ἔσται   ἡ   κληρονομία.   **8** καὶ   λαβόντες
of us   will be   the   inheritance.   And   taking

ἀπέκτειναν   αὐτόν,   καὶ   ἐξέβαλον   αὐτὸν
they killed   him,   and   cast out   him

ἔξω   τοῦ   ἀμπελῶνος.   **9** τί   ποιήσει   ὁ
outside   the   vineyard.   What   will do   the

κύριος   τοῦ   ἀμπελῶνος;   ἐλεύσεται   καὶ
lord   of the   vineyard ?   he will come   and

ἀπολέσει   τοὺς   γεωργούς,   καὶ   δώσει   τὸν
will destroy   the   husbandmen,   and   will give   the

ἀμπελῶνα   ἄλλοις.   **10** οὐδὲ   τὴν   γραφὴν
vineyard   to others.   ²not   -   ⁴scripture

ταύτην   ἀνέγνωτε·   λίθον   ὃν   ἀπεδοκίμασαν
⁵this   ³Read ye :   A stone   which   ³rejected

οἱ   οἰκοδομοῦντες,   οὗτος   ἐγενήθη   εἰς   κεφαλὴν
¹the [ones]   ²building,   this   became   for   head

γωνίας·   **11** παρὰ   κυρίου   ἐγένετο   αὕτη,
of corner ·   from [the] Lord   was   this,

καὶ   ἔστιν   θαυμαστὴ   ἐν   ὀφθαλμοῖς   ἡμῶν;
and   it is   marvellous   in   eyes   of us ?

12 Καὶ   ἐζήτουν   αὐτὸν   κρατῆσαι,   καὶ
And   they sought   him   to seize,   and

ἐφοβήθησαν   τὸν   ὄχλον·   ἔγνωσαν   γὰρ
feared   the   crowd;   for they knew

ὅτι   πρὸς   αὐτοὺς   τὴν   παραβολὴν
that   to   them   the   parable

Chapter 12

The Parable of the Tenants

HE then began to speak to them in parables: "A man planted a vineyard. He put a wall around it, dug a pit for the winepress and built a watchtower. Then he rented the vineyard to some farmers and went away on a journey. 2 At harvest time he sent a servant to the tenants to collect from them some of the fruit of the vineyard. 3 But they seized him, beat him and sent him away empty-handed. 4 Then he sent another servant to them; they struck this man on the head and treated him shamefully. 5 He sent still another, and that one they killed. He sent many others; some of them they beat, others they killed.

6 "He had one left to send, a son, whom he loved. He sent him last of all, saying, 'They will respect my son.' 7 "But the tenants said to one another, 'This is the heir. Come, let's kill him, and the inheritance will be ours.' 8 So they took him and killed him, and threw him out of the vineyard.

9 "What then will the owner of the vineyard do? He will come and kill those tenants and give the vineyard to others. 10 Haven't you read this scripture:

" 'The stone the builders
    rejected
has become the
    capstone[v];
11 the Lord has done this,
    and it is marvelous in
    our eyes'[w]?"

12 Then they looked for a way to arrest him because they knew he had spoken the parable against them.

ᶦOr keystone

ᵛ10 Or cornerstone
ʷ11 Psalm 118:22,23

feared the crowd. So they left him and went away.

The Question about Paying Taxes

13 Then they sent to him some Pharisees and some Herodians to trap him in what he said. 14 And they came and said to him, "Teacher, we know that you are sincere, and show deference to no one; for you do not regard people with partiality, but teach the way of God in accordance with truth. Is it lawful to pay taxes to the emperor, or not? 15 Should we pay them, or should we not?" But knowing their hypocrisy, he said to them, "Why are you putting me to the test? Bring me a denarius and let me see it." 16 And they brought one. Then he said to them, "Whose head is this, and whose title?" They answered, "The emperor's." 17 Jesus said to them, "Give to the emperor the things that are the emperor's, and to God the things that are God's." And they were utterly amazed at him.

The Question about the Resurrection

18 Some Sadducees, who say there is no resurrection, came to him and asked him a question, saying, 19 "Teacher, Moses wrote for us that 'if a man's brother dies, leaving a wife but no child, the man[j] shall marry the widow and raise up children for his brother.' 20 There were seven brothers; the first married and, when he died, left no children; 21 and the second married her and died, leaving no children; and the third likewise; 22 none of the seven left children. Last of all the woman herself died. 23 In the resurrection[k] whose wife will she

---

εἶπεν. καὶ ἀφέντες αὐτὸν ἀπῆλθον.
he told. And leaving him they went away.

13 Καὶ ἀποστέλλουσιν πρὸς αὐτόν τινας τῶν
And they send to him some of the

Φαρισαίων καὶ τῶν Ἡρῳδιανῶν ἵνα αὐτὸν
Pharisees and of the Herodians that him

ἀγρεύσωσιν λόγῳ. 14 καὶ ἐλθόντες
they might catch in a word. And coming

λέγουσιν αὐτῷ· διδάσκαλε, οἴδαμεν ὅτι
they say to him: Teacher, we know that

ἀληθὴς εἶ καὶ οὐ μέλει σοι περὶ
true thou art and it matters not to thee about

οὐδενός· οὐ γὰρ βλέπεις εἰς πρόσωπον
no(any)one; for thou lookest not at [the] face

ἀνθρώπων, ἀλλ' ἐπ' ἀληθείας τὴν ὁδὸν
of men, but on(in) truth the way

τοῦ θεοῦ διδάσκεις· ἔξεστιν δοῦναι κῆνσον
– of God teachest; is it lawful to give tribute

Καίσαρι ἢ οὔ; δῶμεν ἢ μὴ δῶμεν;
to Caesar or no? may we give or may we not give?

15 ὁ δὲ εἰδὼς αὐτῶν τὴν ὑπόκρισιν εἶπεν
But he knowing of them the hypocrisy said

αὐτοῖς· τί με πειράζετε; φέρετέ μοι
to them: Why me tempt ye? bring me

δηνάριον ἵνα ἴδω. 16 οἱ δὲ ἤνεγκαν. καὶ
a denarius that I may see. And they brought. And

λέγει αὐτοῖς· τίνος ἡ εἰκὼν αὕτη καὶ ἡ
he says to them: Of whom – image this and –

ἐπιγραφή; οἱ δὲ εἶπαν αὐτῷ· Καίσαρος.
superscription? And they tell him: Of Caesar.

17 ὁ δὲ Ἰησοῦς εἶπεν αὐτοῖς· τὰ Καίσαρος
– So Jesus said to them: The things of Caesar

ἀπόδοτε Καίσαρι καὶ τὰ τοῦ θεοῦ τῷ
render to Caesar and the things – of God –

θεῷ. καὶ ἐξεθαύμαζον ἐπ' αὐτῷ.
to God. And they marvelled at him.

18 Καὶ ἔρχονται Σαδδουκαῖοι πρὸς αὐτόν,
And come Sadducees to him,

οἵτινες λέγουσιν ἀνάστασιν μὴ εἶναι, καὶ
who say resurrection not to be, and
= that there is no resurrection,

ἐπηρώτων αὐτὸν λέγοντες· 19 διδάσκαλε,
questioned him saying: Teacher,

Μωϋσῆς ἔγραψεν ἡμῖν ὅτι ἐάν τινος
Moses wrote to us that if of anyone

ἀδελφὸς ἀποθάνῃ καὶ καταλίπῃ γυναῖκα
a brother should die and leave behind a wife

καὶ μὴ ἀφῇ τέκνον, ἵνα λάβῃ ὁ ἀδελφὸς
and leave not a child, – ¹may take ¹the ²brother

αὐτοῦ τὴν γυναῖκα καὶ ἐξαναστήσῃ σπέρμα
³of him the wife and may raise up seed

τῷ ἀδελφῷ αὐτοῦ. 20 ἑπτὰ ἀδελφοὶ ἦσαν·
to the brother of him. Seven brothers there were;

καὶ ὁ πρῶτος ἔλαβεν γυναῖκα, καὶ
and the first took a wife, and

ἀποθνῄσκων οὐκ ἀφῆκεν σπέρμα· 21 καὶ
dying left not seed; and

ὁ δεύτερος ἔλαβεν αὐτήν, καὶ ἀπέθανεν μὴ
the second took her, and died not

καταλιπὼν σπέρμα· καὶ ὁ τρίτος ὡσαύτως·
leaving behind seed; and the third similarly;

22 καὶ οἱ ἑπτὰ οὐκ ἀφῆκαν σπέρμα.
and the seven left not seed.

ἔσχατον πάντων καὶ ἡ γυνὴ ἀπέθανεν.
Last of all also the wife died.

23 ἐν τῇ ἀναστάσει, ὅταν ἀναστῶσιν,
In the resurrection, when they rise again,

But they were afraid of the crowd; so they left him and went away.

Paying Taxes to Caesar

13 Later they sent some of the Pharisees and Herodians to Jesus to catch him in his words. 14 They came to him and said, "Teacher, we know you are a man of integrity. You aren't swayed by men, because you pay no attention to who they are; but you teach the way of God in accordance with the truth. Is it right to pay taxes to Caesar or not? 15 Should we pay or shouldn't we?"

But Jesus knew their hypocrisy. "Why are you trying to trap me?" he asked. "Bring me a denarius and let me look at it." 16 They brought the coin, and he asked them, "Whose portrait is this? And whose inscription?"

"Caesar's," they replied.

17 Then Jesus said to them, "Give to Caesar what is Caesar's and to God what is God's."

And they were amazed at him.

Marriage at the Resurrection

18 Then the Sadducees, who say there is no resurrection, came to him with a question. 19 "Teacher," they said, "Moses wrote for us that if a man's brother dies and leaves a wife but no children, the man must marry the widow and have children for his brother. 20 Now there were seven brothers. The first one married and died without leaving any children. 21 The second one married the widow, but he also died, leaving no child. It was the same with the third. 22 In fact, none of the seven left any children. Last of all, the woman died too. 23 At the resurrection[x] whose

---

[j] Gk his brother
[k] Other ancient authorities add when they rise

[x] 23 Some manuscripts resurrection, when men rise from the dead.

be? For the seven had married her."

24 Jesus said to them, "Is not this the reason you are wrong, that you know neither the scriptures nor the power of God? 25 For when they rise from the dead, they neither marry nor are given in marriage, but are like angels in heaven. 26 And as for the dead being raised, have you not read in the book of Moses, in the story about the bush, how God said to him, 'I am the God of Abraham, the God of Isaac, and the God of Jacob'? 27 He is God not of the dead, but of the living; you are quite wrong."

The First Commandment

28 One of the scribes came near and heard them disputing with one another, and seeing that he had answered them well, he asked him, "Which commandment is the first of all?" 29 Jesus answered, "The first is, 'Hear, O Israel: the Lord our God, the Lord is one; 30 you shall love the Lord your God with all your heart, and with all your soul, and with all your mind, and with all your strength.' 31 The second is this, 'You shall love your neighbor as yourself.' There is no other commandment greater than these." 32 Then the scribe said to him, "You are right, Teacher; you have truly said that 'he is one, and besides him there is no other'; 33 and 'to love him with all the heart, and with all the understanding, and with all the strength,' and 'to love one's neighbor as oneself,'—this is much

---

τίνος αὐτῶν ἔσται γυνή; οἱ γὰρ ἑπτὰ
of which of them will she be wife? for the seven

ἔσχον αὐτὴν γυναῖκα. 24 ἔφη αὐτοῖς ὁ
had her [as] wife. Said to them -

'Ἰησοῦς· οὐ διὰ τοῦτο πλανᾶσθε μὴ
Jesus: ¹not ⁴therefore ¹Do ⁴ye ⁵err not

εἰδότες τὰς γραφὰς μηδὲ τὴν δύναμιν
knowing the scriptures nor the power

τοῦ θεοῦ; 25 ὅταν γὰρ ἐκ νεκρῶν
- of God? for when out of [the] dead

ἀναστῶσιν, οὔτε γαμοῦσιν οὔτε γαμίζονται,
they rise again, they neither marry nor are given in marriage,

ἀλλ' εἰσὶν ὡς ἄγγελοι ἐν τοῖς οὐρανοῖς.
but are as angels in the heavens.

26 περὶ δὲ τῶν νεκρῶν ὅτι ἐγείρονται,
But concerning the dead that they are raised,

οὐκ ἀνέγνωτε ἐν τῇ βίβλῳ Μωϋσέως ἐπὶ
did ye not read in the roll of Moses at

τοῦ βάτου πῶς εἶπεν αὐτῷ ὁ θεὸς λέγων·
the bush how said to him - God saying:

ἐγὼ ὁ θεὸς 'Αβραὰμ καὶ θεὸς 'Ισαὰκ
I [am] the God of Abraham and God of Isaac

καὶ θεὸς 'Ιακώβ; 27 οὐκ ἔστιν θεὸς
and God of Jacob? he is not God

νεκρῶν ἀλλὰ ζώντων. πολὺ πλανᾶσθε.
of dead [persons] but of living [ones]. Much ye err.

28 Καὶ προσελθὼν εἷς τῶν γραμματέων,
And ⁴approaching ¹one ²of the ³scribes,

ἀκούσας αὐτῶν συζητούντων, εἰδὼς ὅτι
hearing them debating, knowing that

καλῶς ἀπεκρίθη αὐτοῖς, ἐπηρώτησεν αὐτόν·
well he answered them, questioned him:

ποία ἐστὶν ἐντολὴ πρώτη πάντων;
What is [the] commandment first of all?

29 ἀπεκρίθη ὁ 'Ἰησοῦς ὅτι πρώτη ἐστίν·
Answered - Jesus[,] - [The] first is:

ἄκουε, 'Ισραήλ, κύριος ὁ θεὸς ἡμῶν κύριος
Hear, Israel, Lord the God of us Lord
= The Lord our God is one Lord,

εἷς ἐστιν, 30 καὶ ἀγαπήσεις κύριον τὸν
one is, and thou shalt love Lord the

θεόν σου ἐξ ὅλης τῆς καρδίας σου καὶ
God of thee from(with) all the heart of thee and

ἐξ ὅλης τῆς ψυχῆς σου καὶ ἐξ ὅλης
with all the soul of thee and with all

τῆς διανοίας σου καὶ ἐξ ὅλης τῆς ἰσχύος
the mind of thee and with all the strength

σου. 31 δευτέρα αὕτη· ἀγαπήσεις τὸν
of thee. [The] second [is] this: Thou shalt love the

πλησίον σου ὡς σεαυτόν. μείζων τούτων
neighbour of thee as thyself. Greater [than] these

ἄλλη ἐντολὴ οὐκ ἔστιν. 32 καὶ εἶπεν
other commandment there is not. And said

αὐτῷ ὁ γραμματεύς· καλῶς, διδάσκαλε, ἐπ'
to him the scribe: Well, teacher, on(in)

ἀληθείας εἶπες ὅτι εἷς ἐστιν καὶ οὐκ
truth thou sayest that one there is and not

ἔστιν ἄλλος πλὴν αὐτοῦ· 33 καὶ τὸ
there is another besides him; and -

ἀγαπᾶν αὐτὸν ἐξ ὅλης τῆς καρδίας καὶ ἐξ
to love him with all the heart and with

ὅλης τῆς συνέσεως καὶ ἐξ ὅλης τῆς
all the understanding and with all the

ἰσχύος, καὶ τὸ ἀγαπᾶν τὸν πλησίον ὡς
strength, and - to love the(one's) neighbour as

---

wife will she be, since the seven were married to her?"

24 Jesus replied, "Are you not in error because you do not know the Scriptures or the power of God? 25 When the dead rise, they will neither marry nor be given in marriage; they will be like the angels in heaven. 26 Now about the dead rising—have you not read in the book of Moses, in the account of the bush, how God said to him, 'I am the God of Abraham, the God of Isaac, and the God of Jacob'? 27 He is not the God of the dead, but of the living. You are badly mistaken!"

The Greatest Commandment

28 One of the teachers of the law came and heard them debating. Noticing that Jesus had given them a good answer, he asked him, "Of all the commandments, which is the most important?"

29 "The most important one," answered Jesus, "is this: 'Hear, O Israel, the Lord our God, the Lord is one.ᶻ 30 Love the Lord your God with all your heart and with all your soul and with all your mind and with all your strength.'ᵃ 31 The second is this: 'Love your neighbor as yourself.'ᵇ There is no commandment greater than these."

32 "Well said, teacher," the man replied. "You are right in saying that God is one and there is no other but him. 33 To love him with all your heart, with all your understanding and with all your strength, and to love your neighbor as yourself is

---

ʸ26 Exodus 3:6
ᶻ29 Or *the Lord our God is one Lord*
ᵃ30 Deut. 6:4,5
ᵇ31 Lev. 19:18

more important than all whole burnt offerings and sacrifices." ³⁴When Jesus saw that he answered wisely, he said to him, "You are not far from the kingdom of God." After that no one dared to ask him any question.

The Question about David's Son

35 While Jesus was teaching in the temple, he said, "How can the scribes say that the Messiah¹ is the son of David? ³⁶David himself, by the Holy Spirit, declared,

'The Lord said to my
 Lord,
"Sit at my right hand,
 until I put your
 enemies under
 your feet." '

³⁷David himself calls him Lord; so how can he be his son?" And the large crowd was listening to him with delight.

Jesus Denounces the Scribes

38 As he taught, he said, "Beware of the scribes, who like to walk around in long robes, and to be greeted with respect in the marketplaces, ³⁹and to have the best seats in the synagogues and places of honor at banquets.¹ ⁴⁰They devour widows' houses and for the sake of appearance say long prayers. They will receive the greater condemnation."

The Widow's Offering

41 He sat down opposite the treasury, and watched the crowd putting money into the treasury. Many rich people put in large sums. ⁴²A poor widow came and put in two small copper coins, which are worth a penny. ⁴³Then he called his disciples and said to them, "Truly I tell you, this poor widow has put in more than all those

---

Greek	English
ἑαυτὸν	himself
περισσότερόν	more
ἐστιν	is [than]
πάντων	all
τῶν	the
ὁλοκαυτωμάτων	burnt offerings
καὶ	and
θυσιῶν.	sacrifices.
34 καὶ ὁ	And the

'Ιησοῦς, ἰδὼν αὐτὸν ὅτι νουνεχῶς ἀπεκρίθη,
Jesus, seeing him that sensibly he answered,

εἶπεν αὐτῷ· οὐ μακρὰν εἶ ἀπὸ τῆς
said to him: Not far thou art from the

βασιλείας τοῦ θεοῦ. καὶ οὐδεὶς οὐκέτι
kingdom of God. And no one no(any) more

ἐτόλμα αὐτὸν ἐπερωτῆσαι.
dared him to question.

35 Καὶ ἀποκριθεὶς ὁ 'Ιησοῦς ἔλεγεν
And answering - Jesus said

διδάσκων ἐν τῷ ἱερῷ· πῶς λέγουσιν οἱ
teaching in the temple: How say the

γραμματεῖς ὅτι ὁ χριστὸς υἱὸς Δαυὶδ
scribes that the Christ son of David

ἐστιν; 36 αὐτὸς Δαυὶδ εἶπεν ἐν τῷ πνεύματι
is? himself David said by the Spirit

τῷ ἁγίῳ· εἶπεν κύριος τῷ κυρίῳ μου·
- Holy: said [the] LORD to the Lord of me:

κάθου ἐκ δεξιῶν μου ἕως ἂν θῶ τοὺς
Sit at [the] right [hand] of me until I put the

ἐχθρούς σου ὑποκάτω τῶν ποδῶν σου.
enemies of thee under the feet of thee.

37 αὐτὸς Δαυὶδ λέγει αὐτὸν κύριον, καὶ
himself David says(calls) him Lord, and

πόθεν αὐτοῦ ἐστιν υἱός;
whence of him is he son?

Καὶ ὁ πολὺς ὄχλος ἤκουεν αὐτοῦ
And the much crowd heard him

ἡδέως. 38 Καὶ ἐν τῇ διδαχῇ αὐτοῦ
gladly. And in the teaching of him

ἔλεγεν· βλέπετε ἀπὸ τῶν γραμματέων
he said: Beware from(of) the scribes

τῶν θελόντων ἐν στολαῖς περιπατεῖν καὶ
the [ones] wishing in robes to walk about and

ἀσπασμοὺς ἐν ταῖς ἀγοραῖς 39 καὶ
greetings in the marketplaces and

πρωτοκαθεδρίας ἐν ταῖς συναγωγαῖς καὶ
chief seats in the synagogues and

πρωτοκλισίας ἐν τοῖς δείπνοις· 40 οἱ
chief places in the dinners; the [ones]

κατεσθίοντες τὰς οἰκίας τῶν χηρῶν καὶ
devouring the houses of the widows and

προφάσει μακρὰ προσευχόμενοι, οὗτοι
under pretence long praying, these

λήμψονται περισσότερον κρίμα. 41 Καὶ
will receive greater condemnation. And

καθίσας κατέναντι τοῦ γαζοφυλακείου ἐθεώρει
sitting opposite the treasury he beheld

πῶς ὁ ὄχλος βάλλει χαλκὸν εἰς τὸ
how the crowd puts copper money into the

γαζοφυλακεῖον· καὶ πολλοὶ πλούσιοι ἔβαλλον
treasury; and many rich men put

πολλά· 42 καὶ ἐλθοῦσα μία χήρα πτωχὴ
much; and coming one widow poor

ἔβαλεν λεπτὰ δύο, ὅ ἐστιν κοδράντης.
put lepta two, which is a quadrans.

43 καὶ προσκαλεσάμενος τοὺς μαθητὰς αὐτοῦ
And calling to [him] the disciples of him

εἶπεν αὐτοῖς· ἀμὴν λέγω ὑμῖν ὅτι
he said to them: Truly I tell you that

ἡ χήρα αὕτη ἡ πτωχὴ πλεῖον πάντων
- ³widow ¹this - ²poor ⁵more [than] ⁶all

---

more important than all burnt offerings and sacrifices."

³⁴When Jesus saw that he had answered wisely, he said to him, "You are not far from the kingdom of God." And from then on no one dared ask him any more questions.

Whose Son Is the Christ?

³⁵While Jesus was teaching in the temple courts, he asked, "How is it that the teachers of the law say that the Christ ᶜ is the son of David? ³⁶David himself, speaking by the Holy Spirit, declared:

" 'The Lord said to my
 Lord:
"Sit at my right hand
 until I put your enemies
 under your feet." ' ᵈ

³⁷David himself calls him 'Lord.' How then can he be his son?"

The large crowd listened to him with delight.

³⁸As he taught, Jesus said, "Watch out for the teachers of the law. They like to walk around in flowing robes and be greeted in the marketplaces, ³⁹and have the most important seats in the synagogues and the places of honor at banquets. ⁴⁰They devour widows' houses and for a show make lengthy prayers. Such men will be punished most severely."

The Widow's Offering

⁴¹Jesus sat down opposite the place where the offerings were put and watched the crowd putting their money into the temple treasury. Many rich people threw in large amounts. ⁴²But a poor widow came and put in two very small copper coins, ᵉ worth only a fraction of a penny. ᶠ

⁴³Calling his disciples to him, Jesus said, "I tell you the truth, this poor widow

---

ᶜ35 Or Messiah
ᵈ36 Psalm 110:1
ᵉ42 Greek two lepta
ᶠ42 Greek kodrantes

¹Or the Christ

who are contributing to the treasury. 44 For all of them have contributed out of their abundance; but she out of her poverty has put in everything she had, all she had to live on."

ἔβαλεν τῶν βαλλόντων εἰς τὸ γαζοφυλακεῖον·
⁴put   the [ones] putting into the treasury;

44 πάντες γὰρ ἐκ τοῦ περισσεύοντος αὐτοῖς
for all   out of the abounding   to them⁰
= their abundance

ἔβαλον, αὕτη δὲ ἐκ τῆς ὑστερήσεως αὐτῆς
put, but this woman out of the want of her

πάντα   ὅσα   εἶχεν ἔβαλεν, ὅλον τὸν βίον
¹all things ²how many ⁴she had ¹put,   all   the living

αὐτῆς.
of her.

has put more into the treasury than all the others. 44They all gave out of their wealth; but she, out of her poverty, put in everything —all she had to live on."

Chapter 13

The Destruction of the Temple Foretold

AS he came out of the temple, one of his disciples said to him, "Look, Teacher, what large stones and what large buildings!" 2 Then Jesus asked him, "Do you see these great buildings? Not one stone will be left here upon another; all will be thrown down."

3 When he was sitting on the Mount of Olives opposite the temple, Peter, James, John, and Andrew asked him privately, 4 "Tell us, when will this be, and what will be the sign that all these things are about to be accomplished?" 5 Then Jesus began to say to them, "Beware that no one leads you astray. 6 Many will come in my name and say, 'I am he!'ᵐ and will lead many astray. 7 When you hear of wars and rumors of wars, do not be alarmed; this must take place, but the end is still to come. 8 For nation will rise against nation, and kingdom against kingdom; there will be earthquakes in various places; there will be famines. This is but the beginning of the birth-pangs.

Persecution Foretold

9 "As for yourselves, beware; for they will hand you over to councils; and you will be beaten in synagogues; and you will stand before governors and kings because of me, as a testimony to them. 10 And the

13 Καὶ ἐκπορευομένου αὐτοῦ ἐκ τοῦ
   And   going forth   himᵃ out of the
               = as he went forth

ἱεροῦ λέγει αὐτῷ εἷς τῶν μαθητῶν αὐτοῦ·
temple says to him one of the disciples of him:

διδάσκαλε, ἴδε ποταποὶ λίθοι καὶ ποταπαὶ
Teacher, behold[,] what great stones and what great

οἰκοδομαί. 2 καὶ ὁ Ἰησοῦς εἶπεν αὐτῷ·
buildings.   And   - Jesus   said to him:

βλέπεις ταύτας τὰς μεγάλας οἰκοδομάς;
Seest thou these   -   great   buildings?

οὐ μὴ ἀφεθῇ λίθος ἐπὶ λίθον ὃς οὐ
by no means be left stone on stone which by no
= there shall by no means be left stone on stone which will not

μὴ καταλυθῇ. 3 Καὶ καθημένου αὐτοῦ
means be overthrown. And   sitting   himᵃ
be overthrown.   = as he sat

εἰς τὸ ὄρος τῶν ἐλαιῶν κατέναντι τοῦ
in(on) the mount of the olives   opposite the

ἱεροῦ, ἐπηρώτα αὐτὸν κατ᾽ ἰδίαν Πέτρος
temple, questioned him   privately   Peter

καὶ Ἰάκωβος καὶ Ἰωάννης καὶ Ἀνδρέας·
and James   and John   and Andrew:

4 εἰπὸν ἡμῖν, πότε ταῦτα ἔσται, καὶ τί
  Tell   us,   when these things will be, and what

τὸ σημεῖον ὅταν μέλλῃ ταῦτα συντελεῖσθαι
the sign when ²are about ²these things ⁴to be completed

πάντα; 5 ὁ δὲ Ἰησοῦς ἤρξατο λέγειν
¹all?   - And Jesus   began   to say

αὐτοῖς· βλέπετε μή τις ὑμᾶς πλανήσῃ.
to them: See   lest anyone you lead astray.

6 πολλοὶ ἐλεύσονται ἐπὶ τῷ ὀνόματί μου
  Many   will come   on(in) the name   of me

λέγοντες ὅτι ἐγώ εἰμι, καὶ πολλοὺς
saying[,] -   I   am, and many

πλανήσουσιν. 7 ὅταν δὲ ἀκούσητε πολέμους
they will lead astray. But when ye hear [of] wars

καὶ ἀκοὰς πολέμων, μὴ θροεῖσθε· δεῖ
and rumours of wars, be not disturbed; it behoves

γενέσθαι, ἀλλ᾽ οὔπω τὸ τέλος. 8 ἐγερθήσεται
to happen, but not yet the end.   will be raised

γὰρ ἔθνος ἐπ᾽ ἔθνος καὶ βασιλεία ἐπὶ
For nation against nation and kingdom against

βασιλείαν. ἔσονται σεισμοὶ κατὰ τόπους,
kingdom. There will be earthquakes in places,

ἔσονται λιμοί· ἀρχὴ ὠδίνων ταῦτα.
there will be famines; beginning of birth-pangs these things [are].

9 Βλέπετε δὲ ὑμεῖς ἑαυτούς· παραδώσουσιν
  But see   ye yourselves; they will deliver

ὑμᾶς εἰς συνέδρια καὶ εἰς συναγωγὰς
you   to councils and in synagogues

δαρήσεσθε καὶ ἐπὶ ἡγεμόνων καὶ βασιλέων
ye will be beaten and before rulers and kings

σταθήσεσθε ἕνεκεν ἐμοῦ, εἰς μαρτύριον
ye will stand for the sake of me, for a testimony

Chapter 13

Signs of the End of the Age

AS he was leaving the temple, one of his disciples said to him, "Look, Teacher! What massive stones! What magnificent buildings!"

2 "Do you see all these great buildings?" replied Jesus. "Not one stone here will be left on another; every one will be thrown down."

3 As Jesus was sitting on the Mount of Olives opposite the temple, Peter, James, John and Andrew asked him privately, 4 "Tell us, when will these things happen? And what will be the sign that they are all about to be fulfilled?"

5 Jesus said to them: "Watch out that no one deceives you. 6 Many will come in my name, claiming, 'I am he,' and will deceive many. 7 When you hear of wars and rumors of wars, do not be alarmed. Such things must happen, but the end is still to come. 8 Nation will rise against nation, and kingdom against kingdom. There will be earthquakes in various places, and famines. These are the beginning of birth pains.

9 "You must be on your guard. You will be handed over to the local councils and flogged in the synagogues. On account of me you will stand before governors and kings as wit-

ᵐ Gk *I am*

good news[n] must first be proclaimed to all nations. [11]When they bring you to trial and hand you over, do not worry beforehand about what you are to say; but say whatever is given you at that time, for it is not you who speak, but the Holy Spirit. [12]Brother will betray brother to death, and a father his child, and children will rise against parents and have them put to death; [13]and you will be hated by all because of my name. But the one who endures to the end will be saved.

The Desolating Sacrilege

14 "But when you see the desolating sacrilege set up where it ought not to be (let the reader understand), then those in Judea must flee to the mountains; [15]the one on the housetop must not go down or enter the house to take anything away; [16]the one in the field must not turn back to get a coat. [17]Woe to those who are pregnant and to those who are nursing infants in those days! [18]Pray that it may not be in winter. [19]For in those days there will be suffering, such as has not been from the beginning of the creation that God created until now, no, and never will be. [20]And if the Lord had not cut short those days, no one would be saved; but for the sake of the elect, whom he chose, he has cut short those days. [21]And if anyone says to you at that time, 'Look! Here is the Messiah!'[o] or 'Look! There he is!'—do not believe it. [22]False mes-

---

αὐτοῖς. 10 καὶ εἰς πάντα τὰ ἔθνη πρῶτον
to them.　And　to　all　the nations　first

δεῖ　κηρυχθῆναι　τὸ εὐαγγέλιον. 11 καὶ ὅταν
it behoves to be proclaimed the　gospel.　And when
= the gospel must be proclaimed.

ἄγωσιν ὑμᾶς παραδιδόντες, μὴ προμεριμνᾶτε
they lead you　delivering,　be not anxious beforehand

τί λαλήσητε, ἀλλ' ὃ ἐὰν δοθῇ ὑμῖν ἐν
what ye speak,　but　whatever is given　you　in

ἐκείνῃ τῇ ὥρᾳ, τοῦτο λαλεῖτε· οὐ γάρ
that　- hour,　this　speak ye;　for not

ἐστε ὑμεῖς οἱ λαλοῦντες ἀλλὰ τὸ πνεῦμα
are　ye　the [ones] speaking　but　the Spirit

τὸ ἅγιον. 12 καὶ παραδώσει ἀδελφὸς
-　Holy.　And　²will deliver　¹a brother

ἀδελφὸν εἰς θάνατον καὶ πατὴρ τέκνον, καὶ
a brother to death　and a father a child,　and

ἐπαναστήσονται τέκνα ἐπὶ γονεῖς καὶ
²will rise *against*　¹children against parents and

θανατώσουσιν αὐτούς· 13 καὶ ἔσεσθε
will put to death　them;　and ye will be

μισούμενοι ὑπὸ πάντων διὰ τὸ ὄνομά
being hated　by all men on account of the name

μου· ὁ δὲ ὑπομείνας εἰς τέλος, οὗτος
of me; but the [one] enduring to [the] end, this

σωθήσεται. 14 Ὅταν δὲ ἴδητε τὸ βδέλυγμα
will be saved.　But when ye see the abomination

τῆς ἐρημώσεως ἑστηκότα ὅπου οὐ δεῖ, ὁ
- of desolation stand where he (it) behoves not, the

ἀναγινώσκων νοείτω, τότε οἱ ἐν τῇ
[one] reading let him understand, then the [ones] in

Ἰουδαίᾳ φευγέτωσαν εἰς τὰ ὄρη, 15 ὁ ἐπὶ
Judæa let them flee to the mountains, the [one] on

τοῦ δώματος μὴ καταβάτω μηδὲ εἰσελθάτω
the roof let him not come down nor let him enter

τι ἆραι ἐκ τῆς οἰκίας αὐτοῦ, 16 καὶ ὁ
anything to take out of the house of him, and the [one]

εἰς τὸν ἀγρὸν μὴ ἐπιστρεψάτω εἰς τὰ
in the field let him not return to the things

ὀπίσω ἆραι τὸ ἱμάτιον αὐτοῦ. 17 οὐαὶ
behind to take the garment of him.　woe

δὲ ταῖς ἐν γαστρὶ ἐχούσαις καὶ ταῖς
But to the women　pregnant†　and to the

θηλαζούσαις ἐν ἐκείναις ταῖς ἡμέραις.
[ones] giving suck in those the days.

18 προσεύχεσθε δὲ ἵνα μὴ γένηται χειμῶνος·
But pray ye that it may not happen of(in) winter;

19 ἔσονται γὰρ αἱ ἡμέραι ἐκεῖναι θλῖψις, οἵα
for ²will be - ²days ¹those ⁴affliction, of such a kind

οὐ γέγονεν τοιαύτη ἀπ' ἀρχῆς κτίσεως
²has not happened ¹as from [the] beginning of [the] creation

ἣν ἔκτισεν ὁ θεὸς ἕως τοῦ νῦν καὶ οὐ
which created - God until - now and by

μὴ γένηται. 20 καὶ εἰ μὴ ἐκολόβωσεν
no means may be.　And unless ¹shortened

κύριος τὰς ἡμέρας, οὐκ ἂν ἐσώθη πᾶσα
¹[the] Lord the days,　would not be saved all
= no flesh would be saved;

σάρξ· ἀλλὰ διὰ τοὺς ἐκλεκτοὺς οὓς
flesh;　but on account of the chosen whom

ἐξελέξατο ἐκολόβωσεν τὰς ἡμέρας. 21 καὶ
he chose he shortened the days.　And

τότε ἐάν τις ὑμῖν εἴπῃ· ἴδε ὧδε ὁ
then if anyone ²you ¹tells: Behold here [is] the

χριστός, ἴδε ἐκεῖ, μὴ πιστεύετε· 22 ἐγερθή-
Christ, behold there, believe ye not;　⁵will be

---

nesses to them. [10]And the gospel must first be preached to all nations. [11]Whenever you are arrested and brought to trial, do not worry beforehand about what to say. Just say whatever is given you at the time, for it is not you speaking, but the Holy Spirit.

[12]"Brother will betray brother to death, and a father his child. Children will rebel against their parents and have them put to death. [13]All men will hate you because of me, but he who stands firm to the end will be saved.

[14]"When you see 'the abomination that causes desolation'[g] standing where it[h] does not belong —let the reader understand—then let those who are in Judea flee to the mountains. [15]Let no one on the roof of his house go down or enter the house to take anything out. [16]Let no one in the field go back to get his cloak. [17]How dreadful it will be in those days for pregnant women and nursing mothers! [18]Pray that this will not take place in winter, [19]because those will be days of distress unequaled from the beginning, when God created the world, until now—and never to be equaled again. [20]If the Lord had not cut short those days, no one would survive. But for the sake of the elect, whom he has chosen, he has shortened them. [21]At that time if anyone says to you, 'Look, here is the Christ[i]!' or, 'Look, there he is!' do not believe it. [22]For false

---

[g]14 Daniel 9:27; 11:31; 12:11
[h]14 Or *he*; also in verse 29
[i]21 Or *Messiah*

siahs[p] and false prophets will appear and produce signs and omens, to lead astray, if possible, the elect. 23 But be alert; I have already told you everything.

The Coming of the Son of Man

24 "But in those days, after that suffering,
the sun will be darkened,
and the moon will not give its light,
25 and the stars will be falling from heaven,
and the powers in the heavens will be shaken.
26 Then they will see 'the Son of Man coming in clouds' with great power and glory. 27 Then he will send out the angels, and gather his elect from the four winds, from the ends of the earth to the ends of heaven.

The Lesson of the Fig Tree

28 "From the fig tree learn its lesson: as soon as its branch becomes tender and puts forth its leaves, you know that summer is near. 29 So also, when you see these things taking place, you know that he[q] is near, at the very gates. 30 Truly I tell you, this generation will not pass away until all these things have taken place. 31 Heaven and earth will pass away, but my words will not pass away.

The Necessity for Watchfulness

32 "But about that day or hour no one knows, neither the angels in heaven, nor the Son, but only the Father. 33 Beware, keep alert;[r] for you do not know when the time will come. 34 It is like a man going on a journey, when he leaves home and puts his slaves in charge, each with his work, and commands the door-

---

σονται δὲ ψευδόχριστοι καὶ ψευδοπροφῆται
raised ¹and ²false Christs ³and ⁴false prophets

καὶ ποιήσουσιν σημεῖα καὶ τέρατα πρὸς
and they will do signs and wonders for

τὸ ἀποπλανᾶν, εἰ δυνατόν, τοὺς ἐκλεκτούς.
- to lead astray, if possible, the chosen.

23 ὑμεῖς δὲ βλέπετε· προείρηκα ὑμῖν πάντα.
But ²ye ¹see; ¹I have told ⁴before ²you ³all things.

24 Ἀλλὰ ἐν ἐκείναις ταῖς ἡμέραις μετὰ
But in those - days after

τὴν θλῖψιν ἐκείνην ὁ ἥλιος σκοτισθήσεται,
- affliction that the sun will be darkened,

καὶ ἡ σελήνη οὐ δώσει τὸ φέγγος αὐτῆς,
and the moon will not give the light of her,

25 καὶ οἱ ἀστέρες ἔσονται ἐκ τοῦ οὐρανοῦ
and the stars ¹will be ²out of - ⁴heaven

πίπτοντες, καὶ αἱ δυνάμεις αἱ ἐν τοῖς
³falling, and the powers - in the

οὐρανοῖς σαλευθήσονται. 26 καὶ τότε ὄψονται
heavens will be shaken. And then they will see

τὸν υἱὸν τοῦ ἀνθρώπου ἐρχόμενον ἐν
the Son - of man coming in

νεφέλαις μετὰ δυνάμεως πολλῆς καὶ δόξης.
clouds with power much and glory.

27 καὶ τότε ἀποστελεῖ τοὺς ἀγγέλους καὶ
And then he will send the angels and

ἐπισυνάξει τοὺς ἐκλεκτοὺς [αὐτοῦ] ἐκ τῶν
they will assemble the chosen of him out of the

τεσσάρων ἀνέμων ἀπ' ἄκρου γῆς ἕως
four winds from [the] extremity of earth to

ἄκρου οὐρανοῦ. 28 Ἀπὸ δὲ τῆς συκῆς
[the] extremity of heaven. Now from the fig-tree

μάθετε τὴν παραβολήν· ὅταν ἤδη ὁ
learn the parable: when now the

κλάδος αὐτῆς ἁπαλὸς γένηται καὶ ἐκφύῃ
branch of it tender becomes and puts forth

τὰ φύλλα, γινώσκετε ὅτι ἐγγὺς τὸ θέρος
the leaves, ye know that near the summer

ἐστίν· 29 οὕτως καὶ ὑμεῖς, ὅταν ἴδητε
is; so also ye, when ye see

ταῦτα γινόμενα, γινώσκετε ὅτι ἐγγύς ἐστιν
these things happening, know that near he/it is

ἐπὶ θύραις. 30 ἀμὴν λέγω ὑμῖν ὅτι οὐ
at [the] doors. Truly I tell you that by no

μὴ παρέλθῃ ἡ γενεὰ αὕτη μέχρις οὗ
means passes - generation this until

ταῦτα πάντα γένηται. 31 ὁ οὐρανὸς καὶ
these things all happen. The heaven and

ἡ γῆ παρελεύσονται, οἱ δὲ λόγοι μου
the earth will pass away, but the words of me

οὐ παρελεύσονται. 32 Περὶ δὲ τῆς ἡμέρας
will not pass away. But concerning - day

ἐκείνης ἢ τῆς ὥρας οὐδεὶς οἶδεν, οὐδὲ
that or - hour no one knows, not

οἱ ἄγγελοι ἐν οὐρανῷ οὐδὲ ὁ υἱός, εἰ
the angels in heaven neither the Son, ex-

μὴ ὁ πατήρ. 33 Βλέπετε, ἀγρυπνεῖτε·
cept the Father. Look, be wakeful;

οὐκ οἴδατε γὰρ πότε ὁ καιρός ἐστιν.
for ye know not when the time is.

34 ὡς ἄνθρωπος ἀπόδημος ἀφεὶς τὴν οἰκίαν
As a man away from home leaving the house

αὐτοῦ καὶ δοὺς τοῖς δούλοις αὐτοῦ τὴν
of him and giving to the slaves of him -

ἐξουσίαν, ἑκάστῳ τὸ ἔργον αὐτοῦ, καὶ
authority, to each the work of him, and

Christs and false prophets will appear and perform signs and miracles to deceive the elect—if that were possible. 23 So be on your guard; I have told you everything ahead of time.

24 "But in those days, following that distress,

" 'the sun will be darkened,
and the moon will not give its light;
25 the stars will fall from the sky,
and the heavenly bodies will be shaken.'[j]

26 "At that time men will see the Son of Man coming in clouds with great power and glory. 27 And he will send his angels and gather his elect from the four winds, from the ends of the earth to the ends of the heavens.

28 "Now learn this lesson from the fig tree: As soon as its twigs get tender and its leaves come out, you know that summer is near. 29 Even so, when you see these things happening, you know that it is near, right at the door. 30 I tell you the truth, this generation[k] will certainly not pass away until all these things have happened. 31 Heaven and earth will pass away, but my words will never pass away.

The Day and Hour Unknown

32 "No one knows about that day or hour, not even the angels in heaven, nor the Son, but only the Father. 33 Be on guard! Be alert[l]! You do not know when that time will come. 34 It's like a man going away: He leaves his house and puts his servants in charge, each with his assigned task, and tells the

---

[p] Or christs
[q] Or it
[r] Other ancient authorities add and pray

[j] 25 Isaiah 13:10; 34:4
[k] 30 Or race
[l] 33 Some manuscripts alert and pray

keeper to be on the watch.
35 Therefore, keep awake—
for you do not know when
the master of the house will
come, in the evening, or at
midnight, or at cockcrow,
or at dawn, 36 or else he
may find you asleep when
he comes suddenly. 37 And
what I say to you I say to
all: Keep awake."

Chapter 14

The Plot to Kill Jesus

IT was two days before
the Passover and the
festival of Unleavened
Bread. The chief priests
and the scribes were looking for a way to arrest
Jesus[s] by stealth and kill
him; 2 for they said, "Not
during the festival, or there
may be a riot among the
people."

The Anointing at Bethany

3 While he was at Beth-
any in the house of Simon
the leper,[t] as he sat at the
table, a woman came with
an alabaster jar of very
costly ointment of nard,
and she broke open the jar
and poured the ointment on
his head. 4 But some were
there who said to one an-
other in anger, "Why was
the ointment wasted in this
way? 5 For this ointment
could have been sold for
more than three hundred
denarii,[u] and the money
given to the poor." And
they scolded her. 6 But
Jesus said, "Let her alone;
why do you trouble her?
She has performed a good
service for me. 7 For you always have the poor with
you, and you can show
kindness to them whenever
you wish; but you will not
always have me. 8 She has
done what she could; she
has anointed my body be-
forehand for its burial.
9 Truly I tell you, wherever

[s] Gk him
[t] The terms *leper* and *leprosy* can
refer to several diseases
[u] The denarius was the usual day's
wage for a laborer

Center column (interlinear)

τῷ θυρωρῷ ἐνετείλατο ἵνα γρηγορῇ.
the doorkeeper he commanded that he should watch.

35 γρηγορεῖτε οὖν· οὐκ οἴδατε γὰρ πότε
Watch ye therefore; for ye know not when

ὁ κύριος τῆς οἰκίας ἔρχεται, ἢ ὀψὲ ἢ
the lord of the house comes, either late or

μεσονύκτιον ἢ ἀλεκτοροφωνίας ἢ πρωΐ·
at midnight or at cock-crowing or early;

36 μὴ ἐλθὼν ἐξαίφνης εὕρῃ ὑμᾶς καθεύδ-
lest coming suddenly he find you sleep-

οντας. 37 ὃ δὲ ὑμῖν λέγω, πᾶσιν λέγω,
ing. And what to you I say, to all I say,

γρηγορεῖτε.
watch ye.

14 Ἦν δὲ τὸ πάσχα καὶ τὰ ἄζυμα
Now it was the Passover and [the feast of] the
unleavened bread†

μετὰ δύο ἡμέρας. καὶ ἐζήτουν οἱ ἀρχιερεῖς
after two days. And sought the chief priests

καὶ οἱ γραμματεῖς πῶς αὐτὸν ἐν δόλῳ
and the scribes how ²him ³by ⁴guile

κρατήσαντες ἀποκτείνωσιν. 2 ἔλεγον γάρ·
¹seizing they might kill. For they said:

μὴ ἐν τῇ ἑορτῇ, μήποτε ἔσται θόρυβος
Not at the feast, lest there will be a disturbance

τοῦ λαοῦ.
of the people.

3 Καὶ ὄντος αὐτοῦ ἐν Βηθανίᾳ ἐν τῇ
And being him* in Bethany in the
= when he was

οἰκίᾳ Σίμωνος τοῦ λεπροῦ, κατακειμένου
house of Simon the leper, reclining
= as he reclined

αὐτοῦ ἦλθεν γυνὴ ἔχουσα ἀλάβαστρον
him* came a woman having an alabaster phial

μύρου νάρδου πιστικῆς πολυτελοῦς·
of ointment ²nard ¹of pure ³costly;

συντρίψασα τὴν ἀλάβαστρον κατέχεεν αὐτοῦ
breaking the alabaster phial she poured over of him

τῆς κεφαλῆς. 4 ἦσαν δέ τινες ἀγανακτοῦντες
the head. Now there were some being angry

πρὸς ἑαυτούς· εἰς τί ἡ ἀπώλεια αὕτη
with themselves; Why - waste this

τοῦ μύρου γέγονεν; 5 ἠδύνατο γὰρ τοῦτο
of the ointment has occurred? for ²could ¹this

τὸ μύρον πραθῆναι ἐπάνω δηναρίων
- ²ointment to be sold [for] over denarii

τριακοσίων καὶ δοθῆναι τοῖς πτωχοῖς·
three hundred and to be given to the poor;

καὶ ἐνεβριμῶντο αὐτῇ. 6 ὁ δὲ Ἰησοῦς
and they were indignant with her. - But Jesus

εἶπεν· ἄφετε αὐτήν· τί αὐτῇ κόπους
said: Leave her; why ²to her ¹troubles

παρέχετε; καλὸν ἔργον ἠργάσατο ἐν ἐμοί.
¹cause ye? a good work she wrought in me.

7 πάντοτε γὰρ τοὺς πτωχοὺς ἔχετε μεθ'
For always the poor ye have with

ἑαυτῶν, καὶ ὅταν θέλητε δύνασθε αὐτοῖς
yourselves, and whenever ye wish ye can them

εὖ ποιῆσαι, ἐμὲ δὲ οὐ πάντοτε ἔχετε.
well to do, but me not always ye have.

8 ὃ ἔσχεν ἐποίησεν· προέλαβεν μυρίσαι τὸ
What she had she did; she was beforehand to anoint the

σῶμά μου εἰς τὸν ἐνταφιασμόν. 9 ἀμὴν
body of me for the burial. truly

one at the door to keep
watch.
35 "Therefore keep watch
because you do not know
when the owner of the
house will come back—
whether in the evening, or
at midnight, or when the
rooster crows, or at dawn.
36 If he comes suddenly, do
not let him find you sleeping. 37 What I say to you, I
say to everyone:
'Watch!' "

Chapter 14

Jesus Anointed at Bethany

NOW the Passover and
the Feast of Unleav-
ened Bread were only two
days away, and the chief
priests and the teachers of
the law were looking for
some sly way to arrest
Jesus and kill him. 2 "But
not during the Feast," they
said, "or the people may
riot."

3 While he was in Betha-
ny, reclining at the table in
the home of a man known
as Simon the Leper, a
woman came with an ala-
baster jar of very expensive
perfume, made of pure
nard. She broke the jar and
poured the perfume on his
head.
4 Some of those present
were saying indignantly to
one another, "Why this
waste of perfume? 5 It could
have been sold for more
than a year's wages[m] and
the money given to the
poor." And they rebuked
her harshly.
6 "Leave her alone," said
Jesus. "Why are you both-
ering her? She has done a
beautiful thing to me. 7 The
poor you will always have
with you, and you can help
them any time you want.
But you will not always
have me. 8 She did what she
could. She poured perfume
on my body beforehand to
prepare for my burial. 9 I

[m] 5 Greek *than three hundred
denarii*

the good news[v] is proclaimed in the whole world, what she has done will be told in remembrance of her."

Judas Agrees to Betray Jesus

10 Then Judas Iscariot, who was one of the twelve, went to the chief priests in order to betray him to them. 11 When they heard it, they were greatly pleased, and promised to give him money. So he began to look for an opportunity to betray him.

The Passover with the Disciples

12 On the first day of Unleavened Bread, when the Passover lamb is sacrificed, his disciples said to him, "Where do you want us to go and make the preparations for you to eat the Passover?" 13 So he sent two of his disciples, saying to them, "Go into the city, and a man carrying a jar of water will meet you; follow him, 14 and wherever he enters, say to the owner of the house, 'The Teacher asks, Where is my guest room where I may eat the Passover with my disciples?' 15 He will show you a large room upstairs, furnished and ready. Make preparations for us there." 16 So the disciples set out and went to the city, and found everything as he had told them; and they prepared the Passover meal.

17 When it was evening, he came with the twelve. 18 And when they had taken their places and were eating, Jesus said, "Truly I tell you, one of you will betray me, one who is eating with me." 19 They began to be distressed and to say to him one after another, "Surely, not I?" 20 He said to them, "It is one of the twelve, one who is dipping bread[w] into the bowl[x] with me. 21 For

δὲ λέγω ὑμῖν, ὅπου ἐὰν κηρυχθῇ τὸ
And I tell you, wherever is proclaimed the

εὐαγγέλιον εἰς ὅλον τὸν κόσμον, καὶ ὃ
gospel in all the world, also what

ἐποίησεν αὕτη λαληθήσεται εἰς μνημόσυνον
did this woman will be spoken for a memorial

αὐτῆς. 10 Καὶ Ἰούδας Ἰσκαριώθ, ὁ εἷς
of her. And Judas Iscariot, the one

τῶν δώδεκα, ἀπῆλθεν πρὸς τοὺς ἀρχιερεῖς
of the twelve, went to the chief priests

ἵνα αὐτὸν παραδοῖ αὐτοῖς. 11 οἱ δὲ
that him he might betray to them. And they

ἀκούσαντες ἐχάρησαν καὶ ἐπηγγείλαντο αὐτῷ
hearing rejoiced and promised him

ἀργύριον δοῦναι. καὶ ἐζήτει πῶς αὐτὸν
silver to give. And he sought how him

εὐκαίρως παραδοῖ.
opportunely he might betray.

12 Καὶ τῇ πρώτῃ ἡμέρᾳ τῶν ἀζύμων,
And on the first day of unleavened bread,†

ὅτε τὸ πάσχα ἔθυον, λέγουσιν αὐτῷ οἱ
when the passover they sacrificed, say to him the

μαθηταὶ αὐτοῦ· ποῦ θέλεις ἀπελθόντες
disciples of him: Where wishest thou , going

ἐτοιμάσωμεν ἵνα φάγῃς τὸ πάσχα; 13 καὶ
we may prepare that thou eatest the passover? And

ἀποστέλλει δύο τῶν μαθητῶν αὐτοῦ καὶ
he sends two of the disciples of him and

λέγει αὐτοῖς· ὑπάγετε εἰς τὴν πόλιν, καὶ
tells them: Go ye into the city, and

ἀπαντήσει ὑμῖν ἄνθρωπος κεράμιον ὕδατος
will meet you a man a pitcher of water

βαστάζων· ἀκολουθήσατε αὐτῷ, 14 καὶ ὅπου
carrying; follow him, and wher-

ἐὰν εἰσέλθῃ εἴπατε τῷ οἰκοδεσπότῃ ὅτι ὁ
ever he enters tell the housemaster[,] - The

διδάσκαλος λέγει· ποῦ ἐστιν τὸ κατάλυμά
teacher says: Where is the guest room

μου, ὅπου τὸ πάσχα μετὰ τῶν μαθητῶν
of me, where the passover with the disciples

μου φάγω; 15 καὶ αὐτὸς ὑμῖν δείξει
of me I may eat? And he you will show

ἀνάγαιον μέγα ἐστρωμένον ἕτοιμον· καὶ
upper room a large *having been* spread ready; and

ἐκεῖ ἑτοιμάσατε ἡμῖν. 16 καὶ ἐξῆλθον οἱ
there prepare ye for us. And went forth the

μαθηταὶ καὶ ἦλθον εἰς τὴν πόλιν καὶ
disciples and came into the city and

εὗρον καθὼς εἶπεν αὐτοῖς, καὶ ἡτοίμασαν
found as he told them, and they prepared

τὸ πάσχα. 17 Καὶ ὀψίας γενομένης ἔρχεται
the passover. And evening coming[a] he comes
= when evening came

μετὰ τῶν δώδεκα. 18 καὶ ἀνακειμένων
with the twelve. And reclining
= as they reclined and ate

αὐτῶν καὶ ἐσθιόντων ὁ Ἰησοῦς εἶπεν·
them and eating[a] - Jesus said:

ἀμὴν λέγω ὑμῖν ὅτι εἷς ἐξ ὑμῶν παραδώσει
Truly I tell you that one of you will betray

με, ὁ ἐσθίων μετ' ἐμοῦ. 19 ἤρξαντο
me, the [one] eating with me. They began

λυπεῖσθαι καὶ λέγειν αὐτῷ εἷς κατὰ εἷς·
to grieve and to say to him one by one:

μήτι ἐγώ; 20 ὁ δὲ εἶπεν αὐτοῖς· εἷς τῶν
Not I? And he said to them: One of the

δώδεκα, ὁ ἐμβαπτόμενος μετ' ἐμοῦ εἰς
twelve, the [one] dipping with me in

tell you the truth, wherever the gospel is preached throughout the world, what she has done will also be told, in memory of her."

10 Then Judas Iscariot, one of the Twelve, went to the chief priests to betray Jesus to them. 11 They were delighted to hear this and promised to give him money. So he watched for an opportunity to hand him over.

The Lord's Supper

12 On the first day of the Feast of Unleavened Bread, when it was customary to sacrifice the Passover lamb, Jesus' disciples asked him, "Where do you want us to go and make preparations for you to eat the Passover?"

13 So he sent two of his disciples, telling them, "Go into the city, and a man carrying a jar of water will meet you. Follow him. 14 Say to the owner of the house he enters, 'The Teacher asks: Where is my guest room, where I may eat the Passover with my disciples?' 15 He will show you a large upper room, furnished and ready. Make preparations for us there."

16 The disciples left, went into the city and found things just as Jesus had told them. So they prepared the Passover.

17 When evening came, Jesus arrived with the Twelve. 18 While they were reclining at the table eating, he said, "I tell you the truth, one of you will betray me—one who is eating with me."

19 They were saddened, and one by one they said to him, "Surely not I?"

20 "It is one of the Twelve," he replied, "one who dips bread into the

[v] Or *gospel*
[w] Gk lacks *bread*
[x] Other ancient authorities read *same bowl*

the Son of Man goes as it is written of him, but woe to that one by whom the Son of Man is betrayed! It would have been better for that one not to have been born."

The Institution of the Lord's Supper

22 While they were eating, he took a loaf of bread, and after blessing it he broke it, gave it to them, and said, "Take; this is my body." 23 Then he took a cup, and after giving thanks he gave it to them, and all of them drank from it. 24 He said to them, "This is my blood of the[y] covenant, which is poured out for many. 25 Truly I tell you, I will never again drink of the fruit of the vine until that day when I drink it new in the kingdom of God."

Peter's Denial Foretold

26 When they had sung the hymn, they went out to the Mount of Olives. 27 And Jesus said to them, "You will all become deserters; for it is written,

'I will strike the
shepherd,
and the sheep will
be scattered.'

28 But after I am raised up, I will go before you to Galilee." 29 Peter said to him, "Even though all become deserters, I will not." 30 Jesus said to him, "Truly I tell you, this day, this very night, before the cock crows twice, you will deny me three times." 31 But he said vehemently, "Even though I must die with you, I will not deny you." And all of them said the same.

Jesus Prays in Gethsemane

32 They went to a place

Middle column (interlinear)

τὸ [ἐν] τρύβλιον. 21 ὅτι ὁ μὲν υἱὸς τοῦ
the one dish. Because indeed the Son -

ἀνθρώπου ὑπάγει καθὼς γέγραπται περὶ
of man is going as it has been written concerning

αὐτοῦ· οὐαὶ δε τῷ ἀνθρώπῳ ἐκείνῳ δι᾽
him; but woe to that man through

οὗ ὁ υἱὸς τοῦ ἀνθρώπου παραδίδοται·
whom the Son - of man is betrayed;

καλὸν αὐτῷ εἰ οὐκ ἐγεννήθη ὁ ἄνθρωπος
good for him if was not born - man

ἐκεῖνος. 22 Καὶ ἐσθιόντων αὐτῶν λαβὼν
that. And eating them[a] taking
= as they were eating

ἄρτον εὐλογήσας ἔκλασεν καὶ ἔδωκεν αὐτοῖς
a loaf blessing he broke and gave to them

καὶ εἶπεν· λάβετε· τοῦτό ἐστιν τὸ σῶμά
and said: Take ye; this is the body

μου. 23 καὶ λαβὼν ποτήριον εὐχαριστήσας
of me. And taking a cup giving thanks

ἔδωκεν αὐτοῖς, καὶ ἔπιον ἐξ αὐτοῦ πάντες.
he gave to them, and drank of it all.

24 καὶ εἶπεν αὐτοῖς· τοῦτό ἐστιν τὸ αἷμά
And he said to them: This is the blood

μου τῆς διαθήκης τὸ ἐκχυννόμενον ὑπὲρ
of me of the covenant - being shed for

πολλῶν. 25 ἀμὴν λέγω ὑμῖν ὅτι οὐκέτι
many. Truly I tell you[,] - No more

οὐ μὴ πίω ἐκ τοῦ γενήματος τῆς ἀμπέλου
by no(any) will I drink of the fruit of the vine
means

ἕως τῆς ἡμέρας ἐκείνης ὅταν αὐτὸ πίνω
until - day that when it I drink

καινὸν ἐν τῇ βασιλείᾳ τοῦ θεοῦ.
new in the kingdom - of God.

26 Καὶ ὑμνήσαντες ἐξῆλθον εἰς τὸ
And having sung a hymn they went forth to the

ὄρος τῶν ἐλαιῶν. 27 Καὶ λέγει αὐτοῖς ὁ
mount of the olives. And says to them -

Ἰησοῦς ὅτι πάντες σκανδαλισθήσεσθε, ὅτι
Jesus[,] - [1]All [1]ye [2]will [3]be offended, because

γέγραπται· πατάξω τὸν ποιμένα, καὶ τὰ
it has been written: I will strike the shepherd, and the

πρόβατα διασκορπισθήσονται. 28 ἀλλὰ μετὰ
sheep will be scattered. But after

τὸ ἐγερθῆναί με προάξω ὑμᾶς εἰς τὴν
the to be raised me[b] I will go before you to -
= I am raised

Γαλιλαίαν. 29 ὁ δὲ Πέτρος ἔφη αὐτῷ·
Galilee. - And Peter said to him:

εἰ καὶ πάντες σκανδαλισθήσονται, ἀλλ᾽
If even all men shall be offended, yet

οὐκ ἐγώ. 30 καὶ λέγει αὐτῷ ὁ Ἰησοῦς·
not I. And says to him - Jesus:

ἀμὴν λέγω σοι ὅτι σὺ σήμερον ταύτῃ τῇ
Truly I tell thee[,] - Thou to-day in this

νυκτὶ πρὶν ἢ δὶς ἀλέκτορα φωνῆσαι τρίς
night before twice a cock to sound[b] thrice

με ἀπαρνήσῃ. 31 ὁ δὲ ἐκπερισσῶς ἐλάλει·
me thou wilt deny. But he more exceedingly said:

ἐὰν δέῃ με συναποθανεῖν σοι, οὐ μή
If should behove me to die with thee, by no means
= I must

σε ἀπαρνήσομαι. ὡσαύτως [δὲ] καὶ πάντες
thee will I deny. And similarly also all

ἔλεγον.
said.

32 Καὶ ἔρχονται εἰς χωρίον οὗ τὸ
And they come to a piece of land of which the

bowl with me. 21 The Son of Man will go just as it is written about him. But woe to that man who betrays the Son of Man! It would be better for him if he had not been born."

22 While they were eating, Jesus took bread, gave thanks and broke it, and gave it to his disciples, saying, "Take it; this is my body."

23 Then he took the cup, gave thanks and offered it to them, and they all drank from it.

24 "This is my blood of the[n] covenant, which is poured out for many," he said to them. 25 "I tell you the truth, I will not drink again of the fruit of the vine until that day when I drink it anew in the kingdom of God."

26 When they had sung a hymn, they went out to the Mount of Olives.

Jesus Predicts Peter's Denial

27 "You will all fall away," Jesus told them, "for it is written:

" 'I will strike the
shepherd,
and the sheep will be
scattered.'[o]

28 But after I have risen, I will go ahead of you into Galilee."

29 Peter declared, "Even if all fall away, I will not."

30 "I tell you the truth," Jesus answered, "today— yes, tonight—before the rooster crows twice[p] you yourself will disown me three times."

31 But Peter insisted emphatically, "Even if I have to die with you, I will never disown you." And all the others said the same.

Gethsemane

32 They went to a place

---

[y] Other ancient authorities add new

[n]24 Some manuscripts the new
[o]27 Zech. 13:7
[p]30 Some early manuscripts do not have twice.

called Gethsemane; and he said to his disciples, "Sit here while I pray." ³³ He took with him Peter and James and John, and began to be distressed and agitated. ³⁴ And said to them, "I am deeply grieved, even to death; remain here, and keep awake." ³⁵ And going a little farther, he threw himself on the ground and prayed that, if it were possible, the hour might pass from him. ³⁶ He said, "Abba, ᶻ Father, for you all things are possible; remove this cup from me; yet, not what I want, but what you want." ³⁷ He came and found them sleeping; and he said to Peter, "Simon, are you asleep? Could you not keep awake one hour? ³⁸ Keep awake and pray that you may not come into the time of trial;ᵃ the spirit indeed is willing, but the flesh is weak." ³⁹ And again he went away and prayed, saying the same words. ⁴⁰ And once more he came and found them sleeping, for their eyes were very heavy; and they did not know what to say to him. ⁴¹ He came a third time and said to them, "Are you still sleeping and taking your rest? Enough! The hour has come; the Son of Man is betrayed into the hands of sinners. ⁴² Get up, let us be going. See, my betrayer is at hand."

The Betrayal and Arrest of Jesus

43 Immediately, while he was still speaking, Judas, one of the twelve, arrived; and with him was a crowd with swords and clubs, from the chief priests, the scribes, and the

ὄνομα Γεθσημανί, καὶ λέγει τοῖς μαθηταῖς
name [was] Gethsemane, and he says to the disciples
αὐτοῦ· καθίσατε ὧδε ἕως προσεύξωμαι.
of him: Sit ye here while I pray.
33 καὶ παραλαμβάνει τὸν Πέτρον καὶ τὸν
And he takes - Peter and -
Ἰάκωβον καὶ τὸν Ἰωάννην μετ' αὐτοῦ,
James and - John with him,
καὶ ἤρξατο ἐκθαμβεῖσθαι καὶ ἀδημονεῖν,
and began to be greatly astonished and to be distressed,
34 καὶ λέγει αὐτοῖς· περίλυπός ἐστιν ἡ
and says to them: Deeply grieved is the
ψυχή μου ἕως θανάτου· μείνατε ὧδε καὶ
soul of me unto death; remain ye here and
γρηγορεῖτε. 35 καὶ προελθὼν μικρὸν ἔπιπτεν
watch. And going forward a little he fell
ἐπὶ τῆς γῆς, καὶ προσηύχετο ἵνα εἰ
on the ground, and prayed that if
δυνατόν ἐστιν παρέλθῃ ἀπ' αὐτοῦ ἡ ὥρα,
possible it is might pass away from him the hour,
36 καὶ ἔλεγεν· ἀββὰ ὁ πατήρ, πάντα
and said: Abba - Father, all things
δυνατά σοι· παρένεγκε τὸ ποτήριον τοῦτο
[are] possible to thee; remove - cup this
ἀπ' ἐμοῦ· ἀλλ' οὐ τί ἐγὼ θέλω ἀλλὰ
from me; but not what I wish but
τί σύ. 37 καὶ ἔρχεται καὶ εὑρίσκει
what thou. And he comes and finds
αὐτοὺς καθεύδοντας, καὶ λέγει τῷ Πέτρῳ·
them sleeping, and says - to Peter:
Σίμων, καθεύδεις; οὐκ ἴσχυσας μίαν ὥραν
Simon, sleepest thou? couldest thou not one hour
γρηγορῆσαι; 38 γρηγορεῖτε καὶ προσεύχεσθε,
to watch? Watch ye and pray,
ἵνα μὴ ἔλθητε εἰς πειρασμόν· τὸ μὲν
lest ye come into temptation; indeed the
πνεῦμα πρόθυμον, ἡ δὲ σὰρξ ἀσθενής.
spirit [is] eager, but the flesh weak.
39 καὶ πάλιν ἀπελθὼν προσηύξατο τὸν
And again going away he prayed ᵇthe
αὐτὸν λόγον εἰπών. 40 καὶ πάλιν ἐλθὼν
ᵃsame ᵇword ⁴saying. And again coming
εὗρεν αὐτοὺς καθεύδοντας, ἦσαν γὰρ αὐτῶν
he found them sleeping, for were of them
οἱ ὀφθαλμοὶ καταβαρυνόμενοι, καὶ οὐκ
the eyes becoming heavy, and not
ᾔδεισαν τί ἀποκριθῶσιν αὐτῷ. 41 καὶ
they knew what they might answer him. And
ἔρχεται τὸ τρίτον καὶ λέγει αὐτοῖς·
he comes the third [time] and says to them:
καθεύδετε τὸ λοιπὸν καὶ ἀναπαύεσθε·
Sleep ye now† and rest;
ἀπέχει· ἦλθεν ἡ ὥρα, ἰδοὺ παραδίδοται ὁ
it is enough; came the hour, behold is betrayed the
υἱὸς τοῦ ἀνθρώπου εἰς τὰς χεῖρας τῶν
Son - man into the hands -
ἁμαρτωλῶν. 42 ἐγείρεσθε, ἄγωμεν· ἰδοὺ ὁ
of sinners. Rise ye, let us go; behold the
παραδιδούς με ἤγγικεν. 43 Καὶ εὐθὺς ἔτι
[one] betraying me has drawn near. And immediately yet
αὐτοῦ λαλοῦντοςᵃ παραγίνεται [ὁ] Ἰούδας
him speakingᵃ arrives - Judas
= while he was still speaking
εἷς τῶν δώδεκα, καὶ μετ' αὐτοῦ ὄχλος
one of the twelve, and with him a crowd
μετὰ μαχαιρῶν καὶ ξύλων παρὰ τῶν
with swords and clubs from the

called Gethsemane, and Jesus said to his disciples, "Sit here while I pray." ³³ He took Peter, James and John along with him, and he began to be deeply distressed and troubled. ³⁴ "My soul is overwhelmed with sorrow to the point of death," he said to them. "Stay here and keep watch." ³⁵ Going a little farther, he fell to the ground and prayed that if possible the hour might pass from him. ³⁶ "Abba,�q Father," he said, "everything is possible for you. Take this cup from me. Yet not what I will, but what you will." ³⁷ Then he returned to his disciples and found them sleeping. "Simon," he said to Peter, "are you asleep? Could you not keep watch for one hour? ³⁸ Watch and pray so that you will not fall into temptation. The spirit is willing, but the body is weak." ³⁹ Once more he went away and prayed the same thing. ⁴⁰ When he came back, he again found them sleeping, because their eyes were heavy. They did not know what to say to him. ⁴¹ Returning the third time, he said to them, "Are you still sleeping and resting? Enough! The hour has come. Look, the Son of Man is betrayed into the hands of sinners. ⁴² Rise! Let us go! Here comes my betrayer!"

Jesus Arrested

43 Just as he was speaking, Judas, one of the Twelve, appeared. With him was a crowd armed with swords and clubs, sent from the

---

ᶻ Aramaic for *Father*
ᵃ Or *into temptation*

�q36 Aramaic for *Father*

elders. 44 Now the betrayer had given them a sign, saying, "The one I will kiss is the man; arrest him and lead him away under guard." 45 So when he came, he went up to him at once and said, "Rabbi!" and kissed him. 46 Then they laid hands on him and arrested him. 47 But one of those who stood near drew his sword and struck the slave of the high priest, cutting off his ear. 48 Then Jesus said to them, "Have you come out with swords and clubs to arrest me as though I were a bandit? 49 Day after day I was with you in the temple teaching, and you did not arrest me. But let the scriptures be fulfilled." 50 All of them deserted him and fled.

51 A certain young man was following him, wearing nothing but a linen cloth. They caught hold of him, 52 but he left the linen cloth and ran off naked.

Jesus before the Council

53 They took Jesus to the high priest; and all the chief priests, the elders, and the scribes were assembled. 54 Peter had followed him at a distance, right into the courtyard of the high priest; and he was sitting with the guards, warming himself at the fire. 55 Now the chief priests and the whole council were looking for testimony against Jesus to put him to death; but they found none. 56 For many gave false testimony against him, and their testimony did not agree. 57 Some stood up

---

ἀρχιερέων καὶ τῶν γραμματέων καὶ τῶν
chief priests and the scribes and the
πρεσβυτέρων. 44 δεδώκει δὲ ὁ παραδιδοὺς
elders. [1]Now [2]had given [3]the [one] [3]betraying
αὐτὸν σύσσημον αὐτοῖς λέγων· ὃν ἂν
[4]him [7]a signal [6]them saying: Whomever
φιλήσω αὐτός ἐστιν· κρατήσατε αὐτὸν καὶ
I may kiss he is; seize ye him and
ἀπάγετε ἀσφαλῶς. 45 καὶ ἐλθὼν εὐθὺς
lead away securely. And coming immediately
προσελθὼν αὐτῷ λέγει· ῥαββί, καὶ
approaching to him he says: Rabbi, and
κατεφίλησεν αὐτόν· 46 οἱ δὲ ἐπέβαλαν τὰς
fervently kissed him; and they [1]laid [4]on [3]the(their)
χεῖρας αὐτῷ καὶ ἐκράτησαν αὐτόν. 47 εἷς
[2]hands him and seized him. [4]one
δέ τις τῶν παρεστηκότων σπασάμενος
[1]But [2]a certain of the [ones] standing by drawing
τὴν μάχαιραν ἔπαισεν τὸν δοῦλον τοῦ ἀρχιερέως
the sword struck the slave of the high priest
καὶ ἀφεῖλεν αὐτοῦ τὸ ὠτάριον. 48 καὶ
and cut off of him the ear. And
ἀποκριθεὶς ὁ Ἰησοῦς εἶπεν αὐτοῖς· ὡς
answering - Jesus said to them: As
ἐπὶ λῃστὴν ἐξήλθατε μετὰ μαχαιρῶν καὶ
against a robber came ye forth with swords and
ξύλων συλλαβεῖν με; 49 καθ᾽ ἡμέραν ἤμην
clubs to arrest me? Daily I was
πρὸς ὑμᾶς ἐν τῷ ἱερῷ διδάσκων, καὶ οὐκ
with you in the temple teaching, and not
ἐκρατήσατέ με· ἀλλ᾽ ἵνα πληρωθῶσιν αἱ
ye did seize me; but that may be fulfilled the
γραφαί. 50 καὶ ἀφέντες αὐτὸν ἔφυγον
scriptures. And leaving him they fled
πάντες. 51 Καὶ νεανίσκος τις συνηκολούθει
all. And a certain young man accompanied
αὐτῷ περιβεβλημένος σινδόνα ἐπὶ γυμνοῦ,
him having been clothed [in] a nightgown over [his] naked [body],
καὶ κρατοῦσιν αὐτόν· 52 ὁ δὲ καταλιπὼν
and they seize him; and he leaving
τὴν σινδόνα γυμνὸς ἔφυγεν.
the nightgown naked fled.
53 Καὶ ἀπήγαγον τὸν Ἰησοῦν πρὸς τὸν
And they led away - Jesus to the
ἀρχιερέα, καὶ συνέρχονται πάντες οἱ
high priest, and come together all the
ἀρχιερεῖς καὶ οἱ πρεσβύτεροι καὶ οἱ
chief priests and the elders and the
γραμματεῖς. 54 καὶ ὁ Πέτρος ἀπὸ μακρόθεν
scribes. And - Peter from afar
ἠκολούθησεν αὐτῷ ἕως ἔσω εἰς τὴν αὐλὴν
followed him until within in the court
τοῦ ἀρχιερέως, καὶ ἦν συγκαθήμενος μετὰ
of the high priest, and was sitting with with
τῶν ὑπηρετῶν καὶ θερμαινόμενος πρὸς τὸ
the attendants and warming himself by the
φῶς. 55 Οἱ δὲ ἀρχιερεῖς καὶ ὅλον τὸ
bright fire. Now the chief priests and all the
συνέδριον ἐζήτουν κατὰ τοῦ Ἰησοῦ
council sought against - Jesus
μαρτυρίαν εἰς τὸ θανατῶσαι αὐτόν, καὶ
witness for the to put to death him, and
= so as
οὐχ ηὕρισκον· 56 πολλοὶ γὰρ ἐψευδομαρτύρουν
found not; for many falsely witnessed
κατ᾽ αὐτοῦ, καὶ ἴσαι αἱ μαρτυρίαι οὐκ
against him, and [1]identical [2]the [3]testimonies [4]not

---

chief priests, the teachers of the law, and the elders. 44 Now the betrayer had arranged a signal with them: "The one I kiss is the man; arrest him and lead him away under guard." 45 Going at once to Jesus, Judas said, "Rabbi!" and kissed him. 46 The men seized Jesus and arrested him. 47 Then one of those standing near drew his sword and struck the servant of the high priest, cutting off his ear.

48 "Am I leading a rebellion," said Jesus, "that you have come out with swords and clubs to capture me? 49 Every day I was with you, teaching in the temple courts, and you did not arrest me. But the Scriptures must be fulfilled." 50 Then everyone deserted him and fled.

51 A young man, wearing nothing but a linen garment, was following Jesus. When they seized him, 52 he fled naked, leaving his garment behind.

Before the Sanhedrin

53 They took Jesus to the high priest, and all the chief priests, elders and teachers of the law came together. 54 Peter followed him at a distance, right into the courtyard of the high priest. There he sat with the guards and warmed himself at the fire. 55 The chief priests and the whole Sanhedrin were looking for evidence against Jesus so that they could put him to death, but they did not find any. 56 Many testified falsely against him, but their statements did not agree.

and gave false testimony against him, saying, 58 "We heard him say, 'I will destroy this temple that is made with hands, and in three days I will build another, not made with hands.'" 59 But even on this point their testimony did not agree. 60 Then the high priest stood up before them and asked Jesus, "Have you no answer? What is it that they testify against you?" 61 But he was silent and did not answer. Again the high priest asked him, "Are you the Messiah,[b] the Son of the Blessed One?" 62 Jesus said, "I am;

and

'you will see the Son
of Man
seated at the right
hand of
the Power,'
and 'coming with the
clouds
of heaven.'"

63 Then the high priest tore his clothes and said, "Why do we still need witnesses? 64 You have heard his blasphemy! What is your decision?" All of them condemned him as deserving death. 65 Some began to spit on him, to blindfold him, and to strike him, saying to him, "Prophesy!" The guards also took him over and beat him.

Peter Denies Jesus

66 While Peter was below in the courtyard, one of the servant-girls of the high priest came by. 67 When she saw Peter warming himself, she stared at him and said, "You also were with Jesus, the man from Nazareth." 68 But he denied it, saying, "I do not know or understand what you are talking about." And he went out into the forecourt.[c] Then the cock

---

ἦσαν. 57 καὶ τινες ἀναστάντες ἐψευδομαρτύρουν
were. And some standing up falsely witnessed

κατ’ αὐτοῦ λέγοντες 58 ὅτι ἡμεῖς ἠκούσαμεν
against him saying[,] – We heard

αὐτοῦ λέγοντος ὅτι ἐγὼ καταλύσω τὸν
him saying[,] – I will overthrow –

ναὸν τοῦτον τὸν χειροποίητον καὶ διὰ
shrine ¹this ¹handmade and through(after)

τριῶν ἡμερῶν ἄλλον ἀχειροποίητον οἰκο-
three days another not handmade I will

δομήσω. 59 καὶ οὐδὲ οὕτως ἴση ἦν ἡ
build. And not so identical was the

μαρτυρία αὐτῶν. 60 καὶ ἀναστὰς ὁ
witness of them. And standing up the

ἀρχιερεὺς εἰς μέσον ἐπηρώτησεν τὸν Ἰησοῦν
high priest in [the] midst questioned – Jesus

λέγων· οὐκ ἀποκρίνῃ οὐδὲν τί οὗτοί σου
saying: Answerest thou not no(any)thing what these men ²thee

καταμαρτυροῦσιν; 61 ὁ δὲ ἐσιώπα καὶ
¹testify against? But he was silent and

οὐκ ἀπεκρίνατο οὐδέν. πάλιν ὁ ἀρχιερεὺς
answered not no(any)thing. Again the high priest

ἐπηρώτα αὐτὸν καὶ λέγει αὐτῷ· σὺ εἶ ὁ
questioned him and says to him: Thou art the

χριστὸς ὁ υἱὸς τοῦ εὐλογητοῦ; 62 ὁ δὲ
Christ the Son of the Blessed [one]? – And

Ἰησοῦς εἶπεν· ἐγώ εἰμι, καὶ ὄψεσθε
Jesus said: I am, and ye will see

τὸν υἱὸν τοῦ ἀνθρώπου ἐκ δεξιῶν καθήμενον
the Son – of man ²at [the] right [hand] ¹sitting

τῆς δυνάμεως καὶ ἐρχόμενον μετὰ τῶν
of the Power and coming with the

νεφελῶν τοῦ οὐρανοῦ. 63 ὁ δὲ ἀρχιερεὺς
clouds – of heaven. And the high priest

διαρρήξας τοὺς χιτῶνας αὐτοῦ λέγει· τί
rending the tunics of him says: What

ἔτι χρείαν ἔχομεν μαρτύρων; 64 ἠκούσατε
more need have we of witnesses? ye heard

τῆς βλασφημίας· τί ὑμῖν φαίνεται; οἱ δὲ
the blasphemy; what to you appears it? And they

πάντες κατέκριναν αὐτὸν ἔνοχον εἶναι
all condemned him liable to be

θανάτου. 65 Καὶ ἤρξαντό τινες ἐμπτύειν
of(to) death. And began some to spit at

αὐτῷ καὶ περικαλύπτειν αὐτοῦ τὸ πρόσωπον
him and to cover of him the face

καὶ κολαφίζειν αὐτὸν καὶ λέγειν αὐτῷ·
and to maltreat him and to say to him:

προφήτευσον, καὶ οἱ ὑπηρέται ῥαπίσμασιν
Prophesy, and the attendants with slaps

αὐτὸν ἔλαβον. 66 Καὶ ὄντος τοῦ Πέτρου
³him ¹took. And being – Peter⁴
= as Peter was

κάτω ἐν τῇ αὐλῇ ἔρχεται μία τῶν
below in the court comes one of the

παιδισκῶν τοῦ ἀρχιερέως, 67 καὶ ἰδοῦσα
maidservants of the high priest, and seeing

τὸν Πέτρον θερμαινόμενον ἐμβλέψασα αὐτῷ
– Peter warming himself looking at him

λέγει· καὶ σὺ μετὰ τοῦ Ναζαρηνοῦ ἦσθα
says: And ¹thou ²with ⁴the ⁵Nazarene ³wast

τοῦ Ἰησοῦ. 68 ὁ δὲ ἠρνήσατο λέγων· οὔτε
– ⁶Jesus. But he denied saying: ¹neither

οἶδα οὔτε ἐπίσταμαι σὺ τί λέγεις. καὶ
¹I know ²nor ³understand ⁴thou ⁵what ⁶sayest. And

ἐξῆλθεν ἔξω εἰς τὸ προαύλιον· 69 καὶ ἡ
he went forth outside into the forecourt; and the

---

57 Then some stood up and gave this false testimony against him: 58 "We heard him say, 'I will destroy this man-made temple and in three days will build another, not made by man.'" 59 Yet even then their testimony did not agree.

60 Then the high priest stood up before them and asked Jesus, "Are you not going to answer? What is this testimony that these men are bringing against you?" 61 But Jesus remained silent and gave no answer.

Again the high priest asked him, "Are you the Christ,[r] the Son of the Blessed One?"

62 "I am," said Jesus. "And you will see the Son of Man sitting at the right hand of the Mighty One and coming on the clouds of heaven."

63 The high priest tore his clothes. "Why do we need any more witnesses?" he asked. 64 "You have heard the blasphemy. What do you think?"

They all condemned him as worthy of death. 65 Then some began to spit at him; they blindfolded him, struck him with their fists, and said, "Prophesy!" And the guards took him and beat him.

Peter Disowns Jesus

66 While Peter was below in the courtyard, one of the servant girls of the high priest came by. 67 When she saw Peter warming himself, she looked closely at him.

"You also were with that Nazarene, Jesus," she said.

68 But he denied it. "I don't know or understand what you're talking about," he said, and went out into the entryway.[s]

---

crowed.d 69 And the servant-girl, on seeing him, began again to say to the bystanders, "This man is one of them." 70 But again he denied it. Then after a little while the bystanders again said to Peter, "Certainly you are one of them; for you are a Galilean." 71 But he began to curse, and he swore an oath, "I do not know this man you are talking about." 72 At that moment the cock crowed for the second time. Then Peter remembered that Jesus had said to him, "Before the cock crows twice, you will deny me three times." And he broke down and wept.

Chapter 15
Jesus before Pilate

AS soon as it was morning, the chief priests held a consultation with the elders and scribes and the whole council. They bound Jesus, led him away, and handed him over to Pilate. 2 Pilate asked him, "Are you the King of the Jews?" He answered him, "You say so." 3 Then the chief priests accused him of many things. 4 Pilate asked him again, "Have you no answer? See how many charges they bring against you." 5 But Jesus made no further reply, so that Pilate was amazed.

Pilate Hands Jesus over to Be Crucified

6 Now at the festival he used to release a prisoner for them, anyone for whom they asked. 7 Now a man called Barabbas was in prison with the rebels who had committed murder during the insurrection. 8 So the crowd came and began to ask Pilate to do for them according to his custom. 9 Then he answered them, "Do you want me to release

d Other ancient authorities lack Then the cock crowed

παιδίσκη ἰδοῦσα αὐτὸν ἤρξατο πάλιν λέγειν
maidservant seeing him began again to say

τοῖς παρεστῶσιν ὅτι οὗτος ἐξ αὐτῶν ἐστιν.
to the [ones] standing by[,] – This man of them is.

70 ὁ δὲ πάλιν ἠρνεῖτο. καὶ μετὰ μικρὸν
But he again denied. And after a little

πάλιν οἱ παρεστῶτες ἔλεγον τῷ Πέτρῳ·
again the [ones] standing by said – to Peter:

ἀληθῶς ἐξ αὐτῶν εἶ· καὶ γὰρ Γαλιλαῖος
Truly of them thou art; indeed for a Galilæan

εἶ. 71 ὁ δὲ ἤρξατο ἀναθεματίζειν καὶ
thou art. And he began to curse and

ὀμνύναι ὅτι οὐκ οἶδα τὸν ἄνθρωπον
to swear[,] that I know not – man

τοῦτον ὃν λέγετε. 72 καὶ εὐθὺς ἐκ
this whom ye say. And immediately a

δευτέρου ἀλέκτωρ ἐφώνησεν. καὶ ἀνεμνήσθη
second time a cock crew. And remembered

ὁ Πέτρος τὸ ῥῆμα ὡς εἶπεν αὐτῷ ὁ
– Peter the word as said to him –

Ἰησοῦς ὅτι πρὶν ἀλέκτορα δὶς φωνῆσαι
Jesus[,] – Before a cock twice to crowb

τρίς με ἀπαρνήσῃ· καὶ ἐπιβαλὼν ἔκλαιεν.
thrice me thou wilt deny; and thinking thereon he wept.

15 Καὶ εὐθὺς πρωῒ συμβούλιον ἑτοιμάσαντες
And immediately early a council preparing

οἱ ἀρχιερεῖς μετὰ τῶν πρεσβυτέρων καὶ
the chief priests with the elders and

γραμματέων καὶ ὅλον τὸ συνέδριον, δήσαντες
scribes and all the council, having bound

τὸν Ἰησοῦν ἀπήνεγκαν καὶ παρέδωκαν
– Jesus led [him] away and delivered [him]

Πιλάτῳ. 2 καὶ ἐπηρώτησεν αὐτὸν ὁ
to Pilate. And questioned him –

Πιλᾶτος· σὺ εἶ ὁ βασιλεὺς τῶν Ἰουδαίων;
Pilate: Thou art the king of the Jews?

ὁ δὲ ἀποκριθεὶς αὐτῷ λέγει· σὺ λέγεις.
And he answering him says: Thou sayest.

3 καὶ κατηγόρουν αὐτοῦ οἱ ἀρχιερεῖς πολλά.
And accused him the chief priests many things.

4 ὁ δὲ Πιλᾶτος πάλιν ἐπηρώτα αὐτόν [λέγων]·
– But Pilate again questioned him saying:

οὐκ ἀποκρίνῃ οὐδέν; ἴδε πόσα
Answerest thou not no(any)thing? Behold how many things

σου κατηγοροῦσιν. 5 ὁ δὲ Ἰησοῦς οὐκ-
thee they accuse. – But Jesus no(any)

ἔτι οὐδὲν ἀπεκρίθη, ὥστε θαυμάζειν
more nothing answered, so as to marvel = so that Pilate marvelled

τὸν Πιλᾶτον. 6 Κατὰ δὲ ἑορτὴν ἀπέλυεν
– Pilateb. Now at a feast he released

αὐτοῖς ἕνα δέσμιον ὃν παρῃτοῦντο. 7 ἦν δὲ
to them one prisoner whom they begged. Now there was

ὁ λεγόμενος Βαραββᾶς μετὰ τῶν
the [one] named Barabbas with the

στασιαστῶν δεδεμένος, οἵτινες ἐν τῇ στάσει
rebels having been bound, who* in the rebellion

φόνον πεποιήκεισαν. 8 καὶ ἀναβὰς ὁ ὄχλος
murder had done. And going up the crowd

ἤρξατο αἰτεῖσθαι καθὼς ἐποίει αὐτοῖς.
began to ask as he used to do for them.

9 ὁ δὲ Πιλᾶτος ἀπεκρίθη αὐτοῖς λέγων·
– But Pilate answered them saying:

* Note the plural.

---

69 When the servant girl saw him there, she said again to those standing around, "This fellow is one of them." 70 Again he denied it.

After a little while, those standing near said to Peter, "Surely you are one of them, for you are a Galilean."

71 He began to call down curses on himself, and he swore to them, "I don't know this man you're talking about."

72 Immediately the rooster crowed the second time.f Then Peter remembered the word Jesus had spoken to him: "Before the rooster crows twiceu you will disown me three times." And he broke down and wept.

Chapter 15
Jesus Before Pilate

VERY early in the morning, the chief priests, with the elders, the teachers of the law and the whole Sanhedrin, reached a decision. They bound Jesus, led him away and handed him over to Pilate. 2 "Are you the king of the Jews?" asked Pilate. "Yes, it is as you say," Jesus replied. 3 The chief priests accused him of many things. 4 So again Pilate asked him, "Aren't you going to answer? See how many things they are accusing you of." 5 But Jesus still made no reply, and Pilate was amazed.

6 Now it was the custom at the Feast to release a prisoner whom the people requested. 7 A man called Barabbas was in prison with the insurrectionists who had committed murder in the uprising. 8 The crowd came up and asked Pilate to do for them what he usually did. 9 "Do you want me to release to you the king of the

f 72 Some early manuscripts do not have the second time.
u 72 Some early manuscripts do not have twice.

Left column (RSV)

for you the King of the Jews?" [10] For he realized that it was out of jealousy that the chief priests had handed him over. [11] But the chief priests stirred up the crowd to have him release Barabbas for them instead. [12] Pilate spoke to them again, "Then what do you wish me to do*f* with the man you call*f* the King of the Jews?" [13] They shouted back, "Crucify him!" [14] Pilate asked them, "Why, what evil has he done?" But they shouted all the more, "Crucify him!" [15] So Pilate, wishing to satisfy the crowd, released Barabbas for them; and after flogging Jesus, he handed him over to be crucified.

The Soldiers Mock Jesus

[16] Then the soldiers led him into the courtyard of the palace (that is, the governor's headquarters*g*); and they called together the whole cohort. [17] And they clothed him in a purple cloak; and after twisting some thorns into a crown, they put it on him. [18] And they began saluting him, "Hail, King of the Jews!" [19] They struck his head with a reed, spat upon him, and knelt down in homage to him. [20] After mocking him, they stripped him of the purple cloak and put his own clothes on him. Then they led him out to crucify him.

The Crucifixion of Jesus

[21] They compelled a passer-by, who was coming in from the country, to carry his cross; it was Simon of Cyrene, the father of Alexander and Rufus. [22] Then they brought Jesus*h* to the place called Golgotha (which means the place of a skull). [23] And they offered

Middle column (Greek interlinear)

θέλετε ἀπολύσω ὑμῖν τὸν βασιλέα τῶν
Do ye wish I may release to you the king of the

'Ιουδαίων; 10 ἐγίνωσκεν γὰρ ὅτι διὰ φθόνον
Jews? For he knew that on account of envy

παραδεδώκεισαν αὐτὸν οἱ ἀρχιερεῖς. 11 οἱ
had delivered him the chief priests. the

δὲ ἀρχιερεῖς ἀνέσεισαν τὸν ὄχλον ἵνα
But chief priests stirred up the crowd that

μᾶλλον τὸν Βαραββᾶν ἀπολύσῃ αὐτοῖς.
rather - Barabbas he should release to them.

12 ὁ δὲ Πιλᾶτος πάλιν ἀποκριθεὶς ἔλεγεν
- So Pilate again answering said

αὐτοῖς· τί οὖν ποιήσω [ὃν] λέγετε τὸν
to them: What then may I do [to him] whom ye call the

βασιλέα τῶν 'Ιουδαίων; 13 οἱ δὲ πάλιν
king of the Jews? And they again

ἔκραξαν· σταύρωσον αὐτόν. 14 ὁ δὲ
cried out: Crucify him. - But

Πιλᾶτος ἔλεγεν αὐτοῖς· τί γὰρ ἐποίησεν
Pilate said to them: Indeed what *did he

κακόν; οἱ δὲ περισσῶς ἔκραξαν· σταύρωσον
*evil? and they more cried out: Crucify

αὐτόν. 15 ὁ δὲ Πιλᾶτος βουλόμενος τῷ
him. - And Pilate resolving the

ὄχλῳ τὸ ἱκανὸν ποιῆσαι ἀπέλυσεν αὐτοῖς
crowd to satisfy† released to them

τὸν Βαραββᾶν, καὶ παρέδωκεν τὸν 'Ιησοῦν
- Barabbas, and delivered - Jesus

φραγελλώσας ἵνα σταυρωθῇ.
having scourged [him] that he might be crucified.

16 Οἱ δὲ στρατιῶται ἀπήγαγον αὐτὸν
Then the soldiers led away him

ἔσω τῆς αὐλῆς, ὅ ἐστιν πραιτώριον, καὶ
inside the court, which is prætorium, and

συγκαλοῦσιν ὅλην τὴν σπεῖραν. 17 καὶ
they call together all the cohort. And

ἐνδιδύσκουσιν αὐτὸν πορφύραν καὶ περιτιθέασιν
they put on him a purple [robe] and place round

αὐτῷ πλέξαντες ἀκάνθινον στέφανον· 18 καὶ
him plaiting a thorny crown; and

ἤρξαντο ἀσπάζεσθαι αὐτόν· χαῖρε, βασιλεῦ
they began to salute him: Hail, king

τῶν 'Ιουδαίων· 19 καὶ ἔτυπτον αὐτοῦ τὴν
of the Jews; and they struck of him the

κεφαλὴν καλάμῳ καὶ ἐνέπτυον αὐτῷ, καὶ
head with a reed and spat at him, and

τιθέντες τὰ γόνατα προσεκύνουν αὐτῷ.
placing(bending) the(their) knees worshipped him.

20 καὶ ὅτε ἐνέπαιξαν αὐτῷ, ἐξέδυσαν
And when they mocked him, they took off

αὐτὸν τὴν πορφύραν καὶ ἐνέδυσαν αὐτὸν
him the purple [robe] and put on him

τὰ ἱμάτια αὐτοῦ. Καὶ ἐξάγουσιν αὐτὸν
the garments of him. And they lead forth him

ἵνα σταυρώσωσιν αὐτόν. 21 καὶ ἀγγαρεύουσιν
that they might crucify him. And they impress

παράγοντά τινα Σίμωνα Κυρηναῖον ἐρχόμενον
passing by a certain Simon a Cyrenian coming

ἀπ' ἀγροῦ, τὸν πατέρα 'Αλεξάνδρου καὶ
from [the] country, the father of Alexander and

'Ρούφου, ἵνα ἄρῃ τὸν σταυρὸν αὐτοῦ.
of Rufus, that he might bear the cross of him.

22 καὶ φέρουσιν αὐτὸν ἐπὶ τὸν Γολγοθὰν
And they bring him to the Golgotha

τόπον, ὅ ἐστιν μεθερμηνευόμενος κρανίου
place, which is being interpreted of a skull

Jews?" asked Pilate, [10] knowing it was out of envy that the chief priests had handed Jesus over to him. [11] But the chief priests stirred up the crowd to have Pilate release Barabbas instead.

[12] "What shall I do, then, with the one you call the king of the Jews?" Pilate asked them.

[13] "Crucify him!" they shouted.

[14] "Why? What crime has he committed?" asked Pilate.

But they shouted all the louder, "Crucify him!"

[15] Wanting to satisfy the crowd, Pilate released Barabbas to them. He had Jesus flogged, and handed him over to be crucified.

The Soldiers Mock Jesus

[16] The soldiers led Jesus away into the palace (that is, the Praetorium) and called together the whole company of soldiers. [17] They put a purple robe on him, then twisted together a crown of thorns and set it on him. [18] And they began to call out to him, "Hail, king of the Jews!" [19] Again and again they struck him on the head with a staff and spit on him. Falling on their knees, they paid homage to him. [20] And when they had mocked him, they took off the purple robe and put his own clothes on him. Then they led him out to crucify him.

The Crucifixion

[21] A certain man from Cyrene, Simon, the father of Alexander and Rufus, was passing by on his way in from the country, and they forced him to carry the cross. [22] They brought Jesus to the place called Golgotha (which means The Place of the Skull).

Footnotes

e Other ancient authorities read what should I do
f Other ancient authorities lack the man you call
g Gk the praetorium
h Gk him

him wine mixed with myrrh; but he did not take it. 24 And they crucified him, and divided his clothes among them, casting lots to decide what each should take.

25 It was nine o'clock in the morning when they crucified him. 26 The inscription of the charge against him read, "The King of the Jews." 27 And with him they crucified two bandits, one on his right and one on his left. [i] 29 Those who passed by derided [j] him, shaking their heads and saying, "Aha! You who would destroy the temple and build it in three days, 30 save yourself, and come down from the cross!" 31 In the same way the chief priests, along with the scribes, were also mocking him among themselves and saying, "He saved others; he cannot save himself. 32 Let the Messiah, [k] the King of Israel, come down from the cross now, so that we may see and believe." Those who were crucified with him also taunted him.

The Death of Jesus

33 When it was noon, darkness came over the whole land [l] until three in the afternoon. 34 At three o'clock Jesus cried out with a loud voice, "Eloi, Eloi, lema sabachthani?" which means, "My God, my God, why have you forsaken me?" [m] 35 When some of the bystanders heard it, they said, "Listen, he is calling for Elijah." 36 And someone ran, filled a sponge with sour wine, put it on a stick, and gave it to him to drink, saying, "Wait, let us see whether Elijah will come to take him down." 37 Then Jesus gave

---

τόπος. 23 καὶ ἐδίδουν αὐτῷ ἐσμυρνισμένον
place.   And they gave him   ²having been spiced with myrrh

οἶνον· ὃς δὲ οὐκ ἔλαβεν. 24 καὶ σταυροῦσιν
¹wine; but who(he) received not.   And they crucify

αὐτόν, καὶ διαμερίζονται τὰ ἱμάτια αὐτοῦ,
him,   and divide   the garments of him,

βάλλοντες κλῆρον ἐπ' αὐτὰ τίς τί ἄρῃ.
casting   a lot   on them ²one ¹what might take.

25 ἦν δὲ ὥρα τρίτη καὶ ἐσταύρωσαν
Now it was hour third and they crucified

αὐτόν. 26 καὶ ἦν ἡ ἐπιγραφὴ τῆς αἰτίας
him.   And was the superscription of the accusation

αὐτοῦ ἐπιγεγραμμένη· Ο ΒΑΣΙΛΕΥΣ ΤΩΝ
of him having been written over· THE KING OF THE

ΙΟΥΔΑΙΩΝ. 27 Καὶ σὺν αὐτῷ σταυροῦσιν
JEWS.   And with him they crucify

δύο λῃστάς, ἕνα ἐκ δεξιῶν καὶ ἕνα ἐξ
two robbers, one on [the] right and one on

εὐωνύμων αὐτοῦ. ‡ 29 Καὶ οἱ παραπορευόμενοι
[the] left of him.   And the [ones] passing by

ἐβλασφήμουν αὐτὸν κινοῦντες τὰς κεφαλὰς
blasphemed   him   wagging   the heads

αὐτῶν καὶ λέγοντες· οὐὰ ὁ καταλύων
of them and saying· Ah the [one] overthrowing

τὸν ναὸν καὶ οἰκοδομῶν [ἐν] τρισὶν
the shrine and building in three

ἡμέραις, 30 σῶσον σεαυτὸν καταβὰς ἀπὸ
days,   save thyself coming down from

τοῦ σταυροῦ. 31 ὁμοίως καὶ οἱ ἀρχιερεῖς
the cross.   Likewise also the chief priests

ἐμπαίζοντες πρὸς ἀλλήλους μετὰ τῶν
mocking   to   one another with the

γραμματέων ἔλεγον· ἄλλους ἔσωσεν, ἑαυτὸν
scribes   said· Others he saved, himself

οὐ δύναται σῶσαι· 32 ὁ χριστὸς ὁ βασιλεὺς
he cannot to save;   the Christ the king

Ἰσραὴλ καταβάτω νῦν ἀπὸ τοῦ σταυροῦ,
of Israel let come down now from the cross,

ἵνα ἴδωμεν καὶ πιστεύσωμεν. καὶ οἱ
that we may see and believe.   And the

συνεσταυρωμένοι σὺν αὐτῷ ὠνείδιζον αὐτόν.
[ones] crucified with him   reproached him.

33 Καὶ γενομένης ὥρας ἕκτης σκότος
And becoming   hour sixth⁴ darkness
= when it was the sixth hour

ἐγένετο ἐφ' ὅλην τὴν γῆν ἕως ὥρας
came   over all the land until [the] hour

ἐνάτης. 34 καὶ τῇ ἐνάτῃ ὥρᾳ ἐβόησεν ὁ
ninth.   And at the ninth hour cried   –

Ἰησοῦς φωνῇ μεγάλῃ· ἐλωὶ ἐλωὶ λαμὰ
Jesus with a voice great(loud): Eloi[,] Eloi[,] lama

σαβαχθάνι; ὅ ἐστιν μεθερμηνευόμενον· ὁ
sabachthani? which is being interpreted: The

θεός μου ὁ θεός μου, εἰς τί ἐγκατέλιπές
God of me[,] the God of me, why didst thou forsake

με; 35 καί τινες τῶν παρεστηκότων
me ?   And some of the [ones] standing by

ἀκούσαντες ἔλεγον· ἴδε Ἡλίαν φωνεῖ.
hearing   said· Behold Elias he calls.

36 δραμὼν δέ τις γεμίσας σπόγγον ὄξους
And running one having filled a sponge of(with) vinegar

περιθεὶς καλάμῳ ἐπότιζεν αὐτόν, λέγων·
placing it round a reed ¹gave ²to drink ³him, saying:

ἄφετε ἴδωμεν εἰ ἔρχεται Ἡλίας ·καθελεῖν
Leave[,] let us see if comes Elias ¹to take ²down

‡ Verse 28 omitted by Nestle; cf. NIV footnote.

---

23 Then they offered him wine mixed with myrrh, but he did not take it. 24 And they crucified him. Dividing up his clothes, they cast lots to see what each would get.

25 It was the third hour when they crucified him. 26 The written notice of the charge against him read: THE KING OF THE JEWS. 27 They crucified two robbers with him, one on his right and one on his left. [v] 29 Those who passed by hurled insults at him, shaking their heads and saying, "So! You who are going to destroy the temple and build it in three days, 30 come down from the cross and save yourself!" 31 In the same way the chief priests and the teachers of the law mocked him among themselves. "He saved others," they said, "but he can't save himself! 32 Let this Christ, [w] King of Israel, come down now from the cross, that we may see and believe." Those crucified with him also heaped insults on him.

The Death of Jesus

33 At the sixth hour darkness came over the whole land until the ninth hour. 34 And at the ninth hour Jesus cried out in a loud voice, "Eloi, Eloi, lama sabachthani?" — which means, "My God, my God, why have you forsaken me?" [x] 35 When some of those standing near heard this, they said, "Listen, he's calling Elijah." 36 One man ran, filled a sponge with wine vinegar, put it on a stick, and offered it to Jesus to drink. "Now leave him alone. Let's see if Elijah comes to take him down," he said.

---

[i] Other ancient authorities add verse 28. And the scripture was fulfilled that says, "And he was counted among the lawless."
[j] Or blasphemed
[k] Or the Christ
[l] Or earth
[m] Other ancient authorities read made me a reproach

[v] 27 Some manuscripts left, 28 and the scripture was fulfilled which says, "He was counted with the lawless ones" (Isaiah 53:12)
[w] 32 Or Messiah
[x] 34 Psalm 22:1

a loud cry and breathed his last. 38 And the curtain of the temple was torn in two, from top to bottom. 39 Now when the centurion, who stood facing him, saw that in this way he[n] breathed his last, he said, "Truly this man was God's Son!"[o]

40 There were also women looking on from a distance; among them were Mary Magdalene, and Mary the mother of James the younger and of Joses, and Salome. 41 These used to follow him and provided for him when he was in Galilee; and there were many other women who had come up with him to Jerusalem.

The Burial of Jesus

42 When evening had come, and since it was the day of Preparation, that is, the day before the sabbath, 43 Joseph of Arimathea, a respected member of the council, who was also himself waiting expectantly for the kingdom of God, went boldly to Pilate and asked for the body of Jesus. 44 Then Pilate wondered if he were already dead; and summoning the centurion, he asked him whether he had been dead for some time. 45 When he learned from the centurion that he was dead, he granted the body to Joseph. 46 Then Joseph[p] bought a linen cloth, and taking down the body,[q] wrapped it in the linen cloth, and laid it in a tomb that had been hewn out of the rock. He then rolled a stone against the door of the tomb. 47 Mary Magdalene and Mary the mother of Joses saw where the body[q] was laid.

αὐτόν. **37** ὁ δὲ Ἰησοῦς ἀφεὶς φωνὴν
[h]him.   -   But   Jesus   letting go   voice

μεγάλην ἐξέπνευσεν. **38** Καὶ τὸ καταπέτασμα
a great(loud)   expired.   And the   veil

τοῦ ναοῦ ἐσχίσθη εἰς δύο ἀπ' ἄνωθεν
of the   shrine   was rent   in   two   from   top

ἕως κάτω. **39** Ἰδὼν δὲ ὁ κεντυρίων ὁ
to   bottom.   And [s]seeing   [1]the   [2]centurion   -

παρεστηκὼς ἐξ ἐναντίας αὐτοῦ ὅτι οὕτως
[3]standing by   [4]opposite   [5]him   that   thus

ἐξέπνευσεν, εἶπεν· ἀληθῶς οὗτος ὁ ἄνθρωπος
he expired,   said: Truly   this   -   man

υἱὸς θεοῦ ἦν. **40** Ἦσαν δὲ καὶ γυναῖκες
son   of God was.   Now there were   also   women

ἀπὸ μακρόθεν θεωροῦσαι, ἐν αἷς καὶ
from   afar   beholding,   among whom   both

Μαρία ἡ Μαγδαληνὴ καὶ Μαρία ἡ
Mary   the   Magdalene   and   Mary   the

Ἰακώβου τοῦ μικροῦ καὶ Ἰωσῆτος μήτηρ
[3]of James   [4]the   [5]little   [6]and   [7]of Joses   [1]mother

καὶ Σαλώμη, **41** αἷ ὅτε ἦν ἐν τῇ Γαλιλαίᾳ
and   Salome,   who   when he was in   -   Galilee

ἠκολούθουν αὐτῷ καὶ διηκόνουν αὐτῷ, καὶ
followed   him   and   served   him,   and

ἄλλαι πολλαὶ αἱ συναναβᾶσαι αὐτῷ εἰς
others   many   -   having come up with   him   to

Ἱεροσόλυμα.
Jerusalem.

42 Καὶ ἤδη ὀψίας γενομένης, ἐπεὶ ἦν
And   now   evening   coming,[a]   since   it was
= when it was evening,

παρασκευή, ὅ ἐστιν προσάββατον, **43** ἐλθὼν
[the] preparation,   which is the day before the sabbath,   coming

Ἰωσὴφ ὁ ἀπὸ Ἀριμαθαίας, εὐσχήμων
Joseph   the [one]   from   Arimathæa,   an honourable

βουλευτής, ὃς καὶ αὐτὸς ἦν προσδεχόμενος
councillor,   who   also   [him]self   was   expecting

τὴν βασιλείαν τοῦ θεοῦ, τολμήσας εἰσῆλθεν
the   kingdom   of God,   taking courage   went in

πρὸς τὸν Πιλᾶτον καὶ ᾐτήσατο τὸ σῶμα
to   -   Pilate   and   asked   the   body

τοῦ Ἰησοῦ. **44** ὁ δὲ Πιλᾶτος ἐθαύμασεν
-   of Jesus.   -   And   Pilate   marvelled

εἰ ἤδη τέθνηκεν, καὶ προσκαλεσάμενος τὸν
if   already   he has died,   and   calling to [him]   the

κεντυρίωνα ἐπηρώτησεν αὐτὸν εἰ πάλαι
centurion   questioned   him   [1]f   long ago

ἀπέθανεν· **45** καὶ γνοὺς ἀπὸ τοῦ κεντυρίωνος
he died;   and knowing   from   the   centurion

ἐδωρήσατο τὸ πτῶμα τῷ Ἰωσήφ. **46** καὶ
he granted   the   corpse   -   to Joseph.   And

ἀγοράσας σινδόνα καθελὼν αὐτὸν ἐνείλησεν
having bought   a piece of   taking down   him   he wrapped
unused linen

τῇ σινδόνι καὶ κατέθηκεν αὐτὸν ἐν μνήματι
with the linen   and   deposited   him   in   a tomb

ὃ ἦν λελατομημένον ἐκ πέτρας, καὶ
which was   having been hewn   out of   rock,   and

προσεκύλισεν λίθον ἐπὶ τὴν θύραν τοῦ
rolled   a stone   against   the   door   of the

μνημείου. **47** ἡ δὲ Μαρία ἡ Μαγδαληνὴ
tomb.   -   And   Mary   the   Magdalene

καὶ Μαρία ἡ Ἰωσῆτος ἐθεώρουν ποῦ
and   Mary   the [mother]   of Joses   beheld   where

τέθειται.
he has been laid.

37 With a loud cry, Jesus breathed his last. 38 The curtain of the temple was torn in two from top to bottom. 39 And when the centurion, who stood there in front of Jesus, heard his cry and[y] saw how he died, he said, "Surely this man was the Son[z] of God!"

40 Some women were watching from a distance. Among them were Mary Magdalene, Mary the mother of James the younger and of Joses, and Salome. 41 In Galilee these women had followed him and cared for his needs. Many other women who had come up with him to Jerusalem were also there.

The Burial of Jesus

42 It was Preparation Day (that is, the day before the Sabbath). So as evening approached, 43 Joseph of Arimathea, a prominent member of the Council, who was himself waiting for the kingdom of God, went boldly to Pilate and asked for Jesus' body. 44 Pilate was surprised to hear that he was already dead. Summoning the centurion, he asked him if Jesus had already died. 45 When he learned from the centurion that it was so, he gave the body to Joseph. 46 So Joseph bought some linen cloth, took down the body, wrapped it in the linen, and placed it in a tomb cut out of rock. Then he rolled a stone against the entrance of the tomb. 47 Mary Magdalene and Mary the mother of Joses saw where he was laid.

[n] Other ancient authorities add cried out and
[o] Or a son of God
[p] Gk he
[q] Gk it

[y]39 Some manuscripts do not have heard his cry and.
[z]39 Or a son

Chapter 16

The Resurrection of Jesus

WHEN the sabbath was over, Mary Magdalene, and Mary the mother of James, and Salome bought spices, so that they might go and anoint him. 2 And very early on the first day of the week, when the sun had risen, they went to the tomb. 3 They had been saying to one another, "Who will roll away the stone for us from the entrance to the tomb?" 4 When they looked up, they saw that the stone, which was very large, already had been rolled back. 5 As they entered the tomb, they saw a young man, dressed in a white robe, sitting on the right side; and they were alarmed. 6 But he said to them, "Do not be alarmed; you are looking for Jesus of Nazareth, who was crucified. He has been raised; he is not here. Look, there is the place they laid him. 7 But go, tell his disciples and Peter that he is going ahead of you to Galilee; there you will see him, just as he told you." 8 So they went out and fled from the tomb, for terror and amazement had seized them; and they said nothing to anyone, for they were afraid.[r]

THE SHORTER ENDING OF MARK

[And all that had been commanded them they told briefly to those around Peter. And afterward Jesus himself sent out through them, from east to west, the sacred and imperishable proclamation of eternal salvation.[s]]

THE LONGER ENDING OF MARK

Jesus Appears to Mary Magdalene

9 [Now after he rose early on the first day of the week, he appeared first to Mary Magdalene, from whom he had cast out seven demons. 10 She went out and told those who had been with him, while they were mourning and weeping. 11 But when they heard that he was alive and had been seen by her, they would not believe it.

[r] Some of the most ancient authorities bring the book to a close at the end of verse 8. One authority concludes the book with the shorter ending; others include the shorter ending and then continue with verses 9-20. In most authorities verses 9-20 follow immediately after verse 8, though in some of these authorities the passage is marked as being doubtful.

[s] Other ancient authorities add *Amen*

---

16 Καὶ διαγενομένου τοῦ σαββάτου [ἡ]
And   passing   the   sabbath[a]   -
= when the sabbath was past

Μαρία ἡ Μαγδαληνὴ καὶ Μαρία ἡ [τοῦ]
Mary the Magdalene   and Mary the [mother]

Ἰακώβου καὶ Σαλώμη ἠγόρασαν ἀρώματα
of James   and Salome   bought   spices

ἵνα ἐλθοῦσαι ἀλείψωσιν αὐτόν. 2 καὶ λίαν
that coming they might anoint him.   And   very

πρωὶ [τῇ] μιᾷ τῶν σαββάτων ἔρχονται
early on   the first day of the week†   they come

ἐπὶ τὸ μνῆμα, ἀνατείλαντος τοῦ ἡλίου.
upon the tomb,   rising   the   sun.[a]
= as the sun rose.

3 καὶ ἔλεγον πρὸς ἑαυτάς· τίς ἀποκυλίσει
And   they said to themselves: Who will roll away

ἡμῖν τὸν λίθον ἐκ τῆς θύρας τοῦ μνημείου;
for us the stone out of the door of the tomb?

4 καὶ ἀναβλέψασαι θεωροῦσιν ὅτι ἀνακεκύλισται
And   looking up   they behold that has been rolled back

ὁ λίθος· ἦν γὰρ μέγας σφόδρα. 5 καὶ
the stone;   for it was great   exceedingly.   And

εἰσελθοῦσαι εἰς τὸ μνημεῖον εἶδον νεανίσκον
entering   into the tomb   they saw a young man

καθήμενον ἐν τοῖς δεξιοῖς περιβεβλημένον
sitting   on the right   *having been* clothed

στολὴν λευκήν, καὶ ἐξεθαμβήθησαν. 6 ὁ δὲ
robe [in] a white, and they were greatly astonished. But he

λέγει αὐταῖς· μὴ ἐκθαμβεῖσθε· Ἰησοῦν
says to them: Be not greatly astonished;   Jesus

ζητεῖτε τὸν Ναζαρηνὸν τὸν ἐσταυρωμένον·
ye seek the   Nazarene   - *having been* crucified;

ἠγέρθη, οὐκ ἔστιν ὧδε· ἴδε ὁ τόπος
he was raised, he is not   here; behold[,] the place

ὅπου ἔθηκαν αὐτόν. 7 ἀλλὰ ὑπάγετε εἴπατε
where they put him.   But   go ye   tell

τοῖς μαθηταῖς αὐτοῦ καὶ τῷ Πέτρῳ ὅτι
the disciples of him and   - Peter   that

προάγει ὑμᾶς εἰς τὴν Γαλιλαίαν· ἐκεῖ
he goes before you   to   - Galilee;   there

αὐτὸν ὄψεσθε, καθὼς εἶπεν ὑμῖν. 8 καὶ
him   ye will see,   as   he told you.   And

ἐξελθοῦσαι ἔφυγον ἀπὸ τοῦ μνημείου, εἶχεν
going forth they fled from   the   tomb,   [b]had

γὰρ αὐτὰς τρόμος καὶ ἔκστασις· καὶ
[a]for [b]them [a]trembling [a]and [b]bewilderment; and

οὐδενὶ οὐδὲν εἶπαν· ἐφοβοῦντο γάρ.
no one no(any)thing they told;   for they were afraid.

9 Ἀναστὰς δὲ πρωὶ πρώτη σαββάτου
And rising   early   on the first day of the week†

ἐφάνη πρῶτον Μαρίᾳ τῇ Μαγδαληνῇ, παρ'
he appeared first to Mary the   Magdalene,   from

ἧς ἐκβεβλήκει ἑπτὰ δαιμόνια. 10 ἐκείνη
whom he had expelled seven demons.   That [one]
= She

πορευθεῖσα ἀπήγγειλεν τοῖς μετ' αὐτοῦ
going   reported   to the [ones] with   him
= those who had been with him

γενομένοις πενθοῦσι καὶ κλαίουσιν· 11 κἀκεῖνοι
having been   mourning   and   weeping;   and those

ἀκούσαντες ὅτι ζῇ καὶ ἐθεάθη ὑπ' αὐτῆς
hearing   that he lives and was seen   by   her

Chapter 16

The Resurrection

WHEN the Sabbath was over, Mary Magdalene, Mary the mother of James, and Salome bought spices so that they might go to anoint Jesus' body. 2 Very early on the first day of the week, just after sunrise, they were on their way to the tomb 3 and they asked each other, "Who will roll the stone away from the entrance of the tomb?"

4 But when they looked up, they saw that the stone, which was very large, had been rolled away. 5 As they entered the tomb, they saw a young man dressed in a white robe sitting on the right side, and they were alarmed.

6 "Don't be alarmed," he said. "You are looking for Jesus the Nazarene, who was crucified. He has risen! He is not here. See the place where they laid him. 7 But go, tell his disciples and Peter, 'He is going ahead of you into Galilee. There you will see him, just as he told you.'"

8 Trembling and bewildered, the women went out and fled from the tomb. They said nothing to anyone, because they were afraid.

[The most reliable early manuscripts and other ancient witnesses do not have Mark 16:9-20.]

9 When Jesus rose early on the first day of the week, he appeared first to Mary Magdalene, out of whom he had driven seven demons. 10 She went and told those who had been with him and who were mourning and weeping. 11 When they heard that Jesus was alive and that she had seen him, they did not believe it.

Jesus Appears to Two Disciples

12 After this he appeared in another form to two of them, as they were walking into the country. 13 And they went back and told the rest, but they did not believe them.

Jesus Commissions the Disciples

14 Later he appeared to the eleven themselves as they were sitting at the table; and he upbraided them for their lack of faith and stubbornness, because they had not believed those who saw him after he had risen. [t] 15 And he said to them, "Go into all the world and proclaim the good news [u] to the whole creation. 16 The one who believes and is baptized will be saved; but the one who does not believe will be condemned. 17 And these signs will accompany those who believe: by using my name they will cast out demons; they will speak in new tongues; 18 they will pick up snakes in their hands, [v] and if they drink any deadly thing, it will not hurt them; they will lay their hands on the sick, and they will recover."

The Ascension of Jesus

19 So then the Lord Jesus, after he had spoken to them, was taken up into heaven and sat down at the right hand of God. 20 And they went out and proclaimed the good news everywhere, while the Lord worked with them and confirmed the message by the signs that accompanied it. [w]]

[t] Other ancient authorities add, in whole or in part, *And they excused themselves, saying, "This age of lawlessness and unbelief is under Satan, who does not allow the truth and power of God to prevail over the unclean things of the spirits. Therefore reveal your righteousness now"—thus they spoke to Christ. And Christ replied to them, "The term of years of Satan's power has been fulfilled, but other terrible things draw near. And for those who have sinned I was handed over to death, that they may return to the truth and sin no more, that they may inherit the spiritual and imperishable glory of righteousness that is in heaven."*

[u] Or *gospel*

[v] Other ancient authorities lack *in their hands*

[w] Other ancient authorities add *Amen*

ἠπίστησαν. **12** Μετὰ δὲ ταῦτα δυσὶν ἐξ
disbelieved. And after these things to two of

αὐτῶν περιπατοῦσιν ἐφανερώθη ἐν ἑτέρᾳ
them walking he was manifested in a different

μορφῇ πορευομένοις εἰς ἀγρόν· **13** κἀκεῖνοι
form going into [the] country; and those

ἀπελθόντες ἀπήγγειλαν τοῖς λοιποῖς· οὐδὲ
going reported to the rest; neither

ἐκείνοις ἐπίστευσαν. **14** Ὕστερον [δὲ]
those they believed. And later

ἀνακειμένοις αὐτοῖς τοῖς ἕνδεκα ἐφανερώθη,
to the reclining them the eleven he was manifested,
= to the eleven as they reclined

καὶ ὠνείδισεν τὴν ἀπιστίαν αὐτῶν καὶ
and reproached the disbelief of them and

σκληροκαρδίαν ὅτι τοῖς θεασαμένοις αὐτὸν
hardness of heart because the [ones] beholding him

ἐγηγερμένον οὐκ ἐπίστευσαν. **15** καὶ εἶπεν
having been raised they did not believe. And he said

αὐτοῖς· πορευθέντες εἰς τὸν κόσμον ἅπαντα
to them: Going into ²the ³world ¹all

κηρύξατε τὸ εὐαγγέλιον πάσῃ τῇ κτίσει.
proclaim ye the gospel to all the creation.

16 ὁ πιστεύσας καὶ βαπτισθεὶς σωθήσεται,
The [one] believing and being baptized will be saved,

ὁ δὲ ἀπιστήσας κατακριθήσεται. **17** σημεῖα
but the [one] disbelieving will be condemned. ²signs

δὲ τοῖς πιστεύσασιν ταῦτα παρακολουθήσει·
¹And ⁴the ⁵[ones] ⁶believing ³these ⁷will follow:

ἐν τῷ ὀνόματί μου δαιμόνια ἐκβαλοῦσιν,
in the name of me demons they will expel,

γλώσσαις λαλήσουσιν καιναῖς, **18** ὄφεις
³tongues ¹they will speak ²with new, serpents

ἀροῦσιν κἂν θανάσιμόν τι πίωσιν
they will take and if ²deadly ¹anything ³they drink

οὐ μὴ αὐτοὺς βλάψῃ, ἐπὶ ἀρρώστους χεῖρας
by no means them it will hurt, on sick [ones] hands

ἐπιθήσουσιν καὶ καλῶς ἕξουσιν. **19** Ὁ μὲν
they will place *on* and well they will have. ¹The ⁴there-
= they will recover.

οὖν κύριος [Ἰησοῦς] μετὰ τὸ λαλῆσαι
fore ²Lord ³Jesus after the to speak
= speaking

αὐτοῖς ἀνελήμφθη εἰς τὸν οὐρανὸν καὶ
to them was taken up into – heaven and

ἐκάθισεν ἐκ δεξιῶν τοῦ θεοῦ. **20** ἐκεῖνοι
sat at [the] right [hand] – of God. those

δὲ ἐξελθόντες ἐκήρυξαν πανταχοῦ, τοῦ
But going forth proclaimed everywhere, the

κυρίου συνεργοῦντος καὶ τὸν λόγον
Lord working with and the word
= while the Lord worked with [them] and confirmed the word

βεβαιοῦντος διὰ τῶν ἐπακολουθούντων
confirming² through the accompanying

σημείων.
signs.

---

12 Afterward Jesus appeared in a different form to two of them while they were walking in the country. 13 These returned and reported it to the rest; but they did not believe them either.

14 Later Jesus appeared to the Eleven as they were eating; he rebuked them for their lack of faith and their stubborn refusal to believe those who had seen him after he had risen.

15 He said to them, "Go into all the world and preach the good news to all creation. 16 Whoever believes and is baptized will be saved, but whoever does not believe will be condemned. 17 And these signs will accompany those who believe: In my name they will drive out demons; they will speak in new tongues; 18 they will pick up snakes with their hands; and when they drink deadly poison, it will not hurt them at all; they will place their hands on sick people, and they will get well."

19 After the Lord Jesus had spoken to them, he was taken up into heaven and he sat at the right hand of God. 20 Then the disciples went out and preached everywhere, and the Lord worked with them and confirmed his word by the signs that accompanied it.

Luke

Chapter 1

Dedication to Theophilus

SINCE many have undertaken to set down an orderly account of the events that have been fulfilled among us, [2]just as they were handed on to us by those who from the beginning were eyewitnesses and servants of the word, [3]I too decided, after investigating everything carefully from the very first,[a] to write an orderly account for you, most excellent Theophilus, [4]so that you may know the truth concerning the things about which you have been instructed.

The Birth of John the Baptist Foretold

[5] In the days of King Herod of Judea, there was a priest named Zechariah, who belonged to the priestly order of Abijah. His wife was a descendant of Aaron, and her name was Elizabeth. [6]Both of them were righteous before God, living blamelessly according to all the commandments and regulations of the Lord. [7]But they had no children, because Elizabeth was barren, and both were getting on in years.

[8] Once when he was serving as priest before God and his section was on duty, [9]he was chosen by lot, according to the custom of the priesthood, to enter the sanctuary of the Lord and offer incense. [10]Now at the time of the incense offering, the whole assembly of the people was praying outside. [11]Then there appeared to him an angel of the Lord, standing at the right side of the altar of incense. [12]When Zechariah saw him, he was terrified; and fear overwhelmed him. [13]But the angel said to him, "Do not be afraid, Zechariah, for your prayer has been heard. Your wife

1 Ἐπειδήπερ πολλοὶ ἐπεχείρησαν ἀνατάξασθαι
Since many took in hand to draw up

διήγησιν περὶ τῶν πεπληροφορημένων
a narrative concerning ¹the ²having been fully carried out

ἐν ἡμῖν πραγμάτων, **2** καθὼς παρέδοσαν ἡμῖν
⁴among ⁵us ³matters, as delivered to us

οἱ ἀπ' ἀρχῆς αὐτόπται καὶ ὑπηρέται
the [ones] from [the] beginning eyewitnesses and attendants

γενόμενοι τοῦ λόγου, **3** ἔδοξε κἀμοὶ
becoming of the Word, it seemed good to me also

παρηκολουθηκότι ἄνωθεν πᾶσιν ἀκριβῶς
having investigated from their source all things accurately

καθεξῆς σοι γράψαι, κράτιστε Θεόφιλε,
²in order ³to thee ¹to write, most excellent Theophilus,

4 ἵνα ἐπιγνῶς περὶ ὧν
that thou mightest know ⁴concerning ¹which

κατηχήθης λόγων τὴν ἀσφάλειαν.
⁵thou wast instructed ²of [the] things ³the ³reliability.

5 Ἐγένετο ἐν ταῖς ἡμέραις
There was in the days

Ἡρῴδου βασιλέως τῆς Ἰουδαίας ἱερεύς
of Herod king - of Judæa ¹priest

τις ὀνόματι Ζαχαρίας ἐξ ἐφημερίας Ἀβιά,
¹a certain by name Zacharias of [the] course of Abia,

καὶ γυνὴ αὐτῷ ἐκ τῶν θυγατέρων Ἀαρών,
and wife to him° of the daughters of Aaron,
=his wife

καὶ τὸ ὄνομα αὐτῆς Ἐλισάβετ. **6** ἦσαν δὲ
and the name of her Elisabeth. And they were

δίκαιοι ἀμφότεροι ἐναντίον τοῦ θεοῦ,
righteous both before - God,

πορευόμενοι ἐν πάσαις ταῖς ἐντολαῖς καὶ
going in all the commandments and

δικαιώμασιν τοῦ κυρίου ἄμεμπτοι. **7** καὶ
ordinances of the Lord blameless. And

οὐκ ἦν αὐτοῖς τέκνον, καθότι ἦν ἡ
there was not to them a child,° because ³was -
=they had no child,

Ἐλισάβετ στεῖρα, καὶ ἀμφότεροι προβεβηκότες
¹Elisabeth barren, and both having advanced

ἐν ταῖς ἡμέραις αὐτῶν ἦσαν. **8** Ἐγένετο
in the days of them were. it came to pass

δὲ ἐν τῷ ἱερατεύειν αὐτὸν ἐν τῇ τάξει
Now in the to serve as priest him⁰° in the order
=while he served as priest

τῆς ἐφημερίας αὐτοῦ ἔναντι τοῦ θεοῦ,
of the course of him before - God,

9 κατὰ τὸ ἔθος τῆς ἱερατείας ἔλαχε τοῦ
according to the custom of the priesthood his lot was -

θυμιᾶσαι εἰσελθὼν εἰς τὸν ναὸν τοῦ κυρίου,
to burn incense⁰ entering into the shrine of the Lord,

10 καὶ πᾶν τὸ πλῆθος ἦν τοῦ λαοῦ
and all ¹the ²multitude ⁵was ³of the ⁴people

προσευχόμενον ἔξω τῇ ὥρᾳ τοῦ θυμιάματος.
praying outside at the hour - of incense.

11 ὤφθη δὲ αὐτῷ ἄγγελος κυρίου ἑστὼς
And there appeared to him an angel of [the] Lord standing

ἐκ δεξιῶν τοῦ θυσιαστηρίου τοῦ θυμιάματος.
on [the] right of the altar - of incense.

12 καὶ ἐταράχθη Ζαχαρίας ἰδών, καὶ φόβος
And was troubled Zacharias seeing, and fear

ἐπέπεσεν ἐπ' αὐτόν. **13** εἶπεν δὲ πρὸς
fell on upon him. But said to

αὐτὸν ὁ ἄγγελος· μὴ φοβοῦ, Ζαχαρία,
him the angel: Fear not, Zacharias,

διότι εἰσηκούσθη ἡ δέησίς σου, καὶ ἡ
because was heard the request of thee, and the

Chapter 1

Introduction

MANY have undertaken to draw up an account of the things that have been fulfilled[a] among us, [2]just as they were handed down to us by those who from the first were eyewitnesses and servants of the word. [3]Therefore, since I myself have carefully investigated everything from the beginning, it seemed good also to me to write an orderly account for you, most excellent Theophilus, [4]so that you may know the certainty of the things you have been taught.

The Birth of John the Baptist Foretold

[5]In the time of Herod king of Judea there was a priest named Zechariah, who belonged to the priestly division of Abijah; his wife Elizabeth was also a descendant of Aaron. [6]Both of them were upright in the sight of God, observing all the Lord's commandments and regulations blamelessly. [7]But they had no children, because Elizabeth was barren; and they were both well along in years.

[8]Once when Zechariah's division was on duty and he was serving as priest before God, [9]he was chosen by lot, according to the custom of the priesthood, to go into the temple of the Lord and burn incense. [10]And when the time for the burning of incense came, all the assembled worshipers were praying outside.

[11]Then an angel of the Lord appeared to him, standing at the right side of the altar of incense. [12]When Zechariah saw him, he was startled and was gripped with fear. [13]But the angel said to him: "Do not be afraid, Zechariah; your prayer has been heard. Your wife Elizabeth

---

[a] Or for a long time

[a]1 Or been surely believed

Elizabeth will bear you a son, and you will name him John. 14 You will have joy and gladness, and many will rejoice at his birth, 15 for he will be great in the sight of the Lord. He must never drink wine or strong drink; even before his birth he will be filled with the Holy Spirit. 16 He will turn many of the people of Israel to the Lord their God. 17 With the spirit and power of Elijah he will go before him, to turn the hearts of parents to their children, and the disobedient to the wisdom of the righteous, to make ready a people prepared for the Lord." 18 Zechariah said to the angel, "How will I know that this is so? For I am an old man, and my wife is getting on in years." 19 The angel replied, "I am Gabriel. I stand in the presence of God, and I have been sent to speak to you and to bring you this good news. 20 But now, because you did not believe my words, which will be fulfilled in their time, you will become mute, unable to speak, until the day these things occur."

21 Meanwhile the people were waiting for Zechariah, and wondered at his delay in the sanctuary. 22 When he did come out, he could not speak to them, and they realized that he had seen a vision in the sanctuary. He kept motioning to them and remained unable to speak. 23 When

---

γυνή σου 'Ελισάβετ γεννήσει υἱόν σοι,
wife of thee Elisabeth will bear a son to thee,

καὶ καλέσεις τὸ ὄνομα αὐτοῦ 'Ιωάννην·
and thou shalt call the name of him John;

14 καὶ ἔσται χαρά σοι καὶ ἀγαλλίασις,^e
and there shall be joy to thee and gladness,
=thou shalt have joy and gladness,

καὶ πολλοὶ ἐπὶ τῇ γενέσει αὐτοῦ χαρή-
and many over the birth of him will

σονται. 15 ἔσται γὰρ μέγας ἐνώπιον
rejoice. For he will be great in the eyes of

κυρίου, καὶ οἶνον καὶ σίκερα οὐ μὴ
[the] Lord, and wine and strong drink by no means

πίῃ, καὶ πνεύματος ἁγίου πλησθήσεται
may he drink, and of(with) Spirit [the] Holy he will be filled

ἔτι ἐκ κοιλίας μητρὸς αὐτοῦ, 16 καὶ
even from [the] womb of [the] mother of him, and

πολλοὺς τῶν υἱῶν 'Ισραὴλ ἐπιστρέψει ἐπὶ κύριον
many of the sons of Israel he will turn to [the] Lord

τὸν θεὸν αὐτῶν· 17 καὶ αὐτὸς προελεύσεται
the God of them; and he will go before

ἐνώπιον αὐτοῦ ἐν πνεύματι καὶ δυνάμει
before him in [the] spirit and power

'Ηλίου, ἐπιστρέψαι καρδίας πατέρων ἐπὶ
of Elias, to turn [the] hearts of fathers to

τέκνα καὶ ἀπειθεῖς ἐν φρονήσει
children and disobedient [ones] to [the] understanding

δικαίων, ἑτοιμάσαι κυρίῳ λαὸν κατεσκευασ-
of [the] just, to prepare for [the] Lord a people having been

μένον. 18 καὶ εἶπεν Ζαχαρίας πρὸς τὸν ἄγγελον·
prepared. And said Zacharias to the angel:

κατὰ τί γνώσομαι τοῦτο; ἐγὼ γάρ εἰμι
By what shall I know this? for I am

πρεσβύτης καὶ ἡ γυνή μου προβεβηκυῖα
old and the wife of me having advanced

ἐν ταῖς ἡμέραις αὐτῆς. 19 καὶ ἀποκριθεὶς
in the days of her. And answering

ὁ ἄγγελος εἶπεν αὐτῷ· ἐγώ εἰμι Γαβριὴλ
the angel said to him: I am Gabriel

ὁ παρεστηκὼς ἐνώπιον τοῦ θεοῦ, καὶ
the [one] standing before - God, and

ἀπεστάλην λαλῆσαι πρὸς σὲ καὶ εὐαγ-
I was sent to speak to thee and to

γελίσασθαί σοι ταῦτα· 20 καὶ ἰδοὺ
announce to thee these things; and behold

ἔσῃ σιωπῶν καὶ μὴ δυνάμενος λαλῆσαι
thou shalt be being silent and not being able to speak

ἄχρι ἧς ἡμέρας γένηται ταῦτα, ἀνθ' ὧν οὐκ
until which day happens these things, because not
=the day when these things happen,

ἐπίστευσας τοῖς λόγοις μου, οἵτινες πληρω-
thou believedst the words of me, which will be

θήσονται εἰς τὸν καιρὸν αὐτῶν. 21 καὶ ἦν
fulfilled in the time of them. And was

ὁ λαὸς προσδοκῶν τὸν Ζαχαρίαν, καὶ
the people expecting - Zacharias, and

ἐθαύμαζον ἐν τῷ χρονίζειν ἐν τῷ ναῷ
they marvelled in(at) the to delay in the shrine
=when he delayed in the shrine.

αὐτόν. 22 ἐξελθὼν δὲ οὐκ ἐδύνατο λαλῆσαι
him.^{be} And going out he was not able to speak

αὐτοῖς καὶ ἐπέγνωσαν ὅτι ὀπτασίαν ἑώρακεν
to them, and they knew that a vision he has(had) seen

ἐν τῷ ναῷ· καὶ αὐτὸς ἦν διανεύων
in the shrine; and he was beckoning

αὐτοῖς, καὶ διέμενεν κωφός. 23 καὶ
to them, and remained dumb. And

---

will bear you a son, and you are to give him the name John. 14 He will be a joy and delight to you, and many will rejoice because of his birth, 15 for he will be great in the sight of the Lord. He is never to take wine or other fermented drink, and he will be filled with the Holy Spirit even from birth.^b 16 Many of the people of Israel will he bring back to the Lord their God. 17 And he will go on before the Lord, in the spirit and power of Elijah, to turn the hearts of the fathers to their children and the disobedient to the wisdom of the righteous—to make ready a people prepared for the Lord."

18 Zechariah asked the angel, "How can I be sure of this? I am an old man and my wife is well along in years."

19 The angel answered, "I am Gabriel. I stand in the presence of God, and I have been sent to speak to you and to tell you this good news. 20 And now you will be silent and not able to speak until the day this happens, because you did not believe my words, which will come true at their proper time."

21 Meanwhile, the people were waiting for Zechariah and wondering why he stayed so long in the temple. 22 When he came out, he could not speak to them. They realized he had seen a vision in the temple, for he kept making signs to them but remained unable to speak.

^b15 Or from his mother's womb

his time of service was ended, he went to his home.

24 After those days his wife Elizabeth conceived, and for five months she remained in seclusion. She said, 25 "This is what the Lord has done for me when he looked favorably on me and took away the disgrace I have endured among my people."

The Birth of Jesus Foretold

26 In the sixth month the angel Gabriel was sent by God to a town in Galilee called Nazareth, 27 to a virgin engaged to a man whose name was Joseph, of the house of David. The virgin's name was Mary. 28 And he came to her and said, "Greetings, favored one! The Lord is with you."[b] 29 But she was much perplexed by his words and pondered what sort of greeting this might be. 30 The angel said to her, "Do not be afraid, Mary, for you have found favor with God. 31 And now, you will conceive in your womb and bear a son, and you will name him Jesus. 32 He will be great, and will be called the Son of the Most High, and the Lord God will give to him the throne of his ancestor David. 33 He will reign over the house of Jacob forever, and of his kingdom there will be no end." 34 Mary said to the angel, "How can this be, since I am a virgin?"[c] 35 The angel said to her, "The Holy Spirit will come upon you, and the power of the Most High will overshadow you; therefore the

---

ἐγένετο　ὡς ἐπλήσθησαν αἱ ἡμέραι τῆς
it came to pass when were fulfilled the days of the

λειτουργίας αὐτοῦ, ἀπῆλθεν εἰς τὸν οἶκον
service of him, he went away to the house

αὐτοῦ. 24 Μετὰ δὲ ταύτας τὰς ἡμέρας
of him. And after these - days

συνέλαβεν Ἐλισάβετ ἡ γυνὴ αὐτοῦ, καὶ
conceived Elisabeth the wife of him, and

περιέκρυβεν ἑαυτὴν μῆνας πέντε, λέγουσα
hid herself months five, saying[.]

25 ὅτι οὕτως μοι πεποίηκεν κύριος ἐν
- Thus to me has done [the] Lord in

ἡμέραις αἷς ἐπεῖδεν ἀφελεῖν ὄνειδός
days in which he looked upon to take away reproach

μου ἐν ἀνθρώποις.
of me among men.

26 Ἐν δὲ τῷ μηνὶ τῷ ἕκτῳ ἀπεστάλη
Now in the month - sixth was sent

ὁ ἄγγελος Γαβριὴλ ἀπὸ τοῦ θεοῦ εἰς
the angel Gabriel from - God to

πόλιν τῆς Γαλιλαίας ᾗ ὄνομα[e] Ναζαρέθ,
a city - of Galilee to which name Nazareth,
　　　　　　　　　= the name of which [was]

27 πρὸς παρθένον ἐμνηστευμένην ἀνδρὶ ᾧ ὄνομα
to a virgin having been betrothed to a man to whom name[e]

Ἰωσήφ, ἐξ οἴκου Δαυίδ, καὶ τὸ ὄνομα
Joseph, of [the] house of David, and the name

τῆς παρθένου Μαριάμ. 28 καὶ εἰσελθὼν
of the virgin [was] Mary. And entering

πρὸς αὐτὴν εἶπεν· χαῖρε, κεχαριτωμένη, ὁ
to her he said: Hail, having been favoured [one], the

κύριος μετὰ σοῦ. 29 ἡ δὲ ἐπὶ τῷ λόγῳ
Lord [is] with thee. And she at the saying

διεταράχθη, καὶ διελογίζετο ποταπὸς εἴη
was greatly disturbed, and considered of what sort might be[e]

ὁ ἀσπασμὸς οὗτος. 30 καὶ εἶπεν ὁ ἄγγελος
- greeting[e] this. And said the angel

αὐτῇ· μὴ φοβοῦ, Μαριάμ· εὗρες γὰρ
to her: Fear not, Mary: for thou didst find

χάριν παρὰ τῷ θεῷ. 31 καὶ ἰδοὺ συλλήμψῃ
favour with - God. And behold thou wilt conceive

ἐν γαστρὶ καὶ τέξῃ υἱόν, καὶ καλέσεις τὸ
in womb and bear a son, and thou shalt call the

ὄνομα αὐτοῦ Ἰησοῦν. 32 οὗτος ἔσται μέγας
name of him Jesus. This will be great

καὶ υἱὸς ὑψίστου κληθήσεται, καὶ δώσει
and Son of [the] Most High will be called, and will give

αὐτῷ κύριος ὁ θεὸς τὸν θρόνον Δαυὶδ
him [the] Lord - God the throne of David

τοῦ πατρὸς αὐτοῦ, 33 καὶ βασιλεύσει ἐπὶ
the father of him, and he will reign over

τὸν οἶκον Ἰακὼβ εἰς τοὺς αἰῶνας, καὶ
the house of Jacob unto the ages, and
　　　　　　　　　　　= for ever,

τῆς βασιλείας αὐτοῦ οὐκ ἔσται τέλος.
of the kingdom of him there will not be an end.

34 εἶπεν δὲ Μαριὰμ πρὸς τὸν ἄγγελον·
And said Mary to the angel:

πῶς ἔσται τοῦτο, ἐπεὶ ἄνδρα οὐ γινώσκω;
How will be this, since a man I know not?

35 καὶ ἀποκριθεὶς ὁ ἄγγελος εἶπεν αὐτῇ·
And answering the angel said . to her:

πνεῦμα ἅγιον ἐπελεύσεται ἐπὶ σέ, καὶ
[The] Spirit Holy[1] will come upon upon thee, and

δύναμις ὑψίστου ἐπισκιάσει σοι· διὸ
[the] power of [the] Most High will overshadow thee; wherefore

---

23 When his time of service was completed, he returned home. 24 After this his wife Elizabeth became pregnant and for five months remained in seclusion. 25 "The Lord has done this for me," she said. "In these days he has shown his favor and taken away my disgrace among the people."

The Birth of Jesus Foretold

26 In the sixth month, God sent the angel Gabriel to Nazareth, a town in Galilee, 27 to a virgin pledged to be married to a man named Joseph, a descendant of David. The virgin's name was Mary. 28 The angel went to her and said, "Greetings, you who are highly favored! The Lord is with you." 29 Mary was greatly troubled at his words and wondered what kind of greeting this might be. 30 But the angel said to her, "Do not be afraid, Mary, you have found favor with God. 31 You will be with child and give birth to a son, and you are to give him the name Jesus. 32 He will be great and will be called the Son of the Most High. The Lord God will give him the throne of his father David, 33 and he will reign over the house of Jacob forever; his kingdom will never end." 34 "How will this be," Mary asked the angel, "since I am a virgin?" 35 The angel answered, "The Holy Spirit will come upon you, and the power of the Most High will overshadow you. So the holy

---

[b] Other ancient authorities add Blessed are you among women
[c] Gk I do not know a man

child to be born^d will be holy; he will be called Son of God. 36 And now, your relative Elizabeth in her old age has also conceived a son; and this is the sixth month for her who was said to be barren. 37 For nothing will be impossible with God." 38 Then Mary said, "Here am I, the servant of the Lord; let it be with me according to your word." Then the angel departed from her.

Mary Visits Elizabeth

39 In those days Mary set out and went with haste to a Judean town in the hill country, 40 where she entered the house of Zechariah and greeted Elizabeth. 41 When Elizabeth heard Mary's greeting, the child leaped in her womb. And Elizabeth was filled with the Holy Spirit 42 and exclaimed with a loud cry, "Blessed are you among women, and blessed is the fruit of your womb. 43 And why has this happened to me, that the mother of my Lord comes to me? 44 For as soon as I heard the sound of your greeting, the child in my womb leaped for joy. 45 And blessed is she who believed that there would be^e a fulfillment of what was spoken to her by the Lord."

Mary's Song of Praise

46 And Mary^f said,
47 "My soul magnifies the Lord, and my spirit rejoices in God my Savior,
48 for he has looked with favor on the lowliness of his servant. Surely, from now on all generations will call me blessed;
49 for the Mighty One has done great things for me,

καὶ τὸ γεννώμενον ἅγιον κληθήσεται υἱὸς θεοῦ.
also the thing being born holy will be called[,] Son of God.

36 καὶ ἰδοὺ Ἐλισάβετ ἡ συγγενίς σου καὶ
And behold Elisabeth the relative of thee also

αὐτὴ συνείληφεν υἱὸν ἐν γήρει αὐτῆς, καὶ
she conceived a son in old age of her, and

οὗτος μὴν ἕκτος ἐστὶν αὐτῇ τῇ καλουμένῃ
this month sixth is with her the [one] being called

στεῖρα· 37 ὅτι οὐκ ἀδυνατήσει παρὰ τοῦ
barren; because will not be impossible with -

θεοῦ πᾶν ῥῆμα. 38 εἶπεν δὲ Μαριάμ· ἰδοὺ ἡ
God every word. And said Mary: Behold[,] the

δούλη κυρίου· γένοιτό μοι κατὰ
handmaid of [the]Lord; may it be to me according to

τὸ ῥῆμά σου. καὶ ἀπῆλθεν ἀπ' αὐτῆς
the word of thee. And went away from her

ὁ ἄγγελος. 39 Ἀναστᾶσα δὲ Μαριὰμ ἐν
the angel. And rising up Mary in

ταῖς ἡμέραις ταύταις ἐπορεύθη εἰς τὴν
- days these she went to the

ὀρεινὴν μετὰ σπουδῆς εἰς πόλιν Ἰούδα,
mountain country with haste to a city of Juda,

40 καὶ εἰσῆλθεν εἰς τὸν οἶκον Ζαχαρίου
and entered into the house of Zacharias

καὶ ἠσπάσατο τὴν Ἐλισάβετ. 41 καὶ
and greeted - Elisabeth. And

ἐγένετο ὡς ἤκουσεν τὸν ἀσπασμὸν τῆς
it came to pass when ²heard ³the ⁴greeting -

Μαρίας ἡ Ἐλισάβετ, ἐσκίρτησεν τὸ βρέφος
⁵of Mary ¹Elisabeth, leaped the babe

ἐν τῇ κοιλίᾳ αὐτῆς, καὶ ἐπλήσθη πνεύματος
in the womb of her, and ³was filled ²of(with) ⁵Spirit

ἁγίου ἡ Ἐλισάβετ, 42 καὶ ἀνεφώνησεν
⁴[the] Holy - ¹Elisabeth, and she called out

κραυγῇ μεγάλῃ καὶ εἶπεν· εὐλογημένη
cry with a great and said: Blessed [art]

σὺ ἐν γυναιξίν, καὶ εὐλογημένος ὁ καρπὸς
thou among women, and blessed [is] the fruit

τῆς κοιλίας σου. 43 καὶ πόθεν μοι τοῦτο
of the womb of thee. And whence to me this

ἵνα ἔλθῃ ἡ μήτηρ τοῦ κυρίου μου πρὸς
that comes the mother of the Lord of me to

ἐμέ; 44 ἰδοὺ γὰρ ὡς ἐγένετο ἡ φωνὴ τοῦ
me? For behold when came the sound of the

ἀσπασμοῦ σου εἰς τὰ ὦτά μου, ἐσκίρτησεν
greeting of thee in the ears of me, leaped

ἐν ἀγαλλιάσει τὸ βρέφος ἐν τῇ κοιλίᾳ
in gladness the babe in the womb

μου. 45 καὶ μακαρία ἡ πιστεύσασα ὅτι
of me. And blessed the [one] believing because

ἔσται τελείωσις τοῖς λελαλημένοις αὐτῇ
there shall be a completion to the things *having been* to her
spoken

παρὰ κυρίου. 46 Καὶ εἶπεν Μαριάμ·
from [the] Lord. And said Mary:

Μεγαλύνει ἡ ψυχή μου τὸν κύριον, 47 καὶ
Magnifies the soul of me the Lord, and

ἠγαλλίασεν τὸ πνεῦμά μου ἐπὶ τῷ θεῷ
exulted the spirit of me in - God

τῷ σωτῆρί μου· 48 ὅτι ἐπέβλεψεν ἐπὶ τὴν
the saviour of me; because he looked on upon the

ταπείνωσιν τῆς δούλης αὐτοῦ. ἰδοὺ γὰρ
humiliation of the handmaid of him. For behold

ἀπὸ τοῦ νῦν μακαριοῦσίν με πᾶσαι αἱ
from - now ⁴will ⁵deem ⁷blessed ⁶me ¹all ²the

γενεαί· 49 ὅτι ἐποίησέν μοι μεγάλα ὁ
³generations; because did to me great things the

---

one to be born will be called^c the Son of God. 36 Even Elizabeth your relative is going to have a child in her old age, and she who was said to be barren is in her sixth month. 37 For nothing is impossible with God."
38 "I am the Lord's servant," Mary answered. "May it be to me as you have said." Then the angel left her.

Mary Visits Elizabeth

39 At that time Mary got ready and hurried to a town in the hill country of Judea, 40 where she entered Zechariah's home and greeted Elizabeth. 41 When Elizabeth heard Mary's greeting, the baby leaped in her womb, and Elizabeth was filled with the Holy Spirit. 42 In a loud voice she exclaimed: "Blessed are you among women, and blessed is the child you will bear! 43 But why am I so favored, that the mother of my Lord should come to me? 44 As soon as the sound of your greeting reached my ears, the baby in my womb leaped for joy. 45 Blessed is she who has believed that what the Lord has said to her will be accomplished!"

Mary's Song

46 And Mary said:
"My soul glorifies the Lord
47 and my spirit rejoices in God my Savior,
48 for he has been mindful of the humble state of his servant. From now on all generations will call me blessed,
49 for the Mighty One has done great things for me—

---

^d Other ancient authorities add *of you*
^e Or *believed, for there will be*
^f Other ancient authorities read *Elizabeth*

^c 35 Or *So the child to be born will be called holy.*

and holy is his
name.

50 His mercy is for those
who fear him
from generation to
generation.

51 He has shown
strength with
his arm;
he has scattered the
proud in the
thoughts of their
hearts.

52 He has brought down
the powerful
from their
thrones,
and lifted up the
lowly;

53 he has filled the
hungry with
good things,
and sent the rich
away empty.

54 He has helped his
servant Israel,
in remembrance of
his mercy,

55 according to the
promise he
made to our
ancestors,
to Abraham and to
his descendants
forever."

56 And Mary remained
with her about three
months and then returned
to her home.

*The Birth of John the
Baptist*

57 Now the time came
for Elizabeth to give birth,
and she bore a son. 58 Her
neighbors and relatives
heard that the Lord had
shown her great mercy to
her, and they rejoiced with
her.

59 On the eighth day
they came to circumcise
the child, and they were going to name him Zechariah
after his father. 60 But his
mother said, "No; he is to
be called John." 61 They
said to her, "None of your
relatives has this name."
62 Then they began motioning to his father to find out
what name he wanted to
give him. 63 He asked for a
writing tablet and wrote,
"His name is John." And all
of them were amazed.
64 Immediately his mouth
was opened and his tongue

δυνατός.   καὶ   ἅγιον   τὸ   ὄνομα   αὐτοῦ,
Mighty [one].   And   holy   the   name   of him,

50 καὶ   τὸ   ἔλεος   αὐτοῦ   εἰς   γενεὰς   καὶ
and   the   mercy   of him   to   generations   and

γενεὰς   τοῖς   φοβουμένοις   αὐτόν.   51 Ἐποίησεν
generations   to the [ones] fearing   him.   He did

κράτος   ἐν   βραχίονι   αὐτοῦ,   διεσκόρπισεν
might   with   [the] arm   of him,   he scattered

ὑπερηφάνους   διανοίᾳ   καρδίας   αὐτῶν·
haughty [ones]   in [the] understanding   of [the] heart   of them;

52 καθεῖλεν   δυνάστας   ἀπὸ   θρόνων   καὶ   ὕψω-
he pulled down   potentates   from   thrones   and   exalt-

σεν   ταπεινούς,   53 πεινῶντας   ἐνέπλησεν
ed   humble [ones],   hungering [ones]   he filled

ἀγαθῶν   καὶ   πλουτοῦντας   ἐξαπέστειλεν
of(with) good things   and   rich [ones]   he sent away

κενούς.   54 ἀντελάβετο   Ἰσραὴλ   παιδὸς   αὐτοῦ,
empty.   He succoured   Israel   servant   of him,

μνησθῆναι   ἐλέους,   55 καθὼς   ἐλάλησεν
to remember   mercy,   as   he spoke

πρὸς   τοὺς   πατέρας   ἡμῶν,   τῷ   Ἀβραὰμ
to   the   fathers   of us,   - to Abraham

καὶ   τῷ   σπέρματι   αὐτοῦ   εἰς   τὸν   αἰῶνα.
and   to the   seed   of him   unto   the   age.
= for ever.

56 Ἔμεινεν   δὲ   Μαριὰμ   σὺν   αὐτῇ   ὡς
And remained   Mary   with   her   about

μῆνας   τρεῖς,   καὶ   ὑπέστρεψεν   εἰς   τὸν
months   three,   and   returned   to   the

οἶκον   αὐτῆς.
house   of her.

57 Τῇ   δὲ   Ἐλισάβετ   ἐπλήσθη   ὁ   χρόνος
-   Now   ⁴to Elisabeth   ³was fulfilled   ¹the   ⁴time

τοῦ   τεκεῖν   αὐτήν,   καὶ   ἐγέννησεν   υἱόν.
-   to bear   her,ᵇᵈ   and she brought forth   a son.
= that she should bear,

58 καὶ   ἤκουσαν   οἱ   περίοικοι   καὶ   οἱ
And   heard   the   neighbours   and   the

συγγενεῖς   αὐτῆς   ὅτι   ἐμεγάλυνεν   κύριος   τὸ
relatives   of her   that   magnified   [the] Lord   the

ἔλεος   αὐτοῦ   μετ'   αὐτῆς,   καὶ   συνέχαιρον
mercy   of him   with   her,   and they rejoiced with

αὐτῇ.   59 Καὶ   ἐγένετο   ἐν   τῇ   ἡμέρᾳ   τῇ
her.   And it came to pass   on   the   day   the

ὀγδόῃ   ἦλθον   περιτεμεῖν   τὸ   παιδίον,   καὶ
eighth   they came   to circumcise   the   child,   and

ἐκάλουν   αὐτὸ   ἐπὶ   τῷ   ὀνόματι   τοῦ   πατρὸς
were calling it(him)   by   the   name   of the   father

αὐτοῦ   Ζαχαρίαν.   60 καὶ   ἀποκριθεῖσα   ἡ
of him   Zacharias.   And   answering   the

μήτηρ   αὐτοῦ   εἶπεν·   οὐχί,   ἀλλὰ   κληθήσεται
mother   of him   said :   No,   but he shall be called

Ἰωάννης.   61 καὶ   εἶπαν   πρὸς   αὐτὴν   ὅτι
John.   And   they said   to   her[,]   -

οὐδείς   ἐστιν   ἐκ   τῆς   συγγενείας   σου   ὃς
No one   there is   of   the   kindred   of thee   who

καλεῖται   τῷ   ὀνόματι   τούτῳ.   62 ἐνένευον
is called   -   name   by this.   they nodded

δὲ   τῷ   πατρὶ   αὐτοῦ   τὸ   τί   ἂν   θέλοι
And to the   father   of him   -   what   he might wish

καλεῖσθαι   αὐτό.   63 καὶ   αἰτήσας   πινακίδιον
²to be called   ¹him.   And   asking for   a tablet

ἔγραψεν   λέγων·   Ἰωάννης   ἐστὶν   ὄνομα
he wrote   saying :   John   is   name

αὐτοῦ.   καὶ   ἐθαύμασαν   πάντες.   64 ἀνεῴχθη   δὲ
of him.   And they marvelled   all.   And was opened

τὸ   στόμα   αὐτοῦ   παραχρῆμα   καὶ   ἡ
the   mouth   of him   instantly   and   the

---

holy is his name.
50 His mercy extends to
those who fear him,
from generation to
generation.
51 He has performed
mighty deeds with
his arm;
he has scattered those
who are proud in
their inmost
thoughts.
52 He has brought down
rulers from their
thrones
but has lifted up the
humble.
53 He has filled the hungry
with good things
but has sent the rich
away empty.
54 He has helped his
servant Israel,
remembering to be
merciful
55 to Abraham and his
descendants
forever,
even as he said to our
fathers."

56 Mary stayed with Elizabeth for about three
months and then returned
home.

*The Birth of John the
Baptist*

57 When it was time for
Elizabeth to have her baby,
she gave birth to a son.
58 Her neighbors and relatives heard that the Lord
had shown her great mer-
cy, and they shared her joy.

59 On the eighth day they
came to circumcise the
child, and they were going
to name him after his father
Zechariah, 60 but his mother
spoke up and said, "No!
He is to be called John."
61 They said to her,
"There is no one among
your relatives who has that
name."

62 Then they made signs to
his father, to find out what
he would like to name the
child. 63 He asked for a writing tablet, and to every-
one's astonishment he
wrote, "His name is
John." 64 Immediately his
mouth was opened and his

freed, and he began to speak, praising God. ⁶⁵ Fear came over all their neighbors, and all these things were talked about throughout the entire hill country of Judea. ⁶⁶ All who heard them pondered them and said, "What then will this child become?" For, indeed, the hand of the Lord was with him.

Zechariah's Prophecy

67 Then his father Zechariah was filled with the Holy Spirit and spoke this prophecy:
⁶⁸ "Blessed be the Lord God of Israel, for he has looked favorably on his people and redeemed them.
69 He has raised up a mighty savior[g] for us in the house of his servant David,
70 as he spoke through the mouth of his holy prophets from of old,
71 that we would be saved from our enemies and from the hand of all who hate us.
72 Thus he has shown the mercy promised to our ancestors, and has remembered his holy covenant,
73 the oath that he swore to our ancestor Abraham, to grant us ⁷⁴ that we, being rescued from the hands of our enemies, might serve him without fear, ⁷⁵ in holiness and righteousness before him all our days.
76 And you, child, will be called the prophet of the Most High; for you will go before the Lord to prepare his ways,
77 to give knowledge of salvation to his people by the forgiveness of their sins.
78 By the tender mercy of our God, the dawn from on high will break upon[h] us,
79 to give light to those who sit in darkness and in the shadow of death.

[g] Gk *a horn of salvation*
[h] Other ancient authorities read *has broken upon*

γλῶσσα αὐτοῦ, καὶ ἐλάλει εὐλογῶν τὸν
tongue   of him,   and he spoke blessing   -

θεόν. 65 Καὶ ἐγένετο ἐπὶ πάντας φόβος
God.   And ¹came   ²on ⁴all   ¹fear

τοὺς περιοικοῦντας αὐτούς, καὶ ἐν ὅλῃ τῇ
the [ones] dwelling round them, and in all the

ὀρεινῇ τῆς Ἰουδαίας διελαλεῖτο πάντα
mountain country - of Judæa ⁴were talked over ¹all

τὰ ῥήματα ταῦτα, 66 καὶ ἔθεντο πάντες
  ²facts   ³these,   and   ⁴put   ¹all

οἱ ἀκούσαντες ἐν τῇ καρδίᾳ αὐτῶν,
¹the [ones] ³hearing in the heart   of them,

λέγοντες· τί ἄρα τὸ παιδίον τοῦτο ἔσται;
saying : What then - child   this   will be ?

καὶ γὰρ χεὶρ κυρίου ἦν μετ' αὐτοῦ.
for indeed [the] hand of [the] Lord was with him.

67 Καὶ Ζαχαρίας ὁ πατὴρ αὐτοῦ ἐπλήσθη
   And Zacharias the father of him was filled

πνεύματος ἁγίου καὶ ἐπροφήτευσεν λέγων·
of(with) Spirit [the] Holy and prophesied   saying :

68 Εὐλογητὸς κύριος ὁ θεὸς τοῦ Ἰσραήλ,
   Blessed [be] [the] Lord the God - of Israel,

ὅτι ἐπεσκέψατο καὶ ἐποίησεν λύτρωσιν τῷ
because he visited and wrought redemption for the

λαῷ αὐτοῦ, 69 καὶ ἤγειρεν κέρας σωτηρίας
people of him,   and raised a horn of salvation

ἡμῖν ἐν οἴκῳ Δαυὶδ παιδὸς αὐτοῦ, 70 καθὼς
for us in [the] house of David servant of him,   as

ἐλάλησεν διὰ στόματος τῶν ἁγίων ἀπ'
he spoke through [the] mouth of the ¹holy ⁴from

αἰῶνος προφητῶν αὐτοῦ, 71 σωτηρίαν ἐξ
⁵[the] age ²prophets ³of him,   salvation out of

ἐχθρῶν ἡμῶν καὶ ἐκ χειρὸς πάντων τῶν
[the] enemies of us and out of [the] hand of all the [ones]

μισούντων ἡμᾶς, 72 ποιῆσαι ἔλεος μετὰ
hating   us,   to perform mercy with

τῶν πατέρων ἡμῶν καὶ μνησθῆναι διαθήκης
the fathers of us and to remember [the] covenant

ἁγίας αὐτοῦ, 73 ὅρκον ὃν ὤμοσεν πρὸς Ἀβραὰμ
holy of him, [the] oath which he swore to Abraham

τὸν πατέρα ἡμῶν, 74 τοῦ δοῦναι ἡμῖν
the father of us,   - to give[d] us

ἀφόβως ἐκ χειρὸς ἐχθρῶν ῥυσθέντας
⁶fearlessly ²out of ³[the] hand ⁴of [our] enemies ¹having been delivered

λατρεύειν αὐτῷ 75 ἐν ὁσιότητι καὶ δικαιοσύνῃ
⁵to serve him   in holiness and righteousness

ἐνώπιον αὐτοῦ πάσαις ταῖς ἡμέραις ἡμῶν.
before him   all   the   days[e] of us.

76 Καὶ σὺ δέ, παιδίον, προφήτης ὑψίστου
   And thou also, child, a prophet of [the] Most High

κληθήσῃ προπορεύσῃ γὰρ ἐνώπιον κυρίου
wilt be called; for thou wilt go before before [the] Lord

ἑτοιμάσαι ὁδοὺς αὐτοῦ, 77 τοῦ δοῦναι
to prepare [the] ways of him,   - to give[d]

γνῶσιν σωτηρίας τῷ λαῷ αὐτοῦ ἐν
a knowledge of salvation to the people of him by

ἀφέσει ἁμαρτιῶν αὐτῶν, 78 διὰ σπλάγχνα
forgiveness of sins of them,   because of [the] bowels

ἐλέους θεοῦ ἡμῶν, ἐν οἷς ἐπισκέψεται
of mercy of God of us, whereby will visit

ἡμᾶς ἀνατολὴ ἐξ ὕψους, 79 ἐπιφᾶναι τοῖς
us a [sun]rising from [the] height, to appear ¹to the [ones]

ἐν σκότει καὶ σκιᾷ θανάτου καθημένοις,
²in ⁴darkness ⁵and ⁶in a shadow ⁷of death ¹sitting,

tongue was loosed, and he began to speak, praising God. ⁶⁵The neighbors were all filled with awe, and throughout the hill country of Judea people were talking about all these things. ⁶⁶Everyone who heard this wondered about it, asking, "What then is this child going to be?" For the Lord's hand was with him.

Zechariah's Song

⁶⁷His father Zechariah was filled with the Holy Spirit and prophesied:
⁶⁸"Praise be to the Lord, the God of Israel, because he has come and has redeemed his people.
⁶⁹He has raised up a horn[d] of salvation for us in the house of his servant David
⁷⁰(as he said through his holy prophets of long ago),
⁷¹salvation from our enemies and from the hand of all who hate us—
⁷²to show mercy to our fathers and to remember his holy covenant,
73 the oath he swore to our father Abraham:
⁷⁴to rescue us from the hand of our enemies, and to enable us to serve him without fear
75 in holiness and righteousness before him all our days.
⁷⁶And you, my child, will be called a prophet of the Most High; for you will go on before the Lord to prepare the way for him,
⁷⁷to give his people the knowledge of salvation through the forgiveness of their sins,
⁷⁸because of the tender mercy of our God, by which the rising sun will come to us from heaven
⁷⁹to shine on those living in darkness and in the shadow of death,

[d]69 *Horn* here symbolizes strength.

to guide our feet
into the way
of peace."
80 The child grew and became strong in spirit, and he was in the wilderness until the day he appeared publicly to Israel.

Chapter 2
The Birth of Jesus

IN those days a decree went out from Emperor Augustus that all the world should be registered. 2This was the first registration and was taken while Quirinius was governor of Syria. 3All went to their own towns to be registered. 4Joseph also went from the town of Nazareth in Galilee to Judea, to the city of David called Bethlehem, because he was descended from the house and family of David. 5He went to be registered with Mary, to whom he was engaged and who was expecting a child. 6While they were there, the time came for her to deliver her child. 7And she gave birth to her firstborn son and wrapped him in bands of cloth, and laid him in a manger, because there was no place for them in the inn.

The Shepherds and the Angels

8 In that region there were shepherds living in the fields, keeping watch over their flock by night. 9Then an angel of the Lord stood before them, and the glory of the Lord shone around them, and they were terrified. 10But the angel said to them, "Do not be afraid; for see—I am bringing you good news of

---

τοῦ κατευθῦναι τοὺς πόδας ἡμῶν εἰς ὁδὸν
to guide[d] the feet of us into a way
εἰρήνης.
of peace.
80 Τὸ δὲ παιδίον ηὔξανεν καὶ ἐκραταιοῦτο
And the child grew and became strong
πνεύματι, καὶ ἦν ἐν ταῖς ἐρήμοις ἕως
in spirit, and was in the deserts until
ἡμέρας ἀναδείξεως αὐτοῦ πρὸς τὸν Ἰσραήλ.
[the] days of showing of him to – Israel.

2 Ἐγένετο δὲ ἐν ταῖς ἡμέραις ἐκείναις
Now it came to pass in – days those
ἐξῆλθεν δόγμα παρὰ Καίσαρος Αὐγούστου
went out a decree from Cæsar Augustus
ἀπογράφεσθαι πᾶσαν τὴν οἰκουμένην. 2 αὕτη
to be enrolled all the inhabited earth. This
ἀπογραφὴ πρώτη ἐγένετο ἡγεμονεύοντος τῆς
[1]enrolment [1]first was governing –
= when Cyrenius governed Syria.
Συρίας Κυρηνίου. 3 καὶ ἐπορεύοντο πάντες
Syria Cyrenius.[a] And went all
ἀπογράφεσθαι, ἕκαστος εἰς τὴν ἑαυτοῦ
to be enrolled, each man to the of himself
πόλιν. 4 Ἀνέβη δὲ καὶ Ἰωσὴφ ἀπὸ τῆς
city. So went up also Joseph from –
Γαλιλαίας ἐκ πόλεως Ναζαρὲθ εἰς τὴν
Galilee out of a city Nazareth to the
Ἰουδαίαν εἰς πόλιν Δαυὶδ ἥτις καλεῖται Βηθλέεμ,
Judæa to a city of David which is called Bethlehem,
διὰ τὸ εἶναι αὐτὸν ἐξ οἴκου καὶ
because of the to be him[b] out of [the] house and
= because he was
πατριᾶς Δαυίδ, 5 ἀπογράψασθαι σὺν Μαριὰμ
family of David, to be enrolled with Mary
τῇ ἐμνηστευμένῃ αὐτῷ, οὔσῃ ἐγκύῳ.
the[one] having been betrothed to him, being pregnant.
6 Ἐγένετο δὲ ἐν τῷ εἶναι αὐτοὺς ἐκεῖ
And it came to pass in the to be them[be] there
= while they were
ἐπλήσθησαν αἱ ἡμέραι τοῦ τεκεῖν αὐτήν,
were fulfilled the days – to bear her,[bd]
= for her to bear,
7 καὶ ἔτεκεν τὸν υἱὸν αὐτῆς τὸν πρωτότοκον,
and she bore the son of her the firstborn,
καὶ ἐσπαργάνωσεν αὐτὸν καὶ ἀνέκλινεν
and she swathed him and laid
αὐτὸν ἐν φάτνῃ, διότι οὐκ ἦν αὐτοῖς
him in a manger, because there was not for them
τόπος ἐν τῷ καταλύματι. 8 Καὶ ποιμένες
place in the inn. And shepherds
ἦσαν ἐν τῇ χώρᾳ τῇ αὐτῇ ἀγραυλοῦντες
there were in the country – same living in the fields
καὶ φυλάσσοντες φυλακὰς τῆς νυκτὸς ἐπὶ
and keeping guard of(in) the night over
τὴν ποίμνην αὐτῶν. 9 καὶ ἄγγελος κυρίου
the flock of them. And an angel of [the] Lord
ἐπέστη αὐτοῖς καὶ δόξα κυρίου περιέλαμψεν
came upon them and [the] glory of [the] Lord shone around
αὐτούς, καὶ ἐφοβήθησαν φόβον μέγαν.
them, and they feared fear a great.
= exceedingly.
10 καὶ εἶπεν αὐτοῖς ὁ ἄγγελος· μὴ
And said to them the angel : not
φοβεῖσθε· ἰδοὺ γὰρ εὐαγγελίζομαι ὑμῖν
Fear ye; for behold I announce to you

---

to guide our feet into the path of peace."
80And the child grew and became strong in spirit; and he lived in the desert until he appeared publicly to Israel.

Chapter 2
The Birth of Jesus

IN those days Caesar Augustus issued a decree that a census should be taken of the entire Roman world. 2(This was the first census that took place while Quirinius was governor of Syria.) 3And everyone went to his own town to register.
4So Joseph also went up from the town of Nazareth in Galilee to Judea, to Bethlehem the town of David, because he belonged to the house and line of David. 5He went there to register with Mary, who was pledged to be married to him and was expecting a child. 6While they were there, the time came for the baby to be born, 7and she gave birth to her firstborn, a son. She wrapped him in cloths and placed him in a manger, because there was no room for them in the inn.

The Shepherds and the Angels

8And there were shepherds living out in the fields nearby, keeping watch over their flocks at night. 9An angel of the Lord appeared to them, and the glory of the Lord shone around them, and they were terrified. 10But the angel said to them, "Do not be afraid. I bring you good

great joy for all the people:
11 to you is born this day in the city of David a Savior, who is the Messiah,[i] the Lord. 12 This will be a sign for you: you will find a child wrapped in bands of cloth and lying in a manger." 13 And suddenly there was with the angel a multitude of the heavenly host,[j] praising God and saying, 14 "Glory to God in the highest heaven, and on earth peace among those whom he favors!"[k]

15 When the angels had left them and gone into heaven, the shepherds said to one another, "Let us go now to Bethlehem and see this thing that has taken place, which the Lord has made known to us." 16 So they went with haste and found Mary and Joseph, and the child lying in the manger. 17 When they saw this, they made known what had been told them about this child; 18 and all who heard it were amazed at what the shepherds told them. 19 But Mary treasured all these words and pondered them in her heart. 20 The shepherds returned, glorifying and praising God for all they had heard and seen, as it had been told them.

Jesus Is Named

21 After eight days had passed, it was time to circumcise the child; and he was called Jesus, the name given by the angel before he was conceived in the womb.

Jesus Is Presented in the Temple

22 When the time came for their purification ac-

χαρὰν μεγάλην, ἥτις ἔσται παντὶ τῷ λαῷ,
joy   a great,   which   will be   to all   the people,

11 ὅτι ἐτέχθη ὑμῖν σήμερον σωτήρ, ὅς
because was born to you to-day a Saviour, who

ἐστιν χριστὸς κύριος, ἐν πόλει Δαυίδ.
is   Christ   [the] Lord,   in   a city   of David.

12 καὶ τοῦτο ὑμῖν σημεῖον, εὑρήσετε βρέφος
And   this   to you   a sign,   ye will find   a babe

ἐσπαργανωμένον καὶ κείμενον ἐν φάτνῃ.
having been swathed and lying in a manger.

13 καὶ ἐξαίφνης ἐγένετο σὺν τῷ ἀγγέλῳ
And   suddenly   there was   with   the   angel

πλῆθος στρατιᾶς οὐρανίου αἰνούντων τὸν
a multitude   army   of a heavenly   praising   —

θεὸν καὶ λεγόντων· 14 δόξα ἐν ὑψίστοις
God and saying :   Glory   in highest [places]

θεῷ καὶ ἐπὶ γῆς εἰρήνη ἐν ἀνθρώποις
to God and on earth peace among men

εὐδοκίας. 15 Καὶ ἐγένετο ὡς ἀπῆλθον
of goodwill.   And   it came to pass when went away

ἀπ' αὐτῶν εἰς τὸν οὐρανὸν οἱ ἄγγελοι,
from   them   to   —   heaven   the   angels,

οἱ ποιμένες ἐλάλουν πρὸς ἀλλήλους·
the   shepherds   said   to   one another :

διέλθωμεν δὴ ἕως Βηθλέεμ καὶ ἴδωμεν
Let us go   then   unto   Bethlehem   and   let us see

τὸ ῥῆμα τοῦτο τὸ γεγονὸς ὃ ὁ κύριος
—   thing   this   — having happened which the Lord

ἐγνώρισεν ἡμῖν. 16 καὶ ἦλθαν σπεύσαντες,
made known to us.   And they came hastening,

καὶ ἀνεῦραν τήν τε Μαριὰμ καὶ τὸν
and   found   —   both   Mary   and   —

Ἰωσὴφ καὶ τὸ βρέφος κείμενον ἐν τῇ
Joseph   and   the   babe   lying   in   the

φάτνῃ. 17 ἰδόντες δὲ ἐγνώρισαν περὶ τοῦ
manger;   and seeing they made known concerning the

ῥήματος τοῦ λαληθέντος αὐτοῖς περὶ τοῦ
word   —   spoken   to them concerning —

παιδίου τούτου. 18 καὶ πάντες οἱ ἀκούσαντες
child   this.   And   all   the [ones]   hearing

ἐθαύμασαν περὶ τῶν λαληθέντων ὑπὸ τῶν
marvelled concerning the things spoken   ᵕ   the

ποιμένων πρὸς αὐτούς· 19 ἡ δὲ Μαρία
shepherds   to   them;   — but Mary

πάντα συνετήρει τὰ ῥήματα ταῦτα συμβάλλουσα
²all   ¹kept   —   ⁴things   ³these   pondering

ἐν τῇ καρδίᾳ αὐτῆς. 20 καὶ ὑπέστρεψαν
in   the   heart   of her.   And   returned

οἱ ποιμένες δοξάζοντες καὶ αἰνοῦντες τὸν
the   shepherds   glorifying   and   praising   —

θεὸν ἐπὶ πᾶσιν οἷς ἤκουσαν καὶ εἶδον
God   at   all things   which   they heard   and   saw

καθὼς ἐλαλήθη πρὸς αὐτούς.
as   was spoken   to   them.

21 Καὶ ὅτε ἐπλήσθησαν ἡμέραι ὀκτὼ
And   when   were completed   days   eight

τοῦ περιτεμεῖν αὐτόν, καὶ ἐκλήθη τὸ
—   to circumcise   himᵈ,   *and*   was called   the

ὄνομα αὐτοῦ Ἰησοῦς, τὸ κληθὲν ὑπὸ τοῦ
name   of him   Jesus,   the [name] called   by   the

ἀγγέλου πρὸ τοῦ συλλημφθῆναι αὐτὸν ἐν
angel   before   the   to be conceived   himᵇ   in
                =he was conceived

τῇ κοιλίᾳ.
the womb.

22 Καὶ ὅτε ἐπλήσθησαν αἱ ἡμέραι τοῦ
And   when   were completed   the   days   of the

---

news of great joy that will be for all the people. 11 Today in the town of David a Savior has been born to you; he is Christ[e] the Lord. 12 This will be a sign to you: You will find a baby wrapped in cloths and lying in a manger."

13 Suddenly a great company of the heavenly host appeared with the angel, praising God and saying, 14 "Glory to God in the highest, and on earth peace to men on whom his favor rests."

15 When the angels had left them and gone into heaven, the shepherds said to one another, "Let's go to Bethlehem and see this thing that has happened, which the Lord has told us about."

16 So they hurried off and found Mary and Joseph, and the baby, who was lying in the manger. 17 When they had seen him, they spread the word concerning what had been told them about this child, 18 and all who heard it were amazed at what the shepherds said to them. 19 But Mary treasured up all these things and pondered them in her heart. 20 The shepherds returned, glorifying and praising God for all the things they had heard and seen, which were just as they had been told.

Jesus Presented in the Temple

21 On the eighth day, when it was time to circumcise him, he was named Jesus, the name the angel had given him before he had been conceived.

22 When the time of their

---

[i] Or *the Christ*
[j] Gk *army*
[k] Other ancient authorities read *peace, good will among people*

[e] 11 Or *Messiah.* "The Christ" (Greek) and "the Messiah" (Hebrew) both mean "the Anointed One"; also in verse 26.

cording to the law of Moses, they brought him up to Jerusalem to present him to the Lord 23(as it is written in the law of the Lord, "Every firstborn male shall be designated as holy to the Lord"), 24and they offered a sacrifice according to what is stated in the law of the Lord, "a pair of turtledoves or two young pigeons."

25 Now there was a man in Jerusalem whose name was Simeon;l this man was righteous and devout, looking forward to the consolation of Israel, and the Holy Spirit rested on him. 26It had been revealed to him by the Holy Spirit that he would not see death before he had seen the Lord's Messiah.m 27Guided by the Spirit, Simeonn came into the temple; and when the parents brought in the child Jesus, to do for him what was customary under the law, 28Simeono took him in his arms and praised God, saying,
"Master, now you
      are dismissing
      your servantp in
      peace,
      according to your
      word;
30 for my eyes have seen
      your salvation,
31   which you have
      prepared in the
      presence of all
      peoples,
32 a light for revelation
      to the Gentiles
      and for glory to
      your people
      Israel."
33 And the child's father and mother were amazed at what was being said about him. 34Then Simeonq blessed them and said to his mother Mary, "This child is destined for the falling and the rising of many in Israel, and to be a

---

καθαρισμοῦ αὐτῶν κατὰ τὸν νόμον
cleansing   of them according to the   law
Μωϋσέως, ἀνήγαγον αὐτὸν εἰς Ἱεροσόλυμα
of Moses, they took up him   to   Jerusalem
παραστῆσαι τῷ κυρίῳ, 23 καθὼς γέγραπται
to present to the Lord,   as   it has been written
ἐν νόμῳ κυρίου ὅτι πᾶν ἄρσεν διανοῖγον
in [the] law of the Lord[,] – Every male opening
μήτραν ἅγιον τῷ κυρίῳ κληθήσεται, 24 καὶ
a womb holy to the Lord   shall be called,   and
τοῦ δοῦναι θυσίαν κατὰ τὸ εἰρημένον ἐν
– to gived a sacrifice according to the thing said   in
τῷ νόμῳ κυρίου, ζεῦγος τρυγόνων ἢ δύο
the law of [the] Lord, a pair of turtledoves or two
νοσσοὺς περιστερῶν. 25 Καὶ ἰδοὺ ἄνθρωπος
nestlings   of doves.   And behold[,]   a man
ἦν ἐν Ἱερουσαλὴμ ᾧ ὄνομα Συμεών, καὶ
was in   Jerusalem to whom namee Simeon, and
                          = whose name was
ὁ ἄνθρωπος οὗτος δίκαιος καὶ εὐλαβής,
–   man   this   [was] just   and   devout,
προσδεχόμενος παράκλησιν τοῦ Ἰσραήλ, καὶ
expecting   [the] consolation – of Israel,   and
πνεῦμα ἦν ἅγιον ἐπ' αὐτόν· 26 καὶ ἦν
1[the] 2Spirit 4was 3Holy upon him;   and it was
αὐτῷ κεχρηματισμένον ὑπὸ τοῦ πνεύματος
to him having been communicated by the   Spirit
τοῦ ἁγίου μὴ ἰδεῖν θάνατον πρὶν ἢ ἂν
– Holy not to see death   before
ἴδη τὸν χριστὸν κυρίου. 27 καὶ ἦλθεν
he should see the Christ of [the] Lord.   And he came
ἐν τῷ πνεύματι εἰς τὸ ἱερόν· καὶ ἐν τῷ
by the   Spirit into the temple; and in the
                                = as the(his) parents brought in
εἰσαγαγεῖν τοὺς γονεῖς τὸ παιδίον Ἰησοῦν
to bring in the parentsbe the child   Jesus
τοῦ ποιῆσαι αὐτοὺς κατὰ τὸ εἰθισμένον
– to do   thembd according to the   custom
                  = for them to do
τοῦ νόμου περὶ αὐτοῦ, 28 καὶ αὐτὸς
of the law concerning him,   and   he
ἐδέξατο αὐτὸ εἰς τὰς ἀγκάλας καὶ
received   him   in the(his) arms   and
εὐλόγησεν τὸν θεὸν καὶ εἶπεν· 29 νῦν
blessed   –   God and said :   Now
ἀπολύεις τὸν δοῦλόν σου, δέσποτα, κατὰ
thou releasest the slave of thee, Master, according to
τὸ ῥῆμά σου ἐν εἰρήνῃ· 30 ὅτι εἶδον οἱ
the word of thee in peace;   because saw   the
ὀφθαλμοί μου τὸ σωτήριόν σου, 31 ὃ
eyes   of me the salvation of thee,   which
ἡτοίμασας κατὰ πρόσωπον πάντων τῶν
thou didst prepare before [the] face of all   the
λαῶν, 32 φῶς εἰς ἀποκάλυψιν ἐθνῶν καὶ
peoples, a light for a revelation of [the] nations and
δόξαν λαοῦ σου Ἰσραήλ. 33 καὶ ἦν
a glory of [the] people of thee Israel.   And 7was(were)
ὁ πατὴρ αὐτοῦ καὶ ἡ μήτηρ θαυμάζοντες
1the 2father 3of him 4and 5the 6mother 8marvelling
ἐπὶ τοῖς λαλουμένοις περὶ αὐτοῦ. 34 καὶ
at the things being said concerning him.   And
εὐλόγησεν αὐτοὺς Συμεὼν καὶ εἶπεν πρὸς
blessed   them   Simeon and said to
Μαριὰμ τὴν μητέρα αὐτοῦ· ἰδοὺ οὗτος
Mary   the mother of him : Behold[,] this
κεῖται εἰς πτῶσιν καὶ ἀνάστασιν πολλῶν
is set for fall   and rising again of many

---

purification according to the Law of Moses had been completed, Joseph and Mary took him to Jerusalem to present him to the Lord 23(as it is written in the Law of the Lord, "Every firstborn male is to be consecrated to the Lord"f), 24and to offer a sacrifice in keeping with what is said in the Law of the Lord: "a pair of doves or two young pigeons."g

25Now there was a man in Jerusalem called Simeon, who was righteous and devout. He was waiting for the consolation of Israel, and the Holy Spirit was upon him. 26It had been revealed to him by the Holy Spirit that he would not die before he had seen the Lord's Christ. 27Moved by the Spirit, he went into the temple courts. When the parents brought in the child Jesus to do for him what the custom of the Law required, 28Simeon took him in his arms and praised God, saying:

29"Sovereign Lord, as you
      have promised,
      you now dismissh your
      servant in peace.
30For my eyes have seen
      your salvation,
31   which you have
      prepared in the sight
      of all people,
32a light for revelation to
      the Gentiles
      and for glory to your
      people Israel."

33The child's father and mother marveled at what was said about him. 34Then Simeon blessed them and said to Mary, his mother: "This child is destined to cause the falling and rising of many in Israel, and to be

---

lGk Symeon
mOr the Lord's Christ
nGk In the Spirit, he
oGk he
pGk slave

f23 Exodus 13:2,12
g24 Lev. 12:8
h29 Or promised, / now dismiss

sign that will be opposed 35 so that the inner thoughts of many will be revealed—and a sword will pierce your own soul too."

36 There was also a prophet, Anna[r] the daughter of Phanuel, of the tribe of Asher. She was of a great age, having lived with her husband seven years after her marriage, 37 then as a widow to the age of eighty-four. She never left the temple but worshiped there with fasting and prayer night and day. 38 At that moment she came, and began to praise God and to speak about the child[q] to all who were looking for the redemption of Jerusalem.

The Return to Nazareth

39 When they had finished everything required by the law of the Lord, they returned to Galilee, to their own town of Nazareth. 40 The child grew and became strong, filled with wisdom; and the favor of God was upon him.

The Boy Jesus in the Temple

41 Now every year his parents went to Jerusalem for the festival of the Passover. 42 And when he was twelve years old, they went up as usual for the festival. 43 When the festival was ended and they started to return, the boy Jesus stayed behind in Jerusalem, but his parents did not know it. 44 Assuming that he was in the group of travelers, they went a day's journey. Then they started to look for him among their relatives and friends. 45 When they did not find him, they returned to Jeru-

---

ἐν τῷ Ἰσραὴλ καὶ εἰς σημεῖον ἀντιλεγ-
in   -   Israel   and   for   a sign   spoken

όμενον — 35 καὶ σοῦ δὲ αὐτῆς τὴν ψυχὴν
against —   and ⁶of thee ⁷also ⁸[thy]self ³the ⁴soul

διελεύσεται ῥομφαία—, ὅπως ἂν ἀποκαλυφθῶσιν
²will go through ¹a sword —, so as   -   may be revealed

ἐκ πολλῶν καρδιῶν διαλογισμοί. 36 Καὶ
of many hearts [the] thoughts.   And

ἦν Ἄννα προφῆτις, θυγάτηρ Φανουήλ, ἐκ
there was Anna a prophetess, a daughter of Phanuel, of

φυλῆς Ἀσήρ· αὕτη προβεβηκυῖα ἐν ἡμέραις
[the] tribe of Asher; this having advanced in days

πολλαῖς, ζήσασα μετὰ ἀνδρὸς ἔτη ἑπτὰ
many, having lived with a husband years seven

ἀπὸ τῆς παρθενίας αὐτῆς, 37 καὶ αὐτὴ
from the virginity of her, and she [was]

χήρα ἕως ἐτῶν ὀγδοήκοντα τεσσάρων, ἣ
a widow until years eighty-four, who

οὐκ ἀφίστατο τοῦ ἱεροῦ νηστείαις καὶ
withdrew not from the temple with fastings and

δεήσεσιν λατρεύουσα νύκτα καὶ ἡμέραν.
petitionings serving night and day.

38 καὶ αὐτῇ τῇ ὥρᾳ ἐπιστᾶσα ἀνθωμολογεῖτο
And at the very hour* coming upon she gave thanks

τῷ θεῷ καὶ ἐλάλει περὶ αὐτοῦ πᾶσιν τοῖς
- to God and spoke about him to all the [ones]

προσδεχομένοις λύτρωσιν Ἰερουσαλήμ. 39 Καὶ
expecting redemption in Jerusalem. And

ὡς ἐτέλεσαν πάντα τὰ κατὰ τὸν νόμον
when they finished all things - according to the law

κυρίου, ἐπέστρεψαν εἰς τὴν Γαλιλαίαν εἰς
of [the] Lord, they returned to   -   Galilee to

πόλιν ἑαυτῶν Ναζαρέθ.
a city of them*selves* Nazareth.

40 Τὸ δὲ παιδίον ηὔξανεν καὶ ἐκραταιοῦτο
And the child grew and became strong

πληρούμενον σοφίᾳ, καὶ χάρις θεοῦ ἦν ἐπ'
being filled with wisdom, and [the] grace of God was upon

αὐτό.
him.

41 Καὶ ἐπορεύοντο οἱ γονεῖς αὐτοῦ κατ'
And went the parents of him year

ἔτος εἰς Ἰερουσαλὴμ τῇ ἑορτῇ τοῦ πάσχα.
by year† to Jerusalem at the feast of the Passover.

42 Καὶ ὅτε ἐγένετο ἐτῶν δώδεκα, ἀναβαινόντων
And when he became of years twelve, going up =as they went up

αὐτῶν κατὰ τὸ ἔθος τῆς ἑορτῆς, 43 καὶ
them[a] according to the custom of the feast, and

τελειωσάντων τὰς ἡμέρας, ἐν τῷ ὑποστρέφειν
fulfilling[a] the days, in the to return =when they returned

αὐτοὺς ὑπέμεινεν Ἰησοῦς ὁ παῖς ἐν
them[be] ⁴remained ¹Jesus ²the ³boy in

Ἰερουσαλήμ, καὶ οὐκ ἔγνωσαν οἱ γονεῖς
Jerusalem, and ⁴knew not ¹the ²parents

αὐτοῦ. 44 νομίσαντες δὲ αὐτὸν εἶναι ἐν
³of him. But supposing him to be in

τῇ συνοδίᾳ ἦλθον ἡμέρας ὁδὸν καὶ ἀνεζήτουν
the company they went of a day a journey and sought

αὐτὸν ἐν τοῖς συγγενεῦσιν καὶ τοῖς
him among the(ir) relatives and the(ir)

γνωστοῖς, 45 καὶ μὴ εὑρόντες ὑπέστρεψαν
acquaintances, and not finding returned

---

a sign that will be spoken against, 35 so that the thoughts of many hearts will be revealed. And a sword will pierce your own soul too."

36 There was also a prophetess, Anna, the daughter of Phanuel, of the tribe of Asher. She was very old; she had lived with her husband seven years after her marriage, 37 and then was a widow until she was eighty-four.[i] She never left the temple but worshiped night and day, fasting and praying. 38 Coming up to them at that very moment, she gave thanks to God and spoke about the child to all who were looking forward to the redemption of Jerusalem.

39 When Joseph and Mary had done everything required by the Law of the Lord, they returned to Galilee to their own town of Nazareth. 40 And the child grew and became strong; he was filled with wisdom, and the grace of God was upon him.

The Boy Jesus at the Temple

41 Every year his parents went to Jerusalem for the Feast of the Passover. 42 When he was twelve years old, they went up to the Feast, according to the custom. 43 After the Feast was over, while his parents were returning home, the boy Jesus stayed behind in Jerusalem, but they were unaware of it. 44 Thinking he was in their company, they traveled on for a day. Then they began looking for him among their relatives and friends. 45 When they did not find him, they

---

* Strictly, this construction should mean " the hour itself "; but the context demands " the same hour ". See 10. 7, 21; 12. 12; 13. 1, 31; 20. 19; 23. 12; 24. 13. " Luke seems to be the only N.T. writer who affects the construction " (C. F. D. Moule). See also Acts 16. 18; 22. 13. Of course there is not a great difference between " the hour itself ", " the very hour ", and " the same hour ".

q Gk Symeon
r Gk Hanna

i 37 Or widow for eighty-four years

salem to search for him. [46]After three days they found him in the temple, sitting among the teachers, listening to them and asking them questions. [47]And all who heard him were amazed at his understanding and his answers. [48]When his parents[t] saw him they were astonished; and his mother said to him, "Child, why have you treated us like this? Look, your father and I have been searching for you in great anxiety." [49]He said to them, "Why were you searching for me? Did you not know that I must be in my Father's house?"[u] [50]But they did not understand what he said to them. [51]Then he went down with them and came to Nazareth, and was obedient to them. His mother treasured all these things in her heart. [52] And Jesus increased in wisdom and in years,[v] and in divine and human favor.

εἰς Ἰερουσαλὴμ ἀναζητοῦντες αὐτόν. 46 καὶ
to Jerusalem seeking him. And

ἐγένετο μετὰ ἡμέρας τρεῖς εὗρον αὐτὸν
it came to pass after days three they found him

ἐν τῷ ἱερῷ καθεζόμενον ἐν μέσῳ τῶν
in the temple sitting in [the] midst of the

διδασκάλων καὶ ἀκούοντα αὐτῶν καὶ
teachers both hearing them and

ἐπερωτῶντα αὐτούς· 47 ἐξίσταντο δὲ πάντες
questioning them; and were astonished all

οἱ ἀκούοντες αὐτοῦ ἐπὶ τῇ συνέσει καὶ
the [ones] hearing him at the intelligence and

ταῖς ἀποκρίσεσιν αὐτοῦ. 48 καὶ ἰδόντες
the answers of him. And seeing

αὐτὸν ἐξεπλάγησαν, καὶ εἶπεν πρὸς αὐτὸν
him they were astounded, and said to him

ἡ μήτηρ αὐτοῦ· τέκνον, τί ἐποίησας ἡμῖν
the mother of him : Child, why didst thou to us

οὕτως; ἰδοὺ ὁ πατήρ σου κἀγὼ ὀδυνώμενοι
thus? behold[,] the father of thee and I greatly distressed

ζητοῦμέν σε. 49 καὶ εἶπεν πρὸς αὐτούς·
are seeking thee. And he said to them :

τί ὅτι ἐζητεῖτέ με; οὐκ ᾔδειτε ὅτι ἐν
Why [is it] that ye sought me? did ye not know that in
=I

τοῖς τοῦ πατρός μου δεῖ εἶναί με;
the [affairs] of the Father of me it behoves to be me?
must be about my Father's business?

50 καὶ αὐτοὶ οὐ συνῆκαν τὸ ῥῆμα ὃ
And they did not understand the word which

ἐλάλησεν αὐτοῖς. 51 καὶ κατέβη μετ'
he spoke to them. And he went down with

αὐτῶν καὶ ἦλθεν εἰς Ναζαρέθ, καὶ ἦν
them and came to Nazareth, and was

ὑποτασσόμενος αὐτοῖς. καὶ ἡ μήτηρ
being subject to them. And the mother

αὐτοῦ διετήρει πάντα τὰ ῥήματα ἐν τῇ
of him carefully kept all the matters in the

καρδίᾳ αὐτῆς. 52 Καὶ Ἰησοῦς προέκοπτεν
heart of her. And Jesus progressed

ἐν τῇ σοφίᾳ καὶ ἡλικίᾳ καὶ χάριτι παρὰ
in - wisdom and age and favour before

θεῷ καὶ ἀνθρώποις.
God and men.

---

went back to Jerusalem to look for him. [46]After three days they found him in the temple courts, sitting among the teachers, listening to them and asking them questions. [47]Everyone who heard him was amazed at his understanding and his answers. [48]When his parents saw him, they were astonished. His mother said to him, ''Son, why have you treated us like this? Your father and I have been anxiously searching for you.''
[49]''Why were you searching for me?'' he asked. ''Didn't you know I had to be in my Father's house?'' [50]But they did not understand what he was saying to them. [51]Then he went down to Nazareth with them and was obedient to them. But his mother treasured all these things in her heart. [52]And Jesus grew in wisdom and stature, and in favor with God and men.

Chapter 3

The Proclamation of John the Baptist

IN the fifteenth year of the reign of Emperor Tiberius, when Pontius Pilate was governor of Judea, and Herod was ruler[w] of Galilee, and his brother Philip ruler[w] of the region of Ituraea and Trachonitis, and Lysanias ruler[w] of Abilene, [2]during the high priesthood of Annas and Caiaphas, the word of God came to John son of Zechariah in the wilderness. [3]He went into all the region

---

3 Ἐν ἔτει δὲ πεντεκαιδεκάτῳ τῆς
Now in [the] year fifteenth of the

ἡγεμονίας Τιβερίου Καίσαρος, ἡγεμονεύοντος
government of Tiberius Caesar, governing
=while Pontius Pilate

Ποντίου Πιλάτου τῆς Ἰουδαίας, καὶ
Pontius Pilate[a] - of Judæa, and
was governing

τετρααρχοῦντος τῆς Γαλιλαίας Ἡρῴδου,
ruling as tetrarch - of Galilee Herod,[a]
=while Herod was ruling as tetrarch of Galilee,

Φιλίππου δὲ τοῦ ἀδελφοῦ αὐτοῦ τετρα-
and Philip the brother of him ruling

αρχοῦντος τῆς Ἰτουραίας καὶ Τραχωνίτιδος
as tetrarch[a] [2]of the [3]of Ituræa [4]and [5]of Trachonitis

χώρας, καὶ Λυσανίου τῆς Ἀβιληνῆς
[6]country, and Lysanias - of Abilene

τετρααρχοῦντος, 2 ἐπὶ ἀρχιερέως Ἄννα
ruling as tetrarch[a], in the time of [the] high priest Anna

καὶ Καϊαφᾶ, ἐγένετο ῥῆμα θεοῦ ἐπὶ Ἰωάννην
and Caiaphas, came a word of God to John

τὸν Ζαχαρίου υἱὸν ἐν τῇ ἐρήμῳ. 3 καὶ
the of Zacharias son in the desert. And

Chapter 3

John the Baptist Prepares the Way

IN the fifteenth year of the reign of Tiberius Caesar—when Pontius Pilate was governor of Judea, Herod tetrarch of Galilee, his brother Philip tetrarch of Iturea and Traconitis, and Lysanias tetrarch of Abilene—[2]during the high priesthood of Annas and Caiaphas, the word of God came to John son of Zechariah in the desert. [3]He went

---

s Gk *him*
t Gk *they*
u Or *be about my Father's interests?*
v Or *in stature*
w Gk *tetrarch*

around the Jordan, proclaiming a baptism of repentance for the forgiveness of sins, 4 as it is written in the book of the words of the prophet Isaiah,
"The voice of one
  crying out in
  the wilderness:
'Prepare the way of
  the Lord,
make his paths
  straight.
5 Every valley shall be
  filled,
and every mountain
  and hill shall be
  made low,
and the crooked shall
  be made
  straight,
and the rough ways
  made smooth;
6 and all flesh shall see
  the salvation of
  God.' "
7 John said to the crowds that came out to be baptized by him, "You brood of vipers! Who warned you to flee from the wrath to come? 8 Bear fruits worthy of repentance. Do not begin to say to yourselves, 'We have Abraham as our ancestor'; for I tell you, God is able from these stones to raise up children to Abraham. 9 Even now the ax is lying at the root of the trees; every tree therefore that does not bear good fruit is cut down and thrown into the fire."
10 And the crowds asked him, "What then should we do?" 11 In reply he said to them, "Whoever has two coats must share with anyone who has none; and whoever has food must do likewise." 12 Even tax collectors came to be baptized, and they asked him, "Teacher, what should we do?" 13 He said to them, "Collect no more than the amount prescribed for you." 14 Soldiers also asked him, "And we, what should we do?" He said to them,

ἦλθεν εἰς πᾶσαν τὴν περίχωρον τοῦ
he came into all the neighbourhood of the
Ἰορδάνου κηρύσσων βάπτισμα μετανοίας
Jordan proclaiming a baptism of repentance
εἰς ἄφεσιν ἁμαρτιῶν, 4 ὡς γέγραπται ἐν
for forgiveness of sins, as it has been written in
βίβλῳ λόγων Ἡσαΐου τοῦ προφήτου·
[the] roll of [the] words of Esaias the prophet :
φωνὴ βοῶντος ἐν τῇ ἐρήμῳ· ἑτοιμάσατε
Voice of [one] crying in the desert : Prepare ye
τὴν ὁδὸν κυρίου, εὐθείας ποιεῖτε τὰς
the way of [the] Lord, straight make the
τρίβους αὐτοῦ· 5 πᾶσα φάραγξ πληρωθήσεται
paths of him; every valley shall be filled up
καὶ πᾶν ὄρος καὶ βουνὸς ταπεινωθήσεται,
and every mountain and hill shall be laid low,
καὶ ἔσται τὰ σκολιὰ εἰς εὐθείας καὶ αἱ
and shall be the crooked [places] into straight [ones] and the
τραχεῖαι εἰς ὁδοὺς λείας· 6 καὶ ὄψεται
rough [places] into ways smooth; and ¹shall see
πᾶσα σὰρξ τὸ σωτήριον τοῦ θεοῦ.
¹all ²flesh the salvation – of God.
7 Ἔλεγεν οὖν τοῖς ἐκπορευομένοις ὄχλοις
He said therefore to the ²going out ¹crowds
βαπτισθῆναι ὑπ᾽ αὐτοῦ· γεννήματα ἐχιδνῶν,
to be baptized by him : Offspring of vipers,
τίς ὑπέδειξεν ὑμῖν φυγεῖν ἀπὸ τῆς
who warned you to flee from the
μελλούσης ὀργῆς; 8 ποιήσατε οὖν καρποὺς
coming wrath? Produce therefore fruits
ἀξίους τῆς μετανοίας· καὶ μὴ ἄρξησθε
worthy of repentance; and do not begin
λέγειν ἐν ἑαυτοῖς· πατέρα ἔχομεν τὸν
to say among yourselves : Father we have –
Ἀβραάμ· λέγω γὰρ ὑμῖν ὅτι δύναται ὁ
Abraham; for I tell you that ¹can –
θεὸς ἐκ τῶν λίθων τούτων ἐγεῖραι τέκνα
¹God out of – stones these to raise children
τῷ Ἀβραάμ. 9 ἤδη δὲ καὶ ἡ ἀξίνη πρὸς
– to Abraham. And ²already ¹even the axe at
τὴν ῥίζαν τῶν δένδρων κεῖται· ²πᾶν οὖν
the root of the trees is laid : ²every ¹therefore
δένδρον μὴ ποιοῦν καρπὸν καλὸν
tree not producing fruit good
ἐκκόπτεται καὶ εἰς πῦρ βάλλεται. 10 Καὶ
is being cut down and into fire is being cast. And
ἐπηρώτων αὐτὸν οἱ ὄχλοι λέγοντες· τί
asked him the crowds saying : What
οὖν ποιήσωμεν; 11 ἀποκριθεὶς δὲ ἔλεγεν
then may we do? And answering he told
αὐτοῖς· ὁ ἔχων δύο χιτῶνας μεταδότω
them : The [one] having two tunics let him impart
τῷ μὴ ἔχοντι, καὶ ὁ ἔχων βρώματα
to the [one] not having, and the [one] having foods
ὁμοίως ποιείτω. 12 ἦλθον δὲ καὶ τελῶναι
likewise let him do. And there came also tax-collectors
βαπτισθῆναι καὶ εἶπαν πρὸς αὐτόν·
to be baptized and they said to him :
διδάσκαλε, τί ποιήσωμεν; 13 ὁ δὲ εἶπεν
Teacher, what may we do? And he said
πρὸς αὐτούς· μηδὲν πλέον παρὰ τὸ
to them : Nothing more besides the [thing]
διατεταγμένον ὑμῖν πράσσετε. 14 ἐπηρώτων δὲ
having been commanded you do ye. And asked
αὐτὸν καὶ στρατευόμενοι λέγοντες· τί
him also men serving in the army saying : What

into all the country around the Jordan, preaching a baptism of repentance for the forgiveness of sins. 4 As is written in the book of the words of Isaiah the prophet:

"A voice of one calling
  in the desert,
'Prepare the way for the
  Lord,
make straight paths for
  him.
5 Every valley shall be
  filled in,
every mountain and hill
  made low.
The crooked roads shall
  become straight,
the rough ways
  smooth.
6 And all mankind will see
  God's salvation.' "ʲ
7 John said to the crowds coming out to be baptized by him, "You brood of vipers! Who warned you to flee from the coming wrath? 8 Produce fruit in keeping with repentance. And do not begin to say to yourselves, 'We have Abraham as our father.' For I tell you that out of these stones God can raise up children for Abraham. 9 The ax is already at the root of the trees, and every tree that does not produce good fruit will be cut down and thrown into the fire."
10 "What should we do then?" the crowd asked.
11 John answered, "The man with two tunics should share with him who has none, and the one who has food should do the same."
12 Tax collectors also came to be baptized. "Teacher," they asked, "what should we do?"

/6 Isaiah 40:3-5

"Do not extort money from anyone by threats or false accusation, and be satisfied with your wages."

15 As the people were filled with expectation, and all were questioning in their hearts concerning John, whether he might be the Messiah,ˣ 16 John answered all of them by saying, "I baptize you with water; but one who is more powerful than I is coming; I am not worthy to untie the thong of his sandals. He will baptize you with the Holy Spirit and fire. 17 His winnowing fork is in his hand, to clear his threshing floor and to gather the wheat into his granary; but the chaff he will burn with unquenchable fire."

18 So, with many other exhortations, he proclaimed the good news to the people. 19 But Herod the ruler,ᶻ who had been rebuked by him because of Herodias, his brother's wife, and because of all the evil things that Herod had done, 20 added to them all by shutting up John in prison.

The Baptism of Jesus

21 Now when all the people were baptized, and when Jesus also had been baptized and was praying, the heaven was opened, 22 and the Holy Spirit descended upon him in bodily form like a dove. And a voice came from heaven, "You are my Son, the Beloved;ᵃ with you I am well pleased."ᵇ

The Ancestors of Jesus

23 Jesus was about thirty years old when he began his work. He was the son (as was thought) of Joseph

---

ποιήσωμεν καὶ ἡμεῖς; καὶ εἶπεν αὐτοῖς·
may do also we? And he told them:

μηδένα διασείσητε μηδὲ συκοφαντήσητε,
No one intimidate nor accuse falsely,

καὶ ἀρκεῖσθε τοῖς ὀψωνίοις ὑμῶν.
and be satisfied with the pay of you.

15 Προσδοκῶντος δὲ τοῦ λαοῦ καὶ
Now expecting the peopleᵃ and
= while the people were expecting and all were debating

διαλογιζομένων πάντων ἐν ταῖς καρδίαις
debating allᵃ in the hearts

αὐτῶν περὶ τοῦ Ἰωάννου, μήποτε αὐτὸς
of them concerning - John, perhaps he

εἴη ὁ χριστός, 16 ἀπεκρίνατο λέγων πᾶσιν
might be the Christ, ¹answered ²saying ⁴to all

ὁ Ἰωάννης· ἐγὼ μὲν ὕδατι βαπτίζω ὑμᾶς·
- ³John: I indeed with water baptize you;

ἔρχεται δὲ ὁ ἰσχυρότερός μου, οὗ οὐκ
but there comes the [one] stronger of me, of whom not
= than I,

εἰμὶ ἱκανὸς λῦσαι τὸν ἱμάντα τῶν ὑποδημά-
I am competent to loosen the thong of the san-

των αὐτοῦ· αὐτὸς ὑμᾶς βαπτίσει ἐν
dals of him; he you will baptize with

πνεύματι ἁγίῳ καὶ πυρί· 17 οὗ τὸ πτύον
Spirit [the] Holy and fire; of whom the fan [is]

ἐν τῇ χειρὶ αὐτοῦ διακαθᾶραι τὴν ἅλωνα
in the hand of him thoroughly to cleanse the threshing-floor

αὐτοῦ καὶ συναγαγεῖν τὸν σῖτον εἰς τὴν
of him and to gather the wheat into the

ἀποθήκην αὐτοῦ, τὸ δὲ ἄχυρον κατακαύσει
barn of him, but the chaff he will burn up

πυρὶ ἀσβέστῳ. 18 Πολλὰ μὲν οὖν καὶ
with fire unquenchable. Many things indeed therefore and

ἕτερα παρακαλῶν εὐηγγελίζετο τὸν λαόν·
different exhorting he evangelized the people;

19 ὁ δὲ Ἡρῴδης ὁ τετράρχης, ἐλεγχόμενος
- but Herod the tetrarch, being reproved

ὑπ᾽ αὐτοῦ περὶ Ἡρῳδιάδος τῆς γυναικὸς
by him concerning Herodias the wife

τοῦ ἀδελφοῦ αὐτοῦ καὶ περὶ πάντων ὧν
of the brother of him and concerning ¹all ²things ⁴which

ἐποίησεν πονηρῶν ὁ Ἡρῴδης, 20 προσέθηκεν
⁵did ³evil - ¹Herod, added

καὶ τοῦτο ἐπὶ πᾶσιν, κατέκλεισεν τὸν
also this above all, he shut up

Ἰωάννην ἐν φυλακῇ.
John in prison.

21 Ἐγένετο δὲ ἐν τῷ βαπτισθῆναι ἅπαντα
Now it came to pass in the to be baptized all
= when all the people were baptized

τὸν λαὸν καὶ Ἰησοῦ βαπτισθέντος καὶ
the peopleᵇᵉ and Jesus being baptized and
= as Jesus had been baptized and was praying

προσευχομένου ἀνεῳχθῆναι τὸν οὐρανὸν 22 καὶ
prayingᵃ to be opened the heaven and
= the heaven was opened and the Holy Spirit came down

καταβῆναι τὸ πνεῦμα τὸ ἅγιον σωματικῷ
to come down the Spirit - Holyᵇ in a bodily

εἴδει ὡς περιστερὰν ἐπ᾽ αὐτόν, καὶ φωνὴν
form as a dove upon him, and a voice

ἐξ οὐρανοῦ γενέσθαι· σὺ εἶ ὁ υἱός μου
out of heaven to comeᵇ: Thou art the Son of me

ὁ ἀγαπητός, ἐν σοὶ εὐδόκησα. 23 Καὶ
- beloved, in thee I was well pleased. And

αὐτὸς ἦν Ἰησοῦς ἀρχόμενος ὡσεὶ ἐτῶν
²himself ³was ¹Jesus ⁴beginning about years

---

13 "Don't collect any more than you are required to," he told them.

14 Then some soldiers asked him, "And what should we do?"

He replied, "Don't extort money and don't accuse people falsely—be content with your pay."

15 The people were waiting expectantly and were all wondering in their hearts if John might possibly be the Christ.ᵏ 16 John answered them all, "I baptize you withˡ water. But one more powerful than I will come, the thongs of whose sandals I am not worthy to untie. He will baptize you with the Holy Spirit and with fire. 17 His winnowing fork is in his hand to clear his threshing floor and to gather the wheat into his barn, but he will burn up the chaff with unquenchable fire." 18 And with many other words John exhorted the people and preached the good news to them.

19 But when John rebuked Herod the tetrarch because of Herodias, his brother's wife, and all the other evil things he had done, 20 Herod added this to them all: He locked John up in prison.

The Baptism and Genealogy of Jesus

21 When all the people were being baptized, Jesus was baptized too. And as he was praying, heaven was opened 22 and the Holy Spirit descended on him in bodily form like a dove. And a voice came from heaven: "You are my Son, whom I love; with you I am well pleased."

23 Now Jesus himself was about thirty years old when he began his ministry. He

---

ˣ Or the Christ
ʸ Or in
ᶻ Gk tetrarch
ᵃ Or my beloved Son
ᵇ Other ancient authorities read You are my Son, today I have begotten you

ᵏ 15 Or Messiah
ˡ 16 Or in

son of Heli, 24 son of Matthat, son of Levi, son of Melchi, son of Jannai, son of Joseph, 25 son of Mattathias, son of Amos, son of Nahum, son of Esli, son of Naggai, 26 son of Maath, son of Mattathias, son of Semein, son of Josech, son of Joda, 27 son of Joanan, son of Rhesa, son of Zerubbabel, son of Shealtiel, c son of Neri, 28 son of Melchi, son of Addi, son of Cosam, son of Elmadam, son of Er, 29 son of Joshua, son of Eliezer, son of Jorim, son of Matthat, son of Levi, 30 son of Simeon, son of Judah, son of Joseph, son of Jonam, son of Eliakim, 31 son of Melea, son of Menna, son of Mattatha, son of Nathan, son of David, 32 son of Jesse, son of Obed, son of Boaz, son of Sala, d son of Nahshon, 33 son of Amminadab, son of Admin, son of Arni, e son of Hezron, son of Perez, son of Judah, 34 son of Jacob, son of Isaac, son of Abraham, son of Terah, son of Nahor, 35 son of Serug, son of Reu, son of Peleg, son of Eber, son of Shelah, 36 son of Cainan, son of Arphaxad, son of Shem, son of Noah, son of Lamech, 37 son of Methuselah, son of Enoch, son of Jared, son of Mahalaleel, son of Cainan, 38 son of Enos, son of Seth, son of Adam, son of God.

τριάκοντα, ὢν υἱός, ὡς ἐνομίζετο, Ἰωσήφ,
thirty,   being son,   as   was supposed, of Joseph,

τοῦ Ἠλὶ 24 τοῦ Ματθὰτ τοῦ Λευὶ τοῦ
- of Eli   - of Matthat   - of Levi -

Μελχὶ τοῦ Ἰανναὶ τοῦ Ἰωσὴφ 25 τοῦ
of Melchi   - of Jannai   - of Joseph -

Ματταθίου τοῦ Ἀμὼς τοῦ Ναοὺμ τοῦ
of Mattathias   - of Amos   - of Naum -

Ἐσλὶ τοῦ Ναγγαὶ 26 τοῦ Μάαθ τοῦ
of Hesli   - of Naggai   - of Maath -

Ματταθίου τοῦ Σεμεῒν τοῦ Ἰωσὴχ τοῦ
of Mattathias   - of Semein   - of Josech -

Ἰωδὰ 27 τοῦ Ἰωανὰν τοῦ Ῥησὰ τοῦ
of Jodah   - of Joanan   - of Rhesa -

Ζοροβαβὲλ τοῦ Σαλαθιὴλ τοῦ Νηρὶ 28 τοῦ
of Zorobabel   - of Salathiel   - of Neri -

Μελχὶ τοῦ Ἀδδὶ τοῦ Κωσὰμ τοῦ
of Melchi   - of Addi   - of Kosam -

Ἐλμαδὰμ τοῦ Ἢρ 29 τοῦ Ἰησοῦ τοῦ
of Elmadam   - of Er   - of Jesus -

Ἐλιέζερ τοῦ Ἰωρὶμ τοῦ Ματθὰτ τοῦ
of Eliezer   - of Jorim   - of Matthat -

Λευὶ 30 τοῦ Συμεὼν τοῦ Ἰούδα τοῦ
of Levi   - of Simeon   - of Juda -

Ἰωσὴφ τοῦ Ἰωνὰμ τοῦ Ἐλιακὶμ 31 τοῦ
of Joseph   - of Jonam   - of Eliakim -

Μελεὰ τοῦ Μεννὰ τοῦ Ματταθὰ τοῦ
of Melea   - of Menna   - of Mattatha -

Ναθὰμ τοῦ Δαυὶδ 32 τοῦ Ἰεσσαὶ τοῦ
of Natham   - of David   - of Jesse -

Ἰωβὴδ τοῦ Βόος τοῦ Σάλα τοῦ Ναασσὼν
of Jobed   - of Boos   - of Sala   - of Naasson

33 τοῦ Ἀμιναδὰβ τοῦ Ἀδμὶν τοῦ Ἀρνὶ
- of Aminadab   - of Admin   - of Arni

τοῦ Ἑσρὼμ τοῦ Φάρες τοῦ Ἰούδα
- of Hesrom   - of Phares   - of Juda

34 τοῦ Ἰακὼβ τοῦ Ἰσαὰκ τοῦ Ἀβραὰμ
- of Jacob   - of Isaac   - of Abraham

τοῦ Θάρα τοῦ Ναχὼρ 35 τοῦ Σεροὺχ
- of Thara   - of Nachor   - of Seruch

τοῦ Ῥαγαὺ τοῦ Φάλεκ τοῦ Ἕβερ τοῦ
- of Rhagau   - of Phalek   - of Eber -

Σάλα 36 τοῦ Καϊνὰμ τοῦ Ἀρφαξὰδ τοῦ
of Sala   - of Cainam   - of Arphaxad -

Σὴμ τοῦ Νῶε τοῦ Λάμεχ 37 τοῦ Μαθουσάλα
of Sem   - of Noe   - of Lamech   - of Mathusala

τοῦ Ἐνὼχ τοῦ Ἰάρετ τοῦ Μαλελεὴλ
- of Henoch   - of Jaret   - of Maleleel

τοῦ Καϊνὰμ 38 τοῦ Ἐνὼς τοῦ Σὴθ τοῦ
- of Cainam   - of Enos   - of Seth -

Ἀδὰμ τοῦ θεοῦ.
of Adam   - of God.

was the son, so it was thought, of Joseph, the son of Heli, 24 the son of Levi, the son of Melki, the son of Jannai, the son of Joseph, 25 the son of Mattathias, the son of Amos, the son of Nahum, the son of Esli, the son of Naggai, 26 the son of Maath, the son of Mattathias, the son of Semein, the son of Josech, the son of Joda, 27 the son of Joanan, the son of Rhesa, the son of Zerubbabel, the son of Shealtiel, the son of Neri, 28 the son of Melki, the son of Addi, the son of Cosam, the son of Elmadam, the son of Er, 29 the son of Joshua, the son of Eliezer, the son of Jorim, the son of Matthat, the son of Levi, 30 the son of Simeon, the son of Judah, the son of Joseph, the son of Jonam, the son of Eliakim, 31 the son of Melea, the son of Menna, the son of Mattatha, the son of Nathan, the son of David, 32 the son of Obed, the son of Boaz, the son of Salmon, m the son of Nahshon, 33 the son of Amminadab, the son of Ram, n the son of Hezron, the son of Perez, the son of Judah, 34 the son of Jacob, the son of Isaac, the son of Abraham, the son of Terah, the son of Nahor, 35 the son of Serug, the son of Reu, the son of Peleg, the son of Eber, the son of Shelah, 36 the son of Cainan, the son of Arphaxad, the son of Shem, the son of Noah, the son of Lamech, 37 the son of Methuselah, the son of Enoch, the son of Jared, the son of Mahalalel, the son of Kenan, 38 the son of Enosh, the son of Seth, the son of Adam, the son of God.

Chapter 4

The Temptation of Jesus

JESUS, full of the Holy Spirit, returned from the Jordan and was led by the Spirit in the wilderness, 2 where for forty days he was tempted by the devil.

c Gk Salathiel
d Other ancient authorities read Salmon
e Other ancient authorities read Amminadab, son of Aram; others vary widely

4 Ἰησοῦς δὲ πλήρης πνεύματος ἁγίου
And Jesus   full   of [the] *Spirit   ²Holy

ὑπέστρεψεν ἀπὸ τοῦ Ἰορδάνου, καὶ ἤγετο
returned   from   the   Jordan,   and   was led

ἐν τῷ πνεύματι ἐν τῇ ἐρήμῳ 2 ἡμέρας
by   the   Spirit   in   the   desert   days

τεσσεράκοντα πειραζόμενος ὑπὸ τοῦ διαβόλου.
forty   being tempted   by   the   devil.

m 32 Some early manuscripts Sala
n 33 Some manuscripts Amminadab, the son of Admin, the son of Arni; other manuscripts vary widely.

He ate nothing at all during those days, and when they were over, he was famished. ³The devil said to him, "If you are the Son of God, command this stone to become a loaf of bread." ⁴Jesus answered him, "It is written, 'One does not live by bread alone.'"

5 Then the devil*ᶠ* led him up and showed him in an instant all the kingdoms of the world. ⁶And the devil*ᶠ* said to him, "To you I will give their glory and all this authority; for it has been given over to me, and I give it to anyone I please. ⁷If you, then, will worship me, it will all be yours." ⁸Jesus answered him, "It is written,

'Worship the Lord
   your God,
and serve only
   him.'"

9 Then the devil*ᶠ* took him to Jerusalem, and placed him on the pinnacle of the temple, saying to him, "If you are the Son of God, throw yourself down from here, ¹⁰for it is written,

'He will command his
   angels
concerning you,
   to protect you,'
¹¹and

'On their hands they
   will bear
   you up,
so that you will not
   dash your foot
   against a
   stone.'"

¹²Jesus answered him, "It is said, 'Do not put the Lord your God to the test.'" ¹³When the devil had finished every test, he departed from him until an opportune time.

The Beginning of the Galilean Ministry

14 Then Jesus, filled with the power of the Spirit, returned to Galilee, and a report about him spread through all the surrounding country. ¹⁵He began to teach in their synagogues

ᶠGk he

Καὶ   οὐκ   ἔφαγεν   οὐδὲν   ἐν   ταῖς   ἡμέραις
And   he ate not   no(any)thing   in   –   days
ἐκείναις,   καὶ   συντελεσθεισῶν   αὐτῶν   ἐπεί-
those,   and   being ended   themᵃ   he
=when they were ended
νασεν.   3 εἶπεν   δὲ   αὐτῷ   ὁ   διάβολος·
hungered.   And said   to him   the   devil :
εἰ   υἱὸς   εἶ   τοῦ   θεοῦ,   εἰπὲ   τῷ   λίθῳ
If   Son   thou art   –   of God,   tell   –   stone
τούτῳ   ἵνα   γένηται   ἄρτος.   4 καὶ   ἀπεκρίθη
this   that it become   a loaf.   And made answer
πρὸς   αὐτὸν   ὁ   Ἰησοῦς·   γέγραπται   ὅτι
to   him   –   Jesus :   It has been written[,] –
οὐκ   ἐπ'   ἄρτῳ   μόνῳ   ζήσεται   ὁ   ἄνθρωπος.
Not   on   bread   only   shall live   –   man.
5 Καὶ   ἀναγαγὼν   αὐτὸν   ἔδειξεν   αὐτῷ   πάσας
And   leading up   him   he showed   him   all
τὰς   βασιλείας   τῆς   οἰκουμένης   ἐν   στιγμῇ
the   kingdoms   of the   inhabited earth   in   a moment
χρόνου.   6 καὶ   εἶπεν   αὐτῷ   ὁ   διάβολος·
of time.   And   said   to him   the   devil :
σοὶ   δώσω   τὴν   ἐξουσίαν   ταύτην   ἅπασαν   καὶ
To thee   I will give   –   authority   this   all   and
τὴν   δόξαν   αὐτῶν,   ὅτι   ἐμοὶ   παραδέδοται
the   glory   of them,   because   to me   it has been delivered
καὶ   ᾧ   ἐὰν   θέλω   δίδωμι   αὐτήν· 7 σὺ   οὖν
and to   whomever I wish   I give   it;   ᵃthou   ¹therefore
ἐὰν   προσκυνήσῃς   ἐνώπιον   ἐμοῦ,   ἔσται   σοῦ
²if   worship   before   me,   will be   of thee
πᾶσα.   8 καὶ   ἀποκριθεὶς   ὁ   Ἰησοῦς   εἶπεν
all.   And   answering   –   Jesus   said
αὐτῷ·   γέγραπται·   προσκυνήσεις   κύριον   τὸν
to him : It has been written: Thou shalt worship [the] Lord the
θεόν   σου   καὶ   αὐτῷ   μόνῳ   λατρεύσεις.
God   of thee   and   him   only   shalt thou serve.
9 Ἤγαγεν   δὲ   αὐτὸν   εἰς   Ἰερουσαλὴμ   καὶ
And he led   him   to   Jerusalem   and
ἔστησεν   ἐπὶ   τὸ   πτερύγιον   τοῦ   ἱεροῦ,   καὶ
set   on   the   gable   of the   temple,   and
εἶπεν   αὐτῷ·   εἰ   υἱὸς   εἶ   τοῦ   θεοῦ,   βάλε
said   to him :   If   Son   thou art   –   of God,   throw
σεαυτὸν   ἐντεῦθεν   κάτω· 10 γέγραπται   γὰρ   ὅτι
thyself   hence   down;   for it has been written[,] –
τοῖς   ἀγγέλοις   αὐτοῦ   ἐντελεῖται   περὶ
The   angels   of him   he will command concerning
σοῦ   τοῦ   διαφυλάξαι   σε,   11 καὶ   ὅτι   ἐπὶ
thee   –   to preserveᵈ   thee,   and   on
χειρῶν   ἀροῦσίν   σε,   μήποτε   προσκόψῃς
[their] hands   they will bear   thee,   lest   thou dash
πρὸς   λίθον   τὸν   πόδα   σου.   12 καὶ
against   a stone   the   foot   of thee.   And
ἀποκριθεὶς   εἶπεν   αὐτῷ   ὁ   Ἰησοῦς   ὅτι
answering   said   to him   –   Jesus[,]   –
εἴρηται·   οὐκ   ἐκπειράσεις   κύριον   τὸν
It has been said : Thou shalt not overtempt [the] Lord the
θεόν   σου.   13 Καὶ   συντελέσας   πάντα   πειρασμὸν
God of thee.   And having finished   every   temptation
ὁ   διάβολος   ἀπέστη   ἀπ'   αὐτοῦ   ἄχρι   καιροῦ.
the   devil   went away from   him   until   a season.
14 Καὶ   ὑπέστρεψεν   ὁ   Ἰησοῦς   ἐν   τῇ
And   returned   –   Jesus   in   the
δυνάμει   τοῦ   πνεύματος   εἰς   τὴν   Γαλιλαίαν·
power   of the   Spirit   to   –   Galilee;
καὶ   φήμη   ἐξῆλθεν   καθ'   ὅλης   τῆς   περιχώρου
and   a rumour   went forth   throughout   all   the   neighbourhood
περὶ   αὐτοῦ.   15 καὶ   αὐτὸς   ἐδίδασκεν   ἐν
concerning   him.   And   he   taught   in

Chapter 4

The Temptation of Jesus

JESUS, full of the Holy Spirit, returned from the Jordan and was led by the Spirit in the desert, ²where for forty days he was tempted by the devil. He ate nothing during those days, and at the end of them he was hungry.

³The devil said to him, "If you are the Son of God, tell this stone to become bread."

⁴Jesus answered, "It is written: 'Man does not live on bread alone.'*ᵒ*

⁵The devil led him up to a high place and showed him in an instant all the kingdoms of the world. ⁶And he said to him, "I will give you all their authority and splendor, for it has been given to me, and I can give it to anyone I want to. ⁷So if you worship me, it will all be yours."

⁸Jesus answered, "It is written: 'Worship the Lord your God and serve him only.'*ᵖ*

⁹The devil led him to Jerusalem and had him stand on the highest point of the temple. "If you are the Son of God," he said, "throw yourself down from here. ¹⁰For it is written:

" 'He will command his
   angels concerning
   you
   to guard you carefully;
¹¹they will lift you up in
   their hands,
so that you will not
   strike your foot
   against a stone.'*ᵠ*

¹²Jesus answered, "It says: 'Do not put the Lord your God to the test.'*ʳ*

¹³When the devil had finished all this tempting, he left him until an opportune time.

Jesus Rejected at Nazareth

¹⁴Jesus returned to Galilee in the power of the Spirit, and news about him spread through the whole countryside. ¹⁵He taught in

ᵒ4 Deut. 8:3
ᵖ8 Deut. 6:13
ᵠ11 Psalm 91:11,12
ʳ12 Deut. 6:16

and was praised by every-
one.

*The Rejection of Jesus at
Nazareth*

16 When he came to
Nazareth, where he had
been brought up, he went
to the synagogue on the
sabbath day, as was his
custom. He stood up to
read, 17 and the scroll of the
prophet Isaiah was given to
him. He unrolled the scroll
and found the place where
it was written:
18 "The Spirit of the
    Lord is upon
    me,
  because he has
    anointed me
  to bring good
    news to the
    poor.
  He has sent me to
    proclaim release
    to the captives
  and recovery of
    sight to the
    blind,
  to let the
    oppressed go
    free,
19 to proclaim the year
    of the Lord's
    favor."
20 And he rolled up the
scroll, gave it back to the
attendant, and sat down.
The eyes of all in the synagogue were fixed on him.
21 Then he began to say to
them, "Today this scripture
has been fulfilled in your
hearing." 22 All spoke well
of him and were amazed at
the gracious words that
came from his mouth. They
said, "Is not this Joseph's
son?" 23 He said to them,
"Doubtless you will quote
to me this proverb, 'Doc-
tor, cure yourself!' And
you will say, 'Do here also
in your hometown the
things that we have heard
you did at Capernaum.' "
24 And he said, "Truly I tell
you, no prophet is accepted
in the prophet's hometown.
25 But the truth is, there
were many widows in Isra-
el in the time of Elijah,
when the heaven was shut
up three years and six

ταῖς συναγωγαῖς αὐτῶν, δοξαζόμενος ὑπὸ
the synagogues of them, being glorified by
πάντων.
all.

16 Καὶ ἦλθεν εἰς Ναζαρά, οὗ ἦν
   And he came to Nazareth, where he was
τεθραμμένος, καὶ εἰσῆλθεν κατὰ τὸ εἰωθὸς
having been and entered accord- the custom
brought up,   ing to = his custom
αὐτῷ ἐν τῇ ἡμέρᾳ τῶν σαββάτων εἰς τὴν
to him on the day of the sabbaths into the
συναγωγήν, καὶ ἀνέστη ἀναγνῶναι. 17 καὶ
synagogue, and stood up to read. And
ἐπεδόθη αὐτῷ βιβλίον τοῦ προφήτου
was handed to him a roll of the prophet
Ἠσαΐου, καὶ ἀνοίξας τὸ βιβλίον εὗρεν
Esaias, and having opened the roll he found
[τὸν] τόπον οὗ ἦν γεγραμμένον· 18 πνεῦμα
the place where it was written: [The] Spirit
κυρίου ἐπ᾽ ἐμέ, οὗ εἵνεκεν ἔχρισέν με
of [the] Lord [is] upon me, wherefore he anointed me
εὐαγγελίσασθαι πτωχοῖς, ἀπέσταλκέν με
to evangelize [the] poor, he has sent me
κηρῦξαι αἰχμαλώτοις ἄφεσιν καὶ τυφλοῖς
to proclaim to captives release and to blind [ones]
ἀνάβλεψιν, ἀποστεῖλαι τεθραυσμένους ἐν
sight, to send away having been crushed [ones] in
ἀφέσει, 19 κηρῦξαι ἐνιαυτὸν κυρίου δεκτόν.
release, to proclaim a year of [the] Lord acceptable.
20 καὶ πτύξας τὸ βιβλίον ἀποδοὺς τῷ
   And having closed the roll returning [it] to the
ὑπηρέτῃ ἐκάθισεν· καὶ πάντων οἱ ὀφθαλμοὶ
attendant he sat; and of all the eyes
ἐν τῇ συναγωγῇ ἦσαν ἀτενίζοντες αὐτῷ.
in the synagogue were gazing at him.
21 ἤρξατο δὲ λέγειν πρὸς αὐτοὺς ὅτι
   And he began to say to them[,] –
σήμερον πεπλήρωται ἡ γραφὴ αὕτη ἐν
To-day has been fulfilled the scripture this in
τοῖς ὠσὶν ὑμῶν. 22 καὶ πάντες ἐμαρτύρουν
the ears of you. And all bore witness
αὐτῷ καὶ ἐθαύμαζον ἐπὶ τοῖς λόγοις τῆς
to him and marvelled at the words –
χάριτος τοῖς ἐκπορευομένοις ἐκ τοῦ στόματος
of grace – proceeding out of the mouth
αὐτοῦ, καὶ ἔλεγον· οὐχὶ υἱός ἐστιν Ἰωσὴφ
of him, and they said: ²not ⁴son ¹Is ⁵of Joseph
οὗτος; 23 καὶ εἶπεν πρὸς αὐτούς· πάντως
³this man? And he said to them: To be sure
ἐρεῖτέ μοι τὴν παραβολὴν ταύτην· ἰατρέ,
ye will say to me the parable this: Physician,
θεράπευσον σεαυτόν· ὅσα ἠκούσαμεν γεν-
heal thyself; what things we heard hap-
όμενα εἰς τὴν Καφαρναούμ, ποίησον καὶ
pening in – Capernaum, do also
ὧδε ἐν τῇ πατρίδι σου. 24 εἶπεν δέ·
here in the native place of thee. And he said:
ἀμὴν λέγω ὑμῖν ὅτι οὐδεὶς προφήτης
Truly I tell you that no prophet
δεκτός ἐστιν ἐν τῇ πατρίδι αὐτοῦ. 25 ἐπ᾽
acceptable is in the native place of him. ²on(in)
ἀληθείας δὲ λέγω ὑμῖν, πολλαὶ χῆραι ἦσαν
³truth ¹But I tell you, many widows were
ἐν ταῖς ἡμέραις Ἡλίου ἐν τῷ Ἰσραήλ,
in the days of Elias in – Israel,
ὅτε ἐκλείσθη ὁ οὐρανὸς ἐπὶ ἔτη τρία καὶ
when was shut up the heaven over years three and

their synagogues, and ev-
eryone praised him.
16 He went to Nazareth,
where he had been brought
up, and on the Sabbath day
he went into the syna-
gogue, as was his custom.
And he stood up to read.
17 The scroll of the prophet
Isaiah was handed to him.
Unrolling it, he found the
place where it is written:
18 "The Spirit of the Lord
    is on me,
  because he has
    anointed me
  to preach good news to
    the poor.
  He has sent me to
    proclaim freedom
    for the prisoners
  and recovery of sight
    for the blind,
  to release the oppressed,
19 to proclaim the year of
    the Lord's favor." ˢ
20 Then he rolled up the
scroll, gave it back to the
attendant and sat down.
The eyes of everyone in the
synagogue were fastened
on him, 21 and he began by
saying to them, "Today
this scripture is fulfilled in
your hearing."
22 All spoke well of him
and were amazed at the
gracious words that came
from his lips. "Isn't this Joseph's son?" they asked.
23 Jesus said to them,
"Surely you will quote this
proverb to me: 'Physician,
heal yourself! Do here in
your hometown what we
have heard that you did in
Capernaum.' "
24 "I tell you the truth,"
he continued, "no prophet
is accepted in his home-
town. 25 I assure you that
there were many widows in
Israel in Elijah's time,
when the sky was shut for
three and a half years and

ˢ 19 Isaiah 61:1,2

months, and there was a severe famine over all the land; 26 yet Elijah was sent to none of them except to a widow at Zarephath in Sidon. 27 There were also many lepers[g] in Israel in the time of the prophet Elisha, and none of them was cleansed except Naaman the Syrian." 28 When they heard this, all in the synagogue were filled with rage. 29 They got up, drove him out of the town, and led him to the brow of the hill on which their town was built, so that they might hurl him off the cliff. 30 But he passed through the midst of them and went on his way.

The Man with an Unclean Spirit

31 He went down to Capernaum, a city in Galilee, and was teaching them on the sabbath. 32 They were astounded at his teaching, because he spoke with authority. 33 In the synagogue there was a man who had the spirit of an unclean demon, and he cried out with a loud voice, 34 "Let us alone! What have you to do with us, Jesus of Nazareth? Have you come to destroy us? I know who you are, the Holy One of God." 35 But Jesus rebuked him, saying, "Be silent, and come out of him!" When the demon had thrown him down before them, he came out of him without having done him any harm. 36 They were all amazed and kept saying to one another, "What kind of utterance is this? For with authority and power he commands the unclean spirits, and out they come!" 37 And a report about him began to reach every place in the region.

μῆνας ἕξ, ὡς ἐγένετο λιμὸς μέγας ἐπὶ
months six, when came famine a great over

πᾶσαν τὴν γῆν, 26 καὶ πρὸς οὐδεμίαν
all the land, and to not one

αὐτῶν ἐπέμφθη Ἡλίας εἰ μὴ εἰς Σάρεπτα
of them was sent Elias except to Sarepta

τῆς Σιδωνίας πρὸς γυναῖκα χήραν. 27 καὶ
- of Sidon to a woman a widow. And

πολλοὶ λεπροὶ ἦσαν ἐν τῷ Ἰσραὴλ ἐπὶ
many lepers were in - Israel during

Ἐλισαίου τοῦ προφήτου, καὶ οὐδεὶς αὐτῶν
Elisæus the prophet, and not one of them

ἐκαθαρίσθη εἰ μὴ Ναιμὰν ὁ Σύρος.
was cleansed except Naaman the Syrian.

28 καὶ ἐπλήσθησαν πάντες θυμοῦ ἐν τῇ
And ²were filled ¹all of(with) anger in the

συναγωγῇ ἀκούοντες ταῦτα, 29 καὶ ἀναστάντες
synagogue hearing these things, and rising up

ἐξέβαλον αὐτὸν ἔξω τῆς πόλεως, καὶ
they cast out him outside the city, and

ἤγαγον αὐτὸν ἕως ὀφρύος τοῦ ὄρους ἐφ'
led him to a brow of the hill on

οὗ ἡ πόλις ᾠκοδόμητο αὐτῶν, ὥστε
which the city was built of them, so as

κατακρημνίσαι αὐτόν· 30 αὐτὸς δὲ διελθὼν
to throw down him; but he passing through

διὰ μέσου αὐτῶν ἐπορεύετο.
through [the] midst of them went.

31 Καὶ κατῆλθεν εἰς Καφαρναοὺμ πόλιν
And he went down to Capernaum a city

τῆς Γαλιλαίας. καὶ ἦν διδάσκων αὐτοὺς
- of Galilee. And he was teaching them

ἐν τοῖς σάββασιν· 32 καὶ ἐξεπλήσσοντο
on the sabbaths; and they were astounded

ἐπὶ τῇ διδαχῇ αὐτοῦ, ὅτι ἐν ἐξουσίᾳ
at the teaching of him, because with authority

ἦν ὁ λόγος αὐτοῦ. 33 καὶ ἐν τῇ συναγωγῇ
was the word of him. And in the synagogue

ἦν ἄνθρωπος ἔχων πνεῦμα δαιμονίου
there was a man having a spirit ²demon

ἀκαθάρτου, καὶ ἀνέκραξεν φωνῇ μεγάλῃ·
¹of an unclean, and he shouted voice with a great :

34 ἔα, τί ἡμῖν καὶ σοί, Ἰησοῦ Ναζαρηνέ;
Ah, what to us and to thee, Jesus Nazarene?

ἦλθες ἀπολέσαι ἡμᾶς; οἶδά σε τίς εἶ,
Camest thou to destroy us? I know thee who thou art,

ὁ ἅγιος τοῦ θεοῦ. 35 καὶ ἐπετίμησεν αὐτῷ
the holy one - of God. And rebuked him

ὁ Ἰησοῦς λέγων· φιμώθητι καὶ ἔξελθε
- Jesus saying : Be muzzled and come out

ἀπ' αὐτοῦ. καὶ ῥῖψαν αὐτὸν τὸ δαιμόνιον
from him. And ²throwing ¹him ¹the ²demon

εἰς τὸ μέσον ἐξῆλθεν ἀπ' αὐτοῦ μηδὲν
in the midst came out from him nothing

βλάψαν αὐτόν. 36 καὶ ἐγένετο θάμβος
injuring him. And came astonishment

ἐπὶ πάντας, καὶ συνελάλουν πρὸς ἀλλήλους
on all, and they spoke to one another

λέγοντες· τίς ὁ λόγος οὗτος, ὅτι ἐν
saying : What [is] - word this, because with

ἐξουσίᾳ καὶ δυνάμει ἐπιτάσσει τοῖς
authority and power he commands the

ἀκαθάρτοις πνεύμασιν καὶ ἐξέρχονται; 37 καὶ
unclean spirits and they come out? And

ἐξεπορεύετο ἦχος περὶ αὐτοῦ εἰς πάντα
went forth a rumour concerning him into every

there was a severe famine throughout the land. 26 Yet Elijah was not sent to any of them, but to a widow in Zarephath in the region of Sidon. 27 And there were many in Israel with leprosy[t] in the time of Elisha the prophet, yet not one of them was cleansed—only Naaman the Syrian."
28 All the people in the synagogue were furious when they heard this. 29 They got up, drove him out of the town, and took him to the brow of the hill on which the town was built, in order to throw him down the cliff. 30 But he walked right through the crowd and went on his way.

Jesus Drives Out an Evil Spirit

31 Then he went down to Capernaum, a town in Galilee, and on the Sabbath began to teach the people. 32 They were amazed at his teaching, because his message had authority.
33 In the synagogue there was a man possessed by a demon, an evil[u] spirit. He cried out at the top of his voice, 34 "Ha! What do you want with us, Jesus of Nazareth? Have you come to destroy us? I know who you are—the Holy One of God!"
35 "Be quiet!" Jesus said sternly. "Come out of him!" Then the demon threw the man down before them all and came out without injuring him.
36 All the people were amazed and said to each other, "What is this teaching? With authority and power he gives orders to evil spirits and they come out!" 37 And the news about

g The terms leper and leprosy can refer to several diseases

t 27 The Greek word was used for various diseases affecting the skin—not necessarily leprosy.
u 33 Greek unclean; also in verse 36

Healings at Simon's House

38 After leaving the synagogue he entered Simon's house. Now Simon's mother-in-law was suffering from a high fever, and they asked him about her. 39 Then he stood over her and rebuked the fever, and it left her. Immediately she got up and began to serve them.

40 As the sun was setting, all those who had any who were sick with various kinds of diseases brought them to him; and he laid his hands on each of them and cured them. 41 Demons also came out of many, shouting, "You are the Son of God!" But he rebuked them and would not allow them to speak, because they knew that he was the Messiah. [h]

Jesus Preaches in the Synagogues

42 At daybreak he departed and went into a deserted place. And the crowds were looking for him; and when they reached him, they wanted to prevent him from leaving them. 43 But he said to them, "I must proclaim the good news of the kingdom of God to the other cities also; for I was sent for this purpose." 44 So he continued proclaiming the message in the synagogues of Judea. [i]

Chapter 5

Jesus Calls the First Disciples

ONCE while Jesus[j] was standing beside the lake of Gennesaret, and the crowd was pressing in on him to hear the word of God, 2 he saw two boats there at the shore of the lake; the fishermen had gone out of them and were washing their nets. 3 He got into one of the boats, the

[h] Or the Christ
[i] Other ancient authorities read Galilee
[j] Gk he

τόπον   τῆς   περιχώρου.   **38** Ἀναστὰς   δὲ
place   of the   neighbourhood.   And rising up

ἀπὸ   τῆς   συναγωγῆς   εἰσῆλθεν   εἰς   τὴν
from   the   synagogue   he entered   into   the

οἰκίαν   Σίμωνος.   πενθερὰ   δὲ   τοῦ   Σίμωνος
house   of Simon.   And [the] mother-in-law   -   of Simon

ἦν   συνεχομένη   πυρετῷ   μεγάλῳ,   καὶ
was   being seized   fever   with a great,   and

ἠρώτησαν   αὐτὸν   περὶ   αὐτῆς.   **39** καὶ
they ask   ₊him   about   her.   And

ἐπιστὰς   ἐπάνω   αὐτῆς   ἐπετίμησεν   τῷ   πυρετῷ,
standing   over   her   he rebuked   the   fever,

καὶ   ἀφῆκεν   αὐτήν·   παραχρῆμα   δὲ   ἀναστᾶσα
and   it left   her;   and at once   rising up

διηκόνει   αὐτοῖς.   **40** Δύνοντος   δὲ   τοῦ
she served   them.   And setting   -   the
=as the sun was setting

ἡλίου   ἅπαντες   ὅσοι   εἶχον   ἀσθενοῦντας
sun[a]   all   as many as   had   ailing [ones]

νόσοις   ποικίλαις   ἤγαγον   αὐτοὺς   πρὸς   αὐτόν·
diseases   with various   brought   them   to   him;

ὁ   δὲ   ἑνὶ   ἑκάστῳ   αὐτῶν   τὰς   χεῖρας
and he   ⁵one   ⁴on each   ⁶of them   ³the(his)   ³hands

ἐπιτιθεὶς   ἐθεράπευεν   αὐτούς.   **41** ἐξήρχετο
¹putting on   healed   them.   came out

δὲ   καὶ   δαιμόνια   ἀπὸ   πολλῶν,   κραυγάζοντα
And also   demons   from   many,   crying out

καὶ   λέγοντα   ὅτι   σὺ   εἶ   ὁ   υἱὸς   τοῦ   θεοῦ.
and   saying[,]   -   Thou art   the   Son   -   of God.

καὶ   ἐπιτιμῶν   οὐκ   εἴα   αὐτὰ   λαλεῖν,   ὅτι
And   rebuking   he allowed not   them   to speak,   because

ᾔδεισαν   τὸν   χριστὸν   αὐτὸν   εἶναι.   **42** Γενομένης
they knew   ³the   ⁴Christ   ¹him   ²to be.   coming
=And when

δὲ   ἡμέρας   ἐξελθὼν   ἐπορεύθη   εἰς   ἔρημον
And   day[a]   going forth   he went   to   a desert
day came

τόπον·   καὶ   οἱ   ὄχλοι   ἐπεζήτουν   αὐτόν,   καὶ
place;   and   the   crowds   sought   him,   and

ἦλθον   ἕως   αὐτοῦ,   καὶ   κατεῖχον   αὐτὸν
came   up to   him,   and   detained   him

τοῦ   μὴ   πορεύεσθαι   ἀπ'   αὐτῶν.   **43** ὁ   δὲ
-    not   to go[d]   from   them.   And he
=so that he should not go

εἶπεν   πρὸς   αὐτοὺς   ὅτι   καὶ   ταῖς   ἑτέραις
said   to   them[,]   -   Also   to the   other

πόλεσιν   εὐαγγελίσασθαί   με   δεῖ   τὴν
cities   ²to preach   ³me   ¹it behoves   the

βασιλείαν   τοῦ   θεοῦ,   ὅτι   ἐπὶ   τοῦτο   ἀπεστάλην.
kingdom   -   of God, because on   this   I was sent.

44 καὶ   ἦν   κηρύσσων   εἰς   τὰς   συναγωγὰς
And   he was   proclaiming   in   the   synagogues

τῆς   Ἰουδαίας.
-    of Judæa.

5 Ἐγένετο   δὲ   ἐν   τῷ   τὸν   ὄχλον   ἐπικεῖσθαι
Now it came to pass   in   the   the   crowd   to press upon
=as the crowd pressed upon him and heard

αὐτῷ   καὶ   ἀκούειν   τὸν   λόγον   τοῦ   θεοῦ,
him   and   to hear[be]   the   word   -   of God,

καὶ   αὐτὸς   ἦν   ἑστὼς   παρὰ   τὴν   λίμνην
and   he   was   standing   by   the   lake

Γεννησαρέτ,   **2** καὶ   εἶδεν   δύο   πλοιάρια
Gennesaret,   and   saw   two   boats

ἑστῶτα   παρὰ   τὴν   λίμνην·   οἱ   δὲ   ἁλεεῖς
standing   by   the   lake;   but the   fishermen

ἀπ'   αὐτῶν   ἀποβάντες   ἔπλυνον   τὰ   δίκτυα.
from   them   having gone away   were washing the   nets.

---

him spread throughout the surrounding area.

Jesus Heals Many

38 Jesus left the synagogue and went to the home of Simon. Now Simon's mother-in-law was suffering from a high fever, and they asked Jesus to help her. 39 So he bent over her and rebuked the fever, and it left her. She got up at once and began to wait on them.

40 When the sun was setting, the people brought to Jesus all who had various kinds of sickness, and laying his hands on each one, he healed them. 41 Moreover, demons came out of many people, shouting, "You are the Son of God!" But he rebuked them and would not allow them to speak, because they knew he was the Christ. [v]

42 At daybreak Jesus went out to a solitary place. The people were looking for him and when they came to where he was, they tried to keep him from leaving them. 43 But he said, "I must preach the good news of the kingdom of God to the other towns also, because that is why I was sent." 44 And he kept on preaching in the synagogues of Judea. [w]

Chapter 5

The Calling of the First Disciples

ONE day as Jesus was standing by the Lake of Gennesaret, [x] with the people crowding around him and listening to the word of God, 2 he saw at the water's edge two boats, left there by the fishermen, who were washing their

[v] 41 Or Messiah
[w] 44 Or the land of the Jews; some manuscripts Galilee
[x] 1 That is, Sea of Galilee

one belonging to Simon, and asked him to put out a little way from the shore. Then he sat down and taught the crowds from the boat. 4When he had finished speaking, he said to Simon, "Put out into the deep water and let down your nets for a catch." 5Simon answered, "Master, we have worked all night long but have caught nothing. Yet if you say so, I will let down the nets." 6When they had done this, they caught so many fish that their nets were beginning to break. 7So they signaled their partners in the other boat to come and help them. And they came and filled both boats, so that they began to sink. 8But when Simon Peter saw it, he fell down at Jesus' knees, saying, "Go away from me, Lord, for I am a sinful man!" 9For he and all who were with him were amazed at the catch of fish that they had taken; 10and so also were James and John, sons of Zebedee, who were partners with Simon. Then Jesus said to Simon, "Do not be afraid; from now on you will be catching people." 11When they had brought their boats to shore, they left everything and followed him.

Jesus Cleanses a Leper

12 Once, when he was in one of the cities, there was a man covered with leprosy.[k] When he saw Jesus, he bowed with his face to the ground and begged him, "Lord, if you

3 ἐμβὰς δὲ εἰς ἕν τῶν πλοίων, ὃ ἦν
And embarking in one of the boats, which was

Σίμωνος, ἠρώτησεν αὐτὸν ἀπὸ τῆς γῆς
of Simon, he asked him from the land

ἐπαναγαγεῖν ὀλίγον· καθίσας δὲ ἐκ τοῦ
to put out a little; and sitting ⁴out of ⁵the

πλοίου ἐδίδασκεν τοὺς ὄχλους. 4 ὡς δὲ
⁶boat ¹he taught ²the ³crowds. And when

ἐπαύσατο λαλῶν, εἶπεν πρὸς τὸν Σίμωνα·
he ceased speaking, he said to - Simon :

ἐπανάγαγε εἰς τὸ βάθος, καὶ χαλάσατε
Put out into the deep, and let down

τὰ δίκτυα ὑμῶν εἰς ἄγραν. 5 καὶ
the nets of you for a draught. And

ἀποκριθεὶς Σίμων εἶπεν· ἐπιστάτα, δι᾽
answering Simon said : Master, through

ὅλης νυκτὸς κοπιάσαντες οὐδὲν ἐλάβομεν·
[the] whole night labouring nothing we took;

ἐπὶ δὲ τῷ ῥήματί σου χαλάσω τὰ δίκτυα.
but at the word of thee I will let down the nets.

6 καὶ τοῦτο ποιήσαντες συνέκλεισαν πλῆθος
And this doing they enclosed multitude

ἰχθύων πολύ· διερρήσσετο δὲ τὰ δίκτυα
of fishes a much; and were being torn the nets

αὐτῶν. 7 καὶ κατένευσαν τοῖς μετόχοις
of them. And they nodded to the(ir) partners

ἐν τῷ ἑτέρῳ πλοίῳ τοῦ ἐλθόντας
in the other boat - coming
=that they should come

συλλαβέσθαι αὐτοῖς· καὶ ἦλθαν, καὶ ἔπλησαν
to help[d] them; and they came, and filled

ἀμφότερα τὰ πλοῖα ὥστε βυθίζεσθαι αὐτά.
both the boats so as to be sinking them.[b]
=so that they were sinking.

8 ἰδὼν δὲ Σίμων Πέτρος προσέπεσεν τοῖς
And seeing Simon Peter fell at the

γόνασιν Ἰησοῦ λέγων· ἔξελθε ἀπ᾽ ἐμοῦ,
knees of Jesus saying : Depart from me,

ὅτι ἀνὴρ ἁμαρτωλός εἰμι, κύριε. 9 θάμβος
because man a sinful I am, Lord. astonishment

γὰρ περιέσχεν αὐτὸν καὶ πάντας τοὺς
For seized him and all the [ones]

σὺν αὐτῷ ἐπὶ τῇ ἄγρᾳ τῶν ἰχθύων ᾗ
with him at the draught of the fishes which

συνέλαβον, 10 ὁμοίως δὲ καὶ Ἰάκωβον καὶ
they took, and likewise both James and

Ἰωάννην υἱοὺς Ζεβεδαίου, οἳ ἦσαν κοινωνοὶ
John sons of Zebedee, who were sharers

τῷ Σίμωνι. καὶ εἶπεν πρὸς τὸν Σίμωνα
- with Simon. And said to - Simon

ὁ Ἰησοῦς· μὴ φοβοῦ· ἀπὸ τοῦ νῦν
- Jesus: Fear thou not; from - now

ἀνθρώπους ἔσῃ ζωγρῶν. 11 καὶ καταγαγόντες
men thou wilt be taking alive. And bringing down

τὰ πλοῖα ἐπὶ τὴν γῆν, ἀφέντες πάντα
the boats onto the land, leaving all things

ἠκολούθησαν αὐτῷ.
they followed him.

12 Καὶ ἐγένετο ἐν τῷ εἶναι αὐτὸν ἐν
And it came to pass in the to be him[be] in
=as he was

μιᾷ τῶν πόλεων καὶ ἰδοὺ ἀνὴρ πλήρης
one of the cities and behold[,] a man full

λέπρας· ἰδὼν δὲ τὸν Ἰησοῦν, πεσὼν ἐπὶ
of leprosy; and seeing - Jesus, falling on

πρόσωπον ἐδεήθη αὐτοῦ λέγων· κύριε,
[his] face he begged him saying : Lord,

nets. 3He got into one of the boats, the one belonging to Simon, and asked him to put out a little from shore. Then he sat down and taught the people from the boat.

4When he had finished speaking, he said to Simon, "Put out into deep water, and let down[y] the nets for a catch."

5Simon answered, "Master, we've worked hard all night and haven't caught anything. But because you say so, I will let down the nets."

6When they had done so, they caught such a large number of fish that their nets began to break. 7So they signaled their partners in the other boat to come and help them, and they came and filled both boats so full that they began to sink.

8When Simon Peter saw this, he fell at Jesus' knees and said, "Go away from me, Lord; I am a sinful man!" 9For he and all his companions were astonished at the catch of fish they had taken, 10and so were James and John, the sons of Zebedee, Simon's partners.

Then Jesus said to Simon, "Don't be afraid; from now on you will catch men." 11So they pulled their boats up on shore, left everything and followed him.

The Man With Leprosy

12While Jesus was in one of the towns, a man came along who was covered with leprosy.[z] When he saw Jesus, he fell with his face to the ground and begged him, "Lord, if you

y4 The Greek verb is plural.
z12 The Greek word was used for various diseases affecting the skin—not necessarily leprosy.

choose, you can make me clean." 13Then Jesus[j] stretched out his hand, touched him, and said, "I do choose. Be made clean." The leprosy[k] left him. 14And he ordered him to tell no one. "Go," he said, "and show yourself to the priest, and, as Moses commanded, make an offering for your cleansing, for a testimony to them." 15But now more than ever the word about Jesus[l] spread abroad; many crowds would gather to hear him and to be cured of their diseases. 16But he would withdraw to deserted places and pray.

Jesus Heals a Paralytic

17 One day, while he was teaching, Pharisees and teachers of the law were sitting near by (they had come from every village of Galilee and Judea and from Jerusalem); and the power of the Lord was with him to heal.[m] 18Just then some men came, carrying a paralyzed man on a bed. They were trying to bring him in and lay him before Jesus;[l] 19but finding no way to bring him in because of the crowd, they went up on the roof and let him down with his bed through the tiles into the middle of the crowd[n] in front of Jesus. 20When he saw their faith, he said, "Friend,[o] your sins are forgiven you." 21Then the scribes and the Pharisees began to question, "Who is this who is speaking blasphemies? Who can forgive sins but God alone?" 22When Jesus perceived their questionings, he an-

---

ἐὰν θέλῃς, δύνασαί με καθαρίσαι. 13 καὶ
if thou willest, thou canst me to cleanse. And

ἐκτείνας τὴν χεῖρα ἥψατο αὐτοῦ λέγων·
stretching out the(his) hand he touched him saying:

θέλω, καθαρίσθητι· καὶ εὐθέως ἡ λέπρα
I am willing, be thou cleansed; and immediately the leprosy

ἀπῆλθεν ἀπ' αὐτοῦ. 14 καὶ αὐτὸς παρήγγειλεν
departed from him. And he charged

αὐτῷ μηδενὶ εἰπεῖν, ἀλλὰ ἀπελθὼν δεῖξον
him no one to tell, but going away show

σεαυτὸν τῷ ἱερεῖ, καὶ προσένεγκε περὶ
thyself to the priest, and offer concerning

τοῦ καθαρισμοῦ σου καθὼς προσέταξεν
the cleansing of thee as commanded

Μωϋσῆς, εἰς μαρτύριον αὐτοῖς. 15 διήρχετο
Moses, for a testimony to them. went

δὲ μᾶλλον ὁ λόγος περὶ αὐτοῦ, καὶ
But rather the word concerning him, and

συνήρχοντο ὄχλοι πολλοὶ ἀκούειν καὶ
³accompanied ²crowds ¹many to hear and

θεραπεύεσθαι ἀπὸ τῶν ἀσθενειῶν αὐτῶν·
to be healed from the infirmities of them;

16 αὐτὸς δὲ ἦν ὑποχωρῶν ἐν ταῖς ἐρήμοις
but he was withdrawing in the deserts

καὶ προσευχόμενος.
and praying.

17 Καὶ ἐγένετο ἐν μιᾷ τῶν ἡμερῶν καὶ
And it came to pass on one of the days and

αὐτὸς ἦν διδάσκων, καὶ ἦσαν καθήμενοι
he was teaching, and were sitting

Φαρισαῖοι καὶ νομοδιδάσκαλοι οἳ ἦσαν
Pharisees and law-teachers who were

ἐληλυθότες ἐκ πάσης κώμης τῆς Γαλιλαίας
having come out of every village - of Galilee

καὶ Ἰουδαίας καὶ Ἰερουσαλήμ· καὶ δύναμις
and Judæa and Jerusalem; and [the] power

κυρίου ἦν εἰς τὸ ἰᾶσθαι αὐτόν. 18 καὶ
of [the] Lord was ¹in - ²to cure ²him. And

ἰδοὺ ἄνδρες φέροντες ἐπὶ κλίνης ἄνθρωπον
behold[,] men bearing on a couch a man

ὃς ἦν παραλελυμένος, καὶ ἐζήτουν αὐτὸν
who was *having been* paralysed, and they sought ²him

εἰσενεγκεῖν καὶ θεῖναι [αὐτὸν] ἐνώπιον
¹to carry in and to lay him before

αὐτοῦ. 19 καὶ μὴ εὑρόντες ποίας εἰσ-
him. And not finding how† they

ἐνέγκωσιν αὐτὸν διὰ τὸν ὄχλον, ἀναβάντες
might carry in him because of the crowd, going up

ἐπὶ τὸ δῶμα διὰ τῶν κεράμων καθῆκαν
onto the roof through the tiles they let down

αὐτὸν σὺν τῷ κλινιδίῳ εἰς τὸ μέσον
him with the couch into the midst

ἔμπροσθεν τοῦ Ἰησοῦ. 20 καὶ ἰδὼν τὴν
in front of - Jesus. And seeing the

πίστιν αὐτῶν εἶπεν· ἄνθρωπε, ἀφέωνταί
faith of them he said: Man, have been forgiven

σοι αἱ ἁμαρτίαι σου. 21 καὶ ἤρξαντο
thee the sins of thee. And began

διαλογίζεσθαι οἱ γραμματεῖς καὶ οἱ Φαρισαῖοι
to reason the scribes and the Pharisees

λέγοντες· τίς ἐστιν οὗτος ὃς λαλεῖ
saying: Who is this man who speaks

βλασφημίας; τίς δύναται ἁμαρτίας ἀφεῖναι
blasphemies? Who can sins to forgive

εἰ μὴ μόνος ὁ θεός; 22 ἐπιγνοὺς δὲ ὁ
except only - God? But knowing -

---

are willing, you can make me clean."

13Jesus reached out his hand and touched the man. "I am willing," he said. "Be clean!" And immediately the leprosy left him. 14Then Jesus ordered him, "Don't tell anyone, but go, show yourself to the priest and offer the sacrifices that Moses commanded for your cleansing, as a testimony to them." 15Yet the news about him spread all the more, so that crowds of people came to hear him and to be healed of their sicknesses. 16But Jesus often withdrew to lonely places and prayed.

Jesus Heals a Paralytic

17One day as he was teaching, Pharisees and teachers of the law, who had come from every village of Galilee and from Judea and Jerusalem, were sitting there. And the power of the Lord was present for him to heal the sick. 18Some men came carrying a paralytic on a mat and tried to take him into the house to lay him before Jesus. 19When they could not find a way to do this because of the crowd, they went up on the roof and lowered him on his mat through the tiles into the middle of the crowd, right in front of Jesus.

20When Jesus saw their faith, he said, "Friend, your sins are forgiven."

21The Pharisees and the teachers of the law began thinking to themselves, "Who is this fellow who speaks blasphemy? Who can forgive sins but God alone?"

22Jesus knew what they

---

l Gk him
m Other ancient authorities read *was present to heal them*
n Gk *into the midst*
o Gk *Man*

swered them, "Why do you raise such questions in your hearts? 23 Which is easier, to say, 'Your sins are forgiven you,' or to say, 'Stand up and walk'? 24 But so that you may know that the Son of Man has authority on earth to forgive sins"—he said to the one who was paralyzed—"I say to you, stand up and take your bed and go to your home." 25 Immediately he stood up before them, took what he had been lying on, and went to his home, glorifying God. 26 Amazement seized all of them, and they glorified God and were filled with awe, saying, "We have seen strange things today."

Jesus Calls Levi

27 After this he went out and saw a tax collector named Levi, sitting at the tax booth; and he said to him, "Follow me." 28 And he got up, left everything, and followed him.

29 Then Levi gave a great banquet for him in his house; and there was a large crowd of tax collectors and others sitting at the table *p* with them. 30 The Pharisees and their scribes were complaining to his disciples, saying, "Why do you eat and drink with tax collectors and sinners?" 31 Jesus answered, "Those who are well have no need of a physician, but those who are sick; 32 I have come to call not the righteous but sinners to repentance."

The Question about Fasting

33 Then they said to him, "John's disciples, like the disciples of the Pharisees, frequently fast and pray, but your disciples eat

---

Ἰησοῦς τοὺς διαλογισμοὺς αὐτῶν, ἀποκριθεὶς
Jesus the reasonings of them, answering

εἶπεν πρὸς αὐτούς· τί διαλογίζεσθε ἐν
said to them : Why reason ye in

ταῖς καρδίαις ὑμῶν; 23 τί ἐστιν εὐκοπώτερον,
the hearts of you? What is easier,

εἰπεῖν· ἀφέωνταί σοι αἱ ἁμαρτίαι σου, ἢ
to say : Have been forgiven thee the sins of thee, or

εἰπεῖν· ἔγειρε καὶ περιπάτει; 24 ἵνα δὲ
to say : Rise and walk ? but that

εἰδῆτε ὅτι ὁ υἱὸς τοῦ ἀνθρώπου ἐξουσίαν
ye may know that the Son – of man authority

ἔχει ἐπὶ τῆς γῆς ἀφιέναι ἁμαρτίας, —
has on the earth to forgive sins, —

εἶπεν τῷ παραλελυμένῳ· σοὶ λέγω, ἔγειρε
he said to the paralysed [one] : To thee I say, rise

καὶ ἄρας τὸ κλινίδιόν σου πορεύου εἰς
and taking the pallet of thee go to

τὸν οἶκόν σου. 25 καὶ παραχρῆμα ἀναστὰς
the house of thee. And at once rising up

ἐνώπιον αὐτῶν, ἄρας ἐφ᾽ ὃ κατέκειτο,
before them, taking [that] on which he was lying,

ἀπῆλθεν εἰς τὸν οἶκον αὐτοῦ δοξάζων τὸν
he went away to the house of him glorifying –

θεόν. 26 καὶ ἔκστασις ἔλαβεν ἅπαντας, καὶ
God. And bewilderment took all, and

ἐδόξαζον τὸν θεόν, καὶ ἐπλήσθησαν φόβου
they glorified – God, and were filled of(with) fear

λέγοντες ὅτι εἴδομεν παράδοξα σήμερον.
saying[,] – We saw wonderful things to-day.

27 Καὶ μετὰ ταῦτα ἐξῆλθεν, καὶ ἐθεάσατο
And after these things he went forth, and saw

τελώνην ὀνόματι Λευὶν καθήμενον ἐπὶ τὸ
a tax-collector by name Levi sitting on(in) the

τελώνιον, καὶ εἶπεν αὐτῷ· ἀκολούθει μοι.
custom house, and said to him : Follow me.

28 καὶ καταλιπὼν πάντα ἀναστὰς ἠκολούθει
And abandoning all things rising up he followed

αὐτῷ. 29 Καὶ ἐποίησεν δοχὴν μεγάλην
him. And ³made ⁴feast ²a great

Λευὶς αὐτῷ ἐν τῇ οἰκίᾳ αὐτοῦ· καὶ ἦν
¹Levi for him in the house of him; and there was

ὄχλος πολὺς τελωνῶν καὶ ἄλλων οἳ ἦσαν
crowd a much of tax-collectors and of others who were

μετ᾽ αὐτῶν κατακείμενοι. 30 καὶ ἐγόγγυζον
¹with ²them ¹reclining. And grumbled

οἱ Φαρισαῖοι καὶ οἱ γραμματεῖς αὐτῶν
the Pharisees and the scribes of them

πρὸς τοὺς μαθητὰς αὐτοῦ λέγοντες· διὰ
at the disciples of him saying : Why

τί μετὰ τῶν τελωνῶν καὶ ἁμαρτωλῶν
with the tax-collectors and sinners

ἐσθίετε καὶ πίνετε; 31 καὶ ἀποκριθεὶς ὁ
eat ye and drink ye? And answering –

Ἰησοῦς εἶπεν πρὸς αὐτούς· οὐ χρείαν
Jesus said to them : not need

ἔχουσιν οἱ ὑγιαίνοντες ἰατροῦ ἀλλὰ οἱ
have the [ones] being healthy of a physician but the
                                   =those who are ill;

κακῶς ἔχοντες· 32 οὐκ ἐλήλυθα καλέσαι
[ones] ill having; I have not come to call

δικαίους ἀλλὰ ἁμαρτωλοὺς εἰς μετάνοιαν.
righteous persons but sinners to repentance.

33 Οἱ δὲ εἶπαν πρὸς αὐτόν· οἱ μαθηταὶ
And they said to him : The disciples

Ἰωάννου νηστεύουσιν πυκνὰ καὶ δεήσεις
of John fast often and prayers

---

were thinking and asked, "Why are you thinking these things in your hearts? 23 Which is easier: to say, 'Your sins are forgiven,' or to say, 'Get up and walk'? 24 But that you may know that the Son of Man has authority on earth to forgive sins. . . ." He said to the paralyzed man, "I tell you, get up, take your mat and go home." 25 Immediately he stood up in front of them, took what he had been lying on and went home praising God. 26 Everyone was amazed and gave praise to God. They were filled with awe and said, "We have seen remarkable things today."

The Calling of Levi

27 After this, Jesus went out and saw a tax collector by the name of Levi sitting at his tax booth. "Follow me," Jesus said to him, 28 and Levi got up, left everything and followed him.

29 Then Levi held a great banquet for Jesus at his house, and a large crowd of tax collectors and others were eating with them. 30 But the Pharisees and the teachers of the law who belonged to their sect complained to his disciples, "Why do you eat and drink with tax collectors and 'sinners'?" 31 Jesus answered them, "It is not the healthy who need a doctor, but the sick. 32 I have not come to call the righteous, but sinners to repentance."

Jesus Questioned About Fasting

33 They said to him, "John's disciples often fast and pray, and so do the dis-

---

p Gk *reclining*

and drink. 34 Jesus said to them, "You cannot make wedding guests fast while the bridegroom is with them, can you? 35 The days will come when the bridegroom will be taken away from them, and then they will fast in those days." 36 He also told them a parable: "No one tears a piece from a new garment and sews it on an old garment; otherwise the new will be torn, and the piece from the new will not match the old. 37 And no one puts new wine into old wineskins; otherwise the new wine will burst the skins and will be spilled, and the skins will be destroyed. 38 But new wine must be put into fresh wineskins. 39 And no one after drinking old wine desires new wine, but says, 'The old is good.' " q

ποιοῦνται, ὁμοίως καὶ οἱ τῶν Φαρισαίων,
make, likewise also those of the Pharisees,

οἱ δὲ σοὶ ἐσθίουσιν καὶ πίνουσιν. 34 ὁ
but those to thee° eat and drink. - but thine

δὲ Ἰησοῦς εἶπεν πρὸς αὐτούς· μὴ δύνασθε
And Jesus said to them: not ¹Can ye

τοὺς υἱοὺς τοῦ νυμφῶνος, ἐν ᾧ ὁ νυμφίος
⁸the ⁷sons ⁶of the ⁵bride-chamber, ⁸while ⁹the ¹⁰bridegroom

μετ᾿ αὐτῶν ἐστιν, ποιῆσαι νηστεῦσαι;
¹¹with ¹²them ¹¹is, ²to make ⁴to fast?

35 ἐλεύσονται δὲ ἡμέραι, καὶ ὅταν ἀπαρθῇ
but will come days, and when is taken away

ἀπ᾿ αὐτῶν ὁ νυμφίος, τότε νηστεύσουσιν
from them the bridegroom, then they will fast

ἐν ἐκείναις ταῖς ἡμέραις. 36 Ἔλεγεν δὲ
in those - days. And he told

καὶ παραβολὴν πρὸς αὐτοὺς ὅτι οὐδεὶς
also a parable to them[:] - No one

ἐπίβλημα ἀπὸ ἱματίου καινοῦ σχίσας
²a patch ³from ⁴garment ⁴a new ¹tearing

ἐπιβάλλει ἐπὶ ἱμάτιον παλαιόν· εἰ δὲ μή γε,
⁵puts [it] ⁷on ⁶a garment ⁵an old; otherwise,

καὶ τὸ καινὸν σχίσει καὶ τῷ παλαιῷ
both the new will tear and ⁷with the ⁸old

οὐ συμφωνήσει τὸ ἐπίβλημα τὸ ἀπὸ τοῦ
⁶will not agree ¹the ²patch - ³from ⁴the

καινοῦ. 37 καὶ οὐδεὶς βάλλει οἶνον νέον
⁵new. And no one puts wine new

εἰς ἀσκοὺς παλαιούς· εἰ δὲ μή γε, ῥήξει
into wineskins old; otherwise, ⁴will burst

ὁ οἶνος ὁ νέος τοὺς ἀσκούς, καὶ αὐτὸς
¹the ²wine ¹the ²new ⁶the ⁶wineskins, and it

ἐκχυθήσεται καὶ οἱ ἀσκοὶ ἀπολοῦνται.
will be poured out and the wineskins will perish.

38 ἀλλὰ οἶνον νέον εἰς ἀσκοὺς καινοὺς
But wine new into wineskins new

βλητέον. 39 καὶ οὐδεὶς πιὼν παλαιὸν
one must put. And no one having drunk old

θέλει νέον· λέγει γάρ· ὁ παλαιὸς χρηστός
desires new; for he says: The old good

ἐστιν.
is.

ciples of the Pharisees, but yours go on eating and drinking."

34 Jesus answered, "Can you make the guests of the bridegroom fast while he is with them? 35 But the time will come when the bridegroom will be taken from them; in those days they will fast."

36 He told them this parable: "No one tears a patch from a new garment and sews it on an old one. If he does, he will have torn the new garment, and the patch from the new will not match the old. 37 And no one pours new wine into old wineskins. If he does, the new wine will burst the skins, the wine will run out and the wineskins will be ruined. 38 No, new wine must be poured into new wineskins. 39 And no one after drinking old wine wants the new, for he says, 'The old is better.' "

Chapter 6

The Question about the Sabbath

ONE sabbath r while Jesus s was going through the grainfields, his disciples plucked some heads of grain, rubbed them in their hands, and ate them. 2 But some of the Pharisees said, "Why are you doing what is not lawful ᵗ on the sabbath?" 3 Jesus answered, "Have you not read what David did when he and his companions were hungry? 4 He entered the house of God and took and ate the bread of the Presence, which it is not lawful for any but the priests to eat, and gave

6 Ἐγένετο δὲ ἐν σαββάτῳ διαπορεύεσθαι
And it came to pass on a sabbath to go through
=he went through

αὐτὸν διὰ σπορίμων, καὶ ἔτιλλον οἱ
him ᵇ through cornfields, and ⁴plucked ¹the

μαθηταὶ αὐτοῦ καὶ ἤσθιον τοὺς στάχυας
²disciples ³of him and ate the ears

ψώχοντες ταῖς χερσίν. 2 τινὲς δὲ τῶν
rubbing with the(ir) hands. And some of the

Φαρισαίων εἶπαν· τί ποιεῖτε ὃ οὐκ ἔξεστιν
Pharisees said: Why do ye what is not lawful

τοῖς σάββασιν; 3 καὶ ἀποκριθεὶς πρὸς
on the sabbaths? And replying to

αὐτοὺς εἶπεν ὁ Ἰησοῦς· οὐδὲ τοῦτο ἀνέγνωτε
them said - Jesus: ²not ³this ¹read ye

ὃ ἐποίησεν Δαυίδ, ὁπότε ἐπείνασεν αὐτὸς
which did David, when hungered he

καὶ οἱ μετ᾿ αὐτοῦ ὄντες; 4 ὡς εἰσῆλθεν
and the [ones] with him being? how he entered

εἰς τὸν οἶκον τοῦ θεοῦ καὶ τοὺς ἄρτους
into the house - of God and the loaves

τῆς προθέσεως λαβὼν ἔφαγεν καὶ ἔδωκεν
of the setting forth taking he ate and gave

Chapter 6

Lord of the Sabbath

ONE Sabbath Jesus was going through the grainfields, and his disciples began to pick some heads of grain, rub them in their hands and eat the kernels. 2 Some of the Pharisees asked, "Why are you doing what is unlawful on the Sabbath?"

3 Jesus answered them, "Have you never read what David did when he and his companions were hungry? 4 He entered the house of God, and taking the consecrated bread, he ate what is lawful only for

q Other ancient authorities read better; others lack verse 39
r Other ancient authorities read On the second first sabbath
s Gk he
t Other ancient authorities add to do

some to his companions?"
5Then he said to them,
"The Son of Man is lord of
the sabbath."

*The Man with a Withered
Hand*

6 On another sabbath he
entered the synagogue and
taught, and there was a
man there whose right hand
was withered. 7The scribes
and the Pharisees watched
him to see whether he
would cure on the sabbath,
so that they might find an
accusation against him.
8Even though he knew
what they were thinking,
he said to the man who had
the withered hand, "Come
and stand here." He got up
and stood there. 9Then
Jesus said to them, "I ask
you, is it lawful to do good
or to do harm on the sab-
bath, to save life or to destroy it?" 10After looking
around at all of them, he
said to him, "Stretch out
your hand." He did so, and
his hand was restored.
11But they were filled with
fury and discussed with
one another what they
might do to Jesus.

*Jesus Chooses the Twelve
Apostles*

12 Now during those
days he went out to the
mountain to pray; and he
spent the night in prayer to
God. 13And when day
came, he called his disciples and chose twelve of
them, whom he also named
apostles: 14Simon, whom
he named Peter, and his
brother Andrew, and
James, and John, and Philip, and Bartholomew,
15and Matthew, and Thom-
as, and James son of Al-

τοῖς   μετ᾽ αὐτοῦ, οὓς οὐκ ἔξεστιν φαγεῖν
to the [ones] with him, which it is not lawful to eat

εἰ μὴ μόνους τοὺς ἱερεῖς; 5 καὶ ἔλεγεν
except only   the   priests? And he said

αὐτοῖς· κύριός ἐστιν τοῦ σαββάτου ὁ
to them : Lord   is   of the sabbath the

υἱὸς τοῦ ἀνθρώπου. 6 Ἐγένετο δὲ ἐν
Son   -   of man.   And it came to pass on

ἑτέρῳ σαββάτῳ εἰσελθεῖν αὐτὸν εἰς τὴν
another sabbath to enter   him   into the
                                  =he entered into the synagogue and

συναγωγὴν καὶ διδάσκειν· καὶ ἦν ἄνθρωπος
synagogue and to teach[b]; and there was a man
taught;

ἐκεῖ καὶ ἡ χεὶρ αὐτοῦ ἡ δεξιὰ ἦν ξηρά·
there and the [8]hand [9]of him - [7]right was withered;

7 παρετηροῦντο δὲ αὐτὸν οἱ γραμματεῖς
and carefully watched   him   the scribes

καὶ οἱ Φαρισαῖοι εἰ ἐν τῷ σαββάτῳ
and the Pharisees if in the sabbath

θεραπεύει, ἵνα εὕρωσιν κατηγορεῖν αὐτοῦ.
he heals,   that they might find to accuse him.

8 αὐτὸς δὲ ᾔδει τοὺς διαλογισμοὺς αὐτῶν,
But he   knew the   reasonings   of them,

εἶπεν δὲ τῷ ἀνδρὶ τῷ ξηρὰν ἔχοντι τὴν
and said to the man the [9]withered [1]having [8]the

χεῖρα· ἔγειρε καὶ στῆθι εἰς τὸ μέσον·
[4]hand : Rise and stand in the midst;

καὶ ἀναστὰς ἔστη. 9 εἶπεν δὲ ὁ Ἰησοῦς
and rising up he stood. And said -   Jesus

πρὸς αὐτούς· ἐπερωτῶ ὑμᾶς εἰ ἔξεστιν
to them: I ask   you   if it is lawful

τῷ σαββάτῳ ἀγαθοποιῆσαι ἢ κακοποιῆσαι,
on the sabbath to do good   or to do evil,

ψυχὴν σῶσαι ἢ ἀπολέσαι; 10 καὶ περι-
life   to save or to destroy?   And looking

βλεψάμενος πάντας αὐτοὺς εἶπεν αὐτῷ·
round at   all   them   he said to him :

ἔκτεινον τὴν χεῖρά σου. ὁ δὲ ἐποίησεν,
Stretch out the hand of thee. And he did,

καὶ ἀπεκατεστάθη ἡ χεὶρ αὐτοῦ. 11 αὐτοὶ
and was restored the hand of him. they

δὲ ἐπλήσθησαν ἀνοίας, καὶ διελάλουν πρὸς
But were filled of(with) madness, and talked to

ἀλλήλους τί ἂν ποιήσαιεν τῷ Ἰησοῦ.
one another what they might do - to Jesus.

12 Ἐγένετο δὲ ἐν ταῖς ἡμέραις ταύταις
Now it came to pass in   days   these

ἐξελθεῖν αὐτὸν εἰς τὸ ὄρος προσεύξασθαι,
to go forth him[b] to the mountain to pray,
=he went forth

καὶ ἦν διανυκτερεύων ἐν τῇ προσευχῇ τοῦ
and was spending the whole in the prayer of
         night

θεοῦ. 13 καὶ ὅτε ἐγένετο ἡμέρα, προσεφώνησεν
of God.   And when it became day,   he called to [him]

τοὺς μαθητὰς αὐτοῦ, καὶ ἐκλεξάμενος ἀπ᾽
the disciples of him, and choosing   from

αὐτῶν δώδεκα, οὓς καὶ ἀποστόλους ὠνόμασεν,
them   twelve, whom also apostles   he named,

14 Σίμωνα, ὃν καὶ ὠνόμασεν Πέτρον, καὶ
Simon,   whom also he named Peter,   and

Ἀνδρέαν τὸν ἀδελφὸν αὐτοῦ, καὶ Ἰάκωβον
Andrew the brother   of him, and James

καὶ Ἰωάννην, καὶ Φίλιππον καὶ Βαρθο-
and John,   and Philip   and Bartho-

λομαῖον, 15 καὶ Μαθθαῖον καὶ Θωμᾶν,
lomew,   and Matthew   and Thomas,

priests to eat. And he also
gave some to his compan-
ions." 5Then Jesus said to
them, "The Son of Man is
Lord of the Sabbath."

6On another Sabbath he
went into the synagogue
and was teaching, and a
man was there whose right
hand was shriveled. 7The
Pharisees and the teachers
of the law were looking for
a reason to accuse Jesus, so
they watched him closely
to see if he would heal on
the Sabbath. 8But Jesus
knew what they were
thinking and said to the
man with the shriveled
hand, "Get up and stand in
front of everyone." So he
got up and stood there.

9Then Jesus said to them,
"I ask you, which is lawful
on the Sabbath: to do good
or to do evil, to save life or
to destroy it?"

10He looked around at
them all, and then said to
the man, "Stretch out your
hand." He did so, and his
hand was completely re-
stored. 11But they were furious and began to discuss
with one another what they
might do to Jesus.

The Twelve Apostles

12One of those days Jesus
went out to a mountainside
to pray, and spent the night
praying to God. 13When
morning came, he called
his disciples to him and
chose twelve of them,
whom he also designated
apostles: 14Simon (whom
he named Peter), his brother Andrew, James, John,
Philip, Bartholomew,
15Matthew, Thomas,
James son of Alphaeus, Si-

phaeus, and Simon, who was called the Zealot, 16and Judas son of James, and Judas Iscariot, who became a traitor.

Jesus Teaches and Heals

17 He came down with them and stood on a level place, with a great crowd of his disciples and a great multitude of people from all Judea, Jerusalem, and the coast of Tyre and Sidon. 18They had come to hear him and to be healed of their diseases; and those who were troubled with unclean spirits were cured. 19And all in the crowd were trying to touch him, for power came out from him and healed all of them.

Blessings and Woes

20 Then he looked up at his disciples and said:
"Blessed are you who
   are poor,
   for yours is the
   kingdom of
   God.
21 "Blessed are you who
   are hungry now,
   for you will be
   filled.
"Blessed are you who
   weep now,
   for you will laugh.
22 "Blessed are you
when people hate you, and
when they exclude you, revile you, and defame you[u]
on account of the Son of
Man. 23Rejoice in that day
and leap for joy, for surely
your reward is great in
heaven; for that is what
their ancestors did to the
prophets.
24 "But woe to you who
   are rich,
   for you have
   received your
   consolation.
25 "Woe to you who are
   full now,
   for you will be
   hungry.
"Woe to you who are
   laughing now,
   for you will mourn
   and weep.
26 "Woe to you when all

[καὶ] Ἰάκωβον Ἁλφαίου καὶ Σίμωνα τὸν
and   James [son] of Alphæus and Simon the [one]
καλούμενον ζηλωτήν, 16 καὶ Ἰούδαν Ἰακώβου,
being called a Zealot,   and Judas   of James,
καὶ Ἰούδαν Ἰσκαριώθ, ὃς ἐγένετο προδότης,
and Judas Iscariot, who became   betrayer,
17 καὶ καταβὰς μετ' αὐτῶν ἔστη ἐπὶ
   and coming down with them he stood on
τόπου πεδινοῦ, καὶ ὄχλος πολὺς μαθητῶν
place a level,   and crowd a much of disciples
αὐτοῦ, καὶ πλῆθος πολὺ τοῦ λαοῦ ἀπὸ
of him, and multitude a much of the people from
πάσης τῆς Ἰουδαίας καὶ Ἱερουσαλὴμ καὶ
all   -   Judæa   and   Jerusalem   and
τῆς παραλίου Τύρου καὶ Σιδῶνος, 18 οἳ
the coast country of Tyre and Sidon,   who
ἦλθον ἀκοῦσαι αὐτοῦ καὶ ἰαθῆναι ἀπὸ
came   to hear   him   and to be cured from
τῶν νόσων αὐτῶν, καὶ οἱ ἐνοχλούμενοι
the diseases of them,   and the [ones] being tormented
ἀπὸ πνευμάτων ἀκαθάρτων ἐθεραπεύοντο.
from spirits   unclean   were healed.
19 καὶ πᾶς ὁ ὄχλος ἐζήτουν ἅπτεσθαι
   And all the crowd sought   to touch
αὐτοῦ, ὅτι δύναμις παρ' αὐτοῦ ἐξήρχετο
him, because power from him   went forth
καὶ ἰᾶτο πάντας. 20 Καὶ αὐτὸς ἐπάρας
and cured all.   And he   lifting up
τοὺς ὀφθαλμοὺς αὐτοῦ εἰς τοὺς μαθητὰς
the   eyes   of him to the disciples
αὐτοῦ ἔλεγεν·
of him said :
Μακάριοι οἱ πτωχοί, ὅτι ὑμετέρα ἐστὶν
Blessed [are] the poor, because yours   is
ἡ βασιλεία τοῦ θεοῦ. 21 μακάριοι οἱ
the kingdom - of God.   Blessed [are] the [ones]
πεινῶντες νῦν, ὅτι χορτασθήσεσθε. μακάριοι [are]
hungering now, because ye will be satisfied. Blessed [are]
οἱ κλαίοντες νῦν, ὅτι γελάσετε. 22 μακάριοί
the [ones] weeping now, because ye will laugh. Blessed
ἐστε ὅταν μισήσωσιν ὑμᾶς οἱ ἄνθρωποι,
are ye when   'hate   'you the ¹men.
καὶ ὅταν ἀφορίσωσιν ὑμᾶς καὶ ὀνειδίσωσιν
and when they separate   you   and   reproach
καὶ ἐκβάλωσιν τὸ ὄνομα ὑμῶν ὡς πονηρὸν
and cast out   the name of you as   evil
ἕνεκα τοῦ υἱοῦ τοῦ ἀνθρώπου. 23 χάρητε
for the sake of the Son -   of man.   Rejoice
ἐν ἐκείνῃ τῇ ἡμέρᾳ καὶ σκιρτήσατε·
in that   -   day   and   leap for joy;
ἰδοὺ γὰρ ὁ μισθὸς ὑμῶν πολὺς ἐν τῷ
for behold[,] the reward of you much in -
οὐρανῷ· κατὰ τὰ αὐτὰ γὰρ ἐποίουν τοῖς
heaven; for according to the same things ⁴did ⁵to the
= in the same way
προφήταις οἱ πατέρες αὐτῶν.
⁶prophets ¹the ²fathers ³of them.
24 Πλὴν οὐαὶ ὑμῖν τοῖς πλουσίοις, ὅτι
   But   woe to you the   rich [ones], because
ἀπέχετε τὴν παράκλησιν ὑμῶν. 25 οὐαὶ ὑμῖν,
ye have the   consolation   of you.   Woe to you,
οἱ ἐμπεπλησμένοι νῦν, ὅτι πεινάσετε.
the [ones] having been filled up now, because ye will hunger.
οὐαί, οἱ γελῶντες νῦν, ὅτι πενθήσετε
Woe, the [ones] laughing now, because ye will mourn
καὶ κλαύσετε. 26 οὐαὶ ὅταν καλῶς ὑμᾶς
and lament.   Woe when   well [of] you

---

mon who was called the Zealot, 16Judas son of James, and Judas Iscariot, who became a traitor.

Blessings and Woes

17He went down with them and stood on a level place. A large crowd of his disciples was there and a great number of people from all over Judea, from Jerusalem, and from the coast of Tyre and Sidon, 18who had come to hear him and to be healed of their diseases. Those troubled by evil[a] spirits were cured, 19and the people all tried to touch him, because power was coming from him and healing them all.
20Looking at his disciples, he said:
   "Blessed are you who
      are poor,
      for yours is the
      kingdom of God.
21Blessed are you who
   hunger now,
   for you will be
   satisfied.
Blessed are you who
   weep now,
   for you will laugh.
22Blessed are you when
   men hate you,
   when they exclude you
      and insult you
   and reject your name
      as evil,
      because of the Son of
      Man.
23"Rejoice in that day
and leap for joy, because
great is your reward in
heaven. For that is how
their fathers treated the
prophets.
24"But woe to you who
   are rich,
   for you have already
   received your
   comfort.
25Woe to you who are well
   fed now,
   for you will go hungry.
Woe to you who laugh
   now,
   for you will mourn and
   weep.
26Woe to you when all

---

speak well of you, for that is what their ancestors did to the false prophets.

Love for Enemies

27 "But I say to you that listen, Love your enemies, do good to those who hate you, 28 bless those who curse you; pray for those who abuse you. 29 If anyone strikes you on the cheek, offer the other also; and from anyone who takes away your coat do not withhold even your shirt. 30 Give to everyone who begs from you; and if anyone takes away your goods, do not ask for them again. 31 Do to others as you would have them do to you.

32 "If you love those who love you, what credit is that to you? For even sinners love those who love them. 33 If you do good to those who do good to you, what credit is that to you? For even sinners do the same. 34 If you lend to those from whom you hope to receive, what credit is that to you? Even sinners lend to sinners, to receive as much again. 35 But love your enemies, do good, and lend, expecting nothing in return. *v* Your reward will be great, and you will be children of the Most High; for he is kind to the ungrateful and the wicked. 36 Be merciful, just as your Father is merciful.

Judging Others

37 "Do not judge, and you will not be judged; do

εἴπωσιν πάντες οἱ ἄνθρωποι· κατὰ τὰ
say all – men; for according to
= in the same way

αὐτὰ γὰρ ἐποίουν τοῖς ψευδοπροφήταις οἱ
the same things did to the false prophets the

πατέρες αὐτῶν. 27 Ἀλλὰ ὑμῖν λέγω
fathers of them. But you I tell

τοῖς ἀκούουσιν· ἀγαπᾶτε τοὺς ἐχθροὺς
the [ones] hearing: Love ye the enemies

ὑμῶν, καλῶς ποιεῖτε τοῖς μισοῦσιν ὑμᾶς,
of you, ¹well ¹do to the [ones] hating you,

28 εὐλογεῖτε τοὺς καταρωμένους ὑμᾶς,
bless the [ones] cursing you,

προσεύχεσθε περὶ τῶν ἐπηρεαζόντων ὑμᾶς.
pray about the [ones] insulting you.

29 τῷ τύπτοντί σε ἐπὶ τὴν σιαγόνα
To the [one] striking thee on the cheek

πάρεχε καὶ τὴν ἄλλην, καὶ ἀπὸ τοῦ
turn also the other, and from the [one]

αἴροντός σου τὸ ἱμάτιον καὶ τὸν χιτῶνα
taking of thee the garment also the tunic

μὴ κωλύσῃς. 30 παντὶ αἰτοῦντί σε δίδου,
do not prevent. To everyone asking thee give,

καὶ ἀπὸ τοῦ αἴροντος τὰ σὰ μὴ ἀπαίτει.
and from the [one] taking thy things do not ask back.

31 καὶ καθὼς θέλετε ἵνα ποιῶσιν ὑμῖν
And as ye wish that may do to you

οἱ ἄνθρωποι, ποιεῖτε αὐτοῖς ὁμοίως. 32 καὶ
– men, do ye to them likewise. And

εἰ ἀγαπᾶτε τοὺς ἀγαπῶντας ὑμᾶς, ποία
if ye love the [ones] loving you, what

ὑμῖν χάρις ἐστίν; καὶ γὰρ οἱ ἁμαρτωλοὶ
to you thanks is there?ᶜ for even – sinners
= thanks have ye?

τοὺς ἀγαπῶντας αὐτοὺς ἀγαπῶσιν. 33 καὶ
¹the [ones] ³loving ⁴them ¹love. even

γὰρ ἐὰν ἀγαθοποιῆτε τοὺς ἀγαθοποιοῦντας
For if ye do good to the [ones] doing good to

ὑμᾶς, ποία ὑμῖν χάρις ἐστίν; καὶ οἱ
you, what to you thanks is there?ᶜ even –
= thanks have ye?

ἁμαρτωλοὶ τὸ αὐτὸ ποιοῦσιν. 34 καὶ ἐὰν
sinners the same thing do. And if

δανείσητε παρ' ὧν ἐλπίζετε λαβεῖν, ποία
ye lend from whom ye hope to receive, what

ὑμῖν χάρις [ἐστίν]; καὶ ἁμαρτωλοὶ
to you thanks is there?ᶜ even sinners
= thanks have ye?

ἁμαρτωλοῖς δανείζουσιν ἵνα ἀπολάβωσιν τὰ
to sinners lend that they may receive back the

ἴσα. 35 πλὴν ἀγαπᾶτε τοὺς ἐχθροὺς ὑμῶν
equal things. But love ye the enemies of you

καὶ ἀγαθοποιεῖτε καὶ δανείζετε μηδὲν
and do good and lend nothing

ἀπελπίζοντες· καὶ ἔσται ὁ μισθὸς ὑμῶν
despairing; and will be the reward of you
= despairing not at all;

πολύς, καὶ ἔσεσθε υἱοὶ ὑψίστου, ὅτι
much, and ye will be sons of [the] Most High, because

αὐτὸς χρηστός ἐστιν ἐπὶ τοὺς ἀχαρίστους
he kind is to the unthankful

καὶ πονηρούς. 36 Γίνεσθε οἰκτίρμονες,
and evil. Be ye compassionate,

καθὼς ὁ πατὴρ ὑμῶν οἰκτίρμων ἐστίν.
as the Father of you compassionate is.

37 καὶ μὴ κρίνετε, καὶ οὐ μὴ κριθῆτε· καὶ
And do not judge, and by no means ye may be and
judged;

---

men speak well of you,
for that is how their fathers treated the false prophets.

Love for Enemies

27 "But I tell you who hear me: Love your enemies, do good to those who hate you, 28 bless those who curse you, pray for those who mistreat you. 29 If someone strikes you on one cheek, turn to him the other also. If someone takes your cloak, do not stop him from taking your tunic. 30 Give to everyone who asks you, and if anyone takes what belongs to you, do not demand it back. 31 Do to others as you would have them do to you. 32 "If you love those who love you, what credit is that to you? Even 'sinners' love those who love them. 33 And if you do good to those who are good to you, what credit is that to you? Even 'sinners' do that. 34 And if you lend to those from whom you expect repayment, what credit is that to you? Even 'sinners' lend to 'sinners,' expecting to be repaid in full. 35 But love your enemies, do good to them, and lend to them without expecting to get anything back. Then your reward will be great, and you will be sons of the Most High, because he is kind to the ungrateful and wicked. 36 Be merciful, just as your Father is merciful.

Judging Others

37 "Do not judge, and you will not be judged. Do not

---

v Other ancient authorities read *despairing of no one*

not condemn, and you will not be condemned. Forgive, and you will be forgiven; 38 give, and it will be given to you. A good measure, pressed down, shaken together, running over, will be put into your lap; for the measure you give will be the measure you get back."

39 He also told them a parable: "Can a blind person guide a blind person? Will not both fall into a pit? 40 A disciple is not above the teacher, but everyone who is fully qualified will be like the teacher. 41 Why do you see the speck in your neighbor's w eye, but do not notice the log in your own eye? 42 Or how can you say to your neighbor, x 'Friend, x let me take out the speck in your eye,' when you yourself do not see the log in your own eye? You hypocrite, first take the log out of your own eye, and then you will see clearly to take the speck out of your neighbor's w eye.

A Tree and Its Fruit

43 "No good tree bears bad fruit, nor again does a bad tree bear good fruit; 44 for each tree is known by its own fruit. Figs are not gathered from thorns, nor are grapes picked from a bramble bush. 45 The good person out of the good treasure of the heart produces good, and the evil person out of evil treasure produces evil; for it is out of the abundance of the heart that the mouth speaks.

μὴ καταδικάζετε, καὶ οὐ μὴ καταδικασθῆτε.
do not condemn, and by no means ye may be condemned.

ἀπολύετε, καὶ ἀπολυθήσεσθε· 38 δίδοτε, καὶ
Forgive, and ye will be forgiven; give, and

δοθήσεται ὑμῖν· μέτρον καλὸν πεπιεσμένον
it will be given to you; measure good *having been* pressed down

σεσαλευμένον ὑπερεκχυννόμενον δώσουσιν εἰς
having been shaken running over they will give into

τὸν κόλπον ὑμῶν· ᾧ γὰρ μέτρῳ μετρεῖτε
the bosom of you; for in what measure ye measure

ἀντιμετρηθήσεται ὑμῖν. 39 Εἶπεν δὲ καὶ
it will be measured in return to you. And he told also

παραβολὴν αὐτοῖς· μήτι δύναται τυφλὸς
a parable to them : Not can a blind man

τυφλὸν ὁδηγεῖν; οὐχὶ ἀμφότεροι εἰς βόθυνον
a blind man ¹guide? not both into a ditch

ἐμπεσοῦνται; 40 οὐκ ἔστιν μαθητὴς ὑπὲρ
will fall in? ²not ¹is ¹A disciple above

τὸν διδάσκαλον· κατηρτισμένος δὲ πᾶς
the teacher; ¹but *having been* perfected ²everyone

ἔσται ὡς ὁ διδάσκαλος αὐτοῦ. 41 Τί δὲ
¹will be as the teacher of him. And why

βλέπεις τὸ κάρφος τὸ ἐν τῷ ὀφθαλμῷ
seest thou the mote - in the eye

τοῦ ἀδελφοῦ σου, τὴν δὲ δοκὸν τὴν ἐν
of the brother of thee, but the beam - in

τῷ ἰδίῳ ὀφθαλμῷ οὐ κατανοεῖς; 42 πῶς
thine own eye thou considerest not? how

δύνασαι λέγειν τῷ ἀδελφῷ σου· ἀδελφέ,
canst thou *to* say to the brother of thee : Brother,

ἄφες ἐκβάλω τὸ κάρφος τὸ ἐν τῷ
allow I may take out the mote - in the

ὀφθαλμῷ σου, αὐτὸς τὴν ἐν τῷ ὀφθαλμῷ
eye of thee, ¹[thy]self ⁴the ³in ⁷the ⁸eye

σου δοκὸν οὐ βλέπων; ὑποκριτά, ἔκβαλε
²of thee ⁵beam ⁹not ⁶seeing? hypocrite, take *out*

πρῶτον τὴν δοκὸν ἐκ τοῦ ὀφθαλμοῦ σου,
first the beam out of the eye of thee,

καὶ τότε διαβλέψεις τὸ κάρφος τὸ ἐν τῷ
and then thou wilt see clearly the mote - in the

ὀφθαλμῷ τοῦ ἀδελφοῦ σου ἐκβαλεῖν. 43 Οὐ
eye of the brother of thee to take out. ²no

γάρ ἐστιν δένδρον καλὸν ποιοῦν καρπὸν
¹For ³there is ²tree ⁴good producing fruit

σαπρόν, οὐδὲ πάλιν δένδρον σαπρὸν ποιοῦν
bad, nor again tree a bad producing

καρπὸν καλόν. 44 ἕκαστον γὰρ δένδρον
fruit good. For each tree

ἐκ τοῦ ἰδίου καρποῦ γινώσκεται· οὐ γὰρ
by the(its) own fruit is known; for not

ἐξ ἀκανθῶν συλλέγουσιν σῦκα, οὐδὲ ἐκ
of thorns do they gather figs, nor of

βάτου σταφυλὴν τρυγῶσιν. 45 ὁ ἀγαθὸς
a thorn bush a grape do they pick. The good

ἄνθρωπος ἐκ τοῦ ἀγαθοῦ θησαυροῦ τῆς
man out of the good treasure of the(his)

καρδίας προφέρει τὸ ἀγαθόν, καὶ ὁ
heart brings forth the good, and the
      =that which is good,

πονηρὸς ἐκ τοῦ πονηροῦ προφέρει τὸ
evil man out of the evil brings forth the

πονηρόν· ἐκ γὰρ περισσεύματος καρδίας
evil; for out of [the] abundance of [his] heart
      =that which is evil;

---

condemn, and you will not be condemned. Forgive, and you will be forgiven. 38 Give, and it will be given to you. A good measure, pressed down, shaken together and running over, will be poured into your lap. For with the measure you use, it will be measured to you."

39 He also told them this parable: "Can a blind man lead a blind man? Will they not both fall into a pit? 40 A student is not above his teacher, but everyone who is fully trained will be like his teacher. 41 "Why do you look at the speck of sawdust in your brother's eye and pay no attention to the plank in your own eye? 42 How can you say to your brother, 'Brother, let me take the speck out of your eye,' when you yourself fail to see the plank in your own eye? You hypocrite, first take the plank out of your eye, and then you will see clearly to remove the speck from your brother's eye.

A Tree and Its Fruit

43 "No good tree bears bad fruit, nor does a bad tree bear good fruit. 44 Each tree is recognized by its own fruit. People do not pick figs from thornbushes, or grapes from briers. 45 The good man brings good things out of the good stored up in his heart, and the evil man brings evil things out of the evil stored up in his heart. For out of the overflow of his heart his mouth speaks.

---

w Gk *brother's*
x Gk *brother*

The Two Foundations

46 "Why do you call me 'Lord, Lord,' and do not do what I tell you? 47 I will show you what someone is like who comes to me, hears my words, and acts on them. 48 That one is like a man building a house, who dug deeply and laid the foundation on rock; when a flood arose, the river burst against that house but could not shake it, because it had been well built.[y] 49 But the one who hears and does not act is like a man who built a house on the ground without a foundation. When the river burst against it, immediately it fell, and great was the ruin of that house."

λαλεῖ τὸ στόμα αὐτοῦ. 46 Τί δέ με καλεῖτε·
speaks the mouth of him. And why me call ye:

κύριε κύριε, καὶ οὐ ποιεῖτε ἃ
Lord[,] Lord, and do not [the things] which

λέγω; 47 Πᾶς ὁ ἐρχόμενος πρός με καὶ
I say? Everyone coming to me and

ἀκούων μου τῶν λόγων καὶ ποιῶν αὐτούς,
hearing of me the words and doing them,

ὑποδείξω ὑμῖν τίνι ἐστὶν ὅμοιος. 48 ὅμοιός
I will show to whom he is like. Like

ἐστιν ἀνθρώπῳ οἰκοδομοῦντι οἰκίαν, ὃς
he is to a man building a house, who

ἔσκαψεν καὶ ἐβάθυνεν καὶ ἔθηκεν θεμέλιον
dug and deepened and laid a foundation

ἐπὶ τὴν πέτραν· πλημμύρης δὲ γενομένης
on the rock; and a flood occurring[a]
= when a flood occurred

προσέρρηξεν ὁ ποταμὸς τῇ οἰκίᾳ ἐκείνῃ,
[a]dashed against [the]river house that,

καὶ οὐκ ἴσχυσεν σαλεῦσαι αὐτὴν διὰ
and was not able to shake it because of

τὸ καλῶς οἰκοδομῆσθαι αὐτήν. 49 ὁ δὲ
the well to be built it.[b] But the [one]
= because it was well built.

ἀκούσας καὶ μὴ ποιήσας ὅμοιός ἐστιν
hearing and not doing [a]like [1]is

ἀνθρώπῳ οἰκοδομήσαντι οἰκίαν ἐπὶ τὴν
a man having built a house on the

γῆν χωρὶς θεμελίου, ᾗ προσέρρηξεν ὁ
earth without a foundation, [a]which [a]dashed [1]against [a]the

ποταμός, καὶ εὐθὺς συνέπεσεν, καὶ ἐγένετο
[a]river, and immediately it collapsed, and [a]was

τὸ ῥῆγμα τῆς οἰκίας ἐκείνης μέγα.
[1]the [2]ruin - [a]house [a]of that [a]great.

The Wise and Foolish Builders

46 "Why do you call me, 'Lord, Lord,' and do not do what I say? 47 I will show you what he is like who comes to me and hears my words and puts them into practice. 48 He is like a man building a house, who dug down deep and laid the foundation on rock. When a flood came, the torrent struck that house but could not shake it, because it was well built. 49 But the one who hears my words and does not put them into practice is like a man who built a house on the ground without a foundation. The moment the torrent struck that house, it collapsed and its destruction was complete."

Chapter 7

Jesus Heals a Centurion's Servant

AFTER Jesus[z] had finished all his sayings in the hearing of the people, he entered Capernaum. 2 A centurion there had a slave whom he valued highly, and who was ill and close to death. 3 When he heard about Jesus, he sent some Jewish elders to him, asking him to come and heal his slave. 4 When they came to Jesus, they appealed to him earnestly, saying, "He is worthy of having you do this for him, 5 for he loves our people, and it is he who built our synagogue for us." 6 And Jesus went with them, but when he was not far from the house, the centurion sent friends to say to him,

---

7 Ἐπειδὴ ἐπλήρωσεν πάντα τὰ ῥήματα
When he completed all the words

αὐτοῦ εἰς τὰς ἀκοὰς τοῦ λαοῦ, εἰσῆλθεν
of him in the ears of the people, he entered

εἰς Καφαρναούμ. 2 Ἑκατοντάρχου δέ
into Capernaum. Now [a]of [a]a [a]centurion

τινος δοῦλος κακῶς ἔχων ἤμελλεν τελευτᾶν,
[a]certain [1]a slave [a]ill [a]having(being) [1]was about [1]to die,

ὃς ἦν αὐτῷ ἔντιμος. 3 ἀκούσας δὲ περὶ
[a]who [a]was [1]to him [a]dear. And hearing about

τοῦ Ἰησοῦ ἀπέστειλεν πρὸς αὐτὸν πρε-
- Jesus he sent to him eld-

σβυτέρους τῶν Ἰουδαίων, ἐρωτῶν αὐτὸν
ers of the Jews, asking him

ὅπως ἐλθὼν διασώσῃ τὸν δοῦλον αὐτοῦ.
that coming he might recover the slave of him.

4 οἱ δὲ παραγενόμενοι πρὸς τὸν Ἰησοῦν
And they coming to - Jesus

παρεκάλουν αὐτὸν σπουδαίως, λέγοντες ὅτι ἄξιός
besought him earnestly, saying[,] - Worthy

ἐστιν ᾧ παρέξῃ τοῦτο· 5 ἀγαπᾷ γὰρ
he is for whom thou shouldest grant this; for he loves

τὸ ἔθνος ἡμῶν καὶ τὴν συναγωγὴν
the nation of us and the synagogue

αὐτὸς ᾠκοδόμησεν ἡμῖν. 6 ὁ δὲ Ἰησοῦς
he built for us. - And Jesus

ἐπορεύετο σὺν αὐτοῖς. ἤδη δὲ αὐτοῦ οὐ
went with them. And yet him not
= while he was yet

μακρὰν ἀπέχοντος ἀπὸ τῆς οἰκίας, ἔπεμψεν
far being away[a] from the house, sent
not far away

Chapter 7

The Faith of the Centurion

WHEN Jesus had finished saying all this in the hearing of the people, he entered Capernaum. 2 There a centurion's servant, whom his master valued highly, was sick and about to die. 3 The centurion heard of Jesus and sent some elders of the Jews to him, asking him to come and heal his servant. 4 When they came to Jesus, they pleaded earnestly with him, "This man deserves to have you do this, 5 because he loves our nation and has built our synagogue." 6 So Jesus went with them.

He was not far from the house when the centurion

---

[y] Other ancient authorities read founded upon the rock
[z] Gk he

"Lord, do not trouble yourself, for I am not worthy to have you come under my roof; [7]therefore I did not presume to come to you. But only speak the word, and let my servant be healed. [8]For I also am a man set under authority, with soldiers under me; and I say to one, 'Go,' and he goes, and to another, 'Come,' and he comes, and to my slave, 'Do this,' and the slave does it." [9]When Jesus heard this he was amazed at him, and turning to the crowd that followed him, he said, "I tell you, not even in Israel have I found such faith." [10]When those who had been sent returned to the house, they found the slave in good health.

Jesus Raises the Widow's Son at Nain

[11] Soon afterwards[a] he went to a town called Nain, and his disciples and a large crowd went with him. [12]As he approached the gate of the town, a man who had died was being carried out. He was his mother's only son, and she was a widow; and with her was a large crowd from the town. [13]When the Lord saw her, he had compassion for her and said to her, "Do not weep." [14]Then he came forward and touched the bier, and the bearers stood still. And he said, "Young man, I say to you, rise!" [15]The dead man sat up and began to speak, and Jesus[b] gave him to his mother. [16]Fear seized all of them; and they glorified God, saying, "A great prophet has risen among us!" and "God has looked favorably

---

φίλους ὁ ἑκατοντάρχης λέγων αὐτῷ· κύριε,
friends the centurion saying to him: Lord,
μὴ σκύλλου· οὐ γὰρ ἱκανός εἰμι ἵνα ὑπὸ
do not trouble; for not worthy am I that under
τὴν στέγην μου εἰσέλθῃς· 7 διὸ οὐδὲ
the roof of me thou shouldest enter; wherefore not
ἐμαυτὸν ἠξίωσα πρὸς σὲ ἐλθεῖν· ἀλλὰ εἰπὲ
myself I accounted worthy to thee to come; but say
λόγῳ, καὶ ἰαθήτω ὁ παῖς μου. 8 καὶ
in a word, and let be cured the servant of me. [8]also
γὰρ ἐγὼ ἄνθρωπός εἰμι ὑπὸ ἐξουσίαν
[1]For [3]I [2]a man [4]am [7]under [8]authority
τασσόμενος, ἔχων ὑπ' ἐμαυτὸν στρατιώτας,
[6]being set, having under myself soldiers,
καὶ λέγω τούτῳ· πορεύθητι, καὶ πορεύεται,
and I tell this one: Go, and he goes,
καὶ ἄλλῳ· ἔρχου, καὶ ἔρχεται, καὶ τῷ
and another: Come, and he comes, and the
δούλῳ μου· ποίησον τοῦτο, καὶ ποιεῖ.
slave of me: Do this, and he does.
9 ἀκούσας δὲ ταῦτα ὁ Ἰησοῦς ἐθαύμασεν
And hearing these [words] - Jesus marvelled at
αὐτόν, καὶ στραφεὶς τῷ ἀκολουθοῦντι αὐτῷ
him, and turning to the [2]following [3]him
ὄχλῳ εἶπεν· λέγω ὑμῖν, οὐδὲ ἐν τῷ
[1]crowd said: I tell you, not in -
Ἰσραὴλ τοσαύτην πίστιν εὗρον. 10 καὶ
Israel such faith I found. And
ὑποστρέψαντες εἰς τὸν οἶκον οἱ πεμφθέντες
returning to the house the [ones] sent
εὗρον τὸν δοῦλον ὑγιαίνοντα. 11 Καὶ
found the slave well. And
ἐγένετο ἐν τῷ ἑξῆς ἐπορεύθη εἰς πόλιν
it came to pass on the next day he went into a city
καλουμένην Ναΐν, καὶ συνεπορεύοντο αὐτῷ
being called Nain, and went with him
οἱ μαθηταὶ αὐτοῦ καὶ ὄχλος πολύς.
the disciples of him and crowd a much.
12 ὡς δὲ ἤγγισεν τῇ πύλῃ τῆς πόλεως, καὶ
And as he drew near to the gate of the city, and
ἰδοὺ ἐξεκομίζετο τεθνηκὼς μονογενὴς
behold was being carried out having died an only born
[for burial]
υἱὸς τῇ μητρὶ αὐτοῦ, καὶ αὐτὴ ἦν χήρα,
son to the mother of him, and this was a widow,
καὶ ὄχλος τῆς πόλεως ἱκανὸς ἦν σὺν
and a [2]crowd [3]of the [4]city [1]considerable was with
αὐτῇ. 13 καὶ ἰδὼν αὐτὴν ὁ κύριος
her. And seeing her the Lord
ἐσπλαγχνίσθη ἐπ' αὐτῇ καὶ εἶπεν αὐτῇ·
felt compassion over her and said to her:
μὴ κλαῖε. 14 καὶ προσελθὼν ἥψατο τῆς
Do not weep. And approaching he touched the
σοροῦ, οἱ δὲ βαστάζοντες ἔστησαν, καὶ
bier, and the [ones] bearing stood, and
εἶπεν· νεανίσκε, σοὶ λέγω, ἐγέρθητι. 15 καὶ
he said: Young man, to thee I say, Arise. And
ἀνεκάθισεν ὁ νεκρὸς καὶ ἤρξατο λαλεῖν,
sat up the dead man and began to speak,
καὶ ἔδωκεν αὐτὸν τῇ μητρὶ αὐτοῦ.
and he gave him to the mother of him.
16 ἔλαβεν δὲ φόβος πάντας, καὶ ἐδόξαζον
And [2]took [1]fear [3]all, and they glorified
τὸν θεὸν λέγοντες ὅτι προφήτης μέγας
God saying[,] - prophet A great
ἠγέρθη ἐν ἡμῖν, καὶ ὅτι ἐπεσκέψατο ὁ
was raised among us, and[,] - [2]visited -

---

sent friends to say to him: "Lord, don't trouble yourself, for I do not deserve to have you come under my roof. [7]That is why I did not even consider myself worthy to come to you. But say the word, and my servant will be healed. [8]For I myself am a man under authority, with soldiers under me. I tell this one, 'Go,' and he goes; and that one, 'Come,' and he comes. I say to my servant, 'Do this,' and he does it."

[9]When Jesus heard this, he was amazed at him, and turning to the crowd following him, he said, "I tell you, I have not found such great faith even in Israel." [10]Then the men who had been sent returned to the house and found the servant well.

Jesus Raises a Widow's Son

[11]Soon afterward, Jesus went to a town called Nain, and his disciples and a large crowd went along with him. [12]As he approached the town gate, a dead person was being carried out—the only son of his mother, and she was a widow. And a large crowd from the town was with her. [13]When the Lord saw her, his heart went out to her and he said, "Don't cry."

[14]Then he went up and touched the coffin, and those carrying it stood still. He said, "Young man, I say to you, get up!" [15]The dead man sat up and began to talk, and Jesus gave him back to his mother.

[16]They were all filled with awe and praised God. "A great prophet has appeared among us," they said.

---

[a] Other ancient authorities read *Next day*
[b] Gk *he*

on his people!" 17This word about him spread throughout Judea and all the surrounding country.

Messengers from John the Baptist

18 The disciples of John reported all these things to him. So John summoned two of his disciples 19 and sent them to the Lord to ask, "Are you the one who is to come, or are we to wait for another?" 20 When the men had come to him, they said, "John the Baptist has sent us to you to ask, 'Are you the one who is to come, or are we to wait for another?' " 21 Jesus[c] had just then cured many people of diseases, plagues, and evil spirits, and had given sight to many who were blind. 22 And he answered them, "Go and tell John what you have seen and heard: the blind receive their sight, the lame walk, the lepers[d] are cleansed, the deaf hear, the dead are raised, the poor have good news brought to them. 23 And blessed is anyone who takes no offense at me."

24 When John's messengers had gone, Jesus[b] began to speak to the crowds about John:[e] "What did you go out into the wilderness to look at? A reed shaken by the wind? 25 What then did you go out to see? Someone[f] dressed in soft robes? Look, those who put on fine clothing and live in luxury are in royal palaces. 26 What then did you go out to see? A prophet? Yes, I tell you, and more than a prophet. 27 This is the one about whom it is written,

---

θεὸς τὸν λαὸν αὐτοῦ. 17 καὶ ἐξῆλθεν ὁ
¹God   the   people   of him.   And went forth -

λόγος οὗτος ἐν ὅλῃ τῇ ᾿Ιουδαίᾳ περὶ
word   this   in   all   the   Judæa   ²concerning

αὐτοῦ καὶ πάσῃ τῇ περιχώρῳ.
¹him   ¹and   ²all   ¹the   ⁴neighbourhood.

18 Καὶ ἀπήγγειλαν ᾿Ιωάννῃ οἱ μαθηταὶ
And   reported   to John   the   disciples

αὐτοῦ περὶ πάντων τούτων. καὶ
of him   about   all   these things.   And

προσκαλεσάμενος δύο τινὰς τῶν μαθητῶν
calling to [him]   ²two   ¹a certain   of the   disciples

αὐτοῦ ὁ ᾿Ιωάννης 19 ἔπεμψεν πρὸς τὸν
of him   -   John   sent   to   the

κύριον λέγων· σὺ εἶ ὁ ἐρχόμενος, ἢ ἄλλον
Lord   saying: Thou art the   coming [one],   or   another

προσδοκῶμεν; 20 παραγενόμενοι δὲ πρὸς
may we expect?   And coming   to

αὐτὸν οἱ ἄνδρες εἶπαν· ᾿Ιωάννης ὁ βαπτιστὴς
him   the   men   said: John   the   Baptist

ἀπέστειλεν ἡμᾶς πρὸς σὲ λέγων· σὺ εἶ ὁ
sent   us   to   thee   saying: Thou art the

ἐρχόμενος, ἢ ἄλλον προσδοκῶμεν; 21 ἐν
coming [one],   or   another   may we expect?   In

ἐκείνῃ τῇ ὥρᾳ ἐθεράπευσεν πολλοὺς ἀπὸ
that   -   hour   he healed   many   from(of)

νόσων καὶ μαστίγων καὶ πνευμάτων πονηρῶν,
diseases   and   plagues   and   spirits   evil,

καὶ τυφλοῖς πολλοῖς ἐχαρίσατο βλέπειν.
and   blind persons   to many   he gave   to see.

22 καὶ ἀποκριθεὶς εἶπεν αὐτοῖς· πορευθέντες
And   answering   he said   to them :   Going

ἀπαγγείλατε ᾿Ιωάννῃ ἃ εἴδετε καὶ
report   to John   [the things] which ye saw   and

ἠκούσατε· τυφλοὶ ἀναβλέπουσιν, χωλοὶ
heard: blind men   see again,   lame men

περιπατοῦσιν, λεπροὶ καθαρίζονται, καὶ κωφοὶ
walk,   lepers   are being cleansed,   and   deaf men

ἀκούουσιν, νεκροὶ ἐγείρονται, πτωχοὶ
hear,   dead men   are raised,   poor people

εὐαγγελίζονται· 23 καὶ μακάριός ἐστιν ὃς ἐὰν
are evangelized;   and   blessed   is   whoever

μὴ σκανδαλισθῇ ἐν ἐμοί. 24 ᾿Απελθόντων δὲ
is not offended   in   me.   And going away
                                    =as the

τῶν ἀγγέλων ᾿Ιωάννου ἤρξατο λέγειν πρὸς
the   messengers   of John²   he began   to say   to
messengers of John went away

τοὺς ὄχλους περὶ ᾿Ιωάννου· τί ἐξήλθατε
the   crowds   concerning   John: What went ye forth

εἰς τὴν ἔρημον θεάσασθαι; κάλαμον ὑπὸ
into   the   desert   to see?   a reed   by

ἀνέμου σαλευόμενον; 25 ἀλλὰ τί ἐξήλθατε
wind   being shaken?   But   what went ye forth

ἰδεῖν; ἄνθρωπον ἐν μαλακοῖς ἱματίοις
to see?   a man   in   soft   garments

ἠμφιεσμένον; ἰδοὺ οἱ ἐν ἱματισμῷ ἐνδόξῳ
having been   behold[,] the   ¹in   ²raiment   ³splendid
clothed?   [ones]

καὶ τρυφῇ ὑπάρχοντες ἐν τοῖς βασιλείοις
⁴and   ⁵in luxury   ⁶being   ⁸in   -   ⁹royal palaces

εἰσίν. 26 ἀλλὰ τί ἐξήλθατε ἰδεῖν; προφήτην;
⁷are.   But   what went ye forth to see?   a prophet?

ναὶ λέγω ὑμῖν, καὶ περισσότερον προφήτου.
yes   I tell   you,   and   more [than]   a prophet.

27 οὗτός ἐστιν περὶ οὗ γέγραπται· ἰδοὺ
This   is he   concerning whom   it has been written : Behold

---

"God has come to help his people." 17This news about Jesus spread throughout Judea[b] and the surrounding country.

Jesus and John the Baptist

18John's disciples told him about all these things. Calling two of them, 19he sent them to the Lord to ask, "Are you the one who was to come, or should we expect someone else?"

20When the men came to Jesus, they said, "John the Baptist sent us to you to ask, 'Are you the one who was to come, or should we expect someone else?' "

21At that very time Jesus cured many who had diseases, sicknesses and evil spirits, and gave sight to many who were blind. 22So he replied to the messengers, "Go back and report to John what you have seen and heard: The blind receive sight, the lame walk, those who have leprosy[c] are cured, the deaf hear, the dead are raised, and the good news is preached to the poor. 23Blessed is the man who does not fall away on account of me."

24After John's messengers left, Jesus began to speak to the crowd about John: "What did you go out into the desert to see? A reed swayed by the wind? 25If not, what did you go out to see? A man dressed in fine clothes? No, those who wear expensive clothes and indulge in luxury are in palaces. 26But what did you go out to see? A prophet? Yes, I tell you, and more than a prophet. 27This is the one about whom it is written:

---

c Gk He
d The terms leper and leprosy can refer to several diseases
e Gk him
f Or Why then did you go out? To see someone

b17 Or the land of the Jews
c22 The Greek word was used for various diseases affecting the skin—not necessarily leprosy.

'See, I am sending my messenger ahead of you, who will prepare your way before you.' 28 I tell you, among those born of women no one is greater than John; yet the least in the kingdom of God is greater than he." 29 (And all the people who heard this, including the tax collectors, acknowledged the justice of God,[g] because they had been baptized with John's baptism. 30 But by refusing to be baptized by him, the Pharisees and the lawyers rejected God's purpose for themselves.) 31 "To what then will I compare the people of this generation, and what are they like? 32 They are like children sitting in the marketplace and calling to one another,

'We played the flute
for you, and you
did not dance;
we wailed, and you
did not weep.'

33 For John the Baptist has come eating no bread and drinking no wine, and you say, 'He has a demon'; 34 the Son of Man has come eating and drinking, and you say, 'Look, a glutton and a drunkard, a friend of tax collectors and sinners!' 35 Nevertheless, wisdom is vindicated by all her children."

A Sinful Woman Forgiven

36 One of the Pharisees asked Jesus[e] to eat with him, and he went into the Pharisee's house and took his place at the table. 37 And a woman in the city, who was a sinner, having learned that he was eating in the Pharisee's house, brought an alabaster jar of ointment. 38 She stood behind him at his feet, weeping, and began to bathe his feet with her tears and to dry them with her hair.

ἀποστέλλω τὸν ἄγγελόν μου πρὸ προσώπου
I send the messenger of me before [the] face

σου, ὃς κατασκευάσει τὴν ὁδόν σου
of thee, who will prepare the way of thee

ἔμπροσθέν σου. 28 λέγω ὑμῖν, μείζων
before thee. I tell you, ⁹greater

ἐν γεννητοῖς γυναικῶν Ἰωάννου οὐδείς
¹among ³[those] born ³of women [⁷than] ⁸John ⁴no one

ἐστιν· ὁ δὲ μικρότερος ἐν τῇ βασιλείᾳ τοῦ
⁵is; but the less in the kingdom

θεοῦ μείζων αὐτοῦ ἐστιν. 29 καὶ πᾶς ὁ
of God greater [than] he is. And all the

λαὸς ἀκούσας καὶ οἱ τελῶναι ἐδικαίωσαν
people hearing and the tax-collectors justified

τὸν θεόν, βαπτισθέντες τὸ βάπτισμα
– God, being baptized [with] the baptism

Ἰωάννου· 30 οἱ δὲ Φαρισαῖοι καὶ οἱ
of John; but the Pharisees and the

νομικοὶ τὴν βουλὴν τοῦ θεοῦ ἠθέτησαν εἰς
lawyers ⁴the ⁵counsel ³of God ¹rejected ²for

ἑαυτούς, μὴ βαπτισθέντες ὑπ' αὐτοῦ. 31 Τίνι
³themselves, not being baptized by him. To what

οὖν ὁμοιώσω τοὺς ἀνθρώπους τῆς γενεᾶς
then may I liken the men – generation

ταύτης, καὶ τίνι εἰσὶν ὅμοιοι; 32 ὅμοιοί εἰσιν
of this, and to what are they like? Like are they

παιδίοις τοῖς ἐν ἀγορᾷ καθημένοις καὶ
to children – in a marketplace sitting and

προσφωνοῦσιν ἀλλήλοις ἃ λέγει· ηὐλήσαμεν
calling to one another who says We piped

ὑμῖν καὶ οὐκ ὠρχήσασθε· ἐθρηνήσαμεν καὶ
to you and ye did not dance; we mourned and

οὐκ ἐκλαύσατε. 33 ἐλήλυθεν γὰρ Ἰωάννης
ye did not weep. For has come John

ὁ βαπτιστὴς μὴ ἐσθίων ἄρτον μήτε πίνων
the Baptist not eating bread nor drinking

οἶνον, καὶ λέγετε· δαιμόνιον ἔχει.
wine, and ye say: A demon he has.

34 ἐλήλυθεν ὁ υἱὸς τοῦ ἀνθρώπου ἐσθίων
Has come the Son – of man eating

καὶ πίνων, καὶ λέγετε· ἰδοὺ ἄνθρωπος
and drinking, and ye say: Behold[,] a man

φάγος καὶ οἰνοπότης, φίλος τελωνῶν καὶ
a glutton and a winebibber, a friend of tax-collectors and

ἁμαρτωλῶν. 35 καὶ ἐδικαιώθη ἡ σοφία
of sinners. And was(is) justified – wisdom

ἀπὸ πάντων τῶν τέκνων αὐτῆς.
from(by) all the children of her.

36 Ἠρώτα δέ τις αὐτὸν τῶν Φαρισαίων
And ⁴asked ¹a certain one ⁵him ²of the ³Pharisees

ἵνα φάγῃ μετ' αὐτοῦ· καὶ εἰσελθὼν εἰς
that he would eat with him; and entering into

τὸν οἶκον τοῦ Φαρισαίου κατεκλίθη. 37 καὶ
the house of the Pharisee he reclined. And[,]

ἰδοὺ γυνὴ ἥτις ἦν ἐν τῇ πόλει ἁμαρτωλός,
behold[,] a woman who was in the city a sinner,

καὶ ἐπιγνοῦσα ὅτι κατάκειται ἐν τῇ
and knowing that he reclines in the

οἰκίᾳ τοῦ Φαρισαίου, κομίσασα ἀλάβαστρον
house of the Pharisee, bringing an alabaster box

μύρου 38 καὶ στᾶσα ὀπίσω παρὰ τοὺς
of ointment and standing behind at the

πόδας αὐτοῦ κλαίουσα, τοῖς δάκρυσιν
feet of him weeping, with the(her) tears

ἤρξατο βρέχειν τοὺς πόδας αὐτοῦ, καὶ
began to wet the feet of him, and

'' 'I will send my messenger ahead of you, who will prepare your way before you.'[d] 28 I tell you, among those born of women there is no one greater than John; yet the one who is least in the kingdom of God is greater than he." 29 (All the people, even the tax collectors, when they heard Jesus' words, acknowledged that God's way was right, because they had been baptized by John. 30 But the Pharisees and experts in the law rejected God's purpose for themselves, because they had not been baptized by John.)

31 "To what, then, can I compare the people of this generation? What are they like? 32 They are like children sitting in the marketplace and calling out to each other:

'' 'We played the flute
for you,
and you did not dance;
we sang a dirge,
and you did not cry.'

33 For John the Baptist came neither eating bread nor drinking wine, and you say, 'He has a demon.' 34 The Son of Man came eating and drinking, and you say, 'Here is a glutton and a drunkard, a friend of tax collectors and "sinners." ' 35 But wisdom is proved right by all her children."

Jesus Anointed by a Sinful Woman

36 Now one of the Pharisees invited Jesus to have dinner with him, so he went to the Pharisee's house and reclined at the table. 37 When a woman who had lived a sinful life in that town learned that Jesus was eating at the Pharisee's house, she brought an alabaster jar of perfume, 38 and as she stood behind him at his feet weeping, she began to wet his feet with her

---

[g] Or *praised God*

[d] 27 Mal. 3:1

Then she continued kissing his feet and anointing them with the ointment. ³⁹Now when the Pharisee who had invited him saw it, he said to himself, "If this man were a prophet, he would have known who and what kind of woman this is who is touching him—that she is a sinner." ⁴⁰Jesus spoke up and said to him, "Simon, I have something to say to you." "Teacher," he replied, "Speak." ⁴¹"A certain creditor had two debtors; one owed five hundred denarii,ʰ and the other fifty. ⁴²When they could not pay, he canceled the debts for both of them. Now which of them will love him more?" ⁴³Simon answered, "I suppose the one for whom he canceled the greater debt." And Jesusᵇ said to him, "You have judged rightly." ⁴⁴Then turning toward the woman, he said to Simon, "Do you see this woman? I entered your house; you gave me no water for my feet, but she has bathed my feet with her tears and dried them with her hair. ⁴⁵You gave me no kiss, but from the time I came in she has not stopped kissing my feet. ⁴⁶You did not anoint my head with oil, but she has anointed my feet with ointment. ⁴⁷Therefore, I tell you, her sins, which were many, have been forgiven; hence she has shown great love. But the one to whom little is forgiven, loves little." ⁴⁸Then he said to her, "Your sins are forgiven." ⁴⁹But those who were at the table with him began to say among themselves, "Who is this who even for-

ταῖς θριξὶν τῆς κεφαλῆς αὐτῆς ἐξέμασσεν,
with the hairs of the head of her wiped off,
καὶ κατεφίλει τοὺς πόδας αὐτοῦ καὶ
and fervently kissed the feet of him and
ἤλειφεν τῷ μύρῳ. 39 ἰδὼν δὲ ὁ Φαρισαῖος
anointed with the ointment. But ⁵seeing ¹the ²Pharisee
ὁ καλέσας αὐτὸν εἶπεν ἐν ἑαυτῷ λέγων·
- ³having invited ⁴him spoke within himself saying :
οὗτος εἰ ἦν [ὁ] προφήτης, ἐγίνωσκεν ἂν
This man if he was the prophet, would have known
τίς καὶ ποταπὴ ἡ γυνὴ ἥτις ἅπτεται
who and what sort the woman who is touching
αὐτοῦ, ὅτι ἁμαρτωλός ἐστιν. 40 καὶ
him, because a sinner she is. And
ἀποκριθεὶς ὁ Ἰησοῦς εἶπεν πρὸς αὐτόν·
answering - Jesus said to him :
Σίμων, ἔχω σοί τι εἰπεῖν. ὁ δέ· διδάσκαλε,
Simon, I have to thee something to say. And he : Teacher,
εἰπέ, φησίν. 41 δύο χρεοφειλέται ἦσαν
say, says. Two debtors were
=A certain creditor had two debtors;
δανειστῇ τινι· ὁ εἷς ὤφειλεν δηνάρια
creditor to a certain;ᵉ the one owed denarii
πεντακόσια, ὁ δὲ ἕτερος πεντήκοντα. 42 μὴ
five hundred, and the other fifty. Not
=As they had no[thing]
ἐχόντων αὐτῶν ἀποδοῦναι ἀμφοτέροις
having them to repay ²both
ἐχαρίσατο. τίς οὖν αὐτῶν πλεῖον ἀγαπήσει
¹he freely forgave. Who then of them more will love
αὐτόν; 43 ἀποκριθεὶς Σίμων εἶπεν·
him? Answering Simon said :
ὑπολαμβάνω ὅτι ᾧ τὸ πλεῖον ἐχαρίσατο.
I suppose[,] - to whom the more he freely forgave.
ὁ δὲ εἶπεν αὐτῷ· ὀρθῶς ἔκρινας. 44 καὶ
And he said to him : Rightly thou didst judge. And
στραφεὶς πρὸς τὴν γυναῖκα τῷ Σίμωνι
turning to the woman - to Simon
ἔφη· βλέπεις ταύτην τὴν γυναῖκα; εἰσῆλθόν
he said : Seest thou this - woman? I entered
σου εἰς τὴν οἰκίαν, ὕδωρ μοι ἐπὶ πόδας
of thee into the house, water to me on(for) [my] feet
οὐκ ἔδωκας· αὕτη δὲ τοῖς δάκρυσιν
thou gavest not; but this woman with the(her) tears
ἔβρεξέν μου τοὺς πόδας καὶ ταῖς θριξὶν
wet of me the feet and with the hairs
αὐτῆς ἐξέμαξεν. 45 φίλημά μοι οὐκ ἔδωκας·
of her wiped off. A kiss to me thou gavest not;
αὕτη δὲ ἀφ' ἧς εἰσῆλθον οὐ διέλειπεν
but this woman from [the time] I entered ceased not
which
καταφιλοῦσά μου τοὺς πόδας. 46 ἐλαίῳ
fervently kissing of me the feet. With oil
τὴν κεφαλήν μου οὐκ ἤλειψας· αὕτη δὲ
the head of me thou didst not anoint; but this woman
μύρῳ ἤλειψεν τοὺς πόδας μου. 47 οὗ
with ointment anointed the feet of me. Of which
=Wherefore
χάριν λέγω σοι, ἀφέωνται αἱ ἁμαρτίαι
for the sake of I tell thee, ⁵have been forgiven ¹the ²sins
αὐτῆς αἱ πολλαί, ὅτι ἠγάπησεν πολύ·
⁴of her - ³many, because she loved much;
ᾧ δὲ ὀλίγον ἀφίεται, ὀλίγον ἀγαπᾷ.
but to whom little is forgiven, little he loves.
48 εἶπεν δὲ αὐτῇ· ἀφέωνταί σου αἱ
And he said to her : Have been forgiven of thee the
ἁμαρτίαι. 49 καὶ ἤρξαντο οἱ συνανακείμενοι
sins. And began the [ones] reclining with [him]

tears. Then she wiped them with her hair, kissed them and poured perfume on them.
³⁹When the Pharisee who had invited him saw this, he said to himself, "If this man were a prophet, he would know who is touching him and what kind of woman she is—that she is a sinner."
⁴⁰Jesus answered him, "Simon, I have something to tell you."
"Tell me, teacher," he said.
⁴¹"Two men owed money to a certain moneylender. One owed him five hundred denarii,ᵉ and the other fifty. ⁴²Neither of them had the money to pay him back, so he canceled the debts of both. Now which of them will love him more?"
⁴³Simon replied, "I suppose the one who had the bigger debt canceled."
"You have judged correctly," Jesus said.
⁴⁴Then he turned toward the woman and said to Simon, "Do you see this woman? I came into your house. You did not give me any water for my feet, but she wet my feet with her tears and wiped them with her hair. ⁴⁵You did not give me a kiss, but this woman, from the time I entered, has not stopped kissing my feet. ⁴⁶You did not put oil on my head, but she has poured perfume on my feet. ⁴⁷Therefore, I tell you, her many sins have been forgiven—for she loved much. But he who has been forgiven little loves little."
⁴⁸Then Jesus said to her, "Your sins are forgiven."
⁴⁹The other guests began to say among themselves,

ʰ The denarius was the usual day's wage for a laborer

ᵉ41 A denarius was a coin worth about a day's wages.

gives sins?" 50 And he said to the woman, "Your faith has saved you; go in peace."

Chapter 8

Some Women Accompany Jesus

SOON afterwards he went on through cities and villages, proclaiming and bringing the good news of the kingdom of God. The twelve were with him, 2 as well as some women who had been cured of evil spirits and infirmities: Mary, called Magdalene, from whom seven demons had gone out, 3 and Joanna, the wife of Herod's steward Chuza, and Susanna, and many others, who provided for them[i] out of their resources.

The Parable of the Sower

4 When a great crowd gathered and people from town after town came to him, he said in a parable: 5 "A sower went out to sow his seed; and as he sowed, some fell on the path and was trampled on, and the birds of the air ate it up. 6 Some fell on the rock; and as it grew up, it withered for lack of moisture. 7 Some fell among thorns, and the thorns grew with it and choked it. 8 Some fell into good soil, and when it grew, it produced a hundredfold." As he said this, he called out, "Let anyone with ears to hear listen!"

λέγειν ἐν ἑαυτοῖς· τίς οὗτός ἐστιν, ὃς καὶ
to say among themselves : Who this is, who even

ἁμαρτίας ἀφίησιν; 50 εἶπεν δὲ πρὸς τὴν
sins forgives? But he said to the

γυναῖκα· ἡ πίστις σου σέσωκέν σε·
woman : The faith of thee has saved thee;

πορεύου εἰς εἰρήνην.
go in peace.

8 Καὶ ἐγένετο ἐν τῷ καθεξῆς καὶ αὐτὸς
And it came to pass afterwards and he

διώδευεν κατὰ πόλιν καὶ κώμην κηρύσσων
journeyed through every† city and village proclaiming

καὶ εὐαγγελιζόμενος τὴν βασιλείαν τοῦ
and preaching the kingdom -

θεοῦ, καὶ οἱ δώδεκα σὺν αὐτῷ, **2** καὶ
of God, and the twelve with him, and

γυναῖκές τινες αἳ ἦσαν τεθεραπευμέναι ἀπὸ
women certain who were having been healed from

πνευμάτων πονηρῶν καὶ ἀσθενειῶν, Μαρία
spirits evil and infirmities, Mary

ἡ καλουμένη Μαγδαληνή, ἀφ᾽ ἧς δαιμόνια
- being called Magdalene, from whom demons

ἑπτὰ ἐξεληλύθει, **3** καὶ Ἰωάννα γυνὴ Χουζᾶ
seven had gone out, and Joanna wife of Chuza

ἐπιτρόπου Ἡρῴδου καὶ Σουσάννα καὶ
steward of Herod and Susanna and

ἕτεραι πολλαί, αἵτινες διηκόνουν αὐτοῖς
others many, who ministered to them

ἐκ τῶν ὑπαρχόντων αὐταῖς.ᵉ
out of the possessions to them.ᵉ

4 Συνιόντος δὲ ὄχλου πολλοῦ καὶ τῶν
And coming together crowd a much and the [ones]
=when a great crowd came together and people in each city

κατὰ πόλιν ἐπιπορευομένων πρὸς αὐτὸν
in each city† resorting* to him
resorted

εἶπεν διὰ παραβολῆς· **5** ἐξῆλθεν ὁ σπείρων
he said by a parable : Went forth the [one] sowing

τοῦ σπεῖραι τὸν σπόρον αὐτοῦ. καὶ ἐν τῷ
- to sowᵈ the seed of him. And in the

σπείρειν αὐτὸν ὃ μὲν ἔπεσεν παρὰ τὴν
to sow himᵇᵉ this fell by the
=as he sowed

ὁδὸν καὶ κατεπατήθη, καὶ τὰ πετεινὰ τοῦ
way and was trodden down, and the birds of the

οὐρανοῦ κατέφαγεν αὐτό. **6** καὶ ἕτερον
heaven(air) devoured it. And other [seed]

κατέπεσεν ἐπὶ τὴν πέτραν, καὶ φυὲν
fell on the rock, and grown

ἐξηράνθη διὰ τὸ μὴ ἔχειν ἰκμάδα.
it was withered because of the not to have moisture.
=because it had no moisture.

7 καὶ ἕτερον ἔπεσεν ἐν μέσῳ τῶν ἀκανθῶν, καὶ
And other fell in [the] of the thorns, and
midst

συμφυεῖσαι αἱ ἄκανθαι ἀπέπνιξαν αὐτό.
growing up with [it] the thorns choked it.

8 καὶ ἕτερον ἔπεσεν εἰς τὴν γῆν τὴν
And other fell in the soil -

ἀγαθὴν καὶ φυὲν ἐποίησεν καρπὸν
good and grown it produced fruit

ἑκατονταπλασίονα. ταῦτα λέγων ἐφώνει· ὁ
a hundredfold. These things saying he called: The [one]

ἔχων ὦτα ἀκούειν ἀκουέτω. **9** Ἐπηρώτων δὲ
having ears to hear let him hear. And questioned

"Who is this who even forgives sins?"
50Jesus said to the woman, "Your faith has saved you; go in peace."

Chapter 8

The Parable of the Sower

AFTER this, Jesus traveled about from one town and village to another, proclaiming the good news of the kingdom of God. The Twelve were with him, 2and also some women who had been cured of evil spirits and diseases: Mary (called Magdalene) from whom seven demons had come out; 3Joanna the wife of Cuza, the manager of Herod's household; Susanna; and many others. These women were helping to support them out of their own means.

4While a large crowd was gathering and people were coming to Jesus from town after town, he told this parable: 5"A farmer went out to sow his seed. As he was scattering the seed, some fell along the path; it was trampled on, and the birds of the air ate it up. 6Some fell on rock, and when it came up, the plants withered because they had no moisture. 7Other seed fell among thorns, which grew up with it and choked the plants. 8Still other seed fell on good soil. It came up and yielded a crop, a hundred times more than was sown."

When he said this, he called out, "He who has ears to hear, let him hear."

The Purpose of the Parables

9 Then his disciples asked him what this parable meant. 10 He said, "To you it has been given to know the secrets[j] of the kingdom of God; but to others I speak[k] in parables, so that

'looking they may not perceive,
and listening they may not understand.'

The Parable of the Sower Explained

11 "Now the parable is this: The seed is the word of God. 12 The ones on the path are those who have heard; then the devil comes and takes away the word from their hearts, so that they may not believe and be saved. 13 The ones on the rock are those who, when they hear the word, receive it with joy. But these have no root; they believe only for a while and in a time of testing fall away. 14 As for what fell among the thorns, these are the ones who hear; but as they go on their way, they are choked by the cares and riches and pleasures of life, and their fruit does not mature. 15 But as for that in the good soil, these are the ones who, when they hear the word, hold it fast in an honest and good heart, and bear fruit with patient endurance.

A Lamp under a Jar

16 "No one after lighting a lamp hides it under a jar, or puts it under a bed, but puts it on a lampstand, so that those who enter may see the light. 17 For nothing is hidden that will not be disclosed, nor is anything secret that will not become known and come to light. 18 Then pay attention to how you listen; for to those who have, more will be given; and from those who do not have, even what they seem to have will be taken away."

The True Kindred of Jesus

19 Then his mother and his brothers came to him,

αὐτὸν οἱ μαθηταὶ αὐτοῦ τίς αὕτη εἴη ἡ
him the disciples of him what 'this 'might be -
παραβολή. 10 ὁ δὲ εἶπεν· ὑμῖν δέδοται
'parable. And he said: To you it has been given
γνῶναι τὰ μυστήρια τῆς βασιλείας τοῦ
to know the mysteries of the kingdom -
θεοῦ, τοῖς δὲ λοιποῖς ἐν παραβολαῖς, ἵνα
of God, but to the rest in parables, that
βλέποντες μὴ βλέπωσιν καὶ ἀκούοντες μὴ
seeing they may not see and hearing not
συνιῶσιν. 11 ἔστιν δὲ αὕτη ἡ παραβολή.
they may understand. 'is 'Now 'this - 'parable.
ὁ σπόρος ἐστὶν ὁ λόγος τοῦ θεοῦ.
The seed is the word - of God.
12 οἱ δὲ παρὰ τὴν ὁδόν εἰσιν οἱ ἀκούσαντες,
And the [ones] by the way are the[ones] hearing,
εἶτα ἔρχεται ὁ διάβολος καὶ αἴρει τὸν
then comes the devil and takes the
λόγον ἀπὸ τῆς καρδίας αὐτῶν, ἵνα μὴ
word from the heart of them, lest
πιστεύσαντες σωθῶσιν. 13 οἱ δὲ ἐπὶ τῆς
believing they may be saved. And the [ones] on the
πέτρας οἳ ὅταν ἀκούσωσιν μετὰ χαρᾶς
rock who when they hear with joy
δέχονται τὸν λόγον· καὶ οὗτοι ῥίζαν
receive the word; and these root
οὐκ ἔχουσιν, οἳ πρὸς καιρὸν πιστεύουσιν
have not, who for a time believe
καὶ ἐν καιρῷ πειρασμοῦ ἀφίστανται. 14 τὸ
and in time of trial withdraw. the [one]
δὲ εἰς τὰς ἀκάνθας πεσόν, οὗτοί εἰσιν
And in the thorns falling, these are
οἱ ἀκούσαντες, καὶ ὑπὸ μεριμνῶν καὶ
the [ones] hearing, 'and 'by 'cares 'and
πλούτου καὶ ἡδονῶν τοῦ βίου πορευόμενοι
'riches 'and 'pleasures - 'of life 'going
συμπνίγονται καὶ οὐ τελεσφοροῦσιν. 15 τὸ
'are choked and do not bear [fruit] to maturity. the [one]
δὲ ἐν τῇ καλῇ γῇ, οὗτοί εἰσιν οἵτινες ἐν
And in the good soil, these are [those] who in
καρδίᾳ καλῇ καὶ ἀγαθῇ ἀκούσαντες τὸν
heart a worthy and good hearing the
λόγον κατέχουσιν καὶ καρποφοροῦσιν ἐν
word hold fast and bear fruit in
ὑπομονῇ. 16 Οὐδεὶς δὲ λύχνον ἅψας
patience. Now no one a lamp having lit
καλύπτει αὐτὸν σκεύει ἢ ὑποκάτω κλίνης
hides it with a vessel or underneath a couch
τίθησιν, ἀλλ' ἐπὶ λυχνίας τίθησιν, ἵνα οἱ
puts, but on a lampstand puts, that the
εἰσπορευόμενοι βλέπωσιν τὸ φῶς. 17 οὐ
[ones] coming in may see the light. not
γάρ ἐστιν κρυπτὸν ὃ οὐ φανερὸν
For [anything] is hidden which 'not 'manifest
γενήσεται, οὐδὲ ἀπόκρυφον ὃ οὐ μὴ
'will 'become, nor secret which by no means
γνωσθῇ καὶ εἰς φανερὸν ἔλθῃ. 18 βλέπετε
will be known and to [be] manifest come. See
οὖν πῶς ἀκούετε· ὃς ἂν γὰρ ἔχῃ,
therefore how ye hear; for whoever has,
δοθήσεται αὐτῷ· καὶ ὃς ἂν μὴ ἔχῃ,
it will be given to him; and whoever has not,
καὶ ὃ δοκεῖ ἔχειν ἀρθήσεται ἀπ' αὐτοῦ.
even what he seems to have will be taken from him.
19 Παρεγένετο δὲ πρὸς αὐτὸν ἡ μήτηρ
And came to him the mother

9 His disciples asked him what this parable meant. 10 He said, "The knowledge of the secrets of the kingdom of God has been given to you, but to others I speak in parables, so that,

"'though seeing, they may not see;
though hearing, they may not understand.'[f]

11 "This is the meaning of the parable: The seed is the word of God. 12 Those along the path are the ones who hear, and then the devil comes and takes away the word from their hearts, so that they may not believe and be saved. 13 Those on the rock are the ones who receive the word with joy when they hear it, but they have no root. They believe for a while, but in the time of testing they fall away. 14 The seed that fell among thorns stands for those who hear, but as they go on their way they are choked by life's worries, riches and pleasures, and they do not mature. 15 But the seed on good soil stands for those with a noble and good heart, who hear the word, retain it, and by persevering produce a crop.

A Lamp on a Stand

16 "No one lights a lamp and hides it in a jar or puts it under a bed. Instead, he puts it on a stand, so that those who come in can see the light. 17 For there is nothing hidden that will not be disclosed, and nothing concealed that will not be known or brought out into the open. 18 Therefore consider carefully how you listen. Whoever has will be given more; whoever does not have, even what he thinks he has will be taken from him."

Jesus' Mother and Brothers

19 Now Jesus' mother and brothers came to see him,

j Or mysteries
k Gk lacks I speak

f 10 Isaiah 6:9

but they could not reach him because of the crowd. [20]And he was told, "Your mother and your brothers are standing outside, wanting to see you." [21]But he said to them, "My mother and my brothers are those who hear the word of God and do it."

Jesus Calms a Storm

[22] One day he got into a boat with his disciples, and he said to them, "Let us go across to the other side of the lake." So they put out, [23]and while they were sailing he fell asleep. A windstorm swept down on the lake, and the boat was filling with water, and they were in danger. [24]They went to him and woke him up, shouting, "Master, Master, we are perishing!" And he woke up and rebuked the wind and the raging waves; they ceased, and there was a calm. [25]He said to them, "Where is your faith?" They were afraid and amazed, and said to one another, "Who then is this, that he commands even the winds and the water, and they obey him?"

Jesus Heals the Gerasene Demoniac

[26] Then they arrived at the country of the Gerasenes,[l] which is opposite Galilee. [27]As he stepped out on land, a man of the city who had demons met him. For a long time he had worn[m] no clothes, and he did not live in a house but in the tombs. [28]When he saw Jesus, he fell down before him and shouted at the top of his voice, "What have you to do with me, Jesus, Son of the Most High God? I beg you, do not torment

---

καὶ οἱ ἀδελφοὶ αὐτοῦ, καὶ οὐκ ἠδύναντο
and　the　brothers　of him,　and　were not able
συντυχεῖν αὐτῷ διὰ τὸν ὄχλον. 20 ἀπηγγέλη δὲ
to come up　with him be-　the　crowd.　And it was reported
αὐτῷ· ἡ μήτηρ σου καὶ οἱ ἀδελφοί σου
to him : The mother of thee　and　the　brothers of thee
ἐστήκασιν ἔξω ἰδεῖν θέλοντές σε. 21 ὁ δὲ
are standing outside ²to see ¹wishing　thee.　But he
ἀποκριθεὶς εἶπεν πρὸς αὐτούς· μήτηρ μου
answering　said　to　them :　Mother of me
καὶ ἀδελφοί μου οὗτοί εἰσιν οἱ τὸν λόγον
and　brothers of me ²these ¹are ⁴the [ones] ⁵the ⁶word
τοῦ θεοῦ ἀκούοντες καὶ ποιοῦντες.
-　⁷of God ⁸hearing　⁹and　⁰doing.

22 Ἐγένετο δὲ ἐν μιᾷ τῶν ἡμερῶν καὶ
And it came to pass on　one　of the　days　and
αὐτὸς ἐνέβη εἰς πλοῖον καὶ οἱ μαθηταὶ
he　embarked in　a boat　and　the　disciples
αὐτοῦ, καὶ εἶπεν πρὸς αὐτούς· διέλθωμεν
of him,　and　he said　to　them;　Let us go over
εἰς τὸ πέραν τῆς λίμνης· καὶ ἀνήχθησαν.
to　the　other side of the　lake;　and　they put to sea.
23 πλεόντων δὲ αὐτῶν ἀφύπνωσεν. καὶ
And sailing　　them⁵　he fell asleep.　And
= as they sailed
κατέβη λαῖλαψ ἀνέμου εἰς τὴν λίμνην, καὶ
came down a storm　of wind　to　the　lake,　and
συνεπληροῦντο καὶ ἐκινδύνευον. 24 προσ-
they were filling up　and　were in danger.　ap-
ελθόντες δὲ διήγειραν αὐτὸν λέγοντες·
proaching　And　they awoke　him　saying :
ἐπιστάτα ἐπιστάτα, ἀπολλύμεθα. ὁ δὲ
Master[,]　Master,　we are perishing.　But he
διεγερθεὶς ἐπετίμησεν τῷ ἀνέμῳ καὶ τῷ
being awakened　rebuked　the　wind　and　the
κλύδωνι τοῦ ὕδατος· καὶ ἐπαύσαντο, καὶ ἐγένετο
roughness of the water;　and　they ceased,　and　there was
γαλήνη. 25 εἶπεν δὲ αὐτοῖς· ποῦ ἡ πίστις ὑμῶν;
a calm.　Then he said to them : Where the faith of you?
φοβηθέντες δὲ ἐθαύμασαν, λέγοντες πρὸς
And fearing　they marvelled,　saying　to
ἀλλήλους· τίς ἄρα οὗτός ἐστιν, ὅτι καὶ
one another : . Who then ²this man ¹is,　that　³even
τοῖς ἀνέμοις ἐπιτάσσει καὶ τῷ ὕδατι, καὶ
⁴the　⁵winds　¹he commands and　the　water,　and
ὑπακούουσιν αὐτῷ; 26 Καὶ κατέπλευσαν εἰς
they obey　him?　And　they sailed down　to
τὴν χώραν τῶν Γερασηνῶν, ἥτις ἐστὶν
the　country　of the　Gerasenes,　which　is
ἀντιπέρα τῆς Γαλιλαίας. 27 ἐξελθόντι δὲ
opposite　-　Galilee.　And going out
= as he went out
αὐτῷ ἐπὶ τὴν γῆν ὑπήντησεν ἀνήρ τις
him⁵　onto　the　land　met [him]　man a certain
ἐκ τῆς πόλεως ἔχων δαιμόνια, καὶ χρόνῳ
out of the　city　having　demons,　and　²time
ἱκανῷ οὐκ ἐνεδύσατο ἱμάτιον, καὶ ἐν οἰκίᾳ
¹for a con-　put not on　a garment,　and　in a house
siderable
οὐκ ἔμενεν ἀλλ' ἐν τοῖς μνήμασιν. 28 ἰδὼν
remained not　but among the　tombs.　seeing
δὲ τὸν Ἰησοῦν ἀνακράξας προσέπεσεν αὐτῷ
And -　Jesus　crying out　he fell prostrate before him
καὶ φωνῇ μεγάλῃ εἶπεν· τί ἐμοὶ καὶ σοί,
and　voice in a great(loud) said :　What to me and to thee,
Ἰησοῦ υἱὲ τοῦ θεοῦ τοῦ ὑψίστου; δέομαί
Jesus　Son　-　of God　-　most high?　I beg

---

but they were not able to get near him because of the crowd. [20]Someone told him, "Your mother and brothers are standing outside, wanting to see you." [21]He replied, "My mother and brothers are those who hear God's word and put it into practice."

Jesus Calms the Storm

[22]One day Jesus said to his disciples, "Let's go over to the other side of the lake." So they got into a boat and set out. [23]As they sailed, he fell asleep. A squall came down on the lake, so that the boat was being swamped, and they were in great danger. [24]The disciples went and woke him, saying, "Master, Master, we're going to drown!"

He got up and rebuked the wind and the raging waters; the storm subsided, and all was calm. [25]"Where is your faith?" he asked his disciples.

In fear and amazement they asked one another, "Who is this? He commands even the winds and the water, and they obey him."

The Healing of a Demon-possessed Man

[26]They sailed to the region of the Gerasenes,[g] which is across the lake from Galilee. [27]When Jesus stepped ashore, he was met by a demon-possessed man from the town. For a long time this man had not worn clothes or lived in a house, but had lived in the tombs. [28]When he saw Jesus, he cried out and fell at his feet, shouting at the top of his voice, "What do you want with me, Jesus, Son of the Most High God? I beg you,

---

[l]Other ancient authorities read Gadarenes; others, Gergesenes
[m]Other ancient authorities read a man of the city who had had demons for a long time met him. He wore

[g]26 Some manuscripts Gadarenes; other manuscripts Gergesenes; also in verse 37

me"— 29for Jesus[n] had commanded the unclean spirit to come out of the man. (For many times it had seized him; he was kept under guard and bound with chains and shackles, but he would break the bonds and be driven by the demon into the wilds.) 30Jesus then asked him, "What is your name?" He said, "Legion"; for many demons had entered him. 31They begged him not to order them to go back into the abyss.

32 Now there on the hillside a large herd of swine was feeding; and the demons[o] begged Jesus[p] to let them enter these. So he gave them permission. 33Then the demons came out of the man and entered the swine, and the herd rushed down the steep bank into the lake and was drowned.

34 When the swineherds saw what had happened, they ran off and told it in the city and in the country. 35Then people came out to see what had happened, and when they came to Jesus, they found the man from whom the demons had gone sitting at the feet of Jesus, clothed and in his right mind. And they were afraid. 36Those who had seen it told them how the one who had been possessed by demons had been healed. 37Then all the people of the surrounding country of the Gerasenes[l] asked Jesus[p] to leave them; for they were seized with great fear. So he got into the boat and returned.

[n] Gk he
[o] Gk they
[p] Gk him

σου, μή με βασανίσῃς. 29 παρήγγελλεν
of thee, do not me torment. he charged
γὰρ τῷ πνεύματι τῷ ἀκαθάρτῳ ἐξελθεῖν
For the spirit - unclean to come out
ἀπὸ τοῦ ἀνθρώπου. πολλοῖς γὰρ χρόνοις
from the man. For many times
συνηρπάκει αὐτόν, καὶ ἐδεσμεύετο ἁλύσεσιν
it had seized him, and he was bound with chains
καὶ πέδαις φυλασσόμενος, καὶ διαρήσσων
and fetters being guarded, and tearing asunder
τὰ δεσμὰ ἠλαύνετο ἀπὸ τοῦ δαιμονίου εἰς
the bonds he was driven from(by) the demon into
τὰς ἐρήμους. 30 ἐπηρώτησεν δὲ αὐτὸν ὁ
the deserts. And questioned him .
Ἰησοῦς· τί σοι ὄνομά ἐστιν; ὁ δὲ εἶπεν·
Jesus : What to thee name is?[c] And he said :
λεγιών, ὅτι εἰσῆλθεν δαιμόνια πολλὰ εἰς
Legion, because ³entered ²demons ¹many into
αὐτόν. 31 καὶ παρεκάλουν αὐτὸν ἵνα μὴ
him. And they besought him that not
ἐπιτάξῃ αὐτοῖς εἰς τὴν ἄβυσσον ἀπελθεῖν.
he would order them into the abyss to go away.
32 ἦν δὲ ἐκεῖ ἀγέλη χοίρων ἱκανῶν
Now there was there a herd pigs of many
βοσκομένη ἐν τῷ ὄρει· καὶ παρεκάλεσαν
feeding in the mountain; and they besought
αὐτὸν ἵνα ἐπιτρέψῃ αὐτοῖς εἰς ἐκείνους
him that he would allow them into those
εἰσελθεῖν· καὶ ἐπέτρεψεν αὐτοῖς. 33 ἐξελθόντα
to enter; and he allowed them. ⁴coming out
δὲ τὰ δαιμόνια ἀπὸ τοῦ ἀνθρώπου εἰσῆλθον
¹So ²the ³demons from the man entered
εἰς τοὺς χοίρους, καὶ ὥρμησεν ἡ ἀγέλη
into the pigs, and rushed the herd
κατὰ τοῦ κρημνοῦ εἰς τὴν λίμνην καὶ
down the precipice into the lake and
ἀπεπνίγη. 34 ἰδόντες δὲ οἱ βόσκοντες
was choked. And ²seeing ¹the [ones] ²feeding
τὸ γεγονὸς ἔφυγον καὶ ἀπήγγειλαν εἰς
⁴the thing ³having fled and reported in
happened
= what had happened
τὴν πόλιν καὶ εἰς τοὺς ἀγρούς. 35 ἐξῆλθον
the city and in the farms. they went out
δὲ ἰδεῖν τὸ γεγονός, καὶ ἦλθον πρὸς τὸν
And to see the thing having and came to -
happened,
= what had happened,
Ἰησοῦν, καὶ εὗρον καθήμενον τὸν ἄνθρωπον
Jesus, and found sitting the man
ἀφ' οὗ τὰ δαιμόνια ἐξῆλθεν ἱματισμένον
from whom the demons went out having been clothed
καὶ σωφρονοῦντα παρὰ τοὺς πόδας τοῦ
and being in his senses by the feet -
Ἰησοῦ, καὶ ἐφοβήθησαν. 36 ἀπήγγειλαν δὲ
of Jesus, and they were afraid. And ²reported
αὐτοῖς οἱ ἰδόντες πῶς ἐσώθη ὁ δαιμο-
¹to them ¹the [ones] ²seeing ³how ⁵was healed ⁴the ⁶demon-
νισθείς. 37 καὶ ἠρώτησεν αὐτὸν ἅπαν τὸ
possessed. And asked him all the
πλῆθος τῆς περιχώρου τῶν Γερασηνῶν
multitude of the neighbourhood of the Gerasenes
ἀπελθεῖν ἀπ' αὐτῶν, ὅτι φόβῳ μεγάλῳ
to go away from them, because fear with a great
συνείχοντο· αὐτὸς δὲ ἐμβὰς εἰς πλοῖον
they were seized; so he embarking in a boat

don't torture me!'' 29For Jesus had commanded the evil[h] spirit to come out of the man. Many times it had seized him, and though he was chained hand and foot and kept under guard, he had broken his chains and had been driven by the demon into solitary places.
30Jesus asked him, "What is your name?"
"Legion," he replied, because many demons had gone into him. 31And they begged him repeatedly not to order them to go into the Abyss.
32A large herd of pigs was feeding there on the hillside. The demons begged Jesus to let them go into them, and he gave them permission. 33When the demons came out of the man, they went into the pigs, and the herd rushed down the steep bank into the lake and was drowned.
34When those tending the pigs saw what had happened, they ran off and reported this in the town and countryside, 35and the people went out to see what had happened. When they came to Jesus, they found the man from whom the demons had gone out, sitting at Jesus' feet, dressed and in his right mind; and they were afraid. 36Those who had seen it told the people how the demon-possessed man had been cured. 37Then all the people of the region of the Gerasenes asked Jesus to leave them, because they were overcome with fear. So he got into the boat and left.

[h]29 Greek unclean

Left column (RSV)

[38] The man from whom the demons had gone begged that he might be with him; but Jesus [n] sent him away, saying, [39] "Return to your home, and declare how much God has done for you." So he went away, proclaiming throughout the city how much Jesus had done for him.

A Girl Restored to Life and a Woman Healed

[40] Now when Jesus returned, the crowd welcomed him, for they were all waiting for him. [41] Just then there came a man named Jairus, a leader of the synagogue. He fell at Jesus' feet and begged him to come to his house, [42] for he had an only daughter, about twelve years old, who was dying.

As he went, the crowds pressed in on him. [43] Now there was a woman who had been suffering from hemorrhages for twelve years; and though she had spent all she had on physicians, [q] no one could cure her. [44] She came up behind him and touched the fringe of his clothes, and immediately her hemorrhage stopped. [45] Then Jesus asked, "Who touched me?" When all denied it, Peter [r] said, "Master, the crowds surround you and press in on you." [46] But Jesus said, "Someone touched me; for I noticed that power had gone out from me." [47] When the woman saw that she could not remain hidden, she came trembling; and falling down before him, she declared in the presence of all the people why she had touched him, and how she had been

Middle column (Greek interlinear)

ὑπέστρεψεν. **38** ἐδεῖτο δὲ αὐτοῦ ὁ ἀνὴρ
returned. And begged of him the man

ἀφ' οὗ ἐξεληλύθει τὰ δαιμόνια εἶναι σὺν
from whom had gone out the demons to be with

αὐτῷ· ἀπέλυσεν δὲ αὐτὸν λέγων· **39** ὑπόστρεφε
him; but he dismissed him saying : Return

εἰς τὸν οἶκόν σου, καὶ διηγοῦ ὅσα σοι
to the house of thee, and relate what [²to thee things

ἐποίησεν ὁ θεός. καὶ ἀπῆλθεν καθ' ὅλην
¹did – ¹God. And he went away throughout all

τὴν πόλιν κηρύσσων ὅσα ἐποίησεν αὐτῷ
the city proclaiming what things ¹did ²to him

ὁ Ἰησοῦς.
– ¹Jesus.

40 Ἐν δὲ τῷ ὑποστρέφειν τὸν Ἰησοῦν
Now in the to return – Jesus[be]
=when Jesus returned

ἀπεδέξατο αὐτὸν ὁ ὄχλος· ἦσαν γὰρ
welcomed him the crowd; for they were

πάντες προσδοκῶντες αὐτόν. **41** καὶ ἰδοὺ
all expecting him. And behold

ἦλθεν ἀνὴρ ᾧ ὄνομα Ἰάϊρος, καὶ οὗτος
came a man to whom name Jairus,[c] and this man

ἄρχων τῆς συναγωγῆς ὑπῆρχεν· καὶ πεσὼν
a ruler of the synagogue was; and falling

παρὰ τοὺς πόδας Ἰησοῦ παρεκάλει αὐτὸν
at the feet of Jesus he besought him

εἰσελθεῖν εἰς τὸν οἶκον αὐτοῦ, **42** ὅτι
to enter into the house of him, because

θυγάτηρ μονογενὴς ἦν αὐτῷ ὡς ἐτῶν
daughter an only born was to him[c] about of years
=he had an only daughter

δώδεκα καὶ αὐτὴ ἀπέθνησκεν. Ἐν δὲ τῷ
twelve and this(she) was dying. Now in the
=as he went

ὑπάγειν αὐτὸν οἱ ὄχλοι συνέπνιγον αὐτόν.
to go him[be] the crowds pressed upon him.

43 καὶ γυνὴ οὖσα ἐν ῥύσει αἵματος ἀπὸ
And a woman being in a flow of blood from
=having

ἐτῶν δώδεκα, ἥτις οὐκ ἴσχυσεν ἀπ'
years twelve, who was not able from

οὐδενὸς θεραπευθῆναι, **44** προσελθοῦσα ὄπισθεν
no(any)one to be healed, approaching behind

ἥψατο τοῦ κρασπέδου τοῦ ἱματίου αὐτοῦ,
touched the fringe of the garment of him,

καὶ παραχρῆμα ἔστη ἡ ῥύσις τοῦ αἵματος
and at once stood the flow of the blood

αὐτῆς. **45** καὶ εἶπεν ὁ Ἰησοῦς· τίς ὁ
of her. And said – Jesus : Who the

ἁψάμενός μου; ἀρνουμένων δὲ πάντων
[one] touching me? And denying all[a]
=when all denied

εἶπεν ὁ Πέτρος· ἐπιστάτα, οἱ ὄχλοι
said – Peter : Master, the crowds

συνέχουσίν σε καὶ ἀποθλίβουσιν. **46** ὁ δὲ
press upon thee and jostle. – But

Ἰησοῦς εἶπεν· ἥψατό μού τις· ἐγὼ γὰρ
Jesus said : Touched me someone; for I

ἔγνων δύναμιν ἐξεληλυθυῖαν ἀπ' ἐμοῦ.
knew power having gone forth from me.

47 ἰδοῦσα δὲ ἡ γυνὴ ὅτι οὐκ ἔλαθεν,
And ²seeing ¹the ²woman that she was not hidden,

τρέμουσα ἦλθεν καὶ προσπεσοῦσα αὐτῷ δι'
trembling came and prostrating before him ²for

ἦν αἰτίαν ἥψατο αὐτοῦ ἀπήγγειλεν ἐνώπιον
⁷what ³cause ⁵she touched ¹⁰him ¹declared ⁴before

Right column (NIV)

[38] The man from whom the demons had gone out begged to go with him, but Jesus sent him away, saying, [39] "Return home and tell how much God has done for you." So the man went away and told all over town how much Jesus had done for him.

A Dead Girl and a Sick Woman

[40] Now when Jesus returned, a crowd welcomed him, for they were all expecting him. [41] Then a man named Jairus, a ruler of the synagogue, came and fell at Jesus' feet, pleading with him to come to his house [42] because his only daughter, a girl of about twelve, was dying.

As Jesus was on his way, the crowds almost crushed him. [43] And a woman was there who had been subject to bleeding for twelve years, [i] but no one could heal her. [44] She came up behind him and touched the edge of his cloak, and immediately her bleeding stopped. [45] "Who touched me?" Jesus asked.

When they all denied it, Peter said, "Master, the people are crowding and pressing against you." [46] But Jesus said, "Someone touched me; I know that power has gone out from me." [47] Then the woman, seeing that she could not go unnoticed, came trembling and fell at his feet. In the presence of all the people, she told why she had touched him and how she

Footnotes

[q] Other ancient authorities lack *and had spent all she had on physicians*

[r] Other ancient authorities add *and those who were with him*

[i] 43 Many manuscripts *years, and she had spent all she had on doctors*

immediately healed. [48] He said to her, "Daughter, your faith has made you well; go in peace."

[49] While he was still speaking, someone came from the leader's house to say, "Your daughter is dead; do not trouble the teacher any longer." [50] When Jesus heard this, he replied, "Do not fear. Only believe, and she will be saved." [51] When he came to the house, he did not allow anyone to enter with him, except Peter, John, and James, and the child's father and mother. [52] They were all weeping and wailing for her; but he said, "Do not weep; for she is not dead but sleeping." [53] And they laughed at him, knowing that she was dead. [54] But he took her by the hand and called out, "Child, get up!" [55] Her spirit returned, and she got up at once, and he directed them to give her something to eat. [56] Her parents were astounded; but he ordered them to tell no one what had happened.

παντὸς τοῦ λαοῦ, καὶ ὡς ἰάθη παραχρῆμα.
³all ⁴the ⁵people, and how she was cured at once.

48 ὁ δὲ εἶπεν αὐτῇ· θυγάτηρ, ἡ πίστις
And he said to her: Daughter, the faith

σου σέσωκέν σε· πορεύου εἰς εἰρήνην.
of thee has healed thee; go in peace.

49 Ἔτι αὐτοῦ λαλοῦντος ἔρχεταί τις παρὰ
Yet him speaking³ comes someone from
=While he was yet speaking

τοῦ ἀρχισυναγώγου λέγων ὅτι τέθνηκεν
the synagogue ruler saying[,] — Has died

ἡ θυγάτηρ σου· μηκέτι σκύλλε τὸν
the daughter of thee; no more trouble the

διδάσκαλον. **50** ὁ δὲ Ἰησοῦς ἀκούσας
teacher. But Jesus hearing

ἀπεκρίθη αὐτῷ· μὴ φοβοῦ· μόνον πίστευσον,
answered him: Fear thou not; only believe,

καὶ σωθήσεται. **51** ἐλθὼν δὲ εἰς τὴν
and she will be healed. And coming into the

οἰκίαν οὐκ ἀφῆκεν εἰσελθεῖν τινα σὺν
house he allowed not to enter anyone with

αὐτῷ εἰ μὴ Πέτρον καὶ Ἰωάννην καὶ
him except Peter and John and

Ἰάκωβον καὶ τὸν πατέρα τῆς παιδὸς καὶ
James and the father of the maid and

τὴν μητέρα. **52** ἔκλαιον δὲ πάντες καὶ
the mother. And were weeping all and

ἐκόπτοντο αὐτήν. ὁ δὲ εἶπεν· μὴ κλαίετε·
bewailing her. But he said: Weep ye not;

οὐκ ἀπέθανεν ἀλλὰ καθεύδει. **53** καὶ
she did not die but sleeps. And

κατεγέλων αὐτοῦ, εἰδότες ὅτι ἀπέθανεν.
they ridiculed him, knowing that she died.

54 αὐτὸς δὲ κρατήσας τῆς χειρὸς αὐτῆς
But he holding the hand of her

ἐφώνησεν λέγων· ἡ παῖς, ἔγειρε. **55** καὶ
called saying: – Maid, arise. And

ἐπέστρεψεν τὸ πνεῦμα αὐτῆς, καὶ ἀνέστη
returned the spirit of her, and she rose up

παραχρῆμα, καὶ διέταξεν αὐτῇ δοθῆναι
at once, and he commanded ¹to her ¹to be given

φαγεῖν. **56** καὶ ἐξέστησαν οἱ γονεῖς
to eat. And were amazed the parents

αὐτῆς· ὁ δὲ παρήγγειλεν αὐτοῖς μηδενὶ
of her; but he enjoined them ²no one

εἰπεῖν τὸ γεγονός.
¹to tell the thing having happened.
=what had happened.

---

had been instantly healed. [48] Then he said to her, "Daughter, your faith has healed you. Go in peace."

[49] While Jesus was still speaking, someone came from the house of Jairus, the synagogue ruler. "Your daughter is dead," he said. "Don't bother the teacher any more."

[50] Hearing this, Jesus said to Jairus, "Don't be afraid; just believe, and she will be healed."

[51] When he arrived at the house of Jairus, he did not let anyone go in with him except Peter, John and James, and the child's father and mother. [52] Meanwhile, all the people were wailing and mourning for her. "Stop wailing," Jesus said. "She is not dead but asleep."

[53] They laughed at him, knowing that she was dead. [54] But he took her by the hand and said, "My child, get up!" [55] Her spirit returned, and at once she stood up. Then Jesus told them to give her something to eat. [56] Her parents were astonished, but he ordered them not to tell anyone what had happened.

Chapter 9

The Mission of the Twelve

THEN Jesus ⁿ called the twelve together and gave them power and authority over all demons and to cure diseases, ² and he sent them out to proclaim the kingdom of God and to heal. ³ He said to them, "Take nothing for your journey, no staff, nor bag, nor bread, nor money—not even an extra tunic. ⁴ What-

---

9 Συγκαλεσάμενος δὲ τοὺς δώδεκα ἔδωκεν
And having called together the twelve he gave

αὐτοῖς δύναμιν καὶ ἐξουσίαν ἐπὶ πάντα τὰ
them power and authority over all the

δαιμόνια καὶ νόσους θεραπεύειν· **2** καὶ
demons and diseases to heal; and

ἀπέστειλεν αὐτοὺς κηρύσσειν τὴν βασιλείαν
sent them to proclaim the kingdom

τοῦ θεοῦ καὶ ἰᾶσθαι, **3** καὶ εἶπεν πρὸς
– of God and to cure, and said to

αὐτούς· μηδὲν αἴρετε εἰς τὴν ὁδόν, μήτε
them: Nothing take ye for the way, neither

ῥάβδον μήτε πήραν μήτε ἄρτον μήτε
staff nor wallet nor bread nor

ἀργύριον μήτε ἀνὰ δύο χιτῶνας ἔχειν.
silver nor each two tunics to have.

Chapter 9

Jesus Sends Out the Twelve

WHEN Jesus had called the Twelve together, he gave them power and authority to drive out all demons and to cure diseases, ² and he sent them out to preach the kingdom of God and to heal the sick. ³ He told them: "Take nothing for the journey—no staff, no bag, no bread, no money, no extra tunic.

ever house you enter, stay there, and leave from there. 5 Wherever they do not welcome you, as you are leaving that town shake the dust off your feet as a testimony against them." 6 They departed and went through the villages, bringing the good news and curing diseases everywhere.

Herod's Perplexity

7 Now Herod the ruler[s] heard about all that had taken place, and he was perplexed, because it was said by some that John had been raised from the dead, 8 by some that Elijah had appeared, and by others that one of the ancient prophets had arisen. 9 Herod said, "John I beheaded; but who is this about whom I hear such things?" And he tried to see him.

Feeding the Five Thousand

10 On their return the apostles told Jesus[t] all they had done. He took them with him and withdrew privately to a city called Bethsaida. 11 When the crowds found out about it, they followed him; and he welcomed them, and spoke to them about the kingdom of God, and healed those who needed to be cured.
12 The day was drawing to a close, and the twelve came to him and said, "Send the crowd away, so that they may go into the surrounding villages and countryside, to lodge and get provisions; for we are here in a deserted place." 13 But he said to them, "You give them something to eat." They said, "We have no more than five loaves and two fish—

---

4 καὶ εἰς ἣν ἂν οἰκίαν εἰσέλθητε, ἐκεῖ
And into whatever house ye may enter, there

μένετε καὶ ἐκεῖθεν ἐξέρχεσθε. **5** καὶ
remain and thence go forth. And

ὅσοι ἂν μὴ δέχωνται ὑμᾶς, ἐξερχόμενοι
as many as may not receive you, going forth

ἀπὸ τῆς πόλεως ἐκείνης τὸν κονιορτὸν
from － city that the dust

ἀπὸ τῶν ποδῶν ὑμῶν ἀποτινάσσετε εἰς
from the feet of you shake off for

μαρτύριον ἐπ᾽ αὐτούς. **6** ἐξερχόμενοι δὲ
a testimony against them. And going forth

διήρχοντο κατὰ τὰς κώμας εὐαγγελιζόμενοι
they went throughout the villages evangelizing
through

καὶ θεραπεύοντες πανταχοῦ. **7** Ἤκουσεν
and healing everywhere. ⁵heard

δὲ Ἡρώδης ὁ τετραάρχης τὰ γινόμενα
¹And ²Herod ³the ⁴tetrarch the things happening

πάντα, καὶ διηπόρει διὰ τὸ λέγεσθαι
all, and was in perplexity because of the to be said
=because it was said

ὑπό τινων ὅτι Ἰωάννης ἠγέρθη ἐκ νεκρῶν,
by some that John was raised from [the] dead,

8 ὑπό τινων δὲ ὅτι Ἡλίας ἐφάνη, ἄλλων
and by some that Elias appeared, ⁶others

δὲ ὅτι προφήτης τις τῶν ἀρχαίων ἀνέστη.
¹but that prophet a certain of the ancients rose again.

9 εἶπεν δὲ [ὁ] Ἡρώδης· Ἰωάννην ἐγὼ
But said － Herod: John I

ἀπεκεφάλισα· τίς δέ ἐστιν οὗτος περὶ οὗ
beheaded; but who is this about whom

ἀκούω τοιαῦτα; καὶ ἐζήτει ἰδεῖν αὐτόν.
I hear such things? And he sought to see him.

10 Καὶ ὑποστρέψαντες οἱ ἀπόστολοι
And having returned the apostles

διηγήσαντο αὐτῷ ὅσα ἐποίησαν. Καὶ
narrated to him what things they did. And

παραλαβὼν αὐτοὺς ὑπεχώρησεν κατ᾽ ἰδίαν
taking them he departed privately

εἰς πόλιν καλουμένην Βηθσαϊδά. **11** οἱ δὲ
to a city being called Bethsaida. But the

ὄχλοι γνόντες ἠκολούθησαν αὐτῷ· καὶ
crowds knowing followed him; and

ἀποδεξάμενος αὐτοὺς ἐλάλει αὐτοῖς περὶ
welcoming them he spoke to them about

τῆς βασιλείας τοῦ θεοῦ, καὶ τοὺς χρείαν
the kingdom － of God, and the [ones] ⁷need

ἔχοντας θεραπείας ἰᾶτο. **12** Ἡ δὲ ἡμέρα
¹having of healing he cured. But the day

ἤρξατο κλίνειν· προσελθόντες δὲ οἱ δώδεκα
began to decline; and approaching the twelve

εἶπαν αὐτῷ· ἀπόλυσον τὸν ὄχλον, ἵνα
said to him: Dismiss the crowd, that

πορευθέντες εἰς τὰς κύκλῳ κώμας καὶ
going to ¹the ²around ³villages ⁴and

ἀγροὺς καταλύσωσιν καὶ εὕρωσιν ἐπισιτισμόν,
⁴farms they may lodge and may find provisions,

ὅτι ὧδε ἐν ἐρήμῳ τόπῳ ἐσμέν. **13** εἶπεν
because here in a desert place we are. he said

δὲ πρὸς αὐτούς· δότε αὐτοῖς φαγεῖν
And to them: ¹Give ³them ⁴to eat

ὑμεῖς. οἱ δὲ εἶπαν· οὐκ εἰσὶν ἡμῖν
⁵ye. But they said: There are not to us
=We have not

πλεῖον ἢ ἄρτοι πέντε καὶ ἰχθύες δύο, εἰ
more than loaves five and fishes two, un-

---

4 Whatever house you enter, stay there until you leave that town. 5 If people do not welcome you, shake the dust off your feet when you leave their town, as a testimony against them." 6 So they set out and went from village to village, preaching the gospel and healing people everywhere.

7 Now Herod the tetrarch heard about all that was going on. And he was perplexed, because some were saying that John had been raised from the dead, 8 others that Elijah had appeared, and still others that one of the prophets of long ago had come back to life. 9 But Herod said, "I beheaded John. Who, then, is this I hear such things about?" And he tried to see him.

Jesus Feeds the Five Thousand

10 When the apostles returned, they reported to Jesus what they had done. Then he took them with him and they withdrew by themselves to a town called Bethsaida, 11 but the crowds learned about it and followed him. He welcomed them and spoke to them about the kingdom of God, and healed those who needed healing.
12 Late in the afternoon the Twelve came to him and said, "Send the crowd away so they can go to the surrounding villages and countryside and find food and lodging, because we are in a remote place here."
13 He replied, "You give them something to eat."
They answered, "We have only five loaves of bread and two fish—unless

---

unless we are to go and buy food for all these people." 14 For there were about five thousand men. And he said to his disciples, "Make them sit down in groups of about fifty each." 15 They did so and made them all sit down. 16 And taking the five loaves and the two fish, he looked up to heaven, and blessed and broke them, and gave them to the disciples to set before the crowd. 17 And all ate and were filled. What was left over was gathered up, twelve baskets of broken pieces.

Peter's Declaration about Jesus

18 Once when Jesus[u] was praying alone, with only the disciples near him, he asked them, "Who do the crowds say that I am?" 19 They answered, "John the Baptist; but others, Elijah; and still others, that one of the ancient prophets has arisen." 20 He said to them, "But who do you say that I am?" Peter answered, "The Messiah[v] of God."

Jesus Foretells His Death and Resurrection

21 He sternly ordered and commanded them not to tell anyone, 22 saying, "The Son of Man must undergo great suffering, and be rejected by the elders, chief priests, and scribes, and be killed, and on the third day be raised."

23 Then he said to them all, "If any want to become my followers, let them deny themselves and take up their cross daily and fol-

---

μήτι πορευθέντες ἡμεῖς ἀγοράσωμεν εἰς
less   going   we   may buy   for

πάντα τὸν λαὸν τοῦτον βρώματα. 14 ἦσαν
all   -   people   this   foods.   there were

γὰρ ὡσεὶ ἄνδρες πεντακισχίλιοι. εἶπεν δὲ
For about men   five thousand.   And he said

πρὸς τοὺς μαθητὰς αὐτοῦ· κατακλίνατε
to   the   disciples   of him :   ¹Make ²to recline

αὐτοὺς κλισίας ὡσεὶ ἀνὰ πεντήκοντα.
²them [in] groups ¹about ²each   ¹fifty.

15 καὶ ἐποίησαν οὕτως καὶ κατέκλιναν
And   they did   so   and   made to recline

ἅπαντας. 16 λαβὼν δὲ τοὺς πέντε ἄρτους
all.   And taking   the   five   loaves

καὶ τοὺς δύο ἰχθύας, ἀναβλέψας εἰς τὸν
and the   two   fishes,   looking up to   -

οὐρανὸν εὐλόγησεν αὐτοὺς καὶ κατέκλασεν,
heaven   he blessed   them   and   broke,

καὶ ἐδίδου τοῖς μαθηταῖς παραθεῖναι τῷ
and gave   to the   disciples   to set before   the

ὄχλῳ. 17 καὶ ἔφαγον καὶ ἐχορτάσθησαν
crowd.   And   they ate   and   were satisfied

πάντες· καὶ ἤρθη τὸ περισσεῦσαν αὐτοῖς
all;   and   were taken the   excess   to them

κλασμάτων κόφινοι δώδεκα.
of fragments   baskets   twelve.

18 Καὶ ἐγένετο ἐν τῷ εἶναι αὐτὸν
And   it came to pass in the to be   him[b]
=as he was

προσευχόμενον κατὰ μόνας συνῆσαν αὐτῷ
praying   alone   were with   him

οἱ μαθηταί, καὶ ἐπηρώτησεν αὐτοὺς λέγων·
the disciples, and   he questioned   them   saying :

τίνα με οἱ ὄχλοι λέγουσιν εἶναι; 19 οἱ δὲ
Whom me the crowds   say   to be?   And they
=Whom do the crowds say that I am?

ἀποκριθέντες εἶπαν· Ἰωάννην τὸν βαπτιστήν,
answering   said :   John   the   Baptist,

ἄλλοι δὲ Ἠλίαν, ἄλλοι δὲ ὅτι προφήτης
but others   Elias,   and others that   prophet

τις τῶν ἀρχαίων ἀνέστη. 20 εἶπεν δὲ
a certain of the ancients   rose again.   And he said

αὐτοῖς· ὑμεῖς δὲ τίνα με λέγετε εἶναι;
to them :   But ye whom me   say   to be?
=whom say ye that I am?

Πέτρος δὲ ἀποκριθεὶς εἶπεν· τὸν χριστὸν
And Peter   answering   said: The   Christ

τοῦ θεοῦ. 21 ὁ δὲ ἐπιτιμήσας αὐτοῖς
-   of God.   But he   warning   ²them

παρήγγειλεν μηδενὶ λέγειν τοῦτο, 22 εἰπὼν
¹charged   ⁴no one ²to tell ³this,   saying

ὅτι δεῖ τὸν υἱὸν τοῦ ἀνθρώπου πολλὰ
that it behoves the Son   of man   many things

παθεῖν καὶ ἀποδοκιμασθῆναι ἀπὸ τῶν
to suffer   and   to be rejected   from(by) the

πρεσβυτέρων καὶ ἀρχιερέων καὶ γραμματέων
elders   and   chief priests   and   scribes

καὶ ἀποκτανθῆναι καὶ τῇ τρίτῃ ἡμέρᾳ
and   to be killed   and on the third   day

ἐγερθῆναι. 23 Ἔλεγεν δὲ πρὸς πάντας·
to be raised.   And he said   to   all :

εἴ τις θέλει ὀπίσω μου ἔρχεσθαι, ἀρνησάσθω
If anyone wishes after   me   to come,   let him deny

ἑαυτὸν καὶ ἀράτω τὸν σταυρὸν
himself   and   take   the   cross

αὐτοῦ καθ' ἡμέραν, καὶ ἀκολουθείτω μοι.
of him   daily,   and   let him follow   me.

---

we go and buy food for all this crowd." 14 (About five thousand men were there.) But he said to his disciples, "Have them sit down in groups of about fifty each." 15 The disciples did so, and everybody sat down. 16 Taking the five loaves and the two fish and looking up to heaven, he gave thanks and broke them. Then he gave them to the disciples to set before the people. 17 They all ate and were satisfied, and the disciples picked up twelve basketfuls of broken pieces that were left over.

Peter's Confession of Christ

18 Once when Jesus was praying in private and his disciples were with him, he asked them, "Who do the crowds say I am?" 19 They replied, "Some say John the Baptist; others say Elijah; and still others, that one of the prophets of long ago has come back to life." 20 "But what about you?" he asked. "Who do you say I am?" Peter answered, "The Christ[j] of God." 21 Jesus strictly warned them not to tell this to anyone. 22 And he said, "The Son of Man must suffer many things and be rejected by the elders, chief priests and teachers of the law, and he must be killed and on the third day be raised to life." 23 Then he said to them all: "If anyone would come after me, he must deny himself and take up his cross daily and follow me. 24 For

---

[u] Gk he
[v] Or The Christ
[j] 20 Or Messiah

low me. 24 For those who want to save their life will lose it, and those who lose their life for my sake will save it. 25 What does it profit them if they gain the whole world, but lose or forfeit themselves? 26 Those who are ashamed of me and of my words, of them the Son of Man will be ashamed when he comes in his glory and the glory of the Father and of the holy angels. 27 But truly I tell you, there are some standing here who will not taste death before they see the kingdom of God."

The Transfiguration

28 Now about eight days after these sayings Jesus took with him Peter and John and James, and went up on the mountain to pray. 29 And while he was praying, the appearance of his face changed, and his clothes became dazzling white. 30 Suddenly they saw two men, Moses and Elijah, talking to him. 31 They appeared in glory and were speaking of his departure, which he was about to accomplish at Jerusalem. 32 Now Peter and his companions were weighed down with sleep; but since they had stayed awake, w they saw his glory and the two men who stood with him. 33 Just as they were leaving him, Peter said to Jesus, "Master, it is good for us to be here; let us make three dwellings, x

---

24 ὃς γὰρ ἐὰν θέλῃ τὴν ψυχὴν αὐτοῦ
For whoever wishes the life of him
σῶσαι, ἀπολέσει αὐτήν· ὃς δ᾽ ἂν ἀπολέσῃ
to save, he will lose it; but whoever loses
τὴν ψυχὴν αὐτοῦ ἕνεκεν ἐμοῦ, οὗτος
the life of him for the sake of me, this [one]
σώσει αὐτήν. 25 τί γὰρ ὠφελεῖται
will save it. For what is profited
ἄνθρωπος κερδήσας τὸν κόσμον ὅλον ἑαυτὸν
a man gaining the world whole ²himself
δὲ ἀπολέσας ἢ ζημιωθείς; 26 ὃς γὰρ ἂν
¹but ³losing or suffering loss? For whoever
ἐπαισχυνθῇ με καὶ τοὺς ἐμοὺς λόγους,
is ashamed of me and - my words,
τοῦτον ὁ υἱὸς τοῦ ἀνθρώπου ἐπαι-
this [one] the Son of man will be
σχυνθήσεται, ὅταν ἔλθῃ ἐν τῇ δόξῃ
ashamed of, when he comes in the glory
αὐτοῦ καὶ τοῦ πατρὸς καὶ τῶν ἁγίων
of him and of the Father and of the holy
ἀγγέλων. 27 λέγω δὲ ὑμῖν ἀληθῶς,
angels. But I tell you truly,
εἰσίν τινες τῶν αὐτοῦ ἑστηκότων οἳ
there are some of the [ones] here standing who
οὐ μὴ γεύσωνται θανάτου ἕως ἂν ἴδωσιν
by no means may taste of death until they see
τὴν βασιλείαν τοῦ θεοῦ.
the kingdom - of God.

28 Ἐγένετο δὲ μετὰ τοὺς λόγους τούτους
And it came to pass ⁴after - ⁵these
ὡσεὶ ἡμέραι ὀκτώ, καὶ παραλαβὼν Πέτρον
¹about ³days ²eight, and taking Peter
καὶ Ἰωάννην καὶ Ἰάκωβον ἀνέβη εἰς τὸ
and John and James he went up into the
ὄρος προσεύξασθαι. 29 καὶ ἐγένετο ἐν τῷ
mountain to pray. And ²became in the
=¹as ³he ²prayed
προσεύχεσθαι αὐτὸν τὸ εἶδος τοῦ προσώπου
to pray him ᵇᵉ ⁴the ⁵appearance ⁶of the ⁷face
αὐτοῦ ἕτερον καὶ ὁ ἱματισμὸς αὐτοῦ
⁹of him ¹⁰different and the raiment of him
λευκὸς ἐξαστράπτων. 30 καὶ ἰδοὺ ἄνδρες
⁸white ¹gleaming. And[,] behold[,] men
δύο συνελάλουν αὐτῷ, οἵτινες ἦσαν Μωϋσῆς
two conversed with him, who were Moses
καὶ Ἡλίας, 31 οἳ ὀφθέντες ἐν δόξῃ ἔλεγον
and Elias, who appearing in glory spoke of
τὴν ἔξοδον αὐτοῦ, ἣν ἤμελλεν πληροῦν
the exodus of him, which he was about to accomplish
ἐν Ἰερουσαλήμ. 32 ὁ δὲ Πέτρος καὶ οἱ
in Jerusalem. - But Peter and the [ones]
σὺν αὐτῷ ἦσαν βεβαρημένοι ὕπνῳ· δια-
with him were *having been* burdened with sleep; ²wak-
γρηγορήσαντες δὲ εἶδαν τὴν δόξαν αὐτοῦ
ing thoroughly ¹but they saw the glory of him
καὶ τοὺς δύο ἄνδρας τοὺς συνεστῶτας
and the two men - standing with
αὐτῷ. 33 καὶ ἐγένετο ἐν τῷ διαχωρίζεσθαι
him. And it came to pass in the to part
=when they parted
αὐτοὺς ἀπ᾽ αὐτοῦ εἶπεν ὁ Πέτρος πρὸς
them ᵇᵉ from him said - Peter to
τὸν Ἰησοῦν· ἐπιστάτα, καλόν ἐστιν ἡμᾶς
- Jesus : Master, good it is [for] us
ὧδε εἶναι, καὶ ποιήσωμεν σκηνὰς τρεῖς,
here to be, and let us make tents three,

---

whoever wants to save his life will lose it, but whoever loses his life for me will save it. 25 What good is it for a man to gain the whole world, and yet lose or forfeit his very self? 26 If anyone is ashamed of me and my words, the Son of Man will be ashamed of him when he comes in his glory and in the glory of the Father and of the holy angels. 27 I tell you the truth, some who are standing here will not taste death before they see the kingdom of God."

The Transfiguration

28 About eight days after Jesus said this, he took Peter, John and James with him and went up onto a mountain to pray. 29 As he was praying, the appearance of his face changed, and his clothes became as bright as a flash of lightning. 30 Two men, Moses and Elijah, 31 appeared in glorious splendor, talking with Jesus. They spoke about his departure, which he was about to bring to fulfillment at Jerusalem. 32 Peter and his companions were very sleepy, but when they became fully awake, they saw his glory and the two men standing with him. 33 As the men were leaving Jesus, Peter said to him, "Master, it is good for us to be here. Let us put up three shelters—one for you, one

---

w Or *but when they were fully awake*
x Or *tents*

one for you, one for Moses, and one for Elijah"—not knowing what he said. 34 While he was saying this, a cloud came and overshadowed them; and they were terrified as they entered the cloud. 35 Then from the cloud came a voice that said, "This is my Son, my Chosen;[y] listen to him!" 36 When the voice had spoken, Jesus was found alone. And they kept silent and in those days told no one any of the things they had seen.

Jesus Heals a Boy with a Demon

37 On the next day, when they had come down from the mountain, a great crowd met him. 38 Just then a man from the crowd shouted, "Teacher, I beg you to look at my son; he is my only child. 39 Suddenly a spirit seizes him, and all at once he[z] shrieks. It convulses him until he foams at the mouth; it mauls him and will scarcely leave him. 40 I begged your disciples to cast it out, but they could not." 41 Jesus answered, "You faithless and perverse generation, how much longer must I be with you and bear with you? Bring your son here." 42 While he was coming, the demon dashed him to the ground in convulsions. But Jesus rebuked the unclean spirit, healed the boy, and gave him back to his father. 43 And all were astounded

[y] Other ancient authorities read *my Beloved*
[z] Or *it*

μίαν σοὶ καὶ μίαν Μωϋσεῖ καὶ μίαν
one for thee and one for Moses and one
'Ηλίᾳ, μὴ εἰδὼς ὃ λέγει. 34 ταῦτα δὲ
for Elias, not knowing what he says. And these things
αὐτοῦ λέγοντος ἐγένετο νεφέλη καὶ
him saying[a] came a cloud and
= while he said these things
ἐπεσκίαζεν αὐτούς· ἐφοβήθησαν δὲ ἐν τῷ
overshadowed them; and they feared in the
= as they entered
εἰσελθεῖν αὐτοὺς εἰς τὴν νεφέλην. 35 καὶ
to enter them[b] into the cloud. And
φωνὴ ἐγένετο ἐκ τῆς νεφέλης λέγουσα·
a voice came out of the cloud saying :
οὗτός ἐστιν ὁ υἱός μου ὁ ἐκλελεγμένος,
This is the Son of me - having been chosen,
αὐτοῦ ἀκούετε, 36 καὶ ἐν τῷ γενέσθαι
him hear ye, and in the to become
= when the voice came
τὴν φωνὴν εὑρέθη 'Ιησοῦς μόνος. καὶ
the voice[b] was found Jesus alone. And
αὐτοὶ ἐσίγησαν καὶ οὐδενὶ ἀπήγγειλαν ἐν ἐκείναις
they were silent and to no one reported in those
ταῖς ἡμέραις οὐδὲν ὧν ἑώρακαν.
- days no(any) of [the things] they have
thing which (had) seen.
37 'Εγένετο δὲ τῇ ἑξῆς ἡμέρᾳ κατελ-
And it came to pass on the following day coming
θόντων αὐτῶν ἀπὸ τοῦ ὄρους συνήντησεν
down them[a] from the mountain met
= as they came down
αὐτῷ ὄχλος πολύς. 38 καὶ ἰδοὺ ἀνὴρ
him crowd a much. And[,] behold[,] a man
ἀπὸ τοῦ ὄχλου ἐβόησεν λέγων· διδάσκαλε,
from the crowd called aloud saying : Teacher,
δέομαί σου ἐπιβλέψαι ἐπὶ τὸν υἱόν μου,
I beg of thee to look at at the son of me,
ὅτι μονογενής μοί ἐστιν, 39 καὶ ἰδοὺ
because only born to me he is, and[,] behold[,]
πνεῦμα λαμβάνει αὐτόν, καὶ ἐξαίφνης
a spirit takes him, and suddenly
κράζει καὶ σπαράσσει αὐτὸν μετὰ ἀφροῦ,
cries out and throws him with foam,
καὶ μόλις ἀποχωρεῖ ἀπ' αὐτοῦ συντρῖβον
and scarcely departs from him bruising
αὐτόν· 40 καὶ ἐδεήθην τῶν μαθητῶν σου
him; and I begged the disciples of thee
ἵνα ἐκβάλωσιν αὐτό, καὶ οὐκ ἠδυνήθησαν.
that they would expel it, and they were not able.
41 ἀποκριθεὶς δὲ ὁ 'Ιησοῦς εἶπεν· ὦ
And answering - Jesus said : O
γενεὰ ἄπιστος καὶ διεστραμμένη, ἕως πότε
generation unbelieving and *having been* perverted, until when
ἔσομαι πρὸς ὑμᾶς καὶ ἀνέξομαι ὑμῶν;
shall I be with you and endure you?
προσάγαγε ὧδε τὸν υἱόν σου. 42 ἔτι
Bring here the son of thee. yet
δὲ προσερχομένου αὐτοῦ ἔρρηξεν αὐτὸν τὸ
But approaching him[a] tore him the
= But while he was yet approaching
δαιμόνιον καὶ συνεσπάραξεν· ἐπετίμησεν δὲ
demon and threw violently; but[a] rebuked
ὁ 'Ιησοῦς τῷ πνεύματι τῷ ἀκαθάρτῳ, καὶ
- [1]Jesus [3]the [4]spirit [2]the [5]unclean, and
ἰάσατο τὸν παῖδα καὶ ἀπέδωκεν αὐτὸν τῷ
cured the boy and restored him to the
πατρὶ αὐτοῦ. 43 ἐξεπλήσσοντο δὲ πάντες
father of him. And were astounded all

for Moses and one for Elijah." (He did not know what he was saying.) 34 While he was speaking, a cloud appeared and enveloped them, and they were afraid as they entered the cloud. 35 A voice came from the cloud, saying, "This is my Son, whom I have chosen; listen to him." 36 When the voice had spoken, they found that Jesus was alone. The disciples kept this to themselves, and told no one at that time what they had seen.

The Healing of a Boy With an Evil Spirit

37 The next day, when they came down from the mountain, a large crowd met him. 38 A man in the crowd called out, "Teacher, I beg you to look at my son, for he is my only child. 39 A spirit seizes him and he suddenly screams; it throws him into convulsions so that he foams at the mouth. It scarcely ever leaves him and is destroying him. 40 I begged your disciples to drive it out, but they could not."

41 "O unbelieving and perverse generation," Jesus replied, "how long shall I stay with you and put up with you? Bring your son here."

42 Even while the boy was coming, the demon threw him to the ground in a convulsion. But Jesus rebuked the evil[k] spirit, healed the boy and gave him back to his father. 43 And they were

[k] 42 Greek *unclean*

at the greatness of God.

Jesus Again Foretells His Death

While everyone was amazed at all that he was doing, he said to his disciples, 44 "Let these words sink into your ears: The Son of Man is going to be betrayed into human hands." 45 But they did not understand this saying; its meaning was concealed from them, so that they could not perceive it. And they were afraid to ask him about this saying.

True Greatness

46 An argument arose among them as to which one of them was the greatest. 47 But Jesus, aware of their inner thoughts, took a little child and put it by his side, 48 and said to them, "Whoever welcomes this child in my name welcomes me, and whoever welcomes me welcomes the one who sent me; for the least among all of you is the greatest."

Another Exorcist

49 John answered, "Master, we saw someone casting out demons in your name, and we tried to stop him, because he does not follow with us." 50 But Jesus said to him, "Do not stop him; for whoever is not against you is for you."

A Samaritan Village Refuses to Receive Jesus

51 When the days drew near for him to be taken up, he set his face to go to Jerusalem. 52 And he sent messengers ahead of him. On their way they entered a village of the Samaritans to make ready for him; 53 but they did not receive him,

---

ἐπὶ τῇ μεγαλειότητι τοῦ θεοῦ.
at the majesty - of God.

Πάντων δὲ θαυμαζόντων ἐπὶ πᾶσιν οἷς
And all marvelling[a] at all things which
=while all marvelled

ἐποίει εἶπεν πρὸς τοὺς μαθητὰς αὐτοῦ·
he did he said to the disciples of him:

44 θέσθε ὑμεῖς εἰς τὰ ὦτα ὑμῶν τοὺς
Lay ye in the ears of you -

λόγους τούτους· ὁ γὰρ υἱὸς τοῦ ἀνθρώπου
sayings these; for the Son - of man

μέλλει παραδίδοσθαι εἰς χεῖρας ἀνθρώπων.
is about to be betrayed into [the] hands of men.

45 οἱ δὲ ἠγνόουν τὸ ῥῆμα τοῦτο, καὶ ἦν
But they knew not - word this, and it was

παρακεκαλυμμένον ἀπ' αὐτῶν ἵνα μὴ
having been veiled from them lest

αἴσθωνται αὐτό, καὶ ἐφοβοῦντο ἐρωτῆσαι
they should perceive it, and they feared to ask

αὐτὸν περὶ τοῦ ῥήματος τούτου. 46 Εἰσῆλθεν
him about - word this. entered

δὲ διαλογισμὸς ἐν αὐτοῖς, τὸ τίς ἂν εἴη
And a debate among them, - who might be
=a debate arose

μείζων αὐτῶν. 47 ὁ δὲ Ἰησοῦς εἰδὼς τὸν
greater(est) of them. - And Jesus knowing the

διαλογισμὸν τῆς καρδίας αὐτῶν, ἐπιλαβόμενος
debate of the heart of them, taking

παιδίον ἔστησεν αὐτὸ παρ' ἑαυτῷ, 48 καὶ
a child stood it(him) beside himself, and

εἶπεν αὐτοῖς· ὃς ἐὰν δέξηται τοῦτο τὸ
said to them: Whoever receives this -

παιδίον ἐπὶ τῷ ὀνόματί μου, ἐμὲ δέχεται·
child on(in) the name of me, me receives;

καὶ ὃς ἂν ἐμὲ δέξηται, δέχεται τὸν
and whoever me receives, receives the [one]

ἀποστείλαντά με· ὁ γὰρ μικρότερος ἐν
having sent me; for ¹the [one] ³lesser ⁴among

πᾶσιν ὑμῖν ὑπάρχων, οὗτός ἐστιν μέγας.
⁵all ²you ²being, this [one] is great.

49 Ἀποκριθεὶς δὲ ὁ Ἰωάννης εἶπεν· ἐπιστάτα,
And answering - John said: Master,

εἴδομέν τινα ἐν τῷ ὀνόματί σου ἐκβάλλοντα
we saw someone in the name of thee expelling

δαιμόνια, καὶ ἐκωλύομεν αὐτόν, ὅτι
demons, and we prevented him, because

οὐκ ἀκολουθεῖ μεθ' ἡμῶν. 50 εἶπεν δὲ πρὸς
he does not follow with us. And said to

αὐτὸν Ἰησοῦς· μὴ κωλύετε· ὃς γὰρ οὐκ
him Jesus: Do not prevent; for [he] who not

ἔστιν καθ' ὑμῶν, ὑπὲρ ὑμῶν ἐστιν.
is against you, for you is.

51 Ἐγένετο δὲ ἐν τῷ συμπληροῦσθαι
And it came to pass in the to be fulfilled

τὰς ἡμέρας τῆς ἀναλήμψεως αὐτοῦ καὶ
the days of the assumption of him[be] and
=as the days of his assumption were fulfilled

αὐτὸς τὸ πρόσωπον ἐστήρισεν τοῦ
he the(his) face set -

πορεύεσθαι εἰς Ἰερουσαλήμ, 52 καὶ ἀπέστειλεν
to go[d] to Jerusalem, and sent

ἀγγέλους πρὸ προσώπου αὐτοῦ. καὶ
messengers before face of him. And

πορευθέντες εἰσῆλθον εἰς κώμην Σαμαριτῶν,
going they entered into a village of Samaritans,

ὥστε ἑτοιμάσαι αὐτῷ· 53 καὶ οὐκ ἐδέξαντο
so as to prepare for him; and they did not receive

---

all amazed at the greatness of God.

While everyone was marveling at all that Jesus did, he said to his disciples, 44 "Listen carefully to what I am about to tell you: The Son of Man is going to be betrayed into the hands of men." 45 But they did not understand what this meant. It was hidden from them, so that they did not grasp it, and they were afraid to ask him about it.

Who Will Be the Greatest?

46 An argument started among the disciples as to which of them would be the greatest. 47 Jesus, knowing their thoughts, took a little child and had him stand beside him. 48 Then he said to them, "Whoever welcomes this little child in my name welcomes me; and whoever welcomes me welcomes the one who sent me. For he who is least among you all—he is the greatest."

49 "Master," said John, "we saw a man driving out demons in your name and we tried to stop him, because he is not one of us."

50 "Do not stop him," Jesus said, "for whoever is not against you is for you."

Samaritan Opposition

51 As the time approached for him to be taken up to heaven, Jesus resolutely set out for Jerusalem. 52 And he sent messengers on ahead, who went into a Samaritan village to get things ready for him; 53 but the people there did not

because his face was set to-ward Jerusalem. 54 When his disciples James and John saw it, they said, "Lord, do you want us to command fire to come down from heaven and consume them?" *a* 55 But he turned and rebuked them. 56 Then *b* they went on to another village.

Would-Be Followers of Jesus

57 As they were going along the road, someone said to him, "I will follow you wherever you go." 58 And Jesus said to him, "Foxes have holes, and birds of the air have nests; but the Son of Man has nowhere to lay his head." 59 To another he said, "Follow me." But he said, "Lord, first let me go and bury my father." 60 But Jesus *c* said to him, "Let the dead bury their own dead; but as for you, go and proclaim the kingdom of God." 61 Another said, "I will follow you, Lord; but let me first say farewell to those at my home." 62 Jesus said to him, "No one who puts a hand to the plow and looks back is fit for the kingdom of God."

αὐτόν, ὅτι τὸ πρόσωπον αὐτοῦ ἦν
him, because the face of him was
πορευόμενον εἰς ᾽Ιερουσαλήμ. 54 ἰδόντες
going to Jerusalem. *seeing
δὲ οἱ μαθηταὶ ᾽Ιάκωβος καὶ ᾽Ιωάννης
And ¹the ²disciples ³James ⁴and ⁵John
εἶπαν· κύριε, θέλεις εἴπωμεν πῦρ κατα-
⁷said: Lord, wilt thou we may tell fire to come
βῆναι ἀπὸ τοῦ οὐρανοῦ καὶ ἀναλῶσαι
down from heaven and to destroy
αὐτούς; 55 στραφεὶς δὲ ἐπετίμησεν αὐτοῖς.
them? But turning he rebuked them.
56 καὶ ἐπορεύθησαν εἰς ἑτέραν κώμην.
And they went to another village.
57 Καὶ πορευομένων αὐτῶν ἐν τῇ ὁδῷ
And going them* in the way
=as they went
εἶπέν τις πρὸς αὐτόν· ἀκολουθήσω σοι
said one to him: I will follow thee
ὅπου ἐὰν ἀπέρχη. 58 καὶ εἶπεν αὐτῷ ὁ
wherever thou goest. And said to him -
᾽Ιησοῦς· αἱ ἀλώπεκες φωλεοὺς ἔχουσιν καὶ
Jesus: The foxes holes have and
τὰ πετεινὰ τοῦ οὐρανοῦ κατασκηνώσεις, ὁ
the birds - of heaven nests, ¹the
δὲ υἱὸς τοῦ ἀνθρώπου οὐκ ἔχει ποῦ τὴν
¹but Son - of man has not where the(his)
κεφαλὴν κλίνη. 59 Εἶπεν δὲ πρὸς ἕτερον·
head he may lay. And he said to another:
ἀκολούθει μοι. ὁ δὲ εἶπεν· ἐπίτρεψόν μοι
Follow me. But he said: Allow me
πρῶτον ἀπελθόντι θάψαι τὸν πατέρα μου.
first going to bury the father of me.
60 εἶπεν δὲ αὐτῷ· ἄφες τοὺς νεκροὺς
But he said to him: Leave the dead
θάψαι τοὺς ἑαυτῶν νεκρούς, σὺ δὲ ἀπελθὼν
to bury the of themselves dead, but thou going
=their own dead,
διάγγελλε τὴν βασιλείαν τοῦ θεοῦ. 61 Εἶπεν
announce the kingdom - of God. said
δὲ καὶ ἕτερος· ἀκολουθήσω σοι, κύριε·
And also another: I will follow thee, Lord;
πρῶτον δὲ ἐπίτρεψόν μοι ἀποτάξασθαι τοῖς
but first allow me to say farewell to the [ones]
εἰς τὸν οἶκόν μου. 62 εἶπεν δὲ [πρὸς
in the house of me. But said to
αὐτὸν] ὁ ᾽Ιησοῦς· οὐδεὶς ἐπιβαλὼν τὴν
him - Jesus: No one putting on the(his)
χεῖρα ἐπ᾽ ἄροτρον καὶ βλέπων εἰς τὰ
hand on a plough and looking at the things
ὀπίσω εὔθετός ἐστιν τῇ βασιλείᾳ τοῦ θεοῦ.
behind fit is for the kingdom - of God.

10 Μετὰ δὲ ταῦτα ἀνέδειξεν ὁ κύριος
Now after these things appointed the Lord
ἑτέρους ἑβδομήκοντα [δύο], καὶ ἀπέστειλεν
others seventy-two, and sent
αὐτοὺς ἀνὰ δύο πρὸ προσώπου αὐτοῦ εἰς
them two by two† before face of him into
πᾶσαν πόλιν καὶ τόπον οὗ ἤμελλεν αὐτὸς
every city and place where ²was about ¹he
ἔρχεσθαι. 2 ἔλεγεν δὲ πρὸς αὐτούς· ὁ
to come. And he said to them: -
μὲν θερισμὸς πολύς, οἱ δὲ ἐργάται ὀλίγοι·
Indeed harvest much, but the workmen few;

---

welcome him, because he was heading for Jerusalem. 54 When the disciples James and John saw this, they asked, "Lord, do you want us to call fire down from heaven to destroy them *l* ?" 55 But Jesus turned and rebuked them, 56 and *m* they went to another village.

The Cost of Following Jesus

57 As they were walking along the road, a man said to him, "I will follow you wherever you go." 58 Jesus replied, "Foxes have holes and birds of the air have nests, but the Son of Man has no place to lay his head." 59 He said to another man, "Follow me." But the man replied, "Lord, first let me go and bury my father." 60 Jesus said to him, "Let the dead bury their own dead, but you go and proclaim the kingdom of God." 61 Still another said, "I will follow you, Lord; but first let me go back and say good-by to my family." 62 Jesus replied, "No one who puts his hand to the plow and looks back is fit for service in the kingdom of God."

Chapter 10

The Mission of the Seventy

AFTER this the Lord appointed seventy *d* others and sent them on ahead of him in pairs to every town and place where he himself intended to go. 2 He said to them, "The harvest is plentiful, but the laborers are few; therefore

a Other ancient authorities add *as Elijah did*
b Other ancient authorities read *rebuked them, and said, "You do not know what spirit you are of.* 56 *for the Son of Man has not come to destroy the lives of human beings but to save them." Then*
c Gk *he*
d Other ancient authorities read *seventy-two*

Chapter 10

Jesus Sends Out the Seventy-two

AFTER this the Lord appointed seventy-two *n* others and sent them two by two ahead of him to every town and place where he was about to go. 2 He told them, "The harvest is plentiful, but the workers

l 54 Some manuscripts *them, even as Elijah did*
m 55,56 Some manuscripts *them. And he said, "You do not know what kind of spirit you are of, for the Son of Man did not come to destroy men's lives, but to save them."* 56 *And*
n 1 Some manuscripts *seventy*; also in verse 17

ask the Lord of the harvest to send out laborers into his harvest. 3 Go on your way. See, I am sending you out like lambs into the midst of wolves. 4 Carry no purse, no bag, no sandals; and greet no one on the road. 5 Whatever house you enter, first say, 'Peace to this house!' 6 And if anyone is there who shares in peace, your peace will rest on that person; but if not, it will return to you. 7 Remain in the same house, eating and drinking whatever they provide, for the laborer deserves to be paid. Do no move about from house to house. 8 Whenever you enter a town and its people welcome you, eat what is set before you; 9 cure the sick who are there, and say to them, 'The kingdom of God has come near to you.'ᵉ 10 But whenever you enter a town and they do not welcome you, go out into its streets and say, 11 'Even the dust of your town that clings to our feet, we wipe off in protest against you. Yet know this: the kingdom of God has come near.'ᶠ 12 I tell you, on that day it will be more tolerable for Sodom than for that town.

Woes to Unrepentant Cities

13 "Woe to you, Chorazin! Woe to you, Bethsaida! For if the deeds of power done in you had been done in Tyre and Sidon, they would have repented long ago, sitting in sackcloth and ashes. 14 But at

---

δεήθητε οὖν τοῦ κυρίου τοῦ θερισμοῦ
beg ye therefore of the Lord of the harvest

ὅπως ἐργάτας ἐκβάλῃ εἰς τὸν θερισμὸν
that workmen he would thrust forth into the harvest

αὐτοῦ. 3 ὑπάγετε· ἰδοὺ ἀποστέλλω ὑμᾶς
of him. Go ye; behold I send you

ὡς ἄρνας ἐν μέσῳ λύκων. 4 μὴ βαστάζετε
as lambs in [the] midst of wolves. Do not carry

βαλλάντιον, μὴ πήραν, μὴ ὑποδήματα· καὶ
a purse, nor a wallet, nor sandals; and

μηδένα κατὰ τὴν ὁδὸν ἀσπάσησθε. 5 εἰς
no one by the way greet. ¹into

ἣν δ' ἂν εἰσέλθητε οἰκίαν, πρῶτον λέγετε·
¹And ²whatever ⁵ye enter ⁴house, first say :

εἰρήνη τῷ οἴκῳ τούτῳ. 6 καὶ ἐὰν ἐκεῖ
Peace - house to this. And if there

ᾖ υἱὸς εἰρήνης, ἐπαναπαήσεται ἐπ' αὐτὸν
there is a son of peace, shall rest on it(?him)

ἡ εἰρήνη ὑμῶν· εἰ δὲ μή γε, ἐφ' ὑμᾶς
the peace of you; otherwise, on you

ἀνακάμψει. 7 ἐν αὐτῇ δὲ τῇ οἰκίᾳ μένετε,
it shall return. ²in ¹same ¹And ²the ³house* remain,

ἔσθοντες καὶ πίνοντες τὰ παρ' αὐτῶν·
eating and drinking the things with them;

ἄξιος γὰρ ὁ ἐργάτης τοῦ μισθοῦ αὐτοῦ.
for worthy [is] the workman of the pay of him.

μὴ μεταβαίνετε ἐξ οἰκίας εἰς οἰκίαν.
Do not remove from house to house.

8 καὶ εἰς ἣν ἂν πόλιν εἰσέρχησθε καὶ
And into whatever city ye enter and

δέχωνται ὑμᾶς, ἐσθίετε τὰ παρατιθέμενα
they receive you, eat the things being set before

ὑμῖν, 9 καὶ θεραπεύετε τοὺς ἐν αὐτῇ
you, and heal the ³in ²it

ἀσθενεῖς, καὶ λέγετε αὐτοῖς· ἤγγικεν ἐφ'
¹sick, and tell them : Has drawn near on(to)

ὑμᾶς ἡ βασιλεία τοῦ θεοῦ. 10 εἰς ἣν δ'
you the kingdom - of God. And into what-

ἂν πόλιν εἰσέλθητε καὶ μὴ δέχωνται ὑμᾶς,
ever city ye enter and they do not receive you,

ἐξελθόντες εἰς τὰς πλατείας αὐτῆς εἴπατε·
going forth into the streets of it say :

11 καὶ τὸν κονιορτὸν τὸν κολληθέντα ἡμῖν
Even the dust - adhering to us
=the dust of your city adhering to us, on our feet,

ἐκ τῆς πόλεως ὑμῶν εἰς τοὺς πόδας
of the city of you on the(our) feet

ἀπομασσόμεθα ὑμῖν· πλὴν τοῦτο γινώσκετε,
we shake off to you; nevertheless this know ye,

ὅτι ἤγγικεν ἡ βασιλεία τοῦ θεοῦ. 12 λέγω
that has drawn near the kingdom - of God. I tell

ὑμῖν ὅτι Σοδόμοις ἐν τῇ ἡμέρᾳ ἐκείνῃ
you that for Sodom in the day that

ἀνεκτότερον ἔσται ἢ τῇ πόλει ἐκείνῃ.
more endurable it will be than - city for that.

13 Οὐαί σοι, Χοραζίν, οὐαί σοι, Βηθσαϊδά·
Woe to thee, Chorazin, woe to thee, Bethsaida;

ὅτι εἰ ἐν Τύρῳ καὶ Σιδῶνι ἐγενήθησαν αἱ
because if in Tyre and Sidon happened the

δυνάμεις αἱ γενόμεναι ἐν ὑμῖν, πάλαι ἂν ἐν
powerful deeds - happening in you, long ago - in

σάκκῳ καὶ σποδῷ καθήμενοι μετενόησαν.
sackcloth and ashes sitting they would have repented.

---

are few. Ask the Lord of the harvest, therefore, to send out workers into his harvest field. 3 Go! I am sending you out like lambs among wolves. 4 Do not take a purse or bag or sandals; and do not greet anyone on the road.

5 "When you enter a house, first say, 'Peace to this house.' 6 If a man of peace is there, your peace will rest on him; if not, it will return to you. 7 Stay in that house, eating and drinking whatever they give you, for the worker deserves his wages. Do not move around from house to house.

8 "When you enter a town and are welcomed, eat what is set before you. 9 Heal the sick who are there and tell them, 'The kingdom of God is near you.' 10 But when you enter a town and are not welcomed, go into its streets and say, 11 'Even the dust of your town that sticks to our feet we wipe off against you. Yet be sure of this: The kingdom of God is near.' 12 I tell you, it will be more bearable on that day for Sodom than for that town.

13 "Woe to you, Korazin! Woe to you, Bethsaida! For if the miracles that were performed in you had been performed in Tyre and Sidon, they would have repented long ago, sitting in sackcloth and ashes.

---

* Luke here, and in 2. 38; 10. 21; 12. 12; 13. 31; 24. 13, as well as in Acts 16. 18; 22. 13, ignores the strict idiomatic construction of αὐτός when in apposition. The words here should mean "in the house itself" but obviously do mean "in the same house". So elsewhere. See note on Luke 2. 38.

ᵉ Or is at hand for you
ᶠ Or is at hand

the judgment it will be more tolerable for Tyre and Sidon than for you. 15 And you, Capernaum, will you be exalted to heaven? No, you will be brought down to Hades.

16 "Whoever listens to you listens to me, and whoever rejects you rejects me, and whoever rejects me rejects the one who sent me."

The Return of the Seventy

17 The seventy[g] returned with joy, saying, "Lord, in your name even the demons submit to us!" [18]He said to them, "I watched Satan fall from heaven like a flash of lightning. [19]See, I have given you authority to tread on snakes and scorpions, and over all the power of the enemy; and nothing will hurt you. [20]Nevertheless, do not rejoice at this, that the spirits submit to you, but rejoice that your names are written in heaven."

Jesus Rejoices

21 At that same hour Jesus[h] rejoiced in the Holy Spirit[i] and said, "I thank[j] you, Father, Lord of heaven and earth, because you have hidden these things from the wise and the intelligent and have revealed them to infants; yes, Father, for such was your gracious will.[k] [22]All things have been handed over to me by my Father; and no one knows who the Son is except the Father, or who the Father is except the Son and anyone to whom the Son chooses to reveal him."

23 Then turning to the disciples, Jesus[h] said to them privately, "Blessed are the eyes that see what you see! [24]For I tell you

---

14 πλὴν Τύρῳ καὶ Σιδῶνι ἀνεκτότερον
Nevertheless for Tyre and Sidon more endurable

ἔσται ἐν τῇ κρίσει ἢ ὑμῖν. **15** καὶ σύ,
it will be in the judgment than for you. And thou,

Καφαρναούμ, μὴ ἕως οὐρανοῦ ὑψωθήσῃ;
Capernaum, not to heaven wast thou lifted?

ἕως τοῦ ᾅδου καταβήσῃ. **16** Ὁ ἀκούων
to - hades thou shalt come down. The [one] hearing

ὑμῶν ἐμοῦ ἀκούει, καὶ ὁ ἀθετῶν ὑμᾶς
you me hears, and the [one] rejecting you

ἐμὲ ἀθετεῖ· ὁ δὲ ἐμὲ ἀθετῶν ἀθετεῖ τὸν
me rejects; and the [one] me rejecting rejects the [one]

ἀποστείλαντά με. **17** Ὑπέστρεψαν δὲ οἱ
having sent me. And returned the

ἑβδομήκοντα [δύο] μετὰ χαρᾶς λέγοντες·
seventy-two with joy saying :

κύριε, καὶ τὰ δαιμόνια ὑποτάσσεται ἡμῖν
Lord, even the demons submit to us

ἐν τῷ ὀνόματί σου. **18** εἶπεν δὲ αὐτοῖς·
in the name of thee. And he said to them :

ἐθεώρουν τὸν σατανᾶν ὡς ἀστραπὴν ἐκ
I beheld - Satan as lightning out of

τοῦ οὐρανοῦ πεσόντα. **19** ἰδοὺ δέδωκα
- heaven fall. Behold I have given

ὑμῖν τὴν ἐξουσίαν τοῦ πατεῖν ἐπάνω
you the authority - to tread[d] on

ὄφεων καὶ σκορπίων, καὶ ἐπὶ πᾶσαν τὴν
serpents and scorpions, and on all the

δύναμιν τοῦ ἐχθροῦ, καὶ οὐδὲν ὑμᾶς οὐ μὴ
power of the enemy, and nothing you by no(any) means

ἀδικήσει. **20** πλὴν ἐν τούτῳ μὴ χαίρετε
shall hurt. Nevertheless in this rejoice not

ὅτι τὰ πνεύματα ὑμῖν ὑποτάσσεται, χαίρετε
that the spirits to you submits, ²rejoice

δὲ ὅτι τὰ ὀνόματα ὑμῶν ἐγγέγραπται ἐν
¹but that the names of you have been enrolled in

τοῖς οὐρανοῖς. **21** Ἐν αὐτῇ τῇ ὥρᾳ
the heavens. In ²same ¹the hour

ἠγαλλιάσατο τῷ πνεύματι τῷ ἁγίῳ καὶ
he exulted in(?by) the Spirit - Holy and

εἶπεν· ἐξομολογοῦμαί σοι, πάτερ, κύριε
said: I praise thee, Father, Lord

τοῦ οὐρανοῦ καὶ τῆς γῆς, ὅτι ἀπέκρυψας
- of heaven and - of earth, because thou didst hide

ταῦτα ἀπὸ σοφῶν καὶ συνετῶν, καὶ
these things from wise and intelligent [ones], and

ἀπεκάλυψας αὐτὰ νηπίοις· ναί, ὁ πατήρ,
didst reveal them to infants; yes - Father,

ὅτι οὕτως εὐδοκία ἐγένετο ἔμπροσθέν σου.
because thus good pleasure it was before thee.

22 πάντα μοι παρεδόθη ὑπὸ τοῦ πατρός
All things to me were delivered by the Father

μου, καὶ οὐδεὶς γινώσκει τίς ἐστιν ὁ
of me, and no one knows who is the

υἱὸς εἰ μὴ ὁ πατήρ, καὶ τίς ἐστιν ὁ πατὴρ
Son except the Father, and who is the Father

εἰ μὴ ὁ υἱὸς καὶ ᾧ ἐὰν βούληται
except the Son and [he] to whomever wills

ὁ υἱὸς ἀποκαλύψαι. **23** Καὶ στραφεὶς
the Son to reveal [him]. And turning

πρὸς τοὺς μαθητὰς κατ᾽ ἰδίαν εἶπεν·
to the disciples privately he said :

μακάριοι οἱ ὀφθαλμοὶ οἱ βλέποντες ἃ
Blessed the eyes - seeing the things which

βλέπετε. **24** λέγω γὰρ ὑμῖν ὅτι πολλοὶ
ye see. For I tell you that many

---

[14]But it will be more bearable for Tyre and Sidon at the judgment than for you. [15]And you, Capernaum, will you be lifted up to the skies? No, you will go down to the depths.[o]

[16]"He who listens to you listens to me; he who rejects you rejects me; but he who rejects me rejects him who sent me."

[17]The seventy-two returned with joy and said, "Lord, even the demons submit to us in your name."

[18]He replied, "I saw Satan fall like lightning from heaven. [19]I have given you authority to trample on snakes and scorpions and to overcome all the power of the enemy; nothing will harm you. [20]However, do not rejoice that the spirits submit to you, but rejoice that your names are written in heaven."

[21]At that time Jesus, full of joy through the Holy Spirit, said, "I praise you, Father, Lord of heaven and earth, because you have hidden these things from the wise and learned, and revealed them to little children. Yes, Father, for this was your good pleasure.

[22]"All things have been committed to me by my Father. No one knows who the Son is except the Father, and no one knows who the Father is except the Son and those to whom the Son chooses to reveal him."

[23]Then he turned to his disciples and said privately, "Blessed are the eyes that see what you see. [24]For I tell you that many

---

[g] Other ancient authorities read *seventy-two*
[h] Gk *he*
[i] Other authorities read *in the spirit*
[j] Or *praise*
[k] Or *for so it was well-pleasing in your sight*

[o]15 Greek *Hades*

that many prophets and kings desired to see what you see, but did not see it, and to hear what you hear, but did not hear it."

The Parable of the Good Samaritan

25 Just then a lawyer stood up to test Jesus.[l] "Teacher," he said, "what must I do to inherit eternal life?" 26 He said to him, "What is written in the law? What do you read there?" 27 He answered, "You shall love the Lord your God with all your heart, and with all your soul, and with all your strength, and with all your mind; and your neighbor as yourself." 28 And he said to him, "You have given the right answer; do this, and you will live."

29 But wanting to justify himself, he asked Jesus, "And who is my neighbor?" 30 Jesus replied, "A man was going down from Jerusalem to Jericho, and fell into the hands of robbers, who stripped him, beat him, and went away, leaving him half dead. 31 Now by chance a priest was going down that road; and when he saw him, he passed by on the other side. 32 So likewise a Levite, when he came to the place and saw him, passed by on the other side. 33 But a Samaritan while traveling came near him; and when he saw him, he was moved with pity. 34 He went to him and bandaged his wounds, having poured oil and wine on them. Then he put him on his own animal, brought him to an inn, and took care of him. 35 The next day he took out two denarii,[m] gave them to the innkeeper, and said, 'Take care of him; and

---

προφῆται καὶ βασιλεῖς ἠθέλησαν ἰδεῖν ἃ
prophets and kings desired to see the things which
ὑμεῖς βλέπετε καὶ οὐκ εἶδαν, καὶ ἀκοῦσαι
ye see and did not see, and to hear
ἃ ἀκούετε καὶ οὐκ ἤκουσαν.
the things which ye hear and did not hear.

25 Καὶ ἰδοὺ νομικός τις ἀνέστη
And[,] behold[,] lawyer a certain stood up
ἐκπειράζων αὐτὸν λέγων· διδάσκαλε, τί
tempting him saying: Teacher, what
ποιήσας ζωὴν αἰώνιον κληρονομήσω; **26** ὁ
doing ⁵life ⁴eternal ¹I ¹may ³inherit? he
δὲ εἶπεν πρὸς αὐτόν· ἐν τῷ νόμῳ τί
And said to him: In the law what
γέγραπται; πῶς ἀναγινώσκεις; **27** ὁ δὲ
has been written? how readest thou? And he
ἀποκριθεὶς εἶπεν· ἀγαπήσεις κύριον τὸν
answering said: Thou shalt love [the] Lord the
θεόν σου ἐξ ὅλης τῆς καρδίας σου καὶ
God of thee from all the heart of thee and
ἐν ὅλῃ τῇ ψυχῇ σου καὶ ἐν ὅλῃ τῇ
with all the soul of thee and with all the
ἰσχύϊ σου καὶ ἐν ὅλῃ τῇ διανοίᾳ σου,
strength of thee and with all the mind of thee,
καὶ τὸν πλησίον σου ὡς σεαυτόν. **28** εἶπεν
and the neighbour of thee as thyself. he said
δὲ αὐτῷ· ὀρθῶς ἀπεκρίθης· τοῦτο ποίει
And to him: Rightly thou didst answer; this do
καὶ ζήσῃ. **29** ὁ δὲ θέλων δικαιῶσαι ἑαυτὸν
and thou shalt live. But he wishing to justify himself
εἶπεν πρὸς τὸν Ἰησοῦν· καὶ τίς ἐστίν
said to Jesus: And who is
μου πλησίον; **30** ὑπολαβὼν ὁ Ἰησοῦς
of me neighbour? Taking [him] up Jesus
εἶπεν· ἄνθρωπός τις κατέβαινεν ἀπὸ
said: A certain man was going down from
Ἰερουσαλὴμ εἰς Ἰεριχώ, καὶ λῃσταῖς
Jerusalem to Jericho, and ²robbers
περιέπεσεν, οἳ καὶ ἐκδύσαντες αὐτὸν καὶ
¹fell in with, who both stripping him and
πληγὰς ἐπιθέντες ἀπῆλθον ἀφέντες ἡμιθανῆ.
²blows ¹laying ³on ⁴[him] went away leaving [him] half dead.
31 κατὰ συγκυρίαν δὲ ἱερεύς τις κατέβαινεν
And by a coincidence a certain priest was going down
ἐν τῇ ὁδῷ ἐκείνῃ, καὶ ἰδὼν αὐτὸν
in - way that, and seeing him
ἀντιπαρῆλθεν. **32** ὁμοίως δὲ καὶ Λευίτης
passed by opposite. And likewise also a Levite
κατὰ τὸν τόπον ἐλθὼν καὶ ἰδὼν
upon the place coming and seeing
ἀντιπαρῆλθεν. **33** Σαμαρίτης δέ τις ὁδεύων
passed by opposite. And a certain Samaritan journeying
ἦλθεν κατ' αὐτόν καὶ ἰδὼν ἐσπλαγχνίσθη,
came upon him and seeing was filled with pity,
34 καὶ προσελθὼν κατέδησεν τὰ τραύματα
and approaching bound up the wounds
αὐτοῦ ἐπιχέων ἔλαιον καὶ οἶνον, ἐπιβιβάσας
of him pouring on oil and wine, ²placing
δὲ αὐτὸν ἐπὶ τὸ ἴδιον κτῆνος ἤγαγεν
¹and him on the(his) own beast brought
αὐτὸν εἰς πανδοχεῖον καὶ ἐπεμελήθη αὐτοῦ.
him to an inn and cared for him.
35 καὶ ἐπὶ τὴν αὔριον ἐκβαλὼν δύο
And on the morrow taking out two
δηνάρια ἔδωκεν τῷ πανδοχεῖ καὶ εἶπεν·
denarii he gave to the innkeeper and said:

The Parable of the Good Samaritan

25 On one occasion an expert in the law stood up to test Jesus. "Teacher," he asked, "what must I do to inherit eternal life?"
26 "What is written in the Law?" he replied. "How do you read it?"
27 He answered: " 'Love the Lord your God with all your heart and with all your soul and with all your strength and with all your mind'[p]; and, 'Love your neighbor as yourself.'[q]"
28 "You have answered correctly," Jesus replied. "Do this and you will live."
29 But he wanted to justify himself, so he asked Jesus, "And who is my neighbor?"
30 In reply Jesus said: "A man was going down from Jerusalem to Jericho, when he fell into the hands of robbers. They stripped him of his clothes, beat him and went away, leaving him half dead. 31 A priest happened to be going down the same road, and when he saw the man, he passed by on the other side. 32 So too, a Levite, when he came to the place and saw him, passed by on the other side. 33 But a Samaritan, as he traveled, came where the man was; and when he saw him, he took pity on him. 34 He went to him and bandaged his wounds, pouring on oil and wine. Then he put the man on his own donkey, took him to an inn and took care of him. 35 The next day he took out two silver coins[r] and gave them to the innkeeper. 'Look after him,' he said,

---

l Gk him
m The denarius was the usual day's wage for a laborer

p 27 Deut. 6:5
q 27 Lev. 19:18
r 35 Greek two denarii

when I come back, I will repay you whatever more you spend.' 36 Which of these three, do you think, was a neighbor to the man who fell into the hands of the robbers?" 37 He said, "The one who showed him mercy." Jesus said to him, "Go and do likewise."

Jesus Visits Martha and Mary

38 Now as they went on their way, he entered a certain village, where a woman named Martha welcomed him into her home. 39 She had a sister named Mary, who sat at the Lord's feet and listened to what he was saying. 40 But Martha was distracted by her many tasks; so she came to him and asked, "Lord, do you not care that my sister has left me to do all the work by myself? Tell her then to help me." 41 But the Lord answered her, "Martha, Martha, you are worried and distracted by many things; 42 there is need of only one thing.[n] Mary has chosen the better part, which will not be taken away from her."

Chapter 11

The Lord's Prayer

HE was praying in a certain place, and after he had finished, one of his disciples said to him, "Lord, teach us to pray, as John taught his disciples." 2 He said to them, "When you pray, say: Father,[o] hallowed be

[n] Other ancient authorities read few things are necessary, or only one
[o] Other ancient authorities read Our Father in heaven

ἐπιμελήθητι αὐτοῦ, καὶ ὅ τι ἂν προσδα-
Care thou for him, and whatever thou spendest

πανήσῃς ἐγὼ ἐν τῷ ἐπανέρχεσθαί με
in addition I in the to return me[be]
=when I return

ἀποδώσω σοι. 36 τίς τούτων τῶν τριῶν πλησίον
will repay thee. Who of these – three [neighbour]

δοκεῖ σοι γεγονέναι τοῦ ἐμπεσόντος
[seems] to thee [to have become] of the [one] falling into

εἰς τοὺς λῃστάς; 37 ὁ δὲ εἶπεν· ὁ ποιήσας
among the robbers? And he said : The [one] doing

τὸ ἔλεος μετ' αὐτοῦ. εἶπεν δὲ αὐτῷ ὁ
the mercy with him. And said to him

Ἰησοῦς· πορεύου καὶ σὺ ποίει ὁμοίως.
Jesus : Go and thou do likewise.

38 Ἐν δὲ τῷ πορεύεσθαι αὐτοὺς αὐτὸς
And in the to go them[be] he
=as they went

εἰσῆλθεν εἰς κώμην τινά· γυνὴ δέ τις
entered into a certain village; and a certain woman

ὀνόματι Μάρθα ὑπεδέξατο αὐτὸν εἰς τὴν
by name Martha received him into the

οἰκίαν. 39 καὶ τῇδε ἦν ἀδελφὴ καλουμένη
house. And to this was a sister[o] being called
=she had a sister

Μαριάμ, ἣ καὶ παρακαθεσθεῖσα πρὸς τοὺς
Mary, who also sitting beside at the

πόδας τοῦ κυρίου ἤκουεν τὸν λόγον αὐτοῦ.
feet of the Lord heard the word of him.

40 ἡ δὲ Μάρθα περιεσπᾶτο περὶ πολλὴν
– But Martha was distracted about much

διακονίαν· ἐπιστᾶσα δὲ εἶπεν· κύριε, οὐ
serving; and coming upon [him] she said : Lord, not

μέλει σοι ὅτι ἡ ἀδελφή μου μόνην με
matters it to thee that the sister of me [alone] [me]

κατέλειπεν διακονεῖν; εἰπὸν οὖν αὐτῇ ἵνα
[left] to serve? tell therefore her that

μοι συναντιλάβηται. 41 ἀποκριθεὶς δὲ εἶπεν
[me] [she may help]. And answering said

αὐτῇ ὁ κύριος· Μάρθα Μάρθα, μεριμνᾷς
to her the Lord : Martha[,] Martha, thou art anxious

καὶ θορυβάζῃ περὶ πολλά, 42 ὀλίγων δέ
and disturbed about many things, but of few things

ἐστιν χρεία ἢ ἑνός· Μαριὰμ γὰρ τὴν
there is need or of one; for Mary the

ἀγαθὴν μερίδα ἐξελέξατο, ἥτις οὐκ
good part chose, which not

ἀφαιρεθήσεται αὐτῆς.
shall be taken from her.

11 Καὶ ἐγένετο ἐν τῷ εἶναι αὐτὸν ἐν
And it came to pass in the to be him[be] in
=when he was

τόπῳ τινὶ προσευχόμενον, ὡς ἐπαύσατο,
a certain place praying, as he ceased,

εἶπέν τις τῶν μαθητῶν αὐτοῦ πρὸς
said a certain one of the disciples of him to

αὐτόν· κύριε, δίδαξον ἡμᾶς προσεύχεσθαι,
him : Lord, teach us to pray,

καθὼς καὶ Ἰωάννης ἐδίδαξεν τοὺς μαθητὰς
even as also John taught the disciples

αὐτοῦ. 2 εἶπεν δὲ αὐτοῖς· ὅταν
of him. And he said to them : When

προσεύχησθε, λέγετε· Πάτερ, ἁγιασθήτω τὸ
ye pray, say : Father, let be hallowed the

'and when I return, I will reimburse you for any extra expense you may have.' 36 "Which of these three do you think was a neighbor to the man who fell into the hands of robbers?"

37 The expert in the law replied, "The one who had mercy on him."

Jesus told him, "Go and do likewise."

At the Home of Martha and Mary

38 As Jesus and his disciples were on their way, he came to a village where a woman named Martha opened her home to him. 39 She had a sister called Mary, who sat at the Lord's feet listening to what he said. 40 But Martha was distracted by all the preparations that had to be made. She came to him and asked, "Lord, don't you care that my sister has left me to do the work by myself? Tell her to help me!"

41 "Martha, Martha," the Lord answered, "you are worried and upset about many things, 42 but only one thing is needed.[s] Mary has chosen what is better, and it will not be taken away from her."

Chapter 11

Jesus' Teaching on Prayer

ONE day Jesus was praying in a certain place. When he finished, one of his disciples said to him, "Lord, teach us to pray, just as John taught his disciples."

2 He said to them, "When you pray, say:

" 'Father,[t] hallowed be your name,

[s] 42 Some manuscripts but few things are needed—or only one
[t] 2 Some manuscripts Our Father in heaven

your name.
Your kingdom
come. p
3 Give us each day
our daily
bread. q
4 And forgive us our
sins,
for we ourselves
forgive everyone
indebted to us.
And do not bring us
to the time of
trial.'r

Perseverance in Prayer

5 And he said to them, "Suppose one of you has a friend, and you go to him at midnight and say to him, 'Friend, lend me three loaves of bread; 6for a friend of mine has arrived, and I have nothing to set before him.' 7And he answers from within, 'Do not bother me; the door has already been locked, and my children are with me in bed; I cannot get up and give you anything.' 8I tell you, even though he will not get up and give him anything because he is his friend, at least because of his persistence he will get up and give him whatever he needs.

9 "So I say to you, Ask, and it will be given you; search, and you will find; knock, and the door will be opened for you. 10For everyone who asks receives, and everyone who searches finds, and for everyone who knocks, the door will be opened. 11Is there anyone among you who, if your child asks for s a fish, will give a snake instead of a fish? 12Or if the child asks for an egg, will give a scorpion? 13If you then, who are evil, know how to give good gifts to your children, how much more will the heavenly Father give the Holy Spirit t to those who ask him!"

Jesus and Beelzebul

14 Now he was casting out a demon that was mute; when the demon had gone out, the one who had been

---

p A few ancient authorities read *Your Holy Spirit come upon us and cleanse us.* Other ancient authorities add *Your will be done, on earth as in heaven*
q Or *our bread for tomorrow*
r Or *us into temptation.* Other ancient authorities add *but rescue us from the evil one (or from evil)*
s Other ancient authorities add *bread, will give a stone; or if your child asks for*
t Other ancient authorities read *the Father give the Holy Spirit from heaven*

ὄνομά σου· ἐλθάτω ἡ βασιλεία σου·
name of thee; let come the kingdom of thee;

3 τὸν ἄρτον ἡμῶν τὸν ἐπιούσιον δίδου
the bread of us - belonging to the morrow give

ἡμῖν τὸ καθ᾽ ἡμέραν· 4 καὶ ἄφες ἡμῖν τὰς
us each day†; and forgive us the

ἁμαρτίας ἡμῶν, καὶ γὰρ αὐτοὶ ἀφίομεν
sins of us, for indeed [our]selves we forgive

παντὶ ὀφείλοντι ἡμῖν· καὶ μὴ εἰσενέγκῃς
everyone owing to us; and lead not

ἡμᾶς εἰς πειρασμόν. 5 Καὶ εἶπεν πρὸς
us into temptation. And he said to

αὐτούς· τίς ἐξ ὑμῶν ἕξει φίλον, καὶ
them: Who of you shall have a friend, and

πορεύσεται πρὸς αὐτὸν μεσονυκτίου καὶ
will come to him at midnight and

εἴπῃ αὐτῷ· φίλε, χρῆσόν μοι τρεῖς ἄρτους,
say to him: Friend, lend me three loaves,

6 ἐπειδὴ φίλος μου παρεγένετο ἐξ ὁδοῦ
since a friend of me arrived off a journey

πρός με καὶ οὐκ ἔχω ὃ παραθήσω αὐτῷ·
to me and I have not what I may set before him;

7 κἀκεῖνος ἔσωθεν ἀποκριθεὶς εἴπῃ· μή
and that one within answering may say: Not

μοι κόπους πάρεχε· ἤδη ἡ θύρα κέκλεισται,
me troubles cause; now the door has been shut,

καὶ τὰ παιδία μου μετ᾽ ἐμοῦ εἰς τὴν
and the children of me with me in the

κοίτην εἰσίν· οὐ δύναμαι ἀναστὰς δοῦναί
bed are; I cannot rising up *to* give

σοι. 8 λέγω ὑμῖν, εἰ καὶ οὐ δώσει
thee. I tell you, if even he will not give

αὐτῷ ἀναστὰς διὰ τὸ εἶναι φίλον αὐτοῦ,
him rising up on account of the to be friend of him,
= because he is his friend,

διά γε τὴν ἀναίδειαν αὐτοῦ ἐγερθεὶς
yet on account of the importunity of him rising

δώσει αὐτῷ ὅσων χρῄζει. 9 Κἀγὼ ὑμῖν
he will give him as many as he needs. And I to you

λέγω, αἰτεῖτε, καὶ δοθήσεται ὑμῖν· ζητεῖτε,
[1]tell, ask, and it will be given you; seek,

καὶ εὑρήσετε· κρούετε, καὶ ἀνοιγήσεται
and ye will find; knock, and it will be opened

ὑμῖν. 10 πᾶς γὰρ ὁ αἰτῶν λαμβάνει, καὶ
to you. For everyone asking receives, and

ὁ ζητῶν εὑρίσκει, καὶ τῷ κρούοντι
the [one] seeking finds, and to the [one] knocking

ἀνοιγήσεται. 11 τίνα δὲ ἐξ ὑμῶν τὸν
it will be opened. And [1]what [4]of [5]you the

πατέρα αἰτήσει ὁ υἱὸς ἰχθύν, μὴ
[2]father [3][is there] [6][of whom] [9]will ask [7]the [8]son [10]a fish, *not*

ἀντὶ ἰχθύος ὄφιν αὐτῷ ἐπιδώσει; 12 ἢ
instead of a fish [2]a serpent [3]to him [1]will hand? or

καὶ αἰτήσει ᾠόν, ἐπιδώσει αὐτῷ σκορπίον;
even he will ask an egg, will hand to him a scorpion?

13 εἰ οὖν ὑμεῖς πονηροὶ ὑπάρχοντες οἴδατε δόματα
If therefore ye [2]evil [1]being know gifts

ἀγαθὰ διδόναι τοῖς τέκνοις ὑμῶν, πόσῳ
good to give to the children of you, how much

μᾶλλον ὁ πατὴρ ὁ ἐξ οὐρανοῦ δώσει
more the Father - of heaven will give

πνεῦμα ἅγιον τοῖς αἰτοῦσιν αὐτόν.
Spirit [the] Holy to the [ones] asking him.

14 Καὶ ἦν ἐκβάλλων δαιμόνιον, καὶ αὐτὸ
And he was expelling a demon, and it

ἦν κωφόν· ἐγένετο δὲ τοῦ δαιμονίου
was dumb; and it came to pass the demon
= as the demon went out

---

your kingdom come. u
3Give us each day our
daily bread.
4Forgive us our sins,
for we also forgive
everyone who sins
against us. v
And lead us not into
temptation. w' "

5Then he said to them, "Suppose one of you has a friend, and he goes to him at midnight and says, 'Friend, lend me three loaves of bread, 6because a friend of mine on a journey has come to me, and I have nothing to set before him.'

7"Then the one inside answers, 'Don't bother me. The door is already locked, and my children are with me in bed. I can't get up and give you anything.' 8I tell you, though he will not get up and give him the bread because he is his friend, yet because of the man's boldness x he will get up and give him as much as he needs.

9"So I say to you: Ask and it will be given to you; seek and you will find; knock and the door will be opened to you. 10For everyone who asks receives; he who seeks finds; and to him who knocks, the door will be opened.

11"Which of you fathers, if your son asks for y a fish, will give him a snake instead? 12Or if he asks for an egg, will give him a scorpion? 13If you then, though you are evil, know how to give good gifts to your children, how much more will your Father in heaven give the Holy Spirit to those who ask him!' "

Jesus and Beelzebub

14Jesus was driving out a demon that was mute. When the demon left, the

---

u2 Some manuscripts *come. May your will be done on earth as it is in heaven.*
v4 Greek *everyone who is indebted to us*
w4 Some manuscripts *temptation but deliver us from the evil one*
x8 Or *persistence*
y11 Some manuscripts *for bread, will give him a stone; or if he asks for*

mute spoke, and the crowds were amazed. 15 But some of them said, "He casts out demons by Beelzebul, the ruler of the demons." 16 Others, to test him, kept demanding from him a sign from heaven. 17 But he knew what they were thinking and said to them, "Every kingdom divided against itself becomes a desert, and house falls on house. 18 If Satan also is divided against himself, how will his kingdom stand? —for you say that I cast out the demons by Beelzebul. 19 Now if I cast out the demons by Beelzebul, by whom do your exorcists[u] cast them out? Therefore they will be your judges. 20 But if it is by the finger of God that I cast out the demons, then the kingdom of God has come to you. 21 When a strong man, fully armed, guards his castle, his property is safe. 22 But when one stronger than he attacks him and overpowers him, he takes away his armor in which he trusted and divides his plunder. 23 Whoever is not with me is against me, and whoever does not gather with me scatters.

The Return of the Unclean Spirit

24 "When the unclean spirit has gone out of a person, it wanders through waterless regions looking for a resting place, but not finding any, it says, 'I will return to my house from which I came.' 25 When it comes, it finds it swept and put in order. 26 Then it goes and brings seven other spirits more evil than itself, and

---

ἐξελθόντος ἐλάλησεν ὁ κωφός· καὶ
going out[a] spoke the dumb man; and
ἐθαύμασαν οἱ ὄχλοι· 15 τινὲς δὲ ἐξ
marvelled the crowds; but some of
αὐτῶν εἶπαν· ἐν Βεελζεβοὺλ τῷ ἄρχοντι
them said: By Beelzebub the chief
τῶν δαιμονίων ἐκβάλλει τὰ δαιμόνια·
of the demons he expels the demons;
16 ἕτεροι δὲ πειράζοντες σημεῖον ἐξ οὐρανοῦ
and others tempting a sign out of heaven
ἐζήτουν παρ' αὐτοῦ. 17 αὐτὸς δὲ εἰδὼς
sought from him. But he knowing
αὐτῶν τὰ διανοήματα εἶπεν αὐτοῖς· πᾶσα
of them the thoughts said to them: Every
βασιλεία ἐφ' ἑαυτὴν διαμερισθεῖσα ἐρημοῦται,
kingdom against itself divided is made desolate,
καὶ οἶκος ἐπὶ οἶκον πίπτει. 18 εἰ δὲ
and a house against a house falls. And if
καὶ ὁ σατανᾶς ἐφ' ἑαυτὸν διεμερίσθη,
also — Satan against himself was divided,
πῶς σταθήσεται ἡ βασιλεία αὐτοῦ; ὅτι
how will stand the kingdom of him? because
λέγετε ἐν Βεελζεβοὺλ ἐκβάλλειν με τὰ
ye say by Beelzebub to expel me[b] the
=[that] by Beelzebub I expel
δαιμόνια. 19 εἰ δὲ ἐγὼ ἐν Βεελζεβοὺλ
demons. But if I by Beelzebub
ἐκβάλλω τὰ δαιμόνια, οἱ υἱοὶ ὑμῶν ἐν
expel the demons, the sons of you by
τίνι ἐκβάλλουσιν; διὰ τοῦτο αὐτοὶ ὑμῶν
what do they expel? therefore they of you
κριταὶ ἔσονται. 20 εἰ δὲ ἐν δακτύλῳ
judges shall be. But if by [the] finger
θεοῦ [ἐγὼ] ἐκβάλλω τὰ δαιμόνια, ἄρα
of God I expel the demons, then
ἔφθασεν ἐφ' ὑμᾶς ἡ βασιλεία τοῦ θεοῦ.
came upon you the kingdom - of God.
21 ὅταν ὁ ἰσχυρὸς καθωπλισμένος φυλάσσῃ
When the strong man having been well armed guards
τὴν ἑαυτοῦ αὐλήν, ἐν εἰρήνῃ ἐστὶν τὰ
the of himself palace, in peace is(are) the
ὑπάρχοντα αὐτοῦ· 22 ἐπὰν δὲ ἰσχυρότερος
goods of him; but when a stronger
αὐτοῦ ἐπελθὼν νικήσῃ αὐτόν, τὴν πανοπλίαν
[than] him coming upon overcomes him, the armour
αὐτοῦ αἴρει, ἐφ' ᾗ ἐπεποίθει, καὶ τὰ
of him he takes, on which he had relied, and the
σκῦλα αὐτοῦ διαδίδωσιν. 23 Ὁ μὴ ὢν
arms of him distributes. The [one] not being
μετ' ἐμοῦ κατ' ἐμοῦ ἐστιν, καὶ ὁ μὴ
with me against me is, and the [one] not
συνάγων μετ' ἐμοῦ σκορπίζει. 24 Ὅταν
gathering with me scatters. When
τὸ ἀκάθαρτον πνεῦμα ἐξέλθῃ ἀπὸ τοῦ
the unclean spirit goes out from the
ἀνθρώπου, διέρχεται δι' ἀνύδρων τόπων
man, he goes *through* through dry places
ζητοῦν ἀνάπαυσιν, καὶ μὴ εὑρίσκον λέγει·
seeking rest, and not finding says:
ὑποστρέψω εἰς τὸν οἶκόν μου ὅθεν ἐξῆλθον·
I will return to the house of me whence I came out;
25 καὶ ἐλθὸν εὑρίσκει σεσαρωμένον καὶ
and coming he finds [it] *having been* swept and
κεκοσμημένον. 26 τότε πορεύεται καὶ
having been furnished. Then he goes and
παραλαμβάνει ἕτερα πνεύματα πονηρότερα
takes other spirits more wicked

---

man who had been mute spoke, and the crowd was amazed. 15 But some of them said, "By Beelzebub,[z] the prince of demons, he is driving out demons." 16 Others tested him by asking for a sign from heaven.

17 Jesus knew their thoughts and said to them: "Any kingdom divided against itself will be ruined, and a house divided against itself will fall. 18 If Satan is divided against himself, how can his kingdom stand? I say this because you claim that I drive out demons by Beelzebub. 19 Now if I drive out demons by Beelzebub, by whom do your followers drive them out? So then, they will be your judges. 20 But if I drive out demons by the finger of God, then the kingdom of God has come to you.

21 "When a strong man, fully armed, guards his own house, his possessions are safe. 22 But when someone stronger attacks and overpowers him, he takes away the armor in which the man trusted and divides up the spoils.

23 "He who is not with me is against me, and he who does not gather with me, scatters.

24 "When an evil[a] spirit comes out of a man, it goes through arid places seeking rest and does not find it. Then it says, 'I will return to the house I left.' 25 When it arrives, it finds the house swept clean and put in order. 26 Then it goes and takes seven other spirits more wicked than itself,

---

[z]15 Greek *Beezeboul* or *Beelzeboul*; also in verses 18 and 19
[a]24 Greek *unclean*

they enter and live there; and the last state of that person is worse than the first."

True Blessedness

27 While he was saying this, a woman in the crowd raised her voice and said to him, "Blessed is the womb that bore you and the breasts that nursed you!" 28 But he said, "Blessed rather are those who hear the word of God and obey it!"

The Sign of Jonah

29 When the crowds were increasing, he began to say, "This generation is an evil generation; it asks for a sign, but no sign will be given to it except the sign of Jonah. 30 For just as Jonah became a sign to the people of Nineveh, so the Son of Man will be to this generation. 31 The queen of the South will rise at the judgment with the people of this generation and condemn them, because she came from the ends of the earth to listen to the wisdom of Solomon, and see, something greater than Solomon is here! The people of Nineveh will rise up at the judgment with this generation and condemn it, because they repented at the proclamation of Jonah, and see, something greater than Jonah is here!

The Light of the Body

33 "No one after lighting a lamp puts it in a cellar, [v] but on the lampstand so that those who enter may see the light. 34 Your eye is the lamp of your body. If your eye is healthy, your whole body is full of light; but if it is not healthy, your body is full of darkness. 35 Therefore con-

---

ἑαυτοῦ ἑπτά, καὶ εἰσελθόντα κατοικεῖ
[than] himself seven, and entering he dwells

ἐκεῖ· καὶ γίνεται τὰ ἔσχατα τοῦ ἀνθρώπου
there; and becomes the last things – man

ἐκείνου χείρονα τῶν πρώτων. 27 Ἐγένετο
of that worse [than] the first. it came to pass

δὲ ἐν τῷ λέγειν αὐτὸν ταῦτα ἐπάρασά τις
And in the to say him[be] these things [e]lifting up [a]a certain
=as he said

φωνὴν γυνὴ ἐκ τοῦ ὄχλου εἶπεν αὐτῷ·
[her] [e]voice [a]woman [e]of [a]the [b]crowd said to him:

μακαρία ἡ κοιλία ἡ βαστάσασά σε καὶ
Blessed the womb – having borne thee and

μαστοὶ οὓς ἐθήλασας. 28 αὐτὸς δὲ εἶπεν·
[the] breasts which thou didst suck. But he said:

μενοῦν μακάριοι οἱ ἀκούοντες τὸν λόγον
Nay rather blessed the [ones] hearing the word

τοῦ θεοῦ καὶ φυλάσσοντες.
– of God and keeping.

29 Τῶν δὲ ὄχλων ἐπαθροιζομένων ἤρξατο
And the crowds pressing upon [him]
=as the crowds pressed upon [him] he began

λέγειν· ἡ γενεὰ αὕτη γενεὰ πονηρά ἐστιν·
to say: – [a]generation [1]This [e]generation [a]an evil [e]is;

σημεῖον ζητεῖ, καὶ σημεῖον οὐ δοθήσεται
a sign it seeks, and a sign will not be given

αὐτῇ εἰ μὴ τὸ σημεῖον Ἰωνᾶ. 30 καθὼς
to it except the sign of Jonas. even as

γὰρ ἐγένετο [ὁ] Ἰωνᾶς τοῖς Νινευίταις
For [e]became [a]Jonas [e]to the [a]Ninevites

σημεῖον, οὕτως ἔσται καὶ ὁ υἱὸς τοῦ
[a]a sign, so will be also the Son –

ἀνθρώπου τῇ γενεᾷ ταύτῃ. 31 βασίλισσα
of man – generation to this. [The] queen

νότου ἐγερθήσεται ἐν τῇ κρίσει μετὰ
of [the] south will be raised in the judgment with

ἀνδρῶν τῆς γενεᾶς ταύτης καὶ κατακρινεῖ
men – generation of this and will condemn

αὐτούς· ὅτι ἦλθεν ἐκ τῶν περάτων τῆς
them; because she came from the extremities of the

γῆς ἀκοῦσαι τὴν σοφίαν Σολομῶνος, καὶ
earth to hear the wisdom of Solomon, and

ἰδοὺ πλεῖον Σολομῶνος ὧδε. 32 ἄνδρες
behold a greater [than] Solomon [is] here. Men

Νινευῖται ἀναστήσονται ἐν τῇ κρίσει μετὰ
Ninevites will rise up in the judgment with

τῆς γενεᾶς ταύτης καὶ κατακρινοῦσιν αὐτήν·
– generation this and will condemn it;

ὅτι μετενόησαν εἰς τὸ κήρυγμα Ἰωνᾶ, καὶ
because they repented at the proclamation of Jonas, and

ἰδοὺ πλεῖον Ἰωνᾶ ὧδε. 33 Οὐδεὶς λύχνον
behold a greater [than] Jonas [is] here. No one [a]a lamp

ἅψας εἰς κρύπτην τίθησιν οὐδὲ ὑπὸ τὸν
[1]having lit [e]in [e]secret [e]places [it] nor under the

μόδιον, ἀλλ' ἐπὶ τὴν λυχνίαν, ἵνα οἱ
bushel, but on the lampstand, that the

εἰσπορευόμενοι τὸ φέγγος βλέπωσιν. 34 ὁ
ones] entering the light may see. The

λύχνος τοῦ σώματός ἐστιν ὁ ὀφθαλμός σου.
lamp of the body is the eye of thee.

ὅταν ὁ ὀφθαλμός σου ἁπλοῦς ᾖ, καὶ
When the eye of thee single is, also

ὅλον τὸ σῶμά σου φωτεινόν ἐστιν· ἐπὰν
all the body of thee bright is; [e]when

δὲ πονηρὸς ᾖ, καὶ τὸ σῶμά σου σκοτεινόν.
[1]but evil it is, also the body of thee [is] dark.

---

and they go in and live there. And the final condition of that man is worse than the first."

27 As Jesus was saying these things, a woman in the crowd called out, "Blessed is the mother who gave you birth and nursed you."

28 He replied, "Blessed rather are those who hear the word of God and obey it."

The Sign of Jonah

29 As the crowds increased, Jesus said, "This is a wicked generation. It asks for a miraculous sign, but none will be given it except the sign of Jonah. 30 For as Jonah was a sign to the Ninevites, so also will the Son of Man be to this generation. 31 The Queen of the South will rise at the judgment with the men of this generation and condemn them; for she came from the ends of the earth to listen to Solomon's wisdom, and now one[b] greater than Solomon is here. 32 The men of Nineveh will stand up at the judgment with this generation and condemn it; for they repented at the preaching of Jonah, and now one greater than Jonah is here.

The Lamp of the Body

33 "No one lights a lamp and puts it in a place where it will be hidden, or under a bowl. Instead he puts it on its stand, so that those who come in may see the light. 34 Your eye is the lamp of your body. When your eyes are good, your whole body also is full of light. But when they are bad, your body also is full of

---

[v] Other ancient authorities add *or under the bushel basket*

[b]31 Or *something*; also in verse 32

sider whether the light in you is not darkness. 36 If then your whole body is full of light, with no part of it in darkness, it will be as full of light as when a lamp gives you light with its rays."

Jesus Denounces Pharisees and Lawyers

37 While he was speaking, a Pharisee invited him to dine with him; so he went in and took his place at the table. 38 The Pharisee was amazed to see that he did not first wash before dinner. 39 Then the Lord said to him, "Now you Pharisees clean the outside of the cup and of the dish, but inside you are full of greed and wickedness. 40 You fools! Did not the one who made the outside make the inside also? 41 So give for alms those things that are within; and see, everything will be clean for you.

42 "But woe to you Pharisees! For you tithe mint and rue and herbs of all kinds, and neglect justice and the love of God; it is these you ought to have practiced, without neglecting the others. 43 Woe to you Pharisees! For you love to have the seat of honor in the synagogues and to be greeted with respect in the marketplaces. 44 Woe to you! For you are like unmarked graves, and people walk over them without realizing it."

45 One of the lawyers answered him, "Teacher, when you say these things, you insult us too." 46 And he said, "Woe also to you lawyers! For you load people with burdens hard to bear, and you yourselves do not lift a finger to ease

---

35 σκόπει οὖν μὴ τὸ φῶς τὸ ἐν σοὶ
Watch therefore lest the light – in thee

σκότος ἐστίν. **36** εἰ οὖν τὸ σῶμά σου
darkness is. If therefore ¹the ³body ⁴of thee

ὅλον φωτεινόν, μὴ ἔχον μέρος τι σκοτεινόν,
¹whole [is] bright, not having ²part ¹any dark,

ἔσται φωτεινὸν ὅλον ὡς ὅταν ὁ λύχνος
²will be ³bright ¹all as when the lamp

τῇ ἀστραπῇ φωτίζῃ σε.
with the(its) shining enlightens thee.

37 Ἐν δὲ τῷ λαλῆσαι ἐρωτᾷ αὐτὸν
Now in the to speak° asks him
= as [he] spoke

Φαρισαῖος ὅπως ἀριστήσῃ παρ᾽ αὐτῷ·
a Pharisee that he would dine with him;

εἰσελθὼν δὲ ἀνέπεσεν. **38** ὁ δὲ Φαρισαῖος
and entering he reclined. But the Pharisee

ἰδὼν ἐθαύμασεν ὅτι οὐ πρῶτον ἐβαπτίσθη
seeing marvelled that not first he washed

πρὸ τοῦ ἀρίστου. **39** εἶπεν δὲ ὁ κύριος
before the dinner. But said the Lord

πρὸς αὐτόν· νῦν ὑμεῖς οἱ Φαρισαῖοι τὸ
to him: Now ye – Pharisees the

ἔξωθεν τοῦ ποτηρίου καὶ τοῦ πίνακος
outside of the cup and of the dish

καθαρίζετε, τὸ δὲ ἔσωθεν ὑμῶν γέμει
cleanse, but the inside of you is full

ἁρπαγῆς καὶ πονηρίας. **40** ἄφρονες, οὐχ
of robbery and wickedness. Foolish men, not

ὁ ποιήσας τὸ ἔξωθεν καὶ τὸ ἔσωθεν
the [one] making the outside also the inside

ἐποίησεν; **41** πλὴν τὰ ἐνόντα δότε
made? Nevertheless the things being within give

ἐλεημοσύνην, καὶ ἰδοὺ πάντα καθαρὰ ὑμῖν
alms, and behold all things clean to you

ἐστιν. **42** ἀλλὰ οὐαὶ ὑμῖν τοῖς Φαρισαίοις,
is(are). But woe to you – Pharisees,

ὅτι ἀποδεκατοῦτε τὸ ἡδύοσμον καὶ τὸ
because ye tithe the mint and the

πήγανον καὶ πᾶν λάχανον, καὶ παρέρχεσθε
rue and every herb, and pass by

τὴν κρίσιν καὶ τὴν ἀγάπην τοῦ θεοῦ·
the judgment and the love of God;

ταῦτα δὲ ἔδει ποιῆσαι κἀκεῖνα μὴ
but these things it behoved to do and those not

παρεῖναι. **43** οὐαὶ ὑμῖν τοῖς Φαρισαίοις,
to pass by. Woe to you – Pharisees,

ὅτι ἀγαπᾶτε τὴν πρωτοκαθεδρίαν ἐν ταῖς
because ye love the chief seat in the

συναγωγαῖς καὶ τοὺς ἀσπασμοὺς ἐν ταῖς
synagogues and the greetings in the

ἀγοραῖς. **44** οὐαὶ ὑμῖν, ὅτι ἐστὲ ὡς τὰ
marketplaces. Woe to you, because ye are as the

μνημεῖα τὰ ἄδηλα, καὶ οἱ ἄνθρωποι οἱ
tombs – unseen, and the men

περιπατοῦντες ἐπάνω οὐκ οἴδασιν.
walking over do not know.

45 Ἀποκριθεὶς δέ τις τῶν νομικῶν λέγει
And answering one of the lawyers says

αὐτῷ· διδάσκαλε, ταῦτα λέγων καὶ ἡμᾶς
to him: Teacher, these things saying also us

ὑβρίζεις. **46** ὁ δὲ εἶπεν· καὶ ὑμῖν τοῖς
thou insultest. And he said: Also to you –

νομικοῖς οὐαί, ὅτι φορτίζετε τοὺς ἀνθρώπους
lawyers woe, because ye burden men

φορτία δυσβάστακτα, καὶ αὐτοὶ ἑνὶ τῶν
[with] burdens difficult to carry, and [your]selves with one of the

---

darkness. 35 See to it, then, that the light within you is not darkness. 36 Therefore, if your whole body is full of light, and no part of it dark, it will be completely lighted, as when the light of a lamp shines on you."

Six Woes

37 When Jesus had finished speaking, a Pharisee invited him to eat with him; so he went in and reclined at the table. 38 But the Pharisee, noticing that Jesus did not first wash before the meal, was surprised.

39 Then the Lord said to him, "Now then, you Pharisees clean the outside of the cup and dish, but inside you are full of greed and wickedness. 40 You foolish people! Did not the one who made the outside make the inside also? 41 But give what is inside the dish, ᶜ to the poor, and everything will be clean for you.

42 "Woe to you Pharisees, because you give God a tenth of your mint, rue and all other kinds of garden herbs, but you neglect justice and the love of God. You should have practiced the latter without leaving the former undone.

43 "Woe to you Pharisees, because you love the most important seats in the synagogues and greetings in the marketplaces.

44 "Woe to you, because you are like unmarked graves, which men walk over without knowing it."

45 One of the experts in the law answered him, "Teacher, when you say these things, you insult us also."

46 Jesus replied, "And you experts in the law, woe to you, because you load people down with burdens they can hardly carry, and you yourselves will not lift

ᶜ41 Or *what you have*

them. 47 Woe to you! For you build the tombs of the prophets whom your ancestors killed. 48 So you are witnesses and approve of the deeds of your ancestors; for they killed them, and you build their tombs. 49 Therefore also the Wisdom of God said, 'I will send them prophets and apostles, some of whom they will kill and persecute,' 50 so that this generation may be charged with the blood of all the prophets shed since the foundation of the world, 51 from the blood of Abel to the blood of Zechariah, who perished between the altar and the sanctuary. Yes, I tell you, it will be charged against this generation. 52 Woe to you lawyers! For you have taken away the key of knowledge; you did not enter yourselves, and you hindered those who were entering."

53 When he went outside, the scribes and the Pharisees began to be very hostile toward him and to cross-examine him about many things, 54 lying in wait for him, to catch him in something he might say.

δακτύλων ὑμῶν οὐ προσψαύετε τοῖς φορτίοις.
fingers of you ye do not touch the burdens.

47 οὐαὶ ὑμῖν, ὅτι οἰκοδομεῖτε τὰ μνημεῖα
Woe to you, because ye build the tombs

τῶν προφητῶν, οἱ δὲ πατέρες ὑμῶν
of the prophets, and the fathers of you

ἀπέκτειναν αὐτούς. 48 ἄρα μάρτυρές ἐστε
killed them. Therefore witnesses ye are

καὶ συνευδοκεῖτε τοῖς ἔργοις τῶν πατέρων
and ye entirely approve the works of the fathers

ὑμῶν, ὅτι αὐτοὶ μὲν ἀπέκτειναν αὐτούς,
of you, because they on one hand killed them,

ὑμεῖς δὲ οἰκοδομεῖτε. 49 διὰ τοῦτο καὶ
ye on the other hand build. Therefore also

ἡ σοφία τοῦ θεοῦ εἶπεν· ἀποστελῶ εἰς
the Wisdom - of God said: I will send to

αὐτοὺς προφήτας καὶ ἀποστόλους, καὶ ἐξ
them prophets and apostles, and of

αὐτῶν ἀποκτενοῦσιν καὶ διώξουσιν, 50 ἵνα
them they will kill and persecute, that

ἐκζητηθῇ τὸ αἷμα πάντων τῶν προφητῶν
¹¹may be required ¹the ²blood ³of all ⁴the ⁵prophets

τὸ ἐκκεχυμένον ἀπὸ καταβολῆς κόσμου
- ⁶having been shed ⁷from ⁸[the] ⁹foundation ¹⁰of [the] world

ἀπὸ τῆς γενεᾶς ταύτης, 51 ἀπὸ αἵματος
¹²from - generation this, from [the] blood

Ἄβελ ἕως αἵματος Ζαχαρίου τοῦ
of Abel to [the] blood of Zacharias -

ἀπολομένου μεταξὺ τοῦ θυσιαστηρίου καὶ
destroyed between the altar and

τοῦ οἴκου· ναὶ λέγω ὑμῖν, ἐκζητηθήσεται
the house; yes I tell you, it will be required

ἀπὸ τῆς γενεᾶς ταύτης. 52 οὐαὶ ὑμῖν τοῖς
from - generation this. Woe to you -

νομικοῖς, ὅτι ἤρατε τὴν κλεῖδα τῆς
lawyers, because ye took the key of the

γνώσεως· αὐτοὶ οὐκ εἰσήλθατε καὶ τοὺς
of knowledge; [your]selves ye did not enter and the

εἰσερχομένους ἐκωλύσατε. 53 Κἀκεῖθεν ἐξελ-
[ones] entering ye prevented. And thence going
=as he went forth thence

θόντος αὐτοῦ ἤρξαντο οἱ γραμματεῖς καὶ
forth himᵃ began the scribes and

οἱ Φαρισαῖοι δεινῶς ἐνέχειν καὶ ἀποστοματίζειν
the Pharisees ¹terribly ¹to be ²angry and to ¹draw ²out

αὐτὸν περὶ πλειόνων, 54 ἐνεδρεύοντες
¹him concerning a great number of things, lying in wait for

αὐτὸν θηρεῦσαί τι ἐκ τοῦ στόματος αὐτοῦ.
him to catch something out of the mouth of him.

one finger to help them.

47 "Woe to you, because you build tombs for the prophets, and it was your forefathers who killed them. 48 So you testify that you approve of what your forefathers did; they killed the prophets, and you build their tombs. 49 Because of this, God in his wisdom said, 'I will send them prophets and apostles, some of whom they will kill and others they will persecute.' 50 Therefore this generation will be held responsible for the blood of all the prophets that has been shed since the beginning of the world, 51 from the blood of Abel to the blood of Zechariah, who was killed between the altar and the sanctuary. Yes, I tell you, this generation will be held responsible for it all.

52 "Woe to you experts in the law, because you have taken away the key to knowledge. You yourselves have not entered, and you have hindered those who were entering."

53 When Jesus left there, the Pharisees and the teachers of the law began to oppose him fiercely and to besiege him with questions, 54 waiting to catch him in something he might say.

Chapter 12

A Warning against Hypocrisy

MEANWHILE, when the crowd gathered by the thousands, so that they trampled on one another, he began to speak first to his disciples, "Beware of the yeast of the Pharisees, that is, their hypocrisy. 2 Nothing is covered up that will not be uncovered, and nothing secret that will not become

12 Ἐν οἷς ἐπισυναχθεισῶν τῶν μυριάδων
In which things being assembled the thousands
= Meanwhile as the thousands of the crowd were assembled,

τοῦ ὄχλου, ὥστε καταπατεῖν ἀλλήλους,
of the crowd,ᵃ so as to tread on one another,

ἤρξατο λέγειν πρὸς τοὺς μαθητὰς αὐτοῦ
he began to say to the disciples of him

πρῶτον· προσέχετε ἑαυτοῖς ἀπὸ τῆς ζύμης,
first: Take heed to yourselves from the leaven,

ἥτις ἐστὶν ὑπόκρισις, τῶν Φαρισαίων.
which is hypocrisy, of the Pharisees.

2 οὐδὲν δὲ συγκεκαλυμμένον ἐστὶν ὃ οὐκ
And ³nothing ²having been ¹there is which not
completely covered

ἀποκαλυφθήσεται, καὶ κρυπτὸν ὃ οὐ γνωσθήσεται.
will be uncovered, and hidden which will not be known.

Chapter 12

Warnings and Encouragements

MEANWHILE, when a crowd of many thousands had gathered, so that they were trampling on one another, Jesus began to speak first to his disciples, saying: "Be on your guard against the yeast of the Pharisees, which is hypocrisy. 2 There is nothing concealed that will not be disclosed, or hidden that will not be made known. 3 What known. 3 Therefore whatever you have said in the dark will be heard in the light, and what you have whispered behind closed doors will be proclaimed from the housetops.

Exhortation to Fearless Confession

4 "I tell you, my friends, do not fear those who kill the body, and after that can do nothing more. 5 But I will warn you whom to fear: fear him who, after he has killed, has authority[w] to cast into hell. [x] Yes, I tell you, fear him! 6 Are not five sparrows sold for two pennies? Yet not one of them is forgotten in God's sight. 7 But even the hairs of your head are all counted. Do not be afraid; you are of more value than many sparrows.

8 "And I tell you, everyone who acknowledges me before others, the Son of Man also will acknowledge before the angels of God; 9 but whoever denies me before others will be denied before the angels of God. 10 And everyone who speaks a word against the Son of Man will be forgiven; but whoever blasphemes against the Holy Spirit will not be forgiven. 11 When they bring you before the synagogues, the rulers, and the authorities, do not worry about how[y] you are to defend yourselves or what you are to say; 12 for the Holy Spirit will teach you at that very hour what you ought to say."

The Parable of the Rich Fool

13 Someone in the crowd said to him, "Teacher, tell my brother to divide the family inheritance with

3 ἀνθ' ὧν ὅσα ἐν τῇ σκοτίᾳ εἴπατε ἐν
Therefore what things in the darkness ye said in

τῷ φωτὶ ἀκουσθήσεται, καὶ ὃ πρὸς τὸ
the light will be heard, and what to the

οὓς ἐλαλήσατε ἐν τοῖς ταμείοις κηρυχθήσεται
ear ye spoke in the private rooms will be proclaimed

ἐπὶ τῶν δωμάτων. 4 Λέγω δὲ ὑμῖν τοῖς
on the roofs. And I say to you the

φίλοις μου, μὴ φοβηθῆτε ἀπὸ τῶν
friends of me, do not be afraid from(of) the [ones]

ἀποκτεννόντων τὸ σῶμα καὶ μετὰ ταῦτα
killing the body and after these things

μὴ ἐχόντων περισσότερόν τι ποιῆσαι.
no: having anything more to do.

5 ὑποδείξω δὲ ὑμῖν τίνα φοβηθῆτε·
But I will warn you whom ye may fear:

φοβήθητε τὸν μετὰ τὸ ἀποκτεῖναι ἔχοντα
¹fear ²the [one] ⁵after the ⁴to kill(killing) ³having

ἐξουσίαν ἐμβαλεῖν εἰς τὴν γέενναν. ναὶ
⁴authority ⁷to cast in into — gehenna. Yes[,]

λέγω ὑμῖν, τοῦτον φοβήθητε. 6 οὐχὶ
I say to you, this one fear ye. Not

πέντε στρουθία πωλοῦνται ἀσσαρίων δύο;
five sparrows are sold of(for) farthings two?

καὶ ἓν ἐξ αὐτῶν οὐκ ἔστιν ἐπιλελησμένον
and one of them is not having been forgotten

ἐνώπιον τοῦ θεοῦ. 7 ἀλλὰ καὶ αἱ τρίχες
before God. But even the hairs

τῆς κεφαλῆς ὑμῶν πᾶσαι ἠρίθμηνται.
of the head of you all have been numbered.

μὴ φοβεῖσθε· πολλῶν στρουθίων διαφέρετε.
Fear ye not; from many sparrows ye differ.

8 λέγω δὲ ὑμῖν, πᾶς ὃς ἂν ὁμολογήσῃ
But I tell you, everyone whoever confesses

ἐν ἐμοὶ ἔμπροσθεν τῶν ἀνθρώπων, καὶ ὁ
— me before — men, also the

υἱὸς τοῦ ἀνθρώπου ὁμολογήσει ἐν αὐτῷ
Son of man will confess — him

ἔμπροσθεν τῶν ἀγγέλων τοῦ θεοῦ· 9 ὁ δὲ
before the angels — of God; and the

ἀρνησάμενός με ἐνώπιον τῶν ἀνθρώπων
[one] denying me before — men

ἀπαρνηθήσεται ἐνώπιον τῶν ἀγγέλων τοῦ
will be denied before the angels —

θεοῦ. 10 καὶ πᾶς ὃς ἐρεῖ λόγον εἰς τὸν
of God. And everyone who shall say a word against the

υἱὸν τοῦ ἀνθρώπου, ἀφεθήσεται αὐτῷ· τῷ
Son — of man, it will be forgiven him; ¹the [one]

δὲ εἰς τὸ ἅγιον πνεῦμα βλασφημήσαντι
¹but against the Holy Spirit blaspheming

οὐκ ἀφεθήσεται. 11 ὅταν δὲ εἰσφέρωσιν
will not be forgiven. And when they bring in

ὑμᾶς ἐπὶ τὰς συναγωγὰς καὶ τὰς ἀρχὰς
you before — synagogues and — rulers

καὶ τὰς ἐξουσίας, μὴ μεριμνήσητε πῶς ἢ
and — authorities, do not be anxious how or

τί ἀπολογήσησθε ἢ τί εἴπητε· 12 τὸ γὰρ
what ye may answer or what ye may say; for the

ἅγιον πνεῦμα διδάξει ὑμᾶς ἐν αὐτῇ τῇ
Holy Spirit will teach you in ²same ¹the

ὥρᾳ ἃ δεῖ εἰπεῖν. 13 Εἶπεν δέ τις
hour what things it behoves [you] to say. And said someone

ἐκ τοῦ ὄχλου αὐτῷ· διδάσκαλε, εἰπὲ τῷ
out of the crowd to him: Teacher, tell the

ἀδελφῷ μου μερίσασθαι μετ' ἐμοῦ τὴν
brother of me to divide with me the

you have said in the dark will be heard in the daylight, and what you have whispered in the ear in the inner rooms will be proclaimed from the roofs.

4 "I tell you, my friends, do not be afraid of those who kill the body and after that can do no more. 5 But I will show you whom you should fear: Fear him who, after the killing of the body, has power to throw you into hell. Yes, I tell you, fear him. 6 Are not five sparrows sold for two pennies[d]? Yet not one of them is forgotten by God. 7 Indeed, the very hairs of your head are all numbered. Don't be afraid; you are worth more than many sparrows.

8 "I tell you, whoever acknowledges me before men, the Son of Man will also acknowledge him before the angels of God. 9 But he who disowns me before men will be disowned before the angels of God. 10 And everyone who speaks a word against the Son of Man will be forgiven, but anyone who blasphemes against the Holy Spirit will not be forgiven. 11 "When you are brought before synagogues, rulers and authorities, do not worry about how you will defend yourselves or what you will say, 12 for the Holy Spirit will teach you at that time what you should say."

The Parable of the Rich Fool

13 Someone in the crowd said to him, "Teacher, tell my brother to divide the inheritance with me."

[w] Or *power*
[x] Gk *Gehenna*
[y] Other ancient authorities add *or what*

[d]6 Greek *two assaria*

me." 14But he said to him, "Friend, who set me to be a judge or arbitrator over you?" 15And he said to them, "Take care! Be on your guard against all kinds of greed; for one's life does not consist in the abundance of possessions." 16Then he told them a parable: "The land of a rich man produced abundantly. 17And he thought to himself, 'What should I do, for I have no place to store my crops?' 18Then he said, 'I will do this: I will pull down my barns and build larger ones, and there I will store all my grain and my goods. 19And I will say to my soul, 'Soul, you have ample goods laid up for many years; relax, eat, drink, be merry.' 20But God said to him, 'You fool! This very night your life is being demanded of you. And the things you have prepared, whose will they be?' 21So it is with those who store up treasures for themselves but are not rich toward God."

Do Not Worry

22 He said to his disciples, "Therefore I tell you, do not worry about your life, what you will eat, or about your body, what you will wear. 23 For life is more than food, and the body more than clothing. 24Consider the ravens: they neither sow nor reap, they have neither storehouse nor barn, and yet God feeds them. Of how much more value are you than the birds! 25And can any of you by worrying add a single hour to your span of life?ᶻ

κληρονομίαν. 14 ὁ δὲ εἶπεν αὐτῷ· ἄνθρωπε,
inheritance   But he   said   to him :   Man,

τίς με κατέστησεν κριτὴν ἢ μεριστὴν ἐφ'
who me   appointed   a judge   or   a divider   over

ὑμᾶς; 15 εἶπεν δὲ πρὸς αὐτούς· ὁρᾶτε
you?   And he said   to   them :   Beware

καὶ φυλάσσεσθε ἀπὸ πάσης πλεονεξίας,
and   guard   from(against) all   covetousness,

ὅτι οὐκ ἐν τῷ περισσεύειν τινὶ ἡ ζωὴ
because ⁵not ¹in ⁷the   ⁸to abound ⁹to anyone ¹the ²life

αὐτοῦ ἐστιν ἐκ τῶν ὑπαρχόντων αὐτῷ.
²of him   ³is ¹⁰of the   things existing   to him.ᶜ
        =¹¹his ¹²possessions.

16 Εἶπεν δὲ παραβολὴν πρὸς αὐτοὺς λέγων·
And he told   a parable   to   them   saying :

ἀνθρώπου τινὸς πλουσίου εὐφόρησεν ἡ
²of a certain ⁵man   ⁴rich   ⁶bore well ¹The

χώρα. 17 καὶ διελογίζετο ἐν ἑαυτῷ λέγων·
²land.   And   he reasoned   in himself   saying :

τί ποιήσω, ὅτι οὐκ ἔχω ποῦ συνάξω τοὺς
What may I do, because I have not where I may gather the

καρπούς μου; 18 καὶ εἶπεν· τοῦτο ποιήσω·
fruits   of me?   And   he said :   This   will I do :

καθελῶ μου τὰς ἀποθήκας καὶ μείζονας
I will pull down of me the   barns   and   larger ones

οἰκοδομήσω, καὶ συνάξω ἐκεῖ πάντα τὸν
I will build,   and I will gather there   all   the

σῖτον καὶ τὰ ἀγαθά μου, 19 καὶ ἐρῶ τῇ
wheat and the goods of me,   and I will say to the

ψυχῇ μου· ψυχή, ἔχεις πολλὰ ἀγαθὰ
soul   of me :   Soul,   thou hast   many   goods

κείμενα εἰς ἔτη πολλά· ἀναπαύου, φάγε,
laid [up]   for   years   many;   take rest,   eat,

πίε, εὐφραίνου. 20 εἶπεν δὲ αὐτῷ ὁ
drink,   be glad.   But said   to him   —

θεός· ἄφρων, ταύτῃ τῇ νυκτὶ τὴν ψυχήν
God : Foolish man, in this   —   night   the   soul

σου ἀπαιτοῦσιν ἀπὸ σοῦ· ἃ δὲ
of thee   they demand   from   thee;   then [the] things which

ἡτοίμασας, τίνι ἔσται; 21 οὕτως ὁ
thou preparedst, to whom will they be?ᵉ   So the [one]
        =whose will they be?

θησαυρίζων αὐτῷ καὶ μὴ εἰς θεὸν πλουτῶν.
treasuring to himself and not toward God being rich.

22 Εἶπεν δὲ πρὸς τοὺς μαθητὰς [αὐτοῦ]·διὰ τοῦτο
And he said to the   disciples   of him : Therefore

λέγω ὑμῖν· μὴ μεριμνᾶτε τῇ ψυχῇ τί
I tell   you :   Do not be anxious for the life   what

φάγητε, μηδὲ τῷ σώματι [ὑμῶν] τί
ye may eat,   nor   for the body   of you   what

ἐνδύσησθε. 23 ἡ γὰρ ψυχὴ πλεῖόν ἐστιν
ye may put on.   For the life   more   is

τῆς τροφῆς καὶ τὸ σῶμα τοῦ ἐνδύματος.
[than] the food   and   the body [than] the   clothing.

24 κατανοήσατε τοὺς κόρακας, ὅτι οὔτε
Consider ye   the   ravens,   that   neither

σπείρουσιν οὔτε θερίζουσιν, οἷς οὐκ ἔστιν
they sow   nor   reap,   to which is notᶜ
        =which have not

ταμιεῖον οὐδὲ ἀποθήκη, καὶ ὁ θεὸς τρέφει
storehouse   nor   barn,   and   —   God   feeds

αὐτούς· πόσῳ μᾶλλον ὑμεῖς διαφέρετε τῶν
them; by how much rather   ye   differ   from the

πετεινῶν. 25 τίς δὲ ἐξ ὑμῶν μεριμνῶν
birds.   And who of   you   being anxious

δύναται ἐπὶ τὴν ἡλικίαν αὐτοῦ προσθεῖναι
can   on   the   stature   of him   to add

14Jesus replied, "Man, who appointed me a judge or an arbiter between you?" 15Then he said to them, "Watch out! Be on your guard against all kinds of greed; a man's life does not consist in the abundance of his possessions."

16And he told them this parable: "The ground of a certain rich man produced a good crop. 17He thought to himself, 'What shall I do? I have no place to store my crops.'

18"Then he said, 'This is what I'll do. I will tear down my barns and build bigger ones, and there I will store all my grain and my goods. 19And I'll say to myself, "You have plenty of good things laid up for many years. Take life easy; eat, drink and be merry." '

20"But God said to him, 'You fool! This very night your life will be demanded from you. Then who will get what you have prepared for yourself?'

21"This is how it will be with anyone who stores up things for himself but is not rich toward God."

Do Not Worry

22Then Jesus said to his disciples: "Therefore I tell you, do not worry about your life, what you will eat; or about your body, what you will wear. 23Life is more than food, and the body more than clothes. 24Consider the ravens: They do not sow or reap, they have no storeroom or barn; yet God feeds them. And how much more valuable are you than birds! 25Who of you by worrying can add a single hour to his

---

ᶻ Or add a cubit to your stature

26 If then you are not able to do so small a thing as that, why do you worry about the rest? 27 Consider the lilies, how they grow: they neither toil nor spin;ᵃ yet I tell you, even Solomon in all his glory was not clothed like one of these. 28 But if God so clothes the grass of the field, which is alive to-day and tomorrow is thrown into the oven, how much more will he clothe you—you of little faith! 29 And do not keep striving for what you are to eat and what you are to drink, and do not keep worrying. 30 For it is the nations of the world that strive after all these things, and your Father knows that you need them. 31 Instead, strive for hisᵇ kingdom, and these things will be given to you as well.

32 "Do not be afraid, little flock, for it is your Father's good pleasure to give you the kingdom. 33 Sell your possessions, and give alms. Make purses for yourselves that do not wear out, an unfailing treasure in heaven, where no thief comes near and no moth destroys. 34 For where your treasure is, there your heart will be also.

Watchful Slaves

35 "Be dressed for action and have your lamps lit; 36 be like those who are waiting for their master to return from the wedding banquet, so that they may open the door for him as soon as he comes and knocks. 37 Blessed are those slaves whom the master finds alert when he comes; truly I tell you, he will fasten his belt and have them sit down to eat, and he will come and serve them. 38 If he comes during

---

πῆχυν; 26 εἰ οὖν οὐδὲ ἐλάχιστον δύνασθε,
a cubit? If therefore not [the] least ye can,
τί περὶ τῶν λοιπῶν μεριμνᾶτε; 27 κατα-
why concerning the other things are ye anxious? Con-
νοήσατε τὰ κρίνα, πῶς οὔτε νήθει οὔτε
sider ye the lilies, how neither they spin nor
ὑφαίνει· λέγω δὲ ὑμῖν, οὐδὲ Σολομὼν ἐν
weave; but I tell you, not Solomon in
πάσῃ τῇ δόξῃ αὐτοῦ περιεβάλετο ὡς ἓν
all the glory of him was arrayed as one
τούτων. 28 εἰ δὲ ἐν ἀγρῷ τὸν χόρτον
of these. ¹And ²if ³in ¹⁰a field ⁴the ⁷grass
ὄντα σήμερον καὶ αὔριον εἰς κλίβανον
⁸being ¹¹to-day ¹²and ¹³tomorrow ¹⁵into ¹⁶an oven
βαλλόμενον ὁ θεὸς οὕτως ἀμφιάζει, πόσῳ
¹⁴being thrown - ³God ⁴so ⁵clothes, by how much
μᾶλλον ὑμᾶς, ὀλιγόπιστοι. 29 καὶ ὑμεῖς
rather you, little-faiths. And ye
μὴ ζητεῖτε τί φάγητε καὶ τί πίητε, καὶ
do not seek what ye may eat and what ye may drink, and
μὴ μετεωρίζεσθε· 30 ταῦτα γὰρ πάντα τὰ
do not be in suspense; for these things all the
ἔθνη τοῦ κόσμου ἐπιζητοῦσιν· ὑμῶν δὲ
nations of the world seek after; but of you
ὁ πατὴρ οἶδεν ὅτι χρῄζετε τούτων·
the Father knows that ye have need of them;
31 πλὴν ζητεῖτε τὴν βασιλείαν αὐτοῦ, καὶ
but seek ye the kingdom of him, and
ταῦτα προστεθήσεται ὑμῖν. 32 Μὴ φοβοῦ,
these things will be added to you. Fear not,
τὸ μικρὸν ποίμνιον· ὅτι εὐδόκησεν ὁ
- little flock; because was well pleased the
πατὴρ ὑμῶν δοῦναι ὑμῖν τὴν βασιλείαν.
Father of you to give you the kingdom.
33 Πωλήσατε τὰ ὑπάρχοντα ὑμῶν καὶ
Sell the possessions of you and
δότε ἐλεημοσύνην· ποιήσατε ἑαυτοῖς βαλ-
give alms; make for yourselves
λάντια μὴ παλαιούμενα, θησαυρὸν ἀνέκλειπτον
purses not becoming old, a treasure unfailing
ἐν τοῖς οὐρανοῖς, ὅπου κλέπτης οὐκ
in the heavens, where a thief not
ἐγγίζει οὐδὲ σὴς διαφθείρει· 34 ὅπου γάρ
comes near nor moth corrupts; for where
ἐστιν ὁ θησαυρὸς ὑμῶν, ἐκεῖ καὶ ἡ
is the treasure of you, there also the
καρδία ὑμῶν ἔσται. 35 Ἔστωσαν ὑμῶν αἱ
heart of you will be. Let be of you the
ὀσφύες περιεζωσμέναι καὶ οἱ λύχνοι
loins having been girded and the lamps
καιόμενοι· 36 καὶ ὑμεῖς ὅμοιοι ἀνθρώποις
burning; and ye like men
προσδεχομένοις τὸν κύριον ἑαυτῶν, πότε
awaiting the lord of themselves, when
ἀναλύσῃ ἐκ τῶν γάμων, ἵνα ἐλθόντος
he returns from the wedding festivities, that coming
καὶ κρούσαντος εὐθέως ἀνοίξωσιν αὐτῷ.
and knockingᵃ immediately they may open to him.
37 μακάριοι οἱ δοῦλοι ἐκεῖνοι, οὓς ἐλθὼν
Blessed - slaves those, whom coming
ὁ κύριος εὑρήσει γρηγοροῦντας· ἀμὴν λέγω
the lord will find watching; truly I tell
ὑμῖν ὅτι περιζώσεται καὶ ἀνακλινεῖ αὐτοὺς
you that he will gird himself and ¹make ³to recline ⁴them
καὶ παρελθὼν διακονήσει αὐτοῖς. 38 κἂν
and coming up to will serve them. And if

---

lifeᵉ? 26 Since you cannot do this very little thing, why do you worry about the rest? 27 "Consider how the lilies grow. They do not labor or spin. Yet I tell you, not even Solomon in all his splendor was dressed like one of these. 28 If that is how God clothes the grass of the field, which is here today, and tomorrow is thrown into the fire, how much more will he clothe you, O you of little faith! 29 And do not set your heart on what you will eat or drink; do not worry about it. 30 For the pagan world runs after all such things, and your Father knows that you need them. 31 But seek his kingdom, and these things will be given to you as well.

32 "Do not be afraid, little flock, for your Father has been pleased to give you the kingdom. 33 Sell your possessions and give to the poor. Provide purses for yourselves that will not wear out, a treasure in heaven that will not be exhausted, where no thief comes near and no moth destroys. 34 For where your treasure is, there your heart will be also.

Watchfulness

35 "Be dressed ready for service and keep your lamps burning, 36 like men waiting for their master to return from a wedding banquet, so that when he comes and knocks they can immediately open the door for him. 37 It will be good for those servants whose master finds them watching when he comes. I tell you the truth, he will dress himself to serve, will have them recline at the table and will come and wait on

---

ᵃ Other ancient authorities read *Consider the lilies; they neither spin nor weave*
ᵇ Other ancient authorities read *God's*

ᵉ25 Or *single cubit to his height*

the middle of the night, or near dawn, and finds them so, blessed are those slaves. 39 "But know this: if the owner of the house had known at what hour the thief was coming, he[c] would not have let his house be broken into. 40 You also must be ready, for the Son of Man is coming at an unexpected hour."

The Faithful or the Unfaithful Slave

41 Peter said, "Lord, are you telling this parable for us or for everyone?" 42 And the Lord said, "Who then is the faithful and prudent manager whom his master will put in charge of his slaves, to give them their allowance of food at the proper time? 43 Blessed is that slave whom his master will find at work when he arrives. 44 Truly I tell you, he will put that one in charge of all his possessions. 45 But if that slave says to himself, 'My master is delayed in coming,' and if he begins to beat the other slaves, men and women, and to eat and drink and get drunk, 46 the master of that slave will come on a day when he does not expect him and at an hour that he does not know, and will cut him in pieces,[d] and put him with the unfaithful. 47 That slave who knew what his master wanted, but did not prepare himself or do what was wanted, will receive a severe beating. 48 But the one who did not know and did what deserved a beating will receive a light beating. From everyone to whom much has been given, much will be required; and from the one to whom

ἐν τῇ δευτέρᾳ κἂν ἐν τῇ τρίτῃ φυλακῇ
in the second and if in the third watch
ἔλθῃ καὶ εὕρῃ οὕτως, μακάριοί εἰσιν
he comes and finds so, blessed are
ἐκεῖνοι. 39 τοῦτο δὲ γινώσκετε, ὅτι εἰ
those [slaves]. But this know ye, that if
ᾔδει ὁ οἰκοδεσπότης ποίᾳ ὥρᾳ ὁ κλέπτης
knew the house-master in what hour the thief
ἔρχεται, οὐκ ἂν ἀφῆκεν διορυχθῆναι τὸν
comes, he would not have allowed to be dug through the
οἶκον αὐτοῦ. 40 καὶ ὑμεῖς γίνεσθε ἕτοιμοι,
house of him. And ¹ye ¹be prepared,
ὅτι ᾗ ὥρᾳ οὐ δοκεῖτε ὁ υἱὸς τοῦ
because in what hour ye think not the Son –
ἀνθρώπου ἔρχεται. 41 Εἶπεν δὲ ὁ Πέτρος·
of man comes. And said – Peter :
κύριε, πρὸς ἡμᾶς τὴν παραβολὴν ταύτην
Lord, to us – parable this
λέγεις ἢ καὶ πρὸς πάντας; 42 καὶ εἶπεν
sayest thou or also to all? And said
ὁ κύριος· τίς ἄρα ἐστὶν ὁ πιστὸς
the Lord : Who then is the faithful
οἰκονόμος ὁ φρόνιμος, ὃν καταστήσει ὁ
steward the prudent, whom will appoint the
κύριος ἐπὶ τῆς θεραπείας αὐτοῦ τοῦ
lord over the household attendants of him –
διδόναι ἐν καιρῷ [τὸ] σιτομέτριον;
to give[d] in season the portion of food?
43 μακάριος ὁ δοῦλος ἐκεῖνος, ὃν ἐλθὼν
Blessed – slave that, whom coming
ὁ κύριος αὐτοῦ εὑρήσει ποιοῦντα οὕτως.
the lord of him will find doing so.
44 ἀληθῶς λέγω ὑμῖν ὅτι ἐπὶ πᾶσιν τοῖς
Truly I tell you that over all the
ὑπάρχουσιν αὐτοῦ καταστήσει αὐτόν. 45 ἐὰν
possessions of him he will appoint him. if
δὲ εἴπῃ ὁ δοῦλος ἐκεῖνος ἐν τῇ καρδίᾳ
But says – slave that in the heart
αὐτοῦ· χρονίζει ὁ κύριός μου ἔρχεσθαι,
of him : Delays the lord of me to come,
καὶ ἄρξηται τύπτειν τοὺς παῖδας καὶ τὰς
and begins to strike the menservants and the
παιδίσκας, ἐσθίειν τε καὶ πίνειν καὶ
maidservants, ¹to eat ¹both and to drink and
μεθύσκεσθαι, 46 ἥξει ὁ κύριος τοῦ δούλου
to become drunk, will come the lord – slave
ἐκείνου ἐν ἡμέρᾳ ᾗ οὐ προσδοκᾷ καὶ ἐν
of that in a day in which he does not expect and in
ὥρᾳ ᾗ οὐ γινώσκει, καὶ διχοτομήσει
an hour in which he knows not, and will cut asunder
αὐτόν, καὶ τὸ μέρος αὐτοῦ μετὰ τῶν
him, and the portion of him with the
ἀπίστων θήσει. 47 ἐκεῖνος δὲ ὁ δοῦλος
unbelievers will place. But that – slave
ὁ γνοὺς τὸ θέλημα τοῦ κυρίου αὐτοῦ
– having known the will of the lord of him
καὶ μὴ ἑτοιμάσας ἢ ποιήσας πρὸς τὸ θέλημα
and not having prepared or done according to the will
αὐτοῦ δαρήσεται πολλάς· 48 ὁ δὲ
of him will be beaten [with] many [stripes]; but the [one]
μὴ γνούς, ποιήσας δὲ ἄξια πληγῶν,
not having known, but having done things worthy of stripes,
δαρήσεται ὀλίγας. παντὶ δὲ ᾧ
will be beaten [with] few [stripes]. But to everyone to whom
ἐδόθη πολύ, πολὺ ζητηθήσεται παρ' αὐτοῦ, καὶ
was given much, much will be demanded from him, and

them. 38 It will be good for those servants whose master finds them ready, even if he comes in the second or third watch of the night. 39 But understand this: If the owner of the house had known at what hour the thief was coming, he would not have let his house be broken into. 40 You also must be ready, because the Son of Man will come at an hour when you do not expect him."
41 Peter asked, "Lord, are you telling this parable to us, or to everyone?"
42 The Lord answered, "Who then is the faithful and wise manager, whom the master puts in charge of his servants to give them their food allowance at the proper time? 43 It will be good for that servant whom the master finds doing so when he returns. 44 I tell you the truth, he will put him in charge of all his possessions. 45 But suppose the servant says to himself, 'My master is taking a long time in coming,' and he then begins to beat the menservants and maidservants and to eat and drink and get drunk. 46 The master of that servant will come on a day when he does not expect him and at an hour he is not aware of. He will cut him to pieces and assign him a place with the unbelievers.
47 "That servant who knows his master's will and does not get ready or does not do what his master wants will be beaten with many blows. 48 But the one who does not know and does things deserving punishment will be beaten with few blows. From everyone who has been given much, much will be demanded;

much has been entrusted, even more will be demanded.

Jesus the Cause of Division

49 "I came to bring fire to the earth, and how I wish it were already kindled! 50 I have a baptism with which to be baptized, and what stress I am under until it is completed! 51 Do you think that I have come to bring peace to the earth? No, I tell you, but rather division! 52 From now on five in one household will be divided, three against two and two against three; 53 they will be divided:

father against son
  and son against
    father,
mother against
  daughter
  and daughter against
    mother,
mother-in-law against
  her
    daughter-in-law
  and daughter-in-law
    against
    mother-in-law."

Interpreting the Time

54 He also said to the crowds, "When you see a cloud rising in the west, you immediately say, 'It is going to rain'; and so it happens. 55 And when you see the south wind blowing, you say, 'There will be scorching heat'; and it happens. 56 You hypocrites! You know how to interpret the appearance of earth and sky, but why do you not know how to interpret the present time?

Settling with Your Opponent

57 "And why do you not judge for yourselves what is right? 58 Thus, when you go with your accuser before a magistrate, on the way make an effort to settle the case, e or you may be dragged before the judge, and the judge hand you over to the officer, and the officer throw you in prison. 59 I tell you, you will never get out until you have paid the very last penny."

Chapter 13

Repent or Perish

AT that very time there were some present who told him about the Galileans whose blood Pilate

e Gk settle with him

ᾧ παρέθεντο πολύ, περισσότερον αἰτήσουσιν
with whom was deposited much, more exceedingly they will ask

αὐτόν. 49 Πῦρ ἦλθον βαλεῖν ἐπὶ τὴν γῆν,
him. Fire I came to cast on the earth,

καὶ τί θέλω εἰ ἤδη ἀνήφθη. 50 βάπτισμα
and what will I if already it was kindled. ³a baptism

δὲ ἔχω βαπτισθῆναι, καὶ πῶς συνέχομαι
¹And ²I have to be baptized [with], and how am I pressed

ἕως ὅτου τελεσθῇ. 51 δοκεῖτε ὅτι εἰρήνην
until it is accomplished. Think ye that peace

παρεγενόμην δοῦναι ἐν τῇ γῇ; οὐχί, λέγω
I came to give in the earth? No, I tell

ὑμῖν, ἀλλ' ἢ διαμερισμόν. 52 ἔσονται γὰρ
you, but rather division. For there will be

ἀπὸ τοῦ νῦν πέντε ἐν ἑνὶ οἴκῳ διαμεμε-
from - now five in one house having been

ρισμένοι, τρεῖς ἐπὶ δυσὶν καὶ δύο ἐπὶ
divided, three against two and two against

τρισὶν 53 διαμερισθήσονται, πατὴρ ἐπὶ υἱῷ
three will be divided, father against son

καὶ υἱὸς ἐπὶ πατρί, μήτηρ ἐπὶ θυγατέρα
and son against father, mother against daughter

καὶ θυγάτηρ ἐπὶ τὴν μητέρα, πενθερὰ
and daughter against the mother, mother-in-law

ἐπὶ τὴν νύμφην αὐτῆς καὶ νύμφη ἐπὶ
against the daughter-in-law of her and daughter-in-law against

τὴν πενθεράν. 54 Ἔλεγεν δὲ καὶ τοῖς
the mother-in-law. And he said also to the

ὄχλοις· ὅταν ἴδητε νεφέλην ἀνατέλλουσαν
crowds: When ye see a cloud rising

ἐπὶ δυσμῶν, εὐθέως λέγετε ὅτι ὄμβρος
over [the] west, immediately ye say that a storm

ἔρχεται, καὶ γίνεται οὕτως· 55 καὶ ὅταν
is coming, and it becomes so; and when

νότον πνέοντα, λέγετε ὅτι καύσων ἔσται,
a south wind blowing, ye say that heat there will be,

καὶ γίνεται. 56 ὑποκριταί, τὸ πρόσωπον
and it becomes. Hypocrites, the face

τῆς γῆς καὶ τοῦ οὐρανοῦ οἴδατε δοκιμάζειν,
of the earth and of the heaven ye know* to discern,

τὸν καιρὸν δὲ τοῦτον πῶς οὐ δοκιμάζετε;
- ³time ¹but ²this how do ye not discern?

57 Τί δὲ καὶ ἀφ' ἑαυτῶν οὐ κρίνετε
And why even from yourselves do ye not judge

τὸ δίκαιον; 58 ὡς γὰρ ὑπάγεις μετὰ τοῦ
the righteous thing? For as thou goest with the

ἀντιδίκου σου ἐπ' ἄρχοντα, ἐν τῇ ὁδῷ
adversary of thee to a ruler, in the way

δὸς ἐργασίαν ἀπηλλάχθαι ἀπ' αὐτοῦ, μήποτε
give(take) pains to be rid from(of) him, lest

κατασύρῃ σε πρὸς τὸν κριτήν, καὶ ὁ
he drag thee to the judge, and the

κριτής σε παραδώσει τῷ πράκτορι, καὶ ὁ
judge thee will deliver to the usher, and the

πράκτωρ σε βαλεῖ εἰς φυλακήν. 59 λέγω
usher thee will cast into prison. I tell

σοι, οὐ μὴ ἐξέλθῃς ἐκεῖθεν ἕως
thee, by no means mayest thou come out thence until

καὶ τὸ ἔσχατον λεπτὸν ἀποδῷς.
even the last lepton thou payest.

---

13 Παρῆσαν δέ τινες ἐν αὐτῷ τῷ
And there were present some at ²same ¹the

καιρῷ ἀπαγγέλλοντες αὐτῷ περὶ τῶν
time reporting to him about the

* can, as Mat. 16. 3.

---

and from the one who has been entrusted with much, much more will be asked.

Not Peace but Division

49 "I have come to bring fire on the earth, and how I wish it were already kindled! 50 But I have a baptism to undergo, and how distressed I am until it is completed! 51 Do you think I came to bring peace on earth? No, I tell you, but division. 52 From now on there will be five in one family divided against each other, three against two and two against three. 53 They will be divided, father against son and son against father, mother against daughter and daughter against mother, mother-in-law against daughter-in-law and daughter-in-law against mother-in-law."

Interpreting the Times

54 He said to the crowd: "When you see a cloud rising in the west, immediately you say, 'It's going to rain,' and it does. 55 And when the south wind blows, you say, 'It's going to be hot,' and it is. 56 Hypocrites! You know how to interpret the appearance of the earth and the sky. How is it that you don't know how to interpret this present time?

57 "Why don't you judge for yourselves what is right? 58 As you are going with your adversary to the magistrate, try hard to be reconciled to him on the way, or he may drag you off to the judge, and the judge turn you over to the officer, and the officer throw you into prison. 59 I tell you, you will not get out until you have paid the last penny.f"

Chapter 13

Repent or Perish

NOW there were some present at that time who told Jesus about the

f 59 Greek lepton

had mingled with their sacrifices. 2 He asked them, "Do you think that because these Galileans suffered in this way they were worse sinners than all other Galileans? 3 No, I tell you; but unless you repent, you will all perish as they did. 4 Or those eighteen who were killed when the tower of Siloam fell on them—do you think that they were worse offenders than all the others living in Jerusalem? 5 No, I tell you; but unless you repent, you will all perish just as they did."

The Parable of the Barren Fig Tree

6 Then he told this parable: "A man had a fig tree planted in his vineyard; and he came looking for fruit on it and found none. 7 So he said to the gardener, 'See here! For three years I have come looking for fruit on this fig tree, and still I find none. Cut it down! Why should it be wasting the soil?' 8 He replied, 'Sir, let it alone for one more year, until I dig around it and put manure on it. 9 If it bears fruit next year, well and good; but if not, you can cut it down.'"

Jesus Heals a Crippled Woman

10 Now he was teaching in one of the synagogues on the sabbath. 11 And just then there appeared a woman with a spirit that had crippled her for eighteen years. She was bent over and was quite unable to stand up straight. 12 When Jesus saw her, he called her over and said, "Woman, you are set free from your ailment." 13 When he laid his hands

Γαλιλαίων ὧν τὸ αἷμα Πιλᾶτος ἔμιξεν
Galilæans of whom the blood Pilate mixed
μετὰ τῶν θυσιῶν αὐτῶν. 2 καὶ ἀποκριθεὶς
with the sacrifices of them. And answering
εἶπεν αὐτοῖς· δοκεῖτε ὅτι οἱ Γαλιλαῖοι
he said to them : Think ye that - Galilæans
οὗτοι ἁμαρτωλοὶ παρὰ πάντας τοὺς Γαλι-
these sinners above all the Gali-
λαίους ἐγένοντο, ὅτι ταῦτα πεπόνθασιν;
læans were, because these things they have suffered?
3 οὐχί, λέγω ὑμῖν, ἀλλ᾽ ἐὰν μὴ μετανοῆτε,
No, I tell you, but unless ye repent,
πάντες ὁμοίως ἀπολεῖσθε. 4 ἢ ἐκεῖνοι οἱ
all likewise ye will perish. Or those -
δεκαοκτὼ ἐφ᾽ οὓς ἔπεσεν ὁ πύργος ἐν
eighteen on whom fell the tower in
τῷ Σιλωὰμ καὶ ἀπέκτεινεν αὐτούς, δοκεῖτε
- Siloam and killed them, think ye
ὅτι αὐτοὶ ὀφειλέται ἐγένοντο παρὰ πάντας
that they debtors were above all
τοὺς ἀνθρώπους τοὺς κατοικοῦντας Ἱερου-
the men - dwelling in Jeru-
σαλήμ; 5 οὐχί, λέγω ὑμῖν, ἀλλ᾽ ἐὰν μὴ
salem? No, I tell you, but unless
μετανοήσητε, πάντες ὡσαύτως ἀπολεῖσθε.
ye repent, all similarly ye will perish.
6 Ἔλεγεν δὲ ταύτην τὴν παραβολήν. συκῆν
And he told this - parable. ᵃA fig-tree
εἶχέν τις πεφυτευμένην ἐν τῷ ἀμπελῶνι
¹had ¹a certain man having been planted in the vineyard
αὐτοῦ, καὶ ἦλθεν ζητῶν καρπὸν ἐν αὐτῇ
of him, and came seeking fruit in it
καὶ οὐχ εὗρεν. 7 εἶπεν δὲ πρὸς τὸν
and found not. And he said to the
ἀμπελουργόν· ἰδοὺ τρία ἔτη ἀφ᾽ οὗ
vinedresser : Behold[,] three years [it is] since
ἔρχομαι ζητῶν καρπὸν ἐν τῇ συκῇ ταύτῃ
I come seeking fruit in - fig-tree this
καὶ οὐχ εὑρίσκω· ἔκκοψον αὐτήν· ἱνατί
and find not; cut down it: why
καὶ τὴν γῆν καταργεῖ; 8 ὁ δὲ ἀποκριθεὶς
even the ground it spoils? But he answering
λέγει αὐτῷ· κύριε, ἄφες αὐτὴν καὶ τοῦτο
says to him : Lord, leave it also this
τὸ ἔτος, ἕως ὅτου σκάψω περὶ αὐτὴν καὶ
- year, until I may dig round it and
βάλω κόπρια, 9 κἂν μὲν ποιήσῃ καρπὸν
may throw dung, and if indeed it makes fruit
εἰς τὸ μέλλον· εἰ δὲ μή γε, ἐκκόψεις
in the future; otherwise, thou shalt cut down
αὐτήν.
it.
10 Ἦν δὲ διδάσκων ἐν μιᾷ τῶν συναγωγῶν
And he was teaching in one of the synagogues
ἐν τοῖς σάββασιν. 11 καὶ ἰδοὺ γυνὴ
on the sabbaths. And[,] behold[,] a woman
πνεῦμα ἔχουσα ἀσθενείας ἔτη δεκαοκτώ,
²a spirit ¹having of infirmity years eighteen,
καὶ ἦν συγκύπτουσα καὶ μὴ δυναμένη
and was bending double and not being able
ἀνακύψαι εἰς τὸ παντελές. 12 ἰδὼν δὲ
to become erect entirely.† And seeing
αὐτὴν ὁ Ἰησοῦς προσεφώνησεν καὶ εἶπεν
her - Jesus called to [him] and said
αὐτῇ· γύναι, ἀπολέλυσαι τῆς ἀσθενείας
to her : Woman, thou hast been loosed from the infirmity

Galileans whose blood Pilate had mixed with their sacrifices. 2 Jesus answered, "Do you think that these Galileans were worse sinners than all the other Galileans because they suffered this way? 3 I tell you, no! But unless you repent, you too will all perish. 4 Or those eighteen who died when the tower in Siloam fell on them—do you think they were more guilty than all the others living in Jerusalem? 5 I tell you, no! But unless you repent, you too will all perish."

6 Then he told this parable: "A man had a fig tree, planted in his vineyard, and he went to look for fruit on it, but did not find any. 7 So he said to the man who took care of the vineyard, 'For three years now I've been coming to look for fruit on this fig tree and haven't found any. Cut it down! Why should it use up the soil?'

8 "'Sir,' the man replied, 'leave it alone for one more year, and I'll dig around it and fertilize it. 9 If it bears fruit next year, fine! If not, then cut it down.'"

A Crippled Woman Healed on the Sabbath

10 On a Sabbath Jesus was teaching in one of the synagogues, 11 and a woman was there who had been crippled by a spirit for eighteen years. She was bent over and could not straighten up at all. 12 When Jesus saw her, he called her forward and said to her, "Woman, you are set free from your

on her, immediately she stood up straight and began praising God. 14 But the leader of the synagogue, indignant because Jesus had cured on the sabbath, kept saying to the crowd, "There are six days on which work ought to be done; come on those days and be cured, and not on the sabbath day." 15 But the Lord answered him and said, "You hypocrites! Does not each of you on the sabbath untie his ox or his donkey from the manger, and lead it away to give it water? 16 And ought not this woman, a daughter of Abraham whom Satan bound for eighteen long years, be set free from this bondage on the sabbath day?" 17 When he said this, all his opponents were put to shame; and the entire crowd was rejoicing at all the wonderful things that he was doing.

The Parable of the Mustard Seed

18 He said therefore, "What is the kingdom of God like? And to what should I compare it? 19 It is like a mustard seed that someone took and sowed in the garden; it grew and became a tree, and the birds of the air made nests in its branches."

The Parable of the Yeast

20 And again he said, "To what should I compare the kingdom of God? 21 It is like yeast that a woman took and mixed in with/ three measures of flour until all of it was leavened."

The Narrow Door

22 Jesus g went through one town and village after another, teaching as he made his way to Jerusalem. 23 Someone asked him,

f Gk hid in
g Gk He

σου, 13 καὶ ἐπέθηκεν αὐτῇ τὰς χεῖρας·
of thee, and he put on her the(his) hands;

καὶ παραχρῆμα ἀνωρθώθη, καὶ ἐδόξαζεν
and at once she was straightened, and glorified

τὸν θεόν. 14 ἀποκριθεὶς δὲ ὁ ἀρχι-
God. But answering the syn-

συνάγωγος, ἀγανακτῶν ὅτι τῷ σαββάτῳ
agogue ruler, being angry that *on the* *sabbath*

ἐθεράπευσεν ὁ Ἰησοῦς, ἔλεγεν τῷ ὄχλῳ
¹healed - ¹Jesus, said to the crowd[,]

ὅτι ἐξ ἡμέραι εἰσὶν ἐν αἷς δεῖ ἐργάζεσθαι·
- six days there are on which it behoves to work;

ἐν αὐταῖς οὖν ἐρχόμενοι θεραπεύεσθε καὶ
on them therefore coming be ye healed and

μὴ τῇ ἡμέρᾳ τοῦ σαββάτου. 15 ἀπεκρίθη δὲ
not on the day of the sabbath. But answered

αὐτῷ ὁ κύριος καὶ εἶπεν· ὑποκριταί,
him the Lord and said: Hypocrites,

ἕκαστος ὑμῶν τῷ σαββάτῳ οὐ λύει τὸν
each one of you on the sabbath does he not loosen the

βοῦν αὐτοῦ ἢ τὸν ὄνον ἀπὸ τῆς φάτνης
ox of him or the ass from the manger

καὶ ἀπαγαγὼν ποτίζει; 16 ταύτην δὲ
and leading [it] away give drink? And this woman

θυγατέρα Ἀβραὰμ οὖσαν, ἣν ἔδησεν ὁ
a daughter of Abraham being, whom bound -

σατανᾶς ἰδοὺ δέκα καὶ ὀκτὼ ἔτη, οὐκ ἔδει
Satan behold ten and eight years, behoved it not

λυθῆναι ἀπὸ τοῦ δεσμοῦ τούτου τῇ
to be loosened from - bond this on the

ἡμέρᾳ τοῦ σαββάτου; 17 καὶ ταῦτα λέγοντος
day of the sabbath? And these things saying
=when he said these things

αὐτοῦ κατῃσχύνοντο πάντες οἱ ἀντικείμενοι
him* were put to shame all the [ones] opposing

αὐτῷ, καὶ πᾶς ὁ ὄχλος ἔχαιρεν ἐπὶ
him, and all the crowd rejoiced over

πᾶσιν τοῖς ἐνδόξοις τοῖς γινομένοις ὑπ᾽
all the glorious things happening by

αὐτοῦ. 18 Ἔλεγεν οὖν· τίνι ὁμοία ἐστὶν ἡ
him. He said therefore: To what like is the

βασιλεία τοῦ θεοῦ, καὶ τίνι ὁμοιώσω
kingdom - of God, and to what may I liken

αὐτήν; 19 ὁμοία ἐστὶν κόκκῳ σινάπεως, ὃν
it? Like it is to a grain of mustard, which

λαβὼν ἄνθρωπος ἔβαλεν εἰς κῆπον ἑαυτοῦ,
²taking ¹a man cast into a garden of himself,

καὶ ηὔξησεν καὶ ἐγένετο εἰς δένδρον, καὶ
and it grew and became into a tree, and

τὰ πετεινὰ τοῦ οὐρανοῦ κατεσκήνωσεν
the birds of the heaven(air) lodged

ἐν τοῖς κλάδοις αὐτοῦ. 20 Καὶ πάλιν
in the branches of it. And again

εἶπεν· τίνι ὁμοιώσω τὴν βασιλείαν τοῦ
he said: To what may I liken the kingdom -

θεοῦ; 21 ὁμοία ἐστὶν ζύμῃ, ἣν λαβοῦσα
of God? Like it is to leaven, which ²taking

γυνὴ ἔκρυψεν εἰς ἀλεύρου σάτα τρία,
¹a woman hid in of meal measures three,

ἕως οὗ ἐζυμώθη ὅλον.
until was leavened all.

22 Καὶ διεπορεύετο κατὰ πόλεις καὶ
And he journeyed *through* throughout cities and

κώμας διδάσκων καὶ πορείαν ποιούμενος
villages teaching and journey making

εἰς Ἱεροσόλυμα. 23 Εἶπεν δέ τις αὐτῷ·
to Jerusalem. And said someone to him :

infirmity." 13 Then he put his hands on her, and immediately she straightened up and praised God.

14 Indignant because Jesus had healed on the Sabbath, the synagogue ruler said to the people, "There are six days for work. So come and be healed on those days, not on the Sabbath."

15 The Lord answered him, "You hypocrites! Doesn't each of you on the Sabbath untie his ox or donkey from the stall and lead it out to give it water? 16 Then should not this woman, a daughter of Abraham, whom Satan has kept bound for eighteen long years, be set free on the Sabbath day from what bound her?"

17 When he said this, all his opponents were humiliated, but the people were delighted with all the wonderful things he was doing.

The Parables of the Mustard Seed and the Yeast

18 Then Jesus asked, "What is the kingdom of God like? What shall I compare it to? 19 It is like a mustard seed, which a man took and planted in his garden. It grew and became a tree, and the birds of the air perched in its branches."

20 Again he asked, "What shall I compare the kingdom of God to? 21 It is like yeast that a woman took and mixed into a large amount g of flour until it worked all through the dough."

The Narrow Door

22 Then Jesus went through the towns and villages, teaching as he made his way to Jerusalem. 23 Someone asked him,

g 21 Greek *three satas* (probably about 1/2 bushel or 22 liters)

"Lord, will only a few be saved?" He said to them, 24 "Strive to enter through the narrow door; for many, I tell you, will try to enter and will not be able. 25 When once the owner of the house has got up and shut the door, and you begin to stand outside and to knock at the door, saying, 'Lord, open to us,' then in reply he will say to you, 'I do not know where you come from.' 26 Then you will begin to say, 'We ate and drank with you, and you taught in our streets.' 27 But he will say, 'I do not know where you come from; go away from me, all you evildoers!' 28 There will be weeping and gnashing of teeth when you see Abraham and Isaac and Jacob and all the prophets in the kingdom of God, and you yourselves thrown out. 29 Then people will come from east and west, from north and south, and will eat in the kingdom of God. 30 Indeed, some are last who will be first, and some are first who will be last."

The Lament over Jerusalem

31 At that very hour some Pharisees came and said to him, "Get away from here, for Herod wants to kill you." 32 He said to them, "Go and tell that fox for me,[h] 'Listen, I am casting out demons and performing cures today and tomorrow, and on the third day I finish my work. 33 Yet today, tomorrow, and the next day I must be on my way, because it is impossible for a prophet to be killed outside of Jerusalem.' 34 Jerusalem, Jerusalem, the city that kills the

κύριε, εἰ ὀλίγοι οἱ σωζόμενοι; ὁ δὲ εἶπεν
Lord, if few the [ones] being saved? And he said
πρὸς αὐτούς· 24 ἀγωνίζεσθε εἰσελθεῖν διὰ
to them: Struggle to enter through
τῆς στενῆς θύρας, ὅτι πολλοί, λέγω ὑμῖν,
the strait door, because many, I tell you,
ζητήσουσιν εἰσελθεῖν καὶ οὐκ ἰσχύσουσιν.
will seek to enter and will not be able.
25 ἀφ' οὗ ἂν ἐγερθῇ ὁ οἰκοδεσπότης καὶ
From [the time] when is risen the house-master and
ἀποκλείσῃ τὴν θύραν, καὶ ἄρξησθε ἔξω
he shuts the door, and ye begin outside
ἑστάναι καὶ κρούειν τὴν θύραν λέγοντες·
to stand and to knock the door saying:
κύριε, ἄνοιξον ἡμῖν, καὶ ἀποκριθεὶς ἐρεῖ
Lord, open to us, and answering he will say
ὑμῖν· οὐκ οἶδα ὑμᾶς πόθεν ἐστέ. 26 τότε
to you: I know not you whence ye are. Then
ἄρξεσθε λέγειν· ἐφάγομεν ἐνώπιόν σου καὶ
ye will begin to say: We ate before thee and
ἐπίομεν, καὶ ἐν ταῖς πλατείαις ἡμῶν
drank, and in the streets of us
ἐδίδαξας· 27 καὶ ἐρεῖ λέγων ὑμῖν· οὐκ
thou didst teach; and he will say telling you: not
οἶδα πόθεν ἐστέ· ἀπόστητε ἀπ' ἐμοῦ
I know whence ye are; stand away from me
πάντες ἐργάται ἀδικίας. 28 ἐκεῖ ἔσται ὁ
all workers of unrighteousness. There will be the
κλαυθμὸς καὶ ὁ βρυγμὸς τῶν ὀδόντων,
weeping and the gnashing of the teeth,
ὅταν ὄψησθε Ἀβραὰμ καὶ Ἰσαὰκ καὶ
when ye see Abraham and Isaac and
Ἰακὼβ καὶ πάντας τοὺς προφήτας ἐν τῇ
Jacob and all the prophets in the
βασιλείᾳ τοῦ θεοῦ, ὑμᾶς δὲ ἐκβαλλομένους
kingdom of God, but you being thrust out
ἔξω. 29 καὶ ἥξουσιν ἀπὸ ἀνατολῶν καὶ
outside. And they will come from east and
δυσμῶν καὶ ἀπὸ βορρᾶ καὶ νότου, καὶ
west and from north and south, and
ἀνακλιθήσονται ἐν τῇ βασιλείᾳ τοῦ θεοῦ.
will recline in the kingdom of God.
30 καὶ ἰδοὺ εἰσὶν ἔσχατοι οἳ ἔσονται
And behold there are last [ones] who will be
πρῶτοι, καὶ εἰσὶν πρῶτοι οἳ ἔσονται
first, and there are first [ones] who will be
ἔσχατοι. 31 Ἐν αὐτῇ τῇ ὥρᾳ προσῆλθάν
last. In ²same ¹the hour approached
τινες Φαρισαῖοι λέγοντες αὐτῷ· ἔξελθε καὶ
some Pharisees saying to him: Depart and
πορεύου ἐντεῦθεν, ὅτι Ἡρῴδης θέλει σε
go hence, because Herod wishes thee
ἀποκτεῖναι. 32 καὶ εἶπεν αὐτοῖς· πορευθέντες
to kill. And he said to them: Going
εἴπατε τῇ ἀλώπεκι ταύτῃ· ἰδοὺ ἐκβάλλω
tell - fox this: Behold I expel
δαιμόνια καὶ ἰάσεις ἀποτελῶ σήμερον καὶ
demons and ²cures ¹accomplish to-day and
αὔριον, καὶ τῇ τρίτῃ τελειοῦμαι. 33 πλὴν
to-morrow, and on the third [day] I am perfected. Nevertheless
δεῖ με σήμερον καὶ αὔριον καὶ τῇ ἐχομένῃ
it be- me to-day and to- and on the following
hoves   morrow   [day]
πορεύεσθαι, ὅτι οὐκ ἐνδέχεται προφήτην
to journey, because it is not possible a prophet
ἀπολέσθαι ἔξω Ἰερουσαλήμ. 34 Ἰερουσαλὴμ
to perish outside Jerusalem. Jerusalem[,]

"Lord, are only a few people going to be saved?" He said to them, 24 "Make every effort to enter through the narrow door, because many, I tell you, will try to enter and will not be able to. 25 Once the owner of the house gets up and closes the door, you will stand outside knocking and pleading, 'Sir, open the door for us.'
"But he will answer, 'I don't know you or where you come from.'
26 "Then you will say, 'We ate and drank with you, and you taught in our streets.'
27 "But he will reply, 'I don't know you or where you come from. Away from me, all you evildoers!'
28 "There will be weeping there, and gnashing of teeth, when you see Abraham, Isaac and Jacob and all the prophets in the kingdom of God, but you yourselves thrown out. 29 People will come from east and west and north and south, and will take their places at the feast in the kingdom of God. 30 Indeed there are those who are last who will be first, and first who will be last."

Jesus' Sorrow for Jerusalem

31 At that time some Pharisees came to Jesus and said to him, "Leave this place and go somewhere else. Herod wants to kill you."
32 He replied, "Go tell that fox, 'I will drive out demons and heal people today and tomorrow, and on the third day I will reach my goal.' 33 In any case, I must keep going today and tomorrow and the next day—for surely no prophet can die outside Jerusalem!
34 "O Jerusalem, Jerusa-

---

[h] Gk lacks for me

prophets and stones those who are sent to it! How often have I desired to gather your children together as a hen gathers her brood under her wings, and you were not willing! 35 See, your house is left to you. And I tell you, you will not see me until the time comes when *i* you say, 'Blessed is the one who comes in the name of the Lord.' "

'Ιερουσαλήμ, ἡ ἀποκτείνουσα τοὺς προφήτας
Jerusalem, the [one] killing the prophets

καὶ λιθοβολοῦσα τοὺς ἀπεσταλμένους πρὸς
and stoning the [ones] *having been* sent to

αὐτήν, ποσάκις ἠθέλησα ἐπισυνάξαι τὰ
her, how often I wished to gather the

τέκνα σου ὃν τρόπον ὄρνις τὴν ἑαυτῆς
children of thee as † a bird the of herself

νοσσιὰν ὑπὸ τὰς πτέρυγας, καὶ οὐκ
brood under the(her) wings, and not

ἠθελήσατε. 35 ἰδοὺ ἀφίεται ὑμῖν ὁ οἶκος
ye wished. Behold is left to you the house

ὑμῶν. λέγω [δὲ] ὑμῖν, οὐ μὴ ἴδητέ με
of you. And I tell you, by no means ye may see me

ἕως ἥξει ὅτε εἴπητε· εὐλογημένος ὁ
until shall come [the time] when ye say : Blessed the

ἐρχόμενος ἐν ὀνόματι κυρίου.
[one] coming in [the] name of [the] Lord.

---

lem, you who kill the prophets and stone those sent to you, how often I have longed to gather your children together, as a hen gathers her chicks under her wings, but you were not willing! 35 Look, your house is left to you desolate. I tell you, you will not see me again until you say, 'Blessed is he who comes in the name of the Lord.' *h* "

Chapter 14

Jesus Heals the Man with Dropsy

ON one occasion when Jesus *j* was going to the house of a leader of the Pharisees to eat a meal on the sabbath, they were watching him closely. 2 Just then, in front of him, there was a man who had dropsy. 3 And Jesus asked the lawyers and Pharisees, "Is it lawful to cure people on the sabbath, or not?" 4 But they were silent. So Jesus *j* took him and healed him, and sent him away. 5 Then he said to them, "If one of you has a child *k* or an ox that has fallen into a well, will you not immediately pull it out on a sabbath day?" 6 And they could not reply to this.

Humility and Hospitality

7 When he noticed how the guests chose the places of honor, he told them a parable. 8 "When you are invited by someone to a wedding banquet, do not sit down at the place of honor, in case someone more distinguished than you has been invited by your host; 9 and the host who invited both of you may come and say to you, 'Give this person your place,' and then in disgrace you would start to take the lowest place.

---

14 Καὶ ἐγένετο ἐν τῷ ἐλθεῖν αὐτὸν εἰς
And it came to pass in the to go him^be into
=as he went,

οἶκόν τινος τῶν ἀρχόντων τῶν Φαρισαίων
a house of one of the leaders of the Pharisees

σαββάτῳ φαγεῖν ἄρτον, καὶ αὐτοὶ ἦσαν
on a sabbath to eat bread, *and* they were

παρατηρούμενοι αὐτόν. 2 καὶ ἰδοὺ ἄνθρωπός
carefully watching him. And[,] behold[,] man

τις ἦν ὑδρωπικὸς ἔμπροσθεν αὐτοῦ. 3 καὶ
a certain was dropsical before him. And

ἀποκριθεὶς ὁ Ἰησοῦς εἶπεν πρὸς τοὺς
answering – Jesus spoke to the

νομικοὺς καὶ Φαρισαίους λέγων· ἔξεστιν
lawyers and Pharisees saying : Is it lawful

τῷ σαββάτῳ θεραπεῦσαι ἢ οὔ; 4 οἱ δὲ
on the sabbath to heal or not? And they

ἡσύχασαν. καὶ ἐπιλαβόμενος ἰάσατο αὐτὸν
were silent. And taking he cured him

καὶ ἀπέλυσεν. 5 καὶ πρὸς αὐτοὺς εἶπεν·
and dismissed. And to them he said:

τίνος ὑμῶν υἱὸς ἢ βοῦς εἰς φρέαρ πεσεῖται,
Of whom of you a son or an ox into a pit shall fall,

καὶ οὐκ εὐθέως ἀνασπάσει αὐτὸν ἐν
and not immediately he will pull up it on

ἡμέρᾳ τοῦ σαββάτου; 6 καὶ οὐκ ἴσχυσαν
a day of the sabbath? And they were not able

ἀνταποκριθῆναι πρὸς ταῦτα. 7 Ἔλεγεν δὲ
to reply against these things. And he said

πρὸς τοὺς κεκλημένους παραβολήν, ἐπέχων
to the [ones] *having been* invited a parable, noting

πῶς τὰς πρωτοκλισίας ἐξελέγοντο, λέγων
how ³the ²chief seats ¹they were choosing, saying

πρὸς αὐτούς· 8 ὅταν κληθῇς ὑπό τινος εἰς
to them : When thou art invited by anyone to

γάμους, μὴ κατακλιθῇς εἰς τὴν πρωτοκλισίαν,
wedding festivities, do not recline in the chief seat,

μήποτε ἐντιμότερός σου ᾖ κεκλημένος ὑπ'
lest a more honour- thou be *having been* invited by
able [than]

αὐτοῦ, 9 καὶ ἐλθὼν ὁ σὲ καὶ αὐτὸν καλέσας
him, and coming ¹the [one] ³thee ⁴and ⁵him ²inviting

ἐρεῖ σοι· δός τούτῳ τόπον, καὶ τότε
will say to thee : Give this man place, and then

ἄρξῃ μετὰ αἰσχύνης τὸν ἔσχατον τόπον
thou wilt begin with shame the last place

Chapter 14

Jesus at a Pharisee's House

ONE Sabbath, when Jesus went to eat in the house of a prominent Pharisee, he was being carefully watched. 2 There in front of him was a man suffering from dropsy. 3 Jesus asked the Pharisees and experts in the law, "Is it lawful to heal on the Sabbath or not?" 4 But they remained silent. So taking hold of the man, he healed him and sent him away.

5 Then he asked them, "If one of you has a son *i* or an ox that falls into a well on the Sabbath day, will you not immediately pull him out?" 6 And they had nothing to say.

7 When he noticed how the guests picked the places of honor at the table, he told them this parable: 8 "When someone invites you to a wedding feast, do not take the place of honor, for a person more distinguished than you may have been invited. 9 If so, the host who invited both of you will come and say to you, 'Give this man your seat.' Then, humiliated, you will have to take the least important place. 10 But

---

i Other ancient authorities lack *the time comes when*
j Gk *he*
k Other ancient authorities read *a donkey*

h 35 Psalm 118:26
i 5 Some manuscripts *donkey*

10 But when you are invited, go and sit down at the lowest place, so that when your host comes, he may say to you, 'Friend, move up higher'; then you will be honored in the presence of all who sit at the table with you. 11 For all who exalt themselves will be humbled, and those who humble themselves will be exalted."

12 He said also to the one who had invited him, "When you give a luncheon or a dinner, do not invite your friends or your brothers or your relatives or rich neighbors, in case they may invite you in return, and you would be repaid. 13 But when you give a banquet, invite the poor, the crippled, the lame, and the blind. 14 And you will be blessed, because they cannot repay you, for you will be repaid at the resurrection of the righteous."

The Parable of the Great Dinner

15 One of the dinner guests, on hearing this, said to him, "Blessed is the one who will eat bread in the kingdom of God!" 16 Then Jesus[j] said to him, "Someone gave a great dinner and invited many. 17 At the time for the dinner he sent his slave to say to those who had been invited, 'Come; for everything is ready now.' 18 But they all alike began to make excuses. The first said to him, 'I have bought a piece of land, and I must go out and see it; please accept my regrets.' 19 Another said, 'I have bought five yoke of oxen, and I am going to try them out; please accept my regrets.' 20 Another said, 'I have just been married, and

κατέχειν. 10 ἀλλ' ὅταν κληθῆς, πορευθεὶς
to take.   But   when thou art invited,   going
ἀνάπεσε εἰς τὸν ἔσχατον τόπον, ἵνα ὅταν ἔλθῃ
recline   in the   last   place,   that when ⁴comes
ὁ   κεκληκώς σε ἐρεῖ σοι· φίλε,
¹the [one] ²having invited ³thee he will say to thee : Friend,
προσανάβηθι ἀνώτερον· τότε ἔσται σοι δόξα
  go up   higher;   then there will be to thee⁰ glory
ἐνώπιον πάντων τῶν συνανακειμένων σοι.
before   all the [ones] reclining with   thee.
11 ὅτι πᾶς ὁ ὑψῶν ἑαυτὸν ταπεινωθήσεται,
Because everyone exalting himself   will be humbled,
καὶ ὁ ταπεινῶν ἑαυτὸν ὑψωθήσεται.
and the [one] humbling   himself   will be exalted.
12 Ἔλεγεν δὲ καὶ τῷ κεκληκότι αὐτόν·
And he said also to the [one] having invited   him :
ὅταν ποιῇς ἄριστον ἢ δεῖπνον, μὴ φώνει
When thou makest a dinner or a supper,   do not call
τοὺς φίλους σου μηδὲ τοὺς ἀδελφούς
the   friends of thee nor the   brothers
σου μηδὲ τοὺς συγγενεῖς σου μηδὲ
of thee nor the   relatives of thee nor
γείτονας πλουσίους, μήποτε καὶ αὐτοὶ
neighbours   rich,   lest   also   they
ἀντικαλέσωσίν σε καὶ γένηται ἀνταπόδομά
¹invite ²in ⁴return ³thee and   it becomes   a recompence
σοι. 13 ἀλλ' ὅταν δοχὴν ποιῇς, κάλει
to thee.   But   when a party thou makest, invite
πτωχούς, ἀναπήρους, χωλούς, τυφλούς·
poor [persons],   maimed,   lame,   blind;
14 καὶ μακάριος ἔσῃ, ὅτι οὐκ ἔχουσιν
and   blessed   thou shalt be, because they have not
ἀνταποδοῦναί σοι· ἀνταποδοθήσεται γάρ σοι
to recompense thee;   for it will be recompensed to thee
ἐν τῇ ἀναστάσει τῶν δικαίων. 15 Ἀκούσας
in the resurrection of the just.   ²hearing
δέ τις τῶν συνανακειμένων ταῦτα εἶπεν
¹And ⁴one ⁵of the [ones] ⁶reclining with ³these things said
αὐτῷ· μακάριος ὅστις φάγεται ἄρτον ἐν
to him : Blessed [is he] who   shall eat bread   in
τῇ βασιλείᾳ τοῦ θεοῦ. 16 ὁ δὲ εἶπεν
the   kingdom   -   of God.   And he   said
αὐτῷ· ἄνθρωπός τις ἐποίει δεῖπνον μέγα,
to him :   A certain man   made   supper   a great,
καὶ ἐκάλεσεν πολλούς, 17 καὶ ἀπέστειλεν
and   invited   many,   and   sent
τὸν δοῦλον αὐτοῦ τῇ ὥρᾳ τοῦ δείπνου
the   slave   of him at the hour of the   supper
εἰπεῖν τοῖς κεκλημένοις· ἔρχεσθε, ὅτι ἤδη
to say to the [ones] having been invited : Come, because ¹now
ἕτοιμά ἐστιν. 18 καὶ ἤρξαντο ἀπὸ μιᾶς
²prepared ¹it is.   And they began from one [mind]
πάντες παραιτεῖσθαι. ὁ πρῶτος εἶπεν
all   to beg off.   The   first   said
αὐτῷ· ἀγρὸν ἠγόρασα, καὶ ἔχω ἀνάγκην
to him : ²A farm ¹I bought,   and   I am obliged†
ἐξελθὼν ἰδεῖν αὐτόν· ἐρωτῶ σε, ἔχε με
going out to see   it·   I ask   thee, have   me
παρῃτημένον. 19 καὶ ἕτερος εἶπεν· ζεύγη
begged off.   And another   said : ²Yoke
βοῶν ἠγόρασα πέντε, καὶ πορεύομαι
⁴of oxen ¹I bought ³five,   and   I am going
δοκιμάσαι αὐτά· ἐρωτῶ σε, ἔχε με
to prove   them;   I ask   thee, have   me
παρῃτημένον. 20 καὶ ἕτερος εἶπεν· γυναῖκα
begged off.   And another   said : ¹A wife

when you are invited, take the lowest place, so that when your host comes, he will say to you, 'Friend, move up to a better place.' Then you will be honored in the presence of all your fellow guests. 11 For everyone who exalts himself will be humbled, and he who humbles himself will be exalted."

12 Then Jesus said to his host, "When you give a luncheon or dinner, do not invite your friends, your brothers or relatives, or your rich neighbors; if you do, they may invite you back and so you will be repaid. 13 But when you give a banquet, invite the poor, the crippled, the lame, the blind, 14 and you will be blessed. Although they cannot repay you, you will be repaid at the resurrection of the righteous."

The Parable of the Great Banquet

15 When one of those at the table with him heard this, he said to Jesus, "Blessed is the man who will eat at the feast in the kingdom of God."

16 Jesus replied: "A certain man was preparing a great banquet and invited many guests. 17 At the time of the banquet he sent his servant to tell those who had been invited, 'Come, for everything is now ready.'

18 "But they all alike began to make excuses. The first said, 'I have just bought a field, and I must go and see it. Please excuse me.'

19 "Another said, 'I have just bought five yoke of oxen, and I'm on my way to try them out. Please excuse me.'

20 "Still another said, 'I

therefore I cannot come.' 21 So the slave returned and reported this to his master. Then the owner of the house became angry and said to his slave, 'Go out at once into the streets and lanes of the town and bring in the poor, the crippled, the blind, and the lame.' 22 And the slave said, 'Sir, what you ordered has been done, and there is still room.' 23 Then the master said to the slave, 'Go out into the roads and lanes, and compel people to come in, so that my house may be filled. 24 For I tell you,[/] none of those who were invited will taste my dinner.' "

The Cost of Discipleship

25 Now large crowds were traveling with him; and he turned and said to them, 26 "Whoever comes to me and does not hate father and mother, wife and children, brothers and sisters, yes, and even life itself, cannot be my disciple. 27 Whoever does not carry the cross and follow me cannot be my disciple. 28 For which of you, intending to build a tower, does not first sit down and estimate the cost, to see whether he has enough to complete it? 29 Otherwise, when he has laid a foundation and is not able to finish, all who see it will begin to ridicule him, 30 saying, 'This fellow began to build and was not able to finish.' 31 Or what king, going out to wage war against anoth-

---

ἔγημα, καὶ διὰ τοῦτο οὐ δύναμαι ἐλθεῖν.
¹I married, and therefore I cannot *to* come.

21 καὶ παραγενόμενος ὁ δοῦλος ἀπήγγειλεν
And coming up the slave reported

τῷ κυρίῳ αὐτοῦ ταῦτα. τότε ὀργισθεὶς ὁ
to the lord of him these things. Then being angry the

οἰκοδεσπότης εἶπεν τῷ δούλῳ αὐτοῦ· ἔξελθε
house-master told the slave of him : Go out

ταχέως εἰς τὰς πλατείας καὶ ῥύμας τῆς
quickly into the streets and lanes of the

πόλεως, καὶ τοὺς πτωχοὺς καὶ ἀναπήρους
city, and the poor and maimed

καὶ τυφλοὺς καὶ χωλοὺς εἰσάγαγε ὧδε.
and blind and lame bring in here.

22 καὶ εἶπεν ὁ δοῦλος· κύριε, γέγονεν ὃ
And said the slave : Lord, has happened what

ἐπέταξας, καὶ ἔτι τόπος ἐστίν. 23 καὶ
thou didst command, and yet room there is. And

εἶπεν ὁ κύριος πρὸς τὸν δοῦλον· ἔξελθε εἰς
said the lord to the slave : Go out into

τὰς ὁδοὺς καὶ φραγμοὺς καὶ ἀνάγκασον
the ways and hedges and compel

εἰσελθεῖν, ἵνα γεμισθῇ μου ὁ οἶκος·
to come in, that may be filled of me the house ;

24 λέγω γὰρ ὑμῖν ὅτι οὐδεὶς τῶν ἀνδρῶν
for I tell you that not one of the men

ἐκείνων τῶν κεκλημένων γεύσεταί μου
of those - having been invited shall taste of me

τοῦ δείπνου.
the supper.

25 Συνεπορεύοντο δὲ αὐτῷ ὄχλοι πολλοί,
And came together to him crowds many,

καὶ στραφεὶς εἶπεν πρὸς αὐτούς· 26 εἴ τις
and turning he said to them : If anyone

ἔρχεται πρός με καὶ οὐ μισεῖ τὸν πατέρα
comes to me and hates not the father

αὐτοῦ καὶ τὴν μητέρα καὶ τὴν γυναῖκα
of him and the mother and the wife

καὶ τὰ τέκνα καὶ τοὺς ἀδελφοὺς καὶ τὰς
and the children and the brothers and the

ἀδελφάς, ἔτι τε καὶ τὴν ψυχὴν ἑαυτοῦ,
sisters, and besides also the life of himself,

οὐ δύναται εἶναί μου μαθητής. 27 ὅστις
he cannot *to* be of me a disciple. Who

οὐ βαστάζει τὸν σταυρὸν ἑαυτοῦ καὶ
bears not the cross of himself and

ἔρχεται ὀπίσω μου, οὐ δύναται εἶναί μου
comes after me, he cannot *to* be of me

μαθητής. 28 Τίς γὰρ ἐξ ὑμῶν θέλων
a disciple. For who of you wishing

πύργον οἰκοδομῆσαι οὐχὶ πρῶτον καθίσας
a tower to build not first sitting

ψηφίζει τὴν δαπάνην, εἰ ἔχει εἰς ἀπαρ-
counts the cost, if he has for com-

τισμόν; 29 ἵνα μή ποτε θέντος αὐτοῦ
pletion? Lest when laying him*
=he has laid

θεμέλιον καὶ μὴ ἰσχύοντος ἐκτελέσαι πάντες
a foundation and not being able* to finish all

οἱ θεωροῦντες ἄρξωνται αὐτῷ ἐμπαίζειν
the [ones] seeing begin him to mock

30 λέγοντες ὅτι οὗτος ὁ ἄνθρωπος ἤρξατο
saying[,] - This - man began

οἰκοδομεῖν καὶ οὐκ ἴσχυσεν ἐκτελέσαι.
to build and was not able to finish.

31 Ἢ τίς βασιλεὺς πορευόμενος ἑτέρῳ βασιλεῖ
Or what king ¹going ²another ⁴king

---

just got married, so I can't come.' 21 "The servant came back and reported this to his master. Then the owner of the house became angry and ordered his servant, 'Go out quickly into the streets and alleys of the town and bring in the poor, the crippled, the blind and the lame.' 22 " 'Sir,' the servant said, 'what you ordered has been done, but there is still room.' 23 "Then the master told his servant, 'Go out to the roads and country lanes and make them come in, so that my house will be full. 24 I tell you, not one of those men who were invited will get a taste of my banquet.' "

The Cost of Being a Disciple

25 Large crowds were traveling with Jesus, and turning to them he said: 26 "If anyone comes to me and does not hate his father and mother, his wife and children, his brothers and sisters—yes, even his own life—he cannot be my disciple. 27 And anyone who does not carry his cross and follow me cannot be my disciple. 28 "Suppose one of you wants to build a tower. Will he not first sit down and estimate the cost to see if he has enough money to complete it? 29 For if he lays the foundation and is not able to finish it, everyone who sees it will ridicule him, 30 saying, 'This fellow began to build and was not able to finish.' 31 "Or suppose a king is about to go to war against

er king, will not sit down first and consider whether he is able with ten thousand to oppose the one who comes against him with twenty thousand? ³²If he cannot, then, while the other is still far away, he sends a delegation and asks for the terms of peace. ³³So therefore, none of you can become my disciple if you do not give up all your possessions.

About Salt

34 "Salt is good; but if salt has lost its taste, how can it be restored?ᵐ ³⁵It is fit neither for the soil nor for the manure pile; they throw it away. Let anyone with ears to hear listen!"

συμβαλεῖν εἰς πόλεμον οὐχὶ καθίσας πρῶτον
ᵌto attack ᵌin ⁴war not sitting first

βουλεύσεται εἰ δυνατός ἐστιν ἐν δέκα
will deliberate if able he is with ten

χιλιάσιν ὑπαντῆσαι τῷ μετὰ εἴκοσι χιλιάδων
thousands to meet ᵌthe [one] ⁵with ⁶twenty ⁷thousands

ἐρχομένῳ ἐπ' αὐτόν; 32 εἰ δὲ μή γε, ἔτι
ᵌcoming ᵌupon ⁴him? 32 Otherwise, yet
=while

αὐτοῦ πόρρω ὄντος πρεσβείαν ἀποστείλας
him afar beingᵃ a delegation sending
he is yet at a distance

ἐρωτᾷ τὰ πρὸς εἰρήνην. 33 οὕτως οὖν
he asks the things for peace. 33 So therefore

πᾶς ἐξ ὑμῶν ὃς οὐκ ἀποτάσσεται πᾶσιν
everyone of you who does not say farewell to all

τοῖς ἑαυτοῦ ὑπάρχουσιν οὐ δύναται εἶναί
ᵌthe ᵌof himself ᵌpossessions cannot to be

μου μαθητής. 34 Καλὸν οὖν τὸ ἅλας·
of me a disciple. 34 Good therefore the salt;

ἐὰν δὲ καὶ τὸ ἅλας μωρανθῇ, ἐν τίνι
but if even the salt becomes useless, with what

ἀρτυθήσεται; 35 οὔτε εἰς γῆν οὔτε εἰς
will it be seasoned? 35 neither for soil nor for

κοπρίαν εὔθετόν ἐστιν· ἔξω βάλλουσιν
manure suitable is it; outside they cast

αὐτό. ὁ ἔχων ὦτα ἀκούειν ἀκουέτω.
it The [one] having ears to hear let him hear.

another king. Will he not first sit down and consider whether he is able with ten thousand men to oppose the one coming against him with twenty thousand? ³²If he is not able, he will send a delegation while the other is still a long way off and will ask for terms of peace. ³³In the same way, any of you who does not give up everything he has cannot be my disciple.

³⁴"Salt is good, but if it loses its saltiness, how can it be made salty again? ³⁵It is fit neither for the soil nor for the manure pile; it is thrown out.

"He who has ears to hear, let him hear."

Chapter 15

The Parable of the Lost Sheep

NOW all the tax collectors and sinners were coming near to listen to him. ²And the Pharisees and the scribes were grumbling and saying, "This fellow welcomes sinners and eats with them."
3 So he told them this parable: ⁴"Which one of you, having a hundred sheep and losing one of them, does not leave the ninety-nine in the wilderness and go after the one that is lost until he finds it? ⁵When he has found it, he lays it on his shoulders and rejoices. ⁶And when he comes home, he calls together his friends and neighbors, saying to them, 'Rejoice with me, for I have found my sheep that was lost.' ⁷Just so, I tell you, there will be more joy in heaven over one sinner who repents than over ninety-nine righteous per-

15 Ἦσαν δὲ αὐτῷ ἐγγίζοντες πάντες
15 Now there were to him drawing near all

οἱ τελῶναι καὶ οἱ ἁμαρτωλοὶ ἀκούειν
the tax-collectors and the sinners to hear

αὐτοῦ. 2 καὶ διεγόγγυζον οἵ τε Φαρισαῖοι
him. 2 And greatly murmured both the Pharisees

καὶ οἱ γραμματεῖς λέγοντες ὅτι οὗτος
and the scribes saying[,] – This man

ἁμαρτωλοὺς προσδέχεται καὶ συνεσθίει αὐ-
sinners receives and eats with them.

τοῖς. 3 εἶπεν δὲ πρὸς αὐτοὺς τὴν παρα-
And he spoke to them – para-

βολὴν ταύτην λέγων· 4 τίς ἄνθρωπος ἐξ
ble this saying : 4 What man of

ὑμῶν ἔχων ἑκατὸν πρόβατα καὶ ἀπολέσας
you having a hundred sheep and losing

ἐξ αὐτῶν ἓν οὐ καταλείπει τὰ ἐνενήκοντα
of them one does not leave the ninety-

ἐννέα ἐν τῇ ἐρήμῳ καὶ πορεύεται ἐπὶ
nine in the desert and goes after

τὸ ἀπολωλὸς ἕως εὕρη αὐτό; 5 καὶ
the [one] having been lost until he finds it? 5 and

εὑρὼν ἐπιτίθησιν ἐπὶ τοὺς ὤμους αὐτοῦ
finding places on [it] on the shoulders of him

χαίρων, 6 καὶ ἐλθὼν εἰς τὸν οἶκον
rejoicing, and coming into the house

συγκαλεῖ τοὺς φίλους καὶ τοὺς γείτονας,
he calls together the friends and the neighbours,

λέγων αὐτοῖς· συγχάρητέ μοι, ὅτι εὗρον
saying to them : Rejoice with me, because I found

τὸ πρόβατόν μου τὸ ἀπολωλός. 7 λέγω
the sheep of me – having been lost. 7 I tell

ὑμῖν ὅτι οὕτως χαρὰ ἐν τῷ οὐρανῷ
you that thus joy in – heaven

ἔσται ἐπὶ ἑνὶ ἁμαρτωλῷ μετανοοῦντι ἢ
will be over one sinner repenting than

ἐπὶ ἐνενήκοντα ἐννέα δικαίοις οἵτινες οὐ
over ninety-nine just men who no

Chapter 15

The Parable of the Lost Sheep

NOW the tax collectors and "sinners" were all gathering around to hear him. ²But the Pharisees and the teachers of the law muttered, "This man welcomes sinners and eats with them."
³Then Jesus told them this parable: ⁴"Suppose one of you has a hundred sheep and loses one of them. Does he not leave the ninety-nine in the open country and go after the lost sheep until he finds it? ⁵And when he finds it, he joyfully puts it on his shoulders ⁶and goes home. Then he calls his friends and neighbors together and says, 'Rejoice with me; I have found my lost sheep.' ⁷I tell you that in the same way there will be more rejoicing in heaven over one sinner who repents than over ninety-nine righteous

ᵐ Or how can it be used for seasoning?

sons who need no repentance.

The Parable of the Lost Coin

8 "Or what woman having ten silver coins,[n] if she loses one of them, does not light a lamp, sweep the house, and search carefully until she finds it? 9When she has found it, she calls together her friends and neighbors, saying, 'Rejoice with me, for I have found the coin that I had lost.' 10Just so, I tell you, there is joy in the presence of the angels of God over one sinner who repents."

The Parable of the Prodigal and His Brother

11 Then Jesus[o] said, "There was a man who had two sons. 12The younger of them said to his father, 'Father, give me the share of the property that will belong to me.' So he divided his property between them. 13A few days later the younger son gathered all he had and traveled to a distant country, and there he squandered his property in dissolute living. 14When he had spent everything, a severe famine took place throughout that country, and he began to be in need. 15So he went and hired himself out to one of the citizens of that country, who sent him to his fields to feed the pigs. 16He would gladly have filled himself with[p] the pods that the pigs were eating; and no one gave him anything. 17But when he came to himself he said, 'How many of my father's hired hands have bread enough and to spare, but here I am dying of hunger! 18I will get up and go to my father, and I will say to him, "Father, I have sinned against heaven and before you; 19I am no longer worthy to be called your son;

χρείαν ἔχουσιν μετανοίας. **8** Ἢ τίς γυνὴ
need　　have　of repentance.　　Or　what woman

δραχμὰς ἔχουσα δέκα, ἐὰν ἀπολέσῃ
¹drachmae ¹having ²ten,　if　she loses

δραχμὴν μίαν, οὐχὶ ἅπτει λύχνον καὶ
drachma　one,　does not light　a lamp　and

σαροῖ τὴν οἰκίαν καὶ ζητεῖ ἐπιμελῶς
sweep　the　house　and seek　carefully

ἕως οὗ εὕρῃ; **9** καὶ εὑροῦσα συγκαλεῖ
until she finds?　and　finding she calls together

τὰς φίλας καὶ γείτονας λέγουσα· συγχάρητέ
the friends and neighbours saying :　Rejoice with

μοι, ὅτι εὗρον τὴν δραχμὴν ἣν ἀπώλεσα.
me, because I found　the　drachma which　I lost.

10 οὕτως, λέγω ὑμῖν, γίνεται χαρὰ ἐνώπιον
So,　I tell　you,　is　joy　before

τῶν ἀγγέλων τοῦ θεοῦ ἐπὶ ἑνὶ ἁμαρτωλῷ
the angels　- of God over one sinner

μετανοοῦντι. **11** Εἶπεν δέ· ἄνθρωπός τις
repenting.　And he said:　A certain man

εἶχεν δύο υἱούς. **12** καὶ εἶπεν ὁ νεώτερος
had two sons.　And　said the younger

αὐτῶν τῷ πατρί· πάτερ, δός μοι τὸ
of them to the father:　Father,　give me　the

ἐπιβάλλον μέρος τῆς οὐσίας. ὁ δὲ διεῖλες
falling upon share of the property. And he divided
=share of the property falling to [me].

αὐτοῖς τὸν βίον. **13** καὶ μετ᾽ οὐ πολλὰς
to them the living.　And after not many

ἡμέρας συναγαγὼν πάντα ὁ νεώτερος υἱὸς
days　having gathered all things the younger son

ἀπεδήμησεν εἰς χώραν μακράν, καὶ ἐκεῖ
departed　to country　a far,　and there

διεσκόρπισεν τὴν οὐσίαν αὐτοῦ ζῶν ἀσώτως.
scattered　the property of him living prodigally.

14 δαπανήσαντος δὲ αὐτοῦ πάντα ἐγένετο
But having spent him* all things there came
=when he had spent

λιμὸς ἰσχυρὰ κατὰ τὴν χώραν ἐκείνην,
famine a severe throughout　-　country　that,

καὶ αὐτὸς ἤρξατο ὑστερεῖσθαι. **15** καὶ
and　he　began　to be in want.　And

πορευθεὶς ἐκολλήθη ἑνὶ τῶν πολιτῶν τῆς
going he was joined to one of the citizens

χώρας ἐκείνης, καὶ ἔπεμψεν αὐτὸν εἰς
country of that,　and　he sent　him　into

τοὺς ἀγροὺς αὐτοῦ βόσκειν χοίρους· **16** καὶ
the fields of him to feed pigs;　and

ἐπεθύμει γεμίσαι τὴν κοιλίαν αὐτοῦ ἐκ
he longed to fill the stomach of him out of(with)

τῶν κερατίων ὧν ἤσθιον οἱ χοῖροι, καὶ
the husks　which ³ate ¹the ²pigs,　and

οὐδεὶς ἐδίδου αὐτῷ. **17** εἰς ἑαυτὸν δὲ
no one gave to him.　³to ⁴himself ¹But

ἐλθὼν ἔφη· πόσοι μίσθιοι τοῦ πατρός μου
²coming he said: How many hired servants of the father of me

περισσεύονται ἄρτων, ἐγὼ δὲ λιμῷ ὧδε
abound　of loaves,　but I　with famine here
=have abundance of bread,

ἀπόλλυμαι. **18** ἀναστὰς πορεύσομαι πρὸς
am perishing.　Rising up　I will go　to

τὸν πατέρα μου καὶ ἐρῶ αὐτῷ· πάτερ,
the father of me and I will say to him :　Father,

ἥμαρτον εἰς τὸν οὐρανὸν καὶ ἐνώπιόν σου,
I sinned against　-　heaven　and before thee,

19 οὐκέτι εἰμὶ ἄξιος κληθῆναι υἱός σου·
no longer am I worthy to be called a son of thee;

---

persons who do not need to repent.

The Parable of the Lost Coin

8"Or suppose a woman has ten silver coins[j] and loses one. Does she not light a lamp, sweep the house and search carefully until she finds it? 9And when she finds it, she calls her friends and neighbors together and says, 'Rejoice with me; I have found my lost coin.' 10In the same way, I tell you, there is rejoicing in the presence of the angels of God over one sinner who repents."

The Parable of the Lost Son

11Jesus continued: "There was a man who had two sons. 12The younger one said to his father, 'Father, give me my share of the estate.' So he divided his property between them. 13"Not long after that, the younger son got together all he had, set off for a distant country and there squandered his wealth in wild living. 14After he had spent everything, there was a severe famine in that whole country, and he began to be in need. 15So he went and hired himself out to a citizen of that country, who sent him to his fields to feed pigs. 16He longed to fill his stomach with the pods that the pigs were eating, but no one gave him anything. 17"When he came to his senses, he said, 'How many of my father's hired men have food to spare, and here I am starving to death! 18I will set out and go back to my father and say to him: Father, I have sinned against heaven and against you. 19I am no longer worthy to be called

---

[n] Gk *drachmas*, each worth about a day's wage for a laborer
[o] Gk *he*
[p] Other ancient authorities read *filled his stomach with*

[j] 8 Greek *ten drachmas*, each worth about a day's wages

treat me like one of your hired hands." ' 20 So he set off and went to his father. But while he was still far off, his father saw him and was filled with compassion; he ran and put his arms around him and kissed him. 21 Then the son said to him, 'Father, I have sinned against heaven and before you; I am no longer worthy to be called your son.' *q* 22 But the father said to his slaves, 'Quickly, bring out a robe—the best one—and put it on him; put a ring on his finger and sandals on his feet. 23 And get the fatted calf and kill it, and let us eat and celebrate; 24 for this son of mine was dead and is alive again; he was lost and is found!' And they began to celebrate.

25 "Now his elder son was in the field; and when he came and approached the house, he heard music and dancing. 26 He called one of the slaves and asked what was going on. 27 He replied, 'Your brother has come, and your father has killed the fatted calf, because he has got him back safe and sound.' 28 Then he became angry and refused to go in. His father came out and began to plead with him. 29 But he answered his father, 'Listen! For all these years I have been working like a slave for you, and I have never disobeyed your command; yet you have never given me even a young goat so that I might celebrate with my friends. 30 But when this son of yours came back, who has devoured your property with prostitutes,

Greek	English
ποίησόν με ὡς ἕνα τῶν μισθίων σου.	make me as one of the hired servants of thee.
20 καὶ ἀναστὰς ἦλθεν πρὸς τὸν πατέρα	And rising up he came to the father
ἑαυτοῦ. ἔτι δὲ αὐτοῦ μακρὰν ἀπέχοντος	of himself. But yet him afar being away* =while he was yet far away
εἶδεν αὐτὸν ὁ πατὴρ αὐτοῦ καὶ ἐσπλαγχνίσθη,	saw him the father of him and was moved with pity,
καὶ δραμὼν ἐπέπεσεν ἐπὶ τὸν τράχηλον	and running fell on on the neck
αὐτοῦ καὶ κατεφίλησεν αὐτόν. 21 εἶπεν δὲ	of him and fervently kissed him. And said
ὁ υἱὸς αὐτῷ· πάτερ, ἥμαρτον εἰς τὸν	the son to him: Father, I sinned against -
οὐρανὸν καὶ ἐνώπιόν σου, οὐκέτι εἰμὶ	heaven and before thee, no longer am I
ἄξιος κληθῆναι υἱός σου. 22 εἶπεν δὲ	worthy to be called a son of thee. But said
ὁ πατὴρ πρὸς τοὺς δούλους αὐτοῦ· ταχὺ	the father to the slaves of him: Quickly
ἐξενέγκατε στολὴν τὴν πρώτην καὶ ἐνδύσατε	bring ye out a robe the first and clothe
αὐτόν, καὶ δότε δακτύλιον εἰς τὴν χεῖρα	him, and give(put) a ring to the hand
αὐτοῦ καὶ ὑποδήματα εἰς τοὺς πόδας,	of him and sandals to the feet,
23 καὶ φέρετε τὸν μόσχον τὸν σιτευτόν,	and bring the calf - fattened,
θύσατε, καὶ φαγόντες εὐφρανθῶμεν, 24 ὅτι	kill, and eating let us be merry, because
οὗτος ὁ υἱός μου νεκρὸς ἦν καὶ ἀνέζησεν,	this - son of me dead was and lived again,
ἦν ἀπολωλὼς καὶ εὑρέθη. καὶ ἤρξαντο	was having been lost and was found. And they began
εὐφραίνεσθαι. 25 ἦν δὲ ὁ υἱὸς αὐτοῦ	to be merry. But was the son of him
ὁ πρεσβύτερος ἐν ἀγρῷ· καὶ ὡς ἐρχόμενος	- older in a field; and as coming
ἤγγισεν τῇ οἰκίᾳ, ἤκουσεν συμφωνίας καὶ	he drew near to the house, he heard music and
χορῶν, 26 καὶ προσκαλεσάμενος ἕνα τῶν	dances, and calling to [him] one of the
παίδων ἐπυνθάνετο τί ἂν εἴη ταῦτα.	lads he inquired what might be these things.
27 ὁ δὲ εἶπεν αὐτῷ ὅτι ὁ ἀδελφός σου	And he said to him[,] - The brother of thee
ἥκει, καὶ ἔθυσεν ὁ πατήρ σου τὸν μόσχον τὸν	has come, and ⁴killed ¹the ²father ³of thee ⁵the ⁷calf -
σιτευτόν, ὅτι ὑγιαίνοντα αὐτὸν ἀπέλαβεν.	⁶fattened, because ⁵being in health ³him ¹he ²received ⁴back.
28 ὠργίσθη δὲ καὶ οὐκ ἤθελεν εἰσελθεῖν·	But he was angry and did not wish to enter;
ὁ δὲ πατὴρ αὐτοῦ ἐξελθὼν παρεκάλει	so the father of him coming out besought
αὐτόν. 29 ὁ δὲ ἀποκριθεὶς εἶπεν τῷ	him. But he answering said to the
πατρί· ἰδοὺ τοσαῦτα ἔτη δουλεύω σοι καὶ	father: Behold[,] so many years I serve thee and
οὐδέποτε ἐντολήν σου παρῆλθον, καὶ ἐμοὶ	never a command of thee I transgressed, and to me
οὐδέποτε ἔδωκας ἔριφον ἵνα μετὰ τῶν	never thou gavest a goat that with the
φίλων μου εὐφρανθῶ· 30 ὅτε δὲ ὁ υἱός	friends of me I might be merry; but when - ²son
σου οὗτος ὁ καταφαγών σου τὸν βίον	²of thee ¹this - having devoured of thee the living

your son; make me like one of your hired men.' 20 So he got up and went to his father.

"But while he was still a long way off, his father saw him and was filled with compassion for him; he ran to his son, threw his arms around him and kissed him. 21 "The son said to him, 'Father, I have sinned against heaven and against you. I am no longer worthy to be called your son.' *k* 22 "But the father said to his servants, 'Quick! Bring the best robe and put it on him. Put a ring on his finger and sandals on his feet. 23 Bring the fattened calf and kill it. Let's have a feast and celebrate. 24 For this son of mine was dead and is alive again; he was lost and is found.' So they began to celebrate.

25 "Meanwhile, the older son was in the field. When he came near the house, he heard music and dancing. 26 So he called one of the servants and asked him what was going on. 27 'Your brother has come,' he replied, 'and your father has killed the fattened calf because he has him back safe and sound.'

28 "The older brother became angry and refused to go in. So his father went out and pleaded with him. 29 But he answered his father, 'Look! All these years I've been slaving for you and never disobeyed your orders. Yet you never gave me even a young goat so I could celebrate with my friends. 30 But when this son of yours who has squandered your property

q Other ancient authorities add treat me as one of your hired servants

k 21 Some early manuscripts son. Make me like one of your hired men.

you killed the fatted calf for him!' 31 Then the father[r] said to him, 'Son, you are always with me, and all that is mine is yours. 32 But we had to celebrate and rejoice, because this brother of yours was dead and has come to life; he was lost and has been found.' "

Chapter 16

The Parable of the Dishonest Manager

THEN Jesus[r] said to the disciples, "There was a rich man who had a manager, and charges were brought to him that this man was squandering his property. 2 So he summoned him and said to him, 'What is this that I hear about you? Give me an accounting of your management, because you cannot be my manager any longer.' 3 Then the manager said to himself, 'What will I do, now that my master is taking the position away from me? I am not strong enough to dig, and I am ashamed to beg. 4 I have decided what to do so that, when I am dismissed as manager, people may welcome me into their homes.' 5 So, summoning his master's debtors one by one, he asked the first, 'How much do you owe my master?' 6 He answered, 'A hundred jugs of olive oil.' He said to him, 'Take your bill, sit down quickly, and make it fifty.' 7 Then he asked another, 'And how much do you owe?' He replied, 'A hundred containers of wheat.' He said to him, 'Take your bill and make it eighty.' 8 And his master commended the dishonest manager because he had acted shrewdly; for the children of this age are

[r] Gk he

μετὰ πορνῶν ἦλθεν, ἔθυσας αὐτῷ τὸν
with   harlots   came,   thou killedst   for him   the

σιτευτὸν μόσχον. 31 ὁ δὲ εἶπεν αὐτῷ·
fattened   calf.   And he   said   to him :

τέκνον, σὺ πάντοτε μετ᾽ ἐμοῦ εἶ, καὶ
Child,   thou   always   with   me   art,   and

πάντα τὰ ἐμὰ σά ἐστιν· 32 εὐφρανθῆναι
¹all ³things –   ²my ⁴thine ⁵is(are);   ²to be merry

δὲ καὶ χαρῆναι ἔδει, ὅτι ὁ ἀδελφός
¹And ⁴and ³to rejoice ⁵it be- because – ⁸brother
            hoved [us],

σου οὗτος νεκρὸς ἦν καὶ ἔζησεν, καὶ ἀπο-
⁹of thee ¹this   ⁵dead ⁴was and came to life, and having

λωλὼς καὶ εὑρέθη.
been lost   also   was found.

16 Ἔλεγεν δὲ καὶ πρὸς τοὺς μαθητάς·
   And he said   also   to   the   disciples :

ἄνθρωπός τις ἦν πλούσιος ὃς εἶχεν
³A certain ⁴man ¹there was ²rich   who   had

οἰκονόμον, καὶ οὗτος διεβλήθη αὐτῷ ὡς
a steward,   and   this   was complained of to him   as

διασκορπίζων τὰ ὑπάρχοντα αὐτοῦ. 2 καὶ
wasting   the   possessions   of him.   And

φωνήσας αὐτὸν εἶπεν αὐτῷ· τί τοῦτο
calling   him   he said   to him : What [is] this

ἀκούω περὶ σοῦ; ἀπόδος τὸν λόγον τῆς
I hear   about thee?   render   the   account   of the

οἰκονομίας σου· οὐ γὰρ δύνῃ ἔτι οἰκονομεῖν·
stewardship of thee; for thou canst not longer *to* be steward.

3 εἶπεν δὲ ἐν ἑαυτῷ ὁ οἰκονόμος· τί
  And said   in   himself   the   steward : What

ποιήσω, ὅτι ὁ κύριός μου ἀφαιρεῖται τὴν
may I do, because the   lord   of me   takes away   the

οἰκονομίαν ἀπ᾽ ἐμοῦ; σκάπτειν οὐκ ἰσχύω,
stewardship from   me?   to dig   I am not able,

ἐπαιτεῖν αἰσχύνομαι. 4 ἔγνων τί ποιήσω,
to beg   I am ashamed.   I knew(know) what I may do,

ἵνα ὅταν μετασταθῶ ἐκ τῆς οἰκονομίας
that   when   I am removed   out of   the   stewardship

δέξωνταί με εἰς τοὺς οἴκους ἑαυτῶν.
they may receive me   into   the   houses   of them*selves*.

5 καὶ προσκαλεσάμενος ἕνα ἕκαστον τῶν
  And   calling to [him]   ²one ¹each   of the

χρεοφειλετῶν τοῦ κυρίου ἑαυτοῦ ἔλεγεν τῷ
debtors   of the   lord   of him*self* he said to the

πρώτῳ· πόσον ὀφείλεις τῷ κυρίῳ μου;
first :   How much   owest thou to the   lord   of me?

6 ὁ δὲ εἶπεν· ἑκατὸν βάτους ἐλαίου. ὁ δὲ
  And he   said : A hundred   baths   of oil.   And he

εἶπεν αὐτῷ· δέξαι σου τὰ γράμματα καὶ
told   him :   Take   of thee the   letters(bill)   and

καθίσας ταχέως γράψον πεντήκοντα. 7 ἔπειτα
sitting   quickly   write   fifty.   Then

ἑτέρῳ εἶπεν· σὺ δὲ πόσον ὀφείλεις; ὁ δὲ
to another he said : ²thou ¹And ³how much ⁴owest? And he

εἶπεν· ἑκατὸν κόρους σίτου. λέγει αὐτῷ·
said : A hundred   cors   of wheat. He tells   him :

δέξαι σου τὰ γράμματα καὶ γράψον
Take   of thee the   bill   and   write

ὀγδοήκοντα. 8 καὶ ἐπῄνεσεν ὁ κύριος τὸν
eighty.   And ²praised ¹the ¹lord   the

οἰκονόμον τῆς ἀδικίας ὅτι φρονίμως
steward   the – of unrighteousness because   prudently

ἐποίησεν· ὅτι οἱ υἱοὶ τοῦ αἰῶνος τούτου
he acted;   because the   sons   the –   age   of this

---

with prostitutes comes home, you kill the fattened calf for him!'
31 " 'My son,' the father said, 'you are always with me, and everything I have is yours. 32 But we had to celebrate and be glad, because this brother of yours was dead and is alive again; he was lost and is found.' "

Chapter 16

The Parable of the Shrewd Manager

JESUS told his disciples: "There was a rich man whose manager was accused of wasting his possessions. 2 So he called him in and asked him, 'What is this I hear about you? Give an account of your management, because you cannot be manager any longer.'
3 "The manager said to himself, 'What shall I do now? My master is taking away my job. I'm not strong enough to dig, and I'm ashamed to beg— 4 I know what I'll do so that, when I lose my job here, people will welcome me into their houses.'
5 "So he called in each one of his master's debtors. He asked the first, 'How much do you owe my master?'
6 " 'Eight hundred gallons[l] of olive oil,' he replied.
"The manager told him, 'Take your bill, sit down quickly, and make it four hundred.'
7 "Then he asked the second, 'And how much do you owe?'
" 'A thousand bushels[m] of wheat,' he replied.
"He told him, 'Take your bill and make it eight hundred.'
8 "The master commended the dishonest manager because he had acted shrewdly. For the people of

[l] 6 Greek *one hundred batous* (probably about 3 kiloliters)
[m] 7 Greek *one hundred korous* (probably about 35 kiloliters)

more shrewd in dealing with their own generation than are the children of light. ⁹And I tell you, make friends for yourselves by means of dishonest wealth,ˢ so that when it is gone, they may welcome you into the eternal homes.ᵗ

10 "Whoever is faithful in a very little is faithful also in much; and whoever is dishonest in a very little is dishonest also in much. ¹¹If then you have not been faithful with the dishonest wealth,ˢ who will entrust to you the true riches? ¹²And if you have not been faithful with what belongs to another, who will give you what is your own? ¹³No slave can serve two masters; for a slave will either hate the one and love the other, or be devoted to the one and despise the other. You cannot serve God and wealth."ˢ

The Law and the Kingdom of God

14 The Pharisees, who were lovers of money, heard all this, and they ridiculed him. ¹⁵So he said to them, "You are those who justify yourselves in the sight of others; but God knows your hearts; for what is prized by human beings is an abomination in the sight of God. 16 "The law and the prophets were in effect until John came; since then the good news of the kingdom of God is proclaimed, and everyone tries to enter it by force. ᵘ ¹⁷But it is easier for heaven and earth to pass away, than for one stroke of a letter in the law to be dropped. 18 "Anyone who divorces his wife and marries another commits adultery, and whoever marries a

φρονιμώτεροι ὑπὲρ τοὺς υἱοὺς τοῦ φωτὸς
more prudent   than   the   sons   of the   light
εἰς τὴν γενεὰν τὴν ἑαυτῶν εἰσιν. 9 Καὶ
in   the   generation   – of themselves are.   And
ἐγὼ ὑμῖν λέγω, ἑαυτοῖς ποιήσατε φίλους
I   ¹you   ²tell, To yourselves   make   friends
ἐκ τοῦ μαμωνᾶ τῆς ἀδικίας, ἵνα ὅταν
by   the   mammon   – of unrighteousness, that   when
ἐκλίπῃ δέξωνται ὑμᾶς εἰς τὰς αἰωνίους
it fails   they may receive   you   into   the   eternal
σκηνάς. 10 ὁ πιστὸς ἐν ἐλαχίστῳ καὶ ἐν
tabernacles. The man faithful   in   least   also   in
πολλῷ πιστός ἐστιν, καὶ ὁ ἐν ἐλαχίστῳ
much   faithful   is,   and the man in   least
ἄδικος καὶ ἐν πολλῷ ἄδικός ἐστιν. 11 εἰ
unrighteous also in   much   unrighteous is.   If
οὖν ἐν τῷ ἀδίκῳ μαμωνᾷ πιστοὶ οὐκ
therefore in   the   unrighteous   mammon   faithful   not
ἐγένεσθε, τὸ ἀληθινὸν τίς ὑμῖν πιστεύσει;
ye were,   the   true   who to you   will entrust ?
12 καὶ εἰ ἐν τῷ ἀλλοτρίῳ πιστοὶ οὐκ
And if   in the thing belonging to another faithful   not
ἐγένεσθε, τὸ ἡμέτερον τίς δώσει ὑμῖν;
ye were,   the   ours   who   will give   you?
=that which is ours

13 Οὐδεὶς οἰκέτης δύναται δυσὶ κυρίοις
No   household slave   can   two   lords
δουλεύειν· ἢ γὰρ τὸν ἕνα μισήσει καὶ τὸν
to serve;   for either   the   one he will hate and the
ἕτερον ἀγαπήσει, ἢ ἑνὸς ἀνθέξεται καὶ
other   he will love,   or   one he will hold fast to and
τοῦ ἑτέρου καταφρονήσει. οὐ δύνασθε
the   other   he will despise.   Ye cannot
θεῷ δουλεύειν καὶ μαμωνᾷ. 14 Ἤκουον
God   to serve   and   mammon.   ⁶heard
δὲ ταῦτα πάντα οἱ Φαρισαῖοι φιλάργυροι
¹Now ²these things ³all ⁴the ⁵Pharisees ⁶moneylovers
ὑπάρχοντες, καὶ ἐξεμυκτήριζον αὐτόν. 15 καὶ
⁶being,   and   they scoffed at   him.   And
εἶπεν αὐτοῖς· ὑμεῖς ἐστε οἱ δικαιοῦντες
he said   to them :   Ye   are the [ones] justifying
ἑαυτοὺς ἐνώπιον τῶν ἀνθρώπων, ὁ δὲ
yourselves   before   –   men,   – but
θεὸς γινώσκει τὰς καρδίας ὑμῶν· ὅτι τὸ
God   knows   the   hearts   of you; because the thing
ἐν ἀνθρώποις ὑψηλὸν βδέλυγμα ἐνώπιον
¹among ²men   ¹lofty [is]   an abomination   before
τοῦ θεοῦ. 16 Ὁ νόμος καὶ οἱ προφῆται
–   God.   The   law   and   the   prophets
μέχρι Ἰωάννου· ἀπὸ τότε ἡ βασιλεία τοῦ
[were] until John;   from   then   the   kingdom   of
θεοῦ εὐαγγελίζεται καὶ πᾶς εἰς αὐτὴν
of God   is being preached   and everyone into   it
βιάζεται. 17 εὐκοπώτερον δέ ἐστιν τὸν οὐρανὸν
is pressing.   But easier   it is   the   heaven
καὶ τὴν γῆν παρελθεῖν ἢ τοῦ νόμου μίαν
and the   earth   to pass away than of the   law   one
κεραίαν πεσεῖν. 18 Πᾶς ὁ ἀπολύων τὴν
little horn*   to fall.   Everyone dismissing   the
γυναῖκα αὐτοῦ καὶ γαμῶν ἑτέραν μοιχεύει,
wife   of him and marrying   another commits adultery,
καὶ ὁ ἀπολελυμένην ἀπὸ
and   ¹the [one]   ²a woman having been dismissed   ⁴from

this world are more shrewd in dealing with their own kind than are the people of the light. ⁹I tell you, use worldly wealth to gain friends for yourselves, so that when it is gone, you will be welcomed into eternal dwellings.

¹⁰"Whoever can be trusted with very little can also be trusted with much, and whoever is dishonest with very little will also be dishonest with much. ¹¹So if you have not been trustworthy in handling worldly wealth, who will trust you with true riches? ¹²And if you have not been trustworthy with someone else's property, who will give you property of your own?

¹³"No servant can serve two masters. Either he will hate the one and love the other, or he will be devoted to the one and despise the other. You cannot serve both God and Money."

¹⁴The Pharisees, who loved money, heard all this and were sneering at Jesus. ¹⁵He said to them, "You are the ones who justify yourselves in the eyes of men, but God knows your hearts. What is highly valued among men is detestable in God's sight.

Additional Teachings

¹⁶"The Law and the Prophets were proclaimed until John. Since that time, the good news of the kingdom of God is being preached, and everyone is forcing his way into it. ¹⁷It is easier for heaven and earth to disappear than for the least stroke of a pen to drop out of the Law.

¹⁸"Anyone who divorces his wife and marries another woman commits adultery, and the man who marries a divorced woman commits adultery.

ˢ Gk mammon
ᵗ Gk tents
ᵘ Or everyone is strongly urged to enter it

* The little projection which distinguishes some Hebrew letters from those otherwise similar.

woman divorced from her husband commits adultery.

The Rich Man and Lazarus

19 "There was a rich man who was dressed in purple and fine linen and who feasted sumptuously every day. 20 And at his gate lay a poor man named Lazarus, covered with sores, 21 who longed to satisfy his hunger with what fell from the rich man's table; even the dogs would come and lick his sores. 22 The poor man died and was carried away by the angels to be with Abraham.[v] The rich man also died and was buried. 23 In Hades, where he was being tormented, he looked up and saw Abraham far away with Lazarus by his side.[w] 24 He called out, 'Father Abraham, have mercy on me, and send Lazarus to dip the tip of his finger in water and cool my tongue; for I am in agony in these flames.' 25 But Abraham said, 'Child, remember that during your lifetime you received your good things, and Lazarus in like manner evil things; but now he is comforted here, and you are in agony. 26 Besides all this, between you and us a great chasm has been fixed, so that those who might want to pass from here to you cannot do so, and no one can cross from there to us.' 27 He said, 'Then, father, I beg you to send him to my father's house— 28 for I have five brothers— that he may warn them, so that they will not also come into this place of torment.'

ἀνδρὸς γαμῶν μοιχεύει.
a husband marrying commits adultery.

19 Ἄνθρωπος δέ
Now a certain

τις ἦν πλούσιος, καὶ ἐνεδιδύσκετο πορφύραν
man was rich, and used to put on a purple robe

καὶ βύσσον εὐφραινόμενος καθ᾽ ἡμέραν
and fine linen being merry every day†

λαμπρῶς. 20 πτωχὸς δέ τις ὀνόματι
splendidly. And a certain poor man by name

Λάζαρος ἐβέβλητο πρὸς τὸν πυλῶνα αὐτοῦ
Lazarus had been placed at the gate of him

εἱλκωμένος 21 καὶ ἐπιθυμῶν χορτασθῆναι
being covered with sores and desiring to be satisfied

ἀπὸ τῶν πιπτόντων ἀπὸ τῆς τραπέζης
from the things falling from the table

τοῦ πλουσίου· ἀλλὰ καὶ οἱ κύνες ἐρχόμενοι
of the rich man; but even the dogs coming

ἐπέλειχον τὰ ἕλκη αὐτοῦ. 22 ἐγένετο δὲ
licked the sores of him. And it came to pass

ἀποθανεῖν τὸν πτωχὸν καὶ ἀπενεχθῆναι
to die the poor man and to be carried away
=that the poor man died and he was carried away

αὐτὸν ὑπὸ τῶν ἀγγέλων εἰς τὸν κόλπον
him[b] by the angels into the bosom

Ἀβραάμ· ἀπέθανεν δὲ καὶ ὁ πλούσιος καὶ
of Abraham; and died also the rich man and

ἐτάφη. 23 καὶ ἐν τῷ ᾅδῃ ἐπάρας τοὺς
was buried. And in the hades lifting up the

ὀφθαλμοὺς αὐτοῦ, ὑπάρχων ἐν βασάνοις,
eyes of him, being in torments,

ὁρᾷ Ἀβραὰμ ἀπὸ μακρόθεν καὶ Λάζαρον
he sees Abraham from afar and Lazarus

ἐν τοῖς κόλποις αὐτοῦ. 24 καὶ αὐτὸς
in the bosoms of him. And he

φωνήσας εἶπεν· πάτερ Ἀβραάμ, ἐλέησόν
calling said: Father Abraham, pity

με καὶ πέμψον Λάζαρον ἵνα βάψῃ τὸ
me and send Lazarus that he may dip the

ἄκρον τοῦ δακτύλου αὐτοῦ ὕδατος καὶ
tip of the finger of him of(in) water and

καταψύξῃ τὴν γλῶσσάν μου, ὅτι ὀδυνῶμαι
may cool the tongue of me, because I am suffering

ἐν τῇ φλογὶ ταύτῃ. 25 εἶπεν δὲ Ἀβραάμ·
in the flame this. But said Abraham:

τέκνον, μνήσθητι ὅτι ἀπέλαβες τὰ ἀγαθά
Child, remember that thou didst receive the good things

σου ἐν τῇ ζωῇ σου, καὶ Λάζαρος ὁμοίως
of thee in the life of thee, and Lazarus likewise

τὰ κακά· νῦν δὲ ὧδε παρακαλεῖται, σὺ δὲ
the bad; but now here he is comforted, but thou

ὀδυνᾶσαι. 26 καὶ ἐν πᾶσι τούτοις μεταξὺ
art suffering. And among all these things between

ἡμῶν καὶ ὑμῶν χάσμα μέγα ἐστήρικται,
us and you chasm a great has been firmly fixed,

ὅπως οἱ θέλοντες διαβῆναι ἔνθεν πρὸς
so that the [ones] wishing to pass hence to

ὑμᾶς μὴ δύνωνται, μηδὲ ἐκεῖθεν πρὸς
you cannot, neither thence to

ἡμᾶς διαπερῶσιν. 27 εἶπεν δέ· ἐρωτῶ
us may they cross over. And he said: I ask

σε οὖν, πάτερ, ἵνα πέμψῃς αὐτὸν εἰς
thee therefore, father, that thou mayest send him to

τὸν οἶκον τοῦ πατρός μου· 28 ἔχω γὰρ
the house of the father of me; for I have

πέντε ἀδελφούς· ὅπως διαμαρτύρηται αὐτοῖς,
five brothers; so that he may witness to them,

ἵνα μὴ καὶ αὐτοὶ ἔλθωσιν εἰς τὸν τόπον
lest also they come to - place

The Rich Man and Lazarus

19 "There was a rich man who was dressed in purple and fine linen and lived in luxury every day. 20 At his gate was laid a beggar named Lazarus, covered with sores 21 and longing to eat what fell from the rich man's table. Even the dogs came and licked his sores.

22 "The time came when the beggar died and the angels carried him to Abraham's side. The rich man also died and was buried. 23 In hell,[n] where he was in torment, he looked up and saw Abraham far away, with Lazarus by his side. 24 So he called to him, 'Father Abraham, have pity on me and send Lazarus to dip the tip of his finger in water and cool my tongue, because I am in agony in this fire.'

25 "But Abraham replied, 'Son, remember that in your lifetime you received your good things, while Lazarus received bad things, but now he is comforted here and you are in agony. 26 And besides all this, between us and you a great chasm has been fixed, so that those who want to go from here to you cannot, nor can anyone cross over from there to us.'

27 "He answered, 'Then I beg you, father, send Lazarus to my father's house, 28 for I have five brothers. Let him warn them, so that they will not also come to

29 Abraham replied, 'They have Moses and the prophets; they should listen to them.' 30 He said, 'No, father Abraham; but if someone goes to them from the dead, they will repent.' 31 He said to him, 'If they do not listen to Moses and the prophets, neither will they be convinced even if someone rises from the dead.' "

Chapter 17

Some Sayings of Jesus

JESUS[x] said to his disciples, "Occasions for stumbling are bound to come, but woe to anyone by whom they come! 2 It would be better for you if a millstone were hung around your neck and you were thrown into the sea than for you to cause one of these little ones to stumble. 3 Be on your guard! If another disciple[y] sins, you must rebuke the offender, and if there is repentance, you must forgive. 4 And if the same person sins against you seven times a day, and turns back to you seven times and says, 'I repent,' you must forgive."
5 The apostles said to the Lord, "Increase our faith!" 6 The Lord replied, "If you had faith the size of a[z] mustard seed, you could say to this mulberry tree, 'Be uprooted and planted in the sea,' and it would obey you.
7 "Who among you would say to your slave who has just come in from plowing or tending sheep in the field, 'Come here at once and take your place at the table'? 8 Would you not rather say to him, 'Prepare supper for me, put on your apron and serve me while I eat and drink; later you may eat and drink'? 9 Do you thank the slave for doing what was commanded?

[x] Gk *He*
[y] Gk *your brother*
[z] Gk *faith as a grain of*

τοῦτον τῆς βασάνου. 29 λέγει δὲ 'Αβραάμ·
this   —   of torment.   But says   Abraham :

ἔχουσι Μωϋσέα καὶ τοὺς προφήτας·
They have   Moses   and   the   prophets;

ἀκουσάτωσαν αὐτῶν. 30 ὁ δὲ εἶπεν·
let them hear   them.   But he   said :

οὐχί, πάτερ 'Αβραάμ, ἀλλ' ἐάν τις ἀπὸ
No,   father   Abraham,   but   if someone from

νεκρῶν πορευθῇ πρὸς αὐτούς, μετανοήσουσιν.
[the] dead should go   to   them,   they will repent.

31 εἶπεν δὲ αὐτῷ· εἰ Μωϋσέως καὶ τῶν
But he said   to him :   If   Moses   and   the

προφητῶν οὐκ ἀκούσουσιν, οὐδὲ ἐάν τις
prophets   they do not hear,   neither   if someone

ἐκ νεκρῶν ἀναστῇ πεισθήσονται.
out of [the] dead should rise again will they be persuaded.

17 Εἶπεν δὲ πρὸς τοὺς μαθητὰς αὐτοῦ·
And he said   to   the   disciples   of him :

ἀνένδεκτόν ἐστιν τοῦ τὰ σκάνδαλα μὴ ἐλθεῖν,
Impossible   it is   –   the   offences   not to come,[d]

οὐαὶ δὲ δι' οὗ ἔρχεται· 2 λυσιτελεῖ
but woe [to him] through whom they come;   it profits

αὐτῷ εἰ λίθος μυλικὸς περίκειται περὶ
him   if   a millstone   is put round   round

τὸν τράχηλον αὐτοῦ καὶ ἔρριπται εἰς τὴν
the   neck   of him and he has been thrown into   the

θάλασσαν, ἢ ἵνα σκανδαλίσῃ τῶν μικρῶν
sea,   than   that he should offend   –   ³little ones

τούτων ἕνα. 3 προσέχετε ἑαυτοῖς. ἐὰν
²of these   ¹one.   Take heed   to yourselves.   If

ἁμάρτῃ ὁ ἀδελφός σου, ἐπιτίμησον αὐτῷ,
sins   the   brother   of thee,   rebuke   him,

καὶ ἐὰν μετανοήσῃ, ἄφες αὐτῷ. 4 καὶ
and   if   he repents,   forgive   him.   And

ἐὰν ἑπτάκις τῆς ἡμέρας ἁμαρτήσῃ εἰς σὲ
if   seven times of(in) the   day   he sins   against thee

καὶ ἑπτάκις ἐπιστρέψῃ πρὸς σὲ λέγων·
and   seven times   turns   to   thee   saying :

μετανοῶ, ἀφήσεις αὐτῷ. 5 Καὶ εἶπαν οἱ
I repent, thou shalt forgive him.   And   said   the

ἀπόστολοι τῷ κυρίῳ· πρόσθες ἡμῖν πίστιν.
apostles   to the Lord :   Add   to us   faith.

6 εἶπεν δὲ ὁ κύριος· εἰ ἔχετε πίστιν ὡς
And said   the Lord :   If   ye have   faith   as

κόκκον σινάπεως, ἐλέγετε ἂν τῇ συκαμίνῳ
a grain   of mustard,   ye would have said –   sycamine-tree

ταύτῃ· ἐκριζώθητι καὶ φυτεύθητι ἐν τῇ
to this :   Be thou uprooted   and   be thou planted   in   the

θαλάσσῃ· καὶ ὑπήκουσεν ἂν ὑμῖν. 7 Τίς
sea;   and   it would have obeyed   you.   who

δὲ ἐξ ὑμῶν δοῦλον ἔχων ἀροτριῶντα ἢ
But of   you   ²a slave   ¹having   ploughing   or

ποιμαίνοντα, ὃς εἰσελθόντι ἐκ τοῦ ἀγροῦ
herding,   who on [his] coming in°   out of   the   farm

ἐρεῖ αὐτῷ· εὐθέως παρελθὼν ἀνάπεσε,
will say   to him :   Immediately   coming up   recline,

8 ἀλλ' οὐχὶ ἐρεῖ αὐτῷ· ἑτοίμασον τί
but   will not say   to him :   Prepare something

δειπνήσω, καὶ περιζωσάμενος διακόνει μοι
I may dine,   and   having girded thyself   serve   me

ἕως φάγω καὶ πίω, καὶ μετὰ ταῦτα
until   I eat   and   drink,   and   after these things

φάγεσαι καὶ πίεσαι σύ; 9 μὴ ἔχει χάριν
eat   and   drink   thou?   *Not*   he has   thanks

this place of torment.'
29 "Abraham replied, 'They have Moses and the Prophets; let them listen to them.'
30 " 'No, father Abraham,' he said, 'but if someone from the dead goes to them, they will repent.'
31 "He said to him, 'If they do not listen to Moses and the Prophets, they will not be convinced even if someone rises from the dead.' "

Chapter 17

Sin, Faith, Duty

JESUS said to his disciples: "Things that cause people to sin are bound to come, but woe to that person through whom they come. 2 It would be better for him to be thrown into the sea with a millstone tied around his neck than for him to cause one of these little ones to sin. 3 So watch yourselves.
"If your brother sins, rebuke him, and if he repents, forgive him. 4 If he sins against you seven times in a day, and seven times comes back to you and says, 'I repent,' forgive him."
5 The apostles said to the Lord, "Increase our faith!"
6 He replied, "If you have faith as small as a mustard seed, you can say to this mulberry tree, 'Be uprooted and planted in the sea,' and it will obey you.
7 "Suppose one of you had a servant plowing or looking after the sheep. Would he say to the servant when he comes in from the field, 'Come along now and sit down to eat'? 8 Would he not rather say, 'Prepare my supper, get yourself ready and wait on me while I eat and drink; after that you may eat and drink'? 9 Would he thank the ser-

10 So you also, when you have done all that you were ordered to do, say, 'We are worthless slaves; we have done only what we ought to have done!' "

Jesus Cleanses Ten Lepers

11 On the way to Jerusalem Jesus[a] was going through the region between Samaria and Galilee. 12 As he entered a village, ten lepers[b] approached him. Keeping their distance, 13 they called out, saying, "Jesus, Master, have mercy on us!" 14 When he saw them, he said to them, "Go and show yourselves to the priests." And as they went, they were made clean. 15 Then one of them, when he saw that he was healed, turned back, praising God with a loud voice. 16 He prostrated himself at Jesus'[c] feet and thanked him. And he was a Samaritan. 17 Then Jesus asked, "Were not ten made clean? But the other nine, where are they? 18 Was none of them found to return and give praise to God except this foreigner?" 19 Then he said to him, "Get up and go on your way; your faith has made you well."

The Coming of the Kingdom

20 Once Jesus[a] was asked by the Pharisees when the kingdom of God was coming, and he answered, "The kingdom of God is not coming with things that can be observed; 21 nor will they say, 'Look, here it is!' or 'There it is!' For, in fact, the kingdom of God is among[d] you."

22 Then he said to the disciples, "The days are

τῷ δούλῳ ὅτι ἐποίησεν τὰ διαταχθέντα;
to the slave because he did the things commanded?

10 οὕτως καὶ ὑμεῖς, ὅταν ποιήσητε πάντα
So also ye, when ye do all

τὰ διαταχθέντα ὑμῖν, λέγετε ὅτι δοῦλοι
the things commanded you, say[,] - Slaves

ἀχρεῖοί ἐσμεν, ὃ ὠφείλομεν ποιῆσαι
unprofitable we are, what we ought to do

πεποιήκαμεν.
we have done.

11 Καὶ ἐγένετο ἐν τῷ πορεύεσθαι εἰς
And it came to pass in the to go[e] to
=as [he] went

Ἰερουσαλήμ, καὶ αὐτὸς διήρχετο διὰ μέσον
Jerusalem, and he passed through [the]
through midst

Σαμαρείας καὶ Γαλιλαίας. **12** καὶ εἰσερχομένου
of Samaria and Galilee. And entering
=as he entered

αὐτοῦ εἴς τινα κώμην ἀπήντησαν δέκα
him[a] into a certain village met [him] ten

λεπροὶ ἄνδρες, οἳ ἔστησαν πόρρωθεν, **13** καὶ
leprous men, who stood afar off, and

αὐτοὶ ἦραν φωνὴν λέγοντες· Ἰησοῦ
they lifted voice saying: Jesus

ἐπιστάτα, ἐλέησον ἡμᾶς. **14** καὶ ἰδὼν εἶπεν
Master, pity us. And seeing he said

αὐτοῖς· πορευθέντες ἐπιδείξατε ἑαυτοὺς τοῖς
to them: Going show yourselves to the

ἱερεῦσιν. καὶ ἐγένετο ἐν τῷ ὑπάγειν
priests. And it came to pass in the to go
= as they went

αὐτοὺς ἐκαθαρίσθησαν. **15** εἷς δὲ ἐξ
them[be] they were cleansed. But one of

αὐτῶν, ἰδὼν ὅτι ἰάθη, ὑπέστρεψεν μετὰ
them, seeing that he was cured, returned with

φωνῆς μεγάλης δοξάζων τὸν θεόν, **16** καὶ
voice a great glorifying - God, and

ἔπεσεν ἐπὶ πρόσωπον παρὰ τοὺς πόδας
fell on [his] face at the feet

αὐτοῦ εὐχαριστῶν αὐτῷ· καὶ αὐτὸς ἦν
of him thanking him; and he was

Σαμαρίτης. **17** ἀποκριθεὶς δὲ ὁ Ἰησοῦς
a Samaritan. And answering - Jesus

εἶπεν· οὐχ οἱ δέκα ἐκαθαρίσθησαν; οἱ [δὲ]
said: Not the ten were cleansed? the

ἐννέα ποῦ; **18** οὐχ εὑρέθησαν ὑποστρέψαντες
nine where? were there not found returning

δοῦναι δόξαν τῷ θεῷ εἰ μὴ ὁ ἀλλογενὴς
to give glory - to God only - stranger

οὗτος; **19** καὶ εἶπεν αὐτῷ· ἀναστὰς πορεύου·
this? And he said to him: Rising up go;

ἡ πίστις σου σέσωκέν σε.
the faith of thee has healed thee.

20 Ἐπερωτηθεὶς δὲ ὑπὸ τῶν Φαρισαίων
And being questioned by the Pharisees

πότε ἔρχεται ἡ βασιλεία τοῦ θεοῦ,
when comes the kingdom - of God,

ἀπεκρίθη αὐτοῖς καὶ εἶπεν· οὐκ ἔρχεται
he answered them and said: Comes not

ἡ βασιλεία τοῦ θεοῦ μετὰ παρατηρήσεως,
the kingdom - of God with observation,

21 οὐδὲ ἐροῦσιν· ἰδοὺ ὧδε ἤ· ἐκεῖ· ἰδοὺ
nor will they say: Behold[,] here or: there; [s]behold

γὰρ ἡ βασιλεία τοῦ θεοῦ ἐντὸς ὑμῶν
[f]for the kingdom - of God within you

ἐστίν. **22** Εἶπεν δὲ πρὸς τοὺς μαθητάς·
is. And he said to the disciples:

---

vant because he did what he was told to do? 10 So you also, when you have done everything you were told to do, should say, 'We are unworthy servants; we have only done our duty.' "

Ten Healed of Leprosy

11 Now on his way to Jerusalem, Jesus traveled along the border between Samaria and Galilee. 12 As he was going into a village, ten men who had leprosy[o] met him. They stood at a distance 13 and called out in a loud voice, "Jesus, Master, have pity on us!"

14 When he saw them, he said, "Go, show yourselves to the priests." And as they went, they were cleansed.

15 One of them, when he saw he was healed, came back, praising God in a loud voice. 16 He threw himself at Jesus' feet and thanked him—and he was a Samaritan.

17 Jesus asked, "Were not all ten cleansed? Where are the other nine? 18 Was no one found to return and give praise to God except this foreigner?" 19 Then he said to him, "Rise and go; your faith has made you well."

The Coming of the Kingdom of God

20 Once, having been asked by the Pharisees when the kingdom of God would come, Jesus replied, "The kingdom of God does not come with your careful observation, 21 nor will people say, 'Here it is,' or 'There it is,' because the kingdom of God is within[p] you."

22 Then he said to his dis-

---

[a] Gk he
[b] The terms leper and leprosy can refer to several diseases
[c] Gk his
[d] Or within

[o]12 The Greek word was used for various diseases affecting the skin—not necessarily leprosy.
[p]21 Or among

coming when you will long to see one of the days of the Son of Man, and you will not see it. 23 They will say to you, 'Look there!' or 'Look here!' Do not go, do not set off in pursuit. 24 For as the lightning flashes and lights up the sky from one side to the other, so will the Son of Man be in his day. *e* 25 But first he must endure much suffering and be rejected by this generation. 26 Just as it was in the days of Noah, so too it will be in the days of the Son of Man. 27 They were eating and drinking, and marrying and being given in marriage, until the day Noah entered the ark, and the flood came and destroyed all of them. 28 Likewise, just as it was in the days of Lot: they were eating and drinking, buying and selling, planting and building, 29 but on the day that Lot left Sodom, it rained fire and sulfur from heaven and destroyed all of them 30 —it will be like that on the day that the Son of Man is revealed. 31 On that day, anyone on the housetop who has belongings in the house must not come down to take them away; and likewise anyone in the field must not turn back. 32 Remember Lot's wife. 33 Those who try to make their life secure will lose it, but those who lose their life will keep it. 34 I tell you, on that night there will be two in one bed; one will be taken and the other left.

ἐλεύσονται ἡμέραι ὅτε ἐπιθυμήσετε μίαν
Will come days when ye will long one
τῶν ἡμερῶν τοῦ υἱοῦ τοῦ ἀνθρώπου ἰδεῖν
of the days of the Son - of man to see
καὶ οὐκ ὄψεσθε. 23 καὶ ἐροῦσιν ὑμῖν·
and will not see. And they will say to you :
ἰδοὺ ἐκεῖ, ἰδοὺ ὧδε· μὴ ἀπέλθητε μηδὲ
Behold there, behold here; do not go away nor
διώξητε. 24 ὥσπερ γὰρ ἡ ἀστραπὴ
follow. For as the lightning
ἀστράπτουσα ἐκ τῆς ὑπὸ τὸν οὐρανὸν
flashing out of the [one part] under - heaven
εἰς τὴν ὑπ' οὐρανὸν λάμπει, οὕτως ἔσται
to the [other part] under heaven shines, so will be
ὁ υἱὸς τοῦ ἀνθρώπου ἐν τῇ ἡμέρᾳ αὐτοῦ.
the Son - of man in the day of him.
25 πρῶτον δὲ δεῖ αὐτὸν πολλὰ παθεῖν καὶ
But first it behoves him many things to suffer and
ἀποδοκιμασθῆναι ἀπὸ τῆς γενεᾶς ταύτης.
to be rejected from - generation this.
26 καὶ καθὼς ἐγένετο ἐν ταῖς ἡμέραις
And as it was in the days
Νῶε, οὕτως ἔσται καὶ ἐν ταῖς ἡμέραις
of Noah, so it will be also in the days
τοῦ υἱοῦ τοῦ ἀνθρώπου· 27 ἤσθιον, ἔπινον,
of the Son - of man; they were eating, drinking,
ἐγάμουν, ἐγαμίζοντο, ἄχρι ἧς ἡμέρας
marrying, giving in marriage, until which day
= the day when
εἰσῆλθεν Νῶε εἰς τὴν κιβωτόν, καὶ
entered Noah into the ark, and
ἦλθεν ὁ κατακλυσμὸς καὶ ἀπώλεσεν πάντας.
came the flood and destroyed all.
28 ὁμοίως καθὼς ἐγένετο ἐν ταῖς ἡμέραις
Likewise as it was in the days
Λώτ· ἤσθιον, ἔπινον, ἠγόραζον, ἐπώλουν,
of Lot; they were eating, drinking, buying, selling,
ἐφύτευον, ᾠκοδόμουν· 29 ᾗ δὲ ἡμέρᾳ ἐξῆλθεν
planting, building; but on which day went forth
Λὼτ ἀπὸ Σοδόμων, ἔβρεξεν πῦρ καὶ
Lot from Sodom, it rained fire and
θεῖον ἀπ' οὐρανοῦ καὶ ἀπώλεσεν πάντας.
brimstone from heaven and destroyed all.
30 κατὰ τὰ αὐτὰ ἔσται ᾗ ἡμέρᾳ ὁ υἱὸς
According to the same things it will be in which day the Son
= In the same way = on the day when
τοῦ ἀνθρώπου ἀποκαλύπτεται. 31 ἐν ἐκείνῃ
- of man is revealed. In that
τῇ ἡμέρᾳ ὃς ἔσται ἐπὶ τοῦ δώματος καὶ
- day who will be on the roof and
τὰ σκεύη αὐτοῦ ἐν τῇ οἰκίᾳ, μὴ καταβάτω
the goods of him in the house, let him not come down
ἆραι αὐτά, καὶ ὁ ἐν ἀγρῷ ὁμοίως μὴ
to take them, and the [one] in a field likewise not
ἐπιστρεψάτω εἰς τὰ ὀπίσω. 32 μνημονεύετε
let him turn back to the things behind. Remember
τῆς γυναικὸς Λώτ. 33 ὃς ἐὰν ζητήσῃ
the wife of Lot. Whoever seeks
τὴν ψυχὴν αὐτοῦ περιποιήσασθαι, ἀπολέσει
the life of him to preserve, he will lose
αὐτήν, καὶ ὃς ἂν ἀπολέσει, ζῳογονήσει
it, and whoever will lose, will preserve
αὐτήν. 34 λέγω ὑμῖν, ταύτῃ τῇ νυκτὶ
it. I tell you, in this - night
ἔσονται δύο ἐπὶ κλίνης μιᾶς, ὁ εἷς
there will be two men on couch one, the one
παραλημφθήσεται καὶ ὁ ἕτερος ἀφεθήσεται·
will be taken and the other will be left;

---

ciples, "The time is coming when you will long to see one of the days of the Son of Man, but you will not see it. 23 Men will tell you, 'There he is!' or 'Here he is!' Do not go running off after them. 24 For the Son of Man in his day *a* will be like the lightning, which flashes and lights up the sky from one end to the other. 25 But first he must suffer many things and be rejected by this generation.
26 "Just as it was in the days of Noah, so also will it be in the days of the Son of Man. 27 People were eating, drinking, marrying and being given in marriage up to the day Noah entered the ark. Then the flood came and destroyed them all.
28 "It was the same in the days of Lot. People were eating and drinking, buying and selling, planting and building. 29 But the day Lot left Sodom, fire and sulfur rained down from heaven and destroyed them all.
30 "It will be just like this on the day the Son of Man is revealed. 31 On that day no one who is on the roof of his house, with his goods inside, should go down to get them. Likewise, no one in the field should go back for anything. 32 Remember Lot's wife! 33 Whoever tries to keep his life will lose it, and whoever loses his life will preserve it. 34 I tell you, on that night two people will be in one bed; one will be taken and the other left.

e Other ancient authorities lack *in his day*

*a*24 Some manuscripts do not have *in his day*.

35 There will be two women grinding meal together; one will be taken and the other left."*f* 37 Then they asked him, "Where, Lord?" He said to them, "Where the corpse is, there the vultures will gather."

35 ἔσονται δύο ἀλήθουσαι ἐπὶ τὸ αὐτό, ἡ
there will be two women grinding together,† the

μία παραλημφθήσεται ἡ δὲ ἑτέρα ἀφεθήσεται.‡
one will be taken but the other will be left.

37 καὶ ἀποκριθέντες λέγουσιν αὐτῷ· ποῦ,
And answering they say to him: Where,

κύριε; ὁ δὲ εἶπεν αὐτοῖς· ὅπου τὸ σῶμα,
Lord? And he said to them: Where the body,

ἐκεῖ καὶ οἱ ἀετοὶ ἐπισυναχθήσονται.
there also the eagles will be gathered together.

35 Two women will be grinding grain together; one will be taken and the other left.*r*"
37 "Where, Lord?" they asked.
He replied, "Where there is a dead body, there the vultures will gather."

Chapter 18

The Parable of the Widow and the Unjust Judge

THEN Jesus*g* told them a parable about their need to pray always and not to lose heart. 2 He said, "In a certain city there was a judge who neither feared God nor had respect for people. 3 In that city there was a widow who kept coming to him and saying, 'Grant me justice against my opponent.' 4 For a while he refused; but later he said to himself, 'Though I have no fear of God and no respect for anyone, 5 yet because this widow keeps bothering me, I will grant her justice, so that she may not wear me out by continually coming.' "*h* 6 And the Lord said, "Listen to what the unjust judge says. 7 And will not God grant justice to his chosen ones who cry to him day and night? Will he delay long in helping them? 8 I tell you, he will quickly grant justice to them. And yet, when the Son of Man comes, will he find faith on earth?"

The Parable of the Pharisee and the Tax Collector

9 He also told this parable to some who trusted in themselves that they were righteous and regarded others with contempt: 10 "Two

18 Ἔλεγεν δὲ παραβολὴν αὐτοῖς πρὸς
And he told *a parable* *1* them to
=that

τὸ δεῖν πάντοτε προσεύχεσθαι αὐτοὺς καὶ
the *1* to behove *always* *4* to pray *them* and
they must always pray and not faint,

μὴ ἐγκακεῖν, **2** λέγων· κριτής τις ἦν ἐν
not to faint, saying: *1* judge *a* certain *1* There *4* in
was

τινι πόλει τὸν θεὸν μὴ φοβούμενος καὶ
a certain *city* — *2* God *1* not *3* fearing and

ἄνθρωπον μὴ ἐντρεπόμενος. **3** χήρα δὲ ἦν
2 man *1* not *2* regarding. And *a* widow *1* there was

ἐν τῇ πόλει ἐκείνῃ, καὶ ἤρχετο πρὸς
in — city that, and she came to

αὐτὸν λέγουσα· ἐκδίκησόν με ἀπὸ τοῦ
him saying: Vindicate me from the

ἀντιδίκου μου. **4** καὶ οὐκ ἤθελεν ἐπὶ
opponent of me. And he would not for

χρόνον· μετὰ ταῦτα δὲ εἶπεν ἐν ἑαυτῷ·
a time; but after these things he said in himself:

εἰ καὶ τὸν θεὸν οὐ φοβοῦμαι οὐδὲ ἄνθρωπον
If indeed — God I fear not nor man

ἐντρέπομαι, **5** διά γε τὸ παρέχειν
regard, at least because of — to cause
=because this widow causes me trouble

μοι κόπον τὴν χήραν ταύτην ἐκδικήσω αὐτήν,
me trouble this widow this I will vindicate her,

ἵνα μὴ εἰς τέλος ἐρχομένη ὑπωπιάζῃ με.
lest in [the] end coming she exhausts me.

6 Εἶπεν δὲ ὁ κύριος· ἀκούσατε τί ὁ κριτὴς
And said the Lord: Hear ye what the judge

τῆς ἀδικίας λέγει· **7** ὁ δὲ θεὸς οὐ μὴ
— of unrighteousness says: — and God by no means

ποιήσῃ τὴν ἐκδίκησιν τῶν ἐκλεκτῶν
will he make the vindication of the chosen [ones]

αὐτοῦ τῶν βοώντων αὐτῷ ἡμέρας καὶ
of him — crying to him day and

νυκτός, καὶ μακροθυμεῖ ἐπ᾽ αὐτοῖς; **8** λέγω
night, and be patient over them? I tell

ὑμῖν ὅτι ποιήσει τὴν ἐκδίκησιν αὐτῶν
you that he will make the vindication of them

ἐν τάχει. πλὴν ὁ υἱὸς τοῦ ἀνθρώπου ἐλθὼν
quickly. Nevertheless the Son — of man coming

ἆρα εὑρήσει τὴν πίστιν ἐπὶ τῆς γῆς;
then will he find the faith on the earth?

9 Εἶπεν δὲ καὶ πρός τινας τοὺς
And he said also to some the [ones]

πεποιθότας ἐφ᾽ ἑαυτοῖς ὅτι εἰσὶν
relying on themselves that they are

δίκαιοι καὶ ἐξουθενοῦντας τοὺς λοιποὺς
righteous and despising the rest

τὴν παραβολὴν ταύτην. **10** Ἄνθρωποι δύο
— parable this. Men two

Chapter 18

The Parable of the Persistent Widow

THEN Jesus told his disciples a parable to show them that they should always pray and not give up. 2 He said: "In a certain town there was a judge who neither feared God nor cared about men. 3 And there was a widow in that town who kept coming to him with the plea, 'Grant me justice against my adversary.'

4 "For some time he refused. But finally he said to himself, 'Even though I don't fear God or care about men, 5 yet because this widow keeps bothering me, I will see that she gets justice, so that she won't eventually wear me out with her coming!' "

6 And the Lord said, "Listen to what the unjust judge says. 7 And will not God bring about justice for his chosen ones, who cry out to him day and night? Will he keep putting them off? 8 I tell you, he will see that they get justice, and quickly. However, when the Son of Man comes, will he find faith on the earth?"

The Parable of the Pharisee and the Tax Collector

9 To some who were confident of their own righteousness and looked down on everybody else, Jesus told this parable: 10 "Two

---

f Other ancient authorities add verse 36, *"Two will be in the field; one will be taken and the other left."*
g Gk he
h Or so that she may not finally come and slap me in the face

‡ Verse 36 omitted by Nestle; *cf.* NIV footnote.

r 35 Some manuscripts *left.* 36 Two *men will be in the field; one will be taken and the other left.*

men went up to the temple to pray, one a Pharisee and the other a tax collector. 11 The Pharisee, standing by himself, was praying thus, 'God, I thank you that I am not like other people: thieves, rogues, adulterers, or even like this tax collector. 12 I fast twice a week; I give a tenth of all my income.' 13 But the tax collector, standing far off, would not even look up to heaven, but was beating his breast and saying, 'God, be merciful to me, a sinner!' 14 I tell you, this man went down to his home justified rather than the other; for all who exalt themselves will be humbled, but all who humble themselves will be exalted."

Jesus Blesses Little Children

15 People were bringing even infants to him that he might touch them; and when the disciples saw it, they sternly ordered them not to do it. 16 But Jesus called for them and said, "Let the little children come to me, and do not stop them; for it is to such as these that the kingdom of God belongs. 17 Truly I tell you, whoever does not receive the kingdom of God as a little child will never enter it."

The Rich Ruler

18 A certain ruler asked him, "Good Teacher, what must I do to inherit eternal life?" 19 Jesus said to him, "Why do you call me good? No one is good but God alone. 20 You know the commandments: 'You shall not commit adultery; You shall not murder; You shall not steal; You shall not bear false witness; Honor

---

ἀνέβησαν εἰς τὸ ἱερὸν προσεύξασθαι, ὁ εἷς
went up to the temple to pray, the one

Φαρισαῖος καὶ ὁ ἕτερος τελώνης. 11 ὁ
a Pharisee and the other a tax-collector. The

Φαρισαῖος σταθεὶς ταῦτα πρὸς ἑαυτὸν
Pharisee standing these things to himself

προσηύχετο· ὁ θεός, εὐχαριστῶ σοι ὅτι
prayed : - God, I thank thee that

οὐκ εἰμὶ ὥσπερ οἱ λοιποὶ τῶν ἀνθρώπων,
I am not as the rest - of men,

ἅρπαγες, ἄδικοι, μοιχοί, ἢ καὶ ὡς οὗτος
rapacious, unjust, adulterers, or even as this

ὁ τελώνης· 12 νηστεύω δὶς τοῦ σαββάτου,
- tax-collector; I fast twice of(in) the week,

ἀποδεκατεύω πάντα ὅσα κτῶμαι. 13 ὁ δὲ
I tithe all things how many I get. But the

τελώνης μακρόθεν ἑστὼς οὐκ ἤθελεν οὐδὲ
tax-collector far off standing would not not even

τοὺς ὀφθαλμοὺς ἐπᾶραι εἰς τὸν οὐρανόν,
the(his) eyes to lift up to - heaven,

ἀλλ' ἔτυπτεν τὸ στῆθος αὐτοῦ λέγων· ὁ
but smote the breast of him saying : -

θεός, ἱλάσθητί μοι τῷ ἁμαρτωλῷ. 14 λέγω
God, be propitious to me the sinner. I tell

ὑμῖν, κατέβη οὗτος δεδικαιωμένος εἰς τὸν
you, went down this man having been justified to the

οἶκον αὐτοῦ παρ' ἐκεῖνον· ὅτι πᾶς ὁ
house of him [rather] than that one; because everyone

ὑψῶν ἑαυτὸν ταπεινωθήσεται, ὁ δὲ ταπεινῶν
exalting himself will be humbled, and the [one] humbling

ἑαυτὸν ὑψωθήσεται.
himself will be exalted.

15 Προσέφερον δὲ αὐτῷ καὶ τὰ βρέφη
And they brought to him also the babes

ἵνα αὐτῶν ἅπτηται· ἰδόντες δὲ οἱ μαθηταὶ
that them he might touch; but ²seeing ¹the ³disciples

ἐπετίμων αὐτοῖς. 16 ὁ δὲ Ἰησοῦς
rebuked them. - But Jesus

προσεκαλέσατο αὐτὰ λέγων· ἄφετε τὰ
called to [him] them* saying : Allow the

παιδία ἔρχεσθαι πρός με καὶ μὴ κωλύετε
children to come to me and do not prevent

αὐτά· τῶν γὰρ τοιούτων ἐστὶν ἡ βασιλεία
them; - for of such is the kingdom

τοῦ θεοῦ. 17 ἀμὴν λέγω ὑμῖν, ὃς ἂν
- of God. Truly I tell you, whoever

μὴ δέξηται τὴν βασιλείαν τοῦ θεοῦ ὡς
does not receive the kingdom - of God as

παιδίον, οὐ μὴ εἰσέλθῃ εἰς αὐτήν.
a child, by no means enters into it.

18 Καὶ ἐπηρώτησέν τις αὐτὸν ἄρχων
And ²questioned ¹a certain ⁴him ³ruler

λέγων· διδάσκαλε ἀγαθέ, τί ποιήσας ζωὴν
saying : Teacher good, what doing life

αἰώνιον κληρονομήσω; 19 εἶπεν δὲ αὐτῷ
eternal may I inherit? And said to him

ὁ Ἰησοῦς· τί με λέγεις ἀγαθόν; οὐδεὶς
- Jesus : Why me sayest thou good? no one

ἀγαθὸς εἰ μὴ εἷς [ὁ] θεός. 20 τὰς ἐντολὰς
[is] good except one[,] - God. The commandments

οἶδας· μὴ μοιχεύσῃς, μὴ φονεύσῃς,
thou knowest : Do not commit adultery, Do not kill,

μὴ κλέψῃς, μὴ ψευδομαρτυρήσῃς, τίμα
Do not steal, Do not bear false witness, Honour

---

men went up to the temple to pray, one a Pharisee and the other a tax collector. 11 The Pharisee stood up and prayed about⁵ himself: 'God, I thank you that I am not like other men—robbers, evildoers, adulterers—or even like this tax collector. 12 I fast twice a week and give a tenth of all I get.' 13 "But the tax collector stood at a distance. He would not even look up to heaven, but beat his breast and said, 'God, have mercy on me, a sinner.' 14 "I tell you that this man, rather than the other, went home justified before God. For everyone who exalts himself will be humbled, and he who humbles himself will be exalted."

The Little Children and Jesus

15 People were also bringing babies to Jesus to have him touch them. When the disciples saw this, they rebuked them. 16 But Jesus called the children to him and said, "Let the little children come to me, and do not hinder them, for the kingdom of God belongs to such as these. 17 I tell you the truth, anyone who will not receive the kingdom of God like a little child will never enter it."

The Rich Ruler

18 A certain ruler asked him, "Good teacher, what must I do to inherit eternal life?" 19 "Why do you call me good?" Jesus answered. "No one is good—except God alone. 20 You know the commandments: 'Do not commit adultery, do not murder, do not steal, do not give false testimony, honor

---

* That is, "the babes" (τὰ βρέφη in ver. 15).

LUKE 18

your father and mother.' " 21 He replied, "I have kept all these since my youth." 22 When Jesus heard this, he said to him, "There is still one thing lacking. Sell all that you own and distribute the money[i] to the poor, and you will have treasure in heaven; then come, follow me." 23 But when he heard this, he became sad; for he was very rich. 24 Jesus looked at him and said, "How hard it is for those who have wealth to enter the kingdom of God! 25 Indeed, it is easier for a camel to go through the eye of a needle than for someone who is rich to enter the kingdom of God." 26 Those who heard it said, "Then who can be saved?" 27 He replied, "What is impossible for mortals is possible for God."

28 Then Peter said, "Look, we have left our homes and followed you." 29 And he said to them, "Truly I tell you, there is no one who has left house or wife or brothers or parents or children, for the sake of the kingdom of God, 30 who will not get back very much more in this age, and in the age to come eternal life."

A Third Time Jesus Foretells His Death and Resurrection

31 Then he took the twelve aside and said to them, "See, we are going up to Jerusalem, and everything that is written about the Son of Man by the prophets will be accomplished. 32 For he will be handed over to the Gentiles; and he will be mocked and insulted and spat upon. 33 After they have flogged him, they will kill him, and on the third day he will rise

τὸν πατέρα σου καὶ τὴν μητέρα. 21 ὁ δὲ
the father of thee and the mother. And he
εἶπεν· ταῦτα πάντα ἐφύλαξα ἐκ νεότητος.
said: All these things I kept from youth.
22 ἀκούσας δὲ ὁ Ἰησοῦς εἶπεν αὐτῷ· ἔτι
But hearing – Jesus said to him: Yet
ἕν σοι λείπει· πάντα ὅσα ἔχεις
one thing to thee is lacking; all things how many thou hast
πώλησον καὶ διάδος πτωχοῖς, καὶ ἕξεις
sell and distribute to poor people, and thou wilt have
θησαυρὸν ἐν [τοῖς] οὐρανοῖς, καὶ δεῦρο
treasure in – heavens, and come
ἀκολούθει μοι. 23 ὁ δὲ ἀκούσας ταῦτα
follow me. But he hearing these things
περίλυπος ἐγενήθη, ἦν γὰρ πλούσιος σφόδρα.
very grieved became, for he was rich exceedingly.
24 ἰδὼν δὲ αὐτὸν ὁ Ἰησοῦς εἶπεν· πῶς
And seeing him – Jesus said: How
δυσκόλως οἱ τὰ χρήματα ἔχοντες εἰς τὴν
hardly ¹the [ones] – ²property ³having into the
βασιλείαν τοῦ θεοῦ εἰσπορεύονται· 25 εὐκο-
kingdom – of God go in; ²easi-
πώτερον γάρ ἐστιν κάμηλον διὰ τρήματος
er ¹for it is [for] a camel through [the] eye
βελόνης εἰσελθεῖν ἢ πλούσιον εἰς τὴν
of a needle to enter than a rich man into the
βασιλείαν τοῦ θεοῦ εἰσελθεῖν. 26 εἶπαν
kingdom – of God to enter. said
δὲ οἱ ἀκούσαντες· καὶ τίς δύναται
And the [ones] hearing: And who can
σωθῆναι; 27 ὁ δὲ εἶπεν· τὰ ἀδύνατα παρὰ
to be saved? And he said: The things impossible with
ἀνθρώποις δυνατὰ παρὰ τῷ θεῷ ἐστιν.
men possible with – God is(are).
28 Εἶπεν δὲ ὁ Πέτρος· ἰδοὺ ἡμεῖς ἀφέντες
And said – Peter: Behold[,] we leaving
τὰ ἴδια ἠκολουθήσαμέν σοι. 29 ὁ δὲ
our own things followed thee. And he
εἶπεν αὐτοῖς· ἀμὴν λέγω ὑμῖν ὅτι οὐδείς
said to them: Truly I tell you that no one
ἐστιν ὃς ἀφῆκεν οἰκίαν ἢ γυναῖκα ἢ
there is who left house or wife or
ἀδελφοὺς ἢ γονεῖς ἢ τέκνα εἵνεκεν τῆς
brothers or parents or children for the sake of the
βασιλείας τοῦ θεοῦ, 30 ὃς οὐχὶ μὴ λάβῃ
kingdom – of God, who by no means receives
πολλαπλασίονα ἐν τῷ καιρῷ τούτῳ καὶ ἐν
many times over in – time this and in
τῷ αἰῶνι τῷ ἐρχομένῳ ζωὴν αἰώνιον.
the age – coming life eternal.
31 Παραλαβὼν δὲ τοὺς δώδεκα εἶπεν πρὸς
And taking – the twelve he said to
αὐτούς· ἰδοὺ ἀναβαίνομεν εἰς Ἰερουσαλήμ,
them: Behold we are going up to Jerusalem,
καὶ τελεσθήσεται πάντα τὰ γεγραμ-
and will be accomplished all things – having been
μένα διὰ τῶν προφητῶν τῷ υἱῷ τοῦ
written through the prophets to the Son
ἀνθρώπου· 32 παραδοθήσεται γὰρ τοῖς ἔθνεσιν
of man; for he will be delivered to the nations
καὶ ἐμπαιχθήσεται καὶ ὑβρισθήσεται καὶ
and will be mocked and will be insulted and
ἐμπτυσθήσεται, 33 καὶ μαστιγώσαντες
will be spit at, and having scourged
ἀποκτενοῦσιν αὐτόν, καὶ τῇ ἡμέρᾳ τῇ
they will kill him, and on the day –

your father and mother.'[i] " 21 "All these I have kept since I was a boy," he said. 22 When Jesus heard this, he said to him, "You still lack one thing. Sell everything you have and give to the poor, and you will have treasure in heaven. Then come, follow me." 23 When he heard this, he became very sad, because he was a man of great wealth. 24 Jesus looked at him and said, "How hard it is for the rich to enter the kingdom of God! 25 Indeed, it is easier for a camel to go through the eye of a needle than for a rich man to enter the kingdom of God." 26 Those who heard this asked, "Who then can be saved?" 27 Jesus replied, "What is impossible with men is possible with God." 28 Peter said to him, "We have left all we had to follow you!" 29 "I tell you the truth," Jesus said to them, "no one who has left home or wife or brothers or parents or children for the sake of the kingdom of God 30 will fail to receive many times as much in this age and, in the age to come, eternal life."

Jesus Again Predicts His Death

31 Jesus took the Twelve aside and told them, "We are going up to Jerusalem, and everything that is written by the prophets about the Son of Man will be fulfilled. 32 He will be handed over to the Gentiles. They will mock him, insult him, spit on him, flog him and

[i]Gk lacks the money   [i]20 Exodus 20:12-16; Deut. 5:16-20

again." 34 But they understood nothing about all these things; in fact, what he said was hidden from them, and they did not grasp what was said.

Jesus Heals a Blind Beggar Near Jericho

35 As he approached Jericho, a blind man was sitting by the roadside begging. 36 When he heard a crowd going by, he heard what was happening. 37 They told him, "Jesus of Nazareth[j] is passing by." 38 Then he shouted, "Jesus, Son of David, have mercy on me!" 39 Those who were in front sternly ordered him to be quiet; but he shouted even more loudly, "Son of David, have mercy on me!" 40 Jesus stood still and ordered the man to be brought to him; and when he came near, he asked him, 41 "What do you want me to do for you?" He said, "Lord, let me see again." 42 Jesus said to him, "Receive your sight; your faith has saved you." 43 Immediately he regained his sight and followed him, glorifying God; and all the people, when they saw it, praised God.

τρίτῃ ἀναστήσεται. **34** καὶ αὐτοὶ οὐδὲν
third he will rise again.   And they none

τούτων συνῆκαν, καὶ ἦν τὸ ῥῆμα τοῦτο
of these things understood, and was - the ²utterance ¹this

κεκρυμμένον ἀπ' αὐτῶν, καὶ οὐκ ἐγίνωσκον
⁴having been hidden from them, and they knew not

τὰ λεγόμενα.
the things being said.

35 Ἐγένετο δὲ ἐν τῷ ἐγγίζειν αὐτὸν εἰς
And it came to pass in the to draw near him ᵇᵉ to
=as he drew near

Ἰεριχὼ τυφλός τις ἐκάθητο παρὰ τὴν ὁδὸν
Jericho a certain blind man sat by the way

ἐπαιτῶν. **36** ἀκούσας δὲ ὄχλου διαπορευομένου
begging. And hearing a crowd passing through

ἐπυνθάνετο τί εἴη τοῦτο. **37** ἀπήγγειλαν
he inquired what ²might be ¹this.   And they re-

δὲ αὐτῷ ὅτι Ἰησοῦς ὁ Ναζωραῖος
ported to him[,] - Jesus the Nazarene

παρέρχεται. **38** καὶ ἐβόησεν λέγων· Ἰησοῦ
is passing by. And he cried saying: Jesus

υἱὲ Δαυίδ, ἐλέησόν με. **39** καὶ οἱ
son of David, pity me.   And the [ones]

προάγοντες ἐπετίμων αὐτῷ ἵνα σιγήσῃ·
going before rebuked him that he should be quiet;

αὐτὸς δὲ πολλῷ μᾶλλον ἔκραζεν· υἱὲ
but he by much more cried out : Son

Δαυίδ, ἐλέησόν με. **40** σταθεὶς δὲ ὁ
of David, pity me.   And standing -

Ἰησοῦς ἐκέλευσεν αὐτὸν ἀχθῆναι πρὸς
Jesus commanded him to be brought to

αὐτόν. ἐγγίσαντος δὲ αὐτοῦ ἐπηρώτησεν
him. And drawing near   himᵃ he questioned
=as he drew near

αὐτόν· **41** τί σοι θέλεις ποιήσω; ὁ δὲ
him : What for thee wishest thou I may do? And he

εἶπεν· κύριε, ἵνα ἀναβλέψω. **42** καὶ ὁ Ἰησοῦς
said : Lord, that I may see again. And - Jesus

εἶπεν αὐτῷ· ἀνάβλεψον· ἡ πίστις σου
said to him : See again; the faith of thee

σέσωκέν σε. **43** καὶ παραχρῆμα ἀνέβλεψεν,
has healed thee. And at once he saw again,

καὶ ἠκολούθει αὐτῷ δοξάζων τὸν θεόν.
and followed him glorifying - God.

καὶ πᾶς ὁ λαὸς ἰδὼν ἔδωκεν αἶνον τῷ
And all the people seeing gave praise -

θεῷ.
to God.

---

kill him. 33 On the third day he will rise again."

34 The disciples did not understand any of this. Its meaning was hidden from them, and they did not know what he was talking about.

A Blind Beggar Receives His Sight

35 As Jesus approached Jericho, a blind man was sitting by the roadside begging. 36 When he heard the crowd going by, he asked what was happening. 37 They told him, "Jesus of Nazareth is passing by." 38 He called out, "Jesus, Son of David, have mercy on me!" 39 Those who led the way rebuked him and told him to be quiet, but he shouted all the more, "Son of David, have mercy on me!" 40 Jesus stopped and ordered the man to be brought to him. When he came near, Jesus asked him, 41 "What do you want me to do for you?"

"Lord, I want to see," he replied.

42 Jesus said to him, "Receive your sight; your faith has healed you." 43 Immediately he received his sight and followed Jesus, praising God. When all the people saw it, they also praised God.

Chapter 19

Jesus and Zacchaeus

HE entered Jericho and was passing through it. 2 A man was there named Zacchaeus; he was a chief tax collector and was rich. 3 He was trying to see who Jesus was, but on account of the crowd he could not, because he was short in stature. 4 So he ran ahead and climbed a sycamore tree to see him, because he was going to pass that way.

---

19 Καὶ εἰσελθὼν διήρχετο τὴν Ἰεριχώ.
And having entered he passed through - Jericho.

2 Καὶ ἰδοὺ ἀνὴρ ὀνόματι καλούμενος
And behold[,] a man by name being called

Ζακχαῖος, καὶ αὐτὸς ἦν ἀρχιτελώνης, καὶ
Zacchæus, and he was a chief tax-collector, and

αὐτὸς πλούσιος· **3** καὶ ἐζήτει ἰδεῖν τὸν
he [was] rich;   and he sought to see -

Ἰησοῦν τίς ἐστιν, καὶ οὐκ ἠδύνατο ἀπὸ
Jesus who he is(was), and was not able from

τοῦ ὄχλου, ὅτι τῇ ἡλικίᾳ μικρὸς ἦν.
the crowd, because - ²in stature ¹little ¹he was.

4 καὶ προδραμὼν εἰς τὸ ἔμπροσθεν ἀνέβη
And having run forward to the front he went up

ἐπὶ συκομορέαν, ἵνα ἴδῃ αὐτόν, ὅτι
onto a sycamore-tree, that he might see him, because

ἐκείνης ἤμελλεν διέρχεσθαι. **5** καὶ ὡς
³that [way] ¹he was about ²to pass along.   And as

Chapter 19

Zacchaeus the Tax Collector

JESUS entered Jericho and was passing through. 2 A man was there by the name of Zacchaeus; he was a chief tax collector and was wealthy. 3 He wanted to see who Jesus was, but being a short man he could not, because of the crowd. 4 So he ran ahead and climbed a sycamore-fig tree to see him, since Jesus was coming that way.

ʲ Gk the Nazorean

5 When Jesus came to the place, he looked up and said to him, "Zacchaeus, hurry and come down; for I must stay at your house today." 6 So he hurried down and was happy to welcome him. 7 All who saw it began to grumble and said, "He has gone to be the guest of one who is a sinner." 8 Zacchaeus stood there and said to the Lord, "Look, half of my possessions, Lord, I will give to the poor; and if I have defrauded anyone of anything, I will pay back four times as much." 9 Then Jesus said to him, "Today salvation has come to this house, because he too is a son of Abraham. 10 For the Son of Man came to seek out and to save the lost."

The Parable of the Ten Pounds

11 As they were listening to this, he went on to tell a parable, because he was near Jerusalem, and because they supposed that the kingdom of God was to appear immediately. 12 So he said, "A nobleman went to a distant country to get royal power for himself and then return. 13 He summoned ten of his slaves, and gave them ten pounds,^{k} and said to them, 'Do business with these until I come back.' 14 But the citizens of his country hated him and sent a delegation after him, saying, 'We do not want this man to rule over us.' 15 When he returned, having received

ἦλθεν ἐπὶ τὸν τόπον, ἀναβλέψας ὁ Ἰησοῦς
he came upon the place, looking up – Jesus
εἶπεν πρὸς αὐτόν· Ζακχαῖε, σπεύσας
said to him: Zacchæus, making haste
κατάβηθι· σήμερον γὰρ ἐν τῷ οἴκῳ σου
come down; for to-day in the house of thee
δεῖ με μεῖναι. 6 καὶ σπεύσας κατέβη,
it behoves me to remain. And making haste he came down,
καὶ ὑπεδέξατο αὐτὸν χαίρων. 7 καὶ
and welcomed him rejoicing. And
ἰδόντες πάντες διεγόγγυζον λέγοντες ὅτι
seeing all murmured saying[,] that
παρὰ ἁμαρτωλῷ ἀνδρὶ εἰσῆλθεν καταλῦσαι.
With a sinful man he entered to lodge.
8 σταθεὶς δὲ Ζακχαῖος εἶπεν πρὸς τὸν
And standing Zacchæus said to the
κύριον· ἰδοὺ τὰ ἡμίση μου τῶν ὑπαρχόντων,
Lord: Behold[,] the half of me of the possessions,
κύριε, τοῖς πτωχοῖς δίδωμι, καὶ εἴ τινός
Lord, to the poor I give, and if anyone
τι ἐσυκοφάντησα, ἀποδίδωμι τετραπλοῦν.
anything I accused falsely, I restore fourfold.
9 εἶπεν δὲ πρὸς αὐτὸν ὁ Ἰησοῦς ὅτι
And said to him – Jesus[,] that
σήμερον σωτηρία τῷ οἴκῳ τούτῳ ἐγένετο,
To-day salvation – house to this came,
καθότι καὶ αὐτὸς υἱὸς Ἀβραάμ [ἐστιν]·
because even he a son of Abraham is;
10 ἦλθεν γὰρ ὁ υἱὸς τοῦ ἀνθρώπου ζητῆσαι
for came the Son – of man to seek
καὶ σῶσαι τὸ ἀπολωλός.
and to save the thing having been lost.
11 Ἀκουόντων δὲ αὐτῶν ταῦτα προσθεὶς
And hearing them^a these things adding
=as they heard
εἶπεν παραβολήν, διὰ τὸ ἐγγὺς εἶναι
he told a parable, because of the near to be
=because he was near to Jerusalem and they thought
Ἰερουσαλὴμ αὐτὸν καὶ δοκεῖν αὐτοὺς ὅτι
Jerusalem him and to think them^b that
παραχρῆμα μέλλει ἡ βασιλεία τοῦ θεοῦ
at once is(was) about the kingdom – of God
ἀναφαίνεσθαι· 12 εἶπεν οὖν· ἄνθρωπός τις
to appear; he said therefore: A certain man
εὐγενὴς ἐπορεύθη εἰς χώραν μακρὰν λαβεῖν
well born went to country a far to receive
ἑαυτῷ βασιλείαν καὶ ὑποστρέψαι. 13 καλέσας
for himself a kingdom and to return. having called
δὲ δέκα δούλους ἑαυτοῦ ἔδωκεν αὐτοῖς
And ten slaves of himself he gave them
δέκα μνᾶς, καὶ εἶπεν πρὸς αὐτούς·
ten minas, and said to them:
πραγματεύσασθε ἐν ᾧ ἔρχομαι. 14 οἱ δὲ
Trade ye while I am coming.* But the
πολῖται αὐτοῦ ἐμίσουν αὐτόν, καὶ ἀπέστειλαν
citizens of him hated him, and sent
πρεσβείαν ὀπίσω αὐτοῦ λέγοντες· οὐ θέλομεν
a delegation after him saying: We do not wish
τοῦτον βασιλεῦσαι ἐφ’ ἡμᾶς. 15 καὶ
this man to reign over us. And
ἐγένετο ἐν τῷ ἐπανελθεῖν αὐτὸν λυβόντα
it came to pass in the to return him^{be} having received
=when he returned

5 When Jesus reached the spot, he looked up and said to him, "Zacchaeus, come down immediately. I must stay at your house today." 6 So he came down at once and welcomed him gladly. 7 All the people saw this and began to mutter, "He has gone to be the guest of a 'sinner.'" 8 But Zacchaeus stood up and said to the Lord, "Look, Lord! Here and now I give half of my possessions to the poor, and if I have cheated anybody out of anything, I will pay back four times the amount." 9 Jesus said to him, "To-day salvation has come to this house, because this man, too, is a son of Abraham. 10 For the Son of Man came to seek and to save what was lost."

The Parable of the Ten Minas

11 While they were listening to this, he went on to tell them a parable, because he was near Jerusalem and the people thought that the kingdom of God was going to appear at once. 12 He said: "A man of noble birth went to a distant country to have himself appointed king and then to return. 13 So he called ten of his servants and gave them ten minas.^{u} 'Put this money to work,' he said, 'until I come back.' 14 "But his subjects hated him and sent a delegation after him to say, 'We don't want this man to be our king.' 15 "He was made king,

---

^{k} The mina, rendered here by *pound*, was about three months' wages for a laborer

* **That is, "again."** The present of this verb often has a futurist significance; *cf.* John 14. 3.

^{u}13 A mina was about three months' wages.

royal power, he ordered these slaves, to whom he had given the money, to be summoned so that he might find out what they had gained by trading. 16 The first came forward and said, 'Lord, your pound has made ten more pounds.' 17 He said to him, 'Well done, good slave! Because you have been trustworthy in a very small thing, take charge of ten cities.' 18 Then the second came, saying, 'Lord, your pound has made five pounds.' 19 He said to him, 'And you, rule over five cities.' 20 Then the other came, saying, 'Lord, here is your pound. I wrapped it up in a piece of cloth, 21 for I was afraid of you, because you are a harsh man; you take what you did not deposit, and reap what you did not sow.' 22 He said to him, 'I will judge you by your own words, you wicked slave! You knew, did you, that I was a harsh man, taking what I did not deposit and reaping what I did not sow? 23 Why then did you not put my money into the bank? Then when I returned, I could have collected it with interest.' 24 He said to the bystanders, 'Take the pound from him and give it to the one who has ten pounds.' 25 (And they said to him, 'Lord, he has ten pounds!') 26 'I tell you, to all those who have, more will be given; but from those who have nothing, even what they have will be taken away. 27 But as for these enemies of mine who did not want me to be king over them—bring them here and slaughter them in my presence.' "

Jesus' Triumphal Entry into Jerusalem

28 After he had said this, he went on ahead, going up to Jerusalem.

τὴν βασιλείαν καὶ εἶπεν φωνηθῆναι αὐτῷ
the kingdom *and* he said to be called to him
τοὺς δούλους τούτους οἷς δεδώκει τὸ
- slaves these to whom he had given the
ἀργύριον, ἵνα γνοῖ τίς τί
money, that he might know ²anyone ¹what
διεπραγματεύσατο. 16 παρεγένετο δὲ ὁ πρῶτος
gained by trading. And came the first
λέγων· κύριε, ἡ μνᾶ σου δέκα προσηργάσατο
saying: Lord, the mina of thee ²ten ¹gained
μνᾶς. 17 καὶ εἶπεν αὐτῷ· εὖ γε, ἀγαθὲ δοῦλε,
²minas. And he said to him: Well, good slave,
ὅτι ἐν ἐλαχίστῳ πιστὸς ἐγένου, ἴσθι
because in a least thing faithful thou wast, be thou
ἐξουσίαν ἔχων ἐπάνω δέκα πόλεων. 18 καὶ
²authority ¹having over ten cities. And
ἦλθεν ὁ δεύτερος λέγων· ἡ μνᾶ σου,
came the second saying: The mina of thee,
κύριε, ἐποίησεν πέντε μνᾶς. 19 εἶπεν δὲ
lord, made five minas. And he said
καὶ τούτῳ· καὶ σὺ ἐπάνω γίνου πέντε
also to this one: And ²thou ²over ¹be five
πόλεων. 20 καὶ ὁ ἕτερος ἦλθεν λέγων·
cities. And the other came saying:
κύριε, ἰδοὺ ἡ μνᾶ σου, ἣν εἶχον
Lord, behold[,] the mina of thee, which I had
ἀποκειμένην ἐν σουδαρίῳ· 21 ἐφοβούμην γάρ
being put away in a napkin; for I feared
σε, ὅτι ἄνθρωπος αὐστηρὸς εἶ, αἴρεις ὃ
thee, because man an exacting thou art, thou takest what
οὐκ ἔθηκας, καὶ θερίζεις ὃ οὐκ ἔσπειρας.
thou didst not lay, and thou reapest what thou didst not sow.
22 λέγει αὐτῷ· ἐκ τοῦ στόματός σου
He says to him: Out of the mouth of thee
κρινῶ σε, πονηρὲ δοῦλε. ᾔδεις ὅτι ἐγὼ
I will judge thee, wicked slave. Knewest thou that I
ἄνθρωπος αὐστηρός εἰμι, αἴρων ὃ οὐκ
man an exacting am, taking what not
ἔθηκα, καὶ θερίζων ὃ οὐκ ἔσπειρα; 23 καὶ
I laid, and reaping what I sowed not? And
διὰ τί οὐκ ἔδωκάς μου τὸ ἀργύριον ἐπὶ
why didst thou not give of me the money on
τράπεζαν; κἀγὼ ἐλθὼν σὺν τόκῳ ἂν
a table?* And I coming with interest
αὐτὸ ἔπραξα. 24 καὶ τοῖς παρεστῶσιν
it would have exacted. And to the [ones] standing by
εἶπεν· ἄρατε ἀπ' αὐτοῦ τὴν μνᾶν καὶ
he said: Take from him the mina and
δότε τῷ τὰς δέκα μνᾶς ἔχοντι. 25 καὶ
give ¹to the [one] ²the ⁴ten ³minas ¹having. And
εἶπαν αὐτῷ· κύριε, ἔχει δέκα μνᾶς.
they said to him: Lord, he has ten minas.
26 λέγω ὑμῖν ὅτι παντὶ τῷ ἔχοντι
I tell you that to everyone having
δοθήσεται, ἀπὸ δὲ τοῦ μὴ ἔχοντος καὶ
it will be given, and from the [one] not having even
ὃ ἔχει ἀρθήσεται. 27 πλὴν τοὺς ἐχθρούς
what he has will be taken. Nevertheless - enemies
μου τούτους τοὺς μὴ θελήσαντάς με
of me these the [ones] not wishing me
βασιλεῦσαι ἐπ' αὐτοὺς ἀγάγετε ὧδε καὶ
to reign over them bring ye here and
κατασφάξατε αὐτοὺς ἔμπροσθέν μου.
slay them before me.
28 Καὶ εἰπὼν ταῦτα ἐπορεύετο ἔμπροσθεν
And having said these things he went in front

however, and returned home. Then he sent for the servants to whom he had given the money, in order to find out what they had gained with it.

16 "The first one came and said, 'Sir, your mina has earned ten more.'

17 " 'Well done, my good servant!' his master replied. 'Because you have been trustworthy in a very small matter, take charge of ten cities.'

18 "The second came and said, 'Sir, your mina has earned five more.'

19 "His master answered, 'You take charge of five cities.'

20 "Then another servant came and said, 'Sir, here is your mina; I have kept it laid away in a piece of cloth. 21 I was afraid of you, because you are a hard man. You take out what you did not put in and reap what you did not sow.'

22 "His master replied, 'I will judge you by your own words, you wicked servant! You knew, did you, that I am a hard man, taking out what I did not put in, and reaping what I did not sow? 23 Why then didn't you put my money on deposit, so that when I came back, I could have collected it with interest?'

24 "Then he said to those standing by, 'Take his mina away from him and give it to the one who has ten minas.'

25 " 'Sir,' they said, 'he already has ten!'

26 "He replied, 'I tell you that to everyone who has, more will be given, but as for the one who has nothing, even what he has will be taken away. 27 But those enemies of mine who did not want me to be king over them—bring them here and kill them in front of me.' "

The Triumphal Entry

28 After Jesus had said this, he went on ahead, go-

---

* That is, a moneychanger's or banker's table.

29 When he had come near Bethphage and Bethany, at the place called the Mount of Olives, he sent two of the disciples, 30 saying, "Go into the village ahead of you, and as you enter it you will find tied there a colt that has never been ridden. Untie it and bring it here. 31 If anyone asks you, 'Why are you untying it?' just say this, 'The Lord needs it.' " 32 So those who were sent departed and found it as he had told them. 33 As they were untying the colt, its owners asked them, "Why are you untying the colt?" 34 They said, "The Lord needs it." 35 Then they brought it to Jesus; and after throwing their cloaks on the colt, they set Jesus on it. 36 As he rode along, people kept spreading their cloaks on the road. 37 As he was now approaching the path down from the Mount of Olives, the whole multitude of the disciples began to praise God joyfully with a loud voice for all the deeds of power that they had seen, 38 saying,

"Blessed is the king
  who comes in the
  name of
  the Lord!
Peace in heaven,
  and glory in the
  highest heaven!"

39 Some of the Pharisees in the crowd said to him, "Teacher, order your disciples to stop." 40 He answered, "I tell you, if these were silent, the stones would shout out."

ἀναβαίνων εἰς Ἱεροσόλυμα. 29 Καὶ ἐγένετο
going up to Jerusalem.   And it came to pass

ὡς ἤγγισεν εἰς Βηθφαγὴ καὶ Βηθανίαν
as he drew near to Bethphage and Bethany

πρὸς τὸ ὄρος τὸ καλούμενον ἐλαιῶν,
toward the mount - being called of olives,

ἀπέστειλεν δύο τῶν μαθητῶν λέγων·
he sent two of the disciples saying :

30 ὑπάγετε εἰς τὴν κατέναντι κώμην, ἐν ᾗ
Go ye into the opposite village, in which

εἰσπορευόμενοι εὑρήσετε πῶλον δεδεμένον,
entering ye will find a colt having been tied,

ἐφ' ὃν οὐδεὶς πώποτε ἀνθρώπων ἐκάθισεν,
on which no one ever yet of men sat,

καὶ λύσαντες αὐτὸν ἀγάγετε. 31 καὶ ἐάν
and loosening it bring. And if

τις ὑμᾶς ἐρωτᾷ· διὰ τί λύετε; οὕτως
anyone you asks : Why loosen ye? thus

ἐρεῖτε· ὅτι ὁ κύριος αὐτοῦ χρείαν ἔχει.
shall ye say : Because the Lord of it need has.

32 ἀπελθόντες δὲ οἱ ἀπεσταλμένοι εὗρον
And going the [ones] having been sent found

καθὼς εἶπεν αὐτοῖς. 33 λυόντων δὲ
as he told them. And loosening
                                =as they were

αὐτῶν τὸν πῶλον εἶπαν οἱ κύριοι αὐτοῦ
them[a] the colt said the owners of it
loosening

πρὸς αὐτούς· τί λύετε τὸν πῶλον; 34 οἱ
to them : Why loosen ye the colt? [b]they

δὲ εἶπαν· ὅτι ὁ κύριος αὐτοῦ χρείαν ἔχει.
[1]And said : Because the Lord of it need has.

35 καὶ ἤγαγον αὐτὸν πρὸς τὸν Ἰησοῦν,
And they led it to - Jesus,

καὶ ἐπιρίψαντες αὐτῶν τὰ ἱμάτια ἐπὶ τὸν
and throwing on of them the garments on the

πῶλον ἐπεβίβασαν τὸν Ἰησοῦν. 36 πορευ-
colt they put on [it] - Jesus. And

ομένου δὲ αὐτοῦ ὑπεστρώννυον τὰ ἱμάτια
going him[a] they strewed the garments
=as he went

ἑαυτῶν ἐν τῇ ὁδῷ. 37 ἐγγίζοντος δὲ
of themselves in the way. And drawing near
                                =as he drew near

αὐτοῦ ἤδη πρὸς τῇ καταβάσει τοῦ ὄρους
him[a] now to the descent of the mount

τῶν ἐλαιῶν ἤρξαντο ἅπαν τὸ πλῆθος τῶν
of the olives began all the multitude of the

μαθητῶν χαίροντες αἰνεῖν τὸν θεὸν φωνῇ
disciples rejoicing to praise - God voice

μεγάλῃ περὶ πασῶν ὧν εἶδον δυνάμεων,
with a about [1]all [a]which [a]they saw [a][the] powerful
great   deeds,

38 λέγοντες· εὐλογημένος ὁ ἐρχόμενος, ὁ
saying : Blessed the coming [one], the

βασιλεὺς ἐν ὀνόματι κυρίου· ἐν οὐρανῷ
king in [the] name of [the] Lord; in heaven

εἰρήνη καὶ δόξα ἐν ὑψίστοις. 39 καὶ
peace and glory in highest places. And

τινες τῶν Φαρισαίων ἀπὸ τοῦ ὄχλου
some of the Pharisees from the crowd

εἶπαν πρὸς αὐτόν· διδάσκαλε, ἐπιτίμησον
said to him : Teacher, rebuke

τοῖς μαθηταῖς σου. 40 καὶ ἀποκριθεὶς
the disciples of thee. And answering

εἶπεν· λέγω ὑμῖν, ἐὰν οὗτοι σιωπήσουσιν,
he said : I tell you, if these shall(should) be silent,

---

ing up to Jerusalem. 29 As he approached Bethphage and Bethany at the hill called the Mount of Olives, he sent two of his disciples, 30 "Go to the village ahead of you, and as you enter it, you will find a colt tied there, which no one has ever ridden. Untie it and bring it here. 31 If anyone asks you, 'Why are you untying it?' tell him, 'The Lord needs it.' "

32 Those who were sent ahead went and found it just as he had told them. 33 As they were untying the colt, its owners asked them, "Why are you untying the colt?"

34 They replied, "The Lord needs it."

35 They brought it to Jesus, threw their cloaks on the colt and put Jesus on it. 36 As he went along, people spread their cloaks on the road.

37 When he came near the place where the road goes down the Mount of Olives, the whole crowd of disciples began joyfully to praise God in loud voices for all the miracles they had seen:

38 "Blessed is the king who comes in the name of the Lord!" [v]

"Peace in heaven and glory in the highest!"

39 Some of the Pharisees in the crowd said to Jesus, "Teacher, rebuke your disciples!"

40 "I tell you," he replied, "if they keep quiet, the

---

[v]38 Psalm 118:26

Jesus Weeps over Jerusalem

41 As he came near and saw the city, he wept over it, 42saying, "If you, even you, had only recognized on this day the things that make for peace! But now they are hidden from your eyes. 43Indeed, the days will come upon you, when your enemies will set up ramparts around you and surround you, and hem you in on every side. 44They will crush you to the ground, you and your children within you, and they will not leave within you one stone upon another; because you did not recognize the time of your visitation from God."[l]

Jesus Cleanses the Temple

45 Then he entered the temple and began to drive out those who were selling things there; 46and he said, "It is written,

'My house shall be a house
  of prayer';

but you have made it a den of robbers."

47 Every day he was teaching in the temple. The chief priests, the scribes, and the leaders of the people kept looking for a way to kill him; 48but they did not find anything they could do, for all the people were spellbound by what they heard.

Chapter 20

The Authority of Jesus Questioned

ONE day, as he was teaching the people in the temple and telling the good news, the chief priests and the scribes came with the elders 2and said to him, "Tell us, by what authority are you doing these things? Who is it who gave you this authority?" 3He answered them, "I will also ask you a question, and you tell me: 4Did the baptism of John come from heaven, or was it of

---

οἱ λίθοι κράξουσιν. 41 Καὶ ὡς ἤγγισεν,
the stones will cry out. And as he drew near,

ἰδὼν τὴν πόλιν ἔκλαυσεν ἐπ' αὐτήν,
seeing the city he wept over it,

42 λέγων ὅτι εἰ ἔγνως ἐν τῇ ἡμέρᾳ
saying[,] - If thou knewest in - day

ταύτῃ καὶ σὺ τὰ πρὸς εἰρήνην· νῦν δὲ
this even thou the things for peace; but now

ἐκρύβη ἀπὸ ὀφθαλμῶν σου. 43 ὅτι ἥξουσιν
they were hidden from eyes of thee. Because will come

ἡμέραι ἐπὶ σὲ καὶ παρεμβαλοῦσιν οἱ
days upon thee and ¹will raise up ¹the

ἐχθροί σου χάρακά σοι καὶ περικυκλώσουσίν
²enemies ³of thee ²a rampart to thee and will surround

σε καὶ συνέξουσίν σε πάντοθεν, 44 καὶ
thee and will press * thee on all sides, and

ἐδαφιοῦσίν σε καὶ τὰ τέκνα σου ἐν σοί,
dash to the ground thee and the children of thee in thee,

καὶ οὐκ ἀφήσουσιν λίθον ἐπὶ λίθον ἐν σοί,
and will not leave stone upon stone in thee,

ἀνθ' ὧν οὐκ ἔγνως τὸν καιρὸν τῆς
because† thou knewest not the time of the

ἐπισκοπῆς σου. 45 Καὶ εἰσελθὼν εἰς τὸ
visitation of thee. And entering into the

ἱερὸν ἤρξατο ἐκβάλλειν τοὺς πωλοῦντας,
temple he began to expel the [ones] selling,

46 λέγων αὐτοῖς· γέγραπται· καὶ ἔσται ὁ
telling them : It has been written : And shall be the

οἶκός μου οἶκος προσευχῆς· ὑμεῖς δὲ
house of me a house of prayer; but ye

αὐτὸν ἐποιήσατε σπήλαιον λῃστῶν.
it made a den of robbers.

47 Καὶ ἦν διδάσκων τὸ καθ' ἡμέραν ἐν
And he was teaching - daily† in

τῷ ἱερῷ· οἱ δὲ ἀρχιερεῖς καὶ οἱ
the temple; but the chief priests and the

γραμματεῖς ἐζήτουν αὐτὸν ἀπολέσαι καὶ οἱ
scribes ⁶sought ⁵him ⁷to destroy ¹and ²the

πρῶτοι τοῦ λαοῦ, 48 καὶ οὐχ εὕρισκον
³chief men ⁴of the ⁵people, and did not find

τὸ τί ποιήσωσιν· ὁ λαὸς γὰρ ἅπας
- what they might do; ⁸the ⁹people ⁷for ⁸all

ἐξεκρέματο αὐτοῦ ἀκούων.
hung upon him hearing.

20 Καὶ ἐγένετο ἐν μιᾷ τῶν ἡμερῶν
And it came to pass on one of the days

διδάσκοντος αὐτοῦ τὸν λαὸν ἐν τῷ ἱερῷ
teaching himª the people in the temple
=as he was teaching

καὶ εὐαγγελιζομένου ἐπέστησαν οἱ ἀρχιερεῖς
and preaching good newsª came upon [him] the chief priests

καὶ οἱ γραμματεῖς σὺν τοῖς πρεσβυτέροις,
and the scribes with the elders,

2 καὶ εἶπαν λέγοντες πρὸς αὐτόν· εἰπὸν
and spoke, saying to him : Tell

ἡμῖν ἐν ποίᾳ ἐξουσίᾳ ταῦτα ποιεῖς, ἢ τίς
us by what authority these things thou doest, or who

ἐστιν ὁ δούς σοι τὴν ἐξουσίαν ταύτην;
is the [one] having given thee - authority this?

3 ἀποκριθεὶς δὲ εἶπεν πρὸς αὐτούς·
And answering he said to them :

ἐρωτήσω ὑμᾶς κἀγὼ λόγον, καὶ εἴπατέ
Will ask you I also a word, and tell ye

μοι· 4 τὸ βάπτισμα Ἰωάννου ἐξ οὐρανοῦ
me : The baptism of John from heaven

---

stones will cry out."

41As he approached Jerusalem and saw the city, he wept over it 42and said, "If you, even you, had only known on this day what would bring you peace—but now it is hidden from your eyes. 43The days will come upon you when your enemies will build an embankment against you and encircle you and hem you in on every side. 44They will dash you to the ground, you and the children within your walls. They will not leave one stone on another, because you did not recognize the time of God's coming to you."

Jesus at the Temple

45Then he entered the temple area and began driving out those who were selling. 46"It is written," he said to them, " 'My house will be a house of prayer'[w]; but you have made it 'a den of robbers.'[x]"

47Every day he was teaching at the temple. But the chief priests, the teachers of the law and the leaders among the people were trying to kill him. 48Yet they could not find any way to do it, because all the people hung on his words.

Chapter 20

The Authority of Jesus Questioned

ONE day as he was teaching the people in the temple courts and preaching the gospel, the chief priests and the teachers of the law, together with the elders, came up to him. 2"Tell us by what authority you are doing these things," they said. "Who gave you this authority?" 3He replied, "I will also ask you a question. Tell me, 4John's baptism—was it from heaven, or from men?"

---

human origin?" 5 They discussed it with one another, saying, "If we say, 'From heaven,' he will say, 'Why did you not believe him?' 6 But if we say, 'Of human origin,' all the people will stone us; for they are convinced that John was a prophet." 7 So they answered that they did not know where it came from. 8 Then Jesus said to them, "Neither will I tell you by what authority I am doing these things."

The Parable of the Wicked Tenants

9 He began to tell the people this parable: "A man planted a vineyard, and leased it to tenants, and went to another country for a long time. 10 When the season came, he sent a slave to the tenants in order that they might give him his share of the produce of the vineyard; but the tenants beat him and sent him away empty-handed. 11 Next he sent another slave; that one also they beat and insulted and sent away empty-handed. 12 And he sent still a third; this one also they wounded and threw out. 13 Then the owner of the vineyard said, 'What shall I do? I will send my beloved son; perhaps they will respect him.' 14 But when the tenants saw him, they discussed it among themselves and said, 'This is the heir; let us kill him so that the inheritance may be ours.' 15 So they threw him out of the vineyard and killed him. What then will the owner of the vineyard do to them? 16 He will come and destroy those tenants and give the vineyard to others." When they heard this, they said, "Heaven

---

ἦν ἢ ἐξ ἀνθρώπων; 5 οἱ δὲ συνελογίσαντο
was it or from   men?   And they   debated

πρὸς ἑαυτοὺς λέγοντες ὅτι ἐὰν εἴπωμεν
with themselves   saying[,]   –   If   we say :

ἐξ οὐρανοῦ, ἐρεῖ· διὰ τί οὐκ ἐπιστεύσατε
From heaven, he will say: Why   did ye not believe

αὐτῷ; 6 ἐὰν δὲ εἴπωμεν· ἐξ ἀνθρώπων, ὁ
him?   And if   we say : From   men,   the

λαὸς ἅπας καταλιθάσει ἡμᾶς· πεπεισμένος
people all   will stone   us; for having been per-

γάρ ἐστιν Ἰωάννην προφήτην εἶναι. 7 καὶ
suaded it is*   John   a prophet   to be.   And

ἀπεκρίθησαν μὴ εἰδέναι πόθεν. 8 καὶ ὁ
they answered not   to know   whence.   And –

Ἰησοῦς εἶπεν αὐτοῖς· οὐδὲ ἐγὼ λέγω
Jesus   said   to them: Neither   I   tell

ὑμῖν ἐν ποίᾳ ἐξουσίᾳ ταῦτα ποιῶ. 9 Ἤρξατο
you by what   authority these things I do.   he began

δὲ πρὸς τὸν λαὸν λέγειν τὴν παραβολὴν
And to   the   people to tell   the   parable

ταύτην. ἄνθρωπος ἐφύτευσεν ἀμπελῶνα,
this.   A man   planted   a vineyard,

καὶ ἐξέδοτο αὐτὸν γεωργοῖς, καὶ ἀπεδή-
and let out   it   to husbandmen, and   went

μησεν χρόνους ἱκανούς. 10 καὶ καιρῷ
away   periods for considerable.   And   in time
         =a long time.

ἀπέστειλεν πρὸς τοὺς γεωργοὺς δοῦλον,
he sent   to   the   husbandmen   a slave,

ἵνα ἀπὸ τοῦ καρποῦ τοῦ ἀμπελῶνος
that from   the   fruit   of the   vineyard

δώσουσιν αὐτῷ· οἱ δὲ γεωργοὶ ἐξαπέστειλαν
they will give him;   but the husbandmen ³sent ⁴away out

αὐτὸν δείραντες κενόν. 11 καὶ προσέθετο
²him   ¹beating   ⁴empty.   And   he added

ἕτερον πέμψαι δοῦλον· οἱ δὲ κἀκεῖνον
²another   ¹to send   slave;   but they   that one also
=he sent another slave in addition;

δείραντες καὶ ἀτιμάσαντες ἐξαπέστειλαν
beating   and   insulting   sent away out

κενόν. 12 καὶ προσέθετο τρίτον πέμψαι·
empty.   And   he added   a third   to send;

οἱ δὲ καὶ τοῦτον τραυματίσαντες ἐξέβαλον.
but they also   this one   wounding   threw out.

13 εἶπεν δὲ ὁ κύριος τοῦ ἀμπελῶνος· τί
And said   the   owner   of the   vineyard : What

ποιήσω; πέμψω τὸν υἱόν μου τὸν ἀγαπητόν·
may I do? I will send the   son   of me   –   beloved;

ἴσως τοῦτον ἐντραπήσονται. 14 ἰδόντες δὲ
perhaps this one   they will regard.   But seeing

αὐτὸν οἱ γεωργοὶ διελογίζοντο πρὸς
him   the   husbandmen   debated   with

ἀλλήλους λέγοντες· οὗτός ἐστιν ὁ κληρονόμος·
one another   saying : This   is the   heir;

ἀποκτείνωμεν αὐτόν, ἵνα ἡμῶν γένηται
let us kill   him,   that   of us   may become

ἡ κληρονομία. 15 καὶ ἐκβαλόντες αὐτὸν
the   inheritance.   And   throwing out   him

ἔξω τοῦ ἀμπελῶνος ἀπέκτειναν. τί οὖν
outside the   vineyard   they killed.   What therefore

ποιήσει αὐτοῖς ὁ κύριος τοῦ ἀμπελῶνος;
will do   to them   the   owner   of the   vineyard?

16 ἐλεύσεται καὶ ἀπολέσει τοὺς γεωργοὺς
he will come   and   will destroy   –   husbandmen

τούτους, καὶ δώσει τὸν ἀμπελῶνα ἄλλοις.
these,   and will give the   vineyard   to others.

* That is, the people (a collective singular) have been (=are) persuaded.

---

5 They discussed it among themselves and said, "If we say, 'From heaven,' he will ask, 'Why didn't you believe him?' 6 But if we say, 'From men,' all the people will stone us, because they are persuaded that John was a prophet." 7 So they answered, "We don't know where it was from."

8 Jesus said, "Neither will I tell you by what authority I am doing these things."

The Parable of the Tenants

9 He went on to tell the people this parable: "A man planted a vineyard, rented it to some farmers and went away for a long time. 10 At harvest time he sent a servant to the tenants so they would give him some of the fruit of the vineyard. But the tenants beat him and sent him away empty-handed. 11 He sent another servant, but that one also they beat and treated shamefully and sent away empty-handed. 12 He sent it a third, and they wounded him and threw him out. 13 "Then the owner of the vineyard said, 'What shall I do? I will send my son, whom I love; perhaps they will respect him.' 14 "But when the tenants saw him, they talked the matter over. 'This is the heir,' they said. 'Let's kill him, and the inheritance will be ours.' 15 So they threw him out of the vineyard and killed him. "What then will the owner of the vineyard do to them? 16 He will come and kill those tenants and give the vineyard to others." When the people heard

forbid!" 17But he looked at them and said, "What then does this text mean: 'The stone that the builders rejected has become the cornerstone'?m 18Everyone who falls on that stone will be broken to pieces; and it will crush anyone on whom it falls." 19When the scribes and chief priests realized that he had told this parable against them, they wanted to lay hands on him at that very hour, but they feared the people.

The Question about Paying Taxes

20 So they watched him and sent spies who pretended to be honest, in order to trap him by what he said, so as to hand him over to the jurisdiction and authority of the governor. 21So they asked him, "Teacher, we know that you are right in what you say and teach, and you show deference to no one, but teach the way of God in accordance with truth. 22Is it lawful for us to pay taxes to the emperor, or not?" 23But he perceived their craftiness and said to them, 24"Show me a denarius. Whose head and whose title does it bear?" They said, "The emperor's." 25He said to them, "Then give to the emperor the things that are emperor's, and to God the things that are God's." 26And they were not able in the presence of the people to trap him by what he said; and being amazed by his answer, they became silent.

The Question about the Resurrection

27 Some Sadducees, those who say there is no resurrection, came to him

---

ἀκούσαντες δὲ εἶπαν· μὴ γένοιτο. **17** ὁ δὲ
And hearing they said : May it not be. And he
ἐμβλέψας αὐτοῖς εἶπεν· τί οὖν ἐστιν τὸ
looking at them said : What therefore is –
γεγραμμένον τοῦτο· λίθον ὃν ἀπεδοκίμασαν
having been written this : [The] stone which ²rejected
οἱ οἰκοδομοῦντες, οὗτος ἐγενήθη εἰς κεφαλὴν
¹the [ones] ³building, this came to be for [the] head
γωνίας; **18** πᾶς ὁ πεσὼν ἐπ᾽ ἐκεῖνον τὸν
of [the] corner? Everyone falling on that –
λίθον συνθλασθήσεται· ἐφ᾽ ὃν δ᾽ ἂν πέσῃ,
stone will be broken in pieces; but on whomever it falls,
λικμήσει αὐτόν. **19** Καὶ ἐζήτησαν οἱ
it will crush to powder him. And sought the
γραμματεῖς καὶ οἱ ἀρχιερεῖς ἐπιβαλεῖν ἐπ᾽
scribes and the chief priests to lay on on
αὐτὸν τὰς χεῖρας ἐν αὐτῇ τῇ ὥρᾳ, καὶ
him the(ir) hands in ²same ¹the hour, and
ἐφοβήθησαν τὸν λαόν· ἔγνωσαν γὰρ ὅτι
feared the people; for they knew that
πρὸς αὐτοὺς εἶπεν τὴν παραβολὴν ταύτην.
at them he told – parable this.
20 Καὶ παρατηρήσαντες ἀπέστειλαν ἐγκαθέτους
And watching carefully they sent spies
ὑποκρινομένους ἑαυτοὺς δικαίους εἶναι, ἵνα
pretending themselves righteous to be, that
ἐπιλάβωνται αὐτοῦ λόγου, ὥστε παραδοῦναι
they might seize of him a word, so as to deliver
αὐτὸν τῇ ἀρχῇ καὶ τῇ ἐξουσίᾳ τοῦ
him to the rule and to the authority of the
ἡγεμόνος. **21** καὶ ἐπηρώτησαν αὐτὸν
governor. And they questioned him
λέγοντες· διδάσκαλε, οἴδαμεν ὅτι ὀρθῶς
saying : Teacher, we know that ⁴rightly
λέγεις καὶ διδάσκεις καὶ οὐ λαμβάνεις
¹thou speakest ²and ³teachest and receivest not
=regardest not persons,
πρόσωπον, ἀλλ᾽ ἐπ᾽ ἀληθείας τὴν ὁδὸν τοῦ
a face, but on [the basis of] truth the way –
θεοῦ διδάσκεις· **22** ἔξεστιν ἡμᾶς Καίσαρι
of God teachest; is it lawful for us to Cæsar
φόρον δοῦναι ἢ οὔ; **23** κατανοήσας δὲ
tribute to give or not? And perceiving
αὐτῶν τὴν πανουργίαν εἶπεν πρὸς αὐτούς·
of them the cleverness he said to them :
24 δείξατέ μοι δηνάριον· τίνος ἔχει εἰκόνα
Show me a denarius; of whom has it an image
καὶ ἐπιγραφήν; οἱ δὲ εἶπαν· Καίσαρος.
and superscription? And they said : Of Cæsar.
25 ὁ δὲ εἶπεν πρὸς αὐτούς· τοίνυν ἀπόδοτε
And he said to them : So render
τὰ Καίσαρος Καίσαρι καὶ τὰ τοῦ θεοῦ
the things of Cæsar to Cæsar and the things – of God
τῷ θεῷ. **26** καὶ οὐκ ἴσχυσαν ἐπιλαβέσθαι
– to God. And they were not able to seize
αὐτοῦ ῥήματος ἐναντίον τοῦ λαοῦ, καὶ
of him a word in the presence of the people, and
θαυμάσαντες ἐπὶ τῇ ἀποκρίσει αὐτοῦ
marvelling at the answer of him
ἐσίγησαν.
they were silent.
27 Προσελθόντες δὲ τινες τῶν Σαδ-
And ⁴approaching ¹some ²of the ³Sad-
δουκαίων, οἱ ἀντιλέγοντες ἀνάστασιν μὴ
ducees, the [ones] saying in opposition* a resurrection not

---

this, they said, "May this never be!"

17Jesus looked directly at them and asked, "Then what is the meaning of that which is written:

" 'The stone the builders rejected
has become the capstoney' z?

18Everyone who falls on that stone will be broken to pieces, but he on whom it falls will be crushed."

19The teachers of the law and the chief priests looked for a way to arrest him immediately, because they knew he had spoken this parable against them. But they were afraid of the people.

Paying Taxes to Caesar

20Keeping a close watch on him, they sent spies, who pretended to be honest. They hoped to catch Jesus in something he said so that they might hand him over to the power and authority of the governor. 21So the spies questioned him: "Teacher, we know that you speak and teach what is right, and that you do not show partiality but teach the way of God in accordance with the truth. 22Is it right for us to pay taxes to Caesar or not?"

23He saw through their duplicity and said to them, 24"Show me a denarius. Whose portrait and inscription are on it?"

25"Caesar's," they replied.

He said to them, "Then give to Caesar what is Caesar's, and to God what is God's."

26They were unable to trap him in what he had said there in public. And astonished by his answer, they became silent.

The Resurrection and Marriage

27Some of the Sadducees, who say there is no resurrection, came to Jesus with

---

m Or keystone

*That is, to the Pharisees and to the generally held opinion.

y17 Or cornerstone
z17 Psalm 118:22

28and asked him a question, "Teacher, Moses wrote for us that if a man's brother dies, leaving a wife but no children, the man[n] shall marry the widow and raise up children for his brother. 29Now there were seven brothers; the first married, and died childless; 30then the second 31and the third married her, and so in the same way all seven died childless. 32Finally the woman also died. 33In the resurrection, therefore, whose wife will the woman be? For the seven had married her."

34 Jesus said to them, "Those who belong to this age marry and are given in marriage; 35but those who are considered worthy of a place in that age and in the resurrection from the dead neither marry nor are given in marriage. 36Indeed they cannot die anymore, because they are like angels and are children of God, being children of the resurrection. 37And the fact that the dead are raised Moses himself showed, in the story about the bush, where he speaks of the Lord as the God of Abraham, the God of Isaac, and the God of Jacob. 38Now he is God not of the dead, but of the living; for to him all of them are alive." 39Then some of the scribes answered, "Teacher, you have spoken well." 40For they no longer dared to ask him another question.

The Question about David's Son

41 Then he said to them, "How can they say that the Messiah[o] is David's son? 42For David himself says in the book of Psalms,

---

εἶναι, ἐπηρώτησαν αὐτὸν 28 λέγοντες·
to be, they questioned him saying :

διδάσκαλε, Μωϋσῆς ἔγραψεν ἡμῖν, ἐάν
Teacher, Moses wrote to us, If

τινος ἀδελφὸς ἀποθάνῃ ἔχων γυναῖκα, καὶ
of anyone a brother dies having a wife, and

οὗτος ἄτεκνος ᾖ, ἵνα λάβῃ ὁ ἀδελφὸς
this man childless is, that ²should take ¹the ²brother

αὐτοῦ τὴν γυναῖκα καὶ ἐξαναστήσῃ σπέρμα
³of him ⁴the ⁵wife and raise up seed

τῷ ἀδελφῷ αὐτοῦ. 29 ἑπτὰ οὖν ἀδελφοὶ
to the brother of him. Seven therefore brothers

ἦσαν· καὶ ὁ πρῶτος λαβὼν γυναῖκα
there were; and the first having taken a wife

ἀπέθανεν ἄτεκνος· 30 καὶ ὁ δεύτερος 31 καὶ
died childless; and the second and

ὁ τρίτος ἔλαβεν αὐτήν, ὡσαύτως δὲ καὶ
the third took her, and similarly also

οἱ ἑπτὰ οὐ κατέλιπον τέκνα καὶ ἀπέθανον.
the seven did not leave children and died.

32 ὕστερον καὶ ἡ γυνὴ ἀπέθανεν. 33 ἡ
Lastly also the woman died. The

γυνὴ οὖν ἐν τῇ ἀναστάσει τίνος αὐτῶν
woman therefore in the resurrection of which of them

γίνεται γυνή; οἱ γὰρ ἑπτὰ ἔσχον αὐτὴν
becomes she wife? for the seven had her

γυναῖκα. 34 καὶ εἶπεν αὐτοῖς ὁ Ἰησοῦς·
[as] wife. And said to them – Jesus :

οἱ υἱοὶ τοῦ αἰῶνος τούτου γαμοῦσιν καὶ
The sons – age of this marry and

γαμίσκονται, 35 οἱ δὲ καταξιωθέντες τοῦ
are given in marriage, but the [ones] counted worthy –

αἰῶνος ἐκείνου τυχεῖν καὶ τῆς ἀναστάσεως
²age ¹of that ¹to obtain and of the resurrection

τῆς ἐκ νεκρῶν οὔτε γαμοῦσιν οὔτε
– out of [the] dead neither marry nor

γαμίζονται· 36 οὐδὲ γὰρ ἀποθανεῖν ἔτι
are given in marriage; for not even to die more

δύνανται, ἰσάγγελοι γάρ εἰσιν, καὶ υἱοὶ
can they, for equal to angels they are, and ²sons

εἰσιν θεοῦ τῆς ἀναστάσεως υἱοὶ ὄντες.
¹they are ³of God ⁶of the ⁷resurrection ⁸sons ⁴being.

37 ὅτι δὲ ἐγείρονται οἱ νεκροί, καὶ
But that are raised the dead, even

Μωϋσῆς ἐμήνυσεν ἐπι τῆς βάτου, ὡς
Moses pointed out at the bush, as

λέγει κύριον τὸν θεὸν Ἀβραὰμ καὶ θεὸν
he calls [the] Lord the God of Abraham and God

Ἰσαὰκ καὶ θεὸν Ἰακώβ· 38 θεὸς δὲ οὐκ
of Isaac and God of Jacob; but God not

ἔστιν νεκρῶν ἀλλὰ ζώντων· πάντες γὰρ
he is of dead persons but of living; for all

αὐτῷ ζῶσιν. 39 ἀποκριθέντες δέ τινες
to him live. And answering some

τῶν γραμματέων εἶπαν· διδάσκαλε, καλῶς
of the scribes said : Teacher, well

εἶπας. 40 οὐκέτι γὰρ ἐτόλμων ἐπερωτᾶν
thou sayest. For no more dared they to question

αὐτὸν οὐδέν.
him no(any)thing.

41 Εἶπεν δὲ πρὸς αὐτούς· πῶς λέγουσιν
And he said to them : How say they

τὸν χριστὸν εἶναι Δαυὶδ υἱόν; 42 αὐτὸς
the Christ to be of David son? himself

γὰρ Δαυὶδ λέγει ἐν βίβλῳ ψαλμῶν·
For David says in [the] roll of psalms :

---

a question. 28"Teacher," they said, "Moses wrote for us that if a man's brother dies and leaves a wife but no children, the man must marry the widow and have children for his brother. 29Now there were seven brothers. The first one married a woman and died childless. 30The second 31and then the third married her, and in the same way the seven died, leaving no children. 32Finally, the woman died too. 33Now then, at the resurrection whose wife will she be, since the seven were married to her?"

34Jesus replied, "The people of this age marry and are given in marriage. 35But those who are considered worthy of taking part in that age and in the resurrection from the dead will neither marry nor be given in marriage, 36and they can no longer die; for they are like the angels. They are God's children, since they are children of the resurrection. 37But in the account of the bush, even Moses showed that the dead rise, for he calls Lord 'the God of Abraham, and the God of Isaac, and the God of Jacob.'[a] 38He is not the God of the dead, but of the living, for to him all are alive."

39Some of the teachers of the law responded, "Well said, teacher!" 40And no one dared to ask him any more questions.

Whose Son Is the Christ?

41Then Jesus said to them, "How is it that they say the Christ[b] is the Son of David? 42David himself declares in the Book of

---

'The Lord said to my
Lord,
"Sit at my right hand,
43 until I make your
enemies your
footstool." '
44David thus calls him
Lord; so how can he be his
son?"

Jesus Denounces the Scribes

45 In the hearing of all
the people he said to the*p*
disciples, 46"Beware of the
scribes, who like to walk
around in long robes, and
love to be greeted with respect in the marketplaces,
and to have the best seats in
the synagogues and places
of honor at banquets.
47They devour widows'
houses and for the sake of
appearance say long
prayers. They will receive
the greater condemnation."

Chapter 21

The Widow's Offering

HE looked up and saw
rich people putting
their gifts into the treasury;
2 he also saw a poor widow
put in two small copper
coins. 3 He said, "Truly I
tell you, this poor widow
has put in more than all of
them; 4 for all of them have
contributed out of their
abundance, but she out of
her poverty has put in all
she had to live on."

The Destruction of the Temple Foretold

5 When some were
speaking about the temple,
how it was adorned with
beautiful stones and gifts
dedicated to God, he said,
6"As for these things that
you see, the days will come
when not one stone will be
left upon another; all will
be thrown down."

Signs and Persecutions

7 They asked him,
"Teacher, when will this
be, and what will be the
sign that this is about to
take place?" 8 And he said,

εἶπεν κύριος τῷ κυρίῳ μου· κάθου ἐκ
Said [the] LORD to the Lord of me: Sit thou at

δεξιῶν μου 43 ἕως ἂν θῶ τοὺς ἐχθρούς σου
[the] right of me until I put the enemies of thee

ὑποπόδιον τῶν ποδῶν σου. 44 Δαυὶδ
a footstool of the feet of thee. David

οὖν αὐτὸν κύριον καλεῖ, καὶ πῶς αὐτοῦ
therefore him Lord calls, and how of him

υἱός ἐστιν;
son is he?

45 Ἀκούοντος δὲ παντὸς τοῦ λαοῦ εἶπεν
And hearing all the people* he said
=as all the people heard

τοῖς μαθηταῖς· 46 προσέχετε ἀπὸ τῶν
to the disciples: Beware from(of) the

γραμματέων τῶν θελόντων περιπατεῖν ἐν
scribes – wishing to walk about in

στολαῖς καὶ φιλούντων ἀσπασμοὺς ἐν ταῖς
robes and liking greetings in the

ἀγοραῖς καὶ πρωτοκαθεδρίας ἐν ταῖς
marketplaces and chief seats in the

συναγωγαῖς καὶ πρωτοκλισίας ἐν τοῖς
synagogues and chief couches in the

δείπνοις, 47 οἳ κατεσθίουσιν τὰς οἰκίας
suppers, who devour the houses

τῶν χηρῶν καὶ προφάσει μακρὰ προσεύχονται·
of the widows and under pretence long pray;

οὗτοι λήμψονται περισσότερον κρίμα.
these will receive severer judgment.

21 Ἀναβλέψας δὲ εἶδεν τοὺς βάλλοντας
And looking up he saw ¹the ²putting

εἰς τὸ γαζοφυλακεῖον τὰ δῶρα αὐτῶν
⁴into ⁵the ⁶treasury ⁷the ⁸gifts ⁹of them

πλουσίους. 2 εἶδεν δέ τινα χήραν πενιχρὰν
³rich [ones]. And he saw a certain widow poor

βάλλουσαν ἐκεῖ λεπτὰ δύο, 3 καὶ εἶπεν·
putting there lepta two, and he said:

ἀληθῶς λέγω ὑμῖν ὅτι ἡ χήρα αὕτη ἡ
Truly I tell you that – ²widow ¹this –

πτωχὴ πλεῖον πάντων ἔβαλεν· 4 πάντες
³poor more [than] all put; ²all

γὰρ οὗτοι ἐκ τοῦ περισσεύοντος αὐτοῖς
¹for these out of the abounding to them
=their abundance

ἔβαλον εἰς τὰ δῶρα, αὕτη δὲ ἐκ τοῦ
put into the gifts, but this woman out of

ὑστερήματος αὐτῆς πάντα τὸν βίον ὃν
want of her ²all ¹the ⁴living ⁵which

εἶχεν ἔβαλεν.
⁶she had ³put.

5 Καί τινων λεγόντων περὶ τοῦ ἱεροῦ, ὅτι
And some speaking* about the temple, that
=as some spoke

λίθοις καλοῖς καὶ ἀναθήμασιν κεκόσμηται,
with stones beautiful and gifts it has(had)
been adorned,

εἶπεν· 6 ταῦτα ἃ θεωρεῖτε, ἐλεύσονται
he said: These things which ye behold, will come

ἡμέραι ἐν αἷς οὐκ ἀφεθήσεται λίθος ἐπὶ
days in which there will not be left stone on

λίθῳ ὃς οὐ καταλυθήσεται. 7 ἐπηρώτησαν δὲ
stone which will not be overthrown. And they questioned

αὐτὸν λέγοντες· διδάσκαλε, πότε οὖν
him saying: Teacher, when therefore

ταῦτα ἔσται; καὶ τί τὸ σημεῖον ὅταν
these things will be? And what [will be] the sign when

Psalms:
" 'The Lord said to my
Lord:
"Sit at my right hand
43until I make your
enemies
a footstool for your
feet." ' *c*

44David calls him 'Lord.'
How then can he be his
son?"
45While all the people
were listening, Jesus said
to his disciples, 46"Beware
of the teachers of the law.
They like to walk around in
flowing robes and love to
be greeted in the market-
places and have the most
important seats in the synagogues and the places of
honor at banquets. 47They
devour widows' houses
and for a show make
lengthy prayers. Such men
will be punished most se-
verely."

Chapter 21

The Widow's Offering

AS he looked up, Jesus
saw the rich putting
their gifts into the temple
treasury. 2He also saw a
poor widow put in two very
small copper coins. *d* 3"I
tell you the truth," he said,
"this poor widow has put in
more than all the others.
4All these people gave their
gifts out of their wealth; but
she out of her poverty put
in all she had to live on."

Signs of the End of the Age

5Some of his disciples
were remarking about how
the temple was adorned
with beautiful stones and
with gifts dedicated to God.
But Jesus said, 6"As for
what you see here, the time
will come when not one
stone will be left on another; every one of them will
be thrown down."
7"Teacher," they asked,
"when will these things
happen? And what will be
the sign that they are about

"Beware that you are not led astray; for many will come in my name and say, 'I am he!'[q] and, 'The time is near!'[r] Do not go after them.

9 "When you hear of wars and insurrections, do not be terrified; for these things must take place first, but the end will not follow immediately." 10 Then he said to them, "Nation will rise against nation, and kingdom against kingdom; 11 there will be great earthquakes, and in various places famines and plagues; and there will be dreadful portents and great signs from heaven.

12 "But before all this occurs, they will arrest you and persecute you; they will hand you over to synagogues and prisons, and you will be brought before kings and governors because of my name. 13 This will give you an opportunity to testify. 14 So make up your minds not to prepare your defense in advance; 15 for I will give you words[s] and a wisdom that none of your opponents will be able to withstand or contradict. 16 You will be betrayed even by parents and brothers, by relatives and friends; and they will put some of you to death. 17 You will be hated by all because of my name. 18 But not a hair of your head will perish. 19 By your endurance you will gain your souls.

The Destruction of Jerusalem Foretold

20 "When you see Jerusalem surrounded by armies, then know that its desolation has come near.[t] 21 Then those in Judea must flee to the mountains, and those inside the city must

---

μέλλη ταῦτα γίνεσθαι; 8 ὁ δὲ εἶπεν·
1are about 1these things 2to happen?   And he said:

βλέπετε μὴ πλανηθῆτε· πολλοὶ γὰρ
Beware lest ye be led astray; for many

ἐλεύσονται ἐπὶ τῷ ὀνόματί μου λέγοντες·
will come on(in) the name of me saying:

ἐγώ εἰμι, καί· ὁ καιρὸς ἤγγικεν· μὴ
I am, and: The time has drawn near; not

πορευθῆτε ὀπίσω αὐτῶν. 9 ὅταν δὲ
go ye after them.   And when

ἀκούσητε πολέμους καὶ ἀκαταστασίας, μὴ
ye hear [of] wars and commotions, not

πτοηθῆτε· δεῖ γὰρ ταῦτα γενέσθαι
be ye scared; for it behoves these things to happen

πρῶτον, ἀλλ' οὐκ εὐθέως τὸ τέλος. 10 Τότε
first, but not immediately the end.   Then

ἔλεγεν αὐτοῖς· ἐγερθήσεται ἔθνος ἐπ' ἔθνος
he said to them: Will be raised nation against nation

καὶ βασιλεία ἐπὶ βασιλείαν, 11 σεισμοί τε
and kingdom against kingdom, and earthquakes

μεγάλοι καὶ κατὰ τόπους λοιμοὶ καὶ λιμοὶ
great and from place to place† pestilences and famines

ἔσονται, φόβητρά τε καὶ ἀπ' οὐρανοῦ
there will be, and terrors and 2from 1heaven

σημεῖα μεγάλα ἔσται. 12 πρὸ δὲ τούτων
1signs 1great there will be. But before these things

πάντων ἐπιβαλοῦσιν ἐφ' ὑμᾶς τὰς χεῖρας
all they will lay on on you the hands

αὐτῶν καὶ διώξουσιν, παραδιδόντες εἰς τὰς
of them and will persecute, delivering to the

συναγωγὰς καὶ φυλακάς, ἀπαγομένους ἐπὶ
synagogues and prisons, being led away on(before)

βασιλεῖς καὶ ἡγεμόνας ἕνεκεν τοῦ ὀνόματός
kings and governors for the sake of the name

μου· 13 ἀποβήσεται ὑμῖν εἰς μαρτύριον.
of me; it will turn out to you for a testimony.

14 θέτε οὖν ἐν ταῖς καρδίαις ὑμῶν μὴ
Put therefore in the hearts of you not

προμελετᾶν ἀπολογηθῆναι· 15 ἐγὼ γὰρ
to practise beforehand to defend [yourselves]; for I

δώσω ὑμῖν στόμα καὶ σοφίαν, ᾗ οὐ
will give you a mouth and wisdom, which not

δυνήσονται ἀντιστῆναι ἢ ἀντειπεῖν ἅπαντες οἱ
will be able to withstand or to contradict all the

ἀντικείμενοι ὑμῖν. 16 παραδοθήσεσθε δὲ καὶ
[ones] opposing you. And ye will be betrayed also

ὑπὸ γονέων καὶ ἀδελφῶν καὶ συγγενῶν
by parents and brothers and relatives

καὶ φίλων, καὶ θανατώσουσιν ἐξ ὑμῶν,
and friends, and they will put to death [some] of you,

17 καὶ ἔσεσθε μισούμενοι ὑπὸ πάντων διὰ
and ye will be being hated by all men because of

τὸ ὄνομά μου. 18 καὶ θρὶξ ἐκ τῆς
the name of me. And a hair of the

κεφαλῆς ὑμῶν οὐ μὴ ἀπόληται· 19 ἐν τῇ
head of you by no means will perish; in the

ὑπομονῇ ὑμῶν κτήσεσθε τὰς ψυχὰς ὑμῶν.
endurance of you ye will gain the souls of you.

20 Ὅταν δὲ ἴδητε κυκλουμένην ὑπὸ
But when ye see 1being surrounded 2by

στρατοπέδων Ἰερουσαλήμ, τότε γνῶτε ὅτι
4camps 1Jerusalem, then know ye that

ἤγγικεν ἡ ἐρήμωσις αὐτῆς. 21 τότε οἱ ἐν
has drawn near the desolation of it. Then the [ones] in

τῇ Ἰουδαίᾳ φευγέτωσαν εἰς τὰ ὄρη, καὶ
— Judæa let them flee to the mountains, and

---

to take place?"

8 He replied: "Watch out that you are not deceived. For many will come in my name, claiming, 'I am he,' and, 'The time is near.' Do not follow them. 9 When you hear of wars and revolutions, do not be frightened. These things must happen first, but the end will not come right away."

10 Then he said to them: "Nation will rise against nation, and kingdom against kingdom. 11 There will be great earthquakes, famines and pestilences in various places, and fearful events and great signs from heaven.

12 "But before all this, they will lay hands on you and persecute you. They will deliver you to synagogues and prisons, and you will be brought before kings and governors, and all on account of my name. 13 This will result in your being witnesses to them. 14 But make up your mind not to worry beforehand how you will defend yourselves. 15 For I will give you words and wisdom that none of your adversaries will be able to resist or contradict. 16 You will be betrayed even by parents, brothers, relatives and friends, and they will put some of you to death. 17 All men will hate you because of me. 18 But not a hair of your head will perish. 19 By standing firm you will gain life.

20 "When you see Jerusalem being surrounded by armies, you will know that its desolation is near. 21 Then let those who are in Judea flee to the mountains, let those in the city

---

q Gk *I am*
r Or *at hand*
s Gk *a mouth*
t Or *is at hand*

leave it, and those out in the country must not enter it; 22 for these are days of vengeance, as a fulfillment of all that is written. 23 Woe to those who are pregnant and to those who are nursing infants in those days! For there will be great distress on the earth and wrath against this people; 24 they will fall by the edge of the sword and be taken away as captives among all nations; and Jerusalem will be trampled on by the Gentiles, until the times of the Gentiles are fulfilled.

The Coming of the Son of Man

25 "There will be signs in the sun, the moon, and the stars, and on the earth distress among nations confused by the roaring of the sea and the waves. 26 People will faint from fear and foreboding of what is coming upon the world, for the powers of the heavens will be shaken. 27 Then they will see 'the Son of Man coming in a cloud' with power and great glory. 28 Now when these things begin to take place, stand up and raise your heads, because your redemption is drawing near."

The Lesson of the Fig Tree

29 Then he told them a parable: "Look at the fig tree and all the trees; 30 as soon as they sprout leaves you can see for yourselves and know that summer is already near. 31 So also, when you see these things taking place, you know that the kingdom of God is near. 32 Truly I tell you, this generation will not pass away until all things have taken place. 33 Heaven and earth will pass away, but my words will not pass away.

οἱ   ἐν μέσῳ αὐτῆς ἐκχωρείτωσαν, καὶ
the [ones] in [the] midst of it let them depart out, and

οἱ   ἐν ταῖς χώραις μὴ εἰσερχέσθωσαν εἰς
the [ones] in the districts let them not enter into

αὐτήν, 22 ὅτι ἡμέραι ἐκδικήσεως αὗταί
it,   because days   of vengeance these

εἰσιν τοῦ πλησθῆναι πάντα τὰ γεγραμμένα.
are - to be fulfilled[d] all the things having been written.

23 οὐαὶ ταῖς ἐν γαστρὶ ἐχούσαις καὶ ταῖς
Woe to the   pregnant women†   and to the

θηλαζούσαις ἐν ἐκείναις ταῖς ἡμέραις·
[ones] giving suck in those   -   days;

ἔσται γὰρ ἀνάγκη μεγάλη ἐπὶ τῆς γῆς
for there will be distress great on the land

καὶ ὀργὴ τῷ λαῷ τούτῳ, 24 καὶ πεσοῦνται
and wrath - people to this,   and they will fall

στόματι μαχαίρης καὶ αἰχμαλωτισθή-
by [the] mouth(edge) of [the] sword and will be led

σονται εἰς τὰ ἔθνη πάντα, καὶ Ἰερουσαλὴμ
captive to the nations all,   and Jerusalem

ἔσται πατουμένη ὑπὸ ἐθνῶν, ἄχρι οὗ
will be *being* trodden down by nations, until

πληρωθῶσιν καιροὶ ἐθνῶν. 25 Καὶ ἔσονται
are accomplished [the] times of [the] nations. And there will be

σημεῖα ἐν ἡλίῳ καὶ σελήνῃ καὶ ἄστροις,
signs in sun and moon and stars,

καὶ ἐπὶ τῆς γῆς συνοχὴ ἐθνῶν ἐν ἀπορίᾳ
and on the earth anxiety of nations in perplexity

ἤχους θαλάσσης καὶ σάλου, 26 ἀποψυχόντων
of [the] sound of [the] sea and surf,   fainting
                                    =while men faint

ἀνθρώπων ἀπὸ φόβου καὶ προσδοκίας τῶν
men[a]   from fear and expectation of the

ἐπερχομένων τῇ οἰκουμένῃ· αἱ γὰρ δυνάμεις
things coming on the inhabited earth; for the powers

τῶν οὐρανῶν σαλευθήσονται. 27 καὶ τότε
of the heavens will be shaken. And then

ὄψονται τὸν υἱὸν τοῦ ἀνθρώπου ἐρχόμενον
they will see the Son - of man coming

ἐν νεφέλῃ μετὰ δυνάμεως καὶ δόξης
in a cloud with power   and glory

πολλῆς. 28 ἀρχομένων δὲ τούτων γίνεσθαι
much(great). And beginning these things[a] to happen
                      =when these things begin

ἀνακύψατε καὶ ἐπάρατε τὰς κεφαλὰς ὑμῶν,
stand erect and lift up the heads of you,

διότι ἐγγίζει ἡ ἀπολύτρωσις ὑμῶν. 29 Καὶ
because draws near the redemption of you. And

εἶπεν παραβολὴν αὐτοῖς· ἴδετε τὴν συκῆν
he told [a parable] [b]them : Ye see the fig-tree

καὶ πάντα τὰ δένδρα· 30 ὅταν προβάλωσιν
and all the trees;   when [b]they burst into leaf

ἤδη, βλέποντες ἀφ᾽ ἑαυτῶν γινώσκετε ὅτι
now, seeing from(of) yourselves ye know that

ἤδη ἐγγὺς τὸ θέρος ἐστίν· 31 οὕτως καὶ
now near the summer is;   so also

ὑμεῖς, ὅταν ἴδητε ταῦτα γινόμενα,
ye, when ye see these things happening,

γινώσκετε ὅτι ἐγγύς ἐστιν ἡ βασιλεία
know that near is the kingdom

τοῦ θεοῦ. 32 ἀμὴν λέγω ὑμῖν ὅτι οὐ μὴ
- of God. Truly I tell you that by no means

παρέλθῃ ἡ γενεὰ αὕτη ἕως ἂν πάντα
will pass away - generation this until all things

γένηται. 33 ὁ οὐρανὸς καὶ ἡ γῆ παρ-
happens. The heaven and the earth will

ελεύσονται, οἱ δὲ λόγοι μου οὐ μὴ παρελεύ-
pass away, but the words of me by no means will pass

---

get out, and let those in the country not enter the city. 22 For this is the time of punishment in fulfillment of all that has been written. 23 How dreadful it will be in those days for pregnant women and nursing mothers! There will be great distress in the land and wrath against this people. 24 They will fall by the sword and will be taken as prisoners to all the nations. Jerusalem will be trampled on by the Gentiles until the times of the Gentiles are fulfilled.

25 "There will be signs in the sun, moon and stars. On the earth, nations will be in anguish and perplexity at the roaring and tossing of the sea. 26 Men will faint from terror, apprehensive of what is coming on the world, for the heavenly bodies will be shaken. 27 At that time they will see the Son of Man coming in a cloud with power and great glory. 28 When these things begin to take place, stand up and lift up your heads, because your redemption is drawing near."

29 He told them this parable: "Look at the fig tree and all the trees. 30 When they sprout leaves, you can see for yourselves and know that summer is near. 31 Even so, when you see these things happening, you know that the kingdom of God is near.

32 "I tell you the truth, this generation[e] will certainly not pass away until all these things have happened. 33 Heaven and earth will pass away, but my words will never pass away.

---

[e] 32 Or *race*

Exhortation to Watch

34 "Be on guard so that your hearts are not weighed down with dissipation and drunkenness and the worries of this life, and that day catch you unexpectedly, 35 like a trap. For it will come upon all who live on the face of the whole earth. 36 Be alert at all times, praying that you may have the strength to escape all these things that will take place, and to stand before the Son of Man."

37 Every day he was teaching in the temple, and at night he would go out and spend the night on the Mount of Olives, as it was called. 38 And all the people would get up early in the morning to listen to him in the temple.

σονται. **34** Προσέχετε δὲ ἑαυτοῖς μήποτε
away.   And take heed   to yourselves   lest

βαρηθῶσιν ὑμῶν αἱ καρδίαι ἐν κραιπάλῃ
become burdened of you   the   hearts   with   surfeiting

καὶ μέθῃ καὶ μερίμναις βιωτικαῖς, καὶ
and deep drinking and   anxieties   of life,†   and

ἐπιστῇ ἐφ' ὑμᾶς αἰφνίδιος ἡ ἡμέρα ἐκείνη
come on   on   you   suddenly   –   day   that

35 ὡς παγίς· ἐπεισελεύσεται γὰρ ἐπὶ πάντας
as a snare;   for it will come in on   on   all

τοὺς καθημένους ἐπὶ πρόσωπον πάσης τῆς
the [ones]   sitting   on   [the] face   of all   the

γῆς. **36** ἀγρυπνεῖτε δὲ ἐν παντὶ καιρῷ
earth.   But be ye watchful   at   every   time

δεόμενοι ἵνα κατισχύσητε ἐκφυγεῖν ταῦτα
begging   that   ye may be able   to escape   these things

πάντα τὰ μέλλοντα γίνεσθαι, καὶ σταθῆναι
all   –   being about   to happen,   and   to stand

ἔμπροσθεν τοῦ υἱοῦ τοῦ ἀνθρώπου.
before   the   Son   –   of man.

37 ᾿Ην δὲ τὰς ἡμέρας ἐν τῷ ἱερῷ
Now he was [in] the   days   in   the   temple

διδάσκων, τὰς δὲ νύκτας ἐξερχόμενος
teaching,   and [in] the   nights   going forth

ηὐλίζετο εἰς τὸ ὄρος τὸ καλούμενον
he lodged   in   the   mountain   *being* called

ἐλαιῶν. **38** καὶ πᾶς ὁ λαὸς ὥρθριζεν
of olives.   And   all the   people came in the morning

πρὸς αὐτὸν ἐν τῷ ἱερῷ ἀκούειν αὐτοῦ.
to   him   in   the   temple   to hear   him.

34"Be careful, or your hearts will be weighed down with dissipation, drunkenness and the anxieties of life, and that day will close on you unexpectedly like a trap. 35For it will come upon all those who live on the face of the whole earth. 36Be always on the watch, and pray that you may be able to escape all that is about to happen, and that you may be able to stand before the Son of Man."

37Each day Jesus was teaching at the temple, and each evening he went out to spend the night on the hill called the Mount of Olives, 38and all the people came early in the morning to hear him at the temple.

Chapter 22

The Plot to Kill Jesus

NOW the festival of Unleavened Bread, which is called the Passover, was near. 2 The chief priests and the scribes were looking for a way to put Jesus [u] to death, for they were afraid of the people. 3 Then Satan entered into Judas called Iscariot, who was one of the twelve; 4 he went away and conferred with the chief priests and officers of the temple police about how he might betray him to them. 5 They were greatly pleased and agreed to give him money. 6 So he consented and began to look for an opportunity to betray him to them when no crowd was present.

The Preparation of the Passover

7 Then came the day of Unleavened Bread, on which the Passover lamb had to be sacrificed. 8 So Jesus [v] sent Peter and John, saying, "Go and prepare the Passover meal for us that we may eat it." 9 They asked him, "Where do you want us to make preparations for it?"

22 ᾿Ηγγιζεν δὲ ἡ ἑορτὴ τῶν ἀζύμων ἡ
Now drew near the   feast   of unleavened bread   –

λεγομένη πάσχα. **2** καὶ ἐζήτουν οἱ ἀρχιερεῖς
being called Passover.   And   ᵃsought   ¹the   ¹chief priests

καὶ οἱ γραμματεῖς τὸ πῶς ἀνέλωσιν
²and   ⁴the   ⁵scribes   –   how they might destroy

αὐτόν· ἐφοβοῦντο γὰρ τὸν λαόν. **3** Εἰσῆλθεν δὲ
him;   for they feared   the   people.   And entered

σατανᾶς εἰς ᾿Ιούδαν τὸν καλούμενον
Satan   into   Judas   –   *being* called

᾿Ισκαριώτην, ὄντα ἐκ τοῦ ἀριθμοῦ τῶν
Iscariot,   being   of   the   number   of the

δώδεκα· **4** καὶ ἀπελθὼν συνελάλησεν τοῖς
twelve;   and   going   he conversed with   the

ἀρχιερεῦσιν καὶ στρατηγοῖς τὸ πῶς αὐτοῖς
chief priests   and   captains   –   how   to them

παραδῷ αὐτόν. **5** καὶ ἐχάρησαν, καὶ
he might betray   him.   And   they rejoiced,   and

συνέθεντο αὐτῷ ἀργύριον δοῦναι. **6** καὶ
they agreed   ¹him   ²money   ¹to give.   And

ἐξωμολόγησεν, καὶ ἐζήτει εὐκαιρίαν τοῦ
he fully consented,   and   sought   opportunity   –

παραδοῦναι αὐτὸν ἄτερ ὄχλου αὐτοῖς.
to betray[d]   him   apart from   a crowd   to them.

7 ᾿Ηλθεν δὲ ἡ ἡμέρα τῶν ἀζύμων, ᾗ
And came   the   day   of unleavened bread, on which

ἔδει θύεσθαι τὸ πάσχα· **8** καὶ ἀπέστειλεν
it behoved   to kill   the passover [lamb];   and   he sent

Πέτρον καὶ ᾿Ιωάννην εἰπών· πορευθέντες
Peter   and   John   saying :   Going

ἑτοιμάσατε ἡμῖν τὸ πάσχα, ἵνα φάγωμεν. **9** οἱ
prepare ye   for us   the passover,   that we may eat.   they

δὲ εἶπαν αὐτῷ· ποῦ θέλεις ἑτοιμάσωμεν;
And said   to him :   Where wishest thou [that] we may prepare?

Chapter 22

Judas Agrees to Betray Jesus

NOW the Feast of Unleavened Bread, called the Passover, was approaching, 2and the chief priests and the teachers of the law were looking for some way to get rid of Jesus, for they were afraid of the people. 3Then Satan entered Judas, called Iscariot, one of the Twelve. 4And Judas went to the chief priests and the officers of the temple guard and discussed with them how he might betray Jesus. 5They were delighted and agreed to give him money. 6He consented, and watched for an opportunity to hand Jesus over to them when no crowd was present.

The Last Supper

7Then came the day of Unleavened Bread on which the Passover lamb had to be sacrificed. 8Jesus sent Peter and John, saying, "Go and make preparations for us to eat the Passover."

9"Where do you want us to prepare for it?" they asked.

10 "Listen," he said to them, "when you have entered the city, a man carrying a jar of water will meet you; follow him into the house he enters 11 and say to the owner of the house, 'The teacher asks you, "Where is the guest room, where I may eat the Passover with my disciples?"' 12 He will show you a large room upstairs, already furnished. Make preparations for us there." 13 So they went and found everything as he had told them; and they prepared the Passover meal.

The Institution of the Lord's Supper

14 When the hour came, he took his place at the table, and the apostles with him. 15 He said to them, "I have eagerly desired to eat this Passover with you before I suffer; 16 for I tell you, I will not eat it [w] until it is fulfilled in the kingdom of God." 17 Then he took a cup, and after giving thanks he said, "Take this and divide it among yourselves; 18 for I tell you that from now on I will not drink of the fruit of the vine until the kingdom of God comes." 19 Then he took a loaf of bread, and when he had given thanks, he broke it and gave it to them, saying, "This is my body, which is given for you. Do this in remembrance of me." 20 And he did the same with the cup after supper, saying, "This cup that is poured out for you is the new covenant in my blood. [x] 21 But see, the one who betrays me is with me, and his hand is on

---

10 ὁ δὲ εἶπεν αὐτοῖς· ἰδοὺ εἰσελθόντων
And he told them: Behold[,] entering
= as ye enter

ὑμῶν εἰς τὴν πόλιν συναντήσει ὑμῖν
you[a] into the city will meet you

ἄνθρωπος κεράμιον ὕδατος βαστάζων·
a man a pitcher of water bearing;

ἀκολουθήσατε αὐτῷ εἰς τὴν οἰκίαν εἰς ἣν
follow him into the house into which

εἰσπορεύεται· 11 καὶ ἐρεῖτε τῷ οἰκοδεσπότῃ
he enters; and ye will say to the house-master

τῆς οἰκίας· λέγει σοι ὁ διδάσκαλος·
of the house: Says to thee the teacher:

ποῦ ἐστιν τὸ κατάλυμα ὅπου τὸ πάσχα
Where is the guest room where the passover

μετὰ τῶν μαθητῶν μου φάγω; 12 κἀκεῖνος
with the disciples of me I may eat? And that man

ὑμῖν δείξει ἀνάγαιον μέγα ἐστρωμένον·
you will show upper room a large having been spread;[a]

ἐκεῖ ἑτοιμάσατε. 13 ἀπελθόντες δὲ εὗρον
there prepare ye. And going they found

καθὼς εἰρήκει αὐτοῖς, καὶ ἡτοίμασαν τὸ
as he had told them, and they prepared the

πάσχα. 14 Καὶ ὅτε ἐγένετο ἡ ὥρα,
passover. And when came the hour,

ἀνέπεσεν, καὶ οἱ ἀπόστολοι σὺν αὐτῷ.
he reclined, and the apostles with him.

15 καὶ εἶπεν πρὸς αὐτούς· ἐπιθυμίᾳ
And he said to them: With desire

ἐπεθύμησα τοῦτο τὸ πάσχα φαγεῖν μεθ'
I desired this - passover to eat with

ὑμῶν πρὸ τοῦ με παθεῖν· 16 λέγω γὰρ
you before the me to suffer;[b] for I tell
= I suffer;

ὑμῖν ὅτι οὐκέτι οὐ μὴ φάγω αὐτὸ
you that no more by no(any) means I eat it

ἕως ὅτου πληρωθῇ ἐν τῇ βασιλείᾳ τοῦ θεοῦ.
until it is fulfilled in the kingdom of God.

17 καὶ δεξάμενος ποτήριον εὐχαριστήσας
And taking a cup having given thanks

εἶπεν· λάβετε τοῦτο καὶ διαμερίσατε εἰς
he said: Take this and divide among

ἑαυτούς· 18 λέγω γὰρ ὑμῖν, οὐ μὴ πίω
yourselves; for I tell you, by no means I drink

ἀπὸ τοῦ νῦν ἀπὸ τοῦ γενήματος τῆς
from - now [on] from the produce of the

ἀμπέλου ἕως οὗ ἡ βασιλεία τοῦ θεοῦ
vine until the kingdom of God

ἔλθῃ. 19 καὶ λαβὼν ἄρτον εὐχαριστήσας
comes. And taking a loaf having given thanks

ἔκλασεν καὶ ἔδωκεν αὐτοῖς λέγων· τοῦτό
he broke and gave to them saying: This

ἐστιν τὸ σῶμά μου [τὸ ὑπὲρ ὑμῶν
is the body of me [- for you

διδόμενον· τοῦτο ποιεῖτε εἰς τὴν ἐμὴν
being given; this do ye for - my

ἀνάμνησιν. 20 καὶ τὸ ποτήριον ὡσαύτως
memorial. And the cup similarly

μετὰ τὸ δειπνῆσαι, λέγων· τοῦτο τὸ
after the to sup, saying: This the

ποτήριον ἡ καινὴ διαθήκη ἐν τῷ αἵματί
cup [is] the new covenant in the blood

μου, τὸ ὑπὲρ ὑμῶν ἐκχυννόμενον.] 21 πλὴν
of me, - for you being shed.] However

ἰδοὺ ἡ χεὶρ τοῦ παραδιδόντος με μετ'
behold[,] the hand of the [one] betraying me with

---

10 He replied, "As you enter the city, a man carrying a jar of water will meet you. Follow him to the house that he enters, 11 and say to the owner of the house, 'The Teacher asks: Where is the guest room, where I may eat the Passover with my disciples?' 12 He will show you a large upper room, all furnished. Make preparations there."

13 They left and found things just as Jesus had told them. So they prepared the Passover.

14 When the hour came, Jesus and his apostles reclined at the table. 15 And he said to them, "I have eagerly desired to eat this Passover with you before I suffer. 16 For I tell you, I will not eat it again until it finds fulfillment in the kingdom of God."

17 After taking the cup, he gave thanks and said, "Take this and divide it among you. 18 For I tell you I will not drink again of the fruit of the vine until the kingdom of God comes."

19 And he took bread, gave thanks and broke it, and gave it to them, saying, "This is my body given for you; do this in remembrance of me."

20 In the same way, after the supper he took the cup, saying, "This cup is the new covenant in my blood, which is poured out for you. 21 But the hand of him who is going to betray me is

---

w Other ancient authorities read *never eat it again*
x Other ancient authorities lack, in whole or in part, verses 19b-20 *(which is given . . . in my blood)*

a That is, with carpets, and the dining couches supplied with cushions.

the table. 22 For the Son of Man is going as it has been determined, but woe to that one by whom he is betrayed!" 23 Then they began to ask one another, which one of them it could be who would do this.

The Dispute about Greatness

24 A dispute also arose among them as to which one of them was to be regarded as the greatest. 25 But he said to them, "The kings of the Gentiles lord it over them; and those in authority over them are called benefactors. 26 But not so with you; rather the greatest among you must become like the youngest, and the leader like one who serves. 27 For who is greater, the one who is at the table or the one who serves? Is it not the one at the table? But I am among you as one who serves. 28 "You are those who have stood by me in my trials; 29 and I confer on you, just as my Father has conferred on me, a kingdom, 30 so that you may eat and drink at my table in my kingdom, and you will sit on thrones judging the twelve tribes of Israel.

Jesus Predicts Peter's Denial

31 "Simon, Simon, listen! Satan has demanded y to sift all of you like wheat, 32 but I have prayed for you that your own faith may not fail; and you, when once you have turned back, strengthen your brothers." 33 And he said to him, "Lord, I am ready to go with you to prison and to death!" 34 Jesus z said, "I tell you, Peter, the cock will not crow this day, until you have denied three times that you know me."

ἐμοῦ ἐπὶ τῆς τραπέζης. 22 ὅτι ὁ υἱὸς μὲν
me on the table. Because 2the 3Son 1indeed

τοῦ ἀνθρώπου κατὰ τὸ ὡρισμένον
- of man according to the [thing] having been determined

πορεύεται, πλὴν οὐαὶ τῷ ἀνθρώπῳ ἐκείνῳ
goes, nevertheless woe - man to that

δι᾽ οὗ παραδίδοται. 23 καὶ αὐτοὶ ἤρξαντο
through whom he is betrayed. And they began

συζητεῖν πρὸς ἑαυτοὺς τὸ τίς ἄρα εἴη
to debate with themselves - who then it might be

ἐξ αὐτῶν ὁ τοῦτο μέλλων πράσσειν.
of them the [one] this 1being about 2to do.

24 Ἐγένετο δὲ καὶ φιλονεικία ἐν αὐτοῖς,
And there was also a rivalry among them,

τὸ τίς αὐτῶν δοκεῖ εἶναι μείζων. 25 ὁ δὲ
- who of them seems to be greater. So he

εἶπεν αὐτοῖς· οἱ βασιλεῖς τῶν ἐθνῶν
said to them: The kings of the nations

κυριεύουσιν αὐτῶν, καὶ οἱ ἐξουσιάζοντες
lord it over them, and the [ones] having authority over

αὐτῶν εὐεργέται καλοῦνται. 26 ὑμεῖς δὲ
them benefactors are called. But ye

οὐχ οὕτως, ἀλλ᾽ ὁ μείζων ἐν ὑμῖν
not so, but the greater among you

γινέσθω ὡς ὁ νεώτερος, καὶ ὁ ἡγούμενος
let him become as the younger, and the [one] governing

ὡς ὁ διακονῶν. 27 τίς γὰρ μείζων, ὁ
as the [one] serving. For who [is] greater, the

ἀνακείμενος ἢ ὁ διακονῶν; οὐχὶ ὁ
[one] reclining or the [one] serving? not the

ἀνακείμενος; ἐγὼ δὲ ἐν μέσῳ ὑμῶν εἰμι
[one] reclining? But I in [the] midst of you am

ὡς ὁ διακονῶν. 28 ὑμεῖς δέ ἐστε οἱ
as the [one] serving. But ye are the [ones]

διαμεμενηκότες μετ᾽ ἐμοῦ ἐν τοῖς πειρα-
having remained throughout with me in the tempta-

σμοῖς μου· 29 κἀγὼ διατίθεμαι ὑμῖν καθὼς
tions of me; and I appoint to you as

διέθετό μοι ὁ πατήρ μου βασιλείαν,
appointed to me the Father of me a kingdom,

30 ἵνα ἔσθητε καὶ πίνητε ἐπὶ τῆς τραπέζης
that ye may eat and drink at the table

μου ἐν τῇ βασιλείᾳ μου, καὶ καθήσεσθε
of me in the kingdom of me, and ye will sit

ἐπὶ θρόνων τὰς δώδεκα φυλὰς κρίνοντες
on thrones 2the 1twelve 4tribes 3judging

τοῦ Ἰσραήλ. 31 Σίμων Σίμων, ἰδοὺ ὁ
- of Israel. Simon[,] Simon, behold[,] -

σατανᾶς ἐξητήσατο ὑμᾶς τοῦ σινιάσαι ὡς
Satan begged earnestly for you - to sift d as

τὸν σῖτον· 32 ἐγὼ δὲ ἐδεήθην περὶ σοῦ
the wheat; but I requested concerning thee

ἵνα μὴ ἐκλίπῃ ἡ πίστις σου· καὶ σύ
that might not fail the faith of thee; and thou

ποτε ἐπιστρέψας στήρισον τοὺς ἀδελφούς
when having turned support the brothers

σου. 33 ὁ δὲ εἶπεν αὐτῷ· κύριε, μετὰ
of thee. And he said to him: Lord, with

σοῦ ἔτοιμός εἰμι καὶ εἰς φυλακὴν καὶ εἰς
thee prepared I am both to prison and to

θάνατον πορεύεσθαι. 34 ὁ δὲ εἶπεν· λέγω
death to go. But he said: I tell

σοι, Πέτρε, οὐ φωνήσει σήμερον ἀλέκτωρ
thee, Peter, will not sound to-day a cock

ἕως τρίς με ἀπαρνήσῃ μὴ εἰδέναι. 35 Καὶ
until thrice me thou wilt deny not to know. And

---

with mine on the table. 22 The Son of Man will go as it has been decreed, but woe to that man who betrays him." 23 They began to question among themselves which of them it might be who would do this.

24 Also a dispute arose among them as to which of them was considered to be greatest. 25 Jesus said to them, "The kings of the Gentiles lord it over them; and those who exercise authority over them call themselves Benefactors. 26 But you are not to be like that. Instead, the greatest among you should be like the youngest, and the one who rules like the one who serves. 27 For who is greater, the one who is at the table or the one who serves? Is it not the one who is at the table? But I am among you as one who serves. 28 You are those who have stood by me in my trials. 29 And I confer on you a kingdom, just as my Father conferred one on me, 30 so that you may eat and drink at my table in my kingdom and sit on thrones, judging the twelve tribes of Israel.

31 "Simon, Simon, Satan has asked to sift you f as wheat. 32 But I have prayed for you, Simon, that your faith may not fail. And when you have turned back, strengthen your brothers."

33 But he replied, "Lord, I am ready to go with you to prison and to death."

34 Jesus answered, "I tell you, Peter, before the rooster crows today, you will deny three times that you know me."

Purse, Bag, and Sword

35 He said to them,
"When I sent you out without a purse, bag, or san-
dals, did you lack any-
thing?" They said, "No,
not a thing." 36 He said to
them, "But now, the one
who has a purse must take
it, and likewise a bag. And
the one who has no sword
must sell his cloak and buy
one. 37 For I tell you, this
scripture must be fulfilled
in me, 'And he was counted
among the lawless'; and indeed what is written about
me is being fulfilled."
38 They said, "Lord, look,
here are two swords." He
replied, "It is enough."

Jesus Prays on the Mount of Olives

39 He came out and
went, as was his custom, to
the Mount of Olives; and
the disciples followed him.
40 When he reached the
place, he said to them,
"Pray that you may not
come into the time of trial." [a] 41 Then he withdrew
from them about a stone's
throw, knelt down, and
prayed, 42 "Father, if you
are willing, remove this cup
from me; yet, not my will
but yours be done."
[[43 Then an angel from
heaven appeared to him
and gave him strength. 44 In
his anguish he prayed more
earnestly, and his sweat became like great drops of
blood falling down on the
ground.]] [b] 45 When he got
up from prayer, he came to
the disciples and found
them sleeping because of
grief, 46 and he said to
them, "Why are you sleep-
ing? Get up and pray that
you may not come into the
time of trial." [a]

The Betrayal and Arrest of Jesus

47 While he was still
speaking, suddenly a
crowd came, and the one
called Judas, one of the

εἶπεν αὐτοῖς· ὅτε ἀπέστειλα ὑμᾶς ἄτερ
he said   to them : When I sent   you   without

βαλλαντίου καὶ πήρας καὶ ὑποδημάτων, μή
a purse   and a wallet and   sandals,   **not**

τινος ὑστερήσατε; οἱ δὲ εἶπαν· οὐθενός.
of anything were ye short? And they said :   Of nothing.

36 εἶπεν δὲ αὐτοῖς· ἀλλὰ νῦν ὁ ἔχων
    And he said   to them :   But   now the [one] having

βαλλάντιον ἀράτω, ὁμοίως καὶ πήραν, καὶ
a purse   let him take [it], likewise also a wallet, and

ὁ μὴ ἔχων πωλησάτω τὸ ἱμάτιον αὐτοῦ
the [one] not having let him sell the garment   of him

καὶ ἀγορασάτω μάχαιραν. **37** λέγω γὰρ
and let him buy   a sword.   For I tell

ὑμῖν ὅτι τοῦτο τὸ γεγραμμένον δεῖ
you   that this   -   having been written it behoves

τελεσθῆναι ἐν ἐμοί, τό· Καὶ μετὰ ἀνόμων
to be finished in me,   the· And with lawless men

ἐλογίσθη· καὶ γὰρ τὸ περὶ ἐμοῦ τέλος
he was reckoned; for indeed the thing concerning me   an end

ἔχει. **38** οἱ δὲ εἶπαν· κύριε, ἰδοὺ μάχαιραι
has.   And they said : Lord, behold[,] swords

ὧδε δύο. ὁ δὲ εἶπεν αὐτοῖς· ἱκανόν ἐστιν.
here two. And he said   to them : Enough   it is.

39 Καὶ ἐξελθὼν ἐπορεύθη κατὰ τὸ ἔθος
    And going forth he went according to the(his) habit

εἰς τὸ ὄρος τῶν ἐλαιῶν· ἠκολούθησαν δὲ
to   the mountain of the olives;   and ⁴followed

αὐτῷ καὶ οἱ μαθηταί. **40** γενόμενος δὲ
³him ²also ¹the ³disciples.   And coming

ἐπὶ τοῦ τόπου εἶπεν αὐτοῖς· προσεύχεσθε
upon the place   he said to them :   Pray ye

μὴ εἰσελθεῖν εἰς πειρασμόν. **41** καὶ αὐτὸς
not to enter   into temptation.   And   he

ἀπεσπάσθη ἀπ' αὐτῶν ὡσεὶ λίθου βολήν,
was withdrawn from them   about of a stone a throw,

καὶ θεὶς τὰ γόνατα προσηύχετο **42** λέγων·
and placing the knees   he prayed   saying :

πάτερ, εἰ βούλει παρένεγκε τοῦτο τὸ
Father,   if thou wilt take away   this   -

ποτήριον ἀπ' ἐμοῦ· πλὴν μὴ τὸ θέλημά
cup   from me; nevertheless not the will

μου ἀλλὰ τὸ σὸν γινέσθω. **43** [ὤφθη δὲ
of me but   -   thine let be.   And appeared

αὐτῷ ἄγγελος ἀπ' οὐρανοῦ ἐνισχύων αὐτόν.
to him an angel from heaven   strengthening him.

44 καὶ γενόμενος ἐν ἀγωνίᾳ ἐκτενέστερον
    And becoming   in an agony more earnestly

προσηύχετο· καὶ ἐγένετο ὁ ἱδρὼς αὐτοῦ
he prayed;   and became the sweat   of him

ὡσεὶ θρόμβοι αἵματος καταβαίνοντες ἐπὶ
as   drops   of blood falling down   onto

τὴν γῆν.] **45** καὶ ἀναστὰς ἀπὸ τῆς
the earth.]   And rising up   from the

προσευχῆς, ἐλθὼν πρὸς τοὺς μαθητὰς
prayer,   coming   to   the   disciples

εὗρεν κοιμωμένους αὐτοὺς ἀπὸ τῆς λύπης,
he found ³sleeping   ¹them   from the grief,

46 καὶ εἶπεν αὐτοῖς· τί καθεύδετε;
    and said to them :   Why sleep ye?

ἀναστάντες προσεύχεσθε, ἵνα μὴ εἰσέλθητε
rising up   pray ye,   lest   ye enter

εἰς πειρασμόν. **47** Ἔτι αὐτοῦ λαλοῦντος
into temptation.   Yet   him   speakingᵃ
=While he was yet speaking

ἰδοὺ ὄχλος, καὶ ὁ λεγόμενος Ἰούδας εἷς
behold[,] a crowd, and the [one] being named Judas   one

---

35 Then Jesus asked them,
"When I sent you without
purse, bag or sandals, did
you lack anything?"
"Nothing," they an-
swered.
36 He said to them, "But
now if you have a purse,
take it, and also a bag; and
if you don't have a sword,
sell your cloak and buy
one. 37 It is written: 'And he
was numbered with the
transgressors' [g]; and I tell
you that this must be fulfilled in me. Yes, what is
written about me is reaching its fulfillment."
38 The disciples said,
"See, Lord, here are two
swords."
"That is enough," he re-
plied.

Jesus Prays on the Mount of Olives

39 Jesus went out as usual
to the Mount of Olives, and
his disciples followed him.
40 On reaching the place, he
said to them, "Pray that
you will not fall into temptation." 41 He withdrew
about a stone's throw be-
yond them, knelt down and
prayed, 42 "Father, if you
are willing, take this cup
from me; yet not my will,
but yours be done." 43 An
angel from heaven ap-
peared to him and strengthened him. 44 And being in
anguish, he prayed more
earnestly, and his sweat
was like drops of blood falling to the ground. [h]
45 When he rose from
prayer and went back to the
disciples, he found them
asleep, exhausted from sorrow. 46 "Why are you sleeping?" he asked them. "Get
up and pray so that you will
not fall into temptation."

Jesus Arrested

47 While he was still
speaking a crowd came up,
and the man who was
called Judas, one of the

ᵃ Or into temptation
ᵇ Other ancient authorities lack
verses 43 and 44

ᵍ37 Isaiah 53:12
ʰ44 Some early manuscripts do not
have verses 43 and 44.

twelve, was leading them. He approached Jesus to kiss him; 48 but Jesus said to him, "Judas, is it with a kiss that you are betraying the Son of Man?" 49 When those who were around him saw what was coming, they asked, "Lord, should we strike with the sword?" 50 Then one of them struck the slave of the high priest and cut off his right ear. 51 But Jesus said, "No more of this!" And he touched his ear and healed him. 52 Then Jesus said to the chief priests, the officers of the temple police, and the elders who had come for him, "Have you come out with swords and clubs as if I were a bandit? 53 When I was with you day after day in the temple, you did not lay hands on me. But this is your hour, and the power of darkness!"

Peter Denies Jesus

54 Then they seized him and led him away, bringing him into the high priest's house. But Peter was following at a distance. 55 When they had kindled a fire in the middle of the courtyard and sat down together, Peter sat among them. 56 Then a servant-girl, seeing him in the firelight, stared at him and said, "This man also was with him." 57 But he denied it, saying, "Woman, I do not know him." 58 A little later someone else, on seeing him, said, "You also are one of them." But Peter said, "Man, I am not!" 59 Then about an hour later still another kept insisting,

---

τῶν δώδεκα προήρχετο αὐτούς, καὶ ἤγγισεν
of the twelve came before them, and drew near
τῷ 'Ιησοῦ φιλῆσαι αὐτόν. 48 'Ιησοῦς δὲ
- to Jesus to kiss him. But Jesus
εἶπεν αὐτῷ· 'Ιούδα, φιλήματι τὸν υἱὸν
said to him: Judas, with a kiss the Son
τοῦ ἀνθρώπου παραδίδως; 49 ἰδόντες δὲ
- of man betrayest thou? And ⁵seeing
οἱ περὶ αὐτὸν τὸ ἐσόμενον εἶπαν· κύριε,
¹the [ones] ⁴round ³him the thing going to be said : Lord,
εἰ πατάξομεν ἐν μαχαίρῃ; 50 καὶ ἐπάταξεν
if we shall strike with a sword? And ⁴struck
εἷς τις ἐξ αὐτῶν τοῦ ἀρχιερέως τὸν
¹a certain one ³of ²them ⁷of the ⁸high priest ⁵the
δοῦλον καὶ ἀφεῖλεν τὸ οὖς αὐτοῦ τὸ
⁶slave and cut off ¹the ²ear ⁴of him ³the
δεξιόν. 51 ἀποκριθεὶς δὲ ὁ 'Ιησοῦς εἶπεν·
⁵right. And answering - Jesus said :
ἐᾶτε ἕως τούτου· καὶ ἁψάμενος τοῦ
Permit ye until this; and touching the
ὠτίου ἰάσατο αὐτόν. 52 Εἶπεν δὲ 'Ιησοῦς
ear he cured him. And said Jesus
πρὸς τοὺς παραγενομένους ἐπ' αὐτὸν
to ¹the ²⁰coming ¹¹upon ¹¹him
ἀρχιερεῖς καὶ στρατηγοὺς τοῦ ἱεροῦ καὶ
¹chief priests ²and ⁴captains ⁵of the ⁶temple ⁷and
πρεσβυτέρους· ὡς ἐπὶ λῃστὴν ἐξήλθατε
⁸elders : As against a robber came ye out
μετὰ μαχαιρῶν καὶ ξύλων; 53 καθ' ἡμέραν
with swords and clubs? daily
ὄντος μου μεθ' ὑμῶν ἐν τῷ ἱερῷ οὐκ
being me⁸ with you in the temple not
=while I was
ἐξετείνατε τὰς χεῖρας ἐπ' ἐμέ· ἀλλ' αὕτη
ye stretched out the(your) hands against me; but this
ἐστὶν ὑμῶν ἡ ὥρα καὶ ἡ ἐξουσία τοῦ
is of you the hour and the authority of the
σκότους.
darkness.
54 Συλλαβόντες δὲ αὐτὸν ἤγαγον καὶ
And having arrested him they led and
εἰσήγαγον εἰς τὴν οἰκίαν τοῦ ἀρχιερέως·
brought in into the house of the high priest;
ὁ δὲ Πέτρος ἠκολούθει μακρόθεν. 55 περι-
- and Peter followed afar off. light-
αἰψάντων δὲ πῦρ ἐν μέσῳ τῆς αὐλῆς καὶ
ing And a fire in [the] centre of the court and
=when they had lit a fire . . . and had sat down together
συγκαθισάντων ἐκάθητο ὁ Πέτρος μέσος
sitting down together⁸ sat - Peter among
αὐτῶν. 56 ἰδοῦσα δὲ αὐτὸν παιδίσκη τις
them. And ⁵seeing ³him ¹a certain maidservant
καθήμενον πρὸς τὸ φῶς καὶ ἀτενίσασα
sitting near the light and gazing at
αὐτῷ εἶπεν· καὶ οὗτος σὺν αὐτῷ ἦν. 57 ὁ
him said : And this man with him was. he
δὲ ἠρνήσατο λέγων· οὐκ οἶδα αὐτόν,
But denied saying : I know not him,
γύναι. 58 καὶ μετὰ βραχὺ ἕτερος ἰδὼν
woman. And after a short while another seeing
αὐτὸν ἔφη· καὶ σὺ ἐξ αὐτῶν εἶ. ὁ
him said : And thou of them art. -
δὲ Πέτρος ἔφη· ἄνθρωπε, οὐκ εἰμί.
But Peter said : Man, I am not.
59 καὶ διαστάσης ὡσεὶ ὥρας μιᾶς ἄλλος
And intervening about hour one¹ ⁸other man
=when about an hour had intervened

Twelve, was leading them. He approached Jesus to kiss him, 48 but Jesus asked him, "Judas, are you betraying the Son of Man with a kiss?"

49 When Jesus' followers saw what was going to happen, they said, "Lord, should we strike with our swords?" 50 And one of them struck the servant of the high priest, cutting off his right ear.

51 But Jesus answered, "No more of this!" And he touched the man's ear and healed him.

52 Then Jesus said to the chief priests, the officers of the temple guard, and the elders, who had come for him, "Am I leading a rebellion, that you have come with swords and clubs? 53 Every day I was with you in the temple courts, and you did not lay a hand on me. But this is your hour—when darkness reigns."

Peter Disowns Jesus

54 Then seizing him, they led him away and took him into the house of the high priest. Peter followed at a distance. 55 But when they had kindled a fire in the middle of the courtyard and had sat down together, Peter sat down with them. 56 A servant girl saw him seated there in the firelight. She looked closely at him and said, "This man was with him."

57 But he denied it. "Woman, I don't know him," he said.

58 A little later someone else saw him and said, "You also are one of them."

"Man, I am not!" Peter replied.

59 About an hour later another asserted, "Certainly

"Surely this man also was with him; for he is a Galilean." 60 But Peter said, "Man, I do not know what you are talking about!" At that moment, while he was still speaking, the cock crowed. 61 The Lord turned and looked at Peter. Then Peter remembered the word of the Lord, how he had said to him, "Before the cock crows today, you will deny me three times." 62 And he went out and wept bitterly.

The Mocking and Beating of Jesus

63 Now the men who were holding Jesus began to mock him and beat him; 64 they also blindfolded him and kept asking him, "Prophesy! Who is it that struck you?" 65 They kept heaping many other insults on him.

Jesus before the Council

66 When day came, the assembly of the elders of the people, both chief priests and scribes, gathered together, and they brought him to their council. 67 They said, "If you are the Messiah,c tell us." He replied, "If I tell you, you will not believe; 68 and if I question you, you will not answer. 69 But from now on the Son of Man will be seated at the right hand of the power of God." 70 All of them asked, "Are you, then, the Son of God?" He said to them, "You say that I am." 71 Then they said, "What further testimony do we need? We have heard it ourselves from his own lips!"

τις διϊσχυρίζετο λέγων· ἐπ᾽ ἀληθείας καὶ
¹a certain emphatically asserted saying: Of a truth also

οὗτος μετ᾽ αὐτοῦ ἦν, καὶ γὰρ Γαλιλαῖός
this man with him was, for indeed a Galilæan

ἐστιν. 60 εἶπεν δὲ ὁ Πέτρος· ἄνθρωπε,
he is. But said - Peter: Man,

οὐκ οἶδα ὃ λέγεις. καὶ παραχρῆμα ἔτι
I know not what thou sayest. And at once yet

λαλοῦντος αὐτοῦ ἐφώνησεν ἀλέκτωρ. 61 καὶ
speaking himª sounded a cock. And
=while he was yet speaking

στραφεὶς ὁ κύριος ἐνέβλεψεν τῷ Πέτρῳ,
turning the Lord looked at - Peter,

καὶ ὑπεμνήσθη ὁ Πέτρος τοῦ λόγου τοῦ
and remembered - Peter the word of the

κυρίου, ὡς εἶπεν αὐτῷ ὅτι πρὶν ἀλέκτορα
Lord, as he told him that before a cock

φωνῆσαι σήμερον ἀπαρνήσῃ με τρίς. 62 καὶ
to soundᵇ to-day thou wilt deny me thrice. And

ἐξελθὼν ἔξω ἔκλαυσεν πικρῶς. 63 Καὶ οἱ
going out outside he wept bitterly. And the

ἄνδρες οἱ συνέχοντες αὐτὸν ἐνέπαιζον αὐτῷ
men - having in charge him* mocked him

δέροντες, 64 καὶ περικαλύψαντες αὐτὸν
beating, and covering over him

ἐπηρώτων λέγοντες· προφήτευσον, τίς ἐστιν
questioned saying: Prophesy, who is

ὁ παίσας σε; 65 καὶ ἕτερα πολλὰ
the [one] playing thee? And other things many

βλασφημοῦντες ἔλεγον εἰς αὐτόν.
blaspheming they said against him.

66 Καὶ ὡς ἐγένετο ἡμέρα, συνήχθη τὸ
And when came day, was assembled the

πρεσβυτέριον τοῦ λαοῦ, ἀρχιερεῖς τε καὶ
body of elders of the people, both chief priests and

γραμματεῖς, καὶ ἀπήγαγον αὐτὸν εἰς τὸ
scribes, and led away him to the

συνέδριον αὐτῶν, 67 λέγοντες· εἰ σὺ εἶ ὁ
council of them, saying: If thou art the

χριστός, εἰπὸν ἡμῖν. εἶπεν δὲ αὐτοῖς·
Christ, tell us. And he said to them:

ἐὰν ὑμῖν εἴπω, οὐ μὴ πιστεύσητε· 68 ἐὰν
If you I tell, by no means will ye believe; ⁸if

δὲ ἐρωτήσω, οὐ μὴ ἀποκριθῆτε. 69 ἀπὸ
¹and I question, by no means will ye answer. ⁹from

τοῦ νῦν δὲ ἔσται ὁ υἱὸς τοῦ ἀνθρώπου
- ⁹now ¹But ⁷will be ᵗthe ⁸Son - ⁶of man

καθήμενος ἐκ δεξιῶν τῆς δυνάμεως τοῦ
⁵sitting at [the] right of the power -

θεοῦ. 70 εἶπαν δὲ πάντες· σὺ οὖν εἶ ὁ
of God. And they said all: Thou therefore art the

υἱὸς τοῦ θεοῦ; ὁ δὲ πρὸς αὐτοὺς ἔφη·
Son - of God? And he to them said:

ὑμεῖς λέγετε ὅτι ἐγώ εἰμι. 71 οἱ δὲ
Ye say that I am. And they

εἶπαν· τί ἔτι ἔχομεν μαρτυρίας χρείαν;
said: Why yet have we of witness need?

αὐτοὶ γὰρ ἠκούσαμεν ἀπὸ τοῦ στόματος
for [our]selves we heard from the mouth

αὐτοῦ.
of him.

---

this fellow was with him, for he is a Galilean." 60 Peter replied, "Man, I don't know what you're talking about!" Just as he was speaking, the rooster crowed. 61 The Lord turned and looked straight at Peter. Then Peter remembered the word the Lord had spoken to him: "Before the rooster crows today, you will disown me three times." 62 And he went outside and wept bitterly.

The Soldiers Mock Jesus

63 The men who were guarding Jesus began mocking and beating him. 64 They blindfolded him and demanded, "Prophesy! Who hit you?" 65 And they said many other insulting things to him.

Jesus Before Pilate and Herod

66 At daybreak the council of the elders of the people, both the chief priests and teachers of the law, met together, and Jesus was led before them. 67 "If you are the Christ,ⁱ" they said, "tell us."

Jesus answered, "If I tell you, you will not believe me, 68 and if I asked you, you would not answer. 69 But from now on, the Son of Man will be seated at the right hand of the mighty God."

70 They all asked, "Are you then the Son of God?"

He replied, "You are right in saying I am."

71 Then they said, "Why do we need any more testimony? We have heard it from his own lips."

---

c Or the Christ

* That is, Jesus (as some texts have it).

ⁱ67 Or Messiah

Chapter 23

Jesus before Pilate

THEN the assembly rose as a body and brought Jesus[d] before Pilate. [2] They began to accuse him, saying, "We found this man perverting our nation, forbidding us to pay taxes to the emperor, and saying that he himself is the Messiah, a king."[e] [3] Then Pilate asked him, "Are you the king of the Jews?" He answered, "You say so." [4] Then Pilate said to the chief priests and the crowds, "I find no basis for an accusation against this man." [5] But they were insistent and said, "He stirs up the people by teaching throughout all Judea, from Galilee where he began even to this place."

Jesus before Herod

[6] When Pilate heard this, he asked whether the man was a Galilean. [7] And when he learned that he was under Herod's jurisdiction, he sent him off to Herod, who was himself in Jerusalem at that time. [8] When Herod saw Jesus, he was very glad, for he had been wanting to see him for a long time, because he had heard about him and was hoping to see him perform some sign. [9] He questioned him at some length, but Jesus[f] gave him no answer. [10] The chief priests and the scribes stood by, vehemently accusing him. [11] Even Herod with his soldiers treated him with contempt and mocked him; then he put an elegant robe on him, and sent him back to Pilate. [12] That same day

---

23 Καὶ ἀναστὰν ἅπαν τὸ πλῆθος αὐτῶν
And rising up all the multitude of them

ἤγαγον αὐτὸν ἐπὶ τὸν Πιλᾶτον. **2** ἤρξαντο
led him before - Pilate. they began

δὲ κατηγορεῖν αὐτοῦ λέγοντες· τοῦτον
And to accuse him saying : This man

εὕραμεν διαστρέφοντα τὸ ἔθνος ἡμῶν καὶ
we found perverting the nation of us and

κωλύοντα φόρους Καίσαρι διδόναι, καὶ
forbidding tribute to Cæsar to give, and

λέγοντα ἑαυτὸν χριστὸν βασιλέα εἶναι.
saying himself Christ a king to be.

3 ὁ δὲ Πιλᾶτος ἠρώτησεν αὐτὸν λέγων·
- And Pilate questioned him saying :

σὺ εἶ ὁ βασιλεὺς τῶν Ἰουδαίων; ὁ δὲ
Thou art the king of the Jews? And he

ἀποκριθεὶς αὐτῷ ἔφη· σὺ λέγεις. **4** ὁ δὲ
answering him said : Thou sayest. - And

Πιλᾶτος εἶπεν πρὸς τοὺς ἀρχιερεῖς καὶ
Pilate said to the chief priests and

τοὺς ὄχλους· οὐδὲν εὑρίσκω αἴτιον ἐν
the crowds : ²No ¹I find ³crime in

τῷ ἀνθρώπῳ τούτῳ. **5** οἱ δὲ ἐπίσχυον λέγοντες
- man this. But they insisted saying[,]

ὅτι ἀνασείει τὸν λαόν, διδάσκων καθ᾽
- He excites the people, teaching throughout

ὅλης τῆς Ἰουδαίας, καὶ ἀρξάμενος ἀπὸ
all - Judæa, even beginning from

τῆς Γαλιλαίας ἕως ὧδε. **6** Πιλᾶτος δὲ
- Galilee to here. And Pilate

ἀκούσας ἐπηρώτησεν εἰ ὁ ἄνθρωπος
hearing questioned if the man

Γαλιλαῖός ἐστιν, **7** καὶ ἐπιγνοὺς ὅτι ἐκ
a Galilæan is(was), and perceiving that of

τῆς ἐξουσίας Ἡρώδου ἐστίν, ἀνέπεμψεν
the authority of Herod he is(was), he sent up

αὐτὸν πρὸς Ἡρώδην, ὄντα καὶ αὐτὸν ἐν
him to Herod, being also him(he) in

Ἱεροσολύμοις ἐν ταύταις ταῖς ἡμέραις.
Jerusalem in these - days.

8 ὁ δὲ Ἡρώδης ἰδὼν τὸν Ἰησοῦν ἐχάρη
- And Herod seeing - Jesus rejoiced

λίαν· ἦν γὰρ ἐξ ἱκανῶν χρόνων θέλων
greatly; for he was of a long times wishing

ἰδεῖν αὐτὸν διὰ τὸ ἀκούειν περὶ αὐτοῦ,
to see him because of the to hear[b] about him,
=because he had heard

καὶ ἤλπιζέν τι σημεῖον ἰδεῖν ὑπ᾽ αὐτοῦ
and he hoped some sign to see by him

γινόμενον. **9** ἐπηρώτα δὲ αὐτὸν ἐν λόγοις
brought about. And he questioned him in words

ἱκανοῖς· αὐτὸς δὲ οὐδὲν ἀπεκρίνατο αὐτῷ.
many; but he nothing answered him.

10 εἱστήκεισαν δὲ οἱ ἀρχιερεῖς καὶ οἱ
And stood the chief priests and the

γραμματεῖς εὐτόνως κατηγοροῦντες αὐτοῦ.
scribes vehemently accusing him.

11 ἐξουθενήσας δὲ αὐτὸν ὁ Ἡρώδης σὺν
And despising him - Herod with

τοῖς στρατεύμασιν αὐτοῦ καὶ ἐμπαίξας,
the soldiery of him and mocking,

περιβαλὼν ἐσθῆτα λαμπρὰν ἀνέπεμψεν αὐτὸν
throwing round clothing splendid sent back him

τῷ Πιλάτῳ. **12** ἐγένοντο δὲ φίλοι ὅ τε
- to Pilate. And became friends - both

Chapter 23

THEN the whole assembly rose and led him off to Pilate. [2] And they began to accuse him, saying, "We have found this man subverting our nation. He opposes payment of taxes to Caesar and claims to be Christ,[j] a king."

[3] So Pilate asked Jesus, "Are you the king of the Jews?"

"Yes, it is as you say," Jesus replied.

[4] Then Pilate announced to the chief priests and the crowd, "I find no basis for a charge against this man."

[5] But they insisted, "He stirs up the people all over Judea[k] by his teaching. He started in Galilee and has come all the way here."

[6] On hearing this, Pilate asked if the man was a Galilean. [7] When he learned that Jesus was under Herod's jurisdiction, he sent him to Herod, who was also in Jerusalem at that time.

[8] When Herod saw Jesus, he was greatly pleased, because for a long time he had been wanting to see him. From what he had heard about him, he hoped to see him perform some miracle. [9] He plied him with many questions, but Jesus gave him no answer. [10] The chief priests and the teachers of the law were standing there, vehemently accusing him. [11] Then Herod and his soldiers ridiculed and mocked him. Dressing him in an elegant robe, they sent him back to Pilate.

---

[d] Gk *him*
[e] Or *is an anointed king*
[f] Gk *he*

[j2] Or *Messiah*; also in verses 35 and 39
[k5] Or *over the land of the Jews*

Herod and Pilate became friends with each other; before this they had been enemies.

Jesus Sentenced to Death

13 Pilate then called together the chief priests, the leaders, and the people, 14and said to them, "You brought me this man as one who was perverting the people; and here I have examined him in your presence and have not found this man guilty of any of your charges against him. 15Neither has Herod, for he sent him back to us. Indeed, he has done nothing to deserve death. 16I will therefore have him flogged and release him."*g*

18 Then they all shouted out together, "Away with this fellow! Release Barabbas for us!" 19(This was a man who had been put in prison for an insurrection that had taken place in the city, and for murder.) 20Pilate, wanting to release Jesus, addressed them again; 21but they kept shouting, "Crucify, crucify him!" 22A third time he said to them, "Why, what evil has he done? I have found in him no ground for the sentence of death; I will therefore have him flogged and then release him." 23But they kept urgently demanding with loud shouts that he should be crucified; and their voices prevailed. 24So Pilate gave his verdict that their demand should be granted. 25He released the man they asked for, the one who had been put in prison for insurrection and murder, and he handed Jesus over as they wished.

Ἡρῴδης καὶ ὁ Πιλᾶτος ἐν αὐτῇ τῇ
Herod   and   –   Pilate   on   ²same ¹the

ἡμέρᾳ μετ’ ἀλλήλων· προϋπῆρχον γὰρ ἐν
day   with   each other;   for they were previously   in

ἔχθρᾳ ὄντες πρὸς αὐτούς. 13 Πιλᾶτος δὲ
enmity   being   with   themselves.   And Pilate

συγκαλεσάμενος τοὺς ἀρχιερεῖς καὶ τοὺς
calling together   the   chief priests   and   the

ἄρχοντας καὶ τὸν λαὸν 14 εἶπεν πρὸς
leaders   and   the   people   said   to

αὐτούς· προσηνέγκατέ μοι τὸν ἄνθρωπον
them :   Ye brought   to me   –   man

τοῦτον ὡς ἀποστρέφοντα τὸν λαόν, καὶ
this   as   perverting   the   people,   and

ἰδοὺ ἐγὼ ἐνώπιον ὑμῶν ἀνακρίνας οὐθὲν
behold   I   ³before   ²you   ¹examining   ⁴nothing

εὗρον ἐν τῷ ἀνθρώπῳ τούτῳ αἴτιον ὧν
⁵found   ⁷in   –   ⁸man   ⁸this   ⁶crime   of the [things] which

κατηγορεῖτε κατ’ αὐτοῦ. 15 ἀλλ’ οὐδὲ
ye bring accusation against   him.   And   neither

Ἡρῴδης· ἀνέπεμψεν γὰρ αὐτὸν πρὸς ἡμᾶς·
Herod;   for he sent back   him   to   us;

καὶ ἰδοὺ οὐδὲν ἄξιον θανάτου ἐστὶν
and   behold   nothing   worthy   of death   is

πεπραγμένον αὐτῷ· 16 παιδεύσας οὖν αὐτὸν
having been done   by him;   chastising   therefore   him

ἀπολύσω.‡ 18 ἀνέκραγον δὲ παμπληθεὶ
I will release.   But they shouted   with the whole multitude

λέγοντες· αἶρε τοῦτον, ἀπόλυσον δὲ ἡμῖν
saying :   Take   this man,   and release   to us

τὸν Βαραββᾶν· 19 ὅστις ἦν διὰ στάσιν
–   Barabbas;   who   was because ²insurrec- of ¹tion

τινὰ γενομένην ἐν τῇ πόλει καὶ φόνον
¹some   happening   in   the   city   and   murder

βληθεὶς ἐν τῇ φυλακῇ. 20 πάλιν δὲ
thrown   in   the   prison.   But again

ὁ Πιλᾶτος προσεφώνησεν αὐτοῖς, θέλων
–   Pilate   called   to them,   wishing

ἀπολῦσαι τὸν Ἰησοῦν. 21 οἱ δὲ ἐπεφώνουν
to release   –   Jesus.   But they   shouted

λέγοντες· σταύρου σταύρου αὐτόν. 22 ὁ δὲ
saying :   Crucify[,] crucify thou   him.   But he

τρίτον εἶπεν πρὸς αὐτούς· τί γὰρ κακὸν
a third time said   to   them :   But what   evil

ἐποίησεν οὗτος; οὐδὲν αἴτιον θανάτου
did   this man?   *nothing*   cause   of death

εὗρον ἐν αὐτῷ· παιδεύσας οὖν αὐτὸν
I found   in   him;   chastising   therefore   him

ἀπολύσω. 23 οἱ δὲ ἐπέκειντο φωναῖς
I will release.   But they   insisted   voices

μεγάλαις αἰτούμενοι αὐτὸν σταυρωθῆναι,
with great   asking   him   to be crucified,

καὶ κατίσχυον αἱ φωναὶ αὐτῶν. 24 καὶ
and   prevailed   the   voices   of them.   And

Πιλᾶτος ἐπέκρινεν γενέσθαι τὸ αἴτημα
Pilate   decided   to be [carried out]   the   request

αὐτῶν· 25 ἀπέλυσεν δὲ τὸν διὰ στάσιν
of them;   and he released the [one]   because of insurrection

καὶ φόνον βεβλημένον εἰς φυλακήν, ὃν
and   murder   having been thrown   into   prison,   whom

ᾐτοῦντο, τὸν δὲ Ἰησοῦν παρέδωκεν τῷ
they asked,   –   but   Jesus   he delivered   to the

θελήματι αὐτῶν.
will   of them.

12That day Herod and Pilate became friends—before this they had been enemies.

13Pilate called together the chief priests, the rulers and the people, 14and said to them, "You brought me this man as one who was inciting the people to rebellion. I have examined him in your presence and have found no basis for your charges against him. 15Neither has Herod, for he sent him back to us; as you can see, he has done nothing to deserve death. 16Therefore, I will punish him and then release him.*l*"

18With one voice they cried out, "Away with this man! Release Barabbas to us!" 19(Barabbas had been thrown into prison for an insurrection in the city, and for murder.)

20Wanting to release Jesus, Pilate appealed to them again. 21But they kept shouting, "Crucify him! Crucify him!"

22For the third time he spoke to them: "Why? What crime has this man committed? I have found in him no grounds for the death penalty. Therefore I will have him punished and then release him."

23But with loud shouts they insistently demanded that he be crucified, and their shouts prevailed. 24So Pilate decided to grant their demand. 25He released the man who had been thrown into prison for insurrection and murder, the one they asked for, and surrendered Jesus to their will.

---

g Here, or after verse 19, other ancient authorities add verse 17, *Now he was obliged to release someone for them at the festival*

‡ Ver. 17 omitted by Nestle; *cf.* NIV footnote.

l16 Some manuscripts *him."*
17Now he was obliged to release one man to them at the Feast.

The Crucifixion of Jesus

26 As they led him away, they seized a man, Simon of Cyrene, who was coming from the country, and they laid the cross on him, and made him carry it behind Jesus. 27 A great number of the people followed him, and among them were women who were beating their breasts and wailing for him. 28 But Jesus turned to them and said, "Daughters of Jerusalem, do not weep for me, but weep for yourselves and for your children. 29 For the days are surely coming when they will say, 'Blessed are the barren, and the wombs that never bore, and the breasts that never nursed.' 30 Then they will begin to say to the mountains, 'Fall on us'; and to the hills, 'Cover us.' 31 For if they do this when the wood is green, what will happen when it is dry?"

32 Two others also, who were criminals, were led away to be put to death with him. 33 When they came to the place that is called The Skull, they crucified Jesus[h] there with the criminals, one on his right and one on his left. [34 Then Jesus said, "Father, forgive them; for they do not know what they are doing."][i] And they cast lots to divide his clothing. 35 And the people stood by, watching; but the leaders scoffed at him, saying, "He saved others; let him save himself if he is the Messiah[j] of God, his chosen one!" 36 The soldiers also mocked him, coming up and offering him sour wine, 37 and

---

26 Καὶ ὡς ἀπήγαγον αὐτόν, ἐπιλαβόμενοι
And as they led away him, seizing

Σίμωνά τινα Κυρηναῖον ἐρχόμενον ἀπ'
Simon a certain Cyrenian coming from

ἀγροῦ ἐπέθηκαν αὐτῷ τὸν σταυρὸν φέρειν
[the] country they placed on him the cross to carry

ὄπισθεν τοῦ Ἰησοῦ. **27** Ἠκολούθει δὲ
behind - Jesus. And followed

αὐτῷ πολὺ πλῆθος τοῦ λαοῦ καὶ γυναικῶν
him a much multitude of the people and of women

αἳ ἐκόπτοντο καὶ ἐθρήνουν αὐτόν. **28** στρα-
who mourned and lamented him. turn

φεὶς δὲ πρὸς αὐτὰς Ἰησοῦς εἶπεν·
ing And to them Jesus said :

θυγατέρες Ἰερουσαλήμ, μὴ κλαίετε ἐπ'
Daughters of Jerusalem, do not weep over

ἐμέ· πλὴν ἐφ' ἑαυτὰς κλαίετε καὶ ἐπὶ
me; but over yourselves weep and over

τὰ τέκνα ὑμῶν, **29** ὅτι ἰδοὺ ἔρχονται
the children of you, because behold come

ἡμέραι ἐν αἷς ἐροῦσιν· μακάριαι αἱ
days in which they will say : Blessed the

στεῖραι, καὶ αἱ κοιλίαι αἳ οὐκ ἐγέννησαν,
barren, and the wombs which bare not,

καὶ μαστοὶ οἳ οὐκ ἔθρεψαν. **30** τότε
and breasts which gave not suck. Then

ἄρξονται λέγειν τοῖς ὄρεσιν· πέσατε ἐφ'
they will begin to say to the mountains : Fall on

ἡμᾶς, καὶ τοῖς βουνοῖς· καλύψατε ἡμᾶς,
us, and to the hills : Cover us;

31 ὅτι εἰ ἐν ὑγρῷ ξύλῳ ταῦτα ποιοῦσιν,
because if in [a]full of sap [a]tree these things they do,

ἐν τῷ ξηρῷ τί γένηται; **32** Ἤγοντο δὲ
in the dry what may happen? And were led

καὶ ἕτεροι κακοῦργοι δύο σὺν αὐτῷ
also others* criminals two with him

ἀναιρεθῆναι. **33** Καὶ ὅτε ἦλθον ἐπὶ τὸν
to be killed. And when they came upon the

τόπον τὸν καλούμενον Κρανίον, ἐκεῖ ἐσταύ-
place - being called Skull, there they

ρωσαν αὐτὸν καὶ τοὺς κακούργους, ὃν μὲν
crucified him and the criminals, one†

ἐκ δεξιῶν ὃν δὲ ἐξ ἀριστερῶν. **34** [ὁ δὲ
on [the] right and one† on [the] left. - And

Ἰησοῦς ἔλεγεν· πάτερ, ἄφες αὐτοῖς· οὐ
Jesus said : Father, forgive them; ²not

γὰρ οἴδασιν τί ποιοῦσιν.] διαμεριζόμενοι
¹for ³they know what they are doing.] dividing

δὲ τὰ ἱμάτια αὐτοῦ ἔβαλον κλήρους.
And the garments of him they cast lots.

35 καὶ εἱστήκει ὁ λαὸς θεωρῶν. ἐξεμυκ-
And stood the people beholding. scoff-

τήριζον δὲ καὶ οἱ ἄρχοντες λέγοντες·
ed And also the rulers saying :

ἄλλους ἔσωσεν, σωσάτω ἑαυτόν, εἰ οὗτός
Others he saved, let him save himself, if this man

ἐστιν ὁ χριστὸς τοῦ θεοῦ ὁ ἐκλεκτός.
is the Christ - of God the chosen [one].

36 ἐνέπαιξαν δὲ αὐτῷ καὶ οἱ στρατιῶται
And mocked him also the soldiers

προσερχόμενοι, ὄξος προσφέροντες αὐτῷ
approaching, vinegar offering to him

The Crucifixion

26 As they led him away, they seized Simon from Cyrene, who was on his way in from the country, and put the cross on him and made him carry it behind Jesus. 27 A large number of people followed him, including women who mourned and wailed for him. 28 Jesus turned and said to them, "Daughters of Jerusalem, do not weep for me; weep for yourselves and for your children. 29 For the time will come when you will say, 'Blessed are the barren women, the wombs that never bore and the breasts that never nursed!' 30 Then

" 'they will say to the mountains, "Fall on us!" and to the hills, "Cover us!" ' " [m]

31 For if men do these things when the tree is green, what will happen when it is dry?"

32 Two other men, both criminals, were also led out with him to be executed. 33 When they came to the place called the Skull, there they crucified him, along with the criminals—one on his right, the other on his left. 34 Jesus said, "Father, forgive them, for they do not know what they are doing." [n] And they divided up his clothes by casting lots.

35 The people stood watching, and the rulers even sneered at him. They said, "He saved others; let him save himself if he is the Christ of God, the Chosen One."

36 The soldiers also came up and mocked him. They offered him wine vinegar

---

[h] Gk him
[i] Other ancient authorities lack the sentence *Then Jesus ... what they are doing*
[j] Or *the Christ*

* Luke uses ἕτεροι here with strict accuracy = "different." Jesus was not himself a criminal. Note punctuation of A.V. Cf. Acts 28. 1.

[m]30 Hosea 10:8
[n]34 Some early manuscripts do not have this sentence.

saying, "If you are the King of the Jews, save yourself!" 38 There was also an inscription over him,[k] "This is the King of the Jews."

39 One of the criminals who were hanged there kept deriding[l] him and saying, "Are you not the Messiah?[j] Save yourself and us!" 40 But the other rebuked him, saying, "Do you not fear God, since you are under the same sentence of condemnation? 41 And we indeed have been condemned justly, for we are getting what we deserve for our deeds, but this man has done nothing wrong." 42 Then he said, "Jesus, remember me when you come into[m] your kingdom." 43 He replied, "Truly I tell you, today you will be with me in Paradise."

The Death of Jesus

44 It was now about noon, and darkness came over the whole land[n] until three in the afternoon, 45 while the sun's light failed;[o] and the curtain of the temple was torn in two. 46 Then Jesus, crying with a loud voice, said, "Father, into your hands I commend my spirit." Having said this, he breathed his last. 47 When the centurion saw what had taken place, he praised God and said, "Certainly this man was innocent."[p] 48 And when all the crowds who had gathered there for this spectacle saw what had taken place,. they returned home, beating their breasts. 49 But all his acquaintances, including the women who had followed him from Galilee, stood at a distance, watching these things.

The Burial of Jesus

50 Now there was a good and righteous man named Joseph, who, though a member of the

---

37 καὶ λέγοντες· εἰ σὺ εἶ ὁ βασιλεὺς
and saying: If thou art the king
τῶν Ἰουδαίων, σῶσον σεαυτόν. 38 ἦν δὲ
of the Jews, save thyself. And there was
καὶ ἐπιγραφὴ ἐπ᾽ αὐτῷ· Ο ΒΑΣΙΛΕΥΣ
also a superscription over him: THE KING
ΤΩΝ ΙΟΥΔΑΙΩΝ ΟΥΤΟΣ. 39 Εἷς δὲ
OF THE JEWS THIS. And one
τῶν κρεμασθέντων κακούργων ἐβλασφήμει
of the hanged criminals blasphemed
αὐτόν· οὐχὶ σὺ εἶ ὁ χριστός; σῶσον
him: Not thou art the Christ? save
σεαυτὸν καὶ ἡμᾶς 40 ἀποκριθεὶς δὲ ὁ
thyself and us. But answering the
ἕτερος ἐπιτιμῶν αὐτῷ ἔφη· οὐδὲ φοβῇ σὺ
other rebuking him said: Not fearest thou
τὸν θεόν, ὅτι ἐν τῷ αὐτῷ κρίματι εἶ;
- God, because in the same judgment thou art?
41 καὶ ἡμεῖς μὲν δικαίως, ἄξια γὰρ ὧν
And we indeed justly, for things worthy of what
ἐπράξαμεν ἀπολαμβάνομεν· οὗτος δὲ οὐδὲν
we did we receive back; but this man nothing
ἄτοπον ἔπραξεν. 42 καὶ ἔλεγεν Ἰησοῦ,
amiss did. And he said: Jesus,
μνήσθητί μου ὅταν ἔλθῃς εἰς τὴν βασιλείαν
remember me when thou comest into the kingdom
σου. 43 καὶ εἶπεν αὐτῷ· ἀμήν σοι λέγω,
of thee. And he said to him. Truly thee I tell,
σήμερον μετ᾽ ἐμοῦ ἔσῃ ἐν τῷ παραδείσῳ.
to-day with me thou wilt be in the paradise.
44 Καὶ ἦν ἤδη ὡσεὶ ὥρα ἕκτη καὶ
And it was now about hour sixth and
σκότος ἐγένετο ἐφ᾽ ὅλην τὴν γῆν ἕως
darkness came over all the land until
ὥρας ἐνάτης 45 τοῦ ἡλίου ἐκλιπόντος·
hour ninth the sun failing;[a]
     =as the sun failed;
ἐσχίσθη δὲ τὸ καταπέτασμα τοῦ ναοῦ
and was torn the veil of the shrine
μέσον. 46 καὶ φωνήσας φωνῇ μεγάλῃ ὁ
in the middle. And crying voice with a great -
Ἰησοῦς εἶπεν· πάτερ, εἰς χεῖράς σου
Jesus said: Father, into hands of thee
παρατίθεμαι τὸ πνεῦμά μου. τοῦτο δὲ
I commit the spirit of me. And this
εἰπὼν ἐξέπνευσεν. 47 ἰδὼν δὲ ὁ ἑκατον-
saying he expired. And ²seeing ¹the ²cen-
τάρχης τὸ γενόμενον ἐδόξαζεν τὸν θεὸν
turion the thing happening glorified - God
λέγων· ὄντως ὁ ἄνθρωπος οὗτος δίκαιος
saying: Really - man this righteous
ἦν. 48 καὶ πάντες οἱ συμπαραγενόμενοι
was. And all ¹the ²arriving together
ὄχλοι ἐπὶ τὴν θεωρίαν ταύτην, θεωρήσαντες τὰ
²crowds at - sight this, beholding the things
γενόμενα, τύπτοντες τὰ στήθη ὑπέστρεφον.
happening, smiting the(ir) breasts returned.
49 εἰστήκεισαν δὲ πάντες οἱ γνωστοὶ αὐτῷ
And ⁵stood ¹all ²the [ones] ³known ⁴to him
ἀπὸ μακρόθεν, καὶ γυναῖκες αἱ συνακο-
⁶afar off, and women the [ones] accom-
λουθοῦσαι αὐτῷ ἀπὸ τῆς Γαλιλαίας, ὁρῶσαι
panying him from - Galilee, seeing
ταῦτα.
these things.
50 Καὶ ἰδοὺ ἀνὴρ ὀνόματι Ἰωσὴφ
And behold[,] a man by name Joseph

---

37 and said, "If you are the king of the Jews, save yourself."
38 There was a written notice above him, which read: THIS IS THE KING OF THE JEWS.
39 One of the criminals who hung there hurled insults at him: "Aren't you the Christ? Save yourself and us!"
40 But the other criminal rebuked him. "Don't you fear God," he said, "since you are under the same sentence? 41 We are punished justly, for we are getting what our deeds deserve. But this man has done nothing wrong."
42 Then he said, "Jesus, remember me when you come into your kingdom.[o]"
43 Jesus answered him, "I tell you the truth, today you will be with me in paradise."

Jesus' Death

44 It was now about the sixth hour, and darkness came over the whole land until the ninth hour, 45 for the sun stopped shining. And the curtain of the temple was torn in two. 46 Jesus called out with a loud voice, "Father, into your hands I commit my spirit." When he had said this, he breathed his last.
47 The centurion, seeing what had happened, praised God and said, "Surely this was a righteous man." 48 When all the people who had gathered to witness this sight saw what took place, they beat their breasts and went away. 49 But all those who knew him, including the women who had followed him from Galilee, stood at a distance, watching these things.

Jesus' Burial

50 Now there was a man named Joseph, a member

---

[k] Other ancient authorities add *written in Greek and Latin and Hebrew* (that is, *Aramaic*)
[l] Or *blaspheming*
[m] Other ancient authorities read *in*
[n] Or *earth*
[o] Or *the sun was eclipsed.* Other ancient authorities read *the sun was darkened*
[p] Or *righteous*

[o]42 Some manuscripts *come with your kingly power*

council, 51had not agreed to their plan and action. He came from the Jewish town of Arimathea, and he was waiting expectantly for the kingdom of God. 52This man went to Pilate and asked for the body of Jesus. 53Then he took it down, wrapped it in a linen cloth, and laid it in a rock-hewn tomb where no one had ever been laid. 54It was the day of Preparation, and the sabbath was beginning.*q* 55The women who had come with him from Galilee followed, and they saw the tomb and how his body was laid. 56Then they returned, and prepared spices and ointments.

On the sabbath they rested according to the commandment.

Chapter 24

The Resurrection of Jesus

BUT on the first day of the week, at early dawn, they came to the tomb, taking the spices that they had prepared. 2They found the stone rolled away from the tomb, 3but when they went in, they did not find the body.*r* 4While they were perplexed about this, suddenly two men in dazzling clothes stood beside them. 5The women*s* were terrified and bowed their faces to the ground, but the men*t* said to them, "Why do you look for the living among the dead? He is not here, but has risen.*u* 6Remember how he told you, while he was still in Galilee, 7that the Son of Man must be handed over to sinners, and be crucified, and on the third day

---

βουλευτὴς ὑπάρχων, ἀνὴρ ἀγαθὸς καὶ
a councillor   being,   a man   good   and

δίκαιος, — 51 οὗτος οὐκ ἦν συγκατατεθειμένος
righteous, —   this man   was not   agreeing with

τῇ βουλῇ καὶ τῇ πράξει αὐτῶν, — ἀπὸ
the counsel   and   the   action   of them, — from

'Αριμαθαίας πόλεως τῶν 'Ιουδαίων, ὃς
Arimathæa   a city   of the   Jews,   who

προσεδέχετο τὴν βασιλείαν τοῦ θεοῦ,
was awaiting   the   kingdom   -   of God,

52 οὗτος προσελθὼν τῷ Πιλάτῳ ᾐτήσατο
this man   approaching   to Pilate   asked

τὸ σῶμα τοῦ 'Ιησοῦ, 53 καὶ καθελὼν
the   body   -   of Jesus,   and   taking down

ἐνετύλιξεν αὐτὸ σινδόνι, καὶ ἔθηκεν αὐτὸν
wrapped   it   in linen,   and   placed   him

ἐν μνήματι λαξευτῷ, οὗ οὐκ ἦν οὐδεὶς
in   tomb   a hewn,   where   was not   no(any)one

οὔπω κείμενος. 54 καὶ ἡμέρα ἦν παρασκευῆς,
not yet   laid.   And   day   it was   of preparation,

καὶ σάββατον ἐπέφωσκεν. 55 Κατακολουθήσασαι
and   a sabbath   was coming on.   *6*following after

δὲ αἱ γυναῖκες, αἵτινες ἦσαν συνεληλυθυῖαι
*1*And *2*the *3*women,   who   were   *1*having come *with*

ἐκ τῆς Γαλιλαίας αὐτῷ, ἐθεάσαντο τὸ
*3*out of   -   *4*Galilee   *2*with him,   beheld   the

μνημεῖον καὶ ὡς ἐτέθη τὸ σῶμα αὐτοῦ,
tomb   and   how   was placed   the   body   of him,

56 ὑποστρέψασαι δὲ ἡτοίμασαν ἀρώματα καὶ
and returning   prepared   spices   and

μύρα.
ointment.

Καὶ τὸ μὲν σάββατον ἡσύχασαν κατὰ
And [on] the *2*indeed *1*sabbath   they rested according to

τὴν ἐντολήν. 24 τῇ δὲ μιᾷ τῶν σαββάτων
the commandment.   But on the   one   of the   week

ὄρθρου βαθέως ἐπὶ τὸ μνῆμα ἦλθον φέρουσαι
while still very early† upon   the   tomb   they came   carrying

ἃ ἡτοίμασαν ἀρώματα. 2 εὗρον δὲ τὸν
*2*which *3*they prepared *1*spices.   And they found   the

λίθον ἀποκεκυλισμένον ἀπὸ τοῦ μνημείου,
stone   *having been* rolled away   from   the   tomb,

3 εἰσελθοῦσαι δὲ οὐχ εὗρον τὸ σῶμα
and entering   they found not   the   body

τοῦ κυρίου 'Ιησοῦ. 4 καὶ ἐγένετο ἐν τῷ
of the   Lord   Jesus.   And   it was   in   the
                                                   =as they were perplexed

ἀπορεῖσθαι αὐτὰς περὶ τούτου καὶ ἰδοὺ
to be perplexed   them*b*   about   this   and behold[,]

ἄνδρες δύο ἐπέστησαν αὐταῖς ἐν ἐσθῆτι
men   two   stood by   them   in   clothing

ἀστραπτούσῃ· 5 ἐμφόβων δὲ γενομένων
shining;   and terrified   becoming
                         =as they became terrified and bent their faces

αὐτῶν καὶ κλινουσῶν τὰ πρόσωπα εἰς τὴν
them   and   bending   the(ir)   faces*a*   to   the

γῆν, εἶπαν πρὸς αὐτάς· τί ζητεῖτε τὸν
earth,   they said   to   them·   Why   seek ye   the

ζῶντα μετὰ τῶν νεκρῶν; 6 [οὐκ ἔστιν
living [one] with   the   dead [ones]?   He is not

ὧδε, ἀλλὰ ἠγέρθη.] μνήσθητε ὡς ἐλάλησεν
here,   but   was raised.   Remember   how   he spoke

ὑμῖν ἔτι ὢν ἐν τῇ Γαλιλαίᾳ, 7 λέγων
to you   yet   being   in   -   Galilee,   saying[,]

τὸν υἱὸν τοῦ ἀνθρώπου ὅτι δεῖ παραδο-
The   Son   -   of man   -   it behoves   to be de-

θῆναι εἰς χεῖρας ἀνθρώπων ἁμαρτωλῶν καὶ
livered   into   hands   men   of sinful   and

---

of the Council, a good and upright man, 51who had not consented to their decision and action. He came from the Judean town of Arimathea and he was waiting for the kingdom of God. 52Going to Pilate, he asked for Jesus' body. 53Then he took it down, wrapped it in linen cloth and placed it in a tomb cut in the rock, one in which no one had yet been laid. 54It was Preparation Day, and the Sabbath was about to begin.

55The women who had come with Jesus from Galilee followed Joseph and saw the tomb and how his body was laid in it. 56Then they went home and prepared spices and perfumes. But they rested on the Sabbath in obedience to the commandment.

Chapter 24

The Resurrection

ON the first day of the week, very early in the morning, the women took the spices they had prepared and went to the tomb. 2They found the stone rolled away from the tomb, 3but when they entered, they did not find the body of the Lord Jesus. 4While they were wondering about this, suddenly two men in clothes that gleamed like lightning stood beside them. 5In their fright the women bowed down with their faces to the ground, but the men said to them, "Why do you look for the living among the dead? 6He is not here; he has risen! Remember how he told you, while he was still with you in Galilee: 7'The Son of Man must be delivered into the hands of rise again." [8] Then they remembered his words, [9] and returning from the tomb, they told all this to the eleven and to all the rest. [10] Now it was Mary Magdalene, Joanna, Mary the mother of James, and the other women with them who told this to the apostles. [11] But these words seemed to them an idle tale, and they did not believe them. [12] But Peter got up and ran to the tomb; stooping and looking in, he saw the linen cloths by themselves; then he went home, amazed at what had happened. [v]

The Walk to Emmaus

13 Now on that same day two of them were going to a village called Emmaus, about seven miles [w] from Jerusalem, [14] and talking with each other about all these things that had happened. [15] While they were talking and discussing, Jesus himself came near and went with them, [16] but their eyes were kept from recognizing him. [17] And he said to them, "What are you discussing with each other while you walk along?" They stood still, looking sad. [x] [18] Then one of them, whose name was Cleopas, answered him, "Are you the only stranger in Jerusalem who does not know the things that have taken place there in these days?" [19] He asked them, "What things?" They replied, "The things about Jesus of Nazareth, [y] who was a prophet mighty in deed and word before God and all the people, [20] and how our chief priests and leaders handed him over to be condemned to death and

---

σταυρωθῆναι καὶ τῇ τρίτῃ ἡμέρᾳ ἀναστῆναι.
to be crucified and on the third day to rise again.

8 καὶ ἐμνήσθησαν τῶν ῥημάτων αὐτοῦ,
And they remembered the words of him,

9 καὶ ὑποστρέψασαι ἀπὸ τοῦ μνημείου
and returning from the tomb

ἀπήγγειλαν ταῦτα πάντα τοῖς ἔνδεκα καὶ
reported these things all to the eleven and

πᾶσιν τοῖς λοιποῖς. 10 ἦσαν δὲ ἡ
to all the rest. Now they were the

Μαγδαληνὴ Μαρία καὶ Ἰωάννα καὶ Μαρία
Magdalene Mary and Joanna and Mary

ἡ Ἰακώβου· καὶ αἱ λοιπαὶ* σὺν αὐταῖς*
the [mother] of James; and the rest with them

ἔλεγον πρὸς τοὺς ἀποστόλους ταῦτα. 11 καὶ
told to the apostles these things. And

ἐφάνησαν ἐνώπιον αὐτῶν ὡσεὶ λῆρος
seemed before them as folly

τὰ ῥήματα ταῦτα, καὶ ἠπίστουν αὐταῖς.* ‡
- words these, and they disbelieved them.

13 Καὶ ἰδοὺ δύο ἐξ αὐτῶν ἐν αὐτῇ τῇ
And behold[,] two of them on the same the

ἡμέρᾳ ἦσαν πορευόμενοι εἰς κώμην ἀπέχουσαν
day were journeying to a village being distant

σταδίους ἑξήκοντα ἀπὸ Ἰερουσαλήμ, ᾗ
furlongs sixty from Jerusalem, to which

ὄνομα Ἐμμαοῦς, 14 καὶ αὐτοὶ ὡμίλουν
name Emmaus, and they talked

πρὸς ἀλλήλους περὶ πάντων τῶν συμβεβηκότων
to each other about all - *having occurred

τούτων. 15 καὶ ἐγένετο ἐν τῷ ὁμιλεῖν
*these things. And it came to pass in the to talk

αὐτοὺς καὶ συζητεῖν, καὶ αὐτὸς Ἰησοῦς
them and to discuss[bc], and [him]self Jesus
= as they talked and discussed,

ἐγγίσας συνεπορεύετο αὐτοῖς· 16 οἱ δὲ
drawing near journeyed with them; but the

ὀφθαλμοὶ αὐτῶν ἐκρατοῦντο τοῦ μὴ
eyes of them were held - not

ἐπιγνῶναι αὐτόν. 17 εἶπεν δὲ πρὸς αὐτούς·
to recognize[d] him. And he said to them:

τίνες οἱ λόγοι οὗτοι οὓς ἀντιβάλλετε
What - words these which ye exchange

πρὸς ἀλλήλους περιπατοῦντες; καὶ ἐστάθησαν
with each other walking? And they stood

σκυθρωποί. 18 ἀποκριθεὶς δὲ εἷς ὀνόματι
sad-faced. And answering one by name

Κλεοπᾶς εἶπεν πρὸς αὐτόν· σὺ μόνος
Cleopas said to him: Thou only

παροικεῖς Ἰερουσαλὴμ καὶ οὐκ ἔγνως τὰ
a stranger in Jerusalem and knewest not the things

γενόμενα ἐν αὐτῇ ἐν ταῖς ἡμέραις ταύταις;
happening in it in - days these?

19 καὶ εἶπεν αὐτοῖς· ποῖα; οἱ δὲ εἶπαν
And he said to them: What things? And they said

αὐτῷ· τὰ περὶ Ἰησοῦ τοῦ Ναζαρηνοῦ, ὃς
to him: The things about Jesus the Nazarene, who

ἐγένετο ἀνὴρ προφήτης δυνατὸς ἐν ἔργῳ
was a man prophet powerful in work

καὶ λόγῳ ἐναντίον τοῦ θεοῦ καὶ παντὸς
and word before - God and all

τοῦ λαοῦ, 20 ὅπως τε παρέδωκαν αὐτὸν οἱ
the people, how both ¹delivered ⁵him ¹the

ἀρχιερεῖς καὶ οἱ ἄρχοντες ἡμῶν εἰς
¹chief priests ²and ⁴the ⁴rulers ⁶of us to

* **Note the feminines.**

‡ Verse 12 omitted by Nestle.

---

sinful men, be crucified and on the third day be raised again.' " [8] Then they remembered his words.

[9] When they came back from the tomb, they told all these things to the Eleven and to all the others. [10] It was Mary Magdalene, Joanna, Mary the mother of James, and the others with them who told this to the apostles. [11] But they did not believe the women, because their words seemed to them like nonsense. [12] Peter, however, got up and ran to the tomb. Bending over, he saw the strips of linen lying by themselves, and he went away, wondering to himself what had happened.

On the Road to Emmaus

[13] Now that same day two of them were going to a village called Emmaus, about seven miles [p] from Jerusalem. [14] They were talking with each other about everything that had happened. [15] As they talked and discussed these things with each other, Jesus himself came up and walked along with them; [16] but they were kept from recognizing him. [17] He asked them, "What are you discussing together as you walk along?"

They stood still, their faces downcast. [18] One of them, named Cleopas, asked him, "Are you only a visitor to Jerusalem and do not know the things that have happened there in these days?"

[19] "What things?" he asked.

"About Jesus of Nazareth," they replied. "He was a prophet, powerful in word and deed before God and all the people. [20] The chief priests and our rulers handed him over to be sen-

---

crucified him. 21 But we had hoped that he was the one to redeem Israel. z Yes, and besides all this, it is now the third day since these things took place. 22 Moreover, some women of our group astounded us. They were at the tomb early this morning, 23 and when they did not find his body there, they came back and told us that they had indeed seen a vision of angels who said that he was alive. 24 Some of those who were with us went to the tomb and found it just as the women had said; but they did not see him." 25 Then he said to them, "Oh, how foolish you are, and how slow of heart to believe all that the prophets have declared! 26 Was it not necessary that the Messiah a should suffer these things and then enter into his glory?" 27 Then beginning with Moses and all the prophets, he interpreted to them the things about himself in all the scriptures.

28 As they came near the village to which they were going, he walked ahead as if he were going on. 29 But they urged him strongly, saying, "Stay with us, because it is almost evening and the day is now nearly over." So he went in to stay with them. 30 When he was at the table with them, he took bread, blessed and broke it, and gave it to them. 31 Then their eyes were opened, and they recognized him; and he vanished from their sight. 32 They said to each other, "Were not our hearts

---

κρίμα θανάτου καὶ ἐσταύρωσαν αὐτόν.
[the] judgment of death and crucified him.

21 ἡμεῖς δὲ ἠλπίζομεν ὅτι αὐτός ἐστιν
But we were hoping that he it is(was)

ὁ μέλλων λυτροῦσθαι τὸν Ἰσραήλ· ἀλλά
the [one] being about to redeem - Israel; but

γε καὶ σὺν πᾶσιν τούτοις τρίτην ταύτην
- also with all these things third this
                                              =this is the third day

ἡμέραν ἄγει ἀφ’ οὗ ταῦτα ἐγένετο.
day it leads since these things happened.

22 ἀλλὰ καὶ γυναῖκές τινες ἐξ ἡμῶν
But also ²women ¹some ¹some of us

ἐξέστησαν ἡμᾶς, γενόμεναι ὀρθριναὶ ἐπὶ τὸ
astonished us, being early at the

μνημεῖον, 23 καὶ μὴ εὑροῦσαι τὸ σῶμα
tomb, and not finding the body

αὐτοῦ ἦλθον λέγουσαι καὶ ὀπτασίαν ἀγγέλων
of him came saying also a vision of angels

ἑωρακέναι, οἳ λέγουσιν αὐτὸν ζῆν. 24 καὶ
to have seen, who say him to live. And
                                        =that he lives.

ἀπῆλθόν τινες τῶν σὺν ἡμῖν ἐπὶ τὸ
⁵went ¹some ²of the [ones] ³with ⁴us to the

μνημεῖον, καὶ εὗρον οὕτως καθὼς καὶ αἱ
tomb, and found so as indeed the

γυναῖκες εἶπον, αὐτὸν δὲ οὐκ εἶδον.
women said, but him they saw not.

25 καὶ αὐτὸς εἶπεν πρὸς αὐτούς· ὦ
And he said to them : O

ἀνόητοι καὶ βραδεῖς τῇ καρδίᾳ τοῦ πιστεύειν
foolish [ones] and slow - in heart to believe d

ἐπὶ πᾶσιν οἷς ἐλάλησαν οἱ προφῆται·
on(in) all things which spoke the prophets :

26 οὐχὶ ταῦτα ἔδει παθεῖν τὸν χριστὸν καὶ
²not ⁶these things ¹behoved it ³to suffer ⁵the ⁴Christ and

εἰσελθεῖν εἰς τὴν δόξαν αὐτοῦ; 27 καὶ
to enter into the glory of him? And

ἀρξάμενος ἀπὸ Μωϋσέως καὶ ἀπὸ πάντων
beginning from Moses and from all

τῶν προφητῶν διηρμήνευσεν αὐτοῖς ἐν
the prophets he explained to them in

πάσαις ταῖς γραφαῖς τὰ περὶ ἑαυτοῦ.
all the scriptures the things concerning himself.

28 Καὶ ἤγγισαν εἰς τὴν κώμην οὗ
And they drew near to the village whither

ἐπορεύοντο, καὶ αὐτὸς προσεποιήσατο
they were journeying, and he pretended

πορρώτερον πορεύεσθαι. 29 καὶ παρε-
farther to journey. And they

βιάσαντο αὐτὸν λέγοντες· μεῖνον μεθ’
urged him saying : Remain with

ἡμῶν, ὅτι πρὸς ἑσπέραν ἐστὶν καὶ κέκλικεν
us, because toward evening it is and has declined

ἤδη ἡ ἡμέρα. καὶ εἰσῆλθεν τοῦ μεῖναι
now the day. And he went in - to remain d

σὺν αὐτοῖς. 30 καὶ ἐγένετο ἐν τῷ
with them. And it came to pass in the
                                      =as he reclined

κατακλιθῆναι αὐτὸν μετ’ αὐτῶν λαβὼν τὸν
to recline him b e with them taking the

ἄρτον εὐλόγησεν καὶ κλάσας ἐπεδίδου
loaf he blessed and having broken he handed

αὐτοῖς· 31 αὐτῶν δὲ διηνοίχθησαν οἱ
to them; and of them were opened up the

ὀφθαλμοί, καὶ ἐπέγνωσαν αὐτόν· καὶ αὐτὸς
eyes, and they recognized him; and he

ἄφαντος ἐγένετο ἀπ’ αὐτῶν. 32 καὶ
invisible became from them. And

---

tenced to death, and they crucified him; 21 but we had hoped that he was the one who was going to redeem Israel. And what is more, it is the third day since all this took place. 22 In addition, some of our women amazed us. They went to the tomb early this morning 23 but didn't find his body. They came and told us that they had seen a vision of angels, who said he was alive. 24 Then some of our companions went to the tomb and found it just as the women had said, but him they did not see."

25 He said to them, "How foolish you are, and how slow of heart to believe all that the prophets have spoken! 26 Did not the Christ a have to suffer these things and then enter his glory?" 27 And beginning with Moses and all the Prophets, he explained to them what was said in all the Scriptures concerning himself.

28 As they approached the village to which they were going, Jesus acted as if he were going farther. 29 But they urged him strongly, "Stay with us, for it is nearly evening; the day is almost over." So he went in to stay with them. 30 When he was at the table with them, he took bread, gave thanks, broke it and began to give it to them. 31 Then their eyes were opened and they recognized him, and he disappeared from their sight. 32 They asked each other,

---

z Or to set Israel free
a Or the Christ

a26 Or Messiah; also in verse 46

burning within us[b] while he was talking to us on the road, while he was opening the scriptures to us?" [33] That same hour they got up and returned to Jerusalem; and they found the eleven and their companions gathered together. [34] They were saying, "The Lord has risen indeed, and he has appeared to Simon!" [35] Then they told what had happened on the road, and how he had been made known to them in the breaking of the bread.

Jesus Appears to His Disciples

[36] While they were talking about this, Jesus himself stood among them and said to them, "Peace be with you."[c] [37] They were startled and terrified, and thought that they were seeing a ghost. [38] He said to them, "Why are you frightened, and why do doubts arise in your hearts? [39] Look at my hands and my feet; see that it is I myself. Touch me and see; for a ghost does not have flesh and bones as you see that I have." [40] And when he had said this, he showed them his hands and his feet.[d] [41] While in their joy they were disbelieving and still wondering, he said to them, "Have you anything here to eat?" [42] They gave him a piece of broiled fish, [43] and he took it and ate in their presence.

[44] Then he said to them, "These are my words that I spoke to you while I was still with you, that everything written about me in the law of Moses, the prophets, and the psalms must be fulfilled." [45] Then he opened their minds to understand the scriptures, [46] and he said to them, "Thus it is written, that the Messiah[e] is to suffer and to

---

εἶπαν πρὸς ἀλλήλους· οὐχὶ ἡ καρδία
they said to each other : Not the heart

ἡμῶν καιομένη ἦν ἐν ἡμῖν, ὡς ἐλάλει
of us burning was in us, as he spoke

ἡμῖν ἐν τῇ ὁδῷ, ὡς διήνοιγεν ἡμῖν τὰς
to us in the way, as he opened up to us the

γραφάς; 33 Καὶ ἀναστάντες αὐτῇ τῇ ὥρᾳ
scriptures? And rising up ²same ¹in the hour

ὑπέστρεψαν εἰς Ἰερουσαλήμ, καὶ εὗρον
they returned to Jerusalem, and found

ἠθροισμένους τοὺς ἕνδεκα καὶ τοὺς σὺν
having been collected the eleven and the [ones] with

αὐτοῖς, 34 λέγοντας ὅτι ὄντως ἠγέρθη ὁ
them, saying[.] - Really was raised the

κύριος καὶ ὤφθη Σίμωνι. 35 καὶ αὐτοὶ ἐξηγοῦντο
Lord and appeared to Simon. And they related

τὰ ἐν τῇ ὁδῷ καὶ ὡς ἐγνώσθη
the things in the way and how he was known

αὐτοῖς ἐν τῇ κλάσει τοῦ ἄρτου. 36 Ταῦτα
by them in the breaking of the loaf. these things

δὲ αὐτῶν λαλούντων αὐτὸς ἔστη ἐν
And them saying[a] he stood in
    = as they said these things

μέσῳ αὐτῶν. 37 πτοηθέντες δὲ καὶ
[the] midst of them. But scared and

ἔμφοβοι γενόμενοι ἐδόκουν πνεῦμα θεωρεῖν.
terrified becoming they thought a spirit to behold.

38 καὶ εἶπεν αὐτοῖς· τί τεταραγμένοι ἐστέ,
And he said to them : Why having been troubled are ye,

καὶ διὰ τί διαλογισμοὶ ἀναβαίνουσιν ἐν
and why thoughts come up in

τῇ καρδίᾳ ὑμῶν; 39 ἴδετε τὰς χεῖράς
the heart of you? See the hands

μου καὶ τοὺς πόδας μου, ὅτι ἐγώ εἰμι
of me and the feet of me, that I am

αὐτός· ψηλαφήσατέ με καὶ ἴδετε, ὅτι
[my]self; feel me and see, because

πνεῦμα σάρκα καὶ ὀστέα οὐκ ἔχει καθὼς
a spirit flesh and bones has not as

ἐμὲ θεωρεῖτε ἔχοντα. ‡ 41 ἔτι δὲ ἀπιστούντων
me ye behold having. And yet disbelieving
    = while they yet disbelieved

αὐτῶν ἀπὸ τῆς χαρᾶς καὶ θαυμαζόντων,
them[a] from the joy and marvelling[a],

εἶπεν αὐτοῖς· ἔχετέ τι βρώσιμον ἐνθάδε;
he said to them : Have ye any food here?

42 οἱ δὲ ἐπέδωκαν αὐτῷ ἰχθύος ὀπτοῦ
And they handed to him ²fish ¹of a broiled

μέρος· 43 καὶ λαβὼν ἐνώπιον αὐτῶν ἔφαγεν.
¹part; and taking before them he ate.

44 Εἶπεν δὲ πρὸς αὐτούς· οὗτοι οἱ λόγοι
And he said to them : These - words

μου οὓς ἐλάλησα πρὸς ὑμᾶς ἔτι ὢν σὺν
of me which I spoke to you yet being with

ὑμῖν, ὅτι δεῖ πληρωθῆναι πάντα τὰ
you, that it behoves to be fulfilled all the things

γεγραμμένα ἐν τῷ νόμῳ Μωϋσέως καὶ
having been written in the law of Moses and

τοῖς προφήταις καὶ ψαλμοῖς περὶ ἐμοῦ.
the prophets and psalms concerning me.

45 τότε διήνοιξεν αὐτῶν τὸν νοῦν τοῦ
Then he opened up of them the mind -

συνιέναι τὰς γραφάς· 46 καὶ εἶπεν αὐτοῖς
to understand[d] the scriptures; and said to them[.]

ὅτι οὕτως γέγραπται παθεῖν τὸν χριστὸν
- Thus it has been written ²to suffer ¹the ²Christ

"Were not our hearts burning within us while he talked with us on the road and opened the Scriptures to us?"

[33] They got up and returned at once to Jerusalem. There they found the Eleven and those with them, assembled together [34] and saying, "It is true! The Lord has risen and has appeared to Simon." [35] Then the two told what had happened on the way, and how Jesus was recognized by them when he broke the bread.

Jesus Appears to the Disciples

[36] While they were still talking about this, Jesus himself stood among them and said to them, "Peace be with you."

[37] They were startled and frightened, thinking they saw a ghost. [38] He said to them, "Why are you troubled, and why do doubts rise in your minds? [39] Look at my hands and my feet. It is I myself! Touch me and see; a ghost does not have flesh and bones, as you see I have."

[40] When he had said this, he showed them his hands and feet. [41] And while they still did not believe it because of joy and amazement, he asked them, "Do you have anything here to eat?" [42] They gave him a piece of broiled fish, [43] and he took it and ate it in their presence.

[44] He said to them, "This is what I told you while I was still with you: Everything must be fulfilled that is written about me in the Law of Moses, the Prophets and the Psalms."

[45] Then he opened their minds so they could understand the Scriptures. [46] He told them, "This is what is written: The Christ will suf-

---

‡ Verse 40 omitted by Nestle.

rise from the dead on the third day, 47 and that repentance and forgiveness of sins is to be proclaimed in his name to all nations,^{f} beginning from Jerusalem. 48 You are witnesses of these things. 49 And see, I am sending upon you what my Father promised; so stay here in the city until you have been clothed with power from on high."

The Ascension of Jesus

50 Then he led them out as far as Bethany, and, lifting up his hands, he blessed them. 51 While he was blessing them, he withdrew from them and was carried up into heaven.^{g} 52 And they worshiped him, and^h returned to Jerusalem with great joy; 53 and they were continually in the temple blessing God.^{i}

καὶ ἀναστῆναι ἐκ νεκρῶν τῇ τρίτῃ ἡμέρᾳ,
and to rise again out of [the] dead on the third day,

47 καὶ κηρυχθῆναι ἐπὶ τῷ ὀνόματι αὐτοῦ
and to be proclaimed on(in) the name of him

μετάνοιαν εἰς ἄφεσιν ἁμαρτιῶν εἰς πάντα
repentance unto forgiveness of sins to all

τὰ ἔθνη, — ἀρξάμενοι ἀπὸ Ἰερουσαλήμ.
the nations, — beginning from Jerusalem.

48 ὑμεῖς μάρτυρες τούτων. 49 καὶ ἰδοὺ
Ye [are] witnesses of these things. And behold

ἐγὼ ἐξαποστέλλω τὴν ἐπαγγελίαν τοῦ
I send forth the promise of the

πατρός μου ἐφ’ ὑμᾶς· ὑμεῖς δὲ καθίσατε
Father of me on you; but ye sit

ἐν τῇ πόλει ἕως οὗ ἐνδύσησθε ἐξ ὕψους
in the city until ¹ye are clothed[with]²out of ⁴height

δύναμιν.
²power.

50 Ἐξήγαγεν δὲ αὐτοὺς ἕως πρὸς
And he led out them until toward

Βηθανίαν, καὶ ἐπάρας τὰς χεῖρας αὐτοῦ
Bethany, and lifting up the hands of him

εὐλόγησεν αὐτούς. 51 καὶ ἐγένετο ἐν τῷ
he blessed them. And it came to pass in the

εὐλογεῖν αὐτὸν αὐτοὺς διέστη ἀπ’ αὐτῶν.
to bless him^{be} them he withdrew from them.
=while he blessed

52 καὶ αὐτοὶ ὑπέστρεψαν εἰς Ἰερουσαλὴμ
And they returned to Jerusalem

μετὰ χαρᾶς μεγάλης, 53 καὶ ἦσαν διὰ παντὸς
with joy great, and were continually

ἐν τῷ ἱερῷ εὐλογοῦντες τὸν θεόν.
in the temple blessing - God.

fer and rise from the dead on the third day, 47 and repentance and forgiveness of sins will be preached in his name to all nations, beginning at Jerusalem. 48 You are witnesses of these things. 49 I am going to send you what my Father has promised; but stay in the city until you have been clothed with power from on high.''

The Ascension

50 When he had led them out to the vicinity of Bethany, he lifted up his hands and blessed them. 51 While he was blessing them, he left them and was taken up into heaven. 52 Then they worshiped him and returned to Jerusalem with great joy. 53 And they stayed continually at the temple, praising God.

^{f} Or nations. Beginning from Jerusalem you are witnesses
^{g} Other ancient authorities lack and was carried up into heaven
^{h} Other ancient authorities lack worshiped him, and
^{i} Other ancient authorities add Amen

The Gospel According
to
John

ΚΑΤΑ ΙΩΑΝΝΗΝ
According to John

John

Chapter 1

Chapter 1

The Word Became Flesh

IN the beginning was the Word, and the Word was with God, and the Word was God. ²He was in the beginning with God. ³All things came into being through him, and without him not one thing came into being. What has come into being ⁴in him was life,ᵃ and the life was the light of all people. ⁵The light shines in the darkness, and the darkness did not overcome it.

6 There was a man sent from God, whose name was John. ⁷He came as a witness to testify to the light, so that all might believe through him. ⁸He himself was not the light, but he came to testify to the light. ⁹The true light, which enlightens everyone, was coming into the world.ᵇ

10 He was in the world, and the world came into being through him; yet the world did not know him. ¹¹He came to what was his own,ᶜ and his own people did not accept him. ¹²But to all who received him, who believed in his name, he gave power to become children of God, ¹³who were born, not of blood or of the will of the flesh or of the will of man, but of God.

14 And the Word became flesh and lived among us, and we have seen his glory, the glory as of a father's only son,ᵈ full of grace and truth. ¹⁵(John testified to him and cried out, "This was he of whom I said, 'He who comes after me ranks ahead of me be-

ᵃ Or ³through him. And without him not one thing came into being that has come into being. ⁴In him was life
ᵇ Or He was the true light that enlightens everyone coming into the world
ᶜ Or to his own home
ᵈ Or the Father's only Son

---

1 Ἐν ἀρχῇ ἦν ὁ λόγος, καὶ ὁ λόγος
In [the] beginning was the Word, and the Word
ἦν πρὸς τὸν θεόν, καὶ θεὸς ἦν ὁ λόγος.
was with - God, and God was the Word.*
2 οὗτος ἦν ἐν ἀρχῇ πρὸς τὸν θεόν.
This one was in [the] beginning with - God.
3 πάντα δι' αὐτοῦ ἐγένετο, καὶ χωρὶς
All things through him became, and without
αὐτοῦ ἐγένετο οὐδὲ ἓν ὃ γέγονεν. 4 ἐν
him became not one thing which has become. In
αὐτῷ ζωὴ ἦν, καὶ ἡ ζωὴ ἦν τὸ φῶς
him life was, and the life was the light
τῶν ἀνθρώπων· 5 καὶ τὸ φῶς ἐν τῇ
- of men; and the light in the
σκοτίᾳ φαίνει, καὶ ἡ σκοτία αὐτὸ οὐ
darkness shines, and the darkness it not
κατέλαβεν. 6 Ἐγένετο ἄνθρωπος, ἀπεσταλμένος
overtook. There was a man, having been sent
παρὰ θεοῦ, ὄνομα αὐτῷ Ἰωάννης· 7 οὗτος
from God, name to himᵉ John; this man
ἦλθεν εἰς μαρτυρίαν, ἵνα μαρτυρήσῃ περὶ
came for witness, that he might witness concerning
τοῦ φωτός, ἵνα πάντες πιστεύσωσιν δι'
the light, that all men might believe through
αὐτοῦ. 8 οὐκ ἦν ἐκεῖνος τὸ φῶς, ἀλλ' ἵνα
him. He was not that - light, but that
μαρτυρήσῃ περὶ τοῦ φωτός. 9 Ἦν τὸ φῶς
he might witness concerning the light. It was the light
τὸ ἀληθινόν, ὃ φωτίζει πάντα ἄνθρωπον,
- true, which enlightens every man,
ἐρχόμενον εἰς τὸν κόσμον. 10 ἐν τῷ
coming into the world. In the
κόσμῳ ἦν, καὶ ὁ κόσμος δι' αὐτοῦ
world he was, and the world through him
ἐγένετο, καὶ ὁ κόσμος αὐτὸν οὐκ ἔγνω.
became, and the world him knew not.
11 εἰς τὰ ἴδια ἦλθεν, καὶ οἱ ἴδιοι αὐτὸν
To his own things he came, and his own people him
οὐ παρέλαβον. 12 ὅσοι δὲ ἔλαβον αὐτόν,
received not. But as many as received him,
ἔδωκεν αὐτοῖς ἐξουσίαν τέκνα θεοῦ γεν-
he gave to them right children of God to be-
έσθαι, τοῖς πιστεύουσιν εἰς τὸ ὄνομα αὐτοῦ,
come, to the [ones] believing in the name of him,
13 οἳ οὐκ ἐξ αἱμάτων οὐδὲ ἐκ θελήματος
who not of bloods nor of [the] will
σαρκὸς οὐδὲ ἐκ θελήματος ἀνδρὸς ἀλλ'
of [the] flesh nor of [the] will of a man but
ἐκ θεοῦ ἐγεννήθησαν. 14 Καὶ ὁ λόγος
of God were born. And the Word
σὰρξ ἐγένετο καὶ ἐσκήνωσεν ἐν ἡμῖν,
flesh became and tabernacled among us,
καὶ ἐθεασάμεθα τὴν δόξαν αὐτοῦ, δόξαν
and we beheld the glory of him, glory
ὡς μονογενοῦς παρὰ πατρός, πλήρης χάριτος
as of an only begotten from a father, full of grace
καὶ ἀληθείας. 15 Ἰωάννης μαρτυρεῖ περὶ
and of truth. John witnesses concerning
αὐτοῦ καὶ κέκραγεν λέγων· οὗτος ἦν ὃν
him and has cried out saying : This man was he whom
εἶπον· ὁ ὀπίσω μου ἐρχόμενος ἔμπροσθέν
I said : The [one] after me coming before

* But note that the subject has the article and the predicate has it not; hence translate—" the Word was God ."

The Word Became Flesh

IN the beginning was the Word, and the Word was with God, and the Word was God. ²He was with God in the beginning.

³Through him all things were made; without him nothing was made that has been made. ⁴In him was life, and that life was the light of men. ⁵The light shines in the darkness, but the darkness has not understoodᵃ it.

⁶There came a man who was sent from God; his name was John. ⁷He came as a witness to testify concerning that light, so that through him all men might believe. ⁸He himself was not the light; he came only as a witness to the light. ⁹The true light that gives light to every man was coming into the world.ᵇ

¹⁰He was in the world, and though the world was made through him, the world did not recognize him. ¹¹He came to that which was his own, but his own did not receive him. ¹²Yet to all who received him, to those who believed in his name, he gave the right to become children of God— ¹³children born not of natural descent,ᶜ nor of human decision or a husband's will, but born of God.

¹⁴The Word became flesh and made his dwelling among us. We have seen his glory, the glory of the One and Only,ᵈ who came from the Father, full of grace and truth.

¹⁵John testifies concerning him. He cries out, saying, "This was he of whom I said, 'He who comes after

ᵃ5 Or darkness, and the darkness has not overcome
ᵇ9 Or This was the true light that gives light to every man who comes into the world
ᶜ13 Greek of bloods
ᵈ14,18 Or the Only Begotten

cause he was before me.' ")
16 From his fullness we have all received, grace upon grace. 17 The law indeed was given through Moses; grace and truth came through Jesus Christ. 18 No one has ever seen God. It is God the only Son,*e* who is close to the Father's heart,*f* who has made him known.

The Testimony of John the Baptist

19 This is the testimony given by John when the Jews sent priests and Levites from Jerusalem to ask him, "Who are you?" 20 He confessed and did not deny it, but confessed, "I am not the Messiah."*g* 21 And they asked him, "What then? Are you Elijah?" He said, "I am not." "Are you the prophet?" He answered, "No." 22 Then they said to him, "Who are you? Let us have an answer for those who sent us. What do you say about yourself?" 23 He said,

"I am the voice of
        one crying out
        in the
        wilderness,
'Make straight the
        way of
        the Lord,' "

as the prophet Isaiah said. 24 Now they had been sent from the Pharisees. 25 They asked him, "Why then are you baptizing if you are neither the Messiah,*g* nor Elijah, nor the prophet?" 26 John answered them, "I baptize with water. Among you stands one whom you do not know, 27 the one who is coming after me; I am not worthy to untie the thong of his sandal." 28 This took place in Bethany across the Jordan where John was baptizing.

The Lamb of God

29 The next day he saw

μου γέγονεν, ὅτι πρῶτός μου ἦν. 16 ὅτι
me has become, because first of me he was. Because

ἐκ τοῦ πληρώματος αὐτοῦ ἡμεῖς πάντες
of the fulness of him we all

ἐλάβομεν, καὶ χάριν ἀντὶ χάριτος· 17 ὅτι
received, and grace instead of grace; because

ὁ νόμος διὰ Μωϋσέως ἐδόθη, ἡ χάρις καὶ
the law through Moses was given, the grace and

ἡ ἀλήθεια διὰ Ἰησοῦ Χριστοῦ ἐγένετο.
the truth through Jesus Christ became.

18 Θεὸν οὐδεὶς ἑώρακεν πώποτε· μονογενὴς
God no man has seen never; [the] only begotten

θεὸς ὁ ὢν εἰς τὸν κόλπον τοῦ πατρός,
God the [one] being in the bosom of the Father,

ἐκεῖνος ἐξηγήσατο.
that one declared [?him].

19 Καὶ αὕτη ἐστὶν ἡ μαρτυρία τοῦ
And this is the witness –

Ἰωάννου, ὅτε ἀπέστειλαν πρὸς αὐτὸν οἱ
of John, when ²sent ⁴to ⁵him ¹the

Ἰουδαῖοι ἐξ Ἱεροσολύμων ἱερεῖς καὶ Λευίτας
³Jews ⁶from ⁷Jerusalem ⁶priests ⁷and ⁸Levites

ἵνα ἐρωτήσωσιν αὐτόν· σὺ τίς εἶ; 20 καὶ
that they might ask him: Thou who art? And

ὡμολόγησεν καὶ οὐκ ἠρνήσατο, καὶ
he confessed and denied not, and

ὡμολόγησεν ὅτι ἐγὼ οὐκ εἰμὶ ὁ χριστός.
he confessed[,] that I am not the Christ.

21 καὶ ἠρώτησαν αὐτόν· τί οὖν; Ἠλίας εἶ
And they asked him· · What then? Elias art

σύ; καὶ λέγει· οὐκ εἰμί. ὁ προφήτης εἶ σύ;
thou? And he says: I am not. The prophet art thou?

καὶ ἀπεκρίθη· οὔ. 22 εἶπαν οὖν αὐτῷ·
And he answered: No. They said therefore to him:

τίς εἶ; ἵνα ἀπόκρισιν δῶμεν τοῖς
Who art thou? that an answer we may give to the [ones]

πέμψασιν ἡμᾶς· τί λέγεις περὶ σεαυτοῦ;
having sent us· What sayest thou concerning thyself?

23 ἔφη· ἐγὼ φωνὴ βοῶντος ἐν τῇ ἐρήμῳ·
He said: I [am] a voice of [one] crying in the desert:

εὐθύνατε τὴν ὁδὸν κυρίου, καθὼς εἶπεν
Make straight the way of [the] Lord, as said

Ἠσαΐας ὁ προφήτης. 24 Καὶ ἀπεσταλμένοι
Esaias the prophet. And [the ones] having been sent

ἦσαν ἐκ τῶν Φαρισαίων. 25 καὶ ἠρώτησαν
were of the Pharisees. And they asked

αὐτὸν καὶ εἶπαν αὐτῷ· τι οὖν βαπτίζεις
him and said to him: Why then baptizest thou

εἰ σὺ οὐκ εἶ ὁ χριστὸς οὐδὲ Ἠλίας
if thou art not the Christ nor Elias

οὐδὲ ὁ προφήτης; 26 ἀπεκρίθη αὐτοῖς ὁ
nor the prophet? Answered them –

Ἰωάννης λέγων· ἐγὼ βαπτίζω ἐν ὕδατι·
John saying: I baptize in water;

μέσος ὑμῶν στήκει ὃν ὑμεῖς οὐκ οἴδατε,
among you stands [one] whom ye know not,

27 ὁ ὀπίσω μου ἐρχόμενος, οὗ οὐκ εἰμὶ
the [one] after me coming, of whom am not

ἐγὼ ἄξιος ἵνα λύσω αὐτοῦ τὸν ἱμάντα
I worthy that I should loosen of him the thong

τοῦ ὑποδήματος. 28 Ταῦτα ἐν Βηθανίᾳ
of the sandal. These things in Bethany

ἐγένετο πέραν τοῦ Ἰορδάνου, ὅπου ἦν ὁ
happened beyond the Jordan, where was –

Ἰωάννης βαπτίζων. 29 Τῇ ἐπαύριον βλέπει
John baptizing. On the morrow he sees

me has surpassed me because he was before me.' "
16 From the fullness of his grace we have all received one blessing after another. 17 For the law was given through Moses; grace and truth came through Jesus Christ. 18 No one has ever seen God, but God the One and Only,*d* *e*who is at the Father's side, has made him known.

John the Baptist Denies Being the Christ

19 Now this was John's testimony when the Jews of Jerusalem sent priests and Levites to ask him who he was. 20 He did not fail to confess, but confessed freely, "I am not the Christ.*f*" 21 They asked him, "Then who are you? Are you Elijah?"

He said, "I am not."

"Are you the Prophet?" He answered, "No."

22 Finally they said, "Who are you? Give us an answer to take back to those who sent us. What do you say about yourself?"

23 John replied in the words of Isaiah the prophet, "I am the voice of one calling in the desert, 'Make straight the way for the Lord.'*g*"

24 Now some Pharisees who had been sent 25 questioned him, "Why then do you baptize if you are not the Christ, nor Elijah, nor the Prophet?"

26 "I baptize with*h* water," John replied, "but among you stands one you do not know. 27 He is the one who comes after me, the thongs of whose sandals I am not worthy to untie."

28 This all happened at Bethany on the other side of the Jordan, where John was baptizing.

Jesus the Lamb of God

29 The next day John saw

e Other ancient authorities read It is an only Son, God, or It is the only Son
f Gk bosom
g Or the Christ

e 18 Some manuscripts but the only (or only begotten) Son
f 20 Or Messiah. "The Christ" (Greek) and "the Messiah" (Hebrew) both mean "the Anointed One"; also in verse 25.
g 23 Isaiah 40:3
h 26 Or in; also in verses 31 and 33

Jesus coming toward him and declared, "Here is the Lamb of God who takes away the sin of the world! [30] This is he of whom I said, 'After me comes a man who ranks ahead of me because he was before me.' [31] I myself did not know him; but I came baptizing with water for this reason, that he might be revealed to Israel." [32] And John testified, "I saw the Spirit descending from heaven like a dove, and it remained on him. [33] I myself did not know him, but the one who sent me to baptize with water said to me, 'He on whom you see the Spirit descend and remain is the one who baptizes with the Holy Spirit.' [34] And I myself have seen and have testified that this is the Son of God."[h]

The First Disciples of Jesus

[35] The next day John again was standing with two of his disciples, [36] and as he watched Jesus walk by, he exclaimed, "Look, here is the Lamb of God!" [37] The two disciples heard him say this, and they followed Jesus. [38] When Jesus turned and saw them following, he said to them, "What are you looking for?" They said to him, "Rabbi" (which translated means Teacher), "where are you staying?" [39] He said to them, "Come and see." They came and saw where he was staying, and they re-

τὸν Ἰησοῦν ἐρχόμενον πρὸς αὐτόν, καὶ
-    Jesus   coming   toward him,   and
λέγει· ἴδε ὁ ἀμνὸς τοῦ θεοῦ ὁ αἴρων
says : Behold[,] the Lamb of God - taking
τὴν ἁμαρτίαν τοῦ κόσμου. 30 οὗτός ἐστιν
the   sin   of the world.   This   is he
ὑπὲρ οὗ ἐγὼ εἶπον· ὀπίσω μου ἔρχεται
as to whom I   said :   After   me   comes
ἀνὴρ ὃς ἔμπροσθέν μου γέγονεν, ὅτι
a man who   before   me has become, because
πρῶτός μου ἦν. 31 κἀγὼ οὐκ ᾔδειν
first   of me he was.   And I   knew not
αὐτόν, ἀλλ' ἵνα φανερωθῇ τῷ Ἰσραήλ,
him,   but   that he might be manifested - to Israel,
διὰ τοῦτο ἦλθον ἐγὼ ἐν ὕδατι βαπτίζων.
therefore came   I   in water baptizing.
32 Καὶ ἐμαρτύρησεν Ἰωάννης λέγων ὅτι
   And   witnessed   John   saying[,] -
τεθέαμαι τὸ πνεῦμα καταβαῖνον ὡς
I have beheld the Spirit   coming down   as
περιστερὰν ἐξ οὐρανοῦ, καὶ ἔμεινεν ἐπ'
a dove   out of heaven, and he remained on
αὐτόν. 33 κἀγὼ οὐκ ᾔδειν αὐτόν, ἀλλ'
him.   And I   knew not   him,   but
ὁ πέμψας με βαπτίζειν ἐν ὕδατι, ἐκεῖνός
the [one] having sent me to baptize in water, that [one].
μοι εἶπεν· ἐφ' ὃν ἂν ἴδῃς τὸ πνεῦμα
to me said: On whomever thou seest the Spirit
καταβαῖνον καὶ μένον ἐπ' αὐτόν, οὗτός
coming down   and remaining on him,   this
ἐστιν ὁ βαπτίζων ἐν πνεύματι ἁγίῳ.
is the [one] baptizing in Spirit   Holy.
34 κἀγὼ ἑώρακα, καὶ μεμαρτύρηκα ὅτι
   And I have seen, and have witnessed   that
οὗτός ἐστιν ὁ υἱὸς τοῦ θεοῦ.
this [one] is the Son   - of God.
35 Τῇ ἐπαύριον πάλιν εἱστήκει ὁ Ἰωάννης
   On the morrow   again stood   - John
καὶ ἐκ τῶν μαθητῶν αὐτοῦ δύο, 36 καὶ
and of the disciples of him   two,   and
ἐμβλέψας τῷ Ἰησοῦ περιπατοῦντι λέγει·
looking at   - Jesus   walking   he says:
ἴδε ὁ ἀμνὸς τοῦ θεοῦ. 37 καὶ ἤκουσαν
Behold[,] the Lamb - of God.   And   [4]heard
οἱ δύο μαθηταὶ αὐτοῦ λαλοῦντος καὶ
[1]the [2]two [3]disciples [5]him [6]speaking   and
ἠκολούθησαν τῷ Ἰησοῦ. 38 στραφεὶς δὲ
they followed   - Jesus.   And [2]turning
ὁ Ἰησοῦς καὶ θεασάμενος αὐτοὺς ἀκολουθοῦντας
- [1]Jesus and beholding   them   following
λέγει αὐτοῖς· τί ζητεῖτε; οἱ δὲ εἶπαν
says to them : What seek ye? And they   said
αὐτῷ· ῥαββί (ὃ λέγεται μεθερμηνευόμενον
to him : Rabbi (which is called   being translated
διδάσκαλε), ποῦ μένεις; 39 λέγει αὐτοῖς·
Teacher),   where remainest thou? He says to them :
ἔρχεσθε καὶ ὄψεσθε. ἦλθαν οὖν καὶ εἶδαν
Come   and ye will see. They went therefore and   saw
ποῦ μένει, καὶ παρ' αὐτῷ ἔμειναν τὴν
where he remains(ed), and with   him   remained   -
ἡμέραν ἐκείνην· ὥρα ἦν ὡς δεκάτη.
day   that;   hour was about tenth.
40 Ἦν Ἀνδρέας ὁ ἀδελφὸς Σίμωνος Πέτρου
   It was Andrew the brother   of Simon   Peter
εἷς ἐκ τῶν δύο τῶν ἀκουσάντων παρὰ
one of the two   -   hearing   from

Jesus coming toward him and said, "Look, the Lamb of God, who takes away the sin of the world! [30] This is the one I meant when I said, 'A man who comes after me has surpassed me because he was before me.' [31] I myself did not know him, but the reason I came baptizing with water was that he might be revealed to Israel."

[32] Then John gave this testimony: "I saw the Spirit come down from heaven as a dove and remain on him. [33] I would not have known him, except that the one who sent me to baptize with water told me, 'The man on whom you see the Spirit come down and remain is the one who will baptize with the Holy Spirit.' [34] I have seen and I testify that this is the Son of God."

Jesus' First Disciples

[35] The next day John was there again with two of his disciples. [36] When he saw Jesus passing by, he said, "Look, the Lamb of God!"

[37] When the two disciples heard him say this, they followed Jesus. [38] Turning around, Jesus saw them following and asked, "What do you want?"

They said, "Rabbi" (which means Teacher), "where are you staying?"

[39] "Come," he replied, "and you will see."

So they went and saw

[h] Other ancient authorities read *is God's chosen one*

mained with him that day. It was about four o'clock in the afternoon. 40 One of the two who heard John speak and followed him was Andrew, Simon Peter's brother. 41 He first found his brother Simon and said to him, "We have found the Messiah" (which is translated Anointed*i*). 42 He brought Simon*j* to Jesus, who looked at him and said, "You are Simon son of John. You are to be called Cephas" (which is translated Peter*k*).

Jesus Calls Philip and Nathanael

43 The next day Jesus decided to go to Galilee. He found Philip and said to him, "Follow me." 44 Now Philip was from Bethsaida, the city of Andrew and Peter. 45 Philip found Nathanael and said to him, "We have found him about whom Moses in the law and also the prophets wrote, Jesus son of Joseph from Nazareth." 46 Nathanael said to him, "Can anything good come out of Nazareth?" Philip said to him, "Come and see." 47 When Jesus saw Nathanael coming toward him, he said of him, "Here is truly an Israelite in whom there is no deceit!" 48 Nathanael asked him, "Where did you get to know me?" Jesus answered, "I saw you under the fig tree before Philip called you." 49 Nathanael replied, "Rabbi, you are the Son of God! You are the King of Israel!" 50 Jesus answered, "Do you believe because I told you that I saw you under the fig tree? You will see greater things than these." 51 And he said to him, "Very truly, I tell you,*l* you will see heaven opened and the angels of

Ἰωάννου καὶ ἀκολουθησάντων αὐτῷ·
John and following him;

41 εὑρίσκει οὗτος πρῶτον τὸν ἀδελφὸν τὸν
³finds ¹this one ²first ⁴the(his) ⁶brother

ἴδιον Σίμωνα καὶ λέγει αὐτῷ· εὑρήκαμεν
⁵own Simon and tells him: We have found

τὸν Μεσσίαν (ὅ ἐστιν μεθερμηνευόμενον
the Messiah (which is being translated

χριστός). 42 ἤγαγεν αὐτὸν πρὸς τὸν
Christ). He led him to the

Ἰησοῦν. ἐμβλέψας αὐτῷ ὁ Ἰησοῦς εἶπεν·
Jesus. Looking at him - Jesus said:

σὺ εἶ Σίμων ὁ υἱὸς Ἰωάννου, σὺ κληθήσῃ
Thou art Simon the son of John, thou shalt be called

Κηφᾶς (ὃ ἑρμηνεύεται Πέτρος). 43 Τῇ
Cephas (which is translated Peter). On the

ἐπαύριον ἠθέλησεν ἐξελθεῖν εἰς τὴν Γαλιλαίαν,
morrow he wished to go forth into - Galilee,

καὶ εὑρίσκει Φίλιππον. καὶ λέγει αὐτῷ ὁ
and finds Philip. And says to him -

Ἰησοῦς· ἀκολούθει μοι. 44 ἦν δὲ ὁ
Jesus: Follow me. Now was -

Φίλιππος ἀπὸ Βηθσαϊδά, ἐκ τῆς πόλεως
Philip from Bethsaida, of the city

Ἀνδρέου καὶ Πέτρου. 45 εὑρίσκει Φίλιππος
of Andrew and of Peter. ²Finds ¹Philip

τὸν Ναθαναὴλ καὶ λέγει αὐτῷ· ὃν ἔγραψεν
- ³Nathanael and tells him: [He] whom wrote

Μωϋσῆς ἐν τῷ νόμῳ καὶ οἱ προφῆται
Moses in the law and the prophets

εὑρήκαμεν, Ἰησοῦν υἱὸν τοῦ Ἰωσὴφ τὸν
we have found, Jesus son of Joseph -

ἀπὸ Ναζαρέθ. 46 καὶ εἶπεν αὐτῷ
from Nazareth. And said to him

Ναθαναήλ· ἐκ Ναζαρὲθ δύναταί τι ἀγαθὸν
Nathanael: Out of Nazareth can anything good

εἶναι; λέγει αὐτῷ ὁ Φίλιππος· ἔρχου καὶ
to be? Says to him - Philip: Come and

ἴδε. 47 εἶδεν Ἰησοῦς τὸν Ναθαναὴλ
see. ²Saw ¹Jesus - ³Nathanael

ἐρχόμενον πρὸς αὐτὸν καὶ λέγει περὶ
coming toward him and says concerning

αὐτοῦ· ἴδε ἀληθῶς Ἰσραηλίτης, ἐν ᾧ
him: Behold[,] truly an Israelite, in whom

δόλος οὐκ ἔστιν. 48 λέγει αὐτῷ Ναθαναήλ·
guile is not. Says to him Nathanael:

πόθεν με γινώσκεις; ἀπεκρίθη Ἰησοῦς καὶ
Whence me knowest thou? Answered Jesus and

εἶπεν αὐτῷ· πρὸ τοῦ σε Φίλιππον φωνῆσαι
said to him: Before the thee Philip to call*b*
=Philip called thee

ὄντα ὑπὸ τὴν συκῆν εἶδόν σε. 49 ἀπεκρίθη
being under the fig-tree I saw thee. Answered

αὐτῷ Ναθαναήλ· ῥαββί, σὺ εἶ ὁ υἱὸς τοῦ
him Nathanael: Rabbi, thou art the Son -

θεοῦ, σὺ βασιλεὺς εἶ τοῦ Ἰσραήλ.
of God, thou king art - of Israel.

50 ἀπεκρίθη Ἰησοῦς καὶ εἶπεν αὐτῷ·
Answered Jesus and said to him:

ὅτι εἶπόν σοι ὅτι εἶδόν σε ὑποκάτω τῆς
Because I told thee that I saw thee underneath the

συκῆς, πιστεύεις; μείζω τούτων ὄψῃ.
fig-tree, believest thou? greater [than] these things thou shalt see.

51 καὶ λέγει αὐτῷ· ἀμὴν ἀμὴν λέγω
And he says to him: Truly truly I tell

ὑμῖν, ὄψεσθε τὸν οὐρανὸν ἀνεῳγότα καὶ
you, ye shall see the heaven having been opened and

where he was staying, and spent that day with him. It was about the tenth hour. 40 Andrew, Simon Peter's brother, was one of the two who heard what John had said and who had followed Jesus. 41 The first thing Andrew did was to find his brother Simon and tell him, "We have found the Messiah" (that is, the Christ). 42 And he brought him to Jesus.

Jesus looked at him and said, "You are Simon son of John. You will be called Cephas" (which, when translated, is Peter*i*).

Jesus Calls Philip and Nathanael

43 The next day Jesus decided to leave for Galilee. Finding Philip, he said to him, "Follow me." 44 Philip, like Andrew and Peter, was from the town of Bethsaida. 45 Philip found Nathanael and told him, "We have found the one Moses wrote about in the Law, and about whom the prophets also wrote—Jesus of Nazareth, the son of Joseph." 46 "Nazareth! Can anything good come from there?" Nathanael asked. "Come and see," said Philip. 47 When Jesus saw Nathanael approaching, he said of him, "Here is a true Israelite, in whom there is nothing false." 48 "How do you know me?" Nathanael asked. Jesus answered, "I saw you while you were still under the fig tree before Philip called you." 49 Then Nathanael declared, "Rabbi, you are the Son of God; you are the King of Israel." 50 Jesus said, "You believe*j* because I told you I saw you under the fig tree. You shall see greater things than that." 51 He then added, "I tell you*k* the truth, you*k* shall see heaven

Footnotes:

i Or Christ
j Gk him
k From the word for rock in Aramaic (kepha) and Greek (petra), respectively
l Both instances of the Greek word for you in this verse are plural

i 42 Both Cephas (Aramaic) and Peter (Greek) mean rock.
j 50 Or Do you believe . . . ?
k 51 The Greek is plural.

God ascending and descending upon the Son of Man."

Chapter 2

The Wedding at Cana

ON the third day there was a wedding in Cana of Galilee, and the mother of Jesus was there. 2 Jesus and his disciples had also been invited to the wedding. 3 When the wine gave out, the mother of Jesus said to him, "They have no wine." 4 And Jesus said to her, "Woman, what concern is that to you and to me? My hour has not yet come." 5 His mother said to the servants, "Do whatever he tells you." 6 Now standing there were six stone water jars for the Jewish rites of purification, each holding twenty or thirty gallons. 7 Jesus said to them, "Fill the jars with water." And they filled them up to the brim. 8 He said to them, "Now draw some out, and take it to the chief steward." So they took it. 9 When the steward tasted the water that had become wine, and did not know where it came from (though the servants who had drawn the water knew), the steward called the bridegroom 10 and said to him, "Everyone serves the good wine first, and then the inferior wine after the guests have become drunk. But you have kept the good wine until now." 11 Jesus did this, the first of his signs, in Cana of Galilee, and revealed his glory; and his disciples believed in him.
12 After this he went down to Capernaum with

τοὺς ἀγγέλους τοῦ θεοῦ ἀναβαίνοντας καὶ
the angels - of God going up and

καταβαίνοντας ἐπὶ τὸν υἱὸν τοῦ ἀνθρώπου.
coming down on the Son - of man.

2 Καὶ τῇ ἡμέρᾳ τῇ τρίτῃ γάμος ἐγένετο
And on the day - third a wedding there was

ἐν Κανὰ τῆς Γαλιλαίας, καὶ ἦν ἡ μήτηρ
in Cana - of Galilee, and was the mother

τοῦ Ἰησοῦ ἐκεῖ· **2** ἐκλήθη δὲ καὶ ὁ
- of Jesus there; and was invited both -

Ἰησοῦς καὶ οἱ μαθηταὶ αὐτοῦ εἰς τὸν
Jesus and the disciples of him to the

γάμον. **3** καὶ ὑστερήσαντος οἴνου λέγει ἡ
wedding. And lacking wineᵇ says the
=when wine was lacking

μήτηρ τοῦ Ἰησοῦ πρὸς αὐτόν· οἶνον
mother - of Jesus to him: Wine

οὐκ ἔχουσιν. **4** καὶ λέγει αὐτῇ ὁ Ἰησοῦς·
they have not. And says to her - Jesus:

τί ἐμοὶ καὶ σοί, γύναι; οὔπω ἥκει ἡ
What to me and to thee, woman? not yet is come the

ὥρα μου. **5** λέγει ἡ μήτηρ αὐτοῦ τοῖς
hour of me. Says the mother of him to the

διακόνοις· ὅ τι ἂν λέγῃ ὑμῖν, ποιήσατε.
servants: Whatever he tells you, do ye.

6 ἦσαν δὲ ἐκεῖ λίθιναι ὑδρίαι ἓξ κατὰ
Now there were there stone water-pots six according to

τὸν καθαρισμὸν τῶν Ἰουδαίων κείμεναι,
the purifying of the Jews lying,

χωροῦσαι ἀνὰ μετρητὰς δύο ἢ τρεῖς.
containing each† measures two or three.

7 λέγει αὐτοῖς ὁ Ἰησοῦς· γεμίσατε τὰς
Tells them - Jesus: Fill ye the

ὑδρίας ὕδατος. καὶ ἐγέμισαν αὐτὰς ἕως
water-pots of(with) water. And they filled them up to

ἄνω. **8** καὶ λέγει αὐτοῖς· ἀντλήσατε νῦν
[the] top. And he tells them: Draw now

καὶ φέρετε τῷ ἀρχιτρικλίνῳ. οἱ δὲ
and carry to the master of the feast. And they

ἤνεγκαν. **9** ὡς δὲ ἐγεύσατο ὁ ἀρχιτρίκλινος
carried. But when tasted the master of the feast

τὸ ὕδωρ οἶνον γεγενημένον, καὶ οὐκ ᾔδει
the water ²wine ¹having become, and did not know

πόθεν ἐστίν, οἱ δὲ διάκονοι ᾔδεισαν οἱ
whence it is(was), but the servants knew the [ones]

ἠντληκότες τὸ ὕδωρ, φωνεῖ τὸν νυμφίον
having drawn the water, ²calls ¹the ³bridegroom

ὁ ἀρχιτρίκλινος **10** καὶ λέγει αὐτῷ· πᾶς
¹the ²master of the feast and says to him: Every

ἄνθρωπος πρῶτον τὸν καλὸν οἶνον τίθησιν,
man first the good wine sets forth,

καὶ ὅταν μεθυσθῶσιν τὸν ἐλάσσω· σὺ
and when they become drunk the worse; thou

τετήρηκας τὸν καλὸν οἶνον ἕως ἄρτι.
hast kept the good wine until now.

11 Ταύτην ἐποίησεν ἀρχὴν τῶν σημείων ὁ
¹This ⁵did ²beginning ³of the ⁴signs -

Ἰησοῦς ἐν Κανὰ τῆς Γαλιλαίας καὶ
Jesus in Cana - of Galilee and

ἐφανέρωσεν τὴν δόξαν αὐτοῦ, καὶ ἐπίστευσαν
manifested the glory of him, and believed

εἰς αὐτὸν οἱ μαθηταὶ αὐτοῦ.
in him the disciples of him.

12 Μετὰ τοῦτο κατέβη εἰς Καφαρναοὺμ
After this went down to Capernaum

Chapter 2

Jesus Changes Water to Wine

ON the third day a wedding took place at Cana in Galilee. Jesus' mother was there, 2 and Jesus and his disciples had also been invited to the wedding. 3 When the wine was gone, Jesus' mother said to him, "They have no more wine."

4 "Dear woman, why do you involve me?" Jesus replied. "My time has not yet come."

5 His mother said to the servants, "Do whatever he tells you."

6 Nearby stood six stone water jars, the kind used by the Jews for ceremonial washing, each holding from twenty to thirty gallons.

7 Jesus said to the servants, "Fill the jars with water"; so they filled them to the brim.

8 Then he told them, "Now draw some out and take it to the master of the banquet."

They did so, 9 and the master of the banquet tasted the water that had been turned into wine. He did not realize where it had come from, though the servants who had drawn the water knew. Then he called the bridegroom aside 10 and said, "Everyone brings out the choice wine first and then the cheaper wine after the guests have had too much to drink; but you have saved the best till now."

11 This, the first of his miraculous signs, Jesus performed in Cana of Galilee. He thus revealed his glory, and his disciples put their faith in him.

Jesus Clears the Temple

12 After this he went down to Capernaum with his

ˡ6 Greek *two to three metretes* (probably about 75 to 115 liters) his mother, his brothers, and his disciples; and they remained there a few days.

Jesus Cleanses the Temple

13 The Passover of the Jews was near, and Jesus went up to Jerusalem. 14 In the temple he found people selling cattle, sheep, and doves, and the money changers seated at their tables. 15 Making a whip of cords, he drove all of them out of the temple, both the sheep and the cattle. He also poured out the coins of the money changers and overturned their tables. 16 He told those who were selling the doves, "Take these things out of here! Stop making my Father's house a marketplace!" 17 His disciples remembered that it was written, "Zeal for your house will consume me." 18 The Jews then said to him, "What sign can you show us for doing this?" 19 Jesus answered them, "Destroy this temple, and in three days I will raise it up." 20 The Jews then said, "This temple has been under construction for forty-six years, and will you raise it up in three days?" 21 But he was speaking of the temple of his body. 22 After he was raised from the dead, his disciples remembered that he had said this; and they believed the scripture and the word that Jesus had spoken.

23 When he was in Jerusalem during the Passover festival, many believed in his name because they saw

αὐτὸς   καὶ   ἡ   μήτηρ   αὐτοῦ   καὶ
he   and   the   mother   of him   and

οἱ   ἀδελφοὶ   καὶ   οἱ   μαθηταὶ   αὐτοῦ,   καὶ
the   brothers   and   the   disciples   of him,   and

ἐκεῖ   ἔμειναν   οὐ   πολλὰς   ἡμέρας.
there   remained   not   many   days.

13 Καὶ ἐγγὺς ἦν τὸ πάσχα τῶν Ἰουδαίων,
And near was the Passover of the Jews,

καὶ ἀνέβη εἰς Ἱεροσόλυμα ὁ Ἰησοῦς.
and went up to Jerusalem - Jesus.

14 καὶ εὗρεν ἐν τῷ ἱερῷ τοὺς πωλοῦντας
And he found in the temple the [ones] selling

βόας καὶ πρόβατα καὶ περιστερὰς καὶ τοὺς
oxen and sheep and doves and the

κερματιστὰς καθημένους, **15** καὶ ποιήσας
coindealers sitting, and having made

φραγέλλιον ἐκ σχοινίων πάντας ἐξέβαλεν
a lash out of ropes ²all ¹he expelled

ἐκ τοῦ ἱεροῦ, τά τε πρόβατα καὶ τοὺς
out of the temple, both the sheep and the

βόας, καὶ τῶν κολλυβιστῶν ἐξέχεεν τὰ
oxen, and ⁴of the ⁵moneychangers ¹poured out ³the

κέρματα καὶ τὰς τραπέζας ἀνέτρεψεν,
²coins ⁴and ⁵the ⁶tables ⁷overturned,

16 καὶ τοῖς τὰς περιστερὰς πωλοῦσιν
and ¹to the [ones] ⁴the ³doves ²selling

εἶπεν· ἄρατε ταῦτα ἐντεῦθεν, μὴ ποιεῖτε
¹said : Take these things hence, do not make

τὸν οἶκον τοῦ πατρός μου οἶκον ἐμπορίου.
the house of the Father of me a house of merchandise.

17 ἐμνήσθησαν οἱ μαθηταὶ αὐτοῦ ὅτι
Remembered the disciples of him that

γεγραμμένον ἐστίν· ὁ ζῆλος τοῦ οἴκου
having been written it is : The zeal of the house

σου καταφάγεταί με. **18** ἀπεκρίθησαν οὖν
of thee will consume me. Answered therefore

οἱ Ἰουδαῖοι καὶ εἶπαν αὐτῷ· τί σημεῖον
the Jews and said to him: What sign

δεικνύεις ἡμῖν, ὅτι ταῦτα ποιεῖς;
showest thou to us, because these things thou doest?

19 ἀπεκρίθη Ἰησοῦς καὶ εἶπεν αὐτοῖς· λύσατε τὸν
Answered Jesus and said to them: Destroy -

ναὸν τοῦτον, καὶ ἐν τρισὶν ἡμέραις ἐγερῶ αὐτόν.
shrine this, and in three days I will raise it.

20 εἶπαν οὖν οἱ Ἰουδαῖοι· τεσσεράκοντα
Said therefore the Jews : In forty

καὶ ἓξ ἔτεσιν οἰκοδομήθη ὁ ναὸς οὗτος,
and six years was built - shrine this,

καὶ σὺ ἐν τρισὶν ἡμέραις ἐγερεῖς αὐτόν;
and thou in three days wilt raise it?

21 ἐκεῖνος δὲ ἔλεγεν περὶ τοῦ ναοῦ τοῦ
But that [one]* spoke about the shrine of the

σώματος αὐτοῦ. **22** ὅτε οὖν ἠγέρθη ἐκ
body of him. When therefore he was raised from

νεκρῶν, ἐμνήσθησαν οἱ μαθηταὶ αὐτοῦ
[the] dead, remembered the disciples of him

ὅτι τοῦτο ἔλεγεν, καὶ ἐπίστευσαν τῇ
that this he said, and they believed the

γραφῇ καὶ τῷ λόγῳ ὃν εἶπεν ὁ Ἰησοῦς.
scripture and the word which said - Jesus.

23 Ὡς δὲ ἦν ἐν τοῖς Ἱεροσολύμοις ἐν
And when he was in - Jerusalem at

τῷ πάσχα ἐν τῇ ἑορτῇ, πολλοὶ ἐπίστευσαν
the Passover at the feast, many believed

εἰς τὸ ὄνομα αὐτοῦ, θεωροῦντες αὐτοῦ τὰ
in the name of him, beholding of him the

mother and brothers and his disciples. There they stayed for a few days.

13 When it was almost time for the Jewish Passover, Jesus went up to Jerusalem. 14 In the temple courts he found men selling cattle, sheep and doves, and others sitting at tables exchanging money. 15 So he made a whip out of cords, and drove all from the temple area, both sheep and cattle; he scattered the coins of the money changers and overturned their tables. 16 To those who sold doves he said, "Get these out of here! How dare you turn my Father's house into a market!" 17 His disciples remembered that it is written: "Zeal for your house will consume me." m 18 Then the Jews demanded of him, "What miraculous sign can you show us to prove your authority to do all this?" 19 Jesus answered them, "Destroy this temple, and I will raise it again in three days." 20 The Jews replied, "It has taken forty-six years to build this temple, and you are going to raise it in three days?" 21 But the temple he had spoken of was his body. 22 After he was raised from the dead, his disciples recalled what he had said. Then they believed the Scripture and the words that Jesus had spoken.

23 Now while he was in Jerusalem at the Passover Feast, many people saw

* John repeatedly uses the demonstrative adjective ἐκεῖνος in the sense of " he," referring to Christ.   m 17 Psalm 69:9

the signs that he was doing. 24 But Jesus on his part would not entrust himself to them, because he knew all people 25 and needed no one to testify about anyone; for he himself knew what was in everyone.

Chapter 3

Nicodemus Visits Jesus

NOW there was a Pharisee named Nicodemus, a leader of the Jews. 2 He came to Jesus[m] by night and said to him, "Rabbi, we know that you are a teacher who has come from God; for no one can do these signs that you do apart from the presence of God." 3 Jesus answered him, "Very truly, I tell you, no one can see the kingdom of God without being born from above."[n] 4 Nicodemus said to him, "How can anyone be born after having grown old? Can one enter a second time into the mother's womb and be born?" 5 Jesus answered, "Very truly, I tell you, no one can enter the kingdom of God without being born of water and Spirit. 6 What is born of the flesh is flesh, and what is born of the Spirit is spirit.[o] 7 Do not be astonished that I said to you, 'You[p] must be born from above.'[q] 8 The wind[o] blows where it chooses, and you hear the sound of it, but you do not know where it comes from or where it goes. So it is with everyone who is born of the Spirit." 9 Nicodemus said to him, "How can these

σημεῖα ἃ ἐποίει· 24 αὐτὸς δὲ Ἰησοῦς
signs   which he was doing;   ¹but ³[him]self,   ¹Jesus

οὐκ ἐπίστευεν αὐτὸν αὐτοῖς διὰ τὸ αὐτὸν
did not commit   himself to them because of the   him
=because he knew

γινώσκειν πάντας, 25 καὶ ὅτι οὐ χρείαν εἶχεν
to know[b] all men,   and because no   need he had

ἵνα τις μαρτυρήσῃ περὶ τοῦ ἀνθρώπου·
that anyone should witness concerning   –   man;

αὐτὸς γὰρ ἐγίνωσκεν τί ἦν ἐν τῷ ἀνθρώπῳ.
for he   knew   what was in   –   man.

3 Ἦν δὲ ἄνθρωπος ἐκ τῶν Φαρισαίων,
Now there was   a man   of   the   Pharisees,

Νικόδημος ὄνομα αὐτῷ, ἄρχων τῶν
Nicodemus   name   to him[e],   a ruler   of the

Ἰουδαίων· 2 οὗτος ἦλθεν πρὸς αὐτὸν νυκτὸς
Jews;   this man came   to   him of(by) night

καὶ εἶπεν αὐτῷ· ῥαββί, οἴδαμεν ὅτι ἀπὸ
and said to him : Rabbi, we know that from

θεοῦ ἐλήλυθας διδάσκαλος· οὐδεὶς γὰρ
God thou hast come   a teacher;   for no one

δύναται ταῦτα τὰ σημεῖα ποιεῖν ἃ σὺ
can   these   –   signs to do which thou

ποιεῖς, ἐὰν μὴ ᾖ ὁ θεὸς μετ' αὐτοῦ.
doest, except ²is – ¹God with   him.

3 ἀπεκρίθη Ἰησοῦς καὶ εἶπεν αὐτῷ· ἀμὴν
Answered Jesus and said to him : Truly

ἀμὴν λέγω σοι, ἐὰν μή τις γεννηθῇ
truly I tell thee, except anyone is born

ἄνωθεν, οὐ δύναται ἰδεῖν τὴν βασιλείαν
from above, he cannot to see the   kingdom

τοῦ θεοῦ. 4 λέγει πρὸς αὐτὸν ὁ Νικόδημος·
– of God. Says to   him – Nicodemus·

πῶς δύναται ἄνθρωπος γεννηθῆναι γέρων ὤν;
How can a man to be born old being?

μὴ δύναται εἰς τὴν κοιλίαν τῆς μητρὸς
not can he into the   womb of the mother

αὐτοῦ δεύτερον εἰσελθεῖν καὶ γεννηθῆναι;
of him secondly to enter and to be born?

5 ἀπεκρίθη Ἰησοῦς· ἀμὴν ἀμὴν λέγω σοι,
Answered Jesus : Truly truly I tell thee,

ἐὰν μή τις γεννηθῇ ἐξ ὕδατος καὶ
except anyone is born of water and

πνεύματος, οὐ δύναται εἰσελθεῖν εἰς τὴν
spirit,   he cannot to enter into the

βασιλείαν τοῦ θεοῦ. 6 τὸ γεγεννημένον ἐκ
kingdom   – of God. The thing having been born of

τῆς σαρκὸς σάρξ ἐστιν, καὶ τὸ γεγεννημένον
the flesh   flesh is,   and the thing having been born

ἐκ τοῦ πνεύματος πνεῦμά ἐστιν. 7 μὴ
of the Spirit spirit is.   not

θαυμάσῃς ὅτι εἶπόν σοι· δεῖ ὑμᾶς
Marvel because I told thee : It behoves you

γεννηθῆναι ἄνωθεν. 8 τὸ πνεῦμα ὅπου θέλει
to be born from above. The spirit(?wind) where it wishes

πνεῖ, καὶ τὴν φωνὴν αὐτοῦ ἀκούεις, ἀλλ'
blows, and the sound of it thou hearest, but

οὐκ οἶδας πόθεν ἔρχεται καὶ ποῦ ὑπάγει·
thou knowest not whence it comes and whither it goes;

οὕτως ἐστὶν πᾶς ὁ γεγεννημένος ἐκ τοῦ
so   is everyone having been born of the

πνεύματος. 9 ἀπεκρίθη Νικόδημος καὶ
Spirit.   Answered Nicodemus and

εἶπεν αὐτῷ· πῶς δύναται ταῦτα γενέσθαι;
said to him : How can these things to come about?

the miraculous signs he was doing and believed in his name.[n] 24 But Jesus would not entrust himself to them, for he knew all men. 25 He did not need man's testimony about man, for he knew what was in a man.

Chapter 3

Jesus Teaches Nicodemus

NOW there was a man of the Pharisees named Nicodemus, a member of the Jewish ruling council. 2 He came to Jesus at night and said, "Rabbi, we know you are a teacher who has come from God. For no one could perform the miraculous signs you are doing if God were not with him."

3 In reply Jesus declared, "I tell you the truth, no one can see the kingdom of God unless he is born again. o"

4 "How can a man be born when he is old?" Nicodemus asked. "Surely he cannot enter a second time into his mother's womb to be born!"

5 Jesus answered, "I tell you the truth, no one can enter the kingdom of God unless he is born of water and the Spirit. 6 Flesh gives birth to flesh, but the Spirit[p] gives birth to spirit. 7 You should not be surprised at my saying, 'You[q] must be born again.' 8 The wind blows wherever it pleases. You hear its sound, but you cannot tell where it comes from or where it is going. So it is with everyone born of the Spirit."

9 "How can this be?" Nicodemus asked.

[m] Gk him
[n] Or born anew
[o] The same Greek word means both wind and spirit
[p] The Greek word for you here is plural
[q] Or anew

[n] 23 Or and believed in him
[o] 3 Or born from above; also in verse 7
[p] 6 Or but spirit
[q] 7 The Greek is plural.

things be?" 10 Jesus answered him, "Are you a teacher of Israel, and yet you do not understand these things?
11 "Very truly, I tell you, we speak of what we know and testify to what we have seen; yet you[r] do not receive our testimony. 12 If I have told you about earthly things and you do not believe, how can you believe if I tell you about heavenly things? 13 No one has ascended into heaven except the one who descended from heaven, the Son of Man.[s] 14 And just as Moses lifted up the serpent in the wilderness, so must the Son of Man be lifted up, 15 that whoever believes in him may have eternal life.[t]
16 "For God so loved the world that he gave his only Son, so that everyone who believes in him may not perish but may have eternal life.
17 "Indeed, God did not send the Son into the world to condemn the world, but in order that the world might be saved through him. 18 Those who believe in him are not condemned; but those who do not believe are condemned already, because they have not believed in the name of the only Son of God. 19 And this is the judgment, that the light has come into the world, and people loved darkness rather than light because their deeds were evil. 20 For all who do evil hate the light and do not come to the light, so that their deeds may not be exposed. 21 But those who do what is true come to the light, so that it may be clearly seen that their

10 ἀπεκρίθη Ἰησοῦς καὶ εἶπεν αὐτῷ· σὺ
Answered Jesus and said to him : Thou
εἶ ὁ διδάσκαλος τοῦ Ἰσραὴλ καὶ ταῦτα
art the teacher - of Israel and these things
οὐ γινώσκεις; 11 ἀμὴν ἀμὴν λέγω σοι ὅτι
knowest not? Truly truly I tell thee[,] -
ὃ οἴδαμεν λαλοῦμεν καὶ ὃ ἑωράκαμεν
What we know we speak and what we have seen
μαρτυροῦμεν, καὶ τὴν μαρτυρίαν ἡμῶν
we witness, and the witness of us
οὐ λαμβάνετε. 12 εἰ τὰ ἐπίγεια εἶπον
ye receive not. If the earthly things I told
ὑμῖν καὶ οὐ πιστεύετε, πῶς ἐὰν εἴπω
you and ye believe not, how if I tell
ὑμῖν τὰ ἐπουράνια πιστεύσετε; 13 καὶ
you the heavenly things will ye believe? And
οὐδεὶς ἀναβέβηκεν εἰς τὸν οὐρανὸν εἰ μὴ
no man has gone up into - heaven except
ὁ ἐκ τοῦ οὐρανοῦ καταβάς, ὁ υἱὸς
the[one] out of - heaven having come down, the Son
τοῦ ἀνθρώπου. 14 Καὶ καθὼς Μωϋσῆς ὕψωσεν
- of man. And as Moses lifted up
τὸν ὄφιν ἐν τῇ ἐρήμῳ, οὕτως ὑψωθῆναι
the serpent in the desert, so to be lifted up
δεῖ τὸν υἱὸν τοῦ ἀνθρώπου, 15 ἵνα πᾶς ὁ
it behoves the Son - of man, that everyone
πιστεύων ἐν αὐτῷ ἔχῃ ζωὴν αἰώνιον.
believing in him may have life eternal.
16 οὕτως γὰρ ἠγάπησεν ὁ θεὸς τὸν
For thus [2]loved - [1]God the
κόσμον, ὥστε τὸν υἱὸν τὸν μονογενῆ
world, so as the Son the only begotten
ἔδωκεν, ἵνα πᾶς ὁ πιστεύων εἰς αὐτὸν
he gave, that everyone believing in him
μὴ ἀπόληται ἀλλ' ἔχῃ ζωὴν αἰώνιον.
may not perish but may have life eternal.
17 οὐ γὰρ ἀπέστειλεν ὁ θεὸς τὸν υἱὸν
For [2]not [1]sent - [1]God the Son
εἰς τὸν κόσμον ἵνα κρίνῃ τὸν κόσμον,
into the world that he might judge the world,
ἀλλ' ἵνα σωθῇ ὁ κόσμος δι' αὐτοῦ.
but that [3]might be saved [1]the [2]world through him.
18 ὁ πιστεύων εἰς αὐτὸν οὐ κρίνεται·
The [one] believing in him is not judged;
ὁ μὴ πιστεύων ἤδη κέκριται, ὅτι
the[one]not believing already has been judged, because
μὴ πεπίστευκεν εἰς τὸ ὄνομα τοῦ μονογενοῦς
he has not believed in the name of the only begotten
υἱοῦ τοῦ θεοῦ. 19 αὕτη δέ ἐστιν ἡ
Son - of God. And this is the
κρίσις, ὅτι τὸ φῶς ἐλήλυθεν εἰς τὸν
judgment, that the light has come into the
κόσμον καὶ ἠγάπησαν οἱ ἄνθρωποι μᾶλλον
world and [2]loved - [1]men [3]rather
τὸ σκότος ἢ τὸ φῶς· ἦν γὰρ αὐτῶν
[2]the [4]darkness [5]than the light; for was(were) of them
πονηρὰ τὰ ἔργα. 20 πᾶς γὰρ ὁ φαῦλα
evil the works. For everyone evil things
πράσσων μισεῖ τὸ φῶς καὶ οὐκ ἔρχεται
doing hates the light and does not come
πρὸς τὸ φῶς, ἵνα μὴ ἐλεγχθῇ τὰ ἔργα
to the light, lest is(are) reproved the works
αὐτοῦ· 21 ὁ δὲ ποιῶν τὴν ἀλήθειαν ἔρχεται
of him; but the [one] doing the truth comes
πρὸς τὸ φῶς, ἵνα φανερωθῇ αὐτοῦ τὰ
to the light, that may be manifested of him the

10 "You are Israel's teacher," said Jesus, "and do you not understand these things? 11 I tell you the truth, we speak of what we know, and we testify to what we have seen, but still you people do not accept our testimony. 12 I have spoken to you of earthly things and you do not believe; how then will you believe if I speak of heavenly things? 13 No one has ever gone into heaven except the one who came from heaven—the Son of Man.[r] 14 Just as Moses lifted up the snake in the desert, so the Son of Man must be lifted up, 15 that everyone who believes in him may have eternal life.[s]
16 "For God so loved the world that he gave his one and only Son,[t] that whoever believes in him shall not perish but have eternal life. 17 For God did not send his Son into the world to condemn the world, but to save the world through him. 18 Whoever believes in him is not condemned, but whoever does not believe stands condemned already because he has not believed in the name of God's one and only Son.[u] 19 This is the verdict: Light has come into the world, but men loved darkness instead of light because their deeds were evil. 20 Everyone who does evil hates the light, and will not come into the light for fear that his deeds will be exposed. 21 But whoever lives by the truth comes into the light, so that it may be seen plainly that

---

[r] The Greek word for you here and in verse 12 is plural
[s] Other ancient authorities add who is in heaven
[t] Some interpreters hold that the quotation concludes with verse 15

[r]13 Some manuscripts Man, who is in heaven
[s]15 Or believes may have eternal life in him
[t]16 Or his only begotten Son
[u]18 Or God's only begotten Son

deeds have been done in God."*t*

Jesus and John the Baptist

22 After this Jesus and his disciples went into the Judean countryside, and he spent some time there with them and baptized. 23 John also was baptizing at Aenon near Salim because water was abundant there; and people kept coming and were being baptized 24 —John, of course, had not yet been thrown into prison.

25 Now a discussion about purification arose between John's disciples and a Jew.*u* 26 They came to John and said to him, "Rabbi, the one who was with you across the Jordan, to whom you testified, here he is baptizing, and all are going to him." 27 John answered, "No one can receive anything except what has been given from heaven. 28 You yourselves are my witnesses that I said, 'I am not the Messiah,*v* but I have been sent ahead of him.' 29 He who has the bride is the bridegroom. The friend of the bridegroom, who stands and hears him, rejoices greatly at the bridegroom's voice. For this reason my joy has been fulfilled. 30 He must increase, but I must decrease."*w*

The One Who Comes from Heaven

31 The one who comes from above is above all; the one who is of the earth belongs to the earth and speaks about earthly things. The one who comes from heaven is above all. 32 He testifies to what he has seen and heard, yet no one accepts his testimony. 33 Whoever has accepted

---

ἔργα ὅτι ἐν θεῷ ἐστιν εἰργασμένα.
works that in God they are *having been* wrought.

22 Μετὰ ταῦτα ἦλθεν ὁ Ἰησοῦς καὶ οἱ
After these things came – Jesus and the

μαθηταὶ αὐτοῦ εἰς τὴν Ἰουδαίαν γῆν, καὶ
disciples of him into *the* Judæan land, and

ἐκεῖ διέτριβεν μετ' αὐτῶν καὶ ἐβάπτιζεν.
there continued with them and baptized.

23 ἦν δὲ καὶ Ἰωάννης βαπτίζων ἐν
And was also John baptizing in

Αἰνὼν ἐγγὺς τοῦ Σαλίμ, ὅτι ὕδατα
Ainon near – Salim, because waters

πολλὰ ἦν ἐκεῖ, καὶ παρεγίνοντο καὶ
many was(were) there, and they came and

ἐβαπτίζοντο· 24 οὔπω γὰρ ἦν βεβλημένος
were baptized; for *not yet* *was* *having been* cast

εἰς τὴν φυλακὴν Ἰωάννης. 25 Ἐγένετο
⁵into ⁶the ⁷prison ¹John. There was

οὖν ζήτησις ἐκ τῶν μαθητῶν Ἰωάννου
therefore a questioning of the disciples of John

μετὰ Ἰουδαίου περὶ καθαρισμοῦ. 26 καὶ
with a Jew about purifying. And

ἦλθον πρὸς τὸν Ἰωάννην καὶ εἶπαν αὐτῷ·
they came to – John and said to him:

ῥαββί, ὃς ἦν μετὰ σοῦ πέραν τοῦ
Rabbi, [he] who was with thee beyond the

Ἰορδάνου, ᾧ σὺ μεμαρτύρηκας, ἴδε
Jordan, to whom thou hast borne witness, behold[,]

οὗτος βαπτίζει καὶ πάντες ἔρχονται πρὸς
this man baptizes and all men are coming to

αὐτόν. 27 ἀπεκρίθη Ἰωάννης καὶ εἶπεν·
him. Answered John and said:

οὐ δύναται ἄνθρωπος λαμβάνειν οὐδὲν ἐὰν μὴ
Cannot a man *to* receive no(any)thing unless

ᾖ δεδομένον αὐτῷ ἐκ τοῦ οὐρανοῦ.
it is *having been* given to him out of – heaven.

28 αὐτοὶ ὑμεῖς μοι μαρτυρεῖτε ὅτι εἶπον·
[Your]selves ye to me bear witness that I said:

οὐκ εἰμὶ ἐγὼ ὁ χριστός, ἀλλ' ὅτι
³not ²am ¹I the Christ, but that

ἀπεσταλμένος εἰμὶ ἔμπροσθεν ἐκείνου. 29 ὁ
having been sent I am before that one.* The [one]

ἔχων τὴν νύμφην νυμφίος ἐστίν· ὁ δὲ
having the bride a bridegroom is; but the

φίλος τοῦ νυμφίου, ὁ ἑστηκὼς καὶ ἀκούων
friend of the bridegroom, – standing and hearing

αὐτοῦ, χαρᾷ χαίρει διὰ τὴν φωνὴν τοῦ
him, with joy rejoices because of the voice of the

νυμφίου. αὕτη οὖν ἡ χαρὰ ἡ ἐμὴ
bridegroom. ²This ¹therefore – ⁴joy – ³my

πεπλήρωται. 30 ἐκεῖνον δεῖ αὐξάνειν, ἐμὲ
has been fulfilled. That one it behoves to increase, ²me

δὲ ἐλαττοῦσθαι. 31 Ὁ ἄνωθεν ἐρχόμενος
¹but to decrease. The [one] from above coming

ἐπάνω πάντων ἐστίν· ὁ ὢν ἐκ τῆς γῆς
over all is; the [one] being of the earth

ἐκ τῆς γῆς ἐστιν καὶ ἐκ τῆς γῆς λαλεῖ.
of the earth is and of the earth speaks.

ὁ ἐκ τοῦ οὐρανοῦ ἐρχόμενος ἐπάνω
The [one] of – heaven coming over

πάντων ἐστίν· 32 ὃ ἑώρακεν καὶ ἤκουσεν,
all is; what he has seen and heard,

τοῦτο μαρτυρεῖ, καὶ τὴν μαρτυρίαν αὐτοῦ
this he witnesses [to], and the witness of him

οὐδεὶς λαμβάνει. 33 ὁ λαβὼν αὐτοῦ τὴν
no man receives. The [one] receiving of him the

* See note to 2. 21.

John the Baptist's Testimony About Jesus

22 After this, Jesus and his disciples went out into the Judean countryside, where he spent some time with them, and baptized. 23 Now John also was baptizing at Aenon near Salim, because there was plenty of water, and people were constantly coming to be baptized. 24 (This was before John was put in prison.) 25 An argument developed between some of John's disciples and a certain Jew*w* over the matter of ceremonial washing. 26 They came to John and said to him, "Rabbi, that man who was with you on the other side of the Jordan—the one you testified about—well, he is baptizing, and everyone is going to him."

27 To this John replied, "A man can receive only what is given him from heaven. 28 You yourselves can testify that I said, 'I am not the Christ*x* but am sent ahead of him.' 29 The bride belongs to the bridegroom. The friend who attends the bridegroom waits and listens for him, and is full of joy when he hears the bridegroom's voice. That joy is mine, and it is now complete. 30 He must become greater; I must become less.

31 "The one who comes from above is above all; the one who is from the earth belongs to the earth, and speaks as one from the earth. The one who comes from heaven is above all. 32 He testifies to what he has seen and heard, but no one accepts his testimony. 33 The man who has accept-

---

u Other ancient authorities read *the Jews*
v Or *the Christ*
w Some interpreters hold that the quotation continues through verse 36

v 21 Some interpreters end the quotation after verse 15.
w 25 Some manuscripts *and certain Jews*
x 28 Or *Messiah*

his testimony has certi-
fied*x* this, that God is true.
34 He whom God has sent
speaks the words of God,
for he gives the Spirit without measure. 35 The Father
loves the Son and has
placed all things in his
hands. 36 Whoever believes
in the Son has eternal life;
whoever disobeys the Son
will not see life, but must
endure God's wrath.

Chapter 4

Jesus and the Woman of Samaria

NOW when Jesus*y*
learned that the Phar-
isees had heard, "Jesus is
making and baptizing more
disciples than John"
2 —although it was not
Jesus himself but his disciples who baptized— 3 he
left Judea and started back
to Galilee. 4 But he had to
go through Samaria. 5 So he
came to a Samaritan city
called Sychar, near the plot
of ground that Jacob had
given to his son Joseph.
6 Jacob's well was there,
and Jesus, tired out by his
journey, was sitting by the
well. It was about noon.
7 A Samaritan woman
came to draw water, and
Jesus said to her, "Give me
a drink." 8 (His disciples
had gone to the city to buy
food.) 9 The Samaritan
woman said to him, "How
is it that you, a Jew, ask a
drink of me, a woman of
Samaria?" (Jews do not
share things in common
with Samaritans.) 10 Jesus
answered her, "If you
knew the gift of God, and

μαρτυρίαν   ἐσφράγισεν   ὅτι   ὁ   θεὸς   ἀληθής
witness   sealed   that   -   God   true

ἐστιν.   34   ὃν   γὰρ   ἀπέστειλεν   ὁ   θεὸς   τὰ
is.   For [he] whom   ²sent   -   ¹God   the

ῥήματα   τοῦ   θεοῦ   λαλεῖ·   οὐ   γὰρ   ἐκ
words   -   of God   speaks;   for not   by

μέτρου   δίδωσιν   τὸ   πνεῦμα.   35 ὁ   πατὴρ
measure   he gives   the   Spirit.   The Father

ἀγαπᾷ   τὸν   υἱόν,   καὶ   πάντα   δέδωκεν   ἐν
loves   the   Son,   and   all things   has given   in[to]

τῇ   χειρὶ   αὐτοῦ.   36 ὁ   πιστεύων   εἰς   τὸν
the   hand   of him.   The [one] believing   in   the

υἱὸν   ἔχει   ζωὴν   αἰώνιον·   ὁ   δὲ   ἀπειθῶν
Son   has   life   eternal;   but the [one]   disobeying

τῷ   υἱῷ   οὐκ   ὄψεται   ζωήν,   ἀλλ᾽   ἡ   ὀργὴ
the   Son   will not see   life,   but   the   wrath

τοῦ   θεοῦ   μένει   ἐπ᾽   αὐτόν.
-   of God   remains   on   him.

4 Ὡς   οὖν   ἔγνω   ὁ   κύριος   ὅτι   ἤκουσαν
²When   ¹therefore   ⁵knew   ³the   ⁴Lord   ⁶that   ⁹heard

οἱ   Φαρισαῖοι   ὅτι   Ἰησοῦς   πλείονας   μαθητὰς
⁷the   ⁸Pharisees   that   Jesus   more   disciples

ποιεῖ   καὶ   βαπτίζει   ἢ   Ἰωάννης,   —   2 καίτοι   γε
makes   and   baptizes   than   John,   —   though

Ἰησοῦς   αὐτὸς   οὐκ   ἐβάπτιζεν   ἀλλ᾽   οἱ
Jesus   [him]self   baptized not   but   the

μαθηταὶ   αὐτοῦ,   —   3 ἀφῆκεν   τὴν   Ἰουδαίαν
disciples   of him,   —   he left   -   Judæa

καὶ   ἀπῆλθεν   πάλιν   εἰς   τὴν   Γαλιλαίαν.
and   went away   again   into   -   Galilee.

4 Ἔδει   δὲ   αὐτὸν   διέρχεσθαι   διὰ   τῆς
And it behoved   him   to pass through   through   -

Σαμαρείας.   5 ἔρχεται   οὖν   εἰς   πόλιν   τῆς
Samaria.   He comes   therefore   to   a city   -

Σαμαρείας   λεγομένην   Σύχαρ,   πλησίον   τοῦ
of Samaria   being called   Sychar,   near   the

χωρίου   ὃ   ἔδωκεν   Ἰακὼβ   [τῷ]   Ἰωσὴφ
piece of land   which   ²gave   ¹Jacob   -   to Joseph

τῷ   υἱῷ   αὐτοῦ·   6 ἦν   δὲ   ἐκεῖ   πηγὴ   τοῦ
the   son   of him;   and was   there   a fountain   -

Ἰακώβ.   ὁ   οὖν   Ἰησοῦς   κεκοπιακὼς   ἐκ
of Jacob.   -   Therefore   Jesus   having become wearied   from

τῆς   ὁδοιπορίας   ἐκαθέζετο   οὕτως   ἐπὶ   τῇ
the   journey   sat   thus   at   the

πηγῇ·   ὥρα   ἦν   ὡς   ἕκτη.   7 ἔρχεται   γυνὴ
fountain;   [the] hour was   about   sixth.   Comes   a woman

ἐκ   τῆς   Σαμαρείας   ἀντλῆσαι   ὕδωρ.   λέγει
of   -   Samaria   to draw   water.   Says

αὐτῇ   ὁ   Ἰησοῦς·   δός   μοι   πεῖν.   8 οἱ   γὰρ
to her   -   Jesus: Give   me   to drink.   For the

μαθηταὶ   αὐτοῦ   ἀπεληλύθεισαν   εἰς   τὴν
disciples   of him   had gone away   into   the

πόλιν,   ἵνα   τροφὰς   ἀγοράσωσιν.   9 λέγει
city,   that   foods   they might buy.   Says

οὖν   αὐτῷ   ἡ   γυνὴ   ἡ   Σαμαρῖτις·   πῶς
therefore to him   the   woman   -   Samaritan: How

σὺ   Ἰουδαῖος   ὢν   παρ᾽   ἐμοῦ   πεῖν
thou   ¹a Jew   ¹being   ⁵from   ⁶me   ⁷to drink

αἰτεῖς   γυναικὸς   Σαμαρίτιδος   οὔσης;
²askest   ⁴woman   ⁵a Samaritan   ⁷being?

[οὐ   γὰρ   συγχρῶνται   Ἰουδαῖοι   Σαμαρίταις.]
¹For   ¹not   ²associate   ¹Jews   ¹with Samaritans.

10 ἀπεκρίθη   Ἰησοῦς   καὶ   εἶπεν   αὐτῇ·   εἰ   ᾔδεις
Answered   Jesus   and   said   to her: If thou knewest

Chapter 4

Jesus Talks With a Samaritan Woman

THE Pharisees heard
that Jesus was gaining
and baptizing more disci-
ples than John, 2 although in
fact it was not Jesus who
baptized, but his disciples.
3 When the Lord learned of
this, he left Judea and went
back once more to Galilee.
4 Now he had to go
through Samaria. 5 So he
came to a town in Samaria
called Sychar, near the plot
of ground Jacob had given
to his son Joseph. 6 Jacob's
well was there, and Jesus,
tired as he was from the
journey, sat down by the
well. It was about the sixth
hour.
7 When a Samaritan wom-
an came to draw water,
Jesus said to her, "Will you
give me a drink?" 8 (His disciples had gone into the
town to buy food.)
9 The Samaritan woman
said to him, "You are a Jew
and I am a Samaritan wom-
an. How can you ask me for
a drink?" (For Jews do not
associate with Samari-
tans.*a*)
10 Jesus answered her, "If
you knew the gift of God

---

x Gk set a seal to
y Other ancient authorities read the
Lord
z Other ancient authorities lack this
sentence

*y*34 Greek he
*z*36 Some interpreters end the
quotation after verse 30.

*a*9 Or do not use dishes Samaritans
have used

who it is that is saying to you, 'Give me a drink,' you would have asked him, and he would have given you living water." 11 The woman said to him, "Sir, you have no bucket, and the well is deep. Where do you get that living water? 12 Are you greater than our ancestor Jacob, who gave us the well, and with his sons and his flocks drank from it?" 13 Jesus said to her, "Everyone who drinks of this water will be thirsty again, 14 but those who drink of the water that I will give them will never be thirsty. The water that I will give will become in them a spring of water gushing up to eternal life." 15 The woman said to him, "Sir, give me this water, so that I may never be thirsty or have to keep coming here to draw water.

16 Jesus said to her, "Go, call your husband, and come back." 17 The woman answered him, "I have no husband." Jesus said to her, "You are right in saying, 'I have no husband'; 18 for you have had five husbands, and the one you have now is not your husband. What you have said is true!" 19 The woman said to him, "Sir, I see that you are a prophet. 20 Our ancestors worshiped on this mountain, but you*a* say that the place where people must worship is in Jerusalem." 21 Jesus said to her, "Woman, believe me, the hour is coming when you will worship the Father neither on this mountain nor in Jerusalem. 22 You

τὴν δωρεὰν τοῦ θεοῦ, καὶ τίς ἐστιν ὁ
the gift - of God, and who is the [one]
λέγων σοι· δός μοι πεῖν, σὺ ἂν ᾔτησας
saying to thee: Give me to drink, thou wouldest have asked
αὐτὸν καὶ ἔδωκεν ἄν σοι ὕδωρ ζῶν.
him and he would have given thee water living.
11 λέγει αὐτῷ· κύριε, οὔτε ἄντλημα ἔχεις
She says to him: Sir, no pail thou hast
καὶ τὸ φρέαρ ἐστὶν βαθύ· πόθεν οὖν
and the well is deep; whence then
ἔχεις τὸ ὕδωρ τὸ ζῶν; 12 μὴ σὺ μείζων
hast thou the water - living? not thou greater
εἶ τοῦ πατρὸς ἡμῶν Ἰακώβ, ὃς ἔδωκεν
art [than] the father of us Jacob, who gave
ἡμῖν τὸ φρέαρ, καὶ αὐτὸς ἐξ αὐτοῦ
us the well, and [him]self of it
ἔπιεν καὶ οἱ υἱοὶ αὐτοῦ καὶ τὰ θρέμματα
drank and the sons of him and the cattle
αὐτοῦ; 13 ἀπεκρίθη Ἰησοῦς καὶ εἶπεν αὐτῇ·
of him? Answered Jesus and said to her:
πᾶς ὁ πίνων ἐκ τοῦ ὕδατος τούτου
Everyone drinking of - water this
διψήσει πάλιν· 14 ὃς δ᾽ ἂν πίῃ ἐκ τοῦ
will thirst again; but whoever drinks of the
ὕδατος οὗ ἐγὼ δώσω αὐτῷ, οὐ μὴ
water which I will give him, by no means
διψήσει εἰς τὸν αἰῶνα, ἀλλὰ τὸ ὕδωρ ὃ
will thirst unto the age, but the water which
δώσω αὐτῷ γενήσεται ἐν αὐτῷ πηγὴ
I will give him will become in him a fountain
ὕδατος ἁλλομένου εἰς ζωὴν αἰώνιον. 15 λέγει
of water springing to life eternal. Says
πρὸς αὐτὸν ἡ γυνή· κύριε, δός μοι
to him the woman: Sir, give me
τοῦτο τὸ ὕδωρ, ἵνα μὴ διψῶ μηδὲ
this - water, that I thirst not nor
διέρχωμαι ἐνθάδε ἀντλεῖν. 16 λέγει αὐτῇ·
come through hither to draw. He says to her:
ὕπαγε φώνησον τὸν ἄνδρα σου καὶ ἐλθὲ
Go call the husband of thee and come
ἐνθάδε. 17 ἀπεκρίθη ἡ γυνὴ καὶ εἶπεν·
hither. Answered the woman and said:
οὐκ ἔχω ἄνδρα. λέγει αὐτῇ ὁ Ἰησοῦς·
I have not a husband. Says to her - Jesus:
καλῶς εἶπες ὅτι ἄνδρα οὐκ ἔχω· 18 πέντε
Well sayest thou[,] A husband I have not; *5*five
γὰρ ἄνδρας ἔσχες, καὶ νῦν ὃν ἔχεις
*1*for husbands thou hadst, and now [he] whom thou hast
οὐκ ἔστιν σου ἀνήρ· τοῦτο ἀληθὲς εἴρηκας.
is not of thee husband; this truly thou hast said.
19 λέγει αὐτῷ ἡ γυνή· κύριε, θεωρῶ
Says to him the woman: Sir, I perceive
ὅτι προφήτης εἶ σύ. 20 οἱ πατέρες
that a prophet art thou. The fathers
ἡμῶν ἐν τῷ ὄρει τούτῳ προσεκύνησαν·
of us in - mountain this worshipped;
καὶ ὑμεῖς λέγετε ὅτι ἐν Ἱεροσολύμοις
and ye say that in Jerusalem
ἐστὶν ὁ τόπος ὅπου προσκυνεῖν δεῖ.
is the place where to worship it behoves.
21 λέγει αὐτῇ ὁ Ἰησοῦς· πίστευέ μοι,
Says to her - Jesus: Believe me,
γύναι, ὅτι ἔρχεται ὥρα ὅτε οὔτε ἐν
woman, that is coming an hour when neither in
τῷ ὄρει τούτῳ οὔτε ἐν Ἱεροσολύμοις
- mountain this nor in Jerusalem

and who it is that asks you for a drink, you would have asked him and he would have given you living water."

11 "Sir," the woman said, "you have nothing to draw with and the well is deep. Where can you get this living water? 12 Are you greater than our father Jacob, who gave us the well and drank from it himself, as did also his sons and his flocks and herds?"

13 Jesus answered, "Everyone who drinks this water will be thirsty again, 14 but whoever drinks the water I give him will never thirst. Indeed, the water I give him will become in him a spring of water welling up to eternal life."

15 The woman said to him, "Sir, give me this water so that I won't get thirsty and have to keep coming here to draw water."

16 He told her, "Go, call your husband and come back."

17 "I have no husband," she replied.

Jesus said to her, "You are right when you say you have no husband. 18 The fact is, you have had five husbands, and the man you now have is not your husband. What you have just said is quite true."

19 "Sir," the woman said, "I can see that you are a prophet. 20 Our fathers worshiped on this mountain, but you Jews claim that the place where we must worship is in Jerusalem."

21 Jesus declared, "Believe me, woman, a time is coming when you will worship the Father neither on

a The Greek word for *you* here and in verses 21 and 22 is plural worship what you do not know; we worship what we know, for salvation is from the Jews. 23 But the hour is coming, and is now here, when the true worshipers will worship the Father in spirit and truth, for the Father seeks such as these to worship him. 24 God is spirit, and those who worship him must worship in spirit and truth." 25 The woman said to him, "I know that Messiah is coming" (who is called Christ). "When he comes, he will proclaim all things to us." 26 Jesus said to her, "I am he,b the one who is speaking to you."

27 Just then his disciples came. They were astonished that he was speaking with a woman, but no one said, "What do you want?" or, "Why are you speaking with her?" 28 Then the woman left her water jar and went back to the city. She said to the people, 29 "Come and see a man who told me everything I have ever done! He cannot be the Messiah,c can he?" 30 They left the city and were on their way to him.

31 Meanwhile the disciples were urging him, "Rabbi, eat something." 32 But he said to them, "I have food to eat that you do not know about." 33 So the disciples said to one another, "Surely no one has brought him something to eat?" 34 Jesus said to them, "My food is to do the will of him who sent me and to complete his work. 35 Do you not say, 'Four months more, then comes the har-

---

προσκυνήσετε τῷ πατρί. 22 ὑμεῖς προσκυ-
will ye worship the Father. Ye wor-

νεῖτε ὃ οὐκ οἴδατε, ἡμεῖς προσκυνοῦμεν ὃ
ship what ye know not, we worship what

οἴδαμεν, ὅτι ἡ σωτηρία ἐκ τῶν Ἰουδαίων
we know, because - salvation of the Jews

ἐστίν· 23 ἀλλὰ ἔρχεται ὥρα καὶ νῦν
is; but is coming an hour and now

ἐστιν, ὅτε οἱ ἀληθινοὶ προσκυνηταὶ προσκυνή-
is, when the true worshippers will

σουσιν τῷ πατρὶ ἐν πνεύματι καὶ ἀληθείᾳ·
worship the Father in spirit and truth;

καὶ γὰρ ὁ πατὴρ τοιούτους ζητεῖ τοὺς
for indeed the Father ²such ¹seeks the [ones]

προσκυνοῦντας αὐτόν· 24 πνεῦμα ὁ θεός,*
worshipping him; God [is] spirit,*

καὶ τοὺς προσκυνοῦντας ἐν πνεύματι καὶ
and ¹the [ones] ³worshipping ⁴in ⁵spirit ⁷and

ἀληθείᾳ δεῖ προσκυνεῖν. 25 λέγει αὐτῷ
⁶truth ¹it behoves ²to worship. Says to him

ἡ γυνή· οἶδα ὅτι Μεσσίας ἔρχεται, ὁ
the woman: I know that Messiah is coming, the [one]

λεγόμενος χριστός· ὅταν ἔλθῃ ἐκεῖνος,
being called Christ; when comes that one,

ἀναγγελεῖ ἡμῖν ἅπαντα. 26 λέγει αὐτῇ
he will announce to us all things. Says to her

ὁ Ἰησοῦς· ἐγώ εἰμι, ὁ λαλῶν σοι.
- Jesus: I am, the [one] speaking to thee.

27 Καὶ ἐπὶ τούτῳ ἦλθαν οἱ μαθηταὶ
And on this came the disciples

αὐτοῦ, καὶ ἐθαύμαζον ὅτι μετὰ γυναικὸς
of him, and marvelled that with a woman

ἐλάλει· οὐδεὶς μέντοι εἶπεν· τί ζητεῖς
he was speaking; no one however said: What seekest thou

ἢ τί λαλεῖς μετ' αὐτῆς; 28 ἀφῆκεν οὖν
or why speakest thou with her? ¹Left ²therefore

τὴν ὑδρίαν αὐτῆς ἡ γυνὴ καὶ ἀπῆλθεν
³the ⁵waterpot ⁷of her ¹the ²woman and went away

εἰς τὴν πόλιν, καὶ λέγει τοῖς ἀνθρώποις·
into the city, and says to the men:

29 δεῦτε ἴδετε ἄνθρωπον ὃς εἶπέν μοι
Come see a man who told me

πάντα ἃ ἐποίησα· μήτι οὗτός ἐστιν ὁ
all things which I did; not this is the

χριστός; 30 ἐξῆλθον ἐκ τῆς πόλεως καὶ
Christ? They went forth out of the city and

ἤρχοντο πρὸς αὐτόν. 31 Ἐν τῷ μεταξὺ
came to him. In the meantime

ἠρώτων αὐτὸν οἱ μαθηταὶ λέγοντες· ῥαββί,
asked him the disciples saying: Rabbi,

φάγε. 32 ὁ δὲ εἶπεν αὐτοῖς· ἐγὼ βρῶσιν
eat. But he said to them: I food

ἔχω φαγεῖν ἣν ὑμεῖς οὐκ οἴδατε. 33 ἔλεγον
have to eat which ye do not know. Said

οὖν οἱ μαθηταὶ πρὸς ἀλλήλους· μή τις
therefore the disciples to one another: Not anyone

ἤνεγκεν αὐτῷ φαγεῖν; 34 λέγει αὐτοῖς ὁ
brought him to eat? Says to them -

Ἰησοῦς· ἐμὸν βρῶμά ἐστιν ἵνα ποιῶ τὸ
Jesus: My food is that I may do the

θέλημα τοῦ πέμψαντός με καὶ τελειώσω
will of the [one] having sent me and may finish

αὐτοῦ τὸ ἔργον. 35 οὐχ ὑμεῖς λέγετε ὅτι
of him the work. ³Not ²ye ¹say that

---

this mountain nor in Jerusalem. 22 You Samaritans worship what you do not know; we worship what we do know, for salvation is from the Jews. 23 Yet a time is coming and has now come when the true worshipers will worship the Father in spirit and truth, for they are the kind of worshipers the Father seeks. 24 God is spirit, and his worshipers must worship in spirit and in truth."

25 The woman said, "I know that Messiah" (called Christ) "is coming. When he comes, he will explain everything to us."

26 Then Jesus declared, "I who speak to you am he."

The Disciples Rejoin Jesus

27 Just then his disciples returned and were surprised to find him talking with a woman. But no one asked, "What do you want?" or "Why are you talking with her?"

28 Then, leaving her water jar, the woman went back to the town and said to the people, 29 "Come, see a man who told me everything I ever did. Could this be the Christb?" 30 They came out of the town and made their way toward him.

31 Meanwhile his disciples urged him, "Rabbi, eat something."

32 But he said to them, "I have food to eat that you know nothing about."

33 Then his disciples said to each other, "Could someone have brought him food?"

34 "My food," said Jesus, "is to do the will of him who sent me and to finish his work. 35 Do you not say,

---

b Gk I am
c Or the Christ

* See note on 1. 1.

b29 Or Messiah

vest'? But I tell you, look around you, and see how the fields are ripe for harvesting. 36 The reaper is already receiving^d wages and is gathering fruit for eternal life, so that sower and reaper may rejoice together. 37 For here the saying holds true, 'One sows and another reaps.' 38 I sent you to reap that for which you did not labor. Others have labored, and you have entered into their labor.''

39 Many Samaritans from that city believed in him because of the woman's testimony, ''He told me everything I have ever done.'' 40 So when the Samaritans came to him, they asked him to stay with them; and he stayed there two days. 41 And many more believed because of his word. 42 They said to the woman, ''It is no longer because of what you said that we believe, for we have heard for ourselves, and we know that this is truly the Savior of the world.''

Jesus Returns to Galilee

43 When the two days were over, he went from that place to Galilee 44 (for Jesus himself had testified that a prophet has no honor in the prophet's own country). 45 When he came to Galilee, the Galileans welcomed him, since they had seen all that he had done in Jerusalem at the festival; for they too had gone to the festival.

Jesus Heals an Official's Son

46 Then he came again to Cana in Galilee where he

ἔτι τετράμηνός ἐστιν καὶ ὁ θερισμὸς
yet four months it is and the harvest

ἔρχεται; ἰδοὺ λέγω ὑμῖν, ἐπάρατε τοὺς
comes? Behold I tell you, lift up the

ὀφθαλμοὺς ὑμῶν καὶ θεάσασθε τὰς χώρας,
eyes of you and behold the fields,

ὅτι λευκαί εἰσιν πρὸς θερισμόν. ἤδη
because white they are to harvest. Already

36 ὁ θερίζων μισθὸν λαμβάνει καὶ συνάγει
the [one] reaping wages receives and gathers

καρπὸν εἰς ζωὴν αἰώνιον, ἵνα ὁ σπείρων
fruit to life eternal, that ¹the [one] ²sowing

ὁμοῦ χαίρῃ καὶ ὁ θερίζων. 37 ἐν γὰρ
⁷together ⁶may rejoice ³and ⁴the [one] ⁵reaping. For in

τούτῳ ὁ λόγος ἐστὶν ἀληθινὸς ὅτι ἄλλος
this the word is true that another(one)

ἐστὶν ὁ σπείρων καὶ ἄλλος ὁ θερίζων.
is the [one] sowing and another the [one] reaping.

38 ἐγὼ ἀπέστειλα ὑμᾶς θερίζειν ὃ οὐχ
I sent you to reap what not

ὑμεῖς κεκοπιάκατε· ἄλλοι κεκοπιάκασιν, καὶ
ye have laboured; others have laboured, and

ὑμεῖς εἰς τὸν κόπον αὐτῶν εἰσεληλύθατε.
ye into the labour of them have entered.

39 Ἐκ δὲ τῆς πόλεως ἐκείνης πολλοὶ
And out of - city that many

ἐπίστευσαν εἰς αὐτὸν τῶν Σαμαριτῶν διὰ
believed in him of the Samaritans because of

τὸν λόγον τῆς γυναικὸς μαρτυρούσης ὅτι
the word of the woman witnessing[,] -

εἶπέν μοι πάντα ἃ ἐποίησα. 40 ὡς
He told me all things which I did. When

οὖν ἦλθον πρὸς αὐτὸν οἱ Σαμαρῖται,
therefore came to him the Samaritans,

ἠρώτων αὐτὸν μεῖναι παρ' αὐτοῖς· καὶ
they asked him to remain with them; and

ἔμεινεν ἐκεῖ δύο ἡμέρας. 41 καὶ πολλῷ
he remained there two days. And ²more

πλείους ἐπίστευσαν διὰ τὸν λόγον αὐτοῦ,
¹many believed because of the word of him,

42 τῇ τε γυναικὶ ἔλεγον ὅτι οὐκέτι διὰ
and to the woman they said[,] - No longer because of

τὴν σὴν λαλιὰν πιστεύομεν· αὐτοὶ γὰρ
- thy talk we believe; for [our]selves

ἀκηκόαμεν, καὶ οἴδαμεν ὅτι οὗτός ἐστιν
we have heard, and we know that this man is

ἀληθῶς ὁ σωτὴρ τοῦ κόσμου.
truly the Saviour of the world.

43 Μετὰ δὲ τὰς δύο ἡμέρας ἐξῆλθεν
And after the two days he went forth

ἐκεῖθεν εἰς τὴν Γαλιλαίαν. 44 αὐτὸς γὰρ
thence into - Galilee. For ²[him]self

Ἰησοῦς ἐμαρτύρησεν ὅτι προφήτης ἐν
¹Jesus witnessed that a prophet in

τῇ ἰδίᾳ πατρίδι τιμὴν οὐκ ἔχει. 45 ὅτε
the(his) own native place honour has not. When

οὖν ἦλθεν εἰς τὴν Γαλιλαίαν, ἐδέξαντο
therefore he came into - Galilee, received

αὐτὸν οἱ Γαλιλαῖοι, πάντα ἑωρακότες
him the Galilæans, all things having seen

ὅσα ἐποίησεν ἐν Ἱεροσολύμοις ἐν τῇ
which he did in Jerusalem at the

ἑορτῇ· καὶ αὐτοὶ γὰρ ἦλθον εἰς τὴν
feast; ²also ³they ¹for went to the

ἑορτήν. 46 Ἦλθεν οὖν πάλιν εἰς τὴν
feast. He came therefore again to -

'Four months more and then the harvest'? I tell you, open your eyes and look at the fields! They are ripe for harvest. 36 Even now the reaper draws his wages, even now he harvests the crop for eternal life, so that the sower and the reaper may be glad together. 37 Thus the saying 'One sows and another reaps' is true. 38 I sent you to reap what you have not worked for. Others have done the hard work, and you have reaped the benefits of their labor.''

Many Samaritans Believe

39 Many of the Samaritans from that town believed in him because of the woman's testimony, ''He told me everything I ever did.'' 40 So when the Samaritans came to him, they urged him to stay with them, and he stayed two days. 41 And because of his words many more became believers. 42 They said to the woman, ''We no longer believe just because of what you said; now we have heard for ourselves, and we know that this man really is the Savior of the world.''

Jesus Heals the Official's Son

43 After the two days he left for Galilee. 44 (Now Jesus himself had pointed out that a prophet has no honor in his own country.) 45 When he arrived in Galilee, the Galileans welcomed him. They had seen all that he had done in Jerusalem at the Passover Feast, for they also had been there. 46 Once more he visited Cana in Galilee, where he

---

^{d} Or ³⁵ . . . the fields are already ripe for harvesting. ³⁶The reaper is receiving had changed the water into wine. Now there was a royal official whose son lay ill in Capernaum. ⁴⁷When he heard that Jesus had come from Judea to Galilee, he went and begged him to come down and heal his son, for he was at the point of death. ⁴⁸Then Jesus said to him, "Unless you' see signs and wonders you will not believe." ⁴⁹The official said to him, "Sir, come down before my little boy dies." ⁵⁰Jesus said to him, "Go; your son will live." The man believed the word that Jesus spoke to him and started on his way. ⁵¹As he was going down, his slaves met him and told him that his child was alive. ⁵²So he asked them the hour when he began to recover, and they said to him, "Yesterday at one in the afternoon the fever left him." ⁵³The father realized that this was the hour when Jesus had said to him, "Your son will live." So he himself believed, along with his whole household. ⁵⁴Now this was the second sign that Jesus did after coming from Judea to Galilee.

Κανὰ τῆς Γαλιλαίας, ὅπου ἐποίησεν τὸ
Cana   -   of Galilee,   where   he made   the

ὕδωρ οἶνον. καὶ ἦν τις βασιλικὸς
water   wine.   And there was a certain   courtier

οὗ ὁ υἱὸς ἠσθένει ἐν Καφαρναούμ· 47 οὗτος
of whom the son   ailed   in   Capernaum;   this man

ἀκούσας ὅτι Ἰησοῦς ἥκει ἐκ τῆς Ἰουδαίας
hearing   that   Jesus comes(came) out of -   Judæa

εἰς τὴν Γαλιλαίαν, ἀπῆλθεν πρὸς αὐτὸν καὶ
into   -   Galilee,   went   to   him   and

ἠρώτα ἵνα καταβῇ καὶ ἰάσηται αὐτοῦ
asked   that he would come down and would cure of him

τὸν υἱόν· ἤμελλεν γὰρ ἀποθνήσκειν. 48 εἶπεν
the son;   for he was about   to die.   Said

οὖν ὁ Ἰησοῦς πρὸς αὐτόν· ἐὰν μὴ σημεῖα
therefore -   Jesus   to   him :   Except   signs

καὶ τέρατα ἴδητε, οὐ μὴ πιστεύσητε.
and   prodigies   ye see, by no means ye believe.

49 λέγει πρὸς αὐτὸν ὁ βασιλικός· κύριε,
Says   to   him   the   courtier :   Sir,

κατάβηθι πρὶν ἀποθανεῖν τὸ παιδίον μου.
come down before   to die   the   childᵇ   of me.

50 λέγει αὐτῷ ὁ Ἰησοῦς· πορεύου, ὁ
Tells   him   -   Jesus :   Go,   the

υἱός σου ζῇ. ³ἐπίστευσεν ὁ ⁴ἄνθρωπος ⁴τῷ
son of thee lives. ³Believed ¹the ²man   ⁴the

λόγῳ ὃν εἶπεν αὐτῷ ὁ Ἰησοῦς, καὶ
⁵word ⁶which ⁷said ⁹to him   -   ⁷Jesus,   and

ἐπορεύετο. 51 ἤδη δὲ αὐτοῦ καταβαίνοντοςᵃ
went.   And already him   going downᵃ
                       =while he was going down

οἱ δοῦλοι ὑπήντησαν αὐτῷ λέγοντες ὅτι
the   slaves   met   him   saying   that

ὁ παῖς αὐτοῦ ζῇ. 52 ἐπύθετο οὖν τὴν
the boy   of him lives.   He inquired therefore   the

ὥραν παρ᾽ αὐτῶν ἐν ᾗ κομψότερον ἔσχεν·
hour   from   them   in which   better   he had;
                                =he got better;

εἶπαν οὖν αὐτῷ ὅτι ἐχθὲς ὥραν ἑβδόμην
they said therefore to him[,]   - Yesterday [at] hour seventh

ἀφῆκεν αὐτὸν ὁ πυρετός. 53 ἔγνω οὖν
left   him   the fever.   Knew therefore

ὁ πατὴρ ὅτι ἐκείνῃ τῇ ὥρᾳ ἐν ᾗ εἶπεν
the father that in that   the hour in which told

αὐτῷ ὁ Ἰησοῦς· ὁ υἱός σου ζῇ· καὶ
him   -   Jesus :   The son of thee lives;   and

ἐπίστευσεν αὐτὸς καὶ ἡ οἰκία αὐτοῦ ὅλη.
believed   he   and the household of him whole.

54 Τοῦτο [δὲ] πάλιν δεύτερον σημεῖον
And this   again   a second   sign

ἐποίησεν ὁ Ἰησοῦς ἐλθὼν ἐκ τῆς Ἰουδαίας
did   -   Jesus having come out of -   Judæa

εἰς τὴν Γαλιλαίαν.
into   -   Galilee.

---

had turned the water into wine. And there was a certain royal official whose son lay sick at Capernaum. ⁴⁷When this man heard that Jesus had arrived in Galilee from Judea, he went to him and begged him to come and heal his son, who was close to death.

⁴⁸"Unless you people see miraculous signs and wonders," Jesus told him, "you will never believe."

⁴⁹The royal official said, "Sir, come down before my child dies."

⁵⁰Jesus replied, "You may go. Your son will live."

The man took Jesus at his word and departed. ⁵¹While he was still on the way, his servants met him with the news that his boy was living. ⁵²When he inquired as to the time when his son got better, they said to him, "The fever left him yesterday at the seventh hour."

⁵³Then the father realized that this was the exact time at which Jesus had said to him, "Your son will live." So he and all his household believed.

⁵⁴This was the second miraculous sign that Jesus performed, having come from Judea to Galilee.

Chapter 5

Jesus Heals on the Sabbath

AFTER this there was a festival of the Jews, and Jesus went up to Jerusalem.

2 Now in Jerusalem by the Sheep Gate there is a pool, called in Hebrewᶠ

---

5 Μετὰ ταῦτα ἦν ἑορτὴ τῶν Ἰουδαίων,
After these things there was a feast of the   Jews,

καὶ ἀνέβη Ἰησοῦς εἰς Ἱεροσόλυμα. 2 ἔστιν
and went up Jesus   to   Jerusalem.   there is

δὲ ἐν τοῖς Ἱεροσολύμοις ἐπὶ τῇ προβατικῇ
Now in   -   Jerusalem   at the   sheepgate

κολυμβήθρα, ἡ ἐπιλεγομένη Ἑβραϊστὶ
a pool,   the [one] being called   in Hebrew

Chapter 5

The Healing at the Pool

SOME time later, Jesus went up to Jerusalem for a feast of the Jews. ²Now there is in Jerusalem near the Sheep Gate a pool, which in Aramaic is called

---

ᵉ Both instances of the Greek word for *you* in this verse are plural
ᶠ That is, *Aramaic*

Beth-zatha,[g] which has five porticoes. 3 In these lay many invalids—blind, lame, and paralyzed.[h] 5 One man was there who had been ill for thirty-eight years. 6 When Jesus saw him lying there and knew that he had been there a long time, he said to him, "Do you want to be made well?" 7 The sick man answered him, "Sir, I have no one to put me into the pool when the water is stirred up; and while I am making my way, someone else steps down ahead of me." 8 Jesus said to him, "Stand up, take your mat and walk." 9 At once the man was made well, and he took up his mat and began to walk.

Now that day was a sabbath. 10 So the Jews said to the man who had been cured, "It is the sabbath; it is not lawful for you to carry your mat." 11 But he answered them, "The man who made me well said to me, 'Take up your mat and walk.'" 12 They asked him, "Who is the man who said to you, 'Take it up and walk'?" 13 Now the man who had been healed did not know who it was, for Jesus had disappeared in[i] the crowd that was there. 14 Later Jesus found him in the temple and said to him, "See, you have been made well! Do not sin any more, so that nothing worse happens to you." 15 The man went away and told the Jews that it was Jesus who had made him well.

Βηθζαθά, πέντε στοὰς ἔχουσα. 3 ἐν
Bethzatha, five porches having. In

ταύταις κατέκειτο πλῆθος τῶν ἀσθενούντων,
these lay a multitude of the ailing [ones],

τυφλῶν, χωλῶν, ξηρῶν. ‡ 5 ἦν δέ τις
blind, lame, withered. And there was a

ἄνθρωπος ἐκεῖ τριάκοντα καὶ ὀκτὼ ἔτη
certain man there thirty and eight years

ἔχων ἐν τῇ ἀσθενείᾳ αὐτοῦ· 6 τοῦτον
having in the ailment of him; this man

ἰδὼν ὁ Ἰησοῦς κατακείμενον, καὶ γνοὺς
seeing Jesus lying, and knowing

ὅτι πολὺν ἤδη χρόνον ἔχει, λέγει αὐτῷ·
that much already time he has, says to him:

θέλεις ὑγιὴς γενέσθαι; 7 ἀπεκρίθη αὐτῷ
Wishest thou whole to become? Answered him

ὁ ἀσθενῶν· κύριε, ἄνθρωπον οὐκ ἔχω,
the ailing [one]: Sir, a man I have not,

ἵνα ὅταν ταραχθῇ τὸ ὕδωρ βάλῃ με εἰς
that when is troubled the water he may put me into

τὴν κολυμβήθραν· ἐν ᾧ δὲ ἔρχομαι ἐγώ,
the pool; but while am coming I,

ἄλλος πρὸ ἐμοῦ καταβαίνει. 8 λέγει αὐτῷ
another before me goes down. Says to him

ὁ Ἰησοῦς· ἔγειρε ἆρον τὸν κράβατόν
- Jesus: Rise[,] take the mattress

σου καὶ περιπάτει. 9 καὶ εὐθέως ἐγένετο
of thee and walk. And immediately became

ὑγιὴς ὁ ἄνθρωπος, καὶ ἦρεν τὸν κράβατον
whole the man, and took the mattress

αὐτοῦ καὶ περιεπάτει. Ἦν δὲ σάββατον
of him and walked. And it was a sabbath

ἐν ἐκείνῃ τῇ ἡμέρᾳ. 10 ἔλεγον οὖν οἱ
on that day. Said therefore the

Ἰουδαῖοι τῷ τεθεραπευμένῳ· σάββατόν ἐστιν,
Jews to the [one] having been healed: A sabbath it is,

καὶ οὐκ ἔξεστίν σοι ἆραι τὸν κράβατον.
and it is not lawful for thee to take the mattress.

11 ὃς δὲ ἀπεκρίθη αὐτοῖς· ὁ ποιήσας
But who(he) answered them: The [one] making

με ὑγιῆ, ἐκεῖνός μοι εἶπεν· ἆρον τὸν
me whole, that one me told: Take the

κράβατόν σου καὶ περιπάτει. 12 ἠρώτησαν
mattress of thee and walk. They asked

αὐτόν· τίς ἐστιν ὁ ἄνθρωπος ὁ εἰπών
him: Who is the man the telling

σοι· ἆρον καὶ περιπάτει; 13 ὁ δὲ ἰαθεὶς
thee: Take and walk? But the [one] cured

οὐκ ᾔδει τίς ἐστιν· ὁ γὰρ Ἰησοῦς
did not know who it is(was); - for Jesus

ἐξένευσεν ὄχλου ὄντος ἐν τῷ τόπῳ.
withdrew a crowd being in the place.
    =as there was a crowd

14 μετὰ ταῦτα εὑρίσκει αὐτὸν ὁ Ἰησοῦς
After these things finds him - Jesus

ἐν τῷ ἱερῷ καὶ εἶπεν αὐτῷ· ἴδε ὑγιὴς
in the temple and said to him: Behold[,] whole

γέγονας· μηκέτι ἁμάρτανε, ἵνα μὴ χεῖρόν
thou hast become; no longer sin, lest worse

σοί τι γένηται. 15 ἀπῆλθεν ὁ ἄνθρωπος
to thee something happens. Went away the man

καὶ εἶπεν τοῖς Ἰουδαίοις ὅτι Ἰησοῦς
and told the Jews that Jesus

ἐστιν ὁ ποιήσας αὐτὸν ὑγιῆ. 16 καὶ διὰ
it is(was) the [one] having made him whole. And there-

Bethesda[c] and which is surrounded by five covered colonnades. 3 Here a great number of disabled people used to lie—the blind, the lame, the paralyzed.[d] 5 One who was there had been an invalid for thirty-eight years. 6 When Jesus saw him lying there and learned that he had been in this condition for a long time, he asked him, "Do you want to get well?"

7 "Sir," the invalid replied, "I have no one to help me into the pool when the water is stirred. While I am trying to get in, someone else goes down ahead of me."

8 Then Jesus said to him, "Get up! Pick up your mat and walk." 9 At once the man was cured; he picked up his mat and walked.

The day on which this took place was a Sabbath, 10 and so the Jews said to the man who had been healed, "It is the Sabbath; the law forbids you to carry your mat."

11 But he replied, "The man who made me well said to me, 'Pick up your mat and walk.'"

12 So they asked him, "Who is this fellow who told you to pick it up and walk?"

13 The man who was healed had no idea who it was, for Jesus had slipped away into the crowd that was there.

14 Later Jesus found him at the temple and said to him, "See, you are well again. Stop sinning or something worse may happen to you." 15 The man went away and told the Jews that it was Jesus who had made him well.

---

[g] Other ancient authorities read Bethesda, others Bethsaida
[h] Other ancient authorities add, wholly or in part, waiting for the stirring of the water; [4for an angel of the Lord went down at certain seasons into the pool, and stirred up the water; whoever stepped in first after the stirring of the water was made well from whatever disease that person had.
[i] Or had left because of

‡ End of ver. 3 and ver. 4 omitted by Nestle; cf. NIV footnote.

[c]2 Some manuscripts Bethzatha; other manuscripts Bethsaida
[d]3 Some less important manuscripts paralyzed—and they waited for the moving of the waters. 4 From time to time an angel of the Lord would come down and stir up the waters. The first one into the pool after each such disturbance would be cured of whatever disease he had.

16Therefore the Jews started persecuting Jesus, because he was doing such things on the sabbath. 17But Jesus answered them, "My Father is still working, and I also am working." 18For this reason the Jews were seeking all the more to kill him, because he was not only breaking the sabbath, but was also calling God his own Father, thereby making himself equal to God.

The Authority of the Son

19 Jesus said to them, "Very truly, I tell you, the Son can do nothing on his own, but only what he sees the Father doing; for whatever the Father*j* does, the Son does likewise. 20The Father loves the Son and shows him all that he himself is doing; and he will show him greater works than these, so that you will be astonished. 21Indeed, just as the Father raises the dead and gives them life, so also the Son gives life to whomever he wishes. 22The Father judges no one but has given all judgment to the Son, 23so that all may honor the Son just as they honor the Father. Anyone who does not honor the Son does not honor the Father who sent him. 24Very truly, I tell you, anyone who hears my word and believes him who sent me has eternal life, and does not come under judgment, but has passed from death to life.

j Gk *that one*

τοῦτο	ἐδίωκον	οἱ	Ἰουδαῖοι	τὸν Ἰησοῦν,
fore	³persecuted	¹the	²Jews	⁴Jesus.

ὅτι ταῦτα ἐποίει ἐν σαββάτῳ. 17 ὁ δὲ
because these things he did on a sabbath. But he

ἀπεκρίνατο αὐτοῖς· ὁ πατήρ μου ἕως
answered them: The Father of me until

ἄρτι ἐργάζεται, κἀγὼ ἐργάζομαι· 18 διὰ
now works, and I work; because of

τοῦτο οὖν μᾶλλον ἐζήτουν αὐτὸν οἱ
this therefore ⁴the more ²sought ⁵him ¹the

Ἰουδαῖοι ἀποκτεῖναι, ὅτι οὐ μόνον ἔλυεν
²Jews ³to kill, because not only he broke

τὸ σάββατον, ἀλλὰ καὶ πατέρα ἴδιον
the sabbath, but also Father [his] own

ἔλεγεν τὸν θεόν, ἴσον ἑαυτὸν ποιῶν τῷ
said the God, equal himself making

θεῷ. 19 Ἀπεκρίνατο οὖν ὁ Ἰησοῦς καὶ
to God. Answered therefore - Jesus and

ἔλεγεν αὐτοῖς· ἀμὴν ἀμὴν λέγω· ὑμῖν,
said to them: Truly truly I say to you,

οὐ δύναται ὁ υἱὸς ποιεῖν ἀφ᾽ ἑαυτοῦ
cannot the Son to do from himself

οὐδέν, ἂν μή τι βλέπῃ τὸν πατέρα
no(any)thing, except what he sees the Father

ποιοῦντα· ἃ γὰρ ἂν ἐκεῖνος ποιῇ, ταῦτα
doing; for whatever that one does, these

καὶ ὁ υἱὸς ὁμοίως ποιεῖ. 20 ὁ γὰρ
also the Son likewise does. For the

πατὴρ φιλεῖ τὸν υἱὸν καὶ πάντα δείκνυσιν
Father loves the Son and all things shows

αὐτῷ ἃ αὐτὸς ποιεῖ, καὶ μείζονα τούτων
him which he does, and ¹greater ³[than] ⁴these

δείξει αὐτῷ ἔργα, ἵνα ὑμεῖς θαυμάζητε.
⁵he will show ⁶him ²works, that ye may marvel.

21 ὥσπερ γὰρ ὁ πατὴρ ἐγείρει τοὺς
For as the Father raises the

νεκροὺς καὶ ζωοποιεῖ, οὕτως καὶ ὁ υἱὸς
dead and quickens, so also the Son

οὓς θέλει ζωοποιεῖ. 22 οὐδὲ γὰρ ὁ
whom he wills quickens. For not the

πατὴρ κρίνει οὐδένα, ἀλλὰ τὴν κρίσιν
Father judges no(any) one, but - judgment

πᾶσαν δέδωκεν τῷ υἱῷ, 23 ἵνα πάντες
all he has given to the Son, that all men

τιμῶσι τὸν υἱὸν καθὼς τιμῶσι τὸν πατέρα.
may honour the Son as they honour the Father.

ὁ μὴ τιμῶν τὸν υἱὸν οὐ τιμᾷ τὸν πατέρα
The [one] not honouring the Son honours not the Father

τὸν πέμψαντα αὐτόν. 24 Ἀμὴν ἀμὴν
- having sent him. Truly truly

λέγω ὑμῖν ὅτι ὁ τὸν λόγον μου ἀκούων
I say to you[,] - The [one] the word of me hearing

καὶ πιστεύων τῷ πέμψαντί με ἔχει
and believing the [one] having sent me has

ζωὴν αἰώνιον, καὶ εἰς κρίσιν οὐκ ἔρχεται
life eternal, and into judgment comes not

ἀλλὰ μεταβέβηκεν ἐκ τοῦ θανάτου εἰς
but has passed over out of - death into

τὴν ζωήν. 25 ἀμὴν ἀμὴν λέγω ὑμῖν ὅτι
- life. Truly truly I say to you[,] -

ἔρχεται ὥρα καὶ νῦν ἐστιν ὅτε οἱ νεκροὶ
Comes an hour and now is when the dead

ἀκούσουσιν τῆς φωνῆς τοῦ υἱοῦ τοῦ
will hear the voice of the Son

θεοῦ καὶ οἱ ἀκούσαντες ζήσουσιν. 26 ὥσπερ
of God and the [ones] hearing will live. as

Life Through the Son

16So, because Jesus was doing these things on the Sabbath, the Jews persecuted him. 17Jesus said to them, "My Father is always at his work to this very day, and I, too, am working." 18For this reason the Jews tried all the harder to kill him; not only was he breaking the Sabbath, but he was even calling God his own Father, making himself equal with God.

19Jesus gave them this answer: "I tell you the truth, the Son can do nothing by himself; he can do only what he sees his Father doing, because whatever the Father does the Son also does. 20For the Father loves the Son and shows him all he does. Yes, to your amazement he will show him even greater things than these. 21For just as the Father raises the dead and gives them life, even so the Son gives life to whom he is pleased to give it. 22Moreover, the Father judges no one, but has entrusted all judgment to the Son, 23that all may honor the Son just as they honor the Father. He who does not honor the Son does not honor the Father, who sent him.

24"I tell you the truth, whoever hears my word and believes him who sent me has eternal life and will not be condemned; he has crossed over from death to

25 "Very truly, I tell you, the hour is coming, and is now here, when the dead will hear the voice of the Son of God, and those who hear will live. 26 For just as the Father has life in himself, so he has granted the Son also to have life in himself; 27 and he has given him authority to execute judgment, because he is the Son of Man. 28 Do not be astonished at this; for the hour is coming when all who are in their graves will hear his voice 29 and will come out—those who have done good, to the resurrection of life, and those who have done evil, to the resurrection of condemnation.

Witnesses to Jesus

30 "I can do nothing on my own. As I hear, I judge; and my judgment is just, because I seek to do not my own will but the will of him who sent me.

31 "If I testify about myself, my testimony is not true. 32 There is another who testifies on my behalf, and I know that his testimony to me is true. 33 You sent messengers to John, and he testified to the truth. 34 Not that I accept such human testimony, but I say these things so that you may be saved. 35 He was a burning and shining lamp, and you were willing to rejoice for a while in his light. 36 But I have a testimony greater than John's. The works that the Father has given me to complete, the very works that I am doing, testify on my behalf that the Father has sent me. 37 And the Father who sent me has himself testified on my behalf. You have never heard his voice or seen his form,

---

γὰρ ὁ πατὴρ ἔχει ζωὴν ἐν ἑαυτῷ, οὕτως
For the Father has life in himself, so
καὶ τῷ υἱῷ ἔδωκεν ζωὴν ἔχειν ἐν ἑαυτῷ.
also to the Son he gave life to have in himself.
27 καὶ ἐξουσίαν ἔδωκεν αὐτῷ κρίσιν ποιεῖν,
And authority he gave him judgment to do,
ὅτι υἱὸς ἀνθρώπου ἐστίν. 28 μὴ θαυμάζετε
because son of man* he is. Marvel not [at]
τοῦτο, ὅτι ἔρχεται ὥρα ἐν ᾗ πάντες οἱ
this, because comes an hour in which all the [ones]
ἐν τοῖς μνημείοις ἀκούσουσιν τῆς φωνῆς
in the tombs will hear the voice
αὐτοῦ 29 καὶ ἐκπορεύσονται οἱ τὰ ἀγαθὰ
of him and will come forth the [ones] the good things
ποιήσαντες εἰς ἀνάστασιν ζωῆς, οἱ τὰ
having done to a resurrection of life, the [ones] the
φαῦλα πράξαντες εἰς ἀνάστασιν κρίσεως.
evil things having done to a resurrection of judgment.
30 Οὐ δύναμαι ἐγὼ ποιεῖν ἀπ' ἐμαυτοῦ
Cannot I to do from myself
οὐδέν· καθὼς ἀκούω κρίνω, καὶ ἡ κρίσις
no(any)thing; as I hear I judge, and - judgment
ἡ ἐμὴ δικαία ἐστίν, ὅτι οὐ ζητῶ τὸ
- my just is, because I seek not -
θέλημα τὸ ἐμὸν ἀλλὰ τὸ θέλημα τοῦ
will - my but the will of the [one]
πέμψαντός με. 31 Ἐὰν ἐγὼ μαρτυρῶ
having sent me. If I witness
περὶ ἐμαυτοῦ, ἡ μαρτυρία μου οὐκ ἔστιν
concerning myself, the witness of me is not
ἀληθής· 32 ἄλλος ἐστιν ὁ μαρτυρῶν περὶ
true; another there is the [one] witnessing concerning
ἐμοῦ, καὶ οἶδα ὅτι ἀληθής ἐστιν ἡ
me, and I know that true is the
μαρτυρία ἣν μαρτυρεῖ περὶ ἐμοῦ. 33 ὑμεῖς
witness which he witnesses concerning me. Ye
ἀπεστάλκατε πρὸς Ἰωάννην, καὶ μεμαρ-
have sent to John, and he has
τύρηκεν τῇ ἀληθείᾳ· 34 ἐγὼ δὲ οὐ παρὰ
witnessed to the truth; but I not from
ἀνθρώπου τὴν μαρτυρίαν λαμβάνω, ἀλλὰ
man the witness receive, but
ταῦτα λέγω ἵνα ὑμεῖς σωθῆτε. 35 ἐκεῖνος
these things I say that ye may be saved. That man
ἦν ὁ λύχνος ὁ καιόμενος καὶ φαίνων,
was the lamp - burning and shining,
ὑμεῖς δὲ ἠθελήσατε ἀγαλλιαθῆναι πρὸς
and ye were willing to exult for
ὥραν ἐν τῷ φωτὶ αὐτοῦ. 36 Ἐγὼ δὲ
an hour in the light of him. But I
ἔχω τὴν μαρτυρίαν μείζω τοῦ Ἰωάννου·
have the witness greater [than] - of John;
τὰ γὰρ ἔργα ἃ δέδωκέν μοι ὁ πατὴρ ἵνα
for the works which has given me the Father that
τελειώσω αὐτά, αὐτὰ τὰ ἔργα ἃ ποιῶ,
I may finish them, ³[them]selves ¹the ²works which I do,
μαρτυρεῖ περὶ ἐμοῦ ὅτι ὁ πατήρ με
witnesses concerning me that the Father me
ἀπέσταλκεν. 37 καὶ ὁ πέμψας με πατήρ,
has sent. And ¹the ³having sent ⁴me ²Father,
ἐκεῖνος μεμαρτύρηκεν περὶ ἐμοῦ. οὔτε
that [one] has witnessed concerning me. Neither
φωνὴν αὐτοῦ πώποτε ἀκηκόατε οὔτε εἶδος
voice of him never ye have heard nor form

* Note the absence of the definite article here. See also Rev. 1. 13 and 14. 14.

---

life. 25 I tell you the truth, a time is coming and has now come when the dead will hear the voice of the Son of God and those who hear will live. 26 For as the Father has life in himself, so he has granted the Son to have life in himself. 27 And he has given him authority to judge because he is the Son of Man.

28 "Do not be amazed at this, for a time is coming when all who are in their graves will hear his voice 29 and come out—those who have done good will rise to live, and those who have done evil will rise to be condemned. 30 By myself I can do nothing; I judge only as I hear, and my judgment is just, for I seek not to please myself but him who sent me.

Testimonies About Jesus

31 "If I testify about myself, my testimony is not valid. 32 There is another who testifies in my favor, and I know that his testimony about me is valid.

33 "You have sent to John and he has testified to the truth. 34 Not that I accept human testimony; but I mention it that you may be saved. 35 John was a lamp that burned and gave light, and you chose for a time to enjoy his light.

36 "I have testimony weightier than that of John. For the very work that the Father has given me to finish, and which I am doing, testifies that the Father has sent me. 37 And the Father who sent me has himself testified concerning me. You have never heard his voice nor seen his form,

38and you do not have his word abiding in you, because you do not believe him whom he has sent.

39 "You search the scriptures because you think that in them you have eternal life; and it is they that testify on my behalf. 40Yet you refuse to come to me to have life. 41I do not accept glory from human beings. 42But I know that you do not have the love of God in*k* you. 43I have come in my Father's name, and you do not accept me; if another comes in his own name, you will accept him. 44How can you believe when you accept glory from one another and do not seek the glory that comes from the one who alone is God? 45Do not think that I will accuse you before the Father; your accuser is Moses, on whom you have set your hope. 46If you believed Moses, you would believe me, for he wrote about me. 47But if you do not believe what he wrote, how will you believe what I say?"

αὐτοῦ ἑωράκατε, 38 καὶ τὸν λόγον αὐτοῦ
of him   ye have seen,   and   the   word   of him

οὐκ ἔχετε ἐν ὑμῖν μένοντα, ὅτι ὃν
ye have not   in   you   remaining, because [he] whom

ἀπέστειλεν ἐκεῖνος, τούτῳ ὑμεῖς οὐ πιστεύετε.
²sent   ¹that [one],   this [one]   ye   do not believe.

39 ἐρευνᾶτε τὰς γραφάς, ὅτι ὑμεῖς δοκεῖτε
Ye search   the   scriptures, because   ye   think

ἐν αὐταῖς ζωὴν αἰώνιον ἔχειν· καὶ ἐκεῖναί
in   them   life   eternal   to have; and   those

εἰσιν αἱ μαρτυροῦσαι περὶ ἐμοῦ· 40 καὶ
are the [ones]   witnessing   concerning   me ;   and

οὐ θέλετε ἐλθεῖν πρός με ἵνα ζωὴν
ye wish not   to come   to   me   that   life

ἔχητε. 41 Δόξαν παρὰ ἀνθρώπων οὐ
ye may have.   Glory   from   men   not

λαμβάνω, 42 ἀλλὰ ἔγνωκα ὑμᾶς ὅτι τὴν
I receive,   but   I have known   you   that   the

ἀγάπην τοῦ θεοῦ οὐκ ἔχετε ἐν ἑαυτοῖς.
love   –   of God   ye have not   in   yourselves.

43 ἐγὼ ἐλήλυθα ἐν τῷ ὀνόματι τοῦ πατρός
I   have come   in   the   name   of the   Father

μου, καὶ οὐ λαμβάνετέ με· ἐὰν ἄλλος
of me,   and   ye receive not   me;   if   another

ἔλθῃ ἐν τῷ ὀνόματι τῷ ἰδίῳ, ἐκεῖνον
comes   in   –   name   the(his)   own,   that [one]

λήμψεσθε. 44 πῶς δύνασθε ὑμεῖς πιστεῦσαι,
ye will receive.   How   can   ye   to believe,

δόξαν παρὰ ἀλλήλων λαμβάνοντες, καὶ
glory   from   one another   receiving,   and

τὴν δόξαν τὴν παρὰ τοῦ μόνου θεοῦ
the   glory   –   from   the   only   God

οὐ ζητεῖτε; 45 μὴ δοκεῖτε ὅτι ἐγὼ κατηγορήσω
ye seek not?   Do not think that   I   will accuse

ὑμῶν πρὸς τὸν πατέρα· ἔστιν ὁ κατηγορῶν
you   to   the   Father;   there is the [one] accusing

ὑμῶν Μωϋσῆς, εἰς ὃν ὑμεῖς ἠλπίκατε. 46 εἰ
you[,]   Moses,   in whom   ye   have hoped.   if

γὰρ ἐπιστεύετε Μωϋσεῖ, ἐπιστεύετε ἂν
For   ye believed   Moses,   ye would have believed

ἐμοί· περὶ γὰρ ἐμοῦ ἐκεῖνος ἔγραψεν.
me;   for concerning   me   that [one]   wrote.

47 εἰ δὲ τοῖς ἐκείνου γράμμασιν οὐ
  But ¹if   ⁴the   ⁶of that [one]   ⁵letters   ²not

πιστεύετε, πῶς τοῖς ἐμοῖς ῥήμασιν
³ye believe,   how   –   my   words

πιστεύσετε;
will ye believe?

38nor does his word dwell in you, for you do not believe the one he sent. 39You diligently study*e* the Scriptures because you think that by them you possess eternal life. These are the Scriptures that testify about me, 40yet you refuse to come to me to have life.

41"I do not accept praise from men, 42but I know you. I know that you do not have the love of God in your hearts. 43I have come in my Father's name, and you do not accept me; but if someone else comes in his own name, you will accept him. 44How can you believe if you accept praise from one another, yet make no effort to obtain the praise that comes from the only God*f*?

45"But do not think I will accuse you before the Father. Your accuser is Moses, on whom your hopes are set. 46If you believed Moses, you would believe me, for he wrote about me. 47But since you do not believe what he wrote, how are you going to believe what I say?''

Chapter 6

Feeding the Five Thousand

AFTER this Jesus went to the other side of the Sea of Galilee, also called the Sea of Tiberias.*l* 2A large crowd kept following him, because they saw the signs that he was doing for the sick. 3Jesus went up the mountain and sat down there with his disciples. 4Now the Passover, the festival of the Jews, was near. 5When he looked up and saw a

---

6 Μετὰ ταῦτα ἀπῆλθεν ὁ Ἰησοῦς πέραν
After   these things went away   –   Jesus   across

τῆς θαλάσσης τῆς Γαλιλαίας τῆς Τιβεριάδος.
the   sea   –   of Galilee[,]   –   of Tiberias.

2 ἠκολούθει δὲ αὐτῷ ὄχλος πολύς, ὅτι
And followed   him   crowd   a much, because

ἑώρων τὰ σημεῖα ἃ ἐποίει ἐπὶ τῶν
they saw   the   signs   which   he did   on   the

ἀσθενούντων. 3 ἀνῆλθεν δὲ εἰς τὸ ὄρος
ailing [ones].   And went up   to   the   mountain

Ἰησοῦς, καὶ ἐκεῖ ἐκάθητο μετὰ τῶν
Jesus,   and   there   sat   with   the

μαθητῶν αὐτοῦ. 4 ἦν δὲ ἐγγὺς τὸ πάσχα,
disciples   of him.   And was   near   the   Passover,

ἡ ἑορτὴ τῶν Ἰουδαίων. 5 ἐπάρας οὖν
the   feast   of the   Jews.   Lifting up therefore

Chapter 6

Jesus Feeds the Five Thousand

SOME time after this, Jesus crossed to the far shore of the Sea of Galilee (that is, the Sea of Tiberias), 2and a great crowd of people followed him because they saw the miraculous signs he had performed on the sick. 3Then Jesus went up on a mountainside and sat down with his disciples. 4The Jewish Passover Feast was near.

5When Jesus looked up

e39 Or *Study diligently* (the imperative)
f44 Some early manuscripts *the Only One*

---

k Or *among*
l Gk *of Galilee of Tiberius*

large crowd coming toward him, Jesus said to Philip, "Where are we to buy bread for these people to eat?" 6 He said this to test him, for he himself knew what he was going to do. 7 Philip answered him, "Six months' wages*m* would not buy enough bread for each of them to get a little." 8 One of his disciples, Andrew, Simon Peter's brother, said to him, 9 "There is a boy here who has five barley loaves and two fish. But what are they among so many people?" 10 Jesus said, "Make the people sit down." Now there was a great deal of grass in the place; so they sat down, about five thousand in all. 11 Then Jesus took the loaves, and when he had given thanks, he distributed them to those who were seated; so also the fish, as much as they wanted. 12 When they were satisfied, he told his disciples, "Gather up the fragments left over, so that nothing may be lost." 13 So they gathered them up, and from the fragments of the five barley loaves, left by those who had eaten, they filled twelve baskets. 14 When the people saw the sign that he had done, they began to say, "This is indeed the prophet who is to come into the world."

15 When Jesus realized that they were about to come and take him by force to make him king, he withdrew again to the mountain by himself.

τοὺς ὀφθαλμοὺς ὁ Ἰησοῦς καὶ θεασάμενος
the(his) eyes – Jesus and beholding
ὅτι πολὺς ὄχλος ἔρχεται πρὸς αὐτόν,
that a much crowd is(was) coming toward him,
λέγει πρὸς Φίλιππον· πόθεν ἀγοράσωμεν
he says to Philip: Whence may we buy
ἄρτους ἵνα φάγωσιν οὗτοι; 6 τοῦτο δὲ
loaves that may eat these? And this
ἔλεγεν πειράζων αὐτόν· αὐτὸς γὰρ ᾔδει
he said testing him; for he knew
τί ἔμελλεν ποιεῖν. 7 ἀπεκρίθη αὐτῷ ὁ
what he was about to do. Answered him –
Φίλιππος· διακοσίων δηναρίων ἄρτοι οὐκ
Philip: *Of two hundred *denarii *loaves not
ἀρκοῦσιν αὐτοῖς, ἵνα ἕκαστος βραχύ τι
are enough for them, that each a little
λάβῃ. 8 λέγει αὐτῷ εἷς ἐκ τῶν μαθητῶν
may take. Says to him one of the disciples
αὐτοῦ, Ἀνδρέας ὁ ἀδελφὸς Σίμωνος
of him, Andrew the brother of Simon
Πέτρου· 9 ἔστιν παιδάριον ὧδε ὃς ἔχει
Peter: There is a lad here who has
πέντε ἄρτους κριθίνους καὶ δύο ὀψάρια·
five loaves barley and two fishes;
ἀλλὰ ταῦτα τί ἐστιν εἰς τοσούτους;
but *these *what *is(are) among so many?
10 εἶπεν ὁ Ἰησοῦς· ποιήσατε τοὺς ἀνθρώπους
Said – Jesus: Make the men*
ἀναπεσεῖν. ἦν δὲ χόρτος πολὺς ἐν τῷ
to recline. Now there was grass much in the
τόπῳ. ἀνέπεσαν οὖν οἱ ἄνδρες τὸν ἀριθμὸν
place. Reclined therefore the men the number
ὡς πεντακισχίλιοι. 11 ἔλαβεν οὖν τοὺς
about five thousand. Took therefore the
ἄρτους ὁ Ἰησοῦς καὶ εὐχαριστήσας
loaves – Jesus and having given thanks
διέδωκεν τοῖς ἀνακειμένοις, ὁμοίως καὶ
distributed to the [ones] lying down, likewise also
ἐκ τῶν ὀψαρίων ὅσον ἤθελον. 12 ὡς δὲ
of the fishes as much as they wished. Now when
ἐνεπλήσθησαν, λέγει τοῖς μαθηταῖς αὐτοῦ·
they were filled, he tells the disciples of him:
συναγάγετε τὰ περισσεύσαντα κλάσματα, ἵνα
Gather ye the left over fragments, that
μή τι ἀπόληται. 13 συνήγαγον οὖν, καὶ
not anything is lost. They gathered therefore, and
ἐγέμισαν δώδεκα κοφίνους κλασμάτων ἐκ
filled twelve baskets of fragments of
τῶν πέντε ἄρτων τῶν κριθίνων ἃ ἐπερίσσευσαν
the five loaves – barley which were left over
τοῖς βεβρωκόσιν. 14 Οἱ οὖν ἄνθρωποι
to the [ones] having eaten. Therefore the men*
ἰδόντες ὃ ἐποίησεν σημεῖον ἔλεγον ὅτι
seeing *what *he did *sign said[,] –
οὗτός ἐστιν ἀληθῶς ὁ προφήτης ὁ
This is truly the prophet –
ἐρχόμενος εἰς τὸν κόσμον. 15 Ἰησοῦς
coming into the world. Jesus
οὖν γνοὺς ὅτι μέλλουσιν ἔρχεσθαι καὶ
therefore knowing that they are(were) about to come and
ἁρπάζειν αὐτὸν ἵνα ποιήσωσιν βασιλέα,
seize him that they might make a king,
ἀνεχώρησεν πάλιν εἰς τὸ ὄρος αὐτὸς
departed again to the mountain [him]self

and saw a great crowd coming toward him, he said to Philip, "Where shall we buy bread for these people to eat?" 6 He asked this only to test him, for he already had in mind what he was going to do. 7 Philip answered him, "Eight months' wages*g* would not buy enough bread for each one to have a bite!" 8 Another of his disciples, Andrew, Simon Peter's brother, spoke up, 9 "Here is a boy with five small barley loaves and two small fish, but how far will they go among so many?" 10 Jesus said, "Have the people sit down." There was plenty of grass in that place, and the men sat down, about five thousand of them. 11 Jesus then took the loaves, gave thanks, and distributed to those who were seated as much as they wanted. He did the same with the fish. 12 When they had all had enough to eat, he said to his disciples, "Gather the pieces that are left over. Let nothing be wasted." 13 So they gathered them and filled twelve baskets with the pieces of the five barley loaves left over by those who had eaten.

14 After the people saw the miraculous sign that Jesus did, they began to say, "Surely this is the Prophet who is to come into the world." 15 Jesus, knowing that they intended to come and make him king by force, withdrew again to a mountain by himself.

m Gk *Two hundred denarii;* the denarius was the usual day's wage for a laborer
n Gk *the men*

* That is, people. Compare ἄνδρες in ver. 10.

g 7 Greek *two hundred denarii*

Jesus Walks on the Water

16 When evening came, his disciples went down to the sea, [17] got into a boat, and started across the sea to Capernaum. It was now dark, and Jesus had not yet come to them. [18] The sea became rough because a strong wind was blowing. [19] When they had rowed about three or four miles, [o] they saw Jesus walking on the sea and coming near the boat, and they were terrified. [20] But he said to them, "It is I; [p] do not be afraid." [21] Then they wanted to take him into the boat, and immediately the boat reached the land toward which they were going.

The Bread from Heaven

22 The next day the crowd that had stayed on the other side of the sea saw that there had been only one boat there. They also saw that Jesus had not got into the boat with his disciples, but that his disciples had gone away alone. [23] Then some boats from Tiberias came near the place where they had eaten the bread after the Lord had given thanks. [q] [24] So when the crowd saw that neither Jesus nor his disciples were there, they themselves got into the boats and went to Capernaum looking for Jesus.

25 When they found him on the other side of the sea, they said to him, "Rabbi, when did you come here?" [26] Jesus answered them, "Very truly, I tell you, you are looking for me, not because you saw

---

μόνος. **16** Ὡς δὲ ὀψία ἐγένετο, κατέβησαν
alone. And when evening came, went down

οἱ μαθηταὶ αὐτοῦ ἐπὶ τὴν θάλασσαν,
the disciples of him to the sea,

17 καὶ ἐμβάντες εἰς πλοῖον ἤρχοντο πέραν
and embarking in a boat came across

τῆς θαλάσσης εἰς Καφαρναούμ. καὶ
the sea to Capernaum. And

σκοτία ἤδη ἐγεγόνει καὶ οὔπω ἐληλύθει
darkness now had come and not yet had come

πρὸς αὐτοὺς ὁ Ἰησοῦς, **18** ἥ τε θάλασσα
to them Jesus, and the sea

ἀνέμου μεγάλου πνέοντος διηγείρετο
wind a great blowing[a] was roused.
=as a great wind blew

19 ἐληλακότες οὖν ὡς σταδίους εἴκοσι
Having rowed therefore about furlongs twenty-

πέντε ἢ τριάκοντα θεωροῦσιν τὸν Ἰησοῦν
five or thirty they behold - Jesus

περιπατοῦντα ἐπὶ τῆς θαλάσσης καὶ ἐγγὺς
walking on the sea and near

τοῦ πλοίου γινόμενον, καὶ ἐφοβήθησαν.
the boat becoming, and they feared.

20 ὁ δὲ λέγει αὐτοῖς· ἐγώ εἰμι· μὴ
But he says to them: I am; not

φοβεῖσθε. **21** ἤθελον οὖν λαβεῖν αὐτὸν εἰς
fear ye. They wished therefore to take him into

τὸ πλοῖον, καὶ εὐθέως ἐγένετο τὸ πλοῖον
the boat, and immediately was the boat

ἐπὶ τῆς γῆς εἰς ἣν ὑπῆγον.
at the land to which they were going.

22 Τῇ ἐπαύριον ὁ ὄχλος ὁ ἑστηκὼς
On the morrow the crowd - standing

πέραν τῆς θαλάσσης εἶδον ὅτι πλοιάριον
across the sea saw that boat

ἄλλο οὐκ ἦν ἐκεῖ εἰ μὴ ἕν, καὶ ὅτι
other was not there except one, and that

οὐ συνεισῆλθεν τοῖς μαθηταῖς αὐτοῦ ὁ
[3]did not come in with [3]the [4]disciples [5]of him

Ἰησοῦς εἰς τὸ πλοῖον ἀλλὰ μόνοι οἱ
[1]Jesus in the boat but alone the

μαθηταὶ αὐτοῦ ἀπῆλθον· **23** ἄλλα ἦλθεν
disciples of him went away; [1]other [2]came

πλοιάρια ἐκ Τιβεριάδος ἐγγὺς τοῦ τόπου
[2]boats from Tiberias near the place

ὅπου ἔφαγον τὸν ἄρτον εὐχαριστήσαντος
where they ate the bread having given thanks

τοῦ κυρίου. **24** ὅτε οὖν εἶδεν ὁ ὄχλος
the Lord.[a] When therefore saw the crowd
=when the Lord had given thanks.

ὅτι Ἰησοῦς οὐκ ἔστιν ἐκεῖ οὐδὲ οἱ
that Jesus is(was) not there nor the

μαθηταὶ αὐτοῦ, ἐνέβησαν αὐτοὶ εἰς τὰ
disciples of him, embarked they into the

πλοιάρια καὶ ἦλθον εἰς Καφαρναούμ
boats and came to Capernaum

ζητοῦντες τὸν Ἰησοῦν. **25** καὶ εὑρόντες
seeking - Jesus. And finding

αὐτὸν πέραν τῆς θαλάσσης εἶπον αὐτῷ·
him across the sea they said to him:

ῥαββί, πότε ὧδε γέγονας; **26** ἀπεκρίθη
Rabbi, when here hast thou come? Answered

αὐτοῖς ὁ Ἰησοῦς καὶ εἶπεν· ἀμὴν ἀμὴν
them - Jesus and said: Truly truly

λέγω ὑμῖν, ζητεῖτέ με οὐχ ὅτι εἴδετε
I say to you, ye seek me not because ye saw

Jesus Walks on the Water

[16] When evening came, his disciples went down to the lake, [17] where they got into a boat and set off across the lake for Capernaum. By now it was dark, and Jesus had not yet joined them. [18] A strong wind was blowing and the waters grew rough. [19] When they had rowed three or three and a half miles, [h] they saw Jesus approaching the boat, walking on the water; and they were terrified. "It is I; don't be afraid." [21] Then they were willing to take him into the boat, and immediately the boat reached the shore where they were heading.

[22] The next day the crowd that had stayed on the opposite shore of the lake realized that only one boat had been there, and that Jesus had not entered it with his disciples, but that they had gone away alone. [23] Then some boats from Tiberias landed near the place where the people had eaten the bread after the Lord had given thanks. [24] Once the crowd realized that neither Jesus nor his disciples were there, they got into the boats and went to Capernaum in search of Jesus.

Jesus the Bread of Life

[25] When they found him on the other side of the lake, they asked him, "Rabbi, when did you get here?" [26] Jesus answered, "I tell you the truth, you are looking for me, not because you

---

[o] Gk about twenty-five or thirty stadia

[p] Gk I am

[q] Other ancient authorities lack after the Lord had given thanks

[h] 19 Greek rowed twenty-five or thirty stadia (about 5 or 6 kilometers)

signs, but because you ate your fill of the loaves. 27 Do not work for the food that perishes, but for the food that endures for eternal life, which the Son of Man will give you. For it is on him that God the Father has set his seal." 28 Then they said to him, "What must we do to perform the works of God?" 29 Jesus answered them, "This is the work of God, that you believe in him whom he has sent." 30 So they said to him, "What sign are you going to give us then, so that we may see it and believe you? What work are you performing? 31 Our ancestors ate the manna in the wilderness; as it is written, 'He gave them bread from heaven to eat.' " 32 Then Jesus said to them, "Very truly, I tell you, it was not Moses who gave you the bread from heaven, but it is my Father who gives you the true bread from heaven. 33 For the bread of God is that which comes down from heaven and gives life to the world." 34 They said to him, "Sir, give us this bread always."

35 Jesus said to them, "I am the bread of life. Whoever comes to me will never be hungry, and whoever believes in me will never be thirsty. 36 But I said to you that you have seen me and yet do not believe. 37 Everything that the Father gives me will come to me, and anyone who comes to me I will never drive away; 38 for I have come down

σημεῖα, ἀλλ᾽ ὅτι ἐφάγετε ἐκ τῶν ἄρτων
signs, but because ye ate of the loaves
καὶ ἐχορτάσθητε. 27 ἐργάζεσθε μὴ τὴν
and were satisfied. Work not [for] the
βρῶσιν τὴν ἀπολλυμένην, ἀλλὰ τὴν βρῶσιν
food – perishing, but [for] the food
τὴν μένουσαν εἰς ζωὴν αἰώνιον, ἣν ὁ
– remaining to life eternal, which the
υἱὸς τοῦ ἀνθρώπου ὑμῖν δώσει· τοῦτον γὰρ
Son – of man you will give; for this [one]
ὁ πατὴρ ἐσφράγισεν ὁ θεός. 28 εἶπον
¹the ³Father ⁴sealed – ²God. They said
οὖν πρὸς αὐτόν· τί ποιῶμεν ἵνα ἐργαζ-
therefore to him : What may we do that we may
ώμεθα τὰ ἔργα τοῦ θεοῦ; 29 ἀπεκρίθη
work the works – of God? Answered
Ἰησοῦς καὶ εἶπεν αὐτοῖς· τοῦτό ἐστιν τὸ
Jesus and said to them· This is the
ἔργον τοῦ θεοῦ, ἵνα πιστεύητε εἰς ὃν
work – of God, that ye believe in [him] whom
ἀπέστειλεν ἐκεῖνος. 30 εἶπον οὖν αὐτῷ·
sent that [one]. They said therefore to him :
τί οὖν ποιεῖς σὺ σημεῖον, ἵνα ἴδωμεν
¹What ²then ³doest ⁴thou ⁵sign, that we may see
καὶ πιστεύσωμέν σοι; τί ἐργάζῃ; 31 οἱ
and believe thee? what workest thou? The
πατέρες ἡμῶν τὸ μάννα ἔφαγον ἐν τῇ
fathers of us the manna ate in the
ἐρήμῳ, καθώς ἐστιν γεγραμμένον· ἄρτον
desert, as it is having been written : Bread
ἐκ τοῦ οὐρανοῦ ἔδωκεν αὐτοῖς φαγεῖν.
out of – heaven he gave them to eat.
32 Εἶπεν οὖν αὐτοῖς ὁ Ἰησοῦς· ἀμὴν
Said therefore to them – Jesus : Truly
ἀμὴν λέγω ὑμῖν, οὐ Μωϋσῆς δέδωκεν
truly I say to you, not Moses has given
ὑμῖν τὸν ἄρτον ἐκ τοῦ οὐρανοῦ, ἀλλ᾽ ὁ
you the bread out of – heaven, but the
πατήρ μου δίδωσιν ὑμῖν τὸν ἄρτον ἐκ
Father of me gives you ¹the ²bread ⁴out of
τοῦ οὐρανοῦ τὸν ἀληθινόν· 33 ὁ γὰρ ἄρτος
– ⁵heaven the ³true; for the bread
τοῦ θεοῦ ἐστιν ὁ καταβαίνων ἐκ τοῦ
– of God is the [one] coming down out of –
οὐρανοῦ καὶ ζωὴν διδοὺς τῷ κόσμῳ.
heaven and life giving to the world.
34 εἶπον οὖν πρὸς αὐτόν· κύριε, πάντοτε
They said therefore to him : Lord, always
δὸς ἡμῖν τὸν ἄρτον τοῦτον. 35 εἶπεν
give us – bread this. Said
αὐτοῖς ὁ Ἰησοῦς· ἐγώ εἰμι ὁ ἄρτος τῆς
to them – Jesus : I am the bread
ζωῆς· ὁ ἐρχόμενος πρὸς ἐμὲ οὐ μὴ
of life; the [one] coming to me by no means
πεινάσῃ, καὶ ὁ πιστεύων εἰς ἐμὲ οὐ μὴ
hungers, and the [one] believing in me by no means
διψήσει πώποτε. 36 Ἀλλ᾽ εἶπον ὑμῖν ὅτι
will thirst never. But I told you that
καὶ ἑωράκατέ [με] καὶ οὐ πιστεύετε.
both ye have seen me and do not believe.
37 πᾶν ὃ δίδωσίν μοι ὁ πατὴρ πρὸς
All which gives to me the Father to
ἐμὲ ἥξει, καὶ τὸν ἐρχόμενον πρός με
me will come, and the [one] coming to me
οὐ μὴ ἐκβάλω ἔξω, 38 ὅτι καταβέβηκα
by no means I will cast out outside, because I have come down

saw miraculous signs but because you ate the loaves and had your fill. 27 Do not work for food that spoils, but for food that endures to eternal life, which the Son of Man will give you. On him God the Father has placed his seal of approval."

28 Then they asked him, "What must we do to do the works God requires?"

29 Jesus answered, "The work of God is this: to believe in the one he has sent."

30 So they asked him, "What miraculous sign then will you give that we may see it and believe you? What will you do? 31 Our forefathers ate the manna in the desert; as it is written: 'He gave them bread from heaven to eat.' "

32 Jesus said to them, "I tell you the truth, it is not Moses who has given you the bread from heaven, but it is my Father who gives you the true bread from heaven. 33 For the bread of God is he who comes down from heaven and gives life to the world."

34 "Sir," they said, "from now on give us this bread." 35 Then Jesus declared, "I am the bread of life. He who comes to me will never go hungry, and he who believes in me will never be thirsty. 36 But as I told you, you have seen me and still you do not believe. 37 All that the Father gives me will come to me, and whoever comes to me I will never drive away. 38 For I have come down from

ʳ Or he who

ⁱ31 Exodus 16:4; Neh. 9:15; Psalm 78:24,25

from heaven, not to do my own will, but the will of him who sent me. ³⁹And this is the will of him who sent me, that I should lose nothing of all that he has given me, but raise it up on the last day. ⁴⁰This is indeed the will of my Father, that all who see the Son and believe in him may have eternal life; and I will raise them up on the last day."

⁴¹ Then the Jews began to complain about him because he said, "I am the bread that came down from heaven." ⁴²They were saying, "Is not this Jesus, the son of Joseph, whose father and mother we know? How can he now say, 'I have come down from heaven'?" ⁴³Jesus answered them, "Do not complain among yourselves. ⁴⁴No one can come to me unless drawn by the Father who sent me; and I will raise that person up on the last day. ⁴⁵It is written in the prophets, 'And they shall all be taught by God.' Everyone who has heard and learned from the Father comes to me. ⁴⁶Not that anyone has seen the Father except the one who is from God; he has seen the Father. ⁴⁷Very truly, I tell you, whoever believes has eternal life. ⁴⁸I am the bread of life. ⁴⁹Your ancestors ate the manna in the wilderness, and they died. ⁵⁰This is the bread that comes down from heaven, so that one may eat of it and

ἀπὸ τοῦ οὐρανοῦ οὐχ ἵνα ποιῶ τὸ θέλημα
from — heaven not that I may do *the* ²will
τὸ ἐμὸν ἀλλὰ τὸ θέλημα τοῦ πέμψαντός
— ¹my but the will of the [one] having sent
με. 39 τοῦτο δέ ἐστιν τὸ θέλημα τοῦ
me. And this is the will of the [one]
πέμψαντός με, ἵνα πᾶν ὃ δέδωκέν μοι
having sent me, that all which he has given me
μὴ ἀπολέσω ἐξ αὐτοῦ, ἀλλὰ ἀναστήσω
I shall not lose of it, but shall raise up
αὐτὸ ἐν τῇ ἐσχάτῃ ἡμέρᾳ. 40 τοῦτο
it in the last day. this
γάρ ἐστιν τὸ θέλημα τοῦ πατρός μου,
For is the will of the Father of me,
ἵνα πᾶς ὁ θεωρῶν τὸν υἱὸν καὶ πιστεύων
that everyone beholding the Son and believing
εἰς αὐτὸν ἔχῃ ζωὴν αἰώνιον, καὶ ἀναστήσω
in him may have life eternal, and will raise up
αὐτὸν ἐγὼ ἐν τῇ ἐσχάτῃ ἡμέρᾳ. 41 Ἐγόγ-
him I in the last day. Mur-
γυζον οὖν οἱ Ἰουδαῖοι περὶ αὐτοῦ ὅτι
mured therefore the Jews about him because
εἶπεν· ἐγώ εἰμι ὁ ἄρτος ὁ καταβὰς ἐκ
he said: I am the bread – having come down out
τοῦ οὐρανοῦ, 42 καὶ ἔλεγον· οὐχ οὗτός
– of heaven, and they said: Not this man
ἐστιν Ἰησοῦς ὁ υἱὸς Ἰωσήφ, οὗ ἡμεῖς
is Jesus the son of Joseph, of whom we
οἴδαμεν τὸν πατέρα καὶ τὴν μητέρα;
know the father and the mother?
πῶς νῦν λέγει ὅτι ἐκ τοῦ οὐρανοῦ
how now says he[,] Out of – heaven
καταβέβηκα; 43 ἀπεκρίθη Ἰησοῦς καὶ εἶπεν
I have come down? Answered Jesus and said
αὐτοῖς· μὴ γογγύζετε μετ᾽ ἀλλήλων.
to them: Do not murmur with one another.
44 Οὐδεὶς δύναται ἐλθεῖν πρός με ἐὰν μὴ
No one can to come to me unless
ὁ πατὴρ ὁ πέμψας με ἑλκύσῃ αὐτόν,
the Father the [one] having sent me should draw him,
κἀγὼ ἀναστήσω αὐτὸν ἐν τῇ ἐσχάτῃ
and I will raise up him in the last
ἡμέρᾳ. 45 ἔστιν γεγραμμένον ἐν τοῖς
day. It is *having been* written in the
προφήταις· καὶ ἔσονται πάντες διδακτοὶ
prophets: And they shall be all taught
θεοῦ· πᾶς ὁ ἀκούσας παρὰ τοῦ πατρὸς
of God; everyone hearing from the Father
καὶ μαθὼν ἔρχεται πρὸς ἐμέ. 46 οὐχ
and learning comes to me. Not
ὅτι τὸν πατέρα ἑώρακέν τις, εἰ μὴ ὁ
that ³the ⁴Father ⁵has seen ¹anyone, except the [one]
ὢν παρὰ τοῦ θεοῦ, οὗτος ἑώρακεν τὸν
being from – God, this [one] has seen the
πατέρα. 47 ἀμὴν ἀμὴν λέγω ὑμῖν, ὁ
Father. Truly truly I say to you, the
πιστεύων ἔχει ζωὴν αἰώνιον. 48 Ἐγώ
[one] believing has life eternal. I
εἰμι ὁ ἄρτος τῆς ζωῆς. 49 οἱ πατέρες
am the bread – of life. The fathers
ὑμῶν ἔφαγον ἐν τῇ ἐρήμῳ τὸ μάννα καὶ
of you ate in the desert the manna and
ἀπέθανον· 50 οὗτός ἐστιν ὁ ἄρτος ὁ ἐκ
died; this is the bread – out of
τοῦ οὐρανοῦ καταβαίνων, ἵνα τις ἐξ
– heaven coming down, that anyone of

heaven not to do my will but to do the will of him who sent me. ³⁹And this is the will of him who sent me, that I shall lose none of all that he has given me, but raise them up at the last day. ⁴⁰For my Father's will is that everyone who looks to the Son and believes in him shall have eternal life, and I will raise him up at the last day."

⁴¹At this the Jews began to grumble about him because he said, "I am the bread that came down from heaven." ⁴²They said, "Is this not Jesus, the son of Joseph, whose father and mother we know? How can he now say, 'I came down from heaven'?"

⁴³"Stop grumbling among yourselves," Jesus answered. ⁴⁴"No one can come to me unless the Father who sent me draws him, and I will raise him up at the last day. ⁴⁵It is written in the Prophets: 'They will all be taught by God.' Everyone who listens to the Father and learns from him comes to me. ⁴⁶No one has seen the Father except the one who is from God; only he has seen the Father. ⁴⁷I tell you the truth, he who believes has everlasting life. ⁴⁸I am the bread of life. ⁴⁹Your forefathers ate the manna in the desert, yet they died. ⁵⁰But here is the bread that comes down from heaven, which a man may eat and not die. ⁵¹I am

j45 Isaiah 54:13

not die. ⁵¹I am the living bread that came down from heaven. Whoever eats of this bread will live forever; and the bread that I will give for the life of the world is my flesh."

⁵² The Jews then disputed among themselves, saying, "How can this man give us his flesh to eat?" ⁵³ So Jesus said to them, "Very truly, I tell you, unless you eat the flesh of the Son of Man and drink his blood, you have no life in you. ⁵⁴ Those who eat my flesh and drink my blood have eternal life, and I will raise them up on the last day; ⁵⁵ for my flesh is true food and my blood is true drink. ⁵⁶ Those who eat my flesh and drink my blood abide in me, and I in them. ⁵⁷ Just as the living Father sent me, and I live because of the Father, so whoever eats me will live because of me. ⁵⁸ This is the bread that came down from heaven, not like that which your ancestors ate, and they died. But the one who eats this bread will live forever." ⁵⁹ He said these things while he was teaching in the synagogue at Capernaum.

The Words of Eternal Life

60 When many of his disciples heard it, they said, "This teaching is difficult; who can accept it?" ⁶¹ But Jesus, being aware that his disciples were complaining about it, said to them, "Does this offend you? ⁶² Then what if you

---

αὐτοῦ φάγῃ καὶ μὴ ἀποθάνῃ. **51** ἐγώ
it　 may eat　 and　 may not die.　　　 I

εἰμι ὁ ἄρτος ὁ ζῶν ὁ ἐκ τοῦ οὐρανοῦ
am　 the　 bread　 - living　 the [one] out of - heaven

καταβάς· ἐάν τις φάγῃ ἐκ τούτου τοῦ
having come down; if anyone eats of　 this -

ἄρτου, ζήσει εἰς τὸν αἰῶνα· καὶ ὁ ἄρτος
bread, he will live　 to　 the　 age;　 ²indeed ⁴the ⁴bread

δὲ ὃν ἐγὼ δώσω ἡ σάρξ μού ἐστιν
¹and which　 I　 will give　 the　 flesh　 of me　 is

ὑπὲρ τῆς τοῦ κόσμου ζωῆς. **52** Ἐμάχοντο
for　 ¹the　 ³of the ⁴world　 ²life.　　 Fought

οὖν πρὸς ἀλλήλους οἱ Ἰουδαῖοι λέγοντες·
therefore with　 one another　 the　 Jews　 saying :

πῶς δύναται οὗτος ἡμῖν δοῦναι τὴν
How　 can　 this man　 us　 to give　 the(his)

σάρκα φαγεῖν; **53** εἶπεν οὖν αὐτοῖς ὁ
flesh　 to eat?　　 Said therefore　 to them　 -

Ἰησοῦς· ἀμὴν ἀμὴν λέγω ὑμῖν, ἐὰν μὴ
Jesus :　 Truly　 truly　 I say　 to you,　 unless

φάγητε τὴν σάρκα τοῦ υἱοῦ τοῦ ἀνθρώπου
ye eat　 the　 flesh　 of the Son　 -　 of man

καὶ πίητε αὐτοῦ τὸ αἷμα, οὐκ ἔχετε
and　 drink　 of him　 the　 blood,　 ye have not

ζωὴν ἐν ἑαυτοῖς. **54** ὁ τρώγων μου τὴν
life　 in yourselves.　 The [one] eating　 of me　 the

σάρκα καὶ πίνων μου τὸ αἷμα ἔχει ζωὴν
flesh　 and drinking of me　 the　 blood　 has　 life

αἰώνιον, κἀγὼ ἀναστήσω αὐτὸν τῇ ἐσχάτῃ
eternal,　 and I　 will raise up　 him　 in the　 last

ἡμέρᾳ. **55** ἡ γὰρ σάρξ μου ἀληθής
day.　　 For the　 flesh　 of me　 ³true

ἐστιν βρῶσις, καὶ τὸ αἷμά μου ἀληθής
¹is　 ⁴food,　 and　 the　 blood　 of me　 ²true

ἐστιν πόσις. **56** ὁ τρώγων μου τὴν
¹is　 ³drink.　 The [one] eating　 of me　 the

σάρκα καὶ πίνων μου τὸ αἷμα ἐν ἐμοὶ
flesh　 and drinking of me　 the blood　 in me

μένει κἀγὼ ἐν αὐτῷ. **57** καθὼς ἀπέστειλέν
remains and I　 in　 him.　　 As　　 sent

με ὁ ζῶν πατὴρ κἀγὼ ζῶ διὰ τὸν
me the living　 Father　 and I　 live because of the

πατέρα, καὶ ὁ τρώγων με κἀκεῖνος
Father,　 also　 the [one] eating　 me　 even that one

ζήσει δι' ἐμέ. **58** οὗτός ἐστιν ὁ ἄρτος ὁ
will live because of me.　 This　 is　 the bread　 -

ἐξ οὐρανοῦ καταβάς, οὐ καθὼς ἔφαγον
out of heaven having come down, not as　 ate

οἱ πατέρες καὶ ἀπέθανον· ὁ τρώγων
the fathers　 and　 died;　 the [one] eating

τοῦτον τὸν ἄρτον ζήσει εἰς τὸν αἰῶνα.
this　 - bread　 will live unto the　 age.

59 Ταῦτα εἶπεν ἐν συναγωγῇ διδάσκων ἐν
These things he said in　 a synagogue　 teaching　 in

Καφαρναούμ. **60** Πολλοὶ οὖν ἀκούσαντες
Capernaum.　 ³Many　 ¹therefore ²hearing

ἐκ τῶν μαθητῶν αὐτοῦ εἶπαν· σκληρός·
⁵of ⁴the ⁶disciples ⁷of him said :　 Hard

ἐστιν ὁ λόγος οὗτος· τίς δύναται αὐτοῦ
is　 - word　 this;　 who can　 it

ἀκούειν; **61** εἰδὼς δὲ ὁ Ἰησοῦς ἐν ἑαυτῷ
to hear?　 But knowing - Jesus　 in himself

ὅτι γογγύζουσιν περὶ τούτου οἱ μαθηταὶ
that ⁴are murmuring ⁵about ⁶this ¹the ²disciples

αὐτοῦ, εἶπεν αὐτοῖς· τοῦτο ὑμᾶς σκανδαλίζει;
³of him, said　 to them :　 This	 you　 offends?

---

the living bread that came down from heaven. If anyone eats of this bread, he will live forever. This bread is my flesh, which I will give for the life of the world."

⁵²Then the Jews began to argue sharply among themselves, "How can this man give us his flesh to eat?" ⁵³Jesus said to them, "I tell you the truth, unless you eat the flesh of the Son of Man and drink his blood, you have no life in you. ⁵⁴Whoever eats my flesh and drinks my blood has eternal life, and I will raise him up at the last day. ⁵⁵For my flesh is real food and my blood is real drink. ⁵⁶Whoever eats my flesh and drinks my blood remains in me, and I in him. ⁵⁷Just as the living Father sent me and I live because of the Father, so the one who feeds on me will live because of me. ⁵⁸This is the bread that came down from heaven. Your forefathers ate manna and died, but he who feeds on this bread will live forever." ⁵⁹He said this while teaching in the synagogue in Capernaum.

Many Disciples Desert Jesus

60On hearing it, many of his disciples said, "This is a hard teaching. Who can accept it?"

61Aware that his disciples were grumbling about this, Jesus said to them, "Does this offend you? 62What if were to see the Son of Man ascending to where he was before? 63 It is the spirit that gives life; the flesh is useless. The words that I have spoken to you are spirit and life. 64 But among you there are some who do not believe." For Jesus knew from the first who were the ones that did not believe, and who was the one that would betray him. 65 And he said, "For this reason I have told you that no one can come to me unless it is granted by the Father."

66 Because of this many of his disciples turned back and no longer went about with him. 67 So Jesus asked the twelve, "Do you also wish to go away?" 68 Simon Peter answered him, "Lord, to whom can we go? You have the words of eternal life. 69 We have come to believe and know that you are the Holy One of God." [s] 70 Jesus answered them, "Did I not choose you, the twelve? Yet one of you is a devil." 71 He was speaking of Judas son of Simon Iscariot, [t] for he, though one of the twelve, was going to betray him.

---

62 ἐὰν οὖν θεωρῆτε τὸν υἱὸν τοῦ ἀνθρώπου
If then ye behold the Son — of man

ἀναβαίνοντα ὅπου ἦν τὸ πρότερον; **63** τὸ
ascending where he was at first? † The

πνεῦμά ἐστιν τὸ ζωοποιοῦν, ἡ σὰρξ οὐκ
spirit is the [thing] quickening, the flesh not

ὠφελεῖ οὐδέν· τὰ ῥήματα ἃ ἐγὼ λελάληκα
profits no(any)thing; the words which I have spoken

ὑμῖν πνεῦμά ἐστιν καὶ ζωή ἐστιν. **64** ἀλλ'
to you spirit is(are) and life is(are). But

εἰσὶν ἐξ ὑμῶν τινες οἳ οὐ πιστεύουσιν. ᾔδει
there are of you some who do not believe. knew

γὰρ ἐξ ἀρχῆς ὁ Ἰησοῦς τίνες εἰσὶν
For from [the] beginning — Jesus who are(were)

οἱ μὴ πιστεύοντες καὶ τίς ἐστιν ὁ
the [ones] not believing and who is(was) the

παραδώσων αὐτόν. **65** καὶ ἔλεγεν·
[one] betraying him. And he said :

διὰ τοῦτο εἴρηκα ὑμῖν ὅτι οὐδεὶς δύναται
Therefore I have told you that no one can

ἐλθεῖν πρός με ἐὰν μὴ ᾖ δεδομένον
to come to me unless it is *having been* given

αὐτῷ ἐκ τοῦ πατρός.
to him of the Father.

66 Ἐκ τούτου πολλοὶ τῶν μαθητῶν
From this many of the disciples

αὐτοῦ ἀπῆλθον εἰς τὰ ὀπίσω καὶ οὐκέτι
of him went away back† and no longer

μετ' αὐτοῦ περιεπάτουν. **67** εἶπεν οὖν ὁ
with him walked. Said therefore —

Ἰησοῦς τοῖς δώδεκα· μὴ καὶ ὑμεῖς
Jesus to the twelve : Not also ye

θέλετε ὑπάγειν; **68** ἀπεκρίθη αὐτῷ Σίμων
wish to go? Answered him Simon

Πέτρος· κύριε, πρὸς τίνα ἀπελευσόμεθα;
Peter : Lord, to whom shall we go away?

ῥήματα ζωῆς αἰωνίου ἔχεις· **69** καὶ ἡμεῖς
words of life eternal thou hast; and we

πεπιστεύκαμεν καὶ ἐγνώκαμεν ὅτι σὺ εἶ
have believed and have known that thou art

ὁ ἅγιος τοῦ θεοῦ. **70** ἀπεκρίθη αὐτοῖς ὁ
the holy one — of God. Answered them —

Ἰησοῦς· οὐκ ἐγὼ ὑμᾶς τοὺς δώδεκα
Jesus : [3]Not [2]I [4]you [5]the [6]twelve

ἐξελεξάμην; καὶ ἐξ ὑμῶν εἷς διάβολός
[1]chose? and of you one a devil

ἐστιν. **71** ἔλεγεν δὲ τὸν Ἰούδαν Σίμωνος
is. Now he spoke [of] — Judas [son] of Simon

Ἰσκαριώτου· οὗτος γὰρ ἔμελλεν παραδιδόναι
Iscariot; for this one was about to betray

αὐτόν, εἷς ἐκ τῶν δώδεκα.
him, one of the twelve.

---

you see the Son of Man ascend to where he was before! 63 The Spirit gives life; the flesh counts for nothing. The words I have spoken to you who do not are spirit [k] and they are life. 64 Yet there are some of you who do not believe." For Jesus had known from the beginning which of them did not believe and who would betray him. 65 He went on to say, "This is why I told you that no one can come to me unless the Father has enabled him."

66 From this time many of his disciples turned back and no longer followed him.

67 "You do not want to leave too, do you?" Jesus asked the Twelve.

68 Simon Peter answered him, "Lord, to whom shall we go? You have the words of eternal life. 69 We believe and know that you are the Holy One of God."

70 Then Jesus replied, "Have I not chosen you, the Twelve? Yet one of you is a devil!" 71 (He meant Judas, the son of Simon Iscariot, who, though one of the Twelve, was later to betray him.)

Chapter 7

The Unbelief of Jesus' Brothers

AFTER this Jesus went about in Galilee. He did not wish [u] to go about in Judea because the Jews were looking for an opportunity to kill him. 2 Now the Jewish festival of Booths [v] was near. 3 So his brothers said to him, "Leave here

[s] Other ancient authorities read *the Christ, the Son of the living God*

[t] Other ancient authorities read *Judas Iscariot son of Simon;* others, *Judas son of Simon from Karyot* (Kerioth)

[u] Other ancient authorities read *was not at liberty*

[v] Or *Tabernacles*

---

7 Καὶ μετὰ ταῦτα περιεπάτει ὁ Ἰησοῦς
And after these things walked — Jesus

ἐν τῇ Γαλιλαίᾳ· οὐ γὰρ ἤθελεν ἐν τῇ
in — Galilee; for he did not wish in —

Ἰουδαίᾳ περιπατεῖν, ὅτι ἐζήτουν αὐτὸν οἱ
Judæa to walk, because [3]were seeking [4]him [1]the

Ἰουδαῖοι ἀποκτεῖναι. **2** ἦν δὲ ἐγγὺς ἡ
[2]Jews [5]to kill. Now was near the

ἑορτὴ τῶν Ἰουδαίων ἡ σκηνοπηγία. **3** εἶπον
feast of the Jews the Tabernacles. Said

οὖν πρὸς αὐτὸν οἱ ἀδελφοὶ αὐτοῦ·
therefore to him the brothers of him :

Chapter 7

Jesus Goes to the Feast of Tabernacles

AFTER this, Jesus went around in Galilee, purposely staying away from Judea because the Jews there were waiting to take his life. 2 But when the Jewish Feast of Tabernacles was near, 3 Jesus' brothers said to him, "You

[k] 63 Or *Spirit*

and go to Judea so that your disciples also may see the works you are doing; 4for no one who wants[w] to be widely known acts in secret. If you do these things, show yourself to the world." 5(For not even his brothers believed in him.) 6Jesus said to them, "My time has not yet come, but your time is always here. 7The world cannot hate you, but it hates me because I testify against it that its works are evil. 8Go to the festival yourselves. I am not[x] going to this festival, for my time has not yet fully come." 9After saying this, he remained in Galilee.

Jesus at the Festival of Booths

10 But after his brothers had gone to the festival, then he also went, not publicly but as it were[y] in secret. 11The Jews were looking for him at the festival and saying, "Where is he?" 12And there was considerable complaining about him among the crowds. While some were saying, "He is a good man," others were saying, "No, he is deceiving the crowd." 13Yet no one would speak openly about him for fear of the Jews.

14 About the middle of the festival Jesus went up into the temple and began to teach. 15The Jews were astonished at it, saying, "How does this man have such learning,[z] when he has never been taught?" 16Then Jesus answered them, "My teaching is not

μετάβηθι ἐντεῦθεν καὶ ὕπαγε εἰς τὴν Ἰουδαίαν,
Depart hence and go into - Judaea,

ἵνα καὶ οἱ μαθηταί σου θεωρήσουσιν τὰ
that also the disciples of thee will behold the

ἔργα σου ἃ ποιεῖς· 4 οὐδεὶς γάρ τι ἐν
works of thee which thou doest; for no one anything in

κρυπτῷ ποιεῖ καὶ ζητεῖ αὐτὸς ἐν παρρησίᾳ
secret does and seeks [him]self in [the] open

εἶναι. εἰ ταῦτα ποιεῖς, φανέρωσον σεαυτὸν
to be. If these things thou doest, manifest thyself

τῷ κόσμῳ. 5 οὐδὲ γὰρ οἱ ἀδελφοὶ
to the world. For not the brothers

αὐτοῦ ἐπίστευον εἰς αὐτόν. 6 λέγει οὖν
of him believed in him. Says therefore

αὐτοῖς ὁ Ἰησοῦς· ὁ καιρὸς ὁ ἐμὸς
to them - Jesus: The ²time - ¹my

οὔπω πάρεστιν, ὁ δὲ καιρὸς ὁ ὑμέτερος
not yet is arrived, but the ²time - ¹your

πάντοτέ ἐστιν ἕτοιμος. 7 οὐ δύναται ὁ
always is ready. Cannot the

κόσμος μισεῖν ὑμᾶς, ἐμὲ δὲ μισεῖ, ὅτι
world to hate you, but me it hates, because

ἐγὼ μαρτυρῶ περὶ αὐτοῦ ὅτι τὰ ἔργα
I witness about it that the works

αὐτοῦ πονηρά ἐστιν. 8 ὑμεῖς ἀνάβητε εἰς
of it evil is(are). ¹Ye ²go ³up to

τὴν ἑορτήν· ἐγὼ οὐκ ἀναβαίνω εἰς τὴν
the feast; I am not going up to -

ἑορτὴν ταύτην, ὅτι ὁ ἐμὸς καιρὸς οὔπω
feast this, because the my time not yet

πεπλήρωται. 9 ταῦτα δὲ εἰπὼν αὐτοῖς
has been fulfilled. And these things saying to them

ἔμεινεν ἐν τῇ Γαλιλαίᾳ. 10 Ὡς δὲ
he remained in - Galilee. But when

ἀνέβησαν οἱ ἀδελφοὶ αὐτοῦ εἰς τὴν ἑορτήν,
went up the brothers of him to the feast,

τότε καὶ αὐτὸς ἀνέβη, οὐ φανερῶς ἀλλὰ
then also he went up, not manifestly but

ὡς ἐν κρυπτῷ. 11 οἱ οὖν Ἰουδαῖοι
as in secret. Therefore the Jews

ἐζήτουν αὐτὸν ἐν τῇ ἑορτῇ καὶ ἔλεγον·
sought him at the feast and said:

ποῦ ἐστιν ἐκεῖνος; 12 καὶ γογγυσμὸς περὶ
Where is that man? And ²murmuring ⁴about

αὐτοῦ ἦν πολὺς ἐν τοῖς ὄχλοις· οἱ μὲν
⁵him ¹there was ³much in the crowds; some

ἔλεγον ὅτι ἀγαθός ἐστιν· ἄλλοι [δὲ]
said[,] - A good man he is; but others

ἔλεγον· οὔ, ἀλλὰ πλανᾷ τὸν ὄχλον.
said: No, but he deceives the crowd.

13 οὐδεὶς μέντοι παρρησίᾳ ἐλάλει περὶ
No one however openly spoke about

αὐτοῦ διὰ τὸν φόβον τῶν Ἰουδαίων.
him because of the fear of the Jews.

14 Ἤδη δὲ τῆς ἑορτῆς μεσούσης ἀνέβη
But now the feast being in [its] middle went up
= in the middle of the feast

Ἰησοῦς εἰς τὸ ἱερὸν καὶ ἐδίδασκεν.
Jesus to the temple and taught.

15 ἐθαύμαζον οὖν οἱ Ἰουδαῖοι λέγοντες·
Marvelled therefore the Jews saying:

πῶς οὗτος γράμματα οἶδεν μὴ μεμαθηκώς;
How this man letters knows not having learned?

16 ἀπεκρίθη οὖν αὐτοῖς Ἰησοῦς καὶ εἶπεν·
Answered therefore them Jesus and said:

ought to leave here and go to Judea, so that your disciples may see the miracles you do. 4No one who wants to become a public figure acts in secret. Since you are doing these things, show yourself to the world." 5For even his own brothers did not believe in him.

6Therefore Jesus told them, "The right time for me has not yet come; for you any time is right. 7The world cannot hate you, but it hates me because I testify that what it does is evil. 8You go to the Feast. I am not[l] going up to this Feast, because for me the right time has not yet come." 9Having said this, he stayed in Galilee.

10However, after his brothers had left for the Feast, he went also, not publicly, but in secret. 11Now at the Feast the Jews were watching for him and asking, "Where is that man?"

12Among the crowds there was widespread whispering about him. Some said, "He is a good man." Others replied, "No, he deceives the people." 13But no one would say anything publicly about him for fear of the Jews.

Jesus Teaches at the Feast

14Not until halfway through the Feast did Jesus go up to the temple courts and begin to teach. 15The Jews were amazed and asked, "How did this man get such learning without having studied?"

16Jesus answered, "My

w Other ancient authorities read wants it
x Other ancient authorities add yet
y Other ancient authorities lack as it were
z Or this man know his letters

l Some early manuscripts do not have yet.

mine but his who sent me. 17 Anyone who resolves to do the will of God will know whether the teaching is from God or whether I am speaking on my own. 18 Those who speak on their own seek their own glory; but the one who seeks the glory of him who sent him is true, and there is nothing false in him.

19 "Did not Moses give you the law? Yet none of you keeps the law. Why are you looking for an opportunity to kill me?" 20 The crowd answered, "You have a demon! Who is trying to kill you?" 21 Jesus answered them, "I performed one work, and all of you are astonished. 22 Moses gave you circumcision (it is, of course, not from Moses, but from the patriarchs), and you circumcise a man on the sabbath. 23 If a man receives circumcision on the sabbath in order that the law of Moses may not be broken, are you angry with me because I healed a man's whole body on the sabbath? 24 Do not judge by appearances, but judge with right judgment."

Is This the Christ?

25 Now some of the people of Jerusalem were saying, "Is not this the man whom they are trying to kill? 26 And here he is, speaking openly, but they say nothing to him! Can it be that the authorities really know that this is the Messiah?*a* 27 Yet we know where this man is from; but when the Messiah*a* comes, no one will know where he is from." 28 Then Jesus cried out as he was teaching in the temple, "You

---

ἡ ἐμὴ διδαχὴ οὐκ ἔστιν ἐμὴ ἀλλὰ τοῦ
The my teaching is not mine but of the

πέμψαντός με· 17 ἐάν τις θέλῃ τὸ θέλημα
[one] having sent me; if anyone wishes the will

αὐτοῦ ποιεῖν, γνώσεται περὶ τῆς διδαχῆς,
of him to do, he will know concerning the teaching,

πότερον ἐκ τοῦ θεοῦ ἐστιν ἢ ἐγὼ ἀπ'
whether of – God it is or I from

ἐμαυτοῦ λαλῶ. 18 ὁ ἀφ' ἑαυτοῦ λαλῶν
myself speak. The [one] from himself speaking

τὴν δόξαν τὴν ἰδίαν ζητεῖ· ὁ δὲ ζητῶν
his own glory seeks; but the [one] seeking

τὴν δόξαν τοῦ πέμψαντος αὐτόν, οὗτος
the glory of the [one] having sent him, this man

ἀληθής ἐστιν καὶ ἀδικία ἐν αὐτῷ οὐκ
true is and unrighteousness in him not

ἔστιν. 19 οὐ Μωϋσῆς ἔδωκεν ὑμῖν τὸν
is. Not Moses gave you the

νόμον; καὶ οὐδεὶς ἐξ ὑμῶν ποιεῖ τὸν
law? and no one of you does the

νόμον. τί με ζητεῖτε ἀποκτεῖναι;
law. Why me seek ye to kill?

20 ἀπεκρίθη ὁ ὄχλος· δαιμόνιον ἔχεις·
Answered the crowd : A demon thou hast;

τίς σε ζητεῖ ἀποκτεῖναι; 21 ἀπεκρίθη
who thee seeks to kill? Answered

'Ιησοῦς καὶ εἶπεν αὐτοῖς· ἓν ἔργον ἐποίησα
Jesus and said to them : One work I did

καὶ πάντες θαυμάζετε. 22 διὰ τοῦτο
and all ye marvel. Because of this

Μωϋσῆς δέδωκεν ὑμῖν τὴν περιτομήν, —
Moses has given you circumcision, —

οὐχ ὅτι ἐκ τοῦ Μωϋσέως ἐστιν ἀλλ' ἐκ
not that of – Moses it is but of

τῶν πατέρων, — καὶ ἐν σαββάτῳ
the fathers, — and on a sabbath

περιτέμνετε ἄνθρωπον 23 εἰ περιτομὴν
ye circumcise a man. If ⁸circumcision

λαμβάνει [ὁ] ἄνθρωπος ἐν σαββάτῳ ἵνα
⁸receives – ¹a man on a sabbath that

μὴ λυθῇ ὁ νόμος Μωϋσέως, ἐμοὶ χολᾶτε,
is not broken the law of Moses, with me are ye angry

ὅτι ὅλον ἄνθρωπον ὑγιῆ ἐποίησα ἐν
because a whole man healthy I made on

σαββάτῳ; 24 μὴ κρίνετε κατ' ὄψιν, ἀλλὰ
a sabbath? Judge not according to face, but

τὴν δικαίαν κρίσιν κρίνατε. 25 Ἔλεγον
– righteous judgment judge. Said

οὖν τινες ἐκ τῶν Ἱεροσολυμιτῶν· οὐχ
therefore some of the Jerusalemites : ¹Not

οὗτός ἐστιν ὃν ζητοῦσιν ἀποκτεῖναι; 26 καὶ
³this man ¹is it whom they are seeking to kill? and

ἴδε παρρησίᾳ λαλεῖ, καὶ οὐδὲν αὐτῷ
behold openly he speaks, and nothing to him

λέγουσιν. μήποτε ἀληθῶς ἔγνωσαν οἱ
they say. Perhaps indeed knew the

ἄρχοντες ὅτι οὗτός ἐστιν ὁ χριστός; *
rulers that this is the Christ? *

27 ἀλλὰ τοῦτον οἴδαμεν πόθεν ἐστίν· ὁ δὲ
But this man we know whence he is; but ²the

χριστὸς ὅταν ἔρχηται, οὐδεὶς γινώσκει
³Christ ¹when comes, no one knows

πόθεν ἐστίν. 28 ἔκραξεν οὖν ἐν τῷ ἱερῷ
whence he is. ³Cried out ²therefore ⁴in ⁵the ⁶temple

---

teaching is not my own. It comes from him who sent me. 17 If anyone chooses to do God's will, he will find out whether my teaching comes from God or whether I speak on my own. 18 He who speaks on his own does so to gain honor for himself, but he who works for the honor of the one who sent him is a man of truth; there is nothing false about him. 19 Has not Moses given you the law? Yet not one of you keeps the law. Why are you trying to kill me?"

20 "You are demon-possessed," the crowd answered. "Who is trying to kill you?"

21 Jesus said to them, "I did one miracle, and you are all astonished. 22 Yet, because Moses gave you circumcision (though actually it did not come from Moses, but from the patriarchs), you circumcise a child on the Sabbath. 23 Now if a child can be circumcised on the Sabbath so that the law of Moses may not be broken, why are you angry with me for healing the whole man on the Sabbath? 24 Stop judging by mere appearances, and make a right judgment."

Is Jesus the Christ?

25 At that point some of the people of Jerusalem began to ask, "Isn't this the man they are trying to kill? 26 Here he is, speaking publicly, and they are not saying a word to him. Have the authorities really concluded that he is the Christ*m*? 27 But we know where this man is from; when the Christ comes, no one will know where he is from."

28 Then Jesus, still teaching in the temple courts,

---

a Or the Christ

* As this question is introduced by μήποτε, a negative answer is expected; see page xiii, and note ver. 31 below.

*m*26 Or *Messiah*; also in verses 27, 31, 41 and 42

know me, and you know where I am from. I have not come on my own. But the one who sent me is true, and you do not know him. ²⁹ I know him, because I am from him, and he sent me." ³⁰ Then they tried to arrest him, but no one laid hands on him, because his hour had not yet come. ³¹ Yet many in the crowd believed in him and were saying, "When the Messiah[a] comes, will he do more signs than this man has done?"[b]

Officers Are Sent to Arrest Jesus

32 The Pharisees heard the crowd muttering such things about him, and the chief priests and Pharisees sent temple police to arrest him. ³³ Jesus then said, "I will be with you a little while longer, and then I am going to him who sent me. ³⁴ You will search for me, but you will not find me; and where I am, you cannot come." ³⁵ The Jews said to one another, "Where does this man intend to go that we will not find him? Does he intend to go to the Dispersion among the Greeks and teach the Greeks? ³⁶ What does he mean by saying, 'You will search for me and you will not find me' and 'Where I am, you cannot come'?"

Rivers of Living Water

37 On the last day of the festival, the great day, while Jesus was standing there, he cried out, "Let anyone who is thirsty come to me, ³⁸ and let the one who believes in me drink. As[c] the scripture has said, 'Out of the believer's

---

διδάσκων ὁ Ἰησοῦς καὶ λέγων· κἀμὲ
⁷teaching – ¹Jesus ⁸and ⁹saying : Both me

οἴδατε καὶ οἴδατε πόθεν εἰμί· καὶ ἀπ'
ye know and ye know whence I am; and from

ἐμαυτοῦ οὐκ ἐλήλυθα, ἀλλ' ἔστιν ἀληθινὸς
myself I have not come, but he is true

ὁ πέμψας με, ὃν ὑμεῖς οὐκ οἴδατε·
the [one] having sent me, whom ye know not;

29 ἐγὼ οἶδα αὐτόν, ὅτι παρ' αὐτοῦ εἰμι
I know him, because ¹from ⁹him ¹I am

κἀκεῖνός με ἀπέστειλεν. 30 Ἐζήτουν οὖν
⁴and that one ⁵me ⁶sent. They sought therefore

αὐτὸν πιάσαι, καὶ οὐδεὶς ἐπέβαλεν ἐπ'
him to arrest, and no one laid on on

αὐτὸν τὴν χεῖρα, ὅτι οὔπω ἐληλύθει ἡ
him the hand, because not yet had come the

ὥρα αὐτοῦ. 31 Ἐκ τοῦ ὄχλου δὲ πολλοὶ
hour of him. ³of ⁴the ⁵crowd ¹But ²many

ἐπίστευσαν εἰς αὐτόν, καὶ ἔλεγον· ὁ
believed in him, and said : ²The

χριστὸς ὅταν ἔλθῃ, μὴ πλείονα σημεῖα
³Christ ¹when ⁴comes, *not* more signs

ποιήσει ὧν οὗτος ἐποίησεν; 32 ἤκουσαν
will he do [than] which this man did? ²Heard

οἱ Φαρισαῖοι τοῦ ὄχλου γογγύζοντος περὶ
¹the ²Pharisees ⁴the ⁵crowd ³murmuring ⁶about

αὐτοῦ ταῦτα, καὶ ἀπέστειλαν οἱ ἀρχιερεῖς
⁷him ⁷these things, and ⁸sent ¹the ²chief priests

καὶ οἱ Φαρισαῖοι ὑπηρέτας ἵνα πιάσωσιν
³and ⁴the ⁵Pharisees ⁷attendants that they might arrest

αὐτόν. 33 εἶπεν οὖν ὁ Ἰησοῦς· ἔτι
him. Said therefore – Jesus : Yet

χρόνον μικρὸν μεθ' ὑμῶν εἰμι καὶ ὑπάγω
time a little with you I am and I go

πρὸς τὸν πέμψαντά με. 34 ζητήσετέ με
to the [one] having sent me. Ye will seek me

καὶ οὐχ εὑρήσετε, καὶ ὅπου εἰμὶ ἐγὼ
and will not find, and where am I

ὑμεῖς οὐ δύνασθε ἐλθεῖν. 35 εἶπον οὖν
ye cannot *to* come. Said therefore

οἱ Ἰουδαῖοι πρὸς ἑαυτούς· ποῦ οὗτος
the Jews to themselves : Where this man

μέλλει πορεύεσθαι, ὅτι ἡμεῖς οὐχ εὑρήσομεν
is about to go, that we will not find

αὐτόν; μὴ εἰς τὴν διασπορὰν τῶν Ἑλλήνων
him? *not* to the dispersion of the Greeks

μέλλει πορεύεσθαι καὶ διδάσκειν τοὺς
is he about to go and to teach the

Ἕλληνας; 36 τίς ἐστιν ὁ λόγος οὗτος
Greeks? What is – word this

ὃν εἶπεν· ζητήσετέ με καὶ οὐχ εὑρήσετε,
which he said : Ye will seek me and will not find,

καὶ ὅπου εἰμὶ ἐγὼ ὑμεῖς οὐ δύνασθε
and where am I ye cannot

ἐλθεῖν;
to come?

37 Ἐν δὲ τῇ ἐσχάτῃ ἡμέρᾳ τῇ μεγάλῃ
Now in the last day the great [day]

τῆς ἑορτῆς εἱστήκει ὁ Ἰησοῦς καὶ ἔκραξεν
of the feast stood – Jesus and cried out

λέγων· ἐάν τις διψᾷ, ἐρχέσθω πρός με
saying : If anyone thirsts, let him come to me

καὶ πινέτω. 38 ὁ πιστεύων εἰς ἐμέ,
and drink. The [one] believing in me,

καθὼς εἶπεν ἡ γραφή, ποταμοὶ ἐκ τῆς
as said the scripture, ¹rivers ⁵out of ⁶the

---

cried out, "Yes, you know me, and you know where I am from. I am not here on my own, but he who sent me is true. You do not know him, ²⁹ but I know him because I am from him and he sent me."

³⁰ At this they tried to seize him, but no one laid a hand on him, because his time had not yet come. ³¹ Still, many in the crowd put their faith in him. They said, "When the Christ comes, will he do more miraculous signs than this man?"

³² The Pharisees heard the crowd whispering such things about him. Then the chief priests and the Pharisees sent temple guards to arrest him.

³³ Jesus said, "I am with you for only a short time, and then I go to the one who sent me. ³⁴ You will look for me, but you will not find me; and where I am, you cannot come."

³⁵ The Jews said to one another, "Where does this man intend to go that we cannot find him? Will he go where our people live scattered among the Greeks, and teach the Greeks? ³⁶ What did he mean when he said, 'You will look for me, but you will not find me,' and 'Where I am, you cannot come'?"

³⁷ On the last and greatest day of the Feast, Jesus stood and said in a loud voice, "If anyone is thirsty, let him come to me and drink. ³⁸ Whoever believes in me, as[n] the Scripture has said, streams of

---

[b] Other ancient authorities read *is doing*

[c] Or *come to me and drink.* ³⁸*The one who believes in me, as*

[n]37,38 Or / *If anyone is thirsty, let him come to me.* / *And let him drink,* ³⁸*who believes in me.* / *As*

heart[d] shall flow rivers of living water.'" [39]Now he said this about the Spirit, which believers in him were to receive; for as yet there was no Spirit,[e] because Jesus was not yet glorified.

Division among the People

[40] When they heard these words, some in the crowd said, "This is really the prophet." [41]Others said, "This is the Messiah."[f] But some asked, "Surely the Messiah[f] does not come from Galilee, does he? [42]Has not the scripture said that the Messiah[f] is descended from David and comes from Bethlehem, the village where David lived?" [43]So there was a division in the crowd because of him. [44]Some of them wanted to arrest him, but no one laid hands on him.

The Unbelief of Those in Authority

[45] Then the temple police went back to the chief priests and Pharisees, who asked them, "Why did you not arrest him?" [46]The police answered, "Never has anyone spoken like this!" [47]Then the Pharisees replied, "Surely you have not been deceived too, have you? [48]Has any one of the authorities or of the Pharisees believed in him? [49]But this crowd, which does not know the law—they are accursed." [50]Nicodemus, who had gone to Jesus[g] before, and who was one of them, asked, [51]"Our law does not judge people without first giving them a hearing to find out what they are doing, does it?" [52]They replied, "Surely you are not also from Galilee, are you? Search and you will see that no prophet is to arise from Galilee."

κοιλίας αὐτοῦ ῥεύσουσιν ὕδατος ζῶντος.
[7]belly [6]of him [1]will flow [3]water [2]of living.

39 τοῦτο δὲ εἶπεν περὶ τοῦ πνεύματος
But this he said concerning the Spirit

οὗ ἔμελλον λαμβάνειν οἱ πιστεύσαντες
whom were about to receive the [ones] believing

εἰς αὐτόν· οὔπω γὰρ ἦν πνεῦμα, ὅτι
in him; not yet for was [?the] Spirit, because

Ἰησοῦς οὐδέπω ἐδοξάσθη. 40 Ἐκ τοῦ
Jesus not yet was glorified. [Some] of the

ὄχλου οὖν ἀκούσαντες τῶν λόγων τούτων
crowd therefore hearing - words these

ἔλεγον [ὅτι]· οὗτός ἐστιν ἀληθῶς ὁ
said - : This man is truly the

προφήτης· 41 ἄλλοι ἔλεγον· οὗτός ἐστιν ὁ
prophet; Others said : This man is the

χριστός· οἱ δὲ ἔλεγον· μὴ γὰρ ἐκ τῆς
Christ; But others† said : Not then out of -

Γαλιλαίας ὁ χριστὸς ἔρχεται; 42 οὐχ ἡ
Galilee the Christ comes? not the

γραφὴ εἶπεν ὅτι ἐκ τοῦ σπέρματος Δαυίδ,
scripture said that of the seed of David,

καὶ ἀπὸ Βηθλέεμ τῆς κώμης ὅπου ἦν
and from Bethlehem the village where was

Δαυίδ, ἔρχεται ὁ χριστός; 43 σχίσμα
David, comes the Christ? A division

οὖν ἐγένετο ἐν τῷ ὄχλῳ δι' αὐτόν·
therefore became in the crowd because of him;

44 τινὲς δὲ ἤθελον ἐξ αὐτῶν πιάσαι αὐτόν,
and [1]some [4]wished [2]of [3]them to arrest him,

ἀλλ' οὐδεὶς ἐπέβαλεν ἐπ' αὐτὸν τὰς χεῖρας.
but no one laid on on him the(his) hands.

45 Ἦλθον οὖν οἱ ὑπηρέται πρὸς τοὺς
Came therefore the attendants to the

ἀρχιερεῖς καὶ Φαρισαίους, καὶ εἶπον αὐτοῖς
chief priests and Pharisees, and [2]said [3]to them

ἐκεῖνοι· διὰ τί οὐκ ἠγάγετε αὐτόν;
[1]those: Why did ye not bring him?

46 ἀπεκρίθησαν οἱ ὑπηρέται· οὐδέποτε
Answered the attendants : Never

ἐλάλησεν οὕτως ἄνθρωπος, ὡς οὗτος λαλεῖ
spoke so a man, as [1]this [2]speaks

ὁ ἄνθρωπος. 47 ἀπεκρίθησαν οὖν αὐτοῖς
[2]man. Answered therefore them

οἱ Φαρισαῖοι· μὴ καὶ ὑμεῖς πεπλάνησθε;
the Pharisees : Not also ye have been deceived?

48 μή τις ἐκ τῶν ἀρχόντων ἐπίστευσεν
not anyone of the rulers believed

εἰς αὐτὸν ἢ ἐκ τῶν Φαρισαίων; 49 ἀλλὰ
in him or of the Pharisees? But

ὁ ὄχλος οὗτος ὁ μὴ γινώσκων τὸν
- crowd this - not knowing the

νόμον ἐπάρατοί εἰσιν. 50 λέγει Νικόδημος
law cursed are. Says Nicodemus

πρὸς αὐτούς, ὁ ἐλθὼν πρὸς αὐτὸν πρότερον,
to them, the [one] having come to him firstly,

εἷς ὢν ἐξ αὐτῶν· 51 μὴ ὁ νόμος ἡμῶν
[2]one [1]being of them : Not the law of us

κρίνει τὸν ἄνθρωπον ἐὰν μὴ ἀκούσῃ
judges the man unless it hears

πρῶτον παρ' αὐτοῦ καὶ γνῷ τί ποιεῖ;
first from him and knows what he does?

52 ἀπεκρίθησαν καὶ εἶπαν αὐτῷ· μὴ καὶ
They answered and said to him : Not also

σὺ ἐκ τῆς Γαλιλαίας εἶ; ἐρεύνησον καὶ
thou of - Galilee art? search and

---

living water will flow from within him." [39]By this he meant the Spirit, whom those who believed in him were later to receive. Up to that time the Spirit had not been given, since Jesus had not yet been glorified.

[40]On hearing his words, some of the people said, "Surely this man is the Prophet." [41]Others said, "He is the Christ."

Still others asked, "How can the Christ come from Galilee? [42]Does not the Scripture say that the Christ will come from David's family[o] and from Bethlehem, the town where David lived?" [43]Thus the people were divided because of Jesus. [44]Some wanted to seize him, but no one laid a hand on him.

Unbelief of the Jewish Leaders

[45]Finally the temple guards went back to the chief priests and Pharisees, who asked them, "Why didn't you bring him in?"

[46]"No one ever spoke the way this man does," the guards declared.

[47]"You mean he has deceived you also?" the Pharisees retorted. [48]"Has any of the rulers or of the Pharisees believed in him? [49]No! But this mob that knows nothing of the law—there is a curse on them."

[50]Nicodemus, who had gone to Jesus earlier and who was one of their own number, asked, [51]"Does our law condemn anyone without first hearing him to find out what he is doing?"

[52]They replied, "Are you from Galilee, too? Look

---

[d] Gk out of his belly
[e] Other ancient authorities read for as yet the Spirit (others, Holy Spirit) had not been given
[f] Or the Christ
[g] Gk him

[o]42 Greek seed

The Woman Caught in Adultery

[[53] Then each of them went home, [1] while Jesus went to the Mount of Olives. [2] Early in the morning he came again to the temple. All the people came to him and he sat down and began to teach them. [3] The scribes and the Pharisees brought a woman who had been caught in adultery; and making her stand before all of them, [4] they said to him, "Teacher, this woman was caught in the very act of committing adultery. [5] Now in the law Moses commanded us to stone such women. Now what do you say?" [6] They said this to test him, so that they might have some charge to bring against him. Jesus bent down and wrote with his finger on the ground. [7] When they kept on questioning him, he straightened up and said to them, "Let anyone among you who is without sin be the first to throw a stone at her." [8] And once again he bent down and wrote on the ground. [h] [9] When they heard it, they went away, one by one, beginning with the elders; and Jesus was left alone with the woman standing before him. [10] Jesus straightened up and said to her, "Woman, where are they? Has no one condemned you?" [11] She said, "No one, sir." [i] And Jesus said, "Neither do I condemn you. Go your way, and from now on do not sin again."]][j]

Jesus the Light of the World

[12] Again Jesus spoke to them, saying, "I am the light of the world. Whoever follows me will never walk

[h] Other ancient authorities add *the sins of each of them*
[i] Or *Lord*
[j] The most ancient authorities lack 7.53—8.11; other authorities add the passage here or after 7.36 or after 21.25 or after Luke 21.38, with variations of text; some mark the passage as doubtful.

ἴδε   ὅτι   ἐκ   τῆς   Γαλιλαίας   προφήτης   οὐκ
see   that out of -   Galilee   a prophet   not
ἐγείρεται.
is raised.

53 Καὶ ἐπορεύθησαν ἕκαστος εἰς τὸν οἶκον
   And   they went   each one to   the house
αὐτοῦ,   **8** Ἰησοῦς δὲ   ἐπορεύθη εἰς   τὸ
of him,   but Jesus   went   to   the
Ὄρος τῶν Ἐλαιῶν. **2** Ὄρθρου δὲ πάλιν
Mount of the Olives.   And at dawn   again
παρεγένετο   εἰς   τὸ   ἱερόν [, καὶ   πᾶς   ὁ
he arrived   in   the temple,   and   all   the
λαὸς   ἤρχετο   πρὸς αὐτόν, καὶ   καθίσας
people came   to   him,   and   sitting
ἐδίδασκεν αὐτούς]. **3** Ἄγουσιν δὲ οἱ
he taught   them.   And lead   the
γραμματεῖς καὶ οἱ Φαρισαῖοι γυναῖκα ἐπὶ
scribes   and the Pharisees   a woman   in
μοιχείᾳ κατειλημμένην, καὶ στήσαντες αὐτὴν
adultery *having been* caught, and standing   her
ἐν μέσῳ **4** λέγουσιν αὐτῷ Διδάσκαλε,
in [the] midst   they say   to him[,]   Teacher,
αὕτη ἡ γυνὴ κατείληπται ἐπ' αὐτοφώρῳ
this   - woman has been caught in   the act
μοιχευομένη· **5** ἐν δὲ τῷ νόμῳ [ἡμῖν]
committing adultery;   now in   the   law   to us[e]
Μωϋσῆς ἐνετείλατο τὰς τοιαύτας λιθάζειν·
Moses   enjoined   -   [a]such   [1]to stone;
σὺ   οὖν   τί λέγεις; **6** [τοῦτο δὲ ἔλεγον
thou therefore what sayest thou?   But this   they said
πειράζοντες αὐτόν, ἵνα ἔχωσιν κατηγορεῖν
tempting   him,   that they might have to accuse
αὐτοῦ.] ὁ δὲ Ἰησοῦς κάτω κύψας τῷ
him.   - But Jesus   down   stooping with the
δακτύλῳ κατέγραφεν εἰς τὴν γῆν. **7** ὡς δὲ
finger   wrote   in   the earth.   But as
ἐπέμενον ἐρωτῶντες [αὐτόν], ἀνέκυψεν καὶ
they remained questioning   him,   he stood erect   and
εἶπεν [αὐτοῖς] Ὁ ἀναμάρτητος ὑμῶν
said   to them[,]   The [one] sinless   of you
πρῶτος ἐπ' αὐτὴν βαλέτω λίθον. **8** καὶ
first   on   her   let him cast a stone.   And
πάλιν κατακύψας ἔγραφεν εἰς τὴν γῆν.
again   stooping down   he wrote   in   the earth.
9 οἱ δὲ ἀκούσαντες ἐξήρχοντο εἷς καθ'
   And they   hearing   went out   one by
εἷς ἀρξάμενοι ἀπὸ τῶν πρεσβυτέρων, καὶ
one beginning   from the   older ones,   and
κατελείφθη μόνος, καὶ ἡ γυνὴ ἐν μέσῳ
he was left   alone,   and the woman in [the] midst
οὖσα. **10** ἀνακύψας δὲ ὁ Ἰησοῦς εἶπεν
being.   And standing erect   -   Jesus   said
αὐτῇ Γύναι, ποῦ εἰσίν; οὐδείς σε κατέκρινεν;
to her[,] Woman, where are they? no one thee condemned?
11 ἡ δὲ εἶπεν Οὐδείς, κύριε. εἶπεν δὲ
   And she   said[,]   No one,   sir.   So said
ὁ Ἰησοῦς Οὐδὲ ἐγώ σε κατακρίνω·
-   Jesus[,]   Neither   I   thee condemn;
πορεύου, ἀπὸ τοῦ νῦν μηκέτι ἁμάρτανε.
go,   from the   now no longer   sin.
12 Πάλιν οὖν αὐτοῖς ἐλάλησεν ὁ Ἰησοῦς
   Again therefore to them   spoke   - Jesus
λέγων· ἐγώ εἰμι τὸ φῶς τοῦ κόσμου·
saying :   I   am   the light of the world;
ὁ ἀκολουθῶν μοι οὐ μὴ περιπατήσῃ ἐν
the [one] following   me   by no means   will walk   in

---

into it, and you will find that a prophet[p] does not come out of Galilee."

[The earliest and most reliable manuscripts and other ancient witnesses do not have John 7:53–8:11.]

[53] Then each went to his own home.

Chapter 8

BUT Jesus went to the Mount of Olives. [2] At dawn he appeared again in the temple courts, where all the people gathered around him, and he sat down to teach them. [3] The teachers of the law and the Pharisees brought in a woman caught in adultery. They made her stand before the group [4] and said to Jesus, "Teacher, this woman was caught in the act of adultery. [5] In the Law Moses commanded us to stone such women. Now what do you say?" [6] They were using this question as a trap, in order to have a basis for accusing him.

But Jesus bent down and started to write on the ground with his finger. [7] When they kept on questioning him, he straightened up and said to them, "If any one of you is without sin, let him be the first to throw a stone at her." [8] Again he stooped down and wrote on the ground. [9] At this, those who heard began to go away one at a time, the older ones first, until only Jesus was left, with the woman still standing there. [10] Jesus straightened up and asked her, "Woman, where are they? Has no one condemned you?"

[11] "No one, sir," she said.

"Then neither do I condemn you," Jesus declared. "Go now and leave your life of sin."

The Validity of Jesus' Testimony

[12] When Jesus spoke again to the people, he said, "I am the light of the world. Whoever follows me will never walk in darkness, but

[p] 52 Two early manuscripts *the Prophet*

in darkness but will have the light of life." 13 Then the Pharisees said to him, "You are testifying on your own behalf; your testimony is not valid." 14 Jesus answered, "Even if I testify on my own behalf, my testimony is valid because I know where I have come from and where I am going, but you do not know where I come from or where I am going. 15 You judge by human standards;*k* I judge no one. 16 Yet even if I do judge, my judgment is valid; for it is not I alone who judge, but I and the Father*l* who sent me. 17 In your law it is written that the testimony of two witnesses is valid. 18 I testify on my own behalf, and the Father who sent me testifies on my behalf." 19 Then they said to him, "Where is your Father?" Jesus answered, "You know neither me nor my Father. If you knew me, you would know my Father also." 20 He spoke these words while he was teaching in the treasury of the temple, but no one arrested him, because his hour had not yet come.

Jesus Foretells His Death

21 Again he said to them, "I am going away, and you will search for me, but you will die in your sin. Where I am going, you cannot come." 22 Then the Jews said, "Is he going to kill himself? Is that what he means by saying, 'Where I am going, you cannot come'?" 23 He said to them, "You are from below, I am from above; you are of this

τῇ σκοτίᾳ, ἀλλ' ἕξει τὸ φῶς τῆς ζωῆς.
the darkness, but will have the light - of life.

13 εἶπον οὖν αὐτῷ οἱ Φαρισαῖοι· σὺ περὶ
Said therefore to him the Pharisees; Thou concerning

σεαυτοῦ μαρτυρεῖς· ἡ μαρτυρία σου οὐκ
thyself witnessest; the witness of thee not

ἔστιν ἀληθής. 14 ἀπεκρίθη Ἰησοῦς καὶ
is true. Answered Jesus and

εἶπεν αὐτοῖς· κἂν ἐγὼ μαρτυρῶ περὶ
said to them: Even if I witness concerning

ἐμαυτοῦ, ἀληθής ἐστιν ἡ μαρτυρία μου,
myself, true is the witness of me,

ὅτι οἶδα πόθεν ἦλθον καὶ ποῦ ὑπάγω·
because I know whence I came and where I go;

ὑμεῖς δὲ οὐκ οἴδατε πόθεν ἔρχομαι ἢ
but ye know not whence I come or

ποῦ ὑπάγω. 15 ὑμεῖς κατὰ τὴν σάρκα
where I go. Ye according to the flesh

κρίνετε, ἐγὼ οὐ κρίνω οὐδένα. 16 καὶ
judge, I judge not no(any)one. ²even

ἐὰν κρίνω δὲ ἐγώ, ἡ κρίσις ἡ ἐμὴ
²if ⁴judge ³But ¹I, the ¹judgment - ¹my

ἀληθινή ἐστιν, ὅτι μόνος οὐκ εἰμί, ἀλλ'
true is, because alone I am not, but

ἐγὼ καὶ ὁ πέμψας με. 17 καὶ ἐν τῷ
I and the [one] having sent me. ²even ¹in the

νόμῳ δὲ τῷ ὑμετέρῳ γέγραπται ὅτι δύο
²law ¹And - ¹your it has been written that of two

ἀνθρώπων ἡ μαρτυρία ἀληθής ἐστιν.
men the witness true is.

18 ἐγώ εἰμι ὁ μαρτυρῶν περὶ ἐμαυτοῦ,
I am the [one] witnessing concerning myself,

καὶ μαρτυρεῖ περὶ ἐμοῦ ὁ πέμψας με
and witnesses concerning me ¹the ²having sent ⁴me

πατήρ. 19 ἔλεγον οὖν αὐτῷ· ποῦ ἐστιν ὁ
³Father. They said therefore to him: Where is the

πατήρ σου; ἀπεκρίθη Ἰησοῦς· οὔτε ἐμὲ
Father of thee? Answered Jesus: Neither me

οἴδατε οὔτε τὸν πατέρα μου· εἰ ἐμὲ
ye know nor the Father of me; if me

ᾔδειτε, καὶ τὸν πατέρα μου ἂν ᾔδειτε.
ye knew, also the Father of me ye would have known.

20 Ταῦτα τὰ ῥήματα ἐλάλησεν ἐν τῷ
These - words he spoke in the

γαζοφυλακείῳ διδάσκων ἐν τῷ ἱερῷ· καὶ
treasury teaching in the temple; and

οὐδεὶς ἐπίασεν αὐτόν, ὅτι οὔπω ἐληλύθει
no one seized him, because not yet had come

ἡ ὥρα αὐτοῦ.
the hour of him.

21 Εἶπεν οὖν πάλιν αὐτοῖς· ἐγὼ ὑπάγω
He said therefore again to them: I go

καὶ ζητήσετέ με, καὶ ἐν τῇ ἁμαρτίᾳ
and ye will seek me, and in the sin

ὑμῶν ἀποθανεῖσθε· ὅπου ἐγὼ ὑπάγω ὑμεῖς
of you ye will die; where I go ye

οὐ δύνασθε ἐλθεῖν. 22 ἔλεγον οὖν οἱ
cannot to come. Said therefore the

Ἰουδαῖοι· μήτι ἀποκτενεῖ ἑαυτόν, ὅτι
Jews: Not will he kill himself, because

λέγει· ὅπου ἐγὼ ὑπάγω ὑμεῖς οὐ δύνασθε
he says: Where I go ye cannot

ἐλθεῖν; 23 καὶ ἔλεγεν αὐτοῖς· ὑμεῖς ἐκ
to come? And he said to them: Ye of

τῶν κάτω ἐστέ, ἐγὼ ἐκ τῶν ἄνω εἰμί·
the things below are, I of the things above am;

will have the light of life."
13 The Pharisees challenged him, "Here you are, appearing as your own witness; your testimony is not valid."
14 Jesus answered, "Even if I testify on my own behalf, my testimony is valid, for I know where I came from and where I am going. But you have no idea where I come from or where I am going. 15 You judge by human standards; I pass judgment on no one. 16 But if I do judge, my decisions are right, because I am not alone. I stand with the Father, who sent me. 17 In your own Law it is written that the testimony of two men is valid. 18 I am one who testifies for myself; my other witness is the Father, who sent me."
19 Then they asked him, "Where is your father?"
"You do not know me or my Father," Jesus replied. "If you knew me, you would know my Father also." 20 He spoke these words while teaching in the temple area near the place where the offerings were put. Yet no one seized him, because his time had not yet come.
21 Once more Jesus said to them, "I am going away, and you will look for me, and you will die in your sin. Where I go, you cannot come."
22 This made the Jews ask, "Will he kill himself? Is that why he says, 'Where I go, you cannot come'?"
23 But he continued, "You are from below; I am from above. You are of this

world, I am not of this world. 24 I told you that you would die in your sins, for you will die in your sins unless you believe that I am he."[m] 25 They said to him, "Who are you?" Jesus said to them, "Why do I speak to you at all?[n] 26 I have much to say about you and much to condemn; but the one who sent me is true, and I declare to the world what I have heard from him." 27 They did not understand that he was speaking to them about the Father. 28 So Jesus said, "When you have lifted up the Son of Man, then you will realize that I am he,[m] and that I do nothing on my own, but I speak these things as the Father instructed me. 29 And the one who sent me is with me; he has not left me alone, for I always do what is pleasing to him." 30 As he was saying these things, many believed in him.

True Disciples

31 Then Jesus said to the Jews who had believed in him, "If you continue in my word, you are truly my disciples; 32 and you will know the truth, and the truth will make you free." 33 They answered him, "We are descendants of Abraham and have never been slaves to anyone. What do you mean by saying, 'You will be made free'?" 34 Jesus answered them, "Very truly, I tell you, everyone who commits sin is a slave to sin. 35 The slave does not have a permanent place in the household; the son has a

---

ὑμεῖς ἐκ τούτου τοῦ κόσμου ἐστέ, ἐγὼ
ye   of   this   the   world   are,   I

οὐκ εἰμὶ ἐκ τοῦ κόσμου τούτου. 24 εἶπον
am not -   of the   world   this.   I said

οὖν ὑμῖν ὅτι ἀποθανεῖσθε ἐν ταῖς ἁμαρτίαις
therefore to you that ye will die in the   sins

ὑμῶν· ἐὰν γὰρ μὴ πιστεύσητε ὅτι ἐγώ
of you ; for if ye believe not   that   I

εἰμι, ἀποθανεῖσθε ἐν ταῖς ἁμαρτίαις ὑμῶν.
am,   ye will die   in the   sins   of you.

25 ἔλεγον οὖν αὐτῷ· σὺ τίς εἶ; εἶπεν
  They said therefore to him : ²Thou ¹who ²art?   Said

αὐτοῖς ὁ Ἰησοῦς· τὴν ἀρχὴν ὅ τι καὶ
to them - Jesus :   ⁴at all † ¹Why ²indeed

λαλῶ ὑμῖν; 26 πολλὰ ἔχω περὶ ὑμῶν
²speak I ⁴to you? Many things I have about   you

λαλεῖν καὶ κρίνειν· ἀλλ' ὁ πέμψας με
to speak and to judge; but the [one] having sent me

ἀληθής ἐστιν, κἀγὼ ἃ ἤκουσα παρ'
true   is,   and I what I heard   from

αὐτοῦ, ταῦτα λαλῶ εἰς τὸν κόσμον.
him, these things I speak in the   world.

27 οὐκ ἔγνωσαν ὅτι τὸν πατέρα αὐτοῖς
  They did not know that ³the ²Father ⁴to them

ἔλεγεν. 28 εἶπεν οὖν ὁ Ἰησοῦς· ὅταν
¹he spoke [of]. Said therefore - Jesus : When

ὑψώσητε τὸν υἱὸν τοῦ ἀνθρώπου, τότε
ye lift up the Son of - man,   then

γνώσεσθε ὅτι ἐγώ εἰμι, καὶ ἀπ' ἐμαυτοῦ
ye will know that I am, and from myself

ποιῶ οὐδέν, ἀλλὰ καθὼς ἐδίδαξέν με ὁ
I do nothing, but   as   taught   me the

πατήρ, ταῦτα λαλῶ. 29 καὶ ὁ πέμψας
Father, these things I speak. And the [one] having sent

με μετ' ἐμοῦ ἐστιν· οὐκ ἀφῆκέν με
me with me is;   he did not leave   me

μόνον, ὅτι ἐγὼ τὰ ἀρεστὰ αὐτῷ ποιῶ
alone, because I the things pleasing to him do

πάντοτε.
always.

30 Ταῦτα αὐτοῦ λαλοῦντος πολλοὶ ἐπίσ-
  These things him saying²   many   be-
  = As he said these things

τευσαν εἰς αὐτόν. 31 ἔλεγεν οὖν ὁ Ἰησοῦς
lieved in   him.   Said therefore - Jesus

πρὸς τοὺς πεπιστευκότας αὐτῷ Ἰουδαίους·
to ¹the ³having believed ⁴him ²Jews :

ἐὰν ὑμεῖς μείνητε ἐν τῷ λόγῳ τῷ ἐμῷ,
If   ye   continue in the ²word - ¹my,

ἀληθῶς μαθηταί μού ἐστε, 32 καὶ γνώσεσθε
truly disciples of me ye are, and ye will know

τὴν ἀλήθειαν, καὶ ἡ ἀλήθεια ἐλευθερώσει
the   truth,   and the truth   will free

ὑμᾶς. 33 ἀπεκρίθησαν πρὸς αὐτόν· σπέρμα
you.   They answered to   him :   Seed

Ἀβραάμ ἐσμεν, καὶ οὐδενὶ δεδουλεύκαμεν
of Abraham we are, and to no one have we been enslaved

πώποτε· πῶς σὺ λέγεις ὅτι ἐλεύθεροι
never; how thou sayest that   free

γενήσεσθε; 34 ἀπεκρίθη αὐτοῖς ὁ Ἰησοῦς·
ye will become? Answered them   - Jesus :

ἀμὴν ἀμὴν λέγω ὑμῖν ὅτι πᾶς ὁ ποιῶν
Truly truly I tell you that everyone - doing

τὴν ἁμαρτίαν δοῦλός ἐστιν τῆς ἁμαρτίας.
 -    sin   a slave is   -   of sin.

35 ὁ δὲ δοῦλος οὐ μένει ἐν τῇ οἰκίᾳ
  But the slave does not remain in the house

---

world; I am not of this world. 24 I told you that you would die in your sins; if you do not believe that I am the one I claim to be,[q] you will indeed die in your sins."

25 "Who are you?" they asked.

"Just what I have been claiming all along," Jesus replied. 26 "I have much to say in judgment of you. But he who sent me is reliable, and what I have heard from him I tell the world."

27 They did not understand that he was telling them about his Father. 28 So Jesus said, "When you have lifted up the Son of Man, then you will know that I am the one I claim to be, and that I do nothing on my own but speak just what the Father has taught me. 29 The one who sent me is with me; he has not left me alone, for I always do what pleases him." 30 Even as he spoke, many put their faith in him.

The Children of Abraham

31 To the Jews who had believed him, Jesus said, "If you hold to my teaching, you are really my disciples. 32 Then you will know the truth, and the truth will set you free."

33 They answered him, "We are Abraham's descendants[r] and have never been slaves of anyone. How can you say that we shall be set free?"

34 Jesus replied, "I tell you the truth, everyone who sins is a slave to sin. 35 Now a slave has no permanent place in the family,

---

place there forever. 36 So if the Son makes you free, you will be free indeed. 37 I know that you are descendants of Abraham; yet you look for an opportunity to kill me, because there is no place in you for my word. 38 I declare what I have seen in the Father's presence; as for you, you should do what you have heard from the Father."o

Jesus and Abraham

39 They answered him, "Abraham is our father." Jesus said to them, "If you were Abraham's children, you would be doingp what Abraham did, 40 but now you are trying to kill me, a man who has told you the truth that I heard from God. This is not what Abraham did. 41 You are indeed doing what your father does." They said to him, "We are not illegitimate children; we have one father, God himself." 42 Jesus said to them, "If God were your Father, you would love me, for I came from God and now I am here. I did not come on my own, but he sent me. 43 Why do you not understand what I say? It is because you cannot accept my word. 44 You are from your father the devil, and you choose to do your father's desires. He was a murderer from the beginning, and does not stand in the truth, because there is no truth in him. When he lies, he speaks according to his own nature, for he is a liar and the father of lies. 45 But because I tell the truth, you do not believe me. 46 Which of you

o Other ancient authorities read *you do what you have heard from your father*
p Other ancient authorities read *If you are Abraham's children, then do*

εἰς τὸν αἰῶνα· ὁ υἱὸς μένει εἰς τὸν
unto the age; the son remains unto the

αἰῶνα. 36 ἐὰν οὖν ὁ υἱὸς ὑμᾶς ἐλευθερώσῃ,
age. If therefore the Son you frees,

ὄντως ἐλεύθεροι ἔσεσθε. 37 Οἶδα ὅτι
really free ye will be. I know that

σπέρμα Ἀβραάμ ἐστε· ἀλλὰ ζητεῖτέ με
seed of Abraham ye are; but ye seek me

ἀποκτεῖναι, ὅτι ὁ λόγος ὁ ἐμὸς οὐ χωρεῖ
to kill, because the ¹word - ¹my finds no room

ἐν ὑμῖν. 38 ἃ ἐγὼ ἑώρακα παρὰ τῷ
in you. What I have seen with the

πατρὶ λαλῶ· καὶ ὑμεῖς οὖν ἃ ἠκού-
Father I speak; and ye therefore what ye

σατε παρὰ τοῦ πατρὸς ποιεῖτε. 39 ἀπεκρί-
heard from the father ye do. They

θησαν καὶ εἶπαν αὐτῷ· ὁ πατὴρ ἡμῶν Ἀβραάμ
answered and said to him: The father of us Abraham

ἐστιν. λέγει αὐτοῖς ὁ Ἰησοῦς· εἰ τέκνα
is. Says to them - Jesus: If children

τοῦ Ἀβραάμ ἐστε, τὰ ἔργα τοῦ Ἀβραάμ
- of Abraham ye are, the works - of Abraham

ποιεῖτε· 40 νῦν δὲ ζητεῖτέ με ἀποκτεῖναι,
ye do; but now ye seek me to kill,

ἄνθρωπον ὃς τὴν ἀλήθειαν ὑμῖν λελάληκα,
a man who the truth to you has spoken,

ἣν ἤκουσα παρὰ τοῦ θεοῦ· τοῦτο Ἀβραὰμ
which I heard from - God; this Abraham

οὐκ ἐποίησεν. 41 ὑμεῖς ποιεῖτε τὰ ἔργα
did not. Ye do the works

τοῦ πατρὸς ὑμῶν. εἶπαν αὐτῷ· ἡμεῖς ἐκ
of the father of you. They said to him: We of

πορνείας οὐκ ἐγεννήθημεν, ἕνα πατέρα
fornication were not born, one father

ἔχομεν τὸν θεόν. 42 εἶπεν αὐτοῖς ὁ
we have[,] - God. Said to them -

Ἰησοῦς· εἰ ὁ θεὸς πατὴρ ὑμῶν ἦν,
Jesus: If - God father of you was,

ἠγαπᾶτε ἂν ἐμέ· ἐγὼ γὰρ ἐκ τοῦ θεοῦ
ye would have loved me; for I of - God

ἐξῆλθον καὶ ἥκω· οὐδὲ γὰρ ἀπ' ἐμαυτοῦ
came forth and have come; for not from myself

ἐλήλυθα, ἀλλ' ἐκεῖνός με ἀπέσταλκεν. 43 διὰ τί
I have come, but that one me sent. Why

τὴν λαλιὰν τὴν ἐμὴν οὐ γινώσκετε;
the ²speech - ¹my know ye not?

ὅτι οὐ δύνασθε ἀκούειν τὸν λόγον τὸν
because ye cannot *to hear* the ²word -

ἐμόν. 44 ὑμεῖς ἐκ τοῦ πατρὸς τοῦ
¹my. Ye of the father *of the*

διαβόλου ἐστὲ καὶ τὰς ἐπιθυμίας τοῦ
devil are and the desires of the

πατρὸς ὑμῶν θέλετε ποιεῖν. ἐκεῖνος
father of you ye wish to do. That one

ἀνθρωποκτόνος ἦν ἀπ' ἀρχῆς, καὶ ἐν
a murderer was from [the] beginning, and in

τῇ ἀληθείᾳ οὐκ ἔστηκεν, ὅτι οὐκ ἔστιν
the truth stood not, because not is

ἀλήθεια ἐν αὐτῷ. ὅταν λαλῇ τὸ ψεῦδος,
truth in him. When he speaks the lie,

ἐκ τῶν ἰδίων λαλεῖ, ὅτι ψεύστης ἐστὶν
out of his own things he speaks, because a liar he is

καὶ ὁ πατὴρ αὐτοῦ. 45 ἐγὼ δὲ ὅτι τὴν
and the father of it. But ²I ¹because ⁴the

ἀλήθειαν λέγω, οὐ πιστεύετέ μοι. 46 τίς
³truth ⁵say, ye do not believe me. Who

---

but a son belongs to it forever. 36 So if the Son sets you free, you will be free indeed. 37 I know you are Abraham's descendants. Yet you are ready to kill me, because you have no room for my word. 38 I am telling you what I have seen in the Father's presence, and you do what you have heard from your father.s"

39 "Abraham is our father," they answered.

"If you were Abraham's children," said Jesus, "then youf do the things Abraham did. 40 As it is, you are determined to kill me, a man who has told you the truth that I heard from God. Abraham did not do such things. 41 You are doing the things your own father does."

"We are not illegitimate children," they protested. "The only Father we have is God himself."

The Children of the Devil

42 Jesus said to them, "If God were your Father, you would love me, for I came from God and now am here. I have not come on my own; but he sent me. 43 Why is my language not clear to you? Because you are unable to hear what I say. 44 You belong to your father, the devil, and you want to carry out your father's desire. He was a murderer from the beginning, not holding to the truth, for there is no truth in him. When he lies, he speaks his native language, for he is a liar and the father of lies. 45 Yet because I tell the truth, you do not be-

s38 Or *presence. Therefore do what you have heard from the Father.*
f39 Some early manuscripts *"If you are Abraham's children," said Jesus, "then*

convicts me of sin? If I tell the truth, why do you not believe me? [47]Whoever is from God hears the words of God. The reason you do not hear them is that you are not from God."

[48] The Jews answered him, "Are we not right in saying that you are a Samaritan and have a demon?" [49]Jesus answered, "I do not have a demon; but I honor my Father, and you dishonor me. [50]Yet I do not seek my own glory; there is one who seeks it and he is the judge. [51]Very truly, I tell you, whoever keeps my word will never see death." [52]The Jews said to him, "Now we know that you have a demon. Abraham died, and so did the prophets; yet you say, 'Whoever keeps my word will never taste death.' [53]Are you greater than our father Abraham, who died? The prophets also died. Who do you claim to be?" [54]Jesus answered, "If I glorify myself, my glory is nothing. It is my Father who glorifies me, he of whom you say, 'He is our God,' [55]though you do not know him. But I know him; if I would say that I do not know him, I would be a liar like you. But I do know him and I keep his word. [56]Your ancestor Abraham rejoiced that he would see my day; he saw it and was glad." [57]Then the Jews said to

ἐξ ὑμῶν ἐλέγχει με περὶ ἁμαρτίας; εἰ
of you reproves me concerning sin? If

ἀλήθειαν λέγω, διὰ τί ὑμεῖς οὐ πιστεύετέ
truth I say, why ²ye ¹do not believe

μοι; 47 ὁ ὢν ἐκ τοῦ θεοῦ τὰ ῥήματα
me? The [one] being of - God the words

τοῦ θεοῦ ἀκούει· διὰ τοῦτο ὑμεῖς οὐκ
- of God hears; therefore ye not

ἀκούετε, ὅτι ἐκ τοῦ θεοῦ οὐκ ἐστέ.
hear, because of - God ye are not.

48 Ἀπεκρίθησαν οἱ Ἰουδαῖοι καὶ εἶπαν
Answered the Jews and said

αὐτῷ· οὐ καλῶς λέγομεν ἡμεῖς ὅτι
to him: ³Not ⁴well ¹say ²we ⁵that

Σαμαρίτης εἶ σὺ καὶ δαιμόνιον ἔχεις;
⁶a Samaritan ⁷art ⁸thou ⁹and ¹¹a demon ¹⁰hast?

49 ἀπεκρίθη Ἰησοῦς· ἐγὼ δαιμόνιον οὐκ
Answered Jesus: I a demon not

ἔχω, ἀλλὰ τιμῶ τὸν πατέρα μου, καὶ
have, but I honour the Father of me, and

ὑμεῖς ἀτιμάζετέ με. 50 ἐγὼ δὲ οὐ ζητῶ
ye dishonour me. But I seek not

τὴν δόξαν μου· ἔστιν ὁ ζητῶν καὶ
the glory of me; there is the [one] seeking and

κρίνων. 51 ἀμὴν ἀμὴν λέγω ὑμῖν, ἐάν
judging. Truly truly I tell you, if

τις τὸν ἐμὸν λόγον τηρήσῃ, θάνατον
anyone - my word keeps, death

οὐ μὴ θεωρήσῃ εἰς τὸν αἰῶνα. 52 εἶπαν
by no means will he behold unto the age. Said

αὐτῷ οἱ Ἰουδαῖοι· νῦν ἐγνώκαμεν ὅτι
to him the Jews: Now we have known that

δαιμόνιον ἔχεις. Ἀβραὰμ ἀπέθανεν καὶ οἱ
a demon thou hast. Abraham died and the

προφῆται, καὶ σὺ λέγεις· ἐάν τις τὸν
prophets, and thou sayest: If anyone the

λόγον μου τηρήσῃ, οὐ μὴ γεύσηται
word of me keeps, by no means will he taste

θανάτου εἰς τὸν αἰῶνα. 53 μὴ σὺ μείζων
of death unto the age. Not thou greater

εἶ τοῦ πατρὸς ἡμῶν Ἀβραάμ, ὅστις
art [than] the father of us Abraham, who

ἀπέθανεν; καὶ οἱ προφῆται ἀπέθανον· τίνα
died? and the prophets died;· whom

σεαυτὸν ποιεῖς; 54 ἀπεκρίθη Ἰησοῦς· ἐὰν
thyself makest thou? Answered Jesus: If

ἐγὼ δοξάσω ἐμαυτόν, ἡ δόξα μου οὐδέν
I glorify myself, the glory of me nothing

ἐστιν· ἔστιν ὁ πατήρ μου ὁ δοξάζων με,
is; ⁴is ¹the ²Father ³of me the [one] glorifying me,

ὃν ὑμεῖς λέγετε ὅτι θεὸς ἡμῶν ἐστιν,
whom ye say[,] - God of us he is,

55 καὶ οὐκ ἐγνώκατε αὐτόν, ἐγὼ δὲ
and ye have not known him, but I

οἶδα αὐτόν. κἂν εἴπω ὅτι οὐκ οἶδα
know him. Even if I say that I know not

αὐτόν, ἔσομαι ὅμοιος ὑμῖν ψεύστης· ἀλλὰ
him, I shall be like you a liar; but

οἶδα αὐτὸν καὶ τὸν λόγον αὐτοῦ τηρῶ.
I know him and the word of him I keep.

56 Ἀβραὰμ ὁ πατὴρ ὑμῶν ἠγαλλιάσατο
Abraham the father of you was glad

ἵνα ἴδῃ τὴν ἡμέραν τὴν ἐμήν, καὶ εἶδεν
that he should see the ²day - ¹my, and he saw

καὶ ἐχάρη. 57 εἶπαν οὖν οἱ Ἰουδαῖοι
and rejoiced. Said therefore the Jews

lieve me! [46]Can any of you prove me guilty of sin? If I am telling the truth, why don't you believe me? [47]He who belongs to God hears what God says. The reason you do not hear is that you do not belong to God."

The Claims of Jesus About Himself

[48]The Jews answered him, "Aren't we right in saying that you are a Samaritan and demon-possessed?"

[49]"I am not possessed by a demon," said Jesus, "but I honor my Father and you dishonor me. [50]I am not seeking glory for myself; but there is one who seeks it, and he is the judge. [51]I tell you the truth, if anyone keeps my word, he will never see death."

[52]At this the Jews exclaimed, "Now we know that you are demon-possessed! Abraham died and so did the prophets, yet you say that if anyone keeps your word, he will never taste death. [53]Are you greater than our father Abraham? He died, and so did the prophets. Who do you think you are?"

[54]Jesus replied, "If I glorify myself, my glory means nothing. My Father, whom you claim as your God, is the one who glorifies me. [55]Though you do not know him, I know him. If I said I did not, I would be a liar like you, but I do know him and keep his word. [56]Your father Abraham rejoiced at the thought of seeing my day; he saw it and was glad."

[57]"You are not yet fifty

him, "You are not yet fifty years old, and have you seen Abraham?"[q] 58 Jesus said to them, "Very truly, I tell you, before Abraham was, I am." 59 So they picked up stones to throw at him, but Jesus hid himself and went out of the temple.

πρὸς αὐτόν· πεντήκοντα ἔτη οὔπω ἔχεις
to him: Fifty years not yet thou hast
καὶ Ἀβραὰμ ἑώρακας; 58 εἶπεν αὐτοῖς
and Abraham hast thou seen? Said to them
Ἰησοῦς· ἀμὴν ἀμὴν λέγω ὑμῖν, πρὶν
Jesus: Truly truly I tell you, before
Ἀβραὰμ γενέσθαι ἐγὼ εἰμί. 59 ἦραν
Abraham to become[b] I am. They took
=became
οὖν λίθους ἵνα βάλωσιν ἐπ᾽ αὐτόν·
therefore stones that they might cast on him;
Ἰησοῦς δὲ ἐκρύβη καὶ ἐξῆλθεν ἐκ τοῦ
but Jesus was hidden and went forth out of the
ἱεροῦ.
temple.

years old," the Jews said to him, "and you have seen Abraham!"
58"I tell you the truth," Jesus answered, "before Abraham was born, I am!" 59At this, they picked up stones to stone him, but Jesus hid himself, slipping away from the temple grounds.

Chapter 9
A Man Born Blind Receives Sight

AS he walked along, he saw a man blind from birth. 2His disciples asked him, "Rabbi, who sinned, this man or his parents, that he was born blind?" 3Jesus answered, "Neither this man nor his parents sinned; he was born blind so that God's works might be revealed in him. 4We[r] must work the works of him who sent me[s] while it is day; night is coming when no one can work. 5As long as I am in the world, I am the light of the world." 6When he had said this, he spat on the ground and made mud with the saliva and spread the mud on the man's eyes, 7saying to him, "Go, wash in the pool of Siloam" (which means Sent). Then he went and washed and came back able to see. 8The neighbors and those who had seen him before as a beggar began to ask, "Is this not the man who used to sit and beg?" 9Some were saying, "It is he." Others were saying, "No, but it is someone like him." He kept saying, "I am the man." 10But they kept asking him, "Then how were your eyes opened?" 11He answered, "The man called

9 Καὶ παράγων εἶδεν ἄνθρωπον τυφλὸν
And passing along he saw a man blind
ἐκ γενετῆς. 2 καὶ ἠρώτησαν αὐτὸν οἱ
from birth. And asked him the
μαθηταὶ αὐτοῦ λέγοντες· ῥαββί, τίς ἥμαρτεν,
disciples of him saying: Rabbi, who sinned,
οὗτος ἢ οἱ γονεῖς αὐτοῦ, ἵνα τυφλὸς
this man or the parents of him, that blind
γεννηθῇ; 3 ἀπεκρίθη Ἰησοῦς· οὔτε οὗτος
he was born? Answered Jesus: Neither this man
ἥμαρτεν οὔτε οἱ γονεῖς αὐτοῦ, ἀλλ᾽ ἵνα
sinned nor the parents of him, but that
φανερωθῇ τὰ ἔργα τοῦ θεοῦ ἐν αὐτῷ.
might be manifested the works – of God in him.
4 ἡμᾶς δεῖ ἐργάζεσθαι τὰ ἔργα τοῦ
Us it behoves to work the works of the
πέμψαντός με ἕως ἡμέρα ἐστίν· ἔρχεται
[one] having sent me while day it is; comes
νὺξ ὅτε οὐδεὶς δύναται ἐργάζεσθαι. 5 ὅταν
night when no one can to work. When
ἐν τῷ κόσμῳ ὦ, φῶς εἰμι τοῦ κόσμου.
in the world I am, light I am of the world.
6 ταῦτα εἰπὼν ἔπτυσεν χαμαὶ καὶ ἐποίησεν
These things having said he spat on the ground and made
πηλὸν ἐκ τοῦ πτύσματος, καὶ ἐπέθηκεν
clay out of the spittle, and ¹put on
αὐτοῦ τὸν πηλὸν ἐπὶ τοὺς ὀφθαλμούς,
⁷of him ²the ³clay ⁴on ⁵the ⁶eyes,
7 καὶ εἶπεν αὐτῷ· ὕπαγε νίψαι εἰς τὴν
and said to him: Go wash in the
κολυμβήθραν τοῦ Σιλωάμ (ὃ ἑρμηνεύεται
pool – of Siloam (which is translated
ἀπεσταλμένος). ἀπῆλθεν οὖν καὶ ἐνίψατο,
having been sent). He went therefore and washed,
καὶ ἦλθεν βλέπων. 8 Οἱ οὖν γείτονες
and came seeing. Therefore the neighbours
καὶ οἱ θεωροῦντες αὐτὸν τὸ πρότερον,†
and the [ones] beholding him formerly,†
ὅτι προσαίτης ἦν, ἔλεγον· οὐχ οὗτός
that a beggar he was, said: ¹Not ²this man
ἐστιν ὁ καθήμενος καὶ προσαιτῶν; 9 ἄλλοι
¹is the [one] sitting and begging? Some
ἔλεγον ὅτι οὗτός ἐστιν· ἄλλοι ἔλεγον·
said[,] – This is he; others said:
οὐχί, ἀλλὰ ὅμοιος αὐτῷ ἐστιν. ἐκεῖνος
No, but like to him he is. That [one]
ἔλεγεν ὅτι ἐγώ εἰμι. 10 ἔλεγον
said[,] – I am. They said therefore
αὐτῷ· πῶς [οὖν] ἠνεῴχθησάν σου οἱ
to him: How then were opened of thee the

Chapter 9
Jesus Heals a Man Born Blind

AS he went along, he saw a man blind from birth. 2His disciples asked him, "Rabbi, who sinned, this man or his parents, that he was born blind?"
3"Neither this man nor his parents sinned," said Jesus, "but this happened so that the work of God might be displayed in his life. 4As long as it is day, we must do the work of him who sent me. Night is coming, when no one can work. 5While I am in the world, I am the light of the world."
6Having said this, he spit on the ground, made some mud with the saliva, and put it on the man's eyes. 7"Go," he told him, "wash in the Pool of Siloam" (this word means Sent). So the man went and washed, and came home seeing.
8His neighbors and those who had formerly seen him begging asked, "Isn't this the same man who used to sit and beg?" 9Some claimed that he was.
Others said, "No, he only looks like him."
But he himself insisted, "I am the man."
10"How then were your eyes opened?" they demanded.

[q] Other ancient authorities read *has Abraham seen you?*
[r] Other ancient authorities read *I*
[s] Other ancient authorities read *us*

Jesus made mud, spread it on my eyes, and said to me, 'Go to Siloam and wash.' Then I went and washed and received my sight."
12They said to him, "Where is he?" He said, "I do not know."

The Pharisees Investigate the Healing

13 They brought to the Pharisees the man who had formerly been blind.
14Now it was a sabbath day when Jesus made the mud and opened his eyes.
15Then the Pharisees also began to ask him how he had received his sight. He said to them, "He put mud on my eyes. Then I washed, and now I see."
16Some of the Pharisees said, "This man is not from God, for he does not observe the sabbath." But others said, "How can a man who is a sinner perform such signs?" And they were divided. 17So they said again to the blind man, "What do you say about him? It was your eyes he opened." He said, "He is a prophet."
18 The Jews did not believe that he had been blind and had received his sight until they called the parents of the man who had received his sight 19and asked them, "Is this your son, who you say was born blind? How then does he now see?" 20His parents answered, "We know that this is our son, and that he was born blind; 21but we do not know how it is that now he sees, nor do we know

---

ὀφθαλμοί; 11 ἀπεκρίθη ἐκεῖνος· ὁ ἄνθρωπος
eyes?   Answered   that [one] : The   man
ὁ λεγόμενος Ἰησοῦς πηλὸν ἐποίησεν καὶ
- being named   Jesus   clay   made   and
ἐπέχρισέν μου τοὺς ὀφθαλμοὺς καὶ εἶπέν
anointed of me the   eyes   and told
μοι ὅτι ὕπαγε εἰς τὸν Σιλωὰμ καὶ
me[,] -   Go   to   -   Siloam and
νίψαι· ἀπελθὼν οὖν καὶ νιψάμενος ἀνέβλεψα.
wash;   going   therefore and washing   I saw.
12 καὶ εἶπαν αὐτῷ· ποῦ ἐστιν ἐκεῖνος;
   And they said to him : Where is that [one]?
λέγει· οὐκ οἶδα. 13 Ἄγουσιν αὐτὸν
He says: I do not know.   They lead   him
πρὸς τοὺς Φαρισαίους, τόν ποτε τυφλόν.
to   the   Pharisees,   the at one time blind.
14 ἦν δὲ σάββατον ἐν ᾗ ἡμέρᾳ τὸν
   Now it was a sabbath on which day ³the
πηλὸν ἐποίησεν ὁ Ἰησοῦς καὶ ἀνέῳξεν
⁴clay ²made   - ¹Jesus   and opened
αὐτοῦ τοὺς ὀφθαλμούς. 15 πάλιν οὖν
of him the   eyes.   Again   therefore
ἠρώτων αὐτὸν καὶ οἱ Φαρισαῖοι πῶς
⁵asked ⁴him   ²also ¹the ³Pharisees   how
ἀνέβλεψεν. ὁ δὲ εἶπεν αὐτοῖς· πηλὸν
he saw.   And he said   to them :   Clay
ἐπέθηκέν μου ἐπὶ τοὺς ὀφθαλμούς, καὶ
he put on ⁴of me ¹on ²the ³eyes,   and
ἐνιψάμην, καὶ βλέπω. 16 ἔλεγον οὖν ἐκ
I washed, and I see.   Said   therefore of
τῶν Φαρισαίων τινές· οὐκ ἔστιν οὗτος
the   Pharisees   some : ⁴not ⁵is   ¹This
παρὰ θεοῦ ὁ ἄνθρωπος, ὅτι τὸ σάββατον
²from ⁶God - ²man,   because the   sabbath
οὐ τηρεῖ. ἄλλοι [δὲ] ἔλεγον· πῶς δύναται
he keeps not. But others said :   How   can
ἄνθρωπος ἁμαρτωλὸς τοιαῦτα σημεῖα ποιεῖν;
man   a sinful   such   signs   to do?
καὶ σχίσμα ἦν ἐν αὐτοῖς. 17 λέγουσιν
And a division there was among them.   They say
οὖν τῷ τυφλῷ πάλιν· τί σὺ λέγεις
therefore to the blind man again : What thou sayest
περὶ αὐτοῦ, ὅτι ἠνέῳξέν σου τοὺς
about   him, because he opened of thee the
ὀφθαλμούς; ὁ δὲ εἶπεν ὅτι προφήτης ἐστίν.
eyes?   And he said[,] -   A prophet   he is.
18 οὐκ ἐπίστευσαν οὖν οἱ Ἰουδαῖοι περὶ
   Did not believe therefore the Jews   about
αὐτοῦ ὅτι ἦν τυφλὸς καὶ ἀνέβλεψεν,
him   that he was blind   and   saw,
ἕως ὅτου ἐφώνησαν τοὺς γονεῖς αὐτοῦ
until -   they called the   parents of him
τοῦ ἀναβλέψαντος 19 καὶ ἠρώτησαν αὐτοὺς
of the [one] having seen   and asked   them
λέγοντες· οὗτός ἐστιν ὁ υἱὸς ὑμῶν, ὃν
saying :   This   is the son of you, whom
ὑμεῖς λέγετε ὅτι τυφλὸς ἐγεννήθη; πῶς
ye   say   that blind he was born? how
οὖν βλέπει ἄρτι; 20 ἀπεκρίθησαν οὖν οἱ
then sees he now?   Answered   therefore the
γονεῖς αὐτοῦ καὶ εἶπαν· οἴδαμεν ὅτι
parents of him and   said : We know   that
οὗτός ἐστιν ὁ υἱὸς ἡμῶν καὶ ὅτι τυφλὸς
this   is the son of us and that blind
ἐγεννήθη· 21 πῶς δὲ νῦν βλέπει οὐκ
he was born;   but how now he sees   not

11He replied, "The man they call Jesus made some mud and put it on my eyes. He told me to go to Siloam and wash. So I went and washed, and then I could see."
12"Where is this man?" they asked him.
"I don't know," he said.

The Pharisees Investigate the Healing

13They brought to the Pharisees the man who had been blind. 14Now the day on which Jesus had made the mud and opened the man's eyes was a Sabbath.
15Therefore the Pharisees also asked him how he had received his sight. "He put mud on my eyes," the man replied, "and I washed, and now I see."
16Some of the Pharisees said, "This man is not from God, for he does not keep the Sabbath."
But others asked, "How can a sinner do such miraculous signs?" So they were divided.
17Finally they turned again to the blind man, "What have you to say about him? It was your eyes he opened."
The man replied, "He is a prophet."
18The Jews still did not believe that he had been blind and had received his sight until they sent for the man's parents. 19"Is this your son?" they asked. "Is this the one you say was born blind? How is it that now he can see?"
20"We know he is our son," the parents answered, "and we know he was born blind. 21But how

who opened his eyes. Ask him; he is of age. He will speak for himself." 22 His parents said this because they were afraid of the Jews; for the Jews had already agreed that anyone who confessed Jesus[t] to be the Messiah[u] would be put out of the synagogue. 23 Therefore his parents said, "He is of age; ask him."

24 So for the second time they called the man who had been blind, and they said to him, "Give glory to God! We know that this man is a sinner." 25 He answered, "I do not know whether he is a sinner. One thing I do know, that though I was blind, now I see." 26 They said to him, "What did he do to you? How did he open your eyes?" 27 He answered them, "I have told you already, and you would not listen. Why do you want to hear it again? Do you also want to become his disciples?" 28 Then they reviled him, saying, "You are his disciple, but we are disciples of Moses. 29 We know that God has spoken to Moses, but as for this man, we do not know where he comes from." 30 The man answered, "Here is an astonishing thing! You do not know where he comes from, and yet he opened my eyes. 31 We know that God does not listen to sinners, but he does listen to one who worships him and obeys his will. 32 Never since the world began has it been heard that anyone opened the eyes of a person

---

οἴδαμεν, ἢ τίς ἤνοιξεν αὐτοῦ τοὺς ὀφθαλμοὺς
we know, or who opened of him the eyes

ἡμεῖς οὐκ οἴδαμεν· αὐτὸν ἐρωτήσατε,
we know not; him ask ye,

ἡλικίαν ἔχει, αὐτὸς περὶ ἑαυτοῦ λαλήσει.
age he has, he about himself will speak.

22 ταῦτα εἶπαν οἱ γονεῖς αὐτοῦ ὅτι ἐφο-
These things said the parents of him because they

βοῦντο τοὺς Ἰουδαίους· ἤδη γὰρ συνετέθειντο
feared the Jews; for already had agreed

οἱ Ἰουδαῖοι ἵνα ἐάν τις αὐτὸν ὁμολογήσῃ
the Jews that if anyone him should acknowledge

χριστόν, ἀποσυνάγωγος γένηται.
[to be] Christ, put away from [the] synagogue he would be.

23 διὰ τοῦτο οἱ γονεῖς αὐτοῦ εἶπαν ὅτι
Therefore the parents of him said[,] –

ἡλικίαν ἔχει, αὐτὸν ἐπερωτήσατε. 24 Ἐφώνησαν
Age he has, him question ye. They called

οὖν τὸν ἄνθρωπον ἐκ δευτέρου ὃς ἦν
therefore the man a second time who was

τυφλός, καὶ εἶπαν αὐτῷ· δὸς δόξαν τῷ
blind, and said to him: Give glory –

θεῷ· ἡμεῖς οἴδαμεν ὅτι οὗτος ὁ ἄνθρωπος
to God; we know that this – man

ἁμαρτωλός ἐστιν. 25 ἀπεκρίθη οὖν ἐκεῖνος·
sinful is. Answered therefore that [one]:

εἰ ἁμαρτωλός ἐστιν οὐκ οἶδα· ἓν οἶδα,
If sinful he is I know not; one thing I know,

ὅτι τυφλὸς ὢν ἄρτι βλέπω. 26 εἶπαν
that blind being now I see. They said

οὖν αὐτῷ· τί ἐποίησέν σοι; πῶς ἤνοιξέν
therefore to him: What did he to thee? how opened he

σου τοὺς ὀφθαλμούς; 27 ἀπεκρίθη αὐτοῖς·
of thee the eyes? He answered them:

εἶπον ὑμῖν ἤδη καὶ οὐκ ἠκούσατε· τί
I told you already and ye heard not; why

πάλιν θέλετε ἀκούειν; μὴ καὶ ὑμεῖς
again wish ye to hear? not also ye

θέλετε αὐτοῦ μαθηταὶ γενέσθαι; 28 καὶ
wish of him disciples to become? And

ἐλοιδόρησαν αὐτὸν καὶ εἶπαν· σὺ μαθητὴς
they reviled him and said: Thou a disciple

εἶ ἐκείνου, ἡμεῖς δὲ τοῦ Μωϋσέως ἐσμὲν
art of that man, but we – of Moses are

μαθηταί· 29 ἡμεῖς οἴδαμεν ὅτι Μωϋσεῖ
disciples; we know that by Moses

λελάληκεν ὁ θεός, τοῦτον δὲ οὐκ οἴδαμεν
has spoken – God, but this man we know not

πόθεν ἐστίν. 30 ἀπεκρίθη ὁ ἄνθρωπος
whence he is. Answered the man

καὶ εἶπεν αὐτοῖς· ἐν τούτῳ γὰρ τὸ
and said to them: In this then the

θαυμαστόν ἐστιν, ὅτι ὑμεῖς οὐκ οἴδατε
marvellous thing is, that ye do not know

πόθεν ἐστίν, καὶ ἤνοιξέν μου τοὺς
whence he is, and he opened of me the

ὀφθαλμούς. 31 οἴδαμεν ὅτι ὁ θεὸς
eyes. We know that – God

ἁμαρτωλῶν οὐκ ἀκούει, ἀλλ᾽ ἐάν τις
sinful men does not hear, but if anyone

θεοσεβὴς ᾖ καὶ τὸ θέλημα αὐτοῦ ποιῇ,
godfearing is and the will of him does,

τούτου ἀκούει. 32 ἐκ τοῦ αἰῶνος οὐκ
this man he hears. From the age not

ἠκούσθη ὅτι ἠνέῳξέν τις ὀφθαλμοὺς τυφλοῦ
it was heard that [2]opened [1]anyone eyes of a blind man

---

he can see now, or who opened his eyes, we don't know. Ask him. He is of age; he will speak for himself." 22 His parents said this because they were afraid of the Jews, for already the Jews had decided that anyone who acknowledged that Jesus was the Christ[u] would be put out of the synagogue. 23 That was why his parents said, "He is of age; ask him."

24 A second time they summoned the man who had been blind. "Give glory to God,[v]" they said. "We know this man is a sinner."

25 He replied, "Whether he is a sinner or not, I don't know. One thing I do know. I was blind but now I see!"

26 Then they asked him, "What did he do to you? How did he open your eyes?"

27 He answered, "I have told you already and you did not listen. Why do you want to hear it again? Do you want to become his disciples, too?"

28 Then they hurled insults at him and said, "You are this fellow's disciple! We are disciples of Moses! 29 We know that God spoke to Moses, but as for this fellow, we don't even know where he comes from."

30 The man answered, "Now that is remarkable! You don't know where he comes from, yet he opened my eyes. 31 We know that God does not listen to sinners. He listens to the godly man who does his will. 32 Nobody has ever heard of opening the eyes of a man born blind. 33 If this man

---

[u] 22 Or Messiah
[v] 24 A solemn charge to tell the truth (see Joshua 7:19)

born blind. 33 If this man were not from God, he could do nothing." 34 They answered him, "You were born entirely in sins, and are you trying to teach us?" And they drove him out.

Spiritual Blindness

35 Jesus heard that they had driven him out, and when he found him, he said, "Do you believe in the Son of Man?"ᵛ 36 He answered, "And who is he, sir?"ʷ Tell me, so that I may believe in him." 37 Jesus said to him, "You have seen him, and the one speaking with you is he." 38 He said, "Lord,ʷ I believe." And he worshiped him. 39 Jesus said, "I came into this world for judgment so that those who do not see may see, and those who do see may become blind." 40 Some of the Pharisees near him heard this and said to him, "Surely we are not blind, are we?" 41 Jesus said to them, "If you were blind, you would not have sin. But now that you say, 'We see,' your sin remains.

γεγεννημένου· **33** εἰ μὴ ἦν οὗτος παρὰ
having been born;   if ¹not ²was ¹this man from

θεοῦ, οὐκ ἠδύνατο ποιεῖν οὐδέν. **34** ἀπεκρίθησαν
God, he could not *to* do no(any)thing.   They answered

καὶ εἶπαν αὐτῷ· ἐν ἁμαρτίαις σὺ ἐγεννήθης
and said to him : In   sins   thou wast born

ὅλος, καὶ σὺ διδάσκεις ἡμᾶς; καὶ ἐξέβαλον
wholly, and thou teachest   us?   and they cast *out*

αὐτὸν ἔξω. **35** Ἤκουσεν Ἰησοῦς ὅτι
him   outside.   Heard   Jesus   that

ἐξέβαλον αὐτὸν ἔξω, καὶ εὑρὼν αὐτὸν
they cast *out* him outside, and finding him

εἶπεν· σὺ πιστεύεις εἰς τὸν υἱὸν τοῦ
said : Thou believest in the Son   -

ἀνθρώπου; **36** ἀπεκρίθη ἐκεῖνος καὶ εἶπεν·
of man?   Answered   that [one] and said :

καὶ τίς ἐστιν, κύριε, ἵνα πιστεύσω εἰς
And who is he, sir, that I may believe in

αὐτόν; **37** εἶπεν αὐτῷ ὁ Ἰησοῦς· καὶ
him?   Said to him - Jesus :   Both

ἑώρακας αὐτὸν καὶ ὁ λαλῶν μετὰ σοῦ
thou hast seen him and the [one] speaking with thee

ἐκεῖνός ἐστιν. **38** ὁ δὲ ἔφη· πιστεύω, κύριε·
that [one] is.   And he said : I believe,   sir;

καὶ προσεκύνησεν αὐτῷ. **39** καὶ εἶπεν ὁ
and he worshipped   him.   And said -

Ἰησοῦς· εἰς κρίμα ἐγὼ εἰς τὸν κόσμον
Jesus : For judgment I into -   world

τοῦτον ἦλθον, ἵνα οἱ μὴ βλέποντες
this   came, that the [ones] not   seeing

βλέπωσιν καὶ οἱ βλέποντες τυφλοὶ γένωνται.
may see and the [ones] seeing blind may become.

40 Ἤκουσαν ἐκ τῶν Φαρισαίων ταῦτα
³heard ¹[Some] ²of ³the ⁴Pharisees ⁵these things

οἱ μετ' αὐτοῦ ὄντες, καὶ εἶπαν αὐτῷ·
- ⁶with ⁷him ⁸being, and they said to him :

μὴ καὶ ἡμεῖς τυφλοί ἐσμεν; **41** εἶπεν
Not also we   blind are?   Said

αὐτοῖς ὁ Ἰησοῦς· εἰ τυφλοὶ ἦτε, οὐκ
to them - Jesus : If blind ye were, not

ἂν εἴχετε ἁμαρτίαν· νῦν δὲ λέγετε ὅτι
ye would have had sin; but now ye say[,] -

βλέπομεν· ἡ ἁμαρτία ὑμῶν μένει.
We see; the sin   of you remains.

---

were not from God, he could do nothing."

34 To this they replied, "You were steeped in sin at birth; how dare you lecture us!" And they threw him out.

Spiritual Blindness

35 Jesus heard that they had thrown him out, and when he found him, he said, "Do you believe in the Son of Man?" 36 "Who is he, sir?" the man asked. "Tell me so that I may believe in him." 37 Jesus said, "You have now seen him; in fact, he is the one speaking with you." 38 Then the man said, "Lord, I believe," and he worshiped him. 39 Jesus said, "For judgment I have come into this world, so that the blind will see and those who see will become blind." 40 Some Pharisees who were with him heard him say this and asked, "What? Are we blind too?" 41 Jesus said, "If you were blind, you would not be guilty of sin; but now that you claim you can see, your guilt remains."

Chapter 10

Jesus the Good Shepherd

" VERY truly, I tell you, anyone who does not enter the sheepfold by the gate but climbs in by another way is a thief and a bandit. 2 The one who enters by the gate is the shepherd of the sheep. 3 The gatekeeper opens the gate for him, and the sheep hear his voice. He calls his own sheep by name and leads them out. 4 When he has brought out all his own, he goes ahead of them, and

---

10 Ἀμὴν ἀμὴν λέγω ὑμῖν, ὁ μὴ
Truly truly I say to you, the [one] not

εἰσερχόμενος διὰ τῆς θύρας εἰς τὴν
entering through the door   into the

αὐλὴν τῶν προβάτων ἀλλὰ ἀναβαίνων
fold of the sheep   but   going up

ἀλλαχόθεν, ἐκεῖνος κλέπτης ἐστὶν καὶ
by another way, that [one] a thief is   and

λῃστής· **2** ὁ δὲ εἰσερχόμενος διὰ τῆς
a robber; but the [one] entering through the

θύρας ποιμήν ἐστιν τῶν προβάτων. **3** τούτῳ
door shepherd is of the sheep.   To this [one]

ὁ θυρωρὸς ἀνοίγει, καὶ τὰ πρόβατα τῆς
the doorkeeper opens, and the sheep the

φωνῆς αὐτοῦ ἀκούει, καὶ τὰ ἴδια πρόβατα
voice of him hears, and the(his) own sheep

φωνεῖ κατ' ὄνομα καὶ ἐξάγει αὐτά.
he calls by name and leads out them.

4 ὅταν τὰ ἴδια πάντα ἐκβάλῃ, ἔμπροσθεν
When the(his) own all he puts forth, in front of

Chapter 10

The Shepherd and His Flock

" I TELL you the truth, the man who does not enter the sheep pen by the gate, but climbs in by some other way, is a thief and a robber. 2 The man who enters by the gate is the shepherd of his sheep. 3 The watchman opens the gate for him, and the sheep listen to his voice. He calls his own sheep by name and leads them out. 4 When he has the sheep follow him because they know his voice. 5They will not follow a stranger, but they will run from him because they do not know the voice of strangers." 6Jesus used this figure of speech with them, but they did not understand what he was saying to them.

7 So again Jesus said to them, "Very truly, I tell you, I am the gate for the sheep. 8All who came before me are thieves and bandits; but the sheep did not listen to them. 9I am the gate. Whoever enters by me will be saved, and will come in and go out and find pasture. 10The thief comes only to steal and kill and destroy. I came that they may have life, and have it abundantly.

11 "I am the good shepherd. The good shepherd lays down his life for the sheep. 12The hired hand, who is not the shepherd and does not own the sheep, sees the wolf coming and leaves the sheep and runs away—and the wolf snatches them and scatters them. 13The hired hand runs away because a hired hand does not care for the sheep. 14I am the good shepherd. I know my own and my own know me, 15just as the Father knows me and I know the Father. And I lay down my life for the sheep. 16I have other sheep that do not belong to this fold. I must bring them

αὐτῶν πορεύεται, καὶ τὰ πρόβατα αὐτῷ
them he goes, and the sheep him

ἀκολουθεῖ, ὅτι οἴδασιν τὴν φωνὴν αὐτοῦ·
follows, because they know the voice of him;

5 ἀλλοτρίῳ δὲ οὐ μὴ ἀκολουθήσουσιν,
but a stranger by no means will they follow,

ἀλλὰ φεύξονται ἀπ' αὐτοῦ, ὅτι οὐκ
but will flee from him, because not

οἴδασιν τῶν ἀλλοτρίων τὴν φωνήν.
they know of the strangers the voice.

6 Ταύτην τὴν παροιμίαν εἶπεν αὐτοῖς ὁ
This - allegory told them -

Ἰησοῦς· ἐκεῖνοι δὲ οὐκ ἔγνωσαν τίνα
Jesus; but those men knew not what things

ἦν ἃ ἐλάλει αὐτοῖς. 7 Εἶπεν οὖν πάλιν
they were which he spoke to them. Said therefore again

ὁ Ἰησοῦς· ἀμὴν ἀμὴν λέγω ὑμῖν ὅτι
- Jesus: Truly truly I say to you that

ἐγώ εἰμι ἡ θύρα τῶν προβάτων. 8 πάντες
I am the door of the sheep. All

ὅσοι ἦλθον πρὸ ἐμοῦ κλέπται εἰσὶν καὶ
who came before me thieves are and

λησταί· ἀλλ' οὐκ ἤκουσαν αὐτῶν τὰ
robbers; but did not hear them the

πρόβατα. 9 ἐγώ εἰμι ἡ θύρα· δι' ἐμοῦ
sheep. I am the door; through me

ἐάν τις εἰσέλθῃ, σωθήσεται, καὶ εἰσελεύ-
if anyone enters, he will be saved, and will go

σεται καὶ ἐξελεύσεται καὶ νομὴν εὑρήσει.
in and will go out and pasture will find.

10 ὁ κλέπτης οὐκ ἔρχεται εἰ μὴ ἵνα
The thief comes not except that

κλέψῃ καὶ θύσῃ καὶ ἀπολέσῃ· ἐγὼ ἦλθον
he may steal and kill and destroy; I came

ἵνα ζωὴν ἔχωσιν καὶ περισσὸν ἔχωσιν.
that life they may have and abundantly they may have.

11 Ἐγώ εἰμι ὁ ποιμὴν ὁ καλός. ὁ
I am the shepherd - good. The

ποιμὴν ὁ καλὸς τὴν ψυχὴν αὐτοῦ τίθησιν
shepherd - good the life of him lays down

ὑπὲρ τῶν προβάτων· 12 ὁ μισθωτὸς καὶ
for the sheep; the hireling and

οὐκ ὢν ποιμήν, οὗ οὐκ ἔστιν τὰ πρόβατα
not being a shepherd, of whom is(are) not the sheep

ἴδια, θεωρεῖ τὸν λύκον ἐρχόμενον καὶ
[his] own, beholds the wolf coming and

ἀφίησιν τὰ πρόβατα καὶ φεύγει, — καὶ
leaves the sheep and flees, — and

ὁ λύκος ἁρπάζει αὐτὰ καὶ σκορπίζει· —
the wolf seizes them and scatters; —

13 ὅτι μισθωτός ἐστιν καὶ οὐ μέλει
because a hireling he is and it matters not

αὐτῷ περὶ τῶν προβάτων. 14 ἐγώ εἰμι
to him about the sheep. I am

ὁ ποιμὴν ὁ καλός, καὶ γινώσκω τὰ
the shepherd - good, and I know the

ἐμὰ καὶ γινώσκουσί με τὰ ἐμά, 15 καθὼς
mine and ²know ³me ¹mine, as

γινώσκει με ὁ πατὴρ κἀγὼ γινώσκω τὸν
³knows ⁴me ¹the ²Father and I know the

πατέρα, καὶ τὴν ψυχὴν μου τίθημι ὑπὲρ
Father, and the life of me I lay down for

τῶν προβάτων. 16 καὶ ἄλλα πρόβατα
the sheep. And other sheep

ἔχω ἃ οὐκ ἔστιν ἐκ τῆς αὐλῆς ταύτης·
I have which is(are) not of - fold this;

brought out all his own, he goes on ahead of them, and his sheep follow him because they know his voice. 5But they will never follow a stranger; in fact, they will run away from him because they do not recognize a stranger's voice." 6Jesus used this figure of speech, but they did not understand what he was telling them.

7Therefore Jesus said again, "I tell you the truth, I am the gate for the sheep. 8All who ever came before me were thieves and robbers, but the sheep did not listen to them. 9I am the gate; whoever enters through me will be saved. ʷ He will come in and go out, and find pasture. 10The thief comes only to steal and kill and destroy; I have come that they may have life, and have it to the full.

11"I am the good shepherd. The good shepherd lays down his life for the sheep. 12The hired hand is not the shepherd who owns the sheep. So when he sees the wolf coming, he abandons the sheep and runs away. Then the wolf attacks the flock and scatters it. 13The man runs away because he is a hired hand and cares nothing for the sheep.

14"I am the good shepherd; I know my sheep and my sheep know me— 15just as the Father knows me and I know the Father— and I lay down my life for the sheep. 16I have other sheep that are not of this

ʷ 9 Or kept safe

also, and they will listen to my voice. So there will be one flock, one shepherd. 17 For this reason the Father loves me, because I lay down my life in order to take it up again. 18 No one takes[x] it from me, but I lay it down of my own accord. I have power to lay it down, and I have power to take it up again. I have received this command from my Father."

19 Again the Jews were divided because of these words. 20 Many of them were saying, "He has a demon and is out of his mind. Why listen to him?" 21 Others were saying, "These are not the words of one who has a demon. Can a demon open the eyes of the blind?"

Jesus Is Rejected by the Jews

22 At that time the festival of the Dedication took place in Jerusalem. It was winter, 23 and Jesus was walking in the temple, in the portico of Solomon. 24 So the Jews gathered around him and said to him, "How long will you keep us in suspense? If you are the Messiah,[y] tell us plainly." 25 Jesus answered, "I have told you, and you do not believe. The works that I do in my Father's name testify to me; 26 but you do not believe, because you do not belong to my sheep. 27 My sheep hear my voice. I know them, and they follow me. 28 I give them eternal life, and they will never

Center column (interlinear Greek):

κἀκεῖνα δεῖ με ἀγαγεῖν, καὶ τῆς φωνῆς
those also it behoves me to bring, and the voice
μου ἀκούσουσιν, καὶ γενήσεται μία ποίμνη,
of me they will hear, and there will become one flock,
εἷς ποιμήν. 17 διὰ τοῦτό με ὁ πατὴρ
one shepherd. Therefore me the Father
ἀγαπᾷ ὅτι ἐγὼ τίθημι τὴν ψυχήν μου,
loves because I lay down the life of me,
ἵνα πάλιν λάβω αὐτήν. 18 οὐδεὶς ἦρεν
that again I may take it. No one took
αὐτὴν ἀπ' ἐμοῦ, ἀλλ' ἐγὼ τίθημι αὐτὴν
it from me, but I lay down it
ἀπ' ἐμαυτοῦ. ἐξουσίαν ἔχω θεῖναι αὐτήν,
from myself. Authority I have to lay down it,
καὶ ἐξουσίαν ἔχω πάλιν λαβεῖν αὐτήν·
and authority I have again to take it;
ταύτην τὴν ἐντολὴν ἔλαβον παρὰ τοῦ
this - commandment I received from the
πατρός μου. 19 Σχίσμα πάλιν ἐγένετο ἐν
Father of me. A division again there was among
τοῖς Ἰουδαίοις διὰ τοὺς λόγους τούτους.
the Jews because of - words these.
20 ἔλεγον δὲ πολλοὶ ἐξ αὐτῶν· δαιμόνιον
And said many of them: A demon
ἔχει καὶ μαίνεται· τί αὐτοῦ ἀκούετε;
he has and raves; why him hear ye?
21 ἄλλοι ἔλεγον· ταῦτα τὰ ῥήματα οὐκ
Others said: These - words not
ἔστιν δαιμονιζομένου· μὴ δαιμόνιον δύναται
is(are) of one demon-possessed; not a demon can
τυφλῶν ὀφθαλμοὺς ἀνοῖξαι;
of blind men eyes to open?
22 Ἐγένετο τότε τὰ ἐγκαίνια ἐν τοῖς
There was then the Dedication in -
Ἱεροσολύμοις· χειμὼν ἦν· 23 καὶ περιεπάτει
Jerusalem; winter it was; and walked
ὁ Ἰησοῦς ἐν τῷ ἱερῷ ἐν τῇ στοᾷ τοῦ
- Jesus in the temple in the porch
Σολομῶνος. 24 ἐκύκλωσαν οὖν αὐτὸν οἱ
of Solomon. Surrounded therefore him the
Ἰουδαῖοι καὶ ἔλεγον αὐτῷ· ἕως πότε
Jews and said to him: Until when
τὴν ψυχὴν ἡμῶν αἴρεις; εἰ σὺ εἶ
the life(soul) of us holdest thou *? if thou art
ὁ χριστός, εἰπὸν ἡμῖν παρρησίᾳ. 25 ἀπεκρίθη
the Christ, tell us plainly. Answered
αὐτοῖς ὁ Ἰησοῦς· εἶπον ὑμῖν, καὶ
them - Jesus: I told you, and
οὐ πιστεύετε· τὰ ἔργα ἃ ἐγὼ ποιῶ ἐν τῷ
ye do not believe; the works which I do in the
ὀνόματι τοῦ πατρός μου, ταῦτα μαρτυρεῖ
name of the Father of me, these witnesses
περὶ ἐμοῦ· 26 ἀλλὰ ὑμεῖς οὐ πιστεύετε,
concerning me; but ye do not believe,
ὅτι οὐκ ἐστὲ ἐκ τῶν προβάτων τῶν
because ye are not of the sheep
ἐμῶν. 27 τὰ πρόβατα τὰ ἐμὰ τῆς φωνῆς
my. the sheep - My the voice
μου ἀκούσουσιν, κἀγὼ γινώσκω αὐτά, καὶ
of me hear, and I know them, and
ἀκολουθοῦσίν μοι, 28 κἀγὼ δίδωμι αὐτοῖς
they follow me, and I give to them
ζωὴν αἰώνιον, καὶ οὐ μὴ ἀπόλωνται εἰς
life eternal, and by no means they perish unto

sheep pen. I must bring them also. They too will listen to my voice, and there shall be one flock and one shepherd. 17 The reason my Father loves me is that I lay down my life—only to take it up again. 18 No one takes it from me, but I lay it down of my own accord. I have authority to lay it down and authority to take it up again. This command I received from my Father."

19 At these words the Jews were again divided. 20 Many of them said, "He is demon-possessed and raving mad. Why listen to him?" 21 But others said, "These are not the sayings of a man possessed by a demon. Can a demon open the eyes of the blind?"

The Unbelief of the Jews

22 Then came the Feast of Dedication[z] at Jerusalem. It was winter, 23 and Jesus was in the temple area walking in Solomon's Colonnade. 24 The Jews gathered around him, saying, "How long will you keep us in suspense? If you are the Christ,[y] tell us plainly."

25 Jesus answered, "I did tell you, but you do not believe. The miracles I do in my Father's name speak for me, 26 but you do not believe because you are not my sheep. 27 My sheep listen to my voice; I know them, and they follow me. 28 I give them eternal life, and they shall never perish;

x Other ancient authorities read *has taken*
y Or *the Christ*
* That is, in suspense.
z22 That is, Hanukkah
y24 Or *Messiah*

perish. No one will snatch them out of my hand. ²⁹What my Father has given me is greater than all else, and no one can snatch it out of the Father's hand. ᶻ ³⁰The Father and I are one."

31 The Jews took up stones again to stone him. ³²Jesus replied, "I have shown you many good works from the Father. For which of these are you going to stone me?" ³³The Jews answered, "It is not for a good work that we are going to stone you, but for blasphemy, because you, though only a human being, are making yourself God." ³⁴Jesus answered, "Is it not written in your law,ᵃ 'I said, you are gods'? ³⁵If those to whom the word of God came were called 'gods'—and the scripture cannot be annulled— ³⁶can you say that the one whom the Father has sanctified and sent into the world is blaspheming because I said, 'I am God's Son'? ³⁷If I am not doing the works of my Father, then do not believe me. ³⁸But if I do them, even though you do not believe me, believe the works, so that you may know and understandᵇ that the Father is in me and I am in the Father." ³⁹Then they tried to arrest him again, but he escaped from their hands.

40 He went away again across the Jordan to the place where John had been baptizing earlier, and he remained there. ⁴¹Many came to him, and they were

τὸν αἰῶνα, καὶ οὐχ ἁρπάσει τις αὐτὰ
the age, and ²shall not seize ¹anyone them

ἐκ τῆς χειρός μου. 29 ὁ πατήρ μου ὁ
out of the hand of me. The Father of me who

δέδωκέν μοι πάντων μεῖζόν ἐστιν, καὶ
has given to me [than] all greater is, and

οὐδεὶς δύναται ἁρπάζειν ἐκ τῆς χειρὸς
no one can to seize out of the hand

τοῦ πατρός. 30 ἐγὼ καὶ ὁ πατὴρ ἕν
of the Father. I and the Father one

ἐσμεν. 31 Ἐβάστασαν πάλιν λίθους οἱ
we are. Lifted again stones the

Ἰουδαῖοι ἵνα λιθάσωσιν αὐτόν. 32 ἀπ-
Jews that they might stone him. An-

εκρίθη αὐτοῖς ὁ Ἰησοῦς· πολλὰ ἔργα
swered them Jesus: Many ²works

ἔδειξα ὑμῖν καλὰ ἐκ τοῦ πατρός· διὰ
³I showed ⁴you ¹good of the Father; because of

ποῖον αὐτῶν ἔργον ἐμὲ λιθάζετε;
which ²of them ¹work ⁴me ³stone ye?

33 ἀπεκρίθησαν αὐτῷ οἱ Ἰουδαῖοι· περὶ
Answered him the Jews: Concerning

καλοῦ ἔργου οὐ λιθάζομέν σε ἀλλὰ περὶ
a good work we do not stone thee but concerning

βλασφημίας, καὶ ὅτι σὺ ἄνθρωπος ὢν
blasphemy, and because thou a man being

ποιεῖς σεαυτὸν θεόν. 34 ἀπεκρίθη αὐτοῖς
makest thyself God. Answered them

ὁ Ἰησοῦς· οὐκ ἔστιν γεγραμμένον ἐν τῷ
- Jesus : Is it not *having been* written in the

νόμῳ ὑμῶν ὅτι ἐγὼ εἶπα· θεοί ἐστε;
law of you[,] - I said : Gods ye are?

35 εἰ ἐκείνους εἶπεν θεοὺς πρὸς οὓς ὁ
¹if ²those ³he called ⁴gods with whom the

λόγος τοῦ θεοῦ ἐγένετο, καὶ οὐ δύναται
word - of God was, and cannot

λυθῆναι ἡ γραφή, 36 ὃν ὁ πατὴρ
to be broken the scripture, ²[him] whom ¹the ³Father

ἡγίασεν καὶ ἀπέστειλεν εἰς τὸν κόσμον
⁴sanctified ⁵and ⁶sent ⁷into ¹⁰the ¹¹world

ὑμεῖς λέγετε ὅτι βλασφημεῖς, ὅτι εἶπον·
¹ye ¹tell[,] - Thou blasphemest, because I said :

υἱὸς τοῦ θεοῦ εἰμι; 37 εἰ οὐ ποιῶ τὰ ἔργα
Son - of God I am? If I do not the works

τοῦ πατρός μου, μὴ πιστεύετέ μοι· 38 εἰ δὲ
of the Father of me, do not believe me; but if

ποιῶ, κἂν ἐμοὶ μὴ πιστεύητε, τοῖς ἔργοις
I do, even if me ye do not believe, the works

πιστεύετε, ἵνα γνῶτε καὶ γινώσκητε
believe, that ye may know* and continue to know*

ὅτι ἐν ἐμοὶ ὁ πατὴρ κἀγὼ ἐν τῷ πατρί.
that in me the Father [is] and I in the Father.

39 Ἐζήτουν οὖν αὐτὸν πάλιν πιάσαι· καὶ
They sought therefore him again to arrest; and

ἐξῆλθεν ἐκ τῆς χειρὸς αὐτῶν.
he went forth out of the hand of them.

40 Καὶ ἀπῆλθεν πάλιν πέραν τοῦ
And he went away again across the

Ἰορδάνου εἰς τὸν τόπον ὅπου ἦν Ἰωάννης
Jordan to the place where was John

τὸ πρῶτον βαπτίζων, καὶ ἔμενεν ἐκεῖ.
at first baptizing, and remained there.

41 καὶ πολλοὶ ἦλθον πρὸς αὐτὸν καὶ
And · many came to him and

no one can snatch them out of my hand. ²⁹My Father, who has given them to me, is greater than allᶻ; no one can snatch them out of my Father's hand. ³⁰I and the Father are one."

³¹Again the Jews picked up stones to stone him, ³²but Jesus said to them, "I have shown you many great miracles from the Father. For which of these do you stone me?"

³³"We are not stoning you for any of these," replied the Jews, "but for blasphemy, because you, a mere man, claim to be God."

³⁴Jesus answered them, "Is it not written in your Law, 'I have said you are gods'ᵃ? ³⁵If he called them 'gods,' to whom the word of God came—and the Scripture cannot be broken— ³⁶what about the one whom the Father set apart as his very own and sent into the world? Why then do you accuse me of blasphemy because I said, 'I am God's Son'? ³⁷Do not believe me unless I do what my Father does. ³⁸But if I do it, even though you do not believe me, believe the miracles, that you may know and understand that the Father is in me, and I in the Father." ³⁹Again they tried to seize him, but he escaped their grasp.

⁴⁰Then Jesus went back across the Jordan to the place where John had been baptizing in the early days. Here he stayed ⁴¹and many people came to him. They

ᶻ Other ancient authorities read *My Father who has given them to me is greater than all, and no one can snatch them out of the Father's hand*
ᵃ Other ancient authorities read *in the law*
ᵇ Other ancient authorities lack *and understand*; others read *and believe*

* Different tenses (aorist and present) of the same verb.

ᶻ29 Many early manuscripts *What my Father has given me is greater than all*
ᵃ34 Psalm 82:6

saying, "John performed no sign, but everything that John said about this man was true." 42 And many believed in him there.

Chapter 11

The Death of Lazarus

NOW a certain man was ill, Lazarus of Bethany, the village of Mary and her sister Martha. 2 Mary was the one who anointed the Lord with perfume and wiped his feet with her hair; her brother Lazarus was ill. 3 So the sisters sent a message to Jesus,c "Lord, he whom you love is ill." 4 But when Jesus heard it, he said, "This illness does not lead to death; rather it is for God's glory, so that the Son of God may be glorified through it." 5 Accordingly, though Jesus loved Martha and her sister and Lazarus, 6 after having heard that Lazarusd was ill, he stayed two days longer in the place where he was.

7 Then after this he said to the disciples, "Let us go to Judea again." 8 The disciples said to him, "Rabbi, the Jews were just now trying to stone you, and are you going there again?" 9 Jesus answered, "Are there not twelve hours of daylight? Those who walk during the day do not stumble, because they see the light of this world. 10 But those who walk at night stumble, because the light is not in them." 11 After saying this, he told them, "Our friend Lazarus has

ἔλεγον ὅτι Ἰωάννης μὲν σημεῖον ἐποίησεν
said[,] – John indeed sign did
οὐδέν, πάντα δὲ ὅσα εἶπεν Ἰωάννης περὶ
none, but all things how many said John about
τούτου ἀληθῆ ἦν. 42 καὶ πολλοὶ ἐπίστευσαν
this man true was(were). And many believed
εἰς αὐτὸν ἐκεῖ.
in him there.

11 Ἦν δέ τις ἀσθενῶν, Λάζαρος ἀπὸ
Now there was a certain [man] ailing, Lazarus from
Βηθανίας, ἐκ τῆς κώμης Μαρίας καὶ
Bethany, of the village of Mary and
Μάρθας τῆς ἀδελφῆς αὐτῆς. 2 ἦν δὲ
Martha the sister of her. And it was
Μαριὰμ ἡ ἀλείψασα τὸν κύριον μύρῳ
Mary the [one] anointing the Lord with ointment
καὶ ἐκμάξασα τοὺς πόδας αὐτοῦ ταῖς
and wiping off the feet of him with the
θριξὶν αὐτῆς, ἧς ὁ ἀδελφὸς Λάζαρος
hairs of her, of whom the brother Lazarus
ἠσθένει. 3 ἀπέστειλαν οὖν αἱ ἀδελφαὶ
ailed. Sent therefore the sisters
πρὸς αὐτὸν λέγουσαι· κύριε, ἴδε ὃν
to him saying: Lord, behold[,] [he] whom
φιλεῖς ἀσθενεῖ. 4 ἀκούσας δὲ ὁ Ἰησοῦς
thou lovest ails. And hearing – Jesus
εἶπεν· αὕτη ἡ ἀσθένεια οὐκ ἔστιν πρὸς
said: This – ailment is not to
θάνατον ἀλλ᾽ ὑπὲρ τῆς δόξης τοῦ θεοῦ,
death but for the glory – of God,
ἵνα δοξασθῇ ὁ υἱὸς τοῦ θεοῦ δι᾽ αὐτῆς.
that may be glorified the Son – of God through it.
5 ἠγάπα δὲ ὁ Ἰησοῦς τὴν Μάρθαν καὶ
Now 3loved – 1Jesus – Martha and
τὴν ἀδελφὴν αὐτῆς καὶ τὸν Λάζαρον.
the sister of her and – Lazarus.
6 ὡς οὖν ἤκουσεν ὅτι ἀσθενεῖ, τότε μὲν
When therefore he heard that he ails(ed), then –
ἔμεινεν ἐν ᾧ ἦν τόπῳ δύο ἡμέρας·
he remained 1in 3which 4he was 3place two days;
7 ἔπειτα μετὰ τοῦτο λέγει τοῖς μαθηταῖς·
then after this he says to the disciples:
ἄγωμεν εἰς τὴν Ἰουδαίαν πάλιν. 8 λέγουσιν
Let us go into – Judæa again. Say
αὐτῷ οἱ μαθηταί· ῥαββί, νῦν ἐζήτουν
to him the disciples: Rabbi, 4now 5were 6seeking
σε λιθάσαι οἱ Ἰουδαῖοι, καὶ πάλιν ὑπάγεις
7thee 6to stone 1the 2Jews, and again goest thou
ἐκεῖ; 9 ἀπεκρίθη Ἰησοῦς· οὐχὶ δώδεκα
there? Answered Jesus: Not twelve
ὧραί εἰσιν τῆς ἡμέρας; ἐάν τις περιπατῇ
hours are there of the day? if anyone walks
ἐν τῇ ἡμέρᾳ, οὐ προσκόπτει, ὅτι τὸ φῶς
in the day, he does not stumble, because the light
τοῦ κόσμου τούτου βλέπει· 10 ἐὰν δὲ
– world of this he sees; but if
τις περιπατῇ ἐν τῇ νυκτί, προσκόπτει,
anyone walks in the night, he stumbles,
ὅτι τὸ φῶς οὐκ ἔστιν ἐν αὐτῷ. 11 ταῦτα
because the light is not in him. These things
εἶπεν, καὶ μετὰ τοῦτο λέγει αὐτοῖς·
he said, and after this he says to them:
Λάζαρος ὁ φίλος ἡμῶν κεκοίμηται· ἀλλὰ
Lazarus the friend of us has fallen asleep; but

said, "Though John never performed a miraculous sign, all that John said about this man was true." 42 And in that place many believed in Jesus.

Chapter 11

The Death of Lazarus

NOW a man named Lazarus was sick. He was from Bethany, the village of Mary and her sister Martha. 2 This Mary, whose brother Lazarus now lay sick, was the same one who poured perfume on the Lord and wiped his feet with her hair. 3 So the sisters sent word to Jesus, "Lord, the one you love is sick."

4 When he heard this, Jesus said, "This sickness will not end in death. No, it is for God's glory so that God's Son may be glorified through it." 5 Jesus loved Martha and her sister and Lazarus. 6 Yet when he heard that Lazarus was sick, he stayed where he was two more days.

7 Then he said to his disciples, "Let us go back to Judea."

8 "But Rabbi," they said, "a short while ago the Jews tried to stone you, and yet you are going back there?"

9 Jesus answered, "Are there not twelve hours of daylight? A man who walks by day will not stumble, for he sees by this world's light. 10 It is when he walks by night that he stumbles, for he has no light."

11 After he had said this, he went on to tell them, "Our friend Lazarus has

c Gk him
d Gk he

fallen asleep, but I am going there to awaken him."
12 The disciples said to him, "Lord, if he has fallen asleep, he will be all right."
13 Jesus, however, had been speaking about his death, but they thought that he was referring merely to sleep. 14 Then Jesus told them plainly, "Lazarus is dead. 15 For your sake I am glad I was not there, so that you may believe. But let us go to him." 16 Thomas, who was called the Twin,[e] said to his fellow disciples, "Let us also go, that we may die with him."

Jesus the Resurrection and the Life

17 When Jesus arrived, he found that Lazarus[d] had already been in the tomb four days. 18 Now Bethany was near Jerusalem, some two miles[f] away, 19 and many of the Jews had come to Martha and Mary to console them about their brother. 20 When Martha heard that Jesus was coming, she went and met him, while Mary stayed at home. 21 Martha said to Jesus, "Lord, if you had been here, my brother would not have died. 22 But even now I know that God will give you whatever you ask of him." 23 Jesus said to her, "Your brother will rise again." 24 Martha said to him, "I know that he will rise again in the resurrection on the last day." 25 Jesus said to her, "I am the resurrection and the life.[g] Those who believe in me, even though they die, will live, 26 and everyone who lives and believes in me will never die. Do you believe this?" 27 She said to

---

πορεύομαι ἵνα ἐξυπνίσω αὐτόν. **12** εἶπαν
I am going that I may awaken him.   Said

οὖν οἱ μαθηταὶ αὐτῷ· κύριε, εἰ κεκοίμηται,
there- the disciples to him: Lord, if he has fallen asleep,
fore

σωθήσεται. **13** εἰρήκει δὲ ὁ Ἰησοῦς περὶ
he will be healed. Now had spoken - Jesus concerning

τοῦ θανάτου αὐτοῦ· ἐκεῖνοι δὲ ἔδοξαν ὅτι
the death of him; but those men thought that

περὶ τῆς κοιμήσεως τοῦ ὕπνου λέγει.
concerning the sleep - of slumber he says.

14 τότε οὖν εἶπεν αὐτοῖς ὁ Ἰησοῦς
Then therefore told them - Jesus

παρρησίᾳ· Λάζαρος ἀπέθανεν, **15** καὶ χαίρω
plainly: Lazarus died,   and I rejoice

δι' ὑμᾶς, ἵνα πιστεύσητε, ὅτι οὐκ ἤμην
because of you, that ye may believe, that I was not

ἐκεῖ· ἀλλὰ ἄγωμεν πρὸς αὐτόν. **16** εἶπεν
there; but let us go to him.   Said

οὖν Θωμᾶς ὁ λεγόμενος Δίδυμος τοῖς
therefore Thomas - being called Twin to the(his)

συμμαθηταῖς· ἄγωμεν καὶ ἡμεῖς ἵνα
fellow-disciples : Let go also we(us) that

ἀποθάνωμεν μετ' αὐτοῦ. **17** Ἐλθὼν οὖν
we may die with him.   Coming therefore

ὁ Ἰησοῦς εὗρεν αὐτὸν τέσσαρας ἤδη
- Jesus found him ²four ¹already

ἡμέρας ἔχοντα ἐν τῷ μνημείῳ. **18** ἦν δὲ
³days having(being) in the tomb.   Now was

Βηθανία ἐγγὺς τῶν Ἱεροσολύμων ὡς ἀπὸ
Bethany near - Jerusalem about ²away

σταδίων δεκαπέντε. **19** πολλοὶ δὲ ἐκ τῶν
¹furlongs ¹fifteen.   And many of the

Ἰουδαίων ἐληλύθεισαν πρὸς τὴν Μάρθαν
Jews had come to - Martha

καὶ Μαριάμ, ἵνα παραμυθήσωνται αὐτὰς
and Mary, that they might console them

περὶ τοῦ ἀδελφοῦ. **20** ἡ οὖν Μάρθα ὡς
concerning the(ir) brother. - Therefore Martha when

ἤκουσεν ὅτι Ἰησοῦς ἔρχεται, ὑπήντησεν
she heard that Jesus is(was) coming, met

αὐτῷ· Μαριὰμ δὲ ἐν τῷ οἴκῳ ἐκαθέζετο.
him; but Mary - in the house sat.

21 εἶπεν οὖν ἡ Μάρθα πρὸς Ἰησοῦν·
Said therefore - Martha to Jesus :

κύριε, εἰ ἦς ὧδε, οὐκ ἂν ἀπέθανεν ὁ
Lord, if thou wast here, would not have died the

ἀδελφός μου. **22** καὶ νῦν οἶδα ὅτι ὅσα ἂν
brother of me. And now I know that whatever things

αἰτήσῃ τὸν θεὸν δώσει σοι ὁ θεός.
thou askest - God will give ²thee - ¹God.

23 λέγει αὐτῇ ὁ Ἰησοῦς· ἀναστήσεται ὁ
Says to her - Jesus : Will rise again the

ἀδελφός σου. **24** λέγει αὐτῷ ἡ Μάρθα·
brother of thee. Says to him the Martha :

οἶδα ὅτι ἀναστήσεται ἐν τῇ ἀναστάσει
I know that he will rise again in the resurrection

ἐν τῇ ἐσχάτῃ ἡμέρᾳ. **25** εἶπεν αὐτῇ ὁ
in the last day.   Said to her -

Ἰησοῦς· ἐγώ εἰμι ἡ ἀνάστασις καὶ ἡ
Jesus : I am the resurrection and the

ζωή· ὁ πιστεύων εἰς ἐμὲ κἂν ἀποθάνῃ
life; the [one] believing in me even if he should die

ζήσεται, **26** καὶ πᾶς ὁ ζῶν καὶ πιστεύων
will live, and everyone living and believing

εἰς ἐμὲ οὐ μὴ ἀποθάνῃ εἰς τὸν αἰῶνα·
in me by no means dies unto the age :

---

fallen asleep; but I am going there to wake him up."
12 His disciples replied, "Lord, if he sleeps, he will get better." 13 Jesus had been speaking of his death, but his disciples thought he meant natural sleep.
14 So then he told them plainly, "Lazarus is dead, 15 and for your sake I am glad I was not there, so that you may believe. But let us go to him."
16 Then Thomas (called Didymus) said to the rest of the disciples, "Let us also go, that we may die with him."

Jesus Comforts the Sisters

17 On his arrival, Jesus found that Lazarus had already been in the tomb for four days. 18 Bethany was less than two miles[b] from Jerusalem, 19 and many Jews had come to Martha and Mary to comfort them in the loss of their brother. 20 When Martha heard that Jesus was coming, she went out to meet him, but Mary stayed at home.
21 "Lord," Martha said to Jesus, "if you had been here, my brother would not have died. 22 But I know that even now God will give you whatever you ask."
23 Jesus said to her, "Your brother will rise again."
24 Martha answered, "I know he will rise again in the resurrection at the last day."
25 Jesus said to her, "I am the resurrection and the life. He who believes in me will live, even though he dies; 26 and whoever lives and believes in me will never die. Do you believe this?"

---

e Gk Didymus
f Gk fifteen stadia
g Other ancient authorities lack and the life

b 18 Greek fifteen stadia (about 3 kilometers)

him, "Yes, Lord, I believe that you are the Messiah,[h] the Son of God, the one coming into the world."

Jesus Weeps

28 When she had said this, she went back and called her sister Mary, and told her privately, "The Teacher is here and is calling for you." 29 And when she heard it, she got up quickly and went to him. 30 Now Jesus had not yet come to the village, but was still at the place where Martha had met him. 31 The Jews who were with her in the house, consoling her, saw Mary get up quickly and go out. They followed her because they thought that she was going to the tomb to weep there. 32 When Mary came where Jesus was and saw him, she knelt at his feet and said to him, "Lord, if you had been here, my brother would not have died." 33 When Jesus saw her weeping, and the Jews who came with her also weeping, he was greatly disturbed in spirit and deeply moved. 34 He said, "Where have you laid him?" They said to him, "Lord, come and see." 35 Jesus began to weep. 36 So the Jews said, "See how he loved him!" 37 But some of them said, "Could not he who opened the eyes of the blind man have kept this man from dying?"

Jesus Raises Lazarus to Life

38 Then Jesus, again greatly disturbed, came to the tomb. It was a cave, and a stone was lying

---

πιστεύεις τοῦτο; 27 λέγει αὐτῷ· ναί, κύριε·
believest thou this?　　She says to him: Yes, Lord;

ἐγὼ πεπίστευκα ὅτι σὺ εἶ ὁ χριστὸς ὁ
I　have believed that thou art the Christ the

υἱὸς τοῦ θεοῦ ὁ εἰς τὸν κόσμον ἐρχόμενος.
Son　- of God ¹the ²into ⁴the ³world ⁵[one] coming.

28 καὶ τοῦτο εἰποῦσα ἀπῆλθεν καὶ ἐφώνησεν
And this　saying she went away and called

Μαριὰμ τὴν ἀδελφὴν αὐτῆς λάθρα εἰποῦσα·
Mary the sister of her secretly saying :

ὁ διδάσκαλος πάρεστιν καὶ φωνεῖ σε.
The Teacher　is here and calls thee.

29 ἐκείνη δὲ ὡς ἤκουσεν, ἐγείρεται ταχὺ
And that [one] when she heard,　rose　quickly

καὶ ἤρχετο πρὸς αὐτόν· 30 οὔπω δὲ
and came　to him;　now not yet

ἐληλύθει ὁ Ἰησοῦς εἰς τὴν κώμην, ἀλλ'
had come - Jesus into the village, but

ἦν ἔτι ἐν τῷ τόπῳ ὅπου ὑπήντησεν
was still in the place where met

αὐτῷ ἡ Μάρθα. 31 οἱ οὖν Ἰουδαῖοι
him - Martha. Therefore the Jews

οἱ ὄντες μετ' αὐτῆς ἐν τῇ οἰκίᾳ καὶ
the [ones] being with her in the house and

παραμυθούμενοι αὐτήν, ἰδόντες τὴν Μαριὰμ
consoling her, seeing - Mary

ὅτι ταχέως ἀνέστη καὶ ἐξῆλθεν,
that quickly she rose up and went out,

ἠκολούθησαν αὐτῇ, δόξαντες ὅτι ὑπάγει
followed her, thinking[,] - She is going

εἰς τὸ μνημεῖον ἵνα κλαύσῃ ἐκεῖ. 32 ἡ
to the tomb that she may weep there. -

οὖν Μαριὰμ ὡς ἦλθεν ὅπου ἦν Ἰησοῦς,
Therefore Mary when she came where was Jesus,

ἰδοῦσα αὐτὸν ἔπεσεν αὐτοῦ πρὸς τοὺς
seeing him fell of him at the

πόδας, λέγουσα αὐτῷ· κύριε, εἰ ἧς ὧδε,
feet, saying to him : Lord, if thou wast here,

οὐκ ἄν μου ἀπέθανεν ὁ ἀδελφός.
⁴would not ³of me ⁵have died ¹the ²brother.

33 Ἰησοῦς οὖν ὡς εἶδεν αὐτὴν κλαίουσαν
Jesus therefore when he saw her weeping

καὶ τοὺς συνελθόντας αὐτῇ Ἰουδαίους
and ¹the ²coming with ⁴her ³Jews

κλαίοντας, ἐνεβριμήσατο τῷ πνεύματι καὶ
weeping, groaned in the(his) spirit and

ἐτάραξεν ἑαυτόν, 34 καὶ εἶπεν· ποῦ
troubled himself, and said : Where

τεθείκατε αὐτόν; λέγουσιν αὐτῷ· κύριε,
have ye put him? They say to him : Lord,

ἔρχου καὶ ἴδε. 35 ἐδάκρυσεν ὁ Ἰησοῦς.
come and see. Shed tears - Jesus.

36 ἔλεγον οὖν οἱ Ἰουδαῖοι· ἴδε πῶς
Said therefore the Jews : See how

ἐφίλει αὐτόν. 37 τινὲς δὲ ἐξ αὐτῶν
he loved him. But some of them

εἶπαν· οὐκ ἐδύνατο οὗτος ὁ ἀνοίξας
said : Could not this man the [one] opening

τοὺς ὀφθαλμοὺς τοῦ τυφλοῦ ποιῆσαι ἵνα
the eyes of the blind man to cause that

καὶ οὗτος μὴ ἀποθάνῃ; 38 Ἰησοῦς οὖν
even this man should not die ? Jesus therefore

πάλιν ἐμβριμώμενος ἐν ἑαυτῷ ἔρχεται
again groaning in himself comes

εἰς τὸ μνημεῖον· ἦν δὲ σπήλαιον, καὶ
to the tomb; now it was a cave, and

---

27 "Yes, Lord," she told him, "I believe that you are the Christ,[c] the Son of God, who was to come into the world." 28 And after she had said this, she went back and called her sister Mary aside. "The Teacher is here," she said, "and is asking for you." 29 When Mary heard this, she got up quickly and went to him. 30 Now Jesus had not yet entered the village, but was still at the place where Martha had met him. 31 When the Jews who had been with Mary in the house, comforting her, noticed how quickly she got up and went out, they followed her, supposing she was going to the tomb to mourn there. 32 When Mary reached the place where Jesus was and saw him, she fell at his feet and said, "Lord, if you had been here, my brother would not have died." 33 When Jesus saw her weeping, and the Jews who had come along with her also weeping, he was deeply moved in spirit and troubled. 34 "Where have you laid him?" he asked. "Come and see, Lord," they replied. 35 Jesus wept. 36 Then the Jews said, "See how he loved him!" 37 But some of them said, "Could not he who opened the eyes of the blind man have kept this man from dying?"

Jesus Raises Lazarus From the Dead

38 Jesus, once more deeply moved, came to the tomb. It was a cave with a stone laid across the en-

---

[h] Or *the Christ*　　　　[c]27 Or *Messiah*

against it. 39 Jesus said, "Take away the stone." Martha, the sister of the dead man, said to him, "Lord, already there is a stench because he has been dead four days." 40 Jesus said to her, "Did I not tell you that if you believed, you would see the glory of God?" 41 So they took away the stone. And Jesus looked upward and said, "Father, I thank you for having heard me. 42 I knew that you always hear me, but I have said this for the sake of the crowd standing here, so that they may believe that you sent me." 43 When he had said this, he cried with a loud voice, "Lazarus, come out!" 44 The dead man came out, his hands and feet bound with strips of cloth, and his face wrapped in a cloth. Jesus said to them, "Unbind him, and let him go."

The Plot to Kill Jesus

45 Many of the Jews therefore, who had come with Mary and had seen what Jesus did, believed in him. 46 But some of them went to the Pharisees and told them what he had done. 47 So the chief priests and the Pharisees called a meeting of the council, and said, "What are we to do? This man is performing many signs. 48 If we let him go on like this, everyone will believe in him, and the Romans will come and destroy both our holy place [i] and our nation." 49 But one of them, Caiaphas, who was high priest that year, said to them, "You know

---

λίθος ἐπέκειτο ἐπ' αὐτῷ. **39** λέγει ὁ
a stone was lying on on it. Says –

Ἰησοῦς· ἄρατε τὸν λίθον. λέγει αὐτῷ
Jesus : Lift ye the stone. Says to him

ἡ ἀδελφὴ τοῦ τετελευτηκότος Μάρθα·
the sister of the [one] having died Martha :

κύριε, ἤδη ὄζει· τεταρταῖος γάρ ἐστιν.
Lord, now he smells; for fourth [day] it is.

40 λέγει αὐτῇ ὁ Ἰησοῦς· οὐκ εἶπόν
Says to her – Jesus : Not I told

σοι ὅτι ἐὰν πιστεύσῃς ὄψῃ τὴν δόξαν
thee that if thou believest thou wilt see the glory

τοῦ θεοῦ; **41** ἦραν οὖν τὸν λίθον. ὁ
– of God? They lifted therefore the stone. –

δὲ Ἰησοῦς ἦρεν τοὺς ὀφθαλμοὺς ἄνω
And Jesus lifted the(his) eyes up

καὶ εἶπεν· πάτερ, εὐχαριστῶ σοι ὅτι
and said : Father, I thank thee that

ἤκουσάς μου. **42** ἐγὼ δὲ ᾔδειν ὅτι
thou didst hear me. And I knew that

πάντοτέ μου ἀκούεις· ἀλλὰ διὰ τὸν
always me thou hearest; but because of the

ὄχλον τὸν περιεστῶτα εἶπον, ἵνα
crowd – standing round I said, that

πιστεύσωσιν ὅτι σύ με ἀπέστειλας.
they may believe that thou me didst send.

43 καὶ ταῦτα εἰπὼν φωνῇ μεγάλῃ
And these things saying voice with a great

ἐκραύγασεν· Λάζαρε, δεῦρο ἔξω. **44** ἐξῆλθεν
he cried out : Lazarus, come out. Came out

ὁ τεθνηκὼς δεδεμένος τοὺς πόδας καὶ
the [one] having died *having been* bound the feet and

τὰς χεῖρας κειρίαις, καὶ ἡ ὄψις αὐτοῦ
the hands with bandages, and the face of him

σουδαρίῳ περιεδέδετο. λέγει αὐτοῖς ὁ
with a napkin had been bound round. Says to them –

Ἰησοῦς· λύσατε αὐτὸν καὶ ἄφετε αὐτὸν ὑπάγειν.
Jesus : Loosen him and let him *to go.*

45 Πολλοὶ οὖν ἐκ τῶν Ἰουδαίων, οἱ
Many therefore of the Jews, the [ones]

ἐλθόντες πρὸς τὴν Μαριὰμ καὶ θεασάμενοι
having come to – Mary and having beheld

ὃ ἐποίησεν, ἐπίστευσαν εἰς αὐτόν· **46** τινὲς δὲ
what he did, believed in him; but some

ἐξ αὐτῶν ἀπῆλθον πρὸς τοὺς Φαρισαίους
of them went away to the Pharisees

καὶ εἶπαν αὐτοῖς ἃ ἐποίησεν Ἰησοῦς.
and told them what things did Jesus.

47 συνήγαγον οὖν οἱ ἀρχιερεῖς καὶ οἱ
Assembled therefore the chief priests and the

Φαρισαῖοι συνέδριον, καὶ ἔλεγον· τί
Pharisees a council, and said : What

ποιοῦμεν, ὅτι οὗτος ὁ ἄνθρωπος πολλὰ
are we doing, because this – man [1]many

ποιεῖ σημεῖα; **48** ἐὰν ἀφῶμεν αὐτὸν οὕτως,
[1]does [2]signs? If we leave him thus,

πάντες πιστεύσουσιν εἰς αὐτόν, καὶ
all men will believe in him, and

ἐλεύσονται οἱ Ῥωμαῖοι καὶ ἀροῦσιν ἡμῶν
will come the Romans and will take of us

καὶ τὸν τόπον καὶ τὸ ἔθνος. **49** εἰς
both the place and the nation. [2]one

δέ τις ἐξ αὐτῶν Καϊάφας, ἀρχιερεὺς
[1]But [3]a certain of them[,] Caiaphas, high priest

ὢν τοῦ ἐνιαυτοῦ ἐκείνου, εἶπεν αὐτοῖς·
being – year of that, said to them :

---

trance. 39 "Take away the stone," he said. "But, Lord," said Martha, the sister of the dead man, "by this time there is a bad odor, for he has been there four days." 40 Then Jesus said, "Did I not tell you that if you believed, you would see the glory of God?" 41 So they took away the stone. Then Jesus looked up and said, "Father, I thank you that you have heard me. 42 I knew that you always hear me, but I said this for the benefit of the people standing here, that they may believe that you sent me." 43 When he had said this, Jesus called in a loud voice, "Lazarus, come out!" 44 The dead man came out, his hands and feet wrapped with strips of linen, and a cloth around his face. Jesus said to them, "Take off the grave clothes and let him go."

The Plot to Kill Jesus

45 Therefore many of the Jews who had come to visit Mary, and had seen what Jesus did, put their faith in him. 46 But some of them went to the Pharisees and told them what Jesus had done. 47 Then the chief priests and the Pharisees called a meeting of the Sanhedrin. "What are we accomplishing?" they asked. "Here is this man performing many miraculous signs. 48 If we let him go on like this, everyone will believe in him, and then the Romans will come and take away both our place [d] and our nation." 49 Then one of them, named Caiaphas, who was high priest that year, spoke

---

[i] Or *our temple*; Greek *our place*   [d]48 Or *temple*

nothing at all! 50 You do not understand that it is better for you to have one man die for the people than to have the whole nation destroyed." 51 He did not say this on his own, but being high priest that year he prophesied that Jesus was about to die for the nation, 52 and not for the nation only, but to gather into one the dispersed children of God. 53 So from that day on they planned to put him to death.

54 Jesus therefore no longer walked about openly among the Jews, but went from there to a town called Ephraim in the region near the wilderness; and he remained there with the disciples.

55 Now the Passover of the Jews was near, and many went up from the country to Jerusalem before the Passover to purify themselves. 56 They were looking for Jesus and were asking one another as they stood in the temple, "What do you think? Surely he will not come to the festival, will he?" 57 Now the chief priests and the Pharisees had given orders that anyone who knew where Jesus[j] was should let them know, so that they might arrest him.

ὑμεῖς οὐκ οἴδατε οὐδέν, 50 οὐδὲ λογίζεσθε
Ye know not no(any)thing, nor reckon

ὅτι συμφέρει ὑμῖν ἵνα εἷς ἄνθρωπος
that it is expedient for us that one man

ἀποθάνῃ ὑπὲρ τοῦ λαοῦ καὶ μὴ ὅλον
should die for the people and not all

τὸ ἔθνος ἀπόληται. 51 τοῦτο δὲ ἀφ'
the nation perish. But this from

ἑαυτοῦ οὐκ εἶπεν, ἀλλὰ ἀρχιερεὺς ὢν
himself he said not, but high priest being

τοῦ ἐνιαυτοῦ ἐκείνου ἐπροφήτευσεν ὅτι
- year of that he prophesied that

ἔμελλεν Ἰησοῦς ἀποθνήσκειν ὑπὲρ τοῦ
was about Jesus to die for the

ἔθνους, 52 καὶ οὐχ ὑπὲρ τοῦ ἔθνους
nation, and not for the nation

μόνον, ἀλλ' ἵνα καὶ τὰ τέκνα τοῦ θεοῦ
only, but that also the children - of God

τὰ διεσκορπισμένα συναγάγῃ εἰς ἕν.
- having been scattered he might gather into one.

53 ἀπ' ἐκείνης οὖν τῆς ἡμέρας ἐβουλεύσαντο
From 1that 3therefore - 2day they took counsel

ἵνα ἀποκτείνωσιν αὐτόν. 54 Ὁ οὖν
that they might kill him. - Therefore

Ἰησοῦς οὐκέτι παρρησίᾳ περιεπάτει ἐν
Jesus no longer openly walked among

τοῖς Ἰουδαίοις, ἀλλὰ ἀπῆλθεν ἐκεῖθεν εἰς
the Jews, but went away thence into

τὴν χώραν ἐγγὺς τῆς ἐρήμου, εἰς Ἐφραὶμ
the country near the desert, to 2Ephraim

λεγομένην πόλιν, κἀκεῖ ἔμεινεν μετὰ τῶν
3being called 1a city, and there remained with the

μαθητῶν.
disciples.

55 Ἦν δὲ ἐγγὺς τὸ πάσχα τῶν
Now was near the Passover of the

Ἰουδαίων, καὶ ἀνέβησαν πολλοὶ εἰς
Jews, and went up many to

Ἱεροσόλυμα ἐκ τῆς χώρας πρὸ τοῦ
Jerusalem out of the country before the

πάσχα, ἵνα ἁγνίσωσιν ἑαυτούς.
Passover, that they might purify themselves.

56 ἐζήτουν οὖν τὸν Ἰησοῦν καὶ ἔλεγον
They sought therefore - Jesus and said

μετ' ἀλλήλων ἐν τῷ ἱερῷ ἑστηκότες·
with one another in the temple standing:

τί δοκεῖ ὑμῖν; ὅτι οὐ μὴ ἔλθῃ εἰς
What seems it to you? that by no means he comes to

τὴν ἑορτήν; 57 δεδώκεισαν δὲ οἱ ἀρχιερεῖς
the feast? Now had given the chief priests

καὶ οἱ Φαρισαῖοι ἐντολὰς ἵνα ἐάν τις
and the Pharisees commands that if anyone

γνῷ ποῦ ἐστιν μηνύσῃ, ὅπως πιάσωσιν
knew where he is (was) he should inform, so as they might arrest

αὐτόν. 12 Ὁ οὖν Ἰησοῦς πρὸ ἓξ ἡμερῶν
him. - Therefore Jesus 2before 1six 3days

τοῦ πάσχα ἦλθεν εἰς Βηθανίαν, ὅπου
the Passover came to Bethany, where

ἦν Λάζαρος, ὃν ἤγειρεν ἐκ νεκρῶν
was Lazarus, whom 1raised 2out of [the] 3dead

Ἰησοῦς. 2 ἐποίησαν οὖν αὐτῷ δεῖπνον ἐκεῖ,
1Jesus. They made therefore for him a supper there,

καὶ ἡ Μάρθα διηκόνει, ὁ δὲ Λάζαρος εἷς
and - Martha served, - but Lazarus one

ἦν ἐκ τῶν ἀνακειμένων σὺν αὐτῷ· 3 ἡ
was of the [ones] reclining with him; -

up, "You know nothing at all! 50 You do not realize that it is better for you that one man die for the people than that the whole nation perish."

51 He did not say this on his own, but as high priest that year he prophesied that Jesus would die for the Jewish nation, 52 and not only for that nation but also for the scattered children of God, to bring them together and make them one. 53 So from that day on they plotted to take his life.

54 Therefore Jesus no longer moved about publicly among the Jews. Instead he withdrew to a region near the desert, to a village called Ephraim, where he stayed with his disciples.

55 When it was almost time for the Jewish Passover, many went up from the country to Jerusalem for their ceremonial cleansing before the Passover. 56 They kept looking for Jesus, and as they stood in the temple area they asked one another, "What do you think? Isn't he coming to the Feast at all?" 57 But the chief priests and Pharisees had given orders that if anyone found out where Jesus was, he should report it so that they might arrest him.

Chapter 12

Mary Anoints Jesus

SIX days before the Passover Jesus came to Bethany, the home of Lazarus, whom he had raised from the dead. 2 There they gave a dinner for him. Martha served, and Lazarus was one of those at the table with him. 3 Mary took a pound of

Chapter 12

Jesus Anointed at Bethany

SIX days before the Passover, Jesus arrived at Bethany, where Lazarus lived, whom Jesus had raised from the dead. 2 Here a dinner was given in Jesus' honor. Martha served, while Lazarus was among those reclining at the table with him. 3 Then

[j] Gk he

costly perfume made of pure nard, anointed Jesus' feet, and wiped them[k] with her hair. The house was filled with the fragrance of the perfume. 4 But Judas Iscariot, one of his disciples (the one who was about to betray him), said, 5 "Why was this perfume not sold for three hundred denarii[l] and the money given to the poor?" 6 (He said this not because he cared about the poor, but because he was a thief; he kept the common purse and used to steal what was put into it.) 7 Jesus said, "Leave her alone. She bought it[m] so that she might keep it for the day of my burial. 8 You always have the poor with you, but you do not always have me."

The Plot to Kill Lazarus

9 When the great crowd of the Jews learned that he was there, they came not only because of Jesus but also to see Lazarus, whom he had raised from the dead. 10 So the chief priests planned to put Lazarus to death as well, 11 since it was on account of him that many of the Jews were deserting and were believing in Jesus.

Jesus' Triumphal Entry into Jerusalem

12 The next day the great crowd that had come to the festival heard that Jesus was coming to Jerusalem. 13 So they took branches of palm trees and went out to meet him, shouting,

"Hosanna!

Blessed is the one
who comes in
the name
of the Lord—

οὖν   Μαριὰμ   λαβοῦσα   λίτραν   μύρου
therefore Mary   taking   a pound   ᵃointment

νάρδου   πιστικῆς   πολυτίμου   ἤλειψεν   τοὺς
¹of spikenard ²of pure   ³costly   anointed   the

πόδας   τοῦ   ᾽Ιησοῦ   καὶ   ἐξέμαξεν   ταῖς
feet   of Jesus   and   wiped off   with the

θριξὶν   αὐτῆς   τοὺς   πόδας   αὐτοῦ·   ἡ   δὲ
hairs   of her   the   feet   of him;   and the

οἰκία   ἐπληρώθη   ἐκ   τῆς   ὀσμῆς   τοῦ
house   was filled   of(with)   the   odour   of the

μύρου.   4 λέγει   δὲ   ᾽Ιούδας   ὁ   ᾽Ισκαριώτης
ointment.   And says   Judas   the   Iscariot

εἷς   τῶν   μαθητῶν   αὐτοῦ,   ὁ   μέλλων
one   of the   disciples   of him, the [one] being about

αὐτὸν   παραδιδόναι·   5 διὰ   τί   τοῦτο   τὸ
him   to betray :   Why   this   –

μύρον   οὐκ   ἐπράθη   τριακοσίων   δηναρίων
ointment   not   was sold   of(for) three hundred   denarii

καὶ   ἐδόθη   πτωχοῖς;   6 εἶπεν   δὲ   τοῦτο
and   given   to [the] poor?   But he said   this

οὐχ   ὅτι   περὶ   τῶν   πτωχῶν   ἔμελεν   αὐτῷ,
not because   about   the   poor   it mattered   to him,

ἀλλ᾽   ὅτι   κλέπτης   ἦν   καὶ   τὸ   γλωσσόκομον
but because   a thief   he was   and   ³the   ²bag

ἔχων   τὰ   βαλλόμενα   ἐβάσταζεν. *
¹having   ⁴the things   ⁵being put [in]   ⁶carried. *

7 εἶπεν   οὖν   ὁ   ᾽Ιησοῦς·   ἄφες   αὐτήν,
Said   therefore   –   Jesus :   Leave   her,

ἵνα   εἰς   τὴν   ἡμέραν   τοῦ   ἐνταφιασμοῦ
that   to   the   day   of the   burial

μου   τηρήσῃ   αὐτό·   8 τοὺς   πτωχοὺς   γὰρ
of me   she may keep   it;   ⁴the   ⁵poor   ¹for

πάντοτε   ἔχετε   μεθ᾽   ἑαυτῶν,   ἐμὲ   δὲ
always   ye have   with   yourselves,   but me   –

οὐ   πάντοτε   ἔχετε.   9 Ἔγνω   οὖν   ὁ   ὄχλος
not   always   ye have.   Knew   therefore   the   crowd

πολὺς   ἐκ   τῶν   ᾽Ιουδαίων   ὅτι   ἐκεῖ   ἐστιν,
great   of   the   Jews   that   there   he is(was),

καὶ   ἦλθον   οὐ   διὰ   τὸν   ᾽Ιησοῦν   μόνον,
and   they came   not because of   –   Jesus   only,

ἀλλ᾽   ἵνα   καὶ   τὸν   Λάζαρον   ἴδωσιν   ὃν
but   that   also   –   Lazarus they might see   whom

ἤγειρεν   ἐκ   νεκρῶν.   10 ἐβουλεύσαντο   δὲ
he raised   out of [the] dead.   But took counsel   –

οἱ   ἀρχιερεῖς   ἵνα   καὶ   τὸν   Λάζαρον
the   chief priests   that   also   –   Lazarus

ἀποκτείνωσιν,   11 ὅτι   πολλοὶ   δι᾽   αὐτὸν
they might kill,   because   ¹many   ⁴because of   ⁵him

ὑπῆγον   τῶν   ᾽Ιουδαίων   καὶ   ἐπίστευον   εἰς
⁶went   ²of the   ³Jews   and   believed   in

τὸν   ᾽Ιησοῦν.
–   Jesus.

12 Τῇ   ἐπαύριον   ὁ   ὄχλος   πολὺς   ὁ
On the   morrow   the   crowd   much   –

ἐλθὼν   εἰς   τὴν   ἑορτήν,   ἀκούσαντες   ὅτι
coming   to   the   feast,   hearing   that

ἔρχεται   ᾽Ιησοῦς   εἰς   ᾽Ιεροσόλυμα,   13 ἔλαβον
is(was) coming   Jesus   to   Jerusalem,   took

τὰ   βαΐα   τῶν   φοινίκων   καὶ   ἐξῆλθον   εἰς
the   branches   of the   palm-trees   and   went out   to

ὑπάντησιν   αὐτῷ,   καὶ   ἐκραύγαζον·   ὡσαννά,
a meeting   with him,   and   cried out :   Hosanna,

εὐλογημένος   ὁ   ἐρχόμενος   ἐν   ὀνόματι
being blessed   the [one] coming   in [the]   name

Mary took about a pint[e] of pure nard, an expensive perfume; she poured it on Jesus' feet and wiped his feet with her hair. And the house was filled with the fragrance of the perfume.

4 But one of his disciples, Judas Iscariot, who was later to betray him, objected, 5 "Why wasn't this perfume sold and the money given to the poor? It was worth a year's wages.[f]" 6 He did not say this because he cared about the poor but because he was a thief; as keeper of the money bag, he used to help himself to what was put into it.

7 "Leave her alone," Jesus replied. "It was intended that she should save this perfume for the day of my burial. 8 You will always have the poor among you, but you will not always have me."

9 Meanwhile a large crowd of Jews found out that Jesus was there and came, not only because of him but also to see Lazarus, whom he had raised from the dead. 10 So the chief priests made plans to kill Lazarus as well, 11 for on account of him many of the Jews were going over to Jesus and putting their faith in him.

The Triumphal Entry

12 The next day the great crowd that had come for the Feast heard that Jesus was on his way to Jerusalem. 13 They took palm branches and went out to meet him, shouting,

"Hosanna![g]"

"Blessed is he who
comes in the name
of the Lord!"[h]

---

[k] Gk *his feet*
[l] Three hundred denarii would be nearly a year's wages for a laborer
[m] Gk lacks *She bought it*

* This may mean "stole"; cf. our euphemism for "steal"—to "lift" a thing.

[e]3 Greek *a litra* (probably about 0.5 liter)
[f]5 Greek *three hundred denarii*
[g]13 A Hebrew expression meaning "Save!" which became an exclamation of praise
[h]13 Psalm 118:25, 26

the King of Israel!"
14 Jesus found a young donkey and sat on it; as it is written:
15 "Do not be afraid, daughter of Zion. Look, your king is coming, sitting on a donkey's colt!"
16 His disciples did not understand these things at first; but when Jesus was glorified, then they remembered that these things had been written of him and had been done to him. 17 So the crowd that had been with him when he called Lazarus out of the tomb and raised him from the dead continued to testify.[n] 18 It was also because they heard that he had performed this sign that the crowd went to meet him. 19 The Pharisees said to one another, "You see, you can do nothing. Look, the world has gone after him!"

Some Greeks Wish to See Jesus

20 Now among those who went up to worship at the festival were some Greeks. 21 They came to Philip, who was from Bethsaida in Galilee, and said to him, "Sir, we wish to see Jesus." 22 Philip went and told Andrew; then Andrew and Philip went and told Jesus. 23 Jesus answered them, "The hour has come for the Son of Man to be glorified. 24 Very truly, I tell you, unless a grain of wheat falls into the earth and dies, it remains just a single grain; but if it dies, it bears much fruit. 25 Those who love their life lose it,

---

κυρίου, καὶ ὁ βασιλεὺς τοῦ Ἰσραήλ.
of [the] Lord, and the king - of Israel.
14 εὑρὼν δὲ ὁ Ἰησοῦς ὀνάριον ἐκάθισεν
And ²having found - ¹Jesus a young ass sat
ἐπ' αὐτό, καθώς ἐστιν γεγραμμένον·
on it, as it is *having been* written :
15 μὴ φοβοῦ, θυγάτηρ Σιών· ἰδοὺ ὁ
Fear not, daughter of Sion : behold[,] the
βασιλεύς σου ἔρχεται, καθήμενος ἐπὶ
king of thee comes, sitting on
πῶλον ὄνου. 16 ταῦτα οὐκ ἔγνωσαν
a foal of an ass. These things knew not
αὐτοῦ οἱ μαθηταὶ τὸ πρῶτον, ἀλλ' ὅτε
of him the disciples at first, but when
ἐδοξάσθη Ἰησοῦς, τότε ἐμνήσθησαν ὅτι
was glorified Jesus, then they remembered that
ταῦτα ἦν ἐπ' αὐτῷ γεγραμμένα καὶ
these things were on him *having been* written and
ταῦτα ἐποίησαν αὐτῷ. 17 ἐμαρτύρει οὖν
these things they did to him. Witnessed therefore
ὁ ὄχλος ὁ ὢν μετ' αὐτοῦ ὅτε τὸν
the crowd - being with him when -
Λάζαρον ἐφώνησεν ἐκ τοῦ μνημείου καὶ
Lazarus he called out of the tomb and
ἤγειρεν αὐτὸν ἐκ νεκρῶν. 18 διὰ τοῦτο
raised him out of [the] dead. Therefore
καὶ ὑπήντησεν αὐτῷ ὁ ὄχλος, ὅτι
also met him the crowd, because
ἤκουσαν τοῦτο αὐτὸν πεποιηκέναι τὸ
¹they heard ⁴this ²him ³to have done[b] the
σημεῖον. 19 οἱ οὖν Φαρισαῖοι εἶπαν
⁵sign. Therefore the Pharisees said
πρὸς ἑαυτούς· θεωρεῖτε ὅτι οὐκ ὠφελεῖτε
to themselves : Behold ye that ye profit not
οὐδέν· ἴδε ὁ κόσμος ὀπίσω αὐτοῦ ἀπῆλθεν.
no(any)thing; see[,] the world after him went(is gone).
20 Ἦσαν δὲ Ἕλληνές τινες ἐκ τῶν
Now there were ²Greeks ¹some of the
ἀναβαινόντων ἵνα προσκυνήσωσιν ἐν τῇ
[ones] going up that they might worship at the
ἑορτῇ· 21 οὗτοι οὖν προσῆλθον Φιλίππῳ
feast; these therefore approached *to* Philip
τῷ ἀπὸ Βηθσαϊδὰ τῆς Γαλιλαίας, καὶ
the [one] from Bethsaida of Galilee, and
ἠρώτων αὐτὸν λέγοντες· κύριε, θέλομεν
asked him saying: Sir, we wish
τὸν Ἰησοῦν ἰδεῖν. 22 ἔρχεται ὁ Φίλιππος
- Jesus to see. Comes - Philip
καὶ λέγει τῷ Ἀνδρέᾳ· ἔρχεται Ἀνδρέας
and tells - Andrew; comes Andrew
καὶ Φίλιππος καὶ λέγουσιν τῷ Ἰησοῦ.
and Philip and tell - Jesus.
23 ὁ δὲ Ἰησοῦς ἀποκρίνεται αὐτοῖς λέγων·
- And Jesus answers them saying:
ἐλήλυθεν ἡ ὥρα ἵνα δοξασθῇ ὁ υἱὸς τοῦ
Has come the hour that is glorified the Son -
ἀνθρώπου. 24 ἀμὴν ἀμὴν λέγω ὑμῖν,
of man. Truly truly I say to you,
ἐὰν μὴ ὁ κόκκος τοῦ σίτου πεσὼν εἰς
unless the grain - of wheat falling into
τὴν γῆν ἀποθάνῃ, αὐτὸς μόνος μένει·
the ground dies, it alone remains;
ἐὰν δὲ ἀποθάνῃ, πολὺν καρπὸν φέρει.
but if it dies, much fruit it bears.
25 ὁ φιλῶν τὴν ψυχὴν αὐτοῦ ἀπολλύει
The [one] loving the life of him loses

"Blessed is the King of Israel!"
14 Jesus found a young donkey and sat upon it, as it is written,
15 "Do not be afraid, O Daughter of Zion; see, your king is coming, seated on a donkey's colt."[i]
16 At first his disciples did not understand all this. Only after Jesus was glorified did they realize that these things had been written about him and that they had done these things to him.
17 Now the crowd that was with him when he called Lazarus from the tomb and raised him from the dead continued to spread the word. 18 Many people, because they had heard that he had given this miraculous sign, went out to meet him. 19 So the Pharisees said to one another, "See, this is getting us nowhere. Look how the whole world has gone after him!"

Jesus Predicts His Death

20 Now there were some Greeks among those who went up to worship at the Feast. 21 They came to Philip, who was from Bethsaida in Galilee, with a request. "Sir," they said, "we would like to see Jesus." 22 Philip went to tell Andrew; Andrew and Philip in turn told Jesus.
23 Jesus replied, "The hour has come for the Son of Man to be glorified. 24 I tell you the truth, unless a kernel of wheat falls to the ground and dies, it remains only a single seed. But if it dies, it produces many seeds. 25 The man who loves his life will lose it,

---

[n] Other ancient authorities read *with him began to testify that he had called. . from the dead*

[i]15 Zech. 9:9

and those who hate their life in this world will keep it for eternal life. 26 Whoever serves me must follow me, and where I am, there will my servant be also. Whoever serves me, the Father will honor.

Jesus Speaks about His Death

27 "Now my soul is troubled. And what should I say—'Father, save me from this hour'? No, it is for this reason that I have come to this hour. 28 Father, glorify your name." Then a voice came from heaven, "I have glorified it, and I will glorify it again." 29 The crowd standing there heard it and said that it was thunder. Others said, "An angel has spoken to him." 30 Jesus answered, "This voice has come for your sake, not for mine. 31 Now is the judgment of this world; now the ruler of this world will be driven out. 32 And I, when I am lifted up from the earth, will draw all people*o* to myself." 33 He said this to indicate the kind of death he was to die. 34 The crowd answered him, "We have heard from the law that the Messiah*p* remains forever. How can you say that the Son of Man must be lifted up? Who is this Son of Man?" 35 Jesus said to them, "The light is with you for a little longer. Walk while you have the light, so that the darkness may not overtake you. If you walk in the darkness, you do not know where you are going. 36 While you

αὐτήν, καὶ ὁ μισῶν τὴν ψυχὴν αὐτοῦ
it,　and the [one] hating　the　life　of him

ἐν τῷ κόσμῳ τούτῳ εἰς ζωὴν αἰώνιον
in　-　world　this　unto life　eternal

φυλάξει αὐτήν. 26 ἐὰν ἐμοί τις διακονῇ,
will keep　it.　If　me anyone serves,

ἐμοὶ ἀκολουθείτω, καὶ ὅπου εἰμὶ ἐγώ,
me　let him follow,　and where　am I,

ἐκεῖ καὶ ὁ διάκονος ὁ ἐμὸς ἔσται·
there also *the* ¹servant　-　¹my　will be;

ἐάν τις ἐμοὶ διακονῇ, τιμήσει αὐτὸν
if anyone　me　serves,　will honour　him

ὁ πατήρ. 27 νῦν ἡ ψυχή μου τετάρακται,
the Father.　Now the soul of me has been troubled,

καὶ τί εἴπω; πάτερ, σῶσόν με ἐκ
and what may I say? Father,　save　me out of

τῆς ὥρας ταύτης. ἀλλὰ διὰ τοῦτο ἦλθον
-　hour this.　But　therefore　I came

εἰς τὴν ὥραν ταύτην. 28 πάτερ, δόξασόν
to　-　hour　this.　Father,　glorify

σου τὸ ὄνομα. ἦλθεν οὖν φωνὴ ἐκ
of thee the　name.　Came therefore a voice out of

τοῦ οὐρανοῦ· καὶ ἐδόξασα καὶ πάλιν
-　heaven:　Both I glorified　and　again

δοξάσω. 29 ὁ οὖν ὄχλος ὁ ἑστὼς καὶ
I will glorify.　Therefore the crowd　-　standing　and

ἀκούσας ἔλεγεν βροντὴν γεγονέναι· ἄλλοι
hearing　said　thunder　to have happened; others

ἔλεγον· ἄγγελος αὐτῷ λελάληκεν.
said :　An angel　to him　has spoken.

30 ἀπεκρίθη Ἰησοῦς καὶ εἶπεν· οὐ δι᾽ ἐμὲ
Answered Jesus and said :　Not because of me

ἡ φωνὴ αὕτη γέγονεν ἀλλὰ δι᾽ ὑμᾶς.
-　voice　this has happened but because of you.

31 νῦν κρίσις ἐστὶν τοῦ κόσμου τούτου·
Now judgment is　-　world　of this ;

νῦν ὁ ἄρχων τοῦ κόσμου τούτου
now the ruler　-　world　of this

ἐκβληθήσεται ἔξω· 32 κἀγὼ ἐὰν ὑψωθῶ
shall be cast out　outside;　and I　if I am lifted up

ἐκ τῆς γῆς, πάντας ἑλκύσω πρὸς
out of the earth,　all men will draw　to

ἐμαυτόν. 33 τοῦτο δὲ ἔλεγεν σημαίνων
myself.　And this　he said　signifying

ποίῳ θανάτῳ ἤμελλεν ἀποθνῄσκειν.
by what kind of death he was about to die.

34 ἀπεκρίθη οὖν αὐτῷ ὁ ὄχλος· ἡμεῖς
Answered therefore him the crowd :　We

ἠκούσαμεν ἐκ τοῦ νόμου ὅτι ὁ χριστὸς
heard out of the law　that the Christ

μένει εἰς τὸν αἰῶνα, καὶ πῶς λέγεις
remains unto the　age,　and how sayest

σὺ ὅτι δεῖ ὑψωθῆναι τὸν υἱὸν τοῦ
thou that it behoves to be lifted up the Son　-

ἀνθρώπου; τίς ἐστιν οὗτος ὁ υἱὸς τοῦ
of man? who is this　-　Son　-

ἀνθρώπου; 35 εἶπεν οὖν αὐτοῖς ὁ Ἰησοῦς·
of man?　Said therefore to them　-　Jesus :

ἔτι μικρὸν χρόνον τὸ φῶς ἐν ὑμῖν
Yet a little　time　the light among you

ἐστιν. περιπατεῖτε ὡς τὸ φῶς ἔχετε,
is.　Walk　while the light ye have,

ἵνα μὴ σκοτία ὑμᾶς καταλάβῃ· καὶ
lest darkness　you overtakes; and

ὁ περιπατῶν ἐν τῇ σκοτίᾳ οὐκ οἶδεν
the [one] walking in the darkness knows not

while the man who hates his life in this world will keep it for eternal life. 26 Whoever serves me must follow me; and where I am, my servant also will be. My Father will honor the one who serves me.

27 "Now my heart is troubled, and what shall I say? 'Father, save me from this hour'? No, it was for this very reason I came to this hour. 28 Father, glorify your name!"

Then a voice came from heaven, "I have glorified it, and will glorify it again." 29 The crowd that was there and heard it said it had thundered; others said an angel had spoken to him.

30 Jesus said, "This voice was for your benefit, not mine. 31 Now is the time for judgment on this world; now the prince of this world will be driven out. 32 But I, when I am lifted up from the earth, will draw all men to myself." 33 He said this to show the kind of death he was going to die.

34 The crowd spoke up, "We have heard from the Law that the Christ*j* will remain forever, so how can you say, 'The Son of Man must be lifted up'? Who is this 'Son of Man'?"

35 Then Jesus told them, "You are going to have the light just a little while longer. Walk while you have the light, before darkness overtakes you. The man who walks in the dark does not know where he is go-

have the light, believe in the light, so that you may become children of light."

The Unbelief of the People

After Jesus had said this, he departed and hid from them. 37Although he had performed so many signs in their presence, they did not believe in him. 38This was to fulfill the word spoken by the prophet Isaiah:
"Lord, who has
believed our
message,
and to whom has
the arm of the
Lord been
revealed?"
39And so they could not believe, because Isaiah also said,
40 "He has blinded their
eyes
and hardened their
heart,
so that they might not
look with their
eyes,
and understand with
their heart and
turn—
and I would heal
them."
41Isaiah said this because^a he saw his glory and spoke about him. 42Nevertheless many, even of the authorities, believed in him. But because of the Pharisees they did not confess it, for fear that they would be put out of the synagogue; 43for they loved human glory more than the glory that comes from God.

Summary of Jesus' Teaching

44 Then Jesus cried aloud: "Whoever believes in me believes not in me but in him who sent me. 45And whoever sees me sees him who sent me. 46I have come as light into the world, so that everyone who believes in me should not remain in the darkness. 47I do not judge anyone who hears my words and does not keep them, for I came not to judge the world, but to save the

^a Other ancient witnesses read *when*

ποῦ ὑπάγει. 36 ὡς τὸ φῶς ἔχετε,
where he is going. While the light ye have,

πιστεύετε εἰς τὸ φῶς, ἵνα υἱοὶ φωτὸς
believe in the light, that sons of light

γένησθε.
ye may become.

Ταῦτα ἐλάλησεν Ἰησοῦς, καὶ ἀπελθὼν
These things spoke Jesus, and going away

ἐκρύβη ἀπ' αὐτῶν. 37 Τοσαῦτα δὲ αὐτοῦ
was hidden from them. But so many him

σημεῖα πεποιηκότος* ἔμπροσθεν αὐτῶν οὐκ
signs having done* before them not
=But while he did so many signs

ἐπίστευον εἰς αὐτόν, 38 ἵνα ὁ λόγος
they believed in him, that the word

Ἡσαΐου τοῦ προφήτου πληρωθῇ ὃν
of Esaias the prophet might be fulfilled which

εἶπεν· κύριε, τίς ἐπίστευσεν τῇ ἀκοῇ
he said: Lord, who believed the report

ἡμῶν; καὶ ὁ βραχίων κυρίου τίνι
of us? and the arm of [the] Lord to whom

ἀπεκαλύφθη; 39 διὰ τοῦτο οὐκ ἠδύναντο
was it revealed? Therefore they could not

πιστεύειν, ὅτι πάλιν εἶπεν Ἡσαΐας·
to believe, because again said Esaias:

40 τετύφλωκεν αὐτῶν τοὺς ὀφθαλμοὺς καὶ
He has blinded of them the eyes and

ἐπώρωσεν αὐτῶν τὴν καρδίαν, ἵνα
hardened of them the heart, that

μὴ ἴδωσιν τοῖς ὀφθαλμοῖς καὶ νοήσωσιν
they might not see with the eyes and understand

τῇ καρδίᾳ καὶ στραφῶσιν, καὶ ἰάσομαι
with the heart and might turn, and I will cure

αὐτούς. 41 ταῦτα εἶπεν Ἡσαΐας ὅτι
them. These things said Esaias because

εἶδεν τὴν δόξαν αὐτοῦ, καὶ ἐλάλησεν
he saw the glory of him, and spoke

περὶ αὐτοῦ. 42 ὅμως μέντοι καὶ ἐκ
about him. Nevertheless however even of

τῶν ἀρχόντων πολλοὶ ἐπίστευσαν εἰς αὐτόν,
the rulers many believed in him,

ἀλλὰ διὰ τοὺς Φαρισαίους οὐχ ὡμολόγουν,
but because of the Pharisees did not confess,

ἵνα μὴ ἀποσυνάγωγοι γένωνται·
lest put out of [the] synagogue they should become;

43 ἠγάπησαν γὰρ τὴν δόξαν τῶν ἀνθρώπων
for they loved the glory - of men

μᾶλλον ἤπερ τὴν δόξαν τοῦ θεοῦ.
more than the glory - of God.

44 Ἰησοῦς δὲ ἔκραξεν καὶ εἶπεν· ὁ
But Jesus cried out and said: The

πιστεύων εἰς ἐμὲ οὐ πιστεύει εἰς ἐμὲ
[one] believing in me believes not in me

ἀλλὰ εἰς τὸν πέμψαντά με, 45 καὶ ὁ
but in the [one] having sent me, and the

θεωρῶν ἐμὲ θεωρεῖ τὸν πέμψαντά με.
[one] beholding me beholds the [one] having sent me.

46 ἐγὼ φῶς εἰς τὸν κόσμον ἐλήλυθα,
I a light into the world have come,

ἵνα πᾶς ὁ πιστεύων εἰς ἐμὲ ἐν τῇ
that everyone believing in me in the

σκοτίᾳ μὴ μείνῃ. 47 καὶ ἐάν τίς μου
darkness may not remain. And if anyone of me

ἀκούσῃ τῶν ῥημάτων καὶ μὴ φυλάξῃ,
hears the words and keeps not,

ἐγὼ οὐ κρίνω αὐτόν· οὐ γὰρ ἦλθον
I do not judge him; for I came not

---

ing. 36Put your trust in the light while you have it, so that you may become sons of light." When he had finished speaking, Jesus left and hid himself from them.

The Jews Continue in Their Unbelief

37Even after Jesus had done all these miraculous signs in their presence, they still would not believe in him. 38This was to fulfill the word of Isaiah the prophet:

"Lord, who has believed
our message
and to whom has the
arm of the Lord
been revealed?"^k

39For this reason they could not believe, because, as Isaiah says elsewhere:

40"He has blinded their
eyes
and deadened their
hearts,
so they can neither see
with their eyes,
nor understand with
their hearts,
nor turn—and I would
heal them."^l

41Isaiah said this because he saw Jesus' glory and spoke about him. 42Yet at the same time many even among the leaders believed in him. But because of the Pharisees they would not confess their faith for fear they would be put out of the synagogue; 43for they loved praise from men more than praise from God.
44Then Jesus cried out, "When a man believes in me, he does not believe in me only, but in the one who sent me. 45When he looks at me, he sees the one who sent me. 46I have come into the world as a light, so that no one who believes in me should stay in darkness. 47"As for the person who hears my words but does not keep them, I do not judge him. For I did not

^k38 Isaiah 53:1
^l40 Isaiah 6:10

world. 48 The one who rejects me and does not receive my word has a judge; on the last day the word that I have spoken will serve as judge, 49 for I have not spoken on my own, but the Father who sent me has himself given me a commandment about what to say and what to speak. 50 And I know that his commandment is eternal life. What I speak, therefore, I speak just as the Father has told me."

Chapter 13

Jesus Washes the Disciples' Feet

NOW before the festival of the Passover, Jesus knew that his hour had come to depart from this world and go to the Father. Having loved his own who were in the world, he loved them to the end. 2 The devil had already put it into the heart of Judas son of Simon Iscariot to betray him. And during supper 3 Jesus, knowing that the Father had given all things into his hands, and that he had come from God and was going to God, 4 got up from the table,[r] took off his outer robe, and tied a towel around himself. 5 Then he poured water into a basin and began to wash the disciples' feet and to wipe them with the towel that was tied around him. 6 He came to Simon Peter, who said to him, "Lord, are you going to wash my feet?" 7 Jesus answered,

ἵνα κρίνω τὸν κόσμον, ἀλλ' ἵνα σώσω
that I might judge the world, but that I might save
τὸν κόσμον. 48 ὁ ἀθετῶν ἐμὲ καὶ μὴ
the world. The [one] rejecting me and not
λαμβάνων τὰ ῥήματά μου ἔχει τὸν
receiving the words of me has the
κρίνοντα αὐτόν· ὁ λόγος ὃν ἐλάλησα,
[one] judging him; the word which I spoke,
ἐκεῖνος κρινεῖ αὐτὸν ἐν τῇ ἐσχάτῃ ἡμέρᾳ.
that will judge him in the last day.
49 ὅτι ἐγὼ ἐξ ἐμαυτοῦ οὐκ ἐλάλησα,
Because I of myself did not speak,
ἀλλ' ὁ πέμψας με πατὴρ αὐτός μοι
but ¹the ²having sent ⁴me ³Father ⁵he ⁷me
ἐντολὴν δέδωκεν τί εἴπω καὶ τί
⁶commandment ⁸has given what I may say and what
λαλήσω. 50 καὶ οἶδα ὅτι ἡ ἐντολὴ
I may speak. And I know that the commandment
αὐτοῦ ζωὴ αἰώνιός ἐστιν. ἃ οὖν ἐγὼ
of him life eternal is. What things therefore I
λαλῶ, καθὼς εἴρηκέν μοι ὁ πατήρ,
speak, as has said to me the Father,
οὕτως λαλῶ.
so I speak.

13 Πρὸ δὲ τῆς ἑορτῆς τοῦ πάσχα
Now before the feast of the Passover
εἰδὼς ὁ Ἰησοῦς ὅτι ἦλθεν αὐτοῦ ἡ
²knowing ¹Jesus that came of him the
ὥρα ἵνα μεταβῇ ἐκ τοῦ κόσμου τούτου
hour that he should remove out of – world this
πρὸς τὸν πατέρα, ἀγαπήσας τοὺς ἰδίους
to the Father, loving the(his) own
τοὺς ἐν τῷ κόσμῳ, εἰς τέλος ἠγάπησεν
– in the world, to [the] end he loved
αὐτούς. 2 καὶ δείπνου γινομένου, τοῦ
them. And supper taking place,ᵃ the
=during supper,
διαβόλου ἤδη βεβληκότος εἰς τὴν καρδίαν
devil now having putᵃ into the heart
=as the devil had now put
ἵνα παραδοῖ αὐτὸν Ἰούδας Σίμωνος
that ⁴should betray ⁵him ¹Judas ²[son] of Simon
Ἰσκαριώτης, 3 εἰδὼς ὅτι πάντα ἔδωκεν
³Iscariot, knowing that all things gave
αὐτῷ ὁ πατὴρ εἰς τὰς χεῖρας, καὶ
him the Father into the(his) hands, and
ὅτι ἀπὸ θεοῦ ἐξῆλθεν καὶ πρὸς τὸν
that from God he came forth and to –
θεὸν ὑπάγει, 4 ἐγείρεται ἐκ τοῦ δείπνου
God goes, he rises out of(from) the supper
καὶ τίθησιν τὰ ἱμάτια, καὶ λαβὼν
and places [aside] the(his) garments, and taking
λέντιον διέζωσεν ἑαυτόν· 5 εἶτα βάλλει
a towel he girded himself; then he puts
ὕδωρ εἰς τὸν νιπτῆρα, καὶ ἤρξατο νίπτειν
water into the basin, and began to wash
τοὺς πόδας τῶν μαθητῶν καὶ ἐκμάσσειν
the feet of the disciples and to wipe off
τῷ λεντίῳ ᾧ ἦν διεζωσμένος.
with the towel with which he was *having been* girded.
6 ἔρχεται οὖν πρὸς Σίμωνα Πέτρον·
He comes therefore to Simon Peter;
λέγει αὐτῷ· κύριε, σύ μου νίπτεις τοὺς
he says to him: Lord, thou of me washest the

come to judge the world, but to save it. 48 There is a judge for the one who rejects me and does not accept my words; that very word which I spoke will condemn him at the last day. 49 For I did not speak of my own accord, but the Father who sent me commanded me what to say and how to say it. 50 I know that his command leads to eternal life. So whatever I say is just what the Father has told me to say."

Chapter 13

Jesus Washes His Disciples' Feet

IT was just before the Passover Feast. Jesus knew that the time had come for him to leave this world and go to the Father. Having loved his own who were in the world, he now showed them the full extent of his love.[m]

2 The evening meal was being served, and the devil had already prompted Judas Iscariot, son of Simon, to betray Jesus. 3 Jesus knew that the Father had put all things under his power, and that he had come from God and was returning to God; 4 so he got up from the meal, took off his outer clothing, and wrapped a towel around his waist. 5 After that, he poured water into a basin and began to wash his disciples' feet, drying them with the towel that was wrapped around him.

6 He came to Simon Peter, who said to him, "Lord, are you going to wash my feet?"

---

[r] Gk *from supper*

ᵃ Repeated from ver. 1; the subject is therefore again "Jesus".

[m] 1 Or *he loved them to the last*

"You do not know now what I am doing, but later you will understand." 8 Peter said to him, "You will never wash my feet." Jesus answered, "Unless I wash you, you have no share with me." 9 Simon Peter said to him, "Lord, not my feet only but also my hands and my head!" 10 Jesus said to him, "One who has bathed does not need to wash, except for the feet,$ but is entirely clean. And you$ are clean, though not all of you." 11 For he knew who was to betray him; for this reason he said, "Not all of you are clean."

12 After he had washed their feet, had put on his robe, and had returned to the table, he said to them, "Do you know what I have done to you? 13 You call me Teacher and Lord—and you are right, for that is what I am. 14 So if I, your Lord and Teacher, have washed your feet, you also ought to wash one another's feet. 15 For I have set you an example, that you also should do as I have done to you. 16 Very truly, I tell you, servants" are not greater than their master, nor are messengers greater than the one who sent them. 17 If you know these things, you are blessed if you do them. 18 I am not speaking of all of you; I know whom I have chosen. But it is to fulfill the scripture, 'The one who ate my bread' has lifted his heel

πόδας; 7 ἀπεκρίθη Ἰησοῦς καὶ εἶπεν αὐτῷ·
feet? Answered Jesus and said to him:

ὁ ἐγὼ ποιῶ σὺ οὐκ οἶδας ἄρτι,
What I am doing thou knowest not yet,

γνώσῃ δὲ μετὰ ταῦτα. 8 λέγει αὐτῷ
but thou wilt know after these things. Says to him

Πέτρος· οὐ μὴ νίψῃς μου τοὺς πόδας
Peter: By no means shalt thou wash of me the feet

εἰς τὸν αἰῶνα. ἀπεκρίθη Ἰησοῦς αὐτῷ·
unto the age. Answered Jesus him:

ἐὰν μὴ νίψω σε, οὐκ ἔχεις μέρος μετ'
Unless I wash thee, thou hast no part with

ἐμοῦ. 9 λέγει αὐτῷ Σίμων Πέτρος·
me. Says to him Simon Peter:

κύριε, μὴ τοὺς πόδας μου μόνον ἀλλὰ
Lord, not the feet of me only but

καὶ τὰς χεῖρας καὶ τὴν κεφαλήν. 10 λέγει
also the hands and the head. Says

αὐτῷ Ἰησοῦς· ὁ λελουμένος οὐκ ἔχει
to him Jesus: The [one] having been bathed has not

χρείαν [εἰ μὴ τοὺς πόδας] νίψασθαι,
need except the feet to wash,

ἀλλ' ἔστιν καθαρὸς ὅλος· καὶ ὑμεῖς
but is clean wholly; and ye

καθαροί ἐστε, ἀλλ' οὐχὶ πάντες. 11 ᾔδει
clean are, but not all. he knew

γὰρ τὸν παραδιδόντα αὐτόν· διὰ τοῦτο
For the [one] betraying him; therefore

εἶπεν ὅτι οὐχὶ πάντες καθαροί ἐστε.
he said[,] - Not all clean ye are.

12 Ὅτε οὖν ἔνιψεν τοὺς πόδας αὐτῶν
When therefore he washed the feet of them

καὶ ἔλαβεν τὰ ἱμάτια αὐτοῦ καὶ ἀνέπεσεν
and took the garments of him and reclined

πάλιν, εἶπεν αὐτοῖς· γινώσκετε τί πε-
again, he said to them: Do ye know what I

ποίηκα ὑμῖν; 13 ὑμεῖς φωνεῖτέ με· ὁ
have done to you? Ye call me: The

διδάσκαλος καὶ ὁ κύριος, καὶ καλῶς
Teacher and the Lord, and well

λέγετε· εἰμὶ γάρ. 14 εἰ οὖν ἐγὼ ἔνιψα
ye say; for I am. If therefore I washed

ὑμῶν τοὺς πόδας ὁ κύριος καὶ ὁ
of you the feet the Lord and the

διδάσκαλος, καὶ ὑμεῖς ὀφείλετε ἀλλήλων
Teacher, also ye ought of one another

νίπτειν τοὺς πόδας· 15 ὑπόδειγμα γὰρ
to wash the feet; for an example

ἔδωκα ὑμῖν ἵνα καθὼς ἐγὼ ἐποίησα
I gave you that as I did

ὑμῖν καὶ ὑμεῖς ποιῆτε. 16 ἀμὴν ἀμὴν
to you also ye may do. Truly truly

λέγω ὑμῖν, οὐκ ἔστιν δοῦλος μείζων
I tell you, is not a slave greater [than]

τοῦ κυρίου αὐτοῦ, οὐδὲ ἀπόστολος μείζων
the lord of him, nor a sent one greater [than]

τοῦ πέμψαντος αὐτόν. 17 εἰ ταῦτα
the [one] sending him. If these things

οἴδατε, μακάριοί ἐστε ἐὰν ποιῆτε αὐτά.
ye know, blessed are ye if ye do them.

18 Οὐ περὶ πάντων ὑμῶν λέγω· ἐγὼ
Not concerning all you I speak; I

οἶδα τίνας ἐξελεξάμην· ἀλλ' ἵνα ἡ
know whom I chose; but that the

γραφὴ πληρωθῇ· ὁ τρώγων μου τὸν
scripture may be fulfilled: The [one] eating of me the

7Jesus replied, "You do not realize now what I am doing, but later you will understand."

8"No," said Peter, "you shall never wash my feet." Jesus answered, "Unless I wash you, you have no part with me."

9"Then, Lord," Simon Peter replied, "not just my feet but my hands and my head as well!"

10Jesus answered, "A person who has had a bath needs only to wash his feet; his whole body is clean. And you are clean, though not every one of you."

11For he knew who was going to betray him, and that was why he said not every one was clean.

12When he had finished washing their feet, he put on his clothes and returned to his place. "Do you understand what I have done for you?" he asked them. 13"You call me 'Teacher' and 'Lord,' and rightly so, for that is what I am. 14Now that I, your Lord and Teacher, have washed your feet, you also should wash one another's feet. 15I have set you an example that you should do as I have done for you. 16I tell you the truth, no servant is greater than his master, nor is a messenger greater than the one who sent him. 17Now that you know these things, you will be blessed if you do them.

Jesus Predicts His Betrayal

18"I am not referring to all of you; I know those I have chosen. But this is to fulfill the scripture: 'He who shares my bread has

---

s Other ancient authorities lack *except for the feet*
t The Greek word for *you* here is plural
u Gk *slaves*
v Other ancient authorities read *ate bread with me*

against me.' 19 I tell you this now, before it occurs, so that when it does occur, you may believe that I am he.ʷ 20 Very truly, I tell you, whoever receives one whom I send receives me; and whoever receives me receives him who sent me."

Jesus Foretells His Betrayal

21 After saying this Jesus was troubled in spirit, and declared, "Very truly, I tell you, one of you will betray me." 22 The disciples looked at one another, uncertain of whom he was speaking. 23 One of his disciples—the one whom Jesus loved—was reclining next to him; 24 Simon Peter therefore motioned to him to ask Jesus of whom he was speaking. 25 So while reclining next to Jesus, he asked him, "Lord, who is it?" 26 Jesus answered, "It is the one to whom I give this piece of bread when I have dipped it in the dish."ˣ So when he had dipped the piece of bread, he gave it to Judas son of Simon Iscariot.ʸ 27 After he received the piece of bread,ᶻ Satan entered into him. Jesus said to him, "Do quickly what you are going to do." 28 Now no one at the table knew why he said this to him. 29 Some thought that, because Judas had the common purse, Jesus was telling him, "Buy what we need for the festival"; or, that he should give something to the poor. 30 So, after receiving the piece of bread, he immediately

w Gk *I am*
x Gk *dipped it*
y Other ancient authorities read *Judas Iscariot son of Simon;* others, *Judas son of Simon from Karyot* (Kerioth)
z Gk *After the piece of bread*

ἄρτον ἐπῆρεν ἐπ' ἐμὲ τὴν πτέρναν αὐτοῦ.
bread lifted up against me the heel of him.

19 ἀπ' ἄρτι λέγω ὑμῖν πρὸ τοῦ γενέσθαι,
From now I tell you before the to happen, = it happens,

ἵνα πιστεύητε ὅταν γένηται ὅτι ἐγώ
that ye may believe when it happens that I

εἰμι. 20 ἀμὴν ἀμὴν λέγω ὑμῖν, ὁ
am. Truly truly I say to you, the

λαμβάνων ἄν τινα πέμψω ἐμὲ λαμβάνει,
[one] receiving whomever I may send me receives,

ὁ δὲ ἐμὲ λαμβάνων λαμβάνει τὸν
and the [one] me receiving receives the [one]

πέμψαντά με. 21 ταῦτα εἰπὼν Ἰησοῦς
having sent me. These things saying Jesus

ἐταράχθη τῷ πνεύματι καὶ ἐμαρτύρησεν
was troubled in the(his) spirit and witnessed

καὶ εἶπεν· ἀμὴν ἀμὴν λέγω ὑμῖν ὅτι
and said: Truly truly I tell you that

εἷς ἐξ ὑμῶν παραδώσει με. 22 ἔβλεπον
one of you will betray me. Looked

εἰς ἀλλήλους οἱ μαθηταὶ ἀπορούμενοι περὶ
at one another the disciples being perplexed about

τίνος λέγει. 23 ἦν ἀνακείμενος εἷς ἐκ
whom he speaks. Was reclining one of

τῶν μαθητῶν αὐτοῦ ἐν τῷ κόλπῳ τοῦ
the disciples of him in the bosom

Ἰησοῦ, ὃν ἠγάπα ὁ Ἰησοῦς· 24 νεύει
of Jesus, whom loved - Jesus; nods

οὖν τούτῳ Σίμων Πέτρος καὶ λέγει
therefore to this one Simon Peter and says

αὐτῷ· εἰπὲ τίς ἐστιν περὶ οὗ λέγει.
to him: Say who it is about whom he speaks.

25 ἀναπεσὼν ἐκεῖνος οὕτως ἐπὶ τὸ
Falling back that one thus on the

στῆθος τοῦ Ἰησοῦ λέγει αὐτῷ· κύριε,
breast of Jesus he says to him: Lord,

τίς ἐστιν; 26 ἀποκρίνεται οὖν ὁ Ἰησοῦς·
who is it? Answers therefore Jesus:

ἐκεῖνός ἐστιν ᾧ ἐγὼ βάψω τὸ ψωμίον
That one it is to whom I shall dip the morsel

καὶ δώσω αὐτῷ. βάψας οὖν [τὸ]
and shall give him. Dipping therefore the

ψωμίον λαμβάνει καὶ δίδωσιν Ἰούδᾳ
morsel he takes and gives to Judas

Σίμωνος Ἰσκαριώτου. 27 καὶ μετὰ τὸ
[son] of Simon Iscariot. And after the

ψωμίον τότε εἰσῆλθεν εἰς ἐκεῖνον ὁ
morsel then entered into that one -

σατανᾶς. λέγει οὖν αὐτῷ Ἰησοῦς·
Satan. Says therefore to him Jesus: What

ποιεῖς ποίησον τάχιον. 28 τοῦτο [δὲ]
thou doest do quickly. But this

οὐδεὶς ἔγνω τῶν ἀνακειμένων πρὸς τί
no one knew of the [ones] reclining for what

εἶπεν αὐτῷ· 29 τινὲς γὰρ ἐδόκουν, ἐπεὶ
he told him; for some thought, since

τὸ γλωσσόκομον εἶχεν Ἰούδας, ὅτι λέγει
the bag had Judas, that tells

αὐτῷ Ἰησοῦς· ἀγόρασον ὧν χρείαν
him Jesus: Buy [the] things of which need

ἔχομεν εἰς τὴν ἑορτήν, ἢ τοῖς πτωχοῖς
we have for the feast, or to the poor

ἵνα τι δῷ. 30 λαβὼν οὖν τὸ
that something he should give. Having taken therefore the

---

lifted up his heel against me.'ⁿ

19 "I am telling you now before it happens, so that when it does happen you will believe that I am He. 20 I tell you the truth, whoever accepts anyone I send accepts me; and whoever accepts me accepts the one who sent me."

21 After he had said this, Jesus was troubled in spirit and testified, "I tell you the truth, one of you is going to betray me."

22 His disciples stared at one another, at a loss to know which of them he meant. 23 One of them, the disciple whom Jesus loved, was reclining next to him. 24 Simon Peter motioned to this disciple and said, "Ask him which one he means." 25 Leaning back against Jesus, he asked him, "Lord, who is it?" 26 Jesus answered, "It is the one to whom I will give this piece of bread when I have dipped it in the dish." Then, dipping the piece of bread, he gave it to Judas Iscariot, son of Simon. 27 As soon as Judas took the bread, Satan entered into him.

"What you are about to do, do quickly," Jesus told him, 28 but no one at the meal understood why Jesus said this to him. 29 Since Judas had charge of the money, some thought Jesus was telling him to buy what was needed for the Feast, or to give something to the poor. 30 As soon as Judas had tak-

n 18 Psalm 41:9

The New Commandment

31 When he had gone out, Jesus said, "Now the Son of Man has been glorified, and God has been glorified in him. [32] If God has been glorified in him,[a] God will also glorify him in himself and will glorify him at once. [33] Little children, I am with you only a little longer. You will look for me; and as I said to the Jews so now I say to you, 'Where I am going, you cannot come.' [34] I give you a new commandment, that you love one another. Just as I have loved you, you also should love one another. [35] By this everyone will know that you are my disciples, if you have love for one another."

Jesus Foretells Peter's Denial

36 Simon Peter said to him, "Lord, where are you going?" Jesus answered, "Where I am going, you cannot follow me now; but you will follow afterward." [37] Peter said to him, "Lord, why can I not follow you now? I will lay down my life for you." [38] Jesus answered, "Will you lay down your life for me? Very truly, I tell you, before the cock crows, you will have denied me three times.

ψωμίον   ἐκεῖνος   ἐξῆλθεν   εὐθύς·   ἦν   δὲ
morsel   that one   went out   immediately;   and it was

νύξ.
night.

31 ῞Οτε   οὖν   ἐξῆλθεν,   λέγει   ᾿Ιησοῦς·
When   therefore   he went out,   says   Jesus :

νῦν   ἐδοξάσθη   ὁ   υἱὸς   τοῦ   ἀνθρώπου,
Now   was(is) glorified   the   Son   -   of man,

καὶ   ὁ   θεὸς   ἐδοξάσθη   ἐν   αὐτῷ·   **32** εἰ
and   -   God   was(is) glorified   in   him;   if

ὁ   θεὸς   ἐδοξάσθη   ἐν   αὐτῷ,   καὶ   ὁ   θεὸς
-   God   was(is) glorified   in   him,   both   -   God

δοξάσει   αὐτὸν   ἐν   αὐτῷ,   καὶ   εὐθὺς
will glorify   him   in   him,   and immediately

δοξάσει   αὐτόν.   **33** τεκνία,   ἔτι   μικρὸν
will glorify   him.   Children,   yet a little while

μεθ'   ὑμῶν   εἰμι·   ζητήσετέ   με,   καὶ   καθὼς
with   you   I am;   ye will seek   me,   and   as

εἶπον   τοῖς   ᾿Ιουδαίοις   ὅτι   ὅπου   ἐγὼ
I said   to the   Jews   that   where   I

ὑπάγω   ὑμεῖς   οὐ   δύνασθε   ἐλθεῖν,   καὶ
go   ye   cannot   to come,   also

ὑμῖν   λέγω   ἄρτι.   **34** ᾿Εντολὴν   καινὴν
to you   I say   now.   commandment   A new

δίδωμι   ὑμῖν,   ἵνα   ἀγαπᾶτε   ἀλλήλους,
I give   you,   that   ye love   one another,

καθὼς   ἠγάπησα   ὑμᾶς   ἵνα   καὶ   ὑμεῖς
as   I loved   you   that   also   ye

ἀγαπᾶτε   ἀλλήλους.   **35** ἐν   τούτῳ   γνώσονται
love   one another.   By   this   will know

πάντες   ὅτι   ἐμοὶ   μαθηταί   ἐστε,   ἐὰν
all men   that   to me[e]   disciples   ye are,   if

ἀγάπην   ἔχητε   ἐν   ἀλλήλοις.   **36** Λέγει
love   ye have   among   one another.   Says

αὐτῷ   Σίμων   Πέτρος·   κύριε,   ποῦ   ὑπάγεις;
to him   Simon   Peter :   Lord,   where   goest thou?

ἀπεκρίθη   ᾿Ιησοῦς·   ῞Οπου   ὑπάγω   οὐ   δύνασαί
Answered   Jesus :   Where   I go   thou canst not

μοι   νῦν   ἀκολουθῆσαι,   ἀκολουθήσεις   δὲ
me   now   to follow,   but thou wilt follow

ὕστερον.   **37** λέγει   αὐτῷ   [ὁ]   Πέτρος·
later.   Says   to him   -   Peter :

κύριε,   διὰ   τί   οὐ   δύναμαί   σοι   ἀκολουθῆσαι
Lord,   why   can I not   thee   to follow

ἄρτι;   τὴν   ψυχήν   μου   ὑπὲρ   σοῦ   θήσω.
yet?   the   life   of me   for   thee   I will lay down.

38 ἀποκρίνεται   ᾿Ιησοῦς·   τὴν   ψυχήν   σου
Answers   Jesus :   The   life   of thee

ὑπὲρ   ἐμοῦ   θήσεις;   ἀμὴν   ἀμὴν   λέγω
for   me   wilt thou lay down?   truly   truly   I tell

σοι,   οὐ   μὴ   ἀλέκτωρ   φωνήσῃ   ἕως   οὗ
thee,   by no means   a cock   crows   until

ἀρνήσῃ   με   τρίς.   **14** Μὴ   ταρασσέσθω
thou deniest   me   thrice.   Let not be troubled

ὑμῶν   ἡ   καρδία·   πιστεύετε   εἰς   τὸν   θεόν,   καὶ
of you   the   heart;   believe   in   -   God,   also

εἰς   ἐμὲ   πιστεύετε.   **2** ἐν   τῇ   οἰκίᾳ   τοῦ
in   me   believe.   In   the   house   of the

πατρός   μου   μοναὶ   πολλαί   εἰσιν·   εἰ   δὲ   μή,
Father   of me   abodes   many   there are;   otherwise,

εἶπον   ἂν   ὑμῖν·   ὅτι   πορεύομαι   ἑτοιμάσαι
I would have told   you;   because   I go   to prepare

τόπον   ὑμῖν·   **3** καὶ   ἐὰν   πορευθῶ   καὶ
a place   for you;   and   if   I go   and

Chapter 14

Jesus the Way to the Father

"DO not let your hearts be troubled. Believe[b] in God, believe also in me. [2] In my Father's house there are many dwelling places. If it were not so, would I have told you that I go to prepare a place for you?[c] [3] And if I go and prepare a place for

[a] Other ancient authorities read If God has been glorified in him

[b] Or You believe

[c] Or If it were not so, I would have told you; for I go to prepare a place for you

---

en the bread, he went out. And it was night.

Jesus Predicts Peter's Denial

[31] When he was gone, Jesus said, "Now is the Son of Man glorified and God is glorified in him. [32] If God is glorified in him,[o] God will glorify the Son in himself, and will glorify him at once.

[33] "My children, I will be with you only a little longer. You will look for me, and just as I told the Jews, so I tell you now: Where I am going, you cannot come.

[34] "A new command I give you: Love one another. As I have loved you, so you must love one another. [35] By this all men will know that you are my disciples, if you love one another."

[36] Simon Peter asked him, "Lord, where are you going?"

Jesus replied, "Where I am going, you cannot follow now, but you will follow later."

[37] Peter asked, "Lord, why can't I follow you now? I will lay down my life for you."

[38] Then Jesus answered, "Will you really lay down your life for me? I tell you the truth, before the rooster crows, you will disown me three times!

Chapter 14

Jesus Comforts His Disciples

"DO not let your hearts be troubled. Trust in God[p]; trust also in me. [2] In my Father's house are many rooms; if it were not so, I would have told you. I am going there to prepare a place for you. [3] And if I go and prepare a

[o]32 Many early manuscripts do not have If God is glorified in him.

[p]1 Or You trust in God

you, I will come again and will take you to myself, so that where I am, there you may be also. 4 And you know the way to the place where I am going."d

5 Thomas said to him, "Lord, we do not know where we are going. How can we know the way?" 6 Jesus said to him, "I am the way, and the truth, and the life. No one comes to the Father except through me. 7 If you know me, you will knowe my Father also. From now on you do know him and have seen him."

8 Philip said to him, "Lord, show us the Father, and we will be satisfied." 9 Jesus said to him, "Have I been with you all this time, Philip, and you still do not know me? Whoever has seen me has seen the Father. How can you say, 'Show us the Father'? 10 Do you not believe that I am in the Father and the Father is in me? The words that I say to you I do not speak on my own; but the Father who dwells in me does his works. 11 Believe me that I am in the Father and the Father is in me; but if you do not, then believe me because of the works themselves. 12 Very truly, I tell you, the one who believes in me will also do the works that I do and, in fact, will do greater works than these, because I am going to the Father. 13 I will do whatever you ask in my name, so that the Father may be glorified in the Son. 14 If in my name you ask mef for anything, I will do it.

d Other ancient authorities read *Where I am going you know, and the way you know*
e Other ancient authorities read *If you had known me, you would have known*
f Other ancient authorities lack *me*

ἑτοιμάσω τόπον ὑμῖν, πάλιν ἔρχομαι καὶ
prepare a place for you, again I come and

παραλήμψομαι ὑμᾶς πρὸς ἐμαυτόν, ἵνα
will receive you to myself, that

ὅπου εἰμὶ ἐγὼ καὶ ὑμεῖς ἦτε. 4 Καὶ
where am I also ye may be. And

ὅπου ἐγὼ ὑπάγω οἴδατε τὴν ὁδόν.
where I go ye know the way.

5 λέγει αὐτῷ Θωμᾶς· κύριε, οὐκ οἴδαμεν
Says to him Thomas: Lord, we know not

ποῦ ὑπάγεις· πῶς οἴδαμεν τὴν ὁδόν;
where thou goest; how do we know the way?

6 λέγει αὐτῷ Ἰησοῦς· ἐγώ εἰμι ἡ ὁδὸς
Says to him Jesus: I am the way

καὶ ἡ ἀλήθεια καὶ ἡ ζωή· οὐδεὶς ἔρχεται
and the truth and the life; no one comes

πρὸς τὸν πατέρα εἰ μὴ δι' ἐμοῦ. 7 εἰ
to the Father except through me. If

ἐγνώκειτέ με, καὶ τὸν πατέρα μου
ye had known me, also the Father of me

ἂν ᾔδειτε. ἀπ' ἄρτι γινώσκετε αὐτὸν
ye would have known. From now ye know him

καὶ ἑωράκατε. 8 Λέγει αὐτῷ Φίλιππος·
and have seen. Says to him Philip:

κύριε, δεῖξον ἡμῖν τὸν πατέρα, καὶ
Lord, show us the Father, and

ἀρκεῖ ἡμῖν. 9 λέγει αὐτῷ ὁ Ἰησοῦς·
it suffices for us. Says to him - Jesus:

τοσοῦτον χρόνον μεθ' ὑμῶν εἰμι καὶ
So long time with you I am and

οὐκ ἔγνωκάς με, Φίλιππε; ὁ ἑωρακὼς
thou hast not known me, Philip? The [one] having seen

ἐμὲ ἑώρακεν τὸν πατέρα· πῶς σὺ λέγεις·
me has seen the Father; how thou sayest:

δεῖξον ἡμῖν τὸν πατέρα; 10 οὐ πιστεύεις
Show us the Father? believest thou not

ὅτι ἐγὼ ἐν τῷ πατρὶ καὶ ὁ πατὴρ
that I in the Father and the Father

ἐν ἐμοί ἐστιν; τὰ ῥήματα ἃ ἐγὼ λέγω
in me is? the words which I say

ὑμῖν ἀπ' ἐμαυτοῦ οὐ λαλῶ· ὁ δὲ πατὴρ
to you from myself I speak not; but the Father

ἐν ἐμοὶ μένων ποιεῖ τὰ ἔργα αὐτοῦ.
in me remaining does the works of him.

11 πιστεύετέ μοι ὅτι ἐγὼ ἐν τῷ πατρὶ
Believe ye me that I in the Father

καὶ ὁ πατὴρ ἐν ἐμοί· εἰ δὲ μή, διὰ
and the Father in me; otherwise, because of

τὰ ἔργα αὐτὰ πιστεύετε. 12 ἀμὴν ἀμὴν
the works [them]selves believe ye. Truly truly

λέγω ὑμῖν, ὁ πιστεύων εἰς ἐμὲ τὰ
I tell you, the [one] believing in me the

ἔργα ἃ ἐγὼ ποιῶ κἀκεῖνος ποιήσει,
works which I do that one also will do,

καὶ μείζονα τούτων ποιήσει, ὅτι ἐγὼ
and greater [than] these he will do, because I

πρὸς τὸν πατέρα πορεύομαι· 13 καὶ ὅ τι
to the Father am going; and what-

ἂν αἰτήσητε ἐν τῷ ὀνόματί μου, τοῦτο
ever ye ask in the name of me, this

ποιήσω, ἵνα δοξασθῇ ὁ πατὴρ ἐν τῷ
I will do, that may be glorified the Father in the

υἱῷ. 14 ἐάν τι αἰτήσητέ με ἐν τῷ
Son. If anything ye ask me in the

ὀνόματί μου, ἐγὼ ποιήσω. 15 Ἐὰν
name of me, I will do. If

---

place for you, I will come back and take you to be with me that you also may be where I am. 4 You know the way to the place where I am going."

Jesus the Way to the Father

5 Thomas said to him, "Lord, we don't know where you are going, so how can we know the way?"

6 Jesus answered, "I am the way and the truth and the life. No one comes to the Father except through me. 7 If you really knew me, you would knowq my Father as well. From now on, you do know him and have seen him."

8 Philip said, "Lord, show us the Father and that will be enough for us."

9 Jesus answered: "Don't you know me, Philip, even after I have been among you such a long time? Anyone who has seen me has seen the Father. How can you say, 'Show us the Father'? 10 Don't you believe that I am in the Father, and that the Father is in me? The words I say to you are not just my own. Rather, it is the Father, living in me, who is doing his work. 11 Believe me when I say that I am in the Father and the Father is in me; or at least believe on the evidence of the miracles themselves. 12 I tell you the truth, anyone who has faith in me will do what I have been doing. He will do even greater things than these, because I am going to the Father. 13 And I will do whatever you ask in my name, so that the Son may bring glory to the Father. 14 You may ask me for anything in my name, and I will do it.

q7 Some early manuscripts *If you really have known me, you will know*

The Promise of the Holy Spirit

15 "If you love me, you will keep[g] my commandments. 16 And I will ask the Father, and he will give you another Advocate,[h] to be with you forever. 17 This is the Spirit of truth, whom the world cannot receive, because it neither sees him nor knows him. You know him, because he abides with you, and he will be in[i] you.

18 "I will not leave you orphaned; I am coming to you. 19 In a little while the world will no longer see me, but you will see me; because I live, you also live. 20 On that day you will know that I am in my Father, and you in me, and I in you. 21 They who have my commandments and keep them are those who love me; and those who love me will be loved by my Father, and I will love them and reveal myself to them."

22 Judas (not Iscariot) said to him, "Lord, how is it that you will reveal yourself to us, and not to the world?" 23 Jesus answered him, "Those who love me will keep my word, and my Father will love them, and we will come to them and make our home with them. 24 Whoever does not love me does not keep my words; and the word that you hear is not mine, but is from the Father who sent me.

25 "I have said these

ἀγαπᾶτέ με, τὰς ἐντολὰς τὰς ἐμὰς
ye love me, the ¹commandments - ¹my

τηρήσετε. 16 κἀγὼ ἐρωτήσω τὸν πατέρα
ye will keep. And I will request the Father

καὶ ἄλλον παράκλητον δώσει ὑμῖν, ἵνα
and another Comforter he will give you, that

ᾖ μεθ' ὑμῶν εἰς τὸν αἰῶνα, 17 τὸ
he may be with you unto the age, the

πνεῦμα τῆς ἀληθείας, ὃ ὁ κόσμος
Spirit - of truth, which* the world

οὐ δύναται λαβεῖν, ὅτι οὐ θεωρεῖ αὐτὸ
cannot to receive, because it beholds not it*

οὐδὲ γινώσκει· ὑμεῖς γινώσκετε αὐτό,
nor knows; ye know it,*

ὅτι παρ' ὑμῖν μένει καὶ ἐν ὑμῖν ἔσται.
because with you he remains and in you will be.

18 Οὐκ ἀφήσω ὑμᾶς ὀρφανούς, ἔρχομαι
I will not leave you orphans, I am coming

πρὸς ὑμᾶς. 19 ἔτι μικρὸν καὶ ὁ κόσμος
to you. Yet a little and the world

με οὐκέτι θεωρεῖ, ὑμεῖς δὲ θεωρεῖτέ
me no longer beholds, but ye behold

με, ὅτι ἐγὼ ζῶ καὶ ὑμεῖς ζήσετε.
me, because I live also ye will live.

20 ἐν ἐκείνῃ τῇ ἡμέρᾳ γνώσεσθε ὑμεῖς
In that - day will know ye

ὅτι ἐγὼ ἐν τῷ πατρί μου καὶ ὑμεῖς
that I in the Father of me and ye

ἐν ἐμοὶ κἀγὼ ἐν ὑμῖν. 21 Ὁ ἔχων
in me and I in you. The [one] having

τὰς ἐντολάς μου καὶ τηρῶν αὐτάς,
the commandments of me and keeping them,

ἐκεῖνός ἐστιν ὁ ἀγαπῶν με· ὁ δὲ ἀγαπῶν
that is the [one] loving me; and the [one] loving

με ἀγαπηθήσεται ὑπὸ τοῦ πατρός μου,
me will be loved by the Father of me,

κἀγὼ ἀγαπήσω αὐτὸν καὶ ἐμφανίσω αὐτῷ
and I will love him and will manifest to him

ἐμαυτόν. 22 λέγει αὐτῷ Ἰούδας, οὐχ
myself. Says to him Judas, not

ὁ Ἰσκαριώτης· κύριε, καὶ τί γέγονεν
the Iscariot: Lord, and what has happened

ὅτι ἡμῖν μέλλεις ἐμφανίζειν σεαυτὸν καὶ
that to us thou art about to manifest thyself and

οὐχὶ τῷ κόσμῳ; 23 ἀπεκρίθη Ἰησοῦς
not to the world? Answered Jesus

καὶ εἶπεν αὐτῷ· ἐάν τις ἀγαπᾷ με,
and said to him: If anyone loves me,

τὸν λόγον μου τηρήσει, καὶ ὁ πατήρ
the word of me he will keep, and the Father

μου ἀγαπήσει αὐτόν, καὶ πρὸς αὐτὸν
of me will love him, and to him

ἐλευσόμεθα καὶ μονὴν παρ' αὐτῷ
we will come and abode with him

ποιησόμεθα. 24 ὁ μὴ ἀγαπῶν με τοὺς
we will make. The [one] not loving me the

λόγους μου οὐ τηρεῖ· καὶ ὁ λόγος ὃν
words of me keeps not; and the word which

ἀκούετε οὐκ ἔστιν ἐμὸς ἀλλὰ τοῦ
ye hear is not mine but ¹of the

πέμψαντός με πατρός. 25 Ταῦτα λελάληκα
³having sent ⁴me ³Father. These things I have spoken

Jesus Promises the Holy Spirit

15 "If you love me, you will obey what I command. 16 And I will ask the Father, and he will give you another Counselor to be with you forever— 17 the Spirit of truth. The world cannot accept him, because it neither sees him nor knows him. But you know him, for he lives with you and will be[r] in you. 18 I will not leave you as orphans; I will come to you. 19 Before long, the world will not see me anymore, but you will see me. Because I live, you also will live. 20 On that day you will realize that I am in my Father, and you are in me, and I am in you. 21 Whoever has my commands and obeys them, he is the one who loves me. He who loves me will be loved by my Father, and I too will love him and show myself to him."

22 Then Judas (not Judas Iscariot) said, "But, Lord, why do you intend to show yourself to us and not to the world?"

23 Jesus replied, "If anyone loves me, he will obey my teaching. My Father will love him, and we will come to him and make our home with him. 24 He who does not love me will not obey my teaching. These words you hear are not my own; they belong to the Father who sent me.

25 "All this I have spoken

---

g Other ancient authorities read *me, keep*
h Or *Helper*
i Or *among*

* The gender of these pronouns agrees, of course, with the antecedent πνεῦμα (neuter); and this has been kept though the personal Spirit of God is meant. Elsewhere, masculine pronouns are in fact used.

r 17 Some early manuscripts *and is*

things to you while I am still with you. 26 But the Advocate,[h] the Holy Spirit, whom the Father will send in my name, will teach you everything, and remind you of all that I have said to you. 27 Peace I leave with you; my peace I give to you. I do not give to you as the world gives. Do not let your hearts be troubled, and do not let them be afraid. 28 You heard me say to you, 'I am going away, and I am coming to you.' If you loved me, you would rejoice that I am going to the Father, because the Father is greater than I. 29 And now I have told you this before it occurs, so that when it does occur, you may believe. 30 I will no longer talk much with you, for the ruler of this world is coming. He has no power over me; 31 but I do as the Father has commanded me, so that the world may know that I love the Father. Rise, let us be on our way.

ὑμῖν παρ’ ὑμῖν μένων·
to you with you remaining;

26 ὁ δὲ παρά-
but the Com-

κλητος, τὸ πνεῦμα τὸ ἅγιον ὃ πέμψει ὁ
forter, the Spirit - Holy which will send the

πατὴρ ἐν τῷ ὀνόματί μου, ἐκεῖνος ὑμᾶς
Father in the name of me, that one you

διδάξει πάντα καὶ ὑπομνήσει ὑμᾶς πάντα
will teach all things and remind you [of] all things

ἃ εἶπον ὑμῖν ἐγώ. 27 Εἰρήνην ἀφίημι
which ¹told ²you ¹I. Peace I leave

ὑμῖν, εἰρήνην τὴν ἐμὴν δίδωμι ὑμῖν·
to you, ¹peace - ¹my I give you;

οὐ καθὼς ὁ κόσμος δίδωσιν ἐγὼ δίδωμι
not as the world gives I give

ὑμῖν. μὴ ταρασσέσθω ὑμῶν ἡ καρδία
you. Let not be troubled of you the heart

μηδὲ δειλιάτω. 28 ἠκούσατε ὅτι ἐγὼ
nor let it be fearful. Ye heard that I

εἶπον ὑμῖν· ὑπάγω καὶ ἔρχομαι πρὸς
told you : I go and come to

ὑμᾶς. εἰ ἠγαπᾶτέ με, ἐχάρητε ἂν ὅτι
you. If ye loved me, ye would have rejoiced that

πορεύομαι πρὸς τὸν πατέρα, ὅτι ὁ πατὴρ
I am going to the Father, because the Father

μείζων μού ἐστιν. 29 καὶ νῦν εἴρηκα
greater [than] me(I) is. And now I have told

ὑμῖν πρὶν γενέσθαι, ἵνα ὅταν γένηται
you before to happen, that when it happens
=it happens,

πιστεύσητε. 30 οὐκέτι πολλὰ λαλήσω μεθ’
ye may believe. No longer many things I will speak with

ὑμῶν, ἔρχεται γὰρ ὁ τοῦ κόσμου ἄρχων·
you, for ⁵is coming ¹the ²of the ⁴world ¹ruler;

καὶ ἐν ἐμοὶ οὐκ ἔχει οὐδέν, 31 ἀλλ’
and in me he has not no(any)thing, but

ἵνα γνῷ ὁ κόσμος ὅτι ἀγαπῶ τὸν
that may know the world that I love the

πατέρα, καὶ καθὼς ἐνετείλατό μοι ὁ
Father, and as commanded me the

πατήρ, οὕτως ποιῶ. Ἐγείρεσθε, ἄγωμεν
Father, so I do. Rise, let us go

ἐντεῦθεν.
hence.

while still with you. 26 But the Counselor, the Holy Spirit, whom the Father will send in my name, will teach you all things and will remind you of everything I have said to you. 27 Peace I leave with you; my peace I give to you. I do not give to you as the world gives. Do not let your hearts be troubled, and do not be afraid. 28 "You heard me say, 'I am going away and I am coming back to you.' If you loved me, you would be glad that I am going to the Father, for the Father is greater than I. 29 I have told you now before it happens, so that when it does happen you will believe. 30 I will not speak with you much longer, for the prince of this world is coming. He has no hold on me, 31 but the world must learn that I love the Father and that I do exactly what my Father has commanded me.
"Come now; let us leave.

Chapter 15

Jesus the True Vine

"I am the true vine, and my Father is the vinegrower. 2 He removes every branch in me that bears no fruit. Every branch that bears fruit he prunes[j] to make it bear more fruit. 3 You have already been cleansed[j] by the word that I have spoken to you. 4 Abide in me as I abide in you. Just as the branch cannot bear fruit by itself unless it abides in the vine, neither can you unless you abide in me. 5 I am

15 Ἐγώ εἰμι ἡ ἄμπελος ἡ ἀληθινή,
I am the vine - true,

καὶ ὁ πατήρ μου ὁ γεωργός ἐστιν.
and the Father of me the husbandman is.

2 πᾶν κλῆμα ἐν ἐμοὶ μὴ φέρον καρπόν,
Every branch in me not bearing fruit,

αἴρει αὐτό, καὶ πᾶν τὸ καρπὸν φέρον,
he takes it, and every [branch] the fruit bearing,

καθαίρει αὐτὸ ἵνα καρπὸν πλείονα φέρῃ.
he prunes it that fruit more it may bear.

3 ἤδη ὑμεῖς καθαροί ἐστε διὰ τὸν λόγον
Now ye clean are because of the word

ὃν λελάληκα ὑμῖν· 4 μείνατε ἐν ἐμοί,
which I have spoken to you; remain in me,

κἀγὼ ἐν ὑμῖν. καθὼς τὸ κλῆμα
and I in you. As the branch

οὐ δύναται καρπὸν φέρειν ἀφ’ ἑαυτοῦ ἐὰν μὴ
cannot fruit to bear from itself unless

μένῃ ἐν τῇ ἀμπέλῳ, οὕτως οὐδὲ ὑμεῖς
it remains in the vine, so not ye

ἐὰν μὴ ἐν ἐμοὶ μένητε. 5 ἐγώ εἰμι
unless in me ye remain. I am

Chapter 15

The Vine and the Branches

"I AM the true vine, and my Father is the gardener. 2 He cuts off every branch in me that bears no fruit, while every branch that does bear fruit he prunes[s] so that it will be even more fruitful. 3 You are already clean because of the word I have spoken to you. 4 Remain in me, and I will remain in you. No branch can bear fruit by itself; it must remain in the vine. Neither can you bear fruit unless you remain in me.

---

[j] The same Greek root refers to pruning and cleansing

[s] 2 The Greek for *prunes* also means *cleans.*

the vine, you are the branches. Those who abide in me and I in them bear much fruit, because apart from me you can do nothing. 6Whoever does not abide in me is thrown away like a branch and withers; such branches are gathered, thrown into the fire, and burned. 7If you abide in me, and my words abide in you, ask for whatever you wish, and it will be done for you. 8My Father is glorified by this, that you bear much fruit and become[k] my disciples. 9As the Father has loved me, so I have loved you; abide in my love. 10If you keep my commandments, you will abide in my love, just as I have kept my Father's commandments and abide in his love. 11I have said these things to you so that my joy may be in you, and that your joy may be complete. 12 "This is my commandment, that you love one another as I have loved you. 13No one has greater love than this, to lay down one's life for one's friends. 14You are my friends if you do what I command you. 15I do not call you servants[l] any longer, because the servant[m] does not know what the master is doing; but I have called you friends, because I have made known to you everything that I have heard from my Father. 16You did not choose me but I chose you. And I appointed you to go and bear fruit, fruit that will

ἡ ἄμπελος, ὑμεῖς τὰ κλήματα. ὁ μένων
the vine, ye the branches. The [one] remaining

ἐν ἐμοὶ κἀγὼ ἐν αὐτῷ, οὗτος φέρει
in me and I in him, this one bears

καρπὸν πολύν, ὅτι χωρὶς ἐμοῦ οὐ δύνασθε
fruit much, because apart from me ye cannot

ποιεῖν οὐδέν. 6 ἐὰν μή τις μένῃ ἐν
to do no(any)thing. Unless anyone remains in

ἐμοί, ἐβλήθη ἔξω ὡς τὸ κλῆμα καὶ
me, he was(is) cast outside as the branch and

ἐξηράνθη, καὶ συνάγουσιν αὐτὰ καὶ εἰς
was(is) dried, and they gather them and into

τὸ πῦρ βάλλουσιν, καὶ καίεται. 7 ἐὰν
the fire they cast, and they are burned. If

μείνητε ἐν ἐμοὶ καὶ τὰ ῥήματά μου
ye remain in me and the words of me

ἐν ὑμῖν μείνῃ, ὃ ἐὰν θέλητε αἰτήσασθε,
in you remains, whatever ye wish ask,

καὶ γενήσεται ὑμῖν. 8 ἐν τούτῳ ἐδοξάσθη
and it shall happen to you. By this was glorified

ὁ πατήρ μου, ἵνα καρπὸν πολὺν φέρητε
the Father of me, that fruit much ye bear

καὶ γενήσεσθε ἐμοὶ μαθηταί. 9 καθὼς
and ye will be to me[e] disciples. As

ἠγάπησέν με ὁ πατήρ, κἀγὼ ὑμᾶς
loved me the Father, I also you

ἠγάπησα· μείνατε ἐν τῇ ἀγάπῃ τῇ ἐμῇ.
loved; remain ye in the ²love – ¹my.

10 ἐὰν τὰς ἐντολάς μου τηρήσητε, μενεῖτε
If the commandments of me ye keep, ye will remain

ἐν τῇ ἀγάπῃ μου, καθὼς ἐγὼ τοῦ πατρός
in the love of me, as I of the Father

μου τὰς ἐντολὰς τετήρηκα καὶ μένω
of me the commandments have kept and remain

αὐτοῦ ἐν τῇ ἀγάπῃ. 11 Ταῦτα λελάληκα
of him in the love. These things I have spoken

ὑμῖν ἵνα ἡ χαρὰ ἡ ἐμὴ ἐν ὑμῖν ᾖ
to you that the ²joy – ¹my in you may be

καὶ ἡ χαρὰ ὑμῶν πληρωθῇ. 12 αὕτη
and the joy of you may be filled. This

ἐστὶν ἡ ἐντολὴ ἡ ἐμή, ἵνα ἀγαπᾶτε
is the ²commandment – ¹my, that ye love

ἀλλήλους καθὼς ἠγάπησα ὑμᾶς. 13 μείζονα
one another as I loved you. ¹Greater

ταύτης ἀγάπην οὐδεὶς ἔχει, ἵνα τις
[³than] ⁴this ²love no one has, that anyone

τὴν ψυχὴν αὐτοῦ θῇ ὑπὲρ τῶν φίλων
the life of him should lay down for the friends

αὐτοῦ. 14 ὑμεῖς φίλοι μού ἐστε, ἐὰν
of him. Ye friends of me are, if

ποιῆτε ὃ ἐγὼ ἐντέλλομαι ὑμῖν. 15 οὐκέτι
ye do what I command you. No longer

λέγω ὑμᾶς δούλους, ὅτι ὁ δοῦλος οὐκ οἶδεν
I call you slaves, because the slave knows not

τί ποιεῖ αὐτοῦ ὁ κύριος· ὑμᾶς δὲ
what does of him the lord; but you

εἴρηκα φίλους, ὅτι πάντα ἃ ἤκουσα
I have called friends, because all things which I heard

παρὰ τοῦ πατρός μου ἐγνώρισα ὑμῖν.
from the Father of me I made known to you.

16 οὐχ ὑμεῖς με ἐξελέξασθε, ἀλλ’ ἐγὼ
Not ye me chose, but I

ἐξελεξάμην ὑμᾶς, καὶ ἔθηκα ὑμᾶς ἵνα
chose you, and appointed you that

ὑμεῖς ὑπάγητε καὶ καρπὸν φέρητε καὶ
ye should go and fruit should bear and

5"I am the vine; you are the branches. If a man remains in me and I in him, he will bear much fruit; apart from me you can do nothing. 6If anyone does not remain in me, he is like a branch that is thrown away and withers; such branches are picked up, thrown into the fire and burned. 7If you remain in me and my words remain in you, ask whatever you wish, and it will be given you. 8This is to my Father's glory, that you bear much fruit, showing yourselves to be my disciples. 9"As the Father has loved me, so have I loved you. Now remain in my love. 10If you obey my commands, you will remain in my love, just as I have obeyed my Father's commands and remain in his love. 11I have told you this so that my joy may be in you and that your joy may be complete. 12My command is this: Love each other as I have loved you. 13Greater love has no one than this, that he lay down his life for his friends. 14You are my friends if you do what I command. 15I no longer call you servants, because a servant does not know his master's business. Instead, I have called you friends, for everything that I learned from my Father I have made known to you. 16You did not choose me, but I chose you and appointed you to go and bear

k Or be
l Gk slaves
m Gk slave

last, so that the Father will give you whatever you ask him in my name. 17 I am giving you these commands so that you may love one another.

The World's Hatred

18 "If the world hates you, be aware that it hated me before it hated you. 19 If you belonged to the world, ⁿ the world would love you as its own. Because you do not belong to the world, but I have chosen you out of the world— therefore the world hates you. 20 Remember the word that I said to you, 'Servantsᵒ are not greater than their master.' If they persecuted me, they will persecute you; if they kept my word, they will keep yours also. 21 But they will do all these things to you on account of my name, because they do not know him who sent me. 22 If I had not come and spoken to them, they would not have sin; but now they have no excuse for their sin. 23 Whoever hates me hates my Father also. 24 If I had not done among them the works that no one else did, they would not have sin. But now they have seen and hated both me and my Father. 25 It was to fulfill the word that is written in their law, 'They hated me without a cause.'

26 "When the Advocateᵖ comes, whom I will send to you from the Father, the Spirit of truth who comes from the Father, he will testify on my behalf. 27 You also are to testify because you have been with me from the beginning.

ὁ καρπὸς ὑμῶν μένῃ, ἵνα ὅ τι ἂν
the fruit of you should remain, that whatever
αἰτήσητε τὸν πατέρα ἐν τῷ ὀνόματί
ye may ask the Father in the name
μου δῷ ὑμῖν. 17 ταῦτα ἐντέλλομαι ὑμῖν,
of me he may give you. These things I command you,
ἵνα ἀγαπᾶτε ἀλλήλους. 18 Εἰ ὁ κόσμος
that ye love one another. If the world
ὑμᾶς μισεῖ, γινώσκετε ὅτι ἐμὲ πρῶτον
you hates, ye know that me before
ὑμῶν μεμίσηκεν. 19 εἰ ἐκ τοῦ κόσμου ἦτε,
you it has hated. If of the world ye were,
ὁ κόσμος ἂν τὸ ἴδιον ἐφίλει· ὅτι δὲ
the world ¹would ²the(its) ³own ⁴have loved; but because
ἐκ τοῦ κόσμου οὐκ ἐστέ, ἀλλ' ἐγὼ
of the world ye are not, but I
ἐξελεξάμην ὑμᾶς ἐκ τοῦ κόσμου, διὰ τοῦτο
chose you out of the world, therefore
μισεῖ ὑμᾶς ὁ κόσμος. 20 μνημονεύετε
hates you the world. Remember ye
τοῦ λόγου οὗ ἐγὼ εἶπον ὑμῖν· οὐκ
the word which I said to you: Not
ἔστιν δοῦλος μείζων τοῦ κυρίου αὐτοῦ.
is a slave greater [than] the lord of him.
εἰ ἐμὲ ἐδίωξαν, καὶ ὑμᾶς διώξουσιν·
If me they persecuted, also you they will persecute;
εἰ τὸν λόγον μου ἐτήρησαν, καὶ τὸν
if the word of me they kept, also the
ὑμέτερον τηρήσουσιν. 21 ἀλλὰ ταῦτα πάντα
yours they will keep. But these things all
ποιήσουσιν εἰς ὑμᾶς διὰ τὸ ὄνομά μου,
they will do to you because of the name of me,
ὅτι οὐκ οἴδασιν τὸν πέμψαντά με.
because they know not the [one] having sent me.
22 εἰ μὴ ἦλθον καὶ ἐλάλησα αὐτοῖς, ἁμαρτίαν
Unless I came and spoke to them, sin
οὐκ εἴχοσαν· νῦν δὲ πρόφασιν οὐκ ἔχουσιν
they had not had; but now cloak they have not
περὶ τῆς ἁμαρτίας αὐτῶν. 23 ὁ ἐμὲ
concerning the sin of them. The [one] me
μισῶν καὶ τὸν πατέρα μου μισεῖ. 24 εἰ
hating also the Father of me hates. If
τὰ ἔργα μὴ ἐποίησα ἐν αὐτοῖς ἃ οὐδεὶς
the works I did not among them which no man
ἄλλος ἐποίησεν, ἁμαρτίαν οὐκ εἴχοσαν·
other did, sin they had not had;
νῦν δὲ καὶ ἑωράκασιν καὶ μεμισήκασιν
but now both they have seen and have hated
καὶ ἐμὲ καὶ τὸν πατέρα μου. 25 ἀλλ'
both me and the Father of me. But
ἵνα πληρωθῇ ὁ λόγος ὁ ἐν τῷ νόμῳ
that may be fulfilled the word – in the law
αὐτῶν γεγραμμένος ὅτι ἐμίσησάν με
of them having been written[,] – They hated me
δωρεάν. 26 Ὅταν ἔλθῃ ὁ παράκλητος
freely. When comes the Comforter
ὃν ἐγὼ πέμψω ὑμῖν παρὰ τοῦ πατρός,
whom I will send to you from the Father,
τὸ πνεῦμα τῆς ἀληθείας ὁ παρὰ τοῦ
the Spirit – of truth which from the
πατρὸς ἐκπορεύεται, ἐκεῖνος μαρτυρήσει
Father proceeds, that one will witness
περὶ ἐμοῦ· 27 καὶ ὑμεῖς δὲ μαρτυρεῖτε,
concerning me; ³also ²ye ¹and witness,
ὅτι ἀπ' ἀρχῆς μετ' ἐμοῦ ἐστε.
because from [the] beginning with me ye are.

The World Hates the Disciples

18 "If the world hates you, keep in mind that it hated me first. 19 If you belonged to the world, it would love you as its own. As it is, you do not belong to the world, but I have chosen you out of the world. That is why the world hates you. 20 Remember the words I spoke to you: 'No servant is greater than his master.'ᵗ If they persecuted me, they will persecute you also. If they obeyed my teaching, they will obey yours also. 21 They will treat you this way because of my name, for they do not know the One who sent me. 22 If I had not come and spoken to them, they would not be guilty of sin. Now, however, they have no excuse for their sin. 23 He who hates me hates my Father as well. 24 If I had not done among them what no one else did, they would not be guilty of sin. But now they have seen these miracles, and yet they have hated both me and my Father. 25 But this is to fulfill what is written in their Law: 'They hated me without reason.'ᵘ

26 "When the Counselor comes, whom I will send to you from the Father, the Spirit of truth who goes out from the Father, he will testify about me. 27 And you also must testify, for you have been with me from the beginning.

ⁿ Gk were of the world
ᵒ Gk Slaves
ᵖ Or Helper

ᵗ20 John 13:16
ᵘ25 Psalms 35:19; 69:4

Chapter 16

" I have said these things to you to keep you from stumbling. ²They will put you out of the synagogues. Indeed, an hour is coming when those who kill you will think that by doing so they are offering worship to God. ³And they will do this because they have not known the Father or me. ⁴But I have said these things to you so that when their hour comes you may remember that I told you about them.

The Work of the Spirit

"I did not say these things to you from the beginning, because I was with you. ⁵But now I am going to him who sent me; yet none of you asks me, 'Where are you going?' ⁶But because I have said these things to you, sorrow has filled your hearts. ⁷Nevertheless I tell you the truth: it is to your advantage that I go away, for if I do not go away, the Advocate[p] will not come to you; but if I go, I will send him to you. ⁸And when he comes, he will prove the world wrong about[q] sin and righteousness and judgment: ⁹about sin, because they do not believe in me; ¹⁰about righteousness, because I am going to the Father and you will see me no longer; ¹¹about judgment, because the ruler of this world has been condemned.

12 "I still have many things to say to you, but you cannot bear them now. ¹³When the Spirit of truth comes, he will guide you into all the truth; for he will not speak on his own, but will speak whatever he hears, and he will declare to you the things that are to come. ¹⁴He will glorify me,

---

16 Ταῦτα λελάληκα ὑμῖν ἵνα μὴ
These things I have spoken to you that not
σκανδαλισθῆτε. **2** ἀποσυναγώγους ποιή-
ye be offended. Put away from [the] synagogue they
σουσιν ὑμᾶς· ἀλλ' ἔρχεται ὥρα ἵνα πᾶς ὁ
will make you; but comes an hour that everyone
ἀποκτείνας ὑμᾶς δόξῃ λατρείαν προσφέρειν
killing you thinks service to offer
τῷ θεῷ. **3** καὶ ταῦτα ποιήσουσιν ὅτι
– to God. And these things they will do because
οὐκ ἔγνωσαν τὸν πατέρα οὐδὲ ἐμέ.
they knew not the Father nor me.
4 ἀλλὰ ταῦτα λελάληκα ὑμῖν ἵνα ὅταν
But these things I have spoken to you that when
ἔλθῃ ἡ ὥρα αὐτῶν μνημονεύητε αὐτῶν,
comes the hour of them ye may remember them,
ὅτι ἐγὼ εἶπον ὑμῖν. Ταῦτα δὲ ὑμῖν
that I told you. And these things to you
ἐξ ἀρχῆς οὐκ εἶπον, ὅτι μεθ' ὑμῶν
from [the] beginning I said not, because with you
ἤμην. **5** νῦν δὲ ὑπάγω πρὸς τὸν πέμψαντά
I was. But now I am going to the [one] having sent
με, καὶ οὐδεὶς ἐξ ὑμῶν ἐρωτᾷ με·
me, and not one of you asks me:
ποῦ ὑπάγεις; **6** ἀλλ' ὅτι ταῦτα λελάληκα
Where goest thou? but because these things I have spoken
ὑμῖν, ἡ λύπη πεπλήρωκεν ὑμῶν τὴν
to you, – grief has filled of you the
καρδίαν. **7** ἀλλ' ἐγὼ τὴν ἀλήθειαν λέγω
heart. But I the truth tell
ὑμῖν, συμφέρει ὑμῖν ἵνα ἐγὼ ἀπέλθω.
you, it is expedient for you that I should go away.
ἐὰν γὰρ μὴ ἀπέλθω, ὁ παράκλητος
For if I go not away, the Comforter
οὐ μὴ ἔλθῃ πρὸς ὑμᾶς· ἐὰν δὲ πορευθῶ,
by no means comes to you; but if I go,
πέμψω αὐτὸν πρὸς ὑμᾶς. **8** καὶ ἐλθὼν
I will send him to you. And coming
ἐκεῖνος ἐλέγξει τὸν κόσμον περὶ ἁμαρτίας
that one will reprove the world concerning sin
καὶ περὶ δικαιοσύνης καὶ περὶ κρίσεως·
and concerning righteousness and concerning judgment;
9 περὶ ἁμαρτίας μέν, ὅτι οὐ πιστεύουσιν
concerning sin, – because they believe not
εἰς ἐμέ· **10** περὶ δικαιοσύνης δέ, ὅτι
in me; concerning righteousness, – because that
πρὸς τὸν πατέρα ὑπάγω καὶ οὐκέτι
to the Father I am going and no longer
θεωρεῖτέ με· **11** περὶ δὲ κρίσεως, ὅτι
ye behold me; concerning – judgment, because
ὁ ἄρχων τοῦ κόσμου τούτου κέκριται.
the ruler of the world of this has been judged.
12 Ἔτι πολλὰ ἔχω ὑμῖν λέγειν, ἀλλ'
Yet many things I have you to tell, but
οὐ δύνασθε βαστάζειν ἄρτι· **13** ὅταν δὲ
ye cannot to bear now; but when
ἔλθῃ ἐκεῖνος, τὸ πνεῦμα τῆς ἀληθείας,
comes that one, the Spirit – of truth,
ὁδηγήσει ὑμᾶς εἰς τὴν ἀλήθειαν πᾶσαν·
he will guide you into the truth all;
οὐ γὰρ λαλήσει ἀφ' ἑαυτοῦ, ἀλλ' ὅσα
for not will he speak from himself, but what things
ἀκούει λαλήσει, καὶ τὰ ἐρχόμενα
he hears he will speak, and the coming things
ἀναγγελεῖ ὑμῖν. **14** ἐκεῖνος ἐμὲ δοξάσει,
he will announce to you. That one me will glorify,

Chapter 16

" ALL this I have told you so that you will not go astray. ²They will put you out of the synagogue; in fact, a time is coming when anyone who kills you will think he is offering a service to God. ³They will do such things because they have not known the Father or me. ⁴I have told you this, so that when the time comes you will remember that I warned you. I did not tell you this at first because I was with you.

The Work of the Holy Spirit

⁵"Now I am going to him who sent me, yet none of you asks me, 'Where are you going?' ⁶Because I have said these things, you are filled with grief. ⁷But I tell you the truth: It is for your good that I am going away. Unless I go away, the Counselor will not come to you; but if I go, I will send him to you. ⁸When he comes, he will convict the world of guilt[v] in regard to sin and righteousness and judgment: ⁹in regard to sin, because men do not believe in me; ¹⁰in regard to righteousness, because I am going to the Father, where you can see me no longer; ¹¹and in regard to judgment, because the prince of this world now stands condemned.

12"I have much more to say to you, more than you can now bear. ¹³But when he, the Spirit of truth, comes, he will guide you into all truth. He will not speak on his own; he will speak only what he hears, and he will tell you what is

---

[q] Or convict the world of

[v]8 Or will expose the guilt of the world

because he will take what is
mine and declare it to you.
15 All that the Father has is
mine. For this reason I said
that he will take what is
mine and declare it to you.

Sorrow Will Turn into Joy

16 "A little while, and
you will no longer see me,
and again a little while, and
you will see me." 17 Then
some of his disciples said to
one another, "What does
he mean by saying to us, 'A
little while, and you will no
longer see me, and again a
little while, and you will see
me'; and 'Because I am going to the Father'?" 18 They
said, "What does he mean
by this 'a little while'? We
do not know what he is
talking about." 19 Jesus
knew that they wanted to
ask him, so he said to them,
"Are you discussing among
yourselves what I meant
when I said, 'A little while,
and you will no longer see
me, and again a little while,
and you will see me'?
20 Very truly, I tell you, you
will weep and mourn, but
the world will rejoice; you
will have pain, but your
pain will turn into joy.
21 When a woman is in la-
bor, she has pain, because
her hour has come. But
when her child is born, she
no longer remembers the
anguish because of the joy
of having brought a human
being into the world. 22 So
you have pain now; but I
will see you again, and your
hearts will rejoice, and no
one will take your joy from
you. 23 On that day you will
ask nothing of me.ʳ Very
truly, I tell you, if you ask
anything of the Father in
my name, he will give it to

ὅτι ἐκ τοῦ ἐμοῦ λήμψεται καὶ ἀναγγελεῖ
because of the   of me* he will receive and will announce

ὑμῖν. 15 πάντα ὅσα ἔχει ὁ πατὴρ ἐμά
to you.   All things which has the Father mine

ἐστιν· διὰ τοῦτο εἶπον ὅτι ἐκ τοῦ ἐμοῦ
is(are);   therefore I said that of the of me*

λαμβάνει καὶ ἀναγγελεῖ ὑμῖν. 16 Μικρὸν
he receives and will announce to you.   A little while

καὶ οὐκέτι θεωρεῖτέ με, καὶ πάλιν
and no longer ye behold me, and again

μικρὸν καὶ ὄψεσθέ με. 17 εἶπαν οὖν
a little while and ye will see me. Said therefore

ἐκ τῶν μαθητῶν αὐτοῦ πρὸς ἀλλήλους·
[some] of the disciples of him to one another:

τί ἐστιν τοῦτο ὃ λέγει ἡμῖν· μικρὸν
What is this which he tells us: A little while

καὶ οὐ θεωρεῖτέ με, καὶ πάλιν μικρὸν
and ye behold not me, and again a little while

καὶ ὄψεσθέ με; καί· ὅτι ὑπάγω
and ye will see me? and: Because I am going

πρὸς τὸν πατέρα; 18 ἔλεγον οὖν· τοῦτο
to the Father? They said therefore: ³This

τί ἐστιν ὃ λέγει τὸ μικρόν; οὐκ οἴδαμεν
¹what ²is which he says[,] the "little while"? We do not know

τί λαλεῖ. 19 ἔγνω Ἰησοῦς ὅτι ἤθελον
what he speaks. Knew Jesus that they wished

αὐτὸν ἐρωτᾶν, καὶ εἶπεν αὐτοῖς· περὶ
him to question, and said to them: Concerning

τούτου ζητεῖτε μετ' ἀλλήλων ὅτι εἶπον·
this seek ye with one another because I said:

μικρὸν καὶ οὐ θεωρεῖτέ με, καὶ πάλιν
A little while and ye behold not me, and again

μικρὸν καὶ ὄψεσθέ με; 20 ἀμὴν ἀμὴν
a little while and ye will see me? Truly truly

λέγω ὑμῖν ὅτι κλαύσετε καὶ θρηνήσετε
I tell you that will weep and will lament

ὑμεῖς, ὁ δὲ κόσμος χαρήσεται· ὑμεῖς
ye, and the world will rejoice; ye

λυπηθήσεσθε, ἀλλ' ἡ λύπη ὑμῶν εἰς
will be grieved, but the grief of you into

χαρὰν γενήσεται. 21 ἡ γυνὴ ὅταν τίκτῃ
joy will become. The woman when she gives birth

λύπην ἔχει, ὅτι ἦλθεν ἡ ὥρα αὐτῆς·
grief has, because came the hour of her;

ὅταν δὲ γεννήσῃ τὸ παιδίον, οὐκέτι
but when she brings forth the child, no longer

μνημονεύει τῆς θλίψεως διὰ τὴν χαρὰν
she remembers the distress because of the joy

ὅτι ἐγεννήθη ἄνθρωπος εἰς τὸν κόσμον.
that was born a man into the world.

22 καὶ ὑμεῖς οὖν νῦν μὲν λύπην ἔχετε·
And ye therefore now indeed grief have;

πάλιν δὲ ὄψομαι ὑμᾶς, καὶ χαρήσεται
but again I will see you, and ⁴will rejoice

ὑμῶν ἡ καρδία, καὶ τὴν χαρὰν ὑμῶν
³of you ¹the ²heart, and the joy of you

οὐδεὶς αἴρει ἀφ' ὑμῶν. 23 καὶ ἐν ἐκείνῃ τῇ
no one takes from you. And in that –

ἡμέρα ἐμὲ οὐκ ἐρωτήσετε οὐδέν.
day me ye will not question no(any)thing.

ἀμὴν ἀμὴν λέγω ὑμῖν, ἄν τι αἰτήσητε
Truly truly I tell you, whatever ye ask

τὸν πατέρα δώσει ὑμῖν ἐν τῷ ὀνόματί
the Father he will give you in the name

yet to come. 14 He will bring
glory to me by taking from
what is mine and making it
known to you. 15 All that
belongs to the Father is
mine. That is why I said the
Spirit will take from what is
mine and make it known to
you.

16 "In a little while you
will see me no more, and
then after a little while you
will see me."

*The Disciples' Grief Will
Turn to Joy*

17 Some of his disciples
said to one another, "What
does he mean by saying, 'In
a little while you will see
me no more, and then after
a little while you will see
me,' and 'Because I am going to the Father'?" 18 They
kept asking, "What does
he mean by 'a little while'?
We don't understand what
he is saying."

19 Jesus saw that they
wanted to ask him about
this, so he said to them,
"Are you asking one an-
other what I meant when I
said, 'In a little while you
will see me no more, and
then after a little while you
will see me'? 20 I tell you the
truth, you will weep and
mourn while the world re-
joices. You will grieve, but
your grief will turn to joy.
21 A woman giving birth to a
child has pain because her
time has come; but when
her baby is born she forgets
the anguish because of her
joy that a child is born into
the world. 22 So with you:
Now is your time of grief,
but I will see you again and
you will rejoice, and no one
will take away your joy.
23 In that day you will no
longer ask me anything. I
tell you the truth, my Father will give you whatever
you ask in my name. 24 Un-

ʳ Or will ask me no question

* Understand "that which is mine".

Left column (RSV):

you.[s] 24 Until now you have not asked for anything in my name. Ask and you will receive, so that your joy may be complete.

Peace for the Disciples

25 "I have said these things to you in figures of speech. The hour is coming when I will no longer speak to you in figures, but will tell you plainly of the Father. 26 On that day you will ask in my name. I do not say to you that I will ask the Father on your behalf; 27 for the Father himself loves you, because you have loved me and have believed that I came from God.[t] 28 I came from the Father and have come into the world; again, I am leaving the world and am going to the Father."

29 His disciples said, "Yes, now you are speaking plainly, not in any figure of speech! 30 Now we know that you know all things, and do not need to have anyone question you; by this we believe that you came from God." 31 Jesus answered them, "Do you now believe? 32 The hour is coming, indeed it has come, when you will be scattered, each one to his home, and you will leave me alone. Yet I am not alone because the Father is with me. 33 I have said this to you, so that in me you may have peace. In the world you face persecution. But take courage; I have conquered the world!"

Chapter 17

Jesus Prays for His Disciples

AFTER Jesus had spoken these words, he looked up to heaven and said, "Father, the hour has come; glorify your Son so

[s] Other ancient authorities read *Father, he will give it to you in my name*
[t] Other ancient authorities read *the Father*

Center column (Greek interlinear):

μου. **24** ἕως ἄρτι οὐκ ἠτήσατε οὐδὲν
of me. Until now ye asked not no(any)thing

ἐν τῷ ὀνόματί μου· αἰτεῖτε, καὶ λήμψεσθε,
in the name of me; ask, and ye will receive,

ἵνα ἡ χαρὰ ὑμῶν ᾖ πεπληρωμένη.
that the joy of you may be *having been* filled.

25 Ταῦτα ἐν παροιμίαις λελάληκα ὑμῖν·
These things in allegories I have spoken to you;

ἔρχεται ὥρα ὅτε οὐκέτι ἐν παροιμίαις
comes an hour when no longer in allegories

λαλήσω ὑμῖν, ἀλλὰ παρρησίᾳ περὶ τοῦ
I will speak to you, but plainly concerning the

πατρὸς ἀπαγγελῶ ὑμῖν. **26** ἐν ἐκείνῃ τῇ
Father will declare to you. In that —

ἡμέρᾳ ἐν τῷ ὀνόματί μου αἰτήσεσθε,
day in the name of me ye will ask,

καὶ οὐ λέγω ὑμῖν ὅτι ἐγὼ ἐρωτήσω
and I tell not you that I will request

τὸν πατέρα περὶ ὑμῶν· **27** αὐτὸς γὰρ
the Father concerning you; for [him]self

ὁ πατὴρ φιλεῖ ὑμᾶς, ὅτι ὑμεῖς ἐμὲ
the Father loves you, because ye me

πεφιλήκατε καὶ πεπιστεύκατε ὅτι ἐγὼ
have loved and have believed that I

παρὰ τοῦ θεοῦ ἐξῆλθον. **28** ἐξῆλθον
from — God came forth. I came forth

ἐκ τοῦ πατρὸς καὶ ἐλήλυθα εἰς τὸν
out of the Father and have come into the

κόσμον· πάλιν ἀφίημι τὸν κόσμον καὶ
world; again I leave the world and

πορεύομαι πρὸς τὸν πατέρα. **29** Λέγουσιν
go to the Father. Say

οἱ μαθηταὶ αὐτοῦ· ἴδε νῦν ἐν παρρησίᾳ
the disciples of him: Behold[,] now in plainness

λαλεῖς, καὶ παροιμίαν οὐδεμίαν λέγεις.
thou speakest, and ᵃallegory ¹no thou sayest.

30 νῦν οἴδαμεν ὅτι οἶδας πάντα καὶ
Now we know that thou knowest all things and

οὐ χρείαν ἔχεις ἵνα τίς σε ἐρωτᾷ· ἐν
no need hast that anyone thee should question; by

τούτῳ πιστεύομεν ὅτι ἀπὸ θεοῦ ἐξῆλθες.
this we believe that from God thou camest forth.

31 ἀπεκρίθη αὐτοῖς Ἰησοῦς· ἄρτι πιστεύετε;
Answered them Jesus: Now believe ye?

32 ἰδοὺ ἔρχεται ὥρα καὶ ἐλήλυθεν ἵνα
behold[,] comes an hour and has come that

σκορπισθῆτε ἕκαστος εἰς τὰ ἴδια κἀμὲ
ye are scattered each one to the(his) own and me

μόνον ἀφῆτε· καὶ οὐκ εἰμὶ μόνος, ὅτι
alone ye leave; and I am not alone, because

ὁ πατὴρ μετ' ἐμοῦ ἐστιν. **33** ταῦτα
the Father with me is. These things

λελάληκα ὑμῖν ἵνα ἐν ἐμοὶ εἰρήνην
I have spoken to you that in me peace

ἔχητε. ἐν τῷ κόσμῳ θλῖψιν ἔχετε·
ye may have. In the world distress ye have;

ἀλλὰ θαρσεῖτε, ἐγὼ νενίκηκα τὸν κόσμον.
but cheer ye up, I have overcome the world.

17 Ταῦτα ἐλάλησεν Ἰησοῦς, καὶ ἐπάρας
These things spoke Jesus, and lifting up

τοὺς ὀφθαλμοὺς αὐτοῦ εἰς τὸν οὐρανὸν
the eyes of him to — heaven

εἶπεν· πάτερ, ἐλήλυθεν ἡ ὥρα· δόξασόν
said: Father, has come the hour; glorify

Right column (NEB/other):

til now you have not asked for anything in my name. Ask and you will receive, and your joy will be complete.

25 "Though I have been speaking figuratively, a time is coming when I will no longer use this kind of language but will tell you plainly about my Father. 26 In that day you will ask in my name. I am not saying that I will ask the Father on your behalf. 27 No, the Father himself loves you because you have loved me and have believed that I came from God. 28 I came from the Father and entered the world; now I am leaving the world and going back to the Father."

29 Then Jesus' disciples said, "Now you are speaking clearly and without figures of speech. 30 Now we can see that you know all things and that you do not even need to have anyone ask you questions. This makes us believe that you came from God."

31 "You believe at last!"[w] Jesus answered. 32 "But a time is coming, and has come, when you will be scattered, each to his own home. You will leave me all alone. Yet I am not alone, for my Father is with me.

33 "I have told you these things, so that in me you may have peace. In this world you will have trouble. But take heart! I have overcome the world."

Chapter 17

Jesus Prays for Himself

AFTER Jesus said this, he looked toward heaven and prayed:

"Father, the time has come. Glorify your

[w] 31 Or "Do you now believe?"

that the Son may glorify you, 2 since you have given him authority over all people,ᵘ to give eternal life to all whom you have given him. 3 And this is eternal life, that they may know you, the only true God, and Jesus Christ whom you have sent. 4 I glorified you on earth by finishing the work that you gave me to do. 5 So now, Father, glorify me in your own presence with the glory that I had in your presence before the world existed.

6 "I have made your name known to those whom you gave me from the world. They were yours, and you gave them to me, and they have kept your word. 7 Now they know that everything you have given me is from you; 8 for the words that you gave to me I have given to them, and they have received them and know in truth that I came from you; and they have believed that you sent me. 9 I am asking on their behalf; I am not asking on behalf of the world, but on behalf of those whom you gave me, because they are yours. 10 All mine are yours, and yours are mine; and I have been glorified in them. 11 And now I am no longer in the world, but they are in the world, and I am coming to you. Holy Father, protect them in your name thatᵛ you have given me, so that they may be one, as we are one. 12 While I was with them, I protected them in your name thatᵛ you have given me. I guard-

σου τὸν υἱόν, ἵνα ὁ υἱὸς δοξάσῃ σέ,
of thee the   Son,   that the Son may glorify thee,

2 καθὼς ἔδωκας αὐτῷ ἐξουσίαν πάσης
  as   thou gavest him   authority of(over) all

σαρκός, ἵνα πᾶν ὃ δέδωκας αὐτῷ δώσῃ
flesh, that all which thou hast given him he may give

αὐτοῖς ζωὴν αἰώνιον. 3 αὕτη δέ ἐστιν
to them life eternal.   And this   is

ἡ αἰώνιος ζωή, ἵνα γινώσκωσιν σὲ τὸν
- eternal life, that they may know thee the

μόνον ἀληθινὸν θεὸν καὶ ὃν ἀπέστειλας
only   true   God   and [he] whom thou didst send

Ἰησοῦν Χριστόν. 4 ἐγώ σε ἐδόξασα
Jesus Christ.   I   thee glorified

ἐπὶ τῆς γῆς, τὸ ἔργον τελειώσας ὃ
on the earth, the work finishing which

δέδωκάς μοι ἵνα ποιήσω· 5 καὶ νῦν
thou hast given to me that I should do;   and now

δόξασόν με σύ, πάτερ, παρὰ σεαυτῷ
glorify me thou, Father, with   thyself

τῇ δόξῃ ᾗ εἶχον πρὸ τοῦ τὸν κόσμον
with the glory which I had before the the world
                                      =before the world was

εἶναι παρὰ σοί. 6 Ἐφανέρωσά σου τὸ
to beᵇ with thee.   I manifested   of thee the

ὄνομα τοῖς ἀνθρώποις οὓς ἔδωκάς μοι
name to the men   whom thou gavest to me

ἐκ τοῦ κόσμου. σοὶ ἦσαν κἀμοὶ αὐτοὺς
out of the world. To theeᵉ they were and to me them
                       =Thine

ἔδωκας, καὶ τὸν λόγον σου τετήρηκαν.
thou gavest, and the word of thee they have kept.

7 νῦν ἔγνωκαν ὅτι πάντα ὅσα δέδωκάς
Now they have known that all things as many as thou hast given

μοι παρὰ σοῦ εἰσιν· 8 ὅτι τὰ ῥήματα
to me from thee are;   because the words

ἃ ἔδωκάς μοι δέδωκα αὐτοῖς, καὶ αὐτοὶ
which thou gavest to me I have given to them, and they

ἔλαβον, καὶ ἔγνωσαν ἀληθῶς ὅτι παρὰ
received, and knew   truly   that from

σοῦ ἐξῆλθον, καὶ ἐπίστευσαν ὅτι σύ
thee I came forth, and they believed that thou

με ἀπέστειλας. 9 ἐγὼ περὶ αὐτῶν ἐρωτῶ·
me didst send.   I concerning them make request;

οὐ περὶ τοῦ κόσμου ἐρωτῶ, ἀλλὰ περὶ
not concerning the world do I make request, but concerning

ὧν δέδωκάς μοι, ὅτι σοί εἰσιν,
[those] whom thou hast given to me, because to theeᵉ they are,
                                          =thine

10 καὶ τὰ ἐμὰ πάντα σά ἐστιν καὶ
   and ¹the ²my things ¹all ⁸thine ⁴is(are) and

τὰ σὰ ἐμά, καὶ δεδόξασμαι ἐν αὐτοῖς.
the thy things mine, and I have been glorified in   them.

11 καὶ οὐκέτι εἰμὶ ἐν τῷ κόσμῳ, καὶ
  And no longer am I in the world,   and

αὐτοὶ ἐν τῷ κόσμῳ εἰσίν, κἀγὼ πρὸς
they in the world are,   and I to

σὲ ἔρχομαι. πάτερ ἅγιε, τήρησον αὐτοὺς
thee come.   Father holy, keep   them

ἐν τῷ ὀνόματί σου ᾧ δέδωκάς μοι,
in the name of thee which thou hast given to me,

ἵνα ὦσιν ἓν καθὼς ἡμεῖς. 12 ὅτε ἤμην
that they may be one as   we.   When I was

μετ' αὐτῶν, ἐγὼ ἐτήρουν αὐτοὺς ἐν
with them,   I   kept   them   in

τῷ ὀνόματί σου ᾧ δέδωκάς μοι, καὶ
the name of thee which thou hast given to me, and

Son, that your Son may glorify you. 2 For you granted him authority over all people that he might give eternal life to all those you have given him. 3 Now this is eternal life: that they may know you, the only true God, and Jesus Christ, whom you have sent. 4 I have brought you glory on earth by completing the work you gave me to do. 5 And now, Father, glorify me in your presence with the glory I had with you before the world began.

Jesus Prays for His Disciples

6 "I have revealed youˣ to those whom you gave me out of the world. They were yours; you gave them to me and they have obeyed your word. 7 Now they know that everything you have given me comes from you. 8 For I gave them the words you gave me and they accepted them. They knew with certainty that I came from you, and they believed that you sent me. 9 I pray for them. I am not praying for the world, but for those you have given me, for they are yours. 10 All I have is yours, and all you have is mine. And glory has come to me through them. 11 I will remain in the world no longer, but they are still in the world, and I am coming to you. Holy Father, protect them by the power of your name— the name you gave me —so that they may be one as we are one. 12 While I was with them, I protected them and kept them safe by

ᵘ Gk *flesh*
ᵛ Other ancient authorities read *protected in your name those whom*

ˣ6 Greek *your name*; also in verse 26

ed them, and not one of them was lost except the one destined to be lost, [w] so that the scripture might be fulfilled. 13 But now I am coming to you, and I speak these things in the world so that they may have my joy made complete in themselves. [x] 14 I have given them your word, and the world has hated them because they do not belong to the world, just as I do not belong to the world. 15 I am not asking you to take them out of the world, but I ask you to protect them from the evil one. [y] 16 They do not belong to the world, just as I do not belong to the world. 17 Sanctify them in the truth; your word is truth. 18 As you have sent me into the world, so I have sent them into the world. 19 And for their sakes I sanctify myself, so that they also may be sanctified in truth.

20 "I ask not only on behalf of these, but also on behalf of those who will believe in me through their word, 21 that they may all be one. As you, Father, are in me and I am in you, may they also be in us, [z] so that the world may believe that you have sent me. 22 The glory that you have given me I have given them, so that they may be one, as we are one, 23 I in them and you in me, that they may become completely one, so that the world may know that you have sent me and have loved them even as you have loved me. 24 Father, I desire that those also, whom you have given me, may be with me where

---

ἐφύλαξα, καὶ οὐδεὶς ἐξ αὐτῶν ἀπώλετο
I guarded, and not one of them perished

εἰ μὴ ὁ υἱὸς τῆς ἀπωλείας, ἵνα ἡ
except the son - perdition, that the

γραφὴ πληρωθῇ. 13 νῦν δὲ πρὸς σὲ
scripture might be fulfilled. But now to thee

ἔρχομαι, καὶ ταῦτα λαλῶ ἐν τῷ κόσμῳ
I come, and these things I speak in the world

ἵνα ἔχωσιν τὴν χαρὰν τὴν ἐμὴν
that they may have the ¹joy - ¹my

πεπληρωμένην ἐν ἑαυτοῖς. 14 ἐγὼ δέδωκα
having been fulfilled in themselves. I have given

αὐτοῖς τὸν λόγον σου, καὶ ὁ κόσμος
to them the word of thee, and the world

ἐμίσησεν αὐτούς, ὅτι οὐκ εἰσὶν ἐκ τοῦ
hated them, because they are not of the

κόσμου καθὼς ἐγὼ οὐκ εἰμὶ ἐκ τοῦ
world as I am not of the

κόσμου. 15 οὐκ ἐρωτῶ ἵνα ἄρῃς αὐτοὺς
world. I do not request that thou shouldest take them

ἐκ τοῦ κόσμου, ἀλλ' ἵνα τηρήσῃς αὐτοὺς
out of the world, but that thou shouldest keep them

ἐκ τοῦ πονηροῦ. 16 ἐκ τοῦ κόσμου
out of the evil [?one]. Of the world

οὐκ εἰσὶν καθὼς ἐγὼ οὐκ εἰμὶ ἐκ τοῦ
they are not as I am not of the

κόσμου. 17 ἁγίασον αὐτοὺς ἐν τῇ
world. Sanctify them in(?by) the

ἀληθείᾳ· ὁ λόγος ὁ σὸς ἀλήθειά ἐστιν.
truth; the ¹word ¹thy truth is.

18 καθὼς ἐμὲ ἀπέστειλας εἰς τὸν κόσμον,
As me thou didst send into the world,

κἀγὼ ἀπέστειλα αὐτοὺς εἰς τὸν κόσμον·
I also sent them into the world;

19 καὶ ὑπὲρ αὐτῶν [ἐγὼ] ἁγιάζω ἐμαυτόν,
and on behalf of them I sanctify myself,

ἵνα ὦσιν καὶ αὐτοὶ ἡγιασμένοι ἐν ἀληθείᾳ.
that ²may be ³also ¹they having been sanctified in truth.

20 Οὐ· περὶ τούτων δὲ ἐρωτῶ μόνον,
²Not ³concerning ⁴these ¹but I make request only,

ἀλλὰ καὶ περὶ τῶν πιστευόντων διὰ
but also concerning the [ones] believing through

τοῦ λόγου αὐτῶν εἰς ἐμέ, 21 ἵνα πάντες
the word of them in me, that all

ἐν ὦσιν, καθὼς σύ, πάτερ, ἐν ἐμοὶ
one may be, as thou, Father, in me

κἀγὼ ἐν σοί, ἵνα καὶ αὐτοὶ ἐν ἡμῖν
and I in thee, that also they in us

ὦσιν, ἵνα ὁ κόσμος πιστεύῃ ὅτι σύ
may be, that the world may believe that thou

με ἀπέστειλας. 22 κἀγὼ τὴν δόξαν ἣν
me didst send. And I the glory which

δέδωκάς μοι δέδωκα αὐτοῖς, ἵνα ὦσιν
thou hast given to me have given to them, that they may be

ἓν καθὼς ἡμεῖς ἕν· 23 ἐγὼ ἐν αὐτοῖς
one as we [are] one; I in them

καὶ σὺ ἐν ἐμοί, ἵνα ὦσιν τετελειωμένοι
and thou in me, that they may be having been perfected

εἰς ἕν, ἵνα γινώσκῃ ὁ κόσμος ὅτι σύ
in one, that may know the world that thou

με ἀπέστειλας καὶ ἠγάπησας αὐτοὺς
me didst send and didst love them

καθὼς ἐμὲ ἠγάπησας. 24 Πάτερ, ὃ
as me thou didst love. Father, what

δέδωκάς μοι, θέλω ἵνα ὅπου εἰμὶ ἐγὼ
thou hast given to me, I wish that where am I

---

that name you gave me. None has been lost except the one doomed to destruction so that Scripture would be fulfilled.

13 "I am coming to you now, but I say these things while I am still in the world, so that they may have the full measure of my joy within them. 14 I have given them your word and the world has hated them, for they are not of the world any more than I am of the world. 15 My prayer is not that you take them out of the world but that you protect them from the evil one. 16 They are not of the world, even as I am not of it. 17 Sanctify them by the truth; your word is truth. 18 As you sent me into the world, I have sent them into the world. 19 For them I sanctify myself, that they too may be truly sanctified.

Jesus Prays for All Believers

20 "My prayer is not for them alone. I pray also for those who will believe in me through their message, 21 that all of them may be one, Father, just as you are in me and I am in you. May they also be in us so that the world may believe that you have sent me. 22 I have given them the glory that you gave me, that they may be one as we are one: 23 I in them and you in me. May they be brought to complete unity to let the world know that you sent me and have loved them even as you have loved me.

24 "Father, I want those you have given me to be with me where

---

[w] Gk *except the son of destruction*
[x] Or *among themselves*
[y] Or *from evil*
[z] Other ancient authorities read *be one in us*

[y] 17 Greek *hagiazo* (set apart for sacred use or make holy); also in verse 19

I am, to see my glory, which you have given me because you loved me before the foundation of the world.

25 "Righteous Father, the world does not know you, but I know you; and these know that you have sent me. 26 I made your name known to them, and I will make it known, so that the love with which you have loved me may be in them, and I in them."

Chapter 18

The Betrayal and Arrest of Jesus

AFTER Jesus had spoken these words, he went out with his disciples across the Kidron valley to a place where there was a garden, which he and his disciples entered. 2 Now Judas, who betrayed him, also knew the place, because Jesus often met there with his disciples. 3 So Judas brought a detachment of soldiers together with police from the chief priests and the Pharisees, and they came there with lanterns and torches and weapons. 4 Then Jesus, knowing all that was to happen to him, came forward and asked them, "Whom are you looking for?" 5 They answered, "Jesus of Nazareth."[a] Jesus replied, "I am he."[b] Judas, who betrayed him, was standing with them. 6 When Jesus[c] said to them, "I am he,"[b] they stepped back and fell to the ground. 7 Again he asked them, "Whom are you looking for?" And they said, "Jesus of Nazareth."[a] 8 Jesus answered, "I told you that I am he.[b] So if you are looking for me, let these men go."

κἀκεῖνοι ὦσιν μετ᾽ ἐμοῦ, ἵνα θεωρῶσιν
those also may be with me, that they may behold

τὴν δόξαν τὴν ἐμήν, ἣν δέδωκάς μοι
the 2glory - 1my, which thou hast given to me

ὅτι ἠγάπησάς με πρὸ καταβολῆς κόσμου.
because thou didst love me before [the] foundation of [the] world.

25 πατὴρ δίκαιε, καὶ ὁ κόσμος σε
Father righteous, indeed the world thee

οὐκ ἔγνω, ἐγὼ δέ σε ἔγνων, καὶ οὗτοι
knew not, but I thee knew, and these

ἔγνωσαν ὅτι σύ με ἀπέστειλας· 26 καὶ
knew that thou me didst send; and

ἐγνώρισα αὐτοῖς τὸ ὄνομά σου καὶ
I made known to them the name of thee and

γνωρίσω, ἵνα ἡ ἀγάπη ἣν ἠγάπησάς
will make known, that the love [with] which thou lovedst

με ἐν αὐτοῖς ᾖ κἀγὼ ἐν αὐτοῖς.
me in them may be and I in them.

18 Ταῦτα εἰπὼν Ἰησοῦς ἐξῆλθεν σὺν
These things having said Jesus went forth with

τοῖς μαθηταῖς αὐτοῦ πέραν τοῦ χειμάρρου
the disciples of him across the torrent

τοῦ Κεδρών, ὅπου ἦν κῆπος, εἰς ὃν
- Kedron, where there was a garden, into which

εἰσῆλθεν αὐτὸς καὶ οἱ μαθηταὶ αὐτοῦ.
entered he and the disciples of him.

2 ᾔδει δὲ καὶ Ἰούδας ὁ παραδιδοὺς
3Now 7knew 8also 1Judas 4the [one] 6betraying

αὐτὸν τὸν τόπον, ὅτι πολλάκις συνήχθη
5him 2the 3place, because often assembled

Ἰησοῦς ἐκεῖ μετὰ τῶν μαθητῶν αὐτοῦ.
Jesus there with the disciples of him.

3 ὁ οὖν Ἰούδας λαβὼν τὴν σπεῖραν
- Therefore Judas taking the band

καὶ ἐκ τῶν ἀρχιερέων καὶ [ἐκ] τῶν
and 9from 8the 4chief priests 5and 7from 6the

Φαρισαίων ὑπηρέτας ἔρχεται ἐκεῖ μετὰ
1Pharisees 2attendants comes there with

φανῶν καὶ λαμπάδων καὶ ὅπλων. 4 Ἰησοῦς
lanterns and lamps and weapons. Jesus

οὖν εἰδὼς πάντα τὰ ἐρχόμενα ἐπ᾽ αὐτὸν
therefore knowing all the things coming on him

ἐξῆλθεν καὶ λέγει αὐτοῖς· τίνα ζητεῖτε;
went forth and says to them: Whom seek ye?

5 ἀπεκρίθησαν αὐτῷ· Ἰησοῦν τὸν
They answered him: Jesus the

Ναζωραῖον. λέγει αὐτοῖς· ἐγώ εἰμι.
Nazarene. He tells them: I am.

εἱστήκει δὲ καὶ Ἰούδας ὁ παραδιδοὺς
Now stood also Judas the [one] betraying

αὐτὸν μετ᾽ αὐτῶν. 6 ὡς οὖν εἶπεν
him with them. When therefore he told

αὐτοῖς· ἐγώ εἰμι, ἀπῆλθαν εἰς τὰ ὀπίσω
them: I am, they went away back †

καὶ ἔπεσαν χαμαί. 7 πάλιν οὖν
and fell on the ground. Again therefore

ἐπηρώτησεν αὐτούς· τίνα ζητεῖτε; οἱ δὲ
he questioned them: Whom seek ye? And they

εἶπαν· Ἰησοῦν τὸν Ναζωραῖον. 8 ἀπεκρίθη
said: Jesus the Nazarene. Answered

Ἰησοῦς· εἶπον ὑμῖν ὅτι ἐγώ εἰμι· εἰ
Jesus: I told you that I am; if

οὖν ἐμὲ ζητεῖτε, ἄφετε τούτους ὑπάγειν·
therefore me ye seek, allow these to go;

I am, and to see my glory, the glory you have given me because you loved me before the creation of the world.

25 "Righteous Father, though the world does not know you, I know you, and they know that you have sent me. 26 I have made you known to them, and will continue to make you known in order that the love you have for me may be in them and that I myself may be in them."

Chapter 18

Jesus Arrested

WHEN he had finished praying, Jesus left with his disciples and crossed the Kidron Valley. On the other side there was an olive grove, and he and his disciples went into it.

2 Now Judas, who betrayed him, knew the place, because Jesus had often met there with his disciples. 3 So Judas came to the grove, guiding a detachment of soldiers and some officials from the chief priests and Pharisees. They were carrying torches, lanterns and weapons.

4 Jesus, knowing all that was going to happen to him, went out and asked them, "Who is it you want?"

5 "Jesus of Nazareth," they replied.

"I am he," Jesus said. (And Judas the traitor was standing there with them.) 6 When Jesus said, "I am he," they drew back and fell to the ground.

7 Again he asked them, "Who is it you want?"

And they said, "Jesus of Nazareth."

8 "I told you that I am he," Jesus answered. "If you are looking for me, then let these men go."

---

9 This was to fulfill the word that he had spoken, "I did not lose a single one of those whom you gave me." 10 Then Simon Peter, who had a sword, drew it, struck the high priest's slave, and cut off his right ear. The slave's name was Malchus. 11 Jesus said to Peter, "Put your sword back into its sheath. Am I not to drink the cup that the Father has given me?"

Jesus before the High Priest

12 So the soldiers, their officer, and the Jewish police arrested Jesus and bound him. 13 First they took him to Annas, who was the father-in-law of Caiaphas, the high priest that year. 14 Caiaphas was the one who had advised the Jews that it was better to have one person die for the people.

Peter Denies Jesus

15 Simon Peter and another disciple followed Jesus. Since that disciple was known to the high priest, he went with Jesus into the courtyard of the high priest, 16 but Peter was standing outside at the gate. So the other disciple, who was known to the high priest, went out, spoke to the woman who guarded the gate, and brought Peter in. 17 The woman said to Peter, "You are not also one of this man's disciples, are you?" He said, "I am not." 18 Now the slaves and the police had made a charcoal fire because it was cold, and they were standing around it and warming themselves. Peter also was

9 ἵνα   πληρωθῇ   ὁ   λόγος   ὃν   εἶπεν,   ὅτι
that might be fulfilled the   word   which   he said,   −
οὓς   δέδωκάς   μοι,   οὐκ   ἀπώλεσα   ἐξ
[Those] whom thou hast given to me,   I lost not   of
αὐτῶν   οὐδένα.   10 Σίμων   οὖν   Πέτρος
them   no(any)one.   ¹Simon   ²therefore   ³Peter
ἔχων   μάχαιραν   εἵλκυσεν   αὐτὴν   καὶ   ἔπαισεν
having   a sword   drew   it   and   smote
τὸν   τοῦ   ἀρχιερέως   δοῦλον   καὶ   ἀπέκοψεν
¹the   ²of the   ⁴high priest   ³slave   and   cut off
αὐτοῦ   τὸ   ὠτάριον   τὸ   δεξιόν·   ἦν   δὲ
of him   the   ²ear   −   ¹right;   and was
ὄνομα   τῷ   δούλῳ   Μάλχος.   11 εἶπεν   οὖν
name   to the   slave⁰   Malchus.   Said   therefore
ὁ   Ἰησοῦς   τῷ   Πέτρῳ·   βάλε   τὴν   μάχαιραν
−   Jesus   −   to Peter: Put   the   sword
εἰς   τὴν   θήκην·   τὸ   ποτήριον   ὃ   δέδωκέν
into   the   sheath;   the   cup   which   has given
μοι   ὁ   πατήρ,   οὐ   μὴ   πίω   αὐτό;
to me   the   Father,   by no means   shall I drink   it?
12 Ἡ   οὖν   σπεῖρα   καὶ   ὁ   χιλίαρχος
Therefore the   band   and   the   chiliarch
καὶ   οἱ   ὑπηρέται   τῶν   Ἰουδαίων   συνέλαβον
and   the   attendants   of the   Jews   took
τὸν   Ἰησοῦν   καὶ   ἔδησαν   αὐτόν,   13 καὶ
−   Jesus   and   bound   him,   and
ἤγαγον   πρὸς   Ἄνναν   πρῶτον·   ἦν   γὰρ
led   to   Annas   first;   for he was
πενθερὸς   τοῦ   Καϊάφα,   ὃς   ἦν   ἀρχιερεὺς
father-in-law   −   of Caiaphas,   who   was   high priest
τοῦ   ἐνιαυτοῦ   ἐκείνου·   14 ἦν   δὲ   Καϊάφας
−   year   of that;   now it was   Caiaphas
ὁ   συμβουλεύσας   τοῖς   Ἰουδαίοις   ὅτι
the [one]   having advised   the   Jews   that
συμφέρει   ἕνα   ἄνθρωπον   ἀποθανεῖν   ὑπὲρ
it is(was) expedient one   man   to die   on behalf of
τοῦ   λαοῦ.   15 Ἠκολούθει   δὲ   τῷ   Ἰησοῦ
the   people.   And followed   −   −   Jesus
Σίμων   Πέτρος   καὶ   ἄλλος   μαθητής.   ὁ   δὲ
Simon   Peter   and   another   disciple.   − And
μαθητὴς   ἐκεῖνος   ἦν   γνωστὸς   τῷ   ἀρχιερεῖ,
disciple   that   was   known   to the   high priest,
καὶ   συνεισῆλθεν   τῷ   Ἰησοῦ   εἰς   τὴν   αὐλὴν
and   entered with   −   Jesus   into   the   court
τοῦ   ἀρχιερέως,   16 ὁ   δὲ   Πέτρος   εἱστήκει
of the   high priest,   −   but   Peter   stood
πρὸς   τῇ   θύρᾳ   ἔξω.   ἐξῆλθεν   οὖν   ὁ
at   the   door   outside.   Went out therefore the
μαθητὴς   ὁ   ἄλλος   ὁ   γνωστὸς   τοῦ   ἀρχιερέως
¹disciple   −   ¹other   −   known   of(to) the high priest
καὶ   εἶπεν   τῇ   θυρωρῷ,   καὶ   εἰσήγαγεν
and   told   the   portress,   and   brought in
τὸν   Πέτρον.   17 λέγει   οὖν   τῷ   Πέτρῳ   ἡ
−   Peter.   Says therefore −   to Peter   the
παιδίσκη   ἡ   θυρωρός·   μὴ   καὶ   σὺ   ἐκ
maidservant   the   portress :   Not   also   thou   of
τῶν   μαθητῶν   εἶ   τοῦ   ἀνθρώπου   τούτου;
the   disciples   art   −   man   of this?
λέγει   ἐκεῖνος·   οὐκ   εἰμί.   18 εἱστήκεισαν   δὲ
Says   that one :   I am not.   And stood
οἱ   δοῦλοι   καὶ   οἱ   ὑπηρέται   ἀνθρακιὰν
the   slaves   and   the   attendants   a fire
πεποιηκότες,   ὅτι   ψῦχος   ἦν,   καὶ
having made,   because   cold   it was,   and
ἐθερμαίνοντο·   ἦν   δὲ   καὶ   ὁ   Πέτρος   μετ'
were warming themselves; and was   also   −   Peter   with

9 This happened so that the words he had spoken would be fulfilled: "I have not lost one of those you gave me."²

10 Then Simon Peter, who had a sword, drew it and struck the high priest's servant, cutting off his right ear. (The servant's name was Malchus.)

11 Jesus commanded Peter, "Put your sword away! Shall I not drink the cup the Father has given me?"

Jesus Taken to Annas

12 Then the detachment of soldiers with its commander and the Jewish officials arrested Jesus. They bound him 13 and brought him first to Annas, who was the father-in-law of Caiaphas, the high priest that year. 14 Caiaphas was the one who had advised the Jews that it would be good if one man died for the people.

Peter's First Denial

15 Simon Peter and another disciple were following Jesus. Because this disciple was known to the high priest, he went with Jesus into the high priest's courtyard, 16 but Peter had to wait outside at the door. The other disciple, who was known to the high priest, came back, spoke to the girl on duty there and brought Peter in.

17 "You are not one of his disciples, are you?" the girl at the door asked Peter.

He replied, "I am not."

18 It was cold, and the servants and officials stood around a fire they had made to keep warm. Peter also

²9 John 6:39

standing with them and warming himself.

The High Priest Questions Jesus

19 Then the high priest questioned Jesus about his disciples and about his teaching. 20 Jesus answered, "I have spoken openly to the world; I have always taught in synagogues and in the temple, where all the Jews come together. I have said nothing in secret. 21 Why do you ask me? Ask those who heard what I said to them; they know what I said." 22 When he had said this, one of the police standing nearby struck Jesus on the face, saying, "Is that how you answer the high priest?" 23 Jesus answered, "If I have spoken wrongly, testify to the wrong. But if I have spoken rightly, why do you strike me?" 24 Then Annas sent him bound to Caiaphas the high priest.

Peter Denies Jesus Again

25 Now Simon Peter was standing and warming himself. They asked him, "You are not also one of his disciples, are you?" He denied it and said, "I am not." 26 One of the slaves of the high priest, a relative of the man whose ear Peter had cut off, asked, "Did I not see you in the garden with him?" 27 Again Peter denied it, and at that moment the cock crowed.

Jesus before Pilate

28 Then they took Jesus from Caiaphas to Pilate's headquarters.[d] It was early in the morning. They themselves did not enter the headquarters,[d] so as to avoid ritual defilement and to be able to eat the Passover. 29 So Pilate went out to them and said, "What accusation do you bring against this man?" 30 They answered, "If this man were not a criminal, we would not have handed him over to you." 31 Pilate said

---

αὐτῶν ἑστὼς καὶ θερμαινόμενος. 19 Ὁ
them standing and warming himself. – ¹The

οὖν ἀρχιερεὺς ἠρώτησεν τὸν Ἰησοῦν
²therefore ²high priest questioned the – Jesus

περὶ τῶν μαθητῶν αὐτοῦ καὶ περὶ τῆς
about the disciples of him and about the

διδαχῆς αὐτοῦ. 20 ἀπεκρίθη αὐτῷ Ἰησοῦς·
teaching of him. Answered him Jesus:

ἐγὼ παρρησίᾳ λελάληκα τῷ κόσμῳ· ἐγὼ
I with plainness have spoken to the world; I

πάντοτε ἐδίδαξα ἐν συναγωγῇ καὶ ἐν
always taught in a synagogue and in

τῷ ἱερῷ, ὅπου πάντες οἱ Ἰουδαῖοι
the temple, where all the Jews

συνέρχονται, καὶ ἐν κρυπτῷ ἐλάλησα
come together, and in secret I spoke

οὐδέν. 21 τί με ἐρωτᾷς; ἐρώτησον
nothing. Why me questionest thou? question

τοὺς ἀκηκοότας τί ἐλάλησα αὐτοῖς· ἴδε
the [ones] having heard what I spoke to them; behold[,]

οὗτοι οἴδασιν ἃ εἶπον ἐγώ. 22 ταῦτα
these know what things said I. These things

δὲ αὐτοῦ εἰπόντος εἷς παρεστηκὼς τῶν
and him sayingᵃ one standing by of the
=And as he said this

ὑπηρετῶν ἔδωκεν ῥάπισμα τῷ Ἰησοῦ
attendants gave a blow – to Jesus

εἰπών· οὕτως ἀποκρίνῃ τῷ ἀρχιερεῖ;
saying: Thus answerest thou the high priest?

23 ἀπεκρίθη αὐτῷ Ἰησοῦς· εἰ κακῶς
Answered him Jesus: If ill

ἐλάλησα, μαρτύρησον περὶ τοῦ κακοῦ·
I spoke, witness concerning the evil;

εἰ δὲ καλῶς, τί με δέρεις; 24 ἀπέστειλεν
but if well, why me beatest thou? ²Sent

οὖν αὐτὸν ὁ Ἄννας δεδεμένον πρὸς
²therefore ⁴him – ¹Annas having been bound to

Καϊάφαν τὸν ἀρχιερέα. 25 Ἦν δὲ Σίμων
Caiaphas the high priest. Now was Simon

Πέτρος ἑστὼς καὶ θερμαινόμενος. εἶπον
Peter standing and warming himself. They said

οὖν αὐτῷ· μὴ καὶ σὺ ἐκ τῶν μαθητῶν
therefore to him: Not also thou of the disciples

αὐτοῦ εἶ; ἠρνήσατο ἐκεῖνος καὶ εἶπεν·
of him art? Denied that one and said:

οὐκ εἰμί. 26 λέγει εἷς ἐκ τῶν δούλων τοῦ
I am not. Says one of the slaves of the

ἀρχιερέως, συγγενὴς ὢν οὗ ἀπέκοψεν
high priest, ²a relative ¹being ³[of him] of whom ⁴cut off

Πέτρος τὸ ὠτίον· οὐκ ἐγώ σε εἶδον
⁵Peter ⁶the ⁷ear: ¹Not ²I ⁴thee ³saw

ἐν τῷ κήπῳ μετ' αὐτοῦ; 27 πάλιν οὖν
in the garden with him? Again therefore

ἠρνήσατο Πέτρος, καὶ εὐθέως ἀλέκτωρ
denied Peter, and immediately a cock

ἐφώνησεν.
sounded(crew).

28 Ἄγουσιν οὖν τὸν Ἰησοῦν ἀπὸ τοῦ
They lead therefore – – Jesus from the

Καϊάφα εἰς τὸ πραιτώριον· ἦν δὲ πρωΐ·
Caiaphas to the prætorium; and it was early;

καὶ αὐτοὶ οὐκ εἰσῆλθον εἰς τὸ πραιτώριον,
and they entered not into the prætorium,

ἵνα μὴ μιανθῶσιν ἀλλὰ φάγωσιν τὸ
lest they should be defiled but might eat the

πάσχα. 29 ἐξῆλθεν οὖν ὁ Πιλᾶτος ἔξω
passover. Went forth therefore – Pilate outside

---

was standing with them, warming himself.

The High Priest Questions Jesus

19 Meanwhile, the high priest questioned Jesus about his disciples and his teaching.
20 "I have spoken openly to the world," Jesus replied. "I always taught in synagogues or at the temple, where all the Jews come together. I said nothing in secret. 21 Why question me? Ask those who heard me. Surely they know what I said."
22 When Jesus said this, one of the officials nearby struck him in the face. "Is this the way you answer the high priest?" he demanded.
23 "If I said something wrong," Jesus replied, "testify as to what is wrong. But if I spoke the truth, why did you strike me?" 24 Then Annas sent him, still bound, to Caiaphas the high priest.[a]

Peter's Second and Third Denials

25 As Simon Peter stood warming himself, he was asked, "You are not one of his disciples, are you?"
He denied it, saying, "I am not."
26 One of the high priest's servants, a relative of the man whose ear Peter had cut off, challenged him, "Didn't I see you with him in the olive grove?"
27 Again Peter denied it, and at that moment a rooster began to crow.

Jesus Before Pilate

28 Then the Jews led Jesus from Caiaphas to the palace of the Roman governor. By now it was early morning, and to avoid ceremonial uncleanness the Jews did not enter the palace; they wanted to be able to eat the Passover. 29 So Pilate came out to them and asked, "What charges are you bringing against this man?"
30 "If he were not a criminal," they replied, "we would not have handed him over to you."
31 Pilate said, "Take him

ᵈ Gk the praetorium

ᵃ24 Or (Now Annas had sent him, still bound, to Caiaphas the high priest.)

to them, "Take him yourselves and judge him according to your law." The Jews replied, "We are not permitted to put anyone to death." [32] (This was to fulfill what Jesus had said when he indicated the kind of death he was to die.) [33] Then Pilate entered the headquarters[d] again, summoned Jesus, and asked him, "Are you the King of the Jews?" [34] Jesus answered, "Do you ask this on your own, or did others tell you about me?" [35] Pilate replied, "I am not a Jew, am I? Your own nation and the chief priests have handed you over to me. What have you done?" [36] Jesus answered, "My kingdom is not from this world. If my kingdom were from this world, my followers would be fighting to keep me from being handed over to the Jews. But as it is, my kingdom is not from here." [37] Pilate asked him, "So you are a king?" Jesus answered, "You say that I am a king. For this I was born, and for this I came into the world, to testify to the truth. Everyone who belongs to the truth listens to my voice." [38] Pilate asked him, "What is truth?"

πρὸς αὐτοὺς καὶ φησίν· τίνα κατηγορίαν
to them and says: What accusation

φέρετε τοῦ ἀνθρώπου τούτου; 30 ἀπεκρίθησαν
bring ye - man of this? They answered

καὶ εἶπαν αὐτῷ· εἰ μὴ ἦν
and said to him: Unless was

οὗτος κακὸν ποιῶν, οὐκ ἂν σοι
this man evil doing, ⁹would ⁸not ⁷to thee

παρεδώκαμεν αὐτόν. 31 εἶπεν οὖν αὐτοῖς
¹we ⁴have ⁵delivered ⁶him. Said therefore to them

ὁ Πιλᾶτος· λάβετε αὐτὸν ὑμεῖς, καὶ
- Pilate: Take him ye, and

κατὰ τὸν νόμον ὑμῶν κρίνατε αὐτόν.
according to the law of you judge ye him.

εἶπον αὐτῷ οἱ Ἰουδαῖοι· ἡμῖν οὐκ ἔξεστιν
Said· to him the Jews: For us it is not lawful

ἀποκτεῖναι οὐδένα· 32 ἵνα ὁ λόγος τοῦ
to kill no(any)one; that the word -

Ἰησοῦ πληρωθῇ ὃν εἶπεν σημαίνων ποίῳ
of Jesus might be fulfilled which he said signifying by what

θανάτῳ ἤμελλεν ἀποθνήσκειν. 33 Εἰσῆλθεν
death he was about to die. Entered

οὖν πάλιν εἰς τὸ πραιτώριον ὁ Πιλᾶτος
therefore again into the prætorium - Pilate

καὶ ἐφώνησεν τὸν Ἰησοῦν καὶ εἶπεν
and called - Jesus and said

αὐτῷ· σὺ εἶ ὁ βασιλεὺς τῶν Ἰουδαίων;
to him: Thou art the king of the Jews?

34 ἀπεκρίθη Ἰησοῦς· ἀφ᾽ ἑαυτοῦ σὺ τοῦτο
Answered Jesus: From [thy]self ²thou ¹this

λέγεις, ἢ ἄλλοι εἶπόν σοι περὶ ἐμοῦ;
¹sayest, οι others told thee about me?

35 ἀπεκρίθη ὁ Πιλᾶτος· μήτι ἐγὼ
Answered - Pilate: not I

Ἰουδαῖός εἰμι; τὸ ἔθνος τὸ σὸν καὶ
a Jew am? the ²nation ¹thy and

οἱ ἀρχιερεῖς παρέδωκάν σε ἐμοί· τί
the chief priests delivered thee to me; what

ἐποίησας; 36 ἀπεκρίθη Ἰησοῦς· ἡ βασιλεία
didst thou? Answered Jesus: The ¹kingdom

ἡ ἐμὴ οὐκ ἔστιν ἐκ τοῦ κόσμου τούτου·
- ¹my is not of the world this;

εἰ ἐκ τοῦ κόσμου τούτου ἦν ἡ βασιλεία
if of the world this was the ¹kingdom

ἡ ἐμή, οἱ ὑπηρέται ἂν οἱ ἐμοὶ ἠγωνίζοντο,
- ¹my, the ²attendants ⁴would - ¹my ³have struggled,

ἵνα μὴ παραδοθῶ τοῖς Ἰουδαίοις· νῦν
that I should not be delivered to the Jews; ²now

δὲ ἡ βασιλεία ἡ ἐμὴ οὐκ ἔστιν ἐντεῦθεν.
¹but the ²kingdom - ¹my is not hence.

37 εἶπεν οὖν αὐτῷ ὁ Πιλᾶτος· οὐκοῦν
Said therefore to him - Pilate: Not really

βασιλεὺς εἶ σύ; ἀπεκρίθη [ὁ] Ἰησοῦς·
a king art thou? Answered - Jesus:

σὺ λέγεις ὅτι βασιλεύς εἰμι. ἐγὼ εἰς
Thou sayest that a king I am. I for

τοῦτο γεγέννημαι καὶ εἰς τοῦτο ἐλήλυθα
this have been born and for this I have come

εἰς τὸν κόσμον, ἵνα μαρτυρήσω τῇ
into the world, that I might witness to the

ἀληθείᾳ· πᾶς ὁ ὢν ἐκ τῆς ἀληθείας
truth; everyone being of the truth

ἀκούει μου τῆς φωνῆς. 38 λέγει αὐτῷ
hears of me the voice. Says to him

ὁ Πιλᾶτος· τί ἐστιν ἀλήθεια; Καὶ
- Pilate: What is truth? And

---

yourselves and judge him by your own law."

"But we have no right to execute anyone," the Jews objected. [32] This happened so that the words Jesus had spoken indicating the kind of death he was going to die would be fulfilled.

[33] Pilate then went back inside the palace, summoned Jesus and asked him, "Are you the king of the Jews?"

[34] "Is that your own idea," Jesus asked, "or did others talk to you about me?"

[35] "Am I a Jew?" Pilate replied. "It was your people and your chief priests who handed you over to me. What is it you have done?"

[36] Jesus said, "My kingdom is not of this world. If it were, my servants would fight to prevent my arrest by the Jews. But now my kingdom is from another place."

[37] "You are a king, then!" said Pilate.

Jesus answered, "You are right in saying I am a king. In fact, for this reason I was born, and for this I came into the world, to testify to the truth. Everyone on the side of truth listens to me."

[38] "What is truth?" Pilate asked. With this he went

Jesus Sentenced to Death

After he had said this, he went out to the Jews again and told them, "I find no case against him. 39 But you have a custom that I release someone for you at the Passover. Do you want me to release for you the King of the Jews?" 40 They shouted in reply, "Not this man, but Barabbas!" Now Barabbas was a bandit.

τοῦτο εἰπὼν πάλιν ἐξῆλθεν πρὸς τοὺς
this having said again he went forth to the

'Ιουδαίους, καὶ λέγει αὐτοῖς· ἐγὼ οὐδεμίαν
Jews, and tells them: ¹I ¹no

εὑρίσκω ἐν αὐτῷ αἰτίαν. 39 ἔστιν δὲ
²find ³in ⁵him ⁴crime. But there is

συνήθεια ὑμῖν ἵνα ἕνα ἀπολύσω ὑμῖν
a custom to youᵉ that one I should release to you

ἐν τῷ πάσχα· βούλεσθε οὖν ἀπολύσω
at the Passover; will ye therefore [that] I release

ὑμῖν τὸν βασιλέα τῶν 'Ιουδαίων; 40 ἐκραύ-
to you the king of the Jews? They cried

γασαν οὖν πάλιν λέγοντες· μὴ τοῦτον,
out therefore again saying: Not this man,

ἀλλὰ τὸν Βαραββᾶν. ἦν δὲ ὁ Βαραββᾶς
but - Barabbas. ¹But ³was - ²Barabbas

out again to the Jews and said, "I find no basis for a charge against him. 39 But it is your custom for me to release to you one prisoner at the time of the Passover. Do you want me to release 'the king of the Jews'?" 40 They shouted back, "No, not him! Give us Barabbas!" Now Barabbas had taken part in a rebellion.

Chapter 19

THEN Pilate took Jesus and had him flogged. 2 And the soldiers wove a crown of thorns and put it on his head, and they dressed him in a purple robe. 3 They kept coming up to him, saying, "Hail, King of the Jews!" and striking him on the face. 4 Pilate went out again and said to them, "Look, I am bringing him out to you to let you know that I find no case against him." 5 So Jesus came out, wearing the crown of thorns and the purple robe. Pilate said to them, "Here is the man!" 6 When the chief priests and the police saw him, they shouted, "Crucify him! Crucify him!" Pilate said to them, "Take him yourselves and crucify him; I find no case against him." 7 The Jews answered him, "We have a law, and according to that law he ought to die because he has claimed to be the Son of God." 8 Now when Pilate heard this, he was more afraid than ever. 9 He en-

ληστής. 19 Τότε οὖν ἔλαβεν ὁ Πιλᾶτος
⁴a robber. Then therefore ²took - ¹Pilate

τὸν 'Ιησοῦν καὶ ἐμαστίγωσεν. 2 καὶ οἱ
- ²Jesus and scourged [him]. And the

στρατιῶται πλέξαντες στέφανον ἐξ ἀκανθῶν
soldiers having plaited a wreath out of thorns

ἐπέθηκαν αὐτοῦ τῇ κεφαλῇ, καὶ ἱμάτιον
put [it] on of him the head, and ⁴garment

πορφυροῦν περιέβαλον αὐτόν, 3 καὶ ἤρχοντο
²a purple ¹threw round ³him, and came

πρὸς αὐτὸν καὶ ἔλεγον· χαῖρε ὁ βασιλεὺς
to him and said: Hail[,] - king

τῶν 'Ιουδαίων· καὶ ἐδίδοσαν αὐτῷ
of the Jews; and they gave him

ῥαπίσματα. 4 Καὶ ἐξῆλθεν πάλιν ἔξω
blows. And went forth again outside

ὁ Πιλᾶτος καὶ λέγει αὐτοῖς· ἴδε ἄγω
- Pilate and says to them: Behold ¹I bring

ὑμῖν αὐτὸν ἔξω, ἵνα γνῶτε ὅτι οὐδεμίαν
⁴to you ²him ³out, that ye may know that no

αἰτίαν εὑρίσκω ἐν αὐτῷ. 5 ἐξῆλθεν
crime I find in him. Came forth

οὖν ὁ 'Ιησοῦς ἔξω, φορῶν τὸν ἀκάνθινον
therefore - Jesus outside, wearing the thorny

στέφανον καὶ τὸ πορφυροῦν ἱμάτιον. καὶ
wreath and the purple garment. And

λέγει αὐτοῖς· ἰδοὺ ὁ ἄνθρωπος. 6 ὅτε
he says to them: Behold[,] the man. When

οὖν εἶδον αὐτὸν οἱ ἀρχιερεῖς καὶ οἱ
therefore saw him the chief priests and the

ὑπηρέται, ἐκραύγασαν λέγοντες· σταύρωσον
attendants, they shouted saying: Crucify[,]

σταύρωσον. λέγει αὐτοῖς ὁ Πιλᾶτος·
crucify. Says to them - Pilate:

λάβετε αὐτὸν ὑμεῖς καὶ σταυρώσατε·
¹Take ³him ²ye and crucify;

ἐγὼ γὰρ οὐχ εὑρίσκω ἐν αὐτῷ αἰτίαν.
for I find not in him crime.

7 ἀπεκρίθησαν αὐτῷ οἱ 'Ιουδαῖοι· ἡμεῖς
Answered him the Jews: We

νόμον ἔχομεν, καὶ κατὰ τὸν νόμον
a law have, and according to the law

ὀφείλει ἀποθανεῖν, ὅτι υἱὸν θεοῦ ἑαυτὸν
he ought to die, because Son of God himself

ἐποίησεν. 8 Ὅτε οὖν ἤκουσεν ὁ Πιλᾶτος
he made. When therefore heard - Pilate

τοῦτον τὸν λόγον, μᾶλλον ἐφοβήθη, 9 καὶ
this - word, more he was afraid, and

Chapter 19

Jesus Sentenced to be Crucified

THEN Pilate took Jesus and had him flogged. 2 The soldiers twisted together a crown of thorns and put it on his head. They clothed him in a purple robe 3 and went up to him again and again, saying, "Hail, king of the Jews!" And they struck him in the face.

4 Once more Pilate came out and said to the Jews, "Look, I am bringing him out to you to let you know that I find no basis for a charge against him." 5 When Jesus came out wearing the crown of thorns and the purple robe, Pilate said to them, "Here is the man!"

6 As soon as the chief priests and their officials saw him, they shouted, "Crucify! Crucify!"

But Pilate answered, "You take him and crucify him. As for me, I find no basis for a charge against him."

7 The Jews insisted, "We have a law, and according to that law he must die, because he claimed to be the Son of God."

8 When Pilate heard this, he was even more afraid,

tered his headquarters^d again and asked Jesus, "Where are you from?" But Jesus gave him no answer. 10 Pilate therefore said to him, "Do you refuse to speak to me? Do you not know that I have power to release you, and power to crucify you?" 11 Jesus answered him, "You would have no power over me unless it had been given you from above; therefore the one who handed me over to you is guilty of a greater sin." 12 From then on Pilate tried to release him, but the Jews cried out, "If you release this man, you are no friend of the emperor. Everyone who claims to be a king sets himself against the emperor."

13 When Pilate heard these words, he brought Jesus outside and sat^e on the judge's bench at a place called The Stone Pavement, or in Hebrew^f Gabbatha. 14 Now it was the day of Preparation for the Passover; and it was about noon. He said to the Jews, "Here is your King!" 15 They cried out, "Away with him! Away with him! Crucify him!" Pilate asked them, "Shall I crucify your King?" The chief priests answered, "We have no king but the emperor." 16 Then he handed him over to them to be crucified.

The Crucifixion of Jesus

So they took Jesus; 17 and carrying the cross by himself, he went out to what is called The Place of the Skull, which in Hebrew^f is called Golgotha. 18 There they crucified him, and with him two others, one on either side, with Jesus between them. 19 Pilate also had an inscription

---

εἰσῆλθεν εἰς τὸ πραιτώριον πάλιν καὶ
entered into the prætorium again and

λέγει τῷ Ἰησοῦ· πόθεν εἶ σύ; ὁ δὲ
says to Jesus: Whence art thou? - But

Ἰησοῦς ἀπόκρισιν οὐκ ἔδωκεν αὐτῷ.
Jesus answer did not give him.

10 λέγει οὖν αὐτῷ ὁ Πιλᾶτος· ἐμοὶ
Says therefore to him - Pilate: To me

οὐ λαλεῖς; οὐκ οἶδας ὅτι ἐξουσίαν ἔχω
speakest thou not? knowest thou not that authority I have

ἀπολῦσαί σε καὶ ἐξουσίαν ἔχω σταυρῶσαί
to release thee and authority I have to crucify

σε; 11 ἀπεκρίθη Ἰησοῦς· οὐκ εἶχες
thee? Answered Jesus: Thou hadst not

ἐξουσίαν κατ᾽ ἐμοῦ οὐδεμίαν εἰ μὴ ἦν
¹authority ²against ⁴me ¹no(any) unless it was

δεδομένον σοι ἄνωθεν· διὰ τοῦτο ὁ
having been given thee from above; therefore the [one]

παραδούς μέ σοι μείζονα ἁμαρτίαν ἔχει.
having delivered me to thee a greater sin has.

12 ἐκ τούτου ὁ Πιλᾶτος ἐζήτει ἀπολῦσαι
From this - Pilate sought to release

αὐτόν· οἱ δὲ Ἰουδαῖοι ἐκραύγασαν λέγοντες·
him; but the Jews shouted saying:

ἐὰν τοῦτον ἀπολύσῃς, οὐκ εἶ φίλος τοῦ
If this man thou releasest, thou art not a friend

Καίσαρος· πᾶς ὁ βασιλέα ἑαυτὸν ποιῶν
of Cæsar; everyone a king himself making

ἀντιλέγει τῷ Καίσαρι. 13 Ὁ οὖν Πιλᾶτος
speaks against - Cæsar. - Therefore Pilate

ἀκούσας τῶν λόγων τούτων ἤγαγεν ἔξω
hearing - words these brought outside

τὸν Ἰησοῦν, καὶ ἐκάθισεν ἐπὶ βήματος
- Jesus, and sat on a tribunal

εἰς τόπον λεγόμενον Λιθόστρωτον, Ἑβραϊστὶ δὲ
in a place being called Pavement, but in Hebrew

Γαββαθά. 14 ἦν δὲ παρασκευὴ τοῦ
Gabbatha. Now it was preparation of the

πάσχα, ὥρα ἦν ὡς ἕκτη· καὶ λέγει
Passover, hour it was about sixth; and he says

τοῖς Ἰουδαίοις· ἴδε ὁ βασιλεὺς ὑμῶν.
to the Jews; Behold[,] the king of you.

15 ἐκραύγασαν οὖν ἐκεῖνοι· ἆρον ἆρον,
Shouted therefore those: Take[,] take,

σταύρωσον αὐτόν. λέγει αὐτοῖς ὁ Πιλᾶτος·
crucify him. Says to them - Pilate:

τὸν βασιλέα ὑμῶν σταυρώσω; ἀπεκρίθησαν
The king of you shall I crucify? Answered

οἱ ἀρχιερεῖς· οὐκ ἔχομεν βασιλέα εἰ
the chief priests: We have not a king ex-

μὴ Καίσαρα. 16 τότε οὖν παρέδωκεν
cept Cæsar. Then therefore he delivered

αὐτὸν αὐτοῖς ἵνα σταυρωθῇ.
him to them that he should be crucified.

Παρέλαβον οὖν τὸν Ἰησοῦν· 17 καὶ
They took therefore - Jesus; and

βαστάζων ἑαυτῷ τὸν σταυρὸν ἐξῆλθεν
carrying ²to himself ⁶ ¹the ⁵cross he went forth

εἰς τὸν λεγόμενον κρανίου τόπον, ὃ
to ¹the ²being called ⁴of a skull ³place, which

λέγεται Ἑβραϊστὶ Γολγοθά, 18 ὅπου αὐτὸν
is called in Hebrew Golgotha, where him

ἐσταύρωσαν, καὶ μετ᾽ αὐτοῦ ἄλλους δύο
they crucified, and with him others two

ἐντεῦθεν καὶ ἐντεῦθεν, μέσον δὲ τὸν
on this side and on that, † and in the middle -

---

9 and he went back inside the palace. "Where do you come from?" he asked Jesus, but Jesus gave him no answer. 10 "Do you refuse to speak to me?" Pilate said. "Don't you realize I have power either to free you or to crucify you?"

11 Jesus answered, "You would have no power over me if it were not given to you from above. Therefore the one who handed me over to you is guilty of a greater sin."

12 From then on, Pilate tried to set Jesus free, but the Jews kept shouting, "If you let this man go, you are no friend of Caesar. Anyone who claims to be a king opposes Caesar."

13 When Pilate heard this, he brought Jesus out and sat down on the judge's seat at a place known as the Stone Pavement (which in Aramaic is Gabbatha). 14 It was the day of Preparation of Passover Week, about the sixth hour.

"Here is your king," Pilate said to the Jews.

15 But they shouted, "Take him away! Take him away! Crucify him!"

"Shall I crucify your king?" Pilate asked.

"We have no king but Caesar," the chief priests answered.

16 Finally Pilate handed him over to them to be crucified.

The Crucifixion

So the soldiers took charge of Jesus. 17 Carrying his own cross, he went out to the place of the Skull (which in Aramaic is called Golgotha). 18 Here they crucified him, and with him two others—one on each side and Jesus in the middle.

---

^e Or seated him
^f That is, Aramaic

written and put on the cross. It read, "Jesus of Nazareth,ᵍ the King of the Jews." [20] Many of the Jews read this inscription, because the place where Jesus was crucified was near the city; and it was written in Hebrew,ʰ in Latin, and in Greek. [21] Then the chief priests of the Jews said to Pilate, "Do not write, 'The King of the Jews,' but, 'This man said, I am King of the Jews.' " [22] Pilate answered, "What I have written I have written." [23] When the soldiers had crucified Jesus, they took his clothes and divided them into four parts, one for each soldier. They also took his tunic; now the tunic was seamless, woven in one piece from the top. [24] So they said to one another, "Let us not tear it, but cast lots for it to see who will get it." This was to fulfill what the scripture says,

"They divided my
clothes among
themselves,
and for my clothing
they cast lots."

[25] And that is what the soldiers did.

Meanwhile, standing near the cross of Jesus were his mother, and his mother's sister, Mary the wife of Clopas, and Mary Magdalene. [26] When Jesus saw his mother and the disciple whom he loved standing beside her, he said to his mother, "Woman, here is your son." [27] Then he said to the disciple, "Here is your mother." And from that hour the disciple took

---

Ἰησοῦν. **19** ἔγραψεν   δὲ   καὶ   τίτλον   ὁ
Jesus.   And wrote   also   a title   -

Πιλᾶτος   καὶ   ἔθηκεν   ἐπὶ   τοῦ   σταυροῦ·
Pilate   and   put [it]   on   the   cross;

ἦν   δὲ   γεγραμμένον·   ΙΗΣΟΥΣ   Ο
and it was *having been* written: JESUS   THE

ΝΑΖΩΡΑΙΟΣ   Ο   ΒΑΣΙΛΕΥΣ   ΤΩΝ
NAZARENE   THE   KING   OF THE

ΙΟΥΔΑΙΩΝ. **20** τοῦτον   οὖν   τὸν   τίτλον
JEWS.   ¹This   ²therefore -   ⁴title

πολλοὶ   ἀνέγνωσαν   τῶν   Ἰουδαίων,   ὅτι
³many   ⁵read   ⁶of the ⁷Jews,   because

ἐγγὺς   ἦν   ὁ   τόπος   τῆς   πόλεως   ὅπου
⁷near   ⁶was ⁵the ⁸place ³the ⁴city   ⁹where

ἐσταυρώθη   ὁ   Ἰησοῦς·   καὶ   ἦν   γεγραμμένον
¹was crucified -   ²Jesus;   and it was *having been* written

Ἑβραϊστί,   Ῥωμαϊστί,   Ἑλληνιστί.   **21** ἔλεγον
in Hebrew, in Latin,   in Greek.   Said

οὖν   τῷ   Πιλάτῳ   οἱ   ἀρχιερεῖς   τῶν   Ἰουδαίων·
therefore -   to Pilate the chief priests of the Jews:

μὴ   γράφε·   ὁ   βασιλεὺς   τῶν   Ἰουδαίων,
Write not: The king   of the Jews,

ἀλλ'   ὅτι   ἐκεῖνος   εἶπεν·   βασιλεύς   εἰμι
but   that that man   said: King   I am

τῶν   Ἰουδαίων.   **22** ἀπεκρίθη   ὁ   Πιλᾶτος·
of the Jews.   Answered   -   Pilate:

ὁ   γέγραφα,   γέγραφα.   **23** Οἱ   οὖν
What I have written, I have written. Therefore the

στρατιῶται,   ὅτε   ἐσταύρωσαν   τὸν   Ἰησοῦν,
soldiers,   when they crucified -   Jesus,

ἔλαβον   τὰ   ἱμάτια   αὐτοῦ   καὶ   ἐποίησαν
took   the garments of him   and   made

τέσσερα   μέρη,   ἑκάστῳ   στρατιώτῃ   μέρος,
four   parts, to each   soldier   a part,

καὶ   τὸν   χιτῶνα.   ἦν   δὲ   ὁ   χιτὼν   ἄρραφος,
and the   tunic.   Now was the tunic   seamless,

ἐκ   τῶν   ἄνωθεν   ὑφαντὸς   δι'   ὅλου.   **24** εἶπαν
from the   top   woven   throughout.   They said

οὖν   πρὸς   ἀλλήλους·   μὴ   σχίσωμεν   αὐτόν,
therefore to   one another: Let us not tear   it,

ἀλλὰ   λάχωμεν   περὶ   αὐτοῦ   τίνος   ἔσται·
but   let us cast lots about   it   of whom it shall be;

ἵνα   ἡ   γραφὴ   πληρωθῇ·   διεμερίσαντο   τὰ
that the scripture might be fulfilled: They parted the

ἱμάτιά   μου   ἑαυτοῖς   καὶ   ἐπὶ   τὸν   ἱματισμόν
garments of me to themselves and over   the   raiment

μου   ἔβαλον   κλῆρον.   Οἱ   μὲν   οὖν   στρατιῶται
of me they cast   a lot.   ¹The -* ²therefore ³soldiers

ταῦτα   ἐποίησαν.   **25** εἱστήκεισαν   δὲ   παρὰ
¹these things did.   ²there stood   ¹But   by

τῷ   σταυρῷ   τοῦ   Ἰησοῦ   ἡ   μήτηρ   αὐτοῦ
the   cross   -   of Jesus the mother   of him

καὶ   ἡ   ἀδελφὴ   τῆς   μητρὸς   αὐτοῦ,   Μαρία
and the   sister of the mother   of him,   Mary

ἡ   τοῦ   Κλωπᾶ   καὶ   Μαρία   ἡ   Μαγδαληνή.
the [?wife] - of Clopas and   Mary   the Magdalene.

26 Ἰησοῦς   οὖν   ἰδὼν   τὴν   μητέρα   καὶ
Jesus   therefore seeing the(his) mother   and

τὸν   μαθητὴν   παρεστῶτα   ὃν   ἠγάπα,   λέγει
the   disciple standing by whom he loved,   says

τῇ   μητρί·   γύναι,   ἴδε   ὁ   υἱός   σου.
to the(his) mother: Woman, behold[,] the son of thee.

27 εἶτα   λέγει   τῷ   μαθητῇ·   ἴδε   ἡ   μήτηρ
Then   he says to the disciple: Behold[,] the mother

---

[19] Pilate had a notice prepared and fastened to the cross. It read: JESUS OF NAZARETH, THE KING OF THE JEWS. [20] Many of the Jews read this sign, for the place where Jesus was crucified was near the city, and the sign was written in Aramaic, Latin and Greek. [21] The chief priests of the Jews protested to Pilate, "Do not write 'The King of the Jews,' but that this man claimed to be king of the Jews."

[22] Pilate answered, "What I have written, I have written."

[23] When the soldiers crucified Jesus, they took his clothes, dividing them into four shares, one for each of them, with the undergarment remaining. This garment was seamless, woven in one piece from top to bottom.

[24] "Let's not tear it," they said to one another. "Let's decide by lot who will get it."

This happened that the scripture might be fulfilled which said,

"They divided my
garments among
them
and cast lots for my
clothing."ᵇ

So this is what the soldiers did.

[25] Near the cross of Jesus stood his mother, his mother's sister, Mary the wife of Clopas, and Mary Magdalene. [26] When Jesus saw his mother there, and the disciple whom he loved standing nearby, he said to his mother, "Dear woman, here is your son," [27] and to the disciple, "Here is your mother." From that time

---

ᵍ Gk the Nazorean
ʰ That is, Aramaic

* μέν is scarcely translatable. But note the δέ in ver. 25: John contrasts two groups—the soldiers and the women.

ᵇ24 Psalm 22:18

her into his own home.
28 After this, when Jesus knew that all was now finished, he said (in order to fulfill the scripture), "I am thirsty." 29 A jar full of sour wine was standing there. So they put a sponge full of the wine on a branch of hyssop and held it to his mouth. 30 When Jesus had received the wine, he said, "It is finished." Then he bowed his head and gave up his spirit.

Jesus' Side Is Pierced

31 Since it was the day of Preparation, the Jews did not want the bodies left on the cross during the sabbath, especially because that sabbath was a day of great solemnity. So they asked Pilate to have the legs of the crucified men broken and the bodies removed. 32 Then the soldiers came and broke the legs of the first and of the other who had been crucified with him. 33 But when they came to Jesus and saw that he was already dead, they did not break his legs. 34 Instead, one of the soldiers pierced his side with a spear, and at once blood and water came out. 35 (He who saw this has testified so that you also may believe. His testimony is true, and he knows *i* that he tells the truth.) 36 These things occurred so that the scripture might be fulfilled, "None of his bones shall be broken." 37 And again another passage of scripture says, "They will look on the one whom they have pierced."

The Burial of Jesus

38 After these things, Joseph of Arimathea, who

σου. καὶ ἀπ' ἐκείνης τῆς ὥρας ἔλαβεν
of thee. And from that - hour took

ὁ μαθητὴς αὐτὴν εἰς τὰ ἴδια. 28 Μετὰ
the disciple her to his own [home]. † After

τοῦτο εἰδὼς ὁ Ἰησοῦς ὅτι ἤδη πάντα
this knowing - Jesus that now all things

τετέλεσται, ἵνα τελειωθῇ ἡ γραφή, λέγει·
have been finished, that might be fulfilled the scripture, says:

διψῶ. 29 σκεῦος ἔκειτο ὄξους μεστόν·
I thirst. A vessel was set of vinegar full;

σπόγγον οὖν μεστὸν τοῦ ὄξους ὑσσώπῳ
³a sponge therefore ⁴full ⁵of the ⁶vinegar ¹a hyssop §

περιθέντες προσήνεγκαν αὐτοῦ τῷ ⸀ στόματι.
²putting ²round they brought [it] to of him the mouth.

30 ὅτε οὖν ἔλαβεν τὸ ὄξος [ὁ] Ἰησοῦς
When therefore took the vinegar - Jesus

εἶπεν· τετέλεσται, καὶ κλίνας τὴν κεφαλὴν
he said : It has been finished, and inclining the(his) head

παρέδωκεν τὸ πνεῦμα.
delivered up the(his) spirit.

31 Οἱ οὖν Ἰουδαῖοι, ἐπεὶ παρασκευὴ
The ²therefore ¹Jews, since preparation

ἦν, ἵνα μὴ μείνῃ ἐπὶ τοῦ σταυροῦ τὰ
it was, that might not remain on the cross the

σώματα ἐν τῷ σαββάτῳ, ἦν γὰρ μεγάλη
bodies on the sabbath, for was great

ἡ ἡμέρα ἐκείνου τοῦ σαββάτου, ἠρώτησαν
the day of that - sabbath, they asked

τὸν Πιλᾶτον ἵνα κατεαγῶσιν αὐτῶν τὰ
- Pilate that might be broken of them the

σκέλη καὶ ἀρθῶσιν. 32 ἦλθον οὖν οἱ
legs and they might be taken. Came therefore the

στρατιῶται, καὶ τοῦ μὲν πρώτου κατέαξαν
soldiers, and of the -* first broke

τὰ σκέλη καὶ τοῦ ἄλλου τοῦ
the legs and of the other -

συσταυρωθέντος αὐτῷ· 33 ἐπὶ δὲ τὸν
crucified with him; ²on ¹but -

Ἰησοῦν ἐλθόντες, ὡς εἶδον ἤδη αὐτὸν
⁴Jesus ²coming, when they saw already him

τεθνηκότα, οὐ κατέαξαν αὐτοῦ τὰ σκέλη,
to have died, they did not break of him the legs,

34 ἀλλ' εἷς τῶν στρατιωτῶν λόγχῃ αὐτοῦ
but one of the soldiers with a lance of him

τὴν πλευρὰν ἔνυξεν, καὶ ἐξῆλθεν εὐθὺς αἷμα
the side pricked, and there came immediately blood
out

καὶ ὕδωρ. 35 καὶ ὁ ἑωρακὼς μεμαρτύρηκεν,
and water. And the [one] having seen has witnessed,

καὶ ἀληθινὴ αὐτοῦ ἐστιν ἡ μαρτυρία,
and true of him is the witness,

καὶ ἐκεῖνος οἶδεν ὅτι ἀληθῆ λέγει, ἵνα
and that one knows that truly he says, that

καὶ ὑμεῖς πιστεύητε. 36 ἐγένετο γὰρ
also ye may believe. For happened

ταῦτα ἵνα ἡ γραφὴ πληρωθῇ· ὀστοῦν
these things that the scripture might be fulfilled : A bone

οὐ συντριβήσεται αὐτοῦ. 37 καὶ πάλιν
shall not be broken of him. And again

ἑτέρα γραφὴ λέγει· ὄψονται εἰς ὃν
another scripture says : They shall look at [him] whom

ἐξεκέντησαν. 38 Μετὰ δὲ ταῦτα ἠρώτησεν
they pierced. Now after these things ¹⁴asked

τὸν Πιλᾶτον Ἰωσὴφ ἀπὸ Ἀριμαθαίας,
- ¹⁵Pilate ¹Joseph ²from ³Arimathæa,

§ It has been suggested that ὑσσώπῳ is a graphic error for ὑσσῷ (pilum), pike; but *cf.* Mat. 27. 48.

---

on, this disciple took her into his home.

The Death of Jesus

28 Later, knowing that all was now completed, and so that the Scripture would be fulfilled, Jesus said, "I am thirsty." 29 A jar of wine vinegar was there, so they soaked a sponge in it, put the sponge on a stalk of the hyssop plant, and lifted it to Jesus' lips. 30 When he had received the drink, Jesus said, "It is finished." With that, he bowed his head and gave up his spirit.

31 Now it was the day of Preparation, and the next day was to be a special Sabbath. Because the Jews did not want the bodies left on the crosses during the Sabbath, they asked Pilate to have the legs broken and the bodies taken down. 32 The soldiers therefore came and broke the legs of the first man who had been crucified with Jesus, and then those of the other. 33 But when they came to Jesus and found that he was already dead, they did not break his legs. 34 Instead, one of the soldiers pierced Jesus' side with a spear, bringing a sudden flow of blood and water. 35 The man who saw it has given testimony, and his testimony is true. He knows that he tells the truth, and he testifies so that you also may believe. 36 These things happened so that the scripture would be fulfilled: "Not one of his bones will be broken," *c* 37 and, as another scripture says, "They will look on the one they have pierced." *d*

The Burial of Jesus

38 Later, Joseph of Arimathea asked Pilate for the

---

i Or *there is one who knows*

* See note on 19. 24. Here see ver. 33—two actions contrasted.

c 36 Exodus 12:46; Num. 9:12; Psalm 34:20
d 37 Zech. 12:10

was a disciple of Jesus, though a secret one because of his fear of the Jews, asked Pilate to let him take away the body of Jesus. Pilate gave him permission; so he came and removed his body. 39 Nicodemus, who had at first come to Jesus by night, also came, bringing a mixture of myrrh and aloes, weighing about a hundred pounds. 40 They took the body of Jesus and wrapped it with the spices in linen cloths, according to the burial custom of the Jews. 41 Now there was a garden in the place where he was crucified, and in the garden there was a new tomb in which no one had ever been laid. 42 And so, because it was the Jewish day of Preparation, and the tomb was nearby, they laid Jesus there.

ὤν	μαθητὴς	[τοῦ]	Ἰησοῦ	κεκρυμμένος
⁴being	⁵a disciple	–	⁶of Jesus	⁷having been hidden

δὲ	διὰ	τὸν	φόβον	τῶν	Ἰουδαίων,	ἵνα
⁷but	⁹because	¹⁰the	¹¹fear	¹²of the	¹³Jews,	that

ἄρῃ	τὸ	σῶμα	τοῦ	Ἰησοῦ·	καὶ
he might take the	body	–	of Jesus;	and

ἐπέτρεψεν	ὁ	Πιλᾶτος.	ἦλθεν	οὖν	καὶ	ἦρεν
allowed	–	Pilate.	He came	therefore	and	took

τὸ	σῶμα	αὐτοῦ.	39 ἦλθεν	δὲ	καὶ	Νικόδημος,
the	body	of him.	And came	also	Nicodemus,

ὁ	ἐλθὼν	πρὸς	αὐτὸν	νυκτὸς	τὸ	πρῶτον,
the [one]	having come	to	him	of (by) night	at first,†

φέρων	μίγμα	σμύρνης	καὶ	ἀλόης	ὡς
bearing	a mixture	of myrrh	and	aloes	about

λίτρας	ἑκατόν.	40 ἔλαβον	οὖν	τὸ	σῶμα
pounds	a hundred.	They took	therefore	the	body

τοῦ	Ἰησοῦ	καὶ	ἔδησαν	αὐτὸ	ὀθονίοις
–	of Jesus	and	bound	it	in sheets

μετὰ	τῶν	ἀρωμάτων,	καθὼς	ἔθος	ἐστὶν
with	the	spices,	as	custom	is

τοῖς	Ἰουδαίοις	ἐνταφιάζειν.	41 ἦν	δὲ
with the	Jews	to bury.	Now there was

ἐν	τῷ	τόπῳ	ὅπου	ἐσταυρώθη	κῆπος,
in	the	place	where	he was crucified	a garden,

καὶ	ἐν	τῷ	κήπῳ	μνημεῖον	καινόν,	ἐν
and	in	the	garden	tomb	a new,	in

ᾧ	οὐδέπω	οὐδεὶς	ἦν	τεθειμένος·	42 ἐκεῖ
which	never yet	no(any) one	was	having been put;	there

οὖν	διὰ	τὴν	παρασκευὴν	τῶν	Ἰουδαίων,
therefore	because of	the	preparation	of the	Jews,

ὅτι	ἐγγὺς	ἦν	τὸ	μνημεῖον,	ἔθηκαν	τὸν
because	near	was	the	tomb,	they put	–

Ἰησοῦν.
Jesus.

body of Jesus. Now Joseph was a disciple of Jesus, but secretly because he feared the Jews. With Pilate's permission, he came and took the body away. 39 He was accompanied by Nicodemus, the man who earlier had visited Jesus at night. Nicodemus brought a mixture of myrrh and aloes, about seventy-five pounds.ᵉ 40 Taking Jesus' body, the two of them wrapped it, with the spices, in strips of linen. This was in accordance with Jewish burial customs. 41 At the place where Jesus was crucified, there was a garden, and in the garden a new tomb, in which no one had ever been laid. 42 Because it was the Jewish day of Preparation and since the tomb was nearby, they laid Jesus there.

Chapter 20

The Resurrection of Jesus

EARLY on the first day of the week, while it was still dark, Mary Magdalene came to the tomb and saw that the stone had been removed from the tomb. 2 So she ran and went to Simon Peter and the other disciple, the one whom Jesus loved, and said to them, "They have taken the Lord out of the tomb, and we do not know where they have laid him." 3 Then Peter and the other disciple set out and went toward the tomb. 4 The two were running together, but the other disciple outran Peter and reached the tomb first. 5 He bent down to look in and

20 Τῇ	δὲ	μιᾷ	τῶν	σαββάτων	Μαρία
Now on the one(first)	[day] of the	week	Mary

ἡ	Μαγδαληνὴ	ἔρχεται	πρωῒ	σκοτίας	ἔτι
the	Magdalene	comes	early	darkness	yet
				=while it was yet dark

οὔσης	εἰς	τὸ	μνημεῖον,	καὶ	βλέπει	τὸν
beingᵃ	to	the	tomb,	and	sees	the

λίθον	ἠρμένον	ἐκ	τοῦ	μνημείου.
stone	having been taken	out of	the	tomb.

2 τρέχει	οὖν	καὶ	ἔρχεται	πρὸς	Σίμωνα
She runs	therefore	and	comes	to	Simon

Πέτρον	καὶ	πρὸς	τὸν	ἄλλον	μαθητὴν	ὃν
Peter	and	to	the	other	disciple	whom

ἐφίλει	ὁ	Ἰησοῦς,	καὶ	λέγει	αὐτοῖς·	ἦραν
²loved	–	¹Jesus,	and	says	to them:	They took

τὸν	κύριον	ἐκ	τοῦ	μνημείου,	καὶ	οὐκ	οἴδαμεν
the	Lord	out of	the	tomb,	and	we do not know

ποῦ	ἔθηκαν	αὐτόν.	3 Ἐξῆλθεν	οὖν	ὁ
where	they put	him.	Went forth	therefore	the

Πέτρος	καὶ	ὁ	ἄλλος	μαθητής,	καὶ	ἤρχοντο
Peter	and the	other	disciple,	and	came

εἰς	τὸ	μνημεῖον.	4 ἔτρεχον	δὲ	οἱ	δύο
to	the	tomb.	And ran	the	two

ὁμοῦ·	καὶ	ὁ	ἄλλος	μαθητὴς	προέδραμεν
together;	and	the	other	disciple	ran before

τάχιον	τοῦ	Πέτρου	καὶ	ἦλθεν	πρῶτος
more quickly [than]	–	Peter	and	came	first

εἰς	τὸ	μνημεῖον,	5 καὶ	παρακύψας	βλέπει
to	the	tomb,	and	stooping	sees

Chapter 20

The Empty Tomb

EARLY on the first day of the week, while it was still dark, Mary Magdalene went to the tomb and saw that the stone had been removed from the entrance. 2 So she came running to Simon Peter and the other disciple, the one Jesus loved, and said, "They have taken the Lord out of the tomb, and we don't know where they have put him!"

3 So Peter and the other disciple started for the tomb. 4 Both were running, but the other disciple outran Peter and reached the tomb first. 5 He bent over and looked in at the strips

ʲ Gk lacks to look

ᵏ That is, Aramaic

ᵉ 39 Greek a hundred litrai (about 34 kilograms)

saw the linen wrappings lying there, but he did not go in. 6Then Simon Peter came, following him, and went into the tomb. He saw the linen wrappings lying there, 7and the cloth that had been on Jesus' head, not lying with the linen wrappings but rolled up in a place by itself. 8Then the other disciple, who reached the tomb first, also went in, and he saw and believed; 9for as yet they did not understand the scripture, that he must rise from the dead. 10Then the disciples returned to their homes.

Jesus Appears to Mary Magdalene

11 But Mary stood weeping outside the tomb. As she wept, she bent over to look[j] into the tomb; 12and she saw two angels in white, sitting where the body of Jesus had been lying, one at the head and the other at the feet. 13They said to her, "Woman, why are you weeping?" She said to them, "They have taken away my Lord, and I do not know where they have laid him." 14When she had said this, she turned around and saw Jesus standing there, but she did not know that it was Jesus. 15Jesus said to her, "Woman, why are you weeping? Whom are you looking for?" Supposing him to be the gardener, she said to him, "Sir, if you have carried him away, tell me where you have laid him, and I will take him away." 16Jesus said to her, "Mary!" She turned and said to him in Hebrew,[k] "Rabbouni!" (which means Teacher). 17Jesus said to her, "Do not hold on to me,

κείμενα τὰ ὀθόνια, οὐ μέντοι εἰσῆλθεν.
lying the sheets, not however he entered.
6 ἔρχεται οὖν καὶ Σίμων Πέτρος ἀκο-
Comes therefore also Simon Peter follow-
λουθῶν αὐτῷ, καὶ εἰσῆλθεν εἰς τὸ
ing him, and entered into the
μνημεῖον· καὶ θεωρεῖ τὰ ὀθόνια κείμενα,
tomb; and he beholds the sheets lying,
7 καὶ τὸ σουδάριον, ὃ ἦν ἐπὶ τῆς
and the kerchief, which was on the
κεφαλῆς αὐτοῦ, οὐ μετὰ τῶν ὀθονίων
head of him, not with the sheets
κείμενον ἀλλὰ χωρὶς ἐντετυλιγμένον εἰς
lying but apart having been wrapped up in
ἕνα τόπον. 8 τότε οὖν εἰσῆλθεν καὶ
one place. Then therefore entered also
ὁ ἄλλος μαθητὴς ὁ ἐλθὼν πρῶτος εἰς
the other disciple - having come first to
τὸ μνημεῖον, καὶ εἶδεν καὶ ἐπίστευσεν·
the tomb, and he saw and believed;
9 οὐδέπω γὰρ ᾔδεισαν τὴν γραφήν, ὅτι
for not yet they knew the scripture, that
δεῖ αὐτὸν ἐκ νεκρῶν ἀναστῆναι.
it behoves him from [the] dead to rise again.
10 ἀπῆλθον οὖν πάλιν πρὸς αὐτοὺς οἱ
Went away therefore again to themselves* the
μαθηταί. 11 Μαρία δὲ εἱστήκει πρὸς
disciples. But Mary stood at
τῷ μνημείῳ ἔξω κλαίουσα. ὡς οὖν
the tomb outside weeping. As therefore
ἔκλαιεν, παρέκυψεν εἰς τὸ μνημεῖον,
she was weeping, she stooped into the tomb,
12 καὶ θεωρεῖ δύο ἀγγέλους ἐν λευκοῖς
and beholds two angels in white
καθεζομένους, ἕνα πρὸς τῇ κεφαλῇ καὶ
sitting, one at the head and
ἕνα πρὸς τοῖς ποσίν, ὅπου ἔκειτο τὸ
one at the feet, where lay the
σῶμα τοῦ Ἰησοῦ. 13 καὶ λέγουσιν αὐτῇ
body - of Jesus. And say to her
ἐκεῖνοι· γύναι, τί κλαίεις; λέγει αὐτοῖς
those: Woman, why weepest thou? She says to them[,]
ὅτι ἦραν τὸν κύριόν μου, καὶ οὐκ οἶδα
- They took the Lord of me, and I know not
ποῦ ἔθηκαν αὐτόν. 14 ταῦτα εἰποῦσα
where they put him. These things saying
ἐστράφη εἰς τὰ ὀπίσω, καὶ θεωρεῖ τὸν
she turned back,† and beholds -
Ἰησοῦν ἑστῶτα, καὶ οὐκ ᾔδει ὅτι Ἰησοῦς
Jesus standing, and knew not that Jesus
ἐστιν. 15 λέγει αὐτῇ Ἰησοῦς· γύναι,
it is(was). Says to her Jesus: Woman,
τί κλαίεις; τίνα ζητεῖς; ἐκείνη δοκοῦσα
why weepest thou? whom seekest thou? That one thinking
ὅτι ὁ κηπουρός ἐστιν, λέγει αὐτῷ· κύριε,
that the gardener it is(was), says to him: Sir,
εἰ σὺ ἐβάστασας αὐτόν, εἰπέ μοι ποῦ
if thou didst carry him, tell me where
ἔθηκας αὐτόν, κἀγὼ αὐτὸν ἀρῶ. 16 λέγει
thou didst put him, and I him will take. Says
αὐτῇ Ἰησοῦς· Μαριάμ. στραφεῖσα ἐκείνη
to her Jesus: Mary. Turning that one
λέγει αὐτῷ Ἑβραϊστί· ῥαββουνί (ὃ λέγεται
says to him in Hebrew: Rabboni (which is said
διδάσκαλε). 17 λέγει αὐτῇ Ἰησοῦς· μὴ
Teacher). Says to her Jesus: Not

of linen lying there but did not go in. 6Then Simon Peter, who was behind him, arrived and went into the tomb. He saw the strips of linen lying there, 7as well as the burial cloth that had been around Jesus' head. The cloth was folded up by itself, separate from the linen. 8Finally the other disciple, who had reached the tomb first, also went inside. He saw and believed. 9(They still did not understand from Scripture that Jesus had to rise from the dead.)

Jesus Appears to Mary Magdalene

10Then the disciples went back to their homes, 11but Mary stood outside the tomb crying. As she wept, she bent over to look into the tomb 12and saw two angels in white, seated where Jesus' body had been, one at the head and the other at the foot.

13They asked her, "Woman, why are you crying?"

"They have taken my Lord away," she said, "and I don't know where they have put him." 14At this, she turned around and saw Jesus standing there, but she did not realize that it was Jesus.

15"Woman," he said, "why are you crying? Who is it you are looking for?"

Thinking he was the gardener, she said, "Sir, if you have carried him away, tell me where you have put him, and I will get him."

16Jesus said to her, "Mary."

She turned toward him and cried out in Aramaic, "Rabboni!" (which means Teacher).

17Jesus said, "Do not

---

[j] Gk lacks *to look*
[k] That is, *Aramaic*

* That is, to their own home; cf. 19. 27.

because I have not yet ascended to the Father. But go to my brothers and say to them, 'I am ascending to my Father and your Father, to my God and your God.' " 18 Mary Magdalene went and announced to the disciples, "I have seen the Lord"; and she told them that he had said these things to her.

Jesus Appears to the Disciples

19 When it was evening on that day, the first day of the week, and the doors of the house where the disciples had met were locked for fear of the Jews, Jesus came and stood among them and said, "Peace be with you." 20 After he said this, he showed them his hands and his side. Then the disciples rejoiced when they saw the Lord. 21 Jesus said to them again, "Peace be with you. As the Father has sent me, so I send you." 22 When he had said this, he breathed on them and said to them, "Receive the Holy Spirit. 23 If you forgive the sins of any, they are forgiven them; if you retain the sins of any, they are retained."

Jesus and Thomas

24 But Thomas (who was called the Twin*f*), one of the twelve, was not with them when Jesus came. 25 So the other disciples told him, "We have seen the Lord." But he said to them, "Unless I see the mark of the nails in his hands, and put my finger in the mark of the nails and my hand in his side, I will not believe."

μου ἅπτου, οὔπω γὰρ ἀναβέβηκα πρὸς
me touch, for not yet have I ascended to
τὸν πατέρα· πορεύου δὲ πρὸς τοὺς
the Father; but go thou to the
ἀδελφούς μου καὶ εἰπὲ αὐτοῖς· ἀναβαίνω
brothers of me and tell them: I ascend
πρὸς τὸν πατέρα μου καὶ πατέρα ὑμῶν
to the Father of me and Father of you
καὶ θεόν μου καὶ θεὸν ὑμῶν. 18 ἔρχεται
and God of me and God of you. Comes
Μαριὰμ ἡ Μαγδαληνὴ ἀγγέλλουσα τοῖς
Mary the Magdalene announcing to the
μαθηταῖς ὅτι ἑώρακα τὸν κύριον, καὶ
disciples[,] - I have seen the Lord, and
ταῦτα εἶπεν αὐτῇ.
these things he said to her.

19 Οὔσης οὖν ὀψίας τῇ ἡμέρᾳ ἐκείνῃ
Being therefore early evening* - day on that
=Therefore when it was early evening
τῇ μιᾷ σαββάτων, καὶ τῶν θυρῶν
the one(first) of the week, and the doors
κεκλεισμένων ὅπου ἦσαν οἱ μαθηταὶ διὰ
having been shut* where were the disciples because of
τὸν φόβον τῶν Ἰουδαίων, ἦλθεν ὁ Ἰησοῦς
the fear of the Jews, came - Jesus
καὶ ἔστη εἰς τὸ μέσον, καὶ λέγει αὐτοῖς·
and stood in the midst, and says to them:
εἰρήνη ὑμῖν. 20 καὶ τοῦτο εἰπὼν ἔδειξεν
Peace to you. And this saying he showed
καὶ τὰς χεῖρας καὶ τὴν πλευρὰν αὐτοῖς.
both the(his) hands and the(his) side to them.
ἐχάρησαν οὖν οἱ μαθηταὶ ἰδόντες τὸν
Rejoiced therefore the disciples seeing the
κύριον. 21 εἶπεν οὖν αὐτοῖς [ὁ Ἰησοῦς]
Lord. Said therefore to them [- Jesus]
πάλιν· εἰρήνη ὑμῖν· καθὼς ἀπέσταλκέν
again: Peace to you; as has sent
με ὁ πατήρ, κἀγὼ πέμπω ὑμᾶς. 22 καὶ
me the Father, I also send you. And
τοῦτο εἰπὼν ἐνεφύσησεν καὶ λέγει αὐτοῖς·
this saying he breathed in and says to them:
λάβετε πνεῦμα ἅγιον. 23 ἄν τινων
Receive ye Spirit Holy. Of whomever
ἀφῆτε τὰς ἁμαρτίας, ἀφέωνται αὐτοῖς·
ye forgive the sins, they have been to them;
forgiven
ἄν τινων κρατῆτε, κεκράτηνται.
of whomever ye hold, they have been held.
24 Θωμᾶς δὲ εἷς ἐκ τῶν δώδεκα,
But Thomas one of the twelve,
ὁ λεγόμενος Δίδυμος, οὐκ ἦν μετ' αὐτῶν
- being called Twin, was not with them
ὅτε ἦλθεν Ἰησοῦς. 25 ἔλεγον οὖν αὐτῷ
when came Jesus. Said therefore to him
οἱ ἄλλοι μαθηταί· ἑωράκαμεν τὸν κύριον.
the other disciples: We have seen the Lord.
ὁ δὲ εἶπεν αὐτοῖς· ἐὰν μὴ ἴδω ἐν
But he said to them: Unless I see in
ταῖς χερσὶν αὐτοῦ τὸν τύπον τῶν ἥλων
the hands of him the mark of the nails
καὶ βάλω τὸν δάκτυλόν μου εἰς τὸν
and put the finger of me into the
τόπον τῶν ἥλων καὶ βάλω μου τὴν
place of the nails and put of me the
χεῖρα εἰς τὴν πλευρὰν αὐτοῦ, οὐ μὴ
hand into the side of him, by no means

---

hold on to me, for I have not yet returned to the Father. Go instead to my brothers and tell them, 'I am returning to my Father and your Father, to my God and your God.' "
18 Mary Magdalene went to the disciples with the news: "I have seen the Lord!" And she told them that he had said these things to her.

Jesus Appears to His Disciples

19 On the evening of that first day of the week, when the disciples were together, with the doors locked for fear of the Jews, Jesus came and stood among them and said, "Peace be with you!" 20 After he said this, he showed them his hands and side. The disciples were overjoyed when they saw the Lord.
21 Again Jesus said, "Peace be with you! As the Father has sent me, I am sending you." 22 And with that he breathed on them and said, "Receive the Holy Spirit. 23 If you forgive anyone his sins, they are forgiven; if you do not forgive them, they are not forgiven."

Jesus Appears to Thomas

24 Now Thomas (called Didymus), one of the Twelve, was not with the disciples when Jesus came. 25 So the other disciples told him, "We have seen the Lord!"
But he said to them, "Unless I see the nail marks in his hands and put my finger where the nails were, and put my hand into his side, I will not believe it."

---

f Gk Didymus

26 A week later his disciples were again in the house, and Thomas was with them. Although the doors were shut, Jesus came and stood among them and said, "Peace be with you." 27 Then he said to Thomas, "Put your finger here and see my hands. Reach out your hand and put it in my side. Do not doubt but believe." 28 Thomas answered him, "My Lord and my God!" 29 Jesus said to him, "Have you believed because you have seen me? Blessed are those who have not seen and yet have come to believe."

The Purpose of This Book

30 Now Jesus did many other signs in the presence of his disciples, which are not written in this book. 31 But these are written *m* so that you may come to believe *m* that Jesus is the Messiah, *n* the Son of God, and that through believing you may have life in his name.

πιστεύσω. **26** Καὶ μεθ᾽ ἡμέρας ὀκτὼ
will I believe.   And   after   days   eight
πάλιν ἦσαν ἔσω οἱ μαθηταὶ αὐτοῦ, καὶ
again   were   within the   disciples   of him,   and
Θωμᾶς μετ᾽ αὐτῶν. ἔρχεται ὁ Ἰησοῦς
Thomas   with   them.   Comes   –   Jesus
τῶν θυρῶν κεκλεισμένων, καὶ ἔστη εἰς
the   doors   having been shutᵃ,   and   stood   in
τὸ μέσον καὶ εἶπεν· εἰρήνη ὑμῖν. **27** εἶτα
the   midst   and   said :   Peace   to you.   Then
λέγει τῷ Θωμᾷ· φέρε τὸν δάκτυλόν
he says   –   to Thomas :   Bring   the   finger
σου ὧδε καὶ ἴδε τὰς χεῖράς μου, καὶ
of thee here and   see   the   hands   of me,   and
φέρε τὴν χεῖρά σου καὶ βάλε εἰς τὴν
bring   the   hand   of thee and   put   into   the
πλευράν μου, καὶ μὴ γίνου ἄπιστος
side   of me,   and   be not   faithless
ἀλλὰ πιστός. **28** ἀπεκρίθη Θωμᾶς καὶ
but   faithful.   Answered   Thomas   and
εἶπεν αὐτῷ· ὁ κύριός μου καὶ ὁ θεός
said   to him : The   Lord   of me and   the   God
μου. **29** λέγει αὐτῷ ὁ Ἰησοῦς· ὅτι
of me.   Says   to him   –   Jesus : Because
ἑώρακάς με, πεπίστευκας; μακάριοι οἱ
thou hast seen me,   hast thou believed?   blessed the [ones]
μὴ ἰδόντες καὶ πιστεύσαντες.
not   seeing   and §   believing.

30 Πολλὰ μὲν οὖν καὶ ἄλλα σημεῖα
   Many   –*   therefore and   other   signs
ἐποίησεν ὁ Ἰησοῦς ἐνώπιον τῶν μαθητῶν,
did   –   Jesus   before   the   disciples,
ἃ οὐκ ἔστιν γεγραμμένα ἐν τῷ βιβλίῳ
which is(are) not *having been* written in   –   roll
τούτῳ· **31** ταῦτα δὲ γέγραπται ἵνα
this;   but these*   has(ve) been written   that
πιστεύητε ὅτι Ἰησοῦς ἐστιν ὁ χριστὸς ὁ
ye may believe that   Jesus   is   the   Christ   the
υἱὸς τοῦ θεοῦ, καὶ ἵνα πιστεύοντες ζωὴν
Son   –   of God, and   that   believing   life
ἔχητε ἐν τῷ ὀνόματι αὐτοῦ.
ye may have in   the   name   of him.

---

26 A week later his disciples were in the house again, and Thomas was with them. Though the doors were locked, Jesus came and stood among them and said, "Peace be with you!" 27 Then he said to Thomas, "Put your finger here; see my hands. Reach out your hand and put it into my side. Stop doubting and believe." 28 Thomas said to him, "My Lord and my God!" 29 Then Jesus told him, "Because you have seen me, you have believed; blessed are those who have not seen and yet have believed." 30 Jesus did many other miraculous signs in the presence of his disciples, which are not recorded in this book. 31 But these are written that you may *f* believe that Jesus is the Christ, the Son of God, and that by believing you may have life in his name.

Chapter 21

Jesus Appears to Seven Disciples

AFTER these things Jesus showed himself again to the disciples by the Sea of Tiberias; and he showed himself in this way. 2 Gathered there together were Simon Peter, Thomas called the Twin, *l* Nathanael of Cana in Galilee, the sons of Zebedee, and two others of his disciples. 3 Simon Peter said to them, "I am going fishing." They said to him, "We will go with you." They went out and got into the boat, but that night they caught nothing.

---

21 Μετὰ ταῦτα ἐφανέρωσεν ἑαυτὸν πάλιν
   After these things   manifested   himself   again
Ἰησοῦς τοῖς μαθηταῖς ἐπὶ τῆς θαλάσσης
Jesus   to the   disciples   on   the   sea
τῆς Τιβεριάδος· ἐφανέρωσεν δὲ οὕτως.
–   of Tiberias;   and he manifested [himself]   thus.
2 ἦσαν ὁμοῦ Σίμων Πέτρος καὶ Θωμᾶς
  There were together Simon   Peter   and   Thomas
ὁ λεγόμενος Δίδυμος καὶ Ναθαναὴλ ὁ
–   *being* called   Twin   and   Nathanael   –
ἀπὸ Κανὰ τῆς Γαλιλαίας καὶ οἱ τοῦ
from   Cana   –   of Galilee   and   the [sons]   of
Ζεβεδαίου καὶ ἄλλοι ἐκ τῶν μαθητῶν
of Zebedee   and   others   of   the   disciples
αὐτοῦ δύο. **3** λέγει αὐτοῖς Σίμων Πέτρος·
of him   two.   Says   to them   Simon   Peter :
ὑπάγω ἁλιεύειν. λέγουσιν αὐτῷ· ἐρχόμεθα
I am going to fish.   They say   to him :   Are coming
καὶ ἡμεῖς σὺν σοί. ἐξῆλθον καὶ ἐνέβησαν
also   we   with thee. They went forth and   embarked
εἰς τὸ πλοῖον, καὶ ἐν ἐκείνῃ τῇ νυκτὶ
in   the   boat,   and   in   that   –   night

Chapter 21

Jesus and the Miraculous Catch of Fish

AFTERWARD Jesus appeared again to his disciples, by the Sea of Tiberias. *g* It happened this way: 2 Simon Peter, Thomas (called Didymus), Nathanael from Cana in Galilee, the sons of Zebedee, and two other disciples were together. 3 "I'm going out to fish," Simon Peter told them, and they said, "We'll go with you." So they went out and got into the boat, but that night they

---

m Other ancient authorities read
may continue to believe
n Or *the Christ*

* See note on 19. 24 and 32.

§ καὶ sometimes = and yet; see 5. 40; 8. 55; 9. 30; 16. 32; 17. 11.

f 31 Some manuscripts *may*
continue to
g 1 That is, Sea of Galilee

4 Just after daybreak, Jesus stood on the beach; but the disciples did not know that it was Jesus. 5 Jesus said to them, "Children, you have no fish, have you?" They answered him, "No." 6 He said to them, "Cast the net to the right side of the boat, and you will find some." So they cast it, and now they were not able to haul it in because there were so many fish. 7 That disciple whom Jesus loved said to Peter, "It is the Lord!" When Simon Peter heard that it was the Lord, he put on some clothes, for he was naked, and jumped into the sea. 8 But the other disciples came in the boat, dragging the net full of fish, for they were not far from the land, only about a hundred yards*o* off.

9 When they had gone ashore, they saw a charcoal fire there, with fish on it, and bread. 10 Jesus said to them, "Bring some of the fish that you have just caught." 11 So Simon Peter went aboard and hauled the net ashore, full of large fish, a hundred fifty-three of them; and though there were so many, the net was not torn. 12 Jesus said to them, "Come and have breakfast." Now none of the disciples dared to ask him, "Who are you?" because they knew it was the Lord. 13 Jesus came and took the bread and gave it to them, and did the same with the fish. 14 This was now the third time that Jesus appeared to the disciples after he was raised from the dead.

ἐπίασαν οὐδέν. 4 πρωΐας δὲ ἤδη γινομένης
they caught nothing. Early morning but now becoming*a*
= But when it became early morning

ἔστη Ἰησοῦς εἰς τὸν αἰγιαλόν· οὐ μέντοι
stood Jesus in(on) the shore; not however

ᾔδεισαν οἱ μαθηταὶ ὅτι Ἰησοῦς ἐστιν.
knew the disciples that Jesus it is(was).

5 λέγει οὖν αὐτοῖς Ἰησοῦς· παιδία, μή
Says therefore to them Jesus: Children, not

τι προσφάγιον ἔχετε; ἀπεκρίθησαν αὐτῷ·
any fish have ye? They answered him:

οὔ. 6 ὁ δὲ εἶπεν αὐτοῖς· βάλετε εἰς τὰ
No. So he said to them: Cast in the

δεξιὰ μέρη τοῦ πλοίου τὸ δίκτυον, καὶ
right parts of the boat the net, and

εὑρήσετε. ἔβαλον οὖν, καὶ οὐκέτι αὐτὸ
ye will find. They cast therefore, and *1*no longer *4*it

ἑλκύσαι ἴσχυον ἀπὸ τοῦ πλήθους τῶν
*3*to drag *2*were they able from the multitude of the

ἰχθύων. 7 λέγει οὖν ὁ μαθητὴς ἐκεῖνος
fishes. Says therefore - disciple that

ὃν ἠγάπα ὁ Ἰησοῦς τῷ Πέτρῳ· ὁ κύριός
whom *1*loved - *2*Jesus to Peter: The Lord

ἐστιν. Σίμων οὖν Πέτρος, ἀκούσας ὅτι
it is. *2*Simon *1*therefore *2*Peter, hearing that

ὁ κύριός ἐστιν, τὸν ἐπενδύτην διεζώσατο,
the Lord it is(was), *2*[with]the *4*coat *1*girded himself,

ἦν γὰρ γυμνός, καὶ ἔβαλεν ἑαυτὸν εἰς
for he was naked, and threw himself into

τὴν θάλασσαν· 8 οἱ δὲ ἄλλοι μαθηταὶ
the sea; but the other disciples

τῷ πλοιαρίῳ ἦλθον, οὐ γὰρ ἦσαν μακρὰν
in the little boat came, for not they were far

ἀπὸ τῆς γῆς ἀλλὰ ὡς ἀπὸ πηχῶν
from the land but about from cubits

διακοσίων, σύροντες τὸ δίκτυον τῶν ἰχθύων.
two hundred dragging the net of the fishes.

9 ὡς οὖν ἀπέβησαν εἰς τὴν γῆν, βλέπουσιν
When therefore they disembarked onto the land, they see

ἀνθρακιὰν κειμένην καὶ ὀψάριον ἐπικείμενον
a coal fire lying and a fish lying on

καὶ ἄρτον. 10 λέγει αὐτοῖς ὁ Ἰησοῦς·
and bread. Says to them - Jesus:

ἐνέγκατε ἀπὸ τῶν ὀψαρίων ὧν ἐπιάσατε
Bring from the fishes which ye caught

νῦν. 11 ἀνέβη Σίμων Πέτρος καὶ εἵλκυσεν
now. Went up Simon Peter and dragged

τὸ δίκτυον εἰς τὴν γῆν μεστὸν ἰχθύων
the net to the land full fishes

μεγάλων ἑκατὸν πεντήκοντα τριῶν· καὶ
of great a hundred fifty three; and

τοσούτων ὄντων οὐκ ἐσχίσθη τὸ δίκτυον.
so many being*a* was not torn the net.

12 λέγει αὐτοῖς ὁ Ἰησοῦς· δεῦτε ἀριστήσατε.
Says to them - Jesus: Come breakfast ye.

οὐδεὶς ἐτόλμα τῶν μαθητῶν ἐξετάσαι
No one dared of the disciples to question

αὐτόν· σὺ τίς εἶ; εἰδότες ὅτι ὁ κύριός
him: Thou who art? knowing that the Lord

ἐστιν. 13 ἔρχεται Ἰησοῦς καὶ λαμβάνει
it is(was). Comes Jesus and takes

τὸν ἄρτον καὶ δίδωσιν αὐτοῖς, καὶ τὸ
the bread and gives to them, and the

ὀψάριον ὁμοίως. 14 τοῦτο ἤδη τρίτον
fish likewise. This [was] now [the] third [time]
[that]

ἐφανερώθη Ἰησοῦς τοῖς μαθηταῖς ἐγερθεὶς
*2*was manifested *1*Jesus to the disciples raised

caught nothing.
4 Early in the morning, Jesus stood on the shore, but the disciples did not realize that it was Jesus.
5 He called out to them, "Friends, haven't you any fish?"
"No," they answered.
6 He said, "Throw your net on the right side of the boat and you will find some." When they did, they were unable to haul the net in because of the large number of fish.
7 Then the disciple whom Jesus loved said to Peter, "It is the Lord!" As soon as Simon Peter heard him say, "It is the Lord," he wrapped his outer garment around him (for he had taken it off) and jumped into the water. 8 The other disciples followed in the boat, towing the net full of fish, for they were not far from shore, about a hundred yards.*h* 9 When they landed, they saw a fire of burning coals there with fish on it, and some bread.
10 Jesus said to them, "Bring some of the fish you have just caught."
11 Simon Peter climbed aboard and dragged the net ashore. It was full of large fish, 153, but even with so many the net was not torn. 12 Jesus said to them, "Come and have breakfast." None of the disciples dared ask him, "Who are you?" They knew it was the Lord. 13 Jesus came, took the bread and gave it to them, and did the same with the fish. 14 This was now the third time Jesus appeared to his disciples after he was raised from the dead.

o Gk two hundred cubits

*h*8 Greek about two hundred cubits (about 90 meters)

Jesus and Peter

15 When they had finished breakfast, Jesus said to Simon Peter, "Simon son of John, do you love me more than these?" He said to him, "Yes, Lord; you know that I love you." Jesus said to him, "Feed my lambs." 16 A second time he said to him, "Simon son of John, do you love me?" He said to him, "Yes, Lord; you know that I love you." Jesus said to him, "Tend my sheep." 17 He said to him the third time, "Simon son of John, do you love me?" Peter felt hurt because he said to him the third time, "Do you love me?" And he said to him, "Lord, you know everything; you know that I love you." Jesus said to him, "Feed my sheep. 18 Very truly, I tell you, when you were younger, you used to fasten your own belt and to go wherever you wished. But when you grow old, you will stretch out your hands, and someone else will fasten a belt around you and take you where you do not wish to go." 19 (He said this to indicate the kind of death by which he would glorify God.) After this he said to him, "Follow me."

Jesus and the Beloved Disciple

20 Peter turned and saw the disciple whom Jesus loved following them; he was the one who had reclined next to Jesus at the supper and had said, "Lord, who is it that is going to betray you?" 21 When Peter saw him, he said to Jesus, "Lord, what about him?" 22 Jesus said to him, "If it is my will that he remain until I come, what is that to you? Follow me!" 23 So the rumor spread in the community[p] that this disciple would not die. Yet

[p] Gk among the brothers

ἐκ νεκρῶν.
from [the] dead.

15 Ὅτε οὖν ἠρίστησαν, λέγει τῷ
When therefore they breakfasted, says -

Σίμωνι Πέτρῳ ὁ Ἰησοῦς· Σίμων Ἰωάννου,
to Simon Peter - Jesus: Simon [son] of John,

ἀγαπᾷς με πλέον τούτων; λέγει αὐτῷ·
lovest thou me more [than] these? He says to him:

ναί, κύριε, σὺ οἶδας ὅτι φιλῶ σε. λέγει
Yes, Lord, thou knowest that I love thee. He says

αὐτῷ· βόσκε τὰ ἀρνία μου. 16 λέγει
to him: Feed the lambs of me. He says

αὐτῷ πάλιν δεύτερον· Σίμων Ἰωάννου,
to him again secondly: Simon [son] of John,

ἀγαπᾷς με; λέγει αὐτῷ· ναί, κύριε,
lovest thou me? He says to him: Yes, Lord,

σὺ οἶδας ὅτι φιλῶ σε. λέγει αὐτῷ·
thou knowest that I love thee. He says to him:

ποίμαινε τὰ προβάτιά μου. 17 λέγει
Shepherd the little sheep of me. He says

αὐτῷ τὸ τρίτον· Σίμων Ἰωάννου, φιλεῖς
to him the third [time]: Simon [son] of John, lovest thou

με; ἐλυπήθη ὁ Πέτρος ὅτι εἶπεν αὐτῷ
me? Was grieved - Peter that he said to him

τὸ τρίτον· φιλεῖς με; καὶ εἶπεν αὐτῷ·
the third [time]: Lovest thou me? and said to him:

κύριε, πάντα σὺ οἶδας, σὺ γινώσκεις
Lord, all things thou knowest, thou knowest

ὅτι φιλῶ σε· λέγει αὐτῷ Ἰησοῦς· βόσκε
that I love thee; says to him Jesus: Feed

τὰ προβάτιά μου. 18 ἀμὴν ἀμὴν λέγω
the little sheep of me. Truly truly I tell

σοι, ὅτε ἧς νεώτερος, ἐζώννυες σεαυτὸν
thee, when thou wast younger, thou girdest thyself

καὶ περιεπάτεις ὅπου ἤθελες· ὅταν δὲ
and walkedst where thou wishedst; but when

γηράσῃς, ἐκτενεῖς τὰς χεῖράς σου, καὶ
thou growest old, thou wilt stretch out the hands of thee, and

ἄλλος ζώσει σε καὶ οἴσει ὅπου οὐ θέλεις.
another will gird thee and will carry where thou wishest not.

19 τοῦτο δὲ εἶπεν σημαίνων ποίῳ θανάτῳ
And this he said signifying by what death

δοξάσει τὸν θεόν. καὶ τοῦτο εἰπὼν λέγει
he will glorify - God. And this saying he tells

αὐτῷ· ἀκολούθει μοι. 20 ἐπιστραφεὶς ὁ
him: Follow me. Turning -

Πέτρος βλέπει τὸν μαθητὴν ὃν ἠγάπα ὁ
Peter sees the disciple whom ³loved -

¹Ἰησοῦς ἀκολουθοῦντα, ὃς καὶ ἀνέπεσεν
¹Jesus following, who also leaned

ἐν τῷ δείπνῳ ἐπὶ τὸ στῆθος αὐτοῦ καὶ
at the supper on the breast of him and

εἶπεν· κύριε, τίς ἐστιν ὁ παραδιδούς σε;
said: Lord, who is the[one] betraying thee?

21 τοῦτον οὖν ἰδὼν ὁ Πέτρος λέγει τῷ
⁴This one ³therefore ²seeing - ¹Peter says -

Ἰησοῦ· κύριε, οὗτος δὲ τί; 22 λέγει
to Jesus: Lord, and this one what? Says

αὐτῷ ὁ Ἰησοῦς· ἐὰν αὐτὸν θέλω μένειν
to him - Jesus: If him I wish to remain

ἕως ἔρχομαι, τί πρὸς σέ; σύ μοι
until I come, what to thee? ²thou ⁴me

ἀκολούθει. 23 ἐξῆλθεν οὖν οὗτος ὁ λόγος
¹follow. Went forth therefore this - word

εἰς τοὺς ἀδελφοὺς ὅτι ὁ μαθητὴς ἐκεῖνος
to the brothers that the disciple that

Jesus Reinstates Peter

15 When they had finished eating, Jesus said to Simon Peter, "Simon son of John, do you truly love me more than these?"

"Yes, Lord," he said, "you know that I love you."

Jesus said, "Feed my lambs."

16 Again Jesus said, "Simon son of John, do you truly love me?"

He answered, "Yes, Lord, you know that I love you."

Jesus said, "Take care of my sheep."

17 The third time he said to him, "Simon son of John, do you love me?"

Peter was hurt because Jesus asked him the third time, "Do you love me?" He said, "Lord, you know all things; you know that I love you."

Jesus said, "Feed my sheep. 18 I tell you the truth, when you were younger you dressed yourself and went where you wanted; but when you are old you will stretch out your hands, and someone else will dress you and lead you where you do not want to go." 19 Jesus said this to indicate the kind of death by which Peter would glorify God. Then he said to him, "Follow me!"

20 Peter turned and saw that the disciple whom Jesus loved was following them. (This was the one who had leaned back against Jesus at the supper and had said, "Lord, who is going to betray you?") 21 When Peter saw him, he asked, "Lord, what about him?"

22 Jesus answered, "If I want him to remain alive until I return, what is that to you? You must follow me." 23 Because of this, the rumor spread among the brothers that this disciple

Jesus did not say to him that he would not die, but, "If it is my will that he remain until I come, what is that to you?" [q]

24 This is the disciple who is testifying to these things and has written them, and we know that his testimony is true. 25 But there are also many other things that Jesus did; if every one of them were written down, I suppose that the world itself could not contain the books that would be written.

οὐκ ἀποθνήσκει· οὐκ εἶπεν δὲ αὐτῷ ὁ
does not die; but said not to him -

'Ιησοῦς ὅτι οὐκ ἀποθνήσκει, ἀλλ'· ἐὰν
Jesus that he does not die, but: If

αὐτὸν θέλω μένειν ἕως ἔρχομαι, τί πρὸς
him I wish to remain until I come, what to

σέ;
thee?

24 Οὗτός ἐστιν ὁ μαθητὴς ὁ μαρτυρῶν
This is the disciple - witnessing

περὶ τούτων καὶ ὁ γράψας ταῦτα,
concerning these and - having these
things written things,

καὶ οἴδαμεν ὅτι ἀληθὴς αὐτοῦ ἡ μαρτυρία
and we know that true of him the witness

ἐστίν. 25 Ἔστιν δὲ καὶ ἄλλα πολλὰ ἃ
is. And there are also other many which
things

ἐποίησεν ὁ 'Ιησοῦς, ἅτινα ἐὰν γράφηται
did - Jesus, which if they were written

καθ' ἕν, οὐδ' αὐτὸν οἶμαι τὸν κόσμον
singly,† ²not ⁴[it]self ¹I think ³the ⁵world

χωρήσειν τὰ γραφόμενα βιβλία.
⁶to contain ⁷the ⁸being written ⁹rolls.

would not die. But Jesus did not say that he would not die; he only said, "If I want him to remain alive until I return, what is that to you?"

24 This is the disciple who testifies to these things and who wrote them down. We know that his testimony is true.

25 Jesus did many other things as well. If every one of them were written down, I suppose that even the whole world would not have room for the books that would be written.

The
Acts
of the Apostles

ΠΡΑΞΕΙΣ ΑΠΟΣΤΟΛΩΝ
Acts of Apostles

Acts

Chapter 1

The Promise of the Holy Spirit

IN the first book, Theophilus, I wrote about all that Jesus did and taught from the beginning ²until the day when he was taken up to heaven, after giving instructions through the Holy Spirit to the apostles whom he had chosen. ³ After his suffering he presented himself alive to them by many convincing proofs, appearing to them during forty days and speaking about the kingdom of God. ⁴While staying[a] with them, he ordered them not to leave Jerusalem, but to wait there for the promise of the Father. "This," he said, "is what you have heard from me; ⁵for John baptized with water, but you will be baptized with[b] the Holy Spirit not many days from now."

The Ascension of Jesus

6 So when they had come together, they asked him, "Lord, is this the time when you will restore the kingdom to Israel?" ⁷He replied, "It is not for you to know the times or periods that the Father has set by his own authority. ⁸But you will receive power when the Holy Spirit has come upon you; and you will be my witnesses in Jerusalem, in all Judea and Samaria, and to the ends of the earth." ⁹When he had said this, as they were watching, he was lifted up, and a cloud took him out of their sight. ¹⁰While he was going and they were gazing up toward heaven, suddenly two men in white robes stood by them. ¹¹They

---

1 Τὸν μὲν πρῶτον λόγον ἐποιησάμην
The - first account I made

περὶ πάντων, ὦ Θεόφιλε, ὧν ἤρξατο
concerning all things, O Theophilus, which began

ὁ Ἰησοῦς ποιεῖν τε καὶ διδάσκειν,
- Jesus both to do and to teach,

2 ἄχρι ἧς ἡμέρας ἐντειλάμενος τοῖς
until which day ᵃhaving given injunctions ⁴to the
=the day on which

ἀποστόλοις διὰ πνεύματος ἁγίου οὓς
ᵃapostles ³through ⁵Spirit ⁶Holy ⁷whom

ἐξελέξατο ἀνελήμφθη· **3** οἷς καὶ παρέστησεν
ᵃhe chose ᵃhe was taken up; to whom also he presented

ἑαυτὸν ζῶντα μετὰ τὸ παθεῖν αὐτὸν[b] ἐν
himself living after the to suffer him by
=he suffered

πολλοῖς τεκμηρίοις, δι᾽ ἡμερῶν τεσσεράκοντα
many infallible proofs, through days forty

ὀπτανόμενος αὐτοῖς καὶ λέγων τὰ περὶ
being seen by them and speaking the things concerning

τῆς βασιλείας τοῦ θεοῦ· **4** καὶ συναλιζόμενος
the kingdom - of God; and meeting with [them]

παρήγγειλεν αὐτοῖς ἀπὸ Ἰεροσολύμων μὴ
he charged them from Jerusalem not

χωρίζεσθαι, ἀλλὰ περιμένειν τὴν ἐπαγγελίαν
to depart, but to await the promise

τοῦ πατρὸς ἣν ἠκούσατέ μου· **5** ὅτι
of the Father which ye heard of me: because

Ἰωάννης μὲν ἐβάπτισεν ὕδατι, ὑμεῖς δὲ
John indeed baptized in water, but ye

ἐν πνεύματι βαπτισθήσεσθε ἁγίῳ οὐ μετὰ
in ᵃSpirit ⁶will be baptized ³Holy not after

πολλὰς ταύτας ἡμέρας. **6** Οἱ μὲν οὖν
many these days. ²the [ones] ¹So then

συνελθόντες ἠρώτων αὐτὸν λέγοντες· κύριε,
²coming together questioned him saying: Lord,

εἰ ἐν τῷ χρόνῳ τούτῳ ἀποκαθιστάνεις
if at this time restorest thou

τὴν βασιλείαν τῷ Ἰσραήλ; **7** εἶπεν πρὸς
the kingdom - to Israel? He said to

αὐτούς· οὐχ ὑμῶν ἐστιν γνῶναι χρόνους
them: Not of you it is to know times

ἢ καιροὺς οὓς ὁ πατὴρ ἔθετο ἐν τῇ
or seasons which the Father placed in the(his)

ἰδίᾳ ἐξουσίᾳ, **8** ἀλλὰ λήμψεσθε δύναμιν
own authority, but ye will receive power

ἐπελθόντος τοῦ ἁγίου πνεύματος ἐφ᾽ ὑμᾶς,
coming upon the Holy Spirit[a] upon you,
=when the Holy Spirit comes

καὶ ἔσεσθέ μου μάρτυρες ἔν τε Ἰερουσαλὴμ
and ye will be of me witnesses both in Jerusalem

καὶ ἐν πάσῃ τῇ Ἰουδαίᾳ καὶ Σαμαρείᾳ
and in all - Judæa and Samaria

καὶ ἕως ἐσχάτου τῆς γῆς. **9** καὶ ταῦτα
and unto [the] extremity of the earth. And these things

εἰπὼν βλεπόντων αὐτῶν ἐπήρθη, καὶ
saying looking them[a] he was taken up, and
=as they looked

νεφέλη ὑπέλαβεν αὐτὸν ἀπὸ τῶν ὀφθαλμῶν
a cloud received him from the eyes

αὐτῶν. **10** καὶ ὡς ἀτενίζοντες ἦσαν εἰς
of them. And as gazing they were to

τὸν οὐρανὸν πορευομένου αὐτοῦ, καὶ ἰδοὺ
- heaven going him,[a] - behold[,]
=as he went,

ἄνδρες δύο παρειστήκεισαν αὐτοῖς ἐν ἐσθήσεσι
men two stood by them in garments

Jesus Taken Up Into Heaven

IN my former book, Theophilus, I wrote about all that Jesus began to do and to teach ²until the day he was taken up to heaven, after giving instructions through the Holy Spirit to the apostles he had chosen. ³After his suffering, he showed himself to these men and gave many convincing proofs that he was alive. He appeared to them over a period of forty days and spoke about the kingdom of God. ⁴On one occasion, while he was eating with them, he gave them this command: "Do not leave Jerusalem, but wait for the gift my Father promised, which you have heard me speak about. ⁵For John baptized with[a] water, but in a few days you will be baptized with the Holy Spirit."

⁶So when they met together, they asked him, "Lord, are you at this time going to restore the kingdom to Israel?"

⁷He said to them: "It is not for you to know the times or dates the Father has set by his own authority. ⁸But you will receive power when the Holy Spirit comes on you; and you will be my witnesses in Jerusalem, and in all Judea and Samaria, and to the ends of the earth."

⁹After he said this, he was taken up before their very eyes, and a cloud hid him from their sight.

¹⁰They were looking intently up into the sky as he was going, when suddenly two men dressed in white stood beside them. ¹¹"Men

---

ᵃ Or eating
ᵇ Or by

ᵃ5 Or in

said, "Men of Galilee, why do you stand looking upto-ward heaven? This Jesus, who has been taken up from you into heaven, will come in the same way as you saw him go into heaven."

Matthias Chosen to Replace Judas

12 Then they returned to Jerusalem from the mount called Olivet, which is near Jerusalem, a sabbath day's journey away. 13 When they had entered the city, they went to the room upstairs where they were staying, Peter, and John, and James, and Andrew, Philip and Thomas, Bartholomew and Matthew, James son of Alphaeus, and Simon the Zealot, and Judas son of[c] James. 14 All these were constantly devoting themselves to prayer, together with certain women, including Mary the mother of Jesus, as well as his brothers.

15 In those days Peter stood up among the believers[d] (together the crowd numbered about one hundred twenty persons) and said, 16 "Friends,[e] the scripture had to be fulfilled, which the Holy Spirit through David foretold concerning Judas, who became a guide for those who arrested Jesus— 17 for he was numbered among us and was allotted his share in this ministry." 18 (Now this man acquired a field with the reward of his wickedness; and falling headlong,[f] he burst open in the middle and all his bowels gushed out. 19 This became

---

λευκαῖς, 11 οἳ καὶ εἶπαν· ἄνδρες Γαλιλαῖοι,
white,   who also   said :   Men   Galilæàns,

τί ἑστήκατε βλέποντες εἰς τὸν οὐρανόν;
why stand ye   looking   to   –   heaven ?

οὗτος ὁ Ἰησοῦς ὁ ἀναλημφθεὶς
This   –   Jesus   the [one] having been taken up

ἀφ᾽ ὑμῶν εἰς τὸν οὐρανὸν οὕτως ἐλεύσεται
from you   to   –   heaven   thus   will come

ὃν τρόπον ἐθεάσασθε αὐτὸν πορευόμενον
in the way†   ye beheld   him   going

εἰς τὸν οὐρανόν. 12 Τότε ὑπέστρεψαν
to   –   heaven.   Then   they returned

εἰς Ἰερουσαλὴμ ἀπὸ ὄρους τοῦ καλου-
to   Jerusalem   from [the] mount   the [one]   being

μένου ἐλαιῶνος, ὅ ἐστιν ἐγγὺς Ἰερουσαλὴμ
called of [the] olive grove, which is   near   Jerusalem

σαββάτου ἔχον ὁδόν. 13 καὶ ὅτε εἰσῆλθον,
of a sabbath having a way.   And when they entered,
= a sabbath's journey off.

εἰς τὸ ὑπερῷον ἀνέβησαν οὗ ἦσαν
into   the   upper room   they went up   where they were

καταμένοντες, ὅ τε Πέτρος καὶ Ἰωάννης
waiting,   – both   Peter   and   John

καὶ Ἰάκωβος καὶ Ἀνδρέας, Φίλιππος καὶ
and   James   and   Andrew,   Philip   and

Θωμᾶς, Βαρθολομαῖος καὶ Μαθθαῖος,
Thomas,   Bartholomew   and   Matthew,

Ἰάκωβος Ἀλφαίου καὶ Σίμων ὁ ζηλωτὴς
James [son] of Alphæus   and   Simon   the   zealot

καὶ Ἰούδας Ἰακώβου. 14 οὗτοι πάντες
and   Judas [brother] of James.   These   all

ἦσαν προσκαρτεροῦντες ὁμοθυμαδὸν τῇ
were   continuing steadfastly   with one mind   the

προσευχῇ σὺν γυναιξὶν καὶ Μαριὰμ τῇ
in prayer   with   [the] women   and   Mary   the

μητρὶ [τοῦ] Ἰησοῦ καὶ σὺν τοῖς ἀδελφοῖς
mother   –   of Jesus   and   with   the   brothers

αὐτοῦ.
of him.

15 Καὶ ἐν ταῖς ἡμέραις ταύταις ἀναστὰς
And   in   these days   standing up

Πέτρος ἐν μέσῳ τῶν ἀδελφῶν εἶπεν·
Peter   in [the] midst   of the   brothers   said :

ἦν τε ὄχλος ὀνομάτων ἐπὶ τὸ αὐτὸ
⁶was   ¹and   ²[the] ³crowd   ⁴of names   ⁵together

ὡσεὶ ἑκατὸν εἴκοσι· 16 ἄνδρες ἀδελφοί,
about   a hundred   twenty :   Men   brothers,

ἔδει πληρωθῆναι τὴν γραφὴν ἣν
it behoved   to be fulfilled   the   scripture   which

προεῖπεν τὸ πνεῦμα τὸ ἅγιον διὰ στόματος
spoke before   the   Spirit   –   Holy   through [the] mouth

Δαυὶδ περὶ Ἰούδα τοῦ γενομένου ὁδηγοῦ
of David concerning Judas   the [one]   having become   guide

τοῖς συλλαβοῦσιν Ἰησοῦν, 17 ὅτι κατ-
to the [ones]   taking   Jesus,   because   having

ηριθμημένος ἦν ἐν ἡμῖν καὶ ἔλαχεν τὸν
been numbered   he was among   us   and   obtained   the

κλῆρον τῆς διακονίας ταύτης. 18 οὗτος μὲν οὖν
portion   of this ministry.   This one   therefore

ἐκτήσατο χωρίον ἐκ μισθοῦ τῆς
bought   a field   out of [the]   reward   –

ἀδικίας, καὶ πρηνὴς γενόμενος ἐλάκησεν
of unrighteousness, and swollen up having become he burst asunder

μέσος, καὶ ἐξεχύθη πάντα τὰ σπλάγχ-
in the middle, and   were poured out   all   the   bowel

---

of Galilee," they said, "why do you stand here looking into the sky? This same Jesus, who has been taken from you into heaven, will come back in the same way you have seen him go into heaven."

Matthias Chosen to Replace Judas

12 Then they returned to Jerusalem from the hill called the Mount of Olives, a Sabbath day's walk[b] from the city. 13 When they arrived, they went upstairs to the room where they were staying. Those present were Peter, John, James and Andrew; Philip and Thomas, Bartholomew and Matthew; James son of Alphaeus and Simon the Zealot, and Judas son of James. 14 They all joined together constantly in prayer, along with the women and Mary the mother of Jesus, and with his brothers.

15 In those days Peter stood up among the believers[c] (a group numbering about a hundred and twenty) 16 and said, "Brothers, the Scripture had to be fulfilled which the Holy Spirit spoke long ago through the mouth of David concerning Judas, who served as guide for those who arrested Jesus—17 he was one of our number and shared in this ministry."

18 (With the reward he got for his wickedness, Judas bought a field; there he fell headlong, his body burst open and all his intestines

---

c Or the brother of
d Gk brothers
e Gk Men, brothers
f Or swelling up

known to all the residents of Jerusalem, so that the field was called in their language Hakeldama, that is, Field of Blood.) 20 "For it is written in the book of Psalms,

'Let his homestead become desolate, and let there be no one to live in it';

and

'Let another take his position of overseer.'

21 So one of the men who have accompanied us during all the time that the Lord Jesus went in and out among us, 22 beginning from the baptism of John until the day when he was taken up from us—one of these must become a witness with us to his resurrection." 23 So they proposed two, Joseph called Barsabbas, who was also known as Justus, and Matthias. 24 Then they prayed and said, "Lord, you know everyone's heart. Show us which one of these two you have chosen 25 to take the place *g* in this ministry and apostleship from which Judas turned aside to go to his own place." 26 And they cast lots for them, and the lot fell on Matthias; and he was added to the eleven apostles.

αὐτοῦ· 19 καὶ γνωστὸν ἐγένετο πᾶσι τοῖς
of him; and known it became to all the

κατοικοῦσιν Ἰερουσαλήμ, ὥστε κληθῆναι
[ones] inhabiting Jerusalem, so as to be called

τὸ χωρίον ἐκεῖνο τῇ ἰδίᾳ διαλέκτῳ αὐτῶν
that field in their own language

Ἀκελδαμάχ, τοῦτ' ἔστιν χωρίον
Aceldamach, this is Field

αἵματος. 20 γέγραπται γὰρ ἐν βίβλῳ
of blood. For it has been written in [the] roll

ψαλμῶν· γενηθήτω ἡ ἔπαυλις αὐτοῦ ἔρημος
of Psalms: Let become the estate of him deserted

καὶ μὴ ἔστω ὁ κατοικῶν ἐν αὐτῇ, καὶ·
and let not be the [one] dwelling in it, and:

τὴν ἐπισκοπὴν αὐτοῦ λαβέτω ἕτερος.
The office of him let take another.

21 δεῖ οὖν τῶν συνελθόντων ἡμῖν ἀνδρῶν
It behoves* therefore ¹of the ³accompanying ⁴us ²men

ἐν παντὶ χρόνῳ ᾧ εἰσῆλθεν καὶ
in all [the] time in which went in and

ἐξῆλθεν ἐφ' ἡμᾶς ὁ κύριος Ἰησοῦς,
went out among us the Lord Jesus,

22 ἀρξάμενος ἀπὸ τοῦ βαπτίσματος
beginning from the baptism

Ἰωάννου ἕως τῆς ἡμέρας ἧς ἀνελήμφθη
of John until the day when he was taken up

ἀφ' ἡμῶν, μάρτυρα τῆς ἀναστάσεως
from us, ¹a witness* ²of the ³resurrection

αὐτοῦ σὺν ἡμῖν γενέσθαι ἕνα τούτων.
⁵of him ²with ³us ¹to become ⁴one* ⁶of these.

23 Καὶ ἔστησαν δύο, Ἰωσὴφ τὸν καλού-
And they set two, Joseph the [one] being

μενον Βαρσαββᾶν, ὃς ἐπεκλήθη Ἰοῦστος,
called Barsabbas, who was surnamed Justus,

καὶ Μαθθίαν. 24 καὶ προσευξάμενοι εἶπαν·
and Matthias. And praying they said:

σὺ κύριε καρδιογνῶστα πάντων, ἀνάδειξον
Thou Lord Heart-knower of all men, show

ὃν ἐξελέξω ἐκ τούτων τῶν δύο ἕνα
whom thou didst choose of these the — two one

25 λαβεῖν τὸν τόπον τῆς διακονίας ταύτης
to take the place of this ministry

καὶ ἀποστολῆς, ἀφ' ἧς παρέβη Ἰούδας
and apostleship, from which fell Judas

πορευθῆναι εἰς τὸν τόπον τὸν ἴδιον.
to go to the(his) place — own.

26 καὶ ἔδωκαν κλήρους αὐτοῖς, καὶ ἔπεσεν
And they gave lots for them, and fell

ὁ κλῆρος ἐπὶ Μαθθίαν, καὶ συγκατεψηφίσθη
the lot on Matthias, and he was reckoned along with

μετὰ τῶν ἔνδεκα ἀποστόλων.
with the eleven apostles.

spilled out. 19 Everyone in Jerusalem heard about this, so they called that field in their language Akeldama, that is, Field of Blood.)

20 "For," said Peter, "it is written in the book of Psalms,

" 'May his place be deserted; let there be no one to dwell in it,'*d*

and,

" 'May another take his place of leadership.'*e*

21 Therefore it is necessary to choose one of the men who have been with us the whole time the Lord Jesus went in and out among us, 22 beginning from John's baptism to the time when Jesus was taken up from us. For one of these must become a witness with us of his resurrection."

23 So they proposed two men: Joseph called Barsabbas (also known as Justus) and Matthias. 24 Then they prayed, "Lord, you know everyone's heart. Show us which of these two you have chosen 25 to take over this apostolic ministry, which Judas left to go where he belongs." 26 Then they cast lots, and the lot fell to Matthias; so he was added to the eleven apostles.

Chapter 2

The Coming of the Holy Spirit

WHEN the day of Pentecost had come, they were all together in one place. 2 And suddenly from heaven there came a sound like the rush of a violent wind, and it filled the

2 Καὶ ἐν τῷ συμπληροῦσθαι τὴν ἡμέραν
And in the to be completed the day
=when the day of Pentecost was completed

τῆς πεντηκοστῆς ἦσαν πάντες ὁμοῦ ἐπὶ
— of Pentecost* they were all together to-

τὸ αὐτό· 2 καὶ ἐγένετο ἄφνω ἐκ τοῦ
gether;† and there was suddenly out of —

οὐρανοῦ ἦχος ὥσπερ φερομένης πνοῆς
heaven a sound as ⁵being borne ¹of²a ⁴wind

Chapter 2

The Holy Spirit Comes at Pentecost

WHEN the day of Pentecost came, they were all together in one place. 2 Suddenly a sound like the blowing of a violent

---

g Other ancient authorities read *the share*

* The object (according to the Greek construction) of the verb δεῖ is ἕνα, with μάρτυρα as its complement after γενέσθαι.

d 20 Psalm 69:25
e 20 Psalm 109:8

entire house where they were sitting. 3 Divided tongues, as of fire, appeared among them, and a tongue rested on each of them. 4 All of them were filled with the Holy Spirit and began to speak in other languages, as the Spirit gave them ability.

5 Now there were devout Jews from every nation under heaven living in Jerusalem. 6 And at this sound the crowd gathered and was bewildered, because each one heard them speaking in the native language of each. 7 Amazed and astonished, they asked, "Are not all these who are speaking Galileans? 8 And how is it that we hear, each of us, in our own native language? 9 Parthians, Medes, Elamites, and residents of Mesopotamia, Judea and Cappadocia, Pontus and Asia, 10 Phrygia and Pamphylia, Egypt and the parts of Libya belonging to Cyrene, and visitors from Rome, both Jews and proselytes, 11 Cretans and Arabs—in our own languages we hear them speaking about God's deeds of power." 12 All were amazed and perplexed, saying to one another, "What does this mean?" 13 But others sneered and said, "They are filled with new wine."

Peter Addresses the Crowd

14 But Peter, standing with the eleven, raised his voice and addressed them,

---

βιαίας καὶ ἐπλήρωσεν ὅλον τὸν οἶκον
³violent and it filled all the house

οὗ ἦσαν καθήμενοι, 3 καὶ ὤφθησαν αὐτοῖς
where they were sitting, and there appeared to them

διαμεριζόμεναι γλῶσσαι ὡσεὶ πυρός, καὶ
being distributed tongues as of fire, and

ἐκάθισεν ἐφ' ἕνα ἕκαστον αὐτῶν, 4 καὶ
it sat on ²one ¹each of them, and

ἐπλήσθησαν πάντες πνεύματος ἁγίου, καὶ
they were filled all of(with) Spirit Holy, and

ἤρξαντο λαλεῖν ἑτέραις γλώσσαις καθὼς
began to speak in other tongues as

τὸ πνεῦμα ἐδίδου ἀποφθέγγεσθαι αὐτοῖς.
the Spirit gave ²to speak out ¹them.

5 Ἦσαν δὲ εἰς Ἰερουσαλὴμ κατοικοῦντες
Now there were in Jerusalem dwelling

Ἰουδαῖοι, ἄνδρες εὐλαβεῖς ἀπὸ παντὸς ἔθνους
Jews, men devout from every nation

τῶν ὑπὸ τὸν οὐρανόν· 6 γενομένης
of the [ones] under - heaven; happening

δὲ τῆς φωνῆς ταύτης συνῆλθεν τὸ πλῆθος
and this sound^a came together the multitude
=when this sound happened

καὶ συνεχύθη, ὅτι ἤκουον εἷς ἕκαστος
and were confounded, because they heard ⁴one ³each

τῇ ἰδίᾳ διαλέκτῳ λαλούντων αὐτῶν.
²in his own language ¹speaking ¹them.

7 ἐξίσταντο δὲ καὶ ἐθαύμαζον λέγοντες·
And they were amazed and marvelled saying:

οὐχὶ ἰδοὺ πάντες οὗτοί εἰσιν οἱ λαλοῦντες
³not ¹behold ⁴all ⁵these ²are ⁶the [ones] ⁷speaking

Γαλιλαῖοι; 8 καὶ πῶς ἡμεῖς ἀκούομεν
⁸Galilæans? and how ²we ¹hear

ἕκαστος τῇ ἰδίᾳ διαλέκτῳ ἡμῶν ἐν ᾗ
³each ²in his own language ⁴of us in which

ἐγεννήθημεν, 9 Πάρθοι καὶ Μῆδοι καὶ
we were born, Parthians and Medes and

Ἐλαμῖται, καὶ οἱ κατοικοῦντες τὴν
Elamites, and the [ones] inhabiting the

Μεσοποταμίαν, Ἰουδαίαν τε καὶ Καππα-
Mesopotamia, both Judæa and Cappa-

δοκίαν, Πόντον καὶ τὴν Ἀσίαν, 10 Φρυγίαν
docia, Pontus and - Asia, Phrygia

τε καὶ Παμφυλίαν, Αἴγυπτον καὶ τὰ
both and Pamphylia, Egypt and the

μέρη τῆς Λιβύης τῆς κατὰ Κυρήνην,
regions - of Libya - over against Cyrene,

καὶ οἱ ἐπιδημοῦντες Ῥωμαῖοι, 11 Ἰουδαῖοί
and the temporarily residing Romans, ²Jews

τε καὶ προσήλυτοι, Κρῆτες καὶ Ἄραβες,
¹both and proselytes, Cretans and Arabians,

ἀκούομεν λαλούντων αὐτῶν ταῖς ἡμετέραις
we hear ²speaking ¹them in *the* our

γλώσσαις τὰ μεγαλεῖα τοῦ θεοῦ;
tongues the great deeds - of God?

12 ἐξίσταντο δὲ πάντες καὶ διηπόρουν,
And were amazed all and were troubled,

ἄλλος πρὸς ἄλλον λέγοντες· τί θέλει
other to other saying: What wishes·

τοῦτο εἶναι; 13 ἕτεροι δὲ διαχλευάζοντες
this to be? But others mocking

ἔλεγον ὅτι γλεύκους μεμεστωμένοι εἰσίν.
said[,] - Of(with) sweet wine *having been* filled they are.

14 Σταθεὶς δὲ ὁ Πέτρος σὺν τοῖς ἕνδεκα
But standing - Peter with the eleven

ἐπῆρεν τὴν φωνὴν αὐτοῦ καὶ ἀπεφθέγξατο
lifted up the voice of him and spoke out

---

wind came from heaven and filled the whole house where they were sitting. 3 They saw what seemed to be tongues of fire that separated and came to rest on each of them. 4 All of them were filled with the Holy Spirit and began to speak in other tongues/ as the Spirit enabled them.

5 Now there were staying in Jerusalem God-fearing Jews from every nation under heaven. 6 When they heard this sound, a crowd came together in bewilderment, because each one heard them speaking in his own language. 7 Utterly amazed, they asked: "Are not all these men who are speaking Galileans? 8 Then how is it that each of us hears them in his own native language? 9 Parthians, Medes and Elamites; residents of Mesopotamia, Judea and Cappadocia, Pontus and Asia, 10 Phrygia and Pamphylia, Egypt and the parts of Libya near Cyrene; visitors from Rome 11 (both Jews and converts to Judaism); Cretans and Arabs—we hear them declaring the wonders of God in our own tongues!" 12 Amazed and perplexed, they asked one another, "What does this mean?"

13 Some, however, made fun of them and said, "They have had too much wine. *g*"

Peter Addresses the Crowd

14 Then Peter stood up with the Eleven, raised his voice and addressed the

---

f 4 Or *languages*; also in verse 11
g 13 Or *sweet wine*

"Men of Judea and all who live in Jerusalem, let this be known to you, and listen to what I say. 15 Indeed, these are not drunk, as you suppose, for it is only nine o'clock in the morning. 16 No, this is what was spoken through the prophet Joel:

17 'In the last days it will be, God declares,
that I will pour out my Spirit upon all flesh,
and your sons and your daughters shall prophesy,
and your young men shall see visions,
and your old men shall dream dreams.

18 Even upon my slaves, both men and women,
in those days I will pour out my Spirit;
and they shall prophesy.

19 And I will show portents in the heaven above
and signs on the earth below,
blood, and fire, and smoky mist.

20 The sun shall be turned to darkness
and the moon to blood,
before the coming of the Lord's great and glorious day.

21 Then everyone who calls on the name of the Lord shall be saved.'

22 "You that are Israelites,[h] listen to what I have to say: Jesus of Nazareth,[i] a man attested to you by God with deeds of power, wonders, and signs that God did through him among you, as you yourselves know— 23 this man, handed over to you according to the definite plan and foreknowledge of God, you crucified and killed by the

---

αὐτοῖς·
to them :

Ἄνδρες Ἰουδαῖοι καὶ οἱ κατοικοῦντες
Men Jews and the [ones] inhabiting

Ἰερουσαλὴμ πάντες, τοῦτο ὑμῖν γνωστὸν
Jerusalem all, this to you known

ἔστω, καὶ ἐνωτίσασθε τὰ ῥήματά μου.
let be, and give ear to the words of me.

15 οὐ γὰρ ὡς ὑμεῖς ὑπολαμβάνετε οὗτοι
For not as ye imagine these men

μεθύουσιν, ἔστιν γὰρ ὥρα τρίτη τῆς
are drunk, for it is hour third of the

ἡμέρας, 16 ἀλλὰ τοῦτό ἐστιν τὸ εἰρημένον
day, but this is the thing having been spoken

διὰ τοῦ προφήτου Ἰωήλ· 17 καὶ ἔσται
through the prophet Joel : And it shall be

ἐν ταῖς ἐσχάταις ἡμέραις, λέγει ὁ θεός,
in the last days, says God,

ἐκχεῶ ἀπὸ τοῦ πνεύματός μου ἐπὶ
I will pour out from the Spirit of me on

πᾶσαν σάρκα, καὶ προφητεύσουσιν οἱ υἱοὶ
all flesh, and will prophesy the sons

ὑμῶν καὶ αἱ θυγατέρες ὑμῶν, καὶ οἱ
of you and the daughters of you, and the

νεανίσκοι ὑμῶν ὁράσεις ὄψονται, καὶ οἱ
young men of you visions will see, and the

πρεσβύτεροι ὑμῶν ἐνυπνίοις ἐνυπνιασθήσονται·
old men of you dreams will dream;

18 καὶ γε ἐπὶ τοὺς δούλους μου καὶ ἐπὶ
and - on the male slaves of me and on

τὰς δούλας μου ἐν ταῖς ἡμέραις ἐκείναις
the female slaves of me in those days

ἐκχεῶ ἀπὸ τοῦ πνεύματός μου, καὶ
I will pour out from the Spirit of me, and

προφητεύσουσιν. 19 καὶ δώσω τέρατα ἐν
they will prophesy. And I will give wonders in

τῷ οὐρανῷ ἄνω καὶ σημεῖα ἐπὶ τῆς
the heaven above and signs on the

γῆς κάτω, αἷμα καὶ πῦρ καὶ ἀτμίδα
earth below, blood and fire and vapour

καπνοῦ. 20 ὁ ἥλιος μεταστραφήσεται εἰς
of smoke. The sun will be turned into

σκότος καὶ ἡ σελήνη εἰς αἷμα, πρὶν
darkness and the moon into blood, before

ἐλθεῖν ἡμέραν κυρίου τὴν μεγάλην καὶ
²to come(comes) ⁵day ⁶of [the] Lord ¹the ³great ⁴and

ἐπιφανῆ. 21 καὶ ἔσται πᾶς ὃς ἐὰν
⁷notable.ᵇ And it will be everyone whoever

ἐπικαλέσηται τὸ ὄνομα κυρίου σωθήσεται.
invokes the name of [the] Lord will be saved.

22 Ἄνδρες Ἰσραηλῖται, ἀκούσατε τοὺς
Men Israelites, hear ye -

λόγους τούτους· Ἰησοῦν τὸν Ναζωραῖον,
words these: Jesus the Nazarene,

ἄνδρα ἀποδεδειγμένον ἀπὸ τοῦ θεοῦ εἰς
a man having been approved from - God among

ὑμᾶς δυνάμεσι καὶ τέρασι καὶ σημείοις,
you by powerful deeds and wonders and signs,

οἷς ἐποίησεν δι' αὐτοῦ ὁ θεὸς ἐν μέσῳ
which did through him - God in [the] midst

ὑμῶν, καθὼς αὐτοὶ οἴδατε, 23 τοῦτον
of you, as [your]selves ye know, this man

τῇ ὡρισμένῃ βουλῇ καὶ προγνώσει τοῦ
³by the ¹having been fixed ⁴counsel ⁵and ⁶foreknowledge -

θεοῦ ἔκδοτον διὰ χειρὸς ἀνόμων
⁷of God ¹given up ⁸through ¹⁰[the] ⁹hand ¹¹of lawless men

---

crowd: "Fellow Jews and all of you who live in Jerusalem, let me explain this to you; listen carefully to what I say. 15 These men are not drunk, as you suppose. It's only nine in the morning! 16 No, this is what was spoken by the prophet Joel:

17 " 'In the last days, God says,
I will pour out my Spirit on all people.
Your sons and daughters will prophesy,
your young men will see visions,
your old men will dream dreams.

18 Even on my servants, both men and women,
I will pour out my Spirit in those days,
and they will prophesy.

19 I will show wonders in the heaven above
and signs on the earth below,
blood and fire and billows of smoke.

20 The sun will be turned to darkness
and the moon to blood
before the coming of the great and glorious day of the Lord.

21 And everyone who calls on the name of the Lord will be saved.'[h]

22 "Men of Israel, listen to this: Jesus of Nazareth was a man accredited by God to you by miracles, wonders and signs, which God did among you through him, as you yourselves know. 23 This man was handed over to you by God's set purpose and foreknowledge; and you, with the help of wicked men,[i] put him to death by nailing him

---

ʰ Gk Men, Israelites
ⁱ Gk the Nazorean

ʰ21 Joel 2:28-32
ⁱ23 Or of those not having the law (that is, Gentiles)

hands of those outside the law. 24 But God raised him up, having freed him from death,ʲ because it was impossible for him to be held in its power. 25 For David says concerning him,
'I saw the Lord always before me,
for he is at my right hand so that I will not be shaken;
26 therefore my heart was glad, and my tongue rejoiced;
moreover my flesh will live in hope.
27 For you will not abandon my soul to Hades, or let your Holy One experience corruption.
28 You have made known to me the ways of life; you will make me full of gladness with your presence.'
29 "Fellow Israelites,ᵏ I may say to you confidently of our ancestor David that he both died and was buried, and his tomb is with us to this day. 30 Since he was a prophet, he knew that God had sworn with an oath to him that he would put one of his descendants on his throne. 31 Foreseeing this, Davidˡ spoke of the resurrection of the Messiah,ᵐ saying,
'He was not abandoned to Hades,
nor did his flesh experience corruption.'
32 This Jesus God raised up, and of that all of us are witnesses. 33 Being therefore exalted atⁿ the right hand of God, and having received from the Father the promise of the Holy Spirit, he has poured out this that you both see and hear. 34 For David did not ascend

ʲGk the pains of death
ᵏGk Men, brothers
ˡGk he
ᵐOr the Christ
ⁿOr by

προσπήξαντες ἀνείλατε, 24 ὃν ὁ θεὸς
'fastening' ¹¹ye killed, whom - God
ἀνέστησεν λύσας τὰς ὠδῖνας τοῦ θανάτου,
raised up loosening the pangs - of death,
καθότι οὐκ ἦν δυνατὸν κρατεῖσθαι αὐτὸν
because it was not possible ¹to be held ¹him
ὑπ' αὐτοῦ. 25 Δαυὶδ γὰρ λέγει εἰς
by it. For David says [as] to
αὐτόν· προορώμην τὸν κύριον ἐνώπιόν
him: I foresaw the Lord before
μου διὰ παντός, ὅτι ἐκ δεξιῶν μού
me always, because on right of me
ἐστιν, ἵνα μὴ σαλευθῶ. 26 διὰ τοῦτο
he is, lest I be moved. Therefore
ηὐφράνθη μου ἡ καρδία καὶ ἠγαλλιάσατο
was glad of me the heart and exulted
ἡ γλῶσσά μου, ἔτι δὲ καὶ ἡ σάρξ
the tongue of me, and now also the flesh
μου κατασκηνώσει ἐπ' ἐλπίδι, 27 ὅτι οὐκ
of me will dwell on(in) hope, because not
ἐγκαταλείψεις τὴν ψυχήν μου εἰς ᾅδην
thou wilt abandon the soul of me in hades
οὐδὲ δώσεις τὸν ὅσιόν σου ἰδεῖν
nor wilt thou give the holy one of thee to see
διαφθοράν. 28 ἐγνώρισάς μοι ὁδοὺς ζωῆς,
corruption. Thou madest known to me ways of life,
πληρώσεις με εὐφροσύνης μετὰ τοῦ προσώ-
thou wilt fill me of(with) gladness with the pres-
που σου. 29 Ἄνδρες ἀδελφοί, ἐξὸν εἰπεῖν
ence of thee. Men brothers, it is permitted to speak
μετὰ παρρησίας πρὸς ὑμᾶς περὶ τοῦ
with plainness to you concerning the
πατριάρχου Δαυίδ, ὅτι καὶ ἐτελεύτησεν
patriarch David, that both he died
καὶ ἐτάφη, καὶ τὸ μνῆμα αὐτοῦ ἔστιν
and was buried, and the tomb of him is
ἐν ἡμῖν ἄχρι τῆς ἡμέρας ταύτης.
among us until this day.
30 προφήτης οὖν ὑπάρχων καὶ εἰδὼς ὅτι
A prophet therefore being and knowing that
ὅρκῳ ὤμοσεν αὐτῷ ὁ θεὸς ἐκ καρποῦ
with an oath swore to him - God of [the] fruit
τῆς ὀσφύος αὐτοῦ καθίσαι ἐπὶ τὸν θρόνον
of the loin[s] of him to sit on the throne
αὐτοῦ, 31 προϊδὼν ἐλάλησεν περὶ τῆς
of him, foreseeing he spoke concerning the
ἀναστάσεως τοῦ Χριστοῦ, ὅτι οὔτε
resurrection of the Christ, that neither
ἐγκαταλείφθη εἰς ᾅδην οὔτε ἡ σάρξ
he was abandoned in hades nor the flesh
αὐτοῦ εἶδεν διαφθοράν. 32 τοῦτον τὸν
of him saw corruption. This -
Ἰησοῦν ἀνέστησεν ὁ θεός, οὗ πάντες
Jesus ¹raised up - ¹God, of which all!
ἡμεῖς ἐσμεν μάρτυρες· 33 τῇ δεξιᾷ οὖν
we are witnesses; to the right [hand] therefore
τοῦ θεοῦ ὑψωθεὶς τήν τε ἐπαγγελίαν
- of God having been exalted ²the ¹and ⁷promise
τοῦ πνεύματος τοῦ ἁγίου λαβὼν παρὰ
⁵of the ¹⁰Spirit - ⁹Holy ⁸receiving ⁸from
τοῦ πατρὸς ἐξέχεεν τοῦτο ὃ ὑμεῖς καὶ
⁴the ⁵Father he poured out this which ye both
βλέπετε καὶ ἀκούετε. 34 οὐ γὰρ Δαυὶδ
see and hear. For not David

* That is, to a tree; see ch. 5. 30.

to the cross. 24 But God raised him from the dead, freeing him from the agony of death, because it was impossible for death to keep its hold on him. 25 David said about him:
" 'I saw the Lord always before me.
Because he is at my right hand, I will not be shaken.
26 Therefore my heart is glad and my tongue rejoices;
my body also will live in hope,
27 because you will not abandon me to the grave,
nor will you let your Holy One see decay.
28 You have made known to me the paths of life; you will fill me with joy in your presence.'ʲ
29 "Brothers, I can tell you confidently that the patriarch David died and was buried, and his tomb is here to this day. 30 But he was a prophet and knew that God had promised him on oath that he would place one of his descendants on his throne. 31 Seeing what was ahead, he spoke of the resurrection of the Christ,ᵏ that he was not abandoned to the grave, nor did his body see decay. 32 God has raised this Jesus to life, and we are all witnesses of the fact. 33 Exalted to the right hand of God, he has received from the Father the promised Holy Spirit and has poured out what you now see and hear. 34 For David did not ascend to

ʲ28 Psalm 16:8-11
ᵏ31 Or Messiah. "The Christ" (Greek) and "the Messiah" (Hebrew) both mean "the Anointed One"; also in verse 36.

into the heavens, but he himself says,

'The Lord said to my Lord,

"Sit at my right hand,
35 until I make your enemies your footstool." '

36 Therefore let the entire house of Israel know with certainty that God has made him both Lord and Messiah,[o] this Jesus whom you crucified."

The First Converts

37 Now when they heard this, they were cut to the heart and said to Peter and to the other apostles, "Brothers,[p] what should we do?" 38 Peter said to them, "Repent, and be baptized every one of you in the name of Jesus Christ so that your sins may be forgiven; and you will receive the gift of the Holy Spirit. 39 For the promise is for you, for your children, and for all who are far away, everyone whom the Lord our God calls to him." 40 And he testified with many other arguments and exhorted them, saying, "Save yourselves from this corrupt generation." 41 So those who welcomed his message were baptized, and that day about three thousand persons were added. 42 They devoted themselves to the apostles' teaching and fellowship, to the breaking of bread and the prayers.

Life among the Believers

43 Awe came upon everyone, because many wonders and signs were being done by the apostles. 44 All who believed were together and had all things in common; 45 they would sell their possessions and

---

ἀνέβη εἰς τοὺς οὐρανούς, λέγει δὲ αὐτός·
ascended to the heavens, but says he:

εἶπεν κύριος τῷ κυρίῳ μου· κάθου ἐκ
Said [the] LORD to the Lord of me: Sit at

δεξιῶν μου, 35 ἕως ἂν θῶ τοὺς ἐχθρούς
right of me, until I put the enemies

σου ὑποπόδιον τῶν ποδῶν σου. 36 ἀσφαλῶς
of thee a footstool of the feet of thee. Assuredly

οὖν γινωσκέτω πᾶς οἶκος Ἰσραὴλ ὅτι
therefore ¹let ⁶know ²all³[the] ⁴house ⁵of Israel that

καὶ κύριον αὐτὸν καὶ χριστὸν ἐποίησεν
⁸both ⁵Lord ⁶him ⁶and ⁷Christ ⁴made

ὁ θεός, τοῦτον τὸν Ἰησοῦν ὃν ὑμεῖς
- ¹God, this - Jesus whom ye

ἐσταυρώσατε. 37 Ἀκούσαντες δὲ κατενύγ-
crucified. And hearing they were

ησαν τὴν καρδίαν, εἶπόν τε πρὸς τὸν
stung [in] the heart, and said to -

Πέτρον καὶ τοὺς λοιποὺς ἀποστόλους·
Peter and the remaining apostles:

τί ποιήσωμεν, ἄνδρες ἀδελφοί; 38 Πέτρος
What may we do, men brothers? Peter

δὲ πρὸς αὐτούς· μετανοήσατε, καὶ
And to them: Repent ye, and

βαπτισθήτω ἕκαστος ὑμῶν ἐπὶ τῷ ὀνόματι
let be baptized each of you on the name

Ἰησοῦ Χριστοῦ εἰς ἄφεσιν τῶν
of Jesus Christ [with a view] to forgiveness of the

ἁμαρτιῶν ὑμῶν, καὶ λήμψεσθε τὴν δωρεὰν
sins of you, and ye will receive the gift

τοῦ ἁγίου πνεύματος. 39 ὑμῖν γάρ ἐστιν
of the Holy Spirit. For to you is

ἡ ἐπαγγελία καὶ τοῖς τέκνοις ὑμῶν καὶ
the promise and to the children of you and

πᾶσιν τοῖς εἰς μακράν, ὅσους ἂν
to all the [ones] far away, as many as

προσκαλέσηται κύριος ὁ θεὸς ἡμῶν.
may call to [him] [the] Lord the God of us.

40 ἑτέροις τε λόγοις πλείοσιν διεμαρτύρατο,
And with other words many he solemnly witnessed,

καὶ παρεκάλει αὐτοὺς λέγων· σώθητε
and exhorted them saying: Be ye saved

ἀπὸ τῆς γενεᾶς τῆς σκολιᾶς ταύτης. 41 οἱ
from ²generation ¹perverse ¹this. The [ones]

μὲν οὖν ἀποδεξάμενοι τὸν λόγον αὐτοῦ
- therefore welcoming the word of him

ἐβαπτίσθησαν, καὶ προσετέθησαν ἐν
were baptized, and there were added in

τῇ ἡμέρᾳ ἐκείνῃ ψυχαὶ ὡσεὶ τρισχίλιαι·
that day souls about three thousand;

42 ἦσαν δὲ προσκαρτεροῦντες τῇ διδαχῇ
and they were continuing steadfastly in the teaching

τῶν ἀποστόλων καὶ τῇ κοινωνίᾳ, τῇ
of the apostles and in the fellowship, in the

κλάσει τοῦ ἄρτου καὶ ταῖς προσευχαῖς.
breaking of the loaf and in the prayers.

43 Ἐγίνετο δὲ πάσῃ ψυχῇ φόβος· πολλὰ δὲ
And came to every soul fear; and many

τέρατα καὶ σημεῖα διὰ τῶν ἀποστόλων
wonders and signs through the apostles

ἐγίνετο. 44 πάντες δὲ οἱ πιστεύσαντες
happened. And all the believing [ones]

ἐπὶ τὸ αὐτὸ εἶχον ἅπαντα κοινά, 45 καὶ
together had all things common, and

τὰ κτήματα καὶ τὰς ὑπάρξεις ἐπίπρασκον
the properties and the possessions they sold

---

heaven, and yet he said,

" 'The Lord said to my Lord:
"Sit at my right hand
35 until I make your enemies a footstool for your feet." ' [/]

36 "Therefore let all Israel be assured of this: God has made this Jesus, whom you crucified, both Lord and Christ."

37 When the people heard this, they were cut to the heart and said to Peter and the other apostles, "Brothers, what shall we do?"

38 Peter replied, "Repent and be baptized, every one of you, in the name of Jesus Christ for the forgiveness of your sins. And you will receive the gift of the Holy Spirit. 39 The promise is for you and your children and for all who are far off—for all whom the Lord our God will call."

40 With many other words he warned them; and he pleaded with them, "Save yourselves from this corrupt generation." 41 Those who accepted his message were baptized, and about three thousand were added to their number that day.

The Fellowship of the Believers

42 They devoted themselves to the apostles' teaching and to the fellowship, to the breaking of bread and to prayer. 43 Everyone was filled with awe, and many wonders and miraculous signs were done by the apostles. 44 All the believers were together and had everything in common. 45 Selling their possessions

---

[o] Or Christ
[p] Gk Men, brothers

[/35] Psalm 110:1

goods and distribute the proceeds[q] to all, as any had need. [46]Day by day, as they spent much time together in the temple, they broke bread at home[r] and ate their food with glad and generous[s] hearts, [47]praising God and having the goodwill of all the people. And day by day the Lord added to their number those who were being saved.

καὶ διεμέριζον αὐτὰ πᾶσιν, καθότι ἄν
and distributed them to all, according as

τις χρείαν εἶχεν. 46 καθ᾽ ἡμέραν τε
anyone need had. And from day to day†

προσκαρτεροῦντες ὁμοθυμαδὸν ἐν τῷ ἱερῷ,
continuing steadfastly with one mind in the temple,

κλῶντές τε κατ᾽ οἶκον ἄρτον, μετε-
and ¹breaking ³from house to house† ²bread, they

λάμβανον τροφῆς ἐν ἀγαλλιάσει καὶ
shared food in gladness and

ἀφελότητι καρδίας, 47 αἰνοῦντες τὸν θεὸν
simplicity of heart, praising – God

καὶ ἔχοντες χάριν πρὸς ὅλον τὸν λαόν.
and having favour with all the people.

ὁ δὲ κύριος προσετίθει τοὺς σῳζομένους
And the Lord added the [ones] being saved

καθ᾽ ἡμέραν ἐπὶ τὸ αὐτό.
from day to day† together.†

and goods, they gave to anyone as he had need. [46]Every day they continued to meet together in the temple courts. They broke bread in their homes and ate together with glad and sincere hearts, [47]praising God and enjoying the favor of all the people. And the Lord added to their number daily those who were being saved.

Chapter 3

Peter Heals a Crippled Beggar

ONE day Peter and John were going up to the temple at the hour of prayer, at three o'clock in the afternoon. [2]And a man lame from birth was being carried in. People would lay him daily at the gate of the temple called the Beautiful Gate so that he could ask for alms from those entering the temple. [3]When he saw Peter and John about to go into the temple, he asked them for alms. [4]Peter looked intently at him, as did John, and said, "Look at us." [5]And he fixed his attention on them, expecting to receive something from them. [6]But Peter said, "I have no silver or gold, but what I have I give you; in the name of Jesus Christ of Nazareth,[t] stand up and walk." [7]And he took him by the right hand and raised him up; and immediately his feet and ankles were made strong. [8]Jumping up, he stood and began to walk, and he entered the temple with them, walking and leaping and praising God. [9]All the peo-

3 Πέτρος δὲ καὶ Ἰωάννης ἀνέβαινον
Now Peter and John were going up

εἰς τὸ ἱερὸν ἐπὶ τὴν ὥραν τῆς προσευχῆς
to the temple at the hour of the prayer

τὴν ἐνάτην. 2 καί τις ἀνὴρ χωλὸς ἐκ
the ninth. And a certain man ¹lame ²from

κοιλίας μητρὸς αὐτοῦ ὑπάρχων ἐβαστάζετο,
⁴[the] ⁵of [the] ⁶of him ¹being was being womb mother carried,

ὃν ἐτίθουν καθ᾽ ἡμέραν πρὸς τὴν θύραν
whom they used from day to day† at the door
to put

τοῦ ἱεροῦ τὴν λεγομένην ὡραίαν τοῦ
of the temple – being called Beautiful –

αἰτεῖν ἐλεημοσύνην παρὰ τῶν εἰσπορευομέ-
to ask[d] alms from the [ones] enter-

νων εἰς τὸ ἱερόν· 3 ὃς ἰδὼν Πέτρον καὶ
ing into the temple; who seeing Peter and

Ἰωάννην μέλλοντας εἰσιέναι εἰς τὸ ἱερὸν
John being about to go in into the temple

ἠρώτα ἐλεημοσύνην λαβεῖν. 4 ἀτενίσας δὲ
asked alms to receive. And ²gazing

Πέτρος εἰς αὐτὸν σὺν τῷ Ἰωάννῃ εἶπεν·
¹Peter at him with – John said:

βλέψον εἰς ἡμᾶς. 5 ὁ δὲ ἐπεῖχεν αὐτοῖς
Look at us. And he paid heed to them

προσδοκῶν τι παρ᾽ αὐτῶν λαβεῖν. 6 εἶπεν
expecting something from them to receive. said

δὲ Πέτρος· ἀργύριον καὶ χρυσίον οὐχ
And Peter: Silver and gold not

ὑπάρχει μοι· ὃ δὲ ἔχω, τοῦτό σοι δίδωμι·
is to me[e]; but what I have, this to thee I give;
=I have not;

ἐν τῷ ὀνόματι Ἰησοῦ Χριστοῦ τοῦ
in the name of Jesus Christ the

Ναζωραίου περιπάτει. 7 καὶ πιάσας αὐτὸν τῆς
Nazarene walk. And seizing him of(by)

δεξιᾶς χειρὸς ἤγειρεν αὐτόν· παραχρῆμα
the right hand he raised him; ²at once

δὲ ἐστερεώθησαν αἱ βάσεις αὐτοῦ καὶ τὰ
¹and were made firm the feet of him and the

σφυδρά, 8 καὶ ἐξαλλόμενος ἔστη, καὶ
ankle-bones, and leaping up he stood, and

περιεπάτει, καὶ εἰσῆλθεν σὺν αὐτοῖς εἰς
walked, and entered with them into

τὸ ἱερὸν περιπατῶν καὶ ἀλλόμενος καὶ
the temple walking and leaping and

Chapter 3

Peter Heals the Crippled Beggar

ONE day Peter and John were going up to the temple at the time of prayer —at three in the afternoon. [2]Now a man crippled from birth was being carried to the temple gate called Beautiful, where he was put every day to beg from those going into the temple courts. [3]When he saw Peter and John about to enter, he asked them for money. [4]Peter looked straight at him, as did John. Then Peter said, "Look at us!" [5]So the man gave them his attention, expecting to get something from them.

[6]Then Peter said, "Silver or gold I do not have, but what I have I give you. In the name of Jesus Christ of Nazareth, walk." [7]Taking him by the right hand, he helped him up, and instantly the man's feet and ankles became strong. [8]He jumped to his feet and began to walk. Then he went with them into the temple courts, walking and jump-

[q] Gk them
[r] Or from house to house
[s] Or sincere
[t] Gk the Nazorean

ple saw him walking and praising God, 10 and they recognized him as the one who used to sit and ask for alms at the Beautiful Gate of the temple; and they were filled with wonder and amazement at what had happened to him.

Peter Speaks in Solomon's Portico

11 While he clung to Peter and John, all the people ran together to them in the portico called Solomon's Portico, utterly astonished. 12 When Peter saw it, he addressed the people, "You Israelites,[u] why do you wonder at this, or why do you stare at us, as though by our own power or piety we had made him walk? 13 The God of Abraham, the God of Isaac, and the God of Jacob, the God of our ancestors has glorified his servant[v] Jesus, whom you handed over and rejected in the presence of Pilate, though he had decided to release him. 14 But you rejected the Holy and Righteous One and asked to have a murderer given to you, 15 and you killed the Author of life, whom God raised from the dead. To this we are witnesses. 16 And by faith in his name, his name itself has made this man strong, whom you see and know; and the faith that is through Jesus[w] has given him this perfect health in the presence of all of you.

17 "And now, friends,[x] I know that you acted in ignorance, as did also your rulers. 18 In this way God

αἰνῶν τὸν θεόν. 9 καὶ εἶδεν πᾶς ὁ
praising — God. And ⁴saw ¹all ²the
λαὸς αὐτὸν περιπατοῦντα καὶ αἰνοῦντα
²people him walking and praising
τὸν θεόν· 10 ἐπεγίνωσκον δὲ αὐτόν, ὅτι
— God; and they recognized him, that
οὗτος ἦν ὁ πρὸς τὴν ἐλεημοσύνην
this was the [one] for — alms
καθήμενος ἐπὶ τῇ ὡραίᾳ πύλῃ τοῦ ἱεροῦ,
sitting at the Beautiful gate of the temple,
καὶ ἐπλήσθησαν θάμβους καὶ ἐκστάσεως
and they were filled of(with) and bewilderment
                    amazement
ἐπὶ τῷ συμβεβηκότι αὐτῷ. 11 Κρατοῦντος δὲ
at the thing having happened to him. And holding
                                        =as he held
αὐτοῦ τὸν Πέτρον καὶ τὸν Ἰωάννην
him[a] — Peter and — John
συνέδραμεν πᾶς ὁ λαὸς πρὸς αὐτοὺς
ran together all the people to them
ἐπὶ τῇ στοᾷ τῇ καλουμένῃ Σολομῶντος
at the porch — being called of Solomon
ἔκθαμβοι. 12 ἰδὼν δὲ ὁ Πέτρος ἀπεκρίνατο
greatly amazed. And ²seeing ¹Peter answered
πρὸς τὸν λαόν· ἄνδρες Ἰσραηλῖται, τί
to the people: Men Israelites, why
θαυμάζετε ἐπὶ τούτῳ, ἢ ἡμῖν τί ἀτενίζετε
marvel ye at this man, or at us why gaze ye
ὡς ἰδίᾳ δυνάμει ἢ εὐσεβείᾳ πεποιηκόσιν
as by [our] own power or piety having made
τοῦ περιπατεῖν αὐτόν; 13 ὁ θεὸς Ἀβραὰμ
— to walk[d] him? The God of Abraham
καὶ Ἰσαὰκ καὶ Ἰακώβ, ὁ θεὸς τῶν
and Isaac and Jacob, the God of the
πατέρων ἡμῶν, ἐδόξασεν τὸν παῖδα αὐτοῦ
fathers of us, glorified the servant of him
Ἰησοῦν, ὃν ὑμεῖς μὲν παρεδώκατε καὶ
Jesus, whom ye — delivered and
ἠρνήσασθε κατὰ πρόσωπον Πιλάτου,
denied in [the] presence of Pilate,
κρίναντος ἐκείνου ἀπολύειν· 14 ὑμεῖς δὲ
having decided that one[e] to release [him]; but ye
=when he had decided
τὸν ἅγιον καὶ δίκαιον ἠρνήσασθε, καὶ
the holy and just one denied, and
ᾐτήσασθε ἄνδρα φονέα χαρισθῆναι ὑμῖν,
asked a man a murderer to be granted you,
15 τὸν δὲ ἀρχηγὸν τῆς ζωῆς ἀπεκτείνατε,
and the Author of life ye killed,
ὃν ὁ θεὸς ἤγειρεν ἐκ νεκρῶν, οὗ ἡμεῖς
whom — God raised from [the] dead, of which we
μάρτυρές ἐσμεν. 16 καὶ ἐπὶ τῇ πίστει
witnesses are. And on the faith
τοῦ ὀνόματος αὐτοῦ τοῦτον, ὃν θεωρεῖτε
of(in) name* of him ⁵this man, ⁶whom ⁷ye behold
the
καὶ οἴδατε, ἐστερέωσεν τὸ ὄνομα αὐτοῦ,
⁸and ⁹know, ⁴made firm ¹the ²name ³of him,
καὶ ἡ πίστις ἡ δι᾽ αὐτοῦ ἔδωκεν αὐτῷ
and the faith — through him gave him
τὴν ὁλοκληρίαν ταύτην ἀπέναντι πάντων
this soundness before all
ὑμῶν. 17 καὶ νῦν, ἀδελφοί, οἶδα ὅτι
you. And now, brothers, I know that
κατὰ ἄγνοιαν ἐπράξατε, ὥσπερ καὶ οἱ
by way of ignorance ye acted, as also the

ing, and praising God. 9 When all the people saw him walking and praising God, 10 they recognized him as the same man who used to sit begging at the temple gate called Beautiful, and they were filled with wonder and amazement at what had happened to him.

Peter Speaks to the Onlookers

11 While the beggar held on to Peter and John, all the people were astonished and came running to them in the place called Solomon's Colonnade. 12 When Peter saw this, he said to them: "Men of Israel, why does this surprise you? Why do you stare at us as if by our own power or godliness we had made this man walk? 13 The God of Abraham, Isaac and Jacob, the God of our fathers, has glorified his servant Jesus. You handed him over to be killed, and you disowned him before Pilate, though he had decided to let him go. 14 You disowned the Holy and Righteous One and asked that a murderer be released to you. 15 You killed the author of life, but God raised him from the dead. We are witnesses of this. 16 By faith in the name of Jesus, this man whom you see and know was made strong. It is Jesus' name and the faith that comes through him that has given this complete healing to him, as you can all see.

17 "Now, brothers, I know that you acted in ignorance, as did your lead-

u Gk Men. Israelites
v Or child
w Gk him
x Gk brothers

* Objective genitive; cf. "the fear of God" = the fear which has God for its object; and see Gal. 2. 20, etc.

fulfilled what he had fore-told through all the proph-ets, that his Messiah[y] would suffer. 19 Repent therefore, and turn to God so that your sins may be wiped out, 20 so that times of refreshing may come from the presence of the Lord, and that he may send the Messiah[z] appointed for you, that is, Jesus, 21 who must remain in heaven until the time of universal resto-ration that God announced long ago through his holy prophets. 22 Moses said, 'The Lord your God will raise up for you from your own people[a] a prophet like me. You must listen to whatever he tells you. 23 And it will be that every-one who does not listen to that prophet will be utterly rooted out of the people.' 24 And all the prophets, as many as have spoken, from Samuel and those after him, also predicted these days. 25 You are the de-scendants of the prophets and of the covenant that God gave to your ances-tors, saying to Abraham, 'And in your descendants all the families of the earth shall be blessed.' 26 When God raised up his servant,[b] he sent him first to you, to bless you by turning each of you from your wicked ways."

ἄρχοντες ὑμῶν·   18 ὁ δὲ θεὸς ἃ
rulers of you; — but God the things which

προκατήγγειλεν διὰ στόματος πάντων
he foreannounced through [the] mouth of all

τῶν προφητῶν, παθεῖν τὸν χριστὸν αὐτοῦ,
the prophets, to suffer the Christ of him[b],
= that his Christ was to suffer,

ἐπλήρωσεν οὕτως. 19 μετανοήσατε οὖν
fulfilled thus. Repent ye therefore

καὶ ἐπιστρέψατε πρὸς τὸ ἐξαλειφθῆναι
and turn for the to be wiped away
= that your sins may be wiped away,

ὑμῶν τὰς ἁμαρτίας, 20 ὅπως ἂν ἔλθωσιν
of you the sins, so as may come

καιροὶ ἀναψύξεως ἀπὸ προσώπου τοῦ
times of refreshing from [the] presence of the

κυρίου καὶ ἀποστείλῃ τὸν προκεχειρισμένον
Lord and he may send [the] [3]having been foreappointed

ὑμῖν χριστὸν Ἰησοῦν, 21 ὃν δεῖ οὐρανὸν
[4]for you [1]Christ [2]Jesus, whom it behoves heaven

μὲν δέξασθαι ἄχρι χρόνων ἀποκαταστάσεως
— to receive until [the] times of restitution

πάντων ὧν ἐλάλησεν ὁ θεὸς διὰ στόματος
of all things which [2]spoke — [1]God [3]through [4][the] mouth

τῶν ἁγίων ἀπ᾽ αἰῶνος αὐτοῦ προφητῶν.
[5]of the [6]holy [8]from [10][the] age [9]of him [7]prophets.

22 Μωϋσῆς μὲν εἶπεν ὅτι προφήτην ὑμῖν
Moses indeed said[,] — [4]A prophet [5]for you

ἀναστήσει κύριος ὁ θεὸς ἐκ τῶν ἀδελφῶν
[3]will raise up [1](the) Lord — [2]God of the brothers

ὑμῶν ὡς ἐμέ· αὐτοῦ ἀκούσεσθε κατὰ
of you as me; him shall ye hear according to

πάντα ὅσα ἂν λαλήσῃ πρὸς ὑμᾶς.
all things whatever he may speak to you.

23 ἔσται δὲ πᾶσα ψυχὴ ἥτις ἐὰν μὴ ἀκούσῃ
And it shall be every soul whoever hears not

τοῦ προφήτου ἐκείνου ἐξολεθρευθήσεται
that prophet will be utterly destroyed

ἐκ τοῦ λαοῦ. 24 καὶ πάντες δὲ οἱ
out of the people. [3]also [2]all [1]And the

προφῆται ἀπὸ Σαμουὴλ καὶ τῶν καθεξῆς
prophets from Samuel and the [ones] in order

ὅσοι ἐλάλησαν καὶ κατήγγειλαν τὰς ἡμέρας
as many as spoke also announced — days

ταύτας. 25 ὑμεῖς ἐστε οἱ υἱοὶ τῶν
these. Ye are the sons of the

προφητῶν καὶ τῆς διαθήκης ἧς ὁ θεὸς
prophets and of the covenant which — God

διέθετο πρὸς τοὺς πατέρας ὑμῶν, λέγων
made with the fathers of us, saying

πρὸς Ἀβραάμ· καὶ ἐν τῷ σπέρματί
to Abraham: And in the seed

σου ἐνευλογηθήσονται πᾶσαι αἱ πατριαὶ
of thee shall be blessed all the families

τῆς γῆς. 26 ὑμῖν πρῶτον ἀναστήσας ὁ
of the earth. To you first [2]having raised up [1]

θεὸς τὸν παῖδα αὐτοῦ ἀπέστειλεν αὐτὸν
[1]God the servant of him sent him

εὐλογοῦντα ὑμᾶς ἐν τῷ ἀποστρέφειν
blessing you in the to turn away
= in turning away

ἕκαστον ἀπὸ τῶν πονηριῶν ὑμῶν.
each one from the iniquities of you.

4 Λαλούντων δὲ αὐτῶν πρὸς τὸν λαόν,
And speaking them[a] to the people,
= while they were speaking

ἐπέστησαν αὐτοῖς οἱ ἱερεῖς καὶ ὁ στρατηγὸς
came upon them the priests and the commandant

Chapter 4

Peter and John before the Council

WHILE Peter and John[c] were speak-ing to the people, the priests, the captain of the temple, and the Sadducees

[y] Or his Christ
[z] Or the Christ
[a] Gk brothers
[b] Or child
[c] Gk While they

---

ers. 18 But this is how God fulfilled what he had fore-told through all the proph-ets, saying that his Christ[m] would suffer. 19 Repent, then, and turn to God, so that your sins may be wiped out, that times of re-freshing may come from the Lord, 20 and that he may send the Christ, who has been appointed for you— even Jesus. 21 He must re-main in heaven until the time comes for God to re-store everything, as he promised long ago through his holy prophets. 22 For Moses said, 'The Lord your God will raise up for you a prophet like me from among your own people; you must listen to every-thing he tells you. 23 Any-one who does not listen to him will be completely cut off from among his peo-ple.'[n] 24 "Indeed, all the proph-ets from Samuel on, as many as have spoken, have foretold these days. 25 And you are heirs of the proph-ets and of the covenant God made with your fa-thers. He said to Abraham, 'Through your offspring all peoples on earth will be blessed.'[o] 26 When God raised up his servant, he sent him first to you to bless you by turning each of you from your wicked ways."

Chapter 4

Peter and John Before the Sanhedrin

THE priests and the cap-tain of the temple guard and the Sadducees

[m] 18 Or Messiah; also in verse 20
[n] 23 Deut. 18:15,18,19
[o] 25 Gen. 22:18; 26:4

came to them, 2 much annoyed because they were teaching the people and proclaiming that in Jesus there is the resurrection of the dead. 3 So they arrested them and put them in custody until the next day, for it was already evening. 4 But many of those who heard the word believed; and they numbered about five thousand.

5 The next day their rulers, elders, and scribes assembled in Jerusalem, 6 with Annas the high priest, Caiaphas, John,*d* and Alexander, and all who were of the high-priestly family. 7 When they had made the prisoners*e* stand in their midst, they inquired, "By what power or by what name did you do this?" 8 Then Peter, filled with the Holy Spirit, said to them, "Rulers of the people and elders, 9 if we are questioned today because of a good deed done to someone who was sick and are asked how this man has been healed, 10 let it be known to all of you, and to all the people of Israel, that this man is standing before you in good health by the name of Jesus Christ of Nazareth,*f* whom you crucified, whom God raised from the dead. 11 This Jesus*g* is

'the stone that was
    rejected by you,
    the builders;
it has become the
    cornerstone.'*h*

12 There is salvation in no one else, for there is no other name under heaven giv-

---

τοῦ ἱεροῦ καὶ οἱ Σαδδουκαῖοι, 2 διαπονούμενοι
of the temple and the Sadducees, being greatly troubled

διὰ τὸ διδάσκειν αὐτοὺς τὸν λαὸν καὶ
because of the to teach them*b* the people and
= because they taught ... announced

καταγγέλλειν ἐν τῷ Ἰησοῦ τὴν ἀνάστασιν
to announce*b* by – Jesus the resurrection

τὴν ἐκ νεκρῶν, 3 καὶ ἐπέβαλον αὐτοῖς
from [the] dead, and laid on them

τὰς χεῖρας καὶ ἔθεντο εἰς τήρησιν εἰς
the(ir) hands and put in guard till

τὴν αὔριον· ἦν γὰρ ἑσπέρα ἤδη. 4 πολλοὶ
the morrow, for it was evening now. many

δὲ τῶν ἀκουσάντων τὸν λόγον ἐπίστευσαν,
But of the [ones] hearing the word believed,

καὶ ἐγενήθη ἀριθμὸς τῶν ἀνδρῶν ὡς
and became [the] number of the men about

χιλιάδες πέντε.
thousands five.

5 Ἐγένετο δὲ ἐπὶ τὴν αὔριον
Now it came to pass on the morrow

συναχθῆναι αὐτῶν τοὺς ἄρχοντας καὶ τοὺς
to be assembled of them the rulers and the

πρεσβυτέρους καὶ τοὺς γραμματεῖς ἐν
elders and the scribes in

Ἰερουσαλήμ, 6 καὶ Ἅννας ὁ ἀρχιερεὺς
Jerusalem, and Annas* the high priest

καὶ Καϊάφας καὶ Ἰωάννης καὶ Ἀλέξανδρος
and Caiaphas and John and Alexander

καὶ ὅσοι ἦσαν ἐκ γένους ἀρχιερατικοῦ,
and as many as were of [the] race high-priestly,

7 καὶ στήσαντες αὐτοὺς ἐν τῷ μέσῳ
and having stood them in the midst

ἐπυνθάνοντο· ἐν ποίᾳ δυνάμει ἢ ἐν ποίῳ
inquired : By what power or in what

ὀνόματι ἐποιήσατε τοῦτο ὑμεῖς; 8 τότε
name did this ye? Then

Πέτρος πλησθεὶς πνεύματος ἁγίου εἶπεν
Peter filled of(with) [the] Spirit Holy said

πρὸς αὐτούς· ἄρχοντες τοῦ λαοῦ καὶ
to them : Rulers of the people and

πρεσβύτεροι, 9 εἰ ἡμεῖς σήμερον ἀνα-
elders, if we to-day are be-

κρινόμεθα ἐπὶ εὐεργεσίᾳ ἀνθρώπου ἀσθενοῦς,
ing examined on a good deed man of an infirm,
= [done to] an infirm man,

ἐν τίνι οὗτος σέσωσται, 10 γνωστὸν ἔστω
by what this man has been healed, known let it be

πᾶσιν ὑμῖν καὶ παντὶ τῷ λαῷ Ἰσραήλ,
to all you and to all the people of Israel,

ὅτι ἐν τῷ ὀνόματι Ἰησοῦ Χριστοῦ τοῦ
that in the name of Jesus Christ the

Ναζωραίου, ὃν ὑμεῖς ἐσταυρώσατε, ὃν ὁ
Nazarene, whom ye crucified, whom –

θεὸς ἤγειρεν ἐκ νεκρῶν, ἐν τούτῳ οὗτος
God raised from [the] dead, in this [name] this man

παρέστηκεν ἐνώπιον ὑμῶν ὑγιής. 11 οὗτός
stands before you whole. This

ἐστιν ὁ λίθος ὁ ἐξουθενηθεὶς ὑφ' ὑμῶν
is the stone – despised by you

τῶν οἰκοδόμων, ὁ γενόμενος εἰς κεφαλὴν
the [ones] building, the [one] become *to* head

γωνίας. 12 καὶ οὐκ ἔστιν ἐν ἄλλῳ οὐδενὶ
of [the] corner. And there is not ¹in ³other ²no(any)

ἡ σωτηρία· οὐδὲ γὰρ ὄνομά ἐστιν ἕτερον
the salvation: for neither ²name ¹is there ³other

* The rough breathing in the Greek is ignored in the transliteration of some familiar proper names.

---

came up to Peter and John while they were speaking to the people. 2 They were greatly disturbed because the apostles were teaching the people and proclaiming in Jesus the resurrection of the dead. 3 They seized Peter and John, and because it was evening, they put them in jail until the next day. 4 But many who heard the message believed, and the number of men grew to about five thousand.

5 The next day the rulers, elders and teachers of the law met in Jerusalem. 6 Annas the high priest was there, and so were Caiaphas, John, Alexander and the other men of the high priest's family. 7 They had Peter and John brought before them and began to question them: "By what power or what name did you do this?"

8 Then Peter, filled with the Holy Spirit, said to them: "Rulers and elders of the people! 9 If we are being called to account today for an act of kindness shown to a cripple and are asked how he was healed, 10 then know this, you and all the people of Israel: It is by the name of Jesus Christ of Nazareth, whom you crucified but whom God raised from the dead, that this man stands before you healed. 11 He is

" 'the stone you builders rejected,
which has become the capstone.'*p' q*

12 Salvation is found in no one else, for there is no other name under heaven giv-

---

d Other ancient authorities read *Jonathan*
e Gk *them*
f Gk *the Nazorean*
g Gk *This*
h Or *keystone*

en among mortals by which we must be saved."
13 Now when they saw the boldness of Peter and John and realized that they were uneducated and ordinary men, they were amazed and recognized them as companions of Jesus. 14 When they saw the man who had been cured standing beside them, they had nothing to say in opposition. 15 So they ordered them to leave the council while they discussed the matter with one another. 16 They said, "What will we do with them? For it is obvious to all who live in Jerusalem that a notable sign has been done through them; we cannot deny it. 17 But to keep it from spreading further among the people, let us warn them to speak no more to anyone in this name." 18 So they called them and ordered them not to speak or teach at all in the name of Jesus. 19 But Peter and John answered them, "Whether it is right in God's sight to listen to you rather than to God, you must judge; 20 for we cannot keep from speaking about what we have seen and heard." 21 After threatening them again, they let them go, finding no way to punish them because of the people, for all of them praised God for what had happened. 22 For the man on whom this sign of healing had been performed

---

ὑπὸ τὸν οὐρανὸν τὸ δεδομένον ἐν
under - heaven - having been given among

ἀνθρώποις ἐν ᾧ δεῖ σωθῆναι ἡμᾶς.
men by which it behoves ²to be saved ¹us.

13 Θεωροῦντες δὲ τὴν τοῦ Πέτρου
And beholding the - of Peter

παρρησίαν καὶ Ἰωάννου, καὶ καταλαβόμενοι
boldness and of John, and perceiving

ὅτι ἄνθρωποι ἀγράμματοί εἰσιν καὶ
that men unlettered they are(were) and

ἰδιῶται, ἐθαύμαζον, ἐπεγίνωσκόν τε αὐτοὺς
laymen, they marvelled, and recognized them

ὅτι σὺν τῷ Ἰησοῦ ἦσαν, 14 τόν τε
that with - Jesus they were(had been), ³the ¹and

ἄνθρωπον βλέποντες σὺν αὐτοῖς ἑστῶτα τὸν
⁴man ⁵seeing ⁷with ⁸them ⁶standing -

τεθεραπευμένον, οὐδὲν εἶχον ἀντειπεῖν.
⁵having been healed, nothing they had to say against.

15 κελεύσαντες δὲ αὐτοὺς ἔξω τοῦ συνεδρίου
So having commanded them outside the council

ἀπελθεῖν, συνέβαλλον πρὸς ἀλλήλους
to go, they discussed with with one another

16 λέγοντες· τί ποιήσωμεν τοῖς ἀνθρώποις
saying: What may we do - men

τούτοις; ὅτι μὲν γὰρ γνωστὸν σημεῖον
to these? for that indeed a notable sign

γέγονεν δι᾽ αὐτῶν, πᾶσιν τοῖς κατοικοῦσιν
has happened through them, to all the [ones] inhabiting

Ἰερουσαλὴμ φανερόν, καὶ οὐ δυνάμεθα
Jerusalem [is] manifest, and we cannot

ἀρνεῖσθαι· 17 ἀλλ᾽ ἵνα μὴ ἐπὶ πλεῖον
to deny [it]; but ¹lest ²more†

διανεμηθῇ εἰς τὸν λαόν, ἀπειλησώμεθα
³it is spread abroad ⁴to the people, let us threaten

αὐτοῖς μηκέτι λαλεῖν ἐπὶ τῷ ὀνόματι
them no longer to speak on the name

τούτῳ μηδενὶ ἀνθρώπων. 18 καὶ καλέσαντες
this to no(any)one of men. And calling

αὐτοὺς παρήγγειλαν καθόλου μὴ φθέγγεσθαι
them they charged at all not to utter

μηδὲ διδάσκειν ἐπὶ τῷ ὀνόματι τοῦ
nor to teach on the name the

Ἰησοῦ. 19 ὁ δὲ Πέτρος καὶ Ἰωάννης
of Jesus. - But Peter and John

ἀποκριθέντες εἶπον πρὸς αὐτούς· εἰ
answering said to them: If

δίκαιόν ἐστιν ἐνώπιον τοῦ θεοῦ, ὑμῶν
right it is before - God, you

ἀκούειν μᾶλλον ἢ τοῦ θεοῦ, κρίνατε·
to hear rather than - God, decide ye;

20 οὐ δυνάμεθα γὰρ ἡμεῖς ἃ εἴδαμεν
for cannot we [the] things which we saw

καὶ ἠκούσαμεν μὴ λαλεῖν. 21 οἱ δὲ
and heard not to speak. And they

προσαπειλησάμενοι ἀπέλυσαν αὐτούς, μηδὲν
having added threats released them, nothing

εὑρίσκοντες τὸ πῶς κολάσωνται αὐτούς,
finding - how they might punish them,

διὰ τὸν λαόν, ὅτι πάντες ἐδόξαζον τὸν
because of the people, because all men glorified

θεὸν ἐπὶ τῷ γεγονότι· 22 ἐτῶν γὰρ
God on the thing having happened; of years for

ἦν πλειόνων τεσσεράκοντα ὁ ἄνθρωπος
was more [than] forty the man

ἐφ᾽ ὃν γεγόνει τὸ σημεῖον τοῦτο τῆς
on whom had happened this sign -

---

en to men by which we must be saved."
13 When they saw the courage of Peter and John and realized that they were unschooled, ordinary men, they were astonished and they took note that these men had been with Jesus. 14 But since they could see the man who had been healed standing there with them, there was nothing they could say. 15 So they ordered them to withdraw from the Sanhedrin and then conferred together. 16 "What are we going to do with these men?" they asked. "Everybody living in Jerusalem knows they have done an outstanding miracle, and we cannot deny it. 17 But to stop this thing from spreading any further among the people, we must warn these men to speak no longer to anyone in this name." 18 Then they called them in again and commanded them not to speak or teach at all in the name of Jesus. 19 But Peter and John replied, "Judge for yourselves whether it is right in God's sight to obey you rather than God. 20 For we cannot help speaking about what we have seen and heard." 21 After further threats they let them go. They could not decide how to punish them, because all the people were praising God for what had happened. 22 For the man who was miraculously healed was over forty years old.

was more than forty years old.

The Believers Pray for Boldness

23 After they were released, they went to their friends[i] and reported what the chief priests and the elders had said to them. 24 When they heard it, they raised their voices together to God and said, "Sovereign Lord, who made the heaven and the earth, the sea, and everything in them, 25 it is you who said by the Holy Spirit through our ancestor David, your servant:[b]

'Why did the Gentiles rage,
  and the peoples imagine vain things?
26 The kings of the earth took their stand,
  and the rulers have gathered together
against the Lord
  and against his Messiah.'[j]

27 For in this city, in fact, both Herod and Pontius Pilate, with the Gentiles and the peoples of Israel, gathered together against your holy servant[k] Jesus, whom you anointed, 28 to do whatever your hand and your plan had predestined to take place. 29 And now, Lord, look at their threats, and grant to your servants[l] to speak your word with all boldness, 30 while you stretch out your hand to heal, and signs and wonders are performed through the name of your holy servant[k] Jesus." 31 When they had prayed, the place in which they were gathered together was shaken; and they were all filled with the Holy Spirit and spoke the word of God with boldness.

The Believers Share Their Possessions

32 Now the whole group of those who believed were of one heart

ἰάσεως.
of cure.

23 Ἀπολυθέντες δὲ ἦλθον πρὸς
And being released they went to

τοὺς ἰδίους καὶ ἀπήγγειλαν ὅσα πρὸς
the(ir) own [people] and reported what things to

αὐτοὺς οἱ ἀρχιερεῖς καὶ οἱ πρεσβύτεροι
them the chief priests and the elders

εἶπαν. **24** οἱ δὲ ἀκούσαντες ὁμοθυμαδὸν
said. And they having heard with one mind

ἦραν φωνὴν πρὸς τὸν θεὸν καὶ εἶπαν·
lifted voice to - God and said :

δέσποτα, σὺ ὁ ποιήσας τὸν οὐρανὸν καὶ
Master, thou the [one] having made the heaven and

τὴν γῆν καὶ τὴν θάλασσαν καὶ πάντα
the earth and the sea and all things

τὰ ἐν αὐτοῖς, **25** ὁ τοῦ πατρὸς ἡμῶν
- in them, ¹the ⁸the ⁹father ¹⁰of us
    [one]

διὰ πνεύματος ἁγίου στόματος Δαυὶδ
³through ⁵[the] Spirit ⁴Holy ⁶[by] mouth ⁷of David

παιδός σου εἰπών· ἱνατί ἐφρύαξαν ἔθνη
¹¹servant ¹²of thee ²saying :* Why raged nations

καὶ λαοὶ ἐμελέτησαν κενά; **26** παρέστησαν
and peoples devised vain things? came

οἱ βασιλεῖς τῆς γῆς καὶ οἱ ἄρχοντες
the kings of the earth and the rulers

συνήχθησαν ἐπὶ τὸ αὐτὸ κατὰ τοῦ κυρίου
assembled together against the Lord

καὶ κατὰ τοῦ χριστοῦ αὐτοῦ.
and against the Christ of him.

27 συνήχθησαν γὰρ ἐπ᾿ ἀληθείας ἐν τῇ
For assembled in truth in -

πόλει ταύτῃ ἐπὶ τὸν ἅγιον παῖδά σου
city this against the holy servant of thee

Ἰησοῦν, ὃν ἔχρισας, Ἡρῴδης τε καὶ
Jesus, whom thou didst anoint, both Herod and

Πόντιος Πιλᾶτος σὺν ἔθνεσιν καὶ λαοῖς
Pontius Pilate with nations and peoples

Ἰσραήλ, **28** ποιῆσαι ὅσα ἡ χείρ σου καὶ
of Israel, to do what the hand of thee and
    things

ἡ βουλὴ προώρισεν γενέσθαι. **29** καὶ τὰ
the counsel foreordained to happen. And -

νῦν, κύριε, ἔπιδε ἐπὶ τὰς ἀπειλὰς αὐτῶν,
now, Lord, look on on the threatenings of them,

καὶ δὸς τοῖς δούλοις σου μετὰ παρρησίας
and give to the slaves of thee with ¹boldness

πάσης λαλεῖν τὸν λόγον σου, **30** ἐν τῷ
¹all to speak the word of thee, by the

τὴν χεῖρα ἐκτείνειν σε εἰς ἴασιν καὶ
the hand to stretch forth thee[b] for cure and
=by stretching forth thy hand

σημεῖα καὶ τέρατα γίνεσθαι διὰ τοῦ
signs and wonders to happen through the

ὀνόματος τοῦ ἁγίου παιδός σου Ἰησοῦ.
name of the holy servant of thee Jesus.

31 καὶ δεηθέντων αὐτῶν ἐσαλεύθη ὁ τόπος
And requesting them⁸ was shaken the place
=as they were making request

ἐν ᾧ ἦσαν συνηγμένοι, καὶ ἐπλήσθησαν
in which they were having been and they were filled
    assembled,

ἅπαντες τοῦ ἁγίου πνεύματος, καὶ ἐλάλουν
all of(with) the Holy Spirit, and spoke

τὸν λόγον τοῦ θεοῦ μετὰ παρρησίας.
the word - of God with boldness.

32 Τοῦ δὲ πλήθους τῶν πιστευσάντων
¹Now ⁵of ²the ⁶multitude ⁹of the [ones] ¹⁰having believed

The Believers' Prayer

23 On their release, Peter and John went back to their own people and reported all that the chief priests and elders had said to them. 24 When they heard this, they raised their voices together in prayer to God. "Sovereign Lord," they said, "you made the heaven and the earth and the sea, and everything in them. 25 You spoke by the Holy Spirit through the mouth of your servant, our father David:

" 'Why do the nations rage
  and the peoples plot in vain?
26 The kings of the earth take their stand
  and the rulers gather together
against the Lord
  and against his Anointed One.'[r][s]

27 Indeed Herod and Pontius Pilate met together with the Gentiles and the people[t] of Israel in this city to conspire against your holy servant Jesus, whom you anointed. 28 They did what your power and will had decided beforehand should happen. 29 Now, Lord, consider their threats and enable your servants to speak your word with great boldness. 30 Stretch out your hand to heal and perform miraculous signs and wonders through the name of your holy servant Jesus." 31 After they prayed, the place where they were meeting was shaken. And they were all filled with the Holy Spirit and spoke the word of God boldly.

The Believers Share Their Possessions

32 All the believers were one in heart and mind. No

---

i Gk their own
j Or his Christ
k Or child
l Gk slaves

* It is recognized that there is a primitive error in the text in the first half of ver. 25; it is impossible to construe it as it stands. See ch. 1. 16.

r 26 That is, Christ or Messiah
s 26 Psalm 2:1,2
t 27 The Greek is plural.

and soul, and no one claimed private ownership of any possessions, but everything they owned was held in common. 33 With great power the apostles gave their testimony to the resurrection of the Lord Jesus, and great grace was upon them all. 34 There was not a needy person among them, for as many as owned lands or houses sold them and brought the proceeds of what was sold. 35 They laid it at the apostles' feet, and it was distributed to each as any had need. 36 There was a Levite, a native of Cyprus, Joseph, to whom the apostles gave the name Barnabas (which means "son of encouragement"). 37 He sold a field that belonged to him, then brought the money, and laid it at the apostles' feet.

ἦν καρδία καὶ ψυχὴ μία, καὶ οὐδὲ
[11]was [2][the] [3]heart [4]and [5]soul [13]one, and [1]not

εἷς τι τῶν ὑπαρχόντων αὐτῷ ἔλεγεν
[6]one [5]any- [4]of the [6]possessions [belonging] [3]said
thing [7]to him

ἴδιον εἶναι, ἀλλ᾽ ἦν αὐτοῖς πάντα κοινά.
[9][his] own [8]to be, but were to them° all things common.

33 καὶ δυνάμει μεγάλῃ ἀπεδίδουν τὸ
And [1]with [2]power [3]great [4]gave [7]the

μαρτύριον οἱ ἀπόστολοι τοῦ κυρίου Ἰησοῦ
[8]testimony [9]the [9]apostles [11]of the [12]Lord [13]Jesus

τῆς ἀναστάσεως, χάρις τε μεγάλη ἦν
[9]of the [10]resurrection, and [2]grace [1]great was

ἐπὶ πάντας αὐτούς. 34 οὐδὲ γὰρ ἐνδεής
upon all them. [1]For [3]neither [4]needy

τις ἦν ἐν αὐτοῖς· ὅσοι γὰρ κτήτορες
[4]anyone [2]was among them; for as many as owners

χωρίων ἢ οἰκιῶν ὑπῆρχον, πωλοῦντες
of lands or of houses were, selling

ἔφερον τὰς τιμὰς τῶν πιπρασκομένων
brought the prices of the things being sold

35 καὶ ἐτίθουν παρὰ τοὺς πόδας τῶν
and placed at the feet of the

ἀποστόλων· διεδίδοτο δὲ ἑκάστῳ καθότι ἄν
apostles; and it was distributed to each according as

τις χρείαν εἶχεν. 36 Ἰωσὴφ δὲ ὁ
anyone need had. And Joseph the [one]

ἐπικληθεὶς Βαρναβᾶς ἀπὸ τῶν ἀποστόλων,
surnamed Barnabas from(by) the apostles,

ὃ ἐστιν μεθερμηνευόμενον υἱὸς παρακλήσεως,
which is being translated Son of consolation,

Λευίτης, Κύπριος τῷ γένει, 37 ὑπάρχοντος
a Levite, a Cypriote by race, - being

αὐτῷ ἀγροῦ, πωλήσας ἤνεγκεν τὸ χρῆμα
to him° a field, having sold [it] brought the proceeds
=as he had a field,

καὶ ἔθηκεν πρὸς τοὺς πόδας τῶν ἀποστόλων.
and placed at the feet of the apostles.

one claimed that any of his possessions was his own, but they shared everything they had. 33 With great power the apostles continued to testify to the resurrection of the Lord Jesus, and much grace was upon them all. 34 There were no needy persons among them. For from time to time those who owned lands or houses sold them, brought the money from the sales 35 and put it at the apostles' feet, and it was distributed to anyone as he had need.

36 Joseph, a Levite from Cyprus, whom the apostles called Barnabas (which means Son of Encouragement), 37 sold a field he owned and brought the money and put it at the apostles' feet.

Chapter 5

Ananias and Sapphira

B UT a man named Ananias, with the consent of his wife Sapphira, sold a piece of property; 2 with his wife's knowledge, he kept back some of the proceeds, and brought only a part and laid it at the apostles' feet. 3 "Ananias," Peter asked, "why has Satan filled your heart to lie to the Holy Spirit and to keep back part of the proceeds of the land? 4 While it remained unsold, did it not remain your own? And after it was sold, were not the proceeds at your disposal? How is it that you have contrived this deed in

5 Ἀνὴρ δέ τις Ἀνανίας ὀνόματι σὺν
And a certain man Ananias* by name with

Σαπφίρῃ τῇ γυναικὶ αὐτοῦ ἐπώλησεν
Sapphira the wife of him sold

κτῆμα, 2 καὶ ἐνοσφίσατο ἀπὸ τῆς τιμῆς,
a property, and appropriated from the price,

συνειδυίης καὶ τῆς γυναικός, καὶ ἐνέγκας
aware of [it] also the(his) wife,* and bringing
=his wife also being aware of it,

μέρος τι παρὰ τοὺς πόδας τῶν ἀποστόλων
a certain part at the feet of the apostles

ἔθηκεν. 3 εἶπεν δὲ ὁ Πέτρος· Ἀνανία,
placed [it]. But said - Peter: Ananias,

διὰ τί ἐπλήρωσεν ὁ σατανᾶς τὴν καρδίαν
why filled - Satan the heart

σου, ψεύσασθαί σε τὸ πνεῦμα τὸ ἅγιον
of thee, to deceive thee[b] the Spirit - Holy
=that thou shouldest deceive

καὶ νοσφίσασθαι ἀπὸ τῆς τιμῆς τοῦ
and to appropriate from the price of the

χωρίου; 4 οὐχὶ μένον σοὶ ἔμενεν καὶ
land? Not remaining to thee it remained and

πραθὲν ἐν τῇ σῇ ἐξουσίᾳ ὑπῆρχεν; τί ὅτι
sold in thy authority it was? Why

ἔθου ἐν τῇ καρδίᾳ σου τὸ πρᾶγμα
was put in the heart of thee - action

* See note to 4. 6.

Chapter 5

Ananias and Sapphira

N OW a man named Ananias, together with his wife Sapphira, also sold a piece of property. 2 With his wife's full knowledge he kept back part of the money for himself, but brought the rest and put it at the apostles' feet. 3 Then Peter said, "Ananias, how is it that Satan has so filled your heart that you have lied to the Holy Spirit and have kept for yourself some of the money you received for the land? 4 Didn't it belong to you before it was sold? And after it was sold, wasn't the money at your disposal? What made you think of doing such a thing? You have your heart? You did not lie to us[m] but to God!" 5Now when Ananias heard these words, he fell down and died. And great fear seized all who heard of it. 6The young men came and wrapped up his body,[n] then carried him out and buried him.

7 After an interval of about three hours his wife came in, not knowing what had happened. 8Peter said to her, "Tell me whether you and your husband sold the land for such and such a price." And she said, "Yes, that was the price." 9Then Peter said to her, "How is it that you have agreed together to put the Spirit of the Lord to the test? Look, the feet of those who have buried your husband are at the door, and they will carry you out." 10Immediately she fell down at his feet and died. When the young men came in they found her dead, so they carried her out and buried her beside her husband. 11And great fear seized the whole church and all who heard of these things.

The Apostles Heal Many

12 Now many signs and wonders were done among the people through the apostles. And they were all together in Solomon's Portico. 13None of the rest dared to join them, but the people held them in high esteem. 14Yet more than ever believers were added to the Lord, great numbers of both men and women, 15so that they even carried out the sick into the streets, and laid them on cots and mats, in order that Peter's

---

τοῦτο; οὐκ ἐψεύσω ἀνθρώποις ἀλλὰ
this? thou didst not lie to men but

τῷ θεῷ. 5 ἀκούων δὲ ὁ Ἀνανίας
- to God. And hearing - Ananias

τοὺς λόγους τούτους πεσὼν ἐξέψυξεν· καὶ
these words falling expired; and

ἐγένετο φόβος μέγας ἐπὶ πάντας τοὺς
came fear great on all the [ones]

ἀκούοντας. 6 ἀναστάντες δὲ οἱ νεώτεροι
hearing. And rising up the young men

συνέστειλαν αὐτὸν καὶ ἐξενέγκαντες ἔθαψαν.
wrapped him and carrying out buried [him].

7 Ἐγένετο δὲ ὡς ὡρῶν τριῶν διάστημα
[1]And there was [2]of about [5]hours [4]three [3]an interval

καὶ ἡ γυνὴ αὐτοῦ μὴ εἰδυῖα τὸ γεγονὸς
and the wife of him not knowing the thing having happened

εἰσῆλθεν. . 8 ἀπεκρίθη δὲ πρὸς αὐτὴν
entered. And answered to her

Πέτρος· εἰπέ μοι, εἰ τοσούτου τὸ χωρίον
Peter: Tell me, if of(for) so much the land

ἀπέδοσθε; ἡ δὲ εἶπεν· ναί, τοσούτου.
ye sold? And she said: Yes, of(for) so much.

9 ὁ δὲ Πέτρος πρὸς αὐτήν· τί ὅτι
- And Peter to her: Why

συνεφωνήθη ὑμῖν πειράσαι τὸ πνεῦμα
was it agreed with you to tempt the Spirit

κυρίου; ἰδοὺ οἱ πόδες τῶν θαψάντων τὸν
of [the] behold[,] the feet of the [ones] having Lord? the buried

ἄνδρα σου ἐπὶ τῇ θύρᾳ καὶ ἐξοίσουσίν
husband of thee at the door and they will carry out

σε. 10 ἔπεσεν δὲ παραχρῆμα πρὸς τοὺς
thee. And she fell at once at the

πόδας αὐτοῦ καὶ ἐξέψυξεν· εἰσελθόντες δὲ
feet of him and expired; and entering

οἱ νεανίσκοι εὗρον αὐτὴν νεκράν, καὶ
the young men found her dead, and

ἐξενέγκαντες ἔθαψαν πρὸς τὸν ἄνδρα
carrying out buried [her] beside the husband

αὐτῆς. 11 Καὶ ἐγένετο φόβος μέγας
of her. And came fear great

ἐφ' ὅλην τὴν ἐκκλησίαν καὶ ἐπὶ πάντας
on all the church and on all

τοὺς ἀκούοντας ταῦτα.
the [ones] hearing these things.

12 Διὰ δὲ τῶν χειρῶν τῶν ἀποστόλων
And through the hands of the apostles

ἐγίνετο σημεῖα καὶ τέρατα πολλὰ ἐν
[3]happened [2]signs [3]and [4]wonders [1]many among

τῷ λαῷ· καὶ ἦσαν ὁμοθυμαδὸν πάντες
the people; and were with one mind all

ἐν τῇ στοᾷ Σολομῶντος· 13 τῶν δὲ
in the porch of Solomon; and of the

λοιπῶν οὐδεὶς ἐτόλμα κολλᾶσθαι αὐτοῖς,
rest no one dared to be joined to them,

ἀλλ' ἐμεγάλυνεν αὐτοὺς ὁ λαός· 14 μᾶλλον
but magnified them the people; [2]more

δὲ προσετίθεντο πιστεύοντες τῷ κυρίῳ,
[1]and were added believing [ones] to the Lord,

πλήθη ἀνδρῶν τε καὶ γυναικῶν· 15 ὥστε
multitudes both of men and of women; so as

καὶ εἰς τὰς πλατείας ἐκφέρειν τοὺς
even into the streets to bring out the =they brought out

ἀσθενεῖς καὶ τιθέναι ἐπὶ κλιναρίων καὶ
ailing and to place on pallets and

---

not lied to men but to God."

5When Ananias heard this, he fell down and died. And great fear seized all who heard what had happened. 6Then the young men came forward, wrapped up his body, and carried him out and buried him.

7About three hours later his wife came in, not knowing what had happened. 8Peter asked her, "Tell me, is this the price you and Ananias got for the land?"

"Yes," she said, "that is the price."

9Peter said to her, "How could you agree to test the Spirit of the Lord? Look! The feet of the men who buried your husband are at the door, and they will carry you out also."

10At that moment she fell down at his feet and died. Then the young men came in and, finding her dead, carried her out and buried her beside her husband. 11Great fear seized the whole church and all who heard about these events.

The Apostles Heal Many

12The apostles performed many miraculous signs and wonders among the people. And all the believers used to meet together in Solomon's Colonnade. 13No one else dared join them, even though they were highly regarded by the people. 14Nevertheless, more and more men and women believed in the Lord and were added to their number. 15As a result, people brought the sick into the streets and laid them on beds and mats so that at

---

[m] Gk *to men*
[n] Meaning of Gk uncertain

shadow might fall on some of them as he came by. 16 A great number of people would also gather from the towns around Jerusalem, bringing the sick and those tormented by unclean spirits, and they were all cured.

The Apostles Are Persecuted

17 Then the high priest took action; he and all who were with him (that is, the sect of the Sadducees), being filled with jealousy, 18 arrested the apostles and put them in the public prison. 19 But during the night an angel of the Lord opened the prison doors, brought them out, and said, 20 "Go, stand in the temple and tell the people the whole message about this life." 21 When they heard this, they entered the temple at daybreak and went on with their teaching.

When the high priest and those with him arrived, they called together the council and the whole body of the elders of Israel, and sent to the prison to have them brought. 22 But when the temple police went there, they did not find them in the prison; so they returned and reported, 23 "We found the prison securely locked and the guards standing at the doors, but when we opened them, we found no one inside." 24 Now when the captain of the temple and the chief priests heard these words, they were perplexed about them, wondering what might be going on. 25 Then someone arrived and announced, "Look, the men whom you put in prison are standing in

---

κραβάτων, ἵνα ἐρχομένου Πέτρου κἂν ἡ σκιὰ
mattresses, that ⁵coming ⁴of Peter ¹if even ²the ³shadow
ἐπισκιάσῃ τινὶ αὐτῶν. 16 συνήρχετο δὲ
might overshadow some one of them. And came together
καὶ τὸ πλῆθος τῶν πέριξ πόλεων
also the multitude of the ²round about ¹cities
Ἰερουσαλήμ, φέροντες ἀσθενεῖς καὶ
Jerusalem, carrying ailing [ones] and
ὀχλουμένους ὑπὸ πνευμάτων ἀκαθάρτων,
being tormented by spirits unclean,
οἵτινες ἐθεραπεύοντο ἅπαντες.
who were healed all.

17 Ἀναστὰς δὲ ὁ ἀρχιερεὺς καὶ πάντες
And rising up the high priest and all
οἱ σὺν αὐτῷ, ἡ οὖσα αἵρεσις τῶν
the[ones] with him, the existing sect of the
Σαδδουκαίων, ἐπλήσθησαν ζήλου **18** καὶ
Sadducees, were filled of(with) jealousy and
ἐπέβαλον τὰς χεῖρας ἐπὶ τοὺς ἀποστόλους
laid on the(ir) hands on the apostles
καὶ ἔθεντο αὐτοὺς ἐν τηρήσει δημοσίᾳ.
and put them in custody publicly.

19 Ἄγγελος δὲ κυρίου διὰ νυκτὸς
But an angel of [the] Lord through(during) [the] night
ἤνοιξε τὰς θύρας τῆς φυλακῆς ἐξαγαγών τε
opened the doors of the prison and leading out
αὐτοὺς εἶπεν· **20** πορεύεσθε καὶ σταθέντες
them said : Go ye and standing
λαλεῖτε ἐν τῷ ἱερῷ τῷ λαῷ πάντα
speak in the temple to the people all
τὰ ῥήματα τῆς ζωῆς ταύτης.
the words of this life.

21 ἀκούσαντες δὲ εἰσῆλθον ὑπὸ τὸν ὄρθρον
And having heard they entered about the dawn
εἰς τὸ ἱερὸν καὶ ἐδίδασκον. Παραγενόμενος δὲ
into the temple and taught. And having come
ὁ ἀρχιερεὺς καὶ οἱ σὺν αὐτῷ
the high priest and the [ones] with him
συνεκάλεσαν τὸ συνέδριον καὶ πᾶσαν τὴν
called together the council and all the
γερουσίαν τῶν υἱῶν Ἰσραήλ, καὶ ἀπέστειλαν
senate of the sons of Israel, and sent
εἰς τὸ δεσμωτήριον ἀχθῆναι αὐτούς.ᵇ
to the jail to be brought them.

22 οἱ δὲ παραγενόμενοι ὑπηρέται οὐχ εὗρον
¹But ²the ³having come ³attendants found not
αὐτοὺς ἐν τῇ φυλακῇ· ἀναστρέψαντες δὲ
them in the prison; and having returned
ἀπήγγειλαν **23** λέγοντες ὅτι τὸ δεσμωτήριον
they reported saying[,] - The jail
εὕρομεν κεκλεισμένον ἐν πάσῃ ἀσφαλείᾳ
we found having been shut in all security
καὶ τοὺς φύλακας ἑστῶτας ἐπὶ τῶν
and the guards standing at the
θυρῶν, ἀνοίξαντες δὲ ἔσω οὐδένα εὕρομεν.
doors, but having opened ³inside ²no one ¹we found.
24 ὡς δὲ ἤκουσαν τοὺς λόγους τούτους
And as ⁹heard ¹⁰these ¹¹words
ὅ τε στρατηγὸς τοῦ ἱεροῦ καὶ οἱ ἀρχιερεῖς,
²the ¹both ³commandant ⁴of the ⁵temple ⁶and ⁷the ⁸chief priests,
διηπόρουν περὶ αὐτῶν τί ἂν γένοιτο
they were in doubt about them what ²might become
τοῦτο. **25** παραγενόμενος δέ τις ἀπήγγειλεν
¹this thing. And having come someone reported
αὐτοῖς ὅτι ἰδοὺ οἱ ἄνδρες, οὓς
to them[,] - Behold[,] the men, whom

---

least Peter's shadow might fall on some of them as he passed by. 16 Crowds gathered also from the towns around Jerusalem, bringing their sick and those tormented by evilᵘ spirits, and all of them were healed.

The Apostles Persecuted

17 Then the high priest and all his associates, who were members of the party of the Sadducees, were filled with jealousy. 18 They arrested the apostles and put them in the public jail. 19 But during the night an angel of the Lord opened the doors of the jail and brought them out. 20 "Go, stand in the temple courts," he said, "and tell the people the full message of this new life."
21 At daybreak they entered the temple courts, as they had been told, and began to teach the people.

When the high priest and his associates arrived, they called together the Sanhedrin—the full assembly of the elders of Israel—and sent to the jail for the apostles. 22 But on arriving at the jail, the officers did not find them there. So they went back and reported, 23 "We found the jail securely locked, with the guards standing at the doors; but when we opened them, we found no one inside." 24 On hearing this report, the captain of the temple guard and the chief priests were puzzled, wondering what would come of this.

25 Then someone came and said, "Look! The men you put in jail are standing

ᵘ16 Greek unclean

the temple and teaching the people!" 26 Then the captain went with the temple police and brought them, but without violence, for they were afraid of being stoned by the people.

27 When they had brought them, they had them stand before the council. The high priest questioned them, 28 saying, "We gave you strict orders not to teach in this name,º yet here you have filled Jerusalem with your teaching and you are determined to bring this man's blood on us." 29 But Peter and the apostles answered, "We must obey God rather than any human authority.ᵖ 30 The God of our ancestors raised up Jesus, whom you had killed by hanging him on a tree. 31 God exalted him at his right hand as Leader and Savior that he might give repentance to Israel and forgiveness of sins. 32 And we are witnesses to these things, and so is the Holy Spirit whom God has given to those who obey him."

33 When they heard this, they were enraged and wanted to kill them. 34 But a Pharisee in the council named Gamaliel, a teacher of the law, respected by all the people, stood up and ordered the men to be put outside for a short time. 35 Then he said to them, "Fellow Israelites,q consider carefully what you propose to do to these men.

ἔθεσθε ἐν τῇ φυλακῇ, εἰσὶν ἐν τῷ ἱερῷ
ye put in the prison, are in the temple

ἑστῶτες καὶ διδάσκοντες τὸν λαόν.
standing and teaching the people.

26 Τότε ἀπελθὼν ὁ στρατηγὸς σὺν τοῖς
Then going the commandant with the

ὑπηρέταις ἦγεν αὐτούς, οὐ μετὰ βίας,
attendants brought them, not with force,

ἐφοβοῦντο γὰρ τὸν λαόν, μὴ λιθασθῶσιν·
for they feared the people, lest they should be stoned;

27 ἀγαγόντες δὲ αὐτοὺς ἔστησαν ἐν τῷ
and bringing them they stood in the

συνεδρίῳ. καὶ ἐπηρώτησεν αὐτοὺς ὁ
council. And questioned them the

ἀρχιερεὺς 28 λέγων· παραγγελίᾳ παρηγ-
high priest saying: With charge we
=We strictly

γείλαμεν ὑμῖν μὴ διδάσκειν ἐπὶ
charged you not to teach on(in)

τῷ ὀνόματι τούτῳ, καὶ ἰδοὺ πεπληρώκατε
this name, and behold ye have filled

τὴν Ἰερουσαλὴμ τῆς διδαχῆς ὑμῶν, καὶ
Jerusalem of(with) the teaching of you, and

βούλεσθε ἐπαγαγεῖν ἐφ' ἡμᾶς τὸ αἷμα
intend to bring on on us the blood

τοῦ ἀνθρώπου τούτου. 29 ἀποκριθεὶς δὲ
of this man. And answering

Πέτρος καὶ οἱ ἀπόστολοι εἶπαν· πειθαρχεῖν
Peter and the apostles said: ²to obey

δεῖ θεῷ μᾶλλον ἢ ἀνθρώποις. 30 ὁ
¹It behoves God rather than men. The

θεὸς τῶν πατέρων ἡμῶν ἤγειρεν Ἰησοῦν,
God of the fathers of us raised Jesus,

ὃν ὑμεῖς διεχειρίσασθε κρεμάσαντες ἐπὶ
whom ye killed hanging on

ξύλου· 31 τοῦτον ὁ θεὸς ἀρχηγὸν καὶ
a tree; this man - God a Ruler and

σωτῆρα ὕψωσεν τῇ δεξιᾷ αὐτοῦ τοῦ
a Saviour exalted to the right [hand] of him

δοῦναι μετάνοιαν τῷ Ἰσραὴλ καὶ ἄφεσιν
to give⁴ repentance - to Israel and forgiveness

ἁμαρτιῶν. 32 καὶ ἡμεῖς ἐσμεν μάρτυρες
of sins. And we are witnesses

τῶν ῥημάτων τούτων, καὶ τὸ πνεῦμα
of these words(things), and the Spirit

τὸ ἅγιον ὃ ἔδωκεν ὁ θεὸς τοῖς
- Holy which ²gave - ¹God to the

πειθαρχοῦσιν αὐτῷ. 33 οἱ δὲ ἀκούσαντες
[ones] obeying him. And the [ones] hearing

διεπρίοντο καὶ ἐβούλοντο ἀνελεῖν αὐτούς.
were cut* and intended to kill them.

34 Ἀναστὰς δέ τις ἐν τῷ συνεδρίῳ
¹But ⁴standing up ²a certain ⁵in ⁶the ⁷council

Φαρισαῖος ὀνόματι Γαμαλιήλ, νομοδιδάσκαλος
³Pharisee by name Gamaliel, a teacher of the law

τίμιος παντὶ τῷ λαῷ, ἐκέλευσεν ἔξω
honoured by all the people, commanded ⁴outside

βραχὺ τοὺς ἀνθρώπους ποιῆσαι, 35 εἶπέν
⁵a little ²the ³men ¹to make(put), ²said

τε πρὸς αὐτούς· ἄνδρες Ἰσραηλῖται,
¹and to them: Men Israelites,

προσέχετε ἑαυτοῖς ἐπὶ τοῖς ἀνθρώποις τούτοις
take heed to yourselves ⁴on(to) ⁵these ⁶men

---

in the temple courts teaching the people." 26At that, the captain went with his officers and brought the apostles. They did not use force, because they feared that the people would stone them.

27Having brought the apostles, they made them appear before the Sanhedrin to be questioned by the high priest. 28"We gave you strict orders not to teach in this name," he said. "Yet you have filled Jerusalem with your teaching and are determined to make us guilty of this man's blood."

29Peter and the other apostles replied: "We must obey God rather than men! 30The God of our fathers raised Jesus from the dead —whom you had killed by hanging him on a tree. 31God exalted him to his own right hand as Prince and Savior that he might give repentance and forgiveness of sins to Israel. 32We are witnesses of these things, and so is the Holy Spirit, whom God has given to those who obey him."

33When they heard this, they were furious and wanted to put them to death. 34But a Pharisee named Gamaliel, a teacher of the law, who was honored by all the people, stood up in the Sanhedrin and ordered that the men be put outside for a little while. 35Then he addressed them: "Men of Israel, consider carefully what you in-

---

º Other ancient authorities read Did we not give you strict orders not to teach in this name?
ᵖ Gk than men
q Gk Men, Israelites

* That is, to the heart; cf. 7. 54.

36 For some time ago Theudas rose up, claiming to be somebody, and a number of men, about four hundred, joined him; but he was killed, and all who followed him were dispersed and disappeared. 37 After him Judas the Galilean rose up at the time of the census and got people to follow him; he also perished, and all who followed him were scattered. 38 So in the present case, I tell you, keep away from these men and let them alone; because if this plan or this undertaking is of human origin, it will fail; 39 but if it is of God, you will not be able to overthrow them—in that case you may even be found fighting against God!"

They were convinced by him, 40 and when they had called in the apostles, they had them flogged. Then they ordered them not to speak in the name of Jesus, and let them go. 41 As they left the council, they rejoiced that they were considered worthy to suffer dishonor for the sake of the name. 42 And every day in the temple and at home[r] they did not cease to teach and proclaim Jesus as the Messiah.[s]

r Or from house to house
s Or the Christ

τί   μέλλετε   πράσσειν.   36 πρὸ   γὰρ
¹what   ²ye intend   ³to do.   For before

τούτων   τῶν   ἡμερῶν   ἀνέστη   Θευδᾶς,   λέγων
these   –   days   stood up   Theudas,   saying

εἶναί   τινα   ἑαυτόν,   ᾧ   προσεκλίθη   ἀνδρῶν
to be   someone   himself,   ¹to whom   ⁶were attached   ²of men

ἀριθμὸς   ὡς   τετρακοσίων·   ὃς   ἀνῃρέθη,   καὶ
²a number   ⁴about   ⁵four hundreds;   who   was killed,   and

πάντες   ὅσοι   ἐπείθοντο   αὐτῷ   διελύθησαν
all   as many as   obeyed   him   were dispersed

καὶ   ἐγένοντο   εἰς   οὐδέν.   37 μετὰ   τοῦτον
and   came   to   nothing.   After   this

ἀνέστη   Ἰούδας   ὁ   Γαλιλαῖος   ἐν   ταῖς
stood up   Judas   the   Galilæan   in   the

ἡμέραις   τῆς   ἀπογραφῆς   καὶ   ἀπέστησεν
days   of the   enrolment   and   drew away

λαὸν   ὀπίσω   αὐτοῦ·   κἀκεῖνος   ἀπώλετο,
people   after   him;   and that man   perished,

καὶ   πάντες   ὅσοι   ἐπείθοντο   αὐτῷ
and   all   as many as   obeyed   him

διεσκορπίσθησαν.   38 καὶ   τὰ   νῦν   λέγω
were scattered.   And   –   now   I say

ὑμῖν,   ἀπόστητε   ἀπὸ   τῶν   ἀνθρώπων   τούτων
to you,   stand away   from   these men

καὶ   ἄφετε   αὐτούς·   ὅτι   ἐὰν   ᾖ   ἐξ   ἀνθρώπων
and   leave   them;   because   if   be   of   men

ἡ   βουλὴ   αὕτη   ἢ   τὸ   ἔργον   τοῦτο,
this   counsel   or   the   this work,

καταλυθήσεται·   39 εἰ   δὲ   ἐκ   θεοῦ   ἐστιν,
it will be destroyed;   but if   of   God   it is,

οὐ   δυνήσεσθε   καταλῦσαι   αὐτούς,   μήποτε
ye will not be able   to destroy   them,   lest

καὶ   θεομάχοι   εὑρεθῆτε.   ἐπείσθησαν   δὲ
even   fighters against God   ye be found.   And they obeyed

αὐτῷ,   40 καὶ   προσκαλεσάμενοι   τοὺς
him,   and   having called to [them]   the

ἀποστόλους   δείραντες   παρήγγειλαν   μὴ
apostles   beating   charged   not

λαλεῖν   ἐπὶ   τῷ   ὀνόματι   τοῦ   Ἰησοῦ   καὶ
to speak   on(in)   the   name   –   of Jesus   and

ἀπέλυσαν.   41 Οἱ   μὲν   οὖν   ἐπορεύοντο
released [them].   They   –   therefore   went

χαίροντες   ἀπὸ   προσώπου   τοῦ   συνεδρίου,
rejoicing   from [the]   presence   of the   council,

ὅτι   κατηξιώθησαν   ὑπὲρ   τοῦ   ὀνόματος
because   they were deemed worthy   on behalf of   the   name

ἀτιμασθῆναι·   42 πᾶσάν   τε   ἡμέραν   ἐν   τῷ
to be dishonoured;   and every   day   in   the

ἱερῷ   καὶ   κατ'   οἶκον   οὐκ   ἐπαύοντο
temple   and   from house to house†   they ceased not

διδάσκοντες   καὶ   εὐαγγελιζόμενοι   τὸν   χριστὸν
teaching   and   preaching   the   Christ

Ἰησοῦν.
Jesus.

---

tend to do to these men. 36 Some time ago Theudas appeared, claiming to be somebody, and about four hundred men rallied to him. He was killed, all his followers were dispersed, and it all came to nothing. 37 After him, Judas the Galilean appeared in the days of the census and led a band of people in revolt. He too was killed, and all his followers were scattered. 38 Therefore, in the present case I advise you: Leave these men alone! Let them go. For if their purpose or activity is of human origin, it will fail. 39 But if it is from God, you will not be able to stop these men; you will only find yourselves fighting against God."

40 His speech persuaded them. They called the apostles in and had them flogged. Then they ordered them not to speak in the name of Jesus, and let them go.

41 The apostles left the Sanhedrin, rejoicing because they had been counted worthy of suffering disgrace for the Name. 42 Day after day, in the temple courts and from house to house, they never stopped teaching and proclaiming the good news that Jesus is the Christ.[v]

Chapter 6

Seven Chosen to Serve

NOW during those days, when the disciples were increasing in number, the Hellenists complained against the Hebrews because their widows were being neglected in the daily distribution of food. 2 And the twelve

---

6 Ἐν   δὲ   ταῖς   ἡμέραις   ταύταις
Now in   the   these days

πληθυνόντων   τῶν   μαθητῶν   ἐγένετο
being multiplied   the   disciples*   there was
= as the disciples were multiplied

γογγυσμὸς   τῶν   Ἑλληνιστῶν   πρὸς   τοὺς
a murmuring   of the   Hellenists   against   the

Ἑβραίους,   ὅτι   παρεθεωροῦντο   ἐν   τῇ
Hebrews,   because   ⁴were overlooked   ⁵in   ⁶the

διακονίᾳ   τῇ   καθημερινῇ   αἱ   χῆραι   αὐτῶν.
⁵service   –   ⁷daily   ¹the   ²widows   ³of them.

Chapter 6

The Choosing of the Seven

IN those days when the number of disciples was increasing, the Grecian Jews among them complained against the Hebraic Jews because their widows were being overlooked in the daily distribution of

v 42 Or Messiah

called together the whole community of the disciples and said, "It is not right that we should neglect the word of God in order to wait on tables.¹ ³ Therefore, friends,ᵘ select from among yourselves seven men of good standing, full of the Spirit and of wisdom, whom we may appoint to this task, ⁴ while we, for our part, will devote ourselves to prayer and to serving the word." ⁵ What they said pleased the whole community, and they chose Stephen, a man full of faith and the Holy Spirit, together with Philip, Prochorus, Nicanor, Timon, Parmenas, and Nicolaus, a proselyte of Antioch. ⁶ They had these men stand before the apostles, who prayed and laid their hands on them.

7 The word of God continued to spread; the number of the disciples increased greatly in Jerusalem, and a great many of the priests became obedient to the faith.

The Arrest of Stephen

8 Stephen, full of grace and power, did great wonders and signs among the people. ⁹ Then some of those who belonged to the synagogue of the Freedmen (as it was called), Cyrenians, Alexandrians, and others of those from Cilicia and Asia, stood up and argued with Stephen. ¹⁰ But they could not withstand the wisdom and the Spiritᵛ with which he spoke. ¹¹ Then they secretly instigated some men to say, "We have heard him speak blasphemous words against Moses and God." ¹² They stirred up the people as

2 προσκαλεσάμενοι δὲ οἱ δώδεκα τὸ
⁴having called to [them] ¹And ²the ³twelve the

πλῆθος τῶν μαθητῶν εἶπαν· οὐκ ἀρεστόν
multitude of the disciples said : not pleasing

ἐστιν ἡμᾶς καταλείψαντας τὸν λόγον τοῦ
It is us leaving the word –

θεοῦ διακονεῖν τραπέζαις. 3 ἐπισκέψασθε
of God to serve tables. look ye out

δέ, ἀδελφοί, ἄνδρας ἐξ ὑμῶν μαρτυρουμένους
But, brothers, ²men ³of ⁴you ¹being witnessed to

ἑπτὰ πλήρεις πνεύματος καὶ σοφίας, οὓς
¹seven [as] full of Spirit and of wisdom, whom

καταστήσομεν ἐπὶ τῆς χρείας ταύτης·
we will appoint over this office;

4 ἡμεῖς δὲ τῇ προσευχῇ καὶ τῇ διακονίᾳ
but we to the prayer and to the service

τοῦ λόγου προσκαρτερήσομεν. 5 καὶ ἤρεσεν
of the word will keep. And ²pleased

ὁ λόγος ἐνώπιον παντὸς τοῦ πλήθους,
¹the ²word before all the multitude,

καὶ ἐξελέξαντο Στέφανον, ἄνδρα πλήρη
and they chose Stephen, a man full

πίστεως καὶ πνεύματος ἁγίου, καὶ Φίλιππον
of faith and Spirit of Holy, and Philip

καὶ Πρόχορον καὶ Νικάνορα καὶ Τίμωνα
and Prochorus and Nicanor and Timon

καὶ Παρμενᾶν καὶ Νικόλαον προσήλυτον
and Parmenas and Nicolaus a proselyte

Ἀντιοχέα, 6 οὓς ἔστησαν ἐνώπιον τῶν
of Antioch, whom they set before the

ἀποστόλων, καὶ προσευξάμενοι ἐπέθηκαν
apostles, and having prayed they placed on

αὐτοῖς τὰς χεῖρας.
them the(ir) hands.

7 Καὶ ὁ λόγος τοῦ θεοῦ ηὔξανεν, καὶ
And the word – of God grew, and

ἐπληθύνετο ὁ ἀριθμὸς τῶν μαθητῶν ἐν
was multiplied the number of the disciples in

Ἰερουσαλὴμ σφόδρα, πολύς τε ὄχλος τῶν
Jerusalem greatly, and a much(great) crowd of the

ἱερέων ὑπήκουον τῇ πίστει.
priests obeyed the faith.

8 Στέφανος δὲ πλήρης χάριτος καὶ
And Stephen full of grace and

δυνάμεως ἐποίει τέρατα καὶ σημεῖα μεγάλα
of power did wonders and signs great

ἐν τῷ λαῷ. 9 ἀνέστησαν δέ τινες τῶν
among the people. But rose up some of the
[ones]

ἐκ τῆς συναγωγῆς τῆς λεγομένης
of the synagogue being called

Λιβερτίνων καὶ Κυρηναίων καὶ Ἀλεξ-
of Freedmen and of Cyrenians and of

ανδρέων καὶ τῶν ἀπὸ Κιλικίας καὶ
Alexandrians and of the [ones] from Cilicia and

Ἀσίας συζητοῦντες τῷ Στεφάνῳ, 10 καὶ
Asia discussing with Stephen, and

οὐκ ἴσχυον ἀντιστῆναι τῇ σοφίᾳ καὶ
were not able to withstand the wisdom and

τῷ πνεύματι ᾧ ἐλάλει. 11 τότε ὑπέβαλον
the spirit with which he spoke. Then they suborned

ἄνδρας λέγοντας ὅτι ἀκηκόαμεν αὐτοῦ
men saying[,] – We have heard him

λαλοῦντος ῥήματα βλάσφημα εἰς Μωϋσῆν
speaking words blasphemous against Moses

καὶ τὸν θεόν· 12 συνεκίνησάν τε τὸν
and – God; and they stirred up the

food. ²So the Twelve gathered all the disciples together and said, "It would not be right for us to neglect the ministry of the word of God in order to wait on tables. ³Brothers, choose seven men from among you who are known to be full of the Spirit and wisdom. We will turn this responsibility over to them ⁴and will give our attention to prayer and the ministry of the word."

⁵This proposal pleased the whole group. They chose Stephen, a man full of faith and of the Holy Spirit; also Philip, Procorus, Nicanor, Timon, Parmenas, and Nicolas from Antioch, a convert to Judaism. ⁶They presented these men to the apostles, who prayed and laid their hands on them.

⁷So the word of God spread. The number of disciples in Jerusalem increased rapidly, and a large number of priests became obedient to the faith.

Stephen Seized

⁸Now Stephen, a man full of God's grace and power, did great wonders and miraculous signs among the people. ⁹Opposition arose, however, from members of the Synagogue of the Freedmen (as it was called)—Jews of Cyrene and Alexandria as well as the provinces of Cilicia and Asia. These men began to argue with Stephen, ¹⁰but they could not stand up against his wisdom or the Spirit by whom he spoke. ¹¹Then they secretly persuaded some men to say, "We have heard Stephen speak words of blasphemy against Moses and against God."

¹²So they stirred up the

¹ Or *keep accounts*
ᵘ Gk *brothers*
ᵛ Or *spirit*

well as the elders and the scribes; then they suddenly confronted him, seized him, and brought him before the council. [13] They set up false witnesses who said, "This man never stops saying things against this holy place and the law; [14] for we have heard him say that this Jesus of Nazareth[w] will destroy this place and will change the customs that Moses handed on to us." [15] And all who sat in the council looked intently at him, and they saw that his face was like the face of an angel.

λαὸν	καὶ	τοὺς	πρεσβυτέρους	καὶ	τοὺς
people	and	the	elders	and	the
γραμματεῖς,	καὶ	ἐπιστάντες	συνήρπασαν		
scribes,	and	coming on	they seized		
αὐτὸν	καὶ	ἤγαγον	εἰς	τὸ	συνέδριον,
him	and	led	to	the	council,

13 ἔστησάν τε μάρτυρας ψευδεῖς λέγοντας·
and stood witnesses false saying:

ὁ ἄνθρωπος οὗτος οὐ παύεται λαλῶν
This man ceases not speaking

ῥήματα κατὰ τοῦ τόπου τοῦ ἁγίου [τούτου]
words against - ³place - ²holy ¹this

καὶ τοῦ νόμου· **14** ἀκηκόαμεν γὰρ αὐτοῦ
and the law; for we have heard him

λέγοντος ὅτι Ἰησοῦς ὁ Ναζωραῖος οὗτος
saying that ²Jesus ³the ⁴Nazarene ¹this

καταλύσει τὸν τόπον τοῦτον καὶ ἀλλάξει
will destroy this place and will change

τὰ ἔθη ἃ παρέδωκεν ἡμῖν Μωϋσῆς.
the customs which delivered to us Moses.

15 καὶ ἀτενίσαντες εἰς αὐτὸν πάντες οἱ
And gazing at him all the

καθεζόμενοι ἐν τῷ συνεδρίῳ εἶδον τὸ
[ones] sitting in the council saw the

πρόσωπον αὐτοῦ ὡσεὶ πρόσωπον ἀγγέλου.
face of him as a face of an angel.

people and the elders and the teachers of the law. They seized Stephen and brought him before the Sanhedrin. [13] They produced false witnesses, who testified, "This fellow never stops speaking against this holy place and against the law. [14] For we have heard him say that this Jesus of Nazareth will destroy this place and change the customs Moses handed down to us."

[15] All who were sitting in the Sanhedrin looked intently at Stephen, and they saw that his face was like the face of an angel.

Chapter 7

Stephen's Speech to the Council

THEN the high priest asked him, "Are these things so?" [2] And Stephen replied:

"Brothers[x] and fathers, listen to me. The God of glory appeared to our ancestor Abraham when he was in Mesopotamia, before he lived in Haran, [3] and said to him, 'Leave your country and your relatives and go to the land that I will show you.' [4] Then he left the country of the Chaldeans and settled in Haran. After his father died, God had him move from there to this country in which you are now living. [5] He did not give him any of it as a heritage, not even a foot's length, but promised to give it to him as his possession and to his descendants after him, even though he

7 Εἶπεν δὲ ὁ ἀρχιερεύς· εἰ ταῦτα
And said the high priest: If these things

οὕτως ἔχει; **2** ὁ δὲ ἔφη·
thus have(are)? And he said:

Ἄνδρες ἀδελφοὶ καὶ πατέρες, ἀκούσατε.
Men brothers and fathers, hear ye.

Ὁ θεὸς τῆς δόξης ὤφθη τῷ πατρὶ
The God of glory appeared to the father

ἡμῶν Ἀβραὰμ ὄντι ἐν τῇ Μεσοποταμίᾳ
of us Abraham being in - Mesopotamia

πρὶν ἢ κατοικῆσαι αὐτὸν ἐν Χαρράν,
before to dwell him[b] in Charran,
=he dwelt

3 καὶ εἶπεν πρὸς αὐτόν· ἔξελθε ἐκ τῆς
and said to him: Go forth out of the

γῆς σου καὶ τῆς συγγενείας σου, καὶ
land of thee and the kindred of thee, and

δεῦρο εἰς τὴν γῆν ἣν ἄν σοι δείξω.
come into the land whichever to thee I may show.

4 τότε ἐξελθὼν ἐκ γῆς Χαλδαίων
Then going forth out of [the] land of [the] Chaldæans

κατῴκησεν ἐν Χαρράν. κἀκεῖθεν μετὰ
he dwelt in Charran. And thence after

τὸ ἀποθανεῖν τὸν πατέρα αὐτοῦ μετῴκισεν
the to die the father of him[b] [God] removed
=his father died

αὐτὸν εἰς τὴν γῆν ταύτην εἰς ἣν ὑμεῖς
him into this land in which ye

νῦν κατοικεῖτε, **5** καὶ οὐκ ἔδωκεν αὐτῷ
now dwell, and gave not to him

κληρονομίαν ἐν αὐτῇ οὐδὲ βῆμα ποδός,
an inheritance in it nor a foot's space,

καὶ ἐπηγγείλατο δοῦναι αὐτῷ εἰς
and promised to give him for

κατάσχεσιν αὐτὴν καὶ τῷ σπέρματι αὐτοῦ
a possession it and to the seed of him

μετ' αὐτόν, οὐκ ὄντος αὐτῷ τέκνου.
after him, not being to him[e] a child.[a]
=while he had no child.

Chapter 7

Stephen's Speech to the Sanhedrin

THEN the high priest asked him, "Are these charges true?"

[2] To this he replied: "Brothers and fathers, listen to me! The God of glory appeared to our father Abraham while he was still in Mesopotamia, before he lived in Haran. [3] 'Leave your country and your people,' God said, 'and go to the land I will show you.'[w]

[4] "So he left the land of the Chaldeans and settled in Haran. After the death of his father, God sent him to this land where you are now living. [5] He gave him no inheritance here, not even a foot of ground. But God promised him that he and his descendants after him would possess the land, even though at that time Abraham had no

---

ʷ Gk the Nazorean
ˣ Gk Men, brothers

ᵇ³ Gen. 12:1

had no child. 6 And God spoke in these terms, that his descendants would be resident aliens in a country belonging to others, who would enslave them and mistreat them during four hundred years. 7 'But I will judge the nation that they serve,' said God, 'and after that they shall come out and worship me in this place.' 8 Then he gave him the covenant of circumcision. And so Abraham y became the father of Isaac and circumcised him on the eighth day; and Isaac became the father of Jacob, and Jacob of the twelve patriarchs.

9 "The patriarchs, jealous of Joseph, sold him into Egypt; but God was with him, 10 and rescued him from all his afflictions, and enabled him to win favor and to show wisdom when he stood before Pharaoh, king of Egypt, who appointed him ruler over Egypt and over all his household. 11 Now there came a famine throughout Egypt and Canaan, and great suffering, and our ancestors could find no food. 12 But when Jacob heard that there was grain in Egypt, he sent our ancestors there on their first visit. 13 On the second visit Joseph made himself known to his brothers, and Joseph's family became known to Pharaoh. 14 Then Joseph sent and invited his father Jacob and all his relatives to come to him, seventy-five in all; 15 so Jacob went down to Egypt. He himself died there as

---

6 ἐλάλησεν δὲ οὕτως ὁ θεός, ὅτι ἔσται
And spoke thus — God, that will be

τὸ σπέρμα αὐτοῦ πάροικον ἐν γῇ ἀλλοτρίᾳ,
the seed of him a sojourner in a land belonging to others,

καὶ δουλώσουσιν αὐτὸ καὶ κακώσουσιν
and they will enslave it and will ill-treat

ἔτη τετρακόσια· **7** καὶ τὸ ἔθνος ᾧ ἐὰν
years four hundred; and the nation whichever

δουλεύσουσιν κρινῶ ἐγώ, ὁ θεὸς εἶπεν,
they will serve will judge I, — God said,

καὶ μετὰ ταῦτα ἐξελεύσονται καὶ
and after these things they will come forth and

λατρεύσουσίν μοι ἐν τῷ τόπῳ τούτῳ.
will worship me in this place.

8 καὶ ἔδωκεν αὐτῷ διαθήκην περιτομῆς·
And he gave him a covenant of circumcision;

καὶ οὕτως ἐγέννησεν τὸν Ἰσαὰκ καὶ
and thus he begat — Isaac and

περιέτεμεν αὐτὸν τῇ ἡμέρᾳ τῇ ὀγδόῃ,
circumcised him on the day — eighth,

καὶ Ἰσαὰκ τὸν Ἰακώβ, καὶ Ἰακὼβ
and Isaac [begat] — Jacob, and Jacob [begat]

τοὺς δώδεκα πατριάρχας. **9** Καὶ οἱ
the twelve patriarchs. And the

πατριάρχαι ζηλώσαντες τὸν Ἰωσὴφ
patriarchs becoming jealous — ²Joseph

ἀπέδοντο εἰς Αἴγυπτον· καὶ ἦν ὁ θεὸς
¹sold into Egypt; and was — God

μετ’ αὐτοῦ, **10** καὶ ἐξείλατο αὐτὸν ἐκ
with him, and rescued him out of

πασῶν τῶν θλίψεων αὐτοῦ, καὶ ἔδωκεν
all the afflictions of him, and gave

αὐτῷ χάριν καὶ σοφίαν ἐναντίον Φαραὼ
him favour and wisdom before Pharaoh

βασιλέως Αἰγύπτου, καὶ κατέστησεν αὐτὸν
king of Egypt, and he appointed him

ἡγούμενον ἐπ’ Αἴγυπτον καὶ ὅλον τὸν
governor over Egypt and all the

οἶκον αὐτοῦ. **11** ἦλθεν δὲ λιμὸς ἐφ’
household of him. But came a famine over

ὅλην τὴν Αἴγυπτον καὶ Χανάαν καὶ
all — Egypt and Canaan and

θλῖψις μεγάλη, καὶ οὐχ ηὕρισκον
affliction great, and found not

χορτάσματα οἱ πατέρες ἡμῶν. **12** ἀκούσας
sustenance the fathers of us. ³having heard

δὲ Ἰακὼβ ὄντα σιτία εἰς Αἴγυπτον
¹But ²Jacob ⁶being ⁴corn in Egypt

ἐξαπέστειλεν τοὺς πατέρας ἡμῶν πρῶτον·
sent forth the fathers of us first;

13 καὶ ἐν τῷ δευτέρῳ ἐγνωρίσθη Ἰωσὴφ
and at the second [time] was made known Joseph

τοῖς ἀδελφοῖς αὐτοῦ, καὶ φανερὸν ἐγένετο τῷ
to the brothers of him, and ⁵manifest ⁴became

Φαραὼ τὸ γένος Ἰωσήφ. **14** ἀποστείλας δὲ
⁶to Pharaoh ¹the ²race ³of Joseph. And sending

Ἰωσὴφ μετεκαλέσατο Ἰακὼβ τὸν πατέρα
Joseph called Jacob the father

αὐτοῦ καὶ πᾶσαν τὴν συγγένειαν ἐν
of him and all the(his) kindred in

ψυχαῖς ἑβδομήκοντα πέντε. **15** καὶ κατέβη
souls seventy-five. And went down

Ἰακὼβ εἰς Αἴγυπτον, καὶ ἐτελεύτησεν
Jacob to Egypt, and died

αὐτὸς καὶ οἱ πατέρες ἡμῶν, **16** καὶ
he and the fathers of us, and

---

child. 6 God spoke to him in this way: 'Your descendants will be strangers in a country not their own, and they will be enslaved and mistreated four hundred years. 7 But I will punish the nation they serve as slaves,' God said, 'and afterward they will come out of that country and worship me in this place.' x 8 Then he gave Abraham the covenant of circumcision. And Abraham became the father of Isaac and circumcised him eight days after his birth. Later Isaac became the father of Jacob, and Jacob became the father of the twelve patriarchs.

9 "Because the patriarchs were jealous of Joseph, they sold him as a slave into Egypt. But God was with him 10 and rescued him from all his troubles. He gave Joseph wisdom and enabled him to gain the goodwill of Pharaoh king of Egypt; so he made him ruler over Egypt and all his palace.

11 "Then a famine struck all Egypt and Canaan, bringing great suffering, and our fathers could not find food. 12 When Jacob heard that there was grain in Egypt, he sent our fathers on their first visit. 13 On their second visit, Joseph told his brothers who he was, and Pharaoh learned about Joseph's family. 14 After this, Joseph sent for his father Jacob and his whole family, seventy-five in all. 15 Then Jacob went down to Egypt, where he and our fathers

---

y Gk he　　　　　　　　　x 7 Gen. 15:13,14

well as our ancestors, [16]and their bodies[z] were brought back to Shechem and laid in the tomb that Abraham had bought for a sum of silver from the sons of Hamor in Shechem.

17 "But as the time drew near for the fulfillment of the promise that God had made to Abraham, our people in Egypt increased and multiplied [18]until another king who had not known Joseph ruled over Egypt. [19]He dealt craftily with our race and forced our ancestors to abandon their infants so that they would die. [20]At this time Moses was born, and he was beautiful before God. For three months he was brought up in his father's house; [21]and when he was abandoned, Pharaoh's daughter adopted him and brought him up as her own son. [22]So Moses was instructed in all the wisdom of the Egyptians and was powerful in his words and deeds.

23 "When he was forty years old, it came into his heart to visit his relatives, the Israelites.[a] [24]When he saw one of them being wronged, he defended the oppressed man and avenged him by striking down the Egyptian. [25]He supposed that his kinsfolk would understand that God through him was rescuing them, but they did not understand. [26]The next day he came to some of them as they were quarreling and tried to reconcile them, saying, 'Men, you are brothers; why do you wrong each other?' [27]But

---

μετετέθησαν εἰς Συχὲμ καὶ ἐτέθησαν ἐν
were transferred to Sychem and were put in

τῷ μνήματι ᾧ ὠνήσατο Ἀβραὰμ τιμῆς
the tomb which ²bought ¹Abraham of(for) a price

ἀργυρίου παρὰ τῶν υἱῶν Ἐμμὼρ ἐν
of silver from the sons of Emmor in

Συχέμ. 17 Καθὼς δὲ ἤγγιζεν ὁ χρόνος
Sychem.   And as drew near the time

τῆς ἐπαγγελίας ἧς ὡμολόγησεν ὁ θεὸς
of the promise which ²declared - ¹God

τῷ Ἀβραάμ, ηὔξησεν ὁ λαὸς καὶ
to Abraham, ³grew ¹the ²people and

ἐπληθύνθη ἐν Αἰγύπτῳ, 18 ἄχρι οὗ ἀνέστη
were multiplied in Egypt, until ²rose up

βασιλεὺς ἕτερος ἐπ' Αἴγυπτον, ὃς οὐκ ᾔδει
²king ¹another over Egypt, who did not know

τὸν Ἰωσήφ. 19 οὗτος κατασοφισάμενος
- Joseph. This man dealing craftily with

τὸ γένος ἡμῶν ἐκάκωσεν τοὺς πατέρας
the race of us ill-treated the fathers

τοῦ ποιεῖν τὰ βρέφη ἔκθετα αὐτῶν
- to make[d] ¹the ²babes ⁴exposed ³of them

εἰς τὸ μὴ ζωογονεῖσθαι. 20 Ἐν ᾧ
to the not to be preserved alive. At which
=so that they should not be . . .

καιρῷ ἐγεννήθη Μωϋσῆς, καὶ ἦν ἀστεῖος
time was born Moses, and was fair

τῷ θεῷ· ὃς ἀνετράφη μῆνας τρεῖς ἐν
- to God; who was reared months three in

τῷ οἴκῳ τοῦ πατρός· 21 ἐκτεθέντος δὲ
the house of the(his) father; being exposed and
=and when he was exposed

αὐτοῦ ἀνείλατο αὐτὸν ἡ θυγάτηρ Φαραὼ
him[a] took up him the daughter of Pharaoh

καὶ ἀνεθρέψατο αὐτὸν ἑαυτῇ εἰς υἱόν.
and reared him to herself for a son.
=as her own son.

22 καὶ ἐπαιδεύθη Μωϋσῆς πάσῃ σοφίᾳ
And was trained Moses in all [the] wisdom

Αἰγυπτίων, ἦν δὲ δυνατὸς ἐν λόγοις
of [the] Egyptians, and was powerful in words

καὶ ἔργοις αὐτοῦ. 23 Ὡς δὲ ἐπληροῦτο
and works of him. But when ²was fulfilled

αὐτῷ τεσσερακονταετὴς χρόνος, ἀνέβη ἐπὶ
⁴to him ²of forty years ¹a time, it came up upon

τὴν καρδίαν αὐτοῦ ἐπισκέψασθαι τοὺς
the heart of him to visit the

ἀδελφοὺς αὐτοῦ τοὺς υἱοὺς Ἰσραήλ. 24 καὶ
brothers of him the sons of Israel. And

ἰδών τινα ἀδικούμενον ἠμύνατο, καὶ
seeing one being injured he defended [him], and

ἐποίησεν ἐκδίκησιν τῷ καταπονουμένῳ
he wrought vengeance for the [one] getting the worse

πατάξας τὸν Αἰγύπτιον. 25 ἐνόμιζεν δὲ
striking the Egyptian. Now he supposed

συνιέναι τοὺς ἀδελφοὺς ὅτι ὁ θεὸς διὰ
to understand the(his) brothers[b] that - God through
=that his brothers would understand

χειρὸς αὐτοῦ δίδωσιν σωτηρίαν αὐτοῖς·
hand of him would give salvation to them;

οἱ δὲ οὐ συνῆκαν. 26 τῇ τε ἐπιούσῃ
but they understood not. And on the coming

ἡμέρᾳ ὤφθη αὐτοῖς μαχομένοις, καὶ
day he appeared to them fighting, and

συνήλλασσεν αὐτοὺς εἰς εἰρήνην εἰπών·
attempted to reconcile them in peace saying:

ἄνδρες, ἀδελφοί ἐστε· ἱνατί ἀδικεῖτε
Men, brothers ye are; why injure ye

---

died. [16]Their bodies were brought back to Shechem and placed in the tomb that Abraham had bought from the sons of Hamor at Shechem for a certain sum of money.

[17]"As the time drew near for God to fulfill his promise to Abraham, the number of our people in Egypt greatly increased. [18]Then another king, who knew nothing about Joseph, became ruler of Egypt. [19]He dealt treacherously with our people and oppressed our forefathers by forcing them to throw out their newborn babies so that they would die.

[20]"At that time Moses was born, and he was no ordinary child.[y] For three months he was cared for in his father's house. [21]When he was placed outside, Pharaoh's daughter took him and brought him up as her own son. [22]Moses was educated in all the wisdom of the Egyptians and was powerful in speech and action.

[23]"When Moses was forty years old, he decided to visit his fellow Israelites. [24]He saw one of them being mistreated by an Egyptian, so he went to his defense and avenged him by killing the Egyptian. [25]Moses thought that his own people would realize that God was using him to rescue them, but they did not. [26]The next day Moses came upon two Israelites who were fighting. He tried to reconcile them by saying, 'Men, you are brothers; why do you want to hurt each other?'

---

[z] Gk they
[a] Gk his brothers, the sons of Israel

[y]20 Or was fair in the sight of God

the man who was wronging his neighbor pushed Moses[b] aside, saying, 'Who made you a ruler and a judge over us? 28 Do you want to kill me as you killed the Egyptian yesterday?' 29 When he heard this, Moses fled and became a resident alien in the land of Midian. There he became the father of two sons.

30 "Now when forty years had passed, an angel appeared to him in the wilderness of Mount Sinai, in the flame of a burning bush. 31 When Moses saw it, he was amazed at the sight; and as he approached to look, there came the voice of the Lord: 32 'I am the God of your ancestors, the God of Abraham, Isaac, and Jacob.' Moses began to tremble and did not dare to look. 33 Then the Lord said to him, 'Take off the sandals from your feet, for the place where you are standing is holy ground. 34 I have surely seen the mistreatment of my people who are in Egypt and have heard their groaning, and I have come down to rescue them. Come now, I will send you to Egypt.'

35 "It was this Moses whom they rejected when they said, 'Who made you a ruler and a judge?' and whom God now sent as both ruler and liberator through the angel who appeared to him in the bush. 36 He led them out, having performed wonders and signs in Egypt, at the Red Sea, and in the wilderness for forty years. 37 This is the Moses who said to the

---

ἀλλήλους; 27 ὁ δὲ ἀδικῶν τὸν πλησίον
each other? But the [one] injuring the(his) neighbour

ἀπώσατο αὐτὸν εἰπών· τίς σε κατέστησεν
thrust away him saying: Who thee appointed

ἄρχοντα καὶ δικαστὴν ἐφ' ἡμῶν; 28 μὴ
a ruler and a judge over us? not

ἀνελεῖν με σὺ θέλεις ὃν τρόπον ἀνεῖλες
to kill me thou wishest in the same way as† thou killedst

ἐχθὲς τὸν Αἰγύπτιον; 29 ἔφυγεν δὲ
yesterday the Egyptian? So fled

Μωϋσῆς ἐν τῷ λόγῳ τούτῳ, καὶ ἐγένετο
Moses at this word, and became

πάροικος ἐν γῇ Μαδιάμ, οὗ ἐγέννησεν
a sojourner in [the] land Midian, where he begat

υἱοὺς δύο. 30 Καὶ πληρωθέντων ἐτῶν
sons two. And being fulfilled years
                                     =when forty years were fulfilled

τεσσεράκοντα ὤφθη αὐτῷ ἐν τῇ ἐρήμῳ
forty[a] appeared to him in the desert

τοῦ ὄρους Σινὰ ἄγγελος ἐν φλογὶ πυρὸς
of the mount Sinai an angel in a flame of fire

βάτου. 31 ὁ δὲ Μωϋσῆς ἰδὼν ἐθαύμαζεν
of a thorn bush. - And Moses seeing marvelled at

τὸ ὅραμα· προσερχομένου δὲ αὐτοῦ κατα-
the vision; and approaching him[a] to take
                             =as he approached

νοῆσαι ἐγένετο φωνὴ κυρίου· 32 ἐγὼ ὁ
notice there was a voice of [the] Lord: I the

θεὸς τῶν πατέρων σου, ὁ θεὸς Ἀβραὰμ
God of the fathers of thee, the God of Abraham

καὶ Ἰσαὰκ καὶ Ἰακώβ. ἔντρομος δὲ
and of Isaac and of Jacob. But trembling

γενόμενος Μωϋσῆς οὐκ ἐτόλμα κατανοῆσαι.
becoming Moses dared not to take notice.

33 εἶπεν δὲ αὐτῷ ὁ κύριος· λῦσον τὸ
And said to him the Lord: Loosen the

ὑπόδημα τῶν ποδῶν σου· ὁ γὰρ τόπος
sandal of the feet of thee; for the place

ἐφ' ᾧ ἕστηκας γῆ ἁγία ἐστίν. 34 ἰδὼν
on which thou standest holy is. Seeing

εἶδον τὴν κάκωσιν τοῦ λαοῦ μου τοῦ
I saw the ill-treatment of the people of me -

ἐν Αἰγύπτῳ, καὶ τοῦ στεναγμοῦ αὐτοῦ
in Egypt, and the groan of it

ἤκουσα, καὶ κατέβην ἐξελέσθαι αὐτούς·
I heard, and I came down to rescue them;

καὶ νῦν δεῦρο ἀποστείλω σε εἰς Αἴγυπτον.
and now come I will send thee to Egypt.

35 Τοῦτον τὸν Μωϋσῆν, ὃν ἠρνήσαντο
This Moses, whom they denied

εἰπόντες· τίς σε κατέστησεν ἄρχοντα καὶ
saying: Who thee appointed a ruler and

δικαστήν; τοῦτον ὁ θεὸς καὶ ἄρχοντα
a judge? this man - God both a ruler

καὶ λυτρωτὴν ἀπέσταλκεν σὺν χειρὶ
and a redeemer has sent with [the] hand

ἀγγέλου τοῦ ὀφθέντος αὐτῷ ἐν τῇ βάτῳ.
of [the] angel - appearing to him in the bush.

36 οὗτος ἐξήγαγεν αὐτοὺς ποιήσας τέρατα
This man led forth them doing wonders

καὶ σημεῖα ἐν γῇ Αἰγύπτῳ καὶ ἐν
and signs in [the] land Egypt and in

ἐρυθρᾷ θαλάσσῃ καὶ ἐν τῇ ἐρήμῳ ἔτη
[the] Red Sea and in the desert years

τεσσεράκοντα. 37 οὗτός ἐστιν ὁ Μωϋσῆς
forty. This is the Moses

---

27 "But the man who was mistreating the other pushed Moses aside and said, 'Who made you ruler and judge over us? 28 Do you want to kill me as you killed the Egyptian yesterday?'[z] 29 When Moses heard this, he fled to Midian, where he settled as a foreigner and had two sons.

30 "After forty years had passed, an angel appeared to Moses in the flames of a burning bush in the desert near Mount Sinai. 31 When he saw this, he was amazed at the sight. As he went over to look more closely, he heard the Lord's voice: 32 'I am the God of your fathers, the God of Abraham, Isaac and Jacob.'[a] Moses trembled with fear and did not dare to look.

33 "Then the Lord said to him, 'Take off your sandals; the place where you are standing is holy ground. 34 I have indeed seen the oppression of my people in Egypt. I have heard their groaning and have come down to set them free. Now come, I will send you back to Egypt.'[b]

35 "This is the same Moses whom they had rejected with the words, 'Who made you ruler and judge?' He was sent to be their ruler and deliverer by God himself, through the angel who appeared to him in the bush. 36 He led them out of Egypt and did wonders and miraculous signs in Egypt, at the Red Sea[c] and for forty years in the desert.

37 "This is that Moses

---

[b] Gk him

[z]28 Exodus 2:14
[a]32 Exodus 3:6
[b]34 Exodus 3:5,7,8,10
[c]36 That is, Sea of Reeds

Israelites, 'God will raise up a prophet for you from your own people[c] as he raised me up.' [38] He is the one who was in the congregation in the wilderness with the angel who spoke to him at Mount Sinai, and with our ancestors; and he received living oracles to give to us. [39] Our ancestors were unwilling to obey him; instead, they pushed him aside, and in their hearts they turned back to Egypt, 'Make gods for us who will lead the way for us; as for this Moses who led us out from the land of Egypt, we do not know what has happened to him.' [41] At that time they made a calf, offered a sacrifice to the idol, and reveled in the works of their hands. [42] But God turned away from them and handed them over to worship the host of heaven, as it is written in the book of the prophets:

'Did you offer to me
slain victims and
sacrifices
forty years in the
wilderness,
O house of
Israel?
[43] No; you took along
the tent
of Moloch,
and the star of your
god Rephan,
the images that
you made
to worship;
so I will remove you
beyond
Babylon.'

[44] "Our ancestors had the tent of testimony in the wilderness, as God[d] directed when he spoke to Moses, ordering him to make it according to the pattern he had seen. [45] Our ancestors in turn brought it in with Joshua when they dispossessed the nations that God drove out before

---

ὁ   εἴπας   τοῖς   υἱοῖς   Ἰσραήλ·   προφήτην
–   saying   to the   sons   of Israel :   A prophet

ὑμῖν   ἀναστήσει   ὁ   θεὸς   ἐκ   τῶν   ἀδελφῶν
for you   will raise up   –   God   of   the   brothers

ὑμῶν   ὡς   ἐμέ.   38   οὗτός   ἐστιν   ὁ   γενόμενος
of you   as   me.   This   is   the [one] having been

ἐν   τῇ   ἐκκλησίᾳ   ἐν   τῇ   ἐρήμῳ   μετὰ   τοῦ
in   the   church   in   the   desert   with   the

ἀγγέλου   τοῦ   λαλοῦντος   αὐτῷ   ἐν   τῷ
angel   –   speaking   to him   in   the

ὄρει   Σινὰ   καὶ   τῶν   πατέρων   ἡμῶν,   ὃς
mount   Sinai   and   [with] the   fathers   of us,   who

ἐδέξατο   λόγια   ζῶντα   δοῦναι   ὑμῖν,   39   ᾧ
received   oracles   living   to give   to you,   ¹to whom

οὐκ   ἠθέλησαν   ὑπήκοοι   γενέσθαι   οἱ   πατέρες
¹wished   ⁴not   ⁵obedient   ³to become   ²the   ³fathers

ἡμῶν,   ἀλλὰ   ἀπώσαντο   καὶ   ἐστράφησαν
¹of us,   but   thrust away   and   turned

ἐν   ταῖς   καρδίαις   αὐτῶν   εἰς   Αἴγυπτον,
in   the   hearts   of them   to   Egypt,

40   εἰπόντες   τῷ   Ἀαρών·   ποίησον   ἡμῖν
saying   –   to Aaron :   Make   for us

θεοὺς   οἳ   προπορεύσονται   ἡμῶν·   ὁ   γὰρ
gods   which   will go before   us;   –   for

Μωϋσῆς   οὗτος,   ὃς   ἐξήγαγεν   ἡμᾶς   ἐκ
this Moses,   who   led forth   us   out of

γῆς   Αἰγύπτου,   οὐκ   οἴδαμεν   τί   ἐγένετο
[the] land   Egypt,   we know not   what   happened

αὐτῷ.   41   καὶ   ἐμοσχοποίησαν   ἐν
to him.   And   they made [a model of] a calf   in

ταῖς   ἡμέραις   ἐκείναις   καὶ   ἀνήγαγον   θυσίαν   τῷ
those days   and   brought up   a sacrifice   to the

εἰδώλῳ,   καὶ   εὐφραίνοντο   ἐν   τοῖς   ἔργοις
idol,   and   made merry   in   the   works

τῶν   χειρῶν   αὐτῶν.   42   ἔστρεψεν   δὲ   ὁ
of the   hands   of them.   And   ²turned   –   ¹God

θεὸς   καὶ   παρέδωκεν   αὐτοὺς   λατρεύειν
    and   delivered   them   to worship

τῇ   στρατιᾷ   τοῦ   οὐρανοῦ,   καθὼς   γέγραπται
the   host   –   of heaven,   as   it has been written

ἐν   βίβλῳ   τῶν   προφητῶν·   μὴ   σφάγια
in   [the] roll   of the   prophets :   Not   victims

καὶ   θυσίας   προσηνέγκατέ   μοι   ἔτη
and   sacrifices   ye offered   to me   years

τεσσεράκοντα   ἐν   τῇ   ἐρήμῳ,   οἶκος   Ἰσραήλ,
forty   in   the   desert,   [O] house   of Israel,

43   καὶ   ἀνελάβετε   τὴν   σκηνὴν   τοῦ   Μόλοχ
and   ye took up   the   tent   –   of Moloch

καὶ   τὸ   ἄστρον   τοῦ   θεοῦ   Ῥομφά,   τοὺς
and   the   star   of the   god   Rompha,   the

τύπους   οὓς   ἐποιήσατε   προσκυνεῖν   αὐτοῖς·
models   which   ye made   to worship   them?

καὶ   μετοικιῶ   ὑμᾶς   ἐπέκεινα   Βαβυλῶνος.
and   I will deport   you   beyond   Babylon.

44   Ἡ   σκηνὴ   τοῦ   μαρτυρίου   ἦν   τοῖς
The   tent   –   of witness   was   to the
=Our fathers had the tent of witness

πατράσιν   ἡμῶν   ἐν   τῇ   ἐρήμῳ,   καθὼς
fathers   of us°   in   the   desert,   as

διετάξατο   ὁ   λαλῶν   τῷ   Μωϋσῇ   ποιῆσαι
commanded the   [one] speaking   –   to Moses   to make

αὐτὴν   κατὰ   τὸν   τύπον   ὃν   ἑωράκει·
it   according to   the   model   which   he had seen;

45   ἣν   καὶ   εἰσήγαγον   διαδεξάμενοι   οἱ
which   also   ³brought in   ²having received   ¹the

πατέρες   ἡμῶν   μετὰ   Ἰησοῦ   ἐν   τῇ   κατα-
²fathers   ³of us   with   Jesus   in   the   pos-

---

who told the Israelites, 'God will send you a prophet like me from your own people.'[d] [38] He was in the assembly in the desert, with the angel who spoke to him on Mount Sinai, and with our fathers; and he received living words to pass on to us.

[39] "But our fathers refused to obey him. Instead, they rejected him and in their hearts turned back to Egypt. [40] They told Aaron, 'Make us gods who will go before us. As for this fellow Moses who led us out of Egypt—we don't know what has happened to him!'[e] [41] That was the time they made an idol in the form of a calf. They brought sacrifices to it and held a celebration in honor of what their hands had made. [42] But God turned away and gave them over to the worship of the heavenly bodies. This agrees with what is written in the book of the prophets:

" 'Did you bring me
sacrifices and
offerings
forty years in the
desert, O house of
Israel?
[43] You have lifted up the
shrine of Molech
and the star of your
god Rephan,
the idols you made to
worship.
Therefore I will send you
into exile'[f] beyond
Babylon.

[44] "Our forefathers had the tabernacle of the Testimony with them in the desert. It had been made as God directed Moses, according to the pattern he had seen. [45] Having received the tabernacle, our fathers under Joshua brought it with them when they took the land from the nations God drove out before them. It remained in

---

[c] Gk your brothers
[d] Gk he

[d]37 Deut. 18:15
[e]40 Exodus 32:1
[f]43 Amos 5:25-27

our ancestors. And it was there until the time of David, 46who found favor with God and asked that he might find a dwelling place for the house of Jacob.ᵉ 47But it was Solomon who built a house for him. 48Yet the Most High does not dwell in houses made with human hands;ᶠ as the prophet says,
49 'Heaven is my throne, and the earth is my footstool.
What kind of house will you build for me, says the Lord,
or what is the place of my rest?
50 Did not my hand make all these things?'

51 "You stiff-necked people, uncircumcised in heart and ears, you are forever opposing the Holy Spirit, just as your ancestors used to do. 52Which of the prophets did your ancestors not persecute? They killed those who foretold the coming of the Righteous One, and now you have become his betrayers and murderers. 53You are the ones that received the law as ordained by angels, and yet you have not kept it."

The Stoning of Stephen

54 When they heard these things, they became enraged and ground their teeth at Stephen.ᵍ 55But filled with the Holy Spirit, he gazed into heaven and saw the glory of God and Jesus standing at the right hand of God, 56"Look," he said, "I see the heavens opened and the Son of Man standing at the right hand of God!" 57But they covered their ears, and with a loud shout all rushed together against him. 58Then they

---

σχέσει τῶν ἐθνῶν, ὧν ἐξῶσεν ὁ θεὸς
session of the nations, whom put out - God
ἀπὸ προσώπου τῶν πατέρων ἡμῶν, ἕως
from [the] face of the fathers of us, until
τῶν ἡμερῶν Δαυίδ· 46 ὃς εὗρεν χάριν
the days of David; who found favour
ἐνώπιον τοῦ θεοῦ καὶ ᾐτήσατο εὑρεῖν
before - God and asked to find
σκήνωμα τῷ οἴκῳ Ἰακώβ. 47 Σολομῶν δὲ
a tent for the house of Jacob. But Solomon
οἰκοδόμησεν αὐτῷ οἶκον. 48 ἀλλ'
built for him a house. But
οὐχ ὁ ὕψιστος ἐν χειροποιήτοις κατοικεῖ·
⁴not ¹the ²Most High ⁵in ⁶[places] made by hand ³dwells;
καθὼς ὁ προφήτης λέγει· 49 ὁ οὐρανὸς
as the prophet says: The heaven
μοι θρόνος, ἡ δὲ γῆ ὑποπόδιον τῶν
to me a throne, and the earth a footstool of the
ποδῶν μου· ποῖον οἶκον οἰκοδομήσετέ μοι,
feet of me; what house will ye build for me,
λέγει κύριος, ἢ τίς τόπος τῆς καταπαύσεώς
says [the] Lord, or what place of the rest
μου; 50 οὐχὶ ἡ χείρ μου ἐποίησεν ταῦτα
of me? not the hand of me made these things
πάντα; 51 Σκληροτράχηλοι καὶ ἀπερίτμητοι
all? Hard-necked and uncircumcised
καρδίαις καὶ τοῖς ὠσίν, ὑμεῖς ἀεὶ τῷ
in hearts and - ears, ye always the
πνεύματι τῷ ἁγίῳ ἀντιπίπτετε, ὡς οἱ
Spirit - Holy oppose, as the
πατέρες ὑμῶν καὶ ὑμεῖς. 52 τίνα τῶν
fathers of you also ye. Which of the
προφητῶν οὐκ ἐδίωξαν οἱ πατέρες ὑμῶν;
prophets persecuted not the fathers of you?
καὶ ἀπέκτειναν τοὺς προκαταγγείλαντας
and they killed the [ones] announcing beforehand
περὶ τῆς ἐλεύσεως τοῦ δικαίου, οὗ
concerning the coming of the righteous one, of whom
νῦν ὑμεῖς προδόται καὶ φονεῖς ἐγένεσθε,
now ye betrayers and murderers became,
53 οἵτινες ἐλάβετε τὸν νόμον εἰς διαταγὰς
who received the law in(by) dispositions
ἀγγέλων, καὶ οὐκ ἐφυλάξατε.
of angels, and did not keep [it].
54 Ἀκούοντες δὲ ταῦτα διεπρίοντο ταῖς
And hearing these things they were cut to the
καρδίαις αὐτῶν καὶ ἔβρυχον τοὺς ὀδόντας
hearts of them and gnashed the teeth
ἐπ' αὐτόν. 55 ὑπάρχων δὲ πλήρης
at him. But being full
πνεύματος ἁγίου ἀτενίσας εἰς τὸν οὐρανὸν
of [the] Spirit Holy gazing into - heaven
εἶδεν δόξαν θεοῦ καὶ Ἰησοῦν ἑστῶτα ἐκ
he saw [the] glory of God and Jesus standing at
δεξιῶν τοῦ θεοῦ, 56 καὶ εἶπεν· ἰδοὺ
[the] right [hand] - of God, and said: Behold
θεωρῶ τοὺς οὐρανοὺς διηνοιγμένους καὶ
I see the heavens having been opened up and
τὸν υἱὸν τοῦ ἀνθρώπου ἐκ δεξιῶν ἑστῶτα
the Son - of man at [the] right [hand] standing
τοῦ θεοῦ. 57 κράξαντες δὲ φωνῇ μεγάλῃ
- of God. And crying out voice with a great
συνέσχον τὰ ὦτα αὐτῶν, καὶ ὥρμησαν
they closed the ears of them, and rushed
ὁμοθυμαδὸν ἐπ' αὐτόν, 58 καὶ ἐκβαλόντες
with one mind on him, and casting out

---

the land until the time of David, 46who enjoyed God's favor and asked that he might provide a dwelling place for the God of Jacob.ᵍ 47But it was Solomon who built the house for him.
48"However, the Most High does not live in houses made by men. As the prophet says:
49" 'Heaven is my throne, and the earth is my footstool.
What kind of house will you build for me?
says the Lord.
Or where will my resting place be?
50Has not my hand made all these things?'ʰ

51"You stiff-necked people, with uncircumcised hearts and ears! You are just like your fathers: You always resist the Holy Spirit! 52Was there ever a prophet your fathers did not persecute? They even killed those who predicted the coming of the Righteous One. And now you have betrayed and murdered him— 53you who have received the law that was put into effect through angels but have not obeyed it."

The Stoning of Stephen

54When they heard this, they were furious and gnashed their teeth at him. 55But Stephen, full of the Holy Spirit, looked up to heaven and saw the glory of God, and Jesus standing at the right hand of God. 56"Look," he said, "I see heaven open and the Son of Man standing at the right hand of God."
57At this they covered

ᵉ Other ancient authorities read for the God of Jacob
ᶠ Gk with hands
ᵍ Gk him

ᵍ46 Some early manuscripts the house of Jacob
ʰ50 Isaiah 66:1,2

dragged him out of the city and began to stone him; and the witnesses laid their coats at the feet of a young man named Saul. [59] While they were stoning Stephen, he prayed, "Lord Jesus, receive my spirit." [60] Then he knelt down and cried out in a loud voice, "Lord, do not hold this sin against them." When he had said this, he died. [h] [1] And Saul approved of their killing him.

Saul Persecutes the Church

That day a severe persecution began against the church in Jerusalem, and all except the apostles were scattered throughout the countryside of Judea and Samaria. [2] Devout men buried Stephen and made loud lamentation over him. [3] But Saul was ravaging the church by entering house after house; dragging off both men and women, he committed them to prison.

Philip Preaches in Samaria

[4] Now those who were scattered went from place to place, proclaiming the word. [5] Philip went down to the city[i] of Samaria and proclaimed the Messiah[j] to them. [6] The crowds with one accord listened eagerly to what was said by Philip, hearing and seeing the signs that he did, for unclean spirits, crying with loud shrieks, came out of many who were possessed; and many others who were paralyzed or lame were cured. [8] So there was great

---

ἔξω τῆς πόλεως ἐλιθοβόλουν. καὶ οἱ
outside the city they stoned [him]. And the

μάρτυρες ἀπέθεντο τὰ ἱμάτια αὐτῶν παρὰ
witnesses put off the garments of them at

τοὺς πόδας νεανίου καλουμένου Σαύλου.
the feet of a young man *being* called Saul.

59 καὶ ἐλιθοβόλουν τὸν Στέφανον, ἐπικαλ-
And they stoned - Stephen, invok-

ούμενον καὶ λέγοντα· κύριε Ἰησοῦ, δέξαι
ing [God] and saying: Lord Jesus, receive

τὸ πνεῦμά μου. **60** θεὶς δὲ τὰ γόνατα
the spirit of me. And placing the knees
= kneeling down

ἔκραξεν φωνῇ μεγάλῃ· κύριε, μὴ στήσῃς
he cried voice with a great: Lord, place not

αὐτοῖς ταύτην τὴν ἁμαρτίαν. καὶ τοῦτο
to them this the sin. And ²this

εἰπὼν ἐκοιμήθη. **8** Σαῦλος δὲ ἦν συνευδοκῶν
¹saying he fell asleep. And Saul was consenting

τῇ ἀναιρέσει αὐτοῦ.
to the killing of him.

Ἐγένετο δὲ ἐν ἐκείνῃ τῇ ἡμέρᾳ
And there was in that the day

διωγμὸς μέγας ἐπὶ τὴν ἐκκλησίαν τὴν
persecution a great on(against) the church -

ἐν Ἱεροσολύμοις· πάντες [δὲ] διεσπάρησαν
in Jerusalem; and all were scattered

κατὰ τὰς χώρας τῆς Ἰουδαίας καὶ
throughout the countries of Judæa and

Σαμαρείας πλὴν τῶν ἀποστόλων.
Samaria except the apostles.

2 συνεκόμισαν δὲ τὸν Στέφανον ἄνδρες
And ³recovered - ⁴Stephen ²men

εὐλαβεῖς καὶ ἐποίησαν κοπετὸν μέγαν
¹devout and made lamentation great

ἐπ᾽ αὐτῷ. **3** Σαῦλος δὲ ἐλυμαίνετο τὴν
over him. But Saul ravaged the

ἐκκλησίαν κατὰ τοὺς οἴκους εἰσπορευόμενος,
church house by house† entering,

σύρων τε ἄνδρας καὶ γυναῖκας παρεδίδου
dragging both men and women delivered

εἰς φυλακήν.
to prison.

4 Οἱ μὲν οὖν διασπαρέντες διῆλθον
The [ones] -* therefore being scattered passed through

εὐαγγελιζόμενοι τὸν λόγον. **5** Φίλιππος δὲ
preaching the word. But Philip

κατελθὼν εἰς τὴν πόλιν τῆς
going down to the city the

Σαμαρείας ἐκήρυσσεν αὐτοῖς τὸν Χριστόν.
of Samaria proclaimed to them the Christ.

6 προσεῖχον δὲ οἱ ὄχλοι τοῖς
And gave heed the crowds to the things

λεγομένοις ὑπὸ τοῦ Φιλίππου ὁμοθυμαδὸν
being said by - Philip with one mind

ἐν τῷ ἀκούειν αὐτοὺς καὶ βλέπειν τὰ
in the to hear them and to see[be] the
= as they heard and saw

σημεῖα ἃ ἐποίει. **7** πολλοὶ γὰρ τῶν
signs which he was doing. For many of the

ἐχόντων πνεύματα ἀκάθαρτα βοῶντα φωνῇ
[ones] having spirits unclean crying ²voice

μεγάλῃ ἐξήρχοντο· πολλοὶ δὲ παραλελυμένοι
¹with a great came out; and many *having been* paralysed

καὶ χωλοὶ ἐθεραπεύθησαν· **8** ἐγένετο δὲ
and lame were healed; and there was

* See note on John 19. 24.

---

their ears and, yelling at the top of their voices, they all rushed at him, [58] dragged him out of the city and began to stone him. Meanwhile, the witnesses laid their clothes at the feet of a young man named Saul. [59] While they were stoning him, Stephen prayed, "Lord Jesus, receive my spirit." [60] Then he fell on his knees and cried out, "Lord, do not hold this sin against them." When he had said this, he fell asleep.

Chapter 8

AND Saul was there, giving approval to his death.

The Church Persecuted and Scattered

On that day a great persecution broke out against the church at Jerusalem, and all except the apostles were scattered throughout Judea and Samaria. [2] Godly men buried Stephen and mourned deeply for him. [3] But Saul began to destroy the church. Going from house to house, he dragged off men and women and put them in prison.

Philip in Samaria

[4] Those who had been scattered preached the word wherever they went. [5] Philip went down to a city in Samaria and proclaimed the Christ[i] there. [6] When the crowds heard Philip and saw the miraculous signs he did, they all paid close attention to what he said. [7] With shrieks, evil[j] spirits came out of many, and many paralytics and cripples were healed. [8] So

---

[h] Gk *fell asleep*
[i] Other ancient authorities read *a city*
[j] Or *the Christ*

[i] 5 Or *Messiah*
[j] 7 Greek *unclean*

joy in that city.

9 Now a certain man named Simon had previously practiced magic in the city and amazed the people of Samaria, saying that he was someone great. 10All of them, from the least to the greatest, listened to him eagerly, saying, "This man is the power of God that is called Great." 11And they listened eagerly to him because for a long time he had amazed them with his magic. 12But when they believed Philip, who was proclaiming the good news about the kingdom of God and the name of Jesus Christ, they were baptized, both men and women. 13Even Simon himself believed. After being baptized, he stayed constantly with Philip and was amazed when he saw the signs and great miracles that took place.

14 Now when the apostles at Jerusalem heard that Samaria had accepted the word of God, they sent Peter and John to them. 15The two went down and prayed for them that they might receive the Holy Spirit 16(for as yet the Spirit had not come[k] upon any of them; they had only been baptized in the name of the Lord Jesus. 17Then Peter and John[l] laid their hands on them, and they received the Holy Spirit. 18Now when Simon saw that the Spirit was given through the laying on of the apostles' hands, he offered them money, 19saying, "Give me also this power so that anyone on whom I lay my hands may receive

---

πολλὴ χαρὰ ἐν τῇ πόλει ἐκείνῃ. 9 Ἀνὴρ δέ τις
much   joy   in the city   that.   And a certain man

ὀνόματι Σίμων προϋπῆρχεν ἐν τῇ
by name Simon was previously in the

πόλει μαγεύων καὶ ἐξιστάνων τὸ
city practising sorcery and astonishing the

ἔθνος τῆς Σαμαρείας, λέγων εἶναί τινα
nation - of Samaria, saying ¹to be ²someone

ἑαυτὸν μέγαν, 10 ᾧ προσεῖχον πάντες
¹himself ⁴great, to whom gave heed all

ἀπὸ μικροῦ ἕως μεγάλου λέγοντες· οὗτός
from small to great saying : This man

ἐστιν ἡ δύναμις τοῦ θεοῦ ἡ καλουμένη
is the power of God - being called

μεγάλη. 11 προσεῖχον δὲ αὐτῷ διὰ τὸ
great. And they gave heed to him because of the

ἱκανῷ χρόνῳ ταῖς μαγείαις ἐξεστακέναι
for a considerable time by the sorceries to have astonished
=because for a considerable time he had astonished them by his sorceries.

αὐτούς. 12 ὅτε δὲ ἐπίστευσαν τῷ Φιλίππῳ
them. But when they believed - Philip

εὐαγγελιζομένῳ περὶ τῆς βασιλείας τοῦ
preaching about the kingdom of

θεοῦ καὶ τοῦ ὀνόματος Ἰησοῦ Χριστοῦ,
of God and the name of Jesus Christ,

ἐβαπτίζοντο ἄνδρες τε καὶ γυναῖκες.
they were baptized both men and women.

13 ὁ δὲ Σίμων καὶ αὐτὸς ἐπίστευσεν,
- And Simon also [him]self believed,

καὶ βαπτισθεὶς ἦν προσκαρτερῶν τῷ
and having been baptized was attaching himself -

Φιλίππῳ, θεωρῶν τε σημεῖα καὶ δυνάμεις
to Philip, and beholding signs and powerful deeds

μεγάλας γινομένας ἐξίστατο. 14 Ἀκούσαντες
great happening he was amazed. ⁵hearing

δὲ οἱ ἐν Ἱεροσολύμοις ἀπόστολοι ὅτι
¹And ²the ⁴in ⁶Jerusalem ³apostles that

δέδεκται ἡ Σαμάρεια τὸν λόγον τοῦ
¹has received the Samaria the word of

θεοῦ, ἀπέστειλαν πρὸς αὐτοὺς Πέτρον
of God, they sent to them Peter

καὶ Ἰωάννην, 15 οἵτινες καταβάντες
and John, who going down

προσηύξαντο περὶ αὐτῶν ὅπως λάβωσιν
prayed concerning them so as they might receive

πνεῦμα ἅγιον· 16 οὐδέπω γὰρ ἦν ἐπ᾽
Spirit Holy; for ²not yet ¹he was ⁴on

οὐδενὶ αὐτῶν ἐπιπεπτωκός, μόνον δὲ
⁵no(any)one ⁶of them ³having fallen on, but only

βεβαπτισμένοι ὑπῆρχον εἰς τὸ ὄνομα τοῦ
having been baptized they were in the name of the

κυρίου Ἰησοῦ. 17 τότε ἐπετίθεσαν τὰς
Lord Jesus. Then they laid on the(ir)

χεῖρας ἐπ᾽ αὐτούς, καὶ ἐλάμβανον πνεῦμα
hands on them, and they received ²Spirit

ἅγιον. 18 ἰδὼν δὲ ὁ Σίμων ὅτι διὰ
¹Holy. And ²seeing - ¹Simon that through

τῆς ἐπιθέσεως τῶν χειρῶν τῶν ἀποστόλων
the laying on of the hands of the apostles

δίδοται τὸ πνεῦμα, προσήνεγκεν αὐτοῖς
is(was) given the Spirit, he offered them

χρήματα λέγων· 19 δότε κἀμοὶ τὴν
money saying : Give me also the

ἐξουσίαν ταύτην ἵνα ᾧ ἐὰν ἐπιθῶ τὰς
authority this that whomever I lay on the(my)

---

there was great joy in that city.

Simon the Sorcerer

9Now for some time a man named Simon had practiced sorcery in the city and amazed all the people of Samaria. He boasted that he was someone great, 10and all the people, both high and low, gave him their attention and exclaimed, "This man is the divine power known as the Great Power." 11They followed him because he had amazed them for a long time with his magic. 12But when they believed Philip as he preached the good news of the kingdom of God and the name of Jesus Christ, they were baptized, both men and women. 13Simon himself believed and was baptized. And he followed Philip everywhere, astonished by the great signs and miracles he saw.

14When the apostles in Jerusalem heard that Samaria had accepted the word of God, they sent Peter and John to them. 15When they arrived, they prayed for them that they might receive the Holy Spirit, 16because the Holy Spirit had not yet come upon any of them; they had simply been baptized into[k] the name of the Lord Jesus. 17Then Peter and John placed their hands on them, and they received the Holy Spirit.

18When Simon saw that the Spirit was given at the laying on of the apostles' hands, he offered them money 19and said, "Give me also this ability so that everyone on whom I lay my hands may receive the Holy Spirit."

---

[k] Gk fallen
[l] Gk they

[k] 16 Or in

the Holy Spirit." 20 But Peter said to him, "May your silver perish with you, because you thought you could obtain God's gift with money! 21 You have no part or share in this, for your heart is not right before God. 22 Repent therefore of this wickedness of yours, and pray to the Lord that, if possible, the intent of your heart may be forgiven you. 23 For I see that you are in the gall of bitterness and the chains of wickedness." 24 Simon answered, "Pray for me to the Lord, that nothing of what you[m] have said may happen to me."

25 Now after Peter and John[n] had testified and spoken the word of the Lord, they returned to Jerusalem, proclaiming the good news to many villages of the Samaritans.

Philip and the Ethiopian Eunuch

26 Then an angel of the Lord said to Philip, "Get up and go toward the south[o] to the road that goes down from Jerusalem to Gaza." (This is a wilderness road.) 27 So he got up and went. Now there was an Ethiopian eunuch, a court official of the Candace, queen of the Ethiopians, in charge of her entire treasury. He had come to Jerusalem to worship 28 and was returning home; seated in his chariot, he was reading the prophet Isaiah. 29 Then the Spirit said to Philip, "Go over to this chariot and join it."

χεῖρας λαμβάνῃ πνεῦμα ἅγιον. **20** Πέτρος δὲ
hands he may receive Spirit Holy.   But Peter

εἶπεν πρὸς αὐτόν· τὸ ἀργύριόν σου
said   to   him: The silver   of thee

σὺν σοὶ εἴη εἰς ἀπώλειαν, ὅτι τὴν δωρεὰν
with thee may it be into perdition, because the gift

τοῦ θεοῦ ἐνόμισας διὰ χρημάτων κτᾶσθαι.
– of God thou didst suppose through money   to get.

21 οὐκ ἔστιν σοι μερὶς οὐδὲ κλῆρος
There is not to thee[e] part nor lot
=Thou hast no

ἐν τῷ λόγῳ τούτῳ· ἡ γὰρ καρδία σου
in this matter;   for the heart of thee

οὐκ ἔστιν εὐθεῖα ἔναντι τοῦ θεοῦ.
is not right before   – God.

22 μετανόησον οὖν ἀπὸ τῆς κακίας σου
Repent thou therefore from – ²wickedness ³of thee

ταύτης, καὶ δεήθητι τοῦ κυρίου εἰ ἄρα
¹this, and petition the Lord if perhaps

ἀφεθήσεταί σοι ἡ ἐπίνοια τῆς καρδίας
will be forgiven thee the thought of the heart

σου· **23** εἰς γὰρ χολὴν πικρίας καὶ
of thee; for in gall of bitterness and

σύνδεσμον ἀδικίας ὁρῶ σε ὄντα.
bond of unrighteousness I see thee being.

24 ἀποκριθεὶς δὲ ὁ Σίμων εἶπεν· δεήθητε
And answering – Simon said: Petition

ὑμεῖς ὑπὲρ ἐμοῦ πρὸς τὸν κύριον, ὅπως
ye for me to the Lord, so as

μηδὲν ἐπέλθῃ ἐπ' ἐμὲ ὧν εἰρήκατε.
¹not one ⁴may come on ³on ⁵me ²of the ⁶ye have
                        things which spoken.

25 Οἱ μὲν οὖν διαμαρτυράμενοι καὶ λαλή-
They – therefore having solemnly witnessed and having

σαντες τὸν λόγον τοῦ κυρίου ὑπέστρεφον
spoken the word of the Lord returned

εἰς Ἰεροσόλυμα, πολλάς τε κώμας τῶν
to Jerusalem, and ²many ³villages ⁴of the

Σαμαριτῶν εὐηγγελίζοντο.
⁵Samaritans ¹evangelized.

26 Ἄγγελος δὲ κυρίου ἐλάλησεν πρὸς
But an angel of [the] Lord spoke to

Φίλιππον λέγων· ἀνάστηθι καὶ πορεύου
Philip saying: Rise up and go

κατὰ μεσημβρίαν ἐπὶ τὴν ὁδὸν τὴν
along south on the way the

καταβαίνουσαν ἀπὸ Ἰερουσαλὴμ εἰς Γάζαν·
going down from Jerusalem to Gaza;

αὕτη ἐστὶν ἔρημος. **27** καὶ ἀναστὰς
this is desert. And rising up

ἐπορεύθη. καὶ ἰδοὺ ἀνὴρ Αἰθίοψ εὐνοῦχος
he went. And behold[,] a man Ethiopian a eunuch

δυνάστης Κανδάκης βασιλίσσης Αἰθιόπων,
a courtier of Candace queen of [the]
                                    Ethiopians,

ὃς ἦν ἐπὶ πάσης τῆς γάζης αὐτῆς,
who was over all the treasure of her,

[ὃς] ἐληλύθει προσκυνήσων εἰς Ἰερουσαλήμ,
who had come worshipping in Jerusalem,

28 ἦν δὲ ὑποστρέφων καὶ καθήμενος ἐπὶ
and was returning and sitting on

τοῦ ἅρματος αὐτοῦ καὶ ἀνεγίνωσκεν τὸν
the chariot of him and was reading the

προφήτην Ἠσαΐαν. **29** εἶπεν δὲ τὸ πνεῦμα
prophet Esaias. And said the Spirit

τῷ Φιλίππῳ· πρόσελθε καὶ κολλήθητι
– to Philip: Approach and keep company with

---

20 Peter answered: "May your money perish with you, because you thought you could buy the gift of God with money! 21 You have no part or share in this ministry, because your heart is not right before God. 22 Repent of this wickedness and pray to the Lord. Perhaps he will forgive you for having such a thought in your heart. 23 For I see that you are full of bitterness and captive to sin." 24 Then Simon answered, "Pray to the Lord for me so that nothing you have said may happen to me."

25 When they had testified and proclaimed the word of the Lord, Peter and John returned to Jerusalem, preaching the gospel in many Samaritan villages.

Philip and the Ethiopian

26 Now an angel of the Lord said to Philip, "Go south to the road—the desert road—that goes down from Jerusalem to Gaza." 27 So he started out, and on his way he met an Ethiopian[l] eunuch, an important official in charge of all the treasury of Candace, queen of the Ethiopians. This man had gone to Jerusalem to worship, 28 and on his way home was sitting in his chariot reading the book of Isaiah the prophet. 29 The Spirit told Philip, "Go to

---

m The Greek word for you and the verb pray are plural
n Gk after they
o Or go at noon

l 27 That is, from the upper Nile region

30 So Philip ran up to it and heard him reading the prophet Isaiah. He asked, "Do you understand what you are reading?" 31 He replied, "How can I, unless someone guides me?" And he invited Philip to get in and sit beside him. 32 Now the passage of the scripture that he was reading was this:

"Like a sheep he was
   led to the
   slaughter,
and like a lamb
   silent before
   its shearer,
so he does not
   open his mouth.
33 In his humiliation
   justice was
   denied him.
Who can describe
   his generation?
For his life is
   taken away from
   the earth."

34 The eunuch asked Philip, "About whom, may I ask you, does the prophet say this, about himself or about someone else?" 35 Then Philip began to speak, and starting with this scripture, he proclaimed to him the good news about Jesus. 36 As they were going along the road, they came to some water; and the eunuch said, "Look, here is water! What is to prevent me from being baptized?" p 38 He commanded the chariot to stop, and both of them, Philip and the eunuch, went down into the water, and Philip q baptized him. 39 When they came out of the water, the Spirit of the Lord snatched Philip away; the eunuch saw him no more, and went on his way rejoicing. 40 But Philip found himself at Azotus, and as he was passing through the

---

τῷ ἅρματι τούτῳ.
this chariot.

30 προσδραμὼν δὲ
And running up

ὁ Φίλιππος ἤκουσεν αὐτοῦ ἀναγινώσκοντος
- Philip heard him reading

'Ησαΐαν τὸν προφήτην, καὶ εἶπεν· ἆρά γε
Esaias the prophet, and said: Then

γινώσκεις ἃ ἀναγινώσκεις; **31** ὁ δὲ
knowest thou what things thou art reading? And he

εἶπεν· πῶς γὰρ ἂν δυναίμην ἐὰν μὴ
said: How indeed should I be able unless

τις ὁδηγήσει με; παρεκάλεσέν τε τὸν
someone shall guide me? And he besought -

Φίλιππον ἀναβάντα καθίσαι σὺν αὐτῷ.
Philip coming up to sit with him.

32 ἡ δὲ περιοχὴ τῆς γραφῆς ἦν ἀνεγίνω-
Now the passage of the scripture which he was

σκεν ἦν αὕτη· ὡς πρόβατον ἐπὶ σφαγὴν
reading was this: As a sheep to slaughter

ἤχθη, καὶ ὡς ἀμνὸς ἐναντίον τοῦ κείροντος
he was led, and as a lamb before the [one] shearing

αὐτὸν ἄφωνος, οὕτως οὐκ ἀνοίγει τὸ
it [is] dumb, so he opens not the

στόμα αὐτοῦ. **33** Ἐν τῇ ταπεινώσει
mouth of him. In the humiliation

ἡ κρίσις αὐτοῦ ἤρθη· τὴν γενεὰν αὐτοῦ
the judgment of him was taken away; the generation of him

τίς διηγήσεται; ὅτι αἴρεται ἀπὸ τῆς
who will relate? because is taken from the

γῆς ἡ ζωὴ αὐτοῦ. **34** ἀποκριθεὶς δὲ ὁ
earth the life of him. And answering -

εὐνοῦχος τῷ Φιλίππῳ εἶπεν· δέομαί σου,
eunuch to Philip said: I ask thee,

περὶ τίνος ὁ προφήτης λέγει τοῦτο;
about whom the prophet says this?

περὶ ἑαυτοῦ ἢ περὶ ἑτέρου τινός;
about himself or about other someone?

35 ἀνοίξας δὲ ὁ Φίλιππος τὸ στόμα
And opening - Philip the mouth

αὐτοῦ καὶ ἀρξάμενος ἀπὸ τῆς γραφῆς ταύτης
of him and beginning from this scripture

εὐηγγελίσατο αὐτῷ τὸν Ἰησοῦν.
preached to him - Jesus.

36 ὡς δὲ ἐπορεύοντο κατὰ τὴν ὁδόν,
And as they were going along the way,

ἦλθον ἐπί τι ὕδωρ, καί φησιν ὁ εὐνοῦχος·
they came upon certain water, and says the eunuch:

ἰδοὺ ὕδωρ· τί κωλύει με βαπτισθῆναι;‡
Behold[,] water; what prevents me to be baptized?

38 καὶ ἐκέλευσεν στῆναι τὸ ἅρμα, καὶ
And he commanded to stand the chariot, and

κατέβησαν ἀμφότεροι εἰς τὸ ὕδωρ, ὅ
went down both into the water, -

τε Φίλιππος καὶ ὁ εὐνοῦχος, καὶ ἐβάπτισεν
both Philip and the eunuch, and he baptized

αὐτόν. **39** ὅτε δὲ ἀνέβησαν ἐκ τοῦ ὕδατος,
him. And when they came up out of the water,

πνεῦμα κυρίου ἥρπασεν τὸν Φίλιππον,
[the] Spirit of [the] Lord seized - Philip,

καὶ οὐκ εἶδεν αὐτὸν οὐκέτι ὁ εὐνοῦχος,
and saw not him no(any) more the eunuch,

ἐπορεύετο γὰρ τὴν ὁδὸν αὐτοῦ χαίρων.
for he went the way of him rejoicing.

40 Φίλιππος δὲ εὑρέθη εἰς Ἄζωτον, καὶ
But Philip was found in Azotus, and

---

that chariot and stay near it."
30 Then Philip ran up to the chariot and heard the man reading Isaiah the prophet. "Do you understand what you are reading?" Philip asked.
31 "How can I," he said, "unless someone explains it to me?" So he invited Philip to come up and sit with him.
32 The eunuch was reading this passage of Scripture:

"He was led like a sheep
   to the slaughter,
and as a lamb before
   the shearer is silent,
so he did not open his
   mouth.
33 In his humiliation he was
   deprived of justice.
Who can speak of his
   descendants?
For his life was taken
   from the earth." m

34 The eunuch asked Philip, "Tell me, please, who is the prophet talking about, himself or someone else?"
35 Then Philip began with that very passage of Scripture and told him the good news about Jesus.
36 As they traveled along the road, they came to some water and the eunuch said, "Look, here is water. Why shouldn't I be baptized?" n 38 And he gave orders to stop the chariot. Then both Philip and the eunuch went down into the water and Philip baptized him. 39 When they came up out of the water, the Spirit of the Lord suddenly took Philip away, and the eunuch did not see him again, but went on his way rejoicing. 40 Philip, however, appeared at Azotus and trav-

---

p Other ancient authorities add all or most of verse 37, And Philip said, "If you believe with all your heart, you may." And he replied, "I believe that Jesus Christ is the Son of God."
q Gk he

‡ Verse 37 omitted by Nestle; cf. NIV footnote.

m33 Isaiah 53:7,8
n36 Some late manuscripts baptized?" 37Philip said, "If you believe with all your heart, you may." The eunuch answered, "I believe that Jesus Christ is the Son of God."

region, he proclaimed the good news to all the towns until he came to Caesarea.

Chapter 9

The Conversion of Saul

MEANWHILE Saul, still breathing threats and murder against the disciples of the Lord, went to the high priest 2 and asked him for letters to the synagogues at Damascus, so that if he found any who belonged to the Way, men or women, he might bring them bound to Jerusalem. 3 Now as he was going along and approaching Damascus, suddenly a light from heaven flashed around him. 4 He fell to the ground and heard a voice saying to him, "Saul, Saul, why do you persecute me?" 5 He asked, "Who are you, Lord?" The reply came, "I am Jesus, whom you are persecuting. 6 But get up and enter the city, and you will be told what you are to do." 7 The men who were traveling with him stood speechless because they heard the voice but saw no one. 8 Saul got up from the ground, and though his eyes were open, he could see nothing; so they led him by the hand and brought him into Damascus. 9 For three days he was without sight, and neither ate nor drank.

10 Now there was a disciple in Damascus named Ananias. The Lord said to him in a vision, "Ananias." He answered, "Here I am, Lord." 11 The Lord said to him, "Get up and go to the

---

διερχόμενος εὐηγγελίζετο τὰς πόλεις πάσας
passing through he evangelized the cities all
ἕως τοῦ ἐλθεῖν αὐτὸν[b] εἰς Καισάρειαν.
until the to come him to Cæsarea.
=he came

9 Ὁ δὲ Σαῦλος ἔτι ἐμπνέων ἀπειλῆς
  – But Saul still breathing threatening
καὶ φόνου εἰς τοὺς μαθητὰς τοῦ κυρίου,
and murder against the disciples of the Lord,
προσελθὼν τῷ ἀρχιερεῖ **2** ᾐτήσατο παρ᾽
approaching to the high priest   asked from
αὐτοῦ ἐπιστολὰς εἰς Δαμασκὸν πρὸς τὰς
him letters to Damascus for the
συναγωγάς, ὅπως ἐάν τινας εὕρῃ τῆς
synagogues, so as if ¹any ¹he found ⁴of the
ὁδοῦ ὄντας, ἄνδρας τε καὶ γυναῖκας, δεδεμένους
⁵way ³being, both men and women, ²having been bound
ἀγάγῃ εἰς Ἰερουσαλήμ. **3** Ἐν
¹he might bring [them] to Jerusalem. in
δὲ τῷ πορεύεσθαι ἐγένετο αὐτὸν ἐγγίζειν
Now the to go[e] it came to pass him to draw near[b]
=as he went   =he drew near
τῇ Δαμασκῷ, ἐξαίφνης τε αὐτὸν περιήστ-
  – to Damascus, and suddenly ⁵him ²shone
ραψεν φῶς ἐκ τοῦ οὐρανοῦ, **4** καὶ πεσὼν
round ¹a light ³out of – ⁴heaven, and falling
ἐπὶ τὴν γῆν ἤκουσεν φωνὴν λέγουσαν
on the earth he heard a voice saying
αὐτῷ· Σαοὺλ Σαούλ, τί με διώκεις;
to him : Saul[,] Saul, why me persecutest thou?
5 εἶπεν δέ· τίς εἶ, κύριε; ὁ δέ· ἐγώ
  And he said : Who art thou, Lord? And he [said] : I
εἰμι Ἰησοῦς ὃν σὺ διώκεις· **6** ἀλλὰ
am Jesus whom thou persecutest; but
ἀνάστηθι καὶ εἴσελθε εἰς τὴν πόλιν,
rise thou up, and enter into the city,
καὶ λαληθήσεταί σοι ὅ τί σε δεῖ ποιεῖν.
and it shall be told thee what thee it behoves to do.
7 οἱ δὲ ἄνδρες οἱ συνοδεύοντες αὐτῷ
Now the men – journeying with him
εἱστήκεισαν ἐνεοί, ἀκούοντες μὲν τῆς
stood speechless, hearing indeed the
φωνῆς, μηδένα δὲ θεωροῦντες. **8** ἠγέρθη δὲ
sound, but no man beholding. And was raised
Σαῦλος ἀπὸ τῆς γῆς, ἀνεῳγμένων δὲ
Saul from the ground, and having been opened
=when his eyes were opened
τῶν ὀφθαλμῶν αὐτοῦ οὐδὲν ἔβλεπεν·
the eyes of him[a] nothing he saw;
χειραγωγοῦντες δὲ αὐτὸν εἰσήγαγον εἰς
and leading by the hand   him they brought in into
Δαμασκόν. **9** καὶ ἦν ἡμέρας τρεῖς μὴ
Damascus. And he was days three not
βλέπων, καὶ οὐκ ἔφαγεν οὐδὲ ἔπιεν.
seeing, and ate not nor drank.
10 Ἦν δέ τις μαθητὴς ἐν Δαμασκῷ
Now there was a certain disciple in Damascus
ὀνόματι Ἀνανίας, καὶ εἶπεν πρὸς αὐτὸν
by name Ananias, and said to him
ἐν ὁράματι ὁ κύριος· Ἀνανία. ὁ δὲ
in a vision the Lord : Ananias. And he
εἶπεν· ἰδοὺ ἐγώ, κύριε. **11** ὁ δὲ κύριος
said : Behold[,] I, Lord. And the Lord
πρὸς αὐτόν· ἀναστὰς πορεύθητι ἐπὶ τὴν
[said] to him : Rising up go thou to the

---

eled about, preaching the gospel in all the towns until he reached Caesarea.

Chapter 9

Saul's Conversion

MEANWHILE, Saul was still breathing out murderous threats against the Lord's disciples. He went to the high priest 2 and asked him for letters to the synagogues in Damascus, so that if he found any there who belonged to the Way, whether men or women, he might take them as prisoners to Jerusalem. 3 As he neared Damascus on his journey, suddenly a light from heaven flashed around him. 4 He fell to the ground and heard a voice say to him, "Saul, Saul, why do you persecute me?"

5 "Who are you, Lord?" Saul asked.

"I am Jesus, whom you are persecuting," he replied. 6 "Now get up and go into the city, and you will be told what you must do."

7 The men traveling with Saul stood there speechless; they heard the sound but did not see anyone. 8 Saul got up from the ground, but when he opened his eyes he could see nothing. So they led him by the hand into Damascus. 9 For three days he was blind, and did not eat or drink anything.

10 In Damascus there was a disciple named Ananias. The Lord called to him in a vision, "Ananias!"

"Yes, Lord," he answered.

11 The Lord told him, "Go to the house of Judas on

street called Straight, and at the house of Judas look for a man of Tarsus named Saul. At this moment he is praying, 12 and he has seen in a vision[r] a man named Ananias come in and lay his hands on him so that he might regain his sight." 13 But Ananias answered, "Lord, I have heard from many about this man, how much evil he has done to your saints in Jerusalem; 14 and here he has authority from the chief priests to bind all who invoke your name." 15 But the Lord said to him, "Go, for he is an instrument whom I have chosen to bring my name before Gentiles and kings and before the people of Israel; 16 I will show him how much he must suffer for the sake of my name." 17 So Ananias went and entered the house. He laid his hands on Saul[s] and said, "Brother Saul, the Lord Jesus, who appeared to you on your way here, has sent me so that you may regain your sight and be filled with the Holy Spirit." 18 And immediately something like scales fell from his eyes, and his sight was restored. Then he got up and was baptized, 19 and after taking some food, he regained his strength.

Saul Preaches in Damascus

For several days he was with the disciples in Damascus, 20 and immediately he began to proclaim Jesus in the synagogues, saying, "He is the Son of God." 21 All who heard him were amazed and said, "Is not this the man who made havoc in Jerusalem among those who invoked this name? And has he not

---

ῥύμην τὴν καλουμένην εὐθεῖαν καὶ ζήτησον
street — being called Straight and seek

ἐν οἰκίᾳ Ἰούδα Σαῦλον ὀνόματι Ταρσέα·
in [the] house of Judas ²Saul ³by name ¹a Tarsian;

ἰδοὺ γὰρ προσεύχεται, 12 καὶ εἶδεν ἄνδρα
for behold he is praying, and saw ²a man

[ἐν ὁράματι] Ἀνανίαν ὀνόματι εἰσελθόντα
¹in ²a vision Ananias by name coming in

καὶ ἐπιθέντα αὐτῷ χεῖρας, ὅπως ἀναβλέψῃ.
and putting on him hands, so as he may see again.

13 ἀπεκρίθη δὲ Ἀνανίας· κύριε, ἤκουσα
And answered Ananias: Lord, I heard

ἀπὸ πολλῶν περὶ τοῦ ἀνδρὸς τούτου,
from many about this man,

ὅσα κακὰ τοῖς ἁγίοις σου ἐποίησεν
how many evil things to the saints of thee he did

ἐν Ἰερουσαλήμ· 14 καὶ ὧδε ἔχει ἐξουσίαν
in Jerusalem; and here he has authority

παρὰ τῶν ἀρχιερέων δῆσαι πάντας τοὺς
from the chief priests to bind all the

ἐπικαλουμένους τὸ ὄνομά σου. 15 εἶπεν
[ones] invoking the name of thee. said

δὲ πρὸς αὐτὸν ὁ κύριος· πορεύου, ὅτι
But to him the Lord: Go thou, because

σκεῦος ἐκλογῆς ἐστίν μοι οὗτος τοῦ
²a vessel ³of choice ¹is ⁴to me ⁵this man of

βαστάσαι τὸ ὄνομά μου ἐνώπιον [τῶν]
to bear[d] the name of me ⁶before ⁵the

ἐθνῶν τε καὶ βασιλέων υἱῶν τε Ἰσραήλ·
⁴nations ¹both ²and ³kings ⁶sons ⁷and ⁸of Israel;

16 ἐγὼ γὰρ ὑποδείξω αὐτῷ ὅσα δεῖ
for I will show him how many things it behoves

αὐτὸν ὑπὲρ τοῦ ὀνόματός μου παθεῖν.
him on behalf of the name of me to suffer.

17 Ἀπῆλθεν δὲ Ἀνανίας καὶ εἰσῆλθεν
And went away Ananias and entered

εἰς τὴν οἰκίαν, καὶ ἐπιθεὶς ἐπ᾽ αὐτὸν
into the house, and putting on on him

τὰς χεῖρας εἶπεν· Σαοὺλ ἀδελφέ, ὁ
the(his) hands said: Saul brother, the

κύριος ἀπέσταλκέν με, Ἰησοῦς ὁ ὀφθείς σοι
Lord has sent me, Jesus the [one] appear- to thee
                                     ing

ἐν τῇ ὁδῷ ᾗ ἤρχου, ὅπως ἀναβλέψῃς
in the way which thou camest, so as thou mayest see again

καὶ πλησθῇς πνεύματος ἁγίου. 18 καὶ
and be filled of(with) Spirit Holy. And

εὐθέως ἀπέπεσαν αὐτοῦ ἀπὸ τῶν ὀφθαλμῶν
immediately fell away of him from the eyes

ὡς λεπίδες, ἀνέβλεψέν τε, καὶ ἀναστὰς
as scales, and he saw again, and rising up

ἐβαπτίσθη, 19 καὶ λαβὼν τροφὴν ἐνίσχυσεν.
was baptized, and taking food was strengthened.

Ἐγένετο δὲ μετὰ τῶν ἐν Δαμασκῷ
Now he was with the in Damascus

μαθητῶν ἡμέρας τινάς, 20 καὶ εὐθέως
disciples days some, and immediately

ἐν ταῖς συναγωγαῖς ἐκήρυσσεν τὸν Ἰησοῦν,
in the synagogues he proclaimed — Jesus,

ὅτι οὗτός ἐστιν ὁ υἱὸς τοῦ θεοῦ.
that this one is the Son — of God.

21 ἐξίσταντο δὲ πάντες οἱ ἀκούοντες καὶ
And were amazed all the [ones] hearing and

ἔλεγον· οὐχ οὗτός ἐστιν ὁ πορθήσας
said: Not this man is the [one] having destroyed

εἰς Ἰερουσαλὴμ τοὺς ἐπικαλουμένους
in Jerusalem the [ones] invoking

Straight Street and ask for a man from Tarsus named Saul, for he is praying. 12 In a vision he has seen a man named Ananias come and place his hands on him to restore his sight."
13 "Lord," Ananias answered, "I have heard many reports about this man and all the harm he has done to your saints in Jerusalem. 14 And he has come here with authority from the chief priests to arrest all who call on your name."
15 But the Lord said to Ananias, "Go! This man is my chosen instrument to carry my name before the Gentiles and their kings and before the people of Israel. 16 I will show him how much he must suffer for my name."
17 Then Ananias went to the house and entered it. Placing his hands on Saul, he said, "Brother Saul, the Lord—Jesus, who appeared to you on the road as you were coming here—has sent me so that you may see again and be filled with the Holy Spirit." 18 Immediately, something like scales fell from Saul's eyes, and he could see again. He got up and was baptized, 19 and after taking some food, he regained his strength.

Saul in Damascus and Jerusalem

Saul spent several days with the disciples in Damascus. 20 At once he began to preach in the synagogues that Jesus is the Son of God. 21 All those who heard him were astonished and asked, "Isn't he the man who raised havoc in Jerusalem among those who call on this name? And hasn't

---

[r] Other ancient authorities lack *in a vision*
[s] Gk *him*

come here for the purpose of bringing them bound before the chief priests?" 22 Saul became increasingly more powerful and confounded the Jews who lived in Damascus by proving that Jesus[t] was the Messiah.[u]

Saul Escapes from the Jews

23 After some time had passed, the Jews plotted to kill him, 24 but their plot became known to Saul. They were watching the gates day and night so that they might kill him; 25 but his disciples took him by night and let him down through an opening in the wall,[v] lowering him in a basket.

Saul in Jerusalem

26 When he had come to Jerusalem, he attempted to join the disciples; and they were all afraid of him, for they did not believe that he was a disciple. 27 But Barnabas took him, brought him to the apostles, and described for them how on the road he had seen the Lord, who had spoken to him, and how in Damascus he had spoken boldly in the name of Jesus. 28 So he went in and out among them in Jerusalem, speaking boldly in the name of the Lord. 29 He spoke and argued with the Hellenists; but they were attempting to kill him. 30 When the believers[w] learned of it, they brought him down to Caesarea and sent him off to Tarsus.
31 Meanwhile the church throughout Judea, Galilee, and Samaria had peace and was built up.

τὸ ὄνομα τοῦτο, καὶ ὧδε εἰς τοῦτο ἐληλύθει,
this name,   and   here for   this he had come,
ἵνα δεδεμένους αὐτοὺς ἀγάγῃ ἐπὶ τοὺς
that having been bound them   he might bring before the
ἀρχιερεῖς; 22 Σαῦλος δὲ μᾶλλον ἐνε-
chief priests? But Saul   more   was filled
δυναμοῦτο καὶ συνέχυννεν Ἰουδαίους τοὺς κατ-
with power   and confounded   Jews   the [ones]
οἰκοῦντας ἐν Δαμασκῷ, συμβιβάζων ὅτι οὗτός
dwelling   in Damascus,   proving   that this one
ἐστιν ὁ χριστός. 23 Ὡς δὲ ἐπληροῦντο
is   the Christ.   And when   were fulfilled
ἡμέραι ἱκαναί,   24 συνεβουλεύσαντο
days   considerable(many),   consulted together
οἱ Ἰουδαῖοι ἀνελεῖν αὐτόν· ἐγνώσθη δὲ
the Jews   to kill   him;   but was known
τῷ Σαύλῳ ἡ ἐπιβουλὴ αὐτῶν. παρετη-
- to Saul the plot   of them.   And they
ροῦντο δὲ καὶ τὰς πύλας ἡμέρας τε καὶ
carefully watched also the gates both by day and
νυκτὸς ὅπως αὐτὸν ἀνέλωσιν· 25 λαβόντες δὲ
by night so as him   they might destroy;   but ⁴taking
οἱ μαθηταὶ αὐτοῦ νυκτὸς διὰ τοῦ
¹the ²disciples ³of him by night through the
τείχους καθῆκαν αὐτὸν χαλάσαντες ἐν
wall   let down   him   lowering   in
σπυρίδι. 26 Παραγενόμενος δὲ εἰς
a basket.   And arriving   at
Ἰερουσαλὴμ ἐπείραζεν κολλᾶσθαι τοῖς
Jerusalem   he tried   to be joined to the
μαθηταῖς· καὶ πάντες ἐφοβοῦντο αὐτόν,
disciples;   and   all   feared   him,
μὴ πιστεύοντες ὅτι ἐστὶν μαθητής.
not believing   that he is(was) a disciple.
27 Βαρνάβας δὲ ἐπιλαβόμενος αὐτὸν ἤγαγεν
But Barnabas   taking hold of   him   led
πρὸς τοὺς ἀποστόλους, καὶ διηγήσατο
to   the   apostles,   and   narrated
αὐτοῖς πῶς ἐν τῇ ὁδῷ εἶδεν τὸν κύριον
to them how in the way he saw the Lord
καὶ ὅτι ἐλάλησεν αὐτῷ, καὶ πῶς ἐν
and that he spoke   to him, and how in
Δαμασκῷ ἐπαρρησιάσατο ἐν τῷ ὀνόματι
Damascus   he spoke boldly   in the   name
Ἰησοῦ. 28 καὶ ἦν μετ' αὐτῶν εἰσπορευόμενος
of Jesus. And he was with them   going in
καὶ ἐκπορευόμενος εἰς Ἰερουσαλήμ,
and going out   in Jerusalem,
παρρησιαζόμενος ἐν τῷ ὀνόματι τοῦ
speaking boldly   in the   name   of the
κυρίου, 29 ἐλάλει τε καὶ συνεζήτει πρὸς
Lord,   ²spoke ¹both ³and ⁴discussed with
τοὺς Ἑλληνιστάς· οἱ δὲ ἐπεχείρουν ἀνελεῖν
the Hellenists;   and they attempted   to kill
αὐτόν. 30 ἐπιγνόντες δὲ οἱ ἀδελφοὶ
him.   But ²knowing   ¹the ²brothers
κατήγαγον αὐτὸν εἰς Καισάρειαν καὶ
brought down him   to   Cæsarea   and
ἐξαπέστειλαν αὐτὸν εἰς Ταρσόν.
sent forth   him   to   Tarsus.
31 Ἡ μὲν οὖν ἐκκλησία καθ' ὅλης
²The - ¹therefore ³church throughout all
τῆς Ἰουδαίας καὶ Γαλιλαίας καὶ Σαμαρείας
-   Judæa   and Galilee   and Samaria
εἶχεν εἰρήνην οἰκοδομουμένη καὶ πορευομένη
had   peace   being built   and going

he come here to take them as prisoners to the chief priests?" 22 Yet Saul grew more and more powerful and baffled the Jews living in Damascus by proving that Jesus is the Christ.[o]

23 After many days had gone by, the Jews conspired to kill him, 24 but Saul learned of their plan. Day and night they kept close watch on the city gates in order to kill him. 25 But his followers took him by night and lowered him in a basket through an opening in the wall.
26 When he came to Jerusalem, he tried to join the disciples, but they were all afraid of him, not believing that he really was a disciple. 27 But Barnabas took him and brought him to the apostles. He told them how Saul on his journey had seen the Lord and that the Lord had spoken to him, and how in Damascus he had preached fearlessly in the name of Jesus. 28 So Saul stayed with them and moved about freely in Jerusalem, speaking boldly in the name of the Lord. 29 He talked and debated with the Grecian Jews, but they tried to kill him. 30 When the brothers learned of this, they took him down to Caesarea and sent him off to Tarsus.
31 Then the church throughout Judea, Galilee and Samaria enjoyed a time of peace. It was strengthened; and encouraged by

[t] Gk that this
[u] Or the Christ
[v] Gk through the wall
[w] Gk brothers

[o] 22 Or Messiah

Living in the fear of the Lord and in the comfort of the Holy Spirit, it increased in numbers.

The Healing of Aeneas

32 Now as Peter went here and there among all the believers,ˣ he came down also to the saints living in Lydda. ³³There he found a man named Aeneas, who had been bedridden for eight years, for he was paralyzed. ³⁴Peter said to him, "Aeneas, Jesus Christ heals you; get up and make your bed!" And immediately he got up. ³⁵And all the residents of Lydda and Sharon saw him and turned to the Lord.

Peter in Lydda and Joppa

36 Now in Joppa there was a disciple whose name was Tabitha, which in Greek is Dorcas.ʸ She was devoted to good works and acts of charity. ³⁷At that time she became ill and died. When they had washed her, they laid her in a room upstairs. ³⁸Since Lydda was near Joppa, the disciples, who heard that Peter was there, sent two men to him with the request, "Please come to us without delay." ³⁹So Peter got up and went with them; and when he arrived, they took him to the room upstairs. All the widows stood beside him, weeping and showing tunics and other clothing that Dorcas had made while she was with them. ⁴⁰Peter put all of them outside, and then he knelt down and prayed. He turned to the body and said, "Tabitha, get up."

τῷ φόβῳ τοῦ κυρίου, καὶ τῇ παρακλήσει
in the fear of the Lord, and in the comfort
τοῦ ἁγίου πνεύματος ἐπληθύνετο.
of the Holy Spirit. was multiplied.

32 Ἐγένετο δὲ Πέτρον διερχόμενον διὰ
Now it came to pass Peter passing *through* through
πάντων κατελθεῖν καὶ πρὸς τοὺς ἁγίους
all [quarters] to come downᵇ also to the saints
τοὺς κατοικοῦντας Λύδδα. **33** εὗρεν δὲ
- inhabiting Lydda. And he found
ἐκεῖ ἄνθρωπόν τινα ὀνόματι Αἰνέαν ἐξ
there a certain man by name Aeneas of
ἐτῶν ὀκτὼ κατακείμενον ἐπὶ κραβάτου,
years eight lying on a mattress,
ὃς ἦν παραλελυμένος. **34** καὶ εἶπεν αὐτῷ
who was *having been* paralysed. And said to him
ὁ Πέτρος· Αἰνέα, ἰαταί σε Ἰησοῦς Χριστός·
- Peter: Aeneas, cures thee Jesus Christ;
ἀνάστηθι καὶ στρῶσον σεαυτῷ. καὶ
rise up and gird thyself. And
εὐθέως ἀνέστη. **35** καὶ εἶδαν αὐτὸν
immediately he rose up. And saw him
πάντες οἱ κατοικοῦντες Λύδδα καὶ τὸν
all the [ones] inhabiting Lydda and -
Σαρῶνα, οἵτινες ἐπέστρεψαν ἐπὶ τὸν κύριον.
Saron, who turned to the Lord.
Ἐν Ἰόππῃ δέ τις ἦν μαθήτρια ὀνόματι
²in ³Joppa ¹Now ⁵a certain ⁴was ⁶disciple by name
Ταβιθά, **36** ἣ διερμηνευομένη λέγεται
Tabitha, who being translated is called
Δορκάς· αὕτη ἦν πλήρης ἔργων ἀγαθῶν
Dorcas; this woman was full works of good
καὶ ἐλεημοσυνῶν ὧν ἐποίει. **37** ἐγένετο δὲ
and of alms which she did. And it happened
ἐν ταῖς ἡμέραις ἐκείναις ἀσθενήσασαν
in those days ailing
αὐτὴν ἀποθανεῖν· λούσαντες δὲ ἔθηκαν
she to dieᵇ; and having washed they put [her]
=being ill she died;
ἐν ὑπερῴῳ. **38** ἐγγὺς δὲ οὔσης Λύδδας
in an upper room. Now ²near ¹being ¹Lyddaᵃ
τῇ Ἰόππῃ οἱ μαθηταὶ ἀκούσαντες ὅτι
- to Joppa the disciples having heard that
Πέτρος ἐστὶν ἐν αὐτῇ ἀπέστειλαν δύο
Peter is(was) in it sent two
ἄνδρας πρὸς αὐτὸν παρακαλοῦντες· μὴ
men to him beseeching: ²not
ὀκνήσῃς διελθεῖν ἕως ἡμῶν. **39** ἀναστὰς δὲ
¹hesitate to come to us. And rising up
Πέτρος συνῆλθεν αὐτοῖς· ὃν παραγενόμενον
Peter went with them; whom arriving
ἀνήγαγον εἰς τὸ ὑπερῷον, καὶ παρέστησαν
they led up into the upper room, and stood by
αὐτῷ πᾶσαι αἱ χῆραι κλαίουσαι καὶ
him all the widows weeping and
ἐπιδεικνύμεναι χιτῶνας καὶ ἱμάτια, ὅσα
showing tunics and garments, which
ἐποίει μετ' αὐτῶν οὖσα ἡ Δορκάς.
¹made ⁴with ⁵them ³being - ¹Dorcas.
40 ἐκβαλὼν δὲ ἔξω πάντας ὁ Πέτρος
And ²putting *out* ⁴outside ³all - ¹Peter
καὶ θεὶς τὰ γόνατα προσηύξατο, καὶ
and placing the knees he prayed, and
=kneeling down
ἐπιστρέψας πρὸς τὸ σῶμα εἶπεν· Ταβιθά,
turning to the body said: Tabitha,

---

the Holy Spirit, it grew in numbers, living in the fear of the Lord.

Aeneas and Dorcas

32As Peter traveled about the country, he went to visit the saints in Lydda. ³³There he found a man named Aeneas, a paralytic who had been bedridden for eight years. ³⁴"Aeneas," Peter said to him, "Jesus Christ heals you. Get up and take care of your mat." Immediately Aeneas got up. ³⁵All those who lived in Lydda and Sharon saw him and turned to the Lord.

36In Joppa there was a disciple named Tabitha (which, when translated, is Dorcasᵖ), who was always doing good and helping the poor. ³⁷About that time she became sick and died, and her body was washed and placed in an upstairs room. ³⁸Lydda was near Joppa; so when the disciples heard that Peter was in Lydda, they sent two men to him and urged him, "Please come at once!"

39Peter went with them, and when he arrived he was taken upstairs to the room. All the widows stood around him, crying and showing him the robes and other clothing that Dorcas had made while she was still with them.

40Peter sent them all out of the room; then he got down on his knees and prayed. Turning toward the dead woman, he said,

---

ˣ Gk *all of them*

ᵖ36 Both *Tabitha* (Aramaic) and *Dorcas* (Greek) mean *gazelle.*

Then she opened her eyes, and seeing Peter, she sat up. 41 He gave her his hand and helped her up. Then calling the saints and widows, he showed her to be alive. 42 This became known throughout Joppa, and many believed in the Lord. 43 Meanwhile he stayed in Joppa for some time with a certain Simon, a tanner.

Chapter 10

Peter and Cornelius

IN Caesarea there was a man named Cornelius, a centurion of the Italian Cohort, as it was called. 2 He was a devout man who feared God with all his household; he gave alms generously to the people and prayed constantly to God. 3 One afternoon at about three o'clock he had a vision in which he clearly saw an angel of God coming in and saying to him, "Cornelius." 4 He stared at him in terror and said, "What is it, Lord?" He answered, "Your prayers and your alms have ascended as a memorial before God. 5 Now send men to Joppa for a certain Simon who is called Peter; 6 he is lodging with Simon, a tanner, whose house is by the seaside." 7 When the angel who spoke to him had left, he called two of his slaves and a devout soldier from the ranks of those who served him, 8 and after telling them everything, he

---

ἀνάστηθι. ἡ δὲ ἤνοιξεν τοὺς ὀφθαλμοὺς
rise up. And she opened the eyes
αὐτῆς, καὶ ἰδοῦσα τὸν Πέτρον ἀνεκάθισεν.
of her, and seeing – Peter sat up.
41 δοὺς δὲ αὐτῇ χεῖρα ἀνέστησεν αὐτήν·
And giving her a hand he raised up her;
φωνήσας δὲ τοὺς ἁγίους καὶ τὰς χήρας
and calling the saints and the widows
παρέστησεν αὐτὴν ζῶσαν. 42 γνωστὸν δὲ
he presented her living. And known
ἐγένετο καθ' ὅλης τῆς Ἰόππης, καὶ
it became throughout all – Joppa, and
ἐπίστευσαν πολλοὶ ἐπὶ τὸν κύριον.
believed many on the Lord.
43 Ἐγένετο δὲ ἡμέρας ἱκανὰς μεῖναι ἐν
And it came to pass days several to remain in
                  = he remained many days
Ἰόππῃ παρά τινι Σίμωνι βυρσεῖ.
Joppa with one Simon a tanner.

10 Ἀνὴρ δέ τις ἐν Καισαρείᾳ ὀνόματι
Now a certain man in Cæsarea by name
Κορνήλιος, ἑκατοντάρχης ἐκ σπείρης τῆς
Cornelius, a centurion of a cohort –
καλουμένης Ἰταλικῆς, 2 εὐσεβὴς καὶ
being called Italian, devout and
φοβούμενος τὸν θεὸν σὺν παντὶ τῷ οἴκῳ
fearing – God with all the household
αὐτοῦ, ποιῶν ἐλεημοσύνας πολλὰς τῷ
of him, doing alms many to the
λαῷ καὶ δεόμενος τοῦ θεοῦ διὰ παντός,
people and petitioning – God continually,
3 εἶδεν ἐν ὁράματι φανερῶς, ὡσεὶ περὶ
saw in a vision clearly, as it were around
ὥραν ἐνάτην τῆς ἡμέρας, ἄγγελον τοῦ
hour ninth of the day, an angel –
θεοῦ εἰσελθόντα πρὸς αὐτὸν καὶ εἰπόντα
of God entering to him and saying
αὐτῷ· Κορνήλιε. 4 ὁ δὲ ἀτενίσας αὐτῷ
to him: Cornelius. And he gazing at him
καὶ ἔμφοβος γενόμενος εἶπεν· τί ἐστιν,
and terrified becoming said: What is it,
κύριε; εἶπεν δὲ αὐτῷ· αἱ προσευχαί
lord? And he said to him: The prayers
σου καὶ αἱ ἐλεημοσύναι σου ἀνέβησαν
of thee and the alms of thee went up
εἰς μνημόσυνον ἔμπροσθεν τοῦ θεοῦ. 5 καὶ
for a memorial before – God. And
νῦν πέμψον ἄνδρας εἰς Ἰόππην καὶ
now send men to Joppa and
μετάπεμψαι Σίμωνά τινα ὃς ἐπικαλεῖται
[summon ²Simon ¹one who is surnamed
Πέτρος· 6 οὗτος ξενίζεται παρά τινι
Peter; this man is lodged with one
Σίμωνι βυρσεῖ, ᾧ ἐστιν οἰκία παρὰ
Simon a tanner, to whom is a house^c by
                  = who has a house
θάλασσαν. 7 ὡς δὲ ἀπῆλθεν ὁ ἄγγελος ὁ
[the] sea. And as went away the angel –
λαλῶν αὐτῷ, φωνήσας δύο τῶν οἰκετῶν
speaking to him, calling two of the household slaves
καὶ στρατιώτην εὐσεβῆ τῶν προσκαρτερούν-
and soldier a devout of the [ones] waiting
των αὐτῷ, 8 καὶ ἐξηγησάμενος ἅπαντα
on him, and explaining all things

"Tabitha, get up." She opened her eyes, and seeing Peter she sat up. 41 He took her by the hand and helped her to her feet. Then he called the believers and the widows and presented her to them alive. 42 This became known all over Joppa, and many people believed in the Lord. 43 Peter stayed in Joppa for some time with a tanner named Simon.

Chapter 10

Cornelius Calls for Peter

AT Caesarea there was a man named Cornelius, a centurion in what was known as the Italian Regiment. 2 He and all his family were devout and God-fearing; he gave generously to those in need and prayed to God regularly. 3 One day at about three in the afternoon he had a vision. He distinctly saw an angel of God, who came to him and said, "Cornelius!"
4 Cornelius stared at him in fear. "What is it, Lord?" he asked.
The angel answered, "Your prayers and gifts to the poor have come up as a memorial offering before God. 5 Now send men to Joppa to bring back a man named Simon who is called Peter. 6 He is staying with Simon the tanner, whose house is by the sea."
7 When the angel who spoke to him had gone, Cornelius called two of his servants and a devout soldier who was one of his attendants. 8 He told them ev-

---

sent them to Joppa.

9 About noon the next day, as they were on their journey and approaching the city, Peter went up on the roof to pray. 10 He became hungry and wanted something to eat; and while it was being prepared, he fell into a trance. 11 He saw the heaven opened and something like a large sheet coming down, being lowered to the ground by its four corners. 12 In it were all kinds of four-footed creatures and reptiles and birds of the air. 13 Then he heard a voice saying, "Get up, Peter; kill and eat." 14 But Peter said, "By no means, Lord; for I have never eaten anything that is profane or unclean." 15 The voice said to him again, a second time, "What God has made clean, you must not call profane." 16 This happened three times, and the thing was suddenly taken up to heaven.

17 Now while Peter was greatly puzzled about what to make of the vision that he had seen, suddenly the men sent by Cornelius appeared. They were asking for Simon's house and were standing by the gate. 18 They called out to ask whether Simon, who was called Peter, was staying there. 19 While Peter was still thinking about the vision, the Spirit said to him, "Look, three[z] men are searching for you. 20 Now get up, go down, and go with them without hesitation; for I have sent them."

αὐτοῖς ἀπέστειλεν αὐτοὺς εἰς τὴν Ἰόππην.
to them sent them to — Joppa.

9 Τῇ δὲ ἐπαύριον ὁδοιπορούντων ἐκείνων
And on the morrow journeying those

καὶ τῇ πόλει ἐγγιζόντων ἀνέβη Πέτρος
and to the city drawing near[a] went up Peter
=as they journeyed and drew near to the city

ἐπὶ τὸ δῶμα προσεύξασθαι περὶ ὥραν
onto the roof to pray about hour

ἕκτην. 10 ἐγένετο δὲ πρόσπεινος καὶ
sixth. And he became hungry and

ἤθελεν γεύσασθαι· παρασκευαζόντων δὲ
wished to taste(eat); and preparing
=while they prepared

αὐτῶν ἐγένετο ἐπ' αὐτὸν ἔκστασις, 11 καὶ
them[a] there came on him an ecstasy, and

θεωρεῖ τὸν οὐρανὸν ἀνεῳγμένον καὶ
he beholds the heaven having been opened and

καταβαῖνον σκεῦός τι ὡς ὀθόνην μεγάλην,
coming down a certain vessel like sheet a great,

τέσσαρσιν ἀρχαῖς καθιέμενον ἐπὶ τῆς γῆς,
by four corners being let down onto the earth,

12 ἐν ᾧ ὑπῆρχεν πάντα τὰ τετράποδα
in which were all the quadrupeds

καὶ ἑρπετὰ τῆς γῆς καὶ πετεινὰ τοῦ
and reptiles of the earth and birds of the

οὐρανοῦ. 13 καὶ ἐγένετο φωνὴ πρὸς
heaven(air). And there came a voice to

αὐτόν· ἀναστάς, Πέτρε, θῦσον καὶ φάγε.
him: Rise up, Peter, slay and eat.

14 ὁ δὲ Πέτρος εἶπεν· μηδαμῶς, κύριε,
— But Peter said: Not at all, Lord,

ὅτι οὐδέποτε ἔφαγον πᾶν κοινὸν καὶ
because never did I eat every(any)thing common and

ἀκάθαρτον. 15 καὶ φωνὴ πάλιν ἐκ δευτέρου
unclean. And a voice again a second [time]

πρὸς αὐτόν· ἃ ὁ θεὸς ἐκαθάρισεν σὺ
[came] to him: What things — God cleansed [3]thou

μὴ κοίνου. 16 τοῦτο δὲ ἐγένετο ἐπὶ
[1]not [treat [4]as [5]unclean. And this occurred on

τρίς, καὶ εὐθὺς ἀνελήμφθη τὸ σκεῦος
three [occasions], and immediately was taken up the vessel

εἰς τὸν οὐρανόν. 17 Ὡς δὲ ἐν ἑαυτῷ
into — heaven. Now as in himself

διηπόρει ὁ Πέτρος τί ἂν εἴη τὸ ὅραμα
was doubting — Peter what might be the vision

ὃ εἶδεν, ἰδοὺ οἱ ἄνδρες οἱ ἀπεσταλμένοι
which he saw, behold[,] the men — having been sent

ὑπὸ τοῦ Κορνηλίου διερωτήσαντες τὴν
by — Cornelius asking for the

οἰκίαν τοῦ Σίμωνος ἐπέστησαν ἐπὶ τὸν
house — of Simon stood at at the

πυλῶνα, 18 καὶ φωνήσαντες ἐπυνθάνοντο
porch, and calling inquired

εἰ Σίμων ὁ ἐπικαλούμενος Πέτρος ἐνθάδε
if Simon — being surnamed Peter here

ξενίζεται. 19 Τοῦ δὲ Πέτρου διενθυμουμένου
is lodged. — And Peter pondering[a]
=while Peter pondered

περὶ τοῦ ὁράματος εἶπεν τὸ πνεῦμα·
about the vision [3]said [1]the [2]Spirit:

ἰδοὺ ἄνδρες δύο ζητοῦντές σε· 20 ἀλλὰ
Behold[,] men two seeking thee: but

ἀναστὰς κατάβηθι, καὶ πορεύου σὺν αὐτοῖς
rising up go down, and go with them

μηδὲν διακρινόμενος, ὅτι ἐγὼ ἀπέσταλκα
nothing doubting, because I have sent

---

erything that had happened and sent them to Joppa.

Peter's Vision

9 About noon the following day as they were on their journey and approaching the city, Peter went up on the roof to pray. 10 He became hungry and wanted something to eat, and while the meal was being prepared, he fell into a trance. 11 He saw heaven opened and something like a large sheet being let down to earth by its four corners. 12 It contained all kinds of four-footed animals, as well as reptiles of the earth and birds of the air. 13 Then a voice told him, "Get up, Peter. Kill and eat."

14 "Surely not, Lord!" Peter replied. "I have never eaten anything impure or unclean."

15 The voice spoke to him a second time, "Do not call anything impure that God has made clean."

16 This happened three times, and immediately the sheet was taken back to heaven.

17 While Peter was wondering about the meaning of the vision, the men sent by Cornelius found out where Simon's house was and stopped at the gate. 18 They called out, asking if Simon who was known as Peter was staying there.

19 While Peter was still thinking about the vision, the Spirit said to him, "Simon, three[q] men are looking for you. 20 So get up and go downstairs. Do not hesitate to go with them, for I have sent them."

�q 19 One early manuscript *two*; other manuscripts do not have the number.

21 So Peter went down to the men and said, "I am the one you are looking for; what is the reason for your coming?" 22 They answered, "Cornelius, a centurion, an upright and God-fearing man, who is well spoken of by the whole Jewish nation, was directed by a holy angel to send for you to come to his house and to hear what you have to say." 23 So Peter*a* invited them in and gave them lodging.

The next day he got up and went with them, and some of the believers*b* from Joppa accompanied him. 24 The following day they came to Caesarea. Cornelius was expecting them and had called together his relatives and close friends. 25 On Peter's arrival Cornelius met him, and falling at his feet, worshiped him. 26 But Peter made him get up, saying, "Stand up; I am only a mortal." 27 And as he talked with him, he went in and found that many had assembled; 28 and he said to them, "You yourselves know that it is unlawful for a Jew to associate with or to visit a Gentile; but God has shown me that I should not call anyone profane or unclean. 29 So when I was sent for, I came without objection. Now may I ask why you sent for me?"

30 Cornelius replied, "Four days ago at this very hour, at three o'clock, I was praying in my house

αὐτούς. **21** καταβὰς δὲ Πέτρος πρὸς
them.   And going down   Peter   to
τοὺς ἄνδρας εἶπεν· ἰδοὺ ἐγώ εἰμι ὃν
the   men   said: Behold[,] I   am [he] whom
ζητεῖτε· τίς ἡ αἰτία δι᾽ ἣν πάρεστε;
ye seek; what [is] the cause   for which ye are here?
22 οἱ δὲ εἶπαν· Κορνήλιος ἑκατοντάρχης,
And they   said: Cornelius   a centurion,
ἀνὴρ δίκαιος καὶ φοβούμενος τὸν θεόν,
a man just   and   fearing   -   God,
μαρτυρούμενός τε ὑπὸ ὅλου τοῦ ἔθνους
and being witnessed to by all   the   nation
τῶν Ἰουδαίων, ἐχρηματίσθη ὑπὸ ἀγγέλου
of the Jews,   was warned   by   angel
ἁγίου μεταπέμψασθαί σε εἰς τὸν οἶκον
a holy   to summon   thee to the house
αὐτοῦ καὶ ἀκοῦσαι ῥήματα παρὰ σοῦ.
of him and to hear   words   from   thee.
23 εἰσκαλεσάμενος οὖν αὐτοὺς ἐξένισεν.
Calling in   therefore them   he lodged.
Τῇ δὲ ἐπαύριον ἀναστὰς ἐξῆλθεν σὺν
And on the morrow rising up   he went forth with
αὐτοῖς, καί τινες τῶν ἀδελφῶν τῶν
them,   and some of the brothers   -
ἀπὸ Ἰόππης συνῆλθον αὐτῷ. **24** τῇ δὲ
from Joppa accompanied him.   And on the
ἐπαύριον εἰσῆλθεν εἰς τὴν Καισάρειαν·
morrow   he entered into   -   Caesarea;
ὁ δὲ Κορνήλιος ἦν προσδοκῶν αὐτούς,
- and Cornelius was awaiting   them,
συγκαλεσάμενος τοὺς συγγενεῖς αὐτοῦ καὶ
having called together the relatives   of him and
τοὺς ἀναγκαίους φίλους. **25** Ὡς δὲ
the   intimate   friends.   Now when
ἐγένετο τοῦ εἰσελθεῖν τὸν Πέτρον,*b*
it came to pass the to enter   -   Peter,
= Now it came to pass when Peter entered,
συναντήσας αὐτῷ ὁ Κορνήλιος πεσὼν
²meeting   ³him   -   ¹Cornelius   falling
ἐπὶ τοὺς πόδας προσεκύνησεν. **26** ὁ δὲ
at the(his) feet   worshipped.   - But
Πέτρος ἤγειρεν αὐτὸν λέγων· ἀνάστηθι·
Peter   raised   him   saying;   Stand up;
καὶ ἐγὼ αὐτὸς ἄνθρωπός εἰμι. **27** καὶ
also I   [my]self a man   am.   And
συνομιλῶν αὐτῷ εἰσῆλθεν, καὶ εὑρίσκει
talking with   him   he entered,   and   finds
συνεληλυθότας πολλούς, **28** ἔφη τε πρὸς
having come together many,   and said to
αὐτούς· ὑμεῖς ἐπίστασθε ὡς ἀθέμιτόν ἐστιν
them: Ye   understand   how unlawful   it is
ἀνδρὶ Ἰουδαίῳ κολλᾶσθαι ἢ προσέρχεσθαι
for *a man* a Jew to adhere   or   to approach
ἀλλοφύλῳ· κἀμοὶ ὁ θεὸς ἔδειξεν μηδένα
a foreigner; and to me - God   showed   ²not any
κοινὸν ἢ ἀκάθαρτον λέγειν ἄνθρωπον·
⁴common ⁵or ⁶unclean ¹to call   ³man;
29 διὸ καὶ ἀναντιρρήτως ἦλθον μετα-
wherefore indeed ³unquestioningly ²I came ¹being
πεμφθείς. πυνθάνομαι οὖν, τίνι λόγῳ
summoned.   I inquire   therefore, for what reason
μετεπέμψασθέ με; **30** καὶ ὁ Κορνήλιος
ye summoned   me?   And - Cornelius
ἔφη· ἀπὸ τετάρτης ἡμέρας μέχρι ταύτης τῆς
said; From fourth   day   until   this   -
= Four days ago
ὥρας ἤμην τὴν ἐνάτην προσευχόμενος
hour I was [at] the ninth   praying

21 Peter went down and said to the men, "I'm the one you're looking for. Why have you come?" 22 The men replied, "We have come from Cornelius the centurion. He is a righteous and God-fearing man, who is respected by all the Jewish people. A holy angel told him to have you come to his house so that he could hear what you have to say." 23 Then Peter invited the men into the house to be his guests.

Peter at Cornelius' House

The next day Peter started out with them, and some of the brothers from Joppa went along. 24 The following day he arrived in Caesarea. Cornelius was expecting them and had called together his relatives and close friends. 25 As Peter entered the house, Cornelius met him and fell at his feet in reverence. 26 But Peter made him get up. "Stand up," he said, "I am only a man myself."

27 Talking with him, Peter went inside and found a large gathering of people. 28 He said to them: "You are well aware that it is against our law for a Jew to associate with a Gentile or visit him. But God has shown me that I should not call any man impure or unclean. 29 So when I was sent for, I came without raising any objection. May I ask why you sent for me?"

30 Cornelius answered: "Four days ago I was in my house praying at this hour, at three in the afternoon.

a Gk *he*
b Gk *brothers*

when suddenly a man in dazzling clothes stood before me. 31 He said, 'Cornelius, your prayer has been heard and your alms have been remembered before God. 32 Send therefore to Joppa and ask for Simon, who is called Peter; he is staying in the home of Simon, a tanner, by the sea.' 33 Therefore I sent for you immediately, and you have been kind enough to come. So now all of us are here in the presence of God to listen to all that the Lord has commanded you to say."

Gentiles Hear the Good News

34 Then Peter began to speak to them: "I truly understand that God shows no partiality, 35 but in every nation anyone who fears him and does what is right is acceptable to him. 36 You know the message he sent to the people of Israel, preaching peace by Jesus Christ—he is Lord of all. 37 That message spread throughout Judea, beginning in Galilee after the baptism that John announced; 38 how God anointed Jesus of Nazareth with the Holy Spirit and with power; how he went about doing good and healing all who were oppressed by the devil, for God was with him. 39 We are witnesses to all that he did both in Judea and in Jerusalem. They put him to death by hanging him on a tree; 40 but God raised him on the third day and allowed him

---

ἐν τῷ οἴκῳ μου, καὶ ἰδοὺ ἀνὴρ ἔστη
in the house of me, and behold[,] a man stood

ἐνώπιόν μου ἐν ἐσθῆτι λαμπρᾷ, 31 καὶ
before me in clothing bright, and

φησίν· Κορνήλιε, εἰσηκούσθη σου ἡ
says: Cornelius, was heard of thee the

προσευχὴ καὶ αἱ ἐλεημοσύναι σου ἐμνήσθησαν
prayer and the alms of thee were remembered

ἐνώπιον τοῦ θεοῦ. 32 πέμψον οὖν εἰς
before – God. Send thou therefore to

Ἰόππην καὶ μετακάλεσαι Σίμωνα ὃς ἐπι-
Joppa and send for Simon who is

καλεῖται Πέτρος· οὗτος ξενίζεται ἐν οἰκίᾳ
surnamed Peter; this man is lodged in [the] house

Σίμωνος βυρσέως παρὰ θάλασσαν. 33 ἐξαυτῆς
of Simon a tanner , by [the] sea. At once

οὖν ἔπεμψα πρὸς σέ, σύ τε καλῶς
therefore I sent to thee, and thou well

ἐποίησας παραγενόμενος. νῦν οὖν πάντες
didst arriving. Now therefore all

ἡμεῖς ἐνώπιον τοῦ θεοῦ πάρεσμεν ἀκοῦσαι
we before – God are present to hear

πάντα τὰ προστεταγμένα σοι ὑπὸ τοῦ
all the things having been commanded thee by the

κυρίου. 34 Ἀνοίξας δὲ Πέτρος τὸ στόμα
Lord. And opening Peter the(his) mouth

εἶπεν· ἐπ’ ἀληθείας καταλαμβάνομαι ὅτι
said: On(in) truth I perceive that

οὐκ ἔστιν προσωπολήμπτης ὁ θεός, 35 ἀλλ’
²not ²is ⁴a respecter of persons ¹God, but

ἐν παντὶ ἔθνει ὁ φοβούμενος αὐτὸν καὶ
in every nation the [one] fearing him and

ἐργαζόμενος δικαιοσύνην δεκτὸς αὐτῷ ἐστιν·
working righteousness acceptable to him is;

36 τὸν λόγον ὃν ἀπέστειλεν τοῖς υἱοῖς
the word which he sent to the sons

Ἰσραὴλ εὐαγγελιζόμενος εἰρήνην διὰ Ἰησοῦ
of Israel preaching peace through Jesus

Χριστοῦ· οὗτός ἐστιν πάντων κύριος.
Christ: this one is of all Lord.

37 ὑμεῖς οἴδατε τὸ γενόμενον ῥῆμα καθ’
Ye know the having become thing throughout
=that which took place

ὅλης τῆς Ἰουδαίας, ἀρξάμενος ἀπὸ τῆς
all – Judæa, beginning from –

Γαλιλαίας μετὰ τὸ βάπτισμα ὃ ἐκήρυξεν
Galilee after the baptism which ⁵proclaimed

Ἰωάννης, 38 Ἰησοῦν τὸν ἀπὸ Ναζαρέθ,
¹John, Jesus the one from Nazareth,

ὡς ἔχρισεν αὐτὸν ὁ θεὸς πνεύματι ἁγίῳ
how anointed him – God with Spirit Holy

καὶ δυνάμει, ὃς διῆλθεν εὐεργετῶν καὶ
and power, who went about doing good and

ἰώμενος πάντας τοὺς καταδυναστευομένους
curing all the [ones] being oppressed

ὑπὸ τοῦ διαβόλου, ὅτι ὁ θεὸς ἦν μετ’
by the devil, because – God was with

αὐτοῦ· 39 καὶ ἡμεῖς μάρτυρες πάντων
him; and we [are] witnesses of all things

ὧν ἐποίησεν ἔν τε τῇ χώρᾳ τῶν Ἰουδαίων
which he did both in the country of the Jews

καὶ Ἰερουσαλήμ· ὃν καὶ ἀνεῖλαν
and Jerusalem; whom indeed they killed

κρεμάσαντες ἐπὶ ξύλου. 40 τοῦτον ὁ
hanging on a tree. This one –

θεὸς ἤγειρεν ἐν τῇ τρίτῃ ἡμέρᾳ καὶ
God raised on the third day and

Suddenly a man in shining clothes stood before me 31 and said, 'Cornelius, God has heard your prayer and remembered your gifts to the poor. 32 Send to Joppa for Simon who is called Peter. He is a guest in the home of Simon the tanner, who lives by the sea.' 33 So I sent for you immediately, and it was good of you to come. Now we are all here in the presence of God to listen to everything the Lord has commanded you to tell us.''

34 Then Peter began to speak: "I now realize how true it is that God does not show favoritism 35 but accepts men from every nation who fear him and do what is right. 36 You know the message God sent to the people of Israel, telling the good news of peace through Jesus Christ, who is Lord of all. 37 You know what has happened throughout Judea, beginning in Galilee after the baptism that John preached —38 how God anointed Jesus of Nazareth with the Holy Spirit and power, and how he went around doing good and healing all who were under the power of the devil, because God was with him.

39 "We are witnesses of everything he did in the country of the Jews and in Jerusalem. They killed him by hanging him on a tree, 40 but God raised him from the dead on the third day

to appear, 41 not to all the people but to us who were chosen by God as witnesses, and who ate and drank with him after he rose from the dead. 42 He commanded us to preach to the people and to testify that he is the one ordained by God as judge of the living and the dead. 43 All the prophets testify about him that everyone who believes in him receives forgiveness of sins through his name."

Gentiles Receive the Holy Spirit

44 While Peter was still speaking, the Holy Spirit fell upon all who heard the word. 45 The circumcised believers who had come with Peter were astounded that the gift of the Holy Spirit had been poured out even on the Gentiles, 46 for they heard them speaking in tongues and extolling God. Then Peter said, 47 "Can anyone withhold the water for baptizing these people who have received the Holy Spirit just as we have?" 48 So he ordered them to be baptized in the name of Jesus Christ. Then they invited him to stay for several days.

ἔδωκεν   αὐτὸν   ἐμφανῆ   γενέσθαι,   41 οὐ
gave   him   visible   to become,   not

παντὶ   τῷ   λαῷ,   ἀλλὰ   μάρτυσιν   τοῖς
to all   the   people,   but   to witnesses

προκεχειροτονημένοις   ὑπὸ   τοῦ   θεοῦ,   ἡμῖν,
having been previously appointed by   -   God,   to us,

οἵτινες   συνεφάγομεν   καὶ   συνεπίομεν   αὐτῷ
who   ate with   and   drank with   him

μετὰ   τὸ   ἀναστῆναι   αὐτὸν   ἐκ   νεκρῶν·
after   the to rise again   him[b]   out of [the] dead;
             = he rose again

42 καὶ   παρήγγειλεν   ἡμῖν   κηρύξαι   τῷ   λαῷ
   and   he commanded   us   to proclaim to the people

καὶ   διαμαρτύρασθαι   ὅτι   οὗτός   ἐστιν   ὁ
and   solemnly to witness   that   this man   is the [one]

ὡρισμένος   ὑπὸ   τοῦ   θεοῦ   κριτὴς   ζώντων
having been   by   -   God   judge   of living
designated

καὶ   νεκρῶν.   43 τούτῳ   πάντες   οἱ   προφῆται
and   of dead.   To this man all   the   prophets

μαρτυροῦσιν,   ἄφεσιν   ἁμαρτιῶν   λαβεῖν   διὰ
witness,   [6]forgiveness [7]of sins   [5]to receive [8]through

τοῦ   ὀνόματος   αὐτοῦ   πάντα   τὸν   πιστεύοντα
[9]the [10]name   [11]of him [1]everyone [2]believing

εἰς   αὐτόν.   44 Ἔτι   λαλοῦντος   τοῦ   Πέτρου
[3]in   [4]him.   Yet   speaking   -   Peter[a]
                          = While Peter was still speaking

τὰ   ῥήματα   ταῦτα   ἐπέπεσεν   τὸ   πνεῦμα
these words   [4]fell on   [1]the   [3]Spirit

τὸ   ἅγιον   ἐπὶ   πάντας   τοὺς   ἀκούοντας
-      [2]Holy   on   all   the [ones] hearing

τὸν   λόγον.   45 καὶ   ἐξέστησαν   οἱ   ἐκ
the   discourse.   And   [5]were amazed [1]the [2]of [the]

περιτομῆς   πιστοὶ   ὅσοι   συνῆλθαν   τῷ   Πέτρῳ,
[3]circumcision [4]faithful as many as accompanied -   Peter,

ὅτι   καὶ   ἐπὶ   τὰ   ἔθνη   ἡ   δωρεὰ   τοῦ   ἁγίου
because also   on   the   nations the   gift   of the Holy

πνεύματος   ἐκκέχυται·   46 ἤκουον   γὰρ
Spirit   has been poured out;   for they heard

αὐτῶν   λαλούντων   γλώσσαις   καὶ   μεγαλυνόν-
them   speaking   in tongues   and   magnify-

των   τὸν   θεόν.   τότε   ἀπεκρίθη   Πέτρος·
ing   -   God.   Then   answered   Peter:

47 μήτι   τὸ   ὕδωρ   δύναται   κωλῦσαί   τις
   Not   [4]the [5]water   [1]can   [3]to forbid [2]anyone

τοῦ   μὴ   βαπτισθῆναι   τούτους,   οἵτινες   τὸ
-       [7]not [6]to be baptized[d] [8]these,   who   the

πνεῦμα   τὸ   ἅγιον   ἔλαβον   ὡς   καὶ   ἡμεῖς;
Spirit   -   Holy   received   as   also   we?

48 προσέταξεν   δὲ   αὐτοὺς   ἐν   τῷ   ὀνόματι
   And he commanded   them   in   the   name

Ἰησοῦ   Χριστοῦ   βαπτισθῆναι.   τότε   ἠρώτησαν
of Jesus   Christ   to be baptized.   Then   they asked

αὐτὸν   ἐπιμεῖναι   ἡμέρας   τινάς.
him   to remain   days   some.

and caused him to be seen. 41 He was not seen by all the people, but by witnesses whom God had already chosen—by us who ate and drank with him after he rose from the dead. 42 He commanded us to preach to the people and to testify that he is the one whom God appointed as judge of the living and the dead. 43 All the prophets testify about him that everyone who believes in him receives forgiveness of sins through his name."

44 While Peter was still speaking these words, the Holy Spirit came on all who heard the message. 45 The circumcised believers who had come with Peter were astonished that the gift of the Holy Spirit had been poured out even on the Gentiles. 46 For they heard them speaking in tongues[r] and praising God.

Then Peter said, 47 "Can anyone keep these people from being baptized with water? They have received the Holy Spirit just as we have." 48 So he ordered that they be baptized in the name of Jesus Christ. Then they asked Peter to stay with them for a few days.

Chapter 11

Peter's Report to the Church at Jerusalem

NOW the apostles and the believers[c] who were in Judea heard that the Gentiles had also accepted the word of God. 2 So when Peter went up to Jerusalem, the circumcised

11 Ἤκουσαν   δὲ   οἱ   ἀπόστολοι   καὶ   οἱ
   Now heard   the   apostles   and   the

ἀδελφοὶ   οἱ   ὄντες   κατὰ   τὴν   Ἰουδαίαν
brothers   -   being   throughout -   Judæa

ὅτι   καὶ   τὰ   ἔθνη   ἐδέξαντο   τὸν   λόγον
that   also   the   nations received   the   word

τοῦ   θεοῦ.   2 Ὅτε   δὲ   ἀνέβη   Πέτρος   εἰς
-      of God.   And when   went up   Peter   to

Ἰερουσαλήμ,   διεκρίνοντο   πρὸς   αὐτὸν   οἱ
Jerusalem,   disputed   with   him   the [ones]

Chapter 11

Peter Explains His Actions

THE apostles and the brothers throughout Judea heard that the Gentiles also had received the word of God. 2 So when Peter went up to Jerusalem,

c Gk brothers

r 46 Or other languages

believers*d* criticized him, ³saying, "Why did you go to uncircumcised men and eat with them?" ⁴Then Peter began to explain it to them, step by step, saying, ⁵"I was in the city of Joppa praying, and in a trance I saw a vision. There was something like a large sheet coming down from heaven, being lowered by its four corners; and it came close to me. ⁶As I looked at it closely I saw four-footed animals, beasts of prey, reptiles, and birds of the air. ⁷I also heard a voice saying to me, 'Get up, Peter; kill and eat.' ⁸But I replied, 'By no means, Lord; for nothing profane or unclean has ever entered by mouth.' ⁹But a second time the voice answered from heaven, 'What God has made clean, you must not call profane.' ¹⁰This happened three times; then everything was pulled up again to heaven. ¹¹At that very moment three men, sent to me from Caesarea, arrived at the house where we were. ¹²The Spirit told me to go with them and not to make a distinction between them and us.*e* These six brothers also accompanied me, and we entered the man's house. ¹³He told us how he had seen the angel standing in his house and saying, 'Send to Joppa and bring Simon, who is called Peter; ¹⁴he will give you a message by which you and your entire household will be saved.' ¹⁵And

---

ἐκ περιτομῆς 3 λέγοντες ὅτι εἰσῆλθες
of [the] circumcision   saying[,]   – Thou enteredst

πρὸς ἄνδρας ἀκροβυστίαν ἔχοντας καὶ
to   men   uncircumcision   having   and

συνέφαγες αὐτοῖς. 4 ἀρξάμενος δὲ Πέτρος
didst eat with   them.   And beginning   Peter

ἐξετίθετο αὐτοῖς καθεξῆς λέγων· 5 ἐγὼ
explained   to them   in order   saying: I

ἤμην ἐν πόλει Ἰόππῃ προσευχόμενος, καὶ
was   in [the] city   Joppa   praying,   and

εἶδον ἐν ἐκστάσει ὅραμα, καταβαῖνον
I saw   in   an ecstasy   a vision,   coming down

σκεῦός τι ὡς ὀθόνην μεγάλην τέσσαρσιν
a certain vessel   as   sheet   a great   by four

ἀρχαῖς καθιεμένην ἐκ τοῦ οὐρανοῦ, καὶ
corners   having been let down out of   –   heaven,   and

ἦλθεν ἄχρι ἐμοῦ· 6 εἰς ἣν ἀτενίσας
it came   up to   me;   into   which   gazing

κατενόουν, καὶ εἶδον τὰ τετράποδα τῆς
I perceived,   and   I saw   the   quadrupeds   of the

γῆς καὶ τὰ θηρία καὶ τὰ ἑρπετὰ καὶ τὰ
earth   and   the wild beasts and   the   reptiles   and   the

πετεινὰ τοῦ οὐρανοῦ. 7 ἤκουσα δὲ καὶ
birds   of the heaven(air).   And I heard   also

φωνῆς λεγούσης μοι· ἀναστάς, Πέτρε,
a voice   saying   to me: Rise up,   Peter,

θῦσον καὶ φάγε. 8 εἶπον δέ· μηδαμῶς,
slay   and   eat.   And I said :   Not at all,

κύριε, ὅτι κοινὸν ἢ ἀκάθαρτον οὐδέποτε
Lord,   because a common   or   unclean thing   never

εἰσῆλθεν εἰς τὸ στόμα μου. 9 ἀπεκρίθη δὲ
entered   into   the   mouth   of me.   And answered

ἐκ δευτέρου φωνὴ ἐκ τοῦ οὐρανοῦ·
a second [time]   a voice   out of   –   heaven:

ἃ ὁ θεὸς ἐκαθάρισεν σὺ μὴ κοίνου.
What –   God   cleansed   thou regard not common.
things

10 τοῦτο δὲ ἐγένετο ἐπὶ τρίς, καὶ
And this   happened   on three [occasions], and

ἀνεσπάσθη πάλιν ἅπαντα εἰς τὸν οὐρανόν.
was pulled up   again   all things   to   –   heaven.

11 καὶ ἰδοὺ ἐξαυτῆς τρεῖς ἄνδρες ἐπέστησαν
And behold   at once   three   men   stood *at*

ἐπὶ τὴν οἰκίαν ἐν ᾗ ἦμεν, ἀπεσταλμένοι
at   the   house   in which I was,   having been sent

ἀπὸ Καισαρείας πρός με. 12 εἶπεν δὲ
from   Caesarea   to   me.   And ²told

τὸ πνεῦμά μοι συνελθεῖν αὐτοῖς μηδὲν
¹the   ²Spirit   ⁴me   to go with   them   nothing

διακρίναντα. ἦλθον δὲ σὺν ἐμοὶ καὶ
doubting.   And came   with   me   also

οἱ ἐξ ἀδελφοὶ οὗτοι, καὶ εἰσήλθομεν εἰς
–   six   brothers   these,   and   we entered   into

τὸν οἶκον τοῦ ἀνδρός. 13 ἀπήγγειλεν δὲ
the   house   of the   man.   And he reported

ἡμῖν πῶς εἶδεν τὸν ἄγγελον ἐν τῷ
to us   how   he saw   the   angel   in   the

οἴκῳ αὐτοῦ σταθέντα καὶ εἰπόντα·
house   of him   standing   and   saying:

ἀπόστειλον εἰς Ἰόππην καὶ μετάπεμψαι
Send   to   Joppa   and   summon

Σίμωνα τὸν ἐπικαλούμενον Πέτρον, 14 ὃς
Simon   –   *being* surnamed   Peter,   who

λαλήσει ῥήματα πρὸς σὲ ἐν οἷς σωθήσῃ
will speak   words   to   thee by   which   mayest be saved

σὺ καὶ πᾶς ὁ οἶκός σου. 15 ἐν δὲ
thou   and   all   the   household of thee.   And in

---

the circumcised believers criticized him ³and said, "You went into the house of uncircumcised men and ate with them."

⁴Peter began and explained everything to them precisely as it had happened: ⁵"I was in the city of Joppa praying, and in a trance I saw a vision. I saw something like a large sheet being let down from heaven by its four corners, and it came down to where I was. ⁶I looked into it and saw four-footed animals of the earth, wild beasts, reptiles, and birds of the air. ⁷Then I heard a voice telling me, 'Get up, Peter. Kill and eat.'

⁸"I replied, 'Surely not, Lord! Nothing impure or unclean has ever entered my mouth.'

⁹"The voice spoke from heaven a second time, 'Do not call anything impure that God has made clean.' ¹⁰This happened three times, and then it was all pulled up to heaven again.

¹¹"Right then three men who had been sent to me from Caesarea stopped at the house where I was staying. ¹²The Spirit told me to have no hesitation about going with them. These six brothers also went with me, and we entered the man's house. ¹³He told us how he had seen an angel appear in his house and say, 'Send to Joppa for Simon who is called Peter. ¹⁴He will bring you a message through which you and all your household will be saved.'

---

d Gk lacks believers
e Or not to hesitate

as I began to speak, the Holy Spirit fell upon them just as it had upon us at the beginning. 16 And I remembered the word of the Lord, how he had said, 'John baptized with water, but you will be baptized with the Holy Spirit.' 17 If then God gave them the same gift that he gave us when we believed in the Lord Jesus Christ, who was I that I could hinder God?" 18 When they heard this, they were silenced. And they praised God, saying, "Then God has given even to the Gentiles the repentance that leads to life."

The Church in Antioch

19 Now those who were scattered because of the persecution that took place over Stephen traveled as far as Phoenicia, Cyprus, and Antioch, and they spoke the word to no one except Jews. 20 But among them were some men of Cyprus and Cyrene who, on coming to Antioch, spoke to the Hellenists[f] also, proclaiming the Lord Jesus. 21 The hand of the Lord was with them, and a great number became believers and turned to the Lord. 22 News of this came to the ears of the church in Jerusalem, and they sent Barnabas to Antioch. 23 When he came and saw the grace of God, he rejoiced, and he exhorted them all to remain faithful to the Lord with steadfast devotion; 24 for he was a good man, full of the Holy Spirit and of faith. And a

τῷ   ἄρξασθαί   με   λαλεῖν   ἐπέπεσεν   τὸ
the   to begin   me   to speak   'fell on   'the
=as I began

πνεῦμα   τὸ   ἄγιον   ἐπ'   αὐτοὺς   ὥσπερ   καὶ
'Spirit   -   'Holy   on   them   as   also

ἐφ'   ἡμᾶς   ἐν   ἀρχῇ.   16 ἐμνήσθην   δὲ   τοῦ
on   us   at [the] beginning.   And I remembered   the

ῥήματος   τοῦ   κυρίου,   ὡς   ἔλεγεν·   Ἰωάννης
word   of the   Lord,   how   he said: John

μὲν   ἐβάπτισεν   ὕδατι,   ὑμεῖς   δὲ   βαπτισθήσεσθε
indeed   baptized   with water,   but ye   will be baptized

ἐν   πνεύματι   ἁγίῳ.   17 εἰ   οὖν   τὴν   ἴσην
in   Spirit   Holy.   If   therefore   'the   'equal

δωρεὰν   ἔδωκεν   αὐτοῖς   ὁ   θεὸς   ὡς   καὶ
'gift   'gave   'them   -   'God   as   also

ἡμῖν,   πιστεύσασιν   ἐπὶ   τὸν   κύριον   Ἰησοῦν
to us,   having believed   on   the   Lord   Jesus

Χριστόν,   ἐγὼ   τίς   ἤμην   δυνατὸς   κωλῦσαι
Christ,   'I   'who   'was   [to be] able   to hinder

τὸν   θεόν;   18 ἀκούσαντες   δὲ   ταῦτα   ἡσύχασαν,
-    God?   And hearing   these things   they kept silence

καὶ   ἐδόξασαν   τὸν   θεὸν   λέγοντες·   ἄρα   καὶ
and   glorified   -   God   saying :   Then   also

τοῖς   ἔθνεσιν   ὁ   θεὸς   τὴν   μετάνοιαν   εἰς
to the   nations   -   God   -   repentance   to

ζωὴν   ἔδωκεν.
life   gave.

19 Οἱ   μὲν   οὖν   διασπαρέντες   ἀπὸ   τῆς
The [ones] –   therefore   being scattered   from   the

θλίψεως   τῆς   γενομένης   ἐπὶ   Στεφάνῳ
affliction   -   occurring   over   Stephen

διῆλθον   ἕως   Φοινίκης   καὶ   Κύπρου   καὶ
passed through   to   Phœnicia   and   Cyprus   and

Ἀντιοχείας,   μηδενὶ   λαλοῦντες   τὸν   λόγον
Antioch,   to no one   speaking   the   word

εἰ   μὴ   μόνον   Ἰουδαίοις.   **20** Ἦσαν   δὲ
except   only   to Jews.   But   'were

τινες   ἐξ   αὐτῶν   ἄνδρες   Κύπριοι   καὶ
'some   'of   'them   men   Cypriotes   and

Κυρηναῖοι,   οἵτινες   ἐλθόντες   εἰς   Ἀντιόχειαν
Cyrenians,   who   coming   to   Antioch

ἐλάλουν   καὶ   πρὸς   τοὺς   Ἕλληνας,
spoke   also   to   the   Greeks,

εὐαγγελιζόμενοι   τὸν   κύριον   Ἰησοῦν.   **21** καὶ   ἦν
preaching   the   Lord   Jesus.   And was

χεὶρ   κυρίου   μετ'   αὐτῶν,   πολύς   τε
[the] hand   of [the] Lord   with   them,   and a much(great)

ἀριθμὸς   ὁ   πιστεύσας   ἐπέστρεψεν   ἐπὶ   τὸν
number   -   believing   turned   to   the

κύριον.   **22** Ἠκούσθη   δὲ   ὁ   λόγος   εἰς
Lord.   And was heard   the   account   in

τὰ   ὦτα   τῆς   ἐκκλησίας   τῆς   οὔσης   ἐν
the   ears   of the   church   -   being   in

Ἰερουσαλὴμ   περὶ   αὐτῶν,   καὶ   ἐξαπέστειλαν
Jerusalem   about   them,   and   they sent out

Βαρναβᾶν   ἕως   Ἀντιοχείας·   **23** ὃς   παραγεν-
Barnabas   to   Antioch;   who   arriv-

όμενος   καὶ   ἰδὼν   τὴν   χάριν   τὴν   τοῦ
ing   and   seeing   the   grace   -   -

θεοῦ   ἐχάρη,   καὶ   παρεκάλει   πάντας   τῇ
of God   rejoiced,   and   exhorted   all   -

προθέσει   τῆς   καρδίας   προσμένειν   τῷ
with purpose   -   of heart   to remain with   the

κυρίῳ,   **24** ὅτι   ἦν   ἀνὴρ   ἀγαθὸς   καὶ
Lord,   because   he was   man   a good   and

πλήρης   πνεύματος   ἁγίου   καὶ   πίστεως.
full   of [the] Spirit   Holy   and   of faith.

15 "As I began to speak, the Holy Spirit came on them as he had come on us at the beginning. 16 Then I remembered what the Lord had said: 'John baptized with[s] water, but you will be baptized with the Holy Spirit.' 17 So if God gave them the same gift as he gave us, who believed in the Lord Jesus Christ, who was I to think that I could oppose God?" 18 When they heard this, they had no further objections and praised God, saying, "So then, God has granted even the Gentiles repentance unto life."

The Church in Antioch

19 Now those who had been scattered by the persecution in connection with Stephen traveled as far as Phoenicia, Cyprus and Antioch, telling the message only to Jews. 20 Some of them, however, men from Cyprus and Cyrene, went to Antioch and began to speak to Greeks also, telling them the good news about the Lord Jesus. 21 The Lord's hand was with them, and a great number of people believed and turned to the Lord. 22 News of this reached the ears of the church at Jerusalem, and they sent Barnabas to Antioch. 23 When he arrived and saw the evidence of the grace of God, he was glad and encouraged them all to remain true to the Lord with all their hearts. 24 He was a good man, full of the Holy Spirit and faith, and a great num-

great many people were brought to the Lord. 25 Then Barnabas went to Tarsus to look for Saul, 26 and when he had found him, he brought him to Antioch. So it was that for an entire year they met with g the church and taught a great many people, and it was in Antioch that the disciples were first called "Christians."

27 At that time prophets came down from Jerusalem to Antioch. 28 One of them named Agabus stood up and predicted by the Spirit that there would be a severe famine over all the world; and this took place during the reign of Claudius. 29 The disciples determined that according to their ability, each would send relief to the believers h living in Judea; 30 this they did, sending it to the elders by Barnabas and Saul.

καὶ προσετέθη ὄχλος ἱκανὸς τῷ κυρίῳ.
And was added a crowd considerable to the Lord.

25 ἐξῆλθεν δὲ εἰς Ταρσὸν ἀναζητῆσαι
And he went forth to Tarsus to seek

Σαῦλον, 26 καὶ εὑρὼν ἤγαγεν εἰς Ἀντιόχειαν.
Saul, and finding brought to Antioch.

ἐγένετο δὲ αὐτοῖς καὶ ἐνιαυτὸν ὅλον
And it happened to them also year a whole

συναχθῆναι ἐν τῇ ἐκκλησίᾳ καὶ διδάξαι
to be assembled in the church and to teach

ὄχλον ἱκανόν, χρηματίσαι τε πρώτως ἐν
a crowd considerable, and to call firstly in

Ἀντιοχείᾳ τοὺς μαθητὰς Χριστιανούς.
Antioch the disciples Christians.

27 Ἐν ταύταις δὲ ταῖς ἡμέραις κατῆλθον
And in these - days came down

ἀπὸ Ἱεροσολύμων προφῆται εἰς Ἀντιόχειαν·
from Jerusalem prophets to Antioch;

28 ἀναστὰς δὲ εἷς ἐξ αὐτῶν ὀνόματι
and rising up one of them by name

Ἄγαβος ἐσήμαινεν διὰ τοῦ πνεύματος
Agabus signified through the Spirit

λιμὸν μεγάλην μέλλειν ἔσεσθαι ἐφ' ὅλην τὴν
famine a great to be about to be over all the

οἰκουμένην· ἥτις ἐγένετο ἐπὶ Κλαυδίου.
inhabited earth; which happened in the time of Claudius.

29 τῶν δὲ μαθητῶν καθὼς εὐπορεῖτό
So ²of the ⁴disciples ¹as ³was prosperous

τις, ὥρισαν ἕκαστος αὐτῶν εἰς διακονίαν
¹anyone, they determined each of them for ministration

πέμψαι τοῖς κατοικοῦσιν ἐν τῇ Ἰουδαίᾳ
to send ¹to the ³dwelling ⁴in - ⁵Judæa

ἀδελφοῖς· 30 ὃ καὶ ἐποίησαν ἀποστείλαντες
²brothers; which indeed they did sending

πρὸς τοὺς πρεσβυτέρους διὰ χειρὸς
to the elders through [the] hand

Βαρναβᾶ καὶ Σαύλου.
of Barnabas and of Saul.

ber of people were brought to the Lord. 25 Then Barnabas went to Tarsus to look for Saul, 26 and when he found him, he brought him to Antioch. So for a whole year Barnabas and Saul met with the church and taught great numbers of people. The disciples were called Christians first at Antioch. 27 During this time some prophets came down from Jerusalem to Antioch. 28 One of them, named Agabus, stood up and through the Spirit predicted that a severe famine would spread over the entire Roman world. (This happened during the reign of Claudius.) 29 The disciples, each according to his ability, decided to provide help for the brothers living in Judea. 30 This they did, sending their gift to the elders by Barnabas and Saul.

Chapter 12

James Killed and Peter Imprisoned

ABOUT that time King Herod laid violent hands upon some who belonged to the church. 2 He had James, the brother of John, killed with the sword. 3 After he saw that it pleased the Jews, he proceeded to arrest Peter also. (This was during the festival of Unleavened Bread.) 4 When he had seized him, he put him in prison and handed him over to four squads of soldiers to guard him, intending to bring him out to the people after the Passover. 5 While Peter was kept in prison, the church prayed fervently to

Chapter 12

12 Κατ' ἐκεῖνον δὲ τὸν καιρὸν ἐπέβαλεν
Now at that - time laid on

Ἡρῴδης ὁ βασιλεὺς τὰς χεῖρας κακῶσαι
Herod the king the(his) hands to ill-treat

τινας τῶν ἀπὸ τῆς ἐκκλησίας. 2 ἀνεῖλεν δὲ
some of the [ones] from the church. And he killed

Ἰάκωβον τὸν ἀδελφὸν Ἰωάννου μαχαίρῃ.
James the brother of John with a sword.

3 ἰδὼν δὲ ὅτι ἀρεστόν ἐστιν τοῖς Ἰουδαίοις
And seeing that pleasing it is(was) to the Jews

προσέθετο συλλαβεῖν καὶ Πέτρον, ἦσαν δὲ
he added to arrest also Peter, and they were

ἡμέραι τῶν ἀζύμων, 4 ὃν καὶ πιάσας
days - of unleavened bread, whom also seizing

ἔθετο εἰς φυλακήν, παραδοὺς τέσσαρσιν
he put in prison, delivering to four

τετραδίοις στρατιωτῶν φυλάσσειν αὐτόν,
quaternions of soldiers to guard him,

βουλόμενος μετὰ τὸ πάσχα ἀναγαγεῖν
intending after the Passover to bring up

αὐτὸν τῷ λαῷ. 5 ὁ μὲν οὖν Πέτρος
him to the people. - -* therefore Peter

ἐτηρεῖτο ἐν τῇ φυλακῇ· προσευχὴ δὲ ἦν
was kept in the prison; but prayer was

Peter's Miraculous Escape From Prison

IT was about this time that King Herod arrested some who belonged to the church, intending to persecute them. 2 He had James, the brother of John, put to death with the sword. 3 When he saw that this pleased the Jews, he proceeded to seize Peter also. This happened during the Feast of Unleavened Bread. 4 After arresting him, he put him in prison, handing him over to be guarded by four squads of four soldiers each. Herod intended to bring him out for public trial after the Passover. 5 So Peter was kept in prison, but the church was

g Or were guests of
h Gk brothers

* μέν and δέ are in contrast : "on one hand . . ."—"on the other . . ."

God for him.

Peter Delivered from Prison

6 The very night before Herod was going to bring him out, Peter, bound with two chains, was sleeping between two soldiers, while guards in front of the door were keeping watch over the prison. 7 Suddenly an angel of the Lord appeared and a light shone in the cell. He tapped Peter on the side and woke him, saying, "Get up quickly." And the chains fell off his wrists. 8 The angel said to him, "Fasten your belt and put on your sandals." He did so. Then he said to him, "Wrap your cloak around you and follow me." 9 Peter[i] went out and followed him; he did not realize that what was happening with the angel's help was real; he thought he was seeing a vision. 10 After they had passed the first and the second guard, they came before the iron gate leading into the city. It opened for them of its own accord, and they went outside and walked along a lane, when suddenly the angel left him. 11 Then Peter came to himself and said, "Now I am sure that the Lord has sent his angel and rescued me from the hands of Herod and from all that the Jewish people were expecting." 12 As soon as he realized this, he went to the house of Mary, the mother of John whose other name was Mark, where many had gathered and were praying.

ἐκτενῶς γινομένη ὑπὸ τῆς ἐκκλησίας πρὸς
earnestly being made by the church to
τὸν θεὸν περὶ αὐτοῦ. 6 Ὅτε δὲ ἤμελλεν
– God concerning him. And when ²was about
προαγαγεῖν αὐτὸν ὁ Ἡρῴδης, τῇ νυκτὶ
²to bring forward ⁴him – ¹Herod, – ²night
ἐκείνῃ ἦν ὁ Πέτρος κοιμώμενος μεταξὺ
¹in that was – Peter sleeping between
δύο στρατιωτῶν δεδεμένος ἀλύσεσιν δυσίν,
two soldiers having been bound with chains two,
φύλακές τε πρὸ τῆς θύρας ἐτήρουν τὴν
and guards before the door were keeping the
φυλακήν. 7 καὶ ἰδοὺ ἄγγελος κυρίου
prison. And behold[,] an angel of [the] Lord
ἐπέστη, καὶ φῶς ἔλαμψεν ἐν τῷ οἰκήματι·
came upon, and a light shone in the building;
πατάξας δὲ τὴν πλευρὰν τοῦ Πέτρου
and striking the side – of Peter
ἤγειρεν αὐτὸν λέγων· ἀνάστα ἐν τάχει.
he raised him saying: Rise up in haste.
καὶ ἐξέπεσαν αὐτοῦ αἱ ἀλύσεις ἐκ τῶν
And fell off of him the chains off the(his)
χειρῶν. 8 εἶπεν δὲ ὁ ἄγγελος πρὸς
hands. And said the angel to
αὐτόν· ζῶσαι καὶ ὑπόδησαι τὰ σανδάλιά
him: Gird thyself and put on the sandals
σου. ἐποίησεν δὲ οὕτως. καὶ λέγει
of thee. And he did so. And he tells
αὐτῷ· περιβαλοῦ τὸ ἱμάτιόν σου καὶ
him: Cast round the garment of thee and
ἀκολούθει μοι. 9 καὶ ἐξελθὼν ἠκολούθει,
follow me. And going forth he followed,
καὶ οὐκ ᾔδει ὅτι ἀληθές ἐστιν τὸ
and knew not that ³true ²is(was) ¹the thing
γινόμενον διὰ τοῦ ἀγγέλου, ἐδόκει δὲ
happening through the angel, but he thought
ὅραμα βλέπειν. 10 διελθόντες δὲ πρώτην
a vision to see. And going through [the] first
φυλακὴν καὶ δευτέραν ἦλθαν ἐπὶ τὴν
prison and [the] second they came on the
πύλην τὴν σιδηρᾶν τὴν φέρουσαν εἰς τὴν
gate – iron – leading to the
πόλιν, ἥτις αὐτομάτη ἠνοίγη αὐτοῖς, καὶ
city, which of itself was opened to them, and
ἐξελθόντες προῆλθον ῥύμην μίαν, καὶ
going out they went forward street one, and
εὐθέως ἀπέστη ὁ ἄγγελος ἀπ᾽ αὐτοῦ.
immediately departed the angel from him.
11 καὶ ὁ Πέτρος ἐν ἑαυτῷ γενόμενος
And – Peter in himself having become
εἶπεν· νῦν οἶδα ἀληθῶς ὅτι ἐξαπέστειλεν
said: Now I know truly that sent forth
ὁ κύριος τὸν ἄγγελον αὐτοῦ καὶ ἐξείλατό
the Lord the angel of him and delivered
με ἐκ χειρὸς Ἡρῴδου καὶ πάσης τῆς
me out of [the] hand of Herod and of all the
προσδοκίας τοῦ λαοῦ τῶν Ἰουδαίων.
expectation of the people of the Jews.
12 συνιδών τε ἦλθεν ἐπὶ τὴν οἰκίαν τῆς
And realizing he came on the house of
Μαρίας τῆς μητρὸς Ἰωάννου τοῦ
of Mary the mother of John –
ἐπικαλουμένου Μάρκου, οὗ ἦσαν ἱκανοὶ
being surnamed Mark, where were many
συνηθροισμένοι καὶ προσευχόμενοι. 13 κρού-
having been assembled and praying. And

earnestly praying to God for him.
6 The night before Herod was to bring him to trial, Peter was sleeping between two soldiers, bound with two chains, and sentries stood guard at the entrance. 7 Suddenly an angel of the Lord appeared and a light shone in the cell. He struck Peter on the side and woke him up. "Quick, get up!" he said, and the chains fell off Peter's wrists. 8 Then the angel said to him, "Put on your clothes and sandals." And Peter did so. "Wrap your cloak around you and follow me," the angel told him. 9 Peter followed him out of the prison, but he had no idea that what the angel was doing was really happening; he thought he was seeing a vision. 10 They passed the first and second guards and came to the iron gate leading to the city. It opened for them by itself, and they went through it. When they had walked the length of one street, suddenly the angel left him. 11 Then Peter came to himself and said, "Now I know without a doubt that the Lord sent his angel and rescued me from Herod's clutches and from everything the Jewish people were anticipating." 12 When this had dawned on him, he went to the house of Mary the mother of John, also called Mark, where many people had gathered and were praying.

[i] Gk He

13When he knocked at the outer gate, a maid named Rhoda came to answer. 14On recognizing Peter's voice, she was so overjoyed that, instead of opening the gate, she ran in and announced that Peter was standing at the gate. 15They said to her, "You are out of your mind!" But she insisted that it was so. They said, "It is his angel." 16Meanwhile Peter continued knocking; and when they opened the gate, they saw him and were amazed. 17He motioned to them with his hand to be silent, and described for them how the Lord had brought him out of the prison. And he added, "Tell this to James and to the believers."*h* Then he left and went to another place. 18 When morning came, there was no small commotion among the soldiers over what had become of Peter. 19When Herod had searched for him and could not find him, he examined the guards and ordered them to be put to death. Then Peter*j* went down from Judea to Caesarea and stayed there.

The Death of Herod

20 Now Herod was angry with the people of Tyre and Sidon. So they came to him in a body; and after winning over Blastus, the king's chamberlain, they asked for a reconciliation, because their country depended on the king's country for food. 21On an appointed day Herod put on his royal robes, took his seat on the platform, and delivered a public address to them. 22The people kept shouting, "The voice of a

---

σαντος δὲ αὐτοῦ τὴν θύραν τοῦ πυλῶνος
knocking　him*ª*　the　door　of the　porch
=as he knocked

προσῆλθεν παιδίσκη ὑπακοῦσαι ὀνόματι
approached　a maidservant　to listen　by name

'Ρόδη, 14 καὶ ἐπιγνοῦσα τὴν φωνὴν τοῦ
Rhoda,　and　recognizing　the　voice　—

Πέτρου ἀπὸ τῆς χαρᾶς οὐκ ἤνοιξεν τὸν
of Peter　from　—　joy　she did not open　the

πυλῶνα, εἰσδραμοῦσα δὲ ἀπήγγειλεν ἑστάναι
porch,　but running in　announced　*ª*to stand

τὸν Πέτρον πρὸ τοῦ πυλῶνος. 15 οἱ δὲ
—　*¹*Peter　before　the　porch.　But they

πρὸς αὐτὴν εἶπαν· μαίνῃ. ἡ δὲ διϊσχυρίζετο
to　her　said: Thou ravest. But she emphatically asserted

οὕτως ἔχειν. οἱ δὲ ἔλεγον· ὁ ἄγγελός
so　to have(be). So they　said:　The　angel

ἐστιν αὐτοῦ. 16 ὁ δὲ Πέτρος ἐπέμενεν
it is　of him.　—　But　Peter　continued

κρούων· ἀνοίξαντες δὲ εἶδαν αὐτὸν καὶ
knocking;　and having opened　they saw　him　and

ἐξέστησαν. 17 κατασείσας δὲ αὐτοῖς τῇ
were amazed.　And beckoning　to them with the

χειρὶ σιγᾶν διηγήσατο αὐτοῖς πῶς ὁ
hand　to be quiet　he related　to them　how　the

κύριος αὐτὸν ἐξήγαγεν ἐκ τῆς φυλακῆς,
Lord　him　led *out*　out of the　prison,

εἶπέν τε· ἀπαγγείλατε 'Ιακώβῳ καὶ τοῖς
and said:　Report　to James　and　to the

ἀδελφοῖς ταῦτα. καὶ ἐξελθὼν ἐπορεύθη εἰς
brothers　these things.　And　going out　he went　to

ἕτερον τόπον. 18 Γενομένης δὲ ἡμέρας ἦν
another　place.　And becoming　day*ª*　there was
=when it became day

τάραχος οὐκ ὀλίγος ἐν τοῖς στρατιώταις,
disturbance　not　a little　among　the　soldiers,

τί ἄρα ὁ Πέτρος ἐγένετο. 19 'Ηρῴδης δὲ
what then　[of] Peter　became.　And Herod

ἐπιζητήσας αὐτὸν καὶ μὴ εὑρών,
searching for　him　and　not　finding,

ἀνακρίνας τοὺς φύλακας ἐκέλευσεν ἀπ-
examining　the　guards　commanded　to

αχθῆναι, καὶ κατελθὼν ἀπὸ τῆς 'Ιουδαίας
be led away,*　and　going down　from　—　Judæa

εἰς Καισάρειαν διέτριβεν. 20 *Ην δὲ
to　Cæsarea　stayed.　Now he was

θυμομαχῶν Τυρίοις καὶ Σιδωνίοις·
being furiously angry with　Tyrians　and　Sidonians;

ὁμοθυμαδὸν δὲ παρῆσαν πρὸς αὐτόν, καὶ
and with one mind　they came　to　him,　and

πείσαντες Βλάστον τὸν ἐπὶ τοῦ κοιτῶνος
having persuaded　Blastus　the one over　the　bedchamber

τοῦ βασιλέως ᾐτοῦντο εἰρήνην, διὰ τὸ
of the　king　they asked　peace,　because the

τρέφεσθαι αὐτῶν τὴν χώραν*b* ἀπὸ τῆς
to be fed　of them　the　country*b*　from　the
=their country was fed

βασιλικῆς. 21 τακτῇ δὲ ἡμέρᾳ ὁ 'Ηρῴδης
royal.　And on an appointed day　—　Herod

ἐνδυσάμενος ἐσθῆτα βασιλικὴν καθίσας ἐπὶ
having been arrayed with　clothing　regal　sitting　on

τοῦ βήματος ἐδημηγόρει πρὸς αὐτούς·
the　tribunal　made a public speech　to　them;

22 ὁ δὲ δῆμος ἐπεφώνει· θεοῦ φωνὴ
and the　mob　cried out :　Of a god　a voice

13Peter knocked at the outer entrance, and a servant girl named Rhoda came to answer the door. 14When she recognized Peter's voice, she was so overjoyed she ran back without opening it and exclaimed, "Peter is at the door!" 15"You're out of your mind," they told her. When she kept insisting that it was so, they said, "It must be his angel." 16But Peter kept on knocking, and when they opened the door and saw him, they were astonished. 17Peter motioned with his hand for them to be quiet and described how the Lord had brought him out of prison. "Tell James and the brothers about this," he said, and then he left for another place. 18In the morning, there was no small commotion among the soldiers as to what had become of Peter. 19After Herod had a thorough search for him and did not find him, he cross-examined the guards and ordered that they be executed.

Herod's Death

Then Herod went from Judea to Caesarea and stayed there a while. 20He had been quarreling with the people of Tyre and Sidon; they now joined together and sought an audience with him. Having secured the support of Blastus, a trusted personal servant of the king, they asked for peace, because they depended on the king's country for their food supply. 21On the appointed day Herod, wearing his royal robes, sat on his throne and delivered a public address to the people. 22They shouted, "This is the voice

---

*j*Gk *he*

* That is, to execution.

god, and not of a mortal!" [23]And immediately, because he had not given the glory to God, an angel of the Lord struck him down, and he was eaten by worms and died.

24 But the word of God continued to advance and gain adherents. [25]Then after completing their mission Barnabas and Saul returned to[k] Jerusalem and brought with them John, whose other name was Mark.

καὶ   οὐκ   ἀνθρώπου.   23 παραχρῆμα   δὲ
and   not   of a man.   And at once

ἐπάταξεν   αὐτὸν   ἄγγελος   κυρίου   ἀνθ'   ὧν
smote   him   an angel   of [the] Lord   because

οὐκ   ἔδωκεν   τὴν   δόξαν   τῷ   θεῷ,   καὶ
he gave not   the   glory   -   to God,   and

γενόμενος   σκωληκόβρωτος   ἐξέψυξεν.
becoming   eaten by worms   he expired.

24 Ὁ   δὲ   λόγος   τοῦ   κυρίου   ηὔξανεν
But the   word   of the   Lord   grew

καὶ   ἐπληθύνετο.   25 Βαρναβᾶς   δὲ   καὶ
and   increased.   And Barnabas   and

Σαῦλος   ὑπέστρεψαν   ἐξ   Ἰερουσαλήμ,
Saul   returned   out of   Jerusalem,

πληρώσαντες   τὴν   διακονίαν,   συμπαρα-
having completed   the   ministration,   taking

λαβόντες   Ἰωάννην   τὸν   ἐπικληθέντα   Μᾶρκον.
with [them]   John   -   surnamed   Mark.

---

of a god, not of a man." [23]Immediately, because Herod did not give praise to God, an angel of the Lord struck him down, and he was eaten by worms and died.

[24]But the word of God continued to increase and spread.

[25]When Barnabas and Saul had finished their mission, they returned from[l] Jerusalem, taking with them John, also called Mark.

Chapter 13

Barnabas and Saul Commissioned

NOW in the church at Antioch there were prophets and teachers: Barnabas, Simeon who was called Niger, Lucius of Cyrene, Manaen a member of the court of Herod the ruler,[l] and Saul. [2]While they were worshiping the Lord and fasting, the Holy Spirit said, "Set apart for me Barnabas and Saul for the work to which I have called them." [3]Then after fasting and praying they laid their hands on them and sent them off.

The Apostles Preach in Cyprus

4 So, being sent out by the Holy Spirit, they went down to Seleucia; and from there they sailed to Cyprus. [5]When they arrived at Salamis, they proclaimed the word of God in the synagogues of the Jews. And they had John also to assist them. [6]When they had gone through the whole island as far as Paphos, they met a certain magician, a Jewish false prophet, named Bar-Jesus. [7]He was with the proconsul, Sergius Paulus, an intelligent man,

---

13 Ἦσαν   δὲ   ἐν   Ἀντιοχείᾳ   κατὰ   τὴν
Now there were   in   Antioch   among   the

οὖσαν   ἐκκλησίαν   προφῆται   καὶ   διδάσκαλοι
existing   church   prophets   and   teachers

ὅ   τε   Βαρναβᾶς   καὶ   Συμεὼν   ὁ   καλούμενος
- both   Barnabas   and   Simeon   -   being called

Νίγερ,   καὶ   Λούκιος   ὁ   Κυρηναῖος,   Μαναήν   τε
Niger,   and   Lucius   the   Cyrenian,   and Manaen

Ἡρῴδου   τοῦ   τετραάρχου   σύντροφος
[2]of Herod   [3]the   tetrarch   [1]foster brother

καὶ   Σαῦλος.   2 Λειτουργούντων   δὲ   αὐτῶν
and   Saul.   And ministering   them[a]
           = as they ministered

τῷ   κυρίῳ   καὶ   νηστευόντων   εἶπεν   τὸ
to the   Lord   and   fasting[a]   said   the

πνεῦμα   τὸ   ἅγιον·   ἀφορίσατε   δή   μοι
Spirit   -   Holy: [2]Separate ye   [1]so then   [3]to me

τὸν   Βαρναβᾶν   καὶ   Σαῦλον   εἰς   τὸ   ἔργον
-   Barnabas   and   Saul   for   the   work

ὃ   προσκέκλημαι   αὐτούς·   3 τότε   νηστεύ-
[to] which   I have called   them;   then   having

σαντες   καὶ   προσευξάμενοι   καὶ   ἐπιθέντες
fasted   and   having prayed   and   [1]laying [4]on

τὰς   χεῖρας   αὐτοῖς   ἀπέλυσαν.
[3]the(ir)   [2]hands   [5]them   they dismissed [them].

4 Αὐτοὶ   μὲν   οὖν   ἐκπεμφθέντες   ὑπὸ   τοῦ
They   -   therefore   sent out   by   the

ἁγίου   πνεύματος   κατῆλθον   εἰς   Σελεύκειαν,
Holy   Spirit   went down   to   Seleucia,

ἐκεῖθέν   τε   ἀπέπλευσαν   εἰς   Κύπρον,   5 καὶ
and thence   sailed away   to   Cyprus,   and

γενόμενοι   ἐν   Σαλαμῖνι   κατήγγελλον   τὸν
being   in   Salamis   they announced   the

λόγον   τοῦ   θεοῦ   ἐν   ταῖς   συναγωγαῖς   τῶν
word   -   of God   in   the   synagogues   of the

Ἰουδαίων·   εἶχον   δὲ   καὶ   Ἰωάννην   ὑπηρέτην.
Jews;   and they had   also   John [as]   attendant.

6 Διελθόντες   δὲ   ὅλην   τὴν   νῆσον   ἄχρι
And passing through   all   the   island   unto

Πάφου   εὗρον   ἄνδρα   τινὰ   μάγον   ψευδο-
Paphos   they found   a certain man   a sorcerer   a [2]false

προφήτην   Ἰουδαῖον,   ᾧ   ὄνομα   Βαριησοῦς,
[3]prophet   [1]Jewish,   to whom name[c]   Barjesus,
        = whose name was

7 ὃς   ἦν   σὺν   τῷ   ἀνθυπάτῳ   Σεργίῳ
who   was   with   the   proconsul   Sergius

Chapter 13

Barnabas and Saul Sent Off

IN the church at Antioch there were prophets and teachers: Barnabas, Simeon called Niger, Lucius of Cyrene, Manaen (who had been brought up with Herod the tetrarch) and Saul. [2]While they were worshiping the Lord and fasting, the Holy Spirit said, "Set apart for me Barnabas and Saul for the work to which I have called them." [3]So after they had fasted and prayed, they placed their hands on them and sent them off.

On Cyprus

[4]The two of them, sent on their way by the Holy Spirit, went down to Seleucia and sailed from there to Cyprus. [5]When they arrived at Salamis, they proclaimed the word of God in the Jewish synagogues. John was with them as their helper. [6]They traveled through the whole island until they came to Paphos. There they met a Jewish sorcerer and false prophet named Bar-Jesus, [7]who was an attendant of the proconsul,

---

[k] Other ancient authorities read from

[l] Gk tetrarch

[l]25 Some manuscripts to

who summoned Barnabas and Saul and wanted to hear the word of God. 8 But the magician Elymas (for that is the translation of his name) opposed them and tried to turn the proconsul away from the faith. 9 But Saul, also known as Paul, filled with the Holy Spirit, looked intently at him 10 and said, "You son of the devil, you enemy of all righteousness, full of all deceit and villainy, will you not stop making crooked the straight paths of the Lord? 11 And now listen— the hand of the Lord is against you, and you will be blind for a while, unable to see the sun." Immediately mist and darkness came over him, and he went about groping for someone to lead him by the hand. 12 When the proconsul saw what had happened, he believed, for he was astonished at the teaching about the Lord.

Paul and Barnabas in Antioch of Pisidia

13 Then Paul and his companions set sail from Paphos and came to Perga in Pamphylia. John, however, left them and returned to Jerusalem; 14 but they went on from Perga and came to Antioch in Pisidia. And on the sabbath day they went into the synagogue and sat down. 15 After the reading of the law and the prophets, the officials of the synagogue sent them a message, saying, "Brothers, if you have any word of exhortation for the people, give it." 16 So Paul stood up and with a gesture began to speak:

Παύλῳ, ἀνδρὶ συνετῷ. οὗτος προσ-
Paulus, man an intelligent. This man calling

καλεσάμενος Βαρναβᾶν καὶ Σαῦλον ἐπεζήτησεν
to [him] Barnabas and Saul sought

ἀκοῦσαι τὸν λόγον τοῦ θεοῦ· 8 ἀνθίστατο δὲ
to hear the word – of God; but opposed

αὐτοῖς Ἐλύμας ὁ μάγος, οὕτως γὰρ
them Elymas the sorcerer, for so

μεθερμηνεύεται τὸ ὄνομα αὐτοῦ, ζητῶν
is translated the name of him, seeking

διαστρέψαι τὸν ἀνθύπατον ἀπὸ τῆς
to divert the proconsul from the

πίστεως. 9 Σαῦλος δέ, ὁ καὶ Παῦλος,
faith. But Saul, the [one] also Paul,

πλησθεὶς πνεύματος ἁγίου ἀτενίσας εἰς
filled of(with) Spirit Holy gazing at

αὐτὸν εἶπεν· 10 ὦ πλήρης παντὸς δόλου,
him said: O full of all deceit

καὶ πάσης ῥᾳδιουργίας, υἱὲ διαβόλου,
and of all fraud, son of [the] devil,

ἐχθρὲ πάσης δικαιοσύνης, οὐ παύσῃ
enemy of all righteousness, wilt thou not cease

διαστρέφων τὰς ὁδοὺς τοῦ κυρίου τὰς
perverting the ways of the Lord –

εὐθείας; 11 καὶ νῦν ἰδοὺ χεὶρ κυρίου
right? And now behold[,] [the] hand of [the] Lord

ἐπὶ σέ, καὶ ἔσῃ τυφλὸς μὴ βλέπων
[is] on thee, and thou wilt be blind not seeing

τὸν ἥλιον ἄχρι καιροῦ. παραχρῆμα δὲ
the sun until [such] a time. And at once

ἔπεσεν ἐπ᾽ αὐτὸν ἀχλὺς καὶ σκότος, καὶ
fell on him a mist and darkness, and

περιάγων ἐζήτει χειραγωγούς. 12 τότε
going about he sought leaders by the hand. Then

ἰδὼν ὁ ἀνθύπατος τὸ γεγονὸς
²seeing ¹the ²proconsul the thing having occurred

ἐπίστευσεν, ἐκπλησσόμενος ἐπὶ τῇ διδαχῇ
believed, being astounded at the teaching

τοῦ κυρίου.
of the Lord.

13 Ἀναχθέντες δὲ ἀπὸ τῆς Πάφου οἱ
And setting sail from – Paphos the ones

περὶ Παῦλον ἦλθον εἰς Πέργην τῆς
around(with) Paul came to Perga the

Παμφυλίας· Ἰωάννης δὲ ἀποχωρήσας ἀπ᾽
of Pamphylia; and John departing from

αὐτῶν ὑπέστρεψεν εἰς Ἱεροσόλυμα.
them returned to Jerusalem.

14 Αὐτοὶ δὲ διελθόντες ἀπὸ τῆς Πέργης
And they going through from – Perga

παρεγένοντο εἰς Ἀντιόχειαν τὴν Πισιδίαν,
arrived in Antioch the Pisidian,

καὶ ἐλθόντες εἰς τὴν συναγωγὴν τῇ
and going into the synagogue on the

ἡμέρᾳ τῶν σαββάτων ἐκάθισαν. 15 μετὰ δὲ
day of the sabbaths sat down. And after

τὴν ἀνάγνωσιν τοῦ νόμου καὶ τῶν
the reading of the law and of the

προφητῶν ἀπέστειλαν οἱ ἀρχισυνάγωγοι
prophets sent the synagogue rulers

πρὸς αὐτοὺς λέγοντες· ἄνδρες ἀδελφοί,
to them saying: Men brothers,

εἴ τίς ἐστιν ἐν ὑμῖν λόγος παρακλήσεως
¹if ²any ³there is ²among ⁴you ¹word of exhortation

πρὸς τὸν λαόν, λέγετε. 16 ἀναστὰς δὲ
to the people, say ye. And ¹rising up

Sergius Paulus. The proconsul, an intelligent man, sent for Barnabas and Saul because he wanted to hear the word of God. 8 But Elymas the sorcerer (for that is what his name means) opposed them and tried to turn the proconsul from the faith. 9 Then Saul, who was also called Paul, filled with the Holy Spirit, looked straight at Elymas and said, 10 "You are a child of the devil and an enemy of everything that is right! You are full of all kinds of deceit and trickery. Will you never stop perverting the right ways of the Lord? 11 Now the hand of the Lord is against you. You are going to be blind, and for a time you will be unable to see the light of the sun."

Immediately mist and darkness came over him, and he groped about, seeking someone to lead him by the hand. 12 When the proconsul saw what had happened, he believed, for he was amazed at the teaching about the Lord.

In Pisidian Antioch

13 From Paphos, Paul and his companions sailed to Perga in Pamphylia, where John left them to return to Jerusalem. 14 From Perga they went on to Pisidian Antioch. On the Sabbath they entered the synagogue and sat down. 15 After the reading from the Law and the Prophets, the synagogue rulers sent word to them, saying, "Brothers, if you have a message of encouragement for the people, please speak."

16 Standing up, Paul mo-

"You Israelites,[m] and others who fear God, listen. [17] The God of this people Israel chose our ancestors and made the people great during their stay in the land of Egypt, and with uplifted arm he led them out of it. [18] For about forty years he put up with[n] them in the wilderness. [19] After he had destroyed seven nations in the land of Canaan, he gave them their land as an inheritance [20] for about four hundred fifty years. After that he gave them judges until the time of the prophet Samuel. [21] Then they asked for a king; and God gave them Saul son of Kish, a man of the tribe of Benjamin, who reigned for forty years. [22] When he had removed him, he made David their king. In his testimony about him he said, 'I have found David, son of Jesse, to be a man after my heart, who will carry out all my wishes.' [23] Of this man's posterity God has brought to Israel a Savior, Jesus, as he promised; [24] before his coming John had already proclaimed a baptism of repentance to all the people of Israel. [25] And as John was finishing his work, he said, 'What do you suppose that I am? I am not he. No, but one is coming after me; I am not worthy to untie the thong of the sandals[o] on his feet.'

[26] "My brothers, you descendants of Abraham's family, and others who fear God, to us[p] the message of

Παῦλος καὶ κατασείσας τῇ χειρὶ εἶπεν·
[1]Paul [2]and [3]beckoning [4]with the(his) [5]hand said:

ἄνδρες Ἰσραηλῖται καὶ οἱ φοβούμενοι τὸν
Men Israelites and the [ones] fearing -

θεόν, ἀκούσατε. 17 ὁ θεὸς τοῦ λαοῦ
God, hear ye. The God - people

τούτου Ἰσραὴλ ἐξελέξατο τοὺς πατέρας
of this Israel chose the fathers

ἡμῶν, καὶ τὸν λαὸν ὕψωσεν ἐν τῇ
of us, and [2]the [3]people [1]exalted in the

παροικίᾳ ἐν γῇ Αἰγύπτου, καὶ μετὰ
sojourn in [the] land of Egypt, and with

βραχίονος ὑψηλοῦ ἐξήγαγεν αὐτοὺς ἐξ
arm a high he led forth them out of

αὐτῆς, 18 καὶ ὡς τεσσερακονταέτη χρόνον
it, and about forty years time

ἐτροποφόρησεν αὐτοὺς ἐν τῇ ἐρήμῳ, 19 καὶ
endured them in the desert, and

καθελὼν ἔθνη ἑπτὰ ἐν γῇ Χανάαν
having destroyed nations seven in [the] land Canaan

κατεκληρονόμησεν τὴν γῆν αὐτῶν 20 ὡς
gave as an inheritance the land of them about

ἔτεσιν τετρακοσίοις καὶ πεντήκοντα. καὶ
years four hundred and fifty. And

μετὰ ταῦτα ἔδωκεν κριτὰς ἕως Σαμουὴλ
after these things he gave judges until Samuel

προφήτου. 21 κἀκεῖθεν ᾐτήσαντο βασιλέα,
a prophet. And thence they asked a king,

καὶ ἔδωκεν αὐτοῖς ὁ θεὸς τὸν Σαοὺλ
and gave them - God - Saul

υἱὸν Κίς, ἄνδρα ἐκ φυλῆς Βενιαμίν,
son of Cis, a man of [the] tribe of Benjamin,

ἔτη τεσσεράκοντα· 22 καὶ μεταστήσας
years forty; and removing

αὐτὸν ἤγειρεν τὸν Δαυὶδ αὐτοῖς εἰς
him he raised - David to them for

βασιλέα, ᾧ καὶ εἶπεν μαρτυρήσας·
a king, to whom also he said giving witness:

εὗρον Δαυὶδ τὸν τοῦ Ἰεσσαί, ἄνδρα
I found David the [son] of Jesse, a man

κατὰ τὴν καρδίαν μου, ὃς ποιήσει πάντα
according to the heart of me, who will do all

τὰ θελήματά μου. 23 τούτου ὁ θεὸς
the wishes of me. [4]Of this man - [5]God

ἀπὸ τοῦ σπέρματος κατ' ἐπαγγελίαν
[1]from [2]the [3]seed according to promise

ἤγαγεν τῷ Ἰσραὴλ σωτῆρα Ἰησοῦν,
brought - to Israel a Saviour Jesus,

24 προκηρύξαντος Ἰωάννου πρὸ προσώπου
previously proclaiming John[a] before face
=when John had previously proclaimed

τῆς εἰσόδου αὐτοῦ βάπτισμα μετανοίας
of the entrance of him a baptism of repentance

παντὶ τῷ λαῷ Ἰσραήλ. 25 ὡς δὲ
to all the people of Israel. Now as

ἐπλήρου Ἰωάννης τὸν δρόμον, ἔλεγεν·
completed John the(his) course, he said:

τί ἐμὲ ὑπονοεῖτε εἶναι; οὐκ εἰμὶ ἐγώ·
What me suppose ye to be? [2]Not [1]am [1]I;

ἀλλ' ἰδοὺ ἔρχεται μετ' ἐμὲ οὗ οὐκ εἰμὶ
but behold he comes after me of whom I am not

ἄξιος τὸ ὑπόδημα τῶν ποδῶν λῦσαι.
worthy the sandal of the feet to loosen.

26 Ἄνδρες ἀδελφοί, υἱοὶ γένους Ἀβραὰμ
Men brothers, sons of [the] race of Abraham

καὶ οἱ ἐν ὑμῖν φοβούμενοι τὸν θεόν,
and the [ones] among you fearing - God,

tioned with his hand and said: "Men of Israel and you Gentiles who worship God, listen to me! [17] The God of the people of Israel chose our fathers; he made the people prosper during their stay in Egypt, with mighty power he led them out of that country, [18] he endured their conduct[u] for about forty years in the desert, [19] he overthrew seven nations in Canaan and gave their land to his people as their inheritance. [20] All this took about 450 years.

"After this, God gave them judges until the time of Samuel the prophet. [21] Then the people asked for a king, and he gave them Saul son of Kish, of the tribe of Benjamin, who ruled forty years. [22] After removing Saul, he made David their king. He testified concerning him: 'I have found David son of Jesse a man after my own heart; he will do everything I want him to do.'

[23] "From this man's descendants God has brought to Israel the Savior Jesus, as he promised. [24] Before the coming of Jesus, John preached repentance and baptism to all the people of Israel. [25] As John was completing his work, he said: 'Who do you think I am? I am not that one. No, but he is coming after me, whose sandals I am not worthy to untie.'

[26] "Brothers, children of Abraham, and you God-fearing Gentiles, it is to us

[m] Gk Men, Israelites
[n] Other ancient authorities read cared for
[o] Gk untie the sandals
[p] Other ancient authorities read you

[u] 18 Some manuscripts and cared for them

this salvation has been sent. 27 Because the residents of Jerusalem and their leaders did not recognize him or understand the words of the prophets that are read every sabbath, they fulfilled those words by condemning him. 28 Even though they found no cause for a sentence of death, they asked Pilate to have him killed. 29 When they had carried out everything that was written about him, they took him down from the tree and laid him in a tomb. 30 But God raised him from the dead; 31 and for many days he appeared to those who came up with him from Galilee to Jerusalem, and they are now his witnesses to the people. 32 And we bring you the good news that what God promised to our ancestors 33 he has fulfilled for us, their children, by raising Jesus; as also it is written in the second psalm,

'You are my Son;
today I have
begotten you.'

34 As to his raising him from the dead, no more to return to corruption, he has spoken in this way,

'I will give you the
holy promises
made to David.'

35 Therefore he has also said in another psalm,

'You will not let your
Holy One
experience
corruption.'

36 For David, after he had served the purpose of God in his own generation, died,[q] was laid beside his ancestors, and experienced corruption; 37 but he whom God raised up experienced no corruption. 38 Let it be known to you therefore, my brothers, that through this man forgiveness of sins

[q] Gk fell asleep

ἡμῖν ὁ λόγος τῆς σωτηρίας ταύτης
to us the word of this salvation

ἐξαπεστάλη. 27 οἱ γὰρ κατοικοῦντες ἐν
was sent forth. For the [ones] dwelling in

Ἰερουσαλὴμ καὶ οἱ ἄρχοντες αὐτῶν τοῦτον
Jerusalem and the rulers of them ³this man

ἀγνοήσαντες καὶ τὰς φωνὰς τῶν προφητῶν τὰς
¹not knowing and the voices of the prophets

κατὰ πᾶν σάββατον ἀναγινωσκομένας
²throughout(on) ³every ⁴sabbath ¹being read

κρίναντες ἐπλήρωσαν, 28 καὶ μηδεμίαν
judging they fulfilled, and no

αἰτίαν θανάτου εὑρόντες ᾐτήσαντο Πιλᾶτον
cause of death finding they asked Pilate

ἀναιρεθῆναι αὐτόν· 29 ὡς δὲ ἐτέλεσαν πάντα
to be destroyed him; and when they finished all

τὰ περὶ αὐτοῦ γεγραμμένα, καθελόντες
the things concerning him having been written, taking down

ἀπὸ τοῦ ξύλου ἔθηκαν εἰς μνημεῖον.
from the tree they laid in a tomb.

30 ὁ δὲ θεὸς ἤγειρεν αὐτὸν ἐκ νεκρῶν·
- But God raised him out of [the] dead;

31 ὃς ὤφθη ἐπὶ ἡμέρας πλείους τοῖς
who appeared over days many to the [ones]

συναναβᾶσιν αὐτῷ ἀπὸ τῆς Γαλιλαίας εἰς
having come up with him from the Galilee to

Ἰερουσαλήμ, οἵτινες [νῦν] εἰσιν μάρτυρες
Jerusalem, who now are witnesses

αὐτοῦ πρὸς τὸν λαόν. 32 καὶ ἡμεῖς
of him to the people. And we

ὑμᾶς εὐαγγελιζόμεθα τὴν πρὸς τοὺς
[to] you preach ²the ⁴to ⁵the

πατέρας ἐπαγγελίαν γενομένην, 33 ὅτι
⁶fathers ³promise ¹having come, that

ταύτην ὁ θεὸς ἐκπεπλήρωκεν τοῖς τέκνοις
this [promise] God has fulfilled ²to the ³children

ἡμῖν ἀναστήσας Ἰησοῦν, ὡς καὶ ἐν τῷ
¹to us raising up Jesus, as also in the

ψαλμῷ γέγραπται τῷ δευτέρῳ· υἱός μου
²psalm ³it has been written ¹second: Son of me

εἶ σύ, ἐγὼ σήμερον γεγέννηκά σε. 34 ὅτι δὲ
art thou, I to-day have begotten thee. And that

ἀνέστησεν αὐτὸν ἐκ νεκρῶν μηκέτι
he raised up him out of [the] dead no more

μέλλοντα ὑποστρέφειν εἰς διαφθοράν, οὕτως
being about to return to corruption, thus

εἴρηκεν ὅτι δώσω ὑμῖν τὰ ὅσια Δαυὶδ τὰ
he has said[,] - I will give you the ²holy things ³of David the

πιστά. 35 διότι καὶ ἐν ἑτέρῳ λέγει·
¹faithful. Wherefore also in another [psalm] he says:

οὐ δώσεις τὸν ὅσιόν σου ἰδεῖν διαφθοράν.
Thou wilt not give the holy one of thee to see corruption.

36 Δαυὶδ μὲν γὰρ ἰδίᾳ γενεᾷ ὑπηρετήσας
For David indeed [his] own generation having served

τῇ τοῦ θεοῦ βουλῇ ἐκοιμήθη καὶ προσετέθη
by the - of God counsel fell asleep and was added

πρὸς τοὺς πατέρας αὐτοῦ καὶ εἶδεν
to the fathers of him and saw

διαφθοράν· 37 ὃν δὲ ὁ θεὸς ἤγειρεν,
corruption; but [he] whom - God raised,

οὐκ εἶδεν διαφθοράν. 38 γνωστὸν οὖν
did not see corruption. Known therefore

ἔστω ὑμῖν, ἄνδρες ἀδελφοί, ὅτι διὰ
let it be to you, men brothers, that through

---

that this message of salvation has been sent. 27 The people of Jerusalem and their rulers did not recognize Jesus, yet in condemning him they fulfilled the words of the prophets that are read every Sabbath. 28 Though they found no proper ground for a death sentence, they asked Pilate to have him executed. 29 When they had carried out all that was written about him, they took him down from the tree and laid him in a tomb. 30 But God raised him from the dead, 31 and for many days he was seen by those who had traveled with him from Galilee to Jerusalem. They are now his witnesses to our people.

32 "We tell you the good news: What God promised our fathers 33 he has fulfilled for us, their children, by raising up Jesus. As it is written in the second Psalm:

"'You are my Son;
today I have become
your Father.'[v' w]

34 The fact that God raised him from the dead, never to decay, is stated in these words:

"'I will give you the
holy and sure
blessings promised
to David.'[x]

35 So it is stated elsewhere:

"'You will not let your
Holy One see
decay.'[y]

36 "For when David had served God's purpose in his own generation, he fell asleep; he was buried with his fathers and his body decayed. 37 But the one whom God raised from the dead did not see decay.

38 "Therefore, my brothers, I want you to know that through Jesus the for-

---

[v] 33 Or have begotten you
[w] 33 Psalm 2:7
[x] 34 Isaiah 55:3
[y] 35 Psalm 16:10

is proclaimed to you; 39 by this Jesus' everyone who believes is set free from all those sins' from which you could not be freed by the law of Moses. 40 Beware, therefore, that what the prophets said does not happen to you: 41 'Look, you scoffers! Be amazed and perish, for in your days I am doing a work, a work that you will never believe, even if someone tells you.' "

42 As Paul and Barnabas' were going out, the people urged them to speak about these things again the next sabbath. 43 When the meeting of the synagogue broke up, many Jews and devout converts to Judaism followed Paul and Barnabas, who spoke to them and urged them to continue in the grace of God.

44 The next sabbath almost the whole city gathered to hear the word of the Lord." 45 But when the Jews saw the crowds, they were filled with jealousy; and blaspheming, they contradicted what was spoken by Paul. 46 Then both Paul and Barnabas spoke out boldly, saying, "It was necessary that the word of God should be spoken first to you. Since you reject it and judge yourselves to be unworthy of eternal life, we are now turning to the Gentiles. 47 For so the Lord has commanded us, saying, 'I have set you to be a light for the Gentiles, so that you may bring salvation to the ends of the earth.' "

48 When the Gentiles heard this, they were glad and praised the word of the Lord; and as many as had

τούτου ὑμῖν ἄφεσις ἁμαρτιῶν καταγγέλ-
this man to you forgiveness of sins is an-
λεται, καὶ ἀπὸ πάντων ὧν οὐκ ἠδυνήθητε
nounced, and from all things from which ye could not
ἐν νόμῳ Μωϋσέως δικαιωθῆναι, 39 ἐν
by [the] law of Moses to be justified, 39 by
τούτῳ πᾶς ὁ πιστεύων δικαιοῦται. 40 βλέπετε
this man everyone believing is justified. 40 Look ye
οὖν μὴ ἐπέλθῃ τὸ εἰρημένον
therefore lest come on [you] the thing having been said
ἐν τοῖς προφήταις· 41 ἴδετε, οἱ κατα-
in the prophets: 41 See, the des-
φρονηταί, καὶ θαυμάσατε καὶ ἀφανίσθητε,
pisers, and marvel ye and perish,
ὅτι ἔργον ἐργάζομαι ἐγὼ ἐν ταῖς ἡμέραις
because a work work I in the days
ὑμῶν, ἔργον ὃ οὐ μὴ πιστεύσητε ἐάν
of you, a work which by no means ye believe if
τις ἐκδιηγῆται ὑμῖν. 42 Ἐξιόντων δὲ
anyone declares to you. 42 And going out
=as they went out
αὐτῶν παρεκάλουν εἰς τὸ μεταξὺ σάββατον
them they besought in the intervening sabbath(week)
λαληθῆναι αὐτοῖς τὰ ῥήματα ταῦτα.
to be spoken to them these words.
43 λυθείσης δὲ τῆς συναγωγῆς ἠκολούθησαν
And being broken up the assembly followed
=when the assembly was broken up
πολλοὶ τῶν Ἰουδαίων καὶ τῶν σεβομένων
many of the Jews and of the worshipping
προσηλύτων τῷ Παύλῳ καὶ τῷ Βαρναβᾷ,
proselytes Paul and Barnabas,
οἵτινες προσλαλοῦντες αὐτοῖς ἔπειθον αὐτοὺς
who speaking to them persuaded them
προσμένειν τῇ χάριτι τοῦ θεοῦ. 44 Τῷ δὲ
to continue in the grace of God. 44 And on the
ἐρχομένῳ σαββάτῳ σχεδὸν πᾶσα ἡ
coming sabbath almost all the
πόλις συνήχθη ἀκοῦσαι τὸν λόγον τοῦ
city was assembled to hear the word the
θεοῦ. 45 ἰδόντες δὲ οἱ Ἰουδαῖοι τοὺς
of God. But seeing the Jews the
ὄχλους ἐπλήσθησαν ζήλου, καὶ ἀντέλεγον
crowds were filled of(with) jealousy, and contradicted
τοῖς ὑπὸ Παύλου λαλουμένοις βλασφημοῦντες.
the things by Paul being spoken blaspheming.
46 παρρησιασάμενοί τε ὁ Παῦλος καὶ ὁ
And speaking boldly - Paul and -
Βαρναβᾶς εἶπαν· ὑμῖν ἦν ἀναγκαῖον πρῶτον
Barnabas said: To you it was necessary firstly
λαληθῆναι τὸν λόγον τοῦ θεοῦ· ἐπειδὴ
to be spoken the word of God; since
ἀπωθεῖσθε αὐτὸν καὶ οὐκ ἀξίους κρίνετε
ye put away it and not worthy judge
ἑαυτοὺς τῆς αἰωνίου ζωῆς, ἰδοὺ στρεφόμεθα
yourselves of the eternal life, behold we turn
εἰς τὰ ἔθνη. 47 οὕτως γὰρ ἐντέταλται
to the nations. For thus has commanded
ἡμῖν ὁ κύριος· τέθεικά σε εἰς φῶς
us the Lord: I have set thee for a light
ἐθνῶν τοῦ εἶναί σε εἰς σωτηρίαν ἕως
of nations - to be thee[b] for salvation to
ἐσχάτου τῆς γῆς. 48 ἀκούοντα δὲ τὰ ἔθνη
[the] end of the earth. And hearing the nations
ἔχαιρον καὶ ἐδόξαζον τὸν λόγον τοῦ κυρίου, καὶ
rejoiced and glorified the word of the Lord, and

giveness of sins is proclaimed to you. 39 Through him everyone who believes is justified from everything you could not be justified from by the law of Moses. 40 Take care that what the prophets have said does not happen to you:

41 " 'Look, you scoffers, wonder and perish, for I am going to do something in your days that you would never believe, even if someone told you.' "

42 As Paul and Barnabas were leaving the synagogue, the people invited them to speak further about these things on the next Sabbath. 43 When the congregation was dismissed, many of the Jews and devout converts to Judaism followed Paul and Barnabas, who talked with them and urged them to continue in the grace of God.

44 On the next Sabbath almost the whole city gathered to hear the word of the Lord. 45 When the Jews saw the crowds, they were filled with jealousy and talked abusively against what Paul was saying.

46 Then Paul and Barnabas answered them boldly: "We had to speak the word of God to you first. Since you reject it and do not consider yourselves worthy of eternal life, we now turn to the Gentiles. 47 For this is what the Lord has commanded us:

" 'I have made you[a] a light for the Gentiles, that you[a] may bring salvation to the ends of the earth.' [b] "

48 When the Gentiles heard this, they were glad and honored the word of

---

r Gk this
s Gk all
t Gk they
u Other ancient authorities read God

z41 Hab. 1:5
a47 The Greek is singular.
b47 Isaiah 49:6

been destined for eternal life became believers. [49] Thus the word of the Lord spread throughout the region. [50] But the Jews incited the devout women of high standing and the leading men of the city, and stirred up persecution against Paul and Barnabas, and drove them out of their region. [51] So they shook the dust off their feet in protest against them, and went to Iconium. [52] And the disciples were filled with joy and with the Holy Spirit.

ἐπίστευσαν ὅσοι ἦσαν τεταγμένοι εἰς
believed   [7]as many as   [1]were   [3]having been disposed   [4]to

ζωὴν αἰώνιον· 49 διεφέρετο δὲ ὁ λόγος τοῦ
[5]life   [6]eternal;   and was carried through the word of the

κυρίου δι' ὅλης τῆς χώρας. 50 οἱ δὲ
Lord   through all   the   country.   But the

'Ιουδαῖοι παρώτρυναν τὰς σεβομένας γυναῖκας
Jews   urged on   the   [3]worshipping   [2]women

τὰς εὐσχήμονας καὶ τοὺς πρώτους τῆς
-   [1]honourable   and   the   chief men   of the

πόλεως, καὶ ἐπήγειραν διωγμὸν ἐπὶ τὸν
city,   and   raised up   persecution against   -

Παῦλον καὶ Βαρναβᾶν, καὶ ἐξέβαλον αὐτοὺς
Paul   and   Barnabas,   and   expelled   them

ἀπὸ τῶν ὁρίων αὐτῶν. 51 οἱ δὲ ἐκτιναξάμενοι
from   the   borders of them.   But they   shaking off

τὸν κονιορτὸν τῶν ποδῶν ἐπ' αὐτοὺς ἦλθον
the   dust   of the(ir)   feet   on   them   came

εἰς 'Ικόνιον, 52 οἱ τε μαθηταὶ ἐπλη-
to   Iconium,   and the   disciples   were

ροῦντο χαρᾶς καὶ πνεύματος ἁγίου.
filled   of(with) joy   and   of(with) Spirit   Holy.

---

the Lord; and all who were appointed for eternal life believed.
[49] The word of the Lord spread through the whole region. [50] But the Jews incited the God-fearing women of high standing and the leading men of the city. They stirred up persecution against Paul and Barnabas, and expelled them from their region. [51] So they shook the dust from their feet in protest against them and went to Iconium. [52] And the disciples were filled with joy and with the Holy Spirit.

Chapter 14

Paul and Barnabas in Iconium

THE same thing occurred in Iconium, where Paul and Barnabas went into the Jewish synagogue and spoke in such a way that a great number of both Jews and Greeks became believers. [2] But the unbelieving Jews stirred up the Gentiles and poisoned their minds against the brothers. [3] So they remained for a long time, speaking boldly for the Lord, who testified to the word of his grace by granting signs and wonders to be done through them. [4] But the residents of the city were divided; some sided with the Jews, and some with the apostles. [5] And when an attempt was made by both Gentiles and Jews, with their rulers, to mistreat them and to stone them, [6] the apostles[ᶠ] learned of it and fled to Lystra and Derbe, cities of Lycaonia, and to the surrounding country; [7] and there they continued proclaiming the good news.

Paul and Barnabas in Lystra and Derbe

[8] In Lystra there was a man sitting who could not

---

14 'Εγένετο δὲ ἐν 'Ικονίῳ κατὰ τὸ αὐτὸ
Now it happened in   Iconium   [3]together†

εἰσελθεῖν αὐτοὺς εἰς τὴν συναγωγὴν
[1]to enter   them[ᵇ]   into   the   synagogue
=they entered

τῶν 'Ιουδαίων καὶ λαλῆσαι οὕτως ὥστε
of the   Jews   and   to speak[ᵇ]   so   as

πιστεῦσαι 'Ιουδαίων τε καὶ 'Ελλήνων
to believe   both of Jews   and   of Greeks

πολὺ πλῆθος. 2 οἱ δὲ ἀπειθήσαντες
a much(great) multitude.   But the   disobeying

'Ιουδαῖοι ἐπήγειραν καὶ ἐκάκωσαν τὰς
Jews   excited   and   embittered   the

ψυχὰς τῶν ἐθνῶν κατὰ τῶν ἀδελφῶν.
minds   of the   nations   against   the   brothers.

3 ἱκανὸν μὲν οὖν χρόνον διέτριψαν
A considerable   -   [2]therefore   [1]time   they continued

παρρησιαζόμενοι ἐπὶ τῷ κυρίῳ τῷ μαρ-
speaking boldly   on   the   Lord   -   wit-

τυροῦντι ἐπὶ τῷ λόγῳ τῆς χάριτος αὐτοῦ,
nessing   to the   word   of the   grace   of him,

διδόντι σημεῖα καὶ τέρατα γίνεσθαι διὰ
giving   signs   and   wonders   to happen   through

τῶν χειρῶν αὐτῶν. 4 ἐσχίσθη δὲ τὸ
the   hands   of them.   But was divided   the

πλῆθος τῆς πόλεως, καὶ οἱ μὲν ἦσαν
multitude   of the   city,   and   some   were

σὺν τοῖς 'Ιουδαίοις, οἱ δὲ σὺν τοῖς
with   the   Jews,   but others   with   the

ἀποστόλοις. 5 ὡς δὲ ἐγένετο ὁρμὴ τῶν
apostles.   And when   there was   a rush   [3]of the

ἐθνῶν τε καὶ 'Ιουδαίων σὺν τοῖς ἄρχουσιν
[1]nations   [1]both [4]and   of Jews   with   the   rulers

αὐτῶν ὑβρίσαι καὶ λιθοβολῆσαι αὐτούς,
of them   to insult   and   to stone   them,

6 συνιδόντες κατέφυγον εἰς τὰς πόλεις
perceiving   they escaped   to   the   cities

τῆς Λυκαονίας Λύστραν καὶ Δέρβην καὶ
-   of Lycaonia   Lystra   and   Derbe   and

τὴν περίχωρον· 7 κἀκεῖ εὐαγγελιζόμενοι
the   neighbourhood;   and there   evangelizing

ἦσαν. 8 Καὶ τις ἀνὴρ ἀδύνατος ἐν
they were.   And   a certain   man   impotent   in

Chapter 14

In Iconium

AT Iconium Paul and Barnabas went as usual into the Jewish synagogue. There they spoke so effectively that a great number of Jews and Gentiles believed. [2] But the Jews who refused to believe stirred up the Gentiles and poisoned their minds against the brothers. [3] So Paul and Barnabas spent considerable time there, speaking boldly for the Lord, who confirmed the message of his grace by enabling them to do miraculous signs and wonders. [4] The people of the city were divided; some sided with the Jews, others with the apostles. [5] There was a plot afoot among the Gentiles and Jews, together with their leaders, to mistreat them and stone them. [6] But they found out about it and fled to the Lycaonian cities of Lystra and Derbe and to the surrounding country, [7] where they continued to preach the good news.

In Lystra and Derbe

[8] In Lystra there sat a man crippled in his feet, who

use his feet and had never walked, for he had been crippled from birth. 9He listened to Paul as he was speaking. And Paul, looking at him intently and seeing that he had faith to be healed, 10said in a loud voice, "Stand upright on your feet." And the man[v] sprang up and began to walk. 11When the crowds saw what Paul had done, they shouted in the Lycaonian language, "The gods have come down to us in human form!" 12Barnabas they called Zeus, and Paul they called Hermes, because he was the chief speaker. 13The priest of Zeus, whose temple was just outside the city,[w] brought oxen and garlands to the gates; he and the crowds wanted to offer sacrifice. 14When the apostles Barnabas and Paul heard of it, they tore their clothes and rushed out into the crowd, shouting, 15"Friends,[x] why are you doing this? We are mortals just like you, and we bring you good news, that you should turn from these worthless things to the living God, who made the heaven and the earth and the sea and all that is in them. 16In past generations he allowed all the nations to follow their own ways; 17yet he has not left himself without a witness in doing good—giving you rains from heaven and fruitful seasons, and filling you with food and your hearts with joy." 18Even with

Λύστροις τοῖς ποσὶν ἐκάθητο, χωλὸς ἐκ
Lystra in the feet sat, lame from

κοιλίας μητρὸς αὐτοῦ ὃς οὐδέποτε
[the] womb of [the] mother of him who never

περιεπάτησεν. 9 οὗτος ἤκουεν τοῦ Παύλου
walked. This man heard - Paul

λαλοῦντος· ὃς ἀτενίσας αὐτῷ καὶ ἰδὼν
speaking; who gazing at him and seeing

ὅτι ἔχει πίστιν τοῦ σωθῆναι, 10 εἶπεν
that he has(had) faith - to be healed,[d] said

μεγάλῃ φωνῇ· ἀνάστηθι ἐπὶ τοὺς πόδας
with a voice: Stand up on the feet
great(loud)

σου ὀρθός. καὶ ἥλατο καὶ περιεπάτει.
of thee erect. And he leaped up and walked.

11 οἵ τε ὄχλοι ἰδόντες ὃ ἐποίησεν Παῦλος
And the crowds seeing what did Paul

ἐπῆραν τὴν φωνὴν αὐτῶν Λυκαονιστὶ
lifted up the voice of them in Lycaonian

λέγοντες· οἱ θεοὶ ὁμοιωθέντες ἀνθρώποις
saying: The gods made like men

κατέβησαν πρὸς ἡμᾶς, 12 ἐκάλουν τε τὸν
came down to us, and they called -

Βαρναβᾶν Δία, τὸν δὲ Παῦλον Ἑρμῆν,
Barnabas Zeus, - and Paul Hermes,

ἐπειδὴ αὐτὸς ἦν ὁ ἡγούμενος τοῦ λόγου.
since he was the leader of the discourse.

13 ὅ τε ἱερεὺς τοῦ Διὸς τοῦ ὄντος πρὸ
And the priest - of Zeus - being before

τῆς πόλεως, ταύρους καὶ στέμματα ἐπὶ
the city, bulls and garlands to

τοὺς πυλῶνας ἐνέγκας, σὺν τοῖς ὄχλοις
the gates bringing, with the crowds

ἤθελεν θύειν. 14 ἀκούσαντες δὲ οἱ
wished to sacrifice. But [e]hearing [1]the

ἀπόστολοι Βαρναβᾶς καὶ Παῦλος, διαρ-
[2]apostles [3]Barnabas [4]and [5]Paul, rend-

ρήξαντες τὰ ἱμάτια ἑαυτῶν ἐξεπήδησαν εἰς
ing the garments of themselves rushed out into

τὸν ὄχλον, κράζοντες 15 καὶ λέγοντες·
the crowd, crying out and saying:

ἄνδρες, τί ταῦτα ποιεῖτε; καὶ ἡμεῖς
Men, why these things do ye? [2]also [1]we

ὁμοιοπαθεῖς ἐσμεν ὑμῖν ἄνθρωποι, εὐαγ-
[5]of like nature [3]are [4]to you [6]men, preach-

γελιζόμενοι ὑμᾶς ἀπὸ τούτων τῶν ματαίων
ing [to] you from these - vanities

ἐπιστρέφειν ἐπὶ θεὸν ζῶντα, ὃς ἐποίησεν
to turn to God a living, who made

τὸν οὐρανὸν καὶ τὴν γῆν καὶ τὴν
the heaven and the earth and the

θάλασσαν καὶ πάντα τὰ ἐν αὐτοῖς· 16 ὃς
sea and all the things in them; who

ἐν ταῖς παρῳχημέναις γενεαῖς εἴασεν πάντα
in the having passed generations allowed all

τὰ ἔθνη πορεύεσθαι ταῖς ὁδοῖς αὐτῶν·
the nations to go in the ways of them;

17 καίτοι οὐκ ἀμάρτυρον αὐτὸν ἀφῆκεν
and yet [2]not [4]unwitnessed [3]himself [1]left

ἀγαθουργῶν, οὐρανόθεν ὑμῖν ὑετοὺς διδοὺς
doing good, [4]from heaven [5]us [3]rain [1]giving

καὶ καιροὺς καρποφόρους, ἐμπιπλῶν τροφῆς
and times fruit-bearing, filling of(with) food

καὶ εὐφροσύνης τὰς καρδίας ὑμῶν. 18 καὶ
and of(with) gladness the hearts of us. And

was lame from birth and had never walked. 9He listened to Paul as he was speaking. Paul looked directly at him, saw that he had faith to be healed 10and called out, "Stand up on your feet!" At that, the man jumped up and began to walk.

11When the crowd saw what Paul had done, they shouted in the Lycaonian language, "The gods have come down to us in human form!" 12Barnabas they called Zeus, and Paul they called Hermes because he was the chief speaker. 13The priest of Zeus, whose temple was just outside the city, brought bulls and wreaths to the city gates because he and the crowd wanted to offer sacrifices to them.

14But when the apostles Barnabas and Paul heard of this, they tore their clothes and rushed out into the crowd, shouting: 15"Men, why are you doing this? We too are only men, human like you. We are bringing you good news, telling you to turn from these worthless things to the living God, who made heaven and earth and sea and everything in them. 16In the past, he let all nations go their own way. 17Yet he has not left himself without testimony: He has shown kindness by giving you rain from heaven and crops in their seasons; he provides you with plenty of food and fills your hearts with joy."

[v] Gk he
[w] Or The priest of Zeus-Outside-the-City
[x] Gk Men

these words, they scarcely restrained the crowds from offering sacrifice to them.

19 But Jews came there from Antioch and Iconium and won over the crowds. Then they stoned Paul and dragged him out of the city, supposing that he was dead. 20 But when the disciples surrounded him, he got up and went into the city. The next day he went on with Barnabas to Derbe.

The Return to Antioch in Syria

21 After they had proclaimed the good news to that city and had made many disciples, they returned to Lystra, then on to Iconium and Antioch. 22 There they strengthened the souls of the disciples and encouraged them to continue in the faith, saying, "It is through many persecutions that we must enter the kingdom of God." 23 And after they had appointed elders for them in each church, with prayer and fasting they entrusted them to the Lord in whom they had come to believe. 24 Then they passed through Pisidia and came to Pamphylia. 25 When they had spoken the word in Perga, they went down to Attalia. 26 From there they sailed back to Antioch, where they had been commended to the grace of God for the work ʸ that they had completed. 27 When they arrived, they called the church together and related all that God had done with them, and how he had opened a door of faith for the Gentiles. 28 And they stayed there with the disciples for some time.

ταῦτα λέγοντες μόλις κατέπαυσαν τοὺς
these things saying scarcely they restrained the

ὄχλους τοῦ μὴ θύειν αὐτοῖς. 19 Ἐπῆλθαν
crowds - not to sacrificeᵈ to them.   ᵉcame upon
[the scene]

δὲ ἀπὸ Ἀντιοχείας καὶ Ἰκονίου Ἰουδαῖοι,
And ᵉfrom ³Antioch ⁴and ⁵Iconium   ¹Jews,

καὶ πείσαντες τοὺς ὄχλους καὶ λιθάσαντες
and persuading the crowds and stoning

τὸν Παῦλον ἔσυρον ἔξω τῆς πόλεως,
-   Paul   dragged outside the city,

νομίζοντες αὐτὸν τεθνηκέναι. 20 κυκλω-
supposing him to have died.   But sur-

σάντων δὲ τῶν μαθητῶν αὐτὸν ἀναστὰς
rounding the disciplesª him rising up
=as the disciples surrounded

εἰσῆλθεν εἰς τὴν πόλιν. Καὶ τῇ ἐπαύριον
he entered into the city. And on the morrow

ἐξῆλθεν σὺν τῷ Βαρναβᾷ εἰς Δέρβην.
he went forth with - Barnabas to Derbe.

21 εὐαγγελιζόμενοί τε τὴν πόλιν ἐκείνην
And evangelizing that city

καὶ μαθητεύσαντες ἱκανοὺς ὑπέστρεψαν εἰς
and having made disciples many they returned to

τὴν Λύστραν καὶ εἰς Ἰκόνιον καὶ [εἰς]
-   Lystra   and to Iconium and to

Ἀντιόχειαν, 22 ἐπιστηρίζοντες τὰς ψυχὰς
Antioch,   confirming the minds

τῶν μαθητῶν, παρακαλοῦντες ἐμμένειν τῇ
of the disciples, exhorting to continue in the

πίστει, καὶ ὅτι διὰ πολλῶν θλίψεων
faith, and that through many afflictions

δεῖ ἡμᾶς εἰσελθεῖν εἰς τὴν βασιλείαν τοῦ
it behoves us to enter into the kingdom -

θεοῦ. 23 χειροτονήσαντες δὲ αὐτοῖς κατ'
of God.   And having appointed for them in

ἐκκλησίαν πρεσβυτέρους, προσευξάμενοι
every church elders,   praying

μετὰ νηστειῶν παρέθεντο αὐτοὺς τῷ κυρίῳ
with fastings they committed them to the Lord

εἰς ὃν πεπιστεύκεισαν. 24 καὶ διελθόντες
in whom they had believed. And passing through

τὴν Πισιδίαν ἦλθον εἰς τὴν Παμφυλίαν,
-   Pisidia they came to -   Pamphylia,

25 καὶ λαλήσαντες εἰς τὴν Πέργην τὸν
and speaking in - Perga the

λόγον κατέβησαν εἰς Ἀττάλειαν, κἀκεῖθεν
word they came down to Attalia, and thence

ἀπέπλευσαν εἰς Ἀντιόχειαν, 26 ὅθεν ἦσαν
sailed away to Antioch,   whence they were

παραδεδομένοι τῇ χάριτι τοῦ θεοῦ εἰς
having been commended to the grace - of God for

τὸ ἔργον ὃ ἐπλήρωσαν. 27 Παραγεν-
the work which they accomplished.   And having

όμενοι δὲ καὶ συναγαγόντες τὴν ἐκκλησίαν,
arrived and and assembling the church,

ἀνήγγελλον ὅσα ἐποίησεν ὁ θεὸς μετ'
they reported what things did - God with

αὐτῶν, καὶ ὅτι ἤνοιξεν τοῖς ἔθνεσιν
them, and that he opened to the nations

θύραν πίστεως. 28 διέτριβον δὲ χρόνον
a door of faith.   And they continued time

οὐκ ὀλίγον σὺν τοῖς μαθηταῖς.
not a little with the disciples.

---

18 Even with these words, they had difficulty keeping the crowd from sacrificing to them.

19 Then some Jews came from Antioch and Iconium and won the crowd over. They stoned Paul and dragged him outside the city, thinking he was dead. 20 But after the disciples had gathered around him, he got up and went back into the city. The next day he and Barnabas left for Derbe.

The Return to Antioch in Syria

21 They preached the good news in that city and won a large number of disciples. Then they returned to Lystra, Iconium and Antioch, 22 strengthening the disciples and encouraging them to remain true to the faith. "We must go through many hardships to enter the kingdom of God," they said. 23 Paul and Barnabas appointed elders ᶜ for them in each church and, with prayer and fasting, committed them to the Lord, in whom they had put their trust. 24 After going through Pisidia, they came into Pamphylia, 25 and when they had preached the word in Perga, they went down to Attalia.

26 From Attalia they sailed back to Antioch, where they had been committed to the grace of God for the work they had now completed. 27 On arriving there, they gathered the church together and reported all that God had done through them and how he had opened the door of faith to the Gentiles. 28 And they stayed there a long time with the disciples.

ʸ Or committed in the grace of God to the work

ᶜ 23 Or Barnabas ordained elders; or Barnabas had elders elected

Chapter 15

The Council at Jerusalem

THEN certain individuals came down from Judea and were teaching the brothers, "Unless you are circumcised according to the custom of Moses, you cannot be saved." 2 And after Paul and Barnabas had no small dissension and debate with them, Paul and Barnabas and some of the others were appointed to go up to Jerusalem to discuss this question with the apostles and the elders. 3 So they were sent on their way by the church, and as they passed through Phoenicia and Samaria, they reported the conversion of the Gentiles, and brought great joy to all the believers. 4 When they came to Jerusalem, they were welcomed by the church and the apostles and the elders, and they reported all that they had done with them. 5 But some believers who belonged to the sect of the Pharisees stood up and said, "It is necessary for them to be circumcised and ordered to keep the law of Moses."
6 The apostles and the elders met together to consider this matter. 7 After there had been much debate, Peter stood up and said to them, "My brothers,[a] you know that in the early days God made a choice among you, that I should be the one through whom the Gentiles would hear the message of the good news and become believers. 8 And God, who knows the human heart, testified to them by giving

---

15 Καί τινες κατελθόντες ἀπὸ τῆς
And some going down from –

'Ιουδαίας ἐδίδασκον τοὺς ἀδελφοὺς ὅτι
Judæa taught the brothers[,]

ἐὰν μὴ περιτμηθῆτε τῷ ἔθει τῷ Μωϋσέως,
Unless ye are circumcised by the custom – of Moses,

οὐ δύνασθε σωθῆναι. 2 γενομένης δὲ
ye cannot to be saved. And taking place

στάσεως καὶ ζητήσεως οὐκ ὀλίγης τῷ
discord and questioning not a little[a] –
=when there took place not a little . . .

Παύλῳ καὶ τῷ Βαρναβᾷ πρὸς αὐτούς,
by Paul and – Barnabas with them,

ἔταξαν ἀναβαίνειν Παῦλον καὶ Βαρναβᾶν
they assigned to go up Paul and Barnabas

καὶ τινας ἄλλους ἐξ αὐτῶν πρὸς τοὺς
and some others of them to the

ἀποστόλους καὶ πρεσβυτέρους εἰς 'Ιερουσαλὴμ
apostles and elders in Jerusalem

περὶ τοῦ ζητήματος τούτου. 3 Οἱ μὲν
about this question. They –

οὖν προπεμφθέντες ὑπὸ τῆς ἐκκλησίας
therefore being set forward by the church

διήρχοντο τήν τε Φοινίκην καὶ Σαμάρειαν
passed through – both Phœnicia and Samaria

ἐκδιηγούμενοι τὴν ἐπιστροφὴν τῶν ἐθνῶν,
telling in detail the conversion of the nations,

καὶ ἐποίουν χαρὰν μεγάλην πᾶσιν τοῖς
and caused joy great to all the

ἀδελφοῖς. 4 παραγενόμενοι δὲ εἰς 'Ιεροσόλυμα
brothers. And having arrived in Jerusalem

παρεδέχθησαν ἀπὸ τῆς ἐκκλησίας καὶ τῶν
they were welcomed from the church and the

ἀποστόλων καὶ τῶν πρεσβυτερων, ἀνήγ-
apostles and the elders, and

γειλάν τε ὅσα ὁ θεὸς ἐποίησεν μετ'
reported what things – God did with

αὐτῶν. 5 'Εξανέστησαν δέ τινες τῶν
them. But stood forth some of the [ones]

ἀπὸ τῆς αἱρέσεως τῶν Φαρισαίων
from the sect of the Pharisees

πεπιστευκότες, λέγοντες ὅτι δεῖ περιτέμνειν
having believed, saying[,] – It behoves to circumcise

αὐτοὺς παραγγέλλειν τε τηρεῖν τὸν νόμον
them and to charge to keep the law

Μωϋσέως.
of Moses.

6 Συνήχθησάν τε οἱ ἀπόστολοι καὶ οἱ
And were assembled the apostles and the

πρεσβύτεροι ἰδεῖν περὶ τοῦ λόγου τούτου.
elders to see about this matter.

7 Πολλῆς δὲ ζητήσεως γενομένης ἀναστὰς
And much questioning having taken place[a] rising up
=When much questioning had . . .

Πέτρος εἶπεν πρὸς αὐτούς· ἄνδρες ἀδελφοί,
Peter said to them: Men brothers,

ὑμεῖς ἐπίστασθε ὅτι ἀφ' ἡμερῶν ἀρχαίων
ye understand that from days olden

ἐν ὑμῖν ἐξελέξατο ὁ θεὸς διὰ τοῦ στόματός
[a]among [c]you [b]chose – [1]God through the mouth

μου ἀκοῦσαι τὰ ἔθνη τὸν λόγον τοῦ
of me [a]to hear [1]the [2]nations the word of the

εὐαγγελίου καὶ πιστεῦσαι. 8 καὶ ὁ
gospel and to believe. And [b]the

καρδιογνώστης θεὸς ἐμαρτύρησεν αὐτοῖς
[a]Heart-knower [1]God witnessed to them

Chapter 15

The Council at Jerusalem

SOME men came down from Judea to Antioch and were teaching the brothers: "Unless you are circumcised, according to the custom taught by Moses, you cannot be saved." 2 This brought Paul and Barnabas into sharp dispute and debate with them. So Paul and Barnabas were appointed, along with some other believers, to go up to Jerusalem to see the apostles and elders about this question. 3 The church sent them on their way, and as they traveled through Phoenicia and Samaria, they told how the Gentiles had been converted. This news made all the brothers very glad. 4 When they came to Jerusalem, they were welcomed by the church and the apostles and elders, to whom they reported everything God had done through them.
5 Then some of the believers who belonged to the party of the Pharisees stood up and said, "The Gentiles must be circumcised and required to obey the law of Moses."
6 The apostles and elders met to consider this question. 7 After much discussion, Peter got up and addressed them: "Brothers, you know that some time ago God made a choice among you that the Gentiles might hear from my lips the message of the gospel and believe. 8 God, who knows the heart, showed

---

z Gk brothers
a Gk Men, brothers

them the Holy Spirit, just as he did to us; 9and in cleansing their hearts by faith he has made no distinction between them and us. 10Now therefore why are you putting God to the test by placing on the neck of the disciples a yoke that neither our ancestors nor we have been able to bear? 11On the contrary, we believe that we will be saved through the grace of the Lord Jesus, just as they will."

12 The whole assembly kept silence, and listened to Barnabas and Paul as they told of all the signs and wonders that God had done through them among the Gentiles. 13After they finished speaking, James replied, "My brothers,ᵃ listen to me. 14Simeon has related how God first looked favorably on the Gentiles, to take from among them a people for his name. 15This agrees with the words of the prophets, as it is written,

16 'After this I will return,
and I will rebuild the dwelling of David, which has fallen;
from its ruins I will rebuild it,
and I will set it up,
17 so that all other peoples may seek the Lord—
even all the Gentiles over whom my name has been called.
Thus says the Lord, who has been making these things
18known from long ago.'ᵇ

19Therefore I have reached the decision that we should not trouble those Gentiles who are turning to God, 20but we should write to

---

δοὺς	τὸ	πνεῦμα	τὸ	ἅγιον	καθὼς	καὶ
giving	the	Spirit	-	Holy	as	also

ἡμῖν, 9 καὶ οὐθὲν διέκρινεν μεταξὺ ἡμῶν
to us, and nothing distinguished between ³us

τε καὶ αὐτῶν, τῇ πίστει καθαρίσας τὰς
¹both and them, - by faith cleansing the

καρδίας αὐτῶν. 10 νῦν οὖν τί πειράζετε
hearts of them. Now therefore why test ye

τὸν θεόν, ἐπιθεῖναι ζυγὸν ἐπὶ τὸν
- God, to put on a yoke on the

τράχηλον τῶν μαθητῶν, ὃν οὔτε οἱ
neck of the disciples, which neither the

πατέρες ἡμῶν οὔτε ἡμεῖς ἰσχύσαμεν
fathers of us nor we were able

βαστάσαι; 11 ἀλλὰ διὰ τῆς χάριτος τοῦ
to bear? but through the grace of the

κυρίου Ἰησοῦ πιστεύομεν σωθῆναι καθ'
Lord Jesus we believe to be saved in

ὃν τρόπον κἀκεῖνοι. 12 Ἐσίγησεν δὲ
the same way as† those also. And was silent

πᾶν τὸ πλῆθος, καὶ ἤκουον Βαρναβᾶ
all the multitude, and heard Barnabas

καὶ Παύλου ἐξηγουμένων ὅσα ἐποίησεν
and Paul relating ¹what ²did

ὁ θεὸς σημεῖα καὶ τέρατα ἐν τοῖς
- ³God ¹signs ²and ⁴wonders among the

ἔθνεσιν δι' αὐτῶν. 13 Μετὰ δὲ τὸ σιγῆσαι
nations through them. And after the to keep silence = they kept silence

αὐτοὺς ἀπεκρίθη Ἰάκωβος λέγων· 14 ἄνδρες
themᵇ answered James saying: Men

ἀδελφοί, ἀκούσατέ μου. Συμεὼν ἐξηγήσατο
brothers, hear ye me. Simeon declared

καθὼς πρῶτον ὁ θεὸς ἐπεσκέψατο λαβεῖν ἐξ
even as firstly - God visited to take out of

ἐθνῶν λαὸν τῷ ὀνόματι αὐτοῦ. 15 καὶ
[the] nations a people for the name of him. And

τούτῳ συμφωνοῦσιν οἱ λόγοι τῶν προφητῶν,
to this agree the words of the prophets,

καθὼς γέγραπται· 16 μετὰ ταῦτα
even as it has been written: After these things

ἀναστρέψω καὶ ἀνοικοδομήσω τὴν σκηνὴν
I will return and I will rebuild the tent

Δαυὶδ τὴν πεπτωκυῖαν, καὶ τὰ κατεστραμ-
of David - having fallen, and the things having been

μένα αὐτῆς ἀνοικοδομήσω καὶ ἀνορθώσω
overturned of it I will rebuild and I will rear again = its ruins

αὐτήν, 17 ὅπως ἂν ἐκζητήσωσιν οἱ
it, so as - ⁴may seek ¹the

κατάλοιποι τῶν ἀνθρώπων τὸν κύριον,
²rest - ³of men ⁵the ⁶Lord,

καὶ πάντα τὰ ἔθνη ἐφ' οὓς ἐπικέκληται
even all the nations on whom has been invoked

τὸ ὄνομά μου ἐπ' αὐτούς, λέγει κύριος
the name of me on them, says [the] Lord

ποιῶν ταῦτα 18 γνωστὰ ἀπ' αἰῶνος.
doing these things known from [the] age.

19 διὸ ἐγὼ κρίνω μὴ παρενοχλεῖν τοῖς
Wherefore I decide not to trouble the [ones]

ἀπὸ τῶν ἐθνῶν ἐπιστρέφουσιν ἐπὶ τὸν
from the nations turning to -

θεόν, 20 ἀλλὰ ἐπιστεῖλαι αὐτοῖς τοῦ
God, but to write word to them -

---

that he accepted them by giving the Holy Spirit to them, just as he did to us. 9He made no distinction between us and them, for he purified their hearts by faith. 10Now then, why do you try to test God by putting on the necks of the disciples a yoke that neither we nor our fathers have been able to bear? 11No! We believe it is through the grace of our Lord Jesus that we are saved, just as they are."

12The whole assembly became silent as they listened to Barnabas and Paul telling about the miraculous signs and wonders God had done among the Gentiles through them. 13When they finished, James spoke up: "Brothers, listen to me. 14Simonᵈ has described to us how God at first showed his concern by taking from the Gentiles a people for himself. 15The words of the prophets are in agreement with this, as it is written:

16" 'After this I will return
and rebuild David's fallen tent.
Its ruins I will rebuild,
and I will restore it,
17that the remnant of men may seek the Lord,
and all the Gentiles who bear my name,
says the Lord, who does these things'ᵉ
18 that have been known for ages.ᶠ

19"It is my judgment, therefore, that we should not make it difficult for the Gentiles who are turning to God. 20Instead we should write to them, telling them

---

ᵇOther ancient authorities read things. 18Known to God from of old are all his works.'

ᵈ14 Greek Simeon, a variant of Simon; that is, Peter
ᵉ17 Amos 9:11,12
ᶠ17,18 Some manuscripts things'— / 18known to the Lord for ages is his work

them to abstain only from things polluted by idols and from fornication and from whatever has been strangled[c] and from blood. 21 For in every city, for generations past, Moses has had those who proclaim him, for he has been read aloud every sabbath in the synagogues."

The Council's Letter to Gentile Believers

22 Then the apostles and the elders, with the consent of the whole church, decided to choose men from among their members[d] and to send them to Antioch with Paul and Barnabas. They sent Judas called Barsabbas, and Silas, leaders among the brothers, 23 with the following letter: "The brothers, both the apostles and the elders, to the believers[e] of Gentile origin in Antioch and Syria and Cilicia, greetings. 24 Since we have heard that certain persons who have gone out from us, though with no instructions from us, have said things to disturb you and have unsettled your minds,[f] 25 we have decided unanimously to choose representatives[g] and send them to you, along with our beloved Barnabas and Paul, 26 who have risked their lives for the sake of our Lord Jesus Christ. 27 We have therefore sent Judas and Silas, who themselves will tell you the same things by word of mouth. 28 For it has seemed good to the Holy Spirit and to us to impose on you no further burden than these essentials: 29 that you abstain from what has been sacrificed to idols and from blood and from what is strangled[h] and from fornication. If you keep yourselves from these, you will

---

ἀπέχεσθαι τῶν ἀλισγημάτων τῶν εἰδώλων
to abstain from[d] the   pollutions   -   of idols

καὶ τῆς πορνείας καὶ πνικτοῦ καὶ τοῦ
and   -   fornication   and   a thing strangled   and   -

αἵματος. 21 Μωϋσῆς γὰρ ἐκ γενεῶν
blood.   21 For ¹Moses   ²from ⁴generations

ἀρχαίων κατὰ πόλιν τοὺς κηρύσσοντας
³ancient   ⁶in every city   ⁷the [ones]   ⁸proclaiming

αὐτὸν ἔχει ἐν ταῖς συναγωγαῖς κατὰ
⁹him   ⁵has   ¹¹in   ¹²the   ¹³synagogues   ¹⁴on

πᾶν σάββατον ἀναγινωσκόμενος. 22 Τότε
¹⁵every ¹⁶sabbath   ¹⁰being read.   22 Then

ἔδοξε τοῖς ἀποστόλοις καὶ τοῖς πρεσ-
it seemed [good] to the   apostles   and   to the   el-

βυτέροις σὺν ὅλῃ τῇ ἐκκλησίᾳ ἐκλεξαμένους
ders   with   all   the   church   choosing

ἄνδρας ἐξ αὐτῶν πέμψαι εἰς Ἀντιόχειαν
men   of   them   to send   to   Antioch

σὺν τῷ Παύλῳ καὶ Βαρναβᾷ, Ἰούδαν
with   -   Paul   and   Barnabas,   Judas

τὸν καλούμενον Βαρσαββᾶν καὶ Σιλᾶν,
the   *being* called   Barsabbas   and   Silas,

ἄνδρας ἡγουμένους ἐν τοῖς ἀδελφοῖς,
men   leading   among   the   brothers,

23 γράψαντες διὰ χειρὸς αὐτῶν· Οἱ
writing   through   [the] hand   of them: The

ἀπόστολοι καὶ οἱ πρεσβύτεροι ἀδελφοὶ
apostles   and   the   elder   brothers

τοῖς κατὰ τὴν Ἀντιόχειαν καὶ Συρίαν
¹to the ²throughout -   ⁴Antioch   ⁷and   ⁸Syria

καὶ Κιλικίαν ἀδελφοῖς τοῖς ἐξ ἐθνῶν
⁹and   ¹⁰Cilicia   ⁵brothers   ⁶of [the] ⁵nations

χαίρειν. 24 Ἐπειδὴ ἠκούσαμεν ὅτι τινὲς
¹¹greeting.   24 Since   we heard   that   some

ἐξ ἡμῶν ἐτάραξαν ὑμᾶς λόγοις ἀνασκευάζ-
of   us   troubled   you   with words   unsettl-

οντες τὰς ψυχὰς ὑμῶν, οἷς οὐ διεστειλάμεθα,
ing   the   minds   of you,   to   we did not give whom   commission,

25 ἔδοξεν ἡμῖν γενομένοις ὁμοθυμαδόν,
it seemed [good]   to us   becoming   of one mind,

ἐκλεξαμένους ἄνδρας πέμψαι πρὸς ὑμᾶς
chosen   men   to send   to   you

σὺν τοῖς ἀγαπητοῖς ἡμῶν Βαρναβᾷ καὶ
with   the   beloved   of us   Barnabas   and

Παύλῳ, 26 ἀνθρώποις παραδεδωκόσι τὰς
Paul,   26 men   having given up   the

ψυχὰς αὐτῶν ὑπὲρ τοῦ ὀνόματος τοῦ
lives   of them   on behalf of the   name   of the

κυρίου ἡμῶν Ἰησοῦ Χριστοῦ. 27 ἀπεστάλ-
Lord   of us   Jesus   Christ.   27 We have

καμεν οὖν Ἰούδαν καὶ Σιλᾶν, καὶ αὐτοὺς
sent   therefore Judas   and   Silas,   and   they

διὰ λόγου ἀπαγγέλλοντας τὰ αὐτά.
through   speech   announcing   the   same (by)   things.

28 ἔδοξεν γὰρ τῷ πνεύματι τῷ ἁγίῳ
For it seemed [good]   to the   Spirit   -   Holy

καὶ ἡμῖν μηδὲν πλέον ἐπιτίθεσθαι ὑμῖν
and   to us   ³nothing   ⁴more   ¹to be put on   ²you

βάρος πλὴν τούτων τῶν ἐπάναγκες,
⁵burden   than   these   the   necessary things,

29 ἀπέχεσθαι εἰδωλοθύτων καὶ αἵματος καὶ
to abstain from   idol sacrifices   and   blood   and

πνικτῶν καὶ πορνείας· ἐξ ὧν διατηροῦντες
things   and   fornication;   from which   keeping
strangled

---

to abstain from food polluted by idols, from sexual immorality, from the meat of strangled animals and from blood. 21 For Moses has been preached in every city from the earliest times and is read in the synagogues on every Sabbath."

The Council's Letter to Gentile Believers

22 Then the apostles and elders, with the whole church, decided to choose some of their own men and send them to Antioch with Paul and Barnabas. They chose Judas (called Barsabbas) and Silas, two men who were leaders among the brothers. 23 With them they sent the following letter:

The apostles and elders, your brothers,

To the Gentile believers in Antioch, Syria and Cilicia:

Greetings.

24 We have heard that some went out from us without our authorization and disturbed you, troubling your minds by what they said. 25 So we all agreed to choose some men and send them to you with our dear friends Barnabas and Paul— 26 men who have risked their lives for the name of our Lord Jesus Christ. 27 Therefore we are sending Judas and Silas to confirm by word of mouth what we are writing. 28 It seemed good to the Holy Spirit and to us not to burden you with anything beyond the following requirements: 29 You are to abstain from food sacrificed to idols, from blood, from the meat of strangled animals and from sexual immorality.

---

c Other ancient authorities lack *and from whatever has been strangled*

d Gk *from among them*

e Gk *brothers*

f Other ancient authorities add saying, 'You must be circumcised and keep the law.'

g Gk *men*

h Other ancient authorities lack *and from what is strangled*

do well. Farewell."
30 So they were sent off and went down to Antioch. When they gathered the congregation together, they delivered the letter. 31 When its members[i] read it, they rejoiced at the exhortation. 32 Judas and Silas, who were themselves prophets, said much to encourage and strengthen the believers.[e] 33 After they had been there for some time, they were sent off in peace by the believers[e] to those who had sent them.[j] 35 But Paul and Barnabas remained in Antioch, and there, with many others, they taught and proclaimed the word of the Lord.

Paul and Barnabas Separate

36 After some days Paul said to Barnabas, "Come, let us return and visit the believers[e] in every city where we proclaimed the word of the Lord and see how they are doing." 37 Barnabas wanted to take with them John called Mark. 38 But Paul decided not to take with them one who had deserted them in Pamphylia and had not accompanied them in the work. 39 The disagreement became so sharp that they parted company; Barnabas took Mark with him and sailed away to Cyprus. 40 But Paul chose Silas and set out, the believers[e] commending him to the grace of the Lord. 41 He went through Syria and Cilicia, strengthening the churches.

ἑαυτοὺς εὖ πράξετε. Ἔρρωσθε.
yourselves well ye will do. Farewell.

30 Οἱ μὲν οὖν ἀπολυθέντες κατῆλθον εἰς
They - therefore being dismissed went down to

Ἀντιόχειαν, καὶ συναγαγόντες τὸ πλῆθος
Antioch, and assembling the multitude

ἐπέδωκαν τὴν ἐπιστολήν. **31** ἀναγνόντες δὲ
handed in the letter. And having read

ἐχάρησαν ἐπὶ τῇ παρακλήσει. **32** Ἰούδας τε
they rejoiced at the exhortation. And Judas

καὶ Σιλᾶς, καὶ αὐτοὶ προφῆται ὄντες,
and Silas, also [them]selves prophets being,

διὰ λόγου πολλοῦ παρεκάλεσαν τοὺς
through speech much exhorted the
(by)

ἀδελφοὺς καὶ ἐπεστήριξαν· **33** ποιήσαντες δὲ
brothers and confirmed; and having continued

χρόνον ἀπελύθησαν μετ᾽ εἰρήνης ἀπὸ
a time they were dismissed with peace from

τῶν ἀδελφῶν πρὸς τοὺς ἀποστείλαντας
the brothers to the [ones] having sent

αὐτούς. ‡ **35** Παῦλος δὲ καὶ Βαρνάβας
them. But Paul and Barnabas

διέτριβον ἐν Ἀντιοχείᾳ, διδάσκοντες καὶ
stayed in Antioch, teaching and

εὐαγγελιζόμενοι μετὰ καὶ ἑτέρων πολλῶν
preaching ¹with ⁴also ³others ²many

τὸν λόγον τοῦ κυρίου.
the word of the Lord.

36 Μετὰ δὲ τινας ἡμέρας εἶπεν πρὸς
Now after some days ²said ³to

Βαρνάβαν Παῦλος· ἐπιστρέψαντες δὴ
⁴Barnabas ¹Paul: Returning then

ἐπισκεψώμεθα τοὺς ἀδελφοὺς κατὰ πόλιν
let us visit the brothers throughout ²city

πᾶσαν ἐν αἷς κατηγγείλαμεν τὸν λόγον
¹every in which we announced the word

τοῦ κυρίου, πῶς ἔχουσιν. **37** Βαρναβᾶς
of the Lord, how they have(are). Barnabas

δὲ ἐβούλετο συμπαραλαβεῖν καὶ τὸν
And wished to take with [them] also the

Ἰωάννην τὸν καλούμενον Μᾶρκον· **38** Παῦλος
John - *being* called Mark; ¹Paul

δὲ ἠξίου, τὸν ἀποστάντα ἀπ᾽ αὐτῶν
¹but ²thought fit, - ⁷withdrawing ⁸from ⁹them

ἀπὸ Παμφυλίας καὶ μὴ συνελθόντα αὐτοῖς
¹⁰from ¹¹Pamphylia ¹³and ¹⁵not ¹⁴going with ¹⁶them

εἰς τὸ ἔργον, μὴ συμπαραλαμβάνειν τοῦτον.
¹⁶to ¹⁷the ¹⁸work, ⁴not ⁵to take with [them] ⁶this one.

39 ἐγένετο δὲ παροξυσμός, ὥστε ἀποχωρισ-
And there was sharp feeling, so as to separ-

θῆναι αὐτοὺς ἀπ᾽ ἀλλήλων, τόν τε
ate them from each other, - and

Βαρνάβαν παραλαβόντα τὸν Μᾶρκον
Barnabas taking - Mark

ἐκπλεῦσαι εἰς Κύπρον. **40** Παῦλος δὲ
to sail away to Cyprus. But Paul

ἐπιλεξάμενος Σιλᾶν ἐξῆλθεν, παραδοθεὶς
having chosen Silas went forth, being commended

τῇ χάριτι τοῦ κυρίου ὑπὸ τῶν
to the grace of the Lord by the

ἀδελφῶν· **41** διήρχετο δὲ τὴν Συρίαν
brothers; and he went through - Syria

καὶ Κιλικίαν ἐπιστηρίζων τὰς ἐκκλησίας.
and Cilicia confirming the churches.

You will do well to avoid these things.

Farewell.

30 The men were sent off and went down to Antioch, where they gathered the church together and delivered the letter. 31 The people read it and were glad for its encouraging message. 32 Judas and Silas, who themselves were prophets, said much to encourage and strengthen the brothers. 33 After spending some time there, they were sent off by the brothers with the blessing of peace to return to those who had sent them. [g] 35 But Paul and Barnabas remained in Antioch, where they and many others taught and preached the word of the Lord.

Disagreement Between Paul and Barnabas

36 Some time later Paul said to Barnabas, "Let us go back and visit the brothers in all the towns where we preached the word of the Lord and see how they are doing." 37 Barnabas wanted to take John, also called Mark, with them, 38 but Paul did not think it wise to take him, because he had deserted them in Pamphylia and had not continued with them in the work. 39 They had such a sharp disagreement that they parted company. Barnabas took Mark and sailed for Cyprus, 40 but Paul chose Silas and left, commended by the brothers to the grace of the Lord. 41 He went through Syria and Cilicia, strengthening the churches.

---

i Gk *When they*
j Other ancient authorities add verse 34, *But it seemed good to Silas to remain there*

‡ Verse 34 omitted by Nestle; *cf.* NIV

g 33 Some manuscripts *them; 34 but Silas decided to remain there*

Chapter 16

Timothy Joins Paul and Silas

PAUL[k] went on also to Derbe and to Lystra, where there was a disciple named Timothy, the son of a Jewish woman who was a believer; but his father was a Greek. 2 He was well spoken of by the believers[e] in Lystra and Iconium. 3 Paul wanted Timothy to accompany him; and he took him and had him circumcised because of the Jews who were in those places, for they all knew that his father was a Greek. 4 As they went from town to town, they delivered to them for observance the decisions that had been reached by the apostles and elders who were in Jerusalem. 5 So the churches were strengthened in the faith and increased in numbers daily.

Paul's Vision of the Man of Macedonia

6 They went through the region of Phrygia and Galatia, having been forbidden by the Holy Spirit to speak the word in Asia. 7 When they had come opposite Mysia, they attempted to go into Bithynia, but the Spirit of Jesus did not allow them; 8 so, passing by Mysia, they went down to Troas. 9 During the night Paul had a vision: there stood a man of Macedonia pleading with him and saying, "Come over to Macedonia and help us." 10 When we had seen the vision, we immediately tried to cross over to Macedonia, being convinced that God had called us to proclaim the good news to

---

16 Κατήντησεν δὲ καὶ εἰς Δέρβην καὶ
And he came down also to Derbe and

εἰς Λύστραν. καὶ ἰδοὺ μαθητής τις ἦν
to Lystra. And behold[,] a certain disciple was

ἐκεῖ ὀνόματι Τιμόθεος, υἱὸς γυναικὸς
there by name Timothy, son ⁸woman

Ἰουδαίας πιστῆς πατρὸς δὲ Ἕλληνος,
³Jewish ⁵of a faithful ⁴but ⁶father ⁷of a Greek,

2 ὃς ἐμαρτυρεῖτο ὑπὸ τῶν ἐν Λύστροις
who was witnessed to by ³the ⁴in ⁵Lystra

καὶ Ἰκονίῳ ἀδελφῶν. **3** τοῦτον ἠθέλησεν
⁶and ⁷Iconium ²brothers. ²This one ¹wished

ὁ Παῦλος σὺν αὐτῷ ἐξελθεῖν, καὶ λαβὼν
- ¹Paul with him to go forth, and taking

περιέτεμεν αὐτὸν διὰ τοὺς Ἰουδαίους τοὺς
circumcised him on account the Jews -
of

ὄντας ἐν τοῖς τόποις ἐκείνοις· ᾔδεισαν
being in those places; ²they knew

γὰρ ἅπαντες ὅτι Ἕλλην ὁ πατὴρ αὐτοῦ
¹for all that a Greek the father of him

ὑπῆρχεν. **4** Ὡς δὲ διεπορεύοντο τὰς
was. Now as they went through the

πόλεις, παρεδίδοσαν αὐτοῖς φυλάσσειν τὰ
cities, they delivered to them* to keep the

δόγματα τὰ κεκριμένα ὑπὸ τῶν ἀποστόλων
decrees - having been by the apostles
decided [on]

καὶ πρεσβυτέρων τῶν ἐν Ἱεροσολύμοις.
and elders - in Jerusalem.

5 Αἱ μὲν οὖν ἐκκλησίαι ἐστερεοῦντο
²The - ¹therefore ³churches were strengthened

τῇ πίστει καὶ ἐπερίσσευον τῷ ἀριθμῷ
in the faith and increased - in number

καθ' ἡμέραν.
daily.

6 Διῆλθον δὲ τὴν Φρυγίαν καὶ Γαλατικὴν
And they went through the Phrygian and Galatian

χώραν, κωλυθέντες ὑπὸ τοῦ ἁγίου
country, being prevented by the Holy

πνεύματος λαλῆσαι τὸν λόγον ἐν τῇ
Spirit to speak the word in -
=from speaking

Ἀσίᾳ· **7** ἐλθόντες δὲ κατὰ τὴν Μυσίαν
Asia; but coming against - Mysia

ἐπείραζον εἰς τὴν Βιθυνίαν πορευθῆναι,
they attempted into - Bithynia to go,

καὶ οὐκ εἴασεν αὐτοὺς τὸ πνεῦμα Ἰησοῦ·
and ²not ⁴allowed ³them ¹the ⁵Spirit ⁶of Jesus;

8 παρελθόντες δὲ τὴν Μυσίαν κατέβησαν
so passing by - Mysia they came down

εἰς Τρῳάδα. **9** καὶ ὅραμα διὰ νυκτὸς
to Troas. And a vision through [the]
(during) night

τῷ Παύλῳ ὤφθη, ἀνὴρ Μακεδών τις
- to Paul appeared, a man Macedonian certain

ἦν ἑστὼς καὶ παρακαλῶν αὐτὸν καὶ
was standing and beseeching him and

λέγων· διαβὰς εἰς Μακεδονίαν βοήθησον
saying: Crossing into Macedonia help

ἡμῖν. **10** ὡς δὲ τὸ ὅραμα εἶδεν, εὐθέως
us. So when - the vision he saw, immediately

ἐζητήσαμεν ἐξελθεῖν εἰς Μακεδονίαν,
we sought to go forth to Macedonia,

συμβιβάζοντες ὅτι προσκέκληται ἡμᾶς ὁ
concluding that ²has(had) called ³us ¹the

Chapter 16

Timothy Joins Paul and Silas

HE came to Derbe and then to Lystra, where a disciple named Timothy lived, whose mother was a Jewess and a believer, but whose father was a Greek. 2The brothers at Lystra and Iconium spoke well of him. 3Paul wanted to take him along on the journey, so he circumcised him because of the Jews who lived in that area, for they all knew that his father was a Greek. 4As they traveled from town to town, they delivered the decisions reached by the apostles and elders in Jerusalem for the people to obey. 5So the churches were strengthened in the faith and grew daily in numbers.

Paul's Vision of the Man of Macedonia

6Paul and his companions traveled throughout the region of Phrygia and Galatia, having been kept by the Holy Spirit from preaching the word in the province of Asia. 7When they came to the border of Mysia, they tried to enter Bithynia, but the Spirit of Jesus would not allow them to. 8So they passed by Mysia and went down to Troas. 9During the night Paul had a vision of a man of Macedonia standing and begging him, "Come over to Macedonia and help us." 10After Paul had seen the vision, we got ready at once to leave for Macedonia, concluding that God had called us to

---

[k] Gk He
* Note the gender: πόλις is feminine.

them.

The Conversion of Lydia

11 We set sail from Troas and took a straight course to Samothrace, the following day to Neapolis, 12 and from there to Philippi, which is a leading city of the district[l] of Macedonia and a Roman colony. We remained in this city for some days. 13 On the sabbath day we went outside the gate by the river, where we supposed there was a place of prayer; and we sat down and spoke to the women who had gathered there. 14 A certain woman named Lydia, a worshiper of God, was listening to us; she was from the city of Thyatira and a dealer in purple cloth. The Lord opened her heart to listen eagerly to what was said by Paul. 15 When she and her household were baptized, she urged us, saying, "If you have judged me to be faithful to the Lord, come and stay at my home." And she prevailed upon us.

Paul and Silas in Prison

16 One day, as we were going to the place of prayer, we met a slave girl who had a spirit of divination and brought her owners a great deal of money by fortune-telling. 17 While she followed Paul and us, she would cry out, "These men are slaves of the Most High God, who proclaim to you[m] a way of salvation." 18 She kept doing this for many days. But Paul, very much annoyed, turned and said to the spirit, "I order you in the name of Jesus Christ to come out of her." And it came out that very hour.

[l] Other authorities read a city of the first district
[m] Other ancient authorities read to us

θεὸς εὐαγγελίσασθαι αὐτούς.
¹God　to evangelize　them.

11 Ἀναχθέντες δὲ ἀπὸ Τρῳάδος εὐθυδρο-
And setting sail　from　Troas　we ran a

μήσαμεν εἰς Σαμοθρᾴκην, τῇ δὲ ἐπιούσῃ
straight course to　Samothracia,　and on the next day

εἰς Νέαν πόλιν, 12 κἀκεῖθεν εἰς Φιλίππους,
to　Neapolis,　and thence　to　Philippi,

ἥτις ἐστὶν πρώτη τῆς μερίδος Μακεδονίας
which　is　¹[the] ²first ⁴of the　³part　⁵of Macedonia

πόλις, κολωνία. Ἦμεν δὲ ἐν ταύτῃ τῇ
²city,　a colony.　And we were　in　this　-

πόλει διατρίβοντες ἡμέρας τινάς. 13 τῇ τε
city　staying　days　some.　And on the

ἡμέρᾳ τῶν σαββάτων ἐξήλθομεν ἔξω τῆς
day　of the　sabbaths　we went forth　outside　the

πύλης παρὰ ποταμὸν οὗ ἐνομίζομεν
gate　by　a river　where　we supposed

προσευχὴν εἶναι, καὶ καθίσαντες ἐλαλοῦμεν
a place of prayer to be,　and　sitting　we spoke

ταῖς συνελθούσαις γυναιξίν. 14 καί τις
to the　²coming together　¹women.　And a certain

γυνὴ ὀνόματι Λυδία, πορφυρόπωλις
woman　by name　Lydia,　a dealer in purple-
dyed [garments]

πόλεως Θυατίρων, σεβομένη τὸν θεόν,
of [the] city　of Thyatira,　worshipping　-　God,

ἤκουεν, ἧς ὁ κύριος διήνοιξεν τὴν καρδίαν
heard, of whom the　Lord　opened up　the　heart

προσέχειν τοῖς λαλουμένοις ὑπὸ Παύλου.
to take heed to the things　being spoken　by　Paul.

15 ὡς δὲ ἐβαπτίσθη καὶ ὁ οἶκος αὐτῆς,
And when she was baptized　and　the household of her,

παρεκάλεσεν λέγουσα· εἰ κεκρίκατέ με
she besought　saying:　If　ye have decided　me

πιστὴν τῷ κυρίῳ εἶναι, εἰσελθόντες εἰς
faithful　to the　Lord　to be,　entering　into

τὸν οἶκόν μου μένετε· καὶ παρεβιάσατο
the　house　of me　remain·　and　she urged

ἡμᾶς. 16 Ἐγένετο δὲ πορευομένων ἡμῶν
us.　And it happened　going　us
= as we went

εἰς τὴν προσευχήν, παιδίσκην τινὰ ἔχουσαν
to the　place of prayer,　a certain maid　having

πνεῦμα πύθωνα ὑπαντῆσαι ἡμῖν, ἥτις
a spirit　of a python　to meet　us,　who

ἐργασίαν πολλὴν παρεῖχεν τοῖς κυρίοις
²gain　¹much　³brought　to the　masters

αὐτῆς μαντευομένη. 17 αὕτη κατακολουθοῦσα
of her　practising soothsaying.　This one　following after

τῷ Παύλῳ καὶ ἡμῖν ἔκραζεν λέγουσα·
-　Paul　and　us　cried out　saying:

οὗτοι οἱ ἄνθρωποι δοῦλοι τοῦ θεοῦ τοῦ
These　-　men　slaves　of the　God　-

ὑψίστου εἰσίν, οἵτινες καταγγέλλουσιν ὑμῖν
most high　are,　who　announce　to you

ὁδὸν σωτηρίας. 18 τοῦτο δὲ ἐποίει ἐπὶ
a way　of salvation.　And this　she did　over

πολλὰς ἡμέρας. διαπονηθεὶς δὲ Παῦλος
many　days.　But becoming greatly troubled　Paul

καὶ ἐπιστρέψας τῷ πνεύματι εἶπεν· παραγ-
and　turning　²to the　¹spirit　³he said:　I

γέλλω σοι ἐν ὀνόματι Ἰησοῦ Χριστοῦ
charge　thee　in　[the] name　of Jesus　Christ

ἐξελθεῖν ἀπ' αὐτῆς· καὶ ἐξῆλθεν αὐτῇ
to come out　from　her;　and　it came out　in the

preach the gospel to them.

Lydia's Conversion in Philippi

11 From Troas we put out to sea and sailed straight for Samothrace, and the next day on to Neapolis. 12 From there we traveled to Philippi, a Roman colony and the leading city of that district of Macedonia. And we stayed there several days.

13 On the Sabbath we went outside the city gate to the river, where we expected to find a place of prayer. We sat down and began to speak to the women who had gathered there. 14 One of those listening was a woman named Lydia, a dealer in purple cloth from the city of Thyatira, who was a worshiper of God. The Lord opened her heart to respond to Paul's message. 15 When she and the members of her household were baptized, she invited us to her home. "If you consider me a believer in the Lord," she said, "come and stay at my house." And she persuaded us.

Paul and Silas in Prison

16 Once when we were going to the place of prayer, we were met by a slave girl who had a spirit by which she predicted the future. She earned a great deal of money for her owners by fortune-telling. 17 This girl followed Paul and the rest of us, shouting, "These men are servants of the Most High God, who are telling you the way to be saved." 18 She kept this up for many days. Finally Paul became so troubled that he turned around and said to the spirit, "In the name of Jesus Christ I command you to come out of her!" At that moment the spirit left her.

19 But when her owners saw that their hope of making money was gone, they seized Paul and Silas and dragged them into the marketplace before the authorities. 20 When they had brought them before the magistrates, they said, "These men are disturbing our city; they are Jews 21 and are advocating customs that are not lawful for us as Romans to adopt or observe." 22 The crowd joined in attacking them, and the magistrates had them stripped of their clothing and ordered them to be beaten with rods. 23 After they had given them a severe flogging, they threw them into prison and ordered the jailer to keep them securely. 24 Following these instructions, he put them in the innermost cell and fastened their feet in the stocks.

25 About midnight Paul and Silas were praying and singing hymns to God, and the prisoners were listening to them. 26 Suddenly there was an earthquake, so violent that the foundations of the prison were shaken; and immediately all the doors were opened and everyone's chains were unfastened. 27 When the jailer woke up and saw the prison doors wide open, he drew his sword and was about to kill himself, since he supposed that the prisoners had escaped. 28 But Paul shouted in a loud voice, "Do not harm yourself, for we are all here." 29 The jailer[n] called for lights, and

---

τῇ ὥρᾳ. **19** Ἰδόντες δὲ οἱ κύριοι αὐτῆς
same hour.* And ⁴seeing ¹the ²masters ³of her

ὅτι ἐξῆλθεν ἡ ἐλπὶς τῆς ἐργασίας αὐτῶν,
⁵that ¹¹went out ⁶the ⁷hope ⁸of the ⁹gain ¹⁰of them,

ἐπιλαβόμενοι τὸν Παῦλον καὶ τὸν Σιλᾶν
l:aving seized — Paul and — Silas

εἵλκυσαν εἰς τὴν ἀγορὰν ἐπὶ τοὺς ἄρχοντας,
dragged to the marketplace before the rulers,

20 καὶ προσαγαγόντες αὐτοὺς τοῖς στρατηγοῖς
and ¹bringing ²to ³them the prætors

εἶπαν· οὗτοι οἱ ἄνθρωποι ἐκταράσσουσιν
said: These — men are greatly troubling

ἡμῶν τὴν πόλιν, Ἰουδαῖοι ὑπάρχοντες,
of us the city, ²Jews ¹being,

21 καὶ καταγγέλλουσιν ἔθη ἃ οὐκ ἔξεστιν
and they announce customs which it is not lawful

ἡμῖν παραδέχεσθαι οὐδὲ ποιεῖν Ῥωμαίοις
for us to receive nor to do ²Romans

οὖσιν. **22** καὶ συνεπέστη ὁ ὄχλος κατ'
¹being. And rose up together the crowd against

αὐτῶν, καὶ οἱ στρατηγοὶ περιρήξαντες
them, and the prætors tearing off

αὐτῶν τὰ ἱμάτια ἐκέλευον ῥαβδίζειν,
of them the garments commanded to flog,

23 πολλὰς δὲ ἐπιθέντες αὐτοῖς πληγὰς
and ²many ¹laying on ³them ⁴stripes

ἔβαλον εἰς φυλακήν, παραγγείλαντες τῷ
threw into prison, charging the

δεσμοφύλακι ἀσφαλῶς τηρεῖν αὐτούς· **24** ὃς
jailer securely to keep them; who

παραγγελίαν τοιαύτην λαβὼν ἔβαλεν αὐτοὺς
²a charge ³such ¹having received threw them

εἰς τὴν ἐσωτέραν φυλακὴν καὶ τοὺς
into the inner prison and ²the

πόδας ἠσφαλίσατο αὐτῶν εἰς τὸ ξύλον.
³feet ¹secured ⁴of them in the stocks.

25 Κατὰ δὲ τὸ μεσονύκτιον Παῦλος καὶ
And about — midnight Paul and

Σιλᾶς προσευχόμενοι ὕμνουν τὸν θεόν,
Silas praying ¹praised ²in a hymn — ³God,

ἐπηκροῶντο δὲ αὐτῶν οἱ δέσμιοι· **26** ἄφνω
and ³listened to ⁴them ¹the ²prisoners; and suddenly

σεισμὸς ἐγένετο μέγας, ὥστε σαλευ-
²earthquake ¹there was ³a great, so as to be

θῆναι τὰ θεμέλια τοῦ δεσμωτηρίου·
shaken the foundations of the jail;

ἠνεῴχθησαν δὲ παραχρῆμα αἱ θύραι πᾶσαι,
and ⁵were opened ¹at once ²the ⁴doors ³all,

καὶ πάντων τὰ δεσμὰ ἀνέθη. **27** ἔξυπνος δὲ
and ²of all ¹the ³bonds were And ⁴awake
loosened.

γενόμενος ὁ δεσμοφύλαξ καὶ ἰδὼν
³having become ¹the ²jailer and seeing

ἀνεῳγμένας τὰς θύρας τῆς φυλακῆς,
having been opened the doors of the prison,

σπασάμενος τὴν μάχαιραν ἤμελλεν ἑαυτὸν
having drawn the sword was about himself

ἀναιρεῖν, νομίζων ἐκπεφευγέναι τοὺς
to kill, supposing to have escaped the

δεσμίους. **28** ἐφώνησεν δὲ Παῦλος μεγάλῃ
prisoners. But called Paul with a
great(loud)

φωνῇ λέγων· μηδὲν πράξῃς σεαυτῷ κακόν,
voice saying: ¹Nothing ³do ⁴thyself ²harm,

ἅπαντες γὰρ ἐσμεν ἐνθάδε. **29** αἰτήσας
for ²all ¹we are ³here. asking

---

19 When the owners of the slave girl realized that their hope of making money was gone, they seized Paul and Silas and dragged them into the marketplace to face the authorities. 20 They brought them before the magistrates and said, "These men are Jews, and they are throwing our city into an uproar 21 by advocating customs unlawful for us Romans to accept or practice."

22 The crowd joined in the attack against Paul and Silas, and the magistrates ordered them to be stripped and beaten. 23 After they had been severely flogged, they were thrown into prison, and the jailer was commanded to guard them carefully. 24 Upon receiving such orders, he put them in the inner cell and fastened their feet in the stocks.

25 About midnight Paul and Silas were praying and singing hymns to God, and the other prisoners were listening to them. 26 Suddenly there was such a violent earthquake that the foundations of the prison were shaken. At once all the prison doors flew open, and everybody's chains came loose. 27 The jailer woke up, and when he saw the prison doors open, he drew his sword and was about to kill himself because he thought the prisoners had escaped. 28 But Paul shouted, "Don't harm yourself! We are all here!"

29 The jailer called for

---

rushing in, he fell down
trembling before Paul and
Silas. 30 Then he brought
them outside and said,
"Sirs, what must I do to be
saved?" 31 They answered,
"Believe on the Lord
Jesus, and you will be
saved, you and your household." 32 They spoke the
word of the Lord *o* to him
and to all who were in his
house. 33 At the same hour
of the night he took them
and washed their wounds;
then he and his entire family were baptized without
delay. 34 He brought them
up into the house and set
food before them; and he
and his entire household rejoiced that he had become a
believer in God.

35 When morning
came, the magistrates sent
the police, saying, "Let
those men go." 36 And the
jailer reported the message
to Paul, saying, "The magistrates sent word to let you
go; therefore come out now
and go in peace." 37 But
Paul replied, "They have
beaten us in public, uncondemned, men who are Ro-
man citizens, and have
thrown us into prison; and
now are they going to discharge us in secret? Cer-
tainly not! Let them come
and take us out them-
selves." 38 The police reported these words to the
magistrates, and they were
afraid when they heard that
they were Roman citizens;
39 so they came and apolo-
gized to them. And they
took them out and asked

δὲ φῶτα εἰσεπήδησεν, καὶ ἔντρομος
And lights he rushed in, and trembling

γενόμενος προσέπεσεν τῷ Παύλῳ καὶ
becoming he fell before - Paul and

Σιλᾷ, 30 καὶ προαγαγὼν αὐτοὺς ἔξω ἔφη·
Silas, and ¹leading ³forward ²them outside said:

κύριοι, τί με δεῖ ποιεῖν ἵνα σωθῶ;
Sirs, what ²me ¹behoves it to do that I may
be saved?

31 οἱ δὲ εἶπαν· πίστευσον ἐπὶ τὸν κύριον
And they said: Believe on the Lord

Ἰησοῦν, καὶ σωθήσῃ σὺ καὶ ὁ οἶκός
Jesus, and shalt be saved thou and the household

σου. 32 καὶ ἐλάλησαν αὐτῷ τὸν λόγον
of thee. And they spoke to him the word

τοῦ θεοῦ σὺν πᾶσιν τοῖς ἐν τῇ οἰκίᾳ
- of God with all the [ones] in the house

αὐτοῦ. 33 καὶ παραλαβὼν αὐτοὺς ἐν
of him. And taking them in

ἐκείνῃ τῇ ὥρᾳ τῆς νυκτὸς ἔλουσεν ἀπὸ
that the hour of the night he washed from

τῶν πληγῶν, καὶ ἐβαπτίσθη αὐτὸς καὶ
the stripes, and was baptized he and

οἱ αὐτοῦ ἅπαντες παραχρῆμα, 34 ἀναγαγών
the of him all at once, ²bringing up

τε αὐτοὺς εἰς τὸν οἶκον παρέθηκεν
¹and them to the house he set
before [them]

τράπεζαν, καὶ ἠγαλλιάσατο πανοικεὶ πεπι-
a table, and exulted with all the having
household

στευκὼς τῷ θεῷ. 35 Ἡμέρας δὲ γενομένης
believed - God. And day coming*
=when day came

ἀπέστειλαν οἱ στρατηγοὶ τοὺς ῥαβδούχους
²sent ¹the ²prætors the tipstaffs

λέγοντες· ἀπόλυσον τοὺς ἀνθρώπους
saying: Release - men

ἐκείνους. 36 ἀπήγγειλεν δὲ ὁ δεσμοφύλαξ
those. And announced the jailer

τοὺς λόγους τούτους πρὸς τὸν Παῦλον,
these words to - Paul,

ὅτι ἀπέσταλκαν οἱ στρατηγοὶ ἵνα ἀπολυθῆτε.
- ²have sent ¹The ²prætors that ye may be
released.

νῦν οὖν ἐξελθόντες πορεύεσθε ἐν εἰρήνῃ.
Now therefore going forth proceed in peace.

37 ὁ δὲ Παῦλος ἔφη πρὸς αὐτούς·
- But Paul said to them:

δείραντες ἡμᾶς δημοσίᾳ ἀκατακρίτους,
Having beaten us publicly uncondemned,

ἀνθρώπους Ῥωμαίους ὑπάρχοντας, ἔβαλαν
men ¹Romans ¹being, they threw [us]

εἰς φυλακήν· καὶ νῦν λάθρα ἡμᾶς ἐκβάλ-
into prison; and now secretly us they

λουσιν; οὐ γάρ, ἀλλὰ ἐλθόντες αὐτοὶ
expel? No indeed, but coming [them]selves

ἡμᾶς ἐξαγαγέτωσαν. 38 ἀπήγγειλαν δὲ τοῖς
us let them bring out. And ²reported ⁴to the

στρατηγοῖς οἱ ῥαβδοῦχοι τὰ ῥήματα ταῦτα.
⁵prætors ¹the ²tipstaffs these words.

ἐφοβήθησαν δὲ ἀκούσαντες ὅτι Ῥωμαῖοί
And they were afraid hearing that Romans

εἰσιν, 39 καὶ ἐλθόντες παρεκάλεσαν
they are(were), and coming besought

αὐτούς, καὶ ἐξαγαγόντες ἠρώτων ἀπελθεῖν
them, and bringing out asked to go away

lights, rushed in and fell
trembling before Paul and
Silas. 30 He then brought
them out and asked, "Sirs,
what must I do to be
saved?"
31 They replied, "Believe
in the Lord Jesus, and you
will be saved—you and
your household." 32 Then
they spoke the word of the
Lord to him and to all the
others in his house. 33 At
that hour of the night the
jailer took them and
washed their wounds; then
immediately he and all his
family were baptized.
34 The jailer brought them
into his house and set a
meal before them; he was
filled with joy because he
had come to believe in God
—he and his whole family.

35 When it was daylight,
the magistrates sent their
officers to the jailer with
the order: "Release those
men." 36 The jailer told
Paul, "The magistrates
have ordered that you and
Silas be released. Now you
can leave. Go in peace."
37 But Paul said to the officers: "They beat us publicly without a trial, even
though we are Roman citi-
zens, and threw us into
prison. And now do they
want to get rid of us quietly? No! Let them come
themselves and escort us
out."
38 The officers reported
this to the magistrates, and
when they heard that Paul
and Silas were Roman citizens, they were alarmed.
39 They came to appease
them and escorted them
from the prison, requesting

them to leave the city. 40After leaving the prison they went to Lydia's home; and when they had seen and encouraged the brothers and sisters[p] there, they departed.

Chapter 17

The Uproar in Thessalonica

AFTER Paul and Silas[q] had passed through Amphipolis and Apollonia, they came to Thessalonica, where there was a synagogue of the Jews. 2And Paul went in, as was his custom, and on three sabbath days argued with them from the scriptures, 3explaining and proving that it was necessary for the Messiah[r] to suffer and to rise from the dead, and saying, "This is the Messiah,[r] Jesus whom I am proclaiming to you." 4Some of them were persuaded and joined Paul and Silas, as did a great many of the devout Greeks and not a few of the leading women. 5But the Jews became jealous, and with the help of some ruffians in the marketplaces they formed a mob and set the city in an uproar. While they were searching for Paul and Silas to bring them out to the assembly, they attacked Jason's house. 6When they could not find them, they dragged Jason and some believers[p] before the city authorities,[s] shouting, "These people who have been turning the world upside down have come here also, 7and Jason has entertained them as guests. They are all acting contrary to the decrees of the emperor, saying that there is another king named Jesus." 8The people and the city officials were dis-

---

ἀπὸ τῆς πόλεως. 40 ἐξελθόντες δὲ ἀπὸ
from the city. And going out from

τῆς φυλακῆς εἰσῆλθον πρὸς τὴν Λυδίαν,
the prison they entered to [the – Lydia,
house of]

καὶ ἰδόντες παρεκάλεσαν τοὺς ἀδελφοὺς
and seeing they exhorted the brothers

καὶ ἐξῆλθαν.
and went forth.

17 Διοδεύσαντες δὲ τὴν Ἀμφίπολιν καὶ
And travelling through – Amphipolis and

τὴν Ἀπολλωνίαν ἦλθον εἰς Θεσσαλονίκην,
– Apollonia they came to Thessalonica,

ὅπου ἦν συναγωγὴ τῶν Ἰουδαίων. 2 κατὰ
where was a synagogue of the Jews. according to

δὲ τὸ εἰωθὸς τῷ Παύλῳ εἰσῆλθεν πρὸς
And the custom – with Paul[o] he entered to

αὐτούς, καὶ ἐπὶ σάββατα τρία διελέξατο
them, and on sabbaths three lectured

αὐτοῖς ἀπὸ τῶν γραφῶν, 3 διανοίγων
to them from the scriptures, opening up

καὶ παρατιθέμενος ὅτι τὸν χριστὸν ἔδει
and setting before [them] that [the ¹Christ ¹it behoved

παθεῖν καὶ ἀναστῆναι ἐκ νεκρῶν, καὶ
to suffer and to rise again out of [the] dead, and

ὅτι οὗτός ἐστιν ὁ χριστός, ὁ Ἰησοῦς,
that this is(was) the Christ, – Jesus,

ὃν ἐγὼ καταγγέλλω ὑμῖν. 4 καί τινες
whom I announce to you. And some

ἐξ αὐτῶν ἐπείσθησαν καὶ προσεκληρώθησαν
of them were persuaded and threw in their lot

τῷ Παύλῳ καὶ τῷ Σιλᾷ, τῶν τε
– with Paul and – Silas, both of the

σεβομένων Ἑλλήνων πλῆθος πολύ, γυναικῶν τε
worshipping Greeks ³multitude ¹a much and of ²women
(great),

τῶν πρώτων οὐκ ὀλίγαι. 5 Ζηλώσαντες δὲ
¹the ²chief not a few. But becoming jealous

οἱ Ἰουδαῖοι καὶ προσλαβόμενοι τῶν
the Jews and taking aside of the

ἀγοραίων ἄνδρας τινὰς πονηροὺς καὶ
loungers in the men some wicked and
marketplace

ὀχλοποιήσαντες ἐθορύβουν τὴν πόλιν, καὶ
having gathered a disturbed the city, and
crowd

ἐπιστάντες τῇ οἰκίᾳ Ἰάσονος ἐζήτουν
coming on the house of Jason sought

αὐτοὺς προαγαγεῖν εἰς τὸν δῆμον· 6 μὴ
them to bring forward to the mob; ¹not

εὑρόντες δὲ αὐτοὺς ἔσυρον Ἰάσονα καὶ
³finding ²but them they dragged Jason and

τινας ἀδελφοὺς ἐπὶ τοὺς πολιτάρχας,
some brothers to the politarchs,

βοῶντες ὅτι οἱ τὴν οἰκουμένην ἀναστατώ-
crying[,] – ²the ⁴the ⁵inhabited ²having turned
[ones] earth

σαντες οὗτοι καὶ ἐνθάδε πάρεισιν, 7 οὓς
upside ¹these also here have arrived, whom
down men

ὑποδέδεκται Ἰάσων· καὶ οὗτοι πάντες
³has received ¹Jason; and these all

ἀπέναντι τῶν δογμάτων Καίσαρος
²contrary to ³the ⁴decrees ⁵of Cæsar

πράσσουσιν, βασιλέα ἕτερον λέγοντες εἶναι
¹act, ⁴king ³another ¹saying ²to be

Ἰησοῦν. 8 ἐτάραξαν δὲ τὸν ὄχλον καὶ
⁵Jesus. And they troubled the crowd and

---

them to leave the city. 40After Paul and Silas came out of the prison, they went to Lydia's house, where they met with the brothers and encouraged them. Then they left.

Chapter 17

In Thessalonica

WHEN they had passed through Amphipolis and Apollonia, they came to Thessalonica, where there was a Jewish synagogue. 2As his custom was, Paul went into the synagogue, and on three Sabbath days he reasoned with them from the Scriptures, 3explaining and proving that the Christ[h] had to suffer and rise from the dead. "This Jesus I am proclaiming to you is the Christ,[h]" he said. 4Some of the Jews were persuaded and joined Paul and Silas, as did a large number of God-fearing Greeks and not a few prominent women.

5But the Jews were jealous; so they rounded up some bad characters from the marketplace, formed a mob and started a riot in the city. They rushed to Jason's house in search of Paul and Silas in order to bring them out to the crowd.[i] 6But when they did not find them, they dragged Jason and some other brothers before the city officials, shouting: "These men who have caused trouble all over the world have now come here, 7and Jason has welcomed them into his house. They are all defying Caesar's decrees, saying that there is another king, one called Jesus." 8When they heard this, the crowd and the city

---

[p] Gk brothers
[q] Gk they
[r] Or the Christ
[s] Gk politarchs

[h]3 Or Messiah
[i]5 Or the assembly of the people

turbed when they heard this, 9and after they had taken bail from Jason and the others, they let them go.

Paul and Silas in Beroea

10 That very night the believers*p* sent Paul and Silas off to Beroea; and when they arrived, they went to the Jewish synagogue. 11 These Jews were more receptive to the message than those in Thessalonica, for they welcomed the message very eagerly and examined the scriptures every day to see whether these things were so. 12 Many of them therefore believed, including not a few Greek women and men of high standing. 13 But when the Jews of Thessalonica learned that the word of God had been proclaimed by Paul in Beroea as well, they came there too, to stir up and incite the crowds. 14 Then the believers*p* immediately sent Paul away to the coast, but Silas and Timothy remained behind. 15 Those who conducted Paul brought him as far as Athens; and after receiving instructions to have Silas and Timothy join him as soon as possible, they left him.

Paul in Athens

16 While Paul was waiting for them in Athens, he was deeply distressed to see that the city was full of idols. 17 So he argued in the synagogue with the Jews and the devout persons, and also in the market-

---

τοὺς πολιτάρχας ἀκούοντας ταῦτα, 9 καὶ
the politarchs hearing these things, and

λαβόντες τὸ ἱκανὸν παρὰ τοῦ Ἰάσονος
taking the surety from — Jason

καὶ τῶν λοιπῶν ἀπέλυσαν αὐτούς. 10 Οἱ δὲ
and the rest released them. And the

ἀδελφοὶ εὐθέως διὰ νυκτὸς ἐξεπεμψαν
brothers immediately through [the] night sent forth
(during)

τόν τε Παῦλον καὶ τὸν Σιλᾶν εἰς Βέροιαν,
— both Paul and — Silas to Berœa,

οἵτινες παραγενόμενοι εἰς τὴν συναγωγὴν
who having arrived ²into ³the synagogue

τῶν Ἰουδαίων ἀπῄεσαν· 11 οὗτοι δὲ ἦσαν
⁴of the ⁵Jews ¹went; and these were

εὐγενέστεροι τῶν ἐν Θεσσαλονίκῃ, οἵτινες
more noble [than] the [ones] in Thessalonica, who

ἐδέξαντο τὸν λόγον μετὰ πάσης προθυμίας,
received the word with all eagerness,

[τὸ] καθ' ἡμέραν ἀνακρίνοντες τὰς γραφὰς
daily examining the scriptures

εἰ ἔχοι ταῦτα οὕτως. 12 πολλοὶ μὲν
if ³have(are) ¹these things ²so. Many —

οὖν ἐξ αὐτῶν ἐπίστευσαν, καὶ τῶν
therefore of them believed, and of the

Ἑλληνίδων γυναικῶν τῶν εὐσχημόνων καὶ
²Greek ³women — ¹honourable and

ἀνδρῶν οὐκ ὀλίγοι. 13 Ὡς δὲ ἔγνωσαν
of men not a few. But when ³knew

οἱ ἀπὸ τῆς Θεσσαλονίκης Ἰουδαῖοι ὅτι
¹the ²from — ⁴Thessalonica ³Jews that

καὶ ἐν τῇ Βεροίᾳ κατηγγέλη ὑπὸ τοῦ
also in — Berœa was announced by —

Παύλου ὁ λόγος τοῦ θεοῦ, ἦλθον κἀκεῖ
Paul the word — of God, they came there also

σαλεύοντες καὶ ταράσσοντες τοὺς ὄχλους.
shaking and troubling the crowds.

14 εὐθέως δὲ τότε τὸν Παῦλον ἐξαπέστειλαν
So immediately then — ⁴Paul ³sent away

οἱ ἀδελφοὶ πορεύεσθαι ἕως ἐπὶ τὴν
¹the ²brothers to go as far as to the

θάλασσαν· ὑπέμεινάν τε ὅ τε Σιλᾶς καὶ
sea; ¹but ⁶remained — ²both ³Silas ⁴and

ὁ Τιμόθεος ἐκεῖ. 15 οἱ δὲ καθιστάνοντες
— ⁵Timothy ⁷there. And the [ones] conducting

τὸν Παῦλον ἤγαγον ἕως Ἀθηνῶν, καὶ
— Paul brought [him] as far as Athens, and

λαβόντες ἐντολὴν πρὸς τὸν Σιλᾶν καὶ τὸν
receiving a command to — Silas and —

Τιμόθεον ἵνα ὡς τάχιστα ἔλθωσιν πρὸς
Timothy that as quickly they should to
[as possible] come

αὐτὸν ἐξῄεσαν.
him they departed.

16 Ἐν δὲ ταῖς Ἀθήναις ἐκδεχομένου
And in — Athens awaiting
=while Paul awaited them,

αὐτοὺς τοῦ Παύλου, παρωξύνετο τὸ πνεῦμα
them — Paul,ᵃ ⁴was provoked ¹the ²spirit

αὐτοῦ ἐν αὐτῷ θεωροῦντος κατείδωλον
³of him in him beholding ⁴full of images

οὖσαν τὴν πόλιν. 17 διελέγετο μὲν οὖν
³being ¹the ²city. He addressed —* therefore

ἐν τῇ συναγωγῇ τοῖς Ἰουδαίοις καὶ
in the synagogue the Jews and

---

officials were thrown into turmoil. 9Then they made Jason and the others post bond and let them go.

In Berea

10As soon as it was night, the brothers sent Paul and Silas away to Berea. On arriving there, they went to the Jewish synagogue. 11Now the Bereans were of more noble character than the Thessalonians, for they received the message with great eagerness and examined the Scriptures every day to see if what Paul said was true. 12Many of the Jews believed, as did also a number of prominent Greek women and many Greek men.

13When the Jews in Thessalonica learned that Paul was preaching the word of God at Berea, they went there too, agitating the crowds and stirring them up. 14The brothers immediately sent Paul to the coast, but Silas and Timothy stayed at Berea. 15The men who escorted Paul brought him to Athens and then left with instructions for Silas and Timothy to join him as soon as possible.

In Athens

16While Paul was waiting for them in Athens, he was greatly distressed to see that the city was full of idols. 17So he reasoned in the synagogue with the Jews and the God-fearing

---

* See note on ch. 12. 5.

place[1] every day with those who happened to be there. 18Also some Epicurean and Stoic philosophers debated with him. Some said, "What does this babbler want to say?" Others said, "He seems to be a proclaimer of foreign divinities." (This was because he was telling the good news about Jesus and the resurrection.) 19So they took him and brought him to the Areopagus and asked him, "May we know what this new teaching is that you are presenting? 20It sounds rather strange to us, so we would like to know what it means." 21Now all the Athenians and the foreigners living there would spend their time in nothing but telling or hearing something new. 22 Then Paul stood in front of the Areopagus and said, "Athenians, I see how extremely religious you are in every way. 23For as I went through the city and looked carefully at the objects of your worship, I found among them an altar with the inscription, 'To an unknown god.' What therefore you worship as unknown, this I proclaim to you. 24The God who made the world and everything in it, he who is Lord of heaven and earth, does not live in shrines made by human hands, 25nor is he served by human hands, as though he needed anything, since he himself gives to all mortals life and breath and all things. 26From one ancestor[u] he made all nations to inhabit the whole earth, and he allotted the times of

τοῖς σεβομένοις καὶ ἐν τῇ ἀγορᾷ κατὰ
the [ones] worshipping and in the marketplace –
πᾶσαν ἡμέραν πρὸς τοὺς παρατυγχάνοντας.
every day to the [ones] chancing to be [there].
18 τινὲς δὲ καὶ τῶν Ἐπικουρείων καὶ
But some also of the Epicurean and
Στωϊκῶν φιλοσόφων συνέβαλλον αὐτῷ, καὶ
Stoic philosophers fell in with him, and
τινες ἔλεγον· τί ἂν θέλοι ὁ σπερμολόγος
some said: What may wish – ²ignorant plagiarist
οὗτος λέγειν; οἱ δέ· ξένων δαιμονίων
¹this to say? And others [said]: Of foreign demons
δοκεῖ καταγγελεὺς εἶναι· ὅτι τὸν Ἰησοῦν
he seems an announcer to be; because – Jesus
καὶ τὴν ἀνάστασιν εὐηγγελίζετο. 19 ἐπιλα-
and the resurrection he preached. taking
βόμενοι δὲ αὐτοῦ ἐπὶ τὸν Ἄρειον πάγον
hold And of him to the Areopagus
ἤγαγον, λέγοντες· δυνάμεθα γνῶναι τίς
they led [him], saying: Can we to know what
ἡ καινὴ αὕτη ἡ ὑπὸ σοῦ λαλουμένη
¹this ²new – ³by ⁴thee ⁴being spoken
διδαχή; 20 ξενίζοντα γάρ τινα εἰσφέρεις
³teaching [is]? for ²startling things ¹some thou bringest in
εἰς τὰς ἀκοὰς ἡμῶν· βουλόμεθα οὖν
to the ears of us; we are minded therefore
γνῶναι τίνα θέλει ταῦτα εἶναι. 21 Ἀθηναῖοι
to know what wishes these things to be. ²Athenians
δὲ πάντες καὶ οἱ ἐπιδημοῦντες ξένοι εἰς
Now ¹all ³and ⁴the ⁵dwelling strangers ⁶for
οὐδὲν ἕτερον ηὐκαίρουν ἢ λέγειν τι ἢ
⁸nothing ¹⁰different ⁷have leisure either to say something or
ἀκούειν τι καινότερον. 22 Σταθεὶς δὲ
to hear something newer. And standing
Παῦλος ἐν μέσῳ τοῦ Ἀρείου πάγου
¹Paul ¹in ²[the] midst ³of the ⁴Areopagus
ἔφη· ἄνδρες Ἀθηναῖοι, κατὰ πάντα ὡς
said: Men Athenians, in everything how
δεισιδαιμονεστέρους ὑμᾶς θεωρῶ. 23 διερχόμενος
very religious ²you ¹I behold. passing along
γὰρ καὶ ἀναθεωρῶν τὰ σεβάσματα ὑμῶν
For and looking up at the objects of worship of you
εὗρον καὶ βωμὸν ἐν ᾧ ἐπεγέγραπτο·
I found also an altar in which had been inscribed:
ΑΓΝΩΣΤΩ ΘΕΩ. ὃ οὖν ἀγνοοῦντες
TO AN UNKNOWN GOD. What therefore being ignorant
εὐσεβεῖτε, τοῦτο ἐγὼ καταγγέλλω ὑμῖν.
ye reverence, this I announce to you.
24 ὁ θεὸς ὁ ποιήσας τὸν κόσμον καὶ
The God the [one] having made the world and
πάντα τὰ ἐν αὐτῷ, οὗτος οὐρανοῦ καὶ
all the things in it, this one ³of heaven ⁴and
γῆς ὑπάρχων κύριος οὐκ ἐν χειροποιήτοις
⁵of earth ¹being ²lord ²not ³in ⁴hand-made
ναοῖς κατοικεῖ, 25 οὐδὲ ὑπὸ χειρῶν
¹shrines ¹dwells, nor ²by ⁴hands
ἀνθρωπίνων θεραπεύεται προσδεόμενός
²human ¹is served having need
τινος, αὐτὸς διδοὺς πᾶσι ζωὴν καὶ πνοὴν
of anything, he giving to all life and breath
καὶ τὰ πάντα· 26 ἐποίησέν τε ἐξ ἑνὸς
and – all things; and he made of one
πᾶν ἔθνος ἀνθρώπων κατοικεῖν ἐπὶ παντὸς
every nation of men to dwell on all
προσώπου τῆς γῆς, ὁρίσας προστεταγμένους
[the] face of the earth, fixing having been appointed

Greeks, as well as in the marketplace day by day with those who happened to be there. 18A group of Epicurean and Stoic philosophers began to dispute with him. Some of them asked, "What is this babbler trying to say?" Others remarked, "He seems to be advocating foreign gods." They said this because Paul was preaching the good news about Jesus and the resurrection. 19Then they took him and brought him to a meeting of the Areopagus, where they said to him, "May we know what this new teaching is that you are presenting? 20You are bringing some strange ideas to our ears, and we want to know what they mean." 21(All the Athenians and the foreigners who lived there spent their time doing nothing but talking about and listening to the latest ideas.) 22Paul then stood up in the meeting of the Areopagus and said: "Men of Athens! I see that in every way you are very religious. 23For as I walked around and looked carefully at your objects of worship, I even found an altar with this inscription: TO AN UNKNOWN GOD. Now what you worship as something unknown I am going to proclaim to you. 24"The God who made the world and everything in it is the Lord of heaven and earth and does not live in temples built by hands. 25And he is not served by human hands, as if he needed anything, because he himself gives all men life and breath and everything else. 26From one man he made every nation of men, that they should inhabit the whole earth; and he determined the times set for

[1] Or civic center; Gk agora
[u] Gk From one; other ancient authorities read From one blood

their existence and the boundaries of the places where they would live, 27 so that they would search for God[v] and perhaps grope for him and find him—though indeed he is not far from each one of us. 28 For 'In him we live and move and have our being'; as even some of your own poets have said,

'For we too are his offspring.'

29 Since we are God's offspring, we ought not to think that the deity is like gold, or silver, or stone, an image formed by the art and imagination of mortals. 30 While God has overlooked the times of human ignorance, now he commands all people everywhere to repent, 31 because he has fixed a day on which he will have the world judged in righteousness by a man whom he has appointed, and of this he has given assurance to all by raising him from the dead." 32 When they heard of the resurrection of the dead, some scoffed; but others said, "We will hear you again about this." 33 At that point Paul left them. 34 But some of them joined him and became believers, including Dionysius the Areopagite and a woman named Damaris, and others with them.

καιροὺς	καὶ	τὰς	ὁροθεσίας	τῆς	κατοικίας
seasons	and	the	boundaries	of the	dwelling

αὐτῶν,	27 ζητεῖν	τὸν	θεόν,	εἰ	ἄρα	γε
of them,	to seek	-	God,	if	perchance	

ψηλαφήσειάν	αὐτὸν	καὶ	εὕροιεν,	καὶ	γε
they might feel after	him	and	might find,	though	

οὐ	μακρὰν	ἀπὸ	ἑνὸς	ἑκάστου	ἡμῶν
²not	³far	⁴from	⁵one	⁶each	⁷of us

ὑπάρχοντα.	28 ἐν	αὐτῷ	γὰρ	ζῶμεν	καὶ
¹being.	²in	³him	¹For	we live	and

κινούμεθα	καὶ	ἐσμέν,	ὡς	καὶ	τινες	τῶν
move	and	are,	as	indeed	some	of the

καθ'	ὑμᾶς	ποιητῶν	εἰρήκασιν·	τοῦ	γὰρ
²among	³you	¹poets	have said:	³of him	¹For

καὶ	γένος	ἐσμέν.	29 γένος	οὖν	ὑπάρχοντες
²also	³offspring	⁴we are.	Offspring	therefore	being

τοῦ	θεοῦ	οὐκ	ὀφείλομεν	νομίζειν,	χρυσῷ
-	of God	we ought not	to suppose,	⁵to gold

ἢ	ἀργύρῳ	ἢ	λίθῳ,	χαράγματι	τέχνης
⁶or	⁷to silver	⁸or	⁹to stone,	¹⁰to an engraved work	¹¹of art

καὶ	ἐνθυμήσεως	ἀνθρώπου,	τὸ	θεῖον	εἶναι
¹²and	¹³of meditation	¹⁴of man,	¹the	²divine nature	³to be

ὅμοιον.	30 τοὺς	μὲν	οὖν	χρόνους	τῆς
⁴like.	⁵The	¹so	²then	³times	-

ἀγνοίας	ὑπεριδὼν	ὁ	θεὸς	τὰ	νῦν
⁷of ignorance	⁶having overlooked	-	⁸God	-	now

ἀπαγγέλλει	τοῖς	ἀνθρώποις	πάντας	πανταχοῦ
declares	-	to men	all men	everywhere

μετανοεῖν,	31 καθότι	ἔστησεν	ἡμέραν	ἐν
to repent,	because	he set	a day	in

ᾗ	μέλλει	κρίνειν	τὴν	οἰκουμένην	ἐν
which he is about	to judge	the	inhabited earth	in

δικαιοσύνῃ,	ἐν	ἀνδρὶ	ᾧ	ὥρισεν,	πίστιν
righteousness,	by	a man	whom	he designated,	²a guarantee

παρασχὼν	πᾶσιν	ἀναστήσας	αὐτὸν	ἐκ
¹offering	to all	having raised up	him	out of

νεκρῶν.	32 ἀκούσαντες	δὲ	ἀνάστασιν
[the] dead.	And hearing [of]		a resurrection

νεκρῶν,	οἱ	μὲν	ἐχλεύαζον,	οἱ	δὲ	εἶπαν·
of dead persons,	some		scoffed,	others		said:

ἀκουσόμεθά	σου	περὶ	τούτου	καὶ	πάλιν.
We will hear	thee	concerning	this	also	again.

33 οὕτως	ὁ	Παῦλος	ἐξῆλθεν	ἐκ	μέσου
Thus	-	Paul	went forth	from [the]	midst

αὐτῶν.	34 τινὲς	δὲ	ἄνδρες	κολληθέντες
of them.	But some		men	adhering

αὐτῷ	ἐπίστευσαν,	ἐν	οἷς	καὶ	Διονύσιος
to him	believed,	among	whom	both	Dionysius

ὁ	Ἀρεοπαγίτης	καὶ	γυνὴ	ὀνόματι	Δαμαρὶς
the	Areopagite	and	a woman	by name	Damaris

καὶ	ἕτεροι	σὺν	αὐτοῖς.
and	others	with	them.

them and the exact places where they should live. 27 God did this so that men would seek him and perhaps reach out for him and find him, though he is not far from each one of us. 28 'For in him we live and move and have our being.' As some of your own poets have said, 'We are his offspring.'

29 "Therefore since we are God's offspring, we should not think that the divine being is like gold or silver or stone—an image made by man's design and skill. 30 In the past God overlooked such ignorance, but now he commands all people everywhere to repent. 31 For he has set a day when he will judge the world with justice by the man he has appointed. He has given proof of this to all men by raising him from the dead."

32 When they heard about the resurrection of the dead, some of them sneered, but others said, "We want to hear you again on this subject." 33 At that, Paul left the Council. 34 A few men became followers of Paul and believed. Among them was Dionysius, a member of the Areopagus, also a woman named Damaris, and a number of others.

Chapter 18

Paul in Corinth

AFTER this Paul[w] left Athens and went to Corinth. 2 There he found a Jew named Aquila, a native of Pontus, who had recently come from Italy with his wife Priscilla, because

18 Μετὰ	ταῦτα	χωρισθεὶς	ἐκ	τῶν
After	these things	departing	out of	-

Ἀθηνῶν	ἦλθεν	εἰς	Κόρινθον.	2 καὶ
Athens	he came	to	Corinth.	And

εὑρών	τινα	Ἰουδαῖον	ὀνόματι	Ἀκύλαν,
finding	a certain	Jew	by name	Aquila,

Ποντικὸν	τῷ	γένει,	προσφάτως	ἐληλυθότα
belonging to Pontus	-	by race,	recently	having come

ἀπὸ	τῆς	Ἰταλίας,	καὶ	Πρίσκιλλαν	γυναῖκα
from	-	Italy,	and	Priscilla	wife

Chapter 18

In Corinth

AFTER this, Paul left Athens and went to Corinth. 2 There he met a Jew named Aquila, a native of Pontus, who had recently come from Italy with his wife Priscilla, because

[v] Other ancient authorities read the Lord
[w] Gk he

Claudius had ordered all Jews to leave Rome. Paul* went to see them, ³and, because he was of the same trade, he stayed with them, and they worked together—by trade they were tentmakers. ⁴Every sabbath he would argue in the synagogue and would try to convince Jews and Greeks.

5 When Silas and Timothy arrived from Macedonia, Paul was occupied with proclaiming the word,ʸ testifying to the Jews that the Messiahᶻ was Jesus. ⁶When they opposed and reviled him, in protest he shook the dust from his clothesᵃ and said to them, "Your blood be on your own heads! I am innocent. From now on I will go to the Gentiles." ⁷Then he left the synagogueᵇ and went to the house of a man named Titiusᶜ Justus, a worshiper of God; his house was next door to the synagogue. ⁸Crispus, the official of the synagogue, became a believer in the Lord, together with all his household; and many of the Corinthians who heard Paul became believers and were baptized. ⁹One night the Lord said to Paul in a vision, "Do not be afraid, but speak and do not be silent; ¹⁰for I am with you, and no one will lay a hand on you to harm you, for there are many in this city who are my people." ¹¹He stayed there a year and six months, teaching the word of God among them.

12 But when Gallio was proconsul of Achaia, the

αὐτοῦ, διὰ τὸ διατετάχεναι Κλαύδιον
of him, because of the to have commanded Claudiusᵇ
=because Claudius had commanded

χωρίζεσθαι πάντας τοὺς Ἰουδαίους ἀπὸ
to depart all the Jews from

τῆς Ῥώμης, προσῆλθεν αὐτοῖς, 3 καὶ
- Rome, he came to them, and

διὰ τὸ ὁμότεχνον εἶναι ἔμενεν παρ'
because of the of the same trade to beᵇ he remained with
=because [he] was of the same trade

αὐτοῖς, καὶ ἠργάζοντο· ἦσαν γὰρ σκηνοποιοὶ
them, and they wrought; for they were tentmakers

τῇ τέχνῃ. 4 διελέγετο δὲ ἐν τῇ συναγωγῇ
- by trade. And he lectured in the synagogue

κατὰ πᾶν σάββατον, ἔπειθέν τε Ἰουδαίους
on every sabbath, he persuaded both Jews

καὶ Ἕλληνας. 5 Ὡς δὲ κατῆλθον ἀπὸ
and Greeks. And when came down from

τῆς Μακεδονίας ὅ τε Σιλᾶς καὶ ὁ
- Macedonia both Silas and -

Τιμόθεος, συνείχετο τῷ λόγῳ ὁ Παῦλος,
Timothy, was pressed by the word - Paul,

διαμαρτυρόμενος τοῖς Ἰουδαίοις εἶναι τὸν
solemnly witnessing to the Jews to be the
=that Jesus to be the Christ

χριστὸν Ἰησοῦν. 6 ἀντιτασσομένων δὲ αὐτῶν
Christ Jesus. But resisting them
=when they resisted and blasphemed

καὶ βλασφημούντων ἐκτιναξάμενος τὰ ἱμάτια
and blasphemingᵃ shaking off the(his) garments

εἶπεν πρὸς αὐτούς· τὸ αἷμα ὑμῶν ἐπὶ
he said to them: The blood of you on

τὴν κεφαλὴν ὑμῶν· καθαρὸς ἐγὼ ἀπὸ
the head of you; clean I from

τοῦ νῦν εἰς τὰ ἔθνη πορεύσομαι. 7 καὶ
- now to the nations will go. And

μεταβὰς ἐκεῖθεν ἦλθεν εἰς οἰκίαν τινὸς
removing thence he went into [the] house of one

ὀνόματι Τιτίου Ἰούστου σεβομένου τὸν
by name Titius Justus worshipping the

θεόν, οὗ ἡ οἰκία ἦν συνομοροῦσα τῇ
God, of whom the house was being next door to the

συναγωγῇ. 8 Κρίσπος δὲ ὁ ἀρχισυνάγωγος
synagogue. Now Crispus the synagogue ruler

ἐπίστευσεν τῷ κυρίῳ σὺν ὅλῳ τῷ οἴκῳ
believed the Lord with all the household

αὐτοῦ, καὶ πολλοὶ τῶν Κορινθίων ἀκούοντες
of him, and many of the Corinthians hearing

ἐπίστευον καὶ ἐβαπτίζοντο. 9 Εἶπεν δὲ
believed and were baptized. And said

ὁ κύριος ἐν νυκτὶ δι' ὁράματος τῷ
the Lord in [the] night through a vision -

Παύλῳ· μὴ φοβοῦ, ἀλλὰ λάλει καὶ
to Paul: Do not fear, but speak and

μὴ σιωπήσῃς, 10 διότι ἐγὼ εἰμι μετὰ σοῦ
keep not silence, because I am with thee

καὶ οὐδεὶς ἐπιθήσεταί σοι τοῦ κακῶσαι
and no one shall set on thee - to illtreatᵈ

σε, διότι λαός ἐστί μοι πολὺς ἐν
thee, because people is to me muchᵉ in
=I have a great people

τῇ πόλει ταύτῃ. 11 Ἐκάθισεν δὲ ἐνιαυτὸν
this city. And he sat a year

καὶ μῆνας ἓξ διδάσκων ἐν αὐτοῖς τὸν
and months six teaching among them the

λόγον τοῦ θεοῦ. 12 Γαλλίωνος δὲ
word - of God. And Gallio
=when Gallio

Claudius had ordered all the Jews to leave Rome. Paul went to see them, ³and because he was a tentmaker as they were, he stayed and worked with them. ⁴Every Sabbath he reasoned in the synagogue, trying to persuade Jews and Greeks.

⁵When Silas and Timothy came from Macedonia, Paul devoted himself exclusively to preaching, testifying to the Jews that Jesus was the Christ.ʲ ⁶But when the Jews opposed Paul and became abusive, he shook out his clothes in protest and said to them, "Your blood be on your own heads! I am clear of my responsibility. From now on I will go to the Gentiles."

⁷Then Paul left the synagogue and went next door to the house of Titius Justus, a worshiper of God. ⁸Crispus, the synagogue ruler, and his entire household believed in the Lord; and many of the Corinthians who heard him believed and were baptized.

⁹One night the Lord spoke to Paul in a vision: "Do not be afraid; keep on speaking, do not be silent. ¹⁰For I am with you, and no one is going to attack and harm you, because I have many people in this city." ¹¹So Paul stayed for a year and a half, teaching them the word of God.

¹²While Gallio was pro-

ˣ Gk He
ʸ Gk with the word
ᶻ Or the Christ
ᵃ Gk reviled him, he shook out his clothes
ᵇ Gk left there
ᶜ Other ancient authorities read Titus

Or *Messiah;* also in verse 28

Jews made a united attack on Paul and brought him before the tribunal. 13 They said, "This man is persuading people to worship God in ways that are contrary to the law." 14 Just as Paul was about to speak, Gallio said to the Jews, "If it were a matter of crime or serious villainy, I would be justified in accepting the complaint of you Jews; 15 but since it is a matter of questions about words and names and your own law, see to it yourselves; I do not wish to be a judge of these matters." 16 And he dismissed them from the tribunal. 17 Then all of them*d* seized Sosthenes, the official of the synagogue, and beat him in front of the tribunal. But Gallio paid no attention to any of these things.

Paul's Return to Antioch

18 After staying there for a considerable time, Paul said farewell to the believers*e* and sailed for Syria, accompanied by Priscilla and Aquila. At Cenchreae he had his hair cut, for he was under a vow. 19 When they reached Ephesus, he left them there, but first he himself went into the synagogue and had a discussion with the Jews. 20 When they asked him to stay longer, he declined; 21 but on taking leave of them, he said, "I*f* will return to you, if God wills." Then he set sail from Ephesus. 22 When he had landed at Caesarea, he went up to Jerusalem*g* and greeted the church, and then went

---

ἀνθυπάτου ὄντος τῆς ᾽Αχαΐας κατεπέστησαν
proconsul being*a* — of Achaia   *a*set on
was proconsul

ὁμοθυμαδὸν οἱ ᾽Ιουδαῖοι τῷ Παύλῳ καὶ
*a*with one mind   *1*the   *2*Jews   —   Paul   and

ἤγαγον αὐτὸν ἐπὶ τὸ βῆμα, 13 λέγοντες
brought   him   to   the   tribunal,   saying[,]

ὅτι παρὰ τὸν νόμον ἀναπείθει οὗτος
 — *a*[differently] from *1*the *2*law   *3*urges   *1*This man

τοὺς ἀνθρώπους σέβεσθαι τὸν θεόν.
   *2*men   *4*to worship   —   *5*God.

14 μέλλοντος δὲ τοῦ Παύλου ἀνοίγειν τὸ
And being about   —   Paul*a*   to open the(his)
=when Paul was about

στόμα εἶπεν ὁ Γαλλίων πρὸς τοὺς
mouth   said   — Gallio   to   the

᾽Ιουδαίους· εἰ μὲν ἦν ἀδίκημά τι
Jews: If   indeed   it was   crime   some

ἢ ῥᾳδιούργημα πονηρόν, ὦ ᾽Ιουδαῖοι,
or   villainy   evil,   O   Jews,

κατὰ λόγον ἂν ἀνεσχόμην ὑμῶν· 15 εἰ δὲ ζητή-
rightly   I would endure   you;   but if   ques-

ματά ἐστιν περὶ λόγου καὶ ὀνομάτων καὶ
tions   it is   concerning a word   and   names   and

νόμου τοῦ καθ᾽ ὑμᾶς, ὄψεσθε αὐτοί·
law   the according to you,   ye will see [your]selves;
= your law,

κριτὴς ἐγὼ τούτων οὐ βούλομαι εἶναι.
a judge *1*I *3*of these things *2*do not intend *3*to be.

16 καὶ ἀπήλασεν αὐτοὺς ἀπὸ τοῦ βήματος.
And he drove away   them   from   the   tribunal.

17 ἐπιλαβόμενοι δὲ πάντες Σωσθένην τὸν
But *a*seizing   *1*all   Sosthenes   the

ἀρχισυνάγωγον ἔτυπτον ἔμπροσθεν τοῦ
synagogue ruler   they struck [him]   in front of   the

βήματος· καὶ οὐδὲν τούτων τῷ Γαλλίωνι
tribunal;   and   not one of these things — *2*to Gallio

ἔμελεν. 18 ῾Ο δὲ Παῦλος ἔτι προσμείνας
*1*mattered.   — But   Paul   yet having remained

ἡμέρας ἱκανάς, τοῖς ἀδελφοῖς ἀποταξάμενος
days   many,   to the   brothers   bidding farewell

ἐξέπλει εἰς τὴν Συρίαν, καὶ σὺν αὐτῷ
he sailed away to — Syria,   and   with   him

Πρίσκιλλα καὶ ᾽Ακύλας, κειράμενος ἐν
Priscilla   and   Aquila,   having shorn   in

Κεγχρεαῖς τὴν κεφαλήν· εἶχεν γὰρ εὐχήν.
Cenchrea   the(his)   head;   for he had   a vow.

19 κατήντησαν δὲ εἰς ῎Εφεσον, κἀκείνους
And they came down   to   Ephesus,   and those

κατέλιπεν αὐτοῦ, αὐτὸς δὲ εἰσελθὼν εἰς
he left   there,   but he   entering   into

τὴν συναγωγὴν διελέξατο τοῖς ᾽Ιουδαίοις.
the   synagogue   lectured   to the   Jews.

20 ἐρωτώντων δὲ αὐτῶν ἐπὶ πλείονα
And asking   δὲ   them*a*   over a more(longer)
= as they asked

χρόνον μεῖναι οὐκ ἐπένευσεν, 21 ἀλλὰ
time   to remain   he consented not,   but

ἀποταξάμενος καὶ εἰπών· πάλιν ἀνακάμψω
bidding farewell   and   saying :   Again   I will return

πρὸς ὑμᾶς τοῦ θεοῦ θέλοντος, ἀνήχθη
to   you   —   God   willing,*a*   he set sail
= if God wills,

ἀπὸ τῆς ᾽Εφέσου, 22 καὶ κατελθὼν εἰς
from — Ephesus,   and   coming down   to

Καισάρειαν, ἀναβὰς καὶ ἀσπασάμενος τὴν
Cæsarea,   going up   and   greeting   the

---

consul of Achaia, the Jews made a united attack on Paul and brought him into court. 13 "This man," they charged, "is persuading the people to worship God in ways contrary to the law." 14 Just as Paul was about to speak, Gallio said to the Jews, "If you Jews were making a complaint about some misdemeanor or serious crime, it would be reasonable for me to listen to you. 15 But since it involves questions about words and names and your own law— settle the matter yourselves. I will not be a judge of such things." 16 So he had them ejected from the court. 17 Then they all turned on Sosthenes, the synagogue ruler and beat him in front of the court. But Gallio showed no concern whatever.

Priscilla, Aquila and Apollos

18 Paul stayed on in Corinth for some time. Then he left the brothers and sailed for Syria, accompanied by Priscilla and Aquila. Before he sailed, he had his hair cut off at Cenchrea because of a vow he had taken. 19 They arrived at Ephesus, where Paul left Priscilla and Aquila. He himself went into the synagogue and reasoned with the Jews. 20 When they asked him to spend more time with them, he declined. 21 But as he left, he promised, "I will come back if it is God's will." Then he set sail from Ephesus. 22 When he landed at Caesarea, he went up and greeted the

---

d Other ancient authorities read *all the Greeks*
e Gk *brothers*
f Other ancient authorities read *I must at all costs keep the approaching festival in Jerusalem, but I*
g Gk *went up*

down to Antioch. 23 After spending some time there he departed and went from place to place through the region of Galatia*h* and Phrygia, strengthening all the disciples.

Ministry of Apollos

24 Now there came to Ephesus a Jew named Apollos, a native of Alexandria. He was an eloquent man, well-versed in the scriptures. 25 He had been instructed in the Way of the Lord; and he spoke with burning enthusiasm and taught accurately the things concerning Jesus, though he knew only the baptism of John. 26 He began to speak boldly in the synagogue; but when Priscilla and Aquila heard him, they took him aside and explained the Way of God to him more accurately. 27 And when he wished to cross over to Achaia, the believers*i* encouraged him and wrote to the disciples to welcome him. On his arrival he greatly helped those who through grace had become believers, 28 for he powerfully refuted the Jews in public, showing by the scriptures that the Messiah*j* is Jesus.

ἐκκλησίαν, κατέβη εἰς Ἀντιόχειαν, **23** καὶ
church,　he went down to　Antioch,　　and
ποιήσας χρόνον τινὰ ἐξῆλθεν, διερχόμενος
having spent　time　some　he went forth, passing through
καθεξῆς τὴν Γαλατικὴν χώραν καὶ Φρυγίαν,
in order　the　Galatian　country and　Phrygia,
στηρίζων πάντας τοὺς μαθητάς.
confirming　all　the　disciples.
24 Ἰουδαῖος δέ τις Ἀπολλῶς ὀνόματι,
And a certain Jew　　Apollos　by name,
Ἀλεξανδρεὺς τῷ γένει, ἀνὴρ λόγιος,
an Alexandrian　–　by race,　a man　eloquent,
κατήντησεν εἰς Ἔφεσον, δυνατὸς ὢν ἐν
came　to　Ephesus,　powerful　being in
ταῖς γραφαῖς. **25** οὗτος ἦν κατηχημένος
the　scriptures.　This man　was orally instructed [in]
τὴν ὁδὸν τοῦ κυρίου, καὶ ζέων τῷ
the　way　of the　Lord,　and　burning　the
πνεύματι ἐλάλει καὶ ἐδίδασκεν ἀκριβῶς
in spirit　he spoke and　taught　accurately
τὰ περὶ τοῦ Ἰησοῦ, ἐπιστάμενος
the things concerning　–　Jesus,　understanding
μόνον τὸ βάπτισμα Ἰωάννου· **26** οὗτός τε
only　the　baptism　of John;　and this man
ἤρξατο παρρησιάζεσθαι ἐν τῇ συναγωγῇ.
began　to speak boldly　in　the　synagogue.
ἀκούσαντες δὲ αὐτοῦ Πρίσκιλλα καὶ
And hearing　　him　Priscilla　and
Ἀκύλας προσελάβοντο αὐτὸν καὶ ἀκριβέστε-
Aquila　took　　him　and　more accurate-
ρον αὐτῷ ἐξέθεντο τὴν ὁδὸν τοῦ θεοῦ.
ly　to him　explained　the　way　–　of God.
27 βουλομένου δὲ αὐτοῦ διελθεῖν εἰς τὴν
And intending　　him*a* to go through into　–
=when he intended
Ἀχαΐαν, προτρεψάμενοι οἱ ἀδελφοὶ ἔγραψαν
Achaia,　being encouraged　the　brothers　wrote
τοῖς μαθηταῖς ἀποδέξασθαι αὐτόν· ὃς
to the　disciples　to welcome　him;　who
παραγενόμενος συνεβάλετο πολὺ τοῖς
arriving　contributed　much　to the [ones]
πεπιστευκόσιν διὰ τῆς χάριτος· **28** εὐτόνως
having believed　through　–　grace;　*1*vehemently
γὰρ τοῖς Ἰουδαίοις διακατηλέγχετο δημοσίᾳ
*1*for　*4*the　*6*Jews　*3*he confuted　publicly
ἐπιδεικνὺς διὰ τῶν γραφῶν εἶναι τὸν
proving　through　the　scriptures　*5*to be　*8*the
χριστὸν Ἰησοῦν.
*6*Christ　*7*Jesus.

---

church and then went down to Antioch.
23 After spending some time in Antioch, Paul set out from there and traveled from place to place throughout the region of Galatia and Phrygia, strengthening all the disciples.
24 Meanwhile a Jew named Apollos, a native of Alexandria, came to Ephesus. He was a learned man, with a thorough knowledge of the Scriptures. 25 He had been instructed in the way of the Lord, and he spoke with great fervor*k* and taught about Jesus accurately, though he knew only the baptism of John. 26 He began to speak boldly in the synagogue. When Priscilla and Aquila heard him, they invited him to their home and explained to him the way of God more adequately.
27 When Apollos wanted to go to Achaia, the brothers encouraged him and wrote to the disciples there to welcome him. On arriving, he was a great help to those who by grace had believed. 28 For he vigorously refuted the Jews in public debate, proving from the Scriptures that Jesus was the Christ.

Chapter 19

Paul in Ephesus

WHILE Apollos was in Corinth, Paul passed through the interior regions and came to Ephesus, where he found some disciples. 2 He said to them, "Did you receive the Holy Spirit when you became believers?" They replied, "No, we have not even heard that there is a Holy Spirit." 3 Then he said, "Into what then were you

---

19 Ἐγένετο δὲ ἐν τῷ τὸν Ἀπολλῶ
Now it came to pass　in　the　–　Apollos
=while Apollos was
εἶναι ἐν Κορίνθῳ Παῦλον διελθόντα τὰ
to be*b* in　Corinth　Paul　having passed through the
ἀνωτερικὰ μέρη ἐλθεῖν εἰς Ἔφεσον καὶ
higher　parts　to come*b*　to　Ephesus　and
εὑρεῖν τινας μαθητάς, **2** εἶπέν τε πρὸς
to find*b*　some　disciples,　and said　to
αὐτούς· εἰ πνεῦμα ἅγιον ἐλάβετε πιστεύσαν-
them:　If　Spirit　Holy　ye received　believ-
τες; οἱ δὲ πρὸς αὐτόν· ἀλλ' οὐδ' εἰ
ing?　And they [said]　to　him:　But　*2*not　*3*if
πνεῦμα ἅγιον ἔστιν ἠκούσαμεν. **3** εἶπέν τε·
*6*Spirit　*5*Holy　*4*there is　*1*we heard.　And he said:

Chapter 19

Paul in Ephesus

WHILE Apollos was at Corinth, Paul took the road through the interior and arrived at Ephesus. There he found some disciples 2 and asked them, "Did you receive the Holy Spirit when*l* you believed?"
They answered, "No, we have not even heard that there is a Holy Spirit."
3 So Paul asked, "Then

---

h Gk the Galatian region
i Gk brothers
j Or the Christ

k 25 Or with fervor in the Spirit
l 2 Or after

baptized?" They answered, "Into John's baptism." 4 Paul said, "John baptized with the baptism of repentance, telling the people to believe in the one who was to come after him, that is, in Jesus." 5 On hearing this, they were baptized in the name of the Lord Jesus. 6 When Paul had laid his hands on them, the Holy Spirit came upon them, and they spoke in tongues and prophesied— 7 altogether there were about twelve of them.

8 He entered the synagogue and for three months spoke out boldly, and argued persuasively about the kingdom of God. 9 When some stubbornly refused to believe and spoke evil of the Way before the congregation, he left them, taking the disciples with him, and argued daily in the lecture hall of Tyrannus.ᵏ 10 This continued for two years, so that all the residents of Asia, both Jews and Greeks, heard the word of the Lord.

The Sons of Sceva

11 God did extraordinary miracles through Paul, 12 so that when the handkerchiefs or aprons that had touched his skin were brought to the sick, their diseases left them, and the evil spirits came out of them. 13 Then some itinerant Jewish exorcists tried to use the name of the Lord Jesus over those who had evil spirits, saying, "I ad-

---

εἰς τί οὖν ἐβαπτίσθητε; οἱ δὲ εἶπαν·
To what therefore were ye baptized? And they said:

εἰς τὸ Ἰωάννου βάπτισμα. 4 εἶπεν δὲ
To the of John baptism. And said

Παῦλος· Ἰωάννης ἐβάπτισεν βάπτισμα μετα-
Paul: John baptized [with] a baptism of repent-

νοίας, τῷ λαῷ λέγων εἰς τὸν ἐρχόμενον
ance, ²to the ³people ¹saying ⁴in ⁷the [one] ⁶coming

μετ' αὐτὸν ἵνα πιστεύσωσιν, τοῦτ' ἔστιν
⁸after ¹⁰him ⁴that ⁵they should believe, this is

εἰς τὸν Ἰησοῦν. 5 ἀκούσαντες δὲ ἐβαπτίσ-
in Jesus. And hearing they were

θησαν εἰς τὸ ὄνομα τοῦ κυρίου Ἰησοῦ.
baptized in the name of the Lord Jesus.

6 καὶ ἐπιθέντος αὐτοῖς τοῦ Παύλου χεῖρας
And laying on them Paul hands
=as Paul laid [his] hands on them

ἦλθε τὸ πνεῦμα τὸ ἅγιον ἐπ' αὐτούς,
came the Spirit - Holy on them,

ἐλάλουν τε γλώσσαις καὶ ἐπροφήτευον.
and they spoke in tongues and prophesied.

7 ἦσαν δὲ οἱ πάντες ἄνδρες ὡσεὶ δώδεκα.
And ⁴were ³the ¹all ²men about twelve.

8 Εἰσελθὼν δὲ εἰς τὴν συναγωγὴν
And entering into the synagogue

ἐπαρρησιάζετο ἐπὶ μῆνας τρεῖς διαλεγόμενος
he spoke boldly over months three lecturing

καὶ πείθων περὶ τῆς βασιλείας τοῦ θεοῦ.
and persuading concerning the kingdom - of God.

9 ὡς δὲ τινες ἐσκληρύνοντο καὶ ἠπείθουν
But as some were hardened and disobeyed

κακολογοῦντες τὴν ὁδὸν ἐνώπιον τοῦ
speaking ill [of] the way before the

πλήθους, ἀποστὰς ἀπ' αὐτῶν ἀφώρισεν
multitude, withdrawing from them he separated

τοὺς μαθητάς, καθ' ἡμέραν διαλεγόμενος
the disciples, daily lecturing

ἐν τῇ σχολῇ Τυράννου. 10 τοῦτο δὲ
in the school of Tyrannus. And this

ἐγένετο ἐπὶ ἔτη δύο, ὥστε πάντας τοὺς
happened over years two, so as all the
=so that all who inhabited

κατοικοῦντας τὴν Ἀσίαν ἀκοῦσαι τὸν
[ones] inhabiting - Asia to hearᵇ the
Asia heard

λόγον τοῦ κυρίου, Ἰουδαίους τε καὶ
word of the Lord, ²Jews ¹both and

Ἕλληνας. 11 Δυνάμεις τε οὐ τὰς τυχούσας
Greeks. And powerful deeds not the ordinary

ὁ θεὸς ἐποίει διὰ τῶν χειρῶν Παύλου,
- God did through the hands of Paul,

12 ὥστε καὶ ἐπὶ τοὺς ἀσθενοῦντας
so as even onto the [ones] ailing
=so that there were even brought away from his skin hand-

ἀποφέρεσθαι ἀπὸ τοῦ χρωτὸς αὐτοῦ
to be brought away from the skin of him
kerchiefs or aprons onto those who ailed and the diseases were rid

σουδάρια ἢ σιμικίνθια καὶ ἀπαλλάσσεσθαι
handkerchiefs or aprons and to be rid
from them, and the evil spirits went out.

ἀπ' αὐτῶν τὰς νόσους, τά τε πνεύματα
from them the diseases, and the spirits

τὰ πονηρὰ ἐκπορεύεσθαι. 13 Ἐπεχείρησαν δέ
evil to go out. But ⁷attempted

τινες καὶ τῶν περιερχομένων Ἰουδαίων
¹some ²also ³of the ⁴strolling ⁵Jews

ἐξορκιστῶν ὀνομάζειν ἐπὶ τοὺς ἔχοντας
⁶exorcists to name over the [ones] having

---

what baptism did you receive?" "John's baptism," they replied. 4 Paul said, "John's baptism was a baptism of repentance. He told the people to believe in the one coming after him, that is, in Jesus." 5 On hearing this, they were baptized intoᵐ the name of the Lord Jesus. 6 When Paul placed his hands on them, the Holy Spirit came on them, and they spoke in tonguesⁿ and prophesied. 7 There were about twelve men in all.

8 Paul entered the synagogue and spoke boldly there for three months, arguing persuasively about the kingdom of God. 9 But some of them became obstinate; they refused to believe and publicly maligned the Way. So Paul left them. He took the disciples with him and had discussions daily in the lecture hall of Tyrannus. 10 This went on for two years, so that all the Jews and Greeks who lived in the province of Asia heard the word of the Lord. 11 God did extraordinary miracles through Paul, 12 so that even handkerchiefs and aprons that had touched him were taken to the sick, and their illnesses were cured and the evil spirits left them. 13 Some Jews who went around driving out evil spirits tried to invoke the name of the Lord Jesus over those who were de-

---

ᵏ Other ancient authorities read *of a certain Tyrannus, from eleven o'clock in the morning to four in the afternoon*

ᵐ5 Or *in*
ⁿ6 Or *other languages*

jure you by the Jesus whom Paul proclaims." ¹⁴ Seven sons of a Jewish high priest named Sceva were doing this. ¹⁵ But the evil spirit said to them in reply, "Jesus I know, and Paul I know; but who are you?" ¹⁶ Then the man with the evil spirit leaped on them, mastered them all, and so overpowered them that they fled out of the house naked and wounded. ¹⁷ When this became known to all residents of Ephesus, both Jews and Greeks, everyone was awestruck; and the name of the Lord Jesus was praised. ¹⁸ Also many of those who became believers confessed and disclosed their practices. ¹⁹ A number of those who practiced magic collected their books and burned them publicly; when the value of these books*ʲ* was calculated, it was found to come to fifty thousand silver coins. ²⁰ So the word of the Lord grew mightily and prevailed.

The Riot in Ephesus

21 Now after these things had been accomplished, Paul resolved in the Spirit to go through Macedonia and Achaia, and then to go on to Jerusalem. He said, "After I have gone there, I must also see Rome." ²² So he sent two of his helpers, Timothy and

τὰ πνεύματα τὰ πονηρὰ τὸ ὄνομα τοῦ
the spirits - evil the name of the
κυρίου Ἰησοῦ λέγοντες· ὁρκίζω ὑμᾶς τὸν
Lord Jesus saying: I exorcise you [by] -
Ἰησοῦν ὃν Παῦλος κηρύσσει. 14 ἦσαν δέ
Jesus whom Paul proclaims. And there were
τινος Σκευᾶ Ἰουδαίου ἀρχιερέως ἑπτὰ
⁵of one ⁴Sceva ³a Jewish ²chief priest ¹seven
υἱοὶ τοῦτο ποιοῦντες. 15 ἀποκριθὲν δὲ
⁶sons ⁸this ⁷doing. And answering
τὸ πνεῦμα τὸ πονηρὸν εἶπεν αὐτοῖς·
the spirit - evil said to them:
τὸν [μὲν] Ἰησοῦν γινώσκω καὶ τὸν
- ²indeed ¹Jesus I know and the
Παῦλον ἐπίσταμαι· ὑμεῖς δὲ τίνες ἐστέ;
Paul I understand; but ye who are?
16 καὶ ἐφαλόμενος ὁ ἄνθρωπος ἐπ᾽ αὐτούς,
And ⁹leaping on ¹the ²man ¹⁰on ¹¹them,
ἐν ᾧ ἦν τὸ πνεῦμα τὸ πονηρόν,
³in ⁴whom ⁵was ⁶the ⁷spirit ⁸evil,
κατακυριεύσας ἀμφοτέρων ἴσχυσεν κατ᾽
overmastering both was strong against
αὐτῶν, ὥστε γυμνοὺς καὶ τετραυματισμένους
them, so as naked and *having been* wounded
=so that they escaped out of that house naked and
ἐκφυγεῖν ἐκ τοῦ οἴκου ἐκείνου. 17 τοῦτο
to escape out of that house. this
wounded.
δὲ ἐγένετο γνωστὸν πᾶσιν Ἰουδαίοις τε
And became known to all ²Jews ¹both
καὶ Ἕλλησιν τοῖς κατοικοῦσιν τὴν Ἔφεσον,
and Greeks - inhabiting - Ephesus,
καὶ ἐπέπεσεν φόβος ἐπὶ πάντας αὐτούς,
and ²fell on ¹fear ³on ⁵all ⁴them,
καὶ ἐμεγαλύνετο τὸ ὄνομα τοῦ κυρίου
and was magnified the name of the Lord
Ἰησοῦ· 18 πολλοί τε τῶν πεπιστευκότων
Jesus; and many of the [ones] having believed
ἤρχοντο ἐξομολογούμενοι καὶ ἀναγγέλλοντες
came confessing and telling
τὰς πράξεις αὐτῶν. 19 ἱκανοὶ δὲ τῶν τὰ
the doings of them. And a consider- of the the
able number [ones]
περίεργα πραξάντων συνενέγκαντες τὰς βίβλους
curious things doing bringing together the rolls
κατέκαιον ἐνώπιον πάντων· καὶ συνεψήφισαν
burnt before all; and they reckoned up
τὰς τιμὰς αὐτῶν καὶ εὗρον ἀργυρίου μυριάδας
the prices of them and found [pieces] ²thousand
¹of silver
πέντε. 20 Οὕτως κατὰ κράτος τοῦ κυρίου
¹five. Thus by might ²of the ⁴Lord
ὁ λόγος ηὔξανεν καὶ ἴσχυεν.
¹the ³word increased and was strong.
21 Ὡς δὲ ἐπληρώθη ταῦτα, ἔθετο ὁ
And when were fulfilled these things, purposed -
Παῦλος ἐν τῷ πνεύματι διελθὼν τὴν
Paul in the(his) spirit passing through -
Μακεδονίαν καὶ Ἀχαΐαν πορεύεσθαι εἰς
Macedonia and Achaia to go to
Ἱεροσόλυμα, εἰπὼν ὅτι μετὰ τὸ γενέσθαι
Jerusalem, saying[,] - After the to become
=After I am
με ἐκεῖ δεῖ με καὶ Ῥώμην ἰδεῖν.
me*ᵇ* there it behoves me ²also ¹Rome ³to see.
22 ἀποστείλας δὲ εἰς Μακεδονίαν δύο
And sending into Macedonia two

mon-possessed. They would say, "In the name of Jesus, whom Paul preaches, I command you to come out." ¹⁴ Seven sons of Sceva, a Jewish chief priest, were doing this. ¹⁵ One day the evil spirit answered them, "Jesus I know, and I know about Paul, but who are you?" ¹⁶ Then the man who had the evil spirit jumped on them and overpowered them all. He gave them such a beating that they ran out of the house naked and bleeding. ¹⁷ When this became known to the Jews and Greeks living in Ephesus, they were all seized with fear, and the name of the Lord Jesus was held in high honor. ¹⁸ Many of those who believed now came and openly confessed their evil deeds. ¹⁹ A number who had practiced sorcery brought their scrolls together and burned them publicly. When they calculated the value of the scrolls, the total came to fifty thousand drachmas.*ᵒ* ²⁰ In this way the word of the Lord spread widely and grew in power. ²¹ After all this had happened, Paul decided to go to Jerusalem, passing through Macedonia and Achaia. "After I have been there," he said, "I must visit Rome also." ²² He sent two of his helpers, Timothy

ᵒ19 A drachma was a silver coin worth about a day's wages.

Erastus, to Macedonia, while he himself stayed for some time longer in Asia.

23 About that time no little disturbance broke out concerning the Way. 24 A man named Demetrius, a silversmith who made silver shrines of Artemis, brought no little business to the artisans. 25 These he gathered together, with the workers of the same trade, and said, "Men, you know that we get our wealth from this business. 26 You also see and hear that not only in Ephesus but in almost the whole of Asia this Paul has persuaded and drawn away a considerable number of people by saying that gods made with hands are not gods. 27 And there is danger not only that this trade of ours may come into disrepute but also that the temple of the great goddess Artemis will be scorned, and she will be deprived of her majesty that brought all Asia and the world to worship her."

28 When they heard this, they were enraged and shouted, "Great is Artemis of the Ephesians!" 29 The city was filled with the confusion; and people *m* rushed together to the theater, dragging with them Gaius and Aristarchus, Macedonians who were Paul's travel companions. 30 Paul wished to go into the crowd, but the disciples would not let him; 31 even some officials of the province of Asia, *n* who were

---

τῶν διακονούντων αὐτῷ, Τιμόθεον καὶ
of the [ones] ministering to him, Timothy and

"Ἔραστον, αὐτὸς ἐπέσχεν χρόνον εἰς τὴν
Erastus, he delayed a time in -

'Ασίαν. 23 Ἐγένετο δὲ κατὰ τὸν καιρὸν
Asia. Now there was about - time

ἐκεῖνον τάραχος οὐκ ὀλίγος περὶ τῆς
that ²trouble ¹no ³little concerning the

ὁδοῦ. 24 Δημήτριος γάρ τις ὀνόματι,
way. For ²Demetrius ¹one by name,

ἀργυροκόπος, ποιῶν ναοὺς ἀργυροῦς
a silversmith, making shrines silver

'Αρτέμιδος παρείχετο τοῖς τεχνίταις οὐκ
of Artemis provided the artisans no

ὀλίγην ἐργασίαν, 25 οὓς συναθροίσας καὶ
little trade, ²whom ¹assembling also

τοὺς περὶ τὰ τοιαῦτα ἐργάτας εἶπεν·
¹the ²about(in) - ⁴such things ³workmen said:

ἄνδρες, ἐπίστασθε ὅτι ἐκ ταύτης τῆς
Men, ye understand that from this the

ἐργασίας ἡ εὐπορία ἡμῖν ἐστιν, 26 καὶ
trade the gain to us is,° and
=we have [our] gain,

θεωρεῖτε καὶ ἀκούετε ὅτι οὐ μόνον
ye behold and hear that ⁷not ⁸only

'Εφέσου ἀλλὰ σχεδὸν πάσης τῆς 'Ασίας
⁹of Ephesus ¹⁰but ¹¹almost ¹²of all - ¹³Asia

ὁ Παῦλος οὗτος πείσας μετέστησεν ἱκανὸν
- ²Paul ¹this ⁴having ⁵perverted ⁶a considerable
persuaded

ὄχλον, λέγων ὅτι οὐκ εἰσὶν θεοὶ οἱ διὰ
⁶crowd, saying that they are not gods ¹the ²through
[ones]

χειρῶν γινόμενοι. 27 οὐ μόνον δὲ τοῦτο
⁴hands ²coming into being. ²not ⁵only ¹Now ⁴this

κινδυνεύει ἡμῖν τὸ μέρος εἰς ἀπελεγμὸν
⁶is in danger to us the share° ²into ⁹disrepute
=⁵our share

ἐλθεῖν, ἀλλὰ καὶ τὸ τῆς μεγάλης θεᾶς
⁷to come, but also ¹the ²of the ⁴great ³goddess

'Αρτέμιδος ἱερὸν εἰς οὐθὲν λογισθῆναι,
⁴Artemis ⁵temple ⁶for(as) ⁷nothing ⁸to be reckoned,

μέλλειν τε καὶ καθαιρεῖσθαι τῆς μεγα-
⁵to be about ¹and ²also ⁴to be diminished the great-

λειότητος αὐτῆς, ἣν ὅλη ἡ 'Ασία καὶ
ness of her, whom all - Asia and

ἡ οἰκουμένη σέβεται. 28 ἀκούσαντες δὲ
the inhabited earth worships. And hearing

καὶ γενόμενοι πλήρεις θυμοῦ ἔκραζον
and becoming full of anger they cried out

λέγοντες· μεγάλη ἡ "Αρτεμις 'Εφεσίων.
saying: Great [is] - Artemis of [the] Ephesians.

29 καὶ ἐπλήσθη ἡ πόλις τῆς συγχύσεως,
And was filled the city of(with) the confusion,

ὥρμησάν τε ὁμοθυμαδὸν εἰς τὸ θέατρον,
and they rushed with one mind into the theatre,

συναρπάσαντες Γάϊον καὶ 'Αρίσταρχον
keeping a firm grip on Gaius and Aristarchus[,]

Μακεδόνας, συνεκδήμους Παύλου. 30 Παύλου
Macedonians, travelling companions of Paul. Paul

δὲ βουλομένου εἰσελθεῖν εἰς τὸν δῆμον
And intending° to enter into the mob
=as Paul intended

οὐκ εἴων αὐτὸν οἱ μαθηταί· 31 τινὲς
⁴not ³allowed ⁵him ¹the ²disciples; some

δὲ καὶ τῶν 'Ασιαρχῶν, ὄντες αὐτῷ
and also of the Asiarchs, being to him

---

and Erastus, to Macedonia, while he stayed in the province of Asia a little longer.

The Riot in Ephesus

23 About that time there arose a great disturbance about the Way. 24 A silversmith named Demetrius, who made silver shrines of Artemis, brought in no little business for the craftsmen. 25 He called them together, along with the workmen in related trades, and said: "Men, you know we receive a good income from this business. 26 And you see and hear how this fellow Paul has convinced and led astray large numbers of people here in Ephesus and in practically the whole province of Asia. He says that man-made gods are no gods at all. 27 There is danger not only that our trade will lose its good name, but also that the temple of the great goddess Artemis will be discredited, and the goddess herself, who is worshiped throughout the province of Asia and the world, will be robbed of her divine majesty."

28 When they heard this, they were furious and began shouting: "Great is Artemis of the Ephesians!" 29 Soon the whole city was in an uproar. The people seized Gaius and Aristarchus, Paul's traveling companions from Macedonia, and rushed as one man into the theater. 30 Paul wanted to appear before the crowd, but the disciples would not let him. 31 Even some of the officials of the province,

---

l Gk *them*
m Gk *they*
n Gk *some of the Asiarchs*

friendly to him, sent him a message urging him not to venture into the theater. 32 Meanwhile, some were shouting one thing, some another; for the assembly was in confusion, and most of them did not know why they had come together. 33 Some of the crowd gave instructions to Alexander, whom the Jews had pushed forward. And Alexander motioned for silence and tried to make a defense before the people. 34 But when they recognized that he was a Jew, for about two hours all of them shouted in unison, "Great is Artemis of the Ephesians!" 35 But when the town clerk had quieted the crowd, he said, "Citizens of Ephesus, who is there that does not know that the city of the Ephesians is the temple keeper of the great Artemis and of the statue that fell from heaven?ᵒ 36 Since these things cannot be denied, you ought to be quiet and do nothing rash. 37 You have brought these men here who are neither temple robbers nor blasphemers of ourᵖ goddess. 38 If therefore Demetrius and the artisans with him have a complaint against anyone, the courts are open, and there are proconsuls; let them bring charges there against one another. 39 If there is anything further�q you want to know, it must be settled in the regular assembly. 40 For we are in danger of being charged with rioting today, since there is no cause that we can give to justify this commotion."

φίλοι, πέμψαντες πρὸς αὐτὸν παρεκάλουν
friends, sending to him besought

μὴ δοῦναι ἑαυτὸν εἰς τὸ θέατρον. 32 ἄλλοι
not to give himself in the theatre. Others

μὲν οὖν ἄλλο τι ἔκραζον· ἦν γὰρ
indeed therefore ²different ¹something cried out; for ⁴was

ἡ ἐκκλησία συγκεχυμένη, καὶ οἱ πλείους
¹the ²assembly having been confounded, and the majority

οὐκ ᾔδεισαν τίνος ἕνεκα συνεληλύθεισαν.
knew not ²of what ¹on account they had come together.

33 ἐκ δὲ τοῦ ὄχλου συνεβίβασαν Ἀλέξανδρον,
But [some] of the crowd instructed Alexander,

προβαλόντων αὐτὸν τῶν Ἰουδαίων· ὁ δὲ
putting forward him the Jewsᵃ; – and
=as the Jews put him forward;

Ἀλέξανδρος κατασείσας τὴν χεῖρα ἤθελεν
Alexander waving the(his) hand wished

ἀπολογεῖσθαι τῷ δήμῳ. 34 ἐπιγνόντες δὲ
to defend himself to the mob. But knowing

ὅτι Ἰουδαῖός ἐστιν, φωνὴ ἐγένετο μία
that a Jew he is(was), ²voice ¹there was ²one

ἐκ πάντων, ὡς ἐπὶ ὥρας δύο κραζόντων·
from all, about over hours two crying out:

μεγάλη ἡ Ἄρτεμις Ἐφεσίων. 35 κατα-
Great [is] – Artemis of [the] Ephesians. ⁴having

στείλας δὲ ὁ γραμματεὺς τὸν ὄχλον
quietened ¹And ²the ³town clerk the crowd

φησίν· ἄνδρες Ἐφέσιοι, τίς γάρ ἐστιν
says: Men Ephesians, who indeed is there

ἀνθρώπων ὃς οὐ γινώσκει τὴν Ἐφεσίων
of men who does not know ¹the ²of [the] Ephesians

πόλιν νεωκόρον οὖσαν τῆς μεγάλης
²city ³temple warden ⁴being of the great

Ἀρτέμιδος καὶ τοῦ διοπετοῦς; 36 ἀναντιρ-
Artemis and of the fallen from [image] the sky? undeni-

ρήτων οὖν ὄντων τούτων δέον ἐστὶν
able therefore being these thingsᵃ necessary it is
=as these things are undeniable

ὑμᾶς κατεσταλμένους ὑπάρχειν καὶ μηδὲν
you ²having been quietened ¹to be and ²nothing

προπετὲς πράσσειν. 37 ἠγάγετε γὰρ τοὺς
³rash ¹to do. For ye brought –

ἄνδρας τούτους οὔτε ἱεροσύλους οὔτε
men these neither temple robbers nor

βλασφημοῦντας τὴν θεὸν ἡμῶν. 38 εἰ
blaspheming the goddess of you. If

μὲν οὖν Δημήτριος καὶ οἱ σὺν αὐτῷ
indeed therefore Demetrius and ¹the ²with ³him

τεχνῖται ἔχουσι πρός τινα λόγον, ἀγοραῖοι
¹artisans have against anyone an account, assizes

ἄγονται καὶ ἀνθύπατοί εἰσιν, ἐγκαλείτωσαν
are and proconsuls there are, let them bring a
being(held) charge against

ἀλλήλοις. 39 εἰ δέ τι περαιτέρω ἐπιζητεῖτε,
one another. But if ²anything ³further ¹ye seek,

ἐν τῇ ἐννόμῳ ἐκκλησίᾳ ἐπιλυθήσεται.
in the lawful assembly it will be settled.

40 καὶ γὰρ κινδυνεύομεν ἐγκαλεῖσθαι
For indeed we are in danger to be charged with

στάσεως περὶ τῆς σήμερον, μηδενὸς
insurrection concerning to-day, nothing

αἰτίου ὑπάρχοντος, περὶ οὗ οὐ δυνησόμεθα
cause beingᵃ, concerning which we shall not be able
=there being no cause,

ἀποδοῦναι λόγον περὶ τῆς συστροφῆς
to give account concerning – ²crowding together

friends of Paul, sent him a message begging him not to venture into the theater. 32 The assembly was in confusion: Some were shouting one thing, some another. Most of the people did not even know why they were there. 33 The Jews pushed Alexander to the front, and some of the crowd shouted instructions to him. He motioned for silence in order to make a defense before the people. 34 But when they realized he was a Jew, they all shouted in unison for about two hours: "Great is Artemis of the Ephesians!"

35 The city clerk quieted the crowd and said: "Men of Ephesus, doesn't all the world know that the city of Ephesus is the guardian of the temple of the great Artemis and of her image, which fell from heaven? 36 Therefore, since these facts are undeniable, you ought to be quiet and not do anything rash. 37 You have brought these men here, though they have neither robbed temples nor blasphemed our goddess. 38 If, then, Demetrius and his fellow craftsmen have a grievance against anybody, the courts are open and there are proconsuls. They can press charges. 39 If there is anything further you want to bring up, it must be settled in a legal assembly. 40 As it is, we are in danger of being charged with rioting because of today's events. In that case we would not be able to account for this commotion, since there is no reason for

ᵒ Meaning of Gk uncertain
ᵖ Other ancient authorities read your
q Other ancient authorities read about other matters

41 When he had said this, he dismissed the assembly.

Chapter 20

Paul Goes to Macedonia and Greece

AFTER the uproar had ceased, Paul sent for the disciples; and after encouraging them and saying farewell, he left for Macedonia. 2 When he had gone through those regions and had given the believers' much encouragement, he came to Greece, 3 where he stayed for three months. He was about to set sail for Syria when a plot was made against him by the Jews, and so he decided to return through Macedonia. 4 He was accompanied by Sopater son of Pyrrhus from Beroea, by Aristarchus and Secundus from Thessalonica, by Gaius from Derbe, and by Timothy, as well as by Tychicus and Trophimus from Asia. 5 They went ahead and were waiting for us in Troas; 6 but we sailed from Philippi after the days of Unleavened Bread, and in five days we joined them in Troas, where we stayed for seven days.

Paul's Farewell Visit to Troas

7 On the first day of the week, when we met to break bread, Paul was holding a discussion with them; since he intended to leave the next day, he continued speaking until midnight. 8 There were many lamps in the room upstairs where we were meeting. 9 A young man named Eutychus, who was sitting in the window, began to sink off into a deep sleep while Paul talked still longer.

ταύτης. **41** καὶ ταῦτα εἰπὼν ἀπέλυσεν τὴν
¹this.   And these things saying   he dismissed   the
ἐκκλησίαν.
assembly.

20 Μετὰ δὲ τὸ παύσασθαι τὸν θόρυβον
And after the to cease the uproar[b]
=after the uproar ceased
μεταπεμψάμενος ὁ Παῦλος τοὺς μαθητὰς
¹summoning   - ¹Paul ⁵the ⁶disciples
καὶ παρακαλέσας, ἀσπασάμενος ἐξῆλθεν
³and   ⁴exhorting, taking leave he went forth
πορεύεσθαι εἰς Μακεδονίαν. **2** διελθὼν δὲ
to go to Macedonia. And having gone through
τὰ μέρη ἐκεῖνα καὶ παρακαλέσας αὐτοὺς
those parts and having exhorted them
λόγῳ πολλῷ ἦλθεν εἰς τὴν Ἑλλάδα,
¹with ²speech ²much he came into - Greece,
3 ποιήσας τε μῆνας τρεῖς, γενομένης
and spending months three, there being
ἐπιβουλῆς αὐτῷ ὑπὸ τῶν Ἰουδαίων
a plot[a] [against] him by the Jews
μέλλοντι ἀνάγεσθαι εἰς τὴν Συρίαν, ἐγένετο
being about to set sail to(for) - Syria, he was
=as he was about
γνώμης τοῦ ὑποστρέφειν διὰ Μακεδονίας.
of a mind - to return[d] through Macedonia.
4 συνείπετο δὲ αὐτῷ Σώπατρος Πύρρου
And there accompanied him Sopater [son] of Pyrrhus
Βεροιαῖος, Θεσσαλονικέων δὲ Ἀρίσταρχος
a Berœan, and of Thessalonians Aristarchus
καὶ Σέκουνδος, καὶ Γάϊος Δερβαῖος καὶ
and Secundus, and Gaius a Derbæan and
Τιμόθεος, Ἀσιανοὶ δὲ Τύχικος καὶ
Timothy, and Asians Tychicus and
Τρόφιμος. **5** οὗτοι δὲ προελθόντες ἔμενον
Trophimus. And these men going forward awaited
ἡμᾶς ἐν Τρωάδι· **6** ἡμεῖς δὲ ἐξεπλεύσαμεν
us in Troas; and we sailed away
μετὰ τὰς ἡμέρας τῶν ἀζύμων ἀπὸ
after the days - of unleavened bread from
Φιλίππων, καὶ ἤλθομεν πρὸς αὐτοὺς εἰς
Philippi, and came to them in
τὴν Τρωάδα ἄχρι ἡμερῶν πέντε, ὅπου
- Troas until days five, where
διετρίψαμεν ἡμέρας ἑπτά. **7** Ἐν δὲ τῇ
we stayed days seven. And on the
μιᾷ τῶν σαββάτων συνηγμένων ἡμῶν[a]
one(first) of the sabbaths(week) having been us[a]
[day] assembled
=as we were assembled
κλάσαι ἄρτον ὁ Παῦλος διελέγετο αὐτοῖς,
to break bread - Paul lectured to them,
μέλλων ἐξιέναι τῇ ἐπαύριον, παρέτεινέν τε
being about to depart on the morrow, and continued
τὸν λόγον μέχρι μεσονυκτίου. **8** ἦσαν δὲ
the speech until midnight. Now there were
λαμπάδες ἱκαναὶ ἐν τῷ ὑπερῴῳ οὗ
lamps a considerable in the upper room where
number of
ἦμεν συνηγμένοι. **9** καθεζόμενος δέ τις
we were having been assembled. And sitting a certain
νεανίας ὀνόματι Εὔτυχος ἐπὶ τῆς θυρίδος,
young man by name Eutychus on the window sill,
καταφερόμενος ὕπνῳ βαθεῖ, διαλεγομένου
being overborne sleep by a deep, lecturing

Chapter 20

Through Macedonia and Greece

WHEN the uproar had ended, Paul sent for the disciples and, after encouraging them, said goodby and set out for Macedonia. 2 He traveled through that area, speaking many words of encouragement to the people, and finally arrived in Greece, 3 where he stayed three months. Because the Jews made a plot against him just as he was about to sail for Syria, he decided to go back through Macedonia. 4 He was accompanied by Sopater son of Pyrrhus from Berea, Aristarchus and Secundus from Thessalonica, Gaius from Derbe, Timothy also, and Tychicus and Trophimus from the province of Asia. 5 These men went on ahead and waited for us at Troas. 6 But we sailed from Philippi after the Feast of Unleavened Bread, and five days later joined the others at Troas, where we stayed seven days.

Eutychus Raised From the Dead at Troas

7 On the first day of the week we came together to break bread. Paul spoke to the people and, because he intended to leave the next day, kept on talking until midnight. 8 There were many lamps in the upstairs room where we were meeting. 9 Seated in a window was a young man named Eutychus, who was sinking into a deep sleep as Paul talked on and on. When he

ʳ Gk given them

Overcome by sleep, he fell to the ground three floors below and was picked up dead. 10But Paul went down, and bending over him took him in his arms, and said, "Do not be alarmed, for his life is in him." 11Then Paul went upstairs, and after he had broken bread and eaten, he continued to converse with them until dawn; then he left. 12Meanwhile they had taken the boy away alive and were not a little comforted.

The Voyage from Troas to Miletus

13 We went ahead to the ship and set sail for Assos, intending to take Paul on board there; for he had made this arrangement, intending to go by land himself. 14When he met us in Assos, we took him on board and went to Mitylene. 15 We sailed from there, and on the following day we arrived opposite Chios. The next day we touched at Samos, and⁵ the day after that we came to Miletus. 16For Paul had decided to sail past Ephesus, so that he might not have to spend time in Asia, he was eager to be in Jerusalem, if possible, on the day of Pentecost.

Paul Speaks to the Ephesian Elders

17 From Miletus he sent a message to Ephesus, asking the elders of the church to meet him. 18When they came to him, he said to them:
"You yourselves know how I lived among you the entire time from the first

τοῦ Παύλου ἐπὶ πλεῖον, κατενεχθεὶς ἀπὸ
Paulᵃ for a longer time, having been from
=while Paul lectured overborne

τοῦ ὕπνου ἔπεσεν ἀπὸ τοῦ τριστέγου
the sleep he fell from the third floor*

κάτω καὶ ἤρθη νεκρός. 10 καταβὰς δὲ
down and was taken up dead. But going down

ὁ Παῦλος ἐπέπεσεν αὐτῷ καὶ συμπεριλαβὼν
- Paul fell on him and closely embracing [him]

εἶπεν· μὴ θορυβεῖσθε· ἡ γὰρ ψυχὴ αὐτοῦ
said: Be ye not terrified; for the life of him

ἐν αὐτῷ ἐστιν. 11 ἀναβὰς δὲ καὶ κλάσας
in him is. And going up and breaking

τὸν ἄρτον καὶ γευσάμενος, ἐφ' ἱκανόν τε
the bread and tasting, and over a considerable [time]

ὁμιλήσας ἄχρι αὐγῆς, οὕτως ἐξῆλθεν.
conversing until light [of day], thus he went forth.

12 ἤγαγον δὲ τὸν παῖδα ζῶντα, καὶ
And they brought the lad living, and

παρεκλήθησαν οὐ μετρίως. 13 Ἡμεῖς δὲ
were comforted not moderately. And we

προελθόντες ἐπὶ τὸ πλοῖον ἀνήχθημεν
going before onto the ship set sail

ἐπὶ τὴν Ἄσσον, ἐκεῖθεν μέλλοντες ἀνα-
to(for) Assos, thence intending to

λαμβάνειν τὸν Παῦλον· οὕτως γὰρ
take up Paul; for thus

διατεταγμένος ἦν, μέλλων αὐτὸς πεζεύειν.
having been arranged it was, ²intending ¹he to go afoot.

14 ὡς δὲ συνέβαλλεν ἡμῖν εἰς τὴν Ἄσσον,
Now when he met with us in - Assos,

ἀναλαβόντες αὐτὸν ἤλθομεν εἰς Μιτυλήνην·
taking up him we came to Mitylene;

15 κἀκεῖθεν ἀποπλεύσαντες τῇ ἐπιούσῃ
and thence sailing away on the next [day]

κατηντήσαμεν ἄντικρυς Χίου, τῇ δὲ ἑτέρᾳ
we arrived off Chios, and on the other(next)

παρεβάλομεν εἰς Σάμον, τῇ δὲ ἐχομένῃ
we crossed over to Samos, and on the next

ἤλθομεν εἰς Μίλητον. 16 κέκρικει γὰρ ὁ
we came to Miletus. For had decided -

Παῦλος παραπλεῦσαι τὴν Ἔφεσον, ὅπως
Paul to sail past - Ephesus, so as

μὴ γένηται αὐτῷ χρονοτριβῆσαι ἐν τῇ
not be to him to spend time in -
=so that he should not . . .

Ἀσίᾳ· ἔσπευδεν γάρ, εἰ δυνατὸν εἴη
Asia; for he hasted, if possible it might be

αὐτῷ, τὴν ἡμέραν τῆς πεντηκοστῆς
to him, the day of Pentecost

γενέσθαι εἰς Ἱεροσόλυμα.
to be in Jerusalem.

17 Ἀπὸ δὲ τῆς Μιλήτου πέμψας εἰς
And from - Miletus sending to

Ἔφεσον μετεκαλέσατο τοὺς πρεσβυτέρους
Ephesus he summoned the elders

τῆς ἐκκλησίας. 18 ὡς δὲ παρεγένοντο
of the church. And when they came

πρὸς αὐτόν, εἶπεν αὐτοῖς· ὑμεῖς ἐπίστασθε,
to him, he said to them: Ye understand,

ἀπὸ πρώτης ἡμέρας ἀφ' ἧς ἐπέβην εἰς
from [the] first day from which I set foot on in

was sound asleep, he fell to the ground from the third story and was picked up dead. 10Paul went down, threw himself on the young man and put his arms around him. "Don't be alarmed," he said. "He's alive!" 11Then he went upstairs again and broke bread and ate. After talking until daylight, he left. 12The people took the young man home alive and were greatly comforted.

Paul's Farewell to the Ephesian Elders

13We went on ahead to the ship and sailed for Assos, where we were going to take Paul aboard. He had made this arrangement because he was going there on foot. 14When he met us at Assos, we took him aboard and went on to Mitylene. 15The next day we set sail from there and arrived off Kios. The day after that we crossed over to Samos, and on the following day arrived at Miletus. 16Paul had decided to sail past Ephesus to avoid spending time in the province of Asia, for he was in a hurry to reach Jerusalem, if possible, by the day of Pentecost. 17From Miletus, Paul sent to Ephesus for the elders of the church. 18When they arrived, he said to them: "You know how I lived the whole time I was with you,

⁵Other ancient authorities add *after remaining at Trogyllium*

* Souter remarks that it is uncertain whether the ground floor was counted or not in the enunciation; " if so, we should have to translate ' the second floor '."

day that I set foot in Asia, [19]serving the Lord with all humility and with tears, enduring the trials that came to me through the plots of the Jews. [20]I did not shrink from doing anything helpful, proclaiming the message to you and teaching you publicly and from house to house, [21]as I testified to both Jews and Greeks about repentance toward God and faith toward our Lord Jesus. [22]And now, as a captive to the Spirit,[*t*] I am on my way to Jerusalem, not knowing what will happen to me there, [23]except that the Holy Spirit testifies to me in every city that imprisonment and persecutions are waiting for me. [24]But I do not count my life of any value to myself, if only I may finish my course and the ministry that I received from the Lord Jesus, to testify to the good news of God's grace. [25]"And now I know that none of you, among whom I have gone about proclaiming the kingdom, will ever see my face again. [26]Therefore I declare to you this day that I am not responsible for the blood of any of you, [27]for I did not shrink from declaring to you the whole purpose of God. [28]Keep watch over yourselves and over all the flock, of which the Holy Spirit has made you overseers, to shepherd the church of God[*u*] that he obtained with the blood of his own Son.[*v*] [29]I know that

τὴν Ἀσίαν, πῶς μεθ᾽ ὑμῶν τὸν πάντα
the Asia, how with you the whole
χρόνον ἐγενόμην, 19 δουλεύων τῷ κυρίῳ
time I was, serving the Lord
μετὰ πάσης ταπεινοφροσύνης καὶ δακρύων
with all humility and tears
καὶ πειρασμῶν τῶν συμβάντων μοι ἐν
and trials - happening to me by
ταῖς ἐπιβουλαῖς τῶν Ἰουδαίων, 20 ὡς
the plots of the Jews, as
οὐδὲν ὑπεστειλάμην τῶν συμφερόντων τοῦ
[a]nothing [1]I kept back of the things beneficial -
μὴ ἀναγγεῖλαι ὑμῖν καὶ διδάξαι ὑμᾶς
not to declare[d] to you and to teach[d] you
δημοσίᾳ καὶ κατ᾽ οἴκους, 21 διαμαρτυρόμενος
publicly and from house to house,† solemnly witnessing
Ἰουδαίοις τε καὶ Ἕλλησιν τὴν εἰς θεὸν
[a]to Jews [1]both and to Greeks - toward God
μετάνοιαν καὶ πίστιν εἰς τὸν κύριον
repentance and faith toward(?in) the Lord
ἡμῶν Ἰησοῦν. 22 καὶ νῦν ἰδοὺ δεδεμένος
of us Jesus. And now behold having been bound
ἐγὼ τῷ πνεύματι πορεύομαι εἰς Ἱερου-
I by the Spirit am going to Jeru-
σαλήμ, τὰ ἐν αὐτῇ συναντήσοντά ἐμοὶ
salem, [a]the things [1]in [1]it [a]going to meet [b]me
μὴ εἰδώς, 23 πλὴν ὅτι τὸ πνεῦμα τὸ
[1]not [a]knowing, except that the Spirit the
ἅγιον κατὰ πόλιν διαμαρτύρεταί μοι λέγον
Holy in every city† solemnly witnesses to me saying
ὅτι δεσμὰ καὶ θλίψεις με μένουσιν.
that bonds and afflictions me await.
24 ἀλλ᾽ οὐδενὸς λόγου ποιοῦμαι τὴν ψυχὴν
But [a]of nothing [a]account [1]I make [a]the(my) [a]life
τιμίαν ἐμαυτῷ ὡς τελειώσω τὸν δρόμον
precious to myself so as I may finish the course
μου καὶ τὴν διακονίαν ἣν ἔλαβον παρὰ
of me and the ministry which I received from
τοῦ κυρίου Ἰησοῦ, διαμαρτύρασθαι τὸ
the Lord Jesus, to witness solemnly the
εὐαγγέλιον τῆς χάριτος τοῦ θεοῦ. 25 καὶ
gospel of the grace - of God. And
νῦν ἰδοὺ ἐγὼ οἶδα ὅτι οὐκέτι ὄψεσθε
now behold I know that [a]no more [a]will see
τὸ πρόσωπόν μου ὑμεῖς πάντες ἐν οἷς
[a]the [a]face [a]of me [1]ye [a]all among whom
διῆλθον κηρύσσων τὴν βασιλείαν. 26 διότι
I went about proclaiming the kingdom. Wherefore
μαρτύρομαι ὑμῖν ἐν τῇ σήμερον ἡμέρᾳ
I witness to you on this day
ὅτι καθαρός εἰμι ἀπὸ τοῦ αἵματος πάντων·
that clean I am from the blood of all men;
27 οὐ γὰρ ὑπεστειλάμην τοῦ μὴ ἀναγγεῖλαι
for I kept not back - not to declare[d]
πᾶσαν τὴν βουλὴν τοῦ θεοῦ ὑμῖν.
all the counsel - of God to you.
28 προσέχετε ἑαυτοῖς καὶ παντὶ τῷ
Take heed to yourselves and to all the
ποιμνίῳ, ἐν ᾧ ὑμᾶς τὸ πνεῦμα τὸ
flock, in which [b]you [1]the [a]Spirit the
ἅγιον ἔθετο ἐπισκόπους, ποιμαίνειν τὴν
[1]Holy [a]placed overseers, to shepherd the
ἐκκλησίαν τοῦ θεοῦ, ἣν περιεποιήσατο
church - of God, which he acquired
διὰ τοῦ αἵματος τοῦ ἰδίου.* 29 ἐγὼ
through the blood of the(his) own.* I

from the first day I came into the province of Asia. [19]I served the Lord with great humility and with tears, although I was severely tested by the plots of the Jews. [20]You know that I have not hesitated to preach anything that would be helpful to you but have taught you publicly and from house to house. [21]I have declared to both Jews and Greeks that they must turn to God in repentance and have faith in our Lord Jesus.
[22]"And now, compelled by the Spirit, I am going to Jerusalem, not knowing what will happen to me there. [23]I only know that in every city the Holy Spirit warns me that prison and hardships are facing me. [24]However, I consider my life worth nothing to me, if only I may finish the race and complete the task the Lord Jesus has given me— the task of testifying to the gospel of God's grace.
[25]"Now I know that none of you among whom I have gone about preaching the kingdom will ever see me again. [26]Therefore, I declare to you today that I am innocent of the blood of all men. [27]For I have not hesitated to proclaim to you the whole will of God. [28]Keep watch over yourselves and all the flock of which the Holy Spirit has made you overseers. [*p*] Be shepherds of the church of God,[*q*] which he bought with his own blood. [29]I know that

* This = his own blood or the blood of his own [?Son].

after I have gone, savage wolves will come in among you, not sparing the flock. 30 Some even from your own group will come distorting the truth in order to entice the disciples to follow them. 31 Therefore be alert, remembering that for three years I did not cease night or day to warn everyone with tears. 32 And now I commend you to God and to the message of his grace, a message that is able to build you up and to give you the inheritance among all who are sanctified. 33 I coveted no one's silver or gold or clothing. 34 You know for yourselves that I worked with my own hands to support myself and my companions. 35 In all this I have given you an example that by such work we must support the weak, remembering the words of the Lord Jesus, for he himself said, 'It is more blessed to give than to receive.'"

36 When he had finished speaking, he knelt down with them all and prayed. 37 There was much weeping among them all; they embraced Paul and kissed him, 38 grieving especially because of what he had said, that they would not see him again. Then they brought him to the ship.

οἶδα ὅτι εἰσελεύσονται μετὰ τὴν ἄφιξίν
know that ⁷will come in ¹after ²the ³departure

μου λύκοι βαρεῖς εἰς ὑμᾶς μὴ φειδόμενοι
⁶of me ⁴wolves ⁵grievous ⁸into you not sparing

τοῦ ποιμνίου, 30 καὶ ἐξ ὑμῶν αὐτῶν
the flock, and of you [your]selves

ἀναστήσονται ἄνδρες λαλοῦντες διεστραμμένα
will rise up men speaking *having been perverted things*

τοῦ ἀποσπᾶν τοὺς μαθητὰς ὀπίσω ἑαυτῶν.
– to drag away⁴ the disciples after themselves.

31 διὸ γρηγορεῖτε, μνημονεύοντες ὅτι
Wherefore watch ye, remembering that

τριετίαν νύκτα καὶ ἡμέραν οὐκ ἐπαυσάμην
for three years night and day I ceased not

μετὰ δακρύων νουθετῶν ἕνα ἕκαστον.
with tears admonishing ²one ¹each.

32 καὶ τὰ νῦν παρατίθεμαι ὑμᾶς τῷ
And – now I commend you to the

κυρίῳ καὶ τῷ λόγῳ τῆς χάριτος αὐτοῦ
Lord and to the word of the grace of him

τῷ δυναμένῳ οἰκοδομῆσαι καὶ δοῦναι τὴν
– being able to build and to give the

κληρονομίαν ἐν τοῖς ἡγιασμένοις πᾶσιν.
inheritance among ²the [ones] ³having been ¹all.
                                    sanctified

33 ἀργυρίου ἢ χρυσίου ἢ ἱματισμοῦ οὐδενὸς
Silver or gold or raiment of no one

ἐπεθύμησα· 34 αὐτοὶ γινώσκετε ὅτι ταῖς
I coveted; [your]selves ye know that ⁴to the

χρείαις μου καὶ τοῖς οὖσιν μετ᾽ ἐμοῦ
⁵needs ⁶of me ⁷and ⁸to the [ones] ⁹being ¹⁰with ¹¹me

ὑπηρέτησαν αἱ χεῖρες αὗται. 35 πάντα
³ministered ¹these ²hands. All things

ὑπέδειξα ὑμῖν, ὅτι οὕτως κοπιῶντας δεῖ
I showed you, that thus labouring it behoves

ἀντιλαμβάνεσθαι τῶν ἀσθενούντων, μνημονεύειν
to succour the ailing [ones], ²to remember

τε τῶν λόγων τοῦ κυρίου Ἰησοῦ, ὅτι
¹and the words of the Lord Jesus, that

αὐτὸς εἶπεν· μακάριόν ἐστιν μᾶλλον διδόναι
he said: Blessed it is rather to give

ἢ λαμβάνειν. 36 καὶ ταῦτα εἰπών,
than to receive. And ²these things ¹having said,

θεὶς τὰ γόνατα αὐτοῦ σὺν πᾶσιν αὐτοῖς
placing the knees of him with ²all ¹them
= kneeling down

προσηύξατο. 37 ἱκανὸς δὲ κλαυθμὸς ἐγένετο
he prayed. And ²considerable ³weeping ¹there was

πάντων, καὶ ἐπιπεσόντες ἐπὶ τὸν τράχηλον
of all, and falling *on* on the neck

τοῦ Παύλου κατεφίλουν αὐτόν, 38 ὀδυνώ-
– of Paul they kissed fervently him, suffer-

μενοι μάλιστα ἐπὶ τῷ λόγῳ ᾧ εἰρήκει,
ing most over the word which he had said,

ὅτι οὐκέτι μέλλουσιν τὸ πρόσωπον αὐτοῦ
that no more they are(were) the face of him

θεωρεῖν. προέπεμπον δὲ αὐτὸν εἰς τὸ
to behold. And they escorted him to the

πλοῖον.
ship.

Chapter 21

Paul's Journey to Jerusalem

WHEN we had parted from them and set sail, we came by a straight course to Cos, and the next day to Rhodes, and from

---

21 Ὡς δὲ ἐγένετο ἀναχθῆναι ἡμᾶς
Now when it came to pass to set sail we

ἀποσπασθέντας ἀπ᾽ αὐτῶν, εὐθυδρομήσαντες
having been withdrawn from them, taking a straight course

ἤλθομεν εἰς τὴν Κῶ, τῇ δὲ ἐξῆς εἰς
we came to – Cos, and on the next [day] to

---

after I leave, savage wolves will come in among you and will not spare the flock. 30 Even from your own number men will arise and distort the truth in order to draw away disciples after them. 31 So be on your guard! Remember that for three years I never stopped warning each of you night and day with tears.

32 "Now I commit you to God and to the word of his grace, which can build you up and give you an inheritance among all those who are sanctified. 33 I have not coveted anyone's silver or gold or clothing. 34 You yourselves know that these hands of mine have supplied my own needs and the needs of my companions. 35 In everything I did, I showed you that by this kind of hard work we must help the weak, remembering the words the Lord Jesus himself said: 'It is more blessed to give than to receive.'"

36 When he had said this, he knelt down with all of them and prayed. 37 They all wept as they embraced him and kissed him. 38 What grieved them most was his statement that they would never see his face again. Then they accompanied him to the ship.

Chapter 21

On to Jerusalem

AFTER we had torn ourselves away from them, we put out to sea and sailed straight to Cos. The

412   ACTS 21

there to Patara.ʷ ²When we found a ship bound for Phoenicia, we went on board and set sail. ³We came in sight of Cyprus; and leaving it on our left, we sailed to Syria and landed at Tyre, because the ship was to unload its cargo there. ⁴We looked up the disciples and stayed there for seven days. Through the Spirit they told Paul not to go on to Jerusalem. ⁵When our days there were ended, we left and proceeded on our journey; and all of them, with wives and children, escorted us outside the city. There we knelt down on the beach and prayed ⁶and said farewell to one another. Then we went on board the ship, and they returned home. 7 When we had finishedˣ the voyage from Tyre, we arrived at Ptolemais; and we greeted the believersʸ and stayed with them for one day. ⁸The next day we left and came to Caesarea; and we went into the house of Philip the evangelist, one of the seven, and stayed with him. ⁹He had four unmarried daughtersᶻ who had the gift of prophecy. ¹⁰While we were staying there for several days, a prophet named Agabus came down from Judea. ¹¹He came to us and took Paul's belt, bound his own feet and

τὴν 'Ρόδον κἀκεῖθεν εἰς Πάταρα· 2 καὶ
— Rhodes and thence to Patara; and
εὑρόντες πλοῖον διαπερῶν εἰς Φοινίκην,
having found a ship crossing over to Phœnice,
ἐπιβάντες ἀνήχθημεν. 3 ἀναφάναντες δὲ
embarking we set sail. And sighting
τὴν Κύπρον καὶ καταλιπόντες αὐτὴν
— Cyprus and leaving it
εὐώνυμον ἐπλέομεν εἰς Συρίαν, καὶ κατήλ-
on the left we sailed to Syria, and came
θομεν εἰς Τύρον· ἐκεῖσε γὰρ τὸ πλοῖον
down to Tyre; for there the ship
ἦν ἀποφορτιζόμενον τὸν γόμον. 4 ἀνευρ-
was unloading the cargo. find-
όντες δὲ τοὺς μαθητὰς ἐπεμείναμεν αὐτοῦ
ing And the disciples we remained there
ἡμέρας ἑπτά· οἵτινες τῷ Παύλῳ ἔλεγον
days seven; who — ¹Paul ¹told
διὰ τοῦ πνεύματος μὴ ἐπιβαίνειν εἰς
through the Spirit not to go up to
'Ιεροσόλυμα. 5 ὅτε δὲ ἐγένετο ἐξαρτίσαι
Jerusalem. But when it came to pass to accomplish
= we accomplished
ἡμᾶς τὰς ἡμέρας, ἐξελθόντες ἐπορευόμεθα
usᵇ the days, going forth we journeyed
προπεμπόντων ἡμᾶς πάντων σὺν γυναιξὶ
²escorting ³us ¹all⁴ with women
καὶ τέκνοις ἕως ἔξω τῆς πόλεως, καὶ
and children as far as outside the city, and
θέντες τὰ γόνατα ἐπὶ τὸν αἰγιαλὸν
placing the knees on the shore
= kneeling
προσευξάμενοι 6 ἀπησπασάμεθα ἀλλήλους,
praying we gave parting greetings to one another,
καὶ ἐνέβημεν εἰς τὸ πλοῖον, ἐκεῖνοι δὲ
and embarked in the ship, and those
ὑπέστρεψαν εἰς τὰ ἴδια. 7 'Ημεῖς δὲ
returned to ¹the(ir) ²things ²own. But we
τὸν πλοῦν διανύσαντες ἀπὸ Τύρου κατηντή-
²the ³voyage ¹finishing from Tyre ar-
σαμεν εἰς Πτολεμαΐδα, καὶ ἀσπασάμενοι
rived at Ptolemais, and greeting
τοὺς ἀδελφοὺς ἐμείναμεν ἡμέραν μίαν
the brothers we remained day one
παρ' αὐτοῖς. 8 τῇ δὲ ἐπαύριον ἐξελθόντες
with them. And on the morrow going forth
ἤλθομεν εἰς Καισάρειαν, καὶ εἰσελθόντες
we came to Cæsarea, and entering
εἰς τὸν οἶκον Φιλίππου τοῦ εὐαγγελιστοῦ
into the house of Philip the evangelist
ὄντος ἐκ τῶν ἑπτά, ἐμείναμεν παρ'
being of the seven, we remained with
αὐτῷ. 9 τούτῳ δὲ ἦσαν θυγατέρες
him. Now to this man were daughters
= this man had four daughters
τέσσαρες παρθένοι προφητεύουσαι. 10 'Επιμεν-
fourᵉ virgins prophesying. remain-
όντων δὲ ἡμέρας πλείους κατῆλθέν τις
ingᵃ And days more(many) ¹came down ¹a certain
ἀπὸ τῆς 'Ιουδαίας προφήτης ὀνόματι
⁶from — ⁷Judæa ²prophet ³by name
"Αγαβος, 11 καὶ ἐλθὼν πρὸς ἡμᾶς καὶ
⁴Agabus, and coming to us and
ἄρας τὴν ζώνην τοῦ Παύλου, δήσας
taking the girdle — of Paul, having bound

next day we went to Rhodes and from there to Patara. ²We found a ship crossing over to Phoenicia, went on board and set sail. ³After sighting Cyprus and passing to the south of it, we sailed on to Syria. We landed at Tyre, where our ship was to unload its cargo. ⁴Finding the disciples there, we stayed with them seven days. Through the Spirit they urged Paul not to go on to Jerusalem. ⁵But when our time was up, we left and continued on our way. All the disciples and their wives and children accompanied us out of the city, and there on the beach we knelt to pray. ⁶After saying good-by to each other, we went aboard the ship, and they returned home.

⁷We continued our voyage from Tyre and landed at Ptolemais, where we greeted the brothers and stayed with them for a day. ⁸Leaving the next day, we reached Caesarea and stayed at the house of Philip the evangelist, one of the Seven. ⁹He had four unmarried daughters who prophesied.

¹⁰After we had been there a number of days, a prophet named Agabus came down from Judea. ¹¹Coming over to us, he took Paul's belt, tied his own

ʷ Other ancient authorities add and Myra
ˣ Or continued
ʸ Gk brothers
ᶻ Gk four daughters, virgins.

hands with it, and said, "Thus says the Holy Spirit, 'This is the way the Jews in Jerusalem will bind the man who owns this belt and will hand him over to the Gentiles.' " 12When we heard this, we and the people there urged him not to go up to Jerusalem. 13Then Paul answered, "What are you doing, weeping and breaking my heart? For I am ready not only to be bound but even to die in Jerusalem for the name of the Lord Jesus." 14Since he would not be persuaded, we remained silent except to say, "The Lord's will be done."

15 After these days we got ready and started to go up to Jerusalem. 16Some of the disciples from Caesarea also came along and brought us to the house of Mnason of Cyprus, an early disciple, with whom we were to stay.

Paul Visits James at Jerusalem

17 When we arrived in Jerusalem, the brothers welcomed us warmly. 18The next day Paul went with us to visit James; and all the elders were present. 19After greeting them, he related one by one the things that God had done among the Gentiles through his ministry. 20When they heard it, they praised God. Then they said to him, "You see, brother, how many thousands of believers there are among the

---

ἑαυτοῦ τοὺς πόδας καὶ τὰς χεῖρας εἶπεν·
of himself the feet and the hands said:

τάδε λέγει τὸ πνεῦμα τὸ ἅγιον· τὸν
These things says the Spirit - Holy: 7The

ἄνδρα οὗ ἐστιν ἡ ζώνη αὕτη οὕτως
8man 9of whom 10is 11this 12girdle 1thus

δήσουσιν ἐν Ἰερουσαλὴμ οἱ Ἰουδαῖοι καὶ
4will bind 5in 6Jerusalem 2the 3Jews and

παραδώσουσιν εἰς χεῖρας ἐθνῶν. 12 ὡς
will deliver into [the] hands of [the] nations. when

δὲ ἠκούσαμεν ταῦτα, παρεκαλοῦμεν ἡμεῖς
And we heard these things, 6besought 1we

τε καὶ οἱ ἐντόπιοι τοῦ μὴ ἀναβαίνειν
2both 3and 4the 5residents - 6not 7to go upᵈ

αὐτὸν εἰς Ἰερουσαλήμ. 13 τότε ἀπεκρίθη
7him to Jerusalem. Then answered

ὁ Παῦλος τί ποιεῖτε κλαίοντες καὶ
- Paul: What are ye doing weeping and

συνθρύπτοντές μου τὴν καρδίαν; ἐγὼ γὰρ
weakening of me the heart? For I

οὐ μόνον δεθῆναι ἀλλὰ καὶ ἀποθανεῖν
not only to be bound but also to die

εἰς Ἰερουσαλὴμ ἑτοίμως ἔχω ὑπὲρ τοῦ
in Jerusalem readily have on behalf of the
= am ready

ὀνόματος τοῦ κυρίου Ἰησοῦ. 14 μὴ
name of the Lord Jesus. Not

πειθομένου δὲ αὐτοῦ ἡσυχάσαμεν εἰπόντες·
being persuaded and him* we kept silence having said:
= And when he was not persuaded,

τοῦ κυρίου τὸ θέλημα γινέσθω.
9Of the 1Lord 3the 2will 4let 6be [done].

15 Μετὰ δὲ τὰς ἡμέρας ταύτας
And after these days

ἐπισκευασάμενοι ἀνεβαίνομεν εἰς Ἰεροσόλυμα·
having made ready we went up to Jerusalem;

16 συνῆλθον δὲ καὶ τῶν μαθητῶν ἀπὸ
and went with also [some] of the disciples from

Καισαρείας σὺν ἡμῖν, ἄγοντες παρ' ᾧ
Caesarea with us, bringing [one] with whom

ξενισθῶμεν Μνάσωνί τινι Κυπρίῳ,
we might be lodged Mnason a certain Cypriote,

ἀρχαίῳ μαθητῇ. 17 Γενομένων δὲ ἡμῶν εἰς
an ancient disciple. And being us* in
(early)   = when we were

Ἰεροσόλυμα ἀσμένως ἀπεδέξαντο ἡμᾶς οἱ
Jerusalem 3joyfully 2received 1us 1the

ἀδελφοί. 18 τῇ δὲ ἐπιούσῃ εἰσῄει ὁ
2brothers. And on the next day went in -

Παῦλος σὺν ἡμῖν πρὸς Ἰάκωβον, πάντες
Paul with us to James, 2all

τε παρεγένοντο οἱ πρεσβύτεροι. 19 καὶ
1and 3came 2the 4elders. And

ἀσπασάμενος αὐτοὺς ἐξηγεῖτο καθ' ἓν
having greeted them he related according to one
= singly

ἕκαστον ὧν ἐποίησεν ὁ θεὸς ἐν τοῖς
each of [the] did - God among the
things] which

ἔθνεσιν διὰ τῆς διακονίας αὐτοῦ. 20 οἱ
nations through the ministry of him. they

δὲ ἀκούσαντες ἐδόξαζον τὸν θεόν, εἶπάν τε
And hearing glorified - God, and said

αὐτῷ· θεωρεῖς, ἀδελφέ, πόσαι μυριάδες
to him: Thou beholdest, brother, how many *ten* thousands

εἰσὶν ἐν τοῖς Ἰουδαίοις τῶν πεπιστευκότων,
there are among the Jews - having believed,

---

hands and feet with it and said, "The Holy Spirit says, 'In this way the Jews of Jerusalem will bind the owner of this belt and will hand him over to the Gentiles.' "

12When we heard this, we and the people there pleaded with Paul not to go up to Jerusalem. 13Then Paul answered, "Why are you weeping and breaking my heart? I am ready not only to be bound, but also to die in Jerusalem for the name of the Lord Jesus." 14When he would not be dissuaded, we gave up and said, "The Lord's will be done."

15After this, we got ready and went up to Jerusalem. 16Some of the disciples from Caesarea accompanied us and brought us to the home of Mnason, where we were to stay. He was a man from Cyprus and one of the early disciples.

Paul's Arrival at Jerusalem

17When we arrived at Jerusalem, the brothers received us warmly. 18The next day Paul and the rest of us went to see James, and all the elders were present. 19Paul greeted them and reported in detail what God had done among the Gentiles through his ministry.

20When they heard this, they praised God. Then they said to Paul: "You see, brother, how many thousands of Jews have be-

Jews, and they are all zealous for the law. 21They have been told about you that you teach all the Jews living among the Gentiles to forsake Moses, and that you tell them not to circumcise their children or observe the customs. 22What then is to be done? They will certainly hear that you have come. 23So do what we tell you. We have four men who are under a vow. 24Join these men, go through the rite of purification with them, and pay for the shaving of their heads. Thus all will know that there is nothing in what they have been told about you, but that you yourself observe and guard the law. 25But as for the Gentiles who have become believers, we have sent a letter with our judgment that they should abstain from what has been sacrificed to idols and from blood and from what is strangled[a] and from fornication." 26Then Paul took the men, and the next day, having purified himself, he entered the temple with them, making public the completion of the days of purification when the sacrifice would be made for each of them.

Paul Arrested in the Temple

27 When the seven days were almost completed, the Jews from Asia, who had seen him in the temple, stirred up the whole crowd. They seized him, 28shouting, "Fellow Israelites, help! This is the man who is teaching everyone everywhere against our people,

καὶ πάντες ζηλωταὶ τοῦ νόμου ὑπάρχουσιν·
and all zealots of the law are;

21 κατηχήθησαν δὲ περὶ σοῦ ὅτι ἀποστα-
and they were informed about thee that ⁸apo-

σίαν διδάσκεις ἀπὸ Μωϋσέως τοὺς κατὰ
stasy ¹thou teachest ⁹from ¹⁰Moses ⁵the ⁶throughout

τὰ ἔθνη πάντας 'Ιουδαίους, λέγων μὴ
⁴the ⁷nations ²all ⁴Jews, ¹telling ²not

περιτέμνειν αὐτοὺς τὰ τέκνα μηδὲ τοῖς
⁴to circumcise ²them the children nor in the

ἔθεσιν περιπατεῖν. **22** τί οὖν ἐστιν;
customs to walk. What therefore is it?

πάντως ἀκούσονται ὅτι ἐλήλυθας. **23** τοῦτο
At all events they will hear that thou hast come. This

οὖν ποίησον ὅ σοι λέγομεν· εἰσὶν ἡμῖν
therefore do thou which thee we tell: There are to us⁶
= We have

ἄνδρες τέσσαρες εὐχὴν ἔχοντες ἐφ' ἑαυτῶν·
men four a vow having on themselves;

24 τούτους παραλαβὼν ἁγνίσθητι σὺν αὐτοῖς,
these taking be thou purified with them,

καὶ δαπάνησον ἐπ' αὐτοῖς ἵνα ξυρήσονται
and spend on them that they will shave

τὴν κεφαλήν, καὶ γνώσονται πάντες ὅτι
the head, and will know all men that

ὧν κατήχηνται περὶ σοῦ οὐδέν
³[of the things] ⁴they have been ⁵about ⁶thee ²nothing
of which informed

ἐστιν, ἀλλὰ στοιχεῖς καὶ αὐτὸς φυλάσσων τὸν
¹there is, but thou walkest also [thy]self keeping the

νόμον. **25** περὶ δὲ τῶν πεπιστευκότων
law. And concerning ¹the ²having believed

ἐθνῶν ἡμεῖς ἐπεστείλαμεν κρίναντες φυλάσ-
³nations we joined in writing ¹judging ³to keep

σεσθαι αὐτοὺς τό τε εἰδωλόθυτον καὶ
themselves ²them ⁴[from] ³the ⁵both idol sacrifice and

αἷμα καὶ πνικτὸν καὶ πορνείαν. **26** τότε
blood and a thing strangled and fornication. Then

ὁ Παῦλος παραλαβὼν τοὺς ἄνδρας τῇ
- Paul taking the men on the

ἐχομένῃ ἡμέρᾳ σὺν αὐτοῖς ἁγνισθεὶς εἰσήει
next day with them having been purified went in

εἰς τὸ ἱερόν, διαγγέλλων τὴν ἐκπλήρωσιν
to the temple, announcing the completion

τῶν ἡμερῶν τοῦ ἁγνισμοῦ, ἕως οὗ
of the days of the purification, until

προσηνέχθη ὑπὲρ ἑνὸς ἑκάστου αὐτῶν ἡ
should be offered on behalf of ²one ¹each of them the

προσφορά.
offering.

27 Ὡς δὲ ἔμελλον αἱ ἑπτὰ ἡμέραι
Now when were about the seven days

συντελεῖσθαι, οἱ ἀπὸ τῆς 'Ασίας 'Ιουδαῖοι
to be fulfilled, ¹the ²from - ⁴Asia ³Jews

θεασάμενοι αὐτὸν ἐν τῷ ἱερῷ συνέχεον
seeing him in the temple stirred up

πάντα τὸν ὄχλον, καὶ ἐπέβαλαν ἐπ'
all the crowd, and laid on on

αὐτὸν τὰς χεῖρας, **28** κράζοντες· ἄνδρες
him the(ir) hands, crying out: Men

'Ισραηλῖται, βοηθεῖτε· οὗτός ἐστιν ὁ
Israelites, help: this is the

ἄνθρωπος ὁ κατὰ τοῦ λαοῦ καὶ τοῦ
man ¹the [one] ⁵against ⁴the ⁷people ²and ³the

νόμου καὶ τοῦ τόπου τούτου πάντας
¹⁰law ¹¹and the ¹²this ¹³place ²all men

lieved, and all of them are zealous for the law. 21They have been informed that you teach all the Jews who live among the Gentiles to turn away from Moses, telling them not to circumcise their children or live according to our customs. 22What shall we do? They will certainly hear that you have come, 23so do what we tell you. There are four men with us who have made a vow. 24Take these men, join in their purification rites and pay their expenses, so that they can have their heads shaved. Then everybody will know there is no truth in these reports about you, but that you yourself are living in obedience to the law. 25As for the Gentile believers, we have written to them our decision that they should abstain from food sacrificed to idols, from blood, from the meat of strangled animals and from sexual immorality."

26The next day Paul took the men and purified himself along with them. Then he went to the temple to give notice of the date when the days of purification would end and the offering would be made for each of them.

Paul Arrested

27When the seven days were nearly over, some Jews from the province of Asia saw Paul at the temple. They stirred up the whole crowd and seized him, 28shouting, "Men of Israel, help us! This is the man who teaches all men everywhere against our

[a] Other ancient authorities lack *and from what is strangled*

our law, and this place; more than that, he has actually brought Greeks into the temple and has defiled this holy place." 29 For they had previously seen Trophimus the Ephesian with him in the city, and they supposed that Paul had brought him into the temple. 30 Then all the city was aroused, and the people rushed together. They seized Paul and dragged him out of the temple, and immediately the doors were shut. 31 While they were trying to kill him, word came to the tribune of the cohort that all Jerusalem was in an uproar. 32 Immediately he took soldiers and centurions and ran down to them. When they saw the tribune and the soldiers, they stopped beating Paul. 33 Then the tribune came, arrested him, and ordered him to be bound with two chains; he inquired who he was and what he had done. 34 Some in the crowd shouted one thing, some another; and as he could not learn the facts because of the uproar, he ordered him to be brought into the barracks. 35 When Paul[b] came to the steps, the violence of the mob was so great that he had to be carried by the soldiers. 36 The crowd that followed kept shouting, "Away with him!"

Paul Defends Himself

37 Just as Paul was about to be brought into the barracks, he said to the tribune, "May I say something to you?" The tri-

πανταχῇ διδάσκων, ἔτι τε καὶ Ἕλληνας
'everywhere 'teaching, and even also Greeks
εἰσήγαγεν εἰς τὸ ἱερὸν καὶ κεκοίνωκεν
brought in into the temple and has profaned
τὸν ἅγιον τόπον τοῦτον. 29 ἦσαν γὰρ
- 'holy 'place 'this. For they were
προεωρακότες Τρόφιμον τὸν Ἐφέσιον ἐν
having previously seen Trophimus the Ephesian in
τῇ πόλει σὺν αὐτῷ, ὃν ἐνόμιζον ὅτι
the city with him, whom they supposed that
εἰς τὸ ἱερὸν εἰσήγαγεν ὁ Παῦλος. 30 ἐκινήθη
'into 'the 'temple 'brought in - 'Paul. 'was moved
τε ἡ πόλις ὅλη καὶ ἐγένετο συνδρομὴ
'And 'the 'city 'whole and there was a running together
τοῦ λαοῦ, καὶ ἐπιλαβόμενοι τοῦ Παύλου
of the people, and laying hold - of Paul
εἷλκον αὐτὸν ἔξω τοῦ ἱεροῦ, καὶ εὐθέως
they dragged him outside the temple, and immediately
ἐκλείσθησαν αἱ θύραι. 31 Ζητούντων τε
were shut the doors. And [while they were] seeking²
αὐτὸν ἀποκτεῖναι ἀνέβη φάσις τῷ
²him ¹to kill ⁴came up ³information to the
χιλιάρχῳ τῆς σπείρης ὅτι ὅλη συγχύν-
chiliarch of the cohort that ¹all ³is(was) in
νεται Ἰερουσαλήμ· 32 ὃς ἐξαυτῆς παρα-
confusion ²Jerusalem: who at once tak-
λαβὼν στρατιώτας καὶ ἑκατοντάρχας
ing soldiers and centurions
κατέδραμεν ἐπ' αὐτούς· οἱ δὲ ἰδόντες
ran down on them; and they seeing
τὸν χιλίαρχον καὶ τοὺς στρατιώτας
the chiliarch and the soldiers
ἐπαύσαντο τύπτοντες τὸν Παῦλον. 33 τότε
ceased beating - Paul. Then
ἐγγίσας ὁ χιλίαρχος ἐπελάβετο αὐτοῦ
drawing near the chiliarch laid hold of him
καὶ ἐκέλευσεν δεθῆναι ἁλύσεσι δυσί, καὶ
and commanded to be bound chains with two, and
ἐπυνθάνετο τίς εἴη καὶ τί ἐστιν πεποιηκώς.
inquired who he and what he is having done.
might be
34 ἄλλοι δὲ ἄλλο τι ἐπεφώνουν ἐν τῷ
And ¹others ⁷different ⁶some- ⁵called out ²among ³the
thing
ὄχλῳ· μὴ δυναμένου δὲ αὐτοῦ γνῶναι
⁴crowd; and not being able him³ to know
=as he was not able
τὸ ἀσφαλὲς διὰ τὸν θόρυβον, ἐκέλευσεν
the certain thing because of the uproar, he commanded
ἄγεσθαι αὐτὸν εἰς τὴν παρεμβολήν. 35 ὅτε
to be brought him into the fort. when
δὲ ἐγένετο ἐπὶ τοὺς ἀναβαθμούς, συνέβη
And he was on the steps, it happened
βαστάζεσθαι αὐτὸν ὑπὸ τῶν στρατιωτῶν
to be carried him[b] by he soldiers
=he was carried
διὰ τὴν βίαν τοῦ ὄχλου· 36 ἠκολούθει
because of the violence of the crowd; ⁶followed
γὰρ τὸ πλῆθος τοῦ λαοῦ κράζοντες·
¹for ²the ³multitude ⁴of the ⁵people crying out:
αἶρε αὐτόν. 37 Μέλλων τε εἰσάγεσθαι
Take away him. And being about to be brought in
εἰς τὴν παρεμβολὴν ὁ Παῦλος λέγει τῷ
into the fort - Paul says to the
χιλιάρχῳ· εἰ ἔξεστίν μοι εἰπεῖν τι πρὸς
chiliarch: If it is lawful for me to say something to

people and our law and this place. And besides, he has brought Greeks into the temple area and defiled this holy place." 29(They had previously seen Trophimus the Ephesian in the city with Paul and assumed that Paul had brought him into the temple area.)

30The whole city was aroused, and the people came running from all directions. Seizing Paul, they dragged him from the temple, and immediately the gates were shut. 31While they were trying to kill him, news reached the commander of the Roman troops that the whole city of Jerusalem was in an uproar. 32He at once took some officers and soldiers and ran down to the crowd. When the rioters saw the commander and his soldiers, they stopped beating Paul.

33The commander came up and arrested him and ordered him to be bound with two chains. Then he asked who he was and what he had done. 34Some in the crowd shouted one thing and some another, and since the commander could not get at the truth because of the uproar, he ordered that Paul be taken into the barracks. 35When Paul reached the steps, the violence of the mob was so great he had to be carried by the soldiers. 36The crowd that followed kept shouting, "Away with him!"

Paul Speaks to the Crowd

37As the soldiers were about to take Paul into the barracks, he asked the commander, "May I say something to you?"

b Gk he

bune^c replied, "Do you know Greek? ^38 Then you are not the Egyptian who recently stirred up a revolt and led the four thousand assassins out into the wilderness?" ^39 Paul replied, "I am a Jew, from Tarsus in Cilicia, a citizen of an important city; I beg you, let me speak to the people." ^40 When he had given him permission, Paul stood on the steps and motioned to the people for silence; and when there was a great hush, he addressed them in the Hebrew^d language, saying:

Chapter 22

" "BROTHERS and fathers, listen to the defense that I now make before you."

2 When they heard him addressing them in Hebrew,^d they became even more quiet. Then he said: 3 "I am a Jew, born in Tarsus in Cilicia, but brought up in this city at the feet of Gamaliel, educated strictly according to our ancestral law, being zealous for God, just as all of you are today. ^4 I persecuted this Way up to the point of death by binding both men and women and putting them in prison, ^5 as the high priest and the whole council of elders can testify about me. From them I also received letters to the brothers in Damascus, and I went there in order to bind

σέ;   ὁ   δὲ   ἔφη·   Ἑλληνιστὶ   γινώσκεις;
thee?   And he   said: in Greek   Knowest thou [to speak]?*

38 οὐκ   ἄρα   σὺ   εἶ   ὁ   Αἰγύπτιος   ὁ   πρὸ
²Not   ⁴then   ³thou   ¹art   the   Egyptian   the [one]   before

τούτων   τῶν   ἡμερῶν   ἀναστατώσας   καὶ
these⁵   -   days   unsettling   and

ἐξαγαγὼν   εἰς   τὴν   ἔρημον   τοὺς   τετρα-
leading out   into   the   desert   the   four

κισχιλίους   ἄνδρας   τῶν   σικαρίων;   39 εἶπεν
thousand   men   of the   Sicarii?   said

δὲ   ὁ   Παῦλος·   ἐγὼ   ἄνθρωπος   μέν   εἰμι
And   -   Paul: I   a man   indeed   am

Ἰουδαῖος,   Ταρσεύς,   τῆς   Κιλικίας   οὐκ
a Jew,   a Tarsian,   -   of Cilicia   not

ἀσήμου   πόλεως   πολίτης·   δέομαι   δέ   σου,
of a mean   city   a citizen;   and I beg   of thee,

ἐπίτρεψόν   μοι   λαλῆσαι   πρὸς   τὸν   λαόν.
permit   me   to speak   to   the   people.

40 ἐπιτρέψαντος   δὲ   αὐτοῦ   ὁ   Παῦλος   ἑστὼς
And permitting   him*   -   Paul   standing
=when he gave permission

ἐπὶ   τῶν   ἀναβαθμῶν   κατέσεισεν   τῇ   χειρὶ
on   the   steps   beckoned   with the(his) hand

τῷ   λαῷ·   πολλῆς   δὲ   σιγῆς   γενομένης
to the   people;   and much   silence   becoming*
=when there was great silence

προσεφώνησεν   τῇ   Ἑβραΐδι   διαλέκτῳ   λέγων·
he addressed   in the   Hebrew   language   saying:

22 Ἄνδρες   ἀδελφοὶ   καὶ   πατέρες,   ἀκούσατέ
Men   brothers   and   fathers,   hear ye

μου   τῆς   πρὸς   ὑμᾶς   νυνὶ   ἀπολογίας.
⁵of me   ¹the   ²to   ⁴you   ³now   ⁵defence.

—   2 ἀκούσαντες   δὲ   ὅτι   τῇ   Ἑβραΐδι
(And hearing   that   in the   Hebrew

διαλέκτῳ   προσεφώνει   αὐτοῖς   μᾶλλον
language   he addressed   them   more

παρέσχον   ἡσυχίαν.   καὶ   φησίν·   3 ἐγώ   εἰμι
they showed   quietness.   And   he says:)   I   am

ἀνὴρ   Ἰουδαῖος,   γεγεννημένος   ἐν   Ταρσῷ
a man   a Jew,   having been born   in   Tarsus

τῆς   Κιλικίας,   ἀνατεθραμμένος   δὲ   ἐν   τῇ
-    of Cilicia,   and having been brought up   in   -

πόλει   ταύτῃ,   παρὰ   τοὺς   πόδας   Γαμαλιὴλ
city   this,   at   the   feet   of Gamaliel

πεπαιδευμένος   κατὰ   ἀκρίβειαν   τοῦ   πατρῴου
having been trained   according   exactness   of the   ancestral
to [the]

νόμου,   ζηλωτὴς   ὑπάρχων   τοῦ   θεοῦ   καθὼς
law,   a zealot   being   -   of God   even as

πάντες   ὑμεῖς   ἐστε   σήμερον·   4 ὃς   ταύτην
all   ye   are   to-day;   who   this

τὴν   ὁδὸν   ἐδίωξα   ἄχρι   θανάτου,   δεσμεύων
-    way   persecuted   as far as to   death,   binding

καὶ   παραδιδοὺς   εἰς   φυλακὰς   ἄνδρας   τε
and   delivering   to   prisons   both men

καὶ   γυναῖκας.   5 ὡς   καὶ   ὁ   ἀρχιερεὺς
and   women.   As   even   the   high priest

μαρτυρεῖ   μοι   καὶ   πᾶν   τὸ   πρεσβυτέριον·
witnesses   to me   and   all   the   senate;

παρ'   ὧν   καὶ   ἐπιστολὰς   δεξάμενος   πρὸς
from whom   also   letters   having received   to

τοὺς   ἀδελφοὺς   εἰς   Δαμασκὸν   ἐπορευόμην,
the   brothers   in   Damascus   I journeyed,

"Do you speak Greek?" he replied. ^38 "Aren't you the Egyptian who started a revolt and led four thousand terrorists out into the desert some time ago?"

^39 Paul answered, "I am a Jew, from Tarsus in Cilicia, a citizen of no ordinary city. Please let me speak to the people."

^40 Having received the commander's permission, Paul stood on the steps and motioned to the crowd. When they were all silent, he said to them in Aramaic^r: ¹"Brothers and fathers, listen now to my defense."

²When they heard him speak to them in Aramaic, they became very quiet.

Then Paul said: ³"I am a Jew, born in Tarsus of Cilicia, but brought up in this city. Under Gamaliel I was thoroughly trained in the law of our fathers and was just as zealous for God as any of you are today. ⁴I persecuted the followers of this Way to their death, arresting both men and women and throwing them into prison, ⁵as also the high priest and all the Council can testify. I even obtained letters from them to their brothers in Damascus, and

^c Gk He
^d That is, Aramaic

* See note on page xviii.

^r 40 Or possibly Hebrew; also in 22:2

those who were there and to bring them back to Jerusalem for punishment.

Paul Tells of His Conversion

6 "While I was on my way and approaching Damascus, about noon a great light from heaven suddenly shone about me. 7I fell to the ground and heard a voice saying to me, 'Saul, Saul, why are you persecuting me?' 8I answered, 'Who are you, Lord?' Then he said to me, 'I am Jesus of Nazareth^e whom you are persecuting.' 9Now those who were with me saw the light but did not hear the voice of the one who was speaking to me. 10I asked, 'What am I to do, Lord?' The Lord said to me, 'Get up and go to Damascus; there you will be told everything that has been assigned to you to do.' 11Since I could not see because of the brightness of that light, those who were with me took my hand and led me to Damascus. 12 "A certain Ananias, who was a devout man according to the law and well spoken of by all the Jews living there, 13came to me; and standing beside me, he said, 'Brother Saul, regain your sight!' In that very hour I regained my sight and saw him. 14Then he said, 'The God of our ancestors has chosen you to know his will, to see the Righteous One and to hear his own voice; 15for you will be his witness to all the world of what you have seen and heard. 16And now why do you delay? Get up, be baptized, and have your sins washed away, calling

---

ἄξων καὶ τοὺς ἐκεῖσε ὄντας δεδεμένους
leading also the [ones] ¹there ¹being *having been* bound

εἰς Ἰερουσαλὴμ ἵνα τιμωρηθῶσιν.
to Jerusalem that they might be punished.

6 Ἐγένετο δέ μοι πορευομένῳ καὶ ἐγγίζοντι
Now it happened to me journeying and drawing near

τῇ Δαμασκῷ περὶ μεσημβρίαν ἐξαίφνης ἐκ
– to Damascus about midday suddenly out of

τοῦ οὐρανοῦ περιαστράψαι φῶς ἱκανὸν
– heaven ⁴to shine round ¹a ³light ²considerable

περὶ ἐμέ, 7 ἔπεσά τε εἰς τὸ ἔδαφος
round me, and I fell to the ground

καὶ ἤκουσα φωνῆς λεγούσης μοι· Σαοὺλ
and heard a voice saying to me: Saul[,]

Σαούλ, τί με διώκεις; 8 ἐγὼ δὲ ἀπεκρίθην·
Saul, why me persecutest thou? And I answered:

τίς εἶ, κύριε; εἶπέν τε πρὸς ἐμέ· ἐγώ
Who art thou, Lord? And he said to me: I

εἰμι Ἰησοῦς ὁ Ναζωραῖος, ὃν σὺ διώκεις.
am Jesus the Nazarene, whom thou persecutest.

9 οἱ δὲ σὺν ἐμοὶ ὄντες τὸ μὲν φῶς
Now ¹the [ones] ²with ⁴me ³being ⁷the ⁶indeed ⁵light

ἐθεάσαντο, τὴν δὲ φωνὴν οὐκ ἤκουσαν
⁸beheld, but the voice they heard not

τοῦ λαλοῦντός μοι. 10 εἶπον δέ· τί
of the [one] speaking to me. And I said: What

ποιήσω, κύριε; ὁ δὲ κύριος εἶπεν πρός
may I do, Lord? And the Lord said to

με· ἀναστὰς πορεύου εἰς Δαμασκόν, κἀκεῖ σοι
me: Rising up go into Damascus, and there to thee

λαληθήσεται περὶ πάντων ὧν τέτακταί
it will be told concerning all things which has(ve) been arranged

σοι ποιῆσαι. 11 ὡς δὲ οὐκ ἐνέβλεπον
for thee to do. And as I saw not

ἀπὸ τῆς δόξης τοῦ φωτὸς ἐκείνου,
from the glory of that light,

χειραγωγούμενος ὑπὸ τῶν συνόντων μοι
being led by the hand by the [ones] being with me

ἦλθον εἰς Δαμασκόν. 12 Ἀνανίας δέ τις,
I went into Damascus. And a certain Ananias,

ἀνὴρ εὐλαβὴς κατὰ τὸν νόμον, μαρτυρού-
a man devout according to the law, being witnessed

μενος ὑπὸ πάντων τῶν κατοικούντων
[to] by all ¹the ²dwelling ⁴[there]

Ἰουδαίων, 13 ἐλθὼν πρὸς ἐμὲ καὶ ἐπιστὰς
³Jews, coming to me and standing by

εἶπέν μοι· Σαοὺλ ἀδελφέ, ἀνάβλεψον.
said to me: Saul brother, look up.

κἀγὼ αὐτῇ τῇ ὥρᾳ ἀνέβλεψα εἰς αὐτόν.
And I in that hour* looked up at him.

14 ὁ δὲ εἶπεν· ὁ θεὸς τῶν πατέρων
And he said: The God of the fathers

ἡμῶν προεχειρίσατό σε γνῶναι τὸ θέλημα
of us previously appointed thee to know the will

αὐτοῦ καὶ ἰδεῖν τὸν δίκαιον καὶ ἀκοῦσαι
of him and to see the Just One and to hear

φωνὴν ἐκ τοῦ στόματος αὐτοῦ, 15 ὅτι
a voice out of the mouth of him, because

ἔσῃ μάρτυς αὐτῷ πρὸς πάντας ἀνθρώπους
thou wilt be a witness to him° to all men

ὧν ἑώρακας καὶ ἤκουσας. 16 καὶ νῦν
of things which thou hast seen and didst hear. And now

τί μέλλεις; ἀναστὰς βάπτισαι καὶ ἀπόλου-
what intendest thou? Rising up be baptized and wash

---

went there to bring these people as prisoners to Jerusalem to be punished. 6"About noon as I came near Damascus, suddenly a bright light from heaven flashed around me. 7I fell to the ground and heard a voice say to me, 'Saul! Saul! Why do you persecute me?' 8"'Who are you, Lord?' I asked. "'I am Jesus of Nazareth, whom you are persecuting,' he replied. 9My companions saw the light, but they did not understand the voice of him who was speaking to me. 10"'What shall I do, Lord?' I asked. "'Get up,' the Lord said, 'and go into Damascus. There you will be told all that you have been assigned to do.' 11My companions led me by the hand into Damascus, because the brilliance of the light had blinded me. 12"A man named Ananias came to see me. He was a devout observer of the law and highly respected by all the Jews living there. 13He stood beside me and said, 'Brother Saul, receive your sight!' And at that very moment I was able to see him. 14"Then he said: 'The God of our fathers has chosen you to know his will and to see the Righteous One and to hear words from his mouth. 15You will be his witness to all men of what you have seen and heard. 16And now what are you waiting for? Get up, be baptized and wash your

---

e Gk *the Nazorean*

* See Luke 2. 38.

on his name.'

Paul Sent to the Gentiles

17 "After I had returned to Jerusalem and while I was praying in the temple, I fell into a trance [18] and saw Jesus[f] saying to me, 'Hurry and get out of Jerusalem quickly, because they will not accept your testimony about me.' [19] And I said, 'Lord, they themselves know that in every synagogue I imprisoned and beat those who believed in you. [20] And while the blood of your witness Stephen was shed, I myself was standing by, approving and keeping the coats of those who killed him.' [21] Then he said to me, 'Go, for I will send you far away to the Gentiles.'"

Paul and the Roman Tribune

22 Up to this point they listened to him, but then they shouted, "Away with such a fellow from the earth! For he should not be allowed to live." [23] And while they were shouting, throwing off their cloaks, and tossing dust into the air, [24] the tribune directed that he was to be brought into the barracks, and ordered him to be examined by flogging, to find out the reason for this outcry against him. [25] But when they had tied him up with thongs,[g] Paul said to the centurion who was standing by, "Is it legal for you to flog a Roman citizen who is uncondemned?" [26] When the centurion heard that, he went to the tribune and said to him, "What are you

---

σαι τὰς ἁμαρτίας σου, ἐπικαλεσάμενος τὸ
away the sins of thee, invoking the

ὄνομα αὐτοῦ. 17 Ἐγένετο δέ μοι ὑποστρέ-
name of him. And it happened to me having

ψαντι εἰς Ἰερουσαλὴμ καὶ προσευχομένου
returned to Jerusalem and praying
                                        = as I was praying

μου ἐν τῷ ἱερῷ γενέσθαι με ἐν ἐκστάσει,
me[a] in the temple to become me[b] in an ecstasy,
                                = I became

18 καὶ ἰδεῖν αὐτόν λέγοντά μοι· σπεῦσον
and to see[b] him saying to me; Haste
   = I saw

καὶ ἔξελθε ἐν τάχει ἐξ Ἰερουσαλήμ,
and go forth quickly out of Jerusalem,

διότι οὐ παραδέξονταί σου μαρτυρίαν
because they will not receive of thee witness

περὶ ἐμοῦ. 19 κἀγὼ εἶπον· κύριε, αὐτοὶ
concerning me. And I said: Lord, they

ἐπίστανται ὅτι ἐγὼ ἤμην φυλακίζων καὶ
understand that I was imprisoning and

δέρων κατὰ τὰς συναγωγὰς τοὺς πιστεύον-
beating throughout the synagogues the [ones] believ-

τας ἐπὶ σέ· 20 καὶ ὅτε ἐξεχύννετο τὸ αἷμα
ing on thee; and when was being shed the blood

Στεφάνου τοῦ μάρτυρός σου, καὶ αὐτὸς
of Stephen the witness of thee, even [my]self

ἤμην ἐφεστὼς καὶ συνευδοκῶν καὶ
I was standing by and consenting and

φυλάσσων τὰ ἱμάτια τῶν ἀναιρούντων
keeping the garments of the [ones] killing

αὐτόν. 21 καὶ εἶπεν πρός με· πορεύου,
him. And he said to me: Go,

ὅτι ἐγὼ εἰς ἔθνη μακρὰν ἐξαποστελῶ σε.
because I to nations afar will send forth thee.

22 Ἤκουον δὲ αὐτοῦ ἄχρι τούτου τοῦ
And they heard And him as far as to this

λόγου, καὶ ἐπῆραν τὴν φωνὴν αὐτῶν
word, and lifted up the voice of them

λέγοντες· αἶρε ἀπὸ τῆς γῆς τὸν τοιοῦτον·
saying: Take from the earth such a man;

οὐ γὰρ καθῆκεν αὐτὸν ζῆν. 23 κραυγαζόν-
for not it is fitting him to live. And shout-

των τε αὐτῶν καὶ ῥιπτούντων τὰ ἱμάτια
ing them and tearing[a] the(ir) garments
 = as they shouted and tore

καὶ κονιορτὸν βαλλόντων εἰς τὸν ἀέρα,
and [2]dust [1]throwing[a] in the air,
      = threw dust

24 ἐκέλευσεν ὁ χιλίαρχος εἰσάγεσθαι αὐτὸν
commanded the chiliarch to be brought in him

εἰς τὴν παρεμβολήν, εἴπας μάστιξιν
into the fort, bidding [a]with scourges

ἀνετάζεσθαι αὐτόν, ἵνα ἐπιγνῷ δι’ ἣν
[a]to be examined [1]him, that he might fully know for what

αἰτίαν οὕτως ἐπεφώνουν αὐτῷ. 25 ὡς δὲ
crime thus they were calling against him. But as

προέτειναν αὐτὸν τοῖς ἱμᾶσιν, εἶπεν πρὸς
they stretched him with the thongs, [a]said [a]to
forward

τὸν ἑστῶτα ἑκατόνταρχον ὁ Παῦλος· εἰ
[a]the [a]standing [by] [a]centurion [a]Paul: [1]If

ἄνθρωπον Ῥωμαῖον καὶ ἀκατάκριτον ἔξεστιν
a man [a]a Roman [a]and [a]uncondemned [a]it is lawful

ὑμῖν μαστίζειν; 26 ἀκούσας δὲ ὁ ἑκατον-
[1]for you [a]to scourge? And [a]hearing [1]the [a]cen-

τάρχης προσελθὼν τῷ χιλιάρχῳ ἀπήγγειλεν
turion approaching to the chiliarch reported

---

sins away, calling on his name.'

[17] "When I returned to Jerusalem and was praying at the temple, I fell into a trance [18] and saw the Lord speaking. 'Quick!' he said to me. 'Leave Jerusalem immediately, because they will not accept your testimony about me.'

[19] "'Lord,' I replied, 'these men know that I went from one synagogue to another to imprison and beat those who believe in you. [20] And when the blood of your martyr[s] Stephen was shed, I stood there giving my approval and guarding the clothes of those who were killing him.'

[21] "Then the Lord said to me, 'Go; I will send you far away to the Gentiles.'"

Paul the Roman Citizen

[22] The crowd listened to Paul until he said this. Then they raised their voices and shouted, "Rid the earth of him! He's not fit to live!"

[23] As they were shouting and throwing off their cloaks and flinging dust into the air, [24] the commander ordered Paul to be taken into the barracks. He directed that he be flogged and questioned in order to find out why the people were shouting at him like this. [25] As they stretched him out to flog him, Paul said to the centurion standing there, "Is it legal for you to flog a Roman citizen who hasn't even been found guilty?"

[26] When the centurion heard this, he went to the commander and reported

---

about to do? This man is a Roman citizen." 27 The tribune came and asked Paul,f "Tell me, are you a Roman citizen?" And he said, "Yes." 28 The tribune answered, "It cost me a large sum of money to get my citizenship." Paul said, "But I was born a citizen." 29 Immediately those who were about to examine him drew back from him; and the tribune also was afraid, for he realized that Paul was a Roman citizen and that he had bound him.

Paul before the Council

30 Since he wanted to find out what Paulh was being accused of by the Jews, the next day he released him and ordered the chief priests and the entire council to meet. He brought Paul down and had him stand before them.

Chapter 23

WHILE Paul was looking intently at the council he said, "Brothers,i up to this day I have lived my life with a clear conscience before God." 2 Then the high priest Ananias ordered those standing near him to strike him on the mouth. 3 At this Paul said to him, "God will strike you, you whitewashed wall! Are you sitting there to judge me according to the law, and yet in violation of the law you order me to be struck?" 4 Those standing nearby said, "Do you dare to insult God's high priest?" 5 And Paul said, "I did not realize, brothers, that he was high priest; for it is written, 'You shall not speak evil of a leader of your people.'" 6 When Paul noticed that some were Sadducees

---

λέγων· τί μέλλεις ποιεῖν; ὁ γὰρ ἄνθρωπος
saying: What art thou about to do? - for ¹man

οὗτος Ῥωμαῖός ἐστιν. 27 προσελθὼν δὲ
¹this ⁴a Roman ²is. And approaching

ὁ χιλίαρχος εἶπεν αὐτῷ· λέγε μοι, σὺ
the chiliarch said to him: Tell me, thou

Ῥωμαῖος εἶ; ὁ δὲ ἔφη· ναί. 28 ἀπεκρίθη
a Roman art? And he said: Yes. answered

δὲ ὁ χιλίαρχος· ἐγὼ πολλοῦ κεφαλαίου
And the chiliarch: ¹I ²of(for) ³sum [of money] much(great)

τὴν πολιτείαν ταύτην ἐκτησάμην. ὁ δὲ
⁴this ⁵citizenship ⁶acquired. - So

Παῦλος ἔφη· ἐγὼ δὲ καὶ γεγέννημαι.
Paul said: But I indeed have been born.

29 εὐθέως οὖν ἀπέστησαν ἀπ' αὐτοῦ οἱ
Immediately therefore ⁵stood away ⁶from ⁷him ¹the [ones]

μέλλοντες αὐτὸν ἀνετάζειν· καὶ ὁ χιλίαρχος
²being about ⁴him ³to examine; ⁶also ⁵the ⁷chiliarch

δὲ ἐφοβήθη ἐπιγνοὺς ὅτι Ῥωμαῖός ἐστιν
⁸and feared fully knowing that a Roman he is(was)

καὶ ὅτι αὐτὸν ἦν δεδεκώς.
and that ¹him ¹he was ²having bound.

30 Τῇ δὲ ἐπαύριον βουλόμενος γνῶναι τὸ
And on the morrow being minded to know the

ἀσφαλές, τὸ τί κατηγορεῖται ὑπὸ τῶν
certain thing, - why he was accused by the

Ἰουδαίων, ἔλυσεν αὐτόν, καὶ ἐκέλευσεν
Jews, he released him, and commanded

συνελθεῖν τοὺς ἀρχιερεῖς καὶ πᾶν τὸ
to come together the chief priests and all the

συνέδριον, καὶ καταγαγὼν τὸν Παῦλον
council, and having brought down - Paul

ἔστησεν εἰς αὐτούς. 23 ἀτενίσας δὲ
set [him] among them. And ¹gazing

ὁ Παῦλος τῷ συνεδρίῳ εἶπεν· ἄνδρες
- ¹Paul at the council said: Men

ἀδελφοί, ἐγὼ πάσῃ συνειδήσει ἀγαθῇ
brothers, I in all conscience good

πεπολίτευμαι τῷ θεῷ ἄχρι ταύτης τῆς
have lived - to God until this the

ἡμέρας. 2 ὁ δὲ ἀρχιερεὺς Ἀνανίας
day. And the high priest Ananias

ἐπέταξεν τοῖς παρεστῶσιν αὐτῷ τύπτειν
gave order to the [ones] standing by him to strike

αὐτοῦ τὸ στόμα. 3 τότε ὁ Παῦλος πρὸς
of him the mouth. Then - Paul to

αὐτὸν εἶπεν· τύπτειν σε μέλλει ὁ θεός,
him said: ³To strike ⁴thee ²is about - ¹God,

τοῖχε κεκονιαμένε· καὶ σὺ κάθῃ κρίνων
wall having been whitened; and thou sittest judging

με κατὰ τὸν νόμον, καὶ παρανομῶν
me according to the law, and contravening law

κελεύεις με τύπτεσθαι; 4 οἱ δὲ παρεστῶτες
commandest me to be struck? And the [ones] standing by

εἶπαν· τὸν ἀρχιερέα τοῦ θεοῦ λοιδορεῖς;
said: The high priest - of God revilest thou?

5 ἔφη τε ὁ Παῦλος· οὐκ ᾔδειν, ἀδελφοί,
And said - Paul: I did not know, brothers,

ὅτι ἐστὶν ἀρχιερεύς· γέγραπται γὰρ ὅτι
that he is high priest; for it has been written[,] -

ἄρχοντα τοῦ λαοῦ σου οὐκ ἐρεῖς κακῶς.
A ruler of the people of thee thou shalt not speak evilly.

6 γνοὺς δὲ ὁ Παῦλος ὅτι τὸ ἓν μέρος
And knowing - Paul that the one part

---

it. "What are you going to do?" he asked. "This man is a Roman citizen."
27 The commander went to Paul and asked, "Tell me, are you a Roman citizen?"
"Yes, I am," he answered.
28 Then the commander said, "I had to pay a big price for my citizenship."
"But I was born a citizen," Paul replied.
29 Those who were about to question him withdrew immediately. The commander himself was alarmed when he realized that he had put Paul, a Roman citizen, in chains.

Before the Sanhedrin

30 The next day, since the commander wanted to find out exactly why Paul was being accused by the Jews, he released him and ordered the chief priests and all the Sanhedrin to assemble. Then he brought Paul and had him stand before them.

Chapter 23

PAUL looked straight at the Sanhedrin and said, "My brothers, I have fulfilled my duty to God in all good conscience to this day." 2 At this the high priest Ananias ordered those standing near Paul to strike him on the mouth. 3 Then Paul said to him, "God will strike you, you whitewashed wall! You sit there to judge me according to the law, yet you yourself violate the law by commanding that I be struck!" 4 Those who were standing near Paul said, "You dare to insult God's high priest?" 5 Paul replied, "Brothers, I did not realize that he was the high priest; for it is written: 'Do not speak evil about the ruler of your people.'j" 6 Then Paul, knowing that some of them were Saddu-

---

h Gk he
i Gk Men, brothers
j 5 Exodus 22:28

and others were Pharisees, he called out in the council, "Brothers, I am a Pharisee, a son of Pharisees. I am on trial concerning the hope of the resurrection[j] of the dead." 7 When he said this, a dissension began between the Pharisees and the Sadducees, and the assembly was divided. 8 (The Sadducees say that there is no resurrection, or angel, or spirit; but the Pharisees acknowledge all three.) 9 Then a great clamor arose, and certain scribes of the Pharisees' group stood up and contended, "We find nothing wrong with this man. What if a spirit or an angel has spoken to him?" 10 When the dissension became violent, the tribune, fearing that they would tear Paul to pieces, ordered the soldiers to go down, take him by force, and bring him into the barracks.

11 That night the Lord stood near him and said, "Keep up your courage! For just as you have testified for me in Jerusalem, so you must bear witness also in Rome."

The Plot to Kill Paul

12 In the morning the Jews joined in a conspiracy and bound themselves by an oath neither to eat nor drink until they had killed Paul. 13 There were more than forty who joined in this conspiracy. 14 They went to the chief priests and elders and said, "We have strictly bound ourselves by an oath to taste

---

ἐστὶν Σαδδουκαίων τὸ δὲ ἕτερον Φαρισαίων
is(was) of Sadducees but the other of Pharisees

ἔκραζεν ἐν τῷ συνεδρίῳ· ἄνδρες ἀδελφοί,
cried out in the council: Men brothers,

ἐγὼ Φαρισαῖός εἰμι, υἱὸς Φαρισαίων· περὶ
I a Pharisee am, a son of Pharisees; concerning

ἐλπίδος καὶ ἀναστάσεως νεκρῶν κρίνομαι.
hope and resurrection of dead ones I am being judged.

7 τοῦτο δὲ αὐτοῦ λαλοῦντος ἐγένετο
And this him saying[a] there was
=as he said this

στάσις τῶν Φαρισαίων καὶ Σαδδουκαίων,
a discord of the Pharisees and Sadducees,

καὶ ἐσχίσθη τὸ πλῆθος. 8 Σαδδουκαῖοι
and was divided the multitude. Sadducees

γὰρ λέγουσιν μὴ εἶναι ἀνάστασιν μήτε
For say not to be a resurrection nor

ἄγγελον μήτε πνεῦμα, Φαρισαῖοι δὲ
angel nor spirit, but Pharisees

ὁμολογοῦσιν τὰ ἀμφότερα. 9 ἐγένετο δὲ
confess - both. And there was

κραυγὴ μεγάλη, καὶ ἀναστάντες τινὲς
cry a great, and rising up some

τῶν γραμματέων τοῦ μέρους τῶν Φαρισαίων
of the scribes of the part of the Pharisees

διεμάχοντο λέγοντες· οὐδὲν κακὸν εὑρίσκομεν
strove saying: Nothing evil we find

ἐν τῷ ἀνθρώπῳ τούτῳ· εἰ δὲ πνεῦμα
in this man; and if [a] spirit

ἐλάλησεν αὐτῷ ἢ ἄγγελος —. 10 Πολλῆς δὲ
[b]spoke [c]to him [a]or [a]an angel —. And much

γινομένης στάσεως φοβηθεὶς ὁ χιλίαρχος
arising discord[a] [b]fearing [a]the [c]chiliarch
=when much[b] discord arose

μὴ διασπασθῇ ὁ Παῦλος ὑπ' αὐτῶν,
[a]lest [b]should be - [c]Paul by them,
torn asunder

ἐκέλευσεν τὸ στράτευμα καταβὰν ἁρπάσαι
commanded the soldiery coming down to seize

αὐτὸν ἐκ μέσου αὐτῶν ἄγειν τε εἰς
him out of [the] midst of them and to bring [him] into

τὴν παρεμβολήν. 11 Τῇ δὲ ἐπιούσῃ
the fort. And in the following

νυκτὶ ἐπιστὰς αὐτῷ ὁ κύριος εἶπεν·
night [a]coming on [b]to him [a]the [b]Lord said:

θάρσει· ὡς γὰρ διεμαρτύρω τὰ περὶ
Be of good for as thou didst the concerning
courage; solemnly witness things

ἐμοῦ εἰς Ἰερουσαλήμ, οὕτω σε· δεῖ καὶ
me in Jerusalem, so thee it behoves also

εἰς Ῥώμην μαρτυρῆσαι. 12 Γενομένης δὲ
in Rome to witness. And becoming

ἡμέρας ποιήσαντες συστροφὴν οἱ Ἰουδαῖοι
day[a] [b]making [c]a conspiracy [a]the [b]Jews
=when it became day

ἀνεθεμάτισαν ἑαυτούς, λέγοντες μήτε φαγεῖν
cursed themselves, saying neither to eat

μήτε πεῖν ἕως οὗ ἀποκτείνωσιν τὸν
nor to drink until they should kill -

Παῦλον. 13 ἦσαν δὲ πλείους τεσσεράκοντα
Paul. And there were more [than] forty

οἱ ταύτην τὴν συνωμοσίαν ποιησάμενοι·
the [ones] this - plot making;

14 οἵτινες προσελθόντες τοῖς ἀρχιερεῦσιν
who approaching to the chief priests

καὶ τοῖς πρεσβυτέροις εἶπαν· ἀναθέματι
and to the elders said: With a curse

---

cees and the others Pharisees, called out in the Sanhedrin, "My brothers, I am a Pharisee, the son of a Pharisee. I stand on trial because of my hope in the resurrection of the dead." 7 When he said this, a dispute broke out between the Pharisees and the Sadducees, and the assembly was divided. 8 (The Sadducees say that there is no resurrection, and that there are neither angels nor spirits, but the Pharisees acknowledge them all.)

9 There was a great uproar, and some of the teachers of the law who were Pharisees stood up and argued vigorously. "We find nothing wrong with this man," they said. "What if a spirit or an angel has spoken to him?" 10 The dispute became so violent that the commander was afraid Paul would be torn to pieces by them. He ordered the troops to go down and take him away from them by force and bring him into the barracks.

11 The following night the Lord stood near Paul and said, "Take courage! As you have testified about me in Jerusalem, so you must also testify in Rome."

The Plot to Kill Paul

12 The next morning the Jews formed a conspiracy and bound themselves with an oath not to eat or drink until they had killed Paul. 13 More than forty men were involved in this plot. 14 They went to the chief priests and elders and said, "We have taken a solemn oath not to eat anything un-

---

[j] Gk concerning hope and resurrection

no food until we have killed Paul. 15 Now then, you and the council must notify the tribune to bring him down to you, on the pretext that you want to make a more thorough examination of his case. And we are ready to do away with him before he arrives."

16 Now the son of Paul's sister heard about the ambush; so he went and gained entrance to the barracks and told Paul. 17 Paul called one of the centurions and said, "Take this young man to the tribune, for he has something to report to him." 18 So he took him, brought him to the tribune, and said, "The prisoner Paul called me and asked me to bring this young man to you; he has something to tell you." 19 The tribune took him by the hand, drew him aside privately, and asked, "What is it that you have to report to me?" 20 He answered, "The Jews have agreed to ask you to bring Paul down to the council tomorrow, as though they were going to inquire more thoroughly into his case. 21 But do not be persuaded by them, for more than forty of their men are lying in ambush for him. They have bound themselves by an oath neither to eat nor drink until they kill him. They are ready now and are waiting for your consent." 22 So the tribune dismissed the

---

ἀνεθεματίσαμεν ἑαυτοὺς μηδενὸς γεύσασθαι
we cursed ourselves of nothing to taste

ἕως οὗ ἀποκτείνωμεν τὸν Παῦλον. 15 νῦν
until we may kill - Paul. Now

οὖν ὑμεῖς ἐμφανίσατε τῷ χιλιάρχῳ σὺν
therefore ²ye ¹inform the chiliarch with

τῷ συνεδρίῳ ὅπως καταγάγῃ αὐτὸν εἰς
the council so as he may bring down him to

ὑμᾶς ὡς μέλλοντας διαγινώσκειν ἀκριβέστε-
you as intending to ascertain exactly more accurate-

ρον τὰ περὶ αὐτοῦ· ἡμεῖς δὲ πρὸ τοῦ
ly the things concerning him; and we before -

ἐγγίσαι αὐτὸν ἕτοιμοί ἐσμεν τοῦ ἀνελεῖν
to draw near him[b] ready are - to kill[d]
= he draws near

αὐτόν. 16 Ἀκούσας δὲ ὁ υἱὸς τῆς ἀδελφῆς
him. And ⁴hearing ¹the ²son ³of the ⁴sister

Παύλου τὴν ἐνέδραν, παραγενόμενος καὶ
⁵of Paul the treachery, coming and

εἰσελθὼν εἰς τὴν παρεμβολὴν ἀπήγγειλεν
entering into the fort reported

τῷ Παύλῳ. 17 προσκαλεσάμενος δὲ ὁ
- to Paul. And ²calling to [him]

Παῦλος ἕνα τῶν ἑκατονταρχῶν ἔφη· τὸν
¹Paul one of the centurions said: the

νεανίαν τοῦτον ἄπαγε πρὸς τὸν χιλίαρχον,
³youth ²this ¹Bring up to the chiliarch,

ἔχει γὰρ ἀπαγγειλαί τι αὐτῷ. 18 ὁ
for ¹he has ³to report ²something ⁴to him. He

μὲν οὖν παραλαβὼν αὐτὸν ἤγαγεν πρὸς
- therefore taking ²him ¹brought to

τὸν χιλίαρχον καὶ φησίν· ὁ δέσμιος
the chiliarch and says: The prisoner

Παῦλος προσκαλεσάμενός με ἠρώτησεν
Paul calling to [him] me asked

τοῦτον τὸν νεανίσκον ἀγαγεῖν πρὸς σέ,
²this ¹young man ¹to bring to thee,

ἔχοντά τι λαλῆσαί σοι. 19 ἐπιλαβόμενος
having something to tell thee. ²laying hold

δὲ τῆς χειρὸς αὐτοῦ ὁ χιλίαρχος καὶ
And ⁴of the ³hand ²of him ¹the ⁵chiliarch and

ἀναχωρήσας κατ᾽ ἰδίαν ἐπυνθάνετο· τί
retiring ²privately ¹inquired: What

ἐστιν ὃ ἔχεις ἀπαγγειλαί μοι; 20 εἶπεν
is it which thou hast to report to me? he said[,]

δὲ ὅτι οἱ Ἰουδαῖοι συνέθεντο τοῦ ἐρωτῆσαί
And - The Jews agreed - to ask[d]

σε ὅπως αὔριον τὸν Παῦλον καταγάγῃς
thee so as to-morrow - ¹Paul ¹thou shouldest bring down

εἰς τὸ συνέδριον ὡς μέλλον τι ἀκριβέστερον
to the council as intending some- more accurately thing

πυνθάνεσθαι περὶ αὐτοῦ. 21 σὺ οὖν μὴ
to inquire concerning him. Thou therefore not

πεισθῇς αὐτοῖς· ἐνεδρεύουσιν γὰρ αὐτὸν
be persuaded by them; for there lie in wait for him

ἐξ αὐτῶν ἄνδρες πλείους τεσσεράκοντα,
of them ⁴men ¹more ²[than] ³forty,

οἵτινες ἀνεθεμάτισαν ἑαυτοὺς μήτε φαγεῖν
who cursed themselves neither to eat

μήτε πεῖν ἕως οὗ ἀνέλωσιν αὐτόν, καὶ νῦν
nor to drink until they kill him, and now

εἰσιν ἕτοιμοι προσδεχόμενοι τὴν ἀπὸ σοῦ
they are ⸱ ready awaiting ¹the ³from ⁴thee

ἐπαγγελίαν. 22 ὁ μὲν οὖν χιλίαρχος
²promise. the - Therefore chiliarch

---

til we have killed Paul. 15 Now then, you and the Sanhedrin petition the commander to bring him before you on the pretext of wanting more accurate information about his case. We are ready to kill him before he gets here."

16 But when the son of Paul's sister heard of this plot, he went into the barracks and told Paul.

17 Then Paul called one of the centurions and said, "Take this young man to the commander; he has something to tell him."

18 So he took him to the commander.

The centurion said, "Paul, the prisoner, sent for me and asked me to bring this young man to you because he has something to tell you."

19 The commander took the young man by the hand, drew him aside and asked, "What is it you want to tell me?"

20 He said: "The Jews have agreed to ask you to bring Paul before the Sanhedrin tomorrow on the pretext of wanting more accurate information about him. 21 Don't give in to them, because more than forty of them are waiting in ambush for him. They have taken an oath not to eat or drink until they have killed him. They are ready now, waiting for your consent to their request."

22 The commander dis-

young man, ordering him, "Tell no one that you have informed me of this."

Paul Sent to Felix the Governor

23 Then he summoned two of the centurions and said, "Get ready to leave by nine o'clock tonight for Caesarea with two hundred soldiers, seventy horsemen, and two hundred spearmen. 24 Also provide mounts for Paul to ride, and take him safely to Felix the governor." 25 He wrote a letter to this effect:
26 "Claudius Lysias to his Excellency the governor Felix, greetings. 27 This man was seized by the Jews and was about to be killed by them, but when I had learned that he was a Roman citizen, I came with the guard and rescued him. 28 Since I wanted to know the charge for which they accused him, I had him brought to their council. 29 I found that he was accused concerning questions of their law, but was charged with nothing deserving death or imprisonment. 30 When I was informed that there would be a plot against the man, I sent him to you at once, ordering his accusers also to state before you what they have against him. *"*

31 So the soldiers, according to their instructions, took Paul and brought him during the night to Antipatris. 32 The next day they let the horsemen go on with him, while they returned to the barracks. 33 When they came to Caesarea and delivered

---

ἀπέλυσε τὸν νεανίσκον, παραγγείλας μηδενὶ
dismissed the young man, charging [him] to no one

ἐκλαλῆσαι ὅτι ταῦτα ἐνεφάνισας πρὸς ἐμέ.
to divulge that these things thou reportedst to me.

23 Καὶ προσκαλεσάμενός τινας δύο τῶν
And calling to [him] a certain two of the

ἑκατονταρχῶν εἶπεν· ἑτοιμάσατε στρατιώτας
centurions he said: Prepare ye soldiers

διακοσίους ὅπως πορευθῶσιν ἕως Καισαρείας,
two hundred so as they may go as far as Caesarea,

καὶ ἱππεῖς ἑβδομήκοντα καὶ δεξιολάβους
and horsemen seventy and spearmen

διακοσίους, ἀπὸ τρίτης ὥρας τῆς νυκτός,
two hundred, from third hour of the night,

24 κτήνη τε παραστῆσαι, ἵνα ἐπιβιβάσαντες
and beasts to stand by, that putting on

τὸν Παῦλον διασώσωσι πρὸς Φήλικα τὸν
— Paul they may bring to Felix the

ἡγεμόνα, 25 γράψας ἐπιστολὴν ἔχουσαν
[him] safely governor, writing a letter having

τὸν τύπον τοῦτον· 26 Κλαύδιος Λυσίας τῷ
this pattern: Claudius Lysias to the

κρατίστῳ ἡγεμόνι Φήλικι χαίρειν. 27 Τὸν
most excellent governor Felix greeting.

ἄνδρα τοῦτον συλλημφθέντα ὑπὸ τῶν
man This having been arrested by the

Ἰουδαίων καὶ μέλλοντα ἀναιρεῖσθαι ὑπ᾽
Jews and being about to be killed by

αὐτῶν ἐπιστὰς σὺν τῷ στρατεύματι
them coming on with the soldiery
[the scene]

ἐξειλάμην, μαθὼν ὅτι Ῥωμαῖός ἐστιν·
I rescued, having learned that a Roman he is;

28 βουλόμενός τε ἐπιγνῶναι τὴν αἰτίαν
and being minded to know fully the cause

δι᾽ ἣν ἐνεκάλουν αὐτῷ, κατήγαγον εἰς
on ac- which they were him, I brought to
count of accusing [him] down

τὸ συνέδριον αὐτῶν· 29 ὃν εὗρον ἐγκαλούμενον
the council of them; whom I found being accused

περὶ ζητημάτων τοῦ νόμου αὐτῶν, μηδὲν
about questions of the law of them, ²nothing

δὲ ἄξιον θανάτου ἢ δεσμῶν ἔχοντα
¹but ³worthy ⁴of death ⁵or ⁶of bonds ²having

ἔγκλημα. 30 μηνυθείσης δέ μοι ἐπιβουλῆς
⁴charge. And being revealed to me a plot
=when it was revealed to me that there was a plot

εἰς τὸν ἄνδρα ἔσεσθαι, ἐξαυτῆς ἔπεμψα
against the man to be, at once I sent

πρὸς σέ, παραγγείλας καὶ τοῖς κατηγόροις
to thee, commanding also the accusers

λέγειν πρὸς αὐτὸν ἐπὶ σοῦ. 31 Οἱ μὲν
to say to him before thee. the —

οὖν στρατιῶται κατὰ τὸ διατεταγμένον
Therefore soldiers according the having been
to thing appointed

αὐτοῖς ἀναλαβόντες τὸν Παῦλον ἤγαγον
them taking up — Paul brought

διὰ νυκτὸς εἰς τὴν Ἀντιπατρίδα· 32 τῇ δὲ
through [the] night to — Antipatris; and on the
(during)

ἐπαύριον ἐάσαντες τοὺς ἱππεῖς ἀπέρχεσθαι
morrow allowing the horsemen to depart

σὺν αὐτῷ, ὑπέστρεψαν εἰς τὴν παρεμβολήν·
with him, they returned to the fort;

33 οἵτινες εἰσελθόντες εἰς τὴν Καισάρειαν
who entering into — Caesarea

---

missed the young man and cautioned him, "Don't tell anyone that you have reported this to me."

Paul Transferred to Caesarea

23 Then he called two of his centurions and ordered them, "Get ready a detachment of two hundred soldiers, seventy horsemen and two hundred spearmen *u* to go to Caesarea at nine tonight. 24 Provide mounts for Paul so that he may be taken safely to Governor Felix."
25 He wrote a letter as follows:

26 Claudius Lysias,

To His Excellency, Governor Felix:

Greetings.

27 This man was seized by the Jews and they were about to kill him, but I came with my troops and rescued him, for I had learned that he is a Roman citizen. 28 I wanted to know why they were accusing him, so I brought him to their Sanhedrin. 29 I found that the accusation had to do with questions about their law, but there was no charge against him that deserved death or imprisonment. 30 When I was informed of a plot to be carried out against the man, I sent him to you at once. I also ordered his accusers to present to you their case against him.

31 So the soldiers, carrying out their orders, took Paul with them during the night and brought him as far as Antipatris. 32 The next day they let the cavalry go on with him, while they returned to the barracks. 33 When the cavalry arrived in Caesarea, they

---

k Other ancient authorities add *Farewell*

u 23 The meaning of the Greek for this word is uncertain.

the letter to the governor, they presented Paul also before him. [34]On reading the letter, he asked what province he belonged to, and when he learned that he was from Cilicia, [35]he said, "I will give you a hearing when your accusers arrive." Then he ordered that he be kept under guard in Herod's headquarters. [l]

καὶ ἀναδόντες τὴν ἐπιστολὴν τῷ ἡγεμόνι,
and handing over the letter to the governor,

παρέστησαν καὶ τὸν Παῦλον αὐτῷ.
presented also – Paul to him.

[34] ἀναγνοὺς δὲ καὶ ἐπερωτήσας ἐκ ποίας
And having read and asking of what

ἐπαρχείας ἐστίν, καὶ πυθόμενος ὅτι ἀπὸ
province he is(was), and learning[,] – From

Κιλικίας, [35] διακούσομαί σου, ἔφη, ὅταν
Cilicia, I will hear thee, he said, when

καὶ οἱ κατήγοροί σου παραγένωνται·
also the accusers of thee arrive;

κελεύσας ἐν τῷ πραιτωρίῳ τοῦ Ἡρώδου
commanding in the prætorium – of Herod
= that he be kept in Herod's prætorium.

φυλάσσεσθαι αὐτόν.
to be kept him.

Chapter 24

Paul before Felix at Caesarea

FIVE days later the high priest Ananias came down with some elders and an attorney, a certain Tertullus, and they reported their case against Paul to the governor. [2]When Paul[m] had been summoned, Tertullus began to accuse him, saying: "Your Excellency,[n] because of you, we have long enjoyed peace, and reforms have been made for this people because of your foresight. [3]We welcome this in every way and everywhere with utmost gratitude. [4]But, to detain you no further, I beg you to hear us briefly with your customary graciousness. [5]We have, in fact, found this man a pestilent fellow, an agitator among all the Jews throughout the world, and a ringleader of the sect of the Nazarenes.[o] [6]He even tried to profane the temple, and we seized him.[p] [8]By examining him yourself you will be able to learn from him concerning everything of which we accuse him."

[9] The Jews also joined in the charge by asserting that all this was true.

[24] Μετὰ δὲ πέντε ἡμέρας κατέβη ὁ
And after five days came down the

ἀρχιερεὺς Ἀνανίας μετὰ πρεσβυτέρων τινῶν
high priest Ananias with elders some

καὶ ῥήτορος Τερτύλλου τινός, οἵτινες
and an orator Tertullus one, who

ἐνεφάνισαν τῷ ἡγεμόνι κατὰ τοῦ Παύλου.
informed the governor against – Paul.

[2] κληθέντος δὲ [αὐτοῦ] ἤρξατο κατηγορεῖν
And being called him[a] [1]began [2]to accuse
= when he was called

ὁ Τέρτυλλος λέγων· πολλῆς εἰρήνης
– [1]Tertullus saying: Much peace

τυγχάνοντες διὰ σοῦ καὶ διορθωμάτων
obtaining through thee and reforms

γινομένων τῷ ἔθνει τούτῳ διὰ τῆς σῆς
coming to this nation through thy

προνοίας, [3] πάντῃ τε καὶ πανταχοῦ
forethought, both in everything and everywhere

ἀποδεχόμεθα, κράτιστε Φῆλιξ, μετὰ πάσης
we welcome, most excellent Felix, with all

εὐχαριστίας. [4] ἵνα δὲ μὴ ἐπὶ πλεῖόν
thankfulness. But that [1]not [4]more

σε ἐγκόπτω, παρακαλῶ ἀκοῦσαί σε ἡμῶν
[3]thee [1]I hinder, I beseech [5]to hear [2]thee us

συντόμως τῇ σῇ ἐπιεικείᾳ. [5] εὑρόντες γὰρ
briefly – in thy forbearance. For having found

τὸν ἄνδρα τοῦτον λοιμὸν καὶ κινοῦντα
this man pestilent and moving

στάσεις πᾶσιν τοῖς Ἰουδαίοις τοῖς κατὰ
seditions [among] all the Jews – throughout

τὴν οἰκουμένην πρωτοστάτην τε τῆς τῶν
the inhabited [earth] and a ringleader of the [5]of the

Ναζωραίων αἱρέσεως, [6] ὅς καὶ τὸ ἱερὸν
[3]Nazarenes [1]sect, who also [2]the [4]temple

ἐπείρασεν βεβηλῶσαι, ὃν καὶ ἐκρατήσαμεν,
[1]attempted [2]to profane, whom also we laid hold of,‡

[8] παρ' οὗ δυνήσῃ αὐτὸς ἀνακρίνας
from whom thou wilt be able [thy]self [1]having examined

περὶ πάντων τούτων ἐπιγνῶναι ὧν ἡμεῖς
[2]concerning [3]all [4]these things [1]to know fully of which we

κατηγοροῦμεν αὐτοῦ. [9] συνεπέθεντο δὲ
accuse him. And [4]joined in

καὶ οἱ Ἰουδαῖοι φάσκοντες ταῦτα οὕτως
[2]also [1]the [3]Jews alleging these things thus

‡ Verse 7 omitted by Nestle; *cf.* NIV footnote.

delivered the letter to the governor and handed Paul over to him. [34]The governor read the letter and asked what province he was from. Learning that he was from Cilicia, [35]he said, "I will hear your case when your accusers get here." Then he ordered that Paul be kept under guard in Herod's palace.

Chapter 24

The Trial Before Felix

FIVE days later the high priest Ananias went down to Caesarea with some of the elders and a lawyer named Tertullus, and they brought their charges against Paul before the governor. [2]When Paul was called in, Tertullus presented his case before Felix: "We have enjoyed a long period of peace under you, and your foresight has brought about reforms in this nation. [3]Everywhere and in every way, most excellent Felix, we acknowledge this with profound gratitude. [4]But in order not to weary you further, I would request that you be kind enough to hear us briefly.

[5]"We have found this man to be a troublemaker, stirring up riots among the Jews all over the world. He is a ringleader of the Nazarene sect [6]and even tried to desecrate the temple; so we seized him. [8]By[v] examining him yourself you will be able to learn the truth about all these charges we are bringing against him."

[9]The Jews joined in the accusation, asserting that these things were true.

Paul's Defense before Felix

10 When the governor motioned to him to speak, Paul replied: "I cheerfully make my defense, knowing that for many years you have been a judge over this nation. 11 As you can find out, it is not more than twelve days since I went up to worship in Jerusalem. 12 They did not find me disputing with anyone in the temple or stirring up a crowd either in the synagogues or throughout the city. 13 Neither can they prove to you the charge that they now bring against me. 14 But this I admit to you, that according to the Way, which they call a sect, I worship the God of our ancestors, believing everything laid down according to the law or written in the prophets. 15 I have a hope in God—a hope that they themselves also accept—that there will be a resurrection of both[a] the righteous and the unrighteous. 16 Therefore I do my best always to have a clear conscience toward God and all people. 17 Now after some years I came to bring alms to my nation and to offer sacrifices. 18 While I was doing this, they found me in the temple, completing the rite of purification, without any crowd or disturbance. 19 But there were some Jews from Asia—they ought to be here before you to make an accusation, if they have anything against me. 20 Or let these men here tell what

---

ἔχειν. **10** Ἀπεκρίθη τε ὁ Παῦλος,
to have(be).   And answered   –   Paul,

νεύσαντος αὐτῷ τοῦ ἡγεμόνος λέγειν· ἐκ
³having   ⁴to him ¹the ²governor⁵ to speak: ⁶of
beckoned   (for)

πολλῶν ἐτῶν ὄντα σε κριτὴν τῷ ἔθνει τούτῳ
⁵many   ⁶years ³being ⁴thee ⁷a judge ⁸to ⁹this ¹⁰nation
                 (to be)

ἐπιστάμενος εὐθύμως τὰ περὶ
¹understanding ¹²cheerfully ¹³[as to] ¹⁴the things ¹⁵concerning

ἐμαυτοῦ ἀπολογοῦμαι, **11** δυναμένου σου
¹⁶myself ¹¹I defend myself,   being able   thee⁵
                                =as thou art able

ἐπιγνῶναι ὅτι οὐ πλείους εἰσίν μοι ἡμέραι
to know fully that ²not ⁴more ¹there ⁶to ⁵[than] ⁷days
                           are   me

δώδεκα ἀφ' ἧς ἀνέβην προσκυνήσων εἰς
²twelve from which I went up worshipping   in
       =since

Ἰερουσαλήμ. **12** καὶ οὔτε ἐν τῷ ἱερῷ
Jerusalem.   And neither in the temple

εὗρόν με πρός τινα διαλεγόμενον ἢ
they found me ¹with ²anyone ¹discoursing   or

ἐπίστασιν ποιοῦντα ὄχλου, οὔτε ἐν ταῖς
²collection ¹making of a crowd, neither in the

συναγωγαῖς οὔτε κατὰ τὴν πόλιν, **13** οὐδὲ
synagogues   nor throughout the city,   nor

παραστῆσαι δύναταί σοι περὶ ὧν νυνὶ
²to prove ¹are they able to thee con- [the] things now
                                cerning of which

κατηγοροῦσίν μου. **14** ὁμολογῶ δὲ τοῦτό
they accuse   me.   But I confess   this

σοι, ὅτι κατὰ τὴν ὁδὸν ἣν λέγουσιν
to thee, that according to the way which they say(call)

αἵρεσιν οὕτως λατρεύω τῷ πατρῴῳ θεῷ,
a sect   thus   I worship the ancestral God,

πιστεύων πᾶσι τοῖς κατὰ τὸν νόμον καὶ
believing all   the according the law and
                things to

τοῖς ἐν τοῖς προφήταις γεγραμμένοις,
the things in the prophets *having been* written,

15 ἐλπίδα ἔχων εἰς τὸν θεόν, ἣν καὶ
hope having toward – God, which ²also

αὐτοὶ οὗτοι προσδέχονται, ἀνάστασιν μέλ-
²[them]selves ¹these expect, a resurrection to be

λειν ἔσεσθαι δικαίων τε καὶ ἀδίκων.
about to be both of just and of unjust.

16 ἐν τούτῳ καὶ αὐτὸς ἀσκῶ ἀπρόσκοπον
By this also ²[my]self ¹I exercise ⁴a blameless

συνείδησιν ἔχειν πρὸς τὸν θεὸν καὶ τοὺς
³conscience ³to have toward – God and –

ἀνθρώπους διὰ παντός. **17** δι' ἐτῶν δὲ
men   always.   And after years

πλειόνων ἐλεημοσύνας ποιήσων εἰς τὸ
many   ²alms   ¹making(bringing) ³to ⁴the

ἔθνος μου παρεγενόμην καὶ προσφοράς,
⁵nation ⁶of me ¹I arrived ⁷and ⁸offerings,

18 ἐν αἷς εὗρόν με ἡγνισμένον ἐν τῷ
among which they found me *having been* purified in the

ἱερῷ, οὐ μετὰ ὄχλου οὐδὲ μετὰ θορύβου,
temple, not with a crowd nor with uproar,

19 τινὲς δὲ ἀπὸ τῆς Ἀσίας Ἰουδαῖοι,
but some ²from – ²Asia ¹Jews,

οὓς ἔδει ἐπὶ σοῦ παρεῖναι καὶ κατηγορεῖν
whom it be- before thee to be present and to accuse
hoved

εἴ τι ἔχοιεν πρός ἐμέ. **20** ἢ αὐτοὶ
if anything they have against me.   Or ²[them]selves

---

10 When the governor motioned for him to speak, Paul replied: "I know that for a number of years you have been a judge over this nation; so I gladly make my defense. 11 You can easily verify that no more than twelve days ago I went up to Jerusalem to worship. 12 My accusers did not find me arguing with anyone at the temple, or stirring up a crowd in the synagogues or anywhere else in the city. 13 And they cannot prove to you the charges they are now making against me. 14 However, I admit that I worship the God of our fathers as a follower of the Way, which they call a sect. I believe everything that agrees with the Law and that is written in the Prophets, 15 and I have the same hope in God as these men, that there will be a resurrection of both the righteous and the wicked. 16 So I strive always to keep my conscience clear before God and man.

17 "After an absence of several years, I came to Jerusalem to bring my people gifts for the poor and to present offerings. 18 I was ceremonially clean when they found me in the temple courts doing this. There was no crowd with me, nor was I involved in any disturbance. 19 But there are some Jews from the province of Asia, who ought to be here before you and bring charges if they have anything against me. 20 Or these who are here should

---

crime they had found when I stood before the council, 21 unless it was this one sentence that I called out while standing before them, 'It is about the resurrection of the dead that I am on trial before you today.' "

22 But Felix, who was rather well informed about the Way, adjourned the hearing with the comment, "When Lysias the tribune comes down, I will decide your case." 23 Then he ordered the centurion to keep him in custody, but to let him have some liberty and not to prevent any of his friends from taking care of his needs.

Paul Held in Custody

24 Some days later when Felix came with his wife Drusilla, who was Jewish, he sent for Paul and heard him speak concerning faith in Christ Jesus. 25 And as he discussed justice, self-control, and the coming judgment, Felix became frightened and said, "Go away for the present; when I have an opportunity, I will send for you." 26 At the same time he hoped that money would be given him by Paul, and for that reason he used to send for him very often and converse with him. 27 After two years had passed, Felix was succeeded by Porcius Festus; and since he wanted to grant the Jews a favor, Felix left Paul in prison.

οὗτοι εἰπάτωσαν τί εὗρον ἀδίκημα στάντος
²these ¹let ²say ¹what ²they found ³misdeed standing

μου ἐπὶ τοῦ συνεδρίου, 21 ἢ περὶ μιᾶς
me⁴ before the council, unless concerning ²one
=while I stood

ταύτης φωνῆς ἧς ἐκέκραξα ἐν αὐτοῖς
¹this voice which I have cried out ²among ³them

ἑστὼς ὅτι περὶ ἀναστάσεως νεκρῶν ἐγὼ
¹standing[,] - Concerning a resurrection of dead persons I

κρίνομαι σήμερον ἐφ' ὑμῶν. 22 Ἀνεβάλετο
am being judged to-day before you. ²postponed

δὲ αὐτοὺς ὁ Φῆλιξ, ἀκριβέστερον εἰδὼς
And ³them - ¹Felix, more exactly knowing

τὰ περὶ τῆς ὁδοῦ, εἴπας· ὅταν Λυσίας ὁ
the con- the way, saying: When Lysias the
things cerning

χιλίαρχος καταβῇ, διαγνώσομαι τὰ καθ'
chiliarch comes down, I will determine the things as to

ὑμᾶς· 23 διαταξάμενος τῷ ἑκατοντάρχῃ
you; commanding the centurion

τηρεῖσθαι αὐτὸν ἔχειν τε ἄνεσιν καὶ
to keep him and to have indulgence and

μηδένα κωλύειν τῶν ἰδίων αὐτοῦ ὑπηρετεῖν
²no one ¹to forbid of his own [people] to attend

αὐτῷ. 24 Μετὰ δὲ ἡμέρας τινὰς παραγενό-
him. And after days some ²arriv-

μενος ὁ Φῆλιξ σὺν Δρουσίλλῃ τῇ ἰδίᾳ
ing - ¹Felix with Drusilla the(his) own

γυναικὶ οὔσῃ Ἰουδαίᾳ μετεπέμψατο τὸν
wife being a Jewess he sent for -

Παῦλον, καὶ ἤκουσεν αὐτοῦ περὶ τῆς
Paul, and heard him about ¹the(?his)

εἰς Χριστὸν Ἰησοῦν πίστεως. 25 διαλεγομέ-
²in ⁴Christ ³Jesus ¹faith. discours-
=And as he discoursed

νου δὲ αὐτοῦ περὶ δικαιοσύνης καὶ
ing And him² concerning righteousness and

ἐγκρατείας καὶ τοῦ κρίματος τοῦ μέλλοντος
self-control and the ²judgment - ¹coming

ἔμφοβος γενόμενος ὁ Φῆλιξ ἀπεκρίθη·
afraid becoming - Felix answered:

τὸ νῦν ἔχον πορεύου, καιρὸν δὲ μεταλαβὼν
For the present† go thou, but ²time ¹taking ³later

μετακαλέσομαί σε· 26 ἅμα καὶ ἐλπίζων
I will send for thee; at the also hoping
same time

ὅτι χρήματα δοθήσεται αὐτῷ ὑπὸ τοῦ
that money will be given him by -

Παύλου· διὸ καὶ πυκνότερον αὐτὸν
Paul: wherefore also more frequently him

μεταπεμπόμενος ὡμίλει αὐτῷ. 27 Διετίας δὲ
sending for he conversed him. And two years
with

πληρωθείσης ἔλαβεν διάδοχον ὁ Φῆλιξ
being completed² ²received ³a successor - ¹Felix

Πόρκιον Φῆστον· θέλων τε χάριτα κατα-
Porcius Festus; and wishing a favour to

θέσθαι τοῖς Ἰουδαίοις ὁ Φῆλιξ κατέλιπε
show to the Jews - Felix left

τὸν Παῦλον δεδεμένον.
- Paul *having been* bound.

---

state what crime they found in me when I stood before the Sanhedrin— 21 unless it was this one thing I shouted as I stood in their presence: 'It is concerning the resurrection of the dead that I am on trial before you today.' "

22 Then Felix, who was well acquainted with the Way, adjourned the proceedings. "When Lysias the commander comes," he said, "I will decide your case." 23 He ordered the centurion to keep Paul under guard but to give him some freedom and permit his friends to take care of his needs.

24 Several days later Felix came with his wife Drusilla, who was a Jewess. He sent for Paul and listened to him as he spoke about faith in Christ Jesus. 25 As Paul discoursed on righteousness, self-control and the judgment to come, Felix was afraid and said, "That's enough for now! You may leave. When I find it convenient, I will send for you." 26 At the same time he was hoping that Paul would offer him a bribe, so he sent for him frequently and talked with him.

27 When two years had passed, Felix was succeeded by Porcius Festus, but because Felix wanted to grant a favor to the Jews, he left Paul in prison.

Chapter 25

Paul Appeals to Caesar

THREE days after Festus had arrived in the province, he went up from Caesarea to Jerusalem

---

Chapter 25

The Trial Before Festus

THREE days after arriving in the province, Festus went up from Caesarea to Jerusalem, 2 where

---

25 Φῆστος οὖν ἐπιβὰς τῇ ἐπαρχείῳ
Festus therefore having entered the province

μετὰ τρεῖς ἡμέρας ἀνέβη εἰς Ἱεροσόλυμα
after three days went up to Jerusalem

2 where the chief priests and the leaders of the Jews gave him a report against Paul. They appealed to him 3 and requested, as a favor to them against Paul,ʳ to have him transferred to Jerusalem. They were, in fact, planning an ambush to kill him along the way. 4 Festus replied that Paul was being kept at Caesarea, and that he himself intended to go there shortly. 5 "So," he said, "let those of you who have the authority come down with me, and if there is anything wrong about the man, let them accuse him."

6 After he had stayed among them not more than eight or ten days, he went down to Caesarea; the next day he took his seat on the tribunal and ordered Paul to be brought. 7 When he arrived, the Jews who had gone down from Jerusalem surrounded him, bringing many serious charges against him, which they could not prove. 8 Paul said in his defense, "I have in no way committed an offense against the law of the Jews, or against the temple, or against the emperor." 9 But Festus, wishing to do the Jews a favor, asked Paul, "Do you wish to go up to Jerusalem and be tried there before me on these charges?" 10 Paul said, "I am appealing to the emperor's tribunal; this is where I should be tried. I have done no wrong to the Jews, as you very well know. 11 Now if I am in the wrong and have committed something for which I deserve to die, I am not trying to escape death; but if there is

ἐν ὑμῖν, φησίν, δυνατοὶ συγκαταβάντες,
⁴among ⁵you, ⁶he says, ²able men going down with [me],

ἀπὸ Καισαρείας, 2 ἐνεφάνισάν τε αὐτῷ
from Caesarea, and ²informed ⁶him

οἱ ἀρχιερεῖς καὶ οἱ πρῶτοι τῶν Ἰουδαίων
¹the ²chief priests ³and ⁴the ⁵chiefs ⁶of the ⁷Jews

κατὰ τοῦ Παύλου, καὶ παρεκάλουν αὐτὸν
against - Paul, and they besought him

3 αἰτούμενοι χάριν κατ' αὐτοῦ, ὅπως μετα-
asking a favour against him, so as he might

πέμψηται αὐτὸν εἰς Ἰερουσαλήμ, ἐνέδραν
summon him to Jerusalem, a plot

ποιοῦντες ἀνελεῖν αὐτὸν κατὰ τὴν ὁδόν.
making to kill him by the way.

4 ὁ μὲν οὖν Φῆστος ἀπεκρίθη τηρεῖσθαι
- Therefore Festus answered ²to be kept

τὸν Παῦλον εἰς Καισάρειαν, ἑαυτὸν δὲ
- ¹Paul in Caesarea, and ²himself

μέλλειν ἐν τάχει ἐκπορεύεσθαι· 5 οἱ οὖν
¹to intend shortly to go forth; ²the ¹therefore

εἴ τί ἐστιν ἐν τῷ ἀνδρὶ ἄτοπον,
if anything there is in the man amiss,

κατηγορείτωσαν αὐτοῦ. 6 Διατρίψας δὲ ἐν
let them accuse him. And having stayed among

αὐτοῖς ἡμέρας οὐ πλείους ὀκτὼ ἢ δέκα,
them days not more [than] eight or ten,

καταβὰς εἰς Καισάρειαν, τῇ ἐπαύριον
going down to Caesarea, on the morrow

καθίσας ἐπὶ τοῦ βήματος ἐκέλευσεν τὸν
sitting on the tribunal he commanded -

Παῦλον ἀχθῆναι. 7 παραγενομένου δὲ
Paul to be brought. And arriving
= when he arrived

αὐτοῦ περιέστησαν αὐτὸν οἱ ἀπὸ Ἱεροσο-
himᵃ ⁵stood round ⁷him ¹the ⁴from ⁶Jeru-

λύμων καταβεβηκότες Ἰουδαῖοι, πολλὰ καὶ
salem ³having come down ²Jews, many and

βαρέα αἰτιώματα καταφέροντες, ἃ οὐκ
heavy charges bringing against [him], which not

ἴσχυον ἀποδεῖξαι, 8 τοῦ Παύλου ἀπολογου-
they were able to prove, - Paul defending him-

μένου ὅτι οὔτε εἰς τὸν νόμον τῶν
self [,]ᵃ - Neither against the law of the
= while Paul defended himself,

Ἰουδαίων οὔτε εἰς τὸ ἱερὸν οὔτε εἰς
Jews nor against the temple nor against

Καίσαρά τι ἥμαρτον. 9 ὁ Φῆστος δὲ,
Caesar anything I sinned. - But Festus,

θέλων τοῖς Ἰουδαίοις χάριν καταθέσθαι,
wishing the Jews a favour to show,

ἀποκριθεὶς τῷ Παύλῳ εἶπεν· θέλεις εἰς
answering - Paul said: Dost thou wish ²to

Ἱεροσόλυμα ἀναβὰς ἐκεῖ περὶ τούτων
³Jerusalem ¹going up ⁴there ⁵concerning ⁶these things

κριθῆναι ἐπ' ἐμοῦ; 10 εἶπεν δὲ ὁ Παῦλος·
⁵to be judged ⁶before ⁷me? And said - Paul:

ἑστὼς ἐπὶ τοῦ βήματος Καίσαρός εἰμι,
Standing before the tribunal of Caesar I am,

οὗ με δεῖ κρίνεσθαι. Ἰουδαίους οὐδὲν
where me it behoves to be judged. Jews nothing

ἠδίκηκα, ὡς καὶ σὺ κάλλιον ἐπιγινώσκεις.
I have wronged, as indeed thou very well knowest.

11 εἰ μὲν οὖν ἀδικῶ καὶ ἄξιον θανάτου
If - therefore I do wrong and worthy of death

πέπραχά τι, οὐ παραιτοῦμαι τὸ ἀποθανεῖν·
I have done anything, I do not refuse the to die;

the chief priests and Jewish leaders appeared before him and presented the charges against Paul. 3 They urgently requested Festus, as a favor to them, to have Paul transferred to Jerusalem, for they were preparing an ambush to kill him along the way. 4 Festus answered, "Paul is being held at Caesarea, and I myself am going there soon. 5 Let some of your leaders come with me and press charges against the man there, if he has done anything wrong."

6 After spending eight or ten days with them, he went down to Caesarea, and the next day he convened the court and ordered that Paul be brought before him. 7 When Paul appeared, the Jews who had come down from Jerusalem stood around him, bringing many serious charges against him, which they could not prove.

8 Then Paul made his defense: "I have done nothing wrong against the law of the Jews or against the temple or against Caesar."

9 Festus, wishing to do the Jews a favor, said to Paul, "Are you willing to go up to Jerusalem and stand trial before me there on these charges?"

10 Paul answered: "I am now standing before Caesar's court, where I ought to be tried. I have not done any wrong to the Jews, as you yourself know very well. 11 If, however, I am guilty of doing anything deserving death, I do not refuse to die. But if the

ʳ Gk him

nothing to their charges against me, no one can turn me over to them. I appeal to the emperor." 12 Then Festus, after he had conferred with his council, replied, "You have appealed to the emperor; to the emperor you will go."

Festus Consults King Agrippa

13 After several days had passed, King Agrippa and Bernice arrived at Caesarea to welcome Festus. 14 Since they were staying there several days, Festus laid Paul's case before the king, saying, "There is a man here who was left in prison by Felix. 15 When I was in Jerusalem, the chief priests and the elders of the Jews informed me about him and asked for a sentence against him. 16 I told them that it was not the custom of the Romans to hand over anyone before the accused had met the accusers face to face and had been given an opportunity to make a defense against the charge. 17 So when they met here, I lost no time, but on the next day took my seat on the tribunal and ordered the man to be brought. 18 When the accusers stood up, they did not charge him with any of the crimesˢ that I was expecting. 19 Instead they had certain points of disagreement with him about their own religion and about a certain Jesus, who had died, but whom Paul asserted to be alive. 20 Since I was at a loss how to investigate these questions, I asked whether he wished to go to Jerusalem and be

εἰ δὲ οὐδέν ἐστιν ὧν οὗτοι κατηγοροῦσίν
but if not one there is of [the these accuse
things] which

μου, οὐδείς με δύναται αὐτοῖς χαρίσασθαι·
me, no one ²me ¹can ⁴to them ⁴to grant;

Καίσαρα ἐπικαλοῦμαι. 12 τότε ὁ Φῆστος
²Cæsar ¹I appeal to. Then – Festus

συλλαλήσας μετὰ τοῦ συμβουλίου ἀπεκρίθη·
having talked *with* with the council answered:

Καίσαρα ἐπικέκλησαι, ἐπὶ Καίσαρα πορεύσῃ.
²Cæsar ¹thou hast appealed to, before Cæsar thou shalt go.

13 Ἡμερῶν δὲ διαγενομένων τινῶν
And days passing someᵃ
= when some days had passed

Ἀγρίππας ὁ βασιλεὺς καὶ Βερνίκη
Agrippa the king and Bernice

κατήντησαν εἰς Καισάρειαν ἀσπασάμενοι
arrived at Cæsarea greeting

τὸν Φῆστον. 14 ὡς δὲ πλείους ἡμέρας
– Festus. And as more days

διέτριβον ἐκεῖ, ὁ Φῆστος τῷ βασιλεῖ
they stayed there, – Festus ²to the ³king

ἀνέθετο τὰ κατὰ τὸν Παῦλον λέγων·
¹set forth the matters regarding – Paul saying:

ἀνήρ τίς ἐστιν καταλελειμμένος ὑπὸ
A certain man there is having been left behind by

Φήλικος δέσμιος, 15 περὶ οὗ γενομένου
Felix prisoner, about whom being
= when I was

μου εἰς Ἱεροσόλυμα ἐνεφάνισαν οἱ ἀρχιερεῖς
meᵃ in Jerusalem ³informed ¹the ²chief priests

καὶ οἱ πρεσβύτεροι τῶν Ἰουδαίων,
³and ⁴the ⁵elders ⁶of the ⁷Jews,

αἰτούμενοι κατ' αὐτοῦ καταδίκην· 16 πρὸς
asking against him sentence; to

οὓς ἀπεκρίθην ὅτι οὐκ ἔστιν ἔθος Ῥωμαίοις
whom I answered that it is not a custom with Romans

χαρίζεσθαί τινα ἄνθρωπον πρὶν ἢ ὁ
to grant any man before the

κατηγορούμενος κατὰ πρόσωπον ἔχοι τοὺς
[one] being accused face to face† should have the

κατηγόρους τόπον τε ἀπολογίας λάβοι
accusers ³place* ¹and ⁴of defence ²receive

περὶ τοῦ ἐγκλήματος. 17 συνελθόντων
concerning the charge. Coming togetherᵃ

οὖν ἐνθάδε ἀναβολὴν μηδεμίαν ποιησάμενος
therefore thither ³delay ²no ¹making

τῇ ἐξῆς καθίσας ἐπὶ τοῦ βήματος ἐκέλευσα
on the next [day] sitting on the tribunal I commanded

ἀχθῆναι τὸν ἄνδρα· 18 περὶ οὗ σταθέντες
to be brought the man; concerning whom standing

οἱ κατήγοροι οὐδεμίαν αἰτίαν ἔφερον ὧν
the accusers ²no ³charge ¹brought ⁴of ⁶things
⁷which

ἐγὼ ὑπενόουν πονηρῶν, 19 ζητήματα δέ
⁵I ⁵suspected ⁶evil, but ²questions

τινα περὶ τῆς ἰδίας δεισιδαιμονίας εἶχον
³certain ⁴about ⁵the(ir) own ⁶religion ¹they had

πρὸς αὐτὸν καὶ περὶ τινος Ἰησοῦ
with him and about one Jesus

τεθνηκότος, ὃν ἔφασκεν ὁ Παῦλος ζῆν.
having died, whom ²asserted – ¹Paul to live.

20 ἀπορούμενος δὲ ἐγὼ τὴν περὶ τούτων
And ²being perplexed at ¹I ³the ⁴about ⁵these things

ζήτησιν ἔλεγον εἰ βούλοιτο πορεύεσθαι εἰς
⁴debate said if he wished to go to

charges brought against me by these Jews are not true, no one has the right to hand me over to them. I appeal to Caesar!"

12 After Festus had conferred with his council, he declared: "You have appealed to Caesar. To Caesar you will go!"

Festus Consults King Agrippa

13 A few days later King Agrippa and Bernice arrived at Caesarea to pay their respects to Festus. 14 Since they were spending many days there, Festus discussed Paul's case with the king. He said: "There is a man here whom Felix left as a prisoner. 15 When I went to Jerusalem, the chief priests and elders of the Jews brought charges against him and asked that he be condemned.

16 "I told them that it is not the Roman custom to hand over any man before he has faced his accusers and has had an opportunity to defend himself against their charges. 17 When they came here with me, I did not delay the case, but convened the court the next day and ordered the man to be brought in. 18 When his accusers got up to speak, they did not charge him with any of the crimes I had expected. 19 Instead, they had some points of dispute with him about their own religion and about a dead man named Jesus who Paul claimed was alive. 20 I was at a loss how to investigate such matters; so I asked if he would be willing to go to

---

ˢ Other ancient authorities read *with anything*

* That is, opportunity.

tried there on these charges.¹ 21 But when Paul had appealed to be kept in custody for the decision of his Imperial Majesty, I ordered him to be held until I could send him to the emperor." 22 Agrippa said to Festus, "I would like to hear the man myself." "Tomorrow," he said, "you will hear him."

Paul Brought before Agrippa

23 So on the next day Agrippa and Bernice came with great pomp, and they entered the audience hall with the military tribunes and the prominent men of the city. Then Festus gave the order and Paul was brought in. 24 And Festus said, "King Agrippa and all here present with us, you see this man about whom the whole Jewish community petitioned me, both in Jerusalem and here, shouting that he ought not to live any longer. 25 But I found that he had done nothing deserving death; and when he appealed to his Imperial Majesty, I decided to send him. 26 But I have nothing definite to write to our sovereign about him. Therefore I have brought him before all of you, and especially before you, King Agrippa, so that, after we have examined him, I may have something to write— 27 for it seems to me unreasonable to send a prisoner without indicating the charges against him."

Chapter 26

Paul Defends Himself before Agrippa

AGRIPPA said to Paul, "You have permission to speak for yourself."

¹Gk on them

Ἱεροσόλυμα κἀκεῖ κρίνεσθαι περὶ τούτων.
Jerusalem and there to be judged about these things.

21 τοῦ δὲ Παύλου ἐπικαλεσαμένου τηρηθῆναι
- But Paul having appealedᵃ to be kept
=when Paul appealed

αὐτὸν εἰς τὴν τοῦ Σεβαστοῦ διάγνωσιν,
him to the ²of Augustus ¹decision,

ἐκέλευσα τηρεῖσθαι αὐτὸν ἕως οὗ ἀναπέμψω
I commanded to be kept him until I may send up

αὐτὸν πρὸς Καίσαρα. 22 Ἀγρίππας δὲ
him to Cæsar. And Agrippa

πρὸς τὸν Φῆστον· ἐβουλόμην καὶ αὐτὸς
[said] to - Festus: I was minded also [my]self

τοῦ ἀνθρώπου ἀκοῦσαι. αὔριον, φησίν,
the man to hear. Tomorrow, he says,

ἀκούσῃ αὐτοῦ. 23 Τῇ οὖν ἐπαύριον
thou shalt hear him. ²On the ¹therefore ³morrow

ἐλθόντος τοῦ Ἀγρίππα καὶ τῆς Βερνίκης
coming - Agrippa and - Berniceᵃ
=when Agrippa and Bernice came

μετὰ πολλῆς φαντασίας καὶ εἰσελθόντων
with much display and enteringᵃ

εἰς τὸ ἀκροατήριον σύν τε χιλιάρχοις
into the place of audience with both chiliarchs

καὶ ἀνδράσιν τοῖς κατ' ἐξοχὴν τῆς πόλεως,
and ²men ¹the ³chief † of the city,

καὶ κελεύσαντος τοῦ Φῆστου ἤχθη ὁ
and having commanded - Festusᵃ ²was brought -
=when Festus commanded

Παῦλος. 24 καὶ φησιν ὁ Φῆστος· Ἀγρίππα
¹Paul. And says - Festus: Agrippa

βασιλεῦ καὶ πάντες οἱ συμπαρόντες ἡμῖν
king and all the ²present together with ¹us

ἄνδρες, θεωρεῖτε τοῦτον περὶ οὗ ἅπαν τὸ
¹men, ye behold this man about whom all the

πλῆθος τῶν Ἰουδαίων ἐνέτυχόν μοι ἔν τε
multitude of the Jews petitioned me ²in ¹both

Ἱεροσολύμοις καὶ ἐνθάδε, βοῶντες μὴ
Jerusalem and here, crying not

δεῖν αὐτὸν ζῆν μηκέτι. 25 ἐγὼ δὲ κατε-
ought him to live no longer. But I dis-
=that he ought not to live any longer.

λαβόμην μηδὲν ἄξιον αὐτὸν θανάτου
covered ²nothing ⁴worthy ¹him ⁵of death

πεπραχέναι, αὐτοῦ δὲ τούτου ἐπικαλεσαμένου
³to have done, but [him]self this man appealing toᵃ
=when he himself appealed to

τὸν Σεβαστὸν ἔκρινα πέμπειν. 26 περὶ
- Augustus I decided to send. Concerning

οὗ ἀσφαλές τι γράψαι τῷ κυρίῳ οὐκ
whom ²certain ³anything ¹to write ⁴to the ⁷lord ⁵not

ἔχω· διὸ προήγαγον αὐτὸν ἐφ' ὑμῶν καὶ
⁶I have; where- I brought him before you and
fore forth

μάλιστα ἐπὶ σοῦ, βασιλεῦ Ἀγρίππα, ὅπως
most of all before thee, king Agrippa, so as
=when

τῆς ἀνακρίσεως γενομένης σχῶ τί γράψω·
the examination beingᵃ I may what I may
there has been an examination have write;

27 ἄλογον γάρ μοι δοκεῖ πέμποντα δέσμιον
for ²unreasonable ³to me ¹it seems sending a prisoner

μὴ καὶ τὰς κατ' αὐτοῦ αἰτίας σημᾶναι.
not also ³the ⁴against ⁵him ²charges ¹to signify.

26 Ἀγρίππας δὲ πρὸς τὸν Παῦλον ἔφη·
And Agrippa to - Paul said:

ἐπιτρέπεταί σοι ὑπὲρ σεαυτοῦ λέγειν.
It is permitted to thee on behalf of thyself to speak.

Jerusalem and stand trial there on these charges. 21 When Paul made his appeal to be held over for the Emperor's decision, I ordered him held until I could send him to Caesar." 22 Then Agrippa said to Festus, "I would like to hear this man myself."

He replied, "Tomorrow you will hear him."

Paul Before Agrippa

23 The next day Agrippa and Bernice came with great pomp and entered the audience room with the high ranking officers and the leading men of the city. At the command of Festus, Paul was brought in. 24 Festus said: "King Agrippa, and all who are present with us, you see this man! The whole Jewish community has petitioned me about him in Jerusalem and here in Caesarea, shouting that he ought not to live any longer. 25 I found he had done nothing deserving of death, but because he made his appeal to the Emperor I decided to send him to Rome. 26 But I have nothing definite to write to His Majesty about him. Therefore I have brought him before all of you, and especially before you, King Agrippa, so that as a result of this investigation I may have something to write. 27 For I think it is unreasonable to send on a prisoner without specifying the charges against him."

Chapter 26

THEN Agrippa said to Paul, "You have permission to speak for yourself."

Then Paul stretched out his hand and began to defend himself:
2 "I consider myself fortunate that it is before you, King Agrippa, I am to make my defense today against all the accusations of the Jews, 3 because you are especially familiar with all the customs and controversies of the Jews; therefore I beg of you to listen to me patiently.
4 "All the Jews know my way of life from my youth, a life spent from the beginning among my own people and in Jerusalem. 5 They have known for a long time, if they are willing to testify, that I have belonged to the strictest sect of our religion and lived as a Pharisee. 6 And now I stand here on trial on account of my hope in the promise made by God to our ancestors, 7 a promise that our twelve tribes hope to attain, as they earnestly worship day and night. It is for this hope, your Excellency,[u] that I am accused by Jews! 8 Why is it thought incredible by any of you that God raises the dead?
9 "Indeed, I myself was convinced that I ought to do many things against the name of Jesus of Nazareth.[v] 10 And that is what I did in Jerusalem; with authority received from the chief priests, I not only locked up many of the saints in prison, but I also cast my vote against them when they were being condemned to death. 11 By punishing them often in all the synagogues I tried to force them to blaspheme; and since I was so furiously enraged at them, I pursued

τότε   ὁ   Παῦλος   ἐκτείνας   τὴν   χεῖρα
Then   -   Paul   stretching out   the(his)   hand
ἀπελογεῖτο·   2 Περὶ   πάντων   ὧν   ἐγκαλοῦμαι
defended himself: Concerning   all things   of which   I am being accused
ὑπὸ   Ἰουδαίων,   βασιλεῦ   Ἀγρίππα,   ἥγημαι
by   Jews,   king   Agrippa,   I consider
ἐμαυτὸν   μακάριον   ἐπὶ   σοῦ   μέλλων   σήμερον
myself   happy   ³before   ⁴thee   ¹being about   ²to-day
ἀπολογεῖσθαι,   3 μάλιστα   γνώστην   ὄντα   σε
¹to defend myself,   most of all   ⁴an expert   ²being   ¹thee
πάντων   τῶν   κατὰ   Ἰουδαίους   ἐθῶν   τε
⁵of all   ⁶the   ⁷among   ⁸Jews   ⁷customs   ⁸both
καὶ   ζητημάτων·   διὸ   δέομαι   μακροθύμως
¹⁰and   ¹¹questions;   wherefore   I beg   patiently
ἀκοῦσαί   μου.   4 Τὴν   μὲν   οὖν   βίωσίν
to hear   me.   ²the   ³So   ⁴then   ⁵manner of life
μου   ἐκ   νεότητος   τὴν   ἀπ'   ἀρχῆς   γενομένην
of me   from   youth   -   ²from   ⁴beginning   ¹having been
³[the]
ἐν   τῷ   ἔθνει   μου   ἔν   τε   Ἱεροσολύμοις
in   the   nation   of me   ²in   ¹and   Jerusalem
ἴσασι   πάντες   Ἰουδαίοι,   5 προγινώσκοντές
know   all   Jews,   previously knowing
με   ἄνωθεν,   ἐὰν   θέλωσι   μαρτυρεῖν,   ὅτι
me   from the first,   if   they are willing   to testify,   that
κατὰ   τὴν   ἀκριβεστάτην   αἵρεσιν   τῆς
according to the   most exact   sect   of the
ἡμετέρας   θρησκείας   ἔζησα   Φαρισαῖος.   6 καὶ
of our   religion   I lived   a Pharisee.   And
νῦν   ἐπ'   ἐλπίδι   τῆς   εἰς   τοὺς   πατέρας
now   on(in)   hope   of the   ⁴to   ⁵the   ⁷fathers
ἡμῶν   ἐπαγγελίας   γενομένης   ὑπὸ   τοῦ   θεοῦ
⁵of us   ¹promise   ²having been [made]   ³by   -   ⁶God
ἕστηκα   κρινόμενος,   7 εἰς   ἢν   τὸ   δωδεκά-
I stand   being judged,   to   which   the   twelve
φυλον   ἡμῶν   ἐν   ἐκτενείᾳ   νύκτα   καὶ
tribes   of us   with   earnestness   night   and
ἡμέραν   λατρεῦον   ἐλπίζει   καταντῆσαι·   περὶ
day   worshipping   hopes   to arrive;   concerning
ἧς   ἐλπίδος   ἐγκαλοῦμαι   ὑπὸ   Ἰουδαίων,
which   hope   I am accused   by   Jews,
βασιλεῦ.   8 τί   ἄπιστον   κρίνεται   παρ'
[O] king.   Why   incredible   is it judged   by
ὑμῖν   εἰ   ὁ   θεὸς   νεκροὺς   ἐγείρει;   9 ἐγὼ
you   if   -   God   ²dead persons   ¹raises?   ³I
μὲν   οὖν   ἔδοξα   ἐμαυτῷ   πρὸς   τὸ   ὄνομα
¹indeed   ²then   ⁴thought   ⁵to myself   ¹⁰to   ¹¹the   ¹²name
Ἰησοῦ   τοῦ   Ναζωραίου   δεῖν   πολλὰ   ἐναντία
¹³of Jesus   ¹⁴the   ¹⁵Nazarene   ⁶ought   ⁸many   ⁹contrary
things
πρᾶξαι·   10 ὃ   καὶ   ἐποίησα   ἐν   Ἱεροσολύμοις,
⁷to do;   which indeed   I did   in   Jerusalem,
καὶ   πολλοὺς   τε   τῶν   ἁγίων   ἐγὼ   ἐν
and   many   -   of the   saints   ¹I   ³in
φυλακαῖς   κατέκλεισα   τὴν   παρὰ   τῶν
⁴prisons   ²shut up   ⁵the   ⁸from   ⁹the
ἀρχιερέων   ἐξουσίαν   λαβών,   ἀναιρουμένων   τε
¹⁰chief priests   ⁷authority   ⁶having received,   being killed   and
= and when they were killed
αὐτῶν   κατήνεγκα   ψῆφον,   11 καὶ   κατὰ
them   I cast   a vote,   and   throughout
πάσας   τὰς   συναγωγὰς   πολλάκις   τιμωρῶν
all   the   synagogues   often   punishing
αὐτοὺς   ἠνάγκαζον   βλασφημεῖν,   περισσῶς   τε
them   I compelled [them]   to blaspheme,   and excessively
ἐμμαινόμενος   αὐτοῖς   ἐδίωκον   ἕως   καὶ   εἰς
raging against   them   I persecuted   as far as   even   to

So Paul motioned with his hand and began his defense: 2 "King Agrippa, I consider myself fortunate to stand before you today as I make my defense against all the accusations of the Jews, 3 and especially so because you are well acquainted with all the Jewish customs and controversies. Therefore, I beg you to listen to me patiently.
4 "The Jews all know the way I have lived ever since I was a child, from the beginning of my life in my own country, and also in Jerusalem. 5 They have known me for a long time and can testify, if they are willing, that according to the strictest sect of our religion, I lived as a Pharisee. 6 And now it is because of my hope in what God has promised our fathers that I am on trial today. 7 This is the promise our twelve tribes are hoping to see fulfilled as they earnestly serve God day and night. O king, it is because of this hope that the Jews are accusing me. 8 Why should any of you consider it incredible that God raises the dead?
9 "I too was convinced that I ought to do all that was possible to oppose the name of Jesus of Nazareth. 10 And that is just what I did in Jerusalem. On the authority of the chief priests I put many of the saints in prison, and when they were put to death, I cast my vote against them. 11 Many a time I went from one synagogue to another to have them punished, and I tried to force them to blaspheme. In my obsession against them, I even went

them even to foreign cities.

Paul Tells of His Conversion

12 "With this in mind, I was traveling to Damascus with the authority and commission of the chief priests, 13 when at midday along the road, your Excellency,ᵘ I saw a light from heaven, brighter than the sun, shining around me and my companions. 14 When we had all fallen to the ground, I heard a voice saying to me in the Hebrewʷ language, 'Saul, Saul, why are you persecuting me? It hurts you to kick against the goads.' 15 I asked, 'Who are you, Lord?' The Lord answered, 'I am Jesus whom you are persecuting. 16 But get up and stand on your feet; for I have appeared to you for this purpose, to appoint you to serve and testify to the things in which you have seen meˣ and to those in which I will appear to you. 17 I will rescue you from your people and from the Gentiles—to whom I am sending you 18 to open their eyes so that they may turn from darkness to light and from the power of Satan to God, so that they may receive forgiveness of sins and a place among those who are sanctified by faith in me.'

Paul Tells of His Preaching

19 "After that, King Agrippa, I was not disobedient to the heavenly vision, 20 but declared first to those in Damascus, then in Jerusalem and throughout the countryside of Judea, and also to the Gentiles, that they should repent and turn to God and do deeds consistent with repentance. 21 For this reason the Jews seized me in the tem-

---

τὰς ἔξω πόλεις. **12** Ἐν οἷς πορευόμενος
the outside cities.   In which journeying

εἰς τὴν Δαμασκὸν μετ' ἐξουσίας καὶ
to - Damascus with authority and

ἐπιτροπῆς τῆς τῶν ἀρχιερέων, **13** ἡμέρας
power to decide - of the chief priests, at ³day

μέσης κατὰ τὴν ὁδὸν εἶδον, βασιλεῦ,
¹mid along the way I saw, [O] king,

οὐρανόθεν ὑπὲρ τὴν λαμπρότητα τοῦ ἡλίου
⁵from heaven ⁸above ⁶the ⁷brightness ⁹of the ²sun

περιλάμψαν με φῶς καὶ τοὺς σὺν ἐμοὶ
⁵shining round ⁶me ¹a light ¹⁰and ¹¹the [ones] ¹²with ¹⁴me

πορευομένους· **14** πάντων τε καταπεσόντων
¹³journeying;   and all having fallen down
= when we had all fallen

ἡμῶν εἰς τὴν γῆν ἤκουσα φωνὴν λέγουσαν
usᵃ to the earth I heard a voice saying

πρός με τῇ Ἑβραΐδι διαλέκτῳ Σαοὺλ
to me in the Hebrew language: Saul[,]

Σαούλ, τί με διώκεις; σκληρόν σοι
Saul, why me persecutest thou? hard for thee

πρὸς κέντρα λακτίζειν. **15** ἐγὼ δὲ εἶπα·
against goads to kick. And I said:

τίς εἶ, κύριε; ὁ δὲ κύριος εἶπεν· ἐγώ
Who art thou, Lord? And the Lord said: I

εἰμι Ἰησοῦς ὃν σὺ διώκεις. **16** ἀλλὰ
am Jesus whom thou persecutest. But

ἀνάστηθι καὶ στῆθι ἐπὶ τοὺς πόδας σου·
rise thou up and stand on the feet of thee;

εἰς τοῦτο γὰρ ὤφθην σοι, προχειρίσασθαί
¹for this [purpose] ²for I appeared to thee, to appoint

σε ὑπηρέτην καὶ μάρτυρα ὧν τε
thee an attendant and a witness ²of the things ¹both
which

εἶδές με ὧν τε ὀφθήσομαί σοι,
³thou sawest ⁴me ⁵of the things ⁶and I will appear to thee,
which

17 ἐξαιρούμενός σε ἐκ τοῦ λαοῦ καὶ ἐκ
delivering thee from the people and from

τῶν ἐθνῶν, εἰς οὓς ἐγὼ ἀποστέλλω σε,
the nations, to whom I send thee,

18 ἀνοῖξαι ὀφθαλμοὺς αὐτῶν, τοῦ ἐπιστρέψαι
to open eyes of them, - to turnᵇ

ἀπὸ σκότους εἰς φῶς καὶ τῆς ἐξουσίας
from darkness to light and [from] the authority

τοῦ σατανᾶ ἐπὶ τὸν θεόν, τοῦ λαβεῖν
- of Satan to - God, - to receive
= that they may receive

αὐτοὺς ἄφεσιν ἁμαρτιῶν καὶ κλῆρον ἐν
themᵇᵈ forgiveness of sins and a lot among

τοῖς ἡγιασμένοις πίστει τῇ εἰς ἐμέ.
the [ones] having been sanctified by faith - in me.

19 Ὅθεν, βασιλεῦ Ἀγρίππα, οὐκ ἐγενόμην
Whence, king Agrippa, I was not

ἀπειθὴς τῇ οὐρανίῳ ὀπτασίᾳ, **20** ἀλλὰ
disobedient to the heavenly vision, but

τοῖς ἐν Δαμασκῷ πρῶτόν τε καὶ
to the [ones] in Damascus firstly and also

Ἰεροσολύμοις, πᾶσάν τε τὴν χώραν τῆς
[in] Jerusalem, and all the country -

Ἰουδαίας καὶ τοῖς ἔθνεσιν ἀπήγγελλον
of Judæa and to the nations I announced

μετανοεῖν καὶ ἐπιστρέφειν ἐπὶ τὸν θεόν,
to repent and to turn to - God,

ἄξια τῆς μετανοίας ἔργα πράσσοντας.
³worthy ⁴of the ⁵repentance ²works ¹doing.

21 ἕνεκα τούτων με Ἰουδαῖοι συλλαβόμενοι
On these things ²me ¹Jews ³having seized
account of

---

to foreign cities to persecute them.

12 "On one of these journeys I was going to Damascus with the authority and commission of the chief priests. 13 About noon, O king, as I was on the road, I saw a light from heaven, brighter than the sun, blazing around me and my companions. 14 We all fell to the ground, and I heard a voice saying to me in Aramaic,ʷ 'Saul, Saul, why do you persecute me? It is hard for you to kick against the goads.'

15 "Then I asked, 'Who are you, Lord?'

" 'I am Jesus, whom you are persecuting,' the Lord replied. 16 'Now get up and stand on your feet. I have appeared to you to appoint you as a servant and as a witness of what you have seen of me and what I will show you. 17 I will rescue you from your own people and from the Gentiles. I am sending you to them 18 to open their eyes and turn them from darkness to light, and from the power of Satan to God, so that they may receive forgiveness of sins and a place among those who are sanctified by faith in me.'

19 "So then, King Agrippa, I was not disobedient to the vision from heaven. 20 First to those in Damascus, then to those in Jerusalem and in all Judea, and to the Gentiles also, I preached that they should repent and turn to God and prove their repentance by their deeds. 21 That is why the Jews seized me in the

---

ʷ That is, Aramaic
ˣ Other ancient authorities read the things that you have seen

ʷ14 Or Hebrew

ple and tried to kill me.
²²To this day I have had
help from God, and so I
stand here, testifying to
both small and great, saying nothing but what the
prophets and Moses said
would take place: ²³that
the Messiah^y must suffer,
and that, by being the first
to rise from the dead, he
would proclaim light both
to our people and to the
Gentiles."

*Paul Appeals to Agrippa
to Believe*

24 While he was making
this defense, Festus ex-
claimed, "You are out of
your mind, Paul! Too much
learning is driving you insane!" ²⁵But Paul said, "I
am not out of my mind,
most excellent Festus, but
I am speaking the sober
truth. ²⁶Indeed the king
knows about these things,
and to him I speak freely;
for I am certain that none of
these things has escaped
his notice, for this was not
done in a corner. ²⁷King
Agrippa, do you believe the
prophets? I know that you
believe." ²⁸Agrippa said to
Paul, "Are you so quickly
persuading me to become a
Christian?"^z ²⁹Paul re-
plied, "Whether quickly or
not, I pray to God that not
only you but also all who
are listening to me today
might become such as I
am—except for these
chains."

30 Then the king got up,
and with him the governor
and Bernice and those who
had been seated with them;
³¹and as they were leaving,
they said to one another,
"This man is doing nothing

ἐν   τῷ   ἱερῷ   ἐπειρῶντο   διαχειρίσασθαι.
in   the   temple   tried   to kill [me].
22 ἐπικουρίας   οὖν   τυχὼν   τῆς   ἀπὸ   τοῦ
Succour   therefore   having   -   from   -
        obtained
θεοῦ   ἄχρι   τῆς   ἡμέρας   ταύτης   ἔστηκα
God   until   the   day   this   I stand
μαρτυρόμενος   μικρῷ   τε   καὶ   μεγάλῳ,   οὐδὲν
witnessing   ²to small   ¹both   and   to great,   ⁵nothing
ἐκτὸς   λέγων   ὧν   τε   οἱ   προφῆται
⁶apart   ³saying   ⁴the things   ⁸both   ⁷the   ⁹prophets
from   which
ἐλάλησαν   μελλόντων   γίνεσθαι   καὶ   Μωϋσῆς,
¹⁰said   ¹¹being about   ¹²to happen   ⁸and   ⁸Moses,
23 εἰ   παθητὸς   ὁ   χριστός,   εἰ   πρῶτος
if   subject to suffering   the   Christ,   if   first
ἐξ   ἀναστάσεως   νεκρῶν   φῶς   μέλλει
by   a resurrection   of dead   ²a light   ¹he is
        persons   about
καταγγέλλειν   τῷ   τε   λαῷ   καὶ   τοῖς   ἔθνεσιν.
²to announce   ¹to the   ⁴both   people   and   to the   nations.
24 Ταῦτα   δὲ   αὐτοῦ   ἀπολογουμένου   ὁ   Φῆστος
And these things   him   defending himself⁴   -   Festus
= as he defended himself with these things
μεγάλη   τῇ   φωνῇ   φησιν·   μαίνῃ,   Παῦλε·
⁴great   ¹with the(his)   ²voice   says: Thou ravest,   Paul:
τὰ   πολλά   σε   γράμματα   εἰς   μανίαν
¹the   ²many   ⁵thee   ³letters   ⁶to   ⁴madness
περιτρέπει.   25 ὁ   δὲ   Παῦλος·   οὐ   μαίνομαι,
⁷turn[s].   -   But   Paul: I do not rave,
φησίν,   κράτιστε   Φῆστε,   ἀλλὰ   ἀληθείας
he says,   most excellent   Festus,   but   ³of truth
καὶ   σωφροσύνης   ῥήματα   ἀποφθέγγομαι.
⁴and   ⁵of good sense   ²words   ¹speak forth.
26 ἐπίσταται   γὰρ   περὶ   τούτων   ὁ   βασιλεύς,
For ²understands   ⁴about ⁵these things ¹the   ³king,
πρὸς   ὃν   καὶ   παρρησιαζόμενος   λαλῶ·
to   whom   indeed   being bold of speech   I speak;
λανθάνειν   γὰρ   αὐτὸν   τούτων   οὐ   πείθομαι
for ²to be hidden [from] ³him   ²of these things not   ¹I am persuaded
οὐθέν·   οὐ   γὰρ   ἐστιν   ἐν   γωνίᾳ   πεπραγμένον
¹nothing;   for ¹not   is   ⁵in   ⁴a corner   ²having been done
τοῦτο.   27 πιστεύεις,   βασιλεῦ   Ἀγρίππα,
¹this.   Believest thou,   king   Agrippa,
τοῖς   προφήταις;   οἶδα   ὅτι   πιστεύεις.   28 ὁ
the   prophets?   I know   that   thou believest.
δὲ   Ἀγρίππας   πρὸς   τὸν   Παῦλον·   ἐν
And   Agrippa [said]   to   -   Paul: In
ὀλίγῳ   με   πείθεις   Χριστιανὸν   ποιῆσαι.
a little   ²me   ¹thou persuadest   ⁴a Christian   ³to make(act).
29 ὁ   δὲ   Παῦλος·   εὐξαίμην   ἂν   τῷ   θεῷ
-    And   Paul [said]:   I would pray   -   God
καὶ   ἐν   ὀλίγῳ   καὶ   ἐν   μεγάλῳ   οὐ   μόνον
both   in   a little   and   in   great   not   only
σὲ   ἀλλὰ   καὶ   πάντας   τοὺς   ἀκούοντάς
thee   but   also   all   the [ones]   hearing
μου   σήμερον   γενέσθαι   τοιούτους   ὁποῖος
me   to-day   ²to become   ¹such   of what kind
καὶ   ἐγώ   εἰμι,   παρεκτὸς   τῶν   δεσμῶν
indeed   I   am,   except   -   bonds
τούτων.   30 Ἀνέστη   τε   ὁ   βασιλεὺς   καὶ
these.   Rose up   both   the   king   and
ὁ   ἡγεμὼν   ἥ   τε   Βερνίκη   καὶ   οἱ   συγ-
the   governor   -   and   Bernice   and   the [ones] sit-
καθήμενοι   αὐτοῖς,   31 καὶ   ἀναχωρήσαντες
ting with   them,   and   having left
ἐλάλουν   πρὸς   ἀλλήλους   λέγοντες   ὅτι   οὐδὲν
spoke   to   one another   saying [,]   -   ⁴nothing

temple courts and tried to
kill me. ²²But I have had
God's help to this very day,
and so I stand here and testify to small and great alike.
I am saying nothing beyond
what the prophets and Mo-
ses said would happen—
²³that the Christ^x would
suffer and, as the first to
rise from the dead, would
proclaim light to his own
people and to the Gen-
tiles."

²⁴At this point Festus in-
terrupted Paul's defense.
"You are out of your mind,
Paul!" he shouted. "Your
great learning is driving
you insane."

²⁵"I am not insane, most
excellent Festus," Paul replied. "What I am saying is
true and reasonable. ²⁶The
king is familiar with these
things, and I can speak
freely to him. I am con-
vinced that none of this has
escaped his notice, because
it was not done in a corner.
²⁷King Agrippa, do you believe the prophets? I know
you do."

²⁸Then Agrippa said to
Paul, "Do you think that in
such a short time you can
persuade me to be a Christian?"

²⁹Paul replied, "Short
time or long—I pray God
that not only you but all
who are listening to me to-
day may become what I
am, except for these
chains."

³⁰The king rose, and with
him the governor and Ber-
nice and those sitting with
them. ³¹They left the room,
and while talking with one
another, they said, "This

---

^y Or *the Christ*
^z Or *Quickly you will persuade me
to play the Christian*

^x23 Or *Messiah*

to deserve death or imprisonment." 32 Agrippa said to Festus, "This man could have been set free if he had not appealed to the emperor."

Chapter 27

Paul Sails for Rome

WHEN it was decided that we were to sail for Italy, they transferred Paul and some other prisoners to a centurion of the Augustan Cohort, named Julius. 2 Embarking on a ship of Adramyttium that was about to set sail to the ports along the coast of Asia, we put to sea, accompanied by Aristarchus, a Macedonian from Thessalonica. 3 The next day we put in at Sidon; and Julius treated Paul kindly, and allowed him to go to his friends to be cared for. 4 Putting out to sea from there, we sailed under the lee of Cyprus, because the winds were against us. 5 After we had sailed across the sea that is off Cilicia and Pamphylia, we came to Myra in Lycia. 6 There the centurion found an Alexandrian ship bound for Italy and put us on board. 7 We sailed slowly for a number of days and arrived with difficulty off Cnidus, and as the wind was against us, we sailed under the lee of Crete off Salmone. 8 Sailing past it with difficulty, we came to a place called Fair Havens, near the city of Lasea.

9 Since much time had

θανάτου ἢ δεσμῶν ἄξιον πράσσει ὁ
⁶of death ⁷or ⁸of bonds ⁵worthy ³does

ἄνθρωπος οὗτος. 32 Ἀγρίππας δὲ τῷ
⁴man ¹This. And Agrippa –

Φήστῳ ἔφη· ἀπολελύσθαι ἐδύνατο
to Festus said: ³to have been released ²was able(could)

ὁ ἄνθρωπος οὗτος εἰ μὴ ἐπεκέκλητο Καίσαρα.
¹This man if he had not appealed to Cæsar.

27 Ὡς δὲ ἐκρίθη τοῦ ἀποπλεῖν ἡμᾶς
And when it was decided – to sail us^b
=that we should sail

εἰς τὴν Ἰταλίαν, παρεδίδουν τόν τε
to – Italy, they delivered – both

Παῦλον καί τινας ἑτέρους δεσμώτας
Paul and some other prisoners

ἑκατοντάρχῃ ὀνόματι Ἰουλίῳ σπείρης
to a centurion by name Julius of a cohort

Σεβαστῆς. 2 ἐπιβάντες δὲ πλοίῳ Ἀδρα-
Augustan. And embarking in a ship belonging to

μυττηνῷ μέλλοντι πλεῖν εἰς τοὺς κατὰ
Adramyttium being about to sail ¹for ²the ⁴along [the coast of]

τὴν Ἀσίαν τόπους ἀνήχθημεν, ὄντος σὺν
– ⁵Asia ³places we set sail, being with

ἡμῖν Ἀριστάρχου Μακεδόνος Θεσσαλονικέως·
us Aristarchus a Macedonian^a of Thessalonica;

3 τῇ τε ἑτέρᾳ κατήχθημεν εἰς Σιδῶνα,
and on the next [day] we were brought at Sidon,
to land

φιλανθρώπως τε ὁ Ἰούλιος τῷ Παύλῳ
and ²kindly – ¹Julius – ³Paul

χρησάμενος ἐπέτρεψεν πρὸς τοὺς φίλους
³treating [him] ⁴allowed ⁷to ⁸the ⁹friends

πορευθέντι ἐπιμελείας τυχεῖν. 4 κἀκεῖθεν
⁵going ¹¹attention ¹⁰to obtain. And thence

ἀναχθέντες ὑπεπλεύσαμεν τὴν Κύπρον διὰ
putting to sea we sailed close to – Cyprus because of

τὸ τοὺς ἀνέμους εἶναι ἐναντίους, 5 τό τε
– the winds to be(being) contrary, and ²the

πέλαγος τὸ κατὰ τὴν Κιλικίαν καὶ
³sea – ⁴against – ⁵Cilicia ⁶and

Παμφυλίαν διαπλεύσαντες κατήλθομεν εἰς
⁷Pamphylia ¹sailing over we came down to

Μύρα τῆς Λυκίας. 6 Κἀκεῖ εὑρὼν ὁ
Myra of Lycia. And there ²having found ¹the

ἑκατοντάρχης πλοῖον Ἀλεξανδρῖνον πλέον
²centurion ship an Alexandrian sailing

εἰς τὴν Ἰταλίαν ἐνεβίβασεν ἡμᾶς εἰς
to – Italy he embarked us in

αὐτό. 7 ἐν ἱκαναῖς δὲ ἡμέραις βραδυπλο-
it. And in a number of days sailing

οῦντες καὶ μόλις γενόμενοι κατὰ τὴν
slowly and hardly coming against –

Κνίδον, μὴ προσεῶντος ἡμᾶς τοῦ ἀνέμου,^a
Cnidus, not allowing us the wind,
=as the wind did not allow us,

ὑπεπλεύσαμεν τὴν Κρήτην κατὰ Σαλμώνην,
we sailed close to – Crete against Salmone,

8 μόλις τε παραλεγόμενοι αὐτὴν ἤλθομεν
and hardly sailing along it we came

εἰς τόπον τινὰ καλούμενον Καλοὺς λιμένας,
to place a certain being called Fair Havens,

ᾧ ἐγγὺς ἦν πόλις Λασαία. 9 Ἱκανοῦ δὲ
³to which ¹near was a city Lasæa. And much
=when

---

man is not doing anything that deserves death or imprisonment."

32 Agrippa said to Festus, "This man could have been set free if he had not appealed to Caesar."

Chapter 27

Paul Sails for Rome

WHEN it was decided that we would sail for Italy, Paul and some other prisoners were handed over to a centurion named Julius, who belonged to the Imperial Regiment. 2 We boarded a ship from Adramyttium about to sail for ports along the coast of the province of Asia, and we put out to sea. Aristarchus, a Macedonian from Thessalonica, was with us.

3 The next day we landed at Sidon; and Julius, in kindness to Paul, allowed him to go to his friends so they might provide for his needs. 4 From there we put out to sea again and passed to the lee of Cyprus because the winds were against us. 5 When we had sailed across the open sea off the coast of Cilicia and Pamphylia, we landed at Myra in Lycia. 6 There the centurion found an Alexandrian ship sailing for Italy and put us on board. 7 We made slow headway for many days and had difficulty arriving off Cnidus. When the wind did not allow us to hold our course, we sailed to the lee of Crete, opposite Salmone. 8 We moved along the coast with difficulty and came to a place called Fair Havens, near the town of Lasea.

9 Much time had been

been lost and sailing was now dangerous, because even the Fast had already gone by, 10 saying, "Sirs, I can see that the voyage will be with danger and much heavy loss, not only of the cargo and the ship, but also of our lives." 11 But the centurion paid more attention to the pilot and to the owner of the ship than to what Paul said. 12 Since the harbor was not suitable for spending the winter, the majority was in favor of putting to sea from there, on the chance that somehow they could reach Phoenix, where they could spend the winter. It was a harbor of Crete, facing southwest and northwest.

The Storm at Sea

13 When a moderate south wind began to blow, they thought they could achieve their purpose; so they weighed anchor and began to sail past Crete, close to the shore. 14 But soon a violent wind, called the northeaster, rushed down from Crete. *a* 15 Since the ship was caught and could not be turned head-on into the wind, we gave way to it and were driven. 16 By running under the lee of a small island called Cauda *b* we were scarcely able to get the ship's boat under control. 17 After hoisting it up they took measures *c* to undergird the ship; then, fearing that they would run on the Syrtis, they lowered the sea anchor and so were

---

χρόνου   διαγενομένου   καὶ   ὄντος   ἤδη
time   having passed*   and   being   now
much time had passed   = as the voyage

ἐπισφαλοῦς   τοῦ   πλοὸς   διὰ   τὸ   καὶ   τὴν
dangerous   the   voyage*   on account of – also   the
was now dangerous   = because also the fast had now

νηστείαν   ἤδη   παρεληλυθέναι,   παρῄνει   ὁ
fast   now   to have gone by,   ²advised   –
gone by,

Παῦλος   10 λέγων   αὐτοῖς·   ἄνδρες,   θεωρῶ
¹Paul   saying   to them: Men,   I see

ὅτι   μετὰ   ὕβρεως   καὶ   πολλῆς   ζημίας   οὐ
that   with   injury   and   much   loss   not

μόνον   τοῦ   φορτίου   καὶ   τοῦ   πλοίου   ἀλλὰ
only   of the   cargo   and   of the   ship   but

καὶ   τῶν   ψυχῶν   ἡμῶν   μέλλειν   ἔσεσθαι
also   of the   lives   of us   ³to be about   ⁴to be
                       = will be

τὸν   πλοῦν.   11 ὁ   δὲ   ἑκατοντάρχης   τῷ
¹the   ²voyage.   But the   centurion   ²the

κυβερνήτῃ   καὶ   τῷ   ναυκλήρῳ   μᾶλλον
³steersman   ⁴and   ⁵the   ⁶shipmaster   ⁷rather

ἐπείθετο   ἢ   τοῖς   ὑπὸ   Παύλου   λεγομένοις.
¹was persuaded by   ⁸than   ⁹the   ¹¹by   ¹²Paul   ¹⁰things said.

12 ἀνευθέτου   δὲ   τοῦ   λιμένος   ὑπάρχοντος
But unsuitable   the   port   being*
   = as the port was unsuitable

πρὸς   παραχειμασίαν   οἱ   πλείονες   ἔθεντο
for   wintering   the   majority   placed
                           = decided

βουλὴν   ἀναχθῆναι   ἐκεῖθεν,   εἴ   πως   δύναιντο
counsel   to set sail   thence,   if   some-   they might
                             how   be able

καταντήσαντες   εἰς   Φοίνικα   παραχειμάσαι,
having arrived   at   Phœnix   to pass the winter,

λιμένα   τῆς   Κρήτης   βλέποντα   κατὰ   λίβα
a port   –   of Crete   looking   toward   south-
                                  west

καὶ   κατὰ   χῶρον.   13 Ὑποπνεύσαντος   δὲ
and   toward   north-west.   And blowing gently
                             = when a south wind

νότου   δόξαντες   τῆς   προθέσεως   κεκρατηκέναι,
a south wind*   thinking   ²the(ir)   ³purpose   ¹to have obtained,
blew gently

ἄραντες   ἆσσον   παρελέγοντο   τὴν   Κρήτην.
raising   ²close in-   ¹they coasted by   –   ²Crete.
[anchor]   shore

14 μετ᾽   οὐ   πολὺ   δὲ   ἔβαλεν   κατ᾽   αὐτῆς
And after not much   there beat   down   it

ἄνεμος   τυφωνικὸς   ὁ   καλούμενος   εὐρακύλων·
wind   a tempestuous   *being* called   Euraquilo.

15 συναρπασθέντος   δὲ   τοῦ   πλοίου   καὶ   μὴ
and ³being seized   ¹the   ²ship*   and   not

δυναμένου   ἀντοφθαλμεῖν   τῷ   ἀνέμῳ   ἐπιδόντες
being able*   to beat up against   the   wind   giving way

ἐφερόμεθα.   16 νησίον   δέ   τι   ὑποδραμόντες
we were borne.   And ³islet   ²a certain   ¹running under
                             the lee of

καλούμενον   Κλαῦδα   ἰσχύσαμεν   μόλις
being called   Clauda   we were able   hardly

περικρατεῖς   γενέσθαι   τῆς   σκάφης,   17 ἦν
control   to get   of the   boat,   which

ἄραντες   βοηθείαις   ἐχρῶντο,   ὑποζωννύντες
taking   ³helps   ¹they used,   undergirding

τὸ   πλοῖον·   φοβούμενοί   τε   μὴ   εἰς   τὴν
the   ship;   and fearing   lest   into   –

Σύρτιν   ἐκπέσωσιν,   χαλάσαντες   τὸ   σκεῦος,
Syrtis   they might fall off,*   lowering   the   tackle,

---

lost, and sailing had already become dangerous because by now it was after the Fast. *y* So Paul warned them, 10 "Men, I can see that our voyage is going to be disastrous and bring great loss to ship and cargo, and to our own lives also." 11 But the centurion, instead of listening to what Paul said, followed the advice of the pilot and of the owner of the ship. 12 Since the harbor was unsuitable to winter in, the majority decided that we should sail on, hoping to reach Phoenix and winter there. This was a harbor in Crete, facing both southwest and northwest.

The Storm

13 When a gentle south wind began to blow, they thought they had obtained what they wanted; so they weighed anchor and sailed along the shore of Crete. 14 Before very long, a wind of hurricane force, called the "northeaster," swept down from the island. 15 The ship was caught by the storm and could not head into the wind; so we gave way to it and were driven along. 16 As we passed to the lee of a small island called Cauda, we were hardly able to make the lifeboat secure. 17 When the men had hoisted it aboard, they passed ropes under the ship itself to hold it together. Fearing that they would run aground on the sandbars of Syrtis, they lowered the sea anchor and

---

a Gk it
b Other ancient authorities read Clauda
c Gk helps

* This is the classical Greek word for a ship being driven out of her course on to shoals, rocks, etc. (Page). See also vers 26 and 29.

y 9 That is, the Day of Atonement (Yom Kippur)

driven. 18We were being pounded by the storm so violently that on the next day they began to throw the cargo overboard, 19and on the third day with their own hands they threw the ship's tackle overboard. 20When neither sun nor stars appeared for many days, and no small tempest raged, all hope of our being saved was at last abandoned.

21 Since they had been without food for a long time, Paul then stood up among them and said, "Men, you should have listened to me and not have set sail from Crete and thereby avoided this damage and loss. 22I urge you now to keep up your courage, for there will be no loss of life among you, but only of the ship. 23For last night there stood by me an angel of the God to whom I belong and whom I worship, 24and he said, 'Do not be afraid, Paul; you must stand before the emperor; and indeed, God has granted safety to all those who are sailing with you.' 25So keep up your courage, men, for I have faith in God that it will be exactly as I have been told. 26But we will have to run aground on some island."

27 When the fourteenth night had come, as we were drifting across the sea of Adria, about midnight the sailors suspected that they were nearing land. 28So they took soundings and found twenty fathoms; a little farther on they took

---

οὕτως ἐφέροντο. 18 σφοδρῶς δὲ χειμαζ-
thus they were borne. But exceedingly being in
= as we were exceedingly in . . .

ομένων ἡμῶν τῇ ἑξῆς ἐκβολὴν ἐποιοῦντο,
the grip us* on the next a jettisoning they made,
of a storm [day]

19 καὶ τῇ τρίτῃ αὐτόχειρες τὴν σκευὴν
and on the third with their the tackle
[day] own hands

τοῦ πλοίου ἔρριψαν. 20 μήτε δὲ ἡλίου
of the ship they threw [out]. And neither sun
=when neither . . .

μήτε ἄστρων ἐπιφαινόντων ἐπὶ πλείονας
nor stars appearing* over many
appeared

ἡμέρας, χειμῶνός τε οὐκ ὀλίγου ἐπικειμένου,
days, and stormy weather no little pressing hard,*

λοιπὸν περιῃρεῖτο ἐλπὶς πᾶσα τοῦ σῴζεσθαι
now was taken away ²hope ¹all – to be saved
=that we might

ἡμᾶς. 21 Πολλῆς τε ἀσιτίας ὑπαρχούσης
us.ᵇᵈ And much abstinence being*
be saved. =when there was long abstinence

τότε σταθεὶς ὁ Παῦλος ἐν μέσῳ αὐτῶν εἶπεν·
then ¹standing – ¹Paul in [the] midst of them said:

ἔδει μέν, ὦ ἄνδρες, πειθαρχήσαντάς
It behoved – O men, obeying
[you],

μοι μὴ ἀνάγεσθαι ἀπὸ τῆς Κρήτης
me not to set sail from – Crete

κερδῆσαί τε τὴν ὕβριν ταύτην καὶ τὴν
and to come by – injury this and –

ζημίαν. 22 καὶ τὰ νῦν παραινῶ ὑμᾶς
loss. And – now I advise you

εὐθυμεῖν· ἀποβολὴ γὰρ ψυχῆς οὐδεμία
to be of good for ²throwing away ³of life ¹no
cheer;

ἔσται ἐξ ὑμῶν πλὴν τοῦ πλοίου.
¹there will be of you but of the ship.

23 παρέστη γάρ μοι ταύτῃ τῇ νυκτὶ
For there stood by me in this – night

τοῦ θεοῦ οὗ εἰμι, ᾧ καὶ λατρεύω,
– ²of God ³of whom ⁴I am, ⁵whom ⁶also ⁷I serve,

ἄγγελος 24 λέγων· μὴ φοβοῦ, Παῦλε·
¹an angel saying: Fear not, Paul;

Καίσαρί σε δεῖ παραστῆναι, καὶ ἰδοὺ
⁴Cæsar ¹thee ²it behoves ³to stand before, and behold

κεχάρισταί σοι ὁ θεὸς πάντας τοὺς
²has given ³thee – ¹God all the [ones]

πλέοντας μετὰ σοῦ. 25 διὸ εὐθυμεῖτε,
sailing with thee. Wherefore be ye of
good cheer,

ἄνδρες· πιστεύω γὰρ τῷ θεῷ ὅτι οὕτως
men; for I believe – God that thus

ἔσται καθ᾽ ὃν τρόπον λελάληταί μοι.
it will be in the way in which† it has been spoken to me.

26 εἰς νῆσον δέ τινα δεῖ ἡμᾶς ἐκπεσεῖν.
⁵Onto ⁷island ¹but ⁴a ²it ³us ⁶to fall off.
certain behoves

27 Ὡς δὲ τεσσαρεσκαιδεκάτη νὺξ ἐγένετο
Now when [the] fourteenth night came

διαφερομένων ἡμῶν ἐν τῷ Ἀδρίᾳ, κατὰ
being carried about us in the Adria, about
= while we were being carried about

μέσον τῆς νυκτὸς ὑπενόουν οἱ ναῦται
[the] middle of the night ²supposed ¹the ²sailors

προσάγειν τινὰ αὐτοῖς χώραν. 28 καὶ
⁴to approach ⁵some ⁵to them ⁷country. And

βολίσαντες εὗρον ὀργυιὰς εἴκοσι, βραχὺ δὲ
sounding they found fathoms twenty, and ²a little

---

let the ship be driven along. 18We took such a violent battering from the storm that the next day they began to throw the cargo overboard. 19On the third day, they threw the ship's tackle overboard with their own hands. 20When neither sun nor stars appeared for many days and the storm continued raging, we finally gave up all hope of being saved.

21After the men had gone a long time without food, Paul stood up before them and said: "Men, you should have taken my advice not to sail from Crete; then you would have spared yourselves this damage and loss. 22But now I urge you to keep up your courage, because not one of you will be lost; only the ship will be destroyed. 23Last night an angel of the God whose I am and whom I serve stood beside me 24and said, 'Do not be afraid, Paul. You must stand trial before Caesar; and God has graciously given you the lives of all who sail with you.' 25So keep up your courage, men, for I have faith in God that it will happen just as he told me. 26Nevertheless, we must run aground on some island."

The Shipwreck

27On the fourteenth night we were still being driven across the Adriaticᶻ Sea, when about midnight the sailors sensed they were approaching land. 28They took soundings and found that the water was a hundred and twenty feetᵃ deep. A short time later

---

ᶻ27 In ancient times the name referred to an area extending well south of Italy.
ᵃ28 Greek *twenty orguias* (about 37 meters)

soundings again and found fifteen fathoms. 29 Fearing that we might run on the rocks, they let down four anchors from the stern and prayed for day to come. 30 But when the sailors tried to escape from the ship and had lowered the boat into the sea, on the pretext of putting out anchors from the bow, 31 Paul said to the centurion and the soldiers, "Unless these men stay in the ship, you cannot be saved." 32 Then the soldiers cut away the ropes of the boat and set it adrift.

33 Just before daybreak, Paul urged all of them to take some food, saying, "Today is the fourteenth day that you have been in suspense and remaining without food, having eaten nothing. 34 Therefore I urge you to take some food, for it will help you survive; for none of you will lose a hair from your heads." 35 After he had said this, he took bread; and giving thanks to God in the presence of all, he broke it and began to eat. 36 Then all of them were encouraged and took food for themselves. 37 (We were in all two hundred seventy-six[d] persons in the ship.) 38 After they had satisfied their hunger, they lightened the ship by throwing the wheat into the sea.

The Shipwreck

39 In the morning they did not recognize the land, but they noticed a bay with

---

διαστήσαντες καὶ πάλιν βολίσαντες εὗρον
¹having moved   also   again   sounding   they found

ὀργυιὰς δεκαπέντε·   29 φοβούμενοί τε μή
fathoms   fifteen;   and fearing   lest

που κατὰ τραχεῖς τόπους ἐκπέσωμεν,
¹somewhere ³against ⁴rough ⁵places ²we might fall off,

ἐκ πρύμνης ῥίψαντες ἀγκύρας τέσσαρας
out of [the] stern   throwing   anchors   four

ηὔχοντο ἡμέραν γενέσθαι.   30 Τῶν δὲ
they prayed   day   to become.   And the

ναυτῶν ζητούντων φυγεῖν ἐκ τοῦ πλοίου
sailors   seeking*   to flee   out of the   ship
= when the sailors sought

καὶ χαλασάντων τὴν σκάφην εἰς τὴν
and   lowering*   the   boat   into   the
= lowered

θάλασσαν προφάσει ὡς ἐκ πρώρης ἀγκύρας
sea   under pretence   as   ⁴out of ⁵[the] prow   ³anchors

μελλόντων ἐκτείνειν,   31 εἶπεν ὁ Παῦλος
¹intending   ²to cast out,   said   –   Paul

τῷ ἑκατοντάρχῃ καὶ τοῖς στρατιώταις·
to the   centurion   and   to the   soldiers:

ἐὰν μὴ οὗτοι μείνωσιν ἐν τῷ πλοίῳ,
Unless   these   remain   in   the   ship,

ὑμεῖς σωθῆναι οὐ δύνασθε.   32 τότε
ye   ²to be saved   ¹cannot.   Then

ἀπέκοψαν οἱ στρατιῶται τὰ σχοινία τῆς
cut away   the   soldiers   the   ropes   of the

σκάφης καὶ εἴασαν αὐτὴν ἐκπεσεῖν.
boat   and   let   it   to fall off.

33 Ἄχρι δὲ οὗ ἡμέρα ἤμελλεν γίνεσθαι,
   And until   day   was about   to come,

παρεκάλει ὁ Παῦλος ἅπαντας μεταλαβεῖν
besought   –   Paul   all   to partake

τροφῆς λέγων· τεσσαρεσκαιδεκάτην σήμερον
of food   saying: ²[the] fourteenth   ¹To-day [is]

ἡμέραν προσδοκῶντες ἄσιτοι διατελεῖτε,
³day   ⁵waiting   ⁴without food   ⁴ye continued,

μηθὲν προσλαβόμενοι.   34 διὸ παρακαλῶ
nothing   taking.   Wherefore   I beseech

ὑμᾶς μεταλαβεῖν τροφῆς· τοῦτο γὰρ πρὸς
you   to partake   of food;   for this   to

τῆς ὑμετέρας σωτηρίας ὑπάρχει· οὐδενὸς
–   your   salvation   is;   ²of no one

γὰρ ὑμῶν θρὶξ ἀπὸ τῆς κεφαλῆς ἀπολεῖται.
¹for   of you   a hair   from   the   head   shall perish.

35 εἴπας δὲ ταῦτα καὶ λαβὼν ἄρτον
   And saying   these things   and   taking   bread

εὐχαρίστησεν τῷ θεῷ ἐνώπιον πάντων
he gave thanks   –   to God   before   all

καὶ κλάσας ἤρξατο ἐσθίειν.   36 εὔθυμοι δὲ
and   breaking   began   to eat.   And ⁴in good spirits

γενόμενοι πάντες καὶ αὐτοὶ προσελάβοντο
³becoming   ¹all   ²also   they   took

τροφῆς.   37 ἤμεθα δὲ αἱ πᾶσαι ψυχαὶ
food.   Now we were   ²the   ¹all   souls

ἐν τῷ πλοίῳ διακόσιαι ἑβδομήκοντα ἕξ.
in   the   ship   two hundreds   [and] seventy   six.

38 κορεσθέντες δὲ τροφῆς ἐκούφιζον τὸ
And having been satisfied   of(with) food   they lightened   the

πλοῖον ἐκβαλλόμενοι τὸν σῖτον εἰς τὴν
ship   ⁴throwing out   the   wheat   into   the

θάλασσαν.   39 Ὅτε δὲ ἡμέρα ἐγένετο,
sea.   And when   day   came,

τὴν γῆν οὐκ ἐπεγίνωσκον, κόλπον δέ
²the   ³land   ¹they did not recognize,   but   ²bay

---

they took soundings again and found it was ninety feet[b] deep. 29 Fearing that we would be dashed against the rocks, they dropped four anchors from the stern and prayed for daylight. 30 In an attempt to escape from the ship, the sailors let the lifeboat down into the sea, pretending they were going to lower some anchors from the bow. 31 Then Paul said to the centurion and the soldiers, "Unless these men stay with the ship, you cannot be saved." 32 So the soldiers cut the ropes that held the lifeboat and let it fall away.

33 Just before dawn Paul urged them all to eat. "For the last fourteen days," he said, "you have been in constant suspense and have gone without food—you haven't eaten anything. 34 Now I urge you to take some food. You need it to survive. Not one of you will lose a single hair from his head." 35 After he said this, he took some bread and gave thanks to God in front of them all. Then he broke it and began to eat. 36 They were all encouraged and ate some food themselves. 37 Altogether there were 276 of us on board. 38 When they had eaten as much as they wanted, they lightened the ship by throwing the grain into the sea.

39 When daylight came, they did not recognize the land, but they saw a bay

---

[d] Other ancient authorities read *seventy-six*; others, *about seventy-six*

[b] 28 Greek *fifteen orguias* (about 27 meters)

a beach, on which they planned to run the ship ashore, if they could. 40 So they cast off the anchors and left them in the sea. At the same time they loosened the ropes that tied the steering-oars; then hoisting the foresail to the wind, they made for the beach. 41 But striking a reef,ᵉ they ran the ship aground; the bow stuck and remained immovable, but the stern was being broken up by the force of the waves. 42 The soldiers' plan was to kill the prisoners, so that none might swim away and escape; 43 but the centurion, wishing to save Paul, kept them from carrying out their plan. He ordered those who could swim to jump overboard first and make for the land, 44 and the rest to follow, some on planks and others on pieces of the ship. And so it was that all were brought safely to land.

τινα κατενόουν ἔχοντα αἰγιαλόν, εἰς ὃν
ᵃa certain ¹they noticed having a shore, into which

ἐβουλεύοντο εἰ δύναιντο ἐξῶσαι τὸ πλοῖον.
they were minded if they were able to drive the ship.

40 καὶ τὰς ἀγκύρας περιελόντες εἴων
And ¹the ²anchors ¹having cast off they left [them]

εἰς τὴν θάλασσαν, ἅμα ἀνέντες τὰς
in the sea, at the same time loosening the

ζευκτηρίας τῶν πηδαλίων, καὶ ἐπάραντες
fastenings of the rudders, and raising

τὸν ἀρτέμωνα τῇ πνεούσῃ κατεῖχον εἰς
the foresail to the breeze they held [the ship] to

τὸν αἰγιαλόν. 41 περιπεσόντες δὲ εἰς
the shore. And coming upon to

τόπον διθάλασσον ἐπέκειλαν τὴν ναῦν,
a place between two seas they drove the vessel,

καὶ ἡ μὲν πρῷρα ἐρείσασα ἔμεινεν
and ²the ¹while prow having run aground remained

ἀσάλευτος, ἡ δὲ πρύμνα ἐλύετο ὑπὸ
immovable, ²the ¹yet stern was broken by

τῆς βίας.* 42 Τῶν δὲ στρατιωτῶν βουλὴ
the force.* Now ²of the ³soldiers ¹[the] mind

ἐγένετο ἵνα τοὺς δεσμώτας ἀποκτείνωσιν,
was that ¹the ²prisoners ¹they should kill,

μή τις ἐκκολυμβήσας διαφύγῃ· 43 ὁ δὲ
lest anyone swimming out should escape; but the

ἑκατοντάρχης βουλόμενος διασῶσαι τὸν
centurion being minded to save

Παῦλον ἐκώλυσεν αὐτοὺς τοῦ βουλήματος,
Paul forbade them the(ir) intention,

ἐκέλευσέν τε τοὺς δυναμένους κολυμβᾶν
and commanded the [ones] being able to swim

ἀπορίψαντας πρώτους ἐπὶ τὴν γῆν
casting [themselves] first onto the land
overboard

ἐξιέναι, 44 καὶ τοὺς λοιποὺς οὓς μὲν ἐπὶ
to go out, and the rest some on

σανίσιν, οὓς δὲ ἐπί τινων τῶν ἀπὸ τοῦ
planks, others on some of the things from the

πλοίου. καὶ οὕτως ἐγένετο πάντας
ship. And thus it came to pass all

διασωθῆναι ἐπὶ τὴν γῆν.
to be saved on the land.

---

with a sandy beach, where they decided to run the ship aground if they could. 40 Cutting loose the anchors, they left them in the sea and at the same time untied the ropes that held the rudders. Then they hoisted the foresail to the wind and made for the beach. 41 But the ship struck a sandbar and ran aground. The bow stuck fast and would not move, and the stern was broken to pieces by the pounding of the surf. 42 The soldiers planned to kill the prisoners to prevent any of them from swimming away and escaping. 43 But the centurion wanted to spare Paul's life and kept them from carrying out their plan. He ordered those who could swim to jump overboard first and get to land. 44 The rest were to get there on planks or on pieces of the ship. In this way everyone reached land in safety.

Chapter 28

Paul on the Island of Malta

AFTER we had reached safety, we then learned that the island was called Malta. 2 The natives showed us unusual kindness. Since it had begun to rain and was cold, they kindled a fire and welcomed all of us around it. 3 Paul had gathered a bundle of brushwood and was putting it on the fire, when a viper, driven out by the heat, fastened itself on his hand. 4 When the natives saw the crea-

---

28 Καὶ διασωθέντες τότε ἐπέγνωμεν ὅτι
And having been saved then we found out that

Μελίτη ἡ νῆσος καλεῖται. 2 οἵ τε
Melita the island is(was) called. And the

βάρβαροι παρεῖχον οὐ τὴν τυχοῦσαν
foreigners ¹showed ²not ³the ¹ordinary

φιλανθρωπίαν ἡμῖν· ἅψαντες γὰρ πυρὰν
⁶kindness ⁵us; for having lit a fire

προσελάβοντο πάντας ἡμᾶς διὰ τὸν ὑετὸν
they welcomed ²all ¹us because of the rain

τὸν ἐφεστῶτα καὶ διὰ τὸ ψῦχος. 3 συστρέ-
coming on and because of the cold. col-

ψαντος δὲ τοῦ Παύλου φρυγάνων τι
lecting And - Paul ²of sticks ¹a
=when Paul collected

πλῆθος καὶ ἐπιθέντος ἐπὶ τὴν πυράν,
²quantity and putting onᵃ on the fire,
=put them

ἔχιδνα ἀπὸ τῆς θέρμης ἐξελθοῦσα καθῆψεν
a snake from the heat coming out fastened on

τῆς χειρὸς αὐτοῦ. 4 ὡς δὲ εἶδον οἱ
the hand of him. And when ³saw ¹the

Chapter 28

Ashore on Malta

ONCE safely on shore, we found out that the island was called Malta. 2 The islanders showed us unusual kindness. They built a fire and welcomed us all because it was raining and cold. 3 Paul gathered a pile of brushwood and, as he put it on the fire, a viper, driven out by the heat, fastened itself on his hand. 4 When the islanders saw

---

ᵉ Gk place of two seas

* That is, of the waves, as indeed some MSS have.

ture hanging from his hand, they said to one another, "This man must be a murderer; though he has escaped from the sea, justice has not allowed him to live." 5 He, however, shook off the creature into the fire and suffered no harm. 6 They were expecting him to swell up or drop dead, but after they had waited a long time and saw that nothing unusual had happened to him, they changed their minds and began to say that he was a god.

7 Now in the neighborhood of that place were lands belonging to the leading man of the island, named Publius, who received us and entertained us hospitably for three days. 8 It so happened that the father of Publius lay sick in bed with fever and dysentery. Paul visited him and cured him by praying and putting his hands on him. 9 After this happened, the rest of the people on the island who had diseases also came and were cured. 10 They bestowed many honors on us, and when we were about to sail, they put on board all the provisions we needed.

Paul Arrives at Rome

11 Three months later we set sail on a ship that had wintered at the island, an Alexandrian ship with the Twin Brothers as its figurehead. 12 We put in at Syracuse and stayed there for three days; 13 then we weighed anchor and came to Rhegium. After one day

βάρβαροι κρεμάμενον τὸ θηρίον ἐκ τῆς
²foreigners ⁶hanging ⁴the ⁵beast from the

χειρὸς αὐτοῦ, πρὸς ἀλλήλους ἔλεγον·
hand of him, to one another they said:

πάντως φονεύς ἐστιν ὁ ἄνθρωπος οὗτος,
To be sure ²a murderer ³is ¹this man,

ὃν διασωθέντα ἐκ τῆς θαλάσσης ἡ δίκη
whom having been out of the sea - justice
saved

ζῆν οὐκ εἴασεν. 5 ὁ μὲν οὖν ἀποτινάξας
²to live ¹did not allow. He - then shaking off

τὸ θηρίον εἰς τὸ πῦρ ἔπαθεν οὐδὲν
the beast into the fire suffered no

κακόν· 6 οἱ δὲ προσεδόκων αὐτὸν μέλλειν
harm; but they expected him to be about

πίμπρασθαι ἢ καταπίπτειν ἄφνω νεκρόν.
to swell or to fall down suddenly dead.

ἐπὶ πολὺ δὲ αὐτῶν προσδοκώντων καὶ
But over much [time] they expecting and
= while they expected and beheld

θεωρούντων μηδὲν ἄτοπον εἰς αὐτὸν
beholdingᵃ nothing amiss ²to ³him

γινόμενον, μεταβαλόμενοι ἔλεγον αὐτὸν εἶναι
¹happening, changing their minds they said him to be

θεόν. 7 Ἐν δὲ τοῖς περὶ τὸν τόπον
a god. Now in the [parts] about - place

ἐκεῖνον ὑπῆρχεν χωρία τῷ πρώτῳ τῆς
that were lands to the chief manᵉ of the
= the chief man had lands

νήσου ὀνόματι Ποπλίῳ, ὃς ἀναδεξάμενος
island by name Publius, who welcoming

ἡμᾶς ἡμέρας τρεῖς φιλοφρόνως ἐξένισεν.
us ⁴days ³three ²friendlily ¹lodged [us].

8 ἐγένετο δὲ τὸν πατέρα τοῦ Ποπλίου
Now it happened the father - of Publius

πυρετοῖς καὶ δυσεντερίῳ συνεχόμενον
²feverish attacks ⁴and ⁵dysentery ¹suffering from

κατακεῖσθαι, πρὸς ὃν ὁ Παῦλος εἰσελθὼν
¹to be lying down, to whom - Paul entering

καὶ προσευξάμενος, ἐπιθεὶς τὰς χεῖρας
and praying, ¹putting ⁴on ²the(his) ³hands

αὐτῷ ἰάσατο αὐτόν. 9 τούτου δὲ γενομένου
¹him cured him. And this happeningᵃ
= when this happened

καὶ οἱ λοιποὶ οἱ ἐν τῇ νήσῳ ἔχοντες
²also ¹the ²rest - in the island having

ἀσθενείας προσήρχοντο καὶ ἐθεραπεύοντο,
ailments came up and were healed,

10 οἱ καὶ πολλαῖς τιμαῖς ἐτίμησαν ἡμᾶς
who also with many honours honoured us

καὶ ἀναγομένοις ἐπέθεντο τὰ πρὸς τὰς
and on our putting to sea placed on [us] the things for the(our)

χρείας.
needs.

11 Μετὰ δὲ τρεῖς μῆνας ἀνήχθημεν ἐν
And after three months we embarked in

πλοίῳ παρακεχειμακότι ἐν τῇ νήσῳ,
a ship having passed the winter in the island,

Ἀλεξανδρίνῳ, παρασήμῳ Διοσκούροις. 12 καὶ
an Alexandrian, with a sign Dioscuri. And

καταχθέντες εἰς Συρακούσας ἐπεμείναμεν
being brought to land to(at) Syracuse we remained

ἡμέρας τρεῖς, 13 ὅθεν περιελθόντες κατην-
days three, whence tacking we ar-

τήσαμεν εἰς Ῥήγιον. καὶ μετὰ μίαν
rived at Rhegium. And after one

the snake hanging from his hand, they said to each other, "This man must be a murderer; for though he has escaped from the sea, Justice has not allowed him to live." 5 But Paul shook the snake off into the fire and suffered no ill effects. 6 The people expected him to swell up or suddenly fall dead, but after waiting a long time and seeing nothing unusual happen to him, they changed their minds and said he was a god.

7 There was an estate nearby that belonged to Publius, the chief official of the island. He welcomed us to his home and for three days entertained us hospitably. 8 His father was sick in bed, suffering from fever and dysentery. Paul went in to see him and, after prayer, placed his hands on him and healed him. 9 When this had happened, the rest of the sick on the island came and were cured. 10 They honored us in many ways and when we were ready to sail, they furnished us with the supplies we needed.

Arrival at Rome

11 After three months we put out to sea in a ship that had wintered in the island. It was an Alexandrian ship with the figurehead of the twin gods Castor and Pollux. 12 We put in at Syracuse and stayed there three days. 13 From there we set sail and arrived at Rhegi-

there a south wind sprang up, and on the second day we came to Puteoli. [14]There we found believers[f] and were invited to stay with them for seven days. And so we came to Rome. [15]The believers[f] from there, when they heard of us, came as far as the Forum of Appius and Three Taverns to meet us. On seeing them, Paul thanked God and took courage.

[16] When we came into Rome, Paul was allowed to live by himself, with the soldier who was guarding him.

Paul and Jewish Leaders in Rome

[17] Three days later he called together the local leaders of the Jews. When they had assembled, he said to them, "Brothers, though I had done nothing against our people or the customs of our ancestors, yet I was arrested in Jerusalem and handed over to the Romans. [18]When they had examined me, the Romans[g] wanted to release me, because there was no reason for the death penalty in my case. [19]But when the Jews objected, I was compelled to appeal to the emperor—even though I had no charge to bring against my nation. [20]For this reason therefore I have asked to see you and speak with you,[h] since it is for the sake of the hope of Israel that I am bound with this chain." [21]They replied, "We have received no letters from Judea about you,

ἡμέραν ἐπιγενομένου νότου δευτεραῖοι
day   coming on   a south wind[a] on the
            = as a south wind came on second day

ἤλθομεν εἰς Ποτιόλους, 14 οὗ εὑρόντες
we came to   Puteoli,   where having found

ἀδελφοὺς παρεκλήθημεν παρ' αὐτοῖς ἐπιμεῖναι
brothers we were besought with   them   to remain

ἡμέρας ἑπτά· καὶ οὕτως εἰς τὴν Ῥώμην
days   seven; and thus to   Rome

ἤλθαμεν. 15 κἀκεῖθεν οἱ ἀδελφοὶ ἀκούσαντες
we went.   And thence the brothers   having heard

τὰ περὶ ἡμῶν ἦλθαν εἰς ἀπάντησιν ἡμῖν
the con- us came to a meeting with us
things cerning

ἄχρι Ἀππίου φόρου καὶ Τριῶν ταβερνῶν,
as far as Appii Forum and Three Taverns,

οὓς ἰδὼν ὁ Παῦλος εὐχαριστήσας τῷ
whom seeing Paul   thanking

θεῷ ἔλαβε θάρσος. 16 Ὅτε δὲ εἰσήλθομεν
God he took courage.   And when   we entered

εἰς Ῥώμην, ἐπετράπη τῷ Παύλῳ μένειν
into Rome, he* permitted   –   Paul to remain

καθ' ἑαυτὸν σὺν τῷ φυλάσσοντι αὐτὸν
by himself with ¹the ³guarding   ⁴him

στρατιώτῃ.
²soldier.

17 Ἐγένετο δὲ μετὰ ἡμέρας τρεῖς
  And it came to pass after days three

συγκαλέσασθαι αὐτὸν τοὺς ὄντας τῶν
to call together him[b] the [ones] being of the
= he called together

Ἰουδαίων πρώτους· συνελθόντων δὲ αὐτῶν
Jews   first(chief); and coming together them[a]
                              = and when they came together

ἔλεγεν πρὸς αὐτούς· ἐγώ, ἄνδρες ἀδελφοί,
he said to   them: I,   men   brothers,

οὐδὲν ἐναντίον ποιήσας τῷ λαῷ ἢ τοῖς
²nothing ³contrary ¹having done to the people or to the

ἔθεσι τοῖς πατρῴοις, δέσμιος ἐξ Ἱεροσο-
customs –   ancestral, a prisoner from Jeru-

λύμων παρεδόθην εἰς τὰς χεῖρας τῶν
salem I was delivered into the hands of the

Ῥωμαίων, 18 οἵτινες ἀνακρίναντές με ἐβούλοντο
Romans,   who   having examined me were minded

ἀπολῦσαι διὰ τὸ μηδεμίαν αἰτίαν θανάτου
to release on account –   no   cause of death
          of

ὑπάρχειν ἐν ἐμοί· 19 ἀντιλεγόντων δὲ
to be   in me;   but speaking against [this]
                              = when the Jews spoke

τῶν Ἰουδαίων ἠναγκάσθην ἐπικαλέσασθαι
the Jews[a]   I was compelled to appeal to

Καίσαρα, οὐχ ὡς τοῦ ἔθνους μου ἔχων
Cæsar,   not as ¹the ²nation ⁶of me ¹having

τι κατηγορεῖν. 20 διὰ ταύτην οὖν τὴν
⁵anything ⁴to accuse. ¹On account of ²this ⁴therefore –

αἰτίαν παρεκάλεσα ὑμᾶς ἰδεῖν καὶ προσ-
³cause I called   you to see and to

λαλῆσαι· εἵνεκεν γὰρ τῆς ἐλπίδος τοῦ
speak to; for for the sake of the hope

Ἰσραὴλ τὴν ἄλυσιν ταύτην περίκειμαι.
of Israel ²this ³chain ¹I have round [me].

21 οἱ δὲ πρὸς αὐτὸν εἶπαν· ἡμεῖς οὔτε
  And they to him   said: We   neither

γράμματα περὶ σοῦ ἐδεξάμεθα ἀπὸ τῆς
²letters ³about ⁴thee ¹received from –

um. The next day the south wind came up, and on the following day we reached Puteoli. [14]There we found some brothers who invited us to spend a week with them. And so we came to Rome. [15]The brothers there had heard that we were coming, and they traveled as far as the Forum of Appius and the Three Taverns to meet us. At the sight of these men Paul thanked God and was encouraged. [16]When we got to Rome, Paul was allowed to live by himself, with a soldier to guard him.

Paul Preaches at Rome Under Guard

[17]Three days later he called together the leaders of the Jews. When they had assembled, Paul said to them: "My brothers, although I have done nothing against our people or against the customs of our ancestors, I was arrested in Jerusalem and handed over to the Romans. [18]They examined me and wanted to release me, because I was not guilty of any crime deserving death. [19]But when the Jews objected, I was compelled to appeal to Caesar—not that I had any charge to bring against my own people. [20]For this reason I have asked to see you and talk with you. It is because of the hope of Israel that I am bound with this chain."

[21]They replied, "We have not received any letters from Judea concerning

[f] Gk brothers
[g] Gk they
[h] Or I have asked you to see me and speak with me

* That is, the officer to whom Paul was handed over by the centurion Julius.

and none of the brothers coming here has reported or spoken anything evil about you. 22 But we would like to hear from you what you think, for with regard to this sect we know that everywhere it is spoken against."

Paul Preaches in Rome

23 After they had set a day to meet with him, they came to him at his lodgings in great numbers. From morning until evening he explained the matter to them, testifying to the kingdom of God and trying to convince them about Jesus both from the law of Moses and from the prophets. 24 Some were convinced by what he had said, while others refused to believe. 25 So they disagreed with each other; and as they were leaving, Paul made one further statement: "The Holy Spirit was right in saying to your ancestors through the prophet Isaiah,
26 'Go to this people and say,
　You will indeed listen, but never understand,
　and you will indeed look, but never perceive.
27 For this people's heart has grown dull,
　and their ears are hard of hearing,
　and they have shut their eyes;
　so that they might not look with their eyes,
　and listen with their ears,
　and understand with their heart and turn—
　and I would heal them.'
28 Let it be known to you then that this salvation of God has been sent to the Gentiles; they will listen."[i]
30 He lived there two whole years at his own expense[j] and welcomed all

---

'Ιουδαίας, οὔτε παραγενόμενός τις τῶν
Judæa, nor arriving anyone of the
ἀδελφῶν ἀπήγγειλεν ἢ ἐλάλησέν τι περὶ
brothers told or spoke anything ²about
σοῦ πονηρόν. 22 ἀξιοῦμεν δὲ παρὰ σοῦ
³thee ¹evil. But we think fit from thee
ἀκοῦσαι ἃ φρονεῖς· περὶ μὲν γὰρ τῆς
to hear what thou ²concerning ³indeed ¹for –
　　　things thinkest;
αἱρέσεως ταύτης γνωστὸν ἡμῖν ἐστιν ὅτι
⁵sect ⁴this ⁷known ⁶to us ⁸it is that
πανταχοῦ ἀντιλέγεται. 23 Ταξάμενοι δὲ
everywhere it is spoken against. And arranging
αὐτῷ ἡμέραν ἦλθον πρὸς αὐτὸν εἰς τὴν
with him a day ²came ³to ⁴him ¹in ⁵the(his)
ξενίαν πλείονες, οἷς ἐξετίθετο διαμαρτυρ-
⁷lodging ¹more, to whom he set forth solemnly
όμενος τὴν βασιλείαν τοῦ θεοῦ, πείθων
witnessing the kingdom – of God, ²persuading
τε αὐτοὺς περὶ τοῦ 'Ιησοῦ ἀπό τε τοῦ
¹and them concerning – Jesus from both the
νόμου Μωϋσέως καὶ τῶν προφητῶν, ἀπὸ
law of Moses and the prophets, from
πρωῒ ἕως ἑσπέρας. 24 καὶ οἱ μὲν
morning until evening. And some
ἐπείθοντο τοῖς λεγομένοις, 25 οἱ δὲ
were persuaded by the things being said, others
ἠπίστουν· ἀσύμφωνοι δὲ ὄντες πρὸς ἀλλή-
disbelieved; and ²disagreed ¹being with one an-
λους ἀπελύοντο, εἰπόντος τοῦ Παύλου
other they were dismissed, having said – Paul
　　　=after Paul had said
ῥῆμα ἕν, ὅτι καλῶς τὸ πνεῦμα τὸ ἅγιον
word one, – Well the Spirit the Holy
ἐλάλησεν διὰ 'Ησαΐου τοῦ προφήτου πρὸς
spoke through Esaias the prophet to
τοὺς πατέρας ὑμῶν 26 λέγων· πορεύθητι
the fathers of you saying: Go thou
πρὸς τὸν λαὸν τοῦτον καὶ εἰπόν· ἀκοῇ
to this people and say: In hearing
ἀκούσετε καὶ οὐ μὴ συνῆτε, καὶ βλέποντες
ye will hear and by no means understand, and looking
βλέψετε καὶ οὐ μὴ ἴδητε· 27 ἐπαχύνθη
ye will look and by no means see; ¹was thickened
γὰρ ἡ καρδία τοῦ λαοῦ τούτου, καὶ
¹for the heart of this people, and
τοῖς ὠσὶν βαρέως ἤκουσαν, καὶ τοὺς
with the(ir) ears heavily they heard, and the
ὀφθαλμοὺς αὐτῶν ἐκάμμυσαν· μήποτε ἴδωσιν
eyes of them they closed; lest at any time they see
τοῖς ὀφθαλμοῖς καὶ τοῖς ὠσὶν ἀκούσωσιν
with the eyes and with the ears hear
καὶ τῇ καρδίᾳ συνῶσιν καὶ ἐπιστρέψωσιν,
and with the heart understand and turn,
καὶ ἰάσομαι αὐτούς. 28 γνωστὸν οὖν
and I shall cure them. Known therefore
ἔστω ὑμῖν ὅτι τοῖς ἔθνεσιν ἀπεστάλη
let it be to you that to the nations was sent
τοῦτο τὸ σωτήριον τοῦ θεοῦ· αὐτοὶ καὶ
this – salvation – of God; and they
ἀκούσονται.‡
will hear.

30 'Ενέμεινεν δὲ διετίαν ὅλην ἐν ἰδίῳ
And he remained a whole two years in [his] own
μισθώματι, καὶ ἀπεδέχετο πάντας τοὺς
hired apartment, and welcomed all the

---

you, and none of the brothers who have come from there has reported or said anything bad about you. 22 But we want to hear what your views are, for we know that people everywhere are talking against this sect."

23 They arranged to meet Paul on a certain day, and came in even larger numbers to the place where he was staying. From morning till evening he explained and declared to them the kingdom of God and tried to convince them about Jesus from the Law of Moses and from the Prophets. 24 Some were convinced by what he said, but others would not believe. 25 They disagreed among themselves and began to leave after Paul had made this final statement: "The Holy Spirit spoke the truth to your forefathers when he said through Isaiah the prophet:

26 "'Go to this people and say,
　"You will be ever hearing but never understanding;
　you will be ever seeing but never perceiving."
27 For this people's heart has become calloused;
　they hardly hear with their ears,
　and they have closed their eyes.
Otherwise they might see with their eyes,
　hear with their ears,
　understand with their hearts
and turn, and I would heal them.'[c]

28 "Therefore I want you to know that God's salvation has been sent to the Gentiles, and they will listen!"[d]

30 For two whole years Paul stayed there in his own rented house and wel-

---

[i] Other ancient authorities add verse 29, *And when he had said these words, the Jews departed, arguing vigorously among themselves*
[j] Or *in his own hired dwelling*

‡ Verse 29 omitted by Nestle; *cf.* NIV footnote.

[c]27 Isaiah 6:9,10
[d]28 Some manuscripts *listen!"*
29 *After he said this, the Jews left, arguing vigorously among themselves.*

who came to him, 31 pro-
claiming the kingdom of
God and teaching about the
Lord Jesus Christ with all
boldness and without hin-
drance.

εἰσπορευομένους πρὸς αὐτόν, 31 κηρύσσων
[ones] coming in   to   him,   proclaiming

τὴν βασιλείαν τοῦ θεοῦ καὶ διδάσκων
the   kingdom   –   of God and teaching

τὰ περὶ τοῦ κυρίου Ἰησοῦ Χριστοῦ
the things concerning the Lord Jesus Christ

μετὰ πάσης παρρησίας ἀκωλύτως.
with   all   boldness   unhinderedly.

comed all who came to see
him. 31Boldly and without
hindrance he preached the
kingdom of God and taught
about the Lord Jesus
Christ.

Chapter 1

Salutation

PAUL, a servant[a] of Jesus Christ, called to be an apostle, set apart for the gospel of God, [2] which he promised beforehand through his prophets in the holy scriptures, [3] the gospel concerning his Son, who was descended from David according to the flesh [4] and was declared to be Son of God with power according to the spirit[b] of holiness by resurrection from the dead, Jesus Christ our Lord, [5] through whom we have received grace and apostleship to bring about the obedience of faith among all the Gentiles for the sake of his name, [6] including yourselves who are called to belong to Jesus Christ,

[7] To all God's beloved in Rome, who are called to be saints:

Grace to you and peace from God our Father and the Lord Jesus Christ.

Prayer of Thanksgiving

[8] First, I thank my God through Jesus Christ for all of you, because your faith is proclaimed throughout the world. [9] For God, whom I serve with my spirit by announcing the gospel[c] of his Son, is my witness that without ceasing I remember you always in my prayers, [10] asking that by God's will I may somehow at last succeed in coming to you. [11] For I am longing to see you so that I may share with you some spiritual gift to strengthen you— [12] or rather so that we may be mutually encouraged by each other's faith, both yours and mine.

PAUL, a servant of Christ Jesus, called to be an apostle and set apart for the gospel of God— [2] the gospel he promised beforehand through his prophets in the Holy Scriptures [3] regarding his Son, who as to his human nature was a descendant of David, [4] and who through the Spirit[a] of holiness was declared with power to be the Son of God[b] by his resurrection from the dead: Jesus Christ our Lord. [5] Through him and for his name's sake, we received grace and apostleship to call people from among all the Gentiles to the obedience that comes from faith. [6] And you also are among those who are called to belong to Jesus Christ.

[7] To all in Rome who are loved by God and called to be saints:

Grace and peace to you from God our Father and from the Lord Jesus Christ.

Paul's Longing to Visit Rome

[8] First, I thank my God through Jesus Christ for all of you, because your faith is being reported all over the world. [9] God, whom I serve with my whole heart in preaching the gospel of his Son, is my witness how constantly I remember you [10] in my prayers at all times; and I pray that now at last by God's will the way may be opened for me to come to you.

[11] I long to see you so that I may impart to you some spiritual gift to make you strong— [12] that is, that you and I may be mutually encouraged by each other's

---

1 Παῦλος δοῦλος Χριστοῦ Ἰησοῦ, κλητὸς
Paul a slave of Christ Jesus, called

ἀπόστολος ἀφωρισμένος εἰς εὐαγγέλιον
an apostle *having been* separated to [the] gospel

θεοῦ, **2** ὃ προεπηγγείλατο διὰ τῶν
of God, which he promised beforehand through the

προφητῶν αὐτοῦ ἐν γραφαῖς ἁγίαις **3** περὶ
prophets of him in writings holy concerning

τοῦ υἱοῦ αὐτοῦ τοῦ γενομένου ἐκ
the Son of him — come of

σπέρματος Δαυὶδ κατὰ σάρκα, **4** τοῦ
[the] seed of David according to [the] flesh, —

ὁρισθέντος υἱοῦ θεοῦ ἐν δυνάμει
designated Son of God in power

κατὰ πνεῦμα ἁγιωσύνης ἐξ ἀναστάσεως
according to [the] Spirit of holiness by a resurrection

νεκρῶν, Ἰησοῦ Χριστοῦ τοῦ κυρίου ἡμῶν,
of dead persons, Jesus Christ the Lord of us,

5 δι' οὗ ἐλάβομεν χάριν καὶ ἀποστολὴν
through whom we received grace and apostleship

εἰς ὑπακοὴν πίστεως ἐν πᾶσιν τοῖς
for obedience of faith among all the

ἔθνεσιν ὑπὲρ τοῦ ὀνόματος αὐτοῦ, **6** ἐν
nations on behalf of the name of him, among

οἷς ἐστε καὶ ὑμεῖς κλητοὶ Ἰησοῦ Χριστοῦ,
whom are also ye called of Jesus Christ,

7 πᾶσιν τοῖς οὖσιν ἐν Ῥώμῃ ἀγαπητοῖς
to all the [ones] being in Rome beloved

θεοῦ, κλητοῖς ἁγίοις· χάρις ὑμῖν καὶ
of God, called holy: Grace to you and

εἰρήνη ἀπὸ θεοῦ πατρὸς ἡμῶν καὶ κυρίου
peace from God [the] Father of us and Lord

Ἰησοῦ Χριστοῦ.
Jesus Christ.

8 Πρῶτον μὲν εὐχαριστῶ τῷ θεῷ μου
Firstly — I thank the God of me

διὰ Ἰησοῦ Χριστοῦ περὶ πάντων ὑμῶν,
through Jesus Christ concerning all you,

ὅτι ἡ πίστις ὑμῶν καταγγέλλεται ἐν
because the faith of you is being announced in

ὅλῳ τῷ κόσμῳ. **9** μάρτυς γάρ μου
all the world. For witness of me

ἐστιν ὁ θεός, ᾧ λατρεύω ἐν τῷ πνεύματι
is — God, whom I serve in the spirit

μου ἐν τῷ εὐαγγελίῳ τοῦ υἱοῦ αὐτοῦ,
of me in the gospel of the Son of him,

ὡς ἀδιαλείπτως μνείαν ὑμῶν ποιοῦμαι
how unceasingly mention of you I make

10 πάντοτε ἐπὶ τῶν προσευχῶν μου,
always on(in) the prayers of me,

δεόμενος εἴ πως ἤδη ποτὲ εὐοδωθήσομαι
requesting if somehow now at some time I shall have a happy journey

ἐν τῷ θελήματι τοῦ θεοῦ ἐλθεῖν
in the will — of God to come

πρὸς ὑμᾶς. **11** ἐπιποθῶ γὰρ ἰδεῖν ὑμᾶς,
unto you. For I long to see you,

ἵνα τι μεταδῶ χάρισμα ὑμῖν πνευματικὸν
that ²some ¹I may impart ⁴gift ⁵to you ³spiritual

εἰς τὸ στηριχθῆναι ὑμᾶς, **12** τοῦτο δέ
for the to be established you,[b] and this
=that ye may be established

ἐστιν συμπαρακληθῆναι ἐν ὑμῖν διὰ τῆς
is to be encouraged *with* among you through ¹the

ἐν ἀλλήλοις πίστεως ὑμῶν τε καὶ ἐμοῦ.
³in ⁴one another ²faith ⁶of you ⁵both ⁷and ⁸of me.

---

a Gk slave
b Or Spirit
c Gk my spirit in the gospel

a4 Or who as to his spirit
b4 Or was appointed to be the Son of God with power

13 I want you to know, brothers and sisters,[d] that I have often intended to come to you (but thus far have been prevented), in order that I may reap some harvest among you as I have among the rest of the Gentiles. 14 I am a debtor both to Greeks and to barbarians, both to the wise and to the foolish 15 —hence my eagerness to proclaim the gospel to you also who are in Rome.

The Power of the Gospel

16 For I am not ashamed of the gospel; it is the power of God for salvation to everyone who has faith, to the Jew first and also to the Greek. 17 For in it the righteousness of God is revealed through faith for faith; as it is written, "The one who is righteous will live by faith."[e]

The Guilt of Humankind

18 For the wrath of God is revealed from heaven against all ungodliness and wickedness of those who by their wickedness suppress the truth. 19 For what can be known about God is plain to them, because God has shown it to them. 20 Ever since the creation of the world his eternal power and divine nature, invisible though they are, have been understood and seen through the things he has made. So they are without excuse; 21 for though they knew God, they did not honor him as God or give thanks to him, but they became futile in their thinking, and their senseless minds were darkened. 22 Claiming to be wise, they became fools; 23 and they exchanged the glory of the immortal God for images resembling a mortal human being or birds or four-footed animals or reptiles.

---

[d] Gk brothers
[e] Or The one who is righteous through faith will live

---

13 οὐ θέλω δὲ ὑμᾶς ἀγνοεῖν, ἀδελφοί,
³not ¹I wish ²But   you   to be ignorant, brothers,

ὅτι πολλάκις προεθέμην ἐλθεῖν πρὸς ὑμᾶς,
that often   I purposed to come unto   you,

καὶ ἐκωλύθην ἄχρι τοῦ δεῦρο, ἵνα τινὰ
and was hindered until the present, that some

καρπὸν σχῶ καὶ ἐν ὑμῖν καθὼς καὶ
fruit I may have also among you as indeed

ἐν τοῖς λοιποῖς ἔθνεσιν. **14** Ἕλλησίν
among the remaining nations.   ²to Greeks

τε καὶ βαρβάροις, σοφοῖς τε καὶ ἀνοήτοις
¹Both ³and ⁴to foreigners, ⁵to wise men ⁶both ⁷and ⁸to foolish

ὀφειλέτης εἰμί. **15** οὕτως τὸ κατ᾽ ἐμὲ
¹⁰a debtor ⁹I am;   so   as far as in me lies†

πρόθυμον καὶ ὑμῖν τοῖς ἐν Ῥώμῃ
[I am] eager ²also ³to you ⁴the [ones] ⁵in ⁶Rome

εὐαγγελίσασθαι. **16** οὐ γὰρ ἐπαισχύνομαι
¹to preach.   For I am not ashamed of

τὸ εὐαγγέλιον· δύναμις γὰρ θεοῦ ἐστιν
the gospel;   ²power ¹for of God it is

εἰς σωτηρίαν παντὶ τῷ πιστεύοντι, Ἰουδαίῳ
to salvation to everyone believing, ²to Jew

τε πρῶτον καὶ Ἕλληνι. **17** δικαιοσύνη
¹both firstly and to Greek.   a righteousness

γὰρ θεοῦ ἐν αὐτῷ ἀποκαλύπτεται ἐκ
For of God in it is revealed from

πίστεως εἰς πίστιν, καθὼς γέγραπται·
faith to faith, as it has been written:

ὁ δὲ δίκαιος ἐκ πίστεως ζήσεται.
Now the just man by faith will live.

18 Ἀποκαλύπτεται γὰρ ὀργὴ θεοῦ ἀπ᾽
For ⁴is revealed ¹[the] ²wrath ³of God from

οὐρανοῦ ἐπὶ πᾶσαν ἀσέβειαν καὶ ἀδικίαν
heaven against all impiety and unrighteousness

ἀνθρώπων τῶν τὴν ἀλήθειαν ἐν ἀδικίᾳ
of men – ²the ³truth ⁴in ⁵unrighteousness

κατεχόντων, **19** διότι τὸ γνωστὸν τοῦ θεοῦ
¹holding fast, because the thing known – of God

φανερόν ἐστιν ἐν αὐτοῖς· ὁ θεὸς γὰρ αὐτοῖς
manifest is among them; – for God to them

ἐφανέρωσεν. **20** τὰ γὰρ ἀόρατα αὐτοῦ
manifested [it]. For the invisible things of him

ἀπὸ κτίσεως κόσμου τοῖς ποιήμασιν
²from ³[the] ⁴creation ⁵of [the] world ⁷by the ⁸things made

νοούμενα καθορᾶται, ἥ τε
⁶being understood ¹is(are) clearly seen, ¹⁰the ⁹both

ἀίδιος αὐτοῦ δύναμις καὶ θειότης, εἰς
¹¹everlasting ¹⁵of him ¹²power ¹³and ¹⁴divinity, for

τὸ εἶναι αὐτοὺς ἀναπολογήτους, **21** διότι
the to be them[b] without excuse, because
=so that they are

γνόντες τὸν θεὸν οὐχ ὡς θεὸν ἐδόξασαν
knowing – God ²not ³as ⁴God ¹they glorified [him]

ἢ ηὐχαρίστησαν, ἀλλὰ ἐματαιώθησαν ἐν
¹or ²thanked [him], but became vain in

τοῖς διαλογισμοῖς αὐτῶν, καὶ ἐσκοτίσθη
the reasonings of them, and ³was darkened

ἡ ἀσύνετος αὐτῶν καρδία. **22** φάσκοντες
¹the ²undiscerning ⁴of them ³heart. Asserting

εἶναι σοφοὶ ἐμωράνθησαν, **23** καὶ ἤλλαξαν
to be wise they became foolish, and changed

τὴν δόξαν τοῦ ἀφθάρτου θεοῦ ἐν ὁμοιώματι
the glory of the incorruptible God in[to] a likeness

εἰκόνος φθαρτοῦ ἀνθρώπου καὶ πετεινῶν
of an image of corruptible man and birds

καὶ τετραπόδων καὶ ἑρπετῶν· **24** διὸ
and quadrupeds and reptiles; wherefore

---

faith. 13 I do not want you to be unaware, brothers, that I planned many times to come to you (but have been prevented from doing so until now) in order that I might have a harvest among you, just as I have had among the other Gentiles.

14 I am obligated both to Greeks and non-Greeks, both to the wise and the foolish. 15 That is why I am so eager to preach the gospel also to you who are at Rome.

16 I am not ashamed of the gospel, because it is the power of God for the salvation of everyone who believes: first for the Jew, then for the Gentile. 17 For in the gospel a righteousness from God is revealed, a righteousness that is by faith from first to last,[c] just as it is written: "The righteous will live by faith."[d]

God's Wrath Against Mankind

18 The wrath of God is being revealed from heaven against all the godlessness and wickedness of men who suppress the truth by their wickedness, 19 since what may be known about God is plain to them, because God has made it plain to them. 20 For since the creation of the world God's invisible qualities—his eternal power and divine nature—have been clearly seen, being understood from what has been made, so that men are without excuse.

21 For although they knew God, they neither glorified him as God nor gave thanks to him, but their thinking became futile and their foolish hearts were darkened. 22 Although they claimed to be wise, they became fools 23 and exchanged the glory of the immortal God for images made to look like mortal man and birds and animals and reptiles.

---

[c] 17 Or is from faith to faith
[d] 17 Hab. 2:4

24 Therefore God gave them up in the lusts of their hearts to impurity, to the degrading of their bodies among themselves, 25 because they exchanged the truth about God for a lie and worshiped and served the creature rather than the Creator, who is blessed forever! Amen.
26 For this reason God gave them up to degrading passions. Their women exchanged natural intercourse for unnatural, 27 and in the same way also the men, giving up natural intercourse with women, were consumed with passion for one another. Men committed shameless acts with men and received in their own persons the due penalty for their error.
28 And since they did not see fit to acknowledge God, God gave them up to a debased mind and to things that should not be done. 29 They were filled with every kind of wickedness, evil, covetousness, malice. Full of envy, murder, strife, deceit, craftiness, they are gossips, 30 slanderers, God-haters,[f] insolent, haughty, boastful, inventors of evil, rebellious toward parents, 31 foolish, faithless, heartless, ruthless. 32 They know God's decree, that those who practice such things deserve to die—yet they not only do them but even applaud others who practice them.

παρέδωκεν αὐτοὺς ὁ θεὸς ἐν ταῖς
¹gave up ²them – ¹God in the

ἐπιθυμίαις τῶν καρδιῶν αὐτῶν εἰς ἀκαθαρ-
desires of the hearts of them to unclean-

σίαν τοῦ ἀτιμάζεσθαι τὰ σώματα αὐτῶν
ness – to be dishonoured^d the bodies of them

ἐν αὐτοῖς. 25 Οἵτινες μετήλλαξαν τὴν
among them[selves]. Who changed the

ἀλήθειαν τοῦ θεοῦ ἐν τῷ ψεύδει, καὶ
truth of God in[to] the lie, and

ἐσεβάσθησαν καὶ ἐλάτρευσαν τῇ κτίσει
worshipped and served the creature

παρὰ τὸν κτίσαντα, ὅς ἐστιν εὐλογητὸς
rather than the [one] having created, who is blessed

εἰς τοὺς αἰῶνας· ἀμήν. 26 διὰ τοῦτο
unto the ages: Amen. Therefore

παρέδωκεν αὐτοὺς ὁ θεὸς εἰς πάθη
²gave up ³them – ¹God to passions

ἀτιμίας· αἵ τε γὰρ θήλειαι αὐτῶν
of dishonour; ³the ²even ¹for females of them

μετήλλαξαν τὴν φυσικὴν χρῆσιν εἰς τὴν
changed the natural use to the [use]

παρὰ φύσιν, 27 ὁμοίως τε καὶ οἱ ἄρσενες
against nature, ²likewise ¹and also the males

ἀφέντες τὴν φυσικὴν χρῆσιν τῆς θηλείας
leaving the natural use of the female

ἐξεκαύθησαν ἐν τῇ ὀρέξει αὐτῶν εἰς
burned in the desire of them toward

ἀλλήλους, ἄρσενες ἐν ἄρσεσιν τὴν
one another, males among males ²the

ἀσχημοσύνην κατεργαζόμενοι καὶ τὴν
³unseemliness ¹working and ⁴the

ἀντιμισθίαν ἣν ἔδει τῆς πλάνης αὐτῶν
⁵requital ⁶which¹⁰behoved ⁸of the ⁷error ⁹of them

ἐν ἑαυτοῖς ἀπολαμβάνοντες. 28 Καὶ
²in ³themselves ¹receiving back. And

καθὼς οὐκ ἐδοκίμασαν τὸν θεὸν ἔχειν
as they thought not fit – God to have

ἐν ἐπιγνώσει, παρέδωκεν αὐτοὺς ὁ θεὸς
in knowledge, ²gave up ³them – ¹God

εἰς ἀδόκιμον νοῦν, ποιεῖν τὰ μὴ καθήκοντα,
to a reprobate mind, to do the not being proper, things

29 πεπληρωμένους πάσῃ ἀδικίᾳ πονηρίᾳ
having been filled with all unrighteousness wickedness

πλεονεξίᾳ κακίᾳ, μεστοὺς φθόνου φόνου
covetousness evil, full of envy of murder

ἔριδος δόλου κακοηθείας, ψιθυριστάς,
of strife of guile of malignity, whisperers,*

30 καταλάλους, θεοστυγεῖς, ὑβριστάς, ὑπερ-
railers, God-haters, insolent, arro-

ηφάνους, ἀλαζόνας, ἐφευρετὰς κακῶν,
gant, boasters, inventors of evil things,

γονεῦσιν ἀπειθεῖς, 31 ἀσυνέτους, ἀσυνθέτους,
to parents disobedient, undiscerning, faithless,

ἀστόργους, ἀνελεήμονας· 32 οἵτινες τὸ
without unmerciful; who ²the
natural affection,

δικαίωμα τοῦ θεοῦ ἐπιγνόντες, ὅτι οἱ
³ordinance – ⁴of God ¹knowing, that the

τὰ τοιαῦτα πράσσοντες ἄξιοι θανάτου
the ²such things ¹[ones] practising worthy of death

εἰσίν, οὐ μόνον αὐτὰ ποιοῦσιν, ἀλλὰ
are, not only them do, but

καὶ συνευδοκοῦσιν τοῖς πράσσουσιν.
also consent to the [ones] practising.

24Therefore God gave them over in the sinful desires of their hearts to sexual impurity for the degrading of their bodies with one another. 25They exchanged the truth of God for a lie, and worshiped and served created things rather than the Creator—who is forever praised. Amen.
26Because of this, God gave them over to shameful lusts. Even their women exchanged natural relations for unnatural ones. 27In the same way the men also abandoned natural relations with women and were inflamed with lust for one another. Men committed indecent acts with other men, and received in themselves the due penalty for their perversion.
28Furthermore, since they did not think it worthwhile to retain the knowledge of God, he gave them over to a depraved mind, to do what ought not to be done. 29They have become filled with every kind of wickedness, evil, greed and depravity. They are full of envy, murder, strife, deceit and malice. They are gossips, 30slanderers, God-haters, insolent, arrogant and boastful; they invent ways of doing evil; they disobey their parents; 31they are senseless, faithless, heartless, ruthless. 32Although they know God's righteous decree that those who do such things deserve death, they not only continue to do these very things but also approve of those who practice them.

---

^f Or God-hated

* " In a bad sense " (Abbott-Smith).

Chapter 2

The Righteous Judgment of God

THEREFORE you have no excuse, whoever you are, when you judge others; for in passing judgment on another you condemn yourself, because you, the judge, are doing the very same things. 2 You say,[g] "We know that God's judgment on those who do such things is in accordance with truth." 3 Do you imagine, whoever you are, that when you judge those who do such things and yet do them yourself, you will escape the judgment of God? 4 Or do you despise the riches of his kindness and forbearance and patience? Do you not realize that God's kindness is meant to lead you to repentance? 5 But by your hard and impenitent heart you are storing up wrath for yourself on the day of wrath, when God's righteous judgment will be revealed. 6 For he will repay according to each one's deeds: 7 to those who by patiently doing good seek for glory and honor and immortality, he will give eternal life; 8 while for those who are self-seeking and who obey not the truth but wickedness, there will be wrath and fury. 9 There will be anguish and distress for everyone who does evil, the Jew first and also the Greek, 10 but glory and honor and peace for everyone who does good, the Jew first and also the Greek. 11 For God shows no partiality.

12 All who have sinned apart from the law will also

---

2 Διὸ ἀναπολόγητος εἶ, ὦ ἄνθρωπε
Wherefore inexcusable thou art, O man
πᾶς ὁ κρίνων· ἐν ᾧ γὰρ κρίνεις τὸν
everyone judging; ²in ³what ¹for thou judgest the
ἕτερον, σεαυτὸν κατακρίνεις· τὰ γὰρ αὐτὰ
other, thyself thou condemnest; for the same things
πράσσεις ὁ κρίνων. **2** οἴδαμεν δὲ ὅτι τὸ
thou the judging. But we know that the
practisest [one]
κρίμα τοῦ θεοῦ ἐστιν κατὰ ἀλήθειαν ἐπὶ
judg-   -   of   is accord- truth on
ment God   ing to
τοὺς τὰ τοιαῦτα πράσσοντας. **3** λογίζῃ
the the ²such things ¹[ones] practising. reckonest thou
δὲ τοῦτο, ὦ ἄνθρωπε ὁ κρίνων τοὺς
And this, O man the judging the
[one]   [ones]
τὰ τοιαῦτα πράσσοντας καὶ ποιῶν αὐτά,
the such things practising and doing them,
ὅτι σὺ ἐκφεύξῃ τὸ κρίμα τοῦ θεοῦ;
that thou wilt escape the judgment - of God?
4 ἢ τοῦ πλούτου τῆς χρηστότητος αὐτοῦ
or the riches of the kindness of him
καὶ τῆς ἀνοχῆς καὶ τῆς μακροθυμίας
and the forbearance and the longsuffering
καταφρονεῖς, ἀγνοῶν ὅτι τὸ χρηστὸν τοῦ
despisest thou, not knowing that the kindness -
θεοῦ εἰς μετάνοιάν σε ἄγει; **5** κατὰ δὲ
of God to repentance thee leads? but according to
τὴν σκληρότητά σου καὶ ἀμετανόητον
the hardness of thee and impenitent
καρδίαν θησαυρίζεις σεαυτῷ ὀργὴν ἐν
heart treasurest for thyself wrath in
ἡμέρα ὀργῆς καὶ ἀποκαλύψεως δικαιοκρισίας
a day of wrath and of revelation of a righteous
judgment
τοῦ θεοῦ, **6** ὃς ἀποδώσει ἑκάστῳ κατὰ τὰ
- of God, who will requite to each man accord- the
ing to
ἔργα αὐτοῦ· **7** τοῖς μὲν καθ' ὑπομονὴν
works of him: to the on ²by ¹endurance
[ones] one hand
ἔργου ἀγαθοῦ δόξαν καὶ τιμὴν καὶ
⁵work ⁴of(in) good ⁶glory ⁷and ⁸honour ⁹and
ἀφθαρσίαν ζητοῦσιν ζωὴν αἰώνιον·
¹⁰incorruption ¹seeking ¹¹life ¹¹eternal;
8 τοῖς δὲ ἐξ ἐριθείας καὶ ἀπειθοῦσι τῇ
to the [ones] of self-seeking and disobeying the
on the other
ἀληθείᾳ πειθομένοις δὲ τῇ ἀδικίᾳ, ὀργὴ
truth ²obeying ¹but - unrighteousness, wrath
καὶ θυμός. **9** θλῖψις καὶ στενοχωρία ἐπὶ
and anger. Affliction and anguish on
πᾶσαν ψυχὴν ἀνθρώπου τοῦ κατεργαζομένου
every soul of man - working
τὸ κακόν, Ἰουδαίου τε πρῶτον καὶ
the evil, both of Jew firstly and
Ἕλληνος· **10** δόξα δὲ καὶ τιμὴ καὶ
of Greek; but glory and honour and
εἰρήνη παντὶ τῷ ἐργαζομένῳ τὸ ἀγαθόν,
peace to everyone working the good,
Ἰουδαίῳ τε πρῶτον καὶ Ἕλληνι. **11** οὐ
both to Jew firstly and to Greek. not
γάρ ἐστιν προσωπολημψία παρὰ τῷ θεῷ.
For is respect of persons with - God.
12 Ὅσοι γὰρ ἀνόμως ἥμαρτον, ἀνόμως
For as many as without law sinned, without law

Chapter 2

God's Righteous Judgment

YOU, therefore, have no excuse, you who pass judgment on someone else, for at whatever point you judge the other, you are condemning yourself, because you who pass judgment do the same things. 2 Now we know that God's judgment against those who do such things is based on truth. 3 So when you, a mere man, pass judgment on them and yet do the same things, do you think you will escape God's judgment? 4 Or do you show contempt for the riches of his kindness, tolerance and patience, not realizing that God's kindness leads you toward repentance?

5 But because of your stubbornness and your unrepentant heart, you are storing up wrath against yourself for the day of God's wrath, when his righteous judgment will be revealed. 6 God "will give to each person according to what he has done."[e] 7 To those who by persistence in doing good seek glory, honor and immortality, he will give eternal life. 8 But for those who are self-seeking and who reject the truth and follow evil, there will be wrath and anger. 9 There will be trouble and distress for every human being who does evil: first for the Jew, then for the Gentile; 10 but glory, honor and peace for everyone who does good: first for the Jew, then for the Gentile. 11 For God does not show favoritism.

12 All who sin apart from the law will also perish

---

perish apart from the law, and all who have sinned under the law will be judged by the law. 13For it is not the hearers of the law who are righteous in God's sight, but the doers of the law who will be justified. 14When Gentiles, who do not possess the law, do instinctively what the law requires, these, though not having the law, are a law to themselves. 15They show that what the law requires is written on their hearts, to which their own conscience also bears witness; and their conflicting thoughts will accuse or perhaps excuse them 16on the day when, according to my gospel, God, through Jesus Christ, will judge the secret thoughts of all.

The Jews and the Law

17 But if you call yourself a Jew and rely on the law and boast of your relation to God 18and know his will and determine what is best because you are instructed in the law, 19and if you are sure that you are a guide to those who are in darkness, 20a corrector of the foolish, a teacher of children, having in the law the embodiment of knowledge and truth, 21you, then, that teach others, will you not teach yourself? While you preach against stealing, do you steal? 22You that forbid adultery, do you commit adultery? You that abhor idols, do you rob temples? 23You that boast in the law, do you dishonor God by breaking the law? 24For, as it is written, "The name of God is blasphemed among the Gentiles because of you."

καὶ ἀπολοῦνται· καὶ ὅσοι ἐν νόμῳ
also will perish; and as many as (under) in law

ἥμαρτον, διὰ νόμου κριθήσονται· 13 οὐ
sinned, through law will be judged; ⁹not

γὰρ οἱ ἀκροαταὶ νόμου δίκαιοι παρὰ
¹for the hearers of law [are] just with

[τῷ] θεῷ, ἀλλ' οἱ ποιηταὶ νόμου
God, but the doers of law

δικαιωθήσονται. 14 ὅταν γὰρ ἔθνη τὰ
will be justified. For whenever nations –

μὴ νόμον ἔχοντα φύσει τὰ τοῦ νόμου
¹not ³law ²having by nature the things of the law

ποιῶσιν, οὗτοι νόμον μὴ ἔχοντες ἑαυτοῖς
do, these ³law ¹not ²having to themselves

εἰσιν νόμος· 15 οἵτινες ἐνδείκνυνται τὸ
are a law; who show the

ἔργον τοῦ νόμου γραπτὸν ἐν ταῖς καρδίαις
work of the law written in the hearts

αὐτῶν, συμμαρτυρούσης αὐτῶν τῆς συνει-
of them, witnessing with of them the con-
= while their conscience witnesses with and their

δήσεως καὶ μεταξὺ ἀλλήλων τῶν λογισμῶν
science and between one another the thoughts
thoughts among themselves accuse or even excuse,

κατηγορούντων ἢ καὶ ἀπολογουμένων, 16 ἐν
accusing or even excusing,ᵃ in

ᾗ ἡμέρᾳ κρίνει ὁ θεὸς τὰ κρυπτὰ τῶν
what day judges – God the hidden things

ἀνθρώπων κατὰ τὸ εὐαγγέλιόν μου διὰ
of men according to the gospel of me through

Χριστοῦ Ἰησοῦ. 17 Εἰ δὲ σὺ Ἰουδαῖος
Christ Jesus. But if thou ²a Jew

ἐπονομάζῃ καὶ ἐπαναπαύῃ νόμῳ καὶ
¹art named and restest on law and

καυχᾶσαι ἐν θεῷ 18 καὶ γινώσκεις τὸ
boastest in God and knowest the

θέλημα καὶ δοκιμάζεις τὰ διαφέροντα
will and approvest the things excelling

κατηχούμενος ἐκ τοῦ νόμου, 19 πέποιθάς τε
being instructed out of the law, and having persuaded

σεαυτὸν ὁδηγὸν εἶναι τυφλῶν, φῶς
thyself a guide to be of blind a light
[persons],

τῶν ἐν σκότει, 20 παιδευτὴν ἀφρόνων,
of the in darkness, an instructor of foolish
[ones] [persons],

διδάσκαλον νηπίων, ἔχοντα τὴν μόρφωσιν
a teacher of infants, having the form

τῆς γνώσεως καὶ τῆς ἀληθείας ἐν τῷ
– of knowledge and of the truth in the

νόμῳ· 21 ὁ οὖν διδάσκων ἕτερον σεαυτὸν
law: the there- teaching another thyself
[one] fore

οὐ διδάσκεις; ὁ κηρύσσων μὴ κλέπτειν
teachest thou not? the [one] proclaiming not to steal

κλέπτεις; 22 ὁ λέγων μὴ μοιχεύειν
stealest thou? the [one] saying not to commit adultery

μοιχεύεις; ὁ βδελυσσόμενος τὰ εἴδωλα
dost thou com- the detesting the idols
mit adultery? [one]

ἱεροσυλεῖς; 23 ὃς ἐν νόμῳ καυχᾶσαι, διὰ
dost thou rob who in law boastest, through
temples?

τῆς παραβάσεως τοῦ νόμου τὸν θεὸν
– transgression of the law – ²God

ἀτιμάζεις; 24 τὸ γὰρ ὄνομα τοῦ θεοῦ
¹dishonourest thou? for the name of God

δι' ὑμᾶς βλασφημεῖται ἐν τοῖς ἔθνεσιν,
because you is blasphemed among the nations,
of

---

apart from the law, and all who sin under the law will be judged by the law. 13For it is not those who hear the law who are righteous in God's sight, but it is those who obey the law who will be declared righteous. 14(Indeed, when Gentiles, who do not have the law, do by nature things required by the law, they are a law for themselves, even though they do not have the law, 15since they show that the requirements of the law are written on their hearts, their consciences also bearing witness, and their thoughts now accusing, now even defending them.) 16This will take place on the day when God will judge men's secrets through Jesus Christ, as my gospel declares.

The Jews and the Law

17Now you, if you call yourself a Jew; if you rely on the law and brag about your relationship to God; 18if you know his will and approve of what is superior because you are instructed by the law; 19if you are convinced that you are a guide for the blind, a light for those who are in the dark, 20an instructor of the foolish, a teacher of infants, because you have in the law the embodiment of knowledge and truth— 21you, then, who teach others, do you not teach yourself? You who preach against stealing, do you steal? 22You who say that people should not commit adultery, do you commit adultery? You who abhor idols, do you rob temples? 23You who brag about the law, do you dishonor God by breaking the law? 24As it is written: "God's name is blasphemed among the Gentiles because of you."ᶠ

ᶠ24 Isaiah 52:5; Ezek. 36:22

25 Circumcision indeed is of value if you obey the law; but if you break the law, your circumcision has become uncircumcision. 26 So, if those who are uncircumcised keep the requirements of the law, will not their uncircumcision be regarded as circumcision? 27 Then those who are physically uncircumcised but keep the law will condemn you that have the written code and circumcision but break the law. 28 For a person is not a Jew who is one outwardly, nor is true circumcision something external and physical. 29 Rather, a person is a Jew who is one inwardly, and real circumcision is a matter of the heart—it is spiritual and not literal. Such a person receives praise not from others but from God.

Chapter 3

THEN what advantage has the Jew? Or what is the value of circumcision? 2 Much, in every way. For in the first place the Jews[h] were entrusted with the oracles of God. 3 What if some were unfaithful? Will their faithlessness nullify the faithfulness of God? 4 By no means! Although everyone is a liar, let God be proved true, as it is written,

"So that you may be
    justified in your
    words,
and prevail in your
    judging."[i]

5 But if our injustice serves to confirm the justice of God, what should we say? That God is unjust to inflict wrath on us? (I speak in a human way.) 6 By no means! For then how could God judge the world? 7 But if through my falsehood God's truthfulness abounds to his glory, why

---

καθὼς γέγραπται. **25** περιτομὴ μὲν γὰρ
as   it has been written.   circumcision   indeed   For

ὠφελεῖ ἐὰν νόμον πράσσης· ἐὰν δὲ
profits   if   law   thou practisest;   but if

παραβάτης νόμου ᾖς, ἡ περιτομή σου
a transgressor   of law   thou art,   the   circumcision   of thee

ἀκροβυστία γέγονεν. **26** ἐὰν οὖν ἡ ἀκρο-
uncircumcision   has become.   If   therefore the   uncir-

βυστία τὰ δικαιώματα τοῦ νόμου φυλάσσῃ,
cumcision   the   ordinances   of the   law   keeps,

οὐχ ἡ ἀκροβυστία αὐτοῦ εἰς περιτομὴν
not   the   uncircumcision   of him   for   circumcision

λογισθήσεται; **27** καὶ κρινεῖ ἡ ἐκ φύσεως
will be reckoned?   and ⁸will judge ¹the ²by ⁴nature

ἀκροβυστία τὸν νόμον τελοῦσα σὲ τὸν
²uncircumcision ⁵the ⁷law ⁶keeping ⁹thee ¹⁰the

διὰ γράμματος καὶ περιτομῆς παραβάτην
¹³through ¹⁴letter ¹⁵and ¹⁶circumcision ¹¹transgressor

νόμου. **28** οὐ γὰρ ὁ ἐν τῷ φανερῷ
¹²of law.   For ¹not ³the ⁵in ⁴the ⁶open

Ἰουδαῖός ἐστιν, οὐδὲ ἡ ἐν τῷ φανερῷ
²Jew   ¹he is,   nor ¹the ³in ⁴the ⁵open

ἐν σαρκὶ περιτομή· **29** ἀλλ' ὁ ἐν τῷ
⁶in ⁷flesh ²circumcision;   but ¹the ³in ⁴the

κρυπτῷ Ἰουδαῖος, καὶ περιτομὴ καρδίας
⁵secret ²Jew [is],   and circumcision [is]   of heart

ἐν πνεύματι οὐ γράμματι, οὗ ὁ ἔπαινος
in   spirit   not   letter,   of   the   praise [is]
                                            whom

οὐκ ἐξ ἀνθρώπων ἀλλ' ἐκ τοῦ θεοῦ.
not   from   men   but   from   -   God.

3 Τί οὖν τὸ περισσὸν τοῦ Ἰουδαίου,
What therefore the   advantage   of the   Jew,

ἢ τίς ἡ ὠφέλεια τῆς περιτομῆς; **2** πολὺ
or what the   profit   -   of circumcision?   Much

κατὰ πάντα τρόπον. πρῶτον μὲν [γὰρ]
by   every   way.   ³Firstly ²indeed ¹for

ὅτι ἐπιστεύθησαν τὰ λόγια τοῦ θεοῦ.
because   they were   the   oracles   -   of God.
     entrusted [with]

3 τί γάρ; εἰ ἠπίστησάν τινες, μὴ ἡ
For what?   If ²disbelieved ¹some,   not   the

ἀπιστία αὐτῶν τὴν πίστιν τοῦ θεοῦ
unbelief   of them   the   faith   -   of God

καταργήσει; **4** μὴ γένοιτο· γινέσθω δὲ
will destroy?   May it not be;   but let be

ὁ θεὸς ἀληθής, πᾶς δὲ ἄνθρωπος ψεύστης,
-   God   true,   and every   man   a liar,

καθάπερ γέγραπται· ὅπως ἂν δικαιωθῇς
as   it has been   So as   -   thou mayest
      written: be justified

ἐν τοῖς λόγοις σου καὶ νικήσεις ἐν
in   the   sayings   of thee   and   wilt overcome   in

τῷ κρίνεσθαί σε. **5** εἰ δὲ ἡ ἀδικία
the   to be judged   thee.ᵇᵉ   Now if   the   unright-
=when thou art judged.   eousness

ἡμῶν θεοῦ δικαιοσύνην συνίστησιν, τί
of us ²of God ²a righteousness ¹commends,   what

ἐροῦμεν; μὴ ἄδικος ὁ θεὸς ὁ ἐπιφέρων
shall we say?   not   unrighteous   -   God the [one] inflicting

τὴν ὀργήν; κατὰ ἄνθρωπον λέγω. **6** μὴ
-   wrath? according to   man   I say.   not

γένοιτο· ἐπεὶ πῶς κρινεῖ ὁ θεὸς τὸν
May it be;   otherwise how   will judge   -   God   the

κόσμον; **7** εἰ δὲ ἡ ἀλήθεια τοῦ θεοῦ
world?   But if   the   truth   -   of God

---

25 Circumcision has value if you observe the law, but if you break the law, you have become as though you had not been circumcised. 26 If those who are not circumcised keep the law's requirements, will they not be regarded as though they were circumcised? 27 The one who is not circumcised physically and yet obeys the law will condemn you who, even though you have the[g] written code and circumcision, are a lawbreaker. 28 A man is not a Jew if he is only one outwardly, nor is circumcision merely outward and physical. 29 No, a man is a Jew if he is one inwardly; and circumcision is circumcision of the heart, by the Spirit, not by the written code. Such a man's praise is not from men, but from God.

Chapter 3

God's Faithfulness

WHAT advantage, then, is there in being a Jew, or what value is there in circumcision? 2 Much in every way! First of all, they have been entrusted with the very words of God.

3 What if some did not have faith? Will their lack of faith nullify God's faithfulness? 4 Not at all! Let God be true, and every man a liar. As it is written:

"So that you may be
    proved right when
    you speak
and prevail when you
    judge."[h]

5 But if our unrighteousness brings out God's righteousness more clearly, what shall we say? That God is unjust in bringing his wrath on us? (I am using a human argument.) 6 Certainly not! If that were so, how could God judge the world? 7 Someone might argue, "If my falsehood en-

---

[h] Gk they
[i] Gk when you are being judged

[g] 27 Or who, by means of a
[h] 4 Psalm 51:4

am I still being condemned as a sinner? 8 And why not say (as some people slander us by saying that we say), "Let us do evil so that good may come"? Their condemnation is deserved!

None Is Righteous

9 What then? Are we any better off?[j] No, not at all; for we have already charged that all, both Jews and Greeks, are under the power of sin, 10 as it is written:

"There is no one who is righteous, not even one;
11 there is no one who has understanding, there is no one who seeks God.
12 All have turned aside, together they have become worthless; there is no one who shows kindness, there is not even one."
13 "Their throats are opened graves; they use their tongues to deceive."
"The venom of vipers is under their lips."
14 "Their mouths are full of cursing and bitterness."
15 "Their feet are swift to shed blood;
16 ruin and misery are in their paths,
17 and the way of peace they have not known."
18 "There is no fear of God before their eyes."

19 Now we know that whatever the law says, it speaks to those who are under the law, so that every mouth may be silenced, and the whole world may be held accountable to God. 20 For "no human being will be justified in his sight" by deeds prescribed by the law, for through the law comes the knowledge of sin.

Righteousness through Faith

21 But now, apart from law, the righteousness of God has been disclosed, and is attested by the law

[j] Or at any disadvantage:

ἐν τῷ ἐμῷ ψεύσματι ἐπερίσσευσεν εἰς
by - my lie abounded to
τὴν δόξαν αὐτοῦ, τί ἔτι κἀγὼ ὡς
the glory of him, why still I also as
ἁμαρτωλὸς κρίνομαι; 8 καὶ μὴ καθὼς
a sinner am judged? and not as
βλασφημούμεθα καὶ καθώς φασίν τινες
we are blasphemed and as ²say ¹some
ἡμᾶς λέγειν ὅτι ποιήσωμεν τὰ κακὰ
us to say[,] - Let us do - evil things
=that we say,
ἵνα ἔλθη τὰ ἀγαθά; ὧν τὸ κρίμα
that may come - good things? of whom the judgment
ἔνδικόν ἐστιν. 9 Τί οὖν; προεχόμεθα;
just is. What therefore? Do we excel?
οὐ πάντως· προητιασάμεθα γὰρ Ἰουδαίους
not at all; for we previously accused ²Jews
τε καὶ Ἕλληνας πάντας ὑφ' ἁμαρτίαν
¹both and Greeks all under sin
εἶναι, 10 καθὼς γέγραπται ὅτι οὐκ ἔστιν
to be, as it has been written[,] - There is not
δίκαιος οὐδὲ εἷς, οὐκ ἔστιν ὁ
a righteous man not one, there is not the [one]
συνίων, 11 οὐκ ἔστιν ὁ ἐκζητῶν τὸν θεόν·
under- there is not the seeking - God;
standing, [one]
12 πάντες ἐξέκλιναν, ἅμα ἠχρεώθησαν·
all turned away, together became unprofitable;
οὐκ ἔστιν ὁ ποιῶν χρηστότητα, οὐκ
there is not the [one] doing kindness, not
ἔστιν ἕως ἑνός. 13 τάφος ἀνεῳγμένος
there is so much as one. A grave having been opened
ὁ λάρυγξ αὐτῶν, ταῖς γλώσσαις αὐτῶν
the throat of them, with the tongues of them
ἐδολιοῦσαν, ἰὸς ἀσπίδων ὑπὸ τὰ χείλη
they acted poison of asps under the lips
deceitfully,
αὐτῶν· 14 ὧν τὸ στόμα ἀρᾶς καὶ πικρίας
of them; of whom the mouth ²of cursing ³and ⁴bitterness
γέμει· 15 ὀξεῖς οἱ πόδες αὐτῶν ἐκχέαι
¹is full; swift the feet of them to shed
αἷμα, 16 σύντριμμα καὶ ταλαιπωρία ἐν
blood, ruin and misery in
ταῖς ὁδοῖς αὐτῶν, 17 καὶ ὁδὸν εἰρήνης
the ways of them, and a way of peace
οὐκ ἔγνωσαν. 18 οὐκ ἔστιν φόβος θεοῦ
they knew not. There is not fear of God
ἀπέναντι τῶν ὀφθαλμῶν αὐτῶν. 19 οἴδαμεν
before the eyes of them. we know
δὲ ὅτι ὅσα ὁ νόμος λέγει τοῖς ἐν τῷ
But that whatever the law says to the in the
things [ones]
νόμῳ λαλεῖ, ἵνα πᾶν στόμα φραγῇ καὶ
law it speaks, in order that every mouth may be stopped and
ὑπόδικος γένηται πᾶς ὁ κόσμος τῷ
⁵under ⁴may become ¹all ²the ³world -
judgment
θεῷ· 20 διότι ἐξ ἔργων νόμου οὐ
to God; because by works of law not
δικαιωθήσεται πᾶσα σὰρξ ἐνώπιον αὐτοῦ·
will be justified all flesh* before him;
διὰ γὰρ νόμου ἐπίγνωσις ἁμαρτίας.
for through law [is] full knowledge of sin.
21 Νυνὶ δὲ χωρὶς νόμου δικαιοσύνη
But now without law a righteousness
θεοῦ πεφανέρωται, μαρτυρουμένη ὑπὸ τοῦ
of God has been manifested, being witnessed by the

* That is, no flesh will be justified . . .

---

hances God's truthfulness and so increases his glory, why am I still condemned as a sinner? 8 Why not say—as we are being slanderously reported as saying and as some claim that we say—"Let us do evil that good may result"? Their condemnation is deserved.

No One Is Righteous

9 What shall we conclude then? Are we any better[i]? Not at all! We have already made the charge that Jews and Gentiles alike are all under sin. 10 As it is written:

"There is no one righteous, not even one;
11 there is no one who understands, no one who seeks God.
12 All have turned away, they have together become worthless; there is no one who does good, not even one."[j]
13 "Their throats are open graves; their tongues practice deceit."[k]
"The poison of vipers is on their lips."[l]
14 "Their mouths are full of cursing and bitterness."[m]
15 "Their feet are swift to shed blood;
16 ruin and misery mark their ways,
17 and the way of peace they do not know."[n]
18 "There is no fear of God before their eyes."[o]

19 Now we know that whatever the law says, it says to those who are under the law, so that every mouth may be silenced and the whole world held accountable to God. 20 Therefore no one will be declared righteous in his sight by observing the law; rather, men, so also the result of through the law we become conscious of sin.

Righteousness Through Faith

21 But now a righteousness from God, apart from law, has been made known,

[i] 9 Or worse
[j] 12 Psalms 14:1-3; 53:1-3; Eccles. 7:20
[k] 13 Psalm 5:9
[l] 13 Psalm 140:3
[m] 14 Psalm 10:7
[n] 17 Isaiah 59:7,8
[o] 18 Psalm 36:1

and the prophets, 22the righteousness of God through faith in Jesus Christ[k] for all who believe. For there is no distinction, 23since all have sinned and fall short of the glory of God; 24they are now justified by his grace as a gift, through the redemption that is in Christ Jesus, 25whom God put forward as a sacrifice of atonement[l] by his blood, effective through faith. He did this to show his righteousness, because in his divine forbearance he had passed over the sins previously committed; 26it was to prove at the present time that he himself is righteous and that he justifies the one who has faith in Jesus.[m]

27 Then what becomes of boasting? It is excluded. By what law? By that of works? No, but by the law of faith. 28For we hold that a person is justified by faith apart from works prescribed by the law. 29Or is God the God of Jews only? Is he not the God of Gentiles also? Yes, of Gentiles also, 30since God is one; and he will justify the circumcised on the ground of faith and the uncircumcised through that same faith. 31Do we then overthrow the law by this faith? By no means! On the contrary, we uphold the law.

Chapter 4

The Example of Abraham

WHAT then are we to say was gained by[n] Abraham, our ancestor according to the flesh? 2For if Abraham was justified by works, he has something to boast about, but not before God. 3For what does the scripture say? "Abraham believed God, and it was reckoned to him as righ-

[k] Or through the faith of Jesus Christ
[l] Or a place of atonement
[m] Or who has the faith of Jesus
[n] Other ancient authorities read say about

νόμου   καὶ   τῶν   προφητῶν,   **22** δικαιοσύνη
law   and   the   prophets,   ²a righteousness

δὲ   θεοῦ   διὰ   πίστεως   ['Ιησοῦ]   Χριστοῦ,
¹and of God   through faith   of(in) Jesus Christ,

εἰς   πάντας   τοὺς   πιστεύοντας·   οὐ   γάρ
to   all   the [ones] believing·   for not

ἐστιν   διαστολή·   **23** πάντες   γὰρ   ἥμαρτον
there is difference;   for all   sinned

καὶ   ὑστεροῦνται   τῆς   δόξης   τοῦ   θεοῦ,
and   come short   of the glory   of   God,

24 δικαιούμενοι   δωρεὰν   τῇ   αὐτοῦ   χάριτι
being justified   freely   by the of him grace

διὰ   τῆς   ἀπολυτρώσεως   τῆς   ἐν   Χριστῷ
through the   redemption   -   in   Christ

'Ιησοῦ·   **25** ὃν   προέθετο   ὁ θεὸς   ἱλαστήριον
Jesus;   whom   set forth   - God   a propitiation

διὰ   πίστεως   ἐν   τῷ   αὐτοῦ   αἵματι,   εἰς
through faith   by   the   of him   blood,   for

ἔνδειξιν   τῆς   δικαιοσύνης   αὐτοῦ   διὰ   τὴν
a showing   of the righteousness of him   because of the
forth

πάρεσιν   τῶν   προγεγονότων   ἁμαρτημάτων
passing by of the ²having previously ¹sins
                   occurred

26 ἐν   τῇ   ἀνοχῇ   τοῦ   θεοῦ,   πρὸς   τὴν
in   the forbearance - of God,   for   the

ἔνδειξιν   τῆς   δικαιοσύνης   αὐτοῦ   ἐν   τῷ
showing   of the righteousness of him   in   the
forth

νῦν   καιρῷ,   εἰς   τὸ   εἶναι   αὐτὸν   δίκαιον
present time,   for   the   to be   him[b]   just
                        = that he should be

καὶ   δικαιοῦντα   τὸν   ἐκ   πίστεως   'Ιησοῦ.
and   justifying   the [one] of   faith   of(in) Jesus.

27 Ποῦ   οὖν   ἡ   καύχησις;   ἐξεκλείσθη.   διὰ
Where there- the   boasting?   It was shut out. Through
fore

ποίου   νόμου;   τῶν   ἔργων;   οὐχί,   ἀλλὰ
what   law?   -   of works? no,   but

διὰ   νόμου   πίστεως.   **28** λογιζόμεθα   γὰρ
through a law   of faith.   For we reckon

δικαιοῦσθαι   πίστει   ἄνθρωπον   χωρὶς   ἔργων
²to be justified ³by faith ¹a man   without   works

νόμου.   **29** ἢ   'Ιουδαίων   ὁ   θεὸς   μόνον;
of law.   Or   of Jews [is he] the   God   only?

οὐχὶ   καὶ   ἐθνῶν;   ναὶ   καὶ   ἐθνῶν,   **30** εἴπερ
not   also   of nations? Yes[,] also of nations, since [there is]

εἷς   ὁ   θεὸς   ὃς   δικαιώσει   περιτομὴν   ἐκ
one   -   God   who   will justify   circumcision by

πίστεως   καὶ   ἀκροβυστίαν   διὰ   τῆς   πίστεως.
faith   and   uncircumcision through the   faith.

31 νόμον   οὖν   καταργοῦμεν   διὰ   τῆς
³Law   ²therefore ¹do we destroy through the

πίστεως;   μὴ   γένοιτο,   ἀλλὰ   νόμον   ἱστάνομεν.
faith?   May it not be,   but   ²law   ¹we establish.

4 Τί   οὖν   ἐροῦμεν   εὑρηκέναι   'Αβραὰμ
What therefore shall we say to have found Abraham

τὸν   προπάτορα   ἡμῶν   κατὰ   σάρκα;   **2** εἰ
the   forefather   of us   according to flesh?   if

γὰρ   'Αβραὰμ   ἐξ   ἔργων   ἐδικαιώθη,   ἔχει
For   Abraham   by   works   was justified, he has

καύχημα·   ἀλλ'   οὐ   πρὸς   θεόν.   **3** τί   γὰρ
a boast;   but   not   with   God.   For what

ἡ   γραφὴ   λέγει;   ἐπίστευσεν   δὲ   'Αβραὰμ
the scripture says?   And ²believed   ¹Abraham

τῷ   θεῷ,   καὶ   ἐλογίσθη   αὐτῷ   εἰς
-     God,   and   it was reckoned to him for

---

to which the Law and the Prophets testify. 22This righteousness from God comes through faith in Jesus Christ to all who believe. There is no difference, 23for all have sinned and fall short of the glory of God, 24and are justified freely by his grace through the redemption that came by Christ Jesus. 25God presented him as a sacrifice of atonement,[p] through faith in his blood. He did this to demonstrate his justice, because in his forbearance he had left the sins committed beforehand unpunished— 26he did it to demonstrate his justice at the present time, so as to be just and the one who justifies those who have faith in Jesus.

27Where, then, is boasting? It is excluded. On what principle? On that of observing the law? No, but on that of faith. 28For we maintain that a man is justified by faith apart from observing the law. 29Is God the God of Jews only? Is he not the God of Gentiles too? Yes, of Gentiles too, 30since there is only one God, who will justify the circumcised by faith and the uncircumcised through that same faith. 31Do we, then, nullify the law by this faith? Not at all! Rather, we uphold the law.

Chapter 4

Abraham Justified by Faith

WHAT then shall we say that Abraham, our forefather, discovered in this matter? 2If, in fact, Abraham was justified by works, he had something to boast about—but not before God. 3What does the Scripture say? "Abraham believed God, and it was credited to him as righteousness."[q]

[p]25 Or as the one who would turn aside his wrath, taking away sin
[q]3 Gen. 15:6; also in verse 22

teousness." 4 Now to one who works, wages are not reckoned as a gift but as something due. 5 But to one who without works trusts him who justifies the ungodly, such faith is reckoned as righteousness. 6 So also David speaks of the blessedness of those to whom God reckons righteousness apart from works:

7 "Blessed are those
　　whose iniquities
　　are forgiven,
　　and whose sins are
　　covered;
8 blessed is the one
　　against whom
　　the Lord will
　　not reckon sin."

9 Is this blessedness, then, pronounced only on the circumcision, or also on the uncircumcised? We say, "Faith was reckoned to Abraham as righteousness." 10 How then was it reckoned to him? Was it before or after he had been circumcised? It was not after, but before he was circumcised. 11 He received the sign of circumcision as a seal of the righteousness that he had by faith while he was still uncircumcised. The purpose was to make him the ancestor of all who believe without being circumcised and who thus have righteousness reckoned to them, 12 and likewise the ancestor of the circumcised who are not only circumcised but who also follow the example of the faith that our ancestor Abraham had before he was circumcised.

God's Promise Realized through Faith

13 For the promise that he would inherit the world did not come to Abraham or to his descendants through the law but through the righteousness of faith. 14 If it is the adherents of the law who are to be the heirs, faith is null

δικαιοσύνην. 4 τῷ δὲ ἐργαζομένῳ ὁ
righteousness. Now to the [one] working the

μισθὸς οὐ λογίζεται κατὰ χάριν ἀλλὰ
reward is not reckoned according to grace but

κατὰ ὀφείλημα· 5 τῷ δὲ μὴ ἐργαζομένῳ,
according to debt; but to the [one] not working,

πιστεύοντι δὲ ἐπὶ τὸν δικαιοῦντα τὸν
but believing on the [one] justifying the

ἀσεβῆ, λογίζεται ἡ πίστις αὐτοῦ εἰς
impious man, is reckoned the faith of him for

δικαιοσύνην, 6 καθάπερ καὶ Δαυὶδ λέγει
righteousness, even as also David says

τὸν μακαρισμὸν τοῦ ἀνθρώπου ᾧ ὁ
the blessedness of the man to whom -

θεὸς λογίζεται δικαιοσύνην χωρὶς ἔργων·
God reckons righteousness without works;

7 μακάριοι ὧν ἀφέθησαν αἱ ἀνομίαι
Blessed [are they] of whom were forgiven the lawlessnesses

καὶ ὧν ἐπεκαλύφθησαν αἱ ἁμαρτίαι·
and of whom were covered over the sins;

8 μακάριος ἀνὴρ οὗ οὐ μὴ λογίσηται
blessed [is] a man of whom by no means *may reckon

κύριος ἁμαρτίαν. 9 ὁ μακαρισμὸς οὖν
¹[the] Lord sin. - ²blessedness ³then

οὗτος ἐπὶ τὴν περιτομὴν ἢ καὶ ἐπὶ
¹This on the circumcision or also on

τὴν ἀκροβυστίαν; λέγομεν γάρ· ἐλογίσθη
the uncircumcision? for we say: ³was reckoned

τῷ Ἀβραὰμ ἡ πίστις εἰς δικαιοσύνην.
- ⁴to Abraham ¹The(his) ²faith for righteousness.

10 πῶς οὖν ἐλογίσθη; ἐν περιτομῇ ὄντι
How then was it reckoned? in circumcision being

ἢ ἐν ἀκροβυστίᾳ; οὐκ ἐν περιτομῇ ἀλλ'
or in uncircumcision? not in circumcision but

ἐν ἀκροβυστίᾳ· 11 καὶ σημεῖον ἔλαβεν
in uncircumcision; and ²a sign ¹he received

περιτομῆς σφραγῖδα τῆς δικαιοσύνης τῆς
of circumcision a seal of the righteousness of the

πίστεως τῆς ἐν τῇ ἀκροβυστίᾳ, εἰς
faith - [while] in - uncircumcision, for
=so

τὸ εἶναι αὐτὸν πατέρα πάντων τῶν
the to be him(b) a father of all the
that he should be

πιστευόντων δι' ἀκροβυστίας, εἰς τὸ
[ones] believing through uncircumcision, for the
=that right-

λογισθῆναι αὐτοῖς [τὴν] δικαιοσύνην, 12 καὶ
to be reckoned to them - righteousness,(b) and
eousness should be reckoned to them,

πατέρα περιτομῆς τοῖς οὐκ ἐκ περιτομῆς
a father of circumcision to the not of circumcision
[ones]

μόνον ἀλλὰ καὶ τοῖς στοιχοῦσιν τοῖς
only but also to the [ones] walking in the

ἴχνεσιν τῆς ἐν ἀκροβυστίᾳ πίστεως τοῦ
steps ¹of the ⁷in ⁸uncircumcision ²faith ³of the

πατρὸς ἡμῶν Ἀβραάμ. 13 Οὐ γὰρ διὰ
⁴father ⁵of us ⁶Abraham. For not through

νόμου ἡ ἐπαγγελία τῷ Ἀβραὰμ ἢ τῷ
law the promise - to Abraham or to the

σπέρματι αὐτοῦ, τὸ κληρονόμον αὐτὸν
seed of him, the heir him
=that he should be heir

εἶναι κόσμου, ἀλλὰ διὰ δικαιοσύνης πίστεως.
to be(b) of [the] world, but through a righteousness of faith.

14 εἰ γὰρ οἱ ἐκ νόμου κληρονόμοι,
For if ¹the ³[are] ⁴of ⁶law ⁵heirs,

4 Now when a man works, his wages are not credited to him as a gift, but as an obligation. 5 However, to the man who does not work but trusts God who justifies the wicked, his faith is credited as righteousness. 6 David says the same thing when he speaks of the blessedness of the man to whom God credits righteousness apart from works:

7 "Blessed are they
　　whose transgressions
　　are forgiven,
　　whose sins are
　　covered.
8 Blessed is the man
　　whose sin the Lord will
　　never count against
　　him." r

9 Is this blessedness only for the circumcised, or also for the uncircumcised? We have been saying that Abraham's faith was credited to him as righteousness. 10 Under what circumstances was it credited? Was it after he was circumcised, or before? It was not after, but before! 11 And he received the sign of circumcision, a seal of the righteousness that he had by faith while he was still uncircumcised. So then, he is the father of all who believe but have not been circumcised, in order that righteousness might be credited to them. 12 And he is also the father of the circumcised who not only are circumcised but who also walk in the footsteps of the faith that our father Abraham had before he was circumcised.

13 It was not through law that Abraham and his offspring received the promise that he would be heir of the world, but through the righteousness that comes by faith. 14 For if those who live by law are heirs, faith

r 8 Psalm 32:1,2

and the promise is void. 15 For the law brings wrath; but where there is no law, neither is there violation.

16 For this reason it depends on faith, in order that the promise may rest on grace and be guaranteed to all his descendants, not only to the adherents of the law but also to those who share the faith of Abraham (for he is the father of all of us, 17as it is written, "I have made you the father of many nations")—in the presence of the God in whom he believed, who gives life to the dead and calls into existence the things that do not exist. 18 Hoping against hope, he believed that he would become "the father of many nations," according to what was said, "So numerous shall your descendants be." 19He did not weaken in faith when he considered his own body, which was already° as good as dead (for he was about a hundred years old), or when he considered the barrenness of Sarah's womb. 20 No distrust made him waver concerning the promise of God, but he grew strong in his faith as he gave glory to God, 21being fully convinced that God was able to do what he had promised. 22 Therefore his faithᵖ "was reckoned to him as righteousness." 23 Now the words, "it was reckoned to him," were written not for his sake alone, 24but for ours also. It will be reckoned to us who believe in him who raised Jesus our Lord from the dead, 25 who

κεκένωται ἡ πίστις καὶ κατήργηται
³has been emptied – ¹faith and ³has been destroyed

ἡ ἐπαγγελία· 15 ὁ γὰρ νόμος ὀργὴν
¹the ²promise; for the law ²wrath

κατεργάζεται· οὗ δὲ οὐκ ἔστιν νόμος,
¹works; and where there is not law,

οὐδὲ παράβασις. 16 Διὰ τοῦτο ἐκ πίστεως,
neither [is there] transgression. Therefore [it is] of faith,

ἵνα κατὰ χάριν, εἰς τὸ εἶναι βεβαίαν
in [it may be] grace, for the to be firm
order according =so that the promise shall be firm
that to

τὴν ἐπαγγελίαν παντὶ τῷ σπέρματι, οὐ
the promiseᵇ to all the seed, not

τῷ ἐκ τοῦ νόμου μόνον ἀλλὰ καὶ τῷ
[seed] the of the law only but also to the
to the of the law [seed]

ἐκ πίστεως ᾿Αβραάμ, ὅς ἐστιν πατὴρ
of [the] faith of Abraham, who is father

πάντων ἡμῶν, 17 καθὼς γέγραπται ὅτι
of all us, as it has been written[,] –

πατέρα πολλῶν ἐθνῶν τέθεικά σε,
A father of many nations I have appointed thee,

κατέναντι οὗ ἐπίστευσεν θεοῦ τοῦ ζωο-
before ²whom ³he believed ¹God the [one] quick-

ποιοῦντος τοὺς νεκροὺς καὶ καλοῦντος
ening the dead [ones] and calling

τὰ μὴ ὄντα ὡς ὄντα. 18 ὃς παρ᾽ ἐλπίδα
the not being as being; who beyond hope
things

ἐπ᾽ ἐλπίδι ἐπίστευσεν, εἰς τὸ γενέσθαι
on hope believed, for the to become
=so that he should become

αὐτὸν πατέρα πολλῶν ἐθνῶν κατὰ τὸ
himᵇ a father of many nations accord- the
ing to thing

εἰρημένον· οὕτως ἔσται τὸ σπέρμα σου·
having been said : So shall be the seed of thee;

19 καὶ μὴ ἀσθενήσας τῇ πίστει κατενόησεν
and not weakening – in faith he considered

τὸ ἑαυτοῦ σῶμα νενεκρωμένον, ἑκατονταέτης
¹the ³of himself ²body to have died, a hundred years

που ὑπάρχων, καὶ τὴν νέκρωσιν τῆς
about being, and the death of the

μήτρας Σάρρας· 20 εἰς δὲ τὴν ἐπαγγελίαν
womb of Sarah; but ²against ³the ⁴promise

τοῦ θεοῦ οὐ διεκρίθη τῇ ἀπιστίᾳ, ἀλλὰ
– ¹of God ¹he did not decide ⁵by unbelief, but

ἐνεδυναμώθη τῇ πίστει, δοὺς δόξαν τῷ
was empowered – by faith, giving glory –

θεῷ 21 καὶ πληροφορηθεὶς ὅτι ὃ ἐπήγγελται
to God and being fully that what he has
persuaded promised

δυνατός ἐστιν καὶ ποιῆσαι. 22 διὸ [καὶ]
able he is also to do. Wherefore also

ἐλογίσθη αὐτῷ εἰς δικαιοσύνην. 23 Οὐκ
it was to him for righteousness. not
reckoned

ἐγράφη δὲ δι᾽ αὐτὸν μόνον ὅτι ἐλογίσθη
it was Now because him only that it was
written of reckoned

αὐτῷ, 24 ἀλλὰ καὶ δι᾽ ἡμᾶς, οἷς μέλλει
to him, but also because us, to whom it is
of about

λογίζεσθαι, τοῖς πιστεύουσιν ἐπὶ τὸν
to be reckoned, to the [ones] believing on the [one]

ἐγείραντα ᾿Ιησοῦν τὸν κύριον ἡμῶν ἐκ
having raised Jesus the Lord of us out of

has no value and the promise is worthless, 15because law brings wrath. And where there is no law there is no transgression.

16Therefore, the promise comes by faith, so that it may be by grace and may be guaranteed to all Abraham's offspring—not only to those who are of the law but also to those who are of the faith of Abraham. He is the father of us all. 17As it is written: "I have made you a father of many nations."ˢ He is our father in the sight of God, in whom he believed—the God who gives life to the dead and calls things that are not as though they were.

18Against all hope, Abraham in hope believed and so became the father of many nations, just as it had been said to him, "So shall your offspring be."ᵗ 19Without weakening in his faith, he faced the fact that his body was as good as dead—since he was about a hundred years old—and that Sarah's womb was also dead. 20Yet he did not waver through unbelief regarding the promise of God, but was strengthened in his faith and gave glory to God, 21being fully persuaded that God had power to do what he had promised. 22This is why "it was credited to him as righteousness." 23The words "it was credited to him" were written not for him alone, 24but also for us, to whom God will credit righteousness—for us who believe in him who raised Jesus our Lord from the was handed over to death for our trespasses and was raised for our justification.

Chapter 5

Results of Justification

THEREFORE, since we are justified by faith, we[q] have peace with God through our Lord Jesus Christ, [2]through whom we have obtained access[r] to this grace in which we stand; and we[s] boast in our hope of sharing the glory of God. [3]And not only that, but we[s] also boast in our sufferings, knowing that suffering produces endurance, [4]and endurance produces character, and character produces hope, [5]and hope does not disappoint us, because God's love has been poured into our hearts through the Holy Spirit that has been given to us.

[6] For while we were still weak, at the right time Christ died for the ungodly. [7]Indeed, rarely will anyone die for a righteous person—though perhaps for a good person someone might actually dare to die. [8]But God proves his love for us in that while we still were sinners Christ died for us. [9]Much more surely then, now that we have been justified by his blood, will we be saved through him from the wrath of God.[t] [10]For if while we were enemies, we were reconciled to God through the death of his Son, much more surely, having been reconciled, will we be saved by his life. [11]But more than that, we even

[q] Other ancient authorities read let us
[r] Other ancient authorities add by faith
[s] Or let us
[t] Gk the wrath

νεκρῶν, **25** ὃς παρεδόθη διὰ τὰ παραπ-
[the] dead, who was delivered because of the of-

τώματα ἡμῶν καὶ ἠγέρθη διὰ τὴν
fences of us and was raised because of the

δικαίωσιν ἡμῶν.
justification of us.

5 Δικαιωθέντες οὖν ἐκ πίστεως εἰρήνην
Having been justified therefore by faith peace

ἔχομεν πρὸς τὸν θεὸν διὰ τοῦ κυρίου
we have with - God through the Lord

ἡμῶν Ἰησοῦ Χριστοῦ, **2** δι᾽ οὗ καὶ τὴν
of us Jesus Christ, through whom also the

προσαγωγὴν ἐσχήκαμεν [τῇ πίστει] εἰς
access we have had - by faith into

τὴν χάριν ταύτην ἐν ᾗ ἑστήκαμεν, καὶ
this grace in which we stand, and

καυχώμεθα ἐπ᾽ ἐλπίδι τῆς δόξης τοῦ
boast on hope of the glory -

θεοῦ. **3** οὐ μόνον δέ, ἀλλὰ καὶ καυχώμεθα
of God. And not only [so], but also we boast

ἐν ταῖς θλίψεσιν, εἰδότες ὅτι ἡ θλῖψις
in - afflictions, knowing that - affliction

ὑπομονὴν κατεργάζεται, **4** ἡ δὲ ὑπομονὴ
patience works, - and patience

δοκιμήν, ἡ δὲ δοκιμὴ ἐλπίδα· **5** ἡ δὲ
proof, - and proof hope; - and

ἐλπὶς οὐ καταισχύνει, ὅτι ἡ ἀγάπη
hope does not put to shame, because the love

τοῦ θεοῦ ἐκκέχυται ἐν ταῖς καρδίαις
- of God has been poured out in the hearts

ἡμῶν διὰ πνεύματος ἁγίου τοῦ δοθέντος
of us through Spirit Holy - given

ἡμῖν· **6** εἴ γε Χριστὸς ὄντων ἡμῶν
to us; indeed [7]Christ [2]being [1]us
= when we were weak

ἀσθενῶν ἔτι κατὰ καιρὸν ὑπὲρ ἀσεβῶν
[4]weak[a] [3]yet [b]accord- [6]time [9]on [10]impious
ing to behalf of ones

ἀπέθανεν. **7** μόλις γὰρ ὑπὲρ δικαίου
[8]died. For hardly on behalf of a just man

τις ἀποθανεῖται· ὑπὲρ γὰρ τοῦ ἀγαθοῦ
anyone will die; for on behalf of the good man

τάχα τις καὶ τολμᾷ ἀποθανεῖν· **8** συνίστησιν
perhaps some- even dares to die; [2]commends
one

δὲ τὴν ἑαυτοῦ ἀγάπην εἰς ἡμᾶς ὁ θεὸς
but [3]the [5]of himself [4]love [6]to [7]us - [1]God

ὅτι ἔτι ἁμαρτωλῶν ὄντων ἡμῶν Χριστὸς
that yet sinners being us[a] Christ
= while we were yet sinners

ὑπὲρ ἡμῶν ἀπέθανεν. **9** πολλῷ οὖν μᾶλλον
on be- us died. By much there- rather
half of fore

δικαιωθέντες νῦν ἐν τῷ αἵματι αὐτοῦ
having been justified now by the blood of him

σωθησόμεθα δι᾽ αὐτοῦ ἀπὸ τῆς ὀργῆς.
we shall be saved through him from the wrath.

10 εἰ γὰρ ἐχθροὶ ὄντες κατηλλάγημεν
For if enemies being we were reconciled

τῷ θεῷ διὰ τοῦ θανάτου τοῦ υἱοῦ αὐτοῦ,
- to God through the death of the Son of him,

πολλῷ μᾶλλον καταλλαγέντες σωθησόμεθα
by much rather having been reconciled we shall be saved

ἐν τῇ ζωῇ αὐτοῦ· **11** οὐ μόνον δέ, ἀλλὰ
by the life of him; and not only [so], but

dead. [25]He was delivered over to death for our sins and was raised to life for our justification.

Chapter 5

Peace and Joy

THEREFORE, since we have been justified through faith, we[u] have peace with God through our Lord Jesus Christ, [2]through whom we have gained access by faith into this grace in which we now stand. And we[u] rejoice in the hope of the glory of God. [3]Not only so, but we[u] also rejoice in our sufferings, because we know that suffering produces perseverance; [4]perseverance, character; and character, hope. [5]And hope does not disappoint us, because God has poured out his love into our hearts by the Holy Spirit, whom he has given us.

[6]You see, at just the right time, when we were still powerless, Christ died for the ungodly. [7]Very rarely will anyone die for a righteous man, though for a good man someone might possibly dare to die. [8]But God demonstrates his own love for us in this: While we were still sinners, Christ died for us.

[9]Since we have now been justified by his blood, how much more shall we be saved from God's wrath through him! [10]For if, when we were God's enemies, we were reconciled to him through the death of his Son, how much more, having been reconciled, shall we be saved through his life! [11]Not only is this so,

[u] 1,2,3 Or let us

boast in God through our Lord Jesus Christ, through whom we have now received reconciliation.

Adam and Christ

12 Therefore, just as sin came into the world through one man, and death came through sin, and so death spread to all because all have sinned— 13 sin was indeed in the world before the law, but sin is not reckoned when there is no law. 14 Yet death exercised dominion from Adam to Moses, even over those whose sins were not like the transgression of Adam, who is a type of the one who was to come.

15 But the free gift is not like the trespass. For if the many died through the one man's trespass, much more surely have the grace of God and the free gift in the grace of the one man, Jesus Christ, abounded for the many. 16 And the free gift is not like the effect of the one man's sin. For the judgment following one trespass brought condemnation, but the free gift following many trespasses brings justification. 17 If, because of the one man's trespass, death exercised dominion through that one, much more surely will those who receive the abundance of grace and the free gift of righteousness exercise dominion in life through the one man, Jesus Christ.

18 Therefore just as one man's trespass led to condemnation for all, so one

καὶ καυχώμενοι ἐν τῷ θεῷ διὰ τοῦ
also boasting in - God through the
κυρίου ἡμῶν Ἰησοῦ [Χριστοῦ], δι᾽ οὗ
Lord of us Jesus Christ, through whom
νῦν τὴν καταλλαγὴν ἐλάβομεν.
now the reconciliation we received.

12 Διὰ τοῦτο ὥσπερ δι᾽ ἑνὸς ἀνθρώπου
Therefore as through one man
ἡ ἁμαρτία εἰς τὸν κόσμον εἰσῆλθεν,
- sin into the world entered,
καὶ διὰ τῆς ἁμαρτίας ὁ θάνατος, καὶ
and through - sin - death, ²also
οὕτως εἰς πάντας ἀνθρώπους ὁ θάνατος
¹so to all men - death
διῆλθεν, ἐφ᾽ ᾧ πάντες ἥμαρτον· 13 ἄχρι
passed, inasmuch as all sinned; until
γὰρ νόμου ἁμαρτία ἦν ἐν κόσμῳ, ἁμαρτία
for law sin was in [the] world, sin
δὲ οὐκ ἐλλογεῖται μὴ ὄντος νόμου·
but is not reckoned not being lawᵃ;
=when there is no law;

14 ἀλλὰ ἐβασίλευσεν ὁ θάνατος ἀπὸ Ἀδὰμ
but ²reigned - ¹death from Adam
μέχρι Μωϋσέως καὶ ἐπὶ τοὺς μὴ
until Moses even over the [ones] not
ἁμαρτήσαντας ἐπὶ τῷ ὁμοιώματι τῆς
sinning on the likeness of the
παραβάσεως Ἀδάμ, ὅς ἐστιν τύπος τοῦ
transgression of Adam, who is a type of the
μέλλοντος. 15 Ἀλλ᾽ οὐχ ὡς τὸ παράπτωμα,
[one] coming. But not as the offence,
οὕτως [καὶ] τὸ χάρισμα· εἰ γὰρ τῷ
so also the free gift; for if ¹by the
τοῦ ἑνὸς παραπτώματι οἱ πολλοὶ
³of the ⁴one [man] ²offence the many
ἀπέθανον, πολλῷ μᾶλλον ἡ χάρις τοῦ θεοῦ
died, by much rather the grace - of God
καὶ ἡ δωρεὰ ἐν χάριτι τῇ τοῦ ἑνὸς
and the gift in grace - of the one
ἀνθρώπου Ἰησοῦ Χριστοῦ εἰς τοὺς πολλοὺς
man Jesus Christ to the many
ἐπερίσσευσεν. 16 καὶ οὐχ ὡς δι᾽ ἑνὸς
abounded. And not as through one
[man]
ἁμαρτήσαντος τὸ δώρημα· τὸ μὲν γὰρ
sinning the gift; ³the ²on one hand ¹for
κρίμα ἐξ ἑνὸς εἰς κατάκριμα, τὸ δὲ
judgment [is] of one to condemna- on the other
[offence] tion, the
χάρισμα ἐκ πολλῶν παραπτωμάτων εἰς
free gift [is] of many offences to
δικαίωμα. 17 εἰ γὰρ τῷ τοῦ ἑνὸς
justification. For if ¹by the ²of the ⁴one [man]
παραπτώματι ὁ θάνατος ἐβασίλευσεν διὰ
²offence - death reigned through
τοῦ ἑνός, πολλῷ μᾶλλον οἱ τὴν περισσείαν
the one by much rather the ¹the ²the ⁴abundance
[man], [ones]
τῆς χάριτος καὶ τῆς δωρεᾶς τῆς
⁵of the ⁶grace ⁷and ⁸of the ⁹gift
δικαιοσύνης λαμβάνοντες ἐν ζωῇ βασιλεύ-
¹⁰of righteousness ²receiving ¹²in ¹³life ¹¹will
σουσιν διὰ τοῦ ἑνὸς Ἰησοῦ Χριστοῦ.
reign through the one [man] Jesus Christ.

18 Ἄρα οὖν ὡς δι᾽ ἑνὸς παραπτώματος
So therefore as through one offence
εἰς πάντας ἀνθρώπους εἰς κατάκριμα,
to all men to condemnation,

but we also rejoice in God through our Lord Jesus Christ, through whom we have now received reconciliation.

Death Through Adam, Life Through Christ

12 Therefore, just as sin entered the world through one man, and death through sin, and in this way death came to all men, because all sinned— 13 for before the law was given, sin was in the world. But sin is not taken into account when there is no law. 14 Nevertheless, death reigned from the time of Adam to the time of Moses, even over those who did not sin by breaking a command, as did Adam, who was a pattern of the one to come.

15 But the gift is not like the trespass. For if the many died by the trespass of the one man, how much more did God's grace and the gift that came by the grace of the one man, Jesus Christ, overflow to the many! 16 Again, the gift of God is not like the result of the one man's sin: The judgment followed one sin and brought condemnation, but the gift followed many trespasses and brought justification. 17 For if, by the trespass of the one man, death reigned through that one man, how much more will those who receive God's abundant provision of grace and of the gift of righteousness reign in life through the one man, Jesus Christ.

18 Consequently, just as the result of one trespass was condemnation for all

man's act of righteousness leads to justification and life for all. ¹⁹For just as by the one man's disobedience the many were made sinners, so by the one man's obedience the many will be made righteous. ²⁰But law came in, with the result that the trespass multiplied; but where sin increased, grace abounded all the more, ²¹so that, just as sin exercised dominion in death, so grace might also exercise dominion through justification_u_ leading to eternal life through Jesus Christ our Lord.

οὕτως	καὶ	δι'	ἑνὸς	δικαιώματος	εἰς
so	also	through	one	righteous act	to

πάντας	ἀνθρώπους	εἰς	δικαίωσιν	ζωῆς·
all	men	to	justification	of life;

19 ὥσπερ γὰρ διὰ τῆς παρακοῆς τοῦ
for as through the disobedience of the

ἑνὸς ἀνθρώπου ἁμαρτωλοὶ κατεστάθησαν
one man ⁴sinners ³were constituted

οἱ πολλοί, οὕτως καὶ διὰ τῆς ὑπακοῆς
¹the ²many, so also through the obedience

τοῦ ἑνὸς δίκαιοι κατασταθήσονται οἱ
of the one [man] ⁴righteous ³will be constituted ¹the

πολλοί. **20** νόμος δὲ παρεισῆλθεν ἵνα
²many. But law entered in order that

πλεονάσῃ τὸ παράπτωμα· οὗ δὲ ἐπλεόνασεν
might abound the offence; but where abounded

ἡ ἁμαρτία, ὑπερεπερίσσευσεν ἡ χάρις,
- sin, more abounded - grace,

21 ἵνα ὥσπερ ἐβασίλευσεν ἡ ἁμαρτία ἐν
in order that as reigned - sin by

τῷ θανάτῳ, οὕτως καὶ ἡ χάρις βασιλεύσῃ
- death, so also - grace might reign

διὰ δικαιοσύνης εἰς ζωὴν αἰώνιον διὰ
through righteousness to life eternal through

Ἰησοῦ Χριστοῦ τοῦ κυρίου ἡμῶν.
Jesus Christ the Lord of us.

one act of righteousness was justification that brings life for all men. ¹⁹For just as through the disobedience of the one man the many were made sinners, so also through the obedience of the one man the many will be made righteous.

²⁰The law was added so that the trespass might increase. But where sin increased, grace increased all the more, ²¹so that, just as sin reigned in death, so also grace might reign through righteousness to bring eternal life through Jesus Christ our Lord.

Chapter 6

Dying and Rising with Christ

WHAT then are we to say? Should we continue in sin in order that grace may abound? ²By no means! How can we who died to sin go on living in it? ³Do you not know that all of us who have been baptized into Christ Jesus were baptized into his death? ⁴Therefore we have been buried with him by baptism into death, so that, just as Christ was raised from the dead by the glory of the Father, so we too might walk in newness of life.

5 For if we have been united with him in a death like his, we will certainly be united with him in a resurrection like his. ⁶We know that our old self was crucified with him so that the body of sin might be destroyed, and we might no longer be enslaved to sin. ⁷For whoever has died is freed from sin. ⁸But if we

6 Τί οὖν ἐροῦμεν; ἐπιμένωμεν τῇ
What therefore shall we say? May we continue -

ἁμαρτίᾳ, ἵνα ἡ χάρις πλεονάσῃ; **2** μὴ
in sin, in order that - grace may abound? not

γένοιτο. οἵτινες ἀπεθάνομεν τῇ ἁμαρτίᾳ,
May it be. Who *we died* - to sin,

πῶς ἔτι ζήσομεν ἐν αὐτῇ; **3** ἢ ἀγνοεῖτε
how yet shall we live in it? or are ye ignorant

ὅτι ὅσοι ἐβαπτίσθημεν εἰς Χριστὸν
that as many as *we were baptized* into Christ

Ἰησοῦν, εἰς τὸν θάνατον αὐτοῦ ἐβαπτίσ-
Jesus, into the death of him we were

θημεν; **4** συνετάφημεν οὖν αὐτῷ διὰ τοῦ
baptized? ²We were ¹there him through -
buried with fore

βαπτίσματος εἰς τὸν θάνατον, ἵνα ὥσπερ
baptism into - death, in order as
that

ἠγέρθη Χριστὸς ἐκ νεκρῶν διὰ τῆς
was raised Christ from [the] dead through the

δόξης τοῦ πατρός, οὕτως καὶ ἡμεῖς ἐν
glory of the Father, so also we in

καινότητι ζωῆς περιπατήσωμεν. **5** εἰ γὰρ
newness of life might walk. For if

σύμφυτοι γεγόναμεν τῷ ὁμοιώματι τοῦ
united with we have become in the likeness of the

θανάτου αὐτοῦ, ἀλλὰ καὶ τῆς ἀναστάσεως
death of him, but(so) also of the(his) resurrection

ἐσόμεθα· **6** τοῦτο γινώσκοντες, ὅτι ὁ
we shall be; this knowing, that the

παλαιὸς ἡμῶν ἄνθρωπος συνεσταυρώθη, ἵνα
¹old ³of us ²man was crucified in or-
with [him], der that

καταργηθῇ τὸ σῶμα τῆς ἁμαρτίας, τοῦ
might be the body - of sin, -
destroyed

μηκέτι δουλεύειν ἡμᾶς τῇ ἁμαρτίᾳ· **7** ὁ
no longer to serve us_bd_ - sin; ¹the
=that we should no longer serve (one)

γὰρ ἀποθανὼν δεδικαίωται ἀπὸ τῆς
¹for having died has been justified from -

Chapter 6

Dead to Sin, Alive in Christ

WHAT shall we say, then? Shall we go on sinning so that grace may increase? ²By no means! We died to sin; how can we live in it any longer? ³Or don't you know that all of us who were baptized into Christ Jesus were baptized into his death? ⁴We were therefore buried with him through baptism into death in order that, just as Christ was raised from the dead through the glory of the Father, we too may live a new life.

⁵If we have been united with him like this in his death, we will certainly also be united with him in his resurrection. ⁶For we know that our old self was crucified with him so that the body of sin might be done away with,_v_ that we should no longer be slaves to sin— ⁷because anyone who has died has been freed from sin.

have died with Christ, we believe that we will also live with him. 9 We know that Christ, being raised from the dead, will never die again; death no longer has dominion over him. 10 The death he died, he died to sin, once for all; but the life he lives, he lives to God. 11 So you also must consider yourselves dead to sin and alive to God in Christ Jesus.

12 Therefore, do not let sin exercise dominion in your mortal bodies, to make you obey their passions. 13 No longer present your members to sin as instruments^v of wickedness, but present yourselves to God as those who have been brought from death to life, and present your members to God as instruments^v of righteousness. 14 For sin will have no dominion over you, since you are not under law but under grace.

Slaves of Righteousness

15 What then? Should we sin because we are not under law but under grace? By no means! 16 Do you not know that if you present yourselves to anyone as obedient slaves, you are slaves of the one whom you obey, either of sin, which leads to death, or of obedience, which leads to righteousness? 17 But thanks be to God that you, having once been slaves of sin, have become obedient from the heart to the form of teaching to which you were entrusted, 18 and that you, having been set free from sin, have become slaves of righteousness. 19 I am speaking in human terms because of your natural limitations.^w For just as you once presented your members as slaves to impurity and to greater and greater iniquity, so now

^v Or *weapons*
^w Gk *the weakness of your flesh*

ἁμαρτίας. **8** εἰ δὲ ἀπεθάνομεν σὺν Χριστῷ,
sin.   But if   we died   with   Christ

πιστεύομεν ὅτι καὶ συζήσομεν αὐτῷ,
we believe   that also we shall live with him,

9 εἰδότες ὅτι Χριστὸς ἐγερθεὶς ἐκ νεκρῶν
knowing that Christ   having   from [the] dead
                                been raised

οὐκέτι ἀποθνῄσκει, θάνατος αὐτοῦ οὐκέτι
no more dies,   death   ²of him ¹no more

κυριεύει. **10** ὃ γὰρ ἀπέθανεν, τῇ ἁμαρτίᾳ
²lords it over. For in that† he died,   -   to sin

ἀπέθανεν ἐφάπαξ· ὃ δὲ ζῇ, ζῇ τῷ θεῷ.
he died   once; but in that† he he   -   to
                             lives, lives God.

11 οὕτως καὶ ὑμεῖς λογίζεσθε ἑαυτοὺς
So   also ²ye   ¹reckon   yourselves

εἶναι νεκροὺς μὲν τῇ ἁμαρτίᾳ ζῶντας
to be dead   indeed - to sin   ²living

δὲ τῷ θεῷ ἐν Χριστῷ Ἰησοῦ. **12** μὴ
¹but - to God in Christ   Jesus.   ²not

οὖν βασιλευέτω ἡ ἁμαρτία ἐν τῷ θνητῷ
¹There- ²let ⁵reign   -   ⁴sin   ⁴in ⁷the ⁶mortal
fore

ὑμῶν σώματι εἰς τὸ ὑπακούειν ταῖς
¹⁰of you ⁹body for the to obey   the
                              = to obey its lusts,

ἐπιθυμίαις αὐτοῦ, **13** μηδὲ παριστάνετε τὰ
lusts   of it,   neither present ye   the

μέλη ὑμῶν ὅπλα ἀδικίας τῇ ἁμαρτίᾳ,
members of you weapons of unright- - to sin,
                            eousness

ἀλλὰ παραστήσατε ἑαυτοὺς τῷ θεῷ ὡσεὶ
but   present ye   yourselves - to God   as

ἐκ νεκρῶν ζῶντας καὶ τὰ μέλη ὑμῶν
from [the] dead living   and the members of you

ὅπλα δικαιοσύνης τῷ θεῷ, **14** ἁμαρτία
weapons of righteousness - to God,   ²sin

γὰρ ὑμῶν οὐ κυριεύσει· οὐ γάρ ἐστε
¹for ⁴of you ³shall not lord it over; for ye are not

ὑπὸ νόμον ἀλλὰ ὑπὸ χάριν. **15** Τί οὖν;
under law   but under grace.   What therefore?

ἁμαρτήσωμεν, ὅτι οὐκ ἐσμὲν ὑπὸ νόμον
may we sin,   because we are not under law

ἀλλὰ ὑπὸ χάριν; μὴ γένοιτο. **16** οὐκ
but under grace? May it not be.   not

οἴδατε ὅτι ᾧ παριστάνετε ἑαυτοὺς δούλους
Know ye that to ye present   yourselves slaves
          whom

εἰς ὑπακοήν, δοῦλοί ἐστε ᾧ ὑπακούετε,
for obedience,   slaves   ye are whom ye obey,

ἤτοι ἁμαρτίας εἰς θάνατον ἢ ὑπακοῆς
whether of sin   to   death   or of obedience

εἰς δικαιοσύνην, **17** χάρις δὲ τῷ θεῷ
to   righteousness?   But thanks - to God

ὅτι ἦτε δοῦλοι τῆς ἁμαρτίας, ὑπηκούσατε
that ye were slaves   -   of sin,   ²ye obeyed

δὲ ἐκ καρδίας εἰς ὃν παρεδόθητε τύπον
¹but out of [the] heart ²to ⁴which ⁵ye were delivered ¹a form

διδαχῆς, **18** ἐλευθερωθέντες δὲ ἀπὸ τῆς
²of teaching,   and having been freed   from

ἁμαρτίας ἐδουλώθητε τῇ δικαιοσύνῃ.
sin   ye were enslaved - to righteousness.

19 ἀνθρώπινον λέγω διὰ τὴν ἀσθένειαν
Humanly   I say because of the weakness

τῆς σαρκὸς ὑμῶν. ὥσπερ γὰρ παρεστήσατε
of the flesh   of you. For as   ye presented

τὰ μέλη ὑμῶν δοῦλα τῇ ἀκαθαρσίᾳ καὶ
the members of you slaves   - to uncleanness and

8 Now if we died with Christ, we believe that we will also live with him. 9 For we know that since Christ was raised from the dead, he cannot die again; death no longer has mastery over him. 10 The death he died, he died to sin once for all; but the life he lives, he lives to God. 11 In the same way, count yourselves dead to sin but alive to God in Christ Jesus. 12 Therefore do not let sin reign in your mortal body so that you obey its evil desires. 13 Do not offer the parts of your body to sin, as instruments of wickedness, but rather offer yourselves to God, as those who have been brought from death to life; and offer the parts of your body to him as instruments of righteousness. 14 For sin shall not be your master, because you are not under law, but under grace.

Slaves to Righteousness

15 What then? Shall we sin because we are not under law but under grace? By no means! 16 Don't you know that when you offer yourselves to someone to obey him as slaves, you are slaves to the one whom you obey—whether you are slaves to sin, which leads to death, or to obedience, which leads to righteousness? 17 But thanks be to God that, though you used to be slaves to sin, you wholeheartedly obeyed the form of teaching to which you were entrusted. 18 You have been set free from sin and have become slaves to righteousness.

19 I put this in human terms because you are weak in your natural selves. Just as you used to offer the parts of your body in slavery to impurity and

present your members as slaves to righteousness for sanctification.
20 When you were slaves of sin, you were free in regard to righteousness. 21 So what advantage did you then get from the things of which you now are ashamed? The end of those things is death. 22 But now that you have been freed from sin and enslaved to God, the advantage you get is sanctification. The end is eternal life. 23 For the wages of sin is death, but the free gift of God is eternal life in Christ Jesus our Lord.

τῇ ἀνομίᾳ εἰς τὴν ἀνομίαν, οὕτως νῦν
- to iniquity unto - iniquity, so now

παραστήσατε τὰ μέλη ὑμῶν δοῦλα τῇ
present ye the members of you slaves -

δικαιοσύνῃ εἰς ἁγιασμόν. 20 ὅτε γὰρ
to righteousness unto sanctification. For when

δοῦλοι ἦτε τῆς ἁμαρτίας, ἐλεύθεροι ἦτε
slaves ye were - of sin, free ye were

τῇ δικαιοσύνῃ. 21 τίνα οὖν καρπὸν εἴχετε
- to righteousness. What ²therefore ¹fruit had ye

τότε; ἐφ' οἷς νῦν ἐπαισχύνεσθε· τὸ γὰρ
then? Over which now ye are ashamed; for the
things

τέλος ἐκείνων θάνατος. 22 νυνὶ δὲ ἐλευ-
end of those things [is] death. But now having

θερωθέντες ἀπὸ τῆς ἁμαρτίας δουλωθέντες
been freed from - sin ³having been enslaved

δὲ τῷ θεῷ, ἔχετε τὸν καρπὸν ὑμῶν εἰς
¹and - to God, ye have the fruit of you to

ἁγιασμόν, τὸ δὲ τέλος ζωὴν αἰώνιον.
sanctification, and the end life eternal.

23 τὰ γὰρ ὀψώνια τῆς ἁμαρτίας θάνατος,
For the wages - of sin [is] death,

τὸ δὲ χάρισμα τοῦ θεοῦ ζωὴ αἰώνιος
but the free gift - of God life eternal

ἐν Χριστῷ Ἰησοῦ τῷ κυρίῳ ἡμῶν.
in Christ Jesus the Lord of us.

---

to ever-increasing wickedness, so now offer them in slavery to righteousness leading to holiness. 20 When you were slaves to sin, you were free from the control of righteousness. 21 What benefit did you reap at that time from the things you are now ashamed of? Those things result in death! 22 But now that you have been set free from sin and have become slaves to God, the benefit you reap leads to holiness, and the result is eternal life. 23 For the wages of sin is death, but the gift of God is eternal life in ʷ Christ Jesus our Lord.

Chapter 7

An Analogy from Marriage

DO you not know, brothers and sisters ˣ—for I am speaking to those who know the law—that the law is binding on a person only during that person's lifetime? 2 Thus a married woman is bound by the law to her husband as long as he lives; but if her husband dies, she is discharged from the law concerning the husband. 3 Accordingly, she will be called an adulteress if she lives with another man while her husband is alive. But if her husband dies, she is free from that law, and if she marries another man, she is not an adulteress.

4 In the same way, my friends, ˣ you have died to the law through the body of Christ, so that you may belong to another, to him who has been raised from the dead in order that we may bear fruit for God. 5 While we were living in the flesh, our sinful passions, aroused by the law, were at

---

7 Ἦ ἀγνοεῖτε, ἀδελφοί, γινώσκουσιν γὰρ
Or are ye ignorant, brothers, for to [ones] knowing

νόμον λαλῶ, ὅτι ὁ νόμος κυριεύει τοῦ
law I speak, that the law lords it over the

ἀνθρώπου ἐφ' ὅσον χρόνον ζῇ; 2 ἡ γὰρ
man over such time [as] he lives? For the

ὕπανδρος γυνὴ τῷ ζῶντι ἀνδρὶ δέδεται
²married ¹woman to the living husband has
been bound

νόμῳ· ἐὰν δὲ ἀποθάνῃ ὁ ἀνήρ, κατήργηται
by law; but if dies the husband, she has been
discharged

ἀπὸ τοῦ νόμου τοῦ ἀνδρός. 3 ἄρα οὖν
from the law of the husband. Therefore

ζῶντος τοῦ ἀνδρὸς μοιχαλὶς χρηματίσει
living the husbandª an adulteress she will be called
= while the husband lives

ἐὰν γένηται ἀνδρὶ ἑτέρῳ· ἐὰν δὲ ἀποθάνῃ
if she ²husband ¹to a but if dies
becomes different;

ὁ ἀνήρ, ἐλευθέρα ἐστὶν ἀπὸ τοῦ νόμου,
the husband, free she is from the law,

τοῦ μὴ εἶναι αὐτὴν μοιχαλίδα γενομένην
- not to be herᵈ an adulteress having become
= so that she is not

ἀνδρὶ ἑτέρῳ. 4 ὥστε, ἀδελφοί μου, καὶ
²husband ¹to a So, brothers of me, also
different.

ὑμεῖς ἐθανατώθητε τῷ νόμῳ διὰ τοῦ
ye were put to death to the law through the

σώματος τοῦ Χριστοῦ, εἰς τὸ γενέσθαι
body - of Christ, for the to become
= that ye might belong

ὑμᾶς ἑτέρῳ, τῷ ἐκ νεκρῶν ἐγερθέντι,
youᵇ . to a to the from dead having been
different, [one] [the] raised,

ἵνα καρποφορήσωμεν τῷ θεῷ. 5 ὅτε
in order we may bear fruit - to God. when
that

γὰρ ἦμεν ἐν τῇ σαρκί, τὰ παθήματα
For we were in the flesh, the passions

Chapter 7

An Illustration From Marriage

DO you not know, brothers—for I am speaking to men who know the law—that the law has authority over a man only as long as he lives? 2 For example, by law a married woman is bound to her husband as long as he is alive, but if her husband dies, she is released from the law of marriage. 3 So then, if she marries another man while her husband is still alive, she is called an adulteress. But if her husband dies, she is released from that law and is not an adulteress, even though she marries another man.

4 So, my brothers, you also died to the law through the body of Christ, that you might belong to another, to him who was raised from the dead, in order that we might bear fruit to God. 5 For when we were controlled by the sinful nature, ˣ the sinful passions

ʷ23 Or through
ˣ5 Or the flesh; also in verse 25

work in our members to bear fruit for death. 6 But now we are discharged from the law, dead to that which held us captive, so that we are slaves not under the old written code but in the new life of the Spirit.

The Law and Sin

7 What then should we say? That the law is sin? By no means! Yet, if it had not been for the law, I would not have known sin. I would not have known what it is to covet if the law had not said, "You shall not covet." 8 But sin, seizing an opportunity in the commandment, produced in me all kinds of covetousness. Apart from the law sin lies dead. 9 I was once alive apart from the law, but when the commandment came, sin revived 10 and I died, and the very commandment that promised life proved to be death to me. 11 For sin, seizing an opportunity in the commandment, deceived me and through it killed me. 12 So the law is holy, and the commandment is holy and just and good.

13 Did what is good, then, bring death to me? By no means! It was sin, working death in me through what is good, in order that sin might be shown to be sin, and through the commandment might become sinful beyond measure.

The Inner Conflict

14 For we know that the law is spiritual; but I am of the flesh, sold into slavery under sin. [y] 15 I do not understand my own actions. For I do not do what I

τῶν ἁμαρτιῶν τὰ διὰ τοῦ νόμου ἐνηργεῖτο
\- of sins \- through the law operated

ἐν τοῖς μέλεσιν ἡμῶν εἰς τὸ καρποφορῆσαι
in the members of us to bear fruit

τῷ θανάτῳ· 6 νυνὶ δὲ κατηργήθημεν ἀπὸ
\- to death; but now we were discharged from

τοῦ νόμου, ἀποθανόντες ἐν ᾧ κατειχόμεθα,
the law, having died [to that] in which we were held fast,

ὥστε δουλεύειν [ἡμᾶς] ἐν καινότητι
so as to serve us[b] in newness

πνεύματος καὶ οὐ παλαιότητι γράμματος.
of spirit and not [in] oldness of letter.

7 Τί οὖν ἐροῦμεν; ὁ νόμος ἁμαρτία;
What therefore shall we say? the law sin?

μὴ γένοιτο· ἀλλὰ τὴν ἁμαρτίαν οὐκ
May it not be; yet \- sin not

ἔγνων εἰ μὴ διὰ νόμου· τήν τε γὰρ
I knew except through law; \- [a]also [l]for

ἐπιθυμίαν οὐκ ᾔδειν εἰ μὴ ὁ νόμος
lust I knew not except the law

ἔλεγεν· οὐκ ἐπιθυμήσεις· 8 ἀφορμὴν δὲ
said : Thou shalt not lust; but [a]occasion

λαβοῦσα ἡ ἁμαρτία διὰ τῆς ἐντολῆς
[2]taking \- [1]sin through the commandment

κατειργάσατο ἐν ἐμοὶ πᾶσαν ἐπιθυμίαν·
wrought in me every lust;

χωρὶς γὰρ νόμου ἁμαρτία νεκρά. 9 ἐγὼ
for without law sin [is] dead. I

δὲ ἔζων χωρὶς νόμου ποτέ· ἐλθούσης δὲ
And was living without law then; but coming
= when the

τῆς ἐντολῆς ἡ ἁμαρτία ἀνέζησεν, 10 ἐγὼ
the commandment[a] \- sin revived, [a]I
commandment came

δὲ ἀπέθανον, καὶ εὑρέθη μοι ἡ ἐντολὴ
[1]and died, and [a]was [7]to me [1]the [a]command-
found ment

ἡ εἰς ζωήν, αὕτη εἰς θάνατον· 11 ἡ γὰρ
\- [a]for [4]life, [a]this to death; \- for

ἁμαρτία ἀφορμὴν λαβοῦσα διὰ τῆς
sin [a]occasion [1]taking through the

ἐντολῆς ἐξηπάτησέν με καὶ δι' αὐτῆς
commandment deceived me and through it

ἀπέκτεινεν. 12 ὥστε ὁ μὲν νόμος ἅγιος,
killed [me]. So the \- law [is] holy,

καὶ ἡ ἐντολὴ ἁγία καὶ δικαία καὶ ἀγαθή.
and the command- holy and just and good.
ment

13 Τὸ οὖν ἀγαθὸν ἐμοὶ ἐγένετο θάνατος;
[a]The [1]therefore good to me became death?

μὴ γένοιτο· ἀλλὰ ἡ ἁμαρτία, ἵνα φανῇ
May it not be; yet \- sin, in or- it might appear
der that

ἁμαρτία, διὰ τοῦ ἀγαθοῦ μοι κατεργα-
sin, through the good [a]to me [1]work-

ζομένη θάνατον, ἵνα γένηται καθ' ὑπερβολὴν
ing [a]death, in or- [a]might become [a]excessively†
der that

ἁμαρτωλὸς ἡ ἁμαρτία διὰ τῆς ἐντολῆς.
[7]sinful \- [1]sin [a]through [a]the [a]command-
ment.

14 οἴδαμεν γὰρ ὅτι ὁ νόμος πνευματικός
For we know that the law spiritual

ἐστιν· ἐγὼ δὲ σάρκινός εἰμι, πεπραμένος
is; but I fleshy am, *having been sold*

ὑπὸ τὴν ἁμαρτίαν. 15 ὃ γὰρ κατεργάζομαι
under \- sin. For what I work

οὐ γινώσκω· οὐ γὰρ ὃ θέλω τοῦτο
I know not; for not what I wish this

---

aroused by the law were at work in our bodies, so that we bore fruit for death. 6 But now, by dying to what once bound us, we have been released from the law so that we serve in the new way of the Spirit, and not in the old way of the written code.

Struggling With Sin

7 What shall we say, then? Is the law sin? Certainly not! Indeed I would not have known what sin was except through the law. For I would not have known what coveting really was if the law had not said, "Do not covet." [y] 8 But sin, seizing the opportunity afforded by the commandment, produced in me every kind of covetous desire. For apart from law, sin is dead. 9 Once I was alive apart from law; but when the commandment came, sin sprang to life and I died. 10 I found that the very commandment that was intended to bring life actually brought death. 11 For sin, seizing the opportunity afforded by the commandment, deceived me, and through the commandment put me to death. 12 So then, the law is holy, and the commandment is holy, righteous and good.

13 Did that which is good, then, become death to me? By no means! But in order that sin might be recognized as sin, it produced death in me through what was good, so that through the commandment sin might become utterly sinful.

14 We know that the law is spiritual; but I am unspiritual, sold as a slave to sin. 15 I do not understand what I do. For what I want to do

---

[y]7 Exodus 20:17; Deut. 5:21

want, but I do the very thing I hate. 16 Now if I do what I do not want, I agree that the law is good. 17 But in fact it is no longer I that do it, but sin that dwells within me. 18 For I know that nothing good dwells within me, that is, in my flesh. I can will what is right, but I cannot do it. 19 For I do not do the good I want, but the evil I do not want is what I do. 20 Now if I do what I do not want, it is no longer I that do it, but sin that dwells within me.

21 So I find it to be a law that when I want to do what is good, evil lies close at hand. 22 For I delight in the law of God in my inmost self, 23 but I see in my members another law at war with the law of my mind, making me captive to the law of sin that dwells in my members. 24 Wretched man that I am! Who will rescue me from this body of death? 25 Thanks be to God through Jesus Christ our Lord!

So then, with my mind I am a slave to the law of God, but with my flesh I am a slave to the law of sin.

πράσσω, ἀλλ' ὃ μισῶ τοῦτο ποιῶ. 16 εἰ
I practise, but what I hate this I do. if

δὲ ὃ οὐ θέλω τοῦτο ποιῶ, σύμφημι
But what I wish not this I do, I agree with

τῷ νόμῳ ὅτι καλός. 17 νυνὶ δὲ οὐκέτι
the law that [it is] good. But now no longer

ἐγὼ κατεργάζομαι αὐτὸ ἀλλὰ ἡ ἐνοικοῦσα
I work it but ¹the ²indwelling

ἐν ἐμοὶ ἁμαρτία. 18 οἶδα γὰρ ὅτι οὐκ
¹in ²me ²sin. For I know that not

οἰκεῖ ἐν ἐμοί, τοῦτ' ἔστιν ἐν τῇ σαρκί
dwells in me, this is in the flesh

μου, ἀγαθόν· τὸ γὰρ θέλειν παράκειταί
of me, [that which is] good; for to wish is present

μοι, τὸ δὲ κατεργάζεσθαι τὸ καλὸν
to me, but ²to work the ⁴good

οὔ· 19 οὐ γὰρ ὃ θέλω ποιῶ ἀγαθόν,
¹not; for not what ²I wish ¹I do ¹good,

ἀλλὰ ὃ οὐ θέλω κακὸν τοῦτο πράσσω.
but what ²I wish not ²evil this I practise.

20 εἰ δὲ ὃ οὐ θέλω ἐγὼ τοῦτο ποιῶ,
But if what ²wish not ¹I this I do,

οὐκέτι ἐγὼ κατεργάζομαι αὐτὸ ἀλλὰ ἡ
no longer I work it but ¹the

οἰκοῦσα ἐν ἐμοὶ ἁμαρτία. 21 εὑρίσκω
³dwelling ¹in ²me ²sin. I find

ἄρα τὸν νόμον τῷ θέλοντι ἐμοὶ ποιεῖν
then the law ²the [one] ¹wishing ¹to me to do

τὸ καλόν, ὅτι ἐμοὶ τὸ κακὸν παράκειται·
the good, that to me the evil is present;

22 συνήδομαι γὰρ τῷ νόμῳ τοῦ θεοῦ κατὰ
for I delight in the law - of God according to

τὸν ἔσω ἄνθρωπον, 23 βλέπω δὲ ἕτερον
the inner man, but I see a different

νόμον ἐν τοῖς μέλεσίν μου ἀντιστρατευόμενον
law in the members of me warring against

τῷ νόμῳ τοῦ νοός μου καὶ αἰχμαλωτίζοντά
the law of the mind of me and taking captive

με ἐν τῷ νόμῳ τῆς ἁμαρτίας τῷ ὄντι
me by the law - of sin the [one] being

ἐν τοῖς μέλεσίν μου. 24 Ταλαίπωρος
in the members of me. ¹Wretched

ἐγὼ ἄνθρωπος· τίς με ῥύσεται ἐκ τοῦ
²I ¹man; who me will deliver from the

σώματος τοῦ θανάτου τούτου; 25 χάρις
body of this death? Thanks

τῷ θεῷ διὰ Ἰησοῦ Χριστοῦ τοῦ κυρίου
- to God through Jesus Christ the Lord

ἡμῶν. Ἄρα οὖν αὐτὸς ἐγὼ τῷ μὲν
of us. So then ²[my]self ¹I ⁴with ³on one hand

νοῒ δουλεύω νόμῳ θεοῦ, τῇ δὲ σαρκὶ
⁵mind serve [the] law of God, on the other with the flesh

νόμῳ ἁμαρτίας. 8 οὐδὲν ἄρα νῦν κατάκριμα
[the] law of sin. ⁴No ¹then ²now ³condemnation ³[there is]

τοῖς ἐν Χριστῷ Ἰησοῦ. 2 ὁ γὰρ νόμος τοῦ
to the in Christ Jesus. For the law of the
[ones]

πνεύματος τῆς ζωῆς ἐν Χριστῷ Ἰησοῦ
spirit - of life in Christ Jesus

ἠλευθέρωσέν σε ἀπὸ τοῦ νόμου τῆς
freed thee from the law -

Chapter 8

Life in the Spirit

THERE is therefore now no condemnation for those who are in Christ Jesus. 2 For the law of the Spirit² of life in Christ Jesus has set you⁴ free from the law of sin and of

²Or *spirit*

⁴ Here the Greek word *you* is singular number; other ancient authorities read *me* or *us*

I do not do, but what I hate I do. 16 And if I do what I do not want to do, I agree that the law is good. 17 As it is, it is no longer I myself who do it, but it is sin living in me. 18 I know that nothing good lives in me, that is, in my sinful nature.ᶻ For I have the desire to do what is good, but I cannot carry it out. 19 For what I do is not the good I want to do; no, the evil I do not want to do—this I keep on doing. 20 Now if I do what I do not want to do, it is no longer I who do it, but it is sin living in me that does it.

21 So I find this law at work: When I want to do good, evil is right there with me. 22 For in my inner being I delight in God's law; 23 but I see another law at work in the members of my body, waging war against the law of my mind and making me a prisoner of the law of sin at work within my members. 24 What a wretched man I am! Who will rescue me from this body of death? 25 Thanks be to God—through Jesus Christ our Lord!

So then, I myself in my mind am a slave to God's law, but in the sinful nature a slave to the law of sin.

Chapter 8

Life Through the Spirit

THEREFORE, there is now no condemnation for those who are in Christ Jesus,ᵃ 2 because through Christ Jesus the law of the Spirit of life set me free death. ³For God has done what the law, weakened by the flesh, could not do: by sending his own Son in the likeness of sinful flesh, and to deal with sin,ᵇ he condemned sin in the flesh, ⁴so that the just requirement of the law might be fulfilled in us, who walk not according to the flesh but according to the Spirit. ᶻ ⁵For those who live according to the flesh set their minds on the things of the flesh, but those who live according to the Spiritᶻ set their minds on the things of the Spirit. ᶻ ⁶To set the mind on the flesh is death, but to set the mind on the Spiritᶻ is life and peace. ⁷For this reason the mind that is set on the flesh is hostile to God; it does not submit to God's law—indeed it cannot, ⁸and those who are in the flesh cannot please God.

9 But you are not in the flesh; you are in the Spirit, ᶻ since the Spirit of God dwells in you. Anyone who does not have the Spirit of Christ does not belong to him. ¹⁰But if Christ is in you, though the body is dead because of sin, the Spiritᶻ is life because of righteousness. ¹¹If the Spirit of him who raised Jesus from the dead dwells in you, he who raised Christᶜ from the dead will give life to your mortal bodies also throughᵈ his Spirit that dwells in you.

12 So then, brothers and sisters,ᵉ we are debtors, not to the flesh, to live

---

ἁμαρτίας καὶ τοῦ θανάτου. 3 τὸ γὰρ
of sin　　and　　–　　of death.　　For the

ἀδύνατον τοῦ νόμου, ἐν ᾧ ἠσθένει διὰ
impossible of the law,　in which it was through
thing　　　　　　　　　　　　　　weak

τῆς σαρκός, ὁ θεὸς τὸν ἑαυτοῦ υἱὸν
the flesh,　　–　¹God　³the　⁵of himself ⁴Son

πέμψας ἐν ὁμοιώματι σαρκὸς ἁμαρτίας
²sending in　likeness　of flesh　of sin

καὶ περὶ ἁμαρτίας κατέκρινεν τὴν ἁμαρτίαν
and concerning sin　condemned　–　sin

ἐν τῇ σαρκί, 4 ἵνα τὸ δικαίωμα τοῦ
in the flesh,　in order the ordinance of the
　　　　　　that

νόμου πληρωθῇ ἐν ἡμῖν τοῖς μὴ κατὰ
law　may be　in　us　the　not accord-
　　fulfilled　　　　[ones]　　ing to

σάρκα περιπατοῦσιν ἀλλὰ κατὰ πνεῦμα.
flesh　walking　　but according to spirit.

5 οἱ γὰρ κατὰ σάρκα ὄντες τὰ τῆς
For the [ones] accord- flesh being the of the
　　　　　ing to　　　　　　things

σαρκὸς φρονοῦσιν, οἱ δὲ κατὰ πνεῦμα
flesh　mind,　　but the　accord- spirit
　　　　　　　　[ones]　ing to

τὰ τοῦ πνεύματος. 6 τὸ γὰρ φρόνημα
the of the Spirit.　　For the　mind
things

τῆς σαρκὸς θάνατος, τὸ δὲ φρόνημα
of the flesh [is] death,　but the　mind

τοῦ πνεύματος ζωὴ καὶ εἰρήνη. 7 διότι
of the Spirit life and peace.　Wherefore

τὸ φρόνημα τῆς σαρκὸς ἔχθρα εἰς θεόν·
the mind of the flesh [is] enmity against God;

τῷ γὰρ νόμῳ τοῦ θεοῦ οὐχ ὑποτάσσεται,
for to the law　–　of God it is not subject,

οὐδὲ γὰρ δύναται· 8 οἱ δὲ ἐν σαρκὶ
neither indeed can it; and the [ones] ²in ³flesh

ὄντες θεῷ ἀρέσαι οὐ δύνανται. 9 ὑμεῖς
¹being　⁴God ⁵to please ⁴cannot.　ye

δὲ οὐκ ἐστὲ ἐν σαρκὶ ἀλλὰ ἐν πνεύματι,
But are not in flesh but in Spirit,

εἴπερ πνεῦμα θεοῦ οἰκεῖ ἐν ὑμῖν. εἰ
since [the] Spirit of God dwells in you.　if

δέ τις πνεῦμα Χριστοῦ οὐκ ἔχει, οὗτος
But anyone [the] Spirit of Christ has not, this one

οὐκ ἔστιν αὐτοῦ. 10 εἰ δὲ Χριστὸς
is not　of him.　　But if　Christ

ἐν ὑμῖν, τὸ μὲν σῶμα νεκρὸν διὰ
[is] in you,　³the ¹on one ²body [is] dead because
　　　　　hand　　　　　　　　of

ἁμαρτίαν, τὸ δὲ πνεῦμα ζωὴ διὰ
sin,　　³the ¹on the ²spirit [is] because
　　　　　other　　　life　of

δικαιοσύνην. 11 εἰ δὲ τὸ πνεῦμα τοῦ
righteousness.　But if the　Spirit of the
　　　　　　　　　　　[one]

ἐγείραντος τὸν Ἰησοῦν ἐκ νεκρῶν οἰκεῖ ἐν
having raised　–　Jesus from [the] dead dwells in

ὑμῖν, ὁ ἐγείρας ἐκ νεκρῶν Χριστὸν
you, the having from [the] dead Christ
　　　[one] raised

Ἰησοῦν ζωοποιήσει καὶ τὰ θνητὰ σώματα
Jesus will quicken also the mortal bodies

ὑμῶν διὰ τοῦ ἐνοικοῦντος αὐτοῦ πνεύματος
of you through the ³indwelling ²of him ¹Spirit

ἐν ὑμῖν.
⁴in ⁵you.

12 Ἄρα οὖν, ἀδελφοί, ὀφειλέται ἐσμέν,
So　then, brothers,　debtors　we are,

---

from the law of sin and death. ³For what the law was powerless to do in that it was weakened by the sinful nature,ᵇ God did by sending his own Son in the likeness of sinful man to be a sin offering.ᶜ And so he condemned sin in sinful man,ᵈ ⁴in order that the righteous requirements of the law might be fully met in us, who do not live according to the sinful nature but according to the Spirit.

⁵Those who live according to the sinful nature have their minds set on what that nature desires; but those who live in accordance with the Spirit have their minds set on what the Spirit desires. ⁶The mind of sinful manᵉ is death, but the mind controlled by the Spirit is life and peace; ⁷the sinful mindᶠ is hostile to God. It does not submit to God's law, nor can it do so. ⁸Those controlled by the sinful nature cannot please God.

⁹You, however, are controlled not by the sinful nature but by the Spirit, if the Spirit of God lives in you. And if anyone does not have the Spirit of Christ, he does not belong to Christ. ¹⁰But if Christ is in you, your body is dead because of sin, yet your spirit is alive because of righteousness. ¹¹And if the Spirit of him who raised Jesus from the dead is living in you, he who raised Christ from the dead will also give life to your mortal bodies through his Spirit, who lives in you.

¹²Therefore, brothers, we have an obligation—but it

ᵇ Or and as a sin offering
ᶜ Other ancient authorities read the Christ or Christ Jesus or Jesus Christ
ᵈ Other ancient authorities read on account of
ᵉ Gk brothers

ᵇ3 Or the flesh; also in verses 4, 5, 8, 9, 12 and 13
ᶜ3 Or man, for sin
ᵈ3 Or in the flesh
ᵉ6 Or mind set on the flesh
ᶠ7 Or the mind set on the flesh

according to the flesh—
13for if you live according
to the flesh, you will die;
but if by the Spirit you put
to death the deeds of the
body, you will live. 14For
all who are led by the Spirit
of God are children of God.
15For you did not receive a
spirit of slavery to fall back
into fear, but you have received a spirit of adoption.
When we cry, "Abba!f Fa-
ther!" 16it is that very Spirit
bearing witnessg with our
spirit that we are children
of God, 17and if children,
then heirs, heirs of God and
joint heirs with Christ—if,
in fact, we suffer with him
so that we may also be glorified with him.

Future Glory

18 I consider that the
sufferings of this present
time are not worth comparing with the glory about to
be revealed to us. 19For the
creation waits with eager
longing for the revealing of
the children of God; 20for
the creation was subjected
to futility, not of its own
will but by the will of the
one who subjected it, in
hope 21that the creation itself will be set free from its
bondage to decay and will
obtain the freedom of the
glory of the children of
God. 22We know that the
whole creation has been
groaning in labor pains until now; 23and not only the
creation, but we ourselves,
who have the first fruits of
the Spirit, groan inwardly
while we wait for adoption,
the redemption of our bodies. 24For inh hope we
were saved. Now hope that

οὐ τῇ σαρκὶ τοῦ κατὰ σάρκα ζῆν. 13 εἰ
not to the flesh - accord- flesh to lived. if
                           ing to

γὰρ κατὰ σάρκα ζῆτε, μέλλετε ἀποθνῄσκειν·
For accord- flesh ye live, ye are   to die:
ing to   about

εἰ δὲ πνεύματι τὰς πράξεις τοῦ σώματος
but if by [the] Spirit the practices of the body

θανατοῦτε, ζήσεσθε. 14 ὅσοι γὰρ πνεύματι
ye put to death, ye will live. For as many as by [the] Spirit

θεοῦ ἄγονται, οὗτοι υἱοί εἰσιν θεοῦ.
of God are led, these sons are of God.

15 οὐ γὰρ ἐλάβετε πνεῦμα δουλείας πάλιν
For ye received not a spirit of slavery again

εἰς φόβον, ἀλλὰ ἐλάβετε πνεῦμα υἱοθεσίας,
for fear, but ye received a spirit of adoption,

ἐν ᾧ κράζομεν· ἀββὰ ὁ πατήρ. 16 αὐτὸ
by which we cry: Abba - Father. ³it(him)self

τὸ πνεῦμα συμμαρτυρεῖ τῷ πνεύματι ἡμῶν
¹The ²Spirit witnesses with the spirit of us

ὅτι ἐσμὲν τέκνα θεοῦ. 17 εἰ δὲ τέκνα,
that we are children of God. And if children,

καὶ κληρονόμοι· κληρονόμοι μὲν θεοῦ,
also heirs; heirs on one hand of God,

συγκληρονόμοι δὲ Χριστοῦ, εἴπερ συμπάσ-
joint heirs on the of Christ, since we suffer
            other

χομεν ἵνα καὶ συνδοξασθῶμεν. 18 Λογίζομαι
with[him] in or- also we may be glorified I reckon
der that   with [him].

γὰρ ὅτι οὐκ ἄξια τὰ παθήματα τοῦ
For that ⁷[are] ⁷not ⁸worthy ¹the ²sufferings ³of the

νῦν καιροῦ πρὸς τὴν μέλλουσαν δόξαν
⁴now ⁵time [to with the coming glory
(present) be compared]

ἀποκαλυφθῆναι εἰς ἡμᾶς. 19 ἡ γὰρ
to be revealed to us. For the

ἀποκαραδοκία τῆς κτίσεως τὴν ἀποκάλυψιν
anxious watching· of the creation ²the ³revelation

τῶν υἱῶν τοῦ θεοῦ ἀπεκδέχεται. 20 τῇ
⁴of the ⁵sons ⁶of God ¹is eagerly expecting.

γὰρ ματαιότητι ἡ κτίσις ὑπετάγη, οὐχ
For to vanity the creation was subjected, not

ἑκοῦσα, ἀλλὰ διὰ τὸν ὑποτάξαντα, ἐφ'
willing[ly], but because of the [one] subjecting, in

ἐλπίδι 21 διότι καὶ αὐτὴ ἡ κτίσις
hope because even itself the creation

ἐλευθερωθήσεται ἀπὸ τῆς δουλείας τῆς
will be freed from the slavery -

φθορᾶς εἰς τὴν ἐλευθερίαν τῆς δόξης
of corruption to the freedom of the glory

τῶν τέκνων τοῦ θεοῦ. 22 οἴδαμεν γὰρ
of the children - of God. For we know

ὅτι πᾶσα ἡ κτίσις συστενάζει καὶ
that all the creation groans together and

συνωδίνει ἄχρι τοῦ νῦν· 23 οὐ μόνον δέ,
travails together until - now; and not only [so],

ἀλλὰ καὶ αὐτοὶ τὴν ἀπαρχὴν τοῦ πνεύματος
but also [our]selves ²the ³firstfruit ⁴of the ⁵Spirit

ἔχοντες [ἡμεῖς] καὶ αὐτοὶ ἐν ἑαυτοῖς
¹having we also [our]selves in ourselves

στενάζομεν υἱοθεσίαν ἀπεκδεχόμενοι, τὴν
groan adoption eagerly expecting, the

ἀπολύτρωσιν τοῦ σώματος ἡμῶν. 24 τῇ
redemption of the body of us. -

γὰρ ἐλπίδι ἐσώθημεν· ἐλπὶς δὲ βλεπομένη
For by hope we were saved; but hope being seen

is not to the sinful nature,
to live according to it. 13For
if you live according to the
sinful nature, you will die;
but if by the Spirit you put
to death the misdeeds of
the body, you will live,
14because those who are
led by the Spirit of God are
sons of God. 15For you did
not receive a spirit that
makes you a slave again to
fear, but you received the
Spirit of sonship.g And by
him we cry, "Abba,h Fa-
ther." 16The Spirit himself
testifies with our spirit that
we are God's children.
17Now if we are children,
then we are heirs—heirs of
God and co-heirs with
Christ, if indeed we share
in his sufferings in order
that we may also share in
his glory.

Future Glory

18I consider that our present sufferings are not
worth comparing with the
glory that will be revealed
in us. 19The creation waits
in eager expectation for the
sons of God to be revealed.
20For the creation was subjected to frustration, not by
its own choice, but by the
will of the one who subjected it, in hope 21thati the
creation itself will be liber-
ated from its bondage to decay and brought into the
glorious freedom of the
children of God.
22We know that the whole
creation has been groaning
as in the pains of childbirth
right up to the present time.
23Not only so, but we ourselves, who have the firstfruits of the Spirit, groan inwardly as we wait eagerly
for our adoption as sons,
the redemption of our bodies. 24For in this hope we
were saved. But hope that

fAramaic for Father
gOr 15a spirit of adoption, by
which we cry, "Abba! Father!"
16The Spirit itself bears witness
hOr by

g15 Or adoption
h15 Aramaic for Father
i20,21 Or subjected it in hope.
21For

is seen is not hope. For who hopes[i] for what is seen? 25But if we hope for what we do not see, we wait for it with patience.

26 Likewise the Spirit helps us in our weakness; for we do not know how to pray as we ought, but that very Spirit intercedes[j] with sighs too deep for words. 27And God,[k] who searches the heart, knows what is the mind of the Spirit, because the Spirit[l] intercedes for the saints according to the will of God. [m]

28 We know that all things work together for good[n] for those who love God, who are called according to his purpose. 29For those whom he foreknew he also predestined to be conformed to the image of his Son, in order that he might be the firstborn within a large family.[o] 30And those whom he predestined he also called; and those whom he called he also justified; and those whom he justified he also glorified.

God's Love in Christ Jesus

31 What then are we to say about these things? If God is for us, who is against us? 32He who did not withhold his own Son, but gave him up for all of us, will he not with him also give us everything else? 33Who will bring any charge against God's elect? It is God who justifies. 34Who is to condemn? It is Christ Jesus, who died, yes, who was raised, who is at the right hand of God, who indeed intercedes for us.[p] 35Who will separate us from the love of Christ? Will hardship, or distress, or persecution, or famine,

οὐκ ἔστιν ἐλπίς· ὃ γὰρ βλέπει τις,
is not hope; for what sees anyone,

τί καὶ ἐλπίζει; 25 εἰ δὲ ὃ οὐ βλέπομεν
why also he hopes? but if what we do not see

ἐλπίζομεν, δι' ὑπομονῆς ἀπεκδεχόμεθα.
we hope [for], through patience we eagerly expect.

26 ὡσαύτως δὲ καὶ τὸ πνεῦμα συναντιλαμ-
And similarly also the Spirit takes

βάνεται τῇ ἀσθενείᾳ ἡμῶν· τὸ γὰρ τί
share in the weakness of us; — for what

προσευξώμεθα καθὸ δεῖ οὐκ οἴδαμεν, ἀλλὰ
we may pray as it behoves we know not, but

αὐτὸ τὸ πνεῦμα ὑπερεντυγχάνει στεναγμοῖς
it(him)self the Spirit supplicates on [our] behalf with groanings

ἀλαλήτοις· 27 ὁ δὲ ἐρευνῶν τὰς καρδίας
unutterable; and the [one] searching the hearts

οἶδεν τί τὸ φρόνημα τοῦ πνεύματος,
knows what [is] the mind of the Spirit,

ὅτι κατὰ θεὸν ἐντυγχάνει ὑπὲρ ἁγίων.
be-cause according to God he supplicates on behalf saints.

28 οἴδαμεν δὲ ὅτι τοῖς ἀγαπῶσιν τὸν
And we know that to the [ones] loving —

θεὸν πάντα συνεργεῖ [ὁ θεὸς] εἰς ἀγαθόν,
God ³all things ²works together — ¹God for good,

τοῖς κατὰ πρόθεσιν κλητοῖς οὖσιν. 29 ὅτι
to the ²accord- ⁴purpose ²called ¹being. Because
[ones] ing to

οὓς προέγνω, καὶ προώρισεν συμμόρφους
whom he foreknew, also he foreordained conformed to

τῆς εἰκόνος τοῦ υἱοῦ αὐτοῦ, εἰς τὸ
of the image of the Son of him, for the
=that he should be

εἶναι αὐτὸν πρωτότοκον ἐν πολλοῖς
to be him[b] firstborn among many

ἀδελφοῖς· 30 οὓς δὲ προώρισεν, τούτους
brothers; but whom he foreordained, these

καὶ ἐκάλεσεν· καὶ οὓς ἐκάλεσεν, τούτους
also he called; and whom he called, these

καὶ ἐδικαίωσεν· οὓς δὲ ἐδικαίωσεν, τούτους
also he justified; but whom he justified, these

καὶ ἐδόξασεν. 31 Τί οὖν ἐροῦμεν πρὸς
also he glorified. What therefore shall we say to

ταῦτα; εἰ ὁ θεὸς ὑπὲρ ἡμῶν, τίς καθ'
these things? If — God on behalf of us, who against

ἡμῶν; ὅς γε τοῦ ἰδίου υἱοῦ οὐκ ἐφείσατο,
us? Who indeed the(his) own Son spared not,

32 ἀλλὰ ὑπὲρ ἡμῶν πάντων παρέδωκεν
but on behalf of us all delivered

αὐτόν, πῶς οὐχὶ καὶ σὺν αὐτῷ τὰ πάντα
him, how not also with him — all things

ἡμῖν χαρίσεται; 33 τίς ἐγκαλέσει κατὰ
to us will he freely give? Who will bring a charge against against

ἐκλεκτῶν θεοῦ; θεὸς ὁ δικαιῶν· 34 τίς
chosen ones of God? God [is] the [one] justifying; who

ὁ κατακρινῶν; Χριστὸς Ἰησοῦς ὁ ἀποθανών,
the condemning? Christ Jesus [is] the having died,
[one] [one]

μᾶλλον δὲ ἐγερθείς, ὅς ἐστιν ἐν δεξιᾷ
but rather having been raised, who is at [the] right [hand]

τοῦ θεοῦ, ὃς καὶ ἐντυγχάνει ὑπὲρ ἡμῶν.
— of God, who also supplicates on behalf of us.

35 τίς ἡμᾶς χωρίσει ἀπὸ τῆς ἀγάπης
Who us will separate from the love

τοῦ Χριστοῦ; θλῖψις ἢ στενοχωρία ἢ
— of Christ? affliction or distress or

is seen is no hope at all. Who hopes for what he already has? 25But if we hope for what we do not have, we wait for it patiently.

26In the same way, the Spirit helps us in our weakness. We do not know what we ought to pray for, but the Spirit himself intercedes for us with groans that words cannot express. 27And he who searches our hearts knows the mind of the Spirit, because the Spirit intercedes for the saints in accordance with God's will.

More Than Conquerors

28And we know that in all things God works for the good of those who love him,[j] who[k] have been called according to his purpose. 29For those God foreknew he also predestined to be conformed to the likeness of his Son, that he might be the firstborn among many brothers. 30And those he predestined, he also called; those he called, he also justified; those he justified, he also glorified.

31What, then, shall we say in response to this? If God is for us, who can be against us? 32He who did not spare his own Son, but gave him up for us all—how will he not also, along with him, graciously give us all things? 33Who will bring any charge against those whom God has chosen? It is God who justifies. 34Who is he that condemns? Christ Jesus, who died—more than that, who was raised to life—is at the right hand of God and is also interceding for us. 35Who shall separate us from the love of Christ? Shall trouble or hardship or persecution or famine or

---

[i] Other ancient authorities read awaits
[j] Other ancient authorities add for us
[k] Gk the one
[l] Gk he or it
[m] Gk according to God
[n] Other ancient authorities read God makes all things work together for good, or in all things God works for good
[o] Gk among many brothers
[p] Or Is it Christ Jesus . . . for us?

[j]28 Some manuscripts And we know that all things work together for good to those who love God
[k]28 Or works together with those who love him to bring about what is good—with those who

or nakedness, or peril, or sword? ³⁶As it is written, "For your sake we are being killed all day long; we are accounted as sheep to be slaughtered."

³⁷No, in all these things we are more than conquerors through him who loved us. ³⁸For I am convinced that neither death, nor life, nor angels, nor rulers, nor things present, nor things to come, nor powers, ³⁹nor height, nor depth, nor anything else in all creation, will be able to separate us from the love of God in Christ Jesus our Lord.

διωγμὸς ἢ λιμὸς ἢ γυμνότης ἢ κίνδυνος
persecution or famine or nakedness or peril

ἢ μάχαιρα; 36 καθὼς γέγραπται ὅτι ἕνεκεν
or sword? As it has been For the written[,] — sake

σοῦ θανατούμεθα ὅλην τὴν ἡμέραν,
of thee we are being put to death all the day,

ἐλογίσθημεν ὡς πρόβατα σφαγῆς. 37 ἀλλ'
we were reckoned as sheep of(for) slaughter. But

ἐν τούτοις πᾶσιν ὑπερνικῶμεν διὰ τοῦ
in these things all we overconquer through the

ἀγαπήσαντος ἡμᾶς. 38 πέπεισμαι γὰρ
[one] having loved us. For I have been persuaded

ὅτι οὔτε θάνατος οὔτε ζωὴ οὔτε ἄγγελοι
that not death nor life nor angels

οὔτε ἀρχαὶ οὔτε ἐνεστῶτα οὔτε μέλλοντα
nor rulers nor things present nor things coming

οὔτε δυνάμεις 39 οὔτε ὕψωμα οὔτε βάθος
nor powers nor height nor depth

οὔτε τις κτίσις ἑτέρα δυνήσεται ἡμᾶς
nor any creature other will be able us

χωρίσαι ἀπὸ τῆς ἀγάπης τοῦ θεοῦ τῆς
to separate from the love — of God —

ἐν Χριστῷ Ἰησοῦ τῷ κυρίῳ ἡμῶν.
in Christ Jesus the Lord of us.

---

nakedness or danger or sword? ³⁶As it is written:

"For your sake we face death all day long; we are considered as sheep to be slaughtered."/

³⁷No, in all these things we are more than conquerors through him who loved us. ³⁸For I am convinced that neither death nor life, neither angels nor demons,ᵐ neither the present nor the future, nor any powers, ³⁹neither height nor depth, nor anything else in all creation, will be able to separate us from the love of God that is in Christ Jesus our Lord.

Chapter 9

God's Election of Israel

I am speaking the truth in Christ—I am not lying; my conscience confirms it by the Holy Spirit— ²I have great sorrow and unceasing anguish in my heart. ³For I could wish that I myself were accursed and cut off from Christ for the sake of my own people,�q my kindred according to the flesh. ⁴They are Israelites, and to them belong the adoption, the glory, the covenants, the giving of the law, the worship, and the promises; ⁵to them belong the patriarchs, and from them, according to the flesh, comes the Messiah,ʳ who is over all, God blessed forever.ˢ Amen.

6 It is not as though the word of God had failed. For not all Israelites truly belong to Israel, ⁷and not all of Abraham's children are his true descendants; but "It is through Isaac that descendants shall be named for you." ⁸This means that it is not the children of the flesh who are the children

---

9 Ἀλήθειαν λέγω ἐν Χριστῷ, οὐ
Truth I say in Christ, not

ψεύδομαι, συμμαρτυρούσης μοι τῆς
I lie, witnessing with me the

συνειδήσεώςª μου ἐν πνεύματι ἁγίῳ, 2 ὅτι
conscience of me in [the] Spirit Holy, that

λύπη μοί ἐστιν μεγάλη καὶ ἀδιάλειπτος
grief to me is great and incessant
=I have great grief and . . .

ὀδύνη τῇ καρδίᾳ μου. 3 ηὐχόμην γὰρ
painᵉ in the heart of me. For I was praying

ἀνάθεμα εἶναι αὐτὸς ἐγὼ ἀπὸ τοῦ Χριστοῦ
'a curse ²to be ⁶[my]self ¹I from — Christ

ὑπὲρ τῶν ἀδελφῶν μου τῶν συγγενῶν
on behalf of the brothers of me the kinsmen

μου κατὰ σάρκα, 4 οἵτινές εἰσιν Ἰσραη-
of me according to flesh, who are Israel-

λῖται, ὧν ἡ υἱοθεσία καὶ ἡ δόξα καὶ
ites, of whom the adoption and the glory and

αἱ διαθῆκαι καὶ ἡ νομοθεσία καὶ ἡ
the covenants and the giving of [the] law and the

λατρεία καὶ αἱ ἐπαγγελίαι, 5 ὧν οἱ
service and the promises, of whom the

πατέρες, καὶ ἐξ ὧν ὁ Χριστὸς τὸ κατὰ
fathers, and from whom the Christ — according to

σάρκα· ὁ ὢν ἐπὶ πάντων θεὸς εὐλογητὸς
flesh; the [one] being over all God blessed

εἰς τοὺς αἰῶνας, ἀμήν. 6 Οὐχ οἷον δὲ
unto the ages, amen. Not of course

ὅτι ἐκπέπτωκεν ὁ λόγος τοῦ θεοῦ. οὐ
that has failed the word — of God. not

γὰρ πάντες οἱ ἐξ Ἰσραήλ, οὗτοι Ἰσραήλ·
For all the [ones] of Israel, these [are of] Israel;

7 οὐδ' ὅτι εἰσὶν σπέρμα Ἀβραάμ, πάντες
neither because they are seed of [are they] all
Abraham,

τέκνα, ἀλλ'· ἐν Ἰσαὰκ κληθήσεταί σοι
children, but: in Isaac will be called to thee

σπέρμα. 8 τοῦτ' ἔστιν, οὐ τὰ τέκνα τῆς
seed.ᵉ This is, not the children of the
=thy seed.

Chapter 9

God's Sovereign Choice

I SPEAK the truth in Christ—I am not lying, my conscience confirms it in the Holy Spirit— ²I have great sorrow and unceasing anguish in my heart. ³For I could wish that I myself were cursed and cut off from Christ for the sake of my brothers, those of my own race, ⁴the people of Israel. Theirs is the adoption as sons; theirs the divine glory, the covenants, the receiving of the law, the temple worship and the promises. ⁵Theirs are the patriarchs, and from them is traced the human ancestry of Christ, who is God over all, forever praised!ⁿ Amen.

⁶It is not as though God's word had failed. For not all who are descended from Israel are Israel. ⁷Nor because they are his descendants are they all Abraham's children. On the contrary, "It is through Isaac that your offspring will be reckoned."ᵒ ⁸In other words, it is not the natural children

---

q Gk my brothers
r Or the Christ
s Or Messiah, who is God over all, blessed forever; or Messiah. May he who is God over all be blessed forever

l 36 Psalm 44:22
m 38 Or nor heavenly rulers
n 5 Or Christ, who is over all. God be forever praised! Or Christ. God who is over all be forever praised!
o 7 Gen. 21:12

of God, but the children of the promise are counted as descendants. 9For this is what the promise said, "About this time I will return and Sarah shall have a son." 10Nor is that all; something similar happened to Rebecca when she had conceived children by one husband, our ancestor Isaac. 11Even before they had been born or had done anything good or bad (so that God's purpose of election might continue, 12not by works but by his call) she was told, "The elder shall serve the younger." 13As it is written,

"I have loved Jacob,
but I have hated
Esau."

14 What then are we to say? Is there injustice on God's part? By no means! 15For he says to Moses,

"I will have mercy on
whom I
have mercy,
and I will have
compassion on
whom I have
compassion."

16So it depends not on human will or exertion, but on God who shows mercy. 17For the scripture says to Pharaoh, "I have raised you up for the very purpose of showing my power in you, so that my name may be proclaimed in all the earth." 18So then he has mercy on whomever he chooses, and he hardens the heart of whomever he chooses.

God's Wrath and Mercy

19 You will say to me then, "Why then does he still find fault? For who can resist his will?" 20But who indeed are you, a human being, to argue with God? Will what is molded say to the one who molds it, "Why have you made me like this?" 21Has the potter

---

σαρκὸς   ταῦτα   τέκνα   τοῦ   θεοῦ,   ἀλλὰ
flesh   these   children   of   God,   but

τὰ   τέκνα   τῆς   ἐπαγγελίας   λογίζεται   εἰς
the children   of the   promise   is(are) reckoned   for

σπέρμα.   9 ἐπαγγελίας   γὰρ   ὁ   λόγος   οὗτος·
a seed.   For ²of promise   ³the   ⁴word   ¹this ²[is]:

κατὰ   τὸν   καιρὸν   τοῦτον   ἐλεύσομαι   καὶ
According to   this   time   I will come   and

ἔσται   τῇ   Σάρρᾳ   υἱός.   10 οὐ   μόνον   δέ,
will be   to Sara   a son.ᶜ   And not only [so],

᷉= Sarah will have a son.

ἀλλὰ   καὶ   Ῥεβεκκὰ   ἐξ   ἑνὸς   κοίτην   ἔχουσα,
but   also   Rebecca   ²from   ³one   ¹conceiving,†

Ἰσαὰκ   τοῦ   πατρὸς   ἡμῶν·   11 μήπω   γὰρ
Isaac   the   father   of us;   for not yet

γεννηθέντων   μηδὲ   πραξάντων   τι   ἀγαθὸν
being bornᵃ   nor   practisingᵃ   anything   good

ἢ   φαῦλον,   ἵνα   ἡ   κατ'   ἐκλογὴν   πρόθεσις
or   bad,   in order ¹the ⁴accord-   ⁵choice   ²purpose
that   ing to

τοῦ   θεοῦ   μένῃ,   12 οὐκ   ἐξ   ἔργων   ἀλλ'
-   ³of God   might   not   of   works   but
remain,

ἐκ   τοῦ   καλοῦντος,   ἐρρέθη   αὐτῇ   ὅτι   ὁ
of   the [one]   calling,   it was said   to her[,]   -   The

μείζων   δουλεύσει   τῷ   ἐλάσσονι·   13 καθάπερ
greater   will serve   the   lesser;   even as

γέγραπται·   τὸν   Ἰακὼβ   ἠγάπησα,   τὸν   δὲ
it has been   -   Jacob   I loved,   -   but
written:

Ἠσαῦ   ἐμίσησα.
Esau   I hated.

14 Τί   οὖν   ἐροῦμεν;   μὴ   ἀδικία   παρὰ
What therefore   shall we say?   not unrighteousness   with

τῷ   θεῷ;   μὴ   γένοιτο.   15 τῷ   Μωϋσεῖ
-   God?   May it not be.   -   ²to Moses

γὰρ   λέγει·   ἐλεήσω   ὃν   ἂν   ἐλεῶ,   καὶ
¹For   he says: I will   whomever   I have   and
have mercy on   mercy,

οἰκτιρήσω   ὃν   ἂν   οἰκτίρω.   16 ἄρα   οὖν
I will pity   whomever   I pity.   So therefore
[it is]

οὐ   τοῦ   θέλοντος   οὐδὲ   τοῦ   τρέχοντος,
not of the [one]   wishing   nor   of the [one]   running,

ἀλλὰ   τοῦ   ἐλεῶντος   θεοῦ.   17 λέγει   γὰρ
but of the [one]   having mercy   God.   For says

ἡ   γραφὴ   τῷ   Φαραὼ   ὅτι   εἰς   αὐτὸ   τοῦτο
the scripture   -   to Pharaoh[,]   -   For   this very thing

ἐξήγειρά   σε,   ὅπως   ἐνδείξωμαι   ἐν   σοὶ
I raised up   thee,   so as   I may show forth   in   thee

τὴν   δύναμίν   μου,   καὶ   ὅπως   διαγγελῇ   τὸ
the   power   of me,   and   so as   might be pub-   the
lished abroad

ὄνομά   μου   ἐν   πάσῃ   τῇ   γῇ.   18 ἄρα   οὖν
name   of me   in   all   the   earth.   So therefore

ὃν   θέλει   ἐλεεῖ,   ὃν   δὲ   θέλει   σκληρύνει.
whom   he   he has   but whom   he wishes   he hardens.
wishes   mercy,

19 Ἐρεῖς   μοι   οὖν·   τί   ἔτι   μέμφεται;
Thou wilt say   to me   therefore: Why   still   finds he fault?

τῷ   γὰρ   βουλήματι   αὐτοῦ   τίς   ἀνθέστηκεν;
for ³the   ⁴counsel   ²of him   ¹who   ²resisted?

20 ὦ   ἄνθρωπε,   μενοῦν   γε   σὺ   τίς   εἶ   ὁ
O   man,   nay rather   ³thou   ¹who   ²art the

ἀνταποκρινόμενος   τῷ   θεῷ;   μὴ   ἐρεῖ   τὸ
[one] replying against   -   God?   not   ³Will say   ¹the

πλάσμα   τῷ   πλάσαντι·   τί   με   ἐποίησας
¹thing   to the   having formed: Why   ²me   ¹madest
formed   [one]   thou

---

who are God's children, but it is the children of the promise who are regarded as Abraham's offspring. 9For this was how the promise was stated: "At the appointed time I will return, and Sarah will have a son."ᵖ

10Not only that, but Rebekah's children had one and the same father, our father Isaac. 11Yet, before the twins were born or had done anything good or bad —in order that God's purpose in election might stand: 12not by works but by him who calls—she was told, "The older will serve the younger."ᵍ 13Just as it is written: "Jacob I loved, but Esau I hated."ʳ

14What then shall we say? Is God unjust? Not at all! 15For he says to Moses,

"I will have mercy on
whom I have mercy,
and I will have
compassion on
whom I have
compassion."ˢ

16It does not, therefore, depend on man's desire or effort, but on God's mercy. 17For the Scripture says to Pharaoh: "I raised you up for this very purpose, that I might display my power in you and that my name might be proclaimed in all the earth."ᵗ 18Therefore God has mercy on whom he wants to have mercy, and he hardens whom he wants to harden.

19One of you will say to me: "Then why does God still blame us? For who resists his will?" 20But who are you, O man, to talk back to God? "Shall what is formed say to him who formed it, 'Why did you make me like this?' "ᵘ

ᵖ9 Gen. 18:10,14
ᵍ12 Gen. 25:23
ʳ13 Mal. 1:2,3
ˢ15 Exodus 33:19
ᵗ17 Exodus 9:16
ᵘ20 Isaiah 29:16; 45:9

no right over the clay, to make out of the same lump one object for special use and another for ordinary use? 22 What if God, desiring to show his wrath and to make known his power, has endured with much patience the objects of wrath that are made for destruction; 23 and what if he has done so in order to make known the riches of his glory for the objects of mercy, which he has prepared beforehand for glory— 24 including us whom he has called, not from the Jews only but also from the Gentiles? 25 As indeed he says in Hosea,

"Those who were not
my people I will
call 'my people,'
and her who was
not beloved I
will call
'beloved.' "

26 "And in the very
place where it
was said to
them, 'You are
not my people,'
there they shall be
called children
of the living
God."

27 And Isaiah cries out concerning Israel, "Though the number of the children of Israel were like the sand of the sea, only a remnant of them will be saved; 28 for the Lord will execute his sentence on the earth quickly and decisively." *t* 29 And as Isaiah predicted,

"If the Lord of hosts
had not left
survivors *u* to
us,
we would have
fared like
Sodom
and been made like
Gomorrah."

Israel's Unbelief

30 What then are we to say? Gentiles, who did not strive for righteousness, have attained it, that is, righteousness through faith; 31 but Israel, who did strive for the righteousness that is based on the law, did not succeed in fulfilling that law. 32 Why not? Because they did not strive for it on the basis of faith, but as if it were based on works. They have stumbled over the stumbling stone, 33 as it is

t Other ancient authorities read *for he will finish his work and cut it short in righteousness, because the Lord will make the sentence shortened on the earth*
u Or *descendants*; Gk *seed*

οὕτως; 21 ἢ οὐκ ἔχει ἐξουσίαν ὁ κεραμεὺς
thus? or has not ²authority ¹the ²potter

τοῦ πηλοῦ ἐκ τοῦ αὐτοῦ φυράματος
of the clay out of the same lump

ποιῆσαι ὃ μὲν εἰς τιμὴν σκεῦος, ὃ δὲ
to make ¹this ²to ⁴honour ³vessel, that

εἰς ἀτιμίαν; 22 εἰ δὲ θέλων ὁ θεὸς
to dishonour? But if wishing – God

ἐνδείξασθαι τὴν ὀργὴν καὶ γνωρίσαι τὸ
to show forth the(his) wrath and to make known the

δυνατὸν αὐτοῦ ἤνεγκεν ἐν πολλῇ μακρο-
ability of him bore in much long-

θυμίᾳ σκεύη ὀργῆς κατηρτισμένα εἰς
suffering vessels of wrath *having been* fitted for

ἀπώλειαν, 23 καὶ ἵνα γνωρίσῃ τὸν πλοῦτον
destruction, and in or- he might make known the riches
der that

τῆς δόξης αὐτοῦ ἐπὶ σκεύη ἐλέους, ἃ
of the glory of him on vessels of mercy, which

προητοίμασεν εἰς δόξαν, 24 οὓς καὶ
he previously prepared for glory, whom also

ἐκάλεσεν ἡμᾶς οὐ μόνον ἐξ Ἰουδαίων
he called[,] us not only of Jews

ἀλλὰ καὶ ἐξ ἐθνῶν; 25 ὡς καὶ ἐν τῷ
but also of nations? As also in –

Ὡσηὲ λέγει· καλέσω τὸν οὐ λαόν μου
Osee he says: I will call the ²not ¹people of me

λαόν μου καὶ τὴν οὐκ ἠγαπημένην
a people of me and the not having been loved

ἠγαπημένην· 26 καὶ ἔσται ἐν τῷ τόπῳ
having been loved; and it shall be in the place

οὗ ἐρρέθη [αὐτοῖς]· οὐ λαός μου ὑμεῖς,
where it was said to them: not a people of me ye [are],

ἐκεῖ κληθήσονται υἱοὶ θεοῦ ζῶντος.
there they will be called sons ³God ¹of a living.

27 Ἠσαΐας δὲ κράζει ὑπὲρ τοῦ Ἰσραήλ·
But Esaias cries on behalf of – Israel:

ἐὰν ᾖ ὁ ἀριθμὸς τῶν υἱῶν Ἰσραὴλ
If be the number of the sons of Israel

ὡς ἡ ἄμμος τῆς θαλάσσης, τὸ ὑπόλειμμα
as the sand of the sea, the remnant

σωθήσεται· 28 λόγον γὰρ συντελῶν καὶ
will be saved; for ²an account ¹accomplishing ²and

συντέμνων ποιήσει κύριος ἐπὶ τῆς γῆς.
³cutting short ¹will make ⁴[the] Lord on the earth.

29 καὶ καθὼς προείρηκεν Ἠσαΐας· εἰ μὴ
And as ²has previously said ¹Esaias: Except

κύριος σαβαὼθ ἐγκατέλιπεν ἡμῖν σπέρμα,
[the] Lord of hosts left to us a seed,

ὡς Σόδομα ἂν ἐγενήθημεν καὶ ὡς Γόμορρα
as Sodoma we would have become and as Gomorra

ἂν ὡμοιώθημεν.
we would have been likened.

30 Τί οὖν ἐροῦμεν; ὅτι ἔθνη τὰ μὴ
What therefore shall we say? that nations which not

διώκοντα δικαιοσύνην κατέλαβεν δικαιοσύνην,
pursuing righteousness apprehended righteousness,

δικαιοσύνην δὲ τὴν ἐκ πίστεως· 31 Ἰσραὴλ
but a righteousness – of faith; ²Israel

δὲ διώκων νόμον δικαιοσύνης εἰς νόμον
¹but pursuing a law of righteousness ²to(at) ³a law

οὐκ ἔφθασεν. 32 διὰ τί; ὅτι οὐκ ἐκ
¹did not arrive. Why? Because not of

πίστεως ἀλλ' ὡς ἐξ ἔργων· προσέκοψαν
faith but as of works; they stumbled

τῷ λίθῳ τοῦ προσκόμματος, 33 καθὼς
at the stone – of stumbling, as

---

21 Does not the potter have the right to make out of the same lump of clay some pottery for noble purposes and some for common use? 22 What if God, choosing to show his wrath and make his power known, bore with great patience the objects of his wrath—prepared for destruction? 23 What if he did this to make the riches of his glory known to the objects of his mercy, whom he prepared in advance for glory— 24 even us, whom he also called, not only from the Jews but also from the Gentiles? 25 As he says in Hosea:

"I will call them 'my
people' who are not
my people;
and I will call her 'my
loved one' who is
not my loved
one," *v*

26 and,

"It will happen that in
the very place
where it was said to
them,
'You are not my
people,'
they will be called 'sons
of the living
God.' " *w*

27 Isaiah cries out concerning Israel:

"Though the number of
the Israelites be like
the sand by the sea,
only the remnant will
be saved.
28 For the Lord will carry
out
his sentence on earth
with speed and
finality." *x*

29 It is just as Isaiah said previously:

"Unless the Lord
Almighty
had left us
descendants,
we would have become
like Sodom,
we would have been
like Gomorrah." *y*

Israel's Unbelief

30 What then shall we say? That the Gentiles, who did not pursue righteousness, have obtained it, a righteousness that is by faith; 31 but Israel, who pursued a law of righteousness, has not attained it. 32 Why not? Because they pursued it not by faith but as if it were by works. They stumbled over the *a*stumbling

*v*25 Hosea 2:23
*w*26 Hosea 1:10
*x*28 Isaiah 10:22,23
*y*29 Isaiah 1:9

written,
"See, I am laying in
Zion a stone
that will make
people stumble,
a rock that will
make them fall,
and whoever
believes in him[v]
will not be put
to shame."

Chapter 10

Brothers and sisters,[w] my heart's desire and prayer to God for them is that they may be saved. 2 I can testify that they have a zeal for God, but it is not enlightened. 3 For, being ignorant of the righteousness that comes from God, and seeking to establish their own, they have not submitted to God's righteousness. 4 For Christ is the end of the law so that there may be righteousness for everyone who believes.

Salvation Is for All

5 Moses writes concerning the righteousness that comes from the law, that "the person who does these things will live by them." 6 But the righteousness that comes from faith says, "Do not say in your heart, 'Who will ascend into heaven?'" (that is, to bring Christ down) 7 "or 'Who will descend into the abyss?'" (that is, to bring Christ up from the dead). 8 But what does it say? "The word is near you, on your lips and in your heart" (that is, the word of faith that we proclaim); 9 because[x] if you confess with your lips that Jesus is Lord and believe in your heart that God raised him from the dead, you will be saved. 10 For one believes with the heart and so is justified, and one confesses with the mouth and so is saved. 11 The scripture says, "No one who believes in him

---

γέγραπται· ἰδοὺ τίθημι ἐν Σιὼν λίθον
it has been　Behold　I place　in　Sion　a stone
written:

προσκόμματος καὶ πέτραν σκανδάλου, καὶ
of stumbling　and　a rock　of offence,　and

ὁ πιστεύων ἐπ' αὐτῷ οὐ καταισχυνθήσεται.
the [one] believing　on　him　will not be put to shame.

10 Ἀδελφοί, ἡ μὲν εὐδοκία τῆς ἐμῆς
Brothers,　the　- good pleasure　-　of my

καρδίας καὶ ἡ δέησις πρὸς τὸν θεὸν
heart　and　the　request　to　-　God

ὑπὲρ αὐτῶν εἰς σωτηρίαν. **2** μαρτυρῶ
on behalf of them [is] for　salvation.　I witness

γὰρ αὐτοῖς ὅτι ζῆλον θεοῦ ἔχουσιν, ἀλλ'
For　to them　that　a zeal　of God　they have,　but

οὐ κατ' ἐπίγνωσιν· **3** ἀγνοοῦντες γὰρ τὴν
not according to knowledge;　for not knowing　the

τοῦ θεοῦ δικαιοσύνην, καὶ τὴν ἰδίαν
-　¹of God　¹righteousness,　and　the(ir)　own

ζητοῦντες στῆσαι, τῇ δικαιοσύνῃ τοῦ θεοῦ
seeking　to establish,　to the　righteousness　-　of God

οὐχ ὑπετάγησαν. **4** τέλος γὰρ νόμου
they did not submit.　For end　of law

Χριστὸς εἰς δικαιοσύνην παντὶ τῷ
Christ [is]　for　righteousness　to everyone　-

πιστεύοντι. **5** Μωϋσῆς γὰρ γράφει ὅτι
believing.　For Moses　writes[,]　-

τὴν δικαιοσύνην τὴν ἐκ νόμου ὁ ποιήσας
⁴the　⁵righteousness　-　⁶of　⁷law　¹The　³doing

ἄνθρωπος ζήσεται ἐν αὐτῇ. **6** ἡ δὲ
²man　will live　by　it.　But the

ἐκ πίστεως δικαιοσύνη οὕτως λέγει· μὴ
²of　³faith　¹righteousness　thus　says:　not

εἴπῃς ἐν τῇ καρδίᾳ σου· τίς ἀναβήσεται
Say　in　the　heart　of thee: Who　will ascend

εἰς τὸν οὐρανόν; τοῦτ' ἔστιν Χριστὸν
into　-　heaven?　this　is　Christ

καταγαγεῖν· **7** ἤ· τίς καταβήσεται εἰς
to bring down;　or:　Who　will descend　into

τὴν ἄβυσσον; τοῦτ' ἔστιν Χριστὸν ἐκ
the　abyss?　this　is　Christ　from

νεκρῶν ἀναγαγεῖν. **8** ἀλλὰ τί λέγει;
[the] dead　to bring up.　But　what　says it?

ἐγγύς σου τὸ ῥῆμά ἐστιν, ἐν τῷ στόματί
Near　thee　the　word　is,　in　the　mouth

σου καὶ ἐν τῇ καρδίᾳ σου· τοῦτ' ἔστιν
of thee　and　in　the　heart　of thee;　this　is

τὸ ῥῆμα τῆς πίστεως ὃ κηρύσσομεν.
the　word　-　of faith　which　we proclaim.

9 ὅτι ἐὰν ὁμολογήσῃς ἐν τῷ στόματί
Because　if　thou confessest　with　the　mouth

σου κύριον Ἰησοῦν, καὶ πιστεύσῃς ἐν
of thee　Lord　Jesus,　and　believest　in

τῇ καρδίᾳ σου ὅτι ὁ θεὸς αὐτὸν ἤγειρεν
the　heart　of thee that　-　God　him　raised

ἐκ νεκρῶν, σωθήσῃ· **10** καρδίᾳ γὰρ
from　[the] dead, thou shalt be saved;　for with heart

πιστεύεται εἰς δικαιοσύνην, στόματι δὲ
[one] believes　to　righteousness,　and with mouth

ὁμολογεῖται εἰς σωτηρίαν. **11** λέγει γὰρ
[one] confesses　to　salvation.　For says

ἡ γραφή· πᾶς ὁ πιστεύων ἐπ' αὐτῷ
the　scripture:　Everyone　believing　on　him

---

stone." 33 As it is written:

"See, I lay in Zion a
stone that causes
men to stumble
and a rock that makes
them fall,
and the one who trusts in
him will never be
put to shame."[z]

Chapter 10

Brothers, my heart's desire and prayer to God for the Israelites is that they may be saved. 2 For I can testify about them that they are zealous for God, but their zeal is not based on knowledge. 3 Since they did not know the righteousness that comes from God and sought to establish their own, they did not submit to God's righteousness. 4 Christ is the end of the law so that there may be righteousness for everyone who believes.

5 Moses describes in this way the righteousness that is by the law: "The man who does these things will live by them."[a] 6 But the righteousness that is by faith says: "Do not say in your heart, 'Who will ascend into heaven?'[b]" (that is, to bring Christ down) 7 "or 'Who will descend into the deep?'[c]" (that is, to bring Christ up from the dead). 8 But what does it say? "The word is near you; it is in your mouth and in your heart,"[d] that is, the word of faith we are proclaiming: 9 That if you confess with your mouth, "Jesus is Lord," and believe in your heart that God raised him from the dead, you will be saved. 10 For it is with your heart that you believe and are justified, and it is with your mouth that you confess and are saved. 11 As the Scripture says, "Anyone who trusts

---

v Or *trusts in it*
w Gk *Brothers*
x Or *namely, that*

z33 Isaiah 8:14; 28:16
a5 Lev. 18:5
b6 Deut. 30:12
c7 Deut. 30:13
d8 Deut. 30:14

will be put to shame."
12 For there is no distinction between Jew and Greek; the same Lord is Lord of all and is generous to all who call on him.
13 For, "Everyone who calls on the name of the Lord shall be saved."
14 But how are they to call on one in whom they have not believed? And how are they to believe in one of whom they have never heard? And how are they to hear without someone to proclaim him?
15 And how are they to proclaim him unless they are sent? As it is written, "How beautiful are the feet of those who bring good news!" 16 But not all have obeyed the good news;^y for Isaiah says, "Lord, who has believed our message?"
17 So faith comes from what is heard, and what is heard comes through the word of Christ.^z
18 But I ask, have they not heard? Indeed they have; for

"Their voice has gone
   out to all
   the earth,
and their words to
   the ends of the
   world."

19 Again I ask, did Israel not understand? First Moses says,

"I will make you
   jealous of those
   who are not a
   nation;
with a foolish nation
   I will make you
   angry."

20 Then Isaiah is so bold as to say,

"I have been found by
   those who did
   not seek me;
I have shown
   myself to those
   who did not ask
   for me."

21 But of Israel he says, "All day long I have held out my hands to a disobedient and contrary people."

οὐ καταισχυνθήσεται. 12 οὐ γάρ ἐστιν
will not be put to shame. For there is no

διαστολὴ Ἰουδαίου τε καὶ Ἕλληνος. ὁ
difference ¹of Jew ¹both ²and ⁴of Greek.* the

γὰρ αὐτὸς κύριος πάντων, πλουτῶν εἰς
For same Lord of all, is rich to

πάντας τοὺς ἐπικαλουμένους αὐτόν· 13 πᾶς
all the [ones] calling on him; ²everyone

γὰρ ὃς ἂν ἐπικαλέσηται τὸ ὄνομα κυρίου
¹for whoever calls on the name of [the] Lord

σωθήσεται. 14 Πῶς οὖν ἐπικαλέσωνται εἰς
will be saved. How therefore may they call on in
[one]

ὃν οὐκ ἐπίστευσαν; πῶς δὲ πιστεύσωσιν
whom they believed not? And how may they believe

οὗ οὐκ ἤκουσαν; πῶς δὲ ἀκούσωσιν
of whom they heard not? And how may they hear

χωρὶς κηρύσσοντος; 15 πῶς δὲ κηρύξωσιν
without [one] heralding? And how may they herald

ἐὰν μὴ ἀποσταλῶσιν; καθάπερ γέγραπται·
if they are not sent? As it has been written:

ὡς ὡραῖοι οἱ πόδες τῶν εὐαγγελιζομένων
How beautiful the feet of the [ones] announcing good

ἀγαθά. 16 ἀλλ᾽ οὐ πάντες ὑπήκουσαν τῷ
good things. But not all obeyed the

εὐαγγελίῳ. Ἡσαΐας γὰρ λέγει· κύριε,
gospel. For Esaias says: Lord,

τίς ἐπίστευσεν τῇ ἀκοῇ ἡμῶν; 17 ἄρα
who believed the hearing of us? Then

ἡ πίστις ἐξ ἀκοῆς, ἡ δὲ ἀκοὴ διὰ
- faith [is] from hearing, and the hearing through

ῥήματος Χριστοῦ. 18 ἀλλὰ λέγω, μὴ
a word of Christ. But I say, not

οὐκ ἤκουσαν; μενοῦν γε· εἰς πᾶσαν
did they not hear? Nay rather: To all

τὴν γῆν ἐξῆλθεν ὁ φθόγγος αὐτῶν,
the earth went out the utterance of them,

καὶ εἰς τὰ πέρατα τῆς οἰκουμένης τὰ
and to the ends of the inhabited earth the

ῥήματα αὐτῶν. 19 ἀλλὰ λέγω, μὴ Ἰσραὴλ
words of them. But I say, not Israel

οὐκ ἔγνω; πρῶτος Μωϋσῆς λέγει· ἐγὼ
did not know? First Moses says: I

παραζηλώσω ὑμᾶς ἐπ᾽ οὐκ ἔθνει, ἐπ᾽
will provoke to you on(by) not a nation, on(by)
jealousy

ἔθνει ἀσυνέτῳ παροργιῶ ὑμᾶς. 20 Ἡσαΐας
a nation unintelligent I will anger you. Esaias

δὲ ἀποτολμᾷ καὶ λέγει· εὑρέθην τοῖς
But is quite bold and says: I was found by the
[ones]

ἐμὲ μὴ ζητοῦσιν, ἐμφανὴς ἐγενόμην τοῖς
³me ¹not ²seeking, manifest I became to the
[ones]

ἐμὲ μὴ ἐπερωτῶσιν. 21 πρὸς δὲ τὸν
³me ¹not ²inquiring [for]. But to -

Ἰσραὴλ λέγει· ὅλην τὴν ἡμέραν ἐξεπέτασα
Israel he says: All the day I stretched out

τὰς χεῖράς μου πρὸς λαὸν ἀπειθοῦντα
the hands of me to a people disobeying

καὶ ἀντιλέγοντα.
and contradicting.

---

in him will never be put to shame."^e 12 For there is no difference between Jew and Gentile—the same Lord is Lord of all and richly blesses all who call on him, 13 for, "Everyone who calls on the name of the Lord will be saved."^f
14 How, then, can they call on the one they have not believed in? And how can they believe in the one of whom they have not heard? And how can they hear without someone preaching to them? 15 And how can they preach unless they are sent? As it is written, "How beautiful are the feet of those who bring good news!"^g
16 But not all the Israelites accepted the good news. For Isaiah says, "Lord, who has believed our message?"^h 17 Consequently, faith comes from hearing the message, and the message is heard through the word of Christ. 18 But I ask: Did they not hear? Of course they did:

"Their voice has gone
   out into all the
   earth,
their words to the ends
   of the world."ⁱ

19 Again I ask: Did Israel not understand? First, Moses says,

"I will make you
   envious by those
   who are not a
   nation;
I will make you angry
   by a nation that has
   no
   understanding."^j

20 And Isaiah boldly says,

"I was found by those
   who did not seek
   me;
I revealed myself to
   those who did not
   ask for me."^k

21 But concerning Israel he says,

"All day long I have
   held out my hands
to a disobedient and
   obstinate people."^l

---

^y Or gospel
^z Or about Christ; other ancient authorities read of God

* That is, between these two classes.

^e11 Isaiah 28:16
^f13 Joel 2:32
^g15 Isaiah 52:7
^h16 Isaiah 53:1
ⁱ18 Psalm 19:4
^j19 Deut. 32:21
^k20 Isaiah 65:1
^l21 Isaiah 65:2

Chapter 11

Israel's Rejection Is Not Final

I ask, then, has God rejected his people? By no means! I myself am an Israelite, a descendant of Abraham, a member of the tribe of Benjamin. 2 God has not rejected his people whom he foreknew. Do you not know what the scripture says of Elijah, how he pleads with God against Israel? 3 "Lord, they have killed your prophets, they have demolished your altars; I alone am left, and they are seeking my life." 4 But what is the divine reply to him? "I have kept for myself seven thousand who have not bowed the knee to Baal." 5 So too at the present time there is a remnant, chosen by grace. 6 But if it is by grace, it is no longer on the basis of works, otherwise grace would no longer be grace. [a]

7 What then? Israel failed to obtain what it was seeking. The elect obtained it, but the rest were hardened, 8 as it is written,

"God gave them a
　　sluggish spirit,
eyes that would not
　　see
and ears that would
　　not hear,
down to this very
　　day."

9 And David says,
"Let their table
　　become a snare
　　and a trap,
a stumbling block
　　and a retribution
　　for them;
10 let their eyes be
　　darkened so that
　　they cannot see,
and keep their
　　backs forever
　　bent."

The Salvation of the Gentiles

11 So I ask, have they stumbled so as to fall? By no means! But through their stumbling [b] salvation has come to the Gentiles, so as to make Israel [c] jealous. 12 Now if their stum-

---

11 Λέγω οὖν, μὴ ἀπώσατο ὁ θεὸς
I say therefore, [²did *not* put away] - ¹God

τὸν λαὸν αὐτοῦ; μὴ γένοιτο· καὶ γὰρ
the people of him? May it not be; for even

ἐγὼ Ἰσραηλίτης εἰμί, ἐκ σπέρματος
I an Israelite am, of [the] seed

Ἀβραάμ, φυλῆς Βενιαμίν. **2** οὐκ ἀπώσατο
of Abraham, of [the] tribe of Benjamin. did not put away

ὁ θεὸς τὸν λαὸν αὐτοῦ ὃν προέγνω.
- God the people of him whom he foreknew.

ἢ οὐκ οἴδατε ἐν Ἠλίᾳ τί λέγει ἡ
Or know ye not in Elias what says the

γραφή, ὡς ἐντυγχάνει τῷ θεῷ κατὰ τοῦ
scripture, how he supplicates - God against -

Ἰσραήλ; **3** κύριε, τοὺς προφήτας σου
Israel? Lord, the prophets of thee

ἀπέκτειναν, τὰ θυσιαστήριά σου κατέσκαψαν,
they killed, the altars of thee they dug down,

κἀγὼ ὑπελείφθην μόνος καὶ ζητοῦσιν τὴν
and I was left behind alone and they seek the

ψυχήν μου. **4** ἀλλὰ τί λέγει αὐτῷ ὁ
life of me. But what says to him the

χρηματισμός; κατέλιπον ἐμαυτῷ ἑπτακισ-
[divine] response? I reserved to myself seven

χιλίους ἄνδρας, οἵτινες οὐκ ἔκαμψαν γόνυ
thousands men, who bowed not knee

τῇ Βάαλ. **5** οὕτως οὖν καὶ ἐν τῷ νῦν
- to Baal. So therefore also in the present

καιρῷ λεῖμμα κατ' ἐκλογὴν χάριτος
time a remnant according to a choice of grace

γέγονεν· **6** εἰ δὲ χάριτι, οὐκέτι ἐξ ἔργων,
has become; and if by grace, no more of works,

ἐπεὶ ἡ χάρις οὐκέτι γίνεται χάρις. **7** Τί
since - grace no more becomes grace. What

οὖν; ὃ ἐπιζητεῖ Ἰσραήλ, τοῦτο οὐκ
therefore? What ²seeks after ¹Israel, this not

ἐπέτυχεν, ἡ δὲ ἐκλογὴ ἐπέτυχεν· οἱ δὲ
he obtained, but the choice obtained [it]; and the

λοιποὶ ἐπωρώθησαν, **8** καθάπερ γέγραπται·
rest were hardened, as it has been written:

ἔδωκεν αὐτοῖς ὁ θεὸς πνεῦμα κατανύξεως,
Gave to them - God a spirit of torpor,

ὀφθαλμοὺς τοῦ μὴ βλέπειν καὶ ὦτα
eyes - not to see[d] and ears

τοῦ μὴ ἀκούειν, ἕως τῆς σήμερον ἡμέρας.
- not to hear,[d] until the present† day.

9 καὶ Δαυὶδ λέγει· γενηθήτω ἡ τράπεζα
And David says: Let become the table

αὐτῶν εἰς παγίδα καὶ εἰς θήραν καὶ
of them for a snare and for a net and

εἰς σκάνδαλον καὶ εἰς ἀνταπόδομα αὐτοῖς,
for an offence and for a recompence to them,

10 σκοτισθήτωσαν οἱ ὀφθαλμοὶ αὐτῶν τοῦ
let be darkened the eyes of them -

μὴ βλέπειν, καὶ τὸν νῶτον αὐτῶν διὰ
not to see,[d] and the back of them al-

παντὸς σύγκαμψον.
ways bending.

11 Λέγω οὖν, μὴ ἔπταισαν ἵνα πέσωσιν;
I say therefore, did they *not* stumble in order they might fall?

μὴ γένοιτο· ἀλλὰ τῷ αὐτῶν παραπτώματι
May it not be; but by the ²of them ¹trespass

ἡ σωτηρία τοῖς ἔθνεσιν, εἰς τὸ παραζηλῶσαι
- salvation to the nations, for the to provoke to
[came] jealousy

Chapter 11

The Remnant of Israel

I ASK then: Did God reject his people? By no means! I am an Israelite myself, a descendant of Abraham, from the tribe of Benjamin. 2 God did not reject his people, whom he foreknew. Don't you know what the Scripture says in the passage about Elijah—how he appealed to God against Israel: 3 "Lord, they have killed your prophets and torn down your altars; I am the only one left, and they are trying to kill me"[m]? 4 And what was God's answer to him? "I have reserved for myself seven thousand who have not bowed the knee to Baal."[n] 5 So too, at the present time there is a remnant chosen by grace. 6 And if by grace, then it is no longer by works; if it were, grace would no longer be grace.[o]

7 What then? What Israel sought so earnestly it did not obtain, but the elect did. The others were hardened, 8 as it is written:

"God gave them a spirit
　　of stupor,
eyes so that they could
　　not see
and ears so that they
　　could not hear,
to this very day."[p]

9 And David says:

"May their table become
　　a snare and a trap,
a stumbling block and a
　　retribution for them.
10 May their eyes be
　　darkened so they
　　cannot see,
and their backs be bent
　　forever."[q]

Ingrafted Branches

11 Again I ask: Did they stumble so as to fall beyond recovery? Not at all! Rather, because of their transgression, salvation has come to the Gentiles to make Israel envious. 12 But

---

[a] Other ancient authorities add *But if it is by works, it is no longer on the basis of grace, otherwise work would no longer be work*
[b] Gk *transgression*
[c] Gk *them*

[m] 3　1 Kings 19:10,14
[n] 4　1 Kings 19:18
[o] 6　Some manuscripts *by grace. But if by works, then it is no longer grace; if it were, work would no longer be work.*
[p] 8　Deut. 29:4; Isaiah 29:10
[q] 10　Psalm 69:22,23

bling[b] means riches for the world, and if their defeat means riches for Gentiles, how much more will their full inclusion mean! 13 Now I am speaking to you Gentiles. Inasmuch then as I am an apostle to the Gentiles, I glorify my ministry 14 in order to make my own people[d] jealous, and thus save some of them. 15 For if their rejection is the reconciliation of the world, what will their acceptance be but life from the dead! 16 If the part of the dough offered as first fruits is holy, then the whole batch is holy; and if the root is holy, then the branches also are holy.

17 But if some of the branches were broken off, and you, a wild olive shoot, were grafted in their place to share the rich root[e] of the olive tree, 18 do not boast over the branches. If you do boast, remember that it is not you that support the root, but the root that supports you. 19 You will say, "Branches were broken off so that I might be grafted in." 20 That is true. They were broken off because of their unbelief, but you stand only through faith. So do not become proud, but stand in awe. 21 For if God did not spare the natural branches, perhaps he will not spare you.[f] 22 Note then the kindness and the severity of God: severity toward those who have fallen, but God's kindness toward you, provided you continue in his kindness; otherwise you also will be cut off. 23 And even those of Israel,[g] if they do not persist in unbelief, will be grafted in, for God has the power to

αὐτούς. **12** εἰ δὲ τὸ παράπτωμα αὐτῶν
them.　　　But if the trespass of them
πλοῦτος κόσμου καὶ τὸ ἥττημα αὐτῶν
[is] [the] of [the] and the defect of them
riches　world
πλοῦτος ἐθνῶν, πόσῳ μᾶλλον τὸ πλήρωμα
[is] [the] of [the] by how more the fulness
riches nations, much
αὐτῶν. **13** Ὑμῖν δὲ λέγω τοῖς ἔθνεσιν.
of them.　　But to you ³I say[,] ¹the ²nations.
ἐφ' ὅσον μὲν οὖν εἰμι ἐγὼ ἐθνῶν ἀπόστο-
Forasmuch in- there- ²am ¹I ⁴of ³an apos-
as　deed fore　　　　nations
λος, τὴν διακονίαν μου δοξάζω, **14** εἴ πως
tle, the ministry of me I glorify, if somehow
παραζηλώσω μου τὴν σάρκα καὶ σώσω
I may provoke to of me the flesh and may save
jealousy
τινὰς ἐξ αὐτῶν. **15** εἰ γὰρ ἡ ἀποβολὴ
some of them. For if the casting away
αὐτῶν καταλλαγὴ κόσμου, τίς ἡ πρόσλημψις
of them [is] [the] of [the] what the reception
reconciliation world,
εἰ μὴ ζωὴ ἐκ νεκρῶν; **16** εἰ δὲ ἡ
if not life from [the] dead? And if the
ἀπαρχὴ ἁγία, καὶ τὸ φύραμα· καὶ εἰ
firstfruit [is] holy, also the lump; and if
ἡ ῥίζα ἁγία, καὶ οἱ κλάδοι. **17** Εἰ δέ
the root [is] holy, also the branches. But if
τινες τῶν κλάδων ἐξεκλάσθησαν, σὺ δὲ
some of the branches were broken off, and thou
ἀγριέλαιος ὢν ἐνεκεντρίσθης ἐν αὐτοῖς
²a wild olive ¹being wast grafted in among them
καὶ συγκοινωνὸς τῆς ῥίζης τῆς πιότητος
and ²a partaker ³of the ⁴root* ⁵of the ⁶fatness
τῆς ἐλαίας ἐγένου, **18** μὴ κατακαυχῶ
⁷of the ⁸olive-tree ¹didst become, boast not against
τῶν κλάδων· εἰ δὲ κατακαυχᾶσαι, οὐ
of the branches; but if thou boastest, not
σὺ τὴν ῥίζαν βαστάζεις ἀλλὰ ἡ ῥίζα σέ.
thou the root bearest but the root thee.
19 ἐρεῖς οὖν· ἐξεκλάσθησαν κλάδοι ἵνα
Thou wilt therefore: ²Were broken off ¹branches in order
say　　　　　　　　　　　that
ἐγὼ ἐγκεντρισθῶ. **20** καλῶς· τῇ ἀπιστίᾳ
I might be grafted in. Well: - for unbelief
ἐξεκλάσθησαν, σὺ δὲ τῇ πίστει ἕστηκας.
they were broken off, and thou - by faith standest.
μὴ ὑψηλὰ φρόνει, ἀλλὰ φοβοῦ· **21** εἰ
³Not ³high things ¹mind, but fear; ²if
γὰρ ὁ θεὸς τῶν κατὰ φύσιν κλάδων
¹for - ³God ⁵the ⁷according to ⁸nature ⁶branches
οὐκ ἐφείσατο, οὐδὲ σοῦ φείσεται. **22** ἴδε
⁴spared not. neither thee will he spare. See
οὖν χρηστότητα καὶ ἀποτομίαν θεοῦ· ἐπὶ
therefore [the] kindness and [the] severity of God: ²on
μὲν τοὺς πεσόντας ἀποτομία, ἐπὶ δὲ
¹on one, the having fallen severity, ²on ¹on the
hand [ones]　　　　　　　　　　other
σὲ χρηστότης θεοῦ, ἐὰν ἐπιμένῃς τῇ
thee [the] kindness of God, if thou continuest in the
　　　　　　　　　　　　　　　　(his)
χρηστότητι, ἐπεὶ καὶ σὺ ἐκκοπήσῃ.
kindness, since also thou wilt be cut off.
23 κἀκεῖνοι δέ, ἐὰν μὴ ἐπιμένωσιν τῇ
And those also, if they continue not -
ἀπιστίᾳ, ἐγκεντρισθήσονται· δυνατὸς γάρ
in unbelief, will be grafted in; for ²able

if their transgression means riches for the world, and their loss means riches for the Gentiles, how much greater riches will their fullness bring!

13 I am talking to you Gentiles. Inasmuch as I am the apostle to the Gentiles, I make much of my ministry 14 in the hope that I may somehow arouse my own people to envy and save some of them. 15 For if their rejection is the reconciliation of the world, what will their acceptance be but life from the dead? 16 If the part of the dough offered as firstfruits is holy, then the whole batch is holy; if the root is holy, so are the branches.

17 If some of the branches have been broken off, and you, though a wild olive shoot, have been grafted in among the others and now share in the nourishing sap from the olive root, 18 do not boast over those branches. If you do, consider this: You do not support the root, but the root supports you. 19 You will say then, "Branches were broken off so that I could be grafted in." 20 Granted. But they were broken off because of unbelief, and you stand by faith. Do not be arrogant, but be afraid. 21 For if God did not spare the natural branches, he will not spare you either.

22 Consider therefore the kindness and sternness of God: sternness to those who fell, but kindness to you, provided that you continue in his kindness. Otherwise, you also will be cut off. 23 And if they do not persist in unbelief, they will

---

[d] Gk my flesh
[e] Other ancient authorities read the richness
[f] Other ancient authorities read neither will he spare you
[g] Gk lacks of Israel

* Some MSS insert καί (and) here; as it is, the two nouns in the genitive must be in apposition; cf. Col. 1. 18, 2. 2; John 8. 44.

graft them in again. 24 For if you have been cut from what is by nature a wild olive tree and grafted, contrary to nature, into a cultivated olive tree, how much more will these natural branches be grafted back into their own olive tree.

All Israel Will Be Saved

25 So that you may not claim to be wiser than you are, brothers and sisters,[h] I want you to understand this mystery: a hardening has come upon part of Israel, until the full number of the Gentiles has come in. 26 And so all Israel will be saved; as it is written,
"Out of Zion will
    come the
    Deliverer;
he will banish
    ungodliness
    from Jacob."
27 "And this is my
    covenant
    with them,
when I take away
    their sins."
28 As regards the gospel[i] they are enemies of God[i] for your sake; but as regards election they are beloved, for the sake of their ancestors; 29 for the gifts and the calling of God are irrevocable. 30 Just as you were once disobedient to God but have now received mercy because of their disobedience, 31 so they have now been disobedient in order that, by the mercy shown to you, they too may now[j] receive mercy. 32 For God has imprisoned all in disobedience so that he may be merciful to all.
33 O the depth of the riches and wisdom and knowledge of God! How unsearchable are his judgments and how inscrutable his ways!
34 "For who has known the mind of the Lord? Or who has been his

ἐστιν ὁ θεὸς πάλιν ἐγκεντρίσαι αὐτούς.
²is — ¹God ⁷again ⁴to graft ⁶in ⁵them.
24 εἰ γὰρ σὺ ἐκ τῆς κατὰ φύσιν ἐξεκόπης
For if thou ⁸out ³the ⁸according ⁴nature ¹wast cut
of to
ἀγριελαίου καὶ παρὰ φύσιν ἐνεκεντρίσθης
⁴wild olive and against nature wast grafted in
εἰς καλλιέλαιον, πόσῳ μᾶλλον οὗτοι οἱ
into a cultivated by how more these the
olive, much [ones]
κατὰ φύσιν ἐγκεντρισθήσονται τῇ ἰδίᾳ
according to nature will be grafted in the(ir) own
ἐλαίᾳ. 25 Οὐ γὰρ θέλω ὑμᾶς ἀγνοεῖν,
olive-tree. For I wish not you to be ignorant,
ἀδελφοί, τὸ μυστήριον τοῦτο, ἵνα μὴ
brothers, [of] this mystery, lest
ἦτε ἐν ἑαυτοῖς φρόνιμοι, ὅτι πώρωσις
ye be in yourselves wise, that hardness
ἀπὸ μέρους τῷ Ἰσραὴλ γέγονεν ἄχρι οὗ
from(in) part — to Israel has happened until
τὸ πλήρωμα τῶν ἐθνῶν εἰσέλθῃ, 26 καὶ
the fulness of the nations comes in, and
οὕτως πᾶς Ἰσραὴλ σωθήσεται, καθὼς
so all Israel will be saved, as
γέγραπται· ἥξει ἐκ Σιὼν ὁ ῥυόμενος,
it has been ²will ⁴out ⁵Sion ¹The ³delivering,
written; come of [one]
ἀποστρέψει ἀσεβείας ἀπὸ Ἰακώβ. 27 καὶ
he will turn away impiety from Jacob. And
αὕτη αὐτοῖς ἡ παρ' ἐμοῦ διαθήκη, ὅταν
this [is] ⁶with them ¹the ³from ⁴me ²covenant, when
ἀφέλωμαι τὰς ἁμαρτίας αὐτῶν. 28 κατὰ
I take away the sins of them. ²According to
μὲν τὸ εὐαγγέλιον ἐχθροὶ δι' ὑμᾶς,
¹on one the gospel enemies because you,
hand of
κατὰ δὲ τὴν ἐκλογὴν ἀγαπητοὶ διὰ
²accord- ¹on the the choice beloved because
ing to other of
τοὺς πατέρας· 29 ἀμεταμέλητα γὰρ τὰ
the fathers; for unrepented the
χαρίσματα καὶ ἡ κλῆσις τοῦ θεοῦ.
free gifts and the calling — of God.
30 ὥσπερ γὰρ ὑμεῖς ποτε ἠπειθήσατε
For as ye then disobeyed
τῷ θεῷ, νῦν δὲ ἠλεήθητε τῇ τούτων
— God, but now ye obtained mercy ¹by the ³of these
ἀπειθείᾳ, 31 οὕτως καὶ οὗτοι νῦν ἠπείθησαν
²disobedience, so also these now disobeyed
τῷ ὑμετέρῳ ἐλέει ἵνα καὶ αὐτοὶ νῦν
— ²by your ³mercy ¹in order also they now
that
ἐλεηθῶσιν. 32 συνέκλεισεν γὰρ ὁ θεὸς
may obtain mercy. For ²shut up — ¹God
τοὺς πάντας εἰς ἀπείθειαν ἵνα τοὺς
— all in disobedience in order that —
πάντας ἐλεήσῃ.
to all he may show mercy.
33 Ὦ βάθος πλούτου καὶ σοφίας καὶ
O [the] depth of [the] riches and of [the] wisdom and
γνώσεως θεοῦ· ὡς ἀνεξερεύνητα τὰ κρίματα
of [the] of God; how inscrutable the judgments
knowledge
αὐτοῦ καὶ ἀνεξιχνίαστοι αἱ ὁδοὶ αὐτοῦ.
of him and unsearchable the ways of him.
34 τίς γὰρ ἔγνω νοῦν κυρίου; ἢ τίς
.For who knew [the] mind of [the] Lord? or who

be grafted in, for God is able to graft them in again. 24 After all, if you were cut out of an olive tree that is wild by nature, and contrary to nature were grafted into a cultivated olive tree, how much more readily will these, the natural branches, be grafted into their own olive tree!

All Israel Will Be Saved

25 I do not want you to be ignorant of this mystery, brothers, so that you may not be conceited: Israel has experienced a hardening in part until the full number of the Gentiles has come in. 26 And so all Israel will be saved, as it is written:

"The deliverer will come
    from Zion;
he will turn
    godlessness away
    from Jacob.
27 And this is[r] my
    covenant with them
when I take away their
    sins."[s]

28 As far as the gospel is concerned, they are enemies on your account; but as far as election is concerned, they are loved on account of the patriarchs, 29 for God's gifts and his call are irrevocable. 30 Just as you who were at one time disobedient to God have now received mercy as a result of their disobedience, 31 so they too have now become disobedient in order that they too may now[t] receive mercy as a result of God's mercy to you. 32 For God has bound all men over to disobedience so that he may have mercy on them all.

Doxology

33 Oh, the depth of the riches of the wisdom and[u] knowledge of God!
How unsearchable his judgments,
and his paths beyond tracing out!
34 "Who has known the mind of the Lord?
Or who has been his counselor?"[v]
35 "Who has ever given to God.

h Gk *brothers*
i Gk lacks *of God*
j Other ancient authorities lack *now*

*r*27 Or *will be*
*s*27 Isaiah 59:20,21; 27:9; Jer. 31:33,34
*t*31 Some manuscripts do not have *now*.
*u*33 Or *riches and the wisdom and the*
*v*34 Isaiah 40:13

counselor?"
35 "Or who has given a
gift to him,
to receive a gift in
return?"
36 For from him and
through him and to him are
all things. To him be the
glory forever. Amen.

Chapter 12

The New Life in Christ

I appeal to you therefore,
brothers and sisters, [k]
by the mercies of God, to
present your bodies as a
living sacrifice, holy and
acceptable to God, which is
your spiritual [l] worship.
2 Do not be conformed to
this world, [m] but be transformed by the renewing of
your minds, so that you
may discern what is the will
of God—what is good and
acceptable and perfect. [n]
3 For by the grace given
to me I say to everyone
among you not to think of
yourself more highly than
you ought to think, but to
think with sober judgment,
each according to the measure of faith that God has
assigned. 4 For as in one
body we have many mem-
bers, and not all the members have the same func-
tion, 5 so we, who are
many, are one body in
Christ, and individually we
are members one of anoth-
er. 6 We have gifts that differ according to the grace
given to us: prophecy, in
proportion to faith; 7 ministry, in ministering; the
teacher, in teaching; 8 the
exhorter, in exhortation;
the giver, in generosity; the
leader, in diligence; the

σύμβουλος   αὐτοῦ   ἐγένετο;   **35** ἢ   τίς
counsellor   of him   became?   or   who

προέδωκεν   αὐτῷ,   καὶ   ἀνταποδοθήσεται
previously gave to him,   and   it will be repaid

αὐτῷ;   **36** ὅτι   ἐξ   αὐτοῦ   καὶ   δι'   αὐτοῦ
to him?   Because of   him   and through   him

καὶ   εἰς   αὐτὸν   τὰ   πάντα·   αὐτῷ   ἡ   δόξα
and   to   him   –   all things;   to him   the   glory

εἰς   τοὺς   αἰῶνας·   ἀμήν.
unto   the   ages: Amen.

12 Παρακαλῶ   οὖν   ὑμᾶς,   ἀδελφοί,   διὰ
I beseech   therefore   you,   brothers,   through

τῶν   οἰκτιρμῶν   τοῦ   θεοῦ,   παραστῆσαι   τὰ
the   compassions   –   of God,   to present   the

σώματα   ὑμῶν   θυσίαν   ζῶσαν   ἁγίαν   τῷ
bodies   of you   sacrifice   a living   holy   –

θεῷ   εὐάρεστον,   τὴν   λογικὴν   λατρείαν
²to God ¹well-pleasing,   the   reasonable   service

ὑμῶν·   **2** καὶ   μὴ   συσχηματίζεσθε   τῷ   αἰῶνι
of you;   and   not   be ye not conformed   the   age

τούτῳ,   ἀλλὰ   μεταμορφοῦσθε   τῇ   ἀνακαινώσει
to this,   but   be ye transformed   by the   renewing

τοῦ   νοός,   εἰς   τὸ   δοκιμάζειν   ὑμᾶς   τί   τὸ
of the   mind,   for   the   to prove   you [b]   what   the
                                =so that ye may prove

θέλημα   τοῦ   θεοῦ,   τὸ   ἀγαθὸν   καὶ   εὐάρεστον
will   –   of God,   the   good   and   well-pleasing

καὶ   τέλειον.
and   perfect.

3 Λέγω   γὰρ   διὰ   τῆς   χάριτος   τῆς
For I say   through   the   grace   the

δοθείσης   μοι   παντὶ   τῷ   ὄντι   ἐν   ὑμῖν,
given   to me   to everyone   being   among   you,

μὴ   ὑπερφρονεῖν   παρ'   ὃ   δεῖ   φρονεῖν,
not   to have high   beyond   what   it   to think,
       thoughts   behoves

ἀλλὰ   φρονεῖν   εἰς   τὸ   σωφρονεῖν,   ἑκάστῳ
but   to think   to   the   to be sober-minded, ⁴to each

ὡς   ὁ   θεὸς   ἐμέρισεν   μέτρον   πίστεως.
¹as   –   ²God   ³divided   a measure   of faith.

4 καθάπερ   γὰρ   ἐν   ἑνὶ   σώματι   πολλὰ
For as   in   one   body   many

μέλη   ἔχομεν,   τὰ   δὲ   μέλη   πάντα   οὐ   τὴν
members we have,   but   ²the   ³members   ¹all   ⁵not   ⁴the

αὐτὴν   ἔχει   πρᾶξιν,   **5** οὕτως   οἱ   πολλοὶ
⁷same   ⁴has(ve)   ⁶action,   so   the   many

ἐν   σῶμά   ἐσμεν   ἐν   Χριστῷ,   τὸ   δὲ   καθ'
one   body   we are   in   Christ,   –   and   each

εἰς   ἀλλήλων   μέλη.   **6** ἔχοντες   δὲ   χαρίσματα
one   ²of one   ¹members.   And having   gifts
      another

κατὰ   τὴν   χάριν   τὴν   δοθεῖσαν   ἡμῖν   διάφορα,
²accord- ³the   ⁴grace   –   ⁵given   ⁶to us   ¹differing.
ing to

εἴτε   προφητείαν,   κατὰ   τὴν   ἀναλογίαν   τῆς
whether prophecy,   according to   the   proportion   of the

πίστεως·   **7** εἴτε   διακονίαν,   ἐν   τῇ   διακονίᾳ·
faith;   or   ministry,   in   the   ministry;

εἴτε   ὁ   διδάσκων,   ἐν   τῇ   διδασκαλίᾳ·
or   the [one]   teaching,   in   the   teaching;

8 εἴτε   ὁ   παρακαλῶν,   ἐν   τῇ   παρακλήσει·
or   the [one]   exhorting,   in   the   exhortation;

ὁ   μεταδιδοὺς   ἐν   ἁπλότητι,   ὁ   προϊστάμενος
the [one] sharing   in   simplicity,   the [one] taking the lead

---

that God should repay
him?'' [w]
36 For from him and
through him and to
him are all things.
To him be the glory
forever! Amen.

Chapter 12

Living Sacrifices

THEREFORE, I urge
you, brothers, in view
of God's mercy, to offer
your bodies as living sacrifices, holy and pleasing to
God—this is your spiritu-
al [x] act of worship. 2 Do not
conform any longer to the
pattern of this world, but be
transformed by the renew-
ing of your mind. Then you
will be able to test and approve what God's will is—
his good, pleasing and perfect will.
3 For by the grace given
me I say to every one of
you: Do not think of yourself more highly than you
ought, but rather think of
yourself with sober judg-
ment, in accordance with
the measure of faith God
has given you. 4 Just as each
of us has one body with
many members, and these
members do not all have
the same function, 5 so in
Christ we who are many
form one body, and each
member belongs to all the
others. 6 We have different
gifts, according to the grace
given us. If a man's gift is
prophesying, let him use it
in proportion to his [y] faith.
7 If it is serving, let him
serve; if it is teaching, let
him teach; 8 if it is encouraging, let him encourage; if it
is contributing to the needs
of others, let him give generously; if it is leadership,
let him govern diligently; if

---

[k] Gk brothers
[l] Or reasonable
[m] Gk age
[n] Or what is the good and
acceptable and perfect will of God

[w] 35 Job 41:11
[x] 1 Or reasonable
[y] 6 Or in agreement with the

compassionate, in cheerfulness.

Marks of the True Christian

9 Let love be genuine; hate what is evil, hold fast to what is good; 10 love one another with mutual affection; outdo one another in showing honor. 11 Do not lag in zeal, be ardent in spirit, serve the Lord.ᵒ 12 Rejoice in hope, be patient in suffering, persevere in prayer. 13 Contribute to the needs of the saints; extend hospitality to strangers.

14 Bless those who persecute you; bless and do not curse them. 15 Rejoice with those who rejoice, weep with those who weep. 16 Live in harmony with one another; do not be haughty, but associate with the lowly;ᵖ do not claim to be wiser than you are. 17 Do not repay anyone evil for evil, but take thought for what is noble in the sight of all. 18 If it is possible, so far as it depends on you, live peaceably with all. 19 Beloved, never avenge yourselves, but leave room for the wrath of God;�q for it is written, "Vengeance is mine, I will repay, says the Lord." 20 No, "if your enemies are hungry, feed them; if they are thirsty, give them something to drink; for by doing this you will heap burning coals on their heads." 21 Do not be overcome by evil, but overcome evil with good.

Chapter 13

Being Subject to Authorities

LET every person be subject to the governing authorities; for there is no authority except from God, and those authorities that

ᵒ Other ancient authorities read *serve the opportune time*
ᵖ Or *give yourselves to humble tasks*
q Gk *the wrath*

ἐν σπουδῇ, ὁ ἐλεῶν ἐν ἱλαρότητι. **9** ἡ
in diligence, the showing in cheerfulness. –
[one] mercy

ἀγάπη ἀνυπόκριτος. . ἀποστυγοῦντες τὸ
[Let] love [be] unassumed. Shrinking from the

πονηρόν, κολλώμενοι τῷ ἀγαθῷ· **10** τῇ
evil, cleaving to the good; –

φιλαδελφίᾳ εἰς ἀλλήλους φιλόστοργοι, τῇ
in brotherly love to one another loving warmly, –

τιμῇ ἀλλήλους προηγούμενοι, **11** τῇ σπουδῇ
in one another preferring, – in zeal
honour

μὴ ὀκνηροί, τῷ πνεύματι ζέοντες, τῷ
not slothful, – in spirit burning, the

κυρίῳ δουλεύοντες, **12** τῇ ἐλπίδι χαίροντες,
Lord serving, – in hope rejoicing,

τῇ θλίψει ὑπομένοντες, τῇ προσευχῇ
– in affliction showing endurance, – in prayer

προσκαρτεροῦντες, **13** ταῖς χρείαις τῶν
steadfastly continuing, to the needs of the

ἁγίων κοινωνοῦντες, τὴν φιλοξενίαν
saints imparting, – hospitality

διώκοντες. **14** εὐλογεῖτε τοὺς διώκοντας,
pursuing. Bless ye the [ones] ²persecuting,

εὐλογεῖτε καὶ μὴ καταρᾶσθε. **15** χαίρειν
bless and do not curse. To rejoice

μετὰ χαιρόντων, κλαίειν μετὰ κλαιόντων.
with rejoicing [ones], to weep with weeping [ones].

16 τὸ αὐτὸ εἰς ἀλλήλους φρονοῦντες· μὴ
The same thing toward one another minding; not

τὰ ὑψηλὰ φρονοῦντες ἀλλὰ τοῖς ταπεινοῖς
²the ³high things ¹minding but to the humble

συναπαγόμενοι. μὴ γίνεσθε φρόνιμοι παρ'
condescending. Become not wise with

ἑαυτοῖς. **17** μηδενὶ κακὸν ἀντὶ κακοῦ
yourselves. To no one evil instead of evil

ἀποδιδόντες· προνοούμενοι καλὰ ἐνώπιον
returning; providing for good things before

πάντων ἀνθρώπων· **18** εἰ δυνατόν, τὸ ἐξ
all men; if possible, as far as it

ὑμῶν, μετὰ πάντων ἀνθρώπων εἰρηνεύοντες·
rests with with all men seeking peace;
you,†

19 μὴ ἑαυτοὺς ἐκδικοῦντες, ἀγαπητοί, ἀλλὰ
not ²yourselves ¹avenging, beloved, but

δότε τόπον τῇ ὀργῇ· γέγραπται γάρ·
give place – to wrath; for it has been written:

ἐμοὶ ἐκδίκησις, ἐγὼ ἀνταποδώσω, λέγει
To me vengeance,ᵉ I will repay, says
=Vengeance is mine,

κύριος. **20** ἀλλὰ ἐὰν πεινᾷ ὁ ἐχθρός
[the] Lord. But if hungers the enemy

σου, ψώμιζε αὐτόν· ἐὰν διψᾷ, πότιζε
of thee, feed him; if he thirsts, give ²drink

αὐτόν· τοῦτο γὰρ ποιῶν ἄνθρακας πυρὸς
¹him; for this doing coals of fire

σωρεύσεις ἐπὶ τὴν κεφαλὴν αὐτοῦ. **21** μὴ
thou wilt heap on the head of him. not

νικῶ ὑπὸ τοῦ κακοῦ, ἀλλὰ νίκα
Be conquered by the evil, but conquer

ἐν τῷ ἀγαθῷ τὸ κακόν. **13** Πᾶσα
³by ⁴the ⁵good ¹the ²evil. ²Every

ψυχὴ ἐξουσίαις ὑπερεχούσαις ὑποτασσέσθω.
³soul ⁷authorities ⁶to superior ¹let ⁴be ⁵subject.

οὐ γὰρ ἔστιν ἐξουσία εἰ μὴ
For there is no authority except

ὑπὸ θεοῦ, αἱ δὲ οὖσαι ὑπὸ θεοῦ
by God, and the existing [ones] by God

---

it is showing mercy, let him do it cheerfully.

Love

9 Love must be sincere. Hate what is evil; cling to what is good. 10 Be devoted to one another in brotherly love. Honor one another above yourselves. 11 Never be lacking in zeal, but keep your spiritual fervor, serving the Lord. 12 Be joyful in hope, patient in affliction, faithful in prayer. 13 Share with God's people who are in need. Practice hospitality.

14 Bless those who persecute you; bless and do not curse. 15 Rejoice with those who rejoice; mourn with those who mourn. 16 Live in harmony with one another. Do not be proud, but be willing to associate with people of low position.ᶻ Do not be conceited.

17 Do not repay anyone evil for evil. Be careful to do what is right in the eyes of everybody. 18 If it is possible, as far as it depends on you, live at peace with everyone. 19 Do not take revenge, my friends, but leave room for God's wrath, for it is written: "It is mine to avenge; I will repay,"ᵃ says the Lord. 20 On the contrary:

"If your enemy is hungry, feed him;
if he is thirsty, give him something to drink.
In doing this, you will heap burning coals on his head."ᵇ

21 Do not be overcome by evil, but overcome evil with good.

Chapter 13

Submission to the Authorities

EVERYONE must submit himself to the governing authorities, for there is no authority except that which God has established.

ᶻ16 Or *willing to do menial work*
ᵃ19 Deut. 32:35
ᵇ20 Prov. 25:21,22

exist have been instituted by God. ²Therefore whoever resists authority resists what God has appointed, and those who resist will incur judgment. ³For rulers are not a terror to good conduct, but to bad. Do you wish to have no fear of the authority? Then do what is good, and you will receive its approval; ⁴for it is God's servant for your good. But if you do what is wrong, you should be afraid, for the authority[r] does not bear the sword in vain! It is the servant of God to execute wrath on the wrongdoer. ⁵Therefore one must be subject, not only because of wrath but also because of conscience. ⁶For the same reason you also pay taxes, for the authorities are God's servants, busy with this very thing. ⁷Pay to all what is due them—taxes to whom taxes are due, revenue to whom revenue is due, respect to whom respect is due, honor to whom honor is due.

Love for One Another

8 Owe no one anything, except to love one another; for the one who loves another has fulfilled the law. ⁹The commandments, "You shall not commit adultery; You shall not murder; You shall not steal; You shall not covet"; and any other commandment, are summed up in this word, "Love your neighbor as yourself." ¹⁰Love does no wrong to a neighbor; therefore, love is the fulfilling of the law.

τεταγμέναι εἰσίν. 2 ὥστε ὁ ἀντιτασσόμενος
having been are.   So the [one] resisting
ordained

τῇ ἐξουσίᾳ τῇ τοῦ θεοῦ διαταγῇ ἀνθέστη-
the authority ³the - ⁴of God ²ordinance ¹has op-

κεν· οἱ δὲ ἀνθεστηκότες ἑαυτοῖς κρίμα
posed; and the[ones] having opposed to themselves judgment

λήμψονται. 3 οἱ γὰρ ἄρχοντες οὐκ εἰσὶν
will receive. For the rulers are not

φόβος τῷ ἀγαθῷ ἔργῳ ἀλλὰ τῷ κακῷ.
a fear to the good work but to the evil.

θέλεις δὲ μὴ φοβεῖσθαι τὴν ἐξουσίαν;
And wishest thou not to fear the authority?

τὸ ἀγαθὸν ποίει, καὶ ἕξεις ἔπαινον ἐξ
²the ³good ¹do, and thou wilt praise from
have

αὐτῆς· 4 θεοῦ γὰρ διάκονός ἐστιν σοὶ
it;   for of God a minister he is to thee

εἰς τὸ ἀγαθόν. ἐὰν δὲ τὸ κακὸν ποιῇς,
for the good. But if the evil thou doest,

φοβοῦ· οὐ γὰρ εἰκῇ τὴν μάχαιραν φορεῖ·
fear; for not in vain the sword he bears;

θεοῦ γὰρ διάκονός ἐστιν ἔκδικος εἰς
for of God a minister he is an avenger for

ὀργὴν τῷ τὸ κακὸν πράσσοντι. 5 διὸ
wrath to the[one] ²the ¹evil ¹practising. Wherefore

ἀνάγκη ὑποτάσσεσθαι, οὐ μόνον διὰ τὴν
it is necessary to be subject, not only because of -

ὀργὴν ἀλλὰ καὶ διὰ τὴν συνείδησιν.
wrath but also because of - conscience.

6 διὰ τοῦτο γὰρ καὶ φόρους τελεῖτε·
For therefore also taxes pay ye;

λειτουργοὶ γὰρ θεοῦ εἰσιν εἰς αὐτὸ τοῦτο
for ministers of God they are for this very thing

προσκαρτεροῦντες. 7 ἀπόδοτε πᾶσιν τὰς
attending constantly. Render to all men the

ὀφειλάς, τῷ τὸν φόρον τὸν φόρον,
dues, to the [one] the tax the tax,*

τῷ τὸ τέλος τὸ τέλος, τῷ τὸν φόβον
to the the tribute the tribute, to the the fear
[one]   [one]

τὸν φόβον, τῷ τὴν τιμὴν τὴν τιμήν.
the fear, to the [one] the honour the honour.

8 Μηδενὶ μηδὲν ὀφείλετε, εἰ μὴ τὸ
To no one no(any)thing owe ye, except -

ἀλλήλους ἀγαπᾶν· ὁ γὰρ ἀγαπῶν τὸν
one another to love; for the [one] loving the

ἕτερον νόμον πεπλήρωκεν. 9 τὸ γὰρ
other law has fulfilled. - For

οὐ μοιχεύσεις, οὐ φονεύσεις, οὐ κλέψεις,
Thou shalt not Thou shalt not kill, Thou shalt not
commit adultery,   steal,

οὐκ ἐπιθυμήσεις, καὶ εἴ τις ἑτέρα ἐντολή,
Thou shalt not covet, and if any other command-
[there is]   ment,

ἐν τῷ λόγῳ τούτῳ ἀνακεφαλαιοῦται, [ἐν
²in ³this ⁴word ¹it is summed up, in

τῷ]· ἀγαπήσεις τὸν πλησίον σου ὡς
- : Thou shalt love the neighbour of thee as

σεαυτόν. 10 ἡ ἀγάπη τῷ πλησίον κακὸν
thyself. - Love ³to the ⁴neighbour ²evil
(one's)

οὐκ ἐργάζεται· πλήρωμα οὖν νόμου ἡ
¹works not; ³[is] ⁴fulfilment ¹therefore ⁵of law -

The authorities that exist have been established by God. ²Consequently, he who rebels against the authority is rebelling against what God has instituted, and those who do so will bring judgment on themselves. ³For rulers hold no terror for those who do right, but for those who do wrong. Do you want to be free from fear of the one in authority? Then do what is right and he will commend you. ⁴For he is God's servant to do you good. But if you do wrong, be afraid, for he does not bear the sword for nothing. He is God's servant, an agent of wrath to bring punishment on the wrongdoer. ⁵Therefore, it is necessary to submit to the authorities, not only because of possible punishment but also because of conscience. ⁶This is also why you pay taxes, for the authorities are God's servants, who give their full time to governing. ⁷Give everyone what you owe him: If you owe taxes, pay taxes; if revenue, then revenue; if respect, then respect; if honor, then honor.

Love, for the Day Is Near

⁸Let no debt remain outstanding, except the continuing debt to love one another, for he who loves his fellowman has fulfilled the law. ⁹The commandments, "Do not commit adultery," "Do not murder," "Do not steal," "Do not covet,"[c] and whatever other commandment there may be, are summed up in this one rule: "Love your neighbor as yourself."[d] ¹⁰Love does no harm to its neighbor. Therefore love is the fulfillment of the law.

---

* The phrase between the commas is elliptical; understand—to the [one] demanding] the tax [render] the tax. So of the following phrases.

[r] Gk it

c9 Exodus 20:13-15,17; Deut. 5:17-19,21
d9 Lev. 19:18

An Urgent Appeal

11 Besides this, you know what time it is, how it is now the moment for you to wake from sleep. For salvation is nearer to us now than when we became believers; 12 the night is far gone, the day is near. Let us then lay aside the works of darkness and put on the armor of light; 13 let us live honorably as in the day, not in reveling and drunkenness, not in debauchery and licentiousness, not in quarreling and jealousy. 14 Instead, put on the Lord Jesus Christ, and make no provision for the flesh, to gratify its desires.

ἀγάπη. **11** Καὶ τοῦτο εἰδότες τὸν καιρόν,
²love. And this[,] knowing the time,

ὅτι ὥρα ἤδη ὑμᾶς ἐξ ὕπνου ἐγερθῆναι·
that hour now you out of sleep to be raised;ᵇ
=it is now an hour for you to be raised out of sleep;

νῦν γὰρ ἐγγύτερον ἡμῶν ἡ σωτηρία
for now nearer [is] of us the salvation

ἢ ὅτε ἐπιστεύσαμεν. **12** ἡ νὺξ προέκοψεν,
than when we believed. The night advanced,

ἡ δὲ ἡμέρα ἤγγικεν. ἀποθώμεθα οὖν
and the day has drawn near. Let us cast off therefore

τὰ ἔργα τοῦ σκότους, ἐνδυσώμεθα δὲ
the works of the darkness, and let us put on

τὰ ὅπλα τοῦ φωτός. **13** ὡς ἐν ἡμέρᾳ
the weapons of the light. As in [the] day

εὐσχημόνως περιπατήσωμεν, μὴ κώμοις καὶ
becomingly let us walk, not in revellings and

μέθαις, μὴ κοίταις καὶ ἀσελγείαις, μὴ
in drunken not in beds* and excesses, not
bouts,

ἔριδι καὶ ζήλῳ· **14** ἀλλὰ ἐνδύσασθε τὸν
in strife and in jealousy; but put ye on the

κύριον Ἰησοῦν Χριστόν, καὶ τῆς σαρκὸς
Lord Jesus Christ, and of the flesh

πρόνοιαν μὴ ποιεῖσθε εἰς ἐπιθυμίας.
forethought make not for [its] lusts.

11 And do this, understanding the present time. The hour has come for you to wake up from your slumber, because our salvation is nearer now than when we first believed. 12 The night is nearly over; the day is almost here. So let us put aside the deeds of darkness and put on the armor of light. 13 Let us behave decently, as in the daytime, not in orgies and drunkenness, not in sexual immorality and debauchery, not in dissension and jealousy. 14 Rather, clothe yourselves with the Lord Jesus Christ, and do not think about how to gratify the desires of the sinful nature.ᵉ

Chapter 14

Do Not Judge Another

WELCOME those who are weak in faith,ˢ but not for the purpose of quarreling over opinions. ²Some believe in eating anything, while the weak eat only vegetables. ³Those who eat must not despise those who abstain, and those who abstain must not pass judgment on those who eat; for God has welcomed them. ⁴Who are you to pass judgment on servants of another? It is before their own lord that they stand or fall. And they will be upheld, for the Lord¹ is able to make them stand.

5 Some judge one day to be better than another, while others judge all days to be alike. Let all be fully convinced in their own minds. ⁶Those who observe the day, observe it in honor of the Lord. Also those who eat, eat in honor of the Lord, since they give thanks to God; while those who abstain, abstain in

14 Τὸν δὲ ἀσθενοῦντα τῇ πίστει
Now the [one] being weak in the faith

προσλαμβάνεσθε, μὴ εἰς διακρίσεις διαλογισ-
receive ye, not to judgments of

μῶν. **2** ὃς μὲν πιστεύει φαγεῖν πάντα,
thoughts. One indeed believes to eat all things,
man†

ὁ δὲ ἀσθενῶν λάχανα ἐσθίει. **3** ὁ ἐσθίων
but the being weak herbs eats. ³The ⁴eating
[one] [one]

τὸν μὴ ἐσθίοντα μὴ ἐξουθενείτω, ὁ δὲ
⁵the ⁷not ⁶eating ³not ¹let ²despise, and ⁸the
[one] [one]

μὴ ἐσθίων τὸν ἐσθίοντα μὴ κρινέτω,
³not ⁶eating ⁷the [one] ⁵eating ³not ¹let ²judge,

ὁ θεός· γὰρ αὐτὸν προσελάβετο. **4** σὺ
for God him received. ²Thou

τίς εἶ ὁ κρίνων ἀλλότριον οἰκέτην; τῷ
¹who ²art ⁴the ⁵judging ⁷belonging to ⁸a household to
[one] another servant? the(his)

ἰδίῳ κυρίῳ στήκει ἢ πίπτει· σταθήσεται
own lord he stands or falls; ³he will stand

δέ, δυνατεῖ γὰρ ὁ κύριος στῆσαι αὐτόν.
¹but, for is able the Lord to stand him.

5 ὃς μὲν [γὰρ] κρίνει ἡμέραν παρ’
one man† indeed judges a day above

ἡμέραν, ὃς δὲ κρίνει πᾶσαν ἡμέραν·
a day, another† judges every day;

ἕκαστος ἐν τῷ ἰδίῳ νοῒ πληροφορείσθω.
each man in the(his) own mind let him be fully
persuaded.

6 ὁ φρονῶν τὴν ἡμέραν κυρίῳ φρονεῖ.
The minding the day to [the] he minds
[one] Lord [it].

καὶ ὁ ἐσθίων κυρίῳ ἐσθίει, εὐχαριστεῖ γὰρ
And the eating to [the] he eats, for he gives thanks
[one] Lord

τῷ θεῷ· καὶ ὁ μὴ ἐσθίων κυρίῳ
- to God; and the [one] not eating to [the] Lord

Chapter 14

The Weak and the Strong

ACCEPT him whose faith is weak, without passing judgment on disputable matters. ²One man's faith allows him to eat everything, but another man, whose faith is weak, eats only vegetables. ³The man who eats everything must not look down on him who does not, and the man who does not eat everything must not condemn the man who does, for God has accepted him. ⁴Who are you to judge someone else's servant? To his own master he stands or falls. And he will stand, for the Lord is able to make him stand.

⁵One man considers one day more sacred than another; another man considers every day alike. Each one should be fully convinced in his own mind. ⁶He who regards one day as special, does so to the Lord. He who eats meat, eats to the Lord, for he gives thanks to God; and he who abstains, does so to

---

ˢ Or conviction
¹ Other ancient authorities read for God

* That is, illicit sexual intercourse.

ᵉ14 Or the flesh

honor of the Lord and give thanks to God.
7 We do not live to ourselves, and we do not die to ourselves. 8 If we live, we live to the Lord, and if we die, we die to the Lord; so then, whether we live or whether we die, we are the Lord's. 9 For to this end Christ died and lived again, so that he might be Lord of both the dead and the living.
10 Why do you pass judgment on your brother or sister?[u] Or you, why do you despise your brother or sister?[u] For we will all stand before the judgment seat of God.[v] 11 For it is written,
"As I live, says the Lord, every knee shall bow to me, and every tongue shall give praise to[w] God."
12 So then, each of us will be accountable to God.[x]

Do Not Make Another Stumble

13 Let us therefore no longer pass judgment on one another, but resolve instead never to put a stumbling block or hindrance in the way of another.[y] 14 I know and am persuaded in the Lord Jesus that nothing is unclean in itself; but it is unclean for anyone who thinks it unclean. 15 If your brother or sister[u] is being injured by what you eat, you are no longer walking in love. Do not let what you eat cause the ruin of one for whom Christ died. 16 So do not let your good be spoken of as evil. 17 For the kingdom of God is not food and drink but righteousness and peace and joy in the Holy Spirit. 18 The one who thus serves Christ is acceptable to God and has human ap-

οὐκ ἐσθίει, καὶ εὐχαριστεῖ τῷ θεῷ.
he eats not, and gives thanks – to God.
7 οὐδεὶς γὰρ ἡμῶν ἑαυτῷ ζῇ, καὶ οὐδεὶς
For no one of us to himself lives, and no one
ἑαυτῷ ἀποθνῄσκει· 8 ἐάν τε γὰρ ζῶμεν,
to himself dies; for whether we live,
τῷ κυρίῳ ζῶμεν, ἐάν τε ἀποθνῄσκωμεν,
to the Lord we live, or if we die,
τῷ κυρίῳ ἀποθνῄσκομεν. ἐάν τε οὖν
to the Lord we die. Whether therefore
ζῶμεν ἐάν τε ἀποθνῄσκωμεν, τοῦ κυρίου
we live or if we die, of the Lord
ἐσμέν. 9 εἰς τοῦτο γὰρ Χριστὸς ἀπέθανεν
we are. for this For Christ died
καὶ ἔζησεν, ἵνα καὶ νεκρῶν καὶ ζώντων
and lived [again], in order both of dead and of living
that [ones]
κυριεύσῃ. 10 σὺ δὲ τί κρίνεις τὸν ἀδελφόν
he might be Lord. ³thou And ¹why ²judgest the brother
σου; ἢ καὶ σὺ τί ἐξουθενεῖς τὸν ἀδελφόν
of thee? or ²indeed ⁴thou ¹why ³despisest the brother
σου; πάντες γὰρ παραστησόμεθα τῷ
of thee? for all we shall stand before the
βήματι τοῦ θεοῦ. 11 γέγραπται γάρ·
tribunal – of God. For it has been written:
ζῶ ἐγώ, λέγει κύριος, ὅτι ἐμοὶ κάμψει
Live I, says [the] Lord, that to me will bend
πᾶν γόνυ, καὶ πᾶσα γλῶσσα ἐξομολογήσεται
every knee, and every tongue will confess
τῷ θεῷ. 12 ἄρα [οὖν] ἕκαστος ἡμῶν
– to God. So therefore each one of us
περὶ ἑαυτοῦ λόγον δώσει [τῷ θεῷ].
concerning himself account will give – to God.
13 Μηκέτι οὖν ἀλλήλους κρίνωμεν· ἀλλὰ
No longer therefore one another let us judge; but
τοῦτο κρίνατε μᾶλλον, τὸ μὴ τιθέναι
this judge ye rather, – not to put
πρόσκομμα τῷ ἀδελφῷ ἢ σκάνδαλον.
a stumbling-block to the brother or an offence.
14 οἶδα καὶ πέπεισμαι ἐν κυρίῳ Ἰησοῦ
I know and have been by [the] Lord Jesus
persuaded
ὅτι οὐδὲν κοινὸν δι' ἑαυτοῦ· εἰ μὴ
that nothing [is] common through itself; except
τῷ λογιζομένῳ τι κοινὸν εἶναι, ἐκείνῳ
to the reckoning anything common to be, to that man
[one] [it is]
κοινόν. 15 εἰ γὰρ διὰ βρῶμα ὁ ἀδελφός
common. For if because food the brother
of
σου λυπεῖται, οὐκέτι κατὰ ἀγάπην
of thee is grieved, no longer according to love
περιπατεῖς. μὴ τῷ βρώματί σου ἐκεῖνον
thou walkest. ²Not ³by the ⁴food ⁵of thee ⁶that man
ἀπόλλυε, ὑπὲρ οὗ Χριστὸς ἀπέθανεν.
¹destroy, on behalf of whom Christ died.
16 μὴ βλασφημείσθω οὖν ὑμῶν τὸ ἀγαθόν.
Let not be blasphemed therefore of you the good.
17 οὐ γάρ ἐστιν ἡ βασιλεία τοῦ θεοῦ
For not is the kingdom – of God
βρῶσις καὶ πόσις, ἀλλὰ δικαιοσύνη καὶ
eating and drinking, but righteousness and
εἰρήνη καὶ χαρὰ ἐν πνεύματι ἁγίῳ·
peace and joy in [the] Spirit Holy;
18 ὁ γὰρ ἐν τούτῳ δουλεύων τῷ Χριστῷ
for the [one] in this serving – Christ

the Lord and gives thanks to God. 7 For none of us lives to himself alone and none of us dies to himself alone. 8 If we live, we live to the Lord; and if we die, we die to the Lord. So, whether we live or die, we belong to the Lord.
9 For this very reason, Christ died and returned to life so that he might be the Lord of both the dead and the living. 10 You, then, why do you judge your brother? Or why do you look down on your brother? For we will all stand before God's judgment seat. 11 It is written:

"'As surely as I live,'
    says the Lord,
'every knee will bow
    before me;
every tongue will
    confess to God.'"[f]

12 So then, each of us will give an account of himself to God.
13 Therefore let us stop passing judgment on one another. Instead, make up your mind not to put any stumbling block or obstacle in your brother's way. 14 As one who is in the Lord Jesus, I am fully convinced that no food[g] is unclean in itself. But if anyone regards something as unclean, then for him it is unclean. 15 If your brother is distressed because of what you eat, you are no longer acting in love. Do not by your eating destroy your brother for whom Christ died. 16 Do not allow what you consider good to be spoken of as evil. 17 For the kingdom of God is not a matter of eating and drinking, but of righteousness, peace and joy in the Holy Spirit, 18 because anyone who serves

[u] Gk *brother*
[v] Other ancient authorities read *of Christ*
[w] Or *confess*
[x] Other ancient authorities lack *to God*
[y] Gk *of a brother*

[f] 11 Isaiah 45:23
[g] 14 Or *that nothing*

proval. 19Let us then pursue what makes for peace and for mutual upbuilding. 20Do not, for the sake of food, destroy the work of God. Everything is indeed clean, but it is wrong for you to make others fall by what you eat; 21it is good not to eat meat or drink wine or do anything that makes your brother or sister*u* stumble.*z* 22The faith that you have, have as your own conviction before God. Blessed are those who have no reason to condemn themselves because of what they approve. 23But those who have doubts are condemned if they eat, because they do not act from faith;*s* for whatever does not proceed from faith*s* is sin.*a*

Chapter 15
Please Others, Not Yourselves

WE who are strong ought to put up with the failings of the weak, and not to please ourselves. 2Each of us must please our neighbor for the good purpose of building up the neighbor. 3For Christ did not please himself; but, as it is written, "The insults of those who insult you have fallen on me." 4For whatever was written in former days was written for our instruction, so that by steadfastness and by the encouragement of the scriptures we might have hope. 5May the God of steadfastness and encouragement grant you to live in harmony with one another, in accordance with Christ Jesus, 6so that together you may with one voice glorify the God and

z Other ancient authorities add *or be upset or be weakened*
a Other authorities, some ancient, add here 16.25-27

εὐάρεστος τῷ θεῷ καὶ δόκιμος τοῖς
[is] well-pleasing - to God and approved -

ἀνθρώποις. 19 ἄρα οὖν τὰ τῆς εἰρήνης
by men. So there- the - of peace
fore things

διώκωμεν καὶ τὰ τῆς οἰκοδομῆς τῆς
let us pursue and the things - of building [up] -

εἰς ἀλλήλους. 20 μὴ ἕνεκεν βρώματος
for one another. Not for the sake of food

κατάλυε τὸ ἔργον τοῦ θεοῦ. πάντα
undo thou the work - of God. All things

μὲν καθαρά, ἀλλὰ κακὸν τῷ ἀνθρώπῳ
indeed [are] clean, but evil to the man

τῷ διὰ προσκόμματος ἐσθίοντι. 21 καλὸν
- ³through ²a stumbling-block ¹eating. Good [it is]

τὸ μὴ φαγεῖν κρέα μηδὲ πιεῖν οἶνον
- not to eat flesh nor to drink wine

μηδὲ ἐν ᾧ ὁ ἀδελφός σου προσκόπτει.
nor by which the brother of thee stumbles.
[anything]

22 σὺ πίστιν ἣν ἔχεις κατὰ σεαυτὸν
³Thou ¹faith ²which ⁴hast ⁶by ⁷thyself

ἔχε ἐνώπιον τοῦ θεοῦ. μακάριος ὁ
⁵have before - God. Blessed the
[one]

μὴ κρίνων ἑαυτὸν ἐν ᾧ δοκιμάζει·
not judging himself in what he approves;

23 ὁ δὲ διακρινόμενος ἐὰν φάγῃ κατα-
but the [one] doubting if he eats has been

κέκριται, ὅτι οὐκ ἐκ πίστεως· πᾶν
condemned, because not of faith; ²all

δὲ ὃ οὐκ ἐκ πίστεως ἁμαρτία ἐστίν.
¹and which [is] not of faith sin is.

15 Ὀφείλομεν δὲ ἡμεῖς οἱ δυνατοὶ τὰ
⁵Ought ¹so ⁴we ⁸the ⁶strong ⁷the

ἀσθενήματα τῶν ἀδυνάτων βαστάζειν, καὶ
⁹weaknesses ⁹of the ¹⁰not strong ⁶to bear, and

μὴ ἑαυτοῖς ἀρέσκειν. 2 ἕκαστος ἡμῶν
not [our]selves to please. Each one of us

τῷ πλησίον ἀρεσκέτω εἰς τὸ ἀγαθὸν
the(his) neighbour let him please for - good

πρὸς οἰκοδομήν· 3 καὶ γὰρ ὁ Χριστὸς
to building [up]; for even - Christ

οὐχ ἑαυτῷ ἤρεσεν· ἀλλὰ καθὼς γέ-
²not ³himself ¹pleased; but as it has

γραπται· οἱ ὀνειδισμοὶ τῶν ὀνειδιζόντων
been written: The reproaches of the [ones] reproaching

σε ἐπέπεσαν ἐπ’ ἐμέ. 4 ὅσα γὰρ
thee fell on on me. For whatever things

προεγράφη, εἰς τὴν ἡμετέραν διδασκαλίαν
were previously for - our teaching
written,

ἐγράφη, ἵνα διὰ τῆς ὑπομονῆς καὶ
were in order through - patience and
written, that

διὰ τῆς παρακλήσεως τῶν γραφῶν τὴν
through the comfort of the writings -

ἐλπίδα ἔχωμεν. 5 ὁ δὲ θεὸς τῆς ὑπομονῆς
hope we may have. And the God - of patience

καὶ τῆς παρακλήσεως δῴη ὑμῖν τὸ
and - of comfort give to you ²the

αὐτὸ φρονεῖν ἐν ἀλλήλοις κατὰ Χριστὸν
³same ¹to mind among one another according to Christ

Ἰησοῦν, 6 ἵνα ὁμοθυμαδὸν ἐν ἑνὶ στόματι
Jesus, in order with one accord with one mouth
that

Christ in this way is pleasing to God and approved by men.

19Let us therefore make every effort to do what leads to peace and to mutual edification. 20Do not destroy the work of God for the sake of food. All food is clean, but it is wrong for a man to eat anything that causes someone else to stumble. 21It is better not to eat meat or drink wine or to do anything else that will cause your brother to fall.

22So whatever you believe about these things keep between yourself and God. Blessed is the man who does not condemn himself by what he approves. 23But the man who has doubts is condemned if he eats, because his eating is not from faith; and everything that does not come from faith is sin.

Chapter 15

WE who are strong ought to bear with the failings of the weak and not to please ourselves. 2Each of us should please his neighbor for his good, to build him up. 3For even Christ did not please himself but, as it is written: "The insults of those who insult you have fallen on me."*h* 4For everything that was written in the past was written to teach us, so that through endurance and the encouragement of the Scriptures we might have hope.

5May the God who gives endurance and encouragement give you a spirit of unity among yourselves as you follow Christ Jesus, 6so that with one heart and mouth you may glorify the

h3 Psalm 69:9

Father of our Lord Jesus Christ.

The Gospel for Jews and Gentiles Alike

7 Welcome one another, therefore, just as Christ has welcomed you, for the glory of God. [8]For I tell you that Christ has become a servant of the circumcised on behalf of the truth of God in order that he might confirm the promises given to the patriarchs, [9]and in order that the Gentiles might glorify God for his mercy. As it is written,
"Therefore I will confess[b] you among the Gentiles, and sing praises to your name";
[10]and again he says, "Rejoice, O Gentiles, with his people";
[11]and again, "Praise the Lord, all you Gentiles, and let all the peoples praise him";
[12]and again Isaiah says, "The root of Jesse shall come, the one who rises to rule the Gentiles; in him the Gentiles shall hope."
[13]May the God of hope fill you with all joy and peace in believing, so that you may abound in hope by the power of the Holy Spirit.

Paul's Reason for Writing So Boldly

14 I myself feel confident about you, my brothers and sisters,[c] that you yourselves are full of all knowledge, and able to instruct one another. [15]Nevertheless on some points I have written to you rather boldly by way of reminder, because of the grace given me by God [16]to be a minister of

δοξάζητε   τὸν   θεὸν   καὶ   πατέρα   τοῦ
ye may glorify the   God   and   Father   of the

κυρίου   ἡμῶν   Ἰησοῦ   Χριστοῦ.
Lord   of us   Jesus   Christ.

7 Διὸ   προσλαμβάνεσθε   ἀλλήλους,   καθὼς
Wherefore   receive ye   one another,   as

καὶ   ὁ   Χριστὸς   προσελάβετο   ἡμᾶς   εἰς
also   -   Christ   received   us   to

δόξαν   τοῦ   θεοῦ.   8 λέγω   γὰρ   Χριστὸν
[the] glory   -   of God.   For I say   Christ

διάκονον   γεγενῆσθαι   περιτομῆς   ὑπὲρ
a minister   to have become   of [the]   on be-
circumcision   half of

ἀληθείας   θεοῦ,   εἰς   τὸ   βεβαιῶσαι   τὰς
[the] truth   of God,   -   to confirm   the

ἐπαγγελίας   τῶν   πατέρων,   9 τὰ   δὲ   ἔθνη
promises   of the   fathers,   and [1]the   [2]nations

ὑπὲρ   ἐλέους   δοξάσαι   τὸν   θεόν,   καθὼς
[2]on be-   [1]mercy   [3]to glorify   -   [4]God,   as
half of

γέγραπται·   διὰ   τοῦτο   ἐξομολογήσομαί   σοι
it has been written: Therefore   I will confess   to thee

ἐν   ἔθνεσιν   καὶ   τῷ   ὀνόματί   σου   ψαλῶ.
among nations   and   to the   name   of thee   I will sing
praise.

10 καὶ   πάλιν   λέγει·   εὐφράνθητε,   ἔθνη,
And   again   he says: Be glad,   nations,

μετὰ   τοῦ   λαοῦ   αὐτοῦ.   11 καὶ   πάλιν·
with   the   people   of him.   And   again:

αἰνεῖτε,   πάντα   τὰ   ἔθνη,   τὸν   κύριον,
Praise,   all   the   nations,   the   Lord,

καὶ   ἐπαινεσάτωσαν   αὐτὸν   πάντες   οἱ   λαοί.
and   let praise   him   all   the   peoples.

12 καὶ   πάλιν   Ἡσαΐας   λέγει·   ἔσται
And   again   Esaias   says: There
shall be

ἡ   ῥίζα   τοῦ   Ἰεσσαί,   καὶ   ὁ   ἀνιστάμενος
the   root   -   of Jesse,   and   the [one]   rising up

ἄρχειν   ἐθνῶν·   ἐπ’   αὐτῷ   ἔθνη   ἐλπιοῦσιν.
to rule   nations;   on   him   nations   will hope.

13 Ὁ   δὲ   θεὸς   τῆς   ἐλπίδος   πληρώσαι
Now the   God   -   of hope   fill

ὑμᾶς   πάσης   χαρᾶς   καὶ   εἰρήνης   ἐν   τῷ
you   of(with) all   joy   and   peace   in   -

πιστεύειν,   εἰς   τὸ   περισσεύειν   ὑμᾶς   ἐν
to believe   for   -   to abound   you[b]   in
(believing),

τῇ   ἐλπίδι   ἐν   δυνάμει   πνεύματος   ἁγίου.
-    hope   by   [the] power   of [the] Spirit   Holy.

14 Πέπεισμαι   δέ,   ἀδελφοί   μου,   καὶ
But I have been persuaded,   brothers   of me,   even

αὐτὸς   ἐγὼ   περὶ   ὑμῶν,   ὅτι   καὶ   αὐτοὶ
[2][my]self   [1]I   concerning   you,   that   also   [your]-
selves

μεστοί   ἐστε   ἀγαθωσύνης,   πεπληρωμένοι
full   ye are   of goodness,   having been filled

πάσης   τῆς   γνώσεως,   δυνάμενοι   καὶ
of(with) all   -   knowledge,   being able   also

ἀλλήλους   νουθετεῖν.   15 τολμηροτέρως   δὲ
one another   to admonish.   And more daringly

ἔγραψα   ὑμῖν   ἀπὸ   μέρους,   ὡς   ἐπαναμιμνή-
I wrote   to you   in   part,   as   remind-

σκων   ὑμᾶς   διὰ   τὴν   χάριν   τὴν   δοθεῖσάν
ing   you   by   the   grace   -   given

μοι   ἀπὸ   τοῦ   θεοῦ   16 εἰς   τὸ   εἶναί   με
to me   from   -   God   for   the   to be   me[b]
=that I should be

God and Father of our Lord Jesus Christ.

[7]Accept one another, then, just as Christ accepted you, in order to bring praise to God. [8]For I tell you that Christ has become a servant of the Jews[i] on behalf of God's truth, to confirm the promises made to the patriarchs [9]so that the Gentiles may glorify God for his mercy, as it is written:

"Therefore I will praise you among the Gentiles; I will sing hymns to your name."[j]

[10]Again, it says,

"Rejoice, O Gentiles, with his people."[k]

[11]And again,

"Praise the Lord, all you Gentiles, and sing praises to him, all you peoples."[l]

[12]And again, Isaiah says,

"The Root of Jesse will spring up, one who will arise to rule over the nations; the Gentiles will hope in him."[m]

[13]May the God of hope fill you with all joy and peace as you trust in him, so that you may overflow with hope by the power of the Holy Spirit.

Paul the Minister to the Gentiles

[14]I myself am convinced, my brothers, that you yourselves are full of goodness, complete in knowledge and competent to instruct one another. [15]I have written you quite boldly on some points, as if to remind you of them again, because of the grace God gave me [16]to be a minister of Christ

_____
[b] Or *thank*
[c] Gk *brothers*

[i]8 Greek *circumcision*
[j]9 2 Samuel 22:50; Psalm 18:49
[k]10 Deut. 32:43
[l]11 Psalm 117:1
[m]12 Isaiah 11:10

Christ Jesus to the Gentiles in the priestly service of the gospel of God, so that the offering of the Gentiles may be acceptable, sanctified by the Holy Spirit. 17 In Christ Jesus, then, I have reason to boast of my work for God. 18 For I will not venture to speak of anything except what Christ has accomplished[d] through me to win obedience from the Gentiles, by word and deed, 19 by the power of signs and wonders, by the power of the Spirit of God,[e] so that from Jerusalem and as far around as Illyricum I have fully proclaimed the good news[f] of Christ. 20 Thus I make it my ambition to proclaim the good news,[f] not where Christ has already been named, so that I do not build on someone else's foundation, 21 but as it is written,

"Those who have
  never been told
  of him shall see,
and those who have
  never heard of
  him shall
  understand."

Paul's Plan to Visit Rome

22 This is the reason that I have so often been hindered from coming to you. 23 But now, with no further place for me in these regions, I desire, as I have for many years, to come to you 24 when I go to Spain. For I do hope to see you on my journey and to be sent on by you, once I have enjoyed your company for a little while. 25 At present, however, I am going to Jerusalem in a ministry to the saints; 26 for Macedonia and Achaia have been pleased to share their resources with the poor

---

λειτουργὸν Χριστοῦ Ἰησοῦ εἰς τὰ ἔθνη,
a minister of Christ Jesus to the nations,

ἱερουργοῦντα τὸ εὐαγγέλιον τοῦ θεοῦ,
sacrificing the gospel of God,

ἵνα γένηται ἡ προσφορὰ τῶν ἐθνῶν
in order that may be the offering of the nations

εὐπρόσδεκτος, ἡγιασμένη ἐν πνεύματι
acceptable, having been sanctified by [the] Spirit

ἁγίῳ. 17 ἔχω οὖν τὴν καύχησιν ἐν
Holy. I have therefore the boasting in

Χριστῷ Ἰησοῦ τὰ πρὸς τὸν θεόν· 18 οὐ
Christ Jesus the things with* - God; not

γὰρ τολμήσω τι λαλεῖν ὧν οὐ
for I will dare anything to speak of [the] not things which

κατειργάσατο Χριστὸς δι' ἐμοῦ εἰς ὑπακοὴν
did work out Christ through me for obedience

ἐθνῶν, λόγῳ καὶ ἔργῳ, 19 ἐν δυνάμει
of [the] nations, in word and work, by power

σημείων καὶ τεράτων, ἐν δυνάμει πνεύματος·
of signs and wonders, by power of [the] Spirit;

ὥστε με ἀπὸ Ἰερουσαλὴμ καὶ κύκλῳ
so as me from Jerusalem and around =I should fulfil the gospel . . . from . . . Illyricum.

μέχρι τοῦ Ἰλλυρικοῦ πεπληρωκέναι[b] τὸ
unto - Illyricum to have fulfilled the

εὐαγγέλιον τοῦ Χριστοῦ. 20 οὕτως δὲ
gospel - of Christ. And so

φιλοτιμούμενον εὐαγγελίζεσθαι οὐχ ὅπου
eagerly striving to evangelize not where

ὠνομάσθη Χριστός, ἵνα μὴ ἐπ' ἀλλότριον
was named Christ, in order not on belonging to another

θεμέλιον οἰκοδομῶ, 21 ἀλλὰ καθὼς
a foundation I should build, but as

γέγραπται· ὄψονται οἷς οὐκ ἀνηγγέλη
it has been written: They shall see to whom it was not announced

περὶ αὐτοῦ, καὶ οἳ οὐκ ἀκηκόασιν
concerning him, and [those] who have not heard

συνήσουσιν. 22 διὸ καὶ ἐνεκοπτόμην τὰ
will understand. Wherefore also I was hindered

πολλὰ τοῦ ἐλθεῖν[d] πρὸς ὑμᾶς· 23 νυνὶ
many(much) - to come to you; now

δὲ μηκέτι τόπον ἔχων ἐν τοῖς κλίμασι
but no longer place having in - regions

τούτοις, ἐπιποθίαν δὲ ἔχων τοῦ ἐλθεῖν[d]
these, and a desire having to come

πρὸς ὑμᾶς ἀπὸ ἱκανῶν ἐτῶν, 24 ὡς ἂν
to you from several years, whenever

πορεύωμαι εἰς τὴν Σπανίαν· ἐλπίζω γὰρ
I journey to - Spain; for I hope

διαπορευόμενος θεάσασθαι ὑμᾶς καὶ ὑφ'
journeying through to behold you and by

ὑμῶν προπεμφθῆναι ἐκεῖ, ἐὰν ὑμῶν πρῶτον
you to be set forward there, if of(with) you firstly

ἀπὸ μέρους ἐμπλησθῶ, 25 — νυνὶ δὲ
in part I may be filled, - but now

πορεύομαι εἰς Ἰερουσαλὴμ διακονῶν τοῖς
I am going to Jerusalem ministering to the

ἁγίοις. 26 ηὐδόκησαν γὰρ Μακεδονία καὶ
saints. For thought it good Macedonia and

Ἀχαΐα κοινωνίαν τινὰ ποιήσασθαι εἰς
Achaia contribution some to make for

* That is, the things that have to do with . . .

Jesus to the Gentiles with the priestly duty of proclaiming the gospel of God, so that the Gentiles might become an offering acceptable to God, sanctified by the Holy Spirit. 17 Therefore I glory in Christ Jesus in my service to God. 18 I will not venture to speak of anything except what Christ has accomplished through me in leading the Gentiles to obey God by what I have said and done— 19 by the power of signs and miracles, through the power of the Spirit. So from Jerusalem all the way around to Illyricum, I have fully proclaimed the gospel of Christ. 20 It has always been my ambition to preach the gospel where Christ was not known, so that I would not be building on someone else's foundation. 21 Rather, as it is written:

"Those who were not
  told about him will
  see,
and those who have
  not heard will
  understand."[n]

22 This is why I have often been hindered from coming to you.

Paul's Plan to Visit Rome

23 But now that there is no more place for me to work in these regions, and since I have been longing for many years to see you, 24 I plan to do so when I go to Spain. I hope to visit you while passing through and to have you assist me on my journey there, after I have enjoyed your company for a while. 25 Now, however, I am on my way to Jerusalem in the service of the saints there. 26 For Macedonia and Achaia were pleased to make a contribution for the

---

d Gk *speak of those things that Christ has not accomplished*
e Other ancient authorities read *of the Spirit* or *of the Holy Spirit*
f Or *gospel*

n 21 Isaiah 52:15

among the saints at Jerusalem. 27 They were pleased to do this, and indeed they owe it to them; for if the Gentiles have come to share in their spiritual blessings, they ought also to be of service to them in material things. 28 So, when I have completed this, and have delivered to them what has been collected, *g* I will set out by way of you to Spain; 29 and I know that when I come to you, I will come in the fullness of the blessing *h* of Christ.

30 I appeal to you, brothers and sisters, *c* by our Lord Jesus Christ and by the love of the Spirit, to join me in earnest prayer to God on my behalf, 31 that I may be rescued from the unbelievers in Judea, and that my ministry *i* to Jerusalem may be acceptable to the saints, 32 so that by God's will I may come to you with joy and be refreshed in your company. 33 The God of peace be with all of you. *j* Amen.

τοὺς	πτωχοὺς	τῶν	ἁγίων	τῶν	ἐν	Ἰερου-
the	poor	of the	saints	-	in	Jeru-

σαλήμ.	27 ηὐδόκησαν	γάρ,	καὶ	ὀφειλέται
salem.	For they thought it good,	and	debtors

εἰσὶν	αὐτῶν·	εἰ	γὰρ	τοῖς	πνευματικοῖς
they are	of them;	for if	in the	spiritual things

αὐτῶν	ἐκοινώνησαν	τὰ	ἔθνη,	ὀφείλουσιν
of them	²shared	¹the	³nations,	they ought

καὶ	ἐν	τοῖς	σαρκικοῖς	λειτουργῆσαι	αὐτοῖς.
also	in	the	fleshly things	to minister	to them.

28 τοῦτο	οὖν	ἐπιτελέσας,	καὶ	σφραγισάμενος
This	therefore	having completed,	and	having sealed

αὐτοῖς	τὸν	καρπὸν	τοῦτον,	29 ἀπελεύσομαι
to them		this fruit,		I will go away

δι'	ὑμῶν	εἰς	Σπανίαν·	οἶδα	δὲ	ὅτι
through you		to	Spain;	and I know		that

ἐρχόμενος	πρὸς	ὑμᾶς	ἐν	πληρώματι
coming	to	you	in [the]	fulness

εὐλογίας	Χριστοῦ	ἐλεύσομαι.	30 Παρακαλῶ
of [the] blessing	of Christ	I will come.	I beseech

δὲ	ὑμᾶς,	[ἀδελφοί],	διὰ	τοῦ	κυρίου
Now	you,	brothers,	through	the	Lord

ἡμῶν	Ἰησοῦ	Χριστοῦ	καὶ	διὰ	τῆς	ἀγάπης
of us	Jesus	Christ	and through		the	love

τοῦ	πνεύματος,	συναγωνίσασθαί	μοι	ἐν
of the	Spirit,	to strive with	me	in

ταῖς	προσευχαῖς	ὑπὲρ	ἐμοῦ	πρὸς	τὸν
the	prayers	on behalf of	me	to	-

θεόν,	31 ἵνα	ῥυσθῶ	ἀπὸ	τῶν	ἀπειθούντων
God,	in order that I may be	delivered	from	the [ones]	disobeying

ἐν	τῇ	Ἰουδαίᾳ	καὶ	ἡ	διακονία	μου
in	-	Judæa	and	the	ministry	of me

ἡ	εἰς	Ἰερουσαλὴμ	εὐπρόσδεκτος	τοῖς
-	to	Jerusalem	²acceptable	³to the

ἁγίοις	γένηται,	32 ἵνα	ἐν	χαρᾷ	ἐλθὼν
⁴saints,	¹may be,	in order that	in	joy	coming

πρὸς	ὑμᾶς	διὰ	θελήματος	θεοῦ	συνανα-
to	you	through	[the] will	of God	I may

παύσωμαι	ὑμῖν.	33 ὁ	δὲ	θεὸς	τῆς
rest with	you.	And the		God	-

εἰρήνης	μετὰ	πάντων	ὑμῶν·	ἀμήν.
of peace	[be] with	all	you:	Amen.

poor among the saints in Jerusalem. 27 They were pleased to do it, and indeed they owe it to them. For if the Gentiles have shared in the Jews' spiritual blessings, they owe it to the Jews to share with them their material blessings. 28 So after I have completed this task and have made sure that they have received this fruit, I will go to Spain and visit you on the way. 29 I know that when I come to you, I will come in the full measure of the blessing of Christ.

30 I urge you, brothers, by our Lord Jesus Christ and by the love of the Spirit, to join me in my struggle by praying to God for me. 31 Pray that I may be rescued from the unbelievers in Judea and that my service in Jerusalem may be acceptable to the saints there, 32 so that by God's will I may come to you with joy and together with you be refreshed. 33 The God of peace be with you all. Amen.

Chapter 16

Personal Greetings

I commend to you our sister Phoebe, a deacon *k* of the church at Cenchreae, 2 so that you may welcome her in the Lord as is fitting for the saints, and help her in whatever she may require from you, for she has been a benefactor of many and of myself as well.

3 Greet Prisca and Aquila, who work with me in Christ Jesus, 4 and who

16 Συνίστημι	δὲ	ὑμῖν	Φοίβην	τὴν
Now I commend		to you	Phœbe	the

ἀδελφὴν	ἡμῶν,	οὖσαν	[καὶ]	διάκονον	τῆς
sister	of us,	being	also	a minister	of the

ἐκκλησίας	τῆς	ἐν	Κεγχρεαῖς,	2 ἵνα
church	-	in	Cenchrea,	in order that

αὐτὴν	προσδέξησθε	ἐν	κυρίῳ	ἀξίως	τῶν
²her	¹ye may receive	in	[the] Lord	worthily	of the

ἁγίων,	καὶ	παραστῆτε	αὐτῇ	ἐν	ᾧ	ἂν
saints,	and	may stand by	her	in	¹whatever

ὑμῶν	χρῄζῃ	πράγματι·	καὶ	γὰρ	αὐτὴ
⁴of you	³she may have need	²thing;	for indeed		she

προστάτις	πολλῶν	ἐγενήθη	καὶ	ἐμοῦ	αὐτοῦ.
a protectress	of many	became	and	of myself.

3 Ἀσπάσασθε	Πρίσκαν	καὶ	Ἀκύλαν	τοὺς
Greet ye	Prisca	and	Aquila	the

ˌυνεργούς	μου	ἐν	Χριστῷ	Ἰησοῦ,	4 οἵτινες
ˌfellow-workers of me		in	Christ	Jesus,	who

poor among the saints in Jerusalem. 27 They were pleased to do it, and indeed they owe it to them. For if the Gentiles have shared in the Jews' spiritual blessings, they owe it to the Jews to share with them their material blessings. 28 So after I have completed this task and have made sure that they have received this fruit, I will go to Spain and visit you on the way. 29 I know that when I come to you, I will come in the full measure of the blessing of Christ.

I COMMEND to you our sister Phoebe, a servant *o* of the church in Cenchrea. 2 I ask you to receive her in the Lord in a way worthy of the saints and to give her any help she may need from you, for she has been a great help to many people, including me.

3 Greet Priscilla *p* and Aquila, my fellow workers in Christ Jesus. 4 They

g Gk *have sealed to them this fruit*
h Other ancient authorities add *of the gospel*
i Other ancient authorities read *my bringing of a gift*
j One ancient authority adds 16.25-27 here
k Or *minister*

Chapter 16

Personal Greetings

o 1 Or *deaconess*
p 3 Greek *Prisca*, a variant of *Priscilla*

risked their necks for my life, to whom not only I give thanks, but also all the churches of the Gentiles. [5]Greet also the church in their house. Greet my beloved Epaenetus, who was the first convert[j] in Asia for Christ. [6]Greet Mary, who has worked very hard among you. [7]Greet Andronicus and Junia,[m] my relatives[n] who were in prison with me; they are prominent among the apostles, and they were in Christ before I was. [8]Greet Ampliatus, my beloved in the Lord. [9]Greet Urbanus, our co-worker in Christ, and my beloved Stachys. [10]Greet Apelles, who is approved in Christ. Greet those who belong to the family of Aristobulus. [11]Greet my relative[o] Herodion. Greet those in the Lord who belong to the family of Narcissus. [12]Greet those workers in the Lord, Tryphaena and Tryphosa. Greet the beloved Persis, who has worked hard in the Lord. [13]Greet Rufus, chosen in the Lord; and greet his mother—a mother to me also. [14]Greet Asyncritus, Phlegon, Hermes, Patrobas, Hermas, and the brothers and sisters[p] who are with them. [15]Greet Philologus, Julia, Nereus and his sister, and Olympas, and all the saints who are with them. [16]Greet one another with a holy kiss. All the churches of Christ greet you.

ὑπὲρ τῆς ψυχῆς μου τὸν ἑαυτῶν τράχηλον
on be- the life of me ³the ⁴of   ²neck
half of   themselves

ὑπέθηκαν, οἷς οὐκ ἐγὼ μόνος εὐχαριστῶ
¹risked, to whom not I   only give thanks

ἀλλὰ καὶ πᾶσαι αἱ ἐκκλησίαι τῶν ἐθνῶν,
but also all the churches of the nations,

5 καὶ τὴν κατ' οἶκον αὐτῶν ἐκκλησίαν.
and ¹the ²in ⁴house ⁵of them ²church.

ἀσπάσασθε Ἐπαίνετον τὸν ἀγαπητόν μου,
Greet   Epænetus   the beloved   of me,

ὅς ἐστιν ἀπαρχὴ τῆς Ἀσίας εἰς Χριστόν.
who is firstfruit - of Asia for Christ.

6 ἀσπάσασθε Μαρίαν, ἥτις πολλὰ ἐκοπίασεν
Greet   Mary,   who many things laboured
                                    (much)

εἰς ὑμᾶς. 7 ἀσπάσασθε Ἀνδρόνικον καὶ
for you.   Greet   Andronicus   and

Ἰουνιᾶν τοὺς συγγενεῖς μου καὶ συναιχμα-
Junius the kinsmen   of me and fellow-

λώτους μου, οἵτινές εἰσιν ἐπίσημοι ἐν
captives of me, who   are notable among

τοῖς ἀποστόλοις, οἳ καὶ πρὸ ἐμοῦ γέγοναν
the apostles, who indeed before me have been

ἐν Χριστῷ. 8 ἀσπάσασθε Ἀμπλιᾶτον τὸν
in Christ.   Greet   Ampliatus   the

ἀγαπητόν μου ἐν κυρίῳ. 9 ἀσπάσασθε
beloved   of me in [the] Lord.   Greet

Οὐρβανὸν τὸν συνεργὸν ἡμῶν ἐν Χριστῷ
Urbanus   the fellow-worker of us in Christ

καὶ Στάχυν τὸν ἀγαπητόν μου. 10 ἀσπάσ-
and Stachys the beloved   of me.   Greet

ασθε Ἀπελλῆν τὸν δόκιμον ἐν Χριστῷ.
     Apelles   the approved in Christ.

ἀσπάσασθε τοὺς ἐκ τῶν Ἀριστοβούλου.
Greet   the [ones] of the [family] of Aristobulus.

11 ἀσπάσασθε Ἡρῳδίωνα τὸν συγγενῆ μου.
Greet   Herodion   the kinsman of me.

ἀσπάσασθε τοὺς ἐκ τῶν Ναρκίσσου τοὺς
Greet   the [ones] of the [family] of Narcissus   -

ὄντας ἐν κυρίῳ. 12 ἀσπάσασθε Τρύφαιναν
being in [the] Lord.   Greet   Tryphæna

καὶ Τρυφῶσαν τὰς κοπιώσας ἐν κυρίῳ.
and Tryphosa the [ones] labouring in [the] Lord.

ἀσπάσασθε Περσίδα τὴν ἀγαπητήν, ἥτις
Greet   Persis   the beloved,   who

πολλὰ ἐκοπίασεν ἐν κυρίῳ. 13 ἀσπάσασθε
many things laboured in [the] Lord.   Greet
(much)

Ῥοῦφον τὸν ἐκλεκτὸν ἐν κυρίῳ καὶ
Rufus   the chosen   in [the] Lord and

τὴν μητέρα αὐτοῦ καὶ ἐμοῦ. 14 ἀσπάσασθε
the mother of him and of me.   Greet

Ἀσύγκριτον, Φλέγοντα, Ἑρμῆν, Πατροβᾶν,
Asyncritus,   Phlegon,   Hermes, Patrobas,

Ἑρμᾶν, καὶ τοὺς σὺν αὐτοῖς ἀδελφούς.
Hermas, and the ²with ³them ¹brothers.

15 ἀσπάσασθε Φιλόλογον καὶ Ἰουλίαν,
Greet   Philologus   and Julia,

Νηρέα καὶ τὴν ἀδελφὴν αὐτοῦ, καὶ
Nereus and the sister   of him,   and

Ὀλυμπᾶν, καὶ τοὺς σὺν αὐτοῖς πάντας
Olympas,   and ²the ⁴with ⁵them ¹all

ἁγίους. 16 ἀσπάσασθε ἀλλήλους ἐν φιλήματι
³saints.   Greet   one another with kiss

ἁγίῳ. ἀσπάζονται ὑμᾶς αἱ ἐκκλησίαι
a holy.   ⁵greet   ⁴you ²the ³churches

---

risked their lives for me. Not only I but all the churches of the Gentiles are grateful to them. [5]Greet also the church that meets at their house.
Greet my dear friend Epenetus, who was the first convert to Christ in the province of Asia. [6]Greet Mary, who worked very hard for you. [7]Greet Andronicus and Junias, my relatives who have been in prison with me. They are outstanding among the apostles, and they were in Christ before I was. [8]Greet Ampliatus, whom I love in the Lord. [9]Greet Urbanus, our fellow worker in Christ, and my dear friend Stachys. [10]Greet Apelles, tested and approved in Christ. Greet those who belong to the household of Aristobulus. [11]Greet Herodion, my relative.
Greet those in the household of Narcissus who are in the Lord. [12]Greet Tryphena and Tryphosa, those women who work hard in the Lord.
Greet my dear friend Persis, another woman who has worked very hard in the Lord. [13]Greet Rufus, chosen in the Lord, and his mother, who has been a mother to me, too. [14]Greet Asyncritus, Phlegon, Hermes, Patrobas, Hermas and the brothers with them. [15]Greet Philologus, Julia, Nereus and his sister, and Olympas and all the saints with them. [16]Greet one another with a holy kiss.
All the churches of Christ send greetings.

---

[j] Gk first fruits
[m] Or Junias; other ancient authorities read Julia
[n] Or compatriots
[o] Or compatriot
[p] Gk brothers

Final Instructions

17 I urge you, brothers and sisters,[p] to keep an eye on those who cause dissensions and offenses, in opposition to the teaching that you have learned; avoid them. 18 For such people do not serve our Lord Christ, but their own appetites,[q] and by smooth talk and flattery they deceive the hearts of the simple-minded. 19 For while your obedience is known to all, so that I rejoice over you, I want you to be wise in what is good and guileless in what is evil. 20 The God of peace will shortly crush Satan under your feet. The grace of our Lord Jesus Christ be with you.[r]

21 Timothy, my co-worker, greets you; so do Lucius and Jason and Sosipater, my relatives.[n]

22 I Tertius, the writer of this letter, greet you in the Lord.[s]

23 Gaius, who is host to me and to the whole church, greets you. Erastus, the city treasurer, and our brother Quartus, greet you.[t]

Final Doxology

25 Now to God[u] who is able to strengthen you according to my gospel and the proclamation of Jesus Christ, according to the revelation of the mystery that was kept secret for long ages 26 but is now disclosed, and through the prophetic writings is made known to all the Gentiles, according to the command

---

πᾶσαι τοῦ Χριστοῦ.
¹All   ⁴of Christ.

17 Παρακαλῶ δὲ ὑμᾶς, ἀδελφοί, σκοπεῖν
Now I beseech   you,   brothers,   to watch

τοὺς τὰς διχοστασίας καὶ τὰ σκάνδαλα
¹the[ones] ³the ⁴divisions ⁵and ⁶the ⁷offences

παρὰ τὴν διδαχὴν ἣν ὑμεῖς ἐμάθετε
⁸beside ⁹the ¹⁰teaching ¹¹which ¹²ye ¹³learned

ποιοῦντας, καὶ ἐκκλίνετε ἀπ' αὐτῶν· **18** οἱ
²making, and turn away from them; -

γὰρ τοιοῦτοι τῷ κυρίῳ ἡμῶν Χριστῷ
for such men ²the ⁴Lord ³of us ¹Christ

οὐ δουλεύουσιν ἀλλὰ τῇ ἑαυτῶν κοιλίᾳ,
¹serve not but the of themselves belly,

καὶ διὰ τῆς χρηστολογίας καὶ εὐλογίας
and through - fair speech and flattering speech

ἐξαπατῶσιν τὰς καρδίας τῶν ἀκάκων.
deceive the hearts of the guileless.

19 ἡ γὰρ ὑμῶν ὑπακοὴ εἰς πάντας
²the ¹For ³of you ³obedience ⁶to ⁷all men

ἀφίκετο· ἐφ' ὑμῖν οὖν χαίρω, θέλω
⁵came; over you therefore I rejoice, ¹I wish

δὲ ὑμᾶς σοφοὺς εἶναι εἰς τὸ ἀγαθόν,
¹and you wise to be to the good,

ἀκεραίους δὲ εἰς τὸ κακόν. **20** ὁ δὲ
but simple to the evil. And the

θεὸς τῆς εἰρήνης συντρίψει τὸν σατανᾶν
God - of peace will crush - Satan

ὑπὸ τοὺς πόδας ὑμῶν ἐν τάχει.
under the feet of you soon.

Ἡ χάρις τοῦ κυρίου ἡμῶν Ἰησοῦ
The grace of the Lord of us Jesus [be]

μεθ' ὑμῶν.
with you.

21 Ἀσπάζεται ὑμᾶς Τιμόθεος ὁ συνεργός
⁵greets ⁶you ¹Timothy ²the ³fellow-worker

μου, καὶ Λούκιος καὶ Ἰάσων καὶ
⁴of me, and Lucius and Jason and

Σωσίπατρος οἱ συγγενεῖς μου. **22** ἀσπάζ-
Sosipater the kinsmen of me. ⁷greet

ομαι ὑμᾶς ἐγὼ Τέρτιος ὁ γράψας τὴν
⁸you ¹I ²Tertius ³the [one] ⁴writing ⁵the

ἐπιστολὴν ἐν κυρίῳ. **23** ἀσπάζεται ὑμᾶς
⁶epistle in [the] Lord. ⁹greets ¹⁰you

Γάιος ὁ ξένος μου καὶ ὅλης τῆς
¹Gaius ²the ³host ⁴of me ⁵and ⁶of all ⁷the

ἐκκλησίας. ἀσπάζεται ὑμᾶς Ἔραστος ὁ
⁸church. ⁶greets ⁷you ¹Erastus ²the

οἰκονόμος τῆς πόλεως καὶ Κούαρτος ὁ
³treasurer ⁴of the ⁵city and Quartus the (?his)

ἀδελφός. ‡
brother.

25 Τῷ δὲ δυναμένῳ ὑμᾶς στηρίξαι κατὰ
Now to the being able [one] ²you ¹to establish according to

τὸ εὐαγγέλιόν μου καὶ τὸ κήρυγμα
the gospel of me and the proclamation

Ἰησοῦ Χριστοῦ, κατὰ ἀποκάλυψιν μυστηρίου
of Jesus Christ, according to [the] revelation of [the] mystery

χρόνοις αἰωνίοις σεσιγημένου, **26** φανερω-
²in times ³eternal ¹having been kept silent, ²mani-

θέντος δὲ νῦν διά τε γραφῶν προφητικῶν
fested ¹but now and through writings prophetic

‡ Verse 24 omitted by Nestle; cf. NIV footnote.

---

17 I urge you, brothers, to watch out for those who cause divisions and put obstacles in your way that are contrary to the teaching you have learned. Keep away from them. 18 For such people are not serving our Lord Christ, but their own appetites. By smooth talk and flattery they deceive the minds of naive people. 19 Everyone has heard about your obedience, so I am full of joy over you; but I want you to be wise about what is good, and innocent about what is evil.

20 The God of peace will soon crush Satan under your feet.

The grace of our Lord Jesus be with you.

21 Timothy, my fellow worker, sends his greetings to you, as do Lucius, Jason and Sosipater, my relatives.

22 I, Tertius, who wrote down this letter, greet you in the Lord.

23 Gaius, whose hospitality I and the whole church here enjoy, sends you his greetings.

Erastus, who is the city's director of public works, and our brother Quartus send you their greetings.[q]

25 Now to him who is able to establish you by my gospel and the proclamation of Jesus Christ, according to the revelation of the mystery hidden for long ages past, 26 but now revealed and made known through

---

[q] Gk their own belly

[r] Other ancient authorities lack this sentence

[s] Or I Tertius, writing this letter in the Lord, greet you

[t] Other ancient authorities add verse 24, The grace of our Lord Jesus Christ be with all of you. Amen.

[u] Gk the one

[q23] Some manuscripts their greetings. 24 May the grace of our Lord Jesus Christ be with all of you. Amen.

of the eternal God, to bring about the obedience of faith— [27]to the only wise God, through Jesus Christ, to whom[v] be the glory forever! Amen.[w]

κατ’	ἐπιταγὴν	τοῦ	αἰωνίου	θεοῦ	εἰς
according to	[the] command	of the	eternal	God	*for

ὑπακοὴν	πίστεως	εἰς	πάντα	τὰ	ἔθνη
⁷obedience	⁸of faith	³to	⁴all	⁵the	⁶nations

γνωρισθέντος,	27	μόνῳ	σοφῷ	θεῷ,	διὰ
¹made known,		⁹only	²wise	¹to God, through	

Ἰησοῦ	Χριστοῦ,	ᾧ	ἡ	δόξα	εἰς	τοὺς
Jesus	Christ,	to whom the (him)ᵉ		glory	unto	the

αἰῶνας	τῶν	αἰώνων·	ἀμήν.
ages	of the	ages:	Amen.

the prophetic writings by the command of the eternal God, so that all nations might believe and obey him —[27]to the only wise God be glory forever through Jesus Christ! Amen.

[v] Other ancient authorities lack *to whom*. The verse then reads, *to the only wise God be the glory through Jesus Christ forever. Amen.*

[w] Other ancient authorities lack 16.25-27 or include it after 14.23 or 15.33; others put verse 24 after verse 27

The First Letter of Paul
to the
Corinthians

Chapter 1

Salutation

PAUL, called to be an apostle of Christ Jesus by the will of God, and our brother Sosthenes,

2 To the church of God that is in Corinth, to those who are sanctified in Christ Jesus, called to be saints, together with all those who in every place call on the name of our Lord Jesus Christ, both their Lord[a] and ours:

3 Grace to you and peace from God our Father and the Lord Jesus Christ.

4 I give thanks to my[b] God always for you because of the grace of God that has been given you in Christ Jesus, 5for in every way you have been enriched in him, in speech and knowledge of every kind— 6just as the testimony of[c] Christ has been strengthened among you— 7so that you are not lacking in any spiritual gift as you wait for the revealing of our Lord Jesus Christ. 8He will also strengthen you to the end, so that you may be blameless on the day of our Lord Jesus Christ. 9God is faithful: by him you were called into the fellowship of his Son Jesus Christ our Lord.

Divisions in the Church

10 Now I appeal to you, brothers and sisters,[d] by the name of our Lord Jesus Christ, that all of you be in agreement and that there be no divisions among you, but that you be united in the same mind and the same purpose. 11 For it has been reported to me by Chloe's

---

1 Παῦλος κλητὸς ἀπόστολος Χριστοῦ
Paul   a called   apostle   of Christ

'Ιησοῦ διὰ θελήματος θεοῦ καὶ Σωσθένης
Jesus through [the] will of God and Sosthenes

ὁ ἀδελφὸς **2** τῇ ἐκκλησίᾳ τοῦ θεοῦ
the(?his) brother   to the   church   - of God

τῇ οὔσῃ ἐν Κορίνθῳ, ἡγιασμένοις ἐν
- existing in Corinth,   to [ones]   in
                      having been sanctified

Χριστῷ 'Ιησοῦ, κλητοῖς ἁγίοις, σὺν πᾶσιν
Christ Jesus,   called   saints, with   all

τοῖς ἐπικαλουμένοις τὸ ὄνομα τοῦ κυρίου
the [ones] calling on   the name of the Lord

ἡμῶν 'Ιησοῦ Χριστοῦ ἐν παντὶ τόπῳ,
of us Jesus Christ   in every place,

αὐτῶν καὶ ἡμῶν· **3** χάρις ὑμῖν καὶ
of them and of us: Grace to you and

εἰρήνη ἀπὸ θεοῦ πατρὸς ἡμῶν καὶ κυρίου
peace from God Father of us and Lord

'Ιησοῦ Χριστοῦ.
Jesus   Christ.

4 Εὐχαριστῶ τῷ θεῷ πάντοτε περὶ
I gave thanks   - to God always concerning

ὑμῶν ἐπὶ τῇ χάριτι τοῦ θεοῦ τῇ δοθείσῃ
you   on the grace   - of God - given

ὑμῖν ἐν Χριστῷ 'Ιησοῦ, **5** ὅτι ἐν παντὶ
to you in Christ Jesus, because in everything

ἐπλουτίσθητε ἐν αὐτῷ, ἐν παντὶ λόγῳ
ye were enriched in him, in   all   speech

καὶ πάσῃ γνώσει, **6** καθὼς τὸ μαρτύριον
and all knowledge,   as   the   testimony

τοῦ Χριστοῦ ἐβεβαιώθη ἐν ὑμῖν, **7** ὥστε
- of Christ was confirmed in you,   so as

ὑμᾶς μὴ ὑστερεῖσθαι ἐν μηδενὶ χαρίσματι,
you not to be wanting[b] in no(any) gift,

ἀπεκδεχομένους τὴν ἀποκάλυψιν τοῦ κυρίου
awaiting   the   revelation   of the Lord

ἡμῶν 'Ιησοῦ Χριστοῦ· **8** ὃς καὶ βεβαιώσει
of us Jesus Christ;   who also will confirm

ὑμᾶς ἕως τέλους ἀνεγκλήτους ἐν τῇ
you till [the] end   blameless   in the

ἡμέρᾳ τοῦ κυρίου ἡμῶν 'Ιησοῦ [Χριστοῦ].
day of the Lord of us Jesus   Christ.

9 πιστὸς ὁ θεός, δι' οὗ ἐκλήθητε εἰς
Faithful [is] - God, through whom ye were called to

κοινωνίαν τοῦ υἱοῦ αὐτοῦ 'Ιησοῦ Χριστοῦ
[the] fellowship of the Son of him Jesus Christ

τοῦ κυρίου ἡμῶν.
the Lord   of us.

10 Παρακαλῶ δὲ ὑμᾶς, ἀδελφοί, διὰ
Now I beseech   you,   brothers, through

τοῦ ὀνόματος τοῦ κυρίου ἡμῶν 'Ιησοῦ
the   name   of the Lord of us Jesus

Χριστοῦ, ἵνα τὸ αὐτὸ λέγητε πάντες,
Christ, in order the same ye say   all,
         that   thing

καὶ μὴ ᾖ ἐν ὑμῖν σχίσματα, ἦτε δὲ
and not be among you divisions, but ye may be

κατηρτισμένοι ἐν τῷ αὐτῷ νοΐ καὶ
having been joined in the same mind and
together

ἐν τῇ αὐτῇ γνώμῃ. **11** ἐδηλώθη γάρ μοι
in the same opinion.   For it was shown to me

---

1 Corinthians

Chapter 1

PAUL, called to be an apostle of Christ Jesus by the will of God, and our brother Sosthenes,

2To the church of God in Corinth, to those sanctified in Christ Jesus and called to be holy, together with all those everywhere who call on the name of our Lord Jesus Christ—their Lord and ours:

3Grace and peace to you from God our Father and the Lord Jesus Christ.

Thanksgiving

4I always thank God for you because of his grace given you in Christ Jesus. 5For in him you have been enriched in every way—in all your speaking and in all your knowledge— 6because our testimony about Christ was confirmed in you. 7Therefore you do not lack any spiritual gift as you eagerly wait for our Lord Jesus Christ to be revealed. 8He will keep you strong to the end, so that you will be blameless on the day of our Lord Jesus Christ. 9God, who has called you into fellowship with his Son Jesus Christ our Lord, is faithful.

Divisions in the Church

10I appeal to you, brothers, in the name of our Lord Jesus Christ, that all of you agree with one another so that there may be no divisions among you and that you may be perfectly united in mind and thought. 11My brothers, some from

---

[a] Gk theirs
[b] Other ancient authorities lack my
[c] Or to
[d] Gk brothers

people that there are quarrels among you, my brothers and sisters.[e] 12What I mean is that each of you says, "I belong to Paul," or "I belong to Apollos," or "I belong to Cephas," or "I belong to Christ." 13Has Christ been divided? Was Paul crucified for you? Or were you baptized in the name of Paul? 14I thank God[f] that I baptized none of you except Crispus and Gaius, 15so that no one can say that you were baptized in my name. 16(I did baptize also the household of Stephanas; beyond that, I do not know whether I baptized anyone else.) 17For Christ did not send me to baptize but to proclaim the gospel, and not with eloquent wisdom, so that the cross of Christ might not be emptied of its power.

Christ the Power and Wisdom of God

18 For the message about the cross is foolishness to those who are perishing, but to us who are being saved it is the power of God. 19For it is written,
"I will destroy the
wisdom of
the wise,
and the discernment
of the discerning
I will thwart."
20Where is the one who is wise? Where is the scribe? Where is the debater of this age? Has not God made foolish the wisdom of the world? 21For since, in the wisdom of God, the world did not know God through wisdom, God decided, through the foolishness of our proclamation, to save those who believe. 22For Jews demand signs and Greeks desire wisdom, 23but we proclaim Christ crucified, a stumbling block to Jews and foolish-

---

περὶ ὑμῶν, ἀδελφοί μου, ὑπὸ τῶν
concerning you, brothers of me, by the[ones]

Χλόης, ὅτι ἔριδες ἐν ὑμῖν εἰσιν. 12 λέγω
of Chloe, that strifes among you there are. I say

δὲ τοῦτο, ὅτι ἕκαστος ὑμῶν λέγει· ἐγὼ
Now this, because each of you says: I

μέν εἰμι Παύλου, ἐγὼ δὲ Ἀπολλῶ,
indeed am of Paul, but I of Apollos,

ἐγὼ δὲ Κηφᾶ, ἐγὼ δὲ Χριστοῦ.
but I of Cephas, but I of Christ.

13 μεμέρισται ὁ Χριστός; μὴ Παῦλος
Has been divided – Christ? Not Paul

ἐσταυρώθη ὑπὲρ ὑμῶν, ἢ εἰς τὸ ὄνομα
was crucified on behalf of you, or in the name

Παύλου ἐβαπτίσθητε; 14 εὐχαριστῶ ὅτι
of Paul were ye baptized? I give thanks that

οὐδένα ὑμῶν ἐβάπτισα εἰ μὴ Κρίσπον
not one of you I baptized except Crispus

καὶ Γάϊον· 15 ἵνα μή τις εἴπῃ ὅτι
and Gaius; lest anyone should say that

εἰς τὸ ἐμὸν ὄνομα ἐβαπτίσθητε. 16 ἐβάπτισα δὲ
in – my name ye were baptized. But I baptized

καὶ τὸν Στεφανᾶ οἶκον· λοιπὸν οὐκ οἶδα
also the of Stephanas household; for the rest I know not

εἴ τινα ἄλλον ἐβάπτισα. 17 οὐ
if any other I baptized. ⁵not

γὰρ ἀπέστειλέν με Χριστὸς βαπτίζειν
¹For ³sent ⁴me ²Christ to baptize

ἀλλὰ εὐαγγελίζεσθαι, οὐκ ἐν σοφίᾳ λόγου,
but to evangelize, not in wisdom of speech,

ἵνα μὴ κενωθῇ ὁ σταυρὸς τοῦ Χριστοῦ.
lest ⁴be made vain ¹the ²cross – ³of Christ.

18 Ὁ λόγος γὰρ ὁ τοῦ σταυροῦ τοῖς
For the word – of the cross ⁸to the [ones]

μὲν ἀπολλυμένοις μωρία ἐστίν, τοῖς
¹on one ²perishing ³folly ⁴is, ⁵to the hand [ones]

δὲ σῳζομένοις ἡμῖν δύναμις θεοῦ ἐστιν.
¹on the ⁴being saved ²to us ⁶[the] ⁷power ⁸of God ⁵it is.
other

19 γέγραπται γάρ· ἀπολῶ τὴν σοφίαν
For it has been written: I will destroy the wisdom

τῶν σοφῶν, καὶ τὴν σύνεσιν τῶν συνετῶν
of the wise ones, and the understanding of the prudent

ἀθετήσω. 20 ποῦ σοφός; ποῦ γραμματεύς;
I will set Where [is the] where [is the] scribe?
aside. wise man?

ποῦ συζητητὴς τοῦ αἰῶνος τούτου; οὐχὶ
where disputant of this age? ¹Not
[is the]

ἐμώρανεν ὁ θεὸς τὴν σοφίαν τοῦ κόσμου;
¹made ⁵foolish – ⁸God ⁴the ⁶wisdom ⁸of the ⁷world?

21 ἐπειδὴ γὰρ ἐν τῇ σοφίᾳ τοῦ θεοῦ
for since in the wisdom – of God

οὐκ ἔγνω ὁ κόσμος διὰ τῆς σοφίας
⁸knew ²not ¹the ³world ⁴through ⁵the(its) ⁶wisdom

τὸν θεόν, εὐδόκησεν ὁ θεὸς διὰ τῆς
– ⁹God, ²thought well – ¹God through the

μωρίας τοῦ κηρύγματος σῶσαι τοὺς
folly of the proclamation to save the

πιστεύοντας. 22 ἐπειδὴ καὶ Ἰουδαῖοι σημεῖα
[ones] believing. Seeing that both Jews ²signs

αἰτοῦσιν καὶ Ἕλληνες σοφίαν ζητοῦσιν,
¹ask and Greeks ²wisdom ¹seek,

23 ἡμεῖς δὲ κηρύσσομεν Χριστὸν ἐσταυρωμένον,
²we ¹yet proclaim Christ having been crucified,

Chloe's household have informed me that there are quarrels among you. 12What I mean is this: One of you says, "I follow Paul"; another, "I follow Apollos"; another, "I follow Cephas[a]"; still another, "I follow Christ."

13Is Christ divided? Was Paul crucified for you? Were you baptized into[b] the name of Paul? 14I am thankful that I did not baptize any of you except Crispus and Gaius, 15so no one can say that you were baptized into my name. 16(Yes, I also baptized the household of Stephanas; beyond that, I don't remember if I baptized anyone else.) 17For Christ did not send me to baptize, but to preach the gospel—not with words of human wisdom, lest the cross of Christ be emptied of its power.

Christ the Wisdom and Power of God

18For the message of the cross is foolishness to those who are perishing, but to us who are being saved it is the power of God. 19For it is written:

"I will destroy the
wisdom of the wise;
the intelligence of the
intelligent I will
frustrate."[c]

20Where is the wise man? Where is the scholar? Where is the philosopher of this age? Has not God made foolish the wisdom of the world? 21For since in the wisdom of God the world through its wisdom did not know him, God was pleased through the foolishness of what was preached to save those who believe. 22Jews demand miraculous signs and Greeks look for wisdom, 23but we preach Christ crucified: a stumbling block to Jews

---

e Gk my brothers
f Other ancient authorities read I am thankful

a 12 That is, Peter
b 13 Or in; also in verse 15
c 19 Isaiah 29:14

ness to Gentiles, 24but to those who are the called, both Jews and Greeks, Christ the power of God and the wisdom of God. 25For God's foolishness is wiser than human wisdom, and God's weakness is stronger than human strength.

26 Consider your own call, brothers and sisters:d not many of you were wise by human standards,g not many were powerful, not many were of noble birth. 27But God chose what is foolish in the world to shame the wise; God chose what is weak in the world to shame the strong; 28God chose what is low and despised in the world, things that are not, to reduce to nothing things that are, 29so that no oneh might boast in the presence of God. 30He is the source of your life in Christ Jesus, who became for us wisdom from God, and righteousness and sanctification and redemption, 31in order that, as it is written, "Let the one who boasts, boast ini the Lord."

Chapter 2

Proclaiming Christ Crucified

WHEN I came to you, brothers and sisters,d I did not come proclaiming the mysteryj of God to you in lofty words or wisdom. 2For I decided to know nothing among you except Jesus Christ, and him crucified. 3And I came to you in weakness and in fear and in much

g Gk according to the flesh
h Gk no flesh
i Or of
j Other ancient authorities read testimony

Ἰουδαίοις μὲν σκάνδαλον, ἔθνεσιν δὲ
to Jews on one hand an offence, to nations on the other

μωρίαν, 24 αὐτοῖς δὲ τοῖς κλητοῖς,
folly, but to them the called ones,

Ἰουδαίοις τε καὶ Ἕλλησιν, Χριστὸν θεοῦ
¹to Jews ¹both and to Greeks, Christ of God

δύναμιν καὶ θεοῦ σοφίαν. 25 ὅτι τὸ
power and of God wisdom. Because the

μωρὸν τοῦ θεοῦ σοφώτερον τῶν ἀνθρώπων
foolish - of God wiser [than] - men
thing

ἐστίν, καὶ τὸ ἀσθενὲς τοῦ θεοῦ ἰσχυρότερον
is, and the weak thing - of God stronger [than]

τῶν ἀνθρώπων. 26 Βλέπετε γὰρ τὴν
- men. For ye see the

κλῆσιν ὑμῶν, ἀδελφοί, ὅτι οὐ πολλοὶ
calling of you, brothers, that not many

σοφοὶ κατὰ σάρκα, οὐ πολλοὶ δυνατοί,
wise men according flesh, not many powerful,
to

οὐ πολλοὶ εὐγενεῖς· 27 ἀλλὰ τὰ μωρὰ
not many well born; but the foolish things

τοῦ κόσμου ἐξελέξατο ὁ θεὸς ἵνα καται-
of the world ²chose - ¹God in order he might that

σχύνη τοὺς σοφούς, καὶ τὰ ἀσθενῆ τοῦ
shame the wise men, and the weak things of the

κόσμου ἐξελέξατο ὁ θεὸς ἵνα καταισχύνη
world ²chose - ¹God in order he might shame that

τὰ ἰσχυρά, 28 καὶ τὰ ἀγενῆ τοῦ κόσμου
the strong things, and the base things of the world

καὶ τὰ ἐξουθενημένα ἐξελέξατο ὁ θεός,
and the things being despised ²chose - ¹God,

τὰ μὴ ὄντα, ἵνα τὰ ὄντα καταργήσῃ,
the not being, in order ²the ²being ¹he might
things that things abolish,

29 ὅπως μὴ καυχήσηται πᾶσα σάρξ*
so as not might boast all flesh*

ἐνώπιον τοῦ θεοῦ. 30 ἐξ αὐτοῦ δὲ ὑμεῖς
before - God. And of him ye

ἐστε ἐν Χριστῷ Ἰησοῦ, ὃς ἐγενήθη
are in Christ Jesus, who became

σοφία ἡμῖν ἀπὸ θεοῦ, δικαιοσύνη τε
wisdom to us from God, ²righteousness ¹both

καὶ ἁγιασμὸς καὶ ἀπολύτρωσις, 31 ἵνα καθὼς
and sanctification and redemption, in order that as

γέγραπται· ὁ καυχώμενος ἐν κυρίῳ καυχάσθω.
it has been The [one] boasting ²in ³[the] ¹let him boast.
written: Lord

2 Κἀγὼ ἐλθὼν πρὸς ὑμᾶς, ἀδελφοί,
And I coming to you, brothers,

ἦλθον οὐ καθ' ὑπεροχὴν λόγου ἢ σοφίας
came not accord- excellence of speech or of wisdom
ing to

καταγγέλλων ὑμῖν τὸ μαρτύριον τοῦ θεοῦ.
announcing to you the testimony - of God.

2 οὐ γὰρ ἔκρινά τι εἰδέναι ἐν ὑμῖν
For I decided not anything to know among you

εἰ μὴ Ἰησοῦν Χριστὸν καὶ τοῦτον
except Jesus Christ and this one

ἐσταυρωμένον. 3 κἀγὼ ἐν ἀσθενείᾳ καὶ
having been crucified. And I in weakness and

* That is, so that no flesh might boast. Cf. Mat. 24. 22.

---

and foolishness to Gentiles, 24but to those whom God has called, both Jews and Greeks, Christ the power of God and the wisdom of God. 25For the foolishness of God is wiser than man's wisdom, and the weakness of God is stronger than man's strength.

26Brothers, think of what you were when you were called. Not many of you were wise by human standards; not many were influential; not many were of noble birth. 27But God chose the foolish things of the world to shame the wise; God chose the weak things of the world to shame the strong. 28He chose the lowly things of this world and the despised things—and the things that are not—to nullify the things that are, 29so that no one may boast before him. 30It is because of him that you are in Christ Jesus, who has become for us wisdom from God—that is, our righteousness, holiness and redemption. 31Therefore, as it is written: "Let him who boasts boast in the Lord."d

Chapter 2

WHEN I came to you, brothers, I did not come with eloquence or superior wisdom as I proclaimed to you the testimony about God.e 2For I resolved to know nothing while I was with you except Jesus Christ and him crucified. 3I came to you in weakness and fear, and

d31 Jer. 9:24
e1 Some manuscripts as I proclaimed to you God's mystery

trembling. ⁴My speech and my proclamation were not with plausible words of wisdom,ᵏ but with a demonstration of the Spirit and of power, ⁵so that your faith might rest not on human wisdom but on the power of God.

The True Wisdom of God

6 Yet among the mature we do speak wisdom, though it is not a wisdom of this age or of the rulers of this age, who are doomed to perish. ⁷But we speak God's wisdom, secret and hidden, which God decreed before the ages for our glory. ⁸None of the rulers of this age understood this; for if they had, they would not have crucified the Lord of glory. ⁹But, as it is written,

"What no eye has
    seen, nor
  ear heard,
nor the human heart
    conceived,
what God has
    prepared for
  those who love
    him"—

¹⁰these things God has revealed to us through the Spirit; for the Spirit searches everything, even the depths of God. ¹¹For what human being knows what is truly human except the human spirit that is within? So also no one comprehends what is truly God's except the Spirit of God. ¹²Now we have received not the spirit of the world, but the Spirit that is from God, so that we may understand the gifts bestowed on us by God. ¹³And we speak of these things in words not taught

ἐν φόβῳ καὶ ἐν τρόμῳ πολλῷ ἐγενόμην
in fear   and in trembling much   was
πρὸς ὑμᾶς, 4 καὶ ὁ λόγος μου καὶ τὸ
with you,   and the speech of me and the
κήρυγμά μου οὐκ ἐν πειθοῖς σοφίας
proclamation of me not in ¹persuasive ²of wisdom
λόγοις, ἀλλ' ἐν ἀποδείξει πνεύματος καὶ
¹words,   but   in   demonstration   of spirit   and
δυνάμεως, 5 ἵνα ἡ πίστις ὑμῶν μὴ ᾖ
of power,   in order that the faith   of you may not be
ἐν σοφίᾳ ἀνθρώπων ἀλλ' ἐν δυνάμει
in [the] wisdom of men   but   in [the] power
θεοῦ.
of God.

6 Σοφίαν δὲ λαλοῦμεν ἐν τοῖς τελείοις,
  But ²wisdom ¹we speak among the   perfect ones,
σοφίαν δὲ οὐ τοῦ αἰῶνος τούτου οὐδὲ
yet wisdom not   of this age   neither
τῶν ἀρχόντων τοῦ αἰῶνος τούτου τῶν
of the leaders   of this age   of the
                                         [ones]
καταργουμένων· 7 ἀλλὰ λαλοῦμεν θεοῦ
being brought to naught;   but   we speak ²of God
σοφίαν ἐν μυστηρίῳ, τὴν ἀποκεκρυμμένην,
¹a wisdom in mystery,   -   having been hidden,
ἣν προώρισεν ὁ θεὸς πρὸ τῶν αἰώνων
which ²foreordained - ¹God before the   ages
εἰς δόξαν ἡμῶν· 8 ἣν οὐδεὶς τῶν ἀρχόντων
for glory of us; which not one of the   leaders
τοῦ αἰῶνος τούτου ἔγνωκεν· εἰ γὰρ
   of this age   has known;   for if
ἔγνωσαν, οὐκ ἂν τὸν κύριον τῆς δόξης
they knew,   not - the Lord   - of glory
ἐσταύρωσαν· 9 ἀλλὰ καθὼς γέγραπται· ἃ
they would have but   as   it has been written: Things
crucified;⁺   which
ὀφθαλμὸς οὐκ εἶδεν καὶ οὖς οὐκ ἤκουσεν
eye   saw not   and ear not heard not
καὶ ἐπὶ καρδίαν ἀνθρώπου οὐκ ἀνέβη,
and on   heart   of man   came not up,
ὅσα ἡτοίμασεν ὁ θεὸς τοῖς ἀγαπῶσιν
how many ²prepared - ¹God for the [ones] loving
αὐτόν. 10 ἡμῖν γὰρ ἀπεκάλυψεν ὁ θεὸς
him.   ¹For ⁴to us ²revealed - ³God
διὰ τοῦ πνεύματος· τὸ γὰρ πνεῦμα πάντα
through the Spirit;   for the Spirit all things
ἐρευνᾷ, καὶ τὰ βάθη τοῦ θεοῦ. 11 τίς
searches,   even the deep things - of God.   ²who
γὰρ οἶδεν ἀνθρώπων τὰ τοῦ ἀνθρώπου
¹For ³knows ²of men the things -   of a man
εἰ μὴ τὸ πνεῦμα τοῦ ἀνθρώπου τὸ
except the spirit   -   of a man   -
ἐν αὐτῷ; οὕτως καὶ τὰ τοῦ θεοῦ οὐδεὶς
in   him?   so also the things - of God no one
ἔγνωκεν εἰ μὴ τὸ πνεῦμα τοῦ θεοῦ.
has known except the Spirit   - of God.
12 ἡμεῖς δὲ οὐ τὸ πνεῦμα τοῦ κόσμου
  And we   not the spirit of the world
ἐλάβομεν ἀλλὰ τὸ πνεῦμα τὸ ἐκ τοῦ θεοῦ,
received   but the Spirit   - from - God,
ἵνα εἰδῶμεν τὰ ὑπὸ τοῦ θεοῦ
in order we may the things by   -   God
that   know
χαρισθέντα ἡμῖν· 13 ἃ καὶ λαλοῦμεν οὐκ
freely given to us; which things also we speak   not

with much trembling. ⁴My message and my preaching were not with wise and persuasive words, but with a demonstration of the Spirit's power, ⁵so that your faith might not rest on men's wisdom, but on God's power.

Wisdom From the Spirit

⁶We do, however, speak a message of wisdom among the mature, but not the wisdom of this age or of the rulers of this age, who are coming to nothing. ⁷No, we speak of God's secret wisdom, a wisdom that has been hidden and that God destined for our glory before time began. ⁸None of the rulers of this age understood it, for if they had, they would not have crucified the Lord of glory. ⁹However, as it is written:

"No eye has seen,
    no ear has heard,
  no mind has conceived
what God has prepared
    for those who love
    him"ⁱ—

¹⁰but God has revealed it to us by his Spirit.
  The Spirit searches all things, even the deep things of God. ¹¹For who among men knows the thoughts of a man except the man's spirit within him? In the same way no one knows the thoughts of God except the Spirit of God. ¹²We have not received the spirit of the world but the Spirit who is from God, that we may understand what God has freely given us. ¹³This is what we speak, not in words taught

---

ᵏ Other ancient authorities read *the persuasiveness of wisdom*

⁺ This rendering is demanded by the preceding ἄν.

ⁱ9 Isaiah 64:4

by human wisdom but taught by the Spirit, interpreting spiritual things to those who are spiritual.[l]

14 Those who are unspiritual[m] do not receive the gifts of God's Spirit, for they are foolishness to them, and they are unable to understand them because they are spiritually discerned. 15 Those who are spiritual discern all things, and they are themselves subject to no one else's scrutiny.

16 "For who has known
  the mind
  of the Lord
  so as to instruct
  him?"
But we have the mind of Christ.

ἐν   διδακτοῖς   ἀνθρωπίνης   σοφίας   λόγοις,
in   ²taught   ³of human   ⁴wisdom ¹words,

ἀλλ᾿ ἐν διδακτοῖς πνεύματος,   πνευματικοῖς
but   in [words] taught of [the] Spirit, ³with spiritual things

πνευματικὰ   συγκρίνοντες.   14 ψυχικὸς   δὲ
²spiritual things ¹comparing.   But a natural

ἄνθρωπος   οὐ   δέχεται   τὰ   τοῦ   πνεύματος
man   receives not the things of the Spirit

τοῦ   θεοῦ·   μωρία   γὰρ   αὐτῷ   ἐστιν,   καὶ
-    of God;   for folly   to him   they are,   and

οὐ   δύναται   γνῶναι,   ὅτι   πνευματικῶς
he cannot to know,   because ³spiritually

ἀνακρίνεται.   15 ὁ   δὲ   πνευματικὸς   ἀνακρίνει
¹they are ²discerned. But the spiritual man   ³discerns

μὲν   πάντα,   αὐτὸς   δὲ   ὑπ᾿   οὐδενὸς
¹on one all things, ²he   ¹on the ⁴by   ⁵no one
  hand   other

ἀνακρίνεται.   16 τίς   γὰρ   ἔγνω   νοῦν
³is discerned.   For who   knew   [the] mind

κυρίου,   ὃς   συμβιβάσει   αὐτόν;   ἡμεῖς   δὲ
of [the] who   will instruct him?   But we
Lord,

νοῦν   Χριστοῦ   ἔχομεν.
[the] mind of Christ have.

---

us by human wisdom but in words taught by the Spirit, expressing spiritual truths in spiritual words.[g] 14 The man without the Spirit does not accept the things that come from the Spirit of God, for they are foolishness to him, and he cannot understand them, because they are spiritually discerned. 15 The spiritual man makes judgments about all things, but he himself is not subject to any man's judgment:

16 "For who has known the
  mind of the Lord
  that he may instruct
  him?"[h]

But we have the mind of Christ.

Chapter 3

On Divisions in the Corinthian Church

AND so, brothers and sisters,[n] I could not speak to you as spiritual people, but rather as people of the flesh, as infants in Christ. 2 I fed you with milk, not solid food, for you were not ready for solid food. Even now you are still not ready, 3 for you are still of the flesh. For as long as there is jealousy and quarreling among you, are you not of the flesh, and behaving according to human inclinations? 4 For when one says, "I belong to Paul," and another, "I belong to Apollos," are you not merely human?

5 What then is Apollos? What is Paul? Servants through whom you came to believe, as the Lord assigned to each. 6 I planted, Apollos watered, but God gave the growth. 7 So neither the one who plants nor the one who waters is anything, but only God who gives the growth. 8 The one who plants and the one who waters have a common purpose, and each will receive wages according to the labor of each. 9 For we are God's servants, working together; you are God's field, God's building.

10 According to the grace of God given to me, like a skilled master builder

---

3 Κἀγώ,   ἀδελφοί,   οὐκ   ἠδυνήθην   λαλῆσαι
And I,   brothers,   was not able   to speak

ὑμῖν   ὡς   πνευματικοῖς   ἀλλ᾿   ὡς   σαρκίνοις,
to you as   to spiritual men but   as   to fleshy,

ὡς   νηπίοις   ἐν   Χριστῷ.   2 γάλα   ὑμᾶς
as   to infants in   Christ.   ²Milk   ²you

ἐπότισα,   οὐ   βρῶμα·   οὔπω   γὰρ   ἐδύνασθε.
¹I gave   not   food;   for ye were not then able.
⁴to drink,

ἀλλ᾿   οὐδὲ   [ἔτι]   νῦν   δύνασθε,   3 ἔτι   γὰρ
But   neither yet   now   are ye able,   for still

σαρκικοί   ἐστε.   ὅπου   γὰρ   ἐν   ὑμῖν   ζῆλος
fleshly   ye are.   For whereas among you [there is]
                                            jealousy

καὶ   ἔρις,   οὐχὶ   σαρκικοί   ἐστε   καὶ   κατὰ
and   strife, ²not ¹fleshly   ¹are ye ⁴and ⁵according to

ἄνθρωπον   περιπατεῖτε;   4 ὅταν   γὰρ   λέγῃ
⁷man   walk?   For whenever   says

τις·   ἐγὼ   μὲν   εἰμι   Παύλου,   ἕτερος   δέ·
anyone: I   -   am   of Paul,   and another:

ἐγὼ   ᾿Απολλῶ,   οὐκ   ἄνθρωποί   ἐστε;   5 Τί
I   of Apollos, ²not   ¹men   ¹are ye? What

οὖν   ἐστιν   ᾿Απολλῶς;   τί   δέ   ἐστιν   Παῦλος;
there- is   Apollos?   and what is   Paul?
fore

διάκονοι   δι᾿   ὧν   ἐπιστεύσατε,   καὶ   ἑκάστῳ
Ministers through whom ye believed, even ²to each one

ὡς   ὁ   κύριος   ἔδωκεν.   6 ἐγὼ   ἐφύτευσα,
¹as the Lord   gave.   I   planted,

᾿Απολλῶς   ἐπότισεν,   ἀλλὰ   ὁ   θεὸς   ηὔξανεν·
Apollos   watered,   but   -   God   made to
                                         grow;

7 ὥστε   οὔτε   ὁ   φυτεύων   ἐστίν   τι   οὔτε
so as   neither the [one] planting is   anything nor

ὁ   ποτίζων,   ἀλλ᾿   ὁ   αὐξάνων   θεός.   8 ὁ
the watering,   but   ²the ³making to ¹God.   ²The
[one]   [one] grow   [one]

φυτεύων   δὲ   καὶ   ὁ   ποτίζων   ἕν   εἰσιν,
³planting   ¹so and the [one] watering one* are,

ἕκαστος   δὲ   τὸν   ἴδιον   μισθὸν   λήμψεται
and each one the(his) own   reward   will receive

* Notice the neuter gender, though " thing " cannot very well be
expressed; cf. John 10. 30.

Chapter 3

On Divisions in the Church

BROTHERS, I could not address you as spiritual but as worldly— mere infants in Christ. 2 I gave you milk, not solid food, for you were not yet ready for it. Indeed, you are still not ready. 3 You are still worldly. For since there is jealousy and quarreling among you, are you not worldly? Are you not acting like mere men? 4 For when one says, "I follow Paul," and another, "I follow Apollos," are you not mere men?

5 What, after all, is Apollos? And what is Paul? Only servants, through whom you came to believe—as the Lord has assigned to each his task. 6 I planted the seed, Apollos watered it, but God made it grow. 7 So neither he who plants nor he who waters is anything, but only God, who makes things grow. 8 The man who plants and the man who waters have one purpose, and each will be rewarded according to his own labor. 9 For we are God's fellow workers; you are God's field, God's building.

10 By the grace God has

---

[l] Or interpreting spiritual things in spiritual language, or comparing spiritual things with spiritual
[m] Or natural
[n] Gk brothers

[g] 13 Or Spirit, interpreting spiritual truths to spiritual men
[h] 16 Isaiah 40:13

I laid a foundation, and someone else is building on it. Each builder must choose with care how to build on it. 11 For no one can lay any foundation other than the one that has been laid; that foundation is Jesus Christ. 12 Now if anyone builds on the foundation with gold, silver, precious stones, wood, hay, straw— 13 the work of each builder will become visible, for the Day will disclose it, because it will be revealed with fire, and the fire will test what sort of work each has done. 14 If what has been built on the foundation survives, the builder will receive a reward. 15 If the work is burned up, the builder will suffer loss; the builder will be saved, but only as through fire.

16 Do you not know that you are God's temple and that God's Spirit dwells in you?ᵒ 17 If anyone destroys God's temple, God will destroy that person. For God's temple is holy, and you are that temple.

18 Do not deceive yourselves. If you think that you are wise in this age, you should become fools so that you may become wise. 19 For the wisdom of this world is foolishness with God. For it is written,
"He catches the wise
   in their
   craftiness,"
20 and again,
"The Lord knows the
   thoughts of the
   wise,
   that they are futile."
21 So let no one boast about

Middle column (Greek interlinear):

κατὰ τὸν ἴδιον κόπον. 9 θεοῦ γάρ ἐσμεν
accord- his own labour. For of God we are
ing to

συνεργοί· θεοῦ γεώργιον, θεοῦ οἰκοδομή
fellow-workers; ²of God ¹a tillage, ²of God ⁴a building

ἐστε. 10 Κατὰ τὴν χάριν τοῦ θεοῦ τὴν
¹ye are. According to the grace - of God -

δοθεῖσάν μοι ὡς σοφὸς ἀρχιτέκτων
given to me as a wise master builder

θεμέλιον ἔθηκα, ἄλλος δὲ ἐποικοδομεῖ.
a foundation I laid, but another builds on [it].

ἕκαστος δὲ βλεπέτω πῶς ἐποικοδομεῖ.
But each one let him look how he builds on [it].

11 θεμέλιον γὰρ ἄλλον οὐδεὶς δύναται θεῖναι
For foundation other no one is able to lay

παρὰ τὸν κείμενον, ὅς ἐστιν Ἰησοῦς
beside the [one] being laid, who is Jesus

Χριστός. 12 εἰ δέ τις ἐποικοδομεῖ ἐπὶ
Christ. Now if anyone builds on on

τὸν θεμέλιον χρυσίον, ἀργύριον, λίθους
the foundation gold, silver, stones

τιμίους, ξύλα, χόρτον, καλάμην, 13 ἑκάστου
precious, woods, hay, stubble, of each one

τὸ ἔργον φανερὸν γενήσεται· ἡ γὰρ ἡμέρα
the work manifest will become; for the day

δηλώσει, ὅτι ἐν πυρὶ ἀποκαλύπτεται,
will declare because by fire it is revealed,
[it],

καὶ ἑκάστου τὸ ἔργον ὁποῖόν ἐστιν
and ²of each one ¹the ²work ³of what sort ¹it is

τὸ πῦρ αὐτὸ δοκιμάσει. 14 εἴ τινος
¹the ²fire ¹it ¹will prove. If of anyone

τὸ ἔργον μενεῖ ὃ ἐποικοδόμησεν, μισθὸν
the work remains which he built on, a reward

λήμψεται· 15 εἴ τινος τὸ ἔργον κατακαήσ-
he will receive; if of anyone the work will be con-

εται, ζημιωθήσεται, αὐτὸς δὲ σωθήσεται,
sumed, he will suffer loss, but he will be saved,

οὕτως δὲ ὡς διὰ πυρός. 16 Οὐκ οἴδατε
yet so as through fire. Know ye not

ὅτι ναὸς θεοῦ ἐστε καὶ τὸ πνεῦμα τοῦ
that a shrine of God ye are and the Spirit -

θεοῦ ἐν ὑμῖν οἰκεῖ; 17 εἴ τις τὸν ναὸν
of God in you dwells? If anyone the shrine

τοῦ θεοῦ φθείρει, φθερεῖ τοῦτον ὁ θεός·
- of God defiles, ²will defile ³this man - ¹God;

ὁ γὰρ ναὸς τοῦ θεοῦ ἅγιός ἐστιν, οἵτινές
for the shrine - of God holy is, who(which)

ἐστε ὑμεῖς.
are ye.

18 Μηδεὶς ἑαυτὸν ἐξαπατάτω· εἴ τις
No one himself let deceive; if anyone

δοκεῖ σοφὸς εἶναι ἐν ὑμῖν ἐν τῷ αἰῶνι
thinks wise to be among you in - age

τούτῳ, μωρὸς γενέσθω, ἵνα γένηται
this, foolish let him in order he may
become, that become

σοφός. 19 ἡ γὰρ σοφία τοῦ κόσμοι
wise. For the wisdom - world

τούτου μωρία παρὰ τῷ θεῷ ἐστιν.
of this folly with - God is.

γέγραπται γάρ· ὁ δρασσόμενος τοὺς σοφοὺς
For it has been written: The [one] grasping the wise

ἐν τῇ πανουργίᾳ αὐτῶν· 20 καὶ πάλιν·
in the craftiness of them; and again:

κύριος γινώσκει τοὺς διαλογισμοὺς τῶν
[The] Lord knows the reasonings of the

σοφῶν, ὅτι εἰσὶν μάταιοι. 21 ὥστε μηδεὶς
wise, that they are vain. So as no one

given me, I laid a foundation as an expert builder, and someone else is building on it. But each one should be careful how he builds. 11 For no one can lay any foundation other than the one already laid, which is Jesus Christ. 12 If any man builds on this foundation using gold, silver, costly stones, wood, hay or straw, 13 his work will be shown for what it is, because the Day will bring it to light. It will be revealed with fire, and the fire will test the quality of each man's work. 14 If what he has built survives, he will receive his reward. 15 If it is burned up, he will suffer loss; but he himself will be saved, but only as one escaping through the flames.

16 Don't you know that you yourselves are God's temple and that God's Spirit lives in you? 17 If anyone destroys God's temple, God will destroy him; for God's temple is sacred, and you are that temple.

18 Do not deceive yourselves. If any one of you thinks he is wise by the standards of this age, he should become a "fool" so that he may become wise. 19 For the wisdom of this world is foolishness in God's sight. As it is written: "He catches the wise in their craftiness"ⁱ; 20 and again, "The Lord knows that the thoughts of the wise are futile."ʲ 21 So then, no more boasting

human leaders. For all things are yours, [22] whether Paul or Apollos or Cephas or the world or life or death or the present or the future—all belong to you, [23] and you belong to Christ, and Christ belongs to God.

Chapter 4

The Ministry of the Apostles

THINK of us in this way, as servants of Christ and stewards of God's mysteries. [2] Moreover, it is required of stewards that they be found trustworthy. [3] But with me it is a very small thing that I should be judged by you or by any human court. I do not even judge myself. [4] I am not aware of anything against myself, but I am not thereby acquitted. It is the Lord who judges me. [5] Therefore do not pronounce judgment before the time, before the Lord comes, who will bring to light the things now hidden in darkness and will disclose the purposes of the heart. Then each one will receive commendation from God.

6 I have applied all this to Apollos and myself for your benefit, brothers and sisters,[p] so that you may learn through us the meaning of the saying, "Nothing beyond what is written," so that none of you will be puffed up in favor of one against another. [7] For who sees anything different in you?[q] What do you have that you did not receive? And if you received it, why do you boast as if it were not a gift?

8 Already you have all you want! Already you have become rich! Quite apart from us you have become kings! Indeed, I wish that you had become kings, so that we might be kings with you! [9] For I think that

---

[p] Gk brothers

[q] Or Who makes you different from another?

καυχάσθω ἐν ἀνθρώποις· πάντα γὰρ ὑμῶν
let boast   in   men;   for all things   of you

ἐστιν,   22 εἴτε   Παῦλος   εἴτε   Ἀπολλῶς
is(are),   whether   Paul   or   Apollos

εἴτε   Κηφᾶς,   εἴτε   κόσμος   εἴτε   ζωὴ   εἴτε
or   Cephas,   or   [the] world   or   life   or

θάνατος,   εἴτε   ἐνεστῶτα   εἴτε   μέλλοντα,
death,   or   things present   or   things coming,

πάντα ὑμῶν, 23 ὑμεῖς δὲ Χριστοῦ, Χριστὸς δὲ
all things of you,   and ye   of Christ,   and Christ

θεοῦ. 4 Οὕτως ἡμᾶς λογιζέσθω ἄνθρωπος ὡς
of God.   So   ⁴us   ¹let ²reckon   ³a man   as

ὑπηρέτας Χριστοῦ καὶ οἰκονόμους μυστηρίων
attendants   of Christ   and   stewards   of mysteries

θεοῦ. 2 ὧδε   λοιπὸν   ζητεῖται   ἐν   τοῖς
of God.   Here   for the rest   it is sought   among   -

οἰκονόμοις ἵνα πιστός τις εὑρεθῇ. 3 ἐμοὶ
stewards   in order ²faithful ¹anyone ³be found.   to me

δὲ   εἰς   ἐλάχιστόν   ἐστιν   ἵνα   ὑφ' ὑμῶν
And   for a very little thing   it is   in order that   by   you

ἀνακριθῶ ἢ ὑπὸ ἀνθρωπίνης ἡμέρας· ἀλλ'
I am judged   or   by   a human   day;*   but

οὐδὲ ἐμαυτὸν ἀνακρίνω· 4 οὐδὲν γὰρ
not   myself   I judge;   for nothing

ἐμαυτῷ σύνοιδα, ἀλλ' οὐκ ἐν τούτῳ
against myself I know,   but   not   by   this

δεδικαίωμαι· ὁ δὲ ἀνακρίνων με κύριός
have I been   but the [one] judging   me [the] Lord
justified;

ἐστιν. 5 ὥστε μὴ πρὸ καιροῦ τι κρίνετε,
is.   So as   not   before   time   anything   judge ye,

ἕως ἂν ἔλθῃ ὁ κύριος, ὃς καὶ φωτίσει
until   comes the   Lord,   who both   will shed
  light on

τὰ κρυπτὰ τοῦ σκότους καὶ φανερώσει
the hidden things of the   darkness   and   will manifest

τὰς βουλὰς τῶν καρδιῶν· καὶ τότε ὁ
the   counsels   of the   hearts;   and   then   the

ἔπαινος γενήσεται ἑκάστῳ ἀπὸ τοῦ θεοῦ.
praise   will be   to each one°   from   -   God.

6 Ταῦτα δέ, ἀδελφοί, μετεσχημάτισα εἰς
Now these things,   brothers,   I adapted   to

ἐμαυτὸν καὶ Ἀπολλῶν δι' ὑμᾶς, ἵνα
myself   and   Apollos   because   you,   in order
  of   that

ἐν ἡμῖν μάθητε τὸ μὴ ὑπὲρ ἃ
among us   ye may learn   - not [to think] above what
  things

γέγραπται, ἵνα μὴ εἷς ὑπὲρ τοῦ ἑνὸς
has(ve) been written,   lest   ²one ³on behalf of ⁴the   ⁵one

φυσιοῦσθε κατὰ τοῦ ἑτέρου. 7 τίς γάρ σε
¹ye are puffed up against   the   other.   For who   thee

διακρίνει; τί δὲ ἔχεις ὃ οὐκ ἔλαβες;
distinguishes?   and what hast thou which thou didst not receive?

εἰ δὲ καὶ ἔλαβες, τί καυχᾶσαι ὡς μὴ
and if   indeed   thou didst   why boastest thou   as   not
  receive,

λαβών; 8 ἤδη κεκορεσμένοι ἐστέ· ἤδη
receiving?   Now   having been glutted   ye are;   now

ἐπλουτήσατε· χωρὶς ἡμῶν ἐβασιλεύσατε· καὶ
ye became rich;   without   us   ye reigned;   and

ὄφελόν γε ἐβασιλεύσατε, ἵνα
²an advantage ³really ¹[it is] [that] ye reigned,   in order that

καὶ ἡμεῖς ὑμῖν συμβασιλεύσωμεν. 9 δοκῶ
also   we   ²you   ¹might reign with.   I think

* ? of judgment.

about men! All things are yours, [22] whether Paul or Apollos or Cephas[k] or the world or life or death or the present or the future—all are yours, [23] and you are of Christ, and Christ is of God.

Chapter 4

Apostles of Christ

SO then, men ought to regard us as servants of Christ and as those entrusted with the secret things of God. [2] Now it is required that those who have been given a trust must prove faithful. [3] I care very little if I am judged by you or by any human court; indeed, I do not even judge myself. [4] My conscience is clear, but that does not make me innocent. It is the Lord who judges me. [5] Therefore judge nothing before the appointed time; wait till the Lord comes. He will bring to light what is hidden in darkness and will expose the motives of men's hearts. At that time each will receive his praise from God.

[6] Now, brothers, I have applied these things to myself and Apollos for your benefit, so that you may learn from us the meaning of the saying, "Do not go beyond what is written." Then you will not take pride in one man over against another. [7] For who makes you different from anyone else? What do you have that you did not receive? And if you did receive it, why do you boast as though you did not?

[8] Already you have all you want! Already you have become rich! You have become kings—and that without us! How I wish that you really had become kings so that we might be kings with you! [9] For it

---

[k] 22 That is, Peter

God has exhibited us apostles as last of all, as though sentenced to death, because we have become a spectacle to the world, to angels and to mortals. 10 We are fools for the sake of Christ, but you are wise in Christ. We are weak, but you are strong. You are held in honor, but we in disrepute. 11 To the present hour we are hungry and thirsty, we are poorly clothed and beaten and homeless, 12 and we grow weary from the work of our own hands. When reviled, we bless; when persecuted, we endure; 13 when slandered, we speak kindly. We have become like the rubbish of the world, the dregs of all things, to this very day.

Fatherly Admonition

14 I am not writing this to make you ashamed, but to admonish you as my beloved children. 15 For though you might have ten thousand guardians in Christ, you do not have many fathers. Indeed, in Christ Jesus I became your father through the gospel. 16 I appeal to you, then, be imitators of me. 17 For this reason I sent[r] you Timothy, who is my beloved and faithful child in the Lord, to remind you of my ways in Christ Jesus, as I teach them everywhere in every church. 18 But some of you, thinking that I am not coming to you, have become arrogant. 19 But I will come to you soon, if the Lord wills, and I will find out not the talk of these arrogant people but their power. 20 For the kingdom of God de-

γάρ, ὁ θεὸς ἡμᾶς τοὺς ἀποστόλους
For, - God us the apostles
ἐσχάτους ἀπέδειξεν ὡς ἐπιθανατίους, ὅτι
last showed forth as doomed to death, because
θέατρον ἐγενήθημεν τῷ κόσμῳ καὶ ἀγγέλοις
a spectacle we became to the world both to angels
καὶ ἀνθρώποις. 10 ἡμεῖς μωροὶ διὰ
and to men. We [are] fools because of
Χριστόν, ὑμεῖς δὲ φρόνιμοι ἐν Χριστῷ·
Christ, but ye [are] prudent in Christ;
ἡμεῖς ἀσθενεῖς, ὑμεῖς δὲ ἰσχυροί· ὑμεῖς
we [are] weak, but ye [are] strong; ye [are]
ἔνδοξοι, ἡμεῖς δὲ ἄτιμοι. 11 ἄχρι τῆς
held in honour, but we [are] unhonoured. Until the
ἄρτι ὥρας καὶ πεινῶμεν καὶ διψῶμεν
present hour ²both ¹we ³hunger and thirst
καὶ γυμνιτεύομεν καὶ κολαφιζόμεθα καὶ
and are naked and are buffeted and
ἀστατοῦμεν 12 καὶ κοπιῶμεν ἐργαζόμενοι
are unsettled and labour working
ταῖς ἰδίαις χερσίν· λοιδορούμενοι εὐλο-
with the(our) own hands; being reviled we
γοῦμεν, διωκόμενοι ἀνεχόμεθα, 13 δυσφημού-
bless, being persecuted we endure, being de-
μενοι παρακαλοῦμεν· ὡς περικαθάρματα τοῦ
famed we beseech; as refuse of the
κόσμου ἐγενήθημεν, πάντων περίψημα ἕως
world we became, ²of all things ¹offscouring until
ἄρτι.
now.

14 Οὐκ ἐντρέπων ὑμᾶς γράφω ταῦτα,
Not shaming you I write these things,
ἀλλ' ὡς τέκνα μου ἀγαπητὰ νουθετῶν.
but as children of me beloved admonishing.
15 ἐὰν γὰρ μυρίους παιδαγωγοὺς ἔχητε
For if ten thousand trainers ye have
ἐν Χριστῷ, ἀλλ' οὐ πολλοὺς πατέρας·
in Christ, yet not many fathers;
ἐν γὰρ Χριστῷ Ἰησοῦ διὰ τοῦ εὐαγγελίου
for in Christ Jesus through the gospel
ἐγὼ ὑμᾶς ἐγέννησα. 16 παρακαλῶ οὖν
I ²you ¹begat. I beseech therefore
ὑμᾶς, μιμηταί μου γίνεσθε. 17 Διὰ τοῦτο
you, imitators of me become ye. Because of this
αὐτὸ ἔπεμψα ὑμῖν Τιμόθεον, ὅς ἐστίν
very thing I sent to you Timothy, who is
μου τέκνον ἀγαπητὸν καὶ πιστὸν ἐν
of me a child beloved and faithful in
κυρίῳ, ὃς ὑμᾶς ἀναμνήσει τὰς ὁδούς
[the] Lord, who ²you ¹will remind [of] the ways
μου τὰς ἐν Χριστῷ ['Ιησοῦ], καθὼς
of me - in Christ Jesus, as
πανταχοῦ ἐν πάσῃ ἐκκλησίᾳ διδάσκω.
everywhere in every church I teach.
18 ὡς μὴ ἐρχομένου δέ μου πρὸς ὑμᾶς
When not coming now meˢ to you
= Now when I did not come
ἐφυσιώθησάν τινες· 19 ἐλεύσομαι δὲ ταχέως
³were puffed up ¹some; but I will come shortly
πρὸς ὑμᾶς, ἐὰν ὁ κύριος θελήσῃ, καὶ
to you, if the Lord wills, and
γνώσομαι οὐ τὸν λόγον τῶν πεφυσιωμένων
I will know not the speech of the [ones] having been puffed up
ἀλλὰ τὴν δύναμιν· 20 οὐ γὰρ ἐν λόγῳ
but the power; for ⁴[is] ²not ⁵in ¹speech

seems to me that God has put us apostles on display at the end of the procession, like men condemned to die in the arena. We have been made a spectacle to the whole universe, to angels as well as to men. 10 We are fools for Christ, but you are so wise in Christ! We are weak, but you are strong! You are honored, we are dishonored! 11 To this very hour we go hungry and thirsty, we are in rags, we are brutally treated, we are homeless. 12 We work hard with our own hands. When we are cursed, we bless; when we are persecuted, we endure it; 13 when we are slandered, we answer kindly. Up to this moment we have become the scum of the earth, the refuse of the world.

14 I am not writing this to shame you, but to warn you, as my dear children. 15 Even though you have ten thousand guardians in Christ, you do not have many fathers, for in Christ Jesus I became your father through the gospel. 16 Therefore I urge you to imitate me. 17 For this reason I am sending to you Timothy, my son whom I love, who is faithful in the Lord. He will remind you of my way of life in Christ Jesus, which agrees with what I teach everywhere in every church.

18 Some of you have become arrogant, as if I were not coming to you. 19 But I will come to you very soon, if the Lord is willing, and then I will find out not only how these arrogant people are talking, but what power they have. 20 For the kingdom of God is not a matter

pends not on talk but on power. 21What would you prefer? Am I to come to you with a stick, or with love in a spirit of gentleness?

Chapter 5

Sexual Immorality Defiles the Church

IT is actually reported that there is sexual immorality among you, and of a kind that is not found even among pagans; for a man is living with his father's wife. 2And you are arrogant! Should you not rather have mourned, so that he who has done this would have been removed from among you?

3 For though absent in body, I am present in spirit; and as if present I have already pronounced judgment 4in the name of the Lord Jesus on the man who has done such a thing.s When you are assembled, and my spirit is present with the power of our Lord Jesus, 5you are to hand this man over to Satan for the destruction of the flesh, so that his spirit may be saved in the day of the Lord.t

6 Your boasting is not a good thing. Do you not know that a little yeast leavens the whole batch of dough? 7Clean out the old yeast so that you may be a new batch, as you really are unleavened. For our paschal lamb, Christ, has been sacrificed. 8Therefore, let us celebrate the festival, not with the old yeast, the yeast of malice and evil, but with the unleavened bread of sincerity and truth.

Sexual Immorality Must Be Judged

9 I wrote to you in my letter not to associate with sexually immoral persons— 10not at all meaning the immoral of this world, or the greedy and robbers, or idolaters,

---

ἡ βασιλεία τοῦ θεοῦ, ἀλλ' ἐν δυνάμει.
the ¹kingdom – ²of God, but in power.
21 τί θέλετε; ἐν ῥάβδῳ ἔλθω πρὸς ὑμᾶς,
What will ye? with a rod I come to you,
ἢ ἐν ἀγάπῃ πνεύματί τε πραΰτητος;
or in love and a spirit of meekness?

5 Ὅλως ἀκούεται ἐν ὑμῖν πορνεία,
Actually is heard among you fornication,
καὶ τοιαύτη πορνεία ἥτις οὐδὲ ἐν τοῖς
and such fornication which [is] not among the
ἔθνεσιν, ὥστε γυναῖκά τινα τοῦ πατρὸς
nations, so as ³wife ¹one ⁴of the ²father
ἔχειν. **2** καὶ ὑμεῖς πεφυσιωμένοι ἐστέ,
⁵to have.b And ye having been puffed up are,
καὶ οὐχὶ μᾶλλον ἐπενθήσατε, ἵνα ἀρθῇ
and not rather mourned, in order ⁵might be
                                      that ⁶removed
ἐκ μέσου ὑμῶν ὁ τὸ ἔργον τοῦτο πράξας,
⁴from ¹midst ²of you ¹the ³this ⁴deed ³having done?
⁷[the] [one]
3 ἐγὼ μὲν γάρ, ἀπὼν τῷ σώματι,
For I indeed, being absent in the body,
παρὼν δὲ τῷ πνεύματι, ἤδη κέκρικα
but being present in the spirit, already have judged
ὡς παρὼν τὸν οὕτως τοῦτο κατεργα-
as being present ¹the [one] ³thus ²this thing ¹having
σάμενον **4** ἐν τῷ ὀνόματι τοῦ κυρίου
wrought in the name of the Lord
Ἰησοῦ συναχθέντων ὑμῶν καὶ τοῦ ἐμοῦ
Jesus being assembled you and – my
=when you are assembled . . .
πνεύματος σὺν τῇ δυνάμει τοῦ κυρίου
spirit⁴ with the power of the Lord
ἡμῶν Ἰησοῦ **5** παραδοῦναι τὸν τοιοῦτον
of us Jesus to deliver such a person
τῷ σατανᾷ εἰς ὄλεθρον τῆς σαρκός,
– to Satan for destruction of the flesh,
ἵνα τὸ πνεῦμα σωθῇ ἐν τῇ ἡμέρᾳ τοῦ
in order the spirit may be in the day of the
that saved
κυρίου. **6** Οὐ καλὸν τὸ καύχημα ὑμῶν.
Lord. Not good [is] the boast of you.
οὐκ οἴδατε ὅτι μικρὰ ζύμη ὅλον τὸ
Know ye not that a little leaven all the
φύραμα ζυμοῖ; **7** ἐκκαθάρατε τὴν παλαιὰν
lump leavens? Purge out the old
ζύμην, ἵνα ἦτε νέον φύραμα, καθώς
leaven, in order ye a new lump, as
that may be
ἐστε ἄζυμοι. καὶ γὰρ τὸ πάσχα ἡμῶν
ye are unleavened. For indeed the passover of us
ἐτύθη Χριστός. **8** ὥστε ἑορτάζωμεν μὴ
was Christ. So as let us keep feast not
sacrificed[,]
ἐν ζύμῃ παλαιᾷ μηδὲ ἐν ζύμῃ κακίας
with leaven old nor with leaven of malice
καὶ πονηρίας, ἀλλ' ἐν ἀζύμοις εἰλικρινείας
and of evil, but with unleavened of sincerity
[loaves]
καὶ ἀληθείας. **9** Ἔγραψα ὑμῖν ἐν τῇ
and of truth. I wrote to you in the
ἐπιστολῇ μὴ συναναμίγνυσθαι πόρνοις,
epistle not to associate with
intimately with fornicators,
10 οὐ πάντως τοῖς πόρνοις τοῦ κόσμου
not altogether with the fornicators – world
τούτου ἢ τοῖς πλεονέκταις καὶ ἅρπαξιν
of this or with the covetous and rapacious

Chapter 5

Expel the Immoral Brother!

IT is actually reported that there is sexual immorality among you, and of a kind that does not occur even among pagans: A man has his father's wife. 2And you are proud! Shouldn't you rather have been filled with grief and have put out of your fellowship the man who did this? 3Even though I am not physically present, I am with you in spirit. And I have already passed judgment on the one who did this, just as if I were present. 4When you are assembled in the name of our Lord Jesus and I am with you in spirit, and the power of our Lord Jesus is present, 5hand this man over to Satan, so that the sinful nature¹ may be destroyed and his spirit saved on the day of the Lord.

6Your boasting is not good. Don't you know that a little yeast works through the whole batch of dough? 7Get rid of the old yeast that you may be a new batch without yeast—as you really are. For Christ, our Passover lamb, has been sacrificed. 8Therefore let us keep the Festival, not with the old yeast, the yeast of malice and wickedness, but with bread without yeast, the bread of sincerity and truth.

9I have written you in my letter not to associate with sexually immoral people—10not at all meaning the people of this world who are immoral, or the greedy and swindlers, or idolaters.

---

s Or on the man who has done such a thing in the name of the Lord Jesus
t Other ancient authorities add Jesus

¹5 Or that his body; or that the flesh

since you would then need to go out of the world. 11 But now I am writing to you not to associate with anyone who bears the name of brother or sister" who is sexually immoral or greedy, or is an idolater, reviler, drunkard, or robber. Do not even eat with such a one. 12 For what have I to do with judging those outside? Is it not those who are inside that you are to judge? 13 God will judge those outside. "Drive out the wicked person from among you."

Chapter 6

Lawsuits among Believers

WHEN any of you has a grievance against another, do you dare to take it to court before the unrighteous, instead of taking it before the saints? 2 Do you not know that the saints will judge the world? And if the world is to be judged by you, are you incompetent to try trivial cases? 3 Do you not know that we are to judge angels—to say nothing of ordinary matters? 4 If you have ordinary cases, then, do you appoint as judges those who have no standing in the church? 5 I say this to your shame. Can it be that there is no one among you wise enough to decide between one believer" and another, 6 but a believer" goes to court against a believer"—and before unbelievers at that?

7 In fact, to have lawsuits at all with one another is already a defeat for you. Why not rather be wronged? Why not rather be defrauded? 8 But you yourselves wrong and defraud—and believers" at that.

9 Do you not know that wrongdoers will not inherit the kingdom of God? Do not be deceived! Fornica-

" Gk brother
v Gk brothers

ἢ εἰδωλολάτραις, ἐπεὶ ὠφείλετε ἄρα ἐκ
or idolaters, since ye ought then out of

τοῦ κόσμου ἐξελθεῖν. 11 νῦν δὲ ἔγραψα
the world to go out. But now I wrote

ὑμῖν μὴ συναναμίγνυσθαι ἐάν τις ἀδελφὸς
to you not to associate intimately with if anyone a brother

ὀνομαζόμενος ἦ πόρνος ἢ πλεονέκτης ἢ
being named is a fornicator or a covetous man or

εἰδωλολάτρης ἢ λοίδορος ἢ μέθυσος ἢ
an idolater or a railer or a drunkard or

ἅρπαξ, τῷ τοιούτῳ μηδὲ συνεσθίειν. 12 τί
a rapacious man, with such a man not to eat with. what

γάρ μοι τοὺς ἔξω κρίνειν; οὐχὶ τοὺς
For [is it] to me the ones without to judge? Not the ones

ἔσω ὑμεῖς κρίνετε; 13 τοὺς δὲ ἔξω
within ye judge? But the ones without

ὁ θεὸς κρινεῖ. ἐξάρατε τὸν πονηρὸν ἐξ
God will judge. Remove the evil man out of

ὑμῶν αὐτῶν.
yourselves.

6 Τολμᾷ τις ὑμῶν πρᾶγμα ἔχων πρὸς
Dares anyone of you a matter having against

τὸν ἕτερον κρίνεσθαι ἐπὶ τῶν ἀδίκων,
the(an) other to be judged before the unjust,

καὶ οὐχὶ ἐπὶ τῶν ἁγίων; 2 ἢ οὐκ οἴδατε
and not before the saints? or know ye not

ὅτι οἱ ἅγιοι τὸν κόσμον κρινοῦσιν; καὶ
that the saints the world will judge? and

εἰ ἐν ὑμῖν κρίνεται ὁ κόσμος, ἀνάξιοί
if by you is judged the world, unworthy

ἐστε κριτηρίων ἐλαχίστων; 3 οὐκ οἴδατε
are ye judgments? of very little? Know ye not

ὅτι ἀγγέλους κρινοῦμεν, μήτι γε βιωτικά;
that angels we will judge, not to speak of things of this life?

4 βιωτικὰ μὲν οὖν κριτήρια ἐὰν ἔχητε,
Of this life indeed therefore judgments if ye have,

τοὺς ἐξουθενημένους ἐν τῇ ἐκκλησίᾳ,
the ones being despised in the church,

τούτους καθίζετε; 5 πρὸς ἐντροπὴν ὑμῖν
these sit ye? For shame to you

λέγω. οὕτως οὐκ ἔνι ἐν ὑμῖν οὐδεὶς
I say. Thus there is no room among you [for] no one

σοφός, ὃς δυνήσεται διακρῖναι ἀνὰ μέσον
wise man, who will be able to discern in your midst

τοῦ ἀδελφοῦ αὐτοῦ; 6 ἀλλὰ ἀδελφὸς μετὰ
the brother of him? But brother with

ἀδελφοῦ κρίνεται, καὶ τοῦτο ἐπὶ ἀπίστων;
brother is judged, and this before unbelievers?

7 ἤδη μὲν οὖν ὅλως ἥττημα ὑμῖν ἐστιν
Now indeed there-fore altogether a failure with you there is

ὅτι κρίματα ἔχετε μεθ᾽ ἑαυτῶν. διὰ τί
that lawsuits ye have with yourselves. Why

οὐχὶ μᾶλλον ἀδικεῖσθε; διὰ τί οὐχὶ
not rather be wronged? Why not

μᾶλλον ἀποστερεῖσθε; 8 ἀλλὰ ὑμεῖς ἀδικεῖτε
rather be deprived? But ye do wrong

καὶ ἀποστερεῖτε, καὶ τοῦτο ἀδελφούς.
and deprive, and this brothers.

9 ἢ οὐκ οἴδατε ὅτι ἄδικοι θεοῦ βασιλείαν
Or know ye not that unrighteous of God [the] kingdom
men

οὐ κληρονομήσουσιν; μὴ πλανᾶσθε· οὔτε
will not inherit? Be not led astray; not

In that case you would have to leave this world. 11 But now I am writing you that you must not associate with anyone who calls himself a brother but is sexually immoral or greedy, an idolater or a slanderer, a drunkard or a swindler. With such a man do not even eat.

12 What business is it of mine to judge those outside the church? Are you not to judge those inside? 13 God will judge those outside. "Expel the wicked man from among you." m

Chapter 6

Lawsuits Among Believers

IF any of you has a dispute with another, dare he take it before the ungodly for judgment instead of before the saints? 2 Do you not know that the saints will judge the world? And if you are to judge the world, are you not competent to judge trivial cases? 3 Do you not know that we will judge angels? How much more the things of this life! 4 Therefore, if you have disputes about such matters, appoint as judges even men of little account in the church!n 5 I say this to shame you. Is it possible that there is nobody among you wise enough to judge a dispute between believers? 6 But instead, one brother goes to law against another—and this in front of unbelievers!

7 The very fact that you have lawsuits among you means you have been completely defeated already. Why not rather be wronged? Why not rather be cheated? 8 Instead, you yourselves cheat and do wrong, and you do this to your brothers.

9 Do you not know that the wicked will not inherit the kingdom of God? Do

m13 Deut. 17:7; 19:19; 21:21; 22:21,24; 24:7
n4 Or matters, do you appoint as judges men of little account in the church?

tors, idolaters, adulterers, male prostitutes, sodomites, [10]thieves, the greedy, drunkards, revilers, robbers—none of these will inherit the kingdom of God. [11]And this is what some of you used to be. But you were sanctified, you were justified in the name of the Lord Jesus Christ and in the Spirit of our God.

Glorify God in Body and Spirit

[12] "All things are lawful for me," but not all things are beneficial. "All things are lawful for me," but I will not be dominated by anything. [13]"Food is meant for the stomach and the stomach for food," [w] and God will destroy both one and the other. The body is meant not for fornication but for the Lord, and the Lord for the body. [14]And God raised the Lord and will also raise us by his power. [15]Do you not know that your bodies are members of Christ? Should I therefore take the members of Christ and make them members of a prostitute? Never! [16]Do you not know that whoever is united to a prostitute becomes one body with her? For it is said, "The two shall be one flesh." [17]But anyone united to the Lord becomes one spirit with him. [18]Shun fornication! Every sin that a person commits is outside the body; but the fornicator sins against the body itself. [19]Or do you not know that your body is a temple[x] of

w The quotation may extend to the word *other*
x Or *sanctuary*

πόρνοι οὔτε εἰδωλολάτραι οὔτε μοιχοὶ
fornicators nor idolaters nor adulterers
οὔτε μαλακοὶ οὔτε ἀρσενοκοῖται 10 οὔτε
nor voluptuous nor sodomites nor
persons
κλέπται οὔτε πλεονέκται, οὐ μέθυσοι,
thieves nor covetous persons, not drunkards,
οὐ λοίδοροι, οὐχ ἅρπαγες βασιλείαν θεοῦ
not revilers, not rapacious ²[the] kingdom ³of
persons God
κληρονομήσουσιν. 11 καὶ ταῦτά τινες ἦτε·
¹will inherit. And these ²some ¹ye
things [of you] were;
ἀλλὰ ἀπελούσασθε, ἀλλὰ ἡγιάσθητε, ἀλλὰ
but ye were washed, but ye were sanctified, but
ἐδικαιώθητε ἐν τῷ ὀνόματι τοῦ κυρίου
ye were justified in the name of the Lord
Ἰησοῦ Χριστοῦ καὶ ἐν τῷ πνεύματι
Jesus Christ and by the Spirit
τοῦ θεοῦ ἡμῶν.
of the God of us.
12 Πάντα μοι ἔξεστιν, ἀλλ' οὐ πάντα
All things to me [are] lawful, but not all things
συμφέρει. πάντα μοι ἔξεστιν, ἀλλ' οὐκ
expedient. All things to me [are] lawful, but not
ἐγὼ ἐξουσιασθήσομαι ὑπό τινος. 13 τὰ
I will be ruled by anyone. –
βρώματα τῇ κοιλίᾳ, καὶ ἡ κοιλία τοῖς
Foods for the belly, and the belly –
βρώμασιν· ὁ δὲ θεὸς καὶ ταύτην καὶ
for foods; – but God both this and
ταῦτα καταργήσει. τὸ δὲ σῶμα οὐ τῇ
these will destroy. But the body [is] not –
πορνείᾳ ἀλλὰ τῷ κυρίῳ, καὶ ὁ κύριος
for fornication but for the Lord, and the Lord
τῷ σώματι· 14 ὁ δὲ θεὸς καὶ τὸν κύριον
for the body; – and God both the Lord
ἤγειρεν καὶ ἡμᾶς ἐξεγερεῖ διὰ τῆς
raised and us will raise up through the
δυνάμεως αὐτοῦ. 15 οὐκ οἴδατε ὅτι τὰ
power of him. Know ye not that the
σώματα ὑμῶν μέλη Χριστοῦ ἐστιν; ἄρας
bodies of you members of Christ (is)are? Taking
οὖν τὰ μέλη τοῦ Χριστοῦ ποιήσω πόρνης
there- the members – of Christ shall I make ²of a
fore [them] harlot
μέλη; μὴ γένοιτο. 16 ἢ οὐκ οἴδατε ὅτι
¹members? May it not be. Or know ye not that
ὁ κολλώμενος τῇ πόρνῃ ἓν σῶμά ἐστιν;
the *being* joined – to a harlot one body is?
[one]
ἔσονται γάρ, φησίν, οἱ δύο εἰς σάρκα
For ⁶will be, ³he says, ¹the ⁵two ⁴into ⁷flesh
μίαν. 17 ὁ δὲ κολλώμενος τῷ κυρίῳ
⁸one. But the [one] *being* joined to the Lord
ἓν πνεῦμά ἐστιν. 18 φεύγετε τὴν πορνείαν.
one spirit is. Flee ye – fornication.
πᾶν ἁμάρτημα ὃ ἐὰν ποιήσῃ ἄνθρωπος
Every sin whichever ²may do ¹a man
ἐκτὸς τοῦ σώματός ἐστιν· ὁ δὲ πορνεύων
outside the body is; but the committing
[one] fornication
εἰς τὸ ἴδιον σῶμα ἁμαρτάνει. 19
against the(his) own body sins. Or
οὐκ οἴδατε ὅτι τὸ σῶμα ὑμῶν ναὸς
know ye not that the body of you ²a shrine
τοῦ ἐν ὑμῖν ἁγίου πνεύματός ἐστιν,
³of the ⁴in ⁷you ⁶Holy ⁵Spirit ¹is,

not be deceived: Neither the sexually immoral nor idolaters nor adulterers nor male prostitutes nor homosexual offenders [10]nor thieves nor the greedy nor drunkards nor slanderers nor swindlers will inherit the kingdom of God. [11]And that is what some of you were. But you were washed, you were sanctified, you were justified in the name of the Lord Jesus Christ and by the Spirit of our God.

Sexual Immorality

[12]"Everything is permissible for me"—but not everything is beneficial. "Everything is permissible for me"—but I will not be mastered by anything. [13]"Food for the stomach and the stomach for food"—but God will destroy them both. The body is not meant for sexual immorality, but for the Lord, and the Lord for the body. [14]By his power God raised the Lord from the dead, and he will raise us also. [15]Do you not know that your bodies are members of Christ himself? Shall I then take the members of Christ and unite them with a prostitute? Never! [16]Do you not know that he who unites himself with a prostitute is one with her in body? For it is said, "The two will become one flesh."[o] [17]But he who unites himself with the Lord is one with him in spirit.
[18]Flee from sexual immorality. All other sins a man commits are outside his body, but he who sins sexually sins against his own body. [19]Do you not know that your body is a temple of the Holy Spirit, who is in

o 16 Gen. 2:24

the Holy Spirit within you, which you have from God, and that you are not your own? 20 For you were bought with a price; therefore glorify God in your body.

Chapter 7

Directions concerning Marriage

NOW concerning the matters about which you wrote: "It is well for a man not to touch a woman." 2 But because of cases of sexual immorality, each man should have his own wife and each woman her own husband. 3 The husband should give to his wife her conjugal rights, and likewise the wife to her husband. 4 For the wife does not have authority over her own body, but the husband does; likewise the husband does not have authority over his own body, but the wife does. 5 Do not deprive one another except perhaps by agreement for a set time, to devote yourselves to prayer, and then come together again, so that Satan may not tempt you because of your lack of self-control. 6 This I say by way of concession, not of command. 7 I wish that all were as I myself am. But each has a particular gift from God, one having one kind and another a different kind.

8 To the unmarried and the widows I say that it is well for them to remain unmarried as I am. 9 But if they are not practicing self-control, they should marry. For it is better to marry than to be aflame with passion.

10 To the married I give this command—not I but the Lord—that the wife should not separate from her husband 11 (but if she does separate, let her re-

---

οὗ ἔχετε ἀπὸ θεοῦ, καὶ οὐκ ἐστὲ ἑαυτῶν;
which ye have from God, and ye are not of yourselves?

20 ἠγοράσθητε γὰρ τιμῆς· δοξάσατε δὴ
For ye were bought of(with) a price; glorify ye then

τὸν θεὸν ἐν τῷ σώματι ὑμῶν.
- God in the body of you.

---

7 Περὶ δὲ ὧν ἐγράψατε, καλὸν ἀνθρώπῳ
Now about things ye wrote, [it is] good for a man
of which

γυναικὸς μὴ ἅπτεσθαι· 2 διὰ δὲ τὰς
¹a woman* ¹not ²to touch; but because of the

πορνείας ἕκαστος τὴν ἑαυτοῦ γυναῖκα
fornications each man ²the ⁴of himself ³wife

ἐχέτω, καὶ ἑκάστη τὸν ἴδιον ἄνδρα
¹let him have, and each woman the(her) own husband

ἐχέτω. 3 τῇ γυναικὶ ὁ ἀνὴρ τὴν ὀφειλὴν
let her have. To the wife ²the ³husband ⁴the ⁵debt

ἀποδιδότω, ὁμοίως δὲ καὶ ἡ γυνὴ τῷ
¹let him pay, and likewise also the wife to the

ἀνδρί. 4 ἡ γυνὴ τοῦ ἰδίου σώματος
husband. The wife of the(her) own body

οὐκ ἐξουσιάζει ἀλλὰ ὁ ἀνήρ· ὁμοίως
has not authority but the husband; ²likewise

δὲ καὶ ὁ ἀνὴρ τοῦ ἰδίου σώματος οὐκ
¹and also the husband of the(his) own body not

ἐξουσιάζει ἀλλὰ ἡ γυνή. 5 μὴ ἀποστερεῖτε
has authority but the wife. Deprive not ye

ἀλλήλους, εἰ μήτι ἂν ἐκ συμφώνου πρὸς
each other, unless by agreement for

καιρὸν ἵνα σχολάσητε τῇ προσευχῇ καὶ
a time in order ye may have - for prayer and
that leisure

πάλιν ἐπὶ τὸ αὐτὸ ἦτε, ἵνα μὴ πειράζῃ
²again ¹together ¹ye may be, lest ²tempt

ὑμᾶς ὁ σατανᾶς διὰ τὴν ἀκρασίαν [ὑμῶν].
¹you - ¹Satan because the want of of you.
of self-control

6 τοῦτο δὲ λέγω κατὰ συγγνώμην, οὐ
Now this I say by allowance, not

κατ᾽ ἐπιταγήν. 7 θέλω δὲ πάντας
by command. And I wish all

ἀνθρώπους εἶναι ὡς καὶ ἐμαυτόν· ἀλλὰ
men to be as even myself; but

ἕκαστος ἴδιον ἔχει χάρισμα ἐκ θεοῦ,
each man ²[his] own ¹has gift of God,

ὁ μὲν οὕτως, ὁ δὲ οὕτως.
one thus, another thus.

8 Λέγω δὲ τοῖς ἀγάμοις καὶ ταῖς χήραις,
Now I say to the unmarried men and to the widows,

καλὸν αὐτοῖς ἐὰν μείνωσιν ὡς κἀγώ· 9 εἰ δὲ
[it is] good for them if they remain as I also; but if

οὐκ ἐγκρατεύονται, γαμησάτωσαν· κρεῖττον
they do not exercise self-control, let them marry; better

γάρ ἐστιν γαμεῖν ἢ πυροῦσθαι. 10 τοῖς
for it is to marry than to burn. to the [ones]

δὲ γεγαμηκόσιν παραγγέλλω, οὐκ ἐγὼ
But having married I enjoin, not I

ἀλλὰ ὁ κύριος, γυναῖκα ἀπὸ ἀνδρὸς μὴ
but the Lord, a woman from [her] husband not

χωρισθῆναι, 11 — ἐὰν δὲ καὶ χωρισθῇ,
to be separated,ᵇ but if indeed she is separated,

Chapter 7

Marriage

NOW for the matters you wrote about: It is good for a man not to marry.ᵖ 2 But since there is so much immorality, each man should have his own wife, and each woman her own husband. 3 The husband should fulfill his marital duty to his wife, and likewise the wife to her husband. 4 The wife's body does not belong to her alone but also to her husband. In the same way, the husband's body does not belong to him alone but also to his wife. 5 Do not deprive each other except by mutual consent and for a time, so that you may devote yourselves to prayer. Then come together again so that Satan will not tempt you because of your lack of self-control. 6 I say this as a concession, not as a command. 7 I wish that all men were as I am. But each man has his own gift from God; one has this gift, another has that.

8 Now to the unmarried and the widows I say: It is good for them to stay unmarried, as I am. 9 But if they cannot control themselves, they should marry, for it is better to marry than to burn with passion.

10 To the married I give this command (not I, but the Lord): A wife must not separate from her husband. 11 But if she does, she must

---

* As the same Greek word γυνή means "wife" or "(?married) woman" it is not always easy to differentiate in translating. So also the one Greek word ἀνήρ means "man" or "husband"

ᵖ1 Or "It is good for a man not to have sexual relations with a woman."

main unmarried or else be reconciled to her husband), and that the husband should not divorce his wife.

12 To the rest I say—I and not the Lord—that if any believer[y] has a wife who is an unbeliever, and she consents to live with him, he should not divorce her. 13 And if any woman has a husband who is an unbeliever, and he consents to live with her, she should not divorce him. 14 For the unbelieving husband is made holy through his wife, and the unbelieving wife is made holy through her husband. Otherwise, your children would be unclean, but as it is, they are holy. 15 But if the unbelieving partner separates, let it be so; in such a case the brother or sister is not bound. It is to peace that God has called you.[z] 16 Wife, for all you know, you might save your husband. Husband, for all you know, you might save your wife.

The Life That the Lord Has Assigned

17 However that may be, let each of you lead the life that the Lord has assigned, to which God called you. This is my rule in all the churches. 18 Was anyone at the time of his call already circumcised? Let him not seek to remove the marks of circumcision. Was anyone at the time of his call uncircumcised? Let him not seek circumcision. 19 Circumcision is nothing, and uncircumcision is nothing; but obeying the commandments of God is everything. 20 Let each of you remain in the condition in which you were called. 21 Were you a slave when called? Do not be concerned about it. Even if you can gain your freedom, make use of your present condition now more than ever.[a] 22 For whoever was

Gk *brother*
z Other ancient authorities read *us*
a Or *avail yourself of the opportunity*

μενέτω ἄγαμος ἢ τῷ ἀνδρὶ καταλλαγήτω,
let her remain unmarried or to husband be reconciled, the(her)

— καὶ ἄνδρα γυναῖκα μὴ ἀφιέναι. 12 Τοῖς
and a husband [his] wife not to leave.[b] to the

δὲ λοιποῖς λέγω ἐγώ, οὐχ ὁ κύριος·
And rest say I, not the Lord:

εἴ τις ἀδελφὸς γυναῖκα ἔχει ἄπιστον, καὶ
If any brother ²a wife ¹has unbelieving, and

αὕτη συνευδοκεῖ οἰκεῖν μετ' αὐτοῦ, μὴ
this one consents to dwell with him, not

ἀφιέτω αὐτήν· 13 καὶ γυνὴ ἥτις ἔχει
let him leave her; and a woman who has

ἄνδρα ἄπιστον, καὶ οὗτος συνευδοκεῖ οἰκεῖν
a husband unbelieving, and this one consents to dwell

μετ' αὐτῆς, μὴ ἀφιέτω τὸν ἄνδρα.
with her, let her not leave the(her) husband.

14 ἡγίασται γὰρ ὁ ἀνὴρ ὁ ἄπιστος ἐν
For ²has been sanctified ¹the ³husband – ⁴unbelieving by

τῇ γυναικί, καὶ ἡγίασται ἡ γυνὴ ἡ
the wife, and ²has been sanctified ¹the ³wife –

ἄπιστος ἐν τῷ ἀδελφῷ· ἐπεὶ ἄρα τὰ
²unbelieving by the brother; since then the

τέκνα ὑμῶν ἀκάθαρτά ἐστιν, νῦν δὲ
children of you ²unclean ¹is(are), but now

ἅγιά ἐστιν. 15 εἰ δὲ ὁ ἄπιστος χωρίζ-
²holy ¹they are. But if the unbelieving separates one

εται, χωριζέσθω· οὐ δεδούλωται ὁ
him/herself, let him/her be separated; ²has not been enslaved ¹the

ἀδελφὸς ἢ ἡ ἀδελφὴ ἐν τοῖς τοιούτοις·
²brother ³or ⁴the ⁵sister in such matters;

ἐν δὲ εἰρήνῃ κέκληκεν ὑμᾶς ὁ θεός.
but ²in ³peace ⁴has called ⁵you – ¹God.

16 τί γὰρ οἶδας, γύναι, εἰ τὸν ἄνδρα
For what knowest thou, wife, if the(thy) husband

σώσεις; ἢ τί οἶδας, ἄνερ, εἰ τὴν
thou wilt save? or what knowest husband, if the(thy) thou,

γυναῖκα σώσεις; 17 Εἰ μὴ ἑκάστῳ ὡς
wife thou wilt save? Only ⁵to each ¹as

μεμέρικεν ὁ κύριος, ἕκαστον ὡς κέκληκεν
⁴has divided ²the ³Lord, ⁴each ¹as ²has called

ὁ θεός, οὕτως περιπατείτω. καὶ οὕτως
– ¹God, so let him walk. And so

ἐν ταῖς ἐκκλησίαις πάσαις διατάσσομαι.
²in ⁴the ⁵churches ³all ¹I command.

18 περιτετμημένος τις ἐκλήθη; μὴ
²Having been circumcised ³anyone ¹was ³called? not

ἐπισπάσθω· ἐν ἀκροβυστίᾳ κέκληταί τις;
let him be uncircumcised; in uncircumcision has been anyone? called

μὴ περιτεμνέσθω. 19 ἡ περιτομὴ οὐδέν
let him not be circumcised. – Circumcision nothing

ἐστιν, καὶ ἡ ἀκροβυστία οὐδέν ἐστιν,
is, and – uncircumcision nothing is,

ἀλλὰ τήρησις ἐντολῶν θεοῦ. 20 ἕκαστος
but [the] keeping of commandments of God. Each one

ἐν τῇ κλήσει ᾗ ἐκλήθη, ἐν ταύτῃ
in the calling in which he was called, in this

μενέτω. 21 δοῦλος ἐκλήθης; μή σοι
let him remain. A slave wast thou called? not to thee

μελέτω· ἀλλ' εἰ καὶ δύνασαι ἐλεύθερος
let it matter; but if indeed thou art able ³free

γενέσθαι, μᾶλλον χρῆσαι. 22 ὁ γὰρ ἐν
¹to become, ²rather ³use [it]. For ¹the [one] ⁴in

remain unmarried or else be reconciled to her husband. And a husband must not divorce his wife.

12 To the rest I say this (I, not the Lord): If any brother has a wife who is not a believer and she is willing to live with him, he must not divorce her. 13 And if a woman has a husband who is not a believer and he is willing to live with her, she must not divorce him. 14 For the unbelieving husband has been sanctified through his wife, and the unbelieving wife has been sanctified through her believing husband. Otherwise your children would be unclean, but as it is, they are holy.

15 But if the unbeliever leaves, let him do so. A believing man or woman is not bound in such circumstances; God has called us to live in peace. 16 How do you know, wife, whether you will save your husband? Or, how do you know, husband, whether you will save your wife?

17 Nevertheless, each one should retain the place in life that the Lord assigned to him and to which God has called him. This is the rule I lay down in all the churches. 18 Was a man already circumcised when he was called? He should not become uncircumcised. Was a man uncircumcised when he was called? He should not be circumcised. 19 Circumcision is nothing and uncircumcision is nothing. Keeping God's commands is what counts. 20 Each one should remain in the situation which he was in when God called him. 21 Were you a slave when you were called? Don't let it trouble you—although if you can gain your freedom, do so. 22 For

called in the Lord as a slave is a freed person belonging to the Lord, just as whoever was free when called is a slave of Christ. 23 You were bought with a price; do not become slaves of human masters. 24 In whatever condition you were called, brothers and sisters,ᵇ there remain with God.

The Unmarried and the Widows

25 Now concerning virgins, I have no command of the Lord, but I give my opinion as one who by the Lord's mercy is trustworthy. 26 I think that, in view of the impendingᶜ crisis, it is well for you to remain as you are. 27 Are you bound to a wife? Do not seek to be free. Are you free from a wife? Do not seek a wife. 28 But if you marry, you do not sin, and if a virgin marries, she does not sin. Yet those who marry will experience distress in this life,ᵈ and I would spare you that. 29 I mean, brothers and sisters,ᵇ the appointed time has grown short; from now on, let even those who have wives be as though they had none, 30 and those who mourn as though they were not mourning, and those who rejoice as though they were not rejoicing, and those who buy as though they had no possessions, 31 and those who deal with the world as though they had no dealings with it. For the present form of this world is passing away. 32 I want you to be free from anxieties. The unmarried man is anxious about the affairs of the Lord, how to please the Lord; 33 but the married man is anxious about the affairs of the

ᵇ Gk brothers
ᶜ Or present
ᵈ Gk in the flesh

κυρίῳ κληθεὶς δοῦλος ἀπελεύθερος κυρίου
⁵[the] ²called ³a slave ⁷a freed man ⁸of [the]
Lord   Lord

ἐστίν· ὁμοίως ὁ ἐλεύθερος κληθεὶς δοῦλός
⁶is; likewise ¹the ²a free man ²called ³a slave
[one]

ἐστιν Χριστοῦ. 23 τιμῆς ἠγοράσθητε· μὴ
⁴is ⁵of Christ. Of(with) a price ye were bought; not

γίνεσθε δοῦλοι ἀνθρώπων. 24 ἕκαστος ἐν
become ye slaves of men. Each one in

ᾧ ἐκλήθη, ἀδελφοί, ἐν τούτῳ μενέτω
what he was brothers, in this let him
[state] called,   remain

παρὰ θεῷ.
with God.

25 Περὶ δὲ τῶν παρθένων ἐπιταγὴν
Now about the virgins a command

κυρίου οὐκ ἔχω, γνώμην δὲ δίδωμι ὡς
of [the] Lord I have not, but an opinion I give as

ἠλεημένος ὑπὸ κυρίου πιστὸς εἶναι.
having had mercy by [the] Lord faithful to be.

26 Νομίζω οὖν τοῦτο καλὸν ὑπάρχειν
I suppose therefore this good to be

διὰ τὴν ἐνεστῶσαν ἀνάγκην, ὅτι καλὸν
because of the present necessity, that [it is] good

ἀνθρώπῳ τὸ οὕτως εἶναι. 27 δέδεσαι
for a man - so to be. Hast thou been bound

γυναικί; μὴ ζήτει λύσιν· λέλυσαι ἀπὸ
to a woman? do not seek release; hast thou been from
released

γυναικός; μὴ ζήτει γυναῖκα. 28 ἐὰν
a woman? do not seek a woman. if

δὲ καὶ γαμήσῃς, οὐχ ἥμαρτες, καὶ ἐὰν
But indeed thou marriest, thou sinnedst not, and if

γήμῃ ἡ παρθένος, οὐχ ἥμαρτεν· θλῖψιν
³marries ¹the ²virgin, she sinned not; ³affliction

δὲ τῇ σαρκὶ ἕξουσιν οἱ τοιοῦτοι, ἐγὼ
but ⁴in the ⁵flesh ²will have - ¹such, ²I

δὲ ὑμῶν φείδομαι. 29 Τοῦτο δέ φημι,
¹and ⁴you ³am sparing. But this I say,

ἀδελφοί, ὁ καιρὸς συνεσταλμένος ἐστίν·
brothers, the time having been shortened is;

τὸ λοιπὸν ἵνα καὶ οἱ ἔχοντες γυναῖκας
for the rest in order both the [ones] having wives
that

ὡς μὴ ἔχοντες ὦσιν, 30 καὶ οἱ κλαίοντες
as not having may be, and the [ones] weeping

ὡς μὴ κλαίοντες, καὶ οἱ χαίροντες ὡς
as not weeping, and the [ones] rejoicing as

μὴ χαίροντες, καὶ οἱ ἀγοράζοντες ὡς
not rejoicing, and the [ones] buying as

μὴ κατέχοντες, 31 καὶ οἱ χρώμενοι τὸν
not holding, and the [ones] using the

κόσμον ὡς μὴ καταχρώμενοι· παράγει
world as not abusing [it]; ⁴is passing away

γὰρ τὸ σχῆμα τοῦ κόσμου τούτου.
for ¹the ²fashion ³of this world.

32 Θέλω δὲ ὑμᾶς ἀμερίμνους εἶναι. ὁ
But I wish you without care to be. The

ἄγαμος μεριμνᾷ τὰ τοῦ κυρίου, 33 πῶς
unmarried cares for the of the Lord, how
man   things

ἀρέσῃ τῷ κυρίῳ· ὁ δὲ γαμήσας μεριμνᾷ
he may the Lord; but the having married cares for
please   [one]

---

he who was a slave when he was called by the Lord is the Lord's freedman; similarly, he who was a free man when he was called is Christ's slave. 23 You were bought at a price; do not become slaves of men. 24 Brothers, each man, as responsible to God, should remain in the situation God called him to.

25 Now about virgins: I have no command from the Lord, but I give a judgment as one who by the Lord's mercy is trustworthy. 26 Because of the present crisis, I think that it is good for you to remain as you are. 27 Are you married? Do not seek a divorce. Are you unmarried? Do not look for a wife. 28 But if you do marry, you have not sinned; and if a virgin marries, she has not sinned. But those who marry will face many troubles in this life, and I want to spare you this.

29 What I mean, brothers, is that the time is short. From now on those who have wives should live as if they had none; 30 those who mourn, as if they did not; those who are happy, as if they were not; those who buy something, as if it were not theirs to keep; 31 those who use the things of the world, as if not engrossed in them. For this world in its present form is passing away.

32 I would like you to be free from concern. An unmarried man is concerned about the Lord's affairs—how he can please the Lord. 33 But a married man is concerned about the af-

world, how to please his wife, 34 and his interests are divided. And the unmarried woman and the virgin are anxious about the affairs of the Lord, so that they may be holy in body and spirit; but the married woman is anxious about the affairs of the world, how to please her husband. 35 I say this for your own benefit, not to put any restraint upon you, but to promote good order and unhindered devotion to the Lord.

36 If anyone thinks that he is not behaving properly toward his fiancée,[e] if his passions are strong, and so it has to be, let him marry as he wishes; it is no sin. Let them marry. 37 But if someone stands firm in his resolve, being under no necessity but having his own desire under control, and has determined in his own mind to keep her as his fiancée,[e] he will do well. 38 So then, he who marries his fiancée[e] does well; and he who refrains from marriage will do better.

39 A wife is bound as long as her husband lives. But if the husband dies,[f] she is free to marry anyone she wishes, only in the Lord. 40 But in my judgment she is more blessed if she remains as she is. And I think that I too have the Spirit of God.

τὰ τοῦ κόσμου, πῶς ἀρέσῃ τῇ γυναικί,
the of the world, how he may the(his) wife,
        please

34 καὶ μεμέρισται. καὶ ἡ γυνὴ ἡ ἄγαμος
and has been divided. and the ²woman – ¹unmarried

καὶ ἡ παρθένος μεριμνᾷ τὰ τοῦ κυρίου,
and the virgin cares for the things of the Lord,

ἵνα ᾖ ἁγία καὶ τῷ σώματι καὶ τῷ
in she holy both in the body and in
order may   the
that be

πνεύματι· ἡ δὲ γαμήσασα μεριμνᾷ τὰ
spirit; but the [one] having married cares for the
                                                things

τοῦ κόσμου, πῶς ἀρέσῃ τῷ ἀνδρί.
of the world, how she may please the(her) husband.

35 τοῦτο δὲ πρὸς τὸ ὑμῶν αὐτῶν σύμφορον
And ²this ³for ⁴the ⁶of yourselves ⁵advantage

λέγω, οὐχ ἵνα βρόχον ὑμῖν ἐπιβάλω,
¹I say, not in order ²a restraint ³you ¹I may put on,
              that

ἀλλὰ πρὸς τὸ εὔσχημον καὶ εὐπάρεδρον
but for the thing comely and waiting on

τῷ κυρίῳ ἀπερισπάστως. 36 Εἰ δὲ τις
the Lord undistractedly. But if anyone

ἀσχημονεῖν ἐπὶ τὴν παρθένον αὐτοῦ
²to behave ³toward ⁴the ⁵virgin ⁶of him
dishonourably

νομίζει, ἐὰν ᾖ ὑπέρακμος, καὶ οὕτως
¹thinks, if he/she is past the bloom and so
                            of youth,

ὀφείλει γίνεσθαι, ὃ θέλει ποιείτω· οὐχ
ought to be, what he wishes let him do; not

ἁμαρτάνει· γαμείτωσαν. 37 ὃς δὲ ἕστηκεν
he sins; let them marry. But [he] who stands

ἐν τῇ καρδίᾳ αὐτοῦ ἑδραῖος, μὴ
in the heart of him firm, not

ἔχων ἀνάγκην, ἐξουσίαν δὲ ἔχει περὶ
having necessity, but authority has concerning

τοῦ ἰδίου θελήματος, καὶ τοῦτο κέκρικεν
the(his) own will, and this has decided

ἐν τῇ ἰδίᾳ καρδίᾳ, τηρεῖν τὴν ἑαυτοῦ
in the(his) own heart, to keep the of himself

παρθένον, καλῶς ποιήσει. 38 ὥστε καὶ
virgin, ²well ¹he will do. So as both

ὁ γαμίζων τὴν ἑαυτοῦ παρθένον καλῶς
the marrying the of himself virgin ²well
[one]

ποιεῖ, καὶ ὁ μὴ γαμίζων κρεῖσσον ποιήσει.
¹does, and the not marrying ²better ¹will do.
              [one]

39 Γυνὴ δέδεται ἐφ' ὅσον χρόνον ζῇ
A wife has been bound for so long a time as lives

ὁ ἀνὴρ αὐτῆς· ἐὰν δὲ κοιμηθῇ ὁ ἀνήρ,
the husband of her; but if sleeps the husband,

ἐλευθέρα ἐστὶν ᾧ θέλει γαμηθῆναι, μόνον
²free ¹she is ¹to ⁵she ²to be married, only
                  whom wishes

ἐν κυρίῳ. 40 μακαριωτέρα δέ ἐστιν
in [the] Lord. But happier she is

ἐὰν οὕτως μείνῃ, κατὰ τὴν ἐμὴν γνώμην·
if so she according – my opinion;
        remains, to

δοκῶ δὲ κἀγὼ πνεῦμα θεοῦ ἔχειν.
and I think I also [the] Spirit of God to have.

fairs of this world—how he can please his wife— 34 and his interests are divided. An unmarried woman or virgin is concerned about the Lord's affairs: Her aim is to be devoted to the Lord in both body and spirit. But a married woman is concerned about the affairs of this world—how she can please her husband. 35 I am saying this for your own good, not to restrict you, but that you may live in a right way in undivided devotion to the Lord.

36 If anyone thinks he is acting improperly toward the virgin he is engaged to, and if she is getting along in years and he feels he ought to marry, he should do as he wants. He is not sinning. They should get married. 37 But the man who has settled the matter in his own mind, who is under no compulsion but has control over his own will, and who has made up his mind not to marry the virgin—this man also does the right thing. 38 So then, he who marries the virgin does right, but he who does not marry her does even better.[q]

39 A woman is bound to her husband as long as he lives. But if her husband dies, she is free to marry anyone she wishes, but he must belong to the Lord. 40 In my judgment, she is happier if she stays as she is—and I think that I too have the Spirit of God.

Chapter 8

Food Offered to Idols

NOW concerning food sacrificed to idols: we know that "all of us pos-

Chapter 8

Food Sacrificed to Idols

NOW about food sacrificed to idols: We

q36-38 Or 36If anyone thinks he is not treating his daughter properly, and if she is getting along in years, and he feels she ought to marry, he should do as he wants. He is not sinning. He should let her get married. 37But the man who has settled the matter in his own mind, who is under no compulsion but has control over his own will, and who has made up his mind to keep the virgin unmarried—this man also does the right thing. 38So then, he who gives his virgin in marriage does right, but he who does not give her in marriage does even better.

e Gk virgin
f Gk falls asleep

8 Περὶ δὲ τῶν εἰδωλοθύτων, οἴδαμεν
Now about the idolatrous sacrifices, we know

sess knowledge." Knowledge puffs up, but love builds up. 2 Anyone who claims to know something does not yet have the necessary knowledge; 3 but anyone who loves God is known by him.

4 Hence, as to the eating of food offered to idols, we know that "no idol in the world really exists," and that "there is no God but one." 5 Indeed, even though there may be so-called gods in heaven or on earth—as in fact there is many gods and many lords— 6 yet for us there is one God, the Father, from whom are all things and for whom we exist, and one Lord, Jesus Christ, through whom are all things and through whom we exist.

7 It is not everyone, however, who has this knowledge. Since some have become so accustomed to idols until now, they still think of the food they eat as food offered to an idol; and their conscience, being weak, is defiled. 8 "Food will not bring us close to God." *g* We are no worse off if we do not eat, and no better off if we do. 9 But take care that this liberty of yours does not somehow become a stumbling block to the weak. 10 For if others see you, who possess knowledge, eating in the temple of an idol, might they not, since their conscience is weak, be encouraged to the point of eating food sacrificed to idols? 11 So by your knowledge those weak believers for whom Christ died are destroyed. *h* 12 But when you thus sin against members of your family, *i* and wound their conscience when it is weak, you sin

---

ὅτι πάντες γνῶσιν ἔχομεν. ἡ γνῶσις
that ²all ⁴knowledge ¹we ³have. - Knowledge

φυσιοῖ, ἡ δὲ ἀγάπη οἰκοδομεῖ· εἴ τις
puffs up, - but love builds up; if anyone

δοκεῖ ἐγνωκέναι τι, 2 οὔπω ἔγνω καθὼς
thinks to have known anything, not yet he knew as

δεῖ γνῶναι· 3 εἰ δέ τις ἀγαπᾷ τὸν
it be- to know; but if anyone loves -
hoves [him]

θεόν, οὗτος ἔγνωσται ὑπ' αὐτοῦ. 4 Περὶ
God, this one has been known by him. About

τῆς βρώσεως οὖν τῶν εἰδωλοθύτων
the eating therefore - of idolatrous sacrifices

οἴδαμεν ὅτι οὐδὲν εἴδωλον ἐν κόσμῳ,
we know that [there is] no idol in [the] world,

καὶ ὅτι οὐδεὶς θεὸς εἰ μὴ εἷς. 5 καὶ
and that [there is] no God except one. even

γὰρ εἴπερ εἰσὶν λεγόμενοι θεοὶ εἴτε ἐν
For if there are *being* called gods either in

οὐρανῷ εἴτε ἐπὶ γῆς, ὥσπερ εἰσὶν θεοὶ
heaven or on earth, even as there are gods

πολλοὶ καὶ κύριοι πολλοί, 6 ἀλλ' ἡμῖν
many and lords many, yet to us

εἷς θεὸς ὁ πατήρ, ἐξ οὗ τὰ πάντα καὶ
[there God the Father, of whom - [are] all and
is] one things

ἡμεῖς εἰς αὐτόν, καὶ εἷς κύριος Ἰησοῦς
we in him, and one Lord Jesus

Χριστός, δι' οὗ τὰ πάντα καὶ ἡμεῖς
Christ, through whom - [are] all and we
things

δι' αὐτοῦ. 7 Ἀλλ' οὐκ ἐν πᾶσιν ἡ
through him. But [there is] not in all men the
(this)

γνῶσις· τινὲς δὲ τῇ συνηθείᾳ ἕως ἄρτι
knowledge; and some by *the* habit until now

τοῦ εἰδώλου ὡς εἰδωλόθυτον ἐσθίουσιν,
²of the ¹idol ⁴as ³an idolatrous sacrifice ¹eat,

καὶ ἡ συνείδησις αὐτῶν ἀσθενὴς οὖσα
and the conscience of them ²weak ¹being

μολύνεται. 8 βρῶμα δὲ ἡμᾶς οὐ παραστήσει
is defiled. But food ²us ¹will not commend

τῷ θεῷ· οὔτε ἐὰν μὴ φάγωμεν ὑστερούμεθα,
- to God; neither if we eat not are we behind,

οὔτε ἐὰν φάγωμεν περισσεύομεν. 9 βλέπετε
nor if we eat do we excel. look ye

δὲ μή πως ἡ ἐξουσία ὑμῶν αὕτη
But lest somehow *the* ²authority ³of you ¹this

πρόσκομμα γένηται τοῖς ἀσθενέσιν. 10 ἐὰν
a stumbling-block becomes to the weak ones. if

γάρ τις ἴδῃ σὲ τὸν ἔχοντα γνῶσιν ἐν
For anyone sees thee the [one] having knowledge ²in

εἰδωλείῳ κατακείμενον, οὐχὶ ἡ συνείδησις
²an idol's temple ¹sitting, ¹not ²the ⁴conscience

αὐτοῦ ἀσθενοῦς ὄντος οἰκοδομηθήσεται εἰς
⁵of him ⁷weak ⁶[he]being ¹will ⁸be emboldened -

τὸ τὰ εἰδωλόθυτα ἐσθίειν; 11 ἀπόλλυται
- ¹⁰the ¹¹idolatrous sacrifices ⁹to eat? ²is destroyed

γὰρ ὁ ἀσθενῶν ἐν τῇ σῇ γνώσει, ὁ
For ¹the [one] ³being weak by - thy knowledge, the

ἀδελφὸς δι' ὃν Χριστὸς ἀπέθανεν. 12 οὕτως
brother because whom Christ died. so

δὲ ἁμαρτάνοντες εἰς τοὺς ἀδελφοὺς καὶ
And sinning against the brothers and

τύπτοντες αὐτῶν τὴν συνείδησιν ἀσθενοῦσαν
wounding of them the conscience being weak

---

know that we all possess knowledge. Knowledge puffs up, but love builds up. 2 The man who thinks he knows something does not yet know as he ought to know. 3 But the man who loves God is known by God.

4 So then, about eating food sacrificed to idols: We know that an idol is nothing at all in the world and that there is no God but one. 5 For even if there are so-called gods, whether in heaven or on earth (as indeed there are many "gods" and many "lords"), 6 yet for us there is but one God, the Father, from whom all things came and for whom we live; and there is but one Lord, Jesus Christ, through whom all things came and through whom we live.

7 But not everyone knows this. Some people are still so accustomed to idols that when they eat such food they think of it as having been sacrificed to an idol, and since their conscience is weak, it is defiled. 8 But food does not bring us near to God; we are no worse if we do not eat, and no better if we do.

9 Be careful, however, that the exercise of your freedom does not become a stumbling block to the weak. 10 For if anyone sees you who have this knowledge eating in an idol's temple, won't he be emboldened to eat what has been sacrificed to idols? 11 So this weak brother, for whom Christ died, is destroyed by your knowledge. 12 When you sin against your brothers in this way and wound their weak conscience, you sin against Christ. 13 There-

---

g The quotation may extend to the end of the verse
h Gk *the weak brother . . . is destroyed*
i Gk *against the brothers*

r1 Or *"We all possess knowledge,"* as you say

against Christ. [13] Therefore, if food is a cause of their falling,[j] I will never eat meat, so that I may not cause one of them[k] to fall.

εἰς Χριστὸν ἁμαρτάνετε. [13] διόπερ εἰ
[a]against [3]Christ [1]ye sin. Wherefore if

βρῶμα σκανδαλίζει τὸν ἀδελφόν μου, οὐ
food offends the brother of me, by no

μὴ φάγω κρέα εἰς τὸν αἰῶνα, ἵνα μὴ
means I eat flesh unto the age, lest

τὸν ἀδελφόν μου σκανδαλίσω.
[2]the [3]brother [4]of me [1]I offend.

fore, if what I eat causes my brother to fall into sin, I will never eat meat again, so that I will not cause him to fall.

Chapter 9
The Rights of an Apostle

AM I not free? Am I not an apostle? Have I not seen Jesus our Lord? Are you not my work in the Lord? [2] If I am not an apostle to others, at least I am to you; for you are the seal of my apostleship in the Lord.

[3] This is my defense to those who would examine me. [4] Do we not have the right to our food and drink? [5] Do we not have the right to be accompanied by a believing wife,[l] as do the other apostles and the brothers of the Lord and Cephas? [6] Or is it only Barnabas and I who have no right to refrain from working for a living? [7] Who at any time pays the expenses for doing military service? Who plants a vineyard and does not eat any of its fruit? Or who tends a flock and does not get any of its milk?

[8] Do I say this on human authority? Does not the law also say the same? [9] For it is written in the law of Moses, "You shall not muzzle an ox while it is treading out the grain." Is it for oxen that God is concerned? [10] Or does he not speak entirely for our sake? It was indeed written for our sake, for whoever plows should plow in hope and whoever threshes should thresh in hope of a share in the crop. [11] If we have sown spiritual good among you, is it too much if we reap your material ben-

9 Οὐκ εἰμὶ ἐλεύθερος; οὐκ εἰμὶ ἀπόστολος;
Am I not free? am I not an apostle?

οὐχὶ Ἰησοῦν τὸν κύριον ἡμῶν ἑόρακα;
not Jesus the Lord of us I have seen?

οὐ τὸ ἔργον μου ὑμεῖς ἐστε ἐν κυρίῳ;
not the work of me ye are in [the] Lord?

2 εἰ ἄλλοις οὐκ εἰμὶ ἀπόστολος, ἀλλά
If to others I am not an apostle, yet

γε ὑμῖν εἰμι· ἡ γὰρ σφραγίς μου τῆς
indeed to you I am; for the seal [2]of me [1]of the

ἀποστολῆς ὑμεῖς ἐστε ἐν κυρίῳ. **3** Ἡ
[2]apostleship ye are in [the] Lord.

ἐμὴ ἀπολογία τοῖς ἐμὲ ἀνακρίνουσίν ἐστιν
My defence to the [2]me [1]examining is

αὕτη. **4** μὴ οὐκ ἔχομεν ἐξουσίαν φαγεῖν
this. not Have we not authority to eat

καὶ πεῖν; **5** μὴ οὐκ ἔχομεν ἐξουσίαν
and to drink? not have we not authority

ἀδελφὴν γυναῖκα περιάγειν, ὡς καὶ οἱ
a sister a wife to lead about, as also the

λοιποὶ ἀπόστολοι καὶ οἱ ἀδελφοὶ τοῦ
remaining apostles and the brothers of the

κυρίου καὶ Κηφᾶς; **6** ἢ μόνος ἐγὼ καὶ
Lord and Cephas? or only I and

Βαρναβᾶς οὐκ ἔχομεν ἐξουσίαν μὴ
Barnabas have we not authority not

ἐργάζεσθαι; **7** Τίς στρατεύεται ἰδίοις
to work? Who soldiers at [his] own

ὀψωνίοις ποτέ; τίς φυτεύει ἀμπελῶνα καὶ
wages at any time? who plants a vineyard and

τὸν καρπὸν αὐτοῦ οὐκ ἐσθίει; ἢ τίς
the fruit of it eats not? or who

ποιμαίνει ποίμνην καὶ ἐκ τοῦ γάλακτος
shepherds a flock and of the milk

τῆς ποίμνης οὐκ ἐσθίει; **8** μὴ κατὰ
of the flock eats not? Not according to

ἄνθρωπον ταῦτα λαλῶ, ἢ καὶ ὁ νόμος
man these things I speak, or also the law

ταῦτα οὐ λέγει; **9** ἐν γὰρ τῷ Μωϋσέως
these things says not? for in the of Moses

νόμῳ γέγραπται· οὐ κημώσεις βοῦν
law it has been written: Thou shalt not muzzle an ox

ἀλοῶντα. μὴ τῶν βοῶν μέλει τῷ θεῷ;
threshing. not - of oxen matters it - to God?

10 ἢ δι' ἡμᾶς πάντως λέγει; δι' ἡμᾶς
or because of us altogether he says? because of us

γὰρ ἐγράφη, ὅτι ὀφείλει ἐπ' ἐλπίδι
for it was written, because [2]ought [3]on(in) [4]hope

ὁ ἀροτριῶν ἀροτριᾶν, καὶ ὁ ἀλοῶν ἐπ'
[1]the [2]ploughing [4]to plough, and the threshing on(in)

ἐλπίδι τοῦ μετέχειν. **11** εἰ ἡμεῖς ὑμῖν
hope of the to partake. If we to you
=of partaking.

τὰ πνευματικὰ ἐσπείραμεν, μέγα εἰ ἡμεῖς
- spiritual things sowed, [is it] a great thing if we

Chapter 9
The Rights of an Apostle

AM I not free? Am I not an apostle? Have I not seen Jesus our Lord? Are you not the result of my work in the Lord? [2] Even though I may not be an apostle to others, surely I am to you! For you are the seal of my apostleship in the Lord.

[3] This is my defense to those who sit in judgment on me. [4] Don't we have the right to food and drink? [5] Don't we have the right to take a believing wife along with us, as do the other apostles and the Lord's brothers and Cephas[s]? [6] Or is it only I and Barnabas who must work for a living?

[7] Who serves as a soldier at his own expense? Who plants a vineyard and does not eat of its grapes? Who tends a flock and does not drink of the milk? [8] Do I say this merely from a human point of view? Doesn't the Law say the same thing? [9] For it is written in the Law of Moses: "Do not muzzle an ox while it is treading out the grain."[t] Is it about oxen that God is concerned? [10] Surely he says this for us, doesn't he? Yes, this was written for us, because when the plowman plows and the thresher threshes, they ought to do so in the hope of sharing in the harvest. [11] If we have sown spiritual seed among

---

[j] Gk my brother's falling
[k] Gk cause my brother
[l] Gk a sister as wife

[s] That is, Peter
[t] Deut. 25:4

efits? 12 If others share this rightful claim on you, do not we still more?

Nevertheless, we have not made use of this right, but we endure anything rather than put an obstacle in the way of the gospel of Christ. 13 Do you not know that those who are employed in the temple service get their food from the temple, and those who serve at the altar share in what is sacrificed on the altar? 14 In the same way, the Lord commanded that those who proclaim the gospel should get their living by the gospel.

15 But I have made no use of any of these rights, nor am I writing this so that they may be applied in my case. Indeed, I would rather die than that—no one will deprive me of my ground for boasting! 16 If I proclaim the gospel, this gives me no ground for boasting, for an obligation is laid on me, and woe to me if I do not proclaim the gospel! 17 For if I do this of my own will, I have a reward; but if not of my own will, I am entrusted with a commission. 18 What then is my reward? Just this: that in my proclamation I may make the gospel free of charge, so as not to make full use of my rights in the gospel.

19 For though I am free with respect to all, I have made myself a slave to all, so that I might win more of them. 20 To the Jews I became as a Jew, in order to win Jews. To those under the law I became as one under the law (though I myself am not under the law) so that I might win those under the law. 21 To those

---

ὑμῶν τὰ σαρκικὰ θερίσομεν; **12** εἰ ἄλλοι
of you - fleshly things shall reap? If others

τῆς ὑμῶν ἐξουσίας μετέχουσιν, οὐ
⁵of the ⁶of you ²authority ¹have a share of, not

μᾶλλον ἡμεῖς; ἀλλ' οὐκ ἐχρησάμεθα
rather we? But we did not use

τῇ ἐξουσίᾳ ταύτῃ, ἀλλὰ πάντα στέγομεν
this authority, but ²all things ¹we put up with

ἵνα μή τινα ἐγκοπὴν δῶμεν τῷ εὐαγγελίῳ
lest ²anyone ³an obstacle ¹we should to the gospel
give

τοῦ Χριστοῦ. **13** Οὐκ οἴδατε ὅτι οἱ
- of Christ. Know ye not that the [ones]

τὰ ἱερὰ ἐργαζόμενοι τὰ ἐκ τοῦ ἱεροῦ
- ³sacred things ¹working [at] ⁴the things ⁵of ⁶the ⁷temple

ἐσθίουσιν, οἱ τῷ θυσιαστηρίῳ παρεδρεύοντες
²eat, the ³the ⁴altar ¹attending [on]
[ones]

τῷ θυσιαστηρίῳ συμμερίζονται; **14** οὕτως
⁵the ⁶altar ⁷partake with? So

καὶ ὁ κύριος διέταξεν τοῖς τὸ εὐαγγέλιον
also the Lord ordained the [ones] ²the ³gospel

καταγγέλλουσιν ἐκ τοῦ εὐαγγελίου ζῆν.
¹announcing ⁵of ⁶the ⁷gospel ⁴to live.

15 ἐγὼ δὲ οὐ κέχρημαι οὐδενὶ τούτων.
But I have not used not one of these
things.

Οὐκ ἔγραψα δὲ ταῦτα ἵνα οὕτως γένηται
And I did not write these in order so it might be
things that

ἐν ἐμοί· καλὸν γάρ μοι μᾶλλον ἀποθανεῖν
in me; for good [it is] to me rather to die

ἢ — τὸ καύχημά μου οὐδεὶς κενώσει.
than - the boast of me no man shall empty.

16 ἐὰν γὰρ εὐαγγελίζωμαι, οὐκ ἔστιν
For if I preach good news, there is not
= I have no boast;

μοι καύχημα· ἀνάγκη γάρ μοι ἐπίκειται·
to me boast;° for necessity ¹me ²is laid on;

οὐαὶ γάρ μοί ἐστιν ἐὰν μὴ εὐαγγελίσωμαι.
for woe ¹to me ¹is ²if I do not preach good tidings.

17 εἰ γὰρ ἑκὼν τοῦτο πράσσω, μισθὸν
For if willingly ²this ¹I do, ²a reward

ἔχω· εἰ δὲ ἄκων, οἰκονομίαν πεπίστευμαι.
¹I have; but if unwillingly, ²a stewardship ¹I have been
entrusted [with].

18 τίς οὖν μού ἐστιν ὁ μισθός; ἵνα
What therefore ⁴of me ¹is ²the ³reward? in order
that

εὐαγγελιζόμενος ἀδάπανον θήσω τὸ
preaching good tidings ⁴without charge ¹I may place ²the

εὐαγγέλιον, εἰς τὸ μὴ καταχρήσασθαι
³good tidings, so as† not to use to the full

τῇ ἐξουσίᾳ μου ἐν τῷ εὐαγγελίῳ.
the authority of me in the good tidings.

19 Ἐλεύθερος γὰρ ὢν ἐκ πάντων πᾶσιν
For ²free ¹being of all men ³to all men

ἐμαυτὸν ἐδούλωσα, ἵνα τοὺς πλείονας
¹myself ¹I enslaved, in order that the more

κερδήσω· **20** καὶ ἐγενόμην τοῖς Ἰουδαίοις
I might gain; and I became to the Jews

ὡς Ἰουδαῖος, ἵνα Ἰουδαίους κερδήσω·
as a Jew, in order that Jews I might gain;

τοῖς ὑπὸ νόμον ὡς ὑπὸ νόμον, μὴ ὢν
to the under law as under law, not being
ones

αὐτὸς ὑπὸ νόμον, ἵνα τοὺς ὑπὸ νόμον
[my]self under law, in order the under law
that ones

---

you, is it too much if we reap a material harvest from you? 12 If others have this right of support from you, shouldn't we have it all the more?

But we did not use this right. On the contrary, we put up with anything rather than hinder the gospel of Christ. 13 Don't you know that those who work in the temple get their food from the temple, and those who serve at the altar share in what is offered on the altar? 14 In the same way, the Lord has commanded that those who preach the gospel should receive their living from the gospel.

15 But I have not used any of these rights. And I am not writing this in the hope that you will do such things for me. I would rather die than have anyone deprive me of this boast. 16 Yet when I preach the gospel, I cannot boast, for I am compelled to preach. Woe to me if I do not preach the gospel! 17 If I preach voluntarily, I have a reward; if not voluntarily, I am simply discharging the trust committed to me. 18 What then is my reward? Just this: that in preaching the gospel I may offer it free of charge, and so not make use of my rights in preaching it.

19 Though I am free and belong to no man, I make myself a slave to everyone, to win as many as possible. 20 To the Jews I became like a Jew, to win the Jews. To those under the law I became like one under the law (though I myself am not under the law), so as to win those under the law. 21 To

outside the law I became as one outside the law (though I am not free from God's law but am under Christ's law) so that I might win those outside the law. 22 To the weak I became weak, so that I might win the weak. I have become all things to all people, that I might by all means save some. 23 I do it all for the sake of the gospel, so that I may share in its blessings.

24 Do you not know that in a race the runners all compete, but only one receives the prize? Run in such a way that you may win it. 25 Athletes exercise self-control in all things; they do it to receive a perishable wreath, but we an imperishable one. 26 So I do not run aimlessly, nor do I box as though beating the air; 27 but I punish my body and enslave it, so that after proclaiming to others I myself should not be disqualified.

κερδήσω·	**21** τοῖς	ἀνόμοις	ὡς	ἄνομος,
I might gain;	to the ones	without law	as	without law,

μὴ	ὢν	ἄνομος	θεοῦ	ἀλλ'	ἔννομος	Χριστοῦ,
not	being	without [the] law	of God	but	under [the] law	of Christ,

ἵνα	κερδάνω	τοὺς	ἀνόμους·	**22** ἐγενόμην
in order that	I may gain	the ones	without law;	I became

τοῖς	ἀσθενέσιν	ἀσθενής,	ἵνα	τοὺς	ἀσθενεῖς
²to the	³weak	¹weak,	in order that	the	weak

κερδήσω·	τοῖς	πᾶσιν	γέγονα	πάντα,	ἵνα
I might gain;	–	to all men	I have become	all things,	in order that

πάντως	τινὰς	σώσω.	**23** πάντα	δὲ	ποιῶ
in any case	²some	¹I might save.	But all things		I do

διὰ	τὸ	εὐαγγέλιον,	ἵνα	συγκοινωνὸς	αὐτοῦ
because of	the	good tidings,	in order that	²a joint partaker	³of it

γένωμαι.	**24** Οὐκ	οἴδατε	ὅτι	οἱ	ἐν
¹I may become.		Know ye not	that	the [ones]	²in

σταδίῳ	τρέχοντες	πάντες	μὲν	τρέχουσιν,
³a racecourse	¹running	all	indeed	run,

εἷς	δὲ	λαμβάνει	τὸ	βραβεῖον;	οὕτως
but one		receives	the	prize?	So

τρέχετε	ἵνα	καταλάβητε.	**25** πᾶς	δὲ	ὁ
run	in order that	ye may obtain.		And everyone	

ἀγωνιζόμενος	πάντα	ἐγκρατεύεται,	ἐκεῖνοι
struggling	[in] all things	exercises self-control,	those

μὲν	οὖν	ἵνα	φθαρτὸν	στέφανον	λάβωσιν,
indeed	there-fore	in order that	²a corruptible	³crown	¹they may receive,

ἡμεῖς	δὲ	ἄφθαρτον.	**26** ἐγὼ	τοίνυν	οὕτως
but we		an incorruptible.	I	accordingly	so

τρέχω	ὡς	οὐκ	ἀδήλως,	οὕτως	πυκτεύω
run	as	not	unclearly,	so	I box

ὡς	οὐκ	ἀέρα	δέρων·	**27** ἀλλὰ	ὑπωπιάζω
as	not	²air	¹beating;	but	I treat severely

μου	τὸ	σῶμα	καὶ	δουλαγωγῶ,	μή	πως
of me	the	body	and	lead [it] as a slave,	lest	

ἄλλοις	κηρύξας	αὐτὸς	ἀδόκιμος	γένωμαι.
to others	having proclaimed	²[my]self	⁵disapproved	¹I ³may ⁴become.

---

those not having the law I became like one not having the law (though I am not free from God's law but am under Christ's law), so as to win those not having the law. 22 To the weak I became weak, to win the weak. I have become all things to all men so that by all possible means I might save some. 23 I do all this for the sake of the gospel, that I may share in its blessings.

24 Do you not know that in a race all the runners run, but only one gets the prize? Run in such a way as to get the prize. 25 Everyone who competes in the games goes into strict training. They do it to get a crown that will not last; but we do it to get a crown that will last forever. 26 Therefore I do not run like a man running aimlessly; I do not fight like a man beating the air. 27 No, I beat my body and make it my slave so that after I have preached to others, I myself will not be disqualified for the prize.

Chapter 10

Warnings from Israel's History

I do not want you to be unaware, brothers and sisters, [m] that our ancestors were all under the cloud, and all passed through the sea, 2 and all were baptized into Moses in the cloud and in the sea, 3 and all ate the same spiritual food, 4 and all drank the same spiritual drink. For they drank from the spiritual rock that followed them, and the rock was Christ. 5 Nevertheless, God was not pleased with most of them, and they were struck down in the wilderness.

---

10 Οὐ	θέλω	γὰρ	ὑμᾶς	ἀγνοεῖν,	ἀδελφοί,
For I wish not			you	to be ignorant,	brothers,

ὅτι	οἱ	πατέρες	ἡμῶν	πάντες	ὑπὸ	τὴν
that	the	fathers	of us	all	under	the

νεφέλην	ἦσαν	καὶ	πάντες	διὰ	τῆς	θαλάσσης
cloud	were	and	all	through	the	sea

διῆλθον,	**2** καὶ	πάντες	εἰς	τὸν	Μωϋσῆν
passed *through*,	and	all	²to	–	³Moses

ἐβαπτίσαντο	ἐν	τῇ	νεφέλῃ	καὶ	ἐν	τῇ
¹were baptized	in	the	cloud	and	in	the

θαλάσσῃ,	**3** καὶ	πάντες	τὸ	αὐτὸ	πνευματικὸν
sea,	and	all	²the	³same	⁴spiritual

βρῶμα,	ἔφαγον,	**4** καὶ	πάντες	τὸ	αὐτὸ
⁵food	¹ate,	and	all	²the	³same

πνευματικὸν	ἔπιον	πόμα·	ἔπινον	γὰρ	ἐκ
⁴spiritual	¹drank	⁵drink;	for they drank		of

πνευματικῆς	ἀκολουθούσης	πέτρας,	ἡ	πέτρα
a spiritual	²following	¹rock,	²the	³rock

δὲ	ἦν	ὁ	Χριστός.	**5** Ἀλλ'	οὐκ	ἐν	τοῖς
¹and was		the	Christ.	But	⁷not	¹in(with)	²the

πλείοσιν	αὐτῶν	εὐδόκησεν	ὁ	θεός·
³majority	⁴of them	⁶was ⁸well ⁹pleased	–	⁵God;

κατεστρώθησαν	γὰρ	ἐν	τῇ	ἐρήμῳ.
for they were scattered		in	the	desert.

Chapter 10

Warnings From Israel's History

FOR I do not want you to be ignorant of the fact, brothers, that our forefathers were all under the cloud and that they all passed through the sea. 2 They were all baptized into Moses in the cloud and in the sea. 3 They all ate the same spiritual food 4 and drank the same spiritual drink; for they drank from the spiritual rock that accompanied them, and that rock was Christ. 5 Nevertheless, God was not pleased with most of them; their bodies were scattered over the desert.

---

[m] Gk *brothers*

6 Now these things occurred as examples for us, so that we might not desire evil as they did. 7 Do not become idolaters as some of them did; as it is written, "The people sat down to eat and drink, and they rose up to play." 8 We must not indulge in sexual immorality as some of them did, and twenty-three thousand fell in a single day. 9 We must not put Christ [n] to the test, as some of them did, and were destroyed by serpents. 10 And do not complain as some of them did, and were destroyed by the destroyer. 11 These things happened to them to serve as an example, and they were written down to instruct us, on whom the ends of the ages have come. 12 So if you think you are standing, watch out that you do not fall. 13 No testing has overtaken you that is not common to everyone. God is faithful, and he will not let you be tested beyond your strength, but with the testing he will also provide the way out so that you may be able to endure it.

14 Therefore, my dear friends, [o] flee from the worship of idols. 15 I speak as to sensible people; judge for yourselves what I say. 16 The cup of blessing that we bless, is it not a sharing in the blood of Christ? The bread that we break, is it not a sharing in the body of Christ? 17 Because there is one bread, we who are many are one body, for we

---

6 ταῦτα δὲ τύποι ἡμῶν ἐγενήθησαν, εἰς
Now these things types of us were, for

τὸ μὴ εἶναι ἡμᾶς ἐπιθυμητὰς κακῶν,
the not to be us[b] longers after evil things,
=so that we should not be . . .

καθὼς κἀκεῖνοι ἐπεθύμησαν. **7** μηδὲ
as those indeed longed. Neither

εἰδωλολάτραι γίνεσθε, καθώς τινες αὐτῶν·
idolaters be ye, as some of them;

ὥσπερ γέγραπται· ἐκάθισεν ὁ λαὸς φαγεῖν
as it has been written: Sat the people to eat

καὶ πεῖν, καὶ ἀνέστησαν παίζειν. **8** μηδὲ
and to drink, and stood up to play. Neither

πορνεύωμεν, καθώς τινες αὐτῶν ἐπόρνευσαν
let us commit as some of them committed
fornication, fornication

καὶ ἔπεσαν μιᾷ ἡμέρᾳ εἴκοσι τρεῖς
and fell in one day twenty-three

χιλιάδες. **9** μηδὲ ἐκπειράζωμεν τὸν κύριον,
thousands. Neither let us overtempt the Lord,

καθώς τινες αὐτῶν ἐπείρασαν καὶ ὑπὸ
as some of them tempted and by

τῶν ὄφεων ἀπώλλυντο. **10** μηδὲ γογγύζετε,
the serpents were destroyed. Neither murmur ye,

καθάπερ τινὲς αὐτῶν ἐγόγγυσαν, καὶ
even as some of them murmured, and

ἀπώλοντο ὑπὸ τοῦ ὀλεθρευτοῦ. **11** ταῦτα δὲ
were destroyed by the destroyer. Now these things

τυπικῶς συνέβαινεν ἐκείνοις, ἐγράφη δὲ
³typically ¹happened ²to those men, and was(were)
written

πρὸς νουθεσίαν ἡμῶν, εἰς οὓς τὰ
for admonition of us, to whom the

τέλη τῶν αἰώνων κατήντηκεν. **12** Ὥστε
ends of the ages has(ve) arrived. So as

ὁ δοκῶν ἑστάναι βλεπέτω μὴ πέσῃ.
the thinking to stand let him look lest he falls.
[one]

13 πειρασμὸς ὑμᾶς οὐκ εἴληφεν εἰ μὴ
Temptation you has not taken except

ἀνθρώπινος· πιστὸς δὲ ὁ θεός, ὃς οὐκ
[what is] human; but faithful [is] - God, who not

ἐάσει ὑμᾶς πειρασθῆναι ὑπὲρ ὃ δύνασθε,
will allow you to be tempted beyond what you are able
[to bear],

ἀλλὰ ποιήσει σὺν τῷ πειρασμῷ καὶ τὴν
but will make with the temptation also the

ἔκβασιν τοῦ δύνασθαι ὑπενεγκεῖν.
way out to be able to endure.[d]
=so that ye may be able . . .

14 Διόπερ, ἀγαπητοί μου, φεύγετε ἀπὸ
Wherefore, beloved of me, flee ye from

τῆς εἰδωλολατρίας. **15** ὡς φρονίμοις λέγω·
- idolatry. ¹As ²to prudent men ¹I say;

κρίνατε ὑμεῖς ὅ φημι. **16** Τὸ ποτήριον
judge ye what I say. The cup

τῆς εὐλογίας ὅ εὐλογοῦμεν, οὐχὶ κοινωνία
- of blessing which we bless, ²not ³a communion

ἐστὶν τοῦ αἵματος τοῦ Χριστοῦ; τὸν
¹is it of the blood - of Christ? the

ἄρτον ὃν κλῶμεν, οὐχὶ κοινωνία τοῦ
bread which we break, ²not ³a communion ⁴of the

σώματος τοῦ Χριστοῦ ἐστιν; **17** ὅτι εἰς
⁵body - ⁶of Christ ¹is it? Because ⁴one

ἄρτος, ἓν σῶμα οἱ πολλοί ἐσμεν· οἱ γὰρ
⁵bread, ⁶one ⁷body ²the ³many ¹we are; - for

---

6 Now these things occurred as examples [u] to keep us from setting our hearts on evil things as they did. 7 Do not be idolaters, as some of them were; as it is written: "The people sat down to eat and drink and got up to indulge in pagan revelry." [v] 8 We should not commit sexual immorality, as some of them did—and in one day twenty-three thousand of them died. 9 We should not test the Lord, as some of them did —and were killed by snakes. 10 And do not grumble, as some of them did— and were killed by the destroying angel.

11 These things happened to them as examples and were written down as warnings for us, on whom the fulfillment of the ages has come. 12 So, if you think you are standing firm, be careful that you don't fall! 13 No temptation has seized you except what is common to man. And God is faithful; he will not let you be tempted beyond what you can bear. But when you are tempted, he will also provide a way out so that you can stand up under it.

Idol Feasts and the Lord's Supper

14 Therefore, my dear friends, flee from idolatry. 15 I speak to sensible people; judge for yourselves what I say. 16 Is not the cup of thanksgiving for which we give thanks a participation in the blood of Christ? And is not the bread that we break a participation in the body of Christ? 17 Because there is one loaf, we, who are many, are one

---

[n] Other ancient authorities read *the Lord*

[o] Gk *my beloved*

[u] 6 Or *types*; also in verse 11

[v] 7 Exodus 32:6

all partake of the one bread. 18 Consider the people of Israel; *p* are not those who eat the sacrifices partners in the altar? 19 What do I imply then? That food sacrificed to idols is anything, or that an idol is anything? 20 No, I imply that what pagans sacrifice, they sacrifice to demons and not to God. I do not want you to be partners with demons. 21 You cannot drink the cup of the Lord and the cup of demons. You cannot partake of the table of the Lord and the table of demons. 22 Or are we provoking the Lord to jealousy? Are we stronger than he?

Do All to the Glory of God

23 "All things are lawful," but not all things are beneficial. "All things are lawful," but not all things build up. 24 Do not seek your own advantage, but that of the other. 25 Eat whatever is sold in the meat market without raising any question on the ground of conscience, 26 for "the earth and its fullness are the Lord's." 27 If an unbeliever invites you to a meal and you are disposed to go, eat whatever is set before you without raising any question on the ground of conscience. 28 But if someone says to you, "This has been offered in sacrifice," then do not eat it, out of consideration for the one who informed you, and for the sake of conscience— 29 I mean the other's conscience, not your own. For why should my liberty be subject to the judgment of someone else's conscience? 30 If I partake with thankfulness, why should I

πάντες ἐκ τοῦ ἑνὸς ἄρτου μετέχομεν.
all   of   the   one   bread   we partake.

18 βλέπετε τὸν Ἰσραὴλ κατὰ σάρκα·
See ye   the   Israel   according to [the] flesh;

οὐχ οἱ ἐσθίοντες τὰς θυσίας κοινωνοὶ
²not ³the [ones] ⁴eating ⁵the ⁶sacrifices ⁷sharers

τοῦ θυσιαστηρίου εἰσίν; 19 τί οὖν φημι;
⁸of the ⁹altar ¹are? What there- do I say?
                                 fore

ὅτι εἰδωλόθυτόν τι ἐστιν; ἢ ὅτι εἴδωλόν
that an idolatrous ²anything ¹is? or that an idol
       sacrifice

τί ἐστιν; 20 ἀλλ' ὅτι ἃ θύουσιν,
²anything ¹is? but that [the] things they
                        which sacrifice,

δαιμονίοις καὶ οὐ θεῷ θύουσιν· οὐ θέλω
to demons and not to God they sacrifice; ²not ¹I wish

δὲ ὑμᾶς κοινωνοὺς τῶν δαιμονίων γίνεσθαι.
¹and you sharers of the demons to become.

21 οὐ δύνασθε ποτήριον κυρίου πίνειν
Ye cannot ²a cup ³of [the] Lord ¹to drink

καὶ ποτήριον δαιμονίων· οὐ δύνασθε
and a cup of demons; ye cannot

τραπέζης κυρίου μετέχειν καὶ τραπέζης
²of a table ³of [the] Lord ¹to partake and of a table

δαιμονίων. 22 ἢ παραζηλοῦμεν τὸν κύριον;
of demons. Or do we make jealous the Lord?

μὴ ἰσχυρότεροι αὐτοῦ ἐσμεν;
Not ²stronger [than] ³he ¹are we?

23 Πάντα ἔξεστιν, ἀλλ' οὐ πάντα
All things [are] lawful, but not all things

συμφέρει· πάντα ἔξεστιν, ἀλλ' οὐ πάντα
are] expedient; all things lawful, but not all things
                                        [are]

οἰκοδομεῖ. 24 μηδεὶς τὸ ἑαυτοῦ ζητείτω
edifies(fy). No one the thing of himself let him seek

ἀλλὰ τὸ τοῦ ἑτέρου. 25 Πᾶν τὸ ἐν
but the thing of the other. Everything ²in

μακέλλω πωλούμενον ἐσθίετε μηδὲν
¹a meat market ¹being sold eat ye ²nothing

ἀνακρίνοντες διὰ τὴν συνείδησιν· 26 τοῦ
¹examining because of – conscience; ³of the

κυρίου γὰρ ἡ γῆ καὶ τὸ πλήρωμα
³Lord ¹for the earth and the fulness

αὐτῆς. 27 εἴ τις καλεῖ ὑμᾶς τῶν ἀπίστων
of it. If anyone invites you of the unbelievers

καὶ θέλετε πορεύεσθαι, πᾶν τὸ παρατι-
and ye wish to go, ²everything ³being set

θέμενον ὑμῖν ἐσθίετε μηδὲν ἀνακρίνοντες
before ⁴you ¹eat ⁶nothing ⁵examining

διὰ τὴν συνείδησιν. 28 ἐὰν δέ τις ὑμῖν
because – conscience. But if anyone ²to you
of

εἴπῃ· τοῦτο ἱερόθυτόν ἐστιν, μὴ ἐσθίετε
¹says: This ²slain in sacrifice ³is, do not eat

δι' ἐκεῖνον τὸν μηνύσαντα καὶ τὴν
because that the pointing out and –
of man [one]

συνείδησιν· 29 συνείδησιν δὲ λέγω οὐχὶ
conscience: ²conscience ¹but ³I say not

τὴν ἑαυτοῦ ἀλλὰ τὴν τοῦ ἑτέρου.* ἱνατί
the one of himself but the one of the other.* why

γὰρ ἡ ἐλευθερία μου κρίνεται ὑπὸ ἄλλης
For the freedom of me is judged by ²of another

συνειδήσεως; 30 εἰ ἐγὼ χάριτι μετέχω,
¹conscience? If I by grace partake,

body, for we all partake of the one loaf.
18 Consider the people of Israel: Do not those who eat the sacrifices participate in the altar? 19 Do I mean then that a sacrifice offered to an idol is anything, or that an idol is anything? 20 No, but the sacrifices of pagans are offered to demons, not to God, and I do not want you to be participants with demons. 21 You cannot drink the cup of the Lord and the cup of demons too; you cannot have a part in both the Lord's table and the table of demons. 22 Are we trying to arouse the Lord's jealousy? Are we stronger than he?

The Believer's Freedom

23 "Everything is permissible"—but not everything is beneficial. "Everything is permissible"—but not everything is constructive. 24 Nobody should seek his own good, but the good of others. 25 Eat anything sold in the meat market without raising questions of conscience, 26 for, "The earth is the Lord's, and everything in it." *w* 27 If some unbeliever invites you to a meal and you want to go, eat whatever is put before you without raising questions of conscience. 28 But if anyone says to you, "This has been offered in sacrifice," then do not eat it, both for the sake of the man who told you and for conscience' sake *x*—29 the other man's conscience, I mean, yours. For why should my freedom be judged by another's conscience? 30 If I take part in the meal with

---

* That is, not the conscience of the person invited, to whom the apostle's words are addressed, but the conscience of the person " pointing out."

p Gk Israel according to the flesh

w 26 Psalm 24:1
x 28 Some manuscripts *conscience' sake, for "the earth is the Lord's and everything in it"*

be denounced because of that for which I give thanks?

31 So, whether you eat or drink, or whatever you do, do everything for the glory of God. 32 Give no offense to Jews or to Greeks or to the church of God, 33 just as I try to please everyone in everything I do, not seeking my own advantage, but that of many, so that they may be saved. 1 Be imitators of me, as I am of Christ.

Head Coverings

2 I commend you because you remember me in everything and maintain the traditions just as I handed them on to you. 3 But I want you to understand that Christ is the head of every man, and the husband*q* is the head of his wife,*r* and God is the head of Christ. 4 Any man who prays or prophesies with something on his head disgraces his head, 5 but any woman who prays or prophesies with her head unveiled disgraces her head—it is one and the same thing as having her head shaved. 6 For if a woman will not veil herself, then she should cut off her hair; but if it is disgraceful for a woman to have her hair cut off or to be shaved, she should wear a veil. 7 For a man ought not to have his head veiled, since he is the image and reflection*s* of God; but woman is the reflection*s* of man. 8 Indeed, man was not made from woman, but woman from man. 9 Neither was man created for the sake of

---

τί βλασφημοῦμαι ὑπὲρ οὗ ἐγὼ εὐχαριστῶ;
why   am I evil   because   what   I   give thanks
      spoken of   of   [for]?

31 Εἴτε   οὖν   ἐσθίετε   εἴτε   πίνετε   εἴτε
   Whether therefore ye eat   or   ye drink   or
τι   ποιεῖτε,   πάντα   εἰς   δόξαν   θεοῦ   ποιεῖτε.
what ye do,   all things to [the] glory of God do ye.
[ever]

32 ἀπρόσκοποι   καὶ   Ἰουδαίοις   γίνεσθε   καὶ
   ²Without offence ³both   ⁴to Jews   ¹be ye   ⁵and
Ἕλλησιν   καὶ   τῇ   ἐκκλησίᾳ   τοῦ   θεοῦ,
⁶to Greeks and to the church   -   of God,

33 καθὼς   κἀγὼ   πάντα   πᾶσιν   ἀρέσκω,
   as   I also [in] all things all men please,
μὴ   ζητῶν   τὸ   ἐμαυτοῦ   σύμφορον   ἀλλὰ
not seeking the of myself   advantage   but

τὸ   τῶν   πολλῶν,   ἵνα   σωθῶσιν.   11 μιμηταί
the of the many,   in order that may be saved.   Imitators
(that)   that

μου   γίνεσθε,   καθὼς   κἀγὼ   Χριστοῦ.
of me be ye,   as   I also [am] of Christ.

2 Ἐπαινῶ   δὲ   ὑμᾶς   ὅτι   πάντα   μου
  But I praise   you   because ²all things ¹of me
μέμνησθε   καὶ   καθὼς   παρέδωκα   ὑμῖν   τὰς
¹ye have   and   ⁴as   ⁵I delivered ⁶to you ³the
remembered
παραδόσεις   κατέχετε.   3 Θέλω   δὲ   ὑμᾶς
²traditions   ¹ye hold fast.   But I wish   you
εἰδέναι   ὅτι   παντὸς   ἀνδρὸς   ἡ   κεφαλὴ   ὁ
to know that   ⁵of every   ⁶man   ³the ⁴head   -
Χριστός   ἐστιν,   κεφαλὴ   δὲ   γυναικὸς   ὁ
¹Christ   ²is,   and [the] head   of a woman   the
ἀνήρ,   κεφαλὴ   δὲ   τοῦ   Χριστοῦ   ὁ   θεός.
man,   and [the] head   -   of Christ   -   God.

4 πᾶς   ἀνὴρ   προσευχόμενος   ἢ   προφητεύων
  Every   man   praying   or   prophesying
κατὰ   κεφαλῆς   ἔχων   καταισχύνει   τὴν
³down over ⁴[his] head ¹having   shames   the
²[anything]
κεφαλὴν   αὐτοῦ.   5 πᾶσα   δὲ   γυνὴ   προσ-
head   of him.   But every   woman   pray-
ευχομένη   ἢ   προφητεύουσα   ἀκατακαλύπτῳ
ing   or   prophesying   ³unveiled
τῇ   κεφαλῇ   καταισχύνει   τὴν   κεφαλὴν   αὐτῆς·
¹with ²head   shames   the   head   of her;
the(her)
ἐν   γάρ   ἐστιν   καὶ   τὸ   αὐτὸ   τῇ   ἐξυρημένῃ.
for ²one ¹it is   and   the   same with the having been
                      thing   woman   shaved.
6 εἰ   γὰρ   οὐ   κατακαλύπτεται   γυνή,   καὶ
  For if   ²is not veiled   ¹a woman,   also
κειράσθω·   εἰ   δὲ   αἰσχρὸν   γυναικὶ   τὸ
let her be shorn; but if   shameful   for a woman   -
κείρασθαι   ἢ   ξυρᾶσθαι,   κατακαλυπτέσθω.
to be shorn   or   to be shaved,   let her be veiled.
7 ἀνὴρ   μὲν   γὰρ   οὐκ   ὀφείλει   κατα-
  For a man indeed   ought not   to be
καλύπτεσθαι   τὴν   κεφαλήν,   εἰκὼν   καὶ   δόξα
veiled   the   head,*b*   ²[the] image ³and ⁴glory
θεοῦ   ὑπάρχων·   ἡ   γυνὴ   δὲ   δόξα   ἀνδρός
⁵of God   ¹being·   but the woman   ²[the] glory ³of a man
ἐστιν.   8 οὐ   γάρ   ἐστιν   ἀνὴρ   ἐκ   γυναικός,
¹is.   For ²not   ²is   ¹man   of   woman,
ἀλλὰ   γυνὴ   ἐξ   ἀνδρός·   9 καὶ   γὰρ   οὐκ
but   woman   of   man;   for indeed   ³not

---

thankfulness, why am I denounced because of something I thank God for?

31 So whether you eat or drink or whatever you do, do it all for the glory of God. 32 Do not cause anyone to stumble, whether Jews, Greeks or the church of God— 33 even as I try to please everybody in every way. For I am not seeking my own good but the good of many, so that they may be saved. 1 Follow my example, as I follow the example of Christ.

Propriety in Worship

2 I praise you for remembering me in everything and for holding to the teachings,*y* just as I passed them on to you.

3 Now I want you to realize that the head of every man is Christ, and the head of the woman is man, and the head of Christ is God. 4 Every man who prays or prophesies with his head covered dishonors his head. 5 And every woman who prays or prophesies with her head uncovered dishonors her head—it is just as though her head were shaved. 6 If a woman does not cover her head, she should have her hair cut off; and if it is a disgrace for a woman to have her hair cut or shaved off, she should cover her head. 7 A man ought not to cover his head,*z* since he is the image and glory of God; but the woman is the glory of man. 8 For man did not come from woman, but woman from man; 9 neither was man created for wom-

---

q The same Greek word means man or husband
r Or head of the woman
s Or glory

y 2 Or traditions
z 4-7 Or 4Every man who prays or prophesies with long hair dishonors his head. 5And every woman who prays or prophesies with no covering of hair on her head dishonors her head—she is just like one of the "shorn women." 6If a woman has no covering, let her be for now with short hair, but since it is a disgrace for a woman to have her hair shorn or shaved, she should grow it again. 7A man ought not to have long hair

woman, but woman for the sake of man. 10 For this reason a woman ought to have a symbol of¹ authority on her head, ᵘ because of the angels. 11 Nevertheless, in the Lord woman is not independent of man or man independent of woman. 12 For just as woman came from man, so man comes through woman; but all things come from God. 13 Judge for yourselves: is it proper for a woman to pray to God with her head unveiled? 14 Does not nature itself teach you that if a man wears long hair, it is degrading to him, 15 but if a woman has long hair, it is her glory? For her hair is given to her for a covering. 16 But if anyone is disposed to be contentious—we have no such custom, nor do the churches of God.

Abuses at the Lord's Supper

17 Now in the following instructions I do not commend you, because when you come together it is not for the better but for the worse. 18 For, to begin with, when you come together as a church, I hear that there are divisions among you; and to some extent I believe it. 19 Indeed, there have to be factions among you, for only so will it become clear who among you are genuine. 20 When you come together, it is not really to eat the Lord's supper. 21 For when the time comes to eat, each of you goes ahead with your own supper, and one goes hungry and another

---

ἐκτίσθη ἀνὴρ διὰ τὴν γυναῖκα, ἀλλὰ
²was ⁴created ¹man because of the woman, but

γυνὴ διὰ τὸν ἄνδρα. 10 διὰ τοῦτο
woman because of the man. Therefore

ὀφείλει ἡ γυνὴ ἐξουσίαν ἔχειν ἐπὶ τῆς
ought the woman authority to have on the

κεφαλῆς διὰ τοὺς ἀγγέλους. 11 πλὴν
head because of the angels. Nevertheless

οὔτε γυνὴ χωρὶς ἀνδρὸς οὔτε ἀνὴρ χωρὶς
neither woman without man nor man without

γυναικὸς ἐν κυρίῳ· 12 ὥσπερ γὰρ ἡ
woman in [the] Lord; for as the

γυνὴ ἐκ τοῦ ἀνδρός, οὕτως καὶ ὁ ἀνὴρ
woman of the man, so also the man

διὰ τῆς γυναικός· τὰ δὲ πάντα ἐκ τοῦ
through the woman; – but all things of –

θεοῦ. 13 Ἐν ὑμῖν αὐτοῖς κρίνατε· πρέπον
God. Among you [your]selves judge: ²fitting

ἐστιν γυναῖκα ἀκατακάλυπτον τῷ θεῷ
¹is it ²[for] ⁴a woman ⁷unveiled – ⁶to God

προσεύχεσθαι; 14 οὐδὲ ἡ φύσις αὐτὴ
⁵to pray? Not – nature [her]self

διδάσκει ὑμᾶς ὅτι ἀνὴρ μὲν ἐὰν κομᾷ,
teaches you that a man indeed if he wears his hair long,

ἀτιμία αὐτῷ ἐστιν, 15 γυνὴ δὲ ἐὰν
²a dishonour ³to him ¹it is, but a woman if

κομᾷ, δόξα αὐτῇ ἐστιν· ὅτι ἡ κόμη
she wears ³a glory ⁴to her ¹it is? because the long hair
her hair long,

ἀντὶ περιβολαίου δέδοται αὐτῇ. 16 Εἰ
instead of a veil has been given to her. if

δέ τις δοκεῖ φιλόνεικος εἶναι, ἡμεῖς
But anyone thinks ²contentious ¹to be, we

τοιαύτην συνήθειαν οὐκ ἔχομεν, οὐδὲ αἱ
²such ³a custom ¹have not, neither the

ἐκκλησίαι τοῦ θεοῦ.
churches – of God.

17 Τοῦτο δὲ παραγγέλλων οὐκ ἐπαινῶ
But this charging I do not praise

ὅτι οὐκ εἰς τὸ κρεῖσσον ἀλλὰ εἰς τὸ
because not for the better but for the

ἧσσον συνέρχεσθε. 18 πρῶτον μὲν γὰρ
worse ye come together. For firstly indeed

συνερχομένων ὑμῶν ἐν ἐκκλησίᾳ ἀκούω
coming together youᵃ in church I hear
=when ye come together

σχίσματα ἐν ὑμῖν ὑπάρχειν, καὶ μέρος
divisions among you to be, and ²part

τι πιστεύω. 19 δεῖ γὰρ καὶ αἱρέσεις
¹some I believe. For it behoves indeed sects

ἐν ὑμῖν εἶναι, ἵνα [καὶ] οἱ δόκιμοι
among you to be, in order also the approved
that ones

φανεροὶ γένωνται ἐν ὑμῖν. 20 Συν-
manifest may become among you. Coming

ερχομένων οὖν ὑμῶν ἐπὶ τὸ αὐτὸ οὐκ
together therefore youᵃ together not
=When therefore ye come

ἔστιν κυριακὸν δεῖπνον φαγεῖν· 21 ἕκαστος
it is of the Lord* a supper to eat; ²each one

γὰρ τὸ ἴδιον δεῖπνον προλαμβάνει ἐν
¹for the(his) own supper takes before in

τῷ φαγεῖν, καὶ ὃς μὲν πεινᾷ, ὃς δὲ
– to eat(eating), and one† hungers, another†

---

an, but woman for man. 10 For this reason, and because of the angels, the woman ought to have a sign of authority on her head. 11 In the Lord, however, woman is not independent of man, nor is man independent of woman. 12 For as woman came from man, so also man is born of woman. But everything comes from God. 13 Judge for yourselves: Is it proper for a woman to pray to God with her head uncovered? 14 Does not the very nature of things teach you that if a man has long hair, it is a disgrace to him, 15 but that if a woman has long hair, it is her glory? For long hair is given to her as a covering. 16 If anyone wants to be contentious about this, we have no other practice—nor do the churches of God.

The Lord's Supper

17 In the following directives I have no praise for you, for your meetings do more harm than good. 18 In the first place, I hear that when you come together as a church, there are divisions among you, and to some extent I believe it. 19 No doubt there have to be differences among you to show which of you have God's approval. 20 When you come together, it is not the Lord's Supper you eat, 21 for as you eat, each of you goes ahead without waiting for anybody else. One remains hungry, an-

---

¹ Gk lacks *a symbol of*
ᵘ Or *have freedom of choice regarding her head*

* Note that κυριακός is an adjective, for which no exact English equivalent is available. Only other occurrence in N.T., Rev. 1. 10.

becomes drunk. 22 What! Do you not have homes to eat and drink in? Or do you show contempt for the church of God and humiliate those who have nothing? What should I say to you? Should I commend you? In this matter I do not commend you!

The Institution of the Lord's Supper

23 For I received from the Lord what I also handed on to you, that the Lord Jesus on the night when he was betrayed took a loaf of bread, 24 and when he had given thanks, he broke it and said, "This is my body that is for[v] you. Do this in remembrance of me." 25 In the same way he took the cup also, after supper, saying, "This cup is the new covenant in my blood. Do this, as often as you drink it, in remembrance of me." 26 For as often as you eat this bread and drink the cup, you proclaim the Lord's death until he comes.

Partaking of the Supper Unworthily

27 Whoever, therefore, eats the bread or drinks the cup of the Lord in an unworthy manner will be answerable for the body and blood of the Lord. 28 Examine yourselves, and only then eat of the bread and drink of the cup. 29 For all who eat and drink[w] without discerning the body,[x] eat and drink judgment against themselves. 30 For this reason many of you are weak and ill, and some have died.[y] 31 But if we judged ourselves, we would not be judged. 32 But when we are judged by the Lord, we are disciplined[z] so that we may not be condemned

---

μεθύει. 22 μὴ γὰρ οἰκίας οὐκ ἔχετε
is drunken. *Not* indeed ²houses ¹have ye not

εἰς τὸ ἐσθίειν καὶ πίνειν; ἢ τῆς ἐκκλησίας
- - to eat and to drink? or the church

τοῦ θεοῦ καταφρονεῖτε, καὶ καταισχύνετε
- of God despise ye, and shame

τοὺς μὴ ἔχοντας; τί εἴπω ὑμῖν; ἐπαινέσω
the not having? What may I say to you? shall I praise
[ones]

ὑμᾶς; ἐν τούτῳ οὐκ ἐπαινῶ. 23 Ἐγὼ
you? In this I praise not. I

γὰρ παρέλαβον ἀπὸ τοῦ κυρίου, ὃ καὶ
For received from the Lord, what also

παρέδωκα ὑμῖν, ὅτι ὁ κύριος Ἰησοῦς
I delivered to you, that the Lord Jesus

ἐν τῇ νυκτὶ ᾗ παρεδίδοτο ἔλαβεν ἄρτον
in the night in which he was took bread
betrayed

24 καὶ εὐχαριστήσας ἔκλασεν καὶ εἶπεν·
and having given thanks broke and said:

τοῦτό μού ἐστιν τὸ σῶμα τὸ ὑπὲρ
This of me is the body - on behalf of

ὑμῶν· τοῦτο ποιεῖτε εἰς τὴν ἐμὴν
you; this do ye for - my

ἀνάμνησιν. 25 ὡσαύτως καὶ τὸ ποτήριον
remembrance. Similarly also the cup

μετὰ τὸ δειπνῆσαι, λέγων· τοῦτο τὸ
after the to sup, saying: This -

ποτήριον ἡ καινὴ διαθήκη ἐστὶν ἐν τῷ
cup ²the ¹new ²covenant ¹is in -

ἐμῷ αἵματι· τοῦτο ποιεῖτε, ὁσάκις ἐὰν
my blood; this do ye, as often as

πίνητε, εἰς τὴν ἐμὴν ἀνάμνησιν. 26 ὁσάκις
ye drink, for - my remembrance. as often

γὰρ ἐὰν ἐσθίητε τὸν ἄρτον τοῦτον καὶ
For - ye eat the bread this and

τὸ ποτήριον πίνητε, τὸν θάνατον τοῦ
²the ²cup ¹drink, the death of the

κυρίου καταγγέλλετε, ἄχρι οὗ ἔλθῃ.
Lord ye declare, until he comes.

27 Ὥστε ὃς ἂν ἐσθίῃ τὸν ἄρτον ἢ
So as whoever eats the bread or

πίνῃ τὸ ποτήριον τοῦ κυρίου ἀναξίως,
drinks the cup of the Lord unworthily,

ἔνοχος ἔσται τοῦ σώματος καὶ τοῦ
guilty will be of the body and of the

αἵματος τοῦ κυρίου. 28 δοκιμαζέτω δὲ
blood of the Lord. But ¹let ²prove

ἄνθρωπος ἑαυτόν, καὶ οὕτως ἐκ τοῦ
²a man ⁴himself, and so of the

ἄρτου ἐσθιέτω καὶ ἐκ τοῦ ποτηρίου
bread let him eat and of the cup

πινέτω· 29 ὁ γὰρ ἐσθίων καὶ πίνων
let him drink; for the [one] eating and drinking

κρίμα ἑαυτῷ ἐσθίει καὶ πίνει μὴ διακρίνων
⁴judgment ⁵to ¹eats ²and ³drinks not discerning
himself

τὸ σῶμα. 30 διὰ τοῦτο ἐν ὑμῖν πολλοὶ
the body. Therefore among you many

ἀσθενεῖς καὶ ἄρρωστοι καὶ κοιμῶνται
[are] weak and feeble and ²sleep

ἱκανοί. 31 εἰ δὲ ἑαυτοὺς διεκρίνομεν,
¹a number. But if ourselves we discerned,

οὐκ ἂν ἐκρινόμεθα· 32 κρινόμενοι δὲ ὑπὸ
we should not be judged; but being judged by

τοῦ κυρίου παιδευόμεθα, ἵνα μὴ σὺν
the Lord we are chastened, lest with

---

other gets drunk. 22 Don't you have homes to eat and drink in? Or do you despise the church of God and humiliate those who have nothing? What shall I say to you? Shall I praise you for this? Certainly not!

23 For I received from the Lord what I also passed on to you: The Lord Jesus, on the night he was betrayed, took bread, 24 and when he had given thanks, he broke it and said, "This is my body, which is for you; do this in remembrance of me." 25 In the same way, after supper he took the cup, saying, "This cup is the new covenant in my blood; do this, whenever you drink it, in remembrance of me." 26 For whenever you eat this bread and drink this cup, you proclaim the Lord's death until he comes.

27 Therefore, whoever eats the bread or drinks the cup of the Lord in an unworthy manner will be guilty of sinning against the body and blood of the Lord. 28 A man ought to examine himself before he eats of the bread and drinks of the cup. 29 For anyone who eats and drinks without recognizing the body of the Lord eats and drinks judgment on himself. 30 That is why many among you are weak and sick, and a number of you have fallen asleep. 31 But if we judged ourselves, we would not come under judgment. 32 When we are judged by the Lord, we are being disciplined so that we will not

---

[v] Other ancient authorities read *is broken for*
[w] Other ancient authorities add *in an unworthy manner.*
[x] Other ancient authorities read *the Lord's body*
[y] Gk *fallen asleep*
[z] Or *When we are judged, we are being disciplined by the Lord*

along with the world. 33 So then, my brothers and sisters,[a] when you come together to eat, wait for one another. 34 If you are hungry, eat at home, so that when you come together, it will not be for your condemnation. About the other things I will give instructions when I come.

Chapter 12

Spiritual Gifts

NOW concerning spiritual gifts,[b] brothers and sisters,[a] I do not want you to be uninformed. 2 You know that when you were pagans, you were enticed and led astray to idols that could not speak. 3 Therefore I want you to understand that no one speaking by the Spirit of God ever says "Let Jesus be cursed!" and no one can say "Jesus is Lord" except by the Holy Spirit.

4 Now there are varieties of gifts, but the same Spirit; 5 and there are varieties of services, but the same Lord; 6 and there are varieties of activities, but it is the same God who activates all of them in everyone. 7 To each is given the manifestation of the Spirit for the common good. 8 To one is given through the Spirit the utterance of wisdom, and to another the utterance of knowledge according to the same Spirit, 9 to another faith by the same Spirit, to another gifts of healing by the one Spirit, 10 to another the working of miracles, to another prophecy, to another the discernment of spirits, to another various kinds of tongues, to another the interpretation of tongues. 11 All these are activated by one and the same Spirit, who allots to each one individually just

Middle column (interlinear)

τῷ κόσμῳ κατακριθῶμεν. 33 Ὥστε,
the world we are condemned. So as,

ἀδελφοί μου, συνερχόμενοι εἰς τὸ φαγεῖν
brothers of me, coming together for the to eat

ἀλλήλους ἐκδέχεσθε. 34 εἴ τις πεινᾷ,
one another await ye. If anyone hungers,

ἐν οἴκῳ ἐσθιέτω, ἵνα μὴ εἰς κρίμα
at home let him eat, lest to judgment

συνέρχησθε. τὰ δὲ λοιπὰ ὡς ἂν ἔλθω
ye come together. And the remaining matters whenever I come

διατάξομαι.
I will arrange.

12 Περὶ δὲ τῶν πνευματικῶν, ἀδελφοί,
Now about the spiritual matters, brothers,

οὐ θέλω ὑμᾶς ἀγνοεῖν. 2 Οἴδατε ὅτι
I do not wish you to be ignorant. Ye know that

ὅτε ἔθνη ἦτε πρὸς τὰ εἴδωλα τὰ ἄφωνα
when ¹nations ⁵ye were ⁴to ³the ²idols - ⁶voiceless

ὡς ἂν ἤγεσθε ἀπαγόμενοι. 3 διὸ γνωρίζω
⁸however ⁷ye were led ⁹[ye were] ¹⁰being led away.* Where- I make
fore known

ὑμῖν ὅτι οὐδεὶς ἐν πνεύματι θεοῦ λαλῶν
to you that no one ²by ³[the] Spirit ⁴of God ¹speaking

λέγει· ΑΝΑΘΕΜΑ ΙΗΣΟΥΣ, καὶ οὐδεὶς
says: A CURSE [IS] JESUS, and no one

δύναται εἰπεῖν· ΚΥΡΙΟΣ ΙΗΣΟΥΣ, εἰ μὴ
can to say: LORD JESUS, except

ἐν πνεύματι ἁγίῳ.
by [the] ²Spirit ¹Holy.

4 Διαιρέσεις δὲ χαρισμάτων εἰσίν, τὸ δὲ αὐτὸ
Now differences of gifts there are, but the same

πνεῦμα· 5 καὶ διαιρέσεις διακονιῶν εἰσιν, καὶ
Spirit; and differences of ministries there are, and

ὁ αὐτὸς κύριος· 6 καὶ διαιρέσεις ἐνεργημάτων
the same Lord; and differences of operations

εἰσίν, ὁ δὲ αὐτὸς θεὸς ὁ ἐνεργῶν τὰ
there are, but the same God - operating

πάντα ἐν πᾶσιν. 7 ἑκάστῳ δὲ δίδοται
all things in all. But to each one is given

ἡ φανέρωσις τοῦ πνεύματος πρὸς τὸ
the manifestation of the Spirit to the

συμφέρον. 8 ᾧ μὲν γὰρ διὰ τοῦ πνεύματος
profiting. For to one through the Spirit

δίδοται λόγος σοφίας, ἄλλῳ δὲ λόγος
is given a word of wisdom, and to another a word

γνώσεως κατὰ τὸ αὐτὸ πνεῦμα, 9 ἑτέρῳ
of accord- the same Spirit, to
knowledge ing to another

πίστις ἐν τῷ αὐτῷ πνεύματι, ἄλλῳ δὲ
faith by the same Spirit, and to another

χαρίσματα ἰαμάτων ἐν τῷ ἑνὶ πνεύματι,
gifts of cures by the one Spirit,

10 ἄλλῳ δὲ ἐνεργήματα δυνάμεων, ἄλλῳ
and to another operations of powers, to another

[δὲ] προφητεία, ἄλλῳ δὲ διακρίσεις πνευ-
and prophecy, and to another discernings of

μάτων, ἑτέρῳ γένη γλωσσῶν, ἄλλῳ δὲ
spirits, to another kinds of tongues, and to another

ἑρμηνεία γλωσσῶν· 11 πάντα δὲ ταῦτα
interpretation of tongues: and ⁸all ⁹these things

ἐνεργεῖ τὸ ἓν καὶ τὸ αὐτὸ πνεῦμα,
⁷operates ¹the ²one ³and ⁴the ⁵same ⁶Spirit,

be condemned with the world.
33 So then, my brothers, when you come together to eat, wait for each other. 34 If anyone is hungry, he should eat at home, so that when you meet together it may not result in judgment.
And when I come I will give further directions.

Chapter 12

Spiritual Gifts

NOW about spiritual gifts, brothers, I do not want you to be ignorant. 2 You know that when you were pagans, somehow or other you were influenced and led astray to mute idols. 3 Therefore I tell you that no one who is speaking by the Spirit of God says, "Jesus be cursed," and no one can say, "Jesus is Lord," except by the Holy Spirit.

4 There are different kinds of gifts, but the same Spirit. 5 There are different kinds of service, but the same Lord. 6 There are different kinds of working, but the same God works all of them in all men.

7 Now to each one the manifestation of the Spirit is given for the common good. 8 To one there is given through the Spirit the message of wisdom, to another the message of knowledge by means of the same Spirit, 9 to another faith by the same Spirit, to another gifts of healing by that one Spirit, 10 to another miraculous powers, to another prophecy, to another distinguishing between spirits, to another speaking in different kinds of tongues,[a] and to still another the interpretation of tongues.[a] 11 All these are the work of one and the same Spirit, and he gives

---

* It is thought that there is a scribal error in this verse; see commentaries on the Greek text. We have been guided by G. G. Findlay, *The Expositor's Greek Testament.*

[a]10 Or languages; also in verse 28

as the Spirit chooses.

One Body with Many Members

12 For just as the body is one and has many members, and all the members of the body, though many, are one body, so it is with Christ. 13 For in the one Spirit we were all baptized into one body—Jews or Greeks, slaves or free— and we were all made to drink of one Spirit.

14 Indeed, the body does not consist of one member but of many. 15 If the foot would say, "Because I am not a hand, I do not belong to the body," that would not make it any less a part of the body. 16 And if the ear would say, "Because I am not an eye, I do not belong to the body," that would not make it any less a part of the body. 17 If the whole body were an eye, where would the hearing be? If the whole body were hearing, where would the sense of smell be? 18 But as it is, God arranged the members in the body, each one of them, as he chose. 19 If all were a single member, where would the body be? 20 As it is, there are many members, yet one body. 21 The eye cannot say to the hand, "I have no need of you," nor again the head to the feet, "I have no need of you." 22 On the contrary, the members of the body that seem to be weaker are indispensable, 23 and those members of the body that we think less honorable we clothe with greater honor, and our less respectable members are treated with greater respect; 24 whereas

---

διαιροῦν ἰδίᾳ ἑκάστῳ καθὼς βούλεται.
distributing ²separately† ¹to each one   as   he purposes.

12 Καθάπερ γὰρ τὸ σῶμα ἕν ἐστιν
   For as   the   body   ²one   ¹is

καὶ μέλη πολλὰ ἔχει, πάντα δὲ τὰ
and ³members ²many ¹has,   but all   the

μέλη τοῦ σώματος πολλὰ ὄντα ἕν ἐστιν
members of the   body   ²many ¹being ⁴one ³is(are)

σῶμα, οὕτως καὶ ὁ Χριστός· **13** καὶ γὰρ
body,   so   also the   Christ;   for indeed

ἐν ἑνὶ πνεύματι ἡμεῖς πάντες εἰς ἓν
⁴by ⁵one   ⁶Spirit   ¹we   ²all   ⁷into ⁸one

σῶμα ἐβαπτίσθημεν, εἴτε Ἰουδαῖοι εἴτε
⁹body   ³were baptized,   whether   Jews   or

Ἕλληνες, εἴτε δοῦλοι εἴτε ἐλεύθεροι, καὶ
Greeks,   whether slaves   or   free,   and

πάντες ἓν πνεῦμα ἐποτίσθημεν. **14** καὶ
all   one   Spirit   we were given to drink.   indeed

γὰρ τὸ σῶμα οὐκ ἔστιν ἓν μέλος ἀλλὰ
For   the   body   is not   one member   but

πολλά. **15** ἐὰν εἴπῃ ὁ πούς· ὅτι οὐκ
many.   If   ²says ¹the   ²foot: Because   not

εἰμὶ χείρ, οὐκ εἰμὶ ἐκ τοῦ σώματος,
I am   a hand,   I am not   of   the   body,

οὐ παρὰ τοῦτο οὐκ ἔστιν ἐκ τοῦ σώματος.
not   for   this   it is not   of   the   body.

16 καὶ ἐὰν εἴπῃ τὸ οὖς· ὅτι οὐκ εἰμὶ
  And   if   says   the   ear: Because   I am not

ὀφθαλμός, οὐκ εἰμὶ ἐκ τοῦ σώματος,
an eye,   I am not   of   the   body,

οὐ παρὰ τοῦτο οὐκ ἔστιν ἐκ τοῦ σώματος.
not   for   this   it is not   of   the   body.

17 εἰ ὅλον τὸ σῶμα ὀφθαλμός, ποῦ
  If   all   the   body   [was] an eye,   where

ἡ ἀκοή; εἰ ὅλον ἀκοή, ποῦ ἡ ὄσφρησις;
[would be] the hearing? if   all   hearing, where the   smelling?

18 νῦν δὲ ὁ θεὸς ἔθετο τὰ μέλη, ἓν
  But now   God   set   the members, ²one

ἕκαστον αὐτῶν ἐν τῷ σώματι καθὼς
¹each   of them   in   the   body   as

ἠθέλησεν. **19** εἰ δὲ ἦν τὰ πάντα ἓν
he wished.   And if   ¹was   –   ¹all   one

μέλος, ποῦ τὸ σῶμα; **20** νῦν δὲ πολλὰ
member, where the   body?   But now   many

μὲν μέλη, ἓν δὲ σῶμα. **21** οὐ δύναται
¹indeed ²members, but one   body.   ²cannot

δὲ ὁ ὀφθαλμὸς εἰπεῖν τῇ χειρί· χρείαν
And ¹the⁹   ²eye   to say   to the hand: Need

σου οὐκ ἔχω, ἢ πάλιν ἡ κεφαλὴ τοῖς
of thee I have not,   or   again   the   head   to the

ποσίν· χρείαν ὑμῶν οὐκ ἔχω· **22** ἀλλὰ
feet: Need   of you   I have not;   but

πολλῷ μᾶλλον τὰ δοκοῦντα μέλη τοῦ
by much   more   ¹the   ²seeming   ³members ⁴of the

σώματος ἀσθενέστερα ὑπάρχειν ἀναγκαῖά ἐστιν,
⁵body   ⁷weaker   ⁶to be   ⁹necessary ⁸is(are),

23 καὶ ἃ δοκοῦμεν ἀτιμότερα εἶναι
  and ¹[members] ⁵we think   ⁷less honourable   ⁶to be
   ⁴which

τοῦ σώματος, τούτοις τιμὴν περισσοτέραν
²of the   ³body,   to these   honour   more abundant

περιτίθεμεν, καὶ τὰ ἀσχήμονα ἡμῶν
we put round,   and   the uncomely [members]   of us

εὐσχημοσύνην περισσοτέραν ἔχει, **24** τὰ δὲ
²comeliness   ³more abundant ¹has(ve),   but thᵉ

---

them to each one, just as he determines.

One Body, Many Parts

12 The body is a unit, though it is made up of many parts; and though all its parts are many, they form one body. So it is with Christ. 13 For we were all baptized by[b] one Spirit into one body—whether Jews or Greeks, slave or free—and we were all given the one Spirit to drink.

14 Now the body is not made up of one part but of many. 15 If the foot should say, "Because I am not a hand, I do not belong to the body," it would not for that reason cease to be part of the body. 16 And if the ear should say, "Because I am not an eye, I do not belong to the body," it would not for that reason cease to be part of the body. 17 If the whole body were an eye, where would the sense of hearing be? If the whole body were an ear, where would the sense of smell be? 18 But in fact God has arranged the parts in the body, every one of them, just as he wanted them to be. 19 If they were all one part, where would the body be? 20 As it is, there are many parts, but one body. 21 The eye cannot say to the hand, "I don't need you!" And the head cannot say to the feet, "I don't need you!" 22 On the contrary, those parts of the body that seem to be weaker are indispensable, 23 and the parts that we think are less honorable we treat with special honor. And the parts that are unpresentable are treated with special modesty, 24 while our

---

b 13 Or with; or in

our more respectable members do not need this. But God has so arranged the body, giving the greater honor to the inferior member, 25 that there may be no dissension within the body, but the members may have the same care for one another. 26 If one member suffers, all suffer together with it; if one member is honored, all rejoice together with it.

27 Now you are the body of Christ and individually members of it. 28 And God has appointed in the church first apostles, second prophets, third teachers; then deeds of power, then gifts of healing, forms of assistance, various kinds of tongues. 29 Are all apostles? Are all prophets? Are all teachers? Do all work miracles? 30 Do all possess gifts of healing? Do all speak in tongues? Do all interpret? 31 But strive for the greater gifts. And I will show you a still more excellent way.

εὐσχήμονα ἡμῶν οὐ χρείαν ἔχει. ἀλλὰ ὁ
comely [members] of us ⁴no ³need ¹has(ve). But –

θεὸς συνεκέρασεν τὸ σῶμα, τῷ ὑστερουμένῳ
God blended together the body, ⁴to the [member] ⁵lacking

περισσοτέραν δοὺς τιμήν, 25 ἵνα μὴ ᾖ
²more abundant ¹giving ³honour, lest there be

σχίσμα ἐν τῷ σώματι, ἀλλὰ τὸ αὐτὸ
division in the body, but ⁴the ⁵same

ὑπὲρ ἀλλήλων μεριμνῶσιν τὰ μέλη.
⁶on be- ⁷one ³should care ¹the ²members.
half of another

26 καὶ εἴτε πάσχει ἓν μέλος, συμπάσχει
And whether ²suffers ¹one ³member, ⁴suffers with [it]

πάντα τὰ μέλη· εἴτε δοξάζεται μέλος,
⁴all ⁵the ⁶members; or ²is glorified ¹a member,

συγχαίρει πάντα τὰ μέλη. 27 ὑμεῖς
⁴rejoices with [it] ¹all ²the ³members. ye

δέ ἐστε σῶμα Χριστοῦ καὶ μέλη ἐκ
And are a body of Christ and members in

μέρους. 28 Καὶ οὓς μὲν ἔθετο ὁ θεὸς
part. And ²some† ¹placed – ¹God

ἐν τῇ ἐκκλησίᾳ πρῶτον ἀποστόλους, δεύτε-
in the church firstly apostles, second-

ρον προφήτας, τρίτον διδασκάλους, ἔπειτα
ly prophets, thirdly teachers, then

δυνάμεις, ἔπειτα χαρίσματα ἰαμάτων,
powers, then gifts of cures,

ἀντιλήμψεις, κυβερνήσεις, γένη γλωσσῶν,
helps, governings, kinds of tongues.

29 μὴ πάντες ἀπόστολοι; μὴ πάντες
Not all [are] apostles? not all

προφῆται; μὴ πάντες διδάσκαλοι; μὴ
prophets? not all teachers? not

πάντες δυνάμεις; 30 μὴ πάντες χαρίσματα
all powers? not all ¹gifts

ἔχουσιν ἰαμάτων; μὴ πάντες γλώσσαις
¹have of cures? not all ¹with tongues

λαλοῦσιν; μὴ πάντες διερμηνεύουσιν;
¹speak? not all interpret?

31 ζηλοῦτε δὲ τὰ χαρίσματα τὰ μείζονα.
but desire ye eagerly the ²gifts – ¹greater.

Καὶ ἔτι καθ᾽ ὑπερβολὴν ὁδὸν ὑμῖν
And yet ⁴according to ⁵excellence ²a way ³to you

δείκνυμι. 13 Ἐὰν ταῖς γλώσσαις τῶν ἀνθρώπων
¹I show. If in the tongues – of men

λαλῶ καὶ τῶν ἀγγέλων, ἀγάπην δὲ
I speak and – of angels, ²love but

μὴ ἔχω, γέγονα χαλκὸς ἠχῶν ἢ
¹I have not, I have become ³brass ¹sounding or

κύμβαλον ἀλαλάζον. 2 καὶ ἐὰν ἔχω
cymbal a tinkling. And if I have

προφητείαν καὶ εἰδῶ τὰ μυστήρια πάντα
prophecy and know ²the ³mysteries ¹all

καὶ πᾶσαν τὴν γνῶσιν, κἂν ἔχω πᾶσαν
and all – knowledge, and if I have all

τὴν πίστιν ὥστε ὄρη μεθιστάναι, ἀγάπην
– faith so as mountains to remove, ¹love

δὲ μὴ ἔχω, οὐθέν εἰμι. 3 κἂν ψωμίσω
¹but I have not, nothing I am. And if I dole out

πάντα τὰ ὑπάρχοντά μου, καὶ ἐὰν παραδῶ
all the goods of me, and if I deliver

τὸ σῶμά μου ἵνα καυθήσομαι, ἀγάπην
the body of me in order that I shall be burned, ¹love

δὲ μὴ ἔχω, οὐδὲν ὠφελοῦμαι. 4 Ἡ
¹but I have not, nothing I am profited. –

---

presentable parts need no special treatment. But God has combined the members of the body and has given greater honor to the parts that lacked it, 25 so that there should be no division in the body, but that its parts should have equal concern for each other. 26 If one part suffers, every part suffers with it; if one part is honored, every part rejoices with it.

27 Now you are the body of Christ, and each one of you is a part of it. 28 And in the church God has appointed first of all apostles, second prophets, third teachers, then workers of miracles, also those having gifts of healing, those able to help others, those with gifts of administration, and those speaking in different kinds of tongues. 29 Are all apostles? Are all prophets? Are all teachers? Do all work miracles? 30 Do all have gifts of healing? Do all speak in tongues[c]? Do all interpret[d]? 31 But eagerly desire[d] the greater gifts.

Love
And now I will show you the most excellent way.

Chapter 13

The Gift of Love

IF I speak in the tongues of mortals and of angels, but do not have love, I am a noisy gong or a clanging cymbal. 2 And if I have prophetic powers, and understand all mysteries and all knowledge, and if I have all faith, so as to remove mountains, but do not have love, I am nothing. 3 If I give away all my possessions, and if I hand over my body so that I may boast,[c] but do not have love, I gain nothing.

Chapter 13

IF I speak in the tongues[e] of men and of angels, but have not love, I am only a resounding gong or a clanging cymbal. 2 If I have the gift of prophecy and can fathom all mysteries and all knowledge, and if I have a faith that can move mountains, but have not love, I am nothing. 3 If I give all I possess to the poor and surrender my body to the flames,[f] but have not love, I gain nothing.

---

c Other ancient authorities read *body to be burned*

---

c30 Or *other languages*
d31 Or *But you are eagerly desiring*
e1 Or *languages*
f3 Some early manuscripts *body that I may boast*

4 Love is patient; love is kind; love is not envious or boastful or arrogant [5]or rude. It does not insist on its own way; it is not irritable or resentful; [6]it does not rejoice in wrongdoing, but rejoices in the truth. [7]It bears all things, believes all things, hopes all things, endures all things.

8 Love never ends. But as for prophecies, they will come to an end; as for tongues, they will cease; as for knowledge, it will come to an end. [9]For we know only in part, and we prophesy only in part; [10]but when the complete comes, the partial will come to an end. [11]When I was a child, I spoke like a child, I thought like a child, I reasoned like a child; when I became an adult, I put an end to childish ways. [12]For now we see in a mirror, dimly,[d] but then we will see face to face. Now I know only in part; then I will know fully, even as I have been fully known. [13]And now faith, hope, and love abide, these three; and the greatest of these is love.

Chapter 14
Gifts of Prophecy and Tongues

PURSUE love and strive for the spiritual gifts, and especially that you may prophesy. [2]For those who speak in a tongue do not speak to other people but to God; for nobody understands them, since they are speaking mysteries in the Spirit. [3]On the other hand, those who prophesy speak to other people for their upbuilding and encouragement and consolation. [4]Those who speak in a tongue build up themselves, but those who prophesy build up the

[d]Gk in a riddle

ἀγάπη μακροθυμεῖ, χρηστεύεται ἡ ἀγάπη,
Love   suffers long,   is kind   –   love,

οὐ ζηλοῖ, ἡ ἀγάπη οὐ περπερεύεται,
is not jealous, – love   does not vaunt itself,

οὐ φυσιοῦται, 5 οὐκ ἀσχημονεῖ, οὐ ζητεῖ
is not puffed up,   does not act unbecomingly, does not seek

τὰ ἑαυτῆς, οὐ παροξύνεται, οὐ λογίζεται
the of   is not provoked,   does not reckon
things her(it)self,

τὸ κακόν, 6 οὐ χαίρει ἐπὶ τῇ ἀδικίᾳ,
the evil,   rejoices not over the   wrong,

συγχαίρει δὲ τῇ ἀληθείᾳ· 7 πάντα στέγει,
but rejoices with the truth;   all things covers,

πάντα πιστεύει, πάντα ἐλπίζει, πάντα
all things believes, all things hopes,   all things

ὑπομένει. 8 Ἡ ἀγάπη οὐδέποτε πίπτει·
endures.   –   Love   never   falls;

εἴτε δὲ προφητεῖαι, καταργηθήσονται· εἴτε
but whether prophecies, they will be abolished; or

γλῶσσαι, παύσονται· εἴτε γνῶσις, κατ-
tongues, they will cease; or knowledge, it will

αργηθήσεται. 9 ἐκ μέρους γὰρ γινώσκομεν
be abolished.   For in part   we know

καὶ ἐκ μέρους προφητεύομεν· 10 ὅταν
and in   part   we prophesy;   [2]when

δὲ ἔλθῃ τὸ τέλειον, τὸ ἐκ μέρους
[1]but [2]comes [3]the [4]perfect thing, the thing in part

καταργηθήσεται. 11 ὅτε ἤμην νήπιος,
will be abolished.   When I was   an infant,

ἐλάλουν ὡς νήπιος, ἐφρόνουν ὡς νήπιος,
I spoke as an infant, I thought as an infant,

ἐλογιζόμην ὡς νήπιος· ὅτε γέγονα ἀνήρ,
I reckoned   as an infant; when I have become a man,

κατήργηκα τὰ τοῦ νηπίου. 12 βλέπομεν
I have   the of the infant.   we see
abolished things

γὰρ ἄρτι δι᾽ ἐσόπτρου ἐν αἰνίγματι,
For yet through a mirror in   a riddle,

τότε δὲ πρόσωπον πρὸς πρόσωπον· ἄρτι
but then face   to   face;   yet

γινώσκω ἐκ μέρους, τότε δὲ ἐπιγνώσομαι
I know   in   part,   but then I shall fully know

καθὼς καὶ ἐπεγνώσθην. 13 νυνὶ δὲ μένει
as   also I was fully known.   But now remains

πίστις, ἐλπίς, ἀγάπη, τὰ τρία ταῦτα·
faith,   hope, love,   these three;

μείζων δὲ τούτων ἡ ἀγάπη.
and [the] greater of these [is] – love.

14 Διώκετε τὴν ἀγάπην, ζηλοῦτε δὲ
   Pursue ye   –   love,   but desire eagerly

τὰ πνευματικά, μᾶλλον δὲ ἵνα προφητεύητε.
the spiritual [gifts],   and rather in order ye may prophesy.
                                     that

2 ὁ γὰρ λαλῶν γλώσσῃ οὐκ ἀνθρώποις
For the [one] speaking in a tongue [2]not   to men

λαλεῖ ἀλλὰ θεῷ· οὐδεὶς γὰρ ἀκούει,
[1]speaks but to God; for no one hears,

πνεύματι δὲ λαλεῖ μυστήρια· 3 ὁ δὲ
but in spirit he speaks mysteries; but the [one]

προφητεύων ἀνθρώποις λαλεῖ οἰκοδομὴν καὶ
prophesying to men   speaks edification and

παράκλησιν καὶ παραμυθίαν. 4 ὁ λαλῶν
encouragement and   consolation. The [one] speaking

γλώσσῃ ἑαυτὸν οἰκοδομεῖ· ὁ δὲ προφητεύων
in a tongue himself edifies; but the [one] prophesying

---

[4]Love is patient, love is kind. It does not envy, it does not boast, it is not proud. [5]It is not rude, it is not self-seeking, it is not easily angered, it keeps no record of wrongs. [6]Love does not delight in evil but rejoices with the truth. [7]It always protects, always trusts, always hopes, always perseveres.

[8]Love never fails. But where there are prophecies, they will cease; where there are tongues, they will be stilled; where there is knowledge, it will pass away. [9]For we know in part and we prophesy in part, [10]but when perfection comes, the imperfect disappears. [11]When I was a child, I talked like a child, I thought like a child, I reasoned like a child. When I became a man, I put childish ways behind me. [12]Now we see but a poor reflection as in a mirror; then we shall see face to face. Now I know in part; then I shall know fully, even as I am fully known.

[13]And now these three remain: faith, hope and love. But the greatest of these is love.

Chapter 14
Gifts of Prophecy and Tongues

FOLLOW the way of love and eagerly desire spiritual gifts, especially the gift of prophecy. [2]For anyone who speaks in a tongue[g] does not speak to men but to God. Indeed, no one understands him; he utters mysteries with his spirit.[h] [3]But everyone who prophesies speaks to men for their strengthening, encouragement and comfort. [4]He who speaks in a tongue edifies himself, but he who prophesies edifies the

[g]2 Or another language; also in verses 4, 13, 14, 19, 26 and 27
[h]2 Or by the Spirit

church. 5 Now I would like all of you to speak in tongues, but even more to prophesy. One who prophesies is greater than one who speaks in tongues, unless someone interprets, so that the church may be built up.

6 Now, brothers and sisters,[e] if I come to you speaking in tongues, how will I benefit you unless I speak to you in some revelation or knowledge or prophecy or teaching? 7 It is the same way with lifeless instruments that produce sound, such as the flute or the harp. If they do not give distinct notes, how will anyone know what is being played? 8 And if the bugle gives an indistinct sound, who will get ready for battle? 9 So with yourselves; if in a tongue you utter speech that is not intelligible, how will anyone know what is being said? For you will be speaking into the air. 10 There are doubtless many different kinds of sounds in the world, and nothing is without sound. 11 If then I do not know the meaning of a sound, I will be a foreigner to the speaker and the speaker a foreigner to me. 12 So with yourselves; since you are eager for spiritual gifts, strive to excel in them for building up the church.

13 Therefore, one who speaks in a tongue should pray for the power to interpret. 14 For if I pray in a tongue, my mind is unproductive. 15 What should I do then? I will pray with the spirit, but

---

ἐκκλησίαν οἰκοδομεῖ. 5 θέλω δὲ πάντας
a church edifies. Now I wish all

ὑμᾶς λαλεῖν γλώσσαις, μᾶλλον δὲ ἵνα
you to speak in tongues, but rather in order that

προφητεύητε· μείζων δὲ ὁ προφητεύων ἢ
ye may prophesy; and greater the [one] prophesying than

ὁ λαλῶν γλώσσαις, ἐκτὸς εἰ μὴ διερμηνεύῃ,
the speaking in tongues, except unless he interprets,
[one]

ἵνα ἡ ἐκκλησία οἰκοδομὴν λάβῃ. 6 νῦν δέ,
in or- the church edification may receive. But now,
der that

ἀδελφοί, ἐὰν ἔλθω πρὸς ὑμᾶς γλώσσαις
brothers, if I come to you in tongues

λαλῶν, τί ὑμᾶς ὠφελήσω, ἐὰν μὴ ὑμῖν
speaking, what ²you ¹shall I profit, except ³to you

λαλήσω ἢ ἐν ἀποκαλύψει ἢ ἐν γνώσει
¹I speak either in a revelation or in knowledge

ἢ ἐν προφητείᾳ ἢ διδαχῇ; 7 ὅμως τὰ
or in prophecy or in teaching? Yet –

ἄψυχα φωνὴν διδόντα, εἴτε αὐλὸς εἴτε
lifeless things ²a sound ¹giving, whether pipe or

κιθάρα, ἐὰν διαστολὴν τοῖς φθόγγοις μὴ
harp, if ²a distinction ¹in the ³sounds ⁴not

δῷ, πῶς γνωσθήσεται τὸ αὐλούμενον ἢ
¹they how will it be known the being piped or
give, thing

τὸ κιθαριζόμενον; 8 καὶ γὰρ ἐὰν ἄδηλον
the being harped? For indeed if ²an
thing uncertain

σάλπιγξ φωνὴν δῷ, τίς παρασκευάσεται
¹a trumpet ²sound ¹gives, who will prepare himself

εἰς πόλεμον; 9 οὕτως καὶ ὑμεῖς διὰ
for war? so also ¹ye ²through

τῆς γλώσσης ἐὰν μὴ εὔσημον λόγον
¹the ²tongue ³unless ⁴a clear ⁵word

δῶτε, πῶς γνωσθήσεται τὸ λαλούμενον;
⁶give, how will it be known the thing being said?

ἔσεσθε γὰρ εἰς ἀέρα λαλοῦντες. 10 τοσαῦτα
for ¹ye will be ²into ³air ⁴speaking. ²So many

εἰ τύχοι γένη φωνῶν εἰσιν ἐν κόσμῳ,
¹it may be⁺ ¹kinds ⁴of sounds ¹there are in [the] world,

καὶ οὐδὲν ἄφωνον· 11 ἐὰν οὖν μὴ εἰδῶ
and not one [is] voiceless; if therefore I know not

τὴν δύναμιν τῆς φωνῆς, ἔσομαι τῷ
the power of the sound, I shall be to the

λαλοῦντι βάρβαρος καὶ ὁ λαλῶν ἐν ἐμοὶ
[one] speaking a foreigner and the speaking in(to) me
[one]

βάρβαρος. 12 οὕτως καὶ ὑμεῖς. ἐπεὶ
a foreigner. So also ye, since

ζηλωταί ἐστε πνευμάτων, πρὸς τὴν
zealots ye are of spirit[ual thing]s, ²to ³the

οἰκοδομὴν τῆς ἐκκλησίας ζητεῖτε ἵνα περισ-
⁴edification ⁵of the ⁶church ¹seek ye in order ye may
that

σεύητε. 13 Διὸ ὁ λαλῶν γλώσσῃ προσευχ-
abound. Wherefore the speaking in a tongue let him
[one]

έσθω ἵνα διερμηνεύῃ. 14 ἐὰν γὰρ προσεύχωμαι
pray in order he may For if I pray
that interpret.

γλώσσῃ, τὸ πνεῦμά μου προσεύχεται,
in a tongue, the spirit of me prays,

ὁ δὲ νοῦς μου ἄκαρπός ἐστιν. 15 τί
but the mind of me unfruitful is. What

οὖν ἐστιν; προσεύξομαι τῷ πνεύματι,
therefore is it? I will pray with the spirit,

---

church. 5 I would like every one of you to speak in tongues,[i] but I would rather have you prophesy. He who prophesies is greater than one who speaks in tongues,[i] unless he interprets, so that the church may be edified.

6 Now, brothers, if I come to you and speak in tongues, what good will I be to you, unless I bring you some revelation or knowledge or prophecy or word of instruction? 7 Even in the case of lifeless things that make sounds, such as the flute or harp, how will anyone know what tune is being played unless there is a distinction in the notes? 8 Again, if the trumpet does not sound a clear call, who will get ready for battle? 9 So it is with you. Unless you speak intelligible words with your tongue, how will anyone know what you are saying? You will just be speaking into the air. 10 Undoubtedly there are all sorts of languages in the world, yet none of them is without meaning. 11 If then I do not grasp the meaning of what someone is saying, I am a foreigner to the speaker, and he is a foreigner to me. 12 So it is with you. Since you are eager to have spiritual gifts, try to excel in gifts that build up the church.

13 For this reason anyone who speaks in a tongue should pray that he may interpret what he says. 14 For if I pray in a tongue, my spirit prays, but my mind is unfruitful. 15 So what shall I do? I will pray with my spir-

---

I will pray with the mind also; I will sing praise with the spirit, but I will sing praise with the mind also. 16 Otherwise, if you say a blessing with the spirit, how can anyone in the position of an outsider say the "Amen" to your thanksgiving, since the outsider does not know what you are saying? 17 For you may give thanks well enough, but the other person is not built up. 18 I thank God that I speak in tongues more than all of you; 19 nevertheless, in church I would rather speak five words with my mind, in order to instruct others also, than ten thousand words in a tongue.

20 Brothers and sisters,[e] do not be children in your thinking; rather, be infants in evil, but in thinking be adults. 21 In the law it is written,

"By people of strange tongues
and by the lips of foreigners
I will speak to this people;
yet even then they will not listen to me,"

says the Lord. 22 Tongues, then, are a sign not for believers but for unbelievers, while prophecy is not for unbelievers but for believers. 23 If, therefore, the whole church comes together and all speak in tongues, and outsiders or unbelievers enter, will they not say that you are out of your mind? 24 But if all prophesy, an unbeliever or outsider who enters is reproved by all and called to account by all. 25 After the secrets of the unbeliever's heart are disclosed, that person will bow down before God and worship him, declaring, "God is really among you."

Orderly Worship

26 What should be done

προσεύξομαι δὲ καὶ τῷ νοΐ· ψαλῶ τῷ
¹I will pray ²and ³also with mind; I will with
     the   sing the
πνεύματι, ψαλῶ δὲ καὶ τῷ νοΐ. 16 ἐπεὶ
spirit, . ²I will sing ¹and ³also with the mind. Otherwise
ἐὰν εὐλογῇς [ἐν] πνεύματι, ὁ ἀναπληρῶν
if thou blessest in spirit, the [one] occupying
τὸν τόπον τοῦ ἰδιώτου πῶς ἐρεῖ τὸ
the place of the uninstructed how will he say the
ἀμὴν ἐπὶ τῇ σῇ εὐχαριστίᾳ; ἐπειδὴ τί
"amen" at - thy giving thanks? Since what
λέγεις οὐκ οἶδεν· 17 σὺ μὲν γὰρ καλῶς
thou sayest he knows not; ²thou ³indeed ¹for ⁵well
εὐχαριστεῖς, ἀλλ' ὁ ἕτερος οὐκ οἰκοδομεῖται.
⁴givest thanks, but the other is not edified.
18 εὐχαριστῶ τῷ θεῷ, πάντων ὑμῶν μᾶλ-
I give thanks - to God, ³all ⁴you ²more
λον γλώσσαις λαλῶ· 19 ἀλλὰ ἐν ἐκκλησίᾳ
than ¹in tongues ¹I speak; but in a church
θέλω πέντε λόγους τῷ νοΐ μου λαλῆσαι,
¹I wish ²five ³words ⁴with the ⁵mind ⁶of me ⁷to speak,
ἵνα καὶ ἄλλους κατηχήσω, ἢ μυρίους
in or- also others I may instruct, than ten
der that   thousands
λόγους ἐν γλώσσῃ. 20 Ἀδελφοί, μὴ
words in a tongue. Brothers, ²not
παιδία γίνεσθε ταῖς φρεσίν, ἀλλὰ τῇ
³children ¹be ye in the(your) minds, but -
κακίᾳ νηπιάζετε, ταῖς δὲ φρεσὶν τέλειοι
in malice be ye infantlike, and in the(your) minds mature
γίνεσθε. 21 ἐν τῷ νόμῳ γέγραπται ὅτι
be ye. In the law it has been written that
ἐν ἑτερογλώσσοις καὶ ἐν χείλεσιν ἑτέρων
in other tongues and in lips of others
λαλήσω τῷ λαῷ τούτῳ, καὶ οὐδ' οὕτως
I will speak to this people, and not so
εἰσακούσονταί μου, λέγει κύριος. 22 ὥστε
will they hear me, says [the] Lord. So as
αἱ γλῶσσαι εἰς σημεῖόν εἰσιν οὐ τοῖς
the tongues ²for ³a sign ¹are not to the
πιστεύουσιν ἀλλὰ τοῖς ἀπίστοις, ἡ δὲ
[ones] believing but to the unbelievers, and the
προφητεία οὐ τοῖς ἀπίστοις ἀλλὰ τοῖς
prophecy [is] not to the unbelievers but to the
πιστεύουσιν. 23 Ἐὰν οὖν συνέλθῃ ἡ
[ones] believing. If therefore ⁴comes ¹the
                                   together
ἐκκλησία ὅλη ἐπὶ τὸ αὐτὸ καὶ πάντες
³church ²whole together and all
λαλῶσιν γλώσσαις, εἰσέλθωσιν δὲ ἰδιῶται
speak in tongues, and ⁵enter ¹uninstructed
ἢ ἄπιστοι, οὐκ ἐροῦσιν ὅτι μαίνεσθε;
²or ³unbelievers, will they not say that ye rave?
24 ἐὰν δὲ πάντες προφητεύωσιν, εἰσέλθῃ δέ
but if all prophesy, and ⁴enters
τις ἄπιστος ἢ ἰδιώτης, ἐλέγχεται ὑπὸ
¹some ²unbeliever ³or ⁴uninstructed, he is convicted by
πάντων, ἀνακρίνεται ὑπὸ πάντων, 25 τὰ
all, he is judged by all, the
κρυπτὰ τῆς καρδίας αὐτοῦ φανερὰ γίνεται,
hidden of the heart of him ²manifest ¹becomes,
things
καὶ οὕτως πεσὼν ἐπὶ πρόσωπον προσκυνή-
and so falling on [his] face he will wor-
σει τῷ θεῷ, ἀπαγγέλλων ὅτι ὄντως
ship - God, declaring that really
ὁ θεὸς ἐν ὑμῖν ἐστιν. 26 Τί οὖν ἐστιν,
- God ²among ³you ¹is. What therefore is it,

---

it, but I will also pray with my mind; I will sing with my spirit, but I will also sing with my mind. 16 If you are praising God with your spirit, how can one who finds himself among those who do not understand[j] say "Amen" to your thanksgiving, since he does not know what you are saying? 17 You may be giving thanks well enough, but the other man is not edified. 18 I thank God that I speak in tongues more than all of you. 19 But in the church I would rather speak five intelligible words to instruct others than ten thousand words in a tongue.

20 Brothers, stop thinking like children. In regard to evil be infants, but in your thinking be adults. 21 In the Law it is written:

"Through men of strange tongues
and through the lips of foreigners
I will speak to this people,
but even then they will not listen to me,"[k]

says the Lord. 22 Tongues, then, are a sign, not for believers but for unbelievers; prophecy, however, is for believers, not for unbelievers. 23 So if the whole church comes together and everyone speaks in tongues, and some who do not understand[l] or some unbelievers come in, will they not say that you are out of your mind? 24 But if an unbeliever or someone who does not understand[m] comes in while everybody is prophesying, he will be convinced by all that he is a sinner and will be judged by all, 25 and the secrets of his heart will be laid bare. So he will fall down and worship God, exclaiming, "God is really among you!"

Orderly Worship

26 What then shall we say,

---

j 16 Or among the inquirers
k 21 Isaiah 28:11,12
l 23 Or some inquirers
m 24 Or or some inquirer

then, my friends?ᵉ When you come together, each one has a hymn, a lesson, a revelation, a tongue, or an interpretation. Let all things be done for building up. 27 If anyone speaks in a tongue, let there be only two or at most three, and each in turn; and let one interpret. 28 But if there is no one to interpret, let them be silent in church and speak to themselves and to God. 29 Let two or three prophets speak, and let the others weigh what is said. 30 If a revelation is made to someone else sitting nearby, let the first person be silent. 31 For you can all prophesy one by one, so that all may learn and all be encouraged. 32 And the spirits of prophets are subject to the prophets, 33 for God is a God not of disorder but of peace.

(As in all the churches of the saints, 34 women should be silent in the churches. For they are not permitted to speak, but should be subordinate, as the law also says. 35 If there is anything they desire to know, let them ask their husbands at home. For it is shameful for a woman to speak in church. ᶠ 36 Or did the word of God originate with you? Or are you the only ones it has reached?)

37 Anyone who claims to be a prophet, or to have spiritual powers, must acknowledge that what I am writing to you is a command of the Lord. 38 Anyone who does not recognize this is not to be recognized. 39 So, my friends,ᵍ be eager to prophesy, and do not forbid speaking in tongues; 40 but all things should be done decently and in order.

ἀδελφοί; ὅταν συνέρχησθε, ἕκαστος ψαλμὸν
brothers? whenever ye come together, each one a psalm

ἔχει, διδαχὴν ἔχει, ἀποκάλυψιν ἔχει, γλῶσ-
has, a teaching he has, a revelation he has, a

σαν ἔχει, ἑρμηνείαν ἔχει· πάντα πρὸς
tongue he has, an interpretation he has; ³all things ⁴for

οἰκοδομὴν γινέσθω. 27 εἴτε γλώσσῃ τις
⁵edification ¹let ²be. If in a tongue anyone

λαλεῖ, κατὰ δύο ἢ τὸ πλεῖστον τρεῖς,
speaks, by two or the most three,

καὶ ἀνὰ μέρος, 28 καὶ εἷς διερμηνευέτω·
and in turn,† and ²one ¹let ³interpret;

ἐὰν δὲ μὴ ᾖ διερμηνευτής, σιγάτω ἐν
but if there is not an interpreter, let him be silent in

ἐκκλησίᾳ, ἑαυτῷ δὲ λαλείτω καὶ τῷ
church, and to himself let him speak and -

θεῷ. 29 προφῆται δὲ δύο ἢ τρεῖς λαλεί-
to God. And prophets two or three let them

τωσαν, καὶ οἱ ἄλλοι διακρινέτωσαν·
speak, and the others let discern;

30 ἐὰν δὲ ἄλλῳ ἀποκαλυφθῇ καθημένῳ, ὁ
but if ¹to another ²[something] ³sitting, the
⁴is revealed

πρῶτος σιγάτω. 31 δύνασθε γὰρ καθ'
first let be silent. For ye can ³sin-

ἕνα πάντες προφητεύειν, ἵνα πάντες
gly† ¹all ²to prophesy, in order that all

μανθάνωσιν καὶ πάντες παρακαλῶνται.
may learn and all may be encouraged.

32 καὶ πνεύματα προφητῶν προφήταις
And [the] spirits of prophets to prophets

ὑποτάσσεται· 33 οὐ γάρ ἐστιν ἀκαταστασίας
is(are) subject; for not ²is ⁴of tumult

ὁ θεὸς ἀλλὰ εἰρήνης. Ὡς ἐν πάσαις
- ¹God but of peace. As in all

ταῖς ἐκκλησίαις τῶν ἁγίων, 34 αἱ γυναῖκες
the churches of the saints, ²the ³women

ἐν ταῖς ἐκκλησίαις σιγάτωσαν· οὐ γὰρ
¹in ³the ⁷churches ¹let ³be silent; ⁴not ⁵for

ἐπιτρέπεται αὐταῖς λαλεῖν, ἀλλὰ ὑποτασ-
²it is ⁶permitted to them to speak, but let them

σέσθωσαν, καθὼς καὶ ὁ νόμος λέγει.
be subject, as also the law says.

35 εἰ δέ τι μαθεῖν θέλουσιν, ἐν οἴκῳ
But if ²anything ³to learn ¹they wish, ⁵at home

τοὺς ἰδίους ἄνδρας ἐπερωτάτωσαν· αἰσχρὸν
⁶the(ir) ⁷own ⁸husbands ¹let them question; ²a shame

γὰρ ἐστιν γυναικὶ λαλεῖν ἐν ἐκκλησίᾳ.
¹for ²it is for a woman to speak in a church.

36 ἢ ἀφ' ὑμῶν ὁ λόγος τοῦ θεοῦ ἐξῆλθεν,
Or from you ²the ³word - ⁴of God ¹went forth,

ἢ εἰς ὑμᾶς μόνους κατήντησεν; 37 Εἴ
or to you only did it reach? If

τις δοκεῖ προφήτης εἶναι ἢ πνευματικός,
any- thinks ²a prophet ¹to be or a spiritual man,
one

ἐπιγινωσκέτω ἃ γράφω ὑμῖν ὅτι
let him clearly [the] things I write to you that
know which

κυρίου ἐστὶν ἐντολή· 38 εἰ δέ τις
of [the] Lord they are a commandment; but if anyone

ἀγνοεῖ, ἀγνοεῖται. 39 Ὥστε, ἀδελφοί
is ignorant, let him be ignorant. So as, brothers

μου, ζηλοῦτε τὸ προφητεύειν, καὶ τὸ
of me, be ye eager - to prophesy, and ²the

λαλεῖν μὴ κωλύετε γλώσσαις· 40 πάντα
²to speak ¹forbid not in tongues; ²all things

δὲ εὐσχημόνως καὶ κατὰ τάξιν γινέσθω.
and ⁴becomingly ⁵and ⁶according to ⁷order ¹let ³be done.

brothers? When you come together, everyone has a hymn, or a word of instruction, a revelation, a tongue or an interpretation. All of these must be done for the strengthening of the church. 27 If anyone speaks in a tongue, two—or at the most three—should speak, one at a time, and someone must interpret. 28 If there is no interpreter, the speaker should keep quiet in the church and speak to himself and God. 29 Two or three prophets should speak, and the others should weigh carefully what is said. 30 And if a revelation comes to someone who is sitting down, the first speaker should stop. 31 For you can all prophesy in turn so that everyone may be instructed and encouraged. 32 The spirits of prophets are subject to the control of prophets. 33 For God is not a God of disorder but of peace.

As in all the congregations of the saints, 34 women should remain silent in the churches. They are not allowed to speak, but must be in submission, as the Law says. 35 If they want to inquire about something, they should ask their own husbands at home; for it is disgraceful for a woman to speak in the church.

36 Did the word of God originate with you? Or are you the only people it has reached? 37 If anybody thinks he is a prophet or spiritually gifted, let him acknowledge that what I am writing to you is the Lord's command. 38 If he ignores this, he himself will be ignored. ⁿ

39 Therefore, my brothers, be eager to prophesy, and do not forbid speaking in tongues. 40 But everything should be done in a fitting and orderly way.

ᶠOther ancient authorities put verses 34-35 after verse 40

ᵍGk my brothers

ⁿ38 Some manuscripts If he is ignorant of this, let him be ignorant

Chapter 15

The Resurrection of Christ

NOW I would remind you, brothers and sisters,[e] of the good news[h] that I proclaimed to you, which you in turn received, in which also you stand, 2through which also you are being saved, if you hold firmly to the message that I proclaimed to you—unless you have come to believe in vain.

3 For I handed on to you as of first importance what I in turn had received: that Christ died for our sins in accordance with the scriptures, 4and that he was buried, and that he was raised on the third day in accordance with the scriptures, 5and that he appeared to Cephas, then to the twelve. 6Then he appeared to more than five hundred brothers and sisters[i] at one time, most of whom are still alive, though some have died.[j] 7Then he appeared to James, then to all the apostles. 8Last of all, as to one untimely born, he appeared also to me. 9For I am the least of the apostles, unfit to be called an apostle, because I persecuted the church of God. 10But by the grace of God I am what I am, and his grace toward me has not been in vain. On the contrary, I worked harder than any of them—though it was not I, but the grace of God that is with me. 11Whether then it was I or they, so we proclaim and so you have come to believe.

The Resurrection of the Dead

12 Now if Christ is proclaimed as raised from the dead, how can some of you say there is no resurrection of the dead? 13If there is no resurrection of the dead, then Christ has not been raised; 14and if Christ has not been raised, then our

---

15 Γνωρίζω δὲ ὑμῖν, ἀδελφοί, τὸ
Now I make known to you, brothers, the

εὐαγγέλιον ὃ εὐηγγελισάμην ὑμῖν, ὃ καὶ
good tidings which I preached to you, which also

παρελάβετε, ἐν ᾧ καὶ ἑστήκατε, 2 δι᾽
ye received, in which also ye stand, through

οὗ καὶ σῴζεσθε, τίνι λόγῳ εὐηγγελισάμην
which also ye are saved, ²to what ⁴word ⁵I preached

ὑμῖν εἰ κατέχετε, ἐκτὸς εἰ μὴ εἰκῇ
⁶to you ¹if ³ye hold fast, except unless in vain

ἐπιστεύσατε. 3 παρέδωκα γὰρ ὑμῖν ἐν
ye believed. For I delivered to you among

πρώτοις, ὃ καὶ παρέλαβον, ὅτι Χριστὸς
[the] first what also I received, that Christ
things,

ἀπέθανεν ὑπὲρ τῶν ἁμαρτιῶν ἡμῶν κατὰ
died on be- the sins of us accord-
half of ing to

τὰς γραφάς, 4 καὶ ὅτι ἐτάφη, καὶ ὅτι
the scriptures, and that he was buried, and that

ἐγήγερται τῇ ἡμέρᾳ τῇ τρίτῃ κατὰ
he has on the ²day – ¹third accord-
been raised ing to

τὰς γραφάς, 5 καὶ ὅτι ὤφθη Κηφᾷ,
the scriptures, and that he was seen by Cephas,

εἶτα τοῖς δώδεκα· 6 ἔπειτα ὤφθη ἐπάνω
then by the twelve; afterward he was seen ²over

πεντακοσίοις ἀδελφοῖς ἐφάπαξ, ἐξ ὧν οἱ
¹by ⁵five hundreds brothers at one time, of whom the

πλείονες μένουσιν ἕως ἄρτι, τινὲς δὲ
majority remain until now, though some

ἐκοιμήθησαν· 7 ἔπειτα ὤφθη Ἰακώβῳ, εἶτα
fell asleep; afterward he was seen by James, then

τοῖς ἀποστόλοις πᾶσιν· 8 ἔσχατον δὲ
by the apostles all; and lastly

πάντων ὡσπερεὶ τῷ ἐκτρώματι ὤφθη
of all even as if to the(an) abortion he was seen

κἀμοί. 9 Ἐγὼ γὰρ εἰμι ὁ ἐλάχιστος
by me also. For I am the least

τῶν ἀποστόλων, ὃς οὐκ εἰμὶ ἱκανὸς
of the apostles, who am not sufficient

καλεῖσθαι ἀπόστολος, διότι ἐδίωξα τὴν
to be called an apostle, because I persecuted the

ἐκκλησίαν τοῦ θεοῦ· 10 χάριτι δὲ θεοῦ
church – of God; but by [the] grace of God

εἰμι ὃ εἰμι, καὶ ἡ χάρις αὐτοῦ ἡ εἰς
I am what I am, and the grace of him – to

ἐμὲ οὐ κενὴ ἐγενήθη, ἀλλὰ περισσότερον
me not empty was, but ²more abundantly
[than]

αὐτῶν πάντων ἐκοπίασα, οὐκ ἐγὼ δὲ
³them ⁴all ¹I laboured, ⁵not ¹I ¹yet

ἀλλὰ ἡ χάρις τοῦ θεοῦ σὺν ἐμοί. 11 εἴτε
but the grace – of God with me. Whether

οὖν ἐγὼ εἴτε ἐκεῖνοι, οὕτως κηρύσσομεν
therefore I or those, so we proclaim

καὶ οὕτως ἐπιστεύσατε.
and so ye believed.

12 Εἰ δὲ Χριστὸς κηρύσσεται ὅτι ἐκ
But if Christ is proclaimed that from

νεκρῶν ἐγήγερται, πῶς λέγουσιν ἐν ὑμῖν
[the] dead he has been raised, how say ²among ³you

τινες ὅτι ἀνάστασις νεκρῶν οὐκ ἔστιν;
¹some that a resurrection of dead persons there is not?

13 εἰ δὲ ἀνάστασις νεκρῶν οὐκ ἔστιν,
Now if a resurrection of dead persons there is not,

οὐδὲ Χριστὸς ἐγήγερται· 14 εἰ δὲ Χριστὸς
neither Christ has been raised; and if Christ

Chapter 15

The Resurrection of Christ

NOW, brothers, I want to remind you of the gospel I preached to you, which you received and on which you have taken your stand. 2By this gospel you are saved, if you hold firmly to the word I preached to you. Otherwise, you have believed in vain.

3For what I received I passed on to you as of first importance[o]: that Christ died for our sins according to the Scriptures, 4that he was buried, that he was raised on the third day according to the Scriptures, 5and that he appeared to Peter,[p] and then to the Twelve. 6After that, he appeared to more than five hundred of the brothers at the same time, most of whom are still living, though some have fallen asleep. 7Then he appeared to James, then to all the apostles, 8and last of all he appeared to me also, as to one abnormally born.

9For I am the least of the apostles and do not even deserve to be called an apostle, because I persecuted the church of God. 10But by the grace of God I am what I am, and his grace to me was not without effect. No, I worked harder than all of them—yet not I, but the grace of God that was with me. 11Whether, then, it was I or they, this is what we preach, and this is what you believed.

The Resurrection of the Dead

12But if it is preached that Christ has been raised from the dead, how can some of you say that there is no resurrection of the dead? 13If there is no resurrection of the dead, then not even Christ has been raised. 14And if Christ has not been

---

h Or gospel
i Gk brothers
j Gk fallen asleep

o3 Or you at the first
p5 Greek Cephas

proclamation has been in vain and your faith has been in vain. 15 We are even found to be misrepresenting God, because we testified of God that he raised Christ—whom he did not raise if it is true that the dead are not raised. 16 For if the dead are not raised, then Christ has not been raised. 17 If Christ has not been raised, your faith is futile and you are still in your sins. 18 Then those also who have died[j] in Christ have perished. 19 If for this life only we have hoped in Christ, we are of all people most to be pitied.

20 But in fact Christ has been raised from the dead, the first fruits of those who have died.[j] 21 For since death came through a human being, the resurrection of the dead has also come through a human being; 22 for as all die in Adam, so all will be made alive in Christ. 23 But each in his own order: Christ the first fruits, then at his coming those who belong to Christ. 24 Then comes the end,[k] when he hands over the kingdom to God the Father, after he has destroyed every ruler and every authority and power. 25 For he must reign until he has put all his enemies under his feet. 26 The last enemy to be destroyed is death. 27 For "God[l] has put all things in subjection under his feet." But when it says, "All things are put in subjection," it is plain that this

οὐκ ἐγήγερται, κενὸν ἄρα τὸ κήρυγμα
has not been raised, empty then the proclamation

ἡμῶν, κενὴ καὶ ἡ πίστις ὑμῶν· 15 εὑρισκ-
of us, empty also the faith of you; ⁴we are

όμεθα δὲ καὶ ψευδομάρτυρες τοῦ θεοῦ,
found ¹and also false witnesses - of God,

ὅτι ἐμαρτυρήσαμεν κατὰ τοῦ θεοῦ ὅτι
because we witnessed as to - God that

ἤγειρεν τὸν Χριστόν, ὃν οὐκ ἤγειρεν
he raised - Christ, whom he raised not

εἴπερ ἄρα νεκροὶ οὐκ ἐγείρονται. 16 εἰ
if then dead persons are not raised. if

γὰρ νεκροὶ οὐκ ἐγείρονται, οὐδὲ Χριστὸς
For dead persons are not raised, neither Christ

ἐγήγερται· 17 εἰ δὲ Χριστὸς οὐκ ἐγήγερται,
has been raised; and if Christ has not been raised,

ματαία ἡ πίστις ὑμῶν [ἐστιν], ἔτι ἐστὲ
⁴useless ¹the ²faith ³of you ⁴is, ⁵still ¹ye are

ἐν ταῖς ἁμαρτίαις ὑμῶν. 18 ἄρα καὶ οἱ
in the sins of you. Then also the [ones]

κοιμηθέντες ἐν Χριστῷ ἀπώλοντο. 19 εἰ
having fallen asleep in Christ perished. If

ἐν τῇ ζωῇ ταύτῃ ἐν Χριστῷ ἠλπικότες
in this life ²in ⁴Christ ¹having hoped

ἐσμὲν μόνον, ἐλεεινότεροι πάντων ἀνθρώπων
¹we are ²only, more pitiful [than] all men

ἐσμέν. 20 Νυνὶ δὲ Χριστὸς ἐγήγερται
we are. But now Christ has been raised

ἐκ νεκρῶν, ἀπαρχὴ τῶν κεκοιμημένων.
from [the] dead, firstfruit of the [ones] having fallen asleep.

21 ἐπειδὴ γὰρ δι' ἀνθρώπου θάνατος, καὶ
For since through a man death [came], also

δι' ἀνθρώπου ἀνάστασις νεκρῶν. 22 ὥσπερ
through a man a resurrection of dead persons as [came].

γὰρ ἐν τῷ Ἀδὰμ πάντες ἀποθνῄσκουσιν,
For in - Adam all die,

οὕτως καὶ ἐν τῷ Χριστῷ πάντες ζωοποιη-
so also in - Christ all will be

θήσονται. 23 Ἕκαστος δὲ ἐν τῷ ἰδίῳ
made alive. But each one in the(his) own

τάγματι· ἀπαρχὴ Χριστός, ἔπειτα οἱ τοῦ
order: [the] Christ, afterward the -
firstfruit [ones]

Χριστοῦ ἐν τῇ παρουσίᾳ αὐτοῦ, 24 εἶτα
of Christ in the presence of him, then

τὸ τέλος, ὅταν παραδιδοῖ τὴν βασιλείαν
the end, whenever he delivers the kingdom

τῷ θεῷ καὶ πατρί, ὅταν καταργήσῃ
- to God even [the] Father, whenever he abolishes

πᾶσαν ἀρχὴν καὶ πᾶσαν ἐξουσίαν καὶ
all rule and all authority and

δύναμιν. 25 δεῖ γὰρ αὐτὸν βασιλεύειν
power. For it behoves him to reign

ἄχρι οὗ θῇ πάντας τοὺς ἐχθροὺς ὑπὸ
until he puts all the(his) enemies under

τοὺς πόδας αὐτοῦ. 26 ἔσχατος ἐχθρὸς
the feet of him. [The] last enemy

καταργεῖται ὁ θάνατος· πάντα γὰρ ὑπέταξεν
is abolished - death; for all things he subjected

ὑπὸ τοὺς πόδας αὐτοῦ. 27 ὅταν δὲ
under the feet of him. But whenever

εἴπῃ ὅτι πάντα ὑποτέτακται, δῆλον ὅτι
he says that all things have been subjected, [it is] clear that

raised, our preaching is useless and so is your faith. 15 More than that, we are then found to be false witnesses about God, for we have testified about God, that he raised Christ from the dead. But he did not raise him if in fact the dead are not raised. 16 For if the dead are not raised, then Christ has not been raised either. 17 And if Christ has not been raised, your faith is futile; you are still in your sins. 18 Then those also who have fallen asleep in Christ are lost. 19 If only for this life we have hope in Christ, we are to be pitied more than all men.

20 But Christ has indeed been raised from the dead, the firstfruits of those who have fallen asleep. 21 For since death came through a man, the resurrection of the dead comes also through a man. 22 For as in Adam all die, so in Christ all will be made alive. 23 But each in his own turn: Christ, the firstfruits; then, when he comes, those who belong to him. 24 Then the end will come, when he hands over the kingdom to God the Father after he has destroyed all dominion, authority and power. 25 For he must reign until he has put all his enemies under his feet. 26 The last enemy to be destroyed is death. 27 For he "has put everything under his feet." [q] Now when it says that "everything" has been put under him, it is clear that this does not

does not include the one who put all things in subjection under him. 28 When all things are subjected to him, then the Son himself will also be subjected to the one who put all things in subjection under him, so that God may be all in all.

29 Otherwise, what will those people do who receive baptism on behalf of the dead? If the dead are not raised at all, why are people baptized on their behalf?

30 And why are we putting ourselves in danger every hour? 31 I die every day! That is as certain, brothers and sisters,ⁱ as my boasting of you—a boast that I make in Christ Jesus our Lord. 32 If with merely human hopes I fought with wild animals at Ephesus, what would I have gained by it? If the dead are not raised,

   "Let us eat and drink,
    for tomorrow we
    die."

33 Do not be deceived: "Bad company ruins good morals."
34 Come to a sober and right mind, and sin no more; for some people have no knowledge of God. I say this to your shame.

The Resurrection Body

35 But someone will ask, "How are the dead raised? With what kind of body do they come?"
36 Fool! What you sow does not come to life unless it dies. 37 And as for what you sow, you do not sow the body that is to be, but a bare seed, perhaps of wheat or of some other grain. 38 But God gives it a body as he has chosen, and to each kind of seed its own body. 39 Not all flesh is alike, but there is one flesh for human beings, another for animals, another for birds, and another for fish.

ἐκτὸς τοῦ ὑποτάξαντος αὐτῷ τὰ πάντα.
[it is] the having to him - all
apart from [one] subjected things.

28 ὅταν δὲ ὑποταγῇ αὐτῷ τὰ πάντα,
But whenever is(are) subjected to him - all things,

τότε καὶ αὐτὸς ὁ υἱὸς ὑποταγήσεται
then also ²[him]self ¹the ¹Son will be subjected

τῷ ὑποτάξαντι αὐτῷ τὰ πάντα, ἵνα
to the having to him - all in order
[one] subjected things, that

ᾖ ὁ θεὸς πάντα ἐν πᾶσιν. 29 Ἐπεὶ
²may - ¹God all in all. Other-
be things wise

τί ποιήσουσιν οἱ βαπτιζόμενοι ὑπὲρ τῶν
what will they do the [ones] being baptized on behalf of the

νεκρῶν; εἰ ὅλως νεκροὶ οὐκ ἐγείρονται,
dead? if actually dead persons are not raised,

τί καὶ βαπτίζονται ὑπὲρ αὐτῶν; 30 τί
why indeed are they baptized on behalf of them? why

καὶ ἡμεῖς κινδυνεύομεν πᾶσαν ὥραν;
also ²we ¹are ³in danger every hour?

31 καθ' ἡμέραν ἀποθνήσκω, νὴ τὴν
Daily I die, by -

ὑμετέραν καύχησιν, ἀδελφοί, ἣν ἔχω ἐν
your boasting, brothers, which I have in

Χριστῷ Ἰησοῦ τῷ κυρίῳ ἡμῶν. 32 εἰ
Christ Jesus the Lord of us. If

κατὰ ἄνθρωπον ἐθηριομάχησα ἐν Ἐφέσῳ,
according man I fought with wild in Ephesus,
to beasts

τί μοι τὸ ὄφελος; εἰ νεκροὶ οὐκ ἐγείρονται,
what to me the profit?ᶜ If dead persons are not raised,
=what profit have I?

φάγωμεν καὶ πίωμεν, αὔριον γὰρ ἀποθνή-
let us eat and let us drink, for to-morrow we

σκομεν. 33 μὴ πλανᾶσθε· φθείρουσιν ἤθη
die. Be ye not led astray; ²corrupt ¹customs

χρηστὰ ὁμιλίαι κακαί. 34 ἐκνήψατε δικαίως
²good ²associations ¹bad. Become ye sober righteously

καὶ μὴ ἁμαρτάνετε· ἀγνωσίαν γὰρ θεοῦ
and do not sin; for ³ignorance ⁴of God

τινες ἔχουσιν· πρὸς ἐντροπὴν ὑμῖν λαλῶ.
¹some ²have; ³for ⁴shame ²to you ¹I speak.

35 Ἀλλὰ ἐρεῖ τις· πῶς ἐγείρονται οἱ
But ²will say ¹someone: How are raised the

νεκροί; ποίῳ δὲ σώματι ἔρχονται; 36 ἄφρων,
dead? and with what body do they Foolish
sort [of] come? man,

σὺ ὃ σπείρεις, οὐ ζωοποιεῖται ἐὰν μὴ
²thou ¹what sowest, is not made alive unless

ἀποθάνῃ; 37 καὶ ὃ σπείρεις, οὐ τὸ σῶμα
it dies; and what thou sowest, not the body

τὸ γενησόμενον σπείρεις, ἀλλὰ γυμνὸν
- going to become thou sowest, but a naked

κόκκον εἰ τύχοι σίτου ἤ τινος τῶν
grain it may be† of wheat or some one of the

λοιπῶν· 38 ὁ δὲ θεὸς δίδωσιν αὐτῷ
rest; - but God gives to it

σῶμα καθὼς ἠθέλησεν, καὶ ἑκάστῳ τῶν
a body as he wished, and to each of the

σπερμάτων ἴδιον σῶμα. 39 οὐ πᾶσα
seeds [its] own body. ³[is] not ¹All

σὰρξ ἡ αὐτὴ σάρξ, ἀλλὰ ἄλλη μὲν
²flesh the same flesh, but other(one) indeed

ἀνθρώπων, ἄλλη δὲ σὰρξ κτηνῶν, ἄλλη δὲ
of men, and another flesh of animals, and another

σὰρξ πτηνῶν, ἄλλη δὲ ἰχθύων. 40 καὶ
flesh of birds, and another of fishes. And [there

---

include God himself, who put everything under Christ. 28 When he has done this, then the Son himself will be made subject to him who put everything under him, so that God may be all in all.

29 Now if there is no resurrection, what will those do who are baptized for the dead? If the dead are not raised at all, why are people baptized for them? 30 And as for us, why do we endanger ourselves every hour? 31 I die every day—I mean that, brothers—just as surely as I glory over you in Christ Jesus our Lord. 32 If I fought wild beasts in Ephesus for merely human reasons, what have I gained? If the dead are not raised,

   "Let us eat and drink,
    for tomorrow we
    die."ʳ

33 Do not be misled: "Bad company corrupts good character." 34 Come back to your senses as you ought, and stop sinning; for there are some who are ignorant of God—I say this to your shame.

The Resurrection Body

35 But someone may ask, "How are the dead raised? With what kind of body will they come?" 36 How foolish! What you sow does not come to life unless it dies. 37 When you sow, you do not plant the body that will be, but just a seed, perhaps of wheat or of something else. 38 But God gives it a body as he has determined, and to each kind of seed he gives its own body. 39 All flesh is not the same: Men have one kind of flesh, animals have another, birds another and fish another.

ʳ32 Isaiah 22:13

40There are both heavenly bodies and earthly bodies, but the glory of the heavenly is one thing, and that of the earthly is another. 41There is one glory of the sun, and another glory of the moon, and another glory of the stars; indeed, star differs from star in glory.

42 So it is with the resurrection of the dead. What is sown is perishable, what is raised is imperishable. 43It is sown in dishonor, it is raised in glory. It is sown in weakness, it is raised in power. 44It is sown a physical body, it is raised a spiritual body. If there is a physical body, there is also a spiritual body. 45Thus it is written, "The first man, Adam, became a living being"; the last Adam became a life-giving spirit. 46But it is not the spiritual that is first, but the physical, and then the spiritual. 47The first man was from the earth, a man of dust; the second man is *m* from heaven. 48As was the man of dust, so are those who are of the dust; and as is the man of heaven, so are those who are of heaven. 49Just as we have borne the image of the man of dust, we will *n* also bear the image of the man of heaven.

50 What I am saying, brothers and sisters,*o* is this: flesh and blood cannot inherit the kingdom of God, nor does the perishable inherit the imperishable. 51Listen, I will tell you a mystery! We will not all die,*p* but we will all be changed, 52in a moment, in the twinkling of an eye, at the last trumpet. For the trumpet will sound, and the dead will be raised imper-

σώματα ἐπουράνια, καὶ σώματα ἐπίγεια·
are] bodies heavenly, and bodies earthly;
ἀλλὰ ἑτέρα μὲν ἡ τῶν ἐπουρανίων δόξα,
but ⁷other ⁶[is] ¹the ⁸of the ⁴heavenly ²glory,
(one) ⁹indeed [bodies]
ἑτέρα δὲ ἡ τῶν ἐπιγείων. 41 ἄλλη
and other the [glory] of the earthly [bodies]. Other(one)
δόξα ἡλίου, καὶ ἄλλη δόξα σελήνης,
glory of [the] sun, and another glory of [the] moon,
καὶ ἄλλη δόξα ἀστέρων· ἀστὴρ γὰρ
and another glory of [the] stars; for star
ἀστέρος διαφέρει ἐν δόξῃ. 42 οὕτως καὶ
from star differs in glory. So also
ἡ ἀνάστασις τῶν νεκρῶν. σπείρεται ἐν
the resurrection of the dead. It is sown in
φθορᾷ, ἐγείρεται ἐν ἀφθαρσίᾳ· 43 σπείρεται
corruption, it is raised in incorruption; it is sown
ἐν ἀτιμίᾳ, ἐγείρεται ἐν δόξῃ· σπείρεται
in dishonour, it is raised in glory; it is sown
ἐν ἀσθενείᾳ, ἐγείρεται ἐν δυνάμει· 44 σπείρ-
in weakness, it is raised in power; it is
εται σῶμα ψυχικόν, ἐγείρεται σῶμα
sown body a natural, it is raised body
πνευματικόν Εἰ ἔστιν σῶμα ψυχικόν,
a spiritual. If there is body a natural,
ἔστιν καὶ πνευματικόν. 45 οὕτως καὶ
there is also a spiritual [body]. So also
γέγραπται· ἐγένετο ὁ πρῶτος ἄνθρωπος
it has been written: ⁶became ¹The ²first ³man
Ἀδὰμ εἰς ψυχὴν ζῶσαν· ὁ ἔσχατος
⁴Adam — soul a living; the last
Ἀδὰμ εἰς πνεῦμα ζωοποιοῦν. 46 ἀλλ'
Adam — spirit a life-giving. But
οὐ πρῶτον τὸ πνευματικὸν ἀλλὰ τὸ
not firstly the spiritual [body] but the
ψυχικόν, ἔπειτα τὸ πνευματικόν. 47 ὁ
natural, afterward the spiritual. The
πρῶτος ἄνθρωπος ἐκ γῆς χοϊκός, ὁ
first man [was] out of earth earthy, the
δεύτερος ἄνθρωπος ἐξ οὐρανοῦ. 48 οἷος ὁ
second man [is] out of heaven. Such the
χοϊκός, τοιοῦτοι καὶ οἱ χοϊκοί, καὶ οἷος
earthy man, such also the earthy ones, and such
ὁ ἐπουράνιος, τοιοῦτοι καὶ οἱ ἐπουράνιοι·
the heavenly man, such also the heavenly ones;
49 καὶ καθὼς ἐφορέσαμεν τὴν εἰκόνα τοῦ
and as we bore the image of the
χοϊκοῦ, φορέσομεν καὶ τὴν εἰκόνα τοῦ
earthy man, we shall bear also the image of the
ἐπουρανίου. 50 Τοῦτο δέ φημι, ἀδελφοί,
heavenly man. And this I say, brothers,
ὅτι σὰρξ καὶ αἷμα βασιλείαν θεοῦ κληρο-
that flesh and blood ²[the] kingdom ⁴of God ⁵to
νομῆσαι οὐ δύναται, οὐδὲ ἡ φθορὰ τὴν
inherit ¹cannot, neither - ¹corruption -
ἀφθαρσίαν κληρονομεῖ. 51 ἰδοὺ μυστήριον
²incorruption ²inherits. Behold[,] a mystery
ὑμῖν λέγω· πάντες οὐ κοιμηθησόμεθα,
to you I tell: all We shall not fall asleep,
πάντες δὲ ἀλλαγησόμεθα, 52 ἐν ἀτόμῳ,
but all . we shall be changed, in a moment,
ἐν ῥιπῇ ὀφθαλμοῦ, ἐν τῇ ἐσχάτῃ σάλπιγγι·
in a glance of an eye, at the last trumpet;
σαλπίσει γάρ, καὶ οἱ νεκροὶ ἐγερθήσονται
for a trumpet will and the dead will be raised
sound,

40There are also heavenly bodies and there are earthly bodies; but the splendor of the heavenly bodies is one kind, and the splendor of the earthly bodies is another. 41The sun has one kind of splendor, the moon another and the stars another; and star differs from star in splendor.

42So will it be with the resurrection of the dead. The body that is sown is perishable, it is raised imperishable; 43it is sown in dishonor, it is raised in glory; it is sown in weakness, it is raised in power; 44it is sown a natural body, it is raised a spiritual body.

If there is a natural body, there is also a spiritual body. 45So it is written: "The first man Adam became a living being"*s*; the last Adam, a life-giving spirit. 46The spiritual did not come first, but the natural, and after that the spiritual. 47The first man was of the dust of the earth, the second man from heaven. 48As was the earthly man, so are those who are of the earth; and as is the man from heaven, so also are those who are of heaven. 49And just as we have borne the likeness of the earthly man, so shall we*t* bear the likeness of the man from heaven.

50I declare to you, brothers, that flesh and blood cannot inherit the kingdom of God, nor does the perishable inherit the imperishable. 51Listen, I tell you a mystery: We will not all sleep, but we will all be changed—52in a flash, in the twinkling of an eye, at the last trumpet. For the trumpet will sound, the dead will be raised imper-

m Other ancient authorities add *the Lord*
n Other ancient authorities read *let us*
o Gk *brothers*
p Gk *fall asleep*

*s*45 Gen. 2:7
*t*49 Some early manuscripts *so let us*

ishable, and we will be changed. 53 For this perishable body must put on imperishability, and this mortal body must put on immortality. 54 When this perishable body puts on imperishability, and this mortal body puts on immortality, then the saying that is written will be fulfilled: "Death has been swallowed up in victory." 55 "Where, O death, is your victory? Where, O death, is your sting?" 56 The sting of death is sin, and the power of sin is the law. 57 But thanks be to God, who gives us the victory through our Lord Jesus Christ. 58 Therefore, my beloved,[q] be steadfast, immovable, always excelling in the work of the Lord, because you know that in the Lord your labor is not in vain.

ἄφθαρτοι, καὶ ἡμεῖς ἀλλαγησόμεθα. 53 Δεῖ
incorruptible, and we shall be changed. it behoves

γὰρ τὸ φθαρτὸν τοῦτο ἐνδύσασθαι
For   - corruptible this to put on

ἀφθαρσίαν καὶ τὸ θνητὸν τοῦτο ἐνδύσασθαι
incorruption and the mortal this to put on

ἀθανασίαν. 54 ὅταν δὲ τὸ φθαρτὸν τοῦτο
immortality. And whenever this [that is] corruptible

ἐνδύσηται ἀφθαρσίαν καὶ τὸ θνητὸν τοῦτο
shall put on incorruption and this [that is] mortal

ἐνδύσηται ἀθανασίαν, τότε γενήσεται ὁ
shall put on immortality, then will be the

λόγος ὁ γεγραμμένος· κατεπόθη ὁ θάνατος
word - having been   ²was - ¹Death
         written: swallowed up

εἰς νῖκος. 55 ποῦ σου, θάνατε, τὸ νῖκος;
in victory. Where of thee, [O] death, the victory?

ποῦ σου, θάνατε, τὸ κέντρον; 56 τὸ δὲ
where of thee, [O] death, the sting? Now the

κέντρον τοῦ θανάτου ἡ ἁμαρτία, ἡ δὲ
sting - of death - [is] sin, and the

δύναμις τῆς ἁμαρτίας ὁ νόμος· 57 τῷ
power of sin [is] the law; -

δὲ θεῷ χάρις τῷ διδόντι ἡμῖν τὸ νῖκος
but to God thanks the [one] giving to us the victory

διὰ τοῦ κυρίου ἡμῶν Ἰησοῦ Χριστοῦ.
through the Lord of us Jesus Christ.

58 Ὥστε, ἀδελφοί μου ἀγαπητοί, ἑδραῖοι
So as, brothers of me beloved, firm

γίνεσθε, ἀμετακίνητοι, περισσεύοντες ἐν τῷ
be ye, unmovable, abounding in the

ἔργῳ τοῦ κυρίου πάντοτε, εἰδότες ὅτι
work of the Lord always, knowing that

ὁ κόπος ὑμῶν οὐκ ἔστιν κενὸς ἐν κυρίῳ.
the labour of you is not empty in [the] Lord.

ishable, and we will be changed. 53 For the perishable must clothe itself with the imperishable, and the mortal with immortality. 54 When the perishable has been clothed with the imperishable, and the mortal with immortality, then the saying that is written will come true: "Death has been swallowed up in victory."[u] 55 "Where, O death, is your victory? Where, O death, is your sting?"[v] 56 The sting of death is sin, and the power of sin is the law. 57 But thanks be to God! He gives us the victory through our Lord Jesus Christ. 58 Therefore, my dear brothers, stand firm. Let nothing move you. Always give yourselves fully to the work of the Lord, because you know that your labor in the Lord is not in vain.

Chapter 16

The Collection for the Saints

NOW concerning the collection for the saints: you should follow the directions I gave to the churches of Galatia. 2 On the first day of every week, each of you is to put aside and save whatever extra you earn, so that collections need not be taken when I come. 3 And when I arrive, I will send any whom you approve by letters to take your gift to Jerusalem. 4 If it seems advisable that I should go also, they will accompany me.

Plans for Travel

5 I will visit you after passing through Macedonia—for I intend to pass through Macedonia—

16 Περὶ δὲ τῆς λογείας τῆς εἰς τοὺς
Now about the collection - for the

ἁγίους, ὥσπερ διέταξα ταῖς ἐκκλησίαις
saints, as I charged the churches

τῆς Γαλατίας, οὕτως καὶ ὑμεῖς ποιήσατε.
 - of Galatia, so also ²ye ¹do.

2 κατὰ μίαν σαββάτου ἕκαστος ὑμῶν
Every one of a week each of you
=On the first day of every week

παρ᾽ ἑαυτῷ τιθέτω θησαυρίζων ὅ τι ἐὰν
by himself let him put storing up whatever

εὐοδῶται, ἵνα μὴ ὅταν ἔλθω τότε λογεῖαι
he is prospered, lest whenever I come then ²collections

γίνωνται. 3 ὅταν δὲ παραγένωμαι, οὓς
¹there are. And whenever I arrive, whom-

ἐὰν δοκιμάσητε, δι᾽ ἐπιστολῶν τούτους
ever ye approve, through epistles these

πέμψω ἀπενεγκεῖν τὴν χάριν ὑμῶν εἰς
I will send to carry the grace(gift) of you to

Ἰερουσαλήμ· 4 ἐὰν δὲ ἄξιον ᾖ τοῦ κἀμὲ
Jerusalem; and if ²fitting ¹it is - me also

πορεύεσθαι, σὺν ἐμοὶ πορεύσονται.
to go,[d] with me they shall go.

5 Ἐλεύσομαι δὲ πρὸς ὑμᾶς ὅταν Μακε-
And I will come to you whenever ²Mace-

δονίαν διέλθω· Μακεδονίαν γὰρ διέρχομαι,
donia ¹I pass for ²Macedonia ¹I am passing
      through;   through,*

Chapter 16

The Collection for God's People

NOW about the collection for God's people: Do what I told the Galatian churches to do. 2 On the first day of every week, each one of you should set aside a sum of money in keeping with his income, saving it up, so that when I come no collections will have to be made. 3 Then, when I arrive, I will give letters of introduction to the men you approve and send them with your gift to Jerusalem. 4 If it seems advisable for me to go also, they will accompany me.

Personal Requests

5 After I go through Macedonia, I will come to you— for I will be going through

[q] Gk beloved brothers

* "Futuristic present"; cf. John 14. 3 and ch. 15. 32.

[u] 54 Isaiah 25:8
[v] 55 Hosea 13:14

6and perhaps I will stay with you or even spend the winter, so that you may send me on my way, wherever I go. 7I do not want to see you now just in passing, for I hope to spend some time with you, if the Lord permits. 8But I will stay in Ephesus until Pentecost, 9for a wide door for effective work has opened to me, and there are many adversaries.

10 If Timothy comes, see that he has nothing to fear among you, for he is doing the work of the Lord just as I am; 11therefore let no one despise him. Send him on his way in peace, so that he may come to me; for I am expecting him with the brothers.

12 Now concerning our brother Apollos, I strongly urged him to visit you with the other brothers, but he was not at all willing' to come now. He will come when he has the opportunity.

Final Messages and Greetings

13 Keep alert, stand firm in your faith, be courageous, be strong. 14Let all that you do be done in love.

15 Now, brothers and sisters,⁰ you know that members of the household of Stephanas were the first converts in Achaia, and they have devoted themselves to the service of the saints; 16I urge you to put yourselves at the service of such people, and of everyone who works and toils with them. 17I rejoice at the coming of Stephanas and Fortunatus and Achaicus, because they have made up for your absence; 18for they refreshed my spirit as

' Or it was not at all God's will for him

---

6 πρὸς ὑμᾶς δὲ τυχὸν καταμενῶ ἢ
⁷with ⁸you ¹and ²possibly ³I will remain ⁴or
καὶ παραχειμάσω, ἵνα ὑμεῖς με προπέμ-
⁵even ⁶spend the winter, in order ⁸ye ⁷me may set
that
ψητε οὗ ἐὰν πορεύωμαι. **7** οὐ θέλω γὰρ
forward wherever I may go. For I do not wish
ὑμᾶς ἄρτι ἐν παρόδῳ ἰδεῖν· ἐλπίζω γὰρ
²you ³yet ⁴in ⁵passage ¹to see; for I am hoping
χρόνον τινὰ ἐπιμεῖναι πρὸς ὑμᾶς, ἐὰν
³time ²some ¹to remain with you, if
ὁ κύριος ἐπιτρέψῃ. **8** ἐπιμενῶ δὲ ἐν
the Lord permits. But I will remain in
Ἐφέσῳ ἕως τῆς πεντηκοστῆς· **9** θύρα
Ephesus until - Pentecost; ²door
γάρ μοι ἀνέῳγεν μεγάλη καὶ ἐνεργής,
¹for ⁴to me ³opened ²a great ³and ⁴effective,
καὶ ἀντικείμενοι πολλοί. **10** Ἐὰν δὲ
and ²opposing ¹many. Now if
[there are]
ἔλθῃ Τιμόθεος, βλέπετε ἵνα ἀφόβως
²comes ¹Timothy, see in order that fearlessly
γένηται πρὸς ὑμᾶς· τὸ γὰρ ἔργον κυρίου
he is with you; for the work of [the] Lord
ἐργάζεται ὡς κἀγώ· **11** μή τις οὖν αὐτὸν
he works as I also; ²not ⁵any- ⁴there- ²him
one fore
ἐξουθενήσῃ. προπέμψατε δὲ αὐτὸν ἐν
¹despise. But set ye forward him in
εἰρήνῃ, ἵνα ἔλθῃ πρός με· ἐκδέχομαι γὰρ
peace, in order he may to me; for I am awaiting
that come
αὐτὸν μετὰ τῶν ἀδελφῶν. **12** Περὶ δὲ
him with the brothers. Now about
Ἀπολλῶ τοῦ ἀδελφοῦ, πολλὰ παρεκάλεσα
²Apollos the ¹brother, ²much ¹I besought
αὐτὸν ἵνα ἔλθῃ πρὸς ὑμᾶς μετὰ τῶν
²him in order he would to you with the
that come
ἀδελφῶν· καὶ πάντως οὐκ ἦν θέλημα
brothers; and altogether it was not [his] will
ἵνα νῦν ἔλθῃ, ἐλεύσεται δὲ ὅταν εὐκαιρήσῃ.
in ²now ¹he but he will come whenever he has
order should opportunity.
that come,
13 Γρηγορεῖτε, στήκετε ἐν τῇ πίστει,
Watch ye, stand in the faith,
ἀνδρίζεσθε, κραταιοῦσθε. **14** πάντα ὑμῶν
play the man, be strong. ¹All things ²of you
ἐν ἀγάπῃ γινέσθω.
⁴in ⁵love ¹let be.
15 Παρακαλῶ δὲ ὑμᾶς, ἀδελφοί· οἴδατε
Now I beseech you, brothers: Know ye
τὴν οἰκίαν Στεφανᾶ, ὅτι ἐστὶν ἀπαρχὴ
the household of Stephanas, that it is firstfruit
τῆς Ἀχαΐας καὶ εἰς διακονίαν τοῖς
- of Achaia and to ministry to the
ἁγίοις ἔταξαν ἑαυτούς· **16** ἵνα καὶ ὑμεῖς
saints they themselves; in order also ye
appointed that
ὑποτάσσησθε τοῖς τοιούτοις καὶ παντὶ τῷ
may submit to such ones and to everyone
συνεργοῦντι καὶ κοπιῶντι. **17** χαίρω δὲ
working with [?me] and labouring. Now I rejoice
ἐπὶ τῇ παρουσίᾳ Στεφανᾶ καὶ Φορτουνάτου
at the presence of Stephanas and of Fortunatus
καὶ Ἀχαϊκοῦ, ὅτι τὸ ὑμέτερον ὑστέρημα
and of Achaicus, that - ³your ⁴lack
οὗτοι ἀνεπλήρωσαν· **18** ἀνέπαυσαν γὰρ τὸ
¹these ²supplied; for they refreshed -

Macedonia. 6Perhaps I will stay with you awhile, or even spend the winter, so that you can help me on my journey, wherever I go. 7I do not want to see you now and make only a passing visit; I hope to spend some time with you, if the Lord permits. 8But I will stay on at Ephesus until Pentecost, 9because a great door for effective work has opened to me, and there are many who oppose me.

10If Timothy comes, see to it that he has nothing to fear while he is with you, for he is carrying on the work of the Lord, just as I am. 11No one, then, should refuse to accept him. Send him on his way in peace so that he may return to me. I am expecting him along with the brothers.

12Now about our brother Apollos: I strongly urged him to go to you with the brothers. He was quite unwilling to go now, but he will go when he has the opportunity.

13Be on your guard; stand firm in the faith; be men of courage; be strong. 14Do everything in love.

15You know that the household of Stephanas were the first converts in Achaia, and they have devoted themselves to the service of the saints. I urge you, brothers, 16to submit to such as these and to everyone who joins in the work, and labors at it. 17I was glad when Stephanas, Fortunatus and Achaicus arrived, because they have supplied what was lacking from you. 18For they re-well as yours. So give recognition to such persons.

19 The churches of Asia send greetings. Aquila and Prisca, together with the church in their house, greet you warmly in the Lord. 20 All the brothers and sisters° send greetings. Greet one another with a holy kiss.

21 I, Paul, write this greeting with my own hand. 22 Let anyone be accursed who has no love for the Lord. Our Lord, come!ˢ 23 The grace of the Lord Jesus be with you. 24 My love be with all of you in Christ Jesus.ᵗ

ἐμὸν πνεῦμα καὶ τὸ ὑμῶν. ἐπιγινώσκετε
my spirit and - of you(yours). Recognize ye
οὖν τοὺς τοιούτους.
therefore - such ones.

19 Ἀσπάζονται ὑμᾶς αἱ ἐκκλησίαι τῆς
⁴Greet ⁵you ¹the ²churches -
Ἀσίας. ἀσπάζεται ὑμᾶς ἐν κυρίῳ πολλὰ
³of Asia. ⁴Greets ⁵you ⁷in ⁸[the] Lord ⁶much
Ἀκύλας καὶ Πρίσκα σὺν τῇ κατ' οἶκον
¹Aquila ²and ³Prisca ⁹with ¹⁰the ¹¹in [the] house
αὐτῶν ἐκκλησίᾳ. 20 ἀσπάζονται ὑμᾶς οἱ
¹³of them ¹²church. ⁴Greet ⁵you ²the
ἀδελφοὶ πάντες. Ἀσπάσασθε ἀλλήλους ἐν
³brothers ¹all. Greet ye one another with
φιλήματι ἁγίῳ. 21 Ὁ ἀσπασμὸς τῇ
kiss a holy. ¹The ²greeting -
ἐμῇ χειρὶ Παύλου. 22 εἴ τις οὐ φιλεῖ
⁴with my ³hand ⁵of Paul. If anyone loves not
τὸν κύριον, ἤτω ἀνάθεμα. μαράνα θά.
the Lord, let him be a curse. Marana tha.
23 ἡ χάρις τοῦ κυρίου Ἰησοῦ μεθ' ὑμῶν.
The grace of the Lord Jesus [be] with you.
24 ἡ ἀγάπη μου μετὰ πάντων ὑμῶν ἐν
The love of me [be] with ²all ¹you in
Χριστῷ Ἰησοῦ.
Christ Jesus.

---

freshed my spirit and yours also. Such men deserve recognition.

Final Greetings

19The churches in the province of Asia send you greetings. Aquila and Priscillaʷ greet you warmly in the Lord, and so does the church that meets at their house. 20All the brothers here send you greetings. Greet one another with a holy kiss.

21I, Paul, write this greeting in my own hand.

22If anyone does not love the Lord—a curse be on him. Come, O Lordˣ!

23The grace of the Lord Jesus be with you.

24My love to all of you in Christ Jesus. Amen.ʸ

ˢ Gk Marana tha. These Aramaic words can also be read Maran atha, meaning Our Lord has come
ᵗ Other ancient authorities add Amen

ʷ19 Greek Prisca, a variant of Priscilla
ˣ22 In Aramaic the expression Come, O Lord is Marana tha.
ʸ24 Some manuscripts do not have Amen.

The Second Letter of
Paul to the

Corinthians

Chapter 1

Salutation

PAUL, an apostle of Christ Jesus by the will of God, and Timothy our brother,

To the church of God that is in Corinth, including all the saints throughout Achaia:

2 Grace to you and peace from God our Father and the Lord Jesus Christ.

Paul's Thanksgiving after Affliction

3 Blessed be the God and Father of our Lord Jesus Christ, the Father of mercies and the God of all consolation, 4 who consoles us in all our affliction, so that we may be able to console those who are in any affliction with the consolation with which we ourselves are consoled by God. 5 For just as the sufferings of Christ are abundant for us, so also our consolation is abundant through Christ. 6 If we are being afflicted, it is for your consolation and salvation; if we are being consoled, it is for your consolation, which you experience when you patiently endure the same sufferings that we are also suffering. 7 Our hope for you is unshaken; for we know that as you share in our sufferings, so also you share in our consolation.

8 We do not want you to be unaware, brothers and sisters,[a] of the affliction we experienced in Asia; for we were so utterly, unbearably crushed that we despaired of life itself. 9 Indeed, we felt that we had received the sentence of death so that we would rely

[a] Gk brothers

---

1 Παῦλος ἀπόστολος Χριστοῦ Ἰησοῦ
Paul an apostle of Christ Jesus

διὰ θελήματος θεοῦ καὶ Τιμόθεος ὁ
through [the] will of God and Timothy the

ἀδελφὸς τῇ ἐκκλησίᾳ τοῦ θεοῦ τῇ οὔσῃ
brother to the church - of God - being

ἐν Κορίνθῳ σὺν τοῖς ἁγίοις πᾶσιν τοῖς
in Corinth with ⁸the ⁹saints ¹all -

οὖσιν ἐν ὅλῃ τῇ Ἀχαΐᾳ. **2** χάρις ὑμῖν καὶ
being in all - Achaia: Grace to you and

εἰρήνη ἀπὸ θεοῦ πατρὸς ἡμῶν καὶ κυρίου
peace from God [the] Father of us and [the] Lord

Ἰησοῦ Χριστοῦ.
Jesus Christ.

3 Εὐλογητὸς ὁ θεὸς καὶ πατὴρ τοῦ
Blessed [be] the God and Father of the

κυρίου ἡμῶν Ἰησοῦ Χριστοῦ, ὁ πατὴρ
Lord of us Jesus Christ, the Father

τῶν οἰκτιρμῶν καὶ θεὸς πάσης παρακλήσ-
- of compassions and God of all com-

εως, **4** ὁ παρακαλῶν ἡμᾶς ἐπὶ πάσῃ
fort, the [one] comforting us on(in) all

τῇ θλίψει ἡμῶν, εἰς τὸ δύνασθαι ἡμᾶς
the affliction of us, [with a - to be able usᵇ
view] to =our being able

παρακαλεῖν τοὺς ἐν πάσῃ θλίψει διὰ
to comfort the ones in every affliction through

τῆς παρακλήσεως ἧς παρακαλούμεθα αὐτοὶ
the comfort of(with) we are comforted [our-]
which selves

ὑπὸ τοῦ θεοῦ. **5** ὅτι καθὼς περισσεύει τὰ
by - God. Because as abounds the

παθήματα τοῦ Χριστοῦ εἰς ἡμᾶς, οὕτως
sufferings of Christ in us, so

διὰ τοῦ Χριστοῦ περισσεύει καὶ ἡ παρά-
through - Christ abounds also the com-

κλησις ἡμῶν. **6** εἴτε δὲ θλιβόμεθα, ὑπὲρ
fort of us. Now whether we are on be-
afflicted, half of

τῆς ὑμῶν παρακλήσεως καὶ σωτηρίας· εἴτε
the ⁴of you ¹comfort ⁸and ¹salvation; or

παρακαλούμεθα, ὑπὲρ τῆς ὑμῶν παρακλή-
we are comforted, on behalf of the ⁹of you ¹com-

σεως τῆς ἐνεργουμένης ἐν ὑπομονῇ τῶν
fort - operating in endurance of the

αὐτῶν παθημάτων ὧν καὶ ἡμεῖς πάσχομεν,
same sufferings which also we suffer,

7 καὶ ἡ ἐλπὶς ἡμῶν βεβαία ὑπὲρ ὑμῶν
and the hope of us [is] firm on behalf of you

εἰδότες ὅτι ὡς κοινωνοί ἐστε τῶν παθημά-
knowing that as partakers ye are of the suffer-

των, οὕτως καὶ τῆς παρακλήσεως. **8** Οὐ
ings, so also of the comfort. not

γὰρ θέλομεν ὑμᾶς ἀγνοεῖν, ἀδελφοί, ὑπὲρ
For we wish you to be ignorant, brothers, as to

τῆς θλίψεως ἡμῶν τῆς γενομένης ἐν
the affliction of us - having been in

τῇ Ἀσίᾳ, ὅτι καθ' ὑπερβολὴν ὑπὲρ
- Asia, that excessively† beyond

δύναμιν ἐβαρήθημεν, ὥστε ἐξαπορηθῆναι
power we were burdened, so as to despair
=so that we despaired even

ἡμᾶς καὶ τοῦ ζῆν· **9** ἀλλὰ αὐτοὶ ἐν
usᵇ even - to live; but [our]selves in
of life;

ἑαυτοῖς τὸ ἀπόκριμα τοῦ θανάτου ἐσχήκα-
ourselves the sentence - of death we have

PAUL, an apostle of Christ Jesus by the will of God, and Timothy our brother,

To the church of God in Corinth, together with all the saints throughout Achaia:

2 Grace and peace to you from God our Father and the Lord Jesus Christ.

The God of All Comfort

3 Praise be to the God and Father of our Lord Jesus Christ, the Father of compassion and the God of all comfort, 4 who comforts us in all our troubles, so that we can comfort those in any trouble with the comfort we ourselves have received from God. 5 For just as the sufferings of Christ flow over into our lives, so also through Christ our comfort overflows. 6 If we are distressed, it is for your comfort and salvation; if we are comforted, it is for your comfort, which produces in you patient endurance of the same sufferings we suffer. 7 And our hope for you is firm, because we know that just as you share in our sufferings, so also you share in our comfort.

8 We do not want you to be uninformed, brothers, about the hardships we suffered in the province of Asia. We were under great pressure, far beyond our ability to endure, so that we despaired even of life. 9 Indeed, in our hearts we felt

not on ourselves but on God who raises the dead. ¹⁰He who rescued us from so deadly a peril will continue to rescue us; on him we have set our hope that he will rescue us again, ¹¹ as you also join in helping us by your prayers, so that many will give thanks on our ᵇ behalf for the blessing granted us through the prayers of many.

The Postponement of Paul's Visit

12 Indeed, this is our boast, the testimony of our conscience: we have behaved in the world with frankness ᶜ and godly sincerity, not by earthly wisdom but by the grace of God—and all the more toward you. 13 For we write you nothing other than what you can read and also understand; I hope you will understand until the end—¹⁴ as you have already understood us in part—that on the day of the Lord Jesus we are your boast even as you are our boast.

15 Since I was sure of this, I wanted to come to you first, so that you might have a double favor; ᵈ ¹⁶ I wanted to visit you on my way to Macedonia, and to come back to you from Macedonia and have you send me on to Judea. ¹⁷ Was I vacillating when I wanted to do this? Do I make my plans according to ordinary human standards, ᵉ ready to say "Yes,

---

μεν, ἵνα μὴ πεποιθότες ὦμεν ἐφ' ἑαυτοῖς
had, in order ²not ³having ¹we on ourselves
       that   trusted   might be

ἀλλ' ἐπὶ τῷ θεῷ τῷ ἐγείροντι τοὺς
but on - God the [one] raising the

νεκρούς· 10 ὃς ἐκ τηλικούτου θανάτου
dead; who out of so great a death

ἐρρύσατο ἡμᾶς καὶ ρύσεται, εἰς ὃν
delivered us and will deliver, in whom

ἠλπίκαμεν [ὅτι] καὶ ἔτι ρύσεται, 11 συν-
we have hoped that indeed yet he will deliver, co-

υπουργούντων καὶ ὑμῶν ὑπὲρ ἡμῶν τῇ
operating also youᵃ on behalf of us -
=while ye also coöperate

δεήσει, ἵνα ἐκ πολλῶν προσώπων τὸ
in petition, in order ⁴by ⁵many ⁶persons ⁷[for]
    that   ⁸the

εἰς ἡμᾶς χάρισμα διὰ πολλῶν εὐχαριστηθῇ
¹⁰to ¹¹us ⁹gift ¹²through ¹³many ¹thanks may be given

ὑπὲρ ἡμῶν.
²on behalf of ³us.

12 Ἡ γὰρ καύχησις ἡμῶν αὕτη ἐστίν,
For the boasting of us ²this ¹is,

τὸ μαρτύριον τῆς συνειδήσεως ἡμῶν, ὅτι
the testimony of the conscience of us, because

ἐν ἁγιότητι καὶ εἰλικρινείᾳ τοῦ θεοῦ,
in sanctity and sincerity - of God,

οὐκ ἐν σοφίᾳ σαρκικῇ ἀλλ' ἐν χάριτι
not in wisdom fleshly but in [the] grace

θεοῦ, ἀνεστράφημεν ἐν τῷ κόσμῳ, περισ-
of God, we behaved in the world, ²more

σοτέρως δὲ πρὸς ὑμᾶς. 13 οὐ γὰρ ἄλλα
⁵especially ¹and with you. ³Not ¹for ⁴other things

γράφομεν ὑμῖν ἀλλ' ἢ ἃ ἀναγινώσκετε
²we write to you other than what ye read

ἢ καὶ ἐπιγινώσκετε, ἐλπίζω δὲ ὅτι
or even perceive, and I hope that

ἕως τέλους ἐπιγνώσεσθε, 14 καθὼς καὶ
to [the] end ye will perceive, as also

ἐπέγνωτε ἡμᾶς ἀπὸ μέρους, ὅτι καύχημα
ye perceived us from(in) part, because ²boast

ὑμῶν ἐσμεν καθάπερ καὶ ὑμεῖς ἡμῶν
³of you ¹we are even as also ye of us

ἐν τῇ ἡμέρᾳ τοῦ κυρίου ἡμῶν Ἰησοῦ.
in the day of the Lord of us Jesus.

15 Καὶ ταύτῃ τῇ πεποιθήσει ἐβουλόμην
And in this - persuasion I determined

πρότερον πρὸς ὑμᾶς ἐλθεῖν ἵνα δευτέραν
formerly to you to come in order a second
                           that

χάριν σχῆτε, 16 καὶ δι' ὑμῶν διελθεῖν
grace ye might have, and through you to pass *through*

εἰς Μακεδονίαν, καὶ πάλιν ἀπὸ Μακεδονίας
into Macedonia, and again from Macedonia

ἐλθεῖν πρὸς ὑμᾶς καὶ ὑφ' ὑμῶν
to come to you and by you

προπεμφθῆναι εἰς τὴν Ἰουδαίαν. 17 τοῦτο
to be set forward to - Judæa. This

οὖν βουλόμενος μήτι ἄρα τῇ ἐλαφρίᾳ
therefore determining *not* ²then - ²fickleness

ἐχρησάμην; ἢ ἃ βουλεύομαι κατὰ σάρκα
¹did I use? or [the] I determine according [the]
         things which   to   flesh

βουλεύομαι, ἵνα ᾖ παρ' ἐμοὶ τὸ ναὶ
do I determine, in order there with me the Yes
           that may be

---

the sentence of death. But this happened that we might not rely on ourselves but on God, who raises the dead. ¹⁰He has delivered us from such a deadly peril, and he will deliver us. On him we have set our hope that he will continue to deliver us, ¹¹as you help us by your prayers. Then many will give thanks on our ᵃ behalf for the gracious favor granted us in answer to the prayers of many.

Paul's Change of Plans

¹²Now this is our boast: Our conscience testifies that we have conducted ourselves in the world, and especially in our relations with you, in the holiness and sincerity that are from God. We have done so not according to worldly wisdom but according to God's grace. ¹³For we do not write you anything you cannot read or understand. And I hope that, ¹⁴as you have understood us in part, you will come to understand fully that you can boast of us just as we will boast of you in the day of the Lord Jesus.

¹⁵Because I was confident of this, I planned to visit you first so that you might benefit twice. ¹⁶I planned to visit you on my way to Macedonia and to come back to you from Macedonia, and then to have you send me on my way to Judea. ¹⁷When I planned this, did I do it lightly? Or do I make my plans in a worldly manner so that in the same breath I

ᵇ Other ancient authorities read *your*
ᶜ Other ancient authorities read *holiness*
ᵈ Other ancient authorities read *pleasure*
ᵉ Gk *according to the flesh*

ᵃ11 Many manuscripts *your*

yes" and "No, no" at the same time? 18 As surely as God is faithful, our word to you has not been "Yes and No." 19 For the Son of God, Jesus Christ, whom we proclaimed among you, Silvanus and Timothy and I, was not "Yes and No"; but in him it is always "Yes." 20 For in him every one of God's promises is a "Yes." For this reason it is through him that we say the "Amen," to the glory of God. 21 But it is God who establishes us with you in Christ and has anointed us, 22 by putting his seal on us and giving us his Spirit in our hearts as a first installment.

23 But I call on God as witness against me: it was to spare you that I did not come again to Corinth. 24 I do not mean to imply that we lord it over your faith; rather, we are workers with you for your joy, because you stand firm in the faith. 1 So I made up my mind not to make you another painful visit. 2 For if I cause you pain, who is there to make me glad but the one whom I have pained? 3 And I wrote as I did, so that when I came, I might not suffer pain from those who should have made me rejoice; for I am confident about all of you, that my joy would be the joy of all of you. 4 For I wrote you out of much distress and anguish of heart and with many tears, not to cause you pain, but to let you know the abundant love that I have for you.

ναὶ	καὶ	τὸ	οὔ	οὔ;	**18** πιστὸς	δὲ	ὁ
yes	and	the	No	no?	**But faithful** [is]	–	–

θεὸς	ὅτι	ὁ	λόγος	ἡμῶν	ὁ πρὸς	ὑμᾶς
God	that	the	word	of us –	the to	you

οὐκ	ἔστιν	ναὶ	καὶ	οὔ.	**19** ὁ	τοῦ θεοῦ
is not		yes	and	no.	**¹the**	– ⁴of God

γὰρ	υἱὸς	Χριστὸς	Ἰησοῦς	ὁ	ἐν	ὑμῖν
¹For	³Son	Christ	Jesus	¹the	²among	⁴you [one]

δι'	ἡμῶν	κηρυχθείς,	δι' ἐμοῦ καὶ	Σιλουανοῦ
¹through	²us	²proclaimed,	through me and	Silvanus

καὶ	Τιμοθέου,	οὐκ	ἐγένετο	ναὶ καὶ	οὔ,
and	Timothy,		was not	yes and	no,

ἀλλὰ	ναὶ	ἐν	αὐτῷ	γέγονεν.	**20** ὅσαι γὰρ
but	²Yes	³in	⁴him	¹has been.	**For as many**

ἐπαγγελίαι	θεοῦ,	ἐν	αὐτῷ	τὸ	ναί· διὸ
[as are] promises	of God,	in	him [is]	the	Yes; wherefore

καὶ	δι'	αὐτοῦ	τὸ	ἀμὴν	τῷ θεῷ	πρὸς
also	through	him	the	Amen	– ²to God	¹unto

δόξαν	δι'	ἡμῶν.	**21** ὁ δὲ	βεβαιῶν	ἡμᾶς
²glory	through	us.	**But the [one]**	making firm	us

σὺν	ὑμῖν	εἰς	Χριστὸν	καὶ χρίσας	ἡμᾶς [is]
with	you	in	Christ	and having anointed	us

θεός,	**22** ὁ	καὶ	σφραγισάμενος	ἡμᾶς	καὶ
God,	**the [one]**	both	having sealed	us	and

δοὺς	τὸν	ἀρραβῶνα	τοῦ	πνεύματος	ἐν
having given	the	earnest	of the	Spirit	in

ταῖς	καρδίαις ἡμῶν.
the	hearts of us.

23 Ἐγὼ	δὲ	μάρτυρα	τὸν θεὸν	ἐπικαλοῦμαι
Now ⁴I	δὲ	⁷[as] witness	– ⁶God	⁵invoke

ἐπὶ	τὴν	ἐμὴν	ψυχήν,	ὅτι φειδόμενος
¹on	–	³my	²life,	that sparing

ὑμῶν	οὐκέτι	ἦλθον	εἰς Κόρινθον.	**24** οὐχ ὅτι
you	²no more	¹I came	to Corinth.	**Not that**

κυριεύομεν	ὑμῶν	τῆς	πίστεως,	ἀλλὰ συνεργοὶ
we rule over	²of you	¹the	²faith,	but ²fellow-workers

ἐσμεν	τῆς	χαρᾶς	ὑμῶν·	τῇ γὰρ	πίστει
¹we are	of the	joy	of you;	– for	by faith

ἑστήκατε.	**2** ἔκρινα	δὲ	ἐμαυτῷ	τοῦτο,	τὸ μὴ
ye stand.	**But I decided**		in myself	this,	– not

πάλιν	ἐν	λύπῃ	πρὸς	ὑμᾶς	ἐλθεῖν. **2** εἰ
again	⁴in	³grief	²to	²you	¹to come. **if**

γὰρ	ἐγὼ	λυπῶ	ὑμᾶς,	καὶ τίς	ὁ εὐφραίνων
For	I	grieve	you,	then who	the making glad [one]

με	εἰ	μὴ	ὁ λυπούμενος	ἐξ ἐμοῦ;	**3** καὶ
me	except		the [one] being grieved	by me?	**And**

ἔγραψα	τοῦτο	αὐτὸ	ἵνα μὴ	ἐλθὼν λύπην
I wrote	this	very thing	lest	coming grief

σχῶ	ἀφ'	ὧν	ἔδει με	χαίρειν, πεποιθὼς
I should have	from [those]	whom	it behoved me	to rejoice, having confidence

ἐπὶ	πάντας	ὑμᾶς	ὅτι ἡ	ἐμὴ χαρὰ πάντων
in	²all	¹you	that –	my joy ²all

ὑμῶν	ἐστιν.	**4** ἐκ	γὰρ	πολλῆς θλίψεως
²of you	¹is.	**For out of**		much affliction

καὶ	συνοχῆς	καρδίας	ἔγραψα ὑμῖν διὰ
and	anxiety	of heart	I wrote to you through

πολλῶν	δακρύων,	οὐχ	ἵνα	λυπηθῆτε, ἀλλὰ
many	tears,	not	in order that	ye should be grieved, but

τὴν	ἀγάπην	ἵνα	γνῶτε	ἣν ἔχω περισ-
²the	⁴love	¹in order that	²ye should know	⁵which I have more

say, "Yes, yes" and "No, no"? 18 But as surely as God is faithful, our message to you is not "Yes" and "No." 19 For the Son of God, Jesus Christ, who was preached among you by me and Silas[b] and Timothy, was not "Yes" and "No," but in him it has always been "Yes." 20 For no matter how many promises God has made, they are "Yes" in Christ. And so through him the "Amen" is spoken by us to the glory of God. 21 Now it is God who makes both us and you stand firm in Christ. He anointed us, 22 set his seal of ownership on us, and put his Spirit in our hearts as a deposit, guaranteeing what is to come.

23 I call God as my witness that it was in order to spare you that I did not return to Corinth. 24 Not that we lord it over your faith, but we work with you for your joy, because it is by faith you stand firm.

1 So I made up my mind that I would not make another painful visit to you. 2 For if I grieve you, who is left to make me glad but you whom I have grieved? 3 I wrote as I did so that when I came I should not be distressed by those who ought to make me rejoice. I had confidence in all of you, that you would all share my joy. 4 For I wrote you out of great distress and anguish of heart and with many tears, not to

b 19 Greek *Silvanus*, a variant of *Silas*

Forgiveness for the Offender

5 But if anyone has caused pain, he has caused it not to me, but to some extent—not to exaggerate it—to all of you. 6 This punishment by the majority is enough for such a person; 7 so now instead you should forgive and console him, so that he may not be overwhelmed by excessive sorrow. 8 So I urge you to reaffirm your love for him. 9 I wrote for this reason: to test you and to know whether you are obedient in everything. 10 Anyone whom you forgive, I also forgive. What I have forgiven, if I have forgiven anything, has been for your sake in the presence of Christ. 11 And we do this so that we may not be outwitted by Satan; for we are not ignorant of his designs.

Paul's Anxiety in Troas

12 When I came to Troas to proclaim the good news of Christ, a door was opened for me in the Lord; 13 but my mind could not rest because I did not find my brother Titus there. So I said farewell to them and went on to Macedonia.

14 But thanks be to God, who in Christ always leads us in triumphal procession, and through us spreads in every place the fragrance that comes from knowing him. 15 For we are the aroma of Christ to God among those who are being saved and among those who are perishing; 16 to the one a fragrance from death to death, to the other a fragrance from life to life. Who is sufficient for these things? 17 For we are not peddlers of God's word like

σοτέρως   εἰς   ὑμᾶς.   5 Εἰ   δέ   τις   λελύπηκεν,
abundantly   to   you.   But if   anyone   has grieved,

οὐκ   ἐμὲ   λελύπηκεν,   ἀλλὰ   ἀπὸ   μέρους,
not   me   he has grieved,   but   from(in)   part,

ἵνα   μὴ   ἐπιβαρῶ,   πάντας   ὑμᾶς.   6 ἱκανὸν
lest   I am burdensome,   ²all   ¹you.   Enough

τῷ   τοιούτῳ   ἡ   ἐπιτιμία   αὕτη   ἡ   ὑπὸ
for such a one   this punishment   -   by

τῶν   πλειόνων,   7 ὥστε   τοὐναντίον   μᾶλλον
the   majority,   so as   on the contrary   rather

ὑμᾶς   χαρίσασθαι   καὶ   παρακαλέσαι,   μή   πως
you   to forgive   and   to comfort,ᵇ   lest
=ye should rather forgive and comfort,

τῇ   περισσοτέρᾳ   λύπῃ   καταποθῇ   ὁ   τοιοῦτος.
²by   ⁴more abundant   ⁵grief   ³should be   ¹such a one.
the   swallowed up

8 διὸ   παρακαλῶ   ὑμᾶς   κυρῶσαι   εἰς   αὐτὸν
Wherefore   I beseech   you   to confirm   to   him

ἀγάπην·   9 εἰς   τοῦτο   γὰρ   καὶ   ἔγραψα,
[your] love;   ²to   ³this [end]   ¹for   indeed   I wrote,

ἵνα   γνῶ   τὴν   δοκιμὴν   ὑμῶν,   εἰ   εἰς   πάντα
in or-   I might the   proof   of you,   if   in   all things
der that know

ὑπήκοοί   ἐστε.   10 ᾧ   δέ   τι   χαρίζεσθε,
obedient   ye are.   Now to whom anything   ye forgive,

κἀγώ·   καὶ   γὰρ   ἐγὼ   ὃ   κεχάρισμαι,   εἴ
I also;   for indeed   ²I   ¹what   ³have forgiven,   if

τι   κεχάρισμαι,   δι'   ὑμᾶς   ἐν   προσώπῳ
²any-   ¹I have   [it is] on   you   in   [the] person
thing   forgiven,   account of

Χριστοῦ,   11 ἵνα   μὴ   πλεονεκτηθῶμεν   ὑπὸ
of Christ,   lest   we are taken advantage of   by

τοῦ   σατανᾶ·   οὐ   γὰρ   αὐτοῦ   τὰ   νοήματα
-    Satan;   for ²not   ¹of him   -the   ⁴designs

ἀγνοοῦμεν.   12 Ἐλθὼν   δὲ   εἰς   τὴν   Τρῳάδα   εἰς
¹we ²are ⁴ignorant [of].   But coming   to   -   Troas   in

τὸ   εὐαγγέλιον   τοῦ   Χριστοῦ,   καὶ   θύρας
the   gospel   -   of Christ,   and   a door

μοι   ἀνεῳγμένης   ἐν   κυρίῳ,   13 οὐκ   ἔσχηκα
to me   having been   by [the] Lord,   I have had no
opened*

ἄνεσιν   τῷ   πνεύματί   μου   τῷ   μὴ   εὑρεῖν
rest   to the   spirit   of me   in the   not   to find
=when I did not find ...

με   Τίτον   τὸν   ἀδελφόν   μου,   ἀλλὰ   ἀποτα-
meᵇᵉ   Titus   the   brother   of me,   but   saying

ξάμενος   αὐτοῖς   ἐξῆλθον   εἰς   Μακεδονίαν.
farewell   to them   I went forth   into   Macedonia.

14 Τῷ   δὲ   θεῷ   χάρις   τῷ   πάντοτε
-    But   ²to God   ¹thanks   the [one]   always

θριαμβεύοντι   ἡμᾶς   ἐν   τῷ   Χριστῷ   καὶ
leading in triumph   us   in   -   Christ   and

τὴν   ὀσμὴν   τῆς   γνώσεως   αὐτοῦ   φανεροῦντι
⁴the   ⁵odour   ⁶of the   ⁷knowledge   ⁸of him   ¹manifesting

δι'   ἡμῶν   ἐν   παντὶ   τόπῳ·   15 ὅτι   Χριστοῦ
²through   ³us   in   every   place;   because   of Christ

εὐωδία   ἐσμὲν   τῷ   θεῷ   ἐν   τοῖς   σῳζομένοις
a sweet   we are   -   to God   in   the [ones] being saved
smell

καὶ   ἐν   τοῖς   ἀπολλυμένοις,   16 οἷς   μὲν
and   in   the [ones]   perishing,   to the [latter]†

ὀσμὴ   ἐκ   θανάτου   εἰς   θάνατον,   οἷς   δὲ
an odour out of   death   unto   death,   to the [former]†

ὀσμὴ   ἐκ   ζωῆς   εἰς   ζωήν.   καὶ   πρὸς
an odour out of   life   unto   life.   And   for

ταῦτα   τίς   ἱκανός;   17 οὐ   γὰρ   ἐσμεν
these things   who [is]   competent?   For we are not

ὡς   οἱ   πολλοὶ   καπηλεύοντες   τὸν   λόγον
as   the   many   hawking   the   word

grieve you but to let you know the depth of my love for you.

Forgiveness for the Sinner

5 If anyone has caused grief, he has not so much grieved me as he has grieved all of you, to some extent—not to put it too severely. 6 The punishment inflicted on him by the majority is sufficient for him. 7 Now instead, you ought to forgive and comfort him, so that he will not be overwhelmed by excessive sorrow. 8 I urge you, therefore, to reaffirm your love for him. 9 The reason I wrote you was to see if you would stand the test and be obedient in everything. 10 If you forgive anyone, I also forgive him. And what I have forgiven—if there was anything to forgive—I have forgiven in the sight of Christ for your sake, 11 in order that Satan might not outwit us. For we are not unaware of his schemes.

Ministers of the New Covenant

12 Now when I went to Troas to preach the gospel of Christ and found that the Lord had opened a door for me, 13 I still had no peace of mind, because I did not find my brother Titus there. So I said good-by to them and went on to Macedonia.

14 But thanks be to God, who always leads us in triumphal procession in Christ and through us spreads everywhere the fragrance of the knowledge of him. 15 For we are to God the aroma of Christ among those who are being saved and those who are perishing. 16 To the one we are the smell of death; to the other, the fragrance of life. And who is equal to such a task? 17 Unlike so many, we do not peddle the word of God

so many;*f* but in Christ we speak as persons of sincerity, as persons sent from God and standing in his presence.

Chapter 3

Ministers of the New Covenant

ARE we beginning to commend ourselves again? Surely we do not need, as some do, letters of recommendation to you or from you, do we? ²You yourselves are our letter, written on our*g* hearts, to be known and read by all; ³and you show that you are a letter of Christ, prepared by us, written not with ink but with the Spirit of the living God, not on tablets of stone but on tablets of human hearts.

4 Such is the confidence that we have through Christ toward God. ⁵Not that we are competent of ourselves to claim anything as coming from us; our competence is from God, ⁶who has made us competent to be ministers of a new covenant, not of letter but of spirit; for the letter kills, but the Spirit gives life.

7 Now if the ministry of death, chiseled in letters on stone tablets,*h* came in glory so that the people of Israel could not gaze at Moses' face because of the glory of his face, a glory now set aside, ⁸how much more will the ministry of the Spirit come in glory? ⁹For if there was glory in the ministry of condemnation, much more does the ministry of justification abound in glory! ¹⁰Indeed, what once had glory has lost its

---

τοῦ θεοῦ, ἀλλ' ὡς ἐξ εἰλικρινείας, ἀλλ'
\- of God, but as of sincerity, but

ὡς ἐκ θεοῦ κατέναντι θεοῦ ἐν Χριστῷ
as of God before God in Christ

λαλοῦμεν.
we speak.

3 Ἀρχόμεθα πάλιν ἑαυτοὺς συνιστάνειν;
Do we begin again ourselves to commend?

ἢ μὴ χρῄζομεν ὥς τινες συστατικῶν
or not need we as some commendatory

ἐπιστολῶν πρὸς ὑμᾶς ἢ ἐξ ὑμῶν; 2 ἡ
epistles to you or from you? The

ἐπιστολὴ ἡμῶν ὑμεῖς ἐστε, ἐγγεγραμμένη
epistle of us ye are, *having been* inscribed

ἐν ταῖς καρδίαις ἡμῶν, γινωσκομένη καὶ
in the hearts of us, *being* known and

ἀναγινωσκομένη ὑπὸ πάντων ἀνθρώπων,
being read by all men,

3 φανερούμενοι ὅτι ἐστὲ ἐπιστολὴ Χριστοῦ
being manifested that ye are an epistle of Christ

διακονηθεῖσα ὑφ' ἡμῶν, ἐγγεγραμμένη οὐ
ministered by us, *having been* inscribed not

μέλανι ἀλλὰ πνεύματι θεοῦ ζῶντος, οὐκ
by ink but by [the] Spirit of ³God ¹a living, not

ἐν πλαξὶν λιθίναις ἀλλ' ἐν πλαξὶν καρδίαις
in ¹tablets ¹stony but in tablets [which are]

σαρκίναις.
¹fleshy.
²hearts

4 Πεποίθησιν δὲ τοιαύτην ἔχομεν διὰ
²confidence ¹And ²such we have through

τοῦ Χριστοῦ πρὸς τὸν θεόν. 5 οὐχ
\- Christ toward - God. ³not

ὅτι ἀφ' ἑαυτῶν ἱκανοί ἐσμεν λογίσασθαί
that ³from ⁴ourselves ²competent ¹we are to reckon

τι ὡς ἐξ ἑαυτῶν, ἀλλ' ἡ ἱκανότης
anything as of ourselves, but the competence

ἡμῶν ἐκ τοῦ θεοῦ, 6 ὃς καὶ ἱκάνωσεν
of us [is] - God, who also made competent

ἡμᾶς διακόνους καινῆς διαθήκης, οὐ
us [as] ministers of a new covenant, not

γράμματος ἀλλὰ πνεύματος· τὸ γὰρ γράμμα
of letter but of spirit; for the letter

ἀποκτείνει, τὸ δὲ πνεῦμα ζῳοποιεῖ. 7 Εἰ
kills, but the spirit makes alive. if

δὲ ἡ διακονία τοῦ θανάτου ἐν γράμμασιν
Now the ministry - of death in letters

ἐντετυπωμένη λίθοις ἐγενήθη ἐν δόξῃ,
having been engraved in stones was in glory,

ὥστε μὴ δύνασθαι ἀτενίσαι τοὺς υἱοὺς
so as not to be able to gaze the sons
=so that the sons of Israel were not able to gaze

Ἰσραὴλ εἰς τὸ πρόσωπον Μωϋσέως διὰ
of Israel*b* at the face of Moses on account of

τὴν δόξαν τοῦ προσώπου αὐτοῦ τὴν
the glory of the face of him -

καταργουμένην, 8 πῶς οὐχὶ μᾶλλον ἡ
being done away, how ²not ³rather ⁴the

διακονία τοῦ πνεύματος ἔσται ἐν δόξῃ;
⁵ministry ⁶of the ⁷Spirit ¹will ⁸be in glory?

9 εἰ γὰρ ἡ διακονία τῆς κατακρίσεως
For if the ministry - of condemnation

δόξα, πολλῷ μᾶλλον περισσεύει ἡ διακονία
[was] glory, by much rather ⁴abounds ¹the ²ministry

τῆς δικαιοσύνης δόξῃ. 10 καὶ γὰρ οὐ
\- ³of righteousness in glory. For indeed ²not

---

for profit. On the contrary, in Christ we speak before God with sincerity, like men sent from God.

Chapter 3

ARE we beginning to commend ourselves again? Or do we need, like some people, letters of recommendation to you or from you? ²You yourselves are our letter, written on our hearts, known and read by everybody. ³You show that you are a letter from Christ, the result of our ministry, written not with ink but with the Spirit of the living God, not on tablets of stone but on tablets of human hearts.

⁴Such confidence as this is ours through Christ before God. ⁵Not that we are competent in ourselves to claim anything for ourselves, but our competence comes from God. ⁶He has made us competent as ministers of a new covenant— not of the letter but of the Spirit; for the letter kills, but the Spirit gives life.

The Glory of the New Covenant

⁷Now if the ministry that brought death, which was engraved in letters on stone, came with glory, so that the Israelites could not look steadily at the face of Moses because of its glory, fading though it was, ⁸will not the ministry of the Spirit be even more glorious? ⁹If the ministry that condemns men is glorious, how much more glorious is the ministry that brings righteousness! ¹⁰For what was glorious has no glory

---

f Other ancient authorities read *like the others*
g Other ancient authorities read *your*
h Gk *on stones*

glory because of the greater glory; 11 for if what was set aside came through glory, much more has the permanent come in glory!

12 Since, then, we have such a hope, we act with great boldness, 13 not like Moses, who put a veil over his face to keep the people of Israel from gazing at the end of the glory that[i] was being set aside. 14 But their minds were hardened. Indeed, to this very day, when they hear the reading of the old covenant, that same veil is still there, since only in Christ is it set aside. 15 Indeed, to this very day whenever Moses is read, a veil lies over their minds; 16 but when one turns to the Lord, the veil is removed. 17 Now the Lord is the Spirit, and where the Spirit of the Lord is, there is freedom. 18 And all of us, with unveiled faces, seeing the glory of the Lord as though reflected in a mirror, are being transformed into the same image from one degree of glory to another; for this comes from the Lord, the Spirit.

δεδόξασται τὸ δεδοξασμένον ἐν τούτῳ
has been 'the 'having been in this
glorified [thing] glorified

τῷ μέρει εἴνεκεν τῆς ὑπερβαλλούσης δόξης.
- respect for the the excelling glory.
sake of

11 εἰ γὰρ τὸ καταργούμενον διὰ δόξης,
For if the being done away [was] glory,
[thing] through

πολλῷ μᾶλλον τὸ μένον ἐν δόξῃ.
by much more the [thing] remaining [is] in glory.

12 Ἔχοντες οὖν τοιαύτην ἐλπίδα πολλῇ
Having therefore such hope 'much

παρρησίᾳ χρώμεθα, 13 καὶ οὐ καθάπερ
'boldness 'we use, and not as

Μωϋσῆς ἐτίθει κάλυμμα ἐπὶ τὸ πρόσωπον
Moses put a veil on the face

αὐτοῦ, πρὸς τὸ μὴ ἀτενίσαι τοὺς υἱοὺς
of him, for the 'not 'to gaze 'the 'sons

Ἰσραὴλ εἰς τὸ τέλος τοῦ καταργουμένου.
'of Israel[b] at the end of the [thing] being done away.

14 ἀλλὰ ἐπωρώθη τὰ νοήματα αὐτῶν.
But were hardened the thoughts of them.

ἄχρι γὰρ τῆς σήμερον ἡμέρας τὸ αὐτὸ
For until the present day the same

κάλυμμα ἐπὶ τῇ ἀναγνώσει τῆς παλαιᾶς
veil 'on(at) 'the 'reading 'of the 'old

διαθήκης μένει, μὴ ἀνακαλυπτόμενον ὅτι
'covenant 'remains, not being unveiled* that

ἐν Χριστῷ καταργεῖται. 15 ἀλλ' ἕως
in Christ it is being done away. But until

σήμερον ἡνίκα ἂν ἀναγινώσκηται Μωϋσῆς
to-day whenever 'is being read 'Moses

κάλυμμα ἐπὶ τὴν καρδίαν αὐτῶν κεῖται·
a veil 'on 'the 'heart 'of them 'lies;

16 ἡνίκα δὲ ἐὰν ἐπιστρέψῃ πρὸς κύριον,
but whenever it§ turns to [the] Lord,

περιαιρεῖται τὸ κάλυμμα. 17 ὁ δὲ κύριος
'is taken away 'the 'veil. Now the Lord

τὸ πνεῦμά ἐστιν· οὗ δὲ τὸ πνεῦμα
'the 'Spirit 'is; and where the Spirit

κυρίου, ἐλευθερία. 18 ἡμεῖς δὲ πάντες
of [the] [there is] freedom. But we all
Lord [is],

ἀνακεκαλυμμένῳ προσώπῳ τὴν δόξαν
'having been unveiled 'with face 'the 'glory

κυρίου κατοπτριζόμενοι τὴν αὐτὴν εἰκόνα
'of [the] 'beholding in 'the 'same 'image
Lord a mirror

μεταμορφούμεθα ἀπὸ δόξης εἰς δόξαν,
'are being changed [into] from glory to glory,

καθάπερ ἀπὸ κυρίου πνεύματος.
even as from [the] Lord Spirit.

---

now in comparison with the surpassing glory. 11 And if what was fading away came with glory, how much greater is the glory of that which lasts!

12 Therefore, since we have such a hope, we are very bold. 13 We are not like Moses, who would put a veil over his face to keep the Israelites from gazing at it while the radiance was fading away. 14 But their minds were made dull, for to this day the same veil remains when the old covenant is read. It has not been removed, because only in Christ is it taken away. 15 Even to this day when Moses is read, a veil covers their hearts. 16 But whenever anyone turns to the Lord, the veil is taken away. 17 Now the Lord is the Spirit, and where the Spirit of the Lord is, there is freedom. 18 And we, who with unveiled faces all reflect[c] the Lord's glory, are being transformed into his likeness with ever-increasing glory, which comes from the Lord, who is the Spirit.

Chapter 4

Treasure in Clay Jars

THEREFORE, since it is by God's mercy that we are engaged in this ministry, we do not lose heart. 2 We have renounced the shameful things that one hides; we refuse to practice cunning or to falsify God's word; but by the open statement of the truth we commend ourselves to the

---

4 Διὰ τοῦτο, ἔχοντες τὴν διακονίαν
Therefore, having - ministry

ταύτην, καθὼς ἠλεήθημεν, οὐκ ἐγκακοῦμεν,
this, as we obtained mercy, we faint not,

2 ἀλλὰ ἀπειπάμεθα τὰ κρυπτὰ τῆς αἰσχύνης,
but we have renounced the hidden things - of shame,

μὴ περιπατοῦντες ἐν πανουργίᾳ μηδὲ
not walking in craftiness nor

δολοῦντες τὸν λόγον τοῦ θεοῦ, ἀλλὰ
adulterating the word - of God, but

τῇ φανερώσει τῆς ἀληθείας συνιστάνοντες
by the manifestation of the truth commending

Chapter 4

Treasures in Jars of Clay

THEREFORE, since through God's mercy we have this ministry, we do not lose heart. 2 Rather, we have renounced secret and shameful ways; we do not use deception, nor do we distort the word of God. On the contrary, by setting forth the truth plainly we

---

[i] Gk of what

* That is, revealed (Conybeare and Howson). § ? their heart.

[c] 18 Or contemplate

conscience of everyone in the sight of God. 3 And even if our gospel is veiled, it is veiled to those who are perishing. 4 In their case the god of this world has blinded the minds of the unbelievers, to keep them from seeing the light of the gospel of the glory of Christ, who is the image of God. 5 For we do not proclaim ourselves; we proclaim Jesus Christ as Lord and ourselves as your slaves for Jesus' sake. 6 For it is the God who said, "Let light shine out of darkness," who has shone in our hearts to give the light of the knowledge of the glory of God in the face of Jesus Christ.

7　But we have this treasure in clay jars, so that it may be made clear that this extraordinary power belongs to God and does not come from us. 8 We are afflicted in every way, but not crushed; perplexed, but not driven to despair; 9 persecuted, but not forsaken; struck down, but not destroyed; 10 always carrying in the body the death of Jesus, so that the life of Jesus may also be made visible in our bodies. 11 For while we live, we are always being given up to death for Jesus' sake, so that the life of Jesus may be made visible in our mortal flesh. 12 So death is at work in us, but life in you.

13　But just as we have the same spirit of faith that

ἑαυτοὺς πρὸς πᾶσαν συνείδησιν ἀνθρώπων
ourselves to every conscience of men

ἐνώπιον τοῦ θεοῦ. 3 εἰ δὲ καὶ ἔστιν
before - God. But if indeed ⁴is

κεκαλυμμένον τὸ εὐαγγέλιον ἡμῶν, ἐν
⁵having been hidden ¹the ²gospel ³of us, in

τοῖς ἀπολλυμένοις ἐστὶν κεκαλυμμένον, 4 ἐν
the [ones] perishing it is having been hidden, in

οἷς ὁ θεὸς τοῦ αἰῶνος τούτου ἐτύφλωσεν
whom the god of this age blinded

τὰ νοήματα τῶν ἀπίστων εἰς τὸ μὴ
the thoughts of the unbelieving [with a the not
[ones] view] to
=so that the enlightenment . . . should not shine forth,

αὐγάσαι τὸν φωτισμὸν τοῦ εὐαγγελίου
to shine forth the enlightenment of the gospel

τῆς δόξης τοῦ Χριστοῦ, ὅς ἐστιν εἰκὼν
of the glory - of Christ, who is [the] image

τοῦ θεοῦ. 5 οὐ γὰρ ἑαυτοὺς κηρύσσομεν
- of God. For ³not ²ourselves ¹we proclaim

ἀλλὰ Χριστὸν Ἰησοῦν κύριον, ἑαυτοὺς δὲ
but Christ Jesus [as] Lord, and ourselves

δούλους ὑμῶν διὰ Ἰησοῦν. 6 ὅτι ὁ
slaves of you on account of Jesus. Because the

θεὸς ὁ εἰπών· ἐκ σκότους φῶς λάμψει,
God the [one] saying: Out of darkness light shall shine,

ὃς ἔλαμψεν ἐν ταῖς καρδίαις ἡμῶν πρὸς
[is] [he] shone in the hearts of us for
who

φωτισμὸν τῆς γνώσεως τῆς δόξης τοῦ
enlightenment of the knowledge of the glory -

θεοῦ ἐν προσώπῳ Χριστοῦ.
of God in [the] face of Christ.

7 Ἔχομεν δὲ τὸν θησαυρὸν τοῦτον ἐν
And we have this treasure in

ὀστρακίνοις σκεύεσιν, ἵνα ἡ ὑπερβολὴ
earthenware vessels, in order that the excellence

τῆς δυνάμεως ᾖ τοῦ θεοῦ καὶ μὴ ἐξ
of the power may be - of God and not of

ἡμῶν· 8 ἐν παντὶ θλιβόμενοι ἀλλ' οὐ
us; in every [way] being afflicted but not

στενοχωρούμενοι, ἀπορούμενοι ἀλλ' οὐκ
being restrained, being in difficulties but not

ἐξαπορούμενοι, 9 διωκόμενοι ἀλλ' οὐκ
despairing, being persecuted but not

ἐγκαταλειπόμενοι, καταβαλλόμενοι ἀλλ' οὐκ
being deserted, being cast down but not

ἀπολλύμενοι, 10 πάντοτε τὴν νέκρωσιν τοῦ
perishing, always ³the ⁴dying -

Ἰησοῦ ἐν τῷ σώματι περιφέροντες, ἵνα
⁷of Jesus ²in ³the ⁴body ¹bearing about, in order
that

καὶ ἡ ζωὴ τοῦ Ἰησοῦ ἐν τῷ σώματι
also the life - of Jesus in the body

ἡμῶν φανερωθῇ. 11 ἀεὶ γὰρ ἡμεῖς οἱ
of us might be manifested. For always we the

ζῶντες εἰς θάνατον παραδιδόμεθα διὰ
[ones] living to death are being on ac-
delivered count of

Ἰησοῦν, ἵνα καὶ ἡ ζωὴ τοῦ Ἰησοῦ
Jesus, in order that also the life - of Jesus

φανερωθῇ ἐν τῇ θνητῇ σαρκὶ ἡμῶν.
might be in the mortal flesh of us.
manifested

12 ὥστε ὁ θάνατος ἐν ἡμῖν ἐνεργεῖται,
So as - death in us operates,

ἡ δὲ ζωὴ ἐν ὑμῖν. 13 ἔχοντες δὲ τὸ
- but life in you. And having the

commend ourselves to every man's conscience in the sight of God. 3 And even if our gospel is veiled, it is veiled to those who are perishing. 4 The god of this age has blinded the minds of unbelievers, so that they cannot see the light of the gospel of the glory of Christ, who is the image of God. 5 For we do not preach ourselves, but Jesus Christ as Lord, and ourselves as your servants for Jesus' sake. 6 For God, who said, "Let light shine out of darkness,"ᵈ made his light shine in our hearts to give us the light of the knowledge of the glory of God in the face of Christ.

7 But we have this treasure in jars of clay to show that this all-surpassing power is from God and not from us. 8 We are hard pressed on every side, but not crushed; perplexed, but not in despair; 9 persecuted, but not abandoned; struck down, but not destroyed. 10 We always carry around in our body the death of Jesus, so that the life of Jesus may also be revealed in our body. 11 For we who are alive are always being given over to death for Jesus' sake, so that his life may be revealed in our mortal body. 12 So then, death is at work in us, but life is at work in you.

13 It is written: "I be-

is in accordance with scripture—"I believed, and so I spoke"—we also believe, and so we speak, [14]because we know that the one who raised the Lord Jesus will raise us also with Jesus, and will bring us with you into his presence. [15]Yes, everything is for your sake, so that grace, as it extends to more and more people, may increase thanksgiving, to the glory of God.

Living by Faith

[16] So we do not lose heart. Even though our outer nature is wasting away, our inner nature is being renewed day by day. [17]For this slight momentary affliction is preparing us for an eternal weight of glory beyond all measure, [18]because we look not at what can be seen but at what cannot be seen; for what can be seen is temporary, but what cannot be seen is eternal.

αὐτὸ πνεῦμα τῆς πίστεως, κατὰ τὸ
same spirit - of faith, according to the thing

γεγραμμένον· ἐπίστευσα, διὸ ἐλάλησα, καὶ
having been written: I believed, therefore I spoke, both

ἡμεῖς πιστεύομεν, διὸ καὶ λαλοῦμεν, 14 εἰδότες
we believe, and therefore we speak, knowing

ὅτι ὁ ἐγείρας τὸν κύριον Ἰησοῦν καὶ
that the having the Lord Jesus ²also
[one] raised

ἡμᾶς σὺν Ἰησοῦ ἐγερεῖ καὶ παραστήσει
²us ⁴with ³Jesus ¹will raise and will present [us]

σὺν ὑμῖν. 15 τὰ γὰρ πάντα δι᾽ ὑμᾶς,
with you. - For all things [are] on ac- you,
count of

ἵνα ἡ χάρις πλεονάσασα διὰ τῶν πλειόνων
in or- - grace increased through the majority
der that

τὴν εὐχαριστίαν περισσεύσῃ εἰς τὴν δόξαν
²the ³thanksgiving ¹may cause to abound to the glory

τοῦ θεοῦ. 16 Διὸ οὐκ ἐγκακοῦμεν, ἀλλ᾽
- of God. Wherefore we faint not, but

εἰ καὶ ὁ ἔξω ἡμῶν ἄνθρωπος διαφθείρεται,
if indeed the outward ⁵of us ¹man is being disabled,

ἀλλ᾽ ὁ ἔσω ἡμῶν ἀνακαινοῦται ἡμέρα
yet the inward [man] of us is being renewed day

καὶ ἡμέρᾳ. 17 τὸ γὰρ παραυτίκα ἐλαφρὸν
and(by) day. For the present lightness

τῆς θλίψεως καθ᾽ ὑπερβολὴν εἰς ὑπερβολὴν
of the affliction ³excessively ⁴to ⁵excess

αἰώνιον βάρος δόξης κατεργάζεται ἡμῖν,
⁶an eternal ⁷weight ⁸of glory ¹works ²for us,

18 μὴ σκοπούντων ἡμῶν τὰ βλεπόμενα
not considering us⁴ the things *being* seen
=while we do not consider

ἀλλὰ τὰ μὴ βλεπόμενα· τὰ γὰρ βλεπόμενα
but the not *being* seen; for the things *being* seen
things

πρόσκαιρα, τὰ δὲ μὴ βλεπόμενα αἰώνια.
[are] temporary, but the things not *being* seen [are] eternal.

Chapter 5

5 Οἴδαμεν γὰρ ὅτι ἐὰν ἡ ἐπίγειος
For we know that if the earthly

ἡμῶν οἰκία τοῦ σκήνους καταλυθῇ,
⁴of us ¹house ²of the ³tabernacle is destroyed,

οἰκοδομὴν ἐκ θεοῦ ἔχομεν, οἰκίαν ἀχειρο-
a building of God we have, a house not made

ποίητον αἰώνιον ἐν τοῖς οὐρανοῖς. 2 καὶ
by hands eternal in the heavens. And

γὰρ ἐν τούτῳ στενάζομεν, τὸ οἰκητήριον
For in this⁴ we groan, ²the ⁴dwelling-place

ἡμῶν τὸ ἐξ οὐρανοῦ ἐπενδύσασθαι ἐπιπο-
⁵of us - ⁴out of ⁷heaven ⁸to put on ¹greatly

θοῦντες, 3 εἴ γε καὶ ἐνδυσάμενοι οὐ
desiring, if indeed being clothed not

γυμνοὶ εὑρεθησόμεθα. 4 καὶ γὰρ οἱ
naked we shall be found. For indeed ²the
[ones]

ὄντες ἐν τῷ σκήνει στενάζομεν βαρούμενοι,
³being ⁴in ⁵the ⁶tabernacle ¹we groan being burdened,

ἐφ᾽ ᾧ οὐ θέλομεν ἐκδύσασθαι ἀλλ᾽
inasmuch as we do not wish to put off but

ἐπενδύσασθαι, ἵνα καταποθῇ τὸ θνητὸν
to put on, in order ²may be ¹the ²mortal
that swallowed up

ὑπὸ τῆς ζωῆς. 5 ὁ δὲ κατεργασάμενος
by the life. Now the [one] having wrought

---

lieved; therefore I have spoken."[e] With that same spirit of faith we also believe and therefore speak, [14]because we know that the one who raised the Lord Jesus from the dead will also raise us with Jesus and present us with you in his presence. [15]All this is for your benefit, so that the grace that is reaching more and more people may cause thanksgiving to overflow to the glory of God.

[16]Therefore we do not lose heart. Though outwardly we are wasting away, yet inwardly we are being renewed day by day. [17]For our light and momentary troubles are achieving for us an eternal glory that far outweighs them all. [18]So we fix our eyes not on what is seen, but on what is unseen. For what is seen is temporary, but what is unseen is eternal.

Chapter 5

Our Heavenly Dwelling

NOW we know that if the earthly tent we live in is destroyed, we have a building from God, an eternal house in heaven, not built by human hands. [2]Meanwhile we groan, longing to be clothed with our heavenly dwelling, [3]because when we are clothed, we will not be found naked. [4]For while we are in this tent, we groan and are burdened, because we do not wish to be unclothed but to be clothed with our heavenly dwelling, so that what is mortal may be swallowed up by life. [5]Now it is God

---

* Neuter, going back to σκῆνος in the preceding verse.   ᵉ13 Psalm 116:10

thing is God, who has given us the Spirit as a guarantee.

6 So we are always confident; even though we know that while we are at home in the body we are away from the Lord— 7 for we walk by faith, not by sight. 8 Yes, we do have confidence, and we would rather be away from the body and at home with the Lord. 9 So whether we are at home or away, we make it our aim to please him. 10 For all of us must appear before the judgment seat of Christ, so that each may receive recompense for what has been done in the body, whether good or evil.

The Ministry of Reconciliation

11 Therefore, knowing the fear of the Lord, we try to persuade others; but we ourselves are well known to God, and I hope that we are also well known to your consciences. 12 We are not commending ourselves to you again, but giving you an opportunity to boast about us, so that you may be able to answer those who boast in outward appearance and not in the heart. 13 For if we are beside ourselves, it is for God; if we are in our right mind, it is for you. 14 For the love of Christ urges us on, because we are convinced that one has died for all; therefore all have died. 15 And he died for all, so that those who live might

ἡμᾶς	us
εἰς	for
αὐτὸ	this
τοῦτο	very thing
θεός,	[is] God,
ὁ	the [one]
δοὺς	having given
ἡμῖν	to us
τὸν	the
ἀρραβῶνα	earnest
τοῦ	of the
πνεύματος.	Spirit.
6 Θαρ-	Being of
ροῦντες	good cheer
οὖν	therefore
πάντοτε	always
καὶ	and
εἰδότες	knowing
ὅτι	that
ἐνδημοῦντες	being at home
ἐν	in
τῷ	the
σώματι	body
ἐκδημοῦμεν	we are away from home
ἀπὸ	from
τοῦ	the
κυρίου·	Lord;
7 διὰ	²through
πίστεως	³faith
γὰρ	¹for
περιπατοῦμεν,	we walk,
οὐ	not
διὰ	through
εἴδους·	appearance;
8 θαρροῦμεν	we are of good cheer
δὲ	then
καὶ	and
εὐδοκοῦμεν	think it good
μᾶλλον	rather
ἐκδημῆσαι	to go away
ἐκ	out from home
τοῦ	the
σώματος	body
καὶ	and
ἐνδημῆσαι	to come home
πρὸς	to
τὸν	the
κύριον.	Lord.
9 διὸ	Wherefore
καὶ	also
φιλοτιμούμεθα,	we are ambitious,
εἴτε	whether
ἐνδημοῦντες	being at home
εἴτε	or
ἐκδημοῦντες,	being away from home,
εὐάρεστοι	wellpleasing
αὐτῷ	to him
εἶναι.	to be.
10 τοὺς	-
γὰρ	For
πάντας	³all
ἡμᾶς	²us
φανερωθῆναι	⁴to be manifested
δεῖ	¹it behoves
ἔμπροσθεν	before
τοῦ	the
βήματος	tribunal
τοῦ	-
Χριστοῦ,	of Christ,
ἵνα	in order that
κομίσηται	²may receive
ἕκαστος	¹each one
τὰ	the things
διὰ	through
τοῦ	the
σώματος	body
πρὸς	according to
ἃ	what
ἔπραξεν,	he practised,
εἴτε	either
ἀγαθὸν	good
εἴτε	or
φαῦλον.	worthless.
11 Εἰδότες	Knowing
οὖν	therefore
τὸν	the
φόβον	fear
τοῦ	of the
κυρίου	Lord
ἀνθρώπους	²men
πείθομεν,	¹we persuade,
θεῷ	and to God
δὲ	
πεφανερώμεθα·	we have been made manifest;
ἐλπίζω	and I hope
δὲ	
καὶ	also
ἐν	in
ταῖς	the
συνειδήσεσιν	consciences
ὑμῶν	of you
πεφανερῶσθαι.	to have been made manifest.
12 οὐ	Not
πάλιν	again
ἑαυτοὺς	²ourselves
συνιστάνομεν	¹we commend
ὑμῖν,	to you,
ἀλλὰ	but
ἀφορμὴν	²an occasion
διδόντες	¹giving
ὑμῖν	²to you
καυχήματος	of a boast
ὑπὲρ	on behalf of
ἡμῶν,	us,
ἵνα	in order that
ἔχητε	ye may have [it]
πρὸς	in reference to
τοὺς	the [ones]
ἐν	²in
προσώπῳ	³face
καυχωμένους	¹boasting
καὶ	and
μὴ	not
ἐν	in
καρδίᾳ.	heart.
13 εἴτε	For whether
γὰρ	
ἐξέστημεν,	we are mad,
θεῷ·	[it is] to God;
εἴτε	or
σωφρονοῦμεν,	we are in our senses,
ὑμῖν.	[it is] for you.
14 ἡ	For the
γὰρ	
ἀγάπη	love
τοῦ	-
Χριστοῦ	of Christ
συνέχει	constrains
ἡμᾶς,	us,
κρίναντας	judging
τοῦτο,	this,
ὅτι	that
εἷς	one
ὑπὲρ	on behalf of
πάντων	all men
ἀπέθανεν·	died;
ἄρα	then
οἱ	the
πάντες	all
ἀπέθανον·	died;
15 καὶ	and
ὑπὲρ	²on behalf of
πάντων	³all
ἀπέθανεν	¹he died
ἵνα	in order that
οἱ	the
ζῶντες	living [ones]
μηκέτι	no more

who has made us for this very purpose and has given us the Spirit as a deposit, guaranteeing what is to come.

6 Therefore we are always confident and know that as long as we are at home in the body we are away from the Lord. 7 We live by faith, not by sight. 8 We are confident, I say, and would prefer to be away from the body and at home with the Lord. 9 So we make it our goal to please him, whether we are at home in the body or away from it. 10 For we must all appear before the judgment seat of Christ, that each one may receive what is due him for the things done while in the body, whether good or bad.

The Ministry of Reconciliation

11 Since, then, we know what it is to fear the Lord, we try to persuade men. What we are is plain to God, and I hope it is also plain to your conscience. 12 We are not trying to commend ourselves to you again, but are giving you an opportunity to take pride in us, so that you can answer those who take pride in what is seen rather than in what is in the heart. 13 If we are out of our mind, it is for the sake of God; if we are in our right mind, it is for you. 14 For Christ's love compels us, because we are convinced that one died for all, and therefore all died. 15 And he died for all, that those who live should no

live no longer for themselves, but for him who died and was raised for them.

16 From now on, therefore, we regard no one from a human point of view;[k] even though we once knew Christ from a human point of view,[k] we know him no longer in that way. 17 So if anyone is in Christ, there is a new creation: everything old has passed away; see, everything has become new! 18 All this is from God, who reconciled us to himself through Christ, and has given us the ministry of reconciliation; 19 that is, in Christ God was reconciling the world to himself,[l] not counting their trespasses against them, and entrusting the message of reconciliation to us. 20 So we are ambassadors for Christ, since God is making his appeal through us; we entreat you on behalf of Christ, be reconciled to God. 21 For our sake he made him to be sin who knew no sin, so that in him we might become the righteousness of God.

ἑαυτοῖς ζῶσιν ἀλλὰ τῷ ὑπὲρ αὐτῶν
to themselves may live but to the on behalf them
  [one] of

ἀποθανόντι καὶ ἐγερθέντι. 16 Ὥστε ἡμεῖς
having died and having been raised. So as ²we

ἀπὸ τοῦ νῦν οὐδένα οἴδαμεν κατὰ σάρκα·
¹from - ²now ⁵no man ⁴know according to flesh;

εἰ καὶ ἐγνώκαμεν κατὰ σάρκα Χριστόν,
if indeed ¹we have known ²according to ⁴flesh ³Christ,

ἀλλὰ νῦν οὐκέτι γινώσκομεν. 17 ὥστε
yet now no more we know [him]. So as

εἴ τις ἐν Χριστῷ, καινὴ κτίσις· τὰ
if anyone [is] in Christ, [he is] a new creation: the

ἀρχαῖα παρῆλθεν, ἰδοὺ γέγονεν καινά.
old things passed away, behold they have become new.

18 τὰ δὲ πάντα ἐκ τοῦ θεοῦ τοῦ καταλ-
- And all things [are] of - God the [one] having

λάξαντος ἡμᾶς ἑαυτῷ διὰ Χριστοῦ καὶ
reconciled us to himself through Christ and

δόντος ἡμῖν τὴν διακονίαν τῆς καταλλαγῆς,
having given to us the ministry - of reconciliation,

19 ὡς ὅτι θεὸς ἦν ἐν Χριστῷ κόσμον
as that God was in Christ ²[the] world

καταλλάσσων ἑαυτῷ, μὴ λογιζόμενος αὐτοῖς
¹reconciling to himself, not reckoning to them

τὰ παραπτώματα αὐτῶν, καὶ θέμενος
the trespasses of them, and placing

ἐν ἡμῖν τὸν λόγον τῆς καταλλαγῆς.
in us the word - of reconciliation.

20 Ὑπὲρ Χριστοῦ οὖν πρεσβεύομεν ὡς
On behalf of Christ therefore we are ambassadors as

τοῦ θεοῦ παρακαλοῦντος[a] δι' ἡμῶν· δεόμεθα
- God beseeching through us; we beg

ὑπὲρ Χριστοῦ, καταλλάγητε τῷ θεῷ.
on behalf of Christ, Be ye reconciled - to God.

21 τὸν μὴ γνόντα ἁμαρτίαν ὑπὲρ ἡμῶν
³The [one] ²not ⁴knowing ⁵sin ⁷on behalf of ⁸us

ἁμαρτίαν ἐποίησεν, ἵνα ἡμεῖς γενώμεθα
⁶sin ¹he made, in order that we might become

δικαιοσύνη θεοῦ ἐν αὐτῷ.
[the] righteousness of God in him.

---

longer live for themselves but for him who died for them and was raised again.

16 So from now on we regard no one from a worldly point of view. Though we once regarded Christ in this way, we do so no longer. 17 Therefore, if anyone is in Christ, he is a new creation; the old has gone, the new has come! 18 All this is from God, who reconciled us to himself through Christ and gave us the ministry of reconciliation: 19 that God was reconciling the world to himself in Christ, not counting men's sins against them. And he has committed to us the message of reconciliation. 20 We are therefore Christ's ambassadors, as though God were making his appeal through us. We implore you on Christ's behalf: Be reconciled to God. 21 God made him who had no sin to be sin[f] for us, so that in him we might become the righteousness of God.

Chapter 6

As we work together with him,[m] we urge you also not to accept the grace of God in vain. 2 For he says,

> "At an acceptable
> time I have
> listened to you,
> and on a day of
> salvation I have
> helped you."

See, now is the acceptable time; see, now is the day of salvation! 3 We are putting no obstacle in anyone's way, so that no fault may be found with our ministry, 4 but as servants of God we have commended ourselves in every way: through great endurance, in afflictions, hardships, calamities, 5 beatings, impris-

---

Chapter 6

6 Συνεργοῦντες δὲ καὶ παρακαλοῦμεν μὴ
And working together also we beseech ²not

εἰς κενὸν τὴν χάριν τοῦ θεοῦ δέξασθαι
⁷to no purpose ⁴the ³grace - of God ⁵to receive

ὑμᾶς· 2 λέγει γάρ· καιρῷ δεκτῷ ἐπήκουσά
¹you; for he says: In a time acceptable I heard

σου καὶ ἐν ἡμέρᾳ σωτηρίας ἐβοήθησά
thee and in a day of salvation I helped

σοι· ἰδοὺ νῦν καιρὸς εὐπρόσδεκτος, ἰδοὺ
thee; behold now a time acceptable, behold

νῦν ἡμέρα σωτηρίας· 3 — μηδεμίαν ἐν
now a day of salvation; ²no ⁴in

μηδενὶ διδόντες προσκοπήν, ἵνα μὴ
⁵no(any)thing ¹giving ³cause of stumbling, lest

μωμηθῇ ἡ διακονία, 4 ἀλλ' ἐν παντὶ
³be blamed ¹the ²ministry, but in everything

συνιστάνοντες ἑαυτοὺς ὡς θεοῦ διάκονοι,
commending ourselves as ²of God ¹ministers,

ἐν ὑπομονῇ πολλῇ, ἐν θλίψεσιν, ἐν
in ²endurance ¹much, in afflictions, in

ἀνάγκαις, ἐν στενοχωρίαις, ἐν πληγαῖς,
necessities, in straits, in stripes,

As God's fellow workers we urge you not to receive God's grace in vain. 2 For he says,

> "In the time of my favor
> I heard you,
> and in the day of
> salvation I helped
> you."[g]

I tell you, now is the time of God's favor, now is the day of salvation.

Paul's Hardships

3 We put no stumbling block in anyone's path, so that our ministry will not be discredited. 4 Rather, as servants of God we commend ourselves in every way: in great endurance; in troubles, hardships and dis-

---

k Gk according to the flesh
l Or God was in Christ reconciling the world to himself
m Gk As we work together

f 21 Or be a sin offering
g 2 Isaiah 49:8

onments, riots, labors, sleepless nights, hunger; [6]by purity, knowledge, patience, kindness, holiness of spirit, genuine love, [7]truthful speech, and the power of God; with the weapons of righteousness for the right hand and for the left; [8]in honor and dishonor, in ill repute and good repute. We are treated as impostors, and yet are true; [9]as unknown, and yet are well known; as dying, and see—we are alive; as punished, and yet not killed; [10]as sorrowful, yet always rejoicing; as poor, yet making many rich; as having nothing, and yet possessing everything.

[11] We have spoken frankly to you Corinthians; our heart is wide open to you. [12]There is no restriction in our affections, but only in yours. [13]In return—I speak as to children—open wide your hearts also.

The Temple of the Living God

[14] Do not be mismatched with unbelievers. For what partnership is there between righteousness and lawlessness? Or what fellowship is there between light and darkness? [15]What agreement does Christ have with Belial? Or what does a believer share with an unbeliever? [16]What agreement has the temple of God with idols? For we [n] are the temple of the living God; as God said,
"I will live in them and walk among them,
and I will be their God,
and they shall be my people.

---

5 ἐν φυλακαῖς, ἐν ἀκαταστασίαις, ἐν κόποις,
in   prisons,   in   commotions,   in   labours,

ἐν ἀγρυπνίαις, ἐν νηστείαις, 6 ἐν ἁγνότητι,
in   watchings,   in   fastings,   in   purity,

ἐν γνώσει, ἐν μακροθυμίᾳ, ἐν χρηστότητι,
in knowledge, in long-suffering, in   kindness,

ἐν πνεύματι ἁγίῳ, ἐν ἀγάπῃ ἀνυποκρίτῳ,
in   spirit   a holy,   in   love   unfeigned,

7 ἐν λόγῳ ἀληθείας, ἐν δυνάμει θεοῦ·
in   a word   of truth,   in   power   of God;

διὰ τῶν ὅπλων τῆς δικαιοσύνης τῶν
through the   weapons   of the   righteousness   of the

δεξιῶν καὶ ἀριστερῶν, 8 διὰ δόξης καὶ
right [hand] and   of left,   through   glory   and

ἀτιμίας, διὰ δυσφημίας καὶ εὐφημίας·
dishonour, through   ill report   and   good report;

ὡς πλάνοι καὶ ἀληθεῖς, 9 ὡς ἀγνοούμενοι
as deceivers and*   true men,   as   being unknown

καὶ ἐπιγινωσκόμενοι, ὡς ἀποθνῄσκοντες καὶ
and*   being well known,   as   dying   and

ἰδοὺ ζῶμεν, ὡς παιδευόμενοι καὶ μὴ
behold   we live,   as   being chastened   and   not

θανατούμενοι, 10 ὡς λυπούμενοι ἀεὶ δὲ
being put to death,   as   being grieved   ²always ¹but

χαίροντες, ὡς πτωχοὶ πολλοὺς δὲ πλουτίζ-
rejoicing,   as   poor   ²many   ¹but   ²en-

οντες, ὡς μηδὲν ἔχοντες καὶ πάντα
riching,   as   ²nothing   ¹having   ²and*   ²all things

κατέχοντες.
²possessing.

11 Τὸ στόμα ἡμῶν ἀνέῳγεν πρὸς ὑμᾶς,
The   mouth   of us   has opened   to   you,

Κορίνθιοι, ἡ καρδία ἡμῶν πεπλάτυνται·
Corinthians,   the   heart   of us   has been enlarged;

12 οὐ στενοχωρεῖσθε ἐν ἡμῖν, στενοχωρεῖσθε
ye are not restrained   in   us,   ²ye are restrained

δὲ ἐν τοῖς σπλάγχνοις ὑμῶν· 13 τὴν δὲ
¹but in   the   bowels   of you;   but [for] the

αὐτὴν ἀντιμισθίαν, ὡς τέκνοις λέγω,
same   recompence,   as   to children   I say,

πλατύνθητε καὶ ὑμεῖς.
be enlarged   also   ye.

14 Μὴ γίνεσθε ἑτεροζυγοῦντες ἀπίστοις·
Do not ye become   unequally yoked [with] unbelievers;

τίς γὰρ μετοχὴ δικαιοσύνῃ καὶ ἀνομίᾳ,
for what   share   righteousness^c   and   lawlessness,^c
= have righteousness and lawlessness,

ἢ τίς κοινωνία φωτὶ πρὸς σκότος; 15 τίς
or   what   fellowship   light^c   with   darkness?   what
= has light

δὲ συμφώνησις Χριστοῦ πρὸς Βελιάρ,
and   agreement   of Christ   with   Beliar,

ἢ τίς μερὶς πιστῷ μετὰ ἀπίστου; 16 τίς
or   what   part   a believer^c   with   an unbeliever?   what
= has a believer

δὲ συγκατάθεσις ναῷ θεοῦ μετὰ εἰδώλων;
and   union   a shrine^c of God   with   idols?
= has a shrine

ἡμεῖς γὰρ ναὸς θεοῦ ἐσμεν ζῶντος·
For ¹we   ²a shrine ³God   ¹are   ⁴of a living;

καθὼς εἶπεν ὁ θεὸς ὅτι ἐνοικήσω ἐν
as   said   -   God[,]   -   I will dwell among

αὐτοῖς καὶ ἐμπεριπατήσω, καὶ ἔσομαι
them   and   I will walk among [them], and   I will be

αὐτῶν θεός, καὶ αὐτοὶ ἔσονταί μου λαός.
of them   God,   and   they   shall be   of me a people.

---

tresses; [5]in beatings, imprisonments and riots; in hard work, sleepless nights and hunger; [6]in purity, understanding, patience and kindness; in the Holy Spirit and in sincere love; [7]in truthful speech and in the power of God; with the weapons of righteousness in the right hand and in the left; [8]through glory and dishonor, bad report and good report; genuine, yet regarded as impostors; [9]known, yet regarded as unknown; dying, and yet we live; beaten, and yet not killed; [10]sorrowful, yet always rejoicing; poor, yet making many rich; having nothing, and yet possessing everything.

[11]We have spoken freely to you, Corinthians, and opened wide our hearts to you. [12]We are not withholding our affection from you, but you are withholding yours from us. [13]As a fair exchange—I speak as to my children—open wide your hearts also.

Do Not Be Yoked With Unbelievers

[14]Do not be yoked together with unbelievers. For what do righteousness and wickedness have in common? Or what fellowship can light have with darkness? [15]What harmony is there between Christ and Belial [h]? What does a believer have in common with an unbeliever? [16]What agreement is there between the temple of God and idols? For we are the temple of the living God. As God has said: "I will live with them and walk among them, and I will be their God, and they will be my people." [i]

---

[n] Other ancient authorities read *you*

* Evidently = and yet, as in some other places; *cf.* John 20. 29.

[h]15 Greek *Beliar*, a variant of *Belial*
[i]16 Lev. 26:12; Jer. 32:38; Ezek. 37:27

17 Therefore come out from them,
and be separate from them, says the Lord,
and touch nothing unclean;
then I will welcome you,
18 and I will be your father,
and you shall be my sons and daughters,
says the Lord Almighty."

Chapter 7

SINCE we have these promises, beloved, let us cleanse ourselves from every defilement of body and of spirit, making holiness perfect in the fear of God.

Paul's Joy at the Church's Repentance

2 Make room in your hearts[o] for us; we have wronged no one, we have corrupted no one, we have taken advantage of no one. 3 I do not say this to condemn you, for I said before that you are in our hearts, to die together and to live together. 4 I often boast about you; I have great pride in you; I am filled with consolation; I am overjoyed in all our affliction.
5 For even when we came into Macedonia, our bodies had no rest, but we were afflicted in every way—disputes without and fears within. 6 But God, who consoles the downcast, consoled us by the arrival of Titus, 7 and not only by his coming, but also by the consolation with which he was consoled about you, as he told us of your longing, your mourning, your zeal for me, so that I rejoiced still more. 8 For even if I made you sorry with my letter, I do not regret it (though I did regret it, for I see that I grieved you with

[o] Gk lacks in your hearts

---

17 διὸ ἐξέλθατε ἐκ μέσου αὐτῶν καὶ
Wherefore come ye out from [the] midst of them and
ἀφορίσθητε, λέγει κύριος, καὶ ἀκαθάρτου
be ye separated, says [the] Lord, and an unclean thing
μὴ ἅπτεσθε· 18 κἀγὼ εἰσδέξομαι ὑμᾶς, καὶ
do not touch; and I will welcome in you, and
ἔσομαι ὑμῖν εἰς πατέρα, καὶ ὑμεῖς ἔσεσθέ
I will be to you for a father, and ye shall be
μοι εἰς υἱοὺς καὶ θυγατέρας, λέγει κύριος
to me for sons and daughters, says [the] Lord
παντοκράτωρ. 7 ταύτας οὖν ἔχοντες τὰς ἐπ-
[the] Almighty. These therefore having pro-
αγγελίας, ἀγαπητοί, καθαρίσωμεν ἑαυτοὺς ἀπὸ
mises, beloved, let us cleanse ourselves from
παντὸς μολυσμοῦ σαρκὸς καὶ πνεύματος,
all pollution of flesh and of spirit,
ἐπιτελοῦντες ἁγιωσύνην ἐν φόβῳ θεοῦ.
perfecting holiness in [the] fear of God.
2 Χωρήσατε ἡμᾶς· οὐδένα ἠδικήσαμεν,
Make room for us; no one we wronged,
οὐδένα ἐφθείραμεν, οὐδένα ἐπλεονεκτήσαμεν.
no one we injured, no one we defrauded.
3 πρὸς κατάκρισιν οὐ λέγω· προείρηκα
For condemnation I say not; I have previously said
γὰρ ὅτι ἐν ταῖς καρδίαις ἡμῶν ἐστε
for that in the hearts of us ye are
εἰς τὸ συναποθανεῖν καὶ συζῆν. 4 πολλή
for - to die with [you] and to live with [you]. Much
μοι παρρησία πρὸς ὑμᾶς, πολλή μοι
to me boldness toward you, much to me
=I have much   =I have much
καύχησις ὑπὲρ ὑμῶν· πεπλήρωμαι τῇ
boasting on behalf of you; I have been filled -
παρακλήσει, ὑπερπερισσεύομαι τῇ χαρᾷ ἐπὶ
with comfort, I overflow - with joy on(in)
πάσῃ τῇ θλίψει ἡμῶν. 5 Καὶ γὰρ
all the affliction of us. For indeed
ἐλθόντων ἡμῶν εἰς Μακεδονίαν οὐδεμίαν
coming us into Macedonia no
=when we came
ἔσχηκεν ἄνεσιν ἡ σὰρξ ἡμῶν, ἀλλ’ ἐν
has had rest the flesh of us, but in
παντὶ θλιβόμενοι· ἔξωθεν μάχαι, ἔσωθεν
every way being afflicted; without [were] fightings, within
φόβοι. 6 ἀλλ’ ὁ παρακαλῶν τοὺς ταπεινοὺς
[were] fears. But the [one] comforting the humble
παρεκάλεσεν ἡμᾶς ὁ θεὸς ἐν τῇ παρουσίᾳ
comforted us - God by the presence
Τίτου· 7 οὐ μόνον δὲ ἐν τῇ παρουσίᾳ
of Titus; and not only by the presence
αὐτοῦ, ἀλλὰ καὶ ἐν τῇ παρακλήσει ᾗ
of him, but also by the comfort with which
παρεκλήθη ἐφ’ ὑμῖν, ἀναγγέλλων ἡμῖν
he was comforted over you, reporting to us
τὴν ὑμῶν ἐπιπόθησιν, τὸν ὑμῶν ὀδυρμόν,
the of you eager longing, the of you mourning,
τὸν ὑμῶν ζῆλον ὑπὲρ ἐμοῦ, ὥστε με
the of you zeal on behalf of me, so as me
μᾶλλον χαρῆναι. 8 Ὅτι εἰ καὶ ἐλύπησα
more to rejoice. Because if indeed I grieved
=so that I rejoiced more.
ὑμᾶς ἐν τῇ ἐπιστολῇ, οὐ μεταμέλομαι·
you by the epistle, I do not regret;
εἰ καὶ μετεμελόμην, βλέπω ὅτι ἡ ἐπιστολὴ
if indeed I regretted, I see that - epistle

---

17 "Therefore come out from them
and be separate,
says the Lord.
Touch no unclean thing,
and I will receive you." [j]
18 "I will be a Father to you,
and you will be my sons and daughters,
says the Lord Almighty." [k]

Chapter 7

SINCE we have these promises, dear friends, let us purify ourselves from everything that contaminates body and spirit, perfecting holiness out of reverence for God.

Paul's Joy

2 Make room for us in your hearts. We have wronged no one, we have corrupted no one, we have exploited no one. 3 I do not say this to condemn you; I have said before that you have such a place in our hearts that we would live or die with you. 4 I have great confidence in you; I take great pride in you. I am greatly encouraged; in all our troubles my joy knows no bounds.
5 For when we came into Macedonia, this body of ours had no rest, but we were harassed at every turn —conflicts on the outside, fears within. 6 But God, who comforts the downcast, comforted us by the coming of Titus, 7 and not only by his coming but also by the comfort you had given him. He told us about your longing for me, your deep sorrow, your ardent concern for me, so that my joy was greater than ever.
8 Even if I caused you sorrow by my letter, I do not regret it. Though I did re-

[j] 17 Isaiah 52:11; Ezek. 20:34,41
[k] 18 2 Samuel 7:14; 7:8

that letter, though only briefly). 9 Now I rejoice, not because you were grieved, but because your grief led to repentance; for you felt a godly grief, so that you were not harmed in any way by us. 10 For godly grief produces a repentance that leads to salvation and brings no regret, but worldly grief produces death. 11 For see what earnestness, this godly grief has produced in you, what eagerness to clear yourselves, what indignation, what alarm, what longing, what zeal, what punishment! At every point you have proved yourselves guiltless in the matter. 12 So although I wrote to you, it was not on account of the one who did the wrong, nor on account of the one who was wronged, but in order that your zeal for us might be made known to you before God. 13 In this we find comfort.

In addition to our own consolation, we rejoiced still more at the joy of Titus, because his mind has been set at rest by all of you. 14 For if I have been somewhat boastful about you to him, I was not disgraced; but just as everything we said to you was true, so our boasting to Titus has proved true as well. 15 And his heart goes out all the more to you, as he remembers the obedience of all of you, and how you welcomed him with fear and trembling. 16 I rejoice, because I have complete confidence in you.

ἐκείνη εἰ καὶ πρὸς ὥραν ἐλύπησεν ὑμᾶς,
that   if indeed for   an hour it grieved   you,

9 νῦν   χαίρω,   οὐχ   ὅτι   ἐλυπήθητε,   ἀλλ'
now I rejoice,   not   that ye were grieved,   but

ὅτι   ἐλυπήθητε   εἰς   μετάνοιαν· ἐλυπήθητε
that ye were grieved   to   repentance; ʾye were grieved

γὰρ   κατὰ θεόν, ἵνα ἐν μηδενὶ ζημιωθῆτε
ʾfor according God, in order in nothing ye might suffer
             to   that   loss

ἐξ   ἡμῶν.   10 ἡ   γὰρ   κατὰ θεὸν λύπη
by   us.   For ¹the ²according to ⁴God ⁵grief

μετάνοιαν   εἰς   σωτηρίαν   ἀμεταμέλητον
⁶repentance ⁸to ⁹salvation ⁶unregrettable

ἐργάζεται· ἡ δὲ τοῦ κόσμου λύπη θάνατον
⁵works;   but ¹the ⁵of the ⁴world ²grief ⁶death

κατεργάζεται.   11 ἰδοὺ   γὰρ   αὐτὸ τοῦτο
⁵works out.   For behold   this very thing[,]

τὸ κατὰ θεὸν λυπηθῆναι πόσην κατειργά-
- ²according to ³God ¹to be grieved[,] ¹what   ⁵it worked

σατο ὑμῖν σπουδήν, ἀλλὰ ἀπολογίαν, ἀλλὰ
out ⁴in you ⁶earnestness, but [what] defence, but

ἀγανάκτησιν, ἀλλὰ φόβον, ἀλλὰ ἐπιπόθησιν,
vexation, but fear, but eager desire,

ἀλλὰ ζῆλον, ἀλλὰ ἐκδίκησιν. ἐν παντὶ
but zeal, but vengeance.   In everything

συνεστήσατε ἑαυτοὺς ἁγνοὺς εἶναι τῷ
ye commended yourselves pure to be in the

πράγματι. 12 ἄρα εἰ καὶ ἔγραψα ὑμῖν,
affair.   Then if indeed I wrote to you,

οὐχ ἕνεκεν τοῦ ἀδικήσαντος οὐδὲ ἕνεκεν
not for the the [one] having done nor for the
       sake of   wrong   sake of

τοῦ ἀδικηθέντος, ἀλλ' ἕνεκεν τοῦ φανερω-
the having been but for the   - to be mani-
[one] wronged,   sake of

θῆναι τὴν σπουδὴν ὑμῶν τὴν ὑπὲρ ἡμῶν
fested the earnestnessᵇᵈ of you - on behalf of us

πρὸς ὑμᾶς ἐνώπιον τοῦ θεοῦ. 13 διὰ
toward you before - God.   There-

τοῦτο παρακεκλήμεθα. Ἐπὶ δὲ τῇ
fore we have been comforted. But as to the

παρακλήσει ἡμῶν περισσοτέρως μᾶλλον
comfort of us abundantly more

ἐχάρημεν ἐπὶ τῇ χαρᾷ Τίτου, ὅτι ἀναπέ-
we rejoiced over the joy of Titus, because has been

παυται τὸ πνεῦμα αὐτοῦ ἀπὸ πάντων
rested the spirit of him from(by) all

ὑμῶν· 14 ὅτι εἴ τι αὐτῷ ὑπὲρ ὑμῶν
you;   because if ²anything ³to him ⁴on behalf of ⁵you

κεκαύχημαι, οὐ κατῃσχύνθην, ἀλλ' ὡς
¹I have boasted, I was not shamed, but as

πάντα ἐν ἀληθείᾳ ἐλαλήσαμεν ὑμῖν, οὕτως
²all things ³in ⁴truth ¹we spoke ⁵to you, so

καὶ ἡ καύχησις ἡμῶν ἐπὶ Τίτου ἀλήθεια
also the boasting of us over Titus ³truth

ἐγενήθη. 15 καὶ τὰ σπλάγχνα αὐτοῦ
¹became.   And the bowels of him

περισσοτέρως εἰς ὑμᾶς ἐστιν ἀναμιμνησκομέ-
²abundantly ³toward ⁴you ¹is(are) [he] remember-

νου τὴν πάντων ὑμῶν ὑπακοήν, ὡς μετὰ
ingᵃ ¹the ²of all ⁴you ³obedience, as with

φόβου καὶ τρόμου ἐδέξασθε αὐτόν.
fear and trembling ye received him.

16 χαίρω ὅτι ἐν παντὶ θαρρῶ ἐν ὑμῖν.
I rejoice that in everything I am confident in you.

gret it—I see that my letter hurt you, but only for a little while— 9 yet now I am happy, not because you were made sorry, but because your sorrow led you to repentance. For you became sorrowful as God intended and so were not harmed in any way by us. 10 Godly sorrow brings repentance that leads to salvation and leaves no regret, but worldly sorrow brings death. 11 See what this godly sorrow has produced in you: what earnestness, what eagerness to clear yourselves, what indignation, what alarm, what longing, what concern, what readiness to see justice done. At every point you have proved yourselves to be innocent in this matter. 12 So even though I wrote to you, it was not on account of the one who did the wrong or of the injured party, but rather that before God you could see for yourselves how devoted to us you are. 13 By all this we are encouraged.

In addition to our own encouragement, we were especially delighted to see how happy Titus was, because his spirit has been refreshed by all of you. 14 I had boasted to him about you, and you have not embarrassed me. But just as everything we said to you was true, so our boasting about you to Titus has proved to be true as well. 15 And his affection for you is all the greater when he remembers that you were all obedient, receiving him with fear and trembling. 16 I am glad I can have complete confidence in you.

Chapter 8

Encouragement to Be Generous

WE want you to know, brothers and sisters,[p] about the grace of God that has been granted to the churches of Macedonia; [2] for during a severe ordeal of affliction, their abundant joy and their extreme poverty have overflowed in a wealth of generosity on their part. [3] For, as I can testify, they voluntarily gave according to their means, and even beyond their means, [4] begging us earnestly for the privilege[q] of sharing in this ministry to the saints— [5] and this, not merely as we expected; they gave themselves first to the Lord and, by the will of God, to us, [6] so that we might urge Titus that, as he had already made a beginning, so he should also complete this generous undertaking[r] among you. [7] Now as you excel in everything—in faith, in speech, in knowledge, in utmost eagerness, and in our love for you[s]—so we want you to excel also in this generous undertaking.[r]

[8] I do not say this as a command, but I am testing the genuineness of your love against the earnestness of others. [9] For you know the generous act[t] of our Lord Jesus Christ, that though he was rich, yet for your sakes he became poor, so that by his poverty you might become rich. [10] And in this matter I am giving my advice: it is appropriate for you who began last year not only to do something but even to desire to do something— [11] now finish doing it, so

[p] Gk brothers
[q] Gk grace
[r] Gk this grace
[s] Other ancient authorities read your love for us
[t] Gk the grace

---

8 Γνωρίζομεν δὲ ὑμῖν, ἀδελφοί, τὴν
Now we make known to you, brothers, the

χάριν τοῦ θεοῦ τὴν δεδομένην ἐν ταῖς
grace - of God - *having been* given among the

ἐκκλησίαις τῆς Μακεδονίας, **2** ὅτι ἐν πολλῇ
churches - of Macedonia, that in much

δοκιμῇ θλίψεως ἡ περισσεία τῆς χαρᾶς
proving of affliction the abundance of the joy

αὐτῶν καὶ ἡ κατὰ βάθους πτωχεία
of them and [1]the [2]according to [4]depth [3]poverty
=their extreme poverty

αὐτῶν ἐπερίσσευσεν εἰς τὸ πλοῦτος τῆς
of them abounded to the riches of the

ἁπλότητος αὐτῶν· **3** ὅτι κατὰ δύναμιν,
liberality of them; that according [their] power,
to

μαρτυρῶ, καὶ παρὰ δύναμιν, αὐθαίρετοι
I witness, and beyond [their] power, of their own
accord

4 μετὰ πολλῆς παρακλήσεως δεόμενοι ἡμῶν
with much beseeching requesting of us

τὴν χάριν καὶ τὴν κοινωνίαν τῆς διακονίας
the grace and the fellowship of the ministry

τῆς εἰς τοὺς ἁγίους, **5** καὶ οὐ καθὼς
- to the saints, and not as

ἠλπίσαμεν, ἀλλὰ ἑαυτοὺς ἔδωκαν πρῶτον
we hoped, but themselves gave firstly

τῷ κυρίῳ καὶ ἡμῖν διὰ θελήματος θεοῦ,
to the Lord and to us through [the] will of God,

6 εἰς τὸ παρακαλέσαι ἡμᾶς Τίτον, ἵνα
for - to beseech us[b] Titus, in order
=that we should beseech that

καθὼς προενήρξατο οὕτως καὶ ἐπιτελέσῃ
as previously he began so also he should
complete

εἰς ὑμᾶς καὶ τὴν χάριν ταύτην. **7** ἀλλ᾽
in you also this grace. But

ὥσπερ ἐν παντὶ περισσεύετε, πίστει καὶ
as in everything ye abound, in faith and

λόγῳ καὶ γνώσει καὶ πάσῃ σπουδῇ
in word and in knowledge and in all diligence

κὲ τῇ ἐξ ἡμῶν ἐν ὑμῖν ἀγάπῃ, ἵνα
and - [2]from [1]us [4]in(to) [3]you [1]in love, [see] that

καὶ ἐν ταύτῃ τῇ χάριτι περισσεύητε.
[5]also [3]in [2]this - [4]grace [1]ye may abound.

8 Οὐ κατ᾽ ἐπιταγὴν λέγω, ἀλλὰ διὰ
[1]Not [2]by way of [3]command [1]I say,* but through

τῆς ἑτέρων σπουδῆς καὶ τὸ τῆς ὑμετέρας
[1]the [2]of others [3]diligence also [1]the - [2]of your

ἀγάπης γνήσιον δοκιμάζων· **9** γινώσκετε
[2]love [1]reality [1]proving; [1]ye know

γὰρ τὴν χάριν τοῦ κυρίου ἡμῶν Ἰησοῦ
[1]for the grace of the Lord of us Jesus

[Χριστοῦ], ὅτι δι᾽ ὑμᾶς ἐπτώχευσεν
Christ, that on account you [3]he impoverished
of [himself]

πλούσιος ὤν, ἵνα ὑμεῖς τῇ ἐκείνου πτωχείᾳ
[2]rich [1]being, in or- ye [1]by [2]of that [3]poverty
der that the one

πλουτήσητε. **10** καὶ γνώμην ἐν τούτῳ
might become rich. And [4]an opinion [1]in [3]this

δίδωμι· τοῦτο γὰρ ὑμῖν συμφέρει, οἵτινες
[2]I give; for this [2]for you [1]is expedient, who

οὐ μόνον τὸ ποιῆσαι ἀλλὰ καὶ τὸ θέλειν
not only the to do but also the to will

προενήρξασθε ἀπὸ πέρυσι· **11** νυνὶ δὲ καὶ
previously ye began from last year; but now also
=a year ago;

* That is, Paul is not issuing a command. Cf. I. Cor. 7. 6.

Chapter 8

Generosity Encouraged

AND now, brothers, we want you to know about the grace that God has given the Macedonian churches. [2] Out of the most severe trial, their overflowing joy and their extreme poverty welled up in rich generosity. [3] For I testify that they gave as much as they were able, and even beyond their ability. Entirely on their own, [4] they urgently pleaded with us for the privilege of sharing in this service to the saints. [5] And they did not do as we expected, but they gave themselves first to the Lord and then to us in keeping with God's will. [6] So we urged Titus, since he had earlier made a beginning, to bring also to completion this act of grace on your part. [7] But just as you excel in everything—in faith, in speech, in knowledge, in complete earnestness and in your love for us[1]—see that you also excel in this grace of giving.

[8] I am not commanding you, but I want to test the sincerity of your love by comparing it with the earnestness of others. [9] For you know the grace of our Lord Jesus Christ, that though he was rich, yet for your sakes he became poor, so that you through his poverty might become rich.

[10] And here is my advice about what is best for you in this matter: Last year you were the first not only to give but also to have the desire to do so. [11] Now fin-

[1]7 Some manuscripts *in our love for you*

that your eagerness may be matched by completing it according to your means. 12For if the eagerness is there, the gift is acceptable according to what one has—not according to what one does not have. 13 I do not mean that there should be relief for others and pressure on you, but it is a question of a fair balance between 14your present abundance and their need, so that their abundance may be for your need, in order that there may be a fair balance. 15 As it is written,
"The one who had
　　　much did not
　　　have too much,
and the one who
　　　had little did not
　　　have too little."

Commendation of Titus

16 But thanks be to God who put in the heart of Titus the same eagerness for you that I myself have. 17For he not only accepted our appeal, but since he is more eager than ever, he is going to you of his own accord. 18With him we are sending the brother who is famous among all the churches for his proclaiming the good news;[u] 19and not only that, but he has also been appointed by the churches to travel with us while we are administering this generous undertaking[r] for the glory of the Lord himself[v] and to show our goodwill. 20We intend that no one should blame us about this generous gift that we are administering, 21for we intend to do what is right not only in the Lord's sight but also in the sight of others. 22 And with them we are sending our

---

τὸ	ποιῆσαι	ἐπιτελέσατε,	ὅπως	καθάπερ	ἡ
¹the	**²to do**	¹complete ye,	so as	as	the

προθυμία	τοῦ	θέλειν,	οὕτως	καὶ	τὸ
eagerness	of the	to will,	so	also	the

ἐπιτελέσαι	ἐκ	τοῦ	ἔχειν.	12 εἰ	γὰρ	ἡ
to complete	out of	the	to have. = what ye have.	For if		the

προθυμία	πρόκειται,	καθὸ	ἐὰν	ἔχῃ
eagerness	is already there,	according to	whatever	one has

εὐπρόσδεκτος,	οὐ	καθὸ	οὐκ	ἔχει.	13 οὐ
it is acceptable,	not	according to	not	[what] one has not.	but

γὰρ	ἵνα	ἄλλοις	ἄνεσις,	ὑμῖν	θλῖψις,
For	in order that [there may be]	to others	relief,	to you	distress,

ἀλλ'	ἐξ	ἰσότητος	14 ἐν	τῷ	νῦν	καιρῷ
but	by	equality	at	the	present	time

τὸ	ὑμῶν	περίσσευμα	εἰς	τὸ	ἐκείνων
the	²of you	¹abundance [may be] for	the	the	²of those

ὑστέρημα,	ἵνα	καὶ	τὸ	ἐκείνων	περίσσευμα
¹lack,	in order that	also	the	²of those	¹abundance

γένηται	εἰς	τὸ	ὑμῶν	ὑστέρημα,	ὅπως
may be	for	the	²of you	¹lack,	so as

γένηται	ἰσότης,	15 καθὼς	γέγραπται·	ὁ
there may be	equality,	as	it has been written:	He

τὸ	πολὺ	οὐκ	ἐπλεόνασεν,	καὶ	ὁ	τὸ
the	much	did not abound,		and	he	the

ὀλίγον	οὐκ	ἠλαττόνησεν.	16 Χάρις	δὲ
little	had not less.		But thanks [be]	

τῷ	θεῷ	τῷ	διδόντι	τὴν	αὐτὴν	σπουδὴν
-	to God	-	giving	the	same	diligence

ὑπὲρ	ὑμῶν	ἐν	τῇ	καρδίᾳ	Τίτου,	17 ὅτι
on be-half of	you	in	the	heart	of Titus,	because

τὴν	μὲν	παράκλησιν	ἐδέξατο,	σπουδαιότερος
²the	¹indeed	⁴beseeching	³he received,	⁵more diligent

δὲ	ὑπάρχων	αὐθαίρετος	ἐξῆλθεν	πρὸς	ὑμᾶς.
¹and	⁶being	of his own accord	he went forth	to	you.

18 συνεπέμψαμεν	δὲ	μετ'	αὐτοῦ	τὸν
And we sent *with*		with	him	the

ἀδελφὸν	οὗ	ὁ	ἔπαινος	ἐν	τῷ	εὐαγγελίῳ
brother	of whom the		praise	in	the	gospel

διὰ	πασῶν	τῶν	ἐκκλησιῶν,	19 οὐ	μόνον	δὲ
[is] through[out]	all	the	churches,		and not only [this]	

ἀλλὰ	καὶ	χειροτονηθεὶς	ὑπὸ	τῶν	ἐκκλησιῶν
but	also	⁵having been elected	⁶by	⁷the	⁸churches

συνέκδημος	ἡμῶν	ἐν	τῇ	χάριτι	ταύτῃ
¹a travelling companion	²of us	in		this grace	

τῇ	διακονουμένῃ	ὑφ'	ἡμῶν	πρὸς	τὴν
-	being ministered	by	us	to	¹the

αὐτοῦ	τοῦ	κυρίου	δόξαν	καὶ	προθυμίαν
⁵[him]self	²of the	⁴Lord	³glory	and	eagerness

ἡμῶν,	20 στελλόμενοι	τοῦτο,	μή	τις	ἡμᾶς
of us,	avoiding	this,	lest	anyone	²us

μωμήσηται	ἐν	τῇ	ἁδρότητι	ταύτῃ	τῇ
¹should blame	in		this bounty		-

διακονουμένῃ	ὑφ'	ἡμῶν·	21 προνοοῦμεν	γὰρ
being ministered	by	us;	for we provide	

καλὰ	οὐ	μόνον	ἐνώπιον	κυρίου	ἀλλὰ	καὶ
good things	not	only	before	[the] Lord	but	also

ἐνώπιον	ἀνθρώπων.	22 συνεπέμψαμεν	δὲ
before	men.	And we sent with	

---

ish the work, so that your eager willingness to do it may be matched by your completion of it, according to your means. 12For if the willingness is there, the gift is acceptable according to what one has, not according to what he does not have.

13Our desire is not that others might be relieved while you are hard pressed, but that there might be equality. 14At the present time your plenty will supply what they need, so that in turn their plenty will supply what you need. Then there will be equality, 15as it is written: "He who gathered much did not have too much, and he who gathered little did not have too little."[m]

Titus Sent to Corinth

16I thank God, who put into the heart of Titus the same concern I have for you. 17For Titus not only welcomed our appeal, but he is coming to you with much enthusiasm and on his own initiative. 18And we are sending along with him the brother who is praised by all the churches for his service to the gospel. 19What is more, he was chosen by the churches to accompany us as we carry the offering, which we administer in order to honor the Lord himself and to show our eagerness to help. 20We want to avoid any criticism of the way we administer this liberal gift. 21For we are taking pains to do what is right, not only in the eyes of the Lord but also in the eyes of men.

22In addition, we are

---

m 15 Exodus 16:18

brother whom we have often tested and found eager in many matters, but who is now more eager than ever because of his great confidence in you. 23 As for Titus, he is my partner and co-worker in your service; as for our brothers, they are messengers[w] of the churches, the glory of Christ. 24 Therefore openly before the churches, show them the proof of your love and of our reason for boasting about you.

αὐτοῖς τὸν ἀδελφὸν ἡμῶν, ὃν ἐδοκιμάσαμεν
them   the   brother   of us, whom ¹we proved

ἐν πολλοῖς πολλάκις σπουδαῖον ὄντα, νυνὶ
²in ⁶many things ⁵many times ³diligent ⁴being, ⁷now

δὲ πολὺ σπουδαιότερον πεποιθήσει πολλῇ
⁸and ¹²much more diligent ¹¹in ¹⁰confidence ⁹much

τῇ εἰς ὑμᾶς. 23 εἴτε ὑπὲρ Τίτου, κοινωνὸς
- toward you. Whether as to Titus, ²partner

ἐμὸς καὶ εἰς ὑμᾶς συνεργός· εἴτε ἀδελφοὶ
¹my ³and ⁴for ⁵you ⁶fellow-worker; or   brothers

ἡμῶν, ἀπόστολοι ἐκκλησιῶν, δόξα Χριστοῦ.
of us, apostles   of churches, [the] of Christ.
                                 glory

24 τὴν οὖν ἔνδειξιν τῆς ἀγάπης ὑμῶν
⁷The ¹therefore ⁸demon- ⁹of the ¹⁰love ¹¹of you
             stration

καὶ ἡμῶν καυχήσεως ὑπὲρ ὑμῶν εἰς
¹²and ¹⁴of us ¹³boasting ¹⁵on behalf of ¹⁶you ¹⁷to

αὐτοὺς ἐνδεικνύμενοι εἰς πρόσωπον τῶν
¹⁸them ²showing forth ³in ⁴[the] presence ⁵of the

ἐκκλησιῶν.
⁶churches.

Chapter 9

The Collection for Christians at Jerusalem

NOW it is not necessary for me to write you about the ministry to the saints, 2 for I know your eagerness, which is the subject of my boasting about you to the people of Macedonia, saying that Achaia has been ready since last year; and your zeal has stirred up most of them. 3 But I am sending the brothers in order that our boasting about you may not prove to have been empty in this case, so that you may be ready, as I said you would be; 4 otherwise, if some Macedonians come with me and find that you are not ready, we would be humiliated—to say nothing of you—in this undertaking.[x] 5 So I thought it necessary to urge the brothers to go on ahead to you, and arrange in advance for this bountiful gift that you have promised, so that it may be ready as a voluntary gift and not as an extortion.

6 The point is this: the one who sows sparingly will also reap sparingly,

9 Περὶ μὲν γὰρ τῆς διακονίας τῆς
¹Concerning ²indeed ⁵for the ³ministry -

εἰς τοὺς ἁγίους περισσόν μοί ἐστιν τὸ
to the saints ²superfluous ⁴for me ¹it is   -

γράφειν ὑμῖν· 2 οἶδα γὰρ τὴν προθυμίαν
³to write to you; for I know the eagerness

ὑμῶν ἣν ὑπὲρ ὑμῶν καυχῶμαι Μακε-
of you which on behalf of you I boast to Mace-

δόσιν ὅτι Ἀχαΐα παρεσκεύασται ἀπὸ
donians that Achaia has made preparations from

πέρυσι, καὶ τὸ ὑμῶν ζῆλος ἠρέθισεν
last year, and the ³of you ¹zeal stirred up
=a year ago,

τοὺς πλείονας. 3 ἔπεμψα δὲ τοὺς ἀδελφούς,
the greater number. And I sent the brothers,

ἵνα μὴ τὸ καύχημα ἡμῶν τὸ ὑπὲρ
lest the boast, of us - on behalf

ὑμῶν κενωθῇ ἐν τῷ μέρει τούτῳ, ἵνα
of you should be in this respect, in order
       emptied   that

καθὼς ἔλεγον παρεσκευασμένοι ἦτε, 4 μή
as I said *having been* prepared ye were,

πως ἐὰν ἔλθωσιν σὺν ἐμοὶ Μακεδόνες
lest if ²come ³with ⁴me ¹Macedonians

καὶ εὕρωσιν ὑμᾶς ἀπαρασκευάστους
and find you unprepared

καταισχυνθῶμεν ἡμεῖς, ἵνα μὴ λέγωμεν
²should be shamed ¹we, *in order* we say not
                           that

ὑμεῖς, ἐν τῇ ὑποστάσει ταύτῃ. 5 ἀναγκαῖον
ye, in this confidence. ¹Necessary

οὖν ἡγησάμην παρακαλέσαι τοὺς ἀδελφοὺς
³there- ²I thought [it] to beseech the brothers
fore

ἵνα προέλθωσιν εἰς ὑμᾶς καὶ προκαταρτί-
in order they go to you and arrange before-
that   forward

σωσιν τὴν προεπηγγελμένην εὐλογίαν ὑμῶν,
hand ¹the ⁴having been promised ⁵blessing ⁶of you,

ταύτην ἑτοίμην εἶναι οὕτως ὡς εὐλογίαν
this ready to be thus as a blessing

καὶ μὴ ὡς πλεονεξίαν. 6 Τοῦτο δέ,
and not as greediness. And this,

ὁ σπείρων φειδομένως φειδομένως καὶ
the [one] sowing sparingly ²sparingly ²also

sending with them our brother who has often proved to us in many ways that he is zealous, and now even more so because of his great confidence in you. 23 As for Titus, he is my partner and fellow worker among you; as for our brothers, they are representatives of the churches and an honor to Christ. 24 Therefore show these men the proof of your love and the reason for our pride in you, so that the churches can see it.

Chapter 9

THERE is no need for me to write to you about this service to the saints. 2 For I know your eagerness to help, and I have been boasting about it to the Macedonians, telling them that since last year you in Achaia were ready to give; and your enthusiasm has stirred most of them to action. 3 But I am sending the brothers in order that our boasting about you in this matter should not prove hollow, but that you may be ready, as I said you would be. 4 For if any Macedonians come with me and find you unprepared, we—not to say anything about you—would be ashamed of having been so confident. 5 So I thought it necessary to urge the brothers to visit you in advance and finish the arrangements for the generous gift you had promised. Then it will be ready as a generous gift, not as one grudgingly given.

Sowing Generously

6 Remember this: Whoever sows sparingly will also

and the one who sows bountifully will also reap bountifully. 7Each of you must give as you have made up your mind, not reluctantly or under compulsion, for God loves a cheerful giver. 8And God is able to provide you with every blessing in abundance, so that by always having enough of everything, you may share abundantly in every good work. 9As it is written,

"He scatters abroad,
he gives to
the poor;
his righteousness[y]
endures
forever."

10He who supplies seed to the sower and bread for food will supply and multiply your seed for sowing and increase the harvest of your righteousness.[y] 11You will be enriched in every way for your great generosity, which will produce thanksgiving to God through us; 12for the rendering of this ministry not only supplies the needs of the saints but also overflows with many thanksgivings to God. 13Through the testing of this ministry you glorify God by your obedience to the confession of the gospel of Christ and by the generosity of your sharing with them and with all others, 14while they long for you and pray for you because of the surpassing grace of God that he has given you. 15Thanks be to God for his indescribable gift!

Chapter 10

Paul Defends His Ministry

I myself, Paul, appeal to you by the meekness and gentleness of Christ—I who am humble when face to face with you, but bold

[y] Or benevolence

θερίσει, καὶ ὁ σπείρων ἐπ' εὐλογίαις ἐπ'
will reap, and the [one] sowing on(for) blessings on(for)

εὐλογίαις καὶ θερίσει. 7 ἕκαστος καθὼς
blessings also will reap. Each one as

προῄρηται τῇ καρδίᾳ, μὴ ἐκ λύπης ἢ
he chose in the(his) heart, not of grief or

ἐξ ἀνάγκης· ἱλαρὸν γὰρ δότην ἀγαπᾷ ὁ
of necessity; for a cheerful giver loves -

θεός. 8 δυνατεῖ δὲ ὁ θεὸς πᾶσαν χάριν
God. And is able - God all grace

περισσεῦσαι εἰς ὑμᾶς, ἵνα ἐν παντὶ
to cause to abound toward you, in order that in everything

πάντοτε πᾶσαν αὐτάρκειαν ἔχοντες περισ-
always all self-sufficiency having ye may

σεύητε εἰς πᾶν ἔργον ἀγαθόν, 9 καθὼς
abound to every work good, as

γέγραπται· ἐσκόρπισεν, ἔδωκεν τοῖς πένησιν,
it has been written: He scattered, he gave to the poor,

ἡ δικαιοσύνη αὐτοῦ μένει εἰς τὸν αἰῶνα.
the righteousness of him remains unto the age.

10 ὁ δὲ ἐπιχορηγῶν σπέρμα τῷ σπείροντι
Now the [one] providing seed for the [one] sowing

καὶ ἄρτον εἰς βρῶσιν χορηγήσει καὶ
both bread for food will supply and

πληθυνεῖ τὸν σπόρον ὑμῶν καὶ αὐξήσει
will multiply the seed of you and will increase

τὰ γενήματα τῆς δικαιοσύνης ὑμῶν· 11 ἐν
the fruits of the righteousness of you; in

παντὶ πλουτιζόμενοι εἰς πᾶσαν ἁπλότητα,
everything being enriched to all liberality,

ἥτις κατεργάζεται δι' ἡμῶν εὐχαριστίαν
which works out through us thanksgiving

τῷ θεῷ· 12 ὅτι ἡ διακονία τῆς λειτουργίας
- to God; because the ministry - service

ταύτης οὐ μόνον ἐστὶν προσαναπληροῦσα
of this not only is making up

τὰ ὑστερήματα τῶν ἁγίων, ἀλλὰ καὶ
the things lacking of the saints, but [is] also

περισσεύουσα διὰ πολλῶν εὐχαριστιῶν τῷ
abounding through many thanksgivings -

θεῷ· 13 διὰ τῆς δοκιμῆς τῆς διακονίας
to God; through the proof - ministry

ταύτης δοξάζοντες τὸν θεὸν ἐπὶ τῇ
of this glorifying - God on the

ὑποταγῇ τῆς ὁμολογίας ὑμῶν εἰς τὸ
submission of the confession of you to the

εὐαγγέλιον τοῦ Χριστοῦ καὶ ἁπλότητι
gospel - of Christ and [on the] liberality

τῆς κοινωνίας εἰς αὐτοὺς καὶ εἰς πάντας,
of the fellowship toward them and toward all men,

14 καὶ αὐτῶν δεήσει ὑπὲρ ὑμῶν ἐπιποθούν-
and them with request on behalf of you longing

των ὑμᾶς διὰ τὴν ὑπερβάλλουσαν χάριν
after you on account of the excelling grace

τοῦ θεοῦ ἐφ' ὑμῖν. 15 Χάρις τῷ θεῷ
- of God upon you. Thanks - to God

ἐπὶ τῇ ἀνεκδιηγήτῳ αὐτοῦ δωρεᾷ.
for the indescribable of him gift.

10 Αὐτὸς δὲ ἐγὼ Παῦλος παρακαλῶ
[my]self Now I Paul beseech

ὑμᾶς διὰ τῆς πραΰτητος καὶ ἐπιεικείας
you through the meekness and forbearance

τοῦ Χριστοῦ, ὃς κατὰ πρόσωπον μὲν
- of Christ, who according to face indeed

---

reap sparingly, and whoever sows generously will also reap generously. 7Each man should give what he has decided in his heart to give, not reluctantly or under compulsion, for God loves a cheerful giver. 8And God is able to make all grace abound to you, so that in all things at all times, having all that you need, you will abound in every good work. 9As it is written:

"He has scattered
abroad his gifts to
the poor;
his righteousness
endures forever."[n]

10Now he who supplies seed to the sower and bread for food will also supply and increase your store of seed and will enlarge the harvest of your righteousness. 11You will be made rich in every way so that you can be generous on every occasion, and through us your generosity will result in thanksgiving to God. 12This service that you perform is not only supplying the needs of God's people but is also overflowing in many expressions of thanks to God. 13Because of the service by which you have proved yourselves, men will praise God for the obedience that accompanies your confession of the gospel of Christ, and for your generosity in sharing with them and with everyone else. 14And in their prayers for you their hearts will go out to you, because of the surpassing grace God has given you. 15Thanks be to God for his indescribable gift!

Chapter 10

Paul's Defense of His Ministry

BY the meekness and gentleness of Christ, I appeal to you—I, Paul, who am "timid" when face to face with you, but

[n]9 Psalm 112:9

toward you when I am away!— 2 I ask that when I am present I need not show boldness by daring to oppose those who think we are acting according to human standards.ᶻ 3 Indeed, we live as human beings,ᵃ but we do not wage war according to human standards;ᶻ 4 for the weapons of our warfare are not merely human,ᵇ but they have divine power to destroy strongholds. We destroy arguments 5 and every proud obstacle raised up against the knowledge of God, and we take every thought captive to obey Christ. 6 We are ready to punish every disobedience when your obedience is complete.

7 Look at what is before your eyes. If you are confident that you belong to Christ, remind yourself of this, that just as you belong to Christ, so also do we. 8 Now, even if I boast a little too much of our authority, which the Lord gave for building you up and not for tearing you down, I will not be ashamed of it. 9 I do not want to seem as though I am trying to frighten you with my letters. 10 For they say, "His letters are weighty and strong, but his bodily presence is weak, and his speech contemptible." 11 Let such people understand that what we say by letter when absent, we will also do when present.

12 We do not dare to classify or compare ourselves with some of those who commend themselves. But when they measure

ταπεινὸς ἐν ὑμῖν, ἀπὼν δὲ θαρρῶ εἰς
[am] humble among you, but being absent am bold toward

ὑμᾶς· 2 δέομαι δὲ τὸ μὴ παρὼν θαρρῆσαι
you: now I request - not being present to be bold

τῇ πεποιθήσει ᾗ λογίζομαι τολμῆσαι ἐπί
in the confidence which I reckon to be daring toward

τινας τοὺς λογιζομένους ἡμᾶς ὡς κατὰ
some the [ones] reckoning us as ²according to

σάρκα περιπατοῦντας. 3 Ἐν σαρκὶ γὰρ
²flesh ¹walking. in flesh For

περιπατοῦντες οὐ κατὰ σάρκα στρατευόμεθα,
walking not according to flesh we war,

4 τὰ γὰρ ὅπλα τῆς στρατείας ἡμῶν
for the weapons of the warfare of us [are]

οὐ σαρκικὰ ἀλλὰ δυνατὰ τῷ θεῷ πρὸς
not fleshly but powerful - to God to

καθαίρεσιν ὀχυρωμάτων, λογισμοὺς καθαιροῦν-
overthrow of strongholds, ²reasonings ¹overthrow-

τες 5 καὶ πᾶν ὕψωμα ἐπαιρόμενον κατὰ
ing and every high thing rising up against

τῆς γνώσεως τοῦ θεοῦ, καὶ αἰχμαλωτίζοντες
the knowledge - of God, and taking captive

πᾶν νόημα εἰς τὴν ὑπακοὴν τοῦ Χριστοῦ,
every design to the obedience - of Christ,

6 καὶ ἐν ἑτοίμῳ ἔχοντες ἐκδικῆσαι πᾶσαν
and in readiness having to avenge all
= being ready

παρακοήν, ὅταν πληρωθῇ ὑμῶν ἡ ὑπακοή.
disobedience, whenever ⁴is fulfilled ²of you ¹the ³obedience.

7 Τὰ κατὰ πρόσωπον βλέπετε. εἴ τις
²The ³according ⁴face ¹ye look [at]. If any-
things to (appearance) one

πέποιθεν ἑαυτῷ Χριστοῦ εἶναι, τοῦτο
has persuaded himself ²of Christ ¹to be, this

λογιζέσθω πάλιν ἐφ᾽ ἑαυτοῦ, ὅτι καθὼς
let him reckon again as to himself, that as

αὐτὸς Χριστοῦ, οὕτως καὶ ἡμεῖς. 8 ἐάν
he [is] of Christ, so also [are] we. ²if

τε γὰρ περισσότερόν τι καυχήσωμαι περὶ
²even ¹For ³more abundantly ⁵some- ⁴I should boast concern-
what ing

τῆς ἐξουσίας ἡμῶν, ἧς ἔδωκεν ὁ κύριος
the authority of us, which ²gave ¹the ³Lord

εἰς οἰκοδομὴν καὶ οὐκ εἰς καθαίρεσιν
for edification and not for overthrow

ὑμῶν, οὐκ αἰσχυνθήσομαι, 9 ἵνα μὴ δόξω
of you, I shall not be shamed, in order that I may not seem

ὡσὰν ἐκφοβεῖν ὑμᾶς διὰ τῶν ἐπιστολῶν.
as though to frighten you through the epistles.

10 ὅτι αἱ ἐπιστολαὶ μέν, φησίν, βαρεῖαι
Because the(his) epistles indeed, he says, [are] weighty

καὶ ἰσχυραί, ἡ δὲ παρουσία τοῦ σώματος
and strong, but the presence of the(his) body [is]

ἀσθενὴς καὶ ὁ λόγος ἐξουθενημένος.
weak and the(his) speech being despised.

11 τοῦτο λογιζέσθω ὁ τοιοῦτος, ὅτι οἷοί
This let reckon such a one, that such as

ἐσμεν τῷ λόγῳ δι᾽ ἐπιστολῶν ἀπόντες,
we are - in word through epistles being absent,

τοιοῦτοι καὶ παρόντες τῷ ἔργῳ. 12 Οὐ
such also being present - in work. ²not

γὰρ τολμῶμεν ἐγκρῖναι ἢ συγκρῖναι
¹For ³we dare to class with or to compare

ἑαυτούς τισιν τῶν ἑαυτοὺς συνιστανόντων·
ourselves with some of the ²themselves ¹commending;
[ones]

"bold" when away! 2 I beg you that when I come I may not have to be as bold as I expect to be toward some people who think that we live by the standards of this world. 3 For though we live in the world, we do not wage war as the world does. 4 The weapons we fight with are not the weapons of the world. On the contrary, they have divine power to demolish strongholds. 5 We demolish arguments and every pretension that sets itself up against the knowledge of God, and we take captive every thought to make it obedient to Christ. 6 And we will be ready to punish every act of disobedience, once your obedience is complete.

7 You are looking only on the surface of things.ᵒ If anyone is confident that he belongs to Christ, he should consider again that we belong to Christ just as much as he. 8 For even if I boast somewhat freely about the authority the Lord gave us for building you up rather than pulling you down, I will not be ashamed of it. 9 I do not want to seem to be trying to frighten you with my letters. 10 For some say, "His letters are weighty and forceful, but in person he is unimpressive and his speaking amounts to nothing." 11 Such people should realize that what we are in our letters when we are absent, we will be in our actions when we are present.

12 We do not dare to classify or compare ourselves with some who commend themselves. When they

---

ᶻ Gk according to the flesh
ᵃ Gk in the flesh
ᵇ Gk fleshly

ᵒ7 Or Look at the obvious facts

themselves by one another, and compare themselves with one another, they do not show good sense. 13 We, however, will not boast beyond limits, but will keep within the field that God has assigned to us, to reach out even as far as you. 14 For we were not overstepping our limits when we reached you; we were the first to come all the way to you with the good news[c] of Christ. 15 We do not boast beyond limits, that is, in the labors of others; but our hope is that, as your faith increases, our sphere of action among you may be greatly enlarged, 16 so that we may proclaim the good news[c] in lands beyond you, without boasting of work already done in someone else's sphere of action. 17 "Let the one who boasts, boast in the Lord." 18 For it is not those who commend themselves that are approved, but those whom the Lord commends.

ἀλλὰ	αὐτοὶ	ἐν	ἑαυτοῖς	ἑαυτοὺς	μετροῦντες
but	they	²among	⁴them-selves	³them-selves	¹measuring

καὶ	συγκρίνοντες	ἑαυτοὺς	ἑαυτοῖς	οὐ
and	comparing	themselves	with themselves	not

συνιᾶσιν.	13 ἡμεῖς	δὲ	οὐκ	εἰς	τὰ	ἄμετρα
do understand.	But we		²not			⁴immeasurably†

καυχησόμεθα,	ἀλλὰ	κατὰ	τὸ	μέτρον	τοῦ
¹will ³boast,	but	according to the		measure	of the

κανόνος	οὗ	ἐμέρισεν	ἡμῖν	ὁ	θεὸς	μέτρου,
rule	which	²divided	³to us	-	¹God	of(in) measure,

ἐφικέσθαι	ἄχρι	καὶ	ὑμῶν.	14 οὐ	γὰρ
to reach	as far as	even	you.	For not

ὡς	μὴ	ἐφικνούμενοι	εἰς	ὑμᾶς	ὑπερεκτείνομεν
as	not	reaching	to	you	do we overstretch

ἑαυτούς,	ἄχρι	γὰρ	καὶ	ὑμῶν	ἐφθάσαμεν
ourselves,	for as far as		even	you	we came

ἐν	τῷ	εὐαγγελίῳ	τοῦ	Χριστοῦ,	15 οὐκ
in	the	gospel	-	of Christ,	not

εἰς	τὰ	ἄμετρα	καυχώμενοι	ἐν	ἀλλοτρίοις
		immeasurably†	boasting	in	others'†

κόποις,	ἐλπίδα	δὲ	ἔχοντες	αὐξανομένης
labours,	but ²hope		¹having	growing =as your faith grows

τῆς	πίστεως	ὑμῶν	ἐν	ὑμῖν	μεγαλυνθῆναι
the	faith	of youᵃ	²among	³you	¹to be magnified

κατὰ	τὸν	κανόνα	ἡμῶν	εἰς	περισσείαν,
according the to		rule	of us	in	abundance,

16 εἰς	τὰ	ὑπερέκεινα	ὑμῶν	εὐαγγελίσασθαι,
in	the [parts] beyond		you	to preach good tidings,

οὐκ	ἐν	ἀλλοτρίῳ	κανόνι	εἰς	τὰ	ἕτοιμα
not	²in	³another's†	⁴rule	⁵in	-	⁶things ready

καυχήσασθαι.	17 Ὁ	δὲ	καυχώμενος	ἐν
¹to boast.	But the [one]		boasting	²in

κυρίῳ	καυχάσθω·	18 οὐ	γὰρ	ὁ	ἑαυτὸν
³[the] Lord	¹let him boast;	for not		the [one]	himself

συνιστάνων,	ἐκεῖνός	ἐστιν	δόκιμος,	ἀλλὰ
commending,	that one	is	approved,	but

ὃν	ὁ	κύριος	συνίστησιν.
whom the		Lord	commends.

measure themselves by themselves and compare themselves with themselves, they are not wise. 13 We, however, will not boast beyond proper limits, but will confine our boasting to the field God has assigned to us, a field that reaches even to you. 14 We are not going too far in our boasting, as would be the case if we had not come to you, for we did get as far as you with the gospel of Christ. 15 Neither do we go beyond our limits by boasting of work done by others.[p] Our hope is that, as your faith continues to grow, our area of activity among you will greatly expand, 16 so that we can preach the gospel in the regions beyond you. For we do not want to boast about work already done in another man's territory. 17 But, "Let him who boasts boast in the Lord."[q] 18 For it is not the one who commends himself who is approved, but the one whom the Lord commends.

Chapter 11

Paul and the False Apostles

I wish you would bear with me in a little foolishness. Do bear with me! 2 I feel a divine jealousy for you, for I promised you in marriage to one husband, to present you as a chaste virgin to Christ. 3 But I am afraid that as the serpent deceived Eve by its cunning, your thoughts will be led astray from a sincere and pure[d] devotion to Christ. 4 For if someone comes and proclaims another Jesus than the one we proclaimed, or if you receive a different spirit from

11 Ὄφελον	ἀνείχεσθέ	μου	μικρόν	τι
I would that	ye endured	me	a little [bit]

ἀφροσύνης·	ἀλλὰ	καὶ	ἀνέχεσθέ	μου.
of foolishness;	but	indeed	ye do endure	me.

2 ζηλῶ	γὰρ	ὑμᾶς	θεοῦ	ζήλῳ,	ἡρμοσάμην
For I am jealous [of]	you	²of God	¹with a jealousy,	²I betrothed

γὰρ	ὑμᾶς	ἑνὶ	ἀνδρὶ	παρθένον	ἁγνὴν
¹for	you	to one	husband	²virgin	¹a pure

παραστῆσαι	τῷ	Χριστῷ·	3 φοβοῦμαι	δὲ
¹to present	-	to Christ;	and I fear

μή	πως,	ὡς	ὁ	ὄφις	ἐξηπάτησεν	Εὔαν
lest somehow,	as	the	serpent	deceived	Eve

ἐν	τῇ	πανουργίᾳ	αὐτοῦ,	φθαρῇ	τὰ	νοήματα
by the		cleverness	of him,	²should be seduced	¹the ²thoughts

ὑμῶν	ἀπὸ	τῆς	ἁπλότητος	[καὶ	τῆς
of you	from	the	simplicity	and	the

ἁγνότητος]	τῆς	εἰς	Χριστόν.	4 εἰ	μὲν
purity]	-	in	Christ.	²if	³indeed

γὰρ	ὁ	ἐρχόμενος	ἄλλον	Ἰησοῦν	κηρύσσει
¹For the [one]	coming	²another	³Jesus	¹proclaims

ὃν	οὐκ	ἐκηρύξαμεν,	ἢ	πνεῦμα	ἕτερον
whom	we did not proclaim,	or	³spirit	²a different

Chapter 11

Paul and the False Apostles

I HOPE you will put up with a little of my foolishness; but you are already doing this. 2 I am jealous for you with a godly jealousy. I promised you to one husband, to Christ, so that I might present you as a pure virgin to him. 3 But I am afraid that just as Eve was deceived by the serpent's cunning, your minds may somehow be led astray from your sincere and pure devotion to Christ. 4 For if someone comes to you and preaches a Jesus other than the Jesus we preached, or if you receive a different spir-

ᶜ Or the gospel
ᵈ Other ancient authorities lack and pure

ᵖ 13-15 Or 13We, however, will not boast about things that cannot be measured, but we will boast according to the standard of measurement that the God of measure has assigned us—a measurement that relates even to you, 14 . . . . 15Neither do we boast about things that cannot be measured in regard to the work done by others.
 q 17 Jer. 9:24

the one you received, or a different gospel from the one you accepted, you submit to it readily enough. 5 I think that I am not in the least inferior to these super-apostles. 6 I may be untrained in speech, but not in knowledge; certainly in every way and in all things we have made this evident to you.

7 Did I commit a sin by humbling myself so that you might be exalted, because I proclaimed God's good news[e] to you free of charge? 8 I robbed other churches by accepting support from them in order to serve you. 9 And when I was with you and was in need, I did not burden anyone, for my needs were supplied by the friends[f] who came from Macedonia. So I refrained and will continue to refrain from burdening you in any way. 10 As the truth of Christ is in me, this boast of mine will not be silenced in the regions of Achaia. 11 And why? Because I do not love you? God knows I do!

12 And what I do I will also continue to do, in order to deny an opportunity to those who want an opportunity to be recognized as our equals in what they boast about. 13 For such boasters are false apostles, deceitful workers, disguising themselves as apostles of Christ. 14 And no wonder! Even Satan disguises himself as an angel of light. 15 So it is not strange if his ministers also disguise themselves as ministers of righteousness. Their end will match their deeds.

[e] Gk the gospel of God
[f] Gk brothers

λαμβάνετε ὃ οὐκ ἐλάβετε, ἢ εὐαγγέλιον
¹ye receive which ye did not receive, or ²gospel

ἕτερον ὃ οὐκ ἐδέξασθε, καλῶς ἀνέχεσθε.
¹a different which ye did not receive, ²[him] ³well ¹ye endure.

5 λογίζομαι γὰρ μηδὲν ὑστερηκέναι τῶν
For I reckon nothing to have come behind of the

ὑπερλίαν ἀποστόλων. 6 εἰ δὲ καὶ ἰδιώτης
super- apostles. But if indeed unskilled [I am]

τῷ λόγῳ, ἀλλ' οὐ τῇ γνώσει, ἀλλ' ἐν
- in speech, yet not - in knowledge, but in

παντὶ φανερώσαντες ἐν πᾶσιν εἰς ὑμᾶς.
every having manifested in all things to you.
[way] [ourselves]

7 Ἢ ἁμαρτίαν ἐποίησα ἐμαυτὸν ταπεινῶν
Or ¹sin ¹did I commit ²myself ³humbling

ἵνα ὑμεῖς ὑψωθῆτε, ὅτι δωρεὰν τὸ τοῦ
in order ye might be because ²freely ³the -
that exalted,

θεοῦ εὐαγγέλιον εὐηγγελισάμην ὑμῖν;
⁴of God ⁵gospel ¹I preached good tidings to you?

8 ἄλλας ἐκκλησίας ἐσύλησα λαβὼν ὀψώνιον
Other churches I robbed taking wages

πρὸς τὴν ὑμῶν διακονίαν, 9 καὶ παρὼν
for ¹the ²of you ministry, and being present

πρὸς ὑμᾶς καὶ ὑστερηθεὶς οὐ κατενάρκησα
with you and lacking I was not an encumbrance

οὐθενός· τὸ γὰρ ὑστέρημά μου προσανε-
of no man; for the lack of me ⁴made

πλήρωσαν οἱ ἀδελφοὶ ἐλθόντες ἀπὸ Μακε-
up ¹the ²brothers ³coming ⁴from ⁵Mace-

δονίας· καὶ ἐν παντὶ ἀβαρῆ ἐμαυτὸν
donia; and in every [way] ²unburdensome ³myself

ὑμῖν ἐτήρησα καὶ τηρήσω. 10 ἔστιν
⁴to you ¹I kept and I will keep. ¹is

ἀλήθεια Χριστοῦ ἐν ἐμοί, ὅτι ἡ καύχησις
¹[The] truth ²of Christ in me, that - boasting

αὕτη οὐ φραγήσεται εἰς ἐμὲ ἐν τοῖς
this shall not be stopped in me in the

κλίμασιν τῆς Ἀχαΐας. 11 διὰ τί; ὅτι
regions - of Achaia. Why? because

οὐκ ἀγαπῶ ὑμᾶς; ὁ θεὸς οἶδεν. 12 Ὃ
I love not you? - God knows. what

δὲ ποιῶ, καὶ ποιήσω, ἵνα ἐκκόψω τὴν
But I do, also I will do, in order I may cut the
that off

ἀφορμὴν τῶν θελόντων ἀφορμήν, ἵνα ἐν
occasion of the desiring an occasion, in or- where-
[ones] der that

ᾧ καυχῶνται εὑρεθῶσιν καθὼς καὶ ἡμεῖς.
in they boast they may be found as also we.

13 οἱ γὰρ τοιοῦτοι ψευδαπόστολοι, ἐργάται
- For such [are] false apostles, ²workmen

δόλιοι, μετασχηματιζόμενοι εἰς ἀποστόλους
¹deceitful, transforming themselves into apostles

Χριστοῦ. 14 καὶ οὐ θαῦμα· αὐτὸς γὰρ
of Christ. And no wonder; ²[him]self ¹for

ὁ σατανᾶς μετασχηματίζεται εἰς ἄγγελον
- ¹Satan transforms himself into an angel

φωτός. 15 οὐ μέγα οὖν εἰ καὶ οἱ
of light. No great thing therefore if also the

διάκονοι αὐτοῦ μετασχηματίζονται ὡς
ministers of him transform themselves as

διάκονοι δικαιοσύνης· ὧν τὸ τέλος ἔσται
ministers of righteousness; of whom the end will be

κατὰ τὰ ἔργα αὐτῶν.
according to the works of them.

---

it from the one you received, or a different gospel from the one you accepted, you put up with it easily enough. 5 But I do not think I am in the least inferior to those "super-apostles." 6 I may not be a trained speaker, but I do have knowledge. We have made this perfectly clear to you in every way.

7 Was it a sin for me to lower myself in order to elevate you by preaching the gospel of God to you free of charge? 8 I robbed other churches by receiving support from them so as to serve you. 9 And when I was with you and needed something, I was not a burden to anyone, for the brothers who came from Macedonia supplied what I needed. I have kept myself from being a burden to you in any way, and will continue to do so. 10 As surely as the truth of Christ is in me, nobody in the regions of Achaia will stop this boasting of mine. 11 Why? Because I do not love you? God knows I do! 12 And I will keep on doing what I am doing in order to cut the ground from under those who want an opportunity to be considered equal with us in the things they boast about.

13 For such men are false apostles, deceitful workmen, masquerading as apostles of Christ. 14 And no wonder, for Satan himself masquerades as an angel of light. 15 It is not surprising, then, if his servants masquerade as servants of righteousness. Their end will be what their actions deserve.

Paul's Sufferings as an Apostle

16 I repeat, let no one think that I am a fool; but if you do, then accept me as a fool, so that I too may boast a little. 17 What I am saying in regard to this boastful confidence, I am saying not with the Lord's authority, but as a fool; 18 since many boast according to human standards,[g] I will also boast. 19 For you gladly put up with fools, being wise yourselves! 20 For you put up with it when someone makes slaves of you, or preys upon you, or takes advantage of you, or puts on airs, or gives you a slap in the face. 21 To my shame, I must say, we were too weak for that!

But whatever anyone dares to boast of—I am speaking as a fool—I also dare to boast of that. 22 Are they Hebrews? So am I. Are they Israelites? So am I. Are they descendants of Abraham? So am I. 23 Are they ministers of Christ? I am talking like a madman—I am a better one: with far greater labors, far more imprisonments, with countless floggings, and often near death. 24 Five times I have received from the Jews the forty lashes minus one. 25 Three times I was beaten with rods. Once I received a stoning. Three times I was shipwrecked; for a night and a day I was adrift at sea; 26 on frequent journeys, in danger from rivers, danger from bandits, danger from my own people, danger from Gentiles, danger in the city, danger in the wilderness, danger at sea, danger from false brothers and sisters;[f] 27 in toil and hardship, through many a sleepless night, hungry and thirsty, often without food, cold and naked. 28 And, be-

[g] Gk according to the flesh

---

16 Πάλιν λέγω, μή τίς με δόξη ἄφρονα
Again I say, ²not ³anyone ⁴me ¹think ⁵foolish

εἶναι· εἰ δὲ μή γε, κἂν ὡς ἄφρονα
¹to be; otherwise, even if as foolish

δέξασθέ με, ἵνα κἀγὼ μικρόν τι καυχήσω-
receive ye me, in order I also a little [bit] may

μαι. 17 ὃ λαλῶ, οὐ κατὰ κύριον λαλῶ,
boast. What I speak, not according to [the] Lord I speak,

ἀλλ’ ὡς ἐν ἀφροσύνη, ἐν ταύτη τῇ
but as in folly, in this -

ὑποστάσει τῆς καυχήσεως. 18 ἐπεὶ πολλοὶ
confidence - of boasting. Since many

καυχῶνται κατὰ [τὴν] σάρκα, κἀγὼ
boast according to the flesh, I also

καυχήσομαι. 19 ἡδέως γὰρ ἀνέχεσθε τῶν
will boast. For gladly ye endure -

ἀφρόνων φρόνιμοι ὄντες· 20 ἀνέχεσθε γὰρ
fools ²prudent ¹being; for ye endure

εἴ τις ὑμᾶς καταδουλοῖ, εἴ τις κατεσθίει,
if anyone ²you ¹enslaves, if anyone devours [you],

εἴ τις λαμβάνει, εἴ τις ἐπαίρεται, εἴ
if anyone receives [you],* if anyone lifts himself up, if

τις εἰς πρόσωπον ὑμᾶς δέρει. 21 κατὰ
anyone ³in ⁴[the] face ²you ¹beats(hits). According to

ἀτιμίαν λέγω, ὡς ὅτι ἡμεῖς ἠσθενήκαμεν·
dishonour I say, as that we have been weak;

ἐν ᾧ δ’ ἄν τις τολμᾷ, ἐν ἀφροσύνη
but in whatever [respect] anyone dares, in folly

λέγω, τολμῶ κἀγώ. 22 Ἑβραῖοί εἰσιν;
I say, ²dare ¹I ³also. Hebrews are they?

κἀγώ. Ἰσραηλῖταί εἰσιν; κἀγώ. σπέρμα
I also. Israelites are they? I also. Seed

Ἀβραάμ εἰσιν; κἀγώ. 23 διάκονοι Χριστοῦ
of Abraham are they? I also. Ministers of Christ

εἰσιν; παραφρονῶν λαλῶ, ὑπὲρ ἐγώ· ἐν
are they? being out of I speak, ²beyond ¹I: in
          my mind   (more)

κόποις περισσοτέρως, ἐν φυλακαῖς περισ-
labours more abundantly, in prisons more

σοτέρως, ἐν πληγαῖς ὑπερβαλλόντως, ἐν
abundantly, in stripes excessively, in

θανάτοις πολλάκις. 24 ὑπὸ Ἰουδαίων
deaths many times. By Jews

πεντάκις τεσσεράκοντα παρὰ μίαν ἔλαβον,
five times forty [stripes] less one I received,

25 τρὶς ἐρραβδίσθην, ἅπαξ ἐλιθάσθην, τρὶς
thrice I was beaten with rods, once I was stoned, thrice

ἐναυάγησα, 26 νυχθήμερον ἐν τῷ βυθῷ
I was shipwrecked, a night and a day in the deep

πεποίηκα· ὁδοιπορίαις πολλάκις, κινδύνοις
I have done(been); in travels many times, in perils

ποταμῶν, κινδύνοις λῃστῶν, κινδύνοις ἐκ
of rivers, in perils of robbers, in perils of

γένους, κινδύνοις ἐξ ἐθνῶν, κινδύνοις ἐν
[my] kind, in perils of nations, in perils in

πόλει, κινδύνοις ἐν ἐρημίᾳ, κινδύνοις ἐν
a city, in perils in a desert, in perils in(at)

θαλάσσῃ, κινδύνοις ἐν ψευδαδέλφοις, 27 κόπῳ
sea, in perils among false brothers, in labour

καὶ μόχθῳ, ἐν ἀγρυπνίαις πολλάκις, ἐν
and hardship, in watchings many times, in

λιμῷ καὶ δίψει, ἐν νηστείαις πολλάκις,
famine and thirst, in fastings many times,

Paul Boasts About His Sufferings

16 I repeat: Let no one take me for a fool. But if you do, then receive me just as you would a fool, so that I may do a little boasting. 17 In this self-confident boasting I am not talking as the Lord would, but as a fool. 18 Since many are boasting in the way the world does, I too will boast. 19 You gladly put up with fools since you are so wise! 20 In fact, you even put up with anyone who enslaves you or exploits you or takes advantage of you or pushes himself forward or slaps you in the face. 21 To my shame I admit that we were too weak for that!

What anyone else dares to boast about—I am speaking as a fool—I also dare to boast about. 22 Are they Hebrews? So am I. Are they Israelites? So am I. Are they Abraham's descendants? So am I. 23 Are they servants of Christ? (I am out of my mind to talk like this.) I am more. I have worked much harder, been in prison more frequently, been flogged more severely, and been exposed to death again and again. 24 Five times I received from the Jews the forty lashes minus one. 25 Three times I was beaten with rods, once I was stoned, three times I was shipwrecked, I spent a night and a day in the open sea, 26 I have been constantly on the move. I have been in danger from rivers, in danger from bandits, in danger from my own countrymen, in danger from Gentiles; in danger in the city, in danger in the country, in danger at sea; and in danger from false brothers. 27 I have labored and toiled and have often gone without sleep; I have known hunger and thirst and have often gone

* ? takes [you in].

sides other things, I am under daily pressure because of my anxiety for all the churches. 29 Who is weak, and I am not weak? Who is made to stumble, and I am not indignant?

30 If I must boast, I will boast of the things that show my weakness. 31 The God and Father of the Lord Jesus (blessed be he forever!) knows that I do not lie. 32 In Damascus, the governor[h] under King Aretas guarded the city of Damascus in order to[i] seize me, 33 but I was let down in a basket through a window in the wall,[j] and escaped from his hands.

ἐν ψύχει καὶ γυμνότητι· **28** χωρὶς τῶν
in cold and nakedness; apart from the things

παρεκτὸς ἡ ἐπίστασίς μοι ἡ καθ' ἡμέραν,
without[,] the conspiring me - daily,
against

ἡ μέριμνα πασῶν τῶν ἐκκλησιῶν. **29** τίς
the care of all the churches. Who

ἀσθενεῖ, καὶ οὐκ ἀσθενῶ; τίς σκανδαλίζεται,
is weak, and I am not weak? who is offended,

καὶ οὐκ ἐγὼ πυροῦμαι; **30** εἰ καυχᾶσθαι
and ²not ¹I ¹burn? If to boast

δεῖ, τὰ τῆς ἀσθενείας μου καυχήσομαι.
it be- the of the weakness of me I will boast.
hoves things
[me],

31 ὁ θεὸς καὶ πατὴρ τοῦ κυρίου Ἰησοῦ
The God and Father of the Lord Jesus

οἶδεν, ὁ ὢν εὐλογητὸς εἰς τοὺς αἰῶνας,
knows, the being blessed unto the ages,
[one]

ὅτι οὐ ψεύδομαι. **32** ἐν Δαμασκῷ ὁ
that I am not lying. In Damascus the

ἐθνάρχης Ἀρέτα τοῦ βασιλέως ἐφρούρει
ethnarch of Aretas of the king guarded

τὴν πόλιν Δαμασκηνῶν πιάσαι με, **33** καὶ
the city of [the] Damascenes to seize me, and

διὰ θυρίδος ἐν σαργάνῃ ἐχαλάσθην διὰ
through a window in a basket I was lowered through

τοῦ τείχους καὶ ἐξέφυγον τὰς χεῖρας αὐτοῦ.
the wall and escaped the hands of him.

12 Καυχᾶσθαι δεῖ, οὐ συμφέρον μέν,
To boast it behoves not expedient indeed,
[me],

ἐλεύσομαι δὲ εἰς ὀπτασίας καὶ ἀποκαλύψεις
so I will come to visions and revelations

κυρίου. **2** οἶδα ἄνθρωπον ἐν Χριστῷ
of [the] Lord. I know a man in Christ

πρὸ ἐτῶν δεκατεσσάρων, — εἴτε ἐν
before years fourteen, (whether in

σώματι οὐκ οἶδα, εἴτε ἐκτὸς τοῦ σώματος
[the] body I know not, or outside the body

οὐκ οἶδα, ὁ θεὸς οἶδεν, — ἁρπαγέντα
I know not, - God knows,) ²caught

τὸν τοιοῦτον ἕως τρίτου οὐρανοῦ. **3** καὶ
- ¹such a one to [the] third heaven. And

οἶδα τὸν τοιοῦτον ἄνθρωπον — εἴτε
I know - such a man (whether

ἐν σώματι εἴτε χωρὶς τοῦ σώματος
in [the] body or apart from the body

[οὐκ οἶδα], ὁ θεὸς οἶδεν, — **4** ὅτι
I know not, - God knows,) that

ἡρπάγη εἰς τὸν παράδεισον καὶ ἤκουσεν
he was caught into the paradise and heard

ἄρρητα ῥήματα, ἃ οὐκ ἐξὸν ἀνθρώπῳ
unspeakable words, which it is not for a man
permissible

λαλῆσαι. **5** ὑπὲρ τοῦ τοιούτου καυχήσομαι,
to speak. On behalf of - such a one I will boast,

ὑπὲρ δὲ ἐμαυτοῦ οὐ καυχήσομαι εἰ
but on behalf of myself I will not boast ex-

μὴ ἐν ταῖς ἀσθενείαις. **6** ἐὰν γὰρ θελήσω
cept in the(my) weaknesses. For if I shall wish

καυχήσασθαι, οὐκ ἔσομαι ἄφρων, ἀλήθειαν
to boast, I shall not be foolish, ¹truth

γὰρ ἐρῶ· φείδομαι δέ, μή τις εἰς ἐμὲ
¹for ²I will speak; but I spare, lest anyone to me

λογίσηται ὑπὲρ ὃ βλέπει με ἢ ἀκούει
reckons beyond what he sees me or hears

Chapter 12

Paul's Visions and Revelations

IT is necessary to boast; nothing is to be gained by it, but I will go on to visions and revelations of the Lord. 2 I know a person in Christ who fourteen years ago was caught up to the third heaven—whether in the body or out of the body I do not know; God knows. 3 And I know that such a person—whether in the body or out of the body I do not know; God knows— 4 was caught up into Paradise and heard things that are not to be told, that no mortal is permitted to repeat. 5 On behalf of such a one I will boast, but on my own behalf I will not boast, except of my weaknesses. 6 But if I wish to boast, I will not be a fool, for I will be speaking the truth. But I refrain from it, so that no one may think better of me than what is seen in me or heard from me, 7 even considering the

---

Chapter 12

Paul's Vision and His Thorn

I MUST go on boasting. Although there is nothing to be gained, I will go on to visions and revelations from the Lord. 2 I know a man in Christ who fourteen years ago was caught up to the third heaven. Whether it was in the body or out of the body I do not know—God knows. 3 And I know that this man—whether in the body or apart from the body I do not know, but God knows— 4 was caught up to paradise. He heard inexpressible things, things that man is not permitted to tell. 5 I will boast about a man like that, but I will not boast about myself, except about my weaknesses. 6 Even if I should choose to boast, I would not be a fool, because I would be speaking the truth. But I refrain, so no one will think more of me than is warranted by what I do or say.

---

without food; I have been cold and naked. 28 Besides everything else, I face daily the pressure of my concern for all the churches. 29 Who is weak, and I do not feel weak? Who is led into sin, and I do not inwardly burn?

30 If I must boast, I will boast of the things that show my weakness. 31 The God and Father of the Lord Jesus, who is to be praised forever, knows that I am not lying. 32 In Damascus the governor under King Aretas had the city of the Damascenes guarded in order to arrest me. 33 But I was lowered in a basket from a window in the wall and slipped through his hands.

---

[h] Gk *ethnarch*
[i] Other ancient authorities read *and wanted to*
[j] Gk *through the wall*

exceptional character of the revelations. Therefore, to keep[k] me from being too elated, a thorn was given me in the flesh, a messenger of Satan to torment me, to keep me from being too elated.[l] 8 Three times I appealed to the Lord about this, that it would leave me, 9 but he said to me, "My grace is sufficient for you, for power[m] is made perfect in weakness." So, I will boast all the more gladly of my weaknesses, so that the power of Christ may dwell in me. 10 Therefore I am content with weaknesses, insults, hardships, persecutions, and calamities for the sake of Christ; for whenever I am weak, then I am strong.

Paul's Concern for the Corinthian Church

11 I have been a fool! You forced me to it. Indeed you should have been the ones commending me, for I am not at all inferior to these super-apostles, even though I am nothing. 12 The signs of a true apostle were performed among you with utmost patience, signs and wonders and mighty works. 13 How have you been worse off than the other churches, except that I myself did not burden you? Forgive me this wrong!

14 Here I am, ready to come to you this third time. And I will not be a burden, because I do not want what is yours but you; for children ought not to lay up for their parents, but parents for their children. 15 I will most gladly spend and be spent for you. If I love you

---

ἐξ ἐμοῦ 7 καὶ τῇ ὑπερβολῇ τῶν ἀποκα-
of me   and by the   excess   of the revela

λύψεων. διὸ ἵνα μὴ ὑπεραίρωμαι, ἐδόθη
tions.   Where-   lest   I should be   there was
         fore   exceedingly uplifted,   given

μοι σκόλοψ τῇ σαρκί, ἄγγελος σατανᾶ,
to me a thorn in the flesh, a messenger of Satan,

ἵνα με κολαφίζῃ, ἵνα μὴ ὑπεραίρωμαι.
in order ²me ¹he might buffet, lest I should be
that   exceedingly uplifted.

8 ὑπὲρ τούτου τρὶς τὸν κύριον παρεκάλεσα,
As to this thrice the Lord I besought,

ἵνα ἀποστῇ ἀπ' ἐμοῦ. 9 καὶ εἴρηκέν
in or- it might from me.   And he has said
der that depart

μοι· ἀρκεῖ σοι ἡ χάρις μου· ἡ γὰρ
to me: ⁴Suffices ³thee ¹the ²grace ⁵of me; for the(my)

δύναμις ἐν ἀσθενείᾳ τελεῖται. Ἥδιστα
power   in weakness is perfected. Most gladly

οὖν μᾶλλον καυχήσομαι ἐν ταῖς ἀσθενείαις,
therefore rather I will boast in the(my) weaknesses,

ἵνα ἐπισκηνώσῃ ἐπ' ἐμὲ ἡ δύναμις τοῦ
in order ⁴might over ⁵me ¹the ²power —
that overshadow

Χριστοῦ. 10 διὸ εὐδοκῶ ἐν ἀσθενείαις,
³of Christ. Wherefore I am well in weaknesses,
                         pleased

ἐν ὕβρεσιν, ἐν ἀνάγκαις, ἐν διωγμοῖς
in insults, in necessities, in persecutions

καὶ στενοχωρίαις, ὑπὲρ Χριστοῦ· ὅταν
and difficulties, on behalf of Christ; ¹whenever

γὰρ ἀσθενῶ, τότε δυνατός εἰμι.
¹for I am weak, then ²powerful ¹I am.

11 Γέγονα ἄφρων· ὑμεῖς με ἠναγκάσατε.
I have become foolish; ye   me   compelled.

ἐγὼ γὰρ ὤφειλον ὑφ' ὑμῶν συνίστασθαι.
For I ought by you to be commended.

οὐδὲν γὰρ ὑστέρησα τῶν ὑπερλίαν
For nothing I lacked of the super-

ἀποστόλων, εἰ καὶ οὐδέν εἰμι. 12 τὰ
apostles, ²if ¹even ¹nothing ²I am. ²The

μὲν σημεῖα τοῦ ἀποστόλου κατειργάσθη
¹indeed signs of the apostle were wrought

ἐν ὑμῖν ἐν πάσῃ ὑπομονῇ, σημείοις τε
among you in all endurance, ²by signs ¹both

καὶ τέρασιν καὶ δυνάμεσιν. 13 τί γὰρ
and by wonders and by powerful deeds. For what

ἐστιν ὃ ἡσσώθητε ὑπὲρ τὰς λοιπὰς
is it which ye were less than the remaining

ἐκκλησίας, εἰ μὴ ὅτι αὐτὸς ἐγὼ οὐ
churches, except that ²[my]self ¹I ³not

κατενάρκησα ὑμῶν; χαρίσασθέ μοι τὴν
²encumbered ⁴of you? Forgive ye me   —

ἀδικίαν ταύτην. 14 Ἰδοὺ τρίτον τοῦτο
wrong this. Behold ¹[the] ¹this
                      third [time] [is]

ἑτοίμως ἔχω ἐλθεῖν πρὸς ὑμᾶς, καὶ
I am ready† to come to you, and

οὐ καταναρκήσω· οὐ γὰρ ζητῶ τὰ ὑμῶν
I will not encumber [you]; ²not ¹for ⁴I seek the of
                                       things you

ἀλλὰ ὑμᾶς. οὐ γὰρ ὀφείλει τὰ τέκνα
but you. For ⁴not ¹ought ¹the ²children

τοῖς γονεῦσιν θησαυρίζειν, ἀλλὰ οἱ γονεῖς
for the parents to lay up treasure, but the parents

τοῖς τέκνοις. 15 ἐγὼ δὲ ἥδιστα δαπανήσω
for the children. But I most gladly will spend

καὶ ἐκδαπανηθήσομαι ὑπὲρ τῶν ψυχῶν
and will be spent out on behalf of the souls

---

7 To keep me from becoming conceited because of these surpassingly great revelations, there was given me a thorn in my flesh, a messenger of Satan, to torment me. 8 Three times I pleaded with the Lord to take it away from me. 9 But he said to me, "My grace is sufficient for you, for my power is made perfect in weakness." Therefore I will boast all the more gladly about my weaknesses, so that Christ's power may rest on me. 10 That is why, for Christ's sake, I delight in weaknesses, in insults, in hardships, in persecutions, in difficulties. For when I am weak, then I am strong.

Paul's Concern for the Corinthians

11 I have made a fool of myself, but you drove me to it. I ought to have been commended by you, for I am not in the least inferior to the "super-apostles," even though I am nothing. 12 The things that mark an apostle—signs, wonders and miracles—were done among you with great perseverance. 13 How were you inferior to the other churches, except that I was never a burden to you? Forgive me this wrong!

14 Now I am ready to visit you for the third time, and I will not be a burden to you, because what I want is not your possessions but you. After all, children should not have to save up for their parents, but parents for their children. 15 So I will very gladly spend for you

---

[k] Other ancient authorities read To keep
[l] Other ancient authorities lack to keep me from being too elated
[m] Other ancient authorities read my power

more, am I to be loved less? [16]Let it be assumed that I did not burden you. Nevertheless (you say) since I was crafty, I took you in by deceit. [17]Did I take advantage of you through any of those whom I sent to you? [18]I urged Titus to go, and sent the brother with him. Titus did not take advantage of you, did he? Did we not conduct ourselves with the same spirit? Did we not take the same steps?

[19]Have you been thinking all along that we have been defending ourselves before you? We are speaking in Christ before God. Everything we do, beloved, is for the sake of building you up. [20]For I fear that when I come, I may find you not as I wish, and that you may find me not as you wish; I fear that there may perhaps be quarreling, jealousy, anger, selfishness, slander, gossip, conceit, and disorder. [21]I fear that when I come again, my God may humble me before you, and that I may have to mourn over many who previously sinned and have not repented of the impurity, sexual immorality, and licentiousness that they have practiced.

Chapter 13

Further Warning

THIS is the third time I am coming to you. "Any charge must be sustained by the evidence of two or three witnesses." [2]I warned those who sinned previously and all the others, and I warn them now while absent, as I did when present on my second visit, that if I come again, I will not be lenient— [3]since you desire proof that Christ is

ὑμῶν. εἰ περισσοτέρως ὑμᾶς ἀγαπῶ,
of you. If more abundantly ²you ¹I love,

ἧσσον ἀγαπῶμαι; 16 Ἔστω δέ, ἐγὼ οὐ
[the] less am I loved? But let it be, I not

κατεβάρησα ὑμᾶς· ἀλλὰ ὑπάρχων πανοῦργος
burdened you; but being crafty

δόλῳ ὑμᾶς ἔλαβον. 17 μή τινα ὧν
³with guile ²you ¹I took. Not anyone of whom

ἀπέσταλκα πρὸς ὑμᾶς, 18 δι' αὐτοῦ
I have sent to you, through him

ἐπλεονέκτησα ὑμᾶς; παρεκάλεσα Τίτον καὶ
did I defraud you? I besought Titus and

συναπέστειλα τὸν ἀδελφόν· μήτι ἐπλεο-
sent with [him] the brother; not ²de-

νέκτησεν ὑμᾶς Τίτος; οὐ τῷ αὐτῷ
frauded ²you ¹Titus? ²not ³by the ⁴same

πνεύματι περιεπατήσαμεν; οὐ τοῖς αὐτοῖς
⁵spirit ¹walked we? not in the same

ἴχνεσιν;
steps?

19 Πάλαι δοκεῖτε ὅτι ὑμῖν ἀπολογούμεθα.
Already ye think that to you we are making a defence.

κατέναντι θεοῦ ἐν Χριστῷ λαλοῦμεν· τὰ
Before God in Christ we speak; –

δὲ πάντα, ἀγαπητοί, ὑπὲρ τῆς ὑμῶν
but all things, beloved, [are] on behalf of ¹the ²of you

οἰκοδομῆς. 20 φοβοῦμαι γὰρ μή πως ἐλθὼν
²edification. For I fear lest coming

οὐχ οἵους θέλω εὕρω ὑμᾶς, κἀγὼ εὑρεθῶ
³not ⁴such as ⁵I wish ¹I may find ²you, and I am found

ὑμῖν οἷον οὐ θέλετε, μή πως ἔρις,
by you such as ye wish not, lest strife,

ζῆλος, θυμοί, ἐριθεῖαι, καταλαλιαί, ψιθυρισ-
jealousy, angers, rivalries, detractions, whisper-

μοί, φυσιώσεις, ἀκαταστασίαι· 21 μὴ πάλιν
ings, puffings up, disturbances; lest again

ἐλθόντος μου ταπεινώσῃ με ὁ θεός μου
coming me² ⁴may humble ¹me ¹the ²God ³of me = when I come

πρὸς ὑμᾶς, καὶ πενθήσω πολλοὺς τῶν
with you, and I shall mourn many of the [ones]

προημαρτηκότων καὶ μὴ μετανοησάντων
having previously sinned and not repenting

ἐπὶ τῇ ἀκαθαρσίᾳ καὶ πορνείᾳ καὶ
over the uncleanness and fornication and

ἀσελγείᾳ ᾗ ἔπραξαν. 13 Τρίτον τοῦτο
lewdness which they practised. ²[The] third ¹this [time] [is]

ἔρχομαι πρὸς ὑμᾶς· ἐπὶ στόματος
I am coming to you; at [the] mouth

δύο μαρτύρων καὶ τριῶν σταθήσεται
of two witnesses and of three shall be established

πᾶν ῥῆμα. 2 προείρηκα καὶ προλέγω,
every word. I have previously and I say said beforehand,

ὡς παρὼν τὸ δεύτερον καὶ ἀπὼν
as being present the second [time] and being absent

νῦν, τοῖς προημαρτηκόσιν καὶ τοῖς
now, to the [ones] having previously sinned and ¹to ²the

λοιποῖς πᾶσιν, ὅτι ἐὰν ἔλθω εἰς τὸ
⁴remaining ³all, that if I come in the [ones]

πάλιν οὐ φείσομαι, 3 ἐπεὶ δοκιμὴν ζητεῖτε
again I will not spare, since ²a proof ¹ye seek

everything I have and expend myself as well. If I love you more, will you love me less? [16]Be that as it may, I have not been a burden to you. Yet, crafty fellow that I am, I caught you by trickery! [17]Did I exploit you through any of the men I sent you? [18]I urged Titus to go to you and I sent our brother with him. Titus did not exploit you, did he? Did we not act in the same spirit and follow the same course?

[19]Have you been thinking all along that we have been defending ourselves in the sight of God as those in Christ; and everything we do, dear friends, is for your strengthening. [20]For I am afraid that when I come I may not find you as I want you to be, and you may not find me as you want me to be. I fear that there may be quarreling, jealousy, outbursts of anger, factions, slander, gossip, arrogance and disorder. [21]I am afraid that when I come again my God will humble me before you, and I will be grieved over many who have sinned earlier and have not repented of the impurity, sexual sin and debauchery in which they have indulged.

Chapter 13

Final Warnings

THIS will be my third visit to you. "Every matter must be established by the testimony of two or three witnesses."ʳ [2]I already gave you a warning when I was with you the second time. I now repeat it while absent: On my return I will not spare those who sinned earlier or any of the others, [3]since you are demanding proof that Christ

ʳ1 Deut. 19:15

speaking in me. He is not weak in dealing with you, but is powerful in you. ⁴For he was crucified in weakness, but lives by the power of God. For we are weak in him,ⁿ but in dealing with you we will live with him by the power of God.

5 Examine yourselves to see whether you are living in the faith. Test yourselves. Do you not realize that Jesus Christ is in you?—unless, indeed, you fail to meet the test! ⁶I hope you will find out that we have not failed. ⁷But we pray to God that you may not do anything wrong— not that we may appear to have met the test, but that you may do what is right, though we may seem to have failed. ⁸For we cannot do anything against the truth, but only for the truth. ⁹For we rejoice when we are weak and you are strong. This is what we pray for, that you may become perfect. ¹⁰So I write these things while I am away from you, so that when I come, I may not have to be severe in using the authority that the Lord has given me for building up and not for tearing down.

Final Greetings and Benediction

11 Finally, brothers and sisters,ᵒ farewell.ᵖ Put things in order, listen to my appeal,q agree with one another, live in peace; and the God of love and peace will be with you. ¹²Greet one another with a holy kiss. All the saints greet you.
13 The grace of the Lord Jesus Christ, the love

ⁿ Other ancient authorities read *with him*
ᵒ Gk *brothers*
ᵖ Or *rejoice*
q Or *encourage one another*

τοῦ ἐν ἐμοὶ λαλοῦντος Χριστοῦ, ὃς εἰς
  - ⁵in ⁶me ⁴speaking ³of Christ, who toward

ὑμᾶς οὐκ ἀσθενεῖ ἀλλὰ δυνατεῖ ἐν ὑμῖν.
you is not weak but is powerful in you.

4 καὶ γὰρ ἐσταυρώθη ἐξ ἀσθενείας, ἀλλὰ
For indeed he was crucified out of weakness, but

ζῇ ἐκ δυνάμεως θεοῦ. καὶ γὰρ ἡμεῖς
he lives by [the] power of God. For indeed we

ἀσθενοῦμεν ἐν αὐτῷ, ἀλλὰ ζήσομεν σὺν
are weak in him, but we shall live with

αὐτῷ ἐκ δυνάμεως θεοῦ εἰς ὑμᾶς.
him by [the] power of God toward you.

5 Ἑαυτοὺς πειράζετε εἰ ἐστὲ ἐν τῇ
¹Yourselves ¹test if ye are in the

πίστει, ἑαυτοὺς δοκιμάζετε· ἢ οὐκ
faith, ²yourselves ¹prove; or not

ἐπιγινώσκετε ἑαυτοὺς ὅτι Ἰησοῦς Χριστὸς
perceive ye yourselves that Jesus Christ [is]

ἐν ὑμῖν, εἰ μήτι ἀδόκιμοί ἐστε. 6 ἐλπίζω
in you, unless ²counterfeits ¹ye are. I hope

δὲ ὅτι γνώσεσθε ὅτι ἡμεῖς οὐκ ἐσμὲν
But that ye will know that we are not

ἀδόκιμοι. 7 εὐχόμεθα δὲ πρὸς τὸν θεὸν
counterfeits. Now we pray to - God

μὴ ποιῆσαι ὑμᾶς κακὸν μηδέν, οὐχ
not to do you² evil none, not
=that ye do no ...

ἵνα ἡμεῖς δόκιμοι φανῶμεν, ἀλλ' ἵνα
in order we ²approved ¹may appear, but in order
that that

ὑμεῖς τὸ καλὸν ποιῆτε, ἡμεῖς δὲ ὡς
ye ²the ²good ¹may do, and we ²as

ἀδόκιμοι ὦμεν. 8 οὐ γὰρ δυνάμεθά
²counterfeits ¹may be. For we cannot [do]

τι κατὰ τῆς ἀληθείας, ἀλλὰ ὑπὲρ τῆς
any- against the truth, but on behalf of the
thing

ἀληθείας. 9 χαίρομεν γὰρ ὅταν ἡμεῖς
truth. For we rejoice whenever we

ἀσθενῶμεν, ὑμεῖς δὲ δυνατοὶ ἦτε· τοῦτο
are weak, and ye powerful are; this

καὶ εὐχόμεθα, τὴν ὑμῶν κατάρτισιν. 10 Διὰ
also we pray, the ²of you ¹restoration. There-

τοῦτο ταῦτα ἀπὼν γράφω, ἵνα παρὼν
fore ²these things ³being ¹I write, in order being
absent that present

μὴ ἀποτόμως χρήσωμαι κατὰ τὴν ἐξουσίαν
²not ³sharply ¹I may deal according to the authority

ἣν ὁ κύριος ἔδωκέν μοι εἰς οἰκοδομὴν
which the Lord gave me for edification

καὶ οὐκ εἰς καθαίρεσιν.
and not for overthrow.

11 Λοιπόν, ἀδελφοί, χαίρετε, καταρτίζεσθε,
For the rest,† brothers, rejoice, restore yourselves,

παρακαλεῖσθε, τὸ αὐτὸ φρονεῖτε, εἰρηνεύετε,
admonish yourselves, the same thing think, be at peace,

καὶ ὁ θεὸς τῆς ἀγάπης καὶ εἰρήνης
and the God - of love and of peace

ἔσται μεθ' ὑμῶν. 12 Ἀσπάσασθε ἀλλήλους
will be with you. Greet ye one another

ἐν ἁγίῳ φιλήματι. Ἀσπάζονται ὑμᾶς οἱ
with a holy kiss. ⁴greet ⁵you ³the

ἅγιοι πάντες.
²saints ¹All.

13 Ἡ χάρις τοῦ κυρίου Ἰησοῦ Χριστοῦ
The grace of the Lord Jesus Christ

---

is speaking through me. He is not weak in dealing with you, but is powerful among you. ⁴For to be sure, he was crucified in weakness, yet he lives by God's power. Likewise, we are weak in him, yet by God's power we will live with him to serve you.

⁵Examine yourselves to see whether you are in the faith; test yourselves. Do you not realize that Christ Jesus is in you—unless, of course, you fail the test? ⁶And I trust that you will discover that we have not failed the test. ⁷Now we pray to God that you will not do anything wrong. Not that people will see that we have stood the test but that you will do what is right even though we may seem to have failed. ⁸For we cannot do anything against the truth, but only for the truth. ⁹We are glad whenever we are weak but you are strong; and our prayer is for your perfection. ¹⁰This is why I write these things when I am absent, that when I come I may not have to be harsh in my use of authority—the authority the Lord gave me for building you up, not for tearing you down.

Final Greetings

¹¹Finally, brothers, goodby. Aim for perfection, listen to my appeal, be of one mind, live in peace. And the God of love and peace will be with you.
¹²Greet one another with a holy kiss. ¹³All the saints send their greetings.
¹⁴May the grace of the

of God, and the communion of^r the Holy Spirit be with all of you.

καὶ ἡ ἀγάπη τοῦ θεοῦ καὶ ἡ κοινωνία
and the love – of God and the fellowship
τοῦ ἁγίου πνεύματος μετὰ πάντων ὑμῶν.
of the Holy Spirit [be] with ²all ¹you.

Lord Jesus Christ, and the love of God, and the fellowship of the Holy Spirit be with you all.

The Letter of Paul to the
Galatians

ΠΡΟΣ ΓΑΛΑΤΑΣ
To Galatians

Galatians

Chapter 1
Salutation

PAUL an apostle—sent neither by human commission nor from human authorities, but through Jesus Christ and God the Father, who raised him from the dead— ²and all the members of God's family*a* who are with me,
To the churches of Galatia:
3 Grace to you and peace from God our Father and the Lord Jesus Christ, ⁴who gave himself for our sins to set us free from the present evil age, according to the will of our God and Father, ⁵to whom be the glory forever and ever. Amen.

There Is No Other Gospel

6 I am astonished that you are so quickly deserting the one who called you in the grace of Christ and are turning to a different gospel— ⁷not that there is another gospel, but there are some who are confusing you and want to pervert the gospel of Christ. ⁸But even if we or an angel*b* from heaven should proclaim to you a gospel contrary to what we proclaimed to you, let that one be accursed! ⁹As we have said before, so now I repeat, if anyone proclaims to you a gospel contrary to what you received, let that one be accursed!

Chapter 1

1 Παῦλος ἀπόστολος, οὐκ ἀπ' ἀνθρώπων
Paul an apostle, not from men
οὐδὲ δι' ἀνθρώπου ἀλλὰ διὰ 'Ιησοῦ
nor through man but through Jesus
Χριστοῦ καὶ θεοῦ πατρὸς τοῦ ἐγείραντος
Christ and God [the] Father the [one] having raised
αὐτὸν ἐκ νεκρῶν, 2 καὶ οἱ σὺν ἐμοὶ
him out of [the] dead, and ³the ⁴with ¹me
πάντες ἀδελφοί, ταῖς ἐκκλησίαις τῆς
¹all ²brothers, to the churches –
Γαλατίας· 3 χάρις ὑμῖν καὶ εἰρήνη ἀπὸ
of Galatia: Grace to you and peace from
θεοῦ πατρὸς ἡμῶν καὶ κυρίου 'Ιησοῦ
God Father of us and Lord Jesus
Χριστοῦ, 4 τοῦ δόντος ἑαυτὸν ὑπὲρ τῶν
Christ, the [one] having given himself on behalf of the
ἁμαρτιῶν ἡμῶν, ὅπως ἐξέληται ἡμᾶς ἐκ
sins of us, so as he might deliver us out of
τοῦ αἰῶνος τοῦ ἐνεστῶτος πονηροῦ κατὰ
the ²age – ¹present ²evil according to
τὸ θέλημα τοῦ θεοῦ καὶ πατρὸς ἡμῶν,
the will of the God and Father of us,
5 ᾧ ἡ δόξα εἰς τοὺς αἰῶνας τῶν
to whom [be] the glory unto the ages of the
αἰώνων· ἀμήν.
ages: Amen.

6 Θαυμάζω ὅτι οὕτως ταχέως μετατίθεσθε
I wonder that thus quickly ye are removing
ἀπὸ τοῦ καλέσαντος ὑμᾶς ἐν χάριτι
from the [one] having called you by [the] grace
Χριστοῦ εἰς ἕτερον εὐαγγέλιον, 7 ὃ οὐκ
of Christ to another gospel, which not
ἔστιν ἄλλο· εἰ μή τινές εἰσιν οἱ ταράσ-
is another; only ²some ¹there are – troubl-
σοντες ὑμᾶς καὶ θέλοντες μεταστρέψαι
ing you and wishing to pervert
τὸ εὐαγγέλιον τοῦ Χριστοῦ. 8 ἀλλὰ
the gospel – of Christ. But
καὶ ἐὰν ἡμεῖς ἢ ἄγγελος ἐξ οὐρανοῦ
even if we or an angel out of heaven
εὐαγγελίσηται [ὑμῖν] παρ' ὃ εὐηγγελισάμεθα
should preach to you beside what we preached
a gospel
ὑμῖν, ἀνάθεμα ἔστω. 9 ὡς προειρήκαμεν,
to you, ²a curse ¹let him be. As we have previously said,
καὶ ἄρτι πάλιν λέγω, εἴ τις ὑμᾶς εὐαγ-
also now again I say, if anyone ²you ¹preaches
γελίζεται παρ' ὃ παρελάβετε, ἀνάθεμα
a gospel beside what ye received, ²a curse
ἔστω.
¹let him be.

PAUL, an apostle—sent not from men nor by man, but by Jesus Christ and God the Father, who raised him from the dead— ²and all the brothers with me,

To the churches in Galatia:

³Grace and peace to you from God our Father and the Lord Jesus Christ, ⁴who gave himself for our sins to rescue us from the present evil age, according to the will of our God and Father, ⁵to whom be glory for ever and ever. Amen.

No Other Gospel

⁶I am astonished that you are so quickly deserting the one who called you by the grace of Christ and are turning to a different gospel—⁷which is really no gospel at all. Evidently some people are throwing you into confusion and are trying to pervert the gospel of Christ. ⁸But even if we or an angel from heaven should preach a gospel other than the one we preached to you, let him be eternally condemned! ⁹As we have already said, so now I say again: If anybody is preaching to you a gospel other than what you accepted, let him be eternally condemned!

---

r Or *and the sharing in*
a Gk *all the brothers*
b Or *a messenger*

10 Am I now seeking human approval, or God's approval? Or am I trying to please people? If I were still pleasing people, I would not be a servant[c] of Christ.

Paul's Vindication of His Apostleship

11 For I want you to know, brothers and sisters,[d] that the gospel that was proclaimed by me is not of human origin; 12 for I did not receive it from a human source, nor was I taught it, but I received it through a revelation of Jesus Christ.

13 You have heard, no doubt, of my earlier life in Judaism. I was violently persecuting the church of God and was trying to destroy it. 14 I advanced in Judaism beyond many among my people of the same age, for I was far more zealous for the traditions of my ancestors. 15 But when God, who had set me apart before I was born and called me through his grace, was pleased 16 to reveal his Son to me,[e] so that I might proclaim him among the Gentiles, I did not confer with any human being, 17 nor did I go up to Jerusalem to those who were already apostles before me, but I went away at once into Arabia, and afterwards I returned to Damascus.

18 Then after three years I did go up to Jerusalem to visit Cephas and stayed with him fifteen days; 19 but I did not see any other apostle except James the Lord's brother. 20 In what I am writing to you, before God, I do not lie! 21 Then I went into the

[c] Gk slave
[d] Gk brothers
[e] Gk in me

Middle column (interlinear)

10 Ἄρτι γὰρ ἀνθρώπους πείθω ἢ τὸν
For now men do I persuade or -

θεόν; ἢ ζητῶ ἀνθρώποις ἀρέσκειν; εἰ
God? or do I seek men to please? If

ἔτι ἀνθρώποις ἤρεσκον, Χριστοῦ δοῦλος
still men I pleased, of Christ a slave

οὐκ ἂν ἤμην. **11** γνωρίζω γὰρ ὑμῖν,
I would not have been. For I make known to you,

ἀδελφοί, τὸ εὐαγγέλιον τὸ εὐαγγελισθὲν
brothers, the gospel - preached

ὑπ' ἐμοῦ ὅτι οὐκ ἔστιν κατὰ ἄνθρωπον·
by me that it is not according to man;

12 οὐδὲ γὰρ ἐγὼ παρὰ ἀνθρώπου παρέλαβον
for not I from man received

αὐτὸ οὔτε ἐδιδάχθην, ἀλλὰ δι' ἀποκαλύψεως
it nor was I taught but through a revelation [by man],

Ἰησοῦ Χριστοῦ. **13** Ἠκούσατε γὰρ τὴν
of Jesus Christ. For ye heard the

ἐμὴν ἀναστροφήν ποτε ἐν τῷ Ἰουδαϊσμῷ,
my conduct then in - Judaism,

ὅτι καθ' ὑπερβολὴν ἐδίωκον τὴν ἐκκλησίαν
that excessively† I persecuted the church

τοῦ θεοῦ καὶ ἐπόρθουν αὐτήν, **14** καὶ
- of God and wasted it, and

προέκοπτον ἐν τῷ Ἰουδαϊσμῷ ὑπὲρ πολλοὺς
progressed in - Judaism beyond many

συνηλικιώτας ἐν τῷ γένει μου, περισ-
contemporaries in the race of me, abun-

σοτέρως ζηλωτὴς ὑπάρχων τῶν πατρικῶν
dantly a zealot being of the ancestral

μου παραδόσεων. **15** Ὅτε δὲ εὐδόκησεν
of me traditions. But when was pleased

ὁ ἀφορίσας με ἐκ κοιλίας μητρός μου
the having me from [the] womb of mother of me
[one] separated

καὶ καλέσας διὰ τῆς χάριτος αὐτοῦ
and having called through the grace of him

16 ἀποκαλύψαι τὸν υἱὸν αὐτοῦ ἐν ἐμοί,
to reveal the Son of him in me,

ἵνα εὐαγγελίζωμαι αὐτὸν ἐν τοῖς ἔθνεσιν,
in order I might preach him among the nations, that

εὐθέως οὐ προσανεθέμην σαρκὶ καὶ αἵματι,
immediately I conferred not with flesh and blood,

17 οὐδὲ ἀνῆλθον εἰς Ἰεροσόλυμα πρὸς
neither did I go up to Jerusalem to

τοὺς πρὸ ἐμοῦ ἀποστόλους, ἀλλὰ ἀπῆλθον
the before me apostles, but I went away

εἰς Ἀραβίαν, καὶ πάλιν ὑπέστρεψα εἰς
into Arabia, and again returned to

Δαμασκόν. **18** Ἔπειτα μετὰ τρία ἔτη
Damascus. Then after three years

ἀνῆλθον εἰς Ἰεροσόλυμα ἱστορῆσαι Κηφᾶν,
I went up to Jerusalem to visit Cephas,

καὶ ἐπέμεινα πρὸς αὐτὸν ἡμέρας δεκαπέντε·
and remained with him days fifteen;

19 ἕτερον δὲ τῶν ἀποστόλων οὐκ εἶδον,
but other of the apostles I saw not,

εἰ μὴ Ἰάκωβον τὸν ἀδελφὸν τοῦ κυρίου.
except James the brother of the Lord.

20 ἃ δὲ γράφω ὑμῖν, ἰδοὺ ἐνώπιον τοῦ
Now what I write to you, behold before -
things

θεοῦ ὅτι οὐ ψεύδομαι. **21** ἔπειτα ἦλθον
God - I lie not. Then I went

Paul Called by God

10 Am I now trying to win the approval of men, or of God? Or am I trying to please men? If I were still trying to please men, I would not be a servant of Christ.

11 I want you to know, brothers, that the gospel I preached is not something that man made up. 12 I did not receive it from any man, nor was I taught it; rather, I received it by revelation from Jesus Christ.

13 For you have heard of my previous way of life in Judaism, how intensely I persecuted the church of God and tried to destroy it. 14 I was advancing in Judaism beyond many Jews of my own age and was extremely zealous for the traditions of my fathers. 15 But when God, who set me apart from birth[a] and called me by his grace, was pleased 16 to reveal his Son in me so that I might preach him among the Gentiles, I did not consult any man, 17 nor did I go up to Jerusalem to see those who were apostles before I was, but I went immediately into Arabia and later returned to Damascus.

18 Then after three years, I went up to Jerusalem to get acquainted with Peter[b] and stayed with him fifteen days. 19 I saw none of the other apostles—only James, the Lord's brother. 20 I assure you before God that what I am writing you is no lie. 21 Later I went to Syria and Cilicia. 22 I was personally unknown to the

[a]15 Or from my mother's womb
[b]18 Greek Cephas

regions of Syria and Cilicia, [22] and I was still unknown by sight to the churches of Judea that are in Christ; [23] they only heard it said, "The one who formerly was persecuting us is now proclaiming the faith he once tried to destroy." [24] And they glorified God because of me.

Chapter 2

Paul and the Other Apostles

THEN after fourteen years I went up again to Jerusalem with Barnabas, taking Titus along with me. [2] I went up in response to a revelation. Then I laid before them (though only in a private meeting with the acknowledged leaders) the gospel that I proclaim among the Gentiles, in order to make sure that I was not running, or had not run, in vain. [3] But even Titus, who was with me, was not compelled to be circumcised, though he was a Greek. [4] But because of false believers[f] secretly brought in, who slipped in to spy on the freedom we have in Christ Jesus, so that they might enslave us— [5] we did not submit to them even for a moment, so that the truth of the gospel might always remain with you. [6] And from those who were supposed to be acknowledged leaders (what they actually were makes no difference to me; God shows no partiality)— those leaders contributed nothing to me. [7] On the contrary, when they saw that I had been entrusted with the gospel for the uncircumcised, just as Peter had been entrusted with the gospel for the circumcised [8] (for he who worked through Peter making him an apostle to the circumcised also worked through me in sending me to the Gentiles), [9] and when

---

εἰς τὰ κλίματα τῆς Συρίας καὶ τῆς
into the regions – of Syria and –

Κιλικίας. 22 ἤμην δὲ ἀγνοούμενος τῷ
of Cilicia. And I was *being* unknown –

προσώπῳ ταῖς ἐκκλησίαις τῆς Ἰουδαίας
by face to the churches – of Judæa

ταῖς ἐν Χριστῷ. 23 μόνον δὲ ἀκούοντες
– in Christ. But only hearing

ἦσαν ὅτι ὁ διώκων ἡμᾶς ποτε νῦν
they were that the [one] *persecuting* *us* ¹then now

εὐαγγελίζεται τὴν πίστιν ἥν ποτε ἐπόρθει,
preaches the faith which then he was destroying,

24 καὶ ἐδόξαζον ἐν ἐμοὶ τὸν θεόν.
and they glorified ²in ³me – ¹God.

2 Ἔπειτα διὰ δεκατεσσάρων ἐτῶν πάλιν
Then through fourteen years again

ἀνέβην εἰς Ἱεροσόλυμα μετὰ Βαρναβᾶ,
I went up to Jerusalem with Barnabas,

συμπαραλαβὼν καὶ Τίτον· 2 ἀνέβην δὲ
taking with [me] also Titus; and I went up

κατὰ ἀποκάλυψιν· καὶ ἀνεθέμην αὐτοῖς
according to a revelation; and I put before them

τὸ εὐαγγέλιον ὃ κηρύσσω ἐν τοῖς ἔθνεσιν,
the gospel which I proclaim among the nations,

κατ᾽ ἰδίαν δὲ τοῖς δοκοῦσιν, μή πως
²privately ¹but to the [ones] seeming,* lest

εἰς κενὸν τρέχω ἤ ἔδραμον. 3 ἀλλ᾽
in vain I run or I ran. But

οὐδὲ Τίτος ὁ σὺν ἐμοί, Ἕλλην ὤν,
not Titus the [one] with me, a Greek being,

ἠναγκάσθη περιτμηθῆναι· 4 διὰ δὲ τοὺς
was compelled to be circumcised; but on account of ¹the

παρεισάκτους ψευδαδέλφους, οἵτινες παρεισ-
²brought in secretly ³false brothers, who stole

ἦλθον κατασκοπῆσαι τὴν ἐλευθερίαν ἡμῶν
in to spy on the freedom of us

ἣν ἔχομεν ἐν Χριστῷ Ἰησοῦ, ἵνα ἡμᾶς
which we have in Christ Jesus, in order that ¹us

καταδουλώσουσιν· 5 οἷς οὐδὲ πρὸς ὥραν
²they will(might) enslave; to whom not for an hour

εἴξαμεν τῇ ὑποταγῇ, ἵνα ἡ ἀλήθεια
yielded we – in subjection, in order that the truth

τοῦ εὐαγγελίου διαμείνῃ πρὸς ὑμᾶς. 6 ἀπὸ
of the gospel might continue with you. from

δὲ τῶν δοκούντων εἶναί τι, — ὁποῖοί
But the [ones] seeming to be something, (of what kind

ποτε ἦσαν οὐδέν μοι διαφέρει· πρόσωπον
²then ¹they were ⁴nothing ⁵to me ³matters; ⁶[the] face

[ὁ] θεὸς ἀνθρώπου οὐ λαμβάνει — ἐμοὶ
– ¹God ⁴of a man ²receives not,) ⁵to me

γὰρ οἱ δοκοῦντες οὐδὲν προσανέθεντο,
¹for the [ones] seeming⁶ nothing added,

7 ἀλλὰ τοὐναντίον ἰδόντες ὅτι πεπίστευμαι
but on the contrary seeing that I have been entrusted [with]

τὸ εὐαγγέλιον τῆς ἀκροβυστίας καθὼς
the gospel of the uncircumcision as

Πέτρος τῆς περιτομῆς, 8 ὁ γὰρ ἐνεργήσας
Peter [that] of the circumcision, for the [one] operating

Πέτρῳ εἰς ἀποστολὴν τῆς περιτομῆς
in Peter to an apostleship of the circumcision

ἐνήργησεν καὶ ἐμοὶ εἰς τὰ ἔθνη, 9 καὶ
operated also in me to the nations, and

Chapter 2

Paul Accepted by the Apostles

FOURTEEN years later I went up again to Jerusalem, this time with Barnabas. I took Titus along also. [2] I went up in response to a revelation and set before them the gospel that I preach among the Gentiles. But I did this privately to those who seemed to be leaders, for fear that I was running or had run my race in vain. [3] Yet not even Titus, who was with me, was compelled to be circumcised, even though he was a Greek. [4] This matter arose, because some false brothers had infiltrated our ranks to spy on the freedom we have in Christ Jesus and to make us slaves. [5] We did not give in to them for a moment, so that the truth of the gospel might remain with you.

[6] As for those who seemed to be important—whatever they were makes no difference to me; God does not judge by external appearance—those men added nothing to my message. [7] On the contrary, they saw that I had been entrusted with the task of preaching the gospel to the Gentiles,[c] just as Peter had been to the Jews.[d] [8] For God, who was at work in the ministry of Peter as an apostle to the Jews, was also at work in my ministry as an apostle to the Gentiles. [9] James, Pe-

---

James and Cephas and John, who were acknowledged pillars, recognized the grace that had been given to me, they gave to Barnabas and me the right hand of fellowship, agreeing that we should go to the Gentiles and they to the circumcised. 10 They asked only one thing, that we remember the poor, which was actually what I was[g] eager to do.

Paul Rebukes Peter at Antioch

11 But when Cephas came to Antioch, I opposed him to his face, because he stood self-condemned; 12 for until certain people came from James, he used to eat with the Gentiles. But after they came, he drew back and kept himself separate for fear of the circumcision faction. 13 And the other Jews joined him in this hypocrisy, so that even Barnabas was led astray by their hypocrisy. 14 But when I saw that they were not acting consistently with the truth of the gospel, I said to Cephas before them all, "If you, though a Jew, live like a Gentile and not like a Jew, how can you compel the Gentiles to live like Jews?"[h]

Jews and Gentiles Are Saved by Faith

15 We ourselves are Jews by birth and not Gentile sinners; 16 yet we know that a person is justified[i] not by the works of the law but through faith in Jesus Christ.[j] And we have come to believe in Christ Jesus, so that we might be justified by faith in Christ,[k] and not by doing the works of the law, because no one will be justified by the works of the law. 17 But if, in our effort to be justified in Christ, we ourselves

---

γνόντες τὴν χάριν τὴν δοθεῖσάν μοι,
knowing the grace - given to me,

Ἰάκωβος καὶ Κηφᾶς καὶ Ἰωάννης, οἱ
James and Cephas and John, the

δοκοῦντες στῦλοι εἶναι, δεξιὰς ἔδωκαν
[ones] seeming ³pillars ¹to be, ⁵right [hands] ¹gave

ἐμοὶ καὶ Βαρναβᾳ κοινωνίας, ἵνα ἡμεῖς
²to me ³and ⁴to Barnabas ⁶of fellowship, in order we
                                             that [should

εἰς τὰ ἔθνη, αὐτοὶ δὲ εἰς τὴν περιτομήν·
go] to the nations, but they to the circumcision;

10 μόνον τῶν πτωχῶν ἵνα μνημονεύωμεν,
only ²the ⁴poor in order ¹that ²we might remember,

ὃ καὶ ἐσπούδασα αὐτὸ τοῦτο ποιῆσαι.
which indeed ³I was eager ²this very thing to do.

11 Ὅτε δὲ ἦλθεν Κηφᾶς εἰς Ἀντιόχειαν,
But when ²came ¹Cephas to Antioch,

κατὰ πρόσωπον αὐτῷ ἀντέστην, ὅτι
against [his] face to him I opposed, because

κατεγνωσμένος ἦν. 12 πρὸ τοῦ γὰρ
¹having been condemned ¹he was. Before the for
                                = For before some came ...

ἐλθεῖν τινας ἀπὸ Ἰακώβου μετὰ τῶν
to come some[b] from James ¹with ²the

ἐθνῶν συνήσθιεν· ὅτε δὲ ἦλθον, ὑπέστελλεν
⁴nations ¹he ate *with*; but when they came, he withdrew

καὶ ἀφώριζεν ἑαυτόν, φοβούμενος τοὺς
and separated himself, fearing the [ones]

ἐκ περιτομῆς· 13 καὶ συνυπεκρίθησαν αὐτῷ
of [the] circumcision; and dissembled along with him

[καὶ] οἱ λοιποὶ Ἰουδαῖοι, ὥστε καὶ
also the remaining Jews, so as even

Βαρναβᾶς συναπήχθη αὐτῶν τῇ ὑποκρίσει.
Barnabas was led away with ²of them ¹the ³dissembling.

14 ἀλλ' ὅτε εἶδον ὅτι οὐκ ὀρθοποδοῦσιν
But when I saw that they walk[ed] not straight

πρὸς τὴν ἀλήθειαν τοῦ εὐαγγελίου, εἶπον
with the truth of the gospel, I said

τῷ Κηφᾷ ἔμπροσθεν πάντων· εἰ σὺ
- to Cephas in front of all: If thou

Ἰουδαῖος ὑπάρχων ἐθνικῶς καὶ οὐκ
²a Jew ¹being as a Gentile and not

Ἰουδαϊκῶς ζῇς, πῶς τὰ ἔθνη ἀναγκάζεις
as a Jew livest, how ²the ³nations ¹compellest thou

ἰουδαΐζειν; 15 Ἡμεῖς φύσει Ἰουδαῖοι καὶ
to judaize? We by nature Jews and

οὐκ ἐξ ἐθνῶν ἁμαρτωλοί, 16 εἰδότες δὲ
not ²of ³nations ¹sinners, and knowing

ὅτι οὐ δικαιοῦται ἄνθρωπος ἐξ ἔργων
that ²is not justified ¹a man by works

νόμου, ἐὰν μὴ διὰ πίστεως Χριστοῦ
of law except (but) through faith of (in) Christ

Ἰησοῦ, καὶ ἡμεῖς εἰς Χριστὸν Ἰησοῦν
Jesus,* even we ²in ³Christ ⁴Jesus

ἐπιστεύσαμεν, ἵνα δικαιωθῶμεν ἐκ πίστεως
¹believed, in order that we might be by faith
                            justified

Χριστοῦ καὶ οὐκ ἐξ ἔργων νόμου, ὅτι
of (in) Christ* and not by works of law, because

ἐξ ἔργων νόμου οὐ δικαιωθήσεται πᾶσα
by works of law not will be justified all
                      = no flesh will be justified.

σάρξ. 17 εἰ δὲ ζητοῦντες δικαιωθῆναι
flesh. But if seeking to be justified

---

ter[e] and John, those reputed to be pillars, gave me and Barnabas the right hand of fellowship when they recognized the grace given to me. They agreed that we should go to the Gentiles, and they to the Jews. 10 All they asked was that we should continue to remember the poor, the very thing I was eager to do.

Paul Opposes Peter

11 When Peter came to Antioch, I opposed him to his face, because he was clearly in the wrong. 12 Before certain men came from James, he used to eat with the Gentiles. But when they arrived, he began to draw back and separate himself from the Gentiles because he was afraid of those who belonged to the circumcision group. 13 The other Jews joined him in his hypocrisy, so that by their hypocrisy even Barnabas was led astray.

14 When I saw that they were not acting in line with the truth of the gospel, I said to Peter in front of them all, "You are a Jew, yet you live like a Gentile and not like a Jew. How is it, then, that you force Gentiles to follow Jewish customs?

15 "We who are Jews by birth and not 'Gentile sinners' 16 know that a man is not justified by observing the law, but by faith in Jesus Christ. So we, too, have put our faith in Christ Jesus that we may be justified by faith in Christ and not by observing the law, because by observing the law no one will be justified.

17 "If, while we seek to be justified in Christ, it be-

---

g Or *had been*
h Some interpreters hold that the quotation extends into the following paragraph
i Or *reckoned as righteous;* and so elsewhere
j Or *the faith of Jesus Christ*
k Or *the faith of Christ*

---

* Objective genitive, as is shown by the intervening sentence see also 3. 22, 26). *Cf.* "fear of God".

e9 Greek *Cephas*; also in verses 11 and 14

have been found to be sinners, is Christ then a servant of sin? Certainly not! 18But if I build up again the very things that I once tore down, then I demonstrate that I am a transgressor. 19For through the law I died to the law, so that I might live to God. I have been crucified with Christ; 20and it is no longer I who live, but it is Christ who lives in me. And the life I now live in the flesh I live by faith in the Son of God,*l* who loved me and gave himself for me. 21I do not nullify the grace of God; for if justification*m* comes through the law, then Christ died for nothing.

ἐν Χριστῷ εὑρέθημεν καὶ αὐτοὶ ἁμαρτωλοί,
in Christ we were found also [our]selves sinners,

ἆρα Χριστὸς ἁμαρτίας διάκονος; μὴ
then [is] Christ *²*of sin *¹*a minister? not

γένοιτο. 18 εἰ γὰρ ἃ κατέλυσα ταῦτα
May it be. For if what things I destroyed these things

πάλιν οἰκοδομῶ, παραβάτην ἐμαυτὸν συνισ-
again I build, *²*a transgressor *³*myself *¹*I con-

τάνω. 19 ἐγὼ γὰρ διὰ νόμου νόμῳ
stitute. For I through law *²*to law

ἀπέθανον ἵνα θεῷ ζήσω. 20 Χριστῷ συνεσ-
*¹*died in order to God I might live. With Christ I have
          that

ταύρωμαι· ζῶ δὲ οὐκέτι ἐγώ, ζῇ δὲ
been co-crucified; and *²*live *³*no more *¹*I, but *²*lives

ἐν ἐμοὶ Χριστός· ὃ δὲ νῦν ζῶ ἐν σαρκί,
*¹*in *⁴*me *¹*Christ; and what now I live in [the] flesh,

ἐν πίστει ζῶ τῇ τοῦ υἱοῦ τοῦ θεοῦ
*²*by *³*faith *¹*I live - of(in) the Son - of God

τοῦ ἀγαπήσαντός με καὶ παραδόντος ἑαυτὸν
- loving me and giving up himself

ὑπὲρ ἐμοῦ. 21 Οὐκ ἀθετῶ τὴν χάριν
on behalf of me. I do not set aside the grace

τοῦ θεοῦ· εἰ γὰρ διὰ νόμου δικαιοσύνη,
- of God; for if through law righteousness
          [comes],

ἆρα Χριστὸς δωρεὰν ἀπέθανεν.
then Christ without cause died.

comes evident that we ourselves are sinners, does that mean that Christ promotes sin? Absolutely not! 18If I rebuild what I destroyed, I prove that I am a lawbreaker. 19For through the law I died to the law so that I might live for God. 20I have been crucified with Christ and I no longer live, but Christ lives in me. The life I live in the body, I live by faith in the Son of God, who loved me and gave himself for me. 21I do not set aside the grace of God, for if righteousness could be gained through the law, Christ died for nothing!"*f*

Chapter 3

Law or Faith

YOU foolish Galatians! Who has bewitched you? It was before your eyes that Jesus Christ was publicly exhibited as crucified! 2The only thing I want to learn from you is this: Did you receive the Spirit by doing the works of the law or by believing what you heard? 3Are you so foolish? Having started with the Spirit, are you now ending with the flesh? 4Did you experience so much for nothing?—if it really was for nothing. 5Well then, does God*n* supply you with the Spirit and work miracles among you by your doing the works of the law, or by your believing what you heard?

6 Just as Abraham "believed God, and it was reckoned to him as righteousness," 7so, you see, those who believe are the descendants of Abraham. 8And the scripture, foreseeing that God would justify the Gentiles by faith, declared the gospel beforehand to Abraham, saying, "All the Gentiles shall be

3 Ὦ ἀνόητοι Γαλάται, τίς ὑμᾶς
O foolish Galatians, who you

ἐβάσκανεν, οἷς κατ᾿ ὀφθαλμοὺς Ἰησοῦς
bewitched, to before eyes Jesus
     whom [the]

Χριστὸς προεγράφη ἐσταυρωμένος; 2 τοῦτο
Christ was portrayed having been crucified? This

μόνον θέλω μαθεῖν ἀφ᾿ ὑμῶν, ἐξ ἔργων
only I wish to learn from you, by works

νόμου τὸ πνεῦμα ἐλάβετε ἢ ἐξ ἀκοῆς
of law the Spirit received ye or by hearing

πίστεως; 3 οὕτως ἀνόητοί ἐστε; ἐναρξάμενοι
of faith? thus foolish are ye? having begun

πνεύματι νῦν σαρκὶ ἐπιτελεῖσθε; 4 τοσαῦτα
in [the] Spirit now in [the] flesh are ye being so many things
         perfected?

ἐπάθετε εἰκῇ; 5 εἴ γε καὶ εἰκῇ. ὁ
suffered ye in vain? if indeed in vain. The [one]

οὖν ἐπιχορηγῶν ὑμῖν τὸ πνεῦμα καὶ
therefore supplying to you the Spirit and

ἐνεργῶν δυνάμεις ἐν ὑμῖν ἐξ ἔργων
working powerful deeds among you [is it] by works

νόμου ἢ ἐξ ἀκοῆς πίστεως; 6 Καθὼς
of law or by hearing of faith? As

Ἀβραὰμ ἐπίστευσεν τῷ θεῷ, καὶ ἐλογίσθη
Abraham believed - God, and it was reckoned

αὐτῷ εἰς δικαιοσύνην. 7 γινώσκετε ἄρα
to him for righteousness. Know ye then

ὅτι οἱ ἐκ πίστεως, οὗτοι υἱοί εἰσιν
that the [ones] of faith, *¹*these *²*sons *³*are

Ἀβραάμ. 8 προϊδοῦσα δὲ ἡ γραφὴ ὅτι
*⁵*of Abraham. And *²*foreseeing *¹*the *³*scripture *⁴*that

ἐκ πίστεως δικαιοῖ τὰ ἔθνη ὁ θεός,
*⁹*by *¹⁰*faith *⁸*would justify *⁷*the *⁸*nations - *⁶*God,

προευηγγελίσατο τῷ Ἀβραὰμ ὅτι ἐνευλογη-
preached good tidings - to Abraham that *⁵*will be
before

Chapter 3

Faith or Observance of the Law

YOU foolish Galatians! Who has bewitched you? Before your very eyes Jesus Christ was clearly portrayed as crucified. 2I would like to learn just one thing from you: Did you receive the Spirit by observing the law, or by believing what you heard? 3Are you so foolish? After beginning with the Spirit, are you now trying to attain your goal by human effort? 4Have you suffered so much for nothing—if it really was for nothing? 5Does God give you his Spirit and work miracles among you because you observe the law, or because you believe what you heard?

6Consider Abraham: "He believed God, and it was credited to him as righteousness."*g* 7Understand, then, that those who believe are children of Abraham. 8The Scripture foresaw that God would justify the Gentiles by faith, and announced the gospel in advance to Abraham: "All nations will be blessed

l Or by the faith of the Son of God
m Or righteousness
n Gk he

f 21 Some interpreters end the quotation after verse 14.
g 6 Gen. 15:6

blessed in you." For this reason, those who believe are blessed with Abraham who believed.

10 For all who rely on the works of the law are under a curse; for it is written, "Cursed is everyone who does not observe and obey all the things written in the book of the law." 11 Now it is evident that no one is justified before God by the law; for "The one who is righteous will live by faith." o 12 But the law does not rest on faith; on the contrary, "Whoever does the works of the law p will live by them." 13 Christ redeemed us from the curse of the law by becoming a curse for us—for it is written, "Cursed is everyone who hangs on a tree"— 14 in order that in Christ Jesus the blessing of Abraham might come to the Gentiles, so that we might receive the promise of the Spirit through faith.

The Promise to Abraham

15 Brothers and sisters, q I give an example from daily life: once a person's will r has been ratified, no one adds to it or annuls it. 16 Now the promises were made to Abraham and to his offspring; s it does not say, "And to offsprings," t as of many; but it says, "And to your offspring," s that is, to one person, who is Christ. 17 My point is this: the law, which came four hundred thirty years later, does not annul a covenant previously ratified by God, so as to nullify the promise. 18 For if the inheritance comes from the law, it no longer comes from the promise; but God granted it to Abraham

o Or *The one who is righteous through faith will live*
p Gk *does them*
q Gk *Brothers*
r Or *covenant* (as in verse 17)
s Gk *seed*
t Gk *seeds*

θήσονται ἐν σοὶ πάντα τὰ ἔθνη. 9 ὥστε
blessed ¹in ²thee ³all ⁴the ⁵nations. So as

οἱ ἐκ πίστεως εὐλογοῦνται σὺν τῷ πιστῷ
the[ones]of faith are blessed with the believing

Ἀβραάμ. 10 Ὅσοι γὰρ ἐξ ἔργων νόμου
Abraham. For as many as ²of ³works ⁴of law

εἰσίν, ὑπὸ κατάραν εἰσίν· γέγραπται γὰρ
¹are, ⁴under ⁷a curse ⁵are; for it has been written[,]

ὅτι ἐπικατάρατος πᾶς ὃς οὐκ ἐμμένει
- Accursed everyone who continues not

πᾶσιν τοῖς γεγραμμένοις ἐν τῷ βιβλίῳ
in all the things having been written in the roll

τοῦ νόμου τοῦ ποιῆσαι αὐτά. 11 ὅτι
of the law - to do them.ᵈ that

δὲ ἐν νόμῳ οὐδεὶς δικαιοῦται παρὰ τῷ
Now by law no man is justified before

θεῷ δῆλον, ὅτι ὁ δίκαιος ἐκ πίστεως
God [is] clear, because the just man by faith

ζήσεται· 12 ὁ δὲ νόμος οὐκ ἔστιν ἐκ
will live; and the law is not of

πίστεως, ἀλλ' ὁ ποιήσας αὐτὰ ζήσεται
faith, but the [one] doing them will live

ἐν αὐτοῖς. 13 Χριστὸς ἡμᾶς ἐξηγόρασεν
by them. Christ ²us ¹redeemed

ἐκ τῆς κατάρας τοῦ νόμου γενόμενος
out of the curse of the law becoming

ὑπὲρ ἡμῶν κατάρα, ὅτι γέγραπται·
²on behalf of ³us ¹a curse, because it has been written:

ἐπικατάρατος πᾶς ὁ κρεμάμενος ἐπὶ
Accursed everyone hanging on

ξύλου, 14 ἵνα εἰς τὰ ἔθνη ἡ εὐλογία
a tree, in order that ⁴to ⁵the ⁶nations ¹the ²blessing

τοῦ Ἀβραὰμ γένηται ἐν Ἰησοῦ Χριστῷ,
- ³of Abraham ⁴might be in Jesus Christ,

ἵνα τὴν ἐπαγγελίαν τοῦ πνεύματος λάβωμεν
in order ²the ³promise ⁴of the ⁵Spirit ¹we might
that receive

διὰ τῆς πίστεως. 15 Ἀδελφοί, κατὰ
through the faith. Brothers, according to

ἄνθρωπον λέγω. ὅμως ἀνθρώπου κεκυρω-
man I say. Nevertheless ⁶of man ⁷having been

μένην διαθήκην οὐδεὶς ἀθετεῖ ἢ ἐπιδια-
ratified ⁵a covenant ¹no one ²sets aside ³or ⁴makes

τάσσεται. 16 τῷ δὲ Ἀβραὰμ ἐρρέθησαν
additions [to]. - Now to Abraham were said

αἱ ἐπαγγελίαι καὶ τῷ σπέρματι αὐτοῦ.
the promises and to the seed of him.

οὐ λέγει· καὶ τοῖς σπέρμασιν, ὡς ἐπὶ
It says not: And to the seeds, as concerning

πολλῶν, ἀλλ' ὡς ἐφ' ἑνός· καὶ τῷ
many, but as concerning one: And to the

σπέρματί σου, ὅς ἐστιν Χριστός. 17 τοῦτο δὲ
seed of thee, who is Christ. And this

λέγω· διαθήκην προκεκυρωμένην ὑπὸ
I say: ¹⁰A covenant ¹¹having been previously ratified ¹²by

τοῦ θεοῦ ὁ μετὰ τετρακόσια καὶ τριάκοντα
- ¹³God ¹the ⁴after ⁵four hundred ⁶and ⁷thirty

ἔτη γεγονὼς νόμος οὐκ ἀκυροῖ, εἰς τὸ
²years ³having come ⁸law ⁹does not annul, so as†
into being

καταργῆσαι τὴν ἐπαγγελίαν. 18 εἰ γὰρ
to abolish the promise. For if

ἐκ νόμου ἡ κληρονομία, οὐκέτι ἐξ
⁴of ⁵law ¹the ²inheritance ³[is], no more [is it] of

ἐπαγγελίας· τῷ δὲ Ἀβραὰμ δι' ἐπαγγελίας
promise; - but ⁴to Abraham ⁵through ⁶promise

---

through you." h 9 So those who have faith are blessed along with Abraham, the man of faith.

10 All who rely on observing the law are under a curse, for it is written: "Cursed is everyone who does not continue to do everything written in the Book of the Law." i 11 Clearly no one is justified before God by the law, because, "The righteous will live by faith." j 12 The law is not based on faith; on the contrary, "The man who does these things will live by them." k 13 Christ redeemed us from the curse of the law by becoming a curse for us, for it is written: "Cursed is everyone who is hung on a tree." l 14 He redeemed us in order that the blessing given to Abraham might come to the Gentiles through Christ Jesus, so that by faith we might receive the promise of the Spirit.

The Law and the Promise

15 Brothers, let me take an example from everyday life. Just as no one can set aside or add to a human covenant that has been duly established, so it is in this case. 16 The promises were spoken to Abraham and to his seed. The Scripture does not say "and to seeds," meaning many people, but "and to your seed," m meaning one person, who is Christ. 17 What I mean is this: The law, introduced 430 years later, does not set aside the covenant previously established by God and thus do away with the promise. 18 For if the inheritance depends on the law, then it no longer depends on a promise; but God in his grace gave it to

h8 Gen. 12:3; 18:18; 22:18
i10 Deut. 27:26
j11 Hab. 2:4
k12 Lev. 18:5
l13 Deut. 21:23
m16 Gen. 12:7; 13:15; 24:7

through the promise.

The Purpose of the Law

19 Why then the law? It was added because of transgressions, until the offspring[u] would come to whom the promise had been made; and it was ordained through angels by a mediator. 20 Now a mediator involves more than one party; but God is one.

21 Is the law then opposed to the promises of God? Certainly not! For if a law had been given that could make alive, then righteousness would indeed come through the law. 22 But the scripture has imprisoned all things under the power of sin, so that what was promised through faith in Jesus Christ[v] might be given to those who believe.

23 Now before faith came, we were imprisoned and guarded under the law until faith would be revealed. 24 Therefore the law was our disciplinarian until Christ came, so that we might be justified by faith. 25 But now that faith has come, we are no longer subject to a disciplinarian, 26 for in Christ Jesus you are all children of God through faith. 27 As many of you as were baptized into Christ have clothed yourselves with Christ. 28 There is no longer Jew or Greek, there is no longer slave or free, there is no longer male and female; for all of you are one in Christ Jesus. 29 And if you belong to Christ, then you are Abraham's offspring,[u] heirs according to the promise.

Chapter 4

MY point is this: heirs, as long as they are minors, are no better than slaves, though they are the owners of all the property; 2 but they remain under guardians and trustees until the date set by the father.

[u] Gk seed
[v] Or through the faith of Jesus Christ

κεχάρισται ὁ θεός. **19** Τί οὖν ὁ νόμος;
²has given ³[it] – ¹God.   Why therefore the law?

τῶν παραβάσεων χάριν προσετέθη, ἄχρις
³the ⁴transgressions ²by reason of ¹it was added, until

ἂν ἔλθῃ τὸ σπέρμα ᾧ ἐπήγγελται,
³should come ¹the ²seed to whom it has been promised,

διαταγεὶς δι᾽ ἀγγέλων, ἐν χειρὶ μεσίτου.
being ordained through angels, by [the] hand of a mediator.

20 ὁ δὲ μεσίτης ἑνὸς οὐκ ἔστιν, ὁ
Now the mediator ²of one ¹is not,   the

δὲ θεὸς εἷς ἐστιν. **21** ὁ οὖν νόμος κατὰ
but God ²one ¹is. [Is] the ²therefore ¹law against

τῶν ἐπαγγελιῶν [τοῦ θεοῦ]; μὴ γένοιτο.
the promises – of God? May it not be.

εἰ γὰρ ἐδόθη νόμος ὁ δυνάμενος ζωοποι-
For if ²was given ¹a law – being able to make

ῆσαι, ὄντως ἐκ νόμου ἂν ἦν ἡ δικαιοσύνη·
alive, really ³by ⁴law ²would – ¹righteousness;

22 ἀλλὰ συνέκλεισεν ἡ γραφὴ τὰ πάντα
but ³shut up ¹the ²scripture all mankind†

ὑπὸ ἁμαρτίαν ἵνα ἡ ἐπαγγελία ἐκ πίστεως
under sin in or- the promise by faith
            der that

Ἰησοῦ Χριστοῦ δοθῇ τοῖς πιστεύουσιν.
of(in) Jesus Christ might be given to the [ones] believing.

23 Πρὸ τοῦ δὲ ἐλθεῖν τὴν πίστιν ὑπὸ
before the But to come the faith[b] under
=But before faith came

νόμον ἐφρουρούμεθα συγκλειόμενοι εἰς τὴν
law we were guarded being shut up to the

μέλλουσαν πίστιν ἀποκαλυφθῆναι. **24** ὥστε
³being about ¹faith to be revealed. So as

ὁ νόμος παιδαγωγὸς ἡμῶν γέγονεν εἰς
the law ²a trainer ¹of us ³has become [up] to

Χριστόν, ἵνα ἐκ πίστεως δικαιωθῶμεν·
Christ, in order that by faith we might be justified;

25 ἐλθούσης δὲ τῆς πίστεως οὐκέτι ὑπὸ
but ³having come ¹the ²faith[a] ¹no more ²under

παιδαγωγόν ἐσμεν. **26** Πάντες γὰρ υἱοὶ
³a trainer ⁴we are. For all   sons

θεοῦ ἐστε διὰ τῆς πίστεως ἐν Χριστῷ
of God ye are through the faith in Christ

Ἰησοῦ· **27** ὅσοι γὰρ εἰς Χριστὸν ἐβαπτίσ-
Jesus; for as many as ²into ³Christ ¹ye were

θητε, Χριστὸν ἐνεδύσασθε. **28** οὐκ ἔνι
baptized, ²Christ ¹ye put on. There cannot be

Ἰουδαῖος οὐδὲ Ἕλλην, οὐκ ἔνι δοῦλος
Jew   nor Greek, there cannot be slave

οὐδὲ ἐλεύθερος, οὐκ ἔνι ἄρσεν καὶ θῆλυ·
nor freeman, there cannot be male and female;

πάντες γὰρ ὑμεῖς εἷς ἐστε ἐν Χριστῷ
for ²all ¹ye ⁴one ³are in Christ

Ἰησοῦ. **29** εἰ δὲ ὑμεῖς Χριστοῦ, ἄρα
Jesus. But if ye [are] of Christ, then

τοῦ Ἀβραὰμ σπέρμα ἐστέ, κατ᾽ ἐπαγγελίαν
– ³of Abraham ²a seed ¹are ye, according to promise

κληρονόμοι. **4** Λέγω δέ, ἐφ᾽ ὅσον χρόνον ὁ
heirs.   But I say, over so long a time as the

κληρονόμος νήπιός ἐστιν, οὐδὲν διαφέρει
heir ²an infant ¹is, ³nothing ¹he differs
                          ²[from]

δούλου κύριος πάντων ὤν, **2** ἀλλὰ ὑπὸ
⁴a slave ⁶lord ⁷of all ⁵being, but   ¹under

ἐπιτρόπους ἐστὶν καὶ οἰκονόμους ἄχρι τῆς
²guardians ¹is and stewards   until the

Abraham through a promise.

19 What, then, was the purpose of the law? It was added because of transgressions until the Seed to whom the promise referred had come. The law was put into effect through angels by a mediator. 20 A mediator, however, does not represent just one party; but God is one.

21 Is the law, therefore, opposed to the promises of God? Absolutely not! For if a law had been given that could impart life, then righteousness would certainly have come by the law. 22 But the Scripture declares that the whole world is a prisoner of sin, so that what was promised, being given through faith in Jesus Christ, might be given to those who believe.

23 Before this faith came, we were held prisoners by the law, locked up until faith should be revealed. 24 So the law was put in charge to lead us to Christ[n] that we might be justified by faith. 25 Now that faith has come, we are no longer under the supervision of the law.

Sons of God

26 You are all sons of God through faith in Christ Jesus, 27 for all of you who were baptized into Christ have clothed yourselves with Christ. 28 There is neither Jew nor Greek, slave nor free, male nor female, for you are all one in Christ Jesus. 29 If you belong to Christ, then you are Abraham's seed, and heirs according to the promise.

Chapter 4

WHAT I am saying is that as long as the heir is a child, he is no different from a slave, although he owns the whole estate. 2 He is subject to guardians and trustees until the time set by his father. 3 So also, when we were

[n] 24 Or charge until Christ came

3 So with us; while we were minors, we were enslaved to the elemental spirits[w] of the world. 4 But when the fullness of time had come, God sent his Son, born of a woman, born under the law, 5 in order to redeem those who were under the law, so that we might receive adoption as children. 6 And because you are children, God has sent the Spirit of his Son into our[x] hearts, crying, "Abba![y] Father!" 7 So you are no longer a slave but a child, and if a child then also an heir, through God.[z]

Paul Reproves the Galatians

8 Formerly, when you did not know God, you were enslaved to beings that by nature are not gods. 9 Now, however, that you have come to know God, or rather to be known by God, how can you turn back again to the weak and beggarly elemental spirits?[a] How can you want to be enslaved to them again? 10 You are observing special days, and months, and seasons, and years. 11 I am afraid that my work for you may have been wasted.

12 Friends,[b] I beg you, become as I am, for I also have become as you are. You have done me no wrong. 13 You know that it was because of a physical infirmity that I first announced the gospel to you; 14 though my condition put you to the test, you did not scorn or despise me, but welcomed me as an angel of God, as Christ Jesus. 15 What has become of the good will you felt? For I testify that, had it been possible, you would have torn out your eyes and given

προθεσμίας τοῦ πατρός. 3 οὕτως καὶ
term previously of the father. So also
ἡμεῖς, ὅτε ἦμεν νήπιοι, ὑπὸ τὰ στοιχεῖα
we, when we were infants, under the elements
τοῦ κόσμου ἤμεθα δεδουλωμένοι· 4 ὅτε
of the world we were having been enslaved; when
δὲ ἦλθεν τὸ πλήρωμα τοῦ χρόνου,
but came the fulness of the time,
ἐξαπέστειλεν ὁ θεὸς τὸν υἱὸν αὐτοῦ,
sent forth - God the Son of him,
γενόμενον ἐκ γυναικός, γενόμενον ὑπὸ
becoming of a woman, becoming under
νόμον, 5 ἵνα τοὺς ὑπὸ νόμον ἐξαγοράσῃ,
law, in order that the ones under law he might redeem,
ἵνα τὴν υἱοθεσίαν ἀπολάβωμεν. 6 Ὅτι δὲ
in order the adoption of sons we might receive. And because that
ἐστε υἱοί, ἐξαπέστειλεν ὁ θεὸς τὸ
ye are sons, sent forth - God the
πνεῦμα τοῦ υἱοῦ αὐτοῦ εἰς τὰς καρδίας
Spirit of the Son of him into the hearts
ἡμῶν, κρᾶζον· ἀββὰ ὁ πατήρ. 7 ὥστε
of us, crying: Abba - Father. So as
οὐκέτι εἶ δοῦλος ἀλλὰ υἱός· εἰ δὲ υἱός,
no more art thou a slave but a son; and if a son,
καὶ κληρονόμος διὰ θεοῦ.
also an heir through God.
8 Ἀλλὰ τότε μὲν οὐκ εἰδότες θεὸν
But then indeed not knowing God
ἐδουλεύσατε τοῖς φύσει μὴ οὖσιν θεοῖς·
ye served as slaves the by nature not being gods;
9 νῦν δὲ γνόντες θεόν, μᾶλλον δὲ
but now knowing God, but rather
γνωσθέντες ὑπὸ θεοῦ, πῶς ἐπιστρέφετε
being known by God, how turn ye
πάλιν ἐπὶ τὰ ἀσθενῆ καὶ πτωχὰ στοιχεῖα,
again to the weak and poor elements,
οἷς πάλιν ἄνωθεν δουλεῦσαι θέλετε;
to which again anew to serve ye wish?
10 ἡμέρας παρατηρεῖσθε καὶ μῆνας καὶ
days Ye observe and months and
καιροὺς καὶ ἐνιαυτούς. 11 φοβοῦμαι ὑμᾶς
seasons and years. I fear [for] you
μή πως εἰκῇ κεκοπίακα εἰς ὑμᾶς.
lest in vain I have laboured among you.
12 Γίνεσθε ὡς ἐγώ, ὅτι κἀγὼ ὡς
Be ye as I [am], because I also [am] as
ὑμεῖς, ἀδελφοί, δέομαι ὑμῶν. οὐδέν με
ye [are], brothers, I beg of you. Nothing me
ἠδικήσατε· 13 οἴδατε δὲ ὅτι δι’ ἀσθένειαν
ye wronged; and ye know that on account of weakness
τῆς σαρκὸς εὐηγγελισάμην ὑμῖν τὸ
of the flesh I preached good tidings to you -
πρότερον, 14 καὶ τὸν πειρασμὸν ὑμῶν
formerly, and the trial of you
ἐν τῇ σαρκί μου οὐκ ἐξουθενήσατε οὐδὲ
in the flesh of me ye despised not nor
ἐξεπτύσατε, ἀλλὰ ὡς ἄγγελον θεοῦ ἐδέξασθέ
disdained ye, but as a messenger of God ye received
με, ὡς Χριστὸν Ἰησοῦν. 15 ποῦ οὖν
me, as Christ Jesus. Where therefore
ὁ μακαρισμὸς ὑμῶν; μαρτυρῶ γὰρ ὑμῖν
the felicitation of you?* for I witness to you
ὅτι εἰ δυνατὸν τοὺς ὀφθαλμοὺς ὑμῶν
that if possible the eyes of you

children, we were in slavery under the basic principles of the world. 4 But when the time had fully come, God sent his Son, born of a woman, born under law, 5 to redeem those under law, that we might receive the full rights of sons. 6 Because you are sons, God sent the Spirit of his Son into our hearts, the Spirit who calls out, "Abba,[o] Father." 7 So you are no longer a slave, but a son; and since you are a son, God has made you also an heir.

Paul's Concern for the Galatians

8 Formerly, when you did not know God, you were slaves to those who by nature are not gods. 9 But now that you know God—or rather are known by God—how is it that you are turning back to those weak and miserable principles? Do you wish to be enslaved by them all over again? 10 You are observing special days and months and seasons and years! 11 I fear for you, that somehow I have wasted my efforts on you.

12 I plead with you, brothers, become like me, for I became like you. You have done me no wrong. 13 As you know, it was because of an illness that I first preached the gospel to you. 14 Even though my illness was a trial to you, you did not treat me with contempt or scorn. Instead, you welcomed me as if I were an angel of God, as if I were Christ Jesus himself. 15 What has happened to all your joy? I can testify that, if you could have done so, you would have torn out your eyes and given them

[w] Or the rudiments
[x] Other ancient authorities read your
[y] Aramaic for Father
[z] Other ancient authorities read an heir of God through Christ
[a] Or beggarly rudiments
[b] Gk Brothers

* That is, "your felicitation [of me]".

[o]6 Aramaic for Father

them to me. 16Have I now become your enemy by telling you the truth? 17They make much of you, but for no good purpose; they want to exclude you, so that you may make much of them. 18It is good to be made much of for a good purpose at all times, and not only when I am present with you. 19My little children, for whom I am again in the pain of childbirth until Christ is formed in you, 20I wish I were present with you now and could change my tone, for I am perplexed about you.

The Allegory of Hagar and Sarah

21 Tell me, you who desire to be subject to the law, will you not listen to the law? 22For it is written that Abraham had two sons, one by a slave woman and the other by a free woman. 23One, the child of the slave, was born according to the flesh; the other, the child of the free woman, was born through the promise. 24Now this is an allegory: these women are two covenants. One woman, in fact, is Hagar, from Mount Sinai, bearing children for slavery. 25Now Hagar is Mount Sinai in Arabiaᶜ and corresponds to the present Jerusalem, for she is in slavery with her children. 26But the other woman corresponds to the Jerusalem above; she is free, and she is our mother. 27For it is written,

> "Rejoice, you
>   childless one,
> you who bear
>   no children;
> burst into song and
>   shout, you who
>   endure no
>   birthpangs;
> for the children of the
>   desolate woman
>   are more
>   numerous
> than the children of
>   the one who is
>   married."

28Now you,ᵈ my friends,ᵉ are children of the promise, like Isaac. 29But just as at that time the child who was born according to the flesh

---

ἐξορύξαντες ἐδώκατέ μοι. 16 ὥστε ἐχθρὸς
¹gouging out ye gave [them] to me. So that ²an enemy

ὑμῶν γέγονα ἀληθεύων ὑμῖν; 17 ζηλοῦσιν
³of you ¹have I become speaking truth to you? They are zealous of

ὑμᾶς οὐ καλῶς, ἀλλὰ ἐκκλεῖσαι ὑμᾶς
you not well, but ²to exclude ³you

θέλουσιν, 18 ἵνα αὐτοὺς ζηλοῦτε. καλὸν δὲ
¹wish, in order them ye may be But [it is] good
that zealous of.

ζηλοῦσθαι ἐν καλῷ πάντοτε, καὶ μὴ
to be zealous in a good thing always, and not

μόνον ἐν τῷ παρεῖναί με πρὸς ὑμᾶς,
only in the to be present meᵇᵉ with you,
=when I am present

19 τέκνα μου, οὓς πάλιν ὠδίνω μέχρις οὗ
children of me,[for] whom again I travail until
in birth

μορφωθῇ Χριστὸς ἐν ὑμῖν· 20 ἤθελον δὲ
²is formed ¹Christ in you; and I wished

παρεῖναι πρὸς ὑμᾶς ἄρτι καὶ ἀλλάξαι
to be present with you just now and to change

τὴν φωνήν μου, ὅτι ἀπορούμαι ἐν ὑμῖν.
the voice of me, because I am perplexed in(about) you.

21 Λέγετέ μοι, οἱ ὑπὸ νόμον θέλοντες
Tell me, the [ones] ²under ⁴law ¹wishing

εἶναι, τὸν νόμον οὐκ ἀκούετε; 22 γέγραπται
²to be, ²the ³law ¹hear ye not? ²it has been written

γὰρ ὅτι Ἀβραὰμ δύο υἱοὺς ἔσχεν, ἕνα
¹for that Abraham two sons had, one

ἐκ τῆς παιδίσκης καὶ ἕνα ἐκ τῆς ἐλευ-
of the maidservant and one of the free

θέρας. 23 ἀλλ' ὁ [μὲν] ἐκ τῆς παιδίσκης
woman. But the [one] indeed of the maidservant

κατὰ σάρκα γεγέννηται, ὁ δὲ ἐκ τῆς
according to flesh has been born, and the [one] of the

ἐλευθέρας· διὰ τῆς ἐπαγγελίας. 24 ἅτινά
free woman through the promise. Which things

ἐστιν ἀλληγορούμενα· αὗται γάρ εἰσιν
is(are) being allegorized; for these are

δύο διαθῆκαι, μία μὲν ἀπὸ ὄρους Σινά,
two covenants, one indeed from mount Sina,

εἰς δουλείαν γεννῶσα, ἥτις ἐστὶν Ἀγάρ.
to slavery bringing forth, which is Hagar.

25 τὸ δὲ Ἀγὰρ Σινὰ ὄρος ἐστὶν ἐν
⁴The ¹now ²Hagar ⁴Sina ⁵mount ²is in

τῇ Ἀραβίᾳ· συστοιχεῖ δὲ τῇ νῦν
- Arabia; and corresponds to the now

Ἰερουσαλήμ, δουλεύει γὰρ μετὰ τῶν
Jerusalem, for she serves as a slave with the

τέκνων αὐτῆς. 26 ἡ δὲ ἄνω Ἰερουσαλὴμ
children of her. But the above Jerusalem

ἐλευθέρα ἐστίν, ἥτις ἐστὶν μήτηρ ἡμῶν·
free is, who is mother of us;

27 γέγραπται γάρ· εὐφράνθητι, στεῖρα ἡ
for it has been written: Be thou glad, barren[,] the
[one]

οὐ τίκτουσα, ῥῆξον καὶ βόησον, ἡ οὐκ
not bearing, break forth and shout, the [one] not

ὠδίνουσα· ὅτι πολλὰ τὰ τέκνα τῆς ἐρήμου
travailing; because many [are] the children of the desolate

μᾶλλον ἢ τῆς ἐχούσης τὸν ἄνδρα. 28 ὑμεῖς
rather than of the having the husband. ye
[one]

δέ, ἀδελφοί, κατὰ Ἰσαὰκ ἐπαγγελίας τέκνα
But, brothers, ⁴according to ⁵Isaac ²of promise ¹children

ἐστέ. 29 ἀλλ' ὥσπερ τότε ὁ κατὰ σάρκα
¹are. But even as then the [one] according to flesh

---

to me. 16Have I now become your enemy by telling you the truth?

17Those people are zealous to win you over, but for no good. What they want is to alienate you from us, so that you may be zealous for them. 18It is fine to be zealous, provided the purpose is good, and to be so always and not just when I am with you. 19My dear children, for whom I am again in the pains of childbirth until Christ is formed in you, 20how I wish I could be with you now and change my tone, because I am perplexed about you!

Hagar and Sarah

21Tell me, you who want to be under the law, are you not aware of what the law says? 22For it is written that Abraham had two sons, one by the slave woman and the other by the free woman. 23His son by the slave woman was born in the ordinary way; but his son by the free woman was born as the result of a promise.

24These things may be taken figuratively, for the women represent two covenants. One covenant is from Mount Sinai and bears children who are to be slaves: This is Hagar. 25Now Hagar stands for Mount Sinai in Arabia and corresponds to the present city of Jerusalem, because she is in slavery with her children. 26But the Jerusalem that is above is free, and she is our mother. 27For it is written:

> "Be glad, O barren
>   woman,
> who bears no children;
> break forth and cry
>   aloud,
> you who have no labor
>   pains;
> because more are the
>   children of the
>   desolate woman
> than of her who has a
>   husband." ᵖ

28Now you, brothers, like Isaac, are children of promise. 29At that time the son born in the ordinary way

---

ᶜ Other ancient authorities read
For Sinai is a mountain in Arabia
ᵈ Other ancient authorities read *we*
ᵉ Gk *brothers*

ᵖ27 Isaiah 54:1

persecuted the child who was born according to the Spirit, so it is now also. 30 But what does the scripture say? "Drive out the slave and her child; for the child of the slave will not share the inheritance with the child of the free woman." 31 So then, friends,ᵉ we are children, not of the slave but of the free woman. 1 For freedom Christ has set us free. Stand firm, therefore, and do not submit again to a yoke of slavery.

The Nature of Christian Freedom

2 Listen! I, Paul, am telling you that if you let yourselves be circumcised, Christ will be of no benefit to you. 3 Once again I testify to every man who lets himself be circumcised that he is obliged to obey the entire law. 4 You who want to be justified by the law have cut yourselves off from Christ; you have fallen away from grace. 5 For through the Spirit, by faith, we eagerly wait for the hope of righteousness. 6 For in Christ Jesus neither circumcision nor uncircumcision counts for anything; the only thing that counts is faith workingᶠ through love.

7 You were running well; who prevented you from obeying the truth? 8 Such persuasion does not come from the one who calls you. 9 A little yeast leavens the whole batch of dough. 10 I am confident about you in the Lord that you will not think otherwise. But whoever it is that is confusing you will pay the penalty. 11 But my friends,ᵉ why am I still being persecuted if I am still preaching circumcision? In that case the offense of the cross has been removed. 12 I wish those who unsettle you would castrate themselves!

γεννηθεὶς ἐδίωκεν τὸν κατὰ πνεῦμα, οὕτως
born   persecuted the [one] according spirit,   so
                              [born]   to
καὶ νῦν. 30 ἀλλὰ τί λέγει ἡ γραφή;
also now.   But what says the scripture?
ἔκβαλε τὴν παιδίσκην καὶ τὸν υἱὸν αὐτῆς·
Cast out the maidservant and the son of her;
οὐ γὰρ μὴ κληρονομήσει ὁ υἱὸς τῆς
for by no means ¹shall inherit ¹the ²son ³of the
παιδίσκης μετὰ τοῦ υἱοῦ τῆς ἐλευθέρας.
⁴maidservant with the son of the free woman.
31 διό, ἀδελφοί, οὐκ ἐσμὲν παιδίσκης
Wherefore, brothers, we are not ²of a maidservant
τέκνα ἀλλὰ τῆς ἐλευθέρας.
¹children but of the free woman.

5 Τῇ ἐλευθερίᾳ ἡμᾶς Χριστὸς ἠλευθέρωσεν·
For the freedom ²us ¹Christ ²freed;
στήκετε οὖν καὶ μὴ πάλιν ζυγῷ δουλείας
stand firm therefore and not again with a yoke of slavery
ἐνέχεσθε.
be entangled.
2 Ἴδε ἐγὼ Παῦλος λέγω ὑμῖν ὅτι
Behold[,] I Paul te¹l you that
ἐὰν περιτέμνησθε Χριστὸς ὑμᾶς οὐδὲν
if ye are circumcised Christ ²you ¹nothing
ὠφελήσει. 3 μαρτύρομαι δὲ πάλιν παντὶ
¹will profit. And I testify again to every
ἀνθρώπῳ περιτεμνομένῳ ὅτι ὀφειλέτης ἐστὶν
man being circumcised that ²a debtor ¹he is
ὅλον τὸν νόμον ποιῆσαι. 4 κατηργήθητε
⁴all ¹the ²law ³to do. Ye were discharged
ἀπὸ Χριστοῦ οἵτινες ἐν νόμῳ δικαιοῦσθε,
from Christ who by law are justified,
τῆς χάριτος ἐξεπέσατε. 5 ἡμεῖς γὰρ
the ¹grace ¹ye fell from. For we
πνεύματι ἐκ πίστεως ἐλπίδα δικαιοσύνης
in spirit by faith [the] hope of righteousness
ἀπεκδεχόμεθα. 6 ἐν γὰρ Χριστῷ Ἰησοῦ
eagerly expect. For in Christ Jesus
οὔτε περιτομή τι ἰσχύει οὔτε ἀκροβυστία,
neither circumcision ²anything ¹avails nor uncircumcision,
ἀλλὰ πίστις δι᾽ ἀγάπης ἐνεργουμένη.
but faith ²through ¹love ¹operating.
7 Ἐτρέχετε καλῶς· τίς ὑμᾶς ἐνέκοψεν
Ye were running well: who ²you ¹hindered
ἀληθείᾳ μὴ πείθεσθαι; 8 ἡ πεισμονὴ οὐκ
⁵by truth ²not ⁴to be persuaded? the(this) persuasion not
ἐκ τοῦ καλοῦντος ὑμᾶς. 9 μικρὰ ζύμη
of the [one] calling you. A little leaven
ὅλον τὸ φύραμα ζυμοῖ. 10 ἐγὼ πέποιθα
all the lump leavens. I trust
εἰς ὑμᾶς ἐν κυρίῳ ὅτι οὐδὲν ἄλλο φρο-
as to† you in [the] Lord that ²nothing ³other ¹ye
νήσετε· ὁ δὲ ταράσσων ὑμᾶς βαστάσει
will think; but the [one] troubling you shall bear
τὸ κρίμα, ὅστις ἐὰν ᾖ. 11 Ἐγὼ δέ,
the judgment, whoever he may be. ¹But ⁴I,
ἀδελφοί, εἰ περιτομὴν ἔτι κηρύσσω, τί
²brothers, ³if ¹circumcision ⁵still ⁶proclaim, why
ἔτι διώκομαι; ἄρα κατήργηται τὸ
still am I being persecuted? then has been annulled the
σκάνδαλον τοῦ σταυροῦ. 12 Ὄφελον καὶ
offence of the cross. I would that indeed
ἀποκόψονται οἱ ἀναστατοῦντες ὑμᾶς.
⁴will(might) cut ¹the [ones] ²unsettling ³you.
themselves off

persecuted the son born by the power of the Spirit. It is the same now. 30 But what does the Scripture say? "Get rid of the slave woman and her son, for the slave woman's son will never share in the inheritance with the free woman's son."ᵃ 31 Therefore, brothers, we are not children of the slave woman, but of the free woman.

Chapter 5

Freedom in Christ

IT is for freedom that Christ has set us free. Stand firm, then, and do not let yourselves be burdened again by a yoke of slavery.

2 Mark my words! I, Paul, tell you that if you let yourselves be circumcised, Christ will be of no value to you at all. 3 Again I declare to every man who lets himself be circumcised that he is obligated to obey the whole law. 4 You who are trying to be justified by law have been alienated from Christ; you have fallen away from grace. 5 But by faith we eagerly await through the Spirit the righteousness for which we hope. 6 For in Christ Jesus neither circumcision nor uncircumcision has any value. The only thing that counts is faith expressing itself through love.

7 You were running a good race. Who cut in on you and kept you from obeying the truth? 8 That kind of persuasion does not come from the one who calls you. 9 "A little yeast works through the whole batch of dough." 10 I am confident in the Lord that you will take no other view. The one who is throwing you into confusion will pay the penalty, whoever he may be. 11 Brothers, if I am still preaching circumcision, why am I still being persecuted? In that case the offense of the cross has been abolished. 12 As for those agitators, I wish they would go the whole way and emasculate themselves!

ᶠOr *made effective*

ᵃ30 Gen. 21:10

13 For you were called to freedom, brothers and sisters;[e] only do not use your freedom as an opportunity for self-indulgence,[g] but through love become slaves to one another. 14 For the whole law is summed up in a single commandment, "You shall love your neighbor as yourself." 15 If, however, you bite and devour one another, take care that you are not consumed by one another.

The Works of the Flesh

16 Live by the Spirit, I say, and do not gratify the desires of the flesh. 17 For what the flesh desires is opposed to the Spirit, and what the Spirit desires is opposed to the flesh; for these are opposed to each other, to prevent you from doing what you want. 18 But if you are led by the Spirit, you are not subject to the law. 19 Now the works of the flesh are obvious: fornication, impurity, licentiousness, 20 idolatry, sorcery, enmities, strife, jealousy, anger, quarrels, dissensions, factions, 21 envy,[h] drunkenness, carousing, and things like these. I am warning you, as I warned you before: those who do such things will not inherit the kingdom of God.

The Fruit of the Spirit

22 By contrast, the fruit of the Spirit is love, joy, peace, patience, kindness, generosity, faithfulness, 23 gentleness, and self-control. There is no law against such things. 24 And those who belong to Christ Jesus have crucified the flesh with its passions and desires. 25 If we live by the Spirit, let us also be guided by the Spirit. 26 Let us not become conceited, competing against one another, envying one another.

13 Ὑμεῖς γὰρ ἐπ' ἐλευθερίᾳ ἐκλήθητε,
For ye for freedom were called,
ἀδελφοί· μόνον μὴ τὴν ἐλευθερίαν εἰς
brothers; only [use] not the freedom for
ἀφορμὴν τῇ σαρκί, ἀλλὰ διὰ τῆς ἀγάπης
advantage to the flesh, but through - love
δουλεύετε ἀλλήλοις. 14 ὁ γὰρ πᾶς νόμος
serve ye as slaves one another. For the whole law
ἐν ἑνὶ λόγῳ πεπλήρωται, ἐν τῷ· ἀγα-
in one word has been summed up, in the [word]: Thou
πήσεις τὸν πλησίον σου ὡς σεαυτόν.
shalt love the neighbour of thee as thyself.
15 εἰ δὲ ἀλλήλους δάκνετε καὶ κατεσθίετε,
But if ⁴one another ¹ye bite ²and ³ye devour,
βλέπετε μὴ ὑπ' ἀλλήλων ἀναλωθῆτε.
see lest by one another ye are destroyed.
16 Λέγω δέ, πνεύματι περιπατεῖτε καὶ
Now I say, in spirit walk ye and
ἐπιθυμίαν σαρκὸς οὐ μὴ τελέσητε. 17 ἡ
[the] lust of [the] flesh by no means ye will perform. the
γὰρ σὰρξ ἐπιθυμεῖ κατὰ τοῦ πνεύματος,
For flesh lusts against the spirit,
τὸ δὲ πνεῦμα κατὰ τῆς σαρκός, ταῦτα
and the spirit against the flesh, ²these
γὰρ ἀλλήλοις ἀντίκειται, ἵνα μὴ ἃ ἐὰν
¹for ⁴each other ³opposes, lest whatever things
θέλητε ταῦτα ποιῆτε. 18 εἰ δὲ πνεύματι
ye wish these ye do. But if by [the] Spirit
ἄγεσθε, οὐκ ἐστὲ ὑπὸ νόμον. 19 φανερὰ δέ
ye are led, ye are not under law. Now ³manifest
ἐστιν τὰ ἔργα τῆς σαρκός, ἅτινά ἐστιν
⁵is(are) ¹the ²works ³of the ⁴flesh, which is(are)
πορνεία, ἀκαθαρσία, ἀσέλγεια, 20 εἰδωλο-
fornication, uncleanness, lewdness, idola-
λατρία, φαρμακεία, ἔχθραι, ἔρις, ζῆλος,
try, sorcery, enmities, strife, jealousy,
θυμοί, ἐριθεῖαι, διχοστασίαι, αἱρέσεις,
angers, rivalries, divisions, sects,
21 φθόνοι, μέθαι, κῶμοι, καὶ τὰ ὅμοια
envyings, drunken- revellings, and - like
nesses, things
τούτοις, ἃ προλέγω ὑμῖν καθὼς προεῖπον,
to these, which I tell ²beforehand ¹you as I previously said,
ὅτι οἱ τὰ τοιαῦτα πράσσοντες βασιλείαν
that the [ones] - ²such things ¹practising ⁴[the] kingdom
θεοῦ οὐ κληρονομήσουσιν. 22 ὁ δὲ καρπὸς
⁵of God ³will not inherit. But the fruit
τοῦ πνεύματός ἐστιν ἀγάπη, χαρά, εἰρήνη,
of the Spirit is love, joy, peace,
μακροθυμία, χρηστότης, ἀγαθωσύνη, πίστις,
longsuffering, kindness, goodness, faithfulness,
23 πραΰτης, ἐγκράτεια· κατὰ τῶν τοιούτων
meekness, self-control; against - such things
οὐκ ἔστιν νόμος. 24 οἱ δὲ τοῦ Χριστοῦ
there is no law. Now the ones - of Christ
Ἰησοῦ τὴν σάρκα ἐσταύρωσαν σὺν τοῖς
Jesus ²the ³flesh ¹crucified with the(its)
παθήμασιν καὶ ταῖς ἐπιθυμίαις. 25 Εἰ
passions and the(its) lusts. If
ζῶμεν πνεύματι, πνεύματι καὶ στοιχῶμεν.
we live in [the] Spirit, in [the] Spirit also let us walk.
26 μὴ γινώμεθα κενόδοξοι, ἀλλήλους
Let us not become vainglorious, one another
προκαλούμενοι, ἀλλήλοις φθονοῦντες.
provoking, one another envying.

13 You, my brothers, were called to be free. But do not use your freedom to indulge the sinful nature[r]; rather, serve one another in love. 14 The entire law is summed up in a single command: "Love your neighbor as yourself."[s] 15 If you keep on biting and devouring each other, watch out or you will be destroyed by each other.

Life by the Spirit

16 So I say, live by the Spirit, and you will not gratify the desires of the sinful nature. 17 For the sinful nature desires what is contrary to the Spirit, and the Spirit what is contrary to the sinful nature. They are in conflict with each other, so that you do not do what you want. 18 But if you are led by the Spirit, you are not under law. 19 The acts of the sinful nature are obvious: sexual immorality, impurity and debauchery; 20 idolatry and witchcraft; hatred, discord, jealousy, fits of rage, selfish ambition, dissensions, factions 21 and envy; drunkenness, orgies, and the like. I warn you, as I did before, that those who live like this will not inherit the kingdom of God. 22 But the fruit of the Spirit is love, joy, peace, patience, kindness, goodness, faithfulness, 23 gentleness and self-control. Against such things there is no law. 24 Those who belong to Christ Jesus have crucified the sinful nature with its passions and desires. 25 Since we live by the Spirit, let us keep in step with the Spirit. 26 Let us not become conceited, provoking and envying each other.

Chapter 6

Bear One Another's Burdens

MY friends,[i] if anyone is detected in a transgression, you who have received the Spirit should restore such a one in a spirit of gentleness. Take care that you yourselves are not tempted. 2 Bear one another's burdens, and in this way you will fulfill[j] the law of Christ. 3 For if those who are nothing think they are something, they deceive themselves. 4 All must test their own work; then that work, rather than their neighbor's work, will become a cause for pride. 5 For all must carry their own loads.

6 Those who are taught the word must share in all good things with their teacher.

7 Do not be deceived; God is not mocked, for you reap whatever you sow. 8 If you sow to your own flesh, you will reap corruption from the flesh; but if you sow to the Spirit, you will reap eternal life from the Spirit. 9 So let us not grow weary in doing what is right, for we will reap at harvest-time, if we do not give up. 10 So then, whenever we have an opportunity, let us work for the good of all, and especially for those of the family of faith.

Final Admonitions and Benediction

11 See what large letters I make when I am writing in my own hand! 12 It is those who want to make a good showing in the flesh that try to compel you to be circumcised—only that they may not be persecuted for the cross of Christ. 13 Even the circumcised do not themselves obey the law, but they want you to

i Gk Brothers
j Other ancient authorities read in this way fulfill

---

6 Ἀδελφοί, ἐὰν καὶ προλημφθῇ ἄνθρω-
Brothers, if indeed ¹is overtaken ¹a

πος ἐν τινι παραπτώματι, ὑμεῖς οἱ
man in some trespass, ye the

πνευματικοὶ καταρτίζετε τὸν τοιοῦτον ἐν
spiritual [ones] restore - such a one in

πνεύματι πραΰτητος, σκοπῶν σεαυτόν, μὴ
a spirit of meekness, considering thyself, lest

καὶ σὺ πειρασθῇς. **2** Ἀλλήλων τὰ βάρη
also thou art tempted. Of one another the loads

βαστάζετε, καὶ οὕτως ἀναπληρώσετε τὸν
bear ye, and so ye will fulfil the

νόμον τοῦ Χριστοῦ. **3** εἰ γὰρ δοκεῖ
law - of Christ. For if ¹thinks

τις εἶναί τι μηδὲν ὤν, φρεναπατᾷ ἑαυτόν.
¹anyone ²to be ²some-³no- ⁴being, he deceives himself.
thing thing

4 τὸ δὲ ἔργον ἑαυτοῦ δοκιμαζέτω ἕκαστος,
But the work of himself ¹let ²prove ²each man,

καὶ τότε εἰς ἑαυτὸν μόνον τὸ καύχημα
and then in himself alone the boast

ἕξει καὶ οὐκ εἰς τὸν ἕτερον· **5** ἕκαστος
he will and not in the other man; ¹each man
have

γὰρ τὸ ἴδιον φορτίον βαστάσει. **6** Κοινωνείτω δὲ
¹for the(his) own burden will bear. And ¹let him share

ὁ κατηχούμενος τὸν λόγον τῷ κατη-
¹the ²being instructed [in] ³the ⁴word ⁵with the [one] in-
[one]

χοῦντι ἐν πᾶσιν ἀγαθοῖς. **7** Μὴ πλανᾶσθε,
structing in all good things. Be ye not led astray,

θεὸς οὐ μυκτηρίζεται. ὃ γὰρ ἐὰν σπείρῃ
God is not mocked. For whatever ¹may sow

ἄνθρωπος, τοῦτο καὶ θερίσει· **8** ὅτι ὁ
¹a man, this also he will reap; because the

σπείρων εἰς τὴν σάρκα ἑαυτοῦ ἐκ τῆς
[one] sowing to the flesh of himself of the

σαρκὸς θερίσει φθοράν, ὁ δὲ σπείρων
flesh will reap corruption, but the [one] sowing

εἰς τὸ πνεῦμα ἐκ τοῦ πνεύματος θερίσει
to the spirit of the Spirit will reap

ζωὴν αἰώνιον. **9** τὸ δὲ καλὸν ποιοῦντες
life eternal. And ²the ³good ¹doing

μὴ ἐγκακῶμεν· καιρῷ γὰρ ἰδίῳ
let us not lose heart; for in its own time

θερίσομεν μὴ ἐκλυόμενοι. **10** Ἄρα οὖν
we shall reap not failing. Then therefore

ὡς καιρὸν ἔχομεν, ἐργαζώμεθα τὸ ἀγαθὸν
as ¹time ¹we have, let us do the good

πρὸς πάντας, μάλιστα δὲ πρὸς τοὺς
to all men, and most of all to the

οἰκείους τῆς πίστεως.
members of of the faith.
the family

11 Ἴδετε πηλίκοις ὑμῖν γράμμασιν
Ye see in how large ¹to you ¹letters

ἔγραψα τῇ ἐμῇ χειρί. **12** Ὅσοι θέλουσιν
¹I wrote - with my hand. As many as wish

εὐπροσωπῆσαι ἐν σαρκί, οὗτοι ἀναγκάζουσιν
to look well in [the] flesh, these compel

ὑμᾶς περιτέμνεσθαι, μόνον ἵνα τῷ
you to be circumcised, only in order that ²for the

σταυρῷ τοῦ Χριστοῦ [Ἰησοῦ] μὴ
⁴cross - ²of Christ ⁴Jesus ¹not

διώκωνται. **13** οὐδὲ γὰρ οἱ περιτεμνόμενοι
²they are persecuted. For ⁴not ¹the [ones] ²being circumcised

αὐτοὶ νόμον φυλάσσουσιν, ἀλλὰ θέλουσιν
²themselves ⁴law ³keep, but they wish

Chapter 6

Doing Good to All

BROTHERS, if someone is caught in a sin, you who are spiritual should restore him gently. But watch yourself, or you also may be tempted. 2 Carry each other's burdens, and in this way you will fulfill the law of Christ. 3 If anyone thinks he is something when he is nothing, he deceives himself. 4 Each one should test his own actions. Then he can take pride in himself, without comparing himself to somebody else, 5 for each one should carry his own load.

6 Anyone who receives instruction in the word must share all good things with his instructor.

7 Do not be deceived: God cannot be mocked. A man reaps what he sows. 8 The one who sows to please his sinful nature, from that nature[f] will reap destruction; the one who sows to please the Spirit, from the Spirit will reap eternal life. 9 Let us not become weary in doing good, for at the proper time we will reap a harvest if we do not give up. 10 Therefore, as we have opportunity, let us do good to all people, especially to those who belong to the family of believers.

Not Circumcision but a New Creation

11 See what large letters I use as I write to you with my own hand!

12 Those who want to make a good impression outwardly are trying to compel you to be circumcised. The only reason they do this is to avoid being persecuted for the cross of Christ. 13 Not even those who are circumcised obey the law, yet they want you

f 8 Or his flesh, from the flesh

be circumcised so that they may boast about your flesh. 14 May I never boast of anything except the cross of our Lord Jesus Christ, by which^k the world has been crucified to me, and I to the world. 15 For^l neither circumcision nor uncircumcision is anything; but a new creation is everything! 16 As for those who will follow this rule—peace be upon them, and mercy, and upon the Israel of God. 17 From now on, let no one make trouble for me; for I carry the marks of Jesus branded on my body. 18 May the grace of our Lord Jesus Christ be with your spirit, brothers and sisters.^m Amen.

ὑμᾶς περιτέμνεσθαι ἵνα ἐν τῇ ὑμετέρᾳ
you　to be circumcised　in order that ²in　-　³your
σαρκὶ καυχήσωνται. 14 ἐμοὶ δὲ μὴ γένοιτο
⁴flesh　¹they may boast.　　But to me　may it not be
καυχᾶσθαι εἰ μὴ ἐν τῷ σταυρῷ τοῦ
to boast　except　in　the　cross　of the
κυρίου ἡμῶν Ἰησοῦ Χριστοῦ, δι' οὗ
Lord　of us　Jesus　Christ,　through whom
ἐμοὶ κόσμος ἐσταύρωται κἀγὼ κόσμῳ.
to me [the] world　has been crucified　and I to [the] world.
15 οὔτε γὰρ περιτομή τί ἐστιν οὔτε
For neither　circumcision ²anything ¹is　nor
ἀκροβυστία, ἀλλὰ καινὴ κτίσις. 16 καὶ
uncircumcision,　but　a new　creation.　And
ὅσοι τῷ κανόνι τούτῳ στοιχήσουσιν,
as many as　by this rule　will walk,
εἰρήνη ἐπ' αὐτοὺς καὶ ἔλεος, καὶ ἐπὶ τὸν
peace　on　them　and　mercy,　and　on　the
Ἰσραὴλ τοῦ θεοῦ.
Israel　-　of God.
17 Τοῦ λοιποῦ κόπους μοι μηδεὶς
For the rest　⁵troubles ⁴me ¹no one
παρεχέτω· ἐγὼ γὰρ τὰ στίγματα τοῦ
¹let ²cause;　for ¹I　⁵the　⁴brands　-
Ἰησοῦ ἐν τῷ σώματί μου βαστάζω.
⁶of Jesus ⁶in ⁷the ⁸body ⁹of me ²bear.
18 Ἡ χάρις τοῦ κυρίου ἡμῶν Ἰησοῦ
The　grace　of the　Lord　of us　Jesus
Χριστοῦ μετὰ τοῦ πνεύματος ὑμῶν,
Christ　with　the　spirit　of you,
ἀδελφοί· ἀμήν.
brothers :　Amen.

to be circumcised that they may boast about your flesh. 14May I never boast except in the cross of our Lord Jesus Christ, through which^u the world has been crucified to me, and I to the world. 15Neither circumcision nor uncircumcision means anything; what counts is a new creation. 16Peace and mercy to all who follow this rule, even to the Israel of God. 17Finally, let no one cause me trouble, for I bear on my body the marks of Jesus. 18The grace of our Lord Jesus Christ be with your spirit, brothers. Amen.

The Letter of Paul to the

Ephesians

Chapter 1

Salutation

PAUL, an apostle of Christ Jesus by the will of God,

To the saints who are in Ephesus and are faithful^a in Christ Jesus:

2 Grace to you and peace from God our Father and the Lord Jesus Christ.

Spiritual Blessings in Christ

3 Blessed be the God and Father of our Lord Jesus Christ, who has blessed us in Christ with every spiritual blessing in the heavenly places, 4 just as he chose us in Christ^b before the foundation of the world to be holy and blameless before him in love. 5 He destined us for

ΠΡΟΣ ΕΦΕΣΙΟΥΣ
To Ephesians

1 Παῦλος ἀπόστολος Χριστοῦ Ἰησοῦ διὰ
Paul　an apostle　of Christ　Jesus　through
θελήματος θεοῦ τοῖς ἁγίοις τοῖς οὖσιν
[the] will　of God　to the　saints　-　being
[ἐν Ἐφέσῳ] καὶ πιστοῖς ἐν Χριστῷ
in Ephesus　and　faithful　in　Christ
Ἰησοῦ· 2 χάρις ὑμῖν καὶ εἰρήνη ἀπὸ
Jesus:　Grace　to you　and　peace　from
θεοῦ πατρὸς ἡμῶν καὶ κυρίου Ἰησοῦ
God　Father　of us　and　Lord　Jesus
Χριστοῦ.
Christ.
3 Εὐλογητὸς ὁ θεὸς καὶ πατὴρ τοῦ
Blessed　the　God　and　Father　of the
κυρίου ἡμῶν Ἰησοῦ Χριστοῦ, ὁ εὐλογήσας
Lord　of us　Jesus　Christ,　the　having
[one] blessed
ἡμᾶς ἐν πάσῃ εὐλογίᾳ πνευματικῇ ἐν
us　with　every　blessing　spiritual　in
τοῖς ἐπουρανίοις ἐν Χριστῷ, 4 καθὼς
the　heavenlies　in　Christ,　as
ἐξελέξατο ἡμᾶς ἐν αὐτῷ πρὸ καταβολῆς
he chose　us　in　him　before [the] foundation
κόσμου, εἶναι ἡμᾶς ἁγίους καὶ ἀμώμους
of [the] world,　to be　us　holy　and　unblemished^b
=that we should be . . .
κατενώπιον αὐτοῦ, ἐν ἀγάπῃ 5 προορίσας
before　him,　in　love　predestinating

Ephesians

Chapter 1

PAUL, an apostle of Christ Jesus by the will of God,

To the saints in Ephesus,^a the faithful^b in Christ Jesus:

2Grace and peace to you from God our Father and the Lord Jesus Christ.

Spiritual Blessings in Christ

3Praise be to the God and Father of our Lord Jesus Christ, who has blessed us in the heavenly realms with every spiritual blessing in Christ. 4For he chose us in him before the creation of the world to be holy and blameless in his sight. In love 5he^c predestined us to

^k Or through whom
^l Other ancient authorities add in Christ Jesus
^m Gk brothers
^a Other ancient authorities lack in Ephesus, reading saints who are also faithful
^b Gk in him

^u14 Or whom
^a1 Some early manuscripts do not have in Ephesus.
^b1 Or believers who are
^c4,5 Or sight in love. 5He

adoption as his children through Jesus Christ, according to the good pleasure of his will, 6to the praise of his glorious grace that he freely bestowed on us in the Beloved. 7In him we have redemption through his blood, the forgiveness of our trespasses, according to the riches of his grace 8that he lavished on us. With all wisdom and insight 9he has made known to us the mystery of his will, according to his good pleasure that he set forth in Christ, 10as a plan for the fullness of time, to gather up all things in him, things in heaven and things on earth. 11In Christ we have also obtained an inheritance,c having been destined according to the purpose of him who accomplishes all things according to his counsel and will, 12so that we, who were the first to set our hope on Christ, might live for the praise of his glory. 13In him you also, when you had heard the word of truth, the gospel of your salvation, and had believed in him, were marked with the seal of the promised Holy Spirit; 14thisd is the pledge of our inheritance toward redemption as God's own people, to the praise of his glory.

Paul's Prayer

15 I have heard of your faith in the Lord Jesus and your lovee toward all the saints, and for this reason

ἡμᾶς εἰς υἱοθεσίαν διὰ Ἰησοῦ Χριστοῦ
us to adoption of sons through Jesus Christ
εἰς αὐτόν, κατὰ τὴν εὐδοκίαν τοῦ
to him[self], according to the good pleasure of the
θελήματος αὐτοῦ, 6 εἰς ἔπαινον δόξης
will of him, to [the] praise of [the] glory
τῆς χάριτος αὐτοῦ, ἧς ἐχαρίτωσεν ἡμᾶς
of the grace of him, of(with) he favoured us
                which
ἐν τῷ ἠγαπημένῳ, 7 ἐν ᾧ ἔχομεν τὴν
in the [one] *having been* loved, in whom we have the
ἀπολύτρωσιν διὰ τοῦ αἵματος αὐτοῦ, τὴν
redemption through the blood of him, the
ἄφεσιν τῶν παραπτωμάτων, κατὰ τὸ
forgiveness – of trespasses, according to the
πλοῦτος τῆς χάριτος αὐτοῦ, 8 ἧς ἐπερίσ-
riches of the grace of him, which he made to
σευσεν εἰς ἡμᾶς ἐν πάσῃ σοφίᾳ καὶ
abound to us in all wisdom and
φρονήσει 9 γνωρίσας ἡμῖν τὸ μυστήριον
intelligence making known to us the mystery
τοῦ θελήματος αὐτοῦ, κατὰ τὴν εὐδοκίαν
of the will of him, according to the good pleasure
αὐτοῦ, ἣν προέθετο ἐν αὐτῷ 10 εἰς
of him, which he purposed in him[self] for
οἰκονομίαν τοῦ πληρώματος τῶν καιρῶν,
a stewardship of the fulness of the times,
ἀνακεφαλαιώσασθαι τὰ πάντα ἐν τῷ
to head up – all things in –
Χριστῷ, τὰ ἐπὶ τοῖς οὐρανοῖς καὶ τὰ
Christ, the things on(in) *the* heavens and the
                              things
ἐπὶ τῆς γῆς· ἐν αὐτῷ, 11 ἐν ᾧ καὶ
on the earth; in him, in whom also
ἐκληρώθημεν προορισθέντες κατὰ πρόθεσιν
we were chosen as being predestinated according to [the] purpose
[his] inheritance
τοῦ τὰ πάντα ἐνεργοῦντος κατὰ τὴν
of the – ²all things ¹operating according to the
[one]
βουλὴν τοῦ θελήματος αὐτοῦ, 12 εἰς τὸ
counsel of the will of him, for *the*
εἶναι ἡμᾶς εἰς ἔπαινον δόξης αὐτοῦ
to be us^b to [the] praise of [the] glory of him
= that we should be
τοὺς προηλπικότας ἐν τῷ Χριστῷ· 13 ἐν
the having previously in – Christ; in
[ones] hoped
ᾧ καὶ ὑμεῖς, ἀκούσαντες τὸν λόγον
whom also ye, hearing the word
τῆς ἀληθείας, τὸ εὐαγγέλιον τῆς σωτηρίας
– of truth, the gospel of the salvation
ὑμῶν, ἐν ᾧ καὶ πιστεύσαντες ἐσφραγίσθητε
of you, in whom also believing ye were sealed
τῷ πνεύματι τῆς ἐπαγγελίας τῷ ἁγίῳ,
with ¹the ³Spirit – ⁴of promise – ²holy,
14 ὅς ἐστιν ἀρραβὼν τῆς κληρονομίας
who is an earnest of the inheritance
ἡμῶν, εἰς ἀπολύτρωσιν τῆς περιποιήσεως,
of us, till [the] redemption of the possession,
εἰς ἔπαινον τῆς δόξης αὐτοῦ.
to [the] praise of the glory of him.
15 Διὰ τοῦτο κἀγώ, ἀκούσας τὴν καθ'
Therefore I also, hearing the ²among
ὑμᾶς πίστιν ἐν τῷ κυρίῳ Ἰησοῦ καὶ
³you ¹faith in the Lord Jesus and
τὴν ἀγάπην τὴν εἰς πάντας τοὺς ἁγίους,
the love – to all the saints,

be adopted as his sons through Jesus Christ, in accordance with his pleasure and will— 6to the praise of his glorious grace, which he has freely given us in the One he loves. 7In him we have redemption through his blood, the forgiveness of sins, in accordance with the riches of God's grace 8that he lavished on us with all wisdom and understanding. 9And hed made known to us the mystery of his will according to his good pleasure, which he purposed in Christ, 10to be put into effect when the times will have reached their fulfillment—to bring all things in heaven and on earth together under one head, even Christ.

11In him we were also chosen,e having been predestined according to the plan of him who works out everything in conformity with the purpose of his will, 12in order that we, who were the first to hope in Christ, might be for the praise of his glory. 13And you also were included in Christ when you heard the word of truth, the gospel of your salvation. Having believed, you were marked in him with a seal, the promised Holy Spirit, 14who is a deposit guaranteeing our inheritance until the redemption of those who are God's possession—to the praise of his glory.

Thanksgiving and Prayer

15For this reason, ever since I heard about your faith in the Lord Jesus and your love for all the saints,

c Or been made a heritage
d Other ancient authorities read who
e Other ancient authorities lack *and your love*

d8,9 Or us. With all wisdom and understanding. 9he
e11 Or were made heirs

16I do not cease to give thanks for you as I remember you in my prayers. 17I pray that the God of our Lord Jesus Christ, the Father of glory, may give you a spirit of wisdom and revelation as you come to know him, 18so that, with the eyes of your heart enlightened, you may know what is the hope to which he has called you, what are the riches of his glorious inheritance among the saints, 19and what is the immeasurable greatness of his power for us who believe, according to the working of his great power. 20God*f* put this power to work in Christ when he raised him from the dead and seated him at his right hand in the heavenly places, 21far above all rule and authority and power and dominion, and above every name that is named, not only in this age but also in the age to come. 22And he has put all things under his feet and has made him the head over all things for the church, 23which is his body, the fullness of him who fills all in all.

Chapter 2

From Death to Life

YOU were dead through the trespasses and sins 2in which you once lived, following the course of this world, following the ruler of the power of the air, the spirit that is now at work among those who are disobedient. 3All of us

---

16 οὐ παύομαι εὐχαριστῶν ὑπὲρ ὑμῶν
do not cease giving thanks on behalf of you
μνείαν ποιούμενος ἐπὶ τῶν προσευχῶν
mention making on(in) the prayers
μου, 17 ἵνα ὁ θεὸς τοῦ κυρίου ἡμῶν
of me, in order that the God of the Lord of us
Ἰησοῦ Χριστοῦ, ὁ πατὴρ τῆς δόξης,
Jesus Christ, the Father of glory,
δώῃ ὑμῖν πνεῦμα σοφίας καὶ ἀποκαλύψεως
may give to you a spirit of wisdom and of revelation
ἐν ἐπιγνώσει αὐτοῦ, 18 πεφωτισμένους τοὺς
in a full knowledge of him, having been enlightened the
ὀφθαλμοὺς τῆς καρδίας [ὑμῶν,] εἰς τὸ
eyes of the heart of you, for *the*
εἰδέναι ὑμᾶς τίς ἐστιν ἡ ἐλπὶς τῆς
to know you*b* what is the hope of the
κλήσεως αὐτοῦ, τίς ὁ πλοῦτος τῆς δόξης
calling of him, what the riches of the glory
τῆς κληρονομίας αὐτοῦ ἐν τοῖς ἁγίοις,
of the inheritance of him in the saints,
19 καὶ τί τὸ ὑπερβάλλον μέγεθος τῆς
and what the excelling greatness of the
δυνάμεως αὐτοῦ εἰς ἡμᾶς τοὺς πιστεύοντας
power of him toward us the [ones] believing
κατὰ τὴν ἐνέργειαν τοῦ κράτους τῆς
according to the operation of the might of the
ἰσχύος αὐτοῦ, 20 ἣν ἐνήργηκεν ἐν τῷ
strength of him, which he has operated in –
Χριστῷ ἐγείρας αὐτὸν ἐκ νεκρῶν, καὶ
Christ raising him from [the] dead, and
καθίσας ἐν δεξιᾷ αὐτοῦ ἐν τοῖς ἐπου-
seating [him] at [the] right [hand] of him in the heaven-
ρανίοις 21 ὑπεράνω πάσης ἀρχῆς καὶ
lies far above all rule and
ἐξουσίας καὶ δυνάμεως καὶ κυριότητος
authority and power and lordship
καὶ παντὸς ὀνόματος ὀνομαζομένου οὐ
and every name being named not
μόνον ἐν τῷ αἰῶνι τούτῳ ἀλλὰ καὶ
only in this age but also
ἐν τῷ μέλλοντι· 22 καὶ πάντα ὑπέταξεν
in the coming; and all things subjected
ὑπὸ τοὺς πόδας αὐτοῦ, καὶ αὐτὸν ἔδωκεν
under the feet of him, and *a*him *1*gave
κεφαλὴν ὑπὲρ πάντα τῇ ἐκκλησίᾳ, 23 ἥτις
[to be] head over all things to the church, which
ἐστὶν τὸ σῶμα αὐτοῦ, τὸ πλήρωμα
is the body of him, the fulness
τοῦ τὰ πάντα ἐν πᾶσιν πληρουμένου.
of the – *2*all things *3*with *4*all things *1*filling.
[one]

2 Καὶ ὑμᾶς ὄντας νεκροὺς τοῖς παραπτώ-
And you being dead in the tres-
μασιν καὶ ταῖς ἁμαρτίαις ὑμῶν, 2 ἐν
passes and in the sins of you, in
αἷς ποτε περιεπατήσατε κατὰ τὸν αἰῶνα
which then ye walked according to the age
τοῦ κόσμου τούτου, κατὰ τὸν ἄρχοντα
of this world, according to the ruler
τῆς ἐξουσίας τοῦ ἀέρος, τοῦ πνεύματος
of the authority of the air, of the spirit
τοῦ νῦν ἐνεργοῦντος ἐν τοῖς υἱοῖς τῆς
– now operating in the sons –
ἀπειθείας· 3 ἐν οἷς καὶ ἡμεῖς πάντες
of disobedience; among whom also we all

16I have not stopped giving thanks for you, remembering you in my prayers. 17I keep asking that the God of our Lord Jesus Christ, the glorious Father, may give you the Spirit*f* of wisdom and revelation, so that you may know him better. 18I pray also that the eyes of your heart may be enlightened in order that you may know the hope to which he has called you, the riches of his glorious inheritance in the saints, 19and his incomparably great power for us who believe. That power is like the working of his mighty strength, 20which he exerted in Christ when he raised him from the dead and seated him at his right hand in the heavenly realms, 21far above all rule and authority, power and dominion, and every title that can be given, not only in the present age but also in the one to come. 22And God placed all things under his feet and appointed him to be head over everything for the church, 23which is his body, the fullness of him who fills everything in every way.

Chapter 2

Made Alive in Christ

AS for you, you were dead in your transgressions and sins, 2in which you used to live when you followed the ways of this world and of the ruler of the kingdom of the air, the spirit who is now at work in those who are disobedient. 3All of us once lived among them in the passions of our flesh, following the desires of flesh and senses, and we were by nature children of wrath, like everyone else. 4 But God, who is rich in mercy, out of the great love with which he loved us 5 even when we were dead through our trespasses, made us alive together with Christ *—by grace you have been saved— 6 and raised us up with him and seated us with him in the heavenly places in Christ Jesus, 7 so that in the ages to come he might show the immeasurable riches of his grace in kindness toward us in Christ Jesus. 8 For by grace you have been saved through faith, and this is not your own doing; it is the gift of God— 9 not the result of works, so that no one may boast. 10 For we are what he has made us, created in Christ Jesus for good works, which God prepared beforehand to be our way of life.

One in Christ

11 So then, remember that at one time you Gentiles by birth, *h* called "the uncircumcision" by those who are called "the circumcision"—a physical circumcision made in the flesh by human hands— 12 remember that you were at that time without Christ, being aliens from the commonwealth of Israel, and strangers to the covenants of promise, having no hope and without God in the world. 13 But now in Christ Jesus who once were far off have been brought near by the blood of Christ.

ἀνεστράφημέν ποτε ἐν ταῖς ἐπιθυμίαις
conducted ourselves then in the lusts

τῆς σαρκὸς ἡμῶν, ποιοῦντες τὰ θελήματα
of the flesh of us, doing the wishes

τῆς σαρκὸς καὶ τῶν διανοιῶν, καὶ
of the flesh and of the understandings, and

ἤμεθα τέκνα φύσει ὀργῆς ὡς καὶ οἱ
were ²children ¹by nature of wrath as also the

λοιποί· 4 ὁ δὲ θεὸς πλούσιος ὢν ἐν
rest; – but God ²rich ¹being in

ἐλέει, διὰ τὴν πολλὴν ἀγάπην αὐτοῦ
mercy, because of the much love of his

ἣν ἠγάπησεν ἡμᾶς, 5 καὶ ὄντας ἡμᾶς
[with] he loved us, even being us
which   =when we were

νεκροὺς τοῖς παραπτώμασιν συνεζωοποίησεν
dead – in trespasses quickened [us] with

τῷ Χριστῷ, — χάριτί ἐστε σεσωσμένοι,
– Christ, (by grace ye are *having been* saved,)

— 6 καὶ συνήγειρεν καὶ συνεκάθισεν ἐν
and raised [us] with and seated [us] with in

τοῖς ἐπουρανίοις ἐν Χριστῷ Ἰησοῦ, 7 ἵνα
the heavenlies in Christ Jesus, in order that

ἐνδείξηται ἐν τοῖς αἰῶσιν τοῖς ἐπερχομένοις
he might show in the ages – coming on
                                           forth

τὸ ὑπερβάλλον πλοῦτος τῆς χάριτος αὐτοῦ
the excelling riches of the grace of him

ἐν χρηστότητι ἐφ' ἡμᾶς ἐν Χριστῷ
in kindness toward us in Christ

Ἰησοῦ. 8 τῇ γὰρ χάριτί ἐστε σεσωσμένοι
Jesus. – For by grace ye are *having been* saved

διὰ πίστεως· καὶ τοῦτο οὐκ ἐξ ὑμῶν,
through faith; and this not of you,

θεοῦ τὸ δῶρον· 9 οὐκ ἐξ ἔργων, ἵνα μὴ
of [is] the gift; not of works, lest
God

τις καυχήσηται. 10 αὐτοῦ γάρ ἐσμεν
anyone should boast. For of him we are

ποίημα, κτισθέντες ἐν Χριστῷ Ἰησοῦ
a product, created in Christ Jesus

ἐπὶ ἔργοις ἀγαθοῖς, οἷς προητοίμασεν
unto works good, which ²previously prepared

ὁ θεὸς ἵνα ἐν αὐτοῖς περιπατήσωμεν.
– ¹God in order that in them we might walk.

11 Διὸ μνημονεύετε ὅτι ποτὲ ὑμεῖς τὰ
Wherefore remember ye that when ye the

ἔθνη ἐν σαρκί, οἱ λεγόμενοι ἀκροβυστία
nations in [the] flesh, the [ones] *being* called uncircumcision

ὑπὸ τῆς λεγομένης περιτομῆς ἐν σαρκὶ
by the *being* called circumcision in [the] flesh

χειροποιήτου, 12 ὅτι ἦτε τῷ καιρῷ ἐκείνῳ
made by hand, that ye were at that time

χωρὶς Χριστοῦ, ἀπηλλοτριωμένοι τῆς
without Christ, having been alienated from the

πολιτείας τοῦ Ἰσραὴλ καὶ ξένοι τῶν
commonwealth – of Israel and strangers of(from)
                                                    the

διαθηκῶν τῆς ἐπαγγελίας, ἐλπίδα μὴ
covenants – of promise, hope not

ἔχοντες καὶ ἄθεοι ἐν τῷ κόσμῳ. 13 νυνὶ
having and godless in the world. now

δὲ ἐν Χριστῷ Ἰησοῦ ὑμεῖς οἱ ποτε
But in Christ Jesus ye the [ones] then

ὄντες μακρὰν ἐγενήθητε ἐγγὺς ἐν τῷ
being afar became near by the

---

also lived among them at one time, gratifying the cravings of our sinful nature *and following its desires and thoughts. Like the rest, we were by nature objects of wrath. 4 But because of his great love for us, God, who is rich in mercy, 5 made us alive with Christ even when we were dead in transgressions—it is by grace you have been saved. 6 And God raised us up with Christ and seated us with him in the heavenly realms in Christ Jesus, 7 in order that in the coming ages he might show the incomparable riches of his grace, expressed in his kindness to us in Christ Jesus. 8 For it is by grace you have been saved, through faith—and this not from yourselves, it is the gift of God— 9 not by works, so that no one can boast. 10 For we are God's workmanship, created in Christ Jesus to do good works, which God prepared in advance for us to do.

One in Christ

11 Therefore, remember that formerly you who are Gentiles by birth and called "uncircumcised" by those who call themselves "the circumcision" (that done in the body by the hands of men)— 12 remember that at that time you were separate from Christ, excluded from citizenship in Israel and foreigners to the covenants of the promise, without hope and without God in the world. 13 But now in Christ Jesus you who once were far away have been

---

* Other ancient authorities read *in Christ*
h Gk *in the flesh*

*3 Or *our flesh*

14 For he is our peace; in his flesh he has made both groups into one and has broken down the dividing wall, that is, the hostility between us. 15 He has abolished the law with its commandments and ordinances, that he might create in himself one new humanity in place of the two, thus making peace, 16 and might reconcile both groups to God in one body[i] through the cross, thus putting to death the hostility through it.[j] 17 So he came and proclaimed peace to you who were far off and peace to those who were near; 18 for through him both of us have access in one Spirit to the Father. 19 So then you are no longer strangers and aliens, but you are citizens with the saints and also members of the household of God, 20 built upon the foundation of the apostles and prophets, with Christ Jesus himself as the cornerstone.[k] 21 In him the whole structure is joined together and grows into a holy temple in the Lord; 22 in whom you also are built together spiritually[l] into a dwelling place for God.

[i] Or reconcile both of us in one body for God
[j] Or in him, or in himself
[k] Or keystone
[l] Gk in the Spirit
[m] Or of

Chapter 3

Paul's Ministry to the Gentiles

THIS is the reason that I Paul am a prisoner for[m] Christ Jesus for the sake of you Gentiles— 2 for surely you have already heard of the commission of God's grace that was given me for you, 3 and how the mystery was made known to me by revelation, as I wrote above in a few words, 4 a reading of which will enable you to perceive my understanding of the mystery of Christ. 5 In for-

---

αἵματι τοῦ Χριστοῦ.   14 Αὐτὸς γάρ
blood   -   of Christ.   For he

ἐστιν ἡ εἰρήνη ἡμῶν, ὁ ποιήσας τὰ
is the peace of us, the [one] having made -

ἀμφότερα ἓν καὶ τὸ μεσότοιχον τοῦ
both   one and ²the ³middle wall -

φραγμοῦ λύσας, τὴν ἔχθραν, ἐν τῇ σαρκὶ
⁴of partition ¹having the enmity, ²in ³the ⁴flesh
         broken,

αὐτοῦ 15 τὸν νόμον τῶν ἐντολῶν ἐν
⁵of him   ⁶the ⁷law ⁸of the ⁹commandments ¹⁰in

δόγμασιν καταργήσας, ἵνα τοὺς δύο κτίσῃ
¹¹decrees ¹having abolished, in order ⁴the ⁵two ³he might
                       that   create

ἐν αὐτῷ εἰς ἕνα καινὸν ἄνθρωπον ποιῶν
⁶in ⁷him[self] ⁸into ⁹one ¹⁰new ¹¹man ¹making

εἰρήνην, 16 καὶ ἀποκαταλλάξῃ τοὺς
²peace,   and might reconcile the

ἀμφοτέρους ἐν ἑνὶ σώματι τῷ θεῷ διὰ
both   in one body - to God through

τοῦ σταυροῦ, ἀποκτείνας τὴν ἔχθραν ἐν
the cross,   killing   the enmity in

αὐτῷ· 17 καὶ ἐλθὼν εὐηγγελίσατο εἰρήνην
him[self]. and coming preached peace

ὑμῖν τοῖς μακρὰν καὶ εἰρήνην τοῖς ἐγγύς·
to you the ones afar and peace to the ones near;

18 ὅτι δι' αὐτοῦ ἔχομεν τὴν προσαγωγὴν
because through him ¹we ³have - ⁴access

οἱ ἀμφότεροι ἐν ἑνὶ πνεύματι πρὸς τὸν
- ²both   by one Spirit unto the

πατέρα. 19 ἄρα οὖν οὐκέτι ἐστὲ ξένοι
Father.   Then therefore no more are ye strangers

καὶ πάροικοι, ἀλλὰ ἐστὲ συμπολῖται τῶν
and sojourners, but ye are fellow-citizens of the

ἁγίων καὶ οἰκεῖοι τοῦ θεοῦ, 20 ἐποικοδομη-
saints and members of - of God,   having been
           the family

θέντες ἐπὶ τῷ θεμελίῳ τῶν ἀποστόλων
built *on* on the foundation of the apostles

καὶ προφητῶν, ὄντος ἀκρογωνιαίου αὐτοῦ
and prophets, ⁴being ⁵cornerstone ³[him]self

Χριστοῦ Ἰησοῦ, 21 ἐν ᾧ πᾶσα οἰκοδομὴ
¹Christ ²Jesus,ᵃ in whom all [the] building

συναρμολογουμένη αὔξει εἰς ναὸν ἅγιον
being fitted together grows into shrine a holy

ἐν κυρίῳ, 22 ἐν ᾧ καὶ ὑμεῖς συνοικοδομεῖσθε
in [the] Lord, in whom also ye are being built together

εἰς κατοικητήριον τοῦ θεοῦ ἐν πνεύματι.
into a dwelling-place - of God in spirit.

3 Τούτου χάριν ἐγὼ Παῦλος ὁ δέσμιος
²of this ¹By reason of I Paul the prisoner

τοῦ Χριστοῦ Ἰησοῦ ὑπὲρ ὑμῶν τῶν
- of Christ Jesus on behalf of you the

ἐθνῶν 2 — εἴ γε ἠκούσατε τὴν οἰκονομίαν
nations — if indeed ye heard the stewardship

τῆς χάριτος τοῦ θεοῦ τῆς δοθείσης μοι
of the grace - of God - given to me

εἰς ὑμᾶς, 3 ὅτι κατὰ ἀποκάλυψιν ἐγνωρίσθη
for you,   that by way of revelation was made known

μοι τὸ μυστήριον, καθὼς προέγραψα ἐν
to me the mystery, as I previously wrote in

ὀλίγῳ, 4 πρὸς ὃ δύνασθε ἀναγινώσκοντες
brief,   as to which ²ye can ¹reading

νοῆσαι τὴν σύνεσίν μου ἐν τῷ μυστηρίῳ
to realize the understanding of me in the mystery

---

brought near through the blood of Christ.

14 For he himself is our peace, who has made the two one and has destroyed the dividing wall of hostility, 15 by abolishing in his flesh the law with its commandments and regulations. His purpose was to create in himself one new man out of the two, thus making peace, 16 and in this one body to reconcile both of them to God through the cross, by which he put to death their hostility. 17 He came and preached peace to you who were far away and peace to those who were near. 18 For through him we both have access to the Father by one Spirit.

19 Consequently, you are no longer foreigners and aliens, but fellow citizens with God's people and members of God's household, 20 built on the foundation of the apostles and prophets, with Christ Jesus himself as the chief cornerstone. 21 In him the whole building is joined together and rises to become a holy temple in the Lord. 22 And in him too are being built together to become a dwelling in which God lives by his Spirit.

Chapter 3

Paul the Preacher to the Gentiles

FOR this reason I, Paul, the prisoner of Christ Jesus for the sake of you Gentiles—

2 Surely you have heard about the administration of God's grace that was given to me for you, 3 that is, the mystery made known to me by revelation, as I have already written briefly. 4 In reading this, then, you will be able to understand my insight into the mystery of

mer generations this mystery[n] was not made known to humankind, as it has now been revealed to his holy apostles and prophets by the Spirit: [6]that is, the Gentiles have become fellow heirs, members of the same body, and sharers in the promise in Christ Jesus through the gospel.

[7] Of this gospel I have become a servant according to the gift of God's grace that was given me by the working of his power. [8]Although I am the very least of all the saints, this grace was given to me to bring to the Gentiles the news of the boundless riches of Christ, [9]and to make everyone see[o] what is the plan of the mystery hidden for ages in[p] God who created all things; [10]so that through the church the wisdom of God in its rich variety might now be made known to the rulers and authorities in the heavenly places. [11]This was in accordance with the eternal purpose that he has carried out in Christ Jesus our Lord, [12]in whom we have access to God in boldness and confidence through faith in him.[q] [13]I pray therefore that you[r] may not lose heart over my sufferings for you; they are your glory.

Prayer for the Readers

[14] For this reason I bow my knees before the Father,[s] [15]from whom every family[t] in heaven and on earth takes its name. [16]I pray that, according to the riches of his glory, he may grant that you may be strengthened in your inner being with power through

τοῦ Χριστοῦ, 5 ὃ ἑτέραις γενεαῖς οὐκ
\- of Christ, which in other generations not

ἐγνωρίσθη τοῖς υἱοῖς τῶν ἀνθρώπων ὡς
was made known to the sons \- of men as

νῦν ἀπεκαλύφθη τοῖς ἁγίοις ἀποστόλοις
now it was revealed to the holy apostles

αὐτοῦ καὶ προφήταις ἐν πνεύματι, 6 εἶναι
of him and prophets in spirit, [3]to be

τὰ ἔθνη συγκληρονόμα καὶ σύσσωμα καὶ
[1]the [2]nations joint-heirs and a joint-body and

συμμέτοχα τῆς ἐπαγγελίας ἐν Χριστῷ
joint-sharers of the promise in Christ

'Ιησοῦ διὰ τοῦ εὐαγγελίου, 7 οὗ ἐγενήθην
Jesus through the gospel, of which I became

διάκονος κατὰ τὴν δωρεὰν τῆς χάριτος
a minister according to the gift of the grace

τοῦ θεοῦ τῆς δοθείσης μοι κατὰ τὴν
\- of God given to me according to the

ἐνέργειαν τῆς δυνάμεως αὐτοῦ. 8 ἐμοὶ
operation of the power of him. To me

τῷ ἐλαχιστοτέρῳ πάντων ἁγίων ἐδόθη
the leaster* of all saints was given

ἡ χάρις αὕτη, τοῖς ἔθνεσιν εὐαγγελίσασθαι
this grace, to the nations to preach

τὸ ἀνεξιχνίαστον πλοῦτος τοῦ Χριστοῦ,
the unsearchable riches \- of Christ,

9 καὶ φωτίσαι τίς ἡ οἰκονομία τοῦ
and to bring to light what [is] the stewardship of the

μυστηρίου τοῦ ἀποκεκρυμμένου ἀπὸ τῶν
mystery \- having been hidden from the

αἰώνων ἐν τῷ θεῷ τῷ τὰ πάντα κτίσαντι,
ages in \- God [1]the [one] [3]all things [2]having created,

10 ἵνα γνωρισθῇ νῦν ταῖς ἀρχαῖς καὶ
in order might be made now to the rulers and
that known

ταῖς ἐξουσίαις ἐν τοῖς ἐπουρανίοις διὰ
to the authorities in the heavenlies through

τῆς ἐκκλησίας ἡ πολυποίκιλος σοφία τοῦ
the church the manifold wisdom \-

θεοῦ, 11 κατὰ πρόθεσιν τῶν αἰώνων ἥν
of God, according to [the] purpose of the ages which

ἐποίησεν ἐν τῷ Χριστῷ 'Ιησοῦ τῷ κυρίῳ
he made in \- Christ Jesus the Lord

ἡμῶν, 12 ἐν ᾧ ἔχομεν τὴν παρρησίαν
of us, in whom we have \- boldness

καὶ προσαγωγὴν ἐν πεποιθήσει διὰ τῆς
and ·access in confidence through the

πίστεως αὐτοῦ. 13 διὸ αἰτοῦμαι μὴ
faith of(in) him.* Wherefore I ask [you] not

ἐγκακεῖν ἐν ταῖς θλίψεσίν μου ὑπὲρ
to faint in the afflictions of me on behalf

ὑμῶν, ἥτις ἐστὶν δόξα ὑμῶν. 14 Τούτου
of you, which is glory of you. [2]of this

χάριν κάμπτω τὰ γόνατά μου πρὸς
[1]By reason of I bend the knees of me unto

τὸν πατέρα, 15 ἐξ οὗ πᾶσα πατριὰ
the Father, of whom every fatherhood

ἐν οὐρανοῖς καὶ ἐπὶ γῆς ὀνομάζεται,
in heavens and on earth is named,

16 ἵνα δῷ ὑμῖν κατὰ τὸ πλοῦτος τῆς
in order he may you according to the riches of the
that give

δόξης αὐτοῦ δυνάμει κραταιωθῆναι διὰ
glory of him by power to become mighty through

* This is quite literal!—the apostle coins a word.

* See Gal. 2. 16.

Christ, [5]which was not made known to men in other generations as it has now been revealed by the Spirit to God's holy apostles and prophets. [6]This mystery is that through the gospel the Gentiles are heirs together with Israel, members together of one body, and sharers together in the promise in Christ Jesus.

[7]I became a servant of this gospel by the gift of God's grace given me through the working of his power. [8]Although I am less than the least of all God's people, this grace was given me: to preach to the Gentiles the unsearchable riches of Christ, [9]and to make plain to everyone the administration of this mystery, which for ages past was kept hidden in God, who created all things. [10]His intent was that now, through the church, the manifold wisdom of God should be made known to the rulers and authorities in the heavenly realms, [11]according to his eternal purpose which he accomplished in Christ Jesus our Lord. [12]In him and through faith in him we may approach God with freedom and confidence. [13]I ask you, therefore, not to be discouraged because of my sufferings for you, which are your glory.

A Prayer for the Ephesians

[14]For this reason I kneel before the Father, [15]from whom his whole family[h] in heaven and on earth derives its name. [16]I pray that out of his glorious riches he may strengthen you with

[n] Gk it
[o] Other ancient authorities read to bring to light
[p] Or by
[q] Or the faith of him
[r] Or I
[s] Other ancient authorities add of our Lord Jesus Christ
[t] Gk fatherhood

[h]15 Or whom all fatherhood

his Spirit, 17and that Christ may dwell in your hearts through faith, as you are being rooted and grounded in love. 18I pray that you may have the power to comprehend, with all the saints, what is the breadth and length and height and depth, 19and to know the love of Christ that surpasses knowledge, so that you may be filled with all the fullness of God.

20 Now to him who by the power at work within us is able to accomplish abundantly far more than all we can ask or imagine, 21to him be glory in the church and in Christ Jesus to all generations, forever and ever. Amen.

τοῦ πνεύματος αὐτοῦ εἰς τὸν ἔσω ἄνθρω-
the   Spirit   of him   in   the   inward   man,

πον, 17 κατοικῆσαι τὸν Χριστὸνᵇ διὰ τῆς
    to dwell   Christᵇ   through –
    =that Christ may dwell

πίστεως ἐν ταῖς καρδίαις ὑμῶν, ἐν
faith   in   the   hearts   of you,   in

ἀγάπῃ ἐρριζωμένοι καὶ τεθεμελιωμένοι,
love   having been rooted   and   having been founded,

18 ἵνα ἐξισχύσητε καταλαβέσθαι σὺν πᾶσιν
in order ye may have strength   to apprehend   with   all
that

τοῖς ἁγίοις τί τὸ πλάτος καὶ μῆκος
the   saints   what [is] the   breadth   and   length

καὶ ὕψος καὶ βάθος, 19 γνῶναί τε τὴν
and   height   and   depth,   and to know   ¹the

ὑπερβάλλουσαν τῆς γνώσεως ἀγάπην τοῦ
²excelling   –   ⁴knowledge   ²love   –

Χριστοῦ, ἵνα πληρωθῆτε εἰς πᾶν τὸ
³of Christ,   in order that ye may be filled   to   all   the

πλήρωμα τοῦ θεοῦ.
fulness   –   of God.

20 Τῷ δὲ δυναμένῳ ὑπὲρ πάντα ποιῆσαι
Now to the [one] being able   beyond   all things   to do

ὑπερεκπερισσοῦ ὧν αἰτούμεθα ἢ νοοῦμεν
superabundantly   of which   we ask   or   we think

κατὰ τὴν δύναμιν τὴν ἐνεργουμένην ἐν
according to the   power   the   operating   in

ἡμῖν, 21 αὐτῷ ἡ δόξα ἐν τῇ ἐκκλησίᾳ
us,   to him [be] the   glory   in   the   church

καὶ ἐν Χριστῷ Ἰησοῦ εἰς πάσας τὰς
and   in   Christ   Jesus   unto   all   the

γενεὰς τοῦ αἰῶνος τῶν αἰώνων· ἀμήν.
generations of the   age   of the   ages: Amen.

power through his Spirit in your inner being, 17so that Christ may dwell in your hearts through faith. And I pray that you, being rooted and established in love, 18may have power, together with all the saints, to grasp how wide and long and high and deep is the love of Christ, 19and to know this love that surpasses knowledge—that you may be filled to the measure of all the fullness of God.

20Now to him who is able to do immeasurably more than all we ask or imagine, according to his power that is at work within us, 21to him be glory in the church and in Christ Jesus throughout all generations, for ever and ever! Amen.

Chapter 4

Unity in the Body of Christ

I therefore, the prisoner in the Lord, beg you to lead a life worthy of the calling to which you have been called, 2with all humility and gentleness, with patience, bearing with one another in love, 3making every effort to maintain the unity of the Spirit in the bond of peace. 4There is one body and one Spirit, just as you were called to the one hope of your calling, 5one Lord, one faith, one baptism, 6one God and Father of all, who is above all and through all and in all.

7 But each of us was given grace according to the measure of Christ's gift. 8Therefore it is said, "When he ascended on high he made captivity itself

4 Παρακαλῶ οὖν ὑμᾶς ἐγὼ ὁ δέσμιος
⁷beseech   ⁴therefore   ³you   ¹I   ²the   ³prisoner

ἐν κυρίῳ ἀξίως περιπατῆσαι τῆς κλήσεως
⁴in   ⁵[the] Lord   ¹⁰worthily   ⁹to walk   of the   calling

ἧς ἐκλήθητε, 2 μετὰ πάσης ταπεινοφροσύνης
of(with) ye were   with   all   humility
which   called,

καὶ πραΰτητος, μετὰ μακροθυμίας,
and   meekness,   with   longsuffering,

ἀνεχόμενοι ἀλλήλων ἐν ἀγάπῃ, 3 σπου-
forbearing   one another   in   love,   being

δάζοντες τηρεῖν τὴν ἑνότητα τοῦ πνεύματος
eager   to keep   the   unity   of the   Spirit

ἐν τῷ συνδέσμῳ τῆς εἰρήνης· ἐν σῶμα
in   the   bond   –   of peace; [there is] one body

καὶ ἐν πνεῦμα, 4 καθὼς καὶ ἐκλήθητε
and   one   Spirit,   as   also   ye were called

ἐν μιᾷ ἐλπίδι τῆς κλήσεως ὑμῶν· 5 εἷς
in   one   hope   of the   calling   of you;   one

κύριος, μία πίστις, ἓν βάπτισμα· 6 εἷς
Lord,   one   faith,   one   baptism;   one

θεὸς καὶ πατὴρ πάντων, ὁ ἐπὶ πάντων
God   and   Father   of all,   the [one] over   all

καὶ διὰ πάντων καὶ ἐν πᾶσιν. 7 Ἑνὶ
and   through   all   and   in   all.   ³to ⁴one

δὲ ἑκάστῳ ἡμῶν ἐδόθη ἡ χάρις κατὰ
¹But   ⁵each   of us   was given   –   grace according to

τὸ μέτρον τῆς δωρεᾶς τοῦ Χριστοῦ.
the   measure   of the   gift   –   of Christ.

8 διὸ λέγει· ἀναβὰς εἰς ὕψος ᾐχμαλώτευσεν
Where- he says: Having   to   height   he led captive
fore   ascended

Chapter 4

Unity in the Body of Christ

AS a prisoner for the Lord, then, I urge you to live a life worthy of the calling you have received. 2Be completely humble and gentle; be patient, bearing with one another in love. 3Make every effort to keep the unity of the Spirit through the bond of peace. 4There is one body and one Spirit—just as you were called to one hope when you were called— 5one Lord, one faith, one baptism; 6one God and Father of all, who is over all and through all and in all.

7But to each one of us grace has been given as Christ apportioned it. 8This is why itʲ says:

"When he ascended on high,
he led captives in his

ᵇ8 Or God

a captive;
he gave gifts to his
people."

9(When it says, "He ascended," what does it mean but that he had also descended" into the lower parts of the earth? 10He who descended is the same one who ascended far above all the heavens, so that he might fill all things.) 11The gifts he gave were that some would be apostles, some prophets, some evangelists, some pastors and teachers, 12to equip the saints for the work of ministry, for building up the body of Christ, 13until all of us come to the unity of the faith and of the knowledge of the Son of God, to maturity, to the measure of the full stature of Christ. 14We must no longer be children, tossed to and fro and blown about by every wind of doctrine, by people's trickery, by their craftiness in deceitful scheming. 15But speaking the truth in love, we must grow up in every way into him who is the head, into Christ, 16from whom the whole body, joined and knit together by every ligament with which it is equipped, as each part is working properly, promotes the body's growth in building itself up in love.

The Old Life and the New

17 Now this I affirm and insist on in the Lord: you must no longer live as the Gentiles live, in the futility of their minds. 18They are darkened in their under-

αἰχμαλωσίαν, ἔδωκεν δόματα τοῖς ἀνθρώποις.
captivity, he gave gifts – to men.

9 τὸ δὲ ἀνέβη τί ἐστιν εἰ μὴ ὅτι καὶ
Now the "he what is it except that also
ascended"

κατέβη εἰς τὰ κατώτερα μέρη τῆς γῆς;
he descended into the lower parts of the earth?

10 ὁ καταβὰς αὐτός ἐστιν καὶ ὁ ἀναβὰς
The descending himself is also the ascending
[one] [one]

ὑπεράνω πάντων τῶν οὐρανῶν, ἵνα
far above all the heavens, in order that

πληρώσῃ τὰ πάντα. **11** καὶ αὐτὸς ἔδωκεν
he might fill – all things. And he gave

τοὺς μὲν ἀποστόλους, τοὺς δὲ προφήτας,
some† apostles, some† prophets,

τοὺς δὲ εὐαγγελιστάς, τοὺς δὲ ποιμένας
some† evangelists, some† shepherds

καὶ διδασκάλους, **12** πρὸς τὸν καταρτισμὸν
and teachers, for the perfecting

τῶν ἁγίων εἰς ἔργον διακονίας, εἰς
of the saints to [the] work of ministry, to

οἰκοδομὴν τοῦ σώματος τοῦ Χριστοῦ,
building of the body – of Christ,

13 μέχρι καταντήσωμεν οἱ πάντες εἰς
until ¹we ³arrive – ²all at

τὴν ἑνότητα τῆς πίστεως καὶ τῆς ἐπιγνώ-
the unity of the faith and of the full know-

σεως τοῦ υἱοῦ τοῦ θεοῦ, εἰς ἄνδρα τέλειον,
ledge of the Son – of God, at ²man ¹a complete,

εἰς μέτρον ἡλικίας τοῦ πληρώματος τοῦ
at [the] measure of [the] of the fulness
stature

Χριστοῦ, **14** ἵνα μηκέτι ὦμεν νήπιοι,
of Christ, in order that no more we may be infants,

κλυδωνιζόμενοι καὶ περιφερόμενοι παντὶ ἀνέμῳ
being blown and *being* carried round by every wind

τῆς διδασκαλίας ἐν τῇ κυβείᾳ τῶν ἀνθρώ-
– of teaching in the sleight – of

πων, ἐν πανουργίᾳ πρὸς τὴν μεθοδείαν
men, in cleverness unto the craftiness

τῆς πλάνης, **15** ἀληθεύοντες δὲ ἐν ἀγάπῃ
– of error, but speaking truth in love

αὐξήσωμεν εἰς αὐτὸν τὰ πάντα, ὅς ἐστιν
we may grow into him in all respects,† who is

ἡ κεφαλή, Χριστός, **16** ἐξ οὗ πᾶν τὸ
the head, Christ, of whom all the

σῶμα συναρμολογούμενον καὶ συμβιβαζόμενον
body being fitted together and *being* brought together

διὰ πάσης ἁφῆς τῆς ἐπιχορηγίας κατ'
through every band – of supply according
to

ἐνέργειαν ἐν μέτρῳ ἑνὸς ἑκάστου μέρους
[the] operation in measure of ²one ¹each part

τὴν αὔξησιν τοῦ σώματος ποιεῖται εἰς
¹the ³growth ⁴of the ¹body ¹makes for

οἰκοδομὴν ἑαυτοῦ ἐν ἀγάπῃ.
building of itself in love.

17 Τοῦτο οὖν λέγω καὶ μαρτύρομαι ἐν
This therefore I say and witness in

κυρίῳ, μηκέτι ὑμᾶς περιπατεῖν καθὼς
[the] Lord, no more you to walk as

καὶ τὰ ἔθνη περιπατεῖ ἐν ματαιότητι
also the nations walks in vanity

τοῦ νοὸς αὐτῶν, **18** ἐσκοτωμένοι τῇ
of the mind of them, ²having been darkened ³in the
(their)

train
and gave gifts to
men."ʲ

9(What does "he ascended" mean except that he also descended to the lower, earthly regions*k*? 10He who descended is the very one who ascended higher than all the heavens, in order to fill the whole universe.) 11It was he who gave some to be apostles, some to be prophets, some to be evangelists, and some to be pastors and teachers, 12to prepare God's people for works of service, so that the body of Christ may be built up 13until we all reach unity in the faith and in the knowledge of the Son of God and become mature, attaining to the whole measure of the fullness of Christ.

14Then we will no longer be infants, tossed back and forth by the waves, and blown here and there by every wind of teaching and by the cunning and craftiness of men in their deceitful scheming. 15Instead, speaking the truth in love, we will in all things grow up into him who is the Head, that is, Christ. 16From him the whole body, joined and held together by every supporting ligament, grows and builds itself up in love, as each part does its work.

Living as Children of Light

17So I tell you this, and insist on it in the Lord, that you must no longer live as the Gentiles do, in the futility of their thinking. 18They are darkened in their unstanding, alienated from the life of God because of their ignorance and hardness of heart. 19They have lost all sensitivity and have abandoned themselves to licentiousness, greedy to practice every kind of impurity. 20That is not the way you learned Christ! 21For surely you have heard about him and were taught in him, as truth is in Jesus. 22You were taught to put away your former way of life, your old self, corrupt and deluded by its lusts, 23and to be renewed in the spirit of your minds, 24and to clothe yourselves with the new self, created according to the likeness of God in true righteousness and holiness.

Rules for the New Life

25 So then, putting away falsehood, let all of us speak the truth to our neighbors, for we are members of one another. 26Be angry but do not sin; do not let the sun go down on your anger, 27and do not make room for the devil. 28Thieves must give up stealing; rather let them labor and work honestly with their own hands, so as to have something to share with the needy. 29Let no evil talk come out of your mouths, but only what is useful for building up, v as there is need, so that your words may give grace to those who hear. 30And do not grieve the Holy Spirit of God, with which you were marked with a seal for

---

διανοίᾳ ὄντες, ἀπηλλοτριωμένοι τῆς ζωῆς
⁴intellect ¹being, having been alienated [from] the life

τοῦ θεοῦ, διὰ τὴν ἄγνοιαν τὴν οὖσαν
- of God, through the ignorance - being

ἐν αὐτοῖς, διὰ τὴν πώρωσιν τῆς καρδίας
in them, on account of the hardness of the heart

αὐτῶν, 19 οἵτινες ἀπηλγηκότες ἑαυτοὺς
of them, who having ceased to care ²themselves

παρέδωκαν τῇ ἀσελγείᾳ εἰς ἐργασίαν
¹gave up - to lewdness for work

ἀκαθαρσίας πάσης ἐν πλεονεξίᾳ. 20 ὑμεῖς
²uncleanness ¹of all in greediness. ye

δὲ οὐχ οὕτως ἐμάθετε τὸν Χριστόν,
But not so learned - Christ,

21 εἴ γε αὐτὸν ἠκούσατε καὶ ἐν αὐτῷ
if indeed ³him ¹ye heard and ²by ¹him

ἐδιδάχθητε καθώς ἐστιν ἀλήθεια ἐν τῷ
¹were taught as ²is ¹truth in -

Ἰησοῦ, 22 ἀποθέσθαι ὑμᾶς κατὰ τὴν
Jesus, to put off youᵇ as regards the(your)
=that ye put off

προτέραν ἀναστροφὴν τὸν παλαιὸν ἄνθρωπον
former conduct the old man

τὸν φθειρόμενον κατὰ τὰς ἐπιθυμίας τῆς
- being corrupted according to the lusts -

ἀπάτης, 23 ἀνανεοῦσθαι δὲ τῷ πνεύματι
of deceit, and to be renewed in the spirit

τοῦ νοὸς ὑμῶν 24 καὶ ἐνδύσασθαι τὸν
of the mind of you and to put on the

καινὸν ἄνθρωπον τὸν κατὰ θεὸν κτισθέντα
new man - ²according to ³God ¹created

ἐν δικαιοσύνῃ καὶ ὁσιότητι τῆς ἀληθείας.
in righteousness and holiness - of truth.

25 Διὸ ἀποθέμενοι τὸ ψεῦδος λαλεῖτε
Wherefore putting off the lie speak ye

ἀλήθειαν ἕκαστος μετὰ τοῦ πλησίον αὐτοῦ,
truth each man with the neighbour of him,

ὅτι ἐσμὲν ἀλλήλων μέλη. 26 ὀργίζεσθε
because we are of one another members. Be ye wrathful

καὶ μὴ ἁμαρτάνετε· ὁ ἥλιος μὴ
and do not sin; ⁴the ⁵sun ²not

ἐπιδυέτω ἐπὶ παροργισμῷ ὑμῶν, 27 μηδὲ
¹let ³set on on provocation of you, nor

δίδοτε τόπον τῷ διαβόλῳ. 28 ὁ κλέπτων
give ye place to the devil. The [one] stealing

μηκέτι κλεπτέτω, μᾶλλον δὲ κοπιάτω
no more let him steal, but rather let him labour

ἐργαζόμενος ταῖς ἰδίαις χερσὶν τὸ ἀγαθόν,
working with the(his) own hands the good thing,

ἵνα ἔχῃ μεταδιδόναι τῷ χρείαν ἔχοντι.
in order he may to share [with] the [one] ²need ¹having
that have

29 πᾶς λόγος σαπρὸς ἐκ τοῦ στόματος
Every ²word ¹corrupt out of the mouth

ὑμῶν μὴ ἐκπορευέσθω, ἀλλὰ εἴ τις
of you let not proceed*, but if any

ἀγαθὸς πρὸς οἰκοδομὴν τῆς χρείας, ἵνα
[is] good to improvement of the need, in order
that

δῷ χάριν τοῖς ἀκούουσιν. 30 καὶ μὴ λυπεῖτε
it may grace to the [ones] hearing. And do not grieve
give

τὸ πνεῦμα τὸ ἅγιον τοῦ θεοῦ, ἐν ᾧ
the Spirit - Holy - of God, by whom

ἐσφραγίσθητε εἰς ἡμέραν ἀπολυτρώσεως.
ye were sealed for a day of redemption.

---

derstanding and separated from the life of God because of the ignorance that is in them due to the hardening of their hearts. 19Having lost all sensitivity, they have given themselves over to sensuality so as to indulge in every kind of impurity, with a continual lust for more. 20You, however, did not come to know Christ that way. 21Surely you heard of him and were taught in him in accordance with the truth that is in Jesus. 22You were taught, with regard to your former way of life, to put off your old self, which is being corrupted by its deceitful desires; 23to be made new in the attitude of your minds; 24and to put on the new self, created to be like God in true righteousness and holiness.

25Therefore each of you must put off falsehood and speak truthfully to his neighbor, for we are all members of one body. 26"In your anger do not sin"ˡ: Do not let the sun go down while you are still angry, 27and do not give the devil a foothold. 28He who has been stealing must steal no longer, but must work, doing something useful with his own hands, that he may have something to share with those in need. 29Do not let any unwholesome talk come out of your mouths, but only what is helpful for building others up according to their needs, that it may benefit those who listen. 30And do not grieve the Holy Spirit of God, with whom you were sealed for the day of

---

v Other ancient authorities read *building up faith*

* That is, "let no corrupt word proceed ..."

ˡ26 Psalm 4:4

the day of redemption. 31 Put away from you all bitterness and wrath and anger and wrangling and slander, together with all malice, 32 and be kind to one another, tenderhearted, forgiving one another, as God in Christ has forgiven you. w 1 Therefore be imitators of God, as beloved children, 2 and live in love, as Christ loved us x and gave himself up for us, a fragrant offering and sacrifice to God.

Renounce Pagan Ways

3 But fornication and impurity of any kind, or greed, must not even be mentioned among you, as is proper among saints. 4 Entirely out of place is obscene, silly, and vulgar talk; but instead, let there be thanksgiving. 5 Be sure of this, that no fornicator or impure person, or one who is greedy (that is, an idolater), has any inheritance in the kingdom of Christ and of God.

6 Let no one deceive you with empty words, for because of these things the wrath of God comes on those who are disobedient. 7 Therefore do not be associated with them. 8 For once you were darkness, but now in the Lord you are light. Live as children of light— 9 for the fruit of the light is found in all that is good and right and true. 10 Try to find out what is pleasing to the Lord. 11 Take no part in the unfruitful works of darkness, but instead expose them. 12 For it is shameful even to mention what such people do secretly; 13 but everything exposed by the light

---

31 πᾶσα πικρία καὶ θυμὸς καὶ
All bitterness and anger and

ὀργὴ καὶ κραυγὴ καὶ βλασφημία ἀρθήτω
wrath and clamour and blasphemy let it be removed

ἀφ' ὑμῶν σὺν πάσῃ κακία. **32** γίνεσθε
from you with all evil. be ye

δὲ εἰς ἀλλήλους χρηστοί, εὔσπλαγχνοι,
And to one another kind, tenderhearted,

χαριζόμενοι ἑαυτοῖς καθὼς καὶ ὁ θεὸς
forgiving yourselves as also God

ἐν Χριστῷ ἐχαρίσατο ὑμῖν. **5** Γίνεσθε
in Christ forgave you. Be ye

οὖν μιμηταὶ τοῦ θεοῦ, ὡς τέκνα
therefore imitators - of God, as children

ἀγαπητά, **2** καὶ περιπατεῖτε ἐν ἀγάπῃ,
beloved, and walk ye in love,

καθὼς καὶ ὁ Χριστὸς ἠγάπησεν ὑμᾶς
as also - Christ loved you

καὶ παρέδωκεν ἑαυτὸν ὑπὲρ ἡμῶν
and gave up himself on behalf of us

προσφορὰν καὶ θυσίαν τῷ θεῷ εἰς ὀσμὴν
an offering and a sacrifice - to God for an odour

εὐωδίας. **3** Πορνεία δὲ καὶ ἀκαθαρσία
of sweet smell. But fornication and ⁴uncleanness

πᾶσα ἢ πλεονεξία μηδὲ ὀνομαζέσθω ἐν
¹all or greediness not let it be named among

ὑμῖν, καθὼς πρέπει ἁγίοις, **4** καὶ αἰσχρότης
you, as is fitting for saints, and baseness

καὶ μωρολογία ἢ εὐτραπελία, ἃ οὐκ
and foolish talking or raillery, which things not

ἀνῆκεν, ἀλλὰ μᾶλλον εὐχαριστία. **5** τοῦτο
are becoming, but rather thanksgiving. this

γὰρ ἴστε γινώσκοντες, ὅτι πᾶς πόρνος
For be ye knowing, that every fornicator

ἢ ἀκάθαρτος ἢ πλεονέκτης, ὅ ἐστιν
or unclean man or greedy, who is

εἰδωλολάτρης, οὐκ ἔχει κληρονομίαν ἐν τῇ
an idolater, not has inheritance in the

βασιλείᾳ τοῦ Χριστοῦ καὶ θεοῦ. **6** Μηδεὶς
kingdom - of Christ and of God. ²No man

ὑμᾶς ἀπατάτω κενοῖς λόγοις· διὰ ταῦτα
⁴you ¹let ³deceive with empty words; because these of things

γὰρ ἔρχεται ἡ ὀργὴ τοῦ θεοῦ ἐπὶ τοὺς
for is coming the wrath - of God on the

υἱοὺς τῆς ἀπειθείας. **7** μὴ οὖν γίνεσθε
sons of disobedience. Not therefore be ye

συμμέτοχοι αὐτῶν· **8** ἦτε γὰρ ποτε σκότος,
partakers of them; for ye were then darkness,

νῦν δὲ φῶς ἐν κυρίῳ· ὡς τέκνα φωτὸς
but now light in [the] Lord; as children of light

περιπατεῖτε, **9** — ὁ γὰρ καρπὸς τοῦ
walk ye, (for the fruit of the

φωτὸς ἐν πάσῃ ἀγαθωσύνῃ καὶ δικαιοσύνῃ
light [is] in all goodness and righteousness

καὶ ἀληθείᾳ, — **10** δοκιμάζοντες τί ἐστιν
and truth,) proving what is

εὐάρεστον τῷ κυρίῳ, **11** καὶ μὴ συγκοι-
well-pleasing to the Lord, and do not have fellow-

νωνεῖτε τοῖς ἔργοις τοῖς ἀκάρποις τοῦ
ship with the ²works ¹unfruitful -

σκότους, μᾶλλον δὲ καὶ ἐλέγχετε, **12** τὰ
of darkness, but rather even reprove [them], ⁸the

γὰρ κρυφῇ γινόμενα ὑπ' αὐτῶν αἰσχρόν
for ⁶hidden things ⁷being done ⁸by ⁹them ²shameful

ἐστιν καὶ λέγειν· **13** τὰ δὲ πάντα ἐλεγχόμενα
¹it is ³even ⁴to speak [of]; - but all things being reproved

---

redemption. 31 Get rid of all bitterness, rage and anger, brawling and slander, along with every form of malice. 32 Be kind and compassionate to one another, forgiving each other, just as in Christ God forgave you.

Chapter 5

BE imitators of God, therefore, as dearly loved children 2 and live a life of love, just as Christ loved us and gave himself up for us as a fragrant offering and sacrifice to God. 3 But among you there must not be even a hint of sexual immorality, or of any kind of impurity, or of greed, because these are improper for God's holy people. 4 Nor should there be obscenity, foolish talk or coarse joking, which are out of place, but rather thanksgiving. 5 For of this you can be sure: No immoral, impure or greedy person —such a man is an idolater—has any inheritance in the kingdom of Christ and of God. m 6 Let no one deceive you with empty words, for because of such things God's wrath comes on those who are disobedient. 7 Therefore do not be partners with them.

8 For you were once darkness, but now you are light in the Lord. Live as children of light 9 (for the fruit of the light consists in all goodness, righteousness and truth) 10 and find out what pleases the Lord. 11 Have nothing to do with the fruitless deeds of darkness, but rather expose them. 12 For it is shameful even to mention what the disobedient do in secret. 13 But everything exposed

---

w Other ancient authorities read *us*
x Other ancient authorities read *you*

m 5 Or *kingdom of the Christ and God*

becomes visible, 14for everything that becomes visible is light. Therefore it says,

"Sleeper, awake!
Rise from the dead,
and Christ will shine
on you."

15 Be careful then how you live, not as unwise people but as wise, 16making the most of the time, because the days are evil. 17So do not be foolish, but understand what the will of the Lord is. 18Do not get drunk with wine, for that is debauchery; but be filled with the Spirit, 19as you sing psalms and hymns and spiritual songs among yourselves, singing and making melody to the Lord in your hearts, 20giving thanks to God the Father at all times and for everything in the name of our Lord Jesus Christ.

The Christian Household

21 Be subject to one another out of reverence for Christ.
22 Wives, be subject to your husbands as you are to the Lord. 23For the husband is the head of the wife just as Christ is the head of the church, the body of which he is the Savior. 24Just as the church is subject to Christ, so also wives ought to be, in everything, to their husbands.

25 Husbands, love your wives, just as Christ loved the church and gave himself up for her, 26in order to make her holy by cleansing her with the washing of water by the word, 27so as to present the church to himself in splendor, without a spot or wrinkle or anything of the kind—yes, so that

ὑπὸ τοῦ φωτὸς φανεροῦται· 14 πᾶν γὰρ
by the light is(are) manifested; for everything

τὸ φανερούμενον φῶς ἐστιν. διὸ λέγει·
- being manifested [2]light [1]is. Wherefore he says:

ἔγειρε, ὁ καθεύδων, καὶ ἀνάστα ἐκ τῶν
Rise, the sleeping [one], and stand up out of the

νεκρῶν, καὶ ἐπιφαύσει σοι ὁ Χριστός.
dead [ones], and will shine on thee - Christ.

15 Βλέπετε οὖν ἀκριβῶς πῶς περιπατεῖτε,
See ye therefore carefully how ye walk,

μὴ ὡς ἄσοφοι ἀλλ' ὡς σοφοί, 16 ἐξαγοραζ-
not as unwise but as wise, redeem-

όμενοι τὸν καιρόν, ὅτι αἱ ἡμέραι πονηραί
ing the time, because the days evil

εἰσιν. 17 διὰ τοῦτο μὴ γίνεσθε ἄφρονες,
are. Therefore be ye not foolish,

ἀλλὰ συνίετε τί τὸ θέλημα τοῦ κυρίου.
but understand what the will of the Lord [is].

18 καὶ μὴ μεθύσκεσθε οἴνῳ, ἐν ᾧ ἐστιν
And be ye not drunk with wine, in which is

ἀσωτία, ἀλλὰ πληροῦσθε ἐν πνεύματι,
wantonness, but be filled by [the] Spirit,

19 λαλοῦντες ἑαυτοῖς ψαλμοῖς καὶ ὕμνοις
speaking to yourselves in psalms and hymns

καὶ ᾠδαῖς πνευματικαῖς, ᾄδοντες καὶ
and songs spiritual, singing and

ψάλλοντες τῇ καρδίᾳ ὑμῶν τῷ κυρίῳ,
psalming with the heart of you to the Lord,

20 εὐχαριστοῦντες πάντοτε ὑπὲρ πάντων
giving thanks always for all things

ἐν ὀνόματι τοῦ κυρίου ἡμῶν Ἰησοῦ
in [the] name of the Lord of us Jesus

Χριστοῦ τῷ θεῷ καὶ πατρί, 21 ὑποτασ-
Christ - to God even [the] Father, being

σόμενοι ἀλλήλοις ἐν φόβῳ Χριστοῦ. 22 Αἱ
subject to one another in [the] fear of Christ. The

γυναῖκες τοῖς ἰδίοις ἀνδράσιν ὡς τῷ
wives to the(ir) own husbands as to the

κυρίῳ, 23 ὅτι ἀνήρ ἐστιν κεφαλὴ τῆς
Lord, because a man is head of the

γυναικὸς ὡς καὶ ὁ Χριστὸς κεφαλὴ
woman as also - Christ [is] head

τῆς ἐκκλησίας, αὐτὸς σωτὴρ τοῦ σώματος.
of the church, [him]self Saviour of the body.

24 ἀλλὰ ὡς ἡ ἐκκλησία ὑποτάσσεται τῷ
But as the church is subject -

Χριστῷ, οὕτως καὶ αἱ γυναῖκες τοῖς
to Christ, so also the wives to the(ir)

ἀνδράσιν ἐν παντί. 25 Οἱ ἄνδρες, ἀγαπᾶτε
husbands in everything. The husbands, love ye

τὰς γυναῖκας, καθὼς καὶ ὁ Χριστὸς
the(your) wives, as also - Christ

ἠγάπησεν τὴν ἐκκλησίαν καὶ ἑαυτὸν
loved the church and himself

παρέδωκεν ὑπὲρ αὐτῆς, 26 ἵνα αὐτὴν
gave up on behalf of it, in order that it

ἁγιάσῃ καθαρίσας τῷ λουτρῷ τοῦ
he might sanctify cleansing by the washing of the

ὕδατος ἐν ῥήματι, 27 ἵνα παραστήσῃ αὐτὸς
water by word, in order [2]might present [1]he
that

ἑαυτῷ ἔνδοξον τὴν ἐκκλησίαν, μὴ ἔχουσαν
[4]to himself [3]glorious [2]the [1]church, not having

σπίλον ἢ ῥυτίδα ἤ τι τῶν τοιούτων,
spot or wrinkle or any of the such things,

by the light becomes visible, 14for it is light that makes everything visible. This is why it is said:

"Wake up, O sleeper,
rise from the dead,
and Christ will shine on
you."

15Be very careful, then, how you live—not as unwise but as wise, 16making the most of every opportunity, because the days are evil. 17Therefore do not be foolish, but understand what the Lord's will is. 18Do not get drunk on wine, which leads to debauchery. Instead, be filled with the Spirit. 19Speak to one another with psalms, hymns and spiritual songs. Sing and make music in your heart to the Lord, 20always giving thanks to God the Father for everything, in the name of our Lord Jesus Christ.
21Submit to one another out of reverence for Christ.

Wives and Husbands

22Wives, submit to your husbands as to the Lord. 23For the husband is the head of the wife as Christ is the head of the church, his body, of which he is the Savior. 24Now as the church submits to Christ, so also wives should submit to their husbands in everything.
25Husbands, love your wives, just as Christ loved the church and gave himself up for her 26to make her holy, cleansing[n] her by the washing with water through the word, 27and to present her to himself as a radiant church, without stain or wrinkle or any oth-

n26 Or *having cleansed*

she may be holy and without blemish. 28 In the same way, husbands should love their wives as they do their own bodies. He who loves his wife loves himself. 29 For no one ever hates his own body, but he nourishes and tenderly cares for it, just as Christ does for the church, 30 because we are members of his body.[y] 31 "For this reason a man will leave his father and mother and be joined to his wife, and the two will become one flesh." 32 This is a great mystery, and I am applying it to Christ and the church. 33 Each of you, however, should love his wife as himself, and a wife should respect her husband.

ἀλλ' ἵνα ᾖ ἁγία καὶ ἄμωμος. 28 οὕτως
but *in order* it might holy and unblemished. So
that be

ὀφείλουσιν [καὶ] οἱ ἄνδρες ἀγαπᾶν τὰς
ought also the husbands to love the

ἑαυτῶν γυναῖκας ὡς τὰ ἑαυτῶν σώματα.
of themselves wives as the of themselves bodies.

ὁ ἀγαπῶν τὴν ἑαυτοῦ γυναῖκα ἑαυτὸν
The [one] loving the of himself wife himself

ἀγαπᾷ· 29 οὐδεὶς γάρ ποτε τὴν ἑαυτοῦ
loves; for no man ever the of himself

σάρκα ἐμίσησεν, ἀλλὰ ἐκτρέφει καὶ θάλπει
flesh hated, but nourishes and cherishes

αὐτήν, καθὼς καὶ ὁ Χριστὸς τὴν ἐκ-
it, as also - Christ the

κλησίαν, 30 ὅτι μέλη ἐσμὲν τοῦ σώματος
church, because members we are of the body

αὐτοῦ. 31 ἀντὶ τούτου καταλείψει ἄνθρωπος
of him. For this ²shall leave ¹a man

[τὸν] πατέρα καὶ [τὴν] μητέρα καὶ
the(his) father and the(his) mother and

προσκολληθήσεται πρὸς τὴν γυναῖκα αὐτοῦ,
shall cleave to the wife of him,

καὶ ἔσονται οἱ δύο εἰς σάρκα μίαν.
and ³shall be ¹the ²two ⁴for ⁶flesh ⁵one.

32 τὸ μυστήριον τοῦτο μέγα ἐστίν, ἐγὼ
This mystery great is, ¹I

δὲ λέγω εἰς Χριστὸν καὶ [εἰς] τὴν
¹but say as to Christ and as to the

ἐκκλησίαν. 33 πλὴν καὶ ὑμεῖς οἱ
church. Nevertheless also ye *the*

καθ' ἕνα ἕκαστος τὴν ἑαυτοῦ γυναῖκα
one by one† each ¹the ²of himself ³wife

οὕτως ἀγαπάτω ὡς ἑαυτόν, ἡ δὲ
so let him love as himself, and the

γυνὴ ἵνα φοβῆται τὸν ἄνδρα. 6 Τὰ
wife *in order* that she fears the(her) husband. The
that

τέκνα, ὑπακούετε τοῖς γονεῦσιν ὑμῶν
children, obey ye the parents of you

ἐν κυρίῳ· τοῦτο γάρ ἐστιν δίκαιον.
in [the] Lord; for this is right.

2 τίμα τὸν πατέρα σου καὶ τὴν μητέρα,
Honour the father of thee and the mother,

ἥτις ἐστὶν ἐντολὴ πρώτη ἐν ἐπαγγελίᾳ,
which is ²commandment ¹[the] ³first with a promise,

3 ἵνα εὖ σοι γένηται καὶ ἔσῃ μακρο-
in order well with thee it may be and thou may- long-
that est be

χρόνιος ἐπὶ τῆς γῆς. 4 Καὶ οἱ πατέρες,
timed(lived) on the earth. And the fathers,

μὴ παροργίζετε τὰ τέκνα ὑμῶν, ἀλλὰ
do not ye provoke to wrath the children of you, but

ἐκτρέφετε αὐτὰ ἐν παιδείᾳ καὶ νουθεσίᾳ
nurture them in [the] discipline and admonition

κυρίου. 5 Οἱ δοῦλοι, ὑπακούετε τοῖς
of [the] Lord. The slaves, obey ye ¹the(your)

κατὰ σάρκα κυρίοις μετὰ φόβου καὶ
²according to ⁴flesh ³lords with fear and

τρόμου ἐν ἁπλότητι τῆς καρδίας ὑμῶν
trembling in singleness of the heart of you

ὡς τῷ Χριστῷ, 6 μὴ κατ' ὀφθαλμοδουλίαν
as - to Christ, not by way of eye-service

ὡς ἀνθρωπάρεσκοι, ἀλλ' ὡς δοῦλοι Χριστοῦ
as men-pleasers, but as slaves of Christ

ποιοῦντες τὸ θέλημα τοῦ θεοῦ ἐκ ψυχῆς,
doing the will - of God from [the] soul,

er blemish, but holy and blameless. 28 In this same way, husbands ought to love their wives as their own bodies. He who loves his wife loves himself. 29 After all, no one ever hated his own body, but he feeds and cares for it, just as Christ does the church— 30 for we are members of his body. 31 "For this reason a man will leave his father and mother and be united to his wife, and the two will become one flesh."[o] 32 This is a profound mystery—but I am talking about Christ and the church. 33 However, each one of you also must love his wife as he loves himself, and the wife must respect her husband.

Chapter 6

Children and Parents

CHILDREN, obey your parents in the Lord,[z] for this is right. 2 "Honor your father and mother"— this is the first commandment with a promise: 3 "so that it may be well with you and you may live long on the earth."

4 And, fathers, do not provoke your children to anger, but bring them up in the discipline and instruction of the Lord.

Slaves and Masters

5 Slaves, obey your earthly masters with fear and trembling, in singleness of heart, as you obey Christ; 6 not only while being watched, and in order to please them, but as slaves of Christ, doing the will of God from the heart.

Chapter 6

Children and Parents

CHILDREN, obey your parents in the Lord, for this is right. 2 "Honor your father and mother"— which is the first commandment with a promise— 3 "that it may go well with you and that you may enjoy long life on the earth."[p]

4 Fathers, do not exasperate your children; instead, bring them up in the training and instruction of the Lord.

Slaves and Masters

5 Slaves, obey your earthly masters with respect and fear, and with sincerity of heart, just as you would obey Christ. 6 Obey them not only to win their favor when their eye is on you, but like slaves of Christ, doing the will of God from

---

[y] Other ancient authorities add *of his flesh and of his bones*
[z] Other ancient authorities lack *in the Lord*

[o]31 Gen. 2:24
[p]3 Deut. 5:16

7 Render service with enthusiasm, as to the Lord and not to men and women, 8 knowing that whatever good we do, we will receive the same again from the Lord, whether we are slaves or free.

9 And, masters, do the same to them. Stop threatening them, for you know that both of you have the same Master in heaven, and with him there is no partiality.

The Whole Armor of God

10 Finally, be strong in the Lord and in the strength of his power. 11 Put on the whole armor of God, so that you may be able to stand against the wiles of the devil. 12 For our[a] struggle is not against enemies of blood and flesh, but against the rulers, against the authorities, against the cosmic powers of this present darkness, against the spiritual forces of evil in the heavenly places. 13 Therefore take up the whole armor of God, so that you may be able to withstand on that evil day, and having done everything, to stand firm. 14 Stand therefore, and fasten the belt of truth around your waist, and put on the breastplate of righteousness. 15 As shoes for your feet put on whatever will make you ready to proclaim the gospel of peace. 16 With all of these,[b] take the shield of faith, with which you will be able to quench all the flaming arrows of the evil one. 17 Take the helmet of salvation, and the sword of the

a Other ancient authorities read your
b Or In all circumstances

---

7 μετ' εὐνοίας δουλεύοντες ὡς τῷ κυρίῳ
with goodwill serving as slaves as to the Lord

καὶ οὐκ ἀνθρώποις, 8 εἰδότες ὅτι ἕκαστος
and not to men, knowing that each man

ἐάν τι ποιήσῃ ἀγαθόν, τοῦτο κομίσεται
whatever ³he does ¹good thing, this he will get

παρὰ κυρίου, εἴτε δοῦλος εἴτε ἐλεύθερος.
from [the] Lord, whether a slave or a freeman.

9 Καὶ οἱ κύριοι, τὰ αὐτὰ ποιεῖτε πρὸς
And the lords, the same things do ye toward

αὐτούς, ἀνιέντες τὴν ἀπειλήν, εἰδότες ὅτι
them, forbearing *the* threatening, knowing that

καὶ αὐτῶν καὶ ὑμῶν ὁ κύριός ἐστιν
both of them and of you the Lord is

ἐν οὐρανοῖς, καὶ προσωπολημψία οὐκ
in heavens, and respect of persons not

ἔστιν παρ' αὐτῷ.
is with him.

10 Τοῦ λοιποῦ, ἐνδυναμοῦσθε ἐν κυρίῳ
For the rest,† be ye empowered in [the] Lord

καὶ ἐν τῷ κράτει τῆς ἰσχύος αὐτοῦ.
and in the might of the strength of him.

11 ἐνδύσασθε τὴν πανοπλίαν τοῦ θεοῦ
Put ye on the whole armour – of God

πρὸς τὸ δύνασθαι ὑμᾶς στῆναι πρὸς
for the to be able you[b] to stand against
=so that ye are able . . .

τὰς μεθοδείας τοῦ διαβόλου· 12 ὅτι οὐκ
the craftinesses of the devil; because not

ἔστιν ἡμῖν ἡ πάλη πρὸς αἷμα καὶ σάρκα,
is to us the conflict[c] against blood and flesh,
=our conflict is not

ἀλλὰ πρὸς τὰς ἀρχάς, πρὸς τὰς ἐξουσίας,
but against the rulers, against the authorities,

πρὸς τοὺς κοσμοκράτορας τοῦ σκότους
against the world rulers – darkness

τούτου, πρὸς τὰ πνευματικὰ τῆς πονηρίας
of this, against the spiritual [hosts] – of evil

ἐν τοῖς ἐπουρανίοις. 13 διὰ τοῦτο
in the heavenlies. Therefore

ἀναλάβετε τὴν πανοπλίαν τοῦ θεοῦ, ἵνα
take ye up the whole armour – of God, in order that

δυνηθῆτε ἀντιστῆναι ἐν τῇ ἡμέρᾳ τῇ
ye may be able to resist in the day the

πονηρᾷ καὶ ἅπαντα κατεργασάμενοι στῆναι.
evil and all things having wrought to stand.

14 στῆτε οὖν περιζωσάμενοι τὴν ὀσφὺν
Stand ye therefore girding round the loin[s]

ὑμῶν ἐν ἀληθείᾳ, καὶ ἐνδυσάμενοι τὸν
of you with truth, and putting on the

θώρακα τῆς δικαιοσύνης, 15 καὶ ὑπο-
breastplate – of righteousness, and shoe-

δησάμενοι τοὺς πόδας ἐν ἑτοιμασίᾳ τοῦ
ing the feet with readiness of the

εὐαγγελίου τῆς εἰρήνης, 16 ἐν πᾶσιν
gospel – of peace, in all

ἀναλαβόντες τὸν θυρεὸν τῆς πίστεως, ἐν
taking up the shield – of faith, by

ᾧ δυνήσεσθε πάντα τὰ βέλη τοῦ πονηροῦ
which ye will be able ²all ³the ⁴darts ⁵of the ⁶evil one

τὰ πεπυρωμένα σβέσαι· 17 καὶ τὴν
– ¹having been equipped ¹to quench; and the
with fire

περικεφαλαίαν τοῦ σωτηρίου δέξασθε, καὶ
helmet – of salvation take ye, and

---

your heart. 7 Serve wholeheartedly, as if you were serving the Lord, not men, 8 because you know that the Lord will reward everyone for whatever good he does, whether he is slave or free.

9 And masters, treat your slaves in the same way. Do not threaten them, since you know that he who is both their Master and yours is in heaven, and there is no favoritism with him.

The Armor of God

10 Finally, be strong in the Lord and in his mighty power. 11 Put on the full armor of God so that you can take your stand against the devil's schemes. 12 For our struggle is not against flesh and blood, but against the rulers, against the authorities, against the powers of this dark world and against the spiritual forces of evil in the heavenly realms. 13 Therefore put on the full armor of God, so that when the day of evil comes, you may be able to stand your ground, and after you have done everything, to stand. 14 Stand firm then, with the belt of truth buckled around your waist, with the breastplate of righteousness in place, 15 and with your feet fitted with the readiness that comes from the gospel of peace. 16 In addition to all this, take up the shield of faith, with which you can extinguish all the flaming arrows of the evil one. 17 Take the helmet of salvation and the sword

Spirit, which is the word of God.
18 Pray in the Spirit at all times in every prayer and supplication. To that end keep alert and always persevere in supplication for all the saints. 19 Pray also for me, so that when I speak, a message may be given to me to make known with boldness the mystery of the gospel, *c* 20 for which I am an ambassador in chains. Pray that I may declare it boldly, as I must speak.

Personal Matters and Benediction

21 So that you also may know how I am and what I am doing. Tychicus will tell you everything. He is a dear brother and a faithful minister in the Lord. 22 I am sending him to you for this very purpose, to let you know how we are, and to encourage your hearts.
23 Peace be to the whole community, *d* and love with faith, from God the Father and the Lord Jesus Christ. 24 Grace be with all who have an undying love for our Lord Jesus Christ. *e*

τὴν μάχαιραν τοῦ πνεύματος, ὅ ἐστιν
the   sword   of the Spirit,   which* is
ῥῆμα θεοῦ, 18 διὰ πάσης προσευχῆς καὶ
[the] word of God, by means of all prayer   and
δεήσεως, προσευχόμενοι ἐν παντὶ καιρῷ
petition,   praying   at every   time
ἐν πνεύματι, καὶ εἰς αὐτὸ ἀγρυπνοῦντες
in spirit,   and *to *it   ¹watching
ἐν πάσῃ προσκαρτερήσει καὶ δεήσει περὶ
in all   perseverance   and petition concerning
πάντων τῶν ἁγίων, 19 καὶ ὑπὲρ ἐμοῦ,
all   the   saints,   and on behalf of me,
ἵνα μοι δοθῇ λόγος ἐν ἀνοίξει τοῦ
in order to me may be given speech in opening of the
that
στόματός μου, ἐν παρρησίᾳ γνωρίσαι τὸ
mouth   of me, in   boldness to make known the
μυστήριον τοῦ εὐαγγελίου, 20 ὑπὲρ οὗ
mystery   of the gospel,   on behalf of which
πρεσβεύω ἐν ἁλύσει, ἵνα ἐν αὐτῷ παρ-
I am an   in a chain, in order in it   I may
ambassador   that
ρησιάσωμαι ὡς δεῖ με λαλῆσαι.
speak boldly as it behoves me to speak.
21 "Ἵνα δὲ εἰδῆτε καὶ ὑμεῖς τὰ κατ'
Now in order that *may know *also ¹ye the things about
ἐμέ, τί πράσσω, πάντα γνωρίσει ὑμῖν
me, what I am doing, all things ¹⁰will make ¹¹to you
known
Τύχικος ὁ ἀγαπητὸς ἀδελφὸς καὶ πιστὸς
¹Tychicus *the *beloved *brother *and *faithful
διάκονος ἐν κυρίῳ, 22 ὃν ἔπεμψα πρὸς
⁷minister *in *[the] Lord, whom I sent   to
ὑμᾶς εἰς αὐτὸ τοῦτο, ἵνα γνῶτε τὰ
you for this very thing, in order ye may the
that   know things
περὶ ἡμῶν καὶ παρακαλέσῃ τὰς καρδίας
concerning us and may comfort   the   hearts
ὑμῶν.
of you.
23 Εἰρήνη τοῖς ἀδελφοῖς καὶ ἀγάπη
Peace   to the   brothers   and   love
μετὰ πίστεως ἀπὸ θεοῦ πατρὸς καὶ
with   faith   from God [the] Father and
κυρίου Ἰησοῦ Χριστοῦ. 24 ἡ χάρις μετὰ
[the] Lord Jesus Christ.   - Grace [be] with
πάντων τῶν ἀγαπώντων τὸν κύριον ἡμῶν
all   the [ones] loving   the   Lord   of us
Ἰησοῦν Χριστὸν ἐν ἀφθαρσίᾳ.
Jesus   Christ   in incorruptibility.

of the Spirit, which is the word of God. 18 And pray in the Spirit on all occasions with all kinds of prayers and requests. With this in mind, be alert and always keep on praying for all the saints.
19 Pray also for me, that whenever I open my mouth, words may be given me so that I will fearlessly make known the mystery of the gospel, 20 for which I am an ambassador in chains. Pray that I may declare it fearlessly, as I should.

Final Greetings

21 Tychicus, the dear brother and faithful servant in the Lord, will tell you everything, so that you also may know how I am and what I am doing. 22 I am sending him to you for this very purpose, that you may know how we are, and that he may encourage you.
23 Peace to the brothers, and love with faith from God the Father and the Lord Jesus Christ. 24 Grace to all who love our Lord Jesus Christ with an undying love.

The Letter of Paul to the
Philippians
Chapter 1
Salutation

PAUL and Timothy, servants *a* of Christ Jesus,
To all the saints in Christ Jesus who are in Philippi,

c Other ancient authorities lack *of the gospel*
d Gk *to the brothers*
e Other ancient authorities add *Amen*
a Gk *slaves*

ΠΡΟΣ ΦΙΛΙΠΠΗΣΙΟΥΣ
To Philippians

1 Παῦλος καὶ Τιμόθεος δοῦλοι Χριστοῦ
Paul and Timothy   slaves of Christ
Ἰησοῦ πᾶσιν τοῖς ἁγίοις ἐν Χριστῷ
Jesus to all the   saints in   Christ
Ἰησοῦ τοῖς οὖσιν ἐν Φιλίπποις σὺν
Jesus   -   being in Philippi   with

* Neuter, agreeing with πνεῦμα, not feminine to agree with μάχαιρα.

Philippians
Chapter 1

PAUL and Timothy, servants of Christ Jesus,

To all the saints in Christ Jesus at Philippi, together

with the bishops[b] and deacons:[c]

2 Grace to you and peace from God our Father and the Lord Jesus Christ.

Paul's Prayer for the Philippians

3 I thank my God every time I remember you, [4] constantly praying with joy in every one of my prayers for all of you, [5] because of your sharing in the gospel from the first day until now. [6] I am confident of this, that the one who began a good work among you will bring it to completion by the day of Jesus Christ. [7] It is right for me to think this way about all of you, because you hold me in your heart,[d] for all of you share in God's grace[e] with me, both in my imprisonment and in the defense and confirmation of the gospel. [8] For God is my witness, how I long for all of you with the compassion of Christ Jesus. [9] And this is my prayer, that your love may overflow more and more with knowledge and full insight [10] to help you to determine what is best, so that in the day of Christ you may be pure and blameless, [11] having produced the harvest of righteousness that comes through Jesus Christ for the glory and praise of God.

Paul's Present Circumstances

12 I want you to know, beloved[f] that what has happened to me has actually helped to spread the gospel, [13] so that it has become known throughout the

---

ἐπισκόποις καὶ διακόνοις· 2 χάρις ὑμῖν
bishops and ministers: Grace to you

καὶ εἰρήνη ἀπὸ θεοῦ πατρὸς ἡμῶν καὶ
and peace from God Father of us and

κυρίου Ἰησοῦ Χριστοῦ.
[the] Lord Jesus Christ.

3 Εὐχαριστῶ τῷ θεῷ μου ἐπὶ πάσῃ
I thank the God of me at all

τῇ μνείᾳ ὑμῶν, 4 πάντοτε ἐν πάσῃ
the remembrance of you, always in every

δεήσει μου ὑπὲρ πάντων ὑμῶν μετὰ
petition of me on behalf of all you with

χαρᾶς τὴν δέησιν ποιούμενος, 5 ἐπὶ τῇ
joy the petition making, over the

κοινωνίᾳ ὑμῶν εἰς τὸ εὐαγγέλιον ἀπὸ
fellowship of you in the gospel from

τῆς πρώτης ἡμέρας ἄχρι τοῦ νῦν,
the first day until *the* now,

6 πεποιθὼς αὐτὸ τοῦτο, ὅτι ὁ ἐναρξάμενος
being confident this very thing, that the having begun
[of] [one]

ἐν ὑμῖν ἔργον ἀγαθὸν ἐπιτελέσει ἄχρι
in you work a good will complete [it] until

ἡμέρας Χριστοῦ Ἰησοῦ· 7 καθώς ἐστιν
[the] day of Christ Jesus; as it is

δίκαιον ἐμοὶ τοῦτο φρονεῖν ὑπὲρ πάντων
right for me this to think *on behalf of* all

ὑμῶν, διὰ τὸ ἔχειν με ἐν τῇ καρδίᾳ
you, because of the to have me[b] in the heart
=because I have you in the(my) heart,

ὑμᾶς, ἔν τε τοῖς δεσμοῖς μου καὶ ἐν
you, both in the bonds of me and in

τῇ ἀπολογίᾳ καὶ βεβαιώσει τοῦ εὐαγγελίου
the defence and confirmation of the gospel

συγκοινωνούς μου τῆς χάριτος πάντας
[4]partakers [2]of me [3]of the [5]grace [1]all

ὑμᾶς ὄντας. 8 μάρτυς γάρ μου ὁ θεός,
[1]you [2]being. [4]witness [1]For [5]of me - [3]God
[3][is],

ὡς ἐπιποθῶ πάντας ὑμᾶς ἐν σπλάγχνοις
how I long after all you in [the] bowels

Χριστοῦ Ἰησοῦ. 9 Καὶ τοῦτο προσεύχομαι,
of Christ Jesus. And this I pray,

ἵνα ἡ ἀγάπη ὑμῶν ἔτι μᾶλλον καὶ
in order the love of you yet more and
that

μᾶλλον περισσεύῃ ἐν ἐπιγνώσει καὶ πάσῃ
more may abound in full knowledge and all

αἰσθήσει, 10 εἰς τὸ δοκιμάζειν ὑμᾶς τὰ
perception, for the to prove you[b] the
=that ye may prove things

διαφέροντα, ἵνα ἦτε εἰλικρινεῖς καὶ
differing, in order ye may sincere and
that be

ἀπρόσκοποι εἰς ἡμέραν Χριστοῦ, 11 πεπληρω-
unoffending in [the] day of Christ, having been

μένοι καρπὸν δικαιοσύνης τὸν διὰ Ἰησοῦ
filled [with] [the] fruit of righteousness - through Jesus

Χριστοῦ, εἰς δόξαν καὶ ἔπαινον θεοῦ.
Christ, to [the] glory and praise of God.

12 Γινώσκειν δὲ ὑμᾶς βούλομαι, ἀδελφοί,
Now [2]to know [1]you [1]I wish, brothers,

ὅτι τὰ κατ’ ἐμὲ μᾶλλον εἰς προκοπὴν
that the about me[*] [1]rather [3]to [4][the] advance
things
= my affairs

τοῦ εὐαγγελίου ἐλήλυθεν, 13 ὥστε τοὺς
[5]of the [6]gospel [1]has(ve) come, so as the

---

with the overseers[a] and deacons:

[2]Grace and peace to you from God our Father and the Lord Jesus Christ.

Thanksgiving and Prayer

[3]I thank my God every time I remember you. [4]In all my prayers for all of you, I always pray with joy [5]because of your partnership in the gospel from the first day until now, [6]being confident of this, that he who began a good work in you will carry it on to completion until the day of Christ Jesus.

[7]It is right for me to feel this way about all of you, since I have you in my heart; for whether I am in chains or defending and confirming the gospel, all of you share in God's grace with me. [8]God can testify how I long for all of you with the affection of Christ Jesus.

[9]And this is my prayer: that your love may abound more and more in knowledge and depth of insight, [10]so that you may be able to discern what is best and may be pure and blameless until the day of Christ, [11]filled with the fruit of righteousness that comes through Jesus Christ—to the glory and praise of God.

Paul's Chains Advance the Gospel

[12]Now I want you to know, brothers, that what has happened to me has really served to advance the gospel. [13]As a result, it has

---

[b] Or *overseers*
[c] Or *overseers and helpers*
[d] Or *because I hold you in my heart*
[e] Gk *in grace*
[f] Gk *brothers*

[*] *Cf.* ver. 27; ch. 2. 19, 20, 23; Eph. 6. 21, 22; Col. 4. 7, 8.

[a] *1* Traditionally *bishops*

whole imperial guard ^g and to everyone else that my imprisonment is for Christ; ¹⁴and most of the brothers and sisters, ^f having been made confident in the Lord by my imprisonment, dare to speak the word ^h with greater boldness and without fear.

¹⁵ Some proclaim Christ from envy and rivalry, but others from goodwill. ¹⁶These proclaim Christ out of love, knowing that I have been put here for the defense of the gospel; ¹⁷the others proclaim Christ out of selfish ambition, not sincerely but intending to increase my suffering in my imprisonment. ¹⁸What does it matter? Just this, that Christ is proclaimed in every way, whether out of false motives or true; and in that I rejoice.

Yes, and I will continue to rejoice, ¹⁹for I know that through your prayers and the help of the Spirit of Jesus Christ this will turn out for my deliverance. ²⁰It is my eager expectation and hope that I will not be put to shame in any way, but that by my speaking with all boldness, Christ will be exalted now as always in my body, whether by life or by death. ²¹For to me, living is Christ and dying is gain. ²²If I am to live in the flesh, that means fruitful labor for me; and I do not know which I prefer. ²³I am hard pressed between the two: my desire is to depart and be with Christ, for that is far better; ²⁴but to remain in the flesh is more necessary for you. ²⁵Since I am convinced of this, I know that I will re-

δεσμούς μου φανερούς ἐν Χριστῷ γενέσθαι
bonds of me ²manifest ³in ⁴Christ ¹to become

ἐν ὅλῳ τῷ πραιτωρίῳ καὶ τοῖς λοιποῖς
in all the prætorium and to ²the ³rest

πᾶσιν, 14 καὶ τοὺς πλείονας τῶν ἀδελφῶν
¹all, and the majority of the brothers

ἐν κυρίῳ πεποιθότας τοῖς δεσμοῖς μου
in [the] Lord being confident in the bonds of me

περισσοτέρως τολμᾶν ἀφόβως τὸν λόγον
²more exceedingly ¹to dare ²fearlessly ²the ¹word

τοῦ θεοῦ λαλεῖν. 15 τινὲς μὲν καὶ διὰ
- ²of God ⁴to speak. Some indeed even because

φθόνον καὶ ἔριν, τινὲς δὲ καὶ δι' εὐδοκίαν
envy and strife, but some also because good-
                                        of will

τὸν Χριστὸν κηρύσσουσιν· 16 οἱ μὲν ἐξ
- Christ proclaim; these† from

ἀγάπης, εἰδότες ὅτι εἰς ἀπολογίαν τοῦ
love, knowing that for defence of the

εὐαγγελίου κεῖμαι, 17 οἱ δὲ ἐξ ἐριθείας
gospel I am set, those† from rivalry

τὸν Χριστὸν καταγγέλλουσιν, οὐχ ἁγνῶς,
- ²Christ ¹announce, not purely,

οἰόμενοι θλῖψιν ἐγείρειν τοῖς δεσμοῖς μου.
thinking ²affliction ¹to raise to the bonds of me.

18 Τί γάρ; πλὴν ὅτι παντὶ τρόπῳ,
What then? nevertheless that in every way,

εἴτε προφάσει εἴτε ἀληθείᾳ, Χριστὸς
whether in pretence or in truth, Christ

καταγγέλλεται, καὶ ἐν τούτῳ χαίρω· ἀλλὰ
is announced, and in this I rejoice; yet

καὶ χαρήσομαι· 19 οἶδα γὰρ ὅτι τοῦτό
also I will rejoice; for I know that this

μοι ἀποβήσεται εἰς σωτηρίαν διὰ τῆς
to me will result in salvation through the

ὑμῶν δεήσεως καὶ ἐπιχορηγίας τοῦ
²of you ¹petition and supply of the

πνεύματος Ἰησοῦ Χριστοῦ, 20 κατὰ τὴν
spirit of Jesus Christ, according to the

ἀποκαραδοκίαν καὶ ἐλπίδα μου ὅτι ἐν
eager expectation and hope of me that in

οὐδενὶ αἰσχυνθήσομαι, ἀλλ' ἐν πάσῃ παρ-
nothing I shall be shamed, but with all bold-

ρησίᾳ ὡς πάντοτε καὶ νῦν μεγαλυνθήσεται
ness as always also now shall be magnified

Χριστὸς ἐν τῷ σώματί μου, εἴτε διὰ
Christ in the body of me, whether through

ζωῆς εἴτε διὰ θανάτου. 21 ἐμοὶ γὰρ
life or through death. For to me

τὸ ζῆν Χριστὸς καὶ τὸ ἀποθανεῖν κέρδος.
- to live [is] Christ and - to die [is] gain.

22 εἰ δὲ τὸ ζῆν ἐν σαρκί, τοῦτό μοι
But if - to live in [the] flesh, this to me

καρπὸς ἔργου, καὶ τί αἱρήσομαι οὐ
[is] fruit of [?my] work, and what I shall choose not

γνωρίζω. 23 συνέχομαι δὲ ἐκ τῶν δύο,
I perceive. But I am constrained by the two,

τὴν ἐπιθυμίαν ἔχων εἰς τὸ ἀναλῦσαι καὶ
²the ²desire ¹having for the to depart and

σὺν Χριστῷ εἶναι, πολλῷ γὰρ μᾶλλον
²with ²Christ ¹to be, for by much [this is] rather

κρεῖσσον· 24 τὸ δὲ ἐπιμένειν τῇ σαρκὶ
better; - but to remain in the flesh [is]

ἀναγκαιότερον δι' ὑμᾶς. 25 καὶ τοῦτο
more necessary on account of you. And this

become clear throughout the whole palace guard ^b and to everyone else that I am in chains for Christ. ¹⁴Because of my chains, most of the brothers in the Lord have been encouraged to speak the word of God more courageously and fearlessly.

¹⁵It is true that some preach Christ out of envy and rivalry, but others out of goodwill. ¹⁶The latter do so in love, knowing that I am put here for the defense of the gospel. ¹⁷The former preach Christ out of selfish ambition, not sincerely, supposing that they can stir up trouble for me while I am in chains. ^c ¹⁸But what does it matter? The important thing is that in every way, whether from false motives or true, Christ is preached. And because of this I rejoice.

Yes, and I will continue to rejoice, ¹⁹for I know that through your prayers and the help given by the Spirit of Jesus Christ, what has happened to me will turn out for my deliverance. ^d ²⁰I eagerly expect and hope that I will in no way be ashamed, but will have sufficient courage so that now as always Christ will be exalted in my body, whether by life or by death. ²¹For to me, to live is Christ and to die is gain. ²²If I am to go on living in the body, this will mean fruitful labor for me. Yet what shall I choose? I do not know! ²³I am torn between the two: I desire to depart and be with Christ, which is better by far; ²⁴but it is more necessary for you that I remain in the body. ²⁵Convinced of this, I know

^g Gk whole praetorium
^h Other ancient authorities read word of God

^b13 Or whole palace
^c16,17 Some late manuscripts have verses 16 and 17 in reverse order.
^d19 Or salvation

main and continue with all of you for your progress and joy in faith, 26 so that I may share abundantly in your boasting in Christ Jesus when I come to you again.

27 Only, live your life in a manner worthy of the gospel of Christ, so that, whether I come and see you or am absent and hear about you, I will know that you are standing firm in one spirit, striving side by side with one mind for the faith of the gospel, 28 and are in no way intimidated by your opponents. For them this is evidence of their destruction, but of your salvation. And this is God's doing. 29 For he has graciously granted you the privilege not only of believing in Christ, but of suffering for him as well— 30 since you are having the same struggle that you saw I had and now hear that I still have.

Chapter 2

Imitating Christ's Humility

IF then there is any encouragement in Christ, any consolation from love, any sharing in the Spirit, any compassion and sympathy, 2 make my joy complete: be of the same mind, having the same love, being in full accord and of one mind. 3 Do nothing from selfish ambition or conceit, but in humility regard others as better than yourselves. 4 Let each of you look not to your own interests, but to the interests of others. 5 Let the same mind

---

πεποιθὼς οἶδα, ὅτι μενῶ καὶ παραμενῶ
being I know, that I shall and continue
confident remain

πᾶσιν ὑμῖν εἰς τὴν ὑμῶν προκοπὴν καὶ
with all you for the ²of you ¹advance ²and

χαρὰν τῆς πίστεως, 26 ἵνα τὸ καύχημα
²joy ⁴of the ³faith, in order the boast
that

ὑμῶν περισσεύῃ ἐν Χριστῷ Ἰησοῦ ἐν
of you may abound in Christ Jesus in

ἐμοὶ διὰ τῆς ἐμῆς παρουσίας πάλιν
me through – my presence again

πρὸς ὑμᾶς.
with you.

27 Μόνον ἀξίως τοῦ εὐαγγελίου τοῦ
Only ²worthily ³of the ⁴gospel –

Χριστοῦ πολιτεύεσθε, ἵνα εἴτε ἐλθὼν καὶ
⁵of Christ ¹conduct in order whether coming and
yourselves, that

ἰδὼν ὑμᾶς εἴτε ἀπὼν ἀκούω τὰ περὶ
seeing you or being I hear the con-
absent things cerning

ὑμῶν, ὅτι στήκετε ἐν ἑνὶ πνεύματι,
you, that ye stand in one spirit,

μιᾷ ψυχῇ συναθλοῦντες τῇ πίστει τοῦ
with one soul striving together in the faith of the

εὐαγγελίου, 28 καὶ μὴ πτυρόμενοι ἐν
gospel, and not being terrified in

μηδενὶ ὑπὸ τῶν ἀντικειμένων, ἥτις ἐστὶν
no(any) by the [ones] opposing, which is
thing

αὐτοῖς ἔνδειξις ἀπωλείας, ὑμῶν δὲ
to them a proof of destruction, but of you

σωτηρίας, καὶ τοῦτο ἀπὸ θεοῦ· 29 ὅτι
of salvation, and this from God; because

ὑμῖν ἐχαρίσθη τὸ ὑπὲρ Χριστοῦ, οὐ
to you it was given – on behalf of Christ, not

μόνον τὸ εἰς αὐτὸν πιστεύειν ἀλλὰ καὶ
only – in him to believe but also

τὸ ὑπὲρ αὐτοῦ πάσχειν, 30 τὸν αὐτὸν
– on behalf of him to suffer, the same

ἀγῶνα ἔχοντες οἷον εἴδετε ἐν ἐμοὶ
struggle having which ye saw in me

καὶ νῦν ἀκούετε ἐν ἐμοί. 2 Εἴ τις
and now hear in me. ¹If [there ²any
is]

οὖν παράκλησις ἐν Χριστῷ, εἴ τι
¹therefore comfort in Christ, if any

παραμύθιον ἀγάπης, εἴ τις κοινωνία
consolation of love, if any fellowship

πνεύματος, εἴ τις σπλάγχνα καὶ οἰκτιρμοί,
of spirit, if any compassions and pities,

2 πληρώσατέ μου τὴν χαρὰν ἵνα τὸ
fulfil ye of me the joy in order that the

αὐτὸ φρονῆτε, τὴν αὐτὴν ἀγάπην ἔχοντες,
same thing ye think, the same love having,

σύμψυχοι, τὸ ἓν φρονοῦντες, 3 μηδὲν κατ'
one in soul, the one thinking, [doing] by
thing nothing way of

ἐριθείαν μηδὲ κατὰ κενοδοξίαν, ἀλλὰ τῇ
rivalry nor by way of vainglory, but –

ταπεινοφροσύνῃ ἀλλήλους ἡγούμενοι ὑπερ-
in humility ²one another ¹deeming sur-

ἔχοντας ἑαυτῶν, 4 μὴ τὰ ἑαυτῶν ἕκαστοι
passing themselves, not ³the ⁴of them- ¹each ones
things selves

σκοποῦντες, ἀλλὰ καὶ τὰ ἑτέρων ἕκαστοι.
¹looking at, but ²also ³the ⁴of ¹each ones.
things others

---

that I will remain, and I will continue with all of you for your progress and joy in the faith, 26 so that through my being with you again your joy in Christ Jesus will overflow on account of me. 27 Whatever happens, conduct yourselves in a manner worthy of the gospel of Christ. Then, whether I come and see you or only hear about you in my absence, I will know that you stand firm in one spirit, contending as one man for the faith of the gospel 28 without being frightened in any way by those who oppose you. This is a sign to them that they will be destroyed, but that you will be saved—and that by God. 29 For it has been granted to you on behalf of Christ not only to believe on him, but also to suffer for him, 30 since you are going through the same struggle you saw I had, and now hear that I still have.

Chapter 2

Imitating Christ's Humility

IF you have any encouragement from being united with Christ, if any comfort from his love, if any fellowship with the Spirit, if any tenderness and compassion, 2 then make my joy complete by being like-minded, having the same love, being one in spirit and purpose. 3 Do nothing out of selfish ambition or vain conceit, but in humility consider others better than yourselves. 4 Each of you should look not only to your own interests, but also to the interests of others.

be in you that was[i] in Christ Jesus,
6 who, though he was in the form of God, did not regard equality with God as something to be exploited,
7 but emptied himself, taking the form of a slave, being born in human likeness. And being found in human form,
8 he humbled himself and became obedient to the point of death— even death on a cross.
9 Therefore God also highly exalted him and gave him the name that is above every name,
10 so that at the name of Jesus every knee should bend, in heaven and on earth and under the earth,
11 and every tongue should confess that Jesus Christ is Lord, to the glory of God the Father.

Shining as Lights in the World

12 Therefore, my beloved, just as you have always obeyed me, not only in my presence, but much more now in my absence, work out your own salvation with fear and trembling; 13 for it is God who is at work in you, enabling you both to will and to work for his good pleasure.
14 Do all things without murmuring and arguing, 15 so that you may be blameless and innocent, children of God without blemish in the midst of a crooked and perverse generation, in which you shine like stars in the world. 16 It is by your holding fast to the word of life that I can boast on the day of Christ that I did not run in vain or labor in vain. 17 But even if I am being poured out as a libation over the sacrifice and the offering of your faith, I am glad and rejoice

5 τοῦτο φρονεῖτε ἐν ὑμῖν ὃ καὶ ἐν
This think ye among you which also [was] in
Χριστῷ Ἰησοῦ, 6 ὃς ἐν μορφῇ θεοῦ
Christ Jesus, who in [the] form of God
ὑπάρχων οὐχ ἁρπαγμὸν ἡγήσατο τὸ εἶναι
subsisting ¹not ²robbery ¹deemed [it] the to be
ἴσα θεῷ, 7 ἀλλὰ ἑαυτὸν ἐκένωσεν μορφὴν
equal with God, but himself emptied ²[the] form ¹things
δούλου λαβών, ἐν ὁμοιώματι ἀνθρώπων
²of a slave ¹taking, ²in ²likeness ⁴of men
γενόμενος· καὶ σχήματι εὑρεθεὶς ὡς
¹becoming; and ²in fashion ¹being found as
ἄνθρωπος 8 ἐταπείνωσεν ἑαυτὸν γενόμενος
a man he humbled himself becoming
ὑπήκοος μέχρι θανάτου, θανάτου δὲ σταυροῦ.
obedient until death, and death of a cross.
9 διὸ καὶ ὁ θεὸς αὐτὸν ὑπερύψωσεν
Wherefore also - God ²him ¹highly exalted
καὶ ἐχαρίσατο αὐτῷ τὸ ὄνομα τὸ ὑπὲρ
and gave to him the name - above
πᾶν ὄνομα, 10 ἵνα ἐν τῷ ὀνόματι Ἰησοῦ
every name, in order in the name of Jesus that
πᾶν γόνυ κάμψῃ ἐπουρανίων καὶ ἐπιγείων
every knee should of heavenly and earthly bend [beings] [beings]
καὶ καταχθονίων, 11 καὶ πᾶσα γλῶσσα
and [beings] under the earth, and every tongue
ἐξομολογήσηται ὅτι κυρίος Ἰησοῦς
should acknowledge that ²Lord ¹Jesus
Χριστὸς εἰς δόξαν θεοῦ πατρός.
²Christ [is] to [the] glory of God [the] Father.
12 Ὥστε, ἀγαπητοί μου, καθὼς πάντοτε
So as, beloved of me, as always
ὑπηκούσατε, μὴ ὡς ἐν τῇ παρουσίᾳ
ye obeyed, not as in the presence
μου μόνον ἀλλὰ νῦν πολλῷ μᾶλλον ἐν
of me only but now by more rather in
τῇ ἀπουσίᾳ μου, μετὰ φόβου καὶ τρόμου
the absence of me, with fear and trembling
τὴν ἑαυτῶν σωτηρίαν κατεργάζεσθε· 13 θεὸς
¹the ²of yourselves ²salvation work out; ¹God
γάρ ἐστιν ὁ ἐνεργῶν ἐν ὑμῖν καὶ τὸ
¹for is the [one] operating in you both the
θέλειν καὶ τὸ ἐνεργεῖν ὑπὲρ τῆς εὐδοκίας.
to will and the to operate on behalf of the(his) goodwill.
14 πάντα ποιεῖτε χωρὶς γογγυσμῶν καὶ
All things do ye without murmurings and
διαλογισμῶν, 15 ἵνα γένησθε ἄμεμπτοι καὶ
disputings, in order that ye may be blameless and
ἀκέραιοι, τέκνα θεοῦ ἄμωμα μέσον
harmless, children of God faultless in the midst of
γενεᾶς σκολιᾶς καὶ διεστραμμένης, ἐν
a generation crooked and *having been* perverted, among
οἷς φαίνεσθε ὡς φωστῆρες ἐν κόσμῳ,
whom ye shine as luminaries in [the] world,
16 λόγον ζωῆς ἐπέχοντες, εἰς καύχημα
a word of life holding up, for a boast
ἐμοὶ εἰς ἡμέραν Χριστοῦ, ὅτι οὐκ εἰς
to me[e] in [the] day of Christ, that not in
κενὸν ἔδραμον οὐδὲ εἰς κενὸν ἐκοπίασα.
vain I ran nor in vain laboured.
17 Ἀλλὰ εἰ καὶ σπένδομαι ἐπὶ τῇ θυσίᾳ
But if indeed I am poured out on the sacrifice
καὶ λειτουργίᾳ τῆς πίστεως ὑμῶν, χαίρω
and service of the faith of you, I rejoice

5 Your attitude should be the same as that of Christ Jesus:
6 Who, being in very nature[e] God, did not consider equality with God something to be grasped,
7 but made himself nothing, taking the very nature[f] of a servant, being made in human likeness.
8 And being found in appearance as a man, he humbled himself and became obedient to death— even death on a cross!
9 Therefore God exalted him to the highest place and gave him the name that is above every name,
10 that at the name of Jesus every knee should bow, in heaven and on earth and under the earth,
11 and every tongue confess that Jesus Christ is Lord, to the glory of God the Father.

Shining as Stars

12 Therefore, my dear friends, as you have always obeyed—not only in my presence, but now much more in my absence—continue to work out your salvation with fear and trembling, 13 for it is God who works in you to will and to act according to his good purpose.
14 Do everything without complaining or arguing, 15 so that you may become blameless and pure, children of God without fault in a crooked and depraved generation, in which you shine like stars in the universe 16 as you hold out[g] the word of life—in order that I may boast on the day of Christ that I did not run or labor for nothing. 17 But even if I am being poured out like a drink offering on the sacrifice and service coming from your faith, I

[e]6 Or *in the form of*
[f]7 Or *the form*
[g]16 Or *hold on to*

with all of you— 18 and in the same way you also must be glad and rejoice with me.

Timothy and Epaphroditus

19 I hope in the Lord Jesus to send Timothy to you soon, so that I may be cheered by news of you. 20 I have no one like him who will be genuinely concerned for your welfare. 21 All of them are seeking their own interests, not those of Jesus Christ. 22 But Timothy's*j* worth you know, how like a son with a father he has served with me in the work of the gospel. 23 I hope therefore to send him as soon as I see how things go with me; 24 and I trust in the Lord that I will also come soon.

25 Still, I think it necessary to send to you Epaphroditus—my brother and co-worker and fellow soldier, your messenger*k* and minister to my need; 26 for he has been longing for*l* all of you, and has been distressed because you heard that he was ill. 27 He was indeed so ill that he nearly died. But God had mercy on him, and not only on him but on me also, so that I would not have one sorrow after another. 28 I am the more eager to send him, therefore, in order that you may rejoice at seeing him again, and that I may be less anxious. 29 Welcome him then in the Lord with all joy, and honor such people, 30 because he came close to death for the work of Christ,*m* risking his life to make up for

j Gk *his*
k Gk *apostle*
l Other ancient authorities read *longing to see*
m Other ancient authorities read *of the Lord*

καὶ συγχαίρω πᾶσιν ὑμῖν· 18 τὸ δὲ αὐτὸ
and rejoice with ²all ¹you; and the same
καὶ ὑμεῖς χαίρετε καὶ συγχαίρετέ μοι.
also ye rejoice and rejoice with me.
19 Ἐλπίζω δὲ ἐν κυρίῳ Ἰησοῦ Τιμόθεον
But I hope in [the] Lord Jesus ²Timothy
ταχέως πέμψαι ὑμῖν, ἵνα κἀγὼ εὐψυχῶ
⁴shortly ¹to send ³to you, in order I also may be of
that good cheer
γνοὺς τὰ περὶ ὑμῶν. 20 οὐδένα γὰρ
knowing the con- you. For no one
things cerning
ἔχω ἰσόψυχον, ὅστις γνησίως τὰ περὶ
I have likeminded, who genuinely ²the ³con-
things cerning
ὑμῶν μεριμνήσει· 21 οἱ πάντες γὰρ τὰ
⁴you ¹will care for; the for all ³the
things
ἑαυτῶν ζητοῦσιν, οὐ τὰ Χριστοῦ Ἰησοῦ.
²of them- ¹seek, not the of Christ Jesus.
selves things
22 τὴν δὲ δοκιμὴν αὐτοῦ γινώσκετε, ὅτι
But the character of him ye know, that
ὡς πατρὶ τέκνον σὺν ἐμοὶ ἐδούλευσεν
as ²a father ¹a child²[serves] ⁵with ⁴me ³he served
εἰς τὸ εὐαγγέλιον. 23 τοῦτον μὲν οὖν
in the gospel. This one – therefore
ἐλπίζω πέμψαι ὡς ἂν ἀφίδω τὰ περὶ
I hope to send ²whenever ³I see ⁴the ⁵con-
things cerning
ἐμὲ ἐξαυτῆς· 24 πέποιθα δὲ ἐν κυρίῳ
⁶me ¹immediately; but I trust in [the] Lord
ὅτι καὶ αὐτὸς ταχέως ἐλεύσομαι. 25 Ἀναγ-
that ²also ³[my]self ⁴shortly ¹I will come. ⁸neces-
καῖον δὲ ἡγησάμην Ἐπαφρόδιτον τὸν
sary But ¹I deemed [it] ⁶Epaphroditus ⁷the
ἀδελφὸν καὶ συνεργὸν καὶ συστρατιώτην
⁸brother ⁹and ¹⁰fellow-worker ¹¹and ¹²fellow-soldier
μου, ὑμῶν δὲ ἀπόστολον καὶ λειτουργὸν
¹³of me, ¹⁴and ¹⁵of you ¹⁶apostle ¹⁷and ¹⁸minister
τῆς χρείας μου, πέμψαι πρὸς ὑμᾶς,
¹⁹of the ²⁰need ²¹of me, ⁴to send ⁵to ⁶you,
26 ἐπειδὴ ἐπιποθῶν ἦν πάντας ὑμᾶς, καὶ
since ²longing after ¹he was ⁴all ³you, and
ἀδημονῶν, διότι ἠκούσατε ὅτι ἠσθένησεν.
[was] being because ye heard that he ailed.
troubled,
27 καὶ γὰρ ἠσθένησεν παραπλήσιον θανάτῳ·
For indeed he ailed coming near to death;
ἀλλὰ ὁ θεὸς ἠλέησεν αὐτόν, οὐκ αὐτὸν
but – God had mercy on him, ²not ³him
δὲ μόνον ἀλλὰ καὶ ἐμέ, ἵνα μὴ λύπην
¹and only but also me, lest grief
ἐπὶ λύπην σχῶ. 28 σπουδαιοτέρως οὖν
on grief I should have. More eagerly therefore
ἔπεμψα αὐτόν, ἵνα ἰδόντες αὐτὸν πάλιν
I sent him, in order that seeing him again
χαρῆτε κἀγὼ ἀλυπότερος ὦ. 29 προσδέχεσθε
ye may and ¹I ¹less grieved ²may be. Receive ye
rejoice
οὖν αὐτὸν ἐν κυρίῳ μετὰ πάσης χαρᾶς,
therefore him in [the] Lord with all joy,
καὶ τοὺς τοιούτους ἐντίμους ἔχετε, 30 ὅτι
and – ²such ones ³honoured ¹hold ye, because
διὰ τὸ ἔργον Χριστοῦ μέχρι θανάτου
on ac- the work of Christ ²as far as ³death
count of
ἤγγισεν παραβολευσάμενος τῇ ψυχῇ, ἵνα
¹he drew exposing the(his) life, in or-
near der that

am glad and rejoice with all of you. 18 So you too should be glad and rejoice with me.

Timothy and Epaphroditus

19 I hope in the Lord Jesus to send Timothy to you soon, that I also may be cheered when I receive news about you. 20 I have no one else like him, who takes a genuine interest in your welfare. 21 For everyone looks out for his own interests, not those of Jesus Christ. 22 But you know that Timothy has proved himself, because as a son with his father he has served with me in the work of the gospel. 23 I hope, therefore, to send him as soon as I see how things go with me. 24 And I am confident in the Lord that I myself will come soon.

25 But I think it is necessary to send back to you Epaphroditus, my brother, fellow worker and fellow soldier, who is also your messenger, whom you sent to take care of my needs. 26 For he longs for all of you and is distressed because you heard he was ill. 27 Indeed he was ill, and almost died. But God had mercy on him, and not on him only but also on me, to spare me sorrow upon sorrow. 28 Therefore I am all the more eager to send him, so that when you see him again you may be glad and I may have less anxiety. 29 Welcome him in the Lord with great joy, and honor men like him, 30 because he almost died for the work of

those services that you could not give me.

Chapter 3

FINALLY, my brothers and sisters,[n] rejoice[o] in the Lord.

Breaking with the Past

To write the same things to you is not troublesome to me, and for you it is a safeguard.

2 Beware of the dogs, beware of the evil workers, beware of those who mutilate the flesh![p] 3 For it is we who are the circumcision, who worship in the Spirit of God[q] and boast in Christ Jesus and have no confidence in the flesh— 4 even though I, too, have reason for confidence in the flesh.

If anyone else has reason to be confident in the flesh, I have more: 5 circumcised on the eighth day, a member of the people of Israel, of the tribe of Benjamin, a Hebrew born of Hebrews; as to the law, a Pharisee; 6 as to zeal, a persecutor of the church; as to righteousness under the law, blameless.

7 Yet whatever gains I had, these I have come to regard as loss because of Christ. 8 More than that, I regard everything as loss because of the surpassing value of knowing Christ Jesus my Lord. For his sake I have suffered the loss of all things, and I regard them as rubbish, in order that I may gain Christ 9 and be found in him, not having a righteousness of my own that comes from the law, but one that comes through faith in Christ,[r] the righteousness from God

---

ἀναπληρώσῃ τὸ ὑμῶν ὑστέρημα τῆς πρός
he might fill up ¹the ²of you ³lack – ⁴toward
με λειτουργίας.
⁶me ⁵of service.

3 Τὸ λοιπόν, ἀδελφοί μου, χαίρετε ἐν
For the rest, brothers of me, rejoice ye in
κυρίῳ. τὰ αὐτὰ γράφειν ὑμῖν ἐμοὶ μὲν
[the] Lord. ²The ³same things ¹to write to you for me indeed
οὐκ ὀκνηρόν, ὑμῖν δὲ ἀσφαλές.
[is] not irksome, but for you safe.

2 Βλέπετε τοὺς κύνας, βλέπετε τοὺς
Look [to] the dogs, look [to] the
κακοὺς ἐργάτας, βλέπετε τὴν κατατομήν.*
evil workmen, look [to] the concision.*
3 ἡμεῖς γὰρ ἐσμεν ἡ περιτομή, οἱ
For we are the circumcision, the [ones]
πνεύματι θεοῦ λατρεύοντες καὶ καυχώμενοι
³by [the] Spirit ²of God ¹worshipping and boasting
ἐν Χριστῷ Ἰησοῦ καὶ οὐκ ἐν σαρκὶ
in Christ Jesus and ²not ³in [the] ⁴flesh
πεποιθότες, **4** καίπερ ἐγὼ ἔχων πεποίθησιν
¹trusting, even though I having trust
καὶ ἐν σαρκί. Εἴ τις δοκεῖ ἄλλος
also in [the] flesh. If any ²thinks ¹other man
πεποιθέναι ἐν σαρκί, ἐγὼ μᾶλλον·
to trust in [the] flesh, I more:
5 περιτομῇ ὀκταήμερος, ἐκ γένους Ἰσραήλ,
in circumcision eighth day, of [the] race of Israel,
φυλῆς Βενιαμίν, Ἑβραῖος ἐξ Ἑβραίων,
[the] tribe of Benjamin, a Hebrew of Hebrew [parents],
κατὰ νόμον Φαρισαῖος, **6** κατὰ ζῆλος
according [the] law a Pharisee, by way of zeal
to
διώκων τὴν ἐκκλησίαν, κατὰ δικαιοσύνην
persecuting the church, according [the]
to righteousness
τὴν ἐν νόμῳ γενόμενος ἄμεμπτος. **7** ἀλλὰ
– in [the] law being blameless. But
ἅτινα ἦν μοι κέρδη, ταῦτα ἥγημαι διὰ
what were to me gain, these I have ²on ac-
things deemed count of
τὸν Χριστὸν ζημίαν. **8** ἀλλὰ μενοῦν γε
– ¹Christ ¹loss. But nay rather
καὶ ἡγοῦμαι πάντα ζημίαν εἶναι διὰ
²also ¹I deem ³all things ⁵loss ⁴to be on account of
τὸ ὑπερέχον τῆς γνώσεως Χριστοῦ Ἰησοῦ
the excellency of the knowledge of Christ Jesus
τοῦ κυρίου μου, δι’ ὃν τὰ πάντα
the Lord of me, on ac- whom – all things
count of
ἐζημιώθην, καὶ ἡγοῦμαι σκύβαλα ἵνα
I suffered loss, and deem [them] refuse in order
that
Χριστὸν κερδήσω **9** καὶ εὑρεθῶ ἐν αὐτῷ,
Christ I might gain and be found in him,
μὴ ἔχων ἐμὴν δικαιοσύνην τὴν ἐκ νόμου,
not having my righteousness the [one] of law,
ἀλλὰ τὴν διὰ πίστεως Χριστοῦ, τὴν
but the [one] through faith of(in) Christ,* ¹the

Christ, risking his life to make up for the help you could not give me.

Chapter 3

No Confidence in the Flesh

FINALLY, my brothers, rejoice in the Lord! It is no trouble for me to write the same things to you again, and it is a safeguard for you.

2 Watch out for those dogs, those men who do evil, those mutilators of the flesh. 3 For it is we who are the circumcision, we who worship by the Spirit of God, who glory in Christ Jesus, and who put no confidence in the flesh— 4 though I myself have reasons for such confidence.

If anyone else thinks he has reasons to put confidence in the flesh, I have more: 5 circumcised on the eighth day, of the people of Israel, of the tribe of Benjamin, a Hebrew of Hebrews; in regard to the law, a Pharisee; 6 as for zeal, persecuting the church; as for legalistic righteousness, faultless.

7 But whatever was to my profit I now consider loss for the sake of Christ. 8 What is more, I consider everything a loss compared to the surpassing greatness of knowing Christ Jesus my Lord, for whose sake I have lost all things. I consider them rubbish, that I may gain Christ 9 and be found in him, not having a righteousness of my own that comes from the law, but that which is through faith in Christ—the right-

---

[n] Gk my brothers
[o] Or farewell
[p] Gk the mutilation
[q] Other ancient authorities read worship God in spirit
[r] Or through the faith of Christ

* The apostle uses a " studiously contemptuous paronomasia " (Ellicott). He does not use περιτομή, the proper word for " circumcision ", " as this, though now abrogated in Christ, had still its spiritual aspects."

* See Gal. 2. 20.

based on faith. 10 I want to know Christ [s] and the power of his resurrection and the sharing of his sufferings by becoming like him in his death, 11 if somehow I may attain the resurrection from the dead.

Pressing toward the Goal

12 Not that I have already obtained this or have already reached the goal; [t] but I press on to make it my own, because Christ Jesus has made me his own. 13 Beloved, [u] I do not consider that I have made it my own; [v] but this one thing I do: forgetting what lies behind and straining forward to what lies ahead, 14 I press on toward the goal for the prize of the heavenly [w] call of God in Christ Jesus. 15 Let those of us then who are mature be of the same mind; and if you think differently about anything, this too God will reveal to you. 16 Only let us hold fast to what we have attained.

17 Brothers and sisters, [u] join in imitating me, and observe those who live according to the example you have in us. 18 For many live as enemies of the cross of Christ; I have often told you of them, and now I tell you even with tears. 19 Their end is destruction; their god is the belly; and their glory is in their shame; their minds are set on earthly things. 20 But our citizenship [x] is in heaven, and it is from there that we are expecting a Savior, the Lord Jesus Christ. 21 He will transform the body of our humiliation [y] that it may be conformed to the body of his glory, [z] by the

ἐκ θεοῦ δικαιοσύνην ἐπὶ τῇ πίστει,
of ⁴God ³righteousness [based] on – faith,

10 τοῦ γνῶναι αὐτὸν καὶ τὴν δύναμιν
– to know[d] him and the power

τῆς ἀναστάσεως αὐτοῦ καὶ κοινωνίαν
of the resurrection of him and [the] fellowship

παθημάτων αὐτοῦ, συμμορφιζόμενος τῷ
of sufferings of him, being conformed to the

θανάτῳ αὐτοῦ, 11 εἴ πως καταντήσω εἰς
death of him, if [some]how I may attain to to

τὴν ἐξανάστασιν τὴν ἐκ νεκρῶν. 12 Οὐχ
the out-resurrection – from [the] dead. Not

ὅτι ἤδη ἔλαβον ἢ ἤδη τετελείωμαι,
that already I received or already have been perfected,

διώκω δὲ εἰ καὶ καταλάβω, ἐφ' ᾧ
but I follow if indeed I may lay hold, inasmuch as

καὶ κατελήμφθην ὑπὸ Χριστοῦ Ἰησοῦ.
also I was laid hold of by Christ Jesus.

13 ἀδελφοί, ἐγὼ ἐμαυτὸν οὔπω λογίζομαι
Brothers, ²I ⁴myself ¹not yet ³reckon

κατειληφέναι· ἐν δέ, τὰ μὲν ὀπίσω
to have but one thing ²the ²on one ⁴behind
laid hold; [I do], things hand

ἐπιλανθανόμενος τοῖς δὲ ἔμπροσθεν ἐπεκ-
¹forgetting ²the ¹on the ⁴before ²stretching
things other

τεινόμενος, 14 κατὰ σκοπὸν διώκω εἰς
forward to, according to a mark I follow for

τὸ βραβεῖον τῆς ἄνω κλήσεως τοῦ θεοῦ
the prize of the above calling – of God

ἐν Χριστῷ Ἰησοῦ. 15 Ὅσοι οὖν τέλειοι,
in Christ Jesus. ²As many ¹there- [are]
as fore perfect,

τοῦτο φρονῶμεν· καὶ εἴ τι ἑτέρως
²this ¹let us think; and if anything otherwise

φρονεῖτε, καὶ τοῦτο ὁ θεὸς ὑμῖν ἀποκα-
ye think, even this – God to you will

λύψει· 16 πλὴν εἰς ὃ ἐφθάσαμεν, τῷ
reveal; nevertheless to what we arrived, by the

αὐτῷ στοιχεῖν. 17 Συμμιμηταί μου
same to walk. Fellow-imitators of me

γίνεσθε, ἀδελφοί, καὶ σκοπεῖτε τοὺς οὕτω
be ye, brothers, and mark the [ones] thus

περιπατοῦντας καθὼς ἔχετε τύπον ἡμᾶς.
walking as ye have ²an example ¹us.

18 πολλοὶ γὰρ περιπατοῦσιν οὓς πολλάκις
For many walk [of] whom often

ἔλεγον ὑμῖν, νῦν δὲ καὶ κλαίων λέγω,
I said to you, and now also weeping I say,

τοὺς ἐχθροὺς τοῦ σταυροῦ τοῦ Χριστοῦ,
the enemies of the cross – of Christ,

19 ὧν τὸ τέλος ἀπώλεια, ὧν ὁ θεὸς
of whom the end [is] destruction, of whom the god [is]

ἡ κοιλία καὶ ἡ δόξα ἐν τῇ αἰσχύνῃ
the belly and the glory in the shame

αὐτῶν, οἱ τὰ ἐπίγεια φρονοῦντες. 20 ἡμῶν
of them, the the earthly things thinking. of us
[ones]

γὰρ τὸ πολίτευμα ἐν οὐρανοῖς ὑπάρχει,
For the citizenship in heavens is,

ἐξ οὗ καὶ σωτῆρα ἀπεκδεχόμεθα κύριον
from where also ²a Saviour ¹we await Lord

Ἰησοῦν Χριστόν, 21 ὃς μετασχηματίσει τὸ
Jesus Christ, who will change the

σῶμα τῆς ταπεινώσεως ἡμῶν σύμμορφον
body of the humiliation of us [making it]
conformed

τῷ σώματι τῆς δόξης αὐτοῦ, κατὰ τὴν
to the body of the glory of him, according to the

eousness that comes from God and is by faith. 10 I want to know Christ and the power of his resurrection and the fellowship of sharing in his sufferings, becoming like him in his death, 11 and so, somehow, to attain to the resurrection from the dead.

Pressing on Toward the Goal

12 Not that I have already obtained all this, or have already been made perfect, but I press on to take hold of that for which Christ Jesus took hold of me. 13 Brothers, I do not consider myself yet to have taken hold of it. But one thing I do: Forgetting what is behind and straining toward what is ahead, 14 I press on toward the goal to win the prize for which God has called me heavenward in Christ Jesus. 15 All of us who are mature should take such a view of things. And if on some point you think differently, that too God will make clear to you. 16 Only let us live up to what we have already attained.

17 Join with others in following my example, brothers, and take note of those who live according to the pattern we gave you. 18 For, as I have often told you before and now say again even with tears, many live as enemies of the cross of Christ. 19 Their destiny is destruction, their god is their stomach, and their glory is in their shame. Their mind is on earthly things. 20 But our citizenship is in heaven. And we eagerly await a Savior from there, the Lord Jesus Christ, 21 who, by the power that enables him to bring everything under his control, will transform our

[s] Gk *him*
[t] Or *have already been made perfect*
[u] Gk *Brothers*
[v] Other ancient authorities read *my own yet*
[w] Gk *upward*
[x] Or *commonwealth*
[y] Or *our humble bodies*
[z] Or *his glorious body*

power that also enables him to make all things subject to himself. 1 Therefore, my brothers and sisters,[a] whom I love and long for, my joy and crown, stand firm in the Lord in this way, my beloved.

Exhortations

2 I urge Euodia and I urge Syntyche to be of the same mind in the Lord. 3 Yes, and I ask you also, my loyal companion,[b] help these women, for they have struggled beside me in the work of the gospel, together with Clement and the rest of my co-workers, whose names are in the book of life.
4 Rejoice[c] in the Lord always; again I will say, Rejoice.[c] 5 Let your gentleness be known to everyone. The Lord is near. 6 Do not worry about anything, but in everything by prayer and supplication with thanksgiving let your requests be made known to God. 7 And the peace of God, which surpasses all understanding, will guard your hearts and your minds in Christ Jesus.

8 Finally, beloved,[d] whatever is true, whatever is honorable, whatever is just, whatever is pure, whatever is pleasing, whatever is commendable, if there is any excellence and if there is anything worthy of praise, think about[e] these things. 9 Keep on doing the things that you have learned and received and heard and seen in me, and the God of peace will be with you.

Acknowledgment of the Philippians' Gift

10 I rejoice[f] in the Lord greatly that now at last you have revived your concern for me; indeed, you were

---

ἐνέργειαν τοῦ δύνασθαι αὐτὸν καὶ ὑποτάξαι
operation of the to be able him[b] even to subject
=of his ability
αὐτῷ τὰ πάντα. 4 Ὥστε, ἀδελφοί μου
to him[self] - all things. So as, brothers of me
ἀγαπητοὶ καὶ ἐπιπόθητοι, χαρὰ καὶ
beloved and longed for, joy and
στέφανός μου, οὕτως στήκετε ἐν κυρίῳ, ἀγαπητοί.
crown of me, so stand in [the] Lord, beloved.
2 Εὐοδίαν παρακαλῶ καὶ Συντύχην
¹Euodia ¹I beseech and ²Syntyche
παρακαλῶ τὸ αὐτὸ φρονεῖν ἐν κυρίῳ.
¹I beseech the ²same thing ³to think in [the] Lord.
3 ναὶ ἐρωτῶ καὶ σέ, γνήσιε σύζυγε,
Yes[,] I ask also thee, genuine yoke-fellow,
συλλαμβάνου αὐταῖς, αἵτινες ἐν τῷ εὐαγ-
help them, who ³in ⁴the ⁵gos-
γελίῳ συνήθλησάν μοι μετὰ καὶ Κλήμεντος
pel ¹struggled with ²me with both Clement
καὶ τῶν λοιπῶν συνεργῶν μου, ὧν
and the remaining fellow-workers of me, of whom
τὰ ὀνόματα ἐν βίβλῳ ζωῆς. 4 Χαίρετε
the names [are] in [the] book of life. Rejoice ye
ἐν κυρίῳ πάντοτε· πάλιν ἐρῶ, χαίρετε.
in [the] Lord always; again I will say, rejoice.
5 τὸ ἐπιεικὲς ὑμῶν γνωσθήτω πᾶσιν
The forbearance of you let it be known to all
ἀνθρώποις. ὁ κύριος ἐγγύς. 6 μηδὲν
men. The Lord [is] near. ²Nothing
μεριμνᾶτε, ἀλλ' ἐν παντὶ τῇ προσευχῇ
¹be ye anxious but in everything - by prayer
about,
καὶ τῇ δεήσει μετὰ εὐχαριστίας τὰ
and - by petition with thanksgivings the
αἰτήματα ὑμῶν γνωριζέσθω πρὸς τὸν
requests of you let be made known to -
θεόν. 7 καὶ ἡ εἰρήνη τοῦ θεοῦ ἡ
God. And the peace - of God -
ὑπερέχουσα πάντα νοῦν φρουρήσει τὰς
surpassing all understanding will guard the
καρδίας ὑμῶν καὶ τὰ νοήματα ὑμῶν
hearts of you and the thoughts of you
ἐν Χριστῷ Ἰησοῦ. 8 Τὸ λοιπόν, ἀδελφοί,
in Christ Jesus. For the rest, brothers,
ὅσα ἐστὶν ἀληθῆ, ὅσα σεμνά, ὅσα δίκαια,
whatever are true, whatever grave, whatever just,
things things things
ὅσα ἁγνά, ὅσα προσφιλῆ, ὅσα εὔφημα,
whatever pure, whatever lovable, ⁰whatever well-spoken
things things things of,
εἴ τις ἀρετὴ καὶ εἴ τις ἔπαινος, 9 ταῦτα
if any virtue and if any praise, these things
λογίζεσθε· ἃ καὶ ἐμάθετε καὶ παρελάβετε
consider ye; which ²both ¹ye ³learned and ye received
things
καὶ ἠκούσατε καὶ εἴδετε ἐν ἐμοί, ταῦτα
and ye heard and ye saw in me, these
πράσσετε· καὶ ὁ θεὸς τῆς εἰρήνης ἔσται
practise; and the God - of peace will be
μεθ' ὑμῶν.
with you.
10 Ἐχάρην δὲ ἐν κυρίῳ μεγάλως ὅτι
Now I rejoiced in [the] Lord greatly that
ἤδη ποτὲ ἀνεθάλετε τὸ ὑπὲρ ἐμοῦ φρονεῖν·
al- at one ye revived the on behalf me to think;
ready time of
=now at length =your thought for me;

---

lowly bodies so that they will be like his glorious body.

Chapter 4

THEREFORE, my brothers, you whom I love and long for, my joy and crown, that is how you should stand firm in the Lord, dear friends!

Exhortations

2 I plead with Euodia and I plead with Syntyche to agree with each other in the Lord. 3 Yes, and I ask you, loyal yokefellow,[h] help these women who have contended at my side in the cause of the gospel, along with Clement and the rest of my fellow workers, whose names are in the book of life.
4 Rejoice in the Lord always. I will say it again: Rejoice! 5 Let your gentleness be evident to all. The Lord is near. 6 Do not be anxious about anything, but in everything, by prayer and petition, with thanksgiving, present your requests to God. 7 And the peace of God, which transcends all understanding, will guard your hearts and your minds in Christ Jesus.

8 Finally, brothers, whatever is true, whatever is noble, whatever is right, whatever is pure, whatever is lovely, whatever is admirable—if anything is excellent or praiseworthy—think about such things. 9 Whatever you have learned or received or heard from me, or seen in me—put it into practice. And the God of peace will be with you.

Thanks for Their Gifts

10 I rejoice greatly in the Lord that at last you have renewed your concern for me. Indeed, you have been

---

[a] Gk *my brothers*
[b] Or *loyal Syzygus*
[c] Or *Farewell*
[d] Gk *brothers*
[e] Gk *take account of*
[f] Gk *I rejoiced*

[h] 3 Or *loyal Syzygus*

concerned for me, but had no opportunity to show it. *g*
11 Not that I am referring to being in need; for I have learned to be content with whatever I have. 12 I know what it is to have little, and I know what it is to have plenty. In any and all circumstances I have learned the secret of being well-fed and of going hungry, of having plenty and of being in need. 13 I can do all things through him who strengthens me. 14 In any case, it was kind of you to share my distress.
15 You Philippians indeed know that in the early days of the gospel, when I left Macedonia, no church shared with me in the matter of giving and receiving, except you alone. 16 For even when I was in Thessalonica, you sent me help for my needs more than once. 17 Not that I seek the gift, but I seek the profit that accumulates to your account. 18 I have been paid in full and have more than enough; I am fully satisfied, now that I have received from Epaphroditus the gifts you sent, a fragrant offering, a sacrifice acceptable and pleasing to God. 19 And my God will fully satisfy every need of yours according to his riches in glory in Christ Jesus. 20 To our God and Father be glory forever and ever. Amen.

Final Greetings and Benediction

21 Greet every saint in Christ Jesus. The friends *h* who are with me greet you. 22 All the saints greet you, especially those of the emperor's household.

ἐφ᾽ ᾧ καὶ ἐφρονεῖτε, ἠκαιρεῖσθε δέ.
as to which indeed ye thought, but ye had no opportunity.
11 οὐχ ὅτι καθ᾽ ὑστέρησιν λέγω· ἐγὼ
Not that ²by way of ³lack ¹I say; ⁴I
γὰρ ἔμαθον ἐν οἷς εἰμι αὐτάρκης εἶναι.
¹for learned in what I am ²self- ¹to be.
conditions sufficient
12 οἶδα καὶ ταπεινοῦσθαι, οἶδα καὶ περισ-
I know both to be humbled, and I know to
σεύειν· ἐν παντὶ καὶ ἐν πᾶσιν μεμύημαι,
abound; in everything and in all things I have been
initiated,
καὶ χορτάζεσθαι καὶ πεινᾶν, καὶ περισ-
both to be filled and to hunger, both to
σεύειν καὶ ὑστερεῖσθαι. 13 πάντα ἰσχύω
abound and to lack. ²All things ¹I can do
ἐν τῷ ἐνδυναμοῦντί με. 14 πλὴν καλῶς
in the [one] empowering me. Nevertheless ¹well
ἐποιήσατε συγκοινωνήσαντές μου τῇ θλίψει.
¹ye did having partnership in ²of me ¹the ²affliction.
15 οἴδατε δὲ καὶ ὑμεῖς, Φιλιππήσιοι, ὅτι
And ²know ¹also ¹ye, Philippians, that
ἐν ἀρχῇ τοῦ εὐαγγελίου, ὅτε ἐξῆλθον
in [the] of the gospel, when I went out
beginning
ἀπὸ Μακεδονίας, οὐδεμία μοι ἐκκλησία
from Macedonia, not one ²me ¹church
ἐκοινώνησεν εἰς λόγον δόσεως καὶ λήμψεως
²shared with in matter of giving and receiving
εἰ μὴ ὑμεῖς μόνοι, 16 ὅτι καὶ ἐν
except ye only, because indeed in
Θεσσαλονίκῃ καὶ ἅπαξ καὶ δὶς εἰς τὴν
Thessalonica both once and twice to the
= to my need
χρείαν μοι ἐπέμψατε. 17 οὐχ ὅτι ἐπιζητῶ
need to me*e* ye sent. Not that I seek
τὸ δόμα, ἀλλὰ ἐπιζητῶ τὸν καρπὸν
the gift, but I seek the fruit
τὸν πλεονάζοντα εἰς λόγον ὑμῶν. 18 ἀπέχω
increasing to account of you. I have
δὲ πάντα καὶ περισσεύω· πεπλήρωμαι
But all things and abound; I have been filled
δεξάμενος παρὰ Ἐπαφροδίτου τὰ παρ᾽
receiving from Epaphroditus the things from
ὑμῶν, ὀσμὴν εὐωδίας, θυσίαν δεκτήν,
you, an odour of sweet smell, a sacrifice acceptable,
εὐάρεστον τῷ θεῷ. 19 ὁ δὲ θεός μου
well-pleasing – to God. And the God of me
πληρώσει πᾶσαν χρείαν ὑμῶν κατὰ τὸ
will fill every need of you according to the
πλοῦτος αὐτοῦ ἐν δόξῃ ἐν Χριστῷ Ἰησοῦ.
riches of him in glory in Christ Jesus.
20 τῷ δὲ θεῷ καὶ πατρὶ ἡμῶν ἡ δόξα
to the Now God and Father of us [be] the glory
εἰς τοὺς αἰῶνας τῶν αἰώνων· ἀμήν.
unto the ages of the ages: Amen.
21 Ἀσπάσασθε πάντα ἅγιον ἐν Χριστῷ
Greet ye every saint in Christ
Ἰησοῦ. ἀσπάζονται ὑμᾶς οἱ σὺν ἐμοὶ
Jesus. ²greet ⁴you ³The ⁵with ⁶me
ἀδελφοί. 22 ἀσπάζονται ὑμᾶς πάντες οἱ
¹brothers. ⁴greet ⁵you ¹All ²the
ἅγιοι, μάλιστα δὲ οἱ ἐκ τῆς Καίσαρος
³saints, but most of all the ones of ¹the ²of Cæsar
οἰκίας.
³household.

---

concerned, but you had no opportunity to show it. 11 I am not saying this because I am in need, for I have learned to be content whatever the circumstances. 12 I know what it is to be in need, and I know what it is to have plenty. I have learned the secret of being content in any and every situation, whether well fed or hungry, whether living in plenty or in want. 13 I can do everything through him who gives me strength.
14 Yet it was good of you to share in my troubles. 15 Moreover, as you Philippians know, in the early days of your acquaintance with the gospel, when I set out from Macedonia, not one church shared with me in the matter of giving and receiving, except you only; 16 for even when I was in Thessalonica, you sent me aid again and again when I was in need. 17 Not that I am looking for a gift, but I am looking for what may be credited to your account. 18 I have received full payment and even more; I am amply supplied, now that I have received from Epaphroditus the gifts you sent. They are a fragrant offering, an acceptable sacrifice, pleasing to God. 19 And my God will meet all your needs according to his glorious riches in Christ Jesus.
20 To our God and Father be glory for ever and ever. Amen.

Final Greetings

21 Greet all the saints in Christ Jesus. The brothers who are with me send greetings. 22 All the saints send you greetings, especially those who belong to Caesar's household.

---

g Gk lacks *to show it*
h Gk *brothers*

23 The grace of the Lord Jesus Christ be with your spirit. [i]

The Letter of Paul to the

Colossians

Chapter 1

Salutation

PAUL, an apostle of Christ Jesus by the will of God, and Timothy our brother,

2 To the saints and faithful brothers and sisters[a] in Christ in Colossae: Grace to you and peace from God our Father.

Paul Thanks God for the Colossians

3 In our prayers for you we always thank God, the Father of our Lord Jesus Christ, 4 for we have heard of your faith in Christ Jesus and of the love that you have for all the saints, 5 because of the hope laid up for you in heaven. You have heard of this hope before in the word of the truth, the gospel 6 that has come to you. Just as it is bearing fruit and growing in the whole world, so it has been bearing fruit among yourselves from the day you heard it and truly comprehended the grace of God. 7 This you learned from Epaphras, our beloved fellow servant.[b] He is a faithful minister of Christ on your[c] behalf, 8 and he has made known to us your love in the Spirit.

9 For this reason, since the day we heard it, we have not ceased praying for

Middle column (interlinear Greek)

23 'Η χάρις τοῦ κυρίου 'Ιησοῦ Χριστοῦ
The grace of the Lord Jesus Christ
μετὰ τοῦ πνεύματος ὑμῶν.
[be] with the spirit of you.

ΠΡΟΣ ΚΟΛΟΣΣΑΕΙΣ
To Colossians

1 Παῦλος ἀπόστολος Χριστοῦ 'Ιησοῦ διὰ
Paul an apostle of Christ Jesus through
θελήματος θεοῦ καὶ Τιμόθεος ὁ ἀδελφὸς
[the] will of God and Timothy the brother
2 τοῖς ἐν Κολοσσαῖς ἁγίοις καὶ πιστοῖς
to the in Colossae saints and faithful
ἀδελφοῖς ἐν Χριστῷ· χάρις ὑμῖν καὶ
brothers in Christ: Grace to you and
εἰρήνη ἀπὸ θεοῦ πατρὸς ἡμῶν.
peace from God Father of us.

3 Εὐχαριστοῦμεν τῷ θεῷ πατρὶ τοῦ
We give thanks to God Father of the
κυρίου ἡμῶν 'Ιησοῦ [Χριστοῦ] πάντοτε
Lord of us Jesus Christ always
περὶ ὑμῶν προσευχόμενοι, 4 ἀκούσαντες
²concerning ³you ¹praying, having heard
τὴν πίστιν ὑμῶν ἐν Χριστῷ 'Ιησοῦ
the faith of you in Christ Jesus
καὶ τὴν ἀγάπην ἣν ἔχετε εἰς πάντας
and the love which ye have toward all
τοὺς ἁγίους 5 διὰ τὴν ἐλπίδα τὴν
the saints because of the hope –
ἀποκειμένην ὑμῖν ἐν τοῖς οὐρανοῖς, ἣν
being laid up for you in the heavens, which
προηκούσατε ἐν τῷ λόγῳ τῆς ἀληθείας
ye previously heard in the word of the truth
τοῦ εὐαγγελίου 6 τοῦ παρόντος εἰς ὑμᾶς,
of the gospel – coming to you,
καθὼς καὶ ἐν παντὶ τῷ κόσμῳ ἐστὶν
as also in all the world it is
καρποφορούμενον καὶ αὐξανόμενον καθὼς
bearing fruit and growing as
καὶ ἐν ὑμῖν, ἀφ' ἧς ἡμέρας ἠκούσατε
also in you, from which day ye heard
= the day on which
καὶ ἐπέγνωτε τὴν χάριν τοῦ θεοῦ ἐν
and fully knew the grace – of God in
ἀληθείᾳ· 7 καθὼς ἐμάθετε ἀπὸ 'Επαφρᾶ
truth; as ye learned from Epaphras
τοῦ ἀγαπητοῦ συνδούλου ἡμῶν, ὅς ἐστιν
the beloved fellow-slave of us, who is
πιστὸς ὑπὲρ ὑμῶν διάκονος τοῦ Χριστοῦ,
¹a faithful ⁴on behalf ⁵you ²minister – ³of Christ,
of
8 ὁ καὶ δηλώσας ἡμῖν τὴν ὑμῶν ἀγάπην
the also having shown to us ¹the ²of you ³love
[one]
ἐν πνεύματι.
in spirit.

9 Διὰ τοῦτο καὶ ἡμεῖς, ἀφ' ἧς ἡμέρας
Therefore also we, from which day
= the day on which
ἠκούσαμεν, οὐ παυόμεθα ὑπὲρ ὑμῶν
we heard, do not cease on behalf of you

23 The grace of the Lord Jesus Christ be with your spirit. Amen. [i]

Colossians

Chapter 1

PAUL, an apostle of Christ Jesus by the will of God, and Timothy our brother,

2 To the holy and faithful[a] brothers in Christ at Colosse:

Grace and peace to you from God our Father.[b]

Thanksgiving and Prayer

3 We always thank God, the Father of our Lord Jesus Christ, when we pray for you, 4 because we have heard of your faith in Christ Jesus and of the love you have for all the saints— 5 the faith and love that spring from the hope that is stored up for you in heaven and that you have already heard about in the word of truth, the gospel 6 that has come to you. All over the world this gospel is bearing fruit and growing, just as it has been doing among you since the day you heard it and understood God's grace in all its truth. 7 You learned it from Epaphras, our dear fellow servant, who is a faithful minister of Christ on our[c] behalf, 8 and who also told us of your love in the Spirit.

9 For this reason, since the day we heard about you, we have not stopped

---

[i] Other ancient authorities add Amen
[a] Gk brothers
[b] Gk slave
[c] Other ancient authorities read our

[i]23 Some manuscripts do not have Amen.
[a]2 Or believing
[b]2 Some manuscripts Father and the Lord Jesus Christ
[c]7 Some manuscripts your

you and asking that you may be filled with the knowledge of God's[d] will in all spiritual wisdom and understanding, 10 so that you may lead lives worthy of the Lord, fully pleasing to him, as you bear fruit in every good work and as you grow in the knowledge of God. 11 May you be made strong with all the strength that comes from his glorious power, and may you be prepared to endure everything with patience, while joyfully 12 giving thanks to the Father, who has enabled[e] you[f] to share in the inheritance of the saints in the light. 13 He has rescued us from the power of darkness and transferred us into the kingdom of his beloved Son, 14 in whom we have redemption, the forgiveness of sins.[g]

The Supremacy of Christ

15 He is the image of the invisible God, the firstborn of all creation; 16 for in[h] him all things in heaven and on earth were created, things visible and invisible, whether thrones or dominions or rulers or powers— all things have been created through him and for him. 17 He himself is before all things, and in[h] him all things hold together. 18 He is the head of the body, the church; he is the beginning, the firstborn from the dead, so that he might come to have first place in everything. 19 For in him all the fullness of God was pleased to dwell, 20 and through him God was pleased to reconcile to himself all things,

Greek	English
προσευχόμενοι καὶ αἰτούμενοι ἵνα πληρω-	praying and asking in order ye may be that
θῆτε τὴν ἐπίγνωσιν τοῦ θελήματος αὐτοῦ	filled the full knowledge of the will of him [with]
ἐν πάσῃ σοφίᾳ καὶ συνέσει πνευματικῇ,	in all wisdom and understanding spiritual,
10 περιπατῆσαι ἀξίως τοῦ κυρίου εἰς	to walk worthily of the Lord to
πᾶσαν ἀρεσκείαν, ἐν παντὶ ἔργῳ ἀγαθῷ	all pleasing, in every work good
καρποφοροῦντες καὶ αὐξανόμενοι τῇ	bearing fruit and growing in the
ἐπιγνώσει τοῦ θεοῦ, 11 ἐν πάσῃ δυνάμει	full knowledge - of God, with all power
δυναμούμενοι κατὰ τὸ κράτος τῆς δόξης	being empowered according to the might of the glory
αὐτοῦ εἰς πᾶσαν ὑπομονὴν καὶ μακρο-	of him to all endurance and long-
θυμίαν, μετὰ χαρᾶς 12 εὐχαριστοῦντες τῷ	suffering, with joy giving thanks to the
πατρὶ τῷ ἱκανώσαντι ὑμᾶς εἰς τὴν μερίδα	Father - having made ²fit ¹you for the part
τοῦ κλήρου τῶν ἁγίων ἐν τῷ φωτί·	of the lot of the saints in the light;
13 ὃς ἐρρύσατο ἡμᾶς ἐκ τῆς ἐξουσίας	who delivered us out of the authority
τοῦ σκότους καὶ μετέστησεν εἰς τὴν	of the darkness and transferred into the
βασιλείαν τοῦ υἱοῦ τῆς ἀγάπης αὐτοῦ,	kingdom of the Son of the love of him,
14 ἐν ᾧ ἔχομεν τὴν ἀπολύτρωσιν, τὴν	in whom we have the redemption, the
ἄφεσιν τῶν ἁμαρτιῶν· 15 ὅς ἐστιν εἰκὼν	forgiveness of the sins; who is an image (our)
τοῦ θεοῦ τοῦ ἀοράτου, πρωτότοκος πάσης	of the God - invisible, firstborn of all
κτίσεως, 16 ὅτι ἐν αὐτῷ ἐκτίσθη τὰ	creation, because in him were created -
πάντα ἐν τοῖς οὐρανοῖς καὶ ἐπὶ τῆς	all things in the heavens and on the
γῆς, τὰ ὁρατὰ καὶ τὰ ἀόρατα, εἴτε	earth, the visible and the invisible, whether
θρόνοι εἴτε κυριότητες εἴτε ἀρχαὶ εἴτε	thrones or lordships or rulers or
ἐξουσίαι· τὰ πάντα δι᾽ αὐτοῦ καὶ εἰς	authorities; - all things through him and for
αὐτὸν ἔκτισται· 17 καὶ αὐτός ἐστιν πρὸ	him have been created; and he is before
πάντων καὶ τὰ πάντα ἐν αὐτῷ συνέστηκεν,	all things and - all things in him consisted,
18 καὶ αὐτός ἐστιν ἡ κεφαλὴ τοῦ σώματος,	and he is the head of the body,
τῆς ἐκκλησίας· ὅς ἐστιν ἀρχή, πρωτότοκος	of the church; who is [the] firstborn beginning,
ἐκ τῶν νεκρῶν, ἵνα γένηται ἐν πᾶσιν	from the dead, in order ⁴may be ²in ³all that things
αὐτὸς πρωτεύων, 19 ὅτι ἐν αὐτῷ εὐδόκησεν	¹he ⁵holding the because in him ⁴was well first place, pleased
πᾶν τὸ πλήρωμα κατοικῆσαι 20 καὶ δι᾽	¹all ³the ²fulness to dwell and through
αὐτοῦ ἀποκαταλλάξαι τὰ πάντα εἰς αὐτόν,	him to reconcile - all things to him[?self],

praying for you and asking God to fill you with the knowledge of his will through all spiritual wisdom and understanding. 10 And we pray this in order that you may live a life worthy of the Lord and may please him in every way: bearing fruit in every good work, growing in the knowledge of God, 11 being strengthened with all power according to his glorious might so that you may have great endurance and patience, and joyfully 12 giving thanks to the Father, who has qualified you[d] to share in the inheritance of the saints in the kingdom of light. 13 For he has rescued us from the dominion of darkness and brought us into the kingdom of the Son he loves, 14 in whom we have redemption,[e] the forgiveness of sins.

The Supremacy of Christ

15 He is the image of the invisible God, the firstborn over all creation. 16 For by him all things were created: things in heaven and on earth, visible and invisible, whether thrones or powers or rulers or authorities; all things were created by him and for him. 17 He is before all things, and in him all things hold together. 18 And he is the head of the body, the church; he is the beginning and the firstborn from among the dead, so that in everything he might have the supremacy. 19 For God was pleased to have all his fullness dwell in him, 20 and through him to reconcile to himself all things, whether

[d] Gk his
[e] Other ancient authorities read called
[f] Other ancient authorities read us
[g] Other ancient authorities add through his blood
[h] Or by

[d]12 Some manuscripts us
[e]14 A few late manuscripts redemption through his blood

whether on earth or in heaven, by making peace through the blood of his cross.

21 And you who were once estranged and hostile in mind, doing evil deeds, [22]he has now reconciled[i] in his fleshly body[j] through death, so as to present you holy and blameless and irreproachable before him— [23]provided that you continue securely established and steadfast in the faith, without shifting from the hope promised by the gospel that you heard, which has been proclaimed to every creature under heaven. I, Paul, became a servant of this gospel.

Paul's Interest in the Colossians

24 I am now rejoicing in my sufferings for your sake, and in my flesh I am completing what is lacking in Christ's afflictions for the sake of his body, that is, the church. [25]I became its servant according to God's commission that was given to me for you, to make the word of God fully known, [26]the mystery that has been hidden throughout the ages and generations but has now been revealed to his saints. [27]To them God chose to make known how great among the Gentiles are the riches of the glory of this mystery, which is Christ in you, the hope of glory. [28]It is he whom we proclaim, warning everyone and teaching everyone

εἰρηνοποιήσας διὰ τοῦ αἵματος τοῦ σταυροῦ
making peace through the blood of the cross

αὐτοῦ, δι’ αὐτοῦ εἴτε τὰ ἐπὶ τῆς γῆς
of him, through him whether the on the earth things

εἴτε τὰ ἐν τοῖς οὐρανοῖς. 21 Καὶ ὑμᾶς
or the things in *the* heavens. And you

ποτε ὄντας ἀπηλλοτριωμένους καὶ ἐχθροὺς
then being *having been* alienated and enemies

τῇ διανοίᾳ ἐν τοῖς ἔργοις τοῖς πονηροῖς,
in *the* mind by the(your) works - evil,

22 νυνὶ δὲ ἀποκατήλλαξεν ἐν τῷ σώματι
but now he reconciled in the body

τῆς σαρκὸς αὐτοῦ διὰ τοῦ θανάτου,
of the flesh of him through the(his) death,

παραστῆσαι ὑμᾶς ἁγίους καὶ ἀμώμους
to present you holy and blameless

καὶ ἀνεγκλήτους κατενώπιον αὐτοῦ, 23 εἴ
and irreproachable before him, if

γε ἐπιμένετε τῇ πίστει τεθεμελιωμένοι
indeed ye continue in the faith having been founded

καὶ ἑδραῖοι καὶ μὴ μετακινούμενοι ἀπὸ
and steadfast and not being moved away from

τῆς ἐλπίδος τοῦ εὐαγγελίου οὗ ἠκούσατε,
the hope of the gospel which ye heard,

τοῦ κηρυχθέντος ἐν πάσῃ κτίσει τῇ
- proclaimed in all creation the

ὑπὸ τὸν οὐρανόν, οὗ ἐγενόμην ἐγὼ
under *the* heaven, of which ²became ¹I

Παῦλος διάκονος.
¹Paul a minister.

24 Νῦν χαίρω ἐν τοῖς παθήμασιν ὑπὲρ
Now I rejoice in the(my) sufferings on behalf of

ὑμῶν, καὶ ἀνταναπληρῶ τὰ ὑστερήματα
you, and fill up the things lacking

τῶν θλίψεων τοῦ Χριστοῦ ἐν τῇ σαρκί
of the afflictions - of Christ in the flesh

μου ὑπὲρ τοῦ σώματος αὐτοῦ, ὅ ἐστιν
of me on behalf of the body of him, which is

ἡ ἐκκλησία, 25 ἧς ἐγενόμην ἐγὼ διάκονος
the church, of which became I a minister

κατὰ τὴν οἰκονομίαν τοῦ θεοῦ τὴν
according the stewardship - of God -
to

δοθεῖσάν μοι εἰς ὑμᾶς πληρῶσαι τὸν
given to me for you to fulfil the

λόγον τοῦ θεοῦ, 26 τὸ μυστήριον τὸ
word - of God, the mystery the

ἀποκεκρυμμένον ἀπὸ τῶν αἰώνων καὶ
having been hidden from the ages and

ἀπὸ τῶν γενεῶν — νῦν δὲ ἐφανερώθη
from the generations — but now was manifested

τοῖς ἁγίοις αὐτοῦ, 27 οἷς ἠθέλησεν ὁ
to the saints of him, to whom ²wished -

θεὸς γνωρίσαι τί τὸ πλοῦτος τῆς δόξης
¹God to make known what [is] the riches of the glory

τοῦ μυστηρίου τούτου ἐν τοῖς ἔθνεσιν,
- mystery of this among the nations,

ὅς ἐστιν Χριστὸς ἐν ὑμῖν, ἡ ἐλπὶς τῆς
who is Christ in you, the hope of the

δόξης· 28 ὃν ἡμεῖς καταγγέλλομεν νου-
glory; whom we announce warn-

θετοῦντες πάντα ἄνθρωπον καὶ διδάσκοντες
ing every man and teaching

things on earth or things in heaven, by making peace through his blood, shed on the cross.

[21]Once you were alienated from God and were enemies in your minds because of[f] your evil behavior. [22]But now he has reconciled you by Christ's physical body through death to present you holy in his sight, without blemish and free from accusation— [23]if you continue in your faith, established and firm, not moved from the hope held out in the gospel. This is the gospel that you heard and that has been proclaimed to every creature under heaven, and of which I, Paul, have become a servant.

Paul's Labor for the Church

[24]Now I rejoice in what was suffered for you, and I fill up in my flesh what is still lacking in regard to Christ's afflictions, for the sake of his body, which is the church. [25]I have become its servant by the commission God gave me to present to you the word of God in its fullness— [26]the mystery that has been kept hidden for ages and generations, but is now disclosed to the saints. [27]To them God has chosen to make known among the Gentiles the glorious riches of this mystery, which is Christ in you, the hope of glory.

[28]We proclaim him, admonishing and teaching everyone with all wisdom, so

---

[i]Other ancient authorities read *you have now been reconciled*
[j]Gk *in the body of his flesh*

f21 Or minds, as shown by

in all wisdom, so that we may present everyone mature in Christ. 29For this I toil and struggle with all the energy that he powerfully inspires within me.

Chapter 2

FOR I want you to know how much I am struggling for you, and for those in Laodicea, and for all who have not seen me face to face. 2I want their hearts to be encouraged and united in love, so that they may have all the riches of assured understanding, and have the knowledge of God's mystery, that is, Christ himself,k 3in whom are hidden all the treasures of wisdom and knowledge. 4I am saying this so that no one may deceive you with plausible arguments. 5For though I am absent in body, yet I am with you in spirit, and I rejoice to see your morale and the firmness of your faith in Christ.

Fullness of Life in Christ

6 As you therefore have received Christ Jesus the Lord, continue to live your livesl in him, 7rooted and built up in him and established in the faith, just as you were taught, abounding in thanksgiving.

8 See to it that no one takes you captive through philosophy and empty deceit, according to human tradition, according to the elemental spirits of the universe,m and not according to Christ. 9For in him the whole fullness of deity

---

πάντα ἄνθρωπον ἐν πάσῃ σοφίᾳ,
every man in all wisdom,

ἵνα παραστήσωμεν πάντα ἄνθρωπον
in or- we may present every man
der that

τέλειον ἐν Χριστῷ· 29 εἰς ὃ καὶ κοπιῶ
mature in Christ; for which also I labour

ἀγωνιζόμενος κατὰ τὴν ἐνέργειαν αὐτοῦ
struggling accord- the operation of him
ing to

τὴν ἐνεργουμένην ἐν ἐμοὶ ἐν δυνάμει.
- operating in me in power.

2 Θέλω γὰρ ὑμᾶς εἰδέναι ἡλίκον ἀγῶνα
For I wish you to know how great a struggle

ἔχω ὑπὲρ ὑμῶν καὶ τῶν ἐν Λαοδικείᾳ
I have on behalf of you and the [ones] in Laodicea

καὶ ὅσοι οὐχ ἑόρακαν τὸ πρόσωπόν μου
and as many as have not seen the face of me

ἐν σαρκί, 2 ἵνα παρακληθῶσιν αἱ καρδίαι
in flesh, in order ⁴may be ¹the ²hearts
that comforted

αὐτῶν, συμβιβασθέντες ἐν ἀγάπῃ καὶ εἰς
³of them, being joined together in love and for

πᾶν πλοῦτος τῆς πληροφορίας τῆς
all riches of the full assurance -

συνέσεως, εἰς ἐπίγνωσιν τοῦ μυστηρίου
of under- for full knowledge of the mystery
standing,

τοῦ θεοῦ, Χριστοῦ, 3 ἐν ᾧ εἰσιν πάντες
- of God, of Christ, in whom ¹are ²all

οἱ θησαυροὶ τῆς σοφίας καὶ γνώσεως
⁴the ⁵treasures - ⁶of wisdom ⁷and ⁸of knowledge

ἀπόκρυφοι. 4 Τοῦτο λέγω ἵνα μηδεὶς
³hidden. This I say in order no one
that

ὑμᾶς παραλογίζηται ἐν πιθανολογίᾳ. 5 εἰ
²you ¹may beguile with persuasive speech. if

γὰρ καὶ τῇ σαρκὶ ἄπειμι, ἀλλὰ τῷ
For indeed in the flesh I am absent, yet in the

πνεύματι σὺν ὑμῖν εἰμι, χαίρων καὶ
spirit ²with ³you ¹I am, rejoicing and

βλέπων ὑμῶν τὴν τάξιν καὶ τὸ στερέωμα
seeing ²of you ¹the ²order and the firmness

τῆς εἰς Χριστὸν πίστεως ὑμῶν.
of the ³in ⁴Christ ¹faith ²of you.

6 Ὡς οὖν παρελάβετε τὸν Χριστὸν
As therefore ye received - Christ

Ἰησοῦν τὸν κύριον, ἐν αὐτῷ περιπατεῖτε,
Jesus the Lord, in him walk ye,

7 ἐρριζωμένοι καὶ ἐποικοδομούμενοι ἐν αὐτῷ
having been rooted and being built up in him

καὶ βεβαιούμενοι τῇ πίστει καθὼς ἐδιδάχ-
and being confirmed in the faith as ye were

θητε, περισσεύοντες ἐν εὐχαριστίᾳ.
taught, abounding in thanksgiving.

8 Βλέπετε μή τις ὑμᾶς ἔσται ὁ συλαγωγῶν
Look ye lest ²anyone ⁴you ¹there - ²robbing
shall be

διὰ τῆς φιλοσοφίας καὶ κενῆς ἀπάτης
through - philosophy and empty deceit

κατὰ τὴν παράδοσιν τῶν ἀνθρώπων, κατὰ
accord- the tradition - of men, according to ing to

τὰ στοιχεῖα τοῦ κόσμου καὶ οὐ κατὰ
the elements of the world and not according to

Χριστόν· 9 ὅτι ἐν αὐτῷ κατοικεῖ πᾶν
Christ; because in him dwells all

---

that we may present everyone perfect in Christ. 29To this end I labor, struggling with all his energy, which so powerfully works in me.

Chapter 2

I WANT you to know how much I am struggling for you and for those at Laodicea, and for all who have not met me personally. 2My purpose is that they may be encouraged in heart and united in love, so that they may have the full riches of complete understanding, in order that they may know the mystery of God, namely, Christ, 3in whom are hidden all the treasures of wisdom and knowledge. 4I tell you this so that no one may deceive you by fine-sounding arguments. 5For though I am absent from you in body, I am present with you in spirit and delight to see how orderly you are and how firm your faith in Christ is.

Freedom From Human Regulations Through Life With Christ

6So then, just as you received Christ Jesus as Lord, continue to live in him, 7rooted and built up in him, strengthened in the faith as you were taught, and overflowing with thankfulness.

8See to it that no one takes you captive through hollow and deceptive philosophy, which depends on human tradition and the basic principles of this world rather than on Christ. 9For in Christ all the full-

---

k Other ancient authorities read *of the mystery of God, both of the Father and of Christ*
l Gk *to walk*
m Or *the rudiments of the world*

dwells bodily, 10and you have come to fullness in him, who is the head of every ruler and authority. 11In him also you were circumcised with a spiritual circumcision,ⁿ by putting off the body of the flesh in the circumcision of Christ; 12when you were buried with him in baptism, you were also raised with him through faith in the power of God, who raised him from the dead. 13And when you were dead in trespasses and the uncircumcision of your flesh, Godᵒ made youᵖ alive together with him, when he forgave us all our trespasses, 14erasing the record that stood against us with its legal demands. He set this aside, nailing it to the cross. 15He disarmed� the rulers and authorities and made a public example of them, triumphing over them in it.

16 Therefore do not let anyone condemn you in matters of food and drink or of observing festivals, new moons, or sabbaths. 17These are only a shadow of what is to come, but the substance belongs to Christ. 18Do not let anyone disqualify you, insisting on self-abasement and worship of angels, dwellingʳ on visions,ˢ puffed up without cause by a human way of thinking,ᵗ 19and not holding fast to the head, from whom the whole body, nourished and held together by its ligaments

τὸ πλήρωμα τῆς θεότητος σωματικῶς,
the fulness of the Godhead bodily,

10 καὶ ἐστὲ ἐν αὐτῷ πεπληρωμένοι, ὅς
and ye are in him having been filled, who

ἐστιν ἡ κεφαλὴ πάσης ἀρχῆς καὶ ἐξουσίας,
is the head of all rule and authority,

11 ἐν ᾧ καὶ περιετμήθητε περιτομῇ
in whom also ye were circumcised with a circumcision

ἀχειροποιήτῳ ἐν τῇ ἀπεκδύσει τοῦ σώματος
not handwrought by the putting off of the body

τῆς σαρκός, ἐν τῇ περιτομῇ τοῦ Χριστοῦ,
of the flesh, by the circumcision - of Christ,

12 συνταφέντες αὐτῷ ἐν τῷ βαπτίσματι,
co-buried with him in the baptism,

ἐν ᾧ καὶ συνηγέρθητε διὰ τῆς πίστεως
in whom also ye were co-raised through the faith

τῆς ἐνεργείας τοῦ θεοῦ τοῦ ἐγείραντος
of(in) the operation - of God - raising

αὐτὸν ἐκ νεκρῶν· 13 καὶ ὑμᾶς νεκροὺς
him from [the] dead; and you dead

ὄντας τοῖς παραπτώμασιν καὶ τῇ ἀκρο-
being in the trespasses and in the uncir-

βυστίᾳ τῆς σαρκὸς ὑμῶν, συνεζωοποίησεν
cumcision of the flesh of you, he co-quickened

ὑμᾶς σὺν αὐτῷ, χαρισάμενος ἡμῖν πάντα
you with him, forgiving us all

τὰ παραπτώματα· 14 ἐξαλείψας τὸ καθ᾽
the trespasses; wiping out ¹the ²against

ἡμῶν χειρόγραφον τοῖς δόγμασιν ὃ ἦν
⁴us ²handwriting - in ordinances which was

ὑπεναντίον ἡμῖν, καὶ αὐτὸ ἦρκεν ἐκ
contrary to us, and ²it ¹has taken out of

τοῦ μέσου, προσηλώσας αὐτὸ τῷ σταυρῷ·
the midst(way), nailing it to the cross;

15 ἀπεκδυσάμενος τὰς ἀρχὰς καὶ τὰς
putting off the rulers and the

ἐξουσίας ἐδειγμάτισεν ἐν παρρησίᾳ,
authorities he exposed [them] with openness,

θριαμβεύσας αὐτοὺς ἐν αὐτῷ.
triumphing [over] them in it.

16 Μὴ οὖν τις ὑμᾶς κρινέτω ἐν βρώσει
¹Not ²there-fore ⁴any-one ³you ¹let ²judge in eating

καὶ ἐν πόσει ἢ ἐν μέρει ἑορτῆς ἢ
and in drinking or in respect of a feast or

νεομηνίας ἢ σαββάτων, 17 ἅ ἐστιν σκιὰ
of a new moon or of sabbaths, which is(are) a things shadow

τῶν μελλόντων, τὸ δὲ σῶμα τοῦ Χριστοῦ.
of things coming, but the body [is] - of Christ.

18 μηδεὶς ὑμᾶς καταβραβευέτω θέλων ἐν
²No one ⁴you ¹let ³give judgment wishing in against [to do so]

ταπεινοφροσύνῃ καὶ θρησκείᾳ τῶν ἀγγέλων,
humility* and worship of the angels,

ἃ ἑόρακεν ἐμβατεύων, εἰκῇ φυσιούμενος
²things ³he has ¹intruding into, in vain being puffed up which seen

ὑπὸ τοῦ νοὸς τῆς σαρκὸς αὐτοῦ, 19 καὶ
by the mind of the flesh of him, and

οὐ κρατῶν τὴν κεφαλήν, ἐξ οὗ πᾶν
not holding the head, from whom all

τὸ σῶμα διὰ τῶν ἁφῶν καὶ συνδέσμων
the body ⁴by means ⁵the ⁶joints ⁷and ⁸bands of (its)

ness of the Deity lives in bodily form, 10and you have been given fullness in Christ, who is the head over every power and authority. 11In him you were also circumcised, in the putting off of the sinful nature,ᵍ not with a circumcision done by the hands of men but with the circumcision done by Christ, 12having been buried with him in baptism and raised with him through your faith in the power of God, who raised him from the dead. 13When you were dead in your sins and in the uncircumcision of your sinful nature,ʰ God made youⁱ alive with Christ. He forgave us all our sins, 14having canceled the written code, with its regulations, that was against us and that stood opposed to us; he took it away, nailing it to the cross. 15And having disarmed the powers and authorities, he made a public spectacle of them, triumphing over them by the cross.ʲ

16Therefore do not let anyone judge you by what you eat or drink, or with regard to a religious festival, a New Moon celebration or a Sabbath day. 17These are a shadow of the things that were to come; the reality, however, is found in Christ. 18Do not let anyone who delights in false humility and the worship of angels disqualify you for the prize. Such a person goes into great detail about what he has seen, and his unspiritual mind puffs him up with idle notions. 19He has lost connection with the Head, from whom the whole body, supported and held together by

ⁿ Gk a circumcision made without hands
ᵒ Gk he
ᵖ Other ancient authorities read made us; others, made
ᵐ Or divested himself of
ʳ Other ancient authorities read not dwelling
ˢ Meaning of Gk uncertain
ᵗ Gk by the mind of his flesh

* Ellicott supplies " false ". Cf. ver. 22.

ᵍ11 Or the flesh
ʰ13 Or your flesh
ⁱ13 Some manuscripts us
ʲ15 Or them in him

and sinews, grows with a growth that is from God.

Warnings against False Teachers

20 If with Christ you died to the elemental spirits of the universe, [m] why do you live as if you still belonged to the world? Why do you submit to regulations, 21 "Do not handle, Do not taste, Do not touch"? 22 All these regulations refer to things that perish with use; they are simply human commands and teachings. 23 These have indeed an appearance of wisdom in promoting self-imposed piety, humility, and severe treatment of the body, but they are of no value in checking self-indulgence. [u]

Chapter 3

The New Life in Christ

SO if you have been raised with Christ, seek the things that are above, where Christ is, seated at the right hand of God. 2 Set your minds on things that are above, not on things that are on earth. 3 for you have died, and your life is hidden with Christ in God. 4 When Christ who is your [v] life is revealed, then you also will be revealed with him in glory.

5 Put to death, therefore, whatever in you is earthly: fornication, impurity, passion, evil desire, and greed (which is idolatry). 6 On account of these the wrath of God is coming on those who are disobedient. [w] 7 These are the ways you also once followed, when you were living that life. [x] 8 But now you must get rid of all such things— anger, wrath, malice, slander, and abusive [y] language from your mouth. 9 Do not lie to one another, seeing that you have stripped off the old self with its prac-

[u] Or are of no value, serving only to indulge the flesh
[v] Other authorities read our
[w] Other ancient authorities lack on those who are disobedient (Gk the children of disobedience)
[x] Or living among such people
[y] Or filthy

ἐπιχορηγούμενον   καὶ   συμβιβαζόμενον   αὔξει
[1]being supplied   [2]and   [3]being joined together   will grow
τὴν   αὔξησιν   τοῦ   θεοῦ.
[with] the growth   -   of God.
20 Εἰ   ἀπεθάνετε   σὺν   Χριστῷ   ἀπὸ   τῶν   στοι-
If   ye died   with   Christ   from   the   ele-
χείων   τοῦ   κόσμου,   τί   ὡς   ζῶντες   ἐν   κόσμῳ
ments   of the   world,   why   as   living   in [the] world
δογματίζεσθε·   **21** μὴ   ἅψῃ   μηδὲ   γεύσῃ   μηδὲ
are ye subject to   Do not touch   nor   taste   nor
[its] decrees:
θίγῃς,   **22** ἅ   ἐστιν   πάντα   εἰς   φθορὰν
handle,   which   is(are)   all   for   corruption
         things
τῇ   ἀποχρήσει,   κατὰ   τὰ   ἐντάλματα   καὶ
in the   using,   according to the   injunctions   and
διδασκαλίας   τῶν   ἀνθρώπων;   **23** ἅτινά   ἐστιν
teachings   -   of men?   [1]which   [2]is(are)
                                   things
λόγον   μὲν   ἔχοντα   σοφίας   ἐν   ἐθελοθρησκίᾳ
[3]a repute [2]indeed   [4]having   of wisdom   in   self-imposed
                                                   worship
καὶ   ταπεινοφροσύνῃ   καὶ   ἀφειδίᾳ   σώματος,   οὐκ
and   humility   and   severity   of [the] body,   not
ἐν   τιμῇ   τινι   πρὸς   πλησμονὴν   τῆς   σαρκός.
in   [2]honour [1]any   for   satisfaction   of the   flesh.
3 Εἰ   οὖν   συνηγέρθητε   τῷ   Χριστῷ,   τὰ
If   therefore ye were co-raised   -   with Christ,   the
                                                       things
ἄνω   ζητεῖτε,   οὗ   ὁ   Χριστός   ἐστιν   ἐν
above   seek,   where   -   Christ   [1]is   [2]at
δεξιᾷ   τοῦ   θεοῦ   καθήμενος·   **2** τὰ   ἄνω
[4][the] right   -   [2]of God   [3]sitting;   the   above
[hand]   things
φρονεῖτε,   μὴ   τὰ   ἐπὶ   τῆς   γῆς.   **3** ἀπεθάνετε
mind ye,   not   the   on   the   earth.   ye died
                            things
γάρ,   καὶ   ἡ   ζωὴ   ὑμῶν   κέκρυπται   σὺν
For,   and   the   life   of you   has been hidden   with
τῷ   Χριστῷ   ἐν   τῷ   θεῷ·   **4** ὅταν   ὁ   Χριστὸς
-   Christ   in   the   God;   whenever   -   Christ
φανερωθῇ,   ἡ   ζωὴ   ἡμῶν,   τότε   καὶ   ὑμεῖς
is manifested,   the   life   of us,   then   also   ye
σὺν   αὐτῷ   φανερωθήσεσθε   ἐν   δόξῃ.
with   him   will be manifested   in   glory.
5 Νεκρώσατε   οὖν   τὰ   μέλη   τὰ   ἐπὶ
Put ye to death   therefore   the   members   -   on
                            (your)
τῆς   γῆς,   πορνείαν,   ἀκαθαρσίαν,   πάθος,
the   earth,   fornication,   uncleanness,   passion,
ἐπιθυμίαν   κακήν,   καὶ   τὴν   πλεονεξίαν   ἥτις
desire   bad,   and   -   covetousness   which
ἐστὶν   εἰδωλολατρία,   **6** δι᾽   ἃ   ἔρχεται   ἡ
is   idolatry,   because which   is coming   the
                            of things
ὀργὴ   τοῦ   θεοῦ·   **7** ἐν   οἷς   καὶ   ὑμεῖς
wrath   -   of God;   in   which   indeed   ye
περιεπατήσατέ   ποτε,   ὅτε   ἐζῆτε   ἐν   τούτοις·
walked   then,   when   ye lived   in   these things;
8 νυνὶ   δὲ   ἀπόθεσθε   καὶ   ὑμεῖς   τὰ   πάντα,
but now   [1]put [2]away   [4]also   [3]ye   -   all things,
ὀργήν,   θυμόν,   κακίαν,   βλασφημίαν,   αἰσχρο-
wrath,   anger,   malice,   blasphemy,   a-
λογίαν   ἐκ   τοῦ   στόματος   ὑμῶν·   **9** μὴ
buse   out of   the   mouth   of you;   not
ψεύδεσθε   εἰς   ἀλλήλους,   ἀπεκδυσάμενοι   τὸν
lie ye   to   one another,   having put off   the
παλαιὸν   ἄνθρωπον   σὺν   ταῖς   πράξεσιν
old   man   with   the   practices

its ligaments and sinews, grows as God causes it to grow.
20 Since you died with Christ to the basic principles of this world, why, as though you still belonged to it, do you submit to its rules: 21 "Do not handle! Do not taste! Do not touch!"? 22 These are all destined to perish with use, because they are based on human commands and teachings. 23 Such regulations indeed have an appearance of wisdom, with their self-imposed worship, their false humility and their harsh treatment of the body, but they lack any value in restraining sensual indulgence.

Chapter 3

Rules for Holy Living

SINCE, then, you have been raised with Christ, set your hearts on things above, where Christ is seated at the right hand of God. 2 Set your minds on things above, not on earthly things. 3 For you died, and your life is now hidden with Christ in God. 4 When Christ, who is your [k] life, appears, then you also will appear with him in glory.

5 Put to death, therefore, whatever belongs to your earthly nature: sexual immorality, impurity, lust, evil desires and greed, which is idolatry. 6 Because of these, the wrath of God is coming. [l] 7 You used to walk in these ways, in the life you once lived. 8 But now you must rid yourselves of all such things as these: anger, rage, malice, slander, and filthy language from your lips. 9 Do not lie to each other, since you have taken off your old self with its practices 10 and

[k] 4 Some manuscripts our
[l] 6 Some early manuscripts coming on those who are disobedient

tices ¹⁰and have clothed yourselves with the new self, which is being renewed in knowledge according to the image of its creator. ¹¹In that renewal² there is no longer Greek and Jew, circumcised and uncircumcised, barbarian, Scythian, slave and free; but Christ is all and in all. 12 As God's chosen ones, holy and beloved, clothe yourselves with compassion, kindness, humility, meekness, and patience. ¹³Bear with one another and, if anyone has a complaint against another, forgive each other; just as the Lord ͣ has forgiven you, so you also must forgive. ¹⁴Above all, clothe yourselves with love, which binds everything together in perfect harmony. ¹⁵And let the peace of Christ rule in your hearts, to which indeed you were called in the one body. And be thankful. ¹⁶Let the word of Christ ᵇ dwell in you richly; teach and admonish one another in all wisdom; and with gratitude in your hearts sing psalms, hymns, and spiritual songs to God. ͨ ¹⁷And whatever you do, in word or deed, do everything in the name of the Lord Jesus, giving thanks to God the Father through him.

Rules for Christian Households

18 Wives, be subject to your husbands, as is fitting in the Lord. ¹⁹Husbands, love your wives and never treat them harshly.

20 Children, obey your parents in everything, for

αὐτοῦ, 10 καὶ ἐνδυσάμενοι τὸν νέον τὸν
of him, and having put on the new man –

ἀνακαινούμενον εἰς ἐπίγνωσιν κατ' εἰκόνα
being renewed in full knowledge according [the]
to image

τοῦ κτίσαντος αὐτόν, 11 ὅπου οὐκ ἔνι
of the [one] creating him, where ⁴have no place

Ἕλλην καὶ Ἰουδαῖος, περιτομὴ καὶ
¹Greek ²and ³Jew, circumcision and

ἀκροβυστία, βάρβαρος, Σκύθης, δοῦλος,
uncircumcision, barbarian, Scythian, slave,

ἐλεύθερος, ἀλλὰ πάντα καὶ ἐν πᾶσιν
freeman, but ²all things ⁴and ⁵in ⁶all

Χριστός. 12 Ἐνδύσασθε οὖν, ὡς ἐκλεκτοὶ
¹Christ ²[is]. Put ye on therefore, as chosen ones

τοῦ θεοῦ ἅγιοι καὶ ἠγαπημένοι, σπλάγχνα
– of God holy and having been loved, bowels

οἰκτιρμοῦ, χρηστότητα, ταπεινοφροσύνην,
of compassion, kindness, humility,

πραΰτητα, μακροθυμίαν, 13 ἀνεχόμενοι ἀλ-
meekness, long-suffering, forbearing one

λήλων καὶ χαριζόμενοι ἑαυτοῖς, ἐάν τις
another and forgiving yourselves, if anyone

πρός τινα ἔχῃ μομφήν· καθὼς καὶ ὁ
³against ⁴anyone ¹has ²a complaint; as indeed the

κύριος ἐχαρίσατο ὑμῖν οὕτως καὶ ὑμεῖς·
Lord forgave you so also ye;

14 ἐπὶ πᾶσιν δὲ τούτοις τὴν ἀγάπην,
³over ²all ¹and these things – love,

ὅ ἐστιν σύνδεσμος τῆς τελειότητος. 15 καὶ
which is [the] bond – of completeness. And

ἡ εἰρήνη τοῦ Χριστοῦ βραβευέτω ἐν ταῖς
²the ¹peace – ⁴of Christ ¹let ⁵rule in the

καρδίαις ὑμῶν, εἰς ἣν καὶ ἐκλήθητε
hearts of you, to which indeed ye were called

ἐν ἑνὶ σώματι· καὶ εὐχάριστοι γίνεσθε.
in one body; and thankful be ye.

16 ὁ λόγος τοῦ Χριστοῦ ἐνοικείτω ἐν
²The ³word – ⁴of Christ ¹let ⁵indwell in

ὑμῖν πλουσίως, ἐν πάσῃ σοφίᾳ διδάσκοντες
you richly, in all wisdom teaching

καὶ νουθετοῦντες ἑαυτούς, ψαλμοῖς ὕμνοις
and admonishing yourselves, in psalms[,] hymns[,]

ᾠδαῖς πνευματικαῖς ἐν τῇ χάριτι ᾄδοντες
[and] ²songs ¹spiritual with – grace singing

ἐν ταῖς καρδίαις ὑμῶν τῷ θεῷ· 17 καὶ
in the hearts of you – to God; and

πᾶν ὅ τι ἐὰν ποιῆτε ἐν λόγῳ ἢ ἐν
every- whatever ye do in word or in
thing

ἔργῳ, πάντα ἐν ὀνόματι κυρίου Ἰησοῦ,
work, all things [do] in [the] name of [the] Lord Jesus,

εὐχαριστοῦντες τῷ θεῷ πατρὶ δι' αὐτοῦ.
giving thanks – to God [the] through him.
Father

18 Αἱ γυναῖκες, ὑποτάσσεσθε τοῖς
The wives, be ye subject to the(your)

ἀνδράσιν, ὡς ἀνῆκεν ἐν κυρίῳ. 19 Οἱ
husbands, as is befitting in [the] Lord. The

ἄνδρες, ἀγαπᾶτε τὰς γυναῖκας καὶ μὴ
husbands, love ye the(your) wives and not

πικραίνεσθε πρὸς αὐτάς. 20 Τὰ τέκνα,
be bitter toward them. The children,

ὑπακούετε τοῖς γονεῦσιν κατὰ πάντα,
obey ye the(your) parents in all respects,

---

have put on the new self, which is being renewed in knowledge in the image of its Creator. ¹¹Here there is no Greek or Jew, circumcised or uncircumcised, barbarian, Scythian, slave or free, but Christ is all, and is in all.

¹²Therefore, as God's chosen people, holy and dearly loved, clothe yourselves with compassion, kindness, humility, gentleness and patience. ¹³Bear with each other and forgive whatever grievances you may have against one another. Forgive as the Lord forgave you. ¹⁴And over all these virtues put on love, which binds them all together in perfect unity.

¹⁵Let the peace of Christ rule in your hearts, since as members of one body you were called to peace. And be thankful. ¹⁶Let the word of Christ dwell in you richly as you teach and admonish one another with all wisdom, and as you sing psalms, hymns and spiritual songs with gratitude in your hearts to God. ¹⁷And whatever you do, whether in word or deed, do it all in the name of the Lord Jesus, giving thanks to God the Father through him.

Rules for Christian Households

¹⁸Wives, submit to your husbands, as is fitting in the Lord.

¹⁹Husbands, love your wives and do not be harsh with them.

²⁰Children, obey your parents in everything, for

---

²Gk *its creator.* ¹¹*where*
ͣ Other ancient authorities read *just as Christ*
ᵇ Other ancient authorities read *of God,* or *of the Lord*
ͨ Other ancient authorities read *to the Lord*

this is your acceptable duty in the Lord. 21 Fathers, do not provoke your children, or they may lose heart. 22 Slaves, obey your earthly masters[d] not only while being watched and in order to please them, but wholeheartedly, fearing the Lord.[d] 23 Whatever your task, put yourselves into it, as done for the Lord and not for your masters,[e] 24 since you know that from the Lord you will receive the inheritance as your reward; you serve[f] the Lord Christ. 25 For the wrongdoer will be paid back for whatever wrong has been done, and there is no partiality. 1 Masters, treat your slaves justly and fairly, for you know that you also have a Master in heaven.

Further Instructions

2 Devote yourselves to prayer, keeping alert in it with thanksgiving. 3 At the same time pray for us as well that God will open to us a door for the word, that we may declare the mystery of Christ, for which I am in prison, 4 so that I may reveal it clearly, as I should.

5 Conduct yourselves wisely toward outsiders, making the most of the time.[g] 6 Let your speech always be gracious, seasoned with salt, so that you may know how you ought to answer everyone.

Final Greetings and Benediction

7 Tychicus will tell you all the news about me; he is a beloved brother, a faithful minister, and a fellow

---

τοῦτο γὰρ εὐάρεστόν ἐστιν ἐν κυρίῳ.
for this well-pleasing is in [the] Lord.

21 Οἱ πατέρες, μὴ ἐρεθίζετε τὰ τέκνα
The fathers, do not ye provoke the children

ὑμῶν, ἵνα μὴ ἀθυμῶσιν. 22 Οἱ δοῦλοι,
of you, lest they be disheartened. The slaves,

ὑπακούετε κατὰ πάντα τοῖς κατὰ σάρκα
obey ye in all respects ¹the ²accord- ⁴[the]
(your) ing to flesh

κυρίοις, μὴ ἐν ὀφθαλμοδουλίαις ὡς
³lords, not with eyeservice as

ἀνθρωπάρεσκοι, ἀλλ' ἐν ἁπλότητι καρδίας
men-pleasers, but in singleness of heart

φοβούμενοι τὸν κύριον. 23 ὃ ἐὰν ποιῆτε,
fearing the Lord. Whatever ye do,

ἐκ ψυχῆς ἐργάζεσθε ὡς τῷ κυρίῳ καὶ
from [the] soul work ye as to the Lord and

οὐκ ἀνθρώποις, 24 εἰδότες ὅτι ἀπὸ κυρίου
not to men, knowing that from [the] Lord

ἀπολήμψεσθε τὴν ἀνταπόδοσιν τῆς κλη-
ye will receive the reward of the in-

ρονομίας. τῷ κυρίῳ Χριστῷ δουλεύετε·
heritance. The Lord Christ ye serve;

25 ὁ γὰρ ἀδικῶν κομίσεται ὃ ἠδίκησεν,
for the [one] doing wrong will receive what he did wrong,

καὶ οὐκ ἔστιν προσωπολημψία. 4 Οἱ κύριοι,
and there is no respect of persons. The lords,

τὸ δίκαιον καὶ τὴν ἰσότητα τοῖς δούλοις
²the ³just thing ⁴and ⁵the ⁶equality ⁷to the(your) ⁸slaves

παρέχεσθε, εἰδότες ὅτι καὶ ὑμεῖς ἔχετε
¹supply ye, knowing that also ye have

κύριον ἐν οὐρανῷ.
a Lord in heaven.

2 Τῇ προσευχῇ προσκαρτερεῖτε, γρηγο-
In the prayer continue ye, watch-

ροῦντες ἐν αὐτῇ ἐν εὐχαριστίᾳ, 3 προσευ-
ing in it with thanksgiving, pray-

χόμενοι ἅμα καὶ περὶ ἡμῶν, ἵνα ὁ
ing together also concerning us, in order –
that

θεὸς ἀνοίξῃ ἡμῖν θύραν τοῦ λόγου,
God may open to us a door of the word,

λαλῆσαι τὸ μυστήριον τοῦ Χριστοῦ, δι'
to speak the mystery – of because
Christ, of

ὃ καὶ δέδεμαι, 4 ἵνα φανερώσω αὐτὸ
which indeed I have been in order I may manifest it
bound, that

ὡς δεῖ με λαλῆσαι. 5 Ἐν σοφίᾳ
as it behoves me to speak. In wisdom

περιπατεῖτε πρὸς τοὺς ἔξω, τὸν καιρὸν
walk ye toward the ones outside, ²the ³time

ἐξαγοραζόμενοι. 6 ὁ λόγος ὑμῶν πάντοτε
¹redeeming. The speech of you always
[let it be]

ἐν χάριτι, ἅλατι ἠρτυμένος, εἰδέναι πῶς
in grace, with salt *having been* to know how
seasoned,

δεῖ ὑμᾶς ἑνὶ ἑκάστῳ ἀποκρίνεσθαι.
it be- you ²one ³each ¹to answer.
hoves

7 Τὰ κατ' ἐμὲ πάντα γνωρίσει ὑμῖν Τύχικος
²The ³about ⁴me ¹all ⁶will make ⁷to you ⁵Tychicus
things known

ὁ ἀγαπητὸς ἀδελφὸς καὶ πιστὸς διάκονος
the beloved brother and faithful minister

---

this pleases the Lord. 21 Fathers, do not embitter your children, or they will become discouraged. 22 Slaves, obey your earthly masters in everything; and do it, not only when their eye is on you and to win their favor, but with sincerity of heart and reverence for the Lord. 23 Whatever you do, work at it with all your heart, as working for the Lord, not for men, 24 since you know that you will receive an inheritance from the Lord as a reward. It is the Lord Christ you are serving. 25 Anyone who does wrong will be repaid for his wrong, and there is no favoritism.

Chapter 4

MASTERS, provide your slaves with what is right and fair, because you know that you also have a Master in heaven.

Further Instructions

2 Devote yourselves to prayer, being watchful and thankful. 3 And pray for us, too, that God may open a door for our message, so that we may proclaim the mystery of Christ, for which I am in chains. 4 Pray that I may proclaim it clearly, as I should. 5 Be wise in the way you act toward outsiders; make the most of every opportunity. 6 Let your conversation be always full of grace, seasoned with salt, so that you may know how to answer everyone.

Final Greetings

7 Tychicus will tell you all the news about me. He is a dear brother, a faithful min-

---

[d] In Greek the same word is used for *master* and *Lord*
[e] Gk *not for men*
[f] Or *you are slaves of*, or *be slaves of*
[g] Or *opportunity*

servant[h] in the Lord. [8]I have sent him to you for this very purpose, so that you may know how we are[i] and that he may encourage your hearts; [9]he is coming with Onesimus, the faithful and beloved brother, who is one of you. They will tell you about everything here.

[10] Aristarchus my fellow prisoner greets you, as does Mark the cousin of Barnabas, concerning whom you have received instructions—if he comes to you, welcome him. [11] And Jesus who is called Justus greets you. These are the only ones of the circumcision among my co-workers for the kingdom of God, and they have been a comfort to me. [12]Epaphras, who is one of you, a servant[h] of Christ Jesus, greets you. He is always wrestling in his prayers on your behalf, so that you may stand mature and fully assured in everything that God wills. [13]For I testify for him that he has worked hard for you and for those in Laodicea and in Hierapolis. [14]Luke, the beloved physician, and Demas greet you. [15]Give my greetings to the brothers and sisters[j] in Laodicea, and to Nympha and the church in her house. [16]And when this letter has been read among you, have it read also in the church of the Laodiceans; and see that you read also the letter from Laodicea. [17]And say to Archippus, "See that you complete the

καὶ σύνδουλος ἐν κυρίῳ, **8** ὃν ἔπεμψα
and fellow-slave in [the] Lord, whom I sent

πρὸς ὑμᾶς εἰς αὐτὸ τοῦτο, ἵνα γνῶτε
to you for this very thing, in order ye might
                                                    that know
        know

τὰ περὶ ἡμῶν καὶ παρακαλέσῃ τὰς
the concern- us and he might comfort the
things ing

καρδίας ὑμῶν, **9** σὺν Ὀνησίμῳ τῷ πιστῷ
hearts of you, with Onesimus the faithful

καὶ ἀγαπητῷ ἀδελφῷ, ὅς ἐστιν ἐξ ὑμῶν·
and beloved brother, who is of you;

πάντα ὑμῖν γνωρίσουσιν τὰ ὧδε.
¹all ²to you ⁴they will ³the ⁵here.
               make known things

10 Ἀσπάζεται ὑμᾶς Ἀρίσταρχος ὁ
²greets ⁴you ¹Aristarchus ³the

συναιχμάλωτός μου, καὶ Μᾶρκος ὁ ἀνεψιὸς
⁵fellow-captive ⁶of me, and Mark the cousin

Βαρναβᾶ, (περὶ οὗ ἐλάβετε ἐντολάς, ἐὰν
of Barnabas, (concerning whom ye received commandments, if

ἔλθῃ πρὸς ὑμᾶς, δέξασθε αὐτόν,) **11** καὶ
he comes to you, receive ye him,) and

Ἰησοῦς ὁ λεγόμενος Ἰοῦστος, οἱ ὄντες
Jesus the [one] *being* named Justus, the [ones] being

ἐκ περιτομῆς οὗτοι μόνοι συνεργοὶ εἰς
of [the] circumcision these only fellow-workers for

τὴν βασιλείαν τοῦ θεοῦ, οἵτινες ἐγενή-
the kingdom - of God, who be-

θησάν μοι παρηγορία. **12** ἀσπάζεται ὑμᾶς
came to me a comfort. ²greets ³you

Ἐπαφρᾶς ὁ ἐξ ὑμῶν, δοῦλος Χριστοῦ
¹Epaphras the [one] of you, a slave of Christ

Ἰησοῦ, πάντοτε ἀγωνιζόμενος ὑπὲρ ὑμῶν
Jesus, always struggling on behalf of you

ἐν ταῖς προσευχαῖς, ἵνα σταθῆτε τέλειοι
in the prayers, in order ye may complete
                            that stand

καὶ πεπληροφορημένοι ἐν παντὶ θελήματι
and having been fully assured in all [the] will

τοῦ Θεοῦ. **13** μαρτυρῶ γὰρ αὐτῷ ὅτι
- of God. For I bear witness to him that

ἔχει πολὺν πόνον ὑπὲρ ὑμῶν καὶ τῶν
he has much distress on behalf of you and the ones

ἐν Λαοδικείᾳ καὶ τῶν ἐν Ἱεραπόλει.
in Laodicea and the ones in Hierapolis.

14 ἀσπάζεται ὑμᾶς Λουκᾶς ὁ ἰατρὸς ὁ
²greets ³you ¹Luke ⁵the ⁶physician -

ἀγαπητὸς καὶ Δημᾶς. **15** Ἀσπάσασθε
⁵beloved ⁶and ⁷Demas. Greet ye

τοὺς ἐν Λαοδικείᾳ ἀδελφοὺς καὶ Νύμφαν
¹the ³in ⁴Laodicea ²brothers and Nymphas

καὶ τὴν κατ᾽ οἶκον αὐτῆς ἐκκλησίαν.
and ¹the ²at ⁴[the] house ⁵of her ³church.

16 καὶ ὅταν ἀναγνωσθῇ παρ᾽ ὑμῖν ἡ
And whenever is read before you the(this)

ἐπιστολή, ποιήσατε ἵνα καὶ ἐν τῇ
epistle, cause *in order* that ²also ³in ⁴the

Λαοδικέων ἐκκλησίᾳ ἀναγνωσθῇ, καὶ τὴν
⁶of [the] ⁵church ¹it is read, and ²the
Laodiceans   [one]

ἐκ Λαοδικείας ἵνα καὶ ὑμεῖς ἀναγνῶτε.
⁵of ⁷Laodicea ¹in order ²also ³ye ⁴read.
                         that

17 καὶ εἴπατε Ἀρχίππῳ· βλέπε τὴν
And tell Archippus : Look [to] the

ister and fellow servant in the Lord. [8]I am sending him to you for the express purpose that you may know about our[m] circumstances and that he may encourage your hearts. [9]He is coming with Onesimus, our faithful and dear brother, who is one of you. They will tell you everything that is happening here.

[10]My fellow prisoner Aristarchus sends you his greetings, as does Mark, the cousin of Barnabas. (You have received instructions about him; if he comes to you, welcome him.) [11]Jesus, who is called Justus, also sends greetings. These are the only Jews among my fellow workers for the kingdom of God, and they have proved a comfort to me. [12]Epaphras, who is one of you and a servant of Christ Jesus, sends greetings. He is always wrestling in prayer for you, that you may stand firm in all the will of God, mature and fully assured. [13]I vouch for him that he is working hard for you and for those at Laodicea and Hierapolis. [14]Our dear friend Luke, the doctor, and Demas send greetings. [15]Give my greetings to the brothers and sisters at Laodicea, and to Nympha and the church in her house.

[16]After this letter has been read to you, see that it is also read in the church of the Laodiceans and that you in turn read the letter from Laodicea.

[17]Tell Archippus: "See to it that you complete the

[h] Gk *slave*
[i] Other authorities read *that I may know how you are*
[j] Gk *brothers*

[m]8 Some manuscripts *that he may know about your*

task that you have received in the Lord."

18 I, Paul, write this greeting with my own hand. Remember my chains. Grace be with you. [k]

διακονίαν ἣν παρέλαβες ἐν κυρίῳ, ἵνα
ministry   which thou receivedst in [the] Lord, in order that
αὐτὴν πληροῖς.
[²it]   ¹thou mayest fulfil.
18 Ὁ ἀσπασμὸς τῇ ἐμῇ χειρὶ Παύλου.
The   greeting   – by my hand[,]   of Paul.
μνημονεύετέ μου τῶν δεσμῶν. ἡ χάρις
Remember ye of me   the   bonds.   – Grace [be]
μεθ᾽ ὑμῶν,
with   you.

work you have received in the Lord."

18I, Paul, write this greeting in my own hand. Remember my chains. Grace be with you.

The First Letter of Paul
to the
Thessalonians

Chapter 1

Salutation

PAUL, Silvanus, and Timothy,
To the church of the Thessalonians in God the Father and the Lord Jesus Christ:
Grace to you and peace.

The Thessalonians' Faith and Example

2 We always give thanks to God for all of you and mention you in our prayers, constantly ³remembering before our God and Father your work of faith and labor of love and steadfastness of hope in our Lord Jesus Christ. ⁴For we know, brothers and sisters[a] beloved by God, that he has chosen you, ⁵because our message of the gospel came to you not in word only, but also in power and in the Holy Spirit and with full conviction; just as you know what kind of persons we proved to be among you for your sake. ⁶And you became imitators of us and of the Lord, for in spite of persecution you received the word with joy inspired by the Holy Spirit, ⁷so that you became an example to all the believers in Macedonia and in Achaia.

ΠΡΟΣ ΘΕΣΣΑΛΟΝΙΚΕΙΣ Α
To Thessalonians 1

1 Παῦλος καὶ Σιλουανὸς καὶ Τιμόθεος
Paul   and   Silvanus   and   Timothy
τῇ ἐκκλησίᾳ Θεσσαλονικέων ἐν θεῷ πατρὶ
to the church of [the] Thessalonians in God [the] Father
καὶ κυρίῳ Ἰησοῦ Χριστῷ· χάρις ὑμῖν
and [the] Lord Jesus   Christ: Grace [be] to you
καὶ εἰρήνη.
and   peace.
2 Εὐχαριστοῦμεν τῷ θεῷ πάντοτε περὶ
We give thanks   – to God always   concerning
πάντων ὑμῶν, μνείαν ποιούμενοι ἐπὶ τῶν
²all   ¹you,   mention   making   on(in) the
προσευχῶν ἡμῶν, ἀδιαλείπτως **3** μνημο-
prayers   of us,   unceasingly   remember-
νεύοντες ὑμῶν τοῦ ἔργου τῆς πίστεως
ing   of you   the   work   –   of faith
καὶ τοῦ κόπου τῆς ἀγάπης καὶ τῆς
and   the   labour   –   of love   and   the
ὑπομονῆς τῆς ἐλπίδος τοῦ κυρίου ἡμῶν
endurance   – of hope of(in) the Lord   of us
Ἰησοῦ Χριστοῦ ἔμπροσθεν τοῦ θεοῦ καὶ
Jesus   Christ   before   the   God   and
πατρὸς ἡμῶν, **4** εἰδότες, ἀδελφοὶ ἠγαπημένοι
Father   of us,   knowing,   brothers having been loved
ὑπὸ [τοῦ] θεοῦ, τὴν ἐκλογὴν ὑμῶν,
by   –   God,   the   choice   of you,
5 ὅτι τὸ εὐαγγέλιον ἡμῶν οὐκ ἐγενήθη
because the   gospel   of us became not
εἰς ὑμᾶς ἐν λόγῳ μόνον, ἀλλὰ καὶ ἐν
to   you   in   word   only,   but   also   in
δυνάμει καὶ ἐν πνεύματι ἁγίῳ καὶ
power   and   in   Spirit   Holy   and
πληροφορίᾳ πολλῇ, ᵏκαθὼς οἴδατε οἷοι
²assurance   ¹much,   as   ye know what sort
ἐγενήθημεν ἐν ὑμῖν δι᾽ ὑμᾶς. **6** καὶ
we were   among   you because of you.   And
ὑμεῖς μιμηταὶ ἡμῶν ἐγενήθητε καὶ τοῦ
¹ye   ²imitators   ⁴of us   ³became   and   of the
κυρίου, δεξάμενοι τὸν λόγον ἐν θλίψει
Lord,   welcoming   the   word   in   ²affliction
πολλῇ μετὰ χαρᾶς πνεύματος ἁγίου, **7** ὥστε
¹much   with   joy   of ²Spirit   ¹[the] Holy,   so as
γενέσθαι ὑμᾶς τύπον πᾶσιν τοῖς πιστεύουσιν
to become you[b]   a pattern   to all   the [ones] believing
ἐν τῇ Μακεδονίᾳ καὶ ἐν τῇ Ἀχαΐᾳ.
in   –   Macedonia   and   in   –   Achaia.

---

1 Thessalonians

Chapter 1

PAUL, Silas[a] and Timothy,
To the church of the Thessalonians in God the Father and the Lord Jesus Christ:
Grace and peace to you.[b]

Thanksgiving for the Thessalonians' Faith

²We always thank God for all of you, mentioning you in our prayers. ³We continually remember before our God and Father your work produced by faith, your labor prompted by love, and your endurance inspired by hope in our Lord Jesus Christ.

⁴For we know, brothers loved by God, that he has chosen you, ⁵because our gospel came to you not simply with words, but also with power, with the Holy Spirit and with deep conviction. You know how we lived among you for your sake. ⁶You became imitators of us and of the Lord; in spite of severe suffering, you welcomed the message with the joy given by the Holy Spirit. ⁷And so you became a model to all the believers in Macedonia and

---

[k] Other ancient authorities add *Amen*

[a] Gk *brothers*

[a] 1 Greek *Silvanus*, a variant of *Silas*
[b] 1 Some early manuscripts *you from God our Father and the Lord Jesus Christ*

8 For the word of the Lord has sounded forth from you not only in Macedonia and Achaia, but in every place your faith in God has become known, so that we have no need to speak about it. 9 For the people of those regions[b] report about us what kind of welcome we had among you, and how you turned to God from idols, to serve a living and true God, 10 and to wait for his Son from heaven, whom he raised from the dead—Jesus, who rescues us from the wrath that is coming.

8 ἀφ' ὑμῶν γὰρ ἐξήχηται ὁ λόγος τοῦ
¹from ⁰you ¹For sounded the word of the
κυρίου οὐ μόνον ἐν τῇ Μακεδονίᾳ καὶ
Lord not only in - Macedonia and
'Αχαίᾳ, ἀλλ' ἐν παντὶ τόπῳ ἡ πίστις
Achaia, but in every place the faith
ὑμῶν ἡ πρὸς τὸν θεὸν ἐξελήλυθεν, ὥστε
of you - toward - God has gone out, so as
μὴ χρείαν ἔχειν ἡμᾶς λαλεῖν τι· 9 αὐτοὶ
not need to have us[b] to speak anything; ²[them]-
=so that we have no need   selves
γὰρ περὶ ἡμῶν ἀπαγγέλλουσιν ὁποίαν
¹for ⁴concerning ⁵us ³they relate what sort of
εἴσοδον ἔσχομεν πρὸς ὑμᾶς, καὶ πῶς
entrance we had to you, and how
ἐπεστρέψατε πρὸς τὸν θεὸν ἀπὸ τῶν
ye turned to - God from the
εἰδώλων δουλεύειν θεῷ ζῶντι καὶ ἀληθινῷ,
idols to serve a God living and true,
10 καὶ ἀναμένειν τὸν υἱὸν αὐτοῦ ἐκ
and to await the Son of him from
τῶν οὐρανῶν, ὃν ἤγειρεν ἐκ τῶν νεκρῶν,
the heavens, whom he raised from the dead,
'Ιησοῦν τὸν ῥυόμενον ἡμᾶς ἐκ τῆς ὀργῆς
Jesus the [one] delivering us from the wrath
τῆς ἐρχομένης.
- coming.

Achaia. 8 The Lord's message rang out from you not only in Macedonia and Achaia—your faith in God has become known everywhere. Therefore we do not need to say anything about it, 9 for they themselves report what kind of reception you gave us. They tell how you turned to God from idols to serve the living and true God, 10 and to wait for his Son from heaven, whom he raised from the dead—Jesus, who rescues us from the coming wrath.

Chapter 2

Paul's Ministry in Thessalonica

YOU yourselves know, brothers and sisters,[a] that our coming to you was not in vain, 2 but though we had already suffered and been shamefully mistreated at Philippi, as you know, we had courage in our God to declare to you the gospel of God in spite of great opposition. 3 For our appeal does not spring from deceit or impure motives or trickery, 4 but just as we have been approved by God to be entrusted with the message of the gospel, even so we speak, not to please mortals, but to please God who tests our hearts. 5 As you know and as God is our witness, we never came with words of flattery or with a pretext for greed; 6 nor did we seek praise from mortals, whether from you or from

2 Αὐτοὶ γὰρ οἴδατε, ἀδελφοί, τὴν
For [your]selves ye know, brothers, the
εἴσοδον ἡμῶν τὴν πρὸς ὑμᾶς, ὅτι οὐ
entrance of us - to you, that not
κενὴ γέγονεν, 2 ἀλλὰ προπαθόντες καὶ
in vain it has been, but having previously and
suffered
ὑβρισθέντες καθὼς οἴδατε ἐν Φιλίπποις
having been as ye know in Philippi
insulted
ἐπαρρησιασάμεθα ἐν τῷ θεῷ ἡμῶν λαλῆσαι
we were bold in the God of us to speak
πρὸς ὑμᾶς τὸ εὐαγγέλιον τοῦ θεοῦ ἐν
to you the gospel - of God in
πολλῷ ἀγῶνι. 3 ἡ γὰρ · παράκλησις
much struggle. For the exhortation
ἡμῶν οὐκ ἐκ πλάνης οὐδὲ ἐξ ἀκαθαρσίας
of us not of error nor of uncleanness
οὐδὲ ἐν δόλῳ, 4 ἀλλὰ καθὼς δεδοκιμάσμεθα
nor in guile, but as we have been
approved
ὑπὸ τοῦ θεοῦ πιστευθῆναι τὸ εὐαγγέλιον
by - God to be entrusted [with] the gospel
οὕτως λαλοῦμεν, οὐχ ὡς ἀνθρώποις ἀρέ-
so we speak, not as ¹men ¹pleas-
σκοντες, ἀλλὰ θεῷ τῷ δοκιμάζοντι τὰς
ing, but God the [one] proving the
καρδίας ἡμῶν. 5 οὔτε γάρ ποτε ἐν
hearts of us. For neither then with
λόγῳ κολακείας ἐγενήθημεν, καθὼς οἴδατε,
word of flattery were we, as ye know,
οὔτε ἐν προφάσει πλεονεξίας, θεὸς μάρτυς,
nor with pretext of covetousness, God [is] witness,
6 οὔτε ζητοῦντες ἐξ ἀνθρώπων δόξαν,
nor seeking from men glory,
οὔτε ἀφ' ὑμῶν οὔτε ἀπ' ἄλλων, 7 δυνάμε-
neither from you nor from others, being

Chapter 2

Paul's Ministry in Thessalonica

YOU know, brothers, that our visit to you was not a failure. 2 We had previously suffered and been insulted in Philippi, as you know, but with the help of our God we dared to tell you his gospel in spite of strong opposition. 3 For the appeal we make does not spring from error or impure motives, nor are we trying to trick you. 4 On the contrary, we speak as men approved by God to be entrusted with the gospel. We are not trying to please men but God, who tests our hearts. 5 You know we never used flattery, nor did we put on a mask to cover up greed—God is our witness. 6 We were not looking for praise from men, not from you or anyone else.

---

[b] Gk For they

others, 7though we might have made demands as apostles of Christ. But we were gentle*c* among you, like a nurse tenderly caring for her own children. 8So deeply do we care for you that we are determined to share with you not only the gospel of God but also our own selves, because you have become very dear to us.

9 You remember our labor and toil, brothers and sisters;*a* we worked night and day, so that we might not burden any of you while we proclaimed to you the gospel of God. 10You are witnesses, and God also, how pure, upright, and blameless our conduct was toward you believers. 11As you know, we dealt with each one of you like a father with his children, 12urging and encouraging you and pleading that you lead a life worthy of God, who calls you into his own kingdom and glory.

13 We also constantly give thanks to God for this, that when you received the word of God that you heard from us, you accepted it not as a human word but as what it really is, God's word, which is also at work in you believers. 14For you, brothers and sisters,*a* became imitators of the churches of God in Christ Jesus that are in Judea, for you suffered the same

νοι ἐν βάρει εἶναι ὡς Χριστοῦ ἀπόστολοι·
able *with* *weight* *to be as* *of Christ* *apostles;*

ἀλλὰ ἐγενήθημεν ἤπιοι ἐν μέσῳ ὑμῶν,
but we were gentle in [the] midst of you,

ὡς ἐὰν τροφὸς θάλπῃ τὰ ἑαυτῆς τέκνα·
as if a nurse should *the* *of herself* *children;*
             cherish

8 οὕτως ὁμειρόμενοι ὑμῶν ηὐδοκοῦμεν
so longing for you we were well pleased

μεταδοῦναι ὑμῖν οὐ μόνον τὸ εὐαγγέλιον
to impart to you not only the gospel

τοῦ θεοῦ ἀλλὰ καὶ τὰς ἑαυτῶν ψυχάς,
– of God but also *the* *of ourselves* *souls,*

διότι ἀγαπητοὶ ἡμῖν ἐγενήθητε. 9 μνημο-
because *beloved* *to us* ye became. ye re-

νεύετε γάρ, ἀδελφοί, τὸν κόπον ἡμῶν
member For, brothers, the labour of us

καὶ τὸν μόχθον· νυκτὸς καὶ ἡμέρας
and the toil; night and day

ἐργαζόμενοι πρὸς τὸ μὴ ἐπιβαρῆσαί τινα
working for *the* not to put a burden any-
                      on one

ὑμῶν ἐκηρύξαμεν εἰς ὑμᾶς τὸ εὐαγγέλιον
of you we proclaimed to you the gospel

τοῦ θεοῦ. 10 ὑμεῖς μάρτυρες καὶ ὁ
– of God. Ye [are] witnesses and

θεός, ὡς ὁσίως καὶ δικαίως καὶ ἀμέμπτως
God, how holily and righteously and blamelessly

ὑμῖν τοῖς πιστεύουσιν ἐγενήθημεν, 11 καθά-
to you *the [ones]* *believing* *we were,* even

περ οἴδατε ὡς ἕνα ἕκαστον ὑμῶν ὡς
as ye know how *one* *each* of you as

πατὴρ τέκνα ἑαυτοῦ παρακαλοῦντες ὑμᾶς
a father children of himself exhorting you

καὶ παραμυθούμενοι 12 καὶ μαρτυρόμενοι εἰς
and consoling and witnessing for

τὸ περιπατεῖν ὑμᾶς ἀξίως τοῦ θεοῦ
the to walk you*b* worthily – of God
=that ye should walk

τοῦ καλοῦντος ὑμᾶς εἰς τὴν ἑαυτοῦ
the [one] calling you to *the* *of himself*

βασιλείαν καὶ δόξαν.
kingdom *and* *glory.*

13 Καὶ διὰ τοῦτο καὶ ἡμεῖς εὐχαρισ-
And therefore also we give

τοῦμεν τῷ θεῷ ἀδιαλείπτως, ὅτι παρα-
thanks – to God unceasingly, that having

λαβόντες λόγον ἀκοῆς παρ' ἡμῶν τοῦ
received *[the] word* *of hearing* *from* *us* the

θεοῦ ἐδέξασθε οὐ λόγον ἀνθρώπων ἀλλὰ
of God ye welcomed not [as] a of men but
               [it] word

καθὼς ἀληθῶς ἐστιν λόγον θεοῦ, ὃς
as truly it is a word of God, which

καὶ ἐνεργεῖται ἐν ὑμῖν τοῖς πιστεύουσιν.
also operates in you the [ones] believing.

14 ὑμεῖς γὰρ μιμηταὶ ἐγενήθητε, ἀδελφοί,
For ye *imitators* *became,* brothers,

τῶν ἐκκλησιῶν τοῦ θεοῦ τῶν οὐσῶν ἐν
of the churches – of God – being in

τῇ Ἰουδαίᾳ ἐν Χριστῷ Ἰησοῦ, ὅτι τὰ
– Judæa in Christ Jesus, because *the*

As apostles of Christ we could have been a burden to you, 7but we were gentle among you, like a mother caring for her little children. 8We loved you so much that we were delighted to share with you not only the gospel of God but our lives as well, because you had become so dear to us. 9Surely you remember, brothers, our toil and hardship; we worked night and day in order not to be a burden to anyone while we preached the gospel of God to you.

10You are witnesses, and so is God, of how holy, righteous and blameless we were among you who believed. 11For you know that we dealt with each of you as a father deals with his own children, 12encouraging, comforting and urging you to live lives worthy of God, who calls you into his kingdom and glory.

13And we also thank God continually because, when you received the word of God, which you heard from us, you accepted it not as the word of men, but as it actually is, the word of God, which is at work in you who believe. 14For you, brothers, became imitators of God's churches in Judea, which are in Christ Jesus: You suffered from

* ? dignity, authority.

things from your own compatriots as they did from the Jews, 15 who killed both the Lord Jesus and the prophets,[d] and drove us out; they displease God and oppose everyone 16 by hindering us from speaking to the Gentiles so that they may be saved. Thus they have constantly been filling up the measure of their sins; but God's wrath has overtaken them at last.[e]

Paul's Desire to Visit the Thessalonians Again

17 As for us, brothers and sisters,[a] when, for a short time, we were made orphans by being separated from you—in person, not in heart—we longed with great eagerness to see you face to face. 18 For we wanted to come to you—certainly I, Paul, wanted to again and again—but Satan blocked our way. 19 For what is our hope or joy or crown of boasting before our Lord Jesus at his coming? Is it not you? 20 Yes, you are our glory and joy!

αὐτὰ ἐπάθετε καὶ ὑμεῖς ὑπὸ τῶν ἰδίων
²same ²suffered ³also ¹ye by the(your) own things

συμφυλετῶν, καθὼς καὶ αὐτοὶ ὑπὸ τῶν
fellow-tribesmen, as also they by the

'Ιουδαίων, 15 τῶν καὶ τὸν κύριον
Jews, the [ones] ¹both ²the ⁴Lord

ἀποκτεινάντων 'Ιησοῦν καὶ τοὺς προφήτας,
²killing ³Jesus and the prophets,

καὶ ἡμᾶς ἐκδιωξάντων, καὶ θεῷ μὴ
and ²us ¹chasing ³out, and ²God ¹not

ἀρεσκόντων, καὶ πᾶσιν ἀνθρώποις ἐναντίων,
²pleasing, and to all men contrary,

16 κωλυόντων ἡμᾶς τοῖς ἔθνεσιν λαλῆσαι
hindering us ²to the ³nations ¹to speak =from speaking . . .

ἵνα σωθῶσιν, εἰς τὸ ἀναπληρῶσαι αὐτῶν
in order they may for the to fill up ²of them that be saved,

τὰς ἁμαρτίας πάντοτε. ἔφθασεν δὲ ἐπ'
¹the ²sins always. But ²came ⁴on

αὐτοὺς ἡ ὀργὴ εἰς τέλος.
³them ¹the ²wrath to [the] end.

17 'Ημεῖς δέ, ἀδελφοί, ἀπορφανισθέντες
But we brothers, being bereaved

ἀφ' ὑμῶν πρὸς καιρὸν ὥρας προσώπῳ
from you for time of an hour in face (presence)

οὐ καρδίᾳ, περισσοτέρως ἐσπουδάσαμεν τὸ
not in heart, more abundantly were eager ²the

πρόσωπον ὑμῶν ἰδεῖν ἐν πολλῇ ἐπιθυμίᾳ.
²face ⁴of you ¹to see with much desire.

18 διότι ἠθελήσαμεν ἐλθεῖν πρὸς ὑμᾶς,
Wherefore we wished to come to you,

ἐγὼ μὲν Παῦλος καὶ ἅπαξ καὶ δίς,
I ²indeed ¹Paul both once and twice (again),

καὶ ἐνέκοψεν ἡμᾶς ὁ σατανᾶς. 19 τίς
and ¹hindered ²us - ¹Satan. what

γὰρ ἡμῶν ἐλπὶς ἢ χαρὰ ἢ στέφανος
For [is] ²of us ¹hope or joy or crown

καυχήσεως — ἢ οὐχὶ καὶ ὑμεῖς —
of boasting — - not even ye —

ἔμπροσθεν τοῦ κυρίου ἡμῶν 'Ιησοῦ
before the Lord of us Jesus

ἐν τῇ αὐτοῦ παρουσίᾳ; 20 ὑμεῖς γὰρ
in(at) the ²of him ¹presence? for ye

ἐστε ἡ δόξα ἡμῶν καὶ ἡ χαρά.
are ¹the ²glory ⁴of us ²and ¹the ⁴joy.

3 Διὸ μηκέτι στέγοντες ηὐδοκήσαμεν
Wherefore no longer bearing up we were well pleased

καταλειφθῆναι ἐν 'Αθήναις μόνοι, 2 καὶ
to be left in Athens alone, and

ἐπέμψαμεν Τιμόθεον, τὸν ἀδελφὸν ἡμῶν
we sent Timothy, the brother of us

καὶ συνεργὸν τοῦ θεοῦ ἐν τῷ εὐαγγελίῳ
and fellow-worker - of God in the gospel

τοῦ Χριστοῦ, εἰς τὸ στηρίξαι ὑμᾶς καὶ
- of Christ, for the to establish you and

παρακαλέσαι ὑπὲρ τῆς πίστεως ὑμῶν 3 τὸ
to exhort on behalf of the faith of you -

μηδένα σαίνεσθαι ἐν ταῖς θλίψεσιν ταύταις.
no one to be drawn by these afflictions. aside[b]

αὐτοὶ γὰρ οἴδατε ὅτι εἰς τοῦτο κείμεθα·
For [your]selves ye know that to this we are appointed;

---

your own countrymen the same things those churches suffered from the Jews, 15 who killed the Lord Jesus and the prophets and drove us out. They displease God and are hostile to all men 16 in their effort to keep us from speaking to the Gentiles so that they may be saved. In this way they always heap up their sins to the limit. The wrath of God has come upon them at last.[c]

Paul's Longing to See the Thessalonians

17 But, brothers, when we were torn away from you for a short time (in person, not in thought), out of our intense longing we made every effort to see you. 18 For we wanted to come to you—certainly I, Paul, did, again and again—but Satan stopped us. 19 For what is our hope, our joy, or the crown in which we will glory in the presence of our Lord Jesus when he comes? Is it not you? 20 Indeed, you are our glory and joy.

Chapter 3

SO when we could stand it no longer, we thought it best to be left by ourselves in Athens. 2 We sent Timothy, who is our brother and God's fellow worker[d] in spreading the gospel of Christ, to strengthen and encourage you in your faith, 3 so that no one would be unsettled by these trials. You know quite well that we were destined for them. 4 In fact,

---

Chapter 3

THEREFORE when we could bear it no longer, we decided to be left alone in Athens; 2 and we sent Timothy, our brother and co-worker for God in proclaiming[f] the gospel of Christ, to strengthen and encourage you for the sake of your faith, 3 so that no one would be shaken by these persecutions. Indeed, you yourselves know that this is what we are destined for. 4 In fact, when we

---

[d] Other ancient authorities read *their own prophets*
[e] Or *completely* or *forever*
[f] Gk lacks *proclaiming*

[c] 16 Or *them fully*
[d] 2 Some manuscripts *brother and fellow worker*; other manuscripts *brother and God's servant*

were with you, we told you beforehand that we were to suffer persecution; so it turned out, as you know. 5 For this reason, when I could bear it no longer, I sent to find out about your faith; I was afraid that somehow the tempter had tempted you and that our labor had been in vain.

Timothy's Encouraging Report

6 But Timothy has just now come to us from you, and has brought us the good news of your faith and love. He has told us also that you always remember us kindly and long to see us—just as we long to see you. 7 For this reason, brothers and sisters,[g] during all our distress and persecution we have been encouraged about you through your faith. 8 For we now live, if you continue to stand firm in the Lord. 9 How can we thank God enough for you in return for all the joy that we feel before our God because of you? 10 Night and day we pray most earnestly that we may see you face to face and restore whatever is lacking in your faith.

11 Now may our God and Father himself and our Lord Jesus direct our way to you. 12 And may the Lord make you increase and abound in love for one another and for all, just as we abound in love for you. 13 And may he so strengthen your hearts in holiness that you may be blameless before our God and Father at the coming of our Lord

---

4 καὶ γὰρ ὅτε πρὸς ὑμᾶς ἦμεν,
for even when with you we were,

προελέγομεν ὑμῖν ὅτι μέλλομεν θλίβεσθαι,
we said before to you that we are about to be afflicted,

καθὼς καὶ ἐγένετο καὶ οἴδατε. **5** διὰ
as indeed it happened and ye know. There-

τοῦτο κἀγὼ μηκέτι στέγων ἔπεμψα εἰς
fore I also no longer bearing up sent for

τὸ γνῶναι τὴν πίστιν ὑμῶν, μή πως
the to know the faith of you, lest [some]how

ἐπείρασεν ὑμᾶς ὁ πειράζων καὶ εἰς
²tempted ⁴you ¹the [one] ³tempting and in
= the tempter

κενὸν γένηται ὁ κόπος ἡμῶν. **6** Ἄρτι
vain became the labour of us. now

δὲ ἐλθόντος Τιμοθέου πρὸς ἡμᾶς ἀφ'
But coming Timothy[a] to us from
= when Timothy came

ὑμῶν καὶ εὐαγγελισαμένου ἡμῖν τὴν πίστιν
you and announcing good news[a] to us [of] the faith

καὶ τὴν ἀγάπην ὑμῶν, καὶ ὅτι ἔχετε
and the love of you, and that ye have

μνείαν ἡμῶν ἀγαθὴν πάντοτε, ἐπιποθοῦντες
²remem- ¹of us ¹good always, longing
brance

ἡμᾶς ἰδεῖν καθάπερ καὶ ἡμεῖς ὑμᾶς,
¹us ¹to see even as also we you,

7 διὰ τοῦτο παρεκλήθημεν, ἀδελφοί, ἐφ'
therefore we were comforted, brothers, over

ὑμῖν ἐπὶ πάσῃ τῇ ἀνάγκῃ καὶ θλίψει
you on all the distress and affliction

ἡμῶν διὰ τῆς ὑμῶν πίστεως, **8** ὅτι
of us through the ²of you ¹faith, because

νῦν ζῶμεν ἐὰν ὑμεῖς στήκετε ἐν κυρίῳ.
now we live if ye stand in [the] Lord.

9 τίνα γὰρ εὐχαριστίαν δυνάμεθα τῷ θεῷ
For what thanks are we able - to God

ἀνταποδοῦναι περὶ ὑμῶν ἐπὶ πάσῃ τῇ
to return concerning you over all the

χαρᾷ ᾗ χαίρομεν δι' ὑμᾶς ἔμπροσθεν
joy [with] we rejoice because you before
which of

τοῦ θεοῦ ἡμῶν, **10** νυκτὸς καὶ ἡμέρας
the God of us, night and day

ὑπερεκπερισσοῦ δεόμενοι εἰς τὸ ἰδεῖν ὑμῶν
exceedingly petitioning for the to see of you

τὸ πρόσωπον καὶ καταρτίσαι τὰ ὑστερήματα
the face and to adjust the shortcomings

τῆς πίστεως ὑμῶν; **11** Αὐτὸς δὲ ὁ θεὸς
of the faith of you? Now [him]self the God

καὶ πατὴρ ἡμῶν καὶ ὁ κύριος ἡμῶν
and Father of us and the Lord of us

Ἰησοῦς κατευθύναι τὴν ὁδὸν ἡμῶν πρὸς
Jesus may he direct the way of us to

ὑμᾶς· **12** ὑμᾶς δὲ ὁ κύριος πλεονάσαι
you; and ⁴you ¹the ²Lord ³make ⁵to abound

καὶ περισσεύσαι τῇ ἀγάπῃ εἰς ἀλλήλους
and to exceed - in love to one another

καὶ εἰς πάντας, καθάπερ καὶ ἡμεῖς
and to all men, even as also we

εἰς ὑμᾶς, **13** εἰς τὸ στηρίξαι ὑμῶν τὰς
to you, for the to establish of you the

καρδίας ἀμέμπτους ἐν ἁγιωσύνῃ ἔμπροσθεν
hearts blameless in holiness before

τοῦ θεοῦ καὶ πατρὸς ἡμῶν ἐν τῇ παρουσίᾳ
the God and Father of us in(at) the presence

---

when we were with you, we kept telling you that we would be persecuted. And it turned out that way, as you well know. 5 For this reason, when I could stand it no longer, I sent to find out about your faith. I was afraid that in some way the tempter might have tempted you and our efforts might have been useless.

Timothy's Encouraging Report

6 But Timothy has just now come to us from you and has brought good news about your faith. He has told us that you always have pleasant memories of us and that you long to see us, just as we also long to see you. 7 Therefore, brothers, in all our distress and persecution we were encouraged about you because of your faith. 8 For now we really live, since you are standing firm in the Lord. 9 How can we thank God enough for you in return for all the joy we have in the presence of our God because of you? 10 Night and day we pray most earnestly that we may see you again and supply what is lacking in your faith.

11 Now may our God and Father himself and our Lord Jesus clear the way for us to come to you. 12 May the Lord make your love increase and overflow for each other and for everyone else, just as ours does for you. 13 May he strengthen your hearts so that you will be blameless and holy in the presence of our God and Father when

---

g Gk brothers

Jesus with all his saints.

Chapter 4

A Life Pleasing to God

FINALLY, brothers and sisters,[g] we ask and urge you in the Lord Jesus that, as you learned from us how you ought to live and to please God (as, in fact, you are doing), you should do so more and more. 2 For you know what instructions we gave you through the Lord Jesus. 3 For this is the will of God, your sanctification: that you abstain from fornication; 4 that each one of you know how to control your own body[h] in holiness and honor, 5 not with lustful passion, like the Gentiles who do not know God; 6 that no one wrong or exploit a brother or sister[i] in this matter, because the Lord is an avenger in all these things, just as we have already told you beforehand and solemnly warned you. 7 For God did not call us to impurity but in holiness. 8 Therefore whoever rejects this rejects not human authority but God, who also gives his Holy Spirit to you.

9 Now concerning love of the brothers and sisters,[g] you do not need to have anyone write to you, for you yourselves have been taught by God to love one another; 10 and indeed you do love all the brothers and sisters[g] throughout

---

τοῦ κυρίου ἡμῶν Ἰησοῦ μετὰ πάντων
of the Lord of us Jesus with all
τῶν ἁγίων αὐτοῦ.
the saints of him.

4 Λοιπὸν οὖν, ἀδελφοί, ἐρωτῶμεν ὑμᾶς
For the rest therefore, brothers, we ask you
καὶ παρακαλοῦμεν ἐν κυρίῳ Ἰησοῦ, ἵνα
and we beseech in [the] Lord Jesus, in order that
καθὼς παρελάβετε παρ' ἡμῶν τὸ πῶς
as ye received from us the how
δεῖ ὑμᾶς περιπατεῖν καὶ ἀρέσκειν θεῷ,
it behoves you to walk and to please God,
καθὼς καὶ περιπατεῖτε, ἵνα περισσεύητε
as indeed ye do walk, in order that ye abound
μᾶλλον. **2** οἴδατε γὰρ τίνας παραγγελίας
more. For ye know what injunctions
ἐδώκαμεν ὑμῖν διὰ τοῦ κυρίου Ἰησοῦ.
we gave you through the Lord Jesus.
3 Τοῦτο γάρ ἐστιν θέλημα τοῦ θεοῦ,
For this is [the] will - of God,
ὁ ἁγιασμὸς ὑμῶν, ἀπέχεσθαι ὑμᾶς ἀπὸ
the sanctification of you, to abstain you[b] from
τῆς πορνείας, **4** εἰδέναι ἕκαστον ὑμῶν
fornication, ²to know³ ¹each one[b] ²of you
τὸ ἑαυτοῦ σκεῦος κτᾶσθαι ἐν ἁγιασμῷ
²the ⁷of himself ⁴vessel ⁴to possess in sanctification
καὶ τιμῇ, **5** μὴ ἐν πάθει ἐπιθυμίας
and honour, not in passion of lust
καθάπερ καὶ τὰ ἔθνη τὰ μὴ εἰδότα
even as indeed the nations the not knowing
τὸν θεόν, **6** τὸ μὴ ὑπερβαίνειν καὶ
God, - not to go beyond and
πλεονεκτεῖν ἐν τῷ πράγματι τὸν ἀδελφὸν
to defraud in the matter the brother
αὐτοῦ, διότι ἔκδικος κύριος περὶ πάντων
of him, be- ²[the] ¹[the] Lord con- all
cause avenger [is] cerning
τούτων, καθὼς καὶ προείπαμεν ὑμῖν καὶ
these, as in- we previously you and
deed told
διεμαρτυράμεθα. **7** οὐ γὰρ ἐκάλεσεν ἡμᾶς
solemnly witnessed. For ⁴not ²called ³us
ὁ θεὸς ἐπὶ ἀκαθαρσίᾳ ἀλλ' ἐν ἁγιασμῷ.
- ¹God to uncleanness but in sanctification.
8 τοιγαροῦν ὁ ἀθετῶν οὐκ ἄνθρωπον
Wherefore the [one] rejecting ²not ³man
ἀθετεῖ ἀλλὰ τὸν θεὸν τὸν καὶ διδόντα
¹rejects but - God the in- giving
[one] deed
τὸ πνεῦμα αὐτοῦ τὸ ἅγιον εἰς ὑμᾶς.
the ²Spirit ³of him - ¹Holy to you.
9 Περὶ δὲ τῆς φιλαδελφίας οὐ χρείαν
Now concerning brotherly love not need
ἔχετε γράφειν ὑμῖν· αὐτοὶ γὰρ ὑμεῖς
ye have to write to you; for ²[your]selves ¹ye
[for me]
θεοδίδακτοί ἐστε εἰς τὸ ἀγαπᾶν ἀλλήλους·
⁴taught by God ³are for the to love one another;
10 καὶ γὰρ ποιεῖτε αὐτὸ εἰς πάντας
for indeed ye do it toward all
τοὺς ἀδελφοὺς [τοὺς] ἐν ὅλῃ τῇ Μακεδο-
the brothers - in all the Macedo-

---

our Lord Jesus comes with all his holy ones.

Chapter 4

Living to Please God

FINALLY, brothers, we instructed you how to live in order to please God, as in fact you are living. Now we ask you and urge you in the Lord Jesus to do this more and more. 2 For you know what instructions we gave you by the authority of the Lord Jesus.

3 It is God's will that you should be sanctified: that you should avoid sexual immorality; 4 that each of you should learn to control his own body[e] in a way that is holy and honorable, 5 not in passionate lust like the heathen, who do not know God; 6 and that in this matter no one should wrong his brother or take advantage of him. The Lord will punish men for all such sins, as we have already told you and warned you. 7 For God did not call us to be impure, but to live a holy life. 8 Therefore, he who rejects this instruction does not reject man but God, who gives you his Holy Spirit.

9 Now about brotherly love we do not need to write to you, for you yourselves have been taught by God to love each other. 10 And in fact, you do love all the brothers throughout

---

[h] Or *how to take a wife for himself*
[i] Gk *brother*

* That is, " to be able ": see note on page xvi.

[e]4 Or *learn to live with his own wife;* or *learn to acquire a wife*

Macedonia. But we urge you, beloved,ᵍ to do so more and more, 11 to aspire to live quietly, to mind your own affairs, and to work with your hands, as we directed you, 12 so that you may behave properly toward outsiders and be dependent on no one.

The Coming of the Lord

13 But we do not want you to be uninformed, brothers and sisters,ᵍ about those who have died,ʲ so that you may not grieve as others do who have no hope. 14 For since we believe that Jesus died and rose again, even so, through Jesus, God will bring with him those who have died.ʲ 15 For this we declare to you by the word of the Lord, that we who are alive, who are left until the coming of the Lord, will by no means precede those who have died.ʲ 16 For the Lord himself, with a cry of command, with the archangel's call and with the sound of God's trumpet, will descend from heaven, and the dead in Christ will rise first. 17 Then we who are alive, who are left, will be caught up in the clouds together with them to meet the Lord in the air; and so we will be with the Lord forever. 18 Therefore encourage one another with these words.

νία.   Παρακαλοῦμεν   δὲ   ὑμᾶς,   ἀδελφοί,
nia.   But we exhort   you,   brothers,

περισσεύειν   μᾶλλον,   11 καὶ   φιλοτιμεῖσθαι
to abound   more,   and   to strive eagerly

ἡσυχάζειν   καὶ   πράσσειν   τὰ   ἴδια   καὶ
to be quiet   and   to practise   the   own   and
                           (your) things

ἐργάζεσθαι   ταῖς   χερσὶν   ὑμῶν,   καθὼς   ὑμῖν
to work   with the   hands   of you,   as   ²you

παρηγγείλαμεν,   12 ἵνα   περιπατῆτε   εὐσχη-
¹we enjoined,   in or-   ye may walk   becom-
               der that

μόνως   πρὸς   τοὺς   ἔξω   καὶ   μηδενὸς
ingly   toward   the [ones]   outside   and   ³of nothing

χρείαν   ἔχητε.
²need   ¹ye may have.

13 Οὐ   θέλομεν   δὲ   ὑμᾶς   ἀγνοεῖν,   ἀδελφοί,
Now we do not wish   you   to be   brothers,
                          ignorant,

περὶ   τῶν   κοιμωμένων,   ἵνα   μὴ   λυπῆσθε
con-   the   sleeping,   lest   ye grieve
cerning   [ones]

καθὼς   καὶ   οἱ   λοιποὶ   οἱ   μὴ   ἔχοντες
as   indeed   the   rest   -   not   having

ἐλπίδα.   14 εἰ   γὰρ   πιστεύομεν   ὅτι   Ἰησοῦς
hope.   For if   we believe   that   Jesus

ἀπέθανεν   καὶ   ἀνέστη,   οὕτως   καὶ   ὁ   θεὸς
died   and   rose again,   so   also   -   ⁵God

τοὺς   κοιμηθέντας   διὰ   τοῦ   Ἰησοῦ   ἄξει
¹the   ²having slept   ³through   -   ⁴Jesus   will
[ones]   bring

σὺν   αὐτῷ.   15 Τοῦτο   γὰρ   ὑμῖν   λέγομεν
with   him.   For this   to you   we say

ἐν   λόγῳ   κυρίου,   ὅτι   ἡμεῖς   οἱ   ζῶντες
by   a word   of [the]   that   we   the   living
       Lord,   [ones]

οἱ   περιλειπόμενοι   εἰς   τὴν   παρουσίαν   τοῦ
-   remaining   to   the   presence   of the

κυρίου   οὐ   μὴ   φθάσωμεν   τοὺς   κοιμηθέντας·
Lord   by no   may precede   the   having slept;
      means   [ones]

16 ὅτι   αὐτὸς   ὁ   κύριος   ἐν   κελεύσματι,
be-   ²[him]-   ¹the   ²Lord   with   a word of
cause   self   command,

ἐν   φωνῇ   ἀρχαγγέλου   καὶ   ἐν   σάλπιγγι
with   a voice   of an archangel   and   with   a trumpet

θεοῦ,   καταβήσεται   ἀπ'   οὐρανοῦ,   καὶ   οἱ
of God,   will descend   from   heaven,   and   the

νεκροὶ   ἐν   Χριστῷ   ἀναστήσονται   πρῶτον,
dead   in   Christ   will rise again   first*ly*,

17 ἔπειτα   ἡμεῖς   οἱ   ζῶντες   οἱ   περιλειπόμενοι
then   we   the   living   -   remaining
               [ones]

ἅμα   σὺν   αὐτοῖς   ἁρπαγησόμεθα   ἐν   νεφέλαις
to-   with   them   shall be seized   in   clouds
gether

εἰς   ἀπάντησιν   τοῦ   κυρίου   εἰς   ἀέρα·
to   a meeting   of the   Lord   in   air;

καὶ   οὕτως   πάντοτε   σὺν   κυρίῳ   ἐσόμεθα.
and   so   always   with   [the] Lord   we shall be.

18 Ὥστε   παρακαλεῖτε   ἀλλήλους   ἐν   τοῖς   λόγοις
Therefore   comfort ye   one   with   -   words
                       another

τούτοις.
these.

Macedonia. Yet we urge you, brothers, to do so more and more. 11 Make it your ambition to lead a quiet life, to mind your own business and to work with your hands, just as we told you, 12 so that your daily life may win the respect of outsiders and so that you will not be dependent on anybody.

The Coming of the Lord

13 Brothers, we do not want you to be ignorant about those who fall asleep, or to grieve like the rest of men, who have no hope. 14 We believe that Jesus died and rose again and so we believe that God will bring with Jesus those who have fallen asleep in him. 15 According to the Lord's own word, we tell you that we who are still alive, who are left till the coming of the Lord, will certainly not precede those who have fallen asleep. 16 For the Lord himself will come down from heaven, with a loud command, with the voice of the archangel and with the trumpet call of God, and the dead in Christ will rise first. 17 After that, we who are still alive and are left will be caught up together with them in the clouds to meet the Lord in the air. And so we will be with the Lord forever. 18 Therefore encourage each other with these words.

ʲ Gk *fallen asleep*

Chapter 5

NOW concerning the times and the seasons, brothers and sisters,[g] you do not need to have anything written to you. [2]For you yourselves know very well that the day of the Lord will come like a thief in the night. [3]When they say, "There is peace and security," then sudden destruction will come upon them, as labor pains come upon a pregnant woman, and there will be no escape! [4]But you, beloved,[k] are not in darkness, for that day to surprise you like a thief; [5]for you are all children of light and children of the day; we are not of the night or of darkness. [6]So then let us not fall asleep as others do, but let us keep awake and be sober; [7]for those who sleep sleep at night, and those who are drunk get drunk at night. [8]But since we belong to the day, let us be sober, and put on the breastplate of faith and love, and for a helmet the hope of salvation. [9]For God has destined us not for wrath but for obtaining salvation through our Lord Jesus Christ, [10]who died for us, so that whether we are awake or asleep we may live with him. [11]Therefore encourage one another and build up each other, as indeed you are doing.

Final Exhortations, Greetings, and Benediction

12 But we appeal to you, brothers and sisters,[k] to respect those who labor among you, and have charge of you in the Lord and admonish you; [13]esteem them very highly in love because of their work.

[g] Gk brothers

---

5 Περὶ δὲ τῶν χρόνων καὶ τῶν καιρῶν,
But concerning the times and the seasons,

ἀδελφοί, οὐ χρείαν ἔχετε ὑμῖν γράφεσθαι·
brothers, [2]not [3]need [1]ye have [5]to you [4]to be written;

2 αὐτοὶ γὰρ ἀκριβῶς οἴδατε ὅτι ἡμέρα
[2][your]selves [3]accurately [1]ye know that [the] day

κυρίου ὡς κλέπτης ἐν νυκτὶ οὕτως
of [the] Lord as a thief at night so

ἔρχεται. 3 ὅταν λέγωσιν· εἰρήνη καὶ
it comes. Whenever they say : Peace and

ἀσφάλεια, τότε αἰφνίδιος αὐτοῖς ἐφίσταται
safety, then [1]sudden [4]them [2]comes on

ὄλεθρος ὥσπερ ἡ ὠδὶν τῇ ἐν γαστρὶ
[3]destruction as the birth pang to the pregnant

ἐχούσῃ, καὶ οὐ μὴ ἐκφύγωσιν. 4 ὑμεῖς
woman,† and by no may they escape. ye
means

δέ, ἀδελφοί, οὐκ ἐστὲ ἐν σκότει, ἵνα
But, brothers, are not in darkness, der that

ἡ ἡμέρα ὑμᾶς ὡς κλέπτης καταλάβῃ·
the day you as a thief should overtake;

5 πάντες γὰρ ὑμεῖς υἱοὶ φωτός ἐστε
for all ye [2]sons [3]of light [1]are

καὶ υἱοὶ ἡμέρας. Οὐκ ἐσμὲν νυκτὸς
and sons of [the] day. We are not of [the] night

οὐδὲ σκότους· 6 ἄρα οὖν μὴ καθεύδωμεν
nor of darkness; therefore let us not sleep

ὡς οἱ λοιποί, ἀλλὰ γρηγορῶμεν καὶ
as the rest, but let us watch and

νήφωμεν. 7 οἱ γὰρ καθεύδοντες νυκτὸς
be sober. For the [ones] sleeping by night

καθεύδουσιν, καὶ οἱ μεθυσκόμενοι νυκτὸς
sleep, and the [ones] being drunk by night

μεθύουσιν· 8 ἡμεῖς δὲ ἡμέρας ὄντες
are drunk; but we of [the] day being

νήφωμεν, ἐνδυσάμενοι θώρακα πίστεως καὶ
let us be sober, putting on a breastplate of faith and

ἀγάπης καὶ περικεφαλαίαν ἐλπίδα σωτηρίας·
of love and a helmet hope of salvation;

9 ὅτι οὐκ ἔθετο ἡμᾶς ὁ θεὸς εἰς ὀργὴν
because [2]did not appoint [3]us – [1]God to wrath

ἀλλὰ εἰς περιποίησιν σωτηρίας διὰ τοῦ
but to obtainment of salvation through the

κυρίου ἡμῶν Ἰησοῦ Χριστοῦ, 10 τοῦ
Lord of us Jesus Christ, the

ἀποθανόντος περὶ ἡμῶν, ἵνα εἴτε γρηγορ-
[one] having died concern- us, in or- whether we
ing der that

ὦμεν εἴτε καθεύδωμεν ἅμα σὺν αὐτῷ
watch or we sleep [2]together [3]with [4]him

ζήσωμεν. 11 Διὸ παρακαλεῖτε ἀλλήλους
[1]we may live. There- comfort ye one another
fore

καὶ οἰκοδομεῖτε εἰς τὸν ἕνα, καθὼς καὶ
and edify ye one the one(other), as indeed

ποιεῖτε.
ye do.

12 Ἐρωτῶμεν δὲ ὑμᾶς, ἀδελφοί, εἰδέναι
Now we ask you, brothers, to know

τοὺς κοπιῶντας ἐν ὑμῖν καὶ προϊσταμένους
the [ones] labouring among you and taking the lead

ὑμῶν ἐν κυρίῳ καὶ νουθετοῦντας ὑμᾶς,
of you in [the] Lord and admonishing you,

13 καὶ ἡγεῖσθαι αὐτοὺς ὑπερεκπερισσῶς
and consider them most exceedingly

Chapter 5

NOW, brothers, about times and dates we do not need to write to you, [2]for you know very well that the day of the Lord will come like a thief in the night. [3]While people are saying, "Peace and safety," destruction will come on them suddenly, as labor pains on a pregnant woman, and they will not escape. [4]But you, brothers, are not in darkness so that this day should surprise you like a thief. [5]You are all sons of the light and sons of the day. We do not belong to the night or to the darkness. [6]So then, let us not be like others, who are asleep, but let us be alert and self-controlled. [7]For those who sleep, sleep at night, and those who get drunk, get drunk at night. [8]But since we belong to the day, let us be self-controlled, putting on faith and love as a breastplate, and the hope of salvation as a helmet. [9]For God did not appoint us to suffer wrath but to receive salvation through our Lord Jesus Christ. [10]He died for us so that, whether we are awake or asleep, we may live together with him. [11]Therefore encourage one another and build each other up, just as in fact you are doing.

Final Instructions

[12]Now we ask you, brothers, to respect those who work hard among you, who are over you in the Lord and who admonish you. [13]Hold them in the highest regard in love because of

Be at peace among yourselves. 14 And we urge you, beloved k to admonish the idlers, encourage the faint hearted, help the weak, be patient with all of them. 15 See that none of you repays evil for evil, but always seek to do good to one another and to all. 16 Rejoice always, 17 pray without ceasing, 18 give thanks in all circumstances; for this is the will of God in Christ Jesus for you. 19 Do not quench the Spirit. 20 Do not despise the words of prophets, l 21 but test everything; hold fast to what is good; 22 abstain from every form of evil.
23 May the God of peace himself sanctify you entirely; and may your spirit and soul and body be kept sound m and blameless at the coming of our Lord Jesus Christ. 24 The one who calls you is faithful, and he will do this.
25 Beloved, n pray for us.
26 Greet all the brothers and sisters k with a holy kiss. 27 I solemnly command you by the Lord that this letter be read to all of them. o
28 The grace of our Lord Jesus Christ be with you. p

ἐν ἀγάπῃ διὰ τὸ ἔργον αὐτῶν. εἰρηνεύετε
in love be- the work of them. Be at peace
cause of

ἐν ἑαυτοῖς. 14 Παρακαλοῦμεν δὲ ὑμᾶς,
among yourselves. And we exhort you,

ἀδελφοί, νουθετεῖτε τοὺς ἀτάκτους, παρα-
brothers, admonish the idle, con-

μυθεῖσθε τοὺς ὀλιγοψύχους, ἀντέχεσθε τῶν
sole the faint-hearted, hold on to the [ones]

ἀσθενῶν, μακροθυμεῖτε πρὸς πάντας.
being weak, be longsuffering with all men.

15 ὁρᾶτε μή τις κακὸν ἀντὶ κακοῦ τινι
See lest anyone ³evil ⁴instead ⁵evil ⁶to
of anyone

ἀποδῷ, ἀλλὰ πάντοτε τὸ ἀγαθὸν διώκετε
¹returns, but always ²the ³good ¹follow ye

εἰς ἀλλήλους καὶ εἰς πάντας. 16 Πάντοτε
in re- one another and in re- all men. Always
gard to gard to

χαίρετε, 17 ἀδιαλείπτως προσεύχεσθε, 18 ἐν
rejoice ye, unceasingly pray, in

παντὶ εὐχαριστεῖτε· τοῦτο γὰρ θέλημα
everything give thanks; for this [is] [the] will

θεοῦ ἐν Χριστῷ Ἰησοῦ εἰς ὑμᾶς. 19 τὸ
of God in Christ Jesus in regard to you. The

πνεῦμα μὴ σβέννυτε, 20 προφητείας μὴ
Spirit do not quench, prophecies not

ἐξουθενεῖτε· 21 πάντα δὲ δοκιμάζετε, τὸ
despise; and ³all things ¹prove, the

καλὸν κατέχετε· 22 ἀπὸ παντὸς εἴδους
good hold fast; from every form

πονηροῦ ἀπέχεσθε. 23 Αὐτὸς δὲ ὁ θεὸς
of evil abstain. And ⁴[him]self ¹the ³God

τῆς εἰρήνης ἁγιάσαι ὑμᾶς ὁλοτελεῖς, καὶ
- ²of peace may he sanctify you complete, and

ὁλόκληρον ὑμῶν τὸ πνεῦμα καὶ ἡ ψυχὴ
entire of you the spirit and the soul

καὶ τὸ σῶμα ἀμέμπτως ἐν τῇ παρουσίᾳ
and the body blamelessly in(at) the presence

τοῦ κυρίου ἡμῶν Ἰησοῦ Χριστοῦ τηρηθείη.
of the Lord of us Jesus Christ may be kept.

24 πιστὸς ὁ καλῶν ὑμᾶς, ὃς καὶ ποιήσει.
Faithful [is] the [one] calling you, who indeed will do [it].

25 Ἀδελφοί, προσεύχεσθε [καὶ] περὶ
Brothers, pray ye also concerning

ἡμῶν.
us.

26 Ἀσπάσασθε τοὺς ἀδελφοὺς πάντας
Greet ye ⁴the ³brothers ¹all

ἐν φιλήματι ἁγίῳ. 27 Ἐνορκίζω ὑμᾶς τὸν
with kiss a holy. I adjure you [by] the

κύριον ἀναγνωσθῆναι τὴν ἐπιστολὴν πᾶσιν
Lord ³to be read ¹the(this) ²epistle to all

τοῖς ἀδελφοῖς.
the brothers.

28 Ἡ χάρις τοῦ κυρίου ἡμῶν Ἰησοῦ
The grace of the Lord of us Jesus

Χριστοῦ μεθ᾽ ὑμῶν.
Christ [be] with you.

their work. Live in peace with each other. 14 And we urge you, brothers, warn those who are idle, encourage the timid, help the weak, be patient with everyone. 15 Make sure that nobody pays back wrong for wrong, but always try to be kind to each other and to everyone else. 16 Be joyful always; 17 pray continually; 18 give thanks in all circumstances, for this is God's will for you in Christ Jesus.
19 Do not put out the Spirit's fire; 20 do not treat prophecies with contempt. 21 Test everything. Hold on to the good. 22 Avoid every kind of evil.
23 May God himself, the God of peace, sanctify you through and through. May your whole spirit, soul and body be kept blameless at the coming of our Lord Jesus Christ. 24 The one who calls you is faithful and he will do it.
25 Brothers, pray for us. 26 Greet all the brothers with a holy kiss. 27 I charge you before the Lord to have this letter read to all the brothers.
28 The grace of our Lord Jesus Christ be with you.

l Gk despise prophecies
m Or complete
n Gk Brothers
o Gk to all the brothers
p Other ancient authorities add Amen

The Second Letter of Paul to the Thessalonians

Chapter 1

Salutation

PAUL, Silvanus, and Timothy,
To the church of the Thessalonians in God our Father and the Lord Jesus Christ:
2 Grace to you and peace from God our[a] Father and the Lord Jesus Christ.

Thanksgiving

3 We must always give thanks to God for you, brothers and sisters,[b] as is right, because your faith is growing abundantly, and the love of everyone of you for one another is increasing. 4 Therefore we ourselves boast of you among the churches of God for your steadfastness and faith during all your persecutions and the afflictions that you are enduring.

The Judgment at Christ's Coming

5 This is evidence of the righteous judgment of God, and is intended to make you worthy of the kingdom of God, for which you are also suffering. 6 For it is indeed just of God to repay with affliction those who afflict you, 7 and to give relief to the afflicted as well as to us, when the Lord Jesus is revealed from heaven with his mighty angels 8 in flaming fire, inflicting vengeance on those who do not know God and on those who do not obey the gospel of our Lord Jesus. 9 These will suffer the punishment of eternal destruction, separated from the presence of the Lord and from the glory of his might, 10 when he comes to be glorified by his

---

ΠΡΟΣ ΘΕΣΣΑΛΟΝΙΚΕΙΣ Β

1 Παῦλος καὶ Σιλουανὸς καὶ Τιμόθεος
Paul and Silvanus and Timothy

τῇ ἐκκλησίᾳ Θεσσαλονικέων ἐν θεῷ πατρὶ
to the church of [the] Thessalonians in God Father

ἡμῶν καὶ κυρίῳ Ἰησοῦ Χριστῷ· **2** χάρις
of us and [the] Lord Jesus Christ: Grace [be]

ὑμῖν καὶ εἰρήνη ἀπὸ θεοῦ πατρὸς καὶ
to you and peace from God [the] Father and

κυρίου Ἰησοῦ Χριστοῦ.
[the] Lord Jesus Christ.

3 Εὐχαριστεῖν ὀφείλομεν τῷ θεῷ πάντοτε
To give thanks we ought - to God always

περὶ ὑμῶν, ἀδελφοί, καθὼς ἄξιόν ἐστιν,
concerning you, brothers, as ²meet ¹it is,

ὅτι ὑπεραυξάνει ἡ πίστις ὑμῶν καὶ
because ²grows ¹the ²faith ³of you and
exceedingly

πλεονάζει ἡ ἀγάπη ἑνὸς ἑκάστου πάντων
²increases ¹the ²love ²one ²of each ²all

ὑμῶν εἰς ἀλλήλους, **4** ὥστε αὐτοὺς ἡμᾶς
²of you ⁷to ⁸one another, so as [our]selves us
=so that we ourselves boast

ἐν ὑμῖν ἐγκαυχᾶσθαι[b] ἐν ταῖς ἐκκλησίαις
in you to boast in the churches
in you

τοῦ θεοῦ ὑπὲρ τῆς ὑπομονῆς ὑμῶν καὶ
- of God for the ¹endurance ²of you ²and

πίστεως ἐν πᾶσιν τοῖς διωγμοῖς ὑμῶν
²faith in all the persecutions of you

καὶ ταῖς θλίψεσιν αἷς ἀνέχεσθε, **5** ἔνδειγμα
and the afflictions which ye endure, a plain token

τῆς δικαίας κρίσεως τοῦ θεοῦ, εἰς τὸ
of the just judgment - of God, for the

καταξιωθῆναι ὑμᾶς τῆς βασιλείας τοῦ
to be accounted you[b] of the kingdom -
worthy
=so that ye may be accounted worthy

θεοῦ, ὑπὲρ ἧς καὶ πάσχετε, **6** εἴπερ
of God, on behalf which indeed ye suffer, since
of

δίκαιον παρὰ θεῷ ἀνταποδοῦναι τοῖς
[it is] a just with God to repay ²to the
thing [ones]

θλίβουσιν ὑμᾶς θλῖψιν **7** καὶ ὑμῖν τοῖς
²afflicting ⁴you ¹affliction and ⁴to you ⁵the
[ones]

θλιβομένοις ἄνεσιν μεθ' ἡμῶν, ἐν τῇ
⁶being afflicted ¹rest ²with ³us, at the

ἀποκαλύψει τοῦ κυρίου Ἰησοῦ ἀπ'
revelation of the Lord Jesus from

οὐρανοῦ μετ' ἀγγέλων δυνάμεως αὐτοῦ
heaven with angels of power of him

8 ἐν πυρὶ φλογός, διδόντος ἐκδίκησιν τοῖς
in fire of flame, giving full vengeance to the
[ones]

μὴ εἰδόσιν θεὸν καὶ τοῖς μὴ ὑπακούουσιν
not knowing God and to the not obeying
[ones]

τῷ εὐαγγελίῳ τοῦ κυρίου ἡμῶν Ἰησοῦ,
the gospel of the Lord of us Jesus,

9 οἵτινες δίκην τίσουσιν ὄλεθρον αἰώνιον
who ²[the] penalty ¹will pay ⁴destruction ²eternal

ἀπὸ προσώπου τοῦ κυρίου καὶ ἀπὸ
from [the] face of the Lord and from

τῆς δόξης τῆς ἰσχύος αὐτοῦ, **10** ὅταν
the glory of the strength of him, whenever

---

2 Thessalonians

Chapter 1

PAUL, Silas[a] and Timothy,

To the church of the Thessalonians in God our Father and the Lord Jesus Christ:

2 Grace and peace to you from God the Father and the Lord Jesus Christ.

Thanksgiving and Prayer

3 We ought always to thank God for you, brothers, and rightly so, because your faith is growing more and more, and the love every one of you has for each other is increasing. 4 Therefore, among God's churches we boast about your perseverance and faith in all the persecutions and trials you are enduring.

5 All this is evidence that God's judgment is right, and as a result you will be counted worthy of the kingdom of God, for which you are suffering. 6 God is just: He will pay back trouble to those who trouble you 7 and give relief to you who are troubled, and to us as well. This will happen when the Lord Jesus is revealed from heaven in blazing fire with his powerful angels. 8 He will punish those who do not know God and do not obey the gospel of our Lord Jesus. 9 They will be punished with everlasting destruction and shut out from the presence of the Lord and from the majesty of his power 10 on the day he

---

saints and to be marveled at on that day among all who have believed, because our testimony to you was believed. 11 To this end we always pray for you, asking that our God will make you worthy of his call and will fulfill by his power every good resolve and work of faith, 12 so that the name of our Lord Jesus may be glorified in you, and you in him, according to the grace of our God and the Lord Jesus Christ.

ἔλθη ἐνδοξασθῆναι ἐν τοῖς ἁγίοις αὐτοῦ
he comes to be glorified in the saints of him
καὶ θαυμασθῆναι ἐν πᾶσιν τοῖς πιστεύσασιν,
and to be admired in all the [ones] having believed,
ὅτι ἐπιστεύθη τὸ μαρτύριον ἡμῶν ἐφ᾽
be-⁶was believed ¹the ²testimony ³of us ⁴to
cause
ὑμᾶς, ἐν τῇ ἡμέρᾳ ἐκείνῃ. 11 Εἰς ὃ
⁵you, in that day. For which
καὶ προσευχόμεθα πάντοτε περὶ ὑμῶν,
indeed we pray always concerning you,
ἵνα ὑμᾶς ἀξιώσῃ τῆς κλήσεως ὁ θεὸς
in or-⁶you ⁴may ⁵deem ⁸of the ⁹calling ¹the ²God
der that ⁷worthy
ἡμῶν καὶ πληρώσῃ πᾶσαν εὐδοκίαν
³of us and may fulfil every good pleasure
ἀγαθωσύνης καὶ ἔργον πίστεως ἐν δυνάμει,
of goodness and work of faith in power,
12 ὅπως ἐνδοξασθῇ τὸ ὄνομα τοῦ κυρίου
so as ⁷may be glorified ¹the ²name ³of the ⁴Lord
ἡμῶν Ἰησοῦ ἐν ὑμῖν, καὶ ὑμεῖς ἐν
⁵of us ⁶Jesus in you, and ye in
αὐτῷ, κατὰ τὴν χάριν τοῦ θεοῦ ἡμῶν
him, according to the grace of the ¹God ⁴of us
καὶ κυρίου Ἰησοῦ Χριστοῦ.
²and ³Lord Jesus Christ.

comes to be glorified in his holy people and to be marveled at among all those who have believed. This includes you, because you believed our testimony to you.
11With this in mind, we constantly pray for you, that our God may count you worthy of his calling, and that by his power he may fulfill every good purpose of yours and every act prompted by your faith. 12We pray this so that the name of our Lord Jesus may be glorified in you, and you in him, according to the grace of our God and the Lord Jesus Christ. *b*

Chapter 2

The Man of Lawlessness

AS to the coming of our Lord Jesus Christ and our being gathered together to him, we beg you, brothers and sisters, *b* 2 not to be quickly shaken in mind or alarmed, either by spirit or by word or by letter, as though from us, to the effect that the day of the Lord is already here. 3 Let no one deceive you in any way; for that day will not come unless the rebellion comes first and the lawless one *c* is revealed, the one destined for destruction. *d* 4 He opposes and exalts himself above every so-called god or object of worship, so that he takes his seat in the temple of God, declaring himself to be God. 5 Do you not remember that I told you these things when I was still with you? 6 And you know what is now restraining him, so that he

2 Ἐρωτῶμεν δὲ ὑμᾶς, ἀδελφοί, ὑπὲρ
Now we request you, brothers, by
τῆς παρουσίας τοῦ κυρίου [ἡμῶν] Ἰησοῦ
the presence of the Lord of us Jesus
Χριστοῦ καὶ ἡμῶν ἐπισυναγωγῆς ἐπ᾽ αὐτόν,
Christ and ²of us ¹gathering together to him,
2 εἰς τὸ μὴ ταχέως σαλευθῆναι ὑμᾶς
- - not quickly to be shaken you⁶
ἀπὸ τοῦ νοὸς μηδὲ θροεῖσθαι, μήτε
from the(your) mind nor to be disturbed, neither
διὰ πνεύματος μήτε διὰ λόγου μήτε
through a spirit nor through speech nor
δι᾽ ἐπιστολῆς ὡς δι᾽ ἡμῶν, ὡς ὅτι
through an epistle as through us, as that
ἐνέστηκεν ἡ ἡμέρα τοῦ κυρίου. 3 μή
²is come ¹the ²day ³of the ⁴Lord. Not
τις ὑμᾶς ἐξαπατήσῃ κατὰ μηδένα τρόπον·
anyone ²you ¹may deceive by(in) no(any) way;
ὅτι ἐὰν μὴ ἔλθη ἡ ἀποστασία πρῶτον
because unless ²comes ¹the ²apostasy ⁴first/y
καὶ ἀποκαλυφθῇ ὁ ἄνθρωπος τῆς ἀνομίας,
and ⁴is revealed ¹the ²man - ³of lawlessness,
ὁ υἱὸς τῆς ἀπωλείας, 4 ὁ ἀντικείμενος
the son - of perdition, the [one] setting against
καὶ ὑπεραιρόμενος ἐπὶ πάντα λεγόμενον
and exalting himself over everything *being* called
θεὸν ἢ σέβασμα, ὥστε αὐτὸν εἰς τὸν
God or object of worship, so as him in the
ναὸν τοῦ θεοῦ καθίσαι, ἀποδεικνύντα ἑαυ-
shrine - of God to sit,ᵇ showing him-
τὸν ὅτι ἐστὶν θεός. 5 Οὐ μνημονεύετε
self that he is a god. Do ye not remember
ὅτι ἔτι ὢν πρὸς ὑμᾶς ταῦτα ἔλεγον
that yet being with you ²these ¹I used
things to tell
ὑμῖν; 6 καὶ νῦν τὸ κατέχον οἴδατε,
³you? and now the restraining ye know,
[thing]

Chapter 2

The Man of Lawlessness

CONCERNING the coming of our Lord Jesus Christ and our being gathered to him, we ask you, brothers, 2not to become easily unsettled or alarmed by some prophecy, report or letter supposed to have come from us, saying that the day of the Lord has already come. 3Don't let anyone deceive you in any way, for that day will not come, until the rebellion occurs and the man of lawlessness*c* is revealed, the man doomed to destruction. 4He will oppose and will exalt himself over everything that is called God or is worshiped, so that he sets himself up in God's temple, proclaiming himself to be God. 5Don't you remember that when I was with you I used to tell you these things? 6And now you know what is holding him

c Gk *the man of lawlessness*; other ancient authorities read *the man of sin*
d Gk *the son of destruction*

b 12 Or *God and Lord, Jesus Christ*
c 3 Some manuscripts *sin*

may be revealed when his time comes. 7 For the mystery of lawlessness is already at work, but only until the one who now restrains it is removed. 8 And then the lawless one will be revealed, whom the Lord Jesus[e] will destroy[f] with the breath of his mouth, annihilating him by the manifestation of his coming. 9 The coming of the lawless one is apparent in the working of Satan, who uses all power, signs, lying wonders, 10 and every kind of wicked deception for those who are perishing, because they refused to love the truth and so be saved. 11 For this reason God sends them a powerful delusion, leading them to believe what is false, 12 so that all who have not believed the truth but took pleasure in unrighteousness will be condemned.

Chosen for Salvation

13 But we must always give thanks to God for you, brothers and sisters[b] beloved by the Lord, because God chose you as the first fruits[g] for salvation through sanctification by the Spirit and through belief in the truth. 14 For this purpose he called you through our proclamation of the good news,[h] so that you may obtain the glory of our Lord Jesus Christ. 15 So then, brothers and sisters,[b] stand firm and hold fast to the traditions that you were taught by us, either by word of mouth or by our letter.

16 Now may our Lord Jesus Christ himself and God our Father, who loved us and through grace gave us eternal comfort and

---

εἰς   τὸ   ἀποκαλυφθῆναι   αὐτὸν   ἐν   τῷ
for   the   ²to be revealed   ¹him[b]   in   the

αὐτοῦ   καιρῷ.   7 τὸ   γὰρ   μυστήριον   ἤδη
²of him   ¹time.   For the   mystery   ²already

ἐνεργεῖται   τῆς   ἀνομίας·   μόνον   ὁ   κατέχων
³operates   –   ¹of lawless-   only   the   restraining
                    ness;   [there is] [one]

ἄρτι   ἕως   ἐκ   μέσου   γένηται.   8 καὶ   τότε
just now until   ²out of ²[the] midst ¹it comes.   And   then

ἀποκαλυφθήσεται   ὁ   ἄνομος,   ὃν   ὁ   κύριος
will be revealed   the   lawless   whom   the   Lord
                    one,

['Ιησοῦς]   ἀνελεῖ   τῷ   πνεύματι   τοῦ   στό-
Jesus   will destroy   by the   spirit   of the   mouth

ματος   αὐτοῦ   καὶ   καταργήσει   τῇ   ἐπιφανείᾳ
of him   and   bring to nothing by the   outshining

τῆς   παρουσίας   αὐτοῦ,   9 οὗ   ἐστιν   ἡ
of the   presence   of him,   of whom   ²is   ¹the

παρουσία   κατ'   ἐνέργειαν   τοῦ   σατανᾶ   ἐν
²presence   according   operation   of Satan   with
            to [the]

πάσῃ   δυνάμει   καὶ   σημείοις   καὶ   τέρασιν
all   power   and   signs   and   wonders

ψεύδους   10 καὶ   ἐν   πάσῃ   ἀπάτῃ   ἀδικίας
of a lie   and   with   all   deceit   of unright-
                                eousness

τοῖς   ἀπολλυμένοις,   ἀνθ'   ὧν   τὴν   ἀγάπην
in the [ones] perishing,   because   the   love

τῆς   ἀληθείας   οὐκ   ἐδέξαντο   εἰς   τὸ   σωθῆναι
of the   truth   they received not   for the   ²to be saved

αὐτούς.   11 καὶ   διὰ   τοῦτο   πέμπει   αὐτοῖς
¹them.[b]   And   therefore   ²sends   ¹to them

ὁ   θεὸς   ἐνέργειαν   πλάνης   εἰς   τὸ   πιστεῦσαι
–   ¹God   an operation   of error   for the   ²to believe

αὐτοὺς   τῷ   ψεύδει,   12 ἵνα   κριθῶσιν   πάντες
¹them[b]   the   lie,   in or-   ¹⁶may be   ¹all
                        der that   judged

οἱ   μὴ   πιστεύσαντες   τῇ   ἀληθείᾳ   ἀλλὰ
²the   ³not   ⁴having believed   ⁵the   ⁶truth   ⁷but
[ones]

εὐδοκήσαντες   τῇ   ἀδικίᾳ.
⁸having had pleasure –   ⁹in unrighteousness.

13 Ἡμεῖς   δὲ   ὀφείλομεν   εὐχαριστεῖν   τῷ
But we   ought   to thank   –

θεῷ   πάντοτε   περὶ   ὑμῶν,   ἀδελφοὶ   ἠγαπη-
God   always   concerning   you,   brothers   having been

μένοι   ὑπὸ   κυρίου,   ὅτι   εἴλατο   ὑμᾶς   ὁ
loved   by   [the] Lord,   because   ²chose   ²you   –

θεὸς   ἀπαρχὴν   εἰς   σωτηρίαν   ἐν   ἁγιασμῷ
¹God   firstfruit   to   salvation   by   sanctification

πνεύματος   καὶ   πίστει   ἀληθείας,   14 εἰς
of spirit   and   faith   of(in) [the] truth,   to

ὃ   καὶ   ἐκάλεσεν   ὑμᾶς   διὰ   τοῦ   εὐαγγελίου
which also   he called   you   through the   gospel

ἡμῶν,   εἰς   περιποίησιν   δόξης   τοῦ   κυρίου
of us,   to   obtainment   of [the] glory of the   Lord

ἡμῶν   'Ιησοῦ   Χριστοῦ.   15 Ἄρα   οὖν
of us   Jesus   Christ.   So   then,

ἀδελφοί,   στήκετε,   καὶ   κρατεῖτε   τὰς
brothers,   stand,   and   hold   the

παραδόσεις   ἃς   ἐδιδάχθητε   εἴτε   διὰ   λόγου
traditions   which   ye were taught   either   through   speech

εἴτε   δι'   ἐπιστολῆς   ἡμῶν.   16 Αὐτὸς   δὲ
or   through   an epistle   of us.   And ⁶[him]self

ὁ   κύριος   ἡμῶν   'Ιησοῦς   Χριστὸς   καὶ
¹the   ²Lord   ³of us   ⁴Jesus   ⁵Christ   and

ὁ   θεὸς   ὁ   πατὴρ   ἡμῶν,   ὁ   ἀγαπήσας
the   God   the   Father   of us,   the [one] having loved

---

back, so that he may be revealed at the proper time. 7 For the secret power of lawlessness is already at work; but the one who now holds it back will continue to do so till he is taken out of the way. 8 And then the lawless one will be revealed, whom the Lord Jesus will overthrow with the breath of his mouth and destroy by the splendor of his coming. 9 The coming of the lawless one will be in accordance with the work of Satan displayed in all kinds of counterfeit miracles, signs and wonders, 10 and in every sort of evil that deceives those who are perishing. They perish because they refused to love the truth and so be saved. 11 For this reason God sends them a powerful delusion so that they will believe the lie 12 and so that all who have not believed the truth but have delighted in wickedness.

Stand Firm

13 But we ought always to thank God for you, brothers loved by the Lord, because from the beginning God chose you[d] to be saved through the sanctifying work of the Spirit and through belief in the truth. 14 He called you to this through our gospel, that you might share in the glory of our Lord Jesus Christ. 15 So then, brothers, stand firm and hold to the teachings[e] we passed on to you, whether by word of mouth or by letter.

16 May our Lord Jesus Christ himself and God our Father, who loved us and by his grace gave us eternal

---

e Other ancient authorities lack *Jesus*
f Other ancient authorities read *consume*
g Other ancient authorities read *from the beginning*
h Or *through our gospel*

good hope, 17comfort your hearts and strengthen them in every good work and word.

ἡμᾶς   καὶ   δοὺς   παράκλησιν   αἰωνίαν   καὶ
us   and having given   ²comfort   ¹eternal   ³and

ἐλπίδα   ἀγαθὴν   ἐν   χάριτι,   17 παρακαλέσαι
⁵hope   ⁴a good   by   grace,   may he comfort

ὑμῶν   τὰς   καρδίας   καὶ   στηρίξαι   ἐν   παντὶ
of you   the   hearts   and   *may he   in   every
                                    confirm

ἔργῳ   καὶ   λόγῳ   ἀγαθῷ.
²work   ³and   ⁴word   ¹good.

encouragement and good hope, 17encourage your hearts and strengthen you in every good deed and word.

Chapter 3

Request for Prayer

FINALLY, brothers and sisters,[i] pray for us, so that the word of the Lord may spread rapidly and be glorified everywhere, just as it is among you, ²and that we may be rescued from wicked and evil people; for not all have faith. ³But the Lord is faithful; he will strengthen you and guard you from the evil one.[j] ⁴And we have confidence in the Lord concerning you, that you are doing and will go on doing the things that we command. ⁵May the Lord direct your hearts to the love of God and to the steadfastness of Christ.

Warning against Idleness

6 Now we command you, beloved,[i] in the name of our Lord Jesus Christ, to keep away from believers who are[k] living in idleness and not according to the tradition that they[l] received from us. ⁷For you yourselves know how you ought to imitate us; we were not idle when we were with you, ⁸and we did not eat anyone's bread without paying for it; but with toil and labor we worked night and day, so that we might not burden any of you. ⁹This was not because we do not have that right, but

3 Τὸ   λοιπὸν   προσεύχεσθε,   ἀδελφοί,   περὶ
For the rest   pray ye,   brothers,   concerning

ἡμῶν,   ἵνα   ὁ   λόγος   τοῦ   κυρίου   τρέχῃ
us,   in or-   the   word   of the   Lord   may run
         der that

καὶ   δοξάζηται   καθὼς   καὶ   πρὸς   ὑμᾶς,
and   be glorified   as   indeed   with   you,

2 καὶ   ἵνα   ῥυσθῶμεν   ἀπὸ   τῶν   ἀτόπων
and   in or-   we may be   from   -   perverse
         der that   delivered

καὶ   πονηρῶν   ἀνθρώπων·   οὐ   γὰρ   πάντων
and   evil   men;   for ³[is] not   ⁴of all men

ἡ   πίστις.   3 Πιστὸς   δέ   ἐστιν   ὁ   κύριος,
¹the   ²faith.   But faithful   is   the   Lord,

ὃς   στηρίξει   ὑμᾶς   καὶ   φυλάξει   ἀπὸ   τοῦ
who   will confirm   you   and   will guard   from   the

πονηροῦ.   4 πεποίθαμεν   δὲ   ἐν   κυρίῳ
evil [?one].   And we are persuaded   in   [the] Lord

ἐφ'   ὑμᾶς,   ὅτι   ἃ   παραγγέλλομεν   [καὶ]
as to   you,   that what   we charge   both
              things

ποιεῖτε   καὶ   ποιήσετε.   5 Ὁ   δὲ   κύριος
ye do   and   will do.   And ²the   ¹Lord

κατευθύναι   ὑμῶν   τὰς   καρδίας   εἰς   τὴν
¹may ⁴direct   ⁷of you   ⁵the   ⁶hearts   into   the

ἀγάπην   τοῦ   θεοῦ   καὶ   εἰς   τὴν   ὑπομονὴν
love   -   of God   and   into   the   patience

τοῦ   Χριστοῦ.
-    of Christ.

6 Παραγγέλλομεν   δὲ   ὑμῖν,   ἀδελφοί,   ἐν
Now we charge   you,   brothers,   in

ὀνόματι   τοῦ   κυρίου   Ἰησοῦ   Χριστοῦ,
[the] name   of the   Lord   Jesus   Christ,

στέλλεσθαι   ὑμᾶς   ἀπὸ   παντὸς   ἀδελφοῦ
to draw back   you[b]   from   every   brother

ἀτάκτως   περιπατοῦντος   καὶ   μὴ   κατὰ   τὴν
²idly   ¹walking   and   not   accord-   the
                                ing to

παράδοσιν   ἣν   παρελάβετε   παρ'   ἡμῶν.
tradition   which   ye received   from   us.

7 αὐτοὶ   γὰρ   οἴδατε   πῶς   δεῖ   μιμεῖσθαι
For [your]selves   ye know   how   it be-   to imitate
                         hoves

ἡμᾶς,   ὅτι   οὐκ   ἠτακτήσαμεν   ἐν   ὑμῖν,
us,   because   we were not idle   among   you,

8 οὐδὲ   δωρεὰν   ἄρτον   ἐφάγομεν   παρά   τινος,
nor   ²[as] a gift   ³bread   ¹ate   ³from   ⁴anyone,

ἀλλ'   ἐν   κόπῳ   καὶ   μόχθῳ   νυκτὸς   καὶ
but   by   labour   and   struggle   by night   and

ἡμέρας   ἐργαζόμενοι   πρὸς   τὸ   μὴ   ἐπιβαρῆσαί
by day   working   for   the   not   to emburden

τινα   ὑμῶν·   9 οὐχ   ὅτι   οὐκ   ἔχομεν
anyone   of you;   not   that   we have not

ἐξουσίαν,   ἀλλ'   ἵνα   ἑαυτοὺς   τύπον   δῶμεν
authority,   but   in or-   ²our-   ³an   ¹we might
              der that   selves   example   give

Chapter 3

Request for Prayer

FINALLY, brothers, pray for us that the message of the Lord may spread rapidly and be honored, just as it was with you. ²And pray that we may be delivered from wicked and evil men, for not everyone has faith. ³But the Lord is faithful, and he will strengthen and protect you from the evil one. ⁴We have confidence in the Lord that you are doing and will continue to do the things we command. ⁵May the Lord direct your hearts into God's love and Christ's perseverance.

Warning Against Idleness

⁶In the name of the Lord Jesus Christ, we command you, brothers, to keep away from every brother who is idle and does not live according to the teaching[f] you received from us. ⁷For you yourselves know how you ought to follow our example. We were not idle when we were with you, ⁸nor did we eat anyone's food without paying for it. On the contrary, we worked night and day, laboring and toiling so that we would not be a burden to any of you. ⁹We did this, not because we do not have the right to such help, but in order to make ourselves a

[i] Gk brothers
[j] Or from evil
[k] Gk from every brother who is
[l] Other ancient authorities read you

[f] 6 Or tradition

in order to give you an example to imitate. 10For even when we were with you, we gave you this command: Anyone unwilling to work should not eat. 11For we hear that some of you are living in idleness, mere busybodies, not doing any work. 12Now such persons we command and exhort in the Lord Jesus Christ to do their work quietly and to earn their own living. 13Brothers and sisters,^m do not be weary in doing what is right.

14 Take note of those who do not obey what we say in this letter; have nothing to do with them, so that they may be ashamed. 15Do not regard them as enemies, but warn them as believers.^n

Final Greetings and Benediction

16 Now may the Lord of peace himself give you peace at all times in all ways. The Lord be with all of you.

17 I, Paul, write this greeting with my own hand. This is the mark in every letter of mine; it is the way I write. 18The grace of our Lord Jesus Christ be with all of you.^o

---

ὑμῖν εἰς τὸ μιμεῖσθαι ἡμᾶς. 10 καὶ
to you for the to imitate us. even

γὰρ ὅτε ἦμεν πρὸς ὑμᾶς, τοῦτο παρηγ-
For when we were with you, this we

γέλλομεν ὑμῖν, ὅτι εἴ τις οὐ θέλει
charged you, that if anyone does not wish

ἐργάζεσθαι, μηδὲ ἐσθιέτω. 11 ἀκούομεν
to work, neither let him eat. we hear [of]

γὰρ τινας περιπατοῦντας ἐν ὑμῖν ἀτάκτως,
For some walking among you idly,

μηδὲν ἐργαζομένους ἀλλὰ περιεργαζομένους·
nothing working but working round;

12 τοῖς δὲ τοιούτοις παραγγέλλομεν καὶ
- and to such we charge and

παρακαλοῦμεν ἐν κυρίῳ Ἰησοῦ Χριστῷ
exhort in [the]Lord Jesus Christ

ἵνα μετὰ ἡσυχίας ἐργαζόμενοι τὸν
in or-der that ²with ³quietness ¹working ⁵the

ἑαυτῶν ἄρτον ἐσθίωσιν. 13 Ὑμεῖς δέ,
⁷of them-selves ⁶bread ⁴they may eat. And ye,

ἀδελφοί, μὴ ἐγκακήσητε καλοποιοῦντες
brothers, do not lose heart doing good.

14 εἰ δέ τις οὐχ ὑπακούει τῷ λόγῳ
And if anyone obeys not the word

ἡμῶν διὰ τῆς ἐπιστολῆς, τοῦτον σημειοῦσθε,
of us through the epistle, this man mark,

μὴ συναναμίγνυσθαι αὐτῷ, ἵνα ἐντραπῇ·
not to mix with* him, in or-der that he may be put to shame;

15 καὶ μὴ ὡς ἐχθρὸν ἡγεῖσθε, ἀλλὰ
and yet not as an enemy deem ye [him], but

νουθετεῖτε ὡς ἀδελφόν. 16 Αὐτὸς δὲ
admonish as a brother. And ⁴[him]self

ὁ κύριος τῆς εἰρήνης δῴη ὑμῖν τὴν
¹the ²Lord - ³of peace may he give to you the (?his)

εἰρήνην διὰ παντὸς ἐν παντὶ τρόπῳ.
peace always in every way.

ὁ κύριος μετὰ πάντων ὑμῶν.
The Lord [be] with ²all ¹you.

17 Ὁ ἀσπασμὸς τῇ ἐμῇ χειρὶ Παύλου,
The greeting - by my hand[,] of Paul,

ὃ ἐστιν σημεῖον ἐν πάσῃ ἐπιστολῇ·
which is a sign in every epistle:

οὕτως γράφω. 18 ἡ χάρις τοῦ κυρίου
thus I write. The grace of the Lord

ἡμῶν Ἰησοῦ Χριστοῦ μετὰ πάντων ὑμῶν.
of us Jesus Christ [be] with ²all ¹you.

---

model for you to follow. 10For even when we were with you, we gave you this rule: "If a man will not work, he shall not eat."

11We hear that some among you are idle. They are not busy; they are busybodies. 12Such people we command and urge in the Lord Jesus Christ to settle down and earn the bread they eat. 13And as for you, brothers, never tire of doing what is right.

14If anyone does not obey our instruction in this letter, take special note of him. Do not associate with him, in order that he may feel ashamed. 15Yet do not regard him as an enemy, but warn him as a brother.

Final Greetings

16Now may the Lord of peace himself give you peace at all times and in every way. The Lord be with all of you.

17I, Paul, write this greeting in my own hand, which is the distinguishing mark in all my letters. This is how I write.

18The grace of our Lord Jesus Christ be with you all.

The First Letter of Paul to
Timothy

Chapter 1

Salutation

PAUL, an apostle of Christ Jesus by the command of God our Savior and of Christ Jesus our hope,

2 To Timothy, my loyal child in the faith:

Grace, mercy, and peace

m Gk Brothers
n Gk a brother
o Other ancient authorities add Amen

ΠΡΟΣ ΤΙΜΟΘΕΟΝ Α
To Timothy 1

1 Παῦλος ἀπόστολος Χριστοῦ Ἰησοῦ κατ᾽
Paul an apostle of Christ Jesus according to

ἐπιταγὴν θεοῦ σωτῆρος ἡμῶν καὶ Χριστοῦ
a command of God Saviour of us and of Christ

Ἰησοῦ τῆς ἐλπίδος ἡμῶν 2 Τιμοθέῳ
Jesus the hope of us to Timothy

γνησίῳ τέκνῳ ἐν πίστει· χάρις, ἔλεος,
a true child in [the] faith: Grace, mercy,

* Imperative infinitive, as elsewhere (Phil. 3. 16, etc.).

---

1 Timothy

Chapter 1

PAUL, an apostle of Christ Jesus by the command of God our Savior and of Christ Jesus our hope,

2To Timothy my true son in the faith:

from God the Father and Christ Jesus our Lord.

Warning against False Teachers

3 I urge you, as I did when I was on my way to Macedonia, to remain in Ephesus so that you may instruct certain people not to teach any different doctrine, 4 and not to occupy themselves with myths and endless genealogies that promote speculations rather than the divine training[a] that is known by faith. 5 But the aim of such instruction is love that comes from a pure heart, a good conscience, and sincere faith. 6 Some people have deviated from these and turned to meaningless talk, 7 desiring to be teachers of the law, without understanding either what they are saying or the things about which they make assertions. 8 Now we know that the law is good, if one uses it legitimately. 9 This means understanding that the law is laid down not for the innocent but for the lawless and disobedient, for the godless and sinful, for the unholy and profane, for those who kill their father or mother, for murderers, 10 fornicators, sodomites, slave traders, liars, perjurers, and whatever else is contrary to the sound teaching 11 that conforms to the glorious gospel of the blessed God, which he entrusted to me.

Gratitude for Mercy

12 I am grateful to Christ Jesus our Lord, who has strengthened me, because he judged me faithful and appointed me to his service, 13 even though I was formerly a blasphemer, a persecutor, and a man of violence. But I received mercy because I had acted ignorantly in unbelief,

---

εἰρήνη ἀπὸ θεοῦ πατρὸς καὶ Χριστοῦ
peace from God [the] Father and Christ

Ἰησοῦ τοῦ κυρίου ἡμῶν.
Jesus the Lord of us.

3 Καθὼς παρεκάλεσά σε προσμεῖναι ἐν
As I besought thee to remain in

Ἐφέσῳ, πορευόμενος εἰς Μακεδονίαν, ἵνα
Ephesus, [I] going into Macedonia, in order that

παραγγείλῃς τισὶν μὴ ἑτεροδιδασκαλεῖν
thou mightest charge certain persons not to teach differently

4 μηδὲ προσέχειν μύθοις καὶ γενεαλογίαις
nor to pay attention to tales and to ¹genealogies

ἀπεράντοις, αἵτινες ἐκζητήσεις παρέχουσιν
¹unending, which ²questionings ¹provide

μᾶλλον ἢ οἰκονομίαν θεοῦ τὴν ἐν πίστει·
rather than a stewardship of God – in faith:

5 τὸ δὲ τέλος τῆς παραγγελίας ἐστὶν
now the end of the charge is

ἀγάπη ἐκ καθαρᾶς καρδίας καὶ συνειδήσεως
love out of a clean heart and conscience

ἀγαθῆς καὶ πίστεως ἀνυποκρίτου, 6 ὧν
a good and faith unfeigned, from which things

τινες ἀστοχήσαντες ἐξετράπησαν εἰς
some missing aim turned aside to

ματαιολογίαν, 7 θέλοντες εἶναι νομοδιδάσ-
vain talking, wishing to be law-

καλοι, μὴ νοοῦντες μήτε ἃ λέγουσιν
teachers, not understanding either what things they say

μήτε περὶ τίνων διαβεβαιοῦνται. 8 οἴδαμεν
nor concerning what things they emphatically assert. we know

δὲ ὅτι καλὸς ὁ νόμος, ἐάν τις αὐτῷ
Now that ²[is] ⁴good ¹the ³law, if anyone ⁵it

νομίμως χρῆται, 9 εἰδὼς τοῦτο, ὅτι
³lawfully ¹uses, knowing this, that

δικαίῳ νόμος οὐ κεῖται, ἀνόμοις δὲ
²for a just ¹law ³is not laid down, but for lawless men
man

καὶ ἀνυποτάκτοις, ἀσεβέσι καὶ ἁμαρτωλοῖς,
and for unruly, for impious and for sinners,

ἀνοσίοις καὶ βεβήλοις, πατρολῴαις καὶ
for unholy and for profane, for parricides and

μητρολῴαις, ἀνδροφόνοις, 10 πόρνοις, ἀρ-
for matricides, for menkillers, for fornicators, for

σενοκοίταις, ἀνδραποδισταῖς, ψεύσταις, ἐπιόρ-
paederasts, for menstealers, for liars, for per-

κοις, καὶ εἴ τι ἕτερον τῇ ὑγιαινούσῃ
jurers, and if any other thing ²to the ³being healthful

διδασκαλίᾳ ἀντίκειται, 11 κατὰ τὸ εὐαγ-
⁴teaching ¹opposes, according to the gos-

γέλιον τῆς δόξης τοῦ μακαρίου θεοῦ,
pel of the glory of the blessed God,

ὃ ἐπιστεύθην ἐγώ. 12 Χάριν ἔχω τῷ
which ²was entrusted ¹I. Thanks I have to the
[with]

ἐνδυναμώσαντί. με Χριστῷ Ἰησοῦ τῷ κυρίῳ
[one] empowering me Christ Jesus the Lord

ἡμῶν, ὅτι πιστόν με ἡγήσατο θέμενος
of us, because ³faithful ²me ¹he deemed putting [me]

εἰς διακονίαν, 13 τὸ πρότερον ὄντα
into [the] ministry, formerly being

βλάσφημον καὶ διώκτην καὶ ὑβριστήν·
a blasphemer and a persecutor and insolent;

ἀλλὰ ἠλεήθην, ὅτι ἀγνοῶν ἐποίησα ἐν
but I obtained mercy, because being ignorant I acted in

Grace, mercy and peace from God the Father and Chrst Jesus our Lord.

Warning Against False Teachers of the Law

3 As I urged you when I went into Macedonia, stay there in Ephesus so that you may command certain men not to teach false doctrines any longer 4 nor to devote themselves to myths and endless genealogies. These promote controversies rather than God's work —which is by faith. 5 The goal of this command is love, which comes from a pure heart and a good conscience and a sincere faith. 6 Some have wandered away from these and turned to meaningless talk. 7 They want to be teachers of the law, but they do not know what they are talking about or what they so confidently affirm.

8 We know that the law is good if one uses it properly. 9 We also know that law[a] is made not for the righteous but for lawbreakers and rebels, the ungodly and sinful, the unholy and irreligious; for those who kill their fathers or mothers, for murderers, 10 for adulterers and perverts, for slave traders and liars and perjurers—and for whatever else is contrary to the sound doctrine 11 that conforms to the glorious gospel of the blessed God, which he entrusted to me.

The Lord's Grace to Paul

12 I thank Christ Jesus our Lord, who has given me strength, that he considered me faithful, appointing me to his service. 13 Even though I was once a blasphemer and a persecutor and a violent man, I was shown mercy because I acted in ignorance and un-

14and the grace of our Lord overflowed for me with the faith and love that are in Christ Jesus. 15The saying is sure and worthy of full acceptance, that Christ Jesus came into the world to save sinners—of whom I am the foremost. 16But for that very reason I received mercy, so that in me, as the foremost, Jesus Christ might display the utmost patience, making me an example to those who would come to believe in him for eternal life. 17To the King of the ages, immortal, invisible, the only God, be honor and glory forever and ever.[b] Amen.

18 I am giving you these instructions, Timothy, my child, in accordance with the prophecies made earlier about you, so that by following them you may fight the good fight, 19having faith and a good conscience. By rejecting conscience, certain persons have suffered shipwreck in the faith; 20among them are Hymenaeus and Alexander, whom I have turned over to Satan, so that they may learn not to blaspheme.

ἀπιστίᾳ,   **14** ὑπερεπλεόνασεν   δὲ   ἡ   χάρις
unbelief,   and superabounded   the   grace

τοῦ   κυρίου   ἡμῶν   μετὰ   πίστεως   καὶ
of the   Lord   of us   with   faith   and

ἀγάπης   τῆς   ἐν   Χριστῷ   Ἰησοῦ.   **15** πιστὸς
love   -   in   Christ   Jesus.   Faithful [is]

ὁ   λόγος   καὶ   πάσης   ἀποδοχῆς   ἄξιος,
the   word   and   ²of all   ³acceptance   ¹worthy,

ὅτι   Χριστὸς   Ἰησοῦς   ἦλθεν   εἰς   τὸν   κόσμον
that   Christ   Jesus   came   into   the   world

ἁμαρτωλοὺς   σῶσαι·   ὧν   πρῶτός   εἰμι   ἐγώ·
sinners   to save;   of whom first(chief)   am   I;

16 ἀλλὰ   διὰ   τοῦτο   ἠλεήθην,   ἵνα   ἐν
but   because of   this   I obtained   in or-   in
               mercy,   der that

ἐμοὶ   πρώτῳ   ἐνδείξηται   Ἰησοῦς   Χριστὸς
me   first   might show forth   Jesus   Christ

τὴν   ἅπασαν   μακροθυμίαν,   πρὸς   ὑποτύπωσιν
-     all   longsuffering,   for   a pattern

τῶν   μελλόντων   πιστεύειν   ἐπ᾽   αὐτῷ   εἰς
of the [ones] coming   to believe   on   him   to

ζωὴν   αἰώνιον.   **17** Τῷ   δὲ   βασιλεῖ   τῶν
life   eternal.   Now to the   King   of the

αἰώνων,   ἀφθάρτῳ   ἀοράτῳ   μόνῳ   θεῷ,   τιμὴ
ages,   incorruptible   invisible   only   God,   [be] honour

καὶ   δόξα   εἰς   τοὺς   αἰῶνας   τῶν   αἰώνων·
and   glory   unto   the   ages   of the   ages:

ἀμήν.   **18** Ταύτην   τὴν   παραγγελίαν   παρα-
Amen.   This   -   charge   I com-

τίθεμαί   σοι,   τέκνον   Τιμόθεε,   κατὰ   τὰς
mit   to thee,   child   Timothy,   according to   the

προαγούσας   ἐπὶ   σὲ   προφητείας,   ἵνα
preceding   ³respecting   ²thee   ¹prophecies,   in order that

στρατεύῃ   ἐν   αὐταῖς   τὴν   καλὴν   στρατείαν,
thou   by   them   the   good   warfare,
mightest war

19 ἔχων   πίστιν   καὶ   ἀγαθὴν   συνείδησιν,
having   faith   and   a good   conscience,

ἣν   τινες   ἀπωσάμενοι   περὶ   τὴν   πίστιν
which some   thrusting away   ³concerning   ²the   ⁴faith

ἐναυάγησαν·   **20** ὧν   ἐστιν   Ὑμέναιος   καὶ
¹made ship-   of whom   is   Hymenæus   and
wreck;

Ἀλέξανδρος,   οὓς   παρέδωκα   τῷ   σατανᾷ,
Alexander,   whom   I delivered   -   to Satan,

ἵνα   παιδευθῶσιν   μὴ   βλασφημεῖν.
in or-   they may be taught   not   to blaspheme.
der that

---

belief. 14The grace of our Lord was poured out on me abundantly, along with the faith and love that are in Christ Jesus.

15Here is a trustworthy saying that deserves full acceptance: Christ Jesus came into the world to save sinners—of whom I am the worst. 16But for that very reason I was shown mercy so that in me, the worst of sinners, Christ Jesus might display his unlimited patience as an example for those who would believe on him and receive eternal life. 17Now to the King eternal, immortal, invisible, the only God, be honor and glory for ever and ever. Amen.

18Timothy, my son, I give you this instruction in keeping with the prophecies once made about you, so that by following them you may fight the good fight, 19holding on to faith and a good conscience. Some have rejected these and so have shipwrecked their faith. 20Among them are Hymenaeus and Alexander, whom I have handed over to Satan to be taught not to blaspheme.

Chapter 2

Instructions concerning Prayer

FIRST of all, then, I urge that supplications, prayers, intercessions, and thanksgivings be made for everyone, 2for kings and all who are in high positions, so that we may lead a quiet and peaceable life in all godliness and dignity. 3This is right and is accept-

---

2 Παρακαλῶ   οὖν   πρῶτον   πάντων
I exhort   therefore   firstly   of all

ποιεῖσθαι   δεήσεις,   προσευχάς,   ἐντεύξεις,
to be made   petitions,   prayers,   intercessions,

εὐχαριστίας,   ὑπὲρ   πάντων   ἀνθρώπων,
thanksgivings,   on behalf of   all   men,

2 ὑπὲρ   βασιλέων   καὶ   πάντων   τῶν   ἐν
on behalf of   kings   and   all   the [ones] ²in

ὑπεροχῇ   ὄντων,   ἵνα   ἤρεμον   καὶ   ἡσύχιον
³eminence   ¹being,   in or-   ³a tranquil   ²and   ⁴quiet
             der that

βίον   διάγωμεν   ἐν   πάσῃ   εὐσεβείᾳ   καὶ
⁵life   ¹we may lead   in   all   piety   and

σεμνότητι.   **3** τοῦτο   καλὸν   καὶ   ἀπόδεκτον
gravity.   This [is]   good   and   acceptable

Chapter 2

Instructions on Worship

I URGE, then, first of all, that requests, prayers, intercession and thanksgiving be made for everyone —2for kings and all those in authority, that we may live peaceful and quiet lives in all godliness and holiness. 3This is good, and pleases

able in the sight of God our Savior, 4who desires everyone to be saved and to come to the knowledge of the truth. 5For
    there is one God;
    there is also one
        mediator
        between God
        and humankind,
    Christ Jesus, himself
        human,
6   who gave himself a
        ransom for all
—this was attested at the right time. 7For this I was appointed a herald and an apostle (I am telling the truth,c I am not lying), a teacher of the Gentiles in faith and truth.
8 I desire, then, that in every place the men should pray, lifting up holy hands without anger or argument; 9also that the women should dress themselves modestly and decently in suitable clothing, not with their hair braided, or with gold, pearls, or expensive clothes, 10but with good works, as is proper for women who profess reverence for God. 11 Let a woman d learn in silence with full submission. 12I permit no woman d to teach or to have authority over a man; e she is to keep silent. 13For Adam was formed first, then Eve; 14and Adam was not deceived, but the woman was deceived and became a transgressor. 15Yet she will be saved through childbearing, provided they continue in faith and love and holiness, with modesty.

Chapter 3

Qualifications of Bishops

THE saying is sure:f whoever aspires to the office of bishopg desires a noble task. 2Now a bishoph must be above reproach, married only

c Other ancient authorities add *in Christ*
d Or *wife*
e Or *her husband*
f Some interpreters place these words at the end of the previous paragraph. Other ancient authorities read *The saying is commonly accepted*
g Or *overseer*
h Or *an overseer*

ἐνώπιον	τοῦ	σωτῆρος	ἡμῶν	θεοῦ,	**4** ὅς	
before	the	Saviour	of us	God,	who	

πάντας	ἀνθρώπους	θέλει	σωθῆναι	καὶ εἰς
²all	³men	¹wishes	to be saved	and ²to

ἐπίγνωσιν ἀληθείας ἐλθεῖν. **5** εἶς γὰρ
²a full ⁴of truth ¹to come. For ²one
knowledge

θεός, εἶς καὶ μεσίτης θεοῦ καὶ ἀνθρώπων,
¹[there one also mediator of God and of men,
is] ³God,

ἄνθρωπος Χριστὸς Ἰησοῦς, **6** ὁ δοὺς
a man Christ Jesus, the [one] having
given

ἑαυτὸν ἀντίλυτρον ὑπὲρ πάντων, τὸ
himself a ransom on behalf of all, . the

μαρτύριον καιροῖς ἰδίοις· **7** εἰς ὃ ἐτέθην
testimony in its own times; for which ²was
appointed

ἐγὼ κῆρυξ καὶ ἀπόστολος, ἀλήθειαν λέγω,
¹I a herald and an apostle, ²truth ¹I say,

οὐ ψεύδομαι, διδάσκαλος ἐθνῶν ἐν πίστει
I do not lie, a teacher of nations in faith

καὶ ἀληθείᾳ. **8** Βούλομαι οὖν προσεύχεσθαι
and truth. I desire therefore ²to pray

τοὺς ἄνδρας ἐν παντὶ τόπῳ ἐπαίροντας
¹the ²men in every place lifting up

ὁσίους χεῖρας χωρὶς ὀργῆς καὶ διαλογισμοῦ.
holy hands without wrath and doubting.

9 Ὡσαύτως γυναῖκας ἐν καταστολῇ κοσμίῳ,
Similarly women in clothing orderly,

μετὰ αἰδοῦς καὶ σωφροσύνης κοσμεῖν
³with ⁴modesty ⁵and ⁶sobriety ¹to adorn

ἑαυτάς, μὴ ἐν πλέγμασιν καὶ χρυσίῳ
²themselves, not with plaiting and gold

ἢ μαργαρίταις ἢ ἱματισμῷ πολυτελεῖ,
or pearls or raiment costly,

10 ἀλλ' ὃ πρέπει γυναιξὶν ἐπαγγελλομέναις
but what suits women professing

θεοσέβειαν, δι' ἔργων ἀγαθῶν. **11** γυνὴ
reverence, by ²works ¹good. A woman
means of

ἐν ἡσυχίᾳ μανθανέτω ἐν πάσῃ ὑποταγῇ·
in silence let learn in all subjection;

12 διδάσκειν δὲ γυναικὶ οὐκ ἐπιτρέπω,
but ²to teach ²a woman ¹I do not permit,

οὐδὲ αὐθεντεῖν ἀνδρός, ἀλλ' εἶναι ἐν
nor to exercise of(over) a man, but to be in
authority

ἡσυχίᾳ. **13** Ἀδὰμ γὰρ πρῶτος ἐπλάσθη,
silence. For Adam first was formed,

εἶτα Εὔα. **14** καὶ Ἀδὰμ οὐκ ἠπατήθη,
then Eve. And Adam was not deceived,

ἡ δὲ γυνὴ ἐξαπατηθεῖσα ἐν παραβάσει
but the woman being deceived ²in ³transgression

γέγονεν· **15** σωθήσεται δὲ διὰ τῆς
¹has become; but she will be saved through the(her)

τεκνογονίας, ἐὰν μείνωσιν ἐν πίστει καὶ
childbearing, if they remain in faith and

ἀγάπῃ καὶ ἁγιασμῷ μετὰ σωφροσύνης.
love and sanctification with sobriety.

3 Πιστὸς ὁ λόγος· εἴ τις ἐπισκοπῆς
Faithful [is] the word: If anyone ²oversight

ὀρέγεται, καλοῦ ἔργου ἐπιθυμεῖ. **2** δεῖ
¹aspires to, ²a good ³work ¹he desires. It behoves

οὖν τὸν ἐπίσκοπον ἀνεπίλημπτον εἶναι,
there- the bishop without reproach to be,
fore

God our Savior, 4who wants all men to be saved and to come to a knowledge of the truth. 5For there is one God and one mediator between God and men, the man Christ Jesus, 6who gave himself as a ransom for all men—the testimony given in its proper time. 7And for this purpose I was appointed a herald and an apostle—I am telling the truth, I am not lying—and a teacher of the true faith to the Gentiles.
8I want men everywhere to lift up holy hands in prayer, without anger or disputing.
9I also want women to dress modestly, with decency and propriety, not with braided hair or gold or pearls or expensive clothes, 10but with good deeds, appropriate for women who profess to worship God.
11A woman should learn in quietness and full submission. 12I do not permit a woman to teach or to have authority over a man; she must be silent. 13For Adam was formed first, then Eve. 14And Adam was not the one deceived; it was the woman who was deceived and became a sinner. 15But womenb will be savedc through childbearing—if they continue in faith, love and holiness with propriety.

Chapter 3

Overseers and Deacons

HERE is a trustworthy saying: If anyone sets his heart on being an overseer,d he desires a noble task. 2Now the overseer must be above reproach,

b15 Greek *she*
c15 Or *restored*
d1 Traditionally *bishop*; also in verse 2

once,[i] temperate, sensible, respectable, hospitable, an apt teacher, [3]not a drunkard, not violent but gentle, not quarrelsome, and not a lover of money. [4]He must manage his own household well, keeping his children submissive and respectful in every way— [5]for if someone does not know how to manage his own household, how can he take care of God's church? [6]He must not be a recent convert, or he may be puffed up with conceit and fall into the condemnation of the devil. [7]Moreover, he must be well thought of by outsiders, so that he may not fall into disgrace and the snare of the devil.

Qualifications of Deacons

8 Deacons likewise must be serious, not double-tongued, not indulging in much wine, not greedy for money; [9]they must hold fast to the mystery of the faith with a clear conscience. [10]And let them first be tested; then, if they prove themselves blameless, let them serve as deacons. [11]Women[j] likewise must be serious, not slanderers, but temperate, faithful in all things. [12]Let deacons be married only once,[k] and let them manage their children and their households well; [13]for those who serve well as deacons gain a good standing for themselves and great boldness in the faith that is in Christ Jesus.

The Mystery of Our Religion

14 I hope to come to you soon, but I am writing these instructions to you so that, [15]if I am delayed, you may know how one ought to behave in the household of God, which is the church

μιᾶς γυναικὸς ἄνδρα, νηφάλιον, σώφρονα,
of one   wife   husband,   temperate,   sensible,

κόσμιον, φιλόξενον, διδακτικόν, 3 μὴ
orderly,   hospitable,   apt at teaching,   not

πάροινον, μὴ πλήκτην, ἀλλὰ ἐπιεικῆ,
an excessive   not   a striker,   but   forbearing,
drinker,

ἄμαχον, ἀφιλάργυρον, 4 τοῦ ἰδίου οἴκου
uncontentious,   not avaricious,   [3]the(his) [4]own [5]household

καλῶς προϊστάμενον, τέκνα ἔχοντα ἐν
[1]well   [2]ruling,   children   having   in

ὑποταγῇ μετὰ πάσης σεμνότητος, 5 (εἰ
subjection   with   all   gravity,   [2](if

δέ τις τοῦ ἰδίου οἴκου προστῆναι οὐκ
[1]but [3]anyone [7]the(his) [8]own [9]household   [4]to rule   [5]not[*]

οἶδεν, πῶς ἐκκλησίας θεοῦ ἐπιμελήσεται;)
[6]knows,   how   [2]a church   [3]of God   [1]will he care for ?)

6 μὴ νεόφυτον, ἵνα μὴ τυφωθεὶς εἰς
not   a neophyte(recent   lest   being puffed up   [2]into
  convert),

κρίμα ἐμπέσῃ τοῦ διαβόλου. 7 δεῖ δὲ
[3]judgment [1]he fall *in*   of the   devil.   And it behoves

καὶ μαρτυρίαν καλὴν ἔχειν ἀπὸ τῶν
also   [3]witness   [2]a good   [1]to have   from the [ones]

ἔξωθεν, 7 ἵνα μὴ εἰς ὀνειδισμὸν ἐμπέσῃ
outside,   lest   [2]into   [3]reproach   [1]he fall *in*

καὶ παγίδα τοῦ διαβόλου. 8 Διακόνους
and   a snare   of the   devil.   [It behoves] deacons

ὡσαύτως σεμνούς, μὴ διλόγους, μὴ οἴνῳ
similarly [to be] grave,   not double-tongued,   not   [2]wine

πολλῷ προσέχοντας, μὴ αἰσχροκερδεῖς,
[1]to much   [3]being addicted,   not   fond of base gain,

9 ἔχοντας τὸ μυστήριον τῆς πίστεως ἐν
having   the   mystery   of the   faith   with

καθαρᾷ συνειδήσει. 10 καὶ οὗτοι δὲ
a clean   conscience.   [4]Also   [3]these   [1]and

δοκιμαζέσθωσαν πρῶτον, εἶτα διακονείτωσαν
[2]let [5]be proved   first*ly*,   then   let them minister

ἀνέγκλητοι ὄντες. 11 γυναῖκας ὡσαύτως
[2]irreproachable   [1]being.   [It behoves][*] wives   similarly

σεμνάς, μὴ διαβόλους, νηφαλίους, πιστὰς
[to be] grave, not   slanderers,   sober,   faithful

ἐν πᾶσιν. 12 διάκονοι ἔστωσαν μιᾶς
in   all things.   [2]Deacons   [1]let [3]be   [5]of one

γυναικὸς ἄνδρες, τέκνων καλῶς προϊστάμενοι
[6]wife   [4]husbands,   [2]children   [7]well   [1]ruling

καὶ τῶν ἰδίων οἴκων. 13 οἱ γὰρ καλῶς
[3]and   [4]the(ir)   [5]own [6]households.   For the [ones] [2]well

διακονήσαντες βαθμὸν ἑαυτοῖς καλὸν
[1]having ministered   [6]position   [4]for themselves   [5]a good

περιποιοῦνται καὶ πολλὴν παρρησίαν ἐν
[3]acquire   and   much   boldness   in

πίστει τῇ ἐν Χριστῷ Ἰησοῦ. 14 Ταῦτά
faith   the [one] in   Christ   Jesus.   These things

σοι γράφω ἐλπίζων ἐλθεῖν πρὸς σὲ
to thee   I write   hoping   to come   to   thee

τάχιον· 15 ἐὰν δὲ βραδύνω, ἵνα εἰδῇς
shortly;   but if   I delay,   in order   thou
   that   mayest
    know

πῶς δεῖ ἐν οἴκῳ θεοῦ ἀναστρέφεσθαι,
how   it behoves in   [the]   of God   to behave,
     household

the husband of but one wife, temperate, self-controlled, respectable, hospitable, able to teach, [3]not given to drunkenness, not violent but gentle, not quarrelsome, not a lover of money. He must manage his own family well and see that his children obey him with proper respect. [5](If anyone does not know how to manage his own family, how can he take care of God's church?) [6]He must not be a recent convert, or he may become conceited and fall under the same judgment as the devil. [7]He must also have a good reputation with outsiders, so that he will not fall into disgrace and into the devil's trap.

[8]Deacons, likewise, are to be men worthy of respect, sincere, not indulging in much wine, and not pursuing dishonest gain. [9]They must keep hold of the deep truths of the faith with a clear conscience. [10]They must first be tested; and then if there is nothing against them, let them serve as deacons.

[11]In the same way, their wives[e] are to be women worthy of respect, not malicious talkers but temperate and trustworthy in everything.

[12]A deacon must be the husband of but one wife and must manage his children and his household well. [13]Those who have served well gain an excellent standing and great assurance in their faith in Christ Jesus.

[14]Although I hope to come to you soon, I am writing you these instructions so that, [15]if I am delayed, you will know how people ought to conduct themselves in God's house-

[i] Gk *the husband of one wife*
[j] Or *Their wives*, or *Women deacons*
[k] Gk *be husbands of one wife*

[*] That is, " cannot "; see note on page xvi.

[*] See verses 7 and 8.

[e]11 Or *way, deaconesses*

of the living God, the pillar and bulwark of the truth. [16] Without any doubt, the mystery of our religion is great:

He[l] was revealed in flesh,
vindicated[m] in spirit,[n]
seen by angels,
proclaimed among Gentiles,
believed in throughout the world,
taken up in glory.

Chapter 4

False Asceticism

NOW the Spirit expressly says that in later[o] times some will renounce the faith by paying attention to deceitful spirits and teachings of demons, [2] through the hypocrisy of liars whose consciences are seared with a hot iron. [3] They forbid marriage and demand abstinence from foods, which God created to be received with thanksgiving by those who believe and know the truth. [4] For everything created by God is good, and nothing is to be rejected, provided it is received with thanksgiving; [5] for it is sanctified by God's word and prayer.

A Good Minister of Jesus Christ

[6] If you put these instructions before the brothers and sisters,[p] you will be a good servant[q] of Christ Jesus, nourished on the words of the faith and of the sound teaching that you have followed. [7] Have nothing to do with profane myths and old wives' tales. Train yourself in godliness, [8] for, while physical training is of some value, godliness is valuable in every way, holding promise for both the present life and the life to come. [9] The saying is sure and worthy of full ac-

---

ἥτις ἐστὶν ἐκκλησία θεοῦ ζῶντος, στῦλος
which is [the] church [2]God [1]of [the] living, pillar

καὶ ἑδραίωμα τῆς ἀληθείας. 16 καὶ
and bulwark of the truth. And

ὁμολογουμένως μέγα ἐστὶν τὸ τῆς εὐσεβείας
confessedly great is the - [2]of piety

μυστήριον· ὃς ἐφανερώθη ἐν σαρκί,
[1]mystery: Who was manifested in flesh,

ἐδικαιώθη ἐν πνεύματι, ὤφθη ἀγγέλοις,
was justified in spirit, was seen by angels,

ἐκηρύχθη ἐν ἔθνεσιν, ἐπιστεύθη ἐν κόσμῳ,
was proclaimed among nations, was believed in [the] world,

ἀνελήμφθη ἐν δόξῃ.
was taken up in glory.

4 Τὸ δὲ πνεῦμα ῥητῶς λέγει ὅτι
Now the Spirit [2]in words† [1]says that

ἐν ὑστέροις καιροῖς ἀποστήσονταί τινες
in later times [3]will depart from [1]some

τῆς πίστεως, προσέχοντες πνεύμασιν
the faith, attending to [2]spirits

πλάνοις καὶ διδασκαλίαις δαιμονίων, 2 ἐν
[1]misleading and teachings of demons, [1]in

ὑποκρίσει ψευδολόγων, κεκαυστηριασμένων
[3]hypocrisy [1]of men who speak lies, having been branded on

τὴν ἰδίαν συνείδησιν, 3 κωλυόντων γαμεῖν,
the(ir) own conscience, forbidding to marry,

ἀπέχεσθαι βρωμάτων, ἃ ὁ θεὸς ἔκτισεν
[bidding] to abstain from foods, which - God created

εἰς μετάλημψιν μετὰ εὐχαριστίας τοῖς
for partaking with thanksgiving by the

πιστοῖς καὶ ἐπεγνωκόσι τὴν ἀλήθειαν.
believers and [those] having fully known the truth.

4 ὅτι πᾶν κτίσμα θεοῦ καλόν, καὶ
Because every creature of God [is] good, and

οὐδὲν ἀπόβλητον μετὰ εὐχαριστίας λαμβαν-
nothing to be put away [1]with [2]thanksgiving [1]being

ὅμενον· 5 ἁγιάζεται γὰρ διὰ λόγου θεοῦ
received; for it is being sanctified through a word of God

καὶ ἐντεύξεως. 6 Ταῦτα ὑποτιθέμενος
and petition. [2]These things [1]suggesting

τοῖς ἀδελφοῖς καλὸς ἔσῃ διάκονος Χριστοῦ
[3]to the [4]brothers [6]a good [5]thou [7]minister of Christ
wilt be

Ἰησοῦ, ἐντρεφόμενος τοῖς λόγοις τῆς
Jesus, being nourished by the words of the

πίστεως καὶ τῆς καλῆς διδασκαλίας ᾗ
faith and of the good teaching which

παρηκολούθηκας· 7 τοὺς δὲ βεβήλους καὶ
thou hast followed; but the profane and

γραώδεις μύθους παραιτοῦ. γύμναζε δὲ
old-womanish tales refuse. And exercise

σεαυτὸν πρὸς εὐσέβειαν. 8 ἡ γὰρ σωματικὴ
thyself to piety. - For bodily

γυμνασία πρὸς ὀλίγον ἐστὶν ὠφέλιμος·
exercise [2]for [1]a little [1]is [1]profitable;

ἡ δὲ εὐσέβεια πρὸς πάντα ὠφέλιμός
- but piety [2]for [1]all things [1]profitable

ἐστιν, ἐπαγγελίαν ἔχουσα ζωῆς τῆς νῦν
[1]is, promise having [3]life [1]of the [2]now
(present)

καὶ τῆς μελλούσης. 9 πιστὸς ὁ λόγος
and of the coming. Faithful [is] the word

---

hold, which is the church of the living God, the pillar and foundation of the truth. [16] Beyond all question, the mystery of godliness is great:

He[f] appeared in a body,[g]
was vindicated by the Spirit,
was seen by angels,
was preached among the nations,
was believed on in the world,
was taken up in glory.

Chapter 4

Instructions to Timothy

THE Spirit clearly says that in later times some will abandon the faith and follow deceiving spirits and things taught by demons. [2] Such teachings come through hypocritical liars, whose consciences have been seared as with a hot iron. [3] They forbid people to marry and order them to abstain from certain foods, which God created to be received with thanksgiving by those who believe and who know the truth. [4] For everything God created is good, and nothing is to be rejected if it is received with thanksgiving, [5] because it is consecrated by the word of God and prayer.

[6] If you point these things out to the brothers, you will be a good minister of Christ Jesus, brought up in the truths of the faith and of the good teaching that you have followed. [7] Have nothing to do with godless myths and old wives' tales; rather, train yourself to be godly. [8] For physical training is of some value, but godliness has value for all things, holding promise for both the present life and the life to come. [9] This is a trustworthy

---

[l] Gk Who; other ancient authorities read God; others, Which
[m] Or justified
[n] Or by the Spirit
[o] Or the last
[p] Gk brothers
[q] Or deacon

ceptance. 10 For to this end we toil and struggle,ʳ because we have our hope set on the living God, who is the Savior of all people, especially of those who believe.

11 These are the things you must insist on and teach. 12 Let no one despise your youth, but set the believers an example in speech and conduct, in love, in faith, in purity. 13 Until I arrive, give attention to the public reading of scripture,ˢ to exhorting, to teaching. 14 Do not neglect the gift that is in you, which was given to you through prophecy with the laying on of hands by the council of elders.ᵗ 15 Put these things into practice, devote yourself to them, so that all may see your progress. 16 Pay close attention to yourself and to your teaching; continue in these things, for in doing this you will save both yourself and your hearers.

καὶ πάσης ἀποδοχῆς ἄξιος· 10 εἰς τοῦτο
and ⁶of all ⁵acceptance ⁴worthy; ¹to ³this

γὰρ κοπιῶμεν καὶ ἀγωνιζόμεθα, ὅτι
²for we labour and struggle, because

ἠλπίκαμεν ἐπὶ θεῷ ζῶντι, ὅς ἐστιν
we have set on ²God ¹a living, who is

σωτὴρ πάντων ἀνθρώπων, μάλιστα πιστῶν.
[the] of all men, especially of believers.
Saviour

11 Παράγγελλε ταῦτα καὶ δίδασκε.
Charge thou these things and teach.

12 μηδείς σου τῆς νεότητος καταφρονείτω,
¹No one ²of thee ³the ⁴youth ¹let despise,

ἀλλὰ τύπος γίνου τῶν πιστῶν ἐν λόγῳ,
but ²a pattern ¹become of the believers in speech,
thou

ἐν ἀναστροφῇ, ἐν ἀγάπῃ, ἐν πίστει,
in behaviour, in love, in faith,

ἐν ἁγνείᾳ. 13 ἕως ἔρχομαι πρόσεχε
in purity. Until I come attend

τῇ ἀναγνώσει,* τῇ παρακλήσει, τῇ διδασ-
to the reading,* to the exhortation, to the teach-

καλίᾳ. 14 μὴ ἀμέλει τοῦ ἐν σοὶ
ing. Do not be neglectful ¹of the ²in ³thee

χαρίσματος, ὃ ἐδόθη σοι διὰ προφητείας
²gift, which was to thee by prophecy
given means of

μετὰ ἐπιθέσεως τῶν χειρῶν τοῦ πρε-
with laying on of the hands of the body

σβυτερίου. 15 ταῦτα μελέτα, ἐν τούτοις
of elders. ²These things ¹attend to, ²in ³these things

ἴσθι, ἵνα σου ἡ προκοπὴ φανερὰ ᾖ
¹be in order of thee the advance clear may
thou, that be

πᾶσιν. 16 ἔπεχε σεαυτῷ καὶ τῇ διδασκαλίᾳ,
to all men. Take heed to thyself and to the teaching,

ἐπίμενε αὐτοῖς· τοῦτο γὰρ ποιῶν καὶ
continue in them; for this doing both

σεαυτὸν σώσεις καὶ τοὺς ἀκούοντάς σου.
thyself thou wilt save and the [ones] hearing thee.

---

saying that deserves full acceptance 10 (and for this we labor and strive), that we have put our hope in the living God, who is the Savior of all men, and especially of those who believe.

11 Command and teach these things. 12 Don't let anyone look down on you because you are young, but set an example for the believers in speech, in life, in love, in faith and in purity. 13 Until I come, devote yourself to the public reading of Scripture, to preaching and to teaching. 14 Do not neglect your gift, which was given you through a prophetic message when the body of elders laid their hands on you.

15 Be diligent in these matters; give yourself wholly to them, so that everyone may see your progress. 16 Watch your life and doctrine closely. Persevere in them, because if you do, you will save both yourself and your hearers.

Chapter 5

Duties toward Believers

DO not speak harshly to an older man,ᵘ but speak to him as to a father, to younger men as brothers, 2 to older women as mothers, to younger women as sisters—with absolute purity.

3 Honor widows who are really widows. 4 If a widow has children or grandchildren, they should first learn their religious duty to their own family and make some repayment to their parents; for this is pleasing in God's sight. 5 The real widow, left alone, has set her hope on

---

5 Πρεσβυτέρῳ μὴ ἐπιπλήξῃς, ἀλλὰ
An older man do not rebuke, but

παρακάλει ὡς πατέρα, νεωτέρους ὡς
exhort as a father, younger men as

ἀδελφούς, 2 πρεσβυτέρας ὡς μητέρας,
brothers, older women as mothers,

νεωτέρας ὡς ἀδελφὰς ἐν πάσῃ ἁγνείᾳ.
younger women as sisters with all purity.

3 Χήρας τίμα τὰς ὄντως χήρας. 4 εἰ δέ
¹Widows ¹honour ³the ⁴really ⁴widows. But if

τις χήρα τέκνα ἢ ἔκγονα ἔχει, μαν-
any widow ²children ³or ⁴grandchildren ¹has, let

θανέτωσαν πρῶτον τὸν ἴδιον οἶκον εὐσεβεῖν
them learn firstly ²the(ir) ³own ⁴household ¹to show
piety to

καὶ ἀμοιβὰς ἀποδιδόναι τοῖς προγόνοις·
and ²requitals ¹to return to the(ir) forebears;

τοῦτο γάρ ἐστιν ἀπόδεκτον ἐνώπιον τοῦ
for this is acceptable before

θεοῦ. 5 ἡ δὲ ὄντως χήρα καὶ μεμονωμένη
God. But the really widow and having been left
alone

Advice About Widows, Elders and Slaves

DO not rebuke an older man harshly, but exhort him as if he were your father. Treat younger men as brothers, 2 older women as mothers, and younger women as sisters, with absolute purity.

3 Give proper recognition to those widows who are really in need. 4 But if a widow has children or grandchildren, these should learn first of all to put their religion into practice by caring for their own family and so repaying their parents and grandparents, for this is pleasing to God. 5 The widow who is really in need and left all alone puts her

---

ʳ Other ancient authorities read
　suffer reproach
ˢ Gk to the reading
ᵗ Gk by the presbytery
ᵘ Or an elder, or a presbyter

* That is, the reading aloud in public worship of the Scriptures
(as nearly always in the N.T.).

God and continues in supplications and prayers night and day; 6but the widow[v] who lives for pleasure is dead even while she lives. 7Give these commands as well, so that they may be above reproach. 8And whoever does not provide for relatives, and especially for family members, has denied the faith and is worse than an unbeliever. 9 Let a widow be put on the list if she is not less than sixty years old and has been married only once;[w] 10she must be well attested for her good works, as one who has brought up children, shown hospitality, washed the saints' feet, helped the afflicted, and devoted herself to doing good in every way. 11But refuse to put younger widows on the list; for when their sensual desires alienate them from Christ, they want to marry, 12and so they incur condemnation for having violated their first pledge. 13Besides that, they learn to be idle, gadding about from house to house; and they are not merely idle, but also gossips and busybodies, saying what they should not say. 14So I would have younger widows marry, bear children, and manage their households, so as to give the adversary no occasion to revile us. 15For some have already turned away to follow Satan. 16If any believing woman[x] has relatives who are really widows, let her assist them; let the church not be burdened, so that it can assist those who are real widows.

17 Let the elders who rule well be considered worthy of double honor,[y] especially those who labor

ἤλπικεν ἐπὶ θεὸν καὶ προσμένει ταῖς
has set on God and continues in the
[her] hope

δεήσεσιν καὶ ταῖς προσευχαῖς νυκτὸς καὶ
petitions and the prayers night and

ἡμέρας· 6 ἡ δὲ σπαταλῶσα ζῶσα τέθνηκεν.
day; but the living wantonly ²living ¹has died.
[one]

7 καὶ ταῦτα παράγγελλε, ἵνα ἀνεπίλημπτοι
And these charge thou, in order ²without reproach
things that

ὦσιν. 8 εἰ δέ τις τῶν ἰδίων καὶ μάλιστα
¹they But if anyone ²the(his) ²own ⁴and ⁵especially
may be. [people]

οἰκείων οὐ προνοεῖ, τὴν πίστιν ἤρνηται
[his] ¹provides not [for], ²the ²faith ¹he has
¹family denied

καὶ ἔστιν ἀπίστου χείρων. 9 χήρα
and is ²an unbeliever ¹worse [than]. A widow

καταλεγέσθω μὴ ἔλαττον ἐτῶν ἑξήκοντα
let be enrolled ²not ³less [than] ¹of years ⁴sixty

γεγονυῖα, ἑνὸς ἀνδρὸς γυνή, 10 ἐν ἔργοις
¹having of one man wife, ¹by ²works
become,

καλοῖς μαρτυρουμένη, εἰ ἐτεκνοτρόφησεν,
²good ¹being witnessed, if she brought up children,

εἰ ἐξενοδόχησεν, εἰ ἁγίων πόδας ἔνιψεν,
if she entertained if ²of saints ³feet ¹she
strangers, washed,

εἰ θλιβομένοις ἐπήρκεσεν, εἰ παντὶ ἔργῳ
if ²being afflicted ¹she relieved, if ²every ⁴work
[ones],

ἀγαθῷ ἐπηκολούθησεν. 11 νεωτέρας δὲ
²good ¹she followed after. But younger

χήρας παραιτοῦ· ὅταν γὰρ καταστρηνιάσωσιν
widows refuse; for whenever they grow wanton against

τοῦ Χριστοῦ, γαμεῖν θέλουσιν, 12 ἔχουσαι
- Christ, ²to marry ¹they wish, having

κρίμα ὅτι τὴν πρώτην πίστιν ἠθέτησαν·
judgment because the(ir) ³first ⁴faith ¹they set aside;

13 ἅμα δὲ καὶ ἀργαὶ μανθάνουσιν
and at the same time also ¹idle ¹they learn [to be]

περιερχόμεναι τὰς οἰκίας, οὐ μόνον δὲ
going round the houses, ²not ³only ¹and

ἀργαὶ ἀλλὰ καὶ φλύαροι καὶ περίεργοι,
idle but also gossips and busybodies,

λαλοῦσαι τὰ μὴ δέοντα. 14 βούλομαι
speaking the things not proper. I will

οὖν νεωτέρας γαμεῖν, τεκνογονεῖν,
there- younger women to marry, to bear children,
fore

οἰκοδεσποτεῖν, μηδεμίαν ἀφορμὴν διδόναι
to be mistress of ²no ²occasion ¹to give
a house,

τῷ ἀντικειμένῳ λοιδορίας χάριν· 15 ἤδη
to the [one] opposing ²reproach ¹on account of; ²already

γάρ τινες ἐξετράπησαν ὀπίσω τοῦ σατανᾶ.
¹for some turned aside behind - Satan.

16 εἴ τις πιστὴ ἔχει χήρας, ἐπαρκείτω
If any believing has widows, let her relieve
woman

αὐταῖς, καὶ μὴ βαρείσθω ἡ ἐκκλησία,
them, and not let be burdened the church,

ἵνα ταῖς ὄντως χήραις ἐπαρκέσῃ. 17 Οἱ
in or- ²the ²really ⁴widows ¹it may relieve. ²The
der that

καλῶς προεστῶτες πρεσβύτεροι διπλῆς
²well ⁴ruling ³elders ²of double

hope in God and continues night and day to pray and to ask God for help. 6But the widow who lives for pleasure is dead even while she lives. 7Give the people these instructions, too, so that no one may be open to blame. 8If anyone does not provide for his relatives, and especially for his immediate family, he has denied the faith and is worse than an unbeliever.

9No widow may be put on the list of widows unless she is over sixty, has been faithful to her husband,[h] 10and is well known for her good deeds, such as bringing up children, showing hospitality, washing the feet of the saints, helping those in trouble and devoting herself to all kinds of good deeds.

11As for younger widows, do not put them on such a list. For when their sensual desires overcome their dedication to Christ, they want to marry. 12Thus they bring judgment on themselves, because they have broken their first pledge. 13Besides, they get into the habit of being idle and going about from house to house. And not only do they become idlers, but also gossips and busybodies, saying things they ought not to. 14So I counsel younger widows to marry, to have children, to manage their homes and to give the enemy no opportunity for slander. 15Some have in fact already turned away to follow Satan.

16If any woman who is a believer has widows in her family, she should help them and not let the church be burdened with them, so that the church can help those widows who are really in need.

17The elders who direct the affairs of the church well are worthy of double honor, especially those

[v] Gk she
[w] Gk the wife of one husband
[x] Other ancient authorities read believing man or woman; others, believing man
[y] Or compensation

[h]9 Or has had but one husband

in preaching and teaching;
18for the scripture says,
"You shall not muzzle an
ox while it is treading out
the grain," and, "The laborer deserves to be paid."
19Never accept any accu-
sation against an elder except on the evidence of two
or three witnesses. 20As for
those who persist in sin, rebuke them in the presence
of all, so that the rest also
may stand in fear. 21In the
presence of God and of
Christ Jesus and of the
elect angels, I warn you to
keep these instructions
without prejudice, doing
nothing on the basis of partiality. 22Do not ordain
anyone hastily, and do not
participate in the sins of
others; keep yourself pure.

23 No longer drink only
water, but take a little wine
for the sake of your stomach and your frequent ailments.

24 The sins of some
people are conspicuous and
precede them to judgment,
while the sins of others follow them there. 25So also
good works are conspicu-
ous; and even when they
are not, they cannot remain
hidden.

τιμῆς ἀξιούσθωσαν, μάλιστα οἱ κοπιῶντες
19honour 1let 4be 7deemed especially the labouring
'worthy, [ones]

ἐν λόγῳ καὶ διδασκαλίᾳ. 18 λέγει γὰρ
in speech and teaching. For says

ἡ γραφή· βοῦν ἀλοῶντα οὐ φιμώσεις,
the scripture: An ox threshing thou shalt not muzzle,

καὶ· ἄξιος ὁ ἐργάτης τοῦ μισθοῦ αὐτοῦ.
and: Worthy [is] the workman of the pay of him.

19 κατὰ πρεσβυτέρου κατηγορίαν μὴ παρα-
Against an elder accusation do not re-

δέχου, ἐκτὸς εἰ μὴ ἐπὶ δύο ἢ τριῶν
ceive, except unless on [the two or three
word of]

μαρτύρων. 20 Τοὺς ἁμαρτάνοντας ἐνώπιον
witnesses. The [ones] sinning 2before

πάντων ἔλεγχε, ἵνα καὶ οἱ λοιποὶ φόβον
3all 1reprove in 2also 1the 2rest 4fear
thou, order that

ἔχωσιν. 21 Διαμαρτύρομαι ἐνώπιον τοῦ
1may have. I solemnly witness before –

θεοῦ καὶ Χριστοῦ Ἰησοῦ καὶ τῶν
God and Christ Jesus and the

ἐκλεκτῶν ἀγγέλων ἵνα ταῦτα φυλάξῃς,
chosen angels in order these things thou guard
that

χωρὶς προκρίματος, μηδὲν ποιῶν κατὰ
without prejudgment, 2nothing 1doing by way of

πρόσκλισιν. 22 χεῖρας ταχέως μηδενὶ
inclination. 3Hands 2quickly 4no man

ἐπιτίθει, μηδὲ κοινώνει ἁμαρτίαις ἀλ-
1lay 3on, nor share 2sins 1in

λοτρίαις· σεαυτὸν ἁγνὸν τήρει. 23 Μηκέτι
others'†; 2thyself 3pure 1keep. No longer

ὑδροπότει, ἀλλὰ οἴνῳ ὀλίγῳ χρῶ διὰ
drink water, but 2wine 3a little 1use on account of

τὸν στόμαχον καὶ τὰς πυκνάς σου
the(thy) stomach and the frequent 2of thee

ἀσθενείας. 24 Τινῶν ἀνθρώπων αἱ ἁμαρτίαι
1weaknesses. 2of some 4men 1The 3sins

πρόδηλοί εἰσιν προάγουσαι εἰς κρίσιν,
2clear 1are going before to judgment,
beforehand

τισὶν δὲ καὶ ἐπακολουθοῦσιν· 25 ὡσαύτως
but some indeed they follow on; similarly

καὶ τὰ ἔργα τὰ καλὰ πρόδηλα, καὶ
also the 2works – 1good [are] clear and
beforehand,

τὰ ἄλλως ἔχοντα κρυβῆναι οὐ δύνανται.
the 2otherwise 1having 4to be hidden 3cannot.
[ones] (being)

6 Ὅσοι εἰσὶν ὑπὸ ζυγὸν δοῦλοι, τοὺς
As many as are under a yoke slaves, 2the(ir)
[being]

ἰδίους δεσπότας πάσης τιμῆς ἀξίους ἡγείσ-
2own 4masters 6of all 7honour 5worthy 1let them

θωσαν, ἵνα μὴ τὸ ὄνομα τοῦ θεοῦ καὶ
deem, lest the name – of God and

ἡ διδασκαλία βλασφημῆται. 2 οἱ δὲ
the teaching be blasphemed. And 1the [ones]

πιστοὺς ἔχοντες δεσπότας μὴ καταφρο-
3believing 1having 4masters not let them

νείτωσαν, ὅτι ἀδελφοί εἰσιν, ἀλλὰ μᾶλλον
despise [them], because brothers they are, but rather

δουλευέτωσαν, ὅτι πιστοί εἰσιν καὶ
let them serve as slaves, because 2believing 1are 3and

ἀγαπητοὶ οἱ τῆς εὐεργεσίας ἀντιλαμ-
4beloved 1the [ones] 2of the 3good service 1receiving in

βανόμενοι.
return.

whose work is preaching
and teaching. 18For the
Scripture says, "Do not
muzzle the ox while it is
treading out the grain,"[i]
and "The worker deserves
his wages."[j] 19Do not entertain an accusation
against an elder unless it is
brought by two or three
witnesses. 20Those who sin
are to be rebuked publicly,
so that the others may take
warning.

21I charge you, in the
sight of God and Christ
Jesus and the elect angels,
to keep these instructions
without partiality, and to
do nothing out of favoritism.

22Do not be hasty in the
laying on of hands, and do
not share in the sins of others. Keep yourself pure.

23Stop drinking only wa-
ter, and use a little wine because of your stomach and
your frequent illnesses.

24The sins of some men
are obvious, reaching the
place of judgment ahead of
them; the sins of others trail
behind them. 25In the same
way, good deeds are obvi-
ous, and even those that
are not cannot be hidden.

Chapter 6

LET all who are under the
yoke of slavery regard
their masters as worthy of
all honor, so that the name
of God and the teaching
may not be blasphemed.
2Those who have believing
masters must not be disre-
spectful to them on the
ground that they are mem-
bers of the church;[a] rather
they must serve them all
the more, since those who
benefit by their service are
believers and beloved.[b]

*False Teaching and True
Riches*

Teach and urge these du-

Chapter 6

ALL who are under the
yoke of slavery
should consider their masters worthy of full respect,
so that God's name and our
teaching may not be slan-
dered. 2Those who have
believing masters are not to
show less respect for them
because they are brothers.
Instead, they are to serve
them even better, because
those who benefit from
their service are believers,
and dear to them. These are
the things you are to teach
and urge on them.

z Gk *Do not lay hands on*
a Gk *are brothers*
b Or *since they are believers and
beloved, who devote themselves to
good deeds*

i18 Deut. 25:4
j18 Luke 10:7

ties. [3] Whoever teaches otherwise and does not agree with the sound words of our Lord Jesus Christ and the teaching that is in accordance with godliness, [4] is conceited, understanding nothing, and has a morbid craving for controversy and for disputes about words. From these come envy, dissension, slander, base suspicions, [5] and wrangling among those who are depraved in mind and bereft of the truth, imagining that godliness is a means of gain.[c] [6] Of course, there is great gain in godliness combined with contentment; [7] for we brought nothing into the world, so that[d] we can take nothing out of it; [8] but if we have food and clothing, we will be content with these. [9] But those who want to be rich fall into temptation and are trapped by many senseless and harmful desires that plunge people into ruin and destruction. [10] For the love of money is a root of all kinds of evil, and in their eagerness to be rich some have wandered away from the faith and pierced themselves with many pains.

The Good Fight of Faith

[11] But as for you, man of God, shun all this; pursue righteousness, godliness, faith, love, endurance, gentleness. [12] Fight the good fight of the faith; take hold of the eternal life, to which you were called and for which you made[e] the good confession in the

---

Ταῦτα δίδασκε καὶ παρακάλει. **3** εἰ
These things teach thou and exhort. If

τις ἑτεροδιδασκαλεῖ καὶ μὴ προσέρχεται
anyone teaches differently and consents not

ὑγιαίνουσιν λόγοις τοῖς τοῦ κυρίου ἡμῶν
to *being* healthy words the of the Lord of us
[words]

Ἰησοῦ Χριστοῦ, καὶ τῇ κατ' εὐσέβειαν
Jesus Christ, and [1]to the [2]according [4]piety
ing to

διδασκαλίᾳ, **4** τετύφωται, μηδὲν ἐπιστά-
[3]teaching, he has been puffed up, [2]nothing [1]under-

μενος, ἀλλὰ νοσῶν περὶ ζητήσεις καὶ
standing, but being diseased about questionings and

λογομαχίας, ἐξ ὧν γίνεται φθόνος, ἔρις,
battles of words, out of which comes envy, strife,

βλασφημίαι, ὑπόνοιαι πονηραί, **5** διαπαρα-
blasphemies, [2]suspicions [1]evil, perpetual

τριβαὶ διεφθαρμένων ἀνθρώπων τὸν νοῦν
wranglings [2]having been corrupted [1]of men the mind
=of men with corrupted mind

καὶ ἀπεστερημένων τῆς ἀληθείας, νομιζ-
and *having been* deprived of the truth, sup-

όντων πορισμὸν εἶναι τὴν εὐσέβειαν.
posing [3]gain [2]to be the [1]piety.

6 ἔστιν δὲ πορισμὸς μέγας ἡ εὐσέβεια
But [4]is [3]gain [2]great *the* [1]piety

μετὰ αὐταρκείας· **7** οὐδὲν γὰρ εἰσηνέγκαμεν
[5]with [6]self-sufficiency;* for nothing we have brought *in*

εἰς τὸν κόσμον, ὅτι οὐδὲ ἐξενεγκεῖν
into the world, because neither [1]to carry out

τι δυνάμεθα· **8** ἔχοντες δὲ διατροφὰς καὶ
[3]any- [2]can we; but having foods and
thing

σκεπάσματα, τούτοις ἀρκεσθησόμεθα. **9** οἱ
clothings, with these things we will be satisfied. the

δὲ βουλόμενοι πλουτεῖν ἐμπίπτουσιν εἰς
But [ones] resolving to be rich fall *in* into

πειρασμὸν καὶ παγίδα καὶ ἐπιθυμίας πολλὰς
temptation and a snare and [2]lusts [1]many

ἀνοήτους καὶ βλαβεράς, αἵτινες βυθίζουσιν
[2]foolish [3]and [4]injurious, which [1]cause [2]to sink

τοὺς ἀνθρώπους εἰς ὄλεθρον καὶ ἀπώλειαν.
- [1]men into ruin and destruction.

10 ῥίζα γὰρ πάντων τῶν κακῶν ἐστιν
For [4]a root [5]of all - [6]evils [3]is

ἡ φιλαργυρία, ἧς τινες ὀρεγόμενοι
[1]the [2]love of money,* of which some hankering after

ἀπεπλανήθησαν ἀπὸ τῆς πίστεως καὶ
wandered away from the faith and

ἑαυτοὺς περιέπειραν ὀδύναις πολλαῖς. **11** Σὺ
themselves pierced round [2]pains [1]by many. thou

δέ, ὦ ἄνθρωπε θεοῦ, ταῦτα φεῦγε· δίωκε
But, O man of God, these things flee; [2]pursue

δὲ δικαιοσύνην, εὐσέβειαν, πίστιν, ἀγάπην,
[1]and righteousness, piety, faith, love,

ὑπομονήν, πραϋπαθίαν. **12** ἀγωνίζου τὸν
endurance, meekness. Struggle the

καλὸν ἀγῶνα τῆς πίστεως, ἐπιλαβοῦ τῆς
good struggle of the faith, lay hold on *the*

αἰωνίου ζωῆς, εἰς ἣν ἐκλήθης καὶ ὡμολό-
eternal life, to which thou wast and didst con-
called

γησας τὴν καλὴν ὁμολογίαν ἐνώπιον
fess the good confession before

Love of Money

[3] If anyone teaches false doctrines and does not agree to the sound instruction of our Lord Jesus Christ and to godly teaching, [4] he is conceited and understands nothing. He has an unhealthy interest in controversies and quarrels about words that result in envy, strife, malicious talk, evil suspicions [5] and constant friction between men of corrupt mind, who have been robbed of the truth and who think that godliness is a means to financial gain.

[6] But godliness with contentment is great gain. [7] For we brought nothing into the world, and we can take nothing out of it. [8] But if we have food and clothing, we will be content with that. [9] People who want to get rich fall into temptation and a trap and into many foolish and harmful desires that plunge men into ruin and destruction. [10] For the love of money is a root of all kinds of evil. Some people, eager for money, have wandered from the faith and pierced themselves with many griefs.

Paul's Charge to Timothy

[11] But you, man of God, flee from all this, and pursue righteousness, godliness, faith, love, endurance and gentleness. [12] Fight the good fight of the faith. Take hold of the eternal life to which you were called when you made your good

---

[c] Other ancient authorities add *Withdraw yourself from such people*
[d] Other ancient authorities read *world—it is certain that*
[e] Gk *confessed*

* For order of words see note on John 1. 1.

presence of many witnesses. 13 In the presence of God, who gives life to all things, and of Christ Jesus, who in his testimony before Pontius Pilate made the good confession, I charge you 14to keep the commandment without spot or blame until the manifestation of our Lord Jesus Christ, 15which he will bring about at the right time—he who is the blessed and only Sovereign, the King of kings and Lord of lords. 16It is he alone who has immortality and dwells in unapproachable light, whom no one has ever seen or can see; to him be honor and eternal dominion. Amen.

17 As for those who in the present age are rich, command them not to be haughty, or to set their hopes on the uncertainty of riches, but rather on God who richly provides us with everything for our enjoyment. 18They are to do good, to be rich in good works, generous, and ready to share, 19thus storing up for themselves the treasure of a good foundation for the future, so that they may take hold of the life that really is life.

Personal Instructions and Benediction

20 Timothy, guard what has been entrusted to you. Avoid the profane chatter and contradictions of what is falsely called knowledge; 21by professing it some have missed the mark as regards the faith.
Grace be with you.*f*

πολλῶν μαρτύρων. 13 παραγγέλλω ἐνώπιον
many witnesses.   I charge   before

τοῦ θεοῦ τοῦ ζωογονοῦντος τὰ πάντα
-   God the [one] quickening - all things

καὶ Χριστοῦ Ἰησοῦ τοῦ μαρτυρήσαντος
and Christ Jesus the [one] having witnessed

ἐπὶ Ποντίου Πιλάτου τὴν καλὴν ὁμολογίαν,
in the Pontius Pilate the good confession,
time of

14 τηρῆσαί σε τὴν ἐντολὴν ἄσπιλον
  ¹to keep ¹thee* the(this) commandment unspotted

ἀνεπίλημπτον μέχρι τῆς ἐπιφανείας τοῦ
without reproach until the appearance of the

κυρίου ἡμῶν Ἰησοῦ Χριστοῦ, 15 ἣν
Lord of us Jesus Christ, which§

καιροῖς ἰδίοις δείξει ὁ μακάριος καὶ
²in its/his own times ⁴will show ¹the ³blessed ²and

μόνος δυνάστης, ὁ βασιλεὺς τῶν βασιλευ-
⁴only ⁵Potentate, the King of the [ones] reign-

όντων καὶ κύριος τῶν κυριευόντων, 16 ὁ
ing and Lord of the [ones] ruling,

μόνος ἔχων ἀθανασίαν, φῶς οἰκῶν
only [one] having immortality, ⁴light ¹inhabiting

ἀπρόσιτον, ὃν εἶδεν οὐδεὶς ἀνθρώπων οὐδὲ
unapproach- whom ²saw ¹no one ³of men nor
able,

ἰδεῖν δύναται· ᾧ τιμὴ καὶ κράτος αἰώνιον·
¹to see ¹can; to [be] and might eternal:
whom honour

ἀμήν. 17 Τοῖς πλουσίοις ἐν τῷ νῦν
Amen. ³the ²rich ⁴in ⁵the ⁶now
(present)

αἰῶνι παράγγελλε μὴ ὑψηλοφρονεῖν, μηδὲ
⁷age ¹Charge thou not to be highminded, nor

ἠλπικέναι ἐπὶ πλούτου ἀδηλότητι, ἀλλ'
to have set on ²of riches ¹[the] uncertainty, but
[their] hope

ἐπὶ θεῷ τῷ παρέχοντι ἡμῖν πάντα
on God the [one] offering to us all things

πλουσίως εἰς ἀπόλαυσιν, 18 ἀγαθοεργεῖν,
richly for enjoyment, to work good,

πλουτεῖν ἐν ἔργοις καλοῖς, εὐμεταδότους
to be rich in ²works ¹good, ²ready to impart

εἶναι, κοινωνικούς, 19 ἀποθησαυρίζοντας
¹to be, generous, treasuring away

ἑαυτοῖς θεμέλιον καλὸν εἰς τὸ μέλλον,
for ²foundation ¹a good for the future,
themselves

ἵνα ἐπιλάβωνται τῆς ὄντως ζωῆς. 20 Ὦ
in or- they may lay the real*ly* life. O
der that hold on

Τιμόθεε, τὴν παραθήκην φύλαξον, ἐκτρεπ-
Timothy, ²the ³deposit ¹guard, turning

όμενος τὰς βεβήλους κενοφωνίας καὶ
aside from the profane empty utterances and

ἀντιθέσεις τῆς ψευδωνύμου γνώσεως, 21 ἥν
opposing of the falsely named knowledge, which
tenets

τινες ἐπαγγελλόμενοι περὶ τὴν πίστιν
some promising concerning the faith

ἠστόχησαν.
missed aim.

Ἡ χάρις μεθ' ὑμῶν.
- Grace [be] with you.

confession in the presence of many witnesses. 13In the sight of God, who gives life to everything, and of Christ Jesus, who while testifying before Pontius Pilate made the good confession, I charge you 14to keep this command without spot or blame until the appearing of our Lord Jesus Christ, 15which God will bring about in his own time—God, the blessed and only Ruler, the King of kings and Lord of lords, 16who alone is immortal and who lives in unapproachable light, whom no one has seen or can see. To him be honor and might forever. Amen.

17Command those who are rich in this present world not to be arrogant nor to put their hope in wealth, which is so uncertain, but to put their hope in God, who richly provides us with everything for our enjoyment. 18Command them to do good, to be rich in good deeds, and to be generous and willing to share. 19In this way they will lay up treasure for themselves as a firm foundation for the coming age, so that they may take hold of the life that is truly life.

20Timothy, guard what has been entrusted to your care. Turn away from godless chatter and the opposing ideas of what is falsely called knowledge, 21which some have professed and in so doing have wandered from the faith.

Grace be with you.

---

f The Greek word for *you* here is plural; in other ancient authorities it is singular. Other ancient authorities add *Amen*

* "thee" is the direct object of the verb "charge" in ver. 13: "I charge . . . thee to keep . . ."
§ The antecedent to this relative pronoun is "appearance", not "Jesus Christ".

Timothy

Chapter 1

Salutation

PAUL, an apostle of Christ Jesus by the will of God, for the sake of the promise of life that is in Christ Jesus,

2 To Timothy, my beloved child:

Grace, mercy, and peace from God the Father and Christ Jesus our Lord.

Thanksgiving and Encouragement

3 I am grateful to God— whom I worship with a clear conscience, as my ancestors did—when I remember you constantly in my prayers night and day. 4 Recalling your tears, I long to see you so that I may be filled with joy. 5 I am reminded of your sincere faith, a faith that lived first in your grandmother Lois and your mother Eunice and now, I am sure, lives in you. 6 For this reason I remind you to rekindle the gift of God that is within you through the laying on of my hands; 7 for God did not give us a spirit of cowardice, but rather a spirit of power and of love and of self-discipline.

8 Do not be ashamed, then, of the testimony about our Lord or of me his prisoner, but join with me in suffering for the gospel, relying on the power of God, 9 who saved us and called us with a holy calling, not according to our works but according to his own purpose and grace. This grace was given to us in Christ Jesus before the ages began, 10 but it has now been revealed through

1 Παῦλος ἀπόστολος Χριστοῦ Ἰησοῦ διὰ
Paul   an apostle   of Christ   Jesus through

θελήματος θεοῦ κατ' ἐπαγγελίαν ζωῆς
[the] will   of God by way of   a promise   of life

τῆς ἐν Χριστῷ Ἰησοῦ **2** Τιμοθέῳ ἀγαπητῷ
-   in   Christ   Jesus   to Timothy   beloved

τέκνῳ· χάρις, ἔλεος, εἰρήνη ἀπὸ θεοῦ
child: Grace,   mercy,   peace   from   God

πατρὸς καὶ Χριστοῦ Ἰησοῦ τοῦ κυρίου
[our] Father and   Christ   Jesus   the   Lord

ἡμῶν.
of us.

3 Χάριν ἔχω τῷ θεῷ, ᾧ λατρεύω
Thanks   I have   -   to God, whom   I worship

ἀπὸ προγόνων ἐν καθαρᾷ συνειδήσει, ὡς
from   [my] forebears   in   a clean   conscience,   as

ἀδιάλειπτον ἔχω τὴν περὶ σοῦ μνείαν
unceasingly   I have   ¹the ²concerning ⁴thee   ³remembrance

ἐν ταῖς δεήσεσίν μου νυκτὸς καὶ ἡμέρας,
in   the   petitions   of me   night   and   day,

4 ἐπιποθῶν σε ἰδεῖν, μεμνημένος σου
longing   ²thee   ¹to see,   having been   ³of thee
    reminded

τῶν δακρύων, ἵνα χαρᾶς πληρωθῶ,
¹of the   ²tears,   in order   of(with) joy I may be filled,
    that

5 ὑπόμνησιν λαβὼν τῆς ἐν σοὶ ἀνυποκρίτου
²recollection ¹taking ²of the ³in ⁷thee   ⁴unfeigned

πίστεως, ἥτις ἐνῴκησεν πρῶτον ἐν τῇ
⁵faith,   which   indwelt   firstly   in   the

μάμμη σου Λωΐδι καὶ τῇ μητρί σου
grand-   of thee   Lois   and [in] the   mother of thee
mother

Εὐνίκη, πέπεισμαι δὲ ὅτι καὶ ἐν σοί.
Eunice,   and I have been   that [it dwells] in   thee.
    persuaded   also

6 Δι' ἣν αἰτίαν ἀναμιμνήσκω σε ἀνα-
For which   cause   I remind   thee to fan

ζωπυρεῖν τὸ χάρισμα τοῦ θεοῦ, ὅ ἐστιν
the flame [of] the   gift   -   of God, which   is

ἐν σοὶ διὰ τῆς ἐπιθέσεως τῶν χειρῶν
in   thee through the   laying on   of the   hands

μου. **7** οὐ γὰρ ἔδωκεν ἡμῖν ὁ θεὸς
of me.   ²not For   ³gave   ⁴to us   ¹God

πνεῦμα δειλίας, ἀλλὰ δυνάμεως καὶ ἀγάπης
a spirit   of cowardice, but   of power   and   of love

καὶ σωφρονισμοῦ. **8** μὴ οὖν ἐπαισχυνθῇς
and   of self-control.   ²not ¹Therefore   ⁵be ⁴thou
        ashamed [of]

τὸ μαρτύριον τοῦ κυρίου ἡμῶν μηδὲ
the   testimony   of the   Lord   of us   nor

ἐμὲ τὸν δέσμιον αὐτοῦ, ἀλλὰ συγ-
[of] me   the   prisoner   of him,   but   suffer

κακοπάθησον τῷ εὐαγγελίῳ κατὰ δύναμιν
ill with   the   gospel   according to [the] power

θεοῦ, **9** τοῦ σώσαντος ἡμᾶς καὶ καλέσαντος
of God,   of the   having saved   us   and   having called
    [one]

κλήσει ἁγίᾳ, οὐ κατὰ τὰ ἔργα ἡμῶν
²calling ¹with a holy, not according to the   works   of us

ἀλλὰ κατὰ ἰδίαν πρόθεσιν καὶ χάριν,
but   according to [his] own   purpose   and   grace,

τὴν δοθεῖσαν ἡμῖν ἐν Χριστῷ Ἰησοῦ
-   given   to us   in   Christ   Jesus

πρὸ χρόνων αἰωνίων, **10** φανερωθεῖσαν δὲ
before   times   eternal,   but manifested

Chapter 1

PAUL, an apostle of Christ Jesus by the will of God, according to the promise of life that is in Christ Jesus,

2 To Timothy, my dear son:

Grace, mercy and peace from God the Father and Christ Jesus our Lord.

Encouragement to Be Faithful

3 I thank God, whom I serve, as my forefathers did, with a clear conscience, as night and day I constantly remember you in my prayers. 4 Recalling your tears, I long to see you, so that I may be filled with joy. 5 I have been reminded of your sincere faith, which first lived in your grandmother Lois and in your mother Eunice and, I am persuaded, now lives in you also. 6 For this reason I remind you to fan into flame the gift of God, which is in you through the laying on of my hands. 7 For God did not give us a spirit of timidity, but a spirit of power, of love and of self-discipline.

8 So do not be ashamed to testify about our Lord, or ashamed of me his prisoner. But join with me in suffering for the gospel, by the power of God, 9 who has saved us and called us to a holy life—not because of anything we have done but because of his own purpose and grace. This grace was given us in Christ Jesus before the beginning of time, 10 but it has now been re-

the appearing of our Savior Christ Jesus, who abolished death and brought life and immortality to light through the gospel. 11 For this gospel I was appointed a herald and an apostle and a teacher,a 12 and for this reason I suffer as I do. But I am not ashamed, for I know the one in whom I have put my trust, and I am sure that he is able to guard until that day what I have entrusted to him.b 13 Hold to the standard of sound teaching that you have heard from me, in the faith and love that are in Christ Jesus. 14 Guard the good treasure entrusted to you, with the help of the Holy Spirit living in us.

15 You are aware that all who are in Asia have turned away from me, including Phygelus and Hermogenes. 16 May the Lord grant mercy to the household of Onesiphorus, because he often refreshed me and was not ashamed of my chain; 17 when he arrived in Rome, he eagerlyc searched for me and found me 18 —may the Lord grant that he will find mercy from the Lord on that day! And you know very well how much service he rendered in Ephesus.

νῦν διὰ τῆς ἐπιφανείας τοῦ σωτῆρος
now through the appearance of the Saviour

ἡμῶν Χριστοῦ Ἰησοῦ, καταργήσαντος μὲν
of us Christ Jesus, ²abrogating ¹on one hand

τὸν θάνατον φωτίσαντος δὲ ζωὴν καὶ
- death ⁴bringing to light ³on the other life and

ἀφθαρσίαν διὰ τοῦ εὐαγγελίου, 11 εἰς ὃ
incorruption through the gospel, for which

ἐτέθην ἐγὼ κῆρυξ καὶ ἀπόστολος καὶ
²was appointed ¹I a herald and an apostle and

διδάσκαλος· 12 δι' ἣν αἰτίαν καὶ ταῦτα
a teacher; for which cause also these things

πάσχω, ἀλλ' οὐκ ἐπαισχύνομαι, οἶδα γὰρ
I suffer, but I am not ashamed, for I know

ᾧ πεπίστευκα, καὶ πέπεισμαι ὅτι δυνατός
whom I have believed, and I have been persuaded that ²able

ἐστιν τὴν παραθήκην μου φυλάξαι εἰς
¹he is ⁴the deposit ³of me ⁵to guard into

ἐκείνην τὴν ἡμέραν. 13 ὑποτύπωσιν ἔχε
that - day. ²a pattern ¹Have thou

ὑγιαινόντων λόγων ὧν παρ' ἐμοῦ ἤκουσας
of being healthy words which ²from ¹me ¹thou heardest

ἐν πίστει καὶ ἀγάπῃ τῇ ἐν Χριστῷ
in faith and love - in Christ

Ἰησοῦ· 14 τὴν καλὴν παραθήκην φύλαξον
Jesus; the good deposit guard

διὰ πνεύματος ἁγίου τοῦ ἐνοικοῦντος ἐν
through Spirit [the] Holy - indwelling in

ἡμῖν. 15 Οἶδας τοῦτο, ὅτι ἀπεστράφησάν
us. Thou knowest this, that turned away from

με πάντες οἱ ἐν τῇ Ἀσίᾳ, ὧν ἐστιν
me all the ones in - Asia, of whom is

Φύγελος καὶ Ἑρμογένης. 16 δῴη ἔλεος
Phygelus and Hermogenes. ¹May ²give ³mercy

ὁ κύριος τῷ Ὀνησιφόρου οἴκῳ, ὅτι
²the ³Lord ⁴to the ⁵of Onesiphorus ⁷house-hold ⁶because

πολλάκις με ἀνέψυξεν καὶ τὴν ἅλυσίν
often me he refreshed and the chain

μου οὐκ ἐπαισχύνθη, 17 ἀλλὰ γενόμενος
of me was not ashamed [of], but coming to be

ἐν Ῥώμῃ σπουδαίως ἐζήτησέν με καὶ
in Rome ²diligently ¹he ³sought ⁴me ⁵and

εὗρεν· — 18 δῴη αὐτῷ ὁ κύριος εὑρεῖν
⁵found; (¹May ⁴give ²to him ³the ³Lord to find

ἔλεος παρὰ κυρίου ἐν ἐκείνῃ τῇ ἡμέρᾳ·
mercy from [the] Lord in that - day;)

— καὶ ὅσα ἐν Ἐφέσῳ διηκόνησεν,
and what things in Ephesus he served,

βέλτιον σὺ γινώσκεις.
very well thou knowest.

vealed through the appearing of our Savior, Christ Jesus, who has destroyed death and has brought life and immortality to light through the gospel. 11 And of this gospel I was appointed a herald and an apostle and a teacher. 12 That is why I am suffering as I am. Yet I am not ashamed, because I know whom I have believed, and am convinced that he is able to guard what I have entrusted to him for that day. 13 What you heard from me, keep as the pattern of sound teaching, with faith and love in Christ Jesus. 14 Guard the good deposit that was entrusted to you —guard it with the help of the Holy Spirit who lives in us. 15 You know that everyone in the province of Asia has deserted me, including Phygelus and Hermogenes. 16 May the Lord show mercy to the household of Onesiphorus, because he often refreshed me and was not ashamed of my chains. 17 On the contrary, when he was in Rome, he searched hard for me until he found me. 18 May the Lord grant that he will find mercy from the Lord on that day! You know very well in how many ways he helped me in Ephesus.

Chapter 2

A Good Soldier of Christ Jesus

YOU then, my child, be strong in the grace that is in Christ Jesus; 2 and what you have heard from me through many witnesses entrust to faithful people who will be able to

2 Σὺ οὖν, τέκνον μου, ἐνδυναμοῦ ἐν
Thou therefore, child of me, be empowered by

τῇ χάριτι τῇ ἐν Χριστῷ Ἰησοῦ, 2 καὶ
the grace - in Christ Jesus, and

ἃ ἤκουσας παρ' ἐμοῦ διὰ πολλῶν
what things thou heardest from me through many

μαρτύρων, ταῦτα παράθου πιστοῖς ἀνθρώ-
witnesses, these commit to faithful men,

Chapter 2

YOU then, my son, be strong in the grace that is in Christ Jesus. 2 And the things you have heard me say in the presence of many witnesses entrust to reliable men who will also

a Other ancient authorities add of the Gentiles
b Or what has been entrusted to me
c Or promptly

teach others as well. ³Share in suffering like a good soldier of Christ Jesus. ⁴No one serving in the army gets entangled in everyday affairs; the soldier's aim is to please the enlisting officer. ⁵And in the case of an athlete, no one is crowned without competing according to the rules. ⁶It is the farmer who does the work who ought to have the first share of the crops. ⁷Think over what I say, for the Lord will give you understanding in all things.

⁸Remember Jesus Christ, raised from the dead, a descendant of David—that is my gospel, ⁹for which I suffer hardship, even to the point of being chained like a criminal. But the word of God is not chained. ¹⁰Therefore I endure everything for the sake of the elect, so that they may also obtain the salvation that is in Christ Jesus, with eternal glory. ¹¹The saying is sure:
If we have died with him, we will also live with him;
¹² if we endure, we will also reign with him;
if we deny him, he will also deny us;
¹³ if we are faithless, he remains faithful—
for he cannot deny himself.

A Worker Approved by God

¹⁴ Remind them of this, and warn them before God*d* that they are to avoid wrangling over words, which does no good but only ruins those who are listening. ¹⁵Do your best to present yourself to God as one approved by him, a worker who has no need to be ashamed, rightly explaining the word of truth.

*d*Other ancient authorities read *the Lord*

Middle column (interlinear)

ποις,   οἵτινες   ἱκανοὶ   ἔσονται   καὶ   ἑτέρους
who   ²competent ¹will be   ²also   ⁴others

διδάξαι.   3 Συγκακοπάθησον   ὡς   καλὸς
²to teach.   Suffer ill with*   as   a good

στρατιώτης   Χριστοῦ   Ἰησοῦ.   4 οὐδεὶς
soldier   of Christ   Jesus.   No one

στρατευόμενος   ἐμπλέκεται   ταῖς   τοῦ   βίου
soldiering   is involved   ¹with the   —   ²of life

πραγματείαις,   ἵνα   τῷ   στρατολογήσαντι
²affairs,   in order   ³the   ²having enlisted
        that   [one]   [him]

ἀρέσῃ.   5 ἐὰν   δὲ   καὶ   ἀθλῇ   τις,   οὐ
¹he may   And if   also   ²wrestles   ¹any-   not
please.   one,

στεφανοῦται   ἐὰν   μὴ   νομίμως   ἀθλήσῃ.
he is crowned   unless   ²lawfully   ¹he wrestles.

6 τὸν   κοπιῶντα   γεωργὸν   δεῖ   πρῶτον   τῶν
²the   ³labouring   ⁴husbandman   ¹It be-   ¹firstly   ²of the
        hoves

καρπῶν   μεταλαμβάνειν.   7 νόει   ὃ   λέγω·
³fruits   ⁵to partake.   Consider   what   I say;

δώσει   γάρ   σοι   ὁ   κύριος   σύνεσιν   ἐν
for ²will give   ³thee   ¹the   ²Lord   understanding   in

πᾶσιν.   8 μνημόνευε   Ἰησοῦν   Χριστὸν
all things.   Remember   Jesus   Christ

ἐγηγερμένον   ἐκ   νεκρῶν,   ἐκ   σπέρματος
having been raised   from   [the] dead,   of   [the] seed

Δαυίδ,   κατὰ   τὸ   εὐαγγέλιόν   μου·   9 ἐν
of David,   according to the   gospel   of me;   in

ᾧ   κακοπαθῶ   μέχρι   δεσμῶν   ὡς   κακοῦργος,
which   I suffer ill   unto   bonds   as   an evildoer,

ἀλλὰ   ὁ   λόγος   τοῦ   θεοῦ   οὐ   δέδεται.
but   the   word   —   of God   has not been bound.

10 διὰ   τοῦτο   πάντα   ὑπομένω   διὰ   τοὺς
Therefore   all things   I endure   on ac-   the
        count of

ἐκλεκτούς,   ἵνα   καὶ   αὐτοὶ   σωτηρίας   τύχωσιν
chosen ones,   in or-   ²also   ¹they   ²salvation   ³may obtain
        der that

τῆς   ἐν   Χριστῷ   Ἰησοῦ   μετὰ   δόξης
—   in   Christ   Jesus   with   glory

αἰωνίου.   11 πιστὸς   ὁ   λόγος·   εἰ   γὰρ
eternal.   Faithful [is]   the   word: for if

συναπεθάνομεν,   καὶ   συζήσομεν·   12 εἰ
we died with [him],   also   we shall live with [him];   if

ὑπομένομεν,   καὶ   συμβασιλεύσομεν·   εἰ
we endure,   also   we shall reign with [him];   if

ἀρνησόμεθα,   κἀκεῖνος   ἀρνήσεται   ἡμᾶς·   13 εἰ
we shall deny,   that one also   will deny   us;   if

ἀπιστοῦμεν,   ἐκεῖνος   πιστὸς   μένει,   ἀρνή-
we disbelieve,   that one   ²faithful   ¹remains,   ²to

σασθαι   γὰρ   ἑαυτὸν   οὐ   δύναται.   14 Ταῦτα
deny   ¹for   ⁴himself   ³he cannot.   These things

ὑπομίμνησκε,   διαμαρτυρόμενος   ἐνώπιον   τοῦ
remind thou   solemnly witnessing   before   —
[them] [of],

θεοῦ   μὴ   λογομαχεῖν,   ἐπʼ   οὐδὲν   χρήσιμον,
God   not to fight with words,   ²for   ³nothing   ¹useful,

ἐπὶ   καταστροφῇ   τῶν   ἀκουόντων.   15 σπού-
for   overthrowing   of the [ones] hearing.   ¹Be

δασον   σεαυτὸν   δόκιμον   παραστῆσαι   τῷ
eager   ³thyself   ⁴approved   ²to present   —

θεῷ,   ἐργάτην   ἀνεπαίσχυντον,   ὀρθοτομοῦντα
to God,   a workman   unashamed,   cutting straight

τὸν   λόγον   τῆς   ἀληθείας.   16 τὰς   δὲ
the   word   —   of truth.   —   But

* See 1. 8.

be qualified to teach others. ³Endure hardship with us like a good soldier of Christ Jesus. ⁴No one serving as a soldier gets involved in civilian affairs—he wants to please his commanding officer. ⁵Similarly, if anyone competes as an athlete, he does not receive the victor's crown unless he competes according to the rules. ⁶The hardworking farmer should be the first to receive a share of the crops. ⁷Reflect on what I am saying, for the Lord will give you insight into all this.

⁸Remember Jesus Christ, raised from the dead, descended from David. This is my gospel, ⁹for which I am suffering even to the point of being chained like a criminal. But God's word is not chained. ¹⁰Therefore I endure everything for the sake of the elect, that they too may obtain the salvation that is in Christ Jesus, with eternal glory. ¹¹Here is a trustworthy saying:
If we died with him,
we will also live with him;
¹²if we endure,
we will also reign with him.
If we disown him,
he will also disown us;
¹³if we are faithless,
he will remain faithful,
for he cannot disown himself.

A Workman Approved by God

¹⁴Keep reminding them of these things. Warn them before God against quarreling about words; it is of no value, and only ruins those who listen. ¹⁵Do your best to present yourself to God as one approved, a workman who does not need to be ashamed and who correctly handles the word of truth. ¹⁶Avoid godless

16 Avoid profane chatter, for it will lead people into more and more impiety, 17 and their talk will spread like gangrene. Among them are Hymenaeus and Philetus, 18 who have swerved from the truth by claiming that the resurrection has already taken place. They are upsetting the faith of some. 19 But God's firm foundation stands, bearing this inscription: "The Lord knows those who are his," and, "Let everyone who calls on the name of the Lord turn away from wickedness."

20 In a large house there are utensils not only of gold and silver but also of wood and clay, some for special use, some for ordinary. 21 All who cleanse themselves of the things I have mentioned[e] will become special utensils, dedicated and useful to the owner of the house, ready for every good work. 22 Shun youthful passions and pursue righteousness, faith, love, and peace, along with those who call on the Lord from a pure heart. 23 Have nothing to do with stupid and senseless controversies; you know that they breed quarrels. 24 And the Lord's servant[f] must not be quarrelsome but kindly to everyone, an apt teacher, patient, 25 correcting opponents with gentleness. God may perhaps grant that they will repent and come to know the truth, 26 and that they may escape from the snare of the devil, hav-

βεβήλους κενοφωνίας περιΐστασο· ἐπὶ πλεῖον
profane   empty   shun;   ²to ⁴more
          utterances

γὰρ προκόψουσιν ἀσεβείας, 17 καὶ ὁ λόγος
¹for ³they will advance of impiety, and the word

αὐτῶν ὡς γάγγραινα νομὴν ἕξει· ὧν
of them as a canker   feeding will have; of
                                           whom

ἐστιν 'Υμέναιος καὶ Φίλητος, 18 οἵτινες
is(are) Hymenæus and Philetus,   who

περὶ τὴν ἀλήθειαν ἠστόχησαν, λέγοντες
con- the truth   missed aim,   saying
cerning

ἀνάστασιν ἤδη γεγονέναι, καὶ ἀνατρέπουσιν
[the]   already to have and   overturn
resurrection   become,

τὴν τινων πίστιν. 19 ὁ μέντοι στερεὸς
the ¹of some ²faith.   ³the ¹However firm

θεμέλιος τοῦ θεοῦ ἕστηκεν, ἔχων τὴν
foundation - of God stands,   having -

σφραγῖδα ταύτην· ἔγνω κύριος τοὺς ὄντας
seal   this: ²knew ¹[The] the being
                        Lord   [ones]

αὐτοῦ, καὶ· ἀποστήτω ἀπὸ ἀδικίας πᾶς
of him, and: Let stand away from iniquity every-

ὁ ὀνομάζων τὸ ὄνομα κυρίου. 20 ἐν
one naming   the name of [the] Lord.   ¹in

μεγάλη δὲ οἰκίᾳ οὐκ ἔστιν μόνον σκεύη
²a great ¹Now ⁴house there is(are) not only vessels

χρυσᾶ καὶ ἀργυρᾶ, ἀλλὰ καὶ ξύλινα
golden and silvern, but also wooden

καὶ ὀστράκινα, καὶ ἃ μὲν εἰς τιμὴν ἃ δὲ
and earthen, and some to honour others

εἰς ἀτιμίαν· 21 ἐὰν οὖν τις ἐκκαθάρῃ
to dishonour;   if therefore anyone cleanses

ἑαυτὸν ἀπὸ τούτων, ἔσται σκεῦος εἰς
himself from these [latter], he will be a vessel to

τιμήν, ἡγιασμένον, εὔχρηστον τῷ δεσπότῃ,
honour, having been suitable for the master,
        sanctified;

εἰς πᾶν ἔργον ἀγαθὸν ἡτοιμασμένον.
to every work good   having been prepared.

22 τὰς δὲ νεωτερικὰς ἐπιθυμίας φεῦγε,
   Now the   ²youthful   ³lusts   ¹flee,

δίωκε δὲ δικαιοσύνην, πίστιν, ἀγάπην,
but pursue righteousness, faith,   love,

εἰρήνην μετὰ τῶν ἐπικαλουμένων τὸν
peace   with the [ones] calling on   the

κύριον ἐκ καθαρᾶς καρδίας. 23 τὰς δὲ
Lord out of a clean   heart.   -   But

μωρὰς καὶ ἀπαιδεύτους ζητήσεις παραιτοῦ,
foolish and uninstructed questionings refuse,

εἰδὼς ὅτι γεννῶσιν μάχας· 24 δοῦλον δὲ
knowing that they beget fights; and ²a slave

κυρίου οὐ δεῖ μάχεσθαι ἀλλὰ ἤπιον
³of [the] ¹it behoves not to fight but gentle
Lord

εἶναι πρὸς πάντας, διδακτικόν, ἀνεξίκακον,
to be toward all men, apt to teach, forbearing,

25 ἐν πραΰτητι παιδεύοντα τοὺς ἀντιδιατι-
   in meekness instructing the [ones]   oppos-

θεμένους, μήποτε δώῃ αὐτοῖς ὁ θεὸς
ing,   [if] perhaps ²may ³them - ¹God
                       give

μετάνοιαν εἰς ἐπίγνωσιν ἀληθείας, 26 καὶ
repentance for a full knowledge of truth,   and

ἀνανήψωσιν ἐκ τῆς τοῦ διαβόλου παγίδος,
they may return out of ¹the ³of the ⁴devil ²snare,
to soberness

chatter, because those who indulge in it will become more and more ungodly. 17 Their teaching will spread like gangrene. Among them are Hymenaeus and Philetus, 18 who have wandered away from the truth. They say that the resurrection has already taken place, and they destroy the faith of some. 19 Nevertheless, God's solid foundation stands firm, sealed with this inscription: "The Lord knows those who are his,"[a] and, "Everyone who confesses the name of the Lord must turn away from wickedness."

20 In a large house there are articles not only of gold and silver, but also of wood and clay; some are for noble purposes and some for ignoble. 21 If a man cleanses himself from the latter, he will be an instrument for noble purposes, made holy, useful to the Master and prepared to do any good work.

22 Flee the evil desires of youth, and pursue righteousness, faith, love and peace, along with those who call on the Lord out of a pure heart. 23 Don't have anything to do with foolish and stupid arguments, because you know they produce quarrels. 24 And the Lord's servant must not quarrel; instead, he must be kind to everyone, able to teach, not resentful. 25 Those who oppose him he must gently instruct, in the hope that God will grant them repentance leading them to a knowledge of the truth, 26 and that they will come to their senses and escape from the trap of the

ᵃ19 Num. 16:5 (see Septuagint)

ing been held captive by him to do his will. *g*

Chapter 3

Godlessness in the Last Days

YOU must understand this, that in the last days distressing times will come. 2 For people will be lovers of themselves, lovers of money, boasters, arrogant, abusive, disobedient to their parents, ungrateful, unholy, 3 inhuman, implacable, slanderers, profligates, brutes, haters of good, 4 treacherous, reckless, swollen with conceit, lovers of pleasure rather than lovers of God, 5 holding to the outward form of godliness but denying its power. Avoid them! 6 For among them are those who make their way into households and captivate silly women, overwhelmed by their sins and swayed by all kinds of desires, 7 who are always being instructed and can never arrive at a knowledge of the truth. 8 As Jannes and Jambres opposed Moses, so these people, of corrupt mind and counterfeit faith, also oppose the truth. 9 But they will not make much progress, because, as in the case of those two men, *h* their folly will become plain to everyone.

Paul's Charge to Timothy

10 Now you have observed my teaching, my conduct, my aim in life, my faith, my patience, my love, my steadfastness, 11 my persecutions and suffering the things that happened to me in Antioch,

---

ἐζωγρημένοι ὑπ' αὐτοῦ εἰς τὸ ἐκείνου θέλημα.
having been   by   him[,]   to   ¹the   ²of that   ²will.
caught   one*

3 Τοῦτο δὲ γίνωσκε, ὅτι ἐν ἐσχάταις
And this   know thou,   that   in   [the] last

ἡμέραις ἐνστήσονται καιροὶ χαλεποί·
days   ²will be at hand   ¹times   ¹grievous;

2 ἔσονται γὰρ οἱ ἄνθρωποι φίλαυτοι,
for ²will be   –   ¹men   self-lovers,

φιλάργυροι, ἀλαζόνες, ὑπερήφανοι, βλάσφημοι,
money-lovers,   boasters,   arrogant,   blasphemers,

γονεῦσιν ἀπειθεῖς, ἀχάριστοι, ἀνόσιοι,
²to parents   ¹disobedient,   unthankful,   unholy,

3 ἄστοργοι, ἄσπονδοι, διάβολοι, ἀκρατεῖς,
without natural   implacable,   slanderers,   incontinent,
affection,

ἀνήμεροι, ἀφιλάγαθοι, **4** προδόται, προπετεῖς,
untamed,   haters of good   betrayers,   reckless,
       [things/men],

τετυφωμένοι, φιλήδονοι μᾶλλον ἢ φιλόθεοι,
having been   pleasure-lovers   rather   than   God-lovers,
puffed up,

5 ἔχοντες μόρφωσιν εὐσεβείας τὴν δὲ
having   a form   of piety   but the

δύναμιν αὐτῆς ἠρνημένοι· καὶ τούτους
power   of it   having denied: and   ²these

ἀποτρέπου. **6** ἐκ τούτων γάρ εἰσιν οἱ
²turn away ¹from.   ²of   ¹these   ¹For   are   the

ἐνδύνοντες εἰς τὰς οἰκίας καὶ αἰχμαλωτίζ-
[ones] creeping into   –   houses   and   captur-

οντες γυναικάρια σεσωρευμένα ἁμαρτίαις,
ing   silly women   *having been* heaped*   with sins,

ἀγόμενα ἐπιθυμίαις ποικίλαις, **7** πάντοτε
being led*   lusts   by various,   always

μανθάνοντα καὶ μηδέποτε εἰς ἐπίγνωσιν
learning*   and   never   ²to   ¹a full knowledge

ἀληθείας ἐλθεῖν δυνάμενα. **8** ὃν τρόπον
²of truth   ²to come   ¹being able.*   by what way

δὲ Ἰάννης καὶ Ἰαμβρῆς ἀντέστησαν
Now   Jannes   and   Jambres   opposed

Μωϋσεῖ, οὕτως καὶ οὗτοι ἀνθίστανται τῇ
Moses,   so   *also*   these   oppose   the

ἀληθείᾳ, ἄνθρωποι κατεφθαρμένοι τὸν νοῦν,
truth,   men   having been corrupted   the   mind,
                  =with corrupted mind,

ἀδόκιμοι περὶ τὴν πίστιν. **9** ἀλλ' οὐ
reprobate   as to   the   faith.   But   not

προκόψουσιν ἐπὶ πλεῖον· ἡ γὰρ ἄνοια
they will advance   to   more;   for the   folly
           =farther;

αὐτῶν ἔκδηλος ἔσται πᾶσιν, ὡς καὶ
of them   very clear   will be   to all men,   as   also

ἡ ἐκείνων ἐγένετο. **10** Σὺ δὲ παρηκολού-
the   of those   became.   But thou   hast closely
[folly]

θησάς μου τῇ διδασκαλίᾳ, τῇ ἀγωγῇ,
followed   of me   the   teaching,   the   conduct,

τῇ προθέσει, τῇ πίστει, τῇ μακροθυμίᾳ,
the   purpose,   the   faith,   the   longsuffering,

τῇ ἀγάπῃ, τῇ ὑπομονῇ, **11** τοῖς διωγμοῖς,
the   love,   the   endurance,   the   persecutions,

τοῖς παθήμασιν, οἷά μοι ἐγένετο ἐν
the   sufferings,   which   ²to me   ¹happened   in

---

devil, who has taken them captive to do his will.

Chapter 3

Godlessness in the Last Days

BUT mark this: There will be terrible times in the last days. 2 People will be lovers of themselves, lovers of money, boastful, proud, abusive, disobedient to their parents, ungrateful, unholy, 3 without love, unforgiving, slanderous, without self-control, brutal, not lovers of the good, 4 treacherous, rash, conceited, lovers of pleasure rather than lovers of God— 5 having a form of godliness but denying its power. Have nothing to do with them.

6 They are the kind who worm their way into homes and gain control over weak-willed women, who are loaded down with sins and are swayed by all kinds of evil desires, 7 always learning but never able to acknowledge the truth. 8 Just as Jannes and Jambres opposed Moses, so also these men oppose the truth—men of depraved minds, who, as far as the faith is concerned, are rejected. 9 But they will not get very far because, as in the case of those men, their folly will be clear to everyone.

Paul's Charge to Timothy

10 You, however, know all about my teaching, my way of life, my purpose, faith, patience, love, endurance, 11 persecutions, sufferings —what kinds of things hap-

---

g Or *by him, to do his* (that is, God's) *will*

h Gk lacks *two men*

* That is, of God (the remoter antecedent).

* Agreeing with "silly women" (neut. pl.).

Iconium, and Lystra. What persecutions I endured! Yet the Lord rescued me from all of them. 12 Indeed, all who want to live a godly life in Christ Jesus will be persecuted. 13 But wicked people and impostors will go from bad to worse, deceiving others and being deceived. 14 But as for you, continue in what you have learned and firmly believed, knowing from whom you learned it, 15 and how from childhood you have known the sacred writings that are able to instruct you for salvation through faith in Christ Jesus. 16 All scripture is inspired by God and is *i* useful for teaching, for reproof, for correction, and for training in righteousness, 17 so that everyone who belongs to God may be proficient, equipped for every good work.

'Αντιοχεία, ἐν 'Ικονίῳ, ἐν Λύστροις· οἵους
Antioch,   in Iconium, in Lystra: what
διωγμοὺς ὑπήνεγκα, καὶ ἐκ πάντων με
persecutions I bore, and out of all ⁴me
ἐρρύσατο ὁ κύριος.   12 καὶ πάντες δὲ
³delivered ¹the ²Lord.   ²indeed ²all   ¹And
οἱ θέλοντες ζῆν εὐσεβῶς ἐν Χριστῷ
the [ones] wishing to live piously in Christ
'Ιησοῦ διωχθήσονται. 13 πονηροὶ δὲ ἄν-
Jesus   will be persecuted. But evil men
θρωποι καὶ γόητες προκόψουσιν ἐπὶ τὸ
and impostors will advance to the
χεῖρον, πλανῶντες καὶ πλανώμενοι. 14 σὺ
worse,   deceiving and being deceived. ²thou
δὲ μένε ἐν οἷς ἔμαθες καὶ ἐπιστώθης,
But ¹continue in what thou didst learn and wast assured of,
        things   learn
εἰδὼς παρὰ τίνων ἔμαθες, 15 καὶ ὅτι
knowing from whom* thou didst learn, and that
ἀπὸ βρέφους ἱερὰ γράμματα οἶδας, τὰ
from a babe ²sacred ³letters ¹thou know- the
          est, [ones]
δυνάμενά σε σοφίσαι εἰς σωτηρίαν διὰ
being able thee to make wise to salvation through
πίστεως τῆς ἐν Χριστῷ 'Ιησοῦ. 16 πᾶσα
faith   – in Christ Jesus.   Every
γραφὴ θεόπνευστος καὶ ὠφέλιμος πρὸς
scripture [is] God-breathed and profitable for
διδασκαλίαν, πρὸς ἐλεγμόν, πρὸς ἐπανόρ-
teaching,   for reproof, for cor-
θωσιν, πρὸς παιδείαν τὴν ἐν δικαιοσύνῃ,
rection, for instruction – in righteousness,
17 ἵνα ἄρτιος ᾖ ὁ τοῦ θεοῦ ἄνθρωπος,
in order ⁵fitted ⁴may ¹the – ²of God ³man,
that   be

pened to me in Antioch, Iconium and Lystra, the persecutions I endured. Yet the Lord rescued me from all of them. 12 In fact, everyone who wants to live a godly life in Christ Jesus will be persecuted, 13 while evil men and impostors will go from bad to worse, deceiving and being deceived. 14 But as for you, continue in what you have learned and have become convinced of, because you know those from whom you learned it, 15 and how from infancy you have known the holy Scriptures, which are able to make you wise for salvation through faith in Christ Jesus. 16 All Scripture is God-breathed and is useful for teaching, rebuking, correcting and training in righteousness, 17 so that the man of God may be thoroughly equipped for every good work.

πρὸς πᾶν ἔργον ἀγαθὸν ἐξηρτισμένος.
for every work good *having been* furnished.

Chapter 4

IN the presence of God and of Christ Jesus, who is to judge the living and the dead, and in view of his appearing and his kingdom, I solemnly urge you: 2 proclaim the message; be persistent whether the time is favorable or unfavorable; convince, rebuke, and encourage, with the utmost patience in teaching. 3 For the time is coming when people will not put up with sound doctrine, but having itching ears, they will accumulate for themselves teachers to suit their own desires, 4 and will turn away from listening to the truth and wander away to myths. 5 As for you, always

4 Διαμαρτύρομαι ἐνώπιον τοῦ θεοῦ καὶ
I solemnly witness before – God and
Χριστοῦ 'Ιησοῦ, τοῦ μέλλοντος κρίνειν
Christ Jesus, the [one] being about to judge
ζῶντας καὶ νεκρούς, καὶ τὴν ἐπιφάνειαν
living [ones] and dead, both [by] the appearance
αὐτοῦ καὶ τὴν βασιλείαν αὐτοῦ· 2 κήρυξον
of him and [by] the kingdom of him: proclaim
τὸν λόγον, ἐπίστηθι εὐκαίρως ἀκαίρως,
the word, be attentive seasonably[,] unseasonably,
ἔλεγξον, ἐπιτίμησον, παρακάλεσον, ἐν πάσῃ
reprove, admonish, exhort, with all
μακροθυμίᾳ καὶ διδαχῇ. 3 ἔσται γὰρ
longsuffering and teaching. For there will be
καιρὸς ὅτε τῆς ὑγιαινούσης διδασκαλίας
a time when the ³being healthy ⁴teaching
οὐκ ἀνέξονται, ἀλλὰ κατὰ τὰς ἰδίας
¹they will not bear with, but according to the(ir) own
ἐπιθυμίας ἑαυτοῖς ἐπισωρεύσουσιν διδασ-
lusts   ²to themselves ¹they will heap up ²teach-
κάλους κνηθόμενοι τὴν ἀκοήν, 4 καὶ ἀπὸ
ers   tickling   the ear, and ⁵from
μὲν τῆς ἀληθείας τὴν ἀκοὴν ἀποστρέψουσιν,
¹on ⁶the ⁷truth ⁸the ⁴ear ²will turn away,
one hand
ἐπὶ δὲ τοὺς μύθους ἐκτραπήσονται. 5 σὺ
³to ¹on the *the* ⁴tales ²will be turned aside. ²thou
    other

Chapter 4

IN the presence of God and of Christ Jesus, who will judge the living and the dead, and in view of his appearing and his kingdom, I give you this charge: 2 Preach the Word; be prepared in season and out of season; correct, rebuke and encourage—with great patience and careful instruction. 3 For the time will come when men will not put up with sound doctrine. Instead, to suit their own desires, they will gather around them a great number of teachers to say what their itching ears want to hear. 4 They will turn their ears away from the truth and turn aside to myths.

i Or *Every scripture inspired by God is also*

* Plural.

be sober, endure suffering, do the work of an evangelist, carry out your ministry fully.

6 As for me, I am already being poured out as a libation, and the time of my departure has come. 7 I have fought the good fight, I have finished the race, I have kept the faith. 8 From now on there is reserved for me the crown of righteousness, which the Lord, the righteous judge, will give me on that day, and not only to me but also to all who have longed for his appearing.

Personal Instructions

9 Do your best to come to me soon, 10 for Demas, in love with this present world, has deserted me and gone to Thessalonica; Crescens has gone to Galatia,[j] Titus to Dalmatia. 11 Only Luke is with me. Get Mark and bring him with you, for he is useful in my ministry. 12 I have sent Tychicus to Ephesus. 13 When you come, bring the cloak that I left with Carpus at Troas, also the books, and above all the parchments. 14 Alexander the coppersmith did me great harm; the Lord will pay him back for his deeds. 15 You also must beware of him, for he strongly opposed our message.

16 At my first defense no one came to my support, but all deserted me. May it not be counted against them! 17 But the Lord stood by me and gave me strength, so that through me the message might be fully proclaimed and all the

---

δὲ νῆφε ἐν πᾶσιν, κακοπάθησον, ἔργον
But ¹be in all things, suffer evil, ⁸[the] work
   sober

ποίησον εὐαγγελιστοῦ, τὴν διακονίαν σου
¹do of an evangelist, ²the ³ministry ⁴of thee

πληροφόρησον. 6 Ἐγὼ γὰρ ἤδη σπένδομαι,
¹fulfil. For I already am being
                     poured out,

καὶ ὁ καιρὸς τῆς ἀναλύσεώς μου ἐφέστη-
and the time of the departure of me has

κεν. 7 τὸν καλὸν ἀγῶνα ἠγώνισμαι,
arrived. The good struggle I have struggled,

τὸν δρόμον τετέλεκα, τὴν πίστιν τετήρηκα·
the course I have finished, the faith I have kept:

8 λοιπὸν ἀπόκειταί μοι ὁ τῆς δικαιοσύνης
for the rest there is laid up for me ¹the - ²of righteousness

στέφανος, ὃν ἀποδώσει μοι ὁ κύριος
²crown, which ¹will render ²to me ¹the ²Lord

ἐν ἐκείνῃ τῇ ἡμέρᾳ, ὁ δίκαιος κριτής,
²in ⁹that - ¹⁰day, ³the ¹righteous ²judge,

οὐ μόνον δὲ ἐμοὶ ἀλλὰ καὶ πᾶσι τοῖς
¹not ²only ¹and to me but also to all the [ones]

ἠγαπηκόσι τὴν ἐπιφάνειαν αὐτοῦ.
having loved the appearance of him.

9 Σπούδασον ἐλθεῖν πρός με ταχέως·
Hasten to come to me shortly;

10 Δημᾶς γάρ με ἐγκατέλιπεν ἀγαπήσας
¹Demas ¹For me ²forsook loving

τὸν νῦν αἰῶνα, καὶ ἐπορεύθη εἰς Θεσσαλο-
the now age, and went to Thessalo-
   (present)

νίκην, Κρήσκης εἰς Γαλατίαν, Τίτος εἰς
nica, Crescens to Galatia, Titus to

Δαλματίαν· 11 Λουκᾶς ἐστιν μόνος μετ'
Dalmatia; Luke is alone with

ἐμοῦ. Μάρκον ἀναλαβὼν ἄγε μετὰ σεαυτοῦ·
me. Mark taking bring with thyself;

ἔστιν γάρ μοι εὔχρηστος εἰς διακονίαν.
²he is ¹for ⁴to me ⁵useful for ministry.

12 Τύχικον δὲ ἀπέστειλα εἰς Ἔφεσον.
And Tychicus I sent to Ephesus.

13 τὸν φαιλόνην, ὃν ἀπέλιπον ἐν Τρῳάδι
The cloak, which I left in Troas

παρὰ Κάρπῳ, ἐρχόμενος φέρε, καὶ τὰ
with Carpus, coming bring thou, and the

βιβλία, μάλιστα τὰς μεμβράνας. 14 Ἀλέξ-
scrolls, especially the parchments. Alex-

ανδρος ὁ χαλκεὺς πολλά μοι κακὰ
ander the coppersmith ²many ³to me ⁴evils

ἐνεδείξατο· ἀποδώσει αὐτῷ ὁ κύριος κατὰ
¹showed; ⁵will render ⁴to him ¹the ²Lord accord-
                            ing to

τὰ ἔργα αὐτοῦ· 15 ὃν καὶ σὺ φυλάσσου·
the works of him; whom also ²thou ¹guard
                                ³[against];

λίαν γὰρ ἀντέστη τοῖς ἡμετέροις λόγοις.
for greatly he opposed - our words.

16 Ἐν τῇ πρώτῃ μου ἀπολογίᾳ οὐδείς
At the first ²of me ¹defence no one

μοι παρεγένετο, ἀλλὰ πάντες με ἐγκατέ-
²me ¹was beside, but all men ²me ¹for-

λιπον· μὴ αὐτοῖς λογισθείη· 17 ὁ δὲ
sook; not to them may it be reckoned; but the

κύριός μοι παρέστη καὶ ἐνεδυνάμωσέν με,
Lord ²me ¹stood with and empowered me,

ἵνα δι' ἐμοῦ τὸ κήρυγμα πληροφορηθῇ
in or- through me the proclamation might be
der that   accomplished

---

5 But you, keep your head in all situations, endure hardship, do the work of an evangelist, discharge all the duties of your ministry.

6 For I am already being poured out like a drink offering, and the time has come for my departure. 7 I have fought the good fight, I have finished the race, I have kept the faith. 8 Now there is in store for me the crown of righteousness, which the Lord, the righteous Judge, will award to me on that day—and not only to me, but also to all who have longed for his appearing.

Personal Remarks

9 Do your best to come to me quickly, 10 for Demas, because he loved this world, has deserted me and has gone to Thessalonica. Crescens has gone to Galatia, and Titus to Dalmatia. 11 Only Luke is with me. Get Mark and bring him with you, because he is helpful to me in my ministry. 12 I sent Tychicus to Ephesus. 13 When you come, bring the cloak that I left with Carpus at Troas, and my scrolls, especially the parchments. 14 Alexander the metalworker did me a great deal of harm. The Lord will repay him for what he has done. 15 You too should be on your guard against him, because he strongly opposed our message.

16 At my first defense, no one came to my support, but everyone deserted me. May it not be held against them. 17 But the Lord stood at my side and gave me strength, so that through me the message might be fully proclaimed and all the

---

j Other ancient authorities read *Gaul*

Gentiles might hear it. So I was rescued from the lion's mouth. 18The Lord will rescue me from every evil attack and save me for his heavenly kingdom. To him be the glory forever and ever. Amen.

Final Greetings and Benediction

19 Greet Prisca and Aquila, and the household of Onesiphorus. 20Erastus remained in Corinth; Trophimus I left ill in Miletus. 21Do your best to come before winter. Eubulus sends greetings to you, as do Pudens and Linus and Claudia and all the brothers and sisters.[k] 22 The Lord be with your spirit. Grace be with you.[l]

καὶ ἀκούσωσιν πάντα τὰ ἔθνη, καὶ
and ⁴might hear ¹all ²the ³nations, and
ἐρρύσθην ἐκ στόματος λέοντος. 18 ῥύσεταί
I was out of [the] mouth of [the] lion. ⁴will deliver
delivered
με ὁ κύριος ἀπὸ παντὸς ἔργου πονηροῦ
⁴me ¹The ²Lord from every work wicked
καὶ σώσει εἰς τὴν βασιλείαν αὐτοῦ τὴν
and will save to the ³kingdom ⁵of him –
ἐπουράνιον· ᾧ ἡ δόξα εἰς τοὺς αἰῶνας
¹heavenly: to [be] glory unto the ages
whom
τῶν αἰώνων, ἀμήν.
of the ages, Amen.
19 Ἄσπασαι Πρίσκαν καὶ Ἀκύλαν καὶ
Greet Prisca and Aquila and
τὸν Ὀνησιφόρου οἶκον. 20 Ἔραστος
the ²of Onesiphorus ¹household. Erastus
ἔμεινεν ἐν Κορίνθῳ, Τρόφιμον δὲ ἀπέλιπον
remained in Corinth, but Trophimus I left
ἐν Μιλήτῳ ἀσθενοῦντα. 21 Σπούδασον
in Miletus ailing. Hasten
πρὸ χειμῶνος ἐλθεῖν. Ἀσπάζεταί σε
before winter to come. Greets thee
Εὔβουλος καὶ Πούδης καὶ Λίνος καὶ
Eubulus and Pudens and Linus and
Κλαυδία καὶ οἱ ἀδελφοὶ πάντες.
Claudia and ²the ³brothers ¹all.
22 Ὁ κύριος μετὰ τοῦ πνεύματός σου.
The Lord [be] with the spirit of thee.
ἡ χάρις μεθ᾽ ὑμῶν.
– Grace [be] with you.

Gentiles might hear it. And I was delivered from the lion's mouth. 18The Lord will rescue me from every evil attack and will bring me safely to his heavenly kingdom. To him be glory for ever and ever. Amen.

Final Greetings

19Greet Priscilla[b] and Aquila and the household of Onesiphorus. 20Erastus stayed in Corinth, and I left Trophimus sick in Miletus. 21Do your best to get here before winter. Eubulus greets you, and so do Pudens, Linus, Claudia and all the brothers. 22The Lord be with your spirit. Grace be with you.

The Letter of Paul to
Titus

ΠΡΟΣ ΤΙΤΟΝ
To Titus

Titus

Chapter 1
Salutation

PAUL, a servant[a] of God and an apostle of Jesus Christ, for the sake of the faith of God's elect and the knowledge of the truth that is in accordance with godliness, 2in the hope of eternal life that God, who never lies, promised before the ages began— 3in due time he revealed his word through the proclamation with which I have been entrusted by the command of God our Savior, 4 To Titus, my loyal child in the faith we share: Grace[b] and peace from God the Father and Christ Jesus our Savior.

Chapter 1

1 Παῦλος δοῦλος θεοῦ, ἀπόστολος δὲ
Paul a slave of God, and an apostle
Ἰησοῦ Χριστοῦ κατὰ πίστιν ἐκλεκτῶν
of Jesus Christ according to [the] faith of chosen ones
θεοῦ καὶ ἐπίγνωσιν ἀληθείας τῆς κατ᾽
of God and full know- of [the] – accord-
ledge truth ing to
εὐσέβειαν 2 ἐπ᾽ ἐλπίδι ζωῆς αἰωνίου,
piety on(in) hope life of eternal,
ἣν ἐπηγγείλατο ὁ ἀψευδὴς θεὸς πρὸ
which ⁴promised ¹the ²unlying ³God before
χρόνων αἰωνίων, 3 ἐφανέρωσεν δὲ καιροῖς
times eternal, but ³manifested ¹times
ἰδίοις τὸν λόγον αὐτοῦ ἐν κηρύγματι
¹in [its] own the word of him in a proclamation
ὃ ἐπιστεύθην ἐγὼ κατ᾽ ἐπιταγὴν τοῦ
which ²was entrust- ¹I accord- [the] of the
ed [with] ing to command
σωτῆρος ἡμῶν θεοῦ, 4 Τίτῳ γνησίῳ τέκνῳ
Saviour of us God, to Titus a true child
κατὰ κοινὴν πίστιν· χάρις καὶ εἰρήνη
accord- a common faith: Grace and peace
ing to
ἀπὸ θεοῦ πατρὸς καὶ Χριστοῦ Ἰησοῦ
from God [the] Father and Christ Jesus
τοῦ σωτῆρος ἡμῶν.
the Saviour of us.

PAUL, a servant of God and an apostle of Jesus Christ for the faith of God's elect and the knowledge of the truth that leads to godliness— 2a faith and knowledge resting on the hope of eternal life, which God, who does not lie, promised before the beginning of time, 3and at his appointed season he brought his word to light through the preaching entrusted to me by the command of God our Savior,

4To Titus, my true son in our common faith:

Grace and peace from God the Father and Christ Jesus our Savior.

---

k Gk all the brothers
l The Greek word for you here is plural. Other ancient authorities add Amen
a Gk slave
b Other ancient authorities read Grace, mercy.

b 19 Greek *Prisca*, a variant of *Priscilla*

Titus in Crete

5 I left you behind in Crete for this reason, so that you should put in order what remained to be done, and should appoint elders in every town, as I directed you: 6 someone who is blameless, married only once,[c] whose children are believers, not accused of debauchery and not rebellious. 7 For a bishop,[d] as God's steward, must be blameless; he must not be arrogant or quick-tempered or addicted to wine or violent or greedy for gain; 8 but he must be hospitable, a lover of goodness, prudent, upright, devout, and self-controlled. 9 He must have a firm grasp of the word that is trustworthy in accordance with the teaching, so that he may be able both to preach with sound doctrine and to refute those who contradict it.

10 There are also many rebellious people, idle talkers and deceivers, especially those of the circumcision; 11 they must be silenced, since they are upsetting whole families by teaching for sordid gain what it is not right to teach. 12 It was one of them, their very own prophet, who said,
"Cretans are always
liars, vicious
brutes, lazy
gluttons."
13 That testimony is true. For this reason rebuke them sharply, so that they may become sound in the faith, 14 not paying attention to Jewish myths or to commandments of those who reject the truth. 15 To the pure all things are pure, but to the corrupt and unbelieving nothing is pure.

---

5 Τούτου χάριν ἀπέλιπόν σε ἐν Κρήτῃ,
For this reason†   I left   thee   in   Crete,

ἵνα τὰ λείποντα ἐπιδιορθώσῃ, καὶ
in or- the   the   wanting   thou shouldest   and
der that things   set in order,

καταστήσῃς κατὰ πόλιν πρεσβυτέρους, ὡς ἐγώ
shouldest appoint in each city   elders,   as   I

σοι διεταξάμην, **6** εἴ τίς ἐστιν ἀνέγκλητος,
²thee ¹charged,   if anyone is   unreprovable,

μιᾶς γυναικὸς ἀνήρ, τέκνα ἔχων πιστά,
²of one ³wife ¹husband, ²children ¹having ³believing,

μὴ ἐν κατηγορίᾳ ἀσωτίας ἢ ἀνυπότακτα.*
not in accusation of profligacy or   unruly.*

7 δεῖ γὰρ τὸν ἐπίσκοπον ἀνέγκλητον εἶναι
For it behoves the bishop   ²unreprovable ¹to be

ὡς θεοῦ οἰκονόμον, μὴ αὐθάδη, μὴ
as of God a steward,   not self-pleasing,   not

ὀργίλον, μὴ πάροινον, μὴ πλήκτην, μὴ
passionate, not given to wine, not   a striker,   not

αἰσχροκερδῆ, **8** ἀλλὰ φιλόξενον, φιλάγαθον,
greedy of   but   hospitable, a lover of good
base gain,   [men/things],

σώφρονα, δίκαιον, ὅσιον, ἐγκρατῆ, **9** ἀντεχ-
sensible,   just,   holy, self-controlled,   holding

όμενον τοῦ κατὰ τὴν διδαχὴν πιστοῦ
  ¹the ⁴according to ⁵the ⁶teaching ²faithful

λόγου, ἵνα δυνατὸς ᾖ καὶ παρακαλεῖν
³word, in order ²able ¹he may both   to exhort
        that   be

ἐν τῇ διδασκαλίᾳ τῇ ὑγιαινούσῃ καὶ
by the ²teaching   – ¹being healthy   and

τοὺς ἀντιλέγοντας ἐλέγχειν. **10** Εἰσὶν γὰρ
²the [ones] ²contradicting ¹to convince.   For there are

πολλοὶ ἀνυπότακτοι, ματαιολόγοι καὶ
many   unruly men,   vain talkers   and

φρεναπάται, μάλιστα οἱ ἐκ τῆς περιτομῆς,
deceivers,   specially the ones of the   circumcision,

11 οὓς δεῖ ἐπιστομίζειν, οἵτινες ὅλους
whom it   to stop the   who   ²whole
      behoves   mouth,

οἴκους ἀνατρέπουσιν διδάσκοντες ἃ μὴ
³households ¹overturn   teaching   things ²not
                        which

δεῖ αἰσχροῦ κέρδους χάριν. **12** εἶπέν
¹it be- ⁴base ⁵gain ²for the   ⁷Said
hoves   sake of,

τις ἐξ αὐτῶν ἴδιος αὐτῶν προφήτης·
¹a cer- ²of ³them ⁴an own ⁶of them   ⁸prophet:
tain one

Κρῆτες ἀεὶ ψεῦσται, κακὰ θηρία, γαστέρες
Cretans always liars,   evil   beasts, ²glutton
[are]

ἀργαί. **13** ἡ μαρτυρία αὕτη ἐστὶν ἀληθής.
¹idle.   This witness   is   true.

δι᾽ ἣν αἰτίαν ἔλεγχε αὐτοὺς ἀποτόμως,
For which cause reprove   them   severely,

ἵνα ὑγιαίνωσιν ἐν τῇ πίστει, **14** μὴ
in or- they may in the   faith,   not
der that be healthy

προσέχοντες Ἰουδαϊκοῖς μύθοις καὶ
giving heed   to Jewish   tales   and

ἐντολαῖς ἀνθρώπων ἀποστρεφομένων τὴν
commandments of men   perverting   the

ἀλήθειαν. **15** πάντα καθαρὰ τοῖς καθαροῖς·
truth.   All things [are] clean to the   clean;

τοῖς δὲ μεμιαμμένοις καὶ ἀπίστοις οὐδὲν
but to the *having been* and unfaithful nothing
the [ones] *defiled*

Titus' Task on Crete

5 The reason I left you in Crete was that you might straighten out what was left unfinished and appoint[a] elders in every town, as I directed you. 6 An elder must be blameless, the husband of but one wife, a man whose children believe and are not open to the charge of being wild and disobedient. 7 Since an overseer[b] is entrusted with God's work, he must be blameless—not overbearing, not quick-tempered, not given to drunkenness, not violent, not pursuing dishonest gain. 8 Rather he must be hospitable, one who loves what is good, who is self-controlled, upright, holy and disciplined. 9 He must hold firmly to the trustworthy message as it has been taught, so that he can encourage others by sound doctrine and refute those who oppose it.

10 For there are many rebellious people, mere talkers and deceivers, especially those of the circumcision group. 11 They must be silenced, because they are ruining whole households by teaching things they ought not to teach—and that for the sake of dishonest gain. 12 Even one of their own prophets has said, "Cretans are always liars, evil brutes, lazy gluttons." 13 This testimony is true. Therefore, rebuke them sharply, so that they will be sound in the faith 14 and will pay no attention to Jewish myths or to the commands of those who reject the truth. 15 To the pure, all things are pure, but to those who are corrupted and do not believe,

---

c Gk husband of one wife
d Or an overseer

* In agreement with "children" (neut. pl.).

a 5 Or ordain
b 7 Traditionally bishop

Their very minds and consciences are corrupted. 16They profess to know God, but they deny him by their actions. They are detestable, disobedient, unfit for any good work.

καθαρόν, ἀλλὰ μεμίανται αὐτῶν καὶ ὁ
[is] clean, but ²has(ve) been defiled ⁷of them ¹both ³the
νοῦς καὶ ἡ συνείδησις. 16 θεὸν ὁμολο-
³mind ⁴and ⁵the ⁶conscience. ²God ¹they pro-
γοῦσιν εἰδέναι, τοῖς δὲ ἔργοις ἀρνοῦνται,
fess ²to know, but by the(ir) works they deny [him],
βδελυκτοὶ ὄντες καὶ ἀπειθεῖς καὶ πρὸς
¹abominable ¹being and disobedient and to
πᾶν ἔργον ἀγαθὸν ἀδόκιμοι.
every ²work ¹good reprobate.

nothing is pure. In fact, both their minds and consciences are corrupted. 16They claim to know God, but by their actions they deny him. They are detestable, disobedient and unfit for doing anything good.

Chapter 2
Teach Sound Doctrine

BUT as for you, teach what is consistent with sound doctrine. 2Tell the older men to be temperate, serious, prudent, and sound in faith, in love, and in endurance.

3 Likewise, tell the older women to be reverent in behavior, not to be slanderers or slaves to drink; they are to teach what is good, 4so that they may encourage the young women to love their husbands, to love their children, 5to be self-controlled, chaste, good managers of the household, kind, being submissive to their husbands, so that the word of God may not be discredited.

6 Likewise, urge the younger men to be self-controlled. 7Show yourself in all respects a model of good works, and in your teaching show integrity, gravity, 8and sound speech that cannot be censured; then any opponent will be put to shame, having nothing evil to say of us.

9 Tell slaves to be submissive to their masters and to give satisfaction in every respect; they are not to talk back, 10not to pilfer, but to show complete and perfect fidelity, so that in everything they may be an ornament to the doctrine of God our Savior.

11 For the grace of God has appeared, bringing salvation to all,ᵉ 12training us

2 Σὺ δὲ λάλει ἃ πρέπει τῇ ὑγιαινούσῃ
But ²thou ¹speak things becomes the being which healthy
διδασκαλίᾳ. 2 Πρεσβύτας νηφαλίους εἶναι,
teaching. Aged men ²sober ¹to be,
σεμνούς, σώφρονας, ὑγιαίνοντας τῇ πίστει,
grave, sensible, being healthy in the faith,
τῇ ἀγάπῃ, τῇ ὑπομονῇ· 3 πρεσβύτιδας
- in love, - in endurance; aged women
ὡσαύτως ἐν καταστήματι ἱεροπρεπεῖς, μὴ
similarly in demeanour reverent, not
διαβόλους, μηδὲ οἴνῳ πολλῷ δεδουλωμένας,
slanderers, nor ²wine ²by much ¹having been enslaved,
καλοδιδασκάλους, 4 ἵνα σωφρονίζωσιν τὰς
teachers of what is good, in or- they may train the der that
νέας φιλάνδρους εἶναι, φιλοτέκνους,
young ²lovers of ¹to be, child-lovers,
women [their] husbands
5 σώφρονας, ἁγνάς, οἰκουργούς, ἀγαθάς,
sensible, pure, home-workers, good,
ὑποτασσομένας τοῖς ἰδίοις ἀνδράσιν,
being subject to the(ir) own husbands,
ἵνα μὴ ὁ λόγος τοῦ θεοῦ βλασφημῆται.
lest the word - of God be blasphemed.
6 Τοὺς νεωτέρους ὡσαύτως παρακάλει
The younger men similarly exhort
σωφρονεῖν 7 περὶ πάντα, σεαυτὸν παρ-
to be sensible about all things, ²thyself ¹show-
εχόμενος τύπον καλῶν ἔργων, ἐν τῇ
ing a pattern of good works, in the
διδασκαλίᾳ ἀφθορίαν, σεμνότητα, 8 λόγον
teaching uncorruptness, gravity, ²speech
ὑγιῆ ἀκατάγνωστον, ἵνα ὁ ἐξ ἐναντίας
¹healthy ²irreprehensible, in or- the of contrary
der that man [the] [side]
ἐντραπῇ μηδὲν ἔχων λέγειν περὶ ἡμῶν
may be put ²nothing ¹having ⁴to say ³about ⁴us
to shame
φαῦλον. 9 Δούλους ἰδίοις δεσπόταις
²bad. Slaves to [their] own masters
ὑποτάσσεσθαι ἐν πᾶσιν, εὐαρέστους εἶναι,
to be subject in all things, well-pleasing to be,
μὴ ἀντιλέγοντας, 10 μὴ νοσφιζομένους, ἀλλὰ
not contradicting, not peculating, but
πᾶσαν πίστιν ἐνδεικνυμένους ἀγαθήν, ἵνα
²all ⁴faith ¹showing ³good, in order that
τὴν διδασκαλίαν τὴν τοῦ σωτῆρος ἡμῶν
²the ³teaching - ⁴of the ⁵Saviour ⁶of us
θεοῦ κοσμῶσιν ἐν πᾶσιν. 11 Ἐπεφάνη
⁷God ¹they may adorn in all things. ¹appeared
γὰρ ἡ χάρις τοῦ θεοῦ σωτήριος πᾶσιν
For ¹the ²grace - ³of God ⁴saving to all

Chapter 2
What Must Be Taught to Various Groups

YOU must teach what is in accord with sound doctrine. 2Teach the older men to be temperate, worthy of respect, self-controlled, and sound in faith, in love and in endurance.

3Likewise, teach the older women to be reverent in the way they live, not to be slanderers or addicted to much wine, but to teach what is good. 4Then they can train the younger women to love their husbands and children, 5to be self-controlled and pure, to be busy at home, to be kind, and to be subject to their husbands, so that no one will malign the word of God.

6Similarly, encourage the young men to be self-controlled. 7In everything set them an example by doing what is good. In your teaching show integrity, seriousness 8and soundness of speech that cannot be condemned, so that those who oppose you may be ashamed because they have nothing bad to say about us.

9Teach slaves to be subject to their masters in everything, to try to please them, not to talk back to them, 10and not to steal from them, but to show that they can be fully trusted, so that in every way they will make the teaching about God our Savior attractive.

11For the grace of God that brings salvation has appeared to all men. 12It

ᵉ Or has appeared to all, bringing salvation

to renounce impiety and worldly passions, and in the present age to live lives that are self-controlled, upright, and godly, 13 while we wait for the blessed hope and the manifestation of the glory of our great God and Savior,[f] Jesus Christ. 14 He it is who gave himself for us that he might redeem us from all iniquity and purify for himself a people of his own who are zealous for good deeds.

15 Declare these things; exhort and reprove with all authority.[g] Let no one look down on you.

Chapter 3

Maintain Good Deeds

REMIND them to be subject to rulers and authorities, to be obedient, to be ready for every good work, 2 to speak evil of no one, to avoid quarreling, to be gentle, and to show every courtesy to everyone. 3 For we ourselves were once foolish, disobedient, led astray, slaves to various passions and pleasures, passing our days in malice and envy, despicable, hating one another. 4 But when the goodness and loving kindness of God our Savior appeared, 5 he saved us, not because of any works of righteousness that we had done, but according to his mercy, through the water[h] of rebirth and renewal by the Holy Spirit. 6 This Spirit he poured out on us richly through Jesus Christ our Savior, 7 so that, having been justified by his grace, we might become heirs according to the hope of eternal life. 8 The saying is sure.

ἀνθρώποις, 12 παιδεύουσα ἡμᾶς, ἵνα
men, instructing us, in order that

ἀρνησάμενοι τὴν ἀσέβειαν καὶ τὰς κοσμικὰς
denying - impiety and - worldly

ἐπιθυμίας σωφρόνως καὶ δικαίως καὶ
lusts ²sensibly ¹and ⁴righteously ³and

εὐσεβῶς ζήσωμεν ἐν τῷ νῦν αἰῶνι,
⁵piously ¹we might live in the now(present) age,

13 προσδεχόμενοι τὴν μακαρίαν ἐλπίδα καὶ
expecting the blessed hope and

ἐπιφάνειαν τῆς δόξης τοῦ μεγάλου θεοῦ
appearance of the glory of the great God

καὶ σωτῆρος ἡμῶν Χριστοῦ Ἰησοῦ, 14 ὃς
and Saviour of us Christ Jesus, who

ἔδωκεν ἑαυτὸν ὑπὲρ ἡμῶν ἵνα λυτρώσηται
gave himself on behalf of us in order that he might ransom

ἡμᾶς ἀπὸ πάσης ἀνομίας καὶ καθαρίσῃ
us from all iniquity and might cleanse

ἑαυτῷ λαὸν περιούσιον, ζηλωτὴν καλῶν ἔργων.
for himself a people [his] own possession, zealous of good works.

15 Ταῦτα λάλει καὶ παρακάλει καὶ ἔλεγχε
These things speak thou and exhort and reprove

μετὰ πάσης ἐπιταγῆς· μηδείς σου περιφρονείτω.
with all command; ²no one ⁴of thee ¹let ³despise.

3 Ὑπομίμνησκε αὐτοὺς ἀρχαῖς ἐξουσίαις
Remind thou them ²to rulers ³[and] ⁴authorities

ὑποτάσσεσθαι, πειθαρχεῖν, πρὸς πᾶν ἔργον
¹to be subject, to be obedient, ²to ⁴every ³work

ἀγαθὸν ἑτοίμους εἶναι, 2 μηδένα βλασ-
⁵good ²ready ¹to be, no one to

φημεῖν, ἀμάχους εἶναι, ἐπιεικεῖς, πᾶσαν
rail at, uncontentious to be, forbearing, ²all

ἐνδεικνυμένους πρᾳύτητα πρὸς πάντας
¹showing forth meekness to all

ἀνθρώπους. 3 Ἦμεν γάρ ποτε καὶ ἡμεῖς
men. For ²were ⁴then ³also ¹we

ἀνόητοι, ἀπειθεῖς, πλανώμενοι, δουλεύοντες
senseless, disobedient, being deceived, serving [as slaves]

ἐπιθυμίαις καὶ ἡδοναῖς ποικίλαις, ἐν κακίᾳ
²lusts ³and ⁴pleasures ¹various, ²in ³evil

καὶ φθόνῳ διάγοντες, στυγητοί, μισοῦντες
⁴and ⁵envy ¹living, hateful, hating

ἀλλήλους. 4 ὅτε δὲ ἡ χρηστότης καὶ
one another. But when the kindness and

ἡ φιλανθρωπία ἐπεφάνη τοῦ σωτῆρος ἡμῶν
the love to man ²appeared ¹of the ³Saviour ⁴of us

θεοῦ, 5 οὐκ ἐξ ἔργων τῶν ἐν δικαιοσύνῃ
⁵God, not by works - ²in ³righteousness

ἃ ἐποιήσαμεν ἡμεῖς, ἀλλὰ κατὰ τὸ
¹which ³did ²we, but according to the

αὐτοῦ ἔλεος ἔσωσεν ἡμᾶς διὰ λουτροῦ
of him mercy he saved us through [the] washing

παλιγγενεσίας καὶ ἀνακαινώσεως πνεύματος
of regeneration and renewal ¹Spirit

ἁγίου, 6 οὗ ἐξέχεεν ἐφ᾽ ἡμᾶς πλουσίως
¹of [the] Holy, which he shed on us richly

διὰ Ἰησοῦ Χριστοῦ τοῦ σωτῆρος ἡμῶν,
through Jesus Christ the Saviour of us,

7 ἵνα δικαιωθέντες τῇ ἐκείνου χάριτι
in order that being justified ¹by the ²of that one ³grace

κληρονόμοι γενηθῶμεν κατ᾽ ἐλπίδα ζωῆς
heirs we might become according to a hope of life

---

teaches us to say "No" to ungodliness and worldly passions, and to live self-controlled, upright and godly lives in this present age, 13 while we wait for the blessed hope—the glorious appearing of our great God and Savior, Jesus Christ, 14 who gave himself for us to redeem us from all wickedness and to purify for himself a people that are his very own, eager to do what is good.

15 These, then, are the things you should teach. Encourage and rebuke with all authority. Do not let anyone despise you.

Chapter 3

Doing What Is Good

REMIND the people to be subject to rulers and authorities, to be obedient, to be ready to do whatever is good, 2 to slander no one, to be peaceable and considerate, and to show true humility toward all men.

3 At one time we too were foolish, disobedient, deceived and enslaved by all kinds of passions and pleasures. We lived in malice and envy, being hated and hating one another. 4 But when the kindness and love of God our Savior appeared, 5 he saved us, not because of righteous things we had done, but because of his mercy. He saved us through the washing of rebirth and renewal by the Holy Spirit, 6 whom he poured out on us generously through Jesus Christ our Savior, 7 so that, having been justified by his grace, we might become heirs having the hope of eternal

---

f Or of the great God and our Savior
g Gk commandment
h Gk washing

I desire that you insist on these things, so that those who have come to believe in God may be careful to devote themselves to good works; these things are excellent and profitable to everyone. 9 But avoid stupid controversies, genealogies, dissensions, and quarrels about the law, for they are unprofitable and worthless. 10 After a first and second admonition, have nothing more to do with anyone who causes divisions, 11 since you know that such a person is perverted and sinful, being self-condemned.

Final Messages and Benediction

12 When I send Artemas to you, or Tychicus, do your best to come to me at Nicopolis, for I have decided to spend the winter there. 13 Make every effort to send Zenas the lawyer and Apollos on their way, and see that they lack nothing. 14 And let people learn to devote themselves to good works in order to meet urgent needs, so that they may not be unproductive.

15 All who are with me send greetings to you. Greet those who love us in the faith.

Grace be with all of you. [i]

αἰωνίου.	8 Πιστὸς	ὁ	λόγος,	καὶ	περὶ
eternal.	Faithful [is] the		word,	and	as to

τούτων	βούλομαί	σε	διαβεβαιοῦσθαι,	ἵνα
these things	I wish	thee	to affirm confidently,	in order that

φροντίζωσιν	καλῶν	ἔργων	προΐστασθαι	οἱ
⁶may take thought	⁵of good	⁷works	⁸to maintain	¹the [ones]

πεπιστευκότες	θεῷ.	ταῦτά	ἐστιν	καλὰ
³having believed	²God.	These things	is(are)	good

καὶ	ὠφέλιμα	τοῖς	ἀνθρώποις·	9 μωρὰς
and	profitable	–	to men;	²foolish

δὲ	ζητήσεις	καὶ	γενεαλογίας	καὶ	ἔριν
¹but	questionings	and	genealogies	and	strife

καὶ	μάχας	νομικὰς	περιΐστασο·	εἰσὶν	γὰρ
and	²fights	¹legal	shun thou;	for they are	

ἀνωφελεῖς	καὶ	μάταιοι.	10 αἱρετικὸν
unprofitable	and	vain.	A factious

ἄνθρωπον	μετὰ	μίαν	καὶ	δευτέραν
man	after	one	and	a second

νουθεσίαν	παραιτοῦ,	11 εἰδὼς	ὅτι	ἐξέστραπ-
admonition	avoid,	knowing that	³has been per-	

ται	ὁ	τοιοῦτος	καὶ	ἁμαρτάνει	ὢν	αὐτο-
verted	¹such a man	and	sins	being	self-	

κατάκριτος.
condemned.

12 Ὅταν	πέμψω	Ἀρτεμᾶν	πρὸς	σὲ
Whenever	I send	Artemas	to	thee

ἢ	Τύχικον,	σπούδασον	ἐλθεῖν	πρός	με
or	Tychicus,	hasten	to come	to	me

εἰς	Νικόπολιν·	ἐκεῖ	γὰρ	κέκρικα	παραχειμά-
in	Nicopolis;	for there	I have decided to spend	[the]	

σαι.	13 Ζηνᾶν	τὸν	νομικὸν	καὶ	Ἀπολλῶν
winter.	Zenas	the	lawyer	and	Apollos

σπουδαίως	πρόπεμψον,	ἵνα	μηδὲν	αὐτοῖς
urgently	send forward,	in order that	nothing	to them

λείπῃ.	14 μανθανέτωσαν	δὲ	καὶ	οἱ	ἡμέτεροι
may be lacking.	And ³let ⁴learn	²also	–	¹our [people]	

καλῶν	ἔργων	προΐστασθαι	εἰς	τὰς	ἀναγ-
⁶of good	⁷works	⁸to maintain	for	neces-	

καίας	χρείας,	ἵνα	μὴ	ὦσιν	ἄκαρποι.
sary	wants,	lest	they be	unfruitful.	

15 Ἀσπάζονταί	σε	οἱ	μετ’	ἐμοῦ	πάντες.
⁵greet	⁶thee	²the [ones]	³with	⁴me	¹All.

ἄσπασαι	τοὺς	φιλοῦντας	ἡμᾶς	ἐν	πίστει.
Greet thou	the [ones]	loving	us	in [the] faith.	

Ἡ	χάρις	μετὰ	πάντων	ὑμῶν.
–	Grace [be]	with	²all	¹you.

life. 8 This is a trustworthy saying. And I want you to stress these things, so that those who have trusted in God may be careful to devote themselves to doing what is good. These things are excellent and profitable for everyone.

9 But avoid foolish controversies and genealogies and arguments and quarrels about the law, because these are unprofitable and useless. 10 Warn a divisive person once, and then warn him a second time. After that, have nothing to do with him. 11 You may be sure that such a man is warped and sinful; he is self-condemned.

Final Remarks

12 As soon as I send Artemas or Tychicus to you, do your best to come to me at Nicopolis, because I have decided to winter there. 13 Do everything you can to help Zenas the lawyer and Apollos on their way and see that they have everything they need. 14 Our people must learn to devote themselves to doing what is good, in order that they may provide for daily necessities and not live unproductive lives.

15 Everyone with me sends you greetings. Greet those who love us in the faith.

Grace be with you all.

The Letter of Paul to

Philemon

Salutation

PAUL, a prisoner of Christ Jesus, and Timothy our brother, [a]

To Philemon our dear friend and co-worker, 2 to Apphia our sister, [b] to Archippus our fellow soldier,

[i] Other ancient authorities add Amen
[a] Gk the brother
[b] Gk the sister

ΠΡΟΣ ΦΙΛΗΜΟΝΑ
To Philemon

1 Παῦλος	δέσμιος	Χριστοῦ	Ἰησοῦ	καὶ
Paul	a prisoner	of Christ	Jesus	and

Τιμόθεος	ὁ	ἀδελφὸς	Φιλήμονι	τῷ	ἀγαπητῷ
Timothy	the	brother	to Philemon	the	beloved

καὶ	συνεργῷ	ἡμῶν	2 καὶ	Ἀπφίᾳ	τῇ
and	a fellow-worker	of us	and	to Apphia	the

ἀδελφῇ	καὶ	Ἀρχίππῳ	τῷ	συστρατιώτῃ
sister	and	to Archippus	the	fellow-soldier

Philemon

PAUL, a prisoner of Christ Jesus, and Timothy our brother,

To Philemon our dear friend and fellow worker, 2 to Apphia our sister, to Archippus our fellow sol-

and to the church in your house:

3 Grace to you and peace from God our Father and the Lord Jesus Christ.

Philemon's Love and Faith

4 When I remember you[c] in my prayers, I always thank my God [5]because I hear of your love for all the saints and your faith toward the Lord Jesus. [6]I pray that the sharing of your faith may become effective when you perceive all the good that we[d] may do for Christ. [7]I have indeed received much joy and encouragement from your love, because the hearts of the saints have been refreshed through you, my brother.

Paul's Plea for Onesimus

8 For this reason, though I am bold enough in Christ to command you to do your duty, [9]yet I would rather appeal to you on the basis of love—and I, Paul, do this as an old man, and now also as a prisoner of Christ Jesus.[e] [10]I am appealing to you for my child, Onesimus, whose father I have become during my imprisonment. [11]Formerly he was useless to you, but now he is indeed useful[f] both to you and to me. [12]I am sending him, that is, my own heart, back to you. [13]I wanted to keep him with me, so that he might be of service to me in your place during my imprisonment for the gospel; [14]but I preferred to do nothing without your consent, in order that your good deed might be voluntary and not some-

---

ἡμῶν   καὶ   τῇ   κατ᾽   οἶκόν   σου   ἐκκλησίᾳ·
of us   and   ¹to the   ²at   ⁴house   ⁵of thee   ³church:

3 χάρις   ὑμῖν   καὶ   εἰρήνη   ἀπὸ   θεοῦ   πατρὸς
Grace   to you   and   peace   from   God   Father

ἡμῶν   καὶ   κυρίου   Ἰησοῦ   Χριστοῦ.
of us   and   Lord   Jesus   Christ.

4 Εὐχαριστῶ   τῷ   θεῷ   μου   πάντοτε   μνείαν
I give thanks   to the   God   of me   always   ²mention

σου   ποιούμενος   ἐπὶ   τῶν   προσευχῶν   μου,
³of thee   ¹making   at   the   prayers   of me,

5 ἀκούων   σου   τὴν   ἀγάπην   καὶ   τὴν
hearing   of thee   the   love   and   the

πίστιν   ἣν   ἔχεις   πρὸς   τὸν   κύριον   Ἰησοῦν
faith   which thou hast   toward   the   Lord   Jesus

καὶ   εἰς   πάντας   τοὺς   ἁγίους,   6 ὅπως
and   to   all   the   saints,   so as

ἡ   κοινωνία   τῆς   πίστεώς   σου   ἐνεργὴς
the   fellowship   of the   faith   of thee   ²operative

γένηται   ἐν   ἐπιγνώσει   παντὸς   ἀγαθοῦ   τοῦ
¹may become   in   a full knowledge   of every   good thing   –

ἐν   ἡμῖν   εἰς   Χριστόν.   7 χαρὰν   γὰρ
in   us   for   Christ.   ²joy   ¹For

πολλὴν   ἔσχον   καὶ   παράκλησιν   ἐπὶ   τῇ
²much   ³I had   and   consolation   over   the

ἀγάπῃ   σου,   ὅτι   τὰ   σπλάγχνα   τῶν   ἁγίων
love   of thee,   because   the   bowels   of the   saints

ἀναπέπαυται   διὰ   σοῦ,   ἀδελφέ.   8 Διό,
has(ve) been refreshed   through   thee,   brother.   Wherefore,

πολλὴν   ἐν   Χριστῷ   παρρησίαν   ἔχων   ἐπιτάσ-
²much   ³in   ⁵Christ   ³boldness   ¹having   to

σειν   σοι   τὸ   ἀνῆκον,   9 διὰ   τὴν   ἀγάπην
charge   thee   the   befitting thing,   because of   –   love

μᾶλλον   παρακαλῶ·   τοιοῦτος   ὢν   ὡς   Παῦλος
rather   I beseech;   such a one   being   as   Paul

πρεσβύτης,   νυνὶ   δὲ   καὶ   δέσμιος   Χριστοῦ
an old man,   and now   also   a prisoner   of Christ

Ἰησοῦ,   10 παρακαλῶ   σε   περὶ   τοῦ   ἐμοῦ
Jesus,   I beseech   thee   concerning   –   my

τέκνου,   ὃν   ἐγέννησα   ἐν   τοῖς   δεσμοῖς,
child,   whom   I begat   in   the(my)   bonds,

Ὀνήσιμον,   11 τόν   ποτέ   σοι   ἄχρηστον
Onesimus,   the [one]   then (formerly)   ²to thee   ¹useless

νυνὶ   δὲ   καὶ   σοὶ   καὶ   ἐμοὶ   εὔχρηστον,
but now   ²both   ³to thee   ⁴and   ⁵to me   ¹useful,

12 ὃν   ἀνέπεμψά   σοι,   αὐτόν,   τοῦτ᾽   ἔστιν
whom   I sent back   to thee,   him,   this   is

τὰ   ἐμὰ   σπλάγχνα·   13 ὃν   ἐγὼ   ἐβουλόμην
–   my   bowels;   whom   I   resolved

πρὸς   ἐμαυτὸν   κατέχειν,   ἵνα   ὑπὲρ   σοῦ
with   myself   to retain,   in order that   on behalf of   thee

μοι   διακονῇ   ἐν   τοῖς   δεσμοῖς   τοῦ   εὐαγ-
to me   he might minister   in   the   bonds   of the   gos-

γελίου,   14 χωρὶς   δὲ   τῆς   σῆς   γνώμης
pel,   but without   –   thy   opinion

οὐδὲν   ἠθέλησα   ποιῆσαι,   ἵνα   μὴ   ὡς   κατὰ
²nothing   ¹I was willing   ³to do,   in order that not   ⁴as   ⁵by way of

ἀνάγκην   τὸ   ἀγαθόν   σου   ᾖ   ἀλλὰ   κατὰ
⁷necessity   ¹the   ²good   ³of thee   ⁴might be   but   by way of

---

dier and to the church that meets in your home:

[3]Grace to you and peace from God our Father and the Lord Jesus Christ.

Thanksgiving and Prayer

[4]I always thank my God as I remember you in my prayers, [5]because I hear about your faith in the Lord Jesus and your love for all the saints. [6]I pray that you may be active in sharing your faith, so that you will have a full understanding of every good thing we have in Christ. [7]Your love has given me great joy and encouragement, because you, brother, have refreshed the hearts of the saints.

Paul's Plea for Onesimus

[8]Therefore, although in Christ I could be bold and order you to do what you ought to do, [9]yet I appeal to you on the basis of love. I then, as Paul—an old man and now also a prisoner of Christ Jesus— [10]I appeal to you for my son Onesimus,[a] who became my son while I was in chains. [11]Formerly he was useless to you, but now he has become useful both to you and to me.

[12]I am sending him—who is my very heart—back to you. [13]I would have liked to keep him with me so that he could take your place in helping me while I am in chains for the gospel. [14]But I did not want to do anything without your consent, so that any favor you do will be spontaneous and

---

[c] From verse 4 through verse 21, you is singular
[d] Other ancient authorities read you (plural)
[e] Or as an ambassador of Christ Jesus, and now also his prisoner
[f] The name Onesimus means useful or (compare verse 20) beneficial

[a] 10 Onesimus means useful.

thing forced. 15 Perhaps this is the reason he was separated from you for a while, so that you might have him back forever, 16 no longer as a slave but more than a slave, a beloved brother—especially to me but how much more to you, both in the flesh and in the Lord.

17 So if you consider me your partner, welcome him as you would welcome me. 18 If he has wronged you in any way, or owes you anything, charge that to my account. 19 I, Paul, am writing this with my own hand: I will repay it. I say nothing about your owing me even your own self. 20 Yes, brother, let me have this benefit from you in the Lord! Refresh my heart in Christ. 21 Confident of your obedience, I am writing to you, knowing that you will do even more than I say.

22 One thing more— prepare a guest room for me, for I am hoping through your prayers to be restored to you.

Final Greetings and Benediction

23 Epaphras, my fellow prisoner in Christ Jesus, sends greetings to you, g 24 and so do Mark, Aristarchus, Demas, and Luke, my fellow workers. 25 The grace of the Lord Jesus Christ be with your spirit. h

---

ἑκούσιον. **15** τάχα γὰρ διὰ τοῦτο ἐχωρίσθη
[being] For perhaps therefore he departed
voluntary.

πρὸς ὥραν, ἵνα αἰώνιον αὐτὸν ἀπέχῃς,
for an hour, in order ²eternally ³him ¹thou mightest receive,

16 οὐκέτι ὡς δοῦλον ἀλλὰ ὑπὲρ δοῦλον,
no longer as a slave but beyond a slave,

ἀδελφὸν ἀγαπητόν, μάλιστα ἐμοί, πόσῳ
a brother beloved, specially to me, ²by how much

δὲ μᾶλλον σοὶ καὶ ἐν σαρκὶ καὶ ἐν
¹and more to thee both in [the] flesh and in

κυρίῳ. **17** εἰ οὖν με ἔχεις κοινωνόν,
[the] Lord. If therefore me thou hast [as] a partner,

προσλαβοῦ αὐτὸν ὡς ἐμέ. **18** εἰ δέ
receive him as me. And if

τι ἠδίκησέν σε ἢ ὀφείλει, τοῦτο ἐμοὶ
any- he wronged thee or owes, ²this ³to me
thing

ἐλλόγα· **19** ἐγὼ Παῦλος ἔγραψα τῇ ἐμῇ
¹reckon: I Paul wrote – with my

χειρί, ἐγὼ ἀποτίσω· ἵνα μὴ λέγω σοι
hand, I will repay; lest I say to thee

ὅτι καὶ σεαυτόν μοι προσοφείλεις. **20** ναί,
that indeed ²thyself ³to me ¹thou owest besides. Yes,

ἀδελφέ, ἐγώ σου ὀναίμην ἐν κυρίῳ·
brother, ²I ¹of thee ¹may ²have ³help in [the] Lord;

ἀνάπαυσόν μου τὰ σπλάγχνα ἐν Χριστῷ.
refresh of me the bowels in Christ.

21 Πεποιθὼς τῇ ὑπακοῇ σου ἔγραψά
Having trusted to the obedience of thee I wrote

σοι, εἰδὼς ὅτι καὶ ὑπὲρ ἃ λέγω ποιήσεις.
to thee, knowing that indeed beyond what I say thou wilt do.

22 ἅμα δὲ καὶ ἑτοίμαζέ μοι ξενίαν·
And at the also prepare for me lodging;
same time

ἐλπίζω γὰρ ὅτι διὰ τῶν προσευχῶν
for I hope that through the prayers

ὑμῶν χαρισθήσομαι ὑμῖν.
of you I shall be given to you.

23 Ἀσπάζεταί σε Ἐπαφρᾶς ὁ συναιχμά-
²greets ³thee ¹Epaphras ⁴the ⁵fellow-

λωτός μου ἐν Χριστῷ Ἰησοῦ, **24** Μᾶρκος,
captive ⁴of me ⁵in ⁶Christ ⁷Jesus, [also] Mark,

Ἀρίσταρχος, Δημᾶς, Λουκᾶς, οἱ συνεργοί
Aristarchus, Demas, Luke, the fellow-workers

μου.
of me.

25 Ἡ χάρις τοῦ κυρίου Ἰησοῦ Χριστοῦ
The grace of the Lord Jesus Christ

μετὰ τοῦ πνεύματος ὑμῶν.
[be] with the spirit of you.

---

not forced. 15 Perhaps the reason he was separated from you for a little while was that you might have him back for good— 16 no longer as a slave, but better than a slave, as a dear brother. He is very dear to me but even dearer to you, both as a man and as a brother in the Lord.

17 So if you consider me a partner, welcome him as you would welcome me. 18 If he has done you any wrong or owes you anything, charge it to me. 19 I, Paul, am writing this with my own hand. I will pay it back—not to mention that you owe me your very self. 20 I do wish, brother, that I may have some benefit from you in the Lord; refresh my heart in Christ. 21 Confident of your obedience, I write to you, knowing that you will do even more than I ask.

22 And one thing more: Prepare a guest room for me, because I hope to be restored to you in answer to your prayers.

23 Epaphras, my fellow prisoner in Christ Jesus, sends you greetings. 24 And so do Mark, Aristarchus, Demas and Luke, my fellow workers. 25 The grace of the Lord Jesus Christ be with your spirit.

The Letter to the
Hebrews
Chapter 1
God Has Spoken by His Son

LONG ago God spoke to our ancestors in many and various ways by the prophets, 2 but in these last

g Here *you* is singular
h Other ancient authorities add *Amen*

ΠΡΟΣ ΕΒΡΑΙΟΥΣ
To Hebrews

1 Πολυμερῶς καὶ πολυτρόπως πάλαι ὁ
¹In many ⁴and ²in many ways ⁵of old –
portions

θεὸς λαλήσας τοῖς πατράσιν ἐν τοῖς
God ³having spoken ²to the ⁴fathers by the

Hebrews
Chapter 1
The Son Superior to Angels

IN the past God spoke to our forefathers through the prophets at many times and in various ways, 2 but in days he has spoken to us by a Son,[a] whom he appointed heir of all things, through whom he also created the worlds. [3] He is the reflection of God's glory and the exact imprint of God's very being, and he sustains[b] all things by his powerful word. When he had made purification for sins, he sat down at the right hand of the Majesty on high, [4] having become as much superior to angels as the name he has inherited is more excellent than theirs.

The Son Is Superior to Angels

[5] For to which of the angels did God ever say,
"You are my Son;
today I have
begotten you"?
Or again,
"I will be his Father,
and he will be my
Son"?
[6] And again, when he brings the firstborn into the world, he says,
"Let all God's angels worship him."
[7] Of the angels he says,
"He makes his angels winds,
and his servants flames of fire."
[8] But of the Son he says,
"Your throne,
O God,[c] is forever and ever,
and the righteous scepter is the scepter of your[d] kingdom.
[9] You have loved righteousness and hated wickedness;
therefore God, your God, has anointed you with the oil of gladness beyond your companions."
[10] And,
"In the beginning, Lord, you founded the earth,

προφήταις 2 ἐπ’ ἐσχάτου τῶν ἡμερῶν
prophets   in [the] last   –   days

τούτων ἐλάλησεν ἡμῖν ἐν υἱῷ, ὃν ἔθηκεν
of these spoke to us in a Son, whom he appointed

κληρονόμον πάντων, δι’ οὗ καὶ ἐποίησεν
heir   of all through whom indeed he made
            things,

τοὺς αἰῶνας· 3 ὃς ὢν ἀπαύγασμα τῆς
the   ages;   who being [the] radiance of the
                                          (his)

δόξης καὶ χαρακτὴρ τῆς ὑποστάσεως αὐτοῦ,
glory and [the]   of the reality   of him,
      representation

φέρων τε τὰ πάντα τῷ ῥήματι τῆς
and bearing – all things by the word of the

δυνάμεως αὐτοῦ, καθαρισμὸν τῶν ἁμαρτιῶν
power   of him, ²cleansing –   ¹of sins

ποιησάμενος ἐκάθισεν ἐν δεξιᾷ τῆς
¹having made sat   on [the] right [hand] of the

μεγαλωσύνης ἐν ὑψηλοῖς, 4 τοσούτῳ
greatness   in high places, ²by so much

κρείττων γενόμενος τῶν ἀγγέλων ὅσῳ
¹better ²becoming ³[than] the angels as

διαφορώτερον παρ’ αὐτοὺς κεκληρονόμηκεν
³a more excellent ⁴than ⁵them ¹he has inherited

ὄνομα. 5 Τίνι γὰρ εἶπέν ποτε τῶν
²name.   For to which ²said he ⁴ever ¹of the

ἀγγέλων· υἱός μου εἶ σύ, ἐγὼ σήμερον
³angels: Son my art thou, I to-day

γεγέννηκά σε; καὶ πάλιν· ἐγὼ ἔσομαι
have begotten thee? and again: I will be

αὐτῷ εἰς πατέρα, καὶ αὐτὸς ἔσται μοι
to him for a father, and he shall be to me

εἰς υἱόν; 6 ὅταν δὲ πάλιν εἰσαγάγῃ
for a son? and whenever again he brings in

τὸν πρωτότοκον εἰς τὴν οἰκουμένην, λέγει·
the firstborn into the inhabited [earth], he says:

καὶ προσκυνησάτωσαν αὐτῷ πάντες ἄγγελοι
And let worship   him   all   angels

θεοῦ. 7 καὶ πρὸς μὲν τοὺς ἀγγέλους
of God. And with re- – the angels
          gard to

λέγει· ὁ ποιῶν τοὺς ἀγγέλους αὐτοῦ
he says: The making the   angels   of him
         [one]

πνεύματα, καὶ τοὺς λειτουργοὺς αὐτοῦ
spirits,   and the ministers   of him

πυρὸς φλόγα· 8 πρὸς δὲ τὸν υἱόν· ὁ
²of fire ¹a flame; but with regard to the Son: The

θρόνος σου ὁ θεὸς εἰς τὸν αἰῶνα τοῦ
throne of thee[,] – God[,]*[is] unto the age of the

αἰῶνος, καὶ ἡ ῥάβδος τῆς εὐθύτητος
age,   and the rod   – of uprightness [is]

ῥάβδος τῆς βασιλείας αὐτοῦ. 9 ἠγάπησας
[the] rod of the kingdom of him. Thou lovedst

δικαιοσύνην καὶ ἐμίσησας ἀνομίαν· διὰ
righteousness and hatedst lawlessness; there-

τοῦτο ἔχρισέν σε, ὁ θεός, ὁ θεός σου
fore ⁴anointed ²thee, – ⁵God,* ¹the ³God ⁶of thee

ἔλαιον ἀγαλλιάσεως παρὰ τοὺς μετόχους
[with] oil of gladness above the   partners

σου. 10 καὶ· σὺ κατ’ ἀρχάς, κύριε,
of thee. And: Thou at [the] beginnings, Lord,

τὴν γῆν ἐθεμελίωσας, καὶ ἔργα τῶν
²the ³earth ¹didst found, and ⁴works ⁵of the

---

these last days he has spoken to us by his Son, whom he appointed heir of all things, and through whom he made the universe. [3] The Son is the radiance of God's glory and the exact representation of his being, sustaining all things by his powerful word. After he had provided purification for sins, he sat down at the right hand of the Majesty in heaven. [4] So he became as much superior to the angels as the name he has inherited is superior to theirs.

[5] For to which of the angels did God ever say,

"You are my Son;
today I have become
your Father"[a][b]?

Or again,

"I will be his Father,
and he will be my
Son"[c]?

[6] And again, when God brings his firstborn into the world, he says,

"Let all God's angels worship him."[d]

[7] In speaking of the angels he says,

"He makes his angels winds,
his servants flames of fire."[e]

[8] But about the Son he says,

"Your throne, O God,
will last for ever and ever,
and righteousness will be the scepter of your kingdom.
[9] You have loved righteousness and hated wickedness;
therefore God, your God, has set you above your companions by anointing you with the oil of joy."[f]

[10] He also says,

"In the beginning, O Lord, you laid the foundations of the earth,

---

a Or the Son
b Or bears along
c Or God is your throne
d Other ancient authorities read his

* Articular vocative; see ver. 10.

*a*5 Or have begotten you
*b*5 Psalm 2:7
*c*5 2 Samuel 7:14; 1 Chron. 17:13
*d*6 Deut. 32:43 (see Dead Sea Scrolls and Septuagint)
*e*7 Psalm 104:4
*f*9 Psalm 45:6,7

and the heavens are
the work of
your hands;
11 they will perish, but
you remain;
they will all wear
out like
clothing;
12 like a cloak you will
roll them up,
and like clothing[e]
they will be
changed.
But you are the same,
and your years will
never end."
13 But to which of the angels has he ever said,
"Sit at my right hand
until I make your
enemies a
footstool for
your feet"?
14 Are not all angels[f] spirits
in the divine service, sent
to serve for the sake of
those who are to inherit salvation?

Chapter 2

Warning to Pay Attention

THEREFORE we must
pay greater attention
to what we have heard, so
that we do not drift away
from it. 2 For if the message
declared through angels
was valid, and every transgression or disobedience
received a just penalty,
3 how can we escape if we
neglect so great a salva-
tion? It was declared at first
through the Lord, and it
was attested to us by those
who heard him, 4 while God
added his testimony by
signs and wonders and various miracles, and by gifts
of the Holy Spirit, distributed according to his will.

Exaltation through Abasement

5 Now God[g] did not
subject the coming world,
about which we are speak-
ing, to angels. 6 But someone has testified some-
where,
"What are human
beings that you
are mindful of
them,[h]
or mortals, that you
care for them?[i]
7 You have made them
for a little while
lower[j] than the
angels;

χειρῶν σού εἰσιν οἱ οὐρανοί· 11 αὐτοὶ
hands ⁷of thee *are* ¹the ²heavens; they

ἀπολοῦνται, σὺ δὲ διαμένεις· καὶ πάντες
will perish, but thou remainest; and all

ὡς ἱμάτιον παλαιωθήσονται, 12 καὶ ὡσεὶ
as a garment will become old, and as

περιβόλαιον ἑλίξεις αὐτούς, ὡς ἱμάτιον
a mantle thou wilt roll up them, as a garment

καὶ ἀλλαγήσονται· σὺ δὲ ὁ αὐτὸς εἶ
also they will be changed; but thou the same art

καὶ τὰ ἔτη σου οὐκ ἐκλείψουσιν. 13 πρὸς
and the years of thee will not fail. ⁵to

τίνα δὲ τῶν ἀγγέλων εἴρηκέν ποτε·
²which ¹But of the angels has he said at any time:

κάθου ἐκ δεξιῶν μου ἕως ἂν θῶ τοὺς
Sit at [the] right of me until I put the

ἐχθρούς σου ὑποπόδιον τῶν ποδῶν σου;
enemies of thee a footstool of the feet of thee?

14 οὐχὶ πάντες εἰσὶν λειτουργικὰ πνεύματα
²not ¹all ¹are they ²ministering ¹spirits

εἰς διακονίαν ἀποστελλόμενα διὰ τοὺς
⁷for ⁸service ⁶being sent forth because of the [ones]

μέλλοντας κληρονομεῖν σωτηρίαν; 2 Διὰ
being about to inherit salvation ? There-

τοῦτο δεῖ περισσοτέρως προσέχειν ἡμᾶς
fore ¹it behoves ⁴more abundantly ³to give heed ²us

τοῖς ἀκουσθεῖσιν, μήποτε παραρυῶμεν.
to the things heard, lest we drift away.

2 εἰ γὰρ ὁ δι' ἀγγέλων λαληθεὶς λόγος
For if ¹the ⁴through ⁵angels ⁶spoken ²word

ἐγένετο βέβαιος, καὶ πᾶσα παράβασις
was firm, and every transgression

καὶ παρακοὴ ἔλαβεν ἔνδικον μισθαποδοσίαν,
and disobedience received a just recompence,

3 πῶς ἡμεῖς ἐκφευξόμεθα τηλικαύτης
how ²we ¹shall ³escape ⁵so great

ἀμελήσαντες σωτηρίας; ἥτις ἀρχὴν λαβοῦσα
⁴neglecting ⁶a salvation ? which ²a beginning ¹having received

λαλεῖσθαι διὰ τοῦ κυρίου, ὑπὸ τῶν
to be spoken through the Lord, by the

ἀκουσάντων εἰς ἡμᾶς ἐβεβαιώθη, 4 συνεπι-
[ones] hearing to us was confirmed, ⁴bearing

μαρτυροῦντος τοῦ θεοῦ σημείοις τε καὶ
witness with — ¹God² ⁴by signs ³both and

τέρασιν καὶ ποικίλαις δυνάμεσιν καὶ
by wonders and by various powerful deeds and

πνεύματος ἁγίου μερισμοῖς κατὰ τὴν αὐτοῦ
⁵Spirit ²of [the] ¹by distribu- according to the ⁸of him
Holy tions

θέλησιν.
¹will.

5 Οὐ γὰρ ἀγγέλοις ὑπέταξεν τὴν
For not to angels subjected he the

οἰκουμένην τὴν μέλλουσαν, περὶ ἧς
²inhabited [earth] – ¹coming, about which

λαλοῦμεν. 6 διεμαρτύρατο δέ πού τις
we speak. But ²solemnly witnessed ³some- ¹one where

λέγων· τί ἐστιν ἄνθρωπος ὅτι μιμνήσκῃ
saying: What is man that thou rememberest

αὐτοῦ; ἢ υἱὸς ἀνθρώπου ὅτι ἐπισκέπτῃ
him ? or a son of man that thou observest

αὐτόν; 7 ἠλάττωσας αὐτὸν βραχύ τι παρ'
him ? Thou madest ²less ¹him ²a little than

---

and the heavens are the
work of your hands.
11They will perish, but you
remain;
they will all wear out
like a garment.
12You will roll them up
like a robe;
like a garment they will
be changed.
But you remain the
same,
and your years will
never end."[g]
13To which of the angels
did God ever say,

"Sit at my right hand
until I make your
enemies
a footstool for your
feet"[h]?

14Are not all angels ministering spirits sent to serve
those who will inherit salvation?

Chapter 2

Warning to Pay Attention

WE must pay more
careful attention,
therefore, to what we have
heard, so that we do not
drift away. 2For if the message spoken by angels was
binding, and every viola-
tion and disobedience re-
ceived its just punishment,
3how shall we escape if we
ignore such a great salvation? This salvation, which
was first announced by the
Lord, was confirmed to us
by those who heard him.
4God also testified to it by
signs, wonders and various
miracles, and gifts of the
Holy Spirit distributed according to his will.

Jesus Made Like His Brothers

5It is not to angels that he
has subjected the world to
come, about which we are
speaking. 6But there is a
place where someone has
testified:

"What is man that you
are mindful of him,
the son of man that you
care for him?
7You made him a little[i]
lower than the
angels;

---

e Other ancient authorities lack like
clothing
f Gk all of them
g Gk he
h Gk What is man that you are
mindful of him?
i Gk or the son of man that you
care for him? In the Hebrew of
Psalm 8.4-6 man and son of
man refer to all humankind
j Or them only a little lower

g12 Psalm 102:25-27
h13 Psalm 110:1
i7 Or him for a little while; also in
verse 9

you have crowned them with glory and honor,[k]

8 subjecting all things under their feet."

Now in subjecting all things to them, God[g] left nothing outside their control. As it is, we do not yet see everything in subjection to them, 9but we do see Jesus, who for a little while was made lower[l] than the angels, now crowned with glory and honor because of the suffering of death, so that by the grace of God[m] he might taste death for everyone.

10 It was fitting that God,[n] for whom and through whom all things exist, in bringing many children to glory, should make the pioneer of their salvation perfect through sufferings. 11For the one who sanctifies and those who are sanctified all have one Father.[o] For this reason Jesus[n] is not ashamed to call them brothers and sisters,[p] 12saying,

"I will proclaim your name to my brothers and sisters,[p] in the midst of the congregation I will praise you."

13And again, "I will put my trust in him." And again, "Here am I and the children whom God has given me."

14 Since, therefore, the children share flesh and blood, he himself likewise shared the same things, so that through death he might destroy the one who has the power of death, that is, the devil, 15and free those who all their lives were held in slavery by the fear of death. 16For it is clear

---

ἀγγέλους,　δόξῃ　καὶ　τιμῇ　ἐστεφάνωσας
angels,　with glory　and with honour　thou crownedst

αὐτόν,　8 πάντα　ὑπέταξας　ὑποκάτω　τῶν
him,　all things　thou subjectedst　underneath　the

ποδῶν　αὐτοῦ.　ἐν　τῷ　γὰρ　ὑποτάξαι
feet　of him.　¹in　the　For　²to subject[ing]

[αὐτῷ]　τὰ　πάντα　οὐδὲν　ἀφῆκεν　αὐτῷ
⁴to him　-　³all things　⁶nothing　⁵he left　⁵to him

ἀνυπότακτον.　Νῦν　δὲ　οὔπω　ὁρῶμεν
⁷unsubjected.　But now　not yet　we see

αὐτῷ　τὰ　πάντα　ὑποτεταγμένα·　9 τὸν　δὲ
³to him　-　¹all things　²having been subjected;　³the [one]　¹but

βραχύ　τι　παρ'　ἀγγέλους　ἠλαττωμένον
⁵a little　⁶than　⁷angels　⁴having been made less

βλέπομεν　Ἰησοῦν　διὰ　τὸ　πάθημα　τοῦ
²we see　⁸Jesus　because of the　suffering　-

θανάτου　δόξῃ　καὶ　τιμῇ　ἐστεφανωμένον,
of death　with glory　and with honour　having been crowned,

ὅπως　χάριτι　θεοῦ　ὑπὲρ　παντὸς　γεύσηται
so as　by [the] grace　of God　³on behalf of　⁴every man　¹he might taste

θανάτου.　10 ἔπρεπεν　γὰρ　αὐτῷ,　δι'
of ²death.　For it was fitting　for him, because of

ὃν　τὰ　πάντα　καὶ　δι'　οὗ　τὰ　πάντα,
whom　-　all things　and　through whom　-　all things,

πολλοὺς　υἱοὺς　εἰς　δόξαν　ἀγαγόντα　τὸν
¹⁰many　¹¹sons　¹²to　¹³glory　⁹leading　⁴the

ἀρχηγὸν　τῆς　σωτηρίας　αὐτῶν　διὰ
⁵author　⁶of the　⁷salvation　⁸of them　²through

παθημάτων　τελειῶσαι.　11 ὅ　τε　γὰρ
³sufferings　¹to perfect.　³the [one] ²both　¹For

ἁγιάζων　καὶ　οἱ　ἁγιαζόμενοι　ἐξ　ἑνὸς
sanctifying　and the [ones] being sanctified [are] ²of　³one

πάντες·　δι'　ἣν　αἰτίαν　οὐκ　ἐπαισχύνεται
¹all;　for which cause　he is not ashamed

ἀδελφοὺς　αὐτοὺς　καλεῖν,　12 λέγων·　ἀπαγ-
³brothers　²them　¹to call,　saying:　I will

γελῶ　τὸ　ὄνομά　σου　τοῖς　ἀδελφοῖς　μου,
announce the　name　of thee　to the　brothers　of me,

ἐν　μέσῳ　ἐκκλησίας　ὑμνήσω　σε·　13 καὶ
in [the] midst　of [the] church　I will hymn　thee;　and

πάλιν·　ἐγὼ　ἔσομαι　πεποιθὼς　ἐπ'　αὐτῷ·
again:　I　will be　having trusted　on(in)　him;

καὶ　πάλιν·　ἰδοὺ　ἐγὼ　καὶ　τὰ　παιδία
and　again:　Behold[,]　I　and　the　children

ἅ　μοι　ἔδωκεν　ὁ　θεός.　14 Ἐπεὶ　οὖν
whom ²to me　¹gave　-　¹God.　Since therefore

τὰ　παιδία　κεκοινώνηκεν　αἵματος　καὶ
the　children　has(ve) partaken　of blood　and

σαρκός,　καὶ　αὐτὸς　παραπλησίως　μετέσχεν
of flesh,　²also　³[him]self　⁴in like manner　¹he shared

τῶν　αὐτῶν,　ἵνα　διὰ　τοῦ　θανάτου
the　same things, in order that　through　the(?his)　death

καταργήσῃ　τὸν　τὸ　κράτος　ἔχοντα　τοῦ
he might destroy ¹the [one] ²the　⁴might　⁵having　-

θανάτου,　τοῦτ'　ἔστιν　τὸν　διάβολον,　15 καὶ
of death,　this　is　the　devil,　and

ἀπαλλάξῃ　τούτους,　ὅσοι　φόβῳ　θανάτου
release　these,　as many as　by fear　of death

διὰ　παντὸς　τοῦ　ζῆν　ἔνοχοι　ἦσαν　δουλείας.
through all　the(ir)　to live　²involved　¹were　slavery.
　　　[time]　　　　in

---

you crowned him with glory and honor,

8 and put everything under his feet."[j]

In putting everything under him, God left nothing that is not subject to him. Yet at present we do not see everything subject to him. 9But we see Jesus, who was made a little lower than the angels, now crowned with glory and honor because he suffered death, so that by the grace of God he might taste death for everyone.

10In bringing many sons to glory, it was fitting that God, for whom and through whom everything exists, should make the author of their salvation perfect through suffering. 11Both the one who makes men holy and those who are made holy are of the same family. So Jesus is not ashamed to call them brothers. 12He says,

"I will declare your name to my brothers; in the presence of the congregation I will sing your praises."[k]

13And again,

"I will put my trust in him."[l]

And again he says,

"Here am I, and the children God has given me."[m]

14Since the children have flesh and blood, he too shared in their humanity so that by his death he might destroy him who holds the power of death—that is, the devil—15and free those who all their lives were held in slavery by their fear

---

[k] Other ancient authorities add and set them over the works of your hands
[l] Or who was made a little lower
[m] Other ancient authorities read apart from God
[n] Gk he
[o] Gk are all of one
[p] Gk brothers

[j]8 Psalm 8:4-6
[k]12 Psalm 22:22
[l]13 Isaiah 8:17
[m]13 Isaiah 8:18

that he did not come to help angels, but the descendants of Abraham. 17 Therefore he had to become like his brothers and sisters *p* in every respect, so that he might be a merciful and faithful high priest in the service of God, to make a sacrifice of atonement for the sins of the people. 18 Because he himself was tested by what he suffered, he is able to help those who are being tested.

16 οὐ   γὰρ   δήπου   ἀγγέλων   ἐπιλαμβάνεται,
⁴not.   ¹For ²of course ³of angels   ³he takes hold,

ἀλλὰ   σπέρματος   ᾿Αβραὰμ   ἐπιλαμβάνεται.
but   of [the] seed   of Abraham   he takes hold.

17 ὅθεν   ὤφειλεν   κατὰ   πάντα   τοῖς   ἀδελφοῖς
Whence   he owed   by all means†   ²to the   ³brothers
(ought)   (his)

ὁμοιωθῆναι,   ἵνα   ἐλεήμων   γένηται   καὶ
¹to become like,   in order   ²a merciful   ¹he might become   and
that

πιστὸς   ἀρχιερεὺς   τὰ   πρὸς   τὸν   θεόν,
faithful   high priest   [in] the   in regard   –   God,
things   to

εἰς   τὸ   ἱλάσκεσθαι   τὰς   ἁμαρτίας   τοῦ
for   the   to make propitia-   the   sins   of the
tion for

λαοῦ.   **18** ἐν   ᾧ   γὰρ   πέπονθεν   αὐτὸς
people.   ³in   ⁴what   ¹For   ²has suffered   ⁴he
[way]

πειρασθείς,   δύναται   τοῖς   πειραζομένοις
being tempted,   he is able   ²the [ones]   ³being tempted

βοηθῆσαι.
¹to help.

of death. 16 For surely it is not angels he helps, but Abraham's descendants. 17 For this reason he had to be made like his brothers in every way, in order that he might become a merciful and faithful high priest in service to God, and that he might make atonement for *n* the sins of the people. 18 Because he himself suffered when he was tempted, he is able to help those who are being tempted.

Chapter 3

Moses a Servant, Christ a Son

THEREFORE, brothers and sisters, *p* holy partners in a heavenly calling, consider that Jesus, the apostle and high priest of our confession, 2 was faithful to the one who appointed him, just as Moses also "was faithful in all *q* God's *r* house." 3 Yet Jesus *s* is worthy of more glory than Moses, just as the builder of a house has more honor than the house itself. 4 For every house is built by someone, but the builder of all things is God.) 5 Now Moses was faithful in all God's *r* house as a servant, to testify to the things that would be spoken later. 6 Christ, however, was faithful over God's *r* house as a son, and we are his house if we hold firm *t* the confidence and the pride that belong to hope.

Warning against Unbelief

7 Therefore, as the Holy Spirit says,
  "Today, if you hear his voice,
8   do not harden your hearts as in the rebellion,

3 Ὅθεν,   ἀδελφοὶ   ἅγιοι,   κλήσεως
Whence,   brothers   holy,   ²calling

ἐπουρανίου   μέτοχοι,   κατανοήσατε   τὸν
³of a heavenly   ¹sharers,   consider   the

ἀπόστολον   καὶ   ἀρχιερέα   τῆς   ὁμολογίας
apostle   and   high priest   of the   confession

ἡμῶν   ᾿Ιησοῦν,   **2** πιστὸν   ὄντα   τῷ   ποιήσαντι
of us[,]   Jesus,   faithful   being   to the [one] making

αὐτόν,   ὡς   καὶ   Μωϋσῆς   ἐν   [ὅλῳ]   τῷ
him,   as   also   Moses   in   all   the

οἴκῳ   αὐτοῦ.   **3** πλείονος   γὰρ   οὗτος   δόξης
household of him.   For ²of more   ¹this one   ⁴glory

παρὰ   Μωϋσῆν   ἠξίωται   καθ᾿   ὅσον   πλείονα
⁵than   ⁶Moses   ³has been   by so much as   ⁶more
counted worthy

τιμὴν   ἔχει   τοῦ   οἴκου   ὁ   κατασκευάσας
⁶honour   ⁴has   ⁸the   ⁹house   ¹the   ³having prepared
⁷[than]   [one]

αὐτόν.   **4** πᾶς   γὰρ   οἶκος   κατασκευάζεται
³it.   For every   house   is prepared

ὑπό   τινος,   ὁ   δὲ   πάντα   κατασκευάσας
by   someone, but   ¹the [one]   ²all things   ³having prepared

θεός.   **5** καὶ   Μωϋσῆς   μὲν   πιστὸς   ἐν
[is] God.   And   Moses   on one hand faithful   in
[was]

ὅλῳ   τῷ   οἴκῳ   αὐτοῦ   ὡς   θεράπων   εἰς
all   the   household   of him   as   a servant   for

μαρτύριον   τῶν   λαληθησομένων,   **6** Χριστὸς
a testimony of the things   being spoken   Christ
[in the future],

δὲ   ὡς   υἱὸς   ἐπὶ   τὸν   οἶκον   αὐτοῦ·   οὗ
on the as   a Son   over   the   household   of him;   of
other   whom

οἶκός   ἐσμεν   ἡμεῖς,   ἐὰν   τὴν   παρρησίαν
a household are   we,   if   ²the   ³confidence

καὶ   τὸ   καύχημα   τῆς   ἐλπίδος   [μέχρι
⁴and   ⁵the   ⁴boast   ⁵of the   ⁴hope   ¹⁰until

τέλους   βεβαίαν]   κατάσχωμεν.   **7** Διό,
¹¹[the] end   ⁹firm   ¹we hold fast.   Wherefore,

καθὼς   λέγει   τὸ   πνεῦμα   τὸ   ἅγιον·   σήμερον
as   says   the   Spirit   –   Holy: To-day

ἐὰν   τῆς   φωνῆς   αὐτοῦ   ἀκούσητε,   **8** μὴ
if   ²the   ³voice   of him   ye may   not

σκληρύνητε   τὰς   καρδίας   ὑμῶν   ὡς   ἐν
harden ye   the   hearts   of you   as   in

Chapter 3

Jesus Greater Than Moses

THEREFORE, holy brothers, who share in the heavenly calling, fix your thoughts on Jesus, the apostle and high priest whom we confess. 2 He was faithful to the one who appointed him, just as Moses was faithful in all God's house. 3 Jesus has been found worthy of greater honor than Moses, just as the builder of a house has greater honor than the house itself. 4 For every house is built by someone, but God is the builder of everything. 5 Moses was faithful as a servant in all God's house, testifying to what would be said in the future. 6 But Christ is faithful as a son over God's house. And we are his house, if we hold on to our courage and the hope of which we boast.

Warning Against Unbelief

7 So, as the Holy Spirit says:

  "Today, if you hear his voice,
8   do not harden your hearts
  as you did in the rebellion,

q Other ancient authorities lack *all*
r Gk *his*
s Gk *this one*
t Other ancient authorities add *to the end*

n 17 Or *and that he might turn aside God's wrath, taking away*

as on the day of
  testing in the
  wilderness,
9 where your ancestors
  put me to
  the test,
  though they had
  seen my works
10for forty
  years.
Therefore I was angry
  with that
  generation,
and I said, 'They
  always go astray
  in their hearts,
  and they have not
  known
  my ways.'
11 As in my anger I
  swore,
  'They will not enter
  my rest.'"
12Take care, brothers and
sisters,ᵖ that none of you
may have an evil, unbelieving heart that turns away
from the living God. 13But
exhort one another every
day, as long as it is called
"today," so that none of
you may be hardened by
the deceitfulness of sin.
14For we have become
partners of Christ, if only
we hold our first confi-
dence firm to the end. 15As
it is said,
  "Today, if you hear
    his voice,
  do not harden your
    hearts as in
    the rebellion."
16Now who were they who
heard and yet were rebel-
lious? Was it not all those
who left Egypt under the
leadership of Moses? 17But
with whom was he angry
forty years? Was it not
those who sinned, whose
bodies fell in the wilderness? 18And to whom did
he swear that they would
not enter his rest, if not to
those who were disobedi-
ent? 19So we see that they
were unable to enter be-
cause of unbelief.

τῷ   παραπικρασμῷ κατὰ τὴν ἡμέραν τοῦ
the   provocation   in   the   day   of the
πειρασμοῦ ἐν τῇ ἐρήμῳ, 9 οὗ ἐπείρασαν
temptation   in the   desert,   when ⁴tempted
οἱ πατέρες ὑμῶν ἐν δοκιμασίᾳ καὶ εἶδον
¹the ³fathers ²of you in proving   and   saw
τὰ ἔργα   μου τεσσεράκοντα ἔτη· 10 διὸ
the works of me   forty   years; where-
                                                fore
προσώχθισα τῇ γενεᾷ ταύτῃ καὶ εἶπον·
I was angry   with this generation and   I said:
ἀεὶ πλανῶνται τῇ καρδίᾳ· αὐτοὶ δὲ
Always they err   in the   heart;   and they
οὐκ ἔγνωσαν τὰς ὁδούς, μου, 11 ὡς
knew not   the   ways   of me,   as
ὤμοσα ἐν τῇ ὀργῇ μου· εἰ εἰσελεύσονται
I swore in the wrath of me: If they shall enter
·εἰς τὴν κατάπαυσίν μου. 12 Βλέπετε,
into the   rest   of me.   Look ye,
ἀδελφοί, μήποτε ἔσται ἔν τινι ὑμῶν
brothers,   lest   there shall be in anyone of you
καρδία πονηρὰ ἀπιστίας ἐν τῷ ἀποστῆναι
¹heart   ²an evil of unbelief in the to depart[ing]
ἀπὸ θεοῦ ζῶντος, 13 ἀλλὰ παρακαλεῖτε
from God   a living,   but   exhort
ἑαυτοὺς καθ' ἑκάστην ἡμέραν, ἄχρις οὗ
yourselves –   each   day,   while
τὸ σήμερον καλεῖται, ἵνα μὴ σκληρυνθῇ
the to-day   it is being called, lest   ⁴be hardened
τις ἐξ ὑμῶν ἀπάτῃ τῆς ἁμαρτίας· 14 μέτ-
¹any- ²of ³you by [the]   –   of sin;   ¹shar-
one   deceit
οχοι γὰρ τοῦ Χριστοῦ γεγόναμεν, ἐάνπερ
ers   ¹for ³of ⁴Christ   ²we have   if indeed
      the   become,
τὴν ἀρχὴν τῆς ὑποστάσεως μέχρι τέλους
³the ⁴beginning of the ⁵assurance ²until ¹[the] end
βεβαίαν κατάσχωμεν. 15 ἐν τῷ λέγεσθαι·
⁶firm   ¹we hold fast.   In the   to be said·:
                          =While it is said:
σήμερον ἐὰν τῆς φωνῆς αὐτοῦ ἀκούσητε,
To-day   if   the   voice   of him ye hear,
μὴ σκληρύνητε τὰς καρδίας ὑμῶν ὡς
do not harden   the   hearts of you   as
ἐν τῷ παραπικρασμῷ. 16 τίνες γὰρ
in the   provocation.   For some
ἀκούσαντες παρεπίκραναν; ἀλλ' οὐ πάντες
hearing   provoked ?   yet   not   all
οἱ ἐξελθόντες ἐξ Αἰγύπτου διὰ
the [ones] coming out out of Egypt   through
Μωϋσέως; 17 τίσιν δὲ προσώχθισεν τεσ-
Moses ?   but with whom was he angry for-
σεράκοντα ἔτη; οὐχὶ τοῖς ἁμαρτήσασιν,
ty   years ? [was it] with the [ones] sinning,
                  not
ὧν τὰ κῶλα ἔπεσεν ἐν τῇ ἐρήμῳ;
of the corpses fell   in the   desert ?
whom
18 τίσιν δὲ ὤμοσεν μὴ εἰσελεύσεσθαι εἰς
and to whom sware he not   to enter   into
τὴν κατάπαυσιν αὐτοῦ εἰ μὴ τοῖς
the   rest   of him except   to the
ἀπειθήσασιν; 19 καὶ βλέπομεν ὅτι οὐκ
[ones] disobeying ? and we see   that not
ἠδυνήθησαν εἰσελθεῖν δι' ἀπιστίαν.
they were able to enter because of disbelief.

during the time of
  testing in the desert,
9where your fathers
  tested and tried me
  and for forty years saw
    what I did.
10That is why I was angry
  with that generation,
  and I said, 'Their
    hearts are always
    going astray,
  and they have not
    known my ways.'
11So I declared on oath in
    my anger,
  'They shall never enter
    my rest.'"ᵒ
12See to it, brothers, that
none of you has a sinful,
unbelieving heart that turns
away from the living God.
13But encourage one another daily, as long as it is
called Today, so that none
of you may be hardened by
sin's deceitfulness. 14We
have come to share in
Christ if we hold firmly till
the end the confidence we
had at first. 15As has just
been said:
  "Today, if you hear his
    voice,
  do not harden your
    hearts
  as you did in the
    rebellion."ᵖ
16Who were they who
heard and rebelled? Were
they not all those Moses led
out of Egypt? 17And with
whom was he angry for-
ty years? Was it not with
those who sinned, whose
bodies fell in the desert?
18And to whom did God
swear that they would never enter his rest if not to
those who disobeyedᵍ?
19So we see that they were
not able to enter, because
of their unbelief.

ᵒ11 Psalm 95:7-11
ᵖ15,7 Psalm 95:7,8
ᵍ18 Or disbelieved

Chapter 4

The Rest That God Promised

THEREFORE, while the promise of entering his rest is still open, let us take care that none of you should seem to have failed to reach it. 2 For indeed the good news came to us just as to them; but the message they heard did not benefit them, because they were not united by faith with those who listened. [u] 3 For we who have believed enter that rest, just as God [v] has said,

"As in my anger I
  swore,
'They shall not enter
  my rest,' "

though his works were finished at the foundation of the world. 4 For in one place it speaks about the seventh day as follows, "And God rested on the seventh day from all his works." 5 And again in this place it says, "They shall not enter my rest." 6 Since therefore it remains open for some to enter it, and those who formerly received the good news failed to enter because of disobedience, 7 again he sets a certain day—"today"—saying through David much later, in the words already quoted,

"Today, if you hear
  his voice,
do not harden your
  hearts."

8 For if Joshua had given them rest, God [v] would not speak later about another day. 9 So then, a sabbath rest still remains for the people of God; 10 for those who enter God's rest also cease from their labors as God did from his. 11 Let us

---

4 Φοβηθῶμεν οὖν μήποτε καταλειπομένης
Let us fear therefore lest [2]being left

ἐπαγγελίας εἰσελθεῖν εἰς τὴν κατάπαυσιν
[1]a promise[a] to enter into the rest

αὐτοῦ δοκῇ τις ἐξ ὑμῶν ὑστερηκέναι.
of him [4]seems [1]anyone [3]of [5]you to have come short.

2 καὶ γάρ ἐσμεν εὐηγγελισμένοι καθάπερ
For indeed we are having had good news even as
preached [to us]

κἀκεῖνοι· ἀλλ' οὐκ ὠφέλησεν ὁ λόγος
those also; but [4]did not profit [1]the [2]word

τῆς ἀκοῆς ἐκείνους μὴ συγκεκερασμένος
- [3]of hearing those not having been mixed
together

τῇ πίστει τοῖς ἀκούσασιν. **3** Εἰσερχόμεθα
- with faith in the [ones] hearing. we enter

γὰρ εἰς [τὴν] κατάπαυσιν οἱ πιστεύσαντες,
For into the rest the [ones] believing,

καθὼς εἴρηκεν· ὡς ὤμοσα ἐν τῇ ὀργῇ
as he has said: As I swore in the wrath

μου· εἰ εἰσελεύσονται εἰς τὴν κατάπαυσίν
of me: If they shall enter into the rest

μου, καίτοι τῶν ἔργων ἀπὸ καταβολῆς
of me, though the works [2]from [3][the] foundation

κόσμου γενηθέντων. **4** εἴρηκεν γάρ που
[4]of [the] [1]having come into For he has said some-
world being.[a] where

περὶ τῆς ἑβδόμης οὕτως· καὶ κατέπαυσεν
con- the seventh [day] thus: And [2]rested
cerning

ὁ θεὸς ἐν τῇ ἡμέρᾳ τῇ ἑβδόμῃ ἀπὸ
- [1]God in the [2]day the [3]seventh from

πάντων τῶν ἔργων αὐτοῦ· **5** καὶ ἐν
all the works of him; and in

τούτῳ πάλιν· εἰ εἰσελεύσονται εἰς τὴν
this [place] again: If they shall enter into the

κατάπαυσίν μου. **6** ἐπεὶ οὖν ἀπολείπεται
rest of me. Since therefore it remains

τινὰς εἰσελθεῖν εἰς αὐτήν, καὶ οἱ πρότερον
[for] to enter into it, and the formerly
some [ones]

εὐαγγελισθέντες οὐκ εἰσῆλθον δι' ἀπείθειαν,
having good news did not enter because of disobedience,
preached [to them]

7 πάλιν τινὰ ὁρίζει ἡμέραν, σήμερον, ἐν
again [a certain [1]he de- day, to-day, [2]in
fines

Δαυὶδ λέγων μετὰ τοσοῦτον χρόνον, καθὼς
[3]David [1]saying after such a time, as

προείρηται· σήμερον ἐὰν τῆς φωνῆς αὐτοῦ
he has To-day if the voice of him
previously said:

ἀκούσητε, μὴ σκληρύνητε τὰς καρδίας
ye hear, do not harden the hearts

ὑμῶν. **8** εἰ γὰρ αὐτοὺς Ἰησοῦς κατέπαυσεν,
of you. For if [3]them [1]Jesus(Joshua) [2]rested,

οὐκ ἂν περὶ ἄλλης ἐλάλει μετὰ ταῦτα
[2]not - [5]concerning [6]another [4]he [3]would [7]after [8]these
[1]have spoken things

ἡμέρας. **9** ἄρα ἀπολείπεται σαββατισμὸς
[7]day. Then [2]remains [1]a sabbath rest

τῷ λαῷ τοῦ θεοῦ. **10** ὁ γὰρ εἰσελθὼν
to the people - of God. For the [one] having
entered

εἰς τὴν κατάπαυσιν αὐτοῦ καὶ αὐτὸς
into the rest of him also [him]self

κατέπαυσεν ἀπὸ τῶν ἔργων αὐτοῦ,
rested from the works of him,

ὥσπερ ἀπὸ τῶν ἰδίων ὁ θεός. **11** Σπου-
as from the(his) own - God [did]. Let us

Chapter 4

A Sabbath-Rest for the People of God

THEREFORE, since the promise of entering his rest still stands, let us be careful that none of you be found to have fallen short of it. 2 For we also have had the gospel preached to us, just as they did; but the message they heard was of no value to them, because those who heard did not combine it with faith. [r] 3 Now we who have believed enter that rest, just as God has said,

"So I declared on oath
  in my anger,
'They shall never enter
  my rest.' " [s]

And yet his work has been finished since the creation of the world. 4 For somewhere he has spoken about the seventh day in these words: "And on the seventh day God rested from all his work." [t] 5 And again in the passage above he says, "They shall never enter my rest."

6 It still remains that some will enter that rest, and those who formerly had the gospel preached to them did not go in, because of their disobedience. 7 Therefore God again set a certain day, calling it Today, when a long time later he spoke through David, as was said before:

"Today, if you hear his
  voice,
do not harden your
  hearts." [p]

8 For if Joshua had given them rest, God would not have spoken later about another day. 9 There remains, then, a Sabbath-rest for the people of God; 10 for anyone who enters God's rest also rests from his own work, just as God did from his.

---

[u] Other ancient authorities read it did not meet with faith in those who listened
[v] Gk he

[r]2 Many manuscripts because they did not share in the faith of those who obeyed
[s]3 Psalm 95:11; also in verse 5
[t]4 Gen. 2:2

therefore make every effort to enter that rest, so that no one may fall through such disobedience as theirs.

12 Indeed, the word of God is living and active, sharper than any two-edged sword, piercing until it divides soul from spirit, joints from marrow; it is able to judge the thoughts and intentions of the heart. 13 And before him no creature is hidden, but all are naked and laid bare to the eyes of the one to whom we must render an account.

Jesus the Great High Priest

14 Since, then, we have a great high priest who has passed through the heavens, Jesus, the Son of God, let us hold fast to our confession. 15 For we do not have a high priest who is unable to sympathize with our weaknesses, but we have one who in every respect has been tested[w] as we are, yet without sin. 16 Let us therefore approach the throne of grace with boldness, so that we may receive mercy and find grace to help in time of need.

δάσωμεν οὖν εἰσελθεῖν εἰς ἐκείνην τὴν
be eager therefore to enter into that –

κατάπαυσιν, ἵνα μὴ ἐν τῷ αὐτῷ τις
rest, lest ³in ⁴the ⁵same ¹any-one

ὑποδείγματι πέσῃ τῆς ἀπειθείας. 12 Ζῶν
⁶example ²falls – of dis-obedience. [⁴is] ¹living

γὰρ ὁ λόγος τοῦ θεοῦ καὶ ἐνεργὴς
For ¹the ²word – ³of God and operative

καὶ τομώτερος ὑπὲρ πᾶσαν μάχαιραν
and sharper beyond every ⁵sword

δίστομον καὶ διϊκνούμενος ἄχρι μερισμοῦ
¹two-mouthed and passing through as far as division
(edged)

ψυχῆς καὶ πνεύματος, ἁρμῶν τε καὶ
of soul and of spirit, ⁵of joints ¹both and

μυελῶν, καὶ κριτικὸς ἐνθυμήσεων καὶ
of marrows, and able to judge of thoughts and

ἐννοιῶν καρδίας· 13 καὶ οὐκ ἔστιν κτίσις
intentions of a heart; and there is no creature

ἀφανὴς ἐνώπιον αὐτοῦ, πάντα δὲ γυμνὰ
unmanifest before him, but all things [are] naked

καὶ τετραχηλισμένα τοῖς ὀφθαλμοῖς αὐτοῦ,
and *having been* laid open to the eyes of him,

πρὸς ὃν ἡμῖν ὁ λόγος.⁰
with whom to us [is] the word(account).⁰
=is our account.

14 Ἔχοντες οὖν ἀρχιερέα μέγαν διεληλυ-
Having there- high priest a great having gone
fore

θότα τοὺς οὐρανούς, Ἰησοῦν τὸν υἱὸν
through the heavens, Jesus the Son

τοῦ θεοῦ, κρατῶμεν τῆς ὁμολογίας. 15 οὐ
– of God, let us hold the confession. ²not

γὰρ ἔχομεν ἀρχιερέα μὴ δυνάμενον
¹For ³we have a high priest not being able

συμπαθῆσαι ταῖς ἀσθενείαις ἡμῶν, πεπει-
to suffer with the weaknesses of us, ¹having

ρασμένον δὲ κατὰ πάντα καθ’ ὁμοιότητα
been tempted ¹but in all respects† accord- [our] likeness
ing to

χωρὶς ἁμαρτίας. 16 προσερχώμεθα οὖν
apart from sin. Let us approach therefore

μετὰ παρρησίας τῷ θρόνῳ τῆς χάριτος,
with confidence *to* the throne of grace,

ἵνα λάβωμεν ἔλεος καὶ χάριν εὕρωμεν
in or- we may mercy and ²grace *we* ¹may
der that receive find

εἰς εὔκαιρον βοήθειαν.
for timely help.

---

11 Let us, therefore, make every effort to enter that rest, so that no one will fall by following their example of disobedience.

12 For the word of God is living and active. Sharper than any double-edged sword, it penetrates even to dividing soul and spirit, joints and marrow; it judges the thoughts and attitudes of the heart. 13 Nothing in all creation is hidden from God's sight. Everything is uncovered and laid bare before the eyes of him to whom we must give account.

Jesus the Great High Priest

14 Therefore, since we have a great high priest who has gone through the heavens,[u] Jesus the Son of God, let us hold firmly to the faith we profess. 15 For we do not have a high priest who is unable to sympathize with our weaknesses, but we have one who has been tempted in every way, just as we are—yet was without sin. 16 Let us then approach the throne of grace with confidence, so that we may receive mercy and find grace to help us in our time of need.

Chapter 5

EVERY high priest chosen from among mortals is put in charge of things pertaining to God on their behalf, to offer gifts and sacrifices for sins. 2 He is able to deal gently with the ignorant and wayward, since he himself is subject to weakness; 3 and because

---

5 Πᾶς γὰρ ἀρχιερεὺς ἐξ ἀνθρώπων
For every high priest ³out of ⁴men

λαμβανόμενος ὑπὲρ ἀνθρώπων καθίσταται
¹being taken on behalf of men is appointed [in]

τὰ πρὸς τὸν θεόν, ἵνα προσφέρῃ δῶρά
the in re- – God, in order he may offer ²gifts
things gard to that

τε καὶ θυσίας ὑπὲρ ἁμαρτιῶν, 2 μετριο-
¹both and sacrifices on behalf of sins, ¹to feel in

παθεῖν δυνάμενος τοῖς ἀγνοοῦσιν καὶ
due measure ¹being able for the [ones] not knowing and

πλανωμένοις, ἐπεὶ καὶ αὐτὸς περίκειται
being led astray, since also he is set round
[with]

Chapter 5

EVERY high priest is selected from among men and is appointed to represent them in matters related to God, to offer gifts and sacrifices for sins. 2 He is able to deal gently with those who are ignorant and are going astray, since he himself is subject to weak-

---

ᵂ Or *tempted*

ᵘ14 Or *gone into heaven*

of this he must offer sacrifice for his own sins as well as for those of the people. 4 And one does not presume to take this honor, but takes it only when called by God, just as Aaron was.

5 So also Christ did not glorify himself in becoming a high priest, but was appointed by the one who said to him,

"You are my Son,
today I have
begotten you";

6 as he says also in another place,

"You are a priest
forever,
according to the
order of
Melchizedek."

7 In the days of his flesh, Jesus[v] offered up prayers and supplications, with loud cries and tears, to the one who was able to save him from death, and he was heard because of his reverent submission. 8 Although he was a Son, he learned obedience through what he suffered; 9 and having been made perfect, he became the source of eternal salvation for all who obey him, 10 having been designated by God a high priest according to the order of Melchizedek.

Warning against Falling Away

11 About this[x] we have much to say that is hard to explain, since you have become dull in understanding. 12 For though by this time you ought to be teachers, you need someone to teach you again the basic elements of the oracles of God. You need milk, not solid food; 13 for everyone

---

ἀσθένειαν, 3 καὶ δι' αὐτὴν ὀφείλει, καθὼς
weakness, and because it he ought, as
of

περὶ τοῦ λαοῦ, οὕτως καὶ περὶ ἑαυτοῦ
concern- the people, so also concerning himself
ing

προσφέρειν περὶ ἁμαρτιῶν. 4 καὶ οὐχ
to offer concerning sins. And not

ἑαυτῷ τις λαμβάνει τὴν τιμήν, ἀλλὰ
to him- anyone takes the honour, but
self

καλούμενος ὑπὸ τοῦ θεοῦ, καθώσπερ καὶ
being called by - God, even as indeed

Ἀαρών. 5 Οὕτως καὶ ὁ Χριστὸς οὐχ
Aaron. So also - Christ not

ἑαυτὸν ἐδόξασεν γενηθῆναι ἀρχιερέα, ἀλλ'
himself glorified to become a high priest, but

ὁ λαλήσας πρὸς αὐτόν· υἱός μου εἶ
the [one] speaking to him: Son of me art

σύ, ἐγὼ σήμερον γεγέννηκά σε· 6 καθὼς
thou, I to-day have begotten thee; as

καὶ ἐν ἑτέρῳ λέγει· σὺ ἱερεὺς εἰς τὸν
also in another he says: Thou a priest unto the
[psalm] [art]

αἰῶνα κατὰ τὴν τάξιν Μελχισέδεκ. 7 ὃς
age according the order of Melchisedec. Who
to

ἐν ταῖς ἡμέραις τῆς σαρκὸς αὐτοῦ δεήσεις
in the days of the flesh of him petitions

τε καὶ ἱκετηρίας πρὸς τὸν δυνάμενον
both and entreaties to the [one] being able

σῴζειν αὐτὸν ἐκ θανάτου μετὰ κραυγῆς
to save him out of death with crying

ἰσχυρᾶς καὶ δακρύων προσενέγκας καὶ
strong and tears offering and

εἰσακουσθεὶς ἀπὸ τῆς εὐλαβείας, 8 καίπερ
being heard from(for) the(his) devoutness, though

ὢν υἱός, ἔμαθεν ἀφ' ὧν ἔπαθεν τὴν
being a Son, he from [the] he suffered –
learned things which

ὑπακοήν, 9 καὶ τελειωθεὶς ἐγένετο πᾶσιν
obedience, and being perfected he became to all

τοῖς ὑπακούουσιν αὐτῷ αἴτιος σωτηρίας
the [ones] obeying him [the] cause salvation

αἰωνίου, 10 προσαγορευθεὶς ὑπὸ τοῦ θεοῦ
of eternal, being designated by - God

ἀρχιερεὺς κατὰ τὴν τάξιν Μελχισέδεκ.
a high priest accord- the order of Melchisedec.
ing to

11 Περὶ οὗ πολὺς ἡμῖν ὁ λόγος καὶ
Concern- whom much to us the word and
ing =we have much to say and hard ...

δυσερμήνευτος λέγειν, ἐπεὶ νωθροὶ γεγόνατε
hard to interpret to say, since dull ye have
become

ταῖς ἀκοαῖς. 12 καὶ γὰρ ὀφείλοντες
in the hearings. For indeed owing

εἶναι διδάσκαλοι διὰ τὸν χρόνον, πάλιν
to be teachers because of the time, again

χρείαν ἔχετε τοῦ διδάσκειν ὑμᾶς τινα
need ye have - to teach you someone

τὰ στοιχεῖα τῆς ἀρχῆς τῶν λογίων
the rudiments of the beginning of the oracles

τοῦ θεοῦ, καὶ γεγόνατε χρείαν ἔχοντες
of God, and ye have become need having

γάλακτος, οὐ στερεᾶς τροφῆς. 13 πᾶς
of milk, not of solid food. every

God's word all over again. You need milk, not solid ness. 3 This is why he has to offer sacrifices for his own sins, as well as for the sins of the people.

4 No one takes this honor upon himself; he must be called by God, just as Aaron was. 5 So Christ also did not take upon himself the glory of becoming a high priest. But God said to him,

"You are my Son;
today I have become
your Father." v w

6 And he says in another place,

"You are a priest
forever,
in the order of
Melchizedek." x

7 During the days of Jesus' life on earth, he offered up prayers and petitions with loud cries and tears to the one who could save him from death, and he was heard because of his reverent submission. 8 Although he was a son, he learned obedience from what he suffered 9 and, once made perfect, he became the source of eternal salvation for all who obey him 10 and was designated by God to be high priest in the order of Melchizedek.

Warning Against Falling Away

11 We have much to say about this, but it is hard to explain because you are slow to learn. 12 In fact, though by this time you ought to be teachers, you need someone to teach you the elementary truths of

---

x Or him

* That is, " ye ought ... "

v 5 Or have begotten you
w 5 Psalm 2:7
x 6 Psalm 110:4

who lives on milk, being still an infant, is unskilled in the word of righteousness. 14 But solid food is for the mature, for those whose faculties have been trained by practice to distinguish good from evil.

Chapter 6
The Peril of Falling Away

THEREFORE let us go on toward perfection,^y leaving behind the basic teaching about Christ, and not laying again the foundation: repentance from dead works and faith toward God, 2 instruction about baptisms, laying on of hands, resurrection of the dead, and eternal judgment. 3 And we will do^z this, if God permits. 4 For it is impossible to restore again to repentance those who have once been enlightened, and have tasted the heavenly gift, and have shared in the Holy Spirit, 5 and have tasted the goodness of the word of God and the powers of the age to come, 6 and then have fallen away, since on their own they are crucifying again the Son of God and are holding him up to contempt. 7 Ground that drinks up the rain falling on it repeatedly, and that produces a crop useful to those for whom it is cultivated, receives a blessing from God. 8 But if it produces thorns and thistles, it is worthless and on the verge of being cursed; its end is to be burned over.

9 Even though we speak in this way, beloved, we are confident of better things in your case, things that belong to salvation. 10 For God is not unjust; he

---

γὰρ ὁ μετέχων γάλακτος ἄπειρος λόγου
For one partaking of milk [is] without of [the] experience word

δικαιοσύνης, νήπιος γάρ ἐστιν· 14 τελείων δέ
of righteousness, for ²an infant ¹he is; but ⁴of mature men

ἐστιν ἡ στερεὰ τροφή, τῶν διὰ τὴν
²is the ¹solid ³food, of the because the(ir) [ones] of

ἕξιν τὰ αἰσθητήρια γεγυμνασμένα ἐχόντων
con-dition ²the(ir) ³faculties having been ⁴exercised ¹having

πρὸς διάκρισιν καλοῦ τε καὶ κακοῦ.
for distinction ²of good ¹both and of bad.

6 Διὸ ἀφέντες τὸν τῆς ἀρχῆς τοῦ Χριστοῦ
Wherefore leaving ¹the ²of the ⁴beginning - ³of Christ

λόγον ἐπὶ τὴν τελειότητα φερώμεθα, μὴ
²word ⁷on to - ³maturity ¹let us be borne, not

πάλιν θεμέλιον καταβαλλόμενοι μετανοίας
again ²a foundation ¹laying down of repentance

ἀπὸ νεκρῶν ἔργων, καὶ πίστεως ἐπὶ
from dead works, and of faith toward

θεόν, 2 βαπτισμῶν διδαχῆς, ἐπιθέσεώς τε
God, ²of baptisms ¹of teaching, and of laying on

χειρῶν, ἀναστάσεως νεκρῶν, καὶ κρίματος
of hands, of resurrection of dead persons, and ²judgment

αἰωνίου. 3 καὶ τοῦτο ποιήσομεν, ἐάνπερ
¹of eternal. And this we will do, if indeed

ἐπιτρέπῃ ὁ θεός. 4 Ἀδύνατον γὰρ τοὺς
²permits - ¹God. For [it is] impossible the [for] [ones]

ἅπαξ φωτισθέντας γευσαμένους τε τῆς
once being enlightened and tasting of the

δωρεᾶς τῆς ἐπουρανίου καὶ μετόχους
²gift - ¹heavenly and sharers

γενηθέντας πνεύματος ἁγίου 5 καὶ καλὸν
becoming Spirit of [the] Holy and ²[the] good

γευσαμένους θεοῦ ῥῆμα δυνάμεις τε
¹tasting ⁴of God ³word and powerful deeds

μέλλοντος αἰῶνος, 6 καὶ παραπεσόντας, πάλιν
of a coming age, and falling away, again

ἀνακαινίζειν εἰς μετάνοιαν, ἀνασταυροῦντας
to renew to repentance, crucifying again

ἑαυτοῖς τὸν υἱὸν τοῦ θεοῦ καὶ παρα-
for them-selves the Son - of God and putting

δειγματίζοντας. 7 γῆ γὰρ ἡ πιοῦσα
[him] to open shame. For earth - drinking

τὸν ἐπ' αὐτῆς ἐρχόμενον πολλάκις ὑετὸν
¹the ²upon ³it ²coming ⁴often ¹rain

καὶ τίκτουσα βοτάνην εὔθετον ἐκείνοις
and bearing fodder suitable for those

δι' οὓς καὶ γεωργεῖται, μεταλαμβάνει
on ac-count of whom indeed it is farmed, receives

εὐλογίας ἀπὸ τοῦ θεοῦ· 8 ἐκφέρουσα δὲ
blessing from - God; but bringing forth

ἀκάνθας καὶ τριβόλους ἀδόκιμος καὶ
thorns and thistles [it is] disapproved and

κατάρας ἐγγύς, ἧς τὸ τέλος εἰς καῦσιν.
²a curse ¹near, of which the end [is] for burning.

9 Πεπείσμεθα δὲ περὶ ὑμῶν, ἀγαπητοί,
But we have been persuaded concerning you, beloved,

τὰ κρείσσονα καὶ ἐχόμενα σωτηρίας, εἰ
the better things and having salvation, if

καὶ οὕτως λαλοῦμεν. 10 οὐ γὰρ ἄδικος
indeed ²so ¹we speak. For ²not ²unjust

---

food! 13 Anyone who lives on milk, being still an infant, is not acquainted with the teaching about righteousness. 14 But solid food is for the mature, who by constant use have trained themselves to distinguish good from evil.

Chapter 6

THEREFORE let us leave the elementary teachings about Christ and go on to maturity, not laying again the foundation of repentance from acts that lead to death,^y and of faith in God, 2 instruction about baptisms, the laying on of hands, the resurrection of the dead, and eternal judgment. 3 And God permitting, we will do so. 4 It is impossible for those who have once been enlightened, who have tasted the heavenly gift, who have shared in the Holy Spirit, 5 who have tasted the goodness of the word of God and the powers of the coming age, 6 if they fall away, to be brought back to repentance, because^z to their loss they are crucifying the Son of God all over again and subjecting him to public disgrace. 7 Land that drinks in the rain often falling on it and that produces a crop useful to those for whom it is farmed receives the blessing of God. 8 But land that produces thorns and thistles is worthless and is in danger of being cursed. In the end it will be burned. 9 Even though we speak like this, dear friends, we are confident of better things in your case—things that accompany salvation. 10 God is not unjust; he will

---

y Or toward maturity
z Other ancient authorities read let us do

y 1 Or from useless rituals
z 6 Or repentance while

will not overlook your work and the love that you showed for his sake*a* in serving the saints, as you still do. 11And we want each one of you to show the same diligence so as to realize the full assurance of hope to the very end, 12so that you may not become sluggish, but imitators of those who through faith and patience inherit the promises.

The Certainty of God's Promise

13 When God made a promise to Abraham, because he had no one greater by whom to swear, he swore by himself, "I will surely bless you and multiply you." 15And thus Abraham,*b* having patiently endured, obtained the promise. 16Human beings, of course, swear by someone greater than themselves, and an oath given as confirmation puts an end to all dispute. 17In the same way, when God desired to show even more clearly to the heirs of the promise the unchangeable character of his purpose, he guaranteed it by an oath, 18so that through two unchangeable things, in which it is impossible that God would prove false, we who have taken refuge might be strongly encouraged to seize the hope set before us. 19We have this hope, a sure and steadfast anchor of the soul, a hope that enters the inner shrine behind the curtain, 20where Jesus, a forerunner on our behalf, has entered, having become a high priest forever according to the order of Melchizedek.

ὁ θεὸς ἐπιλαθέσθαι τοῦ ἔργου ὑμῶν
– ¹God [is] to be forgetful of the work of you

καὶ τῆς ἀγάπης ἧς ἐνεδείξασθε εἰς τὸ
and of the love which ye showed to the

ὄνομα αὐτοῦ, διακονήσαντες τοῖς ἁγίοις
name of him, having ministered to the saints

καὶ διακονοῦντες. 11 ἐπιθυμοῦμεν δὲ
and ministering. But we desire

ἕκαστον ὑμῶν τὴν αὐτὴν ἐνδείκνυσθαι
each of you ²the ³same ¹to show

σπουδὴν πρὸς τὴν πληροφορίαν τῆς ἐλπίδος
eagerness to the full assurance of *the* hope

ἄχρι τέλους, 12 ἵνα μὴ νωθροὶ γένησθε,
unto [the] end, lest dull ye become,

μιμηταὶ δὲ τῶν διὰ πίστεως καὶ μακρο-
but imitators of the through faith and long-
[ones]

θυμίας κληρονομούντων τὰς ἐπαγγελίας.
suffering inheriting the promises.

13 Τῷ γὰρ Ἀβραὰμ ἐπαγγειλάμενος ὁ
– For to Abraham ¹making promise –

θεός, ἐπεὶ κατ᾽ οὐδενὸς εἶχεν μείζονος
¹God, since ²by ³no one ¹he had ⁴greater

ὀμόσαι, ὤμοσεν καθ᾽ ἑαυτοῦ, 14 λέγων·
to swear, swore by himself, saying:

εἰ μὴν εὐλογῶν εὐλογήσω σε καὶ πληθύνων
If surely blessing I will bless thee and multiplying

πληθυνῶ σε· 15 καὶ οὕτως μακροθυμήσας
I will multiply thee; and so being longsuffering

ἐπέτυχεν τῆς ἐπαγγελίας. 16 ἄνθρωποι γὰρ
he obtained the promise. For men

κατὰ τοῦ μείζονος ὀμνύουσιν, καὶ πάσης
by the greater swear, and ⁹of all

αὐτοῖς ἀντιλογίας πέρας εἰς βεβαίωσιν ὁ
³[is] ⁴to ⁷contradiction ⁵an end ⁸for ⁹confirmation ¹the
them

ὅρκος· 17 ἐν ᾧ περισσότερον βουλόμενος
²oath; wherein ³more abundantly ²resolving

ὁ θεὸς ἐπιδεῖξαι τοῖς κληρονόμοις τῆς
– ¹God to show to the heirs of the

ἐπαγγελίας τὸ ἀμετάθετον τῆς βουλῆς
promise the unchangeableness of the resolve

αὐτοῦ ἐμεσίτευσεν ὅρκῳ, 18 ἵνα διὰ
of him interposed by an in or- through
oath, der that

δύο πραγμάτων ἀμεταθέτων, ἐν οἷς ἀδύνατον
two ²things ¹unchangeable, in which impossible
[it was]

ψεύσασθαι θεόν, ἰσχυρὰν παράκλησιν ἔχωμεν
²to lie ¹God,*b* ²a strong ³consolation ¹we may
have[,]

οἱ καταφυγόντες κρατῆσαι τῆς προκειμένης
the [ones] having fled to lay hold of the ²set before [us]

ἐλπίδος· 19 ἣν ὡς ἄγκυραν ἔχομεν τῆς
¹hope; which as an anchor we have of the

ψυχῆς ἀσφαλῆ τε καὶ βεβαίαν καὶ
soul ²safe ¹both and firm and

εἰσερχομένην εἰς τὸ ἐσώτερον τοῦ κατα-
entering into the inner [side] of the veil,

πετάσματος, 20 ὅπου πρόδρομος ὑπὲρ ἡμῶν
where a forerunner on us
behalf of

εἰσῆλθεν Ἰησοῦς, κατὰ τὴν τάξιν Μελχισέ-
entered[,] Jesus, ²according ¹the ³order ⁴of Melchise-
to

δεκ ἀρχιερεὺς γενόμενος εἰς τὸν αἰῶνα.
dec ²a high priest ¹becoming ²unto ³the ⁴age.

---

not forget your work and the love you have shown him as you have helped his people and continue to help them. 11We want each of you to show this same diligence to the very end, in order to make your hope sure. 12We do not want you to become lazy, but to imitate those who through faith and patience inherit what has been promised.

The Certainty of God's Promise

13When God made his promise to Abraham, since there was no one greater for him to swear by, he swore by himself, 14saying, "I will surely bless you and give you many descendants."*a* 15And so after waiting patiently, Abraham received what was promised.

16Men swear by someone greater than themselves, and the oath confirms what is said and puts an end to all argument. 17Because God wanted to make the unchanging nature of his purpose very clear to the heirs of what was promised, he confirmed it with an oath. 18God did this so that, by two unchangeable things in which it is impossible for God to lie, we who have fled to take hold of the hope offered to us may be greatly encouraged. 19We have this hope as an anchor for the soul, firm and secure. It enters the inner sanctuary behind the curtain, 20where Jesus, who went before us, has entered on our behalf. He has become a high priest forever, in the order of Melchizedek.

---

a Gk *for his name*
b Gk *he*

*a*14 Gen. 22:17

Chapter 7

The Priestly Order of Melchizedek

THIS "King Melchizedek of Salem, priest of the Most High God, met Abraham as he was returning from defeating the kings and blessed him"; 2 and to him Abraham apportioned "one-tenth of everything." His name, in the first place, means "king of righteousness"; next he is also king of Salem, that is, "king of peace." 3 Without father, without mother, without genealogy, having neither beginning of days nor end of life, but resembling the Son of God, he remains a priest forever.

4 See how great he is! Even[c] Abraham the patriarch gave him a tenth of the spoils. 5 And those descendants of Levi who receive the priestly office have a commandment in the law to collect tithes[d] from the people, that is, from their kindred,[e] though these also are descended from Abraham. 6 But this man, who does not belong to their ancestry, collected tithes[d] from Abraham and blessed him who had received the promises. 7 It is beyond dispute that the inferior is blessed by the superior. 8 In the one case, tithes are received by those who are mortal; in the other, by one of whom it is testified that he lives. 9 One might even say that Levi himself, who receives tithes, paid tithes through Abraham, 10 for he was still in the loins of his ancestor

[c] Other ancient authorities lack *Even*
[d] Or *a tenth*
[e] Gk *brothers*

---

7 Οὗτος γὰρ ὁ Μελχισέδεκ, βασιλεὺς
For this - Melchisedec, king

Σαλήμ, ἱερεὺς τοῦ θεοῦ τοῦ ὑψίστου,
of Salem, priest - ²God ¹of the ¹most high,

ὁ συναντήσας 'Αβραὰμ ὑποστρέφοντι ἀπὸ
the [one] meeting Abraham returning from

τῆς κοπῆς τῶν βασιλέων καὶ εὐλογήσας
the slaughter of the kings and blessing

αὐτόν, **2** ᾧ καὶ δεκάτην ἀπὸ πάντων
him, to whom indeed ²a tenth ⁴from ⁸all

ἐμέρισεν 'Αβραάμ, πρῶτον μὲν ἑρμηνευ-
³divided ¹Abraham, firstly on one being inter-
hand

ομενος βασιλεὺς δικαιοσύνης, ἔπειτα δὲ καὶ
preted King of righteousness, then on the also
other

βασιλεὺς Σαλήμ, ὅ ἐστιν βασιλεὺς εἰρήνης,
King of Salem, which is King of peace,

3 ἀπάτωρ, ἀμήτωρ, ἀγενεαλόγητος, μήτε
without father, without mother, without pedigree, ²neither

ἀρχὴν ἡμερῶν μήτε ζωῆς τέλος ἔχων,
¹beginning ⁴of days ³nor ⁷of life ⁶end ¹having,

ἀφωμοιωμένος δὲ τῷ υἱῷ τοῦ θεοῦ, μένει
but having been made to the Son - of God, remains
like

ἱερεὺς εἰς τὸ διηνεκές. **4** Θεωρεῖτε δὲ
a priest in the perpetuity. Now behold ye

πηλίκος οὗτος, ᾧ δεκάτην 'Αβραὰμ
how great this man to whom ⁵a tenth ²Abraham
[was],

ἔδωκεν ἐκ τῶν ἀκροθινίων ὁ πατριάρχης.
⁴gave ⁶of ⁷the ⁵spoils ¹the ³patriarch.

5 καὶ οἱ μὲν ἐκ τῶν υἱῶν Λευὶ τὴν
And ³the ¹on one ⁸of ⁴the ⁵sons ⁶of Levi ⁸the
[ones] hand

ἱερατείαν λαμβάνοντες ἐντολὴν ἔχουσιν
⁹priesthood ⁷receiving ¹¹a commandment ¹⁰have

ἀποδεκατοῦν τὸν λαὸν κατὰ τὸν νόμον,
to take tithes the people accord- the law,
from ing to

τοῦτ' ἔστιν τοὺς ἀδελφοὺς αὐτῶν, καίπερ
this is the brothers of them, though

ἐξεληλυθότας ἐκ τῆς ὀσφύος 'Αβραάμ·
having come forth out of the loin[s] of Abraham;

6 ὁ δὲ μὴ γενεαλογούμενος ἐξ αὐτῶν
²the ¹on the not counting [his] pedigree from them
[one] other

δεδεκάτωκεν 'Αβραάμ, καὶ τὸν ἔχοντα
has tithed Abraham, and ²the [one] ³having

τὰς ἐπαγγελίας εὐλόγηκεν. **7** χωρὶς δὲ
⁴the ⁵promises ¹has blessed. And without

πάσης ἀντιλογίας τὸ ἔλαττον ὑπὸ τοῦ
all(any) contradiction the less ²by ³the

κρείττονος εὐλογεῖται. **8** καὶ ὧδε μὲν
⁴better ¹is blessed. And here on one
hand

δεκάτας ἀποθνῄσκοντες ἄνθρωποι λαμβά-
⁴tithes ¹dying ²men ³re-

νουσιν, ἐκεῖ δὲ μαρτυρούμενος ὅτι ζῇ.
ceive, there on the being witnessed that lives.
other

9 καὶ ὡς ἔπος εἰπεῖν, δι' 'Αβραὰμ
And as a word to say, through Abraham
=so to speak,

καὶ Λευὶς ὁ δεκάτας λαμβάνων δεδε-
indeed Levi ¹the [one] ³tithes ²receiving has

κάτωται· **10** ἔτι γὰρ ἐν τῇ ὀσφύϊ τοῦ
been tithed; for ³yet ³in ⁴the ⁵loin[s] ¹of
the(his)

Chapter 7

Melchizedek the Priest

THIS Melchizedek was king of Salem and priest of God Most High. He met Abraham returning from the defeat of the kings and blessed him, 2 and Abraham gave him a tenth of everything. First, his name means "king of righteousness"; then also, "king of Salem" means "king of peace." 3 Without father or mother, without genealogy, without beginning of days or end of life, like the Son of God he remains a priest forever.

4 Just think how great he was: Even the patriarch Abraham gave him a tenth of the plunder! 5 Now the law requires the descendants of Levi who become priests to collect a tenth from the people—that is, their brothers—even though their brothers are descended from Abraham. 6 This man, however, did not trace his descent from Levi, yet he collected a tenth from Abraham and blessed him who had the promises. 7 And without doubt the lesser person is blessed by the greater. 8 In the one case, the tenth is collected by men who die; but in the other case, by him who is declared to be living. 9 One might even say that Levi, who collects the tenth, paid the tenth through Abraham, 10 because when Melchizedek

when Melchizedek met him.

Another Priest, Like Melchizedek

11 Now if perfection had been attainable through the levitical priesthood—for the people received the law under this priesthood—what further need would there have been to speak of another priest arising according to the order of Melchizedek, rather than one according to the order of Aaron? 12 For when there is a change in the priesthood, there is necessarily a change in the law as well. 13 Now the one of whom these things are spoken belonged to another tribe, from which no one has ever served at the altar. 14 For it is evident that our Lord was descended from Judah, and in connection with that tribe Moses said nothing about priests.

15 It is even more obvious when another priest arises, resembling Melchizedek, 16 one who has become a priest, not through a legal requirement concerning physical descent, but through the power of an indestructible life. 17 For it is attested of him,

"You are a priest forever, according to the order of Melchizedek."

18 There is, on the one hand, the abrogation of an earlier commandment because it was weak and ineffectual 19 (for the law made nothing perfect); there is, on the other hand, the introduction of a better hope, through which we approach God. 20 This was confirmed with an oath; for others who became priests took their office without an oath, 21 but this one became a priest with an oath, be-

πατρὸς ἦν ὅτε συνήντησεν αὐτῷ Μελχισέ-
⁷father ¹he was ⁸when ¹⁰met ¹¹him ⁹Melchise-

δεκ. 11 Εἰ μὲν οὖν τελείωσις διὰ τῆς
dec. If – therefore perfection ²through ⁴the

Λευιτικῆς ἱερωσύνῃς ἦν, ὁ λαὸς γὰρ
⁴Levitical ³priestly office ¹was, ⁴the ⁵people ¹for

ἐπ' αὐτῆς νενομοθέτηται, τίς ἔτι χρεία
³under* ⁶it has been furnished why yet need

κατὰ τὴν τάξιν Μελχισέδεκ ἕτερον
[was there ⁵the ⁶order ⁷of Melchisedec ¹another
for] ⁴accord-
ing to

ἀνίστασθαι ἱερέα καὶ οὐ κατὰ τὴν τάξιν
²to arise ²priest and not ²accord- ³the ⁴order
ing to

'Ααρὼν λέγεσθαι; 12 μετατιθεμένης γὰρ
¹of Aaron ¹to be said(named)? for ²being changed ³

τῆς ἱερωσύνης ἐξ ἀνάγκης καὶ νόμου
¹the ²priestly office³ ⁵of ⁷necessity ⁵also ⁹of law

μετάθεσις γίνεται. 13 ἐφ' ὃν γὰρ λέγεται
³a change ⁴there ²[he] ³with ⁴whom ¹For ⁶is(are) said
respect to

ταῦτα, φυλῆς ἑτέρας μετέσχηκεν, ἀφ'
⁸these things, ⁹tribe ⁹of another ¹has partaken, from

ἧς οὐδεὶς προσέσχηκεν τῷ θυσιαστηρίῳ·
which no one has devoted himself to the altar;

14 πρόδηλον γὰρ ὅτι ἐξ 'Ιούδα ἀνατέταλκεν
for it is perfectly clear that out of Juda has risen

ὁ κύριος ἡμῶν, εἰς ἣν φυλὴν περὶ ἱερέων
the Lord of us, as to which tribe concerning priests

οὐδὲν Μωϋσῆς ἐλάλησεν. 15 καὶ περισ-
²nothing ¹Moses ³spoke. And more

σότερον ἔτι κατάδηλόν ἐστιν, εἰ κατὰ
abundantly still quite clear is it, if according to

τὴν ὁμοιότητα Μελχισέδεκ ἀνίσταται ἱερεὺς
the likeness of Melchisedec arises priest

ἕτερος, 16 ὃς οὐ κατὰ νόμον ἐντολῆς
another, who not accord- [the] law ³command-
ing to ment

σαρκίνης γέγονεν ἀλλὰ κατὰ δύναμιν ζωῆς
¹of a fleshy has become but accord- [the] power life
ing to

ἀκαταλύτου. 17 μαρτυρεῖται γὰρ ὅτι σὺ
of an indissoluble. For it is witnessed that Thou

ἱερεὺς εἰς τὸν αἰῶνα κατὰ τὴν τάξιν
a priest unto the age according to the order

Μελχισέδεκ. 18 ἀθέτησις μὲν γὰρ γίνεται
of Melchisedec. ⁴an annul- ²on one ¹For ³there
ment hand comes about

προαγούσης ἐντολῆς διὰ τὸ αὐτῆς ἀσθενὲς
of [the] command- because ¹the ⁵of it ²weak[ness]
preceding ment of

καὶ ἀνωφελές, 19 οὐδὲν γὰρ ἐτελείωσεν
²and ⁴unprofitable[ness], for ⁴nothing ³perfected

ὁ νόμος, ἐπεισαγωγὴ δὲ κρείττονος ἐλπίδος,
¹the ²law, ²a bringing in ¹on the of a better hope,
other

δι' ἧς ἐγγίζομεν τῷ θεῷ. 20 καὶ καθ'
through we draw near – to God. And in pro-
which

ὅσον οὐ χωρὶς ὀρκωμοσίας, — οἱ μὲν
portion not without oath-taking, ³the⁴on one
as (they) hand

γὰρ χωρὶς ὀρκωμοσίας εἰσὶν ἱερεῖς
¹for ⁷without ⁶oath-taking ⁴are ⁵priests

met Abraham, Levi was still in the body of his ancestor.

Jesus Like Melchizedek

11 If perfection could have been attained through the Levitical priesthood (for on the basis of it the law was given to the people), why was there still need for another priest to come—one in the order of Melchizedek, not in the order of Aaron? 12 For when there is a change of the priesthood, there must also be a change of the law. 13 He of whom these things are said belonged to a different tribe, and no one from that tribe has ever served at the altar. 14 For it is clear that our Lord descended from Judah, and in regard to that tribe Moses said nothing about priests. 15 And what we have said is even more clear if another priest like Melchizedek appears, 16 one who has become a priest not on the basis of a regulation as to his ancestry but on the basis of the power of an indestructible life. 17 For it is declared:

"You are a priest forever, in the order of Melchizedek."ᵇ

18 The former regulation is set aside because it was weak and useless 19 (for the law made nothing perfect), and a better hope is introduced, by which we draw near to God. 20 And it was not without an oath! Others became priests without any oath,

---

* See note on ch. 9. 15.

ᵇ17,21 Psalm 110:4

cause of the one who said to him,

"The Lord has sworn and will not change his mind.

'You are a priest forever' "—

22 accordingly Jesus has also become the guarantee of a better covenant.

23 Furthermore, the former priests were many in number, because they were prevented by death from continuing in office; 24 but he holds his priesthood permanently, because he continues forever. 25 Consequently he is able for all time to save[f] those who approach God through him, since he always lives to make intercession for them.

26 For it was fitting that we should have such a high priest, holy, blameless, undefiled, separated from sinners, and exalted above the heavens. 27 Unlike the other[g] high priests, he has no need to offer sacrifices day after day, first for his own sins, and then for those of the people; this he did once for all when he offered himself. 28 For the law appoints as high priests those who are subject to weakness, but the word of the oath, which came later than the law, appoints a Son who has been made perfect forever.

γεγονότες,   21 ὁ   δὲ   μετὰ   ὁρκωμοσίας   διὰ
⁵having   the on the with   oath-taking   through
become,   (he) other

τοῦ   λέγοντος   πρὸς   αὐτόν·   ὤμοσεν   κύριος,
the [one] saying   to   him: swore   [The] Lord,

καὶ   οὐ   μεταμεληθήσεται·   σὺ   ἱερεὺς   εἰς
and   will not change [his] mind: Thou [art] a priest   unto

τὸν   αἰῶνα·   —   22 κατὰ   τοσοῦτο   καὶ
the   age;)   by   so much   indeed

κρείττονος   διαθήκης   γέγονεν   ἔγγυος   Ἰησοῦς.
⁵of a better   ⁶covenant   ¹has become ²surety   ¹Jesus.

23 καὶ   οἱ   μὲν   πλείονές   εἰσιν   γεγονότες
And   the on one ²many   ¹are   ³having become
        (they) hand

ἱερεῖς   διὰ   τὸ   θανάτῳ   κωλύεσθαι   παραμέ-
⁴priests because the ²by death ¹to be prevented ³to con-
         of   = being prevented by death from. continuing;

νειν·   24 ὁ   δὲ   διὰ   τὸ   μένειν   αὐτὸν   εἰς
tinue;   the on the because the to remain   him[b]   unto
           (he) other of

τὸν   αἰῶνα   ἀπαράβατον   ἔχει   τὴν   ἱερωσύνην·
the   age   ⁴intransmissible ¹has ²the   ³priestly office;
                                        = because he remains

25 ὅθεν   καὶ   σῴζειν   εἰς   τὸ   παντελὲς
whence   indeed ¹to save   ²to   ³the   ⁵entire
                                  = entirely

δύναται   τοὺς   προσερχομένους   δι'   αὐτοῦ
¹he is able the [ones] ¹approaching   ²through ⁴him

τῷ   θεῷ,   πάντοτε   ζῶν   εἰς   τὸ   ἐντυγχάνειν
-   ⁴to God, always   living for the to intercede

ὑπὲρ   αὐτῶν.   26 τοιοῦτος   γὰρ   ἡμῖν   καὶ
on be- them.   For ³such   ⁴to us ²indeed
half of

ἔπρεπεν   ἀρχιερεύς,   ὅσιος,   ἄκακος,   ἀμίαντος,
¹was   ²a high priest, holy,   harmless,   undefiled,
suitable

κεχωρισμένος   ἀπὸ   τῶν   ἁμαρτωλῶν,   καὶ
having been   from   -   sinners,   and
separated

ὑψηλότερος   τῶν   οὐρανῶν   γενόμενος·   27 ὃς
higher [than] the   heavens   becoming;   who

οὐκ   ἔχει   καθ'   ἡμέραν   ἀνάγκην,   ὥσπερ
has not   ³daily   ¹necessity,   as

οἱ   ἀρχιερεῖς,   πρότερον   ὑπὲρ   τῶν   ἰδίων
the high priests, firstly   on behalf of the(his) own

ἁμαρτιῶν   θυσίας   ἀναφέρειν,   ἔπειτα   τῶν
sins   sacrifices   to offer up,   then   the [sins]

τοῦ   λαοῦ·   τοῦτο   γὰρ   ἐποίησεν   ἐφάπαξ
of the people;   for this   he did   once for all

ἑαυτὸν   ἀνενέγκας.   28 ὁ   νόμος   γὰρ
himself   offering up.   For the law

ἀνθρώπους   καθίστησιν   ἀρχιερεῖς   ἔχοντας
²men   ¹appoints   ⁵high priests   ³having

ἀσθένειαν,   ὁ   λόγος   δὲ   τῆς   ὁρκωμοσίας
⁴weakness,   but the word   of the   oath-taking

τῆς   μετὰ   τὸν   νόμον   υἱὸν   εἰς   τὸν   αἰῶνα
-     after   the   law   a Son ²unto ³the ⁴age
                             [appoints]

τετελειωμένον.
¹having been perfected.

21 but he became a priest with an oath when God said to him:

"The Lord has sworn and will not change his mind:

'You are a priest forever.' "[b]

22 Because of this oath, Jesus has become the guarantee of a better covenant.

23 Now there have been many of those priests, since death prevented them from continuing in office; 24 but because Jesus lives forever, he has a permanent priesthood. 25 Therefore he is able to save completely[c] those who come to God through him, because he always lives to intercede for them.

26 Such a high priest meets our need—one who is holy, blameless, pure, set apart from sinners, exalted above the heavens. 27 Unlike the other high priests, he does not need to offer sacrifices day after day, first for his own sins, and then for the sins of the people. He sacrificed for their sins once for all when he offered himself. 28 For the law appoints as high priests men who are weak; but the oath, which came after the law, appointed the Son, who has been made perfect forever.

Chapter 8

Mediator of a Better Covenant

NOW the main point in what we are saying is this: we have such a high priest, one who is seated at the right hand of the throne of the Majesty in the heav-

8 Κεφάλαιον   δὲ   ἐπὶ   τοῖς   λεγομένοις,
Now a summary   over(of) the things   being said,

τοιοῦτον   ἔχομεν   ἀρχιερέα,   ὃς   ἐκάθισεν
³such   ¹we have   a high priest,   who   sat

ἐν   δεξιᾷ   τοῦ   θρόνου   τῆς   μεγαλωσύνης
at [the] right   of the   throne   of the   greatness

Chapter 8

The High Priest of a New Covenant

THE point of what we are saying is this: We do have such a high priest, who sat down at the right hand of the throne of the Majesty in heaven, 2 and

---

[f] Or able to save completely
[g] Gk lacks other

[c] 25 Or forever

ens, 2 a minister in the sanctuary and the true tent^h that the Lord, and not any mortal, has set up. 3 For every high priest is appointed to offer gifts and sacrifices; hence it is necessary for this priest also to have something to offer. 4 Now if he were on earth, he would not be a priest at all, since there are priests who offer gifts according to the law. 5 They offer worship in a sanctuary that is a sketch and shadow of the heavenly one; for Moses, when he was about to erect the tent,^h was warned, "See that you make everything according to the pattern that was shown you on the mountain." 6 But Jesus^i has now obtained a more excellent ministry, and to that degree he is the mediator of a better covenant, which has been enacted through better promises. 7 For if that first covenant had been faultless, there would have been no need to look for a second one.

8 God^j finds fault with them when he says:
"The days are surely coming, says the Lord,
when I will establish a new covenant with the house of Israel and with the house of Judah;
9 not like the covenant that I made with their ancestors, on the day when I took them by the hand to lead them out of the land of Egypt; for they did not continue in my covenant, and so I had no concern for them, says the Lord.

ἐν τοῖς οὐρανοῖς, 2 τῶν ἁγίων λειτουργὸς
in the heavens, of the holy things a minister

καὶ τῆς σκηνῆς τῆς ἀληθινῆς, ἣν ἔπηξεν
and of the tabernacle - true, which erected

ὁ κύριος, οὐκ ἄνθρωπος. 3 Πᾶς γὰρ
the Lord, not man. For every

ἀρχιερεὺς εἰς τὸ προσφέρειν δῶρά τε
high priest for the to offer gifts both

καὶ θυσίας καθίσταται· ὅθεν ἀναγκαῖον
and sacrifices is appointed; whence [it is] necessary

ἔχειν τι καὶ τοῦτον ὃ προσενέγκῃ. 4 εἰ
to have some- also this which he may offer. If
thing [priest]

μὲν οὖν ἦν ἐπὶ γῆς, οὐδ' ἂν ἦν ἱερεύς,
- there- he on earth, he would not be a priest,
fore were

ὄντων τῶν προσφερόντων κατὰ νόμον
[there] the [ones] offering according to law
being

τὰ δῶρα· 5 οἵτινες ὑποδείγματι καὶ σκιᾷ
the gifts; who an example and a shadow

λατρεύουσιν τῶν ἐπουρανίων, καθὼς
serve of the heavenly things, as

κεχρημάτισται Μωϋσῆς μέλλων ἐπιτελεῖν
has been warned Moses being about to complete

τὴν σκηνήν· ὅρα γάρ φησιν, ποιήσεις
the tabernacle; for See[,] he says, thou shalt make

πάντα κατὰ τὸν τύπον τὸν δειχθέντα
all things according to the pattern - shown

σοι ἐν τῷ ὄρει· 6 νῦν δὲ διαφορωτέρας
to thee in the mount; but now a more excellent

τέτυχεν λειτουργίας, ὅσῳ καὶ κρείττονός
he has obtained ministry, by so indeed of a better
much

ἐστιν διαθήκης μεσίτης, ἥτις ἐπὶ κρείττοσιν
[as] covenant mediator, which on better
he is

ἐπαγγελίαις νενομοθέτηται. 7 εἰ γὰρ ἡ
promises has been enacted. For if -

πρώτη ἐκείνη ἦν ἄμεμπτος, οὐκ ἂν
first [covenant] that was faultless, would not

δευτέρας ἐζητεῖτο τόπος. 8 μεμφόμενος
of(for) a have been place. finding fault [with]
second sought

γὰρ αὐτοὺς λέγει· ἰδοὺ ἡμέραι ἔρχονται,
For them he says: Behold[,] days are coming,

λέγει κύριος, καὶ συντελέσω ἐπὶ τὸν
says [the] Lord, and I will effect over the

οἶκον Ἰσραὴλ καὶ ἐπὶ τὸν οἶκον Ἰούδα
household of Israel and over the household of Juda

διαθήκην καινήν, 9 οὐ κατὰ τὴν διαθήκην
covenant a new, not accord- the covenant
ing to

ἣν ἐποίησα τοῖς πατράσιν αὐτῶν ἐν
which I made with the fathers of them in

ἡμέρᾳ ἐπιλαβομένου μου τῆς χειρὸς αὐτῶν
[the] day taking me of the hand of them
=when I took

ἐξαγαγεῖν αὐτοὺς ἐκ γῆς Αἰγύπτου, ὅτι
to lead forth them out [the] of Egypt, because
of land

αὐτοὶ οὐκ ἐνέμειναν ἐν τῇ διαθήκῃ μου,
they continued not in in the covenant of me,

κἀγὼ ἠμέλησα αὐτῶν, λέγει κύριος. 10 ὅτι
and I disregarded them, says [the] Lord. Because

---

who serves in the sanctuary, the true tabernacle set up by the Lord, not by man.

3 Every high priest is appointed to offer both gifts and sacrifices, and so it was necessary for this one also to have something to offer. 4 If he were on earth, he would not be a priest, for there are already men who offer the gifts prescribed by the law. 5 They serve at a sanctuary that is a copy and shadow of what is in heaven. This is why Moses was warned when he was about to build the tabernacle: "See to it that you make everything according to the pattern shown you on the mountain."^d 6 But the ministry Jesus has received is as superior to theirs as the covenant of which he is mediator is superior to the old one, and it is founded on better promises.

7 For if there had been nothing wrong with that first covenant, no place would have been sought for another. 8 But God found fault with the people and said^e:

"The time is coming, declares the Lord, when I will make a new covenant with the house of Israel and with the house of Judah.
9 It will not be like the covenant I made with their forefathers when I took them by the hand to lead them out of Egypt, because they did not remain faithful to my covenant, and I turned away from them, declares the Lord.

^h Or tabernacle
^i Gk he
^j Gk He

d5 Exodus 25:40
e8 Some manuscripts may be translated fault and said to the people.

10 This is the covenant
   that I will make
   with the house
   of Israel
after those days,
   says the Lord:
I will put my laws in
   their minds,
and write them on
   their hearts,
and I will be their
   God,
and they shall be
   my people.
11 And they shall not
   teach
   one another
   or say to each
   other, 'Know
   the Lord,'
for they shall all know
   me,
   from the least of
   them to
   the greatest.
12 For I will be merciful
   toward their
   iniquities,
   and I will remember
   their sins
   no more."
13 In speaking of "a new
covenant," he has made the
first one obsolete. And
what is obsolete and growing old will soon disappear.

αὕτη ἡ διαθήκη ἣν διαθήσομαι τῷ οἴκῳ
this [is] the covenant which I will with house-
                              covenant the hold
Ἰσραὴλ μετὰ τὰς ἡμέρας ἐκείνας, λέγει
of Israel after the those days, says
κύριος, διδοὺς νόμους μου εἰς τὴν διάνοιαν
[the] Lord, giving laws of me into the mind
αὐτῶν, καὶ ἐπὶ καρδίας αὐτῶν ἐπιγράψω
of them, and on hearts of them I will inscribe
αὐτούς, καὶ ἔσομαι αὐτοῖς εἰς θεὸν
them, and I will be to them for God
καὶ αὐτοὶ ἔσονταί μοι εἰς λαόν. 11 καὶ
and they shall be to me for a people. And
οὐ μὴ διδάξωσιν ἕκαστος τὸν πολίτην
by no means may they teach each man the citizen
αὐτοῦ καὶ ἕκαστος τὸν ἀδελφὸν αὐτοῦ,
of him and each man the brother of him,
λέγων· γνῶθι τὸν κύριον, ὅτι πάντες
saying: Know thou the Lord, because all
εἰδήσουσίν με ἀπὸ μικροῦ ἕως μεγάλου
will know me from little to great
αὐτῶν. 12 ὅτι ἵλεως ἔσομαι ταῖς ἀδικίαις
of them. Because merciful I will be to the unrighteous-
                                              nesses
αὐτῶν, καὶ τῶν ἁμαρτιῶν αὐτῶν οὐ μὴ
of them, and the sins of them by no means
μνησθῶ ἔτι. 13 ἐν τῷ λέγειν καινὴν
I may more. In the to say° ' new '
remember   =When he says
πεπαλαίωκεν τὴν πρώτην· τὸ δὲ παλαι-
he has made old the first; and the thing being
ούμενον καὶ γηράσκον ἐγγὺς ἀφανισμοῦ.
made old and growing aged [is] near vanishing.

10This is the covenant I
will make with the
house of Israel
after that time,
   declares the Lord.
I will put my laws in
   their minds
and write them on their
   hearts.
I will be their God,
and they will be my
   people.
11No longer will a man
   teach his neighbor,
or a man his brother,
   saying, 'Know the
   Lord,'
because they will all
   know me,
from the least of them
   to the greatest.
12For I will forgive their
   wickedness
and will remember
   their sins no
   more."ƒ
13By calling this covenant
"new," he has made the
first one obsolete; and what
is obsolete and aging will
soon disappear.

Chapter 9

The Earthly and the Heavenly Sanctuaries

NOW even the first cov-
enant had regulations
for worship and an earthly
sanctuary. 2For a tent ʰ
was constructed, the first
one, in which were the
lampstand, the table, and
the bread of the Presence; ᵏ
this is called the Holy
Place. 3Behind the second
curtain was a tent ˡ called
the Holy of Holies. 4In it
stood the golden altar of incense and the ark of the
covenant overlaid on all
sides with gold, in which
there were a golden urn
holding the manna, and
Aaron's rod that budded,
and the tablets of the covenant; 5above it were the
cherubim of glory over-
shadowing the mercy
seat. ᵐ Of these things we
cannot speak now in detail.

9 Εἶχε μὲν οὖν καὶ ἡ πρώτη δικαι-
   ⁵had ¹So then ⁶both ⁵the ³first ordin-
                              ⁴[covenant]
ώματα λατρείας τό τε ἅγιον κοσμικόν.
ances of service ⁵the ¹and ⁴holy place ⁹worldly.
2 σκηνὴ γὰρ κατεσκευάσθη ἡ πρώτη,
For a tabernacle was prepared[,] the first,
ἐν ᾗ ἥ τε λυχνία καὶ ἡ τράπεζα καὶ
in which ¹the ⁵both lampstand and the table and
[were]
ἡ πρόθεσις τῶν ἄρτων, ἥτις λέγεται
the setting forth of the loaves, which is called
Ἅγια· 3 μετὰ δὲ τὸ δεύτερον καταπέτασμα
Holy; and after the second veil
σκηνὴ ἡ λεγομένη Ἅγια Ἁγίων, 4 χρυσοῦν
a taber- the being called Holy of Holies, ⁵a golden
nacle [one]
ἔχουσα θυμιατήριον καὶ τὴν κιβωτὸν τῆς
¹having altar and the ark of the
διαθήκης περικεκαλυμμένην πάντοθεν χρυσίῳ,
covenant having been covered round on all sides with gold,
ἐν ᾗ στάμνος χρυσῆ ἔχουσα τὸ μάννα
in which pot a golden having the manna
[were]
καὶ ἡ ῥάβδος Ἀαρὼν ἡ βλαστήσασα
and the rod of Aaron - budded
καὶ αἱ πλάκες τῆς διαθήκης, 5 ὑπεράνω
and the tablets of the covenant, ⁵above
δὲ αὐτῆς Χερουβὶν δόξης κατασκιάζοντα
¹and it cherubim of glory overshadowing
τὸ ἱλαστήριον· περὶ ὧν οὐκ ἔστιν νῦν
the mercy-seat; concern- which there is not now
           ing things [?time]

Chapter 9

Worship in the Earthly Tabernacle

NOW the first covenant
had regulations for
worship and also an earthly
sanctuary. 2A tabernacle
was set up. In its first room
were the lampstand, the table and the consecrated
bread; this was called the
Holy Place. 3Behind the
second curtain was a room
called the Most Holy Place,
4which had the golden altar
of incense and the gold-
covered ark of the cove-
nant. This ark contained
the gold jar of manna, Aaron's staff that had budded,
and the stone tablets of the
covenant. 5Above the ark
were the cherubim of the
Glory, overshadowing the
atonement cover. ᵍ But we

ᵏ Gk the presentation of the loaves
ˡ Or tabernacle
ᵐ Or the place of atonement

ƒ12 Jer. 31:31-34
ᵍ5 Traditionally the mercy seat

6 Such preparations having been made, the priests go continually into the first tent[l] to carry out their ritual duties; 7 but only the high priest goes into the second, and he but once a year, and not without taking the blood that he offers for himself and for the sins committed unintentionally by the people. 8 By this the Holy Spirit indicates that the way into the sanctuary has not yet been disclosed as long as the first tent[l] is still standing. 9 This is a symbol[n] of the present time, during which gifts and sacrifices are offered that cannot perfect the conscience of the worshiper, 10 but deal only with food and drink and various baptisms, regulations for the body imposed until the time comes to set things right.
11 But when Christ came as a high priest of the good things that have come,[o] then through the greater and perfect[p] tent[l] (not made with hands, that is, not of this creation), 12 he entered once for all into the Holy Place, not with the blood of goats and calves, but with his own blood, thus obtaining eternal redemption. 13 For if the blood of goats and bulls, with the sprinkling of the ashes of a heifer, sanctifies those who have been defiled so that their flesh is purified, 14 how much more will the blood of Christ, who through the eternal Spirit[q] offered himself

---

λέγειν κατὰ μέρος.   6 τούτων δὲ οὕτως
to speak in detail.   These things now thus
                         =Now when these things had

κατεσκευασμένων   εἰς   μὲν τὴν πρώτην
having been prepared*   *into ¹on one ⁷the   *first
been thus prepared   hand

σκηνὴν διὰ παντὸς εἰσίασιν οἱ ἱερεῖς
*tabernacle ⁴at all times   *go in   *the *priests

τὰς λατρείας ἐπιτελοῦντες, 7 εἰς δὲ τὴν
¹¹the ¹²services ¹⁰accomplishing,   *into ¹on the *the
                                                    other

δευτέραν ἅπαξ τοῦ ἐνιαυτοῦ μόνος ὁ
⁴second *once *of(in) the ¹⁰year [goes] *the
                                     ⁷alone

ἀρχιερεύς, οὐ χωρὶς αἵματος ὁ προσφέρει
*high priest, not without blood which he offers

ὑπὲρ ἑαυτοῦ καὶ τῶν τοῦ λαοῦ ἀγνοημά-
on be- himself and ¹the *of the ⁴people ²ignor-
half of

των,   8 τοῦτο δηλοῦντος τοῦ πνεύματος
ances,   *this *showing ¹the *Spirit

τοῦ ἁγίου, μήπω πεφανερῶσθαι τὴν τῶν
-    ¹Holy,*   *not yet *to have been ¹the *of the
                         manifested

ἁγίων ὁδὸν ἔτι τῆς πρώτης σκηνῆς
⁴holies *way ¹⁰still ⁷the *first *tabernacle

ἐχούσης στάσιν, 9 ἥτις παραβολὴ εἰς τὸν
¹¹having* ¹²standing, which [was] a parable for the

καιρὸν τὸν ἐνεστηκότα, καθ' ἣν δῶρά
time   -   present,   accord- which *gifts
                                ing to

τε καὶ θυσίαι προσφέρονται μὴ δυνάμεναι
¹both and sacrifices are being offered not being able

κατὰ συνείδησιν τελειῶσαι τὸν λατρεύοντα,
in respect conscience to perfect the [one] serving,
of

10 μόνον ἐπὶ βρώμασιν καὶ πόμασιν καὶ
only on foods and drinks and

διαφόροις βαπτισμοῖς, δικαιώματα σαρκὸς
various washings, ordinances of flesh

μέχρι καιροῦ διορθώσεως ἐπικείμενα.
*until *a time *of amendment ¹being imposed.

11 Χριστὸς δὲ παραγενόμενος ἀρχιερεὺς
But Christ having appeared a high priest

τῶν γενομένων ἀγαθῶν, διὰ τῆς μείζονος
¹of the *having come *good things, through the greater
about

καὶ τελειοτέρας σκηνῆς οὐ χειροποιήτου,
and more perfect tabernacle not made by hand,

τοῦτ' ἔστιν οὐ ταύτης τῆς κτίσεως,
this is not of this - creation,

12 οὐδὲ δι' αἵματος τράγων καὶ μόσχων,
nor through blood of goats and of calves,

διὰ δὲ τοῦ ἰδίου αἵματος εἰσῆλθεν ἐφάπαξ
but the own blood entered once for
through (his)   all

εἰς τὰ ἅγια, αἰωνίαν λύτρωσιν εὑράμενος.
into the holies, eternal redemption having found.

13 εἰ γὰρ τὸ αἷμα τράγων καὶ ταύρων
For if the blood of goats and of bulls

καὶ σποδὸς δαμάλεως ῥαντίζουσα τοὺς
and ashes of a heifer sprinkling the [ones]

κεκοινωμένους ἁγιάζει πρὸς τὴν τῆς
having been polluted sanctifies to ¹the *of the

σαρκὸς καθαρότητα, 14 πόσῳ μᾶλλον τὸ
⁴flesh *cleanness, by how much more the

αἷμα τοῦ Χριστοῦ, ὃς διὰ πνεύματος
blood - of Christ, who through *Spirit

---

cannot discuss these things in detail now.
6 When everything had been arranged like this, the priests entered regularly into the outer room to carry on their ministry. 7 But only the high priest entered the inner room, and that only once a year, and never without blood, which he offered for himself and for the sins the people had committed in ignorance. 8 The Holy Spirit was showing by this that the way into the Most Holy Place had not yet been disclosed as long as the first tabernacle was still standing. 9 This is an illustration for the present time, indicating that the gifts and sacrifices being offered were not able to clear the conscience of the worshiper. 10 They are only a matter of food and drink and various ceremonial washings—external regulations applying until the time of the new order.

The Blood of Christ

11 When Christ came as high priest of the good things that are already here,[h] he went through the greater and more perfect tabernacle that is not man-made, that is to say, not a part of this creation. 12 He did not enter by means of the blood of goats and calves; but he entered the Most Holy Place once for all by his own blood, having obtained eternal redemption. 13 The blood of goats and bulls and the ashes of a heifer sprinkled on those who are ceremonially unclean sanctify them so that they are outwardly clean. 14 How much more, then, will the blood of Christ, who through the eternal Spirit offered him-

---

[n] Gk parable
[o] Other ancient authorities read good things to come
[p] Gk more perfect
[q] Other ancient authorities read Holy Spirit

[h]11 Some early manuscripts are to come

without blemish to God, purify our[r] conscience from dead works to worship the living God!

15 For this reason he is the mediator of a new covenant, so that those who are called may receive the promised eternal inheritance, because a death has occurred that redeems them from the transgressions under the first covenant.[s] 16 Where a will[s] is involved, the death of the one who made it must be established. 17 For a will[s] takes effect only at death, since it is not in force as long as the one who made it is alive. 18 Hence not even the first covenant was inaugurated without blood. 19 For when every commandment had been told to all the people by Moses in accordance with the law, he took the blood of calves and goats,[t] with water and scarlet wool and hyssop, and sprinkled both the scroll itself and all the people, 20 saying, "This is the blood of the covenant that God has ordained for you." 21 And in the same way he sprinkled with the blood both the tent[t] and all the vessels used in worship. 22 Indeed, under the law almost everything is purified with blood, and without the shedding of blood there is no forgiveness of sins.

Christ's Sacrifice Takes Away Sin

23 Thus it was necessary for the sketches of the heavenly things to be purified with these rites, but the

αἰωνίου ἑαυτὸν προσήνεγκεν ἄμωμον τῷ
[the] eternal ⁴himself ⁵offered unblemished –

θεῷ, καθαριεῖ τὴν συνείδησιν ἡμῶν ἀπὸ
to God, will cleanse the conscience of us from

νεκρῶν ἔργων εἰς τὸ λατρεύειν θεῷ
dead works for the to serve ⁸God

ζῶντι. 15 καὶ διὰ τοῦτο διαθήκης καινῆς
[the] living. And therefore ⁴covenant ⁵of a new

μεσίτης ἐστίν, ὅπως θανάτου γενομένου
³mediator ¹he is, so as death having occurred⁸

εἰς ἀπολύτρωσιν τῶν ἐπὶ τῇ πρώτῃ
for redemption ¹of the ³under * ⁴the ⁵first

διαθήκῃ παραβάσεων τὴν ἐπαγγελίαν
⁶covenant ⁹transgressions ¹⁰the ¹¹promise

λάβωσιν οἱ κεκλημένοι τῆς αἰωνίου
⁹may receive ⁷the ⁸having been ¹²of the ¹³eternal
[ones] called

κληρονομίας. 16 Ὅπου γὰρ διαθήκη,
¹⁴inheritance. For where [there is] a covenant,

θάνατον ἀνάγκη φέρεσθαι τοῦ διαθεμένου·
³[the] death ¹[there is] ²to be offered ⁴of the ⁵making
necessity [one] covenant·

17 διαθήκη γὰρ ἐπὶ νεκροῖς βεβαία, ἐπεὶ
for a covenant over dead [? bodies] [is] firm, since

μήποτε ἰσχύει ὅτε ζῇ ὁ διαθέμενος.
never has it when ³lives ¹the ²making
strength [one] covenant.

18 ὅθεν οὐδὲ ἡ πρώτη χωρὶς αἵματος
Whence neither the first [covenant] ²without ³blood

ἐγκεκαίνισται. 19 λαληθείσης γὰρ πάσης
¹has been dedicated. For ³having been spoken ¹every

ἐντολῆς κατὰ τὸν νόμον ὑπὸ Μωϋσέως
²command- ⁹accord- ¹⁰the ¹¹law ⁴by ⁵Moses
ment⁸ ing to

παντὶ τῷ λαῷ, λαβὼν τὸ αἷμα τῶν
⁶to all ⁷the ⁸people, taking the blood of the

μόσχων καὶ τῶν τράγων μετὰ ὕδατος
calves and of the goats with water

καὶ ἐρίου κοκκίνου καὶ ὑσσώπου, αὐτό
and ²wool ¹scarlet and hyssop, ⁸it[self]

τε τὸ βιβλίον καὶ πάντα τὸν λαὸν
⁹both ³the ⁴scroll ⁶and ⁷all ⁸the ⁹people

ἐρράντισεν, 20 λέγων· τοῦτο τὸ αἷμα τῆς
¹he sprinkled, saying: This [is] the blood of the

διαθήκης ἧς ἐνετείλατο πρὸς ὑμᾶς ὁ
covenant which ²enjoined ³to ⁴you ¹

θεός. 21 καὶ τὴν σκηνὴν δὲ καὶ πάντα
¹God. ³both ³the ⁴tabernacle ¹And and all

τὰ σκεύη τῆς λειτουργίας τῷ αἵματι
the vessels of the service with the blood

ὁμοίως ἐρράντισεν. 22 καὶ σχεδὸν ἐν
likewise he sprinkled. And ⁴almost ⁷by

αἵματι πάντα καθαρίζεται κατὰ τὸν νόμον,
⁸blood ⁵all things ⁶is(are) cleansed ¹accord- ²the ³law,
ing to

καὶ χωρὶς αἱματεκχυσίας οὐ γίνεται
and without bloodshedding there becomes no

ἄφεσις. 23 ἀνάγκη οὖν τὰ μὲν ὑπο-
remission. [There was] therefore ²[for] ¹on one ⁴ex-
necessity ³the hand

δείγματα τῶν ἐν τοῖς οὐρανοῖς τούτοις
amples of the in *the* heavens ²by these
things

self unblemished to God, cleanse our consciences from acts that lead to death,[i] so that we may serve the living God!

15 For this reason Christ is the mediator of a new covenant, that those who are called may receive the promised eternal inheritance—now that he has died as a ransom to set them free from the sins committed under the first covenant.

16 In the case of a will,[j] it is necessary to prove the death of the one who made it, 17 because a will is in force only when somebody has died; it never takes effect while the one who made it is living. 18 This is why even the first covenant was not put into effect without blood. 19 When Moses had proclaimed every commandment of the law to all the people, he took the blood of calves, together with water, scarlet wool and branches of hyssop, and sprinkled the scroll and all the people. 20 He said, "This is the blood of the covenant, which God has commanded you to keep."[k] 21 In the same way, he sprinkled with the blood both the tabernacle and everything used in its ceremonies. 22 In fact, the law requires that nearly everything be cleansed with blood, and without the shedding of blood there is no forgiveness.

23 It was necessary, then, for the copies of the heavenly things to be purified with these sacrifices, but

[r] Other ancient authorities read *your*

[s] The Greek word used here means both *covenant* and *will*

[t] Other ancient authorities lack *and goats*

* It may seem strange to translate a preposition which means "on" or "over" by "under"; but ἐπί has the meaning of "during the time of" (see Mark 2. 26; I. Tim. 6. 13).

[i]14 Or *from useless rituals*

[j]16 Same Greek word as *covenant*; also in verse 17

[k]20 Exodus 24:8

heavenly things themselves need better sacrifices than these. 24For Christ did not enter a sanctuary made by human hands, a mere copy of the true one, but he entered into heaven itself, now to appear in the presence of God on our behalf. 25Nor was it to offer himself again and again, as the high priest enters the Holy Place year after year with blood that is not his own; 26for then he would have had to suffer again and again since the foundation of the world. But as it is, he has appeared once for all at the end of the age to remove sin by the sacrifice of himself. 27And just as it is appointed for mortals to die once, and after that the judgment, 28so Christ, having been offered once to bear the sins of many, will appear a second time, not to deal with sin, but to save those who are eagerly waiting for him.

the heavenly things themselves with better sacrifices than these. 24For Christ did not enter a man-made place that was only a copy of the true one; he entered heaven itself, now to appear for us in God's presence. 25Nor did he enter heaven to offer himself again and again, the way the high priest enters the Most Holy Place every year with blood that is not his own. 26Then Christ would have had to suffer many times since the creation of the world. But now he has appeared once for all at the end of the ages to do away with sin by the sacrifice of himself. 27Just as man is destined to die once, and after that to face judgment, 28so Christ was sacrificed once to take away the sins of many people; and he will appear a second time, not to bear sin, but to bring salvation to those who are waiting for him.

καθαρίζεσθαι, αὐτὰ δὲ τὰ ἐπουράνια
[1]to be cleansed, [5][them]-selves [1]on the other [2][for] [3]the [4]heavenly things

κρείττοσιν θυσίαις παρὰ ταύτας. 24 οὐ
by better sacrifices than these. 24 not

γὰρ εἰς χειροποίητα εἰσῆλθεν ἅγια Χριστός,
For into [2]made by hand [4]entered [1]holies [3]Christ,

ἀντίτυπα τῶν ἀληθινῶν, ἀλλ' εἰς αὐτὸν
figures of the true things, but into [3][it]self

τὸν οὐρανόν, νῦν ἐμφανισθῆναι τῷ προσώπῳ
[1]the [2]heaven, now to appear in the presence

τοῦ θεοῦ ὑπὲρ ἡμῶν· 25 οὐδ' ἵνα πολ-
- of God on behalf of us; 25 nor in order that often

λάκις προσφέρῃ ἑαυτόν, ὥσπερ ὁ ἀρχιερεὺς
he should offer himself, even as the high priest

εἰσέρχεται εἰς τὰ ἅγια κατ' ἐνιαυτὸν
enters into the holies year by year†

ἐν αἵματι ἀλλοτρίῳ, 26 ἐπεὶ ἔδει αὐτὸν
with blood belonging to others, 26 since it behoved him

πολλάκις παθεῖν ἀπὸ καταβολῆς κόσμου·
often to suffer from [the] foundation of [the] world;

νυνὶ δὲ ἅπαξ ἐπὶ συντελείᾳ τῶν αἰώνων
but now once at [the] completion of the ages

εἰς ἀθέτησιν τῆς ἁμαρτίας διὰ τῆς θυσίας
for annulment - of sin through the sacrifice

αὐτοῦ πεφανέρωται. 27 καὶ καθ' ὅσον
of him he has been manifested. 27 And as

ἀπόκειται τοῖς ἀνθρώποις ἅπαξ ἀποθανεῖν,
it is reserved - to men once to die,

μετὰ δὲ τοῦτο κρίσις, 28 οὕτως καὶ
and after this judgment, 28 so also

ὁ Χριστός, ἅπαξ προσενεχθεὶς εἰς τὸ
- Christ, once having been offered for the

πολλῶν ἀνενεγκεῖν ἁμαρτίας, ἐκ δευτέρου
[3]of many [1]to bear [2]sins, [2]a second [time]

χωρὶς ἁμαρτίας ὀφθήσεται τοῖς αὐτὸν
[3]without [4]sin [1]will appear [5]to the [ones] [7]him

ἀπεκδεχομένοις εἰς σωτηρίαν.
[6]expecting for salvation.

Chapter 10

Christ's Sacrifice Once for All

SINCE the law has only a shadow of the good things to come and not the true form of these realities, it u can never, by the same sacrifices that are continually offered year after year, make perfect those who approach. 2Otherwise, would they not have ceased being offered, since the worshipers, cleansed once for all, would no longer have any consciousness of sin? 3But in these sacrifices there is a reminder of sin year after year. 4For it is impossible for the blood of bulls and goats to take away sins. 5Consequently, when Christ v came into the world, he said,

10 Σκιὰν γὰρ ἔχων ὁ νόμος τῶν
10 For [4]a shadow [3]having [1]the [2]law of the

μελλόντων ἀγαθῶν, οὐκ αὐτὴν τὴν εἰκόνα
coming good things, not [2][it]self [1]the [2]image

τῶν πραγμάτων, κατ' ἐνιαυτὸν ταῖς αὐταῖς
of the matters, [5]every [6]year† [3]by the [4]same

θυσίαις ἃς προσφέρουσιν εἰς τὸ διηνεκὲς
[5]sacrifices [6]which [7]they offer [10]continually†

οὐδέποτε δύναται τοὺς προσερχομένους
[2]never [1]can [12]the [ones] [13]approaching

τελειῶσαι· 2 ἐπεὶ οὐκ ἂν ἐπαύσαντο
[11]to perfect; 2 since would not they have ceased

προσφερόμεναι, διὰ τὸ μηδεμίαν ἔχειν
being offered, because of the [2]no [4]to have

ἔτι συνείδησιν ἁμαρτιῶν τοὺς λατρεύοντας
[5]still [3]conscience [1]of sins [1]the [ones] [6]serving

ἅπαξ κεκαθαρισμένους; 3 ἀλλ' ἐν αὐταῖς
[2]once [4]having been cleansed? 3 But in them [there

ἀνάμνησις ἁμαρτιῶν κατ' ἐνιαυτόν.
is] a remembrance of sins yearly†;

4 ἀδύνατον γὰρ αἷμα ταύρων καὶ τράγων
4 for [it is] impossible blood of bulls and of goats

ἀφαιρεῖν ἁμαρτίας. 5 Διὸ εἰσερχόμενος εἰς
to take away sins. 5 Wherefore entering into

Chapter 10

Christ's Sacrifice Once for All

THE law is only a shadow of the good things that are coming—not the realities themselves. For this reason it can never, by the same sacrifices repeated endlessly year after year, make perfect those who draw near to worship. 2If it could, would they not have stopped being offered? For the worshipers would have been cleansed once for all, and would no longer have felt guilty for their sins. 3But those sacrifices are an annual reminder of sins, 4because it is impossible for the blood of bulls and goats to take away sins. 5Therefore, when Christ came into the world, he

u Other ancient authorities read they
v Gk he

"Sacrifices and
offerings you
have not
desired,
but a body you have
prepared for me;
6 in burnt offerings and
sin offerings
you have taken no
pleasure.
7 Then I said, 'See,
God, I have
come to do your
will, O God'
(in the scroll of the
book w it is
written of me)."
8 When he said above,
"You have neither desired
nor taken pleasure in sacrifices and offerings and
burnt offerings and sin offerings" (these are offered
according to the law),
9 then he added, "See, I
have come to do your will."
He abolishes the first in order to establish the second.
10 And it is by God's will x
that we have been sancti-
fied through the offering of
the body of Jesus Christ
once for all.
11 And every priest
stands day after day at his
service, offering again and
again the same sacrifices
that can never take away
sins. 12 But when Christ y
had offered for all time a
single sacrifice for sins, "he
sat down at the right hand
of God," 13 and since then
has been waiting "until his
enemies would be made a
footstool for his feet."
14 For by a single offering
he has perfected for all time
those who are sanctified.
15 And the Holy Spirit also
testifies to us, for after saying,
16 "This is the covenant
that I will make
with them

τὸν κόσμον λέγει· θυσίαν καὶ προσφορὰν
the world he says: Sacrifice and offering
οὐκ ἠθέλησας, σῶμα δὲ κατηρτίσω μοι·
thou didst not wish, but a body thou didst prepare for me;
6 ὁλοκαυτώματα καὶ περὶ ἁμαρτίας οὐκ
burnt offerings and concerning sins not
[sacrifices]
εὐδόκησας. 7 τότε εἶπον· ἰδοὺ ἥκω,
thou wast well Then I said: Behold I have
pleased [with]. come,
ἐν κεφαλίδι βιβλίου γέγραπται περὶ ἐμοῦ,
in a heading of a scroll it has been concerning me,
written
τοῦ ποιῆσαι ὁ θεὸς τὸ θέλημά σου.
- to do[,]d - God[,]* the will of thee.
8 ἀνώτερον λέγων ὅτι θυσίας καὶ προσ-
Above saying that sacrifices and offer-
φορὰς καὶ ὁλοκαυτώματα καὶ περὶ ἁμαρτίας
ings and burnt offerings and concerning sins
οὐκ ἠθέλησας οὐδὲ εὐδόκησας, αἵτινες
thou didst not wish nor thou wast well which
pleased [with],
κατὰ νόμον προσφέρονται, 9 τότε εἴρηκεν·
accord- law are offered, then he has said:
ing to
ἰδοὺ ἥκω τοῦ ποιῆσαι τὸ θέλημά σου.
Behold I have - to dod the will of thee.
come
ἀναιρεῖ τὸ πρῶτον ἵνα τὸ δεύτερον
He takes the first in order the second
away that
στήσῃ· 10 ἐν ᾧ θελήματι ἡγιασμένοι ἐσμὲν
he may by which will 3having been 1we are
set up; sanctified
διὰ τῆς προσφορᾶς τοῦ σώματος Ἰησοῦ
through the offering of the body of Jesus
Χριστοῦ ἐφάπαξ. 11 Καὶ πᾶς μὲν ἱερεὺς
Christ once for all. And 5every 1on one 2priest
hand
ἕστηκεν καθ' ἡμέραν λειτουργῶν καὶ τὰς
stands daily† ministering and 3the
αὐτὰς πολλάκις προσφέρων θυσίας, αἵτινες
4same 6often 7offering 5sacrifices, which
οὐδέποτε δύνανται περιελεῖν ἁμαρτίας· 12 οὗτος
never can to take away sins; 2this
[priest]
δὲ μίαν ὑπὲρ ἁμαρτιῶν προσενέγκας
1on the 4one 6on behalf of 7sins 8 having offered
other
θυσίαν εἰς τὸ διηνεκὲς ἐκάθισεν ἐν δεξιᾷ
9sacrifice 9in - 10perpetuity 8sat at [the] right
[hand]
τοῦ θεοῦ, 13 τὸ λοιπὸν ἐκδεχόμενος ἕως
- of God, henceforth expecting till
τεθῶσιν οἱ ἐχθροὶ αὐτοῦ ὑποπόδιον τῶν
4are put 1the 2enemies 3of him a footstool of the
ποδῶν αὐτοῦ. 14 μιᾷ γὰρ προσφορᾷ
feet of him. For by one offering
τετελείωκεν εἰς τὸ διηνεκὲς τοὺς ἁγιαζ-
he has perfected in - perpetuity the [ones] being
ομένους. 15 Μαρτυρεῖ δὲ ἡμῖν καὶ
sanctified. And 5witnesses 4to us 4indeed
τὸ πνεῦμα τὸ ἅγιον· μετὰ γὰρ τὸ
1the 3Spirit - 2Holy; for after the
εἰρηκέναι· 16 αὕτη ἡ διαθήκη ἣν δια-
to have said: This [is] the covenant which I will
=having said:

said:

"Sacrifice and offering
you did not desire,
but a body you
prepared for me;
6with burnt offerings and
sin offerings
you were not pleased.
7Then I said, 'Here I
am—it is written
about me in the
scroll—
I have come to do your
will, O God.' "/
8First he said, "Sacrifices
and offerings, burnt offerings and sin offerings you
did not desire, nor were
you pleased with them"
(although the law required
them to be made). 9Then he
said, "Here I am, I have
come to do your will." He
sets aside the first to establish the second. 10And by
that will, we have been
made holy through the sacrifice of the body of Jesus
Christ once for all.
11Day after day every
priest stands and performs
his religious duties; again
and again he offers the
same sacrifices, which can
never take away sins. 12But
when this priest had of-
fered for all time one sacrifice for sins, he sat down at
the right hand of God.
13Since that time he waits
for his enemies to be made
his footstool, 14because by
one sacrifice he has made
perfect forever those who
are being made holy.
15The Holy Spirit also
testifies to us about this.
First he says:

16"This is the covenant I
will make with them

w Meaning of Gk uncertain
x Gk by that will
y Gk this one

* The "articular vocative"; cf. 1. 8, 9.

/7 Psalm 40:6-8 (see Septuagint)

after those days,
says the Lord:
I will put my laws in
their hearts,
and I will write
them on
their minds,"
17 he also adds,
"I will remember[z]
their sins and
their lawless
deeds no more."
18 Where there is forgiveness of these, there is no
longer any offering for sin.

A Call to Persevere

19 Therefore, my
friends,[a] since we have
confidence to enter the
sanctuary by the blood of
Jesus, 20 by the new and living way that he opened for
us through the curtain (that
is, through his flesh), 21 and
since we have a great priest
over the house of God,
22 let us approach with a
true heart in full assurance
of faith, with our hearts
sprinkled clean from an evil
conscience and our bodies
washed with pure water.
23 Let us hold fast to the
confession of our hope
without wavering, for he
who has promised is faithful. 24 And let us consider
how to provoke one anoth-
er to love and good deeds,
25 not neglecting to meet together, as is the habit of
some, but encouraging one
another, and all the more as
you see the Day approach-
ing.
26 For if we willfully
persist in sin after having
received the knowledge of
the truth, there no longer
remains a sacrifice for sins,
27 but a fearful prospect of
judgment, and a fury of fire
that will consume the ad-
versaries. 28 Anyone who

θήσομαι πρὸς αὐτοὺς μετὰ τὰς ἡμέρας
covenant to them after - days
ἐκείνας, λέγει κύριος· διδοὺς νόμους μου
those, says [the] Lord: Giving laws of me
ἐπὶ καρδίας αὐτῶν, καὶ ἐπὶ τὴν διάνοιαν
on hearts of them, also on the mind
αὐτῶν ἐπιγράψω αὐτούς, 17 καὶ τῶν
of them I will inscribe them, and the
ἁμαρτιῶν αὐτῶν καὶ τῶν ἀνομιῶν αὐτῶν
sins of them and the iniquities of them
οὐ μὴ μνησθήσομαι ἔτι. 18 ὅπου δὲ
by no means I will remember still. Now where
ἄφεσις τούτων, οὐκέτι προσφορὰ περὶ
forgiveness of these [is], no longer offering concerning
[there is]
ἁμαρτίας.
sins.

19 Ἔχοντες οὖν, ἀδελφοί, παρρησίαν εἰς
Having therefore, brothers, confidence for
τὴν εἴσοδον τῶν ἁγίων ἐν τῷ αἵματι
the entering of the holies by the blood
Ἰησοῦ, 20 ἣν ἐνεκαίνισεν ἡμῖν ὁδὸν
of Jesus, which he dedicated for us[,] a way
πρόσφατον καὶ ζῶσαν διὰ τοῦ κατα-
fresh and living through the veil,
πετάσματος, τοῦτ᾽ ἔστιν τῆς σαρκὸς αὐτοῦ,
this is the flesh of him,
21 καὶ ἱερέα μέγαν ἐπὶ τὸν οἶκον τοῦ
and priest a great over the household -
θεοῦ, 22 προσερχώμεθα μετὰ ἀληθινῆς
of God, let us approach with a true
καρδίας ἐν πληροφορίᾳ πίστεως, ῥεραν-
heart in full assurance of faith, having been
τισμένοι τὰς καρδίας ἀπὸ συνειδήσεως
sprinkled [as to] the hearts from [a] conscience
πονηρᾶς καὶ λελουσμένοι τὸ σῶμα ὕδατι
[an] evil and having been [as to] body [with] water
bathed the
καθαρῷ· 23 κατέχωμεν τὴν ὁμολογίαν τῆς
[in] clean; let us hold fast the confession of the
(our)
ἐλπίδος ἀκλινῆ, πιστὸς γὰρ ὁ ἐπαγ-
hope unyieldingly, for faithful [is] the [one] prom-
γειλάμενος, 24 καὶ κατανοῶμεν ἀλλήλους
ising, and let us consider one another
εἰς παροξυσμὸν ἀγάπης καὶ καλῶν ἔργων,
to incitement of love and of good works,
25 μὴ ἐγκαταλείποντες τὴν ἐπισυναγωγὴν
not forsaking the coming together
ἑαυτῶν, καθὼς ἔθος τισίν, ἀλλὰ παρα-
of [our]selves, as custom with some [is], but ex-
καλοῦντες, καὶ τοσούτῳ μᾶλλον ὅσῳ
horting, and by so much more as
βλέπετε ἐγγίζουσαν τὴν ἡμέραν. 26 Ἑκουσίως
ye see drawing near the day. wilfully
γὰρ ἁμαρτανόντων ἡμῶν μετὰ τὸ λαβεῖν
For sinning us after the to receive
=when we sin wilfully =receiving
τὴν ἐπίγνωσιν τῆς ἀληθείας, οὐκέτι περὶ
the full knowledge of the truth, no more concerning
ἁμαρτιῶν ἀπολείπεται θυσία, 27 φοβερὰ
sins remains a sacrifice, fearful
δέ τις ἐκδοχὴ κρίσεως καὶ πυρὸς ζῆλος
but some expectation of judgment and of fire zeal
ἐσθίειν μέλλοντος τοὺς ὑπεναντίους.
to consume being about the adversaries.

after that time, says the
Lord.
I will put my laws in
their hearts,
and I will write them
on their minds."[m]
17 Then he adds:

"Their sins and lawless
acts
I will remember no
more."[n]
18 And where these have
been forgiven, there is no
longer any sacrifice for sin.

A Call to Persevere

19 Therefore, brothers,
since we have confidence
to enter the Most Holy
Place by the blood of Jesus,
20 by a new and living way
opened for us through the
curtain, that is, his body,
21 and since we have a great
priest over the house of
God, 22 let us draw near to
God with a sincere heart in
full assurance of faith, having our hearts sprinkled to
cleanse us from a guilty
conscience and having our
bodies washed with pure
water. 23 Let us hold un-
swervingly to the hope we
profess, for he who prom-
ised is faithful. 24 And let us
consider how we may spur
one another on toward love
and good deeds. 25 Let us
not give up meeting together, as some are in the habit
of doing, but let us encourage one another—and all
the more as you see the
Day approaching.
26 If we deliberately keep
on sinning after we have received the knowledge of
the truth, no sacrifice for
sins is left, 27 but only a
fearful expectation of judgment and of raging fire that
will consume the enemies

[z] Gk on their minds and I will remember
[a] Gk Therefore, brothers

[m]16 Jer. 31:33
[n]17 Jer. 31:34

has violated the law of Moses dies without mercy "on the testimony of two or three witnesses." ²⁹How much worse punishment do you think will be deserved by those who have spurned the Son of God, profaned the blood of the covenant by which they were sanctified, and outraged the Spirit of grace? ³⁰For we know the one who said, "Vengeance is mine, I will repay." And again, "The Lord will judge his people." ³¹It is a fearful thing to fall into the hands of the living God.

³² But recall those earlier days when, after you had been enlightened, you endured a hard struggle with sufferings, ³³sometimes being publicly exposed to abuse and persecution, and sometimes being partners with those so treated. ³⁴For you had compassion for those who were in prison, and you cheerfully accepted the plundering of your possessions, knowing that you yourselves possessed something better and more lasting. ³⁵Do not, therefore, abandon that confidence of yours; it brings a great reward. ³⁶For you need endurance, so that when you have done the will of God, you may receive what was promised.
³⁷ For yet "in a very little while, the one who is coming will come and will not delay; ³⁸ but my righteous one will live by faith. My soul takes no pleasure in anyone who shrinks back."

---

28 ἀθετήσας τις νόμον Μωϋσέως χωρὶς
¹Disregarding ¹anyone ³law ⁴of Moses ⁵without

οἰκτιρμῶν ἐπὶ δυσὶν ἢ τρισὶν μάρτυσιν
⁷compassions ⁶on [the ⁹two ¹⁰or ¹¹three ¹²witnesses
word of]

ἀποθνήσκει· **29** πόσῳ δοκεῖτε χείρονος
⁸dies; by how much think ye ²of worse

ἀξιωθήσεται τιμωρίας ὁ τὸν υἱὸν τοῦ
¹will be thought ³punishment ⁴the ⁶the ⁷Son –
worthy [one]

θεοῦ καταπατήσας καὶ τὸ αἷμα τῆς
⁸of God ⁹having trampled and ²the ⁴blood ⁵of the
[on]

διαθήκης κοινὸν ἡγησάμενος, ἐν ᾧ ἡγιάσθη,
⁶covenant ⁸common ⁷having by which he was
deemed, sanctified,

καὶ τὸ πνεῦμα τῆς χάριτος ἐνυβρίσας.
and ²the ¹Spirit – ⁴of grace ¹having insulted.

30 οἴδαμεν γὰρ τὸν εἰπόντα· ἐμοὶ
For we know the [one] having said: To me
=Vengeance

ἐκδίκησις, ἐγὼ ἀνταποδώσω· καὶ πάλιν·
vengeance,° I will repay; and again:
is mine,

κρινεῖ κύριος τὸν λαὸν αὐτοῦ. **31** φοβερὸν
¹will judge [¹The] the people of him. A fearful
Lord thing [it is]

τὸ ἐμπεσεῖν εἰς χεῖρας θεοῦ ζῶντος.
the to fall in into [the] hands ¹God ¹of a living.

32 Ἀναμιμνήσκεσθε δὲ τὰς πρότερον ἡμέρας,
But remember ye the ¹formerly ²days,

ἐν αἷς φωτισθέντες πολλὴν ἄθλησιν
in which being enlightened ²a much(great) ³struggle

ὑπεμείνατε παθημάτων, **33** τοῦτο μὲν
¹ye endured ⁴of sufferings, this on one hand

ὀνειδισμοῖς τε καὶ θλίψεσιν θεατριζόμενοι,
²to reproaches ³both ⁴and ⁵to afflictions ¹being exposed,

τοῦτο δὲ κοινωνοὶ τῶν οὕτως ἀναστρεφ-
this on the ⁵sharers ⁶of the ⁴thus ⁴liv-
other [ones]

ομένων γενηθέντες. **34** καὶ γὰρ τοῖς
ing ¹having become. For indeed in the

δεσμίοις συνεπαθήσατε, καὶ τὴν ἁρπαγὴν
bonds ye suffered together, and ⁴the ⁵seizure

τῶν ὑπαρχόντων ὑμῶν μετὰ χαρᾶς
⁶of the ⁷possessions ⁸of you ⁹with ¹joy

προσεδέξασθε, γινώσκοντες ἔχειν ἑαυτοὺς
¹ye accepted, knowing ⁴to have ¹[your]selves

κρείσσονα ὕπαρξιν καὶ μένουσαν. **35** Μὴ
²a better ³possession ⁴and ⁵remaining. not

ἀποβάλητε οὖν τὴν παρρησίαν ὑμῶν, ἥτις
Cast ye away therefore the confidence of you, which

ἔχει μεγάλην μισθαποδοσίαν. **36** ὑπομονῆς
has a great recompence. ²of endurance

γὰρ ἔχετε χρείαν ἵνα τὸ θέλημα τοῦ
For ¹ye have ³need in order ⁵the ⁶will –
that

θεοῦ ποιήσαντες κομίσησθε τὴν ἐπαγγελίαν.
⁴of God ¹having ye may obtain the promise.
done

37 ἔτι γὰρ μικρὸν ὅσον ὅσον, ὁ ἐρχόμενος
For yet ¹little ¹a very,* the coming [one]

ἥξει καὶ οὐ χρονίσει· **38** ὁ δὲ δίκαιός
will come and will not delay; but the just man

μου ἐκ πίστεως ζήσεται, καὶ ἐὰν ὑπο-
of me by faith will live, and if he

---

of God. ²⁸Anyone who rejected the law of Moses died without mercy on the testimony of two or three witnesses. ²⁹How much more severely do you think a man deserves to be punished who has trampled the Son of God under foot, who has treated as an unholy thing the blood of the covenant that sanctified him, and who has insulted the Spirit of grace? ³⁰For we know him who said, "It is mine to avenge; I will repay,"° and again, "The Lord will judge his people."ᵖ ³¹It is a dreadful thing to fall into the hands of the living God.

³²Remember those earlier days after you had received the light, when you stood your ground in a great contest in the face of suffering. ³³Sometimes you were publicly exposed to insult and persecution; at other times you stood side by side with those who were so treated. ³⁴You sympathized with those in prison and joyfully accepted the confiscation of your property, because you knew that you yourselves had better and lasting possessions.

³⁵So do not throw away your confidence; it will be richly rewarded. ³⁶You need to persevere so that when you have done the will of God, you will receive what he has promised. ³⁷For in just a very little while,

"He who is coming will come and will not delay.
³⁸ But my righteous one�q will live by faith.
And if he shrinks back,

°30 Deut. 32:35
ᵖ30 Deut. 32:36; Psalm 135:14
�q38 One early manuscript But the righteous

39 But we are not among those who shrink back and so are lost, but among those who have faith and so are saved.

στείληται,   οὐκ   εὐδοκεῖ   ἡ   ψυχή   μου
withdraws,   *is not well pleased   ¹the   ²soul   ³of me

ἐν   αὐτῷ.   39 ἡμεῖς   δὲ   οὐκ   ἐσμὲν   ὑποστολῆς
in   him.   But we   are not   of withdrawal

εἰς   ἀπώλειαν,   ἀλλὰ   πίστεως   εἰς   περιποίησιν
to   destruction,   but   of faith   to   possession

ψυχῆς.
of soul.

I will not be pleased with him."ʳ

39But we are not of those who shrink back and are destroyed, but of those who believe and are saved.

Chapter 11
The Meaning of Faith

NOW faith is the assurance of things hoped for, the conviction of things not seen. ²Indeed, by faith[b] our ancestors received approval. ³By faith we understand that the worlds were prepared by the word of God, so that what is seen was made from things that are not visible.[c]

The Examples of Abel, Enoch, and Noah

4 By faith Abel offered to God a more acceptable[d] sacrifice than Cain's. Through this he received approval as righteous, God himself giving approval to his gifts; he died, but through his faith[e] he still speaks. ⁵By faith Enoch was taken so that he did not experience death; and "he was not found, because God had taken him." For it was attested before he was taken away that "he had pleased God." ⁶And without faith it is impossible to please God, for whoever would approach him must believe that he exists and that he rewards those who seek him. ⁷By faith Noah, warned by God about events as yet unseen, respected the warning and built an ark to save his household; by this he condemned the world and became an heir to the righteousness that is in accordance with faith.

b Gk by this
c Or was not made out of visible things
d Gk greater
e Gk through it

11 "Εστιν   δὲ   πίστις   ἐλπιζομένων   ὑπό-
Now ²is   ¹faith   ⁴of things being hoped   ⁵[the]

στασις,   πραγμάτων   ἔλεγχος   οὐ   βλεπομένων.
reality,   ²of things   ¹[the] proof   not   being seen.

2 ἐν   ταύτῃ   γὰρ   ἐμαρτυρήθησαν   οἱ
by   this   For   ⁵obtained witness   ¹the

πρεσβύτεροι.   3 Πίστει   νοοῦμεν   κατηρτίσθαι
²elders.   By faith we understand   ⁴to have been adjusted

τοὺς   αἰῶνας   ῥήματι   θεοῦ,   εἰς   τὸ   μὴ
¹the   ²ages   by a word   of God,   so as†   ³not

ἐκ   φαινομένων   τὸ   βλεπόμενον   γεγονέναι.
⁵out   ⁶things   ¹the   ²being seen   ⁴to have become.

4 Πίστει   πλείονα   θυσίαν   "Αβελ   παρὰ
By faith   ⁴a greater(? better)   ²sacrifice   ¹Abel   ³than

Κάϊν   προσήνεγκεν   τῷ   θεῷ,   δι'   ἧς
⁷Cain   ⁵offered   -   ⁶to God, through which

ἐμαρτυρήθη   εἶναι   δίκαιος,   μαρτυροῦντος   ἐπὶ
he obtained witness   to be   just,   ²witnessing   ³over

τοῖς   δώροις   αὐτοῦ   τοῦ   θεοῦ,   καὶ   δι'
¹the   ²gifts   ³of him   -   ¹God,*   and through

αὐτῆς   ἀποθανὼν   ἔτι   λαλεῖ.   5 Πίστει
it   having died   still   he speaks.   By faith

'Ενὼχ   μετετέθη   τοῦ   μὴ   ἰδεῖν   θάνατον,
Enoch   was removed   -   not   to see⁴   death,

καὶ   οὐχ   ηὑρίσκετο   διότι   μετέθηκεν   αὐτὸν
and   was not found   because   ²removed   ³him

ὁ   θεός.   6 πρὸ   γὰρ   τῆς   μεταθέσεως
-    ¹God.   For before   the(his)   removal

μεμαρτύρηται   εὐαρεστηκέναι   τῷ   θεῷ·   χωρὶς
he has obtained witness   to have been well-pleasing   -   to God;   ²without

δὲ   πίστεως   ἀδύνατον   εὐαρεστῆσαι·   πιστεῦσαι
¹but faith [it is] impossible to be well-pleasing [to God];   ⁴to believe

γὰρ   δεῖ   τὸν   προσερχόμενον   [τῷ]   θεῷ,
¹for   ³it   ²the [one]   ⁴approaching   -   ⁵to God,
behoves

ὅτι   ἔστιν   καὶ   τοῖς   ἐκζητοῦσιν   αὐτὸν
that   he is   and   ²to the [ones]   ³seeking   ⁴out   ⁵him

μισθαποδότης   γίνεται.   7 Πίστει   χρηματισ-
¹a rewarder   ¹becomes.   By faith   ²having been warned [by

θεὶς   Νῶε   περὶ   τῶν   μηδέπω   βλεπομένων,
God*]   ¹Noah concerning the things not yet   being seen,

εὐλαβηθεὶς   κατεσκεύασεν   κιβωτὸν   εἰς
being devout   prepared   ، an ark   for

σωτηρίαν   τοῦ   οἴκου   αὐτοῦ,   δι'   ἧς
[the] salvation   of the   household   of him,   through which

κατέκρινεν   τὸν   κόσμον,   καὶ   τῆς   κατὰ
he condemned   the   world,   and   ²of the   ³according to

πίστιν   δικαιοσύνης   ἐγένετο   κληρονόμος.
⁴faith   ⁴righteousness   ¹became   ²heir.

Chapter 11
By Faith

NOW faith is being sure of what we hope for and certain of what we do not see. ²This is what the ancients were commended for.
³By faith we understand that the universe was formed at God's command, so that what is seen was not made out of what was visible.
⁴By faith Abel offered God a better sacrifice than Cain did. By faith he was commended as a righteous man, when God spoke well of his offerings. And by faith he still speaks, even though he is dead.
⁵By faith Enoch was taken from this life, so that he did not experience death; he could not be found, because God had taken him away. For before he was taken, he was commended as one who pleased God. ⁶And without faith it is impossible to please God, because anyone who comes to him must believe that he exists and that he rewards those who earnestly seek him.
⁷By faith Noah, when warned about things not yet seen, in holy fear built an ark to save his family. By his faith he condemned the world and became heir of the righteousness that comes by faith.

*This must be understood, as the word always (or at least generally) has reference to a divine communication.

ʳ38 Hab. 2:3,4

The Faith of Abraham

8 By faith Abraham obeyed when he was called to set out for a place that he was to receive as an inheritance; and he set out, not knowing where he was going. 9 By faith he stayed for a time in the land he had been promised, as in a foreign land, living in tents, as did Isaac and Jacob, who were heirs with him of the same promise. 10 For he looked forward to the city that has foundations, whose architect and builder is God. 11 By faith he received power of procreation, even though he was too old—and Sarah herself was barren—because he considered him faithful who had promised.ᶠ 12 Therefore from one person, and this one as good as dead, descendants were born, "as many as the stars of heaven and as the innumerable grains of sand by the seashore."
13 All of these died in faith without having received the promises, but from a distance they saw and greeted them. They confessed that they were strangers and foreigners on the earth, 14 for people who speak in this way make it clear that they are seeking a homeland. 15 If they had been thinking of the land that they had left behind, they would have had opportunity to return. 16 But as it is, they desire a better country, that is, a heavenly one. Therefore God is not ashamed to be called their God; indeed, he has prepared a city for them.
17 By faith Abraham, when put to the test, offered up Isaac. He who had

ᶠ Other ancient authorities read *By faith Sarah herself, though barren, received power to conceive, even when she was too old, because she considered him faithful who had promised.*

---

8 Πίστει   καλούμενος   'Αβραὰμ   ὑπήκουσεν
By faith ²being called ¹Abraham ¹¹obeyed
ἐξελθεῖν   εἰς   τόπον   ὃν   ἤμελλεν   λαμβάνειν
³to go forth ⁴to ⁵a place ⁶which ⁷he was about ⁸to receive
εἰς   κληρονομίαν,   καὶ   ἐξῆλθεν   μὴ   ἐπιστάμε-
⁹for ¹⁰an inheritance, and went forth not understand-
νος   ποῦ   ἔρχεται.   **9** Πίστει   παρῴκησεν
ing where he goes(went). By faith he sojourned
εἰς   γῆν   τῆς   ἐπαγγελίας   ὡς   ἀλλοτρίαν,
in a land - of promise as a foreigner,
ἐν   σκηναῖς   κατοικήσας,   μετὰ   'Ισαὰκ   καὶ
in tents dwelling, with Isaac and
'Ιακὼβ   τῶν   συγκληρονόμων   τῆς   ἐπαγ-
Jacob the co-heirs of the ⁸pro-
γελίας   τῆς   αὐτῆς·   **10** ἐξεδέχετο   γὰρ   τὴν
mise - ¹same; for he expected the
τοὺς   θεμελίους   ἔχουσαν   πόλιν,   ἧς   τεχνίτης
²the ⁴foundations ³having ¹city, of which ²artificer
καὶ   δημιουργὸς   ὁ   θεός.   **11** Πίστει   καὶ
⁴and ⁵maker - ¹God ²[is]. By faith also
αὐτὴ   Σάρρα   δύναμιν   εἰς   καταβολὴν
¹[her]self ¹Sara ⁴power ⁵for ⁶conception
σπέρματος   ἔλαβεν   καὶ   παρὰ   καιρὸν   ἡλικίας,
⁷of seed ²received even beyond time of age,
ἐπεὶ   πιστὸν   ἡγήσατο   τὸν   ἐπαγγειλάμενον.
since ⁴faithful ³she deemed the [one] having promised.
12 διὸ   καὶ   ἀφ'   ἑνὸς   ἐγενήθησαν,   καὶ
Wherefore indeed from one there became, and
ταῦτα   νενεκρωμένου,   καθὼς   τὰ   ἄστρα
that tootᵃ [he] having died,ᵃ as the stars
τοῦ   οὐρανοῦ   τῷ   πλήθει   καὶ   ὡς   ἡ   ἄμμος
of *the* heaven - in multitude and as the ²sand
ἡ   παρὰ   τὸ   χεῖλος   τῆς   θαλάσσης   ἡ
- ³by ⁴the ⁵lip ⁶of the ⁷sea
ἀναρίθμητος.   **13** Κατὰ   πίστιν   ἀπέθανον
¹innumerable. ⁴By way of ⁵faith ³died
οὗτοι   πάντες,   μὴ   κομισάμενοι   τὰς   ἐπαγ-
¹these ²all, not having obtained the pro-
γελίας,   ἀλλὰ   πόρρωθεν   αὐτὰς   ἰδόντες   καὶ
mises, but ⁵from afar ⁴them ¹seeing ²and
ἀσπασάμενοι,   καὶ   ὁμολογήσαντες   ὅτι   ξένοι
³greeting, and confessing that ²strangers
καὶ   παρεπίδημοί   εἰσιν   ἐπὶ   τῆς   γῆς.
²and ⁴sojourners ³they are on the earth
(? land).
14 οἱ   γὰρ   τοιαῦτα   λέγοντες   ἐμφανίζουσιν
For the [ones] ²such things ¹saying make manifest
ὅτι   πατρίδα   ἐπιζητοῦσιν.   **15** καὶ   εἰ   μὲν
that ²a fatherland ¹they seek. And if on one
hand
ἐκείνης   ἐμνημόνευον   ἀφ'   ἧς   ἐξέβησαν,
²that ¹they remembered from which they came out,
εἶχον   ἂν   καιρὸν   ἀνακάμψαι·   **16** νῦν
they might time(opportunity) to return; now
have had
δὲ   κρείττονος   ὀρέγονται,   τοῦτ'   ἔστιν
on the ²a better ¹they aspire to, this is
other
ἐπουρανίου.   διὸ   οὐκ   ἐπαισχύνεται   αὐτοὺς
a heavenly. Wherefore ³is not ashamed [of] ⁴them
ὁ   θεὸς   θεὸς   ἐπικαλεῖσθαι   αὐτῶν·   ἡτοίμασεν
- ¹God ⁵God ²to be called ⁶of them; ¹he prepared
γὰρ   αὐτοῖς   πόλιν.   **17** Πίστει   προσενήνοχεν
¹for for them a city. By faith ³has offered up
'Αβραὰμ   τὸν   'Ισαὰκ   πειραζόμενος,   καὶ
¹Abraham - ⁴Isaac ²being tested, and

---

8 By faith Abraham, when called to go to a place he would later receive as his inheritance, obeyed and went, even though he did not know where he was going. 9 By faith he made his home in the promised land like a stranger in a foreign country; he lived in tents, as did Isaac and Jacob, who were heirs with him of the same promise. 10 For he was looking forward to the city with foundations, whose architect and builder is God.
11 By faith Abraham, even though he was past age—and Sarah herself was barren—was enabled to become a father because heˢ considered him faithful who had made the promise. 12 And so from this one man, and he as good as dead, came descendants as numerous as the stars in the sky and as countless as the sand on the seashore.
13 All these people were still living by faith when they died. They did not receive the things promised; they only saw them and welcomed them from a distance. And they admitted that they were aliens and strangers on earth. 14 People who say such things show that they are looking for a country of their own. 15 If they had been thinking of the country they had left, they would have had opportunity to return. 16 Instead, they were longing for a better country—a heavenly one. Therefore God is not ashamed to be called their God, for he has prepared a city for them.
17 By faith Abraham, when God tested him, offered Isaac as a sacrifice.

ˢ 11 Or *By faith even Sarah, who was past age, was enabled to bear children because she* received the promises was ready to offer up his only son, [18]of whom he had been told, "It is through Isaac that descendants shall be named for you." [19]He considered the fact that God is able even to raise someone from the dead—and figuratively speaking, he did receive him back. [20]By faith Isaac invoked blessings for the future on Jacob and Esau. [21]By faith Jacob, when dying, blessed each of the sons of Joseph, "bowing in worship over the top of his staff." [22]By faith Joseph, at the end of his life, made mention of the exodus of the Israelites and gave instructions about his burial. *g*

The Faith of Moses

[23] By faith Moses was hidden by his parents for three months after his birth, because they saw that the child was beautiful; and they were not afraid of the king's edict. *h* [24]By faith Moses, when he was grown up, refused to be called a son of Pharaoh's daughter, [25]choosing rather to share ill-treatment with the people of God than to enjoy the fleeting pleasures of sin. [26]He considered abuse suffered for the Christ *i* to be greater wealth than the treasures of Egypt, for he was looking ahead to the reward. [27]By faith he left Egypt, unafraid of the king's anger; for he persevered as though *j* he saw him who is invisible. [28]By faith he kept the Passover and the sprinkling of blood, so that the destroyer

---

τὸν μονογενῆ προσέφερεν ὁ τὰς ἐπαγγελίας
[4]the [7]only begotten [6]was [1]the [2]the [4]promises
(his) offering up [one]

ἀναδεξάμενος, 18 πρὸς ὃν ἐλαλήθη ὅτι
[3]having undertaken, as to whom it was spoken[,] –

ἐν Ἰσαὰκ κληθήσεταί σοι σπέρμα,*o*
In Isaac shall be called to thee a seed,*o*
=thy seed,

19 λογισάμενος ὅτι καὶ ἐκ νεκρῶν ἐγείρειν
reckoning that [4]even [5]from [7]dead [5]to raise

δυνατὸς ὁ θεός· ὅθεν αὐτὸν καὶ ἐν
[1][was] [3]able – [1]God; whence [6]him [8]indeed [9]in

παραβολῇ ἐκομίσατο. 20 Πίστει καὶ περὶ
[7]a parable [6]he obtained. By faith also [6]concerning

μελλόντων εὐλόγησεν Ἰσαὰκ τὸν Ἰακὼβ
[7]coming things [2]blessed [1]Isaac [4]Jacob

καὶ τὸν Ἠσαῦ. 21 Πίστει Ἰακὼβ
[4]and – [5]Esau. By faith Jacob

ἀποθνῄσκων ἕκαστον τῶν υἱῶν Ἰωσὴφ
dying [1]each [2]of the [4]sons [3]of Joseph

εὐλόγησεν, καὶ προσεκύνησεν ἐπὶ τὸ ἄκρον
[1]blessed, and worshipped on the tip

τῆς ῥάβδου αὐτοῦ. 22 Πίστει Ἰωσὴφ
of the rod of him. By faith Joseph

τελευτῶν περὶ τῆς ἐξόδου τῶν υἱῶν
[1]dying [2]concerning [3]the [4]exodus [6]of the [7]sons

Ἰσραὴλ ἐμνημόνευσεν καὶ περὶ τῶν
[5]of Israel [1]remembered and [2]concerning [3]the

ὀστέων αὐτοῦ ἐνετείλατο. 23 Πίστει
[4]bones [5]of him [1]gave orders. By faith

Μωϋσῆς γεννηθεὶς ἐκρύβη τρίμηνον ὑπὸ
Moses having been born was hidden three months by

τῶν πατέρων αὐτοῦ, διότι εἶδον ἀστεῖον
the parents of him, because they saw [3][to be] fine

τὸ παιδίον, καὶ οὐκ ἐφοβήθησαν τὸ
[1]the [2]child, and they did not fear the

διάταγμα τοῦ βασιλέως. 24 Πίστει Μωϋσῆς
decree of the king. By faith Moses

μέγας γενόμενος ἠρνήσατο λέγεσθαι υἱὸς
[2]great [1]having become denied to be said(called) son

θυγατρὸς Φαραώ, 25 μᾶλλον ἑλόμενος
of [the] daughter of Pharaoh, rather choosing

συγκακουχεῖσθαι τῷ λαῷ τοῦ θεοῦ ἢ
to be ill treated with the people – of God than

πρόσκαιρον ἔχειν ἁμαρτίας ἀπόλαυσιν,
for a time to have [2]of sin [1]enjoyment,

26 μείζονα πλοῦτον ἡγησάμενος τῶν
[5]greater [6]riches [1]deeming [7][than] [8]the

Αἰγύπτου θησαυρῶν τὸν ὀνειδισμὸν τοῦ
[10]of Egypt [9]treasures [3]the [2]reproach –

Χριστοῦ· ἀπέβλεπεν γὰρ εἰς τὴν μισθ-
[4]of Christ; for he was looking away to the recom-

αποδοσίαν. 27 Πίστει κατέλιπεν Αἴγυπτον,
pence. By faith he left Egypt,

μὴ φοβηθεὶς τὸν θυμὸν τοῦ βασιλέως·
not fearing the anger of the king;

τὸν γὰρ ἀόρατον ὡς ὁρῶν ἐκαρτέρησεν.
for [1]the [4]unseen [one] [2]as [3]seeing [1]he endured.

28 Πίστει πεποίηκεν τὸ πάσχα καὶ τὴν
By faith he has made the passover and the

πρόσχυσιν τοῦ αἵματος, ἵνα μὴ ὁ
affusion of the blood, lest the

ὀλεθρεύων τὰ πρωτότοκα θίγῃ αὐτῶν.
[one] destroying [2]the [3]firstborns [1]should [4]of them.
touch

He who had received the promises was about to sacrifice his one and only son, [18]even though God had said to him, "It is through Isaac that your offspring *t* will be reckoned." *u* [19]Abraham reasoned that God could raise the dead, and figuratively speaking, he did receive Isaac back from death. [20]By faith Isaac blessed Jacob and Esau in regard to their future. [21]By faith Jacob, when he was dying, blessed each of Joseph's sons, and worshiped as he leaned on the top of his staff. [22]By faith Joseph, when his end was near, spoke about the exodus of the Israelites from Egypt and gave instructions about his bones. [23]By faith Moses' parents hid him for three months after he was born, because they saw he was no ordinary child, and they were not afraid of the king's edict. [24]By faith Moses, when he had grown up, refused to be known as the son of Pharaoh's daughter. [25]He chose to be mistreated along with the people of God rather than to enjoy the pleasures of sin for a short time. [26]He regarded disgrace for the sake of Christ as of greater value than the treasures of Egypt, because he was looking ahead to his reward. [27]By faith he left Egypt, not fearing the king's anger; he persevered because he saw him who is invisible. [28]By faith he kept the Passover and the sprinkling of blood, so that the

---

g Gk *his bones*
h Other ancient authorities add *By faith Moses, when he was grown up, killed the Egyptian, because he observed the humiliation of his people* (Gk *brothers*)
i Or *the Messiah*
j Or *because*

t 18 Greek *seed*
u 18 Gen. 21:12

of the firstborn would not touch the firstborn of Israel.[k]

The Faith of Other Israelite Heroes

29 By faith the people passed through the Red Sea as if it were dry land, but when the Egyptians attempted to do so they were drowned. 30 By faith the walls of Jericho fell after they had been encircled for seven days. 31 By faith Rahab the prostitute did not perish with those who were disobedient,[l] because she had received the spies in peace. 32 And what more should I say? For time would fail me to tell of Gideon, Barak, Samson, Jephthah, of David and Samuel and the prophets— 33 who through faith conquered kingdoms, administered justice, obtained promises, shut the mouths of lions, 34 quenched raging fire, escaped the edge of the sword, won strength out of weakness, became mighty in war, put foreign armies to flight. 35 Women received their dead by resurrection. Others were tortured, refusing to accept release, in order to obtain a better resurrection. 36 Others suffered mocking and flogging, and even chains and imprisonment. 37 They were stoned to death, they were sawn in two,[m] they were killed by the sword; they went about in skins of sheep and goats, destitute, persecuted, tormented— 38 of whom the world was not worthy. They wandered in deserts and mountains, and in caves and holes in the ground.

39 Yet all these, though they were commended for

29 Πίστει διέβησαν τὴν ἐρυθρὰν θάλασσαν
By faith they went the Red Sea
through

ὡς διὰ ξηρᾶς γῆς, ἧς πεῖραν λαβόντες
as through dry land, which ⁴trial ³taking

οἱ Αἰγύπτιοι κατεπόθησαν. 30 Πίστει
¹the ²Egyptians were swallowed up. By faith

τὰ τείχη Ἰεριχὼ ἔπεσαν κυκλωθέντα ἐπὶ
the walls of Jericho fell having been during
encircled

ἑπτὰ ἡμέρας. 31 Πίστει Ῥαὰβ ἡ πόρνη
seven days. By faith Rahab the prostitute

οὐ συναπώλετο τοῖς ἀπειθήσασιν, δεξαμένη
did not perish with the [ones] disobeying, having received

τοὺς κατασκόπους μετ᾽ εἰρήνης. 32 Καὶ
the spies with peace. And

τί ἔτι λέγω; ἐπιλείψει με γὰρ διηγούμενον
what more may ⁴will fail ²me ¹for ⁵recounting
I say?

ὁ χρόνος περὶ Γεδεών, Βαράκ, Σαμψών,
²the ³time concerning Gedeon, Barak, Samson,

Ἰεφθάε, Δαυίδ τε καὶ Σαμουὴλ καὶ
Jephthae, ²David ¹both and Samuel and

τῶν προφητῶν, 33 οἳ διὰ πίστεως
the prophets, who through faith

κατηγωνίσαντο βασιλείας, ἠργάσαντο δι-
overcame kingdoms, wrought right-

καιοσύνην, ἐπέτυχον ἐπαγγελιῶν, ἔφραξαν
eousness, obtained promises, stopped

στόματα λεόντων, 34 ἔσβεσαν δύναμιν
mouths of lions, quenched [the] power

πυρός, ἔφυγον στόματα μαχαίρης, ἐδυναμώ-
of fire, escaped mouths(edges) of [the] sword, were em-

θησαν ἀπὸ ἀσθενείας, ἐγενήθησαν ἰσχυροὶ
powered from weakness, became strong

ἐν πολέμῳ, παρεμβολὰς ἔκλιναν ἀλλοτρίων.
in battle, ¹armies ³made to yield ²of foreigners.

35 ἔλαβον γυναῖκες ἐξ ἀναστάσεως τοὺς
²received ¹women ⁵by ³resurrection ⁴the

νεκροὺς αὐτῶν· ἄλλοι δὲ ἐτυμπανίσθησαν,
⁴dead ⁵of them; but others were beaten to death,

οὐ προσδεξάμενοι τὴν ἀπολύτρωσιν, ἵνα
not accepting – deliverance, in order that

κρείττονος ἀναστάσεως τύχωσιν· 36 ἕτεροι
²a better ³resurrection ¹they might others
obtain;

δὲ ἐμπαιγμῶν καὶ μαστίγων πεῖραν ἔλαβον,
and ³of mockings ⁴and ⁵of scourgings ²trial ¹took,

ἔτι δὲ δεσμῶν καὶ φυλακῆς· 37 ἐλιθάσ-
and more of bonds and of prison; they were

θησαν, ἐπειράσθησαν, ἐπρίσθησαν, ἐν φόνῳ
stoned, they were tried, they were ²by ¹murder
sawn asunder,

μαχαίρης ἀπέθανον, περιῆλθον ἐν μηλωταῖς,
⁴of sword ¹they died, they went about in sheepskins,

ἐν αἰγείοις δέρμασιν, ὑστερούμενοι,
in goatskins, being in want,

θλιβόμενοι, κακουχούμενοι, 38 ὧν οὐκ ἦν
being afflicted, being ill treated, of whom was not

ἄξιος ὁ κόσμος, ἐπὶ ἐρημίαις πλανώμενοι
worthy the world, ²over ³deserts ¹wandering

καὶ ὄρεσιν καὶ σπηλαίοις καὶ ταῖς ὁπαῖς
and mountains and caves and the holes

τῆς γῆς. 39 Καὶ οὗτοι πάντες μαρτυρη-
of the earth. And these all having obtained

destroyer of the firstborn would not touch the firstborn of Israel.

29 By faith the people passed through the Red Sea[v] as on dry land; but when the Egyptians tried to do so, they were drowned.

30 By faith the walls of Jericho fell, after the people had marched around them for seven days.

31 By faith the prostitute Rahab, because she welcomed the spies, was not killed with those who were disobedient.[w]

32 And what more shall I say? I do not have time to tell about Gideon, Barak, Samson, Jephthah, David, Samuel and the prophets, 33 who through faith conquered kingdoms, administered justice, and gained what was promised; who shut the mouths of lions, 34 quenched the fury of the flames, and escaped the edge of the sword; whose weakness was turned to strength; and who became powerful in battle and routed foreign armies. 35 Women received back their dead, raised to life again. Others were tortured and refused to be released, so that they might gain a better resurrection. 36 Some faced jeers and flogging, while still others were chained and put in prison. 37 They were stoned[x]; they were sawed in two; they were put to death by the sword. They went about in sheepskins and goatskins, destitute, persecuted and mistreated—38 the world was not worthy of them. They wandered in deserts and mountains, and in caves and holes in the ground.

39 These were all commended for their faith, yet

k Gk *would not touch them*
l Or *unbelieving*
m Other ancient authorities add
they were tempted

v 29 That is, Sea of Reeds
w 31 Or *unbelieving*
x 37 Some early manuscripts
stoned; they were put to the test;

their faith, did not receive what was promised, 40 since God had provided something better so that they would not, apart from us, be made perfect.

θέντες	διὰ	τῆς	πίστεως	οὐκ	ἐκομίσαντο
witness	through	the(ir)	faith		obtained not

τὴν	ἐπαγγελίαν,	40	τοῦ	θεοῦ	περὶ	ἡμῶν
the	promise,		–	God	⁴concerning	⁵us

κρεῖττόν	τι	προβλεψαμένου,	ἵνα	μὴ	χωρὶς
³better	²some-thing	¹having foreseen,ᵃ	in or-der that	not	without

ἡμῶν	τελειωθῶσιν.
us	they should be perfected.

none of them received what had been promised. 40 God had planned something better for us so that only together with us would they be made perfect.

Chapter 12
The Example of Jesus

THEREFORE, since we are surrounded by so great a cloud of witnesses, let us also lay aside every weight and the sin that clings so closely,ⁿ and let us run with perseverance the race that is set before us, 2 looking to Jesus the pioneer and perfecter of our faith, who for the sake ofᵒ the joy that was set before him endured the cross, disregarding its shame, and has taken his seat at the right hand of the throne of God.

3 Consider him who endured such hostility against himself from sinners,ᵖ so that you may not grow weary or lose heart. 4 In your struggle against sin you have not yet resisted to the point of shedding your blood. 5 And you have forgotten the exhortation that addresses you as children—

"My child, do not
   regard lightly
    the discipline of
    the Lord,
   or lose heart when
    you are
    punished by
    him;
6 for the Lord
    disciplines those
    whom he loves,
   and chastises every
    child whom he
    accepts."

7 Endure trials for the sake of discipline. God is treating you as children; for what child is there whom a parent does not discipline? 8 If you do not have that discipline in which all children share, then you are illegitimate and not his children. 9 Moreover, we had human

12	Τοιγαροῦν	καὶ	ἡμεῖς,	τοσοῦτον	ἔχοντες
	So therefore	²also	¹we,	²such	¹having

περικείμενον	ἡμῖν	νέφος	μαρτύρων,	ὄγκον
⁵lying around	⁶us	⁷a cloud	⁴of witnesses,	²encum-brance

ἀποθέμενοι	πάντα	καὶ	τὴν	εὐπερίστατον
¹putting away	³every	⁴and	⁵the	⁷most besetting

ἁμαρτίαν,	δι᾽	ὑπομονῆς	τρέχωμεν	τὸν
⁶sin,	through	endurance	let us run	¹the

προκείμενον	ἡμῖν	ἀγῶνα,	2	ἀφορῶντες	εἰς
³set before	⁴us	²contest(race),		looking away	to

τὸν	τῆς	πίστεως	ἀρχηγὸν	καὶ	τελειωτὴν
¹the	⁶of the	⁷faith	²author	³and	⁴finisher

Ἰησοῦν,	ὃς	ἀντὶ	τῆς	προκειμένης	αὐτῷ
Jesus,	who	³for	the	²set before	⁴him

χαρᾶς	ὑπέμεινεν	σταυρὸν	αἰσχύνης	κατα-
⁵joy	endured	a cross	²shame	¹de-

φρονήσας,	ἐν	δεξιᾷ	τε	τοῦ	θρόνου	τοῦ
spising,	⁴at	⁵the	¹and	⁶of the	⁷throne	–
		right [hand]				

θεοῦ	κεκάθικεν.	3	ἀναλογίσασθε	γὰρ	τὸν
⁷of God	²has taken [his] seat.		For consider ye		¹the [one]

τοιαύτην	ὑπομεμενηκότα	ὑπὸ	τῶν	ἁμαρτω-
³such	²having endured	⁴by	–	⁵of sin-

λῶν	εἰς	ἑαυτὸν	ἀντιλογίαν,	ἵνα	μὴ	κάμητε
ners	⁷against	⁸himself	⁴contradiction,	lest		ye grow weary

ταῖς	ψυχαῖς	ὑμῶν	ἐκλυόμενοι.	4	Οὔπω
²in the	³souls	⁴of you	¹fainting.		Not yet

μέχρις	αἵματος	ἀντικατέστητε	πρὸς	τὴν
²until	³blood	¹ye resisted	⁴against	the

ἁμαρτίαν	ἀνταγωνιζόμενοι,	5	καὶ	ἐκλέλησθε
⁶sin	⁵struggling against,		and	ye have forgotten

τῆς	παρακλήσεως,	ἥτις	ὑμῖν	ὡς	υἱοῖς
the	exhortation,	which	²with you	³as	⁴with sons

διαλέγεται·	υἱέ	μου,	μὴ	ὀλιγώρει	παιδείας
¹discourses:	Son	of me,	do not make light of		[the] discipline

κυρίου,	μηδὲ	ἐκλύου	ὑπ᾽	αὐτοῦ	ἐλεγχόμενος·
of [the] Lord,	nor	faint	²by	³him	¹being reproved;

6	ὃν	γὰρ	ἀγαπᾷ	κύριος	παιδεύει,	μαστιγοῖ
	for whom		²loves	¹[the] Lord	he disciplines,	²scourges

δὲ	πάντα	υἱὸν	ὃν	παραδέχεται.	7	εἰς
¹and	every	son	whom	he receives.		For

παιδείαν	ὑπομένετε·	ὡς	υἱοῖς	ὑμῖν
discipline	endure ye;	⁴as	⁵with sons	³with you

προσφέρεται	ὁ	θεός·	τίς	γὰρ	υἱὸς	ὃν
²is dealing	–	¹God;	for what		son	whom [is there]

οὐ	παιδεύει	πατήρ;	8	εἰ	δὲ	χωρίς	ἐστε
²disciplines not		¹a father?		But if		²without	¹ye are

παιδείας,	ἧς	μέτοχοι	γεγόνασιν	πάντες,
discipline,	of which	³sharers	²have become	¹all,

ἄρα	νόθοι	καὶ	οὐχ	υἱοί	ἐστε.	9	εἶτα
then	bastards	and	not	sons	ye are.		Furthermore

Chapter 12
God Disciplines His Sons

THEREFORE, since we are surrounded by such a great cloud of witnesses, let us throw off everything that hinders and the sin that so easily entangles, and let us run with perseverance the race marked out for us. 2 Let us fix our eyes on Jesus, the author and perfecter of our faith, who for the joy set before him endured the cross, scorning its shame, and sat down at the right hand of the throne of God. 3 Consider him who endured such opposition from sinful men, so that you will not grow weary and lose heart.

4 In your struggle against sin, you have not yet resisted to the point of shedding your blood. 5 And you have forgotten that word of encouragement that addresses you as sons:

"My son, do not make
   light of the Lord's
   discipline,
  and do not lose heart
   when he rebukes
   you,
6 because the Lord
   disciplines those he
   loves,
  and he punishes
   everyone he accepts
   as a son."ʸ

7 Endure hardship as discipline; God is treating you as sons. For what son is there whom his father does not discipline? 8 If you are not disciplined (and everyone undergoes discipline), then you are illegitimate children and not true sons. 9 Moreover, we

ⁿ Other ancient authorities read *sin that easily distracts*
ᵒ Or *who instead of*
ᵖ Other ancient authorities read *such hostility from sinners against themselves*

ʸ6 Prov. 3:11,12

parents to discipline us, and we respected them. Should we not be even more willing to be subject to the Father of spirits and live? 10 For they disciplined us for a short time as seemed best to them, but he disciplines us for our good, in order that we may share his holiness. 11 Now, discipline always seems painful rather than pleasant at the time, but later it yields the peaceful fruit of righteousness to those who have been trained by it.

12 Therefore lift your drooping hands and strengthen your weak knees, 13 and make straight paths for your feet, so that what is lame may not be put out of joint, but rather be healed.

Warnings against Rejecting God's Grace

14 Pursue peace with everyone, and the holiness without which no one will see the Lord. 15 See to it that no one fails to obtain the grace of God; that no root of bitterness springs up and causes trouble, and through it many become defiled. 16 See to it that no one becomes like Esau, an immoral and godless person, who sold his birthright for a single meal. 17 You know that later, when he wanted to inherit the blessing, he was rejected, for he found no chance to repent,*q* even though he sought the blessing*r* with tears.

18 You have not come to something*s* that can be touched, a blazing fire, and darkness, and gloom, and a tempest, 19 and the sound

---

τοὺς   μὲν   τῆς   σαρκὸς   ἡμῶν   πατέρας
the   —   ³of the   ⁴flesh   ²of us   ¹fathers

εἴχομεν   παιδευτὰς   καὶ   ἐνετρεπόμεθα·   οὐ
¹we had   ⁶correctors   and   we respected [them]:   ³not

πολὺ   μᾶλλον   ὑποταγησόμεθα   τῷ   πατρὶ
⁴much   ⁵more   ¹shall ²we   ⁴be ⁵subject   to the   Father

τῶν   πνευμάτων   καὶ   ζήσομεν;   10 οἱ   μὲν
—   of spirits   and   we shall live?   ²they ³indeed

γὰρ   πρὸς   ὀλίγας   ἡμέρας   κατὰ   τὸ   δοκοῦν
¹for   for   a few   days   accord-   the   seeming
ing to   thing   [good]

αὐτοῖς   ἐπαίδευον,   ὁ   δὲ   ἐπὶ   τὸ   συμφέρον
to them   disciplined [us],   but he   for   the(our)   profit

εἰς   τὸ   μεταλαβεῖν   τῆς   ἁγιότητος   αὐτοῦ.
for   the   to partake   of the   sanctity   of him.

11 πᾶσα   μὲν   παιδεία   πρὸς   μὲν   τὸ   παρὸν
²All   ¹on   ³discipline   ⁴for   ⁷in-   ⁵the   ⁶present
one hand   deed

οὐ   δοκεῖ   χαρᾶς   εἶναι   ἀλλὰ   λύπης,   ὕστερον
seems not   ²of joy   ¹to be   but   of grief,   ¹later

δὲ   καρπὸν   εἰρηνικὸν   τοῖς   δι'   αὐτῆς
¹on the   ⁵fruit   ⁴peaceable   ⁷to the   ⁸through   ¹⁰it
other   [ones]

γεγυμνασμένοις   ἀποδίδωσιν   δικαιοσύνης.
⁹having been exercised   ³it gives back   ⁶of righteousness.

12 Διὸ   τὰς   παρειμένας   χεῖρας   καὶ   τὰ
Where-   ²the   ³having been   ⁴hands   ⁵and   ⁶the
fore   wearied

παραλελυμένα   γόνατα   ἀνορθώσατε,   13 καὶ
⁷having been paralysed   ⁸knees   ¹straighten ye,   and

τροχιὰς   ὀρθὰς   ποιεῖτε   τοῖς   ποσὶν   ὑμῶν,
tracks   straight   make   for the   feet   of you,

ἵνα   μὴ   τὸ   χωλὸν   ἐκτραπῇ,   ἰαθῇ   δὲ
lest   the   lame   be turned   ⁴may   ¹but
aside,   be cured

μᾶλλον.   14 Εἰρήνην   διώκετε   μετὰ   πάντων,
²rather.   Peace   follow   with   all men,

καὶ   τὸν   ἁγιασμόν,   οὗ   χωρὶς   οὐδεὶς
and   —   sanctification,   ²which   ¹without   no one·

ὄψεται   τὸν   κύριον,   15 ἐπισκοποῦντες   μή
will see   the   Lord,   observing   not(lest)

τις   ὑστερῶν   ἀπὸ   τῆς   χάριτος   τοῦ   θεοῦ,
anyone   failing   from   the   grace   —   of God,

μή   τις   ῥίζα   πικρίας   ἄνω   φύουσα   ἐνοχλῇ
not   any   root   of bitterness   ²up   ¹growing   disturb
(lest)

καὶ   διὰ   ταύτης   μιανθῶσιν   οἱ   πολλοί,
and   through   this   ²be defiled   *the*   ¹many,

16 μή   τις   πόρνος   ἢ   βέβηλος   ὡς   Ἠσαῦ,
not(lest)   any   fornicator   or   profane man   as   Esau,

ὃς   ἀντὶ   βρώσεως   μιᾶς   ἀπέδοτο   τὰ
who   against   ²eating   ¹one   gave up   the

πρωτοτόκια   ἑαυτοῦ.   17 ἴστε   γὰρ   ὅτι
rights of   of himself.   For ye know   that
the firstborn

καὶ   μετέπειτα   θέλων   κληρονομῆσαι   τὴν
indeed   afterwards   wishing   to inherit   the

εὐλογίαν   ἀπεδοκιμάσθη,   μετανοίας   γὰρ
blessing   he was rejected,   for ⁴of repentance

τόπον   οὐχ   εὗρεν,   καίπερ   μετὰ   δακρύων
²place   ³not   ¹he found,   though   with   tears

ἐκζητήσας   αὐτήν.   18 Οὐ   γὰρ   προσεληλύθατε
seeking out   it.   For ²not   ¹ye ³have ⁴approached

ψηλαφωμένῳ   καὶ   κεκαυμένῳ   πυρὶ   καὶ
to [a mountain]   and   having been   with   and
being felt   ignited   fire

γνόφῳ   καὶ   ζόφῳ   καὶ   θυέλλῃ   19 καὶ
to darkness   and   to deep gloom   and   to whirlwind   and

---

have all had human fathers who disciplined us and we respected them for it. How much more should we submit to the Father of our spirits and live! 10 Our fathers disciplined us for a little while as they thought best; but God disciplines us for our good, that we may share in his holiness. 11 No discipline seems pleasant at the time, but painful. Later on, however, it produces a harvest of righteousness and peace for those who have been trained by it. 12 Therefore, strengthen your feeble arms and weak knees. 13 "Make level paths for your feet,"*z* so that the lame may not be disabled, but rather healed.

Warning Against Refusing God

14 Make every effort to live in peace with all men and to be holy; without holiness no one will see the Lord. 15 See to it that no one misses the grace of God and that no bitter root grows up to cause trouble and defile many. 16 See that no one is sexually immoral, or is godless like Esau, who for a single meal sold his inheritance rights as the oldest son. 17 Afterward, as you know, when he wanted to inherit this blessing, he was rejected. He could bring about no change of mind, though he sought the blessing with tears.

18 You have not come to a mountain that can be touched and that is burning with fire; to darkness, gloom and storm; 19 to a

---

q Or no chance to change his father's mind
r Gk it
s Other ancient authorities read a mountain

z13 Prov. 4:26

of a trumpet, and a voice whose words made the hearers beg that not another word be spoken to them. 20(For they could not endure the order that was given, "If even an animal touches the mountain, it shall be stoned to death." 21Indeed, so terrifying was the sight that Moses said, "I tremble with fear.") 22But you have come to Mount Zion and to the city of the living God, the heavenly Jerusalem, and to innumerable angels in festal gathering, 23and to the assembly¹ of the firstborn who are enrolled in heaven, and to God the judge of all, and to the spirits of the righteous made perfect, 24and to Jesus, the mediator of a new covenant, and to the sprinkled blood that speaks a better word than the blood of Abel.

25 See that you do not refuse the one who is speaking; for if they did not escape when they refused the one who warned them on earth, how much less will we escape if we reject the one who warns from heaven! 26At that time his voice shook the earth; but now he has promised, "Yet once more I will shake not only the earth but also the heaven." 27This phrase, "Yet once more," indicates the removal of what is shaken—that is, created things—so that what cannot be shaken may remain. 28Therefore, since we are receiving a kingdom that cannot be shaken, let us give thanks, by which we offer to God an acceptable worship with reverence and awe; 29for indeed our God is a consuming fire.

σάλπιγγος ἤχῳ καὶ φωνῇ ῥημάτων, ἧς
⁸of trumpet ¹to a sound and to a voice of words, which

οἱ ἀκούσαντες παρῃτήσαντο μὴ προστεθῆναι
the [ones] hearing entreated not to be added

αὐτοῖς λόγον· 20 οὐκ ἔφερον γὰρ τὸ
to them a word; ⁸not ²they bore ¹for the thing

διαστελλόμενον· κἂν θηρίον θίγῃ τοῦ ὄρους,
being charged: If even a beast touches the mountain,

λιθοβοληθήσεται· 21 καί, οὕτω φοβερὸν ἦν
it shall be stoned; and, so fearful was

τὸ φανταζόμενον, Μωϋσῆς εἶπεν· ⁸Terrified
the thing appearing, Moses said:

εἰμι καὶ ἔντρομος· 22 ἀλλὰ προσεληλύθατε
¹I am and trembling; but ye have approached

Σιὼν ὄρει καὶ πόλει θεοῦ ζῶντος,
²Zion ¹to mount and to a city ⁸God ¹of [the] living,

Ἰερουσαλὴμ ἐπουρανίῳ, καὶ μυριάσιν
⁸Jerusalem ¹to a heavenly, and to myriads

ἀγγέλων, 23 πανηγύρει καὶ ἐκκλησίᾳ
of angels, to an assembly and a church

πρωτοτόκων ἀπογεγραμμένων ἐν οὐρανοῖς,
of firstborn [ones] having been enrolled in heavens,

καὶ κριτῇ θεῷ πάντων, καὶ πνεύμασι
and ²judge ¹to God of all men, and to spirits

δικαίων τετελειωμένων, 24 καὶ διαθήκης
of just men having been made perfect, and ⁴covenant

νέας μεσίτῃ Ἰησοῦ, καὶ αἵματι ῥαντισμοῦ
⁸of a ⁸mediator ¹to Jesus, and to blood of sprinkling
new

κρεῖττον λαλοῦντι παρὰ τὸν Ἅβελ.
²a better thing ¹speaking than - Abel.

25 Βλέπετε μὴ παραιτήσησθε τὸν λαλοῦντα·
Look ye [that] ²not ¹ye refuse the [one] speaking;

εἰ γὰρ ἐκεῖνοι οὐκ ἐξέφυγον ἐπὶ γῆς
for if those escaped not ⁸on ⁴earth

παραιτησάμενοι τὸν χρηματίζοντα, πολὺ
¹refusing ⁸the [one] ⁸warning, much

μᾶλλον ἡμεῖς οἱ τὸν ἀπ' οὐρανῶν
more we* ¹the ⁸the [one] ⁴from ⁸heavens
[ones] ⁴[warning]

ἀποστρεφόμενοι· 26 οὗ ἡ φωνὴ τὴν γῆν
¹turning from; of whom the voice ⁸the ⁴earth

ἐσάλευσεν τότε, νῦν δὲ ἐπήγγελται λέγων·
⁸shook ¹then, but now he has promised saying:

ἔτι ἅπαξ ἐγὼ σείσω οὐ μόνον τὴν
Yet once I will shake not only the

γῆν ἀλλὰ καὶ τὸν οὐρανόν. 27 τὸ δὲ
earth but also the heaven. Now the
[phrase]

ἔτι ἅπαξ δηλοῖ τὴν τῶν σαλευομένων
'Yet once' declares ¹the ⁸of the things ⁴being shaken

μετάθεσιν ὡς πεποιημένων, ἵνα μείνῃ τὰ
⁸removal as of things having in or- ⁴may ¹the
been made, der that remain things

μὴ σαλευόμενα. 28 Διὸ βασιλείαν ἀσάλευτος
¹not being shaken. Wherefore ⁸kingdom ²an unshakable

παραλαμβάνοντες ἔχωμεν χάριν, δι' ἧς
¹receiving let us have grace, through which

λατρεύωμεν εὐαρέστως τῷ θεῷ, μετὰ
we may serve ²well-pleasingly - ¹God, with

εὐλαβείας καὶ δέους· 29 καὶ γὰρ ὁ θεὸς
devoutness and awe; for indeed the God

ἡμῶν πῦρ καταναλίσκον.
of us [is] fire a consuming.

* That is, "much more [shall] we [not escape]"; or, putting it in another way, "much less shall we escape."

trumpet blast or to such a voice speaking words that those who heard it begged that no further word be spoken to them, 20because they could not bear what was commanded: "If even an animal touches the mountain, it must be stoned."ᵃ 21The sight was so terrifying that Moses said, "I am trembling with fear."ᵇ

22But you have come to Mount Zion, to the heavenly Jerusalem, the city of the living God. You have come to thousands upon thousands of angels in joyful assembly, 23to the church of the firstborn, whose names are written in heaven. You have come to God, the judge of all men, to the spirits of righteous men made perfect, 24to Jesus the mediator of a new covenant, and to the sprinkled blood that speaks a better word than the blood of Abel.

25See to it that you do not refuse him who speaks. If they did not escape when they refused him who warned them on earth, how much less will we, if we turn away from him who warns us from heaven? 26At that time his voice shook the earth, but now he has promised, "Once more I will shake not only the earth but also the heavens."ᶜ 27The words "once more" indicate the removing of what can be shaken—that is, created things—so that what cannot be shaken may remain.

28Therefore, since we are receiving a kingdom that cannot be shaken, let us be thankful, and so worship God acceptably with reverence and awe, 29for our "God is a consuming fire."ᵈ

ᵃ20 Exodus 19:12,13
ᵇ21 Deut. 9:19
ᶜ26 Haggai 2:6
ᵈ29 Deut. 4:24

Chapter 13

Service Well-Pleasing to God

LET mutual love continue. 2 Do not neglect to show hospitality to strangers, for by doing that some have entertained angels without knowing it. 3 Remember those who are in prison, as though you were in prison with them; those who are being tortured, as though you yourselves were being tortured.ᵘ 4 Let marriage be held in honor by all, and let the marriage bed be kept undefiled; for God will judge fornicators and adulterers. 5 Keep your lives free from the love of money, and be content with what you have; for he has said, "I will never leave you or forsake you." 6 So we can say with confidence,

"The Lord is my helper;
I will not be afraid.
What can anyone do to me?"

7 Remember your leaders, those who spoke the word of God to you; consider the outcome of their way of life, and imitate their faith. 8 Jesus Christ is the same yesterday and today and forever. 9 Do not be carried away by all kinds of strange teachings; for it is well for the heart to be strengthened by grace, not by regulations about food,ᵛ which have not benefited those who observe them. 10 We have an altar from which those who officiate in the tentʷ have no right to eat. 11 For the bodies of those animals whose blood is brought into the sanctuary by the high priest as a sacrifice for sin are burned outside the camp. 12 Therefore Jesus also suffered outside the city gate in order to sanctify the peo-

---

13 ʹΗ   φιλαδελφία   μενέτω.   **2** τῆς
 -     ²brotherly love   ¹Let *it* remain.   -

φιλοξενίας   μὴ   ἐπιλανθάνεσθε·   διὰ   ταύτης
of hospitality   Be ye not forgetful;   ²through   ³this

γὰρ   ἔλαθόν   τινες   ξενίσαντες   ἀγγέλους.
¹for   ⁵unconsciously†   ⁴some   ⁶entertaining(ed)   ⁷angels.

3 μιμνήσκεσθε   τῶν   δεσμίων   ὡς   συνδεδεμένοι,
Be ye mindful   of the   prisoners   as   *having been* bound
with [them],

τῶν   κακουχουμένων   ὡς   καὶ   αὐτοὶ   ὄντες
of the   *being* ill treated   as   also   [your]selves   being
[ones]

ἐν   σώματι.   **4** Τίμιος   ὁ   γάμος   ἐν   πᾶσιν
in [the] body.   ⁴honourable -   ²marriage   in   all
¹[Let]   ³[be]

καὶ   ἡ   κοίτη   ἀμίαντος·   πόρνους   γὰρ
and   the   bed   undefiled;   for fornicators

καὶ   μοιχοὺς   κρινεῖ   ὁ   θεός.   **5** ᾿Αφιλάργυρος
and   adulterers   ²will judge   -   ¹God.   ⁵without love of
money

ὁ   τρόπος,   ἀρκούμενοι   τοῖς   παροῦσιν·
²[Let]   ³way of   being satisfied   the things   present;
³the   life ⁴[be],   with
(your)

αὐτὸς   γὰρ   εἴρηκεν·   οὐ   μή   σε   ἀνῶ   οὐδ'
for he   has said: By no means   thee   will I   nor
leave

οὐ   μή   σε   ἐγκαταλίπω·   **6** ὥστε   θαρροῦντας
by no(any)   thee   I forsake;   so as   being of good
means   cheer

ἡμᾶς   λέγειν·   κύριος   ἐμοὶ   βοηθός,   οὐ
us   to sayᵇ   [The] Lord   to meᶜ   [is] a helper,   not

φοβηθήσομαι·   τί   ποιήσει   μοι   ἄνθρωπος;
I will fear;   what   ¹will ²do   to me   ²man ?

7 Μνημονεύετε   τῶν   ἡγουμένων   ὑμῶν,
Remember   the [ones]   leading   of you,

οἵτινες   ἐλάλησαν   ὑμῖν   τὸν   λόγον   τοῦ
who   spoke   to you   the   word   -

θεοῦ,   ὧν   ἀναθεωροῦντες   τὴν   ἔκβασιν   τῆς
of God,   ²of   ¹looking at   ³the   ⁴result   ⁴of
whom   the

ἀναστροφῆς   μιμεῖσθε   τὴν   πίστιν.   **8** ᾿Ιησοῦς
⁵conduct   imitate ye   the(ir)   faith.   Jesus

Χριστὸς   ἐχθὲς   καὶ   σήμερον   ὁ   αὐτός
Christ   ⁴yesterday   ⁵and   ⁶to-day   ¹[is] ²the   ²same

καὶ   εἰς   τοὺς   αἰῶνας.   **9** Διδαχαῖς   ποικίλαις
and   unto   the   ages.   ⁵teachings   ²by various

καὶ   ξέναις   μὴ   παραφέρεσθε·   καλὸν   γὰρ
and   ³strange   ¹Do not be carried away;   for [it is] good

χάριτι   βεβαιοῦσθαι   τὴν   καρδίαν,   οὐ
⁴by grace   ³to be confirmed   ¹the   ²heart,ᵇ   not

βρώμασιν,   ἐν   οἷς   οὐκ   ὠφελήθησαν   οἱ
by foods,   by   which   ²were not profited   ¹the

περιπατοῦντες.   **10** ἔχομεν   θυσιαστήριον   ἐξ
²[ones] walking.   We have   an altar   of

οὗ   φαγεῖν   οὐκ   ἔχουσιν   ἐξουσίαν   οἱ   τῇ
which   ²to eat   ⁴have not   ⁴authority   ¹the   ³the
[ones]

σκηνῇ   λατρεύοντες.   **11** ὧν   γὰρ   εἰσφέρεται
⁴tabernacle   ²serving.   For ²of what   ¹is brought *in*

ζῴων   τὸ   αἷμα   περὶ   ἁμαρτίας   εἰς   τὰ
⁵animals   ¹the   ²blood   ⁶concerning   ⁵sins   into   the

ἅγια   διὰ   τοῦ   ἀρχιερέως,   τούτων   τὰ
holies   through   the   high priest,   of these   the

σώματα   κατακαίεται   ἔξω   τῆς   παρεμβολῆς.
bodies   is(are) burned   outside   the   camp.

12 διὸ   καὶ   ᾿Ιησοῦς,   ἵνα   ἁγιάσῃ   διὰ
Where-   in-   Jesus,   in order   he might   ²through
fore   deed   that   sanctify

Chapter 13

Concluding Exhortations

KEEP on loving each other as brothers. 2 Do not forget to entertain strangers, for by so doing some people have entertained angels without knowing it. 3 Remember those in prison as if you were their fellow prisoners, and those who are mistreated as if you yourselves were suffering.

4 Marriage should be honored by all, and the marriage bed kept pure, for God will judge the adulterer and all the sexually immoral. 5 Keep your lives free from the love of money and be content with what you have, because God has said,

"Never will I leave you;
never will I forsake you."ᵉ

6 So we say with confidence,

"The Lord is my helper;
I will not be afraid.
What can man do to me?"ᶠ

7 Remember your leaders, who spoke the word of God to you. Consider the outcome of their way of life and imitate their faith. 8 Jesus Christ is the same yesterday and today and forever.

9 Do not be carried away by all kinds of strange teachings. It is good for our hearts to be strengthened by grace, not by ceremonial foods, which are of no value to those who eat them. 10 We have an altar from which those who minister at the tabernacle have no right to eat.

11 The high priest carries the blood of animals into the Most Holy Place as a sin offering, but the bodies are burned outside the camp. 12 And so Jesus also suffered outside the city

---

ᵘ Gk *were in the body*
ᵛ Gk *not by foods*
ʷ Or *tabernacle*

ᵉ5 Deut. 31:6
ᶠ6 Psalm 118:6,7

ple by his own blood. 13 Let us then go to him outside the camp and bear the abuse he endured. 14 For here we have no lasting city, but we are looking for the city that is to come. 15 Through him, then, let us continually offer a sacrifice of praise to God, that is, the fruit of lips that confess his name. 16 Do not neglect to do good and to share what you have, for such sacrifices are pleasing to God.

17 Obey your leaders and submit to them, for they are keeping watch over your souls and will give an account. Let them do this with joy and not with sighing—for that would be harmful to you. 18 Pray for us; we are sure that we have a clear conscience, desiring to act honorably in all things. 19 I urge you all the more to do this, so that I may be restored to you very soon.

Benediction

20 Now may the God of peace, who brought back from the dead our Lord Jesus, the great shepherd of the sheep, by the blood of the eternal covenant, 21 make you complete in everything good so that you may do his will, working among us ˣ that which is pleasing in his sight, through Jesus Christ, to whom be the glory forever and ever. Amen.

τοῦ ἰδίου αἵματος τὸν λαόν, ἔξω τῆς
⁴the(his) ⁵own ⁶blood ¹the ²people, outside the

πύλης ἔπαθεν. 13 τοίνυν ἐξερχώμεθα πρὸς
gate suffered. So let us go forth to

αὐτὸν ἔξω τῆς παρεμβολῆς τὸν ὀνειδισμὸν
him outside the camp the reproach

αὐτοῦ φέροντες· 14 οὐ γὰρ ἔχομεν ὧδε
of him bearing; for ²not ¹we have here

μένουσαν πόλιν, ἀλλὰ τὴν μέλλουσαν
a continuing city, but the [one] coming

ἐπιζητοῦμεν. 15 Δι’ αὐτοῦ οὖν ἀναφέρωμεν
we seek. Through him therefore let us offer up

θυσίαν αἰνέσεως διὰ παντὸς τῷ θεῷ,
a sacrifice of praise always - to God,

τοῦτ’ ἔστιν καρπὸν χειλέων ὁμολογούντων
this is fruit of lips confessing

τῷ ὀνόματι αὐτοῦ. 16 τῆς δὲ εὐποιΐας
to the name of him. But of the doing good

καὶ κοινωνίας μὴ ἐπιλανθάνεσθε· τοιαύταις
and sharing be ye not forgetful; ²with such

γὰρ θυσίαις εὐαρεστεῖται ὁ θεός. 17 Πεί-
¹for sacrifices ²is well pleased - ¹God. Obey

θεσθε τοῖς ἡγουμένοις ὑμῶν καὶ ὑπείκετε·
ye the [ones] leading of you and submit to
[them];

αὐτοὶ γὰρ ἀγρυπνοῦσιν ὑπὲρ τῶν ψυχῶν
for they watch on behalf of the souls

ὑμῶν ὡς λόγον ἀποδώσοντες· ἵνα μετὰ
of you as ²account ¹rendering*; in or- with
der that

χαρᾶς τοῦτο ποιῶσιν καὶ μὴ στενάζ-
joy ²this ¹they may do and not groan-

οντες· ἀλυσιτελὲς γὰρ ὑμῖν τοῦτο.
ing; for profitless to you this
[would be].

18 Προσεύχεσθε περὶ ἡμῶν· πειθόμεθα
Pray ye concerning us; ²we are persuaded

γὰρ ὅτι καλὴν συνείδησιν ἔχομεν, ἐν
¹for that a good conscience we have, ⁴in

πᾶσιν καλῶς θέλοντες ἀναστρέφεσθαι.
²all [respects] ³well ¹wishing ⁵to behave.

19 περισσοτέρως δὲ παρακαλῶ τοῦτο
And more abundantly I beseech [you] this

ποιῆσαι, ἵνα τάχιον ἀποκατασταθῶ ὑμῖν.
to do, in or- sooner I may be restored to you.
der that

20 Ὁ δὲ θεὸς τῆς εἰρήνης, ὁ ἀναγαγὼν
Now the God - of peace, the having led up
[one]

ἐκ νεκρῶν τὸν ποιμένα τῶν προβάτων
out [the] dead the ²shepherd ³of the ⁴sheep
of

τὸν μέγαν ἐν αἵματι διαθήκης αἰωνίου,
the ¹great in (? with) blood ²covenant ¹of an eternal,

τὸν κύριον ἡμῶν Ἰησοῦν, 21 καταρτίσαι
the Lord of us Jesus, may he adjust

ὑμᾶς ἐν παντὶ ἀγαθῷ εἰς τὸ ποιῆσαι
you in every good thing for the to do

τὸ θέλημα αὐτοῦ, ποιῶν ἐν ἡμῖν τὸ
the will of him, doing in us the
[thing]

εὐάρεστον ἐνώπιον αὐτοῦ διὰ Ἰησοῦ
wellpleasing before him through Jesus

Χριστοῦ, ᾧ ἡ δόξα εἰς τοὺς αἰῶνας
Christ, to [be] glory unto the ages
whom the

gate to make the people holy through his own blood. 13 Let us, then, go to him outside the camp, bearing the disgrace he bore. 14 For here we do not have an enduring city, but we are looking for the city that is to come. 15 Through Jesus, therefore, let us continually offer to God a sacrifice of praise—the fruit of lips that confess his name. 16 And do not forget to do good and to share with others, for with such sacrifices God is pleased.

17 Obey your leaders and submit to their authority. They keep watch over you as men who must give an account. Obey them so that their work will be a joy, not a burden, for that would be of no advantage to you. 18 Pray for us. We are sure that we have a clear conscience and desire to live honorably in every way. 19 I particularly urge you to pray so that I may be restored to you soon.

20 May the God of peace, who through the blood of the eternal covenant brought back from the dead our Lord Jesus, that great Shepherd of the sheep, 21 equip you with everything good for doing his will, and may he work in us what is pleasing to him, through Jesus Christ, to whom be glory for ever and

ˣ Other ancient authorities read *you*

* In the future.

Final Exhortation and Greetings

22 I appeal to you, brothers and sisters,[y] bear with my word of exhortation, for I have written to you briefly. 23 I want you to know that our brother Timothy has been set free; and if he comes in time, he will be with me when I see you. 24 Greet all your leaders and all the saints. Those from Italy send you greetings. 25 Grace be with all of you.[z]

The Letter of
JAMES

Chapter 1

Salutation

JAMES, a servant[a] of God and of the Lord Jesus Christ,
To the twelve tribes in the Dispersion:
Greetings.

Faith and Wisdom

2 My brothers and sisters,[b] whenever you face trials of any kind, consider it nothing but joy, 3 because you know that the testing of your faith produces endurance; 4 and let endurance have its full effect, so that you may be mature and complete, lacking in nothing.
5 If any of you is lacking in wisdom, ask God, who gives to all generously and ungrudgingly, and it will be given you. 6 But ask in faith, never doubting, for the one who doubts is like a wave of the sea, driven and tossed by the wind; 7, 8 for the doubter, being double-

[y] Gk brothers
[z] Other ancient authorities add Amen
[a] Gk slave
[b] Gk brothers

Middle column (Greek interlinear)

τῶν αἰώνων· ἀμήν. **22** Παρακαλῶ δὲ
of the ages; Amen. And I beseech

ὑμᾶς, ἀδελφοί, ἀνέχεσθε τοῦ λόγου τῆς
you, brothers, endure the word –

παρακλήσεως· καὶ γὰρ διὰ βραχέων
of beseeching; for indeed through few [words]

ἐπέστειλα ὑμῖν. **23** Γινώσκετε τὸν ἀδελφὸν
I wrote to you. Know ye the brother

ἡμῶν Τιμόθεον ἀπολελυμένον, μεθ' οὗ
of us Timothy having been released, with whom

ἐὰν τάχιον ἔρχηται ὄψομαι ὑμᾶς.
if sooner I come I will see you.

24 Ἀσπάσασθε πάντας τοὺς ἡγουμένους
Greet ye all the [ones] ⁴leading

ὑμῶν καὶ πάντας τοὺς ἁγίους. Ἀσπάζονται
of you and all the saints. ⁴greet

ὑμᾶς οἱ ἀπὸ τῆς Ἰταλίας.
¹you ¹The [ones] ²from the ³Italy.

25 Ἡ χάρις μετὰ πάντων ὑμῶν.
– Grace [be] with all you.

ΙΑΚΩΒΟΥ ΕΠΙΣΤΟΛΗ
²Of James ¹Epistle

1 Ἰάκωβος θεοῦ καὶ κυρίου Ἰησοῦ
James ²of God ³and ⁴of [the] Lord ⁵Jesus

Χριστοῦ δοῦλος ταῖς δώδεκα φυλαῖς ταῖς
⁶Christ ¹a slave to the twelve tribes –

ἐν τῇ διασπορᾷ χαίρειν.*
in the dispersion greeting.*

2 Πᾶσαν χαρὰν ἡγήσασθε, ἀδελφοί μου,
All joy deem [it], brothers of me,

ὅταν πειρασμοῖς περιπέσητε ποικίλοις,
whenever ²trials ¹ye fall ²into various,

3 γινώσκοντες ὅτι τὸ δοκίμιον ὑμῶν τῆς
knowing that the approved part ³of you ¹of the
=that which is approved in your faith

πίστεως κατεργάζεται ὑπομονήν. **4** ἡ δὲ
²faith works endurance. – And

ὑπομονὴ ἔργον τέλειον ἐχέτω, ἵνα ἦτε
endurance ³work ²perfect ¹let it in or- ye may
have, der that be

τέλειοι καὶ ὁλόκληροι, ἐν μηδενὶ λειπόμενοι.
perfect and entire, in nothing wanting.

5 Εἰ δέ τις ὑμῶν λείπεται σοφίας, αἰτείτω
if But any- of you wants wisdom, let him
one ask

παρὰ τοῦ διδόντος θεοῦ πᾶσιν ἁπλῶς
from ²the ²giving ¹God to all unre-
[one] men servedly

καὶ μὴ ὀνειδίζοντος, καὶ δοθήσεται αὐτῷ.
and not reproaching, and it will be given to him.

6 αἰτείτω δὲ ἐν πίστει, μηδὲν διακριν-
But let him ask in faith, nothing doubt-

όμενος· ὁ γὰρ διακρινόμενος ἔοικεν κλύδωνι
ing; for the [one] doubting is like a wave

θαλάσσης ἀνεμιζομένῳ καὶ ῥιπιζομένῳ.
of [the] sea *being* driven by wind and *being* tossed.

7 μὴ γὰρ οἰέσθω ὁ ἄνθρωπος ἐκεῖνος
For let not ²suppose ¹that ²man

ὅτι λήμψεταί τι παρὰ τοῦ κυρίου, **8** ἀνὴρ
that he will any- from the Lord, a man
receive thing

* See note on Phil. 3.16 in Introduction.

ever. Amen.

22 Brothers, I urge you to bear with my word of exhortation, for I have written you only a short letter. 23 I want you to know that our brother Timothy has been released. If he arrives soon, I will come with him to see you. 24 Greet all your leaders and all God's people. Those from Italy send you their greetings. 25 Grace be with you all.

James

Chapter 1

JAMES, a servant of God and of the Lord Jesus Christ,

To the twelve tribes scattered among the nations:

Greetings.

Trials and Temptations

2 Consider it pure joy, my brothers, whenever you face trials of many kinds, 3 because you know that the testing of your faith develops perseverance. 4 Perseverance must finish its work so that you may be mature and complete, not lacking anything. 5 If any of you lacks wisdom, he should ask God, who gives generously to all without finding fault, and it will be given to him. 6 But when he asks, he must believe and not doubt, because he who doubts is like a wave of the sea, blown and tossed by the wind. 7 That man should not think he will receive anything from the Lord;

minded and unstable in every way, must not expect to receive anything from the Lord.

Poverty and Riches

9 Let the believer[c] who is lowly boast in being raised up, 10 and the rich in being brought low, because the rich will disappear like a flower in the field. 11 For the sun rises with its scorching heat and withers the field; its flower falls, and its beauty perishes. It is the same way with the rich; in the midst of a busy life, they will wither away.

Trial and Temptation

12 Blessed is anyone who endures temptation. Such a one has stood the test and will receive the crown of life that the Lord[d] has promised to those who love him. 13 No one, when tempted, should say, "I am being tempted by God"; for God cannot be tempted by evil and he himself tempts no one. 14 But one is tempted by one's own desire, being lured and enticed by it; 15 then, when that desire has conceived, it gives birth to sin, and that sin, when it is fully grown, gives birth to death. 16 Do not be deceived, my beloved.[e]

17 Every generous act of giving, with every perfect gift, is from above, coming down from the Father of lights, with whom there is no variation or shadow due to change.[f] 18 In fulfillment of his own purpose he gave us birth by the word of truth, so that we would become a kind of first fruits of his creatures.

Hearing and Doing the Word

19 You must understand this, my beloved:[e] let everyone be quick to lis-

---

δίψυχος, ἀκατάστατος ἐν πάσαις ταῖς
two-souled, unsettled in all the

ὁδοῖς αὐτοῦ. 9 Καυχάσθω δὲ ὁ ἀδελφὸς
ways of him. But let ⁴boast ¹the ²brother

ὁ ταπεινὸς ἐν τῷ ὕψει αὐτοῦ, 10 ὁ δὲ
– ²humble in the height of him, and the

πλούσιος ἐν τῇ ταπεινώσει αὐτοῦ, ὅτι
rich one in the humiliation of him, because

ὡς ἄνθος χόρτου παρελεύσεται. 11 ἀνέτειλεν
as a flower of grass he will pass away. ⁴rose

γὰρ ὁ ἥλιος σὺν τῷ καύσωνι καὶ ἐξήρανεν
¹For ²the ³sun with the hot wind and dried

τὸν χόρτον, καὶ τὸ ἄνθος αὐτοῦ ἐξέπεσεν
the grass, and the flower of it fell out

καὶ ἡ εὐπρέπεια τοῦ προσώπου αὐτοῦ
and the comeliness of the appearance of it

ἀπώλετο· οὕτως καὶ ὁ πλούσιος ἐν ταῖς
perished; thus also the rich man in the

πορείαις αὐτοῦ μαρανθήσεται. 12 Μακάριος
goings of him will fade away. Blessed

ἀνὴρ ὃς ὑπομένει πειρασμόν, ὅτι δόκιμος
[the] who endures trial, because ²approved
man

γενόμενος λήμψεται τὸν στέφανον τῆς
¹having become he will receive the crown of

ζωῆς, ὃν ἐπηγγείλατο τοῖς ἀγαπῶσιν αὐτόν.
of life, which he promised to the [ones] loving him.

13 Μηδεὶς πειραζόμενος λεγέτω ὅτι ἀπὸ
²no man ³being tempted ¹Let ⁴say[,] – From

θεοῦ πειράζομαι· ὁ γὰρ θεὸς ἀπείραστός
God I am tempted; – for God ²untempted

ἐστιν κακῶν, πειράζει δὲ αὐτὸς οὐδένα.
¹is of(with) and ²tempts ¹he no man.
evil things,

14 ἕκαστος δὲ πειράζεται ὑπὸ τῆς ἰδίας
But each man is tempted by the(his) own

ἐπιθυμίας ἐξελκόμενος καὶ δελεαζόμενος·
lusts being drawn out and *being enticed*;

15 εἶτα ἡ ἐπιθυμία συλλαβοῦσα τίκτει
then – lust having conceived bears

ἁμαρτίαν, ἡ δὲ ἁμαρτία ἀποτελεσθεῖσα
sin, – and sin having been
fully formed

ἀποκύει θάνατον. 16 Μὴ πλανᾶσθε, ἀδελφοί
brings forth death. Do not err, ²brothers

μου ἀγαπητοί.
³of me ¹beloved.

17 Πᾶσα δόσις ἀγαθὴ καὶ πᾶν δώρημα
Every ²giving ¹good and every ²gift

τέλειον ἄνωθέν ἐστιν καταβαῖνον ἀπὸ τοῦ
¹perfect ⁴from above ²is coming down from the

πατρὸς τῶν φώτων, παρ' ᾧ οὐκ ἔνι
Father of the lights, with whom ⁵has no place

παραλλαγὴ ἢ τροπῆς ἀποσκίασμα. 18 βου-
¹change ²or ⁴of turning ³shadow. Having

ληθεὶς ἀπεκύησεν ἡμᾶς λόγῳ ἀληθείας,
purposed he brought forth us by a word of truth,

εἰς τὸ εἶναι ἡμᾶς ἀπαρχήν τινα τῶν
for the to be us[b] ²firstfruit ¹a certain ³of
=that we should be the

αὐτοῦ κτισμάτων.
⁵of him ⁴creatures.

19 Ἴστε, ἀδελφοί μου ἀγαπητοί. ἔστω
Know ye, ²brothers ³of me ¹beloved. ²let be

---

8 he is a double-minded man, unstable in all he does.

9 The brother in humble circumstances ought to take pride in his high position. 10 But the one who is rich should take pride in his low position, because he will pass away like a wild flower. 11 For the sun rises with scorching heat and withers the plant; its blossom falls and its beauty is destroyed. In the same way, the rich man will fade away even while he goes about his business.

12 Blessed is the man who perseveres under trial, because when he has stood the test, he will receive the crown of life that God has promised to those who love him.

13 When tempted, no one should say, "God is tempting me." For God cannot be tempted by evil, nor does he tempt anyone; 14 but each one is tempted when, by his own evil desire, he is dragged away and enticed. 15 Then, after desire has conceived, it gives birth to sin; and sin, when it is full-grown, gives birth to death.

16 Don't be deceived, my dear brothers. 17 Every good and perfect gift is from above, coming down from the Father of the heavenly lights, who does not change like shifting shadows. 18 He chose to give us birth through the word of truth, that we might be a kind of firstfruits of all he created.

Listening and Doing

19 My dear brothers, take note of this: Everyone

---

c Gk brother
d Gk he; other ancient authorities read God
e Gk my beloved brothers
f Other ancient authorities read variation due to a shadow of turning

ten, slow to speak, slow to anger; 20for your anger does not produce God's righteousness. 21 Therefore rid yourselves of all sordidness and rank growth of wickedness, and welcome with meekness the implanted word that has the power to save your souls.

22 But be doers of the word, and not merely hearers who deceive themselves. 23 For if any are hearers of the word and not doers, they are like those who look at themselves *g* in a mirror; 24for they look at themselves and, on going away, immediately forget what they were like. 25 But those who look into the perfect law, the law of liberty, and persevere, being not hearers who forget but doers who act—they will be blessed in their doing.

26 If any think they are religious, and do not bridle their tongues but deceive their hearts, their religion is worthless. 27 Religion that is pure and undefiled before God, the Father, is this: to care for orphans and widows in their distress, and to keep oneself unstained by the world.

δὲ	πᾶς	ἄνθρωπος	ταχὺς	εἰς	τὸ	ἀκοῦσαι,
1But	every	man	swift	for	the	to hear,

βραδὺς	εἰς	τὸ	λαλῆσαι,	βραδὺς	εἰς	ὀργήν·
slow	for	the	to speak,	slow	to	wrath;

20 ὀργὴ γὰρ ἀνδρὸς δικαιοσύνην θεοῦ
for [the] wrath of a man ¹[the] righteousness ²of God

οὐκ ἐργάζεται. **21** διὸ ἀποθέμενοι πᾶσαν
¹works not. Wherefore putting away all

ῥυπαρίαν καὶ περισσείαν κακίας ἐν πραΰ-
filthiness and superfluity of evil in meek-

τητι δέξασθε τὸν ἔμφυτον λόγον τὸν
ness receive ye the implanted word –

δυνάμενον σῶσαι τὰς ψυχὰς ὑμῶν. **22** γίν-
being able to save the souls of you. be-

εσθε δὲ ποιηταὶ λόγου, καὶ μὴ ἀκροαταὶ
come ye And doers of [the] word, and not hearers

μόνον παραλογιζόμενοι ἑαυτούς. **23** ὅτι
only misleading yourselves. Because

εἴ τις ἀκροατὴς λόγου ἐστὶν καὶ οὐ
if anyone ¹a hearer ²of [the] word ³is and not

ποιητής, οὗτος ἔοικεν ἀνδρὶ κατανοοῦντι
a doer, this one is like a man perceiving

τὸ πρόσωπον τῆς γενέσεως αὐτοῦ ἐν
the face of the birth of him in

ἐσόπτρῳ· **24** κατενόησεν γὰρ ἑαυτὸν καὶ
a mirror: for he perceived himself and

ἀπελήλυθεν, καὶ εὐθέως ἐπελάθετο ὁποῖος
has gone away, and straightway forgot what sort

ἦν. **25** ὁ δὲ παρακύψας εἰς νόμον
he was. But the [one] having looked *into* into ³law

τέλειον τὸν τῆς ἐλευθερίας καὶ παραμείνας,
²perfect ¹the – of freedom and remaining,

οὐκ ἀκροατὴς ἐπιλησμονῆς γενόμενος ἀλλὰ
not ²a hearer ³of forgetfulness* ¹becoming but

ποιητὴς ἔργου, οὗτος μακάριος ἐν τῇ
a doer of [the] work, this one ²blessed ³in ⁴the

ποιήσει αὐτοῦ ἔσται. **26** Εἴ τις δοκεῖ
⁵doing ⁶of him ¹will be. If anyone thinks

θρησκὸς εἶναι, μὴ χαλιναγωγῶν γλῶσσαν
²religious ¹to be, not bridling tongue

ἑαυτοῦ ἀλλὰ ἀπατῶν καρδίαν ἑαυτοῦ,
of himself but deceiving heart of himself,

τούτου μάταιος ἡ θρησκεία. **27** θρησκεία
of this one vain the religion. Religion

καθαρὰ καὶ ἀμίαντος παρὰ τῷ θεῷ
clean and undefiled before the God

καὶ πατρὶ αὕτη ἐστίν, ἐπισκέπτεσθαι
and Father ²this ¹is, to visit

ὀρφανοὺς καὶ χήρας ἐν τῇ θλίψει αὐτῶν,
orphans and widows in the affliction of them,

ἄσπιλον ἑαυτὸν τηρεῖν ἀπὸ τοῦ κόσμου.
unspotted himself to keep from the world.

should be quick to listen, slow to speak and slow to become angry, 20for man's anger does not bring about the righteous life that God desires. 21Therefore, get rid of all moral filth and the evil that is so prevalent and humbly accept the word planted in you, which can save you.

22Do not merely listen to the word, and so deceive yourselves. Do what it says. 23Anyone who listens to the word but does not do what it says is like a man who looks at his face in a mirror 24and, after looking at himself, goes away and immediately forgets what he looks like. 25But the man who looks intently into the perfect law that gives freedom, and continues to do this, not forgetting what he has heard, but doing it—he will be blessed in what he does.

26If anyone considers himself religious and yet does not keep a tight rein on his tongue, he deceives himself and his religion is worthless. 27Religion that God our Father accepts as pure and faultless is this: to look after orphans and widows in their distress and to keep oneself from being polluted by the world.

Chapter 2

Warning against Partiality

MY brothers and sisters,*h* do you with your acts of favoritism really believe in our glorious Lord Jesus Christ?*i* 2 For if a person with gold rings and in fine clothes comes into your assembly, and if a

2 Ἀδελφοί μου, μὴ ἐν προσωπολημψίαις
Brothers of me, not in respects of persons

ἔχετε τὴν πίστιν τοῦ κυρίου ἡμῶν Ἰησοῦ
have ye the faith of the Lord of us Jesus

Χριστοῦ τῆς δόξης.* **2** ἐὰν γὰρ εἰσέλθῃ
Christ[,] of the glory.* For if [there] enters

εἰς συναγωγὴν ὑμῶν ἀνὴρ χρυσοδακτύλιος
into a synagogue of you a man gold-fingered

Chapter 2

Favoritism Forbidden

MY brothers, as believers in our glorious Lord Jesus Christ, don't show favoritism. 2Suppose a man comes into your meeting wearing a gold ring

g Gk *at the face of his birth*
h Gk *My brothers*
i Or *hold the faith of our glorious Lord Jesus Christ without acts of favoritism*

* Genitive of quality: " a forgetful hearer."

* That is, taking " the glory " as in apposition to "Jesus Christ"; see Luke 2. 32*b*.

poor person in dirty clothes also comes in. 3 and if you take notice of the one wearing the fine clothes and say, "Have a seat here, please," while to the one who is poor you say, "Stand there," or, "Sit at my feet,"ʲ 4have you not made distinctions among yourselves, and become judges with evil thoughts? 5 Listen, my beloved brothers and sisters.ᵇ Has not God chosen the poor in the world to be rich in faith and to be heirs of the kingdom that he has promised to those who love him? 6 But you have dishonored the poor. Is it not the rich who oppress you? Is it not they who drag you into court? 7 Is it not they who blaspheme the excellent name that was invoked over you?

8 You do well if you really fulfill the royal law according to the scripture, "You shall love your neighbor as yourself." 9 But if you show partiality, you commit sin and are convicted by the law as transgressors. 10 For whoever keeps the whole law but fails in one point has become accountable for all of it. 11 For the one who said, "You shall not commit adultery," also said, "You shall not murder." Now if you do not commit adultery but if you murder, you have become a transgressor of the law. 12 So speak and so act as those who are to be judged by the law of liberty. 13 For judgment will be without mercy to anyone who has shown no mercy; mercy triumphs over judgment.

Faith without Works Is Dead

14 What good is it, my

ἐν   ἐσθῆτι   λαμπρᾷ,   εἰσέλθῃ   δὲ   καὶ   πτωχὸς
in   ²clothing ¹splendid, and [there] enters also a poor man
ἐν   ῥυπαρᾷ   ἐσθῆτι,   3 ἐπιβλέψητε   δὲ   ἐπὶ
in   shabby   clothing,   and ye look on   on
.τὸν   φοροῦντα   τὴν   ἐσθῆτα   τὴν   λαμπρὰν
the [one] wearing   the   clothing   –   splendid
καὶ   εἴπητε·   σὺ   κάθου   ὧδε   καλῶς,   καὶ
and   say: ²thou ¹Sit   here   well,   and
τῷ   πτωχῷ   εἴπητε·   σὺ   στῆθι   ἐκεῖ   ἢ
to the poor man ye say: ²thou ¹Stand there or
κάθου   ὑπὸ   τὸ   ὑποπόδιόν   μου,   4 οὐ
sit   under   the   footstool   of me,   not
διεκρίθητε   ἐν   ἑαυτοῖς   καὶ   ἐγένεσθε   κριταὶ
did ye dis- among yourselves and became   judges
criminate
διαλογισμῶν   πονηρῶν;   5 Ἀκούσατε,   ἀδελφοί
²thoughts   ¹of evil ?§   Hear ye,   brothers
μου   ἀγαπητοί.   οὐχ   ὁ   θεὸς   ἐξελέξατο
of me   beloved. ²not – ³God ¹Chose
τοὺς   πτωχοὺς   τῷ   κόσμῳ   πλουσίους   ἐν
the   poor   in the world   rich   in
πίστει   καὶ   κληρονόμους   τῆς   βασιλείας
faith   and   heirs   of the   kingdom
ἧς   ἐπηγγείλατο   τοῖς   ἀγαπῶσιν   αὐτόν;
which   he promised   to the [ones]   loving   him?
6 ὑμεῖς   δὲ   ἠτιμάσατε   τὸν   πτωχόν.   οὐχ
But ye   dishonoured   the   poor man. [Do] not
οἱ   .πλούσιοι   καταδυναστεύουσιν   ὑμῶν,   καὶ
the   rich men   oppress   you,   and
αὐτοὶ   ἕλκουσιν   ὑμᾶς   εἰς   κριτήρια;   7 οὐκ
they   drag   you   to   tribunals? [Do] not
αὐτοὶ   βλασφημοῦσιν   τὸ   καλὸν   ὄνομα   τὸ
they   blaspheme   the   good   name   –
ἐπικληθὲν   ἐφ'   ὑμᾶς;   8 εἰ   μέντοι   νόμον
called on   on   you ?   If   indeed   ³law
τελεῖτε   βασιλικὸν   κατὰ   τὴν   γραφήν·
¹ye fulfil ²a royal according to the scripture:
ἀγαπήσεις   τὸν   πλησίον   σου   ὡς   σεαυτόν,
Thou shalt love the neighbour of thee as thyself,
καλῶς   ποιεῖτε·   9 εἰ   δὲ   προσωπολημπτεῖτε,
²well   ¹ye do;   but if   ye respect persons,
ἁμαρτίαν   ἐργάζεσθε,   ἐλεγχόμενοι   ὑπὸ   τοῦ
²sin   ¹ye work,   being reproved   by   the
νόμου   ὡς   παραβάται.   10 ὅστις   γὰρ
law   as   transgressors.   For ¹[he] who
ὅλον   τὸν   νόμον   τηρήσῃ,   πταίσῃ   δὲ   ἐν
²all   ⁴the   ³law   ²keeps,   yet stumbles   in
ἑνί,   γέγονεν   πάντων   ἔνοχος.   11 ὁ   γὰρ
one   he has   ²of all   ¹guilty.   For the
thing,   become   [one]
εἰπών·   μὴ   μοιχεύσῃς,   εἶπεν   καὶ·   μὴ
saying: Do not commit adultery, said also: not
φονεύσῃς·   εἰ   δὲ   οὐ   μοιχεύεις,   φονεύεις
Do murder; now if thou dost not ²murderest
commit adultery,
δέ,   γέγονας   παραβάτης   νόμου.   12 οὕτως
¹but, thou hast   a transgressor   of [the]   So
become   law.
λαλεῖτε   καὶ   οὕτως   ποιεῖτε   ὡς   διὰ   νόμου
speak ye   and   so   do ye   as   ³through ⁴a law
ἐλευθερίας   μέλλοντες   κρίνεσθαι.   13 ἡ   γὰρ
⁵of freedom   ¹being about   ²to be judged.   For the
κρίσις   ἀνέλεος   τῷ   μὴ   ποιήσαντι   ἔλεος·
judg- [will unmerci- to the not do(show)ing mercy;
ment be] ful   [one]
κατακαυχᾶται   ἔλεος   κρίσεως.   14 Τί   τὸ
²exults over   ¹mercy   of judgment.   What [is] the

§ Genitive of quality: "evil-thinking judges."

---

and fine clothes, and a poor man in shabby clothes also comes in. 3 If you show special attention to the man wearing fine clothes and say, "Here's a good seat for you," but say to the poor man, "You stand there" or "Sit on the floor by my feet," 4 have you not discriminated among yourselves and become judges with evil thoughts?

5 Listen, my dear brothers: Has not God chosen those who are poor in the eyes of the world to be rich in faith and to inherit the kingdom he promised those who love him? 6 But you have insulted the poor. Is it not the rich who are exploiting you? Are they not the ones who are dragging you into court? 7 Are they not the ones who are slandering the noble name of him to whom you belong?

8 If you really keep the royal law found in Scripture, "Love your neighbor as yourself,"ᵃ you are doing right. 9 But if you show favoritism, you sin and are convicted by the law as lawbreakers. 10 For whoever keeps the whole law and yet stumbles at just one point is guilty of breaking all of it. 11 For he who said, "Do not commit adultery,"ᵇ also said, "Do not murder."ᶜ If you do not commit adultery but do commit murder, you have become a lawbreaker.

12 Speak and act as those who are going to be judged by the law that gives freedom, 13 because judgment without mercy will be shown to anyone who has not been merciful. Mercy triumphs over judgment!

Faith and Deeds

14 What good is it, my

ᵃ8 Lev. 19:18
ᵇ11 Exodus 20:14; Deut. 5:18
ᶜ11 Exodus 20:13; Deut. 5:17

brothers and sisters,[k] if you say you have faith but do not have works? Can faith save you? 15 If a brother or sister is naked and lacks daily food, 16 and one of you says to them, "Go in peace; keep warm and eat your fill," and yet you do not supply their bodily needs, what is the good of that? 17 So faith by itself, if it has no works, is dead.

18 But someone will say, "You have faith and I have works." Show me your faith apart from your works, and I by my works will show you my faith. 19 You believe that God is one; you do well. Even the demons believe—and shudder. 20 Do you want to be shown, you senseless person, that faith apart from works is barren? 21 Was not our ancestor Abraham justified by works when he offered his son Isaac on the altar? 22 You see that faith was active along with his works, and faith was brought to completion by the works. 23 Thus the scripture was fulfilled that says, "Abraham believed God, and it was reckoned to him as righteousness," and he was called the friend of God. 24 You see that a person is justified by works and not by faith alone. 25 Likewise, was not Rahab the prostitute also justified by works when she welcomed the messengers and sent them out by another road? 26 For

---

ὄφελος, ἀδελφοί μου, ἐὰν πίστιν λέγῃ
profit, brothers of me, if ⁴faith ²says

τις ἔχειν ἔργα δὲ μὴ ἔχῃ; μὴ δύναται
¹any- ³to have ⁵works ⁶but ⁷not ⁸has? not can

ἡ πίστις σῶσαι αὐτόν; 15 ἐὰν ἀδελφὸς
the faith to save him? If a brother

ἢ ἀδελφὴ γυμνοὶ ὑπάρχωσιν καὶ λειπόμενοι
or a sister ²naked ¹are and lacking

τῆς ἐφημέρου τροφῆς, 16 εἴπῃ δέ τις
of the daily food, and ⁴says ¹any-
                                                one

αὐτοῖς ἐξ ὑμῶν· ὑπάγετε ἐν εἰρήνῃ,
²to them ³of ²you: Go ye in peace,

θερμαίνεσθε καὶ χορτάζεσθε, μὴ δῶτε
be warmed and filled, ⁴not ³ye give

δὲ αὐτοῖς τὰ ἐπιτήδεια τοῦ σώματος,
¹but ²them the necessaries of the body,

τί τὸ ὄφελος; 17 οὕτως καὶ ἡ πίστις,
what [is] the profit? So indeed - faith,

ἐὰν μὴ ἔχῃ ἔργα, νεκρά ἐστιν καθ'
if it has not works, ²dead ¹is by

ἑαυτήν. 18 ἀλλ' ἐρεῖ τις· σὺ πίστιν
itself. But ²will say ¹someone: Thou ²faith

ἔχεις, κἀγὼ ἔργα ἔχω· δεῖξόν μοι τὴν
¹hast, and I ²works ¹have; show me the

πίστιν σου χωρὶς τῶν ἔργων, κἀγώ
faith of thee without the works, and I

σοι δείξω ἐκ τῶν ἔργων μου τὴν πίστιν.
thee will show ⁴by ³the ⁵works ²of me ¹the ²faith.

19 σὺ πιστεύεις ὅτι εἷς ἐστιν ὁ θεός;
Thou believest that ²one ¹is - ¹God?

καλῶς ποιεῖς· καὶ τὰ δαιμόνια πιστεύουσιν
²well ¹thou doest; also the demons believe

καὶ φρίσσουσιν. 20 θέλεις δὲ γνῶναι,
and shudder. But art thou willing to know,

ὦ ἄνθρωπε κενέ, ὅτι ἡ πίστις χωρὶς
O ²man ¹vain, that - faith without

τῶν ἔργων ἀργή ἐστιν; 21 Ἀβραὰμ ὁ
- works barren is? Abraham the

πατὴρ ἡμῶν οὐκ ἐξ ἔργων ἐδικαιώθη,
father of us not by works was justified,

ἀνενέγκας Ἰσαὰκ τὸν υἱὸν αὐτοῦ ἐπὶ
offering up Isaac the son of him on

τὸ θυσιαστήριον; 22 βλέπεις ὅτι ἡ πίστις
the altar? Thou seest that - faith

συνήργει τοῖς ἔργοις αὐτοῦ, καὶ ἐκ
worked with the works of him, and by

τῶν ἔργων ἡ πίστις ἐτελειώθη, 23 καὶ
the works the faith was perfected, and

ἐπληρώθη ἡ γραφὴ ἡ λέγουσα· ἐπίστευσεν
was fulfilled the scripture - saying: believed

δὲ Ἀβραὰμ τῷ θεῷ, καὶ ἐλογίσθη αὐτῷ
And Abraham - God, and it was reckoned to him

εἰς δικαιοσύνην, καὶ φίλος θεοῦ ἐκλήθη.
for righteousness, and ²friend ³of God ¹he was called.

24 ὁρᾶτε ὅτι ἐξ ἔργων δικαιοῦται ἄνθρωπος
Ye see that by works ²is justified ¹a man

καὶ οὐκ ἐκ πίστεως μόνον. 25 ὁμοίως
and not by faith only. likewise

δὲ καὶ Ῥαὰβ ἡ πόρνη οὐκ ἐξ ἔργων
And also Rahab the prostitute not by works

ἐδικαιώθη, ὑποδεξαμένη τοὺς ἀγγέλους καὶ
was justified, entertaining the messengers and

---

brothers, if a man claims to have faith but has no deeds? Can such faith save him? 15 Suppose a brother or sister is without clothes and daily food. 16 If one of you says to him, "Go, I wish you well; keep warm and well fed," but does nothing about his physical needs, what good is it? 17 In the same way, faith by itself, if it is not accompanied by action, is dead.

18 But someone will say, "You have faith; I have deeds."

Show me your faith without deeds, and I will show you my faith by what I do. 19 You believe that there is one God. Good! Even the demons believe that—and shudder.

20 You foolish man, do you want evidence that faith without deeds is useless[d]? 21 Was not our ancestor Abraham considered righteous for what he did when he offered his son Isaac on the altar? 22 You see that his faith and his actions were working together, and his faith was made complete by what he did. 23 And the scripture was fulfilled that says, "Abraham believed God, and it was credited to him as righteousness,"[e] and he was called God's friend. 24 You see that a person is justified by what he does and not by faith alone.

25 In the same way, was not even Rahab the prostitute considered righteous for what she did when she gave lodging to the spies and sent them off in a dif-

---

[k] Gk brothers

[d]20 Some early manuscripts dead
[e]23 Gen. 15:6

just as the body without the spirit is dead, so faith without works is also dead.

Chapter 3
Taming the Tongue

NOT many of you should become teachers, my brothers and sisters, *k* for you know that we who teach will be judged with greater strictness. [2] For all of us make many mistakes. Anyone who makes no mistakes in speaking is perfect, able to keep the whole body in check with a bridle. [3] If we put bits into the mouths of horses to make them obey us, we guide their whole bodies. [4] Or look at ships: though they are so large that it takes strong winds to drive them, yet they are guided by a very small rudder wherever the will of the pilot directs. [5] So also the tongue is a small member, yet it boasts of great exploits.

How great a forest is set ablaze by a small fire! [6] And the tongue is a fire. The tongue is placed among our members as a world of iniquity; it stains the whole body, sets on fire the cycle of nature, *l* and is itself set on fire by hell. *m* [7] For every species of beast and bird, of reptile and sea creature, can be tamed and has been tamed by the human species, [8] but no one can tame the tongue—a restless evil, full of deadly poison. [9] With it we bless the Lord and Father, and with it we curse those who are made in the likeness of God. [10] From

l Or wheel of birth
m Gk Gehenna

ἑτέρα   ὁδῷ   ἐκβαλοῦσα;   **26** ὥσπερ   γὰρ   τὸ
by a   way   sending [them]   For as   the
different   forth?

σῶμα   χωρὶς   πνεύματος   νεκρόν   ἐστιν,   οὕτως
body   without   spirit   ²dead   ¹is,   so

καὶ   ἡ   πίστις   χωρὶς   ἔργων   νεκρά   ἐστιν.
also   -   faith   without   works   ²dead   ¹is.

3 Μὴ   πολλοὶ   διδάσκαλοι   γίνεσθε,   ἀδελφοί
²not   ³many   ⁴teachers   ¹Become ye,   brothers

μου,   εἰδότες   ὅτι   μεῖζον   κρίμα   λημψόμεθα.
of me,   knowing   that   greater   judgment   we shall receive.

2 πολλὰ   γὰρ   πταίομεν   ἅπαντες·   εἴ   τις
For [in] many [respects] we stumble   all;   if   anyone

ἐν   λόγῳ   οὐ   πταίει,   οὗτος   τέλειος   ἀνήρ,
²in   ³word   ¹stumbles not,   this [is]   a perfect   man,

δυνατὸς   χαλιναγωγῆσαι   καὶ   ὅλον   τὸ   σῶμα.
able   ²to bridle   ¹indeed   all   the   body.

3 εἰ   δὲ   τῶν   ἵππων   τοὺς   χαλινοὺς   εἰς
Now if   -   ⁶of horses   ⁴bridles   ²into

τὰ   στόματα   βάλλομεν   εἰς   τὸ   πείθεσθαι
⁵the   ⁵mouths   ¹we put   for   the   to obey
= to make them obey us,

αὐτοὺς   ἡμῖν,   καὶ   ὅλον   τὸ   σῶμα   αὐτῶν
them*b*   to us,   and   ²all   ³the   ⁴body   ⁵of them

μετάγομεν.   **4** ἰδοὺ   καὶ   τὰ   πλοῖα,   τηλικαῦτα
¹we direct.   Behold   also   the   ships,   ²so great

ὄντα   καὶ   ὑπὸ   ἀνέμων   σκληρῶν   ἐλαυνόμενα,
¹being   ²and   ⁶by   ⁷winds   ⁸hard(strong)   ⁴being driven,

μετάγεται   ὑπὸ   ἐλαχίστου   πηδαλίου   ὅπου
is(are) directed   by   a very little   helm   where

ἡ   ὁρμὴ   τοῦ   εὐθύνοντος   βούλεται·   **5** οὕτως
the impulse of the [one] steering   resolves;   so

καὶ   ἡ   γλῶσσα   μικρὸν   μέλος   ἐστὶν   καὶ
also   the   tongue   ²a little   ³member   ¹is   and

μεγάλα   αὐχεῖ.   ἰδοὺ   ἡλίκον   πῦρ   ἡλίκον
great things   boasts.   Behold   how little   a fire   ²how great

ὕλην   ἀνάπτει·   **6** καὶ   ἡ   γλῶσσα   πῦρ,
³wood   ¹kindles;   and   the   tongue   [is] a fire,

ὁ   κόσμος   τῆς   ἀδικίας,   ἡ   γλῶσσα   καθίστα-
the   world   τῆς   of iniquity,   the   tongue   is

ται   ἐν   τοῖς   μέλεσιν   ἡμῶν,   ἡ   σπιλοῦσα
set   among   the   members   of us,   -   spotting

ὅλον   τὸ   σῶμα   καὶ   φλογίζουσα   τὸν
all   the   body   and   inflaming   the

τροχὸν   τῆς   γενέσεως   καὶ   φλογιζομένη
course   -   of nature   and   being inflamed

ὑπὸ   τῆς   γεέννης.   **7** πᾶσα   γὰρ   φύσις
by   -   gehenna.   For every   nature

θηρίων   τε   καὶ   πετεινῶν,   ἑρπετῶν   τε
²of beasts   ¹both   and   of birds,   ²of reptiles   ¹both

καὶ   ἐναλίων   δαμάζεται   καὶ   δεδάμασται
and   of marine   is tamed   and   has been tamed
creatures

τῇ   φύσει   τῇ   ἀνθρωπίνῃ,   **8** τὴν   δὲ
by the   ²nature   -   ¹human,   but the

γλῶσσαν   οὐδεὶς   δαμάσαι   δύναται   ἀνθρώπων·
tongue   ¹no one   ⁴to tame   ³is able   ²of men;

ἀκατάστατον   κακόν,   μεστὴ   ἰοῦ   θανατηφόρου.
an unruly   evil,   full   ²poison   ¹of death-dealing.

9 ἐν   αὐτῇ   εὐλογοῦμεν   τὸν   κύριον   καὶ
By   this   we bless   the   Lord   and

πατέρα,   καὶ   ἐν   αὐτῇ   καταρώμεθα   τοὺς
Father,   and   by   this   we curse

ἀνθρώπους   τοὺς   καθ’   ὁμοίωσιν   θεοῦ
men   -   ²according to   ³likeness   ⁴of God

---

ferent direction? [26] As the body without the spirit is dead, so faith without deeds is dead.

Chapter 3
Taming the Tongue

NOT many of you should presume to be teachers, my brothers, because you know that we who teach will be judged more strictly. [2] We all stumble in many ways. If anyone is never at fault in what he says, he is a perfect man, able to keep his whole body in check.

[3] When we put bits into the mouths of horses to make them obey us, we can turn the whole animal. [4] Or take ships as an example. Although they are so large and are driven by strong winds, they are steered by a very small rudder wherever the pilot wants to go. [5] Likewise the tongue is a small part of the body, but it makes great boasts. Consider what a great forest is set on fire by a small spark. [6] The tongue also is a fire, a world of evil among the parts of the body. It corrupts the whole person, sets the whole course of his life on fire, and is itself set on fire by hell.

[7] All kinds of animals, birds, reptiles and creatures of the sea are being tamed and have been tamed by man, [8] but no man can tame the tongue. It is a restless evil, full of deadly poison.

[9] With the tongue we praise our Lord and Father, and with it we curse men, who have been made

the same mouth come blessing and cursing. My brothers and sisters,[n] this ought not to be so. 11 Does a spring pour forth from the same opening both fresh and brackish water? 12 Can a fig tree, my brothers and sisters,[o] yield olives, or a grapevine figs? No more can salt water yield fresh.

Two Kinds of Wisdom

13 Who is wise and understanding among you? Show by your good life that your works are done with gentleness born of wisdom. 14 But if you have bitter envy and selfish ambition in your hearts, do not be boastful and false to the truth. 15 Such wisdom does not come down from above, but is earthly, unspiritual, devilish. 16 For where there is envy and selfish ambition, there will also be disorder and wickedness of every kind. 17 But the wisdom from above is first pure, then peaceable, gentle, willing to yield, full of mercy and good fruits, without a trace of partiality or hypocrisy. 18 And a harvest of righteousness is sown in peace for[p] those who make peace.

γεγονότας· 10 ἐκ τοῦ αὐτοῦ στόματος ἐξέρχεται
having become; out of the same mouth comes forth

εὐλογία καὶ κατάρα. οὐ χρή, ἀδελφοί
blessing and cursing. It is not fitting, brothers

μου, ταῦτα οὕτως γίνεσθαι. 11 μήτι
of me, these things so to be. Not

ἡ πηγὴ ἐκ τῆς αὐτῆς ὀπῆς βρύει τὸ
the fountain out of the same hole sends forth the

γλυκὺ καὶ τὸ πικρόν; 12 μὴ δύναται,
sweet and the bitter? Not can,

ἀδελφοί μου, συκῆ ἐλαίας ποιῆσαι ἢ
brothers of me, a fig-tree ²olives ¹to produce or

ἄμπελος σῦκα; οὔτε ἁλυκὸν γλυκὺ
a vine figs? neither ¹salt ⁴sweet

ποιῆσαι ὕδωρ. 13 Τίς σοφὸς καὶ ἐπιστήμων
²to make ³water. Who [is] wise and knowing

ἐν ὑμῖν; δειξάτω ἐκ τῆς καλῆς ἀναστροφῆς
among you? let him show by the(his) good conduct

τὰ ἔργα αὐτοῦ ἐν πραΰτητι σοφίας.*
the works of him in meekness of wisdom.*

14 εἰ δὲ ζῆλον πικρὸν ἔχετε καὶ ἐριθείαν
But if ²jealousy ²bitter ¹ye have and rivalry

ἐν τῇ καρδίᾳ ὑμῶν, μὴ κατακαυχᾶσθε
in the heart of you, do not exult over

καὶ ψεύδεσθε κατὰ τῆς ἀληθείας. 15 οὐκ
and lie against the truth. ⁴not

ἔστιν αὕτη ἡ σοφία ἄνωθεν κατερχομένη,
²is ¹This ¹wisdom ³from above ³coming down,

ἀλλὰ ἐπίγειος, ψυχική, δαιμονιώδης· 16 ὅπου
but [is] earthly, natural, demon-like; ²where

γὰρ ζῆλος καὶ ἐριθεία, ἐκεῖ ἀκαταστασία
¹for jealousy and rivalry [are], there [is] tumult

καὶ πᾶν φαῦλον πρᾶγμα. 17 ἡ δὲ ἄνωθεν
and every worthless practice. But ¹the ³from above

σοφία πρῶτον μὲν ἁγνή ἐστιν, ἔπειτα
²wisdom ⁵firstly - ⁶pure ⁴is, then

εἰρηνική, ἐπιεικής, εὐπειθής, μεστὴ ἐλέους
peaceable, forbearing, compliant, full of mercy

καὶ καρπῶν ἀγαθῶν, ἀδιάκριτος, ἀνυπό-
and ²fruits ¹of good, without uncertainty, un-

κριτος. 18 καρπὸς δὲ δικαιοσύνης ἐν
feigned. And [the] fruit of righteousness ²in

εἰρήνῃ σπείρεται τοῖς ποιοῦσιν εἰρήνην.
³peace ¹is sown for the [ones] making peace.

---

in God's likeness. 10 Out of the same mouth come praise and cursing. My brothers, this should not be. 11 Can both fresh water and salt[f] water flow from the same spring? 12 My brothers, can a fig tree bear olives, or a grapevine bear figs? Neither can a salt spring produce fresh water.

Two Kinds of Wisdom

13 Who is wise and understanding among you? Let him show it by his good life, by deeds done in the humility that comes from wisdom. 14 But if you harbor bitter envy and selfish ambition in your hearts, do not boast about it or deny the truth. 15 Such "wisdom" does not come down from heaven but is earthly, unspiritual, of the devil. 16 For where you have envy and selfish ambition, there you find disorder and every evil practice.

17 But the wisdom that comes from heaven is first of all pure; then peace-loving, considerate, submissive, full of mercy and good fruit, impartial and sincere. 18 Peacemakers who sow in peace raise a harvest of righteousness.

Chapter 4

Friendship with the World

THOSE conflicts and disputes among you, where do they come from? Do they not come from your cravings that are at war within you? 2 You want something and do not have it; so you commit murder. And you covet[q] something and cannot obtain it; so you engage in disputes and conflicts. You do not have, because you do not ask. 3 You ask and do not receive, because you ask wrongly, in

---

Chapter 4

4 Πόθεν πόλεμοι καὶ πόθεν μάχαι ἐν
Whence wars and whence fights among

ὑμῖν; οὐκ ἐντεῦθεν, ἐκ τῶν ἡδονῶν
you? not thence, out of the pleasures

ὑμῶν τῶν στρατευομένων ἐν τοῖς μέλεσιν
of you - soldiering in the members

ὑμῶν; 2 ἐπιθυμεῖτε, καὶ οὐκ ἔχετε·
of you? Ye desire, and have not;

φονεύετε καὶ ζηλοῦτε, καὶ οὐ δύνασθε
ye murder and are jealous, and are not able

ἐπιτυχεῖν· μάχεσθε καὶ πολεμεῖτε. οὐκ
to obtain; ye fight and ye war. not

ἔχετε διὰ τὸ μὴ αἰτεῖσθαι ὑμᾶς· 3 αἰτεῖτε
Ye have be- the not to ask you[b]; ye ask
cause of

καὶ οὐ λαμβάνετε, διότι κακῶς αἰτεῖσθε,
and receive not, because ³ill ¹ye ask,

Chapter 4

Submit Yourselves to God

WHAT causes fights and quarrels among you? Don't they come from your desires that battle within you? 2 You want something but don't get it. You kill and covet, but you cannot have what you want. You quarrel and fight. You do not have, because you do not ask God. 3 When you ask, you do not receive, because you ask with wrong motives, that

---

[n] Gk My brothers
[o] Gk my brothers
[p] Or by
[q] Or you murder and you covet

* Genitive of quality : " a wise meekness."

[f] 11 Greek bitter (see also verse 14)

order to spend what you get on your pleasures. 4 Adulterers! Do you not know that friendship with the world is enmity with God? Therefore whoever wishes to be a friend of the world becomes an enemy of God. 5 Or do you suppose that it is for nothing that the scripture says, "God *r* yearns jealously for the spirit that he has made to dwell in us"? 6 But he gives all the more grace; therefore it says,

"God opposes the proud,
but gives grace to the humble."

7 Submit yourselves therefore to God. Resist the devil, and he will flee from you. 8 Draw near to God, and he will draw near to you. Cleanse your hands, you sinners, and purify your hearts, you double-minded. 9 Lament and mourn and weep. Let your laughter be turned into mourning and your joy into dejection. 10 Humble yourselves before the Lord, and he will exalt you.

Warning against Judging Another

11 Do not speak evil against one another, brothers and sisters. *s* Whoever speaks evil against another or judges another, speaks evil against the law and judges the law; but if you judge the law, you are not a doer of the law but a judge. 12 There is one lawgiver and judge who is able to save and to destroy. So who, then, are you to judge your neighbor?

Boasting about Tomorrow

13 Come now, you who say, "Today or tomorrow we will go to such and such a town and spend a year there, doing business and making money." 14 Yet you do not even know what to-

---

ἵνα ἐν ταῖς ἡδοναῖς ὑμῶν δαπανήσητε.
in or- in the pleasures of you ye may spend.
der that

4 μοιχαλίδες, οὐκ οἴδατε ὅτι ἡ φιλία
Adulteresses, know ye not that the friendship

τοῦ κόσμου ἔχθρα τοῦ θεοῦ ἐστιν; ὃς
of the world ¹enmity - ²of God ¹is? Who-

ἐὰν οὖν βουληθῇ φίλος εἶναι τοῦ κόσμου,
ever therefore ¹resolves ³a friend ²to be of the world,

ἐχθρὸς τοῦ θεοῦ καθίσταται. 5 ἢ δοκεῖτε
²an enemy - ³of God ¹is constituted. Or think ye

ὅτι κενῶς ἡ γραφὴ λέγει· πρὸς φθόνον
that vainly the scripture says: ⁴to ⁵envy

ἐπιποθεῖ τὸ πνεῦμα ὃ κατῴκισεν ἐν
⁷yearns ¹The ²Spirit ³which ⁴dwelt ⁶in

ἡμῖν; 6 μείζονα δὲ δίδωσιν χάριν· διὸ
⁶you? But ²greater ¹he gives ²grace; where- fore

λέγει· ὁ θεὸς ὑπερηφάνοις ἀντιτάσσεται,
it* says: - God ²arrogant men ¹resists,

ταπεινοῖς δὲ δίδωσιν χάριν. 7 ὑποτάγητε
but to humble men he gives grace. Be ye subject

οὖν τῷ θεῷ· ἀντίστητε δὲ τῷ διαβόλῳ,
there- - to God; but oppose the devil,
fore

καὶ φεύξεται ἀφ' ὑμῶν· 8 ἐγγίσατε τῷ
and he will flee from you; draw near

θεῷ, καὶ ἐγγίσει ὑμῖν. καθαρίσατε
to God, and he will draw near to you. Cleanse ye

χεῖρας, ἁμαρτωλοί, καὶ ἁγνίσατε καρδίας,
hands, sinners, and purify hearts,

δίψυχοι. 9 ταλαιπωρήσατε καὶ πενθήσατε
two-souled Be ye distressed and mourn
(double-minded).

καὶ κλαύσατε· ὁ γέλως ὑμῶν εἰς πένθος
and weep; the laughter of you to mourning

μετατραπήτω καὶ ἡ χαρὰ εἰς κατήφειαν.
let it be turned and the joy to dejection.

10 ταπεινώθητε ἐνώπιον κυρίου, καὶ ὑψώσει
Be ye humbled before [the] Lord, and he will exalt

ὑμᾶς. 11 Μὴ καταλαλεῖτε ἀλλήλων, ἀδελφοί.
you. Speak not against one another, brothers.

ὁ καταλαλῶν ἀδελφοῦ ἢ κρίνων τὸν
The speaking a brother or judging the
[one] against

ἀδελφὸν αὐτοῦ καταλαλεῖ νόμου καὶ κρίνει
brother of him speaks against law and judges

νόμον· εἰ δὲ νόμον κρίνεις, οὐκ εἶ
law; and if· law thou judgest, thou art not

ποιητὴς νόμου ἀλλὰ κριτής. 12 εἷς ἐστιν
a doer of law but a judge. One is

ʻομοθέτης καὶ κριτής, ὁ δυνάμενος
lawgiver and judge, the [one] being able

σῶσαι καὶ ἀπολέσαι· σὺ δὲ τίς εἶ, ὁ
to save and to destroy; ²thou ¹and ²who ¹art, the

κρίνων τὸν πλησίον;
[one] judging the(thy) neighbour?

13 Ἄγε νῦν οἱ λέγοντες· σήμερον ἢ
Come now the [ones] saying: To-day or

αὔριον πορευσόμεθα εἰς τήνδε τὴν πόλιν
to-morrow we will go into this - city

καὶ ποιήσομεν ἐκεῖ ἐνιαυτὸν καὶ ἐμπορευ-
and we will do there a year and we will

σόμεθα καὶ κερδήσομεν· 14 οἵτινες οὐκ
trade and we will make a profit; who not

* That is, " the scripture " (as ver. 5).

---

you may spend what you get on your pleasures.
4 You adulterous people, don't you know that friendship with the world is hatred toward God? Anyone who chooses to be a friend of the world becomes an enemy of God. 5 Or do you think Scripture says without reason that the spirit he caused to live in us envies intensely? *g* 6 But he gives us more grace. That is why Scripture says:

"God opposes the proud but gives grace to the humble." *h*

7 Submit yourselves, then, to God. Resist the devil, and he will flee from you. 8 Come near to God and he will come near to you. Wash your hands, you sinners, and purify your hearts, you double-minded. 9 Grieve, mourn and wail. Change your laughter to mourning and your joy to gloom. 10 Humble yourselves before the Lord, and he will lift you up.

11 Brothers, do not slander one another. Anyone who speaks against his brother or judges him speaks against the law and judges it. When you judge the law, you are not keeping it, but sitting in judgment on it. 12 There is only one Lawgiver and Judge, the one who is able to save and destroy. But you—who are you to judge your neighbor?

Boasting About Tomorrow

13 Now listen, you who say, "Today or tomorrow we will go to this or that city, spend a year there, carry on business and make money." 14 Why, you do

---

r Gk *He*
s Gk *brothers*

g 5 Or *that God jealously longs for the spirit that he made to live in us; or that the Spirit he caused to live in us longs jealously*
h 6 Prov. 3:34

morrow will bring. What is your life? For you are a mist that appears for a little while and then vanishes. 15 Instead you ought to say, "If the Lord wishes, we will live and do this or that." 16 As it is, you boast in your arrogance; all such boasting is evil. 17 Anyone, then, who knows the right thing to do and fails to do it, commits sin.

Chapter 5

Warning to Rich Oppressors

COME now, you rich people, weep and wail for the miseries that are coming to you. 2 Your riches have rotted, and your clothes are moth-eaten. 3 Your gold and silver have rusted, and their rust will be evidence against you, and it will eat your flesh like fire. You have laid up treasure[t] for the last days. 4 Listen! The wages of the laborers who mowed your fields, which you kept back by fraud, cry out, and the cries of the harvesters have reached the ears of the Lord of hosts. 5 You have lived on the earth in luxury and in pleasure; you have fattened your hearts in a day of slaughter. 6 You have condemned and murdered the righteous one, who does not resist you.

Patience in Suffering

7 Be patient, therefore, beloved,[s] until the coming of the Lord. The farmer waits for the precious crop from the earth, being patient with it until it receives the early and the late rains.

ἐπίστασθε τῆς αὔριον ποία ἡ ζωὴ ὑμῶν.
ye know *of the ᵇmorrow ¹what ²the ³life ⁴of you
[will be].

ἀτμὶς γάρ ἐστε ἡ πρὸς ὀλίγον φαινομένη,
For ²a vapour ¹ye are – ⁴for ⁵a little while ³appearing,

ἔπειτα καὶ ἀφανιζομένη· 15 ἀντὶ τοῦ
thereafter indeed disappearing; instead of the

λέγειν ὑμᾶς· ἐὰν ὁ κύριος θελήσῃ, καὶ
to say youᵇ: If the Lord wills, both
=your saying:

ζήσομεν καὶ ποιήσομεν τοῦτο ἢ ἐκεῖνο.
we will live and we will do this or that.

16 νῦν δὲ καυχᾶσθε ἐν ταῖς ἀλαζονείαις
But now ye boast in the vauntings

ὑμῶν· πᾶσα καύχησις τοιαύτη πονηρά
of you; all ²boasting ¹such ⁴evil

ἐστιν. **17** εἰδότι οὖν καλὸν ποιεῖν καὶ
³is. ²to [one] ¹There- ⁴good ³to do and
knowing* fore

μὴ ποιοῦντι, ἁμαρτία αὐτῷ ἐστιν.
not doing, ²sin ¹to him ¹it is.

5 Ἄγε νῦν οἱ πλούσιοι, κλαύσατε
Come now the rich men, weep ye

ὀλολύζοντες ἐπὶ ταῖς ταλαιπωρίαις ὑμῶν
crying aloud over the hardships of you

ταῖς ἐπερχομέναις. **2** ὁ πλοῦτος ὑμῶν
– coming upon. The riches of you

σέσηπεν, καὶ τὰ ἱμάτια ὑμῶν σητόβρωτα
have become and the garments of you moth-eaten
corrupted,

γέγονεν, **3** ὁ χρυσὸς ὑμῶν καὶ ὁ ἄργυρος
have become, the gold of you and the silver

κατίωται, καὶ ὁ ἰὸς αὐτῶν εἰς μαρτύριον
has become and the poison of them for a testimony
rusted over,

ὑμῖν ἔσται καὶ φάγεται τὰς σάρκας
to(against) will and will eat the fleshes
you be

ὑμῶν ὡς πῦρ. ἐθησαυρίσατε ἐν ἐσχάταις
of you as fire. Ye treasured in [the] last

ἡμέραις. **4** ἰδοὺ ὁ μισθὸς τῶν ἐργατῶν
days. Behold[,] the wages of the workmen

τῶν ἀμησάντων τὰς χώρας ὑμῶν ὁ
– having reaped the lands of you –

ἀφυστερημένος ἀφ᾽ ὑμῶν κράζει, καὶ αἱ
being kept back from(by) you cries, and the

βοαὶ τῶν θερισάντων εἰς τὰ ὦτα κυρίου
cries of the having reaped ²into ³the ⁴ears ⁵of [the]
[ones] Lord

σαβαὼθ εἰσελήλυθαν. **5** ἐτρυφήσατε ἐπὶ
⁶of hosts ¹have entered. Ye lived daintily on

τῆς γῆς καὶ ἐσπαταλήσατε, ἐθρέψατε τὰς
the earth and lived riotously, ye nourished the

καρδίας ὑμῶν ἐν ἡμέρᾳ σφαγῆς. **6** κατε-
hearts of you in a day of slaughter. Ye

δικάσατε, ἐφονεύσατε τὸν δίκαιον· οὐκ
condemned, ye murdered the righteous man; not

ἀντιτάσσεται ὑμῖν.
he resists you.

7 Μακροθυμήσατε οὖν, ἀδελφοί, ἕως τῆς
Be ye longsuffering therefore, brothers, until the

παρουσίας τοῦ κυρίου. ἰδοὺ ὁ γεωργὸς
presence of the Lord. Behold[,] the farmer

ἐκδέχεται τὸν τίμιον καρπὸν τῆς γῆς,
awaits the precious fruit of the earth,

μακροθυμῶν ἐπ᾽ αὐτῷ ἕως λάβῃ πρόιμον
being over it until he receives early
longsuffering

---

not even know what will happen tomorrow. What is your life? You are a mist that appears for a little while and then vanishes. 15 Instead, you ought to say, "If it is the Lord's will, we will live and do this or that." 16 As it is, you boast and brag. All such boasting is evil. 17 Anyone, then, who knows the good he ought to do and doesn't do it, sins.

Chapter 5

Warning to Rich Oppressors

NOW listen, you rich people, weep and wail because of the misery that is coming upon you. 2 Your wealth has rotted, and moths have eaten your clothes. 3 Your gold and silver are corroded. Their corrosion will testify against you and eat your flesh like fire. You have hoarded wealth in the last days. 4 Look! The wages you failed to pay the workmen who mowed your fields are crying out against you. The cries of the harvesters have reached the ears of the Lord Almighty. 5 You have lived on earth in luxury and self-indulgence. You have fattened yourselves in the day of slaughter.[t] 6 You have condemned and murdered innocent men, who were not opposing you.

Patience in Suffering

7 Be patient, then, brothers, until the Lord's coming. See how the farmer waits for the land to yield its valuable crop and how patient he is for the autumn

---

[t]Or will eat your flesh, since you have stored up fire

*See note on page xvi.

[t]5 Or yourselves as in a day of feasting

8 You also must be patient. Strengthen your hearts, for the coming of the Lord is near.[u] 9 Beloved,[v] do not grumble against one another, so that you may not be judged. See, the Judge is standing at the doors! 10 As an example of suffering and patience, beloved,[s] take the prophets who spoke in the name of the Lord. 11 Indeed we call blessed those who showed endurance. You have heard of the endurance of Job, and you have seen the purpose of the Lord, how the Lord is compassionate and merciful.

12 Above all, my beloved,[s] do not swear, either by heaven or by earth or by any other oath, but let your "Yes" be yes and your "No" be no, so that you may not fall under condemnation.

The Prayer of Faith

13 Are any among you suffering? They should pray. Are any cheerful? They should sing songs of praise. 14 Are any among you sick? They should call for the elders of the church and have them pray over them, anointing them with oil in the name of the Lord. 15 The prayer of faith will save the sick, and the Lord will raise them up; and anyone who has committed sins will be forgiven. 16 Therefore confess your sins to one another, and pray for one another, so that you may be healed. The prayer of the righteous is powerful and effective. 17 Elijah was a human being like us, and he prayed fervently that it might not rain, and for three years and six months it did not

---

καὶ ὄψιμον.   8 μακροθυμήσατε καὶ ὑμεῖς,
and latter [rain].   Be ²longsuffering ²also ¹ye,

στηρίξατε τὰς καρδίας ὑμῶν, ὅτι ἡ
establish the hearts of you, because the

παρουσία τοῦ κυρίου ἤγγικεν. 9 μὴ
presence of the Lord has drawn near.   not

στενάζετε, ἀδελφοί, κατ' ἀλλήλων ἵνα μὴ
Murmur ye, brothers, against one another lest

κριθῆτε· ἰδοὺ ὁ κριτὴς πρὸ τῶν θυρῶν
ye be behold[,] the judge ²before ³the ⁴doors
judged;

ἕστηκεν.   10 ὑπόδειγμα λάβετε, ἀδελφοί,
¹stands.   ²an example ¹Take ye, ²brothers,

τῆς κακοπαθίας καὶ τῆς μακροθυμίας
⁴of suffering ill ³and – ⁵of longsuffering

τοὺς προφήτας, οἳ ἐλάλησαν ἐν τῷ
¹the ²prophets, who spoke in the

ὀνόματι κυρίου. 11 ἰδοὺ μακαρίζομεν τοὺς
name of [the] Lord. Behold we count blessed the

ὑπομείναντας· τὴν ὑπομονὴν Ἰὼβ ἠκούσατε,
[ones] enduring; ²the ³endurance ⁴of Job ¹ye heard [of],

καὶ τὸ τέλος κυρίου εἴδετε, ὅτι πολύ-
and ²the ³end ⁴of [the] Lord ¹ye saw, that ⁴very

σπλαγχνός ἐστιν ὁ κύριος καὶ οἰκτίρμων.
compassionate ³is ¹the ²Lord and pitiful.

12 Πρὸ πάντων δέ, ἀδελφοί μου, μὴ
²before ³all things ¹But, brothers of me, not

ὀμνύετε, μήτε τὸν οὐρανὸν μήτε τὴν
swear ye, neither by the heaven nor by the

γῆν μήτε ἄλλον τινὰ ὅρκον· ἤτω δὲ
earth nor ²other ¹any oath; but let be

ὑμῶν τὸ ναὶ ναί, καὶ τὸ οὒ οὔ, ἵνα μὴ
of you the Yes yes, and the No no, lest

ὑπὸ κρίσιν πέσητε. 13 Κακοπαθεῖ τις
²under ³judgment ¹ye fall.   Suffers ill anyone

ἐν ὑμῖν; προσευχέσθω· εὐθυμεῖ τις;
among you? let him pray; is cheerful anyone?

ψαλλέτω. 14 ἀσθενεῖ τις ἐν ὑμῖν;
let him sing a psalm. Is weak anyone among you?

προσκαλεσάσθω τοὺς πρεσβυτέρους τῆς
let him summon the elders the

ἐκκλησίας, καὶ προσευξάσθωσαν ἐπ' αὐτὸν
church, and let them pray over him

ἀλείψαντες ἐλαίῳ ἐν τῷ ὀνόματι τοῦ
having anointed with oil in the name of the
[him]

κυρίου. 15 καὶ ἡ εὐχὴ τῆς πίστεως
Lord. And the prayer – of faith

σώσει τὸν κάμνοντα, καὶ ἐγερεῖ αὐτὸν
will heal the [one] being sick, and ³will raise ⁴him

ὁ κύριος· κἂν ἁμαρτίας ᾖ πεποιηκώς,
¹the ²Lord; and if ²sins ¹he ³having done,
may be

ἀφεθήσεται αὐτῷ. 16 ἐξομολογεῖσθε οὖν
it will be forgiven him. Confess ye therefore

ἀλλήλοις τὰς ἁμαρτίας, καὶ προσεύχεσθε
to one the(your) sins, and pray ye
another

ὑπὲρ ἀλλήλων, ὅπως ἰαθῆτε. πολὺ
on be- one another, so as ye may ⁵much(very)
half of be cured.

ἰσχύει δέησις δικαίου ἐνεργουμένη.
⁴is ⁶strong ¹a petition ²of a ³being made effective.
righteous man

17 Ἡλίας ἄνθρωπος ἦν ὁμοιοπαθὴς ἡμῖν,
Elias ²a man ¹was of like feeling to us,

---

and spring rains. 8 You too, be patient and stand firm, because the Lord's coming is near. 9 Don't grumble against each other, brothers, or you will be judged. The Judge is standing at the door!

10 Brothers, as an example of patience in the face of suffering, take the prophets who spoke in the name of the Lord. 11 As you know, we consider blessed those who have persevered. You have heard of Job's perseverance and have seen what the Lord finally brought about. The Lord is full of compassion and mercy.

12 Above all, my brothers, do not swear—not by heaven or by earth or by anything else. Let your "Yes" be yes, and your "No," no, or you will be condemned.

The Prayer of Faith

13 Is any one of you in trouble? He should pray. Is anyone happy? Let him sing songs of praise. 14 Is any one of you sick? He should call the elders of the church to pray over him and anoint him with oil in the name of the Lord. 15 And the prayer offered in faith will make the sick person well; the Lord will raise him up. If he has sinned, he will be forgiven. 16 Therefore confess your sins to each other and pray for each other so that you may be healed. The prayer of a righteous man is powerful and effective. 17 Elijah was a man just like us. He prayed earnestly that it would not rain,

---

[u] Or *is at hand*
[v] Gk *Brothers*

rain on the earth. 18 Then he prayed again, and the heaven gave rain and the earth yielded its harvest.

19 My brothers and sisters,[w] if anyone among you wanders from the truth and is brought back by another, 20 you should know that whoever brings back a sinner from wandering will save the sinner's[x] soul from death and will cover a multitude of sins.

καὶ προσευχῇ προσηύξατο τοῦ μὴ βρέξαι,
and ¹in prayer ¹he prayed   –   not   to rain,ᵈ
                      = that it should not rain,

καὶ οὐκ ἔβρεξεν ἐπὶ τῆς γῆς ἐνιαυτοὺς
and   it rained not   on   the   earth   ¹years

τρεῖς καὶ μῆνας ἕξ· 18 καὶ πάλιν προσ-
¹three and ¹months ¹six;   and   again   he

ηύξατο, καὶ ὁ οὐρανὸς ὑετὸν ἔδωκεν καὶ
prayed,   and   the   heaven   ¹rain   ¹gave   and

ἡ γῆ ἐβλάστησεν τὸν καρπὸν αὐτῆς.
the earth   brought forth   the   fruit   of it.

19 Ἀδελφοί μου, ἐάν τις ἐν ὑμῖν πλανηθῇ
Brothers   of me,   if anyone among you   errs

ἀπὸ τῆς ἀληθείας καὶ ἐπιστρέψῃ τις
from   the   truth   and   ¹turns   ¹anyone

αὐτόν, 20 γινώσκετε ὅτι ὁ ἐπιστρέψας
him,   know ye   that   the [one] turning

ἁμαρτωλὸν ἐκ πλάνης ὁδοῦ ·αὐτοῦ σώσει
a sinner   out of [the] error of way   of him   will save

ψυχὴν αὐτοῦ ἐκ θανάτου καὶ καλύψει
soul   of him   out of   death   and   will hide

πλῆθος ἁμαρτιῶν.
a multitude   of sins.

and it did not rain on the land for three and a half years. 18 Again he prayed, and the heavens gave rain, and the earth produced its crops.

19 My brothers, if one of you should wander from the truth and someone should bring him back, 20 remember this: Whoever turns a sinner from the error of his way will save him from death and cover over a multitude of sins.

The First Letter of
Peter

Chapter 1

Salutation

PETER, an apostle of Jesus Christ,
To the exiles of the Dispersion in Pontus, Galatia, Cappadocia, Asia, and Bithynia, 2 who have been chosen and destined by God the Father and sanctified by the Spirit to be obedient to Jesus Christ and to be sprinkled with his blood:
May grace and peace be yours in abundance.

A Living Hope

3 Blessed be the God and Father of our Lord Jesus Christ! By his great mercy he has given us a new birth into a living hope through the resurrection of Jesus Christ from the dead, 4 and into an inheritance that is imperishable, undefiled, and unfading, kept in heaven for you, 5 who are being protected by the power of God through faith for a salvation ready to be revealed in the last time.

1 Πέτρος ἀπόστολος Ἰησοῦ Χριστοῦ
Peter   an apostle   of Jesus   Christ

ἐκλεκτοῖς παρεπιδήμοις διασπορᾶς Πόντου,
to [the] chosen   sojourners   of [the] dispersion of Pontus,

Γαλατίας, Καππαδοκίας, Ἀσίας καὶ
of Galatia,   of Cappadocia,   of Asia   and

Βιθυνίας, 2 κατὰ πρόγνωσιν θεοῦ πατρός,
of Bithynia,   according   foreknowledge   of God   Father,
        to

ἐν ἁγιασμῷ πνεύματος, εἰς ὑπακοὴν καὶ
in   sanctification   of spirit,   to   obedience   and

ῥαντισμὸν αἵματος Ἰησοῦ Χριστοῦ· χάρις
sprinkling   of [the] blood of Jesus   Christ: Grace

ὑμῖν καὶ εἰρήνη πληθυνθείη.
to you   and   peace   may it be multiplied.

3 Εὐλογητὸς ὁ θεὸς καὶ πατὴρ τοῦ
Blessed [be]   the   God   and   Father   of the

κυρίου ἡμῶν Ἰησοῦ Χριστοῦ, ὁ κατὰ τὸ
Lord   of us   Jesus   Christ,   the accord- the
                        [one] ing to

πολὺ αὐτοῦ ἔλεος ἀναγεννήσας ἡμᾶς εἰς
much   of him   mercy   having regenerated   us   to
(great)

ἐλπίδα ζῶσαν δι' ἀναστάσεως Ἰησοῦ
¹hope   ¹a living   through   [the] resurrection   of Jesus

Χριστοῦ ἐκ νεκρῶν, 4 εἰς κληρονομίαν
Christ   from   [the] dead,   to   an inheritance

ἄφθαρτον καὶ ἀμίαντον καὶ ἀμάραντον,
incorruptible   and   undefiled   and   unfading,

τετηρημένην ἐν οὐρανοῖς εἰς ὑμᾶς 5 τοὺς
having been kept   in   heavens   for   you   the [ones]

ἐν δυνάμει θεοῦ φρουρουμένους διὰ πίστεως
²by   ³[the] power ⁴of God   ¹being guarded   through   faith

εἰς σωτηρίαν ἑτοίμην ἀποκαλυφθῆναι ἐν
to   a salvation   ready   to be revealed   at

1 Peter

Chapter 1

PETER, an apostle of Jesus Christ,

To God's elect, strangers in the world, scattered throughout Pontus, Galatia, Cappadocia, Asia and Bithynia, 2 who have been chosen according to the foreknowledge of God the Father, through the sanctifying work of the Spirit, for obedience to Jesus Christ and sprinkling by his blood:

Grace and peace be yours in abundance.

Praise to God for a Living Hope

3 Praise be to the God and Father of our Lord Jesus Christ! In his great mercy he has given us new birth into a living hope through the resurrection of Jesus Christ from the dead, 4 and into an inheritance that can never perish, spoil or fade —kept in heaven for you, 5 who through faith are shielded by God's power until the coming of the salvation that is ready to be revealed in the last time.

6 In this you rejoice,[a] even if now for a little while you have had to suffer various trials, 7 so that the genuineness of your faith—being more precious than gold that, though perishable, is tested by fire—may be found to result in praise and glory and honor when Jesus Christ is revealed. 8 Although you have not seen[b] him, you love him; and even though you do not see him now, you believe in him and rejoice with an indescribable and glorious joy, 9 for you are receiving the outcome of your faith, the salvation of your souls.

10 Concerning this salvation, the prophets who prophesied of the grace that was to be yours made careful search and inquiry, 11 inquiring about the person or time that the Spirit of Christ within them indicated when it testified in advance to the sufferings destined for Christ and the subsequent glory. 12 It was revealed to them that they were serving not themselves but you, in regard to the things that have now been announced to you through those who brought you good news by the Holy Spirit sent from heaven—things into which angels long to look!

A Call to Holy Living

13 Therefore prepare your minds for action;[c] discipline yourselves; set all your hope on the grace that Jesus Christ will bring you when he is revealed. 14 Like obedient children, do not be conformed to the desires that you formerly had in ignorance. 15 Instead, as he who called you is holy, be holy yourselves

---

καιρῷ ἐσχάτῳ. 6 ἐν ᾧ ἀγαλλιᾶσθε,
²time ¹[the] last. In which ye exult,

ὀλίγον ἄρτι εἰ δέον λυπηθέντες ἐν
a little [while] yet if necessary grieving by

ποικίλοις πειρασμοῖς, 7 ἵνα τὸ δοκίμιον
manifold trials, in order that the proving

ὑμῶν τῆς πίστεως πολυτιμότερον χρυσίου
³of you ¹of the ²faith[,] much more precious [than] ⁴gold

τοῦ ἀπολλυμένου, διὰ πυρὸς δὲ δοκιμαζ-
- ¹of perishing, ⁵through ⁶fire ¹yet ⁸being

ομένου, εὑρεθῇ εἰς ἔπαινον καὶ δόξαν
proved, may be found to praise and glory

καὶ τιμὴν ἐν ἀποκαλύψει Ἰησοῦ Χριστοῦ·
and honour at [the] revelation of Jesus Christ;

8 ὃν οὐκ ἰδόντες ἀγαπᾶτε, εἰς ὃν ἄρτι
whom not having seen ye love, in whom yet

μὴ ὁρῶντες πιστεύοντες δὲ ἀγαλλιᾶσθε
not seeing ²believing ¹but ye exult

χαρᾷ ἀνεκλαλήτῳ καὶ δεδοξασμένῃ,
with joy unspeakable and *having been* glorified,

9 κομιζόμενοι τὸ τέλος τῆς πίστεως
obtaining the end of the(your) faith

σωτηρίαν ψυχῶν. 10 περὶ ἧς σωτηρίας
[the] salvation of [your] souls. Concerning which salvation

ἐξεζήτησαν καὶ ἐξηρεύνησαν προφῆται οἱ
⁹sought out ¹⁰and ¹¹searched out ¹prophets ²the

περὶ τῆς εἰς ὑμᾶς χάριτος προφητεύσαντες,
³con- ⁴the ⁷for ⁸you ⁶grace ⁵[ones] prophesying,
cerning

11 ἐρευνῶντες εἰς τίνα ἢ ποῖον καιρὸν
searching for what or what sort of time

ἐδήλου τὸ ἐν αὐτοῖς πνεῦμα Χριστοῦ
⁴made clear ¹the ²in ³them ⁵Spirit ⁶of Christ

προμαρτυρόμενον τὰ εἰς Χριστὸν παθήματα
⁷forewitnessing ⁸the ¹⁰for ¹¹Christ ⁹sufferings

καὶ τὰς μετὰ ταῦτα δόξας. 12 οἷς
¹²and ¹³the ¹⁵after ¹⁶these ¹⁴glories. To whom

ἀπεκαλύφθη ὅτι οὐχ ἑαυτοῖς ὑμῖν δὲ
it was revealed that not to themselves ²to you ¹but

διηκόνουν αὐτά, ἃ νῦν ἀνηγγέλη ὑμῖν
they the same which now were to you
ministered things, announced

διὰ τῶν εὐαγγελισαμένων ὑμᾶς ἐν
through the [ones] having evangelized you by

πνεύματι ἁγίῳ ἀποσταλέντι ἀπ᾽ οὐρανοῦ,
²Spirit ¹[the] Holy sent forth from heaven,

εἰς ἃ ἐπιθυμοῦσιν ἄγγελοι παρακῦψαι.
into ¹which ³long ²angels ⁴to look into.
things

13 Διὸ ἀναζωσάμενοι τὰς ὀσφύας τῆς
Wherefore girding up the loins of the

διανοίας ὑμῶν, νήφοντες, τελείως ἐλπίσατε
mind of you, being sober, perfectly hope

ἐπὶ τὴν φερομένην ὑμῖν χάριν ἐν
on ¹the ²being brought ³to you ²grace at

ἀποκαλύψει Ἰησοῦ Χριστοῦ. 14 ὡς τέκνα
[the] revelation of Jesus Christ. As children

ὑπακοῆς, μὴ συσχηματιζόμενοι ταῖς πρότε-
of obedience,* not fashioning yourselves to the ⁶form-

ρον ἐν τῇ ἀγνοίᾳ ὑμῶν ἐπιθυμίαις, 15 ἀλλὰ
erly ²in ³the ⁴ignorance ⁵of you ¹longings, but

κατὰ τὸν καλέσαντα ὑμᾶς ἅγιον καὶ
accord- ¹the ²having called ⁴you ³holy [one] ⁷also
ing to

---

6 In this you greatly rejoice, though now for a little while you may have had to suffer grief in all kinds of trials. 7 These have come so that your faith—of greater worth than gold, which perishes even though refined by fire—may be proved genuine and may result in praise, glory and honor when Jesus Christ is revealed. 8 Though you have not seen him, you love him; and even though you do not see him now, you believe in him and are filled with an inexpressible and glorious joy, 9 for you are receiving the goal of your faith, the salvation of your souls.

10 Concerning this salvation, the prophets, who spoke of the grace that was to come to you, searched intently and with the greatest care, 11 trying to find out the time and circumstances to which the Spirit of Christ in them was pointing when he predicted the sufferings of Christ and the glories that would follow. 12 It was revealed to them that they were not serving themselves but you, when they spoke of the things that have now been told you by those who have preached the gospel to you by the Holy Spirit sent from heaven. Even angels long to look into these things.

Be Holy

13 Therefore, prepare your minds for action; be self-controlled; set your hope fully on the grace to be given you when Jesus Christ is revealed. 14 As obedient children, do not conform to the evil desires you had when you lived in ignorance. 15 But just as he who called you is holy, so

---

[a] Or Rejoice in this
[b] Other ancient authorities read known
[c] Gk gird up the loins of your mind

* Genitive of quality: " obedient children."

in all your conduct; 16for it is written, "You shall be holy, for I am holy."

17 If you invoke as Father the one who judges all people impartially according to their deeds, live in reverent fear during the time of your exile. 18 You know that you were ransomed from the futile ways inherited from your ancestors, not with perishable things like silver or gold, 19 but with the precious blood of Christ, like that of a lamb without defect or blemish. 20 He was destined before the foundation of the world, but was revealed at the end of the ages for your sake. 21 Through him you have come to trust in God, who raised him from the dead and gave him glory, so that your faith and hope are set on God.

22 Now that you have purified your souls by your obedience to the truth[d] so that you have genuine mutual love, love one another deeply[e] from the heart.[f] 23 You have been born anew, not of perishable but of imperishable seed, through the living and enduring word of God.[g]
24 For

"All flesh is like grass
and all its glory like
the flower
of grass.
The grass withers,
and the flower falls,
25 but the word of the
Lord endures
forever."

That word is the good news that was announced to you.

Chapter 2

The Living Stone and a Chosen People

RID yourselves, therefore, of all malice, and all guile, insincerity, envy, and all slander. 2 Like newborn infants, long for the pure, spiritual milk, so that

[d] Other ancient authorities add through the Spirit
[e] Or constantly
[f] Other ancient authorities read a pure heart
[g] Or through the word of the living and enduring God

αὐτοὶ ἅγιοι ἐν πάσῃ ἀναστροφῇ γενήθητε,
⁶[your]- ⁷holy ⁸in ¹⁰all ¹¹conduct ⁹become ye,
selves

16 διότι γέγραπται· [ὅτι] ἅγιοι ἔσεσθε,
because it has been written: - Holy ye shall be,

ὅτι ἐγὼ ἅγιος. 17 καὶ εἰ πατέρα
because I [am] holy. And if ¹Father

ἐπικαλεῖσθε τὸν ἀπροσωπολήμπτως κρίνοντα
¹ye invoke [as] ²the [one] ⁵without respect to persons ⁴judging

κατὰ τὸ ἑκάστου ἔργον, ἐν φόβῳ τὸν
accord- the ²of each man ¹work, ²in ³fear ⁴the
ing to

τῆς παροικίας ὑμῶν χρόνον ἀναστράφητε,
⁶of the ⁷sojourning ⁸of you ⁵time ¹pass,

18 εἰδότες ὅτι οὐ φθαρτοῖς, ἀργυρίῳ ἢ
knowing that not with corruptible silver or
things,

χρυσίῳ, ἐλυτρώθητε ἐκ τῆς ματαίας ὑμῶν
gold, ye were redeemed from the vain ²of you

ἀναστροφῆς πατροπαραδότου, 19 ἀλλὰ τιμίῳ
¹conduct delivered from but with
[your] fathers, precious

αἵματι ὡς ἀμνοῦ ἀμώμου καὶ ἀσπίλου
blood[,] as of a lamb unblemished and unspotted[,]

Χριστοῦ, 20 προεγνωσμένου μὲν πρὸ κατα-
of Christ, having been foreknown on one from [the]
hand

βολῆς κόσμου, φανερωθέντος δὲ ἐπ' ἐσχάτου
founda- of [the] manifested on the in [the] last
tion world, other

τῶν χρόνων δι' ὑμᾶς 21 τοὺς δι' αὐτοῦ
of the times because of you the ones through him

πιστοὺς εἰς θεὸν τὸν ἐγείραντα αὐτὸν
believing in God the [one] having raised him

ἐκ νεκρῶν καὶ δόξαν αὐτῷ δόντα, ὥστε
from [the] dead and ²glory ³to him ¹having given, so as

τὴν πίστιν ὑμῶν καὶ ἐλπίδα εἶναι εἰς
the ¹faith ²of you and ³hope to be in

θεόν. 22 Τὰς ψυχὰς ὑμῶν ἡγνικότες
God. ²The ³souls ⁴of you ¹having purified

ἐν τῇ ὑπακοῇ τῆς ἀληθείας εἰς φιλαδελφίαν
by - obedience of(to) the truth to ²brotherly love

ἀνυπόκριτον, ἐκ καρδίας ἀλλήλους ἀγαπήσατε
¹unfeigned, ⁴from ⁵[the] heart ³one another ¹love ye

ἐκτενῶς, 23 ἀναγεγεννημένοι οὐκ ἐκ σπορᾶς
²earnestly, having been regenerated not by ²seed

φθαρτῆς ἀλλὰ ἀφθάρτου, διὰ λόγου ζῶντος
¹corruptible but incorruptible, through ⁴word ¹[the] living

θεοῦ καὶ μένοντος. 24 διότι πᾶσα σὰρξ
⁵of God ²and ³remaining. Because all flesh [is]

ὡς χόρτος, καὶ πᾶσα δόξα αὐτῆς ὡς
as grass, and all [the] glory of it as

ἄνθος χόρτου· ἐξηράνθη ὁ χόρτος, καὶ
a flower of grass; was dried the grass, and

τὸ ἄνθος ἐξέπεσεν· 25 τὸ δὲ ῥῆμα κυρίου
the flower fell out; but the word of [the] Lord

μένει εἰς τὸν αἰῶνα. τοῦτο δέ ἐστιν
remains unto the age. And this is

τὸ ῥῆμα τὸ εὐαγγελισθὲν εἰς ὑμᾶς.
the word the - preached [as good news] to you.

2 Ἀποθέμενοι οὖν πᾶσαν κακίαν καὶ
Putting away therefore all malice and

πάντα δόλον καὶ ὑποκρίσεις καὶ φθόνους
all guile and hypocrisies and envies

καὶ πάσας καταλαλιάς, 2 ὡς ἀρτιγέννητα
and all detractions, as new born

βρέφη τὸ λογικὸν ἄδολον γάλα ἐπιποθήσατε,
babes ²the ³spiritual ⁴pure ¹milk ¹desire ye,

---

be holy in all you do; 16for it is written: "Be holy, because I am holy."[a]

17Since you call on a Father who judges each man's work impartially, live your lives as strangers here in reverent fear. 18For you know that it was not with perishable things such as silver or gold that you were redeemed from the empty way of life handed down to you from your forefathers, 19but with the precious blood of Christ, a lamb without blemish or defect. 20He was chosen before the creation of the world, but was revealed in these last times for your sake. 21Through him you believe in God, who raised him from the dead and glorified him, and so your faith and hope are in God.

22Now that you have purified yourselves by obeying the truth so that you have sincere love for your brothers, love one another deeply, from the heart.[b] 23For you have been born again, not of perishable seed, but of imperishable, through the living and enduring word of God. 24For,

"All men are like grass,
and all their glory is
like the flowers of
the field;
the grass withers and the
flowers fall,
25 but the word of the
Lord stands
forever."[c]

And this is the word that was preached to you.

Chapter 2

THEREFORE, rid yourselves of all malice and all deceit, hypocrisy, envy, and slander of every kind. 2Like newborn babies, crave pure spiritual milk,

[a]16 Lev. 11:44,45; 19:2; 20:7
[b]22 Some early manuscripts from a pure heart
[c]25 Isaiah 40:6-8

by it you may grow into salvation— 3 if indeed you have tasted that the Lord is good.

4 Come to him, a living stone, though rejected by mortals yet chosen and precious in God's sight, and 5 like living stones, let yourselves be built[h] into a spiritual house, to be a holy priesthood, to offer spiritual sacrifices acceptable to God through Jesus Christ. 6 For it stands in scripture:

"See, I am laying in Zion a stone,
a cornerstone chosen and precious;
and whoever believes in him[i] will not be put to shame."

7 To you then who believe, he is precious; but for those who do not believe,

"The stone that the builders rejected has become the very head of the corner,"

8 and

"A stone that makes them stumble, and a rock that makes them fall."

They stumble because they disobey the word, as they were destined to do.

9 But you are a chosen race, a royal priesthood, a holy nation, God's own people,[j] in order that you may proclaim the mighty acts of him who called you out of darkness into his marvelous light. 10 Once you were not a people, but now you are God's people; once you had not received mercy, but now you have received mercy.

Live as Servants of God

11 Beloved, I urge you as aliens and exiles to abstain from the desires of the flesh that wage war against the soul. 12 Conduct yourselves honorably among the Gentiles, so that, though they malign you as

h Or you yourselves are being built
i Or it
j Gk a people for his possession

ἵνα ἐν αὐτῷ αὐξηθῆτε εἰς σωτηρίαν,
in or- by it ye may grow to salvation,
der that

3 εἰ ἐγεύσασθε ὅτι χρηστὸς ὁ κύριος.
if ye tasted that ³good ¹the ²Lord [is].

4 πρὸς ὃν προσερχόμενοι, λίθον ζῶντα,
to whom approaching, ²stone ¹a living,

ὑπὸ ἀνθρώπων μὲν ἀποδεδοκιμασμένον παρὰ
by men on one having been rejected ²by
hand

δὲ θεῷ ἐκλεκτὸν ἔντιμον, 5 καὶ
¹on the ⁴God ²chosen[,] precious, ²also
other

αὐτοὶ ὡς λίθοι ζῶντες οἰκοδομεῖσθε οἶκος
¹[your]- ³as ²stones ⁴living are being built ²house
selves

πνευματικὸς εἰς ἱεράτευμα ἅγιον, ἀνενέγκαι
¹a spiritual for ²priesthood ¹a holy, to offer

πνευματικὰς θυσίας εὐπροσδέκτους θεῷ διὰ
spiritual sacrifices acceptable to through
God

Ἰησοῦ Χριστοῦ· 6 διότι περιέχει ἐν γραφῇ·
Jesus Christ; because it is in scripture:
contained

ἰδοὺ τίθημι ἐν Σιὼν λίθον ἐκλεκτὸν
Behold I lay in Sion ⁴stone ¹a chosen

ἀκρογωνιαῖον ἔντιμον, καὶ ὁ πιστεύων
²corner foundation ³precious, and the [one] believing

ἐπ' αὐτῷ οὐ μὴ καταισχυνθῇ. 7 ὑμῖν
on it(him) by no means will be shamed. To you
=Yours

οὖν ἡ τιμὴ τοῖς πιστεύουσιν· ἀπιστοῦσιν
there- ³[is] ⁵honour ¹the [ones] ²believing⁰; ²to unbelieving
fore ⁴the [ones]
therefore who believe is the honour;

δὲ λίθος ὃν ἀπεδοκίμασαν οἱ οἰκοδομοῦντες,
¹but a stone which ³rejected ¹the [ones] ²building,

οὗτος ἐγενήθη εἰς κεφαλὴν γωνίας 8 καὶ
this came to be for head of [the] corner and

λίθος προσκόμματος καὶ πέτρα σκανδάλου·
a stone of stumbling and a rock of offence;

οἱ προσκόπτουσιν τῷ λόγῳ ἀπειθοῦντες,
who stumble at the word disobeying,

9 εἰς ὃ καὶ ἐτέθησαν· ὑμεῖς δὲ γένος
to which indeed they were but ye [are] ²race
appointed;

ἐκλεκτόν, βασίλειον ἱεράτευμα, ἔθνος ἅγιον,
¹a chosen, a royal priesthood, nation a holy,

λαὸς εἰς περιποίησιν, ὅπως τὰς ἀρετὰς
a people for possession, so as ²the ³virtues

ἐξαγγείλητε τοῦ ἐκ σκότους ὑμᾶς καλέ-
¹ye may tell out ⁴of the ⁷out ⁸darkness ⁶you ⁵having
[one] of

σαντος εἰς τὸ θαυμαστὸν αὐτοῦ φῶς·
called into the marvellous ¹of him ¹light;

10 οἳ ποτε οὐ λαός, νῦν δὲ λαὸς θεοῦ,
who then not a but [are] a of
[were] people, now people God,

οἱ οὐκ ἠλεημένοι, νῦν δὲ ἐλεηθέντες.
the not having been pitied, but now pitied.
[ones]

11 Ἀγαπητοί, παρακαλῶ ὡς παροίκους
Beloved, I exhort [you] as sojourners

καὶ παρεπιδήμους ἀπέχεσθαι τῶν σαρκικῶν
and aliens to abstain from – fleshly

ἐπιθυμιῶν, αἵτινες στρατεύονται κατὰ τῆς
lusts, which war against the

ψυχῆς· 12 τὴν ἀναστροφὴν ὑμῶν ἐν τοῖς
soul; ²the ³conduct ¹of you ⁴among ⁵the

ἔθνεσιν ἔχοντες καλήν, ἵνα ἐν ᾧ κατα-
⁷nations ¹having, ⁸good, in order while they
that

so that by it you may grow up in your salvation, 3 now that you have tasted that the Lord is good.

The Living Stone and a Chosen People

4 As you come to him, the living Stone—rejected by men but chosen by God and precious to him— 5 you also, like living stones, are being built into a spiritual house to be a holy priesthood, offering spiritual sacrifices acceptable to God through Jesus Christ. 6 For in Scripture it says:

"See, I lay a stone in Zion,
a chosen and precious cornerstone,
and the one who trusts in him will never be put to shame."[d]

7 Now to you who believe, this stone is precious. But to those who do not believe,

"The stone the builders rejected has become the capstone,"[e][f]

8 and,

"A stone that causes men to stumble and a rock that makes them fall."[g]

They stumble because they disobey the message—which is also what they were destined for.

9 But you are a chosen people, a royal priesthood, a holy nation, a people belonging to God, that you may declare the praises of him who called you out of darkness into his wonderful light. 10 Once you were not a people, but now you are the people of God; once you had not received mercy, but now you have received mercy.

11 Dear friends, I urge you, as aliens and strangers in the world, to abstain from sinful desires, which war against your soul. 12 Live such good lives among the pagans that, though they accuse you of

evildoers, they may see your honorable deeds and glorify God when he comes to judge. [k]

13 For the Lord's sake accept the authority of every human institution, [l] whether of the emperor as supreme, [14] or of governors, as sent by him to punish those who do wrong and to praise those who do right. [15] For it is God's will that by doing right you should silence the ignorance of the foolish. [16] As servants [m] of God, live as free people, yet do not use your freedom as a pretext for evil. [17] Honor everyone. Love the family of believers. [n] Fear God. Honor the emperor.

The Example of Christ's Suffering

18 Slaves, accept the authority of your masters with all deference, not only those who are kind and gentle but also those who are harsh. [19] For it is a credit to you if, being aware of God, you endure pain while suffering unjustly. [20] If you endure when you are beaten for doing wrong, what credit is that? But if you endure when you do right and suffer for it, you have God's approval. [21] For to this you have been called, because Christ also suffered for you, leaving you an example, so that you should follow in his steps. [22] "He committed no sin, and no deceit was found in his mouth." [23] When he was abused, he did not return abuse; when he suffered, he did not threaten; but he entrusted himself to the one who judges justly. [24] He himself

---

λαλοῦσιν ὑμῶν ὡς κακοποιῶν, ἐκ τῶν
speak against you as evildoers, by the (your)

καλῶν ἔργων ἐποπτεύοντες δοξάσωσιν τὸν
good works observing they may glorify –

θεὸν ἐν ἡμέρᾳ ἐπισκοπῆς.
God in a day of visitation.

13 Ὑποτάγητε πάσῃ ἀνθρωπίνῃ κτίσει
Submit to every human ordinance

διὰ τὸν κύριον· εἴτε βασιλεῖ ὡς ὑπερέχοντι,
be- the Lord: whether to a king as being supreme,
cause of

14 εἴτε ἡγεμόσιν ὡς δι' αὐτοῦ πεμπομένοις
or to governors as through him being sent

εἰς ἐκδίκησιν κακοποιῶν ἔπαινον δὲ
for vengeance of(on) evildoers ²praise ¹but

ἀγαθοποιῶν· 15 ὅτι οὕτως ἐστὶν τὸ
of welldoers; because so is the

θέλημα τοῦ θεοῦ, ἀγαθοποιοῦντας φιμοῦν
will – of God, doing good to silence

τὴν τῶν ἀφρόνων ἀνθρώπων ἀγνωσίαν·
¹the – ³of foolish ⁴men ²ignorance;

16 ὡς ἐλεύθεροι, καὶ μὴ ὡς ἐπικάλυμμα
as free, and not ³as ⁴a cloak

ἔχοντες τῆς κακίας τὴν ἐλευθερίαν, ἀλλ'
¹having the ⁵of evil the ²freedom, but

ὡς θεοῦ δοῦλοι. 17 πάντας τιμήσατε,
as of God slaves. ²All men ¹honour ye,

τὴν ἀδελφότητα ἀγαπᾶτε, τὸν θεὸν
²the ³brotherhood ¹love, – ¹God

φοβεῖσθε, τὸν βασιλέα τιμᾶτε. 18 Οἱ
¹fear, ²the ³king ¹honour. –

οἰκέται, ὑποτασσόμενοι ἐν παντὶ φόβῳ
House submitting yourselves in all fear
servants,

τοῖς δεσπόταις, οὐ μόνον τοῖς ἀγαθοῖς
to the(your) masters, not only to the good

καὶ ἐπιεικέσιν ἀλλὰ καὶ τοῖς σκολιοῖς.
and forbearing but also to the perverse.

19 τοῦτο γὰρ χάρις εἰ διὰ συνείδησιν
For this [is] a favour if because of conscience

θεοῦ ὑποφέρει τις λύπας πάσχων ἀδίκως.
of God ²bears ¹anyone griefs suffering unjustly.

20 ποῖον γὰρ κλέος εἰ ἁμαρτάνοντες καὶ
For what glory [is it] if sinning and

κολαφιζόμενοι ὑπομενεῖτε; ἀλλ' εἰ ἀγαθο-
being buffeted ye endure? but if doing

ποιοῦντες καὶ πάσχοντες ὑπομενεῖτε, τοῦτο
good and suffering ye endure, this [is]

χάρις παρὰ θεῷ. 21 εἰς τοῦτο γὰρ
a favour with God. ²to ³this ¹For

ἐκλήθητε, ὅτι καὶ Χριστὸς ἔπαθεν ὑπὲρ
ye were because indeed Christ suffered on be-
called, half of

ὑμῶν, ὑμῖν ὑπολιμπάνων ὑπογραμμὸν ἵνα
you, ²to you ¹leaving behind an example in order that

ἐπακολουθήσητε τοῖς ἴχνεσιν αὐτοῦ· 22 ὃς
ye should follow the steps of him; who

ἁμαρτίαν οὐκ ἐποίησεν οὐδὲ εὑρέθη δόλος
³sin ²not ¹did nor was ²found ¹guile

ἐν τῷ στόματι αὐτοῦ· 23 ὃς λοιδορούμενος
in the mouth of him; who being reviled

οὐκ ἀντελοιδόρει, πάσχων οὐκ ἠπείλει,
reviled not in return, suffering he threatened not,

παρεδίδου δὲ τῷ κρίνοντι δικαίως· 24 ὃς
but delivered to the judging righteously; who
[himself] [one]

---

doing wrong, they may see your good deeds and glorify God on the day he visits us.

Submission to Rulers and Masters

[13] Submit yourselves for the Lord's sake to every authority instituted among men: whether to the king, as the supreme authority, [14] or to governors, who are sent by him to punish those who do wrong and to commend those who do right. [15] For it is God's will that by doing good you should silence the ignorant talk of foolish men. [16] Live as free men, but do not use your freedom as a cover-up for evil; live as servants of God. [17] Show proper respect to everyone: Love the brotherhood of believers, fear God, honor the king.

[18] Slaves, submit yourselves to your masters with all respect, not only to those who are good and considerate, but also to those who are harsh. [19] For it is commendable if a man bears up under the pain of unjust suffering because he is conscious of God. [20] But how is it to your credit if you receive a beating for doing wrong and endure it? But if you suffer for doing good and you endure it, this is commendable before God. [21] To this you were called, because Christ suffered for you, leaving you an example, that you should follow in his steps. [22] "He committed no sin, and no deceit was found in his mouth." [h] [23] When they hurled their insults at him, he did not retaliate; when he suffered, he made no threats. Instead, he entrusted himself to him who judges justly.

---

[k] Gk *God on the day of visitation*
[l] Or *every institution ordained for human beings*
[m] Gk *slaves*
[n] Gk *Love the brotherhood*

[h] 22 Isaiah 53:9

bore our sins in his body on the cross,ᵒ so that, free from sins, we might live for righteousness; by his woundsᵖ you have been healed. 25 For you were going astray like sheep, but now you have returned to the shepherd and guardian of your souls.

Chapter 3

Wives and Husbands

WIVES, in the same way, accept the authority of your husbands, so that, even if some of them do not obey the word, they may be won over without a word by their wives' conduct, 2 when they see the purity and reverence of your lives. 3 Do not adorn yourselves outwardly by braiding your hair, and by wearing gold ornaments or fine clothing; 4 rather, let your adornment be the inner self with the lasting beauty of a gentle and quiet spirit, which is very precious in God's sight. 5 It was in this way long ago that the holy women who hoped in God used to adorn themselves by accepting the authority of their husbands. 6 Thus Sarah obeyed Abraham and called him lord. You have become her daughters as long as you do what is good and never let fears alarm you.

7 Husbands, in the same way, show consideration for your wives in your life together, paying honor to the woman as the weaker sex,�q since they too are also heirs of the gracious gift of life—so that nothing may hinder your prayers.

Suffering for Doing Right

8 Finally, all of you, have unity of spirit, sympathy, love for one another, a

ᵒ Or carried up our sins in his body to the tree
ᵖ Gk bruise
�q Gk vessel

τὰς ἁμαρτίας ἡμῶν αὐτὸς ἀνήνεγκεν ἐν
³the ⁴sins ⁵of us ¹[him]self ²carried up in
τῷ σώματι αὐτοῦ ἐπὶ τὸ ξύλον, ἵνα
the body of him onto the tree, in order that
ταῖς ἁμαρτίαις ἀπογενόμενοι τῇ δικαιοσύνῃ
- ²to sins ¹dying - ²to righteousness
ζήσωμεν· οὗ τῷ μώλωπι ἰάθητε.
³we might live; ²of ¹by ²bruise ye were cured.
whom the

25 ἦτε γὰρ ὡς πρόβατα πλανώμενοι,
²ye were ¹For ⁴as ⁵sheep ³wandering,
ἀλλὰ ἐπεστράφητε νῦν ἐπὶ τὸν ποιμένα
but ye turned now to the shepherd
καὶ ἐπίσκοπον τῶν ψυχῶν ὑμῶν.
and bishop of the souls of you.

3 Ὁμοίως γυναῖκες, ὑποτασσόμεναι τοῖς
Likewise wives, submitting yourselves to the
(your)
ἰδίοις ἀνδράσιν, ἵνα καὶ εἴ τινες ἀπειθοῦσιν
own husbands, in or- even if any disobey
der that
τῷ λόγῳ, διὰ τῆς τῶν γυναικῶν ἀναστροφῆς
the word, through ¹the ²of ⁴wives ²conduct
the(ir)
ἄνευ λόγου κερδηθήσονται, 2 ἐποπτεύσαντες
without a word they will(may) be gained, observing
τὴν ἐν φόβῳ ἁγνὴν ἀναστροφὴν ὑμῶν.
¹the ³in ⁴fear ²pure ³conduct ⁴of you.
3 ὧν ἔστω οὐχ ὁ ἔξωθεν ἐμπλοκῆς
Of whom let it be not ¹the ²outward ⁴of plaiting
τριχῶν καὶ περιθέσεως χρυσίων ἢ ἐνδύσεως
²of hairs ²and ⁷of putting ⁸of gold ⁹or ¹⁰of clothing
round(on) [ornaments]
ἱματίων κόσμος, 4 ἀλλ᾽ ὁ κρυπτὸς τῆς
¹¹of(with) ³adorning, but ¹the ²hidden ⁴of the
garments
καρδίας ἄνθρωπος ἐν τῷ ἀφθάρτῳ τοῦ
⁵heart ³man in(?by) the incorruptible of the
[adorning]
πραέος καὶ ἡσυχίου πνεύματος, ὅ ἐστιν
meek and quiet spirit, which is
ἐνώπιον τοῦ θεοῦ πολυτελές. 5 οὕτως
before - God of great value. so
γάρ ποτε καὶ αἱ ἅγιαι γυναῖκες αἱ
For then indeed the holy women -
ἐλπίζουσαι εἰς θεὸν ἐκόσμουν ἑαυτάς,
hoping in God adorned themselves,
ὑποτασσόμεναι τοῖς ἰδίοις ἀνδράσιν, 6 ὡς
submitting themselves to the(ir) own husbands, as
Σάρρα ὑπήκουσεν τῷ Ἀβραάμ, κύριον
Sara obeyed - Abraham, ³lord
αὐτὸν καλοῦσα· ἧς ἐγενήθητε τέκνα
²him ¹calling; of whom ye became children
ἀγαθοποιοῦσαι καὶ μὴ φοβούμεναι μηδεμίαν
doing good and not fearing no(any)
πτόησιν. 7 Οἱ ἄνδρες ὁμοίως, συνοικοῦντες
terror. - Husbands likewise, dwelling together
κατὰ γνῶσιν ὡς ἀσθενεστέρῳ σκεύει τῷ
accord- knowledge as with a weaker vessel the
ing to
γυναικείῳ, ἀπονέμοντες τιμὴν ὡς καὶ
female, assigning honour as indeed
συγκληρονόμοις χάριτος ζωῆς, εἰς τὸ μὴ
co-heirs of [the] grace of life, for the not
ἐγκόπτεσθαι τὰς προσευχὰς ὑμῶν.ᵇ 8 Τὸ δὲ
to be hindered the prayers of you. Now the
τέλος πάντες ὁμόφρονες, συμπαθεῖς,
end[,] [be ye] all of one mind, sympathetic,

Wives and Husbands

WIVES, in the same way be submissive to your husbands so that, if any of them do not believe the word, they may be won over without words by the behavior of their wives, 2 when they see the purity and reverence of your lives. 3 Your beauty should not come from outward adornment, such as braided hair and the wearing of gold jewelry and fine clothes. 4 Instead, it should be that of your inner self, the unfading beauty of a gentle and quiet spirit, which is of great worth in God's sight. 5 For this is the way the holy women of the past who put their hope in God used to make themselves beautiful. They were submissive to their own husbands, 6 like Sarah, who obeyed Abraham and called him master. You are her daughters if you do what is right and do not give way to fear.

7 Husbands, in the same way be considerate as you live with your wives, and treat them with respect as the weaker partner and as heirs with you of the gracious gift of life, so that nothing will hinder your prayers.

Suffering for Doing Good

8 Finally, all of you, live in harmony with one another; be sympathetic, love as

tender heart, and a humble mind. 9 Do not repay evil for evil or abuse for abuse; but, on the contrary, repay with a blessing. It is for this that you were called—that you might inherit a blessing. 10 For

"Those who desire life
  and desire to see
    good days,
let them keep their
  tongues
    from evil
and their lips from
  speaking deceit;
11 let them turn away
  from evil and do
  good;
let them seek peace
  and pursue it.
12 For the eyes of the
  Lord are on
  the righteous,
and his ears are
  open to
  their prayer.
But the face of the
  Lord is against
  those who do
  evil."

13 Now who will harm you if you are eager to do what is good? 14 But even if you do suffer for doing what is right, you are blessed. Do not fear what they fear,[r] and do not be intimidated, 15 but in your hearts sanctify Christ as Lord. Always be ready to make your defense to anyone who demands from you an accounting for the hope that is in you; 16 yet do it with gentleness and reverence.[s] Keep your conscience clear, so that, when you are maligned, those who abuse you for your good conduct in Christ may be put to shame. 17 For it is better to suffer for doing good, if suffering should be God's will, than to suffer for doing evil. 18 For Christ also suffered[t] for sins once for all, the righteous for the unrighteous, in order to bring you[u] to God. He was

φιλάδελφοι, εὔσπλαγχνοι, ταπεινόφρονες,
loving [the] brothers, compassionate, humble-minded,
9 μὴ ἀποδιδόντες κακὸν ἀντὶ κακοῦ ἢ
not giving back evil instead of evil or
λοιδορίαν ἀντὶ λοιδορίας, τοὐναντίον δὲ
reviling instead of reviling, but on the contrary
εὐλογοῦντες, ὅτι εἰς τοῦτο ἐκλήθητε ἵνα
blessing, because to this ye were called in order that
εὐλογίαν κληρονομήσητε. 10 ὁ γὰρ θέλων
blessing ye might inherit. For the [one] wishing
ζωὴν ἀγαπᾶν καὶ ἰδεῖν ἡμέρας ἀγαθάς,
¹life ¹to love and to see ²days ¹good,
παυσάτω τὴν γλῶσσαν ἀπὸ κακοῦ καὶ
let him the(his) tongue from evil and
restrain
χείλη τοῦ μὴ λαλῆσαι δόλον, 11 ἐκκλινάτω
[his] lips - not to speak[d] guile, ¹let him turn aside
δὲ ἀπὸ κακοῦ καὶ ποιησάτω ἀγαθόν,
¹and from evil and let him do good,
ζητησάτω εἰρήνην καὶ διωξάτω αὐτήν·
let him seek peace and pursue it;
12 ὅτι ὀφθαλμοὶ κυρίου ἐπὶ δικαίους καὶ
because [the] eyes of [the] [are] on [the] and
Lord righteous
ὦτα αὐτοῦ εἰς δέησιν αὐτῶν, πρόσωπον
[the] of him [open] to [the] of them, ²[the] face
ears petition
δὲ κυρίου ἐπὶ ποιοῦντας κακά.
¹but of [the] [is] [ones] doing evil things.
Lord against
13 Καὶ τίς ὁ κακώσων ὑμᾶς ἐὰν τοῦ
And who the harming you if ³of the
[is] [one]
ἀγαθοῦ ζηλωταὶ γένησθε; 14 ἀλλ' εἰ καὶ
⁴good ²zealots ¹ye become? but if indeed
πάσχοιτε διὰ δικαιοσύνην, μακάριοι. τὸν
ye suffer because of righteousness, blessed [are ye]. ³the
δὲ φόβον αὐτῶν μὴ φοβηθῆτε μηδὲ
¹But ⁴fear ⁵of them ²fear ye not nor
ταραχθῆτε, 15 κύριον δὲ τὸν Χριστὸν
be ye troubled, ³but ⁴[as] ¹Lord - ²Christ
ἁγιάσατε ἐν ταῖς καρδίαις ὑμῶν, ἔτοιμοι
²sanctify in the hearts of you, ready
ἀεὶ πρὸς ἀπολογίαν παντὶ τῷ αἰτοῦντι
always for defence to every one asking
ὑμᾶς λόγον περὶ τῆς ἐν ὑμῖν ἐλπίδος,
you a word concerning ¹the ²in ⁴you ¹hope,
16 ἀλλὰ μετὰ πραΰτητος καὶ φόβου,
but with meekness and fear,
συνείδησιν ἔχοντες ἀγαθήν, ἵνα ἐν ᾧ
³conscience ¹having ²a good, in order that while
καταλαλεῖσθε καταισχυνθῶσιν οἱ ἐπηρεάζον-
ye are spoken against ²may be shamed [by] ¹the [ones] ²abusing
τες ὑμῶν τὴν ἀγαθὴν ἐν Χριστῷ
[you] ⁷of you ⁴the ⁵good ³in ⁶Christ
ἀναστροφήν. 17 κρεῖττον γὰρ ἀγαθοποι-
²conduct. For [it is] better doing
οῦντας, εἰ θέλοι τὸ θέλημα τοῦ θεοῦ,
good, if ⁴wills ¹the ²will - ³of God,
πάσχειν ἢ κακοποιοῦντας. 18 ὅτι καὶ
to suffer than doing evil. Because indeed
Χριστὸς ἅπαξ περὶ ἁμαρτιῶν ἀπέθανεν,
Christ once ²concerning ³sins ¹died,
δίκαιος ὑπὲρ ἀδίκων, ἵνα ὑμᾶς προσαγάγῃ
a righteous on be- unrighteous in or- ¹you ¹he might
man half of ones, der that bring

brothers, be compassionate and humble. 9 Do not repay evil with evil or insult with insult, but with blessing, because to this you were called so that you may inherit a blessing. 10 For,

"Whoever would love
  life
and see good days
must keep his tongue
  from evil
and his lips from
  deceitful speech.
11 He must turn from evil
  and do good;
he must seek peace and
  pursue it.
12 For the eyes of the Lord
  are on the righteous
and his ears are
  attentive to their
  prayer,
but the face of the Lord
  is against those who
  do evil."[i]

13 Who is going to harm you if you are eager to do good? 14 But even if you should suffer for what is right, you are blessed. "Do not fear what they fear[j]; do not be frightened."[k] 15 But in your hearts set apart Christ as Lord. Always be prepared to give an answer to everyone who asks you to give the reason for the hope that you have. But do this with gentleness and respect, 16 keeping a clear conscience, so that those who speak maliciously against your good behavior in Christ may be ashamed of their slander. 17 It is better, if it is God's will, to suffer for doing good than for doing evil. 18 For Christ died for sins once for all, the righteous for the unrighteous, to bring you to

r Gk their fear
s Or respect
t Other ancient authorities read died
u Other ancient authorities read us

i12 Psalm 34:12-16
j14 Or not fear their threats
k14 Isaiah 8:12

put to death in the flesh, but made alive in the spirit, [19] in which also he went and made a proclamation to the spirits in prison, [20] who in former times did not obey, when God waited patiently in the days of Noah, during the building of the ark, in which a few, that is, eight persons, were saved through water. [21] And baptism, which this prefigured, now saves you—not as a removal of dirt from the body, but as an appeal to God for [v] a good conscience, through the resurrection of Jesus Christ, [22] who has gone into heaven and is at the right hand of God, with angels, authorities, and powers made subject to him.

τῷ θεῷ, θανατωθεὶς μὲν σαρκὶ ζωοποιηθεὶς
- to | being put to | on one | in [the] | quickened
God, | death | hand | flesh[,]

δὲ πνεύματι· **19** ἐν ᾧ καὶ τοῖς ἐν
on the | in [the] | in | which indeed | ²to the | ⁴in
other | spirit;

φυλακῇ πνεύμασιν πορευθεὶς ἐκήρυξεν,
⁵prison | ³spirits | ¹going | he proclaimed,

20 ἀπειθήσασίν ποτε ὅτε ἀπεξεδέχετο ἡ
to disobeying ones | then | when | ⁴waited | ¹the

τοῦ θεοῦ μακροθυμία ἐν ἡμέραις Νῶε
- | ³of God | ²longsuffering | in | [the] days | of Noe

κατασκευαζομένης κιβωτοῦ, εἰς ἣν ὀλίγοι,
²being prepared | ¹an ark, | in | which | a few,

τοῦτ' ἔστιν ὀκτὼ ψυχαί, διεσώθησαν δι'
this | is | eight | souls, | were | through
| | | | quite saved

ὕδατος. **21** ὃ καὶ ὑμᾶς ἀντίτυπον νῦν
water. | ¹Which | ³also | ⁴us | ²figure | ⁴now

σῴζει βάπτισμα, οὐ σαρκὸς ἀπόθεσις
⁵saves | [even] baptism, | not | ³of [the] | ¹a putting
| | | flesh | away

ῥύπου ἀλλὰ συνειδήσεως ἀγαθῆς ἐπερώτημα
²of [the] | but | ³conscience | ²of a good | ¹an answer
filth

εἰς θεόν, δι' ἀναστάσεως Ἰησοῦ Χριστοῦ,
toward God, | through | [the] resurrection | of Jesus | Christ,

22 ὅς ἐστιν ἐν δεξιᾷ θεοῦ, πορευθεὶς
who | is | at | [the] right | of God, | having gone
| | | [hand]

εἰς οὐρανόν, ὑποταγέντων αὐτῷ ἀγγέλων
into | heaven, | ⁶being subjected | ⁷to him | ¹angels

καὶ ἐξουσιῶν καὶ δυνάμεων.
²and | ³authorities | ⁴and | ⁵powers⁸.

God. He was put to death in the body but made alive by the Spirit, [19] through whom [j] also he went and preached to the spirits in prison [20] who disobeyed long ago when God waited patiently in the days of Noah while the ark was being built. In it only a few people, eight in all, were saved through water, [21] and this water symbolizes baptism that now saves you also—not the removal of dirt from the body but the pledge [m] of a good conscience toward God. It saves you by the resurrection of Jesus Christ, [22] who has gone into heaven and is at God's right hand—with angels, authorities, and powers in submission to him.

Chapter 4
Good Stewards of God's Grace

SINCE therefore Christ suffered in the flesh, [w] arm yourselves also with the same intention (for whoever has suffered in the flesh has finished with sin), [2] so as to live for the rest of your earthly life [x] no longer by human desires but by the will of God. [3] You have already spent enough time in doing what the Gentiles like to do, living in licentiousness, passions, drunkenness, revels, carousing, and lawless idolatry. [4] They are surprised that you no longer join them in the same excesses of dissipation, and so they blaspheme. [y] [5] But they will have to give an accounting to him who stands ready to judge the living and the dead. [6] For this is the reason the gospel was proclaimed even to the dead, so that, though they had

4 Χριστοῦ οὖν παθόντος σαρκὶ καὶ ὑμεῖς
⁵Christ | ¹there- | having | in [the] | ²also | ¹ye
| fore | suffered⁴ | flesh

τὴν αὐτὴν ἔννοιαν ὁπλίσασθε, ὅτι ὁ
⁴the | ⁵same | ⁶mind | ³arm your- | because | the
| | | selves [with], | | [one]

παθὼν σαρκὶ πέπαυται ἁμαρτίας, **2** εἰς
having | in [the] flesh | has ceased | from sin, | | for
suffered

τὸ μηκέτι ἀνθρώπων ἐπιθυμίαις ἀλλὰ
the | ⁷no longer | ⁸of men | ⁹in [the] lusts | ¹⁰but

θελήματι θεοῦ τὸν ἐπίλοιπον ἐν σαρκὶ
¹¹in [the] will | ¹²of God | ³the | ⁴remaining | ⁶in | ⁷[the] flesh

βιῶσαι χρόνον. **3** ἀρκετὸς γὰρ ὁ παρεληλυ-
⁵to live | ²time. | For ³sufficient | ¹the ²having passed

θὼς χρόνος τὸ βούλημα τῶν ἐθνῶν
away | ⁴time | ⁵[is] | ⁷the | ⁸purpose | ⁹of the | ¹⁰nations

κατειργάσθαι, πεπορευμένους ἐν ἀσελγείαις,
⁶to have worked out, | having gone [on] | in | licentiousnesses,

ἐπιθυμίαις, οἰνοφλυγίαις, κώμοις, πότοις
lusts, | debaucheries, | carousals, | drinking
| | | bouts

καὶ ἀθεμίτοις εἰδωλολατρίαις. **4** ἐν ᾧ
and | unlawful | idolatries. | | While

ξενίζονται μὴ συντρεχόντων ὑμῶν εἰς
they are surprised | ²not | ³running with | ¹you⁴ | to

τὴν αὐτὴν τῆς ἀσωτίας ἀνάχυσιν, βλασ-
the | same | - | ²of profligacy | ¹excess, | blas-

φημοῦντες· **5** οἳ ἀποδώσουσιν λόγον τῷ
pheming; | who | will render | account | to the
| | | | [one]

ἑτοίμως ἔχοντι κρῖναι ζῶντας καὶ νεκρούς.
readily | having | to judge | living | and | dead.
= who is ready

6 εἰς τοῦτο γὰρ καὶ νεκροῖς εὐηγγελίσθη,
²for | ³this | ¹For | indeed | ²to | ¹good news
| | | | dead men | was preached,

Chapter 4
Living for God

THEREFORE, since Christ suffered in his body, arm yourselves also with the same attitude, because he who has suffered in his body is done with sin. [2] As a result, he does not live the rest of his earthly life for evil human desires, but rather for the will of God. [3] For you have spent enough time in the past doing what pagans choose to do—living in debauchery, lust, drunkenness, orgies, carousing and detestable idolatry. [4] They think it strange that you do not plunge with them into the same flood of dissipation, and they heap abuse on you. [5] But they will have to give account to him who is ready to judge the living and the dead. [6] For this is the reason the gospel was preached even to those who are now dead, so that

[v] Or a pledge to God from
[w] Other ancient authorities add for us; others, for you
[x] Gk rest of the time in the flesh
[y] Or they malign you

[j] 18,19 Or alive in the spirit.
[19] through which
[m] 21 Or response

been judged in the flesh as everyone is judged, they might live in the spirit as God does.

7 The end of all things is near;² therefore be serious and discipline yourselves for the sake of your prayers. 8 Above all, maintain constant love for one another, for love covers a multitude of sins. 9 Be hospitable to one another without complaining. 10 Like good stewards of the manifold grace of God, serve one another with whatever gift each of you has received. 11 Whoever speaks must do so as one speaking the very words of God; whoever serves must do so with the strength that God supplies, so that God may be glorified in all things through Jesus Christ. To him belong the glory and the power forever and ever. Amen.

Suffering as a Christian

12 Beloved, do not be surprised at the fiery ordeal that is taking place among you to test you, as though something strange were happening insofar as you. 13 But rejoice insofar as you are sharing Christ's sufferings, so that you may also be glad and shout for joy when his glory is revealed. 14 If you are reviled for the name of Christ, you are blessed, because the spirit of glory,ᵃ which is the Spirit of God, is resting on you.ᵇ 15 But let none of you suffer as a murderer, a thief, a criminal, or even as a mischief maker. 16 Yet if any of you suffers as a Christian, do not consider it a disgrace, but glorify God because you bear this name. 17 For the time has

² Or *is at hand*
ᵃ Other ancient authorities add *and of power*
ᵇ Other ancient authorities add *On their part he is blasphemed, but on your part he is glorified*

ἵνα κριθῶσι μὲν κατὰ ἀνθρώπους
in order ²they might ¹on one according to men
that be judged hand

σαρκί, ζῶσι δὲ κατὰ θεὸν πνεύματι.
in [the] ¹might ¹on the according God in [the] spirit.
flesh, live other to

7 Πάντων δὲ τὸ τέλος ἤγγικεν.
Now of all things the end has drawn near.

σωφρονήσατε οὖν καὶ νήψατε εἰς
Be ye soberminded therefore and be ye sober unto

προσευχάς· 8 πρὸ πάντων τὴν εἰς ἑαυτοὺς
prayers; before all things – ⁴to ⁵yourselves

ἀγάπην ἐκτενῆ ἔχοντες, ὅτι ἀγάπη
³love ²fervent ¹having, because love

καλύπτει πλῆθος ἁμαρτιῶν· 9 φιλόξενοι εἰς
covers a multitude of sins; [be] hospitable to

ἀλλήλους ἄνευ γογγυσμοῦ· 10 ἕκαστος καθὼς
one another without murmuring; each one as

ἔλαβεν χάρισμα, εἰς ἑαυτοὺς αὐτὸ διακον-
he received a gift, ³to ⁴yourselves ²it ¹minister-

οῦντες ὡς καλοὶ οἰκονόμοι ποικίλης χάριτος
ing as good stewards of [the] manifold grace

θεοῦ· 11 εἴ τις λαλεῖ, ὡς λόγια θεοῦ·
of God; if anyone speaks, as [the] oracles of God;

εἴ τις διακονεῖ, ὡς ἐξ ἰσχύος ἧς χορηγεῖ
if anyone ministers, as by strength which ¹supplies

ὁ θεός· ἵνα ἐν πᾶσιν δοξάζηται ὁ θεὸς
– ¹God; in or- in all things ²may be glorified – ¹God
der that

διὰ Ἰησοῦ Χριστοῦ, ᾧ ἐστιν ἡ δόξα
through Jesus Christ, to whom isᶜ the glory
=whose is

καὶ τὸ κράτος εἰς τοὺς αἰῶνας τῶν
and the might unto the ages of the

αἰώνων· ἀμήν.
ages : Amen.

12 Ἀγαπητοί, μὴ ξενίζεσθε τῇ ἐν ὑμῖν
Beloved, be not surprised [at] ¹the ⁴among ⁵you

πυρώσει πρὸς πειρασμὸν ὑμῖν γινομένῃ,
²fiery trial ⁶for ⁷trial ³to you ³happening,

ὡς ξένου ὑμῖν συμβαίνοντος, 13 ἀλλὰ
as a surprising ²to you ¹occurringᵃ, but
thing

καθὸ κοινωνεῖτε τοῖς τοῦ Χριστοῦ
²as ³ye share ⁴the – ⁶of Christ

παθήμασιν χαίρετε, ἵνα καὶ ἐν τῇ ἀπο-
⁵sufferings ¹rejoice, in order also at the reve-
that

καλύψει τῆς δόξης αὐτοῦ χαρῆτε ἀγαλ-
lation of the glory of him ye may exult-
rejoice

λιώμενοι. 14 εἰ ὀνειδίζεσθε ἐν ὀνόματι
ing. If ye are reproached in [the] name

Χριστοῦ, μακάριοι, ὅτι τὸ τῆς δόξης
of Christ, blessed [are ye], because ¹the – ²of glory

καὶ τὸ τοῦ θεοῦ πνεῦμα ἐφ’ ὑμᾶς
⁴and ²the(?that) – ⁵of God ³spirit ⁶on ⁹you

ἀναπαύεται. 15 μὴ γάρ τις ὑμῶν πασχέτω
⁷rests. ³Not ¹for ⁴anyone ⁵of you ²let ⁶suffer

ὡς φονεὺς ἢ κλέπτης ἢ κακοποιὸς ἢ
as a murderer or a thief or an evildoer or

ὡς ἀλλοτριεπίσκοπος· 16 εἰ δὲ ὡς
as a pryer into other men's affairs; but if as

Χριστιανός, μὴ αἰσχυνέσθω, δοξαζέτω δὲ
a Christian, let him not be shamed, but let him glorify

τὸν θεὸν ἐν τῷ ὀνόματι τούτῳ. 17 ὅτι
– God by this name. Because

---

they might be judged according to men in regard to the body, but live according to God in regard to the spirit.

7The end of all things is near. Therefore be clear minded and self-controlled so that you can pray. 8Above all, love each other deeply, because love covers over a multitude of sins. 9Offer hospitality to one another without grumbling. 10Each one should use whatever gift he has received to serve others, faithfully administering God's grace in its various forms. 11If anyone speaks, he should do it as one speaking the very words of God. If anyone serves, he should do it with the strength God provides, so that in all things God may be praised through Jesus Christ. To him be the glory and the power for ever and ever. Amen.

Suffering for Being a Christian

12Dear friends, do not be surprised at the painful trial you are suffering, as though something strange were happening to you. 13But rejoice that you participate in the sufferings of Christ, so that you may be overjoyed when his glory is revealed. 14If you are insulted because of the name of Christ, you are blessed, for the Spirit of glory and of God rests on you. 15If you suffer, it should not be as a murderer or thief or any other kind of criminal, or even as a meddler. 16However, if you suffer as a Christian, do not be ashamed, but praise God that you bear that name.

come for judgment to begin with the household of God; if it begins with us, what will be the end for those who do not obey the gospel of God? 18 And

"If it is hard for the righteous to be saved, what will become of the ungodly and the sinners?"

19 Therefore, let those suffering in accordance with God's will entrust themselves to a faithful Creator, while continuing to do good.

[ὁ] καιρὸς τοῦ ἄρξασθαι τὸ κρίμα ἀπὸ
the time — to begin[d] the judgment from
[?has come]
τοῦ οἴκου τοῦ θεοῦ· εἰ δὲ πρῶτον ἀφ'
the household — of God; and if firstly from
ἡμῶν, τί τὸ τέλος τῶν ἀπειθούντων
us, what [will be] the end of the [ones] disobeying
τῷ τοῦ θεοῦ εὐαγγελίῳ; 18 καὶ εἰ ὁ
the — ²of God ¹gospel? and if the
δίκαιος μόλις σῴζεται, ὁ [δὲ] ἀσεβὴς
righteous man scarcely is saved, ³the — ⁴impious
καὶ ἁμαρτωλὸς ποῦ φανεῖται; 19 ὥστε
⁵and ⁶sinner ¹where ²will ⁷appear ? so as
καὶ οἱ πάσχοντες κατὰ τὸ θέλημα τοῦ
indeed the suffering accord- the will —
[ones] ing to
θεοῦ πιστῷ κτίστῃ παρατιθέσθωσαν τὰς
of God ²to a ³Creator ¹let them commit ⁴the
faithful
ψυχὰς αὐτῶν ἐν ἀγαθοποιΐᾳ.
⁵souls ⁶of them in welldoing.

17For it is time for judgment to begin with the family of God; and if it begins with us, what will the outcome be for those who do not obey the gospel of God? 18And,

"If it is hard for the righteous to be saved, what will become of the ungodly and the sinner?" [n]

19So then, those who suffer according to God's will should commit themselves to their faithful Creator and continue to do good.

Chapter 5

Tending the Flock of God

NOW as an elder myself and a witness of the sufferings of Christ, as well as one who shares in the glory to be revealed, I exhort the elders among you [2]to tend the flock of God that is in your charge, exercising the oversight,[c] not under compulsion but willingly, as God would have you do it[d]—not for sordid gain but eagerly. [3]Do not lord it over those in your charge, but be examples to the flock. [4]And when the chief shepherd appears, you will win the crown of glory that never fades away. [5]In the same way, you who are younger must accept the authority of the elders.[e] And all of you must clothe yourselves with humility in your dealings with one another, for

"God opposes the proud, but gives grace to the humble."

6 Humble yourselves therefore under the mighty hand of God, so that he may exalt you in due time. [7]Cast all your anxiety on him, because he cares for

5 Πρεσβυτέρους οὖν ἐν ὑμῖν παρακαλῶ
Elders there- among you I exhort
fore
ὁ συμπρεσβύτερος καὶ μάρτυς τῶν τοῦ
the co-elder and witness ¹of the —
Χριστοῦ παθημάτων, ὁ καὶ τῆς μελλούσης
²of Christ ³sufferings, ¹the ³also ⁴of the ⁵being about
ἀποκαλύπτεσθαι δόξης κοινωνός· 2 ποιμάνατε
⁷to be revealed ⁵glory ²sharer : shepherd
τὸ ἐν ὑμῖν ποίμνιον τοῦ θεοῦ, μὴ
¹the ⁴among ⁵you ²flock — ³of God, not
ἀναγκαστῶς ἀλλὰ ἑκουσίως κατὰ θεόν,
by way of but willingly accord- God,
compulsion ing to
μηδὲ αἰσχροκερδῶς ἀλλὰ προθύμως, 3 μηδ'
nor from eagerness for but eagerly, nor
base gain
ὡς κατακυριεύοντες τῶν κλήρων ἀλλὰ
as exercising lordship over the lots* but
τύποι γινόμενοι τοῦ ποιμνίου· 4 καὶ
²examples ¹becoming of the flock; and
φανερωθέντος τοῦ ἀρχιποίμενος κομιεῖσθε
appearing the chief shepherd[a] ye will receive
=when the chief shepherd appears
τὸν ἀμαράντινον τῆς δόξης στέφανον.
the unfading — ²of glory ¹crown.
5 Ὁμοίως, νεώτεροι, ὑποτάγητε πρεσβυτέ-
Likewise, younger men, submit yourselves to older
ροις· πάντες δὲ ἀλλήλοις τὴν ταπεινοφρο-
men; and all ²to one another — ¹humil-
σύνην ἐγκομβώσασθε, ὅτι ὁ θεὸς ὑπερηφάνοις
ity ¹gird ye on, because — God ²arrogant men
ἀντιτάσσεται, ταπεινοῖς δὲ δίδωσιν χάριν.
¹resists, but to humble men he gives grace.
6 Ταπεινώθητε οὖν ὑπὸ τὴν κραταιὰν
Be ye humbled therefore under the mighty
χεῖρα τοῦ θεοῦ, ἵνα ὑμᾶς ὑψώσῃ ἐν
hand — of God, in order ²you ¹he may exalt in
that
καιρῷ, 7 πᾶσαν τὴν μέριμναν ὑμῶν
time, ²all ³the ⁴anxiety ⁵of you
ἐπιρίψαντες ἐπ' αὐτόν, ὅτι αὐτῷ μέλει
¹casting on him, because ²to him ¹it matters

Chapter 5

To Elders and Young Men

TO the elders among you, I appeal as a fellow elder, a witness of Christ's sufferings and one who also will share in the glory to be revealed: [2]Be shepherds of God's flock that is under your care, serving as overseers—not because you must, but because you are willing, as God wants you to be; not greedy for money, but eager to serve; [3]not lording it over those entrusted to you, but being examples to the flock. [4]And when the Chief Shepherd appears, you will receive the crown of glory that will never fade away.

[5]Young men, in the same way be submissive to those who are older. All of you, clothe yourselves with humility toward one another, because,

"God opposes the proud but gives grace to the humble." [o]

6Humble yourselves, therefore, under God's mighty hand, that he may lift you up in due time. [7]Cast all your anxiety on him because he cares for you.

[c] Other ancient authorities lack *exercising the oversight*
[d] Other ancient authorities lack *as God would have you do it*
[e] Or *of those who are older*

* That is, the various spheres assigned to the elders.

[n]18 Prov. 11:31
[o]5 Prov. 3:34

you. 8 Discipline your-selves, keep alert. *f* Like a roaring lion your adversary the devil prowls around, looking for someone to de-vour. 9 Resist him, stead-fast in your faith, for you know that your brothers and sisters *g* in all the world are undergoing the same kinds of suffering. 10 And after you have suffered for a little while, the God of all grace, who has called you to his eternal glory in Christ, will himself restore, support, strengthen, and establish you. 11 To him be the power forever and ever. Amen.

Final Greetings and Benediction

12 Through Silvanus, whom I consider a faithful brother, I have written this short letter to encourage you and to testify that this is the true grace of God. Stand fast in it. 13 Your sis-ter church *h* in Babylon, chosen together with you, sends you greetings; and so does my son Mark. 14 Greet one another with a kiss of love.

Peace to all of you who are in Christ. *i*

περὶ ὑμῶν.   8 Νήψατε, γρηγορήσατε. ὁ
concerning you.   Be ye sober,   watch ye.   The

ἀντίδικος ὑμῶν διάβολος ὡς λέων ὠρυόμενος
adversary of you [the] devil as a lion roaring

περιπατεῖ ζητῶν τινα καταπιεῖν· 9 ᾧ
walks about seeking whom to devour; whom

ἀντίστητε στερεοὶ τῇ πίστει, εἰδότες τὰ
oppose firm in the faith, knowing the

αὐτὰ τῶν παθημάτων τῇ ἐν τῷ κόσμῳ
same *of the* sufferings ²in ³in ⁴the ⁷world
things

ὑμῶν ἀδελφότητι ἐπιτελεῖσθαι. 10 Ὁ δὲ
⁶of you ³brotherhood ¹to be accomplished. ²the ¹Now

θεὸς πάσης χάριτος, ὁ καλέσας ὑμᾶς
God of all grace, the [one] having called you

εἰς τὴν αἰώνιον αὐτοῦ δόξαν ἐν Χριστῷ,
to the ¹eternal ³of him ²glory in Christ,

ὀλίγον παθόντας αὐτὸς καταρτίσει, στηρίξει,
¹[you] ²having [him]self will adjust, confirm,
²a little suffered

σθενώσει, θεμελιώσει. 11 αὐτῷ τὸ κράτος
strengthen, found. To him [is] *c* the might
= His is*

εἰς τοὺς αἰῶνας τῶν αἰώνων· ἀμήν.
unto the ages of the ages: Amen.

12 Διὰ Σιλουανοῦ ὑμῖν τοῦ πιστοῦ
Through Silvanus to you the faithful

ἀδελφοῦ, ὡς λογίζομαι, δι᾽ ὀλίγων ἔγραψα,
brother, as I reckon, by a few I wrote,
means of [words]

παρακαλῶν καὶ ἐπιμαρτυρῶν ταύτην εἶναι
exhorting and witnessing this to be

ἀληθῆ χάριν τοῦ θεοῦ, εἰς ἣν στῆτε.
[the] true grace – of God, in which ye stand.

13 Ἀσπάζεται ὑμᾶς ἡ ἐν Βαβυλῶνι
¹⁰greets ¹¹you ¹The ³in ⁴Babylon

συνεκλεκτὴ καὶ Μᾶρκος ὁ υἱός μου.
²co-chosen ⁵and ⁶Mark ⁷the ⁸son ⁹of me.
[? church]

14 ἀσπάσασθε ἀλλήλους ἐν φιλήματι ἀγάπης.
Greet ye one another with a kiss of love.

Εἰρήνη ὑμῖν πᾶσιν τοῖς ἐν Χριστῷ.
Peace to you all the ones in Christ.

---

8 Be self-controlled and alert. Your enemy the devil prowls around like a roar-ing lion looking for some-one to devour. 9 Resist him, standing firm in the faith, because you know that your brothers throughout the world are undergoing the same kind of sufferings. 10 And the God of all grace, who called you to his eternal glory in Christ, af-ter you have suffered a lit-tle while, will himself re-store you and make you strong, firm and steadfast. 11 To him be the power for ever and ever. Amen.

Final Greetings

12 With the help of Silas, *p* whom I regard as a faithful brother, I have written to you briefly, encouraging you and testifying that this is the true grace of God. Stand fast in it.

13 She who is in Babylon, chosen together with you, sends you her greetings, and so does my son Mark. 14 Greet one another with a kiss of love.

Peace to all of you who are in Christ.

The Second Letter of
Peter

Chapter 1

Salutation

SIMEON *a* Peter, a ser-vant *b* and apostle of Jesus Christ,

To those who have re-ceived a faith as precious as ours through the righteous-ness of our God and Savior Jesus Christ: *c*

2 May grace and peace be yours in abundance in the knowledge of God and of Jesus our Lord.

The Christian's Call and Election

3 His divine power has given us everything needed

f Or be vigilant
g Gk your brotherhood
h Gk She who is
i Other ancient authorities add Amen
a Other ancient authorities read Simon
b Gk slave
c Or of our God and the Savior Jesus Christ

ΠΕΤΡΟΥ Β
Of Peter 2

1 Συμεὼν Πέτρος δοῦλος καὶ ἀπόστολος
Symeon Peter a slave and an apostle

Ἰησοῦ Χριστοῦ τοῖς ἰσότιμον ἡμῖν
of Jesus Christ ¹to the ³equally ⁴with
[ones] precious us

λαχοῦσιν πίστιν ἐν δικαιοσύνῃ τοῦ θεοῦ
³having ⁴faith in righteousness of the God
obtained [the]

ἡμῶν καὶ σωτῆρος Ἰησοῦ Χριστοῦ·
of us and Saviour Jesus Christ :

2 χάρις ὑμῖν καὶ εἰρήνη πληθυνθείη ἐν
Grace to you and peace *may it* be multiplied by

ἐπιγνώσει τοῦ θεοῦ καὶ Ἰησοῦ τοῦ
a full knowledge – of God and of Jesus the

κυρίου ἡμῶν.
Lord of us.

3 Ὡς τὰ πάντα ἡμῖν τῆς θείας δυνάμεως
As – all things to us the divine power
= his divine power has given us all things . . .

* Cf. 4. 11 (a statement of fact, not a wish).

---

2 Peter

Chapter 1

SIMON Peter, a servant and apostle of Jesus Christ,

To those who through the righteousness of our God and Savior Jesus Christ have received a faith as precious as ours:

2 Grace and peace be yours in abundance through the knowledge of God and of Jesus our Lord.

Making One's Calling and Election Sure

3 His divine power has given us everything we

p 12 Greek Silvanus, a variant of Silas

for life and godliness, through the knowledge of him who called us by[d] his own glory and goodness. [4]Thus he has given us, through these things, his precious and very great promises, so that through them you may escape from the corruption that is in the world because of lust, and may become participants of the divine nature. [5]For this very reason, you must make every effort to support your faith with goodness, and goodness with knowledge, [6]and knowledge with self-control, and self-control with endurance, and endurance with godliness, [7]and godliness with mutual[e] affection, and mutual[e] affection with love. [8]For if these things are yours and are increasing among you, they keep you from being ineffective and unfruitful in the knowledge of our Lord Jesus Christ. [9]For anyone who lacks these things is nearsighted and blind, and is forgetful of the cleansing of past sins. [10]Therefore, brothers and sisters,[f] be all the more eager to confirm your call and election, for if you do this, you will never stumble. [11]For in this way, entry into the eternal kingdom of our Lord and Savior Jesus Christ will be richly provided for you.

12 Therefore I intend to keep on reminding you of these things, though you know them already and are established in the truth that has come to you. [13]I think

---

αὐτοῦ τὰ πρὸς ζωὴν καὶ εὐσέβειαν δεδωρημένης
of him - [belong- life and piety having given[a]
     ing] to

διὰ τῆς ἐπιγνώσεως τοῦ καλέσαντος ἡμᾶς
through the full knowledge of the [one] having called us

ἰδίᾳ δόξῃ καὶ ἀρετῇ, 4 δι᾽ ὧν τὰ τίμια
to [his] glory and virtue, through which the [a]precious
own   things

καὶ μέγιστα ἡμῖν ἐπαγγέλματα δεδώρηται,
[a]and [b]very great [d]to us [c]promises [1]he has given,

ἵνα διὰ τούτων γένησθε θείας κοινωνοὶ
in or- through these ye might [2]of a divine [1]sharers
der that   become

φύσεως, ἀποφυγόντες τῆς ἐν τῷ κόσμῳ
[2]nature, escaping from [1]the [3]in [2]the [4]world

ἐν ἐπιθυμίᾳ φθορᾶς. 5 καὶ αὐτὸ τοῦτο
[6]by [7]lust [5]corruption. [1]also [2]for this very thing
     (reason)

δὲ σπουδὴν πᾶσαν παρεισενέγκαντες
[1]But [6]diligence [5]all [4]bringing in

ἐπιχορηγήσατε ἐν τῇ πίστει ὑμῶν τὴν
supply in the faith of you -

ἀρετήν, ἐν δὲ τῇ ἀρετῇ τὴν γνῶσιν,
virtue, and in - virtue - knowledge,

6 ἐν δὲ τῇ γνώσει τὴν ἐγκράτειαν,
and in - knowledge - self-control,

ἐν δὲ τῇ ἐγκρατείᾳ τὴν ὑπομονήν, ἐν
and in - self-control - endurance, [1]in

δὲ τῇ ὑπομονῇ τὴν εὐσέβειαν, 7 ἐν δὲ
[1]and - endurance - piety, and in

τῇ εὐσεβείᾳ τὴν φιλαδελφίαν, ἐν δὲ
- piety - brotherly friendship, and in

τῇ φιλαδελφίᾳ τὴν ἀγάπην. 8 ταῦτα
- brotherly friendship - love. these things

γὰρ ὑμῖν ὑπάρχοντα καὶ πλεονάζοντα
For [2]in you [1]being and abounding

οὐκ ἀργοὺς οὐδὲ ἀκάρπους καθίστησιν
[3]not [4]barren [5]nor [6]unfruitful [1]makes [2][you]

εἰς τὴν τοῦ κυρίου ἡμῶν Ἰησοῦ Χριστοῦ
in [1]the [2]of the [4]Lord [3]of us [5]Jesus [7]Christ

ἐπίγνωσιν. 9 ᾧ γὰρ μὴ πάρεστιν ταῦτα,
[6]full knowledge; for [he] [2]not [4]is(are) [1]these
     in whom [3]present things,

τυφλός ἐστιν μυωπάζων, λήθην λαβὼν
[2]blind [1]is being short-sighted, forgetfulness taking
     = being forgetful

τοῦ καθαρισμοῦ τῶν πάλαι αὐτοῦ ἁμαρτιῶν.
of the cleansing of the [3]in time [2]of him [1]sins.
     past

10 διὸ μᾶλλον, ἀδελφοί, σπουδάσατε
Wherefore rather, brothers, be ye diligent

βεβαίαν ὑμῶν τὴν κλῆσιν καὶ ἐκλογὴν
[1]firm [2]of you [3]the [4]calling [5]and [6]choice

ποιεῖσθαι· ταῦτα γὰρ ποιοῦντες οὐ μὴ
[1]to make; for these things doing by no means

πταίσητέ ποτε. 11 οὕτως γὰρ πλουσίως
ye will fail ever. For so [2]richly

ἐπιχορηγηθήσεται ὑμῖν ἡ εἴσοδος εἰς τὴν
[1]will be supplied [3]to you the entrance into the

αἰώνιον βασιλείαν τοῦ κυρίου ἡμῶν καὶ
eternal kingdom of the Lord of us and

σωτῆρος Ἰησοῦ Χριστοῦ.
Saviour Jesus Christ.

12 Διὸ μελλήσω ἀεὶ ὑμᾶς ὑπομιμνῄσκειν
Wherefore I will intend always you to remind

περὶ τούτων, καίπερ εἰδότας καὶ
concerning these things, though knowing and

ἐστηριγμένους ἐν τῇ παρούσῃ ἀληθείᾳ.
having been confirmed in the present truth.

---

need for life and godliness through our knowledge of him who called us by his own glory and goodness. [4]Through these he has given us his very great and precious promises, so that through them you may participate in the divine nature and escape the corruption in the world caused by evil desires.

[5]For this very reason, make every effort to add to your faith goodness; and to goodness, knowledge; [6]and to knowledge, self-control; and to self-control, perseverance; and to perseverance, godliness; [7]and to godliness, brotherly kindness; and to brotherly kindness, love. [8]For if you possess these qualities in increasing measure, they will keep you from being ineffective and unproductive in your knowledge of our Lord Jesus Christ. [9]But if anyone does not have them, he is nearsighted and blind, and has forgotten that he has been cleansed from his past sins.

[10]Therefore, my brothers, be all the more eager to make your calling and election sure. For if you do these things, you will never fall, [11]and you will receive a rich welcome into the eternal kingdom of our Lord and Savior Jesus Christ.

Prophecy of Scripture

[12]So I will always remind you of these things, even though you know them and are firmly established in the truth you now have. [13]I

---

[d]Other ancient authorities read *through*
[e]Gk *brotherly*
[f]Gk *brothers*

it right, as long as I am in this body,[g] to refresh your memory, 14since I know that my death[h] will come soon, as indeed our Lord Jesus Christ has made clear to me. 15And I will make every effort so that after my departure you may be able at any time to recall these things.

Eyewitnesses of Christ's Glory

16 For we did not follow cleverly devised myths when we made known to you the power and coming of our Lord Jesus Christ, but we had been eyewitnesses of his majesty. 17For he received honor and glory from God the Father when that voice was conveyed to him by the Majestic Glory, saying, "This is my Son, my Beloved,[i] with whom I am well pleased." 18We ourselves heard this voice come from heaven, while we were with him on the holy mountain.

19 So we have the prophetic message more fully confirmed. You will do well to be attentive to this as to a lamp shining in a dark place, until the day dawns and the morning star rises in your hearts. 20First of all you must understand this, that no prophecy of scripture is a matter of one's own interpretation, 21because no prophecy ever came by human will, but men and women moved by the Holy Spirit spoke from God.[j]

---

13 δίκαιον δὲ ἡγοῦμαι, ἐφ' ὅσον εἰμι
And ²right ¹I deem [it], so long as† I am

ἐν τούτῳ τῷ σκηνώματι, διεγείρειν ὑμᾶς
in this – tabernacle, to rouse you

ἐν ὑπομνήσει, 14 εἰδὼς ὅτι ταχινή ἐστιν
by a reminder, knowing that soon is

ἡ ἀπόθεσις τοῦ σκηνώματός μου, καθὼς
the putting off of the tabernacle of me, as

καὶ ὁ κύριος ἡμῶν Ἰησοῦς Χριστὸς
indeed the Lord of us Jesus Christ

ἐδήλωσέν μοι· 15 σπουδάσω δὲ καὶ
made clear to me; and I will be diligent also

ἑκάστοτε ἔχειν ὑμᾶς μετὰ τὴν ἐμὴν
⁶always ⁷to have ²you ³after – ⁴my

ἔξοδον τὴν τούτων μνήμην ποιεῖσθαι.
⁵exodus ⁸the ¹⁰of these things ⁹memory ¹to cause.

16 οὐ γὰρ σεσοφισμένοις μύθοις ἐξακολου-
For not ³having been ²fables ¹follow-
cleverly devised

θήσαντες ἐγνωρίσαμεν ὑμῖν τὴν τοῦ κυρίου
ing we made known to you ¹the ⁵of the ⁴Lord

ἡμῶν Ἰησοῦ Χριστοῦ δύναμιν καὶ
⁶of us ⁸Jesus ⁹Christ ²power ³and

παρουσίαν, ἀλλ' ἐπόπται γενηθέντες τῆς
⁴presence, but ¹eyewitnesses ¹having become ³of the

ἐκείνου μεγαλειότητος. 17 λαβὼν γὰρ
⁵of that one ⁴majesty. For receiving

παρὰ θεοῦ πατρὸς τιμὴν καὶ δόξαν
from God [the] Father honour and glory

φωνῆς ἐνεχθείσης αὐτῷ τοιᾶσδε ὑπὸ τῆς
¹a voice ³being borne² ⁴to him ¹such by the

μεγαλοπρεποῦς δόξης· ὁ υἱός μου ὁ
magnificent glory: The Son of me the

ἀγαπητός μου οὗτός ἐστιν, εἰς ὃν ἐγὼ
beloved of me this is, in whom I

εὐδόκησα, — 18 καὶ ταύτην τὴν φωνὴν
was wellpleased,— and this – voice

ἡμεῖς ἠκούσαμεν ἐξ οὐρανοῦ ἐνεχθεῖσαν
we heard ³out of ²heaven ¹being borne

σὺν αὐτῷ ὄντες ἐν τῷ ἁγίῳ ὄρει. 19 καὶ
⁵with ⁶him ⁴being in the holy mountain. And

ἔχομεν βεβαιότερον τὸν προφητικὸν λόγον,
we have more firm the prophetic word,

ᾧ καλῶς ποιεῖτε προσέχοντες ὡς λύχνῳ
to which ²well ¹ye do taking heed as to a lamp

φαίνοντι ἐν αὐχμηρῷ τόπῳ, ἕως οὗ
shining in a murky place, until

ἡμέρα διαυγάσῃ καὶ φωσφόρος ἀνατείλῃ
day dawns and [the] daystar rises

ἐν ταῖς καρδίαις ὑμῶν· 20 τοῦτο πρῶτον
in the hearts of you; ²this ³firstly

γινώσκοντες, ὅτι πᾶσα προφητεία γραφῆς
¹knowing, that every prophecy of scripture
=no ... is –

ἰδίας ἐπιλύσεως οὐ γίνεται· 21 οὐ γὰρ
of [its] own solution not becomes; for not

θελήματι ἀνθρώπου ἠνέχθη προφητεία
by will of man ²was borne ¹prophecy

ποτέ, ἀλλὰ ὑπὸ πνεύματος ἁγίου φερόμενοι
at any but ⁶by ⁵Spirit ⁷[the] being borne
time, Holy

ἐλάλησαν ἀπὸ θεοῦ ἄνθρωποι.
²spoke ³from ⁴God ¹men.

---

[g] Gk tent
[h] Gk the putting off of my tent
[i] Other ancient authorities read my beloved Son
[j] Other ancient authorities read but moved by the Holy Spirit saints of God spoke

---

think it is right to refresh your memory as long as I live in the tent of this body, 14because I know that I will soon put it aside, as our Lord Jesus Christ has made clear to me. 15And I will make every effort to see that after my departure you will always be able to remember these things.

16We did not follow cleverly invented stories when we told you about the power and coming of our Lord Jesus Christ, but we were eyewitnesses of his majesty. 17For he received honor and glory from God the Father when the voice came to him from the Majestic Glory, saying, "This is my Son, whom I love; with him I am well pleased."[a] 18We ourselves heard this voice that came from heaven when we were with him on the sacred mountain.

19And we have the word of the prophets made more certain, and you will do well to pay attention to it, as to a light shining in a dark place, until the day dawns and the morning star rises in your hearts. 20Above all, you must understand that no prophecy of Scripture came about by the prophet's own interpretation. 21For prophecy never had its origin in the will of man, but men spoke from God as they were carried along by the Holy Spirit.

[a]17 Matt. 17:5; Mark 9:7; Luke 9:35

Chapter 2

False Prophets and Their Punishment

BUT false prophets also arose among the people, just as there will be false teachers among you, who will secretly bring in destructive opinions. They will even deny the Master who bought them—bringing swift destruction on themselves. 2 Even so, many will follow their licentious ways, and because of these teachers[k] the way of truth will be maligned. 3 And in their greed they will exploit you with deceptive words. Their condemnation, pronounced against them long ago, has not been idle, and their destruction is not asleep.

4 For if God did not spare the angels when they sinned, but cast them into hell[l] and committed them to chains[m] of deepest darkness to be kept until the judgment; 5 and if he did not spare the ancient world, even though he saved Noah, a herald of righteousness, with seven others, when he brought a flood on a world of the ungodly; 6 and if by turning the cities of Sodom and Gomorrah to ashes he condemned them to extinction[n] and made them an example of what is coming to the ungodly;[o] 7 and if he rescued Lot, a righteous man greatly distressed by the licentiousness of the lawless 8 (for that righteous man, living among them day after day, was tormented in his righteous soul by their lawless deeds that he saw and heard), 9 then the Lord knows how to rescue the godly from trial, and to keep the unrighteous under punishment until the day of judgment 10 —especially those who indulge their

---

2 Ἐγένοντο δὲ καὶ ψευδοπροφῆται ἐν
But there were also false prophets among

τῷ λαῷ, ὡς καὶ ἐν ὑμῖν ἔσονται
the people, as indeed among you there will be

ψευδοδιδάσκαλοι, οἵτινες παρεισάξουσιν
false teachers, who will secretly bring in

αἱρέσεις ἀπωλείας, καὶ τὸν ἀγοράσαντα
opinions of destruction,* and ²the ⁴having bought

αὐτοὺς δεσπότην ἀρνούμενοι, ἐπάγοντες
²them ³Master ³denying, bringing on

ἑαυτοῖς ταχινὴν ἀπώλειαν· 2 καὶ πολλοὶ
themselves swift destruction; and many

ἐξακολουθήσουσιν αὐτῶν ταῖς ἀσελγείαις,
will follow ³of them ¹the ²licentiousnesses,

δι᾽ οὓς ἡ ὁδὸς τῆς ἀληθείας βλασφημη-
be- whom the way of the truth will be
cause of

θήσεται· 3 καὶ ἐν πλεονεξίᾳ πλαστοῖς
blasphemed; and by covetousness with fabricated

λόγοις ὑμᾶς ἐμπορεύσονται· οἷς τὸ κρίμα
words ²you ¹they will make for the judg-
merchandise of; whom ment

ἔκπαλαι οὐκ ἀργεῖ, καὶ ἡ ἀπώλεια
of old lingers not, and the destruction

αὐτῶν οὐ νυστάζει. 4 εἰ γὰρ ὁ θεὸς
of them slumbers not. For if – God

ἀγγέλων ἁμαρτησάντων οὐκ ἐφείσατο, ἀλλὰ
²angels ³sinning ¹spared not, but

σιροῖς ζόφου ταρταρώσας παρέδωκεν
²in pits ³of gloom ¹consigning to Tartarus ⁴delivered [them]

εἰς κρίσιν τηρουμένους, 5 καὶ ἀρχαίου
⁶to ⁷judgment ⁵being kept, and ²[the] ancient

κόσμου οὐκ ἐφείσατο, ἀλλὰ ὄγδοον Νῶε
³world ¹spared not, but ²[the] ¹Noe
eighth man

δικαιοσύνης κήρυκα ἐφύλαξεν, κατακλυσμὸν
³of righteousness ⁴a herald ¹guarded, ²a flood

κόσμῳ ἀσεβῶν ἐπάξας, 6 καὶ πόλεις
⁴a world ⁵of impious men ¹bringing ³on, and ²[the] cities

Σοδόμων καὶ Γομόρρας τεφρώσας
⁴of Sodom ⁵and ⁶Gomorra ¹covering [them]
with ashes

καταστροφῇ κατέκρινεν, ὑπόδειγμα μελ-
³by an overthrow ²condemned, ³an example ³of men

λόντων ἀσεβεῖν τεθεικώς, 7 καὶ δίκαιον
intending ⁴to live ¹having set(made), and ²righteous
impiously

Λὼτ καταπονούμενον ὑπὸ τῆς τῶν ἀθέσμων
³Lot ⁴being oppressed ⁵by ⁶the ¹⁰of the ¹¹lawless

ἐν ἀσελγείᾳ ἀναστροφῆς ἐρρύσατο· 8 βλέμ-
³in ⁹licentiousness ⁷conduct ¹delivered; ³in

ματι γὰρ καὶ ἀκοῇ ὁ δίκαιος ἐγκατοικῶν
seeing ¹for and in hear- the righteous dwelling
ing (that) man

ἐν αὐτοῖς ἡμέραν ἐξ ἡμέρας ψυχὴν
among them day after† day ³[his] ⁴soul

δικαίαν ἀνόμοις ἔργοις ἐβασάνιζεν·
³righteous ⁶with [their] lawless ⁵works ¹tormented;

9 οἶδεν κύριος εὐσεβεῖς ἐκ πειρασμοῦ
²knows* ¹[the] Lord ⁴pious men ⁵out of ³trial

ῥύεσθαι, ἀδίκους δὲ εἰς ἡμέραν κρίσεως
¹to deliver, ⁶unjust men ¹but ⁷for ⁸a day ⁷of judgment

κολαζομένους τηρεῖν, 10 μάλιστα δὲ τοὺς
⁶being punished ³to keep, and most of all ¹the

Chapter 2

False Teachers and Their Destruction

BUT there were also false prophets among the people, just as there will be false teachers among you. They will secretly introduce destructive heresies, even denying the sovereign Lord who bought them—bringing swift destruction on themselves. 2 Many will follow their shameful ways and will bring the way of truth into disrepute. 3 In their greed these false teachers will exploit you with stories they have made up. Their condemnation has long been hanging over them, and their destruction has not been sleeping.

4 For if God did not spare angels when they sinned, but sent them to hell,[b] putting them into gloomy dungeons[c] to be held for judgment; 5 if he did not spare the ancient world when he brought the flood on its ungodly people, but protected Noah, a preacher of righteousness, and seven others; 6 if he condemned the cities of Sodom and Gomorrah by burning them to ashes, and made them an example of what is going to happen to the ungodly; 7 and if he rescued Lot, a righteous man, who was distressed by the filthy lives of lawless men 8 (for that righteous man, living among them day after day, was tormented in his righteous soul by the lawless deeds he saw and heard)— 9 if this is so, then the Lord knows how to rescue godly men from trials and to hold the unrighteous for the day of judgment, while continuing their punishment.[d] 10 This is especially true of

---

k Gk *because of them*
l Gk *Tartaros*
m Other ancient authorities read *pits*
n Other ancient authorities lack *to extinction*
o Other ancient authorities read *an example to those who were to be ungodly*

● Genitive of quality : " destructive opinions."

● That is, " the Lord can deliver "; see note on page xviii.

b 4 Greek *Tartarus*
c 4 Some manuscripts *into chains of darkness*
d 9 Or *unrighteous for punishment until the day of judgment*

flesh in depraved lust, and who despise authority.

Bold and willful, they are not afraid to slander the glorious ones,[p] [11]whereas angels, though greater in might and power, do not bring against them a slanderous judgment from the Lord.[q] [12]These people, however, are like irrational animals, mere creatures of instinct, born to be caught and killed. They slander what they do not understand, and when those creatures are destroyed,[r] they also will be destroyed, [13]suffering[s] the penalty for doing wrong. They count it a pleasure to revel in the daytime. They are blots and blemishes, reveling in their dissipation[t] while they feast with you. [14]They have eyes full of adultery, insatiable for sin. They entice unsteady souls. They have hearts trained in greed. Accursed children! [15]They have left the straight road and have gone astray, following the road of Balaam son of Bosor,[u] who loved the wages of doing wrong, [16]but was rebuked for his own transgression; a speechless donkey spoke with a human voice and restrained the prophet's madness. [17] These are waterless springs and mists driven by a storm; for them the deepest darkness has been reserved. [18]For they speak bombastic nonsense, and with licentious desires of the flesh they entice people who have just[v] escaped from those who live in error. [19]They promise them freedom, but they them-

---

ὀπίσω   σαρκὸς   ἐν   ἐπιθυμίᾳ   μιασμοῦ
²after   ³flesh   ⁵in   ⁶lust   ⁷of defilement*

πορευομένους καὶ κυριότητος καταφρονοῦντας.
²[ones] going ¹and ¹⁰dominion   ⁹despising.

τολμηταὶ   αὐθάδεις,   δόξας   οὐ   τρέμουσιν
²darers ¹Self-satisfied,   glories   they do not tremble [at]

βλασφημοῦντες, 11 ὅπου ἄγγελοι ἰσχύϊ καὶ
blaspheming,   where   angels ³in strength ⁴and

δυνάμει   μείζονες   ὄντες   οὐ   φέρουσιν   κατ᾽
¹in power ²greater ¹being   do not bring   against

αὐτῶν   παρὰ   κυρίῳ   βλάσφημον   κρίσιν.
them   before [the] Lord   railing   judgment.

12 οὗτοι   δέ,   ὡς   ἄλογα   ζῷα   γεγεννημένα
But these ¹as ⁴without ²animals ³having been born
men,   reason

φυσικὰ   εἰς   ἅλωσιν   καὶ   φθοράν,   ἐν   οἷς
²natural   for   capture   and   corruption,   ³in ⁵things
                                      which

ἀγνοοῦσιν   βλασφημοῦντες,   ἐν   τῇ   φθορᾷ
⁴they are   ¹railing,   in   the   corruption
ignorant [of]

αὐτῶν   καὶ   φθαρήσονται,   13 ἀδικούμενοι
of them   indeed they will be corrupted,   suffering wrong

μισθὸν   ἀδικίας·   ἡδονὴν   ἡγούμενοι   τὴν
[as] wages of wrong; ⁵[to be] pleasure ¹deeming   –

ἐν   ἡμέρᾳ   τρυφήν,   σπίλοι   καὶ   μῶμοι
³in ⁴[the] day ²luxury,   spots   and   blemishes

ἐντρυφῶντες   ἐν   ταῖς   ἀπάταις   αὐτῶν
revelling   in   the   deceits   of them

συνευωχούμενοι   ὑμῖν,   14 ὀφθαλμοὺς   ἔχοντες
feasting along with   you,   ²eyes   ¹having

μεστοὺς   μοιχαλίδος   καὶ   ἀκαταπαύστους
full   of an adulteress   and   not ceasing from

ἁμαρτίας,   δελεάζοντες   ψυχὰς   ἀστηρίκτους,
sin,   alluring   ²souls   ¹unsteady,

καρδίαν   γεγυμνασμένην   πλεονεξίας   ἔχοντες,
²a heart ¹having been exercised ⁴of(in) covetousness ¹having,

κατάρας   τέκνα·   15 καταλείποντες   εὐθεῖαν
²of curse ¹children;   forsaking   a straight

ὁδὸν   ἐπλανήθησαν,   ἐξακολουθήσαντες   τῇ
way   they erred,   following   the

ὁδῷ   τοῦ   Βαλαὰμ   τοῦ   Βεώρ,   ὃς   μισθὸν
way   –   of Balaam   the [son] of   who   ³[the]
                          Beor,   wages

ἀδικίας   ἠγάπησεν,   16 ἔλεγξιν   δὲ   ἔσχεν
³of wrong ¹loved,   and ²reproof   ¹had

ἰδίας   παρανομίας·   ὑποζύγιον   ἄφωνον   ἐν
of [his] own transgression;   ²ass   ¹a dumb ⁴with

ἀνθρώπου   φωνῇ   φθεγξάμενον   ἐκώλυσεν
⁶of a man   ⁵voice   ³speaking   restrained

τὴν   τοῦ   προφήτου   παραφρονίαν.   17 οὗτοί
¹the ²of the ³prophet   ⁴madness.   These men

εἰσιν   πηγαὶ   ἄνυδροι   καὶ   ὁμίχλαι   ὑπὸ
are   ²springs ¹waterless   and   mists   ²by

λαίλαπος   ἐλαυνόμεναι,   οἷς   ὁ   ζόφος   τοῦ
²storm   ¹being driven,   for whom   the   gloom   of the

σκότους   τετήρηται.   18 ὑπέρογκα   γὰρ
darkness   has been kept.   For ²immoderate [words]

ματαιότητος   φθεγγόμενοι   δελεάζουσιν   ἐν
³of vanity   ¹speaking   they allure   by

ἐπιθυμίαις   σαρκὸς   ἀσελγείαις   τοὺς   ὀλίγως
[the] lusts   of [the] flesh   in excesses   the [ones]   almost

ἀποφεύγοντας   τοὺς   ἐν   πλάνῃ   ἀναστρε-
escaping   ¹the [ones]   ³in   ⁴error   ²liv-

φομένους,   19 ἐλευθερίαν   αὐτοῖς   ἐπαγγελ-
ing,   ³freedom   ²to them   ¹promis-

* Genitive of quality: " defiling lust."

---

those who follow the corrupt desire of the sinful nature[e] and despise authority.

Bold and arrogant, these men are not afraid to slander celestial beings; [11]yet even angels, although they are stronger and more powerful, do not bring slanderous accusations against such beings in the presence of the Lord. [12]But these men blaspheme in matters they do not understand. They are like brute beasts, creatures of instinct, born only to be caught and destroyed, and like beasts they too will perish.

[13]They will be paid back with harm for the harm they have done. Their idea of pleasure is to carouse in broad daylight. They are blots and blemishes, reveling in their pleasures while they feast with you.[f] [14]With eyes full of adultery, they never stop sinning; they seduce the unstable; they are experts in greed— an accursed brood! [15]They have left the straight way and wandered off to follow the way of Balaam son of Beor, who loved the wages of wickedness. [16]But he was rebuked for his wrongdoing by a donkey—a beast without speech— who spoke with a man's voice and restrained the prophet's madness.

[17]These men are springs without water and mists driven by a storm. Blackest darkness is reserved for them. [18]For they mouth empty, boastful words and, by appealing to the lustful desires of sinful human nature, they entice people who are just escaping from those who live in error. [19]They promise them free-

---

[p] Or angels; Gk glories
[q] Other ancient authorities read before the Lord; others lack the phrase
[r] Gk in their destruction
[s] Other ancient authorities read receiving
[t] Other ancient authorities read love feasts
[u] Other ancient authorities read Beor
[v] Other ancient authorities read actually

[e]10 Or the flesh
[f]13 Some manuscripts in their love feasts

selves are slaves of corruption; for people are slaves to whatever masters them. 20 For if, after they have escaped the defilements of the world through the knowledge of our Lord and Savior Jesus Christ, they are again entangled in them and overpowered, the last state has become worse for them than the first. 21 For it would have been better for them never to have known the way of righteousness than, after knowing it, to turn back from the holy commandment that was passed on to them. 22 It has happened to them according to the true proverb,

"The dog turns back
    to its
    own vomit,"

and,

"The sow is washed
    only to wallow
    in the mud."

λόμενοι, αὐτοὶ δοῦλοι ὑπάρχοντες τῆς
ing, [them]selves ⁸slaves ¹being -

φθορᾶς· ᾧ γάρ τις ἥττηται, τούτῳ
of corruption; for by whom anyone has been defeated, to this man

δεδούλωται. 20 εἰ γὰρ ἀποφυγόντες τὰ
he has been enslaved. For if having escaped the

μιάσματα τοῦ κόσμου ἐν ἐπιγνώσει τοῦ
defilements of the world by a full knowledge of the

κυρίου καὶ σωτῆρος Ἰησοῦ Χριστοῦ,
Lord and Saviour Jesus Christ,

τούτοις δὲ πάλιν ἐμπλακέντες ἡττῶνται,
yet by these again having been entangled have been defeated,

γέγονεν αὐτοῖς τὰ ἔσχατα χείρονα τῶν
³have become ⁴to them ¹the ²last things worse [than] the

πρώτων. 21 κρεῖττον γὰρ ἦν αὐτοῖς
first. For better for it was for them

μὴ ἐπεγνωκέναι τὴν ὁδὸν τῆς δικαιοσύνης,
not to have fully known the way - of righteousness,

ἢ ἐπιγνοῦσιν ὑποστρέψαι ἐκ τῆς παρα-
than fully knowing to turn from ¹the ⁴de-

δοθείσης αὐτοῖς ἁγίας ἐντολῆς. 22 συμβέ-
livered ⁵to them ²holy ³commandment. ⁵has

βηκεν αὐτοῖς τὸ τῆς ἀληθοῦς παροιμίας·
happened ⁶to them ¹The ²of the ³true ⁴proverb:
    thing

κύων ἐπιστρέψας ἐπὶ τὸ ἴδιον ἐξέραμα,
[The] dog turning upon the(its) own vomit,

καὶ· ὗς λουσαμένη εἰς κυλισμὸν βορβόρου.
and: [The] washed to wallowing of mud.
    sow

---

dom, while they themselves are slaves of depravity—for a man is a slave to whatever has mastered him. 20 If they have escaped the corruption of the world by knowing our Lord and Savior Jesus Christ and are again entangled in it and overcome, they are worse off at the end than they were at the beginning. 21 It would have been better for them not to have known the way of righteousness, than to have known it and then to turn their backs on the sacred command that was passed on to them. 22 Of them the proverbs are true: "A dog returns to its vomit," g and, "A sow that is washed goes back to her wallowing in the mud."

Chapter 3

The Promise of the Lord's Coming

THIS is now, beloved, the second letter I am writing to you; in them I am trying to arouse your sincere intention by reminding you 2 that you should remember the words spoken in the past by the holy prophets, and the commandment of the Lord and Savior spoken through your apostles. 3 First of all you must understand this, that in the last days scoffers will come, scoffing and indulging their own lusts 4 and saying, "Where is the promise of his coming? For ever since our ancestors died, w all things continue as they were from the beginning of creation!" 5 They deliberately ignore this fact, that by the word of God heavens existed long ago and an earth was

---

3 Ταύτην ἤδη, ἀγαπητοί, δευτέραν ὑμῖν
¹This ⁸now, ⁴beloved, ⁵second ⁷to you

γράφω ἐπιστολήν, ἐν αἷς διεγείρω ὑμῶν
⁶I write ²epistle, in [both] which I rouse ⁹of you

ἐν ὑπομνήσει τὴν εἰλικρινῆ διάνοιαν,
¹⁰by ⁹reminder ¹the ¹sincere ²mind,

2 μνησθῆναι τῶν προειρημένων ῥημάτων
to remember the ²having been ¹words
    previously spoken

ὑπὸ τῶν ἁγίων προφητῶν καὶ τῆς τῶν
by the holy prophets and ¹the ²of the

ἀποστόλων ὑμῶν ἐντολῆς τοῦ κυρίου καὶ
⁴apostles ⁵of you ³commandment of the Lord and

σωτῆρος, 3 τοῦτο πρῶτον γινώσκοντες, ὅτι
Saviour, ²this ¹firstly ³knowing, that

ἐλεύσονται ἐπ' ἐσχάτων τῶν ἡμερῶν
there will come during [the] last of the days ³in

ἐμπαιγμονῇ ἐμπαῖκται κατὰ τὰς ἰδίας
⁴mocking ¹mockers ²according to ⁵the(ir) ⁷own

ἐπιθυμίας αὐτῶν πορευόμενοι 4 καὶ λέγοντες·
⁸lusts of them ⁶going and saying :

ποῦ ἐστιν ἡ ἐπαγγελία τῆς παρουσίας
Where is the promise of the presence

αὐτοῦ; ἀφ' ἧς γὰρ οἱ πατέρες ἐκοι-
of him? ²from ¹which [day] ¹for the fathers fell
    =for from the day when . . .

μήθησαν, πάντα οὕτως διαμένει ἀπ'
asleep, all things so remains from

ἀρχῆς κτίσεως. 5 λανθάνει γὰρ αὐτοὺς
[the] of creation. For ²is concealed ³them
beginning [from]

τοῦτο θέλοντας ὅτι οὐρανοὶ ἦσαν ἔκπαλαι
¹this wishing* that heavens were of old

Chapter 3

The Day of the Lord

DEAR friends, this is now my second letter to you. I have written both of them as reminders to stimulate you to wholesome thinking. 2 I want you to recall the words spoken in the past by the holy prophets and the command given by our Lord and Savior through your apostles. 3 First of all, you must understand that in the last days scoffers will come, scoffing and following their own evil desires. 4 They will say, "Where is this 'coming' he promised? Ever since our fathers died, everything goes on as it has since the beginning of creation." 5 But they deliberately forget that long ago by God's word the heavens existed and the earth was

---

w Gk our fathers fell asleep

* That is, they wish it to be so.

g 22 Prov. 26:11

formed out of water and by means of water, 6through which the world of that time was deluged with water and perished. 7But by the same word the present heavens and earth have been reserved for fire, being kept until the day of judgment and destruction of the godless.

8 But do not ignore this one fact, beloved, that with the Lord one day is like a thousand years, and a thousand years are like one day. 9The Lord is not slow about his promise, as some think of slowness, but is patient with you, *x* not wanting any to perish, but all to come to repentance. 10But the day of the Lord will come like a thief, and then the heavens will pass away with a loud noise, and the elements will be dissolved with fire, and the earth and everything that is done on it will be disclosed. *y*

11 Since all these things are to be dissolved in this way, what sort of persons ought you to be in leading lives of holiness and godliness, 12waiting for and hastening *z* the coming of the day of God, because of which the heavens will be set ablaze and dissolved, and the elements will melt with fire? 13But, in accordance with his promise, we wait for new heavens and a new earth, where righteousness is at home.

Final Exhortation and Doxology

14 Therefore, beloved, while you are waiting for

καὶ   γῆ   ἐξ   ὕδατος   καὶ   δι'   ὕδατος
and   earth   by   water   and   through   water

συνεστῶσα   τῷ   τοῦ   θεοῦ   λόγῳ,   6 δι'
¹having been   ²by   –   ⁴of God   ³word,   through
held together   the

ὧν   ὁ   τότε   κόσμος   ὕδατι   κατακλυσθεὶς
which the   then§   world   ³by water   ¹being inundated
things

ἀπώλετο·   7 οἱ   δὲ   νῦν   οὐρανοὶ   καὶ   ἡ
perished;   but the   now   heavens   and   the

γῆ   τῷ   αὐτῷ   λόγῳ   τεθησαυρισμένοι   εἰσὶν
earth by the   same   word   ¹having been stored up   ¹are

πυρὶ   τηρούμενοι   εἰς   ἡμέραν   κρίσεως   καὶ
¹for fire   ¹being kept   in   a day   of judgment   and

ἀπωλείας   τῶν   ἀσεβῶν   ἀνθρώπων.   8 Ἐν
destruction   of the   impious   men.   ²one

δὲ   τοῦτο   μὴ   λανθανέτω   ὑμᾶς,   ἀγαπητοί,
But   ¹this   let not be concealed   you,   beloved,
²thing   [from]

ὅτι   μία   ἡμέρα   παρὰ   κυρίῳ   ὡς   χίλια
that   one   day   with [the] Lord [is]   as a thousand

ἔτη   καὶ   χίλια   ἔτη   ὡς   ἡμέρα   μία.   9 οὐ
years   and a thousand years   as   ¹day   ¹one.   ³not

βραδύνει   κύριος   τῆς   ἐπαγγελίας,   ὡς   τινες
²is ⁴slow   ¹[The]   of the   promise,   as   some
Lord   (his)

βραδύτητα   ἡγοῦνται,   ἀλλὰ   μακροθυμεῖ   εἰς
¹slowness   ¹deem,   but   is longsuffering toward

ὑμᾶς,   μὴ   βουλόμενός   τινας   ἀπολέσθαι
you,   not   purposing   any   to perish

ἀλλὰ   πάντας   εἰς   μετάνοιαν   χωρῆσαι.
but   all men   ²to   ²repentance   ¹to come.

10 Ἥξει   δὲ   ἡμέρα   κυρίου   ὡς   κλέπτης,
But will come   [the] day   of [the] Lord as   a thief,

ἐν   ᾗ   οἱ   οὐρανοὶ   ῥοιζηδὸν   παρελεύσονται,
in which the   heavens   ²with rushing   ¹will pass away,
sound

στοιχεῖα   δὲ   καυσούμενα   λυθήσεται,   καὶ
and [the] elements   burning   will be dissolved,   and

γῆ   καὶ   τὰ   ἐν   αὐτῇ   ἔργα   εὑρεθήσεται.
[the]   and   ¹the   ³in   ⁴it   ²works   will be
earth   discovered.

11 Τούτων   οὕτως   πάντων   λυομένων
²these things   ³thus   ¹All   ⁴being dissolvedª

ποταποὺς   δεῖ   ὑπάρχειν   [ὑμᾶς]   ἐν   ἁγίαις
what sort   it be-   ²to be   ¹you   in   holy
of men   hoves

ἀναστροφαῖς   καὶ   εὐσεβείαις,   12 προσδοκῶντας
conduct*   and   piety,*   awaiting

καὶ   σπεύδοντας   τὴν   παρουσίαν   τῆς   τοῦ
and   hastening   the   presence   ¹of the

θεοῦ   ἡμέρας,   δι'   ἣν   οὐρανοὶ   πυρούμενοι
²of God   ¹day,   on ac-   which   [the]   being set on fire
count of   heavens

λυθήσονται   καὶ   στοιχεῖα   καυσούμενα
will be dissolved   and   [the] elements   burning

τήκεται.   13 καινοὺς   δὲ   οὐρανοὺς   καὶ
melts.   But new   heavens   and

γῆν   καινὴν   κατὰ   τὸ   ἐπάγγελμα   αὐτοῦ
²earth   ¹a new   accord-   the   promise   of him
ing to

προσδοκῶμεν,   ἐν   οἷς   δικαιοσύνη   κατοικεῖ.
we await,   in   which   righteousness   dwells.

14 Διό,   ἀγαπητοί,   ταῦτα   προσδοκῶντες
Wherefore,   beloved,   ²these things   ¹awaiting

---

formed out of water and by water. 6By these waters also the world of that time was deluged and destroyed. 7By the same word the present heavens and earth are reserved for fire, being kept for the day of judgment and destruction of ungodly men.

8But do not forget this one thing, dear friends: With the Lord a day is like a thousand years, and a thousand years are like a day. 9The Lord is not slow in keeping his promise, as some understand slowness. He is patient with you, not wanting anyone to perish, but everyone to come to repentance.

10But the day of the Lord will come like a thief. The heavens will disappear with a roar; the elements will be destroyed by fire, and the earth and everything in it will be laid bare. *h*

11Since everything will be destroyed in this way, what kind of people ought you to be? You ought to live holy and godly lives 12as you look forward to the day of God and speed its coming. *i* That day will bring about the destruction of the heavens by fire, and the elements will melt in the heat. 13But in keeping with his promise we are looking forward to a new heaven and a new earth, the home of righteousness.

14So then, dear friends, since you are looking for-

---

x Other ancient authorities read *on your account*
y Other ancient authorities read *will be burned up*
z Or *earnestly desiring*

§ This is allowable English : *cf.* " the then Prime Minister."

* The Greek plurals cannot be literally reproduced in English.

*h*10 Some manuscripts *be burned up*
*i*12 Or *as you wait eagerly for the day of God to come*

these things, strive to be found by him at peace, without spot or blemish; [15]and regard the patience of our Lord as salvation. So also our beloved brother Paul wrote to you according to the wisdom given him, [16]speaking of this as he does in all his letters. There are some things in them hard to understand, which the ignorant and unstable twist to their own destruction, as they do the other scriptures. [17]You therefore, beloved, since you are forewarned, beware that you are not carried away with the error of the lawless and lose your own stability. [18]But grow in the grace and knowledge of our Lord and Savior Jesus Christ. To him be the glory both now and to the day of eternity. Amen.[a]

σπουδάσατε ἄσπιλοι καὶ ἀμώμητοι αὐτῷ
be diligent   [5]spotless   [6]and   [7]unblemished   [2]by him

εὑρεθῆναι ἐν εἰρήνῃ, 15 καὶ τὴν τοῦ
[1]to be found   [3]in   [4]peace,   and   [3]the   [4]of the

κυρίου ἡμῶν μακροθυμίαν σωτηρίαν ἡγεῖσθε,
[5]Lord   [6]of us   [3]longsuffering   [2]salvation   [1]deem,

καθὼς καὶ ὁ ἀγαπητὸς ἡμῶν ἀδελφὸς
as   indeed   the   beloved   [3]of us   [1]brother

Παῦλος κατὰ τὴν δοθεῖσαν αὐτῷ σοφίαν
Paul   accord-   [1]the   [3]given   [4]to him   [2]wisdom
     ing to

ἔγραψεν ὑμῖν, 16 ὡς καὶ ἐν πάσαις
wrote   to you,   as   also   in   all [his]

ἐπιστολαῖς λαλῶν ἐν αὐταῖς περὶ τούτων,
epistles   speaking   in   them   concerning   these
     things,

ἐν αἷς ἐστιν δυσνόητά τινα, ἃ οἱ
in   which   is(are)   [3]hard to   [1]some   which   the
     understand   things,

ἀμαθεῖς καὶ ἀστήρικτοι στρεβλοῦσιν ὡς
unlearned   and   unsteady   twist   as

καὶ τὰς λοιπὰς γραφὰς πρὸς τὴν ἰδίαν
also   the   remaining   scriptures   to   the(ir)   own

αὐτῶν ἀπώλειαν. 17 Ὑμεῖς οὖν, ἀγαπητοί,
of them   destruction.   Ye   therefore,   beloved,

προγινώσκοντες φυλάσσεσθε ἵνα μὴ τῇ
knowing before   guard   lest   [2]by the

τῶν ἀθέσμων πλάνῃ συναπαχθέντες ἐκπέ-
[4]of the   [5]lawless   [3]error   [1]being led away with   ye fall

σητε τοῦ ἰδίου στηριγμοῦ, 18 αὐξάνετε
from   the(your)   own   stability,   [2]grow ye

δὲ ἐν χάριτι καὶ γνώσει τοῦ κυρίου
[1]but   in   grace   and   knowledge   of the   Lord

ἡμῶν καὶ σωτῆρος Ἰησοῦ Χριστοῦ.
of us   and   Saviour   Jesus   Christ.

αὐτῷ ἡ δόξα καὶ νῦν καὶ εἰς
To him[c] [is] the   glory   both   now   and   unto
=His is*   =for ever.

ἡμέραν αἰῶνος.
a day   of age.§

ward to this, make every effort to be found spotless, blameless and at peace with him. [15]Bear in mind that our Lord's patience means salvation, just as our dear brother Paul also wrote you with the wisdom that God gave him. [16]He writes the same way in all his letters, speaking in them of these matters. His letters contain some things that are hard to understand, which ignorant and unstable people distort, as they do the other Scriptures, to their own destruction.

[17]Therefore, dear friends, since you already know this, be on your guard so that you may not be carried away by the error of lawless men and fall from your secure position. [18]But grow in the grace and knowledge of our Lord and Savior Jesus Christ. To him be glory both now and forever! Amen.

The First Letter of
John

Chapter 1
The Word of Life

WE declare to you what was from the beginning, what we have heard, what we have seen with our eyes, what we have looked at and touched with our hands, concerning the word of life— [2]this life was revealed, and we have seen it and testify to it, and declare to you the eternal life that was with the Father and was revealed to us— [3]we declare to you what we have seen and

ΙΩΑΝΝΟΥ Α
Of John 1

1 Ὃ ἦν ἀπ' ἀρχῆς, ὃ ἀκηκόαμεν,
What   was   from   [the]   what   we have heard,
     beginning,

ὃ ἑωράκαμεν τοῖς ὀφθαλμοῖς ἡμῶν, ὃ
what   we have seen   with the   eyes   of us,   what

ἐθεασάμεθα καὶ αἱ χεῖρες ἡμῶν ἐψηλάφησαν,
we beheld   and   the   hands   of us   touched,

περὶ τοῦ λόγου τῆς ζωῆς, — 2 καὶ
concern- the   word   of life,   —   and
ing

ἡ ζωὴ ἐφανερώθη, καὶ ἑωράκαμεν καὶ
the   life   was manifested,   and   we have seen   and

μαρτυροῦμεν καὶ ἀπαγγέλλομεν ὑμῖν τὴν
we bear witness   and   *we* announce   to you   the

ζωὴν τὴν αἰώνιον, ἥτις ἦν πρὸς τὸν
life   the   eternal,   which   was   with   the

πατέρα καὶ ἐφανερώθη ἡμῖν, — 3 ὃ
Father   and   was manifested   to us,   —   what

ἑωράκαμεν καὶ ἀκηκόαμεν, ἀπαγγέλλομεν
we have seen   and   *we* have heard,   we announce

1 John

Chapter 1
The Word of Life

THAT which was from the beginning, which we have heard, which we have seen with our eyes, which we have looked at and our hands have touched—this we proclaim concerning the Word of life. [2]The life appeared; we have seen it and testify to it, and we proclaim to you the eternal life, which was with the Father and has appeared to us. [3]We proclaim to you what we have seen

---

[a] Other ancient authorities lack *Amen*

* See note on I. Pet. 5. 11.   § ? "An age-lasting (*i.e.* eternal) day."

heard so that you also may have fellowship with us; and truly our fellowship is with the Father and with his Son Jesus Christ. 4We are writing these things so that our*a* joy may be complete.

God Is Light

5 This is the message we have heard from him and proclaim to you, that God is light and in him there is no darkness at all. 6If we say that we have fellowship with him while we are walking in darkness, we lie and do not do what is true; 7but if we walk in the light as he himself is in the light, we have fellowship with one another, and the blood of Jesus his Son cleanses us from all sin. 8If we say that we have no sin, we deceive ourselves, and the truth is not in us. 9If we confess our sins, he who is faithful and just will forgive us our sins and cleanse us from all unrighteousness. 10If we say that we have not sinned, we make him a liar, and his word is not in us.

Chapter 2

Christ Our Advocate

MY little children, I am writing these things to you so that you may not sin. But if anyone does sin, we have an advocate with the Father, Jesus Christ the righteous; 2and he is the atoning sacrifice for our sins, and not for ours only but also for the sins of the

---

καὶ ὑμῖν, ἵνα καὶ ὑμεῖς κοινωνίαν ἔχητε
also to you, in order that *also* *ye* *fellowship* *may have*

μεθ' ἡμῶν. καὶ ἡ κοινωνία δὲ ἡ ἡμετέρα
with us. *indeed the* *fellowship* *And* – *our*

μετὰ τοῦ πατρὸς καὶ μετὰ τοῦ υἱοῦ
[is] with the Father and with the Son

αὐτοῦ Ἰησοῦ Χριστοῦ. 4 καὶ ταῦτα
of him Jesus Christ. And these things

γράφομεν ἡμεῖς ἵνα ἡ χαρὰ ἡμῶν ᾖ
write we in order that the joy of us may be

πεπληρωμένη.
having been fulfilled.

5 Καὶ ἔστιν αὕτη ἡ ἀγγελία ἣν
And *is* *this* the message which

ἀκηκόαμεν ἀπ' αὐτοῦ καὶ ἀναγγέλλομεν
we have heard from him and *we announce*

ὑμῖν, ὅτι ὁ θεὸς φῶς ἐστιν καὶ σκοτία
to you, that – God *light* *is* and *darkness*

ἐν αὐτῷ οὐκ ἔστιν οὐδεμία. 6 Ἐὰν
in *him* *not* *is* none. If

εἴπωμεν ὅτι κοινωνίαν ἔχομεν μετ' αὐτοῦ
we say that *fellowship* *we have* with him

καὶ ἐν τῷ σκότει περιπατῶμεν, ψευδόμεθα
and *in* *the* *darkness* *we walk,* we lie

καὶ οὐ ποιοῦμεν τὴν ἀλήθειαν· 7 ἐὰν
and are not doing the truth; *if*

δὲ ἐν τῷ φωτὶ περιπατῶμεν ὡς αὐτός
but *in* *the* *light* *we walk* as he

ἐστιν ἐν τῷ φωτί, κοινωνίαν ἔχομεν
is in the light, *fellowship* *we have*

μετ' ἀλλήλων καὶ τὸ αἷμα Ἰησοῦ τοῦ
with each other and the blood of Jesus the

υἱοῦ αὐτοῦ καθαρίζει ἡμᾶς ἀπὸ πάσης
Son of him cleanses us from all

ἁμαρτίας. 8 ἐὰν εἴπωμεν ὅτι ἁμαρτίαν
sin. If we say that sin

οὐκ ἔχομεν, ἑαυτοὺς πλανῶμεν καὶ ἡ
we have not, *ourselves* *we deceive* and the

ἀλήθεια οὐκ ἔστιν ἐν ἡμῖν. 9 ἐὰν
truth is not in us. If

ὁμολογῶμεν τὰς ἁμαρτίας ἡμῶν, πιστός
we confess the sins of us, faithful

ἐστιν καὶ δίκαιος, ἵνα ἀφῇ ἡμῖν τὰς
he is and righteous, in order he may us the
that forgive

ἁμαρτίας καὶ καθαρίσῃ ἡμᾶς ἀπὸ πάσης
sins and *he* may cleanse us from all

ἀδικίας. 10 ἐὰν εἴπωμεν ὅτι οὐχ
iniquity. If we say that not

ἡμαρτήκαμεν, ψεύστην ποιοῦμεν αὐτὸν
we have sinned, a liar we make him

καὶ ὁ λόγος αὐτοῦ οὐκ ἔστιν ἐν ἡμῖν.
and the word of him is not in us.

2 Τεκνία μου, ταῦτα γράφω ὑμῖν ἵνα
Little children of me, these things I write to you in order that

μὴ ἁμάρτητε. καὶ ἐάν τις ἁμάρτῃ,
ye sin not. And if anyone sins,

παράκλητον ἔχομεν πρὸς τὸν πατέρα,
an advocate we have with the Father,

Ἰησοῦν Χριστὸν δίκαιον· 2 καὶ αὐτός
Jesus Christ [the] righteous; and he

ἱλασμός ἐστιν περὶ τῶν ἁμαρτιῶν ἡμῶν,
a propitiation *is* concerning the sins of us,

οὐ περὶ τῶν ἡμετέρων δὲ μόνον ἀλλὰ
not *concerning* – *ours* *but* only but

---

and heard, so that you also may have fellowship with us. And our fellowship is with the Father and with his Son, Jesus Christ. 4We write this to make our*a* joy complete.

Walking in the Light

5This is the message we have heard from him and declare to you: God is light; in him there is no darkness at all. 6If we claim to have fellowship with him yet walk in the darkness, we lie and do not live by the truth. 7But if we walk in the light, as he is in the light, we have fellowship with one another, and the blood of Jesus, his Son, purifies us from all*b* sin.

8If we claim to be without sin, we deceive ourselves and the truth is not in us. 9If we confess our sins, he is faithful and just and will forgive us our sins and purify us from all unrighteousness. 10If we claim we have not sinned, we make him out to be a liar and his word has no place in our lives.

Chapter 2

MY dear children, I write this to you so that you will not sin. But if anybody does sin, we have one who speaks to the Father in our defense—Jesus Christ, the Righteous One. 2He is the atoning sacrifice for our sins, and not only for ours but also for*c* the

*a*4 Some manuscripts *your*
*b*7 Or *every*
*c*2 Or *He is the one who turns aside God's wrath, taking away our sins, and not only ours but also*

a Other ancient authorities read *your*

whole world.

3 Now by this we may be sure that we know him, if we obey his commandments. 4 Whoever says, "I have come to know him," but does not obey his commandments, is a liar, and in such a person the truth does not exist; 5 but whoever obeys his word, truly in this person the love of God has reached perfection. By this we may be sure that we are in him: 6 whoever says, "I abide in him," ought to walk just as he walked.

A New Commandment

7 Beloved, I am writing you no new commandment, but an old commandment that you have had from the beginning; the old commandment is the word that you have heard. 8 Yet I am writing you a new commandment that is true in him and in you, because[b] the darkness is passing away and the true light is already shining. 9 Whoever says, "I am in the light," while hating a brother or sister,[c] is still in the darkness. 10 Whoever loves a brother or sister[d] lives in the light, and in such a person[e] there is no cause for stumbling. 11 But whoever hates another believer[f] is in the darkness, walks in the darkness, and does not know the way to go, because the darkness has brought on blindness.

12 I am writing to you, little children, because your sins are forgiven on

---

καὶ περὶ ὅλου τοῦ κόσμου. 3 καὶ ἐν
also concerning all the world. And by

τούτῳ γινώσκομεν ὅτι ἐγνώκαμεν αὐτόν,
this we know that we have known him,

ἐὰν τὰς ἐντολὰς αὐτοῦ τηρῶμεν. 4 ὁ
if ²the ³command-ments ⁴of him ¹we keep. The [one]

λέγων ὅτι ἔγνωκα αὐτόν, καὶ τὰς ἐντολὰς
saying[,] - I have known him, and ²the ⁴command-ments

αὐτοῦ μὴ τηρῶν, ψεύστης ἐστίν, καὶ
⁵of him ¹not ³keeping, ²a liar ¹is, and

ἐν τούτῳ ἡ ἀλήθεια οὐκ ἔστιν· 5 ὃς δ'
in this man the truth is not; but who-ever

ἂν τηρῇ αὐτοῦ τὸν λόγον, ἀληθῶς ἐν
keeps ³of him ¹the ²word, truly in

τούτῳ ἡ ἀγάπη τοῦ θεοῦ τετελείωται.
this man the love - of God has been perfected.

ἐν τούτῳ γινώσκομεν ὅτι ἐν αὐτῷ ἐσμεν.
By this we know that ²in ³him ¹we are.

6 ὁ λέγων ἐν αὐτῷ μένειν ὀφείλει καθὼς
The [one] saying in him to remain ought as

ἐκεῖνος περιεπάτησεν καὶ αὐτὸς οὕτως
that [one]* walked also [him]self so

περιπατεῖν.
to walk.

7 Ἀγαπητοί, οὐκ ἐντολὴν καινὴν γράφω
Beloved, ²not ¹command-ment ²a new ¹I write

ὑμῖν, ἀλλ' ἐντολὴν παλαιὰν ἣν εἴχετε
to you, but ²commandment ¹an old which ye had

ἀπ' ἀρχῆς· ἡ ἐντολὴ ἡ παλαιά ἐστιν
from [the] beginning; the ²command-ment - ¹old is

ὁ λόγος ὃν ἠκούσατε. 8 πάλιν ἐντολὴν
the word which ye heard. Again ²command-ment

καινὴν γράφω ὑμῖν, ὃ ἐστιν ἀληθὲς
¹a new I write to you, what is true

ἐν αὐτῷ καὶ ἐν ὑμῖν, ὅτι ἡ σκοτία
in him and in you, because the darkness

παράγεται καὶ τὸ φῶς τὸ ἀληθινὸν
is passing and the ²light - ¹true

ἤδη φαίνει. 9 ὁ λέγων ἐν τῷ φωτὶ
already shines. The [one] saying in the light

εἶναι καὶ τὸν ἀδελφὸν αὐτοῦ μισῶν
to be and the brother of him hating

ἐν τῇ σκοτίᾳ ἐστὶν ἕως ἄρτι. 10 ὁ
in the darkness is until now. The

ἀγαπῶν τὸν ἀδελφὸν αὐτοῦ ἐν τῷ φωτὶ
[one] loving the brother of him in the light

μένει, καὶ σκάνδαλον ἐν αὐτῷ οὐκ ἔστιν·
remains, and offence in him is not;

11 ὁ δὲ μισῶν τὸν ἀδελφὸν αὐτοῦ ἐν
but the [one] hating the brother of him in

τῇ σκοτίᾳ ἐστὶν καὶ ἐν τῇ σκοτίᾳ
the darkness is and in the darkness

περιπατεῖ, καὶ οὐκ οἶδεν ποῦ ὑπάγει,
walks, and knows not where he is going,

ὅτι ἡ σκοτία ἐτύφλωσεν τοὺς ὀφθαλμοὺς
be-cause the darkness blinded the eyes

αὐτοῦ. 12 Γράφω ὑμῖν, τεκνία, ὅτι
of him. I write to you, little children, because

ἀφέωνται ὑμῖν αἱ ἁμαρτίαι διὰ τὸ ὄνομα
have been forgiven *to* you the (your) sins on ac-count of the name

---

sins of the whole world.

3 We know that we have come to know him if we obey his commands. 4 The man who says, "I know him," but does not do what he commands is a liar, and the truth is not in him. 5 But if anyone obeys his word, God's love[d] is truly made complete in him. This is how we know we are in him: 6 Whoever claims to live in him must walk as Jesus did.

7 Dear friends, I am not writing you a new command but an old one, which you have had since the beginning. This old command is the message you have heard. 8 Yet I am writing you a new command; its truth is seen in him and you, because the darkness is passing and the true light is already shining.

9 Anyone who claims to be in the light but hates his brother is still in the darkness. 10 Whoever loves his brother lives in the light, and there is nothing in him[e] to make him stumble. 11 But whoever hates his brother is in the darkness and walks around in the darkness; he does not know where he is going, because the darkness has blinded him.

12 I write to you, dear children, because your sins have been forgiven on

---

[b] Or that
[c] Gk hating a brother
[d] Gk loves a brother
[e] Or in it
[f] Gk hates a brother

* In a number of places John uses this demonstrative adjective as a substitute for "Christ": "the remoter antecedent." See also John 2. 21.

[d]5 Or word, love for God
[e]10 Or it

account of his name.
13 I am writing to you, fathers, because you know him who is from the beginning. I am writing to you, young people, because you have conquered the evil one.
14 I write to you, children, because you know the Father. I write to you, fathers, because you know him who is from the beginning. I write to you, young people, because you are strong and the word of God abides in you, and you have overcome the evil one.
15 Do not love the world or the things in the world. The love of the Father is not in those who love the world; 16for all that is in the world—the desire of the flesh, the desire of the eyes, the pride in riches—comes not from the Father but from the world. 17 And the world and its desire* are passing away, but those who do the will of God live forever.

Warning against Antichrists

18 Children, it is the last hour! As you have heard that antichrist is coming, so now many antichrists have come. From this we know that it is the last hour. 19They went out from us, but they did not belong to us; for if they had belonged to us, they would have remained with us. But by going out they made it plain that none of them belongs to us. 20But you have been anointed by the Holy One, and all of you have knowledge.[h] 21 I write to you, not because you do not know the truth, but because you know it, and you know that no lie comes from the truth.

αὐτοῦ. **13** γράφω ὑμῖν, πατέρες, ὅτι
of him.   I write   to you,   fathers,   because

ἐγνώκατε τὸν ἀπ᾽ ἀρχῆς. γράφω ὑμῖν,
ye have   the from [the]   I write   to you,
known   [one]

νεανίσκοι, ὅτι νενικήκατε τὸν πονηρόν.
young men, because ye have overcome the evil one.

14 ἔγραψα ὑμῖν, παιδία, ὅτι ἐγνώκατε
I wrote to you, young   because ye have
children,   known

τὸν πατέρα. ἔγραψα ὑμῖν, πατέρες,
the Father. I wrote to you, fathers,

ὅτι ἐγνώκατε τὸν ἀπ᾽ ἀρχῆς. ἔγραψα
be- ye have   the from [the]   I wrote
cause known   [one]   beginning.

ὑμῖν, νεανίσκοι, ὅτι ἰσχυροί ἐστε καὶ
to you, young men, because strong ye are and

ὁ λόγος τοῦ θεοῦ ἐν ὑμῖν μένει καὶ
the word of God in you remains and

νενικήκατε τὸν πονηρόν. **15** Μὴ ἀγαπᾶτε
ye have overcome the evil one.   Love ye not

τὸν κόσμον μηδὲ τὰ ἐν τῷ κόσμῳ.
the world   nor the things in the world.

ἐάν τις ἀγαπᾷ τὸν κόσμον, οὐκ ἔστιν
If anyone loves the world, ¹not ²is

ἡ ἀγάπη τοῦ πατρὸς ἐν αὐτῷ· **16** ὅτι
¹the ²love ³of the ⁴Father in him; because

πᾶν τὸ ἐν τῷ κόσμῳ, ἡ ἐπιθυμία τῆς
all that in the world, the lust of the
which† [is]

σαρκὸς καὶ ἡ ἐπιθυμία τῶν ὀφθαλμῶν
flesh   and the lust of the eyes

καὶ ἡ ἀλαζονεία τοῦ βίου, οὐκ ἔστιν
and the vainglory - of life, is not

ἐκ τοῦ πατρός, ἀλλὰ ἐκ τοῦ κόσμου
of the Father, but of the world

ἐστίν. **17** καὶ ὁ κόσμος παράγεται καὶ
is.   And the world is passing away and

ἡ ἐπιθυμία αὐτοῦ· ὁ δὲ ποιῶν τὸ θέλημα
the lust of it; but the [one] doing the will

τοῦ θεοῦ μένει εἰς τὸν αἰῶνα.
- of God remains unto the age.

18 Παιδία, ἐσχάτη ὥρα ἐστίν, καὶ
Young children, a last hour it is, and

καθὼς ἠκούσατε ὅτι ἀντίχριστος ἔρχεται,
as   ye heard   that   antichrist is coming,

καὶ νῦν ἀντίχριστοι πολλοὶ γεγόνασιν·
even now ⁴antichrists ¹many have arisen;

ὅθεν γινώσκομεν ὅτι ἐσχάτη ὥρα ἐστίν.
whence we know   that a last hour it is.

19 ἐξ ἡμῶν ἐξῆλθαν, ἀλλ᾽ οὐκ ἦσαν
From us they went out, but they were not

ἐξ ἡμῶν· εἰ γὰρ ἐξ ἡμῶν ἦσαν, μεμενή-
of us; for if of us they were, they would

κεισαν ἂν μεθ᾽ ἡμῶν· ἀλλ᾽ ἵνα φανερω-
have remained with us; but in order it might be
that

θῶσιν ὅτι οὐκ εἰσὶν πάντες ἐξ ἡμῶν.
manifested that they are not all of us.

20 καὶ ὑμεῖς χρῖσμα ἔχετε ἀπὸ τοῦ
And ye an anointing have from the

ἁγίου, καὶ οἴδατε πάντες. **21** οὐκ ἔγραψα
Holy One, and ¹ye ³know ²all.   I wrote not

ὑμῖν ὅτι οὐκ οἴδατε τὴν ἀλήθειαν, ἀλλ᾽
to you because ye know not the truth, but

ὅτι οἴδατε αὐτήν, καὶ ὅτι πᾶν ψεῦδος
because ye know it, and because every lie
=no lie is . . .

account of his name.
13I write to you, fathers, because you have known him who is from the beginning. I write to you, young men, because you have overcome the evil one. I write to you, dear children, because you have known the Father. 14I write to you, fathers, because you have known him who is from the beginning. I write to you, young men, because you are strong, and the word of God lives in you, and you have overcome the evil one.

Do Not Love the World

15Do not love the world or anything in the world. If anyone loves the world, the love of the Father is not in him. 16For everything in the world—the cravings of sinful man, the lust of his eyes and the boasting of what he has and does—comes not from the Father but from the world. 17The world and its desires pass away, but the man who does the will of God lives forever.

Warning Against Antichrists

18Dear children, this is the last hour; and as you have heard that the antichrist is coming, even now many antichrists have come. This is how we know it is the last hour. 19They went out from us, but they did not really belong to us. For if they had belonged to us, they would have remained with us; but their going showed that none of them belonged to us. 20But you have an anointing from the Holy One, and all of you know the truth.[f] 21I do not write to you because you do not know the truth, but because you know it and because no lie comes from the truth.

---

*Or the desire for it
[h] Other ancient authorities read you know all things

[f]20 Some manuscripts and you know all things

22 Who is the liar but the one who denies that Jesus is the Christ?[i] This is the antichrist, the one who denies the Father and the Son. 23 No one who denies the Son has the Father; everyone who confesses the Son has the Father also. 24 Let what you heard from the beginning abide in you. If what you heard from the beginning abides in you, then you will abide in the Son and in the Father. 25 And this is what he has promised us,[j] eternal life.

26 I write these things to you concerning those who would deceive you. 27 As for you, the anointing that you received from him abides in you, and so you do not need anyone to teach you. But as his anointing teaches you about all things, and is true and is not a lie, and just as it has taught you, abide in him.[k]

28 And now, little children, abide in him, so that when he is revealed we may have confidence and not be put to shame before him at his coming.

Children of God

29 If you know that he is righteous, you may be sure that everyone who does right has been born of him. 1 See what love the Father has given us, that we should be called children of God; and that is what we are. The reason the world does not know us is that it

ἐκ   τῆς   ἀληθείας   οὐκ   ἔστιν.   **22** Tίς
of   the   truth   is not.   Who

ἔστιν   ὁ   ψεύστης   εἰ   μὴ   ὁ   ἀρνούμενος
is   the   liar   except   the [one]   denying

ὅτι   Ἰησοῦς   οὐκ   ἔστιν   ὁ   χριστός;   οὗτός
that   Jesus   not   is   the   Christ?   this

ἐστιν   ὁ   ἀντίχριστος,   ὁ   ἀρνούμενος   τὸν
is   the   antichrist,   the [one]   denying   the

πατέρα   καὶ   τὸν   υἱόν.   **23** πᾶς   ὁ   ἀρνούμενος
Father   and   the   Son.   Everyone   denying

τὸν   υἱὸν   οὐδὲ   τὸν   πατέρα   ἔχει·   ὁ
the   Son   ²neither   ³the   ⁴Father   ¹has;   the

ὁμολογῶν   τὸν   υἱὸν   καὶ   τὸν   πατέρα   ἔχει.
[one] confessing   the   Son   ²also   ³the   ⁴Father   ¹has.

24 ὑμεῖς   ὃ   ἠκούσατε   ἀπ'   ἀρχῆς,   ἐν
²Ye   ¹what   heard   from [the] beginning,   in

ὑμῖν   μενέτω.   ἐὰν   ἐν   ὑμῖν   μείνῃ   ὃ   ἀπ'
you   let it remain.   If   ²in   ¹you   ²remains   ¹what   ²from

ἀρχῆς   ἠκούσατε,   καὶ   ὑμεῖς   ἐν   τῷ   υἱῷ
beginning   ²ye heard,   ³both   ¹ye   ⁴in   ⁵the   ⁶Son

καὶ   [ἐν]   τῷ   πατρὶ   μενεῖτε.   **25** καὶ
⁷and   ⁸in   ⁹the   ¹⁰Father   ⁹will remain.   And

αὕτη   ἐστὶν   ἡ   ἐπαγγελία   ἣν   αὐτὸς   ἐπηγ-
this   is   the   promise   which   he   pro-

γείλατο   ἡμῖν,   τὴν   ζωὴν   τὴν   αἰώνιον.
mised   us,   the   life   –   eternal.

26 Ταῦτα   ἔγραψα   ὑμῖν   περὶ   τῶν   πλανών-
These   I wrote   to you   concern-   the   leading
things   ing   [ones]

των   ὑμᾶς.   **27** καὶ   ὑμεῖς   τὸ   χρίσμα
²astray   ¹you.   And   ⁴ye   ¹the   ²anointing

ὃ   ἐλάβετε   ἀπ'   αὐτοῦ   μένει   ἐν   ὑμῖν,
³which   received   from   him   remains   in   you,

καὶ   οὐ   χρείαν   ἔχετε   ἵνα   τις   διδάσκῃ
and   ²no   ³need   ¹ye have   in order   anyone   should
that   teach

ὑμᾶς·   ἀλλ'   ὡς   τὸ   αὐτοῦ   χρίσμα   διδάσκει
you;   but   as   the   ²of him   ¹anointing   teaches

ὑμᾶς   περὶ   πάντων,   καὶ   ἀληθές   ἐστιν
you   concerning   all things,   and   ²true   ¹is

καὶ   οὐκ   ἔστιν   ψεῦδος,   καὶ   καθὼς   ἐδίδαξεν
and   is not   a lie,   and   as   he/it taught

ὑμᾶς,   μένετε   ἐν   αὐτῷ.
you,   remain ye   in   him.

28 Καὶ   νῦν,   τεκνία,   μένετε   ἐν   αὐτῷ,
And   now,   little children,   remain ye   in   him,

ἵνα   ἐὰν   φανερωθῇ   σχῶμεν   παρρησίαν   καὶ
in or-   if   he is manifested   we may   confidence   and
der that   have

μὴ   αἰσχυνθῶμεν   ἀπ'   αὐτοῦ   ἐν   τῇ   παρουσίᾳ
not   be shamed   from   him   in   the   presence

αὐτοῦ.   **29** ἐὰν   εἰδῆτε   ὅτι   δίκαιός   ἐστιν,
of him.   If   ye know   that   ²righteous   ¹he is,

γινώσκετε   ὅτι   καὶ   πᾶς   ὁ   ποιῶν   τὴν
know ye   that   also   every one   doing

δικαιοσύνην   ἐξ   αὐτοῦ   γεγέννηται.
righteousness   ²of   ³him   ¹has been born.

3 Ἴδετε   ποταπὴν   ἀγάπην   δέδωκεν   ἡμῖν
See ye   what manner of   love   ⁴has given   ⁵to us

ὁ   πατὴρ   ἵνα   τέκνα   θεοῦ   κληθῶμεν,
¹the   ²Father   in order   ³children   ⁶of God   ¹we may be
that   called,

καὶ   ἐσμέν.   διὰ   τοῦτο   ὁ   κόσμος   οὐ
and   we are.   Therefore   the   world   ²not

22 Who is the liar? It is the man who denies that Jesus is the Christ. Such a man is the antichrist—he denies the Father and the Son. 23 No one who denies the Son has the Father; whoever acknowledges the Son has the Father also. 24 See that what you have heard from the beginning remains in you. If it does, you also will remain in the Son and in the Father. 25 And this is what he promised us—even eternal life.

26 I am writing these things to you about those who are trying to lead you astray. 27 As for you, the anointing you received from him remains in you, and you do not need anyone to teach you. But as his anointing teaches you about all things and as that anointing is real, and not counterfeit—just as it has taught you, remain in him.

Children of God

28 And now, dear children, continue in him, so that when he appears we may be confident and unashamed before him at his coming.

29 If you know that he is righteous, you know that everyone who does what is right has been born of him.

Chapter 3

HOW great is the love the Father has lavished on us, that we should be called children of God! And that is what we are! The reason the world does

[i] Or *the Messiah*
[j] Other ancient authorities read *you*
[k] Or *it*

did not know him. 2 Beloved, we are God's children now; what we will be has not yet been revealed. What we do know is this: when he[k] is revealed, we will be like him, for we will see him as he is. 3 And all who have this hope in him purify themselves, just as he is pure.

4 Everyone who commits sin is guilty of lawlessness; sin is lawlessness. 5 You know that he was revealed to take away sins, and in him there is no sin. 6 No one who abides in him sins; no one who sins has either seen him or known him. 7 Little children, let no one deceive you. Everyone who does what is right is righteous, just as he is righteous. 8 Everyone who commits sin is a child of the devil; for the devil has been sinning from the beginning. The Son of God was revealed for this purpose, to destroy the works of the devil. 9 Those who have been born of God do not sin, because God's seed abides in them;[l] they cannot sin, because they have been born of God. 10 The children of God and the children of the devil are revealed in this way: all who do not do what is right are not from God, nor are those who do not love their brothers and sisters.[m]

Love One Another

11 For this is the message you have heard from

γινώσκει ἡμᾶς, ὅτι οὐκ ἔγνω αὐτόν.
¹knows ²us, because it knew not him.

2 ἀγαπητοί, νῦν τέκνα θεοῦ ἐσμεν, καὶ
Beloved, ²now ³children ⁴of God ¹we are, and

οὔπω ἐφανερώθη τί ἐσόμεθα. οἴδαμεν
not yet was it manifested what we shall be. We know

ὅτι ἐὰν φανερωθῇ ὅμοιοι αὐτῷ ἐσόμεθα,
that if he(?it) is manifested like him we shall be,

ὅτι ὀψόμεθα αὐτὸν καθὼς ἐστιν. 3 καὶ
because we shall see him as he is. And

πᾶς ὁ ἔχων τὴν ἐλπίδα ταύτην ἐπ'
everyone having this hope on

αὐτῷ ἁγνίζει ἑαυτὸν καθὼς ἐκεῖνος ἁγνός
him purifies himself as that one* ²pure

ἐστιν. 4 πᾶς ὁ ποιῶν τὴν ἁμαρτίαν
¹is. Everyone doing – sin

καὶ τὴν ἀνομίαν ποιεῖ, καὶ ἡ ἁμαρτία
²also – ³lawlessness ¹does, and – sin

ἐστὶν ἡ ἀνομία. 5 καὶ οἴδατε ὅτι ἐκεῖνος
is – lawlessness. And ye know that that one*

ἐφανερώθη ἵνα τὰς ἁμαρτίας ἄρῃ, καὶ
was manifested in order – sins he might and
         that   bear,

ἁμαρτία ἐν αὐτῷ οὐκ ἔστιν. 6 πᾶς ὁ
sin ²in ³him ¹is not. Everyone

ἐν αὐτῷ μένων οὐχ ἁμαρτάνει· πᾶς ὁ
²in ³him ¹remaining sins not; everyone

ἁμαρτάνων οὐχ ἑώρακεν αὐτὸν οὐδὲ
sinning has not seen him nor

ἔγνωκεν αὐτόν. 7 Τεκνία, μηδεὶς πλανάτω
has known him. Little ²no man ¹let ³lead
         children,   ³astray

ὑμᾶς· ὁ ποιῶν τὴν δικαιοσύνην δίκαιός
⁴you; the [one] doing – righteousness ³righteous

ἐστιν, καθὼς ἐκεῖνος δίκαιός ἐστιν· 8 ὁ
¹is, as that one* ²righteous ¹is; the

ποιῶν τὴν ἁμαρτίαν ἐκ τοῦ διαβόλου
[one] doing – sin ²of ³the ⁴devil

ἐστίν, ὅτι ἀπ' ἀρχῆς ὁ διάβολος ἁμαρτάνει.
¹is, because ⁴from ⁵[the] ¹the ²devil ³sins.
              beginning

εἰς τοῦτο ἐφανερώθη ὁ υἱὸς τοῦ θεοῦ,
For this was manifested the Son – of God,

ἵνα λύσῃ τὰ ἔργα τοῦ διαβόλου.
in or- he might the works of the devil.
der that undo

9 Πᾶς ὁ γεγεννημένος ἐκ τοῦ θεοῦ
Everyone having been begotten of – God

ἁμαρτίαν οὐ ποιεῖ, ὅτι σπέρμα αὐτοῦ
²sin ²not ¹does, because seed of him

ἐν αὐτῷ μένει· καὶ οὐ δύναται ἁμαρτάνειν,
in him remains; and he cannot *to* sin,

ὅτι ἐκ τοῦ θεοῦ γεγέννηται. 10 ἐν
because of – God he has been begotten. By

τούτῳ φανερά ἐστιν τὰ τέκνα τοῦ θεοῦ
this ²manifest ¹is(are) the children – of God

καὶ τὰ τέκνα τοῦ διαβόλου· πᾶς ὁ
and the children of the devil; everyone

μὴ ποιῶν δικαιοσύνην οὐκ ἔστιν ἐκ
not doing righteousness is not of

τοῦ θεοῦ, καὶ ὁ μὴ ἀγαπῶν τὸν ἀδελφὸν
– God, and the not loving the brother
              [one]

αὐτοῦ. 11 ὅτι αὕτη ἐστὶν ἡ ἀγγελία
of him. Because this is the message

---

not know us is that it did not know him. 2 Dear friends, now we are children of God, and what we will be has not yet been made known. But we know that when he appears,[g] we shall be like him, for we shall see him as he is. 3 Everyone who has this hope in him purifies himself, just as he is pure.

4 Everyone who sins breaks the law; in fact, sin is lawlessness. 5 But you know that he appeared so that he might take away our sins. And in him is no sin. 6 No one who lives in him keeps on sinning. No one who continues to sin has either seen him or known him.

7 Dear children, do not let anyone lead you astray. He who does what is right is righteous, just as he is righteous. 8 He who does what is sinful is of the devil, because the devil has been sinning from the beginning. The reason the Son of God appeared was to destroy the devil's work. 9 No one who is born of God will continue to sin, because God's seed remains in him; he cannot go on sinning, because he has been born of God. 10 This is how we know who the children of God are and who the children of the devil are: Anyone who does not do what is right is not a child of God; nor is anyone who does not love his brother.

Love One Another

11 This is the message you

---

the beginning, that we should love one another. 12 We must not be like Cain who was from the evil one and murdered his brother. And why did he murder him? Because his own deeds were evil and his brother's righteous. 13 Do not be astonished, brothers and sisters,[n] that the world hates you. 14 We know that we have passed from death to life because we love one another. Whoever does not love abides in death. 15 All who hate a brother or sister[m] are murderers, and you know that murderers do not have eternal life abiding in them. 16 We know love by this, that he laid down his life for us— and we ought to lay down our lives for one another. 17 How does God's love abide in anyone who has the world's goods and sees a brother or sister[o] in need and yet refuses help? 18 Little children, let us love, not in word or speech, but in truth and action. 19 And by this we will know that we are from the truth and will reassure our hearts before him 20 whenever our hearts condemn us; for God is greater than our hearts, and he knows everything. 21 Beloved, if our hearts do not condemn

---

ἦν ἠκούσατε ἀπ' ἀρχῆς, ἵνα ἀγαπῶμεν
which ye heard from [the] in order we should love
                       beginning, that

ἀλλήλους· 12 οὐ καθὼς Κάϊν ἐκ τοῦ
one another;   not   as   Cain ²of ¹the

πονηροῦ ἦν καὶ ἔσφαξεν τὸν ἀδελφὸν
⁴evil one ¹was and slew   the brother

αὐτοῦ· καὶ χάριν τίνος ἔσφαξεν αὐτόν;
of him; and for the what slew he him?
             sake of

ὅτι τὰ ἔργα αὐτοῦ πονηρὰ ἦν, τὰ δὲ
be- the works of him ²evil ¹was(were), but the
cause   [works]

τοῦ ἀδελφοῦ αὐτοῦ δίκαια. 13 μὴ
of the brother of him righteous.   not

θαυμάζετε, ἀδελφοί, εἰ μισεῖ ὑμᾶς ὁ
Marvel ye, brothers, if ³hates ⁴you ¹the

κόσμος. 14 ἡμεῖς οἴδαμεν ὅτι μεταβεβή-
²world.   We   know   that we have re-

καμεν ἐκ τοῦ θανάτου εἰς τὴν ζωήν,
moved out of the death into the life,

ὅτι ἀγαπῶμεν τοὺς ἀδελφούς· ὁ μὴ
because we love the brothers; the [one] not

ἀγαπῶν μένει ἐν τῷ θανάτῳ. 15 πᾶς
loving remains in the death.   Every-

ὁ μισῶν τὸν ἀδελφὸν αὐτοῦ ἀνθρωποκτόνος
one hating the brother of him ²a murderer

ἐστίν, καὶ οἴδατε ὅτι πᾶς ἀνθρωποκτόνος
¹is, and ye know that every murderer
                            =no murderer has ...

οὐκ ἔχει ζωὴν αἰώνιον ἐν αὐτῷ μένουσαν.
has not life eternal in him remaining.

16 ἐν τούτῳ ἐγνώκαμεν τὴν ἀγάπην, ὅτι
By   this we have known -   love, because

ἐκεῖνος ὑπὲρ ἡμῶν τὴν ψυχὴν αὐτοῦ
that one* on behalf of us the life   of him

ἔθηκεν· καὶ ἡμεῖς ὀφείλομεν ὑπὲρ τῶν
laid down; and we   ought   on behalf of the

ἀδελφῶν τὰς ψυχὰς θεῖναι. 17 ὃς δ'
brothers the(our) lives to lay down.   Who-

ἂν ἔχῃ τὸν βίον τοῦ κόσμου καὶ θεωρῇ
ever has the means of the world and beholds
             of life

τὸν ἀδελφὸν αὐτοῦ χρείαν ἔχοντα καὶ
the brother of him ²need ¹having and

κλείσῃ τὰ σπλάγχνα αὐτοῦ ἀπ' αὐτοῦ,
shuts   the bowels of him from him,

πῶς ἡ ἀγάπη τοῦ θεοῦ μένει ἐν αὐτῷ;
how ²the ³love - ⁴of God ¹remains in him?

18 Τεκνία, μὴ ἀγαπῶμεν λόγῳ μηδὲ τῇ
Little children, let us not love in word nor in the

γλώσσῃ, ἀλλὰ ἐν ἔργῳ καὶ ἀληθείᾳ.
tongue, but in work and truth.

19 ἐν τούτῳ γνωσόμεθα ὅτι ἐκ τῆς ἀληθείας
By   this we shall know that ²of ³the ⁴truth

ἐσμέν, καὶ ἔμπροσθεν αὐτοῦ πείσομεν
¹we are, and before   him shall persuade

τὴν καρδίαν ἡμῶν 20 ὅτι ἐὰν καταγινώσκῃ
the heart of us   that if ⁴blames [us]

ἡμῶν ἡ καρδία, ὅτι μείζων ἐστὶν ὁ
³of us ¹the ²heart, that greater is   -

θεὸς τῆς καρδίας ἡμῶν καὶ γινώσκει
God [than] the heart of us and knows

πάντα. 21 Ἀγαπητοί, ἐὰν ἡ καρδία
all things. Beloved,   if the(our) heart

---

heard from the beginning: We should love one another. 12 Do not be like Cain, who belonged to the evil one and murdered his brother. And why did he murder him? Because his own actions were evil and his brother's were righteous. 13 Do not be surprised, my brothers, if the world hates you. 14 We know that we have passed from death to life, because we love our brothers. Anyone who does not love remains in death. 15 Anyone who hates his brother is a murderer, and you know that no murderer has eternal life in him.

16 This is how we know what love is: Jesus Christ laid down his life for us. And we ought to lay down our lives for our brothers. 17 If anyone has material possessions and sees his brother in need but has no pity on him, how can the love of God be in him? 18 Dear children, let us not love with words or tongue but with actions and in truth. 19 This then is how we know that we belong to the truth, and how we set our hearts at rest in his presence 20 whenever our hearts condemn us. For God is greater than our hearts, and he knows everything.

21 Dear friends, if our

---

[n] Gk brothers
[o] Gk brother

* See ch. 2. 6, 3. 3, 5, 7.

us, we have boldness before God; 22 and we receive from him whatever we ask, because we obey his commandments and do what pleases him.

23 And this is his commandment, that we should believe in the name of his Son Jesus Christ and love one another, just as he has commanded us. 24 All who obey his commandments abide in him, and he abides in them. And by this we know that he abides in us, by the Spirit that he has given us.

μὴ καταγινώσκῃ, παρρησίαν ἔχομεν πρὸς
does not blame [us],   confidence   we have   with

τὸν θεόν, 22 καὶ ὃ ἐὰν αἰτῶμεν λαμβάν-
-   God,   and   whatever   we ask   we re-

ομεν ἀπ᾽ αὐτοῦ, ὅτι τὰς ἐντολὰς αὐτοῦ
ceive   from   him,   because ²the ⁵command- ⁴of him
                               ments

τηροῦμεν καὶ τὰ ἀρεστὰ ἐνώπιον αὐτοῦ
¹we keep   and   ³the ²pleasing   ⁴before   ⁵him
           things

ποιοῦμεν. 23 καὶ αὕτη ἐστὶν ἡ ἐντολὴ
¹we do.   And   this   is   the command-
                              ment

αὐτοῦ, ἵνα πιστεύσωμεν τῷ ὀνόματι τοῦ
of him, *in order* we should believe   the   name   of the
       that

υἱοῦ αὐτοῦ Ἰησοῦ Χριστοῦ καὶ ἀγαπῶμεν
Son   of him   Jesus   Christ   and   love

ἀλλήλους καθὼς ἔδωκεν ἐντολὴν ἡμῖν.
one another   as   he gave   commandment   to us.

24 καὶ ὁ τηρῶν τὰς ἐντολὰς αὐτοῦ ἐν
And   the   keeping   the   command-   of him   in
     [one]   ments

αὐτῷ μένει καὶ αὐτὸς ἐν αὐτῷ· καὶ
him   remains   and   he   in   him;   and

ἐν τούτῳ γινώσκομεν ὅτι μένει ἐν ἡμῖν,
by   this   we know   that he remains in   us,

ἐκ τοῦ πνεύματος οὗ ἡμῖν ἔδωκεν.
by   the   Spirit   whom   to us   he gave.

---

hearts do not condemn us, we have confidence before God 22 and receive from him anything we ask, because we obey his commands and do what pleases him. 23 And this is his command: to believe in the name of his Son, Jesus Christ, and to love one another as he commanded us. 24 Those who obey his commands live in him, and he in them. And this is how we know that he lives in us: We know it by the Spirit he gave us.

Chapter 4

Testing the Spirits

B ELOVED, do not believe every spirit, but test the spirits to see whether they are from God; for many false prophets have gone out into the world. 2 By this you know the Spirit of God: every spirit that confesses that Jesus Christ has come in the flesh is from God, 3 and every spirit that does not confess Jesus*ᵖ* is not from God. And this is the spirit of the antichrist, of which you have heard that it is coming; and now it is already in the world. 4 Little children, you are from God, and have conquered them; for the one who is in you is greater than the one who is in the world. 5 They are from the world; therefore what they say is from the world, and the world listens to them. 6 We are

ᵖ Other ancient authorities read does away with Jesus (Gk dissolves Jesus)

---

4 Ἀγαπητοί, μὴ παντὶ πνεύματι
Beloved,   ¹not   ²every   ³spirit

πιστεύετε, ἀλλὰ δοκιμάζετε τὰ πνεύματα
¹believe ye,   but   prove   the   spirits

εἰ ἐκ τοῦ θεοῦ ἐστιν, ὅτι πολλοὶ
if   of   -   God   they are,   because   many

ψευδοπροφῆται ἐξεληλύθασιν εἰς τὸν
false prophets   have gone forth   into   the

κόσμον. 2 ἐν τούτῳ γινώσκετε τὸ πνεῦμα
world.   By   this   know ye   the   Spirit

τοῦ θεοῦ· πᾶν πνεῦμα ὃ ὁμολογεῖ Ἰησοῦν
-   of God: every   spirit   which confesses   Jesus

Χριστὸν ἐν σαρκὶ ἐληλυθότα ἐκ τοῦ
Christ   ²in ³[the] flesh   ¹having come   ⁵of   -

θεοῦ ἐστιν, 3 καὶ πᾶν πνεῦμα ὃ μὴ
⁶God   ⁴is,   and   every   spirit   which   not

ὁμολογεῖ τὸν Ἰησοῦν ἐκ τοῦ θεοῦ οὐκ
confesses   -   Jesus   ³of   -   ⁴God   ¹not

ἔστιν· καὶ τοῦτό ἐστιν τὸ τοῦ ἀντιχρίστου,
²is;   and   this   is   the   of   antichrist,
                               [spirit] the

ὃ ἀκηκόατε ὅτι ἔρχεται, καὶ νῦν ἐν
which   ye have   that   it is coming,   and   ³now   ⁴in
     heard

τῷ κόσμῳ ἐστὶν ἤδη. 4 ὑμεῖς ἐκ τοῦ
⁵the   ⁶world   ¹is   ²already.   Ye   of   -

θεοῦ ἐστε, τεκνία, καὶ νενικήκατε αὐτούς,
God   are,   little   and   have overcome   them,
          children,

ὅτι μείζων ἐστὶν ὁ ἐν ὑμῖν ἢ ὁ ἐν
because greater   is   the   in   you   than   the   in
               [one]   [one]

τῷ κόσμῳ. 5 αὐτοὶ ἐκ τοῦ κόσμου
the   world.   ¹They   ²of   ³the   ⁴world

εἰσίν· διὰ τοῦτο ἐκ τοῦ κόσμου λαλοῦσιν
²are;   therefore   ²of ³the ⁴world   ¹they speak

καὶ ὁ κόσμος αὐτῶν ἀκούει. 6 ἡμεῖς
and   the   world   them   hears.   ¹We

Chapter 4

Test the Spirits

D EAR friends, do not believe every spirit, but test the spirits to see whether they are from God, because many false prophets have gone out into the world. 2 This is how you can recognize the Spirit of God: Every spirit that acknowledges that Jesus Christ has come in the flesh is from God, 3 but every spirit that does not acknowledge Jesus is not from God. This is the spirit of the antichrist, which you have heard is coming and even now is already in the world.

4 You, dear children, are from God and have overcome them, because the one who is in you is greater than the one who is in the world. 5 They are from the world and therefore speak from the viewpoint of the world, and the world listens to them. 6 We are from

from God. Whoever knows God listens to us, and whoever is not from God does not listen to us. From this we know the spirit of truth and the spirit of error.

God Is Love

7 Beloved, let us love one another, because love is from God; everyone who loves is born of God and knows God. 8 Whoever does not love does not know God, for God is love. 9 God's love was revealed among us in this way: God sent his only Son into the world so that we might live through him. 10 In this is love, not that we loved God but that he loved us and sent his Son to be the atoning sacrifice for our sins. 11 Beloved, since God loved us so much, we also ought to love one another. 12 No one has ever seen God; if we love one another, God lives in us, and his love is perfected in us.

13 By this we know that we abide in him and he in us, because he has given us of his Spirit. 14 And we have seen and do testify that the Father has sent his Son as the Savior of the world. 15 God abides in those who confess that Jesus is the Son of God, and they abide in God. 16 So we have known and believe the love that God has for

---

ἐκ τοῦ θεοῦ ἐσμεν· ὁ γινώσκων τὸν
¹of - ⁴God ²are; the [one] knowing

θεὸν ἀκούει ἡμῶν, ὃς οὐκ ἔστιν ἐκ
God hears us, [he] who is not of

τοῦ θεοῦ οὐκ ἀκούει ἡμῶν. ἐκ τούτου
- God hears not us. From this

γινώσκομεν τὸ πνεῦμα τῆς ἀληθείας καὶ
we know the spirit - of truth and

τὸ πνεῦμα τῆς πλάνης.
the spirit - of error.

7 Ἀγαπητοί, ἀγαπῶμεν ἀλλήλους, ὅτι
Beloved, let us love one another, because

ἡ ἀγάπη ἐκ τοῦ θεοῦ ἐστιν, καὶ πᾶς ὁ
- love ²of - ³God ¹is, and everyone

ἀγαπῶν ἐκ τοῦ θεοῦ γεγέννηται καὶ
loving ²of - ³God ¹has been begotten and

γινώσκει τὸν θεόν. 8 ὁ μὴ ἀγαπῶν
knows - God. The [one] not loving

οὐκ ἔγνω τὸν θεόν, ὅτι ὁ θεὸς ἀγάπη
knew not - God, because - God ²love

ἐστίν. 9 ἐν τούτῳ ἐφανερώθη ἡ ἀγάπη
¹is. By this was manifested the love

τοῦ θεοῦ ἐν ἡμῖν, ὅτι τὸν υἱὸν αὐτοῦ
- of God in(to) us, because ³the ⁵Son ⁴of him

τὸν μονογενῆ ἀπέσταλκεν ὁ θεὸς εἰς
- ⁶only begotten ²has sent ¹God into

τὸν κόσμον ἵνα ζήσωμεν δι' αὐτοῦ.
the world in order we might live through him.
that

10 ἐν τούτῳ ἐστὶν ἡ ἀγάπη, οὐχ ὅτι
In this is - love, not that

ἡμεῖς ἠγαπήκαμεν τὸν θεόν, ἀλλ' ὅτι
we have loved - God, but that

αὐτὸς ἠγάπησεν ἡμᾶς καὶ ἀπέστειλεν τὸν
he loved us and sent the

υἱὸν αὐτοῦ ἱλασμὸν περὶ τῶν ἁμαρτιῶν
Son of him a propitiation concerning the sins

ἡμῶν. 11 ἀγαπητοί, εἰ οὕτως ὁ θεὸς
of us. Beloved, if so - God

ἠγάπησεν ἡμᾶς, καὶ ἡμεῖς ὀφείλομεν
loved us, ²also ¹we ³ought

ἀλλήλους ἀγαπᾶν. 12 θεὸν οὐδεὶς πώποτε
⁵one another ⁴to love. ⁶God ¹no man ²ever

τεθέαται· ἐὰν ἀγαπῶμεν ἀλλήλους, ὁ θεὸς
³has beheld; if we love one another, - God

ἐν ἡμῖν μένει καὶ ἡ ἀγάπη αὐτοῦ
in us remains and the love of him

τετελειωμένη ἐν ἡμῖν ἐστιν. 13 Ἐν
²having been perfected ³in ⁴us ¹is. By

τούτῳ γινώσκομεν ὅτι ἐν αὐτῷ μένομεν
this we know that in him we remain

καὶ αὐτὸς ἐν ἡμῖν, ὅτι ἐκ τοῦ πνεύματος
and he in us, because ³of ⁴the ⁵Spirit

αὐτοῦ δέδωκεν ἡμῖν. 14 καὶ ἡμεῖς
⁶of him ¹he has given ²us. And we

τεθεάμεθα καὶ μαρτυροῦμεν ὅτι ὁ πατὴρ
have beheld and bear witness that the Father

ἀπέσταλκεν τὸν υἱὸν σωτῆρα τοῦ κόσμου.
has sent the Son [as] Saviour of the world.

15 ὃς ἐὰν ὁμολογήσῃ ὅτι Ἰησοῦς ἐστιν
Whoever confesses that Jesus is

ὁ υἱὸς τοῦ θεοῦ, ὁ θεὸς ἐν αὐτῷ μένει
the Son - of God, - God in him remains

καὶ αὐτὸς ἐν τῷ θεῷ. 16 καὶ ἡμεῖς
and he in - God. And we

ἐγνώκαμεν καὶ πεπιστεύκαμεν τὴν ἀγάπην
have known and have believed the love

God, and whoever knows God listens to us; but whoever is not from God does not listen to us. This is how we recognize the Spirit [h] of truth and the spirit of falsehood.

God's Love and Ours

7 Dear friends, let us love one another, for love comes from God. Everyone who loves has been born of God and knows God. 8 Whoever does not love does not know God, because God is love. 9 This is how God showed his love among us: He sent his one and only Son [i] into the world that we might live through him. 10 This is love: not that we loved God, but that he loved us and sent his Son as an atoning sacrifice for [j] our sins. 11 Dear friends, since God so loved us, we also ought to love one another. 12 No one has ever seen God; but if we love one another, God lives in us and his love is made complete in us.

13 We know that we live in him and he in us, because he has given us of his Spirit. 14 And we have seen and testify that the Father has sent his Son to be the Savior of the world. 15 If anyone acknowledges that Jesus is the Son of God, God lives in him and he in God. 16 And so we know and rely on the love God has for us.

[h] 6 Or spirit
[i] 9 Or his only begotten Son
[j] 10 Or as the one who would turn aside his wrath, taking away

us.
God is love, and those who abide in love abide in God, and God abides in them. [17] Love has been perfected among us in this: that we may have boldness on the day of judgment, because as he is, so are we in this world. [18] There is no fear in love, but perfect love casts out fear; for fear has to do with punishment, and whoever fears has not reached perfection in love. [19] We love[q] because he first loved us. [20] Those who say, "I love God," and hate their brothers or sisters,[r] are liars; for those who do not love a brother or sister[s] whom they have seen, cannot love God whom they have not seen. [21] The commandment we have from him is this: those who love God must love their brothers and sisters[r] also.

ἣν ἔχει ὁ θεὸς ἐν ἡμῖν. Ὁ θεὸς ἀγάπη
which [2]has - [1]God in(to) us. - God [1]love

ἐστίν, καὶ ὁ μένων ἐν τῇ ἀγάπῃ ἐν
[1]is, and the remaining in - love [1]in
                [one]

τῷ θεῷ μένει καὶ ὁ θεὸς ἐν αὐτῷ
 - [2]God [1]remains and - God [2]in [3]him

μένει. 17 Ἐν τούτῳ τετελείωται ἡ ἀγάπη
[1]remains. By this [2]has been perfected - [1]love

μεθ᾽ ἡμῶν, ἵνα παρρησίαν ἔχωμεν ἐν
with us, in order that [2]confidence [1]we may have in

τῇ ἡμέρᾳ τῆς κρίσεως, ὅτι καθὼς ἐκεῖνός
the day   - of judgment, because as that one•

ἐστιν καὶ ἡμεῖς ἐσμεν ἐν τῷ κόσμῳ
 is [3]also [1]we [2]are in - world

τούτῳ. 18 φόβος οὐκ ἔστιν ἐν τῇ ἀγάπῃ,
this. Fear is not in - love,

ἀλλ᾽ ἡ τελεία ἀγάπη ἔξω βάλλει τὸν
but - perfect love [2]out [1]casts the

φόβον, ὅτι ὁ φόβος κόλασιν ἔχει, ὁ δὲ
fear, because - [2]fear [3]punishment [1]has, and the

φοβούμενος οὐ τετελείωται ἐν τῇ ἀγάπῃ.
[one] fearing has not been perfected in - love.

19 ἡμεῖς ἀγαπῶμεν, ὅτι αὐτὸς πρῶτος
   We   love,   because he   first

ἠγάπησεν ἡμᾶς. 20 ἐάν τις εἴπῃ ὅτι
loved   us.   If anyone says[,] that

ἀγαπῶ τὸν θεόν, καὶ τὸν ἀδελφὸν αὐτοῦ
I love - God, and [2]the [3]brother [4]of him

μισῇ, ψεύστης ἐστίν· ὁ γὰρ μὴ ἀγαπῶν
[1]hates, [2]a liar [1]he is; for the [one] not loving

τὸν ἀδελφὸν αὐτοῦ ὃν ἑώρακεν, τὸν
the brother   of him whom he has seen, -

θεὸν ὃν οὐχ ἑώρακεν οὐ δύναται ἀγαπᾶν.
[2]God [4]whom [3]he has not seen [1]he cannot [2]to love.

21 καὶ ταύτην τὴν ἐντολὴν ἔχομεν ἀπ᾽
And this   the commandment we have from

αὐτοῦ, ἵνα ὁ ἀγαπῶν τὸν θεὸν ἀγαπᾷ
him, in order the loving - God loves
      that [one]

καὶ τὸν ἀδελφὸν αὐτοῦ.
also the brother   of him.

God is love. Whoever lives in love lives in God, and God in him. [17] In this way, love is made complete among us so that we will have confidence on the day of judgment, because in this world we are like him. [18] There is no fear in love. But perfect love drives out fear, because fear has to do with punishment. The one who fears is not made perfect in love.
[19] We love because he first loved us. [20] If anyone says, "I love God," yet hates his brother, he is a liar. For anyone who does not love his brother, whom he has seen, cannot love God, whom he has not seen. [21] And he has given us this command: Whoever loves God must also love his brother.

Chapter 5

Faith Conquers the World

EVERYONE who believes that Jesus is the Christ[t] has been born of God, and everyone who loves the parent loves the child. [2] By this we know that we love the children of God, when we love God and obey his commandments. [3] For the love of God is this, that we obey his commandments. And his commandments are not

5 Πᾶς ὁ πιστεύων ὅτι Ἰησοῦς ἐστιν
Everyone believing that Jesus is

ὁ χριστὸς ἐκ τοῦ θεοῦ γεγέννηται, καὶ
the Christ [2]of - [1]God [1]has been begotten, and

πᾶς ὁ ἀγαπῶν τὸν γεννήσαντα ἀγαπᾷ
everyone loving the [one] begetting loves

τὸν . γεγεννημένον ἐξ αὐτοῦ. 2 ἐν τούτῳ
the having been begotten of him.   By this
[one]

γινώσκομεν ὅτι ἀγαπῶμεν τὰ τέκνα τοῦ
we know   that we love   the children -

θεοῦ, ὅταν τὸν θεὸν ἀγαπῶμεν καὶ τὰς
of God, whenever - [2]God [1]we love and [2]the

ἐντολὰς αὐτοῦ ποιῶμεν. 3 αὕτη γάρ
[3]command- [4]of him [1]we do.   For this
ments

ἐστιν ἡ ἀγάπη τοῦ θεοῦ, ἵνα τὰς ἐντολὰς
is the love   - of   in order [2]the [3]command-
            God, that   ments

αὐτοῦ τηρῶμεν· καὶ αἱ ἐντολαὶ αὐτοῦ
[4]of him [1]we keep; and the commandments of him

Chapter 5

Faith in the Son of God

EVERYONE who believes that Jesus is the Christ is born of God, and everyone who loves the father loves his child as well. [2] This is how we know that we love the children of God: by loving God and carrying out his commands. [3] This is love for God: to obey his commands. And his commands

---

q Other ancient authorities add *him*; others add *God*
r Gk *brothers*
s Gk *brother*
t Or *the Messiah*

• See ch. 2, 6, 3, 3, 5, 7, 16.

burdensome, 4for whatever is born of God conquers the world. And this is the victory that conquers the world, our faith. 5Who is it that conquers the world but the one who believes that Jesus is the Son of God?

Testimony concerning the Son of God

6 This is the one who came by water and blood, Jesus Christ, not with the water only but with the water and the blood. And the Spirit is the one that testifies, for the Spirit is the truth. 7There are three that testify:[u] 8the Spirit and the water and the blood, and these three agree. 9If we receive human testimony, the testimony of God is greater; for this is the testimony of God that he has testified to his Son. 10Those who believe in the Son of God have the testimony in their hearts. Those who do not believe in God[v] have made him a liar by not believing in the testimony that God has given concerning his Son. 11And this is the testimony: God gave us eternal life, and this life is in his Son. 12Whoever has the Son has life; whoever does not have the Son of God does not have life.

Epilogue

13 I write these things to you who believe in the

βαρεῖαι οὐκ εἰσίν, 4 ὅτι πᾶν τὸ γεγεν-
heavy are not, because everything having

νημένον ἐκ τοῦ θεοῦ νικᾷ τὸν κόσμον·
been begotten of – God overcomes the world;

καὶ αὕτη ἐστὶν ἡ νίκη ἡ νικήσασα τὸν
and this is the victory – overcoming the

κόσμον, ἡ πίστις ἡμῶν. 5 Τίς ἐστιν
world, the faith of us. ³Who ²is

[δὲ] ὁ νικῶν τὸν κόσμον εἰ μὴ ὁ
¹and the overcoming the world except the
[one]

πιστεύων ὅτι Ἰησοῦς ἐστιν ὁ υἱὸς τοῦ
[one] believing that Jesus is the Son –

θεοῦ; 6 οὗτός ἐστιν ὁ ἐλθὼν δι᾽ ὕδατος
of God? This is the coming through water
[one]

καὶ αἵματος, Ἰησοῦς Χριστός· οὐκ ἐν
and blood, Jesus Christ; not by

τῷ ὕδατι μόνον, ἀλλ᾽ ἐν τῷ ὕδατι καὶ
the water only, but by the water and

ἐν τῷ αἵματι· καὶ τὸ πνεῦμά ἐστιν τὸ
by the blood; and the Spirit is the

μαρτυροῦν, ὅτι τὸ πνεῦμά ἐστιν ἡ ἀλήθεια.
[one] bearing be- the Spirit is the truth.
witness, cause

7 ὅτι τρεῖς εἰσιν οἱ μαρτυροῦντες, 8 τὸ
Because three there are the bearing witness, the
[ones]

πνεῦμα καὶ τὸ ὕδωρ καὶ τὸ αἷμα, καὶ
Spirit and the water and the blood, and

οἱ τρεῖς εἰς τὸ ἕν εἰσιν. 9 εἰ τὴν
the three ²in *the* ³one ¹are. If ²the

μαρτυρίαν τῶν ἀνθρώπων λαμβάνομεν, ἡ
³witness – ⁴of men ¹we receive, the

μαρτυρία τοῦ θεοῦ μείζων ἐστίν, ὅτι
witness – of God ²greater ¹is, because

αὕτη ἐστὶν ἡ μαρτυρία τοῦ θεοῦ, ὅτι
this is the witness – of God, because

μεμαρτύρηκεν περὶ τοῦ υἱοῦ αὐτοῦ. 10 ὁ
he has borne concern- the Son of him. The
witness ing

πιστεύων εἰς τὸν υἱὸν τοῦ θεοῦ ἔχει
[one] believing in the Son – of God has

τὴν μαρτυρίαν ἐν αὐτῷ. ὁ μὴ πιστεύων
the witness in him. The not believing
[one]

τῷ θεῷ ψεύστην πεποίηκεν αὐτόν, ὅτι
– God ³a liar ¹has made ²him, because

οὐ πεπίστευκεν εἰς τὴν μαρτυρίαν ἣν
he has not believed in the witness which

μεμαρτύρηκεν ὁ θεὸς περὶ τοῦ υἱοῦ
¹has borne witness – ¹God concerning the Son

αὐτοῦ. 11 καὶ αὕτη ἐστὶν ἡ μαρτυρία,
of him. And this is the witness,

ὅτι ζωὴν αἰώνιον ἔδωκεν ὁ θεὸς ἡμῖν,
that ³life ⁴eternal ²gave – ¹God ³to us,

καὶ αὕτη ἡ ζωὴ ἐν τῷ υἱῷ αὐτοῦ
and this – life ²in *the ⁴Son ⁵of him

ἐστιν. 12 ὁ ἔχων τὸν υἱὸν ἔχει τὴν
¹is. The [one] having the Son has *the*

ζωήν· ὁ μὴ ἔχων τὸν υἱὸν τοῦ θεοῦ
life; the not having the Son – of God
[one]

τὴν ζωὴν οὐκ ἔχει.
the life has not.

13 Ταῦτα ἔγραψα ὑμῖν ἵνα εἰδῆτε ὅτι
These I wrote to you in order ye may that
things that know

---

are not burdensome, 4for everyone born of God overcomes the world. This is the victory that has overcome the world, even our faith. 5Who is it that overcomes the world? Only he who believes that Jesus is the Son of God.

6This is the one who came by water and blood—Jesus Christ. He did not come by water only, but by water and blood. And it is the Spirit who testifies, because the Spirit is the truth. 7For there are three that testify: 8the[k] Spirit, the water and the blood; and the three are in agreement. 9We accept man's testimony, but God's testimony is greater because it is the testimony of God, which he has given about his Son. 10Anyone who believes in the Son of God has this testimony in his heart. Anyone who does not believe God has made him out to be a liar, because he has not believed the testimony God has given about his Son. 11And this is the testimony: God has given us eternal life, and this life is in his Son. 12He who has the Son has life; he who does not have the Son of God does not have life.

Concluding Remarks

13I write these things to you who believe in the

---

[u] A few other authorities read (with variations) 7There are three that testify in heaven, the Father, the Word, and the Holy Spirit, and these three are one. 8And there are three that testify on earth:
[v] Other ancient authorities read in the Son

[k] 7,8 Late manuscripts of the Vulgate testify in heaven: the Father, the Word and the Holy Spirit, and these three are one. 8And there are three that testify on earth: the (not found in any Greek manuscript before the sixteenth century)

name of the Son of God, so that you may know that you have eternal life.

14 And this is the boldness we have in him, that if we ask anything according to his will, he hears us. 15 And if we know that he hears us in whatever we ask, we know that we have obtained the requests made of him. 16 If you see your brother or sister[w] committing what is not a mortal sin, you will ask, and God[x] will give life to such a one—to those whose sin is not mortal. There is sin that is mortal; I do not say that you should pray about that. 17 All wrongdoing is sin, but there is sin that is not mortal.

18 We know that those who are born of God do not sin, but the one who was born of God protects them, and the evil one does not touch them. 19 We know that we are God's children, and that the whole world lies under the power of the evil one. 20 And we know that the Son of God has come and has given us understanding so that we may know him who is true;[y] and we are in him who is true, in his Son Jesus Christ. He is the true God and eternal life.

21 Little children, keep yourselves from idols.[z]

ζωὴν ἔχετε αἰώνιον, τοῖς πιστεύουσιν
ᵃlife ¹ye have ²eternal, to the [ones] believing

εἰς τὸ ὄνομα τοῦ υἱοῦ τοῦ θεοῦ. 14 Καὶ
in the name of the Son — of God. And

αὕτη ἐστὶν ἡ παρρησία ἣν ἔχομεν πρὸς
this is the confidence which we have toward

αὐτόν, ὅτι ἐάν τι αἰτώμεθα κατὰ τὸ
him, that if ²anything ¹we ask according to the

θέλημα αὐτοῦ ἀκούει ἡμῶν. 15 καὶ
will of him he hears us. And

ἐὰν οἴδαμεν ὅτι ἀκούει ἡμῶν ὃ ἐὰν
if we know that he hears us whatever

αἰτώμεθα, οἴδαμεν ὅτι ἔχομεν τὰ αἰτήματα
we ask, we know that we have the requests

ἃ ᾐτήκαμεν ἀπ’ αὐτοῦ. 16 Ἐάν τις
which we have from him. If anyone
asked

ἴδῃ τὸν ἀδελφὸν αὐτοῦ ἁμαρτάνοντα
sees the brother of him sinning

ἁμαρτίαν μὴ πρὸς θάνατον, αἰτήσει, καὶ
a sin not unto death, he shall ask, and

δώσει αὐτῷ ζωήν, τοῖς ἁμαρτάνουσιν
he will give to him life, to the [ones] sinning

μὴ πρὸς θάνατον. ἔστιν ἁμαρτία πρὸς
not unto death. There is a sin unto

θάνατον· οὐ περὶ ἐκείνης λέγω ἵνα
death; not concerning that do I say in order
that

ἐρωτήσῃ. 17 πᾶσα ἀδικία ἁμαρτία ἐστίν,
he should inquire. All iniquity ²sin ¹is,

καὶ ἔστιν ἁμαρτία οὐ πρὸς θάνατον.
and there is a sin not unto death.

18 Οἴδαμεν ὅτι πᾶς ὁ γεγεννημένος ἐκ
We know that everyone having been begotten of

τοῦ θεοῦ οὐχ ἁμαρτάνει, ἀλλ’ ὁ γεννηθεὶς
— God sins not, but the [one] begotten

ἐκ τοῦ θεοῦ τηρεῖ αὐτόν, καὶ ὁ πονηρὸς
of — God keeps him, and the evil one

οὐχ ἅπτεται αὐτοῦ. 19 οἴδαμεν ὅτι ἐκ
does not touch him. We know that of

τοῦ θεοῦ ἐσμεν, καὶ ὁ κόσμος ὅλος ἐν
— God we are, and the ²world ¹whole in

τῷ πονηρῷ κεῖται. 20 οἴδαμεν δὲ ὅτι
the evil one lies. ¹we know ¹And that

ὁ υἱὸς τοῦ θεοῦ ἥκει, καὶ δέδωκεν
the Son — of God is come, and has given

ἡμῖν διάνοιαν ἵνα γινώσκωμεν τὸν
to us an understanding in order we might know the
that

ἀληθινόν· καὶ ἐσμὲν ἐν τῷ ἀληθινῷ,
true [one]; and we are in the true [one],

ἐν τῷ υἱῷ αὐτοῦ Ἰησοῦ Χριστῷ. οὗτός
in the Son of him Jesus Christ. This

ἐστιν ὁ ἀληθινὸς θεὸς καὶ ζωὴ αἰώνιος.
is the true God and life eternal.

21 Τεκνία, φυλάξατε ἑαυτὰ ἀπὸ τῶν
Little children, guard yourselves from the

εἰδώλων.
idols.

name of the Son of God so that you may know that you have eternal life. 14 This is the confidence we have in approaching God: that if we ask anything according to his will, he hears us. 15 And if we know that he hears us—whatever we ask —we know that we have what we asked of him.

16 If anyone sees his brother commit a sin that does not lead to death, he should pray and God will give him life. I refer to those whose sin does not lead to death. There is a sin that leads to death. I am not saying that he should pray about that. 17 All wrongdoing is sin, and there is sin that does not lead to death.

18 We know that anyone born of God does not continue to sin; the one who was born of God keeps him safe, and the evil one cannot harm him. 19 We know that we are children of God, and that the whole world is under the control of the evil one. 20 We know also that the Son of God has come and has given us understanding, so that we may know him who is true. And we are in him who is true—even in his Son Jesus Christ. He is the true God and eternal life.

21 Dear children, keep yourselves from idols.

[w] Gk your brother
[x] Gk he
[y] Other ancient authorities read know the true God
[z] Other ancient authorities add Amen

Salutation

THE elder to the elect lady and her children, whom I love in the truth, and not only I but also all who know the truth, 2 because of the truth that abides in us and will be with us forever:

3 Grace, mercy, and peace will be with us from God the Father and from[a] Jesus Christ, the Father's Son, in truth and love.

Truth and Love

4 I was overjoyed to find some of your children walking in the truth, just as we have been commanded by the Father. 5 But now, dear lady, I ask you, not as though I were writing you a new commandment, but one we have had from the beginning, let us love one another. 6 And this is love, that we walk according to his commandments; this is the commandment just as you have heard it from the beginning—you must walk in it.

7 Many deceivers have gone out into the world, those who do not confess that Jesus Christ has come in the flesh; any such person is the deceiver and the antichrist! 8 Be on your guard, so that you do not lose what we[b] have worked for, but may receive a full reward. 9 Everyone who does not abide in the teaching of Christ, but goes beyond it, does not have God; whoever abides in the teaching has

---

1 Ὁ πρεσβύτερος ἐκλεκτῇ κυρίᾳ καὶ
The elder to [the] chosen lady and
τοῖς τέκνοις αὐτῆς, οὓς ἐγὼ ἀγαπῶ ἐν
to the children of her, whom I love in
ἀληθείᾳ, καὶ οὐκ ἐγὼ μόνος ἀλλὰ καὶ
truth, and not I alone but also
πάντες οἱ ἐγνωκότες τὴν ἀλήθειαν, 2 διὰ
all the having known the truth, because of
[ones]
τὴν ἀλήθειαν τὴν μένουσαν ἐν ἡμῖν,
the truth the - remaining among us,
καὶ μεθ᾽ ἡμῶν ἔσται εἰς τὸν αἰῶνα.
and with us will be unto the age.
3 ἔσται μεθ᾽ ἡμῶν χάρις ἔλεος εἰρήνη
⁴will be ⁵with ⁶us ¹Grace[,] ²mercy[,] ³peace
παρὰ θεοῦ πατρός, καὶ παρὰ Ἰησοῦ
from God [the] Father, and from Jesus
Χριστοῦ τοῦ υἱοῦ τοῦ πατρός, ἐν ἀληθείᾳ
Christ the Son of the Father, in truth
καὶ ἀγάπῃ.
and love.
4 Ἐχάρην λίαν ὅτι εὕρηκα ἐκ τῶν
I rejoiced greatly because I have of the
found [some]
τέκνων σου περιπατοῦντας ἐν ἀληθείᾳ,
children of thee walking in truth,
καθὼς ἐντολὴν ἐλάβομεν παρὰ τοῦ πατρός.
as command- we received from the Father.
ment
5 καὶ νῦν ἐρωτῶ σε, κυρία, οὐχ ὡς
And now I request thee, lady, not as
ἐντολὴν γράφων σοι καινήν, ἀλλὰ ἣν
³command- ¹writing ⁴to thee ²a new, but which
ment
εἴχομεν ἀπ᾽ ἀρχῆς, ἵνα ἀγαπῶμεν
we had from [the] in order we should
beginning, that love
ἀλλήλους. 6 καὶ αὕτη ἐστὶν ἡ ἀγάπη,
one another. And this is - love,
ἵνα περιπατῶμεν κατὰ τὰς ἐντολὰς
in order we should walk accord- the command-
that ing to ments
αὐτοῦ· αὕτη ἡ ἐντολή ἐστιν, καθὼς
of him; this ³the ²commandment ¹is, as
ἠκούσατε ἀπ᾽ ἀρχῆς, ἵνα ἐν αὐτῇ
ye heard from [the] in order ²in ³it
beginning, that
περιπατῆτε. 7 ὅτι πολλοὶ πλάνοι ἐξῆλθον
¹ye should walk. Because many deceivers went forth
εἰς τὸν κόσμον, οἱ μὴ ὁμολογοῦντες
into the world, the not confessing
[ones]
Ἰησοῦν Χριστὸν ἐρχόμενον ἐν σαρκί·
Jesus Christ coming in [the] flesh;
οὗτός ἐστιν ὁ πλάνος καὶ ὁ ἀντίχριστος.
this is the deceiver and the antichrist.
8 βλέπετε ἑαυτούς, ἵνα μὴ ἀπολέσητε
See yourselves, lest ye lose
ἃ ἠργασάμεθα, ἀλλὰ μισθὸν πλήρη
[the] we wrought, but ²reward ¹a full
things which
ἀπολάβητε. 9 πᾶς ὁ προάγων καὶ μὴ
¹ye may receive. Everyone going forward and not
μένων ἐν τῇ διδαχῇ τοῦ Χριστοῦ θεὸν
remaining in the teaching - of Christ ²God
οὐκ ἔχει· ὁ μένων ἐν τῇ διδαχῇ, οὗτος
¹not ¹has; the remaining in the teaching, this one
[one]

THE elder,

To the chosen lady and her children, whom I love in the truth—and not I only, but also all who know the truth— 2 because of the truth, which lives in us and will be with us forever:

3 Grace, mercy and peace from God the Father and from Jesus Christ, the Father's Son, will be with us in truth and love.

4 It has given me great joy to find some of your children walking in the truth, just as the Father commanded us. 5 And now, dear lady, I am not writing you a new command but one we have had from the beginning. I ask that we love one another. 6 And this is love: that we walk in obedience to his commands. As you have heard from the beginning, his command is that you walk in love.

7 Many deceivers, who do not acknowledge Jesus Christ as coming in the flesh, have gone out into the world. Any such person is the deceiver and the antichrist. 8 Watch out that you do not lose what you have worked for, but that you may be rewarded fully. 9 Anyone who runs ahead and does not continue in the teaching of Christ does not have God; whoever continues in the teaching

---

[a] Other ancient authorities add the Lord
[b] Other ancient authorities read you

both the Father and the Son. 10 Do not receive into the house or welcome anyone who comes to you and does not bring this teaching; 11 for to welcome is to participate in the evil deeds of such a person.

Final Greetings

12 Although I have much to write to you, I would rather not use paper and ink; instead I hope to come to you and talk with you face to face, so that our joy may be complete.

13 The children of your elect sister send you their greetings. c

καὶ τὸν πατέρα καὶ τὸν υἱὸν ἔχει.
both **the** **'Father** **and** **the** **'Son** **'has.**

10 εἴ τις ἔρχεται πρὸς ὑμᾶς καὶ ταύτην
If anyone comes to you and this

τὴν διδαχὴν οὐ φέρει, μὴ λαμβάνετε
– teaching brings not, do not ye receive

αὐτὸν εἰς οἰκίαν, καὶ χαίρειν αὐτῷ μὴ
him into [your] and 'to rejoice 'him 'not
house,

λέγετε· 11 ὁ λέγων γὰρ αὐτῷ χαίρειν
'tell ye*; 'the 'telling 'for him to rejoice
[one]

κοινωνεῖ τοῖς ἔργοις αὐτοῦ τοῖς πονηροῖς.
shares in the 'works 'of him – 'evil.

12 Πολλὰ ἔχων ὑμῖν γράφειν οὐκ
'Many things 'having 'to you 'to write 'not

ἐβουλήθην διὰ χάρτου καὶ μέλανος, ἀλλὰ
'I purpose by means paper and ink, but
of

ἐλπίζω γενέσθαι πρὸς ὑμᾶς καὶ στόμα
I am hoping to be with you and 'mouth

πρὸς στόμα λαλῆσαι, ἵνα ἡ χαρὰ ἡμῶν
'to 'mouth 'to speak, in or- the joy of us
der that

πεπληρωμένη ᾖ. 13 Ἀσπάζεταί σε τὰ
having been may be. 'greets 'thee 'The
fulfilled

τέκνα τῆς ἀδελφῆς σου τῆς ἐκλεκτῆς.
'children 'of the 'sister 'of thee – 'chosen.

has both the Father and the Son. 10 If anyone comes to you and does not bring this teaching, do not take him into your house or welcome him. 11 Anyone who welcomes him shares in his wicked work.

12 I have much to write to you, but I do not want to use paper and ink. Instead, I hope to visit you and talk with you face to face, so that our joy may be complete.

13 The children of your chosen sister send their greetings.

The Third Letter of
John

Salutation

THE elder to the beloved Gaius, whom I love in truth.

Gaius Commended for His Hospitality

2 Beloved, I pray that all may go well with you and that you may be in good health, just as it is well with your soul. 3 I was overjoyed when some of the friends a arrived and testified to your faithfulness to the truth, namely how you walk in the truth. 4 I have no greater joy than this, to hear that my children are walking in the truth.

5 Beloved, you do faithfully whatever you do for the friends, a even though they are strangers to you; 6 they have testified to your

ΙΩΑΝΝΟΥ Γ
Of John 3

1 Ὁ πρεσβύτερος Γαΐῳ τῷ ἀγαπητῷ,
The elder to Gaius the beloved,

ὃν ἐγὼ ἀγαπῶ ἐν ἀληθείᾳ.
whom I love in truth.

2 Ἀγαπητέ, περὶ πάντων εὔχομαί σε
Beloved, concerning all things I pray thee
= that

εὐοδοῦσθαι καὶ ὑγιαίνειν, καθὼς εὐοδοῦταί
to prosper and to be in health, as 'prospers
thou mayest prosper . . .

σου ἡ ψυχή. 3 ἐχάρην γὰρ λίαν ἐρχομένων
'of 'the 'soul. For I rejoiced greatly coming
thee = when [some]

ἀδελφῶν καὶ μαρτυρούντων σου τῇ
brothers and bearing witness* of thee in the
brothers came and bore witness

ἀληθείᾳ, καθὼς σὺ ἐν ἀληθείᾳ περιπατεῖς.
truth, as thou in truth walkest.

4 μειζοτέραν τούτων οὐκ ἔχω χαράν, ἵνα
'greater '[than] 'these 'I have no 'joy, in or-
things der that

ἀκούω τὰ ἐμὰ τέκνα ἐν τῇ ἀληθείᾳ
I hear – my children 'in 'the 'truth

περιπατοῦντα. 5 Ἀγαπητέ, πιστὸν ποιεῖς
'walking. Beloved, faithfully thou
doest

ὃ ἐὰν ἐργάσῃ εἰς τοὺς ἀδελφοὺς καὶ
whatever thou workest for the brothers and

τοῦτο ξένους, 6 οἳ ἐμαρτύρησάν σου τῇ
this strangers, who bore witness of thee –

3 John

THE elder,
To my dear friend Gaius, whom I love in the truth.

2 Dear friend, I pray that you may enjoy good health and that all may go well with you, even as your soul is getting along well. 3 It gave me great joy to have some brothers come and tell about your faithfulness to the truth and how you continue to walk in the truth. 4 I have no greater joy than to hear that my children are walking in the truth.

5 Dear friend, you are faithful in what you are doing for the brothers, even though they are strangers to you. 6 They have told the

* That is, "do not greet him."

love before the church. You will do well to send them on in a manner worthy of God; 7 for they began their journey for the sake of Christ,[b] accepting no support from non-believers.[c] 8 Therefore we ought to support such people, so that we may become co-workers with the truth.

Diotrephes and Demetrius

9 I have written something to the church; but Diotrephes, who likes to put himself first, does not acknowledge our authority. 10 So if I come, I will call attention to what he is doing in spreading false charges against us. And not content with those charges, he refuses to welcome the friends,[a] and even prevents those who want to do so and expels them from the church.

11 Beloved, do not imitate what is evil but imitate what is good. Whoever does good is from God; whoever does evil has not seen God. 12 Everyone has testified favorably about Demetrius, and so has the truth itself. We also testify for him,[d] and you know that our testimony is true.

Final Greetings

13 I have much to write to you, but I would rather not write with pen and ink; 14 instead I hope to see you soon, and we will talk together face to face.

15 Peace to you. The friends send you their greetings. Greet the friends there, each by name.

ἀγάπη ἐνώπιον ἐκκλησίας, οὓς καλῶς
in love before [the] church, whom well

ποιήσεις προπέμψας ἀξίως τοῦ θεοῦ·
thou wilt do sending forward worthily – of God;

7 ὑπὲρ γὰρ τοῦ ὀνόματος ἐξῆλθαν μηδὲν
for on behalf of the name they went forth ²nothing

λαμβάνοντες ἀπὸ τῶν ἐθνικῶν. 8 ἡμεῖς
¹taking from the Gentiles. We

οὖν ὀφείλομεν ὑπολαμβάνειν τοὺς τοιούτους,
there- ought to entertain – such men,
fore

ἵνα συνεργοὶ γινώμεθα τῇ ἀληθείᾳ.
in or- ²co-workers ¹we may become in the truth.
der that

9 Ἔγραψά τι τῇ ἐκκλησίᾳ· ἀλλ' ὁ
I wrote some- to the church; but the
thing [one]

φιλοπρωτεύων αὐτῶν Διοτρέφης οὐκ
loving to be first of them Diotrephes not

ἐπιδέχεται ἡμᾶς. 10 διὰ τοῦτο, ἐὰν
receives us. Therefore, if

ἔλθω, ὑπομνήσω αὐτοῦ τὰ ἔργα ἃ ποιεῖ
I come, I will remember ²of him ¹the ²works which he does

λόγοις πονηροῖς φλυαρῶν ἡμᾶς, καὶ μὴ
⁴words ³with evil ¹prating against ²us, and not

ἀρκούμενος ἐπὶ τούτοις οὔτε αὐτὸς
being satisfied on(with) these ²neither ¹he

ἐπιδέχεται τοὺς ἀδελφοὺς καὶ τοὺς
²receives the brothers and the

βουλομένους κωλύει καὶ ἐκ τῆς ἐκκλησίας
[ones] purposing he prevents and ²out of ³the ⁴church

ἐκβάλλει.
¹puts out.

11 Ἀγαπητέ, μὴ μιμοῦ τὸ κακὸν ἀλλὰ
Beloved, imitate not the bad but

τὸ ἀγαθόν. ὁ ἀγαθοποιῶν ἐκ τοῦ θεοῦ
the good. The doing good ¹of – ²God
[one]

ἐστιν· ὁ κακοποιῶν οὐχ ἑώρακεν τὸν
¹is; the [one] doing ill has not seen

θεόν. 12 Δημητρίῳ μεμαρτύρηται ὑπὸ
God. To Demetrius witness has been borne by

πάντων καὶ ὑπὸ αὐτῆς τῆς ἀληθείας·
all and by ³[it]self ¹the ²truth;

καὶ ἡμεῖς δὲ μαρτυροῦμεν, καὶ οἶδας
²also ³we ¹and bear witness, and thou
knowest

ὅτι ἡ μαρτυρία ἡμῶν ἀληθής ἐστιν.
that the witness of us ²true ¹is.

13 Πολλὰ εἶχον γράψαι σοι, ἀλλ' οὐ
¹Many things ²I had to write to thee, but not

θέλω διὰ μέλανος καὶ καλάμου σοι
I wish ³by means of ⁴ink ¹and ²pen ¹to thee

γράφειν· 14 ἐλπίζω δὲ εὐθέως σε ἰδεῖν,
¹to write; but I am hoping ²immediately ³thee ¹to see,

καὶ στόμα πρὸς στόμα λαλήσομεν.
and ¹mouth ²to ⁴mouth ¹we will speak.

15 Εἰρήνη σοι. ἀσπάζονταί σε οἱ φίλοι.
Peace to thee. ²greet ⁴thee ¹The ³friends.

ἀσπάζου τοὺς φίλους κατ' ὄνομα.
Greet thou the friends by name.

---

church about your love. You will do well to send them on their way in a manner worthy of God. 7 It was for the sake of the Name that they went out, receiving no help from the pagans. 8 We ought therefore to show hospitality to such men so that we may work together for the truth.

9 I wrote to the church, but Diotrephes, who loves to be first, will have nothing to do with us. 10 So if I come, I will call attention to what he is doing, gossiping maliciously about us. Not satisfied with that, he refuses to welcome the brothers. He also stops those who want to do so and puts them out of the church.

11 Dear friend, do not imitate what is evil but what is good. Anyone who does what is good is from God. Anyone who does what is evil has not seen God. 12 Demetrius is well spoken of by everyone—and even by the truth itself. We also speak well of him, and you know that our testimony is true.

13 I have much to write you, but I do not want to do so with pen and ink. 14 I hope to see you soon, and we will talk face to face.

Peace to you. The friends here send their greetings. Greet the friends there by name.

---

b Gk for the sake of the name
c Gk the Gentiles
d Gk lacks for him

Salutation

J UDE,[a] a servant[b] of Jesus Christ and brother of James,

To those who are called, who are beloved[c] in[d] God the Father and kept safe for[d] Jesus Christ:

2 May mercy, peace, and love be yours in abundance.

Occasion of the Letter

3 Beloved, while eagerly preparing to write to you about the salvation we share, I find it necessary to write and appeal to you to contend for the faith that was once for all entrusted to the saints. 4 For certain intruders have stolen in among you, people who long ago were designated for this condemnation as ungodly, who pervert the grace of our God to licentiousness and deny our only Master and Lord, Jesus Christ.[e]

Judgment on False Teachers

5 Now I desire to remind you, though you are fully informed, that the Lord, who once for all saved[f] a people out of the land of Egypt, afterward destroyed those who did not believe. 6 And the angels who did not keep their own position, but left their proper dwelling, he has kept in eternal chains in deepest darkness for the judgment of the great Day. 7 Likewise, Sodom and Gomorrah and the surrounding cities, which, in the same manner as they, indulged in sexual immorality and pursued unnatural lust,[g] serve as an example by undergoing a punishment of eternal fire.

8 Yet in the same way these dreamers also defile the flesh, reject authority, and slander the glorious ones.[h] 9 But when the arch-

---

1 'Ιούδας 'Ιησοῦ Χριστοῦ δοῦλος, ἀδελφὸς
Jude of Jesus Christ a slave, [2]brother

δὲ 'Ιακώβου, τοῖς ἐν θεῷ πατρὶ
[1]and of James, [3]to the [4]by [5]God [6][the] Father
[ones]

ἠγαπημένοις καὶ 'Ιησοῦ Χριστῷ
[8]having been loved [7]and [9]for Jesus [10]Christ

τετηρημένοις κλητοῖς. 2 ἔλεος ὑμῖν καὶ
[11]having been kept [12]called. Mercy to you and

εἰρήνη καὶ ἀγάπη πληθυνθείη.
peace and love may it be multiplied.

3 'Αγαπητοί, πᾶσαν σπουδὴν ποιούμενος
Beloved, [2]all [3]haste [1]making

γράφειν ὑμῖν περὶ τῆς κοινῆς ἡμῶν
to write to you concerning the common [1]of us

σωτηρίας, ἀνάγκην ἔσχον γράψαι ὑμῖν
[2]salvation, necessity I had to write to you

παρακαλῶν ἐπαγωνίζεσθαι τῇ ἅπαξ
exhorting to contend for [1]the [2]once

παραδοθείσῃ τοῖς ἁγίοις πίστει. 4 παρεισε-
[4]delivered [3]to the [5]saints [2]faith. [2]crept

δύησαν γάρ τινες ἄνθρωποι, οἱ πάλαι
in For [1]certain [3]men, the [ones] of old

προγεγραμμένοι εἰς τοῦτο τὸ κρίμα,
having been for this — judgment,
previously written

ἀσεβεῖς, τὴν τοῦ θεοῦ ἡμῶν χάριτα
impious men, [1]the [2]of the [3]God [4]of us [5]grace

μετατιθέντες εἰς ἀσέλγειαν καὶ τὸν μόνον
[1]making [2]a pretext for wantonness and [3]the [4]only

δεσπότην καὶ κύριον ἡμῶν 'Ιησοῦν Χριστὸν
[5]Master [6]and [7]Lord [8]of us [9]Jesus [10]Christ

ἀρνούμενοι. 5 'Υπομνῆσαι δὲ ὑμᾶς βούλομαι,
[1]denying. But [2]to remind [3]you [1]I purpose,

εἰδότας ἅπαξ πάντα, ὅτι κύριος λαὸν
[3]knowing [1]once all that [the] [1][the]
things, Lord people

ἐκ γῆς Αἰγύπτου σώσας τὸ δεύτερον
[2]out [3][the] [4]of Egypt [1]having in the second place
of land saved

τοὺς μὴ πιστεύσαντας ἀπώλεσεν, 6 ἀγγέλους
[2]the [3]not [4]believing [1]destroyed, [1]angels
[ones]

τε τοὺς μὴ τηρήσαντας τὴν ἑαυτῶν
[1]and — not having kept the [1]of themselves

ἀρχὴν ἀλλὰ ἀπολιπόντας τὸ ἴδιον
[1]rule but having deserted the(ir) own

οἰκητήριον εἰς κρίσιν μεγάλης ἡμέρας
habitation [6]for [7][the] judgment [8]of [the] great [9]day

δεσμοῖς ἀϊδίοις ὑπὸ ζόφον τετήρηκεν·
[3]bonds [2]in everlasting [4]under [5]gloom [1]he has kept;

7 ὡς Σόδομα καὶ Γόμορρα καὶ αἱ περὶ
as Sodom and Gomorrah and [1]the [2]round

αὐτὰς πόλεις, τὸν ὅμοιον τρόπον τούτοις
[4]them [3]cities, in the like manner to these

ἐκπορνεύσασαι καὶ ἀπελθοῦσαι ὀπίσω σαρκὸς
committing and going away after [2]flesh
fornication

ἑτέρας, πρόκεινται δεῖγμα πυρὸς αἰωνίου
[1]different, are set forth an example [4]fire [5]of eternal

δίκην ὑπέχουσαι. 8 'Ομοίως μέντοι καὶ
[2]ven- [1]undergoing. Likewise indeed also
geance

οὗτοι ἐνυπνιαζόμενοι σάρκα μὲν μιαίνουσιν,
these dreaming [ones] [2]flesh [1]on one [3]defile,
hand

κυριότητα δὲ ἀθετοῦσιν, δόξας δὲ
[5]lordship [4]on the other [6]despise, [7]glories [8]and

J UDE, a servant of Jesus Christ and a brother of James,

To those who have been called, who are loved by God the Father and kept by[a] Jesus Christ:

2 Mercy, peace and love be yours in abundance.

The Sin and Doom of Godless Men

3 Dear friends, although I was very eager to write to you about the salvation we share, I felt I had to write and urge you to contend for the faith that was once for all entrusted to the saints. 4 For certain men whose condemnation was written about[b] long ago have secretly slipped in among you. They are godless men, who change the grace of our God into a license for immorality and deny Jesus Christ our only Sovereign and Lord.

5 Though you already know all this, I want to remind you that the Lord[c] delivered his people out of Egypt, but later destroyed those who did not believe. 6 And the angels who did not keep their positions of authority but abandoned their own home—these he has kept in darkness, bound with everlasting chains for judgment on the great Day. 7 In a similar way, Sodom and Gomorrah and the surrounding towns gave themselves up to sexual immorality and perversion. They serve as an example of those who suffer the punishment of eternal fire.

8 In the very same way, these dreamers pollute their own bodies, reject authority and slander celestial

---

[a] Gk *Judas*
[b] Gk *slave*
[c] Other ancient authorities read *sanctified*
[d] Or *by*
[e] Or *the only Master and our Lord Jesus Christ*
[f] Other ancient authorities read *though you were once for all fully informed, that Jesus* (or *Joshua*) *who saved*
[g] Gk *went after other flesh*
[h] Or *angels;* Gk *glories*

[a] 1 Or *for*; or *in*
[b] 4 Or *men who were marked out for condemnation*
[c] 5 Some early manuscripts *Jesus*

angel Michael contended with the devil and disputed about the body of Moses, he did not dare to bring a condemnation of slander[i] against him, but said, "The Lord rebuke you!" 10 But these people slander whatever they do not understand, and they are destroyed by those things that, like irrational animals, they know by instinct. 11 Woe to them! For they go the way of Cain, and abandon themselves to Balaam's error for the sake of gain, and perish in Korah's rebellion. 12 These are blemishes[j] on your lovefeasts, while they feast with you without fear, feeding themselves.[k] They are waterless clouds carried along by the winds; autumn trees without fruit, twice dead, uprooted; 13 wild waves of the sea, casting up the foam of their own shame; wandering stars, for whom the deepest darkness has been reserved forever.

14 It was also about these that Enoch, in the seventh generation from Adam, prophesied, saying, "See, the Lord is coming[l] with ten thousands of his holy ones, 15 to execute judgment on all, and to convict everyone of all the deeds of ungodliness that they have committed in such an ungodly way, and of all the harsh things that ungodly sinners have spoken against him." 16 These are grumblers and malcontents; they indulge their own lusts; they are bombastic in speech, flattering people to their own advantage.

[i] Or condemnation for blasphemy
[j] Or reefs
[k] Or without fear. They are shepherds who care only for themselves
[l] Gk came

βλασφημοῦσιν. 9 Ὁ δὲ Μιχαὴλ ὁ ἀρχάγ-
rail at.   But Michael the arch-

γελος, ὅτε τῷ διαβόλῳ διακρινόμενος
angel, when ²with the ³devil ¹contending

διελέγετο περὶ τοῦ Μωϋσέως σώματος,
he argued about ¹the ²of Moses ³body,

οὐκ ἐτόλμησεν κρίσιν ἐπενεγκεῖν βλασφημίας,
durst not   ²a judgment ¹to bring on   of railing,

ἀλλὰ εἶπεν· ἐπιτιμήσαι σοι κύριος. 10 οὗτοι
but   said :   ²rebuke ³thee ¹[The] Lord.   these men

δὲ ὅσα μὲν οὐκ οἴδασιν βλασφημοῦσιν,
But what on one they know not   they rail at,
   things hand

ὅσα δὲ φυσικῶς ὡς τὰ ἄλογα ζῷα
what on the ¹naturally ²as ⁴the ⁵without ⁶animals
things other   reason

ἐπίστανται, ἐν τούτοις φθείρονται. 11 οὐαὶ
¹they understand, by these they are corrupted.   Woe

αὐτοῖς, ὅτι τῇ ὁδῷ τοῦ Κάϊν ἐπορεύθησαν,
to them, because in the way - of Cain they went,

καὶ τῇ πλάνῃ τοῦ Βαλαὰμ μισθοῦ
and ²to the ³error - ⁴of Balaam ⁵of(for)
                                    reward

ἐξεχύθησαν, καὶ τῇ ἀντιλογίᾳ τοῦ Κόρε
¹gave themselves and ²in the ³dispute - ⁴of
up,   Korah

ἀπώλοντο. 12 Οὗτοί εἰσιν οἱ ἐν ταῖς
¹perished.   These men are ¹the ²in ⁴the

ἀγάπαις ὑμῶν σπιλάδες συνευωχούμενοι
³love feasts ⁵of you ⁶rocks   feasting together

ἀφόβως, ἑαυτοὺς ποιμαίνοντες, νεφέλαι
without fear, ¹themselves ¹feeding,   ²clouds

ἄνυδροι ὑπὸ ἀνέμων παραφερόμεναι, δένδρα
¹waterless ²by ³winds ⁴being carried away, ⁵trees

φθινοπωρινὰ ἄκαρπα δὶς ἀποθανόντα
¹autumn   without fruit twice dying

ἐκριζωθέντα, 13 κύματα ἄγρια θαλάσσης
having been uprooted, ²waves ¹fierce ³of [the] sea

ἐπαφρίζοντα τὰς ἑαυτῶν αἰσχύνας, ἀστέρες
⁴foaming up ⁵the ⁷of themselves ⁶shames,   ¹stars

πλανῆται, οἷς ὁ ζόφος τοῦ σκότους
¹wandering, for whom the gloom   -   of darkness

εἰς αἰῶνα τετήρηται. 14 Ἐπροφήτευσεν
unto [the] age has been kept.   ⁷prophesied

δὲ καὶ τούτοις ἕβδομος ἀπὸ Ἀδὰμ
¹And ²also ³to these men ⁴[the] seventh ⁵from ⁶Adam

Ἐνὼχ λέγων· ἰδοὺ ἦλθεν κύριος ἐν
²Enoch saying : Behold came [the] Lord with

ἁγίαις μυριάσιν αὐτοῦ, 15 ποιῆσαι κρίσιν
saints ten thousands of him,   to do   judgment

κατὰ πάντων καὶ ἐλέγξαι πάντας τοὺς
against all men and to rebuke all the

ἀσεβεῖς περὶ πάντων τῶν ἔργων ἀσεβείας
impious concerning all the works of impiety

αὐτῶν ὧν ἠσέβησαν καὶ περὶ πάντων
of them which they impiously did and concerning all

τῶν σκληρῶν ὧν ἐλάλησαν κατ' αὐτοῦ
the hard things which ³spoke ⁴against ⁵him

ἁμαρτωλοὶ ἀσεβεῖς. 16 Οὗτοί εἰσιν γογ-
²sinners ¹impious.   These men are ¹mur-

γυσταὶ μεμψίμοιροι, κατὰ τὰς ἐπιθυμίας
murers ¹querulous, ²according to ³the ⁴lusts

αὐτῶν πορευόμενοι, καὶ τὸ στόμα αὐτῶν
⁵of them ⁶going,   and the mouth of them

λαλεῖ ὑπέρογκα, θαυμάζοντες πρόσωπα
speaks arrogant things, admiring   faces

beings. 9 But even the archangel Michael, when he was disputing with the devil about the body of Moses, did not dare to bring a slanderous accusation against him, but said, "The Lord rebuke you!" 10 Yet these men speak abusively against whatever they do not understand; and what things they do understand by instinct, like unreasoning animals—these are the very things that destroy them.

11 Woe to them! They have taken the way of Cain; they have rushed for profit into Balaam's error; they have been destroyed in Korah's rebellion.

12 These men are blemishes at your love feasts, eating with you without the slightest qualm—shepherds who feed only themselves. They are clouds without rain, blown along by the wind; autumn trees, without fruit and uprooted—twice dead. 13 They are wild waves of the sea, foaming up their shame; wandering stars, for whom blackest darkness has been reserved forever.

14 Enoch, the seventh from Adam, prophesied about these men: "See, the Lord is coming with thousands upon thousands of his holy ones 15 to judge everyone, and to convict all the ungodly of all the ungodly acts they have done in the ungodly way, and of all the harsh words ungodly sinners have spoken against him." 16 These men are grumblers and faultfinders; they follow their own evil desires; they boast about themselves and flat-

Warnings and Exhortations

17 But you, beloved, must remember the predictions of the apostles of our Lord Jesus Christ; 18 for they said to you, "In the last time there will be scoffers, indulging their own ungodly lusts." 19 It is these worldly people, devoid of the Spirit, who are causing divisions. 20 But you, beloved, build yourselves up on your most holy faith; pray in the Holy Spirit; 21 keep yourselves in the love of God; look forward to the mercy of our Lord Jesus Christ that leads to *m* eternal life. 22 And have mercy on some who are wavering; 23 save others by snatching them out of the fire; and have mercy on still others with fear, hating even the tunic defiled by their bodies. *n*

Benediction

24 Now to him who is able to keep you from falling, and to make you stand without blemish in the presence of his glory with rejoicing, 25 to the only God our Savior, through Jesus Christ our Lord, be glory, majesty, power, and authority, before all time and now and forever. Amen.

ὠφελείας χάριν.
advantage ¹for the sake of.

17 Ὑμεῖς δέ, ἀγαπητοί, μνήσθητε τῶν
But ye, beloved, be mindful of the

ῥημάτων τῶν προειρημένων ὑπὸ τῶν
words – previously spoken by the

ἀποστόλων τοῦ κυρίου ἡμῶν Ἰησοῦ
apostles of the Lord of us Jesus

Χριστοῦ, 18 ὅτι ἔλεγον ὑμῖν· ἐπ' ἐσχάτου
Christ, because they told you: At [the] last

τοῦ χρόνου ἔσονται ἐμπαῖκται κατὰ τὰς
of the time will be mockers ²according to ³the

ἑαυτῶν ἐπιθυμίας πορευόμενοι τῶν ἀσεβειῶν.
⁵of themselves ⁴lusts ¹going – ⁶of impious things.

19 Οὗτοί εἰσιν οἱ ἀποδιορίζοντες, ψυχικοί,
These men are the [ones] making separations, natural,

πνεῦμα μὴ ἔχοντες. 20 ὑμεῖς δέ, ἀγαπητοί,
²spirit ¹not ³having. But ye, beloved,

ἐποικοδομοῦντες ἑαυτοὺς τῇ ἁγιωτάτῃ ὑμῶν
building up yourselves in the most holy ¹ ²of you

πίστει, ἐν πνεύματι ἁγίῳ προσευχόμενοι,
¹faith, ²in ⁴Spirit ³[the] Holy ¹praying.

21 ἑαυτοὺς ἐν ἀγάπῃ θεοῦ τηρήσατε,
²yourselves ³in ⁴[the] love ⁵of God ¹keep,

προσδεχόμενοι τὸ ἔλεος τοῦ κυρίου ἡμῶν
awaiting the mercy of the Lord of us

Ἰησοῦ Χριστοῦ εἰς ζωὴν αἰώνιον. 22 καὶ
Jesus Christ to life eternal. And

οὓς μὲν ἐλεᾶτε διακρινομένους 23 σώζετε
some ²pity ye ¹[who are] wavering ²save

ἐκ πυρὸς ἁρπάζοντες, οὓς δὲ ἐλεᾶτε
³out of ⁴fire ¹seizing, others pity

ἐν φόβῳ, μισοῦντες καὶ τὸν ἀπὸ τῆς
with fear, hating even ¹the ⁴from ⁵the

σαρκὸς ἐσπιλωμένον χιτῶνα.
⁶flesh ³having been spotted ²tunic.

24 Τῷ δὲ δυναμένῳ φυλάξαι ὑμᾶς
Now to the [one] *being* able to guard you

ἀπταίστους καὶ στῆσαι κατενώπιον τῆς
without and to set [you] before the
stumbling

δόξης αὐτοῦ ἀμώμους ἐν ἀγαλλιάσει,
glory of him unblemished with exultation,

25 μόνῳ θεῷ σωτῆρι ἡμῶν διὰ Ἰησοῦ
to [the] only God Saviour of us through Jesus

Χριστοῦ τοῦ κυρίου ἡμῶν δόξα μεγαλωσύνη
Christ the Lord of us [be] glory[,] greatness[,]

κράτος καὶ ἐξουσία πρὸ παντὸς τοῦ
might[,] and authority before all the

αἰῶνος καὶ νῦν καὶ εἰς πάντας τοὺς
age and now and unto all the

αἰῶνας· ἀμήν.
ages: Amen.

ter others for their own advantage.

A Call to Persevere

17But, dear friends, remember what the apostles of our Lord Jesus Christ foretold. 18They said to you, "In the last times there will be scoffers who will follow their own ungodly desires." 19These are the men who divide you, who follow mere natural instincts and do not have the Spirit.

20But you, dear friends, build yourselves up in your most holy faith and pray in the Holy Spirit. 21Keep yourselves in God's love as you wait for the mercy of our Lord Jesus Christ to bring you to eternal life.

22Be merciful to those who doubt; 23snatch others from the fire and save them; to others show mercy, mixed with fear—hating even the clothing stained by corrupted flesh.

Doxology

24To him who is able to keep you from falling and to present you before his glorious presence without fault and with great joy—25to the only God our Savior be glory, majesty, power and authority, through Jesus Christ our Lord, before all ages, now and forevermore! Amen.

---

m Gk *Christ to*
n Gk *by the flesh.* The Greek text of verses 22-23 is uncertain at several points

The
Revelation
to John

ΑΠΟΚΑΛΥΨΙΣ ΙΩΑΝΝΟΥ
A Revelation of John

Revelation

Chapter 1

Introduction and Salutation

THE revelation of Jesus Christ, which God gave him to show his servants[a] what must soon take place; he made[b] it known by sending his angel to his servant[c] John, [2] who testified to the word of God and to the testimony of Jesus Christ, even to all that he saw.

[3] Blessed is the one who reads aloud the words of the prophecy, and blessed are those who hear and who keep what is written in it; for the time is near.

[4] John to the seven churches that are in Asia:

Grace to you and peace from him who is and who was and who is to come, and from the seven spirits who are before his throne, [5] and from Jesus Christ, the faithful witness, the firstborn of the dead, and the ruler of the kings of the earth.

To him who loves us and freed[d] us from our sins by his blood, [6] and made[b] us to be a kingdom, priests serving[e] his God and Father, to him be glory and dominion forever and ever. Amen.

[7] Look! He is coming
with the clouds;
every eye will see him,
even those who
pierced him;
and on his account
all the tribes of
the earth will wail.
So it is to be. Amen.

[8] "I am the Alpha and the Omega," says the Lord

---

[a] Gk *slaves*
[b] Gk *and he made*
[c] Gk *slave*
[d] Other ancient authorities read *washed*
[e] Gk *priests to*

---

1 Ἀποκάλυψις Ἰησοῦ Χριστοῦ, ἣν
A revelation of Jesus Christ, which

ἔδωκεν αὐτῷ ὁ θεός, δεῖξαι τοῖς δούλοις
[2]gave [3]to him – [1]God, to show to the slaves

αὐτοῦ ἃ δεῖ γενέσθαι ἐν τάχει, καὶ
of him things it be- to occur with speed, and
which hoves

ἐσήμανεν ἀποστείλας διὰ τοῦ ἀγγέλου
he signified sending through the angel

αὐτοῦ τῷ δούλῳ αὐτοῦ Ἰωάννῃ, **2** ὃς
of him to the slave of him John, who

ἐμαρτύρησεν τὸν λόγον τοῦ θεοῦ καὶ
bore witness [of] the word – of God and

τὴν μαρτυρίαν Ἰησοῦ Χριστοῦ, ὅσα εἶδεν.
the witness of Jesus Christ, as many he saw.
things as

3 Μακάριος ὁ ἀναγινώσκων καὶ οἱ
Blessed [is] the [one] reading and the

ἀκούοντες τοὺς λόγους τῆς προφητείας
[ones] hearing the words of the prophecy

καὶ τηροῦντες τὰ ἐν αὐτῇ γεγραμμένα·
and keeping the things [2]in [1]it [1]having been written;

ὁ γὰρ καιρὸς ἐγγύς.
[2]the [1]for time [is] near.

4 Ἰωάννης ταῖς ἑπτὰ ἐκκλησίαις ταῖς
John to the seven churches –

ἐν τῇ Ἀσίᾳ· χάρις ὑμῖν καὶ εἰρήνη
in – Asia: Grace to you and peace

ἀπὸ ὁ ὢν καὶ ὁ ἦν καὶ ὁ ἐρχόμενος,
from the being and the was and the [one] coming,
[one] [one who]
= the one who is

καὶ ἀπὸ τῶν ἑπτὰ πνευμάτων ἃ ἐνώπιον
and from the seven spirits which before
[are]

τοῦ θρόνου αὐτοῦ, **5** καὶ ἀπὸ Ἰησοῦ
the throne of him, and from Jesus

Χριστοῦ, ὁ μάρτυς ὁ πιστός, ὁ πρωτότοκος
Christ, the [2]witness – [1]faithful, the firstborn

τῶν νεκρῶν καὶ ὁ ἄρχων τῶν βασιλέων
of the dead and the ruler of the kings

τῆς γῆς. Τῷ ἀγαπῶντι ἡμᾶς καὶ λύσαντι
of the earth. To loving us and having
the [one] loosed

ἡμᾶς ἐκ τῶν ἁμαρτιῶν ἡμῶν ἐν τῷ
us out of the sins of us by the

αἵματι αὐτοῦ, **6** καὶ ἐποίησεν ἡμᾶς
blood of him, and made us

βασιλείαν, ἱερεῖς τῷ θεῷ καὶ πατρὶ
a kingdom, priests to the God and Father

αὐτοῦ, αὐτῷ ἡ δόξα καὶ τὸ κράτος
of him, to him[c] [is] the glory and the might
= his is

εἰς τοὺς αἰῶνας τῶν αἰώνων· ἀμήν.
unto the ages of the ages: Amen.

7 Ἰδοὺ ἔρχεται μετὰ τῶν νεφελῶν,
Behold he comes with the clouds,

καὶ ὄψεται αὐτὸν πᾶς ὀφθαλμὸς καὶ
and [4]will see [3]him [1]every [2]eye and

οἵτινες αὐτὸν ἐξεκέντησαν, καὶ κόψονται
[those] who [2]him [1]pierced, and [3]will wail

ἐπ' αὐτὸν πᾶσαι αἱ φυλαὶ τῆς γῆς.
[1]over [2]him [1]all [2]the [3]tribes [4]of the [5]land.

ναί, ἀμήν.
Yes, amen.

8 Ἐγώ εἰμι τὸ ἄλφα καὶ τὸ ὦ, λέγει
I am the alpha and the omega, says

Chapter 1

Prologue

THE revelation of Jesus Christ, which God gave him to show his servants what must soon take place. He made it known by sending his angel to his servant John, [2] who testifies to everything he saw—that is, the word of God and the testimony of Jesus Christ. [3] Blessed is the one who reads the words of this prophecy, and blessed are those who hear it and take to heart what is written in it, because the time is near.

Greetings and Doxology

[4] John,

To the seven churches in the province of Asia:

Grace and peace to you from him who is, and who was, and who is to come, and from the seven spirits[a] before his throne, [5] and from Jesus Christ, who is the faithful witness, the firstborn from the dead, and the ruler of the kings of the earth.

To him who loves us and has freed us from our sins by his blood, [6] and has made us to be a kingdom and priests to serve his God and Father—to him be glory and power for ever and ever! Amen.

[7] Look, he is coming with
the clouds,
and every eye will see
him,
even those who pierced
him;
and all the peoples of
the earth will mourn
because of him.
So shall it be!
Amen.

[8] "I am the Alpha and the Omega," says the Lord

---

[a] 4 Or *the sevenfold Spirit*

God, who is and who was and who is to come, the Almighty.

A Vision of Christ

9 I, John, your brother who share with you in Jesus the persecution and the kingdom and the patient endurance, was on the island called Patmos because of the word of God and the testimony of Jesus.[f] 10 I was in the spirit[g] on the Lord's day, and I heard behind me a loud voice like a trumpet 11 saying, "Write in a book what you see and send it to the seven churches, to Ephesus, to Smyrna, to Pergamum, to Thyatira, to Sardis, to Philadelphia, and to Laodicea."

12 Then I turned to see whose voice it was that spoke to me, and on turning I saw seven golden lampstands, 13 and in the midst of the lampstands I saw one like the Son of Man, clothed with a long robe and with a golden sash across his chest. 14 His head and his hair were white as white wool, white as snow; his eyes were like a flame of fire, 15 his feet were like burnished bronze, refined as in a furnace, and his voice was like the sound of many waters. 16 In his right hand he held seven stars, and from his mouth came a sharp, two-edged sword, and his face was like the sun shining with full force.

κύριος ὁ θεός, ὁ ὢν καὶ ὁ ἦν
[the] - God, the [one] being and the was
Lord   =the one who is   [one who]

καὶ ὁ ἐρχόμενος, ὁ παντοκράτωρ.
and the [one] coming, the Almighty.

9 Ἐγὼ Ἰωάννης, ὁ ἀδελφὸς ὑμῶν καὶ
I John, the brother of you and

συγκοινωνὸς ἐν τῇ θλίψει καὶ βασιλείᾳ
co-sharer in the affliction and kingdom

καὶ ὑπομονῇ ἐν Ἰησοῦ, ἐγενόμην ἐν
and endurance in Jesus, came to be in

τῇ νήσῳ τῇ καλουμένῃ Πάτμῳ διὰ
the island - being called Patmos on account of

τὸν λόγον τοῦ θεοῦ καὶ τὴν μαρτυρίαν
the word - of God and the witness

Ἰησοῦ. 10 ἐγενόμην ἐν πνεύματι ἐν
of Jesus. I came to be in [the] spirit on

τῇ κυριακῇ ἡμέρᾳ, καὶ ἤκουσα ὀπίσω
the imperial* day, and heard behind

μου φωνὴν μεγάλην ὡς σάλπιγγος
me ¹voice ¹a great(loud) as of a trumpet

11 λεγούσης· ὃ βλέπεις γράψον εἰς βιβλίον
saying: What thou seest write in a scroll

καὶ πέμψον ταῖς ἑπτὰ ἐκκλησίαις, εἰς
and send to the seven churches, to

Ἔφεσον καὶ εἰς Σμύρναν καὶ εἰς Πέργαμον
Ephesus and to Smyrna and to Pergamum

καὶ εἰς Θυάτιρα καὶ εἰς Σάρδεις καὶ
and to Thyatira and to Sardis and

εἰς Φιλαδέλφειαν καὶ εἰς Λαοδίκειαν.
to Philadelphia and to Laodicea.

12 Καὶ ἐπέστρεψα βλέπειν τὴν φωνὴν
And I turned to see the voice

ἥτις ἐλάλει μετ' ἐμοῦ· καὶ ἐπιστρέψας
which spoke with me; and having turned

εἶδον ἑπτὰ λυχνίας χρυσᾶς, 13 καὶ ἐν
I saw seven ¹lampstands ¹golden, and in

μέσῳ τῶν λυχνιῶν ὅμοιον υἱὸν ἀνθρώπου,
[the] of the lampstands [one] like a son of man,*
midst

ἐνδεδυμένον ποδήρη καὶ περιεζωσμένον
having been clothed to the feet and having been girdled round

πρὸς τοῖς μαστοῖς ζώνην χρυσᾶν· 14 ἡ
at the breasts ¹girdle ¹[with] a golden; ¹the

δὲ κεφαλὴ αὐτοῦ καὶ αἱ τρίχες λευκαὶ
¹and head of him and the hairs white

ὡς ἔριον λευκὸν ὡς χιών, καὶ οἱ ὀφθαλμοὶ
as wool white as snow, and the eyes

αὐτοῦ ὡς φλὸξ πυρός, 15 καὶ οἱ πόδες
of him as a flame of fire, and the feet

αὐτοῦ ὅμοιοι χαλκολιβάνῳ ὡς ἐν καμίνῳ
of him like to burnished brass as ¹in ¹a furnace

πεπυρωμένης, καὶ ἡ φωνὴ αὐτοῦ ὡς
¹having been fired, and the voice of him as

φωνὴ ὑδάτων πολλῶν, 16 καὶ ἔχων ἐν
a sound waters of many, and having in

τῇ δεξιᾷ χειρὶ αὐτοῦ ἀστέρας ἑπτά,
the right hand of him ²stars ¹seven,

καὶ ἐκ τοῦ στόματος αὐτοῦ ῥομφαία
and out of the mouth of him ⁴sword

δίστομος ὀξεῖα ἐκπορευομένη, καὶ ἡ ὄψις
³two- ²a sharp ¹proceeding, and the face
mouthed(edged)

God, "who is, and who was, and who is to come, the Almighty."

One Like a Son of Man

9 I, John, your brother and companion in the suffering and kingdom and patient endurance that are ours in Jesus, was on the island of Patmos because of the word of God and the testimony of Jesus. 10 On the Lord's Day I was in the Spirit, and I heard behind me a loud voice like a trumpet, 11 which said: "Write on a scroll what you see and send it to the seven churches: to Ephesus, Smyrna, Pergamum, Thyatira, Sardis, Philadelphia and Laodicea."

12 I turned around to see the voice that was speaking to me. And when I turned I saw seven golden lampstands, 13 and among the lampstands was someone "like a son of man,"[b] dressed in a robe reaching down to his feet and with a golden sash around his chest. 14 His head and hair were white like wool, as white as snow, and his eyes were like blazing fire. 15 His feet were like bronze glowing in a furnace, and his voice was like the sound of rushing waters. 16 In his right hand he held seven stars, and out of his mouth came a sharp double-edged sword. His face was like

---

f Or testimony to Jesus
g Or in the Spirit

* See I. Cor. 11. 20.

* Anarthrous; see also ch. 14. 14 and John 5. 27, and cf. Heb. 2. 6.   b 13 Daniel 7:13

17 When I saw him, I fell at his feet as though dead. But he placed his right hand on me, saying, "Do not be afraid; I am the first and the last, 18 and the living one. I was dead, and see, I am alive forever and ever; and I have the keys of Death and of Hades. 19 Now write what you have seen, what is, and what is to take place after this. 20 As for the mystery of the seven stars that you saw in my right hand, and the seven golden lampstands: the seven stars are the angels of the seven churches, and the seven lampstands are the seven churches.

αὐτοῦ ὡς ὁ ἥλιος φαίνει ἐν τῇ δυνάμει
of him as the sun shines in the power
αὐτοῦ. 17 Καὶ ὅτε εἶδον αὐτόν, ἔπεσα
of it. And when I saw him, I fell
πρὸς τοὺς πόδας αὐτοῦ ὡς νεκρός· καὶ
at the feet of him as dead; and
ἔθηκεν τὴν δεξιὰν αὐτοῦ ἐπ' ἐμὲ λέγων·
he placed the right [hand] of him on me saying:
μὴ φοβοῦ· ἐγώ εἰμι ὁ πρῶτος καὶ
Fear not: I am the first and
ὁ ἔσχατος 18 καὶ ὁ ζῶν, καὶ ἐγενόμην
the last and the living [one], and I became
νεκρὸς καὶ ἰδοὺ ζῶν εἰμι εἰς τοὺς
dead and behold ¹living ¹I am unto the
αἰῶνας τῶν αἰώνων, καὶ ἔχω τὰς κλεῖς
ages of the ages, and I have the keys
τοῦ θανάτου καὶ τοῦ ᾅδου. 19 γράψον
- of death and - of hades. Write thou
οὖν ἃ εἶδες καὶ ἃ εἰσὶν καὶ ἃ
there- [the] thou and [the] are and [the]
fore things sawest which things things
which which
μέλλει γενέσθαι μετὰ ταῦτα. 20 τὸ
(is)are about to occur after these things. The
μυστήριον τῶν ἑπτὰ ἀστέρων οὓς εἶδες
mystery of the seven stars which thou
sawest
ἐπὶ τῆς· δεξιᾶς μου, καὶ τὰς ἑπτὰ
on the right [hand] of me, and the seven
λυχνίας τὰς χρυσᾶς· οἱ ἑπτὰ ἀστέρες
²lampstands - ¹golden: the seven stars
ἄγγελοι τῶν ἑπτὰ ἐκκλησιῶν εἰσιν, καὶ
messengers* of the seven churches are, and
αἱ λυχνίαι αἱ ἑπτὰ ἑπτὰ ἐκκλησίαι εἰσίν.
the ²lampstanus - ¹seven ⁴seven ⁵churches ³are.

the sun shining in all its brilliance.
17 When I saw him, I fell at his feet as though dead. Then he placed his right hand on me and said: "Do not be afraid. I am the First and the Last. 18 I am the Living One; I was dead, and behold I am alive for ever and ever! And I hold the keys of death and Hades.
19 "Write, therefore, what you have seen, what is now and what will take place later. 20 The mystery of the seven stars that you saw in my right hand and of the seven golden lampstands is this: The seven stars are the angels[c] of the seven churches, and the seven lampstands are the seven churches.

Chapter 2

The Message to Ephesus

" "TO the angel of the church in Ephesus write: These are the words of him who holds the seven stars in his right hand, who walks among the seven golden lampstands:
2 "I know your works, your toil and your patient endurance. I know that you cannot tolerate evildoers; you have tested those who claim to be apostles but are not, and have found them to be false. 3 I also know that you are enduring patiently and bearing up for the sake of my name, and that you have not grown weary. 4 But I have this against you, that you have abandoned the love you

2 Τῷ ἀγγέλῳ τῆς ἐν Ἐφέσῳ ἐκκλησίας
To the messenger ¹of the ²in ⁴Ephesus ³church
γράψον·
write thou:
Τάδε λέγει ὁ κρατῶν τοὺς ἑπτὰ
These things says the [one] holding the seven
ἀστέρας ἐν τῇ δεξιᾷ αὐτοῦ, ὁ περιπατῶν
stars in the right [hand] of him, the [one] walking
ἐν μέσῳ τῶν ἑπτὰ λυχνιῶν τῶν
in [the] midst of the seven ²lampstands -
χρυσῶν· 2 οἶδα τὰ ἔργα σου καὶ τὸν
¹golden: I know the works of thee and the
κόπον καὶ τὴν ὑπομονήν σου, καὶ ὅτι
labour and the endurance of thee, and that
οὐ δύνῃ βαστάσαι κακούς, καὶ ἐπείρασας
thou canst not to bear bad men, and didst try
τοὺς λέγοντας ἑαυτοὺς ἀποστόλους καὶ
the [ones] say(call)ing themselves apostles and
οὐκ εἰσίν, καὶ εὗρες αὐτοὺς ψευδεῖς·
are not, and didst find them liars;
3 καὶ ὑπομονὴν ἔχεις, καὶ ἐβάστασας
and ²endurance ¹thou hast, and didst bear
διὰ τὸ ὄνομά μου, καὶ οὐ κεκοπίακας.
be- the name of me, and hast not grown weary.
cause of
4 ἀλλὰ ἔχω κατὰ σοῦ ὅτι τὴν ἀγάπην
But I have against thee that ²the ⁴love

Chapter 2

To the Church in Ephesus

" "TO the angel[d] of the church in Ephesus write:

These are the words of him who holds the seven stars in his right hand and walks among the seven golden lampstands: 2 I know your deeds, your hard work and your perseverance. I know that you cannot tolerate wicked men, that you have tested those who claim to be apostles but are not, and have found them false. 3 You have persevered and have endured hardships for my name, and have not grown weary.
4 Yet I hold this against you: You have

---

* This, of course, is the prime meaning of the word: whether these beings were "messengers" from the churches, or supernatural beings, "angels" as usually understood, is a matter of exegesis.

c20 Or messengers
d1 Or messenger; also in verses 8, 12 and 18

had at first. 5 Remember then from what you have fallen; repent, and do the works you did at first. If not, I will come to you and remove your lampstand from its place, unless you repent. 6 Yet this is to your credit: you hate the works of the Nicolaitans, which I also hate. 7 Let anyone who has an ear listen to what the Spirit is saying to the churches. To everyone who conquers, I will give permission to eat from the tree of life that is in the paradise of God.

The Message to Smyrna

8 "And to the angel of the church in Smyrna write: These are the words of the first and the last, who was dead and came to life: 9 "I know your affliction and your poverty, even though you are rich. I know the slander on the part of those who say that they are Jews and are not, but are a synagogue of Satan. 10 Do not fear what you are about to suffer. Beware, the devil is about to throw some of you into prison so that you may be tested, and for ten days you will have affliction. Be faithful until death, and I will give you the crown of life. 11 Let anyone who has an ear listen to what the Spirit is saying to the churches. Whoever conquers will not be harmed by the second death.

The Message to Pergamum

12 "And to the angel of the church in Pergamum write: These are the words

σου τὴν πρώτην ἀφῆκας.
'of thee - ²first ¹thou didst leave.

οὖν πόθεν πέπτωκας, καὶ
therefore whence thou hast fallen, and

καὶ τὰ πρῶτα ἔργα ποίησον·
and ²the ³first ⁴works ¹do;

μή, ἔρχομαί σοι καὶ κινήσω τὴν λυχνίαν
not, I am coming to thee and will move the lampstand

σου ἐκ τοῦ τόπου αὐτῆς, ἐὰν μὴ
of thee out of the place of it, unless

μετανοήσῃς. 6 ἀλλὰ τοῦτο ἔχεις, ὅτι
thou repentest. But this thou hast, that

μισεῖς τὰ ἔργα τῶν Νικολαϊτῶν, ἃ
thou hatest the works of the Nicolaitans, which

κἀγὼ μισῶ. 7 'Ο ἔχων οὖς ἀκουσάτω
I also hate. The [one] having an ear let him hear

τί τὸ πνεῦμα λέγει ταῖς ἐκκλησίαις.
what the Spirit says to the churches.

Τῷ νικῶντι δώσω αὐτῷ φαγεῖν ἐκ
To overcoming I will give to him to eat of
the [one]

τοῦ ξύλου τῆς ζωῆς, ὅ ἐστιν ἐν τῷ
the tree - of life, which is in the

παραδείσῳ τοῦ θεοῦ.
paradise - of God.

5 μνημόνευε
Remember

καὶ μετανόησον
and repent

εἰ δὲ
¹do; and if

8 Καὶ τῷ ἀγγέλῳ τῆς ἐν Σμύρνῃ
And to the messenger ¹of the ²in ⁴Smyrna

ἐκκλησίας γράψον·
²church write thou:

Τάδε λέγει ὁ πρῶτος καὶ ὁ ἔσχατος,
These things says the first and the last,

ὃς ἐγένετο νεκρὸς καὶ ἔζησεν· 9 οἶδά
who became dead and lived [again]: I know

σου τὴν θλῖψιν καὶ τὴν πτωχείαν, ἀλλὰ
'of thee ¹the ²affliction ³and ⁴the ⁵poverty, but

πλούσιος εἶ, καὶ τὴν βλασφημίαν ἐκ
rich thou art, and the railing of

τῶν λεγόντων Ἰουδαίους εἶναι ἑαυτούς,
the [ones] say(call)ing ³Jews ²to be ¹themselves,

καὶ οὐκ εἰσὶν ἀλλὰ συναγωγὴ τοῦ σατανᾶ.
and they are not but a synagogue - of Satan.

10 μὴ φοβοῦ ἃ μέλλεις πάσχειν. ἰδοὺ
Do not fear [the] thou art to suffer. Behold[,]
things which about

μέλλει βάλλειν ὁ διάβολος ἐξ ὑμῶν
³is about ⁴to cast ¹the ²devil [some] of you

εἰς φυλακὴν ἵνα πειρασθῆτε, καὶ ἕξετε
into prison in order that ye may be tried, and ye will have

θλῖψιν ἡμερῶν δέκα. γίνου πιστὸς ἄχρι
affliction ²days ¹ten. Be thou faithful until

θανάτου, καὶ δώσω σοι τὸν στέφανον
death, and I will give thee the crown

τῆς ζωῆς. 11 'Ο ἔχων οὖς ἀκουσάτω
- of life. The [one] having an ear let him hear

τί τὸ πνεῦμα λέγει ταῖς ἐκκλησίαις.
what the Spirit says to the churches.

'Ο νικῶν οὐ μὴ ἀδικηθῇ ἐκ τοῦ θανάτου
The over- by no will be by the ²death
[one] coming means hurt

τοῦ δευτέρου.
- ¹second.

12 Καὶ τῷ ἀγγέλῳ τῆς ἐν Περγάμῳ
And to the messenger ¹of the ²in ⁴Pergamum

ἐκκλησίας γράψον·
²church write thou:

forsaken your first love. 5 Remember the height from which you have fallen! Repent and do the things you did at first. If you do not repent, I will come to you and remove your lampstand from its place. 6 But you have this in your favor: You hate the practices of the Nicolaitans, which I also hate.

7 He who has an ear, let him hear what the Spirit says to the churches. To him who overcomes, I will give the right to eat from the tree of life, which is in the paradise of God.

To the Church in Smyrna

8 "To the angel of the church in Smyrna write:

These are the words of him who is the First and the Last, who died and came to life again. 9 I know your afflictions and your poverty—yet you are rich! I know the slander of those who say they are Jews and are not, but are a synagogue of Satan. 10 Do not be afraid of what you are about to suffer. I tell you, the devil will put some of you in prison to test you, and you will suffer persecution for ten days. Be faithful, even to the point of death, and I will give you the crown of life.

11 He who has an ear, let him hear what the Spirit says to the churches. He who overcomes will not be hurt at all by the second death.

To the Church in Pergamum

12 "To the angel of the church in Pergamum write:

of him who has the sharp two-edged sword:
13 "I know where you are living, where Satan's throne is. Yet you are holding fast to my name, and you did not deny your faith in me[h] even in the days of Antipas my witness, my faithful one, who was killed among you, where Satan lives. 14 But I have a few things against you: you have some there who hold to the teaching of Balaam, who taught Balak to put a stumbling block before the people of Israel, so that they would eat food sacrificed to idols and practice fornication. 15 So you also have some who hold to the teaching of the Nicolaitans. 16 Repent then. If not, I will come to you soon and make war against them with the sword of my mouth. 17 Let anyone who has an ear listen to what the Spirit is saying to the churches. To everyone who conquers I will give some of the hidden manna, and I will give a white stone, and on the white stone is written a new name that no one knows except the one who receives it.

The Message to Thyatira

18 "And to the angel of the church in Thyatira write: These are the words of the Son of God, who has eyes like a flame of fire, and whose feet are like burnished bronze:
19 "I know your works—your love, faith, service, and patient endurance. I know that your last works are greater than the first. 20 But I have this

---

Τάδε λέγει ὁ ἔχων τὴν ῥομφαίαν τὴν
These things says the having the ²sword
           [one]

δίστομον τὴν ὀξεῖαν· 13 οἶδα ποῦ κατοικεῖς·
¹two-mouthed - ²sharp: I know where thou
(edged)   dwellest;

ὅπου ὁ θρόνος τοῦ σατανᾶ· καὶ κρατεῖς
where the throne - of Satan [is]; and thou holdest

τὸ ὄνομά μου, καὶ οὐκ ἠρνήσω τὴν
the name of me, and didst not deny the

πίστιν μου καὶ ἐν ταῖς ἡμέραις Ἀντιπᾶς
faith of me even in the days of Antipas

ὁ μάρτυς μου ὁ πιστός μου, ὃς
¹the ²witness ⁴of me the ³faithful of me, who

ἀπεκτάνθη παρ' ὑμῖν, ὅπου ὁ σατανᾶς
was killed among you, where - Satan

κατοικεῖ. 14 ἀλλ' ἔχω κατὰ σοῦ ὀλίγα,
dwells. But I have against thee a few
                                 things,

ὅτι ἔχεις ἐκεῖ κρατοῦντας τὴν διδαχὴν
be- thou there [ones] holding the teaching
cause hast

Βαλαάμ, ὃς ἐδίδασκεν τῷ Βαλὰκ βαλεῖν
of Balaam, who taught - Balak to cast

σκάνδαλον ἐνώπιον τῶν υἱῶν Ἰσραήλ,
a stumbling-block before the sons of Israel,

φαγεῖν εἰδωλόθυτα καὶ πορνεῦσαι. 15 οὕτως
to eat idol sacrifices and to commit fornication. So

ἔχεις καὶ σὺ κρατοῦντας τὴν διδαχὴν
²hast ³also ¹thou [ones] holding the teaching

τῶν Νικολαϊτῶν ὁμοίως. 16 μετανόησον
of the Nicolaitans likewise. Repent thou

οὖν· εἰ δὲ μή, ἔρχομαί σοι ταχὺ καὶ
therefore; otherwise, I am coming to thee quickly and

πολεμήσω μετ' αὐτῶν ἐν τῇ ῥομφαίᾳ
will fight with them with the sword

τοῦ στόματός μου. 17 Ὁ ἔχων οὖς
of the mouth of me. The [one] having an ear

ἀκουσάτω τί τὸ πνεῦμα λέγει ταῖς
let him hear what the Spirit says to the

ἐκκλησίαις. Τῷ νικῶντι δώσω αὐτῷ
churches. To the [one] overcoming I will give to him

τοῦ μάννα τοῦ κεκρυμμένου, καὶ δώσω
of the ²manna - ¹having been hidden, and I will give

αὐτῷ ψῆφον λευκήν, καὶ ἐπὶ τὴν ψῆφον
him ²stone ¹a white, and on the stone

ὄνομα καινὸν γεγραμμένον, ὃ οὐδεὶς οἶδεν
¹name ¹a new having been written, which no man knows

εἰ μὴ ὁ λαμβάνων.
except the [one] receiving [it].

18 Καὶ τῷ ἀγγέλῳ τῆς ἐν Θυατίροις
And to the messenger ¹of the ²in ⁴Thyatira

ἐκκλησίας γράψον·
³church write thou:

Τάδε λέγει ὁ υἱὸς τοῦ θεοῦ, ὁ ἔχων
These things says the Son - of God, the having
                                    [one]

τοὺς ὀφθαλμοὺς [αὐτοῦ] ὡς φλόγα πυρός,
the eyes of him as a flame of fire,

καὶ οἱ πόδες αὐτοῦ ὅμοιοι χαλκολιβάνῳ·
and the feet of him like to burnished brass:

19 οἶδά σου τὰ ἔργα καὶ τὴν ἀγάπην
I know of thee the works and the love

καὶ τὴν πίστιν καὶ τὴν διακονίαν καὶ
and the faith and the ministry and

τὴν ὑπομονήν σου, καὶ τὰ ἔργα σου
the endurance of thee, and the ²works ³of thee

τὰ ἔσχατα πλείονα τῶν πρώτων. 20 ἀλλὰ
the ¹last more [than] the first. But

These are the words of him who has the sharp, double-edged sword. 13 I know where you live—where Satan has his throne. Yet you remain true to my name. You did not renounce your faith in me, even in the days of Antipas, my faithful witness, who was put to death in your city—where Satan lives.
14 Nevertheless, I have a few things against you: You have people there who hold to the teaching of Balaam, who taught Balak to entice the Israelites to sin by eating food sacrificed to idols and by committing sexual immorality. 15 Likewise you also have those who hold to the teaching of the Nicolaitans. 16 Repent therefore! Otherwise, I will soon come to you and will fight against them with the sword of my mouth.
17 He who has an ear, let him hear what the Spirit says to the churches. To him who overcomes, I will give some of the hidden manna. I will also give him a white stone with a new name written on it, known only to him who receives it.

To the Church in Thyatira

18 "To the angel of the church in Thyatira write:

These are the words of the Son of God, whose eyes are like blazing fire and whose feet are like burnished bronze. 19 I know your deeds, your love and faith, your service and perseverance, and that you are now doing more than you did at first.

---

[h] Or deny my faith

against you: you tolerate that woman Jezebel, who calls herself a prophet and is teaching and beguiling my servants[i] to practice fornication and to eat food sacrificed to idols. 21 I gave her time to repent, but she refuses to repent of her fornication. 22 Beware, I am throwing her on a bed, and those who commit adultery with her I am throwing into great distress, unless they repent of her doings; 23 and I will strike her children dead. And all the churches will know that I am the one who searches minds and hearts, and I will give to each of you as your works deserve. 24 But to the rest of you in Thyatira, who do not hold this teaching, who have not learned what some call 'the deep things of Satan,' to you I say, I do not lay on you any other burden; 25 only hold fast to what you have until I come. 26 To everyone who conquers and continues to do my works to the end,

I will give authority
over
the nations;
27 to rule[j] them with an
iron rod,
as when clay pots
are shattered—
28 even as I also received authority from my Father. To the one who conquers I will also give the morning star. 29 Let anyone who has an ear listen to what the Spirit is saying to the churches.

ἔχω κατὰ σοῦ ὅτι ἀφεῖς τὴν γυναῖκα
I have against thee that thou permittest the woman
Ἰεζάβελ, ἡ λέγουσα ἑαυτὴν προφῆτιν,
Jezabel, the [one] say(call)ing herself a prophetess,
καὶ διδάσκει καὶ πλανᾷ τοὺς ἐμοὺς
and she teaches and deceives - my
δούλους πορνεῦσαι καὶ φαγεῖν εἰδωλόθυτα·
slaves to commit fornication and to eat idol sacrifices;
21 καὶ ἔδωκα αὐτῇ χρόνον ἵνα μετανοήσῃ,
and I gave her time in order she might
that repent,
καὶ οὐ θέλει μετανοῆσαι ἐκ τῆς πορνείας
and she wishes not to repent of the fornication
αὐτῆς. 22 ἰδοὺ βάλλω αὐτὴν εἰς κλίνην,
of her. Behold[,] I am casting her into a bed,
καὶ τοὺς μοιχεύοντας μετ' αὐτῆς εἰς
and the [ones] committing adultery with her into
θλῖψιν μεγάλην, ἐὰν μὴ μετανοήσουσιν
²affliction ¹great, unless they shall repent
ἐκ τῶν ἔργων αὐτῆς· 23 καὶ τὰ τέκνα
of the works of her; and the children
αὐτῆς ἀποκτενῶ ἐν θανάτῳ· καὶ γνώσονται
of her I will kill with death; and ⁴will know
πᾶσαι αἱ ἐκκλησίαι ὅτι ἐγώ εἰμι ὁ
¹all ²the ³churches that I am the
[one]
ἐρευνῶν νεφροὺς καὶ καρδίας, καὶ δώσω
searching kidneys and hearts, and I will give
ὑμῖν ἑκάστῳ κατὰ τὰ ἔργα ὑμῶν.
to you each one according to the works of you.
24 ὑμῖν δὲ λέγω τοῖς λοιποῖς τοῖς ἐν
But to you I say to the rest - in
Θυατίροις, ὅσοι οὐκ ἔχουσιν τὴν διδαχὴν
Thyatira, as many as have not - teaching
ταύτην, οἵτινες οὐκ ἔγνωσαν τὰ βαθέα
this, who knew not the deep things
τοῦ σατανᾶ, ὡς λέγουσιν· οὐ βάλλω
- of Satan, as they say: I am not casting
ἐφ' ὑμᾶς ἄλλο βάρος· 25 πλὴν ὃ ἔχετε
on you another burden; nevertheless what ye have
κρατήσατε ἄχρι οὗ ἂν ἥξω. 26 Καὶ
hold until I shall come. And
ὁ νικῶν καὶ ὁ τηρῶν ἄχρι τέλους τὰ
the over- and the keeping until [the] the
[one] coming [one] end
ἔργα μου, δώσω αὐτῷ ἐξουσίαν ἐπὶ
works of me, I will give him authority over
τῶν ἐθνῶν, 27 καὶ ποιμανεῖ αὐτοὺς ἐν
the nations, and he will shepherd them with
ῥάβδῳ σιδηρᾷ, ὡς τὰ σκεύη τὰ κεραμικὰ
²staff ¹an iron, as the ²vessels - ¹clay
συντρίβεται, ὡς κἀγὼ εἴληφα παρὰ
is(are) broken, as I also have received from
τοῦ πατρός μου, 28 καὶ δώσω αὐτῷ τὸν
the Father of me, and I will give him the
ἀστέρα τὸν πρωϊνόν. 29 Ὁ ἔχων οὖς
²star - ¹morning. The [one] having an ear
ἀκουσάτω τί τὸ πνεῦμα λέγει ταῖς
let him hear what the Spirit says to the
ἐκκλησίαις.
churches.

---

20 Nevertheless, I have this against you: You tolerate that woman Jezebel, who calls herself a prophetess. By her teaching she misleads my servants into sexual immorality and the eating of food sacrificed to idols. 21 I have given her time to repent of her immorality, but she is unwilling. 22 So I will cast her on a bed of suffering, and I will make those who commit adultery with her suffer intensely, unless they repent of her ways. 23 I will strike her children dead. Then all the churches will know that I am he who searches hearts and minds, and I will repay each of you according to your deeds. 24 Now I say to the rest of you in Thyatira, to you who do not hold to her teaching and have not learned Satan's so-called deep secrets (I will not impose any other burden on you): 25 Only hold on to what you have until I come.
26 To him who overcomes and does my will to the end, I will give authority over the nations—
27 'He will rule them
with an iron
scepter;
he will dash them
to pieces like
pottery'[e]—
just as I have received authority from my Father. 28 I will also give him the morning star. 29 He who has an ear, let him hear what the Spirit says to the churches.

Chapter 3

The Message to Sardis

" "AND to the angel of the church in Sardis write: These are the words of him who has the seven spirits of God and the seven stars: "I know your works; you have a name of being alive, but you are dead. 2 Wake up, and strengthen what remains and is on the point of death, for I have not found your works perfect in the sight of my God. 3 Remember then what you received and heard; obey it, and repent. If you do not wake up, I will come like a thief, and you will not know at what hour I will come to you. 4 Yet you have still a few persons in Sardis who have not soiled their clothes; they will walk with me, dressed in white, for they are worthy. 5 If you conquer, you will be clothed like them in white robes, and I will not blot your name out of the book of life; I will confess your name before my Father and before his angels. 6 Let anyone who has an ear listen to what the Spirit is saying to the churches.

The Message to Philadelphia

7 "And to the angel of the church in Philadelphia write:

These are the words
of the holy one,
the true one,
who has the key of David,
who opens and no one will shut,
who shuts and no one opens:

8 "I know your works. Look, I have set before you an open door, which no one is able to shut. I know that you have but little power, and yet you have kept my word and have not denied my name. 9 I will make those of the synagogue of

---

3 Καὶ   τῷ   ἀγγέλῳ   τῆς   ἐν   Σάρδεσιν
And   to the   messenger   [1]of the   [3]in   [4]Sardis
ἐκκλησίας   γράψον·
[2]church   write thou:

Τάδε   λέγει   ὁ   ἔχων   τὰ   ἑπτὰ   πνεύματα
These things says   the   having   the   seven   Spirits
[one]

τοῦ   θεοῦ   καὶ   τοὺς   ἑπτὰ   ἀστέρας·   οἶδά
-    of God   and   the   seven   stars: I know

σου   τὰ   ἔργα,   ὅτι   ὄνομα   ἔχεις   ὅτι   ζῆς,
[3]of   [1]the   [2]works,   that   a name   thou   that   thou
thee   hast   livest,

καὶ   νεκρὸς   εἶ.   2 γίνου   γρηγορῶν,   καὶ
and [yet]   [2]dead   [1]thou art.   Be thou   watching,   and

στήρισον   τὰ   λοιπὰ   ἃ   ἔμελλον   ἀποθανεῖν·
establish   the   remain-   which   were   to die;
things   ing   about

οὐ   γὰρ   εὕρηκά   σου   ἔργα   πεπληρωμένα
for I have not found   of thee   works   having been fulfilled

ἐνώπιον   τοῦ   θεοῦ   μου·   3 μνημόνευε   οὖν
before   the   God   of me;   remember   therefore

πῶς   εἴληφας   καὶ   ἤκουσας,   καὶ   τήρει
how thou hast received   and   didst hear,   and   keep

καὶ   μετανόησον.   ἐὰν   οὖν   μὴ   γρηγορήσῃς,
and   repent.   If   therefore   thou dost not watch,

ἥξω   ὡς   κλέπτης,   καὶ   οὐ   μὴ   γνῷς   ποίαν
I will   as   a thief,   and   by no   thou   at what
come   means   knowest

ὥραν   ἥξω   ἐπὶ   σέ.   4 ἀλλὰ   ἔχεις   ὀλίγα
hour   I will come   on   thee.   But   thou hast   a few

ὀνόματα   ἐν   Σάρδεσιν   ἃ   οὐκ   ἐμόλυναν   τὰ
names   in   Sardis   which   did not defile   the

ἱμάτια   αὐτῶν,   καὶ   περιπατήσουσιν   μετ'
garments   of them,   and   they shall walk   with

ἐμοῦ   ἐν   λευκοῖς,   ὅτι   ἄξιοί   εἰσιν.   5 Ὁ
me   in   white   because   [3]worthy   [1]they are.   The
[garments],   [one]

νικῶν   οὕτως   περιβαλεῖται   ἐν   ἱματίοις
overcoming   [3]thus   [1]shall be clothed   in   [2]garments

λευκοῖς,   καὶ   οὐ   μὴ   ἐξαλείψω   τὸ   ὄνομα
[1]white,   and   by no means will I blot   out   the   name

αὐτοῦ   ἐκ   τῆς   βίβλου   τῆς   ζωῆς,   καὶ
of him   out of   the   scroll   -   of life,   and

ὁμολογήσω   τὸ   ὄνομα   αὐτοῦ   ἐνώπιον   τοῦ
I will confess   the   name   of him   before   the

πατρός   μου   καὶ   ἐνώπιον   τῶν   ἀγγέλων
Father   of me   and   before   the   angels

αὐτοῦ.   6 Ὁ   ἔχων   οὓς   ἀκουσάτω   τί   τὸ
of him.   The [one] having   an ear   let him hear   what   the

πνεῦμα   λέγει   ταῖς   ἐκκλησίαις.
Spirit   says   to the   churches.

7 Καὶ   τῷ   ἀγγέλῳ   τῆς   ἐν   Φιλαδελφείᾳ
And   to the   messenger   [1]of the   [3]in   [4]Philadelphia
ἐκκλησίας   γράψον·
[2]church   write thou:

Τάδε   λέγει   ὁ   ἅγιος,   ὁ   ἀληθινός,   ὁ
These   says   the   holy   the   true   the
things   [one],   [one],   [one]

ἔχων   τὴν   κλεῖν   Δαυίδ,   ὁ   ἀνοίγων   καὶ
having   the   key   of David,   the [one]   opening   and

οὐδεὶς   κλείσει,   καὶ   κλείων   καὶ   οὐδεὶς
no one   shall shut,   and   shutting   and   no one

ἀνοίγει·   8 οἶδά   σου   τὰ   ἔργα·   ἰδοὺ
opens: I know   of thee   the   works; behold[,]

δέδωκα   ἐνώπιόν   σου   θύραν   ἠνεῳγμένην,
I have given   before   thee   a door   having been   opened,

---

Chapter 3

To the Church in Sardis

" "TO the angel[f] of the church in Sardis write:

These are the words of him who holds the seven spirits[g] of God and the seven stars. I know your deeds; you have a reputation of being alive, but you are dead. 2 Wake up! Strengthen what remains and is about to die, for I have not found your deeds complete in the sight of my God. 3 Remember, therefore, what you have received and heard; obey it, and repent. But if you do not wake up, I will come like a thief, and you will not know at what time I will come to you.

4 Yet you have a few people in Sardis who have not soiled their clothes. They will walk with me, dressed in white, for they are worthy. 5 He who overcomes will, like them, be dressed in white. I will never blot out his name from the book of life, but will acknowledge his name before my Father and his angels. 6 He who has an ear, let him hear what the Spirit says to the churches.

To the Church in Philadelphia

7 "To the angel of the church in Philadelphia write:

These are the words of him who is holy and true, who holds the key of David. What he opens no one can shut, and what he shuts no one can open. 8 I know your deeds. See, I have placed before you an open door that no one can shut. I know that you have little strength, yet you have kept my word and have not denied my name. 9 I will make those who are of the synagogue of Satan,

Satan who say that they are Jews and are not, but are lying—I will make them come and bow down before your feet, and they will learn that I have loved you. 10 Because you have kept my word of patient endurance, I will keep you from the hour of trial that is coming on the whole world to test the inhabitants of the earth. 11 I am coming soon; hold fast to what you have, so that no one may seize your crown. 12 If you conquer, I will make you a pillar in the temple of my God; you will never go out of it. I will write on you the name of my God, and the name of the city of my God, the new Jerusalem that comes down from my God out of heaven, and my own new name. 13 Let anyone who has an ear listen to what the Spirit is saying to the churches.

The Message to Laodicea

14 "And to the angel of the church in Laodicea write: The words of the Amen, the faithful and true witness, the origin[k] of God's creation:

15 "I know your works;

ἦν οὐδεὶς δύναται κλεῖσαι αὐτήν· ὅτι
which no one can *to* shut *it;* because

μικρὰν ἔχεις δύναμιν, καὶ ἐτήρησάς μου
¹a little ¹thou hast power, and didst keep of me

τὸν λόγον καὶ οὐκ ἠρνήσω τὸ ὄνομά
the word and didst not deny the name

μου. 9 ἰδοὺ διδῶ ἐκ τῆς συναγωγῆς
of me. Behold[,] I may [some] the synagogue
(will) give of

τοῦ σατανᾶ, τῶν λεγόντων ἑαυτοὺς
– of Satan, the [ones] say/(call)ing themselves

'Ιουδαίους εἶναι, καὶ οὐκ εἰσὶν ἀλλὰ
Jews to be, and they are not but

ψεύδονται· ἰδοὺ ποιήσω αὐτοὺς ἵνα
they lie; behold[,] I will make them *in order that*

ἥξουσιν καὶ προσκυνήσουσιν ἐνώπιον τῶν
they shall and *they* shall worship before the
come

ποδῶν σου, καὶ γνῶσιν ὅτι ἐγὼ ἠγάπησά
feet of thee, and *they* that I loved
shall know

σε. 10 ὅτι ἐτήρησας τὸν λόγον τῆς
thee. Because thou didst keep the word of the

ὑπομονῆς μου, κἀγώ σε τηρήσω ἐκ
endurance of me, I also ²thee ¹will keep out of

τῆς ὥρας τοῦ πειρασμοῦ τῆς μελλούσης
the hour – of trial – *being about*

ἔρχεσθαι ἐπὶ τῆς οἰκουμένης ὅλης, πειράσαι
to come on ²the ³inhabited [earth] ¹all, to try

τοὺς κατοικοῦντας ἐπὶ τῆς γῆς. 11 ἔρχομαι
the [ones] dwelling on the earth. I am coming

ταχύ· κράτει ὃ ἔχεις, ἵνα μηδεὶς λάβῃ
quickly; hold what thou in order no one takes
hast, that

τὸν στέφανόν σου. 12 'Ο νικῶν, ποιήσω
the crown of thee. The [one] overcoming, I will make

αὐτὸν στῦλον ἐν τῷ ναῷ τοῦ θεοῦ
him a pillar in the shrine of the God

μου, καὶ ἔξω οὐ μὴ ἐξέλθῃ ἔτι, καὶ
of me, and out by no he will [any] and
means go forth longer,

γράψω ἐπ' αὐτὸν τὸ ὄνομα τοῦ θεοῦ
I will write on him the name of the God

μου καὶ τὸ ὄνομα τῆς πόλεως τοῦ
of me and the name of the city of the

θεοῦ μου, τῆς καινῆς 'Ιερουσαλὴμ ἡ
God of me, *of the* new Jerusalem –

καταβαίνουσα ἐκ τοῦ οὐρανοῦ ἀπὸ τοῦ
descending out of heaven from the

θεοῦ μου, καὶ τὸ ὄνομά μου τὸ καινόν.
God of me, and ¹the ³name ⁴of me – ²new.

13 'Ο ἔχων οὖς ἀκουσάτω τί τὸ πνεῦμα
The [one] having an ear let him hear what the Spirit

λέγει ταῖς ἐκκλησίαις.
says to the churches.

14 Καὶ τῷ ἀγγέλῳ τῆς ἐν Λαοδικείᾳ
And to the messenger ¹of the ²in ⁴Laodicea

ἐκκλησίας γράψον·
³church write thou:

Τάδε λέγει ὁ ἀμήν, ὁ μάρτυς ὁ
These things says the Amen, the ⁴witness the

πιστὸς καὶ ἀληθινός, ἡ ἀρχὴ τῆς κτίσεως
¹faithful ²and ³true, the chief of the creation

τοῦ θεοῦ· 15 οἶδά σου τὰ ἔργα, ὅτι
– of God: I know of thee the works, that

---

who claim to be Jews though they are not, but are liars—I will make them come and fall down at your feet, and acknowledge that I have loved you. 10 Since you have kept my command to endure patiently, I will also keep you from the hour of trial that is going to come upon the whole world to test those who live on the earth. 11 I am coming soon. Hold on to what you have, so that no one will take your crown. 12 Him who overcomes I will make a pillar in the temple of my God. Never again will he leave it. I will write on him the name of my God and the name of the city of my God, the new Jerusalem, which is coming down out of heaven from my God; and I will also write on him my new name. 13 He who has an ear, let him hear what the Spirit says to the churches.

To the Church in Laodicea

14 "To the angel of the church in Laodicea write:

These are the words of the Amen, the faithful and true witness, the ruler of God's creation. 15 I know your deeds,

---

you are neither cold nor hot. I wish that you were either cold or hot. ¹⁶ So, because you are lukewarm, and neither cold nor hot, I am about to spit you out of my mouth. ¹⁷ For you say, 'I am rich, I have prospered, and I need nothing.' You do not realize that you are wretched, pitiable, poor, blind, and naked. ¹⁸ Therefore I counsel you to buy from me gold refined by fire so that you may be rich; and white robes to clothe you and to keep the shame of your nakedness from being seen; and salve to anoint your eyes so that you may see. ¹⁹ I reprove and discipline those whom I love. Be earnest, therefore, and repent. ²⁰ Listen! I am standing at the door, knocking; if you hear my voice and open the door, I will come in to you and eat with you, and you with me. ²¹ To the one who conquers I will give a place with me on my throne, just as I myself conquered and sat down with my Father on his throne. ²² Let anyone who has an ear listen to what the Spirit is saying to the churches."

οὔτε ψυχρὸς εἶ οὔτε ζεστός. ὄφελον
neither cold art thou nor hot. I would that†

ψυχρὸς ἦς ἢ ζεστός. **16** οὕτως ὅτι
cold thou wast or hot. So because

χλιαρὸς εἶ, καὶ οὔτε ζεστὸς οὔτε ψυχρός,
lukewarm thou art, and neither hot nor cold,

μέλλω σε ἐμέσαι ἐκ τοῦ στόματός μου.
I am ²thee ¹to vomit out of the mouth of me.
about*

17 ὅτι λέγεις ὅτι πλούσιός εἰμι καὶ
Because thou sayest[,] ²rich ¹I am and

πεπλούτηκα καὶ οὐδὲν χρείαν ἔχω, καὶ
I have become rich and ²no ³need ¹I have, and

οὐκ οἶδας ὅτι σὺ εἶ ὁ ταλαίπωρος
knowest not that thou art the [one] wretched

καὶ ἐλεεινὸς καὶ πτωχὸς καὶ τυφλὸς
and pitiable and poor and blind

καὶ γυμνός, **18** συμβουλεύω σοι ἀγοράσαι
and naked, I counsel thee to buy

παρ' ἐμοῦ χρυσίον πεπυρωμένον ἐκ πυρὸς
from me gold having been refined by fire
by fire

ἵνα πλουτήσῃς, καὶ ἱμάτια λευκὰ ἵνα
in or- thou mayest and ²garments ¹white in order
der that be rich, that

περιβάλῃ καὶ μὴ φανερωθῇ ἡ αἰσχύνη
thou mayest and ²may not be ¹the ²shame
be clothed manifested

τῆς γυμνότητός σου, καὶ κολλύριον
³of the ⁴nakedness ⁵of thee, and eyesalve

ἐγχρῖσαι τοὺς ὀφθαλμούς σου ἵνα βλέπῃς.
to anoint the eyes of in order thou
thee that mayest see.

19 ἐγὼ ὅσους ἐὰν φιλῶ ἐλέγχω καὶ
¹I ¹as many as love I rebuke and

παιδεύω· ζήλευε οὖν καὶ μετανόησον.
I chasten; be hot therefore and repent thou.

20 Ἰδοὺ ἕστηκα ἐπὶ τὴν θύραν καὶ
Behold[,] I stand at the door and

κρούω· ἐάν τις ἀκούσῃ τῆς φωνῆς μου
I knock; if anyone hears the voice of me

καὶ ἀνοίξῃ τὴν θύραν, εἰσελεύσομαι πρὸς
and opens the door, I will enter to

αὐτὸν καὶ δειπνήσω μετ' αὐτοῦ καὶ
him and I will dine with him and

αὐτὸς μετ' ἐμοῦ. **21** Ὁ νικῶν, δώσω
he with me. The [one] overcoming, I will
give

αὐτῷ καθίσαι μετ' ἐμοῦ ἐν τῷ θρόνῳ
him to sit with me in the throne

μου, ὡς κἀγὼ ἐνίκησα καὶ ἐκάθισα
of me, as I also overcame and sat

μετὰ τοῦ πατρός μου ἐν τῷ θρόνῳ
with the Father of me in the throne

αὐτοῦ. **22** Ὁ ἔχων οὖς ἀκουσάτω τί
of him. The [one] having an ear let him hear what

τὸ πνεῦμα λέγει ταῖς ἐκκλησίαις.
the Spirit says to the churches.

Chapter 4
The Heavenly Worship

AFTER this I looked, and there in heaven a door stood open! And the first voice, which I had heard speaking to me like a trumpet, said, "Come up

4 Μετὰ ταῦτα εἶδον, καὶ ἰδοὺ θύρα
After these things I saw, and behold[,] a door

ἠνεῳγμένη ἐν τῷ οὐρανῷ, καὶ ἡ φωνὴ
having been in - heaven, and the ¹voice
opened

ἡ πρώτη ἣν ἤκουσα ὡς σάλπιγγος
- ¹first which I heard as of a trumpet

---

that you are neither cold nor hot. I wish you were either one or the other! ¹⁶ So, because you are lukewarm—neither hot nor cold—I am about to spit you out of my mouth. ¹⁷ You say, 'I am rich; I have acquired wealth and do not need a thing.' But you do not realize that you are wretched, pitiful, poor, blind and naked. ¹⁸ I counsel you to buy from me gold refined in the fire, so you can become rich; and white clothes to wear, so you can cover your shameful nakedness; and salve to put on your eyes, so you can see. ¹⁹ Those whom I love I rebuke and discipline. So be earnest, and repent. ²⁰ Here I am! I stand at the door and knock. If anyone hears my voice and opens the door, I will come in and eat with him, and he with me. ²¹ To him who overcomes, I will give the right to sit with me on my throne, just as I overcame and sat down with my Father on his throne. ²² He who has an ear, let him hear what the Spirit says to the churches."

Chapter 4
The Throne in Heaven

AFTER this I looked, and there before me was a door standing open in heaven. And the voice I had first heard speaking to me like a

---

* As so often (see also ch. 1. 19, 2. 10), this verb does not necessarily connote imminence, but only simple futurity.

here, and I will show you what must take place after this." 2At once I was in the spirit,¹ and there in heaven stood a throne, with one seated on the throne! 3 And the one seated there looks like jasper and carnelian, and around the throne is a rainbow that looks like an emerald. 4 Around the throne are twenty-four thrones, and seated on the thrones are twenty-four elders, dressed in white robes, with golden crowns on their heads. 5 Coming from the throne are flashes of lightning, and rumblings and peals of thunder, and in front of the throne burn seven flaming torches, which are the seven spirits of God; 6 and in front of the throne there is something like a sea of glass, like crystal.

Around the throne, and on each side of the throne, are four living creatures, full of eyes in front and behind: 7 the first living creature like a lion, the second living creature like an ox, the third living creature with a face like a human face, and the fourth living creature like a flying eagle. 8 And the four living creatures, each of them with six wings, are full of eyes all around and inside. Day and night without ceasing they sing,

λαλούσης μετ' ἐμοῦ, λέγων· ἀνάβα ὧδε,
speaking with me, saying: Come up here,

καὶ δείξω σοι ἃ δεῖ γενέσθαι μετὰ
and I will show thee things it be- to occur after
which hoves

ταῦτα. εὐθέως ἐγενόμην ἐν πνεύματι·
these things. Immediately I became in spirit;

2 καὶ ἰδοὺ θρόνος ἔκειτο ἐν τῷ οὐρανῷ,
and behold[,] a throne was set in heaven,

καὶ ἐπὶ τὸν θρόνον καθήμενος, 3 καὶ
and on the throne a sitting [one], and

ὁ καθήμενος ὅμοιος ὁράσει λίθῳ ἰάσπιδι
the [one] sitting [was] like in appearance ⁴stone ¹to a jasper

καὶ σαρδίῳ, καὶ ἶρις κυκλόθεν τοῦ
²and ³a sardius, and a rain- round the
bow [there was]

θρόνου ὅμοιος ὁράσει σμαραγδίνῳ. 4 καὶ
throne like in appearance to an emerald. And

κυκλόθεν τοῦ θρόνου θρόνους εἴκοσι
round the throne [I saw] ²thrones ¹twenty-

τέσσαρας, καὶ ἐπὶ τοὺς θρόνους εἴκοσι
four, and on the thrones twenty-

τέσσαρας πρεσβυτέρους καθημένους περι-
four elders sitting having been

βεβλημένους ἐν ἱματίοις λευκοῖς, καὶ ἐπὶ
clothed in garments white, and on

τὰς κεφαλὰς αὐτῶν στεφάνους χρυσοῦς·
the heads of them ²crowns ¹golden.

5 καὶ ἐκ τοῦ θρόνου ἐκπορεύονται ἀστραπαὶ
And out of the throne come forth lightnings

καὶ φωναὶ καὶ βρονταί· καὶ ἑπτὰ λαμπάδες
and voices* and thunders; and seven lamps

πυρὸς καιόμεναι ἐνώπιον τοῦ θρόνου, ἃ
of fire [are] burning before the throne, which

εἰσιν τὰ ἑπτὰ πνεύματα τοῦ θεοῦ· 6 καὶ
are the seven Spirits – of God; and

ἐνώπιον τοῦ θρόνου ὡς θάλασσα ὑαλίνη
before the throne as ²sea ¹a glassy

ὁμοία κρυστάλλῳ· καὶ ἐν μέσῳ τοῦ
like to crystal; and in [the] midst of the

θρόνου καὶ κύκλῳ τοῦ θρόνου τέσσερα
throne and round the throne four

ζῷα γέμοντα ὀφθαλμῶν ἔμπροσθεν καὶ
living filling(full) of eyes before and
creatures

ὄπισθεν. 7 καὶ τὸ ζῷον τὸ πρῶτον
behind. And the ²living – ¹first
creature

ὅμοιον λέοντι, καὶ τὸ δεύτερον ζῷον
[was] to a lion, and the second living
like creature

ὅμοιον μόσχῳ, καὶ τὸ τρίτον ζῷον ἔχων
like to a calf, and the third living having
creature

τὸ πρόσωπον ὡς ἀνθρώπου, καὶ τὸ
the(its) face as of a man, and the

τέταρτον ζῷον ὅμοιον ἀετῷ πετομένῳ.
fourth living creature like eagle to a flying.

8 καὶ τὰ τέσσερα ζῷα, ἓν καθ' ἓν
And the four living one by one
creatures,

αὐτῶν ἔχων ἀνὰ πτέρυγας ἕξ, κυκλόθεν
of them having each ²wings ¹six, around

καὶ ἔσωθεν γέμουσιν ὀφθαλμῶν· καὶ
and within are full of eyes; and

ἀνάπαυσιν οὐκ ἔχουσιν ἡμέρας καὶ νυκτὸς
respite they have not day and night

trumpet said, "Come up here, and I will show you what must take place after this." 2At once I was in the Spirit, and there before me was a throne in heaven with someone sitting on it. 3And the one who sat there had the appearance of jasper and carnelian. A rainbow, resembling an emerald, encircled the throne. 4Surrounding the throne were twenty-four other thrones, and seated on them were twenty-four elders. They were dressed in white and had crowns of gold on their heads. 5From the throne came flashes of lightning, rumblings and peals of thunder. Before the throne, seven lamps were blazing. These are the seven spiritsʰ of God. 6Also before the throne there was what looked like a sea of glass, clear as crystal.

In the center, around the throne, were four living creatures, and they were covered with eyes, in front and in back. 7The first living creature was like a lion, the second was like an ox, the third had a face like a man, the fourth was like a flying eagle. 8Each of the four living creatures had six wings and was covered with eyes all around, even under his wings. Day and night they never stop saying:

¹Or in the Spirit

* Or "sounds"; and so elsewhere.

ʰ5 Or the sevenfold Spirit

"Holy, holy, holy,
the Lord God the
Almighty,
who was and is and
is to come."
9 And whenever the living
creatures give glory and
honor and thanks to the one
who is seated on the
throne, who lives forever
and ever, 10 the twenty-four
elders fall before the one
who is seated on the throne
and worship the one who
lives forever and ever; they
cast their crowns before
the throne, singing,
11 "You are worthy, our
Lord and God,
to receive glory and
honor
and power,
for you created all
things,
and by your will
they existed and
were created."

λέγοντες·   ἅγιος   ἅγιος   ἅγιος   κύριος   ὁ
saying: Holy[,]   holy[,] holy[,] Lord   –

θεὸς   ὁ   παντοκράτωρ,   ὁ   ἦν   καὶ   ὁ   ὢν
God   the   Almighty,   the was   and   the being
                               [one who]   [one]
                                            = the one who is

καὶ   ὁ   ἐρχόμενος.   9 Καὶ   ὅταν   δώσουσιν
and   the   coming [one].   And   whenever ³shall give

τὰ   ζῷα   δόξαν   καὶ   τιμὴν   καὶ   εὐχαριστίαν
¹the ²living glory   and   honour   and   thanks
      creatures

τῷ   καθημένῳ   ἐπὶ   τῷ   θρόνῳ   τῷ   ζῶντι
to the sitting   on   the   throne[,] to the living
[one]   [one]

εἰς   τοὺς   αἰῶνας   τῶν   αἰώνων,   10 πεσοῦνται
unto   the   ages   of the ages,   ⁴will fall

οἱ   εἴκοσι   τέσσαρες   πρεσβύτεροι   ἐνώπιον
¹the ²twenty-four   ³elders   before

τοῦ   καθημένου   ἐπὶ   τοῦ   θρόνου,   καὶ
the [one] sitting   on   the   throne,   and

προσκυνήσουσιν   τῷ   ζῶντι   εἰς   τοὺς   αἰῶνας
they will worship   the [one] living unto   the   ages

τῶν   αἰώνων,   καὶ   βαλοῦσιν   τοὺς   στεφάνους
of the ages,   and   will cast   the   crowns

αὐτῶν   ἐνώπιον   τοῦ   θρόνου,   λέγοντες·
of them   before   the   throne,   saying:

11 ἄξιος   εἶ,   ὁ   κύριος   καὶ   ὁ   θεὸς   ἡμῶν,
Worthy art thou, the Lord   and   the God   of us,

λαβεῖν   τὴν   δόξαν   καὶ   τὴν   τιμὴν   καὶ
to receive the   glory   and   the   honour   and

τὴν   δύναμιν,   ὅτι   σὺ   ἔκτισας   τὰ   πάντα,*
the   power,   because thou createdst   –   all things,*

καὶ   διὰ   τὸ   θέλημά   σου   ἦσαν   καὶ
and   on ac-   the   will   of thee they were and
       count of

ἐκτίσθησαν.
they were created.

Chapter 5

The Scroll and the Lamb

THEN I saw in the right
hand of the one seated
on the throne a scroll written on the inside and on the
back, sealed ᵐ with seven
seals; 2 and I saw a mighty
angel proclaiming with a
loud voice, "Who is worthy
to open the scroll and break
its seals?" 3 And no one in
heaven or on earth or under
the earth was able to open
the scroll or to look into it.
4 And I began to weep bitterly because no one was
found worthy to open the
scroll or to look into it.
5 Then one of the elders
said to me, "Do not weep.
See, the Lion of the tribe of

---

5 Καὶ   εἶδον   ἐπὶ   τὴν   δεξιὰν   τοῦ
And   I saw   on   the   right   of the
                                  [hand]   [one]

καθημένου   ἐπὶ   τοῦ   θρόνου   βιβλίον
sitting   on   the   throne   a scroll

γεγραμμένον   ἔσωθεν   καὶ   ὄπισθεν,
having been written within   and   on the reverse side,

κατεσφραγισμένον   σφραγῖσιν   ἑπτά.   2 καὶ
having been sealed   with ²seals   ¹seven.   And

εἶδον   ἄγγελον   ἰσχυρὸν   κηρύσσοντα   ἐν
I saw   angel   a strong   proclaiming   in

φωνῇ   μεγάλῃ·   τίς   ἄξιος   ἀνοῖξαι   τὸ
¹voice   ¹a great(loud): Who [is] worthy to open   the

βιβλίον   καὶ   λῦσαι   τὰς   σφραγῖδας   αὐτοῦ;
scroll   and   to loosen   the   seals   of it?

3 καὶ   οὐδεὶς   ἐδύνατο   ἐν   τῷ   οὐρανῷ
And   no one   was able   in   –   heaven

οὐδὲ   ἐπὶ   τῆς   γῆς   οὐδὲ   ὑποκάτω   τῆς
nor   on   the   earth   nor   underneath   the

γῆς   ἀνοῖξαι   τὸ   βιβλίον   οὔτε   βλέπειν
earth   to open   the   scroll   nor to see(look at)

αὐτό.   4 καὶ   ἔκλαιον   πολύ,   ὅτι   οὐδεὶς
it.   And   I wept   much,   because no one

ἄξιος   εὑρέθη   ἀνοῖξαι   τὸ   βιβλίον   οὔτε
worthy   was found   to open   the   scroll   nor

βλέπειν   αὐτό.   5 καὶ   εἷς   ἐκ   τῶν   πρεσ-
to look at   it.   And   one   of   the   el-

βυτέρων   λέγει   μοι·   μὴ   κλαῖε·   ἰδοὺ
ders   says   to me: Weep not;   behold[,]

"Holy, holy, holy
is the Lord God Almighty,
who was, and is, and is to
come."
9 Whenever the living creatures give glory, honor and
thanks to him who sits on
the throne and who lives
for ever and ever, 10 the
twenty-four elders fall
down before him who sits
on the throne, and worship
him who lives for ever and
ever. They lay their crowns
before the throne and say:

11 "You are worthy, our
Lord and God,
to receive glory and
honor and power,
for you created all
things,
and by your will they
were created
and have their being."

Chapter 5

The Scroll and the Lamb

THEN I saw in the right
hand of him who sat on
the throne a scroll with
writing on both sides and
sealed with seven seals.
2 And I saw a mighty angel
proclaiming in a loud voice,
"Who is worthy to break
the seals and open the
scroll?" 3 But no one in
heaven or on earth or under
the earth could open the
scroll or even look inside it.
4 I wept and wept because
no one was found who was
worthy to open the scroll or
look inside. 5 Then one of
the elders said to me, "Do
not weep! See, the Lion of

ᵐ Or written on the inside, and
sealed on the back

* τὰ πάντα = the universe

Judah, the Root of David, has conquered, so that he can open the scroll and its seven seals."

6 Then I saw between the throne and the four living creatures and among the elders a Lamb standing as if it had been slaughtered, having seven horns and seven eyes, which are the seven spirits of God sent out into all the earth. 7 He went and took the scroll from the right hand of the one who was seated on the throne. 8 When he had taken the scroll, the four living creatures and the twenty-four elders fell before the Lamb, each holding a harp and golden bowls full of incense, which are the prayers of the saints. 9 They sing a new song:

"You are worthy to take the scroll and to open its seals, for you were slaughtered and by your blood you ransomed for God saints from[n] every tribe and language and people and nation;

10 you have made them to be a kingdom and priests serving[o] our God, and they will reign on earth."

11 Then I looked, and I heard the voice of many angels surrounding the throne and the living creatures and the elders; they numbered myriads of myriads and thousands of thousands, 12 singing with full voice, "Worthy is the Lamb that was slaughtered to receive power and

---

ἐνίκησεν ὁ λέων ὁ ἐκ τῆς φυλῆς Ἰούδα,
10overcame 1the 2Lion – 3of 4the 5tribe 6Juda,

ἡ ῥίζα Δαυίδ, ἀνοῖξαι τὸ βιβλίον καὶ
7the 8root 9of David, to open the scroll and

τὰς ἑπτὰ σφραγῖδας αὐτοῦ. 6 Καὶ εἶδον
the seven seals of it. And I saw

ἐν μέσῳ τοῦ θρόνου καὶ τῶν τεσσάρων
in [the] midst of the throne and of the four

ζῴων καὶ ἐν μέσῳ τῶν πρεσβυτέρων
living creatures and in [the] midst of the elders

ἀρνίον ἑστηκὸς ὡς ἐσφαγμένον, ἔχων
a Lamb standing as having been slain, having

κέρατα ἑπτὰ καὶ ὀφθαλμοὺς ἑπτά, οἳ
2horns 1seven and 2eyes 1seven, which

εἰσιν τὰ ἑπτὰ πνεύματα τοῦ θεοῦ
are the seven Spirits – of God

ἀπεσταλμένοι εἰς πᾶσαν τὴν γῆν. 7 καὶ
having been sent forth into all the earth. And

ἦλθεν καὶ εἴληφεν ἐκ τῆς δεξιᾶς τοῦ
he came and has taken out of the right [hand] of the

καθημένου ἐπὶ τοῦ θρόνου. 8 Καὶ ὅτε
[one] sitting on the throne. And when

ἔλαβεν τὸ βιβλίον, τὰ τέσσερα ζῷα
he took the scroll, the four living creatures

καὶ οἱ εἴκοσι τέσσαρες πρεσβύτεροι ἔπεσαν
and the twenty-four elders fell

ἐνώπιον τοῦ ἀρνίου, ἔχοντες ἕκαστος
before the Lamb, having each one

κιθάραν καὶ φιάλας χρυσᾶς γεμούσας
a harp and 2bowls 1golden being full

θυμιαμάτων, αἵ εἰσιν αἱ προσευχαὶ τῶν
of incenses, which are the prayers of the

ἁγίων. 9 καὶ ἄδουσιν ᾠδὴν καινὴν
saints. And they sing 2song 1a new

λέγοντες· ἄξιος εἶ λαβεῖν τὸ βιβλίον
saying: Worthy art thou to receive the scroll

καὶ ἀνοῖξαι τὰς σφραγῖδας αὐτοῦ, ὅτι
and to open the seals of it, because

ἐσφάγης καὶ ἠγόρασας τῷ θεῷ ἐν τῷ
thou wast slain and didst purchase – to God by the

αἵματί σου ἐκ πάσης φυλῆς καὶ γλώσσης
blood of thee out of every tribe and tongue

καὶ λαοῦ καὶ ἔθνους, 10 καὶ ἐποίησας
and people and nation, and didst make

αὐτοὺς τῷ θεῷ ἡμῶν βασιλείαν καὶ
them to the God of us a kingdom and

ἱερεῖς, καὶ βασιλεύσουσιν ἐπὶ τῆς γῆς.
priests, and they will reign on(? over) the earth.

11 καὶ εἶδον, καὶ ἤκουσα φωνὴν ἀγγέλων
And I saw, and I heard a sound 2angels

πολλῶν κύκλῳ τοῦ θρόνου καὶ τῶν
1of many round the throne and the

ζῴων καὶ τῶν πρεσβυτέρων, καὶ ἦν
living creatures and the elders, and 4was

ὁ ἀριθμὸς αὐτῶν μυριάδες μυριάδων καὶ
1the 2number 3of them myriads of myriads and

χιλιάδες χιλιάδων, 12 λέγοντες φωνῇ
thousands of thousands, saying 2voice

μεγάλη· ἄξιός ἐστιν τὸ ἀρνίον τὸ
1with a great Worthy is the Lamb –
(loud)

ἐσφαγμένον λαβεῖν τὴν δύναμιν καὶ πλοῦτον
having been slain to receive the power and riches

---

the tribe of Judah, the Root of David, has triumphed. He is able to open the scroll and its seven seals."

6 Then I saw a Lamb, looking as if it had been slain, standing in the center of the throne, encircled by the four living creatures and the elders. He had seven horns and seven eyes, which are the seven spirits[i] of God sent out into all the earth. 7 He came and took the scroll from the right hand of him who sat on the throne. 8 And when he had taken it, the four living creatures and the twenty-four elders fell down before the Lamb. Each one had a harp and they were holding golden bowls full of incense, which are the prayers of the saints. 9 And they sang a new song:

"You are worthy to take the scroll and to open its seals, because you were slain, and with your blood you purchased men for God from every tribe and language and people and nation.

10 You have made them to be a kingdom and priests to serve our God, and they will reign on the earth."

11 Then I looked and heard the voice of many angels, numbering thousands upon thousands, and ten thousand times ten thousand. They encircled the throne and the living creatures and the elders. 12 In a loud voice they sang:

"Worthy is the Lamb, who was slain, to receive power and

---

n Gk ransomed for God from
o Gk priests to

i 6 Or the sevenfold Spirit

wealth and
wisdom and
might
and honor and glory
and blessing!"
13 Then I heard every creature in heaven and on earth and under the earth and in the sea, and all that is in them, singing,
"To the one seated on the throne and to the Lamb
be blessing and honor and glory and might
forever and ever!"
14 And the four living creatures said, "Amen!" And the elders fell down and worshiped.

καὶ σοφίαν καὶ ἰσχὺν καὶ τιμὴν καὶ
and wisdom and strength and honour and

δόξαν καὶ εὐλογίαν. 13 καὶ πᾶν κτίσμα
glory and blessing. And every creature

ὃ ἐν τῷ οὐρανῷ καὶ ἐπὶ τῆς γῆς καὶ
which ²in – ³heaven ⁴and ⁵on ⁶the ⁷earth ⁸and

ὑποκάτω τῆς γῆς καὶ ἐπὶ τῆς θαλάσσης
⁹underneath ¹⁰the ¹¹earth ¹²and ¹³on ¹⁴the ¹⁵sea

[ἐστίν], καὶ τὰ ἐν αὐτοῖς πάντα, ἤκουσα
¹is, and – ²in ³them ¹all things, I heard

λέγοντας· τῷ καθημένῳ ἐπὶ τῷ θρόνῳ
saying: To the [one] sitting on the throne

καὶ τῷ ἀρνίῳ ἡ εὐλογία καὶ ἡ τιμὴ
and to the Lamb the blessing and the honour

καὶ ἡ δόξα καὶ τὸ κράτος εἰς τοὺς
and the glory and the might unto the

αἰῶνας τῶν αἰώνων. 14 καὶ τὰ τέσσερα
ages of the ages. And the four

ζῷα ἔλεγον· ἀμήν, καὶ οἱ πρεσβύτεροι
living creatures said: Amen, and the elders

ἔπεσαν καὶ προσεκύνησαν.
fell and worshipped.

---

wealth and wisdom
and strength
and honor and glory and
praise!"
13 Then I heard every creature in heaven and on earth and under the earth and on the sea, and all that is in them, singing:

"To him who sits on the throne and to the Lamb
be praise and honor and glory and power,
for ever and ever!"

14 The four living creatures said, "Amen," and the elders fell down and worshiped.

Chapter 6

The Seven Seals

THEN I saw the Lamb open one of the seven seals, and I heard one of the four living creatures call out, as with a voice of thunder, "Come!"ᵖ 2 I looked, and there was a white horse! Its rider had a bow, and a crown was given to him, and he came out conquering and to conquer.
3 When he opened the second seal, I heard the second living creature call out, "Come!"ᵖ 4 And out came q another horse, bright red; its rider was permitted to take peace from the earth, so that people would slaughter one another; and he was given a great sword.
5 When he opened the third seal, I heard the third living creature call out, "Come!"ᵖ I looked, and there was a black horse! Its rider held a pair of scales in his hand, 6 and I heard what

---

Chapter 6

The Seals

6 Καὶ εἶδον ὅτε ἤνοιξεν τὸ ἀρνίον
And I saw when ³opened ¹the ²Lamb

μίαν ἐκ τῶν ἑπτὰ σφραγίδων, καὶ ἤκουσα
one of the seven seals, and I heard

ἑνὸς ἐκ τῶν τεσσάρων ζῴων λέγοντος
one of the four living creatures saying

ὡς φωνῇ βροντῆς· ἔρχου. 2 καὶ εἶδον,
as with a sound of thunder: Come. And I saw,

καὶ ἰδοὺ ἵππος λευκός, καὶ ὁ καθήμενος
and behold[,] ²horse ¹a white, and the [one] sitting

ἐπ’ αὐτὸν ἔχων τόξον, καὶ ἐδόθη αὐτῷ
on it having a bow, and was given ²to him

στέφανος, καὶ ἐξῆλθεν νικῶν καὶ ἵνα
¹a crown, and he went forth overcoming and in order that

νικήσῃ. 3 Καὶ ὅτε ἤνοιξεν τὴν σφραγῖδα
he might overcome. And when he opened the ²seal

τὴν δευτέραν, ἤκουσα τοῦ δευτέρου ζῴου
– ¹second, I heard the second living creature

λέγοντος· ἔρχου. 4 καὶ ἐξῆλθεν ἄλλος
saying: Come. And ⁴went forth ¹another

ἵππος πυρρός, καὶ τῷ καθημένῳ ἐπ’
²horse[,] ³red, and to the [one] sitting on

αὐτὸν ἐδόθη αὐτῷ λαβεῖν τὴν εἰρήνην
it was given to him to take – peace

ἐκ τῆς γῆς καὶ ἵνα ἀλλήλους σφάξουσιν,
out of the earth and in order that ²one another ¹they shall slay,

καὶ ἐδόθη αὐτῷ μάχαιρα μεγάλη. 5 Καὶ
and ⁵was given ⁴to him ²sword ¹a great. And

ὅτε ἤνοιξεν τὴν σφραγῖδα τὴν τρίτην,
when he opened the ²seal – ¹third,

ἤκουσα τοῦ τρίτου ζῴου λέγοντος· ἔρχου.
I heard the third living creature saying: Come.

καὶ εἶδον, καὶ ἰδοὺ ἵππος μέλας, καὶ
And I saw, and behold[,] ²horse ¹a black, and

ὁ καθήμενος ἐπ’ αὐτὸν ἔχων ζυγὸν
the [one] sitting on it having a balance

I WATCHED as the Lamb opened the first of the seven seals. Then I heard one of the four living creatures say in a voice like thunder, "Come!" 2 I looked, and there before me was a white horse! Its rider held a bow, and he was given a crown, and he rode out as a conqueror bent on conquest.
3 When the Lamb opened the second seal, I heard the second living creature say, "Come!" 4 Then another horse came out, a fiery red one. Its rider was given power to take peace from the earth and to make men slay each other. To him was given a large sword.
5 When the Lamb opened the third seal, I heard the third living creature say, "Come!" I looked, and there before me was a black horse! Its rider was holding

---

seemed to be a voice in the midst of the four living creatures saying, "A quart of wheat for a day's pay,r and three quarts of barley for a day's pay,r but do not damage the olive oil and the wine!"

7 When he opened the fourth seal, I heard the voice of the fourth living creature call out, "Come!"p 8 I looked and there was a pale green horse! Its rider's name was Death, and Hades followed with him; they were given authority over a fourth of the earth, to kill with sword, famine, and pestilence, and by the wild animals of the earth.

9 When he opened the fifth seal, I saw under the altar the souls of those who had been slaughtered for the word of God and for the testimony they had given; 10 they cried out with a loud voice, "Sovereign Lord, holy and true, how long will it be before you judge and avenge our blood on the inhabitants of the earth?" 11 They were each given a white robe and told to rest a little longer, until the number would be complete both of their fellow servants s and of their brothers and sisters,t who were soon to be killed as they themselves had been killed.

12 When he opened the sixth seal, I looked, and there came a great earth-

---

ἐν τῇ χειρὶ αὐτοῦ. 6 καὶ ἤκουσα ὡς
in the hand of him. And I heard as

φωνὴν ἐν μέσῳ τῶν τεσσάρων ζῴων
a voice in [the] of the four living
midst creatures

λέγουσαν· χοῖνιξ σίτου δηναρίου, καὶ τρεῖς
saying: A of of(for) and three
choenix wheat a denarius,

χοίνικες κριθῶν δηναρίου· καὶ τὸ ἔλαιον
choenixes of barley of(for) and the oil
a denarius;

καὶ τὸν οἶνον μὴ ἀδικήσῃς. 7 Καὶ
and the wine do not harm. And

ὅτε ἤνοιξεν τὴν σφραγῖδα τὴν τετάρτην,
when he opened the seal - fourth,

ἤκουσα φωνὴν τοῦ τετάρτου ζῴου λέγοντος·
I heard [the] voice of the fourth living creature saying:

ἔρχου. 8 καὶ εἶδον, καὶ ἰδοὺ ἵππος
Come. And I saw, and behold[,] horse

χλωρός, καὶ ὁ καθήμενος ἐπάνω αὐτοῦ,
a pale green, and the [one] sitting upon it,

ὄνομα αὐτῷ [ὁ] θάνατος, καὶ ὁ ᾅδης
name to him - death, and hades

ἠκολούθει μετ' αὐτοῦ, καὶ ἐδόθη αὐτοῖς
followed with him, and was to them
given

ἐξουσία ἐπὶ τὸ τέταρτον τῆς γῆς,
authority over the fourth [part] of the earth,

ἀποκτεῖναι ἐν ῥομφαίᾳ καὶ ἐν λιμῷ
to kill with sword and with famine

καὶ ἐν θανάτῳ καὶ ὑπὸ τῶν θηρίων
and with death and by the wild beasts

τῆς γῆς. 9 Καὶ ὅτε ἤνοιξεν τὴν πέμπτην
of the earth. And when he opened the fifth

σφραγῖδα, εἶδον ὑποκάτω τοῦ θυσιαστηρίου
seal, I saw underneath the altar

τὰς ψυχὰς τῶν ἐσφαγμένων διὰ τὸν
the souls of the having been on account the
[ones] slain of

λόγον τοῦ θεοῦ καὶ διὰ τὴν μαρτυρίαν
word - of God and on the witness
account of

ἣν εἶχον. 10 καὶ ἔκραξαν φωνῇ μεγάλῃ
which they had. And they cried voice with a
great(loud)

λέγοντες· ἕως πότε, ὁ δεσπότης ὁ ἅγιος
saying: Until when, the Master - holy

καὶ ἀληθινός, οὐ κρίνεις καὶ ἐκδικεῖς
and true, judgest thou not and avengest

τὸ αἷμα ἡμῶν ἐκ τῶν κατοικούντων
the blood of us of the [ones] dwelling

ἐπὶ τῆς γῆς; 11 καὶ ἐδόθη αὐτοῖς ἑκάστῳ
on the earth? And was to them each one
given

στολὴ λευκή, καὶ ἐρρέθη αὐτοῖς ἵνα
robe a white, and it was said to them in order
that

ἀναπαύσωνται ἔτι χρόνον μικρόν, ἕως
they should rest yet time a little, until

πληρωθῶσιν καὶ οἱ σύνδουλοι αὐτῶν καὶ
should be fulfilled also the fellow-slaves of them and

οἱ ἀδελφοὶ αὐτῶν οἱ μέλλοντες ἀποκτέν-
the brothers of them the [ones] being about to be

νεσθαι ὡς καὶ αὐτοί. 12 Καὶ εἶδον
killed as also they. And I saw

ὅτε ἤνοιξεν τὴν σφραγῖδα τὴν ἕκτην,
when he opened the seal - sixth,

καὶ σεισμὸς μέγας ἐγένετο, καὶ ὁ ἥλιος
and earthquake a great occurred, and the sun

---

a pair of scales in his hand. 6 Then I heard what sounded like a voice among the four living creatures, saying, "A quart j of wheat for a day's wages, k and three quarts of barley for a day's wages, l and do not damage the oil and the wine!"

7 When the Lamb opened the fourth seal, I heard the voice of the fourth living creature say, "Come!" 8 I looked, and there before me was a pale green horse! Its rider was named Death, and Hades was following close behind him. They were given power over a fourth of the earth to kill with sword, famine and plague, and by the wild beasts of the earth.

9 When he opened the fifth seal, I saw under the altar the souls of those who had been slain because of the word of God and the testimony they had maintained. 10 They called out in a loud voice, "How long, Sovereign Lord, holy and true, until you judge the inhabitants of the earth and avenge our blood?" 11 Then each of them was given a white robe, and they were told to wait a little longer, until the number of their fellow servants and brothers who were to be killed as they had been was completed.

12 I watched as he opened the sixth seal. There was a great earthquake. The sun

---

r Gk a denarius
s Gk slaves
t Gk brothers

j6 Greek a choinix (probably about a liter)
k6 Greek a denarius
l6 Greek a denarius

quake; the sun became black as sackcloth, the full moon became like blood, 13and the stars of the sky fell to the earth as the fig tree drops its winter fruit when shaken by a gale. 14The sky vanished like a scroll rolling itself up, and every mountain and island was removed from its place. 15Then the kings of the earth and the magnates and the generals and the rich and the powerful, and everyone, slave and free, hid in the caves and among the rocks of the mountains, 16calling to the mountains and rocks, "Fall on us and hide us from the face of the one seated on the throne and from the wrath of the Lamb; 17for the great day of their wrath has come, and who is able to stand?"

ἐγένετο μέλας ὡς σάκκος τρίχινος, καὶ
became black as sackcloth made of hair, and

ἡ σελήνη ὅλη ἐγένετο ὡς αἷμα, 13 καὶ
the ²moon ¹whole became as blood, and

οἱ ἀστέρες τοῦ οὐρανοῦ ἔπεσαν εἰς τὴν
the stars - of heaven fell to the

γῆν, ὡς συκῆ βάλλει τοὺς ὀλύνθους
earth, as a fig-tree casts the unripe figs

αὐτῆς ὑπὸ ἀνέμου μεγάλου σειομένη,
of it ⁸by ⁴wind ³a great(strong) ¹being shaken,

14 καὶ ὁ οὐρανὸς ἀπεχωρίσθη ὡς βιβλίον
and the heaven departed as a scroll

ἑλισσόμενον, καὶ πᾶν ὄρος καὶ νῆσος
being rolled up, and every mountain and island

ἐκ τῶν τόπων αὐτῶν ἐκινήθησαν. 15 καὶ
out of the places of them were moved. And

οἱ βασιλεῖς τῆς γῆς καὶ οἱ μεγιστᾶνες
the kings of the earth and the great men

καὶ οἱ χιλίαρχοι καὶ οἱ πλούσιοι καὶ
and the chiliarchs and the rich men and

οἱ ἰσχυροὶ καὶ πᾶς δοῦλος καὶ ἐλεύθερος
the strong men and every slave and free man

ἔκρυψαν ἑαυτοὺς εἰς τὰ σπήλαια καὶ
hid themselves in the caves and

εἰς τὰς πέτρας τῶν ὀρέων, 16 καὶ
in the rocks of the mountains, and

λέγουσιν τοῖς ὄρεσιν καὶ ταῖς πέτραις·
they say to the mountains and to the rocks:

πέσετε ἐφ᾽ ἡμᾶς καὶ κρύψατε ἡμᾶς
Fall ye on us and hide us

ἀπὸ προσώπου τοῦ καθημένου ἐπὶ τοῦ
from [the] face of the [one] sitting on the

θρόνου καὶ ἀπὸ τῆς ὀργῆς τοῦ ἀρνίου,
throne and from the wrath of the Lamb,

17 ὅτι ἦλθεν ἡ ἡμέρα ἡ μεγάλη τῆς
because ⁷came ¹the ²day - ³great ⁴of the

ὀργῆς αὐτῶν, καὶ τίς δύναται σταθῆναι;
⁵wrath ⁶of them, and who can to stand ?

turned black like sackcloth made of goat hair, the whole moon turned blood red, 13and the stars in the sky fell to earth, as late figs drop from a fig tree when shaken by a strong wind. 14The sky receded like a scroll, rolling up, and every mountain and island was removed from its place. 15Then the kings of the earth, the princes, the generals, the rich, the mighty, and every slave and every free man hid in caves and among the rocks of the mountains. 16They called to the mountains and the rocks, "Fall on us and hide us from the face of him who sits on the throne and from the wrath of the Lamb! 17For the great day of their wrath has come, and who can stand?"

Chapter 7

The 144,000 of Israel Sealed

AFTER this I saw four angels standing at the four corners of the earth, holding back the four winds of the earth so that no wind could blow on earth or sea or against any tree. 2I saw another angel ascending from the rising of the sun, having the seal of the living God, and he called with a loud voice to the four angels who had been given power to damage earth and sea, 3saying, "Do not damage the earth or the sea or

7 Μετὰ τοῦτο εἶδον τέσσαρας ἀγγέλους
After this I saw four angels

ἑστῶτας ἐπὶ τὰς τέσσαρας γωνίας τῆς
standing on the four corners of the

γῆς, κρατοῦντας τοὺς τέσσαρας ἀνέμους
earth, holding the four winds

τῆς γῆς, ἵνα μὴ πνέῃ ἄνεμος ἐπὶ τῆς
of the earth, in order ³not ¹should ¹wind on the
that ⁴blow

γῆς μήτε ἐπὶ τῆς θαλάσσης μήτε ἐπὶ
earth nor on the sea nor on

πᾶν δένδρον. 2 καὶ εἶδον ἄλλον ἄγγελον
every(any) tree. And I saw another angel

ἀναβαίνοντα ἀπὸ ἀνατολῆς ἡλίου, ἔχοντα
coming up from [the] rising of [the] sun, having

σφραγῖδα θεοῦ ζῶντος, καὶ ἔκραξεν φωνῇ
a seal God of [the] living, and he cried ¹voice

μεγάλῃ τοῖς τέσσαρσιν ἀγγέλοις οἷς
¹with a to the four angels to whom
great(loud)

ἐδόθη αὐτοῖς ἀδικῆσαι τὴν γῆν καὶ
it was given to them to harm the earth and

τὴν θάλασσαν, 3 λέγων· μὴ ἀδικήσητε
the sea, saying: Do not harm

τὴν γῆν μήτε τὴν θάλασσαν μήτε τὰ
the earth nor the sea nor the

Chapter 7

144,000 Sealed

AFTER this I saw four angels standing at the four corners of the earth, holding back the four winds of the earth to prevent any wind from blowing on the land or on the sea or on any tree. 2Then I saw another angel coming up from the east, having the seal of the living God. He called out in a loud voice to the four angels who had been given power to harm the land and the sea: 3"Do not harm the land or the sea or the trees the trees, until we have marked the servants[u] of our God with a seal on their foreheads."

4 And I heard the number of those who were sealed, one hundred forty-four thousand, sealed out of every tribe of the people of Israel:

5 From the tribe of Judah twelve thousand sealed,
from the tribe of Reuben twelve thousand,
from the tribe of Gad twelve thousand,
6 from the tribe of Asher twelve thousand,
from the tribe of Naphtali twelve thousand,
from the tribe of Manasseh twelve thousand,
7 from the tribe of Simeon twelve thousand,
from the tribe of Levi twelve thousand,
from the tribe of Issachar twelve thousand,
8 from the tribe of Zebulun twelve thousand,
from the tribe of Joseph twelve thousand,
from the tribe of Benjamin twelve thousand sealed.

The Multitude from Every Nation

9 After this I looked, and there was a great multitude that no one could count, from every nation, from all tribes and peoples and languages, standing before the throne and before the Lamb, robed in white, with palm branches in their hands. 10 They cried out in a loud voice, saying,

"Salvation belongs to our God who is seated on the throne, and to the Lamb!"

11 And all the angels stood around the throne and around the elders and the four living creatures, and they fell on their faces before the throne and worshiped God, 12 singing,

"Amen! Blessing and

[u] Gk slaves

δένδρα, ἄχρι σφραγίσωμεν τοὺς δούλους
trees, until we may seal the slaves

τοῦ θεοῦ ἡμῶν ἐπὶ τῶν μετώπων αὐτῶν.
of the God of us on the foreheads of them.

4 Καὶ ἤκουσα τὸν ἀριθμὸν τῶν ἐσφραγισ-
And I heard the number of the [ones] having been

μένων, ἑκατὸν τεσσεράκοντα τέσσαρες
sealed, a hundred forty-four

χιλιάδες ἐσφραγισμένοι ἐκ πάσης φυλῆς
thousands having been sealed out of every tribe

υἱῶν Ἰσραήλ· 5 ἐκ φυλῆς Ἰούδα δώδεκα
of sons of Israel: of [the] tribe Juda twelve

χιλιάδες ἐσφραγισμένοι, ἐκ φυλῆς Ῥουβὴν
thousands having been sealed, of [the] tribe Reuben

δώδεκα χιλιάδες, ἐκ φυλῆς Γὰδ δώδεκα
twelve thousands, of [the] tribe Gad twelve

χιλιάδες, 6 ἐκ φυλῆς Ἀσὴρ δώδεκα
thousands, of [the] tribe Aser twelve

χιλιάδες, ἐκ φυλῆς Νεφθαλὶμ δώδεκα
thousands, of [the] tribe Nephthalim twelve

χιλιάδες, ἐκ φυλῆς Μανασσῆ δώδεκα
thousands, of [the] tribe Manasse twelve

χιλιάδες, 7 ἐκ φυλῆς Συμεὼν δώδεκα
thousands, of [the] tribe Symeon twelve

χιλιάδες, ἐκ φυλῆς Λευὶ δώδεκα χιλιάδες,
thousands, of [the] tribe Levi twelve thousands,

ἐκ φυλῆς Ἰσσαχὰρ δώδεκα χιλιάδες,
of [the] tribe Issachar twelve thousands,

8 ἐκ φυλῆς Ζαβουλὼν δώδεκα χιλιάδες,
of [the] tribe Zabulon twelve thousands,

ἐκ φυλῆς Ἰωσὴφ δώδεκα χιλιάδες, ἐκ
of [the] tribe Joseph twelve thousands, of

φυλῆς Βενιαμὶν δώδεκα χιλιάδες ἐσφραγισ-
[the] tribe Benjamin twelve thousands having been

μένοι. 9 Μετὰ ταῦτα εἶδον, καὶ ἰδοὺ ὄχλος
sealed. After these things I saw, and behold[,] [a] crowd

πολύς, ὃν ἀριθμῆσαι αὐτὸν οὐδεὶς ἐδύνατο,
[a much which [a] to number it [a] no one [a] was able,
(great),

ἐκ παντὸς ἔθνους καὶ φυλῶν καὶ λαῶν
out of every nation and tribes and peoples

καὶ γλωσσῶν, ἑστῶτες ἐνώπιον τοῦ θρόνου
and tongues, standing before the throne

καὶ ἐνώπιον τοῦ ἀρνίου, περιβεβλημένους
and before the Lamb, having been clothed [with]

στολὰς λευκάς, καὶ φοίνικες ἐν ταῖς
[a] robes [a] white, and palms in the

χερσὶν αὐτῶν· 10 καὶ κράζουσιν φωνῇ
hands of them; and they cry [a] voice

μεγάλῃ λέγοντες· ἡ σωτηρία τῷ θεῷ
[a] with a great(loud) saying: – Salvation to the God[c]

ἡμῶν τῷ καθημένῳ ἐπὶ τῷ θρόνῳ καὶ
of us to the sitting on the throne and

τῷ ἀρνίῳ. 11 καὶ πάντες οἱ ἄγγελοι
to the Lamb.[c] And all the angels

εἱστήκεισαν κύκλῳ τοῦ θρόνου καὶ τῶν
stood round the throne and the

πρεσβυτέρων καὶ τῶν τεσσάρων ζῴων,
elders and the four living creatures,

καὶ ἔπεσαν ἐνώπιον τοῦ θρόνου ἐπὶ
and fell before the throne on

τὰ πρόσωπα αὐτῶν καὶ προσεκύνησαν
the faces of them and worshipped

τῷ θεῷ, 12 λέγοντες· ἀμήν, ἡ εὐλογία
– God, saying: Amen, – blessing

---

until we put a seal on the foreheads of the servants of our God." 4 Then I heard the number of those who were sealed: 144,000 from all the tribes of Israel.

5 From the tribe of Judah 12,000 were sealed,
from the tribe of Reuben 12,000,
from the tribe of Gad 12,000,
6 from the tribe of Asher 12,000,
from the tribe of Naphtali 12,000,
from the tribe of Manasseh 12,000,
7 from the tribe of Simeon 12,000,
from the tribe of Levi 12,000,
from the tribe of Issachar 12,000,
8 from the tribe of Zebulun 12,000,
from the tribe of Joseph 12,000,
from the tribe of Benjamin 12,000.

The Great Multitude in White Robes

9 After this I looked and there before me was a great multitude that no one could count, from every nation, tribe, people and language, standing before the throne and in front of the Lamb. They were wearing white robes and were holding palm branches in their hands. 10 And they cried out in a loud voice:

"Salvation belongs to our God, who sits on the throne, and to the Lamb."

11 All the angels were standing around the throne and around the elders and the four living creatures. They fell down on their faces before the throne and worshiped God, 12 saying:

"Amen!
Praise and glory

glory
and wisdom
and thanksgiving and
honor
and power and might
be to our God forever
and ever!
Amen."

13 Then one of the el-
ders addressed me, saying,
"Who are these, robed in
white, and where have they
come from?" 14 I said to
him, "Sir, you are the one
that knows." Then he said
to me, "These are they who
have come out of the great
ordeal; they have washed
their robes and made them
white in the blood of the
Lamb.
15 For this reason they
are before the
throne of God,
and worship him
day and night
within his
temple,
and the one who is
seated on the
throne will
shelter them.
16 They will hunger no
more, and thirst
no more;
the sun will not
strike them,
nor any scorching
heat;
17 for the Lamb at the
center of the
throne will be
their shepherd,
and he will guide
them to springs
of the water of
life,
and God will wipe
away every tear
from their
eyes."

καὶ ἡ δόξα καὶ ἡ σοφία καὶ ἡ εὐχαριστία
and – glory and – wisdom and – thanks

καὶ ἡ τιμὴ καὶ ἡ δύναμις καὶ ἡ ἰσχὺς
and – honour and – power and – strength

τῷ θεῷ ἡμῶν εἰς τοὺς αἰῶνας τῶν
to the God⁰ of us unto the ages of the

αἰώνων· ἀμήν. 13 Καὶ ἀπεκρίθη εἷς
ages: Amen. And ⁵answered ¹one

ἐκ τῶν πρεσβυτέρων λέγων μοι· οὗτοι
²of ³the ⁴elders saying to me: These

οἱ περιβεβλημένοι τὰς στολὰς τὰς
the having been clothed the ²robes the
[ones] [with]

λευκὰς τίνες εἰσὶν καὶ πόθεν ἦλθον;
¹white who are they and whence came they?

14 καὶ εἴρηκα αὐτῷ· κύριέ μου, σὺ
And I have said to him: Lord of me, thou

οἶδας. καὶ εἶπέν μοι· οὗτοί εἰσιν οἱ
knowest. And he told me: These are the

ἐρχόμενοι ἐκ τῆς θλίψεως τῆς μεγάλης
[ones] coming out of the ²affliction – ¹great

καὶ ἔπλυναν τὰς στολὰς αὐτῶν καὶ
and washed the robes of them and

ἐλεύκαναν αὐτὰς ἐν τῷ αἵματι τοῦ
whitened them in the blood of the

ἀρνίου. 15 διὰ τοῦτό εἰσιν ἐνώπιον τοῦ
Lamb. Therefore are they before the

θρόνου τοῦ θεοῦ, καὶ λατρεύουσιν αὐτῷ
throne – of God, and serve him

ἡμέρας καὶ νυκτὸς ἐν τῷ ναῷ αὐτοῦ,
day and night in the shrine of him,

καὶ ὁ καθήμενος ἐπὶ τοῦ θρόνου σκηνώσει
and the [one] sitting on the throne will spread
[his] tent

ἐπ᾽ αὐτούς. 16 οὐ πεινάσουσιν ἔτι οὐδὲ
over them. They will not hunger longer nor

διψήσουσιν ἔτι, οὐδὲ μὴ πέσῃ ἐπ᾽ αὐτοὺς
will they thirst longer, neither not fall on them

ὁ ἥλιος οὐδὲ πᾶν καῦμα, 17 ὅτι τὸ
the sun nor every(any) heat, because the

ἀρνίον τὸ ἀνὰ μέσον τοῦ θρόνου ποιμανεῖ
Lamb – in the midst of the throne will shepherd

αὐτοὺς καὶ ὁδηγήσει αὐτοὺς ἐπὶ ζωῆς
them and will lead them upon ³of life

πηγὰς ὑδάτων· καὶ ἐξαλείψει ὁ θεὸς
¹fountains ²of waters; and ²will wipe off – ¹God

πᾶν δάκρυον ἐκ τῶν ὀφθαλμῶν αὐτῶν.
every tear out of the eyes of them.

---

and wisdom and thanks
and honor
and power and strength
be to our God for ever
and ever.
Amen!"

13Then one of the elders
asked me, "These in white
robes—who are they, and
where did they come
from?"
14I answered, "Sir, you
know."
And he said, "These are
they who have come out of
the great tribulation; they
have washed their robes
and made them white in the
blood of the Lamb.
15Therefore,

"they are before the
throne of God
and serve him day and
night in his temple;
and he who sits on the
throne will spread
his tent over them.
16Never again will they
hunger;
never again will they
thirst.
The sun will not beat
upon them,
nor any scorching heat.
17For the Lamb at the
center of the throne
will be their
shepherd;
he will lead them to
springs of living
water.
And God will wipe away
every tear from their
eyes."

Chapter 8

*The Seventh Seal and the
Golden Censer*

WHEN the Lamb
opened the seventh
seal, there was silence in
heaven for about half an
hour. 2 And I saw the seven
angels who stand before
God, and seven trumpets
were given to them.
3 Another angel with a
golden censer came and
stood at the altar; he was
given a great quantity of incense to offer with the
prayers of all the saints on

---

8 Καὶ ὅταν ἤνοιξεν τὴν σφραγῖδα τὴν
And whenever he opened the ²seal

ἑβδόμην, ἐγένετο σιγὴ ἐν τῷ οὐρανῷ
¹seventh, occurred a silence in – heaven

ὡς ἡμίωρον. 2 Καὶ εἶδον τοὺς ἑπτὰ
about a half-hour. And I saw the seven

ἀγγέλους οἳ ἐνώπιον τοῦ θεοῦ ἑστήκασιν,
angels who before – God stood,

καὶ ἐδόθησαν αὐτοῖς ἑπτὰ σάλπιγγες.
and there were given to them seven trumpets.

3 Καὶ ἄλλος ἄγγελος ἦλθεν καὶ ἐστάθη
And another angel came and stood

ἐπὶ τοῦ θυσιαστηρίου ἔχων λιβανωτὸν
on the altar having ²censer

χρυσοῦν, καὶ ἐδόθη αὐτῷ θυμιάματα πολλά,
¹a golden, and there was to him incenses many
given (much),

Chapter 8

*The Seventh Seal and the
Golden Censer*

WHEN he opened the
seventh seal, there
was silence in heaven for
about half an hour.
2And I saw the seven an-
gels who stand before God,
and to them were given
seven trumpets.
3Another angel, who had
a golden censer, came and
stood at the altar. He was
given much incense to of-

the golden altar that is before the throne. ⁴And the smoke of the incense, with the prayers of the saints, rose before God from the hand of the angel. ⁵Then the angel took the censer and filled it with fire from the altar and threw it on the earth; and there were peals of thunder, rumblings, flashes of lightning, and an earthquake.

The Seven Trumpets

6 Now the seven angels who had the seven trumpets made ready to blow them.

7 The first angel blew his trumpet, and there came hail and fire, mixed with blood, and they were hurled to the earth; and a third of the earth was burned up, and a third of the trees were burned up, and all green grass was burned up.

8 The second angel blew his trumpet, and something like a great mountain, burning with fire, was thrown into the sea. ⁹A third of the sea became blood, a third of the living creatures in the sea died, and a third of the ships were destroyed.

10 The third angel blew his trumpet, and a great star fell from heaven, blazing like a torch, and it fell on a third of the rivers and on the springs of water. ¹¹The name of the star is Wormwood. A third of the

---

ἵνα δώσει ταῖς προσευχαῖς τῶν ἁγίων
in order he will with the prayers of ²the ³saints
that give [it]

πάντων ἐπὶ τὸ θυσιαστήριον τὸ χρυσοῦν
¹all on the ²altar - ¹golden

τὸ ἐνώπιον τοῦ θρόνου. 4 καὶ ἀνέβη
- before the throne. And went up

ὁ καπνὸς τῶν θυμιαμάτων ταῖς προσευχαῖς
the smoke of the incenses with the prayers

τῶν ἁγίων ἐκ χειρὸς τοῦ ἀγγέλου ἐνώπιον
of the saints out of [the] hand of the angel before

τοῦ θεοῦ. 5 καὶ εἴληφεν ὁ ἄγγελος
- God. And ³has taken ¹the ²angel

τὸν λιβανωτόν, καὶ ἐγέμισεν αὐτὸν ἐκ
the censer, and filled it from

τοῦ πυρὸς τοῦ θυσιαστηρίου καὶ ἔβαλεν
the fire of the altar and cast

εἰς τὴν γῆν· καὶ ἐγένοντο βρονταὶ καὶ
into the earth; and there occurred thunders and

φωναὶ καὶ ἀστραπαὶ καὶ σεισμός.
sounds and lightnings and an earthquake.

6 Καὶ οἱ ἑπτὰ ἄγγελοι οἱ ἔχοντες
And the seven angels - having

τὰς ἑπτὰ σάλπιγγας ἡτοίμασαν αὐτοὺς
the seven trumpets prepared themselves

ἵνα σαλπίσωσιν. 7 Καὶ ὁ πρῶτος
in order they might And the first
that trumpet.

ἐσάλπισεν· καὶ ἐγένετο χάλαζα καὶ πῦρ
trumpeted; and there occurred hail and fire

μεμιγμένα ἐν αἵματι καὶ ἐβλήθη εἰς
having been in blood and it was cast to
mixed (with)

τὴν γῆν· καὶ τὸ τρίτον τῆς γῆς
the earth; and the third [part] of the earth

κατεκάη, καὶ τὸ τρίτον τῶν δένδρων
was burnt and the third [part] of the trees
down(up),

κατεκάη, καὶ πᾶς χόρτος χλωρὸς κατεκάη.
was burnt and all ²grass ¹green was burnt
down(up), down(up).

8 Καὶ ὁ δεύτερος ἄγγελος ἐσάλπισεν·
And the second angel trumpeted;

καὶ ὡς ὄρος μέγα πυρὶ καιόμενον ἐβλήθη
and as ²mountain ¹a great ⁴with fire ³burning was cast

εἰς τὴν θάλασσαν· καὶ ἐγένετο τὸ τρίτον
into the sea; and ⁵became ¹the ²third
[part]

τῆς θαλάσσης αἷμα, 9 καὶ ἀπέθανεν τὸ
³of the ⁴sea ⁶blood, and ¹⁰died ¹the

τρίτον τῶν κτισμάτων τῶν ἐν τῇ θαλάσσῃ,
²third ⁵of the ⁴creatures - ⁶in ⁸the ⁷sea,
[part]

τὰ ἔχοντα ψυχάς, καὶ τὸ τρίτον τῶν
- ⁹having ⁸souls, and the third [part] of the

πλοίων διεφθάρησαν. 10 Καὶ ὁ τρίτος
ships were destroyed. And the third

ἄγγελος ἐσάλπισεν· καὶ ἔπεσεν ἐκ τοῦ
angel trumpeted; and fell out of -

οὐρανοῦ ἀστὴρ μέγας καιόμενος ὡς
heaven star a great burning as

λαμπάς, καὶ ἔπεσεν ἐπὶ τὸ τρίτον τῶν
a lamp, and it fell onto the third [part] of the

ποταμῶν καὶ ἐπὶ τὰς πηγὰς τῶν ὑδάτων.
rivers and onto the fountains of the waters.

11 καὶ τὸ ὄνομα τοῦ ἀστέρος λέγεται
And the name of the star is said(called)

---

fer, with the prayers of all the saints, on the golden altar before the throne. ⁴The smoke of the incense, together with the prayers of the saints, went up before God from the angel's hand. ⁵Then the angel took the censer, filled it with fire from the altar, and hurled it on the earth; and there came peals of thunder, rumblings, flashes of lightning and an earthquake.

The Trumpets

6Then the seven angels who had the seven trumpets prepared to sound them.

7The first angel sounded his trumpet, and there came hail and fire mixed with blood, and it was hurled down upon the earth. A third of the earth was burned up, a third of the trees were burned up, and all the green grass was burned up.

8The second angel sounded his trumpet, and something like a huge mountain, all ablaze, was thrown into the sea. A third of the sea turned into blood, ⁹a third of the living creatures in the sea died, and a third of the ships were destroyed.

10The third angel sounded his trumpet, and a great star, blazing like a torch, fell from the sky on a third of the rivers and on the springs of water— ¹¹the name of the star is Worm-waters became worm-wood, and many died from the water, because it was made bitter.

12 The fourth angel blew his trumpet, and a third of the sun was struck, and a third of the moon, and a third of the stars, so that a third of their light was darkened; a third of the day was kept from shining, and likewise the night.

13 Then I looked, and I heard an eagle crying with a loud voice as it flew in mid-heaven, "Woe, woe, woe to the inhabitants of the earth, at the blasts of the other trumpets that the three angels are about to blow!"

ὁ Ἄψινθος.   καὶ ἐγένετο τὸ τρίτον τῶν
— Wormwood.   And ²became ¹the ²third ³of
                                    [part]   the

ὑδάτων εἰς ἄψινθον, καὶ πολλοὶ τῶν
⁴waters into wormwood, and many of the

ἀνθρώπων ἀπέθανον ἐκ τῶν ὑδάτων ὅτι
men died from the waters because

ἐπικράνθησαν.   12 Καὶ ὁ τέταρτος ἄγγελος
they were made bitter.   And the fourth angel

ἐσάλπισεν·   καὶ ἐπλήγη τὸ τρίτον τοῦ
trumpeted;   and ²was struck ¹the ²third [part] ³of the

ἡλίου καὶ τὸ τρίτον τῆς σελήνης καὶ
⁴sun and the third [part] of the moon and

τὸ τρίτον τῶν ἀστέρων, ἵνα σκοτισθῇ
the third of the stars, in order ⁴might be
    [part]   that   darkened

τὸ τρίτον αὐτῶν καὶ ἡ ἡμέρα μὴ φάνῃ
¹the ²third [part] ³of them and the day might not appear

τὸ τρίτον αὐτῆς, καὶ ἡ νὺξ ὁμοίως.
the third [part] of it, and the night likewise.

13 Καὶ εἶδον, καὶ ἤκουσα ἑνὸς ἀετοῦ
And I saw, and I heard one eagle

πετομένου ἐν μεσουρανήματι λέγοντος φωνῇ
flying in mid-heaven saying ²voice

μεγάλῃ·   οὐαὶ οὐαὶ οὐαὶ τοὺς κατοικοῦν-
¹with a   Woe[,] woe[,] woe to the [ones] dwell-
great(loud):

τας ἐπὶ τῆς γῆς ἐκ τῶν λοιπῶν φωνῶν
ing on the earth from the remaining voices

τῆς σάλπιγγος τῶν τριῶν ἀγγέλων τῶν
of the trumpet of the three angels —

μελλόντων σαλπίζειν.
being about to trumpet.

---

wood. ᵐ A third of the waters turned bitter, and many people died from the waters that had become bitter.

12 The fourth angel sounded his trumpet, and a third of the sun was struck, a third of the moon, and a third of the stars, so that a third of them turned dark. A third of the day was without light, and also a third of the night.

13 As I watched, I heard an eagle that was flying in midair call out in a loud voice: "Woe! Woe! Woe to the inhabitants of the earth, because of the trumpet blasts about to be sounded by the other three angels!"

Chapter 9

AND the fifth angel blew his trumpet, and I saw a star that had fallen from heaven to earth, and he was given the key to the shaft of the bottomless pit; ²he opened the shaft of the bottomless pit, and from the shaft rose smoke like the smoke of a great furnace, and the sun and the air were darkened with the smoke from the shaft. ³Then from the smoke came locusts on the earth, and they were given authority like the authority of scorpions of the earth. ⁴They were told not to damage the grass of the earth or any green growth or any tree, but only those people who do not have the

---

9 Καὶ ὁ πέμπτος ἄγγελος ἐσάλπισεν·
And the fifth angel trumpeted;

καὶ εἶδον ἀστέρα ἐκ τοῦ οὐρανοῦ πεπτω-
and I saw a star out of — heaven having

κότα εἰς τὴν γῆν, καὶ ἐδόθη αὐτῷ
fallen onto the earth, and was given to it

ἡ κλεὶς τοῦ φρέατος τῆς ἀβύσσου.   2 καὶ
the key of the shaft of the abyss.   And

ἤνοιξεν τὸ φρέαρ τῆς ἀβύσσου·   καὶ
he opened the shaft of the abyss;   and

ἀνέβη καπνὸς ἐκ τοῦ φρέατος ὡς
went up a smoke out of the shaft as

καπνὸς καμίνου μεγάλης, καὶ ἐσκοτώθη
smoke ³furnace ¹of a great, and ²was darkened

ὁ ἥλιος καὶ ὁ ἀὴρ ἐκ τοῦ καπνοῦ
¹the ²sun ³and ⁴the ⁵air by the smoke

τοῦ φρέατος.   3 καὶ ἐκ τοῦ καπνοῦ
of the shaft.   And out of the smoke

ἐξῆλθον ἀκρίδες εἰς τὴν γῆν, καὶ ἐδόθη
came forth locusts to the earth, and ²was given

αὐτοῖς ἐξουσία ὡς ἔχουσιν ἐξουσίαν οἱ
³to them ¹authority as ⁵have ⁴authority ¹the

σκορπίοι τῆς γῆς.   4 καὶ ἐρρέθη αὐτοῖς
²scorpions ³of the ⁴earth.   And it was said to them

ἵνα μὴ ἀδικήσουσιν τὸν χόρτον τῆς
in order that they shall not harm the grass of the

γῆς οὐδὲ πᾶν χλωρὸν οὐδὲ πᾶν δένδρον,
earth nor every (any) greenstuff nor every (any) tree,

εἰ μὴ τοὺς ἀνθρώπους οἵτινες οὐκ ἔχουσιν
except the men who have not

Chapter 9

THE fifth angel sounded his trumpet, and I saw a star that had fallen from the sky to the earth. The star was given the key to the shaft of the Abyss. ²When he opened the Abyss, smoke rose from it like the smoke from a gigantic furnace. The sun and sky were darkened by the smoke from the Abyss. ³And out of the smoke locusts came down upon the earth and were given power like that of scorpions of the earth. ⁴They were told not to harm the grass of the earth or any plant or tree, but only those people who

---

ᵐ11 That is, Bitterness

seal of God on their foreheads. 5They were allowed to torture them for five months, but not to kill them, and their torture was like the torture of a scorpion when it stings someone. 6And in those days people will seek death but will not find it; they will long to die, but death will flee from them.

7 In appearance the locusts were like horses equipped for battle. On their heads were what looked like crowns of gold; their faces were like human faces, 8their hair like women's hair, and their teeth like lions' teeth; 9they had scales like iron breastplates, and the noise of their wings was like the noise of many chariots with horses rushing into battle. 10They have tails like scorpions, with stingers, and in their tails is their power to harm people for five months. 11They have as king over them the angel of the bottomless pit; his name in Hebrew is Abaddon,[v] and in Greek he is called Apollyon.[w]

12 The first woe has passed. There are still two woes to come.

13 Then the sixth angel blew his trumpet, and I heard a voice from the four[x] horns of the golden altar before God, 14saying to the sixth angel who had

---

τὴν σφραγῖδα τοῦ θεοῦ ἐπὶ τῶν μετώπων.
the   seal   - of God   on   the(ir) foreheads.

5 καὶ ἐδόθη αὐτοῖς ἵνα μὴ ἀποκτείνωσιν
And   it was   to them   *in order*   they should not kill
     given   *that*

αὐτούς, ἀλλ' ἵνα βασανισθήσονται μῆνας
them,   but   *in order* they shall be tormented ²months
         that

πέντε· καὶ ὁ βασανισμὸς αὐτῶν ὡς
¹five;   and   the   torment   of them   [is] as

βασανισμος σκορπίου, ὅταν παίσῃ ἄνθρωπον.
[the] torment   of a scorpion,   whenever it stings   a man.

6 καὶ ἐν ταῖς ἡμέραις ἐκείναις ζητήσουσιν
And   in   those days   ²will seek

οἱ ἄνθρωποι τὸν θάνατον καὶ οὐ μὴ
-   ¹men   -   death   and   by no means

εὑρήσουσιν αὐτόν, καὶ ἐπιθυμήσουσιν
will they find   it,   and   they will long

ἀποθανεῖν καὶ φεύγει ὁ θάνατος ἀπ'
to die   and   ²flees   -   ¹death   from

αὐτῶν. 7 καὶ τὰ ὁμοιώματα τῶν ἀκρίδων
them.   And   the   likenesses   of the   locusts

ὅμοιοι ἵπποις ἡτοιμασμένοις εἰς πόλεμον,
like   to horses   *having been* prepared   for   war,

καὶ ἐπὶ τὰς κεφαλὰς αὐτῶν ὡς στέφανοι
and   on   the   heads   of them   as   crowns

ὅμοιοι χρυσῷ, καὶ τὰ πρόσωπα αὐτῶν
like   *to* gold,   and   the   faces   of them

ὡς πρόσωπα ἀνθρώπων, 8 καὶ εἶχον
as   faces   of men,   and   they had

τρίχας ὡς τρίχας γυναικῶν, καὶ οἱ
hairs   as   hairs   of women,   and   the

ὀδόντες αὐτῶν ὡς λεόντων ἦσαν, 9 καὶ
teeth   of them   ²as   ³of lions   ¹were,   and

εἶχον θώρακας ὡς θώρακας σιδηροῦς,
they had   breastplates   as   ²breastplates   ¹iron,

καὶ ἡ φωνὴ τῶν πτερύγων αὐτῶν ὡς
and   the   sound   of the   wings   of them   as

φωνὴ ἁρμάτων ἵππων πολλῶν τρεχόντων
sound   ²chariots   ³of horses   ¹of many   running

εἰς πόλεμον. 10 καὶ ἔχουσιν οὐρὰς ὁμοίας
to   war.   And   they have   tails   like

σκορπίοις καὶ κέντρα, καὶ ἐν ταῖς οὐραῖς
to scorpions   and   stings,   and   ⁶with   ⁷the   ⁸tails

αὐτῶν ἡ ἐξουσία αὐτῶν ἀδικῆσαι τοὺς
⁹of them   ¹the   ²authority   ³of them   ⁴[is] to harm   -

ἀνθρώπους μῆνας πέντε. 11 ἔχουσιν ἐπ'
⁵men   ¹¹months   ¹⁰five.   They have   over

αὐτῶν βασιλέα τὸν ἄγγελον τῆς ἀβύσσου,
them   a king   the   angel   of the   abyss,

ὄνομα αὐτῷ Ἑβραϊστὶ Ἀβαδδών, καὶ
name   to him°   in Hebrew   Abaddon,   and

ἐν τῇ Ἑλληνικῇ ὄνομα ἔχει Ἀπολλύων.
in   the   Greek   ²[the] name   ¹he has   Apollyon.

12 Ἡ οὐαὶ ἡ μία ἀπῆλθεν· ἰδοὺ ἔρχεται
The   ²woe   - ¹one(first) passed away;   behold   ⁴comes

ἔτι δύο οὐαὶ μετὰ ταῦτα.
¹yet   ²two   ³woes   after   these things.

13 Καὶ ὁ ἕκτος ἄγγελος ἐσάλπισεν·
And   the   sixth   angel   trumpeted;

καὶ ἤκουσα φωνὴν μίαν ἐκ τῶν τεσσάρων
and   I heard   ²voice   ¹one out of the   four

κεράτων τοῦ θυσιαστηρίου τοῦ χρυσοῦ
horns   of the   ²altar   -   ¹golden

τοῦ ἐνώπιον τοῦ θεοῦ, 14 λέγοντα τῷ
-     before   -   God,   saying   to the

---

did not have the seal of God on their foreheads. 5They were not given power to kill them, but only to torture them for five months. And the agony they suffered was like that of the sting of a scorpion when it strikes a man. 6During those days men will seek death, but will not find it; they will long to die, but death will elude them.

7The locusts looked like horses prepared for battle. On their heads they wore something like crowns of gold, and their faces resembled human faces. 8Their hair was like women's hair, and their teeth were like lions' teeth. 9They had breastplates like breastplates of iron, and the sound of their wings was like the thundering of many horses and chariots rushing into battle. 10They had tails and stings like scorpions, and in their tails they had power to torment people for five months. 11They had as king over them the angel of the Abyss, whose name in Hebrew is Abaddon, and in Greek, Apollyon.[n]

12The first woe is past; two other woes are yet to come.

13The sixth angel sounded his trumpet, and I heard a voice coming from the horns° of the golden altar that is before God. 14It said to the sixth angel who had

---

[v] That is, *Destruction*
[w] That is, *Destroyer*
[x] Other ancient authorities lack *four*

[n]11 *Abaddon* and *Apollyon* mean *Destroyer.*
[o]13 That is, projections

the trumpet, "Release the four angels who are bound at the great river Euphrates." 15 So the four angels were released, who had been held ready for the hour, the day, the month, and the year, to kill a third of humankind. 16 The number of the troops of cavalry was two hundred million; I heard their number. 17 And this was how I saw the horses in my vision: the riders wore breastplates the color of fire and of sapphire[y] and of sulfur; the heads of the horses were like lions' heads, and fire and smoke and sulfur came out of their mouths. 18 By these three plagues a third of humankind was killed, by the fire and smoke and sulfur coming out of their mouths. 19 For the power of the horses is in their mouths and in their tails; their tails are like serpents, having heads; and with them they inflict harm. 20 The rest of humankind, who were not killed by these plagues, did not repent of the works of their hands or give up worshiping demons and idols of gold and silver and bronze and stone and wood, which cannot see or hear or walk.

ἔκτῳ ἀγγέλῳ, ὁ ἔχων τὴν σάλπιγγα·
sixth angel, – having the trumpet:

λῦσον τοὺς τέσσαρας ἀγγέλους τοὺς
Loose the four angels –

δεδεμένους ἐπὶ τῷ ποταμῷ τῷ μεγάλῳ
having been bound at the ²river – ¹great

Εὐφράτῃ. 15 καὶ ἐλύθησαν οἱ τέσσαρες
Euphrates. And were loosed the four

ἄγγελοι οἱ ἡτοιμασμένοι εἰς τὴν ὥραν
angels – having been prepared for the hour

καὶ ἡμέραν καὶ μῆνα καὶ ἐνιαυτόν,
and day and month and year,

ἵνα ἀποκτείνωσιν τὸ τρίτον τῶν ἀνθρώπων.
in or- they should kill the third – of men.
der that [part]

16 καὶ ὁ ἀριθμὸς τῶν στρατευμάτων τοῦ
And the number of the bodies of soldiers of the

ἱππικοῦ δισμυριάδες μυριάδων· ἤκουσα τὸν
cavalry [was] two myriads of myriads; I heard the

ἀριθμὸν αὐτῶν. 17 καὶ οὕτως εἶδον
number of them. And thus I saw

τοὺς ἵππους ἐν τῇ ὁράσει καὶ τοὺς
the horses in the vision and the

καθημένους ἐπ' αὐτῶν, ἔχοντας θώρακας
[ones] sitting on them, having breastplates

πυρίνους καὶ ὑακινθίνους καὶ θειώδεις·
fire-coloured and dusky red and sulphurous;

καὶ αἱ κεφαλαὶ τῶν ἵππων ὡς κεφαλαὶ
and the heads of the horses as heads

λεόντων, καὶ ἐκ τῶν στομάτων αὐτῶν
of lions, and out of the mouths of them

ἐκπορεύεται πῦρ καὶ καπνὸς καὶ θεῖον.
proceeds fire and smoke and sulphur.

18 ἀπὸ τῶν τριῶν πληγῶν τούτων ἀπεκτάν-
From the ³three ²plagues ¹these were

θησαν τὸ τρίτον τῶν ἀνθρώπων, ἐκ
killed the third [part] – of men, by

τοῦ πυρὸς καὶ τοῦ καπνοῦ καὶ τοῦ
the fire and the smoke and the

θείου τοῦ ἐκπορευομένου ἐκ τῶν στομάτων
sulphur – proceeding out of the mouths

αὐτῶν. 19 ἡ γὰρ ἐξουσία τῶν ἵππων
of them. For the authority of the horses

ἐν τῷ στόματι αὐτῶν ἐστιν καὶ ἐν
¹in ²the ⁴mouth ⁵of them ³is and in

ταῖς οὐραῖς αὐτῶν· αἱ γὰρ οὐραὶ αὐτῶν
the tails of them; for the tails of them

ὅμοιαι ὄφεσιν, ἔχουσαι κεφαλάς, καὶ ἐν
[are] like to serpents, having heads, and with

αὐταῖς ἀδικοῦσιν. 20 καὶ οἱ λοιποὶ τῶν
them they do harm. And the rest –

ἀνθρώπων, οἳ οὐκ ἀπεκτάνθησαν ἐν ταῖς
of men, who were not killed by –

πληγαῖς ταύταις, οὐδὲ μετενόησαν ἐκ
plagues these, not even repented of

τῶν ἔργων τῶν χειρῶν αὐτῶν, ἵνα μὴ
the works of the hands of them, in order not
that

προσκυνήσουσιν τὰ δαιμόνια καὶ τὰ εἴδωλα
they will worship – demons and – idols

τὰ χρυσᾶ καὶ τὰ ἀργυρᾶ καὶ τὰ χαλκᾶ
– golden and – silver and – bronze

καὶ τὰ λίθινα καὶ τὰ ξύλινα, ἃ οὔτε
and – stone and – wooden, which ²neither

βλέπειν δύνανται οὔτε ἀκούειν οὔτε
²to see ¹can nor to hear nor

the trumpet, "Release the four angels who are bound at the great river Euphrates." 15 And the four angels who had been kept ready for this very hour and day and month and year were released to kill a third of mankind. 16 The number of the mounted troops was two hundred million. I heard their number. 17 The horses and riders I saw in my vision looked like this: Their breastplates were fiery red, dark blue, and yellow as sulfur. The heads of the horses resembled the heads of lions, and out of their mouths came fire, smoke and sulfur. 18 A third of mankind was killed by the three plagues of fire, smoke and sulfur that came out of their mouths. 19 The power of the horses was in their mouths and in their tails; for their tails were like snakes, having heads with which they inflict injury. 20 The rest of mankind that were not killed by these plagues still did not repent of the work of their hands; they did not stop worshiping demons, and idols of gold, silver, bronze, stone and wood—idols that cannot see or

21 And they did not repent of their murders or their sorceries or their fornication or their thefts.

περιπατεῖν, 21 καὶ οὐ μετενόησαν ἐκ τῶν
to walk,   and they repented not of the

φόνων αὐτῶν οὔτε ἐκ τῶν φαρμακειῶν
murders of them nor of the sorceries

αὐτῶν οὔτε ἐκ τῆς πορνείας αὐτῶν
of them nor of the fornication of them

οὔτε ἐκ τῶν κλεμμάτων αὐτῶν.
nor of the thefts   of them.

hear or walk. 21Nor did they repent of their murders, their magic arts, their sexual immorality or their thefts.

Chapter 10

The Angel with the Little Scroll

AND I saw another mighty angel coming down from heaven, wrapped in a cloud, with a rainbow over his head; his face was like the sun, and his legs like pillars of fire. 2 He held a little scroll open in his hand. Setting his right foot on the sea and his left foot on the land, he gave a great shout, like a lion roaring. And when he shouted, the seven thunders sounded. 4 And when the seven thunders had sounded, I was about to write, but I heard a voice from heaven saying, "Seal up what the seven thunders have said, and do not write it down." 5 Then the angel whom I saw standing on the sea and the land
raised his right hand
to heaven
6   and swore by him
who lives
forever and
ever,
who created heaven and what is in it, the earth and what is in it, and the sea and what is in it: "There will be no more delay, 7 but in the days when the seventh angel is to blow his trumpet, the mystery of God will be fulfilled, as he

10 Καὶ εἶδον ἄλλον ἄγγελον ἰσχυρὸν
   And I saw another ²angel   ¹strong

καταβαίνοντα ἐκ τοῦ οὐρανοῦ, περιβεβλημέ-
coming down out of the heaven, having been clothed

νον νεφέλην, καὶ ἡ ἶρις ἐπὶ τὴν κεφαλὴν
[with] a cloud, and the rainbow on the head

αὐτοῦ, καὶ τὸ πρόσωπον αὐτοῦ ὡς ὁ
of him, and the face   of him as the

ἥλιος, καὶ οἱ πόδες αὐτοῦ ὡς στῦλοι
sun,   and the feet of him as pillars

πυρός, 2 καὶ ἔχων ἐν τῇ χειρὶ αὐτοῦ
of fire, and having in the ' hand of him

βιβλαρίδιον ἠνεῳγμένον. καὶ ἔθηκεν τὸν
a little scroll having been opened. And he placed ¹the

πόδα αὐτοῦ τὸν δεξιὸν ἐπὶ τῆς θαλάσσης,
²foot ⁴of him - ³right on the sea,

τὸν δὲ εὐώνυμον ἐπὶ τῆς γῆς, 3 καὶ
and the left   on the land, and

ἔκραξεν φωνῇ μεγάλῃ ὥσπερ λέων μυκᾶται.
cried ²voice ¹with a as   a lion roars.
        great(loud)

καὶ ὅτε ἔκραξεν, ἐλάλησαν αἱ ἑπτὰ
And when he cried, ⁴spoke(uttered) ¹the ²seven

βρονταὶ τὰς ἑαυτῶν φωνάς. 4 Καὶ ὅτε
³thunders ⁵the ⁷of themselves ⁶voices. And when

ἐλάλησαν αἱ ἑπτὰ βρονταί, ἤμελλον
spoke   the seven thunders, I was about

γράφειν· καὶ ἤκουσα φωνὴν ἐκ τοῦ
to write; and I heard a voice out of -

οὐρανοῦ λέγουσαν· σφράγισον ἃ ἐλάλησαν
heaven saying: Seal thou [the] ⁴spoke
                          things which

αἱ ἑπτὰ βρονταί, καὶ μὴ αὐτὰ γράψῃς.
¹the ²seven ³thunders, and ³not ²them thou mayest
                                    ¹write.

5 Καὶ ὁ ἄγγελος, ὃν εἶδον ἑστῶτα
  And the angel, whom I saw standing

ἐπὶ τῆς θαλάσσης καὶ ἐπὶ τῆς γῆς,
on the sea   and on the land,

ἦρεν τὴν χεῖρα αὐτοῦ τὴν δεξιὰν εἰς
lifted ¹the ³hand ⁴of him - ²right to

τὸν οὐρανόν, 6 καὶ ὤμοσεν ἐν τῷ ζῶντι
  - heaven, and swore by the [one] living

εἰς τοὺς αἰῶνας τῶν αἰώνων, ὃς ἔκτισεν
unto the ages of the ages, who created

τὸν οὐρανὸν καὶ τὰ ἐν αὐτῷ καὶ τὴν
the heaven and the things in it and the

γῆν καὶ τὰ ἐν αὐτῇ καὶ τὴν θάλασσαν
earth and the in it and the sea
        things

καὶ τὰ ἐν αὐτῇ, ὅτι χρόνος οὐκέτι
and the things in it, that time ²no longer

ἔσται, 7 ἀλλ’ ἐν ταῖς ἡμέραις τῆς
¹shall be, but in the days of the

φωνῆς τοῦ ἑβδόμου ἀγγέλου, ὅταν μέλλῃ
voice of the seventh angel, whenever he is about

σαλπίζειν, καὶ ἐτελέσθη τὸ μυστήριον
to trumpet, even was finished the mystery

Chapter 10

The Angel and the Little Scroll

THEN I saw another mighty angel coming down from heaven. He was robed in a cloud, with a rainbow above his head; his face was like the sun, and his legs were like fiery pillars. 2He was holding a little scroll, which lay open in his hand. He planted his right foot on the sea and his left foot on the land, 3and he gave a loud shout like the roar of a lion. When he shouted, the voices of the seven thunders spoke. 4And when the seven thunders spoke, I was about to write; but I heard a voice from heaven say, "Seal up what the seven thunders have said and do not write it down."
5Then the angel I had seen standing on the sea and on the land raised his right hand to heaven. 6And he swore by him who lives for ever and ever, who created the heavens and all that is in it, the earth and all that is in it, and the sea and all that is in it, and said, "There will be no more delay! 7But in the days when the seventh angel is about to sound his trumpet, the mystery of

announced to his servants ᶻ the prophets."

8 Then the voice that I had heard from heaven spoke to me again, saying, "Go, take the scroll that is open in the hand of the angel who is standing on the sea and on the land." 9 So I went to the angel and told him to give me the little scroll; and he said to me, "Take it, and eat it; it will be bitter to your stomach, but sweet as honey in your mouth." 10 So I took the little scroll from the hand of the angel and ate it; it was sweet as honey in my mouth, but when I had eaten it, my stomach was made bitter.

11 Then they said to me, "You must prophesy again about many peoples and nations and languages and kings."

Chapter 11

The Two Witnesses

THEN I was given a measuring rod like a staff, and I was told, "Come and measure the temple of God and the altar and those who worship there, 2 but do not measure the court outside the temple; leave that out, for it is given over to the nations, and they will trample over the holy city for forty-two months. 3 And I will grant my two witnesses authority to prophesy for one thousand two hundred sixty days, wearing sackcloth."

4 These are the two olive trees and the two lampstands that stand before the

---

τοῦ θεοῦ, ὡς εὐηγγέλισεν τοὺς ἑαυτοῦ
\- of God, as he preached [to] the ¹of himself

δούλους τοὺς προφήτας. 8 Καὶ ἡ φωνὴ
¹slaves the prophets. And the voice

ἦν ἤκουσα ἐκ τοῦ οὐρανοῦ, πάλιν
which I heard out of - heaven, again

λαλοῦσαν μετ᾽ ἐμοῦ καὶ λέγουσαν· ὕπαγε
speaking with me and saying: Go thou

λάβε τὸ βιβλίον τὸ ἠνεῳγμένον ἐν τῇ
take the scroll - having been opened in the

χειρὶ τοῦ ἀγγέλου τοῦ ἑστῶτος ἐπὶ
hand of the angel - standing on

τῆς θαλάσσης καὶ ἐπὶ τῆς γῆς. 9 καὶ
the sea and on the land. And

ἀπῆλθα πρὸς τὸν ἄγγελον, λέγων αὐτῷ
I went away toward the angel, telling him

δοῦναί μοι τὸ βιβλαρίδιον. καὶ λέγει
to give me the little scroll. And he says

μοι· λάβε καὶ κατάφαγε αὐτό, καὶ
to me: Take and devour it, and

πικρανεῖ σου τὴν κοιλίαν, ἀλλ᾽ ἐν τῷ
it will embitter ²of thee ¹the ²stomach, but in the

στόματί σου ἔσται γλυκὺ ὡς μέλι.
mouth of thee it will be sweet as honey.

10 καὶ ἔλαβον τὸ βιβλαρίδιον ἐκ τῆς
And I took the little scroll out of the

χειρὸς τοῦ ἀγγέλου καὶ κατέφαγον αὐτό,
hand of the angel and devoured it,

καὶ ἦν ἐν τῷ στόματί μου ὡς μέλι
and it was in the mouth of me as ²honey

γλυκύ· καὶ ὅτε ἔφαγον αὐτό, ἐπικράνθη
¹sweet; and when I ate it, ⁴was made bitter

ἡ κοιλία μου. 11 καὶ λέγουσίν μοι·
¹the ²stomach ³of me. And they say to me:

δεῖ σε πάλιν προφητεῦσαι ἐπὶ λαοῖς
It behoves thee again to prophesy before peoples

καὶ ἔθνεσιν καὶ γλώσσαις καὶ βασιλεῦσιν
and nations and tongues and ²kings

πολλοῖς. 11 Καὶ ἐδόθη μοι κάλαμος ὅμοιος
¹many. And was given to me a reed like

ῥάβδῳ, λέγων· ἔγειρε καὶ μέτρησον τὸν ναὸν
to a staff, saying: Rise and measure the shrine

τοῦ θεοῦ καὶ τὸ θυσιαστήριον καὶ τοὺς
of God and the altar and the

προσκυνοῦντας ἐν αὐτῷ. 2 καὶ τὴν
[ones] worshipping in it. And the

αὐλὴν τὴν ἔξωθεν τοῦ ναοῦ ἔκβαλε
²court - ¹outside of the shrine cast out

ἔξωθεν καὶ μὴ αὐτὴν μετρήσῃς, ὅτι
outside and ³not ²it thou mayest ¹measure, because

ἐδόθη τοῖς ἔθνεσιν, καὶ τὴν πόλιν τὴν
it was given to the nations, and the ²city -

ἁγίαν πατήσουσιν μῆνας τεσσεράκοντα
¹holy they will trample ³months ¹forty-

[καὶ] δύο. 3 καὶ δώσω τοῖς δυσὶν
and ²two. And I will give to the two

μάρτυσίν μου, καὶ προφητεύσουσιν ἡμέρας
witnesses of me, and they will prophesy ⁵days

χιλίας διακοσίας ἑξήκοντα περιβεβλημένοι
¹a thousand ²two hundred ³[and] ⁴sixty having been clothed

σάκκους. 4 οὗτοί εἰσιν αἱ δύο ἐλαῖαι
[in] sackclothes. These are the two olive-trees

καὶ αἱ δύο λυχνίαι αἱ ἐνώπιον τοῦ
and the two lampstands - ²before ⁸the

God will be accomplished, just as he announced to his servants the prophets."

8 Then the voice that I had heard from heaven spoke to me once more: "Go, take the scroll that lies open in the hand of the angel who is standing on the sea and on the land." 9 So I went to the angel and asked him to give me the little scroll. He said to me, "Take it and eat it. It will turn your stomach sour, but in your mouth it will be as sweet as honey." 10 I took the little scroll from the angel's hand and ate it. It tasted as sweet as honey in my mouth, but when I had eaten it, my stomach turned sour. 11 Then I was told, "You must prophesy again about many peoples, nations, languages and kings."

Chapter 11

The Two Witnesses

I WAS given a reed like a measuring rod and was told, "Go and measure the temple of God and the altar, and count the worshipers there. 2 But exclude the outer court; do not measure it, because it has been given to the Gentiles. They will trample on the holy city for 42 months. 3 And I will give power to my two witnesses, and they will prophesy for 1,260 days, clothed in sackcloth." 4 These are the two olive trees and the two lampstands that stand before the

Lord of the earth. [5]And if anyone wants to harm them, fire pours from their mouth and consumes their foes; anyone who wants to harm them must be killed in this manner. [6]They have authority to shut the sky, so that no rain may fall during the days of their prophesying, and they have authority over the waters to turn them into blood, and to strike the earth with every kind of plague, as often as they desire.

[7] When they have finished their testimony, the beast that comes up from the bottomless pit will make war on them and conquer them and kill them, [8]and their dead bodies will lie in the street of the great city that is prophetically[a] called Sodom and Egypt, where also their Lord was crucified. [9]For three and a half days members of the peoples and tribes and languages and nations will gaze at their dead bodies and refuse to let them be placed in a tomb; [10]and the inhabitants of the earth will gloat over them and celebrate and exchange presents, because these two prophets had been a torment to the inhabitants of the earth.

[11] But after the three and a half days, the breath[b] of life from God entered them, and they stood on their feet, and those who saw them were

---

κυρίου τῆς γῆς ἑστῶτες. **5** καὶ εἴ τις
[1]Lord [6]of the [5]earth [1]standing. And if anyone

αὐτοὺς θέλει ἀδικῆσαι, πῦρ ἐκπορεύεται·
[2]them [1]wishes [2]to harm, fire proceeds

ἐκ τοῦ στόματος αὐτῶν καὶ κατεσθίει
out of the mouth of them and devours

τοὺς ἐχθροὺς αὐτῶν· καὶ εἴ τις θελήσῃ
the enemies of them; and if anyone should wish

αὐτοὺς ἀδικῆσαι, οὕτως δεῖ αὐτὸν
[2]them [1]to harm, thus it behoves him

ἀποκτανθῆναι. **6** οὗτοι ἔχουσιν τὴν ἐξουσίαν
to be killed. These have the authority

κλεῖσαι τὸν οὐρανόν, ἵνα μὴ ὑετὸς
to shut - heaven, in order that [2]not [1]rain

βρέχῃ τὰς ἡμέρας τῆς προφητείας αὐτῶν,
[2]may the days of the prophecy of them,
[1]rain(fall)

καὶ ἐξουσίαν ἔχουσιν ἐπὶ τῶν ὑδάτων
and authority they have over the waters

στρέφειν αὐτὰ εἰς αἷμα καὶ πατάξαι
to turn them into blood and to strike

τὴν γῆν ἐν πάσῃ πληγῇ ὁσάκις ἐὰν
the earth with every [kind of] plague as often as

θελήσωσιν. **7** Καὶ ὅταν τελέσωσιν τὴν
they may wish. And whenever they finish the

μαρτυρίαν αὐτῶν, τὸ θηρίον τὸ ἀναβαῖνον
witness of them, the beast - coming up

ἐκ τῆς ἀβύσσου ποιήσει μετ' αὐτῶν
out of the abyss [1]will make [3]with [4]them

πόλεμον καὶ νικήσει αὐτοὺς καὶ ἀποκτενεῖ
[2]war and will overcome them and will kill

αὐτούς. **8** καὶ τὸ πτῶμα αὐτῶν ἐπὶ
them. And the corpse of them on

τῆς πλατείας τῆς πόλεως τῆς μεγάλης,
the open street of the [1]city [2]great,

ἥτις καλεῖται πνευματικῶς Σόδομα καὶ
which is called spiritually Sodom and

Αἴγυπτος, ὅπου καὶ ὁ κύριος αὐτῶν
Egypt, where indeed the Lord of them

ἐσταυρώθη. **9** καὶ βλέπουσιν ἐκ τῶν
was crucified. And [10]see [1][some] of [9]the

λαῶν καὶ φυλῶν καὶ γλωσσῶν καὶ
[2]peoples [4]and [5]tribes [6]and [7]tongues [8]and

ἐθνῶν τὸ πτῶμα αὐτῶν ἡμέρας τρεῖς
[9]nations the corpse of them [4]days [1]three

καὶ ἥμισυ, καὶ τὰ πτώματα αὐτῶν
[2]and [3]a half, and [1]the [2]corpses [4]of them

οὐκ ἀφίουσιν τεθῆναι εἰς μνῆμα. **10** καὶ
[1]they do not allow to be placed in a tomb. And

οἱ κατοικοῦντες ἐπὶ τῆς γῆς χαίρουσιν
the [ones] dwelling on the earth rejoice

ἐπ' αὐτοῖς καὶ εὐφραίνονται, καὶ δῶρα
over them and are glad, and [2]gifts

πέμψουσιν ἀλλήλοις, ὅτι οὗτοι οἱ δύο
[1]they will send to one another, because these - two

προφῆται ἐβασάνισαν τοὺς κατοικοῦντας
prophets tormented the [ones] dwelling

ἐπὶ τῆς γῆς. **11** Καὶ μετὰ [τὰς] τρεῖς
on the earth. And after the [1]three

ἡμέρας καὶ ἥμισυ πνεῦμα ζωῆς ἐκ τοῦ
[1]days [2]and [3]a half a spirit of life out of -

θεοῦ εἰσῆλθεν ἐν αὐτοῖς, καὶ ἔστησαν
God entered in[to] them, and they stood

ἐπὶ τοὺς πόδας αὐτῶν, καὶ φόβος μέγας
on the feet of them, and [2]fear [1]great

Lord of the earth. [5]If anyone tries to harm them, fire comes from their mouths and devours their enemies. This is how anyone who wants to harm them must die. [6]These men have power to shut up the sky so that it will not rain during the time they are prophesying; and they have power to turn the waters into blood and to strike the earth with every kind of plague as often as they want.

[7]Now when they have finished their testimony, the beast that comes up from the Abyss will attack them, and overpower and kill them. [8]Their bodies will lie in the street of the great city, which is figuratively called Sodom and Egypt, where also their Lord was crucified. [9]For three and a half days men from every people, tribe, language and nation will gaze on their bodies and refuse them burial. [10]The inhabitants of the earth will gloat over them and will celebrate by sending each other gifts, because these two prophets had tormented those who live on the earth.

[11]But after the three and a half days a breath of life from God entered them, and they stood on their feet, and terror struck

---

terrified. 12 Then they^c heard a loud voice from heaven saying to them, "Come up here!" And they went up to heaven in a cloud while their enemies watched them. At that moment there was a great earthquake, and a tenth of the city fell; seven thousand people were killed in the earthquake, and the rest were terrified and gave glory to the God of heaven. 14 The second woe has passed. The third woe is coming very soon.

The Seventh Trumpet

15 Then the seventh angel blew his trumpet, and there were loud voices in heaven, saying,
"The kingdom of the
world has
become the
kingdom of
our Lord
and of his
Messiah,^d
and he will reign
forever and
ever."
16 Then the twenty-four elders who sit on their thrones before God fell on their faces and worshiped God, 17 singing,
"We give you thanks,
Lord
God Almighty,
who are and who
were,
for you have taken
your
great power
and begun to reign.
18 The nations raged,
but your wrath has
come,
and the time for
judging
the dead,
for rewarding your
servants,^e
the prophets
and saints and all
who fear
your name,
both small and

^c Other ancient authorities read I
^d Gk Christ
^e Gk slaves

Middle column (interlinear)

ἐπέπεσεν ἐπὶ τοὺς θεωροῦντας αὐτούς.
fell on on the [ones] beholding them.

12 καὶ ἤκουσαν φωνῆς μεγάλης ἐκ τοῦ
And they heard ²voice ¹a great(loud) out of -

οὐρανοῦ λεγούσης αὐτοῖς· ἀνάβατε ὧδε·
heaven saying to them: Come ye up here;

καὶ ἀνέβησαν εἰς τὸν οὐρανὸν ἐν τῇ
and they went up to - heaven in the

νεφέλῃ, καὶ ἐθεώρησαν αὐτοὺς οἱ ἐχθροὶ
cloud, and ⁴beheld ⁵them ¹the ²enemies

αὐτῶν. 13 Καὶ ἐν ἐκείνῃ τῇ ὥρᾳ ἐγένετο
³of them. And in that - hour ³occurred

σεισμὸς μέγας, καὶ τὸ δέκατον τῆς
¹earthquake ¹a great, and the tenth [part] of the

πόλεως ἔπεσεν, καὶ ἀπεκτάνθησαν ἐν τῷ
city fell, and ⁵were killed ⁶in ⁷the

σεισμῷ ὀνόματα ἀνθρώπων χιλιάδες ἑπτά,
⁸earthquake ²names ³of men ¹thousands ¹seven,

καὶ οἱ λοιποὶ ἔμφοβοι ἐγένοντο καὶ
and the rest ²terrified ¹became and

ἔδωκαν δόξαν τῷ θεῷ τοῦ οὐρανοῦ.
gave glory to the God - of heaven.

14 Ἡ οὐαὶ ἡ δευτέρα ἀπῆλθεν· ἰδοὺ
The ²woe ¹second passed away; behold[,]

ἡ οὐαὶ ἡ τρίτη ἔρχεται ταχύ.
the ²woe - ¹third is coming quickly.

15 Καὶ ὁ ἕβδομος ἄγγελος ἐσάλπισεν·
And the seventh angel trumpeted;

καὶ ἐγένοντο φωναὶ μεγάλαι ἐν τῷ
and there were voices great(loud) in -

οὐρανῷ, λέγοντες· ἐγένετο ἡ βασιλεία
heaven, saying: ²became ¹The ²kingdom

τοῦ κόσμου τοῦ κυρίου ἡμῶν καὶ τοῦ
³of the ⁴world of the Lord of us and of the

χριστοῦ αὐτοῦ, καὶ βασιλεύσει εἰς τοὺς
Christ of him, and he shall reign unto the

αἰῶνας τῶν αἰώνων. 16 καὶ οἱ εἴκοσι
ages of the ages. And the twenty-

τέσσαρες πρεσβύτεροι, οἱ ἐνώπιον τοῦ
four elders, - ²before -

θεοῦ καθήμενοι ἐπὶ τοὺς θρόνους αὐτῶν,
³God ¹sitting on the thrones of them,

ἔπεσαν ἐπὶ τὰ πρόσωπα αὐτῶν καὶ
fell on the faces of them and

προσεκύνησαν τῷ θεῷ, 17 λέγοντες·
worshipped - God, saying:

εὐχαριστοῦμέν σοι, κύριε ὁ θεὸς ὁ
We thank thee, [O] Lord - God the

παντοκράτωρ, ὁ ὢν καὶ ὁ ἦν, ὅτι
Almighty, the [one] being and the was, because
=the one who is [one who]

εἴληφας τὴν δύναμίν σου τὴν μεγάλην
thou hast taken ¹the ³power ⁴of thee - ²great

καὶ ἐβασίλευσας· 18 καὶ τὰ ἔθνη ὠργίσ-
and didst reign; and the nations were

θησαν, καὶ ἦλθεν ἡ ὀργή σου καὶ ὁ
wrathful, and ⁴came ¹the ²wrath ³of thee and the

καιρὸς τῶν νεκρῶν κριθῆναι καὶ δοῦναι
time of the dead to be judged and to give

τὸν μισθὸν τοῖς δούλοις σου τοῖς προφήταις
the reward to the slaves of thee *to* the prophets

καὶ τοῖς ἁγίοις καὶ τοῖς φοβουμένοις
and to the saints and to the [ones] fearing

τὸ ὄνομά σου, τοῖς μικροῖς καὶ τοῖς
the name of thee, to the small and to the

those who saw them. 12 Then they heard a loud voice from heaven saying to them, "Come up here." And they went up to heaven in a cloud, while their enemies looked on.
13 At that very hour there was a severe earthquake and a tenth of the city collapsed. Seven thousand people were killed in the earthquake, and the survivors were terrified and gave glory to the God of heaven.
14 The second woe has passed; the third woe is coming soon.

The Seventh Trumpet

15 The seventh angel sounded his trumpet, and there were loud voices in heaven, which said:

"The kingdom of the
world has become
the kingdom of our
Lord and of his
Christ,
and he will reign for
ever and ever."

16 And the twenty-four elders, who were seated on their thrones before God, fell on their faces and worshiped God, 17 saying:

"We give thanks to you,
Lord God Almighty,
the One who is and
who was,
because you have taken
your great power
and have begun to
reign.
18 The nations were angry;
and your wrath has
come.
The time has come for
judging the dead,
and for rewarding your
servants the
prophets
and your saints and
those who reverence
your name,

great,
and for destroying
those who
destroy the
earth."
19 Then God's temple
in heaven was opened, and
the ark of his covenant was
seen within his temple; and
there were flashes of lightning, rumblings, peals of
thunder, an earthquake,
and heavy hail.

μεγάλοις, καὶ διαφθεῖραι τοὺς διαφθείροντας
great,   and   to destroy the [ones] destroying

τὴν γῆν. 19 καὶ ἠνοίγη ὁ ναὸς τοῦ
the earth.   And was opened the shrine –

θεοῦ ὁ ἐν τῷ οὐρανῷ, καὶ ὤφθη ἡ
of God – in – heaven,   and was seen the

κιβωτὸς τῆς διαθήκης αὐτοῦ ἐν τῷ
ark   of the covenant of him in the

ναῷ αὐτοῦ, καὶ ἐγένοντο ἀστραπαὶ καὶ
shrine of him, and occurred lightnings and

φωναὶ καὶ βρονταὶ καὶ σεισμὸς καὶ
voices and thunders and an earthquake and

χάλαζα μεγάλη.
¹hail ¹a great.

both small and great—
and for destroying those
who destroy the
earth."
19Then God's temple in
heaven was opened, and
within his temple was seen
the ark of his covenant.
And there came flashes of
lightning, rumblings, peals
of thunder, an earthquake
and a great hailstorm.

Chapter 12
The Woman and the Dragon

A great portent appeared
in heaven: a woman
clothed with the sun, with
the moon under her feet,
and on her head a crown of
twelve stars. ²She was
pregnant and was crying
out in birthpangs, in the agony of giving birth. ³Then
another portent appeared
in heaven: a great red dragon, with seven heads and
ten horns, and seven dia-
dems on his heads. ⁴His tail
swept down a third of the
stars of heaven and threw
them to the earth. Then the
dragon stood before the
woman who was about to
bear a child, so that he
might devour her child as
soon as it was born. ⁵And
she gave birth to a son, a
male child, who is to rule^f
all the nations with a rod of
iron. But her child was
snatched away and taken to
God and to his throne; ⁶and
the woman fled into the wilderness, where she has a
place prepared by God, so
that there she can be nourished for one thousand two
hundred sixty days.

12 Καὶ σημεῖον μέγα ὤφθη ἐν τῷ
And ²sign ¹a great was seen in –

οὐρανῷ, γυνὴ περιβεβλημένη τὸν ἥλιον,
heaven, a woman having been clothed [with] the sun,

καὶ ἡ σελήνη ὑποκάτω τῶν ποδῶν αὐτῆς,
and the moon underneath the feet of her,

καὶ ἐπὶ τῆς κεφαλῆς αὐτῆς στέφανος
and on the head of her a crown

ἀστέρων δώδεκα, 2 καὶ ἐν γαστρὶ ἔχουσα,
²stars ¹of twelve, and in womb having,
                                          = being pregnant,

καὶ κράζει ὠδίνουσα καὶ βασανιζομένη
and she cries suffering birth-pains and being distressed

τεκεῖν. 3 καὶ ὤφθη ἄλλο σημεῖον
to bear.   And was seen another sign

ἐν τῷ οὐρανῷ, καὶ ἰδοὺ δράκων μέγας
in – heaven,   and behold[,] ²dragon ¹a great

πυρρός, ἔχων κεφαλὰς ἑπτὰ καὶ κέρατα
²red, having ²heads ¹seven and ²horns

δέκα καὶ ἐπὶ τὰς κεφαλὰς αὐτοῦ ἑπτὰ
¹ten and on the heads of him seven

διαδήματα, 4 καὶ ἡ οὐρὰ αὐτοῦ σύρει
diadems, and the tail of him draws

τὸ τρίτον τῶν ἀστέρων τοῦ οὐρανοῦ,
the third [part] of the stars – of heaven,

καὶ ἔβαλεν αὐτοὺς εἰς τὴν γῆν. Καὶ
and cast them to the earth. And

ὁ δράκων ἔστηκεν ἐνώπιον τῆς γυναικὸς
the dragon stood before the woman

τῆς μελλούσης τεκεῖν, ἵνα ὅταν τέκῃ
– being about to bear, in order whenever she
                                that bears

τὸ τέκνον αὐτῆς καταφάγῃ. 5 καὶ
¹the ³child ⁴of her ¹he might devour. And

ἔτεκεν υἱὸν ἄρσεν, ὃς μέλλει ποιμαίνειν
she bore a son[,] a male, who is about to shepherd

πάντα τὰ ἔθνη ἐν ῥάβδῳ σιδηρᾷ· καὶ
all the nations with ²staff ¹an iron; and

ἡρπάσθη τὸ τέκνον αὐτῆς πρὸς τὸν
⁴was seized ¹the ²child ³of her to –

θεὸν καὶ πρὸς τὸν θρόνον αὐτοῦ. 6 καὶ
God and to the throne of him. And

ἡ γυνὴ ἔφυγεν εἰς τὴν ἔρημον, ὅπου
the woman fled into the desert, where

ἔχει ἐκεῖ τόπον ἡτοιμασμένον ἀπὸ
she has there a place having been prepared from

τοῦ θεοῦ, ἵνα ἐκεῖ τρέφωσιν αὐτὴν
– God, in order that there they might nourish her

ἡμέρας χιλίας διακοσίας ἑξήκοντα.
⁵days ¹a thousand ²two hundred ³[and] ⁴sixty.

Chapter 12
The Woman and the Dragon

A GREAT and wondrous
sign appeared in heav-
en: a woman clothed with
the sun, with the moon under her feet and a crown of
twelve stars on her head.
²She was pregnant and
cried out in pain as she was
about to give birth. ³Then
another sign appeared in
heaven: an enormous red
dragon with seven heads
and ten horns and seven
crowns on his heads. ⁴His
tail swept a third of the
stars out of the sky and
flung them to the earth. The
dragon stood in front of the
woman who was about to
give birth, so that he might
devour her child the mo-
ment it was born. ⁵She gave
birth to a son, a male child,
who will rule all the nations
with an iron scepter. And
her child was snatched up
to God and to his throne.
⁶The woman fled into the
desert to a place prepared
for her by God, where she
might be taken care of for
1,260 days.

^f Or to shepherd

Michael Defeats the Dragon

7 And war broke out in heaven; Michael and his angels fought against the dragon. The dragon and his angels fought back, 8 but they were defeated, and there was no longer any place for them in heaven. 9 The great dragon was thrown down, that ancient serpent, who is called the Devil and Satan, the deceiver of the whole world—he was thrown down to the earth, and his angels were thrown down with him.
10 Then I heard a loud voice in heaven, proclaiming,

"Now have come the
　salvation and
　the power
　and the kingdom of
　　our God
　and the authority of
　　his Messiah,[g]
for the accuser of our
　comrades[h] has
　been thrown
　down,
who accuses them
　day and night
　before our God.
11 But they have
　conquered him
　by the blood of
　　the Lamb
　and by the word of
　　their testimony,
for they did not cling
　to life even in
　the face of
　death.
12 Rejoice then, you
　heavens
　and those who dwell
　　in them!
But woe to the earth
　and the sea,
for the devil has
　come down
　to you
with great wrath,
　because he knows
　that his time
　is short!"

The Dragon Fights Again on Earth

13 So when the dragon saw that he had been thrown down to the earth, he pursued[i] the woman who had given birth to the male child. 14 But the woman was given the two wings of the great eagle, so that she could fly from the serpent into the wilderness, to

---

7 Καὶ ἐγένετο πόλεμος ἐν τῷ οὐρανῷ,
　And occurred war in - heaven,
ὁ Μιχαὴλ καὶ οἱ ἄγγελοι αὐτοῦ τοῦ
　- Michael and the angels of him -
πολεμῆσαι μετὰ τοῦ δράκοντος. καὶ ὁ
to make war[d] with the dragon. And the
δράκων ἐπολέμησεν καὶ οἱ ἄγγελοι αὐτοῦ,
dragon warred and the angels of him,
8 καὶ οὐκ ἴσχυσεν, οὐδὲ τόπος εὑρέθη
　and prevailed not, not even place was found
αὐτῶν ἔτι ἐν τῷ οὐρανῷ. 9 καὶ ἐβλήθη
of them still in - heaven. And was cast
ὁ δράκων ὁ μέγας, ὁ ὄφις ὁ ἀρχαῖος,
¹the ³dragon - ²great, ⁴the ⁵serpent - ⁶old,
ὁ καλούμενος Διάβολος καὶ ὁ Σατανᾶς,
- being called Devil and the Satan,
ὁ πλανῶν τὴν οἰκουμένην ὅλην, ἐβλήθη
the deceiving the ²inhabited ¹whole, was cast
[one] [earth]
εἰς τὴν γῆν, καὶ οἱ ἄγγελοι αὐτοῦ μετ'
to the earth, and the angels of him with
αὐτοῦ ἐβλήθησαν. 10 καὶ ἤκουσα φωνὴν
him were cast. And I heard ²voice
μεγάλην ἐν τῷ οὐρανῷ λέγουσαν ἄρτι
¹a great(loud) in - heaven saying: Now
ἐγένετο ἡ σωτηρία καὶ ἡ δύναμις καὶ
became the salvation and the power and
ἡ βασιλεία τοῦ θεοῦ ἡμῶν καὶ ἡ ἐξουσία
the kingdom of the God of us and the authority
τοῦ χριστοῦ αὐτοῦ, ὅτι ἐβλήθη ὁ κατήγωρ
of the Christ of him, because ⁴was cast ¹the ²accuser
τῶν ἀδελφῶν ἡμῶν, ὁ κατηγορῶν αὐτοὺς
³of the ⁴brothers ⁵of us, the [one] accusing them
ἐνώπιον τοῦ θεοῦ ἡμῶν ἡμέρας καὶ
before the God of us day and
νυκτός. 11 καὶ αὐτοὶ ἐνίκησαν αὐτὸν
night. And they overcame him
διὰ τὸ αἷμα τοῦ ἀρνίου καὶ διὰ τὸν
be- the blood of the Lamb and because the
cause of of
λόγον τῆς μαρτυρίας αὐτῶν, καὶ οὐκ
word of the witness of them, and not
ἠγάπησαν τὴν ψυχὴν αὐτῶν ἄχρι θανάτου.
they loved the life of them until death.
12 διὰ τοῦτο εὐφραίνεσθε, οὐρανοὶ καὶ
　Therefore be ye glad, heavens and
οἱ ἐν αὐτοῖς σκηνοῦντες· οὐαὶ τὴν
the ²in ³them ¹tabernacling; woe [to] the
[ones]
γῆν καὶ τὴν θάλασσαν, ὅτι κατέβη ὁ
earth and the sea, because ²came down ¹the
διάβολος πρὸς ὑμᾶς ἔχων θυμὸν μέγαν,
²devil to you having ²anger ¹great,
εἰδὼς ὅτι ὀλίγον καιρὸν ἔχει. 13 Καὶ
knowing that ²few(short) ³time ¹he has. And
ὅτε εἶδεν ὁ δράκων ὅτι ἐβλήθη εἰς
when ²saw ¹the ³dragon that he was cast to
τὴν γῆν, ἐδίωξεν τὴν γυναῖκα ἥτις
the earth, he pursued the woman who
ἔτεκεν τὸν ἄρσενα. 14 καὶ ἐδόθησαν
bore the male. And were given
τῇ γυναικὶ αἱ δύο πτέρυγες τοῦ ἀετοῦ
to the woman the two wings of the ²eagle
τοῦ μεγάλου, ἵνα πέτηται εἰς τὴν ἔρημον
- ¹great, in order she might to the desert
　　　　　　that fly

---

7 And there was war in heaven. Michael and his angels fought against the dragon, and the dragon and his angels fought back. 8 But he was not strong enough, and they lost their place in heaven. 9 The great dragon was hurled down—that ancient serpent called the devil, or Satan, who leads the whole world astray. He was hurled to the earth, and his angels with him.
10 Then I heard a loud voice in heaven say:

"Now have come the
　salvation and the
　power and the
　kingdom of our
　God,
　and the authority of his
　Christ.
For the accuser of our
　brothers,
　who accuses them
　before our God day
　and night,
　has been hurled down.
11 They overcame him
　by the blood of the
　Lamb
　and by the word of
　their testimony;
　they did not love their
　lives so much
　as to shrink from
　death.
12 Therefore rejoice, you
　heavens
　and you who dwell in
　them!
But woe to the earth and
　the sea,
　because the devil has
　gone down to you!
He is filled with fury,
　because he knows that
　his time is short."

13 When the dragon saw that he had been hurled to the earth, he pursued the woman who had given birth to the male child. 14 The woman was given the two wings of a great eagle, so that she might fly to the

---

g Gk Christ
h Gk brothers
i Or persecuted

her place where she is nourished for a time, and times, and half a time. 15 Then from his mouth the serpent poured water like a river after the woman, to sweep her away with the flood. 16 But the earth came to the help of the woman; it opened its mouth and swallowed the river that the dragon had poured from his mouth. 17 Then the dragon was angry with the woman, and went off to make war on the rest of her children, those who keep the commandments of God and hold the testimony of Jesus.

The First Beast

18 Then the dragon[j] took his stand on the sand of the seashore. 1 And I saw a beast rising out of the sea; and on its horns were ten diadems, and on its heads were blasphemous names. 2 And the beast that I saw was like a leopard, its feet were like a bear's, and its mouth was like a lion's mouth. And the dragon gave it his power and his throne and great authority. 3 One of its heads seemed to have received a death-blow, but its mortal wound[k] had been healed. In amazement the whole earth followed the beast.

εἰς τὸν τόπον αὐτῆς, ὅπου τρέφεται
to the place of her, where she is nourished

ἐκεῖ καιρὸν καὶ καιροὺς καὶ ἥμισυ καιροῦ
there a time and times and half of a time

ἀπὸ προσώπου τοῦ ὄφεως. 15 καὶ ἔβαλεν
from [the] face of the serpent. And ²cast

ὁ ὄφις ἐκ τοῦ στόματος αὐτοῦ ὀπίσω
¹the ²serpent out of the mouth of him behind

τῆς γυναικὸς ὕδωρ ὡς ποταμόν, ἵνα
the woman water as a river, in order that

αὐτὴν ποταμοφόρητον ποιήσῃ. 16 καὶ
¹her ²carried off by [the] river ¹he might make. And

ἐβοήθησεν ἡ γῆ τῇ γυναικί, καὶ ἤνοιξεν
²helped ¹the ²earth the woman, and ²opened

ἡ γῆ τὸ στόμα αὐτῆς καὶ κατέπιεν
¹the ²earth the mouth of it and swallowed

τὸν ποταμὸν ὃν ἔβαλεν ὁ δράκων ἐκ
the river which ²cast ¹the ²dragon out of

τοῦ στόματος αὐτοῦ. 17 καὶ ὠργίσθη
the mouth of him. And ²was enraged

ὁ δράκων ἐπὶ τῇ γυναικί, καὶ ἀπῆλθεν
¹the ²dragon over the woman, and went away

ποιῆσαι πόλεμον μετὰ τῶν λοιπῶν τοῦ
to make war with the rest of the

σπέρματος αὐτῆς, τῶν [ones] τηρούντων τὰς
seed of her, the [ones] keeping the

ἐντολὰς τοῦ θεοῦ καὶ ἐχόντων τὴν
commandments - of God and having the

μαρτυρίαν Ἰησοῦ· (18) καὶ ἐστάθη ἐπὶ τὴν
witness of Jesus; and he stood on the

ἄμμον τῆς θαλάσσης.
sand of the sea.

place prepared for her in the desert, where she would be taken care of for a time, times and half a time, out of the serpent's reach. 15 Then from his mouth the serpent spewed water like a river, to overtake the woman and sweep her away with the torrent. 16 But the earth helped the woman by opening its mouth and swallowing the river that the dragon had spewed out of his mouth. 17 Then the dragon was enraged at the woman and went off to make war against the rest of her offspring—those who obey God's commandments and hold to the testimony of Jesus.

13 Καὶ εἶδον ἐκ τῆς θαλάσσης θηρίον
And I saw ³out of ⁴the ⁵sea ¹a beast

ἀναβαῖνον, ἔχον κέρατα δέκα καὶ κεφαλὰς
²coming up, having ²horns ¹ten and ²heads

ἑπτά, καὶ ἐπὶ τῶν κεράτων αὐτοῦ δέκα
¹seven, and on the horns of it* ten

διαδήματα, καὶ ἐπὶ τὰς κεφαλὰς αὐτοῦ
diadems, and on the heads of it

ὀνόματα βλασφημίας. 2 καὶ τὸ θηρίον
names of blasphemy. And the beast

ὃ εἶδον ἦν ὅμοιον παρδάλει, καὶ οἱ
which I saw was like to a leopard, and the

πόδες αὐτοῦ ὡς ἄρκου, καὶ τὸ στόμα
feet of it as of a bear, and the mouth

αὐτοῦ ὡς στόμα λέοντος. καὶ ἔδωκεν
of it as [the] mouth of a lion. And ²gave

αὐτῷ ὁ δράκων τὴν δύναμιν αὐτοῦ καὶ
⁴to it ¹the ²dragon the power of it and

τὸν θρόνον αὐτοῦ καὶ ἐξουσίαν μεγάλην.
the throne of it and ²authority ¹great.

3 καὶ μίαν ἐκ τῶν κεφαλῶν αὐτοῦ ὡς
And one of the heads of it as

ἐσφαγμένην εἰς θάνατον, καὶ ἡ πληγὴ
having been slain to death, and the stroke

τοῦ θανάτου αὐτοῦ ἐθεραπεύθη. καὶ
of the death of it was healed. And

1 And the dragon[p] stood on the shore of the sea.

The Beast out of the Sea

And I saw a beast coming out of the sea. He had ten horns and seven heads, with ten crowns on his horns, and on each head a blasphemous name. 2 The beast I saw resembled a leopard, but had feet like those of a bear and a mouth like that of a lion. The dragon gave the beast his power and his throne and great authority. 3 One of the heads of the beast seemed to have had a fatal wound, but the fatal wound had been healed. The whole world

* αὐτοῦ, of course, may be neuter or masculine—" of it " or " of him ". δράκων being masculine (=Satan), we have kept to the masculine. But θηρίον is neuter. Yet if it stands for a person, as ἀρνίον certainly does, it too should be treated, as to the pronoun, as a masculine. However, not to enter the province of interpretation, we have rendered αὐτοῦ by " of it ", though it will be seen that αὐτόν (him) is used in ver. 8, τίς (who?) in ver. 4, and ὅς (who) in ver. 14. See also ch. 17. 11.

[j] Gk Then he; other ancient authorities read Then I stood
[k] Gk the plague of its death

[p] 1 Some late manuscripts And I

4 They worshiped the dragon, for he had given his authority to the beast, and they worshiped the beast, saying, "Who is like the beast, and who can fight against it?"

5 The beast was given a mouth uttering haughty and blasphemous words, and it was allowed to exercise authority for forty-two months. 6 It opened its mouth to utter blasphemies against God, blaspheming his name and his dwelling, that is, those who dwell in heaven. 7 Also it was allowed to make war on the saints and to conquer them.[l] It was given authority over every tribe and people and language and nation, 8 and all the inhabitants of the earth will worship it, everyone whose name has not been written from the foundation of the world in the book of life of the Lamb that was slaughtered.[m]

9 Let anyone who has an ear listen:

10 If you are to be taken captive,
　into captivity you
　　go;
if you kill with the
　sword,
　with the sword you
　　must be killed.

Here is a call for the endurance and faith of the saints.

The Second Beast

11 Then I saw another beast that rose out of the earth; it had two horns like a lamb and it spoke like a dragon. 12 It exercises all the authority of the first beast on its behalf, and it

---

ἐθαυμάσθη ὅλη ἡ γῆ ὀπίσω τοῦ θηρίου,
wondered *all* *the* *earth* *after* *the* *beast,*

4 καὶ προσεκύνησαν τῷ δράκοντι, ὅτι
and *they worshipped* *the* *dragon,* *because*

ἔδωκεν τὴν ἐξουσίαν τῷ θηρίῳ, καὶ
he gave *the* *authority* *to the* *beast,* *and*

προσεκύνησαν τῷ θηρίῳ λέγοντες· τίς
they worshipped *the* *beast* *saying:* *Who*

ὅμοιος τῷ θηρίῳ, καὶ τίς δύναται
[is] like *to the* *beast,* *and* *who* *can*

πολεμῆσαι μετ᾽ αὐτοῦ; 5 καὶ ἐδόθη αὐτῷ
to make war *with* *it?* *And* *was given* *to it*

στόμα λαλοῦν μεγάλα καὶ βλασφημίας,
a mouth *speaking* *great things* *and* *blasphemies,*

καὶ ἐδόθη αὐτῷ ἐξουσία ποιῆσαι μῆνας
and *was given* *to it* *authority* *to act* ³*months*

τεσσεράκοντα [καὶ] δύο. 6 καὶ ἤνοιξεν
¹*forty-two.* *And* *it opened*

τὸ στόμα αὐτοῦ εἰς βλασφημίας πρὸς
the *mouth* *of it* *in* *blasphemies* *against*

τὸν θεόν, βλασφημῆσαι τὸ ὄνομα αὐτοῦ
- *God,* *to blaspheme* *the* *name* *of him*

καὶ τὴν σκηνὴν αὐτοῦ, τοὺς ἐν τῷ
and *the* *tabernacle* *of him,* ¹*the [ones]* ²*in* -

οὐρανῷ σκηνοῦντας. 7 καὶ ἐδόθη αὐτῷ
⁴*heaven* ²*tabernacling.* *And* *it was given* *to it*

ποιῆσαι πόλεμον μετὰ τῶν ἁγίων καὶ
to make *war* *with* *the* *saints* *and*

νικῆσαι αὐτούς, καὶ ἐδόθη αὐτῷ ἐξουσία
to overcome *them,* *and* ¹*was given* ²*to it* ¹*authority*

ἐπὶ πᾶσαν φυλὴν καὶ λαὸν καὶ γλῶσσαν
over *every* *tribe* *and* *people* *and* *tongue*

καὶ ἔθνος. 8 καὶ προσκυνήσουσιν αὐτὸν
and *nation.* *And* ²*will worship* ¹*him*

πάντες οἱ κατοικοῦντες ἐπὶ τῆς γῆς,
¹*all* ²*the [ones]* ³*dwelling* ⁴*on* ⁵*the* ⁶*earth,*

οὗ οὐ γέγραπται τὸ ὄνομα αὐτοῦ ἐν
⁵*of* ⁴*has not been written* ¹*the* ²*name* *of him* *in*
whom

τῷ βιβλίῳ τῆς ζωῆς τοῦ ἀρνίου τοῦ
the *scroll* - *of life* *of the* *Lamb* -

ἐσφαγμένου ἀπὸ καταβολῆς κόσμου.
having been slain *from* *[the] foundation* *of [the] world.*

9 Εἴ τις ἔχει οὖς ἀκουσάτω. 10 εἴ
If *anyone* *has* *an ear* *let him hear.* *If*

τις εἰς αἰχμαλωσίαν, εἰς αἰχμαλωσίαν
anyone [is] for *captivity,* *to* *captivity*

ὑπάγει· εἴ τις ἐν μαχαίρῃ ἀποκτενεῖ,
he goes; *if* *anyone* *by* *a sword* *will kill,*

δεῖ αὐτὸν ἐν μαχαίρῃ ἀποκτανθῆναι.
it behoves him *by* *a sword* *to be killed.*

Ὧδέ ἐστιν ἡ ὑπομονὴ καὶ ἡ πίστις
Here *is* *the* *endurance* *and* *the* *faith*

τῶν ἁγίων.
of the *saints.*

11 Καὶ εἶδον ἄλλο θηρίον ἀναβαῖνον
And *I saw* *another* *beast* *coming up*

ἐκ τῆς γῆς, καὶ εἶχεν κέρατα δύο
out of the *earth,* *and* *it had* ²*horns* ¹*two*

ὅμοια ἀρνίῳ, καὶ ἐλάλει ὡς δράκων.
like *'to a lamb,* *and* *spoke* *as* *a dragon.*

12 καὶ τὴν ἐξουσίαν τοῦ πρώτου θηρίου
And ³*the* ⁴*authority* ⁵*of the* ⁶*first* ⁷*beast*

πᾶσαν ποιεῖ ἐνώπιον αὐτοῦ. καὶ ποιεῖ
²*all* ¹*it does(exercises)* *before* *it.* *And* *it makes*

---

was astonished and followed the beast. 4 Men worshiped the dragon because he had given authority to the beast, and they also worshiped the beast and asked, "Who is like the beast? Who can make war against him?"

5 The beast was given a mouth to utter proud words and blasphemies and to exercise his authority for forty-two months. 6 He opened his mouth to blaspheme God, and to slander his name and his dwelling place and those who live in heaven. 7 He was given power to make war against the saints and to conquer them. And he was given authority over every tribe, people, language and nation. 8 All inhabitants of the earth will worship the beast —all whose names have not been written in the book of life belonging to the Lamb that was slain from the creation of the world.[q]

9 He who has an ear, let him hear.

10 If anyone is to go into captivity,
　into captivity he will
　　go.
If anyone is to be killed[r]
　with the sword,
　with the sword he will
　　be killed.

This calls for patient endurance and faithfulness on the part of the saints.

The Beast out of the Earth

11 Then I saw another beast, coming out of the earth. He had two horns like a lamb, but he spoke like a dragon. 12 He exercised all the authority of the first beast on his behalf,

---

[l] Other ancient authorities lack this sentence
[m] Or *written in the book of life of the Lamb that was slaughtered from the foundation of the world*

[q] 8 Or *written from the creation of the world in the book of life belonging to the Lamb that was slain*
[r] 10 Some manuscripts *anyone kills*

makes the earth and its inhabitants worship the first beast, whose mortal wound[n] had been healed. 13 It performs great signs, even making fire come down from heaven to earth in the sight of all; 14 and by the signs that it is allowed to perform on behalf of the beast, it deceives the inhabitants of earth, telling them to make an image for the beast that had been wounded by the sword[o] and yet lived; 15 and it was allowed to give breath[p] to the image of the beast so that the image of the beast could even speak and cause those who would not worship the image of the beast to be killed. 16 Also it causes all, both small and great, both rich and poor, both free and slave, to be marked on the right hand or the forehead, 17 so that no one can buy or sell who does not have the mark, that is, the name of the beast or the number of its name. 18 This calls for wisdom: let anyone with understanding calculate the number of the beast, for it is the number of a person. Its number is six hundred sixty-six.[q]

τὴν γῆν καὶ τοὺς ἐν αὐτῇ κατοικοῦντας
the earth and ¹the [ones] ²in ⁴it ³dwelling

ἵνα προσκυνήσουσιν τὸ θηρίον τὸ πρῶτον,
in or-der that they shall worship the ²beast — ¹first,

οὗ ἐθεραπεύθη ἡ πληγὴ τοῦ θανάτου
of which ⁴was healed · ¹the ⁵stroke — ³of death

αὐτοῦ. 13 καὶ ποιεῖ σημεῖα μεγάλα,
of it. And it does ¹signs ²great,

ἵνα καὶ πῦρ ποιῇ ἐκ τοῦ οὐρανοῦ
in or-der that ²even ⁴fire ¹it ³makes ⁵out of — ⁷heaven

καταβαίνειν εἰς τὴν γῆν ἐνώπιον τῶν
⁶to come down onto the earth before —

ἀνθρώπων. 14 καὶ πλανᾷ τοὺς κατοι-
men. And it deceives the [ones] dwell-

κοῦντας ἐπὶ τῆς γῆς διὰ τὰ σημεῖα
ing on the earth because of the signs

ἃ ἐδόθη αὐτῷ ποιῆσαι ἐνώπιον τοῦ
which it was given to it to do before the

θηρίου, λέγων τοῖς κατοικοῦσιν ἐπὶ τῆς
beast, telling to the [ones] dwelling on the

γῆς ποιῆσαι εἰκόνα τῷ θηρίῳ, ὃς ἔχει
earth to make an image to the beast, who has

τὴν πληγὴν τῆς μαχαίρης καὶ ἔζησεν.
the stroke of the sword and lived [again].

15 καὶ ἐδόθη αὐτῷ δοῦναι πνεῦμα τῇ
And it was given to it to give spirit to the

εἰκόνι τοῦ θηρίου, ἵνα καὶ λαλήσῃ ἡ
image of the beast, in order that ⁶even ¹might ²speak ³the

εἰκὼν τοῦ θηρίου, καὶ ποιήσῃ [ἵνα]
³image ⁴of the ⁴beast, and might make in order that

ὅσοι ἐὰν μὴ προσκυνήσωσιν τῇ εἰκόνι
as many as might not worship the image

τοῦ θηρίου ἀποκτανθῶσιν. 16 καὶ ποιεῖ
of the beast should be killed. And it makes

πάντας, τοὺς μικροὺς καὶ τοὺς μεγάλους,
all men, the small and the great,

καὶ τοὺς πλουσίους καὶ τοὺς πτωχούς,
both the rich and the poor,

καὶ τοὺς ἐλευθέρους καὶ τοὺς δούλους,
both the free men and the slaves,

ἵνα δῶσιν αὐτοῖς χάραγμα ἐπὶ τῆς
in order that they to them a mark on the

χειρὸς αὐτῶν τῆς δεξιᾶς ἢ ἐπὶ τὸ
²hand ³of them — ¹right or on the

μέτωπον αὐτῶν, 17 [καὶ] ἵνα μή τις
forehead of them, and lest anyone

δύνηται ἀγοράσαι ἢ πωλῆσαι εἰ μὴ
could to buy or to sell except

ὁ ἔχων τὸ χάραγμα τὸ ὄνομα τοῦ
the having the mark[,] the name of the
[one]

θηρίου ἢ τὸν ἀριθμὸν τοῦ ὀνόματος
beast or the number of the name

αὐτοῦ. 18 Ὧδε ἡ σοφία ἐστίν. ὁ ἔχων
of it. Here ²wisdom ¹is. The having
[one]

νοῦν ψηφισάτω τὸν ἀριθμὸν τοῦ θηρίου·
reason let him count the number of the beast;

ἀριθμὸς γὰρ ἀνθρώπου ἐστίν. καὶ ὁ
for ²[the] ³number ⁴of a man ¹it is. And the

ἀριθμὸς αὐτοῦ ἑξακόσιοι ἑξήκοντα ἕξ.
number of it [is] six hundreds [and] sixty-six.

---

and made the earth and its inhabitants worship the first beast, whose fatal wound had been healed. 13 And he performed great and miraculous signs, even causing fire to come down from heaven to earth in full view of men. 14 Because of the signs he was given power to do on behalf of the first beast, he deceived the inhabitants of the earth. He ordered them to set up an image in honor of the beast who was wounded by the sword and yet lived. 15 He was given power to give breath to the image of the first beast, so that it could speak and cause all who refused to worship the image to be killed. 16 He also forced everyone, small and great, rich and poor, free and slave, to receive a mark on his right hand or on his forehead, 17 so that no one could buy or sell unless he had the mark, which is the name of the beast or the number of his name. 18 This calls for wisdom. If anyone has insight, let him calculate the number of the beast, for it is man's number. His number is 666.

---

[n] Gk whose plague of its death
[o] Or that had received the plague of the sword
[p] Or spirit
[q] Other ancient authorities read six hundred sixteen

Chapter 14

The Lamb and the 144,000

THEN I looked, and there was the Lamb, standing on Mount Zion! And with him were one hundred forty-four thousand who had his name and his Father's name written on their foreheads. 2 And I heard a voice from heaven like the sound of many waters and like the sound of loud thunder; the voice I heard was like the sound of harpists playing on their harps, 3 and they sing a new song before the throne and before the four living creatures and before the elders. No one could learn that song except the one hundred forty-four thousand who have been redeemed from the earth. 4 It is these who have not defiled themselves with women, for they are virgins; these follow the Lamb wherever he goes. They have been redeemed from humankind as first fruits for God and the Lamb, 5 and in their mouth no lie was found; they are blameless.

The Messages of the Three Angels

6 Then I saw another angel flying in midheaven, with an eternal gospel to proclaim to those who liveʳ on the earth—to every nation and tribe and language and people. 7 He said in a loud voice, "Fear God and give him glory, for the hour of his judgment has come; and worship him who made heaven and earth, the sea and the springs of water."

---

14 Καὶ εἶδον, καὶ ἰδοὺ τὸ ἀρνίον
And I saw, and behold[,] the Lamb

ἑστὸς ἐπὶ τὸ ὄρος Σιών, καὶ μετ' αὐτοῦ
standing on the mount Sion, and with him

ἑκατὸν τεσσεράκοντα τέσσαρες χιλιάδες
a hundred [and] forty-four thousands

ἔχουσαι τὸ ὄνομα αὐτοῦ καὶ τὸ ὄνομα
having the name of him and the name

τοῦ πατρὸς αὐτοῦ γεγραμμένον ἐπὶ τῶν
of the Father of him *having been* written on the

μετώπων αὐτῶν. **2** καὶ ἤκουσα φωνὴν
foreheads of them. And I heard a sound

ἐκ τοῦ οὐρανοῦ ὡς φωνὴν ὑδάτων πολλῶν
out of - heaven as a sound ²waters ¹of many

καὶ ὡς φωνὴν βροντῆς μεγάλης, καὶ
and as a sound ²thunder ¹of great(loud), and

ἡ φωνὴ ἣν ἤκουσα ὡς κιθαρῳδῶν
the sound which I heard [was] as of harpers

κιθαριζόντων ἐν ταῖς κιθάραις αὐτῶν.
harping with the harps of them.

3 καὶ ᾄδουσιν ᾠδὴν καινὴν ἐνώπιον τοῦ
And they sing ²song ¹a new before the

θρόνου καὶ ἐνώπιον τῶν τεσσάρων ζῴων
throne and before the four living creatures

καὶ τῶν πρεσβυτέρων· καὶ οὐδεὶς ἐδύνατο
and the elders; and no man could

μαθεῖν τὴν ᾠδὴν εἰ μὴ αἱ ἑκατὸν
to learn the song except the hundred

τεσσεράκοντα τέσσαρες χιλιάδες, οἱ
[and] forty-four thousands, the

ἠγορασμέναι ἀπὸ τῆς γῆς. **4** οὗτοί εἰσιν
[ones] *having been* purchased from the earth. These are

οἱ μετὰ γυναικῶν οὐκ ἐμολύνθησαν·
[those] ²with ³women ¹were not defiled;

who

παρθένοι γάρ εἰσιν. οὗτοι οἱ ἀκολουθοῦντες
for ²celibates ¹they are. These the [ones] following [are]

τῷ ἀρνίῳ ὅπου ἂν ὑπάγῃ. οὗτοι ἠγοράσ-
the Lamb wherever he may go. These were

θησαν ἀπὸ τῶν ἀνθρώπων ἀπαρχὴ τῷ
purchased from - men firstfruit -

θεῷ καὶ τῷ ἀρνίῳ, **5** καὶ ἐν τῷ στόματι
to God and to the Lamb, and in the mouth

αὐτῶν οὐχ εὑρέθη ψεῦδος· ἄμωμοί εἰσιν.
of them was not found a lie; ²unblemished ¹they are.

6 Καὶ εἶδον ἄλλον ἄγγελον πετόμενον
And I saw another angel flying

ἐν μεσουρανήματι, ἔχοντα εὐαγγέλιον
in mid-heaven, having ¹gospel

αἰώνιον εὐαγγελίσαι ἐπὶ τοὺς καθημένους
¹an eternal to preach over the [ones] sitting

ἐπὶ τῆς γῆς καὶ ἐπὶ πᾶν ἔθνος καὶ
on the earth and over every nation and

φυλὴν καὶ γλῶσσαν καὶ λαόν, **7** λέγων
tribe and tongue and people, saying

ἐν φωνῇ μεγάλῃ· φοβήθητε τὸν θεὸν
in ²voice ¹a great(loud); Fear ye - God

καὶ δότε αὐτῷ δόξαν, ὅτι ἦλθεν ἡ ὥρα
and give ²to him ¹glory, because came the hour

τῆς κρίσεως αὐτοῦ, καὶ προσκυνήσατε
of the judgment of him, and worship

τῷ ποιήσαντι τὸν οὐρανὸν καὶ τὴν γῆν
the [one] having made the heaven and the earth

καὶ θάλασσαν καὶ πηγὰς ὑδάτων. **8** Καὶ
and sea and fountains of waters. And

Chapter 14

The Lamb and the 144,000

THEN I looked, and there before me was the Lamb, standing on Mount Zion, and with him 144,000 who had his name and his Father's name written on their foreheads. 2 And I heard a sound from heaven like the roar of rushing waters and like a loud peal of thunder. The sound I heard was like that of harpists playing their harps. 3 And they sang a new song before the throne and before the four living creatures and the elders. No one could learn the song except the 144,000 who had been redeemed from the earth. 4 These are those who did not defile themselves with women, for they kept themselves pure. They follow the Lamb wherever he goes. They were purchased from among men and offered as firstfruits to God and the Lamb. 5 No lie was found in their mouths; they are blameless.

The Three Angels

6 Then I saw another angel flying in midair, and he had the eternal gospel to proclaim to those who live on the earth—to every nation, tribe, language and people. 7 He said in a loud voice, "Fear God and give him glory, because the hour of his judgment has come. Worship him who made the heavens, the earth, the sea and the springs of water."

ʳ Gk *sit*

8 Then another angel, a second, followed, saying, "Fallen, fallen is Babylon the great! She has made all nations drink of the wine of the wrath of her fornication."
9 Then another angel, a third, followed them, crying with a loud voice, "Those who worship the beast and its image, and receive a mark on their foreheads or on their hands, 10 they will also drink the wine of God's wrath, poured unmixed into the cup of his anger, and they will be tormented with fire and sulfur in the presence of the holy angels and in the presence of the Lamb. 11 And the smoke of their torment goes up forever and ever. There is no rest day or night for those who worship the beast and its image and for anyone who receives the mark of its name.
12 Here is a call for the endurance of the saints, those who keep the commandments of God and hold fast to the faith of[s] Jesus.
13 And I heard a voice from heaven saying, "Write this: Blessed are the dead who from now on die in the Lord." "Yes," says the Spirit, "they will rest from their labors, for their deeds follow them."

Reaping the Earth's Harvest

14 Then I looked, and there was a white cloud, and seated on the cloud was one like the Son of Man, with a golden crown on his head, and a sharp

ἄλλος ἄγγελος δεύτερος ἠκολούθησεν λέγων·
another angel a second followed saying:
ἔπεσεν ἔπεσεν Βαβυλὼν ἡ μεγάλη, ἡ
Fell[,] fell Babylon the great, which
ἐκ τοῦ οἴνου τοῦ θυμοῦ τῆς πορνείας
of the wine of the anger of the fornication
αὐτῆς πεπότικεν πάντα τὰ ἔθνη. 9 Καὶ
of her has made to drink all the nations. And
ἄλλος ἄγγελος τρίτος ἠκολούθησεν αὐτοῖς
another angel a third followed them
λέγων ἐν φωνῇ μεγάλῃ· εἴ τις προσκυνεῖ
saying in ²voice ¹a great(loud): If anyone worships
τὸ θηρίον καὶ τὴν εἰκόνα αὐτοῦ, καὶ
the beast and the image of it, and
λαμβάνει χάραγμα ἐπὶ τοῦ μετώπου αὐτοῦ
receives a mark on the forehead of him
ἢ ἐπὶ τὴν χεῖρα αὐτοῦ, 10 καὶ αὐτὸς
or on the hand of him, even he
πίεται ἐκ τοῦ οἴνου τοῦ θυμοῦ τοῦ
shall drink of the wine of the anger -
θεοῦ τοῦ κεκερασμένου ἀκράτου ἐν τῷ
of God - having been mixed undiluted in the
ποτηρίῳ τῆς ὀργῆς αὐτοῦ, καὶ βασανισθήσε-
cup of the wrath of him, and will be torment-
ται ἐν πυρὶ καὶ θείῳ ἐνώπιον ἀγγέλων
ed by fire and sulphur before ²angels
ἁγίων καὶ ἐνώπιον τοῦ ἀρνίου. 11 καὶ
¹holy and before the Lamb. And
ὁ καπνὸς τοῦ βασανισμοῦ αὐτῶν εἰς
the smoke of the torment of them unto
αἰῶνας αἰώνων ἀναβαίνει, καὶ οὐκ ἔχουσιν
ages of ages goes up, and they have not
ἀνάπαυσιν ἡμέρας καὶ νυκτὸς οἱ προσκυ-
rest day and night the [ones] wor-
νοῦντες τὸ θηρίον καὶ τὴν εἰκόνα αὐτοῦ,
shipping the beast and the image of it,
καὶ εἴ τις λαμβάνει τὸ χάραγμα τοῦ
and if anyone receives the mark of the
ὀνόματος αὐτοῦ. 12 Ὧδε ἡ ὑπομονὴ
name of it. ¹Here ²the ⁴endurance
τῶν ἁγίων ἐστίν, οἱ τηροῦντες τὰς
³of the ⁵saints ²is, the [ones] keeping the
ἐντολὰς τοῦ θεοῦ καὶ τὴν πίστιν Ἰησοῦ.
command- - of God and the faith of Jesus.
ments
13 Καὶ ἤκουσα φωνῆς ἐκ τοῦ οὐρανοῦ
And I heard a voice out of - heaven
λεγούσης· γράψον· μακάριοι οἱ νεκροὶ
saying: Write thou: Blessed [are] the dead
οἱ ἐν κυρίῳ ἀποθνῄσκοντες ἀπ' ἄρτι.
¹the ³in ⁴[the] Lord ²dying from now.
[ones]
ναί, λέγει τὸ πνεῦμα, ἵνα ἀναπαήσονται
Yes, says the Spirit, in order they shall rest
that
ἐκ τῶν κόπων αὐτῶν· τὰ γὰρ ἔργα
from the labours of them; for the work-
αὐτῶν ἀκολουθεῖ μετ' αὐτῶν.
of them follows with them.
14 Καὶ εἶδον, καὶ ἰδοὺ νεφέλη λευκή,
And I saw, and behold[,] ²cloud ¹a white,
καὶ ἐπὶ τὴν νεφέλην καθήμενον ὅμοιον
and on the cloud [one] sitting like
υἱὸν ἀνθρώπου, ἔχων ἐπὶ τῆς κεφαλῆς
a son of man,* having on the head

8 A second angel followed and said, "Fallen! Fallen is Babylon the Great, which made all the nations drink the maddening wine of her adulteries."
9 A third angel followed them and said in a loud voice: "If anyone worships the beast and his image and receives his mark on the forehead or on the hand, 10 he, too, will drink of the wine of God's fury, which has been poured full strength into the cup of his wrath. He will be tormented with burning sulfur in the presence of the holy angels and of the Lamb. 11 And the smoke of their torment rises for ever and ever. There is no rest day or night for those who worship the beast and his image, or for anyone who receives the mark of his name." 12 This calls for patient endurance on the part of the saints who obey God's commandments and remain faithful to Jesus.
13 Then I heard a voice from heaven say, "Write: Blessed are the dead who die in the Lord from now on."
"Yes," says the Spirit, "they will rest from their labor, for their deeds will follow them."

The Harvest of the Earth

14 I looked, and there before me was a white cloud, and seated on the cloud was one "like a son of man"[s] with a crown of gold on his head and a

---

[s] Or *to their faith in*   * See also ch. 1. 13 and John 5. 27.   [s]14 Daniel 7:13

sickle in his hand! 15 Another angel came out of the temple, calling with a loud voice to the one who sat on the cloud, "Use your sickle and reap, for the hour to reap has come, because the harvest of the earth is fully ripe." 16 So the one who sat on the cloud swung his sickle over the earth, and the earth was reaped.

17 Then another angel came out of the temple in heaven, and he too had a sharp sickle. 18 Then another angel came out from the altar, the angel who has authority over fire, and he called with a loud voice to him who had the sharp sickle, "Use your sharp sickle and gather the clusters of the vine of the earth, for its grapes are ripe." 19 So the angel swung his sickle over the earth and gathered the vintage of the earth, and he threw it into the great wine press of the wrath of God. 20 And the wine press was trodden outside the city, and blood flowed from the wine press, as high as a horse's bridle, for a distance of about two hundred miles.[f]

Chapter 15

The Angels with the Seven Last Plagues

THEN I saw another portent in heaven, great and amazing: seven angels with seven plagues, which are the last, for with them the wrath of God is ended.

2 And I saw what appeared to be a sea of glass mixed with fire, and those

[f] Gk one thousand six hundred stadia

αὐτοῦ στέφανον χρυσοῦν καὶ ἐν τῇ χειρὶ
of him crown a golden and in the hand
αὐτοῦ δρέπανον ὀξύ. 15 καὶ ἄλλος ἄγγελος
of him sickle a sharp. And another angel
ἐξῆλθεν ἐκ τοῦ ναοῦ, κράζων ἐν φωνῇ
went forth out of the shrine, crying in ²voice
μεγάλη τῷ καθημένῳ ἐπὶ τῆς νεφέλης·
¹a great to the sitting on the cloud:
(loud) [one]
πέμψον τὸ δρέπανόν σου καὶ θέρισον,
Send(Thrust) the sickle of thee and reap thou,
ὅτι ἦλθεν ἡ ὥρα θερίσαι, ὅτι ἐξηράνθη
because came the hour to reap, because was dried
ὁ θερισμὸς τῆς γῆς. 16 καὶ ἔβαλεν
the harvest of the earth. And ²thrust
ὁ καθήμενος ἐπὶ τῆς νεφέλης τὸ δρέπανον
¹the ²sitting ³on ⁴the ⁵cloud the sickle
[one]
αὐτοῦ ἐπὶ τὴν γῆν, καὶ ἐθερίσθη ἡ
of him over the earth, and ²was reaped ¹the
γῆ. 17 Καὶ ἄλλος ἄγγελος ἐξῆλθεν ἐκ
²earth. And another angel went forth out of
τοῦ ναοῦ τοῦ ἐν τῷ οὐρανῷ, ἔχων καὶ
the shrine - in - heaven, ²having ¹also
αὐτὸς δρέπανον ὀξύ. 18 καὶ ἄλλος ἄγγελος
¹he ²sickle ⁴a sharp. And another angel
ἐξῆλθεν ἐκ τοῦ θυσιαστηρίου, [ὁ] ἔχων
went forth out of the altar, the [one] having
ἐξουσίαν ἐπὶ τοῦ πυρός, καὶ ἐφώνησεν
authority over the fire, and he spoke
φωνῇ μεγάλη τῷ ἔχοντι τὸ δρέπανον
²voice ¹in a great to the having the ²sickle
(loud) [one]
τὸ ὀξὺ λέγων· πέμψον σου τὸ δρέπανον
- ¹sharp saying: Send(Thrust) ²of thee ¹the ²sickle
τὸ ὀξὺ καὶ τρύγησον τοὺς βότρυας τῆς
- ²sharp and gather the clusters of the
ἀμπέλου τῆς γῆς, ὅτι ἤκμασαν αἱ
vine of the earth, because ⁴ripened ¹the
σταφυλαὶ αὐτῆς. 19 καὶ ἔβαλεν ὁ ἄγγελος
²grapes ³of it. And ³thrust ¹the ²angel
τὸ δρέπανον αὐτοῦ εἰς τὴν γῆν, καὶ
the sickle of him into the earth, and
ἐτρύγησεν τὴν ἄμπελον τῆς γῆς καὶ
gathered the vine of the earth and
ἔβαλεν εἰς τὴν ληνὸν τοῦ θυμοῦ τοῦ
cast into the ²winepress ³of the ⁴anger -
θεοῦ τὸν μέγαν. 20 καὶ ἐπατήθη ἡ
⁵of God ¹great. And ³was trodden ¹the
ληνὸς ἔξωθεν τῆς πόλεως, καὶ ἐξῆλθεν
winepress outside the city, and ¹went out
αἷμα ἐκ τῆς ληνοῦ ἄχρι τῶν χαλινῶν
¹blood out of the winepress as far as the bridles
τῶν ἵππων, ἀπὸ σταδίων χιλίων ἑξακοσίων.
of the horses, from ³furlongs ¹a thousand ²six hundred.

15 Καὶ εἶδον ἄλλο σημεῖον ἐν τῷ
And I saw another sign in the
οὐρανῷ μέγα καὶ θαυμαστόν, ἀγγέλους
heaven[,] great and wonderful, ²angels
ἑπτὰ ἔχοντας πληγὰς ἑπτὰ τὰς ἐσχάτας,
¹seven having ²plagues ¹seven the last,
ὅτι ἐν αὐταῖς ἐτελέσθη ὁ θυμὸς τοῦ
because in them ⁴was finished ¹the ²anger -
θεοῦ. 2 Καὶ εἶδον ὡς θάλασσαν ὑαλίνην
³of God. And I saw as ²sea ¹a glassy

---

sharp sickle in his hand. 15 Then another angel came out of the temple and called in a loud voice to him who was sitting on the cloud, "Take your sickle and reap, because the time to reap has come, for the harvest of the earth is ripe." 16 So he who was seated on the cloud swung his sickle over the earth, and the earth was harvested.

17 Another angel came out of the temple in heaven, and he too had a sharp sickle. 18 Still another angel, who had charge of the fire, came from the altar and called in a loud voice to him who had the sharp sickle, "Take your sharp sickle and gather the clusters of grapes from the earth's vine, because its grapes are ripe." 19 The angel swung his sickle on the earth, gathered its grapes and threw them into the great winepress of God's wrath. 20 They were trampled in the winepress outside the city, and blood flowed out of the press, rising as high as the horses' bridles for a distance of 1,600 stadia.[f]

Chapter 15

Seven Angels With Seven Plagues

I SAW in heaven another great and marvelous sign: seven angels with the seven last plagues—last, because with them God's wrath is completed. 2 And I saw what looked like a sea of glass mixed with fire

[f] 20 That is, about 180 miles (about 300 kilometers)

who had conquered the beast and its image and the number of its name, standing beside the sea of glass with harps of God in their hands. 3 And they sing the song of Moses, the servant" of God, and the song of the Lamb:

"Great and amazing
    are your deeds,
Lord God the
    Almighty!
Just and true are your
    ways,
King of the
    nations!ᵛ
4 Lord, who will not
    fear
and glorify your
    name?
For you alone are
    holy.
All nations will
    come
and worship before
    you,
for your judgments
    have been
    revealed."

5 After this I looked, and the temple of the tentʷ of witness in heaven was opened, 6 and out of the temple came the seven angels with the seven plagues, robed in pure bright linen,ˣ with golden sashes across their chests. 7 Then one of the four living creatures gave the seven angels seven golden bowls full of the wrath of God, who lives forever and ever; 8 and the temple was filled with smoke from the glory of God and from his power, and no one could enter the temple until the seven plagues of the seven angels were ended.

Chapter 16
The Bowls of God's Wrath

THEN I heard a loud voice from the temple telling the seven angels, "Go and pour out on the earth the seven bowls of

ᵘ Gk slave
ᵛ Other ancient authorities read the ages
ʷ Or tabernacle
ˣ Other ancient authorities read stone

μεμιγμένην πυρί, καὶ τοὺς νικῶντας
having been mixed with fire, and the [ones] overcoming

ἐκ τοῦ θηρίου καὶ ἐκ τῆς εἰκόνος αὐτοῦ
of the beast and of the image of it

καὶ ἐκ τοῦ ἀριθμοῦ τοῦ ὀνόματος αὐτοῦ
and of the number of the name of it

ἑστῶτας ἐπὶ τὴν θάλασσαν τὴν ὑαλίνην,
standing on the ²sea – ¹glassy,

ἔχοντας κιθάρας τοῦ θεοῦ. 3 καὶ ᾄδουσιν
having harps – of God. And they sing

τὴν ᾠδὴν Μωϋσέως τοῦ δούλου τοῦ
the song of Moses the slave –

θεοῦ καὶ τὴν ᾠδὴν τοῦ ἀρνίου, λέγοντες·
of God and the song of the Lamb, saying:

μεγάλα καὶ θαυμαστὰ τὰ ἔργα σου,
Great and wonderful the works of thee,

κύριε ὁ θεὸς ὁ παντοκράτωρ· δίκαιαι
[O] Lord – God the Almighty; righteous

καὶ ἀληθιναὶ αἱ ὁδοί σου, ὁ βασιλεὺς
and true the ways of thee, the king

τῶν ἐθνῶν· 4 τίς οὐ μὴ φοβηθῇ, κύριε,
of the nations; who will not fear, [O] Lord,

καὶ δοξάσει τὸ ὄνομά σου; ὅτι μόνος
and *will* glorify the name of thee? because [thou] only

ὅσιος, ὅτι πάντα τὰ ἔθνη ἥξουσιν καὶ
[art] holy, because all the nations will come and

προσκυνήσουσιν ἐνώπιόν σου, ὅτι τὰ
will worship before thee, because the

δικαιώματά σου ἐφανερώθησαν. 5 Καὶ
ordinances of thee were made manifest. And

μετὰ ταῦτα εἶδον, καὶ ἠνοίγη ὁ ναὸς
after these things I saw, and was opened the shrine

τῆς σκηνῆς τοῦ μαρτυρίου ἐν τῷ οὐρανῷ,
of the tabernacle of the testimony in – heaven,

6 καὶ ἐξῆλθον οἱ ἑπτὰ ἄγγελοι οἱ ἔχοντες
and ⁸came forth ¹the ²seven ³angels the ⁴having

τὰς ἑπτὰ πληγὰς ἐκ τοῦ ναοῦ, ἐνδεδυμένοι
⁵the ⁶seven ⁷plagues out of the shrine, *having been* clothed [in]

λίνον καθαρὸν λαμπρὸν καὶ περιεζωσμένοι
³linen ¹clean ²bright and *having been* girdled

περὶ τὰ στήθη ζώνας χρυσᾶς. 7 καὶ
round the breasts [with] ²girdles ¹golden. And

ἓν ἐκ τῶν τεσσάρων ζῴων ἔδωκεν τοῖς
one of the four living gave to the
    creatures

ἑπτὰ ἀγγέλοις ἑπτὰ φιάλας χρυσᾶς
seven angels seven ²bowls ¹golden

γεμούσας τοῦ θυμοῦ τοῦ θεοῦ τοῦ ζῶντος
being filled of(with) anger – of – living
    the   God

εἰς τοὺς αἰῶνας τῶν αἰώνων. 8 καὶ
unto the ages of the ages. And

ἐγεμίσθη ὁ ναὸς καπνοῦ ἐκ τῆς δόξης
was filled the shrine of(with) smoke of the glory

τοῦ θεοῦ καὶ ἐκ τῆς δυνάμεως αὐτοῦ,
– of God and of the power of him,

καὶ οὐδεὶς ἐδύνατο εἰσελθεῖν εἰς τὸν
and no one could *to* enter into the

ναὸν ἄχρι τελεσθῶσιν αἱ ἑπτὰ πληγαὶ
shrine until should be finished the seven plagues

τῶν ἑπτὰ ἀγγέλων. 16 Καὶ ἤκουσα
of the seven angels. And I heard

μεγάλης φωνῆς ἐκ τοῦ ναοῦ λεγούσης τοῖς
a great(loud) voice out of the shrine saying to the

ἑπτὰ ἀγγέλοις· ὑπάγετε καὶ ἐκχέετε τὰς ἑπτὰ
seven angels: Go ye and pour out the seven

---

and, standing beside the sea, those who had been victorious over the beast and his image and over the number of his name. They held harps given them by God 3 and sang the song of Moses the servant of God and the song of the Lamb:

"Great and marvelous
    are your deeds,
Lord God Almighty.
Just and true are your
    ways,
King of the ages.
4 Who will not fear you, O
    Lord,
and bring glory to your
    name?
For you alone are holy.
All nations will come
    and worship before
    you,
for your righteous acts
    have been
    revealed."

5 After this I looked and in heaven the temple, that is, the tabernacle of the Testimony, was opened. 6 Out of the temple came, the seven angels with the seven plagues. They were dressed in clean, shining linen and wore golden sashes around their chests. 7 Then one of the four living creatures gave to the seven angels seven golden bowls filled with the wrath of God, who lives for ever and ever. 8 And the temple was filled with smoke from the glory of God and from his power, and no one could enter the temple until the seven plagues of the seven angels were completed.

Chapter 16
The Seven Bowls of God's Wrath

THEN I heard a loud voice from the temple saying to the seven angels, "Go, pour out the seven the wrath of God."

2 So the first angel went and poured his bowl on the earth, and a foul and painful sore came on those who had the mark of the beast and who worshiped its image.

3 The second angel poured his bowl into the sea, and it became like the blood of a corpse, and every living thing in the sea died.

4 The third angel poured his bowl into the rivers and the springs of water, and they became blood. 5 And I heard the angel of the waters say,

"You are just, O Holy One, who are and were,
for you have judged these things;
6 because they shed the blood of saints and prophets,
you have given them blood to drink.
It is what they deserve!"

7 And I heard the altar respond,

"Yes, O Lord God, the Almighty,
your judgments are true and just!"

8 The fourth angel poured his bowl on the sun, and it was allowed to scorch them with fire; 9 they were scorched by the fierce heat, but they cursed the name of God, who had authority over these plagues, and they did not repent and give him glory.

10 The fifth angel poured his bowl on the throne of the beast, and its kingdom was plunged into

---

φιάλας τοῦ θυμοῦ τοῦ θεοῦ εἰς τὴν γῆν.
bowls of the anger - of God onto the earth.

2 Καὶ ἀπῆλθεν ὁ πρῶτος καὶ ἐξέχεεν τὴν
And ²went away ¹the ³first and poured out the

φιάλην αὐτοῦ εἰς τὴν γῆν· καὶ ἐγένετο
bowl of him onto the earth; and ⁵came

ἕλκος κακὸν καὶ πονηρὸν ἐπὶ τοὺς ἀνθρώπους
⁴sore ¹a bad ²and ³evil on the men

τοὺς ἔχοντας τὸ χάραγμα τοῦ θηρίου καὶ
- having the mark of the beast and

τοὺς προσκυνοῦντας τῇ εἰκόνι αὐτοῦ. 3 Καὶ
- worshipping the image of it. And

ὁ δεύτερος ἐξέχεεν τὴν φιάλην αὐτοῦ
the second poured out the bowl of him

εἰς τὴν θάλασσαν· καὶ ἐγένετο αἷμα
onto the sea; and it became blood

ὡς νεκροῦ, καὶ πᾶσα ψυχὴ ζωῆς ἀπέθανεν,
as of a dead man, and every soul of life died,

τὰ ἐν τῇ θαλάσσῃ. 4 Καὶ ὁ τρίτος
the things in the sea. And the third

ἐξέχεεν τὴν φιάλην αὐτοῦ εἰς τοὺς
poured out the bowl of him onto the

ποταμοὺς καὶ τὰς πηγὰς τῶν ὑδάτων·
rivers and the fountains of the waters;

καὶ ἐγένετο αἷμα. 5 Καὶ ἤκουσα τοῦ
and it became blood. And I heard the

ἀγγέλου τῶν ὑδάτων λέγοντος· δίκαιος
angel of the waters saying: Righteous

εἶ, ὁ ὢν καὶ ὁ ἦν, ὁ ὅσιος, ὅτι
art the being and the was, the holy because
thou, [one] [one who] [one],
= the one who is

ταῦτα ἔκρινας, 6 ὅτι αἷμα ἁγίων
²these ¹thou judgedst, because ²[the] blood ³of saints
things

καὶ προφητῶν ἐξέχεαν, καὶ αἷμα αὐτοῖς
⁴and ⁵of prophets ¹they shed, and blood to them

δέδωκας πεῖν· ἄξιοί εἰσιν. 7 Καὶ ἤκουσα
thou hast to drink; ²worthy ¹they are. And I heard
given

τοῦ θυσιαστηρίου λέγοντος· ναί, κύριε
the altar saying: Yes, [O] Lord

ὁ θεὸς ὁ παντοκράτωρ, ἀληθιναὶ καὶ
- God the Almighty, true and

δίκαιαι αἱ κρίσεις σου. 8 Καὶ ὁ τέταρτος
righteous the judgments of thee. And the fourth

ἐξέχεεν τὴν φιάλην αὐτοῦ ἐπὶ τὸν ἥλιον·
poured out the bowl of him onto the sun;

καὶ ἐδόθη αὐτῷ καυματίσαι τοὺς
and it was given to him to burn -

ἀνθρώπους ἐν πυρί. 9 καὶ ἐκαυματίσθησαν
men with fire. And ²were burnt [with]

οἱ ἄνθρωποι καῦμα μέγα, καὶ ἐβλασ-
- ¹men ⁴heat ³great, and they blas-

φήμησαν τὸ ὄνομα τοῦ θεοῦ τοῦ ἔχοντος
phemed the name - of God the [one] having

τὴν ἐξουσίαν ἐπὶ τὰς πληγὰς ταύτας,
the authority over these plagues,

καὶ οὐ μετενόησαν δοῦναι αὐτῷ δόξαν.
and they repented not to give ²to him ¹glory.

10 Καὶ ὁ πέμπτος ἐξέχεεν τὴν φιάλην
And the fifth poured out the bowl

αὐτοῦ ἐπὶ τὸν θρόνον τοῦ θηρίου· καὶ
of him onto the throne of the beast; and

ἐγένετο ἡ βασιλεία αὐτοῦ ἐσκοτωμένη,
⁴became ¹the ²kingdom ³of it having been darkened,

---

bowls of God's wrath on the earth."

2The first angel went and poured out his bowl on the land, and ugly and painful sores broke out on the people who had the mark of the beast and worshiped his image.

3The second angel poured out his bowl on the sea, and it turned into blood like that of a dead man, and every living thing in the sea died.

4The third angel poured out his bowl on the rivers and springs of water, and they became blood. 5Then I heard the angel in charge of the waters say:

"You are just in these judgments,
you who are and who were, the Holy One,
because you have so judged;
6for they have shed the blood of your saints and prophets,
and you have given them blood to drink as they deserve."

7And I heard the altar respond:

"Yes, Lord God Almighty,
true and just are your judgments."

8The fourth angel poured out his bowl on the sun, and the sun was given power to scorch people with fire. 9They were seared by the intense heat and they cursed the name of God, who had control over these plagues, but they refused to repent and glorify him.

10The fifth angel poured out his bowl on the throne of the beast, and his kingdom was plunged into dark-

darkness; people gnawed their tongues in agony, 11and cursed the God of heaven because of their pains and sores, and they did not repent of their deeds.

12 The sixth angel poured his bowl on the great river Euphrates, and its water was dried up in order to prepare the way for the kings from the east. 13And I saw three foul spirits like frogs coming from the mouth of the dragon, from the mouth of the beast, and from the mouth of the false prophet. 14These are demonic spirits, performing signs, who go abroad to the kings of the whole world, to assemble them for battle on the great day of God the Almighty. 15("See, I am coming like a thief! Blessed is the one who stays awake and is clothed, y not going about naked and exposed to shame.") 16And they assembled them at the place that in Hebrew is called Harmagedon.

17 The seventh angel poured his bowl into the air, and a loud voice came out of the temple, from the throne, saying, "It is done!" 18And there came flashes of lightning, rumblings, peals of thunder, and a violent earthquake, such as had not occurred since people were upon the earth, so violent was that earthquake. 19The great city was split into three parts, and the cities of the

---

καὶ ἐμασῶντο τὰς γλώσσας αὐτῶν ἐκ
and they(men) gnawed the tongues of them from

τοῦ πόνου, 11 καὶ ἐβλασφήμησαν τὸν θεὸν
the pain, and *they* blasphemed the God

τοῦ οὐρανοῦ ἐκ τῶν πόνων αὐτῶν καὶ
- of heaven from the pains of them and

ἐκ τῶν ἑλκῶν αὐτῶν, καὶ οὐ μετενόησαν
from the sores of them, and they repented not

ἐκ τῶν ἔργων αὐτῶν. 12 Καὶ ὁ ἕκτος
of the works of them. And the sixth

ἐξέχεεν τὴν φιάλην αὐτοῦ ἐπὶ τὸν ποταμὸν
poured out the bowl of him onto the ²river

τὸν μέγαν Εὐφράτην· καὶ ἐξηράνθη τὸ
- ¹great Euphrates; and ⁴was dried ¹the

ὕδωρ αὐτοῦ, ἵνα ἑτοιμασθῇ ἡ ὁδὸς τῶν
²water ³of it, in order might be ¹the ²way ³of the
that prepared

βασιλέων τῶν ἀπὸ ἀνατολῆς ἡλίου. 13 Καὶ
⁴kings - ⁵from ⁶[the] rising ⁷of [the] sun. And

εἶδον ἐκ τοῦ στόματος τοῦ δράκοντος
I saw out of the mouth of.the dragon

καὶ ἐκ τοῦ στόματος τοῦ θηρίου καὶ
and out of the mouth of the beast and

ἐκ τοῦ στόματος τοῦ ψευδοπροφήτου
out of the mouth of the false prophet

πνεύματα τρία ἀκάθαρτα ὡς βάτραχοι·
²spirits ¹three ²unclean [coming] as frogs;

14 εἰσὶν γὰρ πνεύματα δαιμονίων ποιοῦντα
for they are spirits of demons doing

σημεῖα, ἃ ἐκπορεύεται ἐπὶ τοὺς βασιλεῖς
signs, which goes forth unto the kings

τῆς οἰκουμένης ὅλης, συναγαγεῖν αὐτοὺς
of the ²inhabited [earth] ¹whole, to assemble them

εἰς τὸν πόλεμον τῆς ἡμέρας τῆς μεγάλης
to the war of the ²day ¹great

τοῦ θεοῦ τοῦ παντοκράτορος. 15 Ἰδοὺ
- of God of the Almighty. Behold

ἔρχομαι ὡς κλέπτης· μακάριος ὁ γρηγορῶν
I am coming as a thief: blessed [is] the [one] watching

καὶ τηρῶν τὰ ἱμάτια αὐτοῦ, ἵνα μὴ
and keeping the garments of him, lest

γυμνὸς περιπατῇ καὶ βλέπωσιν τὴν
naked he walk and they(men) see the

ἀσχημοσύνην αὐτοῦ. 16 Καὶ συνήγαγεν
shame of him. And [t]he[y] assembled

αὐτοὺς εἰς τὸν τόπον τὸν καλούμενον
them in the place - being called

Ἑβραϊστὶ Ἁρμαγεδών. 17 Καὶ ὁ ἕβδομος
in Hebrew Harmagedon. And the seventh

ἐξέχεεν τὴν φιάλην αὐτοῦ ἐπὶ τὸν ἀέρα·
poured out the bowl of him on the air;

καὶ ἐξῆλθεν φωνὴ μεγάλη ἐκ τοῦ ναοῦ
and ²came out ²voice ¹a great(loud) out of the shrine

ἀπὸ τοῦ θρόνου λέγουσα· γέγονεν. 18 καὶ
from the throne saying: It has occurred. And

ἐγένοντο ἀστραπαὶ καὶ φωναὶ καὶ βρονταί,
there were lightnings and voices and thunders,

καὶ σεισμὸς ἐγένετο μέγας, οἷος οὐκ
and ²earthquake ³occurred ¹a great, such as not

ἐγένετο ἀφ’ οὗ ἄνθρωπος ἐγένετο ἐπὶ
did occur from when† man was on

τῆς γῆς, τηλικοῦτος σεισμὸς οὕτω μέγας.
the earth, such an earthquake so great.

19 καὶ ἐγένετο ἡ πόλις ἡ μεγάλη εἰς
And ⁴became ¹the ³city - ²great into

---

ness. Men gnawed their tongues in agony 11and cursed the God of heaven because of their pains and their sores, but they refused to repent of what they had done.

12The sixth angel poured out his bowl on the great river Euphrates, and its water was dried up to prepare the way for the kings from the East. 13Then I saw three evil u spirits that looked like frogs; they came out of the mouth of the dragon, out of the mouth of the beast and out of the mouth of the false prophet. 14They are spirits of demons performing miraculous signs, and they go out to the kings of the whole world, to gather them for the battle on the great day of God Almighty.

15"Behold, I come like a thief! Blessed is he who stays awake and keeps his clothes with him, so that he may not go naked and be shamefully exposed."

16Then they gathered the kings together to the place that in Hebrew is called Armageddon.

17The seventh angel poured out his bowl into the air, and out of the temple came a loud voice from the throne, saying, "It is done!" 18Then there came flashes of lightning, rumblings, peals of thunder and a severe earthquake. No earthquake like it has ever occurred since man has been on earth, so tremendous was the quake. 19The great city split into three

---

nations fell. God remembered great Babylon and gave her the wine-cup of the fury of his wrath. 20 And every island fled away, and no mountains were to be found; 21 and huge hailstones, each weighing about a hundred pounds,[z] dropped from heaven on people, until they cursed God for the plague of the hail, so fearful was that plague.

τρία μέρη, καὶ αἱ πόλεις τῶν ἐθνῶν
three parts, and the cities of the nations

ἔπεσαν. καὶ Βαβυλὼν ἡ μεγάλη ἐμνήσθη
fell. And Babylon the great was remembered

ἐνώπιον τοῦ θεοῦ δοῦναι αὐτῇ τὸ ποτήριον
before – God to give to her/it* the cup

τοῦ οἴνου τοῦ θυμοῦ τῆς ὀργῆς αὐτοῦ.
of the wine of the anger of the wrath of him.

20 καὶ πᾶσα νῆσος ἔφυγεν, καὶ ὄρη
And every island fled, and mountains

οὐχ εὑρέθησαν. 21 καὶ χάλαζα μεγάλη
were not found. And ²hail ¹a great

ὡς ταλαντιαία καταβαίνει ἐκ τοῦ οὐρανοῦ
as a talent in size comes down out of – heaven

ἐπὶ τοὺς ἀνθρώπους· καὶ ἐβλασφήμησαν
on – men; and ²blasphemed

οἱ ἄνθρωποι τὸν θεὸν ἐκ τῆς πληγῆς
– ¹men God from the plague

τῆς χαλάζης, ὅτι μεγάλη ἐστὶν ἡ πληγὴ
of the hail, because ²great ⁴is ¹the ³plague

αὐτῆς σφόδρα.
³of it ⁵exceeding.

---

parts, and the cities of the nations collapsed. God remembered Babylon the Great and gave her the cup filled with the wine of the fury of his wrath. 20 Every island fled away and the mountains could not be found. 21 From the sky huge hailstones of about a hundred pounds each fell upon men. And they cursed God on account of the plague of hail, because the plague was so terrible.

Chapter 17

The Great Whore and the Beast

THEN one of the seven angels who had the seven bowls came and said to me, "Come, I will show you the judgment of the great whore who is seated on many waters, 2 with whom the kings of the earth have committed fornication, and with the wine of whose fornication the inhabitants of the earth have become drunk." 3 So he carried me away in the spirit[a] into a wilderness, and I saw a woman sitting on a scarlet beast that was full of blasphemous names, and it had seven heads and ten horns. 4 The woman was clothed in purple and scarlet, and adorned with gold and jewels and pearls, holding in her hand a golden cup full of abominations and the impurities of her fornication; 5 and on her forehead was written a name, a mystery: "Babylon

---

17 Καὶ ἦλθεν εἷς ἐκ τῶν ἑπτὰ ἀγγέλων
And came one of the seven angels

τῶν ἐχόντων τὰς ἑπτὰ φιάλας, καὶ
– having the seven bowls, and

ἐλάλησεν μετ’ ἐμοῦ λέγων· δεῦρο, δείξω
spoke with me saying: Come, I will show

σοι τὸ κρίμα τῆς πόρνης τῆς μεγάλης
thee the judgment of the ²harlot ¹great

τῆς καθημένης ἐπὶ ὑδάτων πολλῶν, 2 μεθ’
– sitting on ²waters ¹many, with

ἧς ἐπόρνευσαν οἱ βασιλεῖς τῆς γῆς,
whom ²practised ¹the ²kings ³of the ⁴earth,
fornication

καὶ ἐμεθύσθησαν οἱ κατοικοῦντες τὴν γῆν
and ²became drunk ¹the ³dwelling [on] ²the ⁴earth
[ones]

ἐκ τοῦ οἴνου τῆς πορνείας αὐτῆς. 3 καὶ
from the wine of the fornication of her. And

ἀπήνεγκέν με εἰς ἔρημον ἐν πνεύματι.
he carried away me into a desert in spirit.

καὶ εἶδον γυναῖκα καθημένην ἐπὶ θηρίον
And I saw a woman sitting on ²beast

κόκκινον, γέμοντα ὀνόματα βλασφημίας,
¹a scarlet, being filled [with] names of blasphemy,

ἔχοντα κεφαλὰς ἑπτὰ καὶ κέρατα δέκα.
having ²heads ¹seven and ²horns ¹ten.

4 καὶ ἡ γυνὴ ἦν περιβεβλημένη πορφυροῦν
And the woman was having been clothed [in] purple

καὶ κόκκινον, καὶ κεχρυσωμένη χρυσίῳ
and scarlet, and having been gilded with gold

καὶ λίθῳ τιμίῳ καὶ μαργαρίταις, ἔχουσα
and ²stone ¹precious and pearls, having

ποτήριον χρυσοῦν ἐν τῇ χειρὶ αὐτῆς
²cup ¹a golden in the hand of her

γέμον βδελυγμάτων καὶ τὰ ἀκάθαρτα
being filled of(with) and the unclean things
abominations

τῆς πορνείας αὐτῆς, 5 καὶ ἐπὶ τὸ
of the fornication of her, and on the

μέτωπον αὐτῆς ὄνομα γεγραμμένον,
forehead of her a name having been written,

Chapter 17

The Woman on the Beast

ONE of the seven angels who had the seven bowls came and said to me, "Come, I will show you the punishment of the great prostitute, who sits on many waters. 2 With her the kings of the earth committed adultery and the inhabitants of the earth were intoxicated with the wine of her adulteries."

3 Then the angel carried me away in the Spirit into a desert. There I saw a woman sitting on a scarlet beast that was covered with blasphemous names and had seven heads and ten horns. 4 The woman was dressed in purple and scarlet, and was glittering with gold, precious stones and pearls. She held a golden cup in her hand, filled with abominable things and the filth of her adulteries. 5 This title was written on her forehead:

---

* Even in English a city is often personified as feminine.

the great, mother of whores and of earth's abominations." 6 And I saw that the woman was drunk with the blood of the saints and the blood of the witnesses to Jesus.

When I saw her, I was greatly amazed. 7 But the angel said to me, "Why are you so amazed? I will tell you the mystery of the woman, and of the beast with seven heads and ten horns that carries her. 8 The beast that you saw was, and is not, and is about to ascend from the bottomless pit and go to destruction. And the inhabitants of the earth, whose names have not been written in the book of life from the foundation of the world, will be amazed when they see the beast, because it was and is not and is to come.

9 "This calls for a mind that has wisdom: the seven heads are seven mountains on which the woman is seated; also, they are seven kings, 10 of whom five have fallen, one is living, and the other has not yet come; and when he comes, he must remain only a little while. 11 As for the beast that was and is not, it is an eighth but it belongs to the seven, and it goes to destruction. 12 And the ten horns that you saw are ten kings who have not yet received a kingdom, but they are to receive authority as kings for one hour, together with the

μυστήριον, **ΒΑΒΥΛΩΝ Η ΜΕΓΑΛΗ,**
a mystery,   BABYLON THE GREAT,

Η ΜΗΤΗΡ ΤΩΝ ΠΟΡΝΩΝ ΚΑΙ
The Mother of the Harlots and

ΤΩΝ ΒΔΕΛΥΓΜΑΤΩΝ ΤΗΣ ΓΗΣ.
of the   Abominations   of the Earth.

6 καὶ εἶδον τὴν γυναῖκα μεθύουσαν ἐκ
And I saw the woman being drunk from

τοῦ αἵματος τῶν ἁγίων καὶ ἐκ τοῦ
the blood of the saints and from the

αἵματος τῶν μαρτύρων Ἰησοῦ. Καὶ
blood of the witnesses of Jesus. And

ἐθαύμασα ἰδὼν αὐτὴν θαῦμα μέγα. 7 καὶ
¹I wondered ²seeing ³her ⁶[with] ⁵wonder ⁴a great. And

εἶπέν μοι ὁ ἄγγελος· διὰ τί ἐθαύμασας;
²said ³to me ¹the ⁴angel: Why didst thou wonder?

ἐγὼ ἐρῶ σοι τὸ μυστήριον τῆς γυναικὸς
I will tell thee the mystery of the woman

καὶ τοῦ θηρίου τοῦ βαστάζοντος αὐτὴν
and of the beast - carrying her

τοῦ ἔχοντος τὰς ἑπτὰ κεφαλὰς καὶ τὰ
- having the seven heads and the

δέκα κέρατα. 8 Τὸ θηρίον ὃ εἶδες ἦν
ten horns. The beast which thou was
                                  sawest

καὶ οὐκ ἔστιν, καὶ μέλλει ἀναβαίνειν
and is not, and is about to come up

ἐκ τῆς ἀβύσσου καὶ εἰς ἀπώλειαν ὑπάγει·
out of the abyss and ²to ³destruction ¹goes;

καὶ θαυμασθήσονται οἱ κατοικοῦντες ἐπὶ
and ⁴will wonder ¹the [ones] ²dwelling ³on

τῆς γῆς, ὧν οὐ γέγραπται τὸ ὄνομα
⁴the ⁵earth, of whom ³has not been written ¹the ²name

ἐπὶ τὸ βιβλίον τῆς ζωῆς ἀπὸ καταβολῆς
on the scroll - of life from [the] foundation

κόσμου, βλεπόντων τὸ θηρίον ὅτι ἦν
of [the] world, seeing the beast that it was

καὶ οὐκ ἔστιν καὶ παρέσται. 9 ὧδε
and is not and is present. Here [is]

ὁ νοῦς ὁ ἔχων σοφίαν. αἱ ἑπτὰ
the mind - having wisdom. The seven

κεφαλαὶ ἑπτὰ ὄρη εἰσίν, ὅπου ἡ γυνὴ
heads ²seven ³mountains ¹are, where the woman

κάθηται ἐπ᾽ αὐτῶν, καὶ βασιλεῖς ἑπτά
sits on them, and ²kings ¹seven

εἰσιν· 10 οἱ πέντε ἔπεσαν, ὁ εἷς ἔστιν,
¹are: the five fell, the one is,

ὁ ἄλλος οὔπω ἦλθεν, καὶ ὅταν ἔλθῃ
the other not yet came, and whenever he comes

ὀλίγον αὐτὸν δεῖ μεῖναι. 11 καὶ τὸ
⁴a little ⁵him ¹it behoves ²to And the
[while]   remain.

θηρίον ὃ ἦν καὶ οὐκ ἔστιν, καὶ αὐτὸς
beast which was and is not, even he

ὄγδοός ἐστιν, καὶ ἐκ τῶν ἑπτά ἐστιν,
²an eighth ¹is, and ²of ³the ⁴seven ¹is,

καὶ εἰς ἀπώλειαν ὑπάγει. 12 καὶ τὰ
and to destruction goes. And the

δέκα κέρατα ἃ εἶδες δέκα βασιλεῖς
ten horns which thou ²ten ¹kings
                  sawest

εἰσιν, οἵτινες βασιλείαν οὔπω ἔλαβον,
¹are, who a kingdom not yet received,

ἀλλὰ ἐξουσίαν ὡς βασιλεῖς μίαν ὥραν
but ²authority ³as ⁴kings ⁵one ⁶hour

λαμβάνουσιν μετὰ τοῦ θηρίου. 13 οὗτοι
¹receive with the beast. These

6 I saw that the woman was drunk with the blood of the saints, the blood of those who bore testimony to Jesus.

When I saw her, I was greatly astonished. 7 Then the angel said to me: "Why are you astonished? I will explain to you the mystery of the woman and of the beast she rides, which has the seven heads and ten horns. 8 The beast, which you saw, once was, is not, and will come up out of the Abyss and go to his destruction. The inhabitants of the earth whose names have not been written in the book of life from the creation of the world will be astonished when they see the beast, because he once was, now is not, and yet will come.

9 "This calls for a mind with wisdom. The seven heads are seven hills on which the woman sits. 10 They are also seven kings. Five have fallen, one is, the other has not yet come; but when he does come, he must remain for a little while. 11 The beast who once was, and now is not, is an eighth king. He belongs to the seven and is going to his destruction.

12 "The ten horns you saw are ten kings who have not yet received a kingdom, but who for one hour will receive authority as kings along with the beast.

beast. 13 These are united in yielding their power and authority to the beast; 14 they will make war on the Lamb, and the Lamb will conquer them, for he is Lord of lords and King of kings, and those with him are called and chosen and faithful."

15 And he said to me, "The waters you saw, where the whore is seated, are peoples and multitudes and nations and languages. 16 And the ten horns that you saw, they and the beast will hate the whore; they will make her desolate and naked; they will devour her flesh and burn her up with fire. 17 For God has put it into their hearts to carry out his purpose by agreeing to give their kingdom to the beast, until the words of God will be fulfilled. 18 The woman you saw is the great city that rules over the kings of the earth."

μίαν   γνώμην   ἔχουσιν,   καὶ   τὴν   δύναμιν
one   mind   have,   and   the   power

καὶ   ἐξουσίαν   αὐτῶν   τῷ   θηρίῳ   διδόασιν.
and   authority   of them   to the   beast   they give.

14 οὗτοι   μετὰ   τοῦ   ἀρνίου   πολεμήσουσιν
These   ²with   ³the   ⁴Lamb   ¹will make war

καὶ   τὸ   ἀρνίον   νικήσει   αὐτούς,   ὅτι   κύριος
and   the   Lamb   will overcome   them,   because   ¹Lord

κυρίων   ἐστὶν   καὶ   βασιλεὺς   βασιλέων,   καὶ
²of lords   ³he is   and   King   of kings,   and

οἱ   μετ'   αὐτοῦ   κλητοὶ   καὶ   ἐκλεκτοὶ   καὶ
the   with   him [are]   called   and   chosen   and
[ones]

πιστοί.   15 Καὶ   λέγει   μοι·   τὰ   ὕδατα
faithful.   And   he says   to me: The   waters

ἃ   εἶδες,   οὗ   ἡ   πόρνη   κάθηται,   λαοὶ
which thou   sawest,   where   the   harlot   sits,   peoples

καὶ   ὄχλοι   εἰσὶν   καὶ   ἔθνη   καὶ   γλῶσσαι.
and   crowds   are   and   nations   and   tongues.

16 καὶ   τὰ   δέκα   κέρατα   ἃ   εἶδες   καὶ
And   the   ten   horns   which thou sawest   and

τὸ   θηρίον,   οὗτοι   μισήσουσιν   τὴν   πόρνην,
the   beast,   these   will hate   the   harlot,

καὶ   ἠρημωμένην   ποιήσουσιν   αὐτὴν   καὶ
and   ²having been desolated   ¹will make   ³her   and

γυμνήν,   καὶ   τὰς   σάρκας   αὐτῆς   φάγονται,
naked,   and   ²the   ²fleshes   ⁴of her   ¹will eat,

καὶ   αὐτὴν   κατακαύσουσιν   [ἐν]   πυρί·   17 ὁ
and   ²her   ¹will consume   with   fire;   —

γὰρ   θεὸς   ἔδωκεν   εἰς   τὰς   καρδίας   αὐτῶν
for   God   gave   into   the   hearts   of them

ποιῆσαι   τὴν   γνώμην   αὐτοῦ,   καὶ   ποιῆσαι
to do   the   mind   of him,   and   to make

μίαν   γνώμην   καὶ   δοῦναι   τὴν   βασιλείαν
one   mind   and   to give   the   kingdom

αὐτῶν   τῷ   θηρίῳ,   ἄχρι   τελεσθήσονται   οἱ
of them   to the   beast,   until   ⁴shall be accomplished   ¹the

λόγοι   τοῦ   θεοῦ.   18 καὶ   ἡ   γυνὴ   ἦν
²words   —   ³of God.   And   the   woman whom

εἶδες   ἔστιν   ἡ   πόλις   ἡ   μεγάλη   ἡ   ἔχουσα
thou   is   the   ²city   —   ¹great   —   having
sawest

βασιλείαν   ἐπὶ   τῶν   βασιλέων   τῆς   γῆς.
a kingdom   over   the   kings   of the   earth.

---

13 They have one purpose and will give their power and authority to the beast. 14 They will make war against the Lamb, but the Lamb will overcome them because he is Lord of lords and King of kings—and with him will be his called, chosen and faithful followers."

15 Then the angel said to me, "The waters you saw, where the prostitute sits, are peoples, multitudes, nations and languages. 16 The beast and the ten horns you saw will hate the prostitute. They will bring her to ruin and leave her naked; they will eat her flesh and burn her with fire. 17 For God has put it into their hearts to accomplish his purpose by agreeing to give the beast their power to rule, until God's words are fulfilled. 18 The woman you saw is the great city that rules over the kings of the earth."

Chapter 18
The Fall of Babylon

AFTER this I saw another angel coming down from heaven, having great authority; and the earth was made bright with his splendor. 2 He called out with a mighty voice, "Fallen, fallen is Babylon the great! It has become a dwelling place of demons, a haunt of every foul and hateful bird, a haunt of every foul and hateful beast. [b] 3 For all the nations have drunk [c] of the wine of the wrath of her fornication,

[b] Some ancient authorities lack a haunt of every foul and hateful beast
[c] Other ancient authorities read she has made all nations drink

---

18 Μετὰ   ταῦτα   εἶδον   ἄλλον   ἄγγελον
After   these things   I saw   another   angel

καταβαίνοντα   ἐκ   τοῦ   οὐρανοῦ,   ἔχοντα
coming down   out of   —   heaven,   having

ἐξουσίαν   μεγάλην,   καὶ   ἡ   γῆ   ἐφωτίσθη
¹authority   ¹great,   and   the   earth was enlightened

ἐκ   τῆς   δόξης   αὐτοῦ.   2 καὶ   ἔκραξεν
from   the   glory   of him.   And   he cried

ἐν   ἰσχυρᾷ   φωνῇ   λέγων·   ἔπεσεν   ἔπεσεν
in   a strong   voice   saying: Fell[,]   fell

Βαβυλὼν   ἡ   μεγάλη,   καὶ   ἐγένετο   κατοικητή-
Babylon   the   great,   and   became   a dwelling-

ριον   δαιμονίων   καὶ   φυλακὴ   παντὸς
place   of demons   and   a prison   of every

πνεύματος   ἀκαθάρτου   καὶ   φυλακὴ   παντὸς
³spirit   ¹unclean   and   a prison   of every

ὀρνέου   ἀκαθάρτου   καὶ   μεμισημένον,   3 ὅτι
⁴bird   ¹unclean   ²and   ³having been hated,   because

ἐκ   τοῦ   οἴνου   τοῦ   θυμοῦ   τῆς   πορνείας
⁵of   ⁶the   ⁷wine   ⁸of the   ⁹anger   ¹⁰of the   ¹¹fornication

---

Chapter 18
The Fall of Babylon

AFTER this I saw another angel coming down from heaven. He had great authority, and the earth was illuminated by his splendor. 2 With a mighty voice he shouted:

"Fallen! Fallen is
    Babylon the Great!
She has become a
    home for demons
and a haunt for every
    evil [v] spirit,
a haunt for every
    unclean and
    detestable bird.
3 For all the nations have
    drunk
the maddening wine of
    her adulteries.

[v] 2 Greek unclean

and the kings of the earth have committed fornication with her, and the merchants of the earth have grown rich from the power[d] of her luxury."
4 Then I heard another voice from heaven saying, "Come out of her, my people, so that you do not take part in her sins, and so that you do not share in her plagues;
5 for her sins are heaped high as heaven, and God has remembered her iniquities.
6 Render to her as she herself has rendered, and repay her double for her deeds; mix a double draught for her in the cup she mixed.
7 As she glorified herself and lived luxuriously, so give her a like measure of torment and grief. Since in her heart she says, 'I rule as a queen; I am no widow, and I will never see grief,'
8 therefore her plagues will come in a single day—pestilence and mourning and famine—and she will be burned with fire; for mighty is the Lord God who judges her."
9 And the kings of the earth, who committed fornication and lived in luxury with her, will weep and wail over her when they see the smoke of her burning;
10 they will stand far off, in fear of her torment, and say, "Alas, alas, the great city, Babylon, the mighty city! For in one hour your

---

αὐτῆς πέπωκαν πάντα τὰ ἔθνη, καὶ
[3]of her [2]have drunk [1]all [the] [1]the [1]nations, and
οἱ βασιλεῖς τῆς γῆς μετ᾽ αὐτῆς ἐπόρνευσαν,
the kings of the earth with her practised fornication,
καὶ οἱ ἔμποροι τῆς γῆς ἐκ τῆς δυνάμεως
and the merchants of the earth [1]from [2]the [4]power
τοῦ στρήνους αὐτῆς ἐπλούτησαν. 4 Καὶ
[3]of the [5]luxury [6]of her [1]became rich. And
ἤκουσα ἄλλην φωνὴν ἐκ τοῦ οὐρανοῦ
I heard another voice out of — heaven
λέγουσαν· ἐξέλθατε ὁ λαός μου ἐξ αὐτῆς,
saying: Come ye out[,] the people of me[,] out of her,
ἵνα μὴ συγκοινωνήσητε ταῖς ἁμαρτίαις
lest ye share in the sins
αὐτῆς, καὶ ἐκ τῶν πληγῶν αὐτῆς ἵνα
of her, and [1]of [2]the [4]plagues [5]of her [3]lest
μὴ λάβητε· 5 ὅτι ἐκολλήθησαν αὐτῆς αἱ
[6]ye receive; because [4]joined together [5]of her [1]the
ἁμαρτίαι ἄχρι τοῦ οὐρανοῦ, καὶ ἐμνημό-
[2]sins up to — heaven, and [1]remem-
νευσεν ὁ θεὸς τὰ ἀδικήματα αὐτῆς.
bered — [1]God the misdeeds of her.
6 ἀπόδοτε αὐτῇ ὡς καὶ αὐτὴ ἀπέδωκεν,
Give ye back to her as indeed she gave back,
καὶ διπλώσατε τὰ διπλᾶ κατὰ τὰ ἔργα
and double ye the double according to the works
αὐτῆς· ἐν τῷ ποτηρίῳ ᾧ ἐκέρασεν
of her; in the cup in which she mixed
κεράσατε αὐτῇ διπλοῦν· 7 ὅσα ἐδόξασεν
mix ye to her double; by what she glorified
αὐτὴν καὶ ἐστρηνίασεν, τοσοῦτον δότε
her[self] and luxuriated, by so much give ye
αὐτῇ βασανισμὸν καὶ πένθος. ὅτι ἐν
to her torment and sorrow. Because in
τῇ καρδίᾳ αὐτῆς λέγει ὅτι κάθημαι
the heart of her she says[,] — I sit
βασίλισσα καὶ χήρα οὐκ εἰμὶ καὶ πένθος
a queen and a widow I am not and sorrow
οὐ μὴ ἴδω· 8 διὰ τοῦτο ἐν μιᾷ ἡμέρᾳ
by no means I see; therefore in one day
ἥξουσιν αἱ πληγαὶ αὐτῆς, θάνατος καὶ
will come the plagues of her, death and
πένθος καὶ λιμός, καὶ ἐν πυρὶ κατακαυ-
sorrow and famine, and with fire she will be
θήσεται· ὅτι ἰσχυρὸς κύριος ὁ θεὸς ὁ
consumed; because strong [is] [the] Lord — God the
κρίνας αὐτήν. 9 καὶ κλαύσουσιν καὶ
[one] judging her. And [1]will weep [2]and
κόψονται ἐπ᾽ αὐτὴν οἱ βασιλεῖς τῆς
[7]wail [8]over [9]her [1]the [2]kings [3]of the
γῆς οἱ μετ᾽ αὐτῆς πορνεύσαντες καὶ
[4]earth [10]the [11]with [13]her [12]having practised and
fornication
στρηνιάσαντες, ὅταν βλέπωσιν τὸν καπνὸν
having luxuriated, whenever they see the smoke
τῆς πυρώσεως αὐτῆς, 10 ἀπὸ μακρόθεν
of the burning of her, [1]from [2]afar
ἑστηκότες διὰ τὸν φόβον τοῦ βασανισμοῦ
[1]standing because of the fear of the torment
αὐτῆς, λέγοντες· οὐαὶ οὐαί, ἡ πόλις
of her, saying: Woe[,] woe, the [2]city
ἡ μεγάλη, Βαβυλὼν ἡ πόλις ἡ ἰσχυρά,
— [1]great, Babylon the [2]city — [1]strong,

The kings of the earth committed adultery with her, and the merchants of the earth grew rich from her excessive luxuries."
4 Then I heard another voice from heaven say:
"Come out of her, my people, so that you will not share in her sins, so that you will not receive any of her plagues;
5 for her sins are piled up to heaven, and God has remembered her crimes.
6 Give back to her as she has given; pay her back double for what she has done. Mix her a double portion from her own cup.
7 Give her as much torture and grief as the glory and luxury she gave herself. In her heart she boasts, 'I sit as queen; I am not a widow, and I will never mourn.'
8 Therefore in one day her plagues will overtake her: death, mourning and famine. She will be consumed by fire, for mighty is the Lord God who judges her.
9 "When the kings of the earth who committed adultery with her and shared her luxury see the smoke of her burning, they will weep and mourn over her. 10 Terrified at her torment, they will stand far off and cry:
" 'Woe! Woe, O great city, O Babylon, city of power!

---

[d] Or resources

judgment
has come."
11 And the merchants
of the earth weep and
mourn for her, since no one
buys their cargo anymore,
12 cargo of gold, silver, jewels and pearls, fine linen,
purple, silk and scarlet, all
kinds of scented wood, all
articles of ivory, all articles
of costly wood, bronze,
iron, and marble, 13 cinnamon, spice, incense,
myrrh, frankincense, wine,
olive oil, choice flour and
wheat, cattle and sheep,
horses and chariots,
slaves—and human lives. *
14 "The fruit for which
  your soul longed
has gone from you,
  and all your dainties
   and
  your splendor
are lost to you,
  never to be found
   again!"
15 The merchants of these
wares, who gained wealth
from her, will stand far off,
in fear of her torment,
weeping and mourning
aloud,
16 "Alas, alas, the great
  city,
  clothed in fine linen,
  in purple and
   scarlet,
  adorned with gold,
  with jewels, and
   with pearls!
17 For in one hour all
this wealth has
been laid
waste!"
And all shipmasters and
seafarers, sailors and all

ὅτι   μιᾷ   ὥρᾳ   ἦλθεν   ἡ   κρίσις   σου.   11 καὶ
be-   in   hour   came   the judgment   of thee.   And
cause   one

οἱ   ἔμποροι   τῆς   γῆς   κλαίουσιν   καὶ
the   merchants   of the   earth   weep   and

πενθοῦσιν   ἐπ᾽   αὐτήν,   ὅτι   τὸν   γόμον
sorrow   over   her,   because   ²the   ²cargo

αὐτῶν   οὐδεὶς   ἀγοράζει   οὐκέτι,   12 γόμον
⁵of them   ¹no one   ³buys   ⁴any more,   cargo

χρυσοῦ   καὶ   ἀργύρου   καὶ   λίθου   τιμίου
of gold   and   of silver   and   ²stone   ¹of valuable

καὶ   μαργαριτῶν   καὶ   βυσσίνου   καὶ   πορφύρας
and   of pearls   and   of fine linen   and   of purple

καὶ   σηρικοῦ   καὶ   κοκκίνου,   καὶ   πᾶν
and   of silk   and   of scarlet,   and   all

ξύλον   θύϊνον   καὶ   πᾶν   σκεῦος   ἐλεφάντινον
²wood   ¹thyine   and   every   ²vessel   ¹ivory

καὶ   πᾶν   σκεῦος   ἐκ   ξύλου   τιμιωτάτου
and   every   vessel   of   ²wood   ¹very valuable

καὶ   χαλκοῦ   καὶ   σιδήρου   καὶ   μαρμάρου,
and   of bronze   and   of iron   and   of marble,

13 καὶ   κιννάμωμον   καὶ   ἄμωμον   καὶ
and   cinnamon   and   spice   and

θυμιάματα   καὶ   μύρον   καὶ   λίβανον   καὶ
incenses   and   ointment   and   frankincense   and

οἶνον   καὶ   ἔλαιον   καὶ   σεμίδαλιν   καὶ   σῖτον
wine   and   oil   and   fine meal   and   corn

καὶ   κτήνη   καὶ   πρόβατα,   καὶ   ἵππων
and beasts of burden and   sheep,   and   of horses

καὶ   ῥεδῶν   καὶ   σωμάτων,   καὶ   ψυχὰς
and   of carriages   and   of bodies,   and   souls

ἀνθρώπων.   14 καὶ   ἡ   ὀπώρα   σου   τῆς
of men.   And   the   fruit   ¹of thee   ²of the

ἐπιθυμίας   τῆς   ψυχῆς   ἀπῆλθεν   ἀπὸ   σοῦ,
¹lust   ²of the   ²soul   went away   from   thee,

καὶ   πάντα   τὰ   λιπαρὰ   καὶ   τὰ   λαμπρὰ
and   all   the   sumptuous   and   the   bright
    things   things

ἀπώλετο   ἀπὸ   σοῦ,   καὶ   οὐκέτι   οὐ   μὴ
perished   from   thee,   and   no more   by no(any)
    means

αὐτὰ   εὑρήσουσιν.   15 οἱ   ἔμποροι   τούτων,
²them   ¹shall they find.   The   merchants   of these
    things,

οἱ   πλουτήσαντες   ἀπ᾽   αὐτῆς,   ἀπὸ   μακρόθεν
the   having been rich   from   her,   ²from   ²afar
[ones]

στήσονται   διὰ   τὸν   φόβον   τοῦ   βασανισμοῦ
¹will stand because of the   fear   of the   torment

αὐτῆς   κλαίοντες   καὶ   πενθοῦντες,   16 λέγοντες·
of her   weeping   and   sorrowing,   saying:

οὐαὶ   οὐαί,   ἡ   πόλις   ἡ   μεγάλη,   ἡ   περι-
Woe[,]   woe,   the   ²city   –   ¹great,   –   having

βεβλημένη   βύσσινον   καὶ   πορφυροῦν   καὶ
been clothed [with] fine linen   and   purple   and

κόκκινον,   καὶ   κεχρυσωμένη   ἐν   χρυσίῳ
scarlet,   and   having been gilded   with   gold

καὶ   λίθῳ   τιμίῳ   καὶ   μαργαρίτῃ,   17 ὅτι
and   ²stone   ¹valuable   and   pearl,   because

μιᾷ   ὥρᾳ   ἠρημώθη   ὁ   τοσοῦτος   πλοῦτος.
in one   hour   ²was made   –   ¹such great   ²wealth.
    desolate

καὶ   πᾶς   κυβερνήτης   καὶ   πᾶς   ὁ   ἐπὶ
And   every   steersman   and   ¹every   ²one   ⁴to

τόπον   πλέων   καὶ   ναῦται   καὶ   ὅσοι   τὴν
²a place   ³sailing   and   sailors   and as many as   ²the

In one hour your doom
has come!'

11 "The merchants of the
earth will weep and mourn
over her because no one
buys their cargoes any
more—12 cargoes of gold,
silver, precious stones and
pearls; fine linen, purple,
silk and scarlet cloth; every
sort of citron wood, and articles of every kind made of
ivory, costly wood,
bronze, iron and marble;
13 cargoes of cinnamon and
spice, of incense, myrrh
and frankincense, of wine
and olive oil, of fine flour
and wheat; cattle and
sheep; horses and car-
riages; and bodies and
souls of men.
14 "They will say, 'The
fruit you longed for is gone
from you. All your riches
and splendor have van-
ished, never to be recov-
ered.' 15 The merchants
who sold these things and
gained their wealth from
her will stand far off, terrified at her torment. They
will weep and mourn 16and
cry out:

  " 'Woe! Woe, O great
   city,
  dressed in fine linen,
   purple and scarlet,
  and glittering with
   gold, precious
   stones and pearls!
17 In one hour such great
  wealth has been
  brought to ruin!'

"Every sea captain, and
all who travel by ship, the
sailors, and all who earn

---

* Or chariots, and human bodies
and souls

whose trade is on the sea,
stood far off [18] and cried out
as they saw the smoke of
her burning,
"What city was like
  the great city?"
[19] And they threw dust on
their heads, as they wept
and mourned, crying out,
"Alas, alas, the great
  city,
  where all who had
    ships at sea
    grew rich by her
    wealth!
For in one hour she
  has been
  laid waste.
[20] Rejoice over her,
  O heaven,
  you saints and
  apostles and
  prophets!
For God has given
  judgment for
  you against
  her."
[21] Then a mighty angel
took up a stone like a great
millstone and threw it into
the sea, saying,
"With such violence
  Babylon the
  great city
  will be thrown
  down,
  and will be found no
  more;
[22] and the sound of
  harpists and
  minstrels and of
  flutists and
  trumpeters
  will be heard in you
  no more;
  and an artisan of any
  trade
  will be found in you
  no more;
  and the sound of the
  millstone
  will be heard in you
  no more;
[23] and the light of a
  lamp
  will shine in you no
  more;
  and the voice of
  bridegroom
  and bride
  will be heard in you
  no more;
for your merchants
  were the
  magnates of the
  earth,
  and all nations were
  deceived by
  your sorcery.
[24] And in you[f] was
  found the blood
  of prophets and
  of saints,
  and of all who have
  been slaughtered
  on earth."

[f] Gk her

Middle column (Greek interlinear):

θάλασσαν ἐργάζονται, ἀπὸ μακρόθεν ἔστησαν
²sea   ¹work.   ²from   ³afar   ¹stood

18 καὶ ἔκραζον βλέποντες τὸν καπνὸν
  and   cried out   seeing   the   smoke

τῆς πυρώσεως αὐτῆς λέγοντες· τίς ὁμοία
of the   burning   of her   saying: Who(What) [is] like

τῇ πόλει τῇ μεγάλῃ; 19 καὶ ἔβαλον
to the ³city – ¹great?   And   they cast

χοῦν ἐπὶ τὰς κεφαλὰς αὐτῶν καὶ ἔκραζον
dust   on   the   heads   of them   and   cried out

κλαίοντες καὶ πενθοῦντες, λέγοντες· οὐαὶ
weeping   and   sorrowing,   saying: Woe[,]

οὐαί, ἡ πόλις ἡ μεγάλη, ἐν ᾗ ἐπλούτησαν
woe, the ²city – ¹great,   by which   ²were rich

πάντες οἱ ἔχοντες τὰ πλοῖα ἐν τῇ
¹all   ³the [ones] ³having ⁴the   ⁵ships   ⁶in   ⁷the

θαλάσσῃ ἐκ τῆς τιμιότητος αὐτῆς, ὅτι
⁸sea   from   the   worth   of her,   because

μιᾷ ὥρᾳ ἠρημώθη. 20 Εὐφραίνου ἐπ'
in one   hour   she was made desolate.   Be thou glad   over

αὐτῇ, οὐρανὲ καὶ οἱ ἅγιοι καὶ οἱ ἀπό-
her,   heaven   and   the   saints   and   the   apost-

στολοι καὶ οἱ προφῆται, ὅτι ἔκρινεν ὁ
les   and   the   prophets,   because   ²judged   –

θεὸς τὸ κρίμα ὑμῶν ἐξ αὐτῆς. 21 Καὶ
¹God   the   judgment of you   by   her.   And

ἦρεν εἷς ἄγγελος ἰσχυρὸς λίθον ὡς
⁴lifted ¹one   ²angel   ³strong   a stone   as

μύλινον μέγαν, καὶ ἔβαλεν εἰς τὴν θά-
²millstone ¹a great,   and   threw   into   the   sea

λασσαν λέγων· οὕτως ὁρμήματι βληθήσεται
saying: Thus   with a rush   ²shall be thrown

Βαβυλὼν ἡ μεγάλη πόλις, καὶ οὐ μὴ
¹Babylon ²the   ³great   ⁴city,   and   by no means

εὑρεθῇ ἔτι. 22 καὶ φωνὴ κιθαρῳδῶν
[shall] be longer.   And   sound   of harpers
found

καὶ μουσικῶν καὶ αὐλητῶν καὶ σαλπιστῶν
and   of musicians   and   of flutists   and   of trumpeters

οὐ μὴ ἀκουσθῇ ἐν σοὶ ἔτι, καὶ πᾶς
by no means [shall] be heard in thee   longer,   and   every

τεχνίτης πάσης τέχνης οὐ μὴ εὑρεθῇ
craftsman   of every   craft   by no means   [shall]
                                            be found

ἐν σοὶ ἔτι, καὶ φωνὴ μύλου οὐ μὴ
in thee   longer,   and   sound   of a mill by no means

ἀκουσθῇ ἐν σοὶ ἔτι, 23 καὶ φῶς
[shall] be heard in   thee   longer,   and   light

λύχνου οὐ μὴ φάνῃ ἐν σοὶ ἔτι, καὶ
of a   by no means [shall] shine   in   thee   longer,   and
lamp

φωνὴ νυμφίου καὶ νύμφης οὐ μὴ
voice   of bridegroom   and   of bride   by no means

ἀκουσθῇ ἐν σοὶ ἔτι· ὅτι [οἱ] ἔμποροί
[shall] be heard in thee   longer; because the   the merchants

σου ἦσαν οἱ μεγιστᾶνες τῆς γῆς, ὅτι
of thee   were   the   great ones   of the   earth, because

ἐν τῇ φαρμακείᾳ σου ἐπλανήθησαν πάντα
by the   sorcery   of thee   ⁴were deceived   ¹all

τὰ ἔθνη, 24 καὶ ἐν αὐτῇ αἷμα προφητῶν
²the ³nations,   and in   her   ²blood ³of prophets

καὶ ἁγίων εὑρέθη καὶ πάντων τῶν
⁴and ⁵of saints ¹was found   and   of all   the [ones]

ἐσφαγμένων ἐπὶ τῆς γῆς.
having been slain   on   the   earth.

their living from the sea,
will stand far off. [18]When
they see the smoke of her
burning, they will exclaim,
'Was there ever a city like
this great city?' [19]They will
throw dust on their heads,
and with weeping and
mourning cry out:

  " 'Woe! Woe, O great
    city,
    where all who had
    ships on the sea
    became rich through
    her wealth!
  In one hour she has been
    brought to ruin!
[20]Rejoice over her, O
    heaven!
  Rejoice, saints and
    apostles and
    prophets!
  God has judged her for
    the way she treated
    you.' "

[21]Then a mighty angel
picked up a boulder the size
of a large millstone and
threw it into the sea, and
said:

  "With such violence
    the great city of
    Babylon will be
    thrown down,
    never to be found
    again.
[22]The music of harpists
    and musicians, flute
    players and
    trumpeters,
    will never be heard in
    you again.
  No workman of any
    trade
    will ever be found in
    you again.
  The sound of a millstone
    will never be heard in
    you again.
[23]The light of a lamp
    will never shine in you
    again.
  The voice of bridegroom
    and bride
    will never be heard in
    you again.
  Your merchants were
    the world's great
    men.
  By your magic spell all
    the nations were led
    astray.
[24]In her was found the
    blood of prophets
    and of the saints,
    and of all who have
    been killed on the
    earth.' "

Chapter 19

The Rejoicing in Heaven

AFTER this I heard what seemed to be the loud voice of a great multitude in heaven, saying, "Hallelujah!
Salvation and glory
and power
to our God,
2 for his judgments
are true
and just;
he has judged the
great whore
who corrupted the
earth with her
fornication,
and he has avenged
on her the blood
of his
servants." g
3 Once more they said,
"Hallelujah!
The smoke goes up
from her forever
and ever."
4 And the twenty-four elders and the four living creatures fell down and worshiped God who is seated on the throne, saying, "Amen. Hallelujah!"
5 And from the throne came a voice saying,
"Praise our God,
all you his
servants, g
and all who fear him,
small and great."
6 Then I heard what seemed to be the voice of a great multitude, like the sound of many waters and like the sound of mighty thunderpeals, crying out,
"Hallelujah!
For the Lord our God
the Almighty reigns.
7 Let us rejoice and
exult
and give him the
glory,
for the marriage of the
Lamb has come,
and his bride has
made
herself ready;
8 to her it has been
granted to
be clothed
with fine linen,
bright and
pure"—
for the fine linen is the righteous deeds of the saints.
9 And the angel said h to me, "Write this: Blessed are those who are invited to

---

19 Μετὰ ταῦτα ἤκουσα ὡς φωνὴν
After these things I heard as ³voice

μεγάλην ὄχλου πολλοῦ ἐν τῷ οὐρανῷ
¹a great ⁴crowd ²of a much in – heaven
(loud) (great)

λεγόντων· ἀλληλουϊά· ἡ σωτηρία καὶ ἡ
saying: Halleluia: The salvation and the

δόξα καὶ ἡ δύναμις τοῦ θεοῦ ἡμῶν,
glory and the power of the God of us,

2 ὅτι ἀληθιναὶ καὶ δίκαιαι αἱ κρίσεις
because true and righteous the judgments

αὐτοῦ· ὅτι ἔκρινεν τὴν πόρνην τὴν
of him; because he judged the ³harlot –

μεγάλην ἥτις ἔφθειρεν τὴν γῆν ἐν τῇ
¹great who defiled the earth with the

πορνείᾳ αὐτῆς, καὶ ἐξεδίκησεν τὸ αἷμα
fornication of her, and *he* avenged the blood

τῶν δούλων αὐτοῦ ἐκ χειρὸς αὐτῆς.
of the slaves of him out of [the] hand of her.

3 καὶ δεύτερον εἴρηκαν· ἀλληλουϊά· καὶ
And secondly they *have* said: Halleluia: and

ὁ καπνὸς αὐτῆς ἀναβαίνει εἰς τοὺς
the smoke of her goes up unto the

αἰῶνας τῶν αἰώνων. **4** καὶ ἔπεσαν οἱ
ages of the ages. And ⁸fell ¹the

πρεσβύτεροι οἱ εἴκοσι τέσσαρες καὶ τὰ
³elders – ¹twenty-four ⁴and ⁵the

τέσσερα ζῷα, καὶ προσεκύνησαν τῷ θεῷ
⁶four ⁷living and worshipped – God
creatures,

τῷ καθημένῳ ἐπὶ τῷ θρόνῳ λέγοντες·
sitting on the throne saying:

ἀμὴν ἀλληλουϊά. **5** καὶ φωνὴ ἀπὸ τοῦ
Amen[,] halleluia. And a voice ⁵from ¹the

θρόνου ἐξῆλθεν λέγουσα· αἰνεῖτε τῷ θεῷ
⁴throne ¹came out saying: Praise ye the God

ἡμῶν, πάντες οἱ δοῦλοι αὐτοῦ, οἱ
of us, all the slaves of him, the

φοβούμενοι αὐτόν, οἱ μικροὶ καὶ οἱ
[ones] fearing him, the small and the

μεγάλοι. **6** Καὶ ἤκουσα ὡς φωνὴν ὄχλου
great. And I heard as a sound ²crowd

πολλοῦ καὶ ὡς φωνὴν ὑδάτων πολλῶν
¹of a and as a sound ³waters ¹of many
much(great)

καὶ ὡς φωνὴν βροντῶν ἰσχυρῶν, λεγόντων·
and as a sound ⁴thunders ¹of strong saying:
(loud),

ἀλληλουϊά, ὅτι ἐβασίλευσεν κύριος ὁ θεὸς
Halleluia, because ²reigned ¹[the] Lord ³the ³God

ἡμῶν ὁ παντοκράτωρ. **7** χαίρωμεν καὶ
²of us ¹the ³Almighty. Let us rejoice and

ἀγαλλιῶμεν, καὶ δώσομεν τὴν δόξαν αὐτῷ,
let *us* exult, and we will give the glory to him,

ὅτι ἦλθεν ὁ γάμος τοῦ ἀρνίου, καὶ
because ²came ¹the ³marriage ⁴of the ⁵Lamb, and

ἡ γυνὴ αὐτοῦ ἡτοίμασεν ἑαυτήν, **8** καὶ
the wife of him prepared herself, and

ἐδόθη αὐτῇ ἵνα περιβάληται βύσσινον
it was to her *in order* she might be ²fine linen
given that clothed [with]

λαμπρὸν καθαρόν· τὸ γὰρ βύσσινον τὰ
¹bright ²clean; for the fine linen ²the

δικαιώματα τῶν ἁγίων ἐστίν. **9** Καὶ
¹righteous deeds ⁴of the ³saints ¹is. And

λέγει μοι· γράψον· μακάριοι οἱ εἰς τὸ
he tells me: Write thou: blessed ²the [ones] ¹to ⁴the

Chapter 19

Hallelujah!

AFTER this I heard what sounded like the roar of a great multitude in heaven shouting:

"Hallelujah!
Salvation and glory and
power belong to our
God,
2 for true and just are his
judgments.
He has condemned the
great prostitute
who corrupted the
earth by her
adulteries.
He has avenged on her
the blood of his
servants.''

3 And again they shouted:

"Hallelujah!
The smoke from her
goes up for ever and
ever.''

4 The twenty-four elders and the four living creatures fell down and worshiped God, who was seated on the throne. And they cried:

"Amen, Hallelujah!''

5 Then a voice came from the throne, saying:

"Praise our God,
all you his servants,
you who fear him,
both small and great!''

6 Then I heard what sounded like a great multitude, like the roar of rushing waters and like loud peals of thunder, shouting:

"Hallelujah!
For our Lord God
Almighty reigns.
7 Let us rejoice and be
glad
and give him glory!
For the wedding of the
Lamb has come,
and his bride has made
herself ready.
8 Fine linen, bright and
clean,
was given her to
wear.''

(Fine linen stands for the righteous acts of the saints.)

9 Then the angel said to me, "Write: 'Blessed are

---

g Gk *slaves*
h Gk *he said*

the marriage supper of the Lamb." And he said to me, "These are true words of God." [10] Then I fell down at his feet to worship him, but he said to me, "You must not do that! I am a fellow servant[i] with you and your comrades[j] who hold the testimony of Jesus.[k] Worship God! For the testimony of Jesus[k] is the spirit of prophecy."

The Rider on the White Horse

[11] Then I saw heaven opened, and there was a white horse! Its rider is called Faithful and True, and in righteousness he judges and makes war. [12] His eyes are like a flame of fire, and on his head are many diadems; and he has a name inscribed that no one knows but himself. [13] He is clothed in a robe dipped in[l] blood, and his name is called The Word of God. [14] And the armies of heaven, wearing fine linen, white and pure, were following him on white horses. [15] From his mouth comes a sharp sword with which to strike down the nations, and he will rule[m] them with a rod of iron; he will tread the winepress of the fury of the wrath of God the Almighty. [16] On his robe and on his thigh he has a name inscribed, "King of kings and Lord of lords."

δεῖπνον τοῦ γάμου τοῦ ἀρνίου κεκλημένοι.
ᵇsupper ᵉof ⁷marriage ⁸of ⁹Lamb ¹having been called.
 the the

καὶ λέγει μοι· οὗτοι οἱ λόγοι ἀληθινοὶ
And he says to me: ¹These - ²words ⁴true

τοῦ θεοῦ εἰσιν. 10 καὶ ἔπεσα ἔμπροσθεν
 - ³of God ⁴are. And I fell before

τῶν ποδῶν αὐτοῦ προσκυνῆσαι αὐτῷ.
the feet of him to worship him.

καὶ λέγει μοι· ὅρα μή· σύνδουλός σου
And he says to me: See thou not; ¹a fellow- ²of
 [do it] slave thee

εἰμι καὶ τῶν ἀδελφῶν σου τῶν ἐχόντων
¹I am and of the brothers of thee - having

τὴν μαρτυρίαν Ἰησοῦ· τῷ θεῷ προσκύνησον.
the witness of Jesus; - ²God ¹worship thou.

ἡ γὰρ μαρτυρία Ἰησοῦ ἐστιν τὸ πνεῦμα
For the witness of Jesus is the spirit

τῆς προφητείας.
 - of prophecy.

11 Καὶ εἶδον τὸν οὐρανὸν ἠνεῳγμένον,
And I saw - heaven having been opened,

καὶ ἰδοὺ ἵππος λευκός, καὶ ὁ καθήμενος
and behold[,] ²horse ¹a white, and the [one] sitting

ἐπ᾽ αὐτὸν πιστὸς καλούμενος καὶ ἀληθινός,
on it ²faithful ¹being called and true,

καὶ ἐν δικαιοσύνῃ κρίνει καὶ πολεμεῖ.
and in righteousness he judges and makes war.

12 οἱ δὲ ὀφθαλμοὶ αὐτοῦ φλὸξ πυρός,
And the eyes of him [are as] a flame of fire,

καὶ ἐπὶ τὴν κεφαλὴν αὐτοῦ διαδήματα
and on the head of him ²diadems

πολλά, ἔχων ὄνομα γεγραμμένον ὃ οὐδεὶς
¹many, having a name having been written which no one

οἶδεν εἰ μὴ αὐτός, 13 καὶ περιβεβλημένος
knows except [him]self, and having been clothed [with]

ἱμάτιον βεβαμμένον αἵματι, καὶ κέκληται
a garment having been in blood, and ⁴has been
 dipped called

τὸ ὄνομα αὐτοῦ ὁ λόγος τοῦ θεοῦ.
¹the ²name ³of him The Word - of God.

14 καὶ τὰ στρατεύματα τὰ ἐν τῷ οὐρανῷ
And the armies - in - heaven

ἠκολούθει αὐτῷ ἐφ᾽ ἵπποις λευκοῖς, ἐνδεδυμένοι
followed him on ²horses ¹white, having been
 dressed [in]

βύσσινον λευκὸν καθαρόν. 15 καὶ ἐκ
²fine linen ¹white ³clean. And out of

τοῦ στόματος αὐτοῦ ἐκπορεύεται ῥομφαία
the mouth of him proceeds ²sword

ὀξεῖα, ἵνα ἐν αὐτῇ πατάξῃ τὰ ἔθνη·
¹a sharp, in order with it he may the nations;
 that smite

καὶ αὐτὸς ποιμανεῖ αὐτοὺς ἐν ῥάβδῳ
and he will shepherd them with ²staff

σιδηρᾷ· καὶ αὐτὸς πατεῖ τὴν ληνὸν
¹an iron; and he treads the winepress

τοῦ οἴνου τοῦ θυμοῦ τῆς ὀργῆς τοῦ
of the wine of the anger[,] of the wrath -

θεοῦ τοῦ παντοκράτορος. 16 καὶ ἔχει
of God of the Almighty. And he has

ἐπὶ τὸ ἱμάτιον καὶ ἐπὶ τὸν μηρὸν
on the garment and on the thigh

αὐτοῦ ὄνομα γεγραμμένον· ΒΑΣΙΛΕΥΣ
of him a name having been written: KING

ΒΑΣΙΛΕΩΝ ΚΑΙ ΚΥΡΙΟΣ ΚΥΡΙΩΝ.
OF KINGS AND LORD OF LORDS.

---

those who are invited to the wedding supper of the Lamb!' '' And he added, "These are the true words of God."

[10] At this I fell at his feet to worship him. But he said to me, "Do not do it! I am a fellow servant with you and with your brothers who hold to the testimony of Jesus. Worship God! For the testimony of Jesus is the spirit of prophecy."

The Rider on the White Horse

[11] I saw heaven standing open and there before me was a white horse, whose rider is called Faithful and True. With justice he judges and makes war. [12] His eyes are like blazing fire, and on his head are many crowns. He has a name written on him that no one knows but himself. [13] He is dressed in a robe dipped in blood, and his name is the Word of God. [14] The armies of heaven were following him, riding on white horses and dressed in fine linen, white and clean. [15] Out of his mouth comes a sharp sword with which to strike down the nations. "He will rule them with an iron scepter.''[w] He treads the winepress of the fury of the wrath of God Almighty. [16] On his robe and on his thigh he has this name written:

KING OF KINGS AND LORD OF LORDS.

---

[i] Gk slave
[j] Gk brothers
[k] Or to Jesus
[l] Other ancient authorities read sprinkled with
[m] Or will shepherd

[w] 15 Psalm 2:9

The Beast and Its Armies Defeated

17 Then I saw an angel standing in the sun, and with a loud voice he called to all the birds that fly in midheaven, "Come, gather for the great supper of God, 18 to eat the flesh of kings, the flesh of captains, the flesh of the mighty, the flesh of horses and their riders—flesh of all, both free and slave, both small and great." 19 Then I saw the beast and the kings of the earth with their armies gathered to make war against the rider on the horse and against his army. 20 And the beast was captured, and with it the false prophet who had performed in its presence the signs by which he deceived those who had received the mark of the beast and those who worshiped its image. These two were thrown alive into the lake of fire that burns with sulfur. 21 And the rest were killed by the sword of the rider on the horse, the sword that came from his mouth; and all the birds were gorged with their flesh.

17 Καὶ εἶδον ἕνα ἄγγελον ἑστῶτα ἐν
   And   I saw   one   angel   standing   in

τῷ ἡλίῳ, καὶ ἔκραξεν ἐν φωνῇ μεγάλῃ
the sun,   and he cried out in ¹voice ¹a great
                                        (loud)

λέγων πᾶσιν τοῖς ὀρνέοις τοῖς πετομένοις
saying to all the   birds   -   flying

ἐν μεσουρανήματι· δεῦτε συνάχθητε εἰς
in   mid-heaven: Come ye[,] assemble ye   to

τὸ δεῖπνον τὸ μέγα τοῦ θεοῦ, 18 ἵνα
the ¹supper - ¹great of God, in order that

φάγητε σάρκας βασιλέων καὶ σάρκας
ye may eat fleshes of kings and fleshes

χιλιάρχων καὶ σάρκας ἰσχυρῶν καὶ σάρκας
of chiliarchs and fleshes of strong men and fleshes

ἵππων καὶ τῶν καθημένων ἐπ' αὐτῶν,
of horses and of the [ones] sitting   on   them,

καὶ σάρκας πάντων ἐλευθέρων τε καὶ
and fleshes of all   free men   ¹both and

δούλων καὶ μικρῶν καὶ μεγάλων. 19 Καὶ
slaves   both small   and great.   And

εἶδον τὸ θηρίον καὶ τοὺς βασιλεῖς τῆς
I saw the beast   and the   kings   of the

γῆς καὶ τὰ στρατεύματα αὐτῶν συνηγμένα
earth and the armies   of them having been assembled

ποιῆσαι τὸν πόλεμον μετὰ τοῦ καθημένου
to make   the   war   with the [one] sitting

ἐπὶ τοῦ ἵππου καὶ μετὰ τοῦ στρατεύματος
on   the   horse and with the   army

αὐτοῦ. 20 καὶ ἐπιάσθη τὸ θηρίον καὶ
of him.   And ³was seized ¹the ²beast   and

μετ' αὐτοῦ ὁ ψευδοπροφήτης ὁ ποιήσας
with   it   the false prophet the [one] having done

τὰ σημεῖα ἐνώπιον αὐτοῦ, ἐν οἷς ἐπλάνη-
the signs   before   it,   by which he de-

σεν τοὺς λαβόντας τὸ χάραγμα τοῦ
ceived the [ones] having received the mark   of the

θηρίου καὶ τοὺς προσκυνοῦντας τῇ εἰκόνι
beast   and the [ones] worshipping the image

αὐτοῦ· ζῶντες ἐβλήθησαν οἱ δύο εἰς
of it;   ⁴living   ³were cast   ¹the ²two into

τὴν λίμνην τοῦ πυρὸς τῆς καιομένης
the   lake   -   of fire   -   burning*

ἐν θείῳ. 21 καὶ οἱ λοιποὶ ἀπεκτάνθησαν
with sulphur. And the rest   were killed

ἐν τῇ ῥομφαίᾳ τοῦ καθημένου ἐπὶ τοῦ
with the sword   of the [one] sitting   on   the

ἵππου τῇ ἐξελθούσῃ ἐκ τοῦ στόματος
horse   - proceeding§ out of the   mouth

αὐτοῦ, καὶ πάντα τὰ ὄρνεα ἐχορτάσθησαν
of him,   and   all   the birds   were filled

ἐκ τῶν σαρκῶν αὐτῶν.
by the   fleshes   of them.

17And I saw an angel standing in the sun, who cried in a loud voice to all the birds flying in midair, "Come, gather together for the great supper of God, 18so that you may eat the flesh of kings, generals, and mighty men, of horses and their riders, and the flesh of all people, free and slave, small and great." 19Then I saw the beast and the kings of the earth and their armies gathered together to make war against the rider on the horse and his army. 20But the beast was captured, and with him the false prophet who had performed the miraculous signs on his behalf. With these signs he had deluded those who had received the mark of the beast and worshiped his image. The two of them were thrown alive into the fiery lake of burning sulfur. 21The rest of them were killed with the sword that came out of the mouth of the rider on the horse, and all the birds gorged themselves on their flesh.

Chapter 20

The Thousand Years

THEN I saw an angel coming down from heaven, holding in his hand the key to the bottomless

20 Καὶ εἶδον ἄγγελον καταβαίνοντα ἐκ
   And I saw an angel coming down out of

τοῦ οὐρανοῦ, ἔχοντα τὴν κλεῖν τῆς
 -   heaven,   having   the   key   of the

ἀβύσσου καὶ ἅλυσιν μεγάλην ἐπὶ τὴν χεῖρα
abyss   and ²chain ¹a great   on   the   hand

Chapter 20

The Thousand Years

AND I saw an angel coming down out of heaven, having the key to the Abyss and holding in his hand a great chain. 2He

---

* Feminine, agreeing with λίμνη, not with the neuter πῦρ.

§ Agreeing, of course, with ῥομφαίᾳ.

pit and a great chain. 2 He seized the dragon, that ancient serpent, who is the Devil and Satan, and bound him for a thousand years, 3 and threw him into the pit, and locked and sealed it over him, so that he would deceive the nations no more, until the thousand years were ended. After that he must be let out for a little while.

4 Then I saw thrones, and those seated on them were given authority to judge. I also saw the souls of those who had been beheaded for their testimony to Jesus [n] and for the word of God. They had not worshiped the beast or its image and had not received its mark on their foreheads or their hands. They came to life and reigned with Christ a thousand years. 5 (The rest of the dead did not come to life until the thousand years were ended.) This is the first resurrection. 6 Blessed and holy are those who share in the first resurrection. Over these the second death has no power, but they will be priests of God and of Christ, and they will reign with him a thousand years.

Satan's Doom

7 When the thousand years are ended, Satan will be released from his prison 8 and will come out to deceive the nations at the four corners of the earth, Gog and Magog, in order to gather them for battle; they are as numerous as the

---

αὐτοῦ. 2 καὶ ἐκράτησεν τὸν δράκοντα,
of him.   And   he laid hold [of] the   dragon,

ὁ ὄφις ὁ ἀρχαῖος, ὅς ἐστιν Διάβολος
the ¹serpent – ¹old,   who is   Devil

καὶ ὁ Σατανᾶς, καὶ ἔδησεν αὐτὸν χίλια
and – Satan,   and bound   him   a thousand

ἔτη, 3 καὶ ἔβαλεν αὐτὸν εἰς τὴν ἄβυσσον,
years,   and cast   him   into the   abyss,

καὶ ἔκλεισεν καὶ ἐσφράγισεν ἐπάνω αὐτοῦ,
and shut   and sealed   over   him,

ἵνα μὴ πλανήσῃ ἔτι τὰ ἔθνη, ἄχρι
in or- he should not deceive longer the nations, until
der that

τελεσθῇ τὰ χίλια ἔτη· μετὰ ταῦτα
⁴are finished ¹the ²thousand ³years; after these things

δεῖ λυθῆναι αὐτὸν μικρὸν χρόνον.
it be- ²to be ¹him a little   time.
hoves loosed

4 Καὶ εἶδον θρόνους, καὶ ἐκάθισαν ἐπ'
And I saw thrones,   and they sat   on

αὐτούς, καὶ κρίμα ἐδόθη αὐτοῖς, καὶ
them,   and judgment was given to them,   and

τὰς ψυχὰς τῶν πεπελεκισμένων διὰ τὴν
the souls of the having been because the
        [ones] beheaded   of

μαρτυρίαν Ἰησοῦ καὶ διὰ τὸν λόγον
witness of Jesus and because of the word

τοῦ θεοῦ, καὶ οἵτινες οὐ προσεκύνησαν
– of God,   and who   did not worship

τὸ θηρίον οὐδὲ τὴν εἰκόνα αὐτοῦ καὶ
the beast   nor the   image   of it   and

οὐκ ἔλαβον τὸ χάραγμα ἐπὶ τὸ μέτωπον
did not receive the mark   on the forehead

καὶ ἐπὶ τὴν χεῖρα αὐτῶν· καὶ ἔζησαν
and on the   hand   of them; and they lived
                                 [again]

καὶ ἐβασίλευσαν μετὰ τοῦ Χριστοῦ χίλια
and reigned   with – Christ   a thousand

ἔτη. 5 οἱ λοιποὶ τῶν νεκρῶν οὐκ ἔζησαν
years. The rest of the dead did not live [again]

ἄχρι τελεσθῇ τὰ χίλια ἔτη. Αὕτη ἡ
until were finished the thousand years. This [is] the

ἀνάστασις ἡ πρώτη. 6 μακάριος καὶ
¹resurrection – ¹first.   Blessed   and

ἅγιος ὁ ἔχων μέρος ἐν τῇ ἀναστάσει
holy [is] the [one] having part in the ²resurrection

τῇ πρώτῃ· ἐπὶ τούτων ὁ δεύτερος θάνατος
– ¹first; over these the second death

οὐκ ἔχει ἐξουσίαν, ἀλλ' ἔσονται ἱερεῖς
has not authority, but they will be priests

τοῦ θεοῦ καὶ τοῦ Χριστοῦ, καὶ βασιλεύ-
– of God and – of Christ, and will

σουσιν μετ' αὐτοῦ [τὰ] χίλια ἔτη.
reign with him the thousand years.

7 Καὶ ὅταν τελεσθῇ τὰ χίλια ἔτη,
And whenever are finished the thousand years,

λυθήσεται ὁ σατανᾶς ἐκ τῆς φυλακῆς
¹will be loosed – ¹Satan out of the prison

αὐτοῦ, 8 καὶ ἐξελεύσεται πλανῆσαι τὰ
of him,   and will go forth to deceive the

ἔθνη τὰ ἐν ταῖς τέσσαρσιν γωνίαις τῆς
nations – in the   four   corners of the

γῆς, τὸν Γὼγ καὶ Μαγώγ, συναγαγεῖν
earth, – Gog and Magog, to assemble

αὐτοὺς εἰς τὸν πόλεμον, ὧν ὁ ἀριθμὸς
them to the   war, of whom the number

---

seized the dragon, that ancient serpent, who is the devil, or Satan, and bound him for a thousand years. 3 He threw him into the Abyss, and locked and sealed it over him, to keep him from deceiving the nations anymore until the thousand years were ended. After that, he must be set free for a short time.

4 I saw thrones on which were seated those who had been given authority to judge. And I saw the souls of those who had been beheaded because of their testimony for Jesus and because of the word of God. They had not worshiped the beast or his image and had not received his mark on their foreheads or their hands. They came to life and reigned with Christ a thousand years. 5 (The rest of the dead did not come to life until the thousand years were ended.) This is the first resurrection. 6 Blessed and holy are those who have part in the first resurrection. The second death has no power over them, but they will be priests of God and of Christ and will reign with him for a thousand years.

Satan's Doom

7 When the thousand years are over, Satan will be released from his prison 8 and will go out to deceive the nations in the four corners of the earth—Gog and Magog—to gather them for battle. In number they are

---

[n] Or *for the testimony of Jesus*

sands of the sea. 9 They marched up over the breadth of the earth and surrounded the camp of the saints and the beloved city. And fire came down from heaven*o* and consumed them. 10 And the devil who had deceived them was thrown into the lake of fire and sulfur, where the beast and the false prophet were, and they will be tormented day and night forever and ever.

The Dead Are Judged

11 Then I saw a great white throne and the one who sat on it; the earth and the heaven fled from his presence, and no place was found for them. 12 And I saw the dead, great and small, standing before the throne, and books were opened. Also another book was opened, the book of life. And the dead were judged according to their works, as recorded in the books. 13 And the sea gave up the dead that were in it, Death and Hades gave up the dead that were in them, and all were judged according to what they had done. 14 Then Death and Hades were thrown into the lake of fire. This is the second death, the lake of fire; 15 and anyone whose name was not found written in the book of life was thrown into the lake of fire.

αὐτῶν ὡς ἡ ἄμμος τῆς θαλάσσης. 9 καὶ
of them [is] as the sand of the sea. And

ἀνέβησαν ἐπὶ τὸ πλάτος τῆς γῆς, καὶ
they went up over the breadth of the land, and

ἐκύκλευσαν τὴν παρεμβολὴν τῶν ἁγίων
encircled the camp of the saints

καὶ τὴν πόλιν τὴν ἠγαπημένην· καὶ
and the ²city - *having been* ¹loved; and

κατέβη πῦρ ἐκ τοῦ οὐρανοῦ καὶ κατέφαγεν
²came ¹fire out of - heaven and devoured
down

αὐτούς· 10 καὶ ὁ διάβολος ὁ πλανῶν αὐτοὺς
them; and the Devil - deceiving them

ἐβλήθη εἰς τὴν λίμνην τοῦ πυρὸς καὶ
was cast into the lake - of fire and

θείου, ὅπου καὶ τὸ θηρίον καὶ ὁ
sulphur, where [were] also the beast and the

ψευδοπροφήτης, καὶ βασανισθήσονται ἡμέρας
false prophet, and they will be tormented day

καὶ νυκτὸς εἰς τοὺς αἰῶνας τῶν αἰώνων.
and night unto the ages of the ages.

11 Καὶ εἶδον θρόνον μέγαν λευκὸν καὶ
And I saw ²throne ¹a great ³white and

τὸν καθήμενον ἐπ᾽ αὐτὸν οὗ ἀπὸ τοῦ
the sitting on it ⁴of ¹from ²the
[one] whom

προσώπου ἔφυγεν ἡ γῆ καὶ ὁ οὐρανός,
³face ⁵fled ¹the ²earth ³and ⁴the ⁵heaven,

καὶ τόπος οὐχ εὑρέθη αὐτοῖς. 12 καὶ
and a place was not found for them. And

εἶδον τοὺς νεκρούς, τοὺς μεγάλους καὶ
I saw the dead, the great and

τοὺς μικρούς, ἑστῶτας ἐνώπιον τοῦ θρόνου,
the small, standing before the throne,

καὶ βιβλία ἠνοίχθησαν· καὶ ἄλλο βιβλίον
and scrolls were opened; and another scroll

ἠνοίχθη, ὅ ἐστιν τῆς ζωῆς· καὶ ἐκρίθησαν
was which is [the - of life; and ³were judged
opened, scroll]

οἱ νεκροὶ ἐκ τῶν γεγραμμένων ἐν τοῖς
¹the ²dead by the *having been* in the
things written

βιβλίοις κατὰ τὰ ἔργα αὐτῶν. 13 καὶ
scrolls accord- the works of them. And
ing to

ἔδωκεν ἡ θάλασσα τοὺς νεκροὺς τοὺς
²gave ¹the ²sea the dead

ἐν αὐτῇ, καὶ ὁ θάνατος καὶ ὁ ᾅδης
in it, and - death and - hades

ἔδωκαν τοὺς νεκροὺς τοὺς ἐν αὐτοῖς,
gave the dead - in them,

καὶ ἐκρίθησαν ἕκαστος κατὰ τὰ ἔργα
and they were judged each one according to the works

αὐτῶν. 14 καὶ ὁ θάνατος καὶ ὁ ᾅδης
of them. And - death and - hades

ἐβλήθησαν εἰς τὴν λίμνην τοῦ πυρός.
were cast into the lake - of fire.

οὗτος ὁ θάνατος ὁ δεύτερός ἐστιν, ἡ
This ²the, ⁴death - ³second ¹is, the

λίμνη τοῦ πυρός. 15 καὶ εἴ τις οὐχ
lake - of fire. And if anyone not

εὑρέθη ἐν τῇ βίβλῳ τῆς ζωῆς γεγραμ-
was found ²in ³the ⁴scroll - ¹of life ¹having been

μένος, ἐβλήθη εἰς τὴν λίμνην τοῦ πυρός.
written, he was cast into the lake - of fire.

like the sand on the seashore. 9 They marched across the breadth of the earth and surrounded the camp of God's people, the city he loves. But fire came down from heaven and devoured them. 10 And the devil, who deceived them, was thrown into the lake of burning sulfur, where the beast and the false prophet had been thrown. They will be tormented day and night for ever and ever.

The Dead Are Judged

11 Then I saw a great white throne and him who was seated on it. Earth and sky fled from his presence, and there was no place for them. 12 And I saw the dead, great and small, standing before the throne, and books were opened. Another book was opened, which is the book of life. The dead were judged according to what they had done as recorded in the books. 13 The sea gave up the dead that were in it, and death and Hades gave up the dead that were in them, and each person was judged according to what he had done. 14 Then death and Hades were thrown into the lake of fire. The lake of fire is the second death. 15 If anyone's name was not found written in the book of life, he was thrown into the lake of fire.

Chapter 21

The New Heaven and the New Earth

THEN I saw a new heaven and a new earth; for the first heaven and the first earth had passed away, and the sea was no more. 2 And I saw the holy city, the new Jerusalem, coming down out of heaven from God, prepared as a bride adorned for her husband. 3 And I heard a loud voice from the throne saying,

"See, the home[p] of
    God is
    among mortals.
He will dwell[p] with
    them as
    their God;[q]
they will be his
    peoples,[r]
and God himself will
    be with them;[s]
4 he will wipe every
    tear from
    their eyes.
Death will be no
    more;
mourning and crying
    and pain will be
    no more,
for the first things
    have
    passed away."

5 And the one who was seated on the throne said, "See, I am making all things new." Also he said, "Write this, for these words are trustworthy and true." 6 Then he said to me, "It is done! I am the Alpha and the Omega, the beginning and the end. To the thirsty I will give water as a gift from the spring of the water of life. 7 Those who conquer will inherit these things, and I will be their God and they will be my children. 8 But as for the cowardly, the faithless,[t] the polluted, the murderers, the fornicators, the sorcerers, the idolaters, and all liars, their place will be in the lake that burns with fire and sulfur, which is the second death."

[p] Gk tabernacle
[q] Other ancient authorities lack *as their God*
[r] Other ancient authorities read *people*
[s] Other ancient authorities add *and be their God*
[t] Or *the unbelieving*

---

21 Καὶ   εἶδον   οὐρανὸν   καινὸν   καὶ   γῆν
And   I saw   [1]heaven   [1]a new   and   [2]earth

καινήν·   ὁ   γὰρ   πρῶτος   οὐρανὸς   καὶ   ἡ
[1]a new;   for   the   first   heaven   and   the

πρώτη   γῆ   ἀπῆλθαν,   καὶ   ἡ   θάλασσα
first   earth   passed away,   and   the   sea

οὐκ   ἔστιν   ἔτι.   **2** καὶ   τὴν   πόλιν   τὴν
is not   longer.   And   [3]the   [4]city   —

ἁγίαν   Ἰερουσαλὴμ   καινὴν   εἶδον   κατα-
[5]holy   [6]Jerusalem   [7]new   [1]I saw   coming

βαίνουσαν   ἐκ   τοῦ   οὐρανοῦ   ἀπὸ   τοῦ   θεοῦ,
down   out of   —   heaven   from   —   God,

ἡτοιμασμένην   ὡς   νύμφην   κεκοσμημένην
having been prepared   as   a bride   *having been* adorned

τῷ   ἀνδρὶ   αὐτῆς.   **3** καὶ   ἤκουσα   φωνῆς
for the husband   of her.   And   I heard   [1]voice

μεγάλης   ἐκ   τοῦ   θρόνου   λεγούσης·   ἰδοὺ
[1]a great(loud)   out of   the   throne   saying: Behold[,]

ἡ   σκηνὴ   τοῦ   θεοῦ   μετὰ   τῶν   ἀνθρώπων,
the tabernacle   —   of God [is]   with   —   men,

καὶ   σκηνώσει   μετ'   αὐτῶν,   καὶ   αὐτοὶ
and   he will tabernacle   with   them,   and   they

λαοὶ   αὐτοῦ   ἔσονται,   καὶ   αὐτὸς   ὁ   θεὸς
[2]peoples   [3]of him   [1]will be,   and   [2][him]self   —   [1]God

μετ'   αὐτῶν   ἔσται,   **4** καὶ   ἐξαλείψει   πᾶν
with   them   will be,   and   will wipe off   every

δάκρυον   ἐκ   τῶν   ὀφθαλμῶν   αὐτῶν,   καὶ
tear   out of   the   eyes   of them,   and

ὁ   θάνατος   οὐκ   ἔσται   ἔτι,   οὔτε   πένθος
—   death   will not be   longer,   nor   sorrow

οὔτε   κραυγὴ   οὔτε   πόνος   οὐκ   ἔσται   ἔτι·
nor   clamour   nor   pain   will *not* be   longer;

ὅτι   τὰ   πρῶτα   ἀπῆλθαν.   **5** καὶ   εἶπεν
because the   first things   passed away.   And   [2]said

ὁ   καθήμενος   ἐπὶ   τῷ   θρόνῳ·   ἰδοὺ   καινὰ
[1]the [one]   [1]sitting   [2]on   [4]the   [3]throne: Behold   [2]new

ποιῶ   πάντα.   καὶ   λέγει·   γράψον,   ὅτι
[1]I make   [3]all things.   And   he says: Write thou,   because

οὗτοι   οἱ   λόγοι   πιστοὶ   καὶ   ἀληθινοί   εἰσιν.
these   —   words   faithful   and   true   are.

6 καὶ   εἶπέν   μοι·   γέγοναν.*   ἐγὼ   τὸ   ἄλφα
And   said   to me: It has occurred.*   I [am]   the   alpha

καὶ   τὸ   ὦ,   ἡ   ἀρχὴ   καὶ   τὸ   τέλος.   ἐγὼ
and   the   omega,   the   beginning   and   the   end.   [1]I

τῷ   διψῶντι   δώσω   ἐκ   τῆς   πηγῆς
[1]to the [one]   [2]thirsting   [4]will give   out of   the   fountain

τοῦ   ὕδατος   τῆς   ζωῆς   δωρεάν.   **7** ὁ   νικῶν
of the   water   —   of life   freely.   The over-
                                                    [one] coming

κληρονομήσει   ταῦτα,   καὶ   ἔσομαι   αὐτῷ
shall inherit   these things,   and   I will be   to him

θεὸς   καὶ   αὐτὸς   ἔσται   μοι   υἱός.   **8** τοῖς   δὲ
God   and   he   shall be to me   a son.   But for the

δειλοῖς   καὶ   ἀπίστοις   καὶ   ἐβδελυγμένοις
cowardly   and   unbelieving   and   *having become* foul

καὶ   φονεῦσιν   καὶ   πόρνοις   καὶ   φαρμακοῖς
and   murderers   and   fornicators   and   sorcerers

καὶ   εἰδωλολάτραις   καὶ   πᾶσιν   τοῖς   ψευδέσιν
and   idolaters   and   all   the   false [ones]

τὸ   μέρος   αὐτῶν   ἐν   τῇ   λίμνῃ   τῇ   καιομένῃ
the   part   of them   in   the   lake   —   burning

πυρὶ   καὶ   θείῳ,   ὅ   ἐστιν   ὁ   θάνατος   ὁ
with fire and   *with* sulphur,   which   is   the   [2]death

δεύτερος.
[1]second [, shall be].

* Collective neuter plural; cf. ch. 16. 17.

Chapter 21

The New Jerusalem

THEN I saw a new heaven and a new earth, for the first heaven and the first earth had passed away, and there was no longer any sea. 2 I saw the Holy City, the new Jerusalem, coming down out of heaven from God, prepared as a bride beautifully dressed for her husband. 3 And I heard a loud voice from the throne saying, "Now the dwelling of God is with men, and he will live with them. They will be his people, and God himself will be with them and be their God. 4 He will wipe every tear from their eyes. There will be no more death or mourning or crying or pain, for the old order of things has passed away."

5 He who was seated on the throne said, "I am making everything new!" Then he said, "Write this down, for these words are trustworthy and true."

6 He said to me: "It is done. I am the Alpha and the Omega, the Beginning and the End. To him who is thirsty I will give to drink without cost from the spring of the water of life. 7 He who overcomes will inherit all this, and I will be his God and he will be my son. 8 But the cowardly, the unbelieving, the vile, the murderers, the sexually immoral, those who practice magic arts, the idolaters and all liars—their place will be in the fiery lake of burning sulfur. This is the second death."

Vision of the New Jerusalem

9 Then one of the seven angels who had the seven bowls full of the seven last plagues came and said to me, "Come, I will show you the bride, the wife of the Lamb." 10 And in the spirit[u] he carried me away to a great, high mountain and showed me the holy city Jerusalem coming down out of heaven from God. 11 It has the glory of God and a radiance like a very rare jewel, like jasper, clear as crystal. 12 It has a great, high wall with twelve gates, and at the gates twelve angels, and on the gates are inscribed the names of the twelve tribes of the Israelites; 13 on the east three gates, on the north three gates, on the south three gates, and on the west three gates. 14 And the wall of the city has twelve foundations, and on them are the twelve names of the twelve apostles of the Lamb. 15 The angel[v] who talked to me had a measuring rod of gold to measure the city and its gates and walls. 16 The city lies foursquare, its length the same as its width; and he measured the city with his rod, fifteen hundred miles;[w] its length and width and height are equal. 17 He also measured its wall, one hundred

---

9 Καὶ ἦλθεν εἷς ἐκ τῶν ἑπτὰ ἀγγέλων
And came one of the seven angels

τῶν ἐχόντων τὰς ἑπτὰ φιάλας, τῶν
- having the seven bowls, -

γεμόντων τῶν ἑπτὰ πληγῶν τῶν ἐσχάτων,
being filled of(with) seven ³plagues - ¹last,
the

καὶ ἐλάλησεν μετ᾽ ἐμοῦ λέγων· δεῦρο,
and spoke with me saying: Come,

δείξω σοι τὴν νύμφην τὴν γυναῖκα
I will show thee the bride[,] the wife

τοῦ ἀρνίου. 10 καὶ ἀπήνεγκέν με ἐν
of the Lamb. And he bore away me in

πνεύματι ἐπὶ ὄρος μέγα καὶ ὑψηλόν,
spirit onto ²mountain ¹a great ³and ⁴high,

καὶ ἔδειξέν μοι τὴν πόλιν τὴν ἁγίαν
and showed me the ²city - ¹holy

Ἰερουσαλὴμ καταβαίνουσαν ἐκ τοῦ οὐρανοῦ
Jerusalem coming down out of heaven

ἀπὸ τοῦ θεοῦ, 11 ἔχουσαν τὴν δόξαν
from - God, having the glory

τοῦ θεοῦ· ὁ φωστὴρ αὐτῆς ὅμοιος λίθῳ
- of God; the light of it [was] like *to a* stone

τιμιωτάτῳ, ὡς λίθῳ ἰάσπιδι κρυσταλλίζοντι·
very valuable, as ³stone ¹to a jasper being clear as crystal;

12 ἔχουσα τεῖχος μέγα καὶ ὑψηλόν,
having ⁴wall ¹a great ²and ³high,

ἔχουσα πυλῶνας δώδεκα, καὶ ἐπὶ τοῖς
having ²gates ¹twelve, and at the

πυλῶσιν ἀγγέλους δώδεκα, καὶ ὀνόματα
gates ²angels ¹twelve, and names

ἐπιγεγραμμένα, ἃ ἐστιν τῶν δώδεκα
having been inscribed, which is(are) of the twelve

φυλῶν υἱῶν Ἰσραήλ. 13 ἀπὸ ἀνατολῆς
tribes of sons of Israel. From east

πυλῶνες τρεῖς, καὶ ἀπὸ βορρᾶ πυλῶνες
²gates ¹three, and from north ²gates

τρεῖς, καὶ ἀπὸ νότου πυλῶνες τρεῖς,
¹three, and from south ²gates ¹three,

καὶ ἀπὸ δυσμῶν πυλῶνες τρεῖς. 14 καὶ
and from west ²gates ¹three. And

τὸ τεῖχος τῆς πόλεως ἔχων θεμελίους
the wall of the city having ²foundations

δώδεκα, καὶ ἐπ᾽ αὐτῶν δώδεκα ὀνόματα
¹twelve, and on them twelve names

τῶν δώδεκα ἀποστόλων τοῦ ἀρνίου. 15 Καὶ
of the twelve apostles of the Lamb. And

ὁ λαλῶν μετ᾽ ἐμοῦ εἶχεν μέτρον κάλαμον
the speak- with me had ²measure ³reed
[one] ing

χρυσοῦν, ἵνα μετρήσῃ τὴν πόλιν καὶ
¹a golden, in order he might the city and
that measure

τοὺς πυλῶνας αὐτῆς καὶ τὸ τεῖχος αὐτῆς.
the gates of it and the wall of it.

16 καὶ ἡ πόλις τετράγωνος κεῖται, καὶ
And the city ²square ¹lies, and

τὸ μῆκος αὐτῆς ὅσον τὸ πλάτος. καὶ
the length of it [is] as much as the breadth. And

ἐμέτρησεν τὴν πόλιν τῷ καλάμῳ ἐπὶ
he measured the city with the reed at

σταδίων δώδεκα χιλιάδων· τὸ μῆκος καὶ
²furlongs ¹twelve ³thousands; the length and

τὸ πλάτος καὶ τὸ ὕψος αὐτῆς ἴσα ἐστίν.
the breadth and the height of it ²equal ¹is(are).

17 καὶ ἐμέτρησεν τὸ τεῖχος αὐτῆς ἑκατὸν
And he measured the wall of it *of* a hundred

---

9 One of the seven angels who had the seven bowls full of the seven last plagues came and said to me, "Come, I will show you the bride, the wife of the Lamb." 10 And he carried me away in the Spirit to a mountain great and high, and showed me the Holy City, Jerusalem, coming down out of heaven from God. 11 It shone with the glory of God, and its brilliance was like that of a very precious jewel, like a jasper, clear as crystal. 12 It had a great, high wall with twelve gates, and with twelve angels at the gates. On the gates were written the names of the twelve tribes of Israel. 13 There were three gates on the east, three on the north, three on the south and three on the west. 14 The wall of the city had twelve foundations, and on them were the names of the twelve apostles of the Lamb.

15 The angel who talked with me had a measuring rod of gold to measure the city, its gates and its walls. 16 The city was laid out like a square, as long as it was wide. He measured the city with the rod and found it to be 12,000 stadia[x] in length, and as wide and high as it is long. 17 He measured its

---

u Or *in the Spirit*
v Gk *He*
w Gk *twelve thousand stadia*

x 16 That is, about 1,400 miles (about 2,200 kilometers)

forty-four cubits ˣ by human measurement, which the angel was using. 18 The wall is built of jasper, while the city is pure gold, clear as glass. 19 The foundations of the wall of the city are adorned with every jewel; the first was jasper, the second sapphire, the third agate, the fourth emerald, 20 the fifth onyx, the sixth carnelian, the seventh chrysolite, the eighth beryl, the ninth topaz, the tenth chrysoprase, the eleventh jacinth, the twelfth amethyst. 21 And the twelve gates are twelve pearls, each of the gates is a single pearl, and the street of the city is pure gold, transparent as glass.

22 I saw no temple in the city, for its temple is the Lord God the Almighty and the Lamb. 23 And the city has no need of sun or moon to shine on it, for the glory of God is its light, and its lamp is the Lamb. 24 The nations will walk by its light, and the kings of the earth will bring their glory into it. 25 Its gates will never be shut by day—and there will be no night there. 26 People will bring into it the glory and the honor of the nations. 27 But nothing unclean will enter it, nor

---

τεσσεράκοντα τεσσάρων πηχῶν, μέτρον
[and]   forty-four   cubits,   a measure

ἀνθρώπου, ὅ ἐστιν ἀγγέλου. 18 καὶ
of a man,   which   is   of an angel.   And

ἡ ἐνδώμησις τοῦ τείχους αὐτῆς ἴασπις,
the   coping   of the   wall   of it [was] jasper,

καὶ ἡ πόλις χρυσίον καθαρὸν ὅμοιον
and   the   city [was] ²gold   ¹clean(pure)   like

ὑάλῳ καθαρῷ. 19 οἱ θεμέλιοι τοῦ τείχους
²glass   ¹to clean(pure).   The foundations of the   wall

τῆς πόλεως παντὶ λίθῳ τιμίῳ κεκοσμημένοι·
of the   city   ⁴with   ⁴stone ³precious   ¹having been
           every   adorned;

ὁ θεμέλιος ὁ πρῶτος ἴασπις, ὁ δεύτερος
the foundation – first   jasper, the   second

σάπφιρος, ὁ τρίτος χαλκηδών, ὁ τέταρτος
sapphire, the   third   chalcedony,   the   fourth

σμάραγδος, 20 ὁ πέμπτος σαρδόνυξ, ὁ
emerald,   the   fifth   sardonyx,   the

ἕκτος σάρδιον, ὁ ἕβδομος χρυσόλιθος,
sixth   sardius,   the   seventh   chrysolite,

ὁ ὄγδοος βήρυλλος, ὁ ἔνατος τοπάζιον,
the   eighth   beryl,   the   ninth   topaz,

ὁ δέκατος χρυσόπρασος, ὁ ἐνδέκατος
the   tenth   chrysoprasus,   the   eleventh

ὑάκινθος, ὁ δωδέκατος ἀμέθυστος. 21 καὶ
hyacinth, the   twelfth   amethyst.   And

οἱ δώδεκα πυλῶνες δώδεκα μαργαρῖται·
the   twelve   gates [were] twelve   pearls;

ἀνὰ εἷς ἕκαστος τῶν πυλώνων ἦν ἐξ
respec- ²one   ¹each   of the   gates   was   of
tively†

ἑνὸς μαργαρίτου. καὶ ἡ πλατεῖα τῆς
one   pearl.   And   the   street   of the

πόλεως χρυσίον καθαρὸν ὡς ὕαλος διαυγής.
city [was] ²gold   ¹clean(pure)   as   ²glass ¹transparent.

22 Καὶ ναὸν οὐκ εἶδον ἐν αὐτῇ· ὁ γὰρ
And a shrine   I saw not   in   it;   for the

κύριος ὁ θεὸς ὁ παντοκράτωρ ναὸς αὐτῆς
Lord   – God   the   Almighty   shrine   of it

ἐστιν, καὶ τὸ ἀρνίον. 23 καὶ ἡ πόλις
is,   and   the   Lamb.   And   the   city

οὐ χρείαν ἔχει τοῦ ἡλίου οὐδὲ τῆς
not   need   has   of the   sun   nor   of the

σελήνης, ἵνα φαίνωσιν αὐτῇ· ἡ γὰρ
moon,   in order   they might   in it;   for the
       that   shine

δόξα τοῦ θεοῦ ἐφώτισεν αὐτήν, καὶ
glory   –   of God   enlightened   it,   and

ὁ λύχνος αὐτῆς τὸ ἀρνίον. 24 καὶ
the   lamp   of it [is]   the   Lamb.   And

περιπατήσουσιν τὰ ἔθνη διὰ τοῦ φωτὸς
²shall walk about   ¹the ²nations through the   light

αὐτῆς, καὶ οἱ βασιλεῖς τῆς γῆς φέρουσιν
of it,   and   the   kings   of the earth   bring

τὴν δόξαν αὐτῶν εἰς αὐτήν· 25 καὶ οἱ
the   glory   of them   into   it;   and   the

πυλῶνες αὐτῆς οὐ μὴ κλεισθῶσιν ἡμέρας,
gates   of it   by no means   may be shut   by day,

νὺξ γὰρ οὐκ ἔσται ἐκεῖ· 26 καὶ οἴσουσιν
for night   shall not be   there;   and   they will
                                   bring

τὴν δόξαν καὶ τὴν τιμὴν τῶν ἐθνῶν
the   glory   and   the   honour   of the   nations

εἰς αὐτήν. 27 καὶ οὐ μὴ εἰσέλθῃ εἰς
into   it.   And   by no means   may enter   into

---

wall and it was 144 cubits ʸ thick, ᶻ by man's measurement, which the angel was using. 18 The wall was made of jasper, and the city of pure gold, as pure as glass. 19 The foundations of the city walls were decorated with every kind of precious stone. The first foundation was jasper, the second sapphire, the third chalcedony, the fourth emerald, 20 the fifth sardonyx, the sixth carnelian, the seventh chrysolite, the eighth beryl, the ninth topaz, the tenth chrysoprase, the eleventh jacinth, and the twelfth amethyst. ᵃ 21 The twelve gates were twelve pearls, each gate made of a single pearl. The great street of the city was of pure gold, like transparent glass.

22 I did not see a temple in the city, because the Lord God Almighty and the Lamb are its temple. 23 The city does not need the sun or the moon to shine on it, for the glory of God gives it light, and the Lamb is its lamp. 24 The nations will walk by its light, and the kings of the earth will bring their splendor into it. 25 On no day will its gates ever be shut, for there will be no night there. 26 The glory and honor of the nations will be brought into it. 27 Nothing impure will ever enter it,

---

ʸ17 That is, about 200 feet (about 65 meters)
ᶻ17 Or high
ᵃ20 The precise identification of some of these precious stones is uncertain.

anyone who practices abomination or falsehood, but only those who are written in the Lamb's book of life.

Chapter 22

The River of Life

THEN the angel[y] showed me the river of the water of life, bright as crystal, flowing from the throne of God and of the Lamb 2 through the middle of the street of the city. On either side of the river, is the tree of life[z] with its twelve kinds of fruit, producing its fruit each month; and the leaves of the tree are for the healing of the nations. 3 Nothing accursed will be found there any more. But the throne of God and of the Lamb will be in it, and his servants[a] will worship him; 4 they will see his face, and his name will be on their foreheads. 5 And there will be no more night; they need no light of lamp or sun, for the Lord God will be their light, and they will reign forever and ever.

6 And he said to me, "These words are trustworthy and true, for the Lord, the God of the spirits of the prophets, has sent his angel to show his servants[a] what must soon take place."

7 "See, I am coming soon! Blessed is the one who keeps the words of the prophecy of this book."

Epilogue and Benediction

8 I, John, am the one who heard and saw these

y Gk he
z Or the Lamb. 2 In the middle of the street of the city, and on either side of the river, is the tree of life
a Gk slaves

Middle column (Greek interlinear):

αὐτὴν πᾶν κοινὸν καὶ [ὁ] ποιῶν
it every(any) profane thing and the [one] making

βδέλυγμα καὶ ψεῦδος, εἰ μὴ οἱ γεγραμ-
an and a lie, except the having been
abomination [ones]

μένοι ἐν τῷ βιβλίῳ τῆς ζωῆς τοῦ ἀρνίου.
written in the scroll - of life of the Lamb.

22 Καὶ ἔδειξέν μοι ποταμὸν ὕδατος
And he showed me a river of water

ζωῆς λαμπρὸν ὡς κρύσταλλον, ἐκπορευόμε-
of life bright as crystal, proceed-

νον ἐκ τοῦ θρόνου τοῦ θεοῦ καὶ τοῦ
ing out of the throne - of God and of the

ἀρνίου. **2** ἐν μέσῳ τῆς πλατείας αὐτῆς
Lamb. In [the] midst of the street of it

καὶ τοῦ ποταμοῦ ἐντεῦθεν καὶ ἐκεῖθεν
and of the river hence and thence

ξύλον ζωῆς ποιοῦν καρποὺς δώδεκα,
a tree of life producing fruits twelve,

κατὰ μῆνα ἕκαστον ἀποδιδοῦν τὸν καρπὸν
accord- ²month ¹each rendering the fruit
ing to

αὐτοῦ, καὶ τὰ φύλλα τοῦ ξύλου εἰς
of it, and the leaves of the tree [will be] for

θεραπείαν τῶν ἐθνῶν. **3** καὶ πᾶν κατάθεμα
healing of the nations. And every curse
=no curse will be any

οὐκ ἔσται ἔτι. καὶ ὁ θρόνος τοῦ θεοῦ
will not be longer. And the throne - of God
longer.

καὶ τοῦ ἀρνίου ἐν αὐτῇ ἔσται, καὶ οἱ
and of the Lamb ²in ³it ¹will be, and the

δοῦλοι αὐτοῦ λατρεύσουσιν αὐτῷ, **4** καὶ
slaves of him will do service to him, and

ὄψονται τὸ πρόσωπον αὐτοῦ, καὶ τὸ
they will see the face of him, and the

ὄνομα αὐτοῦ ἐπὶ τῶν μετώπων αὐτῶν.
name of him [will be] on the foreheads of them.

5 καὶ νὺξ οὐκ ἔσται ἔτι, καὶ οὐκ
And night will not be longer, and not

ἔχουσιν χρείαν φωτὸς λύχνου καὶ φωτὸς
they have need of light of lamp and of light

ἡλίου, ὅτι κύριος ὁ θεὸς φωτίσει ἐπ᾽
of sun, because [the] Lord - God will shed light on

αὐτούς, καὶ βασιλεύσουσιν εἰς τοὺς
them, and they will reign unto the

αἰῶνας τῶν αἰώνων.
ages of the ages.

6 Καὶ εἶπέν μοι· οὗτοι οἱ λόγοι πιστοὶ
And he said to me: These - words [are] faithful

καὶ ἀληθινοί, καὶ ὁ κύριος ὁ θεὸς τῶν
and true, and the Lord the God of the

πνευμάτων τῶν προφητῶν ἀπέστειλεν τὸν
spirits of the prophets sent the

ἄγγελον αὐτοῦ δεῖξαι τοῖς δούλοις αὐτοῦ
angel of him to show to the slaves of him

ἃ δεῖ γενέσθαι ἐν τάχει. **7** καὶ ἰδοὺ
things it be- to occur quickly. And behold
which hoves

ἔρχομαι ταχύ. μακάριος ὁ τηρῶν τοὺς
I am coming quickly. Blessed [is] the [one] keeping the

λόγους τῆς προφητείας τοῦ βιβλίου τούτου.
words of the prophecy of this scroll.

8 Κἀγὼ Ἰωάννης ὁ ἀκούων καὶ βλέπων
And I John [am] the [one] hearing and seeing

ταῦτα. καὶ ὅτε ἤκουσα καὶ ἔβλεψα,
these things. And when I heard and I saw,

nor will anyone who does what is shameful or deceitful, but only those whose names are written in the Lamb's book of life.

Chapter 22

The River of Life

THEN the angel showed me the river of the water of life, as clear as crystal, flowing from the throne of God and of the Lamb 2 down the middle of the great street of the city. On each side of the river stood the tree of life, bearing twelve crops of fruit, yielding its fruit every month. And the leaves of the tree are for the healing of the nations. 3 No longer will there be any curse. The throne of God and of the Lamb will be in the city, and his servants will serve him. 4 They will see his face, and his name will be on their foreheads. 5 There will be no more night. They will not need the light of a lamp or the light of the sun, for the Lord God will give them light. And they will reign for ever and ever.

6 The angel said to me, "These words are trustworthy and true. The Lord, the God of the spirits of the prophets, sent his angel to show his servants the things that must soon take place."

Jesus Is Coming

7 "Behold, I am coming soon! Blessed is he who keeps the words of the prophecy in this book."

8 I, John, am the one who heard and saw these things.

things. And when I heard and saw them, I fell down to worship at the feet of the angel who showed them to me; 9 but he said to me, "You must not do that! I am a fellow servant[b] with you and your comrades[c] the prophets, and with those who keep the words of this book. Worship God!"

10 And he said to me, "Do not seal up the words of the prophecy of this book, for the time is near. 11 Let the evildoer still do evil, and the filthy still be filthy, and the righteous still do right, and the holy still be holy."

12 "See, I am coming soon; my reward is with me, to repay according to everyone's work. 13 I am the Alpha and the Omega, the first and the last, the beginning and the end."

14 Blessed are those who wash their robes,[d] so that they will have the right to the tree of life and may enter the city by the gates. 15 Outside are the dogs and sorcerers and fornicators and murderers and idolaters, and everyone who loves and practices falsehood.

16 "It is I, Jesus, who sent my angel to you with this testimony for the churches. I am the root and the descendant of David, the bright morning star."

17 The Spirit and the
bride say,
"Come."
And let everyone who

Middle column (interlinear)

ἔπεσα προσκυνῆσαι ἔμπροσθεν τῶν ποδῶν
I fell to worship before the feet

τοῦ ἀγγέλου τοῦ δεικνύοντός μοι ταῦτα.
of the angel - showing me these things.

9 καὶ λέγει μοι· ὅρα μή· σύνδουλός
And he tells me: See thou [do] not; ²a fellow-slave

σού εἰμι καὶ τῶν ἀδελφῶν σου τῶν
³of thee ¹I am and of the brothers of thee the

προφητῶν καὶ τῶν τηρούντων τοὺς λόγους
prophets and of the [ones] keeping the words

τοῦ βιβλίου τούτου· τῷ θεῷ προσκύνησον.
of this scroll: - ²God ¹worship thou.

10 Καὶ λέγει μοι· μὴ σφραγίσῃς τοὺς
And he tells me: Seal not the

λόγους τῆς προφητείας τοῦ βιβλίου τούτου·
words of the prophecy of this scroll:

ὁ καιρὸς γὰρ ἐγγύς ἐστιν 11 ὁ ἀδικῶν
²the ³time ¹for ⁴near ⁵is. The acting [one] unjustly

ἀδικησάτω ἔτι, καὶ ὁ ῥυπαρὸς ῥυπανθήτω
let him act still, and the filthy [one] let him act filthily
unjustly

ἔτι, καὶ ὁ δίκαιος δικαιοσύνην ποιησάτω
still, and the righteous [one] ¹righteousness ²let him do

ἔτι, καὶ ὁ ἅγιος ἁγιασθήτω ἔτι.
still, and the holy [one] let him be hallowed still.

12 Ἰδοὺ ἔρχομαι ταχύ, καὶ ὁ μισθός
Behold I am coming quickly, and the reward

μου μετ᾽ ἐμοῦ, ἀποδοῦναι ἑκάστῳ ὡς
of me [is] with me, to render to each man as

τὸ ἔργον ἐστὶν αὐτοῦ. 13 ἐγὼ τὸ ἄλφα
the work ¹is ²of him. I [am] the alpha

καὶ τὸ ὦ, ὁ πρῶτος καὶ ὁ ἔσχατος,
and the omega, the first and the last,

ἡ ἀρχὴ καὶ τὸ τέλος. 14 μακάριοι οἱ
the begin- and the end. Blessed the
ning [are] [ones]

πλύνοντες τὰς στολὰς αὐτῶν, ἵνα ἔσται
washing the robes of them, in or- ⁴will be
der that

ἡ ἐξουσία αὐτῶν ἐπὶ τὸ ξύλον τῆς
¹the ²authority ³of them over the tree

ζωῆς καὶ τοῖς πυλῶσιν εἰσέλθωσιν εἰς
of life and ²by the ³gates ¹they may enter into

τὴν πόλιν. 15 ἔξω οἱ κύνες καὶ οἱ φαρμακοὶ
the city. Outside the dogs and the sorcerers
[are]

καὶ οἱ πόρνοι καὶ οἱ φονεῖς καὶ οἱ
and the fornicators and the murderers and the

εἰδωλολάτραι καὶ πᾶς φιλῶν καὶ ποιῶν
idolaters and everyone loving and making

ψεῦδος.
a lie.

16 Ἐγὼ Ἰησοῦς ἔπεμψα τὸν ἄγγελόν
I Jesus sent the angel

μου μαρτυρῆσαι ὑμῖν ταῦτα ἐπὶ ταῖς
of me to witness to you these things over(in) the

ἐκκλησίαις. ἐγώ εἰμι ἡ ῥίζα καὶ τὸ
churches. I am the root and the

γένος Δαυίδ, ὁ ἀστὴρ ὁ λαμπρὸς ὁ
offspring of David, the ²star - ¹bright -

πρωϊνός.
¹morning.

17 Καὶ τὸ πνεῦμα καὶ ἡ νύμφη λέγουσιν·
And the Spirit and the bride say:

ἔρχου. καὶ ὁ ἀκούων εἰπάτω· ἔρχου.
Come. And the [one] hearing let him say: Come.

And when I had heard and seen them, I fell down to worship at the feet of the angel who had been showing them to me. 9 But he said to me, "Do not do it! I am a fellow servant with you and with your brothers the prophets and of all who keep the words of this book. Worship God!"

10 Then he told me, "Do not seal up the words of the prophecy of this book, because the time is near. 11 Let him who does wrong continue to do wrong; let him who is vile continue to be vile; let him who does right continue to do right; and let him who is holy continue to be holy."

12 "Behold, I am coming soon! My reward is with me, and I will give to everyone according to what he has done. 13 I am the Alpha and the Omega, the First and the Last, the Beginning and the End.

14 "Blessed are those who wash their robes, that they may have the right to the tree of life and may go through the gates into the city. 15 Outside are the dogs, those who practice magic arts, the sexually immoral, the murderers, the idolaters and everyone who loves and practices falsehood.

16 "I, Jesus, have sent my angel to give you[b] this testimony for the churches. I am the Root and the Offspring of David, and the bright Morning Star."

17 The Spirit and the bride say, "Come!" And let him who hears say, "Come!"

b Gk slave
c Gk brothers
d Other ancient authorities read do his commandments

b16 The Greek is plural.

hears say,
"Come."
And let everyone who
is thirsty come.
Let anyone who
wishes take the
water of life as
a gift.

18 I warn everyone who
hears the words of the
prophecy of this book: if
anyone adds to them, God
will add to that person the
plagues described in this
book; 19if anyone takes
away from the words of the
book of this prophecy, God
will take away that per-
son's share in the tree of
life and in the holy city,
which are described in this
book.
20 The one who testifies
to these things says, "Surely I am coming soon."
Amen. Come, Lord
Jesus!
21 The grace of the
Lord Jesus be with all the
saints. Amen. *ᵉ*

καὶ   ὁ   διψῶν   ἐρχέσθω,   ὁ   θέλων   λαβέτω
And   the   thirsting   let him   the   wishing   let him
[one]   come,   [one]   take

ὕδωρ   ζωῆς   δωρεάν.
[the]   of life   freely.
water

18 Μαρτυρῶ   ἐγὼ   παντὶ   τῷ   ἀκούοντι
²witness   ¹I   to everyone   hearing

τοὺς   λόγους   τῆς   προφητείας   τοῦ   βιβλίου
the   words   of the   prophecy   -   ⁴scroll

τούτου·   ἐάν   τις   ἐπιθῇ   ἐπ'   αὐτά,   ἐπιθήσει
¹of this: If   anyone   adds   upon(to) them,*   ¹will add

ὁ   θεὸς   ἐπ'   αὐτὸν   τὰς   πληγὰς   τὰς
-   ¹God   upon   him   the   plagues

γεγραμμένας   ἐν   τῷ   βιβλίῳ   τούτῳ·   19 καὶ
having been written in   this scroll;   and

ἐάν   τις   ἀφέλῃ   ἀπὸ   τῶν   λόγων   τοῦ
if   anyone   takes away   from   the   words   of the

βιβλίου   τῆς   προφητείας   ταύτης,   ἀφελεῖ
scroll   of this prophecy,   ²will take
away

ὁ   θεὸς   τὸ   μέρος   αὐτοῦ   ἀπὸ   τοῦ   ξύλου
-   ¹God   the   part   of him   from   the   tree

τῆς   ζωῆς   καὶ   ἐκ   τῆς   πόλεως   τῆς   ἁγίας,
-   of life   and out of the   ⁶city   -   ¹holy,

τῶν   γεγραμμένων   ἐν   τῷ   βιβλίῳ   τούτῳ.
of the   having been   in   this scroll.
things   written

20 Λέγει   ὁ   μαρτυρῶν   ταῦτα·   ναί,   ἔρχομαι
Says   the   witnessing   these   Yes,   I am
[one]   things: coming

ταχύ.   Ἀμήν,   ἔρχου   κύριε   Ἰησοῦ.
quickly.   Amen,   come[,]   Lord   Jesus.

21 Ἡ   χάρις   τοῦ   κυρίου   Ἰησοῦ   μετὰ
The   grace   of the   Lord   Jesus [be]   with

πάντων.
all.

Whoever is thirsty, let him
come; and whoever wishes,
let him take the free gift of
the water of life.

18I warn everyone who
hears the words of the
prophecy of this book: If
anyone adds anything to
them, God will add to him
the plagues described in
this book. 19And if anyone
takes words away from this
book of prophecy, God will
take away from him his
share in the tree of life and
in the holy city, which are
described in this book.
20He who testifies to
these things says, "Yes, I
am coming soon."
Amen. Come, Lord
Jesus.
21The grace of the Lord
Jesus be with God's peo-
ple. Amen.

*ᵉ*Other ancient authorities lack *all*;
others lack *the saints*; others lack
Amen

* Neuter plural; see last clause of ver. 19.